To Rob and

Our wonderful neighbours.

Lots of love

Guy (& Sharyn!)

THE YEARBOOK OF WORLD SOCCER

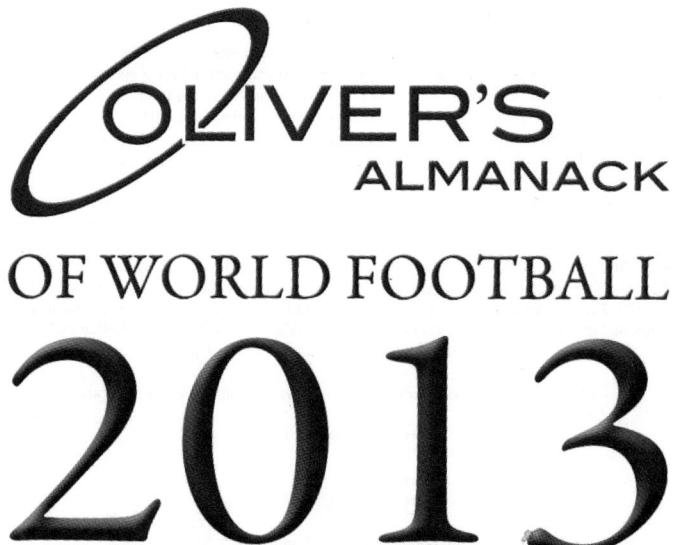

OF WORLD FOOTBALL
2013

GUY OLIVER

HARPASTUM PUBLISHING
OLIVERSALMANACK.COM

Copyright © 2013 Guy Oliver

The right of Guy Oliver to be identified as the Author of
the Work has been asserted by him in accordance with the
Copyright, Designs and Patents Act 1988.

First published in 2013
by HARPASTUM PUBLISHING LIMITED

1

Apart from any use permitted under UK copyright law, this publication may only be
reproduced, stored, or transmitted, in any form, or by any means, with prior permission in writing
of the publishers or, in the case of reprographic production, in accordance with the terms
of licences issued by the Copyright Licensing Agency.

Every effort has been made to fulfil requirements with regard to reproducing copyright material.
The author and publisher will be glad to rectify any omissions at the earliest opportunity.

Front cover photographs: (left) The USA women's team celebrate their gold medal success at the London
Olympics after beating Japan 2-1 in the final - *Action Images*; (centre left) Chelsea become the first team from
London to be crowned European champions after beating Bayern Munich in the UEFA Champions League
final - *Action Images*; (centre right) Lionel Messi celebrates goal number 86 in 2012 to overtake Gerd Muller's
total of 85 in 1972. He went on to score 91 - *Action Images*; (right) Captain Alessandro lifts the FIFA Club
World Cup in Tokyo after Corinthians beat Chelsea 1-0 in the final - *Action Images*

Spine photograph: Spain with the European Championship trophy after beating Italy 4-0 in the final of Euro
2012 in Kyiv - *Action Images*

Back cover photographs: (left) Mohamed Aboutreka of Al Ahly in the 2012 CAF Champions League final
against Tunisia's Esperance - *Action Images*; (centre left) Colombia's Radamel Falcao in action for Atlético
Madrid - *Action Images*; (centre right) Ulsan Hyundai captain Kwak Tae Hwi opens the scoring in the 2012
AFC Champions League final. The Koeans beat Saudi's Al Ahli 3-0 - *AFC*; (right) Andrea Pirlo in action for
Italy during the Euro 2012 finals - *Action Images*

A CIP catalogue record for this title is available from the British Library

ISBN 978-0-9564909-3-3

Design and layout: Guy Oliver
Cover design: Helen Williams

Printed and bound in India at Nutech Print Services

The data within the Almanack of World Football has been obtained from a variety of sources, official
and unofficial. The Author cannot vouch for the accuracy of the data in all cases.

Acknowledgements
The specific text in relation to FIFA Tournaments and the FIFA Ballon d'Or, found within Part One of this
publication on pages 28 to 72, was written and provided by FIFA.com.

Disclaimer
FIFA gives no warranties whatsoever in relation to the accuracy or the completeness of the content or
information contained within this publication and disclaims all responsibility and liability, to the fullest extent
permissible under the applicable law, for any: (i) expenses; (ii) losses; (iii) damages (including consequential
losses and damages); (iv) costs; (v) judgements; or (vi) penalties of any nature which may be incurred by any
person in relation to, or reliance upon, the content or information contained herein.

HARPASTUM PUBLISHING LIMITED
Vatcher's Farm, Thorney Hill
Christchurch, Dorset
United Kingdom, BH23 8DF

CONTENTS

Alphabetical listing of the nations of the world 8
A note for the 2013 edition. 10
How to use Oliver's Almanack. 10

PART ONE – FIFA AND WORLD FOOTBALL

Review of the year at FIFA 17
Map of confederations 18
FIFA national team tournaments. 20
FIFA club tournaments 23
FIFA youth tournaments. 24
FIFA women's tournaments 26
Other FIFA Tournaments. 27
FIFA Ballon d'Or 2012 28
Men's Olympic Football Tournament London 2012. 32
Women's Olympic Football Tournament London 2012 39
FIFA U-20 Women's World Cup Japan 2012. 45
FIFA U-17 Women's World Cup Azerbaijan 2012 52
FIFA Futsal World Cup Thailand 2012. 59
FIFA Club World Cup Japan 2012. 69

PART TWO – THE ASSOCIATIONS

AFG	Afghanistan.	75	BLR	Belarus.	158
AIA	Anguilla	77	BLZ	Belize	162
ALB	Albania.	79	BOL	Bolivia	164
ALG	Algeria	83	BOT	Botswana.	168
AND	Andorra.	87	BRA	Brazil	171
ANG	Angola	90	BRB	Barbados.	196
ARG	Argentina.	93	BRU	Brunei Darussalam	199
ARM	Armenia	109	BUL	Bulgaria	201
ARU	Aruba	112	CAM	Cambodia.	205
ASA	American Samoa	114	CAN	Canada.	207
ATG	Antigua and Barbuda	116	CAY	Cayman Islands.	209
AUS	Australia	118	CGO	Congo	211
AUT	Austria	122	CHA	Chad	214
AZE	Azerbaijan	126	CHI	Chile	216
BAH	Bahamas.	129	CHN	China PR.	221
BAN	Bangladesh.	131	CIV	Côte d'Ivoire	225
BDI	Burundi.	134	CMR	Cameroon.	228
BEL	Belgium	136	COD	Congo DR.	231
BEN	Benin	140	COK	Cook Islands	233
BER	Bermuda	142	COL	Colombia.	235
BFA	Burkina Faso	145	COM	Comoros	240
BHR	Bahrain.	149	CPV	Cape Verde Islands	242
BHU	Bhutan.	152	CRC	Costa Rica	244
BIH	Bosnia-Herzegovina.	154	CRO	Croatia	248

CTA	Central African Republic	252	KSA	Saudi Arabia	495
CUB	Cuba	254	KUW	Kuwait	499
CUW	Curacao	257	LAO	Laos	502
CYP	Cyprus	259	LBR	Liberia	504
CZE	Czech Republic	263	LBY	Libya	506
DEN	Denmark	267	LCA	St Lucia	508
DJI	Djibouti	271	LES	Lesotho	510
DMA	Dominica	273	LIB	Lebanon	512
DOM	Dominican Republic	275	LIE	Liechtenstein	515
ECU	Ecuador	277	LTU	Lithuania	517
EGY	Egypt	280	LUX	Luxembourg	520
ENG	England	283	LVA	Latvia	524
EQG	Equatorial Guinea	306	MAC	Macau	527
ERI	Eritrea	308	MAD	Madagascar	529
ESP	Spain	310	MAR	Morocco	532
EST	Estonia	329	MAS	Malaysia	536
ETH	Ethiopia	333	MDA	Moldova	540
FIJ	Fiji	335	MDV	Maldives	543
FIN	Finland	337	MEX	Mexico	546
FRA	France	341	MKD	Macedonia FYR	550
FRO	Faroe Islands	358	MLI	Mali	554
GAB	Gabon	361	MLT	Malta	557
GAM	Gambia	364	MNE	Montenegro	561
GEO	Georgia	366	MNG	Mongolia	565
GER	Germany	370	MOZ	Mozambique	567
GHA	Ghana	387	MRI	Mauritius	570
GNB	Guinea-Bissau	390	MSR	Montserrat	573
GRE	Greece	392	MTN	Mauritania	575
GRN	Grenada	396	MWI	Malawi	577
GUA	Guatemala	398	MYA	Myanmar	580
GUI	Guinea	402	NAM	Namibia	582
GUM	Guam	405	NCA	Nicaragua	584
GUY	Guyana	407	NCL	New Caledonia	587
HAI	Haiti	410	NED	Netherlands	590
HKG	Hong Kong	413	NEP	Nepal	596
HON	Honduras	416	NGA	Nigeria	598
HUN	Hungary	420	NIG	Niger	602
IDN	Indonesia	424	NIR	Northern Ireland	604
IND	India	429	NOR	Norway	608
IRL	Republic of Ireland	433	NZL	New Zealand	612
IRN	Iran	437	OMA	Oman	615
IRQ	Iraq	441	PAK	Pakistan	618
ISL	Iceland	444	PAN	Panama	621
ISR	Israel	448	PAR	Paraguay	624
ITA	Italy	452	PER	Peru	627
JAM	Jamaica	470	PHI	Philippines	630
JOR	Jordan	473	PLE	Palestine	633
JPN	Japan	476	PNG	Papua New Guinea	635
KAZ	Kazakhstan	483	POL	Poland	637
KEN	Kenya	486	POR	Portugal	641
KGZ	Kyrgyzstan	489	PRK	Korea DPR	648
KOR	Korea Republic	491	PUR	Puerto Rico	650

QAT	Qatar	652	TAN	Tanzania	746
ROU	Romania	656	TCA	Turks and Caicos Islands	748
RSA	South Africa	660	TGA	Tonga	750
RUS	Russia	665	THA	Thailand	752
RWA	Rwanda	670	TJK	Tajikistan	756
SAM	Samoa	673	TKM	Turkmenistan	758
SCO	Scotland	675	TLS	Timor-Leste	761
SDN	Sudan	682	TOG	Togo	763
SEN	Senegal	685	TPE	Chinese Taipei	765
SEY	Seychelles	688	TRI	Trinidad and Tobago	767
SIN	Singapore	691	TUN	Tunisia	770
SKN	St Kitts and Nevis	694	TUR	Turkey	773
SLE	Sierra Leone	697	UAE	United Arab Emirates	778
SLV	El Salvador	699	UGA	Uganda	781
SMR	San Marino	703	UKR	Ukraine	784
SOL	Solomon Islands	706	URU	Uruguay	788
SOM	Somalia	708	USA	United States of America	792
SRB	Serbia	710	UZB	Uzbekistan	797
SRI	Sri Lanka	714	VAN	Vanuatu	800
SSD	South Sudan	716	VEN	Venezuela	802
STP	São Tomé e Príncipe	718	VGB	British Virgin Islands	806
SUI	Switzerland	720	VIE	Vietnam	808
SUR	Surinam	724	VIN	St Vincent and the Grenadines	811
SVK	Slovakia	727	VIR	US Virgin Islands	813
SVN	Slovenia	731	WAL	Wales	815
SWE	Sweden	735	YEM	Yemen	819
SWZ	Swaziland	738	ZAM	Zambia	822
SYR	Syria	741	ZIM	Zimbabwe	825
TAH	Tahiti	743			

PART THREE – THE CONTINENTAL CONFEDERATIONS

ASIA

AFC Review of the Year	831
Map of AFC member nations	832
Asian national team tournaments	833
Asian club tournaments	838
Asian youth tournaments	843
Asian women's tournaments	845
National team tournaments in Asia 2012	847
AFC Challenge Cup Nepal 2012	847
West Asian Federation Championship Kuwait 2012	855
ASEAN Football Championship - AFF Suzuki Cup 2012	859
AFC U-19 Championship UAE 2012	864
AFC U-16 Championship Iran 2012	865
Club tournaments in Asia 2012	866
AFC Champions League 2012	866
AFC President's Cup 2012	881
AFC Cup 2012	882

AFRICA

CAF review of the year 884
Map of CAF member nations 885
African national team tournaments 886
African club tournaments 890
African youth tournaments 897
African women's tournaments 898
National team tournaments in Africa 2012 900
    CAF Africa Cup of Nations Gabon/Equatorial Guinea 2012 900
    CAF Africa Cup of Nations South Africa 2013 928
Regional tournaments in Africa 2012 927
    CECAFA Cup Uganda 2012 927
    CECAFA Kagame Inter-Club Cup Tanzania 2012 939
Club tournaments in Africa 2012 930
    CAF Champions League 2012 930
    CAF Confederations Cup 2012 940

CENTRAL AMERICA, NORTH AMERICA & THE CARIBBEAN

CONCACAF review of the year 942
Map of CONCACAF member nations 943
Central American, North American and Caribbean National Team Tournaments . . . 944
Central American, North American and Caribbean Club Tournaments 946
Central American, North American and Caribbean Youth Tournaments 950
Central American, North American and Caribbean Women's Tournaments 951
National team tournaments in CONCACAF 2012 952
    Caribbean Cup Antigua and Barbuda 2012 952
Club tournaments in CONCACAF 2011–12 962
    CONCACAF Champions League 2011–12 962
    CFU Club Championship 2012 973
Women's tournaments in CONCACAF 2012 977
    CONCACAF U-20 Women's Championship Panama 2012 977
    CONCACAF U-17 Women's Championship Guatemala 2012 978

SOUTH AMERICA

CONMEBOL review of the year 979
Map of CONMEBOL member nations 980
South American national team tournaments 981
South American club tournaments 982
South American youth tournaments 987
South American women's tournaments 987

Club tournaments in South America 2012. 988
    Copa Libertadores 2012 988
    Copa Sudamericana 2012. 1004
Women's tournaments in South America 2012. 1003
    Campeonato Sudamericano Femenino Sub-20 Brazil 2012 1003
    Campeonato Sudamericano Femenino Sub-17 Bolivia 2012. 1003

OCEANIA

OFC review of the year 1006
Map of OFC member nations 1007
Oceania national team Tournaments. 1008
Oceania club tournaments. 1010
Oceania youth tournaments. 1010
Oceania women's tournaments 1012
National team tournaments in Oceania 2012 1013
    OFC Nations Cup Solomon Islands 2012 1013
Club tournaments in Oceania 2011–12. 1016
    OFC Champions League 2011–12. 1016
Women's tournaments in Oceania 2012. 1018
    OFC U-20 Women's Championship New Zealand 2012 1018
    OFC U-17 Women's Championship New Zealand 2012 1018

EUROPE

UEFA review of the year 1019
Map of UEFA member nations. 1020
European national team Tournaments 1021
European club tournaments. 1021
European youth tournaments 1029
European women's tournaments. 1031
National team tournaments in Europe 2012. 1034
    UEFA Euro 2012 Poland/Ukraine Qualifying Tournament 1036
    UEFA Euro 2012 Poland/Ukraine Final Tournament 1060
Club tournaments in Europe 2011–12 1070
    UEFA Champions League 2011–12. 1070
    UEFA Europa League 2011–12. 1092
Youth tournaments in Europe 2012 1098
    UEFA European U-17 Championship Slovenia 2012. 1098
    UEFA European U-19 Championship Estonia 2012 1099
Women's tournaments in Europe 2011–12 1101
    UEFA European Women's U-17 Championship Switzerland 2012 1101
    UEFA Women's Champions League 2011–12 1102
    UEFA European Women's U-19 Championship Turkey 2012. 1104

ALPHABETICAL LISTING OF THE NATIONS OF THE WORLD

COUNTRY		PAGE	COUNTRY		PAGE
Afghanistan	AFG	75	Cyprus	CYP	259
Albania	ALB	79	Czech Republic	CZE	263
Algeria	ALG	83	Denmark	DEN	267
American Samoa	ASA	114	Djibouti	DJI	271
Andorra	AND	87	Dominica	DMA	273
Angola	ANG	90	Dominican Republic	DOM	275
Anguilla	AIA	77	(East Timor) Timor-Leste	TLS	761
Antigua and Barbuda	ATG	116	Ecuador	ECU	277
Argentina	ARG	93	Egypt	EGY	280
Armenia	ARM	109	El Salvador	SLV	699
Aruba	ARU	112	England	ENG	283
Australia	AUS	118	Equatorial Guinea	EQG	306
Austria	AUT	122	Eritrea	ERI	308
Azerbaijan	AZE	126	Estonia	EST	329
Bahamas	BAH	129	Ethiopia	ETH	333
Bahrain	BHR	149	Faroe Islands	FRO	358
Bangladesh	BAN	131	Fiji	FIJ	335
Barbados	BRB	196	Finland	FIN	337
Belarus	BLR	158	France	FRA	341
Belgium	BEL	136	French Polynesia - Tahiti	TAH	743
Belize	BLZ	162	Gabon	GAB	361
Benin	BEN	140	Gambia	GAM	364
Bermuda	BER	142	Georgia	GEO	366
Bhutan	BHU	152	Germany	GER	370
Bolivia	BOL	164	Ghana	GHA	387
Bosnia-Herzegovina	BIH	154	Greece	GRE	392
Botswana	BOT	168	Grenada	GRN	396
Brazil	BRA	171	Guam	GUM	405
British Virgin Islands	VGB	806	Guatemala	GUA	398
Brunei Darussalam	BRU	199	Guinea	GUI	402
Bulgaria	BUL	201	Guinea-Bissau	GNB	390
Burkina Faso	BFA	145	Guyana	GUY	407
(Burma) Myanmar	MYA	580	Haiti	HAI	410
Burundi	BDI	134	(Holland) The Netherlands	NED	590
Cambodia	CAM	205	Honduras	HON	416
Cameroon	CMR	228	Hong Kong	HKG	413
Canada	CAN	207	Hungary	HUN	420
Cape Verde Islands	CPV	242	Iceland	ISL	444
Cayman Islands	CAY	209	India	IND	429
Central African Republic	CTA	252	Indonesia	IDN	424
Chad	CHA	214	Iran	IRN	437
Chile	CHI	216	Iraq	IRQ	441
China PR	CHN	221	Israel	ISR	448
Chinese Taipei (Taiwan)	TPE	765	Italy	ITA	452
Colombia	COL	235	(Ivory Coast) Côte d'Ivoire	CIV	225
Comoros	COM	240	Jamaica	JAM	470
Congo	CGO	211	Japan	JPN	476
Congo DR	COD	231	Jordan	JOR	473
Cook Islands	COK	233	Kazakhstan	KAZ	483
Costa Rica	CRC	244	Kenya	KEN	486
Côte d'Ivoire (Ivory Coast)	CIV	225	Korea DPR (North Korea)	PRK	648
Croatia	CRO	248	Korea Republic (South Korea)	KOR	491
Cuba	CUB	254	Kuwait	KUW	499
Curacao	CUW	257	Kyrgyzstan	KGZ	489

ALPHABETICAL LISTING OF THE NATIONS OF THE WORLD

COUNTRY		PAGE	COUNTRY		PAGE
Laos	LAO	502	San Marino	SMR	703
Latvia	LVA	524	São Tomé e Príncipe	STP	718
Lebanon	LIB	512	Saudi Arabia	KSA	495
Lesotho	LES	510	Scotland	SCO	675
Liberia	LBR	504	Senegal	SEN	685
Libya	LBY	506	Serbia	SRB	710
Liechtenstein	LIE	515	Seychelles	SEY	688
Lithuania	LTU	517	Sierra Leone	SLE	697
Luxembourg	LUX	520	Singapore	SIN	691
Macau	MAC	527	Slovakia	SVK	727
Macedonia FYR	MKD	550	Slovenia	SVN	731
Madagascar	MAD	529	Solomon Islands	SOL	706
Malawi	MWI	577	Somalia	SOM	708
Malaysia	MAS	536	South Africa	RSA	660
Maldives	MDV	543	(South Korea) Korea Republic	KOR	491
Mali	MLI	554	South Sudan	SSD	716
Malta	MLT	557	Spain	ESP	310
Mauritania	MTN	575	Sri Lanka	SRI	714
Mauritius	MRI	570	St Kitts and Nevis	SKN	694
Mexico	MEX	546	St Lucia	LCA	508
Moldova	MDA	540	St Vincent and the Grenadines	VIN	811
Mongolia	MNG	565	Sudan	SDN	682
Montenegro	MNE	561	Surinam	SUR	724
Montserrat	MSR	573	Swaziland	SWZ	738
Morocco	MAR	532	Sweden	SWE	735
Mozambique	MOZ	567	Switzerland	SUI	720
Myanmar (Burma)	MYA	580	Syria	SYR	741
Namibia	NAM	582	Tahiti (French Polynesia)	TAH	743
Nepal	NEP	596	(Taiwan) Chinese Taipei	TPE	765
Netherlands (Holland)	NED	590	Tajikistan	TJK	756
New Caledonia	NCL	587	Tanzania	TAN	746
New Zealand	NZL	612	Thailand	THA	752
Nicaragua	NCA	584	Timor-Leste (East Timor)	TLS	761
Niger	NIG	602	Togo	TOG	763
Nigeria	NGA	598	Tonga	TGA	750
Northern Ireland	NIR	604	Trinidad and Tobago	TRI	767
(North Korea) Korea DPR	PRK	648	Tunisia	TUN	770
Norway	NOR	608	Turkey	TUR	773
Oman	OMA	615	Turkmenistan	TKM	758
Pakistan	PAK	618	Turks and Caicos Islands	TCA	748
Palestine	PLE	633	Uganda	UGA	781
Panama	PAN	621	Ukraine	UKR	784
Papua New Guinea	PNG	635	United Arab Emirates	UAE	778
Paraguay	PAR	624	United States of America	USA	792
Peru	PER	627	Uruguay	URU	788
Philippines	PHI	630	US Virgin Islands	VIR	813
Poland	POL	637	Uzbekistan	UZB	797
Portugal	POR	641	Vanuatu	VAN	800
Puerto Rico	PUR	650	Venezuela	VEN	802
Qatar	QAT	652	Vietnam	VIE	808
Republic of Ireland	IRL	433	Wales	WAL	815
Romania	ROU	656	Yemen	YEM	819
Russia	RUS	665	Zambia	ZAM	822
Rwanda	RWA	670	Zimbabwe	ZIM	825
Samoa	SAM	673			

A NOTE FOR THE 2013 EDITION

Oliver's Almanack of World Football 2013 is a review of football throughout the world in 2012 and once again I have stuck to the formula of including details of tournaments by the year in which they ended. So this edition includes all the matches - qualifiers and finals - for Euro 2012, even though the first of the qualifiers were played at the back end of 2010. With the advent of the internet yearbooks like this have had to adapt. No longer do readers wait for publication to access results that would otherwise have been unavailable. The information contained in the Almanack is available on thousands and thousands of internet pages but what the Almanack does is to distill that information and to provide an editorial overview of the game in each country and on every continent. Below I have included a review from an anonymous Amazon buyer (not me I promise!) which I feel encapsulates what the Almanack is about and the function that it serves.

"Good to see this excellent publication continuing to survive in the here-today-gone-tomorrow world of football reference book publishing. I'm pleased that despite the book's bulk it still remains very easy to navigate. Some sports yearbooks suffer from information overload or an excessively glitzy presentation - all of which leave the poor reader struggling to see the wood for the trees. On the other hand, you can open Guy Oliver's Almanack anywhere and find a comprehensive overview of a FIFA member's recent international and domestic scene, supported by a concise narrative and digestible chunks of statistical data that stops well short of overkill. The ideal blend, in my view. This book is a must for anyone whose horizons extend beyond the trivia and endless gossip of the Barclay's Premier League. As the book's title suggests, it is the perfect point of reference for the global game. Long may it flourish."

ACKNOWLEDGEMENTS

My sincere thanks to Stephanie Fulton at FIFA and the many others there who have helped with the Almanack this year, in particular Mattias Kunz, Matt Stone, Chris Laroche, Christophe Suppiger, Adrian Popp and Nicolas Maingot. My thanks also to Michael Church, Mark Gleeson and Steven Torres for sharing their expertise on Asia, Africa and the CONCACAF region respectively - your contributions are greatly appreciated. Thanks once again to Helen Williams and Michael Oliver for their annual contributions. The Almanack has relied heavily on FIFA.com but also benefits from the thousands of anonymous contributors to the internet along with some notable websites such as soccerway.com, worldfootball.net, wikipedia, eufootball.info, rsssf.com and footballdatabase.eu. This year's Almanack would not have been possible, however, without the invaluable contribution of my wife Sharyn and is dedicated to her and our two boys Ally and Archie. Guy Oliver, The New Forest, April 2013

HOW TO USE OLIVER'S ALMANACK

Oliver's Almanack of World Football contains many traditional techniques used across the world to present information, most of which will be familiar to the seasoned football fan. This guide serves a tool for those who are, perhaps, less familiar. We have tried to be as international in our language as possible - hence, for example, our referring to Red Star Belgrade as Crvena Zvezda Beograd except in written reviews. This may not be to everyone's taste but to see Bayern München and FC København written is becoming much more commonplace. Another tricky area is accents and we have taken the decision to remove them from players names but to keep them for the names of teams and stadia. Inconsistent maybe, but Peñarol just doesn't look right as Penarol. Many players by contrast don't use accents on their names and where do you draw the line with some of the more obscure languages of the world.

HOW TO USE OLIVER'S ALMANACK   11

A word about our football field match graphics... Again, they should be self explanatory. Each player is located on the pitch in his or her position at the start of the match. The two following examples from the Corinthians - Chelsea FIFA Club World Cup final show that Paolo Guerrero was substituted by Juan Martinez in the 87th minute; that Jorge Henrique was booked in the 73rd minute and that Gary Cahill was sent-off in the 90th minute.

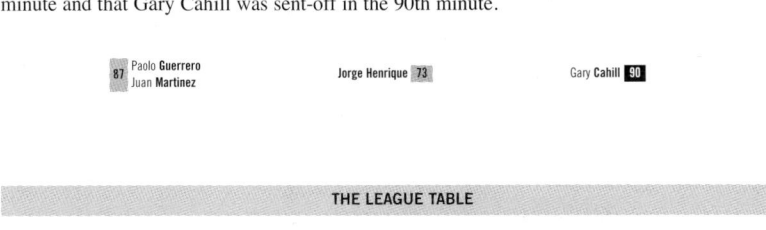

① The club in bold at the top of the league ladder are the league champions. If the club is not in bold it means that there was a further stage to be played. The relegated teams are also listed in bold at the foot of the table.

② This refers to the season in which the league campaign was played. In this instance the Brazilian championship was played through the course of 2009. Other leagues overlap the end of the year - 2008–09 for instance.

③ The league in Brazil is known as Serie A. Sponsors names are also included where applicable whilst (2) after the name means that the league is at the second level. (3) would mean the third level and so on.

④ The scoreline of 1-2 indicated in the box refers to the match between Cruzeiro at home against Palmeiras who were the visiting team. The first number (1) refers to the number of goals the home team Cruzeiro scored, the second (2) to the goals scored by Palmeiras, the away team. So in this instance Cruzeiro lost 1-2 at home to Palmeiras.

⑤ These columns refer to the number of games played during the season (Pl), games won (W), games drawn (D), games lost (L), goals scored (F), goals conceded (A) and the number of points obtained (Pts) during the course of the season by the team listed in each row. Different languages use the annotations listed in the table below.

English	Pl	W	D	L	F	A	Pts
French	J	G	N	P	Bp	Bc	Pts
German	Sp	G	U	V	Tore		Pkte
Italian	G	V	N	P	RF	RS	Pt
Portuguese	J	V	E	D	Gp	Gc	Pt
Spanish	J	G	E	P	Gf	Gc	Pts

HOW TO USE OLIVER'S ALMANACK

CUP BRACKETS

① The name of the Cup tournament and the year in which it was played. In this case the tournament is South Africa's SAA Supa 8 Cup that was played in 2008.

② This shows that Kaiser Chiefs played Santos at home - indicated by the asterisk - in the first round winning 4-0. The brackets are constructed so that the Cup winners always feature as the top bracket in each round with the beaten finalists as the bottom bracket. The winners of each tie are indicated in bold.

③ This bracket shows that Sundowns played SuperSport United in the semi-final over two legs. The asterisk indicates that Sundowns played the first leg at home and won 2-1. In the second leg, played away from home, Sundowns lost 2-3. When a tie finishes level on aggregate, as this tie did, away goals are used to determine the winners unless stated. With two goals scored away from home as opposed to the one goal scored away from home by SuperSport United, Sundowns qualified for the final.

④ This bracket indicates that the final of the 2008 Supa 8 Cup was between Kaiser Chiefs and Sundowns. The match finished 0-0 but Chiefs won the Cup after winning the penalty shoot-out 4-3.

COUNTRY INFORMATION

Most of the items on the front page for each country should be self explanatory. The FIFA Big Count 2006 was a survey conducted by FIFA in 2006 of all of the member associations and followed a similar survey carried out in 2000. The information for the box at the bottom of each page is sourced from the CIA Factbook whilst the population figures for cities and towns are sourced from the World Gazetteer.

① The local football association box contains the following information - the name of the association and its abbreviation, address, phone, fax, email, website - along with the year the FA was formed (FA), the year it joined its continental confederation (CON) and the year it joined FIFA. The names beside 'P' are the president of the FA and the secretary-general 'GS'.

FEDERATA SHQIPTARE E FUTBOLIT (FSHF)
Rruga Labinoti,
Pallati perballe Shkolles, "Gjuhet e Huaja" Tirana
☎ +355 43 46 605
📠 +355 43 46 609
✉ fshf@fshf.org.al
🖥 www.fshf.org
FA 1930 CON 1954 FIFA 1932
P Armand Duka
GS Eduard Prodani

② The information in the country information box is self explanatory. The name of the country is given in its local form first and then in the English form. The figures in brackets are the world rankings of the country according to the CIA Factbook in the category listed. Therefore Albania's population of 3,639,453 (a 2009 estimate) is the 129th largest (out of 228) in the world.

REPUBLIKA E SHQIPERISE • REPUBLIC OF ALBANIA

Capital	Tirana	Population	3 639 453 (129)	% in cities	47%
GDP per capita	$6000 (132)	Area km²	28 748 km² (144)	GMT +/-	+1
Neighbours (km)	Greece 282, Macedonia 151, Montenegro 172, Kosovo 112 • Coast 362					

HOW TO USE OLIVER'S ALMANACK

MATCH BOXES

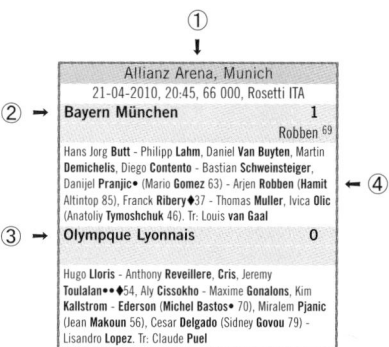

① This match was played at the Allianz Arena in Munich on the 21st April, 2010. Kick-off was at 20:45 in the evening and there were 66,000 fans in the stadium. The match referee was Italy's Rosetti.

② Bayern Munich were the home side and scored one goal. The goalscorer was Arjen Robben in the 69th minute. Had the goal been scored from a penalty the time indicator would have read 69p. A + after the minute of the goal indicates that it was scored in injury-time. Thus 93+ means a goal was scored in the third minute of stoppage time. 93 on the other hand would mean that the goal was scored in the 93rd minute - ie the third minute of extra-time.

③ Olympique Lyonnais were the away team. They did not score and lost the match 0-1.

④ This box indicates the line-up of the Bayern Munich team. Each team is divided by three hyphens into Goalkeepers - Defenders - Midfielders - Forwards where it is possible to gather this information. For the major tournaments we have also listed the players from right to left across the field. Thus in this UEFA Champions League semi-final Philipp Lahm played at right back with Van Buyten and Demichelis in the central defensive positions and Diego Contento at left back. If a player has • after his name it indicates that he was booked. If a player has ♦37 as in the case of Frank Ribery, it means he was sent off in the 37th minute. Jeremy Toulalan on the other hand has ••♦54 after his name indicating that he was sent off in the 54th minute after receiving two yellow cards.

The exact composition of match boxes varies from tournament to tournament - in some tournaments players are listed with shirt numbers for example - but the principles remain the same.

CLUB BY CLUB GUIDES

In the club by club guides - to the leagues in Argentina, Brazil, England, France, Germany, Italy, and Spain - simple annotations are used to describe matches. A competition is given an identifier which is unique to that particular country and is listed at the start of the guide to each country. So in Italy for instance, SA refers to Serie A. The Coppa Italia is referred to IC with ICr1 referring to a first round match, ICqf to a quarter-final, ICsf a semi-final and ICf to the final. A UEFA Champions League match played in group A, for example would be referred to as CLgA. Matches that are shaded are home matches for the club concerned whilst no shading indicates that the match was either played away from home or on a neutral ground. The figures for the player appearances and goals consist of three elements - matches started+appearances as a substitute/goals scored - for league matches only.

PART ONE

FIFA AND WORLD FOOTBALL

FIFA

Fédération Internationale de Football Association

Women's football provided the major focus for FIFA in 2012 with the staging of three tournaments, two of which were won by the United States of America. A record Olympic crowd for women's football of 80,203 saw the USA defeat Japan 2-1 at Wembley to secure gold at the London Olympics - the fourth time since the event was introduced at Atlanta in 1996 that the Americans had won gold. The USA's second title of the year came less than a month later as the U-20 team emulated the success of the senior women's team by winning the 2012 FIFA U-20 Women's World Cup in Japan. In the final they beat defending champions Germany 1-0 to secure the title for the third time. The American U-17 side, however, failed to make it a unique treble after they were knocked out at the group stage of the FIFA U-17 Women's World Cup in Azerbaijan on goal difference. They finished level on points with France and Korea DPR both of whom went on to contest the final which was won by the French after a penalty shoot-out - a first world title won by the French in women's football. There was a very Latin flavour to the winners of the three tournaments contested by the men in 2012. In the men's tournament at the London 2012 Olympics there was a first-ever gold for Mexico who beat Brazil 2-1 - a second world title for Mexico within 13 months following on from their success at the FIFA U-17 World Cup in 2011. The final two FIFA tournaments played in 2012 were both won by Brazilian teams. At the FIFA Futsal World Cup played in Thailand in November, Brazil continued their domination of the sport after winning all seven of their matches and scoring 45 goals on their way to the title. Spain remain the only nation to have seriously challenged the Brazilians in futsal and the two met in a close and dramatic final which Brazil won 3-2 thanks to a Neto goal in the very last minute of extra-time. Japan was once again host to the final action of the year at the FIFA Club World Cup where Copa Libertadores winners Corinthians won the title after beating the UEFA Champions League winners Chelsea 1-0 in the final, much to the delight of the estimated 30,000 of their fans who had made the journey from Brazil for the tournament.

Fédération Internationale de Football Association (FIFA)
FIFA-Strasse 20, PO Box, 8044 Zurich, Switzerland
Tel +41 43 222 7777   Fax +41 43 222 7878
contact@fifa.org   www.fifa.com
President: Joseph S. BLATTER
Secretary General: Jérôme VALCKE   Deputy Secretary General: Markus KATTNER
FIFA Executive Committee see http://www.fifa.com/aboutfifa/organisation/bodies/excoandemergency/index.html

Aerial image of the Home of FIFA, Zurich, Switzerland.
Photo: Foto-net

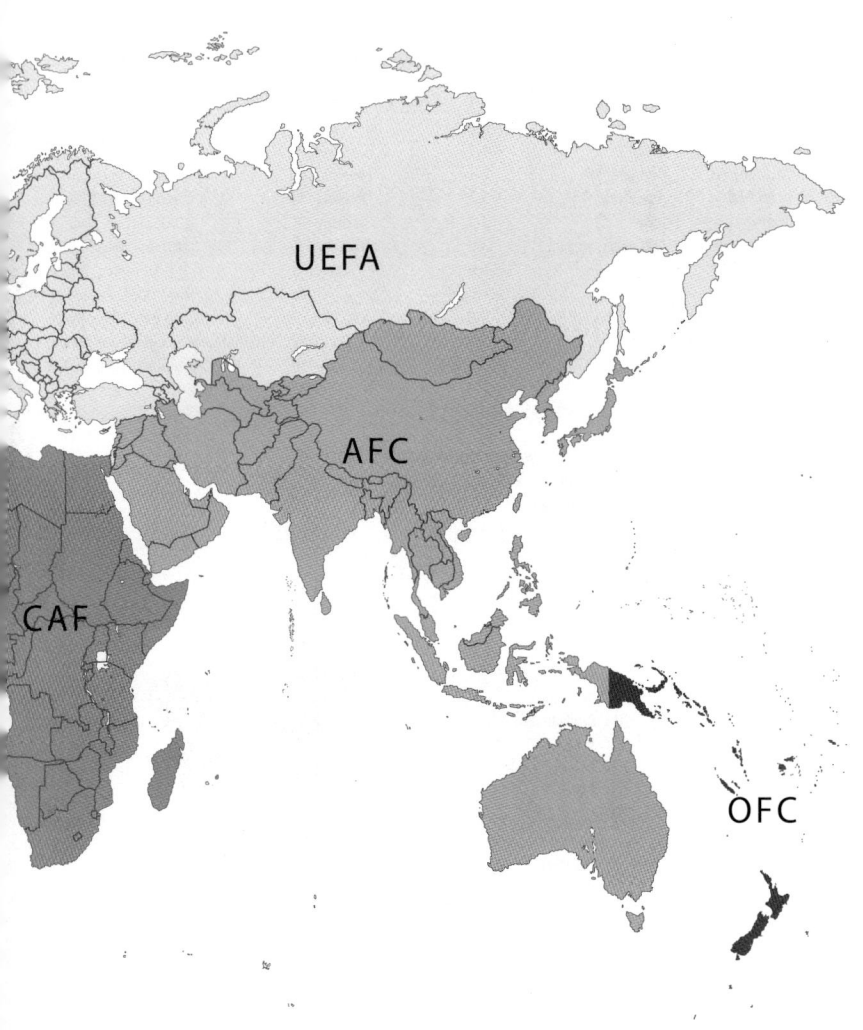

FIFA TOURNAMENTS

FIFA NATIONAL TEAM TOURNAMENTS

FIFA WORLD CUP™

Year	Host country	Winners	Score	Runners-up	Venue
1930	Uruguay	Uruguay	4-2	Argentina	Centenario, Montevideo
1934	Italy	Italy	2-1	Czechoslovakia	PNF, Rome
1938	France	Italy	4-2	Hungary	Colombes, Paris
1950	Brazil	Uruguay	2-1	Brazil	Maracana, Rio de Janeiro
1954	Switzerland	Germany FR	3-2	Hungary	Wankdorf, Berne
1958	Sweden	Brazil	5-2	Sweden	Råsunda, Stockholm
1962	Chile	Brazil	3-1	Czechoslovakia	Estadio Nacional, Santiago
1966	England	England	4-2	Germany FR	Wembley, London
1970	Mexico	Brazil	4-1	Italy	Azteca, Mexico City
1974	Germany FR	Germany FR	2-1	Netherlands	Olympiastadion, Munich
1978	Argentina	Argentina	3-1	Netherlands	Monumental, Buenos Aires
1982	Spain	Italy	3-1	Germany FR	Bernabeu, Madrid
1986	Mexico	Argentina	3-2	Germany FR	Azteca, Mexico City
1990	Italy	Germany FR	1-0	Argentina	Olimpico, Rome
1994	USA	Brazil	0-0 3-2p	Italy	Rose Bowl, Pasadena
1998	France	France	3-0	Brazil	Stade de France, Paris
2002	Korea Rep/Japan	Brazil	2-0	Germany	International Stadium, Yokohama
2006	Germany	Italy	1-1 5-3p	France	Olympiastadion, Berlin
2010	South Africa	Spain	1-0	Netherlands	Soccer City, Johannesburg
2014	Brazil				Maracana, Rio de Janeiro

FIFA WORLD CUP™ MEDALS TABLE

	Country	G	S	B	F	SF
1	Brazil	5	2	2	7	7
2	Italy	4	2	1	6	7
3	Germany	3	4	4	7	11
4	Argentina	2	2		4	3
5	Uruguay	2			2	4
6	France	1	1	2	2	5
7	England	1			1	2
8	Spain	1			1	1
9	Netherlands		3		3	2
10	Czechoslovakia		2		2	2
	Hungary		2		2	2
12	Sweden		1	2	1	3
13	Poland			2		1
14	Austria			1		2
	Portugal			1		2
	Yugoslavia			1		2
17	Chile			1		1
	Croatia			1		1
	Turkey			1		1
	USA			1		1
21	Belgium					1
	Bulgaria					1
	Korea Republic					1
	Soviet Union					1
		19	19	20	38	64

This table represents the Gold (winners), Silver (runners-up) and Bronze (3rd place) wins of nations in the FIFA World Cup™, along with the number of appearances in the final and semi-finals

FIFA NATIONAL TEAM TOURNAMENTS

FIFA CONFEDERATIONS CUP

Year	Host country	Winners	Score	Runners-up	Venue
1992	Saudi Arabia †	Argentina	3-1	Saudi Arabia	King Fahd, Riyadh
1995	Saudi Arabia †	Denmark	2-0	Argentina	King Fahd, Riyadh
1997	Saudi Arabia	Brazil	6-0	Australia	King Fahd, Riyadh
1999	Mexico	Mexico	4-3	Brazil	Azteca, Mexico City
2001	Korea/Japan	France	1-0	Japan	International Stadium, Yokohama
2003	France	France	1-0	Cameroon	Stade de France, Paris
2005	Germany	Brazil	4-1	Argentina	Waldstadion, Frankfurt
2009	South Africa	Brazil	3-2	USA	Ellis Park, Johannesburg
2013	Brazil				Maracana, Rio de Janeiro

† Intercontinental Champions Cup

FIFA CONFEDERATIONS CUP MEDALS TABLE

	Country	G	S	B	F	SF
1	Brazil	3	1		4	5
2	France	2			2	2
3	Argentina	1	2		3	3
4	Mexico	1		1	1	3
5	Denmark	1			1	1
6	USA		1	2	1	3
7	Australia		1	1	1	2
8	Saudi Arabia		1		1	2
9	Cameroon		1		1	1
10	Japan		1		1	1
	Czech Republic			1		1
12	Germany			1		1
13	Turkey			1		1
14	Spain			1		1
	Colombia					1
	Côte d'Ivoire					1
17	Nigeria					1
	South Africa					1
	Uruguay					1
		8	8	8	16	32

MEN'S OLYMPIC FOOTBALL TOURNAMENT

Year	Host city	Winners	Score	Runners-up	Venue
1896	Athens	No football tournament played			
1900	Paris ‡	Great Britain	4-0	France	Vélodrome Municipal, Paris
1904	St Louis ‡	Canada	4-0	USA	Francis Field, St Louis
1906	Athens ‡	Denmark	9-0	Greece	Podilatodromino, Athens
1908	London	Great Britain (England)	2-0	Denmark	White City, London
1912	Stockholm	Great Britain (England)	4-2	Denmark	Stockholms Stadion, Stockholm
1916	Berlin	Games cancelled			
1920	Antwerp	Belgium	2-0	Czechoslovakia †	Olympisch Stadion, Antwerp
1924	Paris	Uruguay	3-0	Switzerland	Colombes, Paris
1928	Amsterdam	Uruguay	1-1 2-1	Argentina	Olympisch Stadion, Amsterdam
1932	Los Angeles	No football tournament played			
1936	Berlin	Italy	2-1	Austria	Olympiastadion, Berlin
1940	Tokyo/Helsinki	Games cancelled			
1944	London	Games cancelled			
1948	London	Sweden	3-1	Yugoslavia	Wembley, London
1952	Helsinki	Hungary	2-0	Yugoslavia	Olympiastadion, Helsinki
1956	Melbourne	Soviet Union	1-0	Yugoslavia	Melbourne Cricket Ground
1960	Rome	Yugoslavia	3-1	Denmark	Flaminio, Rome

MEN'S OLYMPIC FOOTBALL TOURNAMENT (CONT'D)

Year	Host city	Winners	Score	Runners-up	Venue
1964	Tokyo	Hungary	2-1	Czechoslovakia	National Stadium, Tokyo
1968	Mexico City	Hungary	4-1	Bulgaria	Azteca, Mexico City
1972	Munich	Poland	2-1	Hungary	Olympiastadion, Munich
1976	Montreal	German DR	3-1	Poland	Olympic Stadium, Montreal
1980	Moscow	Czechoslovakia	1-0	German DR	Centralny, Moscow
1984	Los Angeles	France	2-0	Brazil	Rose Bowl, Pasadena
1988	Seoul	Soviet Union	2-1	Brazil	Olympic Stadium, Seoul
1992	Barcelona	Spain	3-2	Poland	Camp Nou, Barcelona
1996	Atlanta	Nigeria	3-2	Argentina	Sanford Stadium, Athens
2000	Sydney	Cameroon	2-2 5-3p	Spain	Olympic Stadium, Sydney
2004	Athens	Argentina	1-0	Paraguay	Olympic Stadium, Athens
2008	Beijing	Argentina	1-0	Nigeria	Bird's Nest, Beijing
2012	London	Mexico	2-1	Brazil	Wembley, London
2016	Rio de Janeiro				Maracana, Rio de Janeiro

† Match abandoned and Czechoslovakia disqualified. Spain won an additional tournament for the silver medal • ‡ Tournaments prior to 1908 are unofficial • The 1928 final was replayed after a 1-1 draw in the first match

MEN'S OLYMPIC FOOTBALL TOURNAMENT MEDALS TABLE

	Country	G	S	B	F	SF
1	Hungary	3	1	1	4	5
2	Argentina	2	2		4	4
3	Soviet Union	2		3	2	5
4	Great Britain	2			2	3
5	Uruguay	2			2	2
6	Yugoslavia	1	3	1	4	6
7	Poland	1	2		3	4
8	Spain	1	2		2	3
9	German Democratic Rep	1	1	1	2	4
10	Czechoslovakia	1	1		3	2
	Nigeria	1	1		2	2
12	Italy	1		2	1	6
13	Sweden	1		2	1	4
14	Belgium	1			1	2
	France	1			1	2
	Mexico	1			1	2
17	Cameroon	1			1	1
18	Brazil		3	2	3	6
19	Denmark		3	1	3	4
20	Bulgaria		1	1	1	2
21	Austria		1		1	2
22	Paraguay		1		1	1
	Switzerland		1		1	1
24	Netherlands			3		4
25	Japan			1		2
	German Federal Republic			1		2
27	Chile			1		1
	Ghana			1		1
	Norway			1		1
	Korea Republic			1		1
31	Egypt					2
	Finland					1
	India					1
	Iraq					1
	Portugal					1
	USA					1
		23	23	23	46	92

FIFA CLUB TOURNAMENTS

FIFA CLUB WORLD CUP

Year	Host country	Winners		Score		Runners-up	Venue
2000	Brazil	Corinthians	BRA	0-0 4-3p	BRA	Vasco da Gama	Maracana, Rio de Janeiro
2005	Japan	São Paulo FC	BRA	1-0	ENG	Liverpool	International, Yokohama
2006	Japan	Internacional	BRA	1-0	ESP	Barcelona	International, Yokohama
2007	Japan	Milan	ITA	4-2	ARG	Boca Juniors	International, Yokohama
2008	Japan	Manchester United	ENG	1-0	ECU	LDU Quito	International, Yokohama
2009	UAE	Barcelona	ESP	2-1	ARG	Estudiantes LP	Zayed SC, Abu Dhabi
2010	UAE	Internazionale	ITA	3-0	COD	TP Mazembe	Zayed SC, Abu Dhabi
2011	Japan	Barcelona	ESP	4-0	BRA	Santos	International, Yokohama
2012	Japan	Corinthians	BRA	1-0	ENG	Chelsea	International, Yokohama

FIFA CLUB WORLD CUP MEDALS TABLE

	Country	G	S	B	F	SF
1	Brazil	4	2	1	6	5
2	Spain	2	1		3	3
3	Italy	2			2	2
4	England	1	2		3	3
5	Argentina		2		2	
6	Congo DR			1		1	1
	Ecuador			1	1	1
8	Mexico			2		4
9	Japan			2		3
10	Egypt			1		2
	Korea Republic			1		2
12	Costa Rica			1		1
	Qatar			1		1
14	Saudi Arabia					1
	Tunisia					1
		9	9	9	18	32

FIFA CLUB WORLD CUP MEDALS TABLE – CLUBS

	Club		G	S	B	F	SF
1	Barcelona	ESP	2	1		3	3
2	Corinthians	BRA	2			2	1
3	Internacional	BRA	1		1	1	2
4	Internazionale	ITA	1			1	1
	Manchester United	ENG	1			1	1
	Milan	ITA	1			1	1
	São Paulo FC	BRA	1			1	1
8	Boca Juniors	ARG		1		1	1
	Chelsea	ENG		1		1	1
	Estudiantes LP	ARG		1		1	1
	LDU Quito	ECU		1		1	1
	Liverpool	ENG		1		1	1
	TP Mazembe	COD			1		1	1
	Santos	BRA		1		1	1
	Vasco da Gama	BRA		1		1	

FIFA CLUB WORLD CUP MEDALS TABLE (CONT'D)

	Club		G	S	B	F	SF
16	Al Ahly	EGY			1		2
17	Al Sadd	QAT			1		1
	Deportivo Saprissa	CRC			1		1
	Gamba Osaka	JPN			1		1
	Monterrey	MEX			1		1
	Necaxa	MEX			1		
	Pohang Steelers	KOR			1		1
	Urawa Reds	JPN			1		1
24	Al Ittihad	KSA					1
	América	MEX					1
	Atlante	MEX					1
	Etoile du Sahel	TUN					1
	Kashiwa Reysol	JPN					1
	Pachuca	MEX					1
	Seongnam Ilhwa	KOR					1
			9	9	9	18	32

FIFA YOUTH TOURNAMENTS

FIFA U-20 WORLD CUP

Year	Host Country	Winners	Score	Runners-up	Final Venue
1977	Tunisia	Soviet Union	2-2 9-8p	Mexico	El Menzah, Tunis
1979	Japan	Argentina	3-1	Soviet Union	National Stadium, Tokyo
1981	Australia	Germany FR	4-0	Qatar	Sydney Cricket Ground
1983	Mexico	Brazil	1-0	Argentina	Azteca, Mexico City
1985	Soviet Union	Brazil	1-0	Spain	Centralny, Moscow
1987	Chile	Yugoslavia	1-1 5-4p	Germany FR	Estadio Nacional, Santiago
1989	Saudi Arabia	Portugal	2-0	Nigeria	King Fahd, Riyadh
1991	Portugal	Portugal	0-0 4-2p	Brazil	Da Luz, Lisbon
1993	Australia	Brazil	2-1	Ghana	Sydney Football Stadium, Sydney
1995	Qatar	Argentina	2-0	Brazil	Khalifa, Doha
1997	Malaysia	Argentina	2-1	Uruguay	Shahalam Stadium, Shah Alam
1999	Nigeria	Spain	4-0	Japan	Surulere, Lagos
2001	Argentina	Argentina	3-0	Ghana	Jose Amalfitani, Buenos Aires
2003	UAE	Brazil	1-0	Spain	Zayed Sports City, Abu Dhabi
2005	Netherlands	Argentina	2-1	Nigeria	Galgenwaard, Utrecht
2007	Canada	Argentina	2-1	Czech Republic	National Soccer Stadium, Toronto
2009	Egypt	Ghana	0-0 4-3p	Brazil	International, Cairo
2011	Colombia	Brazil	3-2	Portugal	El Campin, Bogota

FIFA U-20 WORLD CUP MEDALS TABLE

	Country	G	S	B	F	SF
1	Argentina	6	1		7	8
2	Brazil	5	3	3	8	11
3	Portugal	2	1	1	3	4
4	Ghana	1	2		3	4
	Spain	1	2		3	4
6	Soviet Union	1	1	1	2	4
7	German Federal Republic	1	1		2	2
8	Yugoslavia	1			1	1
9	Nigeria		2	1	2	3
10	Uruguay		1	1	1	4
11	Mexico		1	1	1	2
12	Czech Republic		1		1	1
	Japan		1		1	1
	Qatar		1		1	1
15	Chile			1		2
	England			1		2
	Poland			1		2
18	Colombia			1		1
	Egypt			1		1
	German Democratic Rep			1		1
	Hungary			1		1
	Republic of Ireland			1		1
	Mali			1		1
	Romania			1		1
25	Australia					2
26	Austria					1
	Costa Rica					1
	France					1
	Korea Republic					1
	Morocco					1
	Paraguay					1
	USA					1
		18	18	18	36	72

FIFA U-17 WORLD CUP

Year	Host Country	Winners	Score	Runners-up	Final Venue
1985	China PR	Nigeria	2-0	Germany FR	Workers' Stadium, Beijing
1987	Canada	Soviet Union	1-1 3-1p	Nigeria	Varsity Stadium, Toronto
1989	Scotland	Saudi Arabia	2-2 5-4p	Scotland	Hampden Park, Glasgow
1991	Italy	Ghana	1-0	Spain	Comunale, Florence
1993	Japan	Nigeria	2-1	Ghana	National Stadium, Tokyo
1995	Ecuador	Ghana	3-2	Brazil	Monumental, Guayaquil
1997	Egypt	Brazil	2-1	Ghana	National Stadium, Cairo
1999	New Zealand	Brazil	0-0 8-7p	Australia	North Harbour, Auckland
2001	Trinidad & Tobago	France	3-0	Nigeria	Hasely Crawford, Port of Spain
2003	Finland	Brazil	1-0	Spain	Töölö, Helsinki
2005	Peru	Mexico	3-0	Brazil	Estadio Nacional, Lima
2007	Korea Republic	Nigeria	0-0 3-0p	Spain	World Cup Stadium, Seoul
2009	Nigeria	Switzerland	1-0	Nigeria	National Stadium, Abuja
2011	Mexico	Mexico	2-0	Uruguay	Azteca, Mexico City

First three tournaments played as a U-16 event

FIFA U-17 WORLD CUP MEDALS TABLE

	Country	G	S	B	F	SF
1	Nigeria	3	3		6	6
2	Brazil	3	2	1	5	7
3	Ghana	2	2	1	4	6
4	Mexico	2			2	2
5	France	1			1	1
	Saudi Arabia	1			1	1
	Soviet Union	1			1	1
	Switzerland	1			1	1
9	Spain		3	2	3	5
10	Germany (incl FRG)		1	2	1	4
11	Australia		1		1	1
	Scotland		1		1	1
	Uruguay		1		1	1
14	Argentina			3		4
15	Burkina Faso			1		1
	Chile			1		1
	Côte d'Ivoire			1		1
	Netherlands			1		1
	Portugal			1		1
20	Colombia					2
21	Bahrain					1
	Guinea					1
	Italy					1
	Oman					1
	Poland					1
	Qatar					1
	Turkey					1
	USA					1
		14	14	14	28	56

FIFA WOMEN'S TOURNAMENTS

FIFA WOMEN'S WORLD CUP

Year	Host Country	Winners	Score	Runners-up	Venue
1991	China PR	USA	2-1	Norway	Tianhe, Guangzhou
1995	Sweden	Norway	2-0	Germany	Råsunda, Stockholm
1999	USA	USA	0-0 5-4p	China PR	Rose Bowl, Pasadena
2003	USA	Germany	2-1	Sweden	Home Depot Centre, Carson
2007	China PR	Germany	2-0	Brazil	Hongkou, Shanghai
2011	Germany	Japan	2-2 3-1p	USA	Commerzbank, Frankfurt/Main

FIFA WOMEN'S WORLD CUP MEDALS TABLE

	Country	G	S	B	F	SF
1	USA	2	1	3	3	6
2	Germany	2	1		3	4
3	Norway	1	1		2	4
4	Japan	1			1	1
	Brazil		1	1	1	2
6	Sweden		1	2	1	3
7	China PR		1		1	2
	Canada					1
	France					1
		6	6	6	12	24

This table represents the Gold (winners), Silver (runners-up) and Bronze (3rd place) wins of nations in the FIFA Women's World Cup, along with the number of appearances in the final and semi-finals

WOMEN'S OLYMPIC FOOTBALL TOURNAMENT

Year	Host City	Winners	Score	Runners-up	Venue
1996	Atlanta	USA	2-1	China PR	Sanford Stadium, Athens
2000	Sydney	Norway	3-2	USA	Sydney Football Stadium, Sydney
2004	Athens	USA	2-1	Brazil	Karaiskaki, Piraeus
2008	Beijing	USA	1-0	Brazil	Worker's Stadium, Beijing
2012	London	USA	2-1	Japan	Wembley, London

WOMEN'S OLYMPIC FOOTBALL TOURNAMENT MEDALS TABLE

	Country	G	S	B	F	SF
1	USA	4	1		5	5
2	Norway	1		1	1	2
3	Brazil		2		2	4
4	Japan		1		1	2
5	China PR		1		1	1
6	Germany			3		3
7	Canada			1		1
8	France					1
	Sweden					1
		5	5	5	10	20

FIFA U-20 WOMEN'S WORLD CUP

Year	Host Country	Winners	Score	Runners-up	Final Venue
2002	Canada	USA	1-0	Canada	Commonwealth, Edmonton
2004	Thailand	Germany	2-0	China PR	Rajamangala National, Bangkok
2006	Russia	Korea DPR	5-0	China PR	Lokomotiv, Moscow
2008	Chile	USA	2-1	Korea DPR	Municipal, La Florida, Santiago
2010	Germany	Germany	2-0	Nigeria	Schüco Arena, Bielefeld
2012	Japan	USA	1-0	Germany	National Stadium, Tokyo

First two tournaments played as a U-19 event

FIFA U-20 WOMEN'S WORLD CUP MEDALS TABLE

	Country	G	S	B	F	SF
1	USA	3		1	3	5
2	Germany	2	1	2	3	5
3	Korea DPR	1	1		2	2
4	China PR		2		2	2
5	Nigeria		1		1	2
6	Canada		1		1	1
7	Brazil			1		3
8	Japan			1		1
	Korea Republic			1		1
10	Colombia					1
	France					1
		6	6	6	12	24

FIFA U-17 WOMEN'S WORLD CUP

Year	Host Country	Winners	Score	Runners-up	Final Venue
2008	New Zealand	Korea DPR	2-1	USA	North Harbour, Auckland
2010	Trinidad & Tobago	Korea Republic	3-3 5-4p	Japan	Hasely Crawford, Port of Spain
2012	Azerbaijan	France	1-1 7-6p	Korea DPR	Tofig Bahramov, Baku

FIFA U-17 WOMEN'S WORLD CUP MEDALS TABLE

	Country	G	S	B	F	SF
1	Korea DPR	1	1		2	3
2	France	1			1	1
	Korea Republic	1			1	1
4	Japan		1		1	1
	USA		1		1	1
6	Germany			1		2
7	Ghana			1		1
	Spain			1		1
9	England					1
		3	3	3	6	12

OTHER FIFA TOURNAMENTS

FIFA FUTSAL WORLD CUP

Year	Host Country	Winners	Score	Runners-up	Venue
1989	Netherlands	Brazil	2-1	Netherlands	Sportspaleis Ahoy, Rotterdam
1992	Hong Kong	Brazil	4-1	USA	Coliseum, Hong Kong
1996	Spain	Brazil	6-4	Spain	Palau Sant Jordi, Barcelona
2000	Guatemala	Spain	4-3	Brazil	Domo Polideportivo, Guatemala City
2004	Chinese Taipei	Spain	2-1	Italy	NTU, Taipei City
2008	Rio de Janeiro	Brazil	2-2 4-3p	Spain	Maracanazinho, Rio de Janeiro
2012	Thailand	Brazil	3-2	Spain	Huamark, Bangkok

FIFA BEACH SOCCER WORLD CUP

Year	Host Country	Winners	Score	Runners-up	Venue
2005	Brazil	France	3-3 1-0p	Portugal	Rio de Janeiro
2006	Brazil	Brazil	4-1	Uruguay	Rio de Janeiro
2007	Brazil	Brazil	8-2	Mexico	Rio de Janeiro
2008	France	Brazil	5-3	Italy	Marseille
2009	UAE	Brazil	10-5	Switzerland	Main Pitch, Dubai
2011	Italy	Russia	12-8	Brazil	Stadio del Mare, Ravenna

FIFA FUTSAL WORLD CUP MEDALS TABLE

	Country	G	S	B	F	SF
1	Brazil	5	1	1	6	7
2	Spain	2	3	1	5	6
3	Italy		1	2	1	3
4	USA		1	1	1	2
5	Netherlands		1		1	1
6	Russia			1		3
7	Portugal			1		1
8	Argentina					1
	Belgium					1
	Colombia					1
	Iran					1
	Ukraine					1
		7	7	7	14	28

FIFA BEACH SOCCER WORLD CUP MEDALS TABLE

	Country	G	S	B	F	SF
1	Brazil	4	1	1	5	6
2	France	1		1	1	3
3	Russia	1			1	1
4	Portugal		1	3	1	5
5	Uruguay		1	1	1	3
6	Italy		1		1	1
	Mexico		1		1	1
	Switzerland		1		1	1
9	El Salvador					1
	Japan			1		1
	Spain					1
		6	6	6	12	24

FIFA BALLON D'OR 2012

Argentina's Lionel Messi collected a record-breaking fourth consecutive title of best player in the world when he was awarded the **FIFA Ballon d'Or**, while US player Abby Wambach claimed her first **FIFA Women's World Player of the Year** award at the FIFA Ballon d'Or Gala held at the Zurich Kongresshaus in January 2013. Vicente del Bosque, the Spanish national team coach, and Sweden's new women's national team coach and former USA coach Pia Sundhage were the winners of the **FIFA World Coach of the Year awards** for men's and women's football, respectively. Aged 25, Messi concluded 2012 by scoring 91 goals. He also finished top scorer in the UEFA Champions League 2011-2012 season with 14 goals. Meanwhile, Vicente del Bosque added the European title to his 2010 FIFA World Cup crown when leading Spain to victory at EURO 2012. In women's football, 2012 was the US national team's year. Sundhage and Wambach led the US to its fourth Olympic gold medal in London after defeating the Japanese team in the final. The **FIFA Puskás Award** for the most beautiful goal of the year as voted for on FIFA.com, FIFA on YouTube and francefootball.fr by more than five million fans was also presented. This prize, created in 2009 in honour and in memory of Ferenc Puskás, the captain and star of the Hungarian national team during the 1950s, went to Slovakian striker Miroslav Stoch, who superbly hooked a shot into the top corner of the net on 3 March 2012 for his club Fenerbahçe in a Turkish Süper Lig match against Gençlerbirliği. Franz Beckenbauer received the **FIFA Presidential Award** from President Joseph S. Blatter in recognition of his extraordinary achievements and record of service to the world's favourite game. Beckenbauer excelled as a supremely elegant, world-class player, as a charismatic coach and manager on the touchline, and as the figurehead and chief organiser of the 2006 FIFA World Cup. The **FIFA Fair Play Award** was given to the Uzbekistan Football Federation (UFF) for showing that fair play and competition are not mutually exclusive but complement each another. The UFF were chosen ahead of Turkish club Eskisehirspor and the Guatemala Football Federation. Finally, FIFPro, the world players' union, invited 50,000 professional players from all over the world to select their best team of 2012 for the annual FIFA FIFPro World XI with the result that all eleven players chosen play their club football in Spain (see page 29 for the team).

FIFA BALLON D'OR 2012

FIFA BALLON D'OR 2012

	Player	Club	Nat	%
1	Lionel Messi	Barcelona	ARG	41.60
2	Cristiano Ronaldo	Real Madrid	POR	23.68
3	Andres Iniesta	Barcelona	ESP	10.91
4	Xavi	Barcelona	ESP	4.08
5	Radamel Falcao	Atlético Madrid	COL	3.67
6	Iker Casillas	Real Madrid	ESP	3.18
7	Andrea Pirlo	Juventus	ITA	2.66
8	Didier Drogba	Chelsea/Shanghai S	CIV	2.60
9	Robin van Persie	Arsenal/Man Utd	NED	1.45
10	Zlatan Ibrahimovic	Milan/PSG	SWE	1.24
11	Xabi Alonso	Real Madrid	ESP	1.09
12	Yaya Toure	Manchester City	CIV	0.76
13	Neymar	Santos	BRA	0.61
14	Mesut Ozil	Real Madrid	GER	0.41
15	Wayne Rooney	Manchester United	ENG	0.39
16	Gianluigi Buffon	Juventus	ITA	0.35
17	Sergio Aguero	Manchester City	ARG	0.30
18	Sergio Ramos	Real Madrid	ESP	0.22
19	Manuel Neuer	Bayern München	GER	0.21
20	Sergio Busquets	Barcelona	ESP	0.20
21	Gerard Pique	Barcelona	ESP	0.11
22	Karim Benzema	Real Madrid	FRA	0.11
23	Mario Balotelli	Manchester City	ITA	0.07

FIFA WOMEN'S WORLD PLAYER OF THE YEAR 2012

	Player	Club	Nat	%
1	Abby Wambach		USA	20.67
2	Marta	Tyresö FF	BRA	13.50
3	Alex Morgan	Seattle Sounders	USA	10.87
4	Homare Sawa	INAC Kobe Leonessa	JPN	10.85
5	Christine Sinclair		CAN	10.33
6	Carli Lloyd		USA	7.99
7	Camille Abily	Olympique Lyonnais	FRA	7.70
8	Aya Miyama	Yunogo Belle	JPN	7.51
9	Miho Fukumoto	Yunogo Belle	JPN	7.32
10	Megan Rapinoe	Seattle Sounders	USA	2.89

FIFA PUSKAS AWARD 2012

	Player	Club	Nat	%
1	Miroslav Stoch	Fenerbahçe v Gençerbirligi	SVK	78
2	Radamel Falcao	Atlético Madrid v Ath Bilbao	COL	15
3	Neymar	Santos v Internacional	BRA	7

FIFA FAIR PLAY AWARD 2012

1. Uzbekistan Football Federation
2. Eskisehirspor
2. Guatemala Football Federation

FIFA WORLD COACH OF THE YEAR FOR MEN'S FOOTBALL 2012

	Player	Club	Nat	%
1	Vicente Del Bosque	Spain	ESP	34.51
2	Jose Mourinho	Real Madrid	POR	20.49
3	Josep Guardiola	Barcelona	ESP	12.91
4	Roberto Di Matteo	Chelsea	ITA	12.02
5	Alex Ferguson	Manchester United	SCO	5.82
6	Jurgen Klopp	Borussia Dortmund	GER	4.78
7	Cesare Prandelli	Italy	ITA	3.34
8	Roberto Mancini	Manchester City	ITA	3.10
9	Joachim Low	Germany	GER	1.15
10	Jupp Heynckes	Bayern München	GER	1.00

FIFA WORLD COACH OF THE YEAR FOR WOMEN'S FOOTBALL 2012

	Player	Club	Nat	%
1	Pia Sundhage	USA	SWE	28.59
2	Norio Sasaki	Japan	JPN	23.83
3	Bruno Bini	France	FRA	9.02
4	Patrice Lair	Olympique Lyonnais	FRA	7.64
5	Silvia Neid	Germany	GER	6.48
6	John Herdman	Canada	ENG	6.31
7	Hiroshi Yoshida	Japan U-17 & U-20	JPN	5.75
8	Steve Swanson	USA U-20	USA	5.02
9	Maren Meinert	Germany U-20	GER	3.70
10	Hope Powell	England & GBR	ENG	3.29

1 – LIONEL MESSI

24-06-1987, Rosario, ARG (1.69m), Forward

	League				Cup		Europe		CWC		SC		USC		ARG		ARG in WCF		ARG in CA	
	PL	G	Div	Pos	PL	G	PL	G	PL	G	PL	G	PL	G	PL	G	PL	G	PL	G
03-04 Barcelona C	10	5	TD	9																
03-04 Barcelona B	5	0	SB	8																
04-05 Barcelona B	17	6	SB	11																
04-05 Barcelona	7	1	PD	1	1	0	r64		1	0	CL r16									
05-06 Barcelona	17	6	PD	1	2	1	QF		6	1	CL W						10	2	3	1 QF
06-07 Barcelona	26	14	PD	2	2	2	SF		5	1	CL r16		2 0 W		1 0 F		10	4	6	2 F
07-08 Barcelona	28	10	PD	3	3	0	SF		9	6	CL SF						10	3		
08-09 Barcelona	31	23	PD	1	8	6	W		12	9	CL W						9	3		
09-10 Barcelona	35	34	PD	1	3	1	r16		11	8	CL SF		2 2 W		1 2 W		1 0 W		11	1	5	0 QF
10-11 Barcelona	33	31	PD	1	7	7	F		13	12	CL W				2 3 W				11	4	4	0 QF
11-12 Barcelona	37	50	PD	2	7	3	W		11	14	CL SF		2 2 W		2 3 W		1 1 W		9	9		
	246	**180**		**5**	**33**	**20**	**2**		**68**	**51**	**3**		**4**	**4**	**2**		**7**	**8**	**4**	**3 1 2**	**70 26 8 1 0**		**10 2 0**

Other Honours: Olympic Gold 2008 • FIFA U-20 World Cup 2005 • FIFA Ballon D'Or 2009 2010 2011 2012 • FIFA/FIFPro World XI 2007 2008 2009 2010 2011 2012 • Argentina debut: 17-08-2005 v HUN • First Argentina goal: 1-03-2006 v CRO • Barcelona debut: 16-10-2004 v Espanyol • First Barcelona goal: 1-05-2005 v Albacete • (PD = Primera Division • SB = Segunda B • TD = Tercera Division in Spain)

2 – CRISTIANO RONALDO

5-02-1985 Funchal, POR (1.84m), Forward

	League				Cup		Europe		CWC		SC		USC		POR		POR in WCF		POR in ECF	
	PL	G	Div	Pos	PL	G	PL	G	PL	G	PL	G	PL	G	PL	G	PL	G	PL	G
02-03 Sporting CP	25	3	SL	3	3	2	QF		3	0	CL r1										
03-04 Man Utd	29	4	PL	3	5	2	W		5	0	CL r2								13	2	6	2 F
04-05 Man Utd	33	5	PL	3	7	4	F		8	0	CL r2								10	7		
05-06 Man Utd	33	9	PL	2	2	0	r16		8	1	CL r1								15	3	6	1 SF
06-07 Man Utd	34	17	PL	1	7	3	F		11	3	CL SF								8	5		
07-08 Man Utd	34	31	PL	1	3	3	QF		11	8	CL W				1 0 W				12	4	3	1 QF
08-09 Man Utd	33	18	PL	1	2	1	SF		12	4	CL F		2 1 W						7	1		
09-10 Real Madrid	29	26	PD	2					6	7	CL r2								11	1	4	1 r16
10-11 Real Madrid	34	40	PD	2	8	7	W		12	6	CL SF				2 1 F				5	3		
11-12 Real Madrid	38	46	PD	1	5	3	QF		10	10	CL SF								14	9	5	3 SF
	322	**199**		**4**	**42**	**25**	**2**		**86**	**39**	**1**		**2**	**1**	**1**		**3**	**1**	**1**	**0 0 0**	**95 35 10 2 0**		**14 6 0**

Other Honours: FIFA World Player of the Year 2008 • Ballon D'Or 2008 • FIFA/FIFPro World XI 2007 2008 2009 2010 2011 2012 • Portugal debut: 20-08-2003 v KAZ • First Portugal goal: 12-06-2004 v GRE • Sporting debut: 7-10-2002 v Moreiense • First Sporting goal: 7-10-2002 v Moreiense • Man Utd debut: 16-08-2003 v Bolton • First Man Utd goal: 1-11-2003 v Portsmouth • Real Madrid debut: 29-08-2009 v Deportivo • First Real Madrid goal: 29-08-2009 v Deportivo • Cristiano Ronaldo also played 12 games and scored 4 goals for Man Utd in the League Cup
(PL = Premier League in England • SL = Super Liga in Portugal • PD = Primera Division in Spain)

3 – ANDRES INIESTA

11-05-1984, Fuentealbilla, ESP (1.70m), Midfield

	League				Cup		Europe		CWC		SC		USC		ESP		ESP in WCF		ESP in ECF	
	PL	G	Div	Pos	PL	G	PL	G	PL	G	PL	G	PL	G	PL	G	PL	G	PL	G
00-01 Barcelona B	10	1	SB	9																
01-02 Barcelona B	30	2	SB	1																
02-03 Barcelona B	14	3	SB	2																
02-03 Barcelona	6	0	PD	6					3	0	CL QF										
03-04 Barcelona	11	1	PD	2	3	1	QF		3	0	UC r16										
04-05 Barcelona	37	2	PD	1	1	0	r64		8	0	CL r16										
05-06 Barcelona	33	0	PD	1	4	0	QF		11	1	CL W				1 0 W				4	0	1	0 r16
06-07 Barcelona	37	6	PD	2	6	1	SF		8	2	CL r16		2 0 F		2 0 W		1 0 F		9	2		
07-08 Barcelona	31	3	PD	3	7	0	SF		13	1	CL SF								16	2	6	0 W
08-09 Barcelona	26	4	PD	1	6	0	W		9	1	CL W								6	1		
09-10 Barcelona	29	1	PD	1	3	0	r16		9	0	CL SF		1 0 W						14	2	6	2 W
10-11 Barcelona	34	8	PD	1	5	0	F		10	1	CL W				1 0 W				9	1		
11-12 Barcelona	27	2	PD	2	6	2	W		8	3	CL SF		2 0 W		2 1 W		1 0 W		13	2		6	0 W
	325	**32**		**5**	**41**	**4**	**2**		**82**	**9**	**3**		**5**	**0**	**2**		**6**	**1**	**4**	**2 0 1**	**71 10 7 2 1**		**12 0 2**

Other Honours: UEFA U-17 2001 • UEFA U-19 2002 • FIFA/FIFPro World XI 2009 2010 2011 2012 • Spain debut: 27-05-2006 v RUS • First Spain goal: 7-02-2007 v ENG • Barcelona Debut: 13-11-2002 v Club Brugge • First Barcelona goal: 14/01/2004 v Levante

KEY CWC = FIFA Club World Cup • SC = Super Cup • USC = UEFA Super Cup • ARG/POR/ESP = national team statistics • WCF = FIFA World Cup finals • ECF = UEFA European Championship finals • PL = matches played (including substitute appearances) • G = goals scored • Div = division in which playing • Pos = league position • The numbers in the black boxes are the trophies won in each competition

FIFA BALLON D'OR 2012

FRANCE FOOTBALL BALLON D'OR

1956	Stanley Matthews	Blackpool	ENG
1957	Alfredo Di Stefano	Real Madrid	ESP
1958	Raymond Kopa	Real Madrid	FRA
1959	Alfredo Di Stefano	Real Madrid	ESP
1960	Luis Suarez	Barcelona	ESP
1961	Omar Sivori	Juventus	ITA
1962	Josef Masopust	Dukla Praha	CZE
1963	Lev Yashin	Dynamo Moskva	URS
1964	Denis Law	Manchester United	SCO
1965	Eusebio	Benfica	POR
1966	Bobby Charlton	Manchester United	ENG
1967	Florian Albert	Ferencvaros	HUN
1968	George Best	Manchester United	NIR
1969	Gianni Rivera	Milan	ITA
1970	Gerd Müller	Bayern München	FRG
1971	Johan Cruyff	Ajax	NED
1972	Franz Beckenbauer	Bayern München	FRG
1973	Johan Cruyff	Barcelona	NED
1974	Johan Cruyff	Barcelona	NED
1975	Oleg Blokhin	Dynamo Kyiv	URS
1976	Franz Beckenbauer	Bayern München	FRG
1977	Alan Simonsen	B. Mönchengladbach	DEN
1978	Kevin Keegan	Hamburger SV	ENG
1979	Kevin Keegan	Hamburger SV	ENG
1980	Karl-Heinz Rummenigge	Bayern München	FRG
1981	Karl-Heinz Rummenigge	Bayern München	FRG
1982	Paolo Rossi	Juventus	ITA
1983	Michel Platini	Juventus	FRA
1984	Michel Platini	Juventus	FRA
1985	Michel Platini	Juventus	FRA
1986	Igor Belanov	Dynamo Kyiv	URS
1987	Ruud Gullit	Milan	NED
1988	Marco van Basten	Milan	NED
1989	Marco van Basten	Milan	NED
1990	Lothar Matthaus	Internazionale	GER
1991	Jean-Pierre Papin	Olympique Marseille	FRA
1992	Marco van Basten	Milan	NED
1993	Roberto Baggio	Juventus	ITA
1994	Hristo Stoichkov	Barcelona	BUL
1995	George Weah	Milan	LBR
1996	Matthias Sammer	Borussia Dortmund	GER
1997	Ronaldo	Internazionale	BRA
1998	Zinedine Zidane	Juventus	FRA
1999	Rivaldo	Barcelona	BRA
2000	Luis Figo	Real Madrid	POR
2001	Michael Owen	Liverpool	ENG
2002	Ronaldo	Real Madrid	BRA
2003	Pavel Nedved	Juventus	CZE
2004	Andriy Shevchenko	Milan	UKR
2005	Ronaldinho	Barcelona	BRA
2006	Fabio Cannavaro	Real Madrid	ITA
2007	Kaka	Milan	BRA
2008	Cristiano Ronaldo	Manchester United	POR
2009	Lionel Messi	Barcelona	ARG

The France Football Ballon d'Or award merged with the FIFA World Player of the Year award in 2010 to form the FIFA Ballon d'Or. From 1956 to to 1994 it was available only to Europeans. From 1995 until 2006 it was opened up to include any player signed to a European club but for the final three years it was extended to players playing anywhere in the world.

FIFA WORLD PLAYER OF THE YEAR

1991	Lothar Matthaus	Internazionale	GER
1992	Marco van Basten *	Milan	NED
1993	Roberto Baggio *	Juventus	ITA
1994	Romario	Barcelona	BRA
1995	George Weah *	Milan	LBR
1996	Ronaldo	Barcelona	BRA
1997	Ronaldo *	Internazionale	BRA
1998	Zinedine Zidane *	Juventus	FRA
1999	Rivaldo *	Barcelona	BRA
2000	Zinedine Zidane	Juventus	FRA
2001	Luis Figo	Real Madrid	POR
2002	Ronaldo *	Real Madrid	BRA
2003	Zinedine Zidane	Real Madrid	FRA
2004	Ronaldinho	Barcelona	BRA
2005	Ronaldinho *	Barcelona	BRA
2006	Fabio Cannavaro *	Real Madrid	ITA
2007	Kaka *	Milan	BRA
2008	Cristiano Ronaldo *	Manchester United	POR
2009	Lionel Messi *	Barcelona	ARG

* Winner of both the FIFA and France Football awards

FIFA BALLON D'OR

2010	Lionel Messi	Barcelona	ARG
2011	Lionel Messi	Barcelona	ARG
2012	Lionel Messi	Barcelona	ARG

FIFA WOMEN'S WORLD PLAYER OF THE YEAR

2001	Mia Hamm	Washington Freedom	USA
2002	Mia Hamm	Washington Freedom	USA
2003	Birgit Prinz	1.FFC Frankfurt	GER
2004	Birgit Prinz	1.FFC Frankfurt	GER
2005	Birgit Prinz	1.FFC Frankfurt	GER
2006	Marta	Umeå IK	BRA
2007	Marta	Umeå IK	BRA
2008	Marta	Umeå IK	BRA
2009	Marta	Los Angeles Sol/Santos	BRA
2010	Marta	FC Gold Pride/Santos	BRA
2011	Homare Sawa	INAC Kobe Leonessa	JPN
2012	Abby Wambach		USA

FIFA WORLD COACH OF THE YEAR - MEN'S

2010	Jose Mourinho	Inter/Real Madrid	POR
2011	Pep Guardiola	Barcelona	ESP
2012	Vicente Del Bosque	Spain	ESP

FIFA WORLD COACH OF THE YEAR - WOMEN'S

2010	Silvia Neid	Germany	GER
2011	Norio Sasaki	Japan	JPN
2012	Pia Sundhage	USA	SWE

FIFA PUSKAS AWARD WINNERS

2009 Cristiano Ronaldo, **Manchester Utd** v FC Porto 15-04-2009
2010 Hamit Altintop, **Turkey** v Kazakhstan 3-09-2010
2011 Neymar, **Santos** v Flamengo, 28-07-2011
2012 Miroslav Stoch, **Fenerbahçe** v Gençlerbirligi, 3-03-2012

MEN'S OLYMPIC FOOTBALL TOURNAMENT LONDON 2012

MEN'S OLYMPIC FOOTBALL TOURNAMENT LONDON 2012

First round groups

Group A	Pts
Great Britain	7
Senegal	5
Uruguay	3
UAE	1

Group B	Pts
Mexico	7
Korea Republic	5
Gabon	2
Switzerland	1

Group C	Pts
Brazil	9
Egypt	4
Belarus	3
New Zealand	1

Group D	Pts
Japan	7
Honduras	5
Morocco	2
Spain	1

Quarter-finals

Mexico	4
Senegal	2

Egypt	0
Japan	3

Korea Republic	1	5p
Great Britain	1	4p

Honduras	2
Brazil	3

Semi-finals

Mexico	3
Japan	1

Korea Republic	0
Brazil	3

Final

Mexico	2
Brazil	1

Bronze Medal Play-off

Korea Republic	2
Japan	0

Top scorers: **6 - LEANDRO DAMIAO** BRA • **5** - Moussa **KONATE** SEN • **4** - Oribe **PERALTA**, MEX • **3** - Giovanni **DOS SANTOS** MEX; **NEYMAR** BRA; Mohamed Salah EGY; Jerry **BENGTSON** HON & Yuki **OTSU** JPN • **2** - Mohamed **ABOUTRIKA** EGY; **PARK** Chu Young KOR; **ISMAEIL MATAR** UAE; Daniel **STURRIDGE** GBR & Kensuke **NAGAI** JPN
FIFA Fair Play Award: Japan

Mexico's ambition to become a global football superpower took a significant step forward with a thrilling victory over Brazil in the final of the Men's Olympic Football Tournament at London 2012. The Brazilians were hoping to secure the only title never to have been won by the various men's teams over the years but were outdone by a Mexican team that took the lead after just 29 seconds through Oribe Peralta. Peralta scored a second near the end of the second half and although Hulk's injury-time goal pulled one back for Brazil, Oscar spurned the chance of an equaliser moment's later to give the gold medals to the Mexicans - their first ever medal in Olympic football. Brazil must now wait four more years until Rio de Janeiro 2016 for another chance to end their Olympic curse. The final at Wembley was watched by a crowd of 86,162, ensuring a new record aggregate attendance of 1,525,134, which surpassed the previous record set in Los Angeles back in 1984. In the bronze medal match in Cardiff, Korea Republic secured a first-ever medal in the football tournament after beating fierce rivals Japan 2-0. London 2012 witnessed a number of surprises, notably the elimination in the first round of the world and European champions Spain. The Spanish were knocked-out after losing to both Japan and Honduras while a fancied Uruguay team also fell at the first hurdle in a group won by a Great Britain team playing in the Olympics for the first time since 1960. Composed of only Welsh and English players after the refusal of the Scottish and Northern Ireland football communities to be involved, Great Britain won their first round group to set up a tie with the South Koreans in the quarter-finals. There they succumbed to a very English exit after losing the only penalty shoot-out of the tournament.

MEN'S OLYMPIC FOOTBALL TOURNAMENT LONDON 2012

	GROUP A	PL	W	D	L	F	A	PTS	SEN	URU	UAE
1	Great Britain	3	2	1	0	5	2	7	1-1	1-0	3-1
2	Senegal	3	1	2	0	4	2	5		2-0	1-1
3	Uruguay	3	1	0	2	2	4	3			2-1
4	UAE	3	0	1	2	3	6	1			

OLD TRAFFORD, MANCHESTER UNITED
26-07-2012, 17:00, Att: 51 745, Ref: Peter O'Leary NZL

UAE	1	Ismaeil Matar [23]
Uruguay	2	Ramirez [42], Lodeiro [56]

UNITED ARAB EMIRATES

ALI KHASEIF - ABDULAZIZ HUSSAIN, MOHAMED AHMAD•, Hamdan AL KAMALI, ABDELAZIZ SANQOUR - KHAMIS ESMAEEL - OMAR ABDULRAHMAN, AMER ABDULRAHMAN, RASHED EISA (AHMED ALI 73) - AHMED KHALIL, ISMAEIL MATAR(c) (Ismail AL HAMMADI 60). Tr: MAHDI ALI

URUGUAY

Martin CAMPANA - Ramon ARIAS, German ROLIN•, Sebastian COATES, Emiliano ALBIN - Matias AGUIRREGARAY (Nicolas LODEIRO 46), Maximiliano CALZADA (Diego RODRIGUEZ 70), Egidio AREVALO, Gaston RAMIREZ (Jonathan URRETAVISCAYA 81) - Edinson CAVANI, Luis SUAREZ(c). Tr: Oscar TABAREZ

OLD TRAFFORD, MANCHESTER UNITED
26-07-2012, 20:00, Att: 72 176, Ref: Ravshan Irmatov UZB

Great Britain	1	Bellamy [20]
Senegal	1	Konate [82]

GREAT BRITAIN

Jack BUTLAND - Neil TAYLOR, Micah RICHARDS, Steven CAULKER, Ryan BERTRAND - Tom CLEVERLEY, Danny ROSE, Joe ALLEN (Aaron RAMSEY 63) - Craig BELLAMY• (Jack CORK 80), Daniel STURRIDGE (Marvin SORDELL 46), Ryan GIGGS(c). Tr: Stuart PEARCE

SENEGAL

Ousmane MANE - Zargo TOURE, Abdoulaye BA, Papa GUEYE•, Saliou CISS - Sadio MANE•, Idrissa GUEYE (Cheikhou KOUYATE 42), Mohamed DIAME(c), Pape SOUARE• (Kalidou YERO 88) - Ibrahima BALDE (Magaye GUEYE 65), Moussa KONATE. Tr: Abdoukarime DIOUF

WEMBLEY STADIUM, LONDON
29-07-2012, 17:00, Att: 75 093, Ref: Felix Brych GER

Senegal	2	Konate 2 [10] [37]
Uruguay	0	

SENEGAL

Ousmane MANE - Zargo TOURE, Abdoulaye BA•, Papa GUEYE, Saliou CISS - Sadio MANE, Cheikhou KOUYATE•, Mohamed DIAME•(c), Pape SOUARE - Stephane BADJI• (Kara MBODJI 66) - Moussa KONATE (Kalidou YERO 83). Tr: Abdoukarime DIOUF

URUGUAY

Martin CAMPANA - Ramon ARIAS, German ROLIN, Sebastian COATES, Emiliano ALBIN• (Jonathan URRETAVISCAYA 72) - Nicolas LODEIRO (Tabare VIUDEZ 75), Maximiliano CALZADA (Abel HERNANDEZ 46), Egidio AREVALO, Gaston RAMIREZ• - Edinson CAVANI, Luis SUAREZ(c). Tr: Oscar TABAREZ

WEMBLEY STADIUM, LONDON
29-07-2012, 19:45, Att: 85 137, Ref: Roberto Garcia MEX

Great Britain	3	Giggs [16], Sinclair [73], Sturridge [76]
UAE	1	Rashed Eisa [60]

GREAT BRITAIN

Jack BUTLAND - Neil TAYLOR, Micah RICHARDS, Steven CAULKER, James TOMKINS - Tom CLEVERLEY, Aaron RAMSEY, Joe ALLEN - Craig BELLAMY (Jack CORK 83), Marvin SORDELL (Daniel STURRIDGE 46), Ryan GIGGS(c) (Scott SINCLAIR 72). Tr: Stuart PEARCE

UNITED ARAB EMIRATES

ALI KHASEIF - ABDULAZIZ HUSSAIN (SAAD SUROUR 51), MOHAMED AHMAD, Hamdan AL KAMALI, ABDELAZIZ SANQOUR - KHAMIS ESMAEEL• (HABIB FARDAN 79) - OMAR ABDULRAHMAN•, AMER ABDULRAHMAN, RASHED EISA - AHMED KHALIL, ISMAEIL MATAR(c) (AHMED ALI 72). Tr: MAHDI ALI

CITY OF COVENTRY STADIUM, COVENTRY
1-08-2012, 19:45, Att: 28 652, Ref: Svein Moen NOR

Senegal	1	Konate [49]
UAE	1	Ismaeil Matar [21]

SENEGAL

Ousmane MANE - Zargo TOURE, Papa GUEYE, Kara MBODJI - Sadio MANE (Kalidou YERO 83), Cheikhou KOUYATE, Mohamed DIAME(c), Magaye GUEYE (Ibrahima BALDE 46), Pape SOUARE - Stephane BADJI - Moussa KONATE (Ibrahima SECK 91+). Tr: Abdoukarime DIOUF

UNITED ARAB EMIRATES

KHALID EISA - MOHAMED FAWZI, MOHAMED AHMAD, Hamdan AL KAMALI, ABDELAZIZ SANQOUR - KHAMIS ESMAEEL - OMAR ABDULRAHMAN•, AMER ABDULRAHMAN, RASHED EISA (ALI MABKHOOT 65) - AHMED KHALIL (Ismail AL HAMMADI 60), ISMAEIL MATAR(c) (HABIB FARDAN 89). Tr: MAHDI ALI

MILLENNIUM STADIUM, CARDIFF
1-08-2012, 19:45, Att: 70 438, Ref: Yuichi Nishimura JPN

Great Britain	1	Sturridge [45]
Uruguay	0	

GREAT BRITAIN

Jack BUTLAND - Neil TAYLOR•, Micah RICHARDS, Steven CAULKER, Ryan BERTRAND - Tom CLEVERLEY, Aaron RAMSEY•, Joe ALLEN - Craig BELLAMY•(c) (Danny ROSE 78), Daniel STURRIDGE (Craig DAWSON 96+), Scott SINCLAIR (Jack CORK 91+). Tr: Stuart PEARCE

URUGUAY

Martin CAMPANA - Ramon ARIAS•, German ROLIN, Sebastian COATES•, Matias AGUIRREGARAY - Tabare VIUDEZ (Nicolas LODEIRO• 58), Diego RODRIGUEZ, Egidio AREVALO, Gaston RAMIREZ• - Edinson CAVANI, Luis SUAREZ•(c). Tr: Oscar TABAREZ

	GROUP B	PL	W	D	L	F	A	PTS	KOR	GAB	SUI
1	Mexico	3	2	1	0	3	0	7	0-0	2-0	1-0
2	Korea Republic	3	1	2	0	2	1	5		0-0	2-1
3	Gabon	3	0	2	1	1	3	2			1-1
4	Switzerland	3	0	1	2	2	4	1			

ST JAMES' PARK, NEWCASTLE
26-07-2012, 14:30, Att: 15 748, Ref: Slim Jedidi TUN

| Mexico | 0 |
| Korea Republic | 0 |

MEXICO
Jose **CORONA** (c) - Nestor **VIDRIO**, Hiram **MIER**, Diego **REYES**, Darvin **CHAVEZ** - Miguel **PONCE**, Carlos **SALCIDO** - Marco **FABIAN** (Raul **JIMENEZ** 85) - Hector **HERRERA**•, (Jorge **ENRIQUEZ** 71), Oribe **PERALTA** (Giovani **DOS SANTOS** 66), Javier **AQUINO**. Tr: Luis Fernando **TENA**

KOREA REPUBLIC
JUNG Sung Ryong - **KIM** Chang Soo, **HWANG** Seok Ho, **KIM** Young Gwon, **YUN** Suk Young - **NAM** Tae Hee (**JI** Dong Won 87), **KOO** Ja Cheol (c), **KI** Sung Yueng, **KIM** Bo Kyung - **PARK** Chu Young (**BAEK** Sung Dong 76), **PARK** Jong Woo. Tr: **HONG** Myung Bo

---

ST JAMES' PARK, NEWCASTLE
26-07-2012, 17:15, Att: 15 748, Ref: Wilmar Roldan COL

| Gabon | 1 | Aubameyang [45] |
| Switzerland | 1 | Mehmedi [5p] |

GABON
Didier **OVONO** (c) - Franck **ENGONGA**, Mabikou **BOUSSOUGHOU**, Henry **NDONG**, Muller **DINDA** - Merlin **TANDJIGORA**• - Alexander **NDOUMBOU**, Levy **MADINDA**, Jerry **OBIANG** - Allen **NONO**• (Axel **MEYE** 74), Pierre **AUBAMEYANG**. Tr: Claude **MBOUROUNOT**

SWITZERLAND
Diego **BENAGLIO** (c) - Michel **MORGANELLA**, Fabian **SCHAER**, Timm **KLOSE**•, Ricardo **RODRIGUEZ** - Xavier **HOCHSTRASSER**, Fabian **FREI** - Steven **ZUBER** (Pajtim **KASAMI** 68), Oliver **BUFF**••♦78, Innocent **EMEGHARA** (Amir **ABRASHI** 84) - Admir **MEHMEDI**. Tr: Pierluigi **TAMI**

CITY OF COVENTRY STADIUM, COVENTRY
29-07-2012, 14:30, Att: 28 171, Ref: Benjamin Williams AUS

| Mexico | 2 | Dos Santos 2 [63 92+p] |
| Gabon | 0 | |

MEXICO
Jose **CORONA** (c) - Nestor **VIDRIO**, Hiram **MIER**, Diego **REYES**•, Darvin **CHAVEZ** - Miguel **PONCE** (Giovani **DOS SANTOS** 46), Carlos **SALCIDO** - Marco **FABIAN** (Javier **CORTES** 76) - Hector **HERRERA** (Jorge **ENRIQUEZ** 48), Oribe **PERALTA**, Javier **AQUINO**. Tr: Luis Fernando **TENA**

GABON
Didier **OVONO** (c) - Franck **ENGONGA**, Mabikou **BOUSSOUGHOU**, Henry **NDONG**••♦91+, Muller **DINDA**• (Stevy **NZAMBE** 85) - Merlin **TANDJIGORA** - Alexander **NDOUMBOU** (Allen **NONO** 70), Levy **MADINDA**, Jerry **OBIANG** (Samson **MBINGUI** 83) - Pierre **AUBAMEYANG**, Axel **MEYE**. Tr: Claude **MBOUROUNOT**

CITY OF COVENTRY STADIUM, COVENTRY
29-07-2012, 17:15, Att: 30 114, Ref: Raul Orosco BOL

| Korea Republic | 2 | Park Chu Young [57], Kim Bo Kyung [64] |
| Switzerland | 1 | Emeghara [60] |

KOREA REPUBLIC
JUNG Sung Ryong - **KIM** Chang Soo, **HWANG** Seok Ho, **KIM** Young Gwon, **YUN** Suk Young - **NAM** Tae Hee (**BAEK** Sung Dong 61), **KOO** Ja Cheol (c), **KI** Sung Yueng, **KIM** Bo Kyung - **PARK** Chu Young• (**JI** Dong Won 73), **PARK** Jong Woo•. Tr: **HONG** Myung Bo

SWITZERLAND
Diego **BENAGLIO** (c) - Michel **MORGANELLA**•, Fabian **SCHAER**, Timm **KLOSE**, Ricardo **RODRIGUEZ** - Amir **ABRASHI**, Fabian **FREI** - Steven **ZUBER** (Josip **DRMIC**• 71), Pajtim **KASAMI**• (Alain **WISS** 85), Innocent **EMEGHARA**• - Admir **MEHMEDI**. Tr: Pierluigi **TAMI**

MILLENNIUM STADIUM, CARDIFF
1-08-2012, 17:00, Att: 50 000, Ref: Ravshan Irmatov UZB

| Mexico | 1 | Peralta [69] |
| Switzerland | 0 | |

MEXICO
Jose **CORONA** (c) - Nestor **VIDRIO** (Israel **JIMENEZ** 46), Hiram **MIER**, Diego **REYES**, Darvin **CHAVEZ** - Jorge **ENRIQUEZ**, Carlos **SALCIDO** - Marco **FABIAN** (Miguel **PONCE** 79) - Giovani **DOS SANTOS** (Raul **JIMENEZ** 84), Oribe **PERALTA**, Javier **AQUINO**. Tr: Luis Fernando **TENA**

SWITZERLAND
Diego **BENAGLIO** (c) - Fabio **DAPRELA**, Francois **AFFOLTER**, Timm **KLOSE**, Ricardo **RODRIGUEZ** - Amir **ABRASHI** (Alain **WISS** 76), Fabian **FREI** - Steven **ZUBER** (Josip **DRMIC** 61), Pajtim **KASAMI** (Xavier **HOCHSTRASSER** 85), Innocent **EMEGHARA** - Admir **MEHMEDI**. Tr: Pierluigi **TAMI**

WEMBLEY STADIUM, LONDON
1-08-2012, 17:00, Att: 76 927, Ref: Pavel Kralovec CZE

| Korea Republic | 0 |
| Gabon | 0 |

KOREA REPUBLIC
JUNG Sung Ryong• - **KIM** Chang Soo, **HWANG** Seok Ho, **KIM** Young Gwon, **YUN** Suk Young - **BAEK** Sung Dong, **KOO** Ja Cheol (c), **KI** Sung Yueng, **KIM** Bo Kyung (**JI** Dong Won 61) - **PARK** Chu Young (**KIM** Hyun Sung 80), **PARK** Jong Woo (**NAM** Tae Hee 46). Tr: **HONG** Myung Bo

GABON
Didier **OVONO** (c) - Franck **ENGONGA**, Mabikou **BOUSSOUGHOU**, Emmanuel **NDONG**, Muller **DINDA** - Merlin **TANDJIGORA** (Alexander **NDOUMBOU**• 10) - Stevy **NZAMBE**, Levy **MADINDA** (Samson **MBINGUI** 66), Jerry **OBIANG** - Pierre **AUBAMEYANG**, Axel **MEYE** (Allen **NONO** 76). Tr: Claude **MBOUROUNOT**

MEN'S OLYMPIC FOOTBALL TOURNAMENT LONDON 2012

	GROUP C	PL	W	D	L	F	A	PTS	EGY	BLR	NZL
1	Brazil	3	3	0	0	9	3	9	3-2	3-1	3-0
2	Egypt	3	1	1	1	6	5	4		3-1	1-1
3	Belarus	3	1	0	2	3	6	3			1-0
4	New Zealand	3	0	1	2	1	5	1			

CITY OF COVENTRY STADIUM, COVENTRY
26-07-2012, 19:45, Att: 14 457, Ref: Bakary Gassama GAM

Belarus	1	Baga [45]
New Zealand	0	

BELARUS
Aleksandr GUTOR - Aleksei KOZLOV, Sergei POLITEVICH●, Igor KUZMENOK, Denis POLYAKOV - Mikhail GORDEICHUK, Dmitry BAGA, Stanislav DRAGUN(c), Artem SOLOVEI (Ilya ALEKSIEVICH 54) - Renan BARDINI BRESSAN (Andrei VORONKOV 81) - Sergei KORNILENKO (Egor ZUBOVICH 91+). Tr: Georgy KONDRATYEV

NEW ZEALAND
Michael O'KEEFFE - Adam THOMAS (Adam McGEORGE 77), Ryan NELSEN(c), Tommy SMITH●, Ian HOGG - Tim PAYNE - Marco ROJAS (Cameron HOWIESON 73), Michael McGLINCHEY, Kosta BARBAROUSES● - Chris WOOD, Shane SMELTZ. Tr: Neil EMBLEN (ENG)

MILLENNIUM STADIUM, CARDIFF
26-07-2012, 19:45, Att: 26 812, Ref: Gianluca ITA

Brazil	3	Rafael [16], Leandro Damiao [26], Neymar [30]
Egypt	2	Aboutrika [52], Mohamed Salah [76]

BRAZIL
NETO - RAFAEL, THIAGO SILVA(c), JUAN JESUS, MARCELO - ROMULO, OSCAR, SANDRO (DANILO 78) - HULK● (GANSO 72), LEANDRO DAMIAO (ALEXANDRE PATO 77), NEYMAR. Tr: Mano MENEZES

EGYPT
Ahmed ELSHENAWI - AHMED FATHI, Mahmoud ALAA ELDIN●, Ahmed HEGAZI, Eslam RAMADAN● - SALEH GOMAA● (Shehab AHMED 79), HOSSAM HASSAN, Mohamed EL NENY (Ahmed MAGDY 89) - Marwan MOHSEN (MOHAMED SALAH 46), Mohamed ABOUTRIKA(c), EMAD METEAB. Tr: Hany RAMZY

OLD TRAFFORD, MANCHESTER
29-07-2012, 15:00, Att: 66 212, Ref: Yuichi Nishimura JPN

Brazil	3	Alexandre Pato [15], Neymar [65], Oscar [93+]
Belarus	1	Bardini Bressan [8]

BRAZIL
NETO - RAFAEL, THIAGO SILVA(c), JUAN JESUS, MARCELO - ROMULO, OSCAR, SANDRO (GANSO 64) - ALEXANDRE PATO (LUCAS 85), HULK (DANILO 86), NEYMAR. Tr: Mano MENEZES

BELARUS
Aleksandr GUTOR - Aleksei KOZLOV● (Aleksei GAVRILOVICH 80), Sergei POLITEVICH, Igor KUZMENOK, Denis POLYAKOV - Mikhail GORDEICHUK, Dmitry BAGA, Stanislav DRAGUN●(c), Ilya ALEKSIEVICH (Andrei VORONKOV 70) - Renan BARDINI BRESSAN - Sergei KORNILENKO (Egor ZUBOVICH 78). Tr: Georgy KONDRATYEV

OLD TRAFFORD, MANCHESTER
29-07-2012, 12:00, Att: 50 050, Ref: Mark Clattenburg ENG

Egypt	1	Mohamed Salah [40]
New Zealand	1	Wood [17]

EGYPT
Ahmed ELSHENAWI - AHMED FATHI, Mahmoud ALAA ELDIN●, Ahmed HEGAZI, Eslam RAMADAN - SALEH GOMAA (Marwan MOHSEN 88), HOSSAM HASSAN, Mohamed EL NENY (Ahmed MAGDY 68) - MOHAMED SALAH, Mohamed ABOUTRIKA(c) (Shehab AHMED 88), EMAD METEAB. Tr: Hany RAMZY

NEW ZEALAND
Michael O'KEEFFE - Adam THOMAS (Alex FENERIDIS 89), Ryan NELSEN(c), Tommy SMITH, Ian HOGG (James MUSA 63) - Tim PAYNE - Marco ROJAS (Cameron HOWIESON 84), Michael McGLINCHEY, Kosta BARBAROUSES - Chris WOOD, Shane SMELTZ●. Tr: Neil EMBLEN ENG

ST JAMES' PARK, NEWCASTLE
1-08-2012, 14:30, Att: 25 201, Ref: Bakary Gassama GAM

Brazil	3	Danilo [23], Leandro Damiao [29], Sandro [52]
New Zealand	0	

BRAZIL
GABRIEL - RAFAEL, THIAGO SILVA(c), JUAN JESUS, MARCELO - DANILO, SANDRO (ROMULO 82), ALEX SANDRO●●◆76 - LUCAS, LEANDRO DAMIAO (OSCAR 80), NEYMAR (ALEXANDRE PATO 76). Tr: Mano MENEZES

NEW ZEALAND
Michael O'KEEFFE - Adam THOMAS (Cameron HOWIESON 46), Ryan NELSEN(c), Tommy SMITH, Ian HOGG● - Tim PAYNE - Marco ROJAS (Dakota LUCAS 82), Michael McGLINCHEY, Kosta BARBAROUSES (Tim MYERS● 46), Chris WOOD, Shane SMELTZ. Tr: Neil EMBLEN ENG

HAMPDEN PARK, GLASGOW
1-08-2012, 14:30, Att: 8732, Ref: Roberto Garcia MEX

Egypt	3	Mohamed Salah [56], Mohsen [73], Aboutrika [79]
Belarus	1	Voronkov [87]

EGYPT
Ahmed ELSHENAWI - AHMED FATHI (OMAR GABER 69), Saadeldin SAAD, Ahmed HEGAZI, Eslam RAMADAN - MOHAMED SALAH, HOSSAM HASSAN, Mohamed EL NENY - Shehab AHMED (Marwan MOHSEN 46), Mohamed ABOUTRIKA(c), EMAD METEAB (SALEH GOMAA 77). Tr: Hany RAMZY

BELARUS
Aleksandr GUTOR - Aleksei KOZLOV (Andrei VORONKOV 69), Sergei POLITEVICH, Igor KUZMENOK, Denis POLYAKOV - Mikhail GORDEICHUK (Artem SOLOVEI 60), Dmitry BAGA, Stanislav DRAGUN(c), Ilya ALEKSIEVICH - Renan BARDINI BRESSAN (Maksim SKAVYSH 75) - Sergei KORNILENKO●. Tr: Georgy KONDRATYEV

	GROUP D	PL	W	D	L	F	A	PTS		HON	MAR	ESP
1	Japan	3	2	1	0	2	0	7		0-0	1-0	1-0
2	Honduras	3	1	2	0	3	2	5			2-2	1-0
3	Morocco	3	0	2	1	2	3	2				0-0
4	Spain	3	0	1	2	0	2	1				

HAMPDEN PARK, GLASGOW
26-07-2012, 14:45, Att: 37 726, Ref: Mark Geiger USA

Spain	0	
Japan	1	Otsu 34

SPAIN
David DE GEA - Martin MONTOYA, Alvaro DOMINGUEZ•, Inigo MARTINEZ♦41, Jordi ALBA• - ADRIAN LOPEZ (Ander HERRERA 56), KOKE (Cristian TELLO 81), Javier MARTINEZ(c), Juan MATA - RODRIGO - ISCO (Oriol ROMEU 63). Tr: Luis MILLA

JAPAN
Shuichi GONDA - Hiroki SAKAI (Gotoku SAKAI 74), Daisuke SUZUKI, Maya YOSHIDA(c), Yuhei TOKUNAGA - Hotaru YAMAGUCHI, Takahiro OHGIHARA (Kazuya YAMAMURA 86) - Hiroshi KIYOTAKE, Keigo HIGASHI, Yuki OTSU (Manabu SAITO• 46) - Kensuke NAGAI, Tr: Takashi SEKIZUKA

HAMPDEN PARK, GLASGOW
26-07-2012, 12:00, Att: 23 421, Ref: Pavel Kralovec CZE

Honduras	2	Bengtson 2 56 65p
Morocco	2	Barrada 39, Labyad 67

HONDURAS
Jose MENDOZA - Alfredo MEJIA, Jose VELASQUEZ•, Johnny LEVERON (c), Maynor FIGUEROA - Andy NAJAR, Roger ESPINOZA•, Arnold PERALTA•, Mario MARTINEZ (Orlin PERALTA 88) - Alexander LOPEZ (Eddie HERNANDEZ 57) - Jerry BENGTSON (Antony LOZANO 79). Tr: Luis SUAREZ COL

MOROCCO
Mohamed AMSIF - Yassine JEBBOUR, Mohamed ABARHOUN, Abdelhamid EL KAOUTARI, Zakarya BERGDICH♦72 - Soufiane BIDAOUI• (Abdelatif NOUSSIR 75), Houssine KHARJA•, Driss FETTOUHI(c), Zakaria LABYAD - Noureddine AMRABAT (Omar EL KADDOURI 90), Abdelaziz BARRADA (Imad NAJAH 89). Tr: Pim VERBEEK NED

ST JAMES' PARK, NEWCASTLE
29-07-2012, 19:45, Att: 26 523, Ref: Juan Soto VEN

Spain	0	
Honduras	1	Bengtson 7

SPAIN
David DE GEA - Martin MONTOYA•, Alvaro DOMINGUEZ, Alberto BOTIA•, Jordi ALBA - ADRIAN LOPEZ, KOKE (Ander HERRERA 46), Javier MARTINEZ•(c) (Cristian TELLO 83), Iker MUNIAIN•, Juan MATA• - ISCO (RODRIGO 66). Tr: Luis MILLA

HONDURAS
Jose MENDOZA• - Arnold PERALTA•, Jose VELASQUEZ, Johnny LEVERON•(c), Maynor FIGUEROA - Wilmer CRISANTO, Luis GARRIDO•, Roger ESPINOZA• (Orlin PERALTA 72), Mario MARTINEZ - Andy NAJAR (Alfredo MEJIA• 57) - Jerry BENGTSON (Antony LOZANO 81). Tr: Luis SUAREZ COL

ST JAMES' PARK, NEWCASTLE
29-07-2012, 17:00, Att: 24 936, Ref: Svein Moen NOR

Japan	1	Nagai 84
Morocco	0	

JAPAN
Shuichi GONDA - Gotoku SAKAI, Daisuke SUZUKI, Maya YOSHIDA(c), Yuhei TOKUNAGA - Hotaru YAMAGUCHI, Takahiro OHGIHARA - Hiroshi KIYOTAKE (Kenyu SUGIMOTO 90), Keigo HIGASHI, Yuki OTSU (Manabu SAITO 78) - Kensuke NAGAI. Tr: Takashi SEKIZUKA

MOROCCO
Mohamed AMSIF - Yassine JEBBOUR, Mohamed ABARHOUN, Abdelhamid EL KAOUTARI, Abdelatif NOUSSIR• - Soufiane BIDAOUI (Omar EL KADDOURI 74), Houssine KHARJA, Driss FETTOUHI•(c) (Soufian EL HASSNAOUI 88), Zakaria LABYAD - Noureddine AMRABAT (Imad NAJAH 72), Abdelaziz BARRADA•. Tr: Pim VERBEEK NED

CITY OF COVENTRY STADIUM, COVENTRY
1-08-2012, 17:00, Att: 25 862, Ref: Slim Jedidi TUN

Japan	0
Honduras	0

JAPAN
Shuichi GONDA - Gotoku SAKAI, Daisuke SUZUKI, Maya YOSHIDA(c), Kazuya YAMAMURA, Hotaru YAMAGUCHI, Taisuke MURAMATSU, Takashi USAMI, Yuki OTSU (Keigo HIGASHI 87) - Kenyu SUGIMOTO (Hiroshi KIYOTAKE 67), Manabu SAITO (Kensuke NAGAI 81). Tr: Takashi SEKIZUKA

HONDURAS
Jose MENDOZA - Alfredo MEJIA, Jose VELASQUEZ, Johnny LEVERON (c), Maynor FIGUEROA - Wilmer CRISANTO•, Luis GARRIDO, Mario MARTINEZ, Andy NAJAR• (Alexander LOPEZ 60) - Antony LOZANO (Orlin PERALTA 77) - Jerry BENGTSON, Tr: Luis SUAREZ COL

OLD TRAFFORD, MANCHESTER
1-08-2012, 17:00, Att: 35 973, Ref: Benjamin Williams AUS

Spain	0
Morocco	0

SPAIN
David DE GEA - Cesar AZPILICUETA, Alberto BOTIA, Inigo MARTINEZ•, Jordi ALBA - ADRIAN LOPEZ, Iker MUNIAIN (KOKE 66), Javier MARTINEZ(c) (Ander HERRERA 46), Oriol ROMEU, Juan MATA• - ISCO (Cristian TELLO 56). Tr: Luis MILLA

MOROCCO
Mohamed AMSIF - Yassine JEBBOUR, Mohamed ABARHOUN, Zouhair FEDDAL•, Abdelatif NOUSSIR - Soufiane BIDAOUI (Soufian EL HASSNAOUI 70), Houssine KHARJA, Driss FETTOUHI(c), Zakaria LABYAD - Noureddine AMRABAT, Abdelaziz BARRADA. Tr: Pim VERBEEK NED

MEN'S OLYMPIC FOOTBALL TOURNAMENT LONDON 2012   37

QUARTER-FINALS

WEMBLEY STADIUM, LONDON		
4-08-2012, 14:30, Att: 81 855, Ref: Mark Clattenburg ENG		
Mexico	4	Enriquez [10], Aquino [62], Dos Santos [98], Herrera [109]
Senegal	2	Konate [69], Balde [76]

MEXICO

Jose **CORONA**(c) - Israel **JIMENEZ**•, Hiram **MIER**, Diego **REYES**, Darvin **CHAVEZ** - Jorge **ENRIQUEZ**, Carlos **SALCIDO** - Marco **FABIAN** (Miguel **PONCE** 100) - Giovani **DOS SANTOS**, Oribe **PERALTA** (Raul **JIMENEZ** 107), Javier **AQUINO** (Hector **HERRERA**• 75). Tr: Luis Fernando **TENA**

SENEGAL

Ousmane **MANE** - Zargo **TOURE**•, Abdoulaye **BA**•, Papa **GUEYE**, Saliou **CISS** (Magaye **GUEYE** 69) - Sadio **MANE**, Cheikhou **KOUYATE**, Mohamed **DIAME**(c) (Kara **MBODJI** 91+), Pape **SOUARE**• - Kalidou **YERO**• (Ibrahima **BALDE** 60), Moussa **KONATE**. Tr: Abdoukarime **DIOUF**

OLD TRAFFORD, MANCHESTER		
4-08-2012, 12:00, Att: 70 772, Ref: Mark Geiger USA		
Japan	3	Nagai [14], Yoshida [78], Otsu [83]
Egypt	0	

JAPAN

Shuichi **GONDA** - Hiroki **SAKAI**, Daisuke **SUZUKI**, Maya **YOSHIDA**(c), Yuhei **TOKUNAGA**• - Hotaru **YAMAGUCHI**, Takahiro **OHGIHARA** - Hiroshi **KIYOTAKE** (Takashi **USAMI** 84), Keigo **HIGASHI** (Gotoku **SAKAI** 72), Yuki **OTSU** - Kensuke **NAGAI** (Manabu **SAITO** 20). Tr: Takashi **SEKIZUKA**

EGYPT

Ahmed **ELSHENAWI** - **AHMED FATHI**, Saadeldin **SAAD**♦[41], Ahmed **HEGAZI**, Eslam **RAMADAN**, **MOHAMED SALAH** (**OMAR GABER**• 58), **HOSSAM HASSAN**, Mohamed **EL NENY**, Shehab **AHMED** (Mahmoud **ALAA ELDIN**• 46), Mohamed **ABOUTRIKA**(c), **EMAD METEAB** (Marwan **MOHSEN** 74), Tr: Hany **RAMZY**

MILLENNIUM STADIUM, CARDIFF		
4-08-2012, 19:30, Att: 70 171, Ref: Wilmar Roldan COL		
Great Britain	1 4p	Ramsey [36p]
Korea Republic	1 5p	Ji Dong Won [29]

GREAT BRITAIN

Jack **BUTLAND** - Neil **TAYLOR**, Micah **RICHARDS** (Craig **DAWSON** 60), Steven **CAULKER**, Ryan **BERTRAND** - Tom **CLEVERLEY**, Aaron **RAMSEY**, Joe **ALLEN**• - Craig **BELLAMY**(c) (Ryan **GIGGS** 85), Daniel **STURRIDGE**•, Scott **SINCLAIR** (Danny **ROSE** 106). Tr: Stuart **PEARCE**

KOREA REPUBLIC

JUNG Sung Ryong (**LEE** Bum Young 62) - **KIM** Chang Soo (**OH** Jae Suk 7), **HWANG** Seok Ho, **KIM** Young Gwon, **YUN** Suk Young - **NAM** Tae Hee, **KOO** Ja Cheol(c), **KI** Sung Yueng, **PARK** Jong Woo - **PARK** Chu Young, **JI** Dong Won (**BAEK** Sung Dong 104). Tr: Tr: **HONG** Myung Bo

PENALTIES (KOREA WON 5-4)

Ramsey ✓ • Koo Ja Cheol ✓ • Cleverley ✓ • Baek Sung Dong ✓
Dawson ✓ • Hwang Seok Ho ✓ • Park Jong Woo ✓ • Sturridge ✘ [1]
Ki Sung Yeung ✓ • (1 = saved)

ST JAMES' PARK, NEWCASTLE		
4-08-2012, 17:00, Att: 41 166, Ref: Felix Brych GER		
Brazil	3	Leandro Damiao 2 [38 60], Neymar [51p]
Honduras	2	Martinez [12], Espinoza [48]

BRAZIL

GABRIEL - **RAFAEL**, **THIAGO SILVA**(c), **JUAN JESUS**, **MARCELO**• - **ROMULO**•, **OSCAR**, **SANDRO**• (**DANILO** 42) - **HULK** (**LUCAS** 67), **LEANDRO DAMIAO**• (**ALEXANDRE PATO** 89), **NEYMAR**. Tr: Mano **MENEZES**

HONDURAS

Jose **MENDOZA** - Arnold **PERALTA**•, Jose **VELASQUEZ**•, Johnny **LEVERON**(c), Maynor **FIGUEROA**• - Wilmer **CRISANTO**••♦33, Luis **GARRIDO** (Alexander **LOPEZ** 73), Roger **ESPINOZA**••♦90, Mario **MARTINEZ** - Orlin **PERALTA** (Alfredo **MEJIA** 59) - Jerry **BENGTSON** (Antony **LOZANO** 87). Tr: Luis **SUAREZ** COL

SEMI-FINALS

WEMBLEY STADIUM, LONDON		
7-08-2012, 17:00, Att: 82 372, Ref: Gianluca Rocchi ITA		
Mexico	3	Fabian [31], Peralta [65], Cortes [93+]
Japan	1	Otsu [12]

MEXICO

Jose **CORONA**(c) - Israel **JIMENEZ**, Hiram **MIER**, Diego **REYES**, Darvin **CHAVEZ** - Jorge **ENRIQUEZ**, Carlos **SALCIDO** - Marco **FABIAN**• - Giovani **DOS SANTOS** (Raul **JIMENEZ** 46), Oribe **PERALTA**, Javier **AQUINO** (Javier **CORTES** 90). Tr: Luis Fernando **TENA**

JAPAN

Shuichi **GONDA** - Hiroki **SAKAI**•, Daisuke **SUZUKI**, Maya **YOSHIDA**(c), Yuhei **TOKUNAGA** - Hotaru **YAMAGUCHI**, Takahiro **OHGIHARA** (Manabu **SAITO** 83) - Hiroshi **KIYOTAKE** (Takashi **USAMI** 77), Keigo **HIGASHI** (Kenyu **SUGIMOTO** 71), Yuki **OTSU** - Kensuke **NAGAI**, Tr: Takashi **SEKIZUKA**

OLD TRAFFORD, MANCHESTER		
7-08-2012, 19:45, Att: 69 389, Ref: Pavel Kralovec CZE		
Korea Republic	0	
Brazil	3	Romulo [38], Leandro Damiao 2 [57 64]

KOREA REPUBLIC

LEE Bum Young - **OH** Jae Suk, **HWANG** Seok Ho, **KIM** Young Gwon, **YUN** Suk Young - **NAM** Tae Hee, **KOO** Ja Cheol(c) (**JUNG** Woo Young 59), **KI** Sung Yueng, **KIM** Bo Kyung - **KIM** Hyun Sung (**PARK** Chu Young 71), **JI** Dong Won• (**BAEK** Sung Dong 77). Tr: **HONG** Myung Bo

BRAZIL

GABRIEL - **RAFAEL**, **THIAGO SILVA**(c), **JUAN JESUS** (**BRUNO UVINI** 83), **MARCELO** (**HULK** 76) - **ROMULO** - **OSCAR**, **SANDRO**, **ALEX SANDRO** - **LEANDRO DAMIAO** (**ALEXANDRE PATO** 78), **NEYMAR**. Tr: Mano **MENEZES**

BRONZE MEDAL PLAY-OFF

MILLENNIUM STADIUM, CARDIFF
10-08-2012, 19:45, Att: 56 393, Ref: Ravshan Irmatov UZB
Korea Republic 2 Park Chu Young 38, Chu Ja Cheol 57
Japan 0
KOREA REPUBLIC
JUNG Sung Ryong - **OH** Jae Suk●, **HWANG** Seok Ho, **KIM** Young Gwon, **YUN** Suk Young - **PARK** Jong Woo, **KOO** Ja Cheol●(c) (**KIM** Kee Hee 90), **KI** Sung Yueng●, **KIM** Bo Kyung● - **PARK** Chu Young (**KIM** Hyun Sung 86), **JI** Dong Won (**NAM** Tae Hee 69). Tr: **HONG** Myung Bo
JAPAN
Shuichi **GONDA** - Hiroki **SAKAI**, Daisuke **SUZUKI**, Maya **YOSHIDA**(c), Yuhei **TOKUNAGA** - Hotaru **YAMAGUCHI**, Takahiro **OHGIHARA**● (Kazuya **YAMAMURA** 59) - Hiroshi **KIYOTAKE**, Keigo **HIGASHI** (Kenyu **SUGIMOTO**● 62), Yuki **OTSU**● - Kensuke **NAGAI** (Takashi **USAMI** 71). Tr: Takashi **SEKIZUKA**

FINAL

MEN'S OLYMPIC FOOTBALL TOURNAMENT FINAL WEMBLEY STADIUM, LONDON
Saturday, 11-08-2012, 19:30, Att: 86 162, Ref: Mark Clattenburg ENG Assistants: Stephen Child ENG & Simon Beck ENG
MEXICO 2 1 **BRAZIL**
Oribe Peralta 2 1 75 Hulk 91+

MEXICO
Green shirts, green shorts, green socks

Tr: Luis Fernando Tena
Jose **Corona**(c)
Israel **Jimenez** 58 — Hiram **Mier** — Diego **Reyes** 46 — Darvin **Chavez** 81
Nestor **Vidrio** 89
Jorge **Enriquez** — Carlos **Salcido**
Marco **Fabian**
Hector **Herrera** — Oribe **Peralta** 86 / Raul **Jimenez** — Javier **Aquino** 57 / Miguel **Ponce**

Leandro Damiao 91+
Neymar — Oscar
Alex Sandro 32 / Hulk — Sandro 71 / Alexandre Pato — Romulo
Marcelo 42 — Juan Jesus — Thiago Silva(c) — Rafael Lucas 85
Tr: Mano Menezes
Gabriel

Yellow shirts, blue shorts, white socks
BRAZIL

MATCH STATS		
Mexico		Brazil
10	Shots	17
4	Shots on Goal	8
16	Fouls Committed	13
2	Corner Kicks	7
3	Caught Offside	1
40	Possession (%)	60

WOMEN'S OLYMPIC FOOTBALL TOURNAMENT LONDON 2012

WOMEN'S OLYMPIC FOOTBALL TOURNAMENT LONDON 2012

First round groups		Quarter-finals		Semi-finals		Final	
Group E	Pts						
Great Britain	9						
Brazil	6	USA	2				
New Zealand	3	New Zealand	0				
Cameroon	0						
				USA	4		
				Canada	3		
		Great Britain	0				
Group F	Pts	Canada	2				
Sweden	5						
Japan	5					USA	2
Canada	4					Japan	1
South Africa	1						
		France	2				
		Sweden	1				
				France	1		
Group G	Pts			Japan	2		
USA	9						
France	6	Brazil	0			3rd Place Play-off	
Korea DPR	3	Japan	2			Canada	1
Colombia	0					France	0

Top scorers: **6** - Christine **SINCLAIR** CAN • **5** - Abby **WAMBACH** USA • **4** - Melissa **TANCREDI** CAN & Carli **LLOYD** USA • **3** - Alex **MORGAN** USA; Megan **RAPINOE** USA, Stephanie **HOUGHTON** GBR & Yuki **OGIME** JPN • **2** - Elodie **THOMIS** FRA; **CRISTIANE** BRA; **KIM** Song Hui PRK; Nilla **FISCHER** SWE; Lotta **SCHELIN** SWE; **MARTA** BRA; Laura **GEORGES** FRA; Marie-Laure **DELIE** FRA & Wendie **RENARD** FRA
FIFA Fair Play Award: USA

USA won their third consecutive gold medal at London 2012 - their fourth out of a possible five at Women's Olympic Football Tournaments - to cement their status as the undisputed queens of Olympic football. Coach Pia Sundhage retained the core of the squad that took gold in Beijing four years ago, but also added new faces from the group that performed so well at the FIFA Women's World Cup Germany 2011™. Among them was Alex Morgan, long used as an impact substitute but now an integral part of the USA front line. The Stars and Stripes showed an ability to dig deep and salvage results from difficult games, particularly in their group opener against France and their semi-final with Canada. USA's gold-winning campaign ended with the sweet taste of revenge and a 2-1 victory over Japan, their conquerors in the final of Germany 2011. The Japanese, for their part, grew in stature as the tournament progressed, and saved one of their best performances for the gold medal match. An Olympic record 80,203 spectators were at Wembley for the grand finale of the women's competition, and they were treated to a thrilling spectacle. Homare Sawa and Co were not as dazzling at London 2012 as they were at Germany 2011, but their incisive counter-attacks and the predatory finishing of forward Yuki Ogimi were enough to see them progress to the final. Despite the disappointing end to their campaign, Japan appeared more than satisfied with the silver medal, which represents their best finish at an Olympic Women's Football Tournament. Canada were one of the biggest surprise packages at London 2012. A year on from their first-round exit at Germany 2011, they clinched the bronze medal to cap a year of remarkable progress. They beat France 1-0 with Diana Matheson's winning goal coming two minutes into injury-time.

PART ONE – FIFA AND WORLD FOOTBALL

	GROUP E	PL	W	D	L	F	A	PTS	BRA	NZL	CMR
1	Great Britain	3	3	0	0	5	0	9	1-0	1-0	3-0
2	Brazil	3	2	0	1	6	1	6		1-0	5-0
3	New Zealand	3	1	0	2	3	3	3			3-1
4	Cameroon	3	0	0	3	1	11	0			

MILLENNIUM STADIUM, CARDIFF
25-07-2012, 16:00, Att: 24,445, Ref: Kari Seitz USA

Great Britain	1	Houghton 64
New Zealand	0	

GREAT BRITAIN
Karen BARDSLEY - Alex SCOTT, Ifeoma DIEKE, Casey STONEY (c), Stephanie HOUGHTON - Jill SCOTT, Anita ASANTE• - Karen CARNEY (Fara WILLIAMS 89), Kim LITTLE (Ellen WHITE 46), Eniola ALUKO - Kelly SMITH (Rachel YANKEY 68). Tr: Hope POWELL

NEW ZEALAND
Jenny BINDON - Ria PERCIVAL, Rebecca SMITH (c), Abby ERCEG, Ali RILEY - Hayley MOORWOOD (Betsy HASSETT 59), Katie HOYLE, Amber HEARN, Kirsty YALLOP (Annalie LONGO 74) - Hannah WILKINSON•, Sarah GREGORIUS. Tr: Tony READINGS ENG

MILLENNIUM STADIUM, CARDIFF
25-07-2012, 18:45, Att: 30,847, Ref: Jenny Palmqvist SWE

Cameroon	0	
Brazil	5	Francielle 7, Renata Costa 10, Marta 2 73 88p Cristiane 80

CAMEROON
Annette NGO NDOM - Claudine MEFFOMETOU, Christine MANIE•, Augustine EJANGUE, Bebey BEYENE - Raissa FEUDJIO (Francine ZOUGA 64) - Jeannette YANGO•, Francoise BELLA (c) - Madeleine NGONO MANI, Gabrielle ONGUENE, Ajara NCHOUT (Gaelle ENGANAMOUIT 71). Tr: Ngachu ENOW

BRAZIL
ANDREIA - BRUNA, ERIKA, RENATA COSTA - MAURINE, ESTER, THAIS GUEDES (CRISTIANE 46), FRANCIELLE (DAIANE 92+), FORMIGA• (GRAZIELLE 81) - FABIANA, MARTA (c). Tr: Jorge BARCELLOS

MILLENNIUM STADIUM, CARDIFF
28-07-2012, 14:30, Att: 30,103, Ref: Bibiana Steinhaus GER

New Zealand	0	
Brazil	1	Cristiane 86

NEW ZEALAND
Jenny BINDON - Ria PERCIVAL, Rebecca SMITH (c), Abby ERCEG, Ali RILEY - Hayley MOORWOOD (Kirsty YALLOP 77), Katie HOYLE, Amber HEARN, Betsy HASSETT (Annalie LONGO 87) - Hannah WILKINSON (Rosie WHITE 81), Sarah GREGORIUS. Tr: Tony READINGS ENG

BRAZIL
ANDREIA - BRUNA, ERIKA, RENATA COSTA - MAURINE, ESTER, FRANCIELLE (THAIS GUEDES 58), FABIANA (DAIANE 88) - FORMIGA, CRISTIANE, MARTA (c). Tr: Jorge BARCELLOS

MILLENNIUM STADIUM, CARDIFF
28-07-2012, 17:15, Att: 31,141, Ref: Hong Eun Ah KOR

Great Britain	3	Stoney 18, Jill Scott 23, Houghton 82
Cameroon	0	

GREAT BRITAIN
Karen BARDSLEY - Alex SCOTT, Ifeoma DIEKE (Sophie BRADLEY 68), Casey STONEY (c), Stephanie HOUGHTON - Jill SCOTT, Anita ASANTE (Fara WILLIAMS 60) - Karen CARNEY, Kim LITTLE, Eniola ALUKO - Kelly SMITH (Rachel YANKEY 46). Tr: Hope POWELL

CAMEROON
Annette NGO NDOM - Claudine MEFFOMETOU, Christine MANIE•, Augustine EJANGUE, Bebey BEYENE (Bibi MEDOUA• 33) - Francine ZOUGA - Jeannette YANGO (Ajara NCHOUT 62), Francoise BELLA (c) - Madeleine NGONO MANI (Gaelle ENGANAMOUIT 79), Gabrielle ONGUENE, Adrienne IVEN. Tr: Ngachu ENOW

CITY OF COVENTRY STADIUM, COVENTRY
31-07-2012, 19:45, Att: 11,415, Ref: Christina Pedersen NOR

New Zealand	3	Smith 43, Sonkeng OG 49, Gregorius 62
Cameroon	1	Onguene 75

NEW ZEALAND
Jenny BINDON - Ria PERCIVAL, Rebecca SMITH (c), Abby ERCEG, Ali RILEY - Annalie LONGO (Kirsty YALLOP 82), Katie HOYLE, Amber HEARN, Betsy HASSETT - Rosie WHITE, Sarah GREGORIUS (Hayley MOORWOOD 65). Tr: Tony READINGS ENG

CAMEROON
Annette NGO NDOM - Ysis SONKENG, Bibi MEDOUA•, Augustine EJANGUE• - Francine ZOUGA (Gaelle ENGANAMOUIT 78) - Yvonne LEUKO, Raissa FEUDJIO, Francoise BELLA (c) (Jeannette YANGO• 59) - Adrienne IVEN, Gabrielle ONGUENE, Ajara NCHOUT (Madeleine NGONO MANI 46), Tr: Ngachu ENOW

WEMBLEY STADIUM, LONDON
31-07-2012, 19:45, Att: 70,584, Ref: Carol Anne Chenard CAN

Great Britain	1	Houghton 2
Brazil	0	

GREAT BRITAIN
Karen BARDSLEY - Alex SCOTT, Sophie BRADLEY, Casey STONEY (c), Stephanie HOUGHTON - Jill SCOTT, Anita ASANTE - Karen CARNEY (Fara WILLIAMS 84), Kim LITTLE, Eniola ALUKO (Rachel YANKEY 63) - Kelly SMITH (Ellen WHITE 84). Tr: Hope POWELL

BRAZIL
ANDREIA - BRUNA• (ALINE• 46), ERIKA, RENATA COSTA - MAURINE (DAIANE 46), ESTER (GRAZIELLE 72), THAIS GUEDES, ROSANA, FRANCIELLE• - CRISTIANE, MARTA (c). Tr: Jorge BARCELLOS

WOMEN'S OLYMPIC FOOTBALL TOURNAMENT LONDON 2012

	GROUP F	PL	W	D	L	F	A	PTS	JPN	CAN	RSA
1	Sweden	3	1	2	0	6	3	5	0-0	2-2	4-1
2	Japan	3	1	2	0	2	1	5		2-1	0-0
3	Canada	3	1	1	1	6	4	4			3-0
4	South Africa	3	0	1	2	1	7	1			

CITY OF COVENTRY STADIUM, COVENTRY
25-07-2012, 17:00, Att: 14 119, Ref: Kirsi Heikkinen FIN

Japan	2	Kawasumi [33], Miyama [44]
Canada	1	Tancredi [55]

JAPAN
Miho **FUKUMOTO** - Yukari **KINGA**, Azusa **IWASHIMIZU**, Saki **KUMAGAI**, Aya **SAMESHIMA** - Aya **MIYAMA**(c), Mizuho **SAKAGUCHI**, Homare **SAWA** - Nahomi **KAWASUMI**, Yuki **OGIMI**, Shinobu **OHNO** (Kozue **ANDO** 65). Tr: Norio **SASAKI**

CANADA
Erin **McLEOD** - Rhian **WILKINSON** (Robyn **GAYLE** 71), Carmelina **MOSCATO**, Lauren **SESSELMANN** (Chelsea **STEWART** 71), Candace **CHAPMAN** - Kaylyn **KYLE** (Kelly **PARKER** 76), Diana **MATHESON**, Desiree **SCOTT**, Sophie **SCHMIDT** - Christine **SINCLAIR**(c) - Melissa **TANCREDI**. Tr: John **HERDMAN** ENG

CITY OF COVENTRY STADIUM, COVENTRY
25-07-2012, 19:45, Att: 18 290, Ref: Jesica di Iorio ARG

Sweden	4	Fischer [7], Dahlkvist [20], Schelin 2 [21 63]
South Africa	1	Modise [60]

SWEDEN
Hedvig **LINDAHL** - Lina **NILSSON**, Emma **BERGLUND**, Linda **SEMBRANT**, Sara **THUNEBRO** - Sofia **JAKOBSSON**, Lisa **DAHLKVIST**, Caroline **SEGER**, Marie **HAMMARSTROM** (Antonia **GORANSSON** 84), Nilla **FISCHER**(c) - (Johanna **ALMGREN** 61) - Lotta **SCHELIN** (Kosovare **ASLLANI** 73). Tr: Thomas **DENNERBY**

SOUTH AFRICA
Roxanne **BARKER** - Refiloe **JANE**, Amanda **SISTER**, Janine **VAN WYK**, Nothando **VILAKAZI**• - Mpumi **NYANDENI**, Kylie **LOUW**, Amanda **DLAMINI**(c), Portia **MODISE** - Noko **MATLOU** (Marry **NTSWENG** 62), Andisiwe **MGCOYI** (Sanah **MOLLO** 80). Tr: Mkhonzana **MKHONZA**

CITY OF COVENTRY STADIUM, COVENTRY
28-07-2012, 12:00, Att: 14 160, Ref: Quetzalli Alvarado MEX

Japan	0	
Sweden	0	

JAPAN
Miho **FUKUMOTO** - Yukari **KINGA**, Azusa **IWASHIMIZU**, Saki **KUMAGAI**, Aya **SAMESHIMA** - Aya **MIYAMA**(c), Mizuho **SAKAGUCHI**, Homare **SAWA** (Asuna **TANAKA** 59), Nahomi **KAWASUMI** - Yuki **OGIMI** (Kozue **ANDO** 92+), Shinobu **OHNO** (Mana **IWABUCHI** 81). Tr: Norio **SASAKI**

SWEDEN
Hedvig **LINDAHL** - Annica **SVENSSON**, Emma **BERGLUND**, Linda **SEMBRANT**, Sara **THUNEBRO** •(c) - Sofia **JAKOBSSON** (Lina **NILSSON** 78), Lisa **DAHLKVIST** (Antonia **GORANSSON** 87), Caroline **SEGER**, Marie **HAMMARSTROM** - Johanna **ALMGREN** (Kosovare **ASLLANI**) - Lotta **SCHELIN**. Tr: Thomas **DENNERBY**

CITY OF COVENTRY STADIUM, COVENTRY
28-07-2012, 14:45, Att: 14 753, Ref: Christina Pedersen NOR

Canada	3	Tancredi [7], Sinclair 2 [58 86]
South Africa	0	

CANADA
Karina **LeBLANC** - Rhian **WILKINSON**, Carmelina **MOSCATO**, Lauren **SESSELMANN**, Robyn **GAYLE** (Chelsea **STEWART** 68) - Kaylyn **KYLE** (Jonelle **FILIGNO** 74), Diana **MATHESON**, Desiree **SCOTT**, Sophie **SCHMIDT** - Christine **SINCLAIR**(c) - Melissa **TANCREDI** (Brittany **TIMKO** 87). Tr: John **HERDMAN** ENG

SOUTH AFRICA
Thokozile **MNDAWENI** - Refiloe **JANE**, Amanda **SISTER**, Janine **VAN WYK**, Zamandosi **CELE** - Mpumi **NYANDENI**, Kylie **LOUW**, Amanda **DLAMINI**(c), Portia **MODISE**• (Noko **MATLOU** 83), Gabisile **HLUMBANE** - Andisiwe **MGCOYI** (Sanah **MOLLO** 69). Tr: Mkhonzana **MKHONZA**

MILLENNIUM STADIUM, CARDIFF
31-07-2012, 14:30, Att: 24 202, Ref: Thalia Mitsi GRE

Japan	0	
South Africa	0	

JAPAN
Ayumi **KAIHORI** - Yukari **KINGA**, Azusa **IWASHIMIZU**, Saki **KUMAGAI**, Kyoko **YANO** - Aya **MIYAMA**(c) (Mizuho **SAKAGUCHI** 77), Karina **MARUYAMA** (Yuki **OGIMI** 93+), Asuna **TANAKA** - Megumi **TAKASE**, Kozue **ANDO**, Mana **IWABUCHI** (Nahomi **KAWASUMI** 58). Tr: Norio **SASAKI**

SOUTH AFRICA
Thokozile **MNDAWENI** - Refiloe **JANE**, Janine **VAN WYK**, Zamandosi **CELE**, Nothando **VILAKAZI** - Mpumi **NYANDENI**, Kylie **LOUW** (Marry **NTSWENG** 90), Amanda **DLAMINI**(c), Gabisile **HLUMBANE** (Amanda **SISTER** 61), Portia **MODISE** - Noko **MATLOU** (Sanah **MOLLO** 61). Tr: Mkhonzana **MKHONZA**

ST JAMES' PARK, NEWCASTLE
31-07-2012, 14:30, Att: 12 719, Ref: Hong Eun Ah KOR

Canada	2	Tancredi 2 [43 84]
Sweden	2	Hammarstrom [14], Jakobsson [16]

CANADA
Erin **McLEOD** - Rhian **WILKINSON**, Carmelina **MOSCATO**, Lauren **SESSELMANN**, Marie-Eve **NAULT** (Chelsea **STEWART** 86) - Diana **MATHESON**, Desiree **SCOTT**, Sophie **SCHMIDT** (Kelly **PARKER** 88), Christine **SINCLAIR**(c) - Jonelle **FILIGNO** (Kaylyn **KYLE** 75), Melissa **TANCREDI**. Tr: John **HERDMAN** ENG

SWEDEN
Hedvig **LINDAHL** - Lina **NILSSON**, Emma **BERGLUND**, Linda **SEMBRANT**, Sara **THUNEBRO** - Sofia **JAKOBSSON**, Nilla **FISCHER**(c) (Lisa **DAHLKVIST** 53), Marie **HAMMARSTROM**, Caroline **SEGER**, Kosovare **ASLLANI** (Johanna **ALMGREN** 63) - Lotta **SCHELIN**. Tr: Thomas **DENNERBY**

PART ONE – FIFA AND WORLD FOOTBALL

	GROUP G	PL	W	D	L	F	A	PTS		FRA	PRK	COL
1	USA	3	3	0	0	8	2	9		4-2	1-0	3-0
2	France	3	2	0	1	8	4	6			5-0	1-0
3	Korea DPR	3	1	0	2	2	6	3				2-0
4	Colombia	3	0	0	3	0	6	0				

HAMPDEN PARK, GLASGOW
25-07-2012, 17:00, Att: 18 090, Ref: Sachiko Yamagishi JPN

USA	4	Wambach 19, Morgan 2 32 66, Lloyd 56
France	2	Thiney 12, Delie 14

USA
Hope SOLO - Amy LE PEILBET, Christie RAMPONE (c), Rachel BUEHLER, Kelley O'HARA - Megan RAPINOE (Sydney LEROUX 84), Shannon BOXX (Carli LLOYD 17), Tobin HEATH - Lauren CHENEY, Alex MORGAN (Amy RODRIGUEZ 74), Abby WAMBACH. Tr: Pia SUNDHAGE SWE

FRANCE
Sarah BOUHADDI - Corine FRANCO, Ophelie MEILLEROUX (c) (Eugenie LE SOMMER 46), Wendie RENARD, Sonia BOMPASTOR - Elise BUSSAGLIA, Camille ABILY (Sandrine SOUBEYRAND 71) - Elodie THOMIS, Louisa NECIB (Laura GEORGES 46), Gaetane THINEY - Marie-Laure DELIE. Tr: Bruno BINI

HAMPDEN PARK, GLASGOW
25-07-2012, 19:45, Att: 18 900, Ref: Carol Anne Chenard CAN

Colombia	0	
Korea DPR	2	Kim Song Hui 2 39 85

COLOMBIA
Sandra SEPULVEDA - Natalia ARIZA (Ingrid VIDAL 46), Kelis PEDUZINE, Natalia GAITAN (c), Yulieht DOMINGUEZ - Liana SALAZAR (Tatiana ARIZA 77), Catalina USME, Daniela MONTOYA (Nataly ARIAS 46), Carmen RODALLEGA - Orianica VELASQUEZ, Lady ANDRADE. Tr: Ricardo ROZO

KOREA DPR
JO Yun Mi - KIM Nam Hui, KIM Myong Gum, RO Chol Ok, YUN Song Mi, CHOE Un Ju (CHOE Yong Sim 88), RI Ye Gyong, JON Myong Hwa, YUN Hyon Hi•, KIM Chung Sim (c) (KIM Un Hyang 40), KIM Song Hui (CHOE Mi Gyong 92+). Tr: SIN Ui Gun

HAMPDEN PARK, GLASGOW
28-07-2012, 17:00, Att: 11 313, Ref: Thalia Mitsi GRE

USA	3	Rapinoe 33, Wambach 74, Lloyd 77
Colombia	0	

USA
Hope SOLO - Heather MITTS, Christie RAMPONE (c), Rachel BUEHLER, Kelley O'HARA - Megan RAPINOE (Amy RODRIGUEZ 81), Carli LLOYD, Heather O'REILLY (Tobin HEATH 67) - Lauren CHENEY, Alex MORGAN, Abby WAMBACH (Sydney LEROUX 78). Tr: Pia SUNDHAGE SWE

COLOMBIA
Sandra SEPULVEDA - Tatiana ARIZA (Ana MONTOYA 71), Kelis PEDUZINE, Natalia GAITAN (c), Yulieht DOMINGUEZ - Nataly ARIAS, Catalina USME, Ingrid VIDAL (Melissa ORTIZ 86), Carmen RODALLEGA (Liana SALAZAR 71) - Orianica VELASQUEZ, Lady ANDRADE. Tr: Ricardo ROZO

HAMPDEN PARK, GLASGOW
28-07-2012, 19:45, Att: 11 743, Ref: Therese Neguel CMR

France	5	Georges 45, Thomis 70, Delie 71, Renard 81, Catala 87
Korea DPR	0	

FRANCE
Sarah BOUHADDI - Corine FRANCO, Laura GEORGES, Wendie RENARD, Sonia BOMPASTOR• - Elise BUSSAGLIA, Sandrine SOUBEYRAND (c) (Elodie THOMIS 62) - Eugenie LE SOMMER•, (Camille ABILY 62), Louisa NECIB, Gaetane THINEY - Marie-Laure DELIE (Camille CATALA 80). Tr: Bruno BINI

KOREA DPR
JO Yun Mi - KIM Nam Hui, KIM Myong Gum (c), YUN Song Mi, CHOE Un Ju (KIM Song Hui 51), RI Ye Gyong, JON Myong Hwa (O Hui Sun 72), CHOE Mi Gyong, YUN Hyon Hi, KIM Un Hyang (KIM Chung Sim 59), CHOE Yong Sim. Tr: SIN Ui Gun

OLD TRAFFORD, MANCHESTER
31-07-2012, 17:15, Att: 29 522, Ref: Jenny Palmqvist SWE

USA	1	Wambach 25
Korea DPR	0	

USA
Hope SOLO - Amy LE PEILBET, Christie RAMPONE (c), Rachel BUEHLER, (Becky SAUERBRUNN 75), Kelley O'HARA - Megan RAPINOE (Tobin HEATH 46), Carli LLOYD, Heather O'REILLY - Lauren CHENEY• (Amy RODRIGUEZ 84), Alex MORGAN, Abby WAMBACH. Tr: Pia SUNDHAGE SWE

KOREA DPR
O Chang Ran - KIM Nam Hui, KIM Myong Gum, CHOE Un Ju, RI Ye Gyong•, JON Myong Hwa, YUN Hyon Hi (KIM Su Gyong 80), KIM Chung Sim (c) (KIM Un Hyang 80), PONG Son Hwa, KIM Song Hui• (CHOE Mi Gyong 63••♦81), CHOE Yong Sim. Tr: SIN Ui Gun

ST JAMES' PARK, NEWCASTLE
31-07-2012, 17:15, Att: 13 184, Ref: Quetzalli Alvarado MEX

France	1	Thomis 5
Colombia	0	

FRANCE
Sarah BOUHADDI - Corine FRANCO (Sabrina VIGUIER 84), Wendie RENARD, Laura GEORGES, Sonia BOMPASTOR (Laure BOULLEAU 46) - Sandrine SOUBEYRAND (Elise BUSSAGLIA 55), Camille ABILY - Elodie THOMIS, Louisa NECIB•, Gaetane THINEY - Marie-Laure DELIE. Tr: Bruno BINI

COLOMBIA
Sandra SEPULVEDA - Natalia ARIZA, Kelis PEDUZINE, Natalia GAITAN (c), Yulieht DOMINGUEZ• - Nataly ARIAS, Catalina USME (Yoreli RINCON 48), Daniela MONTOYA•, Carmen RODALLEGA - Orianica VELASQUEZ (Melissa ORTIZ 68), Ingrid VIDAL (Tatiana ARIZA 81). Tr: Ricardo ROZO

QUARTER-FINALS

ST JAMES' PARK, NEWCASTLE
3-08-2012, 14:30, Att: 10 441, Ref: Jesica di Iorio ARG

USA	2	Wambach [27], Leroux [87]
New Zealand	0	

USA
Hope SOLO - Amy LE PEILBET, Christie RAMPONE (c), Rachel BUEHLER, Kelley O'HARA - Megan RAPINOE (Heather O'REILLY 71), Carli LLOYD● , Tobin HEATH - Lauren CHENEY (Amy RODRIGUEZ 91), Alex MORGAN (Sydney LEROUX 81), Abby WAMBACH● . Tr: Pia SUNDHAGE SWE

NEW ZEALAND
Jenny BINDON - Ria PERCIVAL, Rebecca SMITH (c), Abby ERCEG, Ali RILEY - Katie HOYLE (Annalie LONGO 95), Amber HEARN, Betsy HASSETT, Kirsty YALLOP (Hayley MOORWOOD 57) - Hannah WILKINSON (Rosie WHITE 77), Sarah GREGORIUS. Tr: Tony READINGS ENG

CITY OF COVENTRY STADIUM, COVENTRY
3-08-2012, 19:30, Att: 28 828, Ref: Sachiko Yamagishi JPN

Great Britain	0	
Canada	2	Filigno [12], Sinclair [26]

GREAT BRITAIN
Karen BARDSLEY - Alex SCOTT, Sophie BRADLEY (Rachel YANKEY 84), Casey STONEY (c), Stephanie HOUGHTON - Jill SCOTT, Anita ASANTE - Karen CARNEY, Kim LITTLE (Rachel WILLIAMS 82), Eniola ALUKO - Ellen WHITE (Fara WILLIAMS 63). Tr: Hope POWELL

CANADA
Erin McLEOD - Rhian WILKINSON, Carmelina MOSCATO, Lauren SESSELMANN, Marie-Eve NAULT● - Diana MATHESON, Desiree SCOTT, Sophie SCHMIDT (Kelly PARKER 78) - Christine SINCLAIR (c) (Brittany TIMKO 88) - Jonelle FILIGNO (Kaylyn KYLE 61), Melissa TANCREDI. Tr: John HERDMAN ENG

HAMPDEN PARK, GLASGOW
3-08-2012, 12:00, Att: 12 869, Ref: Kari Seitz USA

Sweden	1	Fischer [18]
France	2	Georges [29], Renard [39]

SWEDEN
Hedvig LINDAHL - Annica SVENSSON● , Madeleine EDLUND 82), Emma BERGLUND, Linda SEMBRANT, Sara THUNEBRO - Sofia JAKOBSSON (Kosovare ASLLANI 58), Lisa DAHLKVIST, Nilla FISCHER (c), Caroline SEGER, Marie HAMMARSTROM (Antonia GORANSSON 70) - Lotta SCHELIN. Tr: Thomas DENNERBY

FRANCE
Sarah BOUHADDI - Corine FRANCO● , Laura GEORGES, Wendie RENARD, Sonia BOMPASTOR - Elise BUSSAGLIA, Sandrine SOUBEYRAND (c) (Camille ABILY 71) - Elodie THOMIS (Eugenie LE SOMMER 75), Louisa NECIB, Gaetane THINEY (Camille CATALA 88) - Marie-Laure DELIE. Tr: Bruno BINI

MILLENNIUM STADIUM, CARDIFF
3-08-2012, 17:00, Att: 28 528, Ref: Kirsi Heikkinen FIN

Brazil	0	
Japan	2	Ogimi [27], Ohno [73]

BRAZIL
ANDREIA - BRUNA● , ERIKA, RENATA COSTA (GRAZIELE 85) - FABIANA, FORMIGA, THAIS GUEDES, ROSANA (ESTER 80), FRANCIELLE - CRISTIANE, MARTA ●(c). Tr: Jorge BARCELLOS

JAPAN
Miho FUKUMOTO - Yukari KINGA, Azusa IWASHIMIZU, Saki KUMAGAI, Aya SAMESHIMA - Aya MIYAMA (c), Mizuho SAKAGUCHI● , Homare SAWA, Nahomi KAWASUMI - Yuki OGIMI (Megumi TAKASE 89), Shinobu OHNO (Kozue ANDO 85). Tr: Norio SASAKI

SEMI-FINALS

OLD TRAFFORD, MANCHESTER
6-08-2012, 19:45, Att: 26 630, Christina Pedersen NOR

Canada	3	Sinclair 3 [22 67 73]
USA	4	Rapinoe 2 [54 70], Wambach [80p], Morgan [123+]

CANADA
Erin McLEOD - Rhian WILKINSON, Carmelina MOSCATO, Lauren SESSELMANN, Marie-Eve NAULT (Chelsea STEWART 101) - Diana MATHESON, Desiree SCOTT, Sophie SCHMIDT - Christine SINCLAIR (c) - Jonelle FILIGNO (Kaylyn KYLE 67), Melissa TANCREDI. Tr: John HERDMAN ENG

USA
Hope SOLO - Amy LE PEILBET (Sydney LEROUX 76), Christie RAMPONE (c), Rachel BUEHLER (Becky SAUERBRUNN 110), Kelley O'HARA - Megan RAPINOE, Carli LLOYD, Tobin HEATH - Lauren CHENEY (Heather O'REILLY 101), Alex MORGAN, Abby WAMBACH. Tr: Pia SUNDHAGE

WEMBLEY STADIUM, LONDON
6-08-2012, 17:00, Att: 61 482, Ref: Quetzalli Alvarado MEX

France	1	Le Sommer [76]
Japan	2	Ogimi [32], Sakaguchi [49]

FRANCE
Sarah BOUHADDI - Corine FRANCO, Laura GEORGES, Wendie RENARD, Sonia BOMPASTOR - Elise BUSSAGLIA, Sandrine SOUBEYRAND (c) (Camille ABILY 56) - Elodie THOMIS, Louisa NECIB, Gaetane THINEY (Eugenie LE SOMMER 58) - Marie-Laure DELIE. Tr: Bruno BINI

JAPAN
Miho FUKUMOTO - Yukari KINGA, Azusa IWASHIMIZU, Saki KUMAGAI, Aya SAMESHIMA - Aya MIYAMA (c), Mizuho SAKAGUCHI (Asuna TANAKA 84), Homare SAWA, Nahomi KAWASUMI - Yuki OGIMI, Shinobu OHNO (Kozue ANDO 74). Tr: Norio SASAKI

BRONZE MEDAL PLAY-OFF

CITY OF COVENTRY STADIUM, COVENTRY
9-08-2012, 13:00, Att: 12 465, Ref: Jenny Palmqvist SWE
Canada 1 Matheson [92+]
France 0
CANADA
Erin McLEOD - Rhian WILKINSON, Carmelina MOSCATO, Lauren SESSELMANN, Marie-Eve NAULT (Candace CHAPMAN 83) - Diana MATHESON, Desiree SCOTT, Sophie SCHMIDT - Christine SINCLAIR (c) - Jonelle FILIGNO (Kaylyn KYLE 55), Melissa TANCREDI (Brittany TIMKO 77). Tr: John HERDMAN ENG
FRANCE
Sarah BOUHADDI - Corine FRANCO, Laura GEORGES, Wendie RENARD, Sonia BOMPASTOR - Elise BUSSAGLIA, Sandrine SOUBEYRAND (c) (Camille ABILY 54) - Elodie THOMIS (Camille CATALA 92+), Louisa NECIB, Gaetane THINEY - Marie-Laure DELIE (Eugenie LE SOMMER 60). Tr: Bruno BINI

FINAL

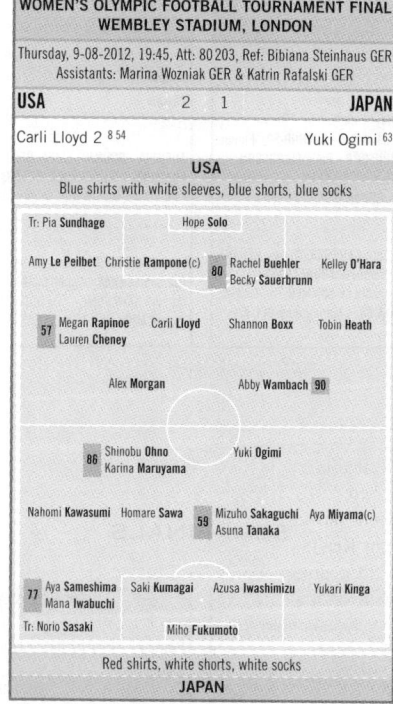

MATCH STATS		
USA		Japan
15	Shots	12
8	Shots on Goal	7
16	Fouls Committed	8
4	Corner Kicks	3
1	Caught Offside	3
42	Possession (%)	58

FIFA U-20 WOMEN'S WORLD CUP JAPAN 2012

FIFA U-20 WOMEN'S WORLD CUP JAPAN 2012

First round groups		Quarter-finals		Semi-finals		Final	
Group A	Pts						
Japan	7						
Mexico	6	USA	2				
New Zealand	4	Korea DPR	1				
Switzerland	0						
				USA	2		
				Nigeria	0		
Group B	Pts						
Nigeria	7						
Korea Republic	6	Mexico	0				
Brazil	2	**Nigeria**	1				
Italy	1						
						USA	1
						Germany	0
Group C	Pts						
Korea DPR	9						
Norway	6	Japan	3				
Canada	3	Korea Republic	1				
Argentina	0						
				Japan	0		
				Germany	3		
Group D	Pts						
Germany	9						
USA	4	Norway	0		Play-off for Third Place		
China PR	4	**Germany**	4		Japan	2	
Ghana	0				Nigeria	1	

Top scorers: 7 - KIM Un Hwa, PRK • 6 - Yoko TANAKA, JPN & Lena LOTZEN, GER • 5 - KIM Su Gyong, PRK • 4 - YUN Hyon Hi, PRK; Francisca ORDEGA, NGA; JEOUN Eun Ha, KOR & Maya HAYES, USA • 3 - Adriana LEON, CAN; Hanae SHIBATA, JPN; Desire OPARANOZIE, NGA; Sofia HUERTA, MEX & Melanie LEUPOLZ, GER
FIFA Fair Play Award: Japan
adidas Golden Ball: 1 - Dzsenifer MAROZSAN, GER • 2 - Hanae SHIBATA, JPN • 3 - Julie JOHNSTON, USA
adidas Golden Boot: 1 - KIM Un Hwa, PRK • 2 - Yoko TANAKA, JPN • 3 - Lena LOTZEN, GER
adidas Golden Glove: Laura BENKARTH, GER

In a battle between the two dominant nations at this level, USA upset the odds to beat defending champions Germany in the final of the FIFA U-20 Women's World Cup in Tokyo. Germany had comprehensively overcome their rivals 3-0 in a Group D encounter just a fortnight previously, and went into the contest without having conceded a goal during all six matches at Japan 2012. However, a lone strike from Kealia Ohai a minute before half-time proved to be the decisive moment of the contest as USA claimed the title for the third time. Earlier in the day Japan proved a popular winner for the majority of the large and colourful Tokyo crowd in the third place play-off against Nigeria. Goals from Yoko Tanaka and Asuka Nishikawa had the Young Nadeshiko on their way but 2010 finalists Nigeria had shown their resilience more than once during the tournament, and a Desire Oparanozie strike caused nerves to jangle for many in the National Stadium. Third place represented Japan's best performance, having never previously appeared in the semi-finals of the tournament. Korea DPR remain the only other nation to have won the U-20 world title aside from Germany and the USA, but despite matching the Germans by winning all of their group games - including a record-breaking 9-0 victory over Argentina - they then lost in the quarter-finals to the USA. Their southern neighbours, Korea Republic, also reached the quarter-finals where they met Japan in what was a rematch of the 2010 FIFA U-17 Women's World Cup final for a number of players on the pitch. They couldn't repeat the victory, however, with the Japanese gaining revenge thanks to a 3-1 victory.

	GROUP A	PL	W	D	L	F	A	PTS	MEX	NZL	SUI
1	Japan	3	2	1	0	10	3	7	4-1	2-2	4-0
2	Mexico	3	2	0	1	7	4	6		4-0	2-0
3	New Zealand	3	1	1	1	4	7	4			2-1
4	Switzerland	3	0	0	3	1	8	0			

MIYAGI STADIUM, MIYAGI
19-08-2012, 19:20, Att: 9542, Ref: Christine Baitinger GER

Japan	4	Shibata [32], Naomoto [56], Yokoyama [77], Yoko Tanaka [89p]
Mexico	1	Huerta [91+]

JAPAN
Sakiko IKEDA - Yushika NAKAMURA (Shiori KINOSHITA 87), Mayo DOKO, Hikari TAKAGI, Haruka HAMADA - Hikaru NAOMOTO, Nozomi FUJITA(c) - Mina TANAKA, Ayu NAKADA (Kumi YOKOYAMA 46), Hanae SHIBATA (Yoko TANAKA● 46) - Ayaka MICHIGAMI. Tr: Hiroshi YOSHIDA

MEXICO
Cecilia SANTIAGO - Arianna ROMERO●, Bianca SIERRA, Christina MURILLO, Valeria MIRANDA - Kenia SANCHEZ●, Nayeli RANGEL(c) - Ariana MARTINEZ (Sofia HUERTA 41), Natalia GOMEZ JUNCO (Yamile FRANCO 77), Tanya SAMARZICH - Daniela SOLIS (Chrystal MARTINEZ 58). Tr: Leonardo CUELLAR

MIYAGI STADIUM, MIYAGI
19-08-2012, 16:20, Att: 9542, Ref: Abirami Apbai SIN

New Zealand	2	Millynn [39], White [52]
Switzerland	1	Aigbogun [91+]

NEW ZEALAND
Erin NAYLER - Holly PATTERSON●, Rebecca BURROWS, Bridgette ARMSTRONG, Ashleigh WARD - Evie MILLYNN, Katie BOWEN, Kate LOYE (Nadia PEARL 89) - Hannah WILKINSON, Rosie WHITE(c), Olivia CHANCE (Steph SKILTON 79). Tr: Aaron McFARLAND

SWITZERLAND
Pascale KUEFFER - Natasha GENSETTER, Lia WAELTI, Carina GERBER(c), Noelle MARITZ - Karin BERNET (Egzona SELJIMI 62), Carmen PULVER, Cinzia JOERG, Audrey WUICHET (Nadine FAESSLER 84) - Mirnije SELIMI (Eseosa AIGBOGUN 75) - Cora CANETTA. Tr: Yannick SCHWERY

MIYAGI STADIUM, MIYAGI
22-08-2012, 16:20, Att: 9061, Ref: Ana Marques BRA

Mexico	2	Huerta [46], Jimenez [91+]
Switzerland	0	

MEXICO
Cecilia SANTIAGO - Arianna ROMERO, Bianca SIERRA, Christina MURILLO●, Valeria MIRANDA - Ashley KOTERO (Kenia SANCHEZ 46), Nayeli RANGEL(c) - Chrystal MARTINEZ (Daniela SOLIS 56) (Olivia JIMENEZ 89), Natalia GOMEZ JUNCO, Tanya SAMARZICH● - Sofia HUERTA. Tr: Leonardo CUELLAR

SWITZERLAND
Pascale KUEFFER - Natasha GENSETTER, Lia WAELTI, Carina GERBER●(c), Noelle MARITZ - Karin BERNET (Egzona SELJIMI● 46), Carmen PULVER, Cinzia JOERG, Audrey WUICHET (Eseosa AIGBOGUN 59) - Mirnije SELIMI (Nadine FAESSLER 74) - Cora CANETTA. Tr: Yannick SCHWERY

MIYAGI STADIUM, MIYAGI
22-08-2012, 19:20, Att: 9061, Ref: Silvia Spinelli ITA

Japan	2	Yoko Tanaka [37], Michigami [71]
New Zealand	2	Nakada OG [11], White [15]

JAPAN
Sakiko IKEDA - Shiori KINOSHITA, Mayo DOKO, Hikari TAKAGI, Haruka HAMADA - Hikaru NAOMOTO, Nozomi FUJITA●(c) (Mina TANAKA 77) - Ayu NAKADA (Asuka NISHIKAWA 29), Yoko TANAKA, Kumi YOKOYAMA (Hanae SHIBATA 60) - Ayaka MICHIGAMI. Tr: Hiroshi YOSHIDA

NEW ZEALAND
Erin NAYLER - Holly PATTERSON, Rebecca BURROWS, Bridgette ARMSTRONG, Ashleigh WARD● - Evie MILLYNN, Katie BOWEN, Nadia PEARL (Kate LOYE 63) - Hannah WILKINSON (Katie ROOD 91+), Rosie WHITE(c), Steph SKILTON (Olivia CHANCE 68). Tr: Aaron McFARLAND

KOBE UNIVER STADIUM, KOBE
26-08-2012, 19:20, Att: 4659, Ref: Teodora Albon ROU

Mexico	4	Huerta [47], Gomez Junco [74], Franco [85], Jimenez [87]
New Zealand	0	

MEXICO
Cecilia SANTIAGO - Arianna ROMERO, Bianca SIERRA, Christina MURILLO, Valeria MIRANDA, Olivia JIMENEZ, Nayeli RANGEL(c) - Ariana MARTINEZ, Natalia GOMEZ JUNCO, Tanya SAMARZICH (Yamile FRANCO 73) - Sofia HUERTA. Tr: Leonardo CUELLAR

NEW ZEALAND
Erin NAYLER - Holly PATTERSON, Rebecca BURROWS, Bridgette ARMSTRONG (Steph SKILTON 83), Ashleigh WARD● (Nadia PEARL 64) - Evie MILLYNN (Katie ROOD 76), Katie BOWEN●, Kate LOYE - Hannah WILKINSON, Rosie WHITE●(c), Olivia CHANCE. Tr: Aaron McFARLAND

NATIONAL STADIUM, TOKYO
26-08-2012, 19:20, Att: 16 914, Ref: Margaret Domka USA

Japan	4	Yoko Tanaka 2 [30] [47], Nishikawa [52], Naomoto [84p]
Switzerland	0	

JAPAN
Sakiko IKEDA - Shiori KINOSHITA(c), Mayo DOKO, Yushika NAKAMURA, Haruka HAMADA - Hikaru NAOMOTO, Hanae SHIBATA - Mina TANAKA, Yoko TANAKA (Yu NAKASATO 53) (Riho SAKAMOTO 72), Kumi YOKOYAMA - Ayaka MICHIGAMI (Asuka NISHIKAWA 46). Tr: Hiroshi YOSHIDA

SWITZERLAND
Nadine BOENI - Natasha GENSETTER, Lia WAELTI, Carina GERBER(c), Noelle MARITZ - Carolyn MALLAUN, Anja THUERIG (Karin BERNET 55), Eseosa AIGBOGUN, Nadine FAESSLER (Fabienne ROCHAIX 63) - Mirnije SELIMI● - Cora CANETTA (Sarina SCHENKEL 76). Tr: Yannick SCHWERY

FIFA U-20 WOMEN'S WORLD CUP JAPAN 2012

	GROUP B	PL	W	D	L	F	A	PTS	KOR	BRA	ITA
1	Nigeria	3	2	1	0	7	1	7	2-0	1-1	4-0
2	Korea Republic	3	2	0	1	4	2	6		2-0	2-0
3	Brazil	3	0	2	1	2	4	2			1-1
4	Italy	3	0	1	2	1	7	1			

KOMABA STADIUM, SAITAMA
19-08-2012, 15:00, Att: 2511, Ref: Margaret Domka USA

Brazil	1	Amanda [92+]
Italy	1	Linari [38]

BRAZIL
DANIELE - GIOVANNA OLIVEIRA, INGRID, TAYLA•, ANDRESSA (CAROL 77) - KETLEN, MARIA• (GLAUCIA 46), AMANDA, GIOVANNA (LUANA 46) - BEATRIZ, THAIS GUEDES(c). Tr: Caio COUTO

ITALY
Laura GIULIANI - Cecilia SALVAI, Elena LINARI, Roberta FILIPPOZZI, Michela LEDRI - Lisa ALBORGHETTI (Federica DI CRISCIO 60••♦74), Michela FRANCO, Claudia MAURI - Elisa LECCE (Sofia LUCIANI 64), Martina ROSUCCI(c), Katia COPPOLA• (Valentina PEDRETTI 82). Tr: Corrado CORRADINI

KOMABA STADIUM, SAITAMA
19-08-2012, 18:00, Att: 2511, Ref: Dianne Ferreira-James GUY

Nigeria	2	Okobi [15], Oparanozie [67]
Korea Republic	0	

NIGERIA
Ibubeleye WHYTE - Ugo NJOKU, Fasilat ADEYEMO, Josephine CHUKWUNONYE, Gloria OFOEGBU(c) - Cecilia NKU, Esther SUNDAY, Charity ADULE (Ebere ORJI 52). Ngozi OKOBI (Asisat OSHOALA 76) - Francisca ORDEGA, Desire OPARANOZIE. Tr: Okon EDWIN

KOREA REPUBLIC
JEON Han Eul - SEO Hyun Sook, KIM Ji Hye•, SHIN Dam Yeong, JANG Sel Gi• - MOON Mi Ra (LEE Jung Eun 61), LEE Young Ju(c) - CHOE Yu Ri (CHOI Yoo Jung 83), JEOUN Eun Ha, LEE Geum Min - YEO Min Ji (LEE So Dam 34). Tr: JONG Song Chon

---

KOMABA STADIUM, SAITAMA
22-08-2012, 15:00, Att: 2539, Ref: Esther Staubli SUI

Brazil	1	Giovanna Oliveira [87]
Nigeria	1	Ordega [44]

BRAZIL
DANIELE - GIOVANNA OLIVEIRA•, INGRID (CAROL 79), TAYLA, ANDRESSA - KETLEN (JUCINARA 59), MARIA, AMANDA•, LUCIMARA• (LUANA 37) - BEATRIZ, THAIS GUEDES(c). Tr: Caio COUTO

NIGERIA
Ibubeleye WHYTE (Chioma NWANKWO• 64) - Ugo NJOKU (Blessing EDOHO• 85), Fasilat ADEYEMO, Josephine CHUKWUNONYE, Gloria OFOEGBU•(c) - Cecilia NKU, Esther SUNDAY, Charity ADULE (Ebere ORJI 78), Ngozi OKOBI - Francisca ORDEGA, Desire OPARANOZIE•. Tr: Okon EDWIN

KOMABA STADIUM, SAITAMA
22-08-2012, 18:00, Att: 2539, Ref: Lucila Venegas MEX

Italy	0	
Korea Republic	2	Lee Geum Min [54], Jeoun Eun Ha [56]

ITALY
Laura GIULIANI - Cecilia SALVAI•, Elena LINARI, Roberta FILIPPOZZI (Francesca VITALE 46), Michela LEDRI - Luisa PUGNALI (Cecilia RE 43), Michela FRANCO••♦89, Claudia MAURI - Sofia LUCIANI (Elisa LECCE 68), Martina ROSUCCI(c), Katia COPPOLA. Tr: Giorgia BRENZAN

KOREA REPUBLIC
JEON Han Eul - SEO Hyun Sook•, KIM Ji Hye, SHIN Dam Yeong•, JANG Sel Gi - KIM Ar Eum (LEE Jung Eun 46), LEE Young Ju(c) - CHOE Yu Ri• (KIM Jie Un 82), LEE So Dam (MOON Mi Ra 66), LEE Geum Min - JEOUN Eun Ha. Tr: JONG Song Chon

---

KOBE UNIVER STADIUM, KOBE
26-08-2012, 16:20, Att: 4659, Ref: Qin Liang CHN

Italy	0	
Nigeria	4	Ordega 3 [22 40 47], Igbinovia [86]

ITALY
Laura GIULIANI - Cecilia SALVAI, Elena LINARI, Roberta FILIPPOZZI•, Michela LEDRI - Lisa ALBORGHETTI (Ana Carolina CANNONE 46), Valentina PEDRETTI (Katia COPPOLA 46), Claudia MAURI - Martina ROSUCCI(c), Federica DI CRISCIO (Cecilia RE 72), Arianna FERRATI. Tr: Corrado CORRADINI

NIGERIA
Ibubeleye WHYTE - Ugo NJOKU, Fasilat ADEYEMO (Jennifer OSAWARU 92+), Josephine CHUKWUNONYE, Gloria OFOEGBU(c) - Cecilia NKU, Esther SUNDAY, Asisat OSHOALA, Ngozi OKOBI (Osarenoma IGBINOVIA 75) - Francisca ORDEGA (Ebere ORJI 82), Desire OPARANOZIE. Tr: Okon EDWIN

NATIONAL STADIUM, TOKYO
26-08-2012, 16:20, Att: 16 914, Ref: Christine Baitinger GER

Korea Republic	2	Jeoun Eun Ha 2 [74 82]
Brazil	0	

KOREA REPUBLIC
JEON Han Eul - SEO Hyun Sook, KIM Ji Hye, SHIN Dam Yeong (CHOI Somi 86), JANG Sel Gi - LEE Jung Eun, LEE Young Ju(c) - MOON Mi Ra (CHOE Yu Ri 68), LEE So Dam (CHOI Yoo Jung 90), LEE Geum Min• - JEOUN Eun Ha. Tr: JONG Song Chon

BRAZIL
DANIELE - GIOVANNA OLIVEIRA, INGRID, TAYLA, ANDRESSA - KETLEN (GLAUCIA 46), MARIA (LUANA• 32), AMANDA• (JUCINARA 77), CAROL• - BEATRIZ, THAIS GUEDES(c). Tr: Caio COUTO

PART ONE – FIFA AND WORLD FOOTBALL

	GROUP C	PL	W	D	L	F	A	PTS		NOR	CAN	ARG
1	Korea DPR	3	3	0	0	15	3	9		4-2	2-1	9-0
2	Norway	3	2	0	1	8	6	6			2-1	4-1
3	Canada	3	1	0	2	8	4	3				6-0
4	Argentina	3	0	0	3	1	19	0				

KOBE UNIVER STADIUM, KOBE
20-08-2012, 16:00, Att: 3468, Ref: Lucila Venegas MEX

Korea DPR	4	Yun Hyon Hi 2 [15] [40p], Kim Un Hwa [72], Kim Su Gyong [77]
Norway	2	Hansen [23], Ada Hegerberg [54]

KOREA DPR
O Chang Ran - PONG Son Hwa, KIM Nam Hui, RI Nam Sil, YUN Song Mi - KIM Un Hyang, O Hui Sun (c) (YU Jong Im 85), JON Myong Hwa, KIM Su Gyong (KIM Un Ju 78), RI Yong Mi (KIM Un Hwa 34) - YUN Hyon Hi●. Tr: SIN Ui Gun

NORWAY
Nora GJOEN - Kristine Wigdahl HEGLAND (c) (Emilie HAAVI 80), Ida AARDALEN● - (Stine REINAS 88), Anette TENGESDAL, Anja SONSTEVOLD - Cathrine DEKKERHUS, Maria THORISDOTTIR - Melissa BJANESOY, Caroline HANSEN, Andrine HEGERBERG - Ada HEGERBERG. Tr: Jarl TORSKE

KOBE UNIVER STADIUM, KOBE
20-08-2012, 19:00, Att: 3468, Ref: Esther Staubli SUI

Canada	6	Zadorsky [7p], Sawicki [20], Leon 3 [22] [42] [45], Charron Delage [86]
Argentina	0	

CANADA
Sabrina D'ANGELO - Vanessa LEGAULT CORDISCO (Jade KOVACEVIC 60), Rachel MELHADO (Nicole SETTERLUND 46), Shelina ZADORSKY (c), Melissa ROY - Jaclyn SAWICKI, Sarah ROBBINS, Adriana LEON● - (Catherine CHARRON DELAGE 46), Danica WU - Jenna RICHARDSON, Christine EXETER. Tr: Andrew OLIVIERI

ARGENTINA
Laurina OLIVEROS (c) - Adriana SACHS, Agustina BARROSO◆6, Noelia ESPINDOLA - Micaela SANDOVAL, Mariana LARROQUETTE, Gabriela IRIBARNE (Yanina HERNANDEZ 29), Camila GOMEZ ARES (Jimena VERA 54), Maria BONSEGUNDO (Erika CABRERA 67) - Betina SORIANO, Yael OVIEDO. Tr: Nestor CALVINO

KOBE UNIVER STADIUM, KOBE
23-08-2012, 16:00, Att: 3144, Ref: Fadouma Dia SEN

Korea DPR	9	Yun Hyon Hi [16], Kim Un Hwa 5 [26] [30] [41] [45] [56], Kim Su Gyong 3 [38] [44] [55]
Argentina	0	

KOREA DPR
O Chang Ran - PONG Son Hwa, KIM Nam Hui, RI Nam Sil, YUN Song Mi - KIM Un Hyang, O Hui Sun (c), KIM Su Gyong (RI Yong Mi 83), JON Myong Hwa (YU Jong Im 36) - KIM Un Hwa, YUN Hyon Hi (KWON Song Hwa 46). Tr: SIN Ui Gun

ARGENTINA
Laurina OLIVEROS (c) - Adriana SACHS, Yanina HERNANDEZ (Dianela ROTELA 27), Noelia ESPINDOLA - Micaela SANDOVAL, Mariana LARROQUETTE, Camila GOMEZ ARES●, Constanza VAZQUEZ (Erika CABRERA 85), Maria BONSEGUNDO - Betina SORIANO (Jimena VERA 59), Yael OVIEDO. Tr: Jose Carlos BORRELLO

KOBE UNIVER STADIUM, KOBE
23-08-2012, 19:00, Att: 3144, Ref: Qin Liang CHN

Norway	2	Ada Hegerberg [52], Andrine Hegerberg [79]
Canada	1	Richardson [44]

NORWAY
Nora GJOEN - Kristine Wigdahl HEGLAND (c), Ida AARDALEN, Anette TENGESDAL, Anja SONSTEVOLD (Emilie HAAVI 46) - Cathrine DEKKERHUS, Maria THORISDOTTIR - Melissa BJANESOY● (Guro REITEN 85), Caroline HANSEN, Andrine HEGERBERG - Ada HEGERBERG. Tr: Jarl TORSKE

CANADA
Sabrina D'ANGELO - Vanessa LEGAULT CORDISCO (Melissa ROY 70), Rachel MELHADO, Shelina ZADORSKY (c) - Kylie DAVIS, Sarah ROBBINS, Adriana LEON, Danica WU (Christine EXETER 71) - Nkem EZURIKE (Constance DE CHANTAL DUMONT 46), Christabel ODURO, Jenna RICHARDSON. Tr: Andrew OLIVIERI

MIYAGI STADIUM, MIYAGI
27-08-2012, 19:00, Att: 1712, Ref: Nami Sato JPN

Norway	4	Haavi [25], Hansen [70], Andrine Hegerberg [85], Skaug [93+]
Argentina	1	Oviedo [82]

NORWAY
Nora GJOEN - Kristine Wigdahl HEGLAND (c), Ida AARDALEN, Anette TENGESDAL, Guro REITEN● - Cathrine DEKKERHUS (Andrine HEGERBERG 69), Stine REINAS - Melissa BJANESOY (Andrea THUN 80), Caroline HANSEN (Ina SKAUG 88) - Ada HEGERBERG, Emilie HAAVI. Tr: Jarl TORSKE

ARGENTINA
Laurina OLIVEROS (c) - Adriana SACHS, Yanina HERNANDEZ, Agustina BARROSO, Noelia ESPINDOLA - Micaela SANDOVAL, Erika CABRERA (Johanna CHAMORRO 63), Mariana LARROQUETTE●, Camila GOMEZ ARES (Betina SORIANO 87), Maria BONSEGUNDO - Yael OVIEDO. Tr: Jose Carlos BORRELLO

KOMABA STADIUM, SAITAMA
27-08-2012, 19:00, Att: 4182, Ref: Pernilla Larsson SWE

Canada	1	Exeter [12]
Korea DPR	2	Kim Un Hwa [33], Yun Hyon Hi [78p]

CANADA
Sabrina D'ANGELO - Vanessa LEGAULT CORDISCO, Rachel MELHADO, Shelina ZADORSKY (c) - Kylie DAVIS (Nkem EZURIKE 56), Sarah ROBBINS, Adriana LEON, Danica WU - Christabel ODURO (Catherine CHARRON DELAGE 46), Jenna RICHARDSON, Christine EXETER (Melissa ROY 56). Tr: Andrew OLIVIERI

KOREA DPR
O Chang Ran - PONG Son Hwa, KIM Nam Hui, RI Nam Sil, YUN Song Mi - KIM Un Hyang, O Hui Sun (c) (KIM Un Ha 89), KIM Su Gyong (KWON Song Hwa● 65), JON Myong Hwa - KIM Un Hwa (YU Jong Im 85), YUN Hyon Hi. Tr: SIN Ui Gun

FIFA U-20 WOMEN'S WORLD CUP JAPAN 2012

	GROUP D	PL	W	D	L	F	A	PTS	USA	CHN	GHA
1	Germany	3	3	0	0	8	0	9	3-0	4-0	1-0
2	USA	3	1	1	1	5	4	4		1-1	4-0
3	China PR	3	1	1	1	2	5	4			1-0
4	Ghana	3	0	0	3	0	6	0			

HIROSHIMA BIG ARCH, HIROSHIMA
20-08-2012, 16:00, Att: 2582, Ref: Teodora Albon ROU

Ghana	0	
USA	4	Addai OG [20], Hayes 3 [50 74 92+]

GHANA
Patricia **MANTEY** - Cynthia **YIADOM** (Faustina **AMPAH** 90), Linda **ADDAI**●, Rosemary **AMPEM**, Grace **ADAMS** - Alice **DANSO** (Jennifer **CUDJOE** 70), Priscilla **SAAHENE** (Candice **OSEI-AGYEMANG** 70), Mercy **MYLES**(c), Beatrice **SESU** - Elizabeth **ADDO**, Florence **DADSON**. Tr: Robert **SACKEY** USA

USA
Bryane **HEABERLIN** - Crystal **DUNN**, Julie **JOHNSTON**(c), Kassey **KALLMAN**, Mollie **PATHMAN** - Sarah **KILLION** (Samantha **MEWIS** 72), Morgan **BRIAN** (Mandy **LADDISH** 81), Vanessa **DI BERNARDO** - Maya **HAYES**, Chioma **UBOGAGU** (Katie **STENGEL** 61), Kealia **OHAI**. Tr: Steve **SWANSON**

HIROSHIMA BIG ARCH, HIROSHIMA
20-08-2012, 19:00, Att: 2582, Ref: Ana Marques BRA

Germany	4	Lotzen [3], Hegenauer [45], Lin Yuping OG [74], Wensing [91+]
China PR	0	

GERMANY
Laura **BENKARTH** - Leonie **MAIER**, Luisa **WENSING**, Jennifer **CRAMER**, Carolin **SIMON** - Melanie **LEUPOLZ**, Kathrin **HENDRICH**, Ramona **PETZELBERGER**(c) (Lina **MAGULL** 81), Anja **HEGENAUER** (Nicole **ROLSER** 66), Dzsenifer **MAROZSAN**, Lena **LOTZEN** (Silvana **CHOJNOWSKI** 75). Tr: Maren **MEINERT**

CHINA PR
SHEN Li - **WU** Haiyan, **LIN** Yuping, **HUANG** Yini, **WANG** Yingying (**LUO** Guiping 78) - **LIU** Shanshan - **ZHANG** Xin (**WANG** Shuang 68), **YAO** Shuangyan (**LI** Ying 61), **SONG** Sicheng(c), **SHEN** Lili - **ZHANG** Jieli. Tr: **YIN** Tiesheng

HIROSHIMA BIG ARCH, HIROSHIMA
23-08-2012, 16:00, Att: 3559, Ref: Nami Sato JPN

Ghana	0	
Germany	1	Magull [91+]

GHANA
Patricia **MANTEY** - Janet **EGYIR**, Linda **ADDAI**, Rosemary **AMPEM** - Alice **DANSO**● (Priscilla **SAAHENE** 54), Jennifer **CUDJOE**● (Deborah **AFRIYIE** 54), Mercy **MYLES**●(c), Beatrice **SESU** - Elizabeth **ADDO**, Candice **OSEI-AGYEMANG**, Florence **DADSON**. Tr: Robert **SACKEY** USA

GERMANY
Laura **BENKARTH** - Leonie **MAIER**, Luisa **WENSING**, Jennifer **CRAMER**, Carolin **SIMON**● - Melanie **LEUPOLZ**, Kathrin **HENDRICH** (Anja **HEGENAUER** 46), Ramona **PETZELBERGER**(c) - Nicole **ROLSER** (Silvana **CHOJNOWSKI** 46), Dzsenifer **MAROZSAN**, Lena **LOTZEN** (Lina **MAGULL** 83). Tr: Maren **MEINERT**

HIROSHIMA BIG ARCH, HIROSHIMA
23-08-2012, 19:00, Att: 3559, Ref: Pernilla Larsson SWE

USA	1	Hayes [36]
China PR	1	Shen Lili [19]

USA
Bryane **HEABERLIN** - Crystal **DUNN**, Julie **JOHNSTON**(c), Cari **ROCCARO**, Mollie **PATHMAN** - Sarah **KILLION**, Morgan **BRIAN**, Vanessa **DI BERNARDO** - Maya **HAYES** (Becca **WANN** 86), Kelly **COBB** (Chioma **UBOGAGU** 46), Kealia **OHAI** (Katie **STENGEL** 65). Tr: Steve **SWANSON**

CHINA PR
SHEN Li - **WU** Haiyan●, **LIN** Yuping●, **HUANG** Yini, **LUO** Guiping - **LIU** Shanshan - **ZHANG** Xin (**ZHAO** Xindi 55), **HAN** Jiayuan (**LI** Ying 82), **SONG** Sicheng●(c), **SHEN** Lili - **ZHANG** Jieli. Tr: **YIN** Tiesheng

MIYAGI STADIUM, MIYAGI
27-08-2012, 16:00, Att: 1712, Ref: Abirami Apbai SIN

USA	0	
Germany	3	Lotzen 2 [35 53], Leupolz [55]

USA
Bryane **HEABERLIN** - Crystal **DUNN**, Julie **JOHNSTON**(c) (Cari **ROCCARO** 59), Kassey **KALLMAN**, Mollie **PATHMAN** - Sarah **KILLION**, Morgan **BRIAN**, Vanessa **DI BERNARDO** (Samantha **MEWIS** 74) - Maya **HAYES**, Katie **STENGEL**, Chioma **UBOGAGU** (Kealia **OHAI** 54). Tr: Steve **SWANSON**

GERMANY
Laura **BENKARTH** - Leonie **MAIER**, Luisa **WENSING**, Jennifer **CRAMER**, Annabel **JAEGER** - Karoline **HEINZE** (Kathrin **HENDRICH** 46), Silvana **CHOJNOWSKI**, Lina **MAGULL**, Ramona **PETZELBERGER**(c) (Melanie **LEUPOLZ** 46) - Dzsenifer **MAROZSAN**, Lena **LOTZEN** (Nicole **ROLSER** 69). Tr: Maren **MEINERT**

KOMABA STADIUM, SAITAMA
27-08-2012, 16:00, Att: 4182, Ref: Dianne Ferreira-James GUY

China PR	1	Zhao Xindi [35]
Ghana	0	

CHINA PR
SHEN Li - **WU** Haiyan, **LIN** Yuping, **HUANG** Yini, **LUO** Guiping● - **LIU** Shanshan - **YAO** Shuangyan, **HAN** Jiayuan (**LI** Ying 80), **SONG** Sicheng(c) (**WANG** Tingting 85), **ZHAO** Xindi (**ZHANG** Jieli 57) - **SHEN** Lili. Tr: **YIN** Tiesheng

GHANA
Patricia **MANTEY** - Janet **EGYIR**, Linda **ADDAI**, Rosemary **AMPEM** - Elizabeth **ADDO**, Deborah **AFRIYIE** (Faustina **AMPAH** 76), Jennifer **CUDJOE**, Mercy **MYLES**(c), Beatrice **SESU** - Candice **OSEI-AGYEMANG** (Alice **DANSO** 53), Florence **DADSON** (Priscilla **SAAHENE** 59). Tr: Robert **SACKEY** USA

QUARTER-FINALS

KOMABA STADIUM, SAITAMA		
31-08-2012, 19:30, Att: 6284, Ref: Silvia Spinelli ITA		
Korea DPR	1	Kim Su Gyong [75]
USA	2	Di Bernardo [52], Ubogagu [98]

KOREA DPR

O Chang Ran - **PONG** Son Hwa, **KIM** Nam Hui, **RI** Nam Sil, **YUN** Song Mi•- **KIM** Un Hyang, O Hui Sun(c), **JON** Myong Hwa, **YU** Jong Im (**KIM** Su Gyong 56) - **KIM** Un Hwa (**KWON** Song Hwa 78) (**RI** Yong Mi 106), **YUN** Hyon Hi. Tr: **SIN** Ui Gun

USA

Bryane **HEABERLIN** - Crystal **DUNN**, Julie **JOHNSTON**(c), Cari **ROCCARO**•, Mollie **PATHMAN** - Sarah **KILLION**, Morgan **BRIAN**, Vanessa **DI BERNARDO** (Kassey **KALLMAN** 108) - Maya **HAYES** (Chioma **UBOGAGU** 71), Kelly **COBB** (Samantha **MEWIS** 61), Kealia **OHAI**•. Tr: Steve **SWANSON**

NATIONAL STADIUM, TOKYO		
30-08-2012, 16:00, Att: 24 097, Ref: Abirami Apbai SIN		
Nigeria	1	Oparanozie [109]
Mexico	0	

NIGERIA

Ibubeleye **WHYTE** - Ugo **NJOKU**, Fasilat **ADEYEMO**, Josephine **CHUKWUNONYE**, Gloria **OFOEGBU**(c) - Cecilia **NKU** (Charity **ADULE** 118), Esther **SUNDAY** (Ebere **ORJI** 107), Asisat **OSHOALA**•, Ngozi **OKOBI** (Osarenoma **IGBINOVIA** 89) - Francisca **ORDEGA**, Desire **OPARANOZIE**. Tr: Okon **EDWIN**

MEXICO

Cecilia **SANTIAGO** - Arianna **ROMERO**, Bianca **SIERRA**, Christina **MURILLO**•, Valeria **MIRANDA** - Olivia **JIMENEZ** (Amanda **PEREZ** 105), Nayeli **RANGEL**(c) - Ariana **MARTINEZ** (Yamile **FRANCO** 88), Natalia **GOMEZ JUNCO**, Tanya **SAMARZICH** (Daniela **SOLIS** 40) - Sofia **HUERTA**. Tr: Leonardo **CUELLAR**

NATIONAL STADIUM, TOKYO		
30-08-2012, 19:30, Att: 24 097, Ref: Teodora Albon ROU		
Japan	3	Shibata 2 [8] [19], Yoko Tanaka [37]
Korea Republic	1	Jeoun Eun Ha [15]

JAPAN

Sakiko **IKEDA** - Shiori **KINOSHITA**, Mayo **DOKO**, Hikari **TAKAGI** (Yushika **NAKAMURA** 45), Haruka **HAMADA** (Kumi **YOKOYAMA** 61) - Hikaru **NAOMOTO**, Nozomi **FUJITA**(c) - Mina **TANAKA**, Yoko **TANAKA**, Hanae **SHIBATA** - Asuka **NISHIKAWA** (Ayaka **MICHIGAMI** 86). Tr: Hiroshi **YOSHIDA**

KOREA REPUBLIC

JEON Han Eul - **SEO** Hyun Sook, **KIM** Ji Hye, **SHIN** Dam Yeong (**CHOI** So Mi 91+), **JANG** Sel Gi - **LEE** Jung Eun (**MOON** Mi Ra• 34), **LEE** Young Ju•(c) - **CHOE** Yu Ri, **JEOUN** Eun Ha, **LEE** Geum Min (**LEE** So Dam 69) - **YEO** Min Ji. Tr: **JONG** Song Chon

KOMABA STADIUM, SAITAMA		
31-08-2012, 16:00, Att: 6284, Ref: Margaret Domka USA		
Germany	4	Lotzen 2 [5] [20], Leupolz [7], Wensing [85]
Norway	0	

GERMANY

Laura **BENKARTH** - Leonie **MAIER**, Luisa **WENSING**, Carolin **SIMON**, Jennifer **CRAMER** - Melanie **LEUPOLZ**• (Marie **PYKO** 71), Kathrin **HENDRICH**, Ramona **PETZELBERGER**(c) (Lina **MAGULL** 77), Anja **HEGENAUER** (Silvana **CHOJNOWSKI** 63) - Dzsenifer **MAROZSAN**, Lena **LOTZEN**. Tr: Maren **MEINERT**

NORWAY

Nora **GJOEN** - Kristine Wigdahl **HEGLAND**(c), Ida **AARDALEN**, Maria **THORISDOTTIR**, Guro **REITEN** (Anja **SONSTEVOLD** 76) - Cathrine **DEKKERHUS**, Andrine **HEGERBERG** - Melissa **BJANESOY**, Caroline **HANSEN**♦80, Emilie **HAAVI** (Anette **TENGESDAL** 59) - Ada **HEGERBERG** (Andrea **THUN** 86). Tr: Jarl **TORSKE**

SEMI-FINALS

NATIONAL STADIUM, TOKYO		
4-09-2012, 16:00, Att: 28 306, Ref: Esther Staubli SUI		
Nigeria	0	
USA	2	Brian [22], Ohai [70]

NIGERIA

Ibubeleye **WHYTE** - Ugo **NJOKU**, Fasilat **ADEYEMO**, Josephine **CHUKWUNONYE**, Gloria **OFOEGBU**(c) - Cecilia **NKU** (Charity **ADULE** 68), Esther **SUNDAY**, Asisat **OSHOALA** (Jennifer **OSAWARU** 79), Ngozi **OKOBI** - Francisca **ORDEGA**, Desire **OPARANOZIE** (Ebere **ORJI** 72). Tr: Okon **EDWIN**

USA

Bryane **HEABERLIN** - Crystal **DUNN**, Julie **JOHNSTON**(c), Cari **ROCCARO**, Mollie **PATHMAN** - Sarah **KILLION**, Morgan **BRIAN** (Mandy **LADDISH** 83), Vanessa **DI BERNARDO** - Maya **HAYES** (Samantha **MEWIS** 66), Kelly **COBB** (Chioma **UBOGAGU** 46), Kealia **OHAI**. Tr: Steve **SWANSON**

NATIONAL STADIUM, TOKYO		
4-09-2012, 19:30, Att: 28 306, Ref: Lucila Venegas MEX		
Japan	0	
Germany	3	Leupolz [1], Marozsan [13], Lotzen [19]

JAPAN

Sakiko **IKEDA** - Shiori **KINOSHITA**, Mayo **DOKO**, Hikari **TAKAGI** (Yushika **NAKAMURA** 86), Haruka **HAMADA** - Hikaru **NAOMOTO**, Nozomi **FUJITA**(c) - Mina **TANAKA** (Kumi **YOKOYAMA** 25), Yoko **TANAKA** (Ayaka **MICHIGAMI** 61), Hanae **SHIBATA** - Asuka **NISHIKAWA**, Tr: Hiroshi **YOSHIDA**

GERMANY

Laura **BENKARTH** - Leonie **MAIER**, Luisa **WENSING**, Jennifer **CRAMER**, Annabel **JAEGER** - Melanie **LEUPOLZ** (Carolin **SIMON** 74), Kathrin **HENDRICH**, Ramona **PETZELBERGER**(c) - Nicole **ROLSER** (Anja **HEGENAUER** 64), Dzsenifer **MAROZSAN**, Lena **LOTZEN** (Lina **MAGULL** 80). Tr: Maren **MEINERT**

PLAY-OFF FOR THIRD PLACE

NATIONAL STADIUM, TOKYO
8-09-2012, 15:30, Att: 31 114, Ref: Margaret Domka USA

Japan	2	Yoko Tanaka [24], Nishikawa [50]
Nigeria	1	Oparanozie [73]

JAPAN

Sakiko **IKEDA** - Yushika **NAKAMURA**, Mayo **DOKO**, Hikari **TAKAGI**, Haruka **HAMADA** - Hikaru **NAOMOTO**, Nozomi **FUJITA** (c) (Shiori **KINOSHITA** 67) - Mina **TANAKA**, Yoko **TANAKA**, Kumi **YOKOYAMA** (Hanae **SHIBATA** 35) - Ayaka **MICHIGAMI** (Asuka **NISHIKAWA** 46), Tr: Hiroshi **YOSHIDA**

NIGERIA

Ibubeleye **WHYTE** - Blessing **EDOHO**, Fasilat **ADEYEMO**•, Josephine **CHUKWUNONYE**, Gloria **OFOEGBU** (c) - Cecilia **NKU** (Charity **ADULE** 46), Esther **SUNDAY**, Asisat **OSHOALA**•, Ngozi **OKOBI** - Francisca **ORDEGA**• (Ebere **ORJI** 46), Desire **OPARANOZIE**. Tr: Okon **EDWIN**

FINAL

MATCH STATS		
USA		Germany
9	Shots	17
4	Shots on Goal	5
5	Fouls Committed	6
6	Corner Kicks	12
2	Caught Offside	2
48	Possession (%)	52

FIFA U-17 WOMEN'S WORLD CUP AZERBAIJAN 2012

FIFA U-17 WOMEN'S WORLD CUP AZERBAIJAN 2012

First round groups

Group A — Pts
- **Nigeria** — 7
- **Canada** — 7
- Colombia — 3
- Azerbaijan — 0

Group B — Pts
- **Korea DPR** — 5
- **France** — 5
- USA — 5
- Gambia — 0

Group C — Pts
- **Japan** — 9
- **Brazil** — 6
- Mexico — 3
- New Zealand — 0

Group D — Pts
- **Germany** — 7
- **Ghana** — 6
- China PR — 4
- Uruguay — 0

Quarter-finals

France	0 5p
Nigeria	0 3p

Japan	0
Ghana	1

Germany	2
Brazil	1

Canada	1
Korea DPR	2

Semi-finals

France	2
Ghana	0

Germany	1
Korea DPR	2

Final

France	1 7p
Korea DPR	1 6p

Play-off for Third Place

Ghana	1
Germany	0

Top scorers: 8 - **RI** Un Sim, PRK • 6 - Chinwendu **IHEZUO**, NGA • 4 - Halimatu **AYINDE**, NGA; Lea **DECLERCQ**, FRA; Kadidiatou **DIANI**, FRA & Jane **AYIEYAM**, GHA • 3 - Yui **NARUMIYA**, JPN; **RI** Kyong Hyang, PRK; Priscilla **OKYERE**, GHA; Sara **DAEBRITZ**, GER; **KIM** So Hyang, PRK & Rebecca **KNAAK**, GER

FIFA Fair Play Award: Japan

adidas Golden Ball: 1 - Griedge **MBOCK BATHY**, FRA • 2 - **RI** Hyang Sim, PRK • 3 - Yui **HASEGAWA**, JPN
adidas Golden Boot: 1 - **RI** Un Sim, PRK • 2 - Chinwendu **IHEZUO**, NGA • 3 - Halimatu **AYINDE**, NGA
adidas Golden Glove: Romane **BRUNEAU**, FRA

The French became the first European nation to be crowned champions at the FIFA U-17 Women's World Cup after beating Korea DPR in a tense final in Baku. The sides could not be separated in normal time, but Les Bleuettes finally overcame the determined and skilful Asians on penalties to seal a first world title for France since the men's team won the FIFA U-17 World Cup in 2001. Lea Declercq had put France ahead in the first half, before a late equaliser from Ri Un Sim forced extra-time and then penalties. After a long shoot-out which saw Kim Un Hwa and Marion Romanelli fail from 12 yards, it was Ri Un Yong's miss that gave the title to France. The game marked a changing of the guard in U-17 women's football with both Europe and Africa mounting a challenge to the domination of Asia that had seen Korea DPR claim the first title in 2008 and Korea Republic the second in 2010. The surprise package of the tournament were Ghana who caused a sensation by beating the 2010 runners-up Japan in the quarter-finals and although they lost to France in the semi-finals the Ghanaians then beat Germany 1-0 to claim third place. Hosts Azerbaijan are likely to reap the rewards of hosting the tournament for some time to come with Baku boasting three new stadia and a refurbished Tofig Bahramov national stadium. On the pitch, however, there is clearly some way for women's football to go with the hosts losing all three of their matches, although fielding a side from a country dominated by men's football represented a significant step forward.

FIFA U-17 WOMEN'S WORLD CUP AZERBAIJAN 2012

	GROUP A	PL	W	D	L	F	A	PTS	CAN	COL	AZE
1	Nigeria	3	2	1	0	15	1	7	1-1	3-0	11-0
2	Canada	3	2	1	0	3	1	7		1-0	1-0
3	Colombia	3	1	0	2	4	4	3			4-0
4	Azerbaijan	3	0	0	3	0	16	0			

TOFIG BAHRAMOV STADIUM, BAKU
22-09-2012, 20:00, Att: 30 250, Ref: Etsuko Fukano JPN

Azerbaijan 0
Colombia 4 Castillo 2 [17] [20], Maldonado [44], Aguirre [73]

AZERBAIJAN
Aytaj SHARIFOVA - Zhala MAHSIMOVA, Amina HEYDAROVA(c), Suheyla ILTAR, Olya SHIOSHVILI - Maia DANGADZE, Shafag NASIROVA - Nigar JALILLI (Aysun ALIYEVA 82), Laman BAGHIROVA (Sabrina RONAGHI 31), Leila SOLMAZ (Aliya VALIYEVA 58) - Melis SARIALTIN. Tr: Sissy RAITH GER

COLOMBIA
Lissa CARDOZO - Anyella MARTINEZ, Maria JARAMILLO, Diana DUARTE, Estefania BOTERO - Carolina ARBELAEZ, Marcela RESTREPO (Pamela PENALOZA 73) - Juliana OCAMPO (Nicole REGNIER 60), Leicy SANTOS, Gabriela MALDONADO (Laura AGUIRRE 66) - Dayana CASTILLO(c). Tr: Fabian TABORDA

TOFIG BAHRAMOV STADIUM, BAKU
22-09-2012, 17:00, Att: 30 250, Ref: Kateryna Monzul UKR

Nigeria 1 Ihezuo [81]
Canada 1 Pierre-Louis [63]

NIGERIA
Gift ANDY - Ebere OKOYE, Victoria AIDELOMON(c), Sarah NNODIM, Jiroro IDIKE - Halimatu AYINDE - Chidinma EDEJI, Tessy BIAHWO, Chinwendu IHEZUO, Mabel EFFIOM (Oluchi OFOEGBU 62) - Yetunde ADEBOYEJO (Aminat YAKUBU 83). Tr: Peter DEDEVBO

CANADA
Kailen SHERIDAN - Lindsay AGNEW, Kadeisha BUCHANAN, Rebecca PONGETTI, Madeline IOZZI - Nicole LONCAR (Jordyn LISTRO 88), Rebecca QUINN, Ashley LAWRENCE• - Jasmin DHANDA (Nichelle PRINCE 61), Amandine PI' RRE-LOUIS (Emily PIETRANGELO 79), Summer CLARKE. Tr: Bryan ROSENFELD

LANKARAN STADIUM, LANKARAN
25-09-2012, 17:00, Att: 10 827, Ref: Alondra Arellano MEX

Azerbaijan 0
Nigeria 11 Ihezuo 5 [5] [32] [37] [56] [70], Ayinde 2 [8] [24], Biawho 2 [20] [74], Yakubu [22], Bokiri [68]

AZERBAIJAN
Aytaj SHARIFOVA - Zhala MAHSIMOVA, Amina HEYDAROVA(c), Suheyla ILTAR, Shafag NASIROVA - Maia DANGADZE - Nigar JALILLI, Sevinj GURBANOVA (Zhala MAMMADOVA 73), Sabrina RONAGHI (Laman BAGHIROVA• 52), Leila SOLMAZ (Aysun ALIYEVA 88) - Aliya VALIYEVA. Tr: Sissy RAITH GER

NIGERIA
Gift ANDY - Ebere OKOYE (Ihuoma ONYEBUCHI 76), Victoria AIDE-LOMON(c), Ugochi EMENAYO, Jiroro IDIKE - Oluchi OFOEGBU, Halimatu AYINDE (Yetunde ADEBOYEJO 73) - Aminat YAKUBU, Chinwendu IHEZUO, Mabel EFFIOM (Joy BOKIRI 62) - Tessy BIAHWO. Tr: Peter DEDEVBO

SHAFA STADIUM, BAKU
25-09-2012, 14:00, Att: 4729, Ref: Carina Vitulano ITA

Colombia 0
Canada 1 Clarke [51]

COLOMBIA
Lissa CARDOZO - Anyella MARTINEZ•, Maria JARAMILLO, Diana DUARTE, Estefania BOTERO - Carolina ARBELAEZ, Marcela RESTREPO (Karen GUTIERREZ 70) - Juliana OCAMPO (Pamela PENALOZA 59), Leicy SANTOS, Gabriela MALDONADO (Nicole REGNIER 46) - Dayana CASTILLO(c). Tr: Fabian TABORDA

CANADA
Kailen SHERIDAN - Lindsay AGNEW, Kadeisha BUCHANAN, Rebecca PONGETTI, Larisa STAUB - Nicole LONCAR, Valerie SANDERSON (Jasmin DHANDA 59), Rebecca QUINN, Ashley LAWRENCE(c) - Nichelle PRINCE, Summer CLARKE (Amandine PIERRE-LOUIS 71). Tr: Bryan ROSENFELD

DALGA ARENA, BAKU
29-09-2012, 20:00, Att: 5000, Ref: Claudia Umpierrez URU

Canada 1 Sanderson [48]
Azerbaijan 0

CANADA
Kailen SHERIDAN - Madeline IOZZI, Kadeisha BUCHANAN, Rebecca PONGETTI, Larisa STAUB - Elissa NEFF (Nicole LONCAR 80), Valerie SANDERSON, Rebecca QUINN, Ashley LAWRENCE(c) - Amandine PIERRE-LOUIS (Summer CLARKE 73), Nichelle PRINCE (Emily PIETRANGELO 92+). Tr: Bryan ROSENFELD

AZERBAIJAN
Aytaj SHARIFOVA - Zhala MAHSIMOVA (Aysun ALIYEVA 64), Amina HEYDAROVA(c), Suheyla ILTAR, Olya SHIOSHVILI - Maia DANGADZE, Shafag NASIROVA - Nigar JALILLI•, Sabrina RONAGHI, Aliya VALIYEVA (Leila SOLMAZ 57) - Melis SARIALTIN (Laman BAGHIROVA 92+). Tr: Sissy RAITH GER

BAYIL STADIUM, BAKU
29-09-2012, 20:00, Att: 2500, Ref: Cardella Samuels JAM

Colombia 0
Nigeria 3 Ayinde 2 [32] [75], Duarte OG [80]

COLOMBIA
Lissa CARDOZO - Anyella MARTINEZ, Maria JARAMILLO, Diana DUARTE, Estefania BOTERO - Carolina ARBELAEZ, Marcela RESTREPO (Juliana OCAMPO 87) - Nicole REGNIER (Daniela TAMAYO 88), Leicy SANTOS, Gabriela MALDONADO (Pamela PENALOZA 83) - Dayana CASTILLO(c). Tr: Fabian TABORDA

NIGERIA
Gift ANDY - Ebere OKOYE, Victoria AIDELOMON(c), Sarah NNODIM, Jiroro IDIKE - Oluchi OFOEGBU, Halimatu AYINDE - Aminat YAKUBU (Yetunde ADEBOYEJO 62), Tessy BIAHWO, Mabel EFFIOM (Joy BOKIRI 85) - Chinwendu IHEZUO. Tr: Peter DEDEVBO

PART ONE – FIFA AND WORLD FOOTBALL

	GROUP B	PL	W	D	L	F	A	PTS	FRA	USA	GAM
1	Korea DPR	3	1	2	0	13	2	5	1-1	1-1	11-0
2	France	3	1	2	0	11	3	5		0-0	10-2
3	USA	3	1	2	0	7	1	5			6-0
4	Gambia	3	0	0	3	2	27	0			

LANKARAN STADIUM, LANKARAN
22-09-2012, 15:00, Att: 8100, Ref: Claudia Umpierrez URU

France	0
USA	0

FRANCE
Romane BRUNEAU - Marion ROMANELLI, Aissatou TOUNKARA, Griedge MBOCK BATHY, Noemie CARAGE - Juliane GATHRAT (Candice GHERBI 92+), Sandie TOLETTI(c), Ghoutia KARCHOUNI - Delphine CASCARINO (Laura BLANCHARD 85), Kadidiatou DIANI, Lea DECLERCQ (Alexandra ATAMANIUK 68). Tr: Guy FERRIER

USA
Jane CAMPBELL - Brittany BASINGER, Maddie BAUER, Mandy FREEMAN (Lizzy RABEN 13), Gabbi MIRANDA - Morgan ANDREWS•(c), Toni PAYNE, Andi SULLIVAN - Summer GREEN•, Margaret PURCE (Emily BRUDER 63), Darian JENKINS. Tr: Albertin MONTOYA

---

8 KM STADIUM, BAKU
22-09-2012, 13:00, Att: 9000, Ref: Carina Vitulano ITA

Korea DPR	11	Choe Yun Gyong [18], Ri Un Sim 3 [19 31 34p], Ri Kyong Hyang 3 [20 63 77], Kim Phyong Hwa [44], Kim So Hyang [68], Ri Hyang Sim 2 [87 91+]
Gambia	0	

KOREA DPR
RIM Yong Hwa - KIM Hyang Mi, RI Un Yong, CHOE Sol Gyong, JON So Yon - RI Hyang Sim, CHOE Chung Bok(c) (KIM Un Hwa 63), CHOE Yun Gyong, KIM Phyong Hwa (CHOE Hyang Mi 70) - RI Kyong Hyang, RI Un Sim (KIM So Hyang 55). Tr: HWANG Yong Bong

GAMBIA
Aminata GAYE - Serreh JATTA, Fatou FATTY, Amie JARJU(c) - Fatou DARBOE, Ndey BEYAI, Fatou COLLEY, Penda BAH (Sainey SISSOHORE 65), Fatoumata GIBBA (Isatou JALLOW 46) - Adama TAMBA, Awa DEMBA (Veronic MALACK 60). Tr: Buba JALLOW

DALGA ARENA, BAKU
25-09-2012, 14:00, Att: 4200, Ref: Gillian Martindale BRB

France	1	Diani [60]
Korea DPR	1	Ri Un Sim [59]

FRANCE
Romane BRUNEAU - Marion ROMANELLI, Aissatou TOUNKARA, Griedge MBOCK BATHY, Noemie CARAGE - Candice GHERBI (Juliane GATHRAT 77), Sandie TOLETTI(c), Ghoutia KARCHOUNI - Pauline COUSIN (Delphine CASCARINO 64), Kadidiatou DIANI, Lea DECLERCQ. Tr: Guy FERRIER

KOREA DPR
RIM Yong Hwa - KIM Hyang Mi, RI Un Yong, CHOE Sol Gyong, JON So Yon - RI Hyang Sim, CHOE Chung Bok(c), CHOE Yun Gyong, KIM Phyong Hwa (KIM Un Hwa 68) - RI Kyong Hyang (JO Ryon Hwa 82), RI Un Sim. Tr: HWANG Yong Bong

---

DALGA ARENA, BAKU
25-09-2012, 17:00, Att: 4200, Ref: Etsuko Fukano JPN

USA	6	Green 2 [25p 71], Munerlyn [46], Jarju OG [61], Stanton [83], Payne [86]
Gambia	0	

USA
Jane CAMPBELL (Cassie MILLER 46) - Brittany BASINGER, Maddie BAUER(c), Lizzy RABEN, Morgan REID - Morgan STANTON, Toni PAYNE, Andi SULLIVAN - Summer GREEN (Lauren KASKIE 82), Amber MUNERLYN (Emily BRUDER 70), Darian JENKINS. Tr: Albertin MONTOYA

GAMBIA
Aminata GAYE - Serreh JATTA, Fatou FATTY, Amie JARJU(c), Awa TAMBA (Anna NYASSI 63) - Fatou DARBOE, Metta SANNEH, Binta COLLEY (Veronic MALACK 72), Sainey SISSOHORE - Adama TAMBA, Awa DEMBA (Isatou JALLOW 55). Tr: Buba JALLOW

DALGA ARENA, BAKU
29-09-2012, 17:00, Att: 5000, Ref: Finau Vulivuli FIJ

Gambia	2	Bah [48], Sissohore [69]
France	10	Cousin 2 [11 81], Sanneh OG [25], Declercq 3 [35 78 85], Gherbi [53], Diani [71], Mbock Bathy [79], Bojang OG [90]

GAMBIA
Mariama Ceesay - Anna NYASSI, Amie JARJU(c) (Fatou FATTY 46), Mariama BOJANG - Fatou DARBOE, Metta SANNEH•, Binta COLLEY•, Sainey SISSOHORE• (Awa TAMBA• 70) - Penda BAH, Veronic MALACK (Adama TAMBA 45), Isatou JALLOW. Tr: Buba JALLOW

FRANCE
Cindy PERRAULT - Marion ROMANELLI, Amandine BLANC, Griedge MBOCK BATHY - Candice GHERBI (Juliane GATHRAT 62), Laura BLANCHARD (Delphine CASCARINO 46), Sandie TOLETTI(c) - Pauline COUSIN, Laurie SAULNIER (Noemie CARAGE 46), Kadidiatou DIANI•, Lea DECLERCQ. Tr: Guy FERRIER

BAYIL STADIUM, BAKU
29-09-2012, 17:00, Att: 2500, Ref: Katalin Kulcsar HUN

USA	1	Jenkins [2]
Korea DPR	1	Ri Un Sim [4]

USA
Jane CAMPBELL - Brittany BASINGER, Maddie BAUER, Mandy FREEMAN, Gabbi MIRANDA - Morgan ANDREWS(c) (Lauren KASKIE 91+), Toni PAYNE, Andi SULLIVAN (Morgan STANTON 82) - Summer GREEN, Amber MUNERLYN (Emily BRUDER 86), Darian JENKINS•. Tr: Albertin MONTOYA

KOREA DPR
RIM Yong Hwa - KIM Hyang Mi•, RI Un Yong, CHOE Sol Gyong•, JON So Yon - RI Hyang Sim, CHOE Chung Bok(c), CHOE Yun Gyong•, KIM Un Hwa (KIM Phyong Hwa 74) - RI Kyong Hyang (KIM So Hyang 88), RI Un Sim. Tr: HWANG Yong Bong

FIFA U-17 WOMEN'S WORLD CUP AZERBAIJAN 2012

	GROUP C	PL	W	D	L	F	A	PTS	BRA	MEX	NZL
1	Japan	3	3	0	0	17	0	9	5-0	9-0	3-0
2	Brazil	3	2	0	1	5	8	6		1-0	4-3
3	Mexico	3	1	0	2	1	10	3			1-0
4	New Zealand	3	0	0	3	3	8	0			

BAYIL STADIUM, BAKU
23-09-2012, 15:00, Att: 1900, Ref: Jana Adamkova CZE

Mexico 1 Perez [36]
New Zealand 0

MEXICO
Gabriela PAZ - Jaqueline RODRIGUEZ, Greta ESPINOZA, Jocelyn OREJEL, Paulina SOLIS - Karla NIETO(c) - Taylor ALVARADO (Natalie RIVAS 68), Cynthia PINEDA, Fernanda PEREZ (Jenny CHIU 82), Hallie HERNANDEZ (Samantha ARELLANO 59) - Luz DUARTE. Tr: Christopher CUELLAR

NEW ZEALAND
Lily ALFELD - Meikayla MOORE, Emily JENSEN, Laura MERRIN - Hannah CARLSEN(c), Briar PALMER (Daisy CLEVERLEY 46) - Jessica INNES (Emma ROLSTON 46), Jasmine PEREIRA, Emma FLETCHER, Megan LEE (Courteney VAN LIESHOUT 70) - Martine PUKETAPU. Tr: Paul TEMPLE

BAYIL STADIUM, BAKU
23-09-2012, 18:00, Att: 1900, Ref: Katalin Kulcsar HUN

Brazil 0
Japan 5 Masuya 2 [2 17], Narumiya 2 [49 67], Sugita [63]

BRAZIL
NICOLE - JULIA, ANA CLARA, CAROLINE, NATANE - GABRIELLY (GABRIELLE 60), BRENA (LETICIA 66), DJENIFER, ANDRESSA(c) - BYANCA, CHAIANE (MAYARA 46). Tr: Edvaldo ERLACHER

JAPAN
Chika HIRAO - Miku KOJIMA (Saki ISHII 82), Shiori MIYAKE, Ruka NORIMATSU, Risa SHIMIZU - Mizuki NAKAMURA, Rin SUMIDA - Ayaka INOUE (Hina SUGITA 46), Yui HASEGAWA (Miki ITO 72), Yui NARUMIYA(c) - Rika MASUYA. Tr: Hiroshi YOSHIDA

8 KM STADIUM, BAKU
26-09-2012, 17:00, Att: 7000, Ref: Kateryna Monzul UKR

Mexico 0
Brazil 1 Byanca [82]

MEXICO
Gabriela PAZ - Jaqueline RODRIGUEZ, Greta ESPINOZA, Jocelyn OREJEL, Paulina SOLIS - Karla NIETO(c) - Taylor ALVARADO, Cynthia PINEDA (Gabriela ALVAREZ 71), Fernanda PEREZ, Hallie HERNANDEZ (Mariana CADENA 52) - Jenny CHIU. Tr: Christopher CUELLAR

BRAZIL
NICOLE - JULIA, ANA CLARA, CAROLINE, LETICIA - CAMILA, BRENA (CHAIANE 69), DJENIFER, ANDRESSA(c) - GABRIELLE (BYANCA 69), JENYFFER (MAYARA 46). Tr: Edvaldo ERLACHER

8 KM STADIUM, BAKU
26-09-2012, 20:00, Att: 7000, Ref: Cardella Samuels JAM

New Zealand 0
Japan 3 Hasegawa 2 [60 78], Sumida [93+]

NEW ZEALAND
Lily ALFELD - Meikayla MOORE, Emily JENSEN, Catherine BOTT(c), Laura MERRIN (Martine PUKETAPU 38) - Hannah CARLSEN, Daisy CLEVERLEY - Jasmine PEREIRA, Emma FLETCHER (Emily OOSTERHOF 84), Megan LEE - Emma ROLSTON (Lauren DABNER 79). Tr: Paul TEMPLE

JAPAN
Chika HIRAO - Saki ISHII, Arisa MATSUBARA, Ruka NORIMATSU, Risa SHIMIZU - Hina SUGITA (Mizuki NAKAMURA 68), Rin SUMIDA - Miki ITO (Yui HASEGAWA 46), Yuka MOMIKI, Yui NARUMIYA(c) - Rika MASUYA (Akari SHIRAKI 84). Tr: Hiroshi YOSHIDA

SHAFA STADIUM, BAKU
30-09-2012, 14:00, Att: 3000, Ref: Morag Pirie SCO

Japan 9 Shimizu [8], Narumiya [18p], Shiraki 2 [22 29], Inoue 2 [28 56], Sugita [69], Momiki [79], Nakamura [86]
Mexico 0

JAPAN
Nene INOUE - Miku KOJIMA, Shiori MIYAKE (Ayaka NISHIKAWA 46), Arisa MATSUBARA, Risa SHIMIZU - Mizuki NAKAMURA, Rin SUMIDA - Yuka MOMIKI 46), Ayaka INOUE, Hina SUGITA, Yui NARUMIYA(c) - (Miho MANYA 71) - Akari SHIRAKI. Tr: Hiroshi YOSHIDA

MEXICO
Gabriela PAZ - Jaqueline RODRIGUEZ, Greta ESPINOZA, Jessica VALADEZ•, Jocelyn OREJEL (Mariana CADENA 39), Paulina SOLIS - Karla NIETO(c) - Taylor ALVARADO, Cynthia PINEDA (Samantha ARELLANO 56), Fernanda PEREZ - Luz DUARTE• (Natalie RIVAS 73). Tr: Christopher CUELLAR

8 KM STADIUM, BAKU
30-09-2012, 14:00, Att: , Ref:

New Zealand 3 Jensen [4], Ana Clara OG [45], Puketapu [77]
Brazil 4 Byanca [10], Brena [26], Andressa [35p], Camila [55]

NEW ZEALAND
Lily ALFELD - Meikayla MOORE, Emily JENSEN, Catherine BOTT, Laura MERRIN(c) (Emma ROLSTON 57) - Hannah CARLSEN, Daisy CLEVERLEY (Jessica INNES 64) - Jasmine PEREIRA (Briar PALMER 76), Emma FLETCHER, Megan LEE - Martine PUKETAPU. Tr: Paul TEMPLE

BRAZIL
NICOLE - JULIA, ANA CLARA, CAROLINE, LETICIA - CAMILA, BRENA (MONICA 73), DJENIFER, ANDRESSA(c) - BYANCA, CHAIANE (MAXINNY 87). Tr: Edvaldo ERLACHER

PART ONE - FIFA AND WORLD FOOTBALL

	GROUP D	PL	W	D	L	F	A	PTS	GHA	CHN	URU
1	Germany	3	2	1	0	8	4	7	2-1	1-1	5-2
2	Ghana	3	2	0	1	8	2	6		2-0	5-0
3	China PR	3	1	1	1	5	3	4			4-0
4	Uruguay	3	0	0	3	2	14	0			

DALGA ARENA, BAKU
23-09-2012, 18:00, Att: 3000, Ref: Morag Pirie SCO

Uruguay	0	
China PR	4	Tang Jiali [23], Zhang Chen 2 [34 41], Lu Yueyun [79]

URUGUAY
Gabriela GONZALEZ♦[51] - Carina FELIPE, Nicole ARAMBULO•(c), Romina SORAVILLA, Yamila DEL PUERTO - Maria GONZALEZ, Pamela GONZALEZ (Sabrina SORAVILLA 46), Carolina BIRIZAMBERRI, Alaides BONILLA (Anabel UBAL 53) - Keisy SILVEIRA (Stephanie TREGARTTEN 60), Yamila BADELL. Tr: Graciela REBOLLO

CHINA PR
LU Feifei - LI Mengwen, WANG Xi, JIANG Tingting(c), SONG Yuqing - LU Yueyun, LEI Jiahui• - ZHANG Zhu (JI Xinyi 68), TANG Jiali (LIU Yanqiu 82) - ZHANG Chen (XIAO Yuyi 79), SONG Duan, Tr: ZHANG Chonglai

---

DALGA ARENA, BAKU
23-09-2012, 15:00, Att: 3000, Ref: Alondra Arellano MEX

Ghana	1	Ayieyam [80]
Germany	2	Beil [13], Bremer [19]

GHANA
Victoria AGYEI - Naomi ANIMA (Laadi ISSAKA 46), Vida OPOKU, Regina ANTWI, Ellen COLEMAN - Fatima ALHASSAN (Alberta AHIALEY 74) - Priscilla OKYERE(c), Rasheda ABDUL-RAHMAN, Sherifatu SUMAILA - Jane AYIEYAM, Wasila DIWURA-SOALE (Ivy KOLLI 46). Tr: Mas-Ud DRAMANI

GERMANY
Merle FROHMS - Johanna TIETGE, Lena LUECKEL, Franziska JASER, Wibke MEISTER - Daria STRENG (Rebecca KNAAK 70) - Vivien BEIL, Theresa PANFIL (Janina MEISSNER 46), Pauline BREMER - Sara DAEBRITZ(c), Venus EL-KASSEM (Ricarda KIESSLING 78). Tr: Anouschka BERNHARD

BAYIL STADIUM, BAKU
26-09-2012, 17:00, Att: 2600, Ref: Ri Hyang Ok PRK

Uruguay	0	
Ghana	5	Ayieyam [8], Okyere 2 [24 79], Ahialey [45], Alhassan [78]

URUGUAY
Anabel UBAL - Carina FELIPE, Nicole ARAMBULO(c), Karen ACOSTA (Romina SORAVILLA 39), Yamila DEL PUERTO - Maria GONZALEZ, Pamela GONZALEZ, Carolina BIRIZAMBERRI, Stephanie TREGARTTEN (Lucia CAPPELLETTI 61), Sabrina SORAVILLA (Alaides BONILLA 44) - Yamila BADELL. Tr: Graciela REBOLLO

GHANA
Victoria AGYEI - Vida OPOKU•, Regina ANTWI, Ivy KOLLI, Ellen COLEMAN - Fatima ALHASSAN - Priscilla OKYERE(c), Sherifatu SUMAILA - Wasila DIWURA-SOALE (Laadi ISSAKA 43) (Lily NIBER-LAWRENCE 72), Alberta AHIALEY (Gladys AMFOBEA 58), Jane AYIEYAM. Tr: Mas-Ud DRAMANI

BAYIL STADIUM, BAKU
26-09-2012, 20:00, Att: 2600, Ref: Aissata Amegee TOG

China PR	1	Miao Siwen [12]
Germany	1	Kiessling [94+]

CHINA PR
LU Feifei - LI Mengwen, WANG Xi, JIANG Tingting(c), SONG Yuqing - LU Yueyun, LEI Jiahui - ZHANG Zhu (XIAO Yuyi 89), TANG Jiali, MIAO Siwen (JI Xinyi 77) - ZHANG Chen (SONG Duan 69). Tr: ZHANG Chonglai

GERMANY
Merle FROHMS - Johanna TIETGE, Lena LUECKEL, Franziska JASER, Wibke MEISTER (Venus EL-KASSEM 76) (Ricarda KIESSLING 87) - Sharon BECK, Daria STRENG - Vivien BEIL (Sarah SCHULTE 69), Theresa PANFIL, Pauline BREMER - Sara DAEBRITZ(c). Tr: Anouschka BERNHARD

LANKARAN STADIUM, LANKARAN
30-09-2012, 17:00, Att: 8610, Ref: Gillian Martindale BRB

Germany	5	Daebritz 2 [14 64], Knaak [48], Kiessling [65], Beck [80p]
Uruguay	2	Badell 2 [42 87]

GERMANY
Merle FROHMS - Johanna TIETGE, Lena LUECKEL•, Franziska JASER, Sharon BECK - Rebecca KNAAK, Daria STRENG• (Ricarda KIESSLING 46) - Vivien BEIL (Manjou WILDE 46), Theresa PANFIL, Pauline BREMER (Janina MEISSNER 83) - Sara DAEBRITZ(c). Tr: Anouschka BERNHARD

URUGUAY
Gabriela GONZALEZ - Gisella DELL OCA, Nicole ARAMBULO(c), Romina SORAVILLA• (Karen ACOSTA 72), Yamila DEL PUERTO - Maria GONZALEZ, Pamela GONZALEZ, Antonella LARRICA (Agustina ARAMBULO• 66) - Keisy SILVEIRA•, Jemina ROLFO (Carolina BIRIZAMBERRI 28), Yamila BADELL. Tr: Graciela REBOLLO

---

8 KM STADIUM, BAKU
30-09-2012, 17:00, Att: 8857, Ref: Jana Adamkova CZE

China PR	0	
Ghana	2	Ayieyam 2 [18 88]

CHINA PR
LU Feifei - LI Mengwen, WANG Xi, JIANG Tingting(c), SONG Yuqing - LU Yueyun (LIU Yanqiu 71), LEI Jiahui - ZHANG Zhu (JI Xinyi 62), TANG Jiali, MIAO Siwen - ZHANG Chen (XIAO Yuyi 83). Tr: ZHANG Chonglai

GHANA
Victoria AGYEI - Vida OPOKU, Regina ANTWI, Ivy KOLLI (Naomi ANIMA 43), Ellen COLEMAN - Fatima ALHASSAN - Priscilla OKYERE(c) (Wasila DIWURA-SOALE 79), Samira ABDUL-RAHMAN, Sherifatu SUMAILA - Alberta AHIALEY (Gladys AMFOBEA 62), Jane AYIEYAM. Tr: Mas-Ud DRAMANI

QUARTER-FINALS

8 KM STADIUM, BAKU
4-10-2012, 20:00, Att: 6852, Ref: Ri Hyank Ok PRK

| Nigeria | 0 3p |
| France | 0 5p |

NIGERIA
Gift ANDY - Ebere OKOYE, Victoria AIDELOMON(c)●●◆74, Sarah NNODIM, Jiroro IDIKE - Oluchi OFOEGBU, Halimatu AYINDE - Aminat YAKUBU (Chidinma EDEJI 71), Chinwendu IHEZUO, Mabel EFFIOM (Tessy BIAHWO 50) - Yetunde ADEBOYEJO (Ugochi EMENAYO 80). Tr: Peter DEDEVBO

FRANCE
Romane BRUNEAU - Marion ROMANELLI●, Aissatou TOUNKARA, Griedge MBOCK BATHY, Noemie CARAGE - Delphine CASCARINO, Sandie TOLETTI(c), Ghoutia KARCHOUNI - Pauline COUSIN (Juliane GATHRAT 56), Kadidiatou DIANI, Lea DECLERCQ. Tr: Guy FERRIER

PENALTIES
Toletti ✓ • Emenayo ✓ • Declercq ✓ • Nnodim ✗[1] • Mbock Bathy ✓ • Ofoegbu ✓ • Cascarino ✓ • Biahwo ✓ • Romanelli ✓
France won 5-3 • ([1] = missed)

8 KM STADIUM, BAKU
5-10-2012, 20:00, Att: 2762, Ref: Kateryna Monzul UKR

| Japan | 0 |
| Ghana | 1 | Sumaila 53 |

JAPAN
Chika HIRAO - Miku KOJIMA (Akari SHIRAKI 82), Shiori MIYAKE, Ruka NORIMATSU, Risa SHIMIZU - Mizuki NAKAMURA (Hina SUGITA 73), Rin SUMIDA - Ayaka INOUE (Yuka MOMIKI 58), Yui HASEGAWA, Yui NARUMIYA(c) - Rika MASUYA. Tr: Hiroshi YOSHIDA

GHANA
Victoria AGYEI - Naomi ANIMA, Vida OPOKU, Regina ANTWI, Ellen COLEMAN - Fatima ALHASSAN (Belinda ANANE● 83) - Samira ABDUL-RAHMAN (Rasheda ABDUL-RAHMAN● 72), Priscilla OKYERE(c) (Laadi ISSAKA 95+), Alberta AHIALEY, Sherifatu SUMAILA - Jane AYIEYAM. Tr: Mas-Ud DRAMANI

8 KM STADIUM, BAKU
5-10-2012, 17:00, Att: 2762, Ref: Alondra Arellano MEX

| Germany | 2 | Daebritz 31, Knaak 92+ |
| Brazil | 1 | Djenifer 13 |

GERMANY
Merle FROHMS - Johanna TIETGE, Lena LUECKEL, Franziska JASER, Wibke MEISTER - Rebecca KNAAK, Janina MEISSNER (Daria STRENG 46) - Vivien BEIL (Sarah SCHULTE 78), Theresa PANFIL, Pauline BREMER (Ricarda KIESSLING 24) - Sara DAEBRITZ(c). Tr: Anouschka BERNHARD

BRAZIL
NICOLE (TAINA 34) - JULIA, ANA CLARA, CAROLINE, LETICIA● - CAMILA, BRENA (GABRIELLY 66), DJENIFER●, ANDRESSA(c) - BYANCA, CHAIANE. Tr: Edvaldo ERLACHER

8 KM STADIUM, BAKU
4-10-2012, 17:00, Att: 6852, Ref: Morag Pirie SCO

| Korea DPR | 2 | Ri Un Sim 2 78 87 |
| Canada | 1 | Prince 91+ |

KOREA DPR
RIM Yong Hwa - KIM Hyang Mi, RI Un Yong, CHOE Sol Gyong - RI Hyang Sim, CHOE Chung Bok(c), CHOE Yun Gyong, RI Kum Suk (JON So Yon 33), KIM Un Hwa (KIM Phyong Hwa 36) - RI Un Sim, RI Kyong Hyang (KIM So Hyang 71). Tr: HWANG Yong Bong

CANADA
Kailen SHERIDAN - Lindsay AGNEW, Kadeisha BUCHANAN, Rebecca PONGETTI (Emily PIETRANGELO 86), Larisa STAUB - Nicole LONCAR, Rebecca QUINN, Valerie SANDERSON (Jasmin DHANDA 66), Ashley LAWRENCE(c) - Nichelle PRINCE, Summer CLARKE (Amandine PIERRE-LOUIS● 73). Tr: Bryan ROSENFELD

SEMI-FINALS

8 KM STADIUM, BAKU
9-10-2012, 17:00, Att: 4651, Ref: Cardella Samuels JAM

| France | 2 | Diani 2 31 89 |
| Ghana | 0 |

FRANCE
Romane BRUNEAU - Marion ROMANELLI, Aissatou TOUNKARA, Griedge MBOCK BATHY, Noemie CARAGE - Juliane GATHRAT, Sandie TOLETTI(c), Ghoutia KARCHOUNI (Candice GHERBI 92+) - Delphine CASCARINO (Alexandra ATAMANIUK 65), Kadidiatou DIANI, Lea DECLERCQ (Ophelie GAHERY 93+). Tr: Guy FERRIER

GHANA
Victoria AGYEI - Naomi ANIMA● (Wasila DIWURA-SOALE 71), Vida OPOKU, Regina ANTWI, Ellen COLEMAN - Fatima ALHASSAN● - Lily NIBER-LAWRENCE (Rasheda ABDUL-RAHMAN 29), Priscilla OKYERE(c) (Laadi ISSAKA 59), Alberta AHIALEY, Sherifatu SUMAILA - Jane AYIEYAM●●◆52. Tr: Mas-Ud DRAMANI

8 KM STADIUM, BAKU
9-10-2012, 20:00, Att: 4651, Ref: Claudia Umpierrez URU

| Korea DPR | 2 | Kim So Hyang 2 39 47 |
| Germany | 1 | Knaak 59 |

KOREA DPR
RIM Yong Hwa - KIM Hyang Mi, RI Un Yong, CHOE Sol Gyong, JON So Yon - RI Hyang Sim, CHOE Chung Bok(c), CHOE Yun Gyong, KIM Phyong Hwa (RI Kyong Hyang 83) - KIM So Hyang, RI Un Sim. Tr: HWANG Yong Bong

GERMANY
Merle FROHMS - Johanna TIETGE, Lena LUECKEL, Franziska JASER, Wibke MEISTER - Rebecca KNAAK●, Daria STRENG (Sharon BECK 80) - Vivien BEIL (Sarah SCHULTE 46), Theresa PANFIL, Ricarda KIESSLING - Sara DAEBRITZ(c). Tr: Anouschka BERNHARD

PLAY-OFF FOR THIRD PLACE

TOFIG BAHRAMOV STADIUM, BAKU
13-10-2012, 17:00, Att: 27 128, Ref: Jana Adamkova CZE

Ghana	1	Okyere 38
Germany	0	

GHANA

Victoria AGYEI - Naomi ANIMA (Belinda ANANE 74), Vida OPOKU, Regina ANTWI•, Ellen COLEMAN - Fatima ALHASSAN••♦32 - Lily NIBER-LAWRENCE (Rasheda ABDUL-RAHMAN 67), Priscilla OKYERE (c) (Gladys AMFOBEA 44), Samira ABDUL-RAHMAN, Sherifatu SUMAILA - Wasila DIWURA-SOALE. Tr: Mas-Ud DRAMANI

GERMANY

Merle FROHMS - Johanna TIETGE, Laura LELUSCHKO, Franziska JASER, Wibke MEISTER - Rebecca KNAAK, Daria STRENG - Vivien BEIL (Ricarda KIESSLING• 46), Theresa PANFIL, Manjou WILDE (Sarah SCHULTE 68) - Sara DAEBRITZ (c). Tr: Anouschka BERNHARD

FINAL

FIFA U-17 WOMEN'S WORLD CUP FINAL 2012
TOFIG BAHRAMOV STADIUM, BAKU

Saturday, 13-10-2012, 20:00, Att: 27 128, Ref: Carina Vitulano ITA
Assistants: Romina Santuari ITA & Giuliana Guarino ITA

FRANCE	1 7p 1 6p	KOREA DPR
Lea Declercq 33		Ri Un Sim 79

FRANCE
Blue shirts, blue shorts, blue socks

Tr: Guy Ferrier
Romane Bruneau
Aissatou Tounkara, Griedge Mbock Bathy
Marion Romanelli, Noemie Carage
Juliane Gathrat, Ghoutia Karchouni
Sandie Toletti (c)
Delphine Cascarino, Lea Declercq
Kadidiatou Diani

Ri Un Sim, Kim So Hyang 73, Ri Kyong Hyang
Kim Phyong Hwa 60, Kim Un Hwa, Ri Hyang Sim
Choe Yun Gyong, Choe Chung Bok (c)
Jon So Yon 56, Ri Kum Suk, Kim Hyang Mi
Choe Sol Gyong, Ri Un Yong 57
Tr: Hwang Yong Bong, Rim Yong Hwa

White shirts, white shorts, white socks
KOREA DPR

MATCH STATS

France		Korea DPR
11	Shots	7
4	Shots on Goal	2
10	Fouls Committed	9
5	Corner Kicks	2
1	Caught Offside	8
48	Possession (%)	52

PENALTIES

France		Korea DPR
✓	Toletti	
	Kim Un Hwa	✗¹
✓	Declercq	
	Choe Chung Bok	✓
✓	Mbock Bathy	
	Choe Yun Gyong	✓
✗¹	Romanelli	
	Kim Hyang Mi	✓

France (cont'd)		Korea DPR
✓	Cascarino	
	Ri Kyong Hyang	✓
✓	Bruneau	
	Ri Un Sim	✓
✓	Carage	
	Ri Kum Suk	✓
✓	Diani	
	Ri Un Yong	✗¹

France won 7-6 (¹ = saved)

FIFA FUTSAL WORLD CUP THAILAND 2012

FIFA FUTSAL WORLD CUP THAILAND 2012

First round groups		Round of 16		Quarter-finals		Semi-finals		Final	
Group A	Pts								
Ukraine	7	**Brazil**	16						
Paraguay	4	Panama	0						
Thailand	3			**Brazil**	3				
Costa Rica	3			Argentina	2				
Group B	Pts	Serbia	1						
Spain	7	**Argentina**	2						
Iran	7					**Brazil**	3		
Panama	3					Colombia	1		
Morocco	0	**Ukraine**	6						
Group C	Pts	Japan	3						
Brazil	9			Ukraine	1				
Portugal	4			**Colombia**	3				
Japan	4	Iran	1						
Libya	0	**Colombia**	2						
								Brazil	3
Group D	Pts							Spain	2
Italy	9	**Italy**	5						
Argentina	6	Egypt	1						
Australia	3			**Italy**	4				
Mexico	0			Portugal	3				
Group E	Pts	Paraguay	1						
Serbia	7	**Portugal**	4						
Czech Republic	4					Italy	1		
Egypt	3					**Spain**	4		
Kuwait	3	**Russia**	3						
Group F	Pts	Czech Republic	0						
Russia	9			Russia	2				
Colombia	3			**Spain**	3			**Play-off for Third Place**	
Guatemala	3	Thailand	1					**Italy**	3
Solomon Islands	3	**Spain**	7					Colombia	0

Top scorers: **9** - **EDER LIMA**, Russia • **8** - Rodolfo **FORTINO**, Italy • **7** - **FERNANDINHO**, Brazil; **CARDINAL**, Portugal; **RICARDINHO**, Portugal, Saad ASSIS, Italy & **NETO**, Brazil • **6** - **JE**, Brazil • **5** - Denys **OVSIANNIKOV**, Ukraine; Ievgen **ROGACHOV**, Ukraine; **SIRILO**, Russia; Sergey **SERGEEV**, Russia; Cristian **BORRUTO**, Argentina & **LOZANO**, Spain
FIFA Fair Play Award: Argentina
adidas Golden Ball: **1** - **NETO**, Brazil • **2** - **KIKE**, Spain • **3** - **RICARDINHO**, Portugal
adidas Golden Boot: **1** - **EDER LIMA**, Russia • **2** - Rodolfo **FORTINO**, Italy • **3** - **FERNANDINHO**, Brazil
adidas Golden Glove: Stefano **MAMMARELLA**, Italy

Brazil became futsal world champions for a fifth time after defeating arch-rivals Spain 3-2 in extra time of a nail-biting final. In a repeat of the 2008 title-decider, the South Americans once again came out on top after superb performances from both teams. The South Americans struck in the final minute to win the encounter at Bangkok's Huamark Indoor Stadium, match-winner Neto scoring the decisive goal 19 seconds from the end. Brazil thus add a fifth world title to their previous triumphs in 1989, 1992, 1996 and 2008. In the match for third place, Italy claimed the final podium berth with a 3-0 victory over debutants Colombia thanks to a double strike from Rodolfo Fortino and a glorious third from Sergio Romano. Hosts Thailand were another team to cause excitement among the fans, drawing roars of approval from the home support with their refreshingly attacking style of play. Despite defeats to Ukraine and Paraguay, victory over Costa Rica took the Thais into the knockout stages, where their dreams were ended by a ruthless Spanish outfit.

PART ONE – FIFA AND WORLD FOOTBALL

	GROUP A	PL	W	D	L	F	A	PTS		PAR	THA	CRC
1	Ukraine	3	2	1	0	14	7	7		3-3	5-3	6-1
2	Paraguay	3	1	1	1	9	11	4			3-2	3-6
3	Thailand	3	1	0	2	8	9	3				3-1
4	Costa Rica	3	1	0	2	8	12	3				

* In starting lineup • ‡ Did not play

INDOOR STADIUM HUAMARK, BANGKOK
1-11-2012, 17:00, Att: 4379, Ref: Wenceslaos Aguilar PAN

Ukraine	3	Pavlenko 2 $^{9'26''\ 39'08''}$, Shoturma $^{34'20''2PG}$
Paraguay	3	Enmanuel Ayala 3 $^{8'53''\ 29'20''\ 36'40''2PG}$

UKRAINE
Ievgen IVANYAK* (GK), Mykhaylo ROMANOV*, Stepan STRUK*, Sergiy ZHURBA*, Dmytro SOROKIN*, Sergiy CHEPORNIUK*, Maksym PAVLENKO*(c), Ievgen ROGACHOV*, Dmytro FEDORCHENKO*•, Petro SHOTURMA*, Denys OVSIANNIKOV*, Kyrylo TSYPUN‡ (GK), Oleksandr SOROKIN, Dmytro LYTVYNENKO‡ (GK). Tr: Gennadiy LISENCHUK

PARAGUAY
Carlos ESPINOLA* (GK), Enmanuel AYALA*•◆38, Fabio ALCARAZ(c), Gabriel AYALA*, Jose Luis SANTANDER•, Adolfo SALAS*, Oscar VELAZQUEZ•, Nelson LEZCANO, Juan SALAS, Walter VILLALBA*, Luis MOLINAS‡ (GK), Marcos BENITEZ*, Gabriel GIMENEZ‡ (GK), Rene VILLALBA. Tr: Fernando LEITE BRA

INDOOR STADIUM HUAMARK, BANGKOK
1-11-2012, 19:00, Att: 4379, Ref: Hector Rojas PER

Thailand	3	Chalaemkhet $^{17'59''}$, Thueanklang $^{28'04''}$, Sornwichian $^{37'54''}$
Costa Rica	1	Zuniga $^{36'39''}$

THAILAND
Prakit DANKHUNTHOD* (GK), Konghla LAKKA‡, Natee JEEPON‡, Piyapan RATANA, Jirawat SORNWICHIAN*, Thananchai CHOMBOON‡, Kritsada WONGKAEO*•, Jetsada CHUDECH*, Suphawut THUEANKLANG*, Apiwat CHAEMCHAROEN•, Nattavut MADYALAN•, Surapong TOMPA (GK)(c), Aref AHAMAH, Keattiyot CHALAEMKHET*. Tr: Victor HERMANS NED

COSTA RICA
Jairo TORUNO* (GK)(c), Adonay VINDAS, Justin WALLACE‡ (GK), Luis NAVARRETE, Edwin CUBILLO*, Jorge ARIAS, Alejandro PANIAGUA*•, Jose GUEVARA, Marco CARVAJAL•, Michael CORDOBA, Aaron JEREZ*, Diego ZUNIGA*, Erick BRENES, Alvaro SANTAMARIA‡ (GK). Tr: Diego SOLIS

INDOOR STADIUM HUAMARK, BANGKOK
4-11-2012, 17:00, Att: 5613, Ref: Francesco Massini ITA

Paraguay	3	Touno OG $^{1'41''}$, Alcaraz $^{10'43''}$, Walter Villalba $^{36'57''}$
Costa Rica	6	Zuniga $^{21'02''}$, Navarrete 2 $^{24'50''\ 27'46''}$, Cubillo 3 $^{26'36''\ 30'41''\ 39'44''}$

PARAGUAY
Carlos ESPINOLA* (GK), Enmanuel AYALA‡, Fabio ALCARAZ*(c), Gabriel AYALA, Jose Luis SANTANDER‡, Adolfo SALAS*, Oscar VELAZQUEZ*, Nelson LEZCANO, Juan SALAS*•, Walter VILLALBA*, Luis MOLINAS‡ (GK), Marcos BENITEZ*, Gabriel GIMENEZ‡ (GK), Rene VILLALBA. Tr: Fernando LEITE BRA

COSTA RICA
Jairo TORUNO* (GK), Adonay VINDAS, Justin WALLACE‡ (GK), Luis NAVARRETE, Edwin CUBILLO*, Jorge ARIAS, Alejandro PANIAGUA*(c), Jose GUEVARA, Marco CARVAJAL*, Michael CORDOBA, Aaron JEREZ••35, Diego ZUNIGA*, Erick BRENES, Alvaro SANTAMARIA‡ (GK). Tr: Diego SOLIS

INDOOR STADIUM HUAMARK, BANGKOK
4-11-2012, 19:00, Att: 5613, Ref: Sergio Cabrera CUB

Thailand	3	Wongkaeo $^{23'14''}$, Thueanklang $^{34'42''2PG}$, Sornwichian $^{38'09''}$
Ukraine	5	Ovsiannikov $^{3'06''}$, Cheporniuk $^{6'54''}$, Rogachov 2 $^{12'04''\ 19'25''}$, Pavlenko $^{19'54''}$

THAILAND
Prakit DANKHUNTHOD (GK), Konghla LAKKA, Natee JEEPON, Piyapan RATANA, Jirawat SORNWICHIAN*, Thananchai CHOMBOON, Kritsada WONGKAEO*•, Jetsada CHUDECH*, Suphawut THUEANKLANG*, Apiwat CHAEMCHAROEN, Nattavut MADYALAN, Surapong TOMPA* (GK)(c), Aref AHAMAH, Keattiyot CHALAEMKHET*•. Tr: Victor HERMANS NED

UKRAINE
Ievgen IVANYAK‡ (GK), Mykhaylo ROMANOV‡, Stepan STRUK‡, Sergiy ZHURBA, Dmytro SOROKIN‡, Sergiy CHEPORNIUK*, Maksym PAVLENKO*(c), Ievgen ROGACHOV*, Dmytro FEDORCHENKO‡, Petro SHOTURMA*, Denys OVSIANNIKOV*, Kyrylo TSYPUN‡ (GK), Oleksandr SOROKIN, Dmytro LYTVYNENKO* (GK). Tr: Gennadiy LISENCHUK

KORAT CHATCHAI HALL, NAKHON RATCHASIMA
7-11-2012, 4200, Att: 4200, Ref: Daniel Rodriguez URU

Costa Rica	1	Cubillo $^{23'11''}$
Ukraine	6	Rogachov 2 $^{6'37''\ 15'49''}$, Ovsiannikov $^{16'44''}$, Sorokin 2 $^{22'59''\ 31'40''}$, Pavlenko $^{28'49''}$

COSTA RICA
Jairo TORUNO‡ (GK), Adonay VINDAS, Justin WALLACE‡ (GK), Luis NAVARRETE*, Edwin CUBILLO*, Jorge ARIAS*, Alejandro PANIAGUA*(c), Jose GUEVARA, Marco CARVAJAL*, Michael CORDOBA, Aaron JEREZ‡, Diego ZUNIGA•, Erick BRENES, Alvaro SANTAMARIA*• (GK). Tr: Diego SOLIS

UKRAINE
Ievgen IVANYAK (GK), Mykhaylo ROMANOV, Stepan STRUK, Sergiy ZHURBA, Dmytro SOROKIN, Sergiy CHEPORNIUK*, Maksym PAVLENKO*(c), Ievgen ROGACHOV*, Dmytro FEDORCHENKO, Petro SHOTURMA*, Denys OVSIANNIKOV*, Kyrylo TSYPUN* (GK), Oleksandr SOROKIN, Dmytro LYTVYNENKO‡ (GK). Tr: Gennadiy LISENCHUK

INDOOR STADIUM HUAMARK, BANGKOK
7-11-2012, 19:00, Att: 5307, Ref: Ivan Shabanov RUS

Paraguay	3	Adolfo Salas $^{3'20''}$, Enmanuel Ayala $^{6'20''}$, Juan Salas $^{9'05''}$
Thailand	2	Thueanklang $^{10'41''}$, Chudech $^{24'59''}$

PARAGUAY
Carlos ESPINOLA* (GK), Enmanuel AYALA, Fabio ALCARAZ*(c), Gabriel AYALA•, Jose Luis SANTANDER*, Adolfo SALAS*, Oscar VELAZQUEZ‡, Nelson LEZCANO, Juan SALAS*•, Walter VILLALBA*, Luis MOLINAS‡ (GK), Marcos BENITEZ*, Gabriel GIMENEZ‡ (GK), Rene VILLALBA•. Tr: Fernando LEITE BRA

THAILAND
Prakit DANKHUNTHOD* (GK), Konghla LAKKA*, Natee JEEPON‡, Piyapan RATANA•, Jirawat SORNWICHIAN*, Thananchai CHOMBOON, Kritsada WONGKAEO*, Jetsada CHUDECH*, Suphawut THUEANKLANG*•, Apiwat CHAEMCHAROEN, Nattavut MADYALAN•, Surapong TOMPA‡ (GK)(c), Aref AHAMAH, Keattiyot CHALAEMKHET*•. Tr: Victor HERMANS NED

FIFA FUTSAL WORLD CUP THAILAND 2012

	GROUP B	PL	W	D	L	F	A	PTS		IRN	PAN	MAR
1	Spain	3	2	1	0	15	6	7		2-2	8-3	5-1
2	Iran	3	2	1	0	8	6	7			4-3	2-1
3	Panama	3	1	0	2	14	15	3				8-3
4	Morocco	3	0	0	3	5	15	0				

* In starting lineup • ‡ Did not play

INDOOR STADIUM HUAMARK, BANGKOK
2-11-2012, 19:00, Att: 3579, Ref: Amitesh Behari FIJ

Panama	8	Perez 19'07", Lasso 2 21'37" 30'06", Mena 2 22'42" 31'09", Galvez 24'26", Hinks 33'23", Goodridge 38'45"
Morocco	3	Jabrane 6'30", Derrou 11'15", Habil 15'26"2PG

PANAMA
Valencio **PARKS**‡ (GK), Miguel **BELLO**‡, Oscar **HINKS***, Augusto **HARRISON**‡, Fernando **MENA**, Edgar **RIVAS**, Claudio **GOODRIDGE***, Carlos **PEREZ**, Miguel **LASSO***, Alquis **ALVARADO***(c), Apolinar **GALVEZ**, Jaime **LONDONO*** (GK), Michael **DE LEON**, Enrique **VALDES**‡. Tr: Agustin **CAMPUZANO** CUB

MOROCCO
Rabie **ZAARI*** (GK), Soufiane **EL MESRAR**•, Hatim **OUAHABI**‡, Mohammed **DAHOU**‡, Youssef **EL MAZRAY***, Yahya **BAYA***(c), Bilal **ASSOUFI**, Adil **HABIL***, Mohammed **TALIBI**, Aziz **DERROU***•, Anouar **CHRAYEH**, Adil **EL BETTACHI**‡ (GK), Yahya **JABRANE**•, Younes **KELKAGHI**‡ (GK). Tr: Hicham **DGUIG**

INDOOR STADIUM HUAMARK, BANGKOK
2-11-2012, 21:00, Att: 3579, Ref: Francesco Rivera MEX

Spain	2	Miguelin 4'03", Lozano 15'34"
Iran	2	Daneshvar 27'50", Tayebi 30'42"

SPAIN
CRISTIAN‡ (GK), **ORTIZ**•, **AICARDO***, **TORRAS**, **FERNANDAO**‡, **ALVARO**, **MIGUELIN**, **KIKE***•(c), **LOZANO**, **BORJA**, **LIN**•, **JUANJO*** (GK), **RAFA**‡ (GK), **ALEMAO***•. Tr: Venancio **LOPEZ**

IRAN
Alireza **SAMIMI**‡ (GK), Ali **KIAEI**‡, Ali **RAHNAMA**, Mohammad **KESHAVARZ***(c), Hamid **AHMADI**•, Afshin **KAZEMI**, Ali **HASSANZADEH***•, Mostafa **TAYYEBI**, Masoud **DANESHVAR***, Mohammad **TAHERI**•, Hossein **TAYEBI**, Mostafa **NAZARI**‡ (GK), Ahmad **ESMAEILPOUR**, Sepehr **MOHAMMADI**‡ (GK). Tr: Ali **SANEI**

INDOOR STADIUM HUAMARK, BANGKOK
5-11-2012, 19:00, Att: 1409, Ref: Carlos Gonzalez GUA

Morocco	1	El Mazray 19'28"
Iran	2	Hassanzadeh 19'17"P, Kazemi 32'05"

MOROCCO
Rabie **ZAARI*** (GK), Soufiane **EL MESRAR**‡•, Hatim **OUAHABI**‡, Mohammed **DAHOU**‡, Youssef **EL MAZRAY**, Yahya **BAYA**(c), Bilal **ASSOUFI**, Adil **HABIL***, Mohammed **TALIBI***, Aziz **DERROU***, Anouar **CHRAYEH***•, Adil **EL BETTACHI**‡ (GK), Yahya **JABRANE**, Younes **KELKAGHI**‡ (GK). Tr: Hicham **DGUIG**

IRAN
Alireza **SAMIMI**‡ (GK), Ali **KIAEI**‡, Ali **RAHNAMA**, Mohammad **KESHAVARZ***(c), Hamid **AHMADI**•, Afshin **KAZEMI**•, Ali **HASSANZADEH***, Mostafa **TAYYEBI**, Masoud **DANESHVAR**‡, Mohammad **TAHERI***•, Hossein **TAYEBI**, Mostafa **NAZARI*** (GK), Ahmad **ESMAEILPOUR***, Sepehr **MOHAMMADI**‡ (GK). Tr: Ali **SANEI**

INDOOR STADIUM HUAMARK, BANGKOK
5-11-2012, 21:00, Att: 1409, Ref: Scott Kidson AUS

Spain	8	Kike 1'44", Lin 7'05", Borja 2 10'20" 21'53", Aicardo 2 13'55" 19'59", Alemao 26'04"P, Miguelin 29'31"
Panama	3	De Leon 2 16'52" 32'34", Alvarado 29'09"

SPAIN
CRISTIAN* (GK), **ORTIZ**•, **AICARDO**, **TORRAS**, **FERNANDAO**‡, **ALVARO**, **MIGUELIN**, **KIKE***•(c), **LOZANO**•, **BORJA**, **LIN**, **JUANJO**‡ (GK), **RAFA**‡ (GK), **ALEMAO**. Tr: Venancio **LOPEZ**

PANAMA
Valencio **PARKS**‡ (GK), Miguel **BELLO**•, Oscar **HINKS***•, Augusto **HARRISON**, Fernando **MENA***, Edgar **RIVAS**•, Claudio **GOODRIDGE**, Carlos **PEREZ**, Miguel **LASSO***, Alquis **ALVARADO***(c), Apolinar **GALVEZ**, Jaime **LONDONO*** (GK), Michael **DE LEON**, Enrique **VALDES**•. Tr: Agustin **CAMPUZANO** CUB

NIMIBUTR STADIUM, BANGKOK
8-11-2012, 19:00, Att: 1400, Ref: Eduardo Fernandes POR

Iran	4	Esmaeilpour 3'00", Kazemi 13'02", Taheri 2 18'44" 37'12"
Panama	3	Goodridge 5'13", Perez 34'12"P, Alvarado 39'21"

IRAN
Alireza **SAMIMI**‡ (GK), Ali **KIAEI**‡, Ali **RAHNAMA**•, Mohammad **KESHAVARZ***(c), Hamid **AHMADI**•, Afshin **KAZEMI**•, Ali **HASSANZADEH***, Mostafa **TAYYEBI**, Masoud **DANESHVAR**‡, Mohammad **TAHERI***•, Hossein **TAYEBI**, Mostafa **NAZARI*** (GK), Ahmad **ESMAEILPOUR***•, Sepehr **MOHAMMADI**‡ (GK). Tr: Ali **SANEI**

PANAMA
Valencio **PARKS**‡ (GK), Miguel **BELLO**‡, Oscar **HINKS***, Augusto **HARRISON**‡, Fernando **MENA***•, Edgar **RIVAS**•, Claudio **GOODRIDGE***, Carlos **PEREZ**, Miguel **LASSO***, Alquis **ALVARADO***(c), Apolinar **GALVEZ**, Jaime **LONDONO*** (GK), Michael **DE LEON**•, Enrique **VALDES**. Tr: Agustin **CAMPUZANO** CUB

INDOOR STADIUM HUAMARK, BANGKOK
8-11-2012, 19:00, Att: 1898, Ref: Naoki Miyatani JPN

Morocco	1	Talibi 21'26"
Spain	5	Lozano 2 9'57" 11'08", Borja 18'31", Fernandao 32'36", Alvaro 33'58"

MOROCCO
Rabie **ZAARI*** (GK), Soufiane **EL MESRAR**, Hatim **OUAHABI**, Mohammed **DAHOU**, Youssef **EL MAZRAY***, Yahya **BAYA**(c), Bilal **ASSOUFI***, Adil **HABIL***, Mohammed **TALIBI**, Aziz **DERROU***, Anouar **CHRAYEH**, Adil **EL BETTACHI**‡ (GK), Yahya **JABRANE**, Younes **KELKAGHI**‡• (GK). Tr: Hicham **DGUIG**

SPAIN
CRISTIAN‡ (GK), **ORTIZ**‡, **AICARDO**, **TORRAS***(c), **FERNANDAO**, **ALVARO**, **MIGUELIN**, **KIKE**•, **LOZANO**•, **BORJA***, **LIN***•, **JUANJO***, **RAFA** (GK), **ALEMAO**‡. Tr: Venancio **LOPEZ**

PART ONE – FIFA AND WORLD FOOTBALL

	GROUP C	PL	W	D	L	F	A	PTS		POR	JPN	LBY
1	Brazil	3	3	0	0	20	2	9		3-1	4-1	13-0
2	Portugal	3	1	1	1	11	9	4			5-5	5-1
3	Japan	3	1	1	1	10	11	4				4-2
4	Libya	3	0	0	3	3	22	0		* In starting lineup • ‡ Did not play		

KORAT CHATCHAI HALL, NAKHON RATCHASIMA
1-11-2012, 19:00, Att: 4298, Ref: Alireza Sohrabi IRN

Libya	1	Ahamed Fathe 5'42"
Portugal	5	Cardinal 3 1'59" 15'58" 17'02", Nandinho 26'43", Marinho 28'13"

LIBYA
Yousef BENSAED* (GK), AHMED FARAJ‡, BADER HASAN*, MOHAMED RAGEB, ABDUSALAM SHERAD, Rabia ABDEL‡, REDA FATHE, Husam AL WAHISHI*, AHAMED FATHE*, MOHAMED RAHOMA*(c), Younis SHAMES, Ramzi AL SHARIF‡ (GK), Salem AGHILA‡, Husam ALTUMI‡ (GK). Tr: Pablo PRIETO ESP

PORTUGAL
JOAO BENEDITO* (GK), PAULINHO*, LEITAO‡, PEDRO CARY•, NANDINHO, ARNALDO*(c), CARDINAL*, DJO‡, GONCALO*, RICARDINHO*, JOAO MATOS, BEBE‡ (GK), MARINHO, ANDRE SOUSA‡ (GK). Tr: Jorge BRAZ

KORAT CHATCHAI HALL, NAKHON RATCHASIMA
1-11-2012, 21:00, Att: 4298, Ref: Gabor Kovacs HUN

Brazil	4	Wilde 2 13'32" 22'11", Neto 20'41", Vinicius 24'47"
Japan	1	Inaba 27'14"

BRAZIL
GUITTA‡ (GK), TIAGO* (GK), FRANKLIN‡ (GK), ARI*, RAFAEL‡, GABRIEL, VINICIUS*(c), SIMI, JE, FERNANDINHO, NETO*, FALCAO, WILDE*, RODRIGO. Tr: Marcos SORATO

JAPAN
Hisamitsu KAWAHARA* (GK), Jun FUJIWARA‡, Wataru KITAHARA‡, Yusuke KOMIYAMA*, Tetsuya MURAKAMI, Nobuya OSODO, Kaoru MORIOKA, Kensuke TAKAHASHI, Shota HOSHI*, Kenichiro KOGURE*(c), Kazu MIURA, Toru FUKUBARA‡ (GK), Katsutoshi HENMI*•, Kotaro INABA. Tr: Miguel RODRIGO ESP

KORAT CHATCHAI HALL, NAKHON RATCHASIMA
4-11-2012, 19:00, Att: 4350, Ref: Daniel Rodriguez URU

Portugal	5	Joao Matos 0'49", Ricardinho 2 1'48" 17'10", Cardinal 2 8'50" 11'56"
Japan	5	Morioka 2 10'36" 32'47", Hoshi 18'15", Kitahara 31'51", Henmi 35'48"

PORTUGAL
JOAO BENEDITO* (GK), PAULINHO*, LEITAO, PEDRO CARY•, NANDINHO, ARNALDO*•(c), CARDINAL*•, DJO, GONCALO*, RICARDINHO*, JOAO MATOS*, BEBE‡ (GK), MARINHO, ANDRE SOUSA‡ (GK). Tr: Jorge BRAZ

JAPAN
Hisamitsu KAWAHARA* (GK), Jun FUJIWARA‡ (GK), Wataru KITAHARA*, Yusuke KOMIYAMA•(c), Tetsuya MURAKAMI*, Nobuya OSODO, Kaoru MORIOKA, Kensuke TAKAHASHI, Shota HOSHI*, Kenichiro KOGURE*•, Kazu MIURA, Toru FUKUBARA‡ (GK), Katsutoshi HENMI*, Kotaro INABA. Tr: Miguel RODRIGO ESP

KORAT CHATCHAI HALL, NAKHON RATCHASIMA
4-11-2012, 21:00, Att: 4350, Ref: Danijel Janosevic CRO

Brazil	13	Gabriel 6'06", Rodrigo 2 7'20" 9'35", Neto 15'00", Fernandinho 4 16'38" 30'38" 32'03" 33'16, Vinicius 24'47", Je 3 30'46" 33'55" 37'38", Rafael 38'41"
Libya	0	

BRAZIL
GUITTA‡ (GK), TIAGO* (GK), FRANKLIN‡ (GK), ARI*, RAFAEL•, GABRIEL, VINICIUS*(c), SIMI, JE, FERNANDINHO, NETO*, FALCAO‡, WILDE*, RODRIGO. Tr: Marcos SORATO

LIBYA
Yousef BENSAED* (GK), AHMED FARAJ, BADER HASAN*•, MOHAMED RAGEB, ABDUSALAM SHERAD‡, Rabia ABDEL‡, REDA FATHE, Husam AL WAHISHI, AHAMED FATHE*, MOHAMED RAHOMA*•(c), Younis SHAMES, Ramzi AL SHARIF‡• (GK), Salem AGHILA*, Husam ALTUMI‡ (GK). Tr: Pablo PRIETO ESP

INDOOR STADIUM HUAMARK, BANGKOK
7-11-2012, 17:00, Att: 5307, Ref: Francesco Massini ITA

Japan	4	Inaba 2 17'41" 25'39", Hoshi 24'53", Osodo 31'26"
Libya	2	Mohamed Rahoma 2 17'55" 37'43"p

JAPAN
Hisamitsu KAWAHARA* (GK), Jun FUJIWARA‡ (GK), Wataru KITAHARA*, Yusuke KOMIYAMA, Tetsuya MURAKAMI*, Nobuya OSODO, Kaoru MORIOKA*•, Kensuke TAKAHASHI‡, Shota HOSHI*, Kenichiro KOGURE(c), Kazu MIURA, Toru FUKUBARA‡ (GK), Katsutoshi HENMI*•, Kotaro INABA. Tr: Miguel RODRIGO ESP

LIBYA
Yousef BENSAED* (GK), AHMED FARAJ‡, BADER HASAN*•, MOHAMED RAGEB, ABDUSALAM SHERAD•, Rabia ABDEL‡, REDA FATHE, Husam AL WAHISHI, AHAMED FATHE*, MOHAMED RAHOMA*•(c), Younis SHAMES‡, Ramzi AL SHARIF‡ (GK), Salem AGHILA*, Husam ALTUMI‡ (GK). Tr: Pablo PRIETO ESP

KORAT CHATCHAI HALL, NAKHON RATCHASIMA
7-11-2012, 17:00, Att: 4200, Ref: Wenceslaos Aguilar PAN

Portugal	1	Cardinal 13'27"
Brazil	3	Simi 11'47", Fernandinho 28'12", Neto 39'15"

PORTUGAL
JOAO BENEDITO*♦32 (GK), PAULINHO*, LEITAO‡, PEDRO CARY‡, NANDINHO•, ARNALDO*(c), CARDINAL*, DJO, GONCALO*, RICARDINHO*, JOAO MATOS, BEBE‡ (GK), MARINHO, ANDRE SOUSA (GK). Tr: Jorge BRAZ

BRAZIL
GUITTA‡ (GK), TIAGO* (GK), FRANKLIN‡ (GK), ARI*, RAFAEL, GABRIEL*, VINICIUS•(c), SIMI*, JE, FERNANDINHO*, NETO, FALCAO‡, WILDE‡, RODRIGO*•. Tr: Marcos SORATO

FIFA FUTSAL WORLD CUP THAILAND 2012

	GROUP D	PL	W	D	L	F	A	PTS	ARG	AUS	MEX
1	Italy	3	3	0	0	17	5	9	3-2	9-1	5-2
2	Argentina	3	2	0	1	14	5	6		7-1	5-1
3	Australia	3	1	0	2	5	17	3			3-1
4	Mexico	3	0	0	3	4	13	0	* In starting lineup • ‡ Did not play

NIMIBUTR STADIUM, BANGKOK
2-11-2012, 17:00, Att: 3000, Ref: Eduardo Mahumane MOZ

Italy	9	Fortino 14'05", Assis 2 15'19" 23'34", Lima 17'11", Forte 19'05", Romano 20'57", Honorio 26'12", Mentasti 28'25", Merlim 30'27"
Australia	1	Ngaluafe 33'00"

ITALY
Stefano **MAMMARELLA*** (GK), Marco **ERCOLESSI**, Marcio **FORTE**(c), Sergio **ROMANO***•, Luca **LEGGIERO**, Humberto **HONORIO**, Giuseppe **MENTASTI**, Rodolfo **FORTINO**, Alex **MERLIM***, Jairo **DOS SANTOS**, Saad **ASSIS***, Valerio **BARIGELLI**‡ (GK), Gabriel **LIMA***, Michele **MIARELLI**‡ (GK). Tr: Riccardo **MANNO**

AUSTRALIA
Peter **SPATHIS*** (GK), Aaron **CIMITILE**, Jarrod **BASGER***, Gregory **GIOVENALI***(c), Nathan **NISKI**, Daniel **FOGARTY**‡, Tobias **SEETO***, **FERNANDO***, Chris **ZEBALLOS**, Lachlan **WRIGHT**, Danny **NGALUAFE**, Gavin **O'BRIEN**‡ (GK), Angelo **KONSTANTINOU**‡ (GK), Keenan **DUIMPIES**. Tr: Steven **KNIGHT**

NIMIBUTR STADIUM, BANGKOK
2-11-2012, 19:00, Att: 2400, Ref: Eduardo Fernandes POR

Argentina	5	Basile 4'27", Rescia 13'11", Amas 25'33", Borruto 2 28'27" 30'01"
Mexico	1	Jorge Rodriguez 36'57"

ARGENTINA
Santiago **ELIAS*** (GK)(c), Damian **STAZZONE**, Matias **LUCUIX**, Pablo **BELSITO**, Pablo **TABORDA**, Maximiliano **RESCIA***, Leandro **CUZZOLINO***, Hernan **GARCIAS***, Cristian **BORRUTO***, Martin **AMAS**, Santiago **BASILE**, Matias **QUEVEDO**‡ (GK), Alamiro **VAPORAKI**, Alan **CALO**. Tr: Fernando **LARRANAGA** ESP

MEXICO
Alonso **SAAVEDRA**‡ (GK), Angel **RODRIGUEZ***, Benjamin **MOSCO**‡, Francisco **CATI***(c), Adrian **GONZALEZ***•, Miguel **LIMON**‡, Jorge **RODRIGUEZ**, Victor **QUIROZ**, Carlos **RAMIREZ***, Gustavo **ROSALES**, Morgan **PLATA***, Miguel **ESTRADA*** (GK), Jorge **QUIROZ**, Omar **CERVANTES**. Tr: Ramon **RAYA**

NIMIBUTR STADIUM, BANGKOK
5-11-2012, 17:00, Att: 3800, Ref: Fernando Gutierrez Lumbreras ESP

Australia	3	Seeto 26'04", Cimitile 26'22", Giovenali 35'14"
Mexico	1	Victor Quiroz 6'05"

AUSTRALIA
Peter **SPATHIS*** (GK), Aaron **CIMITILE**, Jarrod **BASGER***, Gregory **GIOVENALI***(c), Nathan **NISKI**, Daniel **FOGARTY***, Tobias **SEETO***, **FERNANDO***, Chris **ZEBALLOS**, Lachlan **WRIGHT**, Danny **NGALUAFE**‡, Gavin **O'BRIEN**‡ (GK), Angelo **KONSTANTINOU**‡ (GK), Keenan **DUIMPIES**‡. Tr: Steven **KNIGHT**

MEXICO
Alonso **SAAVEDRA**‡ (GK), Angel **RODRIGUEZ***, Benjamin **MOSCO**‡, Francisco **CATI***(c), Adrian **GONZALEZ***•, Miguel **LIMON**, Jorge **RODRIGUEZ**, Victor **QUIROZ**, Carlos **RAMIREZ***•, Gustavo **ROSALES**, Morgan **PLATA***, Miguel **ESTRADA*** (GK), Jorge **QUIROZ**, Omar **CERVANTES**. Tr: Ramon **RAYA**

NIMIBUTR STADIUM, BANGKOK
5-11-2012, 19:00, Att: 3800, Ref: Nurdin Bukuev KGZ

Argentina	2	Rescia 2'02", Cuzzolino 40'00"
Italy	3	Lima 12'43", Fortino 18'15", Assis 37'20"

ARGENTINA
Santiago **ELIAS*** (GK)(c), Damian **STAZZONE**, Matias **LUCUIX**, Pablo **BELSITO**‡, Pablo **TABORDA**, Maximiliano **RESCIA***, Leandro **CUZZOLINO***, Hernan **GARCIAS***, Cristian **BORRUTO***•, Martin **AMAS**‡, Santiago **BASILE**, Matias **QUEVEDO**‡ (GK), Alamiro **VAPORAKI**, Alan **CALO**. Tr: Fernando **LARRANAGA** ESP

ITALY
Stefano **MAMMARELLA*** (GK), Marco **ERCOLESSI**, Marcio **FORTE***(c), Sergio **ROMANO***•, Luca **LEGGIERO**‡, Humberto **HONORIO**, Giuseppe **MENTASTI**‡, Rodolfo **FORTINO**, Alex **MERLIM***, Jairo **DOS SANTOS**, Saad **ASSIS***, Valerio **BARIGELLI**‡ (GK), Gabriel **LIMA**, Michele **MIARELLI**‡ (GK). Tr: Riccardo **MANNO**

INDOOR STADIUM HUAMARK, BANGKOK
8-11-2012, 17:00, Att: 1898, Ref: Sandro Brechane BRA

Mexico	2	Plata 2 22'20" 33'50"
Italy	5	Ercolessi 2 17'07" 23'51", Fortino 2 25'58" 34'42", Leggiero 35'56"

MEXICO
Alonso **SAAVEDRA**‡ (GK), Angel **RODRIGUEZ***, Benjamin **MOSCO**, Francisco **CATI**(c), Adrian **GONZALEZ***, Miguel **LIMON**, Jorge **RODRIGUEZ**, Victor **QUIROZ**, Carlos **RAMIREZ***, Gustavo **ROSALES**, Morgan **PLATA***, Miguel **ESTRADA*** (GK), Jorge **QUIROZ**‡, Omar **CERVANTES**. Tr: Ramon **RAYA**

ITALY
Stefano **MAMMARELLA**‡ (GK), Marco **ERCOLESSI**, Marcio **FORTE***(c), Sergio **ROMANO***, Luca **LEGGIERO**, Humberto **HONORIO**, Giuseppe **MENTASTI***, Rodolfo **FORTINO**, Alex **MERLIM***, Jairo **DOS SANTOS**, Saad **ASSIS***, Valerio **BARIGELLI*** (GK), Gabriel **LIMA**, Michele **MIARELLI**‡ (GK). Tr: Riccardo **MANNO**

NIMIBUTR STADIUM, BANGKOK
8-11-2012, 17:00, Att: 1400, Ref: Marc Birkett ENG

Australia	1	Seeto 5'31"
Argentina	7	Borruto 2 0'43" 38'41", Cuzzolino 6'54", Lucuix 14'39", Vaporaki 21'43", Garcias 27'29", Amas 36'28"

AUSTRALIA
Peter **SPATHIS***• (GK), Aaron **CIMITILE**, Jarrod **BASGER***, Gregory **GIOVENALI***(c), Nathan **NISKI**, Daniel **FOGARTY***•, Tobias **SEETO***, **FERNANDO***, Chris **ZEBALLOS**, Lachlan **WRIGHT**, Danny **NGALUAFE**, Gavin **O'BRIEN**‡ (GK), Angelo **KONSTANTINOU**‡ (GK), Keenan **DUIMPIES**. Tr: Steven **KNIGHT**

ARGENTINA
Santiago **ELIAS*** (GK)(c), Damian **STAZZONE**, Matias **LUCUIX**, Pablo **BELSITO**, Pablo **TABORDA**, Maximiliano **RESCIA***, Leandro **CUZZOLINO***, Hernan **GARCIAS***, Cristian **BORRUTO***•, Martin **AMAS**, Santiago **BASILE**, Matias **QUEVEDO** (GK), Alamiro **VAPORAKI**, Alan **CALO**. Tr: Fernando **LARRANAGA** ESP

PART ONE – FIFA AND WORLD FOOTBALL

	GROUP E	PL	W	D	L	F	A	PTS	CZE	EGY	KUW
1	Serbia	3	2	1	0	12	5	7		2-2	3-1	7-2
2	Czech Republic	3	1	1	1	7	11	4			2-7	3-2
3	Egypt	3	1	0	2	11	9	3				3-4
4	Kuwait	3	1	0	2	8	13	3	* In starting lineup • ‡ Did not play

INDOOR STADIUM HUAMARK, BANGKOK
3-11-2012, 19:00, Att: 1407, Ref: Dario Santamaria ARG

Czech Republic 3 Kopecky 4'26", Belej 22'50", Koudelka 34'55"

Kuwait 2 Al Awadhi 37'15, Altawail 39'21

CZECH REPUBLIC
Jakub ZDANSKY‡ (GK), Tomas KOUDELKA, David CUPAK‡, Matej SLOVACEK*•, Michal KOVACS•, Jiri NOVOTNY*, Lukas RESETAR*, Marek KOPECKY*•, David FRIC‡, Michal SEIDLER‡, Michal BELEJ*, Libor GERCAK* (GK), Zdenek SLAMA(c), Jan JANOVSKY•. Tr: Tomas NEUMANN

KUWAIT
Abdullah HAYAT‡ (GK), Mohammed ALBEDAIH‡ (GK), Abdulrahman ALMOSABEHI*•, Ahmad ALFARSI*, Hayat HAMAD, Abdulrahman ALWADI, Abdulrahman ALTAWAIL*, Aman SALEM(c), Ali ALBUTAI‡, Shaker ALMUTAIRI*••♦39, Abdullah DABI‡, Hamad AL AWADHI, Hani MHISEN* (GK), Mohammad MOHAMMAD. Tr: Luis FONSECA ESP

INDOOR STADIUM HUAMARK, BANGKOK
3-11-2012, 21:00, Att: 1407, Ref: Joel Ruiz PAR

Egypt 1 Mohamed 39'34"

Serbia 3 Bojovic 22'34", Janjic 36'19"P, Kocic 38'56"

EGYPT
HEMA* (GK), Ahmed EL AGOUZ‡(c), Eslam SHALABY, Mohamed EDREES*, BOUGY*, Mostafa NADER*, Ahmed ABOU SERIE*, MIZO•, Ramadan SAMASRY*•, Islam EL DARWJ‡, Ahmed HUSSEIN, Hussein GHARIB‡ (GK), Islam GAMILA‡, Ahmed MOHAMED. Tr: Badr KHALIL

SERBIA
Miodrag AKSENTIJEVIC* (GK), Stefan RAKIC, Aleksandar ZIVANOVIC‡, Vladimir MILOSAVAC, Bojan PAVICEVIC*(c), Boris CIZMAR‡, Slobodan JANJIC, Marko PRSIC*, Vladimir LAZIC*, Mladen KOCIC, Dragan DORDEVIC‡, Aleksa ANTONIC‡ (GK), Vidan BOJOVIC*, Slobodan RAJCEVIC. Tr: Aca KOVACEVIC

INDOOR STADIUM HUAMARK, BANGKOK
6-11-2012, 19:00, Att: 552, Ref: Renata Leite BRA

Kuwait 2 Alfarsi 2 21'20" 36'37"

Serbia 7 Kocic 2 6'36 17'28, Lazic 2 19'28" 24'04", Rajcevic 27'24", Bojovic 31'51", Pavicevic 38'33"

KUWAIT
Abdullah HAYAT‡ (GK), Mohammed ALBEDAIH (GK), Abdulrahman ALMOSABEHI*•, Ahmad ALFARSI, Hayat HAMAD*, Abdulrahman ALWADI*, Abdulrahman ALTAWAIL*, Aman SALEM•(c), Ali ALBUTAI, Shaker ALMUTAIRI‡, Abdullah DABI, Hamad AL AWADHI, Hani MHISEN* (GK), Mohammad MOHAMMAD. Tr: Luis FONSECA ESP

SERBIA
Miodrag AKSENTIJEVIC* (GK), Stefan RAKIC*, Aleksandar ZIVANOVIC, Vladimir MILOSAVAC, Bojan PAVICEVIC*(c), Boris CIZMAR, Slobodan JANJIC, Marko PRSIC*, Vladimir LAZIC*, Mladen KOCIC•, Dragan DORDEVIC, Aleksa ANTONIC‡ (GK), Vidan BOJOVIC*, Slobodan RAJCEVIC. Tr: Aca KOVACEVIC

INDOOR STADIUM HUAMARK, BANGKOK
6-11-2012, 21:00, Att: 552, Ref: Alireza Sohrabi IRN

Egypt 7 Samasry 3 10'19" 30'50" 36'55", Bougy 18'47", Mohamed 21'21", Nader 33'35", Mizo 38'12"

Czech Republic 2 Slovacek 4'12", Resetar 25'27"

EGYPT
HEMA* (GK), Ahmed EL AGOUZ‡(c), Eslam SHALABY, Mohamed EDREES‡, BOUGY•, Mostafa NADER, Ahmed ABOU SERIE*, MIZO*, Ramadan SAMASRY•, Islam EL DARWJ•, Ahmed HUSSEIN*, Hussein GHARIB• (GK), Islam GAMILA‡, Ahmed MOHAMED*. Tr: Badr KHALIL

CZECH REPUBLIC
Jakub ZDANSKY‡ (GK), Tomas KOUDELKA‡, David CUPAK‡, Matej SLOVACEK*, Michal KOVACS‡, Jiri NOVOTNY‡, Lukas RESETAR•, Marek KOPECKY, David FRIC‡, Michal SEIDLER, Michal BELEJ*, Libor GERCAK*• (GK), Zdenek SLAMA*(c), Jan JANOVSKY*. Tr: Tomas NEUMANN

NIMIBUTR STADIUM, BANGKOK
9-11-2012, 19:00, Att: 1370, Ref: Fernando Gutierrez Lumbreras ESP

Serbia 2 Kocic 5'52", Bojovic 35'08"

Czech Republic 2 Seidler 32'26", Belej 35'54"

SERBIA
Miodrag AKSENTIJEVIC* (GK), Stefan RAKIC*, Aleksandar ZIVANOVIC, Vladimir MILOSAVAC, Bojan PAVICEVIC*(c), Boris CIZMAR*, Slobodan JANJIC, Marko PRSIC*, Vladimir LAZIC*, Mladen KOCIC*, Dragan DORDEVIC‡, Aleksa ANTONIC (GK), Vidan BOJOVIC*, Slobodan RAJCEVIC. Tr: Aca KOVACEVIC

CZECH REPUBLIC
Jakub ZDANSKY‡ (GK), Tomas KOUDELKA, David CUPAK*, Matej SLOVACEK, Michal KOVACS, Jiri NOVOTNY‡, Lukas RESETAR*, Marek KOPECKY, David FRIC*, Michal SEIDLER, Michal BELEJ*, Libor GERCAK* (GK), Zdenek SLAMA(c), Jan JANOVSKY. Tr: Tomas NEUMANN

INDOOR STADIUM HUAMARK, BANGKOK
9-11-2012, 19:00, Att: 1152, Ref: Sergio Cabrera CUB

Kuwait 4 Alfarsi 2'06", Almutairi 2 5'14" 6'19", Altawail 19'21"

Egypt 3 Bougy 14'51", Mohamed 2 36'01" 38'54"

KUWAIT
Abdullah HAYAT‡ (GK), Mohammed ALBEDAIH‡ (GK), Abdulrahman ALMOSABEHI*•, Ahmad ALFARSI*•, Hayat HAMAD•, Abdulrahman ALWADI*•, Abdulrahman ALTAWAIL*•, Aman SALEM‡(c), Ali ALBUTAI‡, Shaker ALMUTAIRI, Abdullah DABI‡, Hamad AL AWADHI, Hani MHISEN* (GK), Mohammad MOHAMMAD. Tr: Luis FONSECA ESP

EGYPT
HEMA* (GK), Ahmed EL AGOUZ•(c), Eslam SHALABY*, Mohamed EDREES*, BOUGY*, Mostafa NADER*, Ahmed ABOU SERIE, MIZO•, Ramadan SAMASRY‡, Islam EL DARWJ•, Ahmed HUSSEIN, Hussein GHARIB‡ (GK), Islam GAMILA, Ahmed MOHAMED•. Tr: Badr KHALIL

	GROUP F	PL	W	D	L	F	A	PTS	COL	GUA	SOL
1	Russia	3	3	0	0	27	0	9	2-0	9-0	16-0
2	Colombia	3	1	0	2	13	10	3		2-5	11-3
3	Guatemala	3	1	0	2	8	15	3			3-4
4	Solomon Islands	3	1	0	2	7	30	3			

* In starting lineup • ‡ Did not play

NIMIBUTR STADIUM, BANGKOK
3-11-2012, 17:00, Att: 2300, Ref: Karel Henych CZE

Guatemala	5	Gonzalez 12'00", Escobar 28'12", Aguilar 30'36"2PG, Acevedo 31'31", Enriquez 39'22"
Colombia	2	Serna 6'57", Reyes 18'43"

GUATEMALA
Carlos MERIDA* (GK), Manuel ARISTONDO, Miguel SANTIZO‡, Jose GONZALEZ, Edgar SANTIZO••◆18, Daniel TEJADA, Billy PINEDA, Armando ESCOBAR*, Walter ENRIQUEZ, Erick ACEVEDO*, Alan AGUILAR*, William RAMIREZ‡ (GK), Estuardo DE LEON*(c), Edgar MACAL*. Tr: Carlos ESTRADA

COLOMBIA
Juan LOZANO* (GK), Johann PRADO‡, Luis BARRENECHE, Yefri DUQUE•, Jose QUIROZ, Miguel SIERRA*, Jhonathan TORO, Jorge ABRIL*(c), Andres REYES*, Angellott CARO*, Alejandro SERNA, Carlos NANEZ‡ (GK), Diego BARNEY‡, Yeisson FONNEGRA‡. Tr: Arney FONNEGRA

NIMIBUTR STADIUM, BANGKOK
3-11-2012, 19:00, Att: 2300, Ref: Kim Jang Kwan KOR

Russia	16	Sirilo 2'13", Pula 2'50", Eder Lima 7 4'47" 10'10" 17'24" 19'08" 19'49" 33'15" 39'26", Prudnikov 18'25", Sergeev 2 21'03" 29'35", Robinho 24'23", Suchilin 26'10", Fukin 2 27'22" 35'08"
Solomon Islands	0	

RUSSIA
Leonid KLIMOVSKIY (GK), Vladislav SHAYAKHMETOV*, Nikolay PEREVERZEV*, Dmitrii PRUDNIKOV, Sergey SERGEEV*(c), Pavel SUCHILIN, PULA*, EDER LIMA, Pavel CHISTOPOLOV, ROBINHO, SIRILO*, GUSTAVO* (GK), Alexander FUKIN*, Nikolay MALTSEV. Tr: Sergey SKOROVICH

SOLOMON ISLANDS
Anthony TALO‡ (GK), Paul HUIA* (GK), Elliot RAGOMO*(c), George STEVENSON•, Stanley PUAIRANA, Moffat SIKWAAE, James EGETA*, Jeffery BULE•, Micah LEAALAFA*, Samuel OSIFELO*, Coleman MAKAU, Mathias SARU, Dickson RAMO‡. Tr: Dickson KADAU

NIMIBUTR STADIUM, BANGKOK
6-11-2012, 17:00, Att: 1300, Ref: Borut Sivic SVN

Colombia	11	Toro 3 6'25" 19'36" 37'41", Quiroz 7'03", Reyes 2 21'49" 32'18", Duque 29'56", Abril 34'49", Caro 39'32", Fonnegra 39'49", Prado 39'59"P
Solomon Islands	3	Ragomo 13'50"P, Osifelo 14'50", Leaalafa 19'47"

COLOMBIA
Juan LOZANO* (GK), Johann PRADO, Luis BARRENECHE, Yefri DUQUE, Jose QUIROZ, Miguel SIERRA*, Jhonathan TORO, Jorge ABRIL*(c), Andres REYES*, Angellott CARO*, Alejandro SERNA*, Carlos NANEZ (GK), Diego BARNEY, Yeisson FONNEGRA. Tr: Arney FONNEGRA

SOLOMON ISLANDS
Anthony TALO• (GK), Paul HUIA*◆19 (GK), Elliot RAGOMO*(c), George STEVENSON*, Stanley PUAIRANA, Moffat SIKWAAE•, James EGETA*, Jeffery BULE•, Micah LEAALAFA*, Samuel OSIFELO*, Coleman MAKAU, Mathias SARU, Dickson RAMO‡. Tr: Dickson KADAU

NIMIBUTR STADIUM, BANGKOK
6-11-2012, 19:00, Att: 1300, Ref: Hector Rojas PER

Russia	9	Sergeev 3 0'34" 15'03"2PG 15'31", Shayakhmetov 2'54", Sirilo 7'08", Prudnikov 2 11'29 34'39", Eder Lima 26'47", Suchilin 34'15"
Guatemala	0	

RUSSIA
Leonid KLIMOVSKIY (GK), Vladislav SHAYAKHMETOV*, Nikolay PEREVERZEV‡, Dmitrii PRUDNIKOV, Sergey SERGEEV*(c), Pavel SUCHILIN, PULA*, EDER LIMA, Pavel CHISTOPOLOV, ROBINHO, SIRILO*, GUSTAVO* (GK), Alexander FUKIN*, Nikolay MALTSEV. Tr: Sergey SKOROVICH

GUATEMALA
Carlos MERIDA*• (GK), Manuel ARISTONDO, Miguel SANTIZO, Jose GONZALEZ, Edgar SANTIZO‡, Daniel TEJADA, Billy PINEDA‡, Armando ESCOBAR*, Walter ENRIQUEZ, Erick ACEVEDO, Alan AGUILAR*, William RAMIREZ‡ (GK), Estuardo DE LEON*(c), Edgar MACAL*. Tr: Carlos ESTRADA

INDOOR STADIUM HUAMARK, BANGKOK
9-11-2012, 17:00, Att: 1152, Ref: Francesco Massini ITA

Solomon Islands	4	Stevenson 14'42", Bule 16'56", Leaalafa 28'10", Talo 35'38"
Guatemala	3	De Leon 8'30", Aguilar 21'59", Enriquez 39'48"

SOLOMON ISLANDS
Anthony TALO* (GK), Paul HUIA‡ (GK), Elliot RAGOMO*(c), George STEVENSON, Stanley PUAIRANA‡, Moffat SIKWAAE, James EGETA*•, Jeffery BULE, Micah LEAALAFA*, Samuel OSIFELO*, Coleman MAKAU, Mathias SARU, Dickson RAMO‡. Tr: Dickson KADAU

GUATEMALA
Carlos MERIDA (GK), Manuel ARISTONDO•, Miguel SANTIZO‡, Jose GONZALEZ◆17, Edgar SANTIZO, Daniel TEJADA, Billy PINEDA‡, Armando ESCOBAR*, Walter ENRIQUEZ, Erick ACEVEDO*, Alan AGUILAR*, William RAMIREZ‡ (GK), Estuardo DE LEON*(c), Edgar MACAL*. Tr: Carlos ESTRADA

NIMIBUTR STADIUM, BANGKOK
9-11-2012, 17:00, Att: 1370, Ref: Scott Kidson AUS

Colombia	0	
Russia	2	Sirilo 3'39", Robinho 23'14"

COLOMBIA
Juan LOZANO* (GK), Johann PRADO‡, Luis BARRENECHE, Yefri DUQUE, Jose QUIROZ‡, Miguel SIERRA*, Jhonathan TORO, Jorge ABRIL*(c), Andres REYES*, Angellott CARO*, Alejandro SERNA, Carlos NANEZ‡ (GK), Diego BARNEY‡, Yeisson FONNEGRA. Tr: Arney FONNEGRA

RUSSIA
Leonid KLIMOVSKIY‡ (GK), Vladislav SHAYAKHMETOV*, Nikolay PEREVERZEV, Dmitrii PRUDNIKOV, Sergey SERGEEV*(c), Pavel SUCHILIN, PULA*, EDER LIMA, Pavel CHISTOPOLOV•, ROBINHO, SIRILO*, GUSTAVO* (GK), Alexander FUKIN‡, Nikolay MALTSEV‡. Tr: Sergey SKOROVICH

ROUND OF 16

KORAT CHATCHAI HALL, NAKHON RATCHASIMA
12-11-2012, 18:30, Att: 3644, Ref: Fernando Gutierrez Lumbreras ESP

Brazil	16	Fernandinho 2 $^{3'16''\,37'32''}$, Je 3 $^{5'31''\,18'21''\,34'45''}$, Rodrigo 2 $^{6'58''\,32'10''}$, Ari 3 $^{7'38''\,9'40''\,38'12''}$, Simi $^{11'19''}$, Neto $^{12'31''}$, Vinicius $^{22'50''}$, Rafael 2 $^{29'31''\,33'49''}$, Falcao $^{36'''}$
Panama	0	

BRAZIL

GUITTA‡ (GK), TIAGO* (GK), FRANKLIN (GK), ARI, RAFAEL, GABRIEL*, VINICIUS(c), SIMI*, JE, FERNANDINHO*, NETO*, FALCAO, WILDE, RODRIGO. Tr: Marcos SORATO

PANAMA

Valencio PARKS (GK), Miguel BELLO, Oscar HINKS*●, Augusto HARRISON●, Fernando MENA*●, Edgar RIVAS‡, Claudio GOODRIDGE*, Carlos PEREZ●●♦35, Miguel LASSO, Alquis ALVARADO*(c), Apolinar GALVEZ, Jaime LONDONO* (GK), Michael DE LEON, Enrique VALDES. Tr: Agustin CAMPUZANO CUB

INDOOR STADIUM HUAMARK, BANGKOK
12-11-2012, 21:00, Att: 1355, Ref: Hector Rojas PER

Serbia	1	Rajcevic $^{36'54''}$
Argentina	2	Cuzzolino $^{10'26''}$, Rescia $^{16'21''}$

SERBIA

Miodrag AKSENTIJEVIC* (GK), Stefan RAKIC, Aleksandar ZIVANOVIC, Vladimir MILOSAVAC, Bojan PAVICEVIC*(c), Boris CIZMAR‡, Slobodan JANJIC●●♦38, Marko PRSIC*, Vladimir LAZIC*, Mladen KOCIC, Dragan DORDEVIC, Aleksa ANTONIC‡ (GK), Vidan BOJOVIC*, Slobodan RAJCEVIC●. Tr: Aca KOVACEVIC

ARGENTINA

Santiago ELIAS* (GK)(c), Damian STAZZONE, Matias LUCUIX‡, Pablo BELSITO*, Pablo TABORDA, Maximiliano RESCIA*, Leandro CUZZOLINO*, Hernan GARCIAS*, Cristian BORRUTO‡, Martin AMAS, Santiago BASILE●, Matias QUEVEDO‡ (GK), Alamiro VAPORAKI‡, Alan CALO. Tr: Fernando LARRANAGA ESP

INDOOR STADIUM HUAMARK, BANGKOK
11-11-2012, 18:30, Att: 3579, Ref: Renata Leite BRA

Ukraine	6	Cheporniuk $^{2'16''}$, Fedorchenko $^{4'33''}$, Zhurba $^{9'34''}$, Rogachov $^{12'11''}$, Ocsiannikov 2 $^{15'05''\,15'43''}$
Japan	3	Morioka 2 $^{29'53''\,30'20''}$, Kitahara $^{31'17''}$

UKRAINE

Ievgen IVANYAK* (GK), Mykhaylo ROMANOV, Stepan STRUK●, Sergiy ZHURBA, Dmytro SOROKIN, Sergiy CHEPORNIUK*, Maksym PAVLENKO*(c), Ievgen ROGACHOV*, Dmytro FEDORCHENKO, Petro SHOTURMA, Denys OVSIANNIKOV*, Kyrylo TSYPUN‡ (GK), Oleksandr SOROKIN, Dmytro LYTVYNENKO‡ (GK). Tr: Gennadiy LISENCHUK

JAPAN

Hisamitsu KAWAHARA* (GK), Jun FUJIWARA‡ (GK), Wataru KITAHARA*, Yusuke KOMIYAMA(c), Tetsuya MURAKAMI, Nobuya OSODO*, Kaoru MORIOKA, Kensuke TAKAHASHI‡, Shota HOSHI*●, Kenichiro KOGURE*, Kazu MIURA, Toru FUKIMBARA (GK), Katsutoshi HENMI‡, Kotaro INABA♦14. Tr: Miguel RODRIGO ESP

NIMIBUTR STADIUM, BANGKOK
11-11-2012, 21:00, Att: 4170, Ref: Ivan Shabanov RUS

Iran	1	Rahnama $^{34'33''}$
Colombia	2	Duque $^{29'59''}$, Caro $^{33'41''}$

IRAN

Alireza SAMIMI‡ (GK), Ali KIAEI, Ali RAHNAMA, Mohammad KESHAVARZ*(c), Hamid AHMADI‡, Afshin KAZEMI, Ali HASSANZADEH*, Mostafa TAYYEBI♦32, Masoud DANESHVAR, Mohammad TAHERI*, Hossein TAYEBI*, Mostafa NAZARI* (GK), Ahmad ESMAEILPOUR, Sepehr MOHAMMADI* (GK). Tr: Ali SANEI

COLOMBIA

Juan LOZANO* (GK), Johann PRADO‡, Luis BARRENECHE, Yefri DUQUE, Jose QUIROZ‡, Miguel SIERRA*●, Jhonathan TORO, Jorge ABRIL*(c), Andres REYES*, Angellott CARO*, Alejandro SERNA, Carlos NANEZ‡ (GK), Diego BARNEY‡, Yeisson FONNEGRA. Tr: Arney FONNEGRA

KORAT CHATCHAI HALL, NAKHON RATCHASIMA
12-11-2012, 16:00, Att: 3644, Ref: Nurdin Bukuev KGZ

Italy	5	Assis 3 $^{3'28''\,10'50''\,30'44''}$, Dos Santos $^{19'03''}$, Fortino $^{32'20''}$
Egypt	1	Abou Serie $^{10'15''}$

ITALY

Stefano MAMMARELLA* (GK), Marco ERCOLESSI, Marcio FORTE*(c), Sergio ROMANO*, Luca LEGGIERO, Humberto HONORIO*, Giuseppe MENTASTI, Rodolfo FORTINO, Alex MERLIM‡, Jairo DOS SANTOS, Saad ASSIS*, Valerio BARIGELLI‡ (GK), Gabriel LIMA, Michele MIARELLI‡ (GK). Tr: Riccardo MANNO

EGYPT

HEMA* (GK), Ahmed EL AGOUZ(c), Eslam SHALABY, Mohamed EDREES, BOUGY*, Mostafa NADER*, Ahmed ABOU SERIE, MIZO‡, Ramadan SAMASRY*, Islam EL DARWJ‡, Ahmed HUSSEIN‡, Hussein GHARIB‡ (GK), Islam GAMILA‡, Ahmed MOHAMED*. Tr: Badr KHALIL

INDOOR STADIUM HUAMARK, BANGKOK
11-11-2012, 16:00, Att: 3579, Ref: Daniel Rodriguez URU URU

Paraguay	1	Juan Salas $^{35'03''}$
Portugal	4	Cardinal $^{11'32''}$, Joao Matos $^{19'33''}$, Ricardinho 2 $^{38'42''\,39'54''}$

PARAGUAY

Carlos ESPINOLA* (GK), Enmanuel AYALA, Fabio ALCARAZ*(c), Gabriel AYALA●, Jose Luis SANTANDER*, Adolfo SALAS*, Oscar VELAZQUEZ, Nelson LEZCANO‡, Juan SALAS*, Walter VILLALBA, Luis MOLINAS‡ (GK), Marcos BENITEZ, Gabriel GIMENEZ‡ (GK), Rene VILLALBA. Tr: Fernando LEITE BRA

PORTUGAL

JOAO BENEDITO‡ (GK), PAULINHO, LEITAO‡, PEDRO CARY, NANDINHO‡, ARNALDO*(c), CARDINAL*, DJO, GONCALO*, RICARDINHO*, JOAO MATOS, BEBE‡ (GK), MARINHO, ANDRE SOUSA* (GK). Tr: Jorge BRAZ

INDOOR STADIUM HUAMARK, BANGKOK				NIMIBUTR STADIUM, BANGKOK			
12-11-2012, 18:30, Att: 1355, Ref: Wenceslaos Aguilar PAN				11-11-2012, 18:30, Att: 4170, Ref: Alexander Kline PAN			
Russia	3	Eder Lima $^{6'43''}$, Pula $^{9'20''}$, Sirilo $^{28'20''}$		Spain	7	Torras 2 $^{9'17''\ 16'35''}$, Fernando 2 $^{24'59''\ 27'44''}$, Aicardo $^{29'42''}$, Ortiz $^{33'36''}$, Alvaro $^{37'39''}$	
Czech Republic	0			Thailand	1	Wongkaeo $^{38'48''}$	
RUSSIA				SPAIN			
Leonid KLIMOVSKIY‡ (GK), Vladislav SHAYAKHMETOV*, Nikolay PEREVERZEV, Dmitrii PRUDNIKOV*, Sergey SERGEEV*(c), Pavel SUCHILIN, PULA, EDER LIMA•, Pavel CHISTOPOLOV, ROBINHO, SIRILO*, GUSTAVO* (GK), Alexander FUKIN‡, Nikolay MALTSEV‡. Tr: Sergey SKOROVICH				CRISTIAN‡ (GK), ORTIZ, AICARDO, TORRAS*, FERNANDAO, ALVARO, MIGUELIN*, KIKE*(c), LOZANO, BORJA*, LIN‡, JUANJO* (GK), RAFA‡ (GK), ALEMAO. Tr: Venancio LOPEZ			
CZECH REPUBLIC				THAILAND			
Jakub ZDANSKY‡ (GK), Tomas KOUDELKA‡, David CUPAK*, Matej SLOVACEK*, Michal KOVACS, Jiri NOVOTNY‡, Lukas RESETAR*, Marek KOPECKY‡, David FRIC*, Michal SEIDLER*, Michal BELEJ, Libor GERCAK* (GK), Zdenek SLAMA(c), Jan JANOVSKY. Tr: Tomas NEUMANN				Prakit DANKHUNTHOD* (GK), Konghla LAKKA*, Natee JEEPON, Piyapan RATANA•, Jirawat SORNWICHIAN*, Thananchai CHOMBOON, Kritsada WONGKAEO*, Jetsada CHUDECH, Suphawut THUEANKLANG*, Apiwat CHAEMCHAROEN, Nattavut MADYALAN‡, Surapong TOMPA (GK)(c), Aref AHAMAH‡, Keattiyot CHALAEMKHET‡. Tr: Victor HERMANS NED			

QUARTER-FINALS

INDOOR STADIUM HUAMARK, BANGKOK				INDOOR STADIUM HUAMARK, BANGKOK			
14-11-2012, 16:00, Att: 3007, Ref: Wenceslaos Aguilar PAN				14-11-2012, 18:30, Att: 3007, Ref: Sergio Cabrera CUB			
Argentina	2	Rescia $^{16'30''}$, Borruto $^{17'07''}$		Colombia	3	Reyes $^{22'18''}$, Caro $^{39'07''}$, Abril $^{39'44''}$	
Brazil	3	Neto $^{32'42''}$, Falcao 2 $^{33'55''\ 44'42''}$		Ukraine	1	Ovsiannikov $^{39'54''}$	
ARGENTINA				COLOMBIA			
Santiago ELIAS* (GK)(c), Damian STAZZONE, Matias LUCUIX‡, Pablo BELSITO, Pablo TABORDA, Maximiliano RESCIA*•, Leandro CUZZOLINO*, Hernan GARCIAS*, Cristian BORRUTO*•, Martin AMAS, Santiago BASILE, Matias QUEVEDO‡ (GK), Alamiro VAPORAKI‡, Alan CALO. Tr: Fernando LARRANAGA ESP				Juan LOZANO* (GK), Johann PRADO•, Luis BARRENECHE, Yefri DUQUE•, Jose QUIROZ, Miguel SIERRA*, Jhonathan TORO, Jorge ABRIL*(c), Andres REYES*, Angellott CARO*•, Alejandro SERNA, Carlos NANEZ‡ (GK), Diego BARNEY‡, Yeisson FONNEGRA. Tr: Arney FONNEGRA			
BRAZIL				UKRAINE			
GUITTA‡ (GK), TIAGO* (GK), FRANKLIN‡ (GK), ARI•, RAFAEL, GABRIEL*, VINICIUS(c), SIMI*, JE••◆9, FERNANDINHO*, NETO*, FALCAO, WILDE, RODRIGO. Tr: Marcos SORATO				Ievgen IVANYAK* (GK), Mykhaylo ROMANOV, Stepan STRUK‡, Sergiy ZHURBA, Dmytro SOROKIN, Sergiy CHEPORNIUK*, Maksym PAVLENKO*(c), Ievgen ROGACHOV*, Dmytro FEDORCHENKO‡, Petro SHOTURMA, Denys OVSIANNIKOV*•, Kyrylo TSYPUN‡ (GK), Oleksandr SOROKIN, Dmytro LYTVYNENKO‡ (GK). Tr: Gennadiy LISENCHUK			

NIMIBUTR STADIUM, BANGKOK				NIMIBUTR STADIUM, BANGKOK			
14-11-2012, 18:30, Att: 3100, Ref: Karel Henych CZE				14-11-2012, 21:00, Att: 3100, Ref: Marc Birkett ENG			
Portugal	3	Ricardinho 3 $^{1'02''\ 10'53''\ 11'01''}$		Spain	3	Ortiz $^{3'18''}$, Fernandao $^{13'13''}$, Lozano $^{18'47''}$	
Italy	4	Assis $^{21'24''P}$, Lima $^{37'32''}$, Fortino $^{39'14''}$, Honorio $^{42'00''}$		Russia	2	Sirilo $^{1'14''}$, Alemao OG $^{33'06''}$	
PORTUGAL				SPAIN			
JOAO BENEDITO‡ (GK), PAULINHO, LEITAO‡, PEDRO CARY, NANDINHO, ARNALDO*•(c), CARDINAL*••◆11, DJO•, GONCALO*, RICARDINHO*•, JOAO MATOS, BEBE (GK), MARINHO, ANDRE SOUSA* (GK). Tr: Jorge BRAZ				CRISTIAN‡ (GK), ORTIZ, AICARDO, TORRAS•, FERNANDAO*, ALVARO, MIGUELIN, KIKE*•(c), LOZANO, BORJA, LIN•, JUANJO*, RAFA‡ (GK), ALEMAO*. Tr: Venancio LOPEZ			
ITALY				RUSSIA			
Stefano MAMMARELLA* (GK), Marco ERCOLESSI, Marcio FORTE*(c), Sergio ROMANO*•, Luca LEGGIERO‡, Humberto HONORIO*, Giuseppe MENTASTI*, Rodolfo FORTINO, Alex MERLIM, Jairo DOS SANTOS, Saad ASSIS*, Valerio BARIGELLI‡ (GK), Gabriel LIMA, Michele MIARELLI‡ (GK). Tr: Riccardo MANNO				Leonid KLIMOVSKIY‡ (GK), Vladislav SHAYAKHMETOV*, Nikolay PEREVERZEV, Dmitrii PRUDNIKOV*, Sergey SERGEEV*(c), Pavel SUCHILIN, PULA, EDER LIMA•, Pavel CHISTOPOLOV, ROBINHO•, SIRILO*•, GUSTAVO* (GK), Alexander FUKIN‡, Nikolay MALTSEV‡. Tr: Sergey SKOROVICH			

SEMI-FINALS

INDOOR STADIUM HUAMARK, BANGKOK		
16-11-2012, 19:30, Att: 4597, Ref: Daniel Rodriguez URU		
Brazil	3	Gabriel 2 0'41" 27'15", Toro OG 28'47"
Colombia	1	Toro 18'13"
BRAZIL		
GUITTA‡ (GK), TIAGO* (GK), FRANKLIN‡ (GK), ARI, RAFAEL, GABRIEL*, VINICIUS(c), SIMI*, JE‡, FERNANDINHO*, NETO*, FALCAO, WILDE, RODRIGO•. Tr: Marcos SORATO		
COLOMBIA		
Juan LOZANO* (GK), Johann PRADO, Luis BARRENECHE, Yefri DUQUE‡, Jose QUIROZ, Miguel SIERRA*, Jhonathan TORO, Jorge ABRIL*(c), Andres REYES*, Angellott CARO*, Alejandro SERNA•, Carlos NANEZ‡ (GK), Diego BARNEY‡, Yeisson FONNEGRA. Tr: Arney FONNEGRA		

INDOOR STADIUM HUAMARK, BANGKOK		
16-11-2012, 17:00, Att: 4597, Ref: Nurdin Bukuev KGZ		
Italy	1	Merlim 29'26"
Spain	4	Assis OG 8'02", Alemao 29'37", Lozano 33'03", Lin 37'37"
ITALY		
Stefano MAMMARELLA* (GK), Marco ERCOLESSI, Marcio FORTE*(c), Sergio ROMANO*, Luca LEGGIERO‡, Humberto HONORIO, Giuseppe MENTASTI‡, Rodolfo FORTINO*, Alex MERLIM, Jairo DOS SANTOS, Saad ASSIS*•, Valerio BARIGELLI‡ (GK), Gabriel LIMA, Michele MIARELLI‡ (GK). Tr: Riccardo MANNO		
SPAIN		
CRISTIAN‡ (GK), ORTIZ, AICARDO*•, TORRAS, FERNANDAO*, ALVARO, MIGUELIN•, KIKE*(c), LOZANO, BORJA, LIN, JUANJO* (GK), RAFA‡ (GK), ALEMAO*. Tr: Venancio LOPEZ		

PLAY-OFF FOR THIRD PLACE

INDOOR STADIUM HUAMARK, BANGKOK		
18-11-2012, 17:00, Att: 5685, Ref: Jose Katemo ANG		
Italy	3	Romano 27'53", Fortino 2 32'32" 39'57"
Colombia	0	
ITALY		
Stefano MAMMARELLA* (GK), Marco ERCOLESSI, Marcio FORTE*•(c), Sergio ROMANO*, Luca LEGGIERO‡, Humberto HONORIO, Giuseppe MENTASTI‡, Rodolfo FORTINO, Alex MERLIM*, Jairo DOS SANTOS, Saad ASSIS*, Valerio BARIGELLI‡ (GK), Gabriel LIMA, Michele MIARELLI‡ (GK). Tr: Riccardo MANNO		
COLOMBIA		
Juan LOZANO*♦31 (GK), Johann PRADO, Luis BARRENECHE, Yefri DUQUE, Jose QUIROZ, Miguel SIERRA*, Jhonathan TORO, Jorge ABRIL*(c), Andres REYES*, Angellott CARO*, Alejandro SERNA, Carlos NANEZ (GK), Diego BARNEY‡, Yeisson FONNEGRA. Tr: Arney FONNEGRA		

FINAL

INDOOR STADIUM HUAMARK, BANGKOK		
18-11-2012, 19:30, Att: 5685, Ref: Hector Rojas PER		
Spain	2	Torras 29'55", Aicardo 30'56"
Brazil	3	Neto 2 24'11" 49'41", Falcao 36'18"
SPAIN		
CRISTIAN‡ (GK), ORTIZ, AICARDO*, TORRAS, FERNANDAO*•, ALVARO, MIGUELIN, KIKE*•(c), LOZANO, BORJA, LIN, JUANJO* (GK), RAFA‡ (GK), ALEMAO*. Tr: Venancio LOPEZ		
BRAZIL		
GUITTA‡ (GK), TIAGO*• (GK), FRANKLIN‡ (GK), ARI•, RAFAEL, GABRIEL*, VINICIUS(c), SIMI*, JE, FERNANDINHO*, NETO*•, FALCAO, WILDE‡, RODRIGO. Tr: Marcos SORATO		

FIFA CLUB WORLD CUP JAPAN 2012

FIFA CLUB WORLD CUP JAPAN 2012

Quarter-finals

Corinthians	BRA	Bye
Sanfrecce Hiroshima	JPN	1
Al Ahly Cairo	**EGY**	**2**
Monterrey	**MEX**	**3**
Ulsan Hyundai	KOR	1
Chelsea	ENG	Bye

Semi-finals

Corinthians	**1**
Al Ahly Cairo	0
Monterrey	1
Chelsea	**3**

Final

Corinthians	**1**
Chelsea	0

Preliminary round

Sanfrecce Hiroshima	**JPN**	**1**
Auckland City	NZL	0

Play-off for fifth place

Sanfrecce Hiroshima	**3**
Ulsan Hyundai	2

Play-off for Third Place

Monterrey	**2**
Al Ahly Cairo	0

Top scorers: 3 - Cesar **DELGADO** ARG, Monterrey & Hisalu **SATO**, JPN, Sanfrecce • 2 Paolo **GUERRERO** PFR, Corinthians & Jesus **CORONA** MEX, Monterrey
FIFA Fair Play Award: Monterrey
adidas Golden Ball: 1 - **CASSIO** BRA, Corinthians • 2 - **DAVID LUIZ** BRA, Chelsea • 3 - Paolo **GUERRERO** PER, Corinthians

---

Paolo Guerrero scored his second goal of Japan 2012 to earn Corinthians a 1-0 win over English Premier League side Chelsea and a second world club crown. In the International Stadium in Yokohama, the South American champions made the breakthrough after 69 minutes. Danilo dribbled across the face of goal and fired in a shot, which was blocked by Gary Cahill. The deflection, however, took the ball straight up in the air and into the path of the foraging Guerrero, who leapt to head into the net to an almighty roar from the Brazilians fans behind the goal. Having beaten African champions Al Ahly 1-0 in the semi-final, Corinthians' triumph was founded on teamwork, the sheer commitment of an experienced group of players and the extraordinary support of their fans who descended on Japan in their thousands to create an amazing spectacle. Five years previously Corinthians were a club in crisis. Relegated for the first time in 2007, their Club World Cup triumph completed a remarkable turnaround for the club and which also ended a five-year run of success for European clubs in the competition and brought the world title back to Brazil and South America for the first time since 2006. Corinthians had been the winners of the first tournament, staged at home in 2000, the first of three successive triumphs for Brazilian clubs. All that changed in 2007, when Milan initiated a spell of European domination that was continued by Manchester United, Internazionale and Barcelona, who won it twice. The reigning European champions Chelsea had arrived in Japan determined to atone for their early UEFA Champions League exit and extend the winning run of European sides but they had no answer to Corinthians' application and work rate. In the third place play-off, Monterrey ensured a podium finish for Mexico after beating Al Ahly 2-0 but it wasn't a good tournament for Asia with the continent's two representatives - AFC Champions League winners Ulsan Hyundai from Korea and hosts Sanfrecce Hiroshima left to battle it out for fifth place, a match won by the Koreans 3-2. In the first match of the competition Sanfrecce had beaten OFC Champions League winners Auckland City 1-0.

PRELIMINARY ROUND

INTERNATIONAL STADIUM, YOKOHAMA
6-12-2012, 19:45, Att: 25 174, Ref: Djamel Haimoudi ALG

| SANFRECCE | 1 | 0 | AUCKLAND CITY |

Toshihiro Aoyama 66

SANFRECCE HIROSHIMA

Tr: Hajime Moriyasu
Shusaku Nishikawa
Ryota Moriwaki — Kazuhiko Chiba — Hiroki Mizumoto 47
Kazuyuki Morisaki — Toshihiro Aoyama
82 Mihael Mikic / Hwang Seok Ho — 61 Kohei Shimizu / Satoru Yamagishi 47
Yojiro Takahagi — 93+ Koji Morisaki / Naoki Ishihara
Hisato Sato (c)

78 Manuel Exposito / Emiliano Tade — 67 Jesus Koprivcic / Luis Corrales — Adam Dickinson
Alex Feneridis — Christopher Bale — Albert Riera 50
Takuya Iwata — Ivan Vicelich (c) — Angel Berlanga 38 — Andrew Milne
Tr: Ramon Tribulietx
Tamati Williams

AUCKLAND CITY

QUARTER-FINALS

TOYOTA STADIUM, TOYOTA
9-12-2012, 19:30, Att: 27 314, Ref: Carlos Vera ECU

| SANFRECCE | 1 | 2 | AL AHLY |

Hisato Sato 32 — Elsayed Hamdi 15, Mohamed Aboutrika 57

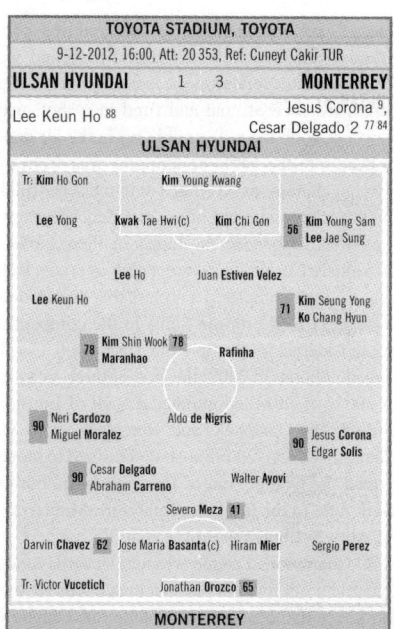

TOYOTA STADIUM, TOYOTA
9-12-2012, 16:00, Att: 20 353, Ref: Cuneyt Cakir TUR

| ULSAN HYUNDAI | 1 | 3 | MONTERREY |

Lee Keun Ho 88 — Jesus Corona 9, Cesar Delgado 2 77 84

FIFA CLUB WORLD CUP JAPAN 2012

SEMI-FINALS

TOYOTA STADIUM, TOYOTA
12-12-2012, 19:30, Att: 31 417, Ref: Marco Rodriguez MEX

AL AHLY 0 – 1 CORINTHIANS

Paolo Guerrero 30

AL AHLY
- Tr: Hossam El Badry
- Sherif Ekramy 65 / Mahmoud Abou Elseoud
- Ahmed Kenawi, Mohamed Naguib, Wael Gomaa (c), Ahmed Fathi
- Ramy Rabia, Hossam Ashour
- Walid Soliman, Abdalla Said 55 / Mohamed Aboutrika, Gedo 80 / Emad Meteab
- Elsayed Hamdi

CORINTHIANS
- Emerson 75 / Romarinho, Paolo Guerrero 92+ / Guilherme Andrade, Danilo
- Ralf, Douglas 80 / Jorge Henrique, Paulinho
- Fabio Santos, Paulo Andre, Chicao, Alessandro (c)
- Cassio
- Tr: Tite

INTERNATIONAL STADIUM, YOKOHAMA
13-12-2012, 19:30, Att: 36 648, Ref: Carlos Vera ECU

MONTERREY 1 – 3 CHELSEA

Aldo De Nigris 91+ | Juan Mata 17, Fernando Torres 46, Darvin Chavez OG 48

MONTERREY
- Tr: Victor Vucetich
- Jonathan Orozco
- Sergio Perez 57 / Ricardo Osorio, Hiram Mier, Jose Maria Basanta (c), Darvin Chavez
- Severo Meza 83 / Edgar Solis
- Walter Ayovi, Neri Cardozo
- Jesus Corona, Cesar Delgado 83 / Abraham Carreno
- Aldo de Nigris

CHELSEA
- Fernando Torres 79 / Victor Moses
- Eden Hazard, Oscar, Juan Mata 74 / Paulo Ferreira
- David Luiz 63 / Frank Lampard, John Obi Mikel
- Ashley Cole, Branislav Ivanovic, Gary Cahill, Cesar Azpilicueta
- Tr: Rafael Benitez
- Petr Cech (c)

PLAY-OFFS FOR FIFTH AND THIRD PLACE

TOYOTA STADIUM, TOYOTA
5th Place. 12-12-2012, 16:30, Att: 17 581, Ref: Nawaf Shukralla BHR

ULSAN HYUNDAI 2 – 3 SANFRECCE

Hiroki Mizumoto OG 17, Lee Yong 95+ | Satoru Yamagishi 35, Hisato Sato 2 56 72

ULSAN HYUNDAI
- Tr: Kim Ho Gon
- Kim Young Kwang
- Lee Yong, Kwak Tae Hwi (c) 52 / Lee Jae Sung, Kim Chi Gon, Kim Young Sam
- Lee Ho 34 / Ko Seul Ki
- Lee Keun Ho, Kim Seung Yong 76 / Maranhao
- Rafinha 90 / Kim Shin Wook

SANFRECCE HIROSHIMA
- Hisato Sato (c)
- Yojiro Takahagi, Koji Morisaki
- Satoru Yamagishi 75 / Kohei Shimizu, Hironori Ishikawa 95+ / Kazuhiko Chiba
- Kazuyuki Morisaki 79 / Toshihiro Aoyama, Naoki Ishihara
- Hiroki Mizumoto, Tsukasa Shiotani 66, Hwang Seok Ho 66
- Shusaku Nishikawa 90
- Tr: Hajime Moriyasu

INTERNATIONAL STADIUM, YOKOHAMA
3rd Place. 16-12-2012, 16:30, Att: 56 301, Ref: Peter O'Leary NZL

AL AHLY 0 – 2 MONTERREY

Jesus Corona 3, Cesar Delgado 66

AL AHLY
- Tr: Hossam El Badry
- Mahmoud Abou Elseoud
- Ahmed Fathi 62 / Mohamed Barakat, Wael Gomaa (c) 80 / Mohamed Naguib, Sayed Moawad
- Hossam Ashour 8, Ramy Rabia
- Abdalla Said, Mohamed Aboutrika, Walid Soliman 77 / Gedo
- Emad Meteab 53 / Elsayed Hamdi

MONTERREY
- Aldo de Nigris
- Cesar Delgado 79 / Miguel Morales, Jesus Corona 63 / Abraham Carreno
- Neri Cardozo 84 / Edgar Solis, Walter Ayovi, Severo Mezo
- Darvin Chavez, Jose Maria Basanta (c), Hiram Mier, Ricardo Osorio
- Jonathan Orozco
- Tr: Victor Vucetich

FINAL

FIFA CLUB WORLD CUP FINAL 2012
INTERNATIONAL STADIUM, YOKOHAMA

Sunday, 16-12-2012, 19:30, Att: 68,275, Ref: Cuneyt Cakir TUR
Assistants: Bahattin Duran TUR & Tarik Ongun TUR

CORINTHIANS	1	0	CHELSEA

Paolo Guerrero 67

CORINTHIANS
White shirts, black shorts, white socks

Tr: Tite
Cassio
Alessandro (c) — Chicao — Paulo Andre — Fabio Santos
Ralf — Danilo — Paulinho
Jorge Henrique 73 — Emerson Wallace 91+
Paolo Guerrero 87
Juan Martinez

Fernando Torres
Eden Hazard 87 — Victor Moses 73
Marko Marin — Juan Mata — Oscar
Ramires — Frank Lampard (c)
Ashley Cole — David Luiz 72 — Gary Cahill 90 83 — Branislav Ivanovic
Cesar Azpilicueta
Tr: Rafael Benitez
Petr Cech

Blue shirts, blue shorts, blue socks
CHELSEA

MATCH STATS

Corinthians		Chelsea
9	Shots	14
2	Shots on Goal	6
17	Fouls Committed	12
4	Corner Kicks	2
1	Caught Offside	4
46	Possession (%)	54

There are a lot of reasons for this victory, but the most important were our teamwork and our fans. Winning this title teaches us some very important lessons. In football, the team is more important than individual talent. Teamwork is more important. Our fans have been very good for us. In the stadium we were able to hear they were turning up the heat. Corinthians were able to come this far thanks to them.

Tite, coach of Corinthians

We could have won the game had we taken our chances, but we didn't. South American teams at this level are really good teams. Corinthians are a good team, and have good players. It was a positive experience for us to play against a top South American side in the stadium of a different country. We played a great game. We did some very good moves, still have a few things to improve but I think this is quite positive for the future.

Rafael Benitez, coach of Chelsea

PART TWO

THE ASSOCIATIONS

PART TWO

THE ASSOCIATIONS

AFG – AFGHANISTAN

FIFA/COCA-COLA WORLD RANKING

'93	'94	'95	'96	'97	'98	'99	'00	'01	'02	'03	'04	'05	'06	'07	'08	'09	'10	'11	'12
-	-	-	-	-	-	-	-	-	-	196	200	189	180	191	183	193	195	177	186

2012

Jan	Feb	Mar	Apr	May	Jun	Jul	Aug	Sep	Oct	Nov	Dec	High	Low	Av
177	178	178	168	170	168	162	164	165	166	167	186	164	204	188

After the 12 games played in 2011, the Afghanistan national team went through the whole of 2012 without any action at all, having been knocked out of both the 2014 FIFA World Cup and the 2012 AFC Challenge Cup. Instead the focus was on the launch of a new national league which kicked off in September 2012 - due in no small part to a reality show broadcast on local television called Maidan-e-Shabz, which means Green Field. The show sought out players for the new eight-team league, eventually selecting 18 for each of the new clubs. The league was given national television coverage and was played out in front of capacity crowds in the national stadium in Kabul - a long way from the days when the sport was banned under the Taliban regime. Played over the duration of a month, the teams were divided into two groups of four with the top two progressing to the championship semi-finals. Toofaan Harirod claimed the title, winning their group before seeing off De Spin Ghar Bazan 10-0 in the semi-finals and then handing Simorgh Alborz - who finished as runners-up in their group - a 2-1 defeat in the final. Ghuam Raza Yaqubi scored what turned out to be the winner in a game his side won despite playing the entire second half with only 10 men while team mate Hamidullah Karimi was the league's top scorer with nine goals.

FIFA WORLD CUP RECORD
1930-2002 DNE   2006-2014 DNQ

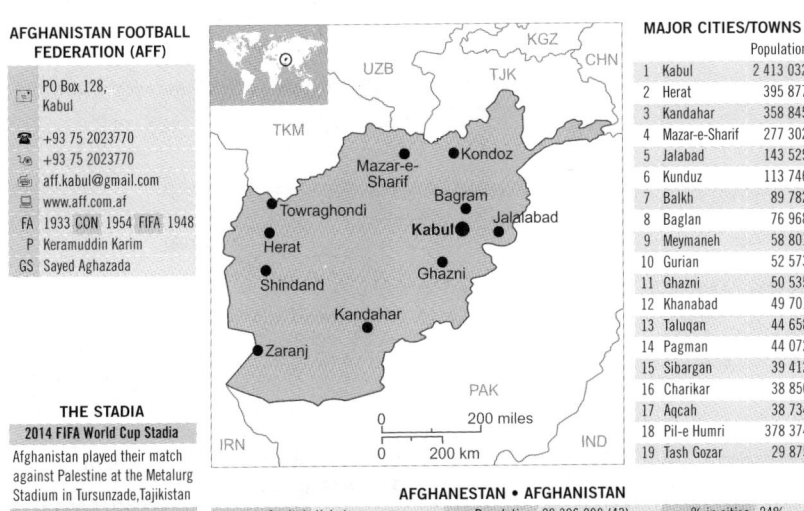

AFGHANISTAN FOOTBALL FEDERATION (AFF)

PO Box 128, Kabul
+93 75 2023770
+93 75 2023770
aff.kabul@gmail.com
www.aff.com.af
FA 1933 CON 1954 FIFA 1948
P Keramuddin Karim
GS Sayed Aghazada

THE STADIA

2014 FIFA World Cup Stadia
Afghanistan played their match against Palestine at the Metalurg Stadium in Tursunzade, Tajikistan

Other Main Stadia
National Stadium 'Ghazi'
Kabul   25 000

MAJOR CITIES/TOWNS

		Population
1	Kabul	2 413 032
2	Herat	395 877
3	Kandahar	358 845
4	Mazar-e-Sharif	277 302
5	Jalabad	143 525
6	Kunduz	113 746
7	Balkh	89 782
8	Baglan	76 968
9	Meymaneh	58 801
10	Gurian	52 573
11	Ghazni	50 535
12	Khanabad	49 701
13	Taluqan	44 658
14	Pagman	44 072
15	Sibargan	39 412
16	Charikar	38 850
17	Aqcah	38 734
18	Pil-e Humri	378 374
19	Tash Gozar	29 875

AFGHANESTAN • AFGHANISTAN

Capital	Kabul	Population	28 396 000 (43)	% in cities	24%
GDP per capita	$700 (219)	Area km²	652 230 km² (41)	GMT +/-	+4.5

Neighbours (km) China 76, Iran 936, Pakistan 2430, Tajikistan 1206, Turkmenistan 744, Uzbekistan 137

RECENT INTERNATIONALS PLAYED BY AFGHANISTAN

2008	Opponents	Score		Venue	Comp	Scorers	Att	Referee
30-07	India	L	0-1	Hyderabad	CCr1		300	Iemoto JPN
1-08	Turkmenistan	L	0-5	Hyderabad	CCr1		350	Shamsuzzaman BAN
3-08	Tajikistan	L	0-4	Hyderabad	CCr1		150	Vo Minh Tri VIE
17-10	Nepal	D	2-2	Petaling Jaya	Fr	Hashmatullah Barekzai 2 [62 72]		
20-10	Malaysia	L	0-6	Petaling Jaya	Fr			
2009								
5-12	India †	L	0-1	Dhaka	SAFr1			
7-12	Maldives	L	1-3	Dhaka	SAFr1	Hashmatullah Barekzai [30]		
9-12	Nepal	L	0-3	Dhaka	SAFr1			
2010								
17-11	Tajikistan	L	0-1	Dushanbe	Fr			
2011								
23-03	Bhutan	W	3-0	Gurgaon	CCq	Sediq Walizada 3 [2 36 80]	200	Mahapab THA
25-03	Bhutan	W	2-0	Gurgaon	CCq	Wahid Nadeem [61], Israfeel Kohistani [65]	2 000	Mombeni IRN
7-04	Nepal	L	0-1	Kathmandu	CCq		9 100	Abdul Baki OMA
9-04	Sri Lanka	W	1-0	Kathmandu	CCq	Mustafa Hadid [82]	1 800	Adday IRQ
11-04	Korea DPR	L	0-2	Kathmandu	CCq		1 000	Abdul Baki OMA
29-06	Palestine	L	0-2	Tursunzade	WCq		5 000	Al Ghafari JOR
3-07	Palestine	D	1-1	Al Ram	WCq	Mohammad Arezou [63]	9 000	Al Dosari QAT
3-12	India	D	1-1	New Delhi	SAFr1	Mohammad Arezou [5]		Noor Mohamed MAS
5-12	Sri Lanka	W	3-1	New Delhi	SAFr1	Sanjar Ahmadi 2 [22 36], Ata Yamrali [78]		Faizullin KGZ
7-12	Bhutan	W	8-1	New Delhi	SAFr1	Ata Yamrali [4], Zohib Amiri [10], Mohammad Arezou 4 [15 18 45 83], Mohammad Mashriqi [60], Djelaludin Sharityar [48]		Gamini SRI
9-12	Nepal	W	1-0	New Delhi	SAFsf	Mohammad Arezou [101]		Tufaylieh SYR
11-12	India	L	0-4	New Delhi	SAFf		20 000	Singh SIN
2012								

No international matches played in 2012

SAF = South Asian Football Federation Cup • AC = Asian Cup • CC = AFC Challenge Cup • WC = FIFA World Cup
q = qualifier • r1 = first round group • † Not a full international

AFGHANISTAN NATIONAL TEAM HISTORICAL RECORDS

Caps
31 - Israfeel Kohistani 2005-

Goals
7 - Mohammad Balal Arezou 2011-

Coaches
Holger Obermann GER 2003 • Mir Ali Akbarzada 2003 • Ali Askar Lali 2003-05 • Klaus Stark 2005-08 • Mohammad Yousef Kargar 2008-09 • Mohammad Farid 2009 • Mohammad Yousef Kargar 2010-

AFGHANISTAN 2012
AFGHAN PREMIER LEAGUE

First Stage

Group A

	Pl	W	D	L	F	A	Pts	DSGB	SA	DAS
De Maiwand Atalan	3	2	1	0	7	2	7	1-1	3-1	3-0
De Spin Ghar Bazan	3	2	1	0	3	1	7		1-0	1-0
Shaheen Asmayee	3	1	0	2	4	4	3			3-0
De Abasin Sape	3	0	0	3	0	7	0			

Final

Toofaan Harirod	10
De Spin Ghar Bazan	0

Toofaan Harirod	2
Simorgh Alborz	1

Group B

	Pl	W	D	L	F	A	Pts	SA	OH	MU
Toofaan Harirod	3	3	0	0	12	1	9	2-1	4-0	4-0
Simorgh Alborz	3	2	0	1	7	7	6		2-1	4-2
Oqaban Hindukush	3	0	1	2	3	8	1			2-2
Mawjhai Amu	3	0	1	2	4	10	1			

De Maiwand Atalan	1
Simorgh Alborz	2

FINAL

AFF Stadium, Kabul
19-10-2012

18/09/2012 - 19/10/2012

AIA – ANGUILLA

FIFA/COCA-COLA WORLD RANKING

'93	'94	'95	'96	'97	'98	'99	'00	'01	'02	'03	'04	'05	'06	'07	'08	'09	'10	'11	'12
-	-	-	-	190	197	202	197	194	196	198	197	198	196	198	201	203	203	201	205

2012

Jan	Feb	Mar	Apr	May	Jun	Jul	Aug	Sep	Oct	Nov	Dec	High	Low	Av
201	200	200	200	200	201	202	203	203	204	205	205	189	205	197

It is now more than a decade since Anguilla last tasted victory in a competitive international and their 4-3 victory over Montserrat in a Caribbean Cup qualifier in 2001 is now a distant memory. There looked to be little prospect of another win when they were drawn against hosts St Kitts and Nevis, Trinidad and Tobago and French Guiana in the qualifiers for the 2012 Caribbean Cup and that turned out to be the case. Coach Colin Johnson saw his side concede two early goals in their opening match in Basseterre against St Kitts and although Anguilla battled on to keep the score to 2-0, it was the first of three defeats in the qualifying group. In the next match against French Guiana, Terrence Rodgers managed to get on the score sheet for Anguilla in a 4-1 defeat but unfortunately for him as French Guiana are not members of FIFA, the match does not count towards official records. The hardest task was always going to be how many goals Anguilla could restrict Trinidad to in the final match and they were grateful that their opponents took their foot off the peddle in the second half after leading 7-0 at the break. They did get to double figures, however, with the match finishing 10-0. At home, Kicks United secured a league and cup double, repeating their success of 2011.

CFU CARIBBEAN CUP RECORD

1989 DNE **1991-1998** DNQ **1999** DNE **2001** DNQ **2005** DNE (withdrew) **2007-2012** DNQ

ANGUILLA FOOTBALL ASSOCIATION (AFA)

2 Queen Elizabeth Avenue, PO Box 1318, The Valley, Anguilla AI-2640
☎ +1 264 497 7323
 +1 264 497 7324
 axafa@yahoo.com
 None
FA 1990 CON 1996 FIFA 1996
P Raymond Guishard
GS Rogers Alkins

THE STADIA

2014 FIFA World Cup Stadia
Anguilla played their match against the Dominican Republic at the Estadio Panamericano in San Cristobal, Dominican Rep

Other Main Stadia
National Stadium
The Valley   1 000

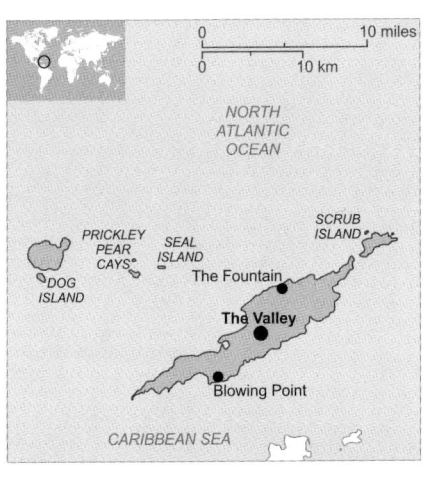

MAJOR CITIES/TOWNS

		Population
1	The Valley	1767
2	The Quarter	1500
3	Stoney Ground	1435
4	Island Harbour	1048
5	George Hill	1040
6	The Farrington	977
7	West End	940
8	Blowing Point	911
9	Sandy Hill	872
10	East End	689
11	North Hill	507
12	Sandy Ground	425

ANGUILLA

Capital	The Valley	Population	14 436 (221)	% in cities	100%
GDP per capita	$8800 (113)	Area km²	91 km² (226)	GMT +/-	-4
Neighbours (km)	Coast 61				

RECENT INTERNATIONALS PLAYED BY ANGUILLA

2004	Opponents		Score	Venue	Comp	Scorers	Att	Referee
19-03	Dominican Republic	D	0-0	Santo Domingo	WCq		400	Mattus CRC
21-03	Dominican Republic	L	0-6	Santo Domingo	WCq		850	Porras CRC
2005								
No international matches played in 2005								
2006								
20-09	Antigua and Barbuda	L	3-5	St John's	CCq	Gaekwad St Hillaire [13], Kapil Assent [51], Richard O'Connor [90]	300	Wijngaarde SUR
22-09	St Kitts and Nevis	L	1-6	St John's	CCq	Richard O'Connor [22]	500	Phillips GRN
24-09	Barbados	L	1-7	St John's	CCq	Girdon Connor [48]	2 800	Wijngaarde SUR
2007								
No international matches played in 2007								
2008								
6-02	El Salvador	L	0-12	San Salvador	WCq		15 000	Jauregui ANT
26-03	El Salvador	L	0-4	Washington DC	WCq		22 670	Bedeau GRN
17-09	St Vincent/Grenadines	L	1-3	Fort de France	CCq	Troy Jeffers OG [38]	100	Fanus LCA
19-09	Martinique †	L	1-3	Fort de France	CCq	Kapil Battice [83]	500	George LCA
2009								
No international matches played in 2009								
2010								
18-09	British Virgin Islands	L	1-2	Saint Martin	Fr			
2-10	Puerto Rico	L	1-3	Bayamon	CCq	Walwyn Benjamin [54p]	2 050	Thomas JAM
4-10	Cayman Islands	L	1-4	Bayamon	CCq	Javille Brooks [32]	500	Davis TRI
6-10	Saint Martin †	W	2-1	Bayamon	CCq	Javille Brooks [19], Terrence Rogers [38]	500	Davis TRI
2011								
19-06	US Virgin Islands	D	0-0	The Valley	Fr		550	Burton AIA
8-07	Dominican Republic	L	0-2	San Cristobal	WCq		1 000	Brizan TRI
10-07	Dominican Republic	L	0-4	San Cristobal	WCq		1 500	Brea CUB
2012								
7-07	British Virgin Islands	L	0-1	Road Town	Fr			
10-10	St Kitts and Nevis	L	0-2	Basseterre	CCq		700	Johnson GUY
12-10	French Guiana †	L	1-4	Basseterre	CCq	Terrence Rogers [59]	600	Hidalgo DOM
14-10	Trinidad and Tobago	L	0-10	Basseterre	CCq		40	Johnson GUY

Fr = Friendly match • WC = FIFA World Cup • CC = Digicel Caribbean Cup • q = qualifier • † Not a full international

ALB – ALBANIA

FIFA/COCA-COLA WORLD RANKING

'93	'94	'95	'96	'97	'98	'99	'00	'01	'02	'03	'04	'05	'06	'07	'08	'09	'10	'11	'12
92	100	91	116	116	106	83	72	96	93	89	86	82	87	80	81	96	65	74	63

2012

Jan	Feb	Mar	Apr	May	Jun	Jul	Aug	Sep	Oct	Nov	Dec	High	Low	Av
77	78	80	84	84	79	75	74	84	84	67	63	50	124	88

Where the league and cup double was once a routine achievement for the top Albanian clubs, in recent years it has become more elusive and in 2012 it fell just beyond the reach of Skenderbeu who lost 1-0 to KF Tiranë in the cup final a week after having clinched the championship ahead of Teuta Durres. Skenderbeu had sacked their 2011 title-winning coach Shpetim Duro after a slow start to their 2012 campaign and replaced him with Czech coach Stanislav Levy and it paid dividends. A 3-1 home win over neighbours Pogradeci on the final day of the season saw Skenderbeu retain their title and send their rivals down. Also relegated were 18-time champions Dinamo Tiranë who dropped into the second division for the first time in their 62 year history. With Partizan Tiranë winning promotion from the third division, what once was the most fiercely contested derby in the country will be renewed once again and for the first time out of the top flight. National team coach Giovanni de Biasi made a solid start to his tenure in charge with six points from the first four 2014 FIFA World Cup qualifiers. A 2-1 defeat at home to Iceland dampened expectations but with the federation actively seeking to persuade ethnic Albanians born abroad to join the national team set-up, there are hopes of a stronger player pool for future qualification campaigns.

UEFA EUROPEAN CHAMPIONSHIP RECORD
1960 DNE 1964-1972 DNQ 1976-1980 DNE 1984-2012 DNQ

FEDERATA SHQIPTARE E FUTBOLIT (FSHF)
Rruga Labinoti,
Pallati perballe Shkolles,
"Gjuhet e Huaja" Tirana
☎ +355 423 46 605
+355 423 46 609
fshf@fshf.org.al
www.fshf.org
FA 1930 CON 1954 FIFA 1932
P Armand Duka
GS Ilir Shulku

THE STADIA
2014 FIFA World Cup Stadia
Stadiumi Qemal Stafa
Tirana — 19 600
Other Main Stadia
Stadiumi Loro Borici
Shkoder — 16 000
Stadiumi Tomori
Berat — 14 500
Stadiumi Ruzhdi Bizhuta
Elbasan — 12 500
Stadiumi Selman Stërmasi
Tirana — 12 500

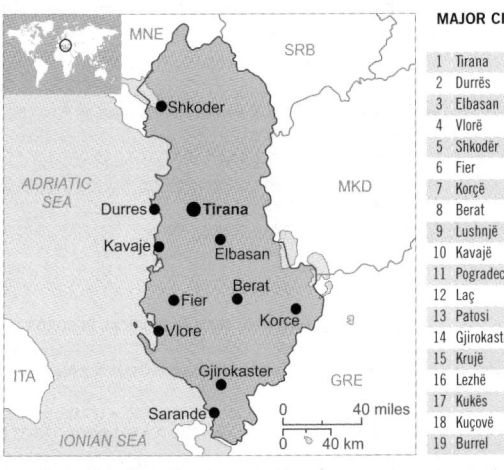

MAJOR CITIES/TOWNS
		Population
1	Tirana	406 936
2	Durrës	132 655
3	Elbasan	107 323
4	Vlorë	95 033
5	Shkodër	91 257
6	Fier	66 600
7	Korçë	57 494
8	Berat	48 385
9	Lushnjë	45 171
10	Kavajë	31 014
11	Pogradec	28 333
12	Laç	27 055
13	Patosi	24 749
14	Gjirokastër	24 278
15	Krujë	23 734
16	Lezhë	21 371
17	Kukës	19239
18	Kuçovë	18 448
19	Burrel	17 100

REPUBLIKA E SHQIPERISE • REPUBLIC OF ALBANIA
Capital Tirana   Population 3 639 453 (129)   % in cities 47%
GDP per capita $6000 (132)   Area km² 28 748 km² (144)   GMT +/- +1
Neighbours (km) Greece 282, Macedonia 151, Montenegro 172, Kosovo 112 • Coast 362

RECENT INTERNATIONALS PLAYED BY ALBANIA

2009	Opponents	Score		Venue	Comp	Scorers	Att	Referee
11-02	Malta	D	0-0	Ta'Qali	WCq		2041	Deaconu ROU
28-03	Hungary	L	0-1	Tirana	WCq		12 000	Kuipers NED
1-04	Denmark	L	0-3	Copenhagen	WCq		24 320	Skomina SVN
6-06	Portugal	L	1-2	Tirana	WCq	Erjon Bogdani [29]	13 320	Meyer GER
10-06	Georgia	D	1-1	Tirana	Fr	Agolli [58]	2 000	Stavrev MKD
12-08	Cyprus	W	6-1	Tirana	Fr	Skela 2 [25p 44p], Erjon Bogdani [65], OG [67], Agolli [71], Emiljano Vila [75]		Yildirim TUR
9-09	Denmark	D	1-1	Tirana	WCq	Erjon Bogdani [51]	8 000	Cakir TUR
14-10	Sweden	L	1-4	Stockholm	WCq	Hamdi Salihi [57]	25 342	Ivanov.N RUS
14-11	Estonia	D	0-0	Tallinn	Fr		2 110	Kancleris LTU
2010								
3-03	Northern Ireland	W	1-0	Tirana	Fr	Skela [25]	7 500	Pilav BIH
25-05	Montenegro	W	1-0	Podgorica	Fr	Hamdi Salihi [79]	7 000	Strahonja CRO
2-06	Andorra	W	1-0	Tirana	Fr	Hamdi Salihi [44]	3 000	Meckarovski MKD
11-08	Uzbekistan	W	1-0	Durres	Fr	Hamdi Salihi [14]	8 000	Radovanovic MNE
3-09	Romania	D	1-1	Piatra-Neamt	ECq	Muzaka [87]	13 000	Schorgenhofer AUT
7-09	Luxembourg	W	1-0	Shkoder	ECq	Hamdi Salihi [37]	11 800	Trutz SVK
8-10	Bosnia-Herzegovina	D	1-1	Tirana	ECq	Duro [45]	11 300	Jakobsson ISL
12-10	Belarus	L	0-2	Minsk	ECq		7 000	Rasmussen DEN
17-11	Macedonia FYR	D	0-0	Korce	Fr		12 000	Gocek TUR
2011								
9-02	Slovenia	L	1-2	Tirana	Fr	Bulku [62]		Koukoulakis GRE
26-03	Belarus	W	1-0	Tirana	ECq	Hamdi Salihi [62]	13 826	Strombergsson SWE
7-06	Bosnia-Herzegovina	L	0-2	Zenica	ECq		9 000	Blom NED
20-06	Argentina	L	0-4	Buenos Aires	Fr		21 000	Larrionda URU
10-08	Montenegro	W	3-2	Tirana	Fr	Erjon Bogdani [33], Hyka [64], Hamdi Salihi [69]	5 500	Genov BUL
2-09	France	L	1-2	Tirana	ECq	Erjon Bogdani [46]	15 600	Nikolaev RUS
6-09	Luxembourg	L	1-2	Luxembourg	ECq	Erjon Bogdani [64]	2 132	Kari FIN
7-10	France	L	0-3	Paris	ECq		65 239	Koukoulakis GRE
11-10	Romania	D	1-1	Tirana	ECq	Hamdi Salihi [24]	3 000	Mazeika LTU
11-11	Azerbaijan	L	0-1	Tirana	Fr		1 200	Mazzoleni ITA
15-11	Macedonia FYR	D	0-0	Prilep	Fr		4 500	Vincic SVN
2012								
29-02	Georgia	L	1-2	Tbilisi	Fr	Edgar Cani [3]	18 000	Sidenco MDA
22-05	Qatar	W	2-1	Madrid	Fr	Elis Bakaj [46], Erjon Bogdani [50]	100	Velasco ESP
27-05	Iran	W	1-0	Istanbul	Fr	Emiljano Vila [60]	8 500	Gocek TUR
15-08	Moldova	D	0-0	Tirana	Fr		5 500	Yildirim TUR
7-09	Cyprus	W	3-1	Tirana	WCq	Armando Sadiku [36], Edgar Cani [84], Erjon Bogdani [87]	9 400	Kuchin KAZ
11-09	Switzerland	L	0-2	Lucerne	WCq		16 500	Hategan ROU
12-10	Iceland	L	1-2	Tirana	WCq	Edgar Cani [28]	8 200	Asumaa FIN
16-10	Slovenia	W	1-0	Tirana	WCq	Odise Roshi [37]	9 000	Hansson SWE
14-11	Cameroon	D	0-0	Geneva	Fr			Studer SUI

Fr = Friendly match • EC = UEFA EURO 2012 • WC = FIFA World Cup • q = qualifier

ALBANIA NATIONAL TEAM HISTORICAL RECORDS

Caps
79 - Altin Lala 1998- • 77 - Klodian Duro 2000- • 75 - Ervin Skela 2000- • 73 - Foto Strakosha 1990-2004 • 68 - Igli Tare 1997-2007 • 67 - Alban Bushi 1995-2007 • 66 - Altin Haxhi 1995-2009 • 65 - Erjon Bogdani 1996- • 63 - Altin Rraklli 1992-2005 • 59 - Rudi Vata 1990-2000

Goals
15 - Erjon Bogdani 1996- • 14 - Alban Bushi 1995-2007 • 13 - Ervin Skela 2000- • 11 - Altin Rraklli 1992-2005 • 10 - Sokol Kushta 1987-96, Igli Tare 1997-2007 • 9 - Hamdi Salihi 2006- • 8 - Adrian Aliaj 2002-06 • 6 - Loro Borici 1946-58, Edmond Kapllani 2004-08, Bledar Kola 1994-2001 & Klodian Duro 2000-

Coaches
Ljubisa Brocic YUG 1946 • Adem Karapici 1947 • Sllave Llambi 1948-50 • Miklos Vadas HUN 1953 • Zyber Konci 1963-65 • Loro Borici 1965-72 • Myslym Alla 1972-73 • Ilia Shuke 1973 • Zyber Konci 1980 • Loro Borici 1981 • Shyqyri Rreli 1982-85 • Agron Sulaj 1985-88 • Shyqyri Rreli 1988-90 • Agron Sulaj 1990 • Bejkush Birce 1990-94 • Neptun Bajko 1994-96 • Astrit Hafizi 1996-99 • Medin Zhega 2000-01 • Sulejman Demollari 2001-02 • Giuseppe Dossena ITA 2002 • Hans-Peter Briegel GER 2002-06 • Otto Baric CRO 2006-07 • Slavko Kovacic 2007 • Arie Haan NED 2008-09 • Josip Kuze CRO 2009-11 • Gianni De Biasi ITA 2011-

ALBANIA 2011-12

SUPERLIGA
KATEGORIA SUPERIORE

	Pl	W	D	L	F	A	Pts	Skënderbeu	Teuta	KF Tirana	Flamurtari	Kastrioti	Bylis	Vllaznia	Laçi	Shkumbini	Tomori	Kamza	Apolonia	Pogradeci	Dinamo
Skënderbeu Korçë †	26	17	6	3	45	16	57		0-1	2-0	2-1	1-0	3-2	2-1	3-0	3-1	0-0	0-0	2-0	3-0	2-0
Teuta Durrës ‡	26	17	5	4	33	18	56	0-0		1-2	1-0	1-1	1-0	0-1	1-0	2-1	1-0	0-0	2-1	5-3	2-0
KF Tirana ‡	26	16	5	5	33	21	53	0-0	0-1		2-0	1-0	3-2	0-0	1-0	1-1	1-0	1-0	1-0	3-1	1-0
Flamurtari Vlorë ‡	26	13	7	6	42	20	46	1-0	1-1	0-1		3-1	2-0	1-0	0-0	5-0	1-1	2-1	1-1	2-0	5-0
Kastrioti Krujë	26	11	5	10	37	30	38	1-2	1-2	2-3	1-1		4-2	2-1	0-1	0-1	3-1	3-2	2-0	4-0	1-0
Bylis Ballshi	26	9	8	9	40	37	35	0-0	0-0	1-0	1-3	0-1		1-0	3-0	5-2	4-2	2-1	2-1	1-0	3-1
Vllaznia Shkodër	26	10	5	11	39	33	35	0-2	3-1	2-2	2-1	2-4	3-3		3-1	4-4	0-0	4-0	1-0	1-0	2-1
Laçi §6	26	11	7	8	26	28	34	2-1	1-0	0-1	0-0	1-1	2-2	1-0		3-2	2-0	1-0	1-0	2-0	1-0
Shkumbini Peqin	26	8	7	11	37	45	31	2-4	1-2	3-2	0-3	0-1	1-1	2-1	1-1		6-2	3-1	2-0	2-1	1-0	
Tomori Berat ‡‡	26	8	4	14	36	47	28	2-4	0-2	0-1	3-2	2-1	2-2	1-0	0-1	1-0		4-1	2-0	4-1	2-1
Kamza ‡‡	26	7	6	13	22	32	27	0-1	1-2	0-0	0-1	1-1	1-0	1-2	3-1	1-0	2-1		0-1	2-1	1-1
Apolonia Fier ‡‡	26	5	6	15	27	46	21	1-5	0-1	1-2	1-3	1-0	2-1	1-4	1-1	1-1	6-5	0-0		2-3	2-0
Pogradeci §3	26	4	6	16	25	47	19	1-3	1-2	1-2	0-2	1-1	1-1	2-1	3-1	0-0	1-0	2-1	1-1		1-0
Dinamo Tiranë §3	26	3	7	16	19	41	13	0-0	0-1	3-2	1-1	0-1	1-1	0-3	2-2	0-0	4-1	0-2	3-3	1-0	

10/09/2011 - 12/05/2012 • † Qualified for the UEFA Champions League • ‡ Qualified for the Europa League • ‡‡ Relegation play-off • § Points deducted • Relegation play-offs: Kamza 0-2 **Besa Kavajë** • **Tomori Berat** 0-0 3-2p Beselidhja Lezhë • **Apolonia Fier** 3-0 Lushnja
Top scorers: 20 - Ronald **DERVISHI**, Shkumbini • 19 - Endri **BAKIU**, Tomori • 14 - Bruce **INKANGO** FRA, Kastrioti • 13 - Bekim **BALA**, Tirana

ALBANIA 2011-12
KATEGORIA E PARE (2)

	Pl	W	D	L	F	A	Pts
Luftëtari Gjirokastër	30	23	3	4	59	22	72
Përparimi Kukës	30	21	4	5	63	24	67
Lushnja ‡‡	30	19	7	4	49	16	64
Besa Kavajë ‡‡	30	17	4	9	44	33	55
Beselidhja Lezhë ‡‡	30	16	6	8	38	16	54
Elbasani	30	11	6	13	44	48	39
Burreli	30	12	3	15	36	43	39
Gramshi	30	10	8	12	37	44	38
Butrinti Sarandë	30	10	7	13	32	36	37
Ada Velipojë	30	9	9	12	34	35	36
Iliria Fushë-Krujë	30	11	3	16	38	44	36
Adriatiku Mamurrasi	30	10	4	16	35	48	34
Himarë ‡‡	30	9	5	16	38	43	32
Gramozi Ersekë ‡‡	30	9	2	19	25	60	29
Vlora	30	6	6	18	24	54	18
Skrapari	30	4	9	17	22	52	18

10/09/2011 - 12/05/2012 • ‡‡ Play-offs • Promotion (see Superliga) • Relegation: **Himara** 3-0 Sukthi • Gramozi 1-2 **Naftëtari Kuçova**

MEDALS TABLE

		Overall			League			Cup	
		G	S	B	G	S	B	G	S
1	KF Tirana	39	21	13	24	13	13	15	8
2	Partizani Tiranë	30	27	8	15	19	8	15	8
3	Dinamo Tiranë	31	15	11	18	9	11	13	6
4	Vllaznia Shkodër	15	19	15	9	11	15	6	8
5	Flamurtari Vlorë	4	15	3	1	7	3	3	8
6	Teuta Durrës	4	12	5	1	6	5	3	6
7	SK Elbasani	4	2	1	2	1	1	2	1
8	Skënderbeu Korçë	3	7	2	3	3	2		4
9	Besa Kavajë	2	8	10		2	10	2	6
10	Apolonia Fier	1						1	
11	Lushnja	3						3	
12	Tomori Berat	2		1			1	2	
13	Albpetrol Patosi	1						1	
	Luftëtari Gjirokastër	1						1	
15	Bylis Ballshi			1			1		

ALBANIA 2011-12
KATEGORIA E DYTE (3)
GROUP A

	Pl	W	D	L	F	A	Pts
Tërbuni Pukë	16	13	3	0	36	9	42
Sukthi ‡‡	16	12	2	2	41	16	38
Veleçiku Koplik	16	8	3	5	23	19	27
Luzi 2008	16	7	3	6	24	23	24
Olimpiku Tiranë	16	6	5	5	24	18	23
Egnatia Rrogozhinë	16	5	3	8	13	18	18
Korabi Peshkopi	16	2	4	10	15	27	10
Erzeni Shijak	16	3	3	10	20	38	9
Pashtriku Has	16	2	2	12	15	43	5

25/09/2011 - 13/05/2012 • ‡‡ Play-offs (see level 2)

KATEGORIA E DYTE FINAL
Selman Stermasi, Tirana, 17-05-2012
Partizani Tiranë 1-2 **Tërbuni Pukë**

ALBANIA 2011-12
KATEGORIA E DYTE (3)
GROUP B

	Pl	W	D	L	F	A	Pts
Partizani Tiranë	22	16	4	2	34	10	52
Naftëtari Kuçovë ‡‡	22	16	3	3	47	8	51
Tepelena	22	12	2	8	36	28	38
Turbina Cërrik	22	10	5	7	36	29	35
Albpetrol Patos	22	9	7	6	26	18	34
Bilisht Sport	22	9	2	11	29	31	29
Sopoti Librazhd	22	7	6	9	23	31	27
Delvina	22	7	2	13	27	36	23
Përmeti	22	7	4	11	24	34	22
Memaliaj	22	6	3	13	25	34	21
Domosdova Prrenjas	22	6	3	13	18	40	18
Këlcyra	22	5	3	14	20	46	18

25/09/2011 - 13/05/2012 • ‡‡ Play-offs (see level 2)

KUPA E SHQIPERISE 2011-12

First Round

KF Tirana	3	7
Himarë *	0	1
Skrapari *	0	2
Laçi	3	8
Apolonia Fier	5	3
Gramozi Ersekë *	1	1
Burreli *	2	0
Shkumbini Peqin	1	7
Flamurtari Vlorë	4	11
Bilisht Sporti *	1	0
Lushnja *	2	0
Kamza	1	1
Teuta Durrës	1	3
Përparimi Kukës *	1	1
Ada Velipojë *	1	0
Pogradeci	2	2
Kastrioti Krujë *	2	2
Gramshi *	1	0
Tërbuni Pukë *	1	0
Skënderbeu Korçë *	2	3
Luftëtari Gj'kastër *	1	0
Tomori Berat	0	0
Besëlidhja Lezhë *	0	0
Besa Kavajë	2	2
Vllaznia Shkodër	3	2
Butrinti Sarandë *	2	0
Iliria Fushë-Krujë *	1	1
Bylis Ballshi	6	1
Elbasani	0	3
Adriatiku M'rrasi *	1	1
Vlora *	0	0
Dinamo Tiranë	3	3

Second round groups

	Pl	W	D	L	F	A	Pts
KF Tirana	6	6	0	0	13	4	**18**
Laçi	6	2	2	2	7	5	**8**
Apolonia	6	2	1	3	11	13	**7**
Shkumbini	6	0	1	5	10	19	**1**

KF Tirana 1-0 3-0 3-1
Laçi 0-1 0-0 3-1
Apolonia 1-2 1-3 5-2
Shkumbini 2-3 1-1 3-4

	Pl	W	D	L	F	A	Pts
Flamurtari	6	3	1	2	6	3	**10**
Kamza	6	2	3	1	9	4	**9**
Teuta	6	2	3	1	4	2	**9**
Pogradeci	6	1	1	4	4	10	**4**

Flamurtari Fl Km Te Po
Kamza 0-0 1-0 3-0
Teuta 1-0 0-0 6-0
Pogradeci 1-0 1-1 0-0
        1-2 3-1 0-2

	Pl	W	D	L	F	A	Pts
Kastrioti	6	4	1	1	15	8	**13**
Skënderbeu	6	4	0	2	10	7	**12**
Luftëtari	6	2	1	3	9	12	**7**
Besa	6	1	0	5	3	10	**3**

Kastrioti Ks Sk Lu Be
Skënderbeu 3-1 4-1 2-0
Luftëtari 2-0 2-0 3-0
Besa 3-3 4-1 1-0
        1-3 0-1 2-0

	Pl	W	D	L	F	A	Pts
Vllaznia	6	5	1	0	19	7	**16**
Bylis	6	4	1	1	13	8	**13**
Elbasani	6	1	0	5	7	16	**3**
Dinamo	6	1	0	5	6	14	**3**

Vllaznia Vl By El Di
Bylis 0-0 3-1 5-2
Elbasani 2-4 4-1 2-1
Dinamo 2-4 1-3 0-1
        0-3 1-2 1-2

Quarter-final groups

	Pl	W	D	L	F	A	Pts
KF Tirana	6	3	2	1	8	4	**11**
Kastrioti	6	3	1	2	9	9	**10**
Bylis Ballsh	6	2	3	1	11	7	**9**
Kamza	6	0	2	4	3	11	**2**

KF Tirana Ti Ks BB Km
Kastrioti 2-0 1-1 2-0
Bylis Ballsh 4-2 0-0 0-0
Kamza 0-0 0-3 5-1
        1-2 1-2 0-0

	Pl	W	D	L	F	A	Pts
Flamurtari	6	3	2	1	8	5	**11**
Skënderbeu	6	3	2	1	8	6	**11**
Vllaznia	6	1	2	3	3	5	**5**
Laçi	6	1	2	3	6	6	**5**

Flamurtari Fl Sk Vl La
Skënderbeu 3-0 2-0 1-1
Vllaznia 4-1 1-1 1-0
Laçi 0-1 0-0 2-0
        0-0 1-2 1-0

Semi-finals

KF Tirana	3	2
Flamurtari *	0	2
Kastrioti	1	0
Skënderbeu *	3	0

Final

KF Tirana ‡	1
Skënderbeu Korçë	0

CUP FINAL

Qemal Stafa, Tirana, 17-05-2012, 19:00
Att: 5000. Ref: Lorenc Jemini
Scorer - Bekim Balaj [107] for Tirana
Tirana - Ilion Lika●- Nertil Ferraj (Rezart Dabulla 113), Arjan Pisha●, Elvis Sina (Gerhard Tushe● 24), Julian Ahmataj●- (Klodian Duro 103), Erjon Dushku, Erindo Karabeci, Sokol Cikalleshi, Renaldo Kalari●- Afrim Taku, Bekim Balaj. Tr: Julian Rubio
Skënderbeu - Orges Shehi - Ivan Gvozdenovic, Marko Radas●- Renato Arapi●, Erbim Fagu, Nurudeen Orelesi, Igli Allmuca●, Gjergj Muzaka (Davor Bratic 38) (Luko Biskup 60), Bledi Shkembi●- (Dorian Kerciku● 92+.), Sebino Plaku, Daniel Xhafaj. Tr: Stanislav Levy

* Home team in the first leg · ‡ Qualified for the Europa League

ALG – ALGERIA

FIFA/COCA-COLA WORLD RANKING

'93	'94	'95	'96	'97	'98	'99	'00	'01	'02	'03	'04	'05	'06	'07	'08	'09	'10	'11	'12
35	57	48	49	59	71	86	82	75	68	62	73	80	80	79	64	26	35	30	19

2012

Jan	Feb	Mar	Apr	May	Jun	Jul	Aug	Sep	Oct	Nov	Dec	High	Low	Av
32	36	35	38	38	32	35	34	28	24	19	19	19	103	61

Algeria went to the 2013 Africa Cup of Nations in South Africa ranked as the continent's second best side and with high hopes. Dominated by players from the French-based Diaspora, they had won six of the eight internationals played in 2012 under coach Vahid Halilhodzic and added several key players, like former French junior international Sofiane Feghouli, to their squad. However, a lack of firepower saw them fail to convert chances in all three of their matches and they suffered surprising losses to both Tunisia and Togo before ending with a draw with Cote d'Ivoire - after they were already mathematically eliminated. Halilhodzic called it a major "deception". A victory over Rwanda in mid-2012 had got their 2014 FIFA World Cup qualifying campaign off to a good start but that was followed by a defeat at the hands of Mali in neutral Burkina Faso as the two looked set for a tight battle to top the group. In club football Entente Setif won the championship by the narrowest of margins from JSM Bejaia after USM Alger had thrown away an advantageous position in the closing stages of the season. Setif, former African champions, then completed the double by beating Chabab Belouizdad in the cup final - a record-breaking eighth success and their first double since 1968 as they maintained their one hundred per cent record in the final.

CAF AFRICA CUP OF NATIONS RECORD

1957-1965 DNE **1968** r1 1970-1978 DNQ **1980** 2 F **1982** 4 SF **1984** 3 SF **1986** r1 **1988** 3 SF **1990** 1 Winners (Hosts) **1992** r1 **1994** Disqualified **1996** 5 QF **1998** r1 **2000** 6 QF **2002** r1 **2004** 8 QF **2006-2008** DNQ **2010** 4 SF **2012** DNQ **2013** 13 r1

FEDERATION ALGERIENNE DE FOOTBALL (FAF)

Chemin Ahmed Ouaked,
Boite Postale 39
16000 Dely Ibrahim, Alger
☎ +213 21 984306
📠 +213 21 984308
✉ faffoot@yahoo.fr
🖥 www.faf.dz
FA 1962 CON 1964 FIFA 1963
P Mohamed Raouraoua
GS Nadir Bouzenad

THE STADIA

2014 FIFA World Cup Stadia
Stade Mustapha Tchaker
Blida 35 000

Other Main Stadia
Stade 5 Juillet 1962
Algiers 66 000
Stade 19 Mai 1956
Annaba 50 000
Stade Ahmed Zabana
Oran 50 000
Stade Mohamed-Hamlaoui
Constantine 40 000

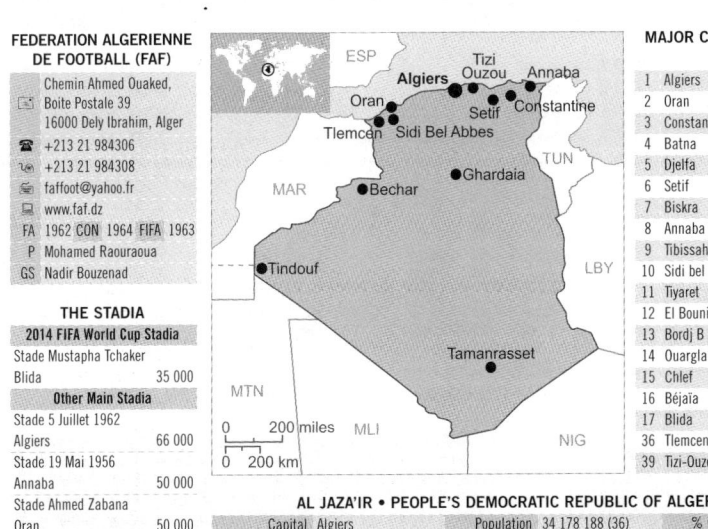

MAJOR CITIES/TOWNS

		Population
1	Algiers	2 203 698
2	Oran	679 877
3	Constantine	462 779
4	Batna	297 835
5	Djelfa	261 026
6	Setif	233 913
7	Biskra	211 890
8	Annaba	205 597
9	Tibissah	197 636
10	Sidi el Abbès	197 603
11	Tiyaret	194 392
12	El Bouni	193 422
13	Bordj B Arreridj	179 969
14	Ouargla	174 122
15	Chlef	171 815
16	Béjaïa	171 673
17	Blida	170 773
36	Tlemcen	122 329
39	Tizi-Ouzou	116 318

AL JAZA'IR • PEOPLE'S DEMOCRATIC REPUBLIC OF ALGERIA

Capital Algiers	Population 34 178 188 (36)	% in cities 65%
GDP per capita $6900 (126)	Area km² 2 381 741 km² (11)	GMT +/- +1

Neighbours (km) Libya 982, Mali 1376, Mauritania 463, Morocco 1559, Niger 956, Tunisia 965 • Coast 998

RECENT INTERNATIONALS PLAYED BY ALGERIA

2010	Opponents	Score	Venue	Comp	Scorers	Att	Referee
11-01	Malawi	L 0-3	Luanda	CNr1		1 000	Diatta SEN
14-01	Mali	W 1-0	Luanda	CNr1	Rafik Halliche 43	4 000	Ssegonga UGA
18-01	Angola	D 0-0	Luanda	CNr1		40 000	Damon RSA
24-01	Côte d'Ivoire	W 3-2	Cabinda	CNqf	Karim Matmour 39, Madjid Bougherra 92+, Hameur Bouazza 92	10 000	Maillet SEY
28-01	Egypt	L 0-4	Benguela	CNsf		30 000	Codjia BEN
30-01	Nigeria	L 0-1	Benguela	CN3p		12 000	Diatta SEN
3-03	Algeria	L 0-3	Algiers	Fr		65 000	Diatta SEN
28-05	Republic of Ireland	L 0-3	Dublin	Fr		16 800	Braamhaar NED
5-06	UAE	W 1-0	Fürth	Fr	Karim Ziani 51p	12 500	Grafe GER
13-06	Slovenia	L 0-1	Polokwane	WCr1		30 325	Batres GUA
18-06	England	D 0-0	Cape Town	WCr1		64 100	Irmatov UZB
23-06	USA	L 0-1	Pretoria	WCr1		35 827	De Bleeckere BEL
11-08	Gabon	L 1-2	Algiers	Fr	Rafik Djebbour 85	55 000	Rouaissi MAR
3-09	Tanzania	D 1-1	Blida	CNq	Adlene Guedioura 44	30 000	Djaoupe TOG
8-10	Central African Rep	L 0-2	Bangui	CNq		25 000	Carvalho ANG
17-11	Luxembourg	D 0-0	Luxembourg	Fr		7 033	Sippel GER
2011							
27-03	Morocco	W 1-0	Annaba	CNq	Hassan Yebda 7p	60 000	Seechurn MRI
4-06	Morocco	L 0-4	Marrakech	CNq			Doue CIV
3-09	Tanzania	D 1-1	Dar es Salaam	CNq	Hameur Bouazza 52		Djaoupe TOG
9-10	Central African Rep	W 2-0	Blida	CNq	Hassan Yebda 2, Foued Kadir 30		Fall SEN
12-11	Tunisia	W 1-0	Algiers	Fr		25 000	Laachiri MAR
2012							
29-02	Gambia	W 2-1	Bakau	CNq	Anthar Yahia 55, Sofiane Feghouli 58		Coulibaly MLI
26-05	Niger	W 3-0	Blida	Fr	OG 33, Rafik Djebbour 38, El Arabi Soudani 82		
2-06	Rwanda	W 4-0	Blida	WCq	Sofiane Feghouli 26, El Arabi Soudani 2 31 82, Islam Slimani 79	20 000	Gassama GAM
10-06	Mali	L 1-2	Ouagadougou	WCq	Islam Slimani 6	5 847	Bennett RSA
15-06	Gambia	W 4-1	Blida	CNq	Foued Kadir 1, Islam Slimani 2 60 50, El Arabi Soudani 66		Jedidi TUN
9-09	Libya	W 1-0	Casablanca	CNq	El Arabi Soudani 88		Diatta SEN
14-10	Libya	W 2-0	Blida	CNq	El Arabi Soudani 6, Islam Slimani 7		Bangoura GUI
14-11	Bosnia-Herzegovina	L 0-1	Algiers	Fr			Coulibaly MLI
2013							
12-01	South Africa	D 0-0	Johannesburg	Fr		14 558	Koto LES
22-01	Tunisia	L 0-1	Rustenburg	CNr1		10 000	Gassama GAM
26-01	Togo	L 0-2	Rustenburg	CNr1		35 000	Nampiandraza MAD
30-01	Côte d'Ivoire	D 2-2	Rustenburg	CNr1	Sofiane Feghouli 64p, El Arabi Soudani 70	5 000	Otogo-Castane GAB

Fr = Friendly match • CN = CAF African Cup of Nations • WC = FIFA World Cup • q = qualifier • r1 = first round group • qf = quarter-final

ALGERIA NATIONAL TEAM HISTORICAL RECORDS

Caps: 89 - Lakhdar Belloumi 1978-89 • 86 - Rabah Madjer 1978-92 • 81 - Billel Dziri 1992-2005 • 80 - Djamel Menad 1980-95 • 79 - Abdelhafid Tasfaout 1991-2002 • 77 - Mahieddine Meftah 1989-2002 • 75 - Mahmoud Guendouz 1977-86 • 69 - Salah Assad 1977-89 • 68 - Fodil Megharia 1984-92 • 67 - Yazid Mansouri 2001-

Goals: 35 - Abdelhafid Tasfaout 1990-2002 • 34 - Lakhdar Belloumi 1978-89 • 29 - Rabah Madjer 1978-92 • 24 - Djamel Menad 1982-95 • 22 - Tedj Bensaoula 1979-86 • 18 - Rafik Saifi 1999- • 13 - Salah Assad 1978-88 • 12 - Hacene Lalmas 1964-74 • 10 - Ali Mecabih 1995-2003 • 9 - Billel Dziri 1993-2002

Coaches: For coaches pre 1989 see Oliver's Almanack 2012 • Abdelhamid Kermali & Ali Fergani 1989-92 • Meziane Ighil 1992-93 • Rabah Madjer 1993-95 • Ali Fergani & Mourad Abdelouahab 1995-96 • Hamid Zouba & Abdelhamid Kermali 1996-97 • Abderrahmane Mehdaoui 1997-98 • Meziane Ighil & Marcel Pigulea ROU 1998-99 • Boualem Charef & Rabah Saadane 1999 • Nacer Sandjak 1999-2000 • Abdelghani Djaadaoui 2000-01 • Hamid Zouba & Abdelhamid Kermali 2001 • Rabah Madjer 2001-02 • Hamid Zouba 2002-03 • Rachid Bouaratta 2003 • George Leekens BEL 2003 • Rabah Saadane 2003-04 • Robert Waseige BEL 2004 • Ali Fergani & Lakhdar Belloumi 2004-05 • Meziane Ighil 2005-06 • Jean-Michel Cavalli FRA 2006-07 • Rabah Saadane 2007-10 • Abdelhak Benchikha 2010-11 • Vahid Halilhodzic BIH 2011-

ALGERIA 2011-12

LIGUE PROFESSIONNELLE 1

	Pl	W	D	L	F	A	Pts	ESS	JSMB	USMA	CRB	ASO	MCA	CAB	WAT	JSK	USMH	MCEE	CSC	MCO	ASK	NAHD	MCS
ES Sétif †	30	16	5	9	53	40	53		1-2	3-2	0-2	3-1	0-1	2-1	3-1	2-1	1-0	1-1	4-2	1-1	2-0	3-2	3-1
JSM Béjaïa †	30	15	8	7	40	26	53	2-3		2-0	4-0	1-0	1-0	1-0	0-0	1-0	1-1	1-1	3-0	1-3	2-0	1-0	3-1
USM Alger ‡	30	15	7	8	37	25	52	2-0	3-4		2-0	1-0	3-1	1-0	2-1	1-0	0-1	1-0	1-1	2-0	2-0	2-0	3-2
CR Bélouizdad ‡	30	13	9	8	34	28	48	1-3	1-2	0-0		2-1	2-0	0-2	0-0	1-0	1-1	2-0	0-0	4-1	4-1	1-0	3-1
ASO Chlef	30	14	5	11	41	34	47	0-0	2-1	1-0	3-1		4-2	1-1	3-0	2-1	0-2	2-0	3-1	2-1	2-0	2-1	1-0
MC Alger	30	11	11	8	35	33	44	1-0	1-1	1-0	1-1	0-0		2-1	3-1	0-0	2-1	2-0	2-2	1-1	3-1	1-1	2-0
CA Batna	30	12	8	10	38	25	44	1-0	0-0	0-1	0-2	2-1	3-0		1-0	0-0	3-2	3-1	0-0	5-1	0-0	0-0	1-0
WA Tlemcen	30	12	8	10	39	37	44	1-0	2-0	1-1	1-1	2-1	2-3	2-1		1-0	2-1	2-0	4-2	4-2	1-1	0-0	2-2
JS Kabylie	30	10	11	9	29	23	41	2-2	1-0	0-0	0-1	3-2	1-0	1-1	2-0		0-1	1-1	1-0	2-2	1-0	3-1	4-0
USM El Harrach	30	11	5	14	28	31	38	3-2	2-2	0-1	0-0	0-1	0-1	1-0	0-1	1-0		3-1	0-1	0-1	1-1	1-0	2-0
MC El Eulma	30	10	8	12	38	39	38	1-3	1-2	2-1	1-2	1-1	2-2	1-0	3-1	1-1	1-0		1-0	3-0	1-1	4-0	1-0
CS Constantine	30	8	12	10	35	42	36	3-2	0-0	1-1	0-0	1-3	1-0	2-1	1-1	0-0	4-1	1-2		3-1	2-1	3-3	2-1
MC Oran	30	9	8	13	38	51	35	2-4	1-0	1-1	1-0	3-1	0-0	1-5	1-3	1-2	1-2	1-1	2-1		3-0	1-0	4-0
AS Khroub	30	7	10	13	23	46	31	2-2	0-0	1-0	0-0	1-0	2-1	0-3	0-2	0-0	1-0	1-5	3-0	1-1		2-1	1-0
NA Hussein Dey	30	5	11	14	29	39	26	1-2	1-0	1-2	1-2	1-1	2-2	1-2	2-1	0-0	2-0	3-1	0-0	0-0	1-1		3-0
MC Saïda	30	6	6	18	28	46	24	0-1	1-2	1-1	2-0	2-0	0-0	1-1	1-0	1-2	0-1	1-0	1-1	2-0	6-1	1-1	

6/09/2011 - 19/05/2012 • † Qualified for the CAF Champions League • ‡ Qualified for the CAF Confederation Cup
Top scorers: 19 - Mohamed **MESSAOUD**, ASO Chlef • 12 - Mohamed Amine **AOUDIA**, ES Sétif & Ahmed **MESSADIA**, CA Batna • 11 - Djamel **BOUAICHA**, MC El Eulma; Lamouri **DJEDIAT**, USM Alger & Ahmed **GASMI**, JSM Béjaïa

MEDALS TABLE

			Overall G S B	League G S B	Cup G S	Africa G S B
1	JS Kabylie	JSK	25 14 6	14 10 4	5 4	6 2
2	ES Sétif	ESS	14 4 6	5 3 5	8	1 1 1
3	MC Alger	MCA	14 2 4	7 2 4	6	1
4	USM Alger	USMA	12 13 4	5 4 2	7 9	2
5	CR Bélouizdad	CRB	12 6 3	6 3 2	6 3	1
6	MC Oran	MCO	8 12 4	4 9 3	4 2	1 1
7	USM El Harrach	USMH	3 3	1 2	2 1	
8	NA Hussein Dey	NAHD	2 8 5	1 4 4	1 3	1 1
9	WA Tlemcem	WAT	2 3 3		3	2 3
10	ASO Chlef	ASO	2 2 3	1 1 3	1 1	
11	Hamra Annaba		2	1	1	
12	MO Constantine	MOC	1 4 2	1 1 2	3	

ALGERIA 2011-12

LIGUE PROFESSIONNELLE 2

	Pl	W	D	L	F	A	Pts	CABBA	JSS	USMBA	MOB	USMB	ESM	ASMO	USMAn	MSPB	ABM	MOC	Olympique	SAM	PAC	RCK	USB
CA Bordj Bou Arréridj	30	17	6	7	36	21	57		2-0	1-0	2-1	2-1	2-1	2-0	0-0	1-0	1-1	1-0	3-0	1-0	1-1	2-0	0-1
JS Saoura	30	17	5	8	48	26	56	0-1		1-0	4-1	2-1	2-1	3-0	1-0	2-0	4-0	5-0	2-0	4-1	2-1	1-1	3-1
USM Bel Abbès	30	14	8	8	34	24	50	1-0	0-0		2-1	3-1	2-1	0-0	3-0	2-0	1-0	1-1	1-0	3-0	0-2	2-1	2-0
MO Béjaïa	30	15	4	11	43	30	49	1-2	1-0	1-1		5-0	2-1	2-1	1-0	2-0	2-1	1-0	5-1	3-0	1-0	1-2	1-0
USM Blida	30	12	9	9	40	36	45	3-1	1-2	0-0	2-1		1-1	0-0	1-0	4-1	2-1	1-0	0-0	4-1	1-0	1-0	5-2
ES Mostaganem	30	12	8	10	38	32	44	0-0	2-1	4-0	1-0	2-2		3-1	0-0	0-0	4-1	2-1	0-0	2-1	2-1	3-1	1-1
ASM Oran	30	10	11	9	34	36	41	2-1	2-0	1-0	0-0	2-2	2-3		2-1	2-2	2-1	0-0	2-1	5-3	2-1	1-1	2-1
USM Annaba	30	10	7	12	31	34	40	1-2	4-2	2-1	1-1	2-0	2-1	2-1		1-1	1-1	1-0	1-0	2-0	1-0	1-2	2-1
MSP Batna	30	10	10	10	24	27	40	0-1	0-0	0-0	1-0	1-0	1-0	0-0	2-2		1-0	2-2	1-0	1-0	1-0	3-0	2-1
AB Mérouana	30	10	9	11	24	29	39	0-0	1-0	1-0	0-1	0-0	1-1	0-0	4-1	0-0		1-0	2-0	1-0	1-1	0-1	1-0
MO Constantine	30	10	8	12	36	40	38	2-1	0-2	1-2	2-2	1-2	2-0	3-1	2-0	2-1	3-1		1-1	1-1	2-2	2-2	1-0
Olympique Médéa	30	9	11	10	24	29	38	1-0	1-1	2-2	2-1	2-0	3-0	0-0	1-0	0-0	0-0	2-1		0-0	2-1	1-0	1-0
SA Mohamadia	30	8	13	16	30	48	36	0-3	0-0	0-2	1-0	1-0	1-0	2-1	2-1	0-1	0-1	3-1	2-1		2-1	1-0	4-1
Paradou AC	30	9	8	13	34	34	35	2-1	2-2	2-1	1-3	1-1	1-0	1-0	1-1	1-0	2-0	0-1	1-1	1-2		1-1	5-2
RC Kouba	30	8	8	14	29	39	32	1-1	2-0	1-1	1-2	2-4	0-1	1-1	0-1	3-2	0-1	1-2	1-0	2-1	1-1		1-0
US Biskra	30	6	3	21	26	46	21	1-2	1-2	0-1	1-0	0-0	0-1	0-1	1-0	1-0	1-2	1-2	1-1	6-1	0-1	1-0	

9/09/2011 - 27/04/2012

COUPE D'ALGERIE 2011-12

Round of 32		Round of 16		Quarter-finals		Semi-finals		Final	
ES Sétif	2	**ES Sétif** *	4						
US Tébessa *	0	US Tébessa *							
RC Arba	2	JS Saoura	2						
JS Saoura *	3			**ES Sétif**	3				
WA Boufarik *	2	WA Boufarik	1	CRB Aïn Oussera	1				
CRB El Milia	0								
MB Constantine	1	**CRB Aïn Oussera** *	3			**ES Sétif** *	3		
CRB Aïn Oussera *	2					USM El Harrach	2		
USM Alger *	0 5p	**USM Alger** *	1						
JS Djijel	0 4p	JS Kabylie	0						
MB Hassasna	1			USM Alger	0 1p				
JS Kabylie *	3			**USM El Harrach**	0 4p			**ES Sétif**	2
IR Bir Mourad Raïs	2	IR Bir Mourad Raïs *	1					CR Bélouizdad ‡	1
ES Ben Aknoun	1								
ES Azzefoun	0	**USM El Harrach**	3						
USM El Harrach *	2								
CS Constantine *	3	**CS Constantine** *	2						
Olympique Médéa	1	AS Khroub	0						
AS Khroub	1			**CS Constantine**	1				
MC El Eulma	0			WA Tlemcen	0				
MC Alger *	2	MC Alger	0						
MC Aïn Beïda	1					CS Constantine	0		
WA Ramdane Djamel	0	**WA Tlemcen** *	1			**CR Bélouizdad** *	1		
WA Tlemcen *	1								
ASO Chlef	1 4p	**ASO Chlef** *	4						
CA Bordj Bou Arréridj *	1 2p	CRB Aïn Djasser	0						
IB Khémis El Khechna	2 7p			ASO Chlef	0				
CRB Aïn Djasser *	2 8p			**CR Bélouizdad**	1				
MC Saïda *	2	MC Saïda	0 4p						
RC Relizane	1	**CR Bélouizdad**	0 5p						
JSM Sidi Salem	0								
CR Bélouizdad *	5								

* Home team • ‡ Qualified for the CAF Confederation Cup

CUP FINAL
Stade 5 Juillet, Algiers
1-05-2012, Att: 55 000, Ref: Mokhtar Amalou
Scorers - Hachoud 22, Benmoussa 96 for ESS; Ammour 82 for CRB

ESS - Mohamed Benhainou● - Abderahmane Hachoud - Mokhtar Megueni (Adel Lakhdari 54), Farouk Belkaid, Riad Benchadi - Amir Karaoui●, Mohamed El Amine Tiouli (Rachid Nadji 90), Mourad Delhoum (c), Mokhtar Benmoussa●, Abdelmoumene Djabou - Mohamed Amine Aoudia (Akram Djahnit 72). Tr. Alain Geiger

CRB - Mohamed Ousserir - Abdelkrim Mameri (c), Fayçal Abdat●, Amine Aksas, Khalil Boukerdjane - Ahmed Mekehout●, Billel Naili● (Mohamed Smain Kherbache 64), Mohamed El Amine Aouad (Mohamed Billel Benaldjia 78), Amar Ammour - Abouaker Rebih, Islam Slimani. Tr: Djamel Menad

AND – ANDORRA

FIFA/COCA-COLA WORLD RANKING

'93	'94	'95	'96	'97	'98	'99	'00	'01	'02	'03	'04	'05	'06	'07	'08	'09	'10	'11	'12
-	-	-	187	185	171	145	145	140	137	147	138	125	164	175	194	202	202	206	204

2012

Jan	Feb	Mar	Apr	May	Jun	Jul	Aug	Sep	Oct	Nov	Dec	High	Low	Av
206	205	205	205	205	199	198	200	199	201	203	204	125	206	166

The Andorra national team celebrated a first draw after six years of consecutive defeats with their opponents Azerbaijan unable to overcome the bottom ranked team in world football. The 0-0 draw in Kelsterbach in Germany saw the Andorrans haul themselves up seven places in the FIFA/Coca-Cola World Ranking although after a fruitless start to the FIFA World Cup qualifying campaign they were quickly back down to within touching distance of the bottom again. October 2004 was the date of their last victory and the chances of them ending that eight year wait for another looked slim after being drawn in a very tough group with no easy looking fixtures. Andorra did come away from Rotterdam having limited the Dutch to just three goals but failed to score in their first four qualifying matches. At home there was a first league title for Lusitanos, the team of the Portuguese community in the country. Going into the final round of fixtures just one point separated the top four teams. The two Santa Coloma's could only draw with each other which meant a 3-1 victory over Sant Julia saw Lusitanos home. They failed to do the double, however, after losing the cup final to FC Santa Coloma, an own goal by Luis Felipe giving their opponents the victory - their eighth in just 12 seasons.

UEFA EUROPEAN CHAMPIONSHIP RECORD
1960-1996 DNE 2000-2012 DNQ

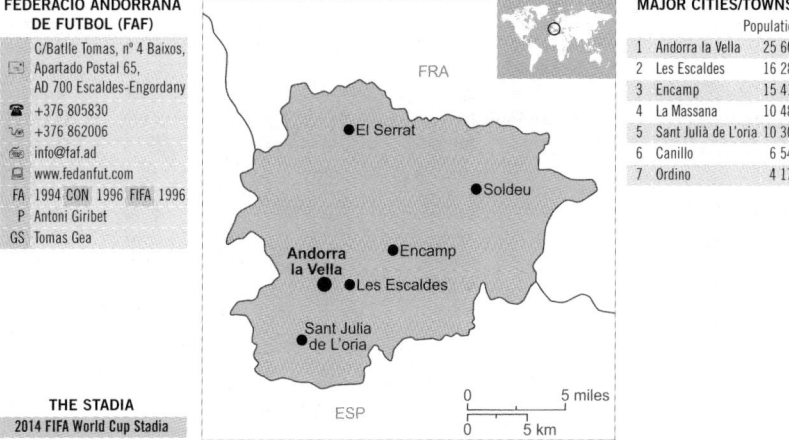

FEDERACIO ANDORRANA DE FUTBOL (FAF)
C/Batlle Tomas, nº 4 Baixos,
Apartado Postal 65,
AD 700 Escaldes-Engordany
+376 805830
+376 862006
info@faf.ad
www.fedanfut.com
FA 1994 CON 1996 FIFA 1996
P Antoni Giribet
GS Tomas Gea

MAJOR CITIES/TOWNS
Population
1 Andorra la Vella 25 608
2 Les Escaldes 16 285
3 Encamp 15 416
4 La Massana 10 480
5 Sant Julià de L'oria 10 305
6 Canillo 6 542
7 Ordino 4 179

THE STADIA
2014 FIFA World Cup Stadia
Estadio Comunal
Andorra La Vella 1 299
Other Main Stadia
Estadio Aixovall
Andorra La Vella 1 000

PRINCIPAT D'ANDORRA • ANDORRA

Capital	Andorra La Vella	Population	83 888 (199)	% in cities	89%
GDP per capita	$42 500 (15)	Area km²	468 km² (195)	GMT +/-	+1
Neighbours (km)	France 56, Spain 63				

RECENT INTERNATIONALS PLAYED BY ANDORRA

2007	Opponents	Score	Venue	Comp	Scorers	Att	Referee
7-02	Armenia	D 0-0	Andorra la Vella	Fr			
28-03	England	L 0-3	Barcelona	ECq		12 800	Duarte Paixao POR
2-06	Russia	L 0-4	St Petersburg	ECq		21 520	Skjerven NOR
6-06	Israel	L 0-2	Andorra la Vella	ECq		680	Stokes IRL
22-08	Estonia	L 1-2	Tallinn	ECq	Fernando Silva 82	7 500	McCourt NIR
12-09	Croatia	L 0-6	Andorra la Vella	ECq		925	Thual FRA
17-10	FYR Macedonia	L 0-3	Skopje	ECq		17 500	Malzinskas LTU
17-11	Estonia	L 0-2	Andorra la Vella	ECq		700	Collum SCO
21-11	Russia	L 0-1	Andorra la Vella	ECq		780	Hauge NOR
2008							
26-03	Latvia	L 0-3	Andorra la Vella	Fr			Perez ESP
4-06	Azerbaijan	L 1-2	Andorra la Vella	Fr	Ildefons Lima 71		Gomes POR
20-08	Kazakhstan	L 0-3	Almaty	WCq		7 700	Banari MDA
6-09	England	L 0-2	Barcelona	WCq		10 300	Cakir TUR
10-09	Belarus	L 1-3	Andorra la Vella	WCq	Marc Pujol 67p	600	Evans WAL
15-10	Croatia	L 0-4	Zagreb	WCq		14 441	Vad HUN
2009							
11-02	Lithuania	L 1-3	Albufeira	Fr	Ildefons Lima 78p		Xistra POR
1-04	Croatia	L 0-2	Andorra la Vella	WCq		1 100	Trattou CYP
6-06	Belarus	L 1-5	Grodno	WCq	Ildefons Lima 93+p	8 500	Kranjc SVN
10-06	England	L 0-6	London	WCq		57 897	Nijhuis NED
5-09	Ukraine	L 0-5	Kyiv	WCq		14 870	Sipailo LVA
9-09	Kazakhstan	L 1-3	Andorra la Vella	WCq	Oscar Sonejee 70	510	Toussaint LUX
14-10	Ukraine	L 0-6	Andorra la Vella	WCq		820	Thomson SCO
2010							
29-05	Iceland	L 0-4	Reykjavik	Fr		2 567	Reinert FRO
2-06	Albania	L 0-1	Tirana	Fr		3 000	Meckarovski MKD
11-08	Cyprus	L 0-1	Larnaca	Fr		1 700	Spathas GRE
3-09	Russia	L 0-2	Andorra la Vella	ECq		1 100	Borg MLT
7-09	Republic of Ireland	L 1-3	Dublin	ECq	Cristian Martinez 45	40 283	Trattou CYP
8-10	FYR Macedonia	L 0-2	Andorra La Vella	ECq		550	Mazeika LTU
12-10	Armenia	L 0-4	Yerevan	ECq		12 000	Mikulski POL
2011							
9-02	Moldova	L 1-2	Lagos	Fr	Josep Ayala 52		Lopes POR
26-03	Slovakia	L 0-1	Andorra la Vella	ECq		850	Masiah ISR
4-06	Slovakia	L 0-1	Bratislava	ECq		4 300	Jemini ALB
2-09	Armenia	L 0-3	Andorra la Vella	ECq		750	Kostadinov BUL
6-09	FYR Macedonia	L 0-1	Skopje	ECq		5 000	Whitby WAL
7-10	Republic of Ireland	L 0-2	Andorra La Vella	ECq		860	Kovarik CZE
11-10	Russia	L 0-6	Moscow	ECq		38 790	Hacmon ISR
2012							
30-05	Azerbaijan	D 0-0	Kelsterbach	Fr			Weiner GER
2-06	Poland	L 0-4	Warsaw	Fr		26 000	Delferiere BEL
14-08	Liechtenstein	L 0-1	Vaduz	Fr		847	Klossner SUI
7-09	Hungary	L 0-5	Andorra La Vella	WCq		815	Aleckovic BIH
11-09	Romania	L 0-4	Bucharest	WCq		24 630	Radovanovic MNE
12-10	Netherlands	L 0-3	Rotterdam	WCq		43 000	Kulbakou BLR
16-10	Estonia	L 0-1	Andorra La Vella	WCq		723	Meckarovski MKD
14-11	Iceland	L 0-2	Andorra La Vella	Fr			Buquet FRA

Fr = Friendly match • EC = UEFA EURO 2008/2012 • WC = FIFA World Cup • q = qualifier

ANDORRA NATIONAL TEAM HISTORICAL RECORDS

App 85 - Oscar Sonejee 1997- • 78 - Koldo 1998-2009 • 75 - Manolo Jimenez 1998- • 71 - Josep Txema 1997- • 67 - Ildefons Lima 1997- • 65 - Justo Ruiz 1996-2008 & Jordi Escura 1998-

G 7 - Ildefons Lima 1997- • 3 - Oscar Sonejee 1997-, Fernando Silva 2002-, Jesus Julian Lucendo 1996-2003

Tr Isidrea Codina 1996 • Manuel Miloie 1997-99, David Rodrigo 1999-2010 • Koldo Alvarez 2010-

ANDORRA 2011-12
LLIGA ANDORRANA PRIMERA DIVISIO

	Pl	W	D	L	F	A	Pts	Lusitanos	Santa Coloma	UE Santa Coloma	Sant Julià	Principat	Engordany	Inter Escaldes	Ranger's
Lusitanos †	20	11	7	2	48	18	**40**		2-0 2-0	1-1 0-0	2-2 2-1	2-1	5-0	3-0	6-0
Santa Coloma ‡	20	11	5	4	56	17	**38**	1-1 1-1		2-0 3-1	0-1 1-1	3-2	5-0	2-1	10-0
UE Santa Coloma ‡	20	10	7	3	61	20	**37**	2-1 2-2	1-3 0-0		2-2 2-2	1-1	5-1	5-1	10-0
Sant Julià	20	10	6	4	57	22	**36**	1-2 2-1	1-1 3-0	0-1 1-2		3-2	9-0	12-3	6-0
Principat	20	8	3	9	32	32	**27**	0-3	0-2	0-6	0-0		0-3 1-0	2-0 1-2	4-1 5-2
Engordany	20	6	4	10	32	51	**22**	2-2	0-2	0-10	1-2	1-1 0-2		1-1 2-1	3-0 3-0
Inter Escaldes ‡‡	20	5	3	12	34	65	**18**	0-5	0-7	0-5	0-3	1-0 1-3	3-2 2-2		0-3 5-5
Ranger's	20	1	1	18	16	111	**4**	2-5	0-13	0-5	0-5	1-4 0-3	0-3 0-8	1-3 1-10	

18/09/2011 - 22/04/2012 • † Qualified for the UEFA Champions League • ‡ Qualified for the Europa League • ‡‡ Relegation play-off
Relegation play-off: **Inter Escaldes** 2-0 1-0 Extremenya
Top scorers: **14** - Victor **BERNAT**, UE Santa Coloma • **12** - JULI **SANCHEZ**, Santa Coloma • **11** - Alejandro **IZQUIERDO**, Inter Escaldes

ANDORRA 2011-12
SEGONA DIVISIO (2)

	Pl	W	D	L	F	A	Pts
Encamp	18	14	0	4	57	22	**42**
Extremenya ‡	18	13	2	3	62	17	**41**
Lusitanos B	18	12	2	4	54	18	**38**
Athlètic Escaldes	18	10	1	7	31	37	**31**
Santa Coloma B	18	9	3	6	63	32	**30**
UE Santa Coloma B	18	9	3	6	50	42	**30**
Casa del Benfica	18	8	1	9	33	48	**25**
Principat B	18	3	2	13	22	57	**11**
Penya Encarnada	18	2	3	13	26	62	**9**
La Massana	18	1	1	16	17	80	**4**

17/09/2011 - 6/05/2012 • ‡ Qualified for play-off (see Primera Divisio

MEDALS TABLE

		Overall			League			Cup	
		G	S	B	G	S	B	G	S
1	Santa Coloma	15	9	4	**6**	6	4	**9**	3
2	Principat	9	1	1	3	1	1	6	
3	Sant Julià	5	12	3	2	6	3	3	6
4	Lusitanos	2	3	1	1		1	1	3
5	Encamp	2	2	3	2	1	3		1
6	Ranger's	2	2	2	2	1	2		1
7	Constelacio	2			1			1	
8	UE Santa Coloma		3	1		1	1		2
9	Inter Escaldes		1	2			2		1
10	Veterans		1			1			

COPA CONSTITUCIO 2011-12

Round of 16		Quarter-finals		Semi-finals		Final	
Santa Coloma	Bye						
		Santa Coloma	7 10				
Extremenya *	1	Ranger's *	0 0				
Ranger's	4			Santa Coloma	3 2		
Principat	7			Sant Julià *	0 0		
Santa Coloma B *	0	Principat *	0 1				
		Sant Julià	3 6				
Sant Julià	Bye					Santa Coloma	1
UE Santa Coloma	Bye					Lusitanos	0
		UE Santa Coloma	6 6				
Engordany	1	UE Santa Coloma B *	2 0			CUP FINAL	
UE Santa Coloma B *	2			UE Santa Coloma *	1 1		
Inter Escaldes	3			Lusitanos	1 2	DEVK-Arena, Sant Julia de Loria	
Principat B *	0	Inter Escaldes *	0 0			27-05-2012, Ref: Villamayor	
		Lusitanos	1 6			Scorer - Luis Felipe OG [42]	
Lusitanos	Bye	* Home team in the first leg • ‡ Qualified for the Europa League					

Cup Final line-ups: **Santa Coloma** - Fernandez - Oriol Fite, Oscar Sonejee, Javi Sanchez, Ribolleda, Txema Garcia, Christopher Pousa, Manolo Jimenez (Albert Mercade 66), Samir Bousenine, Renato Mota (Genis Garcia 90), Alejandro Romero (Juli Sanchez 80). Tr: Luis Torrado
Lusitanos - Jordi Rodriguez - Franclim Soares (Gaby Meza 70), Hugo Veloso, Yael, Leonel Maciel, Bruno Silva (Jamal Zarioh 45), Luis Felipe, Sebastia Bertran, Pedro Reis, Luis Miguel (Juan Guijo Raya 48), Victor Hugo. Tr: Vicenc Marques

ANG – ANGOLA

FIFA/COCA-COLA WORLD RANKING

'93	'94	'95	'96	'97	'98	'99	'00	'01	'02	'03	'04	'05	'06	'07	'08	'09	'10	'11	'12
102	106	80	70	58	50	52	55	55	76	83	72	61	55	73	70	95	88	83	84

2012

Jan	Feb	Mar	Apr	May	Jun	Jul	Aug	Sep	Oct	Nov	Dec	High	Low	Av
85	83	81	78	78	84	86	85	80	83	79	84	45	124	73

Angola suffered another early exit at the 2013 Africa Cup of Nations finals in South Africa, condemned to last place in Group A after failing to win a game. Their defeat to Lusophone rivals Cape Verde Islands marked a low for 'Palancas Negras' who have evolved into regular qualifiers for the finals but have not been able to progress from their quarter-final appearances in 2008 and 2010. Their failure at the previous finals in 2012, where a spate of missed chances proved their undoing, cost coach Lito Vidigal his job and saw the appointment in June of Uruguayan Gustavo Ferrin who had previously won acclaim working at youth level in South America. Angola fumbled through the start of the 2014 FIFA World Cup qualifiers where they drew at home with Uganda and away to Liberia in their opening two matches while in the 2013 Nations Cup qualifiers they squeezed past Zimbabwe on the away goals rule. Zimbabwe had won the first leg 3-1 at home in September but two goals in the first six minutes of the return match in Luanda from Spanish-based striker Manucho saw Angola qualify. In club football Recreativo Libolo went through the season with just a single loss as they romped to the Girabola title for a second successive year, led to the championship this time by Zeca Amaral who had been axed as Angola coach in 2011.

CAF AFRICA CUP OF NATIONS RECORD
1957-1982 DNE 1984 DNQ 1986 DNE 1988-1994 DNQ **1996** 13 r1 **1998** 13 r1 2000-2004 DNQ **2006** 9 r1 **2008** 6 QF **2010** 6 QF (Hosts) **2012** 11 r1 **2013** 14 r1

FEDERACAO ANGOLANA DE FUTEBOL (FAF)
Senado de Camara, Compl. da Cidadela Desportiva, Luanda - 3449,
☎ +244 222 264948
✉ untonesa_faf@yahoo.com
🌐 www.fafutebol-angola.og.ao
FA 1979 CON 1996 FIFA 1980
P Pedro Neto
GS Jose Manuel Cardoso

THE STADIA
2014 FIFA World Cup Stadia
Estádio 11 de Novembro
Luanda — 50 000
Other Main Stadia
Estadio da Cidadela
Luanda — 40 000
Estádio de Ombaka
Benguela — 35 000
Estádio do Chiazi
Cabinda — 20 000
Estádio da Tundavala
Lubango — 20 000

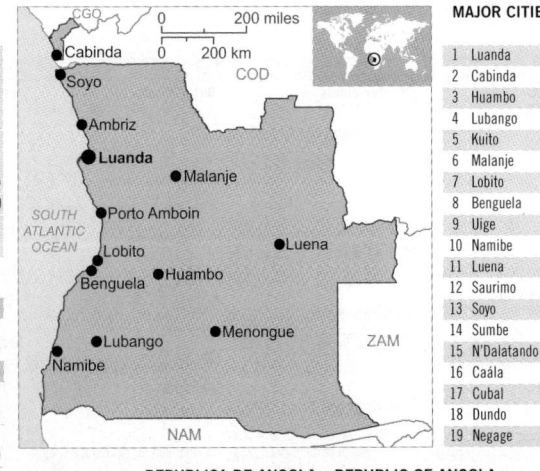

MAJOR CITIES/TOWNS
		Population
1	Luanda	2 583 981
2	Cabinda	377 931
3	Huambo	333 387
4	Lubango	250 921
5	Kuito	180 764
6	Malanje	156 829
7	Lobito	145 652
8	Benguela	131 281
9	Uige	116 751
10	Namibe	89 442
11	Luena	84 619
12	Saurimo	78 417
13	Soyo	75 224
14	Sumbe	50 458
15	N'Dalatando	45 295
16	Caála	41 181
17	Cubal	41 142
18	Dundo	40 055
19	Negage	37 622

REPUBLICA DE ANGOLA • REPUBLIC OF ANGOLA

Capital	Luanda	Population	12 799 293 (69)	% in cities	57%
GDP per capita	$8800 (112)	Area km²	1 246 700 km² (23)	GMT +/-	+1
Neighbours (km)	Congo DR 2511, Congo 201, Namibia 1376, Zambia 1110 • Coast 1600				

ANG – ANGOLA

RECENT INTERNATIONALS PLAYED BY ANGOLA

2010	Opponents	Score	Venue	Comp	Scorers	Att	Referee
3-01	Gambia	D 1-1	Vila Real	Fr	Manucho [29]		
10-01	Mali	D 4-4	Luanda	CNr1	Flavio 2 [36 42], Gilberto [67p], Manucho [74p]	45 000	Abd El Fatah EGY
14-01	Malawi	W 2-0	Luanda	CNr1	Flavio [49], Manucho [55]	48 500	Doue CIV
18-01	Algeria	D 0-0	Luanda	CNr1		40 000	Damon RSA
24-01	Ghana	L 0-1	Luanda	CNqf		50 000	Benouza ALG
13-05	Mexico	L 0-1	Houston	Fr		70 099	Toledo USA
11-08	Uruguay	L 0-2	Lisbon	Fr		1 000	Hugo Miguel POR
4-09	Uganda	L 0-3	Kampala	CNq			Osman EGY
9-10	Guinea-Bissau	W 1-0	Luanda	CNq	Gilberto [22p]		Coulibaly MLI
12-10	UAE	W 2-0	Abu Dhabi	Fr	Rasca [23], Vado [89]		
2011							
2-01	Iran	L 0-1	Al Rayyan	Fr		BCD	
4-01	Saudi Arabia	D 0-0	Dammam	Fr			
26-03	Kenya	L 1-2	Nairobi	CNq	Manucho [18]		
5-06	Kenya	W 1-0	Luanda	CNq	Manucho [69]		Maillet SEY
10-08	Liberia	D 0-0	Monrovia	Fr			
27-08	Congo DR	L 1-2	Dundo	Fr	Joao Martins [13]		
4-09	Uganda	W 2-0	Luanda	CNq	Manucho [57], Flavio [73]		El Ahrach MAR
8-10	Guinea-Bissau	W 2-0	Bissau	CNq	Manucho [8], Mateus [70]		
14-12	Cameroon	D 1-1	Cabinda	Fr	Love [21]		
18-12	Zambia	W 1-0	Dundo	Fr	Love [59]		
22-12	Namibia	D 0-0	Lubango	Fr			
2012							
11-01	Nigeria	D 0-0	Abuja	Fr			
14-01	Sierra Leone	W 3-1	Cabinda	Fr	Manucho [15], Galiano [39], Flavio [76]		
22-01	Burkina Faso	W 2-1	Malabo	CNr1	Mateus [47], Manucho [68]	17 000	Seechurn MRI
26-01	Sudan	D 2-2	Malabo	CNr1	Manucho 2 [4 50p]	2 500	Lemghaifry MTN
30-01	Côte d'Ivoire	L 0-2	Malabo	CNr1		1 500	Jedidi TUN
16-05	Zambia	D 0-0	Luanda	Fr			
29-05	FYR Macedonia	D 0-0	Lisbon	Fr		200	Proenca POR
3-06	Uganda	D 1-1	Luanda	WCq	Djalma [7]	48 000	Grisha EGY
10-06	Liberia	D 0-0	Monrovia	WCq		15 000	Lemghaifry MTN
9-09	Zimbabwe	L 1-3	Harare	CNq	Djalma [56]		Nampiandraza MAD
14-10	Zimbabwe	W 2-0	Luanda	CNq	Manucho 2 [5 7]		Kirwa KEN
14-11	Congo	D 1-1	Estoril	Fr	Yano [2]		
2013							
19-01	Morocco	D 0-0	Johannesburg	CNr1		25 000	Diatta SEN
23-01	South Africa	L 0-2	Durban	CNr1		40 000	Coulibaly MLI
27-01	Cape Verde Islands	L 1-2	Port Elizabeth	CNr1	OG [33]	20 000	Jedidi TUN

Fr = Friendly match • CN = CAF African Cup of Nations • WC = FIFA World Cup • q = qualifier • r1 = first round group • qf = quarter-final

ANGOLA SQUAD FOR THE 2012 CAF AFRICA CUP OF NATIONS

	Player		Ap	G	Club	Date of Birth		Player		Ap	G	Club	Date of Birth
1	Wilson Alegre	GK	1		1° de Agosto	22 07 1984	12	Jaime Linares	MF	0+1		Progresso	21 05 1982
2	Marco Airosa	DF	3		AEL Limassol	6 08 1984	13	Carlos	GK	2		Unattached	8 12 1979
3	Osorio	MF	0		Recreativo Caála	24 07 1981	14	Amaro	DF	0		1° de Agosto	12 11 1986
4	Dani	DF	3		1° de Agosto	1 05 1986	15	Miguel Quiame	MF	3		Petro Atlético	17 09 1991
5	Kali	DF	0		1° de Agosto	11 10 1978	16	Flavio Amado	FW	2		Lierse BEL	30 12 1979
6	Dede	MF	1+1		AEL Lim'sol CYP	4 07 1981	17	Mateus	FW	3	1	Nacional POR	19 06 1984
7	Djalma	FW	3		Porto POR	30 05 1987	18	Love	FW	0+1		Petro Atlético	14 03 1979
8	Andre Macanga (c)	MF	3		Al Jahra KUW	14 05 1978	19	Nando Rafael	FW	0+2		Augsburg GER	10 01 1984
9	Manucho	FW	3	3	Valladolid ESP	7 03 1983	20	Manucho Barros	FW	0+1		InterClube	19 04 1986
10	Francisco Zuela	DF	3		Atromitos GRE	3 08 1983	21	Mingo Bile	DF	0		1° de Agosto	15 06 1987
11	Gilberto	MF	3		Lierse BEL	21 09 1982	22	Hugo Marques	GK	0		Kabuscorp	15 01 1986
							23	Jose Vunguidica	FW	0+3		Pr. Münster GER	3 01 1990

Tr: Lito Vidigal 11-07-1969

ANGOLA 2012

CAMPEONATO NACIONAL XXXIV GIRABOLA 1° DIVISAO

	Pl	W	D	L	F	A	Pts	Libolo	1° Agosto	Petro Atlético	Kabuscorp	InterClube	ASA	Onze Bravos	Progresso	Atlético	Caála	Sagrada	Benfica	Santos	Académica	Sp Cabinda	Nacional
Recreativo Libolo †	30	19	10	1	51	14	**67**		0-0	0-0	2-0	0-0	1-0	3-0	1-0	4-0	3-2	1-0	1-1	1-0	3-0	7-0	6-1
Primeiro de Agosto †	30	17	7	6	42	21	**58**	0-1		0-2	1-0	0-1	0-1	3-1	1-1	4-1	1-0	1-0	0-2	2-0	1-0	4-1	4-0
Petro Atlético ‡	30	14	12	4	34	17	**54**	2-2	0-2		1-1	1-0	1-0	0-0	0-1	3-0	0-0	2-1	3-2	0-0	1-0	2-0	0-0
Kabuscorp Palanca	30	14	9	7	43	32	**51**	1-2	0-0	1-1		0-2	0-2	4-1	0-1	2-0	3-1	3-2	0-0	1-0	5-3	2-0	2-1
InterClube	30	13	10	7	36	23	**49**	0-1	1-1	1-0	1-1		0-0	1-1	0-0	4-1	3-0	1-0	1-2	2-3	1-0	2-1	3-0
Atlético Aviação	30	10	11	9	24	22	**41**	0-1	0-1	0-0	0-0	3-1		1-1	1-0	0-3	0-0	1-0	0-1	1-1	1-0	2-0	2-0
Onze Bravos Maqui	30	11	7	12	41	41	**40**	0-1	0-1	0-3	0-1	0-1	0-1		2-0	4-2	2-1	1-1	3-1	4-0	5-2	4-2	2-1
Progresso Sambizanga	30	9	13	8	30	26	**40**	1-1	1-1	3-1	1-2	0-2	1-1	1-1		0-0	2-0	2-0	3-1	3-2	1-1	1-1	0-0
Atlético do Namibie	30	10	7	13	37	48	**37**	1-3	0-1	0-0	3-1	1-1	1-1	2-1	0-2		2-1	1-0	1-1	0-1	0-1	3-0	2-1
Recreativo Caála	30	9	8	13	26	31	**35**	0-0	1-1	0-0	2-3	1-1	2-0	2-0	1-0	1-0		0-0	3-2	2-0	0-1	1-0	2-0
Sagrada Esperança	30	8	10	12	29	32	**34**	1-1	2-1	0-0	2-2	0-1	1-2	1-1	1-0	0-2	2-1		2-1	1-0	1-0	3-0	0-0
Benfica Luanda	30	7	13	10	32	37	**34**	0-0	1-1	0-1	0-3	1-0	2-1	1-1	0-0	2-3	0-0	2-2		2-2	0-0	2-2	2-0
Santos	30	9	7	14	41	46	**34**	4-2	2-3	0-1	1-1	2-0	1-1	1-2	0-0	5-3	0-1	1-3	1-1		4-2	2-3	3-2
Académica Soyo	30	9	5	16	31	46	**32**	0-1	0-3	0-2	1-1	1-1	1-0	0-2	1-1	2-3	3-1	2-1	1-0	0-2		3-2	1-0
Sporting Cabinda	30	5	7	18	28	61	**22**	0-2	1-2	0-3	0-1	1-1	1-1	3-1	2-3	0-0	1-0	1-1	2-1	1-3	0-3		2-0
Nacional Benguela	30	4	8	18	24	52	**20**	0-0	1-2	3-4	1-2	1-3	1-1	0-1	2-1	2-2	1-0	1-1	0-1	1-0	3-2	1-1	

3/03/2012 - 4/11/2012 • † Qualified for CAF Champions League • ‡ Qualified for CAF Confederation Cup

MEDALS TABLE

		Overall G S B	League G S B	Cup G S	Africa G S B	City
1	Petro Atlético	24 6 7	**15** 3 7	**9** 2	1	Luanda
2	Primeiro de Agosto	14 10 4	9 4 4	5 5	1	Luanda
3	Atlético Sport Aviação	6 7 2	3 5 1	3 2	1	Luanda
4	Primeiro de Maio	5 8	2 5	3 2	1	Benguela
5	Inter Clube	5 7 4	2 1 4	3 5	1	Luanda
6	Sagrada Esperança	3 5	1 3	2 2		Dundo
7	Recreativo Libolo	2 2 1	2 1 1	1		Calulo
8	Ferroviário Huila	2 1 1		1 2 1		Lubango
9	Atlético Petróleas Namibe	2		2		Namibe
10	Progresso Sambiganza	1		1		Luanda
	Santos	1		1		Viana
12	Petro Huambo	2 3	1 3	1		Huambo
13	SL Benfica Luanda	2 1	1	2		Luanda
	Independente	2 1		1 2		Tombwa
15	Recreativo Caála	2	1	1		Caála
16	Nacional Benguela	1 1	1 1			Benguela

TACA NACIONAL 2012

Round of 16
Petro Atlético — 1 5p
Primeiro de Agosto — 1 4p
Evale — 0
Recreativo Libolo — 4
Académica Soyo — 2
Domant — 1
Kabuscorp Palanca — 0 2p
Progresso Sambizanga — 0 4p
Sagrada Esperança — 0 4p
Onze Bravos Maqui — 0 3p
Atlético Aviação — 0 1p
Benfica Luanda — 0 4p
InterClube — 3
Norberto de Castro — 1
Santos — 0 3p
Recreativo Caála — 0 4p

Quarter-finals
Petro Atlético — 0 6p
Recreativo Libolo — 0 5p

Académica Soyo — 0
Progresso Sambizanga — 1

Sagrada Esperança — 2
Benfica Luanda — 1

InterClube — 0 2p
Recreativo Caála — 0 4p

Semi-finals
Petro Atlético — 2
Progresso Sambizanga — 0

Sagrada Esperança — 1 4p
Recreativo Caála — 1 5p

Final
Petro Atlético — 2
Recreativo Caála — 0

CUP FINAL
Estadio 11 de Novembro, Luanda,
11-11-2012
Scorers - Mabululo 2 [73] [92+]

* Home team • ‡ Qualified for CAF Confederation Cup

ARG – ARGENTINA

FIFA/COCA-COLA WORLD RANKING

'93	'94	'95	'96	'97	'98	'99	'00	'01	'02	'03	'04	'05	'06	'07	'08	'09	'10	'11	'12
8	10	7	22	17	5	6	3	2	5	5	3	4	3	1	6	8	5	10	3

2012

Jan	Feb	Mar	Apr	May	Jun	Jul	Aug	Sep	Oct	Nov	Dec	High	Low	Av
10	11	8	10	9	7	7	7	4	3	3	3	1	24	6

Lionel Messi brought some of his inspirational club form to the Argentina national team in 2012, scoring at over a goal a game during a year in which Alejandro Sabella's team lost just one match - away to Brazil in Goiania with a second string team without any European-based players. After a shaky start to the 2014 FIFA World Cup qualifying campaign at the start of his tenure as coach, Sabella steered Argentina to the top of the nine-team qualifying group by the halfway stage with thoughts turning to the possibility of a third world title. In club football there was disappointment for Boca Juniors who just missed out on a record-equalling seventh Copa Libertadores title after losing to Brazil's Corinthians 3-1 on aggregate in the final and there was controversy in the Copa Sudamericana when finalists Tigre refused to finish the second leg of the game against Sao Paulo. At home there was a change to the format of the championship with the return to the system of one champion a year. Arsenal won the last clausura title in June 2012 and although the season will continue to be split into two halves, the winners of the Torneo Inicial and Torneo Final will meet in a play-off to decide the champions. Further changes also saw the re-introduction of the Copa Argentina after a gap of 40 years, with Boca Juniors beating Racing Club 2-1 in the final.

FIFA WORLD CUP RECORD

1930 2 Finalists **1934** 9 r1 **1938-1954** DNE **1958** 13 r1 **1962** 10 r1 **1966** 5 QF **1970** DNQ **1974** 8 r2 **1978** (hosts) 1 Winners **1982** 11 r2 **1986** 1 Winners **1990** 2 Finalists **1994** 10 r2 **1998** 6 QF **2002** 18 r1 **2006** 6 QF **2010** 5 QF

ASOCIACION DEL FUTBOL ARGENTINO (AFA)

Viamonte 1366/76, Buenos Aires - 1053
☏ +54 11 43719400
✆ +54 11 43754410
✉ gerencia@afa.org.ar
🖥 www.afa.org.ar
FA 1893 CON 1916 FIFA 1912
P Julio Grondona
GS Miguel Silva

THE STADIA

2014 FIFA World Cup Stadia
El Monumental
Buenos Aires 65 645
Estadio Mario Alberto Kempes
Cordoba 57 000
Estadio Malvinas Argentinas
Mendoza 34 875

Other Main Stadia
La Bombonera
Buenos Aires 49 446
Estadio Ciudad de La Plata
La Plata 36 000

MAJOR CITIES/TOWNS

		Population
1	Buenos Aires	12 197 347
2	Córdoba	1 531 510
3	Rosario	1 235 558
4	Mendoza	929 045
5	Tucumán	830 370
6	La Plata	736 954
7	Mar del Plata	589 291
8	Salta	551 284
9	Santa Fé	506 360
10	San Juan	486 553
11	Resistencia	402 921
12	Santiago dE	370 074
13	Corrientes	360 299
14	Posadas	339 003
15	Jujuy	332 900
16	Bahía Blanca	292 636
17	Paraná	279 923
18	Neuquén	261 426
19	Formosa	239 770

REPUBLICA ARGENTINA • ARGENTINE REPUBLIC

Capital	Buenos Aires	Population	40 913 584 (31)	% in cities	92%
GDP per capita	$14 200 (80)	Area km²	2 780 400 km² (8)	GMT + / -	-3
Neighbours (km)	Bolivia 832, Brazil 1261, Chile 5308, Paraguay 1880, Uruguay 580 • Coast 4989				

RECENT INTERNATIONAL MATCHES PLAYED BY ARGENTINA

2010	Opponents	Score	Venue	Comp	Scorers	Att	Referee
11-08	Republic of Ireland	W 1-0	Dublin	Fr	Di Maria [20]	49 500	Rasmussen DEN
7-09	Spain	W 4-1	Buenos Aires	Fr	Messi [10], Higuain [13], Tevez [34], Aguero [90]	53 000	Ruiz COL
8-10	Japan	L 0-1	Saitama	Fr		57 735	Gil POL
17-11	Brazil	W 1-0	Doha	Fr	Messi [92+]	40 000	Balideh QAT
2011							
9-02	Portugal	W 2-1	Geneva	Fr	Di Maria [14], Messi [90p]	30 000	Busacca SUI
16-03	Venezuela	W 4-1	San Juan	Fr	Chavez [20], Mouche 2 [35 53], Aued [75]	25 000	Puga CHI
26-03	USA	D 1-1	New York	Fr	Cambiasso [42]	78 936	Garcia MEX
29-03	Costa Rica	D 0-0	San Jose	Fr		35 000	Rodriguez.M MEX
20-04	Ecuador	D 2-2	Mar Del Plata	Fr	Yacob [31], Hauche [34]	9 000	Silvera URU
25-05	Paraguay	W 4-2	Resistencia	Fr	Hauche 2 [12 45], Fernandez [37], Perez [74]	24 000	Silvera URU
1-06	Nigeria	L 1-4	Abuja	Fr	Boselli [98+p]	30 000	Chaibou NIG
5-06	Poland	L 1-2	Warsaw	Fr	Ruben [47]	12 000	Grafe GER
20-06	Albania	W 4-0	Buenos Aires	Fr	Lavezzi [6], Messi [43], Aguero [75], Tevez [90]	21 000	Larrionda URU
1-07	Bolivia	D 1-1	La Plata	CAr1	Aguero [76]	52 700	Silvera URU
7-07	Colombia	D 0-0	Cordoba	CAr1		47 000	Fagundes BRA
11-07	Costa Rica	W 3-0	Cordoba	CAr1	Aguero 2 [45 52], Di Maria [63]	57 000	Rivera PER
16-07	Uruguay	D 1-1	Santa Fe	CAqf	Higuain [18]. L 4-5p	47 000	Amarilla PAR
2-09	Venezuela	W 1-0	Calcutta	Fr	Otamendi [70]	90 000	Rowan IND
6-09	Nigeria	W 3-1	Dhaka	Fr	Higuain [24], Di Maria [26], OG [65]	36 000	Shamsuzzaman BAN
14-09	Brazil	D 0-0	Cordoba	Fr		50 000	Osses CHI
28-09	Brazil	L 0-2	Belem	Fr		43 038	Larrionda URU
7-10	Chile	W 4-1	Buenos Aires	WCq	Higuain 3 [7 52 63], Messi [25]	26 161	Roldan COL
11-10	Venezuela	L 0-1	Puerto La Cruz	WCq		35 600	Silvera URU
11-11	Bolivia	D 1-1	Buenos Aires	WCq	Lavezzi [60]	27 592	Vera ECU
15-11	Colombia	W 2-1	Barranquilla	WCq	Messi [60], Aguero [83]	49 600	Fagundes BRA
2012							
29-02	Switzerland	W 3-1	Berne	Fr	Messi 3 [20 88 93+p]	30 250	Meyer GER
2-06	Ecuador	W 4-0	Buenos Aires	WCq	Aguero [19], Higuain [29], Messi [31], Di Maria [76]	50 000	Rivera PER
9-06	Brazil	W 4-3	New York	Fr	Messi 3 [32 34 84], Fernandez [75]	81 994	Marrufo USA
15-08	Germany	W 3-1	Frankfurt	Fr	OG [45], Messi [52], Di Maria [73]	48 808	Eriksson SWE
7-09	Paraguay	W 3-1	Cordoba	WCq	Di Maria [3], Higuain [30], Messi [64]	51 000	Seneme BRA
11-09	Peru	D 1-1	Lima	WCq	Higuain [37]	34 111	Roldan COL
19-09	Brazil	L 1-2	Goiania	Fr	Martinez [20]	37 871	Amarilla PAR
12-10	Uruguay	W 3-0	Mendoza	WCq	Messi 2 [65 79], Aguero [74]	31 997	Pedro BRA
16-10	Chile	W 2-1	Santiago	WCq	Messi [28], Higuain [31]	45 000	Arias PAR
14-11	Saudi Arabia	D 0-0	Riyadh	Fr		51 000	Abdulnabi BHR
21-11	Brazil	W 2-1	Buenos Aires	Fr	Scocco 2 [82p 90]. L 3-4p	32 000	Osses CHI

Fr = Friendly match • CA = Copa América • WC = FIFA World Cup
q = qualifier • r1 = 1st round group stage • r2 = first knockout round • qf = quarter-final • sf = semi-final • f = final

ARGENTINA NATIONAL TEAM HISTORICAL RECORDS

Caps
145 - Javier Zanetti 1994- • **115** - Roberto Ayala 1994-2007 • **106** - Diego Simeone 1988-2002 • **97** - Oscar Ruggeri 1983-94 • **91** - Diego Maradona 1977-94 • **87** - Ariel Ortega 1993-2010 • **86** - Javier Mascherano 2003- • **78** - Gabriel Batistuta 1991-2002 • **76** - Juan Pablo Sorin 1995-2006 & Lionel Messi 2005- • **73** - Americo Gallego 1975-82 & Juan Sebastian Veron 1996-

Goals
56 - Gabriel Batistuta 1991-2002 • **35** - Hernan Crespo 1995-2007 • **34** - Diego Maradona 1977-94 • **31** - Lionel Messi 2005- • **24** - Luis Artime 1961-67 • **22** - Leopoldo Luque 1975-81 & Daniel Passarella 1976-86 • **21** - Jose Sanfilippo 1956-62 & Herminio Masantonio 1935-42 • **20** - Mario Kempes 1973-82 • **19** - Norberto Mendez 1945-56, Jose Manuel Moreno 1936-50 & Rene Pontoni 1942-47

Coaches
Angel Vazquez 1924-25 • Jose Lago Millan 1927-28 • Francisco Olazar 1928-29 • Francisco Olazar & Juan Jose Tramutola 1929-30 • Felipe Pascucci 1934 • Manuel Seoane 1934-37 • Angel Roca 1937-39 • Guillermo Stabile 1939-60 • Victorio Spinetto 1960-61 • Jose D'Amico 1961 • Juan Carlos Lorenzo 1962-63 • Alejandro Galan 1963 • Horacio Torres 1963-64 • Jose Maria Minella 1964-68 • Renato Cesarini 1968 • Humberto Maschio 1968-69 • Adolfo Pedernera 1969 • Juan Jose Pizzuti 1969-72 • Enrique Sivori 1972-74 • Vladislao Cap & Jose Varacka 1974 • Cesar Luis Menotti 1974-83 • Carlos Bilardo 1983-90 • Alfio Basile 1990-94 • Daniel Passarella 1994-98 • Marcelo Bielsa 1998-2004 • Jose Pekerman 2004-06 • Alfio Basile 2006-08 • Diego Maradona 2008-10 • Sergio Batista 2010-11 • Alejandro Sabella 2011-

ARGENTINA 2011-12
PRIMERA A APERTURA

	Pl	W	D	L	F	A	Pts
Boca Juniors †	19	12	7	0	25	6	**43**
Racing Club	19	7	10	2	16	8	**31**
Vélez Sarsfield	19	9	4	6	22	17	**31**
Belgrano Córdoba	19	8	7	4	21	16	**31**
Colón Santa Fe	19	8	7	4	19	15	**31**
Lanús	19	7	8	4	20	14	**29**
Tigre	19	7	6	6	22	19	**27**
Independiente	19	7	6	6	18	17	**27**
San Martín San Juan	19	6	8	5	17	14	**26**
Atlético Rafaela	19	8	2	9	22	26	**26**
Unión Santa Fe	19	6	7	6	14	18	**25**
Godoy Cruz	19	6	6	7	28	24	**24**
Arsenal	19	6	6	7	21	20	**24**
Estudiantes LP	19	6	5	8	24	24	**23**
Argentinos Juniors	19	5	7	7	18	24	**22**
All Boys	19	4	9	6	15	23	**21**
San Lorenzo	19	5	4	10	13	19	**19**
Newell's Old Boys	19	1	13	5	13	18	**16**
Olimpo	19	2	10	7	15	25	**16**
Banfield	19	3	2	14	13	29	**11**

5/08/2011 - 4/02/2012 • † Qualified for Copa Libertadores
Top scorers: **12** - Ruben **RAMIREZ**, Godoy Cruz • **7** - Mauro **MATOS**, All Boys; Cesar **PEREYRA**, Belgrano & Santiago **SALCEDO** PAR, Argentinos Juniors • **6** - Alexis **CASTRO**, Rafaela; Facundo **FERREYRA**, Banfield; Dario **GANDIN**, Rafaela; Teofilo **GUTIERREZ** COL, Racing & Martin **ROLLE**, Olimpo

ARGENTINA 2011-12
PRIMERA A CLAUSURA

	Pl	W	D	L	F	A	Pts
Arsenal †	19	11	5	3	30	15	**38**
Tigre	19	10	6	3	29	15	**36**
Vélez Sarsfield	19	9	6	4	26	15	**33**
Boca Juniors	19	9	6	4	30	20	**33**
All Boys	19	9	6	4	21	13	**33**
Newell's Old Boys	19	9	5	5	26	19	**32**
Colón Santa Fe	19	7	8	4	24	18	**29**
Argentinos Juniors	19	7	6	6	17	15	**27**
Estudiantes LP	19	7	6	6	23	24	**27**
Lanús	19	7	5	7	19	18	**26**
Unión Santa Fe	19	5	10	4	21	20	**25**
San Lorenzo	19	6	7	6	22	23	**25**
Atlético Rafaela	19	6	6	7	26	24	**24**
Belgrano Córdoba	19	6	6	7	17	20	**24**
San Martín San Juan	19	6	4	9	21	29	**22**
Independiente	19	5	5	9	22	28	**20**
Racing Club	19	5	4	10	19	27	**19**
Godoy Cruz	19	2	8	9	11	25	**14**
Olimpo	19	3	4	12	20	34	**13**
Banfield	19	2	5	12	15	37	**11**

10/02/2012 - 24/06/2012 • † Qualified for Copa Libertadores
Top scorers: **12** - Carlos **LUNA**, Tigre • **8** - Gaston **CAPRARI**, San Martín • **7** - Ernesto **FARIAS**, Independiente; Esteban **FUERTES**, Colón; Dario **GANDIN**, Rafaela; Emanuel **GIGLIOTTI**, San Lorenzo & Mariano **PAVONE**, Lanús

ARGENTINA 2011-12
PRIMERA A APERTURA & CLAUSURA RESULTS AND RELEGATION TABLE

	09-10	10-11	11-12	Pts	Pl	RA	Vélez Sarsfield	Estudiantes LP	Lanús	Boca Juniors	Argentinos Jun	Arsenal	Belgrano	Colón Santa Fe	Newell's	Independiente	All Boys	Godoy Cruz	Unión Santa Fé	Atlético Rafaela	Racing Club	Tigre	San Martín SJ	San Lorenzo	Banfield	Olimpo
Vélez Sarsfield †	61	82	64	207	114	**1.816**		1-0	0-0	0-0	0-2	3-2	0-1	1-1	0-1	1-1	0-1	1-1	0-1	2-1	1-0	0-1	1-0	1-2	3-0	1-0
Estudiantes LP †	71	69	50	190	114	**1.667**	0-2		1-0	0-3	4-3	1-1	2-3	2-2	1-1	2-0	3-0	1-0	2-0	3-0	0-0	1-3	2-2	0-2	2-1	1-0
Lanús †	60	63	55	178	114	**1.561**	1-2	2-1		1-2	0-1	0-1	1-1	2-2	1-1	0-1	2-1	0-0	1-0	2-1	0-1	1-0	1-3	4-1	2-1	0-0
Boca Juniors †	47	53	76	176	114	**1.544**	0-0	1-0	2-2		2-1	0-3	0-0	1-0	2-0	4-5	1-0	3-0	4-0	3-3	1-0	0-1	1-1	1-3	0-2	2-0
Argentinos Juniors ‡	73	54	49	176	114	**1.544**	3-1	1-2	0-4	0-0		2-1	0-0	0-0	1-1	0-0	1-0	1-0	0-0	0-0	2-1	0-1	1-1	0-1	1-0	1-0
Arsenal †	46	57	62	165	114	**1.447**	0-1	1-2	3-1	2-2	3-1		1-0	1-2	1-1	3-1	1-2	1-2	2-2	0-1	1-0	2-0	1-0	2-0	1-0	1-0	2-1
Belgrano Córdoba	0	0	55	55	38	**1.447**	1-3	2-1	0-0	1-1	1-2	1-0		0-1	2-3	2-0	0-0	1-1	1-0	1-1	0-1	1-1	1-1	2-3	1-1
Colón Santa Fe ‡	55	47	60	162	114	**1.421**	0-2	1-1	1-0	0-2	1-0	0-0	2-0		0-3	3-0	1-1	2-0	0-2	1-0	0-2	1-1	0-0	3-1	4-1	3-1
Newell's Old Boys	69	42	48	159	114	**1.395**	1-1	0-0	0-0	0-1	1-0	0-0	0-2	0-0		2-1	1-1	1-3	1-1	3-1	1-0	2-0	0-1	0-0	0-0	3-0	2-2
Independiente ‡	68	43	47	158	114	**1.386**	0-0	3-1	4-3	1-1	0-3	0-0	2-0	0-1	1-1		0-3	2-1	0-0	2-0	4-1	2-1	2-1	0-0	2-0	3-0
All Boys	0	51	54	105	76	**1.382**	0-0	3-1	0-0	3-1	1-0	0-1	1-2	0-1	1-2	0-2		1-1	2-0	1-2	0-4	2-1	2-1	0-0	0-0	0-1	1-2
Godoy Cruz	53	63	38	154	114	**1.351**	1-1	3-1	0-1	1-2	1-1	0-2	1-1	0-1	1-1	0-0	6-1		1-1	1-3	1-0	0-2	2-2	2-0	1-0	1-1
Unión Santa Fé	0	0	50	50	38	**1.316**	3-3	2-2	0-1	0-0	1-1	1-0	0-0	2-2	2-1	0-0	1-1	1-1		0-1	1-1	1-1	0-0	1-0	1-0	2-0
Atlético Rafaela	0	0	50	50	38	**1.316**	2-1	2-2	2-2	3-1	1-3	0-0	0-0	0-1	3-0	1-0	0-2	2-2		4-2	1-1	3-1	2-1	3-3	0-3	1-0
Racing Club ‡	46	52	50	148	114	**1.298**	1-2	1-0	1-1	0-2	1-0	0-0	2-3	1-1	1-0	1-1	3-0	3-0	0-3	1-0		0-0	1-0	1-1	1-2	1-0
Tigre ‡	32	50	63	145	114	**1.272**	1-3	1-1	0-2	1-1	2-2	0-1	2-1	3-1	2-2	1-1	2-1	4-0	3-0	1-1		3-1	3-1	1-0	1-0
San Martín SJ ‡‡	0	0	48	48	38	**1.263**	1-3	0-1	0-0	0-1	0-0	1-4	0-1	2-2	1-1	1-0	0-1	1-0	2-0	2-1	0-0	2-1		1-0	2-1	3-2
San Lorenzo ‡‡	52	47	44	143	114	**1.254**	0-2	1-1	0-1	0-2	3-1	2-0	0-1	1-3	2-0	0-1	0-1	3-2	0-0	0-1	1-3	0-0	1-0		3-1	1-1
Banfield	73	47	22	142	114	**1.246**	0-4	0-3	1-2	1-1	2-2	0-1	0-2	0-3	2-0	0-0	0-1	1-1	0-0	1-0	1-1	1-2	2-0	1-0		1-1
Olimpo	0	48	29	77	76	**1.013**	2-1	0-0	2-2	0-0	0-0	2-2	4-1	0-1	1-2	1-2	2-2	0-1	2-1	0-3	1-1	0-3	1-1	2-5		

† Qualified for the Copa Libertadores • ‡ Qualified for the Copa Sudamericana • Apertura results are in the shaded boxes • RA = Relegation average based on the average number of points per game over the past three seasons • ‡‡ play-off against Primera B Nacional team
Relegation play-offs: **San Martin San Juan** 0-0 0-0 Rosario Central • **San Lorenzo** 2-0 1-1 Instituto Córdoba

ARGENTINA 2011-12

PRIMERA B NACIONAL (2)

	Pl	W	D	L	F	A	Pts
River Plate	38	20	13	5	66	28	**73**
Quilmes	38	20	12	6	62	21	**72**
Instituto Córboba †	38	19	13	6	56	28	**70**
Rosario Central †	38	20	9	9	49	33	**69**
Boca Unidos	38	16	9	13	55	48	**57**
Ferro Carril Oeste	38	14	14	10	29	28	**56**
Patronato	38	15	11	12	42	39	**56**
Almirante Brown	38	14	13	11	36	30	**55**
Gimnasia LP	38	14	12	12	38	33	**54**
Defensa y Justicia	38	14	12	12	50	50	**54**
Aldosiví	38	13	14	11	50	47	**53**
Huracán	38	12	10	16	43	51	**46**
Independiente R'via	38	11	12	15	36	51	**45**
Deportivo Merlo	38	10	13	15	28	38	**43**
Atlético Tucumán	38	11	9	18	33	48	**42**
Guillermo Brown ‡	38	9	11	18	46	63	**38**
Desamparados	38	9	10	19	34	55	**37**
Gimnasia y Esg Jujuy	38	8	10	20	33	51	**34**
Atlanta	38	6	16	16	28	50	**34**
Chacarita Juniors ‡	38	6	15	17	24	46	**33**

6/08/2011 – 23/06/2012 • † Promotion play-off (see Primera A)
‡ Relegation play-off: Chacarita Juniors 0-1 1-1 **Nueva Chicago** • Guillermo Brown 0-0 0-1 **Crucero del Norte**

ARGENTINA 2011-12
PRIMERA DIVISION B METROPOLITANA (3)

	Pl	W	D	L	F	A	Pts
Sarmiento Junín	40	24	8	8	52	25	**80**
Colegiales	40	21	10	9	54	33	**73**
Estudiantes BA †	40	20	12	8	49	29	**72**
Nueva Chicago - P †	40	20	10	10	56	36	**70**
Brown Adrogué †	40	19	12	9	64	34	**69**
Platense †	40	16	13	11	44	32	**61**
Los Andes †	40	16	13	11	44	38	**61**
Comunicaciones †	40	18	6	16	42	38	**60**
Acassuso †	40	15	10	15	43	47	**55**
Almagro	40	13	15	12	43	39	**54**
Villa San Carlos	40	14	12	14	32	41	**54**
Deportivo Armenio	40	12	14	14	45	49	**50**
Flandria	40	12	14	14	36	43	**50**
San Telmo	40	11	14	15	29	37	**47**
Temperley	40	11	13	16	40	45	**46**
Sportivo Italiano - R ‡	40	10	16	14	32	42	**46**
Tristán Suárez	40	12	9	19	48	57	**45**
Defensores de Belgrano	40	10	11	19	31	43	**41**
Barracas Central	40	10	10	20	36	51	**40**
Deportivo Morón	40	9	8	23	39	60	**35**
General Lamadrid	40	7	10	23	28	68	**31**

6/08/2011 – 22/06/2012
† Promotion play-offs (See Primera B Metropolitana for final)
General Lamadrid relegated on three season average
‡ Relegation play-off • **Central Córdoba** 3-1 Sportivo Italiano

PROMOTION PLAY-OFFS
Quarter-finals: **N. Chicago** 3-0 Los Andes; Brown 1-3 **Platense**;
Estudiantes 1-0 Comunicaciones; Colegiales 2-3 **Acassuso**
Semi-finals: Platense 0-0 0-3 **Nueva Chicago**;
Acassuso 1-0 2-1 Estudiantes
Final: Acassuso 2-2 0-1 **Nueva Chicago**

ARGENTINA 2011-12
PRIMERA DIVISION C METROPOLITANA (4)

	Pl	W	D	L	F	A	Pts
Villa Dálmine	38	20	11	7	61	30	**71**
UAI-Urquiza †	38	19	12	7	47	33	**69**
Defensores Cambaceres†	38	16	12	10	40	33	**60**
Justo Jose de Urquiza †	38	15	14	9	47	27	**59**
Deportivo Laferrere †	38	15	13	10	43	33	**58**
Central Córdoba - P †	38	14	15	9	51	36	**57**
Sportivo Dock Sud †	38	15	9	14	37	38	**54**
F.C. Midland †	38	14	11	13	42	39	**53**
Berazategui †	38	14	10	14	50	47	**52**
Talleres R de Escalada	38	13	11	14	47	44	**50**
Excursionistas	38	12	13	13	41	38	**49**
Leandro N. Alem - R	38	14	11	13	37	40	**47**
San Miguel	38	9	17	12	26	35	**44**
Argentino Merlo	38	10	14	14	31	45	**44**
Luján	38	9	16	13	28	37	**43**
Deportivo Español	38	11	10	17	31	42	**43**
El Porvenir	38	9	15	14	40	44	**42**
Sacachispas	38	9	13	16	36	54	**40**
Defensores Unidos	38	9	13	16	29	47	**40**
Liniers	38	9	11	18	28	50	**38**

6/08/2011 – 22/06/2012
† Promotion play-offs (See Primera B Metropolitana for final)
Leandro N. Alem relegated on three season average • ‡ relegation play-off • Lujan 0-1 **D. Español** • Argentino 1-0 1-3 **Lujan**

PLAY-OFFS
Quarter-finals: Central Córdoba 1-1 3-1 Dep Laferrere;
Berazategui 1-1 3-1 UAI Urquiza; Dock Sud 1-0 1-0 JJ Urquiza;
F.C. Midland 4-1 0-1 Defensores Cambaceres
Semi-finals: Berazategui 0-1 0-1 **Central Cordoba**;
F.C. Midland 1-0 0-0 Dock Sud
Final: F.C. Midland 1-2 0-0 **Central Córdoba**

ARGENTINA 2011-12
PRIMERA DIVISIÓN D METROPOLITANA (5)

	Pl	W	D	L	F	A	Pts
Fénix	34	21	10	3	60	18	73
Argentino Quilmes †	34	19	10	5	58	29	67
Atlas †	34	17	13	4	44	25	64
Centro Español †	34	16	11	7	38	21	59
Deportivo Riestra †	34	15	12	7	40	27	57
San Martín Burzaco †	34	14	14	6	44	29	56
Cañuelas †	34	12	12	10	31	22	48
Yupanqui †	34	14	6	14	40	49	48
Victoriano Arenas †	34	11	11	12	46	56	44
Juventud Unida	34	10	10	14	34	40	40
Argentino Rosario	34	7	14	13	35	42	35
Claypole	34	7	14	13	35	45	35
Ituzaingó	34	7	13	14	20	27	34
Atlético Lugano	34	7	13	14	31	34	34
Deportivo Paraguayo	34	9	7	18	24	41	34
Muñiz	34	9	7	18	21	55	34
Central Ballester	34	7	9	18	33	48	30
Sp. Barracas Bolívar	34	6	10	18	33	49	28

6/08/2011 - 22/06/2012
† Promotion play-offs (See Primera C Metropolitana for final)
Sportivo Barracas relegated on three season average

PLAY-OFFS
Quarter-finals: Victoriano Arenas 0-1 1-1 **Argentino Quilmes**;
San Martín Burzaco 0-0 1-0 Dep. Riestra;
Cañuelas 0-0 1-2 **Centro Español**; Yupanqui 0-2 0-3 **Atlas**
Semi-finals: San Martín Burzaco 2-2 1-4 **Argentino Quilmes**;
Centro Español 1-0 0-2 **Atlas**
Final: Atlas 0-0 0-3 **Argentino Quilmes**

ARGENTINA 2011-12
TORNEO ARGENTINA A (3) SECOND STAGE

	Pl	W	D	L	F	A	Pts
Douglas Haig - P	10	6	3	1	19	9	21
Crucero del Norte †	10	6	2	2	11	3	20
Sportivo Belgrano †	10	6	2	2	19	11	20
Talleres Córdoba ‡	10	4	4	2	20	11	16
Santamarina †	10	4	2	4	12	10	14
San Martín Tucumán ‡	10	4	2	4	10	13	14
Defensores de Belgrano ‡	10	2	4	4	8	10	10
Racing Olavarría ‡	10	3	1	6	9	17	10
Unión Mar del Plata ‡	10	2	3	5	7	13	9
Racing Córdoba ‡	10	1	5	4	10	18	8
Central Córdoba ‡	10	2	2	6	9	21	8

11/03/2012 - 14/05/2012 • Douglas Haig promoted to Primera B Nacional • ‡ Third stage • † Fourth stage

THIRD STAGE PLAY-OFFS
Central Córdoba 2-0 1-3 **Racing Olavarría**;
Racing Córdoba 1-1 2-0 Unión Mar del Plata
Central Norte 2-0 2-1 San Martín Tucumán
Juventud Universitario 4-1 0-2 Defensores Belgrano
Winners qualify for the fourth stage

ARGENTINA 2011-12
TORNEO ARGENTINA A (3) FOURTH STAGE

Quarter-finals: J. Universitario 0-1 1-2 **Crucero del Norte**;
Racing Córdoba 1-1 1-1 **Talleres Córdoba**; Racing Olavarría 2-2 2-2 **Santamarina**; Central Norte 3-2 1-2 **Sportivo Belgrano**
Semi-finals: Talleres Córdoba 0-0 1-2 **Crucero del Norte**;
Santamarina 0-3 0-3 **Sportivo Belgrano**
Final: **Crucero del Norte** 3-1 0-0 Sportivo Belgrano

ARGENTINA 2011-12
TORNEO ARGENTINA A (3) FIRST STAGE

North	Pl	W	D	L	F	A	Pts
Crucero del Norte †	24	11	8	5	31	21	41
San Martín Tucumán †	24	8	13	3	29	23	37
Sportivo Belgrano †	24	10	7	7	32	27	37
Talleres Córdoba †	24	8	11	5	35	31	35
Racing Córdoba †	24	10	4	10	29	28	34
Central Córdoba †	24	7	11	6	21	20	32
Tiro Federal	24	8	8	8	26	28	32
Libertad Sunchales	24	7	10	7	30	25	31
Central Norte	24	7	10	7	24	25	31
Gimnasia y Tiro	24	8	7	9	27	30	31
Juventud Antoniana	24	7	9	8	28	27	30
Alumni Villa María	24	5	6	13	25	34	21
Unión Sunchales	24	4	8	12	16	34	20

South	Pl	W	D	L	F	A	Pts
Santamarina †	22	9	11	2	37	20	38
Defensores de Belgrano †	22	10	6	6	35	25	36
Douglas Haig †	22	10	5	7	33	20	35
Racing Olavarría †	22	10	4	8	21	18	34
Unión Mar del Plata †	22	9	5	8	27	26	32
Deportivo Maipú	22	8	7	7	21	21	31
Huracán Tres Arroyos	22	7	7	8	22	27	28
Cipolletti	22	7	5	10	29	35	26
Gimnasia C. del Uruguay	22	6	7	9	20	27	25
Rivadavia Lincoln	22	6	6	10	25	31	24
Juventud Universitario	22	5	8	9	23	29	23
CAI	22	4	9	9	22	37	21

20/08/2011 - 7/03/2012 • † Qualified for the second stage
The rest take part in the Revalida

ARGENTINA 2011-12
TORNEO ARGENTINA A (3) REVALIDA

North	Pl	W	D	L	F	A	Pts
Libertad Sunchales †	30	11	11	8	40	30	44
Central Norte †	30	10	10	10	31	33	40
Gimnasia y Tiro †	30	10	9	11	33	36	39
Juventud Antoniana †	30	9	11	10	35	36	38
Tiro Federal	30	9	9	12	32	35	36
Alumni Villa María	30	7	8	15	35	45	29
Unión Sunchales - R	30	6	10	14	23	41	28

South	Pl	W	D	L	F	A	Pts
Deportivo Maipú †	28	9	8	11	24	27	35
Rivadavia Lincoln †	28	9	7	12	32	35	34
Juventud Universitario †	28	8	10	10	29	33	34
Cipolletti †	28	9	7	12	36	41	34
Gimnasia C. del Uruguay	28	8	10	10	26	32	34
CAI	28	7	12	9	31	41	33
Huracán Tres Arroyos	28	7	9	12	22	36	30

10/03/2012 - 13/05/2012 • † Qualified for the second round
Second round: Gimnasia y Tiro 0-1 **Rivadavia**; Cipolletti 0-2 2-2 **Libertad**; J. Antoniana 1-1 0-1 **J. Universitario**; Ginmasia Concepcion 0-0 1-3 **Central Norte** • Third round: Rivadavia 1-0 0-3 **J. Universitario**; **Central Norte** 2-0 1-1 Libertad
J. Universitario & Central Norte qualified for the third stage

Douglas Haig promoted to Primera B Nacional as Torneo Argentina A champions • Crucero del Norte qualified to meet Guillermo Brown in a play-off (see Primera B Nacional)
Fourth stage played from 26/05/2012 - 23/06/2012

COPA ARGENTINA 2011-12

Fifth Round

Boca Juniors	1	4p
Santamarina	1	3p
Boca Unidos	1	5p
Central Córdoba	1	6p
Excursionistas	0	4p
Huracán	0	3p
Central Norte	1	
Olimpo	2	
Belgrano Córdoba	3	
Sacachispas	0	
Colegiales	0	
Independiente	4	
Vélez Sarsfield	2	
Racing Trelew	0	
Guillermo Brown	0	
Rosario Central	1	
Tigre	4	
Defensa y Justicia	2	
Desamparados	0	
Gimnasia LP	1	
Aldosivi	1	5p
Independiente Rivadavia	1	3p
Racing Olavarría	0	
Argentinos Juniors	3	
Sarmiento Junín	1	
San Martín SJ	0	
Talleres Córdoba	1	
Colón Santa Fe	2	
Estudiantes LP	2	
Unión Villa Krause	1	
Guaymallén	0	
Deportivo Merlo	2	
River Plate	1	
Defensores de Belgrano	0	
Almirante Brown	2	3p
Sportivo Belgrano	2	5p
Atlanta	1	4p
All Boys	1	3p
Deportivo Riestra	0	3p
Quilmes	0	5p
Barracas Central	0	8p
Lanús	0	7p
Instituto Córboba	1	
Atlético Policial	4	
Chacarita Juniors	2	
Unión Santa Fé	1	
Villa Dálmine	1	
San Lorenzo	2	
Atlético Tucumán	3	
Estudiantes BA	2	
Godoy Cruz	1	2p
Sportivo Italiano	1	4p
Banfield	2	
Atlético Paraná	1	
Ferro Carril Oeste	0	2p
Atlético Rafaela	0	4p
Sarmiento Resistencia	1	
Gimnasia y Esg Jujuy	0	
General Lamadrid	1	
Arsenal	2	
Patronato	0	5p
Newell's Old Boys	0	4p
El Porvenir	0	
Racing Club	2	

Sixth Round

Boca Juniors	2	
Central Córdoba	0	
Excursionistas	1	4p
Olimpo	1	5p
Belgrano Córdoba	2	
Independiente	0	
Vélez Sarsfield	1	4p
Rosario Central	1	5p
Tigre	1	4p
Gimnasia LP	1	1p
Aldosivi	0	
Argentinos Juniors	2	
Sarmiento Junín	1	
Colón Santa Fe	0	
Estudiantes LP	0	4p
Deportivo Merlo	0	5p
River Plate	2	
Sportivo Belgrano	0	
Atlanta	1	
Quilmes	2	
Barracas Central	4	
Atlético Policial	0	
Chacarita Juniors	1	1p
San Lorenzo	1	3p
Atlético Tucumán	0	4p
Sportivo Italiano	0	3p
Banfield	0	
Atlético Rafaela	2	
Sarmiento Resistencia	2	
Arsenal	1	
Patronato	1	
Racing Club	3	

Round of 16

Boca Juniors ‡‡	1	11p
Olimpo	1	10p
Belgrano Córdoba	1	
Rosario Central ††	2	
Tigre	1	
Argentinos Juniors	0	
Sarmiento Junín	1	
Deportivo Merlo	2	
River Plate ††	2	
Quilmes	1	
Barracas Central	1	4p
San Lorenzo	1	5p
Atlético Tucumán ‡‡	0	4p
Atlético Rafaela	0	3p
Sarmiento Resistencia	0	
Racing Club	2	

Matches played at a variety of neutral grounds

COPA ARGENTINA 2011-12

Quarter-finals	Semi-finals	Final

Boca Juniors †† 1 4p
Rosario Central 1 2p

       Boca Juniors ‡‡ 1 5p
       Deportivo Merlo 1 4p

Tigre 1
Deportivo Merlo ‡† 2

              Boca Juniors 2
              Racing Club 1

River Plate †‡ 2
San Lorenzo 0

       River Plate 0 4p
       Racing Club †‡ 0 5p

Atlético Tucumán 0
Racing Club ‡‡ 1

†† Played at Bicentenario, San Juan
‡‡ Played at Bicentenario, Catamarca
†‡ Played at Padre Martearena, Salta
‡† Played at Tres de Febrero, Jose Ingenieros

COPA ARGENTINA FINAL 2012
Bicentenario, San Juan, 8-08-2012, Att: 25 000, Ref: Pablo Lunati

Boca Juniors	2	Silva [21], Viatri [62]
Racing Club	1	Viola [68]

BOCA
Oscar **USTARI** - Franco **SOSA**, Rolando **SCHIAVI** (c), Matias **CARUZZO**, Clemente **RODRIGUEZ**• - Pablo **LEDESMA**, Leandro **SOMOZA**, Walter **ERVITI** (Juan **SANCHEZ MINO** 52) - Cristian **CHAVEZ**• (Cristian **ALVAREZ** 88) - Lucas **VIATRI** (Christian **CELLAY** 93+), Tanque **SILVA**. Tr: Julio Cesar **FALCIONI**

RACING
Sebastian **SAJA** - Matias **MARTINEZ**, Fernando **ORTIZ**, Matias **CAHAIS**, Claudio **CORVALAN**• (Luis **FARINA** 66) - Diego **VILLAR**• (Gabriel **HAUCHE** 81), Agustin **PELLETIERI** (Javier **CAMPORA** 73), Mauro **CAMORANESI**, Ricardo **CENTURION** - Valentin **VIOLA**, Jose **SAND**. Tr: Luis **ZUBELDIA**

MEDALS TABLE

		Overall			League			Amateur			Pro			National			Metro			AP/CL			South Am		
		G	S	B	G	S	B	G	S	B	G	S	B	G	S	B	G	S	B	G	S	B	G	S	B
1	Boca Juniors	39	26	21	30	21	17	6	3	5	10	8	5	3			2	2	3	9	8	4	9	5	4
2	River Plate	37	34	29	**34**	30	14	1	5	4	14	11	5	3	7		4	2		12	5	5	3	4	15
3	Independiente	26	17	14	16	16	9	2	2	3	6	8	6	3	1		3	2		2	3		10	1	5
4	Racing Club	18	9	14	16	8	12	9	1	1	6	3	7			1		2		1	2	3	2	1	2
5	San Lorenzo	15	13	22	13	13	16	3	2	2	3	7	5	2	1	3	2	1	2	3	2	4	2		6
6	Velez Sarsfield	10	8	14	8	8	10		1			1	1	1	1	2		2	1	7	3	6	2		4
7	Alumni	10	2		10	2		10	2																
8	Estudiantes La Plata	9	9	11	5	7	9	1	3	2			3	1	2		2	1	2	1	1	2	4	2	2
9	Huracán	5	6	8	5	6	7	4	2	3			3				1	2	1		2				1
10	Rosario Central	5	5	5	4	4	2				1			3	2			1			1	2	1	1	3
11	Newell's Old Boys	5	5	3	5	3	3				2	2	1					1		1	2	1	1		2	
12	Lomas Athletic	5	2	3	5	2	3	5	2	3															
13	Argentinos Juniors	4	2	4	3	2	1		1				1	1			1	1		1					3
14	Belgrano Athletic	3	3	3	3	3	3	3	3	3															
15	Lanús	2	5	5	1	4	5			1	1									1	3	4	1	1	
16	Ferro Carril Oeste	2	3	1	2	3	1							2	1			2	1						
17	CA Porteño	2	2		2	2		2	2																
18	Quilmes	2	1	3	2	1	3	1		3					1		1								
19	Estudantil Porteño	2			2			2																	
	Arsenal Sarandi	2			1															1			1		
21	Gimnasia y Esgrima LP	1	6	4	1	6	3	1	1				1								5	2			1
22	Banfield	1	4	4	1	4	4		2	2	1									1	1	2			
23	Talleres Córdoba	1	1	2		1	2								1				1			1	1		
24	Lomas Academy	1	1		1	1		1	1																
25	Chacarita Juniors	1		1	1		1										1		1						
	Sportivo Barracas	1		1	1		1	1		1															
	Sportivo Doc Sud	1		1	1		1	1		1															
28	St Andrews	1			1			1																	
	Old Caledonians	1			1			1																	
30	Tigre		4			3												3				1			
31	San Isidro		3	3		3	3		3	3															
32	Estudiantes BA		2	2		2	2		2	2															
33	Flores AC		2	1		2	1		2	1															
34	Lobos AC		2			2			2																
	Nueva Chicago		2			2			2																
36	Platense		1	4		1	4		1	3			1												
37	Colón Santa Fe		1	3		1	2														1	2			1
38	Unión Santa Fe		1	1		1	1								1				1						
	Barracas AC		1	1		1	1		1	1															
	Godoy Cruz		1	1		1	1														1	1			
41	Almagro		1			1			1																
	Barracas Central		1			1			1																
	Colegiales		1			1			1																
	Del Plata		1			1			1																
	Gimnasia y Esgrima BA		1			1			1																
	Lanus AC		1			1			1																
	Racing Cordoba		1			1									1										
	Rosario AC		1			1			1																
	Sportivo Palermo		1			1			1																
	Temperley		1			1			1																
51	Deportivo Español			3			3									2						1			
52	Atlanta			2			2			1					1										
	Argentino Quilmes			2			2			2															
	Quilmes Rowers			2			2			2															
55	Belgrano A			1			1			1															
	El Porvenir			1			1			1															
	Defensores Belgrano			1			1			1															
	Old Boys			1			1			1															
	Rosario Railway			1			1			1															
	Sporting Almagro			1			1			1															
	Sportivo Buenos Aires			1			1			1															

Amateur = Amateur Championship 1891-1934 • Pro = Professional Championship 1931-66 & 1986-91 • National = National Championship 1967-85 • Metro = Metropoltian Championship 1967-84 • AP/CL = Apertura and Clausura tournaments 1991- • League column is a combination of all

ARG – ARGENTINA

ALL BOYS
2012 CLAUSURA

Feb	11	Belgrano	D	0-0	Ca	9		20 000
	18	Colón	W	2-0	Ca	5	Ferreyra [11], Rodriguez [96+]	14 000
	24	At. Rafaela	W	1-0	Ca	4	Garcia [92+]	12 000
Mar	3	Vélez	D	0-0	Ca	5		17 000
	10	Racing	L	0-3	Ca	5		18 000
	16	Godoy Cruz	D	1-1	Ca	7	Matos [47]	10 000
	23	Banfield	D	0-0	Ca	8		9 000
Apr	1	Arsenal	L	0-2	Ca	11		7 000
	7	Tigre	W	2-0	Ca	9	Zapata [33], Rodriguez [94+]	8 000
	14	Olimpo	W	2-1	Ca	7	Matos 6, Zapata [67]	6 500
	22	Unión	W	2-1	Ca	6	Perea 6, Zapata [22p]	8 000
	28	Newells OB	D	1-1	Ca	5	Matos 5	33 000
May	6	S. Lorenzo	D	0-0	Ca	6		18 000
	12	Indep'iente	W	3-0	Ca	6	Morel [22], Rudler [61], Matos [81]	24 000
	19	San Martin	W	1-0	Ca	5	Matos [17]	8 000
	26	Lanús	L	0-1	Ca	6		9 000
Jun	10	Estudiantes	W	3-1	Ca	6	Dominguez [32], Ferrari [47], Matos [73]	9 000
	17	Arg Juniors	L	0-1	Ca	6		6 500
	24	Boca Jun	W	3-1	Ca	5	Perea 3 [14] [40] [52]	15 000
5th							Att: 114 000 • Av: 11 400 • Islas Malvinas 21 000

ALL BOYS LEAGUE APPEARANCES/GOALS 2012
Goalkeepers Nicolas Cambiasso 18 • Bernardo Leyenda 1
Defenders Maximiliano Coronel 11/0 • Eduardo Dominguez 17/1
Jonathan Ferrari 9+1/1 • Francisco Martinez 2+4/0 • Facundo Quiroga 11+2/0 • Matias Rudler 2/1 • Carlos Soto 16/0 • Cristian Vella 10+4/0
Midfield Hugo Barrientos 14/0 • Juan Cruz Careaga 0+2/0 • Martin Morel 6+5/1 • Emanuel Perea 8+6/4 • Matias Perez Garcia 10+5/1 • Juan Pablo Rodriguez URU 15/2 • Fernando Sanchez 10+3/0 • Dario Stefanatto 1+5/0 • Martin Zapata 18/3
Forwards Juan Ferreyra 6+2/1 • Mauro Matos 18/6 • Henry Rui 0+3/0 • Carlos Salom 0+3/0 • Javier Soner 0+3/0 • Agustin Torassa 6+5/0
Coach Jose Santos Romero

ARGENTINOS JUNIORS
2012 CLAUSURA

Feb	7	R Olavarria	W	3-0	ACr5		Morales 2 [43] [79], Penalba [79]	
	12	Unión	D	0-0	Ca	9		4 000
	18	Newells OB	L	0-1	Ca	14		34 000
	25	S. Lorenzo	L	0-1	Ca	19		
Mar	3	Indep'iente	W	3-1	Ca	13	Batista [9], Bordagaray [45], Barzola [61]	20 000
	10	San Martin	D	1-1	Ca	15	OG [27]	4 000
	16	Lanús	W	1-0	Ca	9	Hernandez [59]	8 000
	25	Estudiantes	L	1-2	Ca	11	Berardo [26]	7 000
	28	Aldovisi	W	2-0	ACr6		Balsas [23], Escudero [91+p]	2 500
	31	Tigre	W	2-1	Ca	8	Bordagaray 2 [13] [22]	17 000
Apr	7	Boca Jun	L	1-2	Ca	11	Hernandez 1	36 000
	11	Tigre	L	0-1	ACr7			2 000
	15	Belgrano	D	0-0	Ca	12		11 000
	21	Colón	L	0-1	Ca	14		22 000
	29	At. Rafaela	D	0-0	Ca	15		4 000
May	5	Vélez	W	2-0	Ca	13	Naguel [51], Hernandez [82p]	19 000
	13	Racing	W	2-1	Ca	9	Ramirez [8], Morales [89]	18 000
	18	Godoy Cruz	D	1-1	Ca	11	Rius [87]	4 500
	26	Banfield	W	1-0	Ca	7	Barzola [75p]	6 000
Jun	8	Arsenal	L	1-3	Ca	10	Morales [60]	8 000
	17	All Boys	W	1-0	Ca	8	Morales [73]	6 500
	22	Olimpo	D	0-0	Ca	8		3 000
8th							Att: 60 500 • Av: 7 563 • Diego Armando Maradona 24 800

ARGENTINOS LEAGUE APPEARANCES/GOALS 2012
Goalkeepers Nereo Fernandez 6+1 • Luis Ojeda 13
Defenders Pablo Barzola 13/2 • Nicoas Batista 3+2/1 • Nicolas Berardo 2+3/1 • Sergio Escudero 16/0 • Franco Flores 1/0 • Gonzalo Prosperi 11+2/0 • Lucas Rodriguez 1/0 • Juan Sabia 16/0 • Miguel Torren 17/0
Midfield German Basualdo 6+4/0 • Rodrigo Diaz Ponce 0+1/0 • Pablo Hernandez 19/3 • Gaspar Inguez 15/0 • Matias Laba 15/0 • Santiago Naguel 7+2/1 • Gustavo Oberman 12+1/0 • Gabriel Penalba 0+5/0 • Juan Ramirez 2+8/1 • Ciro Rius 1+8/1 • Maximiliano Rodriguez 1+1/0 • Fabio Vazquez 0+1/0
Forwards Sebastian Balsas URU 4+2/0 • Leandro Barrera 0+4/0 • Fabian Bordagaray 13+5/3 • Lucas Cano 4+4/0 • Juan Morales 10+1/3 • Gabriel Perez Tarifa 1+1/0
Coach Nestor Gorosito • Leonardo Astrada (1/03/2012)

The guide to club football in Argentina in this year's Almanack is shortened because of the decision to revert to a single championship for the 2013-13 season. Only the 2011-12 Clausura is covered here. For the 2011-12 Apertura see Oliver's Almanack of World Football 2012. Oliver's Almanack of World Football 2014 will cover the 2012-13 championship which runs from August 2012 to May 2013.
Ca = Clausura • CL = Copa Libertadores • AC = Copa Argentina. For further details see the key on page 13.

ARSENAL
2012 CLAUSURA

Jan	24	Huancayo	W	3-0	CLpr	Cordoba [21], Zelaya [35], Mosca [87]	721
	31	Huancayo	D	1-1	CLpr	Leguizamon [85]	13 000
	7	Fluminense	L	0-1	CLg4		28 928
	13	Colón	D	0-0	Ca	9	25 000
Feb	18	At. Rafaela	D	2-2	Ca	11 Leguizamon [14], Caffa [65p]	2 000
	21	Zamora	W	3-0	CLg4	Ortiz [1], Carbonero [15], Leguizamon [43]	390
	26	Vélez	L	2-3	Ca	16 Zelaya [67], Leguizamon [82]	18 000
	29	Lamadrid	W	2-1	ACr5	Cuesta [41], Sena [89]	
	4	Racing	D	0-0	Ca	17	10 000
	11	Godoy Cruz	W	1-0	Ca	12 Ortiz [6]	3 500
	14	Boca Jun	L	1-2	CLg4	OG [9]	5 829
Mar	18	Banfield	W	1-0	Ca	6 Ortiz [8]	4 500
	21	Sarmineto	L	1-2	ACr6	6 Mosca [72]	500
	25	Tigre	W	1-0	Ca	4 Burdisso [65]	12 000
	29	Boca Jun	L	0-2	CLg4		28 224
	1	All Boys	W	2-0	Ca	2 Leschuk [22], Torres [63]	7 000
	6	Olimpo	W	2-1	Ca	4 Aguirre [39], Ortiz [75]	2 500
	10	Zamora	W	1-0	CLg4	Caffa [29]	2 853
Apr	15	Unión	L	0-1	Ca	5	19 000
	18	Fluminense	L	1-2	CLg4	6 Aguirre [80]	204
	23	Newells OB	D	1-1	Ca	5 Benedetto [46]	8 000
	29	S. Lorenzo	L	0-2	Ca	6	21 000
	5	Indep'iente	W	3-1	Ca	5 Burdisso [8], OG [26], Zelaya [41]	11 000
May	11	San Martin	W	4-1	Ca	4 Zelaya [5p], Perez [17], Aguirre [53], Carbonero [59]	BCD
	21	Lanús	W	3-1	Ca	3 Aguirre [14], Zelaya [25], Ortiz [38]	8 000
	28	Estudiantes	D	1-1	Ca	3 Zelaya [16p]	18 000
Jun	8	Arg Juniors	W	3-1	Ca	3 Lopez [3], OG [21], Leguizamon [76p]	8 000
	17	Boca Jun	W	3-0	Ca	1 Zelaya [2], Leguizamon [23 85]	40 000
	24	Belgrano	W	2-0	Ca	1 Lopez [27]	15 000

1st   Att: 81 000 • Av: 8 100 • El Viaducto 16 300

ARSENAL LEAGUE APPEARANCES/GOALS 2012
Goalkeepers Christian Campestrini 18 • Catriel Orcellet 1
Defenders Guillermo Burdisso 17/2 • Victor Cuesta 6/0
Danilo Gerlo 1+3/0 • Lisandro Lopez 15/2 • Hugo Nervo 14+2/0
Cristian Trombetta 2/0
Midfield Nicolas Aguirre 13+5/3 • Dario Benedetto 5+4/1
Juan Caffa 9+9/1 • Carlos Carbonero COL 15/1
Gaston Esmerado 3+3/0 • Adrian Gonzalez 6+9/0 • Ivan Marcone 18/0
Jorge Ortiz 14+1/4 • Damian Perez 17/1
Forwards Gustavo Blanco Leschuk 2+2/1 • Jorge Cordoba 3+8/0
Luciano Leguizamon 14+2/5 • Diego Torres 2+7/1
Emilio Zelaya 14+2/6
Coach Gustavo Alfaro

ATLETICO RAFAELA
2012 CLAUSURA

Feb	12	Banfield	W	3-0	Ca	2 Fissore [16], Gandin 2 [61p 90]	9 000
	18	Arsenal	D	2-2	Ca	3 Castro [51], Gandin [69p]	2 000
	24	All Boys	L	0-1	Ca	8	12 000
	3	Olimpo	L	1-2	Ca	12 Gandin [41p]	12 000
	11	Unión	L	0-2	Ca	18	15 000
Mar	15	Banfield	W	2-0	ACr5	Capellino [56], Pavetti [70]	5 000
	18	Newells OB	L	0-1	Ca	19	36 000
	24	S. Lorenzo	W	2-1	Ca	15 Fontanini [38], Carrera [85]	15 000
	31	Indep'iente	L	0-2	Ca	19	25 000
	7	San Martin	W	3-1	Ca	12 Carrera [40], Castro [44], Gandin [85]	12 000
Apr	12	At Tucumán	L	0-0	ACr6	L 3-4p	8 000
	16	Lanús	L	0-1	Ca	15	4 000
	21	Estudiantes	W	3-2	Ca	12 Carniello [14], Fissore [19], Carignano [54p]	12 500
	29	Arg Juniors	D	0-0	Ca	13	4 000
	6	Boca Jun	D	2-2	Ca	15 Fontanini [61], Gandin [93+p]	17 000
May	12	Belgrano	D	1-1	Ca	15 Castro [88]	15 000
	20	Colón	D	0-0	Ca	14	15 000
	27	Tigre	D	1-1	Ca	14 Castro [53]	13 000
	9	Vélez	L	1-2	Ca	16 Carignano [63]	8 000
Jun	17	Racing	W	4-2	Ca	15 Carignano 2 [37p 66], Castro [57], Gonzalez [72]	14 000
	24	Godoy Cruz	W	3-1	Ca	12 Fontanini [13], Carrera [30], Castro [59]	8 000

13th   Att: 134 500 • Av: 13 450 • Nuevo Monumental 16 000

RAFAELA LEAGUE APPEARANCES/GOALS 2012
Goalkeepers Guillermo Sara 19
Defenders Lucas Bovaglio 19/0 • Oscar Carniello 17/1 • Francisco
Dutari 5+2/0 • Juan Fernandez 1+1/0 • Fabricio Fontanini 18/3 • Hugo
Iriarte 1+6/0 • Martin Zbrun 15/0
Midfield German Caceres 3+6/0 • Sebastian Carrera 14+4/3 • Nicolas
Castro 18/6 • Rodrigo Depetris 0+3/0 • Matias Fissore 15+1/2 • Walter
Gaitan 1+2/0 • Ivan Juarez 8+5/0 • Alexis Niz 0+1/0 • Pablo
Pavetti 0+6/0 • German Rodriguez Rojas 0+2/0 • Walter Serrano 18/0
Forwards Nicolas Capellino 0+5/0 • Cesar Carignano 12+5/4 • Lucio
Filomeno 2+1/0 • Dario Gandin 14+1/6 • Federico Gonzalez 9+4/1
Coach Carlos Trullet • Ruben Forestello (13/03/2012)

BANFIELD
2012 CLAUSURA

	4	Estudiantes	L	1-2	Ap	Lopez [9]	10 000
Feb	12	At. Rafaela	L	0-3	Ca	20	9 000
	17	Vélez	L	0-4	Ca	20	15 000
	26	Racing	W	2-1	Ca	15 Chavez [12], Lopez [91+]	30 000
	2	Godoy Cruz	D	1-1	Ca	16 Lopez [64]	11 000
	11	Tigre	L	0-2	Ca	19	14 000
	15	At. Rafaela	L	0-2	ACr5		5 000
Mar	18	Arsenal	L	0-1	Ca	19	4 500
	23	All Boys	D	0-0	Ca	20	9 000
	31	Olimpo	W	5-2	Ca	16 Reta [12], Chavez 2 [46 67], Brum [73], Gomez [81]	8 000
	7	Unión	D	2-2	Ca	17 Lopez [27p], Ferreyra [90p]	8 000
Apr	15	Newells OB	L	0-3	Ca	19	36 000
	22	S. Lorenzo	D	1-1	Ca	18 Tagliafico [93+]	18 000
	28	Indep'iente	L	0-2	Ca	19	16 000
	4	San Martin	L	1-2	Ca	19 Quinteros [39]	4 500
May	13	Lanús	L	1-2	Ca	19 Ferreyra [79]	30 000
	19	Estudiantes	L	0-3	Ca	20	8 000
	26	Arg Juniors	L	0-1	Ca	20	6 000
	9	Boca Jun	D	1-1	Ca	20 Alayes [46]	20 000
Jun	16	Belgrano	L	1-3	Ca	20 De Souza [1]	12 000
	24	Colón	L	0-3	Ca	20	12 000

20th   Att: 119 500 • Av: 11 950 • Florencia Sola 34 901

BANFIELD LEAGUE APPEARANCES/GOALS 2012
Goalkeepers Cristian Lucchetti 19 • Pablo Santillo 0+1
Defenders Agustin Alayes 15/1 • Marcelo Bustamante 7+2/0
Alejandro Delfino 4+3/0 • Mauro Dos Santos 16/0
Santiago Ladino 6+1/0 • Adrian Reta 9+1/1 • Nicolas Tagliafico 18/1
Gustavo Toledo 3+2/0
Midfield Walter Acevedo 8+3/0 • Alejandro Barbaro 0+3/0 • Roberto
Brum URU 10+1/1 • Diego De Souza URU 6+5/1
Juan Eluchans 9+5/0 • Jonatan Gomez 11+1/1 • Rodrigo Pepe 1+1/0
Marcelo Quinteros 17+2/0 • Julian Rojas COL 13+3/0
Forwards Jorge Achucarro PAR 7+3/0 • Andres Chavez 12+6/3
Facundo Ferreyra 12+3/2 • Rodrigo Lopez URU 5+8/3
Emiliano Terzaghi 0+1/0
Coach Jorge da Silva • Eduardo Acevedo URU (10/03/2012)

BELGRANO CORDOBA
2012 CLAUSURA

	11	All Boys	D	0-0	Ca	9		20 000
Feb	17	Olimpo	L	1-4	Ca	18	Mansanelli [45p]	12 000
	24	Unión	W	1-0	Ca	13	Parodi [67]	18 000
	2	Newells OB	W	2-0	Ca	6	Silvera [31], Pereyra [36]	34 000
	7	Indep'iente	W	2-0	ACr5	Maldonado [4], Lollo [70]	3 000
Mar	10	S. Lorenzo	L	1-2	Ca	8	Gimenez [10]	20 000
	17	Indep'iente	L	0-2	Ca	12		25 000
	24	San Martin	D	1-1	Ca	13	Perez [90p]	15 000
	30	Lanus	W	1-0	Ca	9	Perez [82p]	9 000
	8	Estudiantes	W	2-1	Ca	7	Gonzalez 2 [50 82]	18 000
	15	Arg Juniors	D	0-0	Ca	9		11 000
Apr	22	Boca Jun	D	1-1	Ca	9	Gimenez [22]	57 000
	25	Rosario C	L	1-2	ACr6	Almerares [93+]	3 000
	30	Tigre	D	1-1	Ca	10	Farre [49]	17 000
	7	Colón	L	0-2	Ca	13		20 000
May	12	At. Rafaela	D	1-1	Ca	13	Perez [5p]	15 000
	20	Vélez	W	1-0	Ca	10	Silvera [61]	19 000
	26	Racing	L	0-1	Ca	13		25 000
Jun	10	Godoy Cruz	L	1-2	Ca	13	Perez [90p]	7 000
	16	Banfield	W	3-1	Ca	12	Almerares [40], Melano 2 [66 67]	12 000
	24	Arsenal	L	0-1	Ca	14		15 000

14th Att: 217 000 • Av: 21 700 • Gigante de Alberdi 28 000

BELGRANO LEAGUE APPEARANCES/GOALS 2012
Goalkeepers Juan Olave **18** • Cesar Rigamonti **1**
Defenders Pier Barrios **3+3/0** • Hernan Grana **8+2/0**
Daniel Lembo URU **9+2/0** • Claudio Perez **17/4** • Juan Quiroga **6/0**
Gaston Turus **18/0**
Midfield Guillermo Farre **16/1** • Matias Gimenez **11+6/2** • Esteban
Gonzalez **16+1/2** • Luciano Lollo **15+1/0** • Juan Maldonado **3+3/0**
Federico Mancuello **5+4/0** • Cesar Mansanelli **9+6/1** • Lucas
Parodi **5+6/1** • Lucas Pittinari **0+3/0** • Ribair Rodriguez URU **15/0**
Forwards Federico Almerares ITA **4+4/1** • Tobias Figueroa **0+1/0**
Lucas Melano **2+5/2** • Cesar Pereyra **8/1** • Marco Perez COL **6+10/0**
Andres Silvera **14/2**
Coach Ricardo Zielinski

BOCA JUNIORS
2012 CLAUSURA

	2	Santamar'a	D	1-1	ACr5		Roncaglia [63]. W 4-3p	
	10	Olimpo	W	2-0	Ca	3	Cvitanich [40], Mouche [66]	30 000
Feb	14	Zamora	D	0-0	CLg4			15 853
	19	Unión	D	0-0	Ca	5		22 000
	26	Newells OB	W	2-0	Ca	3	Cvitanich [44], Riquelme [80]	40 000
	29	C. Córdoba	W	2-0	ACr6		Blandi [41], Araujo [67]	18 000
	4	S. Lorenzo	W	2-0	Ca	1	Sanchez Mino [58], Mouche [86]	35 000
	7	Fluminense	L	1-2	CLg4		Somoza [47]	35 592
	11	Indep'iente	L	4-5	Ca	4	Roncaglia 2 [12 51], Riquelme [45], Ledesma [74]	43 000
Mar	14	Arsenal	W	2-1	CLg4		Mouche [28], Ledesma [67]	5 829
	18	San Martin	W	1-0	Ca	2	Erviti [70]	25 000
	25	Lanús	D	2-2	Ca	2	Mouche [39], Riquelme [42]	40 000
	29	Arsenal	W	2-0	CLg4		Ledesma [49], Sanchez Mino [67]	28 224
	1	Estudiantes	W	3-0	Ca	1	Silva [8], Ledesma [23], Mouche [68]	37 000
	7	Arg Juniors	W	2-1	Ca	1	Insaurralde [44], Cvitanich [65]	36 000
	11	Fluminense	W	2-0	CLg4		Cvitanich [33], Sanchez Mino [74]	36 263
Apr	15	Tigre	L	1-2	Ca	1	Insaurralde [79]	25 000
	18	Zamora	W	2-0	CLg4		Blandi [67], Riquelme [74]	31 705
	22	Belgrano	D	1-1	Ca	1	Erviti [49]	57 000
	25	Olimpo	D	1-1	ACr7		Mouche [61]. W 11-10p	17 000
	28	Colón	W	1-0	Ca	1	Silva [35]	30 000
	2	U. Española	W	2-1	CLr2		Riquelme [24], Silva [89]	32 715
	4	At. Rafaela	D	2-2	Ca	1	Mouche [30], Blandi [96+]	15 000
	9	U. Española	W	3-2	CLr2		Insaurralde [25], Mouche [49], Riquelme [67]	18 454
May	13	Vélez	D	0-0	Ca	2		40 000
	17	Fluminense	W	1-0	CLqf		Mouche [51]	45 320
	20	Racing	W	2-0	Ca	2	Viatri [69], Blandi [81]	35 000
	23	Fluminense	D	1-1	CLqf		Silva [91+]	36 276
	27	Godoy Cruz	W	3-0	Ca	1	Insaurralde [15], Cvitanich [43], Mouche [81]	40 000
	30	Rosario C	D	1-1	ACqf		Blandi [74]. W 4-2p	18 000
	3	Dep Merlo	D	1-1	ACsf		Riquelme [57]. W 5-4p	22 000
	9	Banfield	D	1-1	Ca	1	OG [50]	20 000
	14	U de Chile	W	2-0	CLsf		Silva [15], Sanchez Mino [54]	42 983
Jun	17	Arsenal	L	0-3	Ca	3		40 000
	21	U de Chile	D	0-0	CLsf			51 000
	24	All Boys	L	1-3	Ca	4	Sauro [89]	15 000
	27	Corinthians	D	1-1	CLf		Roncaglia [78]	41 901
Jly	4	Corinthians	L	0-2	CLf			37 500
Aug	4	Quilmes	L	0-3	Tl			20 000
	8	Racing	W	2-1	ACf		Silva [21], Viatri [62]	25 000

4th Att: 339 000 • Av: 37 667 • La Bombonera 49 000

BOCA LEAGUE APPEARANCES/GOALS 2012
Goalkeepers Agustin Orion **16** • Sebastian Sosa URU **3**
Defenders Alan Aguirre **1/0** • Matias Caruzzo **6+2/0**
Juan Insaurralde **15/3** • Emanuel Insua **1/0** • Clemente Rodriguez **8+1/0**
Facundo Roncaglia **11/2** • Enzo Ruiz **2+1/0** • Gaston Sauro **2/1**
Rolando Schiavi **14/0** • Franco Sosa **10+4/0**
Midfield Cristian Alvarez **0+2/0** • Ezequiel Benavidez **2/0**
Cristian Chavez **7+6/0** • Nicolas Colazo **0+1/0** • Cristian Erbes **6+2/0**
Walter Erviti **12/2** • Paul Fernandez **3+2/0** • Pablo Ledesma **9+5/2**
Jonathan Mazzola **0+1/0** • Leandro Paredes **1/0** • Juan Roman
Riquelme **12/3** • Diego Rivero **7+2/0** • Juan Sanchez Mino **11+6/1**
Leandro Somoza **11/0**
Forwards Sergio Araujo **0+4/0** • Nicolas Blandi **4+3/2** • Dario
Cvitanich **14/4** • Orlando Gaona PAR **1+1/0** • Pablo Mouche **10+7/6**
Tanque Silva URU **10/2** • Lucas Viatri **0+4/0**
Coach Julio Falcioni

COLON SANTA FE
2012 CLAUSURA

Feb| 13	Arsenal	D	0-0	Ca	9		25 000
	18	All Boys	L	0-2	Ca	16		14 000
	25	Olimpo	W	3-1	Ca	9	Higuain [15], Fabianesi [74], Fuertes [93+]	22 000
Mar| 4	Unión	D	2-2	Ca	10	Fabianesi 2 [22 32]	22 000
	9	Newells OB	L	0-3	Ca	17		21 000
	13	Sarmiento	L	0-1	ACr5			4 500
	18	S. Lorenzo	D	1-1	Ca	7	Garce [69]	27 000
	25	Indep'iente	W	3-0	Ca	9	Chevanton [42], Fabianesi [55], Mugni [60]	25 000
Apr| 1	San Martin	D	2-2	Ca	10	Chevanton [38], Gonzalez [86]	11 000
	8	Lanús	W	1-0	Ca	8	Chevanton [86]	23 000
	13	Estudiantes	D	2-2	Ca	10	Fabianesi [51], Alcoba [65]	18 000
	21	Arg Juniors	W	1-0	Ca	7	Fuertes [32]	22 000
	28	Boca Jun	L	0-1	Ca	9		30 000
May| 7	Belgrano	W	2-0	Ca	8	Alcoba [1], Fuertes [71]	20 000
	13	Tigre	D	1-1	Ca	7	Prediger [2]	25 000
	20	At. Rafaela	D	0-0	Ca	7		15 000
	28	Vélez	L	0-2	Ca	11		25 000
Jun| 11	Racing	D	1-1	Ca	8	Higuain [89]	18 000
	18	Godoy Cruz	W	2-0	Ca	7	Fuertes 2 [22 51]	32 500
	24	Banfield	W	3-0	Ca	7	Prediger [10] Fuertes 2 [28 30]	12 000

7th Att: 240 500 • Av: 24 050 • Cementerio de los Elefantes 33 458

ESTUDIANTES
2012 CLAUSURA

Feb| 4	Banfield	W	2-1	Ap	5	Boselli [58], Mercado [80]	10 000
	11	Newells OB	D	1-1	Ca	11	Boselli [35p]	25 000
	19	S. Lorenzo	D	1-1	Ca	7	Cellay [18]	30 000
	25	Indep'iente	W	2-0	Ca	4	Fernandez [21], Carrillo [79]	28 000
Mar| 3	San Martin	W	1-0	Ca	3	OG [17]	13 000
	9	Lanús	W	1-0	Ca	4	Sarulyte [65]	25 000
	13	Dep Merlo	D	0-0	ACr5		L 4-5p	3 500
	17	Tigre	D	1-1	Ca		Boselli [17]	15 000
	25	Arg Juniors	W	2-1	Ca	1	Boselli [3p], Iberia [57]	7 000
Apr| 1	Boca Jun	L	0-3	Ca	5		37 000
	8	Belgrano	L	1-2	Ca	5	Boselli [12]	18 000
	13	Colón	D	2-2	Ca	6	Fernandez [44], Boselli [92+]	18 000
	21	At. Rafaela	L	2-3	Ca	8	Boselli [45], Zapata [61]	12 500
	27	Vélez	L	0-2	Ca	12		15 000
May| 6	Racing	L	0-2	Ca	14		8 000
	11	Godoy Cruz	W	1-0	Ca	10	Desabato [45]	15 000
	19	Banfield	W	3-0	Ca	8	Sarulyte [11], Zapata [32], Fernandez [76]	8 000
	28	Arsenal	D	1-1	Ca	9	Zapata [42]	18 000
Jun| 30	All Boys	L	1-3	Ca	11	Fernandez [70p]	9 000
	16	Olimpo	W	1-0	Ca	9	Mercado [52]	40 000
	24	Unión	D	2-2	Ca	9	Fernandez [12], Zapata [61]	20 000

9th Att: 221 000 • Av: 24 556 • Unico 57 000

COLON LEAGUE APPEARANCES/GOALS 2012
Goalkeepers Marcos Diaz 2+1 • Diego Pozo 17
Defenders Gerardo Alcoba URU 14/2 • Julio Barraza 1+1/0 • Maximiliano Caire 15+1/0 • Santiago Fosgt URU 2/0 • Ariel Garce 18/1 • Gabriel Graciani 15+3/0 • Maximiliano Pellegrino 17/0 • Bruno Urribarri 9+3/0
Midfield Adran Bastia 17/0 • Tomas Costa 1+5/0 • Leandro Gracian 2+5/0 • Federico Higuain 19/2 • Federico Jourdan 0+1/0 • Ivan Moreno y Fabianesi 13+2/5 • Lucas Mugni 13+1/1 • Sebastian Prediger 13+4/2
Forwards Lucas Alario 1+5/0 • Ernesto Chevanton URU 5+3/3 • Facundo Curuchet 0+2/0 • Esteban Fuertes 13+3/7 • Leandro Gonzalez 1+6/1 • Carlos Luque 1+10/0
Coach Mario Sciaqua • Roberto Sensini (21/02/2012)

ESTUDIANTES LEAGUE APPEARANCES/GOALS 2012
Goalkeepers Mariano Andujar 18 • Agustin Silva 1
Defenders Christian Cellay 12/1 • Leandro Desabato 16/1 Raul Iberbia 17/1 • Gabriel Mercado 16/1 • Matias Sarulyte 14+3/2 Jonathan Silva 3/0 • Emmanuel Tarabini 0+1/0
Midfield Carlos Auzqui 0+1/0 • Leandro Benitez 9+3/0 Rodrigo Brana 8/0 • Facundo Coria 0+2/0 • Joaquin Correa 0+3/0 Gaston Gil Romero 0+6/0 • Mariano Gonzalez 7+6/0 Leonardo Jara 14/0 • Sergio Modon 1+5/0 • Enzo Perez 13+1/0 Matias Sanchez 12+1/0 • Juan Sebastian Veron 9/0
Forwards Mauro Boselli 14/6 • Guido Carrillo 1+12/1 Gaston Fernandez 16+1/5 • Mauro Fernandez 2+5/0 Duvan Zapata COL 6+2/4
Coach Juan Azconzabal • Martin Zuccarelli (27/04/2012)

GODOY CRUZ
2012 CLAUSURA

Feb| 12	Vélez	D	1-1	Ca	5	Castillon [25]	23 000
	16	Peñarol	W	1-0	CLg8		Villar [52]	12 153
	19	Racing	W	1-0	Ca	7	Sigali [84]	15 000
	22	U de Chile	L	1-5	CLg8		Sigali [53]	14 230
	26	Tigre	L	0-2	Ca	10		7 000
Mar| 2	Banfield	D	1-1	Ca	11	Navarro [11]	11 000
	8	At Nacional	D	4-4	CLg8		Caruso 3 [8 68 90], Ramirez [33]	5 315
	11	Arsenal	L	0-1	Ca	16		3 500
	16	All Boys	D	1-1	Ca	15	Castillon [71]	10 000
	22	At Nacional	D	2-2	CLg8		Curbelo [23], Castillon [34]	37 602
	26	Olimpo	D	1-1	Ca	17	Ramirez [79]	28 000
	31	Unión	D	1-1	Ca	15	Ramirez [41]	19 000
Apr| 4	U de Chile	L	0-1	CLg8			11 628
	8	Newells OB	D	1-1	Ca	15	Garro [51]	11 000
	14	S. Lorenzo	L	0-3	Ca	18		18 000
	19	Peñarol	L	2-4	CLg8		Sanchez [12], Sevillano [19]	24 011
	22	Indep'iente	D	0-0	Ca	17		10 000
	28	San Martin	L	0-1	Ca	18		16 000
May| 6	Lanús	L	0-1	Ca	18		2 500
	11	Estudiantes	L	0-1	Ca	18		15 000
	18	Arg Juniors	D	1-1	Ca	18	Ramirez [65]	4 500
	27	Boca Jun	L	0-3	Ca	18		40 000
Jun| 10	Belgrano	W	2-1	Ca	18	Navarro [15], Ramirez [32]	7 000
	18	Colón	L	0-2	Ca	18		32 500
	24	At. Rafaela	L	1-3	Ca	18	Ramirez [4p]	8 000

18th Att: 96 500 • Av: 9 650 • Malvinas Argentinos 45 268

GODOY CRUZ LEAGUE APPEARANCES/GOALS 2012
Goalkeepers Nelson Ibanez 18 • Sebastian Torrico 1
Defenders Marcelo Cardozo 3+1/0 • Lucas Ceballos 14+2/0 Jorge Curbelo URU 11+2/0 • Zelmar Garcia 14/0 • Claudio Ojeda 1+4/0 Sebastian Olivares 1/0 • Roberto Russo 2/0 • Nicolas Sanchez 17/0 Leonardo Sigali 17/1
Midfield Gonzalo Cabrera 5+4/0 • Armando Cooper PAN 0+6/0 Juan Carlos Falcon 5/0 • Federico Lertora 14+1/0 • Sergio Lopez 1+5/0 Nicolas Olmedo 10/0 • Ariel Rojas 16+2/0 • Sergio Sanchez 1+3/0 Adrian Torres 2+1/0 • Diego Villar 6/1
Forwards Leandro Caruso 9+5/0 • Facundo Castillon 8+8/2 Juan Garro 3+5/1 • Alvaro Navarro URU 6+4/2 • Ruben Ramirez 13/5 Jesus Vera 1+1/0
Coach Nery Pumpido • Daniel Oldra (15/04/2012) Omar Asad (24/04/2012)

INDEPENDIENTE
2012 CLAUSURA

Feb	12	San Martin	L	0-1	Ca	17	25 000
Feb	19	Lanús	L	0-1	Ca	19	25 000
Feb	25	Estudiantes	L	0-2	Ca	20	28 000
Mar	3	Arg Juniors	L	1-3	Ca	20	Battion [63]	20 000
Mar	8	Belgrano	L	0-2	ACr5		3 000
Mar	11	Boca Jun	W	5-4	Ca	20	Vidal [1], Ferreyra [6], Farias 3 [32 88 93+]	43 000
Mar	17	Belgrano	W	2-0	Ca	16	Farias [75], Monserrat [86]	25 000
Mar	25	Colón	L	0-3	Ca	19	25 000
Mar	31	At. Rafaela	W	2-0	Ca	13	Parra [56], Monserrat [79]	25 000
Apr	7	Vélez	D	1-1	Ca	13	Parra [4]	25 000
Apr	14	Racing	W	4-1	Ca	11	Parra 2 [36 58p], Vidal [92+], Rodriguez [94+]	35 000
Apr	22	Godoy Cruz	D	0-0	Ca	11		10 000
Apr	29	Banfield	L	0-2	Ca	8	Ferreyra [70], Farias [80]	16 000
May	5	Arsenal	L	1-3	Ca	10	Parra [68]	11 000
May	12	All Boys	L	0-3	Ca	14		24 000
May	20	Olimpo	L	1-2	Ca	15	Farias [20]	7 000
May	27	Unión	D	0-0	Ca	15		22 000
Jun	9	Newells OB	L	1-2	Ca	17	Farias [35]	36 000
Jun	17	S. Lorenzo	D	0-0	Ca	16		20 000
Jun	24	Tigre	D	2-2	Ca	16	Rodriguez 2 [50 55]	25 000

16th Att: 212 000 • Av: 23 556 • Libertadores de América 46 000

INDEPENDIENTE LEAGUE APPEARANCES/GOALS 2012
Goalkeepers Adrian Gabbarini 10 • Hilario Navarro 6+1
Diego Rodriguez 3
Defenders Adrian Argacha URU 7/0 • Leonel Galeano 10+2/0
Lucas Kruspzky 3/0 • Carlos Matheu 1/0 • Gabriel Militi 13/0
Eduardo Tuzzio 16/0 • Gabriel Valles 4+6/0 • Julian Velazquez 15/0
Midfield Roberto Battion 4+1/1 • Walter Busse 4+1/0
Nicolas Delmonte 0+1/0 • Osmar Ferreyra 15+1/2
Hernan Fredes 11+2/0 • Fernando Godoy 13+3/0
Fabian Monserrat 14+1/2 • Cristian Pellerano 4+5/0
Ivan Perez 1+4/0 • Patricio Rodriguez 14+3/3
Forwards Martin Benitez 2+3/0 • Diego Churin 0+1/0
Matias Defederico 2+1/0 • Ernesto Farias 16/7 • Leonel Nunez 1+1/0
Facundo Parra 6+9/5 • Francisco Pizzini 1+2/0 • Patricio Vidal 4+6/0
Lucas Villafanez 9+2/0
Coach Ramon Diaz • Christian Diaz (5/03/2012)

LANUS
2012 CLAUSURA

Feb	7	Barracas C	D	0-0	ACr5	L 7-8p	
Feb	10	S. Lorenzo	W	4-1	Ca	1	Braghieri [9], Fritzler [15], Pavone 2 [24 50]	15 000
Feb	15	Flamengo	D	1-1	CLg2	Carranza [74]	12 153
Feb	19	Indep'iente	W	1-0	Ca	1	Pavone [87]	25 000
Feb	23	Olimpia	L	1-2	CLg2	Araujo [71]	6 625
Feb	27	San Martin	L	1-3	Ca	5	Carranza [92+]	4 000
Mar	4	Tigre	L	0-1	Ca	7		20 000
Mar	9	Estudiantes	L	0-1	Ca	11		25 000
Mar	13	Emelec	W	1-0	CLg2	Pavone [71]	3 872
Mar	16	Arg Juniors	L	0-1	Ca	14		8 000
Mar	20	Emelec	W	2-0	CLg2	Regueiro 2 [5 87p]	12 874
Mar	25	Boca Jun	D	2-2	Ca	15	Pavone [43], Goltz [55]	40 000
Mar	30	Belgrano	L	0-1	Ca	18		9 000
Apr	3	Olimpia	W	6-0	CLg2	Pavone 2 [13 54], Camoranesi [29], Regueiro [70], Valeri [77], Romero [84]	12 141
Apr	7	Colón	L	0-1	Ca	19		23 000
Apr	12	Flamengo	L	0-3	CLg2		15 932
Apr	16	At. Rafaela	W	1-0	Ca	14	Regueiro [36p]	4 000
Apr	21	Vélez	D	0-0	Ca	16		17 000
Apr	27	Racing	W	3-1	Ca	14	Izquierdoz [16], Pavone [36], Romero [64]	16 000
May	2	Vasco	L	1-2	CLr2	Regueiro [62]	13 017
May	6	Godoy Cruz	W	1-0	Ca	9	Carranza [7]	2 500
May	9	Vasco	W	2-1	CLr2	Pavone [60], Gutierrez [78]	6 408
May	13	Banfield	W	2-1	Ca	8	Braghieri [7], Pavone [13]	30 000
May	21	Arsenal	L	1-3	Ca	12	Regueiro [37p]	8 000
May	26	All Boys	W	1-0	Ca	8	Pavone [52]	9 000
Jun	10	Olimpo	D	2-2	Ca	7	Regueiro 2 [3p 38]	500
Jun	15	Unión	D	0-0	Ca	10		800
Jun	22	Newells OB	D	0-0	Ca	10		28 000

10th Att: 95 800 • Av: 10 644 • La Fortaleza 46 519

LANUS LEAGUE APPEARANCES/GOALS 2012
Goalkeepers Mauricio Caranta 1 • Agustin Marchesin 18
Defenders Carlos Araujo 10/0 • Luciano Balbi 5+2/0
Diego Braghieri 9/2 • Gaston Diaz 10+1/0 • Paolo Goltz 15/1
Carlos Izquierdoz 10+1/1 • Carlos Quintana 4/0 • Matias Valdez 1/0
Maximiliano Velazquez 13/0
Midfield Oscar Benitez 0+2/0 • Mauro Camoranesi ITA 5+2/0
Cesar Carranza 4+6/2 • Matias Fritzler 15/1 • Diego Gonzalez 7+1/0
Juan Jaime 1/0 • Eduardo Ledesma PAR 12+6/0 • Juan Neira 6+2/0
Mauricio Pereyra URU 8+3/0 • Guido Pizarro 11+3/0
Mario Regueiro URU 9+4/4 • Diego Valeri 10+4/0
Forwards Mariano Pavone 12+4/7 • Silvio Romero 12+6/1
Bruno Vides 1+4/0
Coach Gabriel Schurrer • Guillermo & Gustavo Barros Schelotto (20/06/12)

NEWELL'S OLD BOYS
2012 CLAUSURA

Feb	11	Estudiantes	D	1-1	Ca	5	Urruti [49]	25 000
Feb	18	Arg Juniors	W	1-0	Ca	7	Urruti [66]	34 000
Feb	26	Boca Jun	L	0-2	Ca	10		40 000
Mar	2	Belgrano	L	0-2	Ca	14		34 000
Mar	9	Colón	W	3-0	Ca	7	Perez.P [45], Tonso [87], Urruti [94+]	21 000
Mar	18	At. Rafaela	W	1-0	Ca	5	Sperdutti [24]	36 000
Mar	26	Vélez	W	1-0	Ca	4	Pellerano [90]	12 000
Apr	1	Racing	W	2-0	Ca	2	Urruti [60], Perez.P [69]	34 000
Apr	8	Godoy Cruz	D	1-1	Ca	3	Urruti [89]	11 000
Apr	15	Banfield	W	3-0	Ca	2	Vergini [69], Munoz [87], Aquino [91+]	36 000
Apr	23	Arsenal	D	1-1	Ca	5	Figueroa [54]	8 000
Apr	28	All Boys	D	1-1	Ca	3	Tonso [91+]	33 000
May	6	Olimpo	W	2-1	Ca	2	Figueroa [18], Perez.P [74]	10 000
May	12	Unión	W	3-1	Ca	1	Figueroa [5], Vergini [38], Urruti [42]	38 000
May	18	Tigre	L	1-3	Ca	4	Figueroa [19]	15 000
May	27	S. Lorenzo	L	2-3	Ca	4	Perez.P [14], Munoz [30]	35 000
Jun	3	Indep'iente	W	2-1	Ca	4	Perez.P [45], Aquino [82]	36 000
Jun	15	San Martin	L	1-2	Ca	4	Perez.P [32]	18 000
Jun	22	Lanús	D	0-0	Ca	6		28 000

6th Att: 309 000 • Av: 34 333 • El Coloso del Parque 38 095

NEWELL'S LEAGUE APPEARANCES/GOALS 2012
Goalkeepers Sebastian Peratta 19
Defenders Cristian Diaz 4+2/0 • Juan Dominguez COL 7+2/0
Victor Lopez 13/0 • Guillermo Ortiz 6+3/0 • Hernan Pellerano 17/1
Santiago Vergini 17/2
Midfield Lucas Bernardi 19/0 • Victor Figueroa 16/4
Diego Mateo 5+1/0 • Fabian Munoz 4+4/2 • Marcos Perez 0+1/0
Pablo Perez 16/6 • Mauricio Sperdutti 13+2/1 • Martin Tonso 2+15/2
Leandro Torres 4+7/0 • Leonel Vangioni 13+2/0 • Raul Villalba 14+2/0
Forwards Victor Aquino PAR 0+14/2 • Ricardo Noir 1+1/0
Maximiliano Urruti 19/6 • Maximiliano Velasco 0+1/0
Coach Gerardo Martino

OLIMPO
2012 CLAUSURA

Feb	11	Boca Jun	L	0-2	Ca	18		30 000
Feb	17	Belgrano	W	4-1	Ca	9	Perozo [19], Franzoia 2 [59][71], Bareiro [90]	12 000
Mar	25	Colón	L	1-3	Ca	14	Franzoia [18]	22 000
Mar	6	At. Rafaela	W	2-1	Ca	8	Franzoia [19], Rolle [95p]	12 000
Mar	13	Vélez	L	0-1	Ca	13		12 000
Mar	17	Racing	L	0-3	Ca	18		14 000
Mar	23	Excur'istas	D	1-1	ACr5		Pavlovich [22], W 5-4p	2 000
Mar	26	Godoy Cruz	D	1-1	Ca	18	Rolle [72]	28 000
Mar	31	Banfield	L	2-5	Ca	20	Franzoia [4], Perez Guedes [76]	8 000
Apr	6	Arsenal	L	1-2	Ca	20	Perez Guedes [70]	2 500
Apr	14	All Boys	L	1-2	Ca	20	Bareiro [21]	6 500
Apr	21	Tigre	L	0-1	Ca	20		18 000
Apr	26	Boca Jun	D	1-1	ACr6		Rolle [70p], L 10-11p	17 000
Apr	29	Unión	L	0-2	Ca	20		18 000
May	6	Newells OB	L	1-2	Ca	20	Laso [15]	10 000
May	13	S. Lorenzo	D	1-1	Ca	20	Bareiro [72]	21 000
May	20	Indep'iente	W	2-1	Ca	19	Bareiro 2 [7][69]	7 000
May	6	San Martin	L	2-3	Ca	19	Perez Guedes 2 [9][52]	12 000
May	10	Lanús	D	2-2	Ca	19	Franzoia [51], Perez Guedes [76]	55 000
Jun	16	Estudiantes	L	0-1	Ca	19		40 000
Jun	22	Arg Juniors	D	0-0	Ca	19		3 000

19th Att: 73 000 • Av: 8 111 • Roberto Carminatti 20 000

OLIMPO LEAGUE APPEARANCES/GOALS 2012
Goalkeepers Matias Ibanez 19
Defenders Eduardo Casais 14/0 • Gabriel Diaz 7+1/0
Emir Faccioli 6+1/0 • Matias Lopez 1/0 • Federico Mancinelli 14+1/0
Ezequiel Parnisari 8/0 • Grenddy Perozo VEN 7/1 • Walter Sanchez 1/0
Juan Tejera URU 2/0 • Eric Veron 0+1/0 • Cristian Villanueva 12/0
Midfield Leandro Filippini 0+1/0 • Andres Franzoia 16/6
Maximiliano Laso 5+6/1 • Juan Mauri 0+1/0 • Damian Musto 16/0
Martin Perez Guedes 14+2/5 • Martin Rolle 18/2 • Emiliano Romero 4/0
Javier Rosada 17/0 • Juan Schefer 4+5/0 • David Vega 5+4/0
Forwards Nestor Bareiro PAR 12+2/5 • Julio Furch 7+5/0
Marcos Litre 0+10/0 • Nicolas Pavlovich 0+6/0
Coach Hector Rivoira • Walter Perazzo (4/04/2012)

RACING CLUB
2012 CLAUSURA

Feb	12	Tigre	D	0-0	Ca	9		35 000
Feb	19	Godoy Cruz	L	0-1	Ca	14		15 000
Feb	26	Banfield	L	1-2	Ca	18	Gutierrez [3p]	30 000
Mar	4	Arsenal	D	0-0	Ca	19		10 000
Mar	10	All Boys	W	3-0	Ca	14	Castro 3 [18][35][79]	25 000
Mar	17	Olimpo	W	3-0	Ca	8	OG [60], Hauche [70], Castro [75]	14 000
Mar	21	Patronato	W	3-1	ACr6	Farina 2 [11][57], Licht [86]	5 500
Mar	24	Unión	L	0-3	Ca	10		25 000
Apr	1	Newells OB	L	0-2	Ca	14		34 000
Apr	9	S. Lorenzo	D	1-1	Ca	4	Martinez [32]	30 000
Apr	16	Indep'iente	L	1-4	Ca	16	Gutierrez [26]	35 000
Apr	18	Sarmiento	W	2-0	ACr7	Moreno [22p], Castro [62]	22 000
Apr	21	San Martin	W	1-0	Ca	15	Caballero [83]	19 000
Apr	27	Lanús	L	1-3	Ca	17	Viola [84]	16 000
May	6	Estudiantes	W	2-0	Ca	16	Aveldano [37]	8 000
May	9	At Tucumán	W	1-0	ACqf	OG [89]	24 000
May	13	Arg Juniors	L	1-2	Ca	16	Viola [14]	18 000
May	20	Boca Jun	L	0-2	Ca	16		35 000
May	27	Belgrano	W	1-0	Ca	16	Moreno [60]	25 000
Jun	3	River Plate	D	0-0	ACsf	W 5-4p	28 000
Jun	12	Colón	D	1-1	Ca	14	Viola [11]	18 000
Jun	17	At. Rafaela	L	2-4	Ca	17	Zuculini [45], Castro [56]	14 000
Jun	24	Vélez	L	1-2	Ca	17	Pillud [81]	18 000
Aug	4	At. Rafaela	D	1-1	TI		Ortiz [12]	28 000
Aug	8	Boca Jun	L	1-2	ACf		Viola [68]	25 000

17th Att: 243 000 • Av: 24 300 • El Cilindro 51 389

RACING LEAGUE APPEARANCES/GOALS 2012
Goalkeepers Sebastian Saja 19
Defenders Lucas Aveldano 12/1 • Marcos Caceres PAR 12+2/0
Matias Cahais 14+1/0 • Lucas Licht 6/0 • Braian Lluy 2+3/0
Matias Martinez 14+1/1 • Ivan Pillud 17/1 • Nicolas Sainz 1/0
Esteban Saveljich 1/0
Midfield Luciano Aued 5+2/0 • Lucas Castro 15+1/5
Ricardo Centurion 2/0 • Luis Farina 2+5/0
Giovanni Moreno COL 14+2/2 • Agustin Pelletieri 16/0
Patricio Toranzo 5+5/0 • Luciano Vietto 0+1/0
Claudio Yacob 2+3/0 • Bruno Zuculini 12+3/1
Forwards Pablo Caballero 4+1/1 • Teofilo Gutierrez COL 9/2
Gabriel Hauche 12+2/1 • Federico Santander PAR 5+10/0
Valentin Viola 8+11/3
Coach Alfio Basile • Luis Zubeldia (15/04/2012)

ARG – ARGENTINA

SAN LORENZO
2012 CLAUSURA

Feb	10	Lanús	L	1-4	Ca	19	Bueno [59]	15 000
	19	Estudiantes	D	1-1	Ca	17	Ortigoza [55p]	30 000
	25	Arg Juniors	W	1-0	Ca	12	Benitez [49]	BCD
Mar	4	Boca Jun	L	0-2	Ca	15		35 000
	10	Belgrano	W	2-1	Ca	9	Alvarado [63], Ortigoza [68p]	20 000
	14	Chacarita J	D	1-1	ACr6		Chavez [68]. W 3-1p	1 000
	18	Colón	D	1-1	Ca	10	OG [45]	27 000
	24	At. Rafaela	L	1-2	Ca	14	Bueno [6]	15 000
Apr	1	Vélez	L	0-2	Ca	18		BCD
	9	Racing	D	1-1	Ca	18	Gigliotti [41]	30 000
	14	Godoy Cruz	W	3-0	Ca	13	Gigliotti 2 [8 30], Chavez [82]	18 000
	22	Banfield	D	1-1	Ca	13	Bueno [62]	18 000
	29	Arsenal	W	2-0	Ca	11	Salgueiro [31], Gigliotti [78]	21 000
May	2	Barracas C	D	1-1	ACr7		Romeo [38]. W 5-4p	5 000
	6	All Boys	D	0-0	Ca	11		18 000
	12	Olimpo	D	1-1	Ca	12	Gigliotti [90]	21 000
	16	River Plate	L	0-2	ACqf			25 000
	19	Unión	L	0-1	Ca	13		20 000
	27	Newells OB	W	3-2	Ca	12	Gigliotti 2 [50 87], Bueno [54]	35 000
Jun	10	Tigre	L	1-3	Ca	12	Romagnoli [62]	20 000
	17	Indep'iente	D	0-0	Ca	13		20 000
	24	San Martin	W	3-1	Ca	12	Bueno 2 [28 81], Kannemann [55]	35 000
	28	Instituto	W	2-0	Capo		Bueno 2 [47 61]	23 000
Jy	1	Instituto	D	1-1	Capo		Ortigoza [78p]	42 000

12th — Att: 222 000 • Av: 24 667 • Nuevo Gasómetro 43 494

SAN LORENZO LEAGUE APPEARANCES/GOALS 2012
Goalkeepers Nereo Champagne 7 • Pablo Migliore 12
Defenders Nicolas Bianchi Arce 10+2/0 • Jonathan Bottinelli 13/0
Walter Kannemann 4/1 • Sebastian Luna 1/0 • Adrian Martinez 6/0
Damian Martinez 1+2/0 • Fernando Meza 12+3/0
Jose Palomino 11+2/0 • German Voboril 5+3/0
Pablo Alvarado 17/1 • Gonzalo Bazan 9+4/0
Julio Buffarini 11+1/0 • Enzo Kalinski 14/0 • Gabriel Mendez 1+7/0
Nestor Ortigoza 17/2 • Jonathan Pacheco 1/0
Leandro Romagnoli 11+6/1 • Emiliano Tellechea URU 2+1/0
Forwards Nahuel Benitez 2+3/1 • Carlos Bueno URU 10+5/6
Cristian Chavez 3+8/1 • Emanuel Gigliotti 12+3/7
Diego Martinez 0+1/0 • Bernardo Romeo 0+3/0
Juan Salgueiro URU 17+1/1
Coach Leonardo Madelon • Ricardo Caruso Lombardi (3/04/2012)

SAN MARTIN SAN JUAN
2012 CLAUSURA

Feb	11	Indep'iente	W	1-0	Ca	4	Caprari [61]	25 000
	20	Tigre	L	1-3	Ca	10	Caprari [95+p]	16 000
	27	Lanús	W	3-1	Ca	6	Caprari 2 [33 76], Penco [72]	4 000
Mar	3	Estudiantes	L	0-1	Ca	9		13 000
	10	Arg Juniors	D	1-1	Ca	6	Caprari [66]	4 000
	18	Boca Jun	L	0-1	Ca	11		25 000
	24	Belgrano	D	1-1	Ca	12	Alvarez [88p]	15 000
	1	Colón	D	2-2	Ca	12	Carrusca [35], Roberval [87]	11 000
Apr	7	At. Rafaela	L	1-3	Ca	16	Bogado [21]	12 000
	14	Vélez	L	1-3	Ca	17	Affranchino [43]	10 000
	21	Racing	L	0-1	Ca	19		19 000
	28	Godoy Cruz	W	1-0	Ca	16	Carrusca [17]	16 000
May	4	Banfield	W	2-1	Ca	16	Garcia 2 [5 43]	4 500
	11	Arsenal	L	1-4	Ca	17	Penco [54]	BCD
	19	All Boys	L	0-1	Ca	17		8 000
	25	Olimpo	W	3-2	Ca	17	Penco [73], Caprari [82], Alvarez [92+p]	12 000
Jun	9	Unión	D	0-0	Ca	15		19 000
	15	Newells OB	W	2-1	Ca	14	Garcia [2], Caprari [27]	18 000
	24	S. Lorenzo	L	1-3	Ca	15	Caprari [27]	35 000
	28	Rosario C	D	0-0	PDpo			39 000
Jy	1	Rosario C	D	0-0	PDpo			20 000

15th — Att: 130 000 • Av: 14 444 • Ingeniero Hilario Sanchez 19 000

SAN MARTIN LEAGUE APPEARANCES/GOALS 2012
Goalkeepers Luis Ardente 1 • Leonardo Corti 2 • Luciano Pocrnjic 16
Defenders Cristian Alvarez 12+1/2 • Marcos Galarza 6+1/0
Cristian Grabinski 16+1/0 • Lucas Landa 18/0 • Juan Mattia 1+1/0
Raul Saavedra 8+1/0 • Diego Sosa 6+1/0 • Ruben Zamponi 0+1/0
Midfield Facundo Affranchino 7+10/1 • Mauro Bogado 18/1
Maximiliano Bustos 9+1/0 • Pablo Cantero 4+1/0
Damian Canuto 3+1/0 • Marcelo Carrusca 10+8/2
Emanuel Mas 11+2/0 • Maximiliano Nunez 5+3/0
Federico Poggi 9+1/0 • Jonathan Tejada 0+2/0 • Martin Wagner 10+1/0
Forwards Gaston Caprari 14+4/8 • Diego Garcia 7+6/3
Claudio Graf 1+5/0 • Sebastian Penco 15+2/3 • Roberval BRA 0+3/1
Coach Daniel Garnero • Facundo Sava (23/04/2012)

TIGRE
2012 CLAUSURA

Feb	12	Racing	D	0-0	Ca	9		35 000
	21	San Martin	W	3-1	Ca	4	Castano [2], Luna [69], Escobar [77]	16 000
	26	Godoy Cruz	W	2-0	Ca	2	Luna [14], Diaz [86]	7 000
Mar	4	Lanús	W	1-0	Ca	2	Morales [3p]	20 000
	11	Banfield	W	2-0	Ca	1	Maggiolo [84], Luna [90]	14 000
	17	Estudiantes	D	1-1	Ca	1	Morales [27p]	15 000
	21	Gimn'sia LP	D	1-1	ACr5		Escobar [84]. W 4-1p	5 000
	25	Arsenal	L	0-2	Ca	3		12 000
Apr	1	Arg Juniors	L	1-2	Ca	6	Luna [78]	17 000
	7	All Boys	L	0-2	Ca	6		8 000
	11	Arg Juniors	W	1-0	ACr6		Lema [27p]	2 000
	16	Boca Jun	W	2-1	Ca	6	Morales [26], OG [88]	25 000
	21	Olimpo	W	1-0	Ca	4	Galmarini [39]	18 000
	30	Belgrano	D	1-1	Ca	2	Maggiolo [21]	11 000
May	6	Unión	W	4-0	Ca	2	Maggiolo 2 [16 51], Luna 2 [28 44]	10 000
	13	Colón	D	1-1	Ca	3	Luna [13]	25 000
	18	Newells OB	W	3-1	Ca	2	Luna 3 [16 39 82]	15 000
	23	Dep Merlo	L	1-2	ACr7		Martinez [50]	
	27	At. Rafaela	D	1-1	Ca	2	Echeverria [67]	13 000
Jun	10	S. Lorenzo	W	3-1	Ca	2	Maggiolo [35], Martinez 2 [54 84]	20 000
	17	Vélez	W	1-0	Ca	2	Luna [7]	15 000
	24	Indep'iente	D	2-2	Ca	2	Luna [21], Morales [80p]	25 000

2nd — Att: 181 000 • Av: 18 100 • Monumental de Victoria 26 282

TIGRE LEAGUE APPEARANCES/GOALS 2011
Goalkeepers Javier Garcia 18 • Daniel Islas 1
Defenders Juan Blengio 2+1/0 • Carlos Castegliore 5+5/0
Mariano Echeverria 15/1 • Christian Lema 6+1/0 • Lucas Orban 17/0
Norberto Paparatto 12/0
Midfield Ruben Botta 1+2/0 • Javier Carrasco 0+9/0
Diego Castano 17/1 • Gaston Diaz 4+8/0 • Matias Escobar 2+10/1
Martin Galmarini 18/1 • Ramiro Leone 15/0 • Roman Martinez 18/2
Diego Morales 19/4 • Emmanuel Pio 5+2/0
Forwards Leandro Diaz 5+4/1 • Diego Ftacla 1+4/0
Carlos Luna 18/12 • Ezequiel Maggiolo 10+5/5
Coach Rodolfo Arruabarrena

UNION SANTA FE
2012 CLAUSURA

Feb	12	Arg Juniors	D	0-0	Ca	9	4 000
	19	Boca Jun	D	0-0	Ca	13	22 000
	24	Belgrano	L	0-1	Ca	17	18 000
Mar	4	Colón	D	2-2	Ca	18	Jara [63], Correa [68]	22 000
	11	At. Rafaela	W	2-0	Ca	10	Jara [40], Magnin [56]	15 000
	17	Vélez	D	3-3	Ca	13	Erramuspe 2 [18 64], Magnin [79]	20 000
	24	Racing	W	3-0	Ca	7	OG [1], Velazquez [18], Jara [48]	25 000
	31	Godoy Cruz	D	1-1	Ca	7	Velazquez [35]	19 000
Apr	7	Banfield	D	2-2	Ca	10	Barisone [72], Jara [92+p]	8 000
	15	Arsenal	W	1-0	Ca	8	Cavallero [51]	19 000
	22	All Boys	L	1-2	Ca	10	Erramuspe [34]	8 000
	29	Olimpo	W	2-0	Ca	7	Velasquez [71], Donnet [83]	18 000
May	5	Tigre	L	0-4	Ca	8		10 000
	12	Newells OB	L	1-3	Ca	11	Donnet [58]	38 000
	19	S. Lorenzo	W	1-0	Ca	9	Barisone [88]	20 000
	27	Indep'iente	D	0-0	Ca	10		22 000
Jun	9	San Martín	D	0-0	Ca	8		19 000
	15	Lanús	D	0-0	Ca	11		800
	24	Estudiantes	D	2-2	Ca	11	Montero [14], Erramuspe [50]	20 000

11th Att: 179 000 • Av: 19 889 • Estadio 15 de Abril 22 852

UNION LEAGUE APPEARANCES/GOALS 2012
Goalkeepers Enrique Bologna 15 • Oscar Limia 4
Defenders Juan Avendano 16/0 • Diego Barisone 1+1/2
Juan Pablo Cardenas 12/0 • Nicolas Correa URU 18/1
Rodrigo Erramuspe 17/4 • Mauro Maidana 5+2/0 • Renzo Vera 5/0
Midfield Pablo Bruna 0+1/0 • Juan Cavallero 4+3/1
Matias Donnet 18/2 • Alexis Fernandez 3+9/0
Pablo Miguez URU 16+1/0 • Fausto Montero 10+1/1
Emanuel Moreno 0+1/0 • Alejandro Perez 2+5/0 • Paulo Rosales 17/0
Matias Soto Torres 0+1/0 • Jorge Velazquez 18+1/3
Sebastian Vidal 6/0
Forwards Jeronimo Barrales 8+6/0 • Diego Jara 12+5/4
Pablo Magnin 2+11/2 • Fabricio Nunez URU 0+3/0 • Juan Pereyra 0+2/0
Coach Frank Kudelka

VELEZ SARSFIELD
2012 CLAUSURA

Feb	7	Defensor	W	3-0	CLg7		Ramirez [41], Obolo [81], Dominguez [85]	6 812
	12	Godoy Cruz	D	1-1	Ca	5	Obolo [15]	23 000
	17	Banfield	W	4-0	Ca	2	Insua [32], Dominguez [41], Obolo [48], Bella [86]	15 000
	22	Guadalajara	W	3-0	CLg7		Obolo 67, Insua 2 [81 82]	8 661
	26	Arsenal	W	3-2	Ca	1	Fernandez 2 [33 61], Martinez.J [36p]	18 000
	29	R Trelew	W	2-0	ACr5		Bella [9], Canteros [29]	
Mar	3	All Boys	D	0-0	Ca	3		17 000
	7	Dep Quito	L	0-3	CLg7			9 849
	12	Olimpo	W	1-0	Ca	2	Bella [62]	12 000
	17	Unión	D	3-3	Ca	3	Martinez.J [22p], Bella [33], Insua [53]	20 000
	22	Dep Quito	W	1-0	CLg7		Martinez.J [89]	7 300
	26	Newells OB	L	0-1	Ca	5		12 000
	29	Rosario C	D	1-1	ACr6		Pratto [2], L 4-5p	2 500
Apr	1	S. Lorenzo	W	2-0	Ca	3	Cabral [7], Bella [83]	BCD
	6	Indep'iente	D	1-1	Ca	4	Pratto [22]	25 000
	11	Guadalajara	W	2-0	CLg7		Fernandez.A [69], Pratto [89]	16 730
	14	San Martin	W	3-1	Ca	3	OG [31], Velazquez [79], Pratto [84]	10 000
	17	Defensor	L	1-3	CLg7		Insua [63p]	8 000
	21	Lanús	D	0-0	Ca	3		17 000
	27	Estudiantes	W	2-0	Ca	2	Insua 22, Martinez.J [34]	15 000
May	1	At Nacional	W	1-0	CLr2		Bella [8]	33 242
	5	Arg Juniors	L	0-2	Ca	4		19 000
	8	At Nacional	D	1-1	CLr2		Fernandez [52]	10 731
	13	Boca Jun	D	0-0	Ca	5		40 000
	17	Santos	W	1-0	CLqf		Obolo [35]	21 847
	20	Belgrano	L	0-1	Ca	6		19 000
	24	Santos	L	0-1	CLqf		L 2-4p	13 908
	28	Colón	W	2-0	Ca	5	Martinez.J [52], Fernandez [89]	25 000
Jun	9	At. Rafaela	W	2-1	Ca	5	Martinez.J [53], Obolo [58]	8 000
	16	Tigre	L	0-1	Ca	5		20 000
	23	Racing	W	2-1	Ca	3	Insua [37], Fernandez [86]	18 000

3rd Att: 173 000 • Av: 17 300 • José Amalfitani 49 540

VELEZ LEAGUE APPEARANCES/GOALS 2012
Goalkeepers Marcelo Barovero 18 • German Montoya 1
Defenders Mariano Bittolo 2/0 • Sebastian Dominguez 17/1
Lautaro Gianetti 2/0 • David Lencina 1/0 • Fernando Ortiz 16/0
Gino Peruzzi 4+4/0 • Fernando Tobio 5+1/0
Midfield Agustin Allione 0+2/0 • Ivan Bella 6+5/4
Alejandro Cabral 8+7/1 • Hector Canteros 6+5/0 • Francisco Cerro 12/0
Fabian Cubero 13/0 • Leandro Desabato 3+2/0
Augusto Fernandez 12/4 • Brian Ferreira 0+1/0 • Federico Freire 0+3/0
Federico Insua 10+4/4 • Emiliano Papa 17/0 • David Ramirez 5+5/0
Leandro Velazquez 1+4/1 • Victor Zapata 13/0
Forwards Martin Blanco 1/0 • Juan Martinez 13+2/5 • Ivan Obolo 18/3
Lucas Pratto 4+8/2 • Eduardo Pucheta 0+1/0
Jonathan Ramirez URU 1+2/0
Coach Ricardo Gareca

ARM – ARMENIA

FIFA/COCA-COLA WORLD RANKING

'93	'94	'95	'96	'97	'98	'99	'00	'01	'02	'03	'04	'05	'06	'07	'08	'09	'10	'11	'12
-	141	113	106	105	100	85	90	95	107	113	119	108	123	93	113	100	60	46	75

2012

Jan	Feb	Mar	Apr	May	Jun	Jul	Aug	Sep	Oct	Nov	Dec	High	Low	Av
45	41	44	47	51	47	55	56	53	64	82	75	41	159	100

With the change in the timing of the Armenian league season to an Autumn/Spring schedule in order to be in line with much of the rest of Europe, Armenian fans were treated to an extra-long season played over 15 months. That meant the only trophy on offer during the course of 2012 was the Armenian Cup. In the event it produced a major surprise with Shirak finally getting their hands on the trophy after their four previous appearances in the final had all ended in defeat. They beat holders Mika in the semi-final to set up a tie with first-time finalists Impuls in a match played in their home stadium in Gyumri. A first-half goal from Senegalese midfielder Yoro Lamine Ly saw Shirak claim the trophy, much to the delight of their supporters who had packed into their small stadium to watch the game. The national team had a positive start to their 2014 FIFA World Cup qualifying campaign with a win away in Malta but with Italy, Denmark and the Czech Republic in their group - all three of whom qualified for the finals of Euro 2012 - the campaign was never going to be easy despite their rapidly improving form in recent years. A defeat at the hands of Bulgaria in Sofia in the second match was followed by a 3-1 defeat at home to Italy as hopes of making a strong impression in the group quickly faded.

UEFA EUROPEAN CHAMPIONSHIP RECORD
1960-1992 DNE (Played as part of the Soviet Union)   **1996-2012** DNQ

FOOTBALL FEDERATION OF ARMENIA (FFA)

Khanjyan Street 27, Yerevan 0010

☎ +374 10 568883
📠 +374 10 547173
✉ ffarm@arminco.com
🖥 www.ffa.am

FA 1992 CON 1993 FIFA 1992
P Ruben Hayrapetyan
GS Armen Minasyan

THE STADIA

2014 FIFA World Cup Stadia

Hrazdan Yerevan	53 849

Other Main Stadia

Hanrapetakan 'Republican' Yerevan	14 968
Mika Yerevan	7 000
Lori Vanadzor	5 000
Banants Yerevan	3 600

MAJOR CITIES/TOWNS

		Population
1	Yerevan	1 201 322
2	Gyumri	172 053
3	Vanadzor	119 739
4	Vagharshapat	52 567
5	Hrazdan	41 557
6	Abovyan	36 021
7	Ararat	35 093
8	Kapan	34 857
9	Armavir	25 777
10	Gavar	22 143
11	Goris	21 932
12	Masis	20 609
13	Artashat	20 544
14	Ashtarak	20 465
15	Stepanavan	20 143
16	Spitak	18 885
17	Charentsavan	17 287
18	Sevan	17 042
19	Sisian	16 976

HAYASTANI HANRAPETUT'YUN • REPUBLIC OF ARMENIA

Capital	Yerevan	Population	2 967 004 (137)	% in cities	64%
GDP per capita	$6300 (128)	Area km²	29 743 km² (142)	GMT +/-	+4
Neighbours (km)	Azerbaijan 787, Georgia 164, Iran 35, Turkey 268		

RECENT INTERNATIONALS PLAYED BY ARMENIA

2008	Opponents		Score	Venue	Comp	Scorers	Att	Referee
6-09	Turkey	L	0-2	Yerevan	WCq		30 000	Ovrebo NOR
10-09	Spain	L	0-4	Albacete	WCq		16 996	Asumaa FIN
11-10	Belgium	L	0-2	Brussels	WCq		20 949	Rasmussen DEN
15-10	Bosnia-Herzegovina	L	1-4	Zenica	WCq	Minasyan [85]	13 000	Kenan ISR
2009								
11-02	Latvia	D	0-0	Limassol	Fr		150	
28-03	Estonia	D	2-2	Yerevan	WCq	Mkhitaryan [33], Ghazaryan [87]	3 000	Wilmes LUX
1-04	Estonia	L	0-1	Tallinn	WCq		5 200	Zimmermann SUI
12-08	Moldova	L	1-4	Yerevan	Fr	Arakelyan [75]	1 000	Silagava GEO
5-09	Bosnia-Herzegovina	L	0-2	Yerevan	WCq		1 800	Braamhaar NED
9-09	Belgium	W	2-1	Yerevan	WCq	Goharyan [23], Hovsepyan [50]	2 300	Stavrev MKD
10-10	Spain	L	1-2	Yerevan	WCq	Arzumanyan [58]	10 500	Jech CZE
14-10	Turkey	L	0-2	Bursa	WCq		16 200	Hansson SWE
2010								
3-03	Belarus	L	1-3	Antalya	Fr	Pachajyan [59]	BCD	
25-05	Uzbekistan	W	3-1	Yerevan	Fr	Mkhitaryan [7], Manucharyan 2 [18p 27]	20 000	Kvaratskhelia GEO
11-08	Iran	L	1-3	Yerevan	Fr	Mkrtchyan [37]	3 000	Kvaratskhelia GEO
3-09	Republic of Ireland	L	0-1	Yerevan	ECq		8 600	Szabo HUN
7-09	Macedonia FYR	D	2-2	Skopje	ECq	Movsisyan [41], Manucharyan [91+]	9 000	Berntsen NOR
8-10	Slovakia	W	3-1	Yerevan	ECq	Movsisyan [23], Ghazaryan [50], Mkhitaryan [89]	8 500	Orsato ITA
12-10	Andorra	W	4-0	Yerevan	ECq	Ghazaryan [4], Mkhitaryan [16], Movsisyan [33], Pizzelli [33]	12 000	Undiano ESP
2011								
9-02	Georgia	L	1-2	Limassol	Fr	Manucharyan [60p]	300	Giannis CYP
26-03	Russia	D	0-0	Yerevan	ECq		14 800	Thomson SCO
4-06	Russia	L	1-3	St Petersburg	ECq	Pizzelli [25]	18 000	Lannoy FRA
10-08	Lithuania	L	0-3	Kaunas	Fr		500	Sipailo LVA
2-09	Andorra	W	3-0	Andora La Vella	ECq	Pizzelli [35], Ghazaryan [75], Mkhitaryan [91+p]	750	Kostadinov BUL
6-09	Slovakia	W	4-0	Zilina	ECq	Movsisyan [57], Mkhitaryan [70], Ghazaryan [80], Sarkisov [91+]	7 238	Borski POL
7-10	Macedonia FYR	W	4-1	Yerevan	ECq	Pizzelli [28], Mkhitaryan [34], Ghazaryan [69], Sarkisov [91+]	14 403	Schorgenhofer AUT
11-10	Republic of Ireland	L	1-2	Dublin	ECq	Mkhitaryan [62]	45 200	Iturralde ESP
2012								
28-02	Serbia	L	0-2	Limassol	Fr		150	Trattou CYP
29-02	Canada	W	3-1	Limassol	Fr	Pizzelli 2 [22 67], Ozbiliz [90p]	100	Panayi CYP
31-05	Greece	L	0-1	Kufstein	Fr		600	Harkam AUT
5-06	Kazakhstan	W	3-0	Yerevan	Fr	Ghazaryan 2 [9 39], Movsisyan [43]	7500	Kvaratskhelia GEO
15-08	Belarus	L	1-2	Yerevan	Fr	OG [72]	6500	Kharitonashvili GEO
7-09	Malta	W	1-0	Ta'Qali	WCq	Sarkisov [70]	3517	Eisner AUT
11-09	Bulgaria	L	0-1	Sofia	WCq		7883	Studer SUI
12-10	Italy	L	1-3	Yerevan	WCq	Mkhitaryan [28]	25 000	Strahonja CRO
14-11	Lithuania	W	4-2	Yerevan	Fr	Manucharyan [7], Mkrtchyan [50], Mkhitaryan [55], Ozbiliz [72]	10 500	Silagava GEO

Fr = Friendly match • EC = UEFA EURO 2012 • WC = FIFA World Cup • q = qualifier

ARMENIA NATIONAL TEAM HISTORICAL RECORDS

Caps 132 - Sargis Hovsepyan 1992-2012 • 75 - Roman Berezovsky 1996- • 69 - Arthur Petrosyan 1992-2005 • 62 - Harutyun Vardanyan 1994-2004 • 56 - Hamlet Mkhitaryan 1994-2008 & Robert Arzumanyan 2005- • 54 - Romik Khachatryan 1997-2008 • 53 - Arthur Voskanyan 1999 & Armen Shahgeldyan 1992-2007 • 50 - Artavazd Karamyan 2000-10 • 48 - Karen Dokhoyan 1999-2008 & Arman Karamyan 2000-

Goals 11 - Arthur Petrosyan 1992-2005 • 10 - Henrikh Mkhitaryan 2007- • 8 - Gevorg Ghazaryan 2007- • 7 - Ara Hakobyan 1998-2008; Edgar Manucharyan 2000- & Marcos Pizzelli 2008- • 6 - Armen Shahgeldyan 1992-2007 • 5 - Arman Karamyan 2000- & Yura Movsisyan 2010- • 4 - Robert Arzumanyan 2005- & Tigran Yesayan 1996-99

Coaches Eduard Markarov 1992-1994 • Samvel Darbinyan 1995-1996 • Khoren Hovhannisyan 1996-1997 • Souren Barseghyan 1998-1999 • Varuzhan Sukiasyan 2000-2001 • Andranik Adamyan 2002 • Oscar Lopez ARG 2002 • Andranik Adamyan 2003 • Mihai Stoichita ROU 2003-2004 • Bernard Casoni FRA 2004-2005 • Henk Wisman NED 2005-2006 • Ian Porterfield SCO 2006-2007 • Vardan Minasyan & Tom Jones ENG 2007 • Jan Poulsen DEN 2008-2009 • Vardan Minasyan 2009-

ARM – ARMENIA

The Armenian league season has been adjusted from playing over the calendar year to an autumn - spring schedule. There were no champions crowned in 2012. Instead the season was scheduled to run from March 2012 to May 2013.

FFA CUP 2012

1st Round			Semi-finals			Final		
Shirak Gyumri *	2	0						
Banants Yerevan	1	0	**Shirak Gyumri** *	0	2			
Pyunik Yerevan *	0	1	Mika Ashtarak	1	1			
Mika Ashtarak	0	3				**Shirak Gyumri** ‡		1
Ulysses Yerevan *	3	2				Impuls Dilijan		0
Ararat Yerevan	1	3	Ulysses Yerevan	1	0			
Gandzasar Kapan *	0	0	**Impuls Dilijan** *	2	0			
Impuls Dilijan	1	1						

* Home team in the first leg • ‡ Qualified for the Europa League

CUP FINAL 2012

Gyumri City Stadium, Gyumri, 29-04-2012
Att: 5500, Ref: Andrea De Marco ITA

Shirak Gyumri	1	Lamine Ly [38]
Impuls Dilijan	0	

SHIRAK
Artur HARUTYUNYAN - Hovhannes GRIGORYAN (Armen TIGRANYAN 74), Gevorg HOVHANNISYAN, Didier KADIO - Ismael FOFANA, Karen ALEKSANYAN••♦90, Tigran DAVTYAN, David HAKOBYAN (Ararat HARUTYUNYAN 79), Yoro Lamine LY, Karen MURADYAN - Andranik BARIKYAN• (Ara MKRTCHYAN 86). Tr: Vardan BICHAKHCHYAN

IMPULS
Gor ELYAZYAN - Alhassan SHILLA Illiasu, Juliano GIMENEZ, Vachik YEGHIAZARYAN• - Eduard KAKOSYAN, Narek DAVTYAN, Artur BARSEGHYAN (Samvel HAKOBYAN 89), Rumyan HOVSEPYAN (Aghvan HAYRAPETYAN 76), Filip TIMOV (Vahagn AYVAZYAN 61) - Norayr GYOZALYAN, Constantin MANDRICENCO. Tr: Armen GYULBUDAGHYANTS

MEDALS TABLE

		Overall			League			Cup	
		G	S	B	G	S	B	G	S
1	Pyunik Yerevan	16	4	1	13	1	1	5	3
2	Ararat Yerevan	6	6	1	1	4	1	5	2
3	Mika Ashtarak	6	3	2		3	2	6	
4	Shirak Gyumri	4	9	2	3	5	2	1	4
5	Tsement Yerevan	3		1	1		1	2	
6	Banants Yerevan	2	9	3		4	3	2	5
7	FK Yerevan	1	1	3	1		3		1
8	Ulysses Yerevan	1		2	1		2		
9	Araks Ararat	1			1				
10	Zvartnots Yerevan		3			1			2
11	Kotayk Abovyan		2	2		2			2
12	Gandzasar Kapan		1	1		1	1		
13	Impuls Dilijan		1						1
	Kilikia Yerevan		1						1
15	Homenmen Yerevan			1			1		
	Spartak Yerevan			1			1		

ARMENIAN CLUBS IN THE SOVIET UNION

| 8 | Ararat Yerevan | 3 | 4 | | 1 | 2 | | 2 | 2 |

ARU – ARUBA

FIFA/COCA-COLA WORLD RANKING

'93	'94	'95	'96	'97	'98	'99	'00	'01	'02	'03	'04	'05	'06	'07	'08	'09	'10	'11	'12
165	173	171	181	177	180	191	184	185	189	195	198	200	198	201	193	198	199	164	151

2012

Jan	Feb	Mar	Apr	May	Jun	Jul	Aug	Sep	Oct	Nov	Dec	High	Low	Av
164	165	164	167	167	165	164	157	158	154	154	151	151	202	185

Aruba finished bottom of their 2012 Caribbean Cup qualifying group but they were very competitive and were undone in each match by their inability to build on promising situations. They twice took the lead against group winners Dominican Republic in their opening match and looked to be heading for a win before an Erick Ozuna equaliser 15 minutes from time denied them all three points. Against Dominica in the second match, Aruba twice fought back to equalise only for Kurlson Benjamin to score the winner for Dominica with 13 minutes to go while the final match saw hosts Barbados edge to a 2-1 win. Earlier in the year Aruba had won the third edition of the annual ABCS Tournament for the former Dutch Caribbean territories. In the semi-finals they beat Curacao 3-2 before overcoming Suriname 1-0 in the final - a first half Rashidi Gilkes goal securing an impressive win over the favourites. At home it was a double winning year for Racing Club Aruba. In January they thrashed Dakota 5-1 to win the Copa Betico Croes for the first time in the eight year history of the cup and then in June added the league title after beating La Fama 5-3 on aggregate in the final. It was the first time since the late 1980s that Racing had successfully defended their league crown and it took them to within just two of Dakota's record total of 15 titles.

CFU CARIBBEAN CUP RECORD

1989 DNQ **1991** DNE **1992** DNQ **1993** DNE (withdrew) **1994** DNE **1995** DNQ **1996** DNE **1997-1998** DNQ **1999** DNE (withdrew) **2001** DNQ **2005** DNE (withdrew) **2007** DNE **2008** DNQ **2010** DNE **2012** DNQ

ARUBAANSE VOETBAL BOND (AVB)

Technical Centre "Angel Botta", Shaba 24, PO Box 376 Noord
☎ +297 5877357
+297 5876496
avbaruba@hotmail.com
www.avbaruba.aw
FA 1932 CON 1961 FIFA 1988
P Rufo Kelly
GS Egbert Lacle

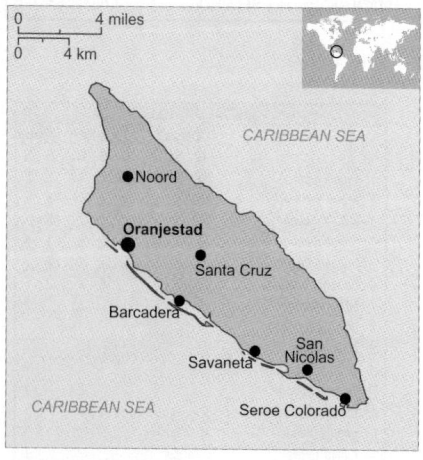

MAJOR CITIES/TOWNS

		Population
1	Oranjestad	33 575
2	San Nicolas	18 395
3	Noord	16 944
4	Santa Cruz	12 326
5	Savaneta	9 996
6	Paradera	9 037

THE STADIA

2014 FIFA World Cup Stadia
Guillermo Prospero Trinidad
Oranjestad 5 000
Other Main Stadia
Frans Figaroa Field
Noord 1 000

ARUBA

Capital Oranjestad
GDP per capita $21 800 (57)
Neighbours (km) Coast 68
Population 103 065 (193)
Area km² 180 km² (217)
% in cities 47%
GMT +/- -5

RECENT INTERNATIONALS PLAYED BY ARUBA

2011	Opponents	Score	Venue	Comp	Scorers	Att	Referee
8-07	St Lucia	W 4-2	Oranjestad	WCq	Erik Santos [13], Maurice Escalona [48], Frederick Gomez [76], David Abdul [85]	300	Foster CAY
12-07	St Lucia	L 2-4	Castries	WCq	Frederick Gomez [44], Rensy Barradas [76]. L 4-5p	500	Lancaster GUY
2-12	Suriname	D 0-0	Paramaribo	Fr	W 5-3p	150	Jauregui CUW
4-12	Bonaire †	D 2-2	Paramaribo	Fr	Jean-Luc Bergen [52], Frederick Gomez [76]. L 3-4p	50	Wijngaarde SUR
2012							
13-07	Curacao	W 3-2	Oranjestad	Fr	Rashidi Gilkes [2], Dwaynalex Raven [44], Rensy		Pinas SUR
15-07	Suriname	W 1-0	Oranjestad	Fr	Rashidi Gilkes [35] Barradas [76]		Jauregui CUW
23-09	Dominican Republic	D 2-2	Bridgetown	CCq	Raymond Baten [6], Rensy Barradas [30]	300	Lancaster GUY
25-09	Dominica	L 2-3	Bridgetown	CCq	Jean-Luc Bergen [40], Frederick Gomez [55]	150	Clarke LCA
27-09	Barbados	L 1-2	Bridgetown	CCq	Jean-Luc Bergen [32]	300	Lancaster GUY

Fr = Friendly match • CC = Digicel Caribbean Cup • WCq = FIFA World Cup • q = qualifier • † Not an official international

ARUBA 2011-12

DIVISION DI HONOR FIRST STAGE

	Pl	W	D	L	F	A	Pts	RCA	La Fama	Britannia	Estrella	Bubali	Nacional	Dakota	Riverplate	Caravel	Juventud
Racing Club Aruba †	18	14	2	2	58	13	44		4-0	3-2	2-1	0-0	3-0	3-0	4-2	5-1	8-0
La Fama †	18	12	3	3	57	25	39	2-4		3-0	0-1	1-2	1-0	6-3	2-1	7-2	5-0
Britannia †	18	11	3	4	53	26	36	1-2	1-3		3-5	1-1	3-2	3-1	6-2	2-1	4-0
Estrella †	18	9	4	5	39	28	31	1-3	2-3	1-1		3-2	0-2	3-0	0-3	0-0	0-1
Bubali	18	8	3	7	33	25	27	1-2	1-2	1-5	2-3		1-2	0-0	2-1	3-1	2-0
Nacional	18	7	3	8	22	22	24	0-2	3-2	1-2	1-1	0-1		0-0	2-3	0-0	1-0
Dakota	18	5	6	7	27	35	21	1-0	0-2	0-4	3-4	1-1	2-1		1-1	3-0	6-2
Riverplate	18	4	3	11	27	48	15	0-3	1-7	1-7	1-4	1-2	0-2	2-2		1-1	3-1
Independiente Caravel	18	1	6	11	15	53	9	0-4	0-6	1-1	1-3	0-8	1-2	2-2	0-3		2-2
Juventud T'ki Leendert	18	2	1	15	11	67	7	0-10	0-4	0-5	0-5	1-4	0-3	1-2	2-1	1-2	

29/09/2011 - 6/05/2012 • † Qualified for the championship play-off

DIVISION DI HONOR CHAMPIONSHIP PLAY-OFF

	Pl	W	D	L	F	A	Pts	LF	RCA	Es	Br
La Fama †	6	3	1	2	8	5	10		2-1	0-1	2-0
Racing Club Aruba †	6	3	1	2	11	9	10	1-1		1-0	2-3
Estrella	6	3	1	2	5	5	10	1-0	1-3		1-0
Britannia	6	1	1	4	7	12	4	1-3	2-3	1-1	

16/05/2012 - 7/06/2012 • † Qualified for the final

FINAL
1st leg. Guillermo Trinidad, 17-06-2012
2nd leg. Guillermo Trinidad, 20-06-2012
Racing Club Aruba 1-1 4-2 La Fama

MEDALS TABLE

		All	Lge	Cp	Town
		G	G	G	
1	Dakota	16	15	1	Oranjestad
2	Racing Club	14	13	1	Oranjestad
3	Estrella	12	12		Santa Cruz
4	Britannia	7	3	4	Paradera
5	Nacional	4	4		Noord
6	Riverplate	2	2		Oranjestad
7	Bubali	1	1		Noord
	Estudiantes	1		1	Oranjestad
	San Luis	1	1		Savaneta
	Sportboys	1		1	Santa Cruz

COPA BETICO CROES 2011-12

First Round		Quarter-finals		Semi-finals		Final	
Racing Club Aruba	8						
Brazil Juniors	0	Racing Club Aruba	3				
Unistars	1	Nacional	0				
Nacional	5			Racing Club Aruba	0 4p		
Juventud TL	1			La Fama	0 3p		
Caiquetio	0	Juventud TL	0				
Bubali	0 4p	La Fama	7			Racing Club Aruba	5
La Fama	0 5p					Dakota	1
Estrella	8						
Sporting	1	Estrella	0 4p			CUP FINAL	
Caravel	2	Britannia	0 3p				
Britannia	10			Estrella	0	Frans Figaroa, Oranjestad	
Arsenal	2			Dakota	1	25-01-2012	
Riverplate	1	Arsenal	1				
Trupial	0	Dakota	3				
Dakota	9	3rd place: **Estrella** 5-3 La Fama					

ASA – AMERICAN SAMOA

FIFA/COCA-COLA WORLD RANKING

'93	'94	'95	'96	'97	'98	'99	'00	'01	'02	'03	'04	'05	'06	'07	'08	'09	'10	'11	'12
-	-	-	-	-	193	199	203	201	201	202	204	205	198	201	201	203	203	186	193

2012

Jan	Feb	Mar	Apr	May	Jun	Jul	Aug	Sep	Oct	Nov	Dec		High	Low	Av
186	187	187	186	186	186	183	182	173	175	178	193		173	205	199

After the heroics of 2011 and their first-ever win in an international match, the American Samoa national team did not see any action in 2012 as attention focused on club football and a first appearance by an American Samoan team in the OFC Champions League. The decision by the Oceania Football Confederation to open up the tournament to all of its 11 member countries will now give the leagues in the weaker nations a positive goal and it was the 2011 champions Pago Youth who earned the honour of becoming American Samoa's first-ever OFC Champions League entrants. They had won the title thanks to a comfortable 3-1 victory over Vailoatai Youth in the final - their 12th victory in 12 games - but domination at home was one never likely to be matched at the preliminary Champions League group staged in Tonga. A 5-1 opening defeat by Samoan champions Liwi was followed by a 6-1 reverse at the hands of Tonga's Lotoha'apai United and they finished by going down 9-0 to Tupapa Maraerenga of the Cook Islands. It was not exactly the most auspicious start to Pago's international career but it should stand them in good stead as they prepare to enter the 2013-14 OFC Champions League after having won the 2012 championship at home. For the third season in a row they didn't lose a match to secure a hat trick of titles.

FIFA WORLD CUP RECORD
1930-1998 DNE 2002-2014 DNQ

FOOTBALL FEDERATION AMERICAN SAMOA (FFAS)

Pago Park,
PO Box 982413,
Pago Pago 96799
☎ +684 6447104
+689 6447102
ffas@blueskynet.as
www.ffas.as
FA 1984 CON 1994 FIFA 1998
P Alex Godinet
GS Tavita Taumua

THE STADIA
2014 FIFA World Cup Stadia
American Samoa played their qualifying group at the Toleafoa J. S. Blatter Complex in Apia, Samoa

Other Main Stadia
Veterans Memorial Stadium
Pago Pago 10 000
Pago Park
Pago Pago 1 000

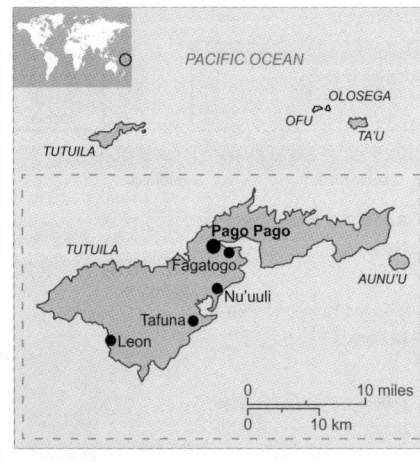

MAJOR CITIES/TOWNS

		Population
1	Tafuna	14 221
2	Nu'uuli	5 934
3	Faleniu	4 778
4	Leone	4 639
5	Pago Pago	4 533
6	Ili'ili	3 791
7	Pava'ia'i	3 107
8	Mapusagafou	2 547
9	Aua	2 264
10	Fagatogo	1 835
11	Vaitogi	1 560
12	Malaeimi	1 493
13	Vailoatai	1 331
14	Aoloau	1 194
15	Faga'alu	1 104
16	Fagasa	997
17	Lauli'i	963
18	Taputimu	863
19	Futiga	834

AMERICAN SAMOA

Capital	Pago Pago	Population	65 628 (204)	% in cities	92%
GDP per capita	$8000 (120)	Area km²	199 km² (215)	GMT +/-	-10
Neighbours (km)	Coast 116				

ASA – AMERICAN SAMOA 115

INTERNATIONALS PLAYED BY AMERICAN SAMOA

2011	Opponents	Score	Venue	Comp	Scorers	Att	Referee
27-08	Tuvalu †	L 0-4	Noumea	PGr1			Jacques TAH
30-08	Solomon Islands	L 0-4	Noumea	PGr1			Jacques TAH
1-09	Guam	L 0-2	Noumea	PGr1			George VAN
3-09	New Caledonia	L 0-8	Noumea	PGr1			Varman FIJ
5-09	Vanuatu	L 0-8	Noumea	PGr1			Achari FIJ
22-11	Tonga	W 2-1	Apia	WCq	Ramin Ott 43, Shalom Luani 74	150	Achari FIJ
24-11	Cook Islands	D 1-1	Apia	WCq	Shalom Luani 24	300	George VAN
26-11	Samoa	L 0-1	Apia	WCq		800	O'Leary NZL
2012							

No international matches played in 2012

WC = FIFA World Cup • ON = OFC Nations Cup • PG = Pacific Games • q = qualifier • † Unofficial match as opponents were not members of FIFA

AMERICAN SAMOA NATIONAL TEAM HISTORICAL RECORDS

Coach: Anthony Langkilde 2001 • Tunoa Lui 2001-02 • Ian Crook ENG 2004 • Nathan Mease 2007 • David Brand ENG 2007-10 • Iofi Lalogafuafua 2011 • Thomas Rongen NED 2011

AMERICAN SAMOA 2011 FFAS SENIOR LEAGUE FIRST ROUND GROUP A

	Pl	W	D	L	F	A	Pts
Pago Youth A †	8	8	0	0	56	2	24
Vaitogi United †	8	6	0	2	42	16	18
Fagasa Youth	8	6	0	2	33	12	18
Kiwi Soccers	8	6	0	2	28	11	18
Vaiala Tongan	8	3	1	4	10	36	10
Fagatogo Blue	8	3	0	5	31	19	9
Lion Heart B	8	1	2	5	8	27	5
Ilaoa & To'omata ‡	8	1	1	6	15	25	4
Atu'u Broncos B ‡	8	0	0	8	0	75	0

23/09/2011 - 3/12/2011 • † Qualified for the semi-finals

AMERICAN SAMOA 2011 FFAS SENIOR LEAGUE FIRST ROUND GROUP B

	Pl	W	D	L	F	A	Pts
Vailoatai Youth †	8	8	0	0	33	8	24
Pago Youth B †	8	4	3	1	18	8	15
Black Roses	8	4	2	2	25	10	14
Utulei Youth	8	3	3	2	22	16	12
Lion Heart A	8	3	3	2	9	8	12
Tafuna Jets	8	2	4	2	22	21	10
PanSa	8	2	1	5	20	28	7
Atu'u Broncos A	8	1	1	6	11	39	4
Green Bay	8	0	1	7	9	31	1

23/09/2011 - 3/12/2011 • † Qualified for the semi-finals

AMERICAN SAMOA 2011 FFAS SENIOR LEAGUE FINAL ROUNDS

Semi-finals

Pago Youth A	5
Pago Youth B	1

Vaitogi United	2
Vailoatai Youth	3

Finals

Pago Youth A	3
Vailoatai Youth	1

Third place play-off:
Pago Youth B 3-2 Vaitogi United

All matches played at the Kananafou Theological Seminary College Sports Field. Final played 17-12-2011

AMERICAN SAMOA 2012 FFAS SENIOR LEAGUE DIVISION ONE

	Pl	W	D	L	F	A	Pts	Pago Youth A	Black Roses	Utulei Youth	Lion Heart A	Tafuna Jets	Vaitogi Utd	Pago Youth B	Kiwi Soccers
Pago Youth A †	14	12	2	0	43	9	38		3-0	1-0	2-0	3-1	5-1	3-1	3-0
Black Roses	14	10	1	3	28	13	31	0-1		3-0	2-0	0-0	2-1	4-2	3-0
Utulei Youth	14	9	0	5	55	19	27	2-5	0-1		4-1	2-1	2-4	2-1	16-0
Lion Heart A	14	5	3	6	27	34	18	1-1	1-3	1-9		3-0	2-1	3-1	3-0
Tafuna Jets	14	5	2	7	22	29	17	1-1	2-0	1-3	1-3		3-6	2-1	2-0
Vaitogi United	14	5	0	9	37	35	15	1-2	0-3	0-3	6-5	2-3		5-1	n/p
Pago Youth B	14	3	1	10	23	47	10	0-7	3-4	0-9	1-1	3-0	4-2		2-5
Kiwi Soccers	14	1	1	12	11	60	4	1-6	0-3	1-3	3-3	2-5	0-8	0-3	

10/08/2012 - 1/12/2012 • † Qualified for the OFC Champions League

ATG – ANTIGUA AND BARBUDA

FIFA/COCA-COLA WORLD RANKING

'93	'94	'95	'96	'97	'98	'99	'00	'01	'02	'03	'04	'05	'06	'07	'08	'09	'10	'11	'12
117	136	137	145	159	137	147	144	157	155	170	153	154	132	151	128	130	106	87	115

2012

Jan	Feb	Mar	Apr	May	Jun	Jul	Aug	Sep	Oct	Nov	Dec	High	Low	Av
84	90	95	100	100	105	106	100	101	106	121	115	83	170	138

2012 was one of the busiest years for football in Antigua with the national team taking part in the penultimate round of qualifying for the 2014 FIFA World Cup and the country hosting the finals of the 2012 Caribbean Cup. At club level there was a debut for pro outfit Antigua Barracuda in the CFU Club championship where they reached the semi-finals although their second season in the USL Pro League in America ended as the first had with the wooden spoon. The national team won just two matches all season - the first in a friendly in St Vincent before the competitive action got underway. It was disappointing given the team's success in 2011 but the step up in the calibre of opposition from the previous year was too much to handle. Antigua finished bottom of their World Cup group with a draw at home to Jamaica the only point they picked up while at the end of the year they failed to make it through the group stage of the Caribbean Cup finals after surprisingly losing their opening game to the Dominican Republic, a result which cost them dear. Had they not conceded a last minute goal they would have made it through to the semi-finals after beating Trinidad in the next game. In club football at home there was a first league title for Old Road who were comfortable winners of the Premier Division ahead of All Saints United.

CFU CARIBBEAN CUP RECORD

1989 DNQ 1991 DNE **1992** 7 r1 1993-1994 DNQ **1995** 6 r1 1996 DNE (withdrew) **1997** 6 r1 (hosts) **1998** 4 SF 1999-2007 DNQ
2008 7 r1 **2010** 5 r1 **2012** 5 r1 (hosts)

ANTIGUA AND BARBUDA FA (ABFA)

Suite 19, Vendors Mall,
Heritage Quay, PO Box 773,
St John's
☎ +1 268 5626012
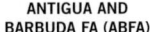 +1 268 5626016
abfa@candw.ag
www.antiguafootball.org
FA 1928 CON 1980 FIFA 1970
P Everton Gonsalves
GS Gordon Derrick

THE STADIA

2014 FIFA World Cup Stadia
Sir Vivian Richards Stadium
St John's

Other Main Stadia
Antigua Recreation Ground
St John's 12 000
Stanford Cricket Ground
Osbourn 5 000
Police Ground
St George's 2 000
Yasco Sports Complex
St John's 1 000

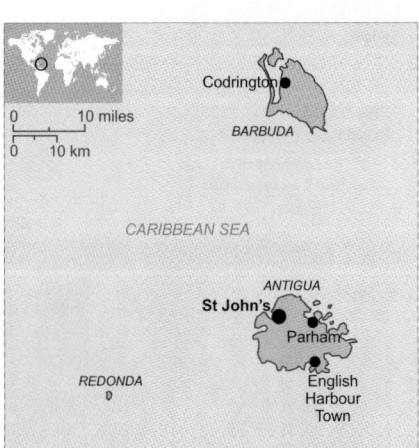

MAJOR CITIES/TOWNS

		Population
1	St John's	21 969
2	All Saints	4 602
3	Liberta	2 986
4	Potters Village	2 933
5	Bolands	2 056
6	Seaview Farm	1 881
7	Swetes	1 775
8	Pigotts	1 726
9	Clare Hill	1 402
10	Carlisle	1 253
11	New Winthropes	1 189
12	Bendals	1 174
13	Willikies	1 145
14	Old Road	1 108
15	Jennings	1 005
16	Freemans Village	953
17	Cedar Grove	897
18	Urlings	869
19	Parham	821

ANTIGUA AND BARBUDA

Capital	St John's	Population	85 632 (198)	% in cities	30%
GDP per capita	$19 600 (64)	Area km^2	442 km^2 (199)	GMT +/-	-4.5
Neighbours (km)	Coast 153				

RECENT INTERNATIONALS PLAYED BY ANTIGUA AND BARBUDA

2010	Opponents	Score	Venue	Comp	Scorers	Att	Referee
27-11	Jamaica	L 1-3	Riviere-Pilote	CCr1	Gayson Gregory [49]	3 000	Wijngaarde SUR
29-11	Guyana	W 1-0	Riviere-Pilote	CCr1	Gayson Gregory [69]	3 000	Wijngaarde SUR
1-12	Guadeloupe †	L 0-1	Riviere-Pilote	CCr1		3 000	Lopez GUA
2011							
27-05	Grenada	D 2-2	St George's	Fr	Randolph Burton [51], Kimoi Alexander [73]	3 500	Bedeau GRN
26-08	St Vincent/Grenadines	W 1-0	St John's	Fr	Kerry Skepple [11]	2 000	Willett ATG
28-08	St Vincent/Grenadines	D 2-2	St John's	Fr	George Dublin [45], Jamie Thomas [89]	2 500	Charles ATG
2-09	Curacao	W 5-2	St John's	WCq	Marc Joseph [42], Quinton Griffith [45], Tamarley Thomas [54], Peter Byers 2 [75 80]	2 000	Santos PUR
6-09	US Virgin Islands	W 8-1	Fredericksted	WCq	Ranja Christian [18], Peter Byers 3 [38p 51 57], Justin Cochrane [47], George Dublin [54], Randolph Burton 2 [68 74]	250	Lancaster GUY
7-10	Curacao	W 1-0	Willemstad	WCq	Tamarley Thomas [73]	2 563	Reyna GUA
11-10	US Virgin Islands	W 10-0	St John's	WCq	Tamarley Thomas 3 [7 41 78], Peter Byers 3 [24 31 40], Randolph Burton 2 [55 65], Jamie Thomas [86], Keiran Murtagh [92+]	1 500	Matthew SKN
11-11	Haiti	W 1-0	St John's	WCq	Kerry Skepple [81]	8 000	Pineda HON
15-11	Haiti	L 1-2	Port-au-Prince	WCq	Tamarley Thomas [10]	3 000	Toledo USA
2012							
29-02	Trinidad and Tobago	L 0-4	St John's	Fr		2 500	Baptiste DMA
3-03	St Kitts and Nevis	L 0-1	Basseterre	Fr			
30-03	St Vincent/Grenadines	L 0-1	Kingstown	Fr		550	Clarke LCA
1-04	St Vincent/Grenadines	W 2-1	Kingstown	Fr	Lawson Robinson [19], Peter Byers [51]	250	Brizan TRI
8-06	USA	L 1-3	Tampa	WCq	Peter Byers [65]	23 971	Cruz CRC
12-06	Jamaica	D 0-0	St John's	WCq		8 500	Lancaster GUY
7-09	Guatemala	L 1-3	Guatemala City	WCq	Peter Byers [39]	8 000	Brea CUB
11-09	Guatemala	L 0-1	St John's	WCq		5 000	Gantar CAN
12-10	USA	L 1-2	St John's	WCq	Dexter Blackstock [25]	7 000	Brizan TRI
16-10	Jamaica	L 1-4	Kingston	WCq	Quinton Griffith [61]	8 000	Quesada CRC
7-12	Dominican Republic	L 1-2	St John's	CCr1	Peter Byers [17]	150	Dacosta BAH
9-12	Trinidad and Tobago	W 2-0	St John's	CCr1	Quinton Griffith [51], Peter Byers [73]	2 000	Rubalcaba CUB
11-12	Haiti	L 0-1	St John's	CCr1		800	Brea CUB

Fr = Friendly match • CC = Digicel Caribbean Cup • WC = FIFA World Cup • q = qualifier • † Not an official FIFA international

ANTIGUA AND BARBUDA NATIONAL TEAM HISTORICAL RECORDS

Coach: Rolston Williams 2004 • Vernon Edwards 2004-05 • Derrick Edwards 2005-08 • Rowan Benjamin 2008-11 • Tom Curtis ENG 2011-12 • Rolston Williams 2012 • Lee Harrington ENG 2013-

ANTIGUA AND BARBUDA 2011-12

DIGICEL, HADEED AND OBSERVER GROUP PREMIER DIVISION	Pl	W	D	L	F	A	Pts	Old Road	All Saints	Hoppers	Parham	Sap	Sea View	Willikies	Bassa	Empire	Bullets
Old Road	18	13	3	2	37	16	42		0-1	2-2	1-1	2-0	2-1	7-2	1-0	2-0	1-0
All Saints United	18	10	3	5	33	21	33	1-4		0-1	0-0	3-4	0-1	1-0	2-2	0-0	6-1
Hoppers	18	8	7	3	33	23	31	1-2	2-3		1-0	4-1	1-2	2-1	2-2	2-0	2-2
Parham	18	8	5	5	31	22	29	3-1	1-2	3-3		0-3	2-0	1-2	0-0	1-1	3-1
Sap	18	8	3	7	27	26	27	1-1	4-2	2-3	0-2			0-3	2-0	2-0	3-0
Sea View Farm	18	6	4	8	19	24	22	1-2	1-3	1-1	1-3	0-1		4-1	0-2	1-1	1-0
Willikies	18	6	2	10	22	32	20	0-1	0-3	1-1	0-2	2-0	2-2		0-1	1-0	3-1
Bassa †	18	5	4	9	22	27	19	1-2	0-1	1-2	2-1	1-1	1-2	3-2		1-2	2-2
Empire	18	3	6	9	13	22	15	0-4	0-2	0-0	1-3	0-1	0-0	2-0	1-2		3-0
Bullets	18	3	3	12	18	42	12	1-2	0-3	0-3	3-3	3-2	0-1	0-2	2-1	2-1	

15/10/2011 - 22/02/2012 • † Promotion/relegation play-offs: Bassa 2-1 Ottos Rangers; Bassa 2-2 Villa Lions; Villa Lions 2-1 Ottos Rangers; Bassa 2-0 Villa Lions. Bassa remain in the Premier Division

AUS – AUSTRALIA

FIFA/COCA-COLA WORLD RANKING

'93	'94	'95	'96	'97	'98	'99	'00	'01	'02	'03	'04	'05	'06	'07	'08	'09	'10	'11	'12
49	58	51	50	35	39	89	73	48	50	82	58	48	39	48	28	21	26	23	36

2012

Jan	Feb	Mar	Apr	May	Jun	Jul	Aug	Sep	Oct	Nov	Dec	High	Low	Av
21	22	20	21	21	24	23	24	25	34	33	36	14	92	46

The A-League's profile took a significant jump ahead of the 2012-13 season with the high profile signing of former Italy and Juventus star Alessandro Del Piero by Sydney FC. The 2006 FIFA World Cup winner signed for the struggling club after a season in which Sydney had, once again, struggled, finishing in fifth place to only just scrape into the championship playoffs, where they lost out to Wellington Phoenix. Central Coast Mariners finished on top of the A-League standings - and as a result secured the country's only guaranteed berth in the AFC Champions League group stage for 2013 after Australia's allocation was cut - but lost out to Perth Glory in the Preliminary Final. That left the way clear for Brisbane Roar to retain their title after they beat Perth 2-1 in a gripping final thanks to two late goals from Besart Berisha - the second coming four minutes into injury-time. Holger Osieck's national side, meanwhile, struggled to reach their usual levels in qualifying for the FIFA World Cup finals, drawing their opening matches in the final phase of Asia's qualifying tournament for Brazil 2014 against Oman and Japan before slipping to a 2-1 loss against Jordan. A come-from-behind win over Iraq - inspired by the ever-green Tim Cahill - averted a catastrophe and kept the Socceroos' hopes of qualifying for a third straight World Cup alive.

FIFA WORLD CUP RECORD
1930-1962 DNE 1966-1970 DNQ **1974** 14 r1 1978-2002 DNQ **2006** 16 r2 **2010** 21 r1

FOOTBALL FEDERATION AUSTRALIA (FFA)

Level 22, 1 Oxford Street, Darlinghurst, NSW 2010
+61 2 80204000
+61 2 80204100
info@footballaustralia.com.au
www.footballaustralia.com.au
FA 1961 CON 2006 FIFA 1963
P Frank Lowy
GS David Gallop

THE STADIA
2014 FIFA World Cup Stadia
ANZ Stadium 'Stadium Australia'		
Sydney		83 500
Suncorp Stadium		
Brisbane		52 500
AAMI Park		
Melbourne		30 050

Other Main Stadia
Melbourne Cricket Ground	
Melbourne	100 000
Hunter Stadium	
Newcastle	33 000

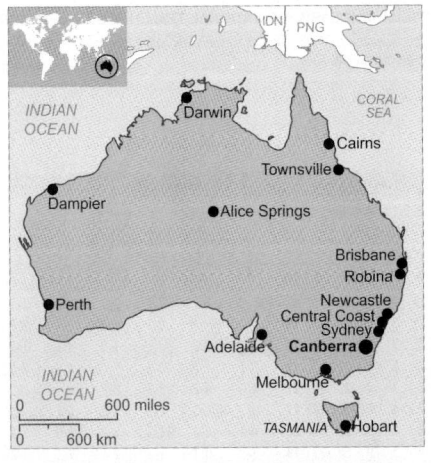

MAJOR CITIES/TOWNS
		Population
1	Melbourne	3 676 105
2	Sydney	3 653 646
3	Brisbane	1 855 083
4	Perth	1 272 193
5	Adelaide	1 040 987
6	Gold Coast	566 739
7	Canberra	331 755
8	Central Coast	302 341
9	Newcastle	292 516
10	Wollongong	232 310
11	Sunshine Coast	182 861
12	Geelong	134 145
13	Townsville	132 225
14	Hobart	125 305
15	Cairns	114 586
16	Toowoomba	99 767
17	Bunbury	94 163
18	Rockingham	83 584
66	Robina	19 182

COMMONWEALTH OF AUSTRALIA
Capital	Canberra	Population	21 262 641 (54)	% in cities	89%
GDP per capita	$38 100 (25)	Area km²	7 741 220 M² (6)	GMT +/-	+10
Neighbours (km)	Coast 25 760				

RECENT INTERNATIONALS PLAYED BY AUSTRALIA

2010	Opponents	Score	Venue	Comp	Scorers	Att	Referee
13-06	Germany	L 0-4	Durban	WCr1		62 660	Rodriguez MEX
19-06	Ghana	D 1-1	Rustenburg	WCr1	Holman [11]	34 812	Rosetti ITA
23-06	Serbia	W 2-1	Nelspruit	WCr1	Cahill [69], Holman [73]	37 836	Larrionda URU
11-08	Slovenia	L 0-2	Ljubljana	Fr		16 135	Tagliavento ITA
3-09	Switzerland	D 0-0	St Gall	Fr		14 660	Einwaller AUT
7-09	Poland	W 2-1	Krakow	Fr	Holman [15], Wilkshire [26p]	17 000	Bebek CRO
9-10	Paraguay	W 1-0	Sydney	Fr	Carney [53]	25 210	Nishimura JPN
17-11	Egypt	L 0-3	Cairo	Fr			Genov BUL
2011							
5-01	UAE	D 0-0	Al Ain	Fr		13 300	Shaban KUW
10-01	India	W 4-0	Doha	ACr1	Cahill 2 [12 65], Kewell [25], Holman [45]	9 783	Albadwawi UAE
14-01	Korea Republic	D 1-1	Doha	ACr1	Jedinak [62]	15 526	Abdou QAT
18-01	Bahrain	W 1-0	Doha	ACr1	Jedinak [37]	3 919	Nishimura JPN
22-01	Iraq	W 1-0	Doha	ACqf	Kewell [118]	7 889	Abdou QAT
25-01	Uzbekistan	W 6-0	Doha	ACsf	Kewell [5], Ognenovski [35], Carney [65], Emerton [73], Valeri [82], Kruse [83]	24 826	Albadwawi UAE
29-01	Japan	L 0-1	Doha	ACf		37 174	Irmatov UZB
29-03	Germany	W 2-1	Monchengladbach	Fr	Carney [61], Wilkshire [64p]	30 152	Lannoy FRA
5-06	New Zealand	W 3-0	Adelaide	Fr	Kennedy 2 [10 59], Troisi [90p]	21 281	Tojo JPN
7-06	Serbia	D 0-0	Melbourne	Fr		28 149	Tojo JPN
10-08	Wales	W 2-1	Cardiff	Fr	Cahill [43], Kruse [60]	6 378	Tohver EST
2-09	Thailand	W 2-1	Brisbane	WCq	Kennedy [58], Brosque [86]	24 540	Balideh QAT
6-09	Saudi Arabia	W 3-1	Dammam	WCq	Kennedy 2 [40 56], Wilkshire [77p]	15 000	Nishimura JPN
7 10	Malaysia	W 5 0	Canberra	Fr	Wilkshire [3], Kennedy 2 [33 45], Brosque 2 [39 69]	10 041	Lee Min Hu KOR
11-10	Oman	W 3-0	Sydney	WCq	Holman [8], Kennedy [65], Jedinak [85]	24 732	Kovalenko UZB
11-11	Oman	L 0-1	Muscat	WCq		4 500	Abdulnabi BHR
15-11	Thailand	W 1-0	Bangkok	WCq	Holman [77]	19 400	Mozaffari IRN
2012							
29-02	Saudi Arabia	W 4-2	Melbourne	WCq	Brosque 2 [43 75], Kewell [73], Emerton [76]	24 240	Kim Dong Jin KOR
2-06	Denmark	L 0-2	Copenhagen	Fr		16 888	Damato ITA
8-06	Oman	D 0-0	Muscat	WCq		11 000	Faghani IRN
12-06	Japan	D 1-1	Brisbane	WCq	Wilkshire [70p]	40 189	Al Ghamdi KSA
15-08	Scotland	L 1-3	Edinburgh	Fr		11 110	Hagen NOR
6-09	Lebanon	W 3-0	Beirut	Fr	Cahill [20], McKay [23], Thompson [88]	7 000	Nikolaidis GRE
11-09	Jordan	L 1-2	Amman	WCq	Thompson [86]	16 000	Balideh QAT
16-10	Iraq	W 2-1	Doha	WCq	Cahill [80], Thompson [84]	2 183	Lee Min Hu KOR
14-11	Korea Republic	W 2-1	Hwaseong	Fr	Rukavytsya [44], Cornthwaite [87]	15 000	Wang Zhe CHN
3-12	Hong Kong	W 1-0	Hong Kong	EAq	Emerton [85]	4 160	Iida JPN
5-12	Korea DPR	D 1-1	Hong Kong	EAq	Thompson [4]	989	Pechsri THA
7-12	Guam	W 9-0	Hong Kong	EAq	Mooy [12], Babalj 2 [20 56], Marrone [43], Thompson 3 [59 63 65p], Milligan [71], Garcia [83]	2 315	Wang Zhe CHN
9-12	Chinese Taipei	W 8-0	Hong Kong	EAq	Garcia [11], Cornthwaite [17], Taggart 2 [20 29], Behich 2 [34 57], Mooy [47], OG [82]	3 345	Kim Dae Yong KOR

Fr = Friendly match • AC = AFC Asian Cup • EA = EAFF EAst Asian Cup • WC = FIFA World Cup
q = qualifier • r1 = first round group • qf = quarter-final • sf = semi-final • f = final

AUSTRALIA NATIONAL TEAM HISTORICAL RECORDS

Caps
103 - Mark Schwarzer 1993- • **95** - Brett Emerton 1998- • **88** - Lucas Neill 1996- • **87** - Alex Tobin 1988-98 • **84** - Paul Wade 1986-96 • **76** - Tony Vidmar 1991-2006 • **73** - Luke Wilkshire 2005- • **68** - Scott Chipperfield 1998-2010 • **64** - Peter Wilson 1970-79 & Mark Bresciano 2001- • **61** - Attila Abonyi 1967-77 • **60** - John Kosmina 1976-88; Stan Lazaridis 1993-2006 & Tim Cahill 2004-

Goals
29 - Damian Mori 1992-2002 • **28** - Archie Thompson 2001- • **27** - John Aloisi 1997-2008 • **26** - Tim Cahill 2004- • **25** - John Kosmina 1976-88 & Attila Abonyi 1967-77 • **20** - David Zdrilic 1997-2005 & Brett Emerton 1998- • **19** - Graham Arnold 1985-97 • **18** - Ray Baartz 1967-74 • **17** - Gary Cole 1978-82; Aurelio Vidmar 1991-2001 & Harry Kewell 1996-

Coaches
Tiko Jelisavcvic YUG 1965 • Jozef Venglos CZE 1965-67 • Joe Vlatsis YUG 1967-69 • Rale Rasic YUG 1970-74 • Brian Green ENG 1976 • Jim Shoulder ENG 1976-78 • Rudi Gutendorf GER 1979-81 • Les Scheinflug 1981-83 • Frank Arok YUG 1983-89 • Eddie Thomson SCO 1990-96 • Raul Blanco 1996 • Terry Venables ENG 1997-98 • Raul Blanco 1998-99 • Frank Farina 1999-2005 • Guus Hiddink NED 2005-06 • Graham Arnold 2006-07 • Pim Verbeek NED 2007-10 • Holger Osieck GER 2010-

AUSTRALIA 2011-12

HYUNDAI A-LEAGUE

	Pl	W	D	L	F	A	Pts	C. Coast	Brisbane	Perth	Wellington	Sydney	M. Heart	Newcastle	M. Victory	Adelaide	Gold Coast
Central Coast Mariners†	27	15	6	6	40	24	51		0-2	2-1	2-0 2-0	1-1	3-1	2-0 1-1	0-0	3-2 1-0	0-0 1-1
Brisbane Roar †	27	14	7	6	50	28	49	1-0 1-2		4-0	1-1	2-1	1-2 1-1	0-1	3-1 3-2	7-1 1-1	3-0
Perth Glory ‡	27	13	4	10	40	35	43	1-3 1-0	3-3 0-3		1-0	0-1	1-2	2-0 2-0	4-1 4-2	1-0	2-0 4-0
Wellington Phoenix ‡	27	12	4	11	34	32	40	1-2 1-2	2-0 0-2	1-0 0-1		2-1 4-2	3-1	2-0 5-2	1-2	1-1	2-0
Sydney FC ‡	27	10	8	9	37	42	38	2-3 0-1	0-2 2-0	1-1 2-1	0-1 0-1		0-4	2-5 3-2	1-0	2-2	3-2 2-1
Melbourne Heart ‡	27	9	10	8	35	34	37	0-1 1-0	1-1	1-2 1-2	1-0 1-1	1-1 2-2		3-0	3-2 0-0	1-3	1-0
Newcastle Jets	27	10	5	12	38	41	35	1-0	1-2 1-2	2-0 1-1	0-1	1-2	3-2 3-0		3-1	1-0 1-0	3-2 1-1
Melbourne Victory	27	6	11	10	35	43	29	2-1	2-2	2-2	3-1 3-0	0-0 2-2	0-0	2-1 1-3		1-1	3-2 1-1
Adelaide United	27	5	10	12	26	44	25	0-4	1-1	0-3 0-2	0-1 2-1	2-1 2-1	1-1 1-1	0-0 1-1	1-0		2-1 0-3
Gold Coast United	27	4	9	14	30	42	21	3-3 3-3	1-0 1-2	3-0	1-1 0-1	0-0	1-2 1-1	3-1	2-0 1-1	1-2	

8/10/2011 - 25/03/2012 • † Qualified for the Minor Semi-final • ‡ Qualified for the final series • Attendance (inc play-offs): 1,536,131 @ 10,817
Top scorers: **21** - Besart **BERISHA** ALB, Brisbane • **17** - Shane **SMELTZ** NZL, Perth • **10** - Carlos **HERNANDEZ** CRC, Melbourne Victory & Mitch **NICHOLS**, Brisbane • **9** - Eli **BABALJ**, Melbourne Heart; Jeremy **BROCKIE** NZL, Newcastle & Ryan **GRIFFITHS**, Newcastle
Brisbane Roar and Central Coast Mariners qualified for the 2012 AFC Champions League

A-LEAGUE FINALS SERIES 2011-12

Minor Semi-final
Brisbane Roar 2
Central Coast Mariners 0

Major Semi-final
Brisbane Roar 3
Central Coast Mariners 2

Grand Final
Brisbane Roar 2
Perth Glory 1

Preliminary Final
Central Coast Mariners 1 3p
Perth Glory 1 5p

First Round
Wellington Phoenix 3
Sydney FC 2

Minor Semi-final
Wellington Phoenix 2
Perth Glory 3

Melbourne Heart 0
Perth Glory 3

30/03/2012 - 22/04/2012 • The loser of the Major Semi-final meets the winner of the Minor Semi-final in the Preliminary Final • The winners of the Major Semi-final and the Preliminary Final meet in the Grand Final

GRAND FINAL 2012

Suncorp Stadium, Brisbane, 22-04-2012, 16:00
Att: 50,334, Ref: Jarred Gillett

Brisbane Roar	2	Berisha 2 [84] [94+]
Perth Glory	1	Franjic OG [53]

BRISBANE ROAR
Michael **THEOKLITOS** - Ivan **FRANJIC**●, Matt **SMITH** (c), Sayed Mohamed **ADNAN**, Shane **STEFANUTTO** - Erik **PAARTALU** (Luke **BRATTAN** 64) - **HENRIQUE** (James **MEYER** 73), Mitch **NICHOLS**, Massimo **MURDOCCA** (Nicholas **FITZGERALD** 64), Thomas **BROICH** - Besart **BERISHA**. Tr: Ange **POSTECOGLOU**

PERTH GLORY
Danny **VUKOVIC**● - Joshua **RISDON**, Steve **PANTELIDIS**, Bas **VAN DEN BRINK**, Dean **HEFFERNAN**●● ♦90 - Travis **DODD** (Scott **NEVILLE** 75), Liam **MILLER**●, Jacob **BURNS**●, Todd **HOWARTH** - Shane **SMELTZ** (Steven **MCGARRY** 79), Billy **MEHMET**●. Tr: Ian **FERGUSON**

MEDALS TABLE SINCE A-LEAGUE

		Overall G S B	A-Lge G S	Asia G S B	City/Town
1	Melbourne Victory	2 1	2 1		Melbourne
2	Sydney FC	2	2		Sydney
3	Brisbane Roar	2	2		Brisbane
	Newcastle Jets	1	1		Newcastle
5	Adelaide United	3	2	1	Adelaide
	Central Coast Mariners	3	3		Gosford
7	Perth Glory	1	1		Perth
	Gold Coast United				Gold Coast
	Melbourne Heart				Melbourne
	Wellington Phoenix				Wellington
		7 8	7 7	1	

MEDALS TABLE PRE A-LEAGUE

		Overall G S B	League G S B	Cup G S	CL G	ST G	City
1	Sydney City	7 4 1	4 3 1	3 1		5	Sydney
2	South Melbourne	7 3 2	4 2 2	2 1	1	7	Melbourne
3	Adelaide City	7 3	3 2	3 1	1	12	Adelaide
4	Marconi Stallions	5 6	4 3	1 3			Sydney
5	Sydney Olympic	4 6	2 4	2 2			Sydney
6	APIA Leichhardt Tigers	4 3	1	3 3		4	Sydney
7	Melbourne Knights	3 4	2 3	1 1		1	Melbourne
8	Wollongong City Wolves	3 1	2 1		1		Wollongong
9	Heidelberg United	2 6 1	2 1	2 4		1	Melbourne
10	Perth Glory	2 2	2 2				Perth
11	Parramatta Eagles	2 1		2 1			Sydney
	Brisbane City	2 1	1	2			Brisbane
13	Sydney United	1 4	3	1 1			Sydney
14	St George Saints	1 3 1	1 1 1	2		3	Sydney
15	West Adelaide	1 2	1	2		7	Adelaide
16	Brunswick	1 1	1	1		7	Melbourne
17	Newcastle Jets	1 1		1 1			Newcastle
	Brisbane Strikers	1	1				Brisbane
	George Cross	1		1			Melbourne
	Melbourne HSC	1		1			Melbourne
	Slavia Melbourne	1		1			Melbourne
	SSC Yugal	1		1			Sydney
	Preston Lions	3 1	1 1	2			Melbourne

League = League championship 1977-2004 • Cup = Cup tournament 1962-77 • CL = OFC Champions Cup • ST = State Championship pre 1977

AUT – AUSTRIA

FIFA/COCA-COLA WORLD RANKING

'93	'94	'95	'96	'97	'98	'99	'00	'01	'02	'03	'04	'05	'06	'07	'08	'09	'10	'11	'12
36	49	39	34	25	22	28	44	56	65	67	83	69	65	94	92	61	46	70	70

2012													High	Low	Av
Jan	Feb	Mar	Apr	May	Jun	Jul	Aug	Sep	Oct	Nov	Dec				
71	71	71	73	73	58	60	60	49	59	68	70		17	105	56

Dietrich Mateschitz's Red Bull Salzburg won a fourth Bundesliga title in six seasons but what made 2012 especially memorable for the club was a first triumph in the Austrian cup final. Four times Salzburg had previously lost in the final but by beating Reid 3-0 in Vienna they finally got their hands on the elusive trophy. Under Dutch coach Ricardo Moniz, Salzburg finished six points ahead of Rapid in the league thanks to a run of six victories in their final six games. In the cup they had an easier time after facing just one Bundesliga club during their campaign - Reid in the final. Salzburg have stated that qualifying for the UEFA Champions League group stage is not an overriding priority for the club but even though they navigated the group stage of the 2011-12 Europa League before losing heavily to Ukraine's Metalist Kharkiv in the round of 32, there is some surprise that more progress has not been made in the Champions League since Mateschitz took over the club in 2005. Austria's 2014 FIFA World Cup qualifying campaign got off to a poor start with defeat at home to Germany and a draw away in Kazakhstan and under their Swiss coach Marcel Koller, they face an uphill struggle to qualify for the finals from a group that contains three Euro 2012 finalists in Sweden, Germany and the Republic of Ireland.

UEFA EUROPEAN CHAMPIONSHIP RECORD
1960 QF 1964 r1 1968-2004 DNQ **2008** r1 (co-hosts) 2012 DNQ

OSTERREICHISCHER FUSSBALL-BUND (OFB)

Ernst Happel Stadion,
Sektor A/F, Postfach 340,
Meiereistrasse 7, Wien 1021
☎ +43 1 727180
📠 +43 1 7281632
✉ office@oefb.at
🌐 www.oefb.at
FA 1904 CON 1954 FIFA 1907
P Leo Windtner
GS Alfred Ludwig

THE STADIA

2014 FIFA World Cup Stadia

Ernst Happel Stadion Vienna	48 844

Other Main Stadia

Hypo Group Arena Klagenfurt	32 000
Red Bull Arena Salzburg	31 835
Gerhard Hanappi Stadium Vienna	17 500
Tivoli Neu Stadion Innsbruck	16 008

MAJOR CITIES/TOWNS

		Population
1	Vienna	1 690 103
2	Graz	253 554
3	Linz	189 612
4	Salzburg	150 112
5	Innsbruck	119 092
6	Klagenfurt	92 895
7	Wels	58 939
8	Villach	58 822
9	Sankt Pölten	51 908
10	Dornbirn	44 954
11	Wiener Neustadt	40 557
12	Steyr	38 780
13	Feldkirch	30 545
14	Bregenz	27 107
15	Baden	25 456
16	Klosterneuburg	25 388
17	Wolfsberg	25 356
18	Leoben	24 879
19	Krems	24 229

REPUBLIK OESTERREICH • REPUBLIC OF AUSTRIA

Capital	Wien (Vienna)	Population	8 210 281 (92)	% in cities	67%
GDP per capita	$40 200 (20)	Area km²	83 871 km² (113)	GMT +/-	+1
Neighbours (km)	Czech Republic 362, Germany 784, Hungary 366, Italy 430, Liechtenstein 35, Slovakia 91, Slovenia 330, Switzerland 164

AUT – AUSTRIA

RECENT INTERNATIONALS PLAYED BY AUSTRIA

2009	Opponents		Score	Venue	Comp	Scorers	Att	Referee
11-02	Sweden	L	0-2	Graz	Fr		11 800	Kassai HUN
1-04	Romania	W	2-1	Klagenfurt	WCq	Hoffer 2 [26 44]	23 000	Thomas SCO
6-06	Serbia	L	0-1	Belgrade	WCq		41 000	Vink NED
12-08	Cameroon	L	0-2	Klagenfurt	Fr		28 800	Olsiak SVK
5-09	Faroe Islands	W	3-1	Graz	WCq	Maierhofer [1], Janko 2 [15 58p]	12 300	Borg MLT
9-09	Romania	D	1-1	Bucharest	WCq	Schiemer [83]	7 505	Atkinson ENG
10-10	Lithuania	W	2-1	Innsbruck	WCq	Janko [16], Wallner [80p]	14 200	Gumienny BEL
14-10	France	L	1-3	Paris	WCq	Janko [49]	78 099	Proença POR
18-11	Spain	L	1-5	Vienna	Fr	Jantscher [8]	32 000	Meyer GER
2010								
3-03	Denmark	W	2-1	Vienna	Fr	Schiemer [11], Wallner [37]	13 500	Kralovec CZE
19-05	Croatia	L	0-1	Klagenfurt	Fr		20 000	Blom NED
11-08	Switzerland	L	0-1	Klagenfurt	Fr		18 000	Rubinos ESP
7-09	Kazakhstan	W	2-0	Salzburg	ECq	Linz [91+], Hoffer [92+]	22 500	Strahonja CRO
8-10	Azerbaijan	W	3-0	Vienna	ECq	Prödl [3], Arnautovic 2 [53 92+]	26 500	Vollquartz DEN
12-10	Belgium	D	4-4	Brussels	ECq	Schiemer 2 [14 62], Arnautovic [29], Harnik [93+]	24 231	Dean ENG
17-11	Greece	L	1-2	Vienna	Fr	Fuchs [67]	16 200	Kever SUI
2011								
9-02	Netherlands	L	1-3	Eindhoven	Fr	Arnautovic [84p]	35 000	Brych GER
25-03	Belgium	L	0-2	Vienna	ECq		44 300	Bezborodov RUS
29-03	Turkey	L	0-2	Istanbul	ECq		40 420	Kralovec CZE
3-06	Germany	L	1-2	Vienna	ECq	OG [50]	47 500	Busacca SUI
7-06	Latvia	W	3-1	Graz	Fr	Dibon [75], Harnik 2 [81 94+p]	8 500	Evans WAL
10-08	Slovakia	L	1-2	Klagenfurt	Fr	Hoffer [62]	13 000	Ceferin SVN
2-09	Germany	L	2-6	Gelsenkirchen	ECq	Arnautovic [42], Harnik [51]	53 313	Tagliavento ITA
6-09	Turkey	D	0-0	Vienna	ECq		47 500	Undiano ESP
7-10	Azerbaijan	W	4-1	Baku	ECq	Ivanschitz [34], Janko 2 [52 62], Junuzovic [91+]	6 000	Studer SUI
11-10	Kazakhstan	D	0-0	Astana	ECq		11 000	Kaasik EST
15-11	Ukraine	L	1-2	Lviv	Fr	OG [71]	31 879	Moen NOR
2012								
29-02	Finland	W	3-1	Klagenfurt	Fr	Janko [32], Harnik [54], Ivanschitz [73p]	10 200	Valeri ITA
1-06	Ukraine	W	3-2	Innsbruck	Fr	Junuzovic [3], Arnautovic 2 [62 89]	13 000	Zwayer GER
5-06	Romania	D	0-0	Innsbruck	Fr		12 500	Makkelie NED
15-08	Turkey	W	2-0	Vienna	Fr	Kavlak [2], Ivanschitz [6p]	23 000	Valasek SVK
11-09	Germany	L	1-2	Vienna	WCq	Junuzovic [57]	47 000	Kuipers NED
12-10	Kazakhstan	D	0-0	Astana	WCq		12 900	Bognar HUN
16-10	Azerbaijan	W	4-0	Vienna	WCq	Janko 2 [24 63], Alaba [71], Harnik [93+]	43 000	Kehlet DEN
14-11	Côte d'Ivoire	L	0-3	Linz	Fr		13 832	Kralovec CZE

Fr = Friendly match • EC = UEFA EURO 2008/2012 • WC = FIFA World Cup • q = qualifier • r1 = first round group

AUSTRIA NATIONAL TEAM HISTORICAL RECORDS

Caps
103 - Andreas Herzog 1988-2003 • 95 - Anton Polster 1982-2000 • 93 - Gerhard Hanappi 1948-62 • 86 - Karl Koller 1952-65 • 84 - Friedrich Koncilia 1970-85 & Bruno Pezzey 1975-90 • 83 - Herbert Prohaska 1974-89 • 69 - Hans Krankl 1973-85 • 68 - Heribert Weber 1976-89 • 65 - Peter Stoger 1988-99 • 64 - Walter Schachner 1976-94 • 63 - Andreas Ogris 1986-97, Anton Pfeffer 1988-99 & Peter Schottel

Goals
44 - Anton Polster 1982-2000 • 34 - Hans Krankl 1973-85 • 29 - Hans Horvath 1924-34 • 28 - Eric Hof 1957-69 • 27 - Anton Schall 1927-34 • 26 - Matthias Sindelar 1926-37 & Andreas Herzog 1988-2003 • 24 - Karl Zischek 1931-45 • 23 - Walter Schachner 1976-94 • 22 - Theodor Wagner 1946-57 • 19 - Karl Decker 1945-52 • 18 - Erich Probst 1951-60, Ferdinand Swatosch 1914-25 & Jan Studnicka 1902-18

Coaches
Hugo Meisl 1912-1914 • Heinrich Retschury 1914-19 • Hugo Meisl 1919-37 • Heinrich Retschury 1937 • Karl Zankl 1945 • Edi Bauer 1945-48 • Eduard Fruhwirth 1948 • Walter Nausch 1948-54 (1954 World Cup) • Hans Kaulich 1954-55 • Josef Molzer 1955 • Karl Geyer 1955-56 • Josef Argauer & Josef Molzer 1956-58 (1958 World Cup) • Alfred Frey, Franz Putzendopler, Egon Selzer & Josef Molzer 1958 • Karl Decker 1958-64 • Josef Walter & Bela Guttmann HUN 1964 • Eduard Fruhwirth 1964-67 • Erwin Alge & Hans Pesser 1967-68 • Leopold Stasny CZE 1968-75 • Branko Elsner YUG 1975 • Helmut Senekowitsch 1976-78 (1978 World Cup) • Karl Stotz 1978-81 • Georg Schmidt & Felix Latzke 1982 (1982 World Cup) • Erich Hof 1982-84 • Branko Elsner YUG 1985-87 • Josef Hickersberger 1988-90 (1990 World Cup) • Alfred Riedl 1990-91 • Dietmar Constantini 1991 • Ernst Happel 1992 • Dietmar Constantini 1992 • Herbert Prohaska 1993-99 (1998 World Cup) • Otto Bari 1999-2001 • Hans Krankl 2002-05 • Willibald Ruttensteiner, Andreas Herzog & Slavko Kovacic 2005 • Josef Hickersberger 2006-08 (Euro 2008) • Karel Bruckner CZE 2008-09 • Dietmar Constantini 2009-11 • Willibald Ruttensteiner 2011 • Marcel Koller SUI 2011-

AUSTRIA 2011–12

TIPP 3 BUNDESLIGA POWERED BY T-MOBILE

	Pl	W	D	L	F	A	Pts	Salzburg	Rapid Wien	Admira	FK Austria	Sturm Graz	Ried	Wacker	Mattersburg	W Neustadt	Kapfenberg
FC RB Salzburg †	36	19	11	6	60	30	**68**		0-0 3-1	2-1 2-0	2-0 3-0	1-1 0-0	1-1 2-0	1-1 2-0	0-0 0-1	3-0 2-1	6-0 2-0
SK Rapid Wien ‡	36	16	14	6	52	30	**62**	4-2 0-1		2-0 2-1	0-3 0-0	3-2 1-1	0-0 1-0	0-0 2-0	1-1 1-1	1-1 2-1	5-1 3-0
FCT Admira ‡	36	15	10	11	59	52	**55**	2-1 2-2	4-3 0-4		0-3 3-2	4-2 2-0	1-1 1-1	3-2 1-1	2-1 0-1	3-0 2-0	1-1 3-1
FK Austria Wien	36	14	12	10	51	43	**54**	3-2 1-1	1-1 0-0	2-4 2-1		2-1 1-1	2-1 2-0	2-2 3-0	0-0 1-0	2-2 3-1	5-0 0-1
SK Sturm Graz	36	12	15	9	47	41	**51**	2-1 2-2	1-0 0-0	3-1 0-3	5-1 3-1		1-0 0-0	1-1 1-0	2-2 1-0	5-0 0-1	1-0 2-1
SV Ried ‡	36	11	15	10	44	38	**48**	1-3 0-1	1-1 2-3	1-1 2-1	2-1 0-1	1-1 1-1		1-0 1-1	1-0 2-0	2-0 2-2	1-0 3-0
FC Wacker Innsbruck	36	10	15	11	36	45	**45**	0-1 1-1	0-3 2-1	2-2 2-1	0-0 0-1	1-0 1-1	0-5 0-0		1-1 3-6	2-0 2-0	3-1 2-0
SV Mattersburg	36	9	11	16	41	43	**38**	3-0 0-1	1-2 0-1	0-0 1-2	2-4 2-0	3-3 0-2	2-3 4-1	1-1 0-1		1-2 0-1	2-0 2-0
SCM Wiener Neustadt	36	6	15	15	26	51	**33**	0-0 1-5	0-2 0-0	0-0 1-4	1-1 0-0	3-1 0-0	2-2 1-1	0-0 0-0	1-2 0-0		2-0 0-0
SV Kapfenberg	36	5	8	23	21	64	**23**	1-3 0-1	0-0 0-2	0-0 2-3	2-2 1-0	3-0 0-0	1-3 0-0	2-3 0-1	1-0 1-1	0-2 1-0	

16/07/2011 - 17/05/2012 • † Qualified for the UEFA Champions League • ‡ Qualified for the Europa League • Attendance: 1,271,856 @ 7,066
Top scorers: **14** - Jakob **JANTSCHER**, Salzburg & Stefan **MAIERHOFER**, Salzburg • **12** - Patrick **BURGER**, Mattersburg & Roland **LINZ**, FK Austria
11 - Darko **BODUL** CRO, Sturm Graz & Patrik **JEZEK** CZE, Admira • **10** - Philipp **HOSINER**, Admira • **9** - Deni **ALAR**, Rapid Wien

AUSTRIA 2011–12

ADEG ERSTE LIGA (2)

	Pl	W	D	L	F	A	Pts	St Andrä	R'dorf Altach	LASK	Lustenau	Sankt Pölten	Blau-Weiß	Grödig	First Vienna	Lustenau	Hartberg
WAC St Andrä	36	19	11	6	71	49	**68**		0-0 3-1	2-1 2-0	2-0 3-0	1-1 0-0	1-1 2-0	1-1 2-0	0-0 0-1	3-0 2-1	6-0 2-0
SC Rheindorf Altach	36	18	8	10	62	39	**62**	4-2 0-1		2-0 2-1	0-3 0-0	3-2 1-1	0-0 1-0	0-0 2-0	1-1 1-1	1-1 2-1	5-1 3-0
LASK Linz - R	36	16	13	7	55	40	**61**	2-1 2-2	4-3 0-4		0-3 3-2	4-2 2-0	1-1 1-1	3-2 1-1	2-1 0-1	3-0 2-0	1-1 3-1
SC Austria Lustenau	36	16	10	10	59	47	**58**	3-2 1-1	1-1 0-0	2-4 2-1		2-1 1-1	2-1 2-0	2-2 3-0	0-0 1-0	2-2 3-1	5-0 0-1
SKN Sankt Pölten	36	14	9	13	45	45	**51**	2-1 2-2	1-0 0-0	3-1 0-3	5-1 3-1		1-0 0-0	1-1 1-0	2-2 1-0	5-0 0-1	1-0 2-1
FC Blau-Weiß Linz	36	13	10	13	49	52	**49**	1-3 0-1	1-1 2-3	1-1 2-1	2-1 0-1	1-1 1-1		1-0 1-1	2-0 2-0	2-0 2-2	1-0 2-0
SV Grödig	36	11	9	16	46	52	**42**	0-1 1-1	0-3 2-1	2-2 2-1	0-0 0-1	1-0 1-1	0-5 0-0		1-1 3-6	2-0 2-0	3-1 2-0
First Vienna FC	36	9	10	17	44	56	**37**	3-0 0-1	1-2 0-1	0-0 1-2	2-4 2-0	3-3 0-2	2-3 4-1	1-1 0-1		1-2 0-1	2-0 2-0
FC Lustenau 07	36	9	10	17	51	66	**37**	0-0 1-5	0-2 0-0	0-0 1-4	1-1 0-0	3-1 0-0	2-2 1-1	0-0 0-0	1-2 0-0		2-0 0-0
TSV Hartberg	36	7	6	23	38	74	**27**	1-3 0-1	0-0 0-2	0-0 2-3	2-2 1-0	3-0 0-0	1-3 0-0	2-3 0-1	1-0 1-1	0-2 1-0	

11/07/2011 - 18/05/2012 • LASK Linz relegated
Top scorer: **19** - David **POLJANEC** SVN, Blau-Weiß Linz • **18** - Christian **FALK**, WAC St Andrä • **17** - Daniel **LUCAS** ESP, St. Pölten

MEDALS TABLE

		Overall	League	Cup	Europe	City	
		G S B	G S B	G S	G S B		
1	FK Austria Wien	52 28 18	23 18 14	27 9	2 1 4	Vienna	
2	SK Rapid Wien	47 40 22	32 24 20	14 12	1 4 2	Vienna	
3	FC Wacker Innsbruck	17 11 7	10 5 6	7 6	1	Innsbruck	
4	Admira Wien	13 6 6	8 5 5	5	1 1	Vienna	1905-71
5	First Vienna FC	10 12 13	6 6 11	3 6	1 2	Vienna	
6	FC RB Salzburg	8 11 1	7 6 1	1 4	1	Salzburg	
7	SK Sturm Graz	7 9 4	3 5 4	4 4		Graz	
8	Grazer AK	5 4 6	1 2 6	4 2		Graz	
9	Wiener Sport-Club	4 14 5	3 7 5	1 7		Vienna	
10	Wiener AC	4 5 6	1 1 6	3 3	1	Vienna	
11	Wacker Wien	2 8 3	1 7 3	1 1		Vienna	1908-71
12	Linzer ASK	2 5 4	1 1 4	1 4		Linz	
13	Wiener AF	2 2 3	1 2 3	1		Vienna	1912-35
14	SV Ried	2 2		1	2 1	Ried	
15	FC Linz	1 4 1	1 2 1	2		Linz	1949-97
16	Floridsdorfer AC	1 3 1	1 3 1			Vienna	1901-39
17	FC Kärnten	1 1			1 1	Klagenfurt	
	Hakoah Wien	1 1	1 1			Vienna	
19	Kremser SC	1		1		Krems	
	SV Stockerau	1		1		Stockerau	
21	FCT Admira		6 4	1 4	5	Mödling	

European medals include those won in the Mitropa Cup 1927-1939

OFB SAMSUNG CUP 2011–12

Second Round

FC RB Salzburg*	4
SAK Klagenfurt	0
FK Austria Wien Amat*	0
LASK Linz	5
FC Blau-Weiß Linz	2
Union St Florian*	0
SV Mattersburg	1 5p
FC RB Salzburg Amat*	1 6p
SK Sturm Graz	3
SC Weiz*	0
SV-ESV Parndorf 1919*	0
FCT Admira	1
SK Rapid Wien Amat*	4
WAC St Andrä	2
Villach*	1
TSV Hartberg	2
FK Austria Wien	3
Allerheiligen*	1
SV Kapfenberg	1
Reichenau*	2
FC Lustenau 07	4
SKU Amstetten*	2
Union Innsbruck*	0
SC Austria Lustenau	7
SV Grödig	2
FC Dornbirn 1913*	0
St Margarethen*	0
FC Wacker Innsbruck	3
SK Rapid Wien	4
Bad Vöslau*	1
Götzendorf*	2
SV Ried	3

Round of 16

FC RB Salzburg*	2
LASK Linz	1
FC Blau-Weiß Linz	1
FC RB Salzburg Amat*	3
SK Sturm Graz*	3
FCT Admira	1
SK Rapid Wien Amat*	0
TSV Hartberg	2
FK Austria Wien	2
Reichenau*	0
FC Lustenau 07	1
SC Austria Lustenau*	4
SV Grödig	1
FC Wacker Innsbruck*	0
SK Rapid Wien*	1
SV Ried	2

Quarter-finals

FC RB Salzburg*	4
FC RB Salzburg Amateure	1
SK Sturm Graz*	2
TSV Hartberg	4
FK Austria Wien	2
SC Austria Lustenau*	1
SV Grödig*	2
SV Ried	3

Semi-finals

FC RB Salzburg	1
TSV Hartberg*	0
FK Austria Wien	0
SV Ried*	2

Final

FC RB Salzburg	3
SV Ried ‡	0

CUP FINAL

Ernst-Happel-Stadion, Vienna, 20-05-2012, 16:00, Att: 16 000, Ref: Thomas Einwaller
Scorers - Leonardo 10p, Schiemer 14, Hierländer 91+ for Salzburg
Salzburg - Alexander Walke - Christian Schwegler, Franz Schiemer, Ibrahim Sekagya●, Andreas Ulmer (Martin Hinteregger● 46) - Mendes, Christoph Leitgeb●, Gonzalo Zarate● (Stefan Hierländer 87), Leonardo●, Dusan Svento - Stefan Maierhofer (Cristiano● 73). Tr: Ricardo Moniz
Ried - Thomas Gebauer - Marcel Ziegl●, Thomas Reifeltshammer, Jan-Marc Riegler - Thomas Hinum, Anel Hadzic●, Emanuel Schreiner (Ivan Carril● 54) - Daniel Beichler, Robert Zulj●, Marco Meilinger (Stefan Lexa● 41) - Guillem (Casanova 70). Tr: Gerhard Schweitzer

* Home team ‡ Qualified for the Europa League

AZE – AZERBAIJAN

FIFA/COCA-COLA WORLD RANKING

'93	'94	'95	'96	'97	'98	'99	'00	'01	'02	'03	'04	'05	'06	'07	'08	'09	'10	'11	'12
-	147	141	125	123	99	97	115	113	113	119	113	114	125	115	134	114	98	112	118

2012

Jan	Feb	Mar	Apr	May	Jun	Jul	Aug	Sep	Oct	Nov	Dec	High	Low	Av
111	109	116	110	109	112	108	108	107	111	123	118	90	170	118

Azerbaijan stepped into the international limelight in September 2012 when the country hosted the FIFA U-17 Women's World Cup, staging matches in both the capital Baku and Lenkoran. It was the first time the country had staged a major international sporting event and although their women's U-17 team crashed out at the group stage without winning a point, it was a positive experience for a country that failed to see Baku become a candidate city to host the 2020 Olympic Games. There was disappointment also when the idea of a joint bid to host Euro 2020 with Georgia had to be dropped when UEFA decided to stage the finals in 12 or 13 cities across the whole continent. National team coach Bertie Vogts continues to try and build a side capable of making an impact to match the ambitions of the country off the pitch, but the only two victories in 2012 came against Asian countries in friendlies and with just two points from their first four games in the qualifiers for the 2014 FIFA World Cup, Azerbaijan were left comfortably off the pace. At home, Neftchi Baku retained their league title after finishing four points ahead of Khazar Lenkoran. They failed to do the double, however, losing to neighbours FK Baku in the cup final a week after the end of the league campaign, beaten 2-0 in the new Dalga Arena.

UEFA EUROPEAN CHAMPIONSHIP RECORD
1960-1992 DNE (part of the Soviet Union) **1996-2012** DNQ

ASSOCIATION OF FOOTBALL FEDERATIONS OF AZERBAIJAN (AFFA)

2208 Nobel prospekti,
Baku AZ-1025
☎ +994 12 4908721
📠 +994 12 4908722
✉ info@affa.az
🌐 www.affa.az
FA 1992 CON 1994 FIFA 1994
P Rovnag Abdullayev
GS Elkhan Mammadov

THE STADIA
2014 FIFA World Cup Stadia
Tofig Bahramov Stadionu
Baku — 31 200

Other Main Stadia
Lenkoran City Stadionu
Lenkoran — 15 000
8 Km Stadionu
Baku — 11 000
Shafa Stadionu
Baku — 8 152
Dalga Arena
Baku — 6 500

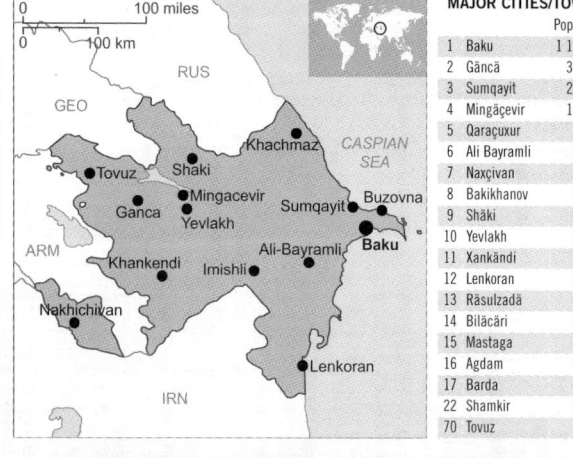

MAJOR CITIES/TOWNS

		Population
1	Baku	1 194 524
2	Gäncä	323 760
3	Sumqayit	282 280
4	Mingäçevir	100 778
5	Qaraçuxur	78 730
6	Ali Bayramli	76 648
7	Naxçivan	75 972
8	Bakikhanov	71 836
9	Shäki	65 616
10	Yevlakh	57 449
11	Xankändi	55 282
12	Lenkoran	50 534
13	Räsulzadä	48 716
14	Biläcäri	45 678
15	Mastaga	42 635
16	Agdam	42 587
17	Barda	40 741
22	Shamkir	38 331
70	Tovuz	13 612

AZARBAYCAN RESPUBLIKASI • REPUBLIC OF AZERBAIJAN

Capital Baku Population 8 238 672 (91) % in cities 52%
GDP per capita $9 500 (107) Area km² 86 600 km² (112) GMT +/- +5
Neighbours (km) Armenia 787, Georgia 322, Iran 611, Russia 284, Turkey 9 • Coast 713 (Caspian Sea)

RECENT INTERNATIONALS PLAYED BY AZERBAIJAN

2009	Opponents	Score	Venue	Comp	Scorers	Att	Referee
12-08	Germany	L 0-2	Baku	WCq		22 500	Kelly IRL
5-09	Finland	L 1-2	Lenkoran	WCq	Elvin Mammadov [49]	12 000	Trifonos CYP
9-09	Germany	L 0-4	Hanover	WCq		35 369	Kakos GRE
10-10	Liechtenstein	W 2-0	Vaduz	WCq	Vagif Javadov [55], Elvin Mammadov [82]	1 635	Radovanovic MNE
14-10	Russia	D 1-1	Baku	WCq	Vagif Javadov [53]	17 000	Webb ENG
15-11	Iraq	L 0-1	Al Ain	Fr			
18-11	Czech Republic	W 2-0	Al Ain	Fr	Vagif Javadov [24], Samir Abasov [89]		Al Marzouqi UAE
2010							
25-02	Jordan	W 2-0	Amman	Fr	Fabio Ramin [1], Afran Ismaylov [31]		Shaaban EGY
3-03	Luxembourg	W 2-1	Luxembourg	Fr	Farid Guliyev [28], Elvin Mammadov [37]	874	Kari FIN
26-05	Moldova	D 1-1	Seekirchen	Fr	Elvin Mammadov [21]	200	Lechner AUT
29-05	FYR Macedonia	L 1-3	Villach	Fr	Elvin Mammadov [89]	100	Drabek AUT
2-06	Honduras	D 0-0	Zell Am See	Fr		500	Brandner AUT
11-08	Kuwait	D 1-1	Baku	Fr	Elvin Mammadov [42]	9 000	Karasev RUS
7-09	Germany	L 1-6	Cologne	ECq	Vagif Javadov [57]	43 751	Strombergsson SWE
8-10	Austria	L 0-3	Vienna	ECq		26 500	Vollquartz DEN
12-10	Turkey	W 1-0	Baku	ECq	Rashad F. Sadygov [38]	29 500	Deaconu ROU
17-11	Montenegro	L 0-2	Podgorica	Fr		3 000	Stavrev MKD
2011							
9-02	Hungary	L 0-2	Dubai	Fr		500	Al Zarooni UAE
29-03	Belgium	L 1-4	Brussels	ECq	Ruslan Abishov [16]	34 985	Stalhammar SWE
3-06	Kazakhstan	L 1-2	Astana	ECq	Vuqar Nadirov [63]	10 000	Norris SCO
7-06	Germany	L 1-3	Baku	ECq	Murad Huseynov [89]	29 858	Koukoulakis GRE
10-08	Macedonia FYR	L 0-1	Baku	Fr			Kulbakov BLR
2-09	Belgium	D 1-1	Baku	ECq	Rauf Aliyev [86]	9 300	Probert ENG
6-09	Kazakhstan	W 3-2	Baku	ECq	Rauf Aliyev [53], Mahir Shukurov [62], Vagif Javadov [67]	9 112	Hermansen DEN
7-10	Austria	L 1-4	Baku	ECq	Vuqar Nadirov [74]	6 000	Studer SUI
11-10	Turkey	L 0-1	Istanbul	ECq		32 174	Rasmussen DEN
11-11	Albania	W 1-0	Tirana	Fr	Rauf Aliyev [22]	1 200	Mazzoleni ITA
2012							
24-02	Singapore	D 2-2	Dubai	Fr	Rauf Aliyev [15], Mahir Shukurov [62]	50	Banihammad UAE
27-02	India	W 3-0	Dubai	Fr	Vuqar Nadirov [3], Mahir Shukurov [43p], Nizami Haciyev [84]	50	Hashmi UAE
23-05	Japan	L 0-2	Shizuoka	Fr		30 276	Bashir SIN
30-05	Andorra	D 0-0	Kelsterbach	Fr			Weiner GER
15-08	Bahrain	W 3-0	Baku	Fr	Branimir Subasic [35], Cihan Ozkara [59], Javid Huseynov [79]		Vadachkoria GEO
7-09	Israel	D 1-1	Baku	WCq	Ruslan Abishov [65]	22 211	Jug SVN
11-09	Portugal	L 0-3	Braga	WCq		29 971	Marciniak POL
16-10	Russia	L 0-1	Moscow	WCq		15 033	Stavrev MKD
14-11	Northern Ireland	D 1-1	Belfast	WCq	Rauf Aliyev [5]	12 372	Shvetsov UKR

Fr = Friendly match • EC = UEFA EURO 2012 • WCq = FIFA World Cup • q = qualifier

AZERBAIJAN NATIONAL TEAM HISTORICAL RECORDS

Caps
80 - Rashad F. Sadygov 2001- • 79 - Aslan Kerimov 1994-2007 • 73 - Tarlan Akhmedov 1992-2005 • 72 - Makhmud Gurbanov 1994-2008
68 - Gurban Gurbanov 1992-2005 • 65 - Emin Agaev 1994-2005 • 62 - Mahir Sukurov 2004- • 54 - Aleksandr Chertoganov 2006-
49 - Emin Guliyev 2000-08 • 46 - Kamal Guliyev 2000-05 • 45 - Vyacheslav Lichkin 1995-2001

Goals
12 - Gurban Gurbanov 1992-2005 • 7 - Elvin Mammadov 2008- & Vagif Javadov 2006- • 6 - Branimir Subasic 2007-09 & Zaur Tagizade 1997-2005 • 5 - Farrukh Ismayilov 1998-2006, Vidadi Rzayev 1992-2001, Nazim Suleymanov 1992-98 & Rauf Aliyev 2010-

Coaches
Alakbar Mammadov 1992-1993 • Kazbek Tuayev 1993-1994 • Agaselim Mirjavadov 1994-1995 • Kazbek Tuayev 1995-1997 • Vagif Sadygov 1997-1998 • Ahmad Alaskarov 1998-2000 • Igor Ponomaryov 2000-2001 • Vagif Sadygov 2002 • Asgar Abdullayev 2003-2004 • Carlos Alberto Torres BRA 2004-2005 • Vagif Sadygov 2005 • Shahin Diniyev 2005-2007 • Gjoko Hadzievski MKD 2007-2008 • Berti Vogts GER 2008-

AZERBAIJAN 2011-12

UNIBANK PREMYER LIGA (1)

	Pl	W	D	L	F	A	Pts	Neftchi	Khazar	Inter	Karabakh	Gabala	FK Baku	AZAL Baku	Ravan Baku	Simurq	Kapaz	Turan	Sumgayit
Neftchi Baku †	32	20	3	9	55	30	63		5-0 1-1 0-1	2-1 3-2	2-1 2-0 0-0	1-1 0-2	2-1	7-1	1-0	4-2	2-0	1-0	4-0
Khazar Lenkoran ‡	32	17	8	7	44	28	59	1-0 1-0		0-1 2-0 0-0	4-1 2-1 1-1	3-0 0-0	1-1	1-0	1-1	1-0	1-0	3-1	2-1
Inter Baku ‡	32	16	8	8	29	21	56	2-1 1-2 1-0 0-0	0-0 1-1 1-1		2-1 0-3 1-0	1-1	1-1	1-0	1-0	0-0	1-0	2-0
Karabakh Agdam	32	15	8	9	37	28	53	1-2 0-0 0-1	1-1 0-1 0-1 0	0-0 1-1 1-2	1-2 4	1-0	2-0	2-0	1-0	3-1	1-2
FK Gabala	32	15	7	10	43	32	52	1-0 4-1 2-1 0	1-0 0-2 2-1 0	0-1 0	0-0 4-0	1-1	2-3	0-2	2-0	2-1	3-1
FK Baku ‡	32	15	5	12	42	37	50	1-3 2-0 2-2 4	1-1 0-0 1-0	3-1 2-2 1-2 1	0-0	3-2	0-0	0-3	5-0	1-0
AZAL Baku	32	12	8	12	44	44	44	3-1	0-3	1-1	1-3	3-0	1-0	1-2 1-1 5-1	0-0 2-0 2-0	3-2 1-0 6-3 1-1
Ravan Baku	32	10	11	11	39	39	41	0-1	1-1	1-2	1-1	0-4	0-0	3-1 2-0	1-1 0-0 1-2 5-1	2-1 2-2 0-0 3-2
Simurq Zaqatala	32	8	10	14	27	41	34	1-2	2-2	0-2	0-1	0-1	0-2	0-3 1-2 1-1 1-1	4-2 1-1 2-1 1-1 1-0 2-1
Kapaz Gança	32	9	5	18	35	55	32	1-1	1-4	0-1	1-2	3-2	1-3	3-1 0-2 3-2 1-0 2-0 0-1	1-1 2-1 1-1 4-1
Turan Tovuz	32	6	7	19	26	42	25	0-1	0-1	0-1	0-1	0-1	0-2	0-0 3-0 0-1 2-1 1-0 0-0 3-1 2-0	1-0 1-1
FC Sumgayit	32	6	6	20	27	52	24	0-3	0-3	0-2	0-0	1-2	0-1	2-1 1-0 0-1 0-1 0-1 1-2 4-1 2-0 1-0 1-1

6/08/2011 – 11/05/2012 • † Qualified for the UEFA Champions League • ‡ Qualified for the Europa League • No teams relegated
Top scorers: **16** - Bakhodir **NASIMOV** UZB, Neftchi • **11** - Yuriy **FOMENKO** UKR, Kapaz • **10** - Tales **SCHUTZ** BRA, AZAL; **FLAVINHO** BRA, Neftchi & Zouhir **BENOUAHI** MAR, AZAL • **9** - **DODO** BRA, Gabala & Yannick **KAMANAN** FRA, Gabala

AZERBAIJAN 2011-12 BIRINCI DASTA (2)

	Pl	W	D	L	F	A	Pts
Kharadag Lökbatan	26	21	2	3	45	9	65
FK Neftçala	26	17	4	5	55	22	55
Karvan Yevlakh	26	16	7	3	42	16	55
Shahdag Khusar	26	13	6	7	46	33	45
Bakili Baku	26	11	5	10	36	28	38
Lokomotiv-Bilajary	26	10	6	10	37	33	36
MTK-Araz Imishli	26	11	3	12	35	43	36
FK Shamkir	26	9	6	11	38	38	33
Tarragi Ganja	26	9	4	13	28	30	31
Mugan Salyan	26	9	4	13	26	43	31
Shusha Baku	26	7	8	11	21	23	29
Energetik Mingacevir	26	6	7	13	21	45	25
MOIK Baku	26	7	4	15	34	44	25
Geyazan Gazakh	26	1	4	21	17	74	7

10/09/2011 – 12/05/2012

MEDALS TABLE

		Overall			League			Cup	
		G	S	B	G	S	B	G	S
1	Neftchi Baku	12	4	4	7	2	4	5	2
2	Kapaz Gança	7	1	2	3	1	2	4	
3	FK Baku	5	1	1	2	1	1	3	
4	Karabakh Agdam	4	6	3	1	3	3	3	3
5	Khazar Lenkoran	4	5		1	3		3	2
6	Inter Baku	2	5	1	2	1	1		4
7	FK Shamkir	2	4	1	2	1	1		3
8	Turan Tovuz	1	1	1	1	1	1		
9	Inshaatchi Baku	1							
	Shafa Baku	1						1	
11	Karvan Yevlakh		2	1		1	1		1
	Khazri Buznova		2	1		1	1		1
13	Khazar Sumgayit		2			2			
	Kur-Nur Mingaçevir		2						2
15	Dinamo Baku		1	1		1	1		
16	Inshaatchi Sabirabad		1						1
	MTK-Araz Imishli		1						
	AZAL Baku (ex Olimpik)		1			1			
19	Simurq Zaqatala			1			1		

AZERBAIJAN KUBOKU 2011-12

First Round		Quarter-finals		Semi-finals		Final	
FK Baku *	0 3p						
Ravan Baku	0 2p	FK Baku *	3 2				
Shahdag Khusar	0	AZAL Baku	1 1				
AZAL Baku *	2			FK Baku *	0 1 5p		
FK Gabala *	3			Karabakh Agdam	1 0 4p		
FK Neftçala	0	FK Gabala *	2 0				
FC Sumgayit	0	Karabakh Agdam	2 0			FK Baku ‡	2
Karabakh Agdam *	3					Neftchi Baku	0
Inter Baku *	3						
Turan Tovuz	0	Inter Baku *	3 1			**CUP FINAL**	
Kharadag Lökbatan	0	Khazar Lenkoran	2 1				
Khazar Lenkoran *	3			Inter Baku *	0 0	Dalga Arena, Baku	
Kapaz Gança *	2			Neftchi Baku	0 1	17-05-2012, 4300, Agayev	
Bakili Baku	0	Kapaz Gança *	1 1			Scorers - Koke [9], Juninho [28] for Baku	
Simurq Zaqatala *	0	Neftchi Baku	2 1				
Neftchi Baku	1						

* Home team in the first leg • ‡ Qualified for the Europa League

Preliminary Round: **Shahdag** 4-1 Mugan • Tarragi 0-1 **Neftçala** • Shusha 2-3 **Kharadag** • **Bakili** 2-1 Karvan • Lokomotiv 0-2 **Sumgayit**

BAH – BAHAMAS

FIFA/COCA-COLA WORLD RANKING

'93	'94	'95	'96	'97	'98	'99	'00	'01	'02	'03	'04	'05	'06	'07	'08	'09	'10	'11	'12
167	-	-	-	-	-	189	178	184	187	193	192	193	146	174	170	180	194	154	174

2012

Jan	Feb	Mar	Apr	May	Jun	Jul	Aug	Sep	Oct	Nov	Dec	High	Low	Av
155	154	155	161	161	162	171	180	180	181	183	174	138	197	178

The withdrawal of the Bahamas national team from the 2014 FIFA World Cup qualifiers after their 10-0 aggregate first round victory over the Turks and Caicos Islands deprived the national team of valuable international experience although it did mean the Bahamas will almost certainly finish as the only team in the tournament with a 100 per cent record! The national team went into further hibernation when the BFA decided not to enter a team into the qualifiers for the 2012 Caribbean Cup - academic studies amongst the players once again seen as a priority - leaving the team with no fixtures during 2012 and having played just two matches in four years. It was the third time in succession that the Bahamas had failed to enter the most prestigious tournament in the region, despite the opening of the new national stadium in Nassau in February 2012. There was no international representation for the Bahamas at the 2012 CFU Club Championship either with 2011 champions Bears content to reinforce their aura of invincibility by staying at home where once again they won the championship in style. The 2012 title was their fourth in a row and since the introduction of the BFA Senior League in 2009, Bears have lost just four matches in four seasons. Predictably Bears also won the 2012 BFA Knock Out Cup, beating Baha Juniors 7-2 in the final.

CFU CARIBBEAN CUP RECORD
1989-1998 DNE 1999 DNQ 2001 DNE (withdrew) 2005 DNE 2007 DNQ 2008-2012 DNE

BAHAMAS FOOTBALL ASSOCIATION (BFA)
Rosetta Street,
PO Box N-8434
Nassau, NP
☎ +1 242 3943117
✆ +1 242 3946284
✉ info@bahamasfa.com
🌐 bahamasfa.com
FA 1967 CON 1981 FIFA 1968
P Anton Sealey
GS Fred Lunn

THE STADIA
2014 FIFA World Cup Stadia
BFA National Development Center
Nassau
Other Main Stadia
Thomas Robinson National Stadium
Nassau　　　　　　　　15 023
Grand Bahama Stadium
Freeport　　　　　　　　3 100
Roscow A. L. Davies Soccer Field
Nassau　　　　　　　　1 700

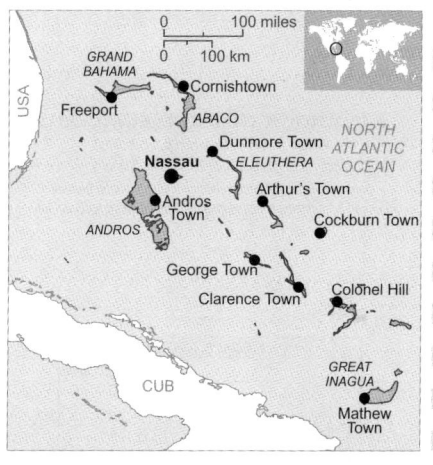

MAJOR CITIES/TOWNS

		Population
1	Nassau	238 132
2	Freeport	47 085
3	West End	13 004
4	Coopers Town	9 069
5	Marsh Harbour	5 728
6	Freetown	4 222
7	High Rock	3 827
8	Andros Town	2 318
9	Spanish Wells	1 805
10	Clarence Town	1 705
11	Dunmore Town	1 578
12	Rock Sound	1 447
13	Arthur's Town	1 216
14	Cockburn Town	1 045
15	George Town	1 038
16	Alice Town	936
17	Sweeting Cay	494
18	Matthew Town	435
19	Snug Corner	402

THE BAHAMAS

Capital	Nassau	Population	309 156 (176)	% in cities	84%
GDP per capita	$29 600 (46)	Area km²	13 880 km² (160)	GMT +/-	-5
Neighbours (km)	Coast 3542				

RECENT INTERNATIONAL MATCHES PLAYED BY BAHAMAS

2007	Opponents	Score	Venue	Comp	Scorers	Att	Referee
No international matches played in 2007							
2008							
26-03	British Virgin Islands	D 1-1	Nassau	WCq	St Fleur [47]	450	Moreno PAN
30-03	British Virgin Islands	D 2-2	Nassau	WCq	Bethel [41], Mitchell [57]	940	Suazo DOM
15-06	Jamaica	L 0-7	Kingston	WCq		20 000	Navarro CAN
18-06	Jamaica	L 0-6	Greenfield-Tr'wny	WCq		10 500	Archundia MEX
2009							
No international matches played in 2009							
2010							
No international matches played in 2010							
2011							
2-07	Turks and Caicos Isl	W 4-0	Providenciales	WCq	Nesley Jean 2 [32 61], Cameron Hepple [36p], Jackner Louis [92+]	1 021	Cruz CRC
9-07	Turks and Caicos Isl	W 6-0	Nassau	WCq	Gibson OG [4], Lesley St Fleur 5 [17 64 73 84 90]	1 600	Santos PUR
2012							
No international matches played in 2012							

Fr = Friendly match • CC = Digicel Caribbean Cup • WC = FIFA World Cup • q = qualifier

BAHAMAS 2012

BFA SENIOR LEAGUE

	Pl	W	D	L	F	A	Pts	Bears	Cavalier	Lyford Cay	Dynamos	United	Baha Juniors	COB	VBS
Bears	14	12	1	1	47	12	**37**		4-1	1-1	2-0	3-0	4-0	3-1	13-2
Cavalier	14	9	2	3	33	18	**29**	1-2		4-2	1-2	1-0	3-3	1-1	5-0
Lyford Cay	14	8	3	3	38	16	**27**	0-3	1-2		4-0	1-1	7-3	1-1	5-1
Dynamos	14	8	2	4	25	20	**26**	3-2	1-1	0-3		3-1	1-3	3-0	5-1
United	14	6	2	6	20	21	**20**	0-2	0-3	0-2	1-1		5-0	3-1	2-1
Baha Juniors	14	5	1	8	26	39	**16**	2-4	1-2	0-4	1-3	1-2		2-1	4-2
College of Bahamas	14	1	1	12	13	37	**4**	1-3	2-3	0-5	0-2	0-1	1-3		4-0
VBS	14	1	0	13	12	51	**3**	0-1	0-1	0-2	0-1	2-4	**0-3**	3-1	

27/11/2011 - 6/06/2012

BFA KNOCK-OUT CUP FINAL 2012
Roscow AL Davies Soccer Field, 11-06-2012

Bears 7-2 Baha Juniors

Scorers - Domingo Hurston, Nesley Jean 2, Mareus, Demont Mitchell 3 for Bears; Alkin Delancy, Nick Constantine for Baha Jun

MEDALS TABLE

		Overall G	Lge G	Cup G
1	Bears	14	8	6
2	Cavalier	6	4	2
3	Britam United	4	4	
4	Caledonia Celtic	3	2	1
5	Abacom United	1	1	
	Freeport	1	1	
	JJ Johnson	1		1

BAN – BANGLADESH

FIFA/COCA-COLA WORLD RANKING

'93	'94	'95	'96	'97	'98	'99	'00	'01	'02	'03	'04	'05	'06	'07	'08	'09	'10	'11	'12
116	130	138	136	141	157	130	151	146	159	151	167	160	144	168	174	149	159	157	168

2012

Jan	Feb	Mar	Apr	May	Jun	Jul	Aug	Sep	Oct	Nov	Dec	High	Low	Av
158	157	164	152	152	152	151	169	170	169	171	168	110	183	150

Abahani Dhaka claimed the Bangladesh league title by a single point from Muktijoddha Sangsad after the two clubs met in a winner-takes-all game on the final day of the season. Muktijoddha twice led their rivals in search of the victory which would have secured them the league crown but goals from Sakhawat Rony and Zahid Hossain levelled the scores to give Abahani the point they needed - the second coming just six minutes from the end. It was the fourth time that the club had won the Bangladesh League in the five years since the tournament was launched and was their fifth national title overall. Defending champions Sheikh Jamal, who won the title for the first time in 2011, struggled as they attempted to retain their title, finishing a distant 20 points adrift of Abahani in sixth place and they also missed out on winning the Federation Cup after losing 2-1 in the final to Sheikh Russell. Their title triumph in 2011 had entitled Sheikh Jamal to represent Bangladesh in the 2012 AFC President's Cup but they did not participate after being drawn to face Pakistan's KRL, Taiwan Power Company and Erchim of Mongolia, withdrawing due to security concerns after Pakistan was named as host for the group matches. The national team played just three friendly international matches in 2012 - none of them at home and none of which were won.

FIFA WORLD CUP RECORD
1930-1982 DNE **1986-2014** DNQ

BANGLADESH FOOTBALL FEDERATION (BFF)

- BFF House,
- Motijheel, Dhaka 1000
- ☎ +880 2 7161582
- 📠 +880 2 7160270
- ✉ info@bff.com.bd
- 🌐 www.bff.com.bd
- FA 1972 CON 1974 FIFA 1976
- P Mohammed Salahuddin Kazi
- GS Shohag Nayeem

THE STADIA

2014 FIFA World Cup Stadia

Bangabandhu National Stadium Dhaka	36 000

Other Main Stadia

MA Aziz Stadium Chittagong	20 000
Kamlapur Stadium Dhaka	20 000
Bangladesh Army Stadium Dhaka	15 000
M.A.G. Osmani Stadium Sylhet	15 000

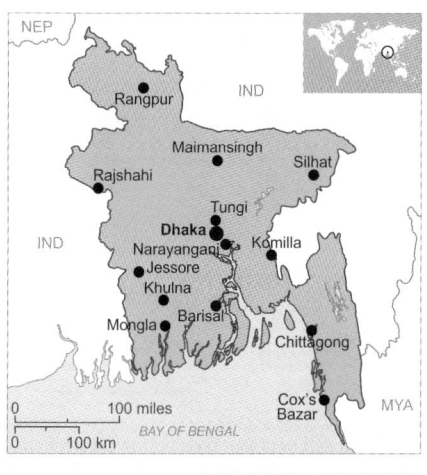

MAJOR CITIES/TOWNS

		Population
1	Dhaka	10 468 510
2	Chittagong	3 761 337
3	Narayanganj	1 448 975
4	Khulna	1 406 963
5	Gazipur	1 159 557
6	Rajshahi	791 051
7	Tungi	417 507
8	Silhat	399 381
9	Maimansingh	388 598
10	Narsingdi	351 538
11	Komilla	337 854
12	Rangpur	323 001
13	Barisal	267 423
14	Jessor	255 716
15	Bogra	254 635
16	Pabna	180 400
17	Dinajpur	180 301
18	Nawabganj	175 363
19	Brahman	157 089

BANLADESH • BANGLADESH

Capital	Dhaka	Population	156 050 883 (7)	% in cities	27%
GDP per capita	$1500 (196)	Area km²	143 998 km² (94)	GMT + / -	+6
Neighbours (km)	Myanmar 193, India 4053 • Coast 580				

RECENT INTERNATIONAL MATCHES PLAYED BY BANGLADESH

2006	Opponents	Score	Venue	Comp	Scorers	Att	Referee
16-08	Qatar	L 1-4	Chittagong	ACq	Mohamad Arman [23]	7 000	Al Yarimi YEM
6-09	Qatar	L 0-3	Doha	ACq		500	Najm LIB
11-10	Uzbekistan	L 0-4	Dhaka	ACq		120	Tan Hai CHN
15-11	Hong Kong	L 0-2	Hong Kong	ACq		1 273	Kim Dong Jin KOR
2007							
18-08	Syria	L 0-2	New Delhi	Fr			
20-08	India	L 0-1	New Delhi	Fr			
22-08	Cambodia	D 1-1	New Delhi	Fr	Abdul Hossain [30]		
24-08	Kyrgyzstan	L 0-3	New Delhi	Fr			
8-10	Tajikistan	D 1-1	Dhaka	WCq	Zumratul Hossain Mithu [50]	700	Al Hilali OMA
28-10	Tajikistan	L 0-5	Dushanbe	WCq		10 000	Chynybekov KGZ
2008							
5-05	Afghanistan	D 0-0	Bishkek	CCq		3 000	Al Senan UAE
9-05	Kyrgyzstan	L 1-2	Bishkek	CCq		5 000	Al Enezi KUW
4-06	Bhutan	D 1-1	Colombo	SAFr1	Arup Baidya [26]		
6-06	Afghanistan	D 2-2	Colombo	SAFr1	Hasan Ameli [52], Mamunul Islam Mamun [76]		
8-06	Sri Lanka	L 0-1	Colombo	SAFr1			
18-10	Myanmar	L 0-1	Kuala Lumpur	Fr			
11-11	Myanmar	D 0-0	Yangon	Fr			
13-11	Indonesia	L 0-2	Yangon	Fr			
2009							
26-04	Cambodia	W 1-0	Dhaka	CCq	Anamul Hoque [73]	8 060	Yazdi IRN
28-04	Myanmar	L 1-2	Dhaka	CCq	Anamul Hoque [12]	14 000	Matsuo JPN
30-04	Macau	W 3-0	Dhaka	CCq	Mamunul Islam Mamun [38], Zahid Hossain 2 [68 71]	8 700	Mashentsev KGZ
4-12	Bhutan	W 4-1	Dhaka	SAFr1	Das [11], Anamul Hoque 2 [22 51], Ameli [72]		
6-12	Pakistan	D 0-0	Dhaka	SAFr1			
8-12	Sri Lanka	W 2-1	Dhaka	SAFr1	Anamul Hoque 2 [8 64]		
11-12	India †	L 0-1	Dhaka	SAFsf			
2010							
16-02	Tajikistan	W 2-1	Colombo	CCr1	Anamul Hoque [67], Atiqur Meshu [74]	1 000	Matsuo JPN
18-02	Myanmar	L 1-2	Colombo	CCr1	Mohammed Hossain [49]	500	Al Yarimi YEM
20-02	Sri Lanka	L 0-3	Colombo	CCr1		600	Mahapab THA
2011							
21-03	Palestine	L 0-2	Yangon	CCq		1 000	
23-03	Myanmar	W 2-0	Yangon	CCq	Ahmed Shakil [10], Abdulbaten Mojumder [88]	3 000	
25-03	Philippines	L 0-3	Yangon	CCq		200	Kim Jong Hyeok KOR
29-06	Pakistan	W 3-0	Dhaka	WCq	Jahid Hasan [1], Zahid Hossain [22], Karim Razaul [56]	5 326	Abu Loum JOR
3-07	Pakistan	D 0-0	Lahore	WCq		3 500	Abdulnabi BHR
23-07	Lebanon	L 0-4	Beirut	WCq		2 000	Auda IRQ
28-07	Lebanon	W 2-0	Dhaka	WCq	Mithun Chowdhury [52], Jahid Hassan [87]	11 000	Aonrak THA
2-12	Pakistan	D 0-0	New Delhi	SAFr1			Faizullin KGZ
4-12	Nepal	L 0-1	New Delhi	SAFr1			Kumar IND
6-12	Maldives	L 1-3	New Delhi	SAFr1	Alam Shahed [29]		Tufaylieh SYR
2012							
20-09	Nepal	D 1-1	Kathmandu	Fr	Zahid Hossain [43]		
17-11	Thailand	L 0-5	Bangkok	Fr			
20-11	Malaysia	D 1-1	Kuala Lumpur	Fr	Jahid Hasan [83]		

SAF = South Asian Football Federation Cup • AC = AFC Asian Cup • CC = AFC Challenge Cup • WCq = FIFA World Cup
q = qualifier • r1 = first round group • sf = semi-final • f = final

BANGLADESH NATIONAL TEAM HISTORICAL RECORDS

Past Coaches: Hamzah Hussain Wahid 1992 • Kazi Salahuddin 1993 • Oldrich Svab SUI • Man Yang Kang KOR 1994 • Otto Pfister GER 1994-97 • Samir Shakir IRQ 1998-99 • Mark Harrison ENG 2000 • Aurel Ticleanu ROU 2002 • Gyorgy Kottan AUT 2002-03 • Andres Cruciani ARG 2005-07 • Syed Nayeemuddin IND 2007 • Sayeed Hassan Kanan 2007-08 • Abu Yusuf Mohammad Bilal 2008 • Shafiq Islam Malik 2008 • Dido BRA 2009 • Rizwan Ali Jahed 2009 • Zoran Djordjevic SRB 2010 • Saiful Bari Titu 2010 • Robert Rupcic CRO 2010-11 • Gjore Jovanovski MKD 2011 • Nikola Olievski MKD 2011 • Saiful Bari Titu 2012 • Lodewijk de Kruif NED 2013-

BANGLADESH 2012

GRAMEENPHONE BANGLADESH LEAGUE

	Pl	W	D	L	F	A	Pts	Abahani Dhaka	Muktijoddha	Mohammedan	BJMC	Sheikh Russell	Sheikh Jamal	Brothers Union	Arambagh	Feni	Farashganj	Rahmatganj
Abahani Dhaka †	20	13	6	1	42	15	45		2-2	1-1	1-0	1-0	3-0	4-2	2-0	5-0	0-0	3-0
Muktijoddha Sangsad	20	13	5	2	43	10	44	1-1		0-0	2-0	1-0	3-0	3-0	4-1	5-0	2-0	3-0
Mohammedan	20	9	7	4	33	21	34	2-0	2-2		1-1	0-3	1-2	2-1	3-1	3-1	2-0	4-0
BJMC	20	9	6	5	32	20	33	2-3	0-0	2-2		0-1	1-1	3-1	2-1	2-0	1-1	1-0
Sheikh Russell	20	9	5	6	30	20	32	1-1	0-2	0-2	3-2		2-3	0-1	3-0	1-1	3-0	3-2
Sheikh Jamal	20	7	4	9	27	33	25	1-2	0-2	4-2	1-3	0-0		1-3	0-3	1-1	0-2	4-2
Brothers Union	20	6	6	8	25	35	24	1-1	2-1	1-1	1-1	1-4	2-2		1-2	1-1	1-0	2-1
Arambagh	20	5	4	11	20	37	19	1-4	1-4	0-1	0-5	0-0	0-2	3-4		1-1	2-0	1-1
Feni	20	5	4	11	15	32	19	0-1	0-2	2-1	0-2	0-1	0-3	1-0	0-1		1-2	3-0
Farashganj	20	4	6	10	15	26	18	1-3	1-0	0-0	1-3	2-4	0-2	0-0	0-0	0-1		4-0
Rahmatganj	20	2	3	15	13	46	9	0-4	0-4	0-3	0-1	1-1	1-0	4-0	0-2	0-2	1-1	

1/02/2012 - 3/07/2012 • † Qualified for the AFC President's Cup

MEDALS TABLE

		Overall		Nat		Fed Cup		Dhaka	
		G	S	G	B	G	S	G	City
1	Mohammedan SC	31	9	2	5	10	4	19	Dhaka
2	Abahani Ltd	24	9	5	2	8	7	11	Dhaka
3	Dhaka Wanderers	7	1				1	7	Dhaka
4	Muktijoddha SKC	6	5	1	2	3	3	2	Dhaka
5	Brothers Union	6	2	1		3	2	2	Dhaka
6	Bangladesh IDC	4						4	Dhaka
7	Victoria SC	3						3	Dhaka
8	Sheikh Jamal Dhanmondi Club	2	2	1		1	2		Dhaka
9	Azad	1						1	Dhaka
10	Bangladesh Jute Mill Corp.	1	1				1	1	Dhaka
11	Bengal Government Press	1						1	Dhaka
	East Pakistan Gymkhana	1						1	Dhaka
	Fakirerpool Young Men's Club	1						1	Dhaka
	Sheikh Russell	1				1			

Nat = National Championship 2000-05 & Bangladesh League 2007-12

FEDERATION CUP 2012

First Round Groups

Group A	Pl	W	D	L	F	A	Pts	Mo	PC	RB
Sheikh Russell	3	3	0	0	13	0	9	2-0	5-0	6-0
Mohammedan	3	2	0	1	7	2	6		3-0	4-0
Police Club	3	0	1	2	1	9	1			1-1
Rampur Boys	3	0	1	2	1	11	1			

Group B	Pl	W	D	L	F	A	Pts	Mu	No
Sheikh Jamal	2	2	0	0	7	0	6	3-0	4-0
Muktijoddha	2	1	0	1	7	4	3		7-1
Noakhali	2	0	0	2	1	11	0		

Group C	Pl	W	D	L	F	A	Pts	AD	Ra	Je
Brothers Union	3	2	1	0	3	0	7	1-0	0-0	2-0
Abahani Dhaka	3	2	0	1	4	1	6		2-0	2-0
Rahmatganj	3	1	1	1	6	3	4			6-1
Jessore DFA	3	0	0	3	1	10	0			

Group D	Pl	W	D	L	F	A	Pts	Fe	Ar	AK
BJMC	3	2	1	0	3	0	7	2-0	0-0	1-0
Feni	3	2	0	1	4	2	6		3-0	1-0
Arambagh	3	1	1	1	2	3	4			2-0
Abahani Khulna	3	0	0	3	0	4	0			

Quarter-finals

Sheikh Russell 1
Feni 0

BJMC 2 0p
Mohammedan 2 3p

Muktijoddha 2
Brothers Union 0

Abahani Dhaka 1
Sheikh Jamal 2

Semi-finals

Sheikh Russell 2
Mohammedan 1

Muktijoddha 0
Sheikh Jamal 2

5/10/2012-22/10/2012

Final

Sheikh Russell 2
Sheikh Jamal 1

CUP FINAL

Bangabandhu, Dhaka
22-10-2012
Scorers: Jahid Hasan [114], Sony Node [121+] for Sheikh Russell; Mike Otojareri [95] for Sheikh Jamal

BDI – BURUNDI

FIFA/COCA-COLA WORLD RANKING

'93	'94	'95	'96	'97	'98	'99	'00	'01	'02	'03	'04	'05	'06	'07	'08	'09	'10	'11	'12
101	126	146	137	152	141	133	126	139	135	145	152	147	117	109	136	126	128	140	104

2012

Jan	Feb	Mar	Apr	May	Jun	Jul	Aug	Sep	Oct	Nov	Dec	High	Low	Av
141	143	132	127	127	131	136	133	134	135	128	104	96	160	134

Burundi Football Federation president Lydia Nsekere broke new ground for women in the sport when she was co-opted onto the FIFA Executive Committee in May as its first female member. She was brought in at the FIFA Congress in Hungary and will be a candidate when the first election for a female member is held at the 2013 Congress in Mauritius. Nsekere has been head of football in Burundi since 2004 and is also an IOC member. A momentous year for her was crowned in September when her club Lydia Lyric Burundi Academic beat traditional powerhouse Vital'O 1-0 in the cup final to secure a first-ever trophy. The dominance of Vital'O in the league continued, however, as they won back the championship and took a fifth title in the last seven years. The Bujumbura-based club, who were runners-up in the old-style African Cup Winners Cup two decades ago, extended to 18 their record number of league successes as they finished three points ahead of defending champions Atletico Olympique. Egyptian-born Nassem Lotfi returned as national coach in April to replace Adel Amrouche but could not prevent Burundi being knocked out of the 2013 Africa Cup of Nations qualifiers by Zimbabwe. But they did reach the quarter-finals of the CECAFA Cup in Uganda at the end of the year, losing to Zanzibar on penalties.

CAF AFRICA CUP OF NATIONS RECORD
1957-1974 DNE 1976 DNQ 1978-1992 DNQ 1994 DNQ 1996-1998 DNE 2000-2013 DNQ

FEDERATION DE FOOTBALL DU BURUNDI (FFB)

Avenue Muyinga,
Boite postale 3426,
Bujumbura
☎ +257 79 928762
+257 22 242892
lydiansekera@yahoo.fr

FA 1948 CON 1972 FIFA 1972
P Lydia Nsekere
GS Jeremie Manirakiza

THE STADIA

2014 FIFA World Cup Stadia
Stade Prince Louis Rwagasore
Bujumbura   22 000

Other Main Stadia
The Stade Prince Louis Rwagasore is the only major stadium in Burundi

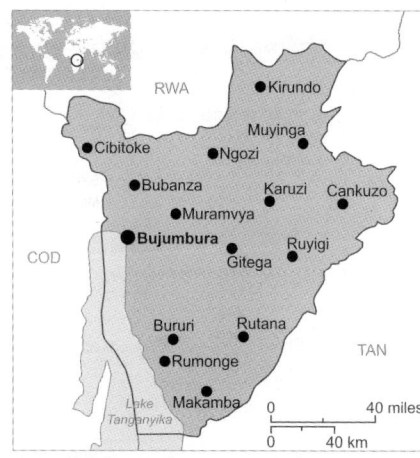

MAJOR CITIES/TOWNS

		Population
1	Bujumbura	367 544
2	Muyinga	95 840
3	Ruyigi	44 854
4	Makamba	25 231
5	Gitega	24 794
6	Rutana	24 150
7	Ngozi	23 779
8	Bururi	21 862
9	Muramvya	21 287
10	Kayanza	20 647
11	Cibitoke	17 142
12	Bubanza	14 945
13	Karuzi	12 729
14	Cankuzo	7 498
15	Kirundo	7 034
16	Rumonge	6 727
17	Mwaro	5 270

REPUBLIKA Y'U BURUNDI • REPUBLIC OF BURUNDI

Capital	Bujumbura	Population	8 988 091 (89)	% in cities	10%
GDP per capita	$400 (227)	Area km²	27 830 km² (146)	GMT +/−	+2
Neighbours (km)	Congo DR 233, Rwanda 290, Tanzania 451				

RECENT INTERNATIONAL MATCHES PLAYED BY BURUNDI

2011	Opponents	Score	Venue	Comp	Scorers	Att	Referee
26-03	Rwanda	L 1-3	Kigali	CNq	Faty Papy [37]		
5-06	Rwanda	W 3-1	Bujumbura	CNq	Saidi Ntibazonkiza 2 [29 53], Didier Kavumbagu [84]		
4-09	Benin	D 1-1	Bujumbura	CNq	Faty Papy [92+]		
9-10	Côte d'Ivoire	L 1-2	Abidjan	CNq	Claude Nahimana [77]		
11-11	Lesotho	L 0-1	Maseru	WCq		5 000	Shikongo NAM
15-11	Lesotho	D 2-2	Bujumbura	WCq	Cedric Amissi [29], Yamin Ndikumana [88p]	7 200	Raphael MWI
25-11	Somalia	W 4-1	Dar es Salaam	CCr1	Floribert Ndayisaba [30], Faty Papy [45], Cedric Amissi [54], Fuadi Ndayisenga [86]		
27-11	Zanzibar †	D 0-0	Dar es Salaam	CCr1			
1-12	Uganda	W 1-0	Dar es Salaam	CCr1	Cedric Amissi [40]		
5-12	Sudan	L 0-2	Dar es Salaam	CCqf			
2012							
29-02	Zimbabwe	W 2-1	Bujumbura	CNq	Laudy Mavugo [49], Valery Nahayo [95+]		
17-06	Zimbabwe	L 0-1	Harare	CNq			
25-11	Somalia	W 5-1	Kampala	CCr1	Christophe Nduwaragira 2 [34 84], Yamin Ndikumana [41], Selemani Ndikumana 2 [78 88]		
28-11	Tanzania	W 1-0	Kampala	CCr1	Selemani Ndikumana [53p]		
1-12	Sudan	W 1-0	Kampala	CCr1	Christophe Nduwaragira [16]		
3-12	Zanzibar †	D 0-0	Kampala	CCqf	L 5-6p		
16-12	Kenya	W 1-0	Bujumbura	Fr	Christophe Nduwaragira [30]		

Fr = Friendly match • CN = CAF African Cup of Nations qualifier • CC = CECAFA Cup • WCq = FIFA World Cup • † Not a full international

BURUNDI 2011-12

LIGUE A

	Pl	W	D	L	F	A	Pts	Vital'O	At. Olympique	Académic	Flambeau	Inter Star	Muzinga	Royal FC	Acad. Tchité	Espoir	Kamenge	Flamengo	Union Sp'ting
Vital'O †	22	16	5	1	54	14	53		1-1	2-2	1-3	1-0	8-2	2-0	2-1	5-0	7-0	3-0	3-0
Atlético Olympique	22	15	5	2	45	12	50	0-0		0-1	1-0	2-0	3-0	1-0	2-1	5-0	6-0	4-1	3-2
LLB Académic ‡	22	12	8	2	37	17	38	0-1	1-0		1-1	3-1	1-3	0-0	3-1	0-0	3-1	6-1	1-0
Flambeau de l'Est	22	9	8	5	23	17	35	0-1	0-0	1-1		0-0	1-0	1-0	0-0	1-1	2-1	2-0	2-0
Inter Star	22	9	5	8	33	25	32	2-2	3-4	0-2	1-1		1-2	4-1	0-1	2-0	4-1	0-0	3-1
Muzinga	22	7	8	7	26	32	29	1-3	1-1	1-1	1-2	0-1		1-1	0-0	1-0	0-3	3-2	1-1
Royal FC Muramvya	22	6	10	6	24	23	28	1-1	0-1	0-0	3-1	2-1	2-2		2-0	1-2	1-1	2-0	3-1
Académie Tchité	22	4	6	12	17	31	18	0-2	0-2	2-4	0-1	0-1	0-0	1-1		2-1	1-1	1-2	3-2
Espoir Gatumba	22	3	9	10	10	29	18	0-3	0-0	0-1	0-0	0-1	0-4	0-0	1-1		2-0	0-0	0-0
Kamenge	22	4	5	13	20	44	17	1-2	0-3	0-1	3-2	1-1	1-1	1-2	1-0	0-1		0-1	2-0
Flamengo de Ngagara	22	4	5	13	19	45	17	0-3	1-2	1-4	2-1	1-5	0-1	1-1	1-2	1-1	2-1		2-2
Union Sporting	22	2	8	12	17	36	14	0-1	0-4	1-1	1-1	0-2	0-1	1-1	2-0	1-1	1-1	1-0	

2/12/2011 - 5/08/2012 • † Qualified for the CAF Champions League • ‡ Qualified for the CAF Confederation Cup

COUPE DU PRESIDENT DE LA REPUBLIQUE 2012

First Round		Quarter-finals		Semi-finals		Final	
LLB Académic	5						
Wazee Rumonge	0	LLB Académic	2				
Union Sporting	0	Volontaires	1				
Volontaires	2			LLB Académic	0 3p		
Le Messager Ngozi	4			Atlético Olympique	0 2p		
Abawigeze	0	Le Messager Ngozi	0 2p				
Olympique Muremera	1	**Atlético Olympique**	0 3p			LLB Académic ‡	1
Atlético Olympique	2					Vital'O	0
Flambeau de l'Est	3						
Espoir Gatumba	1	Flambeau de l'Est	2			**CUP FINAL**	
Royal FC Muramvya	1	Inter FC	1			Stade Prince Louis, Bujumbura	
Inter FC	2			Flambeau de l'Est	0	15-09-2012	
Inter Star	3			**Vital'O**	1	Scorer - Saidi Kayumba [75] for LLB Académic	
Les Amis	0	Inter Star	0 3p				
Delta Star	1	**Vital'O**	0 5p				
Vital'O	2			‡ Qualified for the CAF Confederation Cup			

BEL – BELGIUM

FIFA/COCA-COLA WORLD RANKING

'93	'94	'95	'96	'97	'98	'99	'00	'01	'02	'03	'04	'05	'06	'07	'08	'09	'10	'11	'12
25	24	24	42	41	35	33	27	20	17	16	45	55	53	49	54	66	57	41	21

2012

Jan	Feb	Mar	Apr	May	Jun	Jul	Aug	Sep	Oct	Nov	Dec	High	Low	Av
40	39	40	44	54	53	53	40	30	20	21		16	71	37

After a decade in the doldrums the Belgium national team has finally found its feet again and after a positive year in 2011 with just one defeat, new coach Marc Wilmots got their 2014 FIFA World Cup qualifying campaign off to a positive start in 2012 with three wins and a draw in the first four games. Wilmots moved up from assistant coach in May 2012 after George Leekens left for Club Brugge and he will need the experience he gained from a brief spell as a politician to manage an increasingly talented player pool, a number of whom are starting to make their mark with clubs abroad. Captain Vincent Kompany proved to be a hugely influential figure as Manchester City won their first English title for 44 years, but he was just one of 10 regular squad members playing for clubs across the channel. At home, Anderlecht reclaimed the title from Genk, their 31st triumph, but there was a new name on the Belgian cup with neither of the finalists - Lokeren or Kortrijk - having won a single trophy of any description between them. Despite being reduced to 10-men early on, Lokeren won the final 1-0 thanks to a late goal from their Tunisian striker Hamdi Harbaoui. Anderlecht, Club Brugge and Standard all made it through the group stage of the 2011-12 Europa League in a sign of the growing stature of Belgian clubs in Europe.

UEFA EUROPEAN CHAMPIONSHIP RECORD

1960 DNE 1964 DNQ 1968 DNQ **1972** 3 SF 1976 DNQ **1980** 2 F **1984** 6 r1 1988-1996 DNQ **2000** 12 r1 (co-hosts) 2004-2012 DNQ

URBSFA/KBVB

- 145 Avenue Houba de Strooper, Bruxelles 1020
- ☎ +32 2 4771211
- +32 2 4782391
- urbsfa.kbvb@footbel.com
- www.footbel.com
- FA 1895 CON 1954 FIFA 1904
- P Francois De Keersmaecker
- GS Steven Martens

THE STADIA

2014 FIFA World Cup Stadia

Koning Boudewijn Stadion Brussels	50 024

Other Main Stadia

Stade Maurice Dufrasne Liège	30 200
Jan Breydelstadion Brugge	29 042
Stade Constant Vanden Stock Brussels	28 361
Stade du Pays de Charleroi Charleroi	25 149
Fénix Stadion Genk	24 604

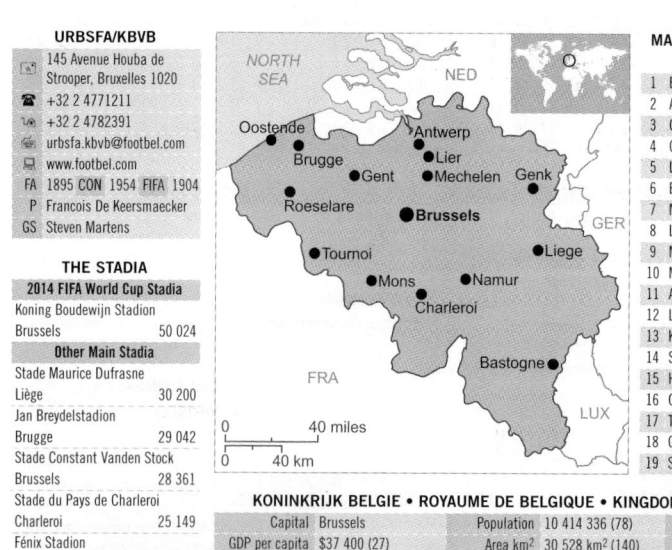

MAJOR CITIES/TOWNS

		Population
1	Brussels	1 050 143
2	Antwerp	472 355
3	Gent	238 634
4	Charleroi	200 487
5	Liège	190 302
6	Brugge	116 737
7	Namur	108 228
8	Leuven	92 894
9	Mons	91 180
10	Mechelen	80 531
11	Aalst	78 353
12	La Louvière	78 031
13	Kortrijk	73 615
14	Sint-Niklaas	71 502
15	Hasselt	71 401
16	Ostend	69 783
17	Tournai	67 471
18	Genk	64 282
19	Seraing	60 702

KONINKRIJK BELGIE • ROYAUME DE BELGIQUE • KINGDOM OF BELGIUM

Capital	Brussels	Population	10 414 336 (78)	% in cities	97%
GDP per capita	$37 400 (27)	Area km²	30 528 km² (140)	GMT +/-	+1

Neighbours (km) France 620, Germany 167, Luxembourg 148, Netherlands 450 • Coast 66

RECENT INTERNATIONAL MATCHES PLAYED BY BELGIUM

2009	Opponents	Score	Venue	Comp	Scorers	Att	Referee
11-02	Slovenia	W 2-0	Genk	Fr	Van Buyten 2 [21] [86]	13 135	Kever SUI
28-03	Bosnia-Herzegovina	L 2-4	Genk	WCq	Dembele [66], Sonck [85p]	20 041	Ivanov.N RUS
1-04	Bosnia-Herzegovina	L 1-2	Zenica	WCq	Swerts [88]	13 800	Hrinak SVK
29-05	Chile	D 1-1	Chiba	Fr	Roelandts [15]	9 700	Tojo JPN
31-05	Japan	L 0-4	Chiba	Fr		42 520	Styles ENG
12-08	Czech Republic	L 1-3	Teplice	Fr	Vertonghen [12]	13 890	Sippel GER
5-09	Spain	L 0-5	La Coruña	WCq		30 441	Layec FRA
9-09	Armenia	L 1-2	Yerevan	WCq	Van Buyten [92+]	2 300	Stavrev MKD
10-10	Turkey	W 2-0	Brussels	WCq	Mpenza.E 2 [7] [84]	30 131	Trefolini ITA
14-10	Estonia	L 0-2	Tallinn	WCq		4 680	Vollquartz DEN
14-11	Hungary	W 3-0	Gent	Fr	Fellaini [39], Vermaelen [55], Mirallas [61p]	8 000	Picirillo FRA
17-11	Qatar	W 2-0	Sedan	Fr	Witsel [20], Sonck [54]	3 000	Buquet FRA
2010							
19-05	Bulgaria	W 2-1	Brussels	Fr	Lepoint [89], Kompany [91+]	15 000	Weiner GER
11-08	Finland	L 0-1	Turku	Fr		7 451	Hamer LUX
3-09	Germany	L 0-1	Brussels	ECq		41 126	Hauge NOR
7-09	Turkey	L 2-3	Istanbul	ECq	Van Buyten 2 [28] [69]	43 538	Skomina SVN
8-10	Kazakhstan	W 2-0	Astana	ECq	Ogunjimi 2 [52] [70]	8 500	Borski POL
12-10	Austria	D 4-4	Brussels	ECq	Vossen [11], Fellaini [47], Ogunjimi [87], Lombaerts [90]	24 231	Dean ENG
17-11	Russia	W 2-0	Voronezh	Fr	Lukaku 2 [2] [73]	31 743	Kaasik EST
2011							
9-02	Finland	D 1-1	Gent	Fr	Witsel [60]	12 000	Zimmerman SUI
25-03	Austria	W 2-0	Vienna	ECq	Witsel 2 [6] [50]	44 300	Bezborodov RUS
29-03	Azerbaijan	W 4-1	Brussels	ECq	Vertonghen [12], Simons [32p], Chadli [45], Vossen [74]	34 985	Stalhammar SWE
3-06	Turkey	D 1-1	Brussels	ECq	Ogunjimi [4]	44 185	Rizzoli ITA
10-08	Slovenia	D 0-0	Ljubljana	Fr		12 230	Strahonja CRO
2-09	Azerbaijan	D 1-1	Baku	ECq	Simons [55p]	9 300	Probert ENG
6-09	USA	W 1-0	Brussels	Fr	Lombaerts [55]	21 946	Collum SCO
7-10	Kazakhstan	W 4-1	Brussels	ECq	Simmons [40p], Hazard [43], Kompany [49], Ogunjimi [84]	29 758	Mazic SRB
11-10	Germany	L 1-3	Dusseldorf	ECq	Fellaini [86]	48 483	Moen NOR
11-11	Romania	W 2-1	Liege	Fr	Van Buyten [11], OG [43]	20 000	Ennjimi FRA
15-11	France	D 0-0	Paris	Fr		52 825	Muniz ESP
2012							
29-02	Greece	D 1-1	Heraklion	Fr	Chadli [32]	15 000	Stalhammar SWE
25-05	Montenegro	D 2-2	Brussels	Fr	Mirallas [25], Hazard [34p]	21 110	Turpin FRA
2-06	England	L 0-1	London	Fr		85 091	Rasmussen DEN
15-08	Netherlands	W 4-2	Brussels	Fr	Benteke [20], Mertens [75], Lukaku [77], Vertonghen [80]	50 000	Atkinson ENG
7-09	Wales	W 2-0	Cardiff	WCq	Kompany [42], Vertonghen [83]	16 557	Johannesson SWE
11-09	Croatia	D 1-1	Brussels	WCq	Gillet [45]	39 987	Undiano ESP
12-10	Serbia	W 3-0	Belgrade	WCq	Benteke [34], De Bruyne [68], Mirallas [91+]	21 650	Kralovec CZE
16-10	Scotland	W 2-0	Brussels	WCq	Benteke [68], Kompany [71]	44 132	Hagen NOR
14-11	Romania	L 1-2	Bucharest	Fr	Benteke [23]	4 000	Bergonzi ITA

Fr = Friendly match • EC = UEFA EURO 2012 • WCq = FIFA World Cup • q = qualifier

BELGIUM NATIONAL TEAM HISTORICAL RECORDS

Caps: 96 - Jan Ceulemans 1977-91 • 91 - Timmy Simons 2001- • 86 - Eric Gerets 1975-91 & Franky Van der Elst 1984-98 • 84 - Enzo Scifo 1984-99 • 81 - Paul Van Himst 1960-74 • 78 - Bart Goor 1999-2008 • 77 - Georges Grun 1984-95 • 70 - Lorenzo Staelens 1990-2000 & Marc Wilmots 1990-2002 • 68 - Victor Mees 1949-60 & Daniel Van Buyten 2001- • 67 - Georges Heylens 1961-73 • 66 - • 64 - Joseph Jurion 1955-67 & Jean-Marie Pfaff 1976-87 • 63 - Franky Vercauteren 1977-8 & Marc Degryse 1984-2002 • 63 - Bernard Voorhoof 1928-40

Goals: 30 - Bernard Voorhoof 1928-40 & Paul van himst 1960-74 • 28 - Marc Wilmots 1990-2002 • 27 - Joseph Mermans 1945-56 • 26 - Robert de Veen 1906-13 & Raymond Braine 1925-39 • 24 - Wesley Sonck 2001-10 • 23 - Marc Degryse 1984-96 & Jan Ceulemans 1976-91 • 21 - Henri 'Rik' Coppens 1949-59 • 20 - Leopold Anoul 1947-54 & Erwin Vandenbergh 1979-91

Coaches: William Maxwell SCO 1910-13 • Charles Bunyan ENG 1914 • William Maxwell SCO 1920-28 • Victor Lowenfelt 1928-30 •Hector Goetinck 1930-34 • Jules Turnauer 1935 • Jack Butler ENG 1935-40 • François Demol 1944-46 • Bill Gormlie ENG 1947-53 • Dougall Livingstone SCO 1953-54 • Andre Vandeweyer 1955-57 • Louis Nicolay 1957 • Geza Toldi HUN 1957-58 • Constant Vanden Stock 1958-68 • Raymond Goethals 1968-76 • Guy Thys 1976-89 • Walter Meeuws 1989-90 • Guy Thys 1990-91 • Paul Van Himst 1991-96 • Wilfried Van Moer 1996 • Georges Leekens 1997-99 • Robert Waseige 1999-2002 • Aime Anthuenis 2002-05 • Rene Vandereycken 2006-09 • Franky Vercauteren 2009 • Dick Advocaat NED 2009-10 • Georges Leekens 2010-12 • Marc Wilmots 2012-

BELGIUM 2011-12

JUPILER PRO LEAGUE FIRST ROUND

	Pl	W	D	L	F	A	Pts	Anderlecht	Brugge	Gent	Standard	Genk	Kortrijk	Cercle	Lokeren	Mechelen	Mons	Beerschot	Lierse	Z-Waregem	Leuven	Westerlo	St-Truiden
RSC Anderlecht †	30	20	7	3	61	26	67		3-0	3-1	5-0	4-2	2-0	4-0	3-2	3-1	2-2	3-2	4-0	2-1	0-0	3-1	3-1
Club Brugge †	30	19	4	7	51	32	61	1-1		2-0	1-0	4-5	2-1	1-0	3-0	0-1	2-1	5-1	1-0	1-0	1-0	5-0	1-0
KAA Gent †	30	17	5	8	63	35	56	0-1	1-3		3-1	2-0	3-1	0-1	3-1	6-2	2-0	0-1	1-0	0-0	6-1	3-1	6-0
Standard Club Liège †	30	14	9	7	43	33	51	1-2	2-1	0-0		0-0	3-1	0-0	3-1	3-2	2-1	6-1	2-0	1-0	4-0	1-0	0-0
KRC Genk †	30	13	7	10	60	44	46	0-1	3-0	3-1	3-0		2-2	4-2	0-1	0-0	2-0	3-1	4-0	2-2	5-0	3-0	2-1
KV Kortrijk †	30	13	7	10	39	36	46	0-1	2-1	0-4	2-0	3-2		2-0	2-5	1-0	2-2	2-0	1-1	0-0	2-0	1-0	4-0
Cercle Brugge ‡	30	13	7	10	36	37	46	1-0	1-2	0-1	0-1	3-2	1-2		1-1	1-0	1-1	2-1	0-0	1-0	2-0	3-1	2-2
KSC Lokeren ‡	30	11	11	8	48	40	44	0-1	1-2	1-1	1-1	3-1	1-4	1-0		3-2	3-1	1-1	2-0	0-0	0-1	4-0	0-0
KV Mechelen ‡	30	10	7	13	40	50	37	2-1	1-2	0-2	1-2	3-2	0-0	1-2	0-2		4-1	2-1	1-1	2-2	1-0	2-1
RAEC Mons ‡	30	9	9	12	50	55	36	1-1	0-2	1-1	1-1	1-2	3-1	0-2	3-3	5-1		4-2	2-1	3-1	2-2	2-1	4-2
Germinal Beerschot ‡	30	9	9	12	45	51	36	0-0	1-1	2-2	1-1	0-0	1-0	4-0	2-2	2-2	2-0		0-0	2-0	2-1	3-1	3-2
Lierse SK ‡	30	6	13	11	24	36	31	0-0	0-1	2-1	0-2	0-0	2-0	2-2	1-1	2-2	1-1	1-1		2-1	3-1	0-0	0-2
Zulte-Waregem ‡	30	6	12	12	32	38	30	2-3	1-1	1-3	4-2	1-1	1-0	1-1	1-1	2-0	2-3	1-0	1-2		2-3	1-0	1-2
Oud-Heverlee Leuven ‡	30	7	8	15	38	58	29	2-1	3-1	2-3	1-3	1-1	0-2	2-3	1-1	1-2	3-1	3-2	0-0	2-2		1-1	3-1
KVC Westerlo ‡†	30	5	5	20	29	59	20	1-2	0-1	2-3	0-0	3-2	0-0	1-3	2-4	1-3	2-1	3-1	0-2	1-1	1-3		2-0
Sint-Truiden VV ‡†	30	3	10	17	32	61	19	2-2	3-3	3-4	1-1	3-4	0-4	0-1	1-1	0-2	2-2	2-4	1-1	1-0	2-1	0-3	

29/07/2011 - 21/03/2012 • †/‡† Qualified for the Championship/play-off II round • ‡† Relegation play-off • Attendance (all): 3,567,520 @ 11,812
Points totals were halved and rounded up for the second round • Top scorers (all rounds): **25** - Jeremy **PERBET** FRA, Mons • **20** - Jelle **VOSSEN**, Genk • **16** - Christian **BENTEKE**, Genk • **15** - Joseph **AKPALA** NGA, Club Brugge; Dieumerci **MBOKANI** COD, Anderlecht & Jordan **REMACLE**, Leuven

JUPILER PRO LEAGUE PLAY-OFFS

Championship	Pl	W	D	L	F	A	Pts	An	CB	Gk	Gt	St	Ko
RSC Anderlecht †	10	5	3	2	16	8	52		1-1	1-3	1-0	3-0	1-1
Club Brugge †	10	5	2	3	14	11	48	0-1		2-0	1-0	2-0	3-2
KRC Genk ‡	10	6	0	4	19	19	41	0-4	1-2		2-0	3-2	2-0
KAA Gent ‡	10	4	0	6	16	16	40	1-4	2-1	3-1		3-0	2-3
Standard CL	10	2	3	5	10	17	35	0-0	1-1	2-3	2-1		2-0
KV Kortrijk	10	3	2	5	16	20	34	1-2	0-4	3-4	1-4	1-1	

Play-off 2 Group A	Pl	W	D	L	F	A	Pts	CB	OHL	Li	Me
Cercle Brugge ‡‡	6	3	2	1	16	10	11		6-4	0-0	3-1
OH Leuven	6	3	1	2	15	14	10	3-2		1-1	4-2
Lierse SK	6	1	4	1	7	7	7	2-2	1-2		2-1
KV Mechelen	6	1	1	4	7	14	4	0-3	2-1	1-1	

Play-off 2 Group B	Pl	W	D	L	F	A	Pts	Mo	ZW	GB	Lo
RAEC Mons ‡‡	6	3	2	1	8	4	11		0-1	2-0	1-1
Zulte-Waregem	6	2	2	2	7	8	8	0-2		2-0	2-2
Germ. Beerschot	6	2	1	3	9	10	7	1-1	3-1		4-1
KSC Lokeren	6	1	3	2	9	11	6	1-2	1-1	3-1	

30/03/2012 - 13/05/2012 • † Qualified for the UEFA Champions League • ‡ Qualified for the Europa League • ‡‡ Qualified for Play-off 2 final
Final: Mons 0-1 2-3 **Cercle Brugge** • Cercle qualified for a play-off against Gent
Pla-off: Cercle Brugge 1-5 1-2 **Gent**. Gent qualified for the Europa League

Relegation play-off: **Westerlo** 3-2 1-3 4-0 4-1 Sint Truiden (Played as best of five matches. The team with the least points - Sint-Truiden - were relegated. Westerlo started with three bonus points having finished higher in the league. They joined three Tweede Classe teams in the promotion/relegation playoffs

BELGIUM 2011-12 TWEEDE CLASSE (2)

	Pl	W	D	L	F	A	Pts
RSC Charleroi	34	23	5	6	64	34	74
Waasland-Beveren ‡	34	21	5	8	61	34	68
AS Eupen ‡	34	19	11	4	61	34	68
KV Oostende ‡	34	19	9	6	61	29	66
Lommel United	34	15	7	12	48	42	52
White Star Woluwe	34	14	9	11	48	43	51
Eendracht Aalst	34	13	7	14	46	52	46
KSK Heist	34	11	13	10	46	46	46
CS Visé	34	12	8	14	44	44	44
Royal Antwerp	34	12	7	15	39	42	43
Boussu Dour Borinage	34	12	6	16	44	54	42
AFC Tubize	34	12	5	17	36	55	41
KSV Roeselare	34	9	13	12	46	51	40
FC Brussels	34	9	11	14	44	46	38
Sportkring Sint-Niklaas	34	8	10	16	41	54	34
KVK Tienen	34	9	6	19	34	61	33
Verbroedering Dender	34	6	15	13	43	33	33
Standaard Wetteren	34	4	9	21	19	54	21

17/08/2011 - 29/04/2012 • ‡ Qualified for promotion play-off

MEDALS TABLE

		Overall		League		Cup		Europe
		G S B		G S B		G S		G S B
1	RSC Anderlecht	43 27 10		31 20 8		9 3		3 4 2
2	Club Brugge	23 26 15		13 18 13		10 6		2 2
3	Standard Liège	16 21 21		10 11 19		6		1 2
4	Union St Gilloise	13 8 8		11 8 7		2		1
5	Beerschot VAV	9 8 5		7 7 5		2 1		
6	Racing CB	7 5 3		6 5 3		1		
7	Royal Antwerp	6 14 7		4 12 7		2 1		1
8	KV Mechelen	6 9 4		4 5 3		1 4		1 1
9	Royal FC Liègeois	6 4 5		5 3 4		1 1		1
10	Lierse SK	6 3 2		4 2 2		2 1		
11	KRC Genk	6 2 1		3 2 1		3		
12	Daring CB	5 5 4		5 4 4		1		
13	Cercle Brugge	3 4 6		3 3 6		2 4		
14	SK Beveren	4 3 1		2		2 3		1
15	KAA Gent	3 3 6		2 6		3 1		

PROMOTION/RELEGATION PLAY-OFFS

	Pl	W	D	L	F	A	Pts	WB	Eu	We	Oo
W'land-Beveren	6	5	1	0	14	5	**16**		2-0	3-1	4-1
AS Eupen	6	3	1	2	8	7	**10**	1-2		2-1	1-0
KVC Westerlo	6	1	2	3	9	9	**5**	1-2	1-1		5-1
KV Oostende	6	0	2	4	4	14	**2**	1-1	1-3	0-0	

6/05/2012 - 24/05/2012 • Waasland-Beveren promoted, Westerlo relegated

COUPE DE BELGIQUE/BEKER VAN BELGIE 2011–12

Round of 32		Round of 16		Quarter-finals		Semi-finals		Final	
KSC Lokeren *	3	**KSC Lokeren** *	3	**KSC Lokeren** *	1 3	**KSC Lokeren** *	1 3	**KSC Lokeren** ‡	1
AS Eupen	0	KVC Westerlo	1	KAA Gent	1 3	Lierse SK	0 0	KV Kortrijk	0
Géants Athois	0								
KVC Westerlo *	1								
Club Brugge	3	**Club Brugge**	4 2p						
Dessel Sport *	2	**KAA Gent** *	4 4p						
KSV Roeselare	0								
KAA Gent *	4								
Standard Club Liège	8	**Standard Club Liège**	2	**Standard Club Liège**	2 2				
Hoogstraten VV *	2	Zulte-Waregem *	1	**Lierse SK** *	1 4				
KSK Ronse *	0								
Zulte-Waregem	6								
KRC Genk	6	**KRC Genk** *	0						
KMSK Deinze *	2	**Lierse SK**	2						
KV Turnhout *	0								
Lierse SK	1								
RAEC Mons	3	**RAEC Mons** *	1	**RAEC Mons** *	3 2				
AFC Tubize *	0	KV Mechelen	0	Rupel Boom	1 2				
KV Oostende *	0					**RAEC Mons** *	1 2		
KV Mechelen	3					**KV Kortrijk**	2 2		
RSC Anderlecht	4	RSC Anderlecht *	1						
Lommel United *	0	**Rupel Boom**	2						
Oud-Heverlee Leuven *	1								
Rupel Boom	2								
Germinal Beerschot *	1 4p	**Germinal Beerschot**	1	**Germinal Beerschot**	0 2				
Mouscron-Peruwelz	1 3p	Cercle Brugge *	0	**KV Kortrijk** *	2 1				
RC Mechelen	0								
Cercle Brugge *	2								
Sint-Truiden VV *	3	Sint-Truiden VV	0						
Waasland-Beveren	0	**KV Kortrijk** *	1						
Royal Antwerp	1 5p								
KV Kortrijk *	1 6p								

* Home team/home team in 1st leg ‡ Qualified for the Europa League

CUP FINAL

Roi Baudouin, Brussels, 24-03-2012, 20:30
Att: 35,000, Ref: Jerome Efong Nzolo
Scorer - Harbaoui 77

Lokeren - Copa - Georgios Galitsios, Ibrahima Gueye, Jeremy Taravel, Laurens De Bock - Killian Overmeire, Koen Persoons, Ivan Leko (Baye Djiby Fall 62) - Nill De Pauw (Geir Ludvig Fevang 93+), Hamdi Harbaoui (Hassan El Mouataz 86), Benjamin De Ceulaer● **19**. Tr: Peter Maes

Kortrijk - Darren Keet - Brecht Capon, Baptiste Martin●, Ervin Zukanovic - Mustapha Oussalah, Nebojsa Pavlovic, Gertjan De Mets●, Ernest Nfor (Steven Joseph-Monrose 69), Mohamed Messoudi - Pablo Chavarria● (Brecht Dejaeghere 81), Dalibor Veselinovic. Tr: Hein Vanhaezebrouck

BEN – BENIN

FIFA/COCA-COLA WORLD RANKING

'93	'94	'95	'96	'97	'98	'99	'00	'01	'02	'03	'04	'05	'06	'07	'08	'09	'10	'11	'12
130	143	161	143	137	127	140	148	152	146	121	122	113	114	97	101	59	71	124	75

2012														
Jan	Feb	Mar	Apr	May	Jun	Jul	Aug	Sep	Oct	Nov	Dec	High	Low	Av
136	136	127	125	124	72	78	77	71	74	77	75	59	165	120

Having qualified for three out of four Africa Cup of Nations finals between 2004 and 2010, Benin failed to make it to the 2013 tournament in South Africa after being knocked out by outsiders Ethiopia on the away goals rule. It was the second tournament in succession that this small west African nation had missed out on - a major disappointment for the former French international defender Manuel Amoros who took over at the start of the year as the national team coach. Benin had seemingly done the hard work against Ethiopia by returning from Addis Abeba with a 0-0 draw but the Ethiopians scored the vital away goal in a 1-1 draw in Cotonou to progress. There was much better news for Amoros, however, with a fine 1-0 victory over Mali at the start of their campaign to qualify for the finals of the 2014 FIFA World Cup in Brazil. In club football, AS Port Autonome Cotonou - or ASPAC as they are more commonly known - won the league championship in 2012 as the tournament was completed without the politically-inspired problems of the previous season which had seen widespread disruption. Indeed, it was only the fourth time in ten years that the championship had been finished. Mogas '90 added to their record haul of nine cup triumphs with a 2-1 victory over Dragons in the final of the Coupe de l'Independance.

CAF AFRICA CUP OF NATIONS RECORD

1957-1970 DNE 1972 DNQ 1974-1978 DNE 1980 DNQ 1982 DNE 1984-1994 DNQ 1996 DNE 1998-2002 DNQ **2004** 16 r1 2006 DNQ **2008** 15 r1 **2010** 14 r1 2012-2013 DNQ

FEDERATION BENINOISE DE FOOTBALL (FBF)

- Boite Postale 112
- Porto-Novo 01
- Benin
- ☎ +229 20 214142
- +229 20 215455
- infofebefoot@yahoo.fr
- www.febefoot.net
- FA 1962 CON 1969 FIFA 1962
- P Moucharafou Anjorin
- GS Quentin Didavi

THE STADIA

2014 FIFA World Cup Stadia

Stade de l'Amitie	
Cotonou	35 000

Other Main Stadia

Stade Municipale	
Porto Novo	20 000
Stade Charles de Gaulle	
Porto Novo	15 000
Stade Municipal de Parakou	
Parakou	8 000
Stade Goho	
Abomey	7 500

MAJOR CITIES/TOWNS

		Population
1	Cotonou	745 726
2	Abomey	518 256
3	Porto Novo	254 627
4	Djougou	235 934
5	Parakou	188 853
6	Bohicon	144 634
7	Kandi	126 944
8	Lokossa	102 149
9	Natitingou	92 101
10	Ouidah	91 726
11	Savé	89 745
12	Abomey	88 649
13	Nikki	65 874
14	Dogbo	47 411
15	Malanville	41 454
16	Cové	41 282
17	Pobé	36 840
18	Kérou	34 733
19	Comé	33 147

REPUBLIQUE DU BENIN • REPUBLIC OF BENIN

Capital	Porto-Novo	Population	8 791 832 (90)	% in cities	41%
GDP per capita	$1500 (198)	Area km²	112 622 km² (101)	GMT +/-	+1
Neighbours (km)	Burkina Faso 306, Niger 266, Nigeria 773, Togo 644 • Coast 121				

RECENT INTERNATIONAL MATCHES PLAYED BY BENIN

2010	Opponents	Score	Venue	Comp	Scorers	Att	Referee
6-01	Libya	W 1-0	Cotonou	Fr	Stephane Sessegnon [19]		
12-01	Mozambique	D 2-2	Benguela	CNr1	Razak Omotoyossi [14p], Khan OG [20]	15 000	Abdel Rahman SUD
16-01	Nigeria	L 0-1	Benguela	CNr1		8 000	Carvalho ANG
20-01	Egypt	L 0-2	Benguela	CNr1		12 500	Bennett RSA
11-08	Niger	D 0-0	Porto Novo	Fr			
5-09	Burundi	D 1-1	Cotonou	CNq	Mickael Pote [2]		Bennett RSA
9-10	Rwanda	W 3-0	Kigali	CNq	Seidath Tchomogo [68], Razak Omotoyossi [81], Stephane Sessegnon [88]		Haimoudi ALG
2011							
9-02	Libya	L 2-3	Tripoli	Fr			
27-03	Côte d'Ivoire	L 1-2	Accra	CNq	Seidath Tchomogo [13]		Kayindi-Ngobi UGA
5-06	Côte d'Ivoire	L 2-6	Cotonou	CNq	Stephane Sessegnon 2 [55 60p]		Benouza ALG
4-09	Burundi	D 1-1	Bujumbura	CNq	Guy Akpagba [55]		
9-10	Rwanda	L 0-1	Cotonou	CNq			
2012							
29-02	Ethiopia	D 0-0	Addis Abeba	CNq			
26-05	Burkina Faso	D 2-2	Ouagadougou	Fr	David Djigla [51], Mickael Pote [58]		
3-06	Mali	W 1-0	Cotonou	WCq	Razak Omotoyossi [18]	20 000	Sikazwe ZAM
10-06	Rwanda	D 1-1	Kigali	WCq	Razak Omotoyossi [74]	15 000	Bamlak ETH
17-06	Ethiopia	D 1-1	Cotonou	CNq	Mickael Pote [20]		
19-12	Oman	L 0-2	Sur	Fr			

Fr = Friendly match • CN = CAF African Cup of Nations • WCq = FIFA World Cup • q = qualifier • r1 = first round group

BENIN NATIONAL TEAM HISTORICAL RECORDS

Coach: Cecil Jones Attuquayefio GHA 2003-04 • Herve Revelli FRA 2004 • Edme Codjo 2005-07 • Didier Notheaux FRA 2007 • Reinhard Fabisch GER 2007-08 • Michel Dussuyer FRA 2008-10 • Jean-Marc Nobilo FRA 2011 • Denis Goavec FRA 2011 • Manuel Amoros 2012-

BENIN 2011-12

PREMIERE DIVISION

	Pl	W	D	L	F	A	Pts	ASPAC	Tonnerre	JAP	Dragons	ASOS	Mogas 90	Panthères	Kraké	Buffles	Avrankou	Soleil	Adjobi
ASPAC †	22	15	6	1	34	13	51		1-0	1-0	0-0	3-2	3-2	4-0	1-0	2-0	3-0	2-1	0-0
Tonnerre d'Abomey	22	12	4	6	24	17	40	3-0		2-0	1-0	0-2	0-0	2-1	2-1	1-0	2-1	0-0	1-0
JA Plateau	22	10	7	5	22	16	37	1-1	0-0		2-0	1-1	0-0	2-1	1-0	4-0	2-0	2-1	2-1
Dragons de l'Ouémé	22	8	9	5	17	13	33	0-3	2-0	0-0		0-1	0-0	0-0	2-0	1-0	2-2	1-1	1-0
ASOS	22	8	6	8	24	24	30	0-1	1-0	3-0	0-0		1-1	2-1	1-4	1-2	1-2	0-2	1-1
Mogas 90 ‡	22	6	9	7	17	18	27	1-1	1-0	0-1	0-2	1-0		1-1	1-2	1-1	0-0	1-0	3-1
Panthères Djougou	22	6	8	8	19	20	26	1-1	0-2	3-0	1-0	0-1	1-0		1-0	1-0	4-0	0-1	0-0
USS Kraké	22	7	4	11	24	25	25	1-2	3-1	0-0	1-2	2-1	1-0	1-1		0-0	1-2	4-2	1-1
Buffles du Borgou	22	4	11	7	13	20	23	0-0	1-2	1-3	1-1	0-0	2-1	1-1	2-0		1-0	0-0	1-1
Avrankou Omnisport	22	5	8	9	15	25	23	0-1	1-1	1-0	0-1	2-2	0-1	1-0	1-0	0-0		0-0	1-1
Soleil FC	22	4	9	9	16	22	21	1-2	2-3	0-0	0-2	0-1	1-2	0-0	1-0	0-0	2-1		0-0
Adjobi	22	0	13	9	9	21	13	0-2	0-1	0-1	0-0	1-2	0-0	1-1	0-2	0-0	0-0	1-1	

26/11/2011 - 3/06/2012 • † Qualified for the CAF Champions League • ‡ Qualified for the CAF Confederation Cup • No relegation

COUPE DE L'INDEPENDANCE
Final. Stade de l'Amite, Cotonou, 2-08-2012
Mogas 90 2-1 Dragons de l'Ouémé
Scorers - Loic Kiki [25], Fadel Suanon 2 [61 81] for Mogas 90

MEDALS TABLE

		Overall	Lge	Cup	Africa	City/Town
		G	G	G	G S B	
1	Dragons de l'Ouémé	17	12	5	1	Porto-Novo
2	Mogas 90	13	3	10		Porto-Novo
3	Requins de l'Atlantique	8	3	5		Cotonou
4	Buffles du Borgou	5	2	3		Parakou
5	AS Porto Novo	3	3			Porto-Novo
	ASPAC	3	2	1		Cotonou
7	Etoile Sportive	2	1	1		Porto-Novo
	Univ National de Benin	2		2		Porto-Novo

BER – BERMUDA

FIFA/COCA-COLA WORLD RANKING

'93	'94	'95	'96	'97	'98	'99	'00	'01	'02	'03	'04	'05	'06	'07	'08	'09	'10	'11	'12
84	102	140	167	176	185	163	153	166	172	183	157	161	107	147	124	142	175	107	157

2012													High	Low	Av
Jan	Feb	Mar	Apr	May	Jun	Jul	Aug	Sep	Oct	Nov	Dec		High	Low	Av
106	105	103	108	97	109	117	120	102	120	135	157		76	189	147

Dandy Town Hornets enjoyed their best-ever season in 2011-12 after winning three trophies - all of which came at the expense of North Village Rams. Although North Village finished just two points behind Dandy Town in the league, the outcome of the title race was a little more clear cut than the points suggest. After losing two of their first four games, Dandy Town then won their next eleven to take an unassailable lead before losing to both North Village and Devonshire Cougars in their final two matches. Shaun Goater's North Village did break their run of three runners-up spots with victory over Somerset Trojans in the Friendship Trophy final on New Year's Day but they lost to Dandy Town in the Dudley Eve Trophy final at the start of the season and in the FA Challenge Cup final at the end. Shortly after conceding their league title, North Village took part in a first round group in the 2012 CFU Club Championship in the Cayman Islands. They held hosts George Town to a draw in the first match but then lost to Elite in the next to finish bottom of the group. The national team took part in the qualifiers for the Caribbean Cup but despite a hefty win over Saint-Martin - which unfortunately for four-goal hero Tyrell Burgess does not count as a full international - defeats at the hands of Puerto Rico and Haiti ended their campaign.

CFU CARIBBEAN CUP RECORD
1989-1996 DNE **1997-1999** DNQ **2001** DNE (withdrew) **2005-2008** DNQ **2010** DNE **2012** DNQ

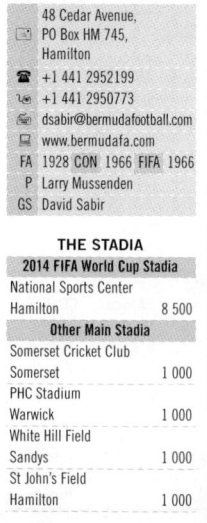

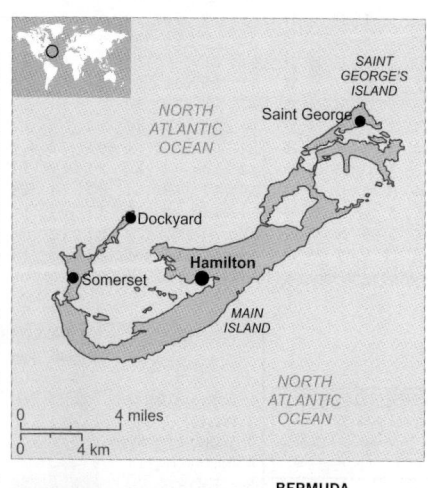

BERMUDA FOOTBALL ASSOCIATION (BFA)
48 Cedar Avenue,
PO Box HM 745,
Hamilton
☎ +1 441 2952199
📠 +1 441 2950773
✉ dsabir@bermudafootball.com
🖥 www.bermudafa.com
FA 1928 CON 1966 FIFA 1966
P Larry Mussenden
GS David Sabir

THE STADIA

2014 FIFA World Cup Stadia	
National Sports Center Hamilton	8 500
Other Main Stadia	
Somerset Cricket Club Somerset	1 000
PHC Stadium Warwick	1 000
White Hill Field Sandys	1 000
St John's Field Hamilton	1 000

MAJOR CITIES/TOWNS

		Population
1	Saint George	1 648
2	Hamilton	1 100

BERMUDA

Capital	Hamilton	Population	67 837 (202)	% in cities	100%
GDP per capita	$69 900 (4)	Area km²	54 km² (231)	GMT +/-	-4
Neighbours (km)	Coast 103				

RECENT INTERNATIONAL MATCHES PLAYED BY BERMUDA

2009	Opponents	Score		Venue	Comp	Scorers	Att	Referee
\multicolumn{9}{l}{No international matches played in 2009}

2010
No international matches played in 2010

2011

	Opponents	Score		Venue	Comp	Scorers	Att	Referee
2-09	Trinidad and Tobago	L	0-1	Port of Spain	WCq		6 000	Perea PAN
6-09	Guyana	L	1-2	Georgetown	WCq	Khano Smith [90]	3 500	Geiger USA
7-10	Trinidad and Tobago	W	2-1	Prospect	WCq	Antwan Russell [52], Nahki Wells [63]	2 243	Solis CRC
11-10	Guyana	D	1-1	Prospect	WCq	John Nusum [71]	2 573	Angela ARU
11-11	Barbados	W	2-1	Prospect	WCq	Khano Smith [28p], Kwame Steede [49]	1 000	Barrios GUA
14-11	Barbados	W	2-1	Prospect	WCq	Nahki Wells [46], Khano Smith [72p]	1 000	Moreno PAN

2012

7-09	Puerto Rico	L	1-2	Port-au-Prince	CCq	Antwan Russell [78p]	2 000	Taylor BRB
9-09	Haiti	L	1-3	Port-au-Prince	CCq	Antwan Russell [9]	10 500	Skeete BRB
11-09	Saint-Martin †	W	8-0	Port-au-Prince	CCq	Tyrell Burgess 4 [18 31 49 76], Antwan Russell [52], Taurean Manders [61], Ian Coke [80], LeJuan Simmons [87]	3 000	Royal JAM

Fr = Friendly match • CC = Digicel Caribbean Cup • WC = FIFA World Cup • q = qualifier • † Not a full international

BERMUDA 2011-12
CINGULAR WIRELESS PREMIER DIVISION

	Pl	W	D	L	F	A	Pts	Hornets	Rams	Cougars	Zebras	Colts	Trojans	Robin Hood	Rangers	Blazers	Warriors
Dandy Town Hornets	18	13	1	4	49	26	40		3-2	1-3	3-2	3-2	5-1	2-0	1-0	2-3	2-0
North Village Rams	18	12	2	4	55	28	38	5-2		2-0	5-3	0-1	3-0	5-2	4-0	5-0	3-2
Devonshire Cougars	18	12	1	5	35	25	37	0-4	3-5		3-0	2-2	1-0	2-1	4-1	2-0	4-1
PHC Zebras	18	10	2	6	43	28	32	3-2	2-1	3-0		6-2	3-0	1-0	1-2	0-0	1-1
St George's Colts	18	9	2	7	38	35	29	2-3	1-2	0-1	2-1		2-1	0-3	5-2	6-3	1-1
Somerset Trojans	18	9	2	7	43	42	29	2-2	4-2	4-3	1-4	4-1		3-2	6-2	3-3	3-2
Robin Hood	18	6	2	10	22	29	20	0-3	1-1	0-1	3-2	0-2	1-2		3-0	1-0	2-0
Southampton Rangers	18	2	6	10	20	41	12	1-2	2-2	0-1	1-3	0-1	4-3	1-1		0-0	1-1
Boulevard Blazers	18	3	3	12	20	48	12	0-7	2-4	0-3	2-5	1-3	2-3	3-0	2-2		2-0
St David's Warriors	18	1	5	12	18	41	8	0-2	0-4	1-2	0-3	3-3	1-2	1-1	2-0		

25/09/2011 - 18/03/2012 • Top scorers: **19** – Antwan RUSSELL, Zebras • **15** – Jonathan BEAN, Trojans • **13** – Dion STOVELL, Trojans

BERMUDA 2011-12
SECOND DIVISION (2)

	Pl	W	D	L	F	A	Pts
Wolves	20	16	3	1	67	21	51
MR Onions	20	15	1	4	81	22	46
BAA Wanderers	20	14	1	5	79	29	43
Hamilton Parish	20	12	2	6	53	30	38
X'roads Warriors	20	11	2	7	60	25	35
YMSC Bluebirds	20	9	6	5	57	32	33
Devonshire Colts	20	6	5	9	49	43	23
Somerset Eagles	20	7	2	11	47	41	23
Prospect United	20	4	5	11	32	56	17
Ireland Rangers	20	1	1	18	9	122	4
Paget Lions	20	0	2	18	7	120	2

25/09/2011 - 18/03/2012

MEDALS TABLE

		Overall	Lge	Cup	FT	Mart	DE
		G S	G S	G S	G S	G S	G S
1	North Village Rams	45 25	8 11	10 3	11 2	8 5	8 4
2	PHC Zebras	38 27	9 5	10 8	10 5	3 6	6 3
3	Somerset Trojans	37 26	9 9	9 3	9 4	7 4	3 6
4	Dandy Town Hornets	22 25	6 8	2 8	4 4	6 2	4 3
5	Devonshire Colts	17 33	3 4	5 10	4 11	2 6	3 2
6	Vasco da Gama	16 9	3 1	5 2	1 3	3 2	4 1
7	Boulevard Blazers	12 8	2 2	5 1	1 1	3 3	1 1
8	Devonshire Cougars	10 15	3 2	2 2	1 5	3 3	1 3
9	Hotels International	7 6	2 2	1	2 2	2 2	
10	YMSC	6 5	3 1	3 1		2	1
11	Southampton Rangers	5 11	1	1 5	3 3	3	1
12	Wolves	2 2		1		1 1	1
13	Dock Hill Rangers	1 4		1	1 3		
14	BAA Wanderers	1 1			1 1		
	Casuals SC	1 1		1 1		1 1	
	St George's Colts	1 1				1 1	
	Wellington Rovers	1 1		1		1	
18	Somerset Eagles	3			1	2	

FRIENDSHIP TROPHY 2011-12

First Round
North Village Rams	4
PHC Zebras	2
St George's Colts	3
St David's Warriors	6
Devonshire Cougars	4
Robin Hood	1
Dandy Town Hornets	1
Somerset Trojans	2

Semi-finals
North Village Rams	3
St David's Warriors	2
Devonshire Cougars	1
Somerset Trojans	2

Final
North Village Rams	4
Somerset Trojans	0

National Stadium, 1/01/2012
Ref: Mouchette
Scorers - Keishen Bean [23], Vernon Tankard [48], DeGraff [85p], Ralph Bean [89]

Prelim Round: Southampton Rangers 2-4 **Dandy Town Hornets** • Somerset Trojans w/o Boulevard Blazers
Rams - Jason Williams - Dakai Grant, Kofi Dill, DeVrae Tankard, Vernon Tankard (Jemeiko Jennings, 51), Jamaul Boyles (J Briers 51), Jason Davis, Sammy DeGraff, Ralph Bean Jr, Logan Alexander, Keishan Bean (Jason Lee, 77). Tr: Shaun Goater
Trojans - Shaquille Bean - T Harvey (T Wade, 50), J Rogers, D Seymour, Treven Ming•, A Trott, J Butterfield (J Simmons, 58), J Scott, Malachi Jones (J Bean, 50), Justin Corday, Chikosi Basden

DUDLEY EVE TROPHY 2011

First Round Group Stage

Group A	Pl	W	D	L	F	A	Pts	DC	PHC
Southampton Rangers	2	2	0	0	9	2	6	4-1	5-1
Devonshire Cougars	2	1	0	1	7	6	3		6-2
PHC Zebras	2	0	0	2	3	11	0		

Group B	Pl	W	D	L	F	A	Pts	DT	SG
North Village Rams	2	2	0	0	7	2	6	2-1	5-1
Dandy Town Hornets	2	0	1	1	2	3	1		1-1
St George's Colts	2	0	1	1	2	6	1		

Semi-finals
Dandy Town Hornets	4
Southampton Rangers	1
Devonshire Cougars	2
North Village Rams	3

Final
Dandy Town Hornets	1
North Village Rams	0

National Stadium, 26-10-2011
Scorer - Jahmal Swan [84]

Hornets - Ireadwell Gibbons - George Dyer, Kamen Tucker (K'Wonde Lathan 10), Antionio Lowe, Anthony Rocker, Seion Darrell, Jahmel Swan, Fabian Frankson, Damon Ming, Heyes Wolfe, Raymond Beach
Rams - Jason Williams - DeVrae Tankard, Tyrell Burgess, Kofi Dill, Dakai Grant, Jason Davis, Kaiwon Dill, Sammy DeGraff, Ralph Bean Jr, Lashun Dill (Pierre Smith), Jason Lee. Tr: Shaun Goater

FA CHALLENGE CUP 2011-12

First Round
Dandy Town Hornets	7	
Prospect United	0	
St George's Colts	3	
PHC Zebras	4	
Flanagan's Onions	2	2
YMSC Bluebirds	2	1
Somerset Eagles	3	
Wolves	5	
Robin Hood	1	2
Somerset Trojans	1	1
St David's Warriors	3	
Devonshire Colts	4	
Devonshire Cougars	3	
Boulevard Blazers	2	
Southampton Rangers	2	
North Village Rams	4	

Quarter-finals
Dandy Town Hornets	6
PHC Zebras	1
Flanagan's Onions	0
Wolves	2
Robin Hood	1 3
Devonshire Colts	1 0
Devonshire Cougars	1 1
North Village Rams	1 3

Semi-finals
Dandy Town Hornets	1
Wolves	0
Robin Hood	0
North Village Rams	1

Final
Dandy Town Hornets	5
North Village Rams	2

CUP FINAL
National Stadium, 15-04-2012
Ref: R Cann
Scorers - Lyn Tucker [15], Seion Darrell [19], Raymond Beach 2 [30 63], Damon Ming [80] for Hornets; Keishen Bean [72], Ralph Bean [83] for Rams

Elimination round: BAA 2-2 2-2 4-5p Prospect United • Hamilton Parish 1-2 **Somerset Eagles** • Paget Lions 0-4 **Devonshire Colts** • Crossroads 0-1 **Flanagan's Onions** • YMSC 4-0 Ireland Rangers

Hornets - Treadwell Gibbons - A Lowe, George Dyer, Kamen Tucker (K'Wonde Lathan 75), Anthony Rocker, Jahmel Swan, Lyn Tucker• (Fabian Frankson 53), Angelo Simmons, Seion Darrell, Damon Ming, Raymond Beach (W Place 77)
Rams - Jason Williams - Kofi Dill, Sean Fubler (Jahquan Smith-Deshields 75), Logan Alexander, Tyrell Burgess, Ralph Bean Jr, Lashun Dill (Jemeiko Jennings 38), Kaiwon Dill (Jason Lee 38), Keishan Bean, Jason Davis, Sammy DeGraff. Tr: Shaun Goater

BFA – BURKINA FASO

FIFA/COCA-COLA WORLD RANKING

'93	'94	'95	'96	'97	'98	'99	'00	'01	'02	'03	'04	'05	'06	'07	'08	'09	'10	'11	'12
127	97	101	107	106	75	71	69	78	75	78	84	87	61	113	62	49	41	62	89

2012

Jan	Feb	Mar	Apr	May	Jun	Jul	Aug	Sep	Oct	Nov	Dec	High	Low	Av
66	75	77	80	80	86	87	87	85	91	89	89	37	127	78

A stunning run against all the odds to the final of the 2013 Africa Cup of Nations in South Africa represented Burkina Faso's best footballing achievement to date. 'Les Etalons' might have been consistent in qualifying for past editions with eight appearances in the last 10 tournaments, but this was only the second time they had managed to get past the first round group stage. Their first-ever appearance in the final itself was also a far cry from the 2012 tournament when they went home early after losing all three group matches. This time they finished top of their group ahead of Nigeria, eliminating defending champions Zambia. Burkina Faso then beat Togo and Ghana in thrilling contests to get to the final, where they lost by a single goal to the Nigerians. It was a huge triumph for Belgian coach Paul Put who was appointed in March to replace Paulo Duarte after the 2012 disaster. His job started badly with FIFA stripping Burkina Faso of a point in the 2014 FIFA World Cup qualifiers for their use of the ineligible Cameroon-born defender Herve Zengue. But that was all forgotten amid the delirium of their unlikely progress to the final in South Africa, where Jonathan Pitroipa was named player of the tournament after an unusual ruling had allowed him to play in the final at Soccer City despite being sent off in the semi-final against Ghana.

CAF AFRICA CUP OF NATIONS RECORD

1957-1965 DNE 1968 DNQ 1970-1972 DNE 1974 DNQ 1976 DNE **1978** 8 r1 1980 DNE 1982 DNQ 1984-1988 DNE 1990-1992 DNQ 1994 DNE **1996** 15 r1 **1998** 4 SF (Hosts) **2000** 15 r1 **2002** 13 r1 **2004** 14 r1 2006-2008 DNQ **2010** 13 r1 **2012** 14 r1 **2013** 2 F

FEDERATION BURKINABE DE FOOT-BALL (FBF)

Centre Technique National, Ouaga 2000, Boite Postale 57, Ouagadougou 01
☎ +226 50 417802
📠 +226 50 417801
✉ febefoo@fasonet.bf
🌐 www.fasofoot.org
FA 1960 CON 1964 FIFA 1964
P Sita Sangare
GS Bertrand Kabore

THE STADIA

2014 FIFA World Cup Stadia
Stade du 4 août
Ouagadougou — 40 000

Other Main Stadia
Stade Municipal
Bobo-Dioulasso — 30 000
Stade Municipal
Ouagadougou — 15 000
Stade de Kadiogo
Kadiogo — 8 000
Stade Balibiè
Koudougou — 5 000

MAJOR CITIES/TOWNS

		Population
1	Ouagadougou	1 351 245
2	Bobo Dioulasso	471 426
3	Koudougou	85 157
4	Banfora	80 491
5	Ouahigouya	76 392
6	Pouytenga	71 278
7	Kaya	57 295
8	Garango	55 851
9	Fada N'gourma	44 629
10	Tenkodogo	43 447
11	Houndé	39 575
12	Dédougou	39 187
13	Tanghin-D'ouri	37 477
14	Kindi	31 614
15	Léo	28 541
16	Réo	28 401
17	Kongoussi	27 155
18	Gaoua	26 835
19	Gourcy	26 527

BURKINA FASO

Capital: Ouagadougou   Population: 15 746 232 (61)   % in cities: 20%
GDP per capita: $1200 (208)   Area km²: 274 200 km² (74)   GMT +/−: 0
Neighbours (km): Benin 306, Cote d'Ivoire 584, Ghana 549, Mali 1000, Niger 628, Togo 126

RECENT INTERNATIONAL MATCHES PLAYED BY BURKINA FASO

2011	Opponents	Score	Venue	Comp	Scorers	Att	Referee
9-02	Cape Verde Islands	L 0-1	Obidos	Fr			
26-03	Namibia	W 4-0	Ouagadougou	CNq	Alain Traore 3 [25] [45] [80], OG [73]		Cordier CHA
4-06	Namibia	W 4-1	Windhoek	CNq	Abdou Razak Traore [12], Aristide Bance [57p], Alain Traore [80], Jonathan Pitroipa [92+]		
10-08	South Africa	L 0-3	Johannesburg	Fr			
3-09	Equatorial Guinea	W 1-0	Bobo-Dioulasso	Fr	Alain Traore [61]		
8-10	Gambia	D 1-1	Bakau	CNq	Moumouni Dagano [90]		
11-11	Mali	D 1-1	St Leu La Foret	Fr	Aristide Bance [55]		
15-11	Guinea	D 1-1	Mantes La Jolie	Fr	Moumouni Dagano [10]		
2012							
9-01	Gabon	D 0-0	Bitam	Fr			
22-01	Angola	L 1-2	Malabo	CNr1	Alain Traore [58]	17 000	Benouza ALG
26-01	Côte d'Ivoire	L 0-2	Malabo	CNr1		4 000	Grisha EGY
30-01	Sudan	L 1-2	Bata	CNr1	Issiakka Ouedraogo [95+]	132	Otogo-Castane GAB
29-02	Morocco	L 0-2	Marrakech	Fr			Ould MTN
26-05	Benin	D 2-2	Ouagadougou	Fr	Prejuce Nakoulma 2 [41] [63]		
2-06	Congo	D 0-0	Ouagadougou	WCq	Match awarded 3-0 to Congo	23 904	El Ahrach MAR
9-06	Gabon	L 0-1	Libreville	WCq		23 000	Fall SEN
8-09	Central African Rep	L 0-1	Bangui	CNq			Gassama GAM
14-10	Central African Rep	W 3-1	Ouagadougou	CNq	Alain Traore 2 [17] [96+], Moumouni Dagano [70p]	40 000	El Ahrach MAR
14-11	Congo DR	W 1-0	Kinshasa	Fr	Aristide Bance [25p]		
1-12	Togo	W 2-1	Ouagadougou	Fr			
16-12	Togo	W 1-0	Lome	Fr			
2013							
17-01	Swaziland	W 3-0	Nelspruit	Fr	Aristide Bance [36], Abdou Traore [51], Wilfried Sanou [66]		
21-01	Nigeria	D 1-1	Nelspruit	CNr1	Alain Traore [94+]	8 500	Benouza ALG
25-01	Ethiopia	W 4-0	Nelspruit	CNr1	Alain Traore 2 [34] [74], Djakaridja Kone [79], Jonathan Pitroipa [95+]	35 000	Camille SEY
29-01	Zambia	D 0-0	Nelspruit	CNr1		8 000	Alioum CMR
3-02	Togo	W 1-0	Nelspruit	CNqf	Jonathan Pitroipa [105]	27 000	Diatta SEN
6-02	Ghana	D 1-1	Nelspruit	CNsf	Aristide Bance [60]. W 3-2p	35 000	Jedidi TUN
10-02	Nigeria	L 0-1	Johannesburg	CNf		85 000	Haimoudi ALG

Fr = Friendly match • CN = CAF African Cup of Nations • WC = FIFA World Cup • q = qualifier, r1 = first round group

BURKINA FASO NATIONAL TEAM HISTORICAL RECORDS

Coaches: Moussa Namoko 1961-65 • Guy Fabre 1966-71 • Bernard Bayala 1971-73 • Jacques Yameogo 1973-76 • Otto Pfister GER 1976-78 • Daniel Coulibaly 1980-82 • Soumaila Diallo 1984 • Piourhi Webonga 1987-88 • Heinz-Peter Uberjahn 1988-90 • Carlo Barrios BRA 1990-91 • Amokrane Waliken ALG 1991-92 • Idrissa Traore 1992-96 • Calixte Zagre 1996 • Ivan Vutov BUL 1996-97 • Malik Jabir GHA 1997 • Philippe Troussier FRA 1997-98 • Didier Notheaux FRA 1998-99 • Rene Taelman BEL 2000 • Sidiki Diarra 2000-01 • Oscar Fullone ARG 2001-02 • Jacques Yameogo & Pihouri Weboanga 2002 • Jean-Paul Rabier FRA 2002-04 • Ivica Todorov SRB 2004-05 • Bernard Simondi FRA 2005-06 • Idrissa Traore 2006-07 • Didier Notheaux FRA & Sidiki Diarra 2007 • Paulo Duarte POR 2008-12 • Paul Put 2012-

BURKINA FASO SQUAD FOR THE 2012 CAF AFRICA CUP OF NATIONS

	Player		Ap	G	Club	Date of Birth		Player		Ap	G	Club	Date of Birth
1	Daouda Diakite	GK	3		Turnhout BEL	30 03 1983	12	Prejuce Nakoulma	FW	2		G. Zabrze POL	21 04 1987
2	Ibrahim Gnanou	DF	1		Alania RUS	8 11 1986	13	Aristide Bance	FW	0+2		Samsunspor TUR	19 09 1984
3	Djakaridja Kone	MF	2		D Bucuresti ROU	22 07 1986	14	Benjamin Balima	MF	0+1		Sheriff MDV	20 03 1985
4	Mamadou Tall	DF	3		Persepolis IRN	4 12 1982	15	Narcisse Yameogo	FW	1+1		Camacha POR	19 11 1980
5	Mohamed Koffi	MF	3		PetroJet EGY	30 12 1986	16	Adama Sawadogo	GK	0		Missile GAB	20 01 1990
6	Bakary Kone	DF	2		Lyon FRA	27 04 1988	17	Keba Paul Koulibaly	DF	1		Ol. Charleroi BEL	24 03 1986
7	Florent Rouamba	MF	1+1		Sheriff MDV	31 12 1986	18	Charles Kabore	MF	3		Marseille FRA	9 02 1988
8	Mahamoudou Kere	MF	1		Konyaspor TUR	2 01 1982	19	Bertrand Traore	MF	0+1		Unattached	6 09 1995
9	Moumouni Dagano (c)	FW	3		Al Khor QAT	1 01 1981	20	Issiaka Ouedraogo	FW	0+1		Admira AUT	19 08 1988
10	Alain Traore	MF	2	1	Auxerre FRA	31 12 1988	21	Abdou Razak Traore	MF	0		L. Gdansk POL	28 12 1988
11	Jonathan Pitroipa	MF	3		Rennes FRA	12 04 1986	22	Saidou Panandetiguiri	DF	2+1		Valletta MLT	22 03 1984
	Tr: Paulo Duarte POR 6-04-1969						23	Germain Sanou	GK	0		St-Etienne FRA	26 05 1992

BURKINA FASO 2011-12

PREMIERE DIVISION FIRST ROUND

Group A

	Pl	W	D	L	F	A	Pts	SONABEL	ASFA/Y	USFA	EFO	RCK	USO	Santos	ASK	Canon	SFC	RCB
AS SONABEL	18	10	4	4	25	11	34		2-0	0-1	0-1	1-0	0-0	0-1	3-2	2-0	3-1	
ASFA/Yennenga	18	9	6	3	28	9	33	1-0		1-2	1-0	0-0	1-0	0-0	8-1	4-0	1-0	
US Forces Armées	18	9	5	4	22	10	32	1-1	1-1		0-1	1-1	1-0	0-0	2-0	1-1	3-0	
Etoile Filante	18	8	6	4	22	8	30	0-0	0-0	2-0		0-0	0-0	1-1	4-0	1-1	5-1	
Rail Club Kadiogo	18	7	9	2	18	12	30	1-1	2-1	0-2	1-0		2-0	2-2	0-0	1-1	2-0	
US Ouagadougou	18	7	5	6	18	12	26	1-2	0-0	2-1	0-1	1-1		0-1	3-0	4-1	0-0	
Santos	18	5	4	9	13	23	19	0-5	0-1	0-2	0-5	1-2	0-1		0-1	0-1	5-0	
AS Koupèla	18	4	6	8	13	28	18	1-2	0-0	1-0	0-2	1-1	1-2	2-0		0-0	2-0	
Canon du Sud	18	3	7	8	14	29	16	0-2	0-5	1-0	0-0	0-1	0-3	0-1	1-1		6-2	
Sanmatinga Kaya	18	0	4	14	6	37	4	0-1	1-1	0-3	0-1	0-1	0-1	0-1	0-0	1-1		

Group B

	Pl	W	D	L	F	A	Pts								Bobo Sport	US Yatenga	Maya	US Comoé	ASFB	ASEC-K	USFRAN	Sourou
Racing Club B-D	18	8	8	2	14	8	32								1-1	0-0	0-2	1-1	2-1	1-0	1-0	1-1
Bouloumpokou FC	18	7	10	1	19	8	31								0-0		1-0	0-0	1-1	1-0	1-1	0-0	4-1	0-1
Bobo Sport	18	7	8	3	12	9	29									0-0	1-1		0-1	1-0	2-0	1-0	1-0	2-1	1-1
US Yatenga	18	6	9	3	18	13	27									0-2	1-1	1-1		1-1	0-0	1-1	1-0	2-0	2-0
AS Maya B-D	18	6	7	5	13	15	25								0-1	0-2	0-0	1-0		3-1	2-0	0-0	1-0	2-1
US Comoé	18	5	7	6	17	18	22								1-2	0-0	3-0	3-3	0-0		0-0	2-2	0-1	1-0
ASF Bobo-Dioulasso	18	4	8	6	10	10	20								0-0	0-0	1-0	0-0	0-0	1-0	0-1		3-1	0-0	2-0
ASEC Koudougou	18	4	7	7	14	14	19								0-1	0-2	0-0	2-1	5-0	1-1	0-0		1-0	0-0
USFRAN	18	4	3	11	7	19	15								0-0	0-2	0-1	0-1	0-0	0-0	1-0	0-2	1-0		2-1
Sourou Sport	18	3	5	10	10	20	14								1-0	1-1	0-1	1-1	1-0	1-2	0-1	0-2	0-1	

29/03/2012 - 20/07/2012 • † Qualified for the championship round

BURKINA FASO 2011-12

PREMIERE DIVISION SECOND ROUND (SUPER DIVISION)

	Pl	W	D	L	F	A	Pts	ASFA/Y	SONABEL	RCB	USFA	BFC	EFO	Bobo Sport	US Yatenga
ASFA/Yennenga †	14	9	3	2	19	7	30		0-2	1-0	2-0	0-0	1-0	3-0	3-1
AS SONABEL	14	8	5	1	16	3	29	2-0		0-1	1-0	4-0	2-0	1-1	1-0
Racing Club B-D	14	8	3	3	13	6	27	0-2	0-0		1-0	1-0	2-0	1-1	3-0
US Forces Armées	14	6	3	5	12	9	21	1-2	0-0	2-0		2-0	1-0	2-1	2-0
Bouloumpokou FC	14	2	8	4	5	9	14	0-0	1-1	0-0	0-1		1-0	0-0	0-0
Etoile Filante	14	2	6	6	6	11	12	0-0	0-0	0-1	0-0	0-0		2-2	2-0
Bobo Sport	14	2	5	7	14	21	11	1-3	0-1	0-1	1-1	0-3	1-2		3-0
US Yatenga	14	1	3	10	3	22	6	0-2	0-1	0-2	1-0	0-0	0-0	1-3	

12/08/2012 - 13/10/2012 • † Qualified for the CAF Champions League

MEDALS TABLE

		All	Lge	Cup	Africa		Town
		G	G	G	G	S B	
1	Etoile Filante	33	12	21			Ougadougou
2	ASFA/Yennega	15	12	3			Ougadougou
3	USFA	10	7	3			Ougadougou
4	Silures	8	7	1			Bobo-Dioulasso
5	RCB	8	3	5			Bobo-Dioulasso
6	USFRAN	8	3	5			Bobo-Dioulasso
7	ASFB	7	2	5			Bobo-Dioulasso
8	USO	3	2	1			Ougadougou
9	RCK	3	1	2		2	Kadiogo
10	Commune	2	1	1			Ougadougou

COUPE NATIONALE DU FASO XXVI 2011-12

First Round		Round of 16		Quarter-finals		Semi-finals		Final	
Rail Club Kadiogo †	3	Rail Club Kadiogo	2	Rail Club Kadiogo	0 4p	Rail Club Kadiogo	1	Rail Club Kadiogo ‡	2
ASEC Koudougou	0	Bobo Sport	1	AS Maya B-D	0 3p	US Yatenga	0	ASFA/Yennenga	1
Racing Club B-D	1 8p								
Bobo Sport	1 9p								
ASF Bobo-Dioulasso	1	ASF Bobo-Dioulasso	3 1p						
Kioghin FC	0	AS Maya B-D	3 3p						
Alliance Koudougou	0								
AS Maya B-D †	3								
Canon du Sud	3	Canon du Sud	2	Canon du Sud	0 4p				
Bafudji	0	Santos FC	0	US Yatenga	0 5p				
Djelgodji FC	0								
Santos FC †	3								
Bouloumpokou FC	3	Bouloumpokou FC	1 1p						
Sourou Sport	0	US Yatenga	1 3p						
AS Dafra	0								
US Yatenga	1								
AS SONABEL †	3	AS SONABEL	7	AS SONABEL	1	AS SONABEL	1		
Jeunesse Bam	0	Nalambou FC	0	AS Koupèla	0	ASFA/Yennenga	2		
Siyossin Juniors	3								
Nalambou FC †	3								
Centre Naaba Kango	0 5p	Centre Naaba Kango	0						
Zempasgho	0 4p	AS Koupèla	1						
US Ouagadougou	0 2p								
AS Koupèla	0 4p								
US Comoé	1	US Comoé	1	US Comoé	0				
USFRAN	0	US Forces Armées	0	ASFA/Yennenga	1				
Sanmatinga Kaya	0								
US Forces Armées †	3								
Espoir FC	1	Espoir FC	0						
Fabao	0	ASFA/Yennenga	2						
Etoile Filante	1 3p								
ASFA/Yennenga	1 4p								

† Match awarded • 3rd Place Play-off: **AS SONABEL** 5-1 US Yatenga • ‡ Qualified for the CAF Confederation Cup

CUP FINAL

Stade du 4 Août, Ouagadougou
5-08-2012, Ref: Tangba Kambou CIV
Scorers - Blaise Yameogo [48], Wahabou Yameogo [51] for RCK; Aime Sirima [81] for ASFA/Y
RCK - Mohamed Diarra - Aime Sirima(c), Abdoulaye Traore, Aboubacar Zerbo, Saidou Simpore, Elisee To, Soumaila Diao (Ousmane Sylla 92+), Blaise Yameogo (Apollinaire Coulibaly 98+), Mahamadi Bande, Wahabou Yameogo, Andre Yameogo. Tr: Maio Kamou
ASFA/Y - Ibrahima Sakande - Aly Zoungrana(c), Moumouni Traore, Kader Kamagate, Darlaine Coulibaly (Issa Gouo 79), Ishola Wassiyou (Simplice Yameogo 60), Yacouba Ouedraogo, Karim Nikiema, Hermann Fallet, Louckmane Ouedraogo, Abubacar Usman (Daniel Yovo 62). Tr: Maxime Gouamene

BHR – BAHRAIN

FIFA/COCA-COLA WORLD RANKING

'93	'94	'95	'96	'97	'98	'99	'00	'01	'02	'03	'04	'05	'06	'07	'08	'09	'10	'11	'12
78	73	99	118	121	119	136	138	110	105	64	49	52	97	102	80	60	93	101	119

2012

Jan	Feb	Mar	Apr	May	Jun	Jul	Aug	Sep	Oct	Nov	Dec	High	Low	Av
95	97	93	93	94	95	103	102	112	115	124	119	44	139	94

The Bahrain national team may have developed a reputation as the 'nearly' men of Asian football after narrowly missing out on the FIFA World Cups finals in 2006 and 2010, but there were to be no such close calls for the 2014 FIFA World Cup in Brazil after failing to make it through to the final round of qualifying in Asia. They did sign off their campaign in some style, however, with a 10-0 thrashing of Indonesia at the start of 2012 in what was comfortably a record margin of victory for the team. Englishman Peter Taylor left his position as coach and was replaced by former Saudi Arabia and Oman coach Gabriel Calderon. Calderon lead his side to fourth place at the West Asian Championship in Kuwait at the end of the year, losing to Syria on penalties in the semi-finals, before slipping up against Oman in the third place play-off. In club football Riffa were crowned league champions for the first time in seven seasons in what was a landmark tenth title for the team. They finished well clear of second-placed Muharraq - sweet revenge for their 3-1 defeat at the start of April in the King's Cup final at the hands of Muharraq. Both clubs were eligible to compete in the 2012 AFC Cup but chose not to take part, entering the Gulf Champions League instead, a tournament won by Muharraq for the first time.

FIFA WORLD CUP RECORD
1930-1974 DNE 1978-1986 DNQ 1990 DNE 1994-2014 DNQ

BAHRAIN FOOTBALL ASSOCIATION (BFA)

Bahrain National Stadium,
PO Box 5464,
Manama
☎ +973 17 689569
+973 17 781188
bhrfa@batelco.com.bh
www.bfa.bh
FA 1957 CON 1970 FIFA 1966
P Shk. Salman Al Khalifa
GS Ali Al Bouanain

THE STADIA

2014 FIFA World Cup Stadia
National Stadium
Manama — 35 000

Other Main Stadia
Khalifa Sports City 'Isa Town'
Isa Town — 20 000
Al Muharraq Stadium
Muharraq — 20 000
Al Ahli Stadium
Manama — 10 000

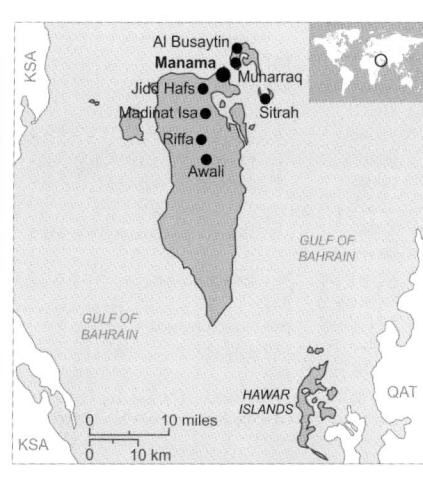

MAJOR CITIES/TOWNS

		Population
1	Manama	156 872
2	ar-Rifa'a	116 568
3	Muharraq	108 180
4	Madinat Hamad	84 709
5	Ali	66 113
6	Sitra	42 223
7	Isa Town	40 637
8	al-Budayyi	38 438
9	Jidhaf	34 757
10	al-Malikiyah	16 116
11	al-Hidd	14 703

MAMLAKAT AL BAHRAYN • KINGDOM OF BAHRAIN

Capital	Manama	Population	727 785 (162)	% in cities	89%
GDP per capita	$37 300 (28)	Area km²	741 km² (190)	GMT +/-	+3
Neighbours (km)	Coast 161				

RECENT INTERNATIONAL MATCHES PLAYED BY BAHRAIN

2010	Opponents	Score	Venue	Comp	Scorers	Att	Referee
24-09	Iran	L 0-3	Amman	WAr1		8 000	Darwish JOR
26-09	Oman	W 2-0	Amman	WAr1	Ismaeel Latif 2 [63 67]	500	
8-10	Kuwait	W 3-1	Kuwait City	Fr	Ismaeel Latif [9], Faouzi Aaish [47], Salman Isa [51]	10 000	
12-10	Uzbekistan	L 2-4	Manama	Fr	Faouzi Aaish [30], Hussein Salman [53]		
10-11	Uganda	D 0-0	Manama	Fr			
14-11	Syria	L 0-2	Manama	Fr			
23-11	Oman	D 1-1	Aden	GCr1	Ebrahim Moshkhas [67]		Al Enezi KUW
26-11	Iraq	L 2-3	Aden	GCr1	Faouzi Aaish [44], Ismaeel Latif [96+p]		Allabany YEM
29-11	UAE	L 1-3	Aden	GCr1	Abdulla Fatadi [35]		Al Marry BHR
28-12	Jordan	W 2-1	Dubai	Fr	Faouzi Aaish [32p], Ismaeel Latif [69]		
31-12	Saudi Arabia	L 0-1	Riffa	Fr			
2011							
4-01	Korea DPR	L 0-1	Riffa	Fr			
10-01	Korea Republic	L 1-2	Doha	ACr1	Faouzi Aaish [86p]	6 669	Al Hilali OMA
14-01	India	W 5-2	Doha	ACr1	Faouzi Aaish [8p], Ismaeel Latif 4 [16 20 35 77]	11 032	Mohd Salleh MAS
18-01	Australia	L 0-1	Doha	ACr1		3 919	Nishimura JPN
14-02	Kuwait	D 0-0	Manama	Fr			
10-08	Oman	D 1-1	Dubai	Fr	Mahmood Abdulrahman [34]		
26-08	Sudan	W 1-0	Manama	Fr	Mahmood Abdulrahman [14]		
2-09	Qatar	D 0-0	Manama	WCq		5 000	Zarouni UAE
6-09	Indonesia	W 2-0	Jakarta	WCq	Sayed Dhiya 45, Ismaeel Latif [70]	85 000	Lee Min Hu KOR
11-10	Iran	L 0-6	Tehran	WCq		82 000	Green AUS
4-11	Kuwait	W 1-0	Kuwait City	Fr	Mahmood Abdulrahman [45]		
11-11	Iran	D 1-1	Manama	WCq	Mohamed Tayeb [45]	18 000	Bashir SIN
15-11	Qatar	D 0-0	Doha	WCq		10 509	Nishimura JPN
6-12	Palestine	L 0-1	Al Muharraq	Fr			
10-12	Qatar	D 2-2	Doha	PGr1	Sami Al Husaini 2 [71 89]		Jiyed MAR
13-12	Iraq	W 3-0	Doha	PGr1	Fahad Hardan [41], Ismaeel Latif 2 [63p 70]		Haimoudi ALG
20-12	Palestine	W 3-1	Doha	PGsf	Mohamed Al Alawi [6], Salman Isa [44], OG [58]		El Haddad LIB
23-12	Jordan	W 1-0	Doha	PGf	Ismaeel Latif [89]		Balida QAT
2012							
18-01	Sweden	L 0-2	Doha	Fr			Al Dosari QAT
29-02	Indonesia	W 10-0	Manama	WCq	Ismaeel Latif 3 [5p 71 75], Mohamed Tayeb 2 [16 61], Mahmood Abdulrahman 2 [35p 42], Sayed Dhiya 3 [63 82 94+]	3 000	El Haddad LIB
23-06	Morocco	L 0-4	Jeddah	ARr1			
26-06	Yemen	L 0-2	Jeddah	ARr1			
15-08	Azerbaijan	L 0-3	Baku	Fr			Vadachkoria GEO
12-10	Philippines	D 0-0	Manama	Fr			
16-10	UAE	L 2-6	Dubai	Fr	Ismaeel Latif [8p], Hussain Baba [29]		
8-11	Jordan	W 3-0	Manama	Fr	Salman Isa [59], Faouzi Aaish [83], Hussain [88]		
14-11	Kuwait	D 1-1	Kuwait City	Fr			
29-11	Palestine	W 2-0	Al Wakrah	Fr	Sami Al Husaini [20], Jaycee Okwunwanne [64]		
3-12	Iraq	D 0-0	Doha	Fr			
9-12	Yemen	W 1-0	Al Farwaniyah	WAr1	Jaycee Okwunwanne [87]	150	Sabbagh LIB
12-12	Iran	D 0-0	Kuwait City	WAr1		1 000	Al Dosari QAT
15-12	Saudi Arabia	W 1-0	Al Farwaniyah	WAr1	Jaycee Okwunwanne [77]	200	Al Ghafari JOR
18-12	Syria	D 1-1	Kuwait City	WAsf	Abdulwahab Ali [67]. L 2-3p	6 000	Shaban KUW
20-12	Oman	L 0-1	Al Farwaniyah	WA3p		100	Al Dosari QAT

Fr = Friendly match • AC = AFC Asian Cup • GC = Gulf Cup • WA = West Asian Championship • WC = FIFA World Cup • PG = Pan Arab Games
q = qualifier • r1 = first round group • qf = quarter-final • sf = semi-final • f = final • 3p = third place play-off • po = play-off

BAHRAIN NATIONAL TEAM HISTORICAL RECORDS

Coaches: (Since 2003) Wolfgang Sidka GER 2000-03 • Yves Herbet FRA 2003 • Srecko Juricic CRO 2004-05 • Wolfgang Sidka GER 2005 • Luka Peruzovic CRO 2005-06 • Riyadh Al Thawadi BHR 2006 • Hans-Peter Briegel GER 2006-07 • Milan Macala CZE 2007-10 • Josef Hickersberger AUT 2010 • Salman Sharida 2010-11 • Peter Taylor ENG 2011-12 • Gabriel Calderon ARG 2012-

BAHRAIN 2011-12

PREMIER LEAGUE

	Pl	W	D	L	F	A	Pts	Riffa	Muharraq	Busaiteen	Al Hadd	Al Najma	Al Hala	Manama	Bahrain	Al Ahli	East Riffa
Riffa †	18	14	3	1	34	16	**45**		2-0	1-1	1-0	4-3	2-2	2-0	1-0	2-0	1-0
Muharraq	18	12	2	4	41	13	**38**	1-2		1-2	0-0	3-1	6-1	2-1	3-0	2-0	3-0
Busaiteen	18	10	4	4	34	25	**34**	0-2	0-2		3-1	1-0	1-5	4-2	4-2	5-1	2-2
Al Hadd	18	5	7	6	23	26	**22**	2-2	0-1	1-1		1-0	1-1	1-0	0-4	0-0	4-2
Al Najma	18	6	3	9	24	24	**21**	1-2	0-1	0-4	3-1		1-1	2-3	1-0	3-2	1-0
Al Hala	18	6	3	9	29	33	**21**	1-2	0-2	1-2	2-5	2-1		2-1	2-0	3-1	1-2
Manama	18	6	2	10	20	29	**20**	1-0	2-1	1-2	1-1	0-1	1-3		0-1	1-0	1-0
Bahrain Club	18	5	4	9	23	29	**19**	2-4	1-5	1-2	2-2	2-0	2-1	2-2		0-1	3-0
Al Ahli ‡	18	5	3	10	16	28	**18**	0-1	1-1	1-4	1-0	2-1	1-0	4-1	0-0		0-1
East Riffa	18	4	3	11	19	36	**15**	0-2	0-7	1-1	2-3	1-1	2-1	1-2	1-3	3-0	

1/12/2011 - 27/05/2012 • ‡ Relegation play-off • Relegation play-off: Al Ahli 2-0 1-4 **Malkiya** • † Qualified for the AFC Cup

MEDALS TABLE

		All G	Lge G	KC G	FAC	CPC	Asia G S B
1	Muharraq	68	32	29	2	5	2
2	Riffa	22	10	5	3	4	
3	Al Ahli	14	5	8	1		
4	Bahrain Club	7	5	2			
5	Al Hala	4	1	3			
6	East Riffa	3	1	2			
	Al Wahda	3		3			
8	Al Arabi	2	1	1			
	Al Najma	2		2			
10	Al Shabab	1		1			
	Busaiteen	1			1		
	Al Nasr	1	1				

KINGS CUP 2011-12

First Round		Quarter-finals		Semi-finals		Final	
Muharraq	1						
Al Hadd	0	**Muharraq**	2				
Al Hadd		East Riffa	1				
East Riffa	w/o			**Muharraq**	2		
Malikiya	3			Busaiteen	1		
Al Ittihad	2	Malikiya	0 1p				
Al Shabab	0	**Busaiteen**	0 3p				
Busaiteen	3					**Muharraq** †	3
Al Najma	4					Riffa	1
Budaia	0	**Al Najma**	0 5p				
Essa Town	2	Manama	0 3p			CUP FINAL	
Manama	3			Al Najma	0		
Bahrain Club	0 4p			**Riffa**	1	National Stadium, Manama	
Al Ahli	0 3p	Bahrain Club	1			8-04-2012	
Al Tadamun	0	**Riffa**	6				
Riffa	9			† Qualified for the AFC Cup			

Preliminary Round: **Budaia** 3-1 Qalali • Sitra 0-3 **Essa Town** • **Al Tadamun** 2-0 Al Ittifaq

BHU – BHUTAN

FIFA/COCA-COLA WORLD RANKING

'93	'94	'95	'96	'97	'98	'99	'00	'01	'02	'03	'04	'05	'06	'07	'08	'09	'10	'11	'12
-	-	-	-	-	-	-	201	202	199	187	187	190	192	198	187	196	197	202	207

2012

Jan	Feb	Mar	Apr	May	Jun	Jul	Aug	Sep	Oct	Nov	Dec	High	Low	Av
202	201	201	201	201	203	205	206	206	207	207	207	187	207	195

Bhutan's status as one of the most remote outposts of the global game continued in 2012 as the national team made just one appearance during the year - a 5-0 loss at the hands of Thailand in an international friendly in Bangkok. It was the 16th consecutive defeat for the team, a run that has seen Bhutan slip down to an all-time low of 207th in the FIFA/Coca-Cola World Ranking - equal bottom alongside San Marino and the Turks and Caicos Islands. In club football Drukpol won the championship in the six-team national league, finishing just one point ahead of Zimdra, while defending champions Yeedzin finished in third place, a further four points adrift in what turned out to be a three-way battle for the title. That saw Drukpol qualify to represent Bhutan in the 2013 AFC President's Cup, the Asian Football Confederation's third tier continental club competition. Yeedzin represented the nation at the 2012 edition of the tournament, but were unable to progress beyond the group stage. A 6-0 defeat at the hands of Phnom Penh Crown was followed by an 11-2 loss at the hands of Dordoi Bishkek in which Tshering Wangdi and Chenco Gyeltshen found the net for Yeedzin. The club's involvement ended with a 4-0 loss against Nepal Police Club that left them well adrift at the bottom of their group.

FIFA WORLD CUP RECORD
1930-2014 DNE

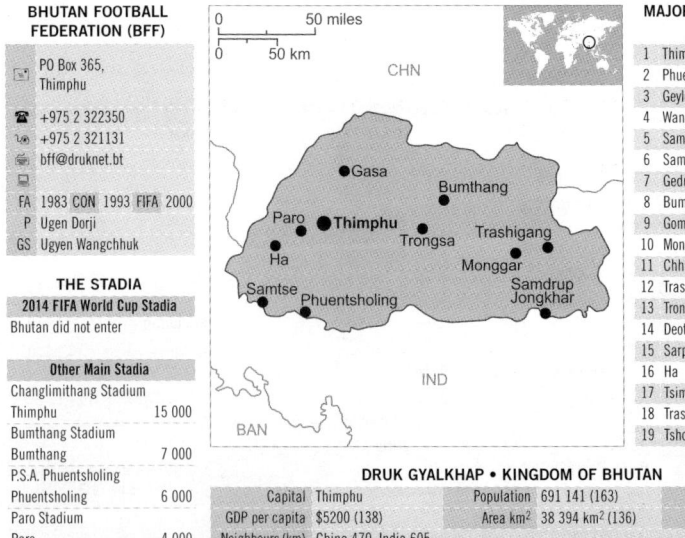

BHUTAN FOOTBALL FEDERATION (BFF)

PO Box 365, Thimphu
+975 2 322350
+975 2 321131
bff@druknet.bt

FA 1983 CON 1993 FIFA 2000
P Ugen Dorji
GS Ugyen Wangchhuk

THE STADIA
2014 FIFA World Cup Stadia
Bhutan did not enter

Other Main Stadia
Changlimithang Stadium
Thimphu 15 000
Bumthang Stadium
Bumthang 7 000
P.S.A. Phuentsholing
Phuentsholing 6 000
Paro Stadium
Paro 4 000

MAJOR CITIES/TOWNS
Population
1 Thimphu 90 300
2 Phuentsholing 22 467
3 Geylegphug 9 901
4 Wangdue 7 174
5 Samdrup Jongkhar 6 389
6 Samtse 5 272
7 Gedu 4 691
8 Bumthang 4 507
9 Gomtu 4 503
10 Monggar 3 722
11 Chhukha 3 123
12 Trashiyangtse 2 900
13 Trongsa 2 866
14 Deothang 2 838
15 Sarpang 2 819
16 Ha 2 657
17 Tsimalakha 2 583
18 Trashigang 2 513
19 Tshongdue 2 477

DRUK GYALKHAP • KINGDOM OF BHUTAN

Capital Thimphu
GDP per capita $5200 (138)
Neighbours (km) China 470, India 605
Population 691 141 (163)
Area km² 38 394 km² (136)
% in cities 35%
GMT +/- +6

RECENT INTERNATIONAL MATCHES PLAYED BY BHUTAN

2005	Opponents	Score	Venue	Comp	Scorers	Att	Referee
8-12	Bangladesh	L 0-3	Karachi	SAFr1			
10-12	India	L 0-3	Karachi	SAFr1			
12-12	Nepal	L 1-3	Karachi	SAFr1	Pradhan [47]		
2006							
2-04	Nepal	L 0-2	Chittagong	CCr1		3 500	Gosh BAN
4-04	Sri Lanka	L 0-1	Chittagong	CCr1			Saidov UZB
6-04	Brunei Darussalam	D 0-0	Chittagong	CCr1		2 000	Al Ghatrifi OMA
2007							
No international matches played in 2007							
2008							
13-05	Tajikistan	L 1-3	Barotac	CCq	Pasang Tshering [69]	5 000	Ng Chiu Kok HGK
15-05	Brunei Darussalam	D 1-1	Barotac	CCq	Nawang Dendup [12]	4 000	Mahapab THA
17-05	Philippines	L 0-3	Barotac	CCq		7 000	Saleem MDV
4-06	Bangladesh	D 1-1	Colombo	SAFr1	Nima Sanghe [79]		
6-06	Sri Lanka	L 0-2	Colombo	SAFr1			
8-06	Afghanistan	W 3-1	Colombo	SAFr1	Kinlay Dorji [13], Gyeltshen 2 [31 80]		
11-06	India	L 1-2	Male	SAFsf	Kinlay Dorji [18]		
2009							
14-04	Philippines	L 0-1	Male	CCq		200	Lazeem IRQ
16-04	Turkmenistan	L 0-7	Male	CCq		300	Perera SRI
18-04	Maldives	L 0-5	Male	CCq		9 000	Lazeem IRQ
29-11	Nepal	L 1-2	Calcutta	Fr	Pasang Tshering [59p]		
4-12	Bangladesh	L 1-4	Dhaka	SAFr1	Nawang Dendup [42p]		
6-12	Sri Lanka	L 0-6	Dhaka	SAFr1			
8-12	Pakistan	L 0-7	Dhaka	SAFr1			
2010							
No international matches played in 2010							
2011							
17-03	Nepal	L 0-1	Pokhara	Fr			
19-03	Nepal	L 1-2	Pokhara	Fr	Chencho Gyeltshen [91+]		
23-03	Afghanistan	L 0-3	Gurgaon	CCq		200	Mahapab THA
25-03	Afghanistan	L 0-2	Gurgaon	CCq		2 000	Mombeni IRN
3-12	Sri Lanka	L 0-3	New Delhi	SAFr1			Tufaylieh SYR
5-12	India	L 0-5	New Delhi	SAFr1			Singh SIN
7-12	Afghanistan	L 1-8	New Delhi	SAFr1	Chencho Gyeltshen [22]		Robesh SRI
2012							
14-11	Thailand	L 0-5	Bangkok	Fr			

SAF = South Asian Football Federation Cup • AC = AFC Asian Cup • CC = AFC Challenge Cup • q = qualifier • r1 = first round group

BHUTAN NATIONAL TEAM HISTORICAL RECORDS

Coach: Kang Byung Chan KOR 2000-02 • Yoo Kee Heung KOR 2002 • Aric Schanz NED 2002 • Henk Walk NED 2002-03 • Kharga Basnet 2005-06 • Koji Gyotoku JPN 2008-11 • Hiroaki Matsuyama JPN 2011

BHUTAN 2012

12TH NATIONAL LEAGUE

	Pl	W	D	L	F	A	Pts	Drukpol	Zimdra	Yeedzin	Dzongrig	Transport	Nangpa
Drukpol †	10	8	1	1	50	7	25		1-1	3-2	3-0	3-0	7-0
Zimdra	10	7	3	0	22	6	24	2-0		0-0	2-1	2-0	4-0
Yeedzin	10	6	2	2	54	9	20	0-1	3-3		6-0	5-1	16-0
Dzongrig	10	3	0	7	15	25	9	1-3	0-2	1-4		3-0	3-1
Transport United	10	2	0	8	14	38	6	1-10	1-2	0-6	2-5		5-2
Nangpa	10	1	0	9	5	75	3	0-19	0-4	0-12	2-1	0-4	

31/08/2012 - 6/10/2012 • † Qualified for the AFC President's Cup

BIH – BOSNIA-HERZEGOVINA

FIFA/COCA-COLA WORLD RANKING

'93	'94	'95	'96	'97	'98	'99	'00	'01	'02	'03	'04	'05	'06	'07	'08	'09	'10	'11	'12
-	-	-	152	99	96	75	78	69	87	59	79	65	59	51	61	51	44	20	27

2012

Jan	Feb	Mar	Apr	May	Jun	Jul	Aug	Sep	Oct	Nov	Dec	High	Low	Av
19	19	21	27	27	29	30	31	30	29	31	27	19	173	69

Amar Osim's Zeljeznicar team swept the board in domestic football in 2012 by winning both the league and cup for a first double in 11 years and only their second overall. They consigned Siroki Brijeg to the runners-up spot in both competitions, finishing eight points clear in the league and beating them 1-0 on aggregate in the cup final. Their cup final success was their third in a row without losing a game - an unbeaten run stretching back to August 2008 over 27 matches. Zeljeznicar were also hugely impressive in the league, going on a run of 26 matches unbeaten until a defeat on the final day of the season. During that time veteran goalkeeper Adnan Guso remained unbeaten for a new league record of 1180 minutes. Indeed, in both league and cup Zeljeznicar didn't concede a goal from the start of November until the beginning of May - 18 matches in all. Guso played in 17 of those, remaining unbeaten for an extraordinary 1630 minutes - only Brazil's Mazaropi has gone longer. The national team made a confident start to the 2014 FIFA World Cup qualifiers with Safet Susic hoping to lead his team to top spot in the group to avoid the possibility of another play-off heartbreak with star player Edin Dzeko hoping to add a World Cup finals appearance to the English championship medal he won with Manchester City in 2012.

UEFA EUROPEAN CHAMPIONSHIP RECORD
1960-1992 DNE (part of Yugoslavia) **1996** DNE **2000-2012** DNQ

FOOTBALL FEDERATION OF BOSNIA–HERZEGOVINA (FFBH/NSBIH)

Ferhadija 30,
Sarajevo - 71000
☎ +387 33 276660
📠 +387 33 444332
✉ nsbih@bih.net.ba
🌐 www.nfsbih.ba
FA 1992 CON 1996 FIFA 1996
P Elvedin Begic
GS Jasmin Bakovic

THE STADIA

2014 FIFA World Cup Stadia

| Bilino Polje | |
| Zenica | 13 632 |

Other Main Stadia

Asim Ferhatovic Hase 'Kosovo'	
Sarajevo	34 630
Bijeli Brijeg Stadion	
Mostar	15 000
Grbavica Stadion	
Sarajevo	12 000
Tusanj Stadion	
Tuzla	11 000

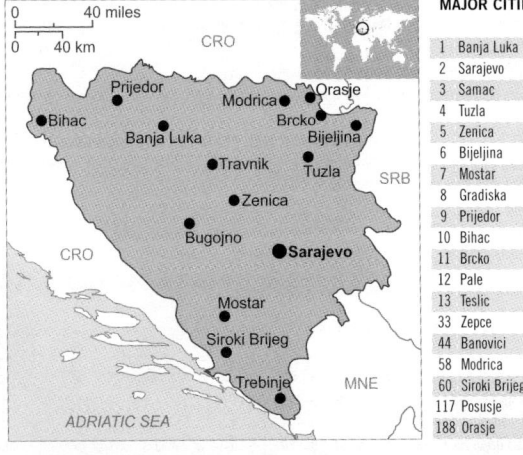

MAJOR CITIES/TOWNS

		Population
1	Banja Luka	221 686
2	Sarajevo	192 264
3	Samac	110 246
4	Tuzla	97 038
5	Zenica	93 043
6	Bijeljina	70 528
7	Mostar	70 270
8	Gradiska	42 262
9	Prijedor	41 938
10	Bihac	39 683
11	Brcko	36 483
12	Pale	34 617
13	Teslic	34 556
33	Zepce	12 504
44	Banovici	10 619
58	Modrica	8 763
60	Siroki Brijeg	8 434
117	Posusje	4 137
188	Orasje	3 088

BOSNA I HERCEGOVINA • BOSNIA AND HERZEGOVINA

Capital	Sarajevo	Population	4 613 414 (119)	% in cities	47%
GDP per capita	$6500 (127)	Area km²	51 197 km² (128)	GMT +/-	+1
Neighbours (km)	Croatia 932, Montenegro 249, Serbia 357 • Coast 20				

BIH – BOSNIA-HERZEGOVINA

RECENT INTERNATIONAL MATCHES PLAYED BY BOSNIA-HERZEGOVINA

2009	Opponents	Score	Venue	Comp	Scorers	Att	Referee
28-03	Belgium	W 4-2	Genk	WCq	Dzeko 7, Jahic 75, Bajramovic 77, Misimovic 81	20 041	Ivanov.N RUS
1-04	Belgium	W 2-1	Zenica	WCq	Dzeko 2 12 14	13 800	Hrinak SVK
1-06	Uzbekistan	D 0-0	Tashkent	Fr		15 000	Kovalenko UZB
9-06	Oman	W 2-1	Cannes	Fr	Dzeko 14, Salihovic 85		
12-08	Iran	L 2-3	Sarajevo	Fr	Dzeko 2 52 69		
5-09	Armenia	W 2-0	Yerevan	WCq	Ibricic 6, Muslimovic 74	1 800	Braamhaar NED
9-09	Turkey	D 1-1	Zenica	WCq	Salihovic 25	14 000	Benquerença POR
10-10	Estonia	W 2-0	Tallinn	WCq	Dzeko 30, Ibisevic 64	6 450	Rizzoli ITA
14-10	Spain	L 2-5	Zenica	WCq	Dzeko 90, Misimovic 92+	13 500	Plautz AUT
14-11	Portugal	L 0-1	Lisbon	WCpo		60 588	Atkinson ENG
18-11	Portugal	L 0-1	Zenica	WCpo		15 000	Rosetti ITA
2010							
3-03	Ghana	W 2-1	Sarajevo	Fr	Ibisevic 40, Pjanic 65	10 000	Batinic CRO
29-05	Sweden	L 2-4	Stockholm	Fr	Salihovic 47, Zec 90	22 589	Grafe GER
3-06	Germany	L 1-3	Frankfurt	Fr	Dzeko 15	48 000	Rizzoli ITA
10-08	Qatar	D 1-1	Sarajevo	Fr	Ibisevic 9	18 000	Vuckov CRO
3-09	Luxembourg	W 3-1	Luxembourg	ECq	Ibricic 6, Pjanic 12, Dzeko 16	7 327	Banari MDA
7-09	France	L 0-2	Sarajevo	ECq		28 000	Brych GER
8-10	Albania	D 1-1	Tirana	ECq	Ibisevic 21	14 220	Jakobsson ISL
17-11	Slovakia	W 3-2	Bratislava	Fr	Medunjanin 28, Pjanic 50, Dzeko 60	7 822	Mikulski POL
10-12	Poland	D 2-2	Antalya	Fr	Subasic 23, Misimovic 56p	100	Ogretmenoglu TUR
2011							
9-02	Mexico	L 0-2	Atlanta	Fr		45 000	Murrufo USA
26-03	Romania	W 2-1	Zenica	ECq	Ibisevic 63, Dzeko 83	13 000	Teixeira ESP
3-06	Romania	L 0-3	Bucharest	ECq		8 200	Eriksson SWE
7-06	Albania	W 2-0	Zenica	ECq	Medunjanin 67, Maletic 91+	9 000	Blom NED
10-08	Greece	D 0-0	Sarajevo	Fr		10 000	Dabanovic MNE
2-09	Belarus	W 2-0	Minsk	ECq	Salihovic 22p, Medunjanin 24	28 500	Kassai HUN
6-09	Belarus	W 1-0	Zenica	ECq	Misimovic 87	12 000	Atkinson ENG
7-10	Luxembourg	W 5-0	Zenica	ECq	Dzeko 12, Misimovic 2 15 22p, Pjanic 36, Medunjanin 51	12 000	Evans WAL
11-10	France	D 1-1	Paris	ECq	Dzeko 40	78 467	Thomson SCO
11-11	Portugal	D 0-0	Zenica	ECpo		12 352	Webb ENG
15-11	Portugal	L 2-6	Lisbon	ECpo	Misimovic 41p, Spahic 65	47 728	Stark GER
2012							
28-02	Brazil	L 1-2	St Gall	Fr	Ibisevic 13	17 500	Kever SUI
26-05	Republic of Ireland	L 0-1	Dublin	Fr		37 100	Haenni SUI
31-05	Mexico	L 1-2	Chicago	Fr	Dzeko 29	51 240	Jurisevic USA
15-08	Wales	W 2-0	Llanelli	Fr	Ibisevic 21, Stevanovic 54	6 253	Borg MLT
7-09	Liechtenstein	W 8-1	Vaduz	WCq	Misimovic 2 26 31, Ibisevic 3 33 39 82, Dzeko 3 46 64 80	5 900	Borg MLT
11-09	Latvia	W 4-1	Zenica	WCq	Misimovic 2 12 54, Pjanic 44, Dzeko 92+	11 900	Aytekin GER
12-10	Greece	D 0-0	Piraeus	WCq		26 211	Damato ITA
16-10	Lithuania	W 3-0	Zenica	WCq	Ibisevic 29, Dzeko 35, Pjanic 41	11 920	Zelinka CZE
14-11	Algeria	W 1-0	Algiers	Fr	Svraka 93+	30 000	Coulibaly MLI

Fr = Friendly match • EC = UEFA EURO 2012 • WC = FIFA World Cup • q = qualifier • po = play-off

BOSNIA-HERZEGOVINA NATIONAL TEAM HISTORICAL RECORDS

Caps
72 - Zvjezdan Misimovic 2004- • 63 - Emir Spahic 2003- • 51 - Edin Dzeko 2007- & Elvir Bolic 1996-2006 • 47 - Sergej Barbarez 1998-2006 • 45 - Vedin Music 1995-2007 • 44 - Vedad Ibisevic 2007- & Kenan Hasagic 2002- • 43 - Hasan Salihamidzic 1996-2006 • 40 - Muhamed Konjic 1995-2004 • 39 - Miralem Pjanic 2008- ; Senijad Ibricic 2005- & Elvir Baljic 1996-2005 • 38 - Sasa Papac 2002-

Goals
26 - Edin Dzeko 2007- • 24 - Zvjezdan Misimovic 2004- • 22 - Elvir Bolic 1996-2006 • 17 - Sergej Barbarez 1998-2006 • 15 - Vedad Ibisevic 2007- • 14 - Elvir Baljic 1996- 2005 • 11 - Zlatan Muslimovic 2006- • 7 - Miralem Pjanic 2008-

Coaches
Mirsad Fazlagic 1992-1993 • Fuad Muzurovic 1993-1998 • Dzemaludin Musovic 1998-99 • Faruk Hadzibegic 1999 • Miso Smajlovic 1999-2002 • Blaz Sliskovic 2002-2006 • Fuad Muzurovic 2006-2007 • Meho Kodro 2008 • Miroslav Blazevic 2008-2009 • Safet Susic 2009-

BOSNIA-HERZEGOVINA 2011-12

PREMIJER LIGA

	Pl	W	D	L	F	A	Pts	Zeljeznicar	Siroki Brijeg	Borac	Sarajevo	Olimpik	Zrinjski	Zvijezda	Travnik	Celik	Rudar	Velez	Leotar	GOSK	Slavija	Sloboda	Kozara
Zeljeznicar Sarajevo †	30	22	5	3	68	17	71		1-0	1-0	1-0	0-0	3-3	1-0	1-0	5-0	3-0	4-1	2-0	5-0	3-1	4-0	2-1
Siroki Brijeg ‡	30	18	9	3	48	17	63	2-1		1-1	3-1	1-1	1-1	0-0	3-1	1-0	3-0	2-0	5-1	2-0	5-0	2-0	1-0
Borac Banja Luka ‡	30	17	4	9	46	26	55	0-3	0-0		2-0	1-0	2-1	1-2	1-0	2-0	3-1	3-0	3-1	6-0	3-2	4-1	1-0
Sarajevo ‡	30	16	6	8	48	31	54	2-2	0-1	2-2		2-0	2-0	3-2	1-0	4-2	3-1	1-1	1-0	0-2	2-1	2-1	4-0
Olimpik Sarajevo	30	15	7	8	44	23	52	0-1	0-0	2-1	1-0		3-0	2-0	1-2	1-0	1-0	0-0	4-1	0-0	2-0	2-0	2-0
Zrinjski Mostar	30	12	9	9	47	41	45	0-0	0-1	1-0	1-1	2-4		4-1	2-0	1-1	3-1	1-0	1-0	4-2	3-1	2-0	2-3
Zvijezda Gradacac	30	13	6	11	37	35	45	0-3	0-2	2-0	2-0	1-0	1-1		3-2	2-1	2-0	2-0	4-1	0-0	4-2	1-0	1-0
Travnik	30	10	5	15	42	53	35	2-1	3-5	0-3	1-2	2-1	2-2	2-1		3-4	3-0	3-2	2-0	1-1	3-0	3-0	0-0
Celik Zenica	30	8	10	12	31	39	34	1-1	0-0	0-0	1-1	1-0	1-3	2-1	2-2		3-0	1-1	2-3	2-0	1-2	1-0	2-0
Rudar Prijedor	30	10	4	16	30	46	34	0-5	1-1	1-3	1-2	1-1	3-2	1-0	4-0	0-0		1-0	2-0	3-0	0-1	2-0	3-0
Velez Mostar	30	8	9	13	28	35	33	1-2	0-2	1-0	0-0	1-3	3-1	1-1	4-1	2-1	0-1		1-1	1-2	3-0	3-0	0-0
Leotar Trebinje	30	9	6	15	27	40	33	2-1	0-0	3-0	1-0	0-1	1-2	0-0	1-1	0-0	1-0	0-1		0-0	2-0	2-0	1-0
GOSK Gabela	30	8	9	13	26	43	33	0-1	1-2	1-0	1-4	3-0	0-0	2-1	3-0	0-0	3-0	0-0	2-1		1-2	1-4	0-0
Slavija Sarajevo	30	10	2	18	36	61	32	1-5	2-0	0-2	0-4	2-2	1-2	3-1	3-0	2-0	1-1	0-1	2-3	1-0		2-0	2-1
Sloboda Tuzla	30	10	2	18	23	48	32	0-4	1-0	0-1	0-1	1-4	3-2	0-0	1-0	1-0	1-2	2-0	2-1	2-1	1-0		1-0
Kozara Gradiska	30	4	7	19	19	45	19	0-2	1-2	0-1	1-3	0-6	0-0	1-2	1-2	1-2	1-0	0-0	1-0	0-0	6-2	1-1	

6/08/2011 - 23/05/2012 • † Qualified for the UEFA Champions League • ‡ Qualified for the Europa League
Top scorers: 20 - Eldin **ADILOVIC**, Zeljeznicar • 10 - Igor **ANICIC** SRB, Leotar; Haris **HARBA**, Olimpik; Dejan **RASEVIC**, Slavija & Muamer **SVRAKA**, Zeljeznicar

BOSNIA 2011-12 PRVA LIGA NS FBIH (2)

	Pl	W	D	L	F	A	Pts
Gradina Srebrenik	30	19	4	7	59	30	61
Buducnost Banovici	30	17	3	10	47	32	54
Vitez	30	15	7	8	55	31	52
Rudar Kakanj	30	15	7	8	51	33	52
Krajina Cazin	30	14	8	8	39	28	50
Bratstvo Gracanica	30	14	7	9	63	30	49
Iskra Bugojno	30	14	6	10	42	34	48
Capljina	30	15	3	12	42	34	48
Gorazde	30	13	3	14	38	43	42
Branitelj Rodoc	30	12	4	14	43	42	40
Jedinstvo Bihac	30	11	6	13	48	46	39
Krajisnik	30	12	5	13	41	42	38
Orasje	30	12	2	16	41	61	38
SASK Napredak	30	10	7	13	34	38	37
UNIS Vogosca	30	4	2	24	23	64	14
Omladinac Mionica	30	5	2	23	18	96	17

13/08/2011 - 6/06/2012

BOSNIA 2011-12 PRVA LIGA FS RS (2)

	Pl	W	D	L	F	A	Pts
Radnik Bijeljina	26	14	8	4	31	19	50
Sloga Doboj	26	14	7	5	48	31	49
Sloboda Mrkonjic Grad	26	14	4	8	40	21	46
Sutjeska Foca	26	11	5	10	34	36	38
Crvena Zemlja	26	11	4	11	40	35	37
Modrica Maksima	26	10	6	10	31	22	36
Drina Visegrad	26	10	6	10	22	25	36
Podrinje Janja	26	9	7	10	32	29	34
Drina Zvornik	26	9	6	11	24	23	33
Mladost Gacko	26	9	6	11	25	33	33
Rudar Ugljevik	26	8	8	10	27	30	32
Sloboda Novi Grad	26	8	8	10	24	32	32
Laktasi	26	8	4	14	34	55	28
Proleter Teslic	26	5	5	16	34	55	20

13/08/2011 - 26/05/2012
Relegation play-off: Jedinstvo 0-2 0-3 **Sloboda Novi Grad**

MEDALS TABLE

	Overall			League			Cup			Europe		
	G	S	B	G	S	B	G	S	B	G	S	B
1 Zeljeznicar Sarajevo	10	6	1	5	3	1	5	3				
2 FK Sarajevo	5	7	3	1	5	3	4	2				
3 Celik Zenica	5	1	1	3		1	2	1				
4 NK Siroki Brijeg	3	7	1	2	4	1	1	3				
5 Zrinjski Mostar	3	1	1	2	1	1	1					
6 Borac Banja Luka	2	1	2	1		2	1	1				
7 FK Modrica Maxima	2			1			1					
8 Slavija Sarajevo	1	2	1			1	1	1	1			
9 Brotnjo Citluk	1	1	1	1	1	1						
10 Leotar Trebinje	1	1					1			1		
11 Bosna Visoko	1		2				2		1			
12 NK Orasje	1						1					
13 Sloboda Tuzla		5	2			2		5				
14 Buducnost Banovici		1				1						
Radniki Lukavac		1				1						

BOSNIAN CLUBS IN YUGOSLAV FOOTBALL

	G	S	B	G	S	B	G	S	B	G	S	B
7 Velez Mostar	2	5	4				3	4	2	2		
9 FK Sarajevo	2	4		2	2			2				
13 Zeljeznicar Sarajevo	1	2	2	1	1	2			1			1
14 Borac Banja Luka	1	1					1	1				
21 Slavia		1	1		1	1						
21 Sloboda Tuzla		1					1			1		
23 SASK Sarajevo		1			1							

KUP BIH 2011-12

First Round

Zeljeznicar Sarajevo*	2
Leotar Trebinje	0
Mladost Gacko	0
Olimpik Sarajevo*	3
GOSK Gabela	1
Vitez*	0
Podrinje Janja	0
Celik Zenica*	4
Sarajevo	1
Sloga Doboj*	0
UNIS Vogosca	0
Rudar Prijedor*	1
Zvijezda Gradacac*	2
Sloboda Tuzla	0
Brotnjo Citluk	1
Borac Banja Luka*	3
Velez Mostar	3
Travnik*	2
Sutjeska Foca	0
Zrinjski Mostar*	3
Rudar Kakanj	1
Iskra Bugojno*	0
Dizdarusa	1
Branitelj Rodoc*	4
Krajisnik*	6
Mladost Zupca	0
Radnik Bijeljina	0
Mramor*	1
Slavija Sarajevo*	3
Modrica Maksima	0
Kozara Gradiska	0
Siroki Brijeg*	3

Round of 16

Zeljeznicar Sarajevo*	3 1
Olimpik Sarajevo	0 1
GOSK Gabela*	1 0
Celik Zenica	3 3
Sarajevo*	3 4
Rudar Prijedor	0 5
Zvijezda Gradacac*	0 0
Borac Banja Luka*	2 0
Velez Mostar* †	3 2
Zrinjski Mostar*	0 0
Rudar Kakanj*	0 1
Branitelj Rodoc*	1 2
Krajisnik	1 2
Mramor*	1 1
Slavija Sarajevo*	1 2
Siroki Brijeg	2 4

† 1st leg awarded 3-0 after match abandoned at 1-0 • * Home team/Home team in the 1st leg ‡ Qualified for the Europa League

Quarter-finals

Zeljeznicar Sarajevo*	2 0
Celik Zenica	0 0
Sarajevo*	0 0 5p
Borac Banja Luka	0 0 6p
Velez Mostar*	2 1
Branitelj Rodoc	0 1
Krajisnik*	1 0
Siroki Brijeg	1 0

Semi-finals

Zeljeznicar Sarajevo*	1 3
Borac Banja Luka	0 0
Velez Mostar	0 0
Siroki Brijeg*	1 1

Final

Zeljeznicar Sarajevo ‡	1 0
Siroki Brijeg	0 0

CUP FINAL 1ST LEG
Grbavica, Sarajevo, 25-04-2012
Att: 4000, Ref: Vladimir Bjelica
Scorer - Svarka 33 for Zeljeznicar
Zeljeznicar - Adnan Guso - Josip Kvesic, Jadranko Bogicevic, Velibor Vasilic, Benjamin Colic - Patrick Nyema●, Muamer Svraka● - Vernes Selimovic - Samir Bekric (Mirsad Beslija 62), Eldin Adilovic (Elvir Colic 74), Zajko Zeba (c) (Nermin Jamak 87). Tr: Amar Osim
Siroki - Luka Bilobrk - Mateo Bertosa, Vedran Jese, Slavko Brekalo, Dino Coric● - Jefthon● (Mario Kvesic 90), Marciano - Goran Zakaric (Mateo Roskam 62) - Juan Manuel Varea (Jure Ivankovic 75), Dalibor Silic, Wagner. Tr: Marijan Bloudek

CUP FINAL 2ND LEG
Pecara, Siroki Brijeg, 16-05-2012
Att: 2000, Ref: Radoslav Vukasovic
Siroki - Luka Bilobrk - Mateo Bertosa, Vedran Jese, Slavko Brekalo●, Dino Coric● - Marciano - Ricardo Baiano (Goran Zakaric 60), Jure Ivankovic - Juan Manuel Varea (Mateo Roskam 66), Dalibor Silic, Wagner (Mario Kvesic 77). Tr: Marijan Bloudek
Zeljeznicar - Adnan Guso● - Jadranko Bogicevic, Josip Kvesic, Velibor Vasilic, Benjamin Colic, Semir Kerla - Zajko Zeba (Srdan Stanic 90), Samir Bekric (Nermin Jamak 85), Muamer Svraka●- Nermin Zolotic - Eldin Adilovic (Mirsad Beslija 17), Vernes Selimovic●. Tr: Amar Osim

BLR – BELARUS

FIFA/COCA-COLA WORLD RANKING

'93	'94	'95	'96	'97	'98	'99	'00	'01	'02	'03	'04	'05	'06	'07	'08	'09	'10	'11	'12
137	121	88	90	110	104	95	96	85	74	90	69	61	70	60	84	80	38	64	65

2012

Jan	Feb	Mar	Apr	May	Jun	Jul	Aug	Sep	Oct	Nov	Dec	High	Low	Av
65	67	69	68	69	69	77	76	76		87	74	65	36	142	84

2012 saw BATE Borisov win the Belarus championship for the seventh year in a row as the rest of the clubs in the league struggled to keep pace. The title took their trophy haul in both the league and cup since independence to eleven, one more than Dinamo Minsk - the traditional giants of club football in the country and the only team from Belarus to win the old Soviet league. BATE had overtaken Dinamo's haul of seven championships when they won the league in 2011 and it is a sobering thought for Dinamo fans that after winning six of the first seven titles post independence, they have won just one in the 15 years since. Indeed, for the fourth year in a row, both the league and cup were won by provincial teams with Naftan from the northern city of Novopolotsk winning the cup after beating FK Minsk on penalties in the final. In Europe BATE continued their progress by qualifying for the group stage of the 2012-13 UEFA Champions League where they beat both Bayern Munich and Lille. It was the fifth time that the club had made it to the group stage with the money earned helping to reinforce their position at home. The national team knew from the outset that their 2014 FIFA World Cup qualifying group was going to be hard work and they duly lost to both France and Spain before a morale boosting victory over Georgia at the end of the year.

UEFA EUROPEAN CHAMPIONSHIP RECORD
1960-1992 DNE (Played as part of the Soviet Union) **1996-2012** DNQ

BELARUS FOOTBALL FEDERATION (BFF)

Prospekt Pobeditelei 20/3
Minsk 220 020

☎ +375 172 545600
📠 +375 172 544483
✉ info@bff.by
🌐 www.bff.by
FA 1989 CON 1993 FIFA 1992
P Sergei Roumas
GS TBD

THE STADIA
2014 FIFA World Cup Stadia
Dinamo Stadion
Minsk 42 375

Other Main Stadia
Traktor Stadion
Minsk 17 586
Central Stadion
Gomel 14 307
Dinamo Stadion
Brest 10 310
Torpedo Stadion
Zhodino 6 542

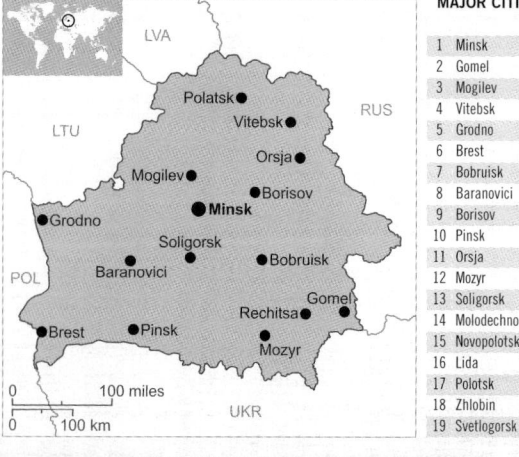

MAJOR CITIES/TOWNS
		Population
1	Minsk	1 758 453
2	Gomel	476 151
3	Mogilev	367 786
4	Vitebsk	341 713
5	Grodno	327 496
6	Brest	309 934
7	Bobruisk	218 294
8	Baranovici	169 390
9	Borisov	150 634
10	Pinsk	131 382
11	Orsja	125 947
12	Mozyr	112 318
13	Soligorsk	102 557
14	Molodechno	98 614
15	Novopolotsk	98 563
16	Lida	96 717
17	Polotsk	79 884
18	Zhlobin	73 525
19	Svetlogorsk	68 634

RESPUBLIKA BYELARUS • REPUBLIC OF BELARUS

Capital Minsk	Population 9 648 533 (86)	% in cities 73%
GDP per capita $11 800 (93)	Area km² 207 600 km² (85)	GMT + / - +2
Neighbours (km) Latvia 171, Lithuania 680, Poland 605, Russia 959, Ukraine 891		

RECENT INTERNATIONAL MATCHES PLAYED BY BELARUS

2009	Opponents	Score	Venue	Comp	Scorers	Att	Referee
1-04	Kazakhstan	W 5-1	Almaty	WCq	Hleb.A [48], Kalachev 2 [54 64], Stasevich [57], Rodionov [88]	19 000	Jech CZE
6-06	Andorra	W 5-1	Grodno	WCq	Blizniuk 2 [1 76], Kalachev [44], Kornilenko 2 [50 65]	8 500	Kranjc SVN
10-06	Moldova	D 2-2	Borisov	Fr	Rodionov [4], Bliznyuk [27]	2 000	Mazeika LTU
12-08	Croatia	L 1-3	Minsk	WCq	Verkhovtsov [81]	21 651	Brych GER
5-09	Croatia	L 0-1	Zagreb	WCq		25 628	Plautz AUT
9-09	Ukraine	D 0-0	Minsk	WCq		21 727	Kassai HUN
10-10	Kazakhstan	W 4-0	Brest	WCq	Bordachev [23], Kalachev 2 [69 92+], Kovel [86]	9 530	Ennjimmi FRA
14-10	England	L 0-3	London	WCq		76 897	Batista POR
14-11	Saudi Arabia	D 1-1	Dammam	Fr	Bordachev [20]		
18-11	Montenegro	L 0-1	Podgorica	Fr		5 000	Stavrev MKD
2010							
3-03	Armenia	W 3-1	Antalya	Fr	Putsila [58], Hleb [73], Rodionov [86]	BCD	
27-05	Honduras	D 2-2	Villach	Fr	Putsila 2 [57 60]	400	Eisner AUT
30-05	Korea Republic	W 1-0	Kufstein	Fr	Kislyak [53]	1 000	Brugger AUT
2-06	Sweden	L 0-1	Minsk	Fr		12 000	Nikolaev RUS
11-08	Lithuania	W 2-0	Kaunas	Fr	Hleb.V 2 [49 90]	3 500	Satchi MDA
3-09	France	W 1-0	Paris	ECq	Kislyak [86]	76 395	Collum SCO
7-09	Romania	D 0-0	Minsk	ECq		26 354	Kralovec CZE
8-10	Luxembourg	D 0-0	Luxembourg	ECq		1 857	Stavrev MKD
12-10	Albania	W 2-0	Minsk	ECq	Rodionov [10], Krivets [77]	7 000	Rasmussen DEN
17-11	Oman	W 4-0	Muscat	Fr	Martynovich 2 [5 11], Hleb.V [35], Rodionov [57p]	1 000	Al Amri KSA
2011							
9-02	Kazakhstan	D 1-1	Antalya	Fr	Hleb.V [44p]	1 500	Banari MDA
26-03	Albania	L 0-1	Tirana	ECq		13 826	Strombergsson SWE
29-03	Canada	L 0-1	Antalya	Fr		100	Yildirim TUR
3-06	France	D 1-1	Minsk	ECq	OG [20]	26 500	Fernandez ESP
7-06	Luxembourg	W 2-0	Minsk	ECq	Kornilenko [48p], Putilo [73]	9 500	Salmanov AZE
10-08	Bulgaria	W 1-0	Minsk	Fr	Kislyak [33]	6 500	Dunauskas LTU
2-09	Bosnia-Herzegovina	L 0-2	Minsk	ECq		28 500	Kassai HUN
6-09	Bosnia-Herzegovina	L 0-1	Zenica	ECq		12 000	Atkinson ENG
7-10	Romania	D 2-2	Bucharest	ECq	Kornilenko [45], Dragun [82]	29 486	Kelly IRL
11-10	Poland	L 0-2	Wiesbaden	Fr		5 116	Sippel GER
15-11	Libya	D 1-1	Dubai	Fr	Kornilenko [77]	250	Mohamed UAE
2012							
29-02	Moldova	D 0-0	Antalya	Fr		100	Mazeika LTU
7-06	Lithuania	D 1-1	Minsk	Fr	Dragun [79]	2 000	Satchi MDA
15-08	Armenia	W 2-1	Yerevan	Fr	Bressan 2 [44 66]	6 500	Kharitonashvili GEO
7-09	Georgia	L 0-1	Tbilisi	WCq		20 000	Todorov BUL
11-09	France	L 1-3	Paris	WCq	Putilo [71]	52 552	Gocek TUR
12-10	Spain	L 0-4	Minsk	WCq		28 800	Gumienny BEL
16-10	Georgia	W 2-0	Minsk	WCq	Bressan [6], Dragun [28]	15 300	Schoergenhofer AUT
14-11	Israel	W 2-1	Jerusalem	Fr	Kislyak [45], Balanovich [46]	8 000	Evans WAL

Fr = Friendly match • EC = UEFA EURO 2012 • WC = FIFA World Cup • q = qualifier

BELARUS NATIONAL TEAM HISTORICAL RECORDS

Caps
102 - Aleksandr Kulchiy 1996-• 80 - Sergei Gurenko 1994-2006 • 74 - Sergei Omelyanchuk 2002-• 71 - Sergei Shtanyuk 1995-2007 •
64 - Maksim Romaschenko 1998-2008 • 57 - Aleksandr Hleb 2001-• 56 - Valentin Byalkevich 1992-2005 & Sergei Kornilenko 2003-•
53 - Timofei Kalachev 2004- & Yuri Zhenov 2003-• 52 - Vitaly Kutuzov 2002- & Andrei Ostrovskiy 1994-2005-

Goals
20 - Maksim Romaschenko 1998-2008 • 13 - Vitaly Kutuzov 2002-• 12 - Vyacheslav Hleb 2004- & Sergei Kornilenko 2003-• 10 - Valentin Byalkevich 1992-2005 & Roman Vasilyuk 2000-08 • 8 - Vitaly Bulyga 2003-08 • 7 - Sergei Gerasimets 1992-99 & Timofei Kalachev 2004-

Coaches
Mihail Verhejenka 1992-1994 • Siarhej Barouski 1994-1996 • Mihail Verhejenka 1997-1999 • Siarhej Barouski 1999-2000 • Eduard Malofeev 2000-2003 • Anatoly Baidachny RUS 2003-2005 • Yuri Puntus 2006-2007 • Bernd Stange GER 2007-11 • Georgy Kondratiev 2011-

BELARUS 2012

VYSSHAYA LIGA

	Pl	W	D	L	F	A	Pts	BATE	Shakhter	Dinamo M	Gomel	Neman	FK Minsk	Belshina	Dinamo B	Naftan	Slavija	Torpedo
BATE Borisov †	30	21	5	4	51	16	68		1-0 2-1	1-3	0-0	2-0 5-1	2-0 5-1	3-1	0-1 3-1	3-0	2-1	0-0 2-0
Shakhter Soligorsk ‡	30	18	7	5	59	24	61	1-1		1-0 1-1	1-2 4-1	1-1	7-0 0-2	2-1 3-1	0-1 4-2	0-0	5-0	1-0
Dinamo Minsk ‡	30	16	8	6	37	19	56	0-2 0-0	1-2		0-1 1-0	1-1 1-0	1-0	1-0	1-0	4-2 1-1	3-1 4-2	2-0
FC Gomel	30	14	8	8	39	24	50	0-1 1-2	1-1	0-0		1-1 0-1	2-2	1-0	2-0	0-0 2-0	3-0 4-1	2-0 3-0
Neman Grodno	30	10	11	9	43	36	41	1-2	1-1 0-4	0-0	0-3		0-1 2-1	1-0 0-0	1-1 3-0	3-0	8-0	1-1 2-1
FK Minsk	30	11	6	13	36	46	39	1-0	0-2	0-0 0-2	1-2 1-1	4-4		3-0 2-2	2-1 0-0	1-0	3-2 3-0	1-2
Belshina Bobruisk	30	7	9	14	26	40	30	0-1 0-1	0-4	1-0 0-2	1-1 3-1	0-0	3-0		3-1	0-0 3-2	3-0 0-0	0-0
Dinamo Brest	30	8	5	17	27	38	29	0-2	1-2	1-2 2-0	0-1 2-1	1-1	0-1	1-1 4-0		2-1 0-1	1-2 2-0	1-0
Naftan Novopolotsk	30	7	8	15	23	40	29	0-4 2-0	1-2 1-2	0-2	0-1	2-1 1-0	1-3 1-2	3-0	1-0		0-0	0-0 1-1
Slavija Moazyr	30	7	6	17	22	58	27	1-2 0-0	0-2 0-0	0-2	0-2	1-3 0-1	1-0	1-0	2-1	2-1 1-1		1-0 3-2
Torpedo Zhodino	30	5	9	16	17	39	24	0-2	2-3 0-2	0-0 0-2	1-0	1-5	2-1 1-0	0-1 2-2	1-0 0-0	0-1	0-0	

24/03/2012 - 25/11/2012 • † Qualified for the UEFA Champions League • ‡ Qualified for the Europa League
Relegation/promotion play-off: Gorodeya 1-0 0-4 Torpedo Zhodino. Torpedo remain in the Vysshaya Liga
Top scorers: **14** - Dzmitry **ASIPENKA**, Shakhter • **11** - Renan **BRESSAN**, BATE; Roman Volkov, Slavija Moazyr & Dzmitry Kamarovski, Shakhter

BELARUS 2012
PERSHAYA LIGA (2)

	Pl	W	D	L	F	A	Pts
Dnepr Mogilev	28	20	3	5	75	22	63
FC Gorodeya	28	18	6	4	49	21	60
FK Vitebsk	28	19	2	7	57	30	59
SKVICh Minsk	28	16	7	5	61	19	55
FC Slutsk	28	15	7	6	59	27	52
Granit Mikashevichi	28	14	8	6	41	23	50
Vedrich-97 Rechitsa	28	9	12	7	40	24	39
Volna Pinsk	28	8	10	10	24	45	34
FC Bereza-2010	28	9	6	13	41	48	33
FC Smorgon	28	7	10	11	23	32	31
FC Lida	28	8	6	14	32	49	30
FC Polotsk	28	7	5	16	24	55	26
Khimik Svetlogorsk	28	5	9	14	29	52	24
DSK Gomel	28	1	5	22	9	62	8
FK Rudensk	28	4	4	20	15	70	7

21/04/2012 - 17/11/2012

BELARUS 2012
DRUHAJA LIGA (3)

	Pl	W	D	L	F	A	Pts
FC Smolevichy	36	26	9	1	113	22	87
Beltransgaz Slonim	36	24	6	6	95	35	78
FC Isloch	36	21	7	8	61	30	70
FC Gomelzheldortrans	36	20	9	7	64	27	69
FK Minsk-2	36	21	5	10	60	33	68
Dinamo Minsk-2	36	19	3	14	52	44	60
Zorka-BDU Minsk	36	18	4	14	54	41	58
Kommunalnik Slonim	36	16	7	13	61	55	55
Belcard Grodno	36	15	8	13	54	45	53
FC Zhlobin	36	16	3	17	53	66	51
Neman Mosty	36	13	7	16	50	54	46
Dnepr Mogilev-2	36	13	4	19	49	60	43
FC Baranovichi	36	10	10	16	33	42	40
Livadyya Dzerzhinsk	36	12	3	21	47	72	39
Zabudova-2007	36	12	2	22	45	86	38
FC Miory	36	9	8	19	47	82	35
MOFK	36	9	8	19	30	72	35
FC Osipovichy	36	8	9	19	47	74	33
FK Vitebsk-2	36	2	4	30	24	99	10

21/04/2012 - 27/11/2012

MEDALS TABLE

		Overall			League			Cup	
		G	S	B	G	S	B	G	S
1	BATE Borisov	11	/	1	9	4	1	2	3
2	Dinamo Minsk	10	8	3	7	6	3	3	2
3	Slavija Mozyr	4	4		2	2		2	2
4	Belshina Bobruisk	4	2	2	1	1	2	3	1
5	FC Gomel	3	2	2	1	1	2	2	1
6	Shakhter Soligorsk	2	6	4	1	3	4	1	3
7	Partizan Minsk (ex MTZ)	2		2			2	2	
8	Naftan Novopolotsk	2						2	
9	Dinamo-93 Minsk	1	2	3		1	3	1	1
10	Lokomotiv Vitebsk	1	2	2		2	2	1	
11	Dnepr-Transmash	1	2		1	1			1
	Neman Grodno	1	2			1		1	1
13	Dinamo Brest	1		1			1	1	
14	FK Minsk		1	1			1		1
15	Lokomotiv Minsk		1				1		
	Torpedo Mogilev		1						1
	Torpedo-SKA Minsk		1						1
	Torpedo Zhodino		1						1
	Vedrich Rechitsa		1						1
20	Dnepr Mogilev			1			1		

BELARUS CLUBS IN THE SOVIET ERA

| 14 | Dinamo Minsk | 1 | 1 | 3 | 1 | | 3 | | 1 |

KUBOK BELARUSII 2011-12

Round of 32

Naftan Novopolotsk	4
Beltransgaz Slonim *	2
FC Baranovichi *	2
Partizan Minsk	3
Vedrich-97 Rechitsa	3
Volna Pinsk *	1
Slavija Mozyr	2
FC Lida *	3
FC Brest	3
Granit Mikashevichi *	0
FC Gorodeya *	0
BATE Borisov	7
Shakhter Soligorsk	6
Khimik Svetlogorsk *	0
FC Polatsak *	0 4p
FC Gomel	0 5p
Neman Grodno	2
FC Smorgon *	0
FC Slutsk *	1
Dinamo Minsk	2
FK Rudensk *	1 7p
Torpedo Zhodino	1 8p
Dnepr Mogilev	0 4p
Klechesk Kletsk *	0 3p
SKVICh Minsk	2
DSK Gomel *	1
FK Vitebsk	0
Belcard Grodno *	2
Belshina Bobruisk	5
Gomelzheldortrans *	1
Partizan Minsk B *	2
FK Minsk	4

Round of 16

Naftan Novopolotsk *	2
Partizan Minsk	1
Vedrich-97 Rechitsa *	1
FC Lida	2
FC Brest *	3
BATE Borisov	1
Shakhter Soligorsk *	0 4p
FC Gomel	0 5p
Neman Grodno *	2
Dinamo Minsk	1
FK Rudensk *	1
Klechesk Kletsk	3
SKVICh Minsk	2
Belcard Grodno *	1
Belshina Bobruisk	0
FK Minsk *	3

Quarter-finals

Naftan Novopolotsk	2
FC Lida *	1
FC Brest *	1
FC Gomel	2
Neman Grodno *	6
Klechesk Kletsk	0
SKVICh Minsk *	2
FK Minsk	3

Semi-finals

Naftan Novopolotsk	0 3p
FC Gomel	0 1p
Neman Grodno *	0
FK Minsk	2

Final

Naftan Novopolotsk ‡	2 4p
FK Minsk	2 3p

PENALTIES

	Mi	NN
	✓ Kovb	
		Shkabara ✓
	✗ Vasilyuk	
		Kovalenko ✓
	✗ Makas	
		Zhukovski ✓
	✓ Sachivko	
		Harbachov ✗
	✓ Rakhmanov	
		Gavrilovich ✓

CUP FINAL
Dinamo Stadium, Minsk
20-05-2012, 13:30. Att: 9800. Ref: Tsinkevich
Scorers - Shkabara [27], Cernych [58] for Naftan; Vasilyuk [52], Kovel [76] for Minsk
Naftan - Nikolai Romanyuk - Mikhail Gorbachev, Denis Obrazov, Aleksei Gavrilovich, Nikita Bukatkin●, Igor Trukhov (Valery Zhukovsky 81), Oleg Shkabara, Aleksandr Kobets, Roman Sorokin, Yegor Zubovich, Fedor Chernykh. Tr: Igor Kovalevich
Minsk - Artur Lesko● - Yuri Ostroukh, Oleh Karamushka, Roman Begunov● (Marius Cinikas 61), Andrey Razin (Aleksandr Makas 64), Sergey Gigevich (Dmitriy Kovb 73), Artem Rakhmanov, Aleksandr Sachivko, Ivan Maevski, Leonid Kovel, Roman Vasilyuk. Tr: Vadim Skripchenko

Vysshaya Liga clubs enter in the round of 32. ● * Home team ● ‡ Qualified for the Europa League

BLZ – BELIZE

FIFA/COCA-COLA WORLD RANKING

'93	'94	'95	'96	'97	'98	'99	'00	'01	'02	'03	'04	'05	'06	'07	'08	'09	'10	'11	'12
-	-	173	182	179	186	190	186	167	158	174	181	180	198	201	173	173	172	141	167

2012

Jan	Feb	Mar	Apr	May	Jun	Jul	Aug	Sep	Oct	Nov	Dec	High	Low	Av
133	135	136	140	140	135	131	132	145	144	144	167	134	201	175

They may well be the weakest team in Central America but Belize caused an almighty surprise at the 2013 Copa Centroamericana after reaching the semi-finals. Prior to the tournament in Costa Rica, Belize had never won a match in the 22-year history of the competition. A 2-1 victory over Nicaragua in the first round group stage changed all that and thanks to an earlier draw with Guatemala they found themselves in the semi-finals and with a place at the 2013 CONCACAF Gold Cup in America. Belize's star player Deon McCauley was the hero with an injury-time winner over the Nicaraguans but even he could not inspire his team to further triumphs and they were beaten by Honduras in the semi-final and by El Salvador in the third place play-off. The performance of the national team was certainly helped by the return of some stability to the club scene in the country. The new Premier League of Belize was launched in October 2011 and kicked off in February 2012 with 12 clubs divided into two groups of six with the top two in each qualifying for the play-offs. Placencia Assassins were widely regarded as national champions in 2011 after their Super-League success and they reinforced their status by winning the first Premier League title in May 2012 after beating Police United 3-2 on aggregate in the final.

FIFA WORLD CUP RECORD
1930-1994 DNE **1998-2014** DNQ

FOOTBALL FEDERATION OF BELIZE (FFB)

26 Hummingbird Highway,
Belmopan, PO Box 1742,
Belize City
☎ +501 822 3410
+501 822 3377
bzefederation@gmail.com
www.belizefootball.bz
FA 1980 CON 1986 FIFA 1986
P Ruperto Vicente
GS Michael Blease

THE STADIA

2014 FIFA World Cup Stadia
FFB Field
Belmopan 5 000
Belize also used the Estadio Olimpico in San Pedro Sula, Honduras

Other Main Stadia
Marion Jones Sports Complex
Belize City 7 500
People's Stadium
Orange Walk 3 000

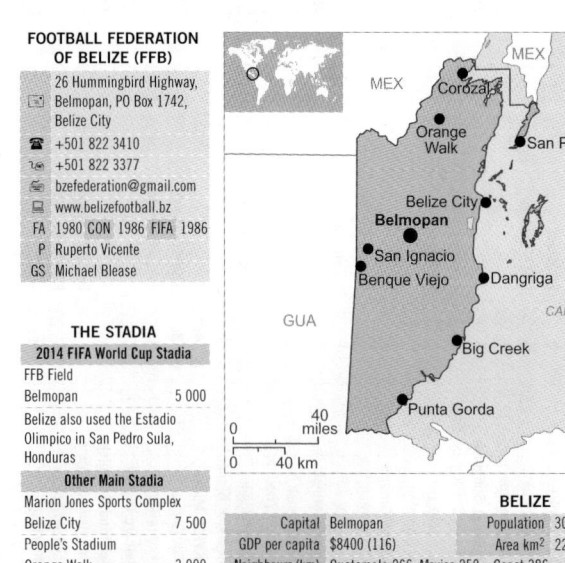

MAJOR CITIES/TOWNS

		Population
1	Belize City	68 170
2	San Ignacio	19 906
3	Belmopan	19 151
4	Orange Walk	16 530
5	San Pedro	12 535
6	Dangriga	12 431
7	Corozal	9 458
8	Benque Viejo	9 300
9	Punta Gorda	5 469

BELIZE

Capital Belmopan Population 307 899 (177) % in cities 52%
GDP per capita $8400 (116) Area km² 22 966 km² (151) GMT +/- -6
Neighbours (km) Guatemala 266, Mexico 250 • Coast 386

BLZ – BELIZE

RECENT INTERNATIONAL MATCHES PLAYED BY BELIZE

2011	Opponents	Score	Venue	Comp	Scorers	Att	Referee
14-01	Panama	L 0-2	Panama City	UCr1		10 000	Pineda HON
16-01	El Salvador	L 2-5	Panama City	UCr1	Elroy Smith [45p], Orlando Jimenez [76]	1 500	Cerdas CRC
18-01	Nicaragua	D 1-1	Panama City	UCr1	Daniel Jimenez [81]	10 000	Brea CUB
15-06	Montserrat	W 5-2	Couva	WCq	Deon McCauley 3 [24 75 83], Harrison Roches [50], Elroy Kuylen [53]	100	Willett ATG
17-07	Montserrat	W 3-1	San Pedro Sula	WCq	Daniel Jimenez [23], Deon McCauley [59], Luis Mendez [61]	150	Reyna GUA
2-09	Grenada	W 3-0	St George's	WCq	Deon McCauley 2 [11 79], Harrison Roches [35]	2 600	Rubalcaba CUB
6-09	Guatemala	L 1-2	Belmopan	WCq	Deon McCauley [77]	3 027	Mejia SLV
7-10	Grenada	L 1-4	Belmopan	WCq	Ryan Simpson [90]	1 200	Jarquin NCA
11-10	Guatemala	L 1-3	Guatemala City	WCq	Deon McCauley [31]	21 107	Penaloza MEX
11-11	St Vincent/Grenadines	D 1-1	Belmopan	WCq	Deon McCauley [22]	300	Skeete BRB
15-11	St Vincent/Grenadines	W 2-0	Kingstown	WCq	Deon McCauley 2 [78 81p]	500	Thomas JAM
2012							
No international matches played in 2012							
2013							
18-01	Costa Rica	L 0-1	San Jose	UCr1		5 484	Rodriguez HON
20-01	Guatemala	D 0-0	San Jose	UCr1		250	Bonilla SLV
22-01	Nicaragua	W 2-1	San Jose	UCr1	Trevor Lennen [29], Deon McCauley [90]	750	Aguilar SLV
25-01	Honduras	L 0-1	San Jose	UCsf		1 644	Lopez GUA
17-01	El Salvador	L 0-1	San Jose	UC3p		1 997	Vasquez DOM

UC = UNCAF Cup/Copa Centroamericana • WC = FIFA World Cup • q = qualifier

BELIZE NATIONAL TEAM HISTORICAL RECORDS

Caps 15 - Deon McCauley 2007- • 5 - Dion Fraser 2000-08 • 4 - Harrison Roches 2004- • 3 - Norman Nunez 1995-2005; Vallan Symms 2000- & Bent Burgess 2000-02 • 2 - David MacCauley 1995-96; Aaron Nolberto 1999-2001; Elroy Smith 2004-; Elroy Kuylen 2009- & Daniel Jimenez

Coach Michael Winston 1995-96 • Manuel Bilches ARG 2000 • Leroy Sherrier CRC 2001 • Eduardo Santana BRA 2003 • Anthony Adderly 2004-06 • Antonio Carlos Vieira BRA • Jose Palmiro Salas GUA 2008 • Ian Mork USA 2008 • Renan Couch MEX 2008-09 • Jose de la Paz HON 2010-11 • LeRoy Sherrier CRC 2012-

BELIZE 2012

PREMIER LEAGUE

North

	Pl	W	D	L	F	A	Pts	Defence	FC Belize	San Pedro	San Felipe	Juventus	World FC
Defence Force †	10	7	2	1	24	5	23		1-0	2-2	2-1	2-0	7-0
FC Belize †	10	5	4	1	12	5	19	1-1		0-0	1-0	2-0	1-0
San Pedro Sea Dogs	10	4	3	3	20	15	15	0-3	0-0		4-0	6-0	4-2
San Felipe Barcelona	10	4	3	3	14	16	15	1-0	1-1	2-1		2-2	3-2
Suga Boys Juventus	10	3	1	6	14	18	10	0-1	2-4	4-0	0-1		3-0
World FC	10	0	1	9	9	34	1	0-5	0-2	2-3	3-3	0-3	

South

	Pl	W	D	L	F	A	Pts	Police	Assassins	San Ignacio	Fighters	Bandits	Hankook
Police United †	10	9	1	0	23	3	28		1-0	0-0	2-1	3-0	6-0
Placencia Assassins †	10	6	2	2	20	8	20	1-2		2-1	5-1	3-1	4-0
San Ignacio United	10	3	4	3	11	12	13	1-3	1-2		1-0	1-1	2-1
Freedom Fighters	10	2	3	5	13	20	9	0-2	1-1	1-1		1-1	6-0
Belmopan Bandits	10	1	4	5	6	13	7	0-1	0-0	1-1	0-1		1-0
Hankook Verdes Utd	10	2	0	8	11	28	6	0-3	0-2	1-2	7-1	2-1	

11/02/2012 - 15/04/2012 • † Qualified for the semi-finals
Top scorers (including play-offs): **8** - Jesse **SMITH**, San Pedro Seadogs • **6** - six players with six goals

PREMIER LEAGUE PLAY-OFFS

Semi-finals
Placencia Assassins 0 2 4p
Defence Force 0 2 2p

Finals
Placencia Assassins 2 1
Police United 1 1

FC Belize 2 0
Police United 2 1

PREMIER LEAGUE FINAL

1st leg. Michael Ashcroft Stadium, Independence, 5-05-2012
2nd leg. FFB Field, Belmopan, 12-05-2012
Placencia Assassins 2-1 1-1 Police United
1st leg scorers - Luis Torres [35], Ashley Torres [43] for Assassins;
Evan Mariano [84] for Police • 2nd leg scorers - Evan Mariano [92+] for Police; Elias Donaire [12] for Assassins

BOL – BOLIVIA

FIFA/COCA-COLA WORLD RANKING

'93	'94	'95	'96	'97	'98	'99	'00	'01	'02	'03	'04	'05	'06	'07	'08	'09	'10	'11	'12
58	44	53	39	24	61	61	65	70	92	99	94	96	101	108	58	56	97	108	42

2012

Jan	Feb	Mar	Apr	May	Jun	Jul	Aug	Sep	Oct	Nov	Dec	High	Low	Av
109	107	106	109	108	110	83	73	63	72	51	42	18	115	72

After a less than inspiring start to the 2014 FIFA World Cup qualifying campaign, Bolivia coach Gustavo Quinteros resigned in July 2012 to take over at Ecuadorian club Emelec and was replaced by the Spaniard Xabier Azcargorta - the man who had lead the Bolivians to the finals of the 1994 World Cup in the USA. The move certainly helped re-invigorate the campaign and by the end of the year Bolivia were closing the gap on the teams in the qualifying places, helped in no small measure by a superb 4-1 victory over Uruguay in La Paz. In the1994 qualifiers it had been their invincibility at altitude at home in La Paz that had seen the Bolivians through to the finals, a factor they would need exploit in order to reach the finals in neighbouring Brazil. In club football, The Strongest lived up to their name after winning both tournaments played during 2012 to complete a hat trick of titles - the first time they had done that since the mid-1920s. The first of those was an extraordinarily close run affair with just one point separating the top five teams. Going into the final round The Strongest trailed leaders San Jose by three points but a late Luis Melgar goal gave them a 2-1 victory over them and the title on goal difference - but only thanks to an even later goal conceded by Oriente Petrolero which deprived them of a win against Nacional Potosi.

FIFA WORLD CUP RECORD

1930 12 r1 **1934-1938** DNE **1950** 15 r1 **1954-1958** DNE **1962-1990** DNQ **1994** 20 r1 **1998-2010** DNQ

FEDERACION BOLIVIANA DE FÚTBOL (FBF)

Av. Libertador Bolívar 1168, Cochabamba
☎ +591 4 4488600
+591 4 4282132
secretaria.cba@fbf.com.bo
www.fbf.com.bo
FA 1925 CON 1926 FIFA 1926
P Carlos Alberto Chavez
GS Jose Pedro Zambrano

THE STADIA

2014 FIFA World Cup Stadia
Estadio Hernando Siles
La Paz   42 000

Other Main Stadia
Ramón Tahuichi Aguilera
Santa Cruz   38 000
Estadio Felix Capriles
Cochabamba   32 000
Estadio Olimpico Patria
Sucre   30 000
Estadio Jesus Bermudez
Oruro   28 000

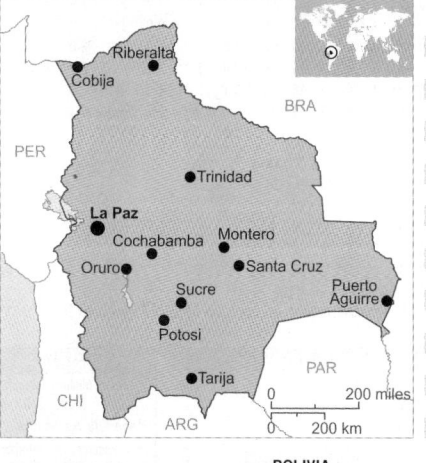

MAJOR CITIES/TOWNS

		Population
1	Santa Cruz	1 614 618
2	El Alto	949 912
3	La Paz	887 512
4	Cochabamba	616 943
5	Sucre	295 455
6	Oruro	232 114
7	Tarija	204 423
8	Potosí	164 600
9	Sacaba	105 105
10	Montero	100 911
11	Trinidad	94 348
12	Riberalta	88 059
13	Yacuiba	87 914
14	Quillacollo	85 224
15	Colcapirhua	47 430
16	Cobija	43 813
17	Guayaramerín	37 612
18	Viacha	35 968
19	Villazón	34 787

BOLIVIA

Capital La Paz; Sucre	Population 9 775 246 (84)	% in cities 66%
GDP per capita $4 500 (148)	Area km² 1 098 581 km² (28)	GMT +/- -4
Neighbours (km) Argentina 832, Brazil 3423, Chile 860, Paraguay 750, Peru 1075		

RECENT INTERNATIONAL MATCHES PLAYED BY BOLIVIA

2009	Opponents	Score	Venue	Comp	Scorers	Att	Referee
11-03	Mexico	L 1-5	Commerce City	Fr	Didi Torrico [68]	20 000	Toledo USA
28-03	Colombia	L 0-2	Bogota	WCq		22 044	Intriago ECU
1-04	Argentina	W 6-1	La Paz	WCq	Marcelo Martins [12], Joaquin Botero 3 [34p 55 66], Alex Da Rosa [45], Didi Torrico [87]	30 487	Vazquez URU
6-06	Venezuela	L 0-1	La Paz	WCq		23 427	Vera ECU
10-06	Chile	L 0-4	Santiago	WCq		60 214	Silvera URU
5-09	Paraguay	L 0-1	Asuncion	WCq		25 094	Carrillo PER
9-09	Ecuador	L 1-3	La Paz	WCq	Gerardo Yecerotte [85]	10 200	Baldassi ARG
11-10	Brazil	W 2-1	La Paz	WCq	Edgar Olivares [10], Marcelo Martins [32]	16 557	Pozo CHI
14-10	Peru	L 0-1	Lima	WCq		4 373	Soto VEN
2010							
24-02	Mexico	L 0-5	San Francisco	Fr		34 244	Vaughn USA
11-08	Colombia	D 1-1	La Paz	Fr	Roberto Galindo [64]	4 000	Favale ARG
7-10	Venezuela	L 1-3	Santa Cruz	Fr	Marcelo Martins [53]	35 000	Chaibou NIG
2011							
25-03	Panama	L 0-2	Panama City	Fr		4 000	Lopez GUA
28-03	Guatemala	D 1-1	Mazatenango	Fr	Ricardo Pedriel [72]	6 154	Aguilar SLV
4-06	Paraguay	L 0-2	Santa Cruz	Fr		27 000	Garay PER
7-06	Paraguay	D 0-0	Ciudad del Este	Fr		15 000	Heber BRA
1-07	Argentina	D 1-1	La Plata	CAr1	Edivaldo Rojas [48]	52 700	Silvera URU
7-07	Costa Rica	L 0-2	Jujuy	CAr1		23 000	Vera ECU
10-07	Colombia	L 0-2	Santa Fe	CAr1		12 000	Chacon MEX
10-08	Panama	L 1-3	Santa Cruz	Fr	Juan Carlos Arce [7]	10 000	Carrillo PER
2-09	Peru	D 2-2	Lima	Fr	Pablo Escobar [6], Rudy Cardozo [70]	35 000	Soto VEN
5-09	Peru	D 0-0	La Paz	Fr		16 670	Quintana PAR
7-10	Uruguay	L 2-4	Montevideo	WCq	Rudy Cardozo [17], Marcelo Martins [87p]	25 500	Carrillo PER
11-10	Colombia	L 1-2	La Paz	WCq	Walter Flores [85]	33 155	Amarilla PAR
11-11	Argentina	D 1-1	Buenos Aires	WCq	Marcelo Martins [55]	27 592	Vera ECU
15-11	Venezuela	L 0-1	San Cristobal	WCq		33 351	Buckley PER
2012							
29-02	Cuba	W 1-0	Cochabamba	Fr	Ricardo Pedriel [52]	14 494	Caceres PAR
2-06	Chile	L 0-2	La Paz	WCq		34 389	Intriago ECU
9-06	Paraguay	W 3-1	La Paz	WCq	Alcides Pena [9], Pablo Escobar 2 [69 80]	17 320	Silvera URU
15-08	Guyana	W 2-0	Santa Cruz	Fr	Gualberto Mojica [87p], Miguel Suarez [90]	12 000	Caceres PAR
7-09	Ecuador	L 0-1	Quito	WCq		32 213	Soto VEN
12-10	Peru	D 1-1	La Paz	WCq	Alejandro Chumacero [51]	36 500	Vera ECU
16-10	Uruguay	W 4-1	La Paz	WCq	Carlos Saucedo 3 [5 50 54], Gualberto Mojica [26]	25 402	Rivera PER
14-11	Costa Rica	D 1-1	Santa Cruz	Fr	Carlos Saucedo [90]	10 000	Henrique BRA

Fr = Friendly match • CA = Copa America • WC = FIFA World Cup • q = qualifier • r1 = first round group

BOLIVIA NATIONAL TEAM HISTORICAL RECORDS

Caps
93 - Luis Hector Cristaldo 1989-2005 & Marco Antonio Sandy 1993-2003 • **89** - Jose Milton Melgar 1980-97 • **88** - Carlos Fernando Borja 1979-97 • **85** - Julio Cesar Baldivieso 1991-2005 & Juan Manuel Pena 1991-2009 • **80** - Miguel Angel Rimba 1989-2000 • **78** - Oscar Sanchez 1994-2006 • **75** - Jaime Moreno 1991-2008 • **71** - Marco Antonio Etcheverry 1989-2003

Goals
20 - Joaquin Botero 1999-2009 • **16** - Victor Agustin Ugarte 1947-63 • **15** - Carlos Aragones 1977-81, Julio Cesar Baldivieso 1991-2005 & Erwin Sanchez 1989-2005 • **13** - Marco Antonio Etcheverry 1989-2003 & Maximo Alcocer 1953-63 • **10** - Miguel Aguilar 1977-83 & Marcelo Martins 2007- • **9** - Jaime Moreno 1991-2008 & William Ramallo 1989-97

Coaches
Jorge Luis Valderrama 1927 • Ulises Sauchedo 1930 • Julio Borelli 1938 & 1945 • Diogenes Lara 1946-47 • Felix Deheza 1948-49 • Mario Pretto ITA 1950 • Cesar Vicino 1953 • Vicente Arraya 1959 • Danilo Alvim BRA 1963 • Freddy Valda 1965 • Carlos Trigo 1967 • Freddy Valda 1969 & 1973 • Carlos Trigo 1973 • Freddy Valda 1975 • Wilfredo Camacho 1977 • Ramiro Blacutt 1979-81 • Jose Saldanha BRA 1981 • Wilfredo Camacho 1983 • Carlos Rodrigues ARG 1985 • Osvaldo Veiga ARG 1987 • Jorge Habbegger ARG 1989 • Ramiro Blacutt 1991 • Xabier Azkargorta ESP 1993-94 • Antoino Lopez ESP 1995 • Dusan Draskovic YUG 1996 • Antoino Lopez ESP 1996-97 • Hector Veira ARG 1999 • Carlos Aragones 2000-01 • Jorge Habbegger ARG 2001 • Carlos Trucco 2001-02 • Vladimir Soria 2002 • Walter Roque 2003 • Dalcio Giovagnoli 2003 • Nelson Acosta CHI 2003-04 • Ramiro Blacutt 2004 • Ovidio Messa 2004-06 • Erwin Sanchez 2006-09 • Eduardo Villegas 2009-10 • Gustavo Quinteros 2010-12 • Xabier Azcargorta ESP 2012-

BOLIVIA 2011-12
CAMPEONATO CLAUSURA

	Pl	W	D	L	F	A	Pts	The Strongest	San José	O. Petrolero	Universitario	Blooming	Real Potosí	Aurora	Nacional	Bolívar	La Paz FC	Real Mamoré	Guabirá
The Strongest †	22	11	5	6	47	28	38		2-2	5-1	2-1	2-0	3-3	1-2	3-1	1-1	1-0	4-0	8-1
San José †	22	11	5	6	43	27	38	1-2		2-2	1-1	2-0	1-0	1-2	3-0	3-0	2-1	3-0	6-2
Oriente Petrolero ‡	22	11	5	6	38	30	38	1-1	2-1		2-1	2-0	0-2	4-1	2-0	1-1	4-0	1-2	2-0
Universitario Sucre	22	11	4	7	36	21	37	2-1	2-2	1-2		0-1	5-0	2-1	1-1	3-0	2-1	2-1	4-1
Blooming ‡	22	11	4	7	28	23	37	3-0	2-0	2-2	0-1		2-0	2-0	2-0	2-0	2-2	1-1	2-0
Real Potosí	22	11	2	9	36	32	35	2-1	2-1	3-2	2-1	0-1		2-1	1-2	2-0	1-2	4-0	6-2
Aurora	22	10	4	8	38	30	34	3-2	1-1	3-1	0-2	3-0	2-0		4-0	2-2	1-1	5-0	3-1
Nacional Potosí	22	10	4	8	33	36	34	1-0	1-4	2-2	0-2	3-1	2-0	2-0		1-1	2-1	4-2	4-1
Bolívar	22	6	10	6	34	27	28	0-1	2-0	1-2	0-0	5-0	2-2	1-1	4-3		4-0	6-0	0-0
La Paz FC	22	7	3	12	29	39	24	1-3	1-3	0-1	2-1	0-4	0-2	2-1	0-1	1-1		6-0	4-1
Real Mamoré	22	5	3	14	16	47	18	0-1	2-1	1-0	0-1	1-0	1-2	1-2	1-2	0-1			0-0
Guabirá	22	1	5	16	19	57	8	1-3	2-3	0-1	0-2	0-0	1-2	2-0	1-1	1-1	2-3	0-2	

28/01/2012 - 13/05/2012 • † Qualified for the Copa Libertadores • ‡ Qualified for the Copa Sudamericana
Top scorers: 17 - Carlos **SAUCEDO**, San José • 13 - Gualberto **MOJICA**, O. Petrolero • 11 - Pablo **ESCOBAR**, The Strongest • 10 - Alcides **PENA**, Petrolero

RELEGATION TABLE AT END OF 2011-12

	2011	2011 Ap	2012 Cl	Pl	Pts	Av
Oriente Petrolero	36	23	38	56	97	1.732
Aurora	33	24	34	56	91	1.625
Real Potosí	38	17	35	56	90	1.607
San José	34	18	38	56	90	1.607
The Strongest	35	15	38	56	88	1.571
Bolívar	40	19	28	56	87	1.554
Universitario Sucre	29	19	37	56	85	1.518
Blooming	35	10	37	56	82	1.464
Nacional Potosí	28	16	34	56	78	1.393
Guabirá †	29	19	8	56	56	1
La Paz FC †	17	14	24	56	55	0.982
Real Mamoré	20	6	18	56	44	0.786

† Relegation play-off • Play-offs: Guabirá 2-0 0-2 0-1 **Jorge Wilstermann** •
La Paz 6-1 1-3 1-0 Destroyers

BOLIVIA 2011-12
LIGA NACIONAL B (2)
FIRST ROUND GROUP A

	Pl	W	D	L	F	A	Pts
Petrolero Yacuiba	12	7	3	2	22	11	24
Destroyers	12	6	3	3	21	12	21
Flamengo	12	5	4	3	21	15	19
García Agreda	12	4	5	3	13	10	17
Oruro Royal	12	3	3	6	20	22	12
ABB	12	3	2	7	14	25	11
Stormers San Lorenzo	12	2	4	6	17	33	10

† Qualified for the final cuadrangular

BOLIVIA 2011-12
LIGA NACIONAL B (2)
FIRST ROUND GROUP B

	Pl	W	D	L	F	A	Pts
Univ'dad Santa Cruz	10	7	0	3	22	11	21
Jorge Wilstermann	10	6	3	1	14	6	21
Enrique Happ	10	5	3	2	18	14	18
JV Mariscal	10	3	1	6	15	22	10
Universitario Beni	10	2	3	5	12	19	9
Vaca Diez	10	1	2	7	8	17	5

† Qualified for the final cuadrangular

BOLIVIA 2011-12
LIGA NACIONAL B (2)
FINAL CUADRANGULAR

	Pl	W	D	L	F	A	Pts
Petrolero Yacuiba †	6	2	3	1	5	4	9
Destroyers †	6	2	3	1	9	9	9
Jorge Wilstermann	6	2	2	2	10	10	8
Univ'dad Santa Cruz	6	1	3	2	8	9	6

† Championship play-off (22-04-2012):
Destroyers 1-3 Petrolero
Petrolero promoted; Destroyers and Wilstermann to play-offs

BOL – BOLIVIA

BOLIVIA 2012-13

CAMPEONATO APERTURA

	Pl	W	D	L	F	A	Pts	The Strongest	San José	Bolívar	Blooming	Real Potosí	O. Petrolero	Wilstermann	Universitario	Nacional	Petrolero Y	Aurora	La Paz FC
The Strongest †	22	13	6	3	53	31	**45**		4-1	1-1	4-2	1-0	3-0	1-3	2-1	4-2	3-1	7-2	4-3
San José †	22	12	5	5	51	35	**41**	1-2		2-1	4-0	1-1	5-2	3-3	3-2	2-0	4-3	4-0	6-3
Bolívar	22	11	4	7	46	31	**37**	2-3	2-4		1-0	1-0	4-1	4-1	0-0	4-2	0-1	3-1	3-0
Blooming	22	11	2	9	29	30	**35**	2-1	3-2	1-0		3-1	1-1	3-0	2-0	1-0	2-0	3-2	3-0
Real Potosí	22	9	5	8	30	27	**32**	2-2	4-1	2-1	3-0		4-1	1-1	2-0	1-0	0-0	2-1	4-2
Oriente Petrolero	22	7	10	5	28	32	**31**	1-1	0-0	1-3	3-0	1-0		1-1	2-1	1-1	0-0	1-1	0-0
Jorge Wilstermann	22	7	7	8	34	35	**28**	2-2	1-2	3-2	3-1	2-3	1-2		3-3	1-2	2-1	0-2	0-0
Universitario Sucre	22	5	10	7	31	32	**25**	1-0	0-0	3-3	1-1	1-0	1-1	0-2		2-2	3-0	3-3	3-1
Nacional Potosí	22	6	7	9	26	28	**25**	2-2	0-2	0-1	0-1	0-0	1-1	1-0	2-2		3-0	2-0	0-0
Petrolero Yacuiba	22	6	6	10	21	30	**24**	1-1	2-0	1-3	1-0	0-0	1-2	0-0	1-1	1-0		3-0	0-1
Aurora	22	6	4	12	31	47	**22**	0-2	0-2	3-3	1-0	3-0	0-2	0-3	2-1	2-4	1-1		4-1
La Paz FC	22	4	4	14	28	50	**16**	1-3	2-2	1-4	2-0	3-0	3-4	1-2	0-2	0-2	4-1	0-3	

27/07/2012 - 16/12/2012 • † Qualified for the Copa Libertadores • ‡ Qualified for the Copa Sudamericana

Top scorers: **23** - Carlos **SAUCEDO**, San José • **21** - Pablo **ESCOBAR**, The Strongest • **11** - Juan **FIERRO**, Universitario • **10** - Harold **REINA** COL, The Strongest • **9** - Vladimir **CASTELLON**, Aurora; Marcos **OVEJERO** ARG, La Paz

MEDALS TABLE

		Overall			Pro		Nat		LL		Sth Am		City
		G	S	B	G	S	G	S	G	S	G	S	B	
1	Bolívar	21	11	2	17	8	4	2	12	11		1	2	La Paz
2	The Strongest	11	8		10	6	1	2	18	10				La Paz
3	Jorge Wilstermann	10	7	1	5	5	5	2	12	3			1	Cochabamba
4	Oriente Petrolero	5	13		4	11	1	2	7	3				Santa Cruz
5	Blooming	5	3	1	5	3			1	2			1	Santa Cruz
6	San José	3	4		2	4	1		9	2				Oruro
7	Real Potosí	1	4		1	4								Potosí
	Deportivo Municipal	1	4				1	4	4	3				La Paz
9	Always Ready	1	2				1	2	2	5				La Paz
	Guabirá	1	2				1	1	1	1				Montero
11	Aurora	1	1		1	1			3	8				Cochabamba
	Chaco Petrolero	1	1				1	1	1					La Paz
	Universitario	1	1		1	1								Sucre
14	Litoral	1					1		4	1				La Paz
	Universitario	1					1		1	4				La Paz
16	La Paz FC		2			2								La Paz
17	31 de Octubre		1					1	1	2				La Paz
	Deportivo Chaco		1					1	1					La Paz
19	Destroyers								2	1				Santa Cruz
	Real Santa Cruz													Santa Cruz
	Union Central													Tarija

Pro = the Professional League played since 1977 • Nat = the various national competitions played between 1954 and 1976 • LL = the local leagues played throughout the country until 1976 (not included in total)

BOT – BOTSWANA

FIFA/COCA-COLA WORLD RANKING

'93	'94	'95	'96	'97	'98	'99	'00	'01	'02	'03	'04	'05	'06	'07	'08	'09	'10	'11	'12
140	145	155	161	162	155	165	150	153	136	112	102	101	108	103	117	118	53	95	121

2012

Jan	Feb	Mar	Apr	May	Jun	Jul	Aug	Sep	Oct	Nov	Dec	High	Low	Av
94	104	100	107	106	116	113	112	123	120	117	121	53	165	127

Botswana's failure in their maiden Africa Cup of Nations appearance at the start of 2012 had surprisingly bitter recriminations throughout the rest of the year for a country that had exceeded all expectations in getting to the tournament in Equatorial Guinea and Gabon in the first place. There were heated calls for coach Stanley Tshosane to go as realism seemed to desert the supporters of one of the smallest countries, in terms of population size, ever to reach the finals. Army officer Tshosane kept his job but defeat at the hands of the Central African Republic at the start of the 2014 FIFA World Cup qualifiers was followed by a home draw with neighbours South Africa - a fixture always eagerly anticipated but forced to be played at the 8,000-capacity University stadium rather than the National Stadium next door which was still closed over a dispute about the re-laying of the pitch. Botswana then lost to Mali, both home and away, in the 2013 Nations Cup qualifiers after being thoroughly outplayed in both matches. The year also marked the retirement from international football of captain Dipsy Selolwane, for so long a symbol for the Zebras and the only Botswanan footballer to have played for a club in Europe. In club football Mochudi Centre Chiefs were runaway winners of the league title but lost on penalties in the cup final to Gaborone United.

CAF AFRICA CUP OF NATIONS RECORD
1957-1992 DNE **1994-2010** DNQ **2012** 16 r1 **2013** DNQ

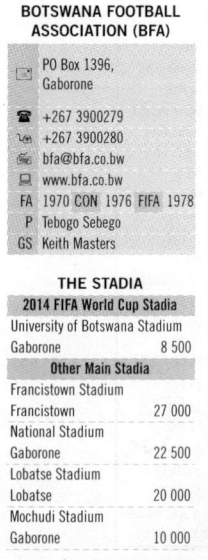

BOTSWANA FOOTBALL ASSOCIATION (BFA)

PO Box 1396, Gaborone

☎ +267 3900279
📠 +267 3900280
✉ bfa@bfa.co.bw
🖥 www.bfa.co.bw
FA 1970 CON 1976 FIFA 1978
P Tebogo Sebego
GS Keith Masters

THE STADIA

2014 FIFA World Cup Stadia
University of Botswana Stadium
Gaborone 8 500

Other Main Stadia
Francistown Stadium
Francistown 27 000
National Stadium
Gaborone 22 500
Lobatse Stadium
Lobatse 20 000
Mochudi Stadium
Gaborone 10 000

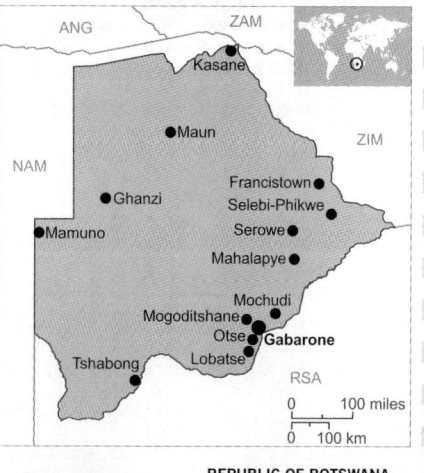

MAJOR CITIES/TOWNS

		Population
1	Gaborone	230 936
2	Francistown	96 292
3	Molepolole	72 122
4	Selibe Phikwe	57 161
5	Mogoditshane	56 251
6	Maun	56 043
7	Serowe	52 324
8	Mahalapye	49 050
9	Kanye	48 362
10	Mochudi	46 715
11	Palapye	35 114
12	Lobatse	31 660
13	Tlokweng	30 384
14	Thamaga	23 296
15	Moshupa	22 243
16	Bobonong	22 175
17	Ramotswa	21 708
18	Letlhakane	21 681
19	Tonota	19 853

REPUBLIC OF BOTSWANA

Capital Gaborone   Population 1 990 876 (146)   % in cities 60%
GDP per capita $13 900 (83)   Area km^2 581 730 km^2 (71)   GMT +/- +2
Neighbours (km) Namibia 1360, South Africa 1840, Zimbabwe 813

RECENT INTERNATIONAL MATCHES PLAYED BY BOTSWANA

2010	Opponents	Score	Venue	Comp	Scorers	Att	Referee
3-03	Mozambique	W 1-0	Maputo	Fr	Michael Mogaladi [6p]		
21-03	Namibia	D 0-0	Windhoek	Fr			
1-07	Tunisia	W 1-0	Tunis	CNq	Jerome Ramatlhakwane [31]		Ditta SEN
9-07	Chad	W 1-0	Gaborone	CNq	Phenyo Mongala [49]		Seechurn MRI
4-08	Zimbabwe	W 2-0	Selibe-Phikwe	Fr	Mokgathi Mokgathi [9], Jerome Ramatlhakwane [14]		
11-08	Malawi	D 1-1	Blantyre	CNq	Jerome Ramatlhakwane [62]		Martins ANG
4-09	Togo	W 2-1	Gaborone	CNq	Joel Mogorosi [6], Jerome Ramatlhakwane [47]		Kagabo RWA
12-10	Equatorial Guinea	W 2-0	Malabo	Fr	Mogogi Gabonamong, Phenyo Mongala		
17-11	Tunisia	W 1-0	Gaborone	CNq	Jerome Ramatlhakwane [45]		
2011							
19-01	Sweden	L 1-2	Cape Town	Fr	Joel Mogorosi [47]		
9-02	Mozambique	D 1-1	Maputo	Fr	Moemedi Moatlhaping [35]		
16-03	Namibia	D 1-1	Maun	Fr	Lemponye Tshireletso [65]		
26-03	Chad	W 1-0	N'Djamena	CNq	Jerome Ramatlhakwane [52]		
25-05	Swaziland	D 0-0	Manzini	Fr			
5-06	Malawi	D 0-0	Lobatse	CNq			Diatta SEN
31-07	Swaziland	W 2-0	Pretoria	Fr	Onalethata Tshekiso [29], Bakang Moeng [88]		
10-08	Kenya	W 1-0	Gaborone	Fr	Moemedi Moatlhaping [87p]		
30-08	Lesotho	L 1-2	Gaborone	Fr			
4-09	Togo	L 0-1	Lome	CNq			Dembele CIV
12-11	Nigeria	D 0-0	Benin City	Fr			
15-11	Niger	D 1-1	Niamey	Fr	Patrick Motsepe [23]		
21-12	Lesotho	W 3-0	Rustenburg	Fr	Jerome Ramatlhakwane 2, Pontsho Moloi		
2012							
7-01	Zimbabwe	D 0-0	Gaborone	Fr			
24-01	Ghana	L 0-1	Franceville	CNr1		5 000	Diatta SEN
28-01	Guinea	L 1-6	Franceville	CNr1	Diphetogo Selolwane [23p]	4 000	El Ahrach MAR
1-02	Mali	L 1-2	Libreville	CNr1	Mogakolodi Ngele [50]	5 500	Bennett RSA
23-05	Lesotho	W 3-0	Gaborone	Fr	Joel Mogorosi [9], Mara Mobi [32], Jerome Ramatlhakwane [90]		
28-05	Iraq	D 1-1	Istanbul	Fr			
2-06	Central African Rep	L 0-2	Bangui	WCq		20 000	Camille SEY
9-06	South Africa	D 1-1	Gaborone	WCq	Ofentse Nato [38]	7 500	Keita MLI
12-07	Kenya	L 1-3	Nairobi	Fr			
16-07	Zimbabwe	W 1-0	Molepolole	Fr	Tebogo Sembowa [50]		
18-07	Lesotho	D 0-0	Molepolole	Fr			
15-08	Tanzania	D 3-3	Molepolole	Fr	Lemponye Tshireletso 2 [26 37], Michael Mogaladi [69]		
26-08	Uganda	D 0-0	Gaborone	Fr			
8-09	Mali	L 0-3	Bamako	CNq			Jedidi TUN
13-10	Mali	L 1-4	Lobatse	CNq	Tebogo Sembowa [88]		Nampiandraza MAD

Fr = Friendly match • CN = CAF African Cup of Nations • CC = COSAFA Cup • WC = FIFA World Cup • q = qualifier • r1 = first round group

BOTSWANA SQUAD FOR THE 2012 CAF AFRICA CUP OF NATIONS

	Player		Ap	G	Club	Date of Birth		Player		Ap	G	Club	Date of Birth
1	Noah Maposa	GK	0		Gaborone Utd	3 06 1985	12	Patrick Motsepe	MF	1+1		BMC	1 07 1981
2	Ndiapo Letsholathebe	DF	3		Police	25 02 1983	13	Boitumelo Mafoko	MF	1+1		Santos RSA	11 02 1982
3	Mosimanegape Ramohibidu	DF	1		BMC	15 06 1985	14	Onalethata Thekiso	FW	0+1		Township Rollers	14 05 1981
4	Mmusa Ohilwe	DF	2		Gaborone Utd	17 04 1986	15	Monametsi Kelebale	DF	0		Nico Utd	15 07 1981
5	Mompati Thuma (c)	DF	3		BDF	5 04 1980	16	Modiri Marumo	GK	3		Bay Utd RSA	6 07 1976
6	Ofentse Nato	MF	2		Gaborone Utd	1 10 1989	17	Abednico Powell	MF	0		Township Rollers	28 01 1983
7	Pontsho Moloi	FW	1		Centre Chiefs	28 11 1981	18	Mogogi Gabonamong	MF	3		SuperSport RSA	10 09 1982
8	Phenyo Mongala	MF	2+1		B. Celtic RSA	10 06 1985	19	Mogakolodi Ngele	MF	1+2	1	Township Rollers	6 10 1990
9	Jerome Ramatlhakwane	FW	3		Unattached	29 10 1985	20	Kabelo Dembe	GK	0		Township Rollers	10 05 1990
10	Moemedi Moatlhaping	FW	2		Bay United	14 07 1985	21	Lemponye Tshireletso	MF	1		BMC	21 09 1984
11	Dipsy Selolwane	FW	1+1		SuperSport RSA	27 01 1978	22	Tshepo Motlhabankwe	DF	3		Centre Chiefs	17 03 1980
							23	Othusitse Pilane	MF	0		Centre Chiefs	26 03 1984

Tr: Stanley Tshosane 16-01-1957

BOTSWANA 2011-12

PREMIER LEAGUE

	Pl	W	D	L	F	A	Pts	Centre Chiefs	BMC	Rollers	Gaborone Utd	Nico Utd	Greens	Defence	Fighters	Gunners	Police	Miscellaneous	TAFIC	UF Santos	Notwane	GNT	Satmos
Centre Chiefs †	30	25	3	2	95	30	78		2-0	2-0	1-0	2-1	3-2	3-4	8-1	3-1	3-1	5-0	4-0	4-1	2-0	5-0	2-0
Bot. Meat Commission	30	17	7	6	35	21	58	0-1		0-0	0-0	3-1	2-1	0-0	1-2	2-1	1-0	3-2	1-0	1-0	1-0	2-0	2-1
Township Rollers	30	16	9	5	57	24	57	2-5	0-0		2-0	0-0	2-2	0-1	1-0	0-0	6-1	4-0	2-1	1-0	2-0	1-0	7-1
Gaborone United	30	17	6	7	60	33	57	1-1	3-2	1-2		2-0	2-4	3-2	3-0	1-1	3-2	1-2	2-1	0-0	2-0	2-0	4-1
Nico United	30	16	4	10	57	41	52	0-2	0-0	2-0	1-3		2-4	4-1	3-1	1-2	1-0	4-3	3-1	1-2	1-0	3-1	4-2
ECCO City Greens	30	13	9	8	51	37	48	3-3	0-3	0-0	1-0	2-2		0-0	1-2	2-0	1-2	1-0	2-2	3-0	1-0	1-1	2-2
Defence Force	30	13	7	10	41	37	46	1-1	3-2	2-1	1-0	0-1	1-4		2-0	1-1	0-2	0-1	0-2	0-1	0-0	0-0	4-0
Mogoditshane Fighters	30	12	4	14	37	60	40	3-2	1-0	0-6	0-4	2-2	2-0	0-2		2-2	2-2	0-1	3-0	2-1	2-1	1-0	2-1
Extension Gunners	30	10	8	12	40	44	38	0-3	0-1	0-0	0-3	1-3	1-0	2-3	2-3		1-0	0-1	2-2	3-0	3-0	0-1	3-1
Police	30	9	9	12	35	48	36	2-7	0-0	1-1	1-1	0-4	0-2	2-1	3-0	1-2		1-2	1-1	2-1	2-1	0-0	1-1
Miscellaneous Serowe	30	11	1	18	34	52	34	0-4	0-1	0-2	1-2	2-0	1-3	0-1	0-2	2-3	1-2		1-2	2-2	2-1	3-0	2-1
TAFIC	30	9	6	15	40	53	33	0-1	1-2	3-4	0-4	1-3	0-1	3-2	1-1	2-2	0-1	1-3		3-1	2-2	2-1	2-1
Uniao Flamengo Santos	30	8	4	18	31	55	28	1-3	1-1	0-4	2-3	1-3	2-3	1-3	2-0	0-1	2-1	1-0	2-1		0-3	1-1	0-3
Notwane FC	30	8	2	20	35	51	26	2-3	1-2	0-2	1-4	2-1	0-2	1-2	3-2	2-3	2-3	0-1	2-1	2-4		4-2	1-0
Great North Tigers	30	5	9	16	23	50	24	0-5	0-1	1-1	3-3	1-3	0-0	1-1	1-0	3-2	0-0	2-1	0-2	1-0	0-2		1-2
FC Satmos	30	5	4	21	37	72	19	3-5	0-1	1-4	1-0	0-3	1-4	1-3	5-3	1-1	1-1	3-0	0-2	0-2	1-2	2-1	

12/08/2011 - 7/07/2012 • † Qualified for the CAF Champions League

MASCOM 'TSE DI TONA' TOP 8 2011-12

Quarter-finals
- T. Rollers 3 1
- Defence 1 2
- UF Santos 0 2
- Gaborone U 1 2
- Centre Chiefs 5 0
- Nico United 1 2
- BMC 1 1
- ECCO City 3 2

Semi-finals
- T. Rollers 2 2
- Gaborone U 1 1
- Centre Chiefs 0 1
- ECCO City 0 1

Final
- Township Rollers 3
- ECCO City Greens 1

UB Stadium, 30-12-2012
Ref: Bondo

Scorers - Tebogo Sembowa [2], Onalethata Tshekiso [50], Sekhana Koko [56] for Rollers; Tendai Nyumasi [58] for ECCO • **Rollers**: Dambe - Ncenga, Ramaabya, Bolweleng, Mathumo - Simanyana (Lesego Molemogi 77) - Majawa, Godirwang (Tshekiso 45), Olerile, Koko - Sembowa (Balepi 74) • **ECCO**: Madamombe - Nko, Ntesa, Nlu - Kafuko (Legoreng 62), Jenamiso, Makafiri, Tafa••♦36, Lenyeletse, Nyumasi - Murirwa (Manuel 70)

MEDALS TABLE

		All G	Lge G	Cup G	City
1	Township Rollers	17	11	6	Gaborone
2	Gaborone United	13	6	7	Gaborone
3	Defence Force	10	7	3	Gaborone
4	M'shane Fighters	7	4	3	Mogoditshane
5	Notwane FC	6	3	3	Gaborone
	Extension Gunners	6	3	3	Lobatse
7	Centre Chiefs	4	2	2	Mochudi
	Police XI	2	1	1	Otse
	TASC	2		2	Francistown
10	BMC	1		1	Lobatse
	ECCO City Greens	1	1		Francistown
	Nico United	1		1	Selibe-Pikwe
	TAFIC	1		1	Francistown
	UF Santos	1		1	Gabane

COCA-COLA CUP 2011-12

Round of 16
- Gaborone United 1
- Motlakase 0
- Notwane FC
- Molapo Green Birds
- Santos
- Miscellaneous
- Extension Gunners 0
- Defence Force 3
- Township Rollers 4
- Mogoditshane Fighters 2
- No Mathata 0
- Bot. Meat Commission 8
- ECCO City Greens 3
- Police 0
- TASC 0
- Centre Chiefs 5

Quarter-finals
- Gaborone United 3
- Molapo Green Birds 1
- Santos 1 3p
- Defence Force 1 4p
- Township Rollers 1
- Bot. Meat Commission 0
- ECCO City Greens 2
- Centre Chiefs 3

Semi-finals
- Gaborone United 2
- Defence Force 1
- Township Rollers 0
- Centre Chiefs 1

Final
- Gaborone United ‡ 0 4p
- Centre Chiefs 0 2p

‡ Qualified for the CAF Confederation Cup

CUP FINAL
5-08-2012
Ref: Omphile Phuthego

Cup Final line-ups: **Gaborone Utd** - Maposa - Mpho Kgaswane, Kaelo Kgaswane, Seosenyeng, Sekanonyane - Mgadla, Modisaotsile, Sandaka (Pako Moloi 71), Maiketso, Maposa (Moeng 67) - Chikomo (Sakala 79) • **Chiefs** - Sephekolo - Motlhabankwe, Chaka, Mpoeleng, Khunwane - Meleka, Galenamotlhale (Pilane 64), Dirang, (Ngele 57), Pontsho, Galabgwe (Maikano 117) - Kekaetswe

BRA – BRAZIL

FIFA/COCA-COLA WORLD RANKING

'93	'94	'95	'96	'97	'98	'99	'00	'01	'02	'03	'04	'05	'06	'07	'08	'09	'10	'11	'12
3	1	1	1	1	1	1	1	3	1	1	1	1	1	2	5	2	4	6	18

2012

Jan	Feb	Mar	Apr	May	Jun	Jul	Aug	Sep	Oct	Nov	Dec	High	Low	Av
6	7	5	6	5	11	13	12	14	13	18		1	18	2

Corinthians ended the year on a high note for Brazilian football by winning the FIFA Club World Cup in Tokyo in front of an estimated 30,000 travelling fans. The rest of the year, however, was a mixed tale with the failure to win gold at the London Olympics compounded by the national team falling out of the top ten of the FIFA/Coca-Cola World Ranking for the first time since its creation in 1993. The CBF lost faith in national team coach Mano Menezes who was sacked after the defeat to Argentina in November. He was replaced by the 2002 World Cup winning coach Luiz Felipe Scolari - despite Scolari having just overseen the relegation of Palmeiras. While the national team struggles to find its feet in the build up to the 2014 FIFA World Cup, club football is flourishing with Brazilian teams winning both continental titles played in 2012 - Corinthians the Copa Libertadores for the first time in their history after beating Boca Juniors in the final; and Sao Paulo the Copa Sudamericana. Domestic success went to Fluminense who won Serie A for the second time in three seasons. They were coached by Abel Braga who had previously taken Internacional to continental and world titles, while the Copa do Brasil was won by Scolari's Palmeiras, who beat Coritiba 3-1 on aggregate in the final before their season fell apart.

FIFA WORLD CUP RECORD

1930 6 r1 **1934** 14 r1 **1938** 3 SF **1950** 2 Finalists (hosts) **1954** 5 QF **1958** 1 Winners **1962** 1 Winners **1966** 11 r1 **1970** 1 Winners **1974** 4 r2 **1978** 3 r2 **1982** 5 r2 **1986** 5 QF **1990** 9 r2 **1994** 1 Winners **1998** 2 Finalists **2002** 1 Winners **2006** 5 QF **2010** 6 QF

CONFEDERACAO BRASILEIRA DE FUTEBOL

Rua Victor Civita 66, Bloco 1 - Edificio 5 - 5 Andar, Barra da Tijuca, Rio de Janeiro
☎ +55 21 35721900
📠 +55 21 35721989
✉ cbf@cbf.com.br
🌐 www.cbf.com.br
FA 1914 CON 1916 FIFA 1923
P Jose Maria Marin
GS Julio Cesar Avelleda

THE STADIA

FIFA Confederations Cup Stadia

Maracanã Rio de Janeiro	76 935
Estadio Nacional Brasilia	70 042
Estadio Castelao Fortaleza	64 846
Estadio Mineirão Belo Horizonte	62 547
Arena Fonte Nova Salvador	56 000
Arena Pernambuco Recife	43 921

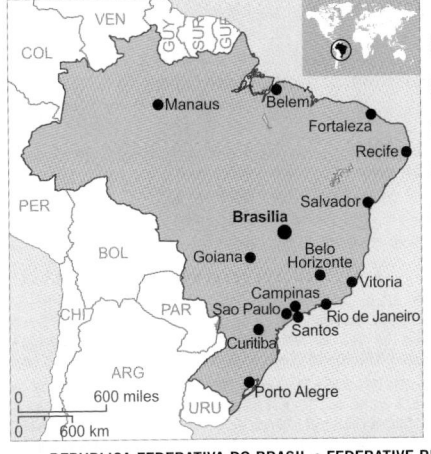

MAJOR CITIES/TOWNS

		Population
1	São Paulo	10 328 094
2	Rio de Janeiro	6 227 355
3	Salvador	2 949 222
4	Fortaleza	2 513 812
5	Belo Horizonte	2 506 025
6	Brasilia	2 463 923
7	Curitiba	1 871 087
8	Manaus	1 817 778
9	Belém	1 554 295
10	Recife	1 542 678
11	Porto Alegre	1 421 272
12	Guarulhos	1 325 997
13	Goiânia	1 267 151
14	Campinas	1 111 854
15	Maceió	1 111 536
16	Nova Iguaçu	1 087 086
17	São Luís	1 007 604
18	São Gonçalo	998 325
19	Natal	821 794

REPUBLICA FEDERATIVA DO BRASIL • FEDERATIVE REPUBLIC OF BRAZIL

Capital	Brasilia	Population	198 739 269 (5)
GDP per capita	$10 200 (102)	Area km²	8 514 877 km² (5)
		% in cities	86%
		GMT +/-	-3
Neighbours (km)	Argentina 1261, Bolivia 3423, Colombia 1644, French Guiana 730, Guyana 1606, Paraguay 1365, Peru 2995, Suriname 593, Uruguay 1068, Venezuela 2200 • Coast 7491		

RECENT INTERNATIONAL MATCHES PLAYED BY BRAZIL

2010	Opponents	Score	Venue	Comp	Scorers	Att	Referee
15-06	Korea DPR	W 2-1	Johannesburg	WCr1	Maicon [55], Elano [72]	54 331	Kassai HUN
20-06	Côte d'Ivoire	W 3-1	Johannesburg	WCr1	Luis Fabiano 2 [25 50], Elano [62]	84 445	Lannoy FRA
25-06	Portugal	D 0-0	Durban	WCr1		62 712	Archundia MEX
28-06	Chile	W 3-0	Johannesburg	WCr2	Juan [35], Luis Fabiano [38], Robinho [59]	54 096	Webb ENG
2-07	Netherlands	L 1-2	Port Elizabeth	WCqf	Robinho [10]	40 186	Nishimura JPN
10-08	USA	W 2-0	New Jersey	Fr	Neymar [29], Pato [45]	77 223	Petrescu CAN
7-10	Iran	W 3-0	Abu Dhabi	Fr	Dani Alves [14], Pato [69], Nilmar [90]	49 000	Al Marzouqi UAE
11-10	Ukraine	W 2-0	Derby	Fr	Dani Alves [25], Pato [64]	13 088	Atkinson ENG
17-11	Argentina	L 0-1	Doha	Fr		50 000	Balideh QAT
2011							
9-02	France	L 0-1	Paris	Fr		79 712	Stark GER
27-03	Scotland	W 2-0	London	Fr	Neymar 2 [43 77p]	53 087	Webb ENG
4-06	Netherlands	D 0-0	Goiania	Fr		36 449	Amarilla PAR
7-06	Romania	W 1-0	São Paulo	Fr	Fred [23]	30 059	Pezzotta ARG
3-07	Venezuela	D 0-0	La Plata	CAr1		35 000	Orozco BOL
9-07	Paraguay	D 2-2	Cordoba	CAr1	Jadson [38], Fred [89]	57 000	Roldan COL
13-07	Ecuador	W 4-2	Cordoba	CAr1	Pato 2 [28 61], Neymar 2 [48 71]	39 000	Silvera URU
17-07	Paraguay	D 0-0	La Plata	CAqf	L 0-2p	36 000	Pezzotta ARG
10-08	Germany	L 2-3	Stuttgart	Fr	Robinho [71], Neymar [90]	54 767	Kassai HUN
5-09	Ghana	W 1-0	London	Fr	Leandro Damiao [45]	25 700	Dean ENG
14-09	Argentina	D 0-0	Cordoba	Fr		50 000	Osses CHI
28-09	Argentina	W 2-0	Belem	Fr		43 038	Larrionda URU
7-10	Costa Rica	W 1-0	San Jose	Fr		25 000	Lopez GUA
11-10	Mexico	W 2-1	Torreon	Fr	Ronaldinho [79], Marcelo Vieira [89]	30 000	Mejia SLV
10-11	Gabon	W 2-0	Libreville	Fr	Sandro [11], Hernanes [34]		Hlungwani RSA
14-11	Egypt	W 2-0	Al Rayyan	Fr	Jonas 2 [38 59]	18 000	Al Dosari QAT
2012							
28-02	Bosnia-Herzegovina	W 2-1	St Gall	Fr	Marcelo [4], OG [90]	17 500	Kever SUI
26-05	Denmark	W 3-1	Hamburg	Fr	Hulk 2 [9 40], OG [13]	51 000	Brych GER
30-05	USA	W 4-1	Washington DC	Fr	Neymar [12p], Thiago Silva [26], Marcelo [52], Pato [87]	67 619	Calderon CRC
3-06	Mexico	L 0-2	Arlington	Fr		84 519	Petrescu CAN
9-06	Argentina	L 3-4	New York	Fr	Romulo [23], Oscar [56], Hulk [73]	81 994	Marrufo USA
15-08	Sweden	W 3-0	Stockholm	Fr	Leandro Damiao [32], Pato 2 [84 86]	32 781	Kassai HUN
7-09	South Africa	W 1-0	Sao Paulo	Fr	Hulk [74]	51 500	Pitana ARG
10-09	China PR	W 8-0	Recife	Fr	Ramires [22], Neymar 3 [25 53 59], Lucas Moura [48], Hulk [51], OG [69], Oscar [75p]	29 658	Silvera URU
19-09	Argentina	W 2-1	Goiania	Fr	Paulinho [26], Neymar [93+p]	37 871	Amarilla PAR
11-10	Iraq	W 6-0	Malmo	Fr	Oscar 2 [22 26], Kaka [48], Hulk [56], Neymar [76], Lucas Moura [80]	14 147	Hansson SWE
16-10	Japan	W 4-0	Wroclaw	Fr	Paulinho [12], Neymar 2 [25p 48], Kaka [76]	36 000	Borski POL
14-11	Colombia	D 1-1	New York	Fr	Neymar [64]	38 624	Geiger USA
21-11	Argentina	L 1-2	Buenos Aires	Fr	Fred [84], W 4-3p	32 000	Osses CHI

Fr = Friendly match • CA = Copa America • CC = FIFA Confederations Cup • WC = FIFA World Cup
q = qualifier • r1 = 1st round group • r2 = second round • qf = quarter-final • sf = semi-final • f = final

BRAZIL NATIONAL TEAM HISTORICAL RECORDS

Caps
142 - Cafu 1990-2006 • 125 - Roberto Carlos 1992-2006 • 105 - Lucio 2000- • 101 - Claudio Taffarel 1988-98 • 98 - Djalma Santos 1952-68 & Ronaldo 1994-2011 • 95 - Ronaldinho 1999- • 94 - Gilmar 1953-69 • 93 - Gilberto Silva 2001-10 • 92 - Pele 1957-71 & Rivelino 1965-78 • 91 - Dunga 1987-98 & Dida 1995-2006 • 90 - Robinho 2003- • 85 - Kaka 2002- • 84 - Ze Roberto 1995-2006 • 81 - Jairzinho 1964-82 & Aldair 1989-2000 • 80 - Emerson Leao 1970-86 • 79 - Juan 2001- • 75 - Bebeto 1985-98 & Nilton Santos 1949-62

Goals
77 - Pele 1957-71 • 62 - Ronaldo 1994-2006 • 55 - Romario 1987-2005 • 52 - Zico 1976-86 • 39 - Bebeto 1985-98 • 34 - Rivaldo 1993-2003 • 33 - Jairzinho 1964-82 & Ronaldinho 1999- • 32 - Ademir 1945-53 & Tostao 1966-72 • 30 - Zizinho 1942-57 • 29 - Careca 1982-93 & Kaka 2002- • 28 - Luis Fabiano 2003- • 27 - Adriano 2000- • 26 - Rivelino 1965-78 & Robinho 2003- • 22 - Jair 1940-50 & Socrates 1979-86 • 21 - Leonidas 1932-46 • 20 - Didi 1952-62 & Roberto Dinamite 1975-84 • 17 - Neymar 2010-

Coaches
For coaches pre 1970 see Oliver's Almanack 2012 • Mario Zagallo 1970-74 • Osvaldo Brandao 1975-77 • Claudio Coutinho 1977-79 • Tele Santana 1980-82 • Carlos Alberto Parreira 1983 • Edu 1984 • Evaristo de Macedo 1985 • Tele Santana 1985-86 • Carlos Alberto Silva 1987-88 • Sebastiao Lazaroni 1989-90 • Paulo Roberto Falcao 1990-91 • Ernesto Paulo 1991 • Carlos Alberto Parreira 1991-94 • Mario Zagallo 1994-98 • Vanderlei Luxemburgo 1998-2000 • Candido 2000 • Emerson Leao 2000-01 • Luiz Felipe Scolari 2001-02 • Mario Zagallo 2002 • Carlos Alberto Parreira 2001-06 • Dunga 2006-10 • Mano Menezes 2010-12 • Luiz Felipe Scolari 2012-

BRAZIL 2012

SERIE A

	Pl	W	D	L	F	A	Pts	Fluminense	Atlético MG	Grêmio	São Paulo FC	Vasco	Corinthians	Botafogo	Santos	Cruzeiro	Internacional	Flamengo	Náutico	Coritiba	Ponte Preta	Bahia	Portuguesa	Sport Recife	Palmeiras	Atlético GO	Figueirense
Fluminense †	38	22	11	5	61	33	77		0-0	2-2	2-1	1-2	1-1	1-0	3-1	0-2	0-0	1-0	2-1	2-1	2-1	4-0	4-1	1-0	1-0	1-2	2-2
Atlético Mineiro †	38	20	12	6	64	37	72	3-2		0-0	1-0	1-0	1-0	3-2	2-0	3-2	3-1	1-1	5-1	1-0	2-2	1-1	2-0	2-1	3-0	2-2	6-0
Grêmio †	38	20	11	7	56	33	71	1-0	0-1		2-1	2-0	2-0	1-1	1-1	2-1	0-0	2-0	2-0	0-0	1-0	3-1	1-2	3-1	1-0	2-1	4-0
São Paulo FC † ‡	38	20	6	12	59	37	66	1-1	1-0	1-2		0-1	3-1	4-0	1-0	1-0	1-1	4-1	2-1	3-1	3-0	1-0	3-1	1-0	3-2	0-0
Vasco da Gama	38	16	10	12	45	44	58	1-2	1-1	2-1	0-2		0-0	1-0	2-0	1-3	1-2	1-1	4-2	2-2	3-2	0-4	2-0	0-3	3-1	1-0	3-1
Corinthians †	38	15	12	11	51	39	57	0-1	1-0	3-1	1-2	1-0		1-3	1-1	2-0	1-0	3-2	2-1	5-1	1-1	1-1	1-3	0-2	1-1	1-1
Botafogo	38	15	10	13	60	50	55	1-1	2-3	0-1	4-2	3-2	2-2		0-2	2-3	1-1	0-0	3-1	2-0	1-2	3-0	3-0	2-0	1-2	4-0	1-0
Santos	38	13	14	11	50	44	53	1-1	2-2	4-2	0-0	2-0	3-2	0-0		4-2	1-1	2-0	0-0	2-2	2-1	1-3	1-3	0-0	3-1	2-2	2-0
Cruzeiro	38	15	7	16	47	51	52	1-1	2-2	1-3	2-3	1-1	2-0	1-3	0-4		0-0	1-0	3-0	2-1	1-2	3-1	2-0	1-0	2-1	0-0	1-0
Internacional	38	13	13	12	44	40	52	0-1	3-0	0-1	1-0	0-0	2-1	2-0	0-2	1-1		4-1	0-0	2-0	2-1	3-1	0-2	2-2	2-1	4-1	2-3
Flamengo	38	12	14	12	38	45	50	0-1	2-1	1-1	1-1	1-0	1-0	0-3	2-2	1-0	1-1		3-3	2-0	3-1	0-1	0-0	0-0	1-1	1-1	3-2	1-0
Náutico	38	14	7	17	44	51	49	0-2	1-0	1-0	3-0	1-1	2-1	3-2	3-0	0-0	3-0	0-1		3-4	3-0	1-0	0-0	1-0	1-0	2-0	3-2
Coritiba	38	14	6	18	53	60	48	0-2	1-0	2-1	1-1	1-2	1-2	2-3	1-2	4-0	1-0	3-0	2-1		1-0	2-1	2-0	2-3	1-1	3-0	3-0
Ponte Preta	38	12	12	14	37	44	48	1-2	0-1	0-0	0-0	0-0	1-0	0-0	0-1	0-1	0-1	0-2	2-2	1-4		1-1	0-2	2-1	1-1	1-0	3-1	2-2
Bahia	38	11	14	13	37	41	47	0-2	0-0	1-1	1-1	0-2	2-0	0-0	0-0	0-1	1-1	1-2	1-1	2-2	1-0		0-0	2-1	0-1	1-1	2-1
Portuguesa	38	10	15	13	39	41	45	0-2	1-1	2-2	1-0	0-1	1-1	1-1	0-0	0-2	1-1	0-0	3-3	1-0	3-0	0-0	0-1		5-1	3-0	2-0	2-0
Sport Recife	38	10	11	17	39	56	41	1-1	1-4	1-3	2-4	0-2	1-1	2-0	2-1	2-1	0-2	1-0	0-1	0-1	1-0	1-0	3-1	1-1	2-1		2-1	0-0	0-1
Palmeiras †	38	9	7	22	39	54	34	2-3	0-1	0-0	1-1	1-1	0-2	2-2	1-2	2-0	0-1	1-0	3-0	0-1	3-0	0-2	1-1	3-1		1-2	3-1
Atlético Goiânense	38	7	9	22	37	67	30	1-4	1-1	0-1	4-3	0-1	0-2	1-2	2-1	0-2	3-1	1-2	0-1	1-3	0-0	1-1	1-0	1-1	1-0	1-1		3-2
Figueirense	38	7	9	22	39	72	30	2-2	3-4	2-4	0-2	1-1	1-0	0-2	1-3	2-0	0-1	0-2	2-1	3-1	0-0	1-1	0-0	1-1	1-3	3-1	

19/05/2012 - 2/12/2012 • † Qualified for the Copa Libertadores • ‡ Qualified for the Copa Sudamericana • Attendance: 5,116,692 @ 13,465
Top scorers: **20 - FRED**, Fluminense • **17 - LUIS FABIAN**, São Paulo • **14 - ALOISIO**, Figueirense; Hernan **BARCOS** ARG, Palmeiras; **BRUNO MINEIRO**, Portuguesa & **NEYMAR**, Santos • **13 - KIEZA**, Náutico & **VAGNER LOVE**, Flamengo • **11 - BERNARD**, Atlético MG & **ELKESON**, Botafogo • **10 - ALECSANDRO**, Vasco; **RONALDINHO**, Atlético MG; **JO**, Atlético MG; Marcelo **MARTINS** BOL, Grêmio & **WELLINGTON PAULISTA**, Cruzeiro

BRAZIL 2012

SERIE B

	Pl	W	D	L	F	A	Pts	Goiás	Criciúma	Atlético PR	Vitória	São Caetano	Joinville	Avaí	América MG	América RN	Paraná	Ceará	ABC	ASA	Bragantino	Boa Esporte	Guaratinguetá	CRB	Guarani	Ipatinga	Grêmio Barueri
Goiás	38	23	9	6	75	37	78		1-0	3-2	4-3	0-0	2-1	2-0	1-0	2-0	0-0	1-1	4-0	1-0	2-0	1-1	1-0	5-0	4-0	3-0
Criciúma	38	22	7	9	78	57	73	3-0		0-0	2-1	2-2	2-0	0-4	4-3	2-1	2-1	2-0	2-1	3-2	4-3	4-1	2-0	2-1	3-3	3-4
Atlético Paranaense	38	21	8	9	65	37	71	0-0	1-0		0-1	0-1	1-1	3-1	5-4	1-1	1-1	2-1	2-1	1-0	0-0	2-1	3-0	4-1	1-1	1-0	3-0
Vitória	38	21	8	9	59	43	71	3-1	2-2	0-2		0-1	2-1	2-0	5-3	2-2	4-3	1-1	1-0	2-0	0-1	3-2	2-0	1-0	1-0	4-0	1-0
São Caetano	38	20	11	7	58	38	71	1-1	1-1	1-3	0-0		1-0	1-0	1-1	3-2	1-1	2-0	0-1	0-1	2-0	4-2	1-0	3-2	1-2	1-1	3-0
Joinville	38	17	9	12	58	40	60	1-0	3-1	1-4	1-1	0-0		1-0	2-2	1-0	3-1	1-1	0-0	1-0	1-0	3-0	2-1	3-1	2-0	6-0	4-0
Avaí	38	18	5	15	44	42	59	1-4	1-1	1-2	2-0	1-0	1-2		2-0	2-2	3-1	2-1	3-1	2-0	1-0	0-2	2-0	4-0	1-1	3-1	1-2	2-1
América Mineiro	38	16	7	15	63	58	55	1-2	3-0	3-2	1-2	2-5	0-2	1-0		1-1	0-0	1-3	3-3	0-1	3-2	3-2	2-1	4-0	1-1	3-1	1-2
América Natal	38	14	12	12	60	61	54	5-2	1-4	0-2	2-2	0-2	3-1	1-0	1-1		2-1	1-1	1-0	2-0	2-1	4-4	4-1	3-3	1-0	2-1	2-1
Paraná	38	14	9	15	49	46	51	1-3	1-1	2-3	1-2	1-2	0-1	1-0	1-1	1-0		1-0	1-2	2-0	2-0	2-0	3-2	4-0	1-1	2-0	1-1
Ceará	38	12	11	15	51	52	47	2-2	2-1	0-1	3-2	2-4	3-0	1-1	2-4	0-0	1-1		4-2	3-2	1-2	1-1	1-1	1-1	2-1	1-0	1-2	1-0
ABC	38	11	12	15	50	52	45	3-2	2-2	0-1	0-1	0-1	0-0	1-2	0-2	2-2	2-0	0-1		1-1	1-0	1-2	3-0	4-2	3-1	2-2	2-1
ASA Arapiraca	38	13	5	20	48	56	44	0-1	1-2	2-3	2-3	4-1	1-0	1-0	3-2	0-2	1-1	3-0	3-1		1-1	3-2	3-1	2-4	1-0	3-0	1-1
Bragantino	38	12	8	18	45	53	44	3-3	3-4	2-1	3-0	2-3	1-0	1-0	2-0	1-0	3-3	1-3	1-2	2-2		3-0	1-0	0-2	0-0	0-2	2-2
Boa Esporte	38	11	16	15	51	63	44	2-2	0-4	2-1	1-2	1-3	0-0	2-2	2-1	1-1	2-1	1-0	0-0	3-2	3-0		0-1	0-0	1-2	2-1	4-1
Guaratinguetá	38	13	4	21	41	63	43	0-3	2-1	0-1	1-0	0-1	0-3	1-1	1-2	0-2	2-0	2-1	2-1	2-1	2-0	0-0		1-2	2-1	3-1	2-1
CRB	38	12	6	20	47	67	42	0-2	0-2	2-0	0-1	2-2	4-3	2-0	0-1	4-2	0-2	0-2	3-3	0-1	0-2	0-0	3-1		2-1	2-0	2-1
Guarani	38	10	11	17	36	47	41	1-2	1-2	2-1	0-0	1-2	2-1	0-2	0-3	0-0	0-0	4-1	1-1	2-1	1-2	0-0	2-1	4-0		1-0	1-0
Ipatinga	38	8	7	23	38	73	31	0-6	2-3	1-1	1-2	1-0	1-2	1-0	4-0	2-0	1-2	1-1	1-0	2-1	1-1	2-2	3-3	2-0	0-0		0-3
Grêmio Barueri	38	7	9	22	38	69	30	2-0	1-4	0-6	0-1	1-2	1-1	2-0	0-1	2-3	1-2	0-0	0-3	1-0	0-1	1-2	2-3	0-0	2-2	2-0	

19/05/2012 - 24/11/2012 • Top scorers: **27 - ZE CARLOS**, Criciúma • **20 - ISAC**, América RN • **17 - LIMA**, Joinville

BRAZIL 2012
SERIE C (3) FIRST ROUND GROUP A

	Pl	W	D	L	F	A	Pts	Fortaleza	Luverdense	Icasa	Paysandu	Treze	Santa Cruz	Aguia	Cuiabá	Salgueiro	Guarany
Fortaleza †	18	11	6	1	28	11	39		3-3	1-0	3-1	2-1	2-0	0-0	3-0	2-1	4-1
Luverdense †	18	10	4	4	32	26	34	2-0		2-1	2-2	0-2	2-1	5-1	1-0	3-2	1-1
Icasa †	18	7	3	8	18	19	24	0-2	0-1		1-0	3-0	3-1	2-1	0-0	2-0	1-0
Paysandu †	18	5	9	4	26	19	24	0-1	2-0	1-1		5-1	0-0	0-0	2-1	4-0	1-1
Treze	18	7	1	10	24	33	22	0-2	1-2	2-1	1-0		2-1	4-0	0-0	4-0	3-1
Santa Cruz	18	5	7	6	26	22	22	1-2	2-1	4-0	3-3	2-1		6-1	1-0	0-0	1-1
Aguia	18	5	7	6	22	32	22	0-0	2-2	1-0	1-1	5-1	1-0		2-1	2-2	2-1
Cuiabá	18	4	8	6	20	21	20	0-0	0-2	0-0	1-1	5-1	0-0	3-1		1-1	2-1
Salgueiro	18	4	8	6	25	29	20	0-0	6-2	2-1	1-1	2-0	2-2	1-1	2-2		3-0
Guarany de Sobral	18	3	5	10	21	30	14	1-1	0-1	1-2	1-2	2-0	1-1	3-1	3-4	2-0	

1/07/2012 - 28/10/2012 • † Qualified for the second round

BRAZIL 2012
SERIE C (3) FIRST ROUND GROUP B

	Pl	W	D	L	F	A	Pts	Macaé	Duque de Caxias	Chapecoense	Oeste	Caxias	Brasiliense	Vila Nova	Madureira	Santo André	Tupi
Macaé †	18	9	5	4	33	17	32		2-1	0-0	0-2	4-1	2-2	3-0	0-0	3-1	4-2
Duque de Caxias †	18	9	2	7	22	23	29	2-1		0-1	0-2	2-1	1-0	1-1	0-2	3-2	2-1
Chapecoense †	18	8	5	5	24	12	29	1-1	3-1		1-0	4-0	3-0	3-2	1-0	0-0	5-0
Oeste †	18	8	5	5	22	19	29	1-1	1-0	1-0		1-2	2-1	3-1	0-0	2-1	1-0
Caxias	18	8	3	7	23	26	27	0-4	0-1	2-0	3-2		3-0	2-1	2-0	0-0	1-0
Brasiliense	18	7	2	9	25	29	23	1-3	3-2	1-1	3-2	2-1		4-2	2-0	1-2	2-1
Vila Nova	18	6	5	7	27	26	23	1-0	4-1	1-0	4-1	0-1	1-0		5-1	2-2	0-0
Madureira	18	6	5	7	17	21	23	2-1	1-2	2-1	1-1	1-1	1-0	3-1		1-1	1-0
Santo André	18	3	9	6	14	22	18	0-3	0-1	0-0	1-1	2-1	0-3	0-0	1-0		1-1
Tupi	18	3	5	10	13	25	14	0-1	0-2	1-0	0-1	2-2	2-0	1-1	2-1	0-0	

30/06/2012 - 27/10/2012 • † Qualified for the second round

BRAZIL 2012
SERIE C (3) FINAL ROUNDS

Quarter-finals			Semi-finals			Final		
Oeste *	1	3						
Fortaleza	1	1	**Oeste**	1	0			
Luverdense	0	1	Chapecoense *	0	0			
Chapecoense *	3	0				**Oeste**	0	2
Paysandu *	2	2				Icasa *	0	0
Macaé	0	3	Paysandu *	3	1			
Duque de Caxias	1	0	**Icasa**	2	2			
Icasa *	2	0						

1/11/2012 - 1/12/2012 • Oeste, Icasa, Chapecoense & Paysandu promoted to Serie B • * Home team in 1st leg

BRAZIL 2012

SERIE D (4) GROUP A1

	Pl	W	D	L	F	A	Pts	Remo	VEC	Atlético	Peñarol	Náutico
Remo †	8	5	1	2	20	16	16		2-1	2-2	4-2	4-0
Vilhena †	8	5	0	3	17	10	15	4-2		4-0	2-1	3-1
Atlético Acreano	8	4	1	3	19	15	13	2-3	0-2		3-2	4-0
Peñarol	8	3	0	5	16	16	9	4-1	1-0	1-3		4-0
Náutico RR	8	2	0	6	9	24	6	1-2	3-1	1-5	3-1	

SERIE D (4) GROUP A2

	Pl	W	D	L	F	A	Pts	Sampaio	Mixto	Comercial	Santos	Araguaína
Sampaio Corrêa †	8	8	0	0	25	2	24		1-0	4-0	6-0	3-0
Mixto †	8	3	3	2	13	9	12	1-3		4-0	1-1	1-1
Comercial AC	8	2	2	4	6	13	5	0-1	0-2		3-1	1-1
Santos Macapá	8	1	4	3	9	16	4	1-3	2-2	0-0		4-1
Araguaína	8	0	3	5	4	17	3	0-4	1-2	0-2	0-0	

SERIE D (4) GROUP A3

	Pl	W	D	L	F	A	Pts	Baraúnas	Campinense	Horizonte	Ypiranga	Petrolina
Baraúnas †	8	4	3	1	12	7	15		2-1	0-0	3-1	1-1
Campinense †	8	4	2	2	11	8	14	2-1		1-0	1-1	2-1
Horizonte	8	3	4	1	9	5	13	0-0	0-0		2-1	2-0
Ypiranga PE	8	2	2	4	13	15	8	1-2	2-1	1-3		3-0
Petrolina	8	0	3	5	9	19	3	1-3	1-3	2-2	3-3	

SERIE D (4) GROUP A4

	Pl	W	D	L	F	A	Pts	CSA	Sousa	Feirense	Itabaiana	Vitória
CSA †	8	6	2	0	15	3	20		2-1	5-0	1-0	3-1
Sousa †	8	3	4	1	7	5	13	0-0		0-0	2-1	2-1
Feirense	8	3	2	3	9	12	11	1-3	1-1		2-0	1-0
Itabaiana	8	1	3	4	5	10	6	0-0	0-0	2-1		2-2
Vitória Conquista	8	1	1	6	7	13	4	0-1	0-1	1-3	2-0	

SERIE D (4) GROUP A5

	Pl	W	D	L	F	A	Pts	CRAC	Ceilândia	CENE	Aparecidense	Sobradinho
CRAC †	8	4	3	1	15	9	15		2-2	4-2	3-0	3-2
Ceilândia †	8	4	2	2	14	14	14	1-0		3-2	2-4	1-1
CENE	8	4	1	3	17	11	13	1-1	3-1		4-1	2-0
Aparecidense	8	3	1	4	11	15	10	1-2	1-0	0-0		1-0
Sobradinho	8	0	3	5	8	16	3	0-0	2-3	0-3	3-3	

SERIE D (4) GROUP A6

	Pl	W	D	L	F	A	Pts	Friburguense	Nacional	Aracruz	V. Redonda	Guarani
Friburguense †	8	4	4	0	13	4	16		1-1	2-1	1-0	6-0
Nacional MG †	8	3	4	1	7	5	13	1-1		0-0	3-2	0-0
Aracruz	8	2	3	3	5	7	9	1-1	1-0		1-0	0-2
Volta Redonda	8	2	2	4	5	6	8	0-0	0-1	1-0		0-0
Guarani MG	8	1	3	4	3	11	6	0-1	0-1	1-1	0-2	

SERIE D (4) GROUP A7

	Pl	W	D	L	F	A	Pts	Cianorte	Mogi Mirim	Cerâmica	Marília	Concórdia
Cianorte †	8	5	3	0	14	4	18		0-0	2-1	6-0	2-1
Mogi Mirim †	8	3	4	1	10	7	13	0-0		2-1	1-1	3-1
Cerâmica	8	3	2	3	10	7	11	1-2	0-0		2-0	3-1
Marília	8	1	4	3	7	15	7	1-1	2-3	0-0		1-0
Concórdia	8	1	1	6	7	15	4	0-1	2-1	0-2	2-2	

SERIE D (4) GROUP A8

	Pl	W	D	L	F	A	Pts	M'politano	Juventude	Arapongas	Brasil	Mirassol
Metropolitano †	8	4	2	2	8	7	14		2-1	2-1	2-0	2-1
Juventude RS †	8	3	3	2	7	4	12	0-0		0-0	1-0	4-0
Arapongas	8	2	4	2	6	6	10	2-0	2-0		0-0	0-0
Brasil de Pelotas	8	2	3	3	6	7	9	2-0	0-1	0-0		2-1
Mirassol	8	1	4	3	8	11	7	0-0	0-0	4-1	2-2	

23/06/2012 - 30/08/2012 • † Qualified for the round of 16

SERIE D (4) FINAL ROUNDS

Round of 16
- Sampaio Corrêa — 2 4
- Vilhena * — 2 1
- Remo — 0 2
- **Mixto *** — 2 1
- **Campinense *** — 2 0
- CSA — 1 0
- Sousa * — 0 0
- **Baraúnas** — 1 2
- **Mogi Mirim *** — 0 2
- Metropolitano — 1 1
- Juventude RS * — 3 0
- **Cianorte** — 1 3
- **Friburguense** — 0 2
- Ceilândia * — 0 1
- Nacional MG * — 2 0
- **CRAC** — 1 1

Quarter-finals
- Sampaio Corrêa — 1 0
- Mixto * — 1 0
- Campinense * — 1 0
- Baraúnas — 1 2
- Mogi Mirim * — 1 2 4p
- Cianorte — 2 1 2p
- Friburguense — 0 3
- CRAC * — 2 1

Semi-finals
- Sampaio Corrêa — 1 1
- Baraúnas * — 1 0
- Mogi Mirim * — 1 0
- CRAC — 1 2

Final
- Sampaio Corrêa — 1 2
- CRAC * — 0 1

* Home team in the 1st leg

1/09/2012 - 21/10/2012 • Sampaio Corrêa, CRAC, Baraúnas and Mogi Mirim are promoted

BRAZIL STATE CHAMPIONSHIPS 2012

State	Winners	Score	Runners-up	State	Winners	Score	Runners-up
Acre	Atlético Acreano	4-2 4-2	Rio Branco	Paraíba	Campinense	1-1 4-0	Sousa
Alagoas	CRB	2-1 0-0	ASA	Paraná	Coritiba	2-2 0-0 5-4p	Atlético PR
Amapá	Oratório			Pernambuco	Santa Cruz	0-0 3-2	Sport Recife
Amazonas	Nacional AM	2-2 2-1	Fast Clube	Piauí	Parnahyba	1-0 0-1	Flamengo PI
Bahia	Bahia	0-0 3-3	Vitória	Rio de Janeiro	Fluminense	4-1 1-0	Botafogo
Ceará	Ceará	0-0 1-1	Fortaleza	Rio Grande Nor.	América RN	2-1 2-0	ABC
Distrito Federal	Celiândia	1-0 0-1	Luziânia	Rio Grande Sul	Internacional	1-1 2-1	Caxias
Espírito Santo	Aracruz	1-2 4-1	Botafogo ES	Rondônia	Ji-Paraná	2-2 4-1	Espigão
Goiás	Goiás	2-2 1-1	Atlético GO	Roraima	São Raimundo	2-0	Náutico RR
Maranhão	Sampaio Corrêa	3-0 2-1	Maranhão	Santa Catarina	Avai	3-0 2-1	Figueirense
Mato Grosso	Luverdense	1-0 0-1 3-0p	Cuiabá	São Paulo	Santos	3-0 4-2	Guarani
Mato Grosso Sul	Aguia Negra	1-1 0-0	Naviraiense	Sergipe	Itabaiana	3-1 0-1	Confiança
Minas Gerais	Atlético MG	1-1 3-0	América MG	Tocantins	Gurupi	‡	Tocantinópolis
Pará	Cametá	2-1 2-2	Remo				

‡ Won both stages so no final needed • † Played on a league basis

BRAZIL STATE CHAMPIONSHIPS 2012 – RIO DE JANEIRO

TAÇA GUANABARA

Group A

	Pl	W	D	L	F	A	Pts
Botafogo †	7	4	3	0	17	4	15
Flamengo †	7	4	3	0	10	1	15
Resende	7	4	0	3	11	13	12
Nova Iguçu	7	2	3	2	6	7	9
Macaé	7	2	2	3	6	8	8
Bonsucesso	7	1	3	3	7	13	6
Madureira	7	1	2	4	8	12	5
Olaria	7	1	2	4	5	12	5

Group B

	Pl	W	D	L	F	A	Pts
Vasco da Gama †	7	7	0	0	16	3	21
Fluminense †	7	4	1	2	15	7	13
Boavista	7	3	3	1	13	12	12
Friburgense	7	3	2	2	10	10	11
Volta Redonda	7	3	2	2	10	11	11
Duque de Caxias	7	2	2	3	9	12	8
Americano	7	1	1	5	6	13	4
Bangu	7	0	0	7	7	18	0

21/01/2012 – 18/02/2012 • † Qualified for the semis

GUANABARA PLAY-OFFS

Semi-finals		**Final**	
Fluminense	1 4p		
Botafogo	1 3p	Fluminense	3
Flamengo	1	Vasco da Gama	1
Vasco da Gama	2		

Engenhão, Rio, 26-02-2012, Att: 36 374, Ref: Marcelo de Lima. Scorers: Fred 2 [35p] [55], Deco 41 for Flu; Eduardo Costa [82] for Vasco

CARIOCA FINAL

1st leg. Engenhão, Rio de Janeiro, 6-05-2012, Att: 28 182, Ref: Silva

Fluminense 4-1 Botafogo

Scorers – Fred [42], Rafael Sobis 2 [56] [65], Marcos Junior [83] for Fluminense; Renato [8] for Botafogo

TAÇA RIO

Group A

	Pl	W	D	L	F	A	Pts
Flamengo †	8	7	0	1	17	8	21
Botafogo †	8	5	3	0	18	8	18
Resende	8	3	4	1	9	8	13
Macaé	8	4	0	4	3	14	12
Madureira	8	3	1	4	11	13	10
Olaria	8	2	3	3	8	12	9
Nova Iguçu	8	2	2	4	8	13	8
Bonsucesso	8	1	4	3	10	13	7

Group B

	Pl	W	D	L	F	A	Pts
Bangu †	8	4	3	1	10	5	15
Vasco da Gama †	8	4	2	2	17	10	14
Fluminense	8	4	1	3	15	10	13
Volta Redonda	8	3	2	3	10	11	11
Duque de Caxias	8	2	2	4	7	12	8
Friburgense	8	1	3	4	6	11	6
Americano	8	1	2	5	13	18	5
Boavista	8	1	2	5	11	17	5

29/02/2012 – 15/04/2012 • † Qualified for the semis

TAÇA RIO PLAY-OFFS

Semi-finals		**Final**	
Botafogo	4		
Bangu	2	Botafogo	3
Flamengo	2	Vasco da Gama	1
Vasco da Gama	3		

Engenhão, Rio, 29-04-2012, Att: 41 387, Ref: Wagner. Scorers – Abreu 2 [3] [45], Maicosuel [52] for Botafogo; Carlos Alberto [80] for Vasco

CARIOCA FINAL

2nd leg. Engenhão, Rio de Janeiro, 13-05-2012, Att: 25 016, Ref: Lima

Botafogo 0-1 Fluminense

Scorer – Rafael Moura [62]

BRAZIL STATE CHAMPIONSHIPS 2012 - RIO DE JANEIRO

CAMPEONATO CARIOCA 2012 RESULTS

	Fluminense	Botafogo	Flamengo	Vasco	Resende	V. Redonda	Macaé	Friburgense	Nova Iguçu	Boavista	Duque de Caxias	Madureira	Bangu	Olaria	Bonsucesso	Americano
Fluminense		1-1					1-3	3-0	3-0	1-2	1-1			3-0	5-1	
Botafogo			0-0	3-1	3-1	3-1		3-1							5-0	4-1
Flamengo	2-0								2-0	1-2		1-0	2-1	0-0	4-0	3-1
Vasco da Gama	2-1		1-2		1-1	3-0		2-0			3-0				2-2	2-0
Resende	2-1		1-3							2-0		2-1	0-3	3-2	1-0	2-1
Volta Redonda	0-3		2-4		1-1			2-2			3-0				2-1	2-0
Macaé		0-3	0-0	1-4	3-0	0-1		3-1			2-1					
Friburgense		5-2	0-1		0-0					0-0	1-1	2-1		0-0		
Nova Iguçu		0-0		1-3	1-3	0-0	2-0	2-1		0-1						
Boavista	1-1			0-1		1-1	2-3		1-2		3-1		4-2	1-2		
Duque de Caxias			1-2	1-3	1-1	1-3						1-4			2-1	3-1
Madureira	1-2	2-2					1-0		2-2	3-1				0-1		2-1
Bangu		1-1		1-3			1-2	1-0		2-1		1-2		0-0		
Olaria				0-2		2-0	0-1	1-2	0-1		0-0	2-1			1-1	
Bonsucesso	0-2						2-2		0-0	3-3		3-1	1-1			2-1
Americano		2-3	2-4				3-1	0-1	2-2	1-1			2-1	2-2		

Clubs listed according to overall position • Taça Guanabara results in shaded boxes • Taça Rio results in unshaded boxes
Top scorers (overall): **12 - ALECSANDRO**, Vasco & **SOMALIA**, Boavista

BRAZIL STATE CHAMPIONSHIPS 2012 - SÃO PAULO

CAMPEONATO PAULISTA SERIE A1 FIRST ROUND

	Pl	W	D	L	F	A	Pts	Corinthians	São Paulo	Santos	Guarani	Palmeiras	Mogi Mirim	Bragantino	Ponte Preta	Mirassol	Oeste	Linense	São Caetano	Paulista	Ituano	Botafogo RP	XV Piracicaba	Portuguesa	Guaratinguetá	Catanduvense	Comercial
Corinthians ‡	19	14	4	1	28	11	46		1-0		1-1	2-1		1-1		2-1		1-0		1-0	1-0	1-0				2-1	
São Paulo FC ‡	19	13	4	2	42	21	43			3-2	1-1	2-0								2-1	3-1		4-0		2-1	3-0	2-0	1-1
Santos ‡	19	12	3	4	46	18	39	1-0				1-2		2-0	6-1		1-1	4-1			2-1					5-0	5-0	2-0
Guarani ‡	19	11	3	5	26	18	36		0-2	3-1				2-0	2-1	2-1		2-1	2-0				2-0	1-0				
Palmeiras ‡	19	10	6	3	37	24	36	3-3			2-0		2-1	0-1	1-1		0-0		3-0		3-2	1-1				2-2		
Mogi Mirim ‡	19	10	5	4	32	22	35	1-1		3-1	3-0			1-3				1-0	3-1	2-2		2-2	3-0					
Bragantino ‡	19	8	5	6	33	33	29				3-3		1-0	1-2	2-0			1-4		2-0		1-1		1-1			2-1	
Ponte Preta ‡	19	8	4	7	34	31	28	1-2	1-3		1-1				5-1		2-2	2-1		4-1	1-0			3-1				1-0
Mirassol	19	6	7	6	31	25	25		0-1	1-3		2-2	2-3	3-3					1-2		3-0	3-0	4-2		1-1			
Oeste	19	6	7	6	32	30	25	0-3	2-3			1-2			0-0		1-1		2-1	4-2	2-3			3-2	2-1			
Linense	19	6	5	8	31	40	23		2-1			1-3	0-2	2-1		1-1		3-3			1-3	0-4	4-2					
São Caetano	19	5	8	6	24	25	23	0-1		2-1	0-1			1-0	2-2	2-2						1-1	1-1		0-1	2-0		
Paulista	19	7	1	11	26	29	22				1-1		0-1	2-0			1-2	1-2				0-1	2-1		2-1	3-1	3-0	
Ituano	19	5	5	9	25	34	20	0-1	2-4				1-4		1-1		2-3	2-2	3-2						3-0	1-1		
Botafogo RP	19	6	1	12	24	40	19			1-4	2-1	2-6	0-1		1-2			2-3		0-1	2-1			1-2				
XV de Piracicaba	19	5	3	11	23	29	18		0-1	1-1				2-3	2-1		2-1			1-2					2-0	0-2	2-1	
Portuguesa	19	4	6	9	22	29	18	0-2		0-2							2-2		0-2	1-1	3-0	1-0				2-1	0-0	3-0
Guaratinguetá	19	4	3	12	22	43	15	0-2			2-1	2-3	1-1	2-2	2-1	0-4			2-2		2-1							
Catanduvense	19	2	7	10	19	36	13				1-2	1-1	0-2	2-4	1-1		1-1	2-2			2-4					1-3		
Comercial	19	3	3	13	18	37	12	3-3			0-2		1-3		0-1	0-2	3-4			0-1						2-1	2-1	

15/01/2010 - 17/04/2011 • ‡ Qualified for the quarter-finals • Top scorers (overall): **20 - NEYMAR**, Santos • **16 - HERNANE**, Mogi Mirim

PAULISTA 2012 FINAL ROUNDS

Quarter-finals		Semi-finals		Final	
Santos *	2				
Mogi Mirim	0	**Santos**	3		
Bragantino	1	São Paulo FC*	1		
São Paulo FC*	4			**Santos**	3 4
Ponte Preta	3			Guarani	0 2
Corinthians *	2	Ponte Preta	1		
Palmeiras	2	**Guarani***	3		
Guarani*	3	* Home team			

1st leg. Morumbi, São Paulo, 6-05-2012, Att: 40 146, Ref: Seneme.
Scorers - Ganso [42], Neymar 2 [65 91+] for Santos
2nd leg. Morumbi, São Paulo, 13-05-2012, 13-05-2012, Att: 53 749, Ref: Oliveira. Scorers - Alan Kardac 2 [1 91+], Neymar 2 [8p 71] for Santos; Fabinho [4], Bruno Mendes [16] for Guarani.
Santos are the 2012 São Paulo state champions

COPA DO BRASIL 2012

First Round			Second Round			Third Round		
Palmeiras	1	3						
Coruripe *	0	0	Palmeiras	3				
América Natal	0 2	2p	Horizonte *	1				
Horizonte *	2 0	4p				Palmeiras	2	4
Ceará	2					Paraná *	1	0
Gama *	0		Ceará *	2	1			
Luverdense *	2	0	Paraná	2	1			
Paraná	2	2						
Cruzeiro	6							
Rio Branco *	0		Cruzeiro	1	4			
São Mateus *	2	1	Chapecoense *	1	1			
Chapecoense	1	3				Cruzeiro	0	1
Criciúma	2					Atlético Paranaense *	1	2
Madureira *	0		Criciúma *	1	1			
Sampaio Corrêa *	2	0	Atlético Paranaense	2	5			
Atlético Paranaense	1	1						
Bahia	3							
Auto Esporte *	0		Bahia	1	4			
AE Real *	0	0	Remo *	2	0			
Remo	0	3				Bahia	0	2
Juventude	4					Portuguesa *	0	0
Operário PR *	0		Juventude *	2	0			
Cuiabá *	1	0	Portuguesa	0	4			
Portuguesa	1	4						
Fortaleza	3	3						
Comercial PI *	2	0	Fortaleza *	4	1			
Santa Cruz RN *	1		Náutico	0	2			
Náutico	3					Fortaleza *	0	0
Ipatinga	2					Grêmio	2	2
Real Noroeste *	0		Ipatinga *	0	0			
River Plate *	2	1	Grêmio	1	3			
Grêmio	3	3						
São Paulo FC	1	4						
Independente PA *	0	0	São Paulo FC	5				
Aquidauanense *	1	0	Bahia de Feira *	2				
Bahia de Feira	0	2				São Paulo FC	0	3
Atlético Goianiense	1	4				Ponte Preta *	1	1
Gurupi *	0	2	Atlético Goianiense *	2 1	3p			
Sapucaiense *	0	2	Ponte Preta	1 2	4p			
Ponte Preta	0	5						
Atlético Mineiro	3							
CENE *	1		Atlético Mineiro	5				
Santa Cruz	2	2	Peñarol *	0				
Peñarol *	1	3				Atlético Mineiro	0	2
América Mineiro	0	1				Goiás *	2	1
Boavista *	0	2	América Mineiro *	0	3			
Paulista *	2	0	Goiás	0	4			
Goiás	3	3						
Vitória	0	2						
São Domingos *	0	0	Vitória	1	3			
Trem *	0		ABC *	1	2			
ABC	5					Vitória *	1	2
Guarani	0	3				Botafogo	1	1
Brasiliense *	2	0	Guarani *	1	0			
Treze *	1 1	2p	Botafogo	2	0			
Botafogo	1 1	3p						
Paysandu	3							
Espigão *	1		Paysandu *	2	4			
4 de Julho *	0		Sport Recife	1	1			
Sport Recife	2					Paysandu	1	0
ASA	3	2				Coritiba *	4	1
Santa Quitéria *	2	1	ASA *	1	0			
Nacional AM *	0	0	Coritiba	0	3			
Coritiba	0	2						

If the away team wins the first leg by two goals in the first or second round no second leg is played

COPA DO BRASIL 2012

Quarter-finals	Semi-finals	Final

COPA DO BRASIL FINAL 1ST LEG
Arena Barueri, Barueri, São Paulo, 5-07-2012, Att: 28 557, Ref: Sampaio

Palmeiras	2	Valdivia 45p, Thiago Heleno 65
Coritiba	0	

PALMEIRAS
BRUNO CORTEZ - THIAGO HELENO, MAURICIO RAMOS, ARTUR, JUNINHO BARBOSA, Jorge VALDIVIA●●♦57, MARCIO ARAUJO●, JOAO VITOR, MARCOS ASSUNCAO (c), MAZINHO (MAIKON LEITE 81), BETINHO. Tr: Luiz Felipe SCOLARI

CORITIBA
VANDERLEI - PEREIRA (c), EMERSON●, JONAS●, LUCAS MENDES, EVERTON RIBEIRO (LINCOLN 57), RAFINHA, WILLIAN FARIAS, GIL (ANDERSON AQUINO 69), JUNIOR URSO● (TCHECO● 75), EVERTON COSTA. Tr: MARCELO OLIVEIRA

Palmeiras	2	1
Grêmio *	0	1

Bahia *	1	0
Grêmio	2	2

Palmeiras * †	2	1
Coritiba	0	1

São Paulo FC *	2	2
Goiás.	0	2

São Paulo FC *	1	0
Coritiba	0	2

COPA DO BRASIL FINAL 2ND LEG
Antônio Couto Pereira, Curitiba, 11-07-2012, Att: 35 122, Ref: Ricci

Coritiba	1	Ayrton 62
Palmeiras	1	Betinho 66

CORITIBA
VANDERLEI - PEREIRA●●♦92+ (c), JONAS (AYRTON 46), LUCAS MENDES, DEMERSON, EVERTON RIBEIRO, RAFINHA●, WILLIAN FARIAS, SERGIO MANOEL (LINCOLN 60), EVERTON COSTA, ROBERTO (ANDERSON AQUINO 67). Tr: MARCELO OLIVEIRA

PALMEIRAS
BRUNO CORTEZ - THIAGO HELENO (LEANDRO AMARO 38), HENRIQUE●, MAURICIO RAMOS, ARTUR●, JUNINHO BARBOSA●, DANIEL CARVALHO (LUAN 57), JOAO VITOR● (MARCIO ARAUJO 71), MARCOS ASSUNCAO● (c), MAZINHO, BETINHO. Tr: Luiz Felipe SCOLARI

Vitória *	0	1
Coritiba	0	4

† Qualified for the Copa Libertadores
* Home team in the first leg

PART TWO – THE ASSOCIATIONS

MEDALS TABLE

		Overall G S B	Nat G S B	Cup G S	TRGP G S B	CW G	Rio-SP G S B	SL G S	Sth Am G S B	City
1	São Paulo FC	13 10 8	6 5 3	1		1	1 5 1	21 17	6 4 5	São Paulo
2	Santos	13 7 5	2 4	6 2	1		5 1	20 9	4 1 5	Santos
3	Palmeiras	12 9 3	4 2	4 1	2 1		5 1 3	22 23	2 5 3	São Paulo
4	Corinthians	11 5 6	5 3 1	3 2		2 2	5 3 2	26 19	1 3	São Paulo
5	Cruzeiro	10 11 5	4 1	5 1	1			37	4 5 4	Belo Horizonte
6	Flamengo	10 7 4	6 1	2 4			1 3 2	32 25	2 3 3	Rio de Janeiro
7	Internacional	8 10 3	3 5	1 2	2	1		41	3 1 3	Porto Alegre
8	Grêmio	8 6 7	2 2 2	4 2				36	2 2 5	Porto Alegre
9	Vasco da Gama	7 5 3	4 3	1 2	1		3 5 2	22 21	2 2	Rio de Janeiro
10	Fluminense	5 4 1	3	1 2	1		2 1 1	31 21	2	Rio de Janeiro
11	Atlético Mineiro	3 5 5	1 4		1			41	2 1 4	Belo Horizonte
12	Botafogo	3 4 2	1 2	1 2			4 3 1	18 16	1 2	Rio de Janeiro
13	EC Bahia	2 2	1	1 2				46		Salvador
14	Sport Recife	2 1	1	1 1				38		Recife
15	Guarani	1 2 1	1 2					2	1	Campinas
	Atlético Paranaense	1 2 1	1 1					22	1 1	Curitiba
17	Coritiba	1 2	1	2				36		Curitiba
18	Criciúma	1		1				8		Criciúma
	Juventude	1		1				1		Caxias do Sul
	Paulista	1		1						Jundiai
	Santo André	1		1				1		Santo Andre
22	São Caetano	3	2					1 1	1	São Caetano
23	Goiás AC	2 1	1	1				23	1	Goiânia
24	Fortaleza	2		2				39		Fortaleza
	Vitória	2	1	1				26		Salvador
26	Portuguesa	1	1				2 3	3 4		São Paulo
	Bangu	1	1				1	2 6		Rio de Janeiro
	Bragantino	1	1					1		Bragança Paul.
	Brasiliense	1		1				7		Taguatinga
	Ceará SC	1						41		Fortaleza
	CSA	1						37	1	Maceió
	Figueirense	1		1				15		Florianópolis
	Nautico	1		1				21		Recife
34	Sampaio Corrêa	1						30	1	São Luis
	São Raimundo	1						7	1	Manaus
		114 109 57	43 43 10	34 34	4 4 4	4	28 22 16		29 28 43	

Nat = the national championship played since 1971 • Cup = the Copa do Brasil played between 1959-68 and since 1989 • TRGP = Torneio Roberto Gomes Pedrosa played from 1967-70 • CW = FIFA Club World Cup • Rio-SP = Torneio Rio-São Paulo played in 1933, 1950-66, 1993 & 1997-2002 • SL = the state leagues played throughout the country • The totals for the Torneio Rio-São Paulo and the state leagues are not included in the overall totals as they are not national competitions

CLUB BY CLUB GUIDE TO 2012 IN BRAZIL

The following guide covers the state championships played in Brazil in the first half of the year along with Serie A in the second half of the year SA = Serie A • CB = Copa do Brasil • CL = Copa Libertadores • CS = Copa Sudamericana • g1 = group 1 etc • r1 = first round etc • qf = quarter-final • sf = semi-final • f = final

State championship abbreviations

CG = Campeonato Goiano (Atlético GO & Goiás) • CM = Campeonato Mineiro (Atlético MG & Cruzeiro) • CP = Campeonato Paranaense (Atlético PR) • CC = Campeonato Catarinense (Avai) • TG & TR = Taça Guanabara & Taça Rio (Botafogo, Flamengo, Fluminense & Vasco) • CC1 = Campeonato Cearense round 1 etc (Ceara) • CP = Campeonato Paulista (Corinthians, Grêmio Prudente, Palmeiras, Santos & São Paulo. Guarani played the 2010 season at the second) • CG = Campeonato Gaúcho (Grêmio & Internacional) • TB = Campeonato Baiano (Vitória)

ATLETICO GOIANIENSE 2012

Jan	21	Rio Verde	W 4-2	CG	Gilson [46], Marcao 2 [52 64], Marino [59]	4 327
	24	Anapolina	W 2-1	CG	Marcao [27], Thiaguinho [91+]	1 085
	29	Goianésia	L 1-2	CG	Elias [53]	1 334
Feb	1	CRAC	W 4-2	CG	Diogo Campos [50], Gabriel [55], Marcao 2 [86 93+]	1 852
	5	Goiás	L 0-1	CG		11 155
	8	Apar'dense	W 6-1	CG	Marcio [20], William 2 [22 30], Emandes [36], Bida [64], Gilson [70]	1 364
	11	Vila Nova	W 1-0	CG	Bida [64]	3 169
	22	Morrinhos	W 2-0	CG	Felipe [17], Joilson [25]	1 670
	26	Itumbiara	D 1-1	CG	Marcao [60]	3 029
	29	Itumbiara	W 1-0	CG	William [51]	26 079
Mar	4	Apar'dense	W 2-0	CG	Marino [49], OG [59]	2 762
	7	Gurupi	W 1-0	CBr1	Marino [50]	1 941
	11	Vila Nova	D 2-2	CG	Marcao 2 [61 85]	8 702
	15	Gurupi	W 4-2	CBr1	Joilson [12], Fabio Lima 2 [22 33], Marcao [87]	1 976
	19	Morrinhos	W 2-1	CG	Marcao [69], Diogo Campos [72]	4 056
	25	Goiás	L 0-2	CG		14 219
	28	CRAC	W 4-1	CG	Bida 2 [41 44], Fernando Bob [55], Felipe [85]	1 868
	31	Goianésia	W 3-0	CG	Bida [11], Marcao [14], Emandes [24]	3 459
Apr	5	Ponte Preta	W 2-1	CBr2	Gilson [61], William [70]	2 138
	8	Anapolina	W 2-0	CG	Bida [31], Felipe [46]	7 163
	15	Rio Verde	W 3-0	CG	Marcio [72], Bida [76], Marcao [78]	2 604
	18	Ponte Preta	L 1-2	CBr2	Marcao [74], L 3-4p	4 205
	22	CRAC	W 4-1	CGsf	Marcao 2 2 [50], Pituca [34], Paulinho [86]	7 230
	28	CRAC	W 8-0	CGsf	Elias 3 2p [44 50], OG [10], Emandes [41], Felipe 2 [52 87], Gilson [59]	3 899
May	6	Goiás	D 2-2	CGf	Bida [31], Elias [54p]	18 345
	13	Goiás	D 1-1	CGf	Bida [7]	32 387
	20	Cruzeiro	D 0-0	SA 11		3 952
	26	Ponte Preta	D 1-1	SA 10	Bida [11]	1 703
Jun	6	Grêmio	L 0-1	SA 15		2 965
	10	Portuguesa	L 0-2	SA 18		1 407
	17	Coritiba	L 0-3	SA 19		7 392
	24	Fluminense	L 1-4	SA 20	Ernandes [13]	5 240
	1	Flamengo	L 2-3	SA 20	Felipe 2 [27 80]	4 200
	7	Náutico	L 0-1	SA 20		2 048
	15	Vasco	L 0-1	SA 20		9 624
Jul	19	Figueirense	W 3-2	SA 20	Marcio [38p], Felipe [58], Joilson [82]	1 112
	22	Inter	L 0-1	SA 20	Renie [27]	8 344
	25	São Paulo	W 4-3	SA 19	Marino [17], Marcio [24p], Patric [31], Wesley [43]	6 236
	29	Sport Recife	D 0-0	SA 19		12 860
	1	Figueirense	D 1-1	CSr1	Marcio [37p]	
	4	Botafogo	L 1-2	SA 19	Marcio [23p]	7 309
	8	Corinthians	D 1-1	SA 19	Ricardo Bueno [56]	24 372
	11	Santos	D 2-2	SA 20	Patric [4], Wesley [37]	9 432
Aug	15	Atlético MG	D 1-1	SA 19	Ernandes [10]	7 729
	19	Palmeiras	W 2-1	SA 18	Eron [17], Raylan [80]	9 955
	23	Figueirense	D 1-1	CSr1	Gustavo [58], W 4-2p	
	26	Bahia	D 1-1	SA 18	Diogo Campos [81]	10 901
	29	Cruzeiro	L 0-2	SA 19		2 675
Sep	2	Ponte Preta	L 1-3	SA 19	Diogo Giaretta [9]	4 762
	5	Grêmio	L 1-2	SA 20	Marino [25]	21 832
	9	Portuguesa	D 1-1	SA 20	Marcos [36]	891
	12	Coritiba	L 1-2	SA 20	Patric [10]	697
	15	Fluminense	W 2-1	SA 20	Diogo Giaretta [18], Renie [42]	8 269
	23	Flamengo	L 1-2	SA 20	Joilson [11]	23 887
	29	Náutico	L 0-1	SA 20		11 884
Oct	3	Un Catolica	L 0-2	CSr2		
	6	Vasco	L 0-1	SA 20		13 212
	10	Figueirense	L 1-3	SA 20	Diogo Giaretta [12]	2 600
	13	Inter	W 3-1	SA 20	Felipe [55], Ricardo Bueno [69], Luciano [76]	1 476
	18	São Paulo	L 0-2	SA 20		27 098
	21	Sport Recife	L 0-1	SA 20		449
	24	Un Catolica	W 3-1	CSr2	Joilson [13], Renie [35], Marcio [49p]	
	27	Botafogo	L 0-4	SA 20		8 303

ATLETICO GOIANIENSE 2012

Nov	4	Corinthians	L 0-2	SA 20		8 931
	10	Santos	W 2-1	SA 20	Diogo Campos [83], Marci [89p]	7 276
	18	Atlético MG	D 2-2	SA 20	Raylan [4], Patric [16]	15 342
Dec	25	Palmeiras	W 2-1	SA 19	Raylan [17], Ernandes [58]	4 579
	2	Bahia	L 0-1	SA 19		2 358

19th Att: 106 149 • Av: 5 587 (-41.2%) • Serra Dourada 50 049

ATLETICO GO SERIE A APPEARANCES/GOALS 2012

Goalkeepers Marcio 33/4 • Roberto 5
Defenders Adriano 8+2/0 • Bruninho 2/0 • Diego Giaretta 12+4/3
Ernandes 27+5/3 • Eron 26/1 • Gabriel 7+2/0 • Gilson 12+1/0
Gustavo 21+2/0 • Marcos 17+2/1 • Paulo Henrique 6/0
Rafael Cruz 3+1/0 • Renie 22+2/2
Midfield Bida 11/1 • Carlos 4+6/0 • Danilinho 6+8/0 • Dodo 23+2/0
Elias 4+2/0 • Fernando Bob 4+1/0 • Joilson 19+2/2 • Luciano 2+3/1
Mahatma 5+2/0 • Marino 28+3/2 • Pituca 21+1/0 • Raylan 6+5/3
Reis 0+2/0 • Wesley 17+2/2
Forwards Alexandre Oliveira 4+5/0 • Diogo Campos 17+10/2
Felipe 8+8/4 • Marcao 2+2/0 • Patric 19+8/4 • Ricardo Bueno 13+2/2
Vanderlei 1+7/0 • Watthimen 0+4/0 • William Souza 2+2/0
Coach Adilson Batista • Helio dos Anjos 29/05/12) • Jairo Araujo
(9/07/12) • Arthur Neto (13/09/12)

ATLETICO MINEIRO 2012

Jan	29	Boa	W 2-0	CM	Andre [10], Bernard [38]	4 419
	5	América TO	W 2-1	CM	Andre [52], Mancini [84]	2 875
Feb	11	Caldense	W 2-0	CM	Rafael Marques [29], Bernard [43]	3 752
	26	Guarani MG	W 4-0	CM	Mancini [25], Andre 3 [36 65 75]	2 653
	4	América MG	W 2-1	CM	Guilherme [80], Marcos Rocha [84]	4 067
Mar	10	Nacional	W 4-2	CM	Marcos Rocha [12], Andre 2 [59 72], Guilherme [68]	3 659
	14	CENE	W 3-1	CBr1	Andre [61], Rever [77], Mancini [84]	2 288
	18	Villa Nova	W 2-1	CM	Neto Berola [73], Rafael Marques [78]	2 320
	24	Democrata	W 3-0	CM	Guilherme [41], Neto Barola 2 [78 88]	3 881
	1	Uberaba	W 3-0	CM	Guilherme [11], Danilinho [57], Mancini [69]	5 210
	8	Cruzeiro	D 2-2	CM	Danilinho [24], Andre [38]	17 724
Apr	11	Peñarol	W 5-0	CBr2	Fillipe Soutto [2], Guilherme [39], Andre 3 [18 77 79]	3 500
	15	Tupi	D 0-0	CM		14 942
	22	Tupi	D 1-1	CMsf	Danilinho [52]	10 178
	25	Goias	L 0-2	CBr3		12 762
	28	Tupi	W 1-0	CMsf	Andre [71]	7 301
May	3	Goias	W 2-1	CBr3	Neto Berola [7], Mancini [26p]	18 628
	6	América MG	D 1-1	CMf	Andre [79]	14 543
	13	América MG	W 3-0	CMf	Serginho [31], Bernard 2 [38 76]	17 112

ATLETICO MINEIRO 2012 (CONT'D)

May	20	Ponte Preta	W	1-0	SA	5	Escudero [91+]	4 911
	27	Corinthians	W	1-0	SA	3	Danilinho [64]	14 740
Jun	6	Bahia	D	1-1	SA	3	Jo [52p]	16 580
	9	Palmeiras	D	1-0	SA	2	Jo [48]	7 268
	17	São Paulo	L	0-1	SA	3	Luis Fabiano [43]	11 656
	23	Náutico	W	5-1	SA	2	Bernard [1], Ronaldinho [34p], Danilinho 2 [36 61], Escudero [92+]	16 367
Jul	1	Grêmio	W	1-0	SA	1	Jo [26]	34 550
	8	Portuguesa	W	2-0	SA	1	Marcos Rocha [24], Leonardo Silva [52]	18 875
	14	Figueirense	W	4-3	SA	1	Leonardo Silva [64], Bernard [68], Guilherme [73]	10 303
	18	Inter	W	3-1	SA	1	Guilherme [45], Leonardo Silva [59], Escudero [92+]	19 181
	21	Sport Recife	W	4-1	SA	1	Danilinho [31], Ronaldinho [59], Jo [64], Bernard [72]	16 230
	24	Santos	W	2-0	SA	1	Danilinho [43], Rever [66]	20 418
	29	Fluminense	D	0-0	SA	1		16 175
Aug	9	Coritiba	W	1-0	SA	1	Rever [47]	19 288
	12	Vasco	W	1-0	SA	1	Jo [70]	19 650
	15	Atlético GO	D	1-1	SA	1	Bernard [28]	7 729
	19	Botafogo	W	3-2	SA	1	Escudero [43], Jo [54], Neto Berola [81p]	19 903
	26	Cruzeiro	D	2-2	SA	1	Leonardo Silva [45], Ronaldinho [90]	17 901
	29	Ponte Preta	D	2-2	SA	1	Danilinho [14], Guilherme [49]	18 644
Sep	2	Corinthians	L	0-1	SA	1		33 375
	5	Bahia	D	0-0	SA	2		19 629
	9	Palmeiras	W	3-0	SA	2	Leonardo Silva [53], Bernard 2 [84 93+]	18 003
	12	São Paulo	W	1-0	SA	2	Leonardo [64]	18 025
	16	Náutico	L	0-1	SA	2		15 013
	23	Grêmio	D	0-0	SA	2		19 668
	26	Flamengo	L	1-2	SA	2	Jo [50]	39 060
	29	Portuguesa	D	1-1	SA	2	Bernard [66]	5 971
Oct	6	Figueirense	W	6-0	SA	2	Ronaldinho 3 [12 32 63p], Rever [24], Bernard [68], Carlo Cesar [82]	16 952
	10	Inter	L	0-3	SA	3		3 372
	14	Sport Recife	W	2-1	SA	2	Leonardo 2 [77 91+]	14 265
	17	Santos	D	2-2	SA	2	Bernard [18], Jo [27]	10 553
	21	Fluminense	W	3-2	SA	2	Jo 2 [69 82], Leonardo Silva [93+]	20 096
	31	Flamengo	D	1-1	SA	2	Leonardo [57]	19 945
Nov	4	Coritiba	L	0-1	SA	2		18 216
	11	Vasco	D	1-1	SA	3	Ronaldinho [27p]	7036
	18	Atlético GO	D	2-2	SA	3	Rever [18], Ronaldinho [91+]	15 342
	25	Botafogo	W	3-2	SA	3	Bernard [15], Richarlyson [82], Rever [90]	3 039
Dc	2	Cruzeiro	W	3-2	SA	2	Bernard [5], OG [60], Rever [74]	21 232

2nd Att: 347 174 • Av: 18 272 (+29.7%) • Arena Independência 25 000

ATLETICO MG SERIE A APPEARANCES/GOALS 2012

Goalkeepers Giovanni 9 • Victor 29
Defenders Carlos Cesar 4+7/1 • Junior Cesar 31+1/0
Leonardo Silva 30+3/6 • Marcos Rocha 32+2/1
Rafael Marques 18+2/0 • Rever 28/6
Midfield Bernard 36/11 • Danilinho 20+1/6 • Dudu Cearense 2/0
Damian Escudero ARG 9+18/4 • Fillipe Soutto 4+4/0 • Leandro
Donizete 28+2/0 • Leleu 0+1/0 • Mancini 2+1/0 • Pierre 32/0
Richarlyson 11+12/1 • Ronaldinho 32/9 • Serginho 10+15/0
Forwards Andre 2+4/0 • Guilherme 15+11/3 • Jo 29/10
Juninho 0+3/0 • Leonardo 5+8/4 • Neto Berola 0+15/1
Paulo Henrique 0+2/0
Coach Cuca

BAHIA
2012

	18	Alagoinhas	D	3-3	TB		Junior Pipoca 2 [14 78], Rafael [66]	11 264
Jan	22	B. de Feira	L	0-1	TB			4 928
	25	Juazeirense	W	2-0	TB		Fahel [12], Lulinha [45]	5 460
	29	Serrano	W	3-1	TB		Lulinha [19], Rafael [81], Souza [88]	1 796
Feb	1	Feirense	W	3-2	TB		Souza 2 [14 81], Lulinha [86]	6 969
	5	Itabuna	W	4-3	TB		Fabinho [34], Souza 3 [52 86 97+p]	756
	8	V.Conquista	W	2-0	TB		Souza [37p], Gabriel [48]	4 808
	12	Vitória	D	0-0	TB			29 388
	16	Juazeiro	W	4-1	TB		Souza 2 [16 45], Gabriel [31], Junior Pipoca [34]	2 748
	23	Fluminense	W	4-0	TB		Magno [50], Fahel [80], Helder [88], Lenine [90]	8 130
	26	Camaçari	W	3-0	TB		Titi [44], Ciro [50], Junior Pipoca [55]	2 667
	29	Camaçari	W	5-1	TB		Junior Pipoca [24], Magno [34], Rafael Donato [51], Souza 2 [55 76]	8 849
Mar	4	Fluminense	W	2-0	TB		Junior Pipoca [17], Gabriel [70]	5 475
	8	AutoEsporte	W	3-0	CBr1		Rafael Donato [23], Souza [67], Gabriel [75]	773
	11	Juazeiro	D	1-1	TB		Rafael [86]	10 985
	18	Vitória	L	2-3	TB		Souza [21], Gabriel [22]	23 093
	22	V.Conquista	W	2-1	TB		Danny Morais [28], Souza [91+]	1 308
	25	Itabuna	W	7-1	TB		Souza 4 [1 12 49p 51], Magno [58], Junior Pipoca [85], Lenine [91+]	6 584
	29	Feirense	W	1-0	TB		Souza [39]	2 932
	1	Serrano	W	3-2	TB		Ciro 2 [4 16], Coelho [21p]	6 855
	5	Juazeirense	D	1-1	TB		Gabriel [18]	1 084
	8	B. de Feira	W	3-2	TB		Rafael Donato 2 [15 95+], Lulinha [90]	9 284
	12	Remo	L	1-2	CBr2		Diones [23]	23 449
Apr	15	Alagoinhas	W	2-1	TB		Junior Pipoca 2 [10 57]	4 018
	19	Remo	W	4-0	CBr2		Lulinha [59], Rafael Donato [73], Junior Pipoca [76], Vander [80]	14 896
	22	V.Conquista	L	0-1	TBsf			4 859
	25	Portuguesa	D	0-0	CBr3			2 369
	29	V.Conquista	W	1-0	TBsf		Rafael Donato [90]	19 358
	6	Vitória	D	0-0	TBf			31 263
	10	Portuguesa	W	2-0	CBr3		Fabinho [15], Junior Pipoca [71]	13 513
May	13	Vitória	D	3-3	TBf		Rafael [9], Gabriel [45], Diones [72]	32 157
	18	Grêmio	L	1-2	CBqf		Junior Pipoca [21]	11 807
	20	Santos	D	0-0	SA	11		8 908
	25	Grêmio	L	0-2	CBqf			35 726
	27	São Paulo	L	0-1	SA	18		10 305
	6	Atlético MG	D	1-1	SA	15	Fahel [68]	16 580
Jun	10	Vasco	L	1-2	SA	17	Jose Junior [90]	17 908
	17	Sport Recife	W	2-1	SA	14	Elias [14], Fahel [85]	11 031
	24	Fluminense	L	1-1	SA	15	Vander [78]	7 232
	1	Inter	D	1-1	SA	15	Gabriel [44]	13 474
	8	Botafogo	L	0-3	SA	17		16 718
	15	Flamengo	L	1-2	SA	19	Kleberson [38]	29 206
Jul	19	Fluminense	L	0-4	SA	19		5 393
	22	Coritiba	D	2-2	SA	19	Souza [9], Mancini [46]	8 380
	26	Palmeiras	W	2-0	SA	15	Souza 2 [69p 82]	7 515
	29	Corinthians	D	0-0	SA	17		24 648
	2	São Paulo	L	0-2	CSr2			
	5	Grêmio	L	1-3	SA	17	Fahel [64]	23 268
	8	Portuguesa	D	0-0	SA	18		8 166
	11	Cruzeiro	L	0-1	SA	18		8 946
Aug	15	Ponte Preta	W	2-0	SA	17	Gabriel [11], Souza [90]	4 259
	18	Náutico	L	0-1	SA	17		12 558
	22	São Paulo	L	0-2	CSr2			9 791
	26	Atlético GO	D	1-1	SA	16	Fabinho [7]	10 901
	29	Santos	W	3-1	SA	16	Souza [58], Neto [62], Gabriel [72]	8 612
Sep	2	São Paulo	L	1-0	SA	15	Gabriel [71]	25 945
	5	Atlético MG	D	0-0	SA	17	Fabinho [7]	10 901
	9	Vasco	W	4-0	SA	14	Souza 2 [41 70], Jones 2 [49 70]	5 018
	12	Sport Recife	D	1-1	SA	15	Helder [84]	17 107
	16	Figueirense	W	2-1	SA	15	Helder [72], Claudio Pitbull [90]	22 041
	23	Inter	L	1-3	SA	15	Kleberson [90]	9 052
	30	Botafogo	W	2-0	SA	12	Fahel [18], Helder [85]	22 708
Oct	4	Flamengo	D	0-0	SA	13		25 777
	10	Fluminense	L	0-2	SA	16		21 998

BAHIA 2012 (CONT'D)

Oct	14	Coritiba	L	1-2	SA 16	Alysson [14]	11 148
	17	Palmeiras	L	0-1	SA 16		18 459
	20	Corinthians	D	1-1	SA 16	Fahel [33]	21 757
	27	Grêmio	D	1-1	SA 16	Gabriel [40]	32 157
Nov	4	Portuguesa	W	1-0	SA 16	Souza [78]	4 340
	11	Cruzeiro	L	1-3	SA 16	Fahel [28]	7 772
	18	Ponte Preta	W	1-0	SA 15	Neto [81]	24 004
	25	Náutico	D	1-1	SA 16	Gabriel [51]	32 157
Dc	2	Atlético GO	W	1-0	SA 15	Rafael [89]	2 358

15th   Att: 360 666 • Av: 18 982 (-17.1%) • Pituaçu 32 179

BAHIA SERIE A APPEARANCES/GOALS 2012

Goalkeepers Marcelo Lomba 36 • Omar 2
Defenders Avine 8/0 • Alysson 3/1 • Danny Morais 28/0 • Dudu 0+1/0 • Gerley 2+1/0 • Gil Bahia 2+1/0 • Jussandro 18/0 • Madson 1/0
Neto 19/2 • Rafael Donato 2/0 • Romario 2+1/0 • Titi 34/0
Midfield Caio 1+5/0 • Diones 30+4/0 • Fabinho 25+5/1 • Fahel 34/6
Helder 30+2/3 • Jeferson 0+2/0 • Jones 15+3/2 • Kleberson 8+11/2
Lucas Fonseca 8+2/0 • Lulinha 6+16/0 • Magno 3+4/0
Mancini 10+5/1 • Morais 1/0 • Ryder Matos 0+1/0 • Vander 1+6/1
Victor Lemos 2+5/0 • Ze Roberto 21+5/0
Forwards Ciro 2+6/0 • Claudio Pitbull 0+7/1 • Diego Oliveira 2/0
Elias 10+6/1 • Gabriel 24+1/6 • Jose Junior 6+5/1 • Rafael 3+6/1
Souza 19/8
Coach Falcao • Caio Junior (20/07/12) • Jorginho (27/08/2012)

BOTAFOGO 2012

Jan	22	Resende	W	3-1	TG	Abreu 2 [29 67], Maicosuel [66]	8 238
	29	Nova Iguaçu	D	0-0	TG		3 166
	2	Madureira	D	2-2	TG	Herrera [75], OG [85]	1 957
	5	Flamengo	D	0-0	TG		12 439
Feb	8	Olaria	W	5-0	TG	Abreu 2 [12 65], Elkeson 2 [23 39], Maicosuel [86]	3 054
	11	Bonsucesso	W	4-1	TG	Maicosuel [43], Abreu [47], Herrera 2 [72 90]	5 762
	18	Macaé	W	3-0	TG	Herrera [27], Felipe Menezes [35], Elkeson [87]	3 990
	23	Fluminense	D	1-1	TGsf	Elkeson [74]. L 3-4p	21 143
	1	Americano	W	4-2	TR	Fellype Gabriel [31], Renato [73], Herrera [77], Caio [90]	3 960
	4	V. Redonda	W	3-1	TR	Herrera 2 [16 75], Antonio Carlos [88]	2 062
Mar	10	Bangu	D	1-1	TR	Cidinho [74]	4 482
	14	Treze	D	1-1	CBr1	Herrera [67]	6 007
	18	Vasco	W	3-1	TR	Fellype Gabriel 3 [33 37 71]	11 941
	21	Treze	D	1-1	CBr1	Abreu [23]. W 3-2p	4 414
	24	D de Caxias	W	2-0	TR	Fellype Gabriel [36], Jobson [68]	4 762
	1	Fluminense	W	2-0	TR	Elkeson [18]	11 340
	4	Guarani	W	2-1	CBr2	Renato [44], Herrera [67]	3 612
	8	Friburgense	W	3-2	TR	Abreu [34], Herrera 2 [81 86]	4 452
Apr	15	Boavista	D	1-1	TR	Caio [53]	1 295
	18	Guarani	D	0-0	CBr2		5 295
	21	Bangu	W	4-2	TRsf	Abreu 3 [39 47 59], Maicosuel [91+]	19 786
	29	Vasco	W	3-1	TRf	Abreu 2 [3 45], Maicosuel [52]	41 387
May	2	Vitória	D	1-1	CBr3	Elkeson [28]	11 371
	6	Fluminense	L	1-4	TG/Rf	Renato [8]	28 182
	9	Vitória	L	1-2	CBr3	Elkeson [21]	8 246
	13	Fluminense	L	0-1	TG/Rf		25 016

BOTAFOGO 2012 (CONT'D)

May	20	São Paulo	W	4-2	SA 1	German Herrera 3 [49 67p 77], Vitor Junior [72]	9 180
	27	Coritiba	W	3-2	SA 1	Lucas 2 [18 87], Vitor Junior [26]	14 369
	7	Cruzeiro	L	2-3	SA 4	OG [20], German Herrera [69]	6 900
Jun	10	Náutico	L	2-3	SA 6	Marcio Azevedo [47], Fabio Ferreira [59]	12 354
	16	Inter	W	2-1	SA 4	Andrezinho [58], Fellype Gabriel [73]	12 419
	24	Ponte Preta	L	1-2	SA 7	Andrezinho [44p]	6 713
	3	Bahia	W	3-0	SA 5	Cidinho 2 [5 45], Elkeson [48]	16 718
	11	Corinthians	W	3-1	SA 4	OG [28], Elkeson 2 [57 69]	25 900
	15	Fluminense	D	1-1	SA 4	Andrezinho [66]	17 122
Jul	18	Santos	D	0-0	SA 5		7 069
	22	Grêmio	L	0-1	SA 8		29 943
	25	Vasco	L	0-1	SA 8		17 778
	28	Figueirense	W	1-0	SA 8	Andrezinho [61]	3 401
	2	Palmeiras	L	0-2	CSr2		
	4	Atlético GO	W	2-1	SA 7	Clarence Seedorf [64], Fellype Gabriel [75]	7 309
	8	Palmeiras	L	1-2	SA 7	Andrezinho [58]	3 550
	12	Portuguesa	D	1-1	SA 8	Elkeson [19]	3 108
Aug	15	Sport Recife	W	2-0	SA 6	Elkeson [66], Seedorf [76]	2 457
	19	Atlético MG	L	2-3	SA 7	Andrezinho 2 [36 81p]	19 903
	23	Palmeiras	W	3-1	CSr2	Seedorf [34], Renato [56], Lodeiro [73]	
	26	Flamengo	D	0-0	SA 7		15 090
	30	São Paulo	L	0-4	SA 8		15 576
	2	Coritiba	W	2-0	SA 8	Elkeson [14], Lodeiro [28]	2 616
	5	Cruzeiro	W	3-1	SA 7	Seedorf 2 [35 37], Jadson [56]	13 957
	9	Náutico	W	3-1	SA 5	Elkeson 2 [1 34], Andrezinho [90]	14 612
Sep	13	Inter	D	1-1	SA 5	Cicinho [77]	9 148
	16	Ponte Preta	D	0-0	SA 6		5 922
	23	Corinthians	D	2-2	SA 6	Seedorf 2 [6 75]	13 775
	30	Bahia	L	0-2	SA 7		22 708
	6	Fluminense	L	0-1	SA 7		16 919
	10	Santos	L	0-2	SA 6		2 986
	14	Grêmio	D	1-1	SA 8	Bruno Mendes [90]	27 529
Oct	18	Vasco	W	3-2	SA 7	Elkeson [30], Bruno Mendes 2 [75 90]	7 525
	24	Figueirense	W	2-0	SA 6	Bruno Mendes [14], Seedorf [32]	8 117
	27	Atlético GO	W	4-0	SA 6	Seedorf [21], Doria [45], Gabriel [48], Bruno Mendes [80]	8 303
	4	Palmeiras	D	2-2	SA 4	Lodeiro [20], Elkeson [64]	13 228
Nov	10	Portuguesa	W	3-0	SA 5	Bruno Mendes [13], Fellype Gabriel [67], Vitor Junior [70]	5 794
	18	Sport Recife	L	0-2	SA 6		25 126
	25	Atlético MG	L	2-3	SA 7	Antonio Carlos [29], Elkeson [31]	3 039
Dc	2	Flamengo	D	2-2	SA 7	Sassa [5], Vitor Junior [48]	6 674

7th   Att: 178 872 • Av: 9 414 (-33.6%) • Engenhão 46 931

BOTAFOGO SERIE A APPEARANCES/GOALS 2012

Goalkeepers Jefferson 30 • Milton Raphael 2 • Renan 6
Defenders Antonio Carlos 20/1 • Brinner 10+5/0 • Doria 18+2/1
Fabio Ferreira 28/1 • Gabriel 17+5/1 • Gilberto 0+2/0
Jonh Lennon 6+2/0 • Lima 4+2/0 • Lucas 32/2 • Marcio Azevedo 33/1
Vinicius 0+1/0
Midfield Amaral 4+2/0 • Andrezinho 31+1/8 • Cidinho 4+9/3
Elkeson 23+8/11 • Fellype Gabriel 25+7/3 • Jadson 22+7/1 • Jeferson Filho 0+3/0 • Nicolas Lodeiro URU 14+4/2 • Lucas Zen 7+4/0
Maicosuel 4+2/0 • Marcelo Mattos 0+2/0 • Renato 26+2/0
Rodriguinho 0+3/0 • Clarence Seedorf NED 21+3/8
Vitor Junior 13+11/4
Forwards Sebastian Abreu URU 2/0 • Bruno Mendes 6+2/6 • German Herrera ARG 4+1/4 • Rafael 5+10/0 • Sassa 1+2/1 • Willian 0+5/0
Coach Oswaldo de Oliveira

CORINTHIANS
2012

Jan	21	Mirassol	W 2-1	CP	Elton [75], OG [88]	16 117
	25	Guarati'ta	W 2-0	CP	Chicao [27], Alessandro [42]	11 003
	29	Linense	W 1-0	CP	Emerson [79]	15 105
Feb	1	Ituano	W 1-0	CP	Paulinho [32]	11 269
	5	Bragantino	D 1-1	CP	Ramirez [51]	16 282
	8	Mogi Mirim	D 1-1	CP	Emerson [14]	7 313
	12	São Paulo	W 1-0	CP	Danilo [21]	26 166
	15	Dep Táchira	D 1-1	CLg6	Ralf [94+]	12 532
	18	S. Caetano	W 1-0	CP	Willian [63]	5 609
	22	Portuguesa	W 2-0	CP	Willian [29], Ramirez [78]	6 167
	25	Botafogo RP	W 1-0	CP	Adriano [3]	17 162
	29	Catan'ense	W 2-1	CP	Paulinho [80], Danilo [91+]	9 496
Mar	4	Santos	L 0-1	CP		12 818
	7	Nacional	W 2-0	CLg6	Danilo [38], Jorge Henrique [67]	32 336
	10	Guarani	D 1-1	CP	Fumagalli [87]	15 412
	14	Cruz Azul	D 0-0	CLg6		29 333
	18	Comercial	D 3-3	CP	Emerson [35], Gilsinho [91+], Ramon [93+]	12 870
	21	Cruz Azul	W 1-0	CLg6	Danilo [35]	29 931
	25	Palmeiras	W 2-1	CP	Paulinho [48], OG [51]	29 284
	28	Piracicaba	W 1-0	CP	Ramon [46]	6 960
Apr	1	Oeste	W 3-0	CP	Liedson 2 [54 90], Willian [63]	8 438
	8	Paulista	W 1-0	CP	Willian [79]	13 006
	11	Nacional	W 3-1	CLg6	Jorge Henrique [28], Emerson [51], Elton [71]	7 000
	15	Ponte Preta	W 2-1	CP	Chicao [46p], Welder [50]	7 418
	18	Dep Táchira	W 6-0	CLg6	Danilo [17], Paulinho [26], Jorge Henrique [62], Emerson [70], Liedson [72], Douglas [83p]	27 379
	22	Ponte Preta	L 2-3	CPqf	Willian [74], Alex [90]	24 254
May	2	Emelec	D 0-0	CLr2		16 974
	9	Emelec	W 3-0	CLr2	Fabio Santos [7], Paulinho [64], Alex [85]	32 577
	16	Vasco	D 0-0	CLqf		20 510
	20	Fluminense	L 0-1	SA 17		14 791
	23	Vasco	W 1-0	CLqf	Paulinho [87]	35 974
	27	Atlético MG	D 0-1	SA 19		14 740
Jun	7	Figueirense	D 1-1	SA 18	Danilo [38]	21 912
	10	Grêmio	L 0-2	SA 20		16 803
	13	Santos	W 1-0	CLsf	Emerson [28]	14 788
	17	Ponte Preta	L 0-1	SA 20		6 316
	20	Santos	D 1-1	CLsf	Danilo [47]	35 873
	24	Palmeiras	W 2-1	SA 17	Romarinho 2 [34 56]	17 519
	27	Boca Jun	D 1-1	CLf	Romarinho [84]	41 901
Jul	4	Boca Jun	W 2-0	CLf	Emerson 2 [53 72]	37 500
	8	Sport Recife	D 1-1	SA 19	Liedson [75]	23 009
	11	Botafogo	L 1-3	SA 19	Chicao [90p]	25 900
	14	Náutico	W 2-1	SA 14	Danilo 2 [22 49]	23 198
	18	Flamengo	W 3-0	SA 13	Douglas 2 [28 40], Danilo [55]	12 027
	21	Portuguesa	D 1-1	SA 13	Douglas [49]	31 106
	25	Cruzeiro	W 2-0	SA 11	Chicao [23p], Paulinho [94+]	28 759
	29	Bahia	D 0-0	SA 9		24 648
Aug	5	Vasco	W 1-0	SA 10		15 655
	8	Atlético GO	D 1-1	SA 11	Paulinho [78]	24 372
	12	Coritiba	W 2-1	SA 10	Paulinho [65], Romarinho [90]	16 139
	16	Inter	W 1-0	SA 9	Paulo Andre [69]	27 282
	19	Santos	L 2-3	SA 10	Danilo [09], Bruno Rodrigo [84]	12 413
	26	São Paulo	L 1-2	SA 10	Emerson [5]	34 843
	29	Fluminense	D 1-1	SA 12	Emerson [36]	7 358
Sep	2	Atlético MG	W 1-0	SA 9	Paulo Andre [64]	33 375
	5	Figueirense	L 0-1	SA 12		11 142
	8	Grêmio	W 3-1	SA 8	Ralf [6], Guilherme [11], Giovanni [90]	24 850
	12	Ponte Preta	D 1-1	SA 9	Emerson [90]	19 844
	16	Palmeiras	W 2-0	SA 9	Romarinho [22], Paulinho [54]	26 068
	23	Botafogo	D 2-2	SA 8	Guerrero [8], Douglas [13p]	13 775
	30	Sport Recife	W 3-0	SA 8	Paulinho [55], Romarinho 2 [70 84]	25 277
Oct	6	Náutico	L 1-2	SA 8	Guerrero [45]	19 005
	10	Flamengo	W 3-2	SA 7	Edenilson [61], Paulo Andre [75], Emerson [90]	25 395
	13	Portuguesa	D 1-1	SA 7	Douglas [17]	7 397
	17	Cruzeiro	L 0-2	SA 9		7 223
	20	Bahia	W 1-0	SA 8	Douglas [12p]	21 757
	27	Vasco	W 1-0	SA 8	Guerrero [57]	24 376

CORINTHIANS 2012 (CONT'D)

Nov	4	Atlético GO	W 2-0	SA 8	Martinez [54], Guilherme [91+]	8 931
	10	Coritiba	W 5-1	SA 6	Chicao [5p], Fabio Santos [18], Paulinho 2 [20 68], Guerrero [64]	23 420
	18	Inter	W 2-0	SA 5	Guerrero [45], Edenilson [91+]	6 850
	24	Santos	D 1-1	SA 5	Wallace [80]	36 482
Dc	2	São Paulo	L 1-3	SA 6	Guerrero [13]	22 436
	12	Al Ahly	W 1-0	CWsf	Guerrero [30]	31 417
	16	Chelsea	W 1-0	CWf	Guerrero [67]	68 275
6th					Att: 484 458 • Av: 25 498 (-14.9%) • Pacaembu 37 952	

CORINTHIANS SERIE A APPEARANCES/GOALS 2012

Goalkeepers Cassio 32 • Danilo Fernandes 1 • Julio Cesar 4
Defenders Alessandro 26/0 • Anderson Polga 2+1/0
Antonio Carlos 3/0 • Chicao 20/3 • Denner 1+2/0 • Fabio Santos 29/1
Felipe Monteiro 0+3/0 • Guilherme 7+5/2 • Leandro Castan 2/0
Marquinhos 5+1/0 • Paulo Andre 29/3 • Ramon 6/0 • Rodinei 0+1/0
Wallace 20+2/1 • Welder 8+2/0
Midfield Alex 4/0 • Chiquinho 0+3/0 • Danilo 24+1/5
Douglas 31+4/6 • Edenilson 10+11/2 • Giovanni 0+9/1 • Paulinho 23/7
Ralf 29/1 • Luis Ramirez PER 3+7/0 • Willian Arao 8/0
Forwards Adilson 1+10/0 • Chen 0+1/0 • Elton 4+4/0
Emerson QAT 13+1/4 • Gilsinho 1+2/0 • Paolo Guerrero PER 11+4/6
Jorge Henrique 8+9/0 • Liedson POR 3+3/1 • Juan Martinez ARG 11+7/2
Romarinho 28+4/6 • Willian 5/0
Coach Tite

CORITIBA
2012

Jan	22	Toledo	W 2-0	CP	Rafinha [3], Emerson [89]	3 889
	25	Corinthians	W 2-0	CP	Lincoln [31], Marcel [88]	10 998
	28	Iraty	W 5-1	CP	Davi 2 [37 47], Renan Oliveira 2 [71 91+], Jackson [72]	9 104
	31	Paranavai	W 3-1	CP	Marcel [23], Willian Farias [60], Renan Oliveira [89]	2 169
Feb	4	Arapongas	W 4-1	CP	Lincoln [8], Marcel [41], Rafinha [50], Emerson [89]	9 665
	8	Londrina	D 1-1	CP	Everton Ribeiro [87]	2 646
	12	Rio Branco	D 1-1	CP	Davi [29]	9 924
	15	Cianorte	D 1-1	CP	Junior Urso [45]	1 693
	19	Operário	W 4-1	CP	Caio Vinicius [1], Renan Oliveira [3], Jackson [59], Gil [85]	4 971
	22	Atlético PR	D 0-0	CP		5 397
	26	Roma	W 5-0	CP	Rafinha 2 [10 29], OG [46], Lincoln [60], Emerson [72]	6 976
Mar	1	Toledo	W 1-0	CP	Marcel [88]	9 076
	4	Corinthians	W 2-1	CP	Pereira [36], Emerson [40]	113
	11	Iraty	W 5-1	CP	Lincoln 3 [17 69 72], Emerson [41], Junior Urso [75]	1 564
	14	Nacional	D 0-0	CBr1		1 502
	18	Paranavai	W 3-1	CP	Anderson Aquino 2 [58 81], Lincoln [70]	9 550
	22	Nacional	W 2-0	CBr1	Anderson Aquino 2 [19 91+]	12 339
	25	Arapongas	L 0-2	CP		1 966
	28	Londrina	W 1-0	CP	Roberto [50]	11 382
	1	Rio Branco	W 2-1	CP	Emerson [36], Demerson [76]	1 835
	4	ASA	L 0-1	CBr2		5 428
	8	Cianorte	W 3-1	CP	Emerson [30], Roberto [75], Everton Ribeiro [85]	6 924
	11	ASA	W 3-0	CBr2	Tcheco [38p], Anderson Aquino [45], Everton Ribeiro [71]	11 811
Apr	15	Operário	D 2-2	CP	Roberto [4], Everton Ribeiro [60]	5 817
	22	Atlético PR	W 4-2	CP	Everton Ribeiro [2], Lincoln [59], Roberto [76], Renan Oliveira [93+]	18 572
	26	Paysandu	W 4-1	CBr3	Anderson Aquino [33], Roberto [34], Everton Ribeiro [43], Tcheco [94+p]	9 228
	29	Roma	W 3-1	CP	Rafael Silva [26], Vaio Vinicius [78], Renan Oliveira [85]	153
May	3	Paysandu	W 1-0	CBr3	Tcheco [9]	36 515
	6	Atlético PR	D 2-2	CPf	Everton Ribeiro [19], Anderson Aquino [79]	8 460
	13	Atlético PR	D 0-0	CPf	W 5-4p	23 605

CORITIBA 2012 (CONT'D)

	16 Vitória	D	0-0	CBqf		8 632
	20 Inter	L	0-2	SA 20		19 000
May	23 Vitória	W	4-1	CBqf	Everton Costa 2 [29 88], Everton Ribeiro [44p], Roberto [62]	15 692
	27 Botafogo	L	2-3	SA 20	Lincoln [1], Lucas Mendes [51]	14 369
	6 Portuguesa	W	2-0	SA 10	Ayrton [18], Everton Costa [44]	8 959
	9 Flamengo	L	1-3	SA 14	Emerson [24]	6 142
	14 São Paulo	L	0-1	CBsf		40 448
Jun	17 Atlético GO	W	3-0	SA 11	Pereira [24], Marcel [72], Tcheco [74]	8 704
	20 São Paulo	W	2-0	CBsf	Emerson [29], Everton Ribeiro [62]	28 244
	24 Santos	D	2-2	SA 11	Rafinha [50], Lincoln [75p]	5 120
	1 Sport Recife	L	2-3	SA 13	Anderson Aquino [13], Tcheco [25]	12 447
	5 Palmeiras	L	0-2	CBf		28 557
	8 São Paulo	L	1-3	SA 16	Robinho [71p]	21 336
	11 Palmeiras	D	1-1	CBf	Ayrton [62]	35 122
Jul	14 Ponte Preta	L	1-4	SA 17	Pereira [39]	2 857
	19 Palmeiras	D	1-1	SA 15	Anderson Aquino [67]	11 998
	22 Bahia	D	2-2	SA 16	Everton Costa [64], Emerson [68]	8 380
	25 Náutico	W	4-3	SA 14	Robson [15], Leonardo 2 [46 56p], Pereira [77]	11 453
	28 Grêmio	W	2-1	SA 12	Ayrton [61], Leonardo [90]	17 619
	1 Grêmio	L	0-1	CSr2		
	5 Fluminense	L	0-2	SA 14		16 523
	9 Atlético MG	L	0-1	SA 15		19 288
	11 Corinthians	L	1-2	SA 15	Everton Ribeiro [45]	16 139
Aug	16 Vasco	D	2-2	SA 16	Junior Urso [22], Everton Ribeiro [90]	5 013
	19 Cruzeiro	W	4-0	SA 15	Lucas Mendes [20], Ayrton [37], Roberto [49], And. Aquino [78]	11 739
	22 Grêmio	W	3-2	CSr2	Everton Ribeiro [22], Roberto [52], Pereira [66]	
	26 Figueirense	L	1-3	SA 15	Anderson Aquino [32]	5 145
	29 Inter	W	1-0	SA 15	Rafinha [55]	12 200
	2 Botafogo	L	0-2	SA 16		2 616
	5 Portuguesa	L	0-3	SA 16		1 600
Sep	8 Flamengo	W	3-0	SA 16	Lincoln [16], Rafinha [56], Everton Ribeiro [71]	12 003
	12 Atlético GO	W	2-1	SA 13	Robson [1], Deivid [59]	697
	16 Santos	L	1-2	SA 15	Deivid [9]	20 274
	23 Sport Recife	L	0-1	SA 16		17 075
	30 São Paulo	D	1-1	SA 16	Everton Ribeiro [60p]	15 061
	4 Ponte Preta	W	1-0	SA 16	Deivid [42]	10 141
	7 Palmeiras	W	1-0	SA 14	Deivid [89p]	10 655
Oct	14 Bahia	W	2-1	SA 12	Lucas Claro [10], Deivid [71]	11 148
	17 Náutico	W	2-1	SA 11	OG [1], Deivid [37]	12 174
	20 Grêmio	D	0-0	SA 10		20 676
	25 Fluminense	L	1-2	SA 12	Everton Ribeiro [82]	29 994
	4 Atlético MG	W	1-0	SA 10	Deivid [9p]	18 216
Nov	7 Corinthians	L	1-5	SA 14	Deivid [31]	23 420
	10 Vasco	L	1-2	SA 14	Lincoln [10]	10 545
	25 Cruzeiro	L	1-2	SA 14	Everton Ribeiro [91+]	12 448
Dc	2 Figueirense	W	3-0	SA 13	Everton Ribeiro 2 [9 88], Denis [63]	3 770

13th Att: 244 172 • Av: 12 851 (-30.7%) • Couto Pereira 37 182

CORITIBA SERIE A APPEARANCES/GOALS 2012
Goalkeepers Bruno 1 • Vanderlei 36 • Victor Brasil 1
Defenders Ayrton 17+2/3 • Demerson 15/0 • Denis 11/1
Eltinho 8+2/0 • Emerson 10+2/2 • Sergio Escudero ARG 20/0
Everton Ribeiro 27+2/8 • Jonas 5+1/0 • Lucas Claro 15+2/1
Lucas Mendes 13/2 • Pereira 12+3/3 • Victor Ferraz 13+1/0
Midfield Chico 10+6/0 • Franca 3+1/0 • Geraldo 0+1/0 • Gil 18+6/0
Junior Urso 16+8/1 • Lincoln 26+7/4 • Rafael Silva 0+7/0
Rafinha 22+1/3 • Renan Oliveira 1+2/0 • Robson 18+7/3 • Sergio
Manoel 8+1/0 • Tcheco 3+1/2 • Thiago Primao 2+9/0 • Vinicius 3+1/0
Willian 28/0 • Willian Leandro 1+1/0
Forwards Alex 1+2/0 • Anderson Aquino 5+8/4 • Deivid 13/8
Everton Costa 12+3/2 • Leonardo 5+1/3 • Marcel 6+6/1
Roberto 8+9/1 • Raul Ruidiaz PER 0+8/0
Coach Marcelo Oliveira • Marquinhos dos Santos ((6/09/12)

CRUZEIRO 2012

	5 Guarani MG	L	0-1	CM		4 825
Feb	12 Tupi	W	3-0	CM	Wellington Paulista [3], Anselmo Ramon 2 [67 69]	1 923
	16 Nacional	W	4-2	CM	Wellington Paulista 3 [17 72 73], Wallyson [91+]	3 120
	25 Democrata	W	2-0	CM	Montillo 2 [46 78]	8 650
	3 América TO	W	2-0	CM	Wellington Paulista 2 [24 43]	3 098
	7 Rio Branco	W	6-0	CBr1	Wallyson 3 [7 50 82], Anselmo Ramon [38], Leo [68], Rudnei [77]	5 173
	11 Villa Nova	W	2-0	CM	Walter [38], Montillo [76]	3 561
Mar	18 Caldense	W	5-0	CM	Wellington Paulista [20], Victorino [38], Anselmo Ramon 2 [46 72], Wallyson [59]	7 200
	25 América MG	W	2-1	CM	Anselmo Ramon [41], Walter [73]	10 337
	31 Boa	W	2-0	CM	Wellington Paulista [57], Montillo [66]	11 186
	8 Atlético MG	D	2-2	CM	Anselmo Ramon 2 [60 79]	17 724
	11 Chap'oense	D	1-1	CBr2	Walter [61]	7 085
	15 Uberaba	W	3-2	CM	Wellington Paulista 2 [67 89], Victorino [84]	3 439
Apr	18 Chap'oense	W	4-1	CBr2	Thiago Carvalho [44], Wellington Paulista 2 [66 78], Anselmo Ramon [75]	4 078
	22 América MG	L	2-3	CMsf	Bobo [85], Roger [88]	4 587
	29 América MG	L	1-2	CMsf	Wellington Paulista [28]	17 780
	2 Atlético PR	L	0-1	CBr3		6 581
May	9 Atlético PR	L	1-2	CBr3	Wellington Paulista [40p]	8 769
	20 Atlético GO	D	0-0	SA 11		3 952
	26 Náutico	D	0-0	SA 12		13 605
	7 Botafogo	D	3-2	SA 8	Anselmo Ramon [74], Everton [75], Wellington Paulista [80p]	6 900
	10 Sport Recife	W	1-0	SA 5	Wellington Paulista [70p]	4 574
Jun	16 Figueirense	W	1-0	SA 2	Wellington Paulista [67]	12 883
	23 Vasco	W	3-1	SA 1	Montillo [41], Wellington Paulista [64], Anselmo Ramon [80]	18 337
	30 São Paulo	L	2-3	SA 4	Rafael Donato 2 [13 54]	17 695
	7 Inter	L	1-2	SA 7	Leo [65]	9 349
	15 Grêmio	L	1-3	SA 10	Wellington Paulista [94+p]	15 523
Jul	18 Portuguesa	W	2-0	SA 6	Wellington Paulista [79p], Diego Renan [84]	2 409
	22 Flamengo	W	1-0	SA 5	Borges [44]	16 277
	25 Corinthians	L	0-2	SA 6		28 759
	29 Palmeiras	W	2-1	SA 5	Borges 2 [36p 55]	11 512
	5 Ponte Preta	L	1-2	SA 8	Borges [45]	15 103
	8 Santos	L	2-4	SA 8	Borges [28], Ceara [31]	3 215
	11 Bahia	W	1-0	SA 6	Montillo [8]	8 946
Aug	15 Fluminense	D	1-1	SA 7	Wellington Paulista [2]	13 551
	19 Coritiba	L	0-4	SA 8		11 739
	26 Atlético MG	D	2-2	SA 8	Wallyson [18], Mateus [102+]	17 901
	29 Atlético GO	W	2-0	SA 6	Borges [26], Wellington Paulista [70p]	2 675
	2 Náutico	W	3-0	SA 6	Borges [75], Elber [87], Wellington Paulista [90]	11 673
	5 Botafogo	L	1-3	SA 8	Tinga [20]	13 957
Sep	9 Sport Recife	L	1-2	SA 8	Wallyson [10]	12 165
	12 Figueirense	L	0-2	SA 8		6 917
	16 Vasco	D	1-1	SA 8	OG [4]	9 753
	23 São Paulo	L	0-1	SA 9		40 457
	29 Inter	D	0-0	SA 9		7 395
	6 Grêmio	L	1-2	SA 10	Anselmo Ramon [27]	27 843
	10 Portuguesa	W	2-0	SA 9	Montillo [36p], Souza [94+]	2 344
	13 Flamengo	D	1-1	SA 11	Everton [19]	15 992
Oct	17 Corinthians	W	2-0	SA 8	Anselmo Ramon [20], Martinuccio [60]	7 223
	20 Palmeiras	L	0-2	SA 9		9 873
	28 Ponte Preta	L	0-1	SA 9		6 480
	3 Santos	L	0-4	SA 13		16 331
Nov	11 Bahia	W	3-1	SA 10	Martinuccio 2 [53 68], Willian Magrao [89]	7 772
	18 Fluminense	W	2-0	SA 8	Walter Montillo [24p], Elber [48]	35 167
	25 Coritiba	W	2-1	SA 8	Tinga [7], Leandro Guerrero [60]	12 448
Dc	2 Atlético MG	L	2-3	SA 9	Martinuccio [45], Everton [50]	21 232

9th Att: 200 347 • Av: 11 467 (+8.7%) • Arena do Jacaré 25 000

CRUZEIRO SERIE A APPEARANCES/GOALS 2012

Goalkeepers Fabio 37 • Rafael 1
Defenders Alex Silva 1/0 • Ceara 20/1 • Diego Renan 15+10/1
Leo 26/1 • Marcos 1/0 • Mateus 18+2/1 • Rafael Donato 10+1/2
Thiago Carvalho 18/0 • Mauricio Victorino URU 8+1/0
Midfield Alisson 0+1/0 • Amaral 5/0 • Diego Arias COL 2/0
Charles 23+2/0 • Eber 0+1/0 • Elber 1+9/2 • Everton 26+3/3
Leandro Guerreiro 29+1/1 • Lucas Silva 4+4/0 • Marcelo
Oliveira 19+6/0 • Walter Montillo ARG 32/4 • Sandro Silva 9+2/0
Souza 9+20/1 • Tinga 22+4/2 • Willian Magrao 9+9/1
Forwards Anselmo Ramon 12+12/4 • Borges 15+2/7 • Fabinho 9+6/0
• Alejandro Martinuccio ARG 8+2/4 • Wallyson 10+7/2
Wellington Paulista 19+8/9
Coach Celso Roth

FIGUEIRENSE 2012 (CONT'D)

May	19	Náutico	W	2-1	SA	3	Fernandes [75], Caio [94+]	5 185
	27	Fluminense	D	2-2	SA	5	Caio [57], Pablo Barros [74]	7 462
	7	Corinthians	D	1-1	SA	6	Caio [79]	21 912
Jun	10	Ponte Preta	D	0-0	SA	9		5 901
	16	Cruzeiro	L	0-1	SA	12		12 883
	24	Bahia	D	1-1	SA	14	Julio Cesar [51]	7 232
	1	Palmeiras	L	1-3	SA	16	Julio Cesar [30]	2 580
	8	Vasco	D	1-1	SA	15	Roni [74]	15 526
	14	Atlético MG	L	3-4	SA	16	Anderson Conceicao [37], Julio Cesar [45], Roni [59]	10 303
Jul	19	Atlético GO	L	2-3	SA	17	Caio 2 [23p 62]	1 112
	22	São Paulo	L	0-2	SA	18		9 445
	25	Inter	L	0-1	SA	20		8 944
	28	Botafogo	L	0-1	SA	20		3 401
	1	Atlético GO	D	1-1	CSr2			
	4	Portuguesa	L	0-2	SA	20		1 600
	8	Flamengo	L	0-2	SA	20		11 307
	11	Sport Recife	W	1-0	SA	19	Aloisio [55]	11 258
Aug	16	Santos	L	1-3	SA	20	Fernandes [48]	10 993
	19	Grêmio	L	0-4	SA	20		18 205
	23	Atlético GO	D	1-1	CSr2			
	26	Coritiba	W	3-1	SA	20	Aloisio 3 [20 25 51]	5 145
	29	Náutico	L	2-3	SA	20	Caio [10], Aloisio [20]	10 880
	1	Fluminense	D	2-2	SA	20	Aloisio [68], Joao Paulo [87]	8 943
	5	Corinthians	W	1-0	SA	19	Caio [47]	11 142
	8	Ponte Preta	D	2-2	SA	19	Aloisio [16], Caio [45]	4 541
Sep	12	Cruzeiro	W	2-0	SA	18	Joao Paulo [35], Aloisio [86]	6 917
	16	Bahia	L	1-2	SA	18	Julio Cesar [33]	22 041
	22	Palmeiras	L	1-3	SA	19	Aloisio [65]	11 062
	29	Vasco	L	1-3	SA	19	Caio [12]	5 062
	6	Atlético MG	L	0-6	SA	19		16 952
	10	Atlético GO	W	3-1	SA	19	Aloisio [11], Roni 2 [33 82]	2 600
	14	São Paulo	L	0-2	SA	19		27 641
Oct	17	Inter	W	3-2	SA	19	Aloisio 2 [45 90], Roni [88]	4 649
	24	Botafogo	L	0-2	SA	19		8 117
	27	Portuguesa	D	0-0	SA	19		3 118
	3	Flamengo	L	0-1	SA	19		6 776
Nov	11	Sport Recife	D	1-1	SA	19	Julio Cesar [63]	3 122
	17	Santos	L	0-1	SA	19		10 013
	25	Grêmio	L	2-4	SA	20	Aloisio 2 [65p 69]	7 756
Dc	2	Coritiba	L	0-3	SA	20		3 770

20th Att: 152 758 • Av: 8 040 (-30.5%) • Orlando Scarpelli 19 908

FIGUEIRENSE 2012

Jan	21	Marc'o Dias	W	5-0	CC1	Ygor [19], Aloisio 2 [22 55], Julio Cesar [32], Luiz Fernando [79]	5 689
	25	H. Aichinger	D	1-1	CC1	Aloisio [70]	1 711
	29	Joinville	D	2-2	CC1	Luiz Fernando [22], Aloisio [79]	8 312
	2	Met'politano	W	3-1	CC1	Julio Cesar [11], OG [41], Niell [78]	7 423
	5	Chap'oense	L	1-3	CC1	Roni [56]	5 175
	8	Criciúma	W	5-4	CC1	Aloisio 2 [8 22], Canuto 2 [36 48], Fred [65]	6 773
Feb	12	Avai	W	1-0	CC1	Roni [62]	9 121
	22	Brusque	W	4-0	CC1	Julio Cesar 3 [28 39 77], Heber [73]	6 857
	26	Camboriú	W	5-1	CC1	Luiz Fernando [21], Fred [37], Roni 2 [48 64], Toro [81]	3 300
	29	Marc'o Dias	W	4-0	CC2	Rafhael [3], OG [36], Aloisio [48], Guilherme Santos [75]	1 059
	4	H. Aichinger	W	2-1	CC2	Roni 2 [5 63], Aloisio [39]	7 047
	11	Joinville	D	3-3	CC2	Canuto [17], Botti [35], Pablo [41]	9 833
Mar	18	Met'politano	W	4-0	CC2	Aloisio 2 [48 81], Julio Cesar [58p], Tulio [68]	4 471
	25	Chap'oense	W	3-0	CC2	Julio Cesar [12p], Luiz Fernando [70], Guilherme Santos [86]	8 471
	28	Criciúma	L	0-2	CC2		8 166
	1	Avai	D	2-2	CC2	Aloisio [2], Julio Cesar [48p]	14 734
	8	Brusque	W	2-1	CC2	Aloisio [50], Roni [74]	444
Apr	15	Camboriú	W	3-2	CC2	Botti [2], Fernandes [31], Luiz Fernando [74]	6 741
	22	Joinville	D	1-1	CCsf	Guilherme Santos [49]	14 437
	29	Joinville	W	3-1	CCsf	Fernandes [24], Aloisio 2 [81 89]	11 381
May	6	Avai	L	0-3	CCf		15 102
	13	Avai	L	1-2	CCf	Jean Deretti [88]	16 994

FIGUEIRENSE SERIE A APPEARANCES/GOALS 2012

Goalkeepers Ricardo 7 • Tiago Volpi 3 • Wilson 28
Defenders Americo 3/0 • Anderson Conceicao 13/1 • Burgel Xavier 10/0
• Edson 10+1/0 • Elsinho 16+2/0 • Ignacio Canuto ARG 13+1/0 •
Dorival 11+9/0 • Guilherme Santos 15/0 • Guti 7+1/0 • Helder 21/0 •
Joao Paulo 15+1/2 • Leonardo 6/0 • Marquinhos 4+1/0 • Pablo 1/0 •
Pablo Barros 7/1 • Roger Deniro 1/0 • Sandro 7+2/0 • Tiaguinho 0+1/0
Midfield Botti 7+7/0 • Bruno Nazario 3/0 • Claudinei 22+1/0 •
Coutinho 9+6/0 • Diguinho 0+1/0 • Diogo 3+3/0 • Fabiano Silva 2/0 •
Fernandes 8+5/2 • Guilherme Lazaroni 3+7/0 • Jackson Sousa 22+3/0
• Jean Deretti 3+4/1 • Jefferson 0+1/0 • Luiz Fernando 1+6/0 • Wilson
Pittoni PAR 3+2/0 • Roni 14+9/5 • Ryan 2/0 • Mario Saldivar PAR
0+1/0 • Toro 2/0 • Tulio 28/0 • Vanderson 0+1/0 • Ygor 6/0
Forwards Almir 8+5/0 • Aloisio 23+7/13 • Caio 26/9 • Cleitinho 0+1/0
• Heber 1+3/0 • Julio Cesar 18+11/5 • William Pottker 1+5/0
Coach Sebastian Abreu URU 5/0 • Argel • Helios dos Anjos (20/07/2012)
• Marcio Goiano (24/08/12) • Adilson Batista (5/11/12)

FLAMENGO
2012

Jan	21	Bonsucesso	W	4-0	TG	Jael 2 [28 31], Camacho [73], Adryan [85]	6 079
	25	Real Potosí	L	1-2	CLpr	Luiz Antonio [29]	19 100
	28	Macaé	D	0-0	TG		5 843
Feb	1	Real Potosí	W	2-0	CLpr	Leo Moura [39], Ronaldinho [93+]	32 004
	3	Olaria	D	0-0	TG		3 131
	5	Botafogo	D	0-0	TG		12 439
	9	Madureira	W	1-0	TG	OG [52]	4 376
	12	Novalguaçu	W	2-0	TG	Deivid [13], Renato Abreu [59]	9 269
	15	Lanús	D	1-1	CLg2	Leo Moura [45]	12 153
	18	Resende	W	3-1	TG	Ronaldinho [57], Vagner Love [62], Negueba [82]	10 959
Mar	22	Vasco	L	1-2	TGsf	Vagner Love [3]	21 492
	29	Boavista	L	1-2	TR	Vagner Love [5]	2 461
	4	D de Caxias	W	2-1	TR	Vagner Love [9], Ronaldinho [82]	5 596
	8	Emelec	W	1-0	CLg2	Vagner Love [48]	31 859
	11	Fluminense	W	2-0	TR	Ronaldinho [22p], Kleberson [24]	14 753
	15	Olimpia	D	3-3	CLg2	Bottinelli [37], Ronaldinho [56p], Luiz Antonio [63]	30 755
	18	Friburgense	W	1-0	TR	Kleberson [80]	2 267
	24	V. Redonda	W	4-2	TR	David Braz [33], Vagner Love 2 [48 75], Leo Moura [92+]	10 301
	28	Olimpia	L	2-3	CLg2	Vagner Love [48], Bottinelli [77]	31 154
Apr	1	Bangu	W	2-1	TR	Vagner Love 2 [17 35]	5 127
	4	Emelec	L	2-3	CLg2	OG [8], Deivid [42]	16 701
	7	Vasco	W	2-1	TR	Deivid [16], Ronaldinho [92+]	14 152
	12	Lanús	W	3-0	CLg2	Welinton Souza [17], Deivid [41], Luiz Antonio [49]	15 932
	15	Americano	W	3-1	TR	Deivid 2 [9p 86], Kleberson [76]	4 104
	22	Vasco	L	2-3	TRsf	Vagner Love [2], Kleberson [52]	20 067
May	19	Sport Recife	D	1-1	SA 7	Vagner Love [73]	26 699
	26	Inter	D	3-3	SA 9	Airton [5], Ronaldinho [16p], Vagner Love [48]	24 310
Jun	6	Ponte Preta	D	2-2	SA 12	Renato 28, Vagner Love [94+]	5 365
	9	Coritiba	W	3-1	SA 8	Vagner Love [6], Luiz Antonio [13], Hernane [92+]	6 142
	17	Santos	W	1-0	SA 8	Dario Bottinelli [89p]	17 373
Jul	24	Grêmio	L	0-2	SA 9		18 601
	1	Atlético GO	W	3-2	SA 9	Renato 2 [34 61], Adryan [57]	4 200
	8	Fluminense	L	0-1	SA 9		38 862
	15	Bahia	W	2-1	SA 9	Hernane [31], Renato [72p]	29 206
	18	Corinthians	L	0-3	SA 10	Douglas 3 [28 40 55]	12 027
	22	Cruzeiro	L	0-1	SA 10		16 277
	26	Portuguesa	D	0-0	SA 10		5 732
	29	São Paulo	L	1-4	SA 10	Ramon [66]	35 049
Aug	8	Figueirense	W	2-0	SA 10	Vagner Love 2 [62 87]	11 307
	11	Náutico	W	2-0	SA 9	Vagner Love 2 [14 43]	7 043
	15	Palmeiras	L	0-1	SA 10		7 500
	19	Vasco	W	1-0	SA 9	Vagner Love [38]	15 459
	26	Botafogo	D	0-0	SA 9		15 090
	30	Sport Recife	D	1-1	SA 10	Ibson [13]	6 035
Sep	2	Inter	L	1-4	SA 12	Vagner Love [15]	10 413
	5	Ponte Preta	L	0-1	SA 13		2 627
	8	Coritiba	L	0-3	SA 13		12 003
	12	Santos	L	0-2	SA 16		8 015
	16	Grêmio	D	1-1	SA 16	Adryan [61]	15 625
	23	Atlético GO	W	2-1	SA 14	Cleber Santana [35], Liedson [67]	23 887
	26	Atlético MG	W	2-1	SA	Vagner Love [21], Liedson [56]	39 060
	30	Fluminense	L	0-1	SA 11		25 313
Oct	4	Bahia	D	0-0	SA 12		25 777
	10	Corinthians	L	2-3	SA 16	Renato Santos [30], Liedson [93+]	25 395
	13	Cruzeiro	D	1-1	SA 15	Liedson [11]	15 992
	17	Portuguesa	D	0-0	SA 15		5 892
	21	São Paulo	W	1-0	SA 14	Gonzalez [73]	21 631
	31	Atlético MG	D	1-1	SA 14	Renato Santos [27]	19 945
Nov	3	Figueirense	W	1-0	SA 12	Hernane [72]	6 776
	11	Náutico	W	1-0	SA 9	Renato Santos [81p]	19 252
	18	Palmeiras	D	1-1	SA 11	Vagner Love [89]	7 333
	24	Vasco	D	1-1	SA 11	Gonzalez [87]	5 971
Dc	2	Botafogo	D	2-2	SA 11	Nixson [31], Vagner Love [55]	6 674

11th Att: 265 159 • Av: 13 956 (-28.7%) • Engenhão 46 931

FLAMENGO SERIE A APPEARANCES/GOALS 2012
Goalkeepers Felipe 20 • Paulo Victor 18+1
Defenders Arthur Sanches 2+1/0 • Felipe Dias 1/0 • Fernando 0+1/0
Marcos Gonzalez CHI 26/2 • Leo Moura 23/0 • Magal 12+2/0
Marllon 11+1/0 • Ramon 25/1 • Renato Santos POR 10/3
Rodrigo Frauches 9/0 • Thiago Medeiros 2/0 • Welinton Souza 16+1/0
Wellington Silva 18+1/0
Midfield Airton 13/1 • Amaral 14+4/0 • Dario Bottinelli ARG 5+16/1
Victor Caceres PAR 10/0 • Camacho 1+2/0 • Cleber Santana 12/1
Ibson 29+4/1 • Kleberson 3/0 • Luiz Antonio 24+2/1 • Muralha 2+5/0
Renato 22+3/4 • Romulo 1/0 • Ronaldinho 2/1
Forwards Adryan 7+16/2 • Deivid 2+4/0 • Diego Mauricio 4+1/0
Hernane 7+7/3 • Liedson POR 10+6/4 • Matthues 3+8/0
Negueba 8+5/0 • Nixson 1+6/1 • Paulo Sergio 0+3/0 • Thomas 7+3/0
Vagner Love 36/13 • Wellington Bruno 2+9/0
Coach Joel Santana • Dorival Junior (23/07/12)

FLUMINENSE
2012

Jan	21	Friburgense	W	3-0	TG	Araujo [15], Rafael Moura [36], Thiago Carleto [51]	6 459
	28	V. Redonda	W	3-0	TG	Anderson [72], Wellington Nem [74], Araujo [90]	5 536
Feb	1	Boavista	L	1-2	TG	Deco [36]	2 784
	4	D de Caxias	D	1-1	TG	Thiago Carleto [73]	3 309
	7	Arsenal	W	1-0	CLg4	Fred [2]	28 928
	12	Vasco	L	1-2	TG	Thiago Neves [7]	10 416
	15	Americano	W	3-2	TG	Rafael Moura [13p], Thiago Neves [49], Wellington Nem [69]	3 791
	18	Bangu	W	3-0	TG	Fred [30], Araujo [36], Wellington Nem [65]	1 987
	23	Botafogo	D	1-1	TGsf	Leandro Euzebio [79]. W 4-3p	21 143
	26	Vasco	W	3-1	TGf	Fred 2 [35p 55], Deco [41]	36 374
	29	Resende	L	1-2	TR	Rafael Sobis [30]	1 447
Mar	3	Novalguaçu	W	3-0	TR	Rafael Sobis 2 [26 74], Matheus [78]	1 981
	7	Boca Jun	W	2-1	CLg4	Fred [9], Deco [54]	35 592
	11	Flamengo	L	0-2	TR		14 753
	14	Zamora	W	1-0	CLg4	Anderson [57]	24 769
	17	Macaé	L	1-3	TR	Matheus [89]	2 252
	24	Bonsucesso	W	2-0	TR	Fred 2 [5 16p]	2 426
	29	Zamora	W	1-0	CLg4	Rafael Sobis [78]	7 000
	1	Botafogo	D	1-1	TR	Fred [36]	11 340
	7	Madureira	W	2-1	TR	Lanzini [20], Thiago Neves [43]	2 493
	11	Boca Jun	L	0-2	CLg4		36 263
Apr	15	Olaria	W	5-1	TR	Rafael Moura 2 [16 31], Deco [17], Anderson [79], Thiago Neves [82]	2 231
	18	Arsenal	W	2-1	CLg4	Carlinhos [34], Rafael Moura [92+]	204
	21	Macaé	W	2-1	TR	Lanzini [43], Marcos Junior [61]	186
	25	Inter	D	0-0	CLr2		32 278
	28	V. Redonda	W	1-0	TR	Fabio [51], Arajo [91+]	418
May	6	Botafogo	W	4-1	TG/Rf	Fred [42], Rafael Sobis 2 [56 65], Marcos Junior [83]	28 182
	10	Inter	W	2-1	CLr2	Leandro Euzebio [15], Fred [45]	33 386
	13	Botafogo	W	1-0	TG/Rf	Rafael Moura [62]	25 016

FLUMINENSE 2012 (CONT'D)

May	17	Boca Jun	L	0-1	CLqf		45 320
May	20	Corinthians	W	1-0	SA	5	Leandro Euzebio [72]	14 791
May	23	Boca Jun	D	1-1	CLqf		Thiago Carleto [16]	36 276
May	27	Figueirense	D	2-2	SA	6	Marcos Junior 16, Wagner 66	7 462
Jun	6	Santos	D	1-1	SA	7	Carlinhos 25p	4 080
Jun	10	Inter	D	0-0	SA	10		5 728
Jun	16	Portuguesa	W	4-1	SA	7	Wellington Nem [41], Anderson [52], Fred [78], Lanzini [86]	4 564
Jun	24	Atlético GO	W	4-1	SA	5	Samuel Rosa [19], Gum [25], OG [52], Deco [94+p]	5 240
Jun	30	Náutico	W	2-0	SA	3		14 501
Jun	8	Flamengo	W	1-0	SA	2	Fred 12	38 862
Jun	15	Botafogo	D	1-1	SA	3		17 122
Jul	19	Bahia	W	4-0	SA	3	Fred 2 [48p 73p], Thiago Neves [65], Wallace [88]	5 393
Jul	22	Ponte Preta	W	2-1	SA	3	Thiago Neves [45], Fred [90p]	5 890
Jul	25	Grêmio	L	0-1	SA	3		27 405
Jul	29	Atlético MG	D	0-0	SA	3		16 175
Aug	1	Coritiba	W	2-0	SA	3	Fred [83], OG [84]	16 523
Aug	9	São Paulo	W	2-1	SA	3	Leandro Euzebio [35], Fred [50]	3 938
Aug	12	Palmeiras	W	1-0	SA	2	Rafael Sobis [84]	6 079
Aug	15	Cruzeiro	D	1-1	SA	2	Fred [43]	13 551
Aug	18	Sport Recife	W	1-0	SA	2	Samuel Rosa [83]	5 298
Aug	22	Vasco	W	2-1	SA	2	Thiago Neves 2 [72 86]	9 729
Aug	29	Corinthians	D	1-1	SA	2	Fred [83]	7 358
Sep	1	Figueirense	D	2-2	SA	2	Digao [47], Rafael Sobis [53]	8 943
Sep	6	Santos	W	3-1	SA	1	Wellington Nem 2 [20 44], Samuel Rosa [78]	13 007
Sep	9	Inter	W	1-0	SA	1	Fred [29]	6 060
Sep	12	Portuguesa	W	2-0	SA	1	Jean [74], Wellington Nem [76]	3 613
Sep	15	Atlético GO	L	1-2	SA	1	Michael [64]	8 269
Sep	22	Náutico	W	2-1	SA	1	Leandro Euzebio [41], Fred [45]	6 132
Sep	30	Flamengo	W	1-0	SA	1	Fred [18]	25 313
Oct	6	Botafogo	W	1-0	SA	1	Fred [72]	16 919
Oct	10	Bahia	W	2-0	SA	1		21 998
Oct	14	Ponte Preta	W	2-1	SA	1	Fred [80p], Gum [89]	16 029
Oct	17	Grêmio	D	2-2	SA	1	Diego [59], Rafael Sobis [63]	35 217
Oct	21	Atlético MG	L	2-3	SA	1	Wellington Nem [56], Fred [85]	20 096
Oct	25	Coritiba	W	2-1	SA	1	Wellington Nem [15], Thiago Neves [71]	29 994
Nov	4	São Paulo	D	1-1	SA	1	Fred [68]	54 118
Nov	11	Palmeiras	W	3-2	SA	1	Fred 3 [45 53 88]	8 461
Nov	18	Cruzeiro	L	0-2	SA	1		35 167
Nov	25	Sport Recife	D	1-1	SA	1	Fred [28]	32 937
Dec	2	Vasco	L	1-2	SA	1	Carleto [86p]	5 470

1st Att: 267 061 • Av: 14 056 (+3.1%) • Engenhão 46 931

FLUMINENSE SERIE A APPEARANCES/GOALS 2012
Goalkeepers Berna 3 • Diego Cavalieri 35
Defenders Anderson 11/1 • Carleto 7+1/1 • Carlinhos 31+1/1
Digao 14+3/2 • Eliveltom 1+1/0 • Gum 34/2 • Igor Juliao 0+1/0
Leandro Euzebio 18+1/3 • Rafinha 0+1/0 • Wallace 11+7/1
Wellington Carvalho 1/0
Midfield Deco POR 17/1 • Diguinho 4+10/0 • Edinho 32/0
Fabio 3+5/0 • Higor 1+6/0 • Jean 34+1/1 • Manuel Lanzini ARG 2+4/1
Lucas Patinho 0+1/0 • Thiago Neves 27+2/5
Edwin Valencia COL 4+5/0 • Wagner 18+11/1 • Wellington Nem 26+1/6
Forwards Biro Biro 0+1/0 • Bruno 27/1 • Fred 28/21
Marcos Junior 4+12/1 • Matheus Carvalho 1+7/0 • Michael 0+5/1
Rafael Moura 0+3/0 • Rafael Sobis 12+9/4 • Samuel Rosa 12+11/5
Coach Abel Braga (8/06/2011)

GREMIO 2012

Jan	21	Lajeadense	L	0-2	CG			15 294
Jan	25	Canoas	W	3-1	CG		Kleber [2], Gabriel [51], Moreno [87]	1 919
Jan	29	Juventude	L	1-2	CG		Kleber [90]	8 276
Feb	2	São Luiz	W	1-0	CG		Kleber [41]	6 675
Feb	5	Inter	D	2-2	CG		Marquinhos [27], Moreno [32p]	16 063
Feb	9	Ypiranga	W	2-1	CG		Moreno [57], Douglas Grolli [93+]	7 167
Feb	11	Santa Cruz	W	4-1	CG		Naldo 2 [18 53], Douglas Grolli [24], Kleber [76]	5 405
Feb	18	São José	L	1-2	CG		OG [91+]	1 206
Feb	22	Inter	W	2-1	CGqf		Leo Gago [17], Kleber [65]	14 459
Feb	26	Caxias	D	1-1	CGsf		Kleber [63]. L 4-5p	9 251
Mar	4	Cerâmica	W	2-1	CG		Kleber [13], Marco Antonio [49]	5 148
Mar	7	River Plate	W	3-2	CBr1		OG [67], Kleber [91+], Facundo [93+]	3 712
Mar	11	N Hamburgo	W	5-0	CG		Andre Lima [6], Kleber [53], Souza [67], Fernando [83], Facundo [86]	10 565
Mar	18	Veranópolis	W	4-1	CG		Gilberto Silva [2], Moreno [19], Fernando [23], Gabriel [41]	3 964
Mar	21	River Plate	W	3-1	CBr1		Moreno [34], Werley [78], Leo Gago [85]	16 719
Mar	25	Cruzeiro RS	W	2-1	CG		Fernando [9], Moreno [94+]	3 143
Mar	29	Avenida	W	4-0	CG		Moreno 2 [1 14p], Leo Gago [68], Facundo [81]	6 376
Apr	1	Pelotas	L	0-1	CG			5 597
Apr	4	Ipatinga	W	1-0	CBr2		Leo Gago [72]	2 083
Apr	8	Caxias	W	3-1	CG		Miralles [13], Naldo [34], Andre Lima [39]	9 211
Apr	11	Ipatinga	W	3-0	CBr2		Facundo [2], Miralles [77], Leo Gago [85]	15 775
Apr	15	Ypiranga	W	4-0	CGqf		Werley 2 [34 84], Andre Lima [35], Fernando [53]	12 233
Apr	21	Canoas	W	1-0	CGsf		Andre Lima [6]	15 282
Apr	29	Inter	L	1-2	CGf		Werley [55]	18 921
May	2	Fortaleza	W	2-0	CBr3		Moreno [12], Marco Antonio [13]	18 414
May	9	Fortaleza	W	2-0	CBr3		Leo Gago [55], Facundo [86]	20 949
May	17	Bahia	W	2-1	CBqf		Fernando [39], Naldo [73]	11 807
May	20	Vasco	L	1-2	SA	15	Fernando [26]	5 826
May	24	Bahia	W	2-0	CBqf		Miralles [13], Moreno [55]	35 726
May	27	Palmeiras	W	1-0	SA	7	Andre Lima [72]	18 277
May	6	Atlético GO	W	1-0	SA	5	Miralles [59]	2 965
Jun	10	Corinthians	W	2-0	SA	3	Marco Antonio [22], Andre Lima [29]	16 803
Jun	13	Palmeiras	L	0-2	CBsf			43 508
Jun	17	Náutico	L	0-1	SA	5		14 006
Jun	21	Palmeiras	D	1-1	CBsf		Fernando [67]	26 255
Jun	24	Flamengo	W	2-0	SA	4	Moreno [33]	18 601
Jul	1	Atlético MG	L	0-1	SA	6		34 550
Jul	8	Santos	L	2-4	SA	8	Vilson [78], Marquinhos [93+]	9 402
Jul	15	Cruzeiro	W	3-1	SA	7	Moreno 2 [26 65], Kleber [29]	15 523
Jul	18	Sport Recife	W	3-1	SA	4	Moreno [64], Leandro 2 [74 80]	15 179
Jul	22	Botafogo	W	1-0	SA	4	Moreno [48]	29 943
Jul	25	Fluminense	W	1-0	SA	4	Edilson [69]	27 405
Jul	28	Coritiba	L	1-2	SA	4	Andre Lima [64]	17 619
Aug	1	Coritiba	W	1-0	CSr2		Andre Lima [71]	
Aug	5	Bahia	W	3-1	SA	4	Elano [33p], Souza [88], Moreno [93+]	23 268
Aug	9	Ponte Preta	D	0-0	SA	4		9 010
Aug	12	São Paulo	W	2-1	SA	4	Werley [66], Andre Lima [92+]	15 386
Aug	15	Portuguesa	L	1-2	SA	4	Kleber [88]	15 798
Aug	19	Figueirense	W	4-0	SA	4	Elano [36], Leandro 2 [41 48], Andre Lima [90]	18 205
Aug	22	Coritiba	L	2-3	CSr2		Elano [40p], Moreno [90]	
Aug	26	Inter	W	1-0	SA	3	Elano [7]	8 844
Aug	29	Vasco	W	2-0	SA	3	Moreno [42], Kleber [59]	21 758
Sep	1	Palmeiras	D	0-0	SA	3		11 586
Sep	5	Atlético GO	W	2-1	SA	3	Elano 2 [11 20]	21 832
Sep	8	Corinthians	L	1-3	SA	3	Leandro [58]	24 850
Sep	13	Náutico	W	2-0	SA	3	Moreno [61], Kleber [93+]	17 942
Sep	16	Flamengo	D	1-1	SA	3	Moreno [18]	15 625
Sep	23	Atlético MG	D	0-0	SA	3		19 668
Sep	27	Barcelona	W	1-0	CSr3		Werley [93+]	
Sep	30	Santos	D	1-1	SA	3	Werley [34]	38 212
Oct	6	Cruzeiro	W	2-1	SA	3	Moreno [66], Marquinhos [77]	27 843
Oct	11	Sport Recife	W	3-1	SA	2	Anderson Pico [43], Leandro [51], Marquinhos [56]	11 210

GREMIO 2012 (CONT'D)

	14	Botafogo	D	1-1	SA	3	Leo Gago [51]	27 529
	17	Fluminense	D	2-2	SA	3	Elano [55], Ze Roberto [86]	35 217
Oct	20	Coritiba	D	0-0	SA	3		20 676
	25	Barcelona	W	2-1	CSr3		OG [65], Ze Roberto [91+]	
	27	Bahia	D	1-1	SA	3	Kleber [42]	32 157
	30	Millonarios	W	1-0	CSqf		Marco Antonio [36]	
	3	Ponte Preta	W	1-0	SA	3	Andre Lima [91+]	40 760
	11	São Paulo	W	2-1	SA	2	Andre Lima [61], Moreno [85]	40 217
Nov	16	Millonarios	L	1-3	CSqf		Werley [12]	
	18	Portuguesa	D	2-2	SA	2	Andre Lima [73], Ze Roberto [75]	3 993
	25	Figueirense	W	4-2	SA	3	Elano [24], Ze Roberto [43], Souza [45], Leandro [71]	7 756
Dc	2	Inter	D	0-0	SA	3		46 209

3rd   Att: 491 064 • Av: 25 845 (+37.3%) • Olímpico 45 000

GREMIO SERIE A APPEARANCES/GOALS 2012
Goalkeepers Marcelo Grohe 32 • Victor 6
Defenders Anderson Pico 19+2/1 • Douglas Grolli 0+1/0 • Edilson 12/1
Gabriel 3+1/0 • Julio Cesar 1+1/0 • Naldo 15+1/0 • Para 34/0
Saimon 2+1/0 • Tony Ewerton 5+5/0 • Vilson 8+9/1 • Werley 30/3
Midfield Facundo Bertoglio ARG 0+1/0 • Elano 24+1/7 • Fernando 32/1
Gilberto Silva 25+1/0 • Leo Gago 13+14/1 • Marco Antonio 16+7/2
Marquinhos 6+22/3 • Rondinelly 0+11/0 • Souza 33/2
Ze Roberto 29/3
Forwards Andre Lima 11+16/8 • Kleber 24+2/5 • Leandro 9+13/7
Ezequiel Miralles ARG 5/1 • Marcelo Moreno BOL 24+4/10
Coach Vanderlei Luxemburgo

INTERNACIONAL 2012

	18	N Hamburgo	W	1-0	CG		Oscar [11]	7 847
	22	Avenida	L	2-3	CG		Gilberto [11], Fabricio [35]	1 191
Jan	25	O. Caldas	W	1-0	CLpr		Leandro Damiao [11]	33 058
	26	Cerâmica	L	1-2	CG		Lucas Lima [61]	1 201
	28	Veranópolis	W	3-1	CG		Marcos Aurelio [4], Fabricio [10], Elton [59]	2 038
	1	O. Caldas	D	2-2	CLpr		D'Alessandro [11p], Tinga [21]	14 295
	5	Grêmio	D	2-2	CG		Datolo [22], Bolivar [74]	16 063
	9	Juan Aurich	W	2-0	CLg1		Oscar [23], Datolo [89]	28 968
Feb	12	Caxias	W	2-0	CG		Dagoberto [2 4 35]	7 306
	15	Cruzeiro RS	W	2-0	CG		Dagoberto [20], Rodrigo Moledo [65]	6 979
	18	Pelotas	W	3-1	CG		Jo 2 [17 51], Elton [36]	2 128
	22	Grêmio	L	1-2	CGqf		Leandro Damiao [27]	14 459
	3	Ypiranga	W	2-1	CG		Oscar [29], Leandro Damiao [60]	4 002
	7	Santos	L	1-3	CLg1		Leandro Damiao [63]	12 857
	10	Santa Cruz	W	2-1	CG		Datolo [18], Leandro Damiao [53]	1 700
Mar	13	Strongest	W	5-0	CLg1		Dagoberto [3], Leandro Damiao 3 [6 56 72], Jo [80]	25 098
	17	Juventude	W	7-0	CG		Leandro Damiao 2 [17 64], Datolo [55], Jaja 2 [76 80], Jo [82], Oscar [84]	9 576
	21	Strongest	D	1-1	CLg1		Gilberto [88]	11 176
	25	São José	W	3-0	CG		Datolo [7], Leandro Damiao 2 [46 90]	1 265
	28	Lajeadense	D	0-0	CG			2 603
Apr	1	Canoas	W	1-0	CG		Leandro Damiao [15]	4 790
	4	Santos	D	1-1	CLg1		Nei [8]	35 530

INTERNACIONAL 2012 (CONT'D)

	8	São Luiz	W	3-0	CG		Joao Paulo [30], Datolo [45], Gilberto [77]	1 542
	14	Cerâmica	W	3-0	CGqf		Gilberto [57], Leandro Damiao [86], D'Alessandro [91+]	3 563
Apr	19	Juan Aurich	L	0-1	CLg1			3 000
	22	Veranópolis	W	4-0	CGsf		Datolo 2 [17 39], Leandro Damiao [53], Indio [65]	9 472
	25	Fluminense	D	0-0	CLr2			32 278
	29	Grêmio	W	2-1	CGf		Datolo [35], Fabricio [78]	18 921
	6	Caxias	D	1-1	CGf		Oscar [56]	12 042
	10	Fluminense	L	1-2	CLr2		Leandro Damiao [13]	33 386
May	13	Caxias	W	2-1	CGf		Sandro Silva [66], Leandro Damiao [71]	23 028
	20	Coritiba	W	2-0	SA	2	Leandro Damiao [8], Dagoberto [37]	19 000
	26	Flamengo	D	3-3	SA	4	Gilberto [33], Fabricio [67], Jesus Datolo [69]	24 310
	6	São Paulo	W	1-0	SA	2	D'Alessandro [21]	12 348
Jun	10	Fluminense	D	0-0	SA	4		5 728
	16	Botafogo	L	1-2	SA	9	Dagoberto [31]	12 419
	24	Sport Recife	W	2-0	SA	6	OG [14], Leandro Damiao [39]	15 249
	1	Bahia	D	1-1	SA	8	Indio [62]	13 474
	7	Cruzeiro	W	2-1	SA	6	Oscar [8], Leandro Damiao [7]	9 349
	15	Santos	D	0-0	SA	6		11 791
	18	Atlético MG	L	1-3	SA	8	Fred [65]	19 181
Jul	22	Atlético GO	W	4-1	SA	7	Elton [20], Dagoberto [47], Jaja [57], Fred [75]	8 344
	25	Figueirense	W	1-0	SA	5	Dagoberto [24]	8 944
	29	Vasco	D	0-0	SA	6		15 462
	4	Palmeiras	W	1-0	SA	5	Ygor [35]	8 387
	8	Náutico	D	0-0	SA	5		9 716
	12	Ponte Preta	W	2-1	SA	5	Jaja [59], Mike [92+]	9 274
Aug	16	Corinthians	L	0-1	SA	5		27 282
	19	Portuguesa	D	1-1	SA	5	Juan [75]	4 365
	26	Grêmio	L	0-1	SA	6		8 844
	29	Coritiba	L	0-1	SA	7		12 200
	2	Flamengo	W	4-1	SA	7	Forlan 2 [29 67], Josimar [40], Leandro Damiao [75]	10 413
	5	São Paulo	D	1-1	SA	6	Dagoberto [8]	14 171
	9	Fluminense	L	0-1	SA	7		6 060
Sep	13	Botafogo	D	1-1	SA	7	Leandro Damiao [69]	9 148
	16	Sport Recife	D	2-2	SA	7	Cassiano [62], Leandro Damiao [75]	4 481
	23	Bahia	W	3-1	SA	7	Fred [13], Forlan [38], Leandro Damiao [53]	9 052
	29	Cruzeiro	L	0-1	SA	6		7 395
	6	Santos	D	1-1	SA	6	Cassiano [51]	9 965
	10	Atlético MG	W	3-0	SA	6	Jackson Souza [67], Fred [80], Cassiano [88]	3 372
Oct	13	Atlético GO	L	1-3	SA	6	Fred [15]	1 476
	17	Figueirense	L	2-3	SA	6	Dagoberto [39], Rafael Moura [70]	4 649
	24	Vasco	W	2-1	SA	6	Forlan 2 [34 45]	14 774
	27	Palmeiras	W	2-1	SA	5	Fred [33], Rafael Moura [54]	11 339
	4	Náutico	L	0-3	SA	6		15 439
Nov	11	Ponte Preta	L	0-1	SA	8		8 435
	18	Corinthians	L	0-2	SA	6		6 850
	25	Portuguesa	L	0-2	SA	9		6 442
Dc	2	Grêmio	D	0-0	SA	10		46 209

10th   Att: 179 205 • Av: 9 432 (-54.8%) • Olímpico 45 000

INTER SERIE A APPEARANCES/GOALS 2012
Goalkeepers Muriel 38 • Renan 0+1
Defenders Bolivar 16/0 • Dalton 1/0 • Fabricio 23+5/1 • Indio 29+1/1
Jackson Souza 3+2/1 • Juan 5+1/1 • Kleber 14/0 • Lima 2/0 • Nei 27/0
Ratinho 9/0 • Rodrigo Moledo 21+1/0 • William Massari 1/0
Midfield Mario Bolatti ARG 3+6/0 • Andres D'Alessandro ARG 19+2/1
Jesus Datolo ARG 7+3/1 • Elton 22+4/1 • Pablo Guinazu ARG 28/0
Joao Paulo 0+4/0 • Josimar 11+4/1 • Lucas Lima 2+10/0 • Oscar 5/1
Otavio 1+6/0 • Rodrigo 1/0 • Sandro Silva 3/0 • Ygor 21/1
Ze Mario 2/0
Forwards Cassiano 6+10/3 • Dagoberto 15+4/6
Diego Forlan URU 17+5/5 • Fred 25+3/6 • Gilberto 3+3/1 • Jaja 10+6/2
Leandro Damiao 19/7 • Marcos Aurelio 1+11/0 • Maurides 0+7/0
Mike 1+6/1 • Rafael Moura 7+7/2 • Rafael Pernao 0+1/0
Coach Dorival Junior • Fernandao (20/07/12) • Osmar Loss (20/11/12)

NAUTICO
2012

	15	Porto	W	2-0	CP	Ronaldo Alves [18], Souza [38]	8 420
	18	Petrolina	W	2-0	CP	Souza [50], Cascata [64]	13 452
Jan	21	Ararpina	W	1-0	CP	Rogerio [29]	5 490
	25	América PE	W	2-0	CP	Marlon [56], Siloe [63]	11 451
	29	Sport Recife	L	3-4	CP	Souza [27], Jefferson [73], Lenon [85]	19 943
	1	Ypiranga	W	3-1	CP	Souza [10], Derley 2 [11][31]	10 461
	4	Santa Cruz	D	2-2	CP	Cascata [24], Souza [94+]	15 072
	8	Salgueiro	L	2-3	CP	Siloe 2 [22][86]	8 768
	12	S. Talhada	W	1-0	CP	Marcos Vinicius [78]	4 402
Feb	15	Central	W	2-0	CP	Siloe 2 [60][83]	9 595
	22	Belo Jardim	L	0-2	CP		5 002
	26	Belo Jardim	W	3-1	CP	Derley [29], Douglas Santos [34], Siloe [72]	10 065
	29	América PE	D	2-2	CP	Souza 2 [55][70]	5 253
	3	Ararpina	W	3-0	CP	Siloe [8], Gustavo [45], Dori [60]	10 409
	7	Porto	W	2-0	CP	Dori [65], Siloe [67]	9 418
	11	Petrolina	D	1-1	CP	Eduardo Ramos [65]	4 510
Mar	15	S. Cruz RN	W	3-1	CBr1	Cesinha [15], OG [61], Derley [91+]	1 045
	18	Ypiranga	D	0-0	CP		4 951
	25	Sport Recife	D	0-0	CP		17 559
	28	Salgueiro	L	0-1	CP		10 344
	1	Santa Cruz	L	0-1	CP		27 068
	7	S. Talhada	L	1-2	CP	Marlon [74p]	6 005
	12	Fortaleza	L	0-4	CBr2		17 887
Apr	15	Central	W	2-1	CP	Lenon [6], Rodrigo Tiui [7]	1 349
	18	Fortaleza	W	2-1	CBr2	Marlon [47], Leo Santos [80]	2 308
	22	Sport Recife	L	1-2	CPsf	Ronaldo Alves [31]	12 594
	29	Sport Recife	D	0-0	CPsf		17 040
May	19	Figueirense	L	1-2	SA	15 Araujo [79p]	5 185
	26	Cruzeiro	D	0-0	SA	14	13 605
	6	Vasco	L	2-4	SA	19 Martinez [66], Araujo [87]	7 541
Jun	10	Botafogo	W	3-2	SA	14 Araujo [17], Lucio [32], Derley [83]	12 354
	17	Grêmio	W	1-0	SA	10 Ronaldo Alves [92+]	12 767
	23	Atlético MG	L	1-5	SA	13 Araujo [12]	16 367
	30	Fluminense	L	0-2	SA	14	14 501
	7	Atlético GO	W	1-0	SA	11 Araujo [21]	2 048
	14	Corinthians	L	1-2	SA	12 Elicarlos [21]	23 198
	18	Ponte Preta	W	3-0	SA	11 Kieza [36], Souza [60], Kieza [87]	11 443
Jul	22	Palmeiras	L	0-3	SA	11	7 407
	25	Coritiba	L	3-4	SA	12 Souza [13], Kieza [17], Rico [85]	11 453
	29	Portuguesa	L	1-3	SA	14 Kieza [2]	1 910
	5	Santos	W	3-0	SA	11 Patric [59], Kim [86], Kieza [91+]	11 086
	8	Inter	D	0-0	SA	12	9 716
	11	Flamengo	L	0-2	SA	13	7 073
Aug	15	São Paulo	W	3-0	SA	12 Kieza [13p], Araujo [28], OG [61]	12 172
	18	Bahia	W	1-0	SA	11 Martinez [87]	12 558
	26	Sport Recife	D	0-0	SA	11	17 066
	29	Figueirense	W	3-2	SA	9 Elicarlos 2 [59][65], Souza [76]	10 880
	2	Cruzeiro	L	0-3	SA	10	11 673
	5	Vasco	D	1-1	SA	10 Kieza [41]	11 541
Sep	8	Botafogo	L	1-3	SA	12 Araujo [55p]	14 612
	13	Grêmio	L	0-2	SA	14	17 942
	16	Atlético MG	W	1-0	SA	12 Souza [49]	15 013
	22	Fluminense	L	1-2	SA	13 Kim [82]	6 132
	29	Atlético GO	W	2-0	SA	10 Kieza 2 [20p][42]	11 884
	6	Corinthians	W	2-1	SA	9 Kieza [30], OG [86]	19 005
	10	Ponte Preta	L	1-2	SA	11 Douglas Santos [4]	6 856
Oct	14	Palmeiras	W	1-0	SA	10 Kieza [14]	13 439
	17	Coritiba	L	1-2	SA	12 Kieza [88]	12 174
	21	Portuguesa	D	0-0	SA	12	13 199
	25	Santos	D	0-0	SA	13	6 256
	4	Inter	W	3-0	SA	11 Souza 2 [23][33], Kieza [62]	15 439
Nov	11	Flamengo	L	0-1	SA	13	19 252
	18	São Paulo	L	1-2	SA	13 Souza [49]	62 207
	25	Bahia	D	1-1	SA	13 Dimba [78]	32 157
Dc	2	Sport Recife	W	1-0	SA	12 Araujo [65]	20 100

12th — Att: 261 691 • Av: 13 773 • Aflitos 23 000

NAUTICO SERIE A APPEARANCES/GOALS 2011–12

Goalkeepers Felipe 21 • Gideao 17
Defenders Alemao 13+1/0 • Alessandro 10/0 • Alison 5+5/0 • Cesinha 1+1/0 • Douglas 21+1/1 • Gustavo 2+1/0 • Jean Rolt 24+1/0 • Joao Paulo 4+9/0 • Marcio Rosario 6+2/0 • Marlon 9/0 • Patric 22/1 • Ronaldo Alves 21+3/1
Midfield Auremir 5+1/0 • Breitner VEN 0+5/0 • Cleverson 5+5/0 • Dada 4+4/0 • Derley 7/1 • Elicarlos 31/3 • Glaydson 2+2/0 • Josa 7+6/0 • Lucio 14+9/1 • Martinez 26/2 • Ramirez 1+7/0 • Rhayner 32+2/0 • Rogerinho 1+6/0 • Andres Romero ARG 0+6/0 • Souza 33+2/7
Forwards Araujo 31+2/8 • Dimba 1+4/1 • Kieza 20/13 • Kim 8+12/2 • Ramon 3/0 • Reis 0+3/0 • Rico 0+4/1 • Rodrigo Tiui 0+1/0 • Rogerio 11+4/0 • Siloe 0+1/0
Coach Alexandre Gallo

PALMEIRAS
2012

	22	Bragantino	W	2-1	CP	Leandro Amaro [6], Maikon Leite [84]	8 180
Jan	25	Portuguesa	D	1-1	CP	Ricardo Bueno [81]	7 993
	29	Catan'ense	D	1-1	CP	Fernandao [82]	5 422
	1	Mogi Mirim	W	2-0	CP	Marcos Assuncao 2 [2][87]	3 551
	5	Santos	W	2-1	CP	Fernandao [88], Juninho Barbosa [92+]	25 933
	8	Piracicaba	W	3-2	CP	Daniel Carvalho [15], Marcos Assuncao [47], Artur [72]	7 352
	11	Ituano	W	3-0	CP	Patrik Camilo [6], Barcos [22], Artur [67]	11 193
Feb	17	Guarati'nta	W	3-2	CP	Artur [18], Barcos [45], Joao Vitor [86]	7 002
	23	Oeste	D	1-1	CP	Maikon Leite [40]	9 005
	26	São Paulo	D	3-3	CP	Daniel Carvalho [5], Barcos 2 [37][72]	19 161
	29	Linense	W	3-1	CP	Maikon Leite [2], Barcos [33], Daniel Carvalho [35]	6 798
	4	S. Caetano	D	0-0	CP		19 437
	11	Botafogo RP	W	6-2	CP	OG [23], Maikon Leite [36], Barcos 2 [54][92+p], Ricardo Bueno [80], Jun'ho Barbosa [91+]	17 947
	14	Coruripe	W	1-0	CBr1	Barcos [3]	10 017
Mar	17	Ponte Preta	W	2-1	CP	Juninho Barbosa [2], Marcos Assuncao [11]	19 152
	21	Coruripe	W	3-0	CBr1	Marcos Assuncao [55], Barcos [58], Jun'ho Barbosa [84]	11 143
	25	Corinthians	L	1-2	CP	Marcos Assuncao [17]	29 284
	28	Paulista	W	1-0	CP	Joao Vitor [87]	4 219
	31	Mirassol	L	0-1	CP		8 502
	4	Horizonte	W	3-1	CBr2	Leandro Amaro 2 [34][67], Maikon Leite [72]	8 361
	8	Guarani	L	1-3	CP	Barcos [18p]	9 399
Apr	15	Comercial	D	2-2	CP	Fernandao [88], Henrique [93+]	5 363
	22	Guarani	L	2-3	CPqf	Marcos Assuncao [53], Henrique [92+]	15 005
	25	Paraná	W	2-1	CBr3	Marcos Assuncao [22], Henrique [79p]	12 065

PALMEIRAS 2012 (CONT'D)

	9	Paraná	W	4-0	CBr3	Mazinho 2 [26 52], Valdivia [63], Maikon Leite [73]	10 855
May	16	Atlético PR	D	2-2	CBqf	Barcos [22], Maikon Leite [60]	7 307
	19	Portuguesa	D	1-1	SA	Luan [38]	8 939
	23	Atlético PR	W	2-0	CBqf	Luan [69], Henrique [83]	17 574
	27	Grêmio	L	0-1	SA	14	18 277
	6	Sport Recife	L	1-2	SA	17 Barcos [38]	19 096
	9	Atlético MG	L	0-1	SA	19	7 268
Jun	13	Grêmio	W	2-0	CBsf	Mazinho [87], Barcos [91+]	43 508
	17	Vasco	D	1-1	SA	18 Mazinho [57]	6 651
	21	Grêmio	D	1-1	CBsf	Valdivia [73]	26 255
	24	Corinthians	L	1-2	SA	19 Mazinho [4]	17 519
	1	Figueirense	W	3-1	SA	17 Roman [38], Barcos [85], Maikon Leite [87]	2 580
	5	Coritiba	W	2-0	CBf	Valdivia [45p], Thiago Heleno [65]	28 557
	8	Ponte Preta	L	0-1	SA	18	5 271
Jul	11	Coritiba	D	1-1	CBf	Betinho [66]	35 122
	15	São Paulo	D	1-1	SA	19 Mazinho [82]	8 374
	19	Coritiba	D	1-1	SA	18 Patrik [5]	11 998
	22	Náutico	W	3-0	SA	19 Obina [19], Mazinho [29], Marcio Araujo [51]	7 407
	26	Bahia	L	0-2	SA	16	7 515
	29	Cruzeiro	L	1-2	SA	18 Barcos [69p]	11 512
	2	Botafogo	W	2-0	CSr2	Barcos 2 [46 65]	
	4	Inter	L	0-1	SA	18	8 387
	8	Botafogo	W	2-1	SA	17 Barcos 2 [14 73]	3 550
	12	Fluminense	L	0-1	SA	17	6 079
Aug	15	Flamengo	W	1-0	SA	15 Barcos [32]	7 500
	19	Atlético GO	L	1-2	SA	16 Barcos [23]	9 955
	23	Botafogo	L	1-3	CSr2	Patrik [43]	
	25	Santos	L	1-2	SA	17 Correa [39]	21 171
	29	Portuguesa	L	0-3	SA	17	7 531
	1	Grêmio	D	0-0	SA	18	11 586
	6	Sport Recife	W	3-1	SA	17 Correa [53], Thiago Real [63], Obina [68]	29 409
	9	Atlético MG	L	0-3	SA	18	18 003
Sep	12	Vasco	L	1-3	SA	19 Luan [24]	1 996
	16	Corinthians	L	0-2	SA	19	26 068
	22	Figueirense	W	3-1	SA	18 Thiago Heleno [8], Henrique [10], Marcos Assuncao [67]	11 062
	29	Ponte Preta	W	3-0	SA	18 Barcos 2 [13 15], Marcos Assuncao [60]	29 739
	3	Millonarios	W	3-1	CSr3	Obina [12], Thiago Real [53], Luan [87]	
	6	São Paulo	L	0-3	SA	18	34 941
	11	Coritiba	L	0-1	SA	18	10 655
Oct	14	Náutico	L	0-1	SA	18	13 439
	17	Bahia	W	1-0	SA	18 Betinho [19]	18 459
	20	Cruzeiro	W	2-0	SA	18 Barcos 2 [67 77]	9 873
	24	Millonarios	L	0-3	CSr2		
	27	Inter	L	1-2	SA	18 Luan [21]	11 339
	4	Botafogo	D	2-2	SA	18 Barcos 2 [28 90]	13 228
Nov	11	Fluminense	L	2-3	SA	18 Barcos [61], Patrik Vieira [65]	8 461
	18	Flamengo	D	1-1	SA	18 Vinicius [62]	7 333
	25	Atlético GO	L	1-2	SA	18 Patrik Vieira [25]	4 579
Dc	1	Santos	L	1-3	SA	18 Maikon Leite [5]	11 641

18th Att: 229 390 • Av: 12 073 (-5.2%) • Pacaembu 37 952

PALMEIRAS SERIE A APPEARANCES/GOALS 2011-12
Goalkeepers Bruno 34 • Deola 2 • Raphael Alemao 2
Defenders Artur 23+2/0 • Cicinho 7+2/0 • Fernandinho 8+3/0
Henrique 28/1 • Leandro 3 • Leandro Amaro 17+1/0
Luiz Gustavo 1+2/0 • Mauricio Ramos 25+1/0 • Adalberto Roman 5+2/1
Thiago Heleno 14/1 • Wellington Silva 5+1/0
Midfield Bruno Dybal 2+1/0 • Correa 13+3/2 • Diego Souza 0+2/0
Felipe 4+1/0 • Joao Arthur 0+1/0 • Joao Denoni 7+6/0
Joao Vitor 17+2/0 • Juninho 30+1/0 • Luan 16+2/3
Marcio Araujo 21+7/1 • Marcos Assuncao 18/2 • Mazinho 15+9/4
Patrik Vieira 6+1/2 • Tiago Real 7+5/1 • Jorge Valdivia CHI 14+3/0
Wesley 3+1/0
Forwards Hernan Barcos ARG 28+1/14 • Betinho 6+7/1
Bruno Oliveira 1/0 • Caio 0+1/0 • Daniel Carvalho 9+5/0 • Indio 0+1/0
Maikon Leite 7+16/2 • Obina 10+14/2 • Patrik 9+3/1 • Vinicius 1+6/1
Coach Luiz Felipe Scolari • Narciso (13/09/12)

PONTE PRETA
2012

	22	S. Caetano	L	0-1	CP		636
Jan	25	Bragantino	W	5-1	CP	Leandro 2 [11 91+], Renato Caja [18], Uendel [88], Rodrigo Pimpao [92+]	3 245
	29	Mogi Mirim	W	3-1	CP	Willian Magrao [24], Joao Paulo Silva [43], Renato Caja [83p]	3 027
	2	Linense	W	2-1	CP	Rodrigo Pimpao [8], Leandro [11]	3 345
	5	São Paulo	L	1-3	CP	Guilherme [52]	8 415
	8	Catan'ense	D	1-1	CP	Gian [57]	1 558
Feb	11	Mirassol	D	3-3	CP	Bruno Nunes 2 [3 6], Marcio Diogo [57]	1 246
	17	Oeste	D	2-2	CP	Renato Caja [8], Guilherme [29]	2 985
	22	Ituano	W	1-0	CP	Rodrigo Pimpao [87]	2 766
	25	Santos	L	1-6	CP	Uendel [51]	10 252
	1	Botafogo RP	W	2-1	CP	Uendel 2 [23 38]	1 816
	4	Comercial	W	1-0	CP	Enrico [30]	3 802
	11	Paulista	W	4-1	CP	Roger [33], Guilherme [36], Gerson [45], Rodrigo Pimpao [65]	5 293
	14	Sapuc'ense	D	0-0	CBr1		296
Mar	17	Palmeiras	L	1-2	CP	Ferron [36]	19 152
	21	Sapuc'ense	W	5-2	CBr1	Roger [21], Enrico 3 [22 59 79], Rodrigo Pimpao [87]	3 226
	24	Guarani	D	1-1	CP	Sacoman [77]	7 143
	28	Portuguesa	W	3-1	CP	Roger 2 [5 50], Renato Caja [77]	2 731
	1	Guaratin'ta	L	1-2	CP	Joao Paulo Silva [11]	1 319
	5	Atlético GO	L	1-2	CBr2	Roger [7]	2 138
	8	Piracicaba	L	1-2	CP	Gerson [45]	4 756
Apr	15	Corinthians	L	1-2	CP	Renato Caja [85p]	7 418
	18	Atlético GO	W	2-1	CBr2	Uendel [63], Renato Caja [70], W 4-3p	4 205
	22	Corinthians	W	3-2	CPqf	Willian Magrao [12], Roger [34], Rodrigo Pimpao [89]	24 254
	29	Guarani	L	1-3	CPsf	Caio [39]	15 179
	2	São Paulo	W	1-0	CBr3	Roger [63]	1 206
May	5	São Paulo	L	1-3	CBr3	Somalia [13]	26 438
	20	Atlético MG	L	0-1	SA	17	4 911
	26	Atlético GO	D	1-1	SA	14 Roger [52]	1 703
	6	Flamengo	D	2-2	SA	14 Rene [14], Joao Paulo [52]	5 365
	10	Figueirense	D	0-0	SA	15	5 901
Jun	17	Corinthians	W	3-1	SA	13 Andre Luis [42]	6 316
	24	Botafogo	W	2-1	SA	10 Nikao [16], Ricardinho [54]	6 713
	30	Vasco	L	2-3	SA	10 Roger 2 [16 26]	7 547
	8	Palmeiras	L	1-0	SA	10 Ricardinho [16]	5 271
	14	Coritiba	W	4-1	SA	8 Roger 3 [35 52 90], Ricardinho [48]	2 857
Jul	18	Náutico	L	0-3	SA	9	11 443
	22	Fluminense	L	1-2	SA	9 Ferron [84]	5 890
	25	Sport Recife	D	1-1	SA	9 Andre Luis [6]	4 117
	29	Santos	L	1-2	SA	10 Roger [82]	4 261
	5	Cruzeiro	W	2-1	SA	9 Cicinho [17], Marcinho [47]	15 103
	9	Grêmio	D	0-0	SA	9	9 010
	11	Inter	L	1-2	SA	11 Cicinho [40]	9 274
Aug	15	Bahia	L	0-2	SA	13	4 259
	18	São Paulo	L	0-3	SA	14	9 900
	25	Portuguesa	W	2-1	SA	13 Giancarlo 2 [6 85]	3 376
	29	Atlético MG	D	2-2	SA	14 Cicinho 2 [42 82]	18 644
	2	Atlético GO	W	3-1	SA	11 Giancarlo [58], Ferron [68], Cleber [85]	4 762
	5	Flamengo	W	1-0	SA	9 Uendel [21]	2 627
Sep	8	Figueirense	D	2-2	SA	10 Giancarlo [9], Marcinho [79]	4 541
	12	Corinthians	D	1-1	SA	10 Tiago [68]	19 844
	16	Botafogo	D	0-0	SA	11	5 922
	23	Vasco	D	0-0	SA	10	7 161
	29	Palmeiras	L	0-3	SA	14	29 739
	4	Coritiba	L	0-1	SA	15	10 141
	10	Náutico	W	2-1	SA	12 Rildo [73], Marcinho [77p]	6 856
Oct	14	Fluminense	L	1-2	SA	14 Luan [2]	16 029
	18	Sport Recife	L	1-3	SA	14 Giancarlo [45]	10 280
	21	Santos	W	1-0	SA	13 Luan [13]	13 468
	25	Cruzeiro	W	1-0	SA	10 Roger [33]	6 480
	3	Grêmio	L	0-1	SA	14	40 760
Nov	7	Inter	W	1-0	SA	11 Roger [26]	8 435
	18	Bahia	L	1-2	SA	12	24 004
	25	São Paulo	D	0-0	SA	12	9 471
Dc	2	Portuguesa	D	0-0	SA	14	5 739

14th Att: 118 468 • Av: 6 235 • Majestoso 19 722

PONTE PRETA SERIE A APPEARANCES/GOALS 2012

Goalkeepers Edson Bastos 30 • Lauro 2 • Roberto 6
Defenders Cicinho 31+1/4 • Cleber 7+1/1 • Diego Sacoman 18+1/0
Ferron 29+1/2 • Geronimo 9+2/0 • Gustavo Araujo 5/0 • Joao Paulo 8/0
Tiago 28+1/1 • Uendel 15+6/1
Midfield Baraka 37/0 • Bruninho 0+5/0 • Caio 3+8/0 • Enrico 1+1/0
Joao Paulo 23+1/1 • Lucas 2+3/0 • Marcinho 18+9/3 • Nadson 0+1/0
Nikao 20+9/1 • Rene 26+5/1 • Ricardinho 9+6/3 • Somalia 7+6/0
Wendel 9/0 • Xaves 1+2/0
Forwards Andre Luis 14+6/2 • Bruno Nunes 0+2/0 • Giancarlo 7+7/5
Luan 11+6/2 • Maranhao 0+1/0 • Rildo 13+10/1
Rodrigo Pimpao 0+1/0 • Roger 27+2/9 • Rossi 0+3/0 • Tony 2+4/0
Coach Gilson Kleina • Guto Ferreira (19/09/12)

PORTUGUESA 2012 (CONT'D)

	4 Figueirense	W	2-0	SA	12	Bruno Mineiro [54], Ananias [85]	1 600
	8 Bahia	D	0-0	SA	13		8 166
	12 Botafogo	D	1-1	SA	12	Bruno Mineiro [39]	3 108
Aug	15 Grêmio	W	2-1	SA	11	Ananias [27], Bruno Mineiro [82]	15 798
	19 Inter	D	1-1	SA	13	Marcelo Cordeiro [82p]	4 365
	25 Ponte Preta	L	1-2	SA	14	Bruno Mineiro [25]	3 376
	29 Palmeiras	W	3-0	SA	13	Bruno Mineiro 2 [49 70], Moises [84]	7 531
	1 Vasco	L	0-2	SA	14		2 464
	5 Coritiba	W	3-0	SA	11	Bruno Mineiro 2 [12 47], Ananias [55]	1 600
	9 Atlético GO	D	1-1	SA	11	Valdomiro [53]	891
Sep	12 Fluminense	L	0-2	SA	12		3 613
	15 São Paulo	L	1-3	SA	12	Bruno Mineiro [37]	18 957
	22 Santos	W	3-1	SA	12	Bruno Mineiro 2 [38 63], Leo Silva [44]	15 774
	29 Atlético MG	D	1-1	SA	15	Leo Silva [51]	5 971
	4 Sport Recife	W	5-1	SA	11	Bruno Mineiro 4 [24 48 66 90], Moises [81]	2 054
	10 Cruzeiro	L	0-2	SA	13		2 344
Oct	13 Corinthians	D	1-1	SA	13	Marcelo Cordeiro [13]	7 397
	17 Flamengo	D	0-0	SA	13		5 892
	21 Náutico	D	0-0	SA	15		13 199
	27 Figueirense	D	0-0	SA	15		3 118
	4 Bahia	L	0-2	SA	15		4 340
	10 Botafogo	L	0-3	SA	15		5 794
Nov	18 Grêmio	D	2-2	SA	16	Moises [52p], Leo Silva [60]	3 993
	25 Inter	W	2-0	SA	15	Luiz Ricardo [36], Marcelo Cordeiro [55p]	6 442
Dc	2 Ponte Preta	D	0-0	SA	16		5 739

16th Att: 80 500 • Av: 4 237 • Caninde 25 470

PORTUGUESA SERIE A APPEARANCES/GOALS 2012

Goalkeepers Dida 32 • Gledson 5 • Weverton 1
Defenders Andre Luis 1/0 • Diego 1+2/0 • Gustavo 31/0 • Ivan 7+1/1
Lima 11+6/0 • Marcelo Cordeiro 23+1/3 • Rai 5+1/0 • Renato 2/0
Rogerio 24+4/0 • Valdomiro 23+1/1
Midfield Ananias 31/4 • Boquita 27+4/0 • Bruninho 1+4/0
Diguinho 0+7/0 • Ferdinando 26+1/0 • Guilherme 6/0 • Henrique 3+5/0
Heverton 7+5/1 • Leo Silva 36/3 • Maylson 1+2/0 • Michael 1+4/0
Moises 34/6 • Wilson Mathias 1/0 • Ze Antonio 2+5/0
Forwards Bruno Mineiro 23/14 • Diego Viana 6+18/1
Luiz Ricardo 33/1 • Ricardo Jesus 7+2/2 • Rodriguinho 3+16/2
Vandinho 3+1/0 • William 1+4/0
Coach Geninho

PORTUGUESA 2012

	21 Paulista	L	0-2	CP		2 267
Jan	25 Palmeiras	D	1-1	CP	Maylson [49]	7 993
	28 Guaratin'ta	W	2-1	CP	Henrique [47], Marcelo Cordeiro [57p]	1 779
	1 Bragantino	D	1-1	CP	Ananias [81]	2 557
	4 Ituano	D	1-1	CP	Rai [79]	2 006
	8 Guarani	L	0-1	CP		4 399
Feb	12 BotafogoRP	W	3-0	CP	Luis Ricardo [1], Renato Chaves [46], Leo Silva [80p]	905
	17 Piracicaba	W	1-0	CP	Danilo [58]	894
	22 Corinthians	L	0-2	CP		6 167
	26 S. Caetano	D	1-1	CP	Vandinho [67p]	786
	29 Mogi Mirim	L	1-3	CP	Henrique [3]	1 756
	3 Catan'ense	D	0-0	CP		1 188
	8 Cuiabá	D	1-1	CBr1	Ricardo Jesus [19]	3 561
	11 São Paulo	L	1-2	CP	Ricardo Jesus [47]	16 883
Mar	18 Oeste	L	2-3	CP	Ricardo Jesus [25p], Henrique [41]	1 234
	21 Cuiabá	W	4-0	CBr1	Diego Souza [45], Ananias [82], Danilo 2 [86 88]	987
	24 Comercial	W	3-0	CP	Luis Ricardo [19], Guilherme [35], Ricardo Jesus [80]	1 460
	28 Ponte Preta	L	1-3	CP	Rodriguinho [43]	2 731
	1 Santos	L	0-2	CP		4 078
	4 Juventude	L	0-2	CBr2		2 851
Apr	7 Linense	D	2-2	CP	Leo Silva [7], Ananias [13]	1 181
	12 Juventude	W	4-0	CBr2	Ricardo Jesus 3 [36p 65 84], Rai [90]	719
	15 Mirassol	L	2-4	CP	Ananias [59], Luis Ricardo [65]	2 824
	25 Bahia	D	0-0	CBr3		2 369
	10 Bahia	L	0-2	CBr3		13 513
May	19 Palmeiras	D	1-1	SA	7	Rodriguinho [86]	8 939
	26 Vasco	L	0-1	SA	17		4 638
	6 Coritiba	L	0-2	SA	20		8 959
	10 Atlético GO	W	2-0	SA	12	Ricardo Jesus [48], Moises [64]	1 407
Jun	16 Fluminense	L	1-4	SA	16	Ricardo Jesus [62]	4 564
	23 São Paulo	W	1-0	SA	12	Ivan [57]	4 554
	1 Santos	D	0-0	SA	12		8 379
	8 Atlético MG	L	0-2	SA	13		18 875
	15 Sport Recife	L	1-2	SA	15	Moises [71]	15 770
Jul	18 Cruzeiro	L	0-2	SA	16		2 409
	21 Corinthians	D	1-1	SA	17	Heverton [30]	31 106
	26 Flamengo	D	0-0	SA	17		5 732
	29 Náutico	W	3-1	SA	15	Moises [30], Ananias [57], Diego Viana [86]	1 910

SANTOS 2012

	21 Piracicaba	D	1-1	CP	Alan Kardec [32]	11 282
Jan	26 Ituano	W	2-1	CP	Alan Kardec 2 [73 90]	2 203
	29 Paulista	D	1-1	CP	Alan Kardec [74]	3 029
	2 Oeste	D	1-1	CP	Ibson [71]	10 364
	5 Palmeiras	L	1-2	CP	Neymar [70]	25 933
	9 BotafogoRP	W	4-1	CP	Neymar 3 [76 79p 90], Felipe Anderson [93+]	12 489
Feb	12 Linense	W	4-1	CP	Bruno Rodrigo [26], Vinicius Simon [61], Anderson Carvalho [73], Dimba [75]	4 226
	15 Strongest	L	1-2	CLg1	Henrique [10]	19 084
	18 Mirassol	W	3-1	CP	Juan [12], Borges [48p], Edu Dracena [64]	8 116
	22 Comercial	W	2-0	CP	Ibson [28], Durval [81]	5 100
	25 Ponte Preta	W	6-1	CP	Neymar 2 [27 77], Ganso [34], OG [56], Edu Dracena 2 [58 67]	10 252
	29 Guarani	W	2-0	CP	Ibson [6], Arouca [89]	10 720

SANTOS 2012 (CONT'D)

	4 Corinthians	W	1-0	CP	Ibson [57]	12 818
	7 Inter	W	3-1	CLg1	Neymar 3 [18 53 64]	12 857
	10 Mogi Mirim	L	1-3	CP	Dimba [3]	3 422
Mar	15 Juan Aurich	W	3-1	CLg1	Fucile [35], Ganso [39], Borges [68]	10 264
	18 São Paulo	L	2-3	CP	Edu Dracena [51], Neymar [76]	31 972
	22 Juan Aurich	W	2-0	CLg1	Edu Dracena [15], Neymar [58]	24 435
	25 Bragantino	W	2-0	CP	Alan Kardec [18], Borges [55]	5 416
	29 Guarati'ta	W	5-0	CP	Neymar 3 [3 42p 88p], Borges [25], Juan [36]	4 449
	1 Portuguesa	W	2-0	CP	Rafael Caldeira [49], Dimba [58]	4 078
	4 Inter	D	1-1	CLg1	Alan Kardec [66]	35 530
	8 S. Caetano	L	1-2	CP	Neymar [30]	4 283
Apr	15 Catan'ense	W	5-0	CP	Ganso 2 [24 71], Borges 2 [33 84], Neymar [65]	11 650
	19 Strongest	W	2-0	CLg1	Alan Kardec [85], Neymar [87]	11 761
	22 Mogi Mirim	W	2-0	CPqf	Maranhao [22], Neymar [71]	10 635
	25 Bolivar	L	1-2	CLr2	Maranhao [34]	20 127
	29 São Paulo	W	3-1	CPsf	Neymar 3 [3 31 77]	47 771
	6 Guarani	W	3-0	CPf	Ganso [42], Neymar 2 [65 91+]	40 146
	10 Bolivar	W	8-0	CLr2	Elano 2 [6 50], Neymar 2 [21p 36], Ganso 2 [27 52], Alan Kardec [29], Borges [60]	15 000
May	13 Guarani	W	4-2	CPf	Alan Kardec 2 [1 91+], Neymar 2 [8p 71]	53 749
	17 Vélez	L	0-1	CLqf		21 847
	20 Bahia	D	0-0	SA	11	8 908
	24 Vélez	W	1-0	CLqf	Alan Kardec [78], W 4-2p	13 908
	27 Sport	D	0-0	SA	12	5 294
	6 Fluminense	D	1-1	SA	13 Wason Renteria [4]	4 080
	10 São Paulo	L	0-1	SA	16	6 505
	13 Corinthians	L	0-1	CLsf		14 788
Jun	17 Flamengo	L	0-1	SA	17	17 373
	20 Corinthians	D	1-1	CLsf	Neymar [39]	35 873
	24 Coritiba	D	2-2	SA	18 Edu Dracena [32], Neymar [71]	5 120
	1 Portuguesa	D	0-0	SA	18	8 379
	8 Grêmio	W	4-2	SA	14 Edu Dracena [27], Felipe Anderson 2 [39 70], Neymar [62]	9 402
Jul	15 Inter	D	0-0	SA	13	11 791
	18 Botafogo	D	0-0	SA	14	7 069
	21 Vasco	L	0-2	SA	15	13 392
	25 Atlético MG	L	0-2	SA	18	20 418
	29 Ponte Preta	W	2-1	SA	16 Bruno Peres [37], Miralles [85]	4 261
	5 Náutico	L	0-3	SA	16	11 086
	8 Cruzeiro	W	4-2	SA	14 Felipe Anderson 2 [21], Victor Andrade 2 [31 60], Bill [78]	3 215
	11 Atlético GO	D	2-2	SA	14	20 418
Aug	16 Figueirense	W	3-1	SA	14 Neymar [51], Bruno Peres [78], Ganso [85]	10 993
	19 Corinthians	W	3-2	SA	12 Andre 2 [37 50], Bruno Rodrigo [84]	12 413
	25 Palmeiras	W	2-1	SA	10 Neymar 2 [43 63]	21 171
	29 Bahia	L	1-3	SA	11 Andre [14]	8 612
	2 Sport Recife	L	1-2	SA	13 Andre [51]	20 171
	5 Fluminense	L	1-3	SA	14 Andre [30]	13 007
	9 São Paulo	D	0-0	SA	15	6 379
Sep	12 Flamengo	W	2-0	SA	11 Victor Andrade [85], Neymar [88]	8 015
	16 Coritiba	W	2-1	SA	10 Neymar 2 [70 82]	20 274
	22 Portuguesa	L	1-3	SA	11 Andre [75]	15 774
	30 Grêmio	D	1-1	SA	13 Bruno Rodrigo [58]	38 212
	3 Inter	D	1-1	SA	14 Bernardo [16]	9 965
	10 Botafogo	W	2-0	SA	10 Andre [53], Miralles [56]	2 986
Oct	14 Vasco	W	2-0	SA	9 Miralles 2 [10 47]	6 555
	17 Atlético MG	D	2-2	SA	10 Miralles [1], Neymar [11]	10 553
	21 Ponte Preta	L	0-1	SA	11	13 468
	25 Náutico	D	0-0	SA	11	6 256
	3 Cruzeiro	W	4-0	SA	9 Neymar 3 [10 35 81], Felipe Anderson [53]	16 331
Nov	10 Atlético GO	L	1-2	SA	10 Bruno Rodrigo [44]	7 276
	17 Figueirense	W	2-0	SA	10 Rodriguez [42], Felipe Anderson [63]	10 013
	24 Corinthians	D	1-1	SA	10 Felipe Anderson [36]	36 482
Dc	2 Palmeiras	W	3-1	SA	8 Victor Andrade [13], Neymar 2 [25p 38]	11 641

8th Att: 154 049 • Av: 8 108 (-8.9%) • Vila Belmiro 20 120

SANTOS SERIE A APPEARANCES/GOALS 2012

Goalkeepers Aranha 13 • Rafael 25
Defenders Bruno Peres 24+1/2 • Bruno Rodrigo 31+2/3 • Crystian 1/0
David 5+2/0 • Douglas 2+1/0 • Durval 33/0 • Edu Dracena 6/2
Emerson 1/0 • Ewerton Pascoa 9+2/0 • Geuvanio 0+4/0
Gustavo Vernes 1/0 • Juan 15+3/0 • Leo 17/0 • Maranhao 3+3/0
Rafael Galhardo 5/0 • Vinicius 0+1/0
Midfield Adriano 28+1/0 • Alan 1+3/0 • Anderson Carvalho 1/0
Arouca 31/0 • Bernardo 4+10/1 • Elano 2+1/0
Felipe Anderson 30+5/6 • Ganso 5/1 • Gerson Magrao 15+9/0
Henrique 19+3/0 • Joao Pedro 1+9/0 • Leandro 3/0 • Pedro Castro 1/0
Patricio Rodriguez ARG 14+6/2
Forwards Alan Kardec 4/0 • Andre 18+1/7 • Bill 7+9/1 • Borges 3/0
Dimba 3+3/0 • Ezequiel Miralles ARG 8+8/6 • Neymar 17/14
Wason Renteria COL 4+1/1 • Victor Andrade 8+11/4
Coach Muricy Ramalho

SAO PAULO FC 2012

	22 Botafogo RP	W	4-0	CP	Rhodolfo [36], Cicero [43], Edson Silva [56], OG [70]	15 586
Jan	25 Oeste	W	3-2	CP	OG [31], Wellington [32], Lucas [76]	8 001
	28 S. Caetano	W	2-1	CP	Luis Fabiano [14], Lucas [77]	12 647
	2 Guarani	D	1-1	CP	Willian Jose [38]	9 407
	5 Ponte Preta	W	3-1	CP	Willian Jose 2 [4 75], Lucas [65]	8 415
	9 Comercial	D	1-1	CP	Willian Jose [4]	8 185
Feb	12 Corinthians	L	0-1	CP		26 166
	19 Paulista	W	3-1	CP	Willian Jose 3 [12p 18 75]	5 825
	22 Bragantino	D	3-3	CP	Jadson [27p], Cicero 2 [35 59]	8 180
	26 Palmeiras	D	3-3	CP	Cicero [30], Willian Jose [54p], Fernandinho [75]	19 161
	1 Guarati'ta	W	3-0	CP	Lucas [41], Willian Jose [59], Fernandinho [62]	6 229
	4 Piracicaba	W	1-0	CP	Cicero [89]	13 982
	7 Indep'ente	W	1-0	CBr1	Cicero [14]	22 184
Mar	11 Portuguesa	W	2-1	CP	Jadson [49], Luis Fabiano [71]	16 883
	14 Indep'ente	W	4-0	CBr1	Luis Fabiano 4 [31 33 55 65]	15 404
	18 Santos	W	3-2	CP	Casemiro [8], Luis Fabiano [64p], Lucas [86]	31 972
	25 Mirassol	W	1-0	CP	Rhodolfo [64]	10 651
	29 Catan'ense	W	2-0	CP	Fernandinho [75], OG [93+]	14 009
	1 Ituano	W	4-2	CP	Rhodolfo 2 [55 59], Lucas [61], Willian Jose [75]	10 521
	7 Mogi Mirim	W	2-0	CP	Casemiro [28], Fernandinho [40]	12 919
Apr	11 B. de Feira	W	5-2	CBr2	Rhodolfo [9], Maicon [78], Luis Fabiano 2 [35p 58p], Osvaldo [87]	15 834
	15 Linense	L	1-2	CP	Rhodolfo [23]	8 410
	21 Bragantino	W	4-1	CPqf	Fernandinho [19], Osvaldo [83], Luis Fabiano 2 [52 68]	25 555
	29 Santos	L	1-3	CPsf	Willian Jose [63]	47 771
	2 Ponte Preta	L	0-1	CBr1		1 206
	10 Ponte Preta	W	3-1	CBr3	Casemiro [39], Lucas [41], Luis Fabiano [67]	26 438
May	16 Goiás	W	2-0	CBqf	Luis Fabiano [32], Douglas [52]	21 567
	20 Botafogo	L	2-4	SA	19 Jadson [12], Luis Fabiano [61]	7 008
	23 Goiás	D	2-2	CBqf	Jadson [30], Cortez [62]	22 232
	27 Bahia	W	1-0	SA	8 Luis Fabiano [58]	10 305
	6 Inter	L	0-1	SA	11	12 348
	10 Santos	W	1-0	SA	7 Paulo Miranda [8]	6 505
	14 Coritiba	W	1-0	CBsf	Lucas [89]	40 448
	17 Atlético MG	W	1-0	SA	6 Luis Fabiano [42]	11 656
	20 Coritiba	L	0-2	CBsf		28 244
	23 Portuguesa	D	0-1	SA	8	4 554
Jun	30 Cruzeiro	W	3-2	SA	7 Luis Fabiano [12], Lucas [16], Jadson [50]	17 695

SAO PAULO FC 2012 (CONT'D)

	Opponent	Res	Score	Comp	Att	Scorers	Gate
Jul	8 Coritiba	W	3-1	SA	5	Jadson [16], Maicon [41], Osvaldo [80]	21 336
	15 Palmeiras	D	1-1	SA	5	Luis Fabiano [12]	8 374
	18 Vasco	L	0-1	SA	7		10 428
	22 Figueirense	W	2-0	SA	6	Ademilson [2], Willian Jose [90]	9 445
	25 Atlético GO	L	3-4	SA	7	Ademilson [40], Jadson [50p], Rafael Toloi [63]	6 236
	29 Flamengo	W	4-1	SA	5	Maicon [41], Luis Fabiano 2 [45 58], Jadson [90]	35 049
Aug	2 Bahia	W	2-0	CSr2		Rogerio Ceni [6], Ademilson [68]	
	5 Sport Recife	W	1-0	SA	6	Ademilson [79]	23 402
	9 Fluminense	L	1-2	SA	6	Cicero [43]	3 938
	12 Grêmio	L	1-2	SA	7	Cicero [40]	15 386
	15 Náutico	L	0-3	SA	8		12 172
	18 Ponte Preta	W	3-0	SA	6	Rogerio Ceni [22p], Lucas [27], Osvaldo [88]	9 900
	22 Bahia	W	2-0	CSr2		Willian Jose [64], Maicon [58]	9 791
	26 Corinthians	W	2-1	SA	5	Luis Fabiano 2 [23 61]	34 843
	30 Botafogo	W	4-0	SA	5	Luis Fabiano [4], Osvaldo [58], Lucas [61], Cicero [88]	15 576
Sep	2 Bahia	L	0-1	SA	5		25 945
	5 Inter	D	1-1	SA	5	Maicon [19]	14 171
	9 Santos	D	0-0	SA	6		6 379
	12 Atlético MG	L	0-1	SA	6		18 025
	15 Portuguesa	W	3-1	SA	5	Osvaldo [6], Bruno Cortes [57], Luis Fabiano [78]	18 957
	23 Cruzeiro	W	1-0	SA	5	Osvaldo [67]	40 457
	27 LDU Loja	D	1-1	CSr3		OG [36]	
	30 Coritiba	D	1-1	SA	5	Osvaldo [84]	15 061
Oct	6 Palmeiras	W	3-0	SA	5	Luis Fabiano 2 [34 69], Denilson [42]	34 941
	10 Vasco	W	2-0	SA	5	Luis Fabiano [21], Osvaldo [48]	8 677
	14 Figueirense	W	2-0	SA	4	Luis Fabiano [14], Douglas [21]	27 641
	18 Atlético GO	W	2-0	SA	4	Paulo Miranda [29], Osvaldo [39]	27 098
	21 Flamengo	L	0-1	SA	4		21 631
	25 LDU Loja	D	0-0	CSr3			
	27 Sport Recife	W	4-2	SA	4	Lucas 3 [19 30 59], OG [34]	31 599
	31 Un de Chile	W	2-0	CSqf		Willian Jose 2 [8 18]	
Nov	4 Fluminense	D	1-1	SA	4	Luis Fabiano [51]	54 118
	7 Un de Chile	W	5-0	CSqf		Jadson 2 [4 76], Lucas [21], Luis Fabiano [28], Rafael Toloi [64]	32 934
	11 Grêmio	L	1-2	SA	4	Rogerio Ceni [44p]	40 217
	18 Náutico	W	2-1	SA	4	Luis Fabiano [55], Rogerio Ceni [72p]	62 207
	22 Un Catolica	D	1-1	CSsf		Rafael Toloi [21]	
	25 Ponte Preta	D	0-0	SA	4		9 471
	28 Un Catolica	W	0-0	CSsf			55 286
Dc	2 Corinthians	W	3-1	SA	4	Douglas [14], Maicon 2 [23 77]	22 436
	5 Tigre	D	0-0	CSf			49 000
	12 Tigre	W	2-0	CSf		Lucas [22], Osvaldo [28]	67 042

4th Att: 461 569 • Av: 24 293 (+13.3%) • Morumbi 67 428

SAO PAULO SERIE A APPEARANCES/GOALS 2012

Goalkeepers Denis 14 • Rogerio Ceni 24/3
Defenders Bruno Cortes 35/1 • Douglas 29+4/2 • Edson Silva 8+4/0
Henrique 2/0 • Joao Filipe 10+1/0 • Lucas Farias 1+1/0
Paulo Miranda 19+1/2 • Ivan Piris PAR 1+2/0 • Rafael Toloi 26/1
Rhodolfo 30/0 • Rodrigo Caio 3+4/0
Midfield Marcelo Canete ARG 0+2/0 • Casemiro 10+12/0
Cicero 14+16/3 • Denilson 31/1 • Fabricio 1/0 • Ganso 2+1/0
Jadson 35/5 • Joao Schmidt 2+4/0 • Lucas 21/6 • Maicon 23+9/5
Paulo Assuncao 7+4/0 • Wellington 10+4/0
Forwards Ademilson 9+14/3 • Fernandinho 2+4/0
Luis Fabiano 22/17 • Osvaldo 18+6/8 • Rafinha 1+3/0
Willian Jose 8+11/1
Coach Emerson Leao • Ney Franco (26/06/12)

SPORT RECIFE 2012

	Opponent	Res	Score	Comp	Att	Scorers	Gate
Jan	15 Araripina	D	1-1	CP		Renato Silva [72]	6 360
	19 América PE	D	0-0	CP			22 834
	23 Petrolina	W	2-1	CP		Marcelinho [6], Jheimy [43]	11 497
	26 Belo Jardim	W	3-0	CP		Jheimy [20], Marquinhos [50], Willian Rocha [73]	5 462
	29 Náutico	W	4-3	CP		Roberson 2 [6 13], Willian Rocha [11], Tobi [60]	19 943
Feb	1 Salgueiro	L	0-2	CP			9 044
	5 S. Talhada	W	2-1	CP		Rene [55], Marcelinho [70]	4 438
	8 Ypiranga	L	0-1	CP			13 650
	11 Porto	W	4-2	CP		OG [33], Marcelinho 3 [72 84p 87p]	12 243
	16 Santa Cruz	W	3-1	CP		Jheimy [43], Marcelinho [66], Milton Junior [90]	45 109
	23 Central	W	2-1	CP		Rivaldo [23], Jael [48]	18 554
	26 Central	D	1-1	CP		Jael [72]	12 653
	29 Belo Jardim	W	3-2	CP		Marcelinho [6], Tobi [51], Willians [77]	14 476
Mar	4 Petrolina	W	1-0	CP		Jael [89]	5 300
	7 Araripina	W	2-1	CP		Marcelinho 2 [39 57]	12 873
	10 América PE	W	4-2	CP		Bruno Aguiar [20], Tobi [30], Willians [47], Marcelinho [82]	10 498
	14 4 de Julho	W	2-0	CBr1		Marcelinho [37], Renato Silva [92+]	2 528
	17 Salgueiro	D	0-0	CP			21 487
	25 Náutico	D	0-0	CP			17 559
	28 Ypiranga	W	2-1	CP		Willians [68], Jheimy [76]	5 033
	31 S. Talhada	W	5-0	CP		Marcelinho 2 [10 61], Jael [66], Ruan [77], Jheimy [81]	14 660
Apr	4 Paysandu	L	1-2	CBr2		Jael [45]	7 702
	8 Porto	W	3-1	CP		Jheimy [3], Ruan [44p], Milton Junior [85]	6 262
	11 Paysandu	L	1-4	CBr2		Bruno Aguiar [76]	13 029
	15 Santa Cruz	W	2-1	CP		Bruno Aguiar 2 [35 51]	18 252
	22 Náutico	W	2-1	CPsf		Marcelinho 2 [23 81]	12 594
	29 Náutico	D	0-0	CPsf			17 040
May	6 Santa Cruz	D	0-0	CPf			44 082
	13 Santa Cruz	L	2-3	CPf		Moacir [14], Edcarlos [82]	29 932
	19 Flamengo	D	1-1	SA	7	Marquinhos [57]	26 699
	27 Santos	D	0-0	SA	10		5 294
Jun	6 Palmeiras	W	2-1	SA	8	Marquinhos Parana [14], Felipe Azevedo [71]	19 096
	10 Cruzeiro	L	0-1	SA	11		4 574
	17 Bahia	L	1-2	SA	15	Bruno Aguiar [69]	11 031
	24 Inter	L	0-2	SA	16		15 249
Jul	1 Coritiba	W	3-2	SA	11	Henrique [36], Marquinhos [75], Felipe Azevedo [86]	13 902
	8 Corinthians	D	1-1	SA	12	Marquinhos [90]	23 009
	15 Portuguesa	W	2-1	SA	11	Henrique [15], Gilberto [68]	15 770
	18 Grêmio	L	1-2	SA	12	Felipe Azevedo [39]	15 179
	21 Atlético MG	L	1-4	SA	13	Gilberto [25]	16 230
	25 Ponte Preta	D	1-1	SA	13	Marquinhos [23]	4 117
	29 Atlético GO	D	0-0	SA	13		12 860
Aug	5 São Paulo	L	0-1	SA	15		23 402
	9 Vasco	L	0-2	SA	16		13 786
	11 Figueirense	L	0-1	SA	16		11 258
	15 Botafogo	L	0-2	SA	18		2 457
	18 Fluminense	L	0-1	SA	19		5 298
	26 Náutico	D	0-0	SA	19		17 066
	30 Flamengo	D	1-1	SA	18	Felipe Azevedo [20]	6 035
Sep	2 Santos	W	2-1	SA	17	Hugo [3], Felipe Azevedo [37]	20 171
	6 Palmeiras	L	1-3	SA	18	Rivaldo [62]	29 409
	9 Cruzeiro	W	2-1	SA	17	Rithely [32], Gilberto [62]	12 165
	12 Bahia	D	1-1	SA	17	Hugo [6]	17 107
	16 Inter	D	2-2	SA	17	Rithely [35], Gilsinho [42]	4 481
	23 Coritiba	W	1-0	SA	17	Gilberto [90p]	17 075
	30 Corinthians	L	0-3	SA	17		25 277
Oct	4 Portuguesa	L	1-5	SA	17	Hugo [15]	2 054
	11 Grêmio	L	1-3	SA	17	Hugo [80p]	11 210
	14 Atlético MG	L	1-2	SA	17	Hugo [16]	14 265
	18 Ponte Preta	W	3-1	SA	17	Rithely [34], Tobi [39], Gilsinho [82]	10 280
	21 Atlético GO	W	1-0	SA	17	Hugo [47]	449
	27 São Paulo	L	2-4	SA	17	Gilberto [14], Hugo [81p]	31 599

SPORT RECIFE 2012 (CONT'D)

Nov	4	Vasco	W 3-0	SA 17	Felipe Azevedo [40], Hugo [53], Henrique [87]	3 809
	11	Figueirense	D 1-1	SA 17	Gilberto [23]	3 122
	18	Botafogo	W 2-0	SA 17	Gilberto [57], Henrique [89]	25 126
	25	Fluminense	D 1-1	SA 17	Felipe Azevedo [45]	32 937
Dc	2	Náutico	L 0-1	SA 17		20 100

17th Att: 348,693 • Av: 18 352 • Ilha do Retiro 45 500

SPORT SERIE A APPEARANCES/GOALS 2012
Goalkeepers Magrao 26 • Matheus 0+1 • Saulo 12
Defenders Ailson 19+1/0 • Bruno Aguiar 18+4/1 • Cicinho 23+1/0
Diego Ivo 21+1/0 • Edcarlos 18+1/0 • Moacir 26+7/0
Reinaldo 18+6/0 • Renato 2+4/0 • Rene 9+4/0 • Thiaguinho 6+1/0
Tobi 34+1/1 • Welton 1/0 • Willian 5+1/0
Midfield Diogo 0+1/0 • Felipe Azevedo 37/7 • Felipe Menezes 1+6/0
Gilberto 16+9/7 • Hamilton TOG 1+1/0 • Hugo 22+2/8
Marquinhos Parana 8/1 • Milton Junior 0+2/0 • Naldinho 3+2/0
Renan 6+4/0 • Rithely 30+3/3 • Rivaldo 13+3/1
Willians Santana 3+12/0
Forwards Gilsinho 18+4/2 • Henrique 4+12/4 • Jael 0+1/0
Jheimy 1+2/0 • Magno Alves 1+3/0 • Marquinhos 16+5/4
Roberson 0+4/0 • Ruan 0+2/0 • Sandrinho 0+1/0
Coach Vagner Mancini • Waldemar Lemos (11/08/12)
Sergio Guedes (6/10/12)

VASCO DA GAMA 2012

Jan	22	Americano	W 2-0	TG	Alecsandro [30], Fagner [41]	6 920
	29	D de Caxias	W 3-1	TG	Juninho [27], Alecsandro [58], Diego Souza [73]	3 598
	1	Bangu	W 3-1	TG	Alecsandro [22], Thiago Feltri [27], Bernardo [58]	6 611
	5	Friburgense	W 2-0	TG	Diego Souza 2 [44 59]	8 540
	8	Nacional	L 1-2	CLg5	Alecsandro [73]	27 300
	12	Fluminense	W 2-1	TG	Alecsandro 2 [59 78]	10 416
Feb	15	V. Redonda	W 3-0	TG	Alecsandro 2 [14 38p], William Barbio [16]	3 687
	18	Boavista	W 1-0	TG	Kim [77]	3 002
	22	Flamengo	W 2-1	TGsf	Alecsandro [14], Diego Souza [77]	21 492
	26	Fluminense	L 1-3	TGf	Eduardo Costa [82]	36 374
	29	Bonsucesso	D 2-2	TR	Alecsandro [2], Felipe [58]	2 428
	3	Olaria	W 2-0	TR	Tenorio [11], Eder Luis [25]	1 354
	6	Alianza	W 3-2	CLg5	OG [18], Dede [59], Juninho [80p]	29 900
	11	Madureira	W 3-0	TR	Juninho [58], Fellipe Bastos [66], Allan [88]	4 489
Mar	14	Libertad	D 1-1	CLg5	Diego Souza [16]	3 847
	18	Botafogo	L 1-3	TR	Fellipe Bastos [47]	11 941
	21	Libertad	W 2-0	CLg5	Juninho [52], Alecsandro [61]	15 799
	25	Resende	D 1-1	TR	Alecsandro [80]	6 608
	31	Macae	W 4-1	TR	Diego Souza [11], Juninho 2 [14 45], Eder Luis [37]	4 877
	3	Alianza	W 2-1	CLg5	Fellipe Bastos 2 [17 70]	7 736
	7	Flamengo	L 1-2	TR	Diego Souza [51]	14 152
Apr	12	Nacional	W 1-0	CLg5	Diego Souza [56]	4 302
	15	Nova Iguçu	W 3-1	TR	Romulo [3], Alecsandro 2 [40 91+]	2 060
	22	Flamengo	W 3-2	TRsf	Eder Luis [12], Felipe 2 [40 48]	20 067
	29	Botafogo	L 1-3	TRf	Carlos Alberto [80]	41 387

VASCO DA GAMA 2012 (CONT'D)

May	2	Lanús	W 2-1	CLr2	Alecsandro [25], Diego Souza [42]	13 017
	9	Lanús	L 1-2	CLr2	Nilton [18]. W 5-4p	6 408
	16	Corinthians	D 0-0	CLqf		20 510
	20	Grêmio	W 2-1	SA 3	Felipe Bastos [22], Alecsandro [68]	8 304
	23	Corinthians	L 0-1	CLqf		35 974
	26	Portuguesa	W 1-0	SA 2	Alecsandro [21]	4 638
Jun	6	Náutico	W 4-2	SA 1	Alecsandro 2 [22 69], Felipe [35], Juninho Pernambucano [62]	7 541
	10	Bahia	W 2-1	SA 1	Juninho Pernambucano [8], Diego Souza 31	17 908
	17	Palmeiras	D 1-1	SA 1	Juninho Pernambucano [84]	6 651
	23	Cruzeiro	L 1-3	SA 3	Rodolfo 66	18 337
	30	Ponte Preta	W 3-2	SA 2	Alecsandro [20], Eder Luis [48], Diego Souza [76b]	7 547
	8	Figueirense	D 1-1	SA 3	Diego Souza [21]	15 526
	15	Atlético GO	W 1-0	SA 2	OG [13]	9 624
Jul	18	São Paulo	W 1-0	SA 2	Fagner [49]	10 428
	21	Santos	W 2-0	SA 2	Douglas [12], Alecsandro [47]	13 392
	25	Botafogo	W 1-0	SA 2	Alecsandro [87]	17 778
	28	Inter	D 0-0	SA 2		15 462
	5	Corinthians	D 0-0	SA 2		15 655
	8	Sport Recife	W 2-0	SA 2	Juninho Pernambucano [68], Carlos Tenorio [85]	13 786
Aug	12	Atlético MG	L 0-1	SA 3		19 650
	16	Coritiba	D 2-2	SA 3	Felipe [49], Wendel [88]	5 013
	19	Flamengo	L 0-1	SA 3		15 459
	25	Fluminense	L 1-2	SA 4	OG [74]	9 729
	29	Grêmio	L 0-2	SA 4		21 758
	1	Portuguesa	W 2-0	SA 4	Alecsandro [37]	2 464
	5	Náutico	D 1-1	SA 4	Fellipe Bastos [54]	11 541
	9	Bahia	L 0-4	SA 4		5 018
Sep	12	Palmeiras	W 3-1	SA 4	Carlos Tenorio [30], Nilton [52], Juninho Pernambucano [72]	1 996
	16	Cruzeiro	D 1-1	SA 4	Nilton [27]	9 753
	23	Ponte Preta	D 0-0	SA 4		7 161
	29	Figueirense	W 3-1	SA 4	Luan [34], Carlos Tenorio [51], Juninho Pernambucano [80]	5 062
	6	Atlético GO	W 1-0	SA 4	Juninho Pernambucano [86]	13 212
	10	São Paulo	L 0-2	SA 4		8 677
Oct	14	Santos	L 0-2	SA 5		6 555
	18	Botafogo	L 2-3	SA 5	Carlos Alberto 2 [25 39]	7 525
	24	Inter	L 1-2	SA 5	Jonas [22]	14 774
	27	Corinthians	L 0-1	SA 7		24 376
	4	Sport Recife	L 0-3	SA 7		3 809
Nov	11	Atlético MG	D 1-1	SA 7	Alecsandro [69]	7 036
	17	Coritiba	W 2-1	SA 7	Romario Correia [22], Nilton [58]	10 545
	24	Flamengo	D 1-1	SA 6	Nilton [34]	5 971
Dc	2	Fluminense	W 2-1	SA 5	Eder Luis 2 [71 80]	5 470

5th Att: 167 727 • Av: 8 828 (-42.9%) • São Januário 20 150

VASCO SERIE A APPEARANCES/GOALS 2012
Goalkeepers Alessandro 1 • Fernando Prass 37
Defenders Dede 22+1/0 • Dieyson 2/0 • Douglas 25+1/1
Fabricio 6+3/0 • Fagnar 7/1 • Jonas 14+2/1 • Luan Teixeira 2+2/1
Max 3+4/0 • Renato Silva 15+1/0 • Rodolfo 8/1 • Thiago Feltri 7+5/0
William 19+2/0
Midfield Abuda 2+1/0 • Aueremir 12+3/0 • Allan 3+1/0
Carlos Alberto 17+11/2 • Leandro Chaparro ARG 0+2/0 • Dakson 0+2/0
Diego Rosa 0+3/0 • Diego Souza 8+1/3 • Eduardo Costa 6+5/0
Felipe 16+7/2 • Fellipe Bastos 15+12/2
Juninho Pernambucano 28+1/7 • Maicon Assis 0+3/0 • Marlone 5+4/0
Nilton 34/4 • Renato Augusto 0+1/0 • Romulo 2+1/0 • Wendel 25+1/1
Forwards Alecsandro 30+1/9 • Eder Luis 25+2/3 • Jhon Cley 4+6/0
Jonathan 0+1/0 • Kim 1/0 • Pipico 0+7/0 • Romario Correia 2+1/1
Carlos Tenorio ECU 8+6/4 • William Barbio 7+5/0
Coach Cristavo Borges • Marcelo Oliveira (9/09/12) Gaucho (5/11/12)

BRB – BARBADOS

FIFA/COCA-COLA WORLD RANKING

'93	'94	'95	'96	'97	'98	'99	'00	'01	'02	'03	'04	'05	'06	'07	'08	'09	'10	'11	'12
114	107	103	110	113	121	113	104	107	99	124	121	115	98	128	122	129	131	165	143

2012

Jan	Feb	Mar	Apr	May	Jun	Jul	Aug	Sep	Oct	Nov	Dec	High	Low	Av
165	169	170	171	171	178	170	171	175	152	153	143	92	178	117

The Barbados national team fell to its lowest position in the FIFA/Coca-Cola World Ranking in June 2012 as a result of just three wins since the start of 2009 and six straight defeats in a 2014 FIFA World Cup qualifying group at the end of 2011. The position had improved by the end of the year thanks to a brace of wins in their 2012 Caribbean Cup qualifying group. Unfortunately for the Bajans, six points wasn't enough to take them through to the second round of qualifying. A defeat at the hands of an improving Dominican Republic team at the Kensington Oval in Bridgetown saw them finish second in the group. In the Bajan league the years were rolled back with the return to winning ways of Weymouth Wales, a team that dominated the club scene until the mid-1980s. In 2011 they had won their first trophy for nearly a quarter of a century by winning the cup but completed their rise from the ashes by claiming the league title in 2012 - their first since 1986. In a close race with Barbados Defence Force they clinched the title after a 0-0 draw between the two in the penultimate game of the season. There was consolation for BDF when a month later they knocked Weymouth Wales out of the cup with a 4-2 victory in the semi-finals and then went on to beat Brittons Hill in a thrilling final that finshed 4-3 - the winner from Shamar Edwards coming nine minutes from the end of extra-time.

CFU CARIBBEAN CUP RECORD

1989 5 r1 **1991** DNE **1992-1993** DNQ **1994** 6 r1 **1995-1999** DNQ **2001** 8 r1 **2005** 4 (hosts) **2007** 8 r1 **2008** 8 r1 **2010-2012** DNQ

BARBADOS FOOTBALL ASSOCIATION (BFA)

Bottom Floor,
ABC Marble Complex,
PO Box 1362, Fontabelle
☎ +1 246 2281707
+1 246 2286484
office@barbadosfa.com
www.barbadosfa.com
FA 1910 CON 1968 FIFA 1968
P Randolph Harris
GS Chris Graham

THE STADIA

2014 FIFA World Cup Stadia
Waterford National Stadium
Bridgetown   7 500
Other Main Stadia
Kensington Oval
Bridgetown   32 000
Empire Ground
Bridgetown   1 000
Wildey Astro Turf
Bridgetown   1 000

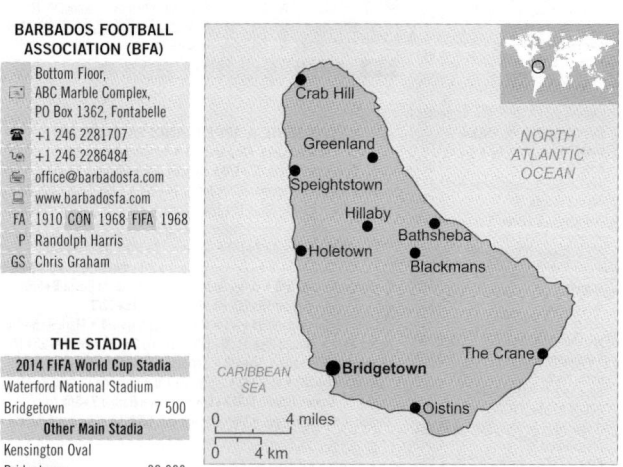

MAJOR CITIES/TOWNS

		Population
1	Bridgetown	93 312
2	Speightstown	2 402
3	Bathsheba	1 575
4	Holetown	1 494
5	Oistins	1 444
6	Bulkeley	1 115
7	Crane	1 016
8	Crab Hill	716
9	Blackmans	550
10	Greenland	524
11	Hillaby	509

BARBADOS

Capital	Bridgetown	Population	284 589 (180)	% in cities	40%
GDP per capita	$19 100 (66)	Area km²	430 km² (200)	GMT +/-	-4
Neighbours (km)	Coast 97				

RECENT INTERNATIONAL MATCHES PLAYED BY BARBADOS

2007	Opponents		Score	Venue	Comp	Scorers	Att	Referee
12-01	Trinidad and Tobago	D	1-1	Port of Spain	CCr1	Harvey [66]		Moreno PAN
15-01	Haiti	L	0-2	Port of Spain	CCr1			Jauregua ANT
17-01	Martinique	L	2-3	Port of Spain	CCr1	Harvey [27], Soares [42]		Jauregua ANT
25-03	Guatemala	D	0-0	Bridgetown	Fr		2 500	Forde BRB
2008								
13-01	Antigua & Barbuda	W	3-2	Black Rock	Fr	Vaughan [17], Straker [39], Lynch [63]	2 700	Small BRB
6-02	Dominica	D	1-1	Roseau	WCq	Rashida Williams [43]	4 200	Quesada CRC
13-03	St Vincent/Grenadines	W	2-0	Kingstown	Fr	Stanford [38], Norman Forde [87]	1 050	Cambridge VIN
15-03	Grenada	D	1-1	St George's	Fr	Worrell [75]	2 500	Phillip GRN
26-03	Dominica	W	1-0	Bridgetown	WCq	Stanford [80]	4 150	Batres GUA
11-05	Trinidad and Tobago	L	0-3	Macoya	Fr		1 200	Brizan TRI
6-06	Bermuda	L	1-2	Hamilton	Fr	Norman Forde [44]	2 000	Raynor BER
9-06	Bermuda	L	0-3	Hamilton	Fr		2 200	Francis BER
15-06	USA	L	0-8	Carson	WCq		11 500	Rodriguez MEX
22-06	USA	L	0-1	Bridgetown	WCq		2 000	Moreno PAN
26-09	British Virgin Isles	W	2-1	Basseterre	CCq	Rashida Williams [11], Norman Forde [53]	150	Baptiste DMA
28-09	St Kitts and Nevis	W	3-1	Basseterre	CCq	Straker [35], Skeete [45], Rashida Williams [80]	500	Charles DMA
23-10	Surinam	W	3-2	Havana	CCq	Norman Forde 3 [62 65 70]	100	Morrison JAM
25-10	Cuba	D	1-1	Havana	CCq	Doyle [66]	1 000	Campbell JAM
27-10	Netherlands Antilles	W	2-1	Havana	CCq	Norman Forde [6p], Parris [20]	1 000	Morrison JAM
3-12	Jamaica	L	1-2	Kingston	CCr1	Riviere Williams [45]	20 000	Aguilar SLV
5-12	Trinidad and Tobago	L	1-2	Montego Bay	CCr1	Goodridge [17]	2 000	Jauregui ANT
7-12	Grenada	L	2-4	Trelawny	CCr1	Riviere Williams 2 [71 79]	9 000	Aguilar SLV
2009								
8-02	Grenada	W	5-0	Bridgetown	Fr	Jeffrey Williams 2 [35 68], Stanford [43], Harte [44], Chandler [88]	3 000	Forde BRB
2010								
25-09	Dominica	L	0-2	Bridgetown	Fr		625	Taylor BRB
26-09	Dominica	L	1-3	Bridgetown	Fr	Harte [21]	580	Skeete DMA
6-10	St Kitts and Nevis	D	1-1	Kingstown	CCq	Rashida Williams [14]	250	Elskampr SUR
8-10	Montserrat	W	5-0	Kingstown	CCq	Norman Forde 2 [19 83], Riviere Williams [36], Terry Adamson [53], Kadeem Atkins [90]	350	Pinas SUR
10-10	St Vincent/Grenadines	D	0-0	Kingstown	CCq		5 420	Jauregui ANT
2011								
20-05	Guyana	L	0-1	Linden	Fr		300	Lancaster GUY
22-05	Guyana	L	2-3	Georgetown	Fr	Mardona Lavine [1], Riviere Williams [15]	2 500	Young GUY
27-05	St Vincent/Grenadines	D	0-0	Bridgetown	Fr		3 500	Skeete BRB
29-05	Guyana	D	1-1	Bridgetown	Fr	Rashida Williams [24]	2 055	Taylor BRB
21-08	St Lucia	W	4-0	Bridgetown	Fr	Riviere Williams [35], Kadeem Atkins 2 [45 56], Kyle Gibson [90]	3 500	Skeete BRB
2-09	Guyana	L	0-2	Georgetown	WCq		4 500	St Catherine LCA
6-09	Trinidad and Tobago	L	0-2	Bridgetown	WCq		775	Bonilla SLV
7-10	Guyana	L	0-2	Bridgetown	WCq		2 500	Georges HAI
11-10	Trinidad and Tobago	L	0-4	Port of Spain	WCq		3 000	Bogle JAM
11-11	Bermuda	L	1-2	Prospect	WCq	Diquan Adamson [7]	1 000	Barrios GUA
14-11	Bermuda	L	1-2	Prospect	WCq	Sheridan Grosvenor [92+]	1 000	Moreno PAN
2012								
1-09	St Vincent/Grenadines	L	0-2	Kingstown	Fr		200	Delves VIN
2-09	St Vincent/Grenadines	D	1-1	Kingstown	Fr	Jeffrey Williams [31]	500	Cambridge VIN
23-09	Dominica	W	1-0	Bridgetown	CNq	Rashida Williams [35]	300	Brizan TRI
25-09	Dominican Republic	L	0-1	Bridgetown	CNq		750	Elskamp SUR
27-09	Aruba	W	2-1	Bridgetown	CNq	Barry Skeete [21], Mario Harte [56]	300	Lancaster GUY

Fr = Friendly match • CC = Digicel Caribbean Cup • WC = FIFA World Cup • q = qualifier • r1 = first round group

BARBADOS 2012

DIGICEL PREMIER LEAGUE

	Pl	W	D	L	F	A	Pts	Weymouth W	Brittons Hill	BDF	Gall Hill	Youth Milan	Notre Dame	Paradise	Dayrells Road	Bagatelle	Pinelands Utd
Weymouth Wales	18	12	4	2	40	10	40		2-1	0-0	0-0	5-1	0-1	1-1	2-0	2-2	2-0
Brittons Hill	18	11	5	2	26	9	38	0-1		2-0	0-0	1-1	1-1	2-1	1-0	4-0	1-0
Bar'dos Defence Force	18	12	2	4	31	17	38	0-4	1-2		1-0	0-0	3-0	1-0	1-0	3-0	3-2
Pride of Gall Hill	18	8	3	7	26	21	27	1-3	0-0	1-3		2-0	4-2	1-0	0-1	2-1	3-1
Youth Milan	18	7	4	7	27	28	25	0-4	0-1	1-6	0-1		3-2	2-0	1-1	0-1	5-0
Notre Dame	18	7	3	8	32	25	24	1-2	0-1	3-1	0-1	0-3		0-0	2-1	4-1	7-0
Paradise	18	6	4	8	17	20	22	2-1	1-1	0-2	1-0	0-1	1-0		0-2	1-0	0-2
Dayrells Road	18	5	6	7	22	23	21	0-1	0-2	1-2	3-2	2-2	2-2	4-4		1-0	1-1
Bagatelle	18	4	1	13	19	38	13	0-3	0-1	0-1	1-0	0-2	1-2	0-3	0-3		6-5
Pinelands United	18	1	2	15	20	69	5	0-7	1-5	1-3	4-8	2-5	0-5	0-2	0-0	1-6	

26/02/2012 - 5/07/2012

BARBADOS 2012 DIVISION ONE

	Pl	W	D	L	F	A	Pts
St Peter's Cosmos	22	13	4	5	49	23	43
Ellerton	22	13	3	6	39	23	42
St John's Sonnets	22	11	6	5	42	29	39
Empire	22	10	5	7	43	23	35
Silver Sands	22	10	5	7	26	19	35
Maxwell	22	8	5	9	25	47	29
Univ. West Indies	22	7	6	9	24	23	27
Deacons	22	5	10	7	27	35	25
Benfica	22	7	4	11	23	35	25
Clarkes Hill	22	7	4	11	24	41	25
Parish Land	22	6	6	10	21	29	24
Road View	22	5	2	15	29	45	17

27/02/2012 - 20/06/2012

MEDALS TABLE

		Overall G	Lge G	Cup G	Town
1	Weymouth Wales	24	16	8	Carrington
2	Notre Dame	15	9	6	Bayville
3	Everton	9	5	4	
4	Paradise	9	4	5	Dover
5	Pride of Gall Hill	6	2	4	Gall Hill
6	Youth Milan	4	2	2	Checker Hall
7	Pinelands	4	3	1	Pinelands
8	BDF	2	2	2	Paragon
9	Brittons Hill	3	2	1	Brittons Hill

FA CUP 2012

Round of 16		Quarter-finals		Semi-finals		Final	
Bar'dos Defence Force	3						
Cosmos	0	**Bar'dos Defence Force**					
Oxley	1	Paradise					
Paradise	4			**Bar'dos Defence Force**	1 4p		
Kick Start	1			Weymouth Wales	1 2p		
Univ. West Indies	0	Kick Start	0				
St John's Sonnets	0	**Weymouth Wales**	2				
Weymouth Wales	1					**Bar'dos Defence Force**	4
Silver Sands	2					Brittons Hill	3
Pride of Gall Hill	1	**Silver Sands**	2				
Bagatelle	0	Rendezvous	0				
Rendezvous	3			Silver Sands	0		
Notre Dame	3			**Brittons Hill**	2		
Dayrells Road	2	Notre Dame	1				
Wooten	1	**Brittons Hill**	3				
Brittons Hill	2			3rd place: Weymouth Wales 5-0 Silver Sands			

CUP FINAL
National Stadium, Waterford
15-07-2012. Scorers - Kemar Dottin [34], Chai Lloyd [78], Mario Harte [109], Shamar Edwards [111] for BDF; Luther Watson [48], Arantees Lawrence [63], Walton Burrowes [92] for BH

BRU – BRUNEI DARUSSALAM

FIFA/COCA-COLA WORLD RANKING

'93	'94	'95	'96	'97	'98	'99	'00	'01	'02	'03	'04	'05	'06	'07	'08	'09	'10	'11	'12
151	165	167	170	178	183	185	193	189	194	194	199	199	175	188	181	191	197	202	182

2012

Jan	Feb	Mar	Apr	May	Jun	Jul	Aug	Sep	Oct	Nov	Dec	High	Low	Av
202	201	201	202	201	202	201	202	202	203	187	182	145	203	184

Brunei returned to international competition in 2012 after the creation of the National Football Association of Brunei Darussalam and the lifting of the ban put in place by FIFA due to government interference. Despite the lifting of the ban in mid-2011, Brunei did not make a return to competitive football at full international level until September 2012 as they tuned up for the qualifying rounds of the AFF Suzuki Cup with a 5-0 defeat at the hands of Indonesia. In the qualifiers in Yangon, Myanmar, Brunei followed up an opening day 1-0 loss against the hosts with a 3-2 win over Cambodia before a 3-1 loss against Laos and a 2-1 victory over Timor-Leste. Those results left them fourth in the five-team group, but just one point shy of securing what would have been a surprise berth in the finals. There was also a welcome return to action for club side Brunei DPMM in Singapore's S-League, where they went on to lift the S-League Cup, a tournament they won previously in 2009 prior to their suspension. At home the new Brunei Super League got underway in December 2012 after a qualifying tournament had whittled down 32 hopefuls to a final ten. 2012 also saw the return of the FA Cup which was won by ABDB. They beat Indira 1-0 to land the trophy for the third time in a row following on from their triumphs in 2008 and 2010.

FIFA WORLD CUP RECORD
1930-1982 DNE **1986** DNQ **1990-1998** DNE **2002** DNQ **2006-2014** DNE

NATIONAL FOOTBALL ASSOCIATION OF BRUNEI DARUSSALAM (NAFBD)

✉ NFABD House, Jalan Pusat Persidangan, Bandar Seri Begawan, BB 4313, Brunei
☎ +673 2 380047
📠 +673 2 380057
✉ nfabd@hotmail.com

FA 1959 CON 1970 FIFA 1969
P Dato Abdul Rahman Mohiddin
GS Mohd Noor bin Haji Abdullah

THE STADIA
2014 FIFA World Cup Stadia
Brunei did not enter the 2014 FIFA World Cup

Main Stadia
Sultan Hassal Bolkiah Stadium
Bandar Seri Begawan 30 000
Track and Field Sports Complex
Bandar Seri Begawan 1 700
Berakas Sports Complex
Bandar Seri Begawan 500

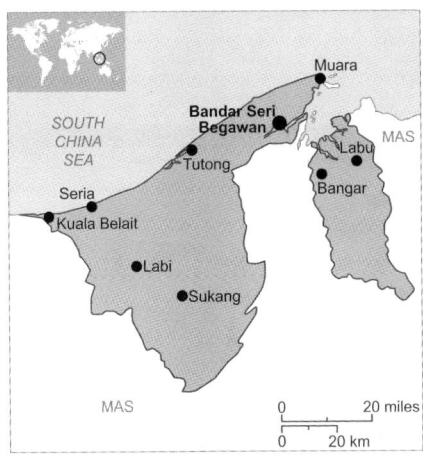

MAJOR CITIES/TOWNS
Population
1 Bandar S Begawan 33 026
2 Kuala Belait 27 726
3 Seria 27 620
4 Tutong 20 962
5 Bangar 3 501

NEGARA BRUNEI DARUSSALAM • BRUNEI DARUSSALAM

Capital Bandar Seri Begawan	Population 388 190 (175)	% in cities 75%
GDP per capita $53 100 (8)	Area km² 5 765 km² (172)	GMT +/- +8
Neighbours (km) Malaysia 381 • Coast 161		

RECENT INTERNATIONAL MATCHES PLAYED BY BRUNEI DARUSSALAM

2007 Opponents	Score	Venue	Comp	Scorers	Att	Referee
No international matches played in 2007						
2008						
13-05 Philippines	L 0-1	Iloilo City	CCq		3 500	Saleem MDV
15-05 Bhutan	D 1-1	Barotac	CCq	Muhammad Khayrun Bin Salleh [76]	4 000	Mahapab THA
17-05 Tajikistan	L 0-4	Iloilo City	CCq		450	Al Badwawi UAE
19-10 Philippines	D 1-1	Phnom Penh	AFFq	Shahraezn Said [17]	12 000	
21-10 Timor-Leste	W 4-1	Phnom Penh	AFFq	Shahraezn Said 2 [9] [26], Azwan Salleh [57], Sallehuddin Damit [76p]		
23-10 Laos	L 2-3	Phnom Penh	AFFq	Hardi Bujang [28], Abu Bakar Mahari [84]		
25-10 Cambodia	L 1-2	Phnom Penh	AFFq	Hardi Bujang [28],	15 000	
2009						
4-04 Sri Lanka	L 1-5	Colombo	CCq	Kamarul Ariffin Ramlee [82]	700	Zhao Liang CHN
6-04 Pakistan	L 0-6	Colombo	CCq		200	Orzuev TJK
8-04 Chinese Taipei	L 0-5	Colombo	CCq		1 000	Al Zahrani KSA
2010						
No international matches played in 2010						
2011						
No international matches played in 2011						
2012						
26-09 Indonesia	L 0-5	B. Seri Begawan	Fr			
5-10 Myanmar	L 0-1	Yangon	AFFq		7 000	Aslam MDV
9-10 Cambodia	W 3-2	Yangon	AFFq	Aminuddin Tahir [56], Helmi Zambrin [62], Azwan Salleh [69]		Takayama JPN
11-10 Laos	L 1-3	Yangon	AFFq	Rosmin Khamis [26]		Shamsuzzaman BAN
13-10 Timor-Leste	W 2-1	Yangon	AFFq	Adi Said [16], Ali Rahman [74]		Takayama JPN

CC = AFC Challenge Cup • AFF = ASEAN Championship • q = qualifier

DST BRUNEI FA CUP 2012

Round of 16		Quarter-finals		Semi-finals		Final	
ABDB	1						
Sporting FT	0	**ABDB**	3				
BSRC	3	Majra United	1				
Majra United	4			**ABDB**	3		
Tunas	3			IKLS	1		
Rimba Star	2	Tunas	0				
Jerudong	1	**IKLS**	1				
IKLS	2					**ABDB**	1
MS PDB	3					Indera	0
Muara Vella	1	**MS PDB**	2				
Besa	1	Kilanas	0				
Kilanas	5			MS PDB	2 3p		
LLRC FT	6			**Indera**	2 5p		
Setia Perdana	2	LLRC FT	3				
KKSJ Penjara	1	**Indera**	5				
Indera	4						

FA CUP FINAL

Sultan Hassal Bolkiah Stadium, Berakas, 10-12-2012
Scorer - Mohammad Hardi bin Matassan [115] for ABDB

BUL – BULGARIA

FIFA/COCA-COLA WORLD RANKING

'93	'94	'95	'96	'97	'98	'99	'00	'01	'02	'03	'04	'05	'06	'07	'08	'09	'10	'11	'12
31	16	17	15	36	49	37	53	51	42	34	37	39	43	18	27	30	49	84	50

2012													High	Low	Av
Jan	Feb	Mar	Apr	May	Jun	Jul	Aug	Sep	Oct	Nov	Dec				
83	88	85	96	96	90	92	94	89	55	40	50		8	96	37

In 2012 Ludogorets, from the small city of Razgrad, became the 15th different team to win the Bulgarian championship but what made their title triumph remarkable was the fact that just two seasons previously they had been playing at the third level. Successive promotions saw them make their debut at the top level and by winning the championship they completed a remarkable hat trick - the first team in the 87-year history of the Bulgarian League to win the title after being promoted. But the incredible rise of Ludogorets didn't stop there. Bought by businessman Kiril Domuschiev in 2010, Ludogorets achieved more than he could have ever dreamed by also winning the cup to complete an extraordinary double. Domuschiev has the aim of revitalising the whole of Bulgarian football and it was with a mixture of imported players, notably from Brazil, and home grown players that Ludogorets achieved their success. They clinched the title thanks to a Miroslav Ivanov goal in a 1-0 victory in the winner takes all clash against CSKA on the final day of the season - the first time in 28 years that the title had gone down to the wire. The previous week they had beaten Lokomotiv Plovdiv 2-1 in Burgas in the cup final to set the trophy quest rolling, Brazilian striker Marcelinho scoring twice in the last 15 minutes.

UEFA EUROPEAN CHAMPIONSHIP RECORD
1960 r1   1964 r2   1968-1992 DNQ   **1996** 11 r1   2000 DNQ   **2004** 16 r1   2008-2012 DNQ

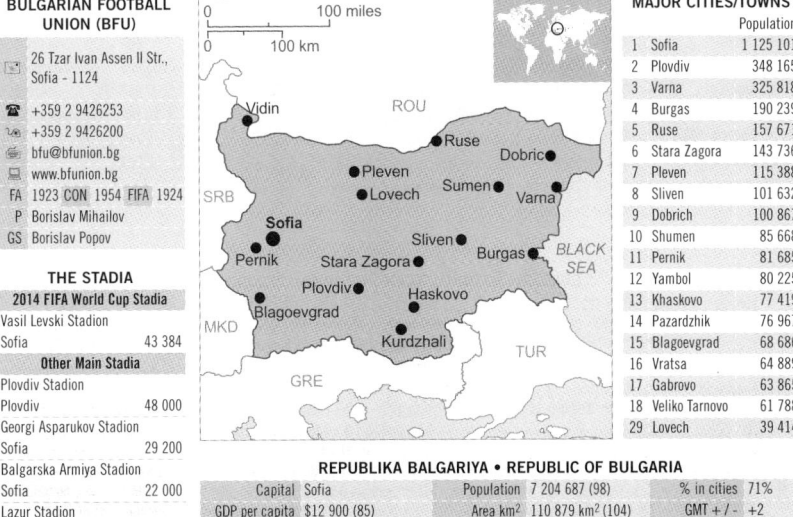

BULGARIAN FOOTBALL UNION (BFU)

26 Tzar Ivan Assen II Str., Sofia - 1124

☎ +359 2 9426253
+359 2 9426200
bfu@bfunion.bg
www.bfunion.bg
FA 1923 CON 1954 FIFA 1924
P Borislav Mihailov
GS Borislav Popov

THE STADIA
2014 FIFA World Cup Stadia
Vasil Levski Stadion
Sofia   43 384
Other Main Stadia
Plovdiv Stadion
Plovdiv   48 000
Georgi Asparukov Stadion
Sofia   29 200
Balgarska Armiya Stadion
Sofia   22 000
Lazur Stadion
Burgas   18 037

MAJOR CITIES/TOWNS
		Population
1	Sofia	1 125 101
2	Plovdiv	348 165
3	Varna	325 818
4	Burgas	190 239
5	Ruse	157 671
6	Stara Zagora	143 736
7	Pleven	115 388
8	Sliven	101 632
9	Dobrich	100 867
10	Shumen	85 668
11	Pernik	81 685
12	Yambol	80 225
13	Khaskovo	77 419
14	Pazardzhik	76 967
15	Blagoevgrad	68 686
16	Vratsa	64 889
17	Gabrovo	63 865
18	Veliko Tarnovo	61 788
29	Lovech	39 414

REPUBLIKA BALGARIYA • REPUBLIC OF BULGARIA
Capital Sofia   Population 7 204 687 (98)   % in cities 71%
GDP per capita $12 900 (85)   Area km² 110 879 km² (104)   GMT +/- +2
Neighbours (km) Greece 494, Macedonia 148, Romania 608, Serbia 318, Turkey 240 • Coast 354

RECENT INTERNATIONAL MATCHES PLAYED BY BULGARIA

2009	Opponents	Score	Venue	Comp	Scorers	Att	Referee
11-02	Switzerland	D 1-1	Geneva	Fr	Popov [34]	9 500	Duarte POR
28-03	Republic of Ireland	D 1-1	Dublin	WCq	Kilbane OG [74]	60 002	Bebek CRO
1-04	Cyprus	W 2-0	Sofia	WCq	Popov [8], Makriev [94+]	16 916	Ingvarsson SWE
6-06	Republic of Ireland	D 1-1	Sofia	WCq	Telkiyski [29]	38 000	Larsen DEN
12-08	Latvia	W 1-0	Sofia	Fr	Rangelov [54]	2 000	Pamporidis GRE
5-09	Montenegro	W 4-1	Sofia	WCq	Kishishev [45], Telkiyski [49], Berbatov [83], Domovchiyski [91+]	7 543	Asumaa FIN
9-09	Italy	L 0-2	Turin	WCq		26 122	Meyer GER
10-10	Cyprus	L 1-4	Larnaca	WCq	Berbatov [44]	3 700	Allaerts BEL
14-10	Georgia	W 6-2	Sofia	WCq	Berbatov 3 [6 23 35], Petrov.M 2 [14 44], Angelov [31]	700	Jakobsson ISL
18-11	Malta	W 4-1	Paola	Fr	Bozhinov [5], Berbabtov 2 [76 83], Georgiev [81]		Nijhuis NED
2010							
3-03	Poland	L 0-2	Warsaw	Fr		6 800	Kever SUI
19-05	Belgium	L 1-2	Brussels	Fr	Popov [31]	15 000	Weiner GER
24-05	South Africa	D 1-1	Johannesburg	Fr	Bojinov [31]	25 000	Fagla TOG
11-08	Russia	L 0-1	St. Petersburg	Fr		8 200	Rizzoli ITA
3-09	England	L 0-4	London	ECq		73 426	Kassai HUN
7-09	Montenegro	L 0-1	Sofia	ECq		9 470	Bezborodov RUS
8-10	Wales	W 1-0	Cardiff	ECq	Popov [48]	14 061	Eriksson SWE
12-10	Saudi Arabia	W 2-0	Istanbul	Fr	Rangelov [39], Domovchiyski [44]	100	Gocek TUR
17-11	Serbia	L 0-1	Sofia	Fr		1 500	Avram ROU
2011							
9-02	Estonia	D 2-2	Antalya	Fr	Popov 2 [40p 83p]		
26-03	Switzerland	D 0-0	Sofia	ECq		9 600	Collum SCO
29-03	Cyprus	W 1-0	Larnaca	Fr	Petrov [35]	120	Borg MLT
4-06	Montenegro	D 1-1	Podgorica	ECq	Popov [66]	11 500	Yefet ISR
10-08	Belarus	L 0-1	Minsk	Fr		6 500	Dunauskas LTU
2-09	England	L 0-3	Sofia	ECq		27 230	De Bleeckere BEL
6-09	Switzerland	L 1-3	Basel	ECq	Ivanov.I [9]	16 880	Kralovec CZE
7-10	Ukraine	L 0-3	Kyiv	Fr		10 000	Kralovec CZE
11-10	Wales	L 0-1	Sofia	ECq		1 672	Gil POL
2012							
29-02	Hungary	D 1-1	Gyor	Fr	Bozhinov [87]	15 000	Eriksson SWE
26-05	Netherlands	W 2-1	Amsterdam	Fr	Popov 49p, Micanski [93+]	45 000	Teixeira ESP
29-05	Turkey	L 0-2	Salzburg	Fr		2 000	Grobelnik AUT
15-08	Cyprus	W 1-0	Sofia	Fr	Micanski [66]	400	Lautier MLT
7-09	Italy	D 2-2	Sofia	WCq	Manolev [30], Milanov.G [66]	12 993	Atkinson ENG
11-09	Armenia	W 1-0	Sofia	WCq	Manolev [43]	7 883	Studer SUI
12-10	Denmark	D 1-1	Sofia	WCq	Rangelov [7]	20 780	Chapron FRA
16-10	Czech Republic	D 0-0	Prague	WCq		16 163	Bezborodov RUS
14-11	Ukraine	L 0-1	Sofia	Fr		2 000	Mazic SRB

Fr = Friendly match • EC = UEFA EURO 2012 • WC = FIFA World Cup • q = qualifier

BULGARIA NATIONAL TEAM HISTORICAL RECORDS

Caps
106 - Stilian Petrov 1998- • 102 - Borislav Mihaylov 1983-98 • 96 - Hristo Bonev 1967-79 • 92 - Krasimir Balakov 1988-2003 • 91 - Martin Petrov 1999- • 90 - Dimitar Penev 1965-74 • 88 - Radostin Kishishev 1996-2009 • 83 - Hristo Stoichkov 1986-99 • 80 - Zlatko Yankov 1989-99 • 79 - Anyo Sadkov 1981-91 • 78 - Dimitar Berbatov 1999- & Nasko Sirakov 1983-96 • 77 - Georgi Dimitrov 1978-87

Goals
48 - Dimitar Berbatov 1999- • 47 - Hristo Bonev 1967-79 • 37 - Hristo Stoichkov 1986-99 • 26 - Emil Kostadinov 1988-98 • 25 - Lyubomir Angelov 1931-40, Ivan Kolev 1950-63 & Petar Jekov 1963-72 • 23 - Nasko Sirakov 1983-96 • 20 - Dimitar Milanov 1948-59 • 19 - Georgi Asparukov 1962-70, Dinko Dermendjiev 1966-77 & Martin Petrov 1999- • 16 - Krasimir Balakov 1988-2003 & Todor Diev 1955-65

Coaches
For coaches pre 1963 see Oliver's Almanack 2012 • Stoyan Ormandzhiev 1963 • Bella Volentik HUN 1963-64 • Rudolf Vytlacil CZE 1965-66 • Dobromir Tashkov 1966 • Stefan Bozhkov 1967-70 • Vasil Spasov 1970-72 • Hristo Mladenov 1972-74 • Stoyan Ormandzhiev 1974-77 • Cvetan Ilchev 1978-80 • Atanas Purzhelov 1980-82 • Ivan Vutsov 1982-86 • Hristo Mladenov 1986-87 • Boris Angelov 1988-89 • Ivan Vutsov 1989-91 • Krasimir Borisov 1991 • Dimitar Penev 1991-96 • Hristo Bonev 1996-98 • Dimitar Dimitrov 1998-99 • Stoycho Mladenov 2000-01 • Plamen Markov 2002-04 • Hristo Stoichkov 2004-07 • Stanimir Stoilov 2007 • Dimitar Penev 2007 • Plamen Markov 2008 • Stanimir Stoilov 2009-10 • Lothar Matthaus GER 2010-11 • Michail Madanski 2011 • Luboslav Penev 2011-

BULGARIA 2011-12 'A' PFG

	Pl	W	D	L	F	A	Pts	Ludogorets	CSKA	Levski	Chernomorets	Litex	Lokomotiv P	Cherno More	Slavia	Minyor	Beroe Stara	Montana	Botev	Lokomotiv S	Vidima	Kaliakra	Svetkavitsa
Ludogorets Razgrad †	30	22	4	4	73	16	70		1-0	2-1	3-1	1-1	0-0	0-2	6-0	4-1	3-0	3-0	3-0	4-0	4-0	2-0	5-0
CSKA Sofia ‡	30	22	3	5	60	19	69	2-2		1-0	1-0	4-1	3-0	4-1	1-2	3-1	1-0	2-0	2-0	4-0	4-1	3-1	3-0
Levski Sofia ‡	30	20	2	8	61	28	62	0-1	1-0		2-2	3-2	2-1	1-0	0-1	2-0	1-0	3-0	4-0	2-1	3-2	3-2	7-0
Chernomorets Burgas	30	17	9	4	57	23	60	0-0	2-0	2-0		1-1	2-0	3-2	2-3	1-0	2-2	2-0	3-1	1-1	4-0	1-0	6-0
Litex Lovech	30	17	8	5	57	28	59	2-1	0-2	1-0	0-0		6-2	1-0	1-0	2-2	2-1	0-0	3-1	2-0	3-0	5-0	6-0
Lokomotiv Plovdiv ‡	30	17	6	7	44	39	57	1-0	0-3	3-2	2-0	2-1		1-0	2-1	1-1	4-2	1-0	2-1	2-1	3-2	2-0	2-0
Cherno More Varna	30	16	4	10	46	25	52	0-1	0-3	1-0	0-3	0-2	0-1		1-2		2-0	2-0	2-0	2-0	1-0	3-0	2-1	7-1	1-0
Slavia Sofia	30	15	6	9	42	36	51	3-2	0-1	0-3	1-1	0-2	3-0	1-1		2-1	0-0	1-1	3-2	2-1	1-1	3-0	2-0
Minyor Pernik	30	8	12	10	35	40	36	0-7	2-0	0-1	1-1	2-2	0-0	0-1	1-1		1-1	3-1	1-3	1-2	1-0	1-1	3-0
Beroe Stara Zagora	30	9	8	13	28	37	35	1-2	0-1	1-2	1-2	1-1	1-1	2-0	1-0	0-0		2-0	1-2	1-0	1-0	3-1	2-0
Montana	30	8	7	15	29	51	31	1-4	0-5	0-3	2-4	1-0	2-2	1-3	1-2	1-2	0-0		2-0	1-1	1-0	2-1	0-0
Botev Vratsa	30	7	8	15	24	30	29	0-1	2-2	0-2	0-0	1-3	1-1	0-1	0-1	0-0	1-1	2-4		2-0	2-2	6-2	1-0
Lokomotiv Sofia	30	5	9	16	26	50	24	0-1	1-2	1-1	0-4	1-2	2-0	0-0	0-3	1-1	3-0	1-1	0-1		0-1	3-2	4-1
Vidima-Rakovski	30	3	6	21	19	59	15	0-5	0-1	1-6	0-1	1-1	0-3	0-0	1-2	0-3	0-1	1-2	0-1	2-2		1-0	1-0
Kaliakra Kavarna	30	2	5	23	26	77	11	0-4	1-2	1-4	0-4	0-2	1-2	0-5	1-2	2-2	3-1	2-2	0-1	0-0	3-2		1-1
Svetkavitsa Targovishte	30	1	5	24	8	71	8	0-1	0-3	0-1	0-3	1-3	0-1	1-3	0-3	0-3	1-3	1-2	0-0	1-1	0-0	1-0	

6/08/2011 - 23/05/2012 • † Qualified for the UEFA Champions League • ‡ Qualified for the Europa League • Attendance: 485,839 @ 2,033
Top scorers: **16** - **JUNIOR MORAES** BRA, CSKA & Ivan **STOYANOV**, Ludogorets • **13** - Emil **GARGOROV**, Ludogorets & Ianis **ZICU** ROU, CSKA
12 - **JOSE JUNIOR** BRA, Slavia/Levski • **11** - Svetoslav **TODOROV**, Litex; Ivan **TSVETKOV**, Levski & Gerasim **ZAKOV**, Kaliakra • **10** - **LOURIVAL ASSIS** BRA, Chernomorets; Aatif **CHAHECHOUHE** MAR, Chernomorets; Georgi **ILIEV**, Cherno More & **MARCELO NICACIO** BRA, Litex

BULGARIA 2011-12 WESTERN 'B' PFG (2)

	Pl	W	D	L	F	A	Pts
Pirin Gotse Delchev	27	19	5	3	41	12	62
Sportist Svoge †	27	17	5	5	44	23	56
Bdin Vidin	27	15	6	6	42	20	51
Bansko 1951	27	10	10	7	36	24	40
Chavdar Etropole	27	10	9	8	36	33	39
Septemvri Simitli	27	8	10	9	35	33	34
Akademik 1947 Sofia	27	9	4	14	25	33	31
Slivnishki Geroi	27	7	4	16	28	48	25
Malesh Mikrevo	27	6	4	17	19	38	22
Chavdar Byala Slatina	27	4	3	20	14	56	12

13/08/2011 - 23/05/2012 • † Play-off

'B' PFG PROMOTION PLAY-OFF
Slavia, Sofia, 30-05-2012
Sportist Svoge 0-2 **Botev Plovdiv**

BULGARIA 2011-12 EASTERN 'B' PFG (2)

	Pl	W	D	L	F	A	Pts
Etar Veliko Tarnovo	27	15	8	4	31	14	53
Botev Plovdiv †	27	14	9	4	40	17	51
Neftochimic Burgas	27	14	7	6	46	29	49
Lyubimets	27	14	6	7	42	22	48
Ch'morets Pomorie - R	27	10	7	10	38	29	37
Sliven 2000	27	10	6	11	29	23	36
Spartak Varna	27	10	6	11	27	35	36
Dobrudzha Dobrich	27	8	8	11	22	28	32
Nesebar	27	7	5	15	24	44	26
Dorostol Silistra	27	1	2	24	6	66	2

13/08/2011 - 23/05/2012 • † Play-off

MEDALS TABLE

	Overall	League	Cup	SAC	Europe
	G S B	G S B	G S		G S B
1 Levski Sofia	51 40 9	26 31 9	12 5	13 4	
2 CSKA Sofia	50 33 7	31 21 4	10 6	9 6	3
3 Slavia Sofia	14 11 13	7 9 12	1	6 2	1
4 Lokomotiv Sofia	8 8 9	4 6 9	1	3 2	
5 Litex Lovech	8 4 2	4 1 2	4 3		
6 Botev Plovdiv	4 10 11	2 2 11	4	2 4	
7 Cherno More Varna	4 8 3	4 6 3	2		
8 Spartak Sofia	3 4	2	2	1 2	
9 Beroe Stara Zagora	2 4 1	1	1	4	
10 Spartak Plovdiv	2 3	1 1		1 2	
11 AC 23 Sofia	2 1	1			
Ludogorets Razgrad	2	1		1	
13 Lokomotiv Plovdiv	1 6 4	1 1 4	1	4	
14 Spartak Varna	1 4 1	1 2 1		1	
15 SC Sofia	1 1	1 1			
16 Etar Veliko Tarnovo	1	1		1	
Marek	1		1		1
Shipka Sofia	1		1 1		
Sliven	1		1 1		
20 Septemvri CDW	1				1
21 Dunav Ruse	5	1		3	1
22 Pirin Blagoevgrad	4			3	1
23 Naftex Burgas	2	1		1	
Sportclub Plovdiv	2			2	
25 Velbazhd Kjustendil	1 3		3	1	
26 Akademik Sofia	1 2		2		1
27 Spartak Pleven	1 1		1		1
28 Ch'morets Burgas	1			1	
Ch'morets Pomorie	1			1	
Ch'morets Popovo	1				1
Macedonia Skopje	1		1		
Minior Pernik	1				
Slavia Sofia	1			1	
33 Botev Vratsa		1		1	

KUPA NA BULGARIYA 2011-12

Second Round

Ludogorets Razgrad	1	
Beroe Stara Zagora *	0	
Vidima-Rakovski *	1 4p	
Svetkavitsa Targovishte	1 5p	
Chernomorets Burgas	3	
Pirin Gotse Delchev *	1	
Botev Vratsa	0	
Botev Plovdiv *	1	
CSKA Sofia	1	
Slavia Sofia *	0	
Lyubimets	1	
Spartak Pleven *	4	
Slivnishki Geroi	4	
Vereya Stara Zagora *	1	
Botev Kozloduy *	2 7p	
Septemvri Simitli	2 6p	
Litex Lovech	5	
Sportist Svoge *	0	
Lokomotiv Sofia	1 3p	
Kaliakra Kavarna *	1 4p	
Tundzha Yambol *	0 5p	
Montana	0 4p	
Cherno More Varna	1 5p	
Minyor Pernik *	1 3p	
Levski Sofia	1	
Bansko 1951 *	0	
Neftochimic Burgas	0	
Etar Veliko Tarnovo *	2	
Dobrudzha Dobrich *	1	
Nesebar	0	
Chavdar Etropole *	0	
Lokomotiv Plovdiv	2	

Round of 16

Ludogorets Razgrad *	5
Svetkavitsa Targovishte	1
Chernomorets Burgas	1
Botev Plovdiv	2
CSKA Sofia	3
Spartak Pleven *	0
Slivnishki Geroi	0
Septemvri Simitli *	3
Litex Lovech *	0
Kaliakra Kavarna	5
Tundzha Yambol *	
Minyor Pernik	
Levski Sofia	3
Etar Veliko Tarnovo *0	0
Dobrudzha Dobrich *	0
Lokomotiv Plovdiv	4

Quarter-finals

Ludogorets Razgrad	3
Botev Plovdiv *	0
CSKA Sofia	1
Septemvri Simitli *	2
Litex Lovech *	2
Minyor Pernik	0
Levski Sofia	1
Lokomotiv Plovdiv *	2

Semi-finals

Ludogorets Razgrad	4
Septemvri Simitli *	1
Litex Lovech *	0
Lokomotiv Plovdiv	1

Final

Ludogorets Razgrad	2
Lokomotiv Plovdiv ‡	1

CUP FINAL

Lazur, Burgas, 16-05-2012
Att: 13 103, Ref: Stanislav Todorov
Scorers - Marcelinkho 2 ²⁷ ⁷⁹ for Ludogorets; Dakson ¹⁸ for Lokomotiv
Ludogorets – Uros Golubovic - Choko, Alexandre Barthe, Lubomir Guldan●, Yordan Minev - Stanislav Genchev, Svetoslav Dyakov - Ivan Stoyanov (Dimo Bakalov 90), Marcelinho, Miroslav Ivanov● (Mihail Aleksandrov 59) - Emil Gargorov (c). Tr: Ivaylo Petev
Lokomotiv – Ivan Karadzhov - Jeremie Rodrigues●, Youness Bengellaoun◆89, Tanko Dyakov (Angel Yoshev 52), Mihail Venkov - Hristo Zlatinski (Yordan Todorov 83) - Daniel Georgiev, Dakson (Lyubomir Vitanov 60), Serginho - Zdravko Lazarov (c), Basile de Carvalho. Tr: Emil Velev

*A PFG teams enter at the second round • * Home team • ‡ Qualified for the Europa League

CAM – CAMBODIA

FIFA/COCA-COLA WORLD RANKING

'93	'94	'95	'96	'97	'98	'99	'00	'01	'02	'03	'04	'05	'06	'07	'08	'09	'10	'11	'12
-	-	180	186	170	162	168	169	169	176	178	184	188	174	183	178	175	166	170	

2012

Jan	Feb	Mar	Apr	May	Jun	Jul	Aug	Sep	Oct	Nov	Dec	High	Low	Av
170	172	166	173	175	175	192	191	188	189	191	184	154	192	176

Cambodia's poor showing in the preliminary rounds of the AFF Suzuki Cup in October 2012 saw the reign of Hok Sochetra at the helm of the national team come to an end. Hok, the nation's leading scorer during his playing days, oversaw a desperately disappointing campaign that saw the Cambodians lose all four of their qualifiers - against Laos, Myanmar and most embarrassingly against minnows Timor-Leste and Brunei Darussalam - to finish bottom of the group. It was a performance that saw them sink to 191 in the FIFA/Coca-Cola World Ranking, just 18 places off the bottom. At home Naga Corp finished on top of the C-League standings at the end of the regular season but missed out on the title when Boeung Ket defeated them 3-1 in the final. Naga Corp's season of near misses was then completed when they lost 2-1 in the final of the Hun Sen Cup to Preah Khan Reach. Defending champions Phnom Penh Crown had a disappointing campaign, finishing in fifth place and 11 points behind the new champions, but they managed to progress to the finals of the 2012 AFC President's Cup. Wins over Nepal Police Club and Yeedzin from Bhutan secured the Cambodian side a place in the finals in Tajikistan but heavy defeats against both hosts Esteghlal and Dordoi Bishkek ended their involvement at the group stage.

FIFA WORLD CUP RECORD
1930-1994 DNE 1998-2002 DNQ 2006 DNE 2010-2014 DNQ

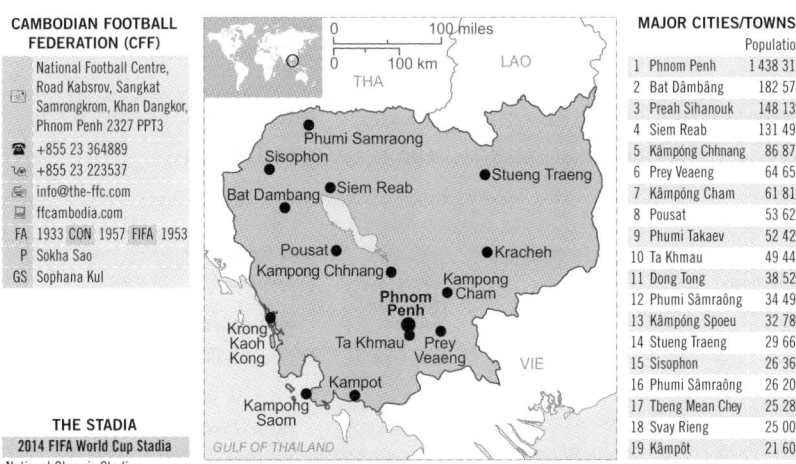

CAMBODIAN FOOTBALL FEDERATION (CFF)
National Football Centre, Road Kabsrov, Sangkat Samrongkrom, Khan Dangkor, Phnom Penh 2327 PPT3
☎ +855 23 364889
📠 +855 23 223537
✉ info@the-ffc.com
🌐 ffcambodia.com
FA 1933 CON 1957 FIFA 1953
P Sokha Sao
GS Sophana Kul

THE STADIA
2014 FIFA World Cup Stadia
National Olympic Stadium
Phnom Penh   50 000
Other Main Stadia
RCAF Old Stadium
Phnom Penh   7 000

MAJOR CITIES/TOWNS

		Population
1	Phnom Penh	1 438 317
2	Bat Dâmbâng	182 574
3	Preah Sihanouk	148 139
4	Siem Reab	131 497
5	Kâmpóng Chhnang	86 876
6	Prey Veaeng	64 659
7	Kâmpóng Cham	61 814
8	Pousat	53 622
9	Phumi Takaev	52 422
10	Ta Khmau	49 443
11	Dong Tong	38 524
12	Phumi Sâmraông	34 494
13	Kâmpóng Spoeu	32 782
14	Stueng Traeng	29 665
15	Sisophon	26 364
16	Phumi Sâmraông	26 201
17	Tbeng Mean Chey	25 286
18	Svay Rieng	25 002
19	Kâmpôt	21 601

PREAHREACHEANACHAKR KAMPUCHEA • KINGDOM OF CAMBODIA

Capital	Phnom Penh	Population	14 494 293 (65)	% in cities	22%
GDP per capita	$2000 (187)	Area km²	181 035 km² (89)	GMT +/-	+7
Neighbours (km)	Laos 541, Thailand 803, Vietnam 1228 • Coast 443				

RECENT INTERNATIONAL MATCHES PLAYED BY CAMBODIA

2010	Opponents	Score		Venue	Comp	Scorers	Att	Referee
22-10	Laos	D	0-0	Vientiane	AFFq			Abdul Wahab MAS
24-10	Timor-Leste	W	4-2	Vientiane	AFFq	Khim Borey 3 [26 29 40], Nuth Sinoun [75]		Phung VIE
26-10	Philippines	D	0-0	Vientiane	AFFq			Abdul Wahab MAS
2011								
9-02	Macau	W	3-1	Phnom Penh	CCq	Samel Nasa 2 [48 53], Khuon Laboravy [59]	2 000	Win Cho MYA
16-02	Macau	L	2-3	Macau	CCq	Khim Borey [45], Samel Nasa [107]	100	Perera SRI
21-03	Maldives	L	0-4	Male	CCq		8 000	Zhao Liang CHN
23-03	Tajikistan	L	0-3	Male	CCq		550	Patwal IND
25-03	Kyrgyzstan	L	3-4	Male	CCq	Kouch Sokumpheak 2 [39 49], Sok Rithy [89]	1 000	Zhao Liang CHN
29-06	Laos	W	4-2	Phnom Penh	WCq	Khuon Laboravy [52], Samel Nasa 2 [59 89], Kouch Sokumpheak [68]	25 000	Jahanbazi IRN
3-07	Laos	L	2-6	Vientiane	WCq	Chhin Chhoeun [45], Kouch Sokumpheak [75]	9 000	Sato JPN
2012								
5-10	Timor-Leste	L	1-5	Yangon	AFFq	Keo Sokngon [91+]	500	Al Yarimi YEM
7-10	Laos	L	0-1	Yangon	AFFq		100	Alzaabi UAE
9-10	Brunei Darussalam	L	2-3	Yangon	AFFq	Prak Udom [25], Khim Borey [91+]		Takayama JPN
11-10	Myanmar	L	0-3	Yangon	AFFq			Al Yarimi YEM

Fr = Friendly match • AFF = ASEAN Football Federation Championship • CC = AFC Challenge Cup • WC = FIFA World Cup • r1 = first round group

CAMBODIA NATIONAL TEAM HISTORICAL RECORDS

Coach: Scott O'Donnell AUS 2005-08 • Som Saran 2008 • Yoo Kee Heung KOR 2008 • Prak Sovannara 2008-09 • Scott O'Donnell AUS 2009-10 • Lee Tae Hong KOR 2010-12 • Hok Sochetra 2012 • Prak Sovannara 2012-

CAMBODIA 2012

METFONE C-LEAGUE

	Pl	W	D	L	F	A	Pts	Naga Corp	Boeung Ket	Preah Khan R	Police	PP Crown	Build Bright	Defence	Kirivon Sok SC	Chhlam Samuth	Western Univ
Naga Corp †	18	11	5	2	49	21	38		2-1	4-3	2-4	2-1	4-0	1-1	1-1	7-0	3-1
Boeung Ket †	18	11	3	4	51	22	36	0-3		2-2	1-1	5-1	2-0	1-1	3-2	7-0	4-1
Preah Khan Reach †	18	10	3	5	49	27	33	1-2	3-5		4-3	2-2	0-0	1-3	2-1	6-0	4-0
Police †	18	9	6	3	42	27	33	2-2	2-1	3-2		1-1	4-0	0-0	1-1	6-7	1-0
Phnom Penh Crown	18	8	3	7	39	30	27	1-1	1-2	0-3	4-3		3-0	1-2	1-3	5-1	5-0
Build Bright United	18	8	3	7	24	29	27	1-2	1-0	1-5	1-1	0-3		1-0	1-1	2-0	1-0
Defence Ministry	18	6	5	7	24	27	23	1-0	0-2	1-2	1-3	1-3	1-3		1-0	5-2	0-0
Kirivon Sok Sen Chey	18	4	5	9	22	28	17	1-1	1-3	0-2	0-2	3-1	0-1	3-1		2-2	0-1
Chhlam Samuth	18	3	2	13	28	74	11	1-8	0-7	0-1	0-3	1-4	2-4	3-3	4-0		4-1
Western University	18	2	1	15	11	54	7	1-4	1-5	0-6	0-2	0-2	1-7	1-2	0-3	3-1	

10/03/2012 - 19/08/2012 • † Qualified for the final rounds
Top scorers: **20** - Nwakuna **FRIDAY** NGA, Boeung Ket • **19** - Nelson **OLADIJI** NGA, Police • **17** - Choun **CHUN**, Nagacorp

METFONE C-LEAGUE FINALS

Semi-finals
Boeung Ket 4
Preah Khan Reach 1

Finals
Boeung Ket † 3
Naga Corp 1

Police 0 1p
Naga Corp 0 3p

9/09 - 15/09/2012 • † Qualified for the AFC President's Cup

HUN SEN CUP 2012

Quarter-finals
Preah Khan R 4
Phnom P Crown 0
Build Bright U 1
Police 2
Chhlam Samuth 1 6p
Defence 1 5p
Kirivon Sok SC 0
Naga Corp 1

Semi-finals
Preah Khan R 4
Police 0
Chhlam Samuth 0
Naga Corp 4

Final
Preah Khan R 2
Naga Corp 1

National Olympic
12-02-2012

First round played in four groups of four • 3rd place: Police 3-0 Chhlam Samuth

CAN – CANADA

FIFA/COCA-COLA WORLD RANKING

'93	'94	'95	'96	'97	'98	'99	'00	'01	'02	'03	'04	'05	'06	'07	'08	'09	'10	'11	'12
44	63	65	40	66	101	81	63	92	70	87	90	84	82	55	90	56	84	72	64

2012															
Jan	Feb	Mar	Apr	May	Jun	Jul	Aug	Sep	Oct	Nov	Dec	**High**	**Low**	**Av**
74	71	79	75	75	77	68	79	73	61	60	64	40	105	73

Canada's World Cup ambitions came crashing down in spectacular fashion when the Canucks lost 8-1 to Honduras in a match both needed to win to progress to the final round of qualifiers for Brazil. Only a late Iain Hume goal spared Canada a record-equalling heaviest defeat. Their campaign had been progressing well but there was little consolation for coach Stephen Hart that his team finished just one point behind both Honduras and Panama and he resigned two days later. The national team's prospects should be helped in the future by Canada's ever-increasing profile in MLS. In 2012 Montreal Impact joined Toronto and Vancouver in the league and had an encouraging first season in which their average attendance of 22,772 was bettered only by Seattle and LA Galaxy. Toronto again found themselves stranded at the bottom of the standings but they did have an excellent campaign in the 2011-12 CONCACAF Champions League. After qualifying from their group they faced LA Galaxy in the quarter-finals who were dispatched 4-3 on aggregate. Having drawn the first match 2-2 at home, Toronto pulled off a major surprise when they beat their opponents 2-1 away from home in Los Angeles. Hopes of a first appearance in the final were dashed, however, by Mexico's Santos Laguna who won 7-3 on aggregate in the semi-final.

CONCACAF GOLD CUP RECORD

1991 r1 1993 r1 1996 r1 1998 DNQ **2000** Winners 2002 3p SF 2003 r1 2005 r1 2007 SF 2009 QF 2011 r1

THE CANADIAN SOCCER ASSOCIATION (CSA)

Place Soccer Canada,
237 Metcalfe Street,
Ottawa, Ontario, K2P 1R2
☎ +1 613 2377678
📠 +1 613 2371516
✉ info@soccercan.ca
🖥 www.canadasoccer.com
FA 1912 CON 1978 FIFA 1912
P Dominique Maestracci
GS Peter Montopoli

THE STADIA

2014 FIFA World Cup Stadia
BMO Field
Toronto   21 800

Other Main Stadia
Olympic Stadium
Montreal   65 255
Commonwealth Stadium
Edmonton   60 217
BC Place
Vancouver   21 000
Saputo Stadium
Montreal   20 341

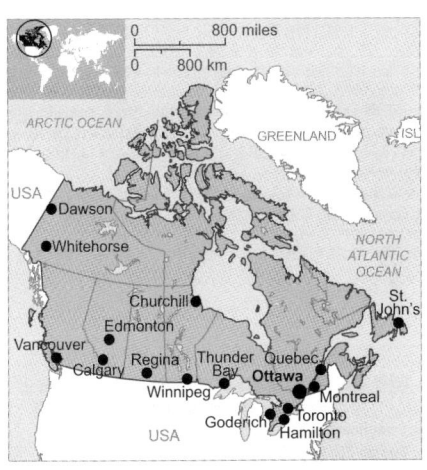

MAJOR CITIES/TOWNS

		Population
1	Toronto	4 977 164
2	Montreal	3 402 994
3	Vancouver	2 021 735
4	Calgary	1 055 546
5	Edmonton	912 067
6	Ottawa	875 097
7	Quebec	672 755
8	Hamilton	663 099
9	Winnipeg	647 411
10	Kitchener	443 774
11	London	360 894
12	Victoria	313 928
13	St Catharines	313 261
14	Windsor	286 329
15	Oshawa	286 310
16	Halifax	286 141
17	Saskatoon	204 931
18	Barrie	181 252
19	Regina	178 960

CANADA

Capital Ottawa	Population 33 487 208 (37)	% in cities 80%
GDP per capita $39 100 (22)	Area km² 9 984 670 km² (2)	GMT +/- -3.5 to -8
Neighbours (km) USA 8893 • Coast 202 080		

RECENT INTERNATIONAL MATCHES PLAYED BY CANADA

2010	Opponents	Score	Venue	Comp	Scorers	Att	Referee
31-01	Jamaica	L 0-1	Kingston	Fr		18 000	Hospedales TRI
24-05	Argentina	L 0-5	Buenos Aires	Fr		60 000	Rivera PER
29-05	Venezuela	D 1-1	Merida	Fr	McCallum [90]	20 000	Buitrago COL
4-09	Peru	L 0-2	Toronto	Fr		10 619	Jurisevic USA
7-09	Honduras	W 2-1	Montreal	Fr	Simpson [29], McKenna [42]	7 525	Geiger USA
8-10	Ukraine	D 2-2	Kyiv	Fr	Jackson [13], Hutchinson [29]	10 000	Mikulski POL
2011							
9-02	Greece	L 0-1	Larissa	Fr		14 800	Moen NOR
29-03	Belarus	W 1-0	Antalya	Fr	Hainault [58]	2 500	Yildirim TUR
1-06	Ecuador	D 2-2	Toronto	Fr	Dunfield [23], Ricketts [90]	14 356	Bogle JAM
7-06	USA	L 0-2	Detroit	GCr1		28 209	Lopez GUA
11-06	Guadeloupe	W 1-0	Tampa	GCr1	De Rosario [50p]	27 731	Taylor BRB
14-06	Panama	D 1-1	Kansas City	GCr1	De Rosario [62p]	20 109	Lopez GUA
2-09	St Lucia	W 4-1	Toronto	WCq	Simpson 2 [6 61], De Rosario [50], Johnson [91+]	11 500	Marrufo USA
6-09	Puerto Rico	W 3-0	Bayamon	WCq	Hume [42], Jackson [84], Ricketts [93+]	4 000	Wijngaarde SUR
7-10	St Lucia	W 7-0	Gros Islet	WCq	Jackson 3 [18 28 40], Occean 2 [34 51], Hume 2 [72 86]	1 005	Vidal PAN
11-10	Puerto Rico	D 0-0	Toronto	WCq		12 178	Lancaster GUY
11-11	St Kitts and Nevis	D 0-0	Basseterre	WCq		4 000	Bonilla SLV
15-11	St Kitts and Nevis	W 4-0	Toronto	WCq	Occean [28], De Rosario [36p], Simpson [45], Ricketts [88]	10 235	Cerdas CRC
2012							
29-02	Armenia	L 1-3	Limassol	Fr	Mckenna [4]	200	Panayi CYP
3-06	USA	D 0-0	Toronto	Fr		15 247	Morales MEX
8-06	Cuba	W 1-0	Havana	WCq	Occean [54]	7 000	Campbell JAM
12-06	Honduras	D 0-0	Toronto	WCq		16 132	Wijngaard SUR
15-08	Trinidad and Tobago	W 2-0	Fort Lauderdale	Fr	Ricketts [58], Johnson [86p]	BCD	Marrufo USA
7-09	Panama	W 1-0	Toronto	WCq	De Rosario [77]	17 586	Solis CRC
11-09	Panama	L 0-2	Panama City	WCq		20 000	Bonilla SLV
12-10	Cuba	W 3-0	Toronto	WCq	Ricketts [14], Johnson [73], Edgar [78]	17 712	Santos PUR
16-10	Honduras	L 1-8	San Pedro Sula	WCq	Hume [77]	38 000	Morales MEX

Fr = Friendly match • GC = CONCACAF Gold Cup • WC = FIFA World Cup • † Not a full international
q = qualifier • r1 = first round group • qf = quarter-final • sf = semi-final

CANADA NATIONAL TEAM HISTORICAL RECORDS

Caps
84 - Paul Stalteri 1997- • **82** - Randy Samuel 1983-97 • **78** - Mark Watson 1991-2004 • **71** - Dwayne DeRosario 2000- • **67** - Lyndon Hooper 1986-97 • **66** - Alex Bunbury 1986-97 • **63** - Kevin McKenna 2000- & Nick Dasovic 1992-2004 • **62** - Atiba Hutchinson 2003- • **61** - Julian De Guzman 2002- ; Colin Miller 1983-97 & Mike Sweeney 1980-93 • **59** - Carlo Corazzin 1994-2004 & Richard Hastings 1998- • **58** - Pat Onstad 1988- • **57** - Bruce Wilson 1974-86 • **56** - Craig Forrest 1988-2001 • **55** - Dale Mitchell 1980-93 • **54** - Paul Dolan 1984-97 • **53** - Paul Peschisolido 1992-2004 • **52** - & Frank Yallop 1990-97 • **51** - Dave Norman 1983-94

Goals
20 - Dwayne DeRosario 2000- • **19** - Dale Mitchell 1980-93 • **18** - John Catliff 1984-94 • **16** - Alex Bunbury 1986-97 • **15** - Ali Gerba 2005- • **12** - Igor Vrablic 1984-86 • **11** - Carlo Corazzin 1994-2004 & Kevin McKenna 2000- • **10** - Tomasz Radzinski 1995-2009 & Paul Peschisolido 1992-2004 • **7** - Paul Stalteri

Coaches
Don Petrie 1957 • Peter Dinsdale ENG 1968-70 • Frank Pike ENG 1970-73 • Bill McAllister 1973 • Eckhard Krautzun GER 1973-75 • Bill McAllister 1975 • Eckhard Krautzun GER 1975-77 • Barrie Clarke 1978-81 • Tony Waiters ENG 1981-86 • Bob Bearpark ENG 1986-87 • Tony Taylor SCO 1988-89 • Bob Lenarduzzi 1989-90 • Tony Waiters ENG 1990-91 • Bob Lenarduzzi 1992-97 • Bruce Twamley 1998 • Holger Osieck GER 1999-2003 • Colin Miller 2003 • Frank Yallop 2004-06 • Stephen Hart TRI 2006-07 • Dale Mitchell 2007-09 • Stephen Hart TRI 2009-12 • Colin Miller 2013-

CANADA 2012
Amway Canadian Championship

Semi-finals			Finals		
Toronto FC	0	2			
Montreal Impact	0	0	**Toronto FC** †	1	1
FC Edmonton	0	1	Vancouver Whitecaps	1	0
Vancouver Whitecaps	2	3			

† Qualified for CONCACAF Champions League • See USA for MLS details

CAY – CAYMAN ISLANDS

FIFA/COCA-COLA WORLD RANKING

'93	'94	'95	'96	'97	'98	'99	'00	'01	'02	'03	'04	'05	'06	'07	'08	'09	'10	'11	'12
154	150	131	148	164	153	148	159	165	164	181	176	181	189	192	172	183	157	183	192

	2012													
Jan	Feb	Mar	Apr	May	Jun	Jul	Aug	Sep	Oct	Nov	Dec	High	Low	Av
183	185	184	185	185	185	178	176	181	183	189	192	127	192	167

With the Cayman national team declining to enter the 2012 Caribbean Cup, it was the clubs who flew the flag for the country after entering the CFU Club championship for only the second time. On the previous occasion ten years earlier George Town found the going tough and they didn't find it any easier in the 2012 tournament which they entered along with Elite. There was a straightforward introduction when the pair were joined by Bermuda's North Village Rams in a preliminary group staged in George Town, where a late Limberg Cuevas-Ebanks goal in the match between the two Cayman teams saw George Town top the group and progress to the second round. There, however, it was a different story and despite home advantage they lost 5-0 to Trinidad's Caledonia AIA and 8-0 to the USA-based Puerto Rico Islanders. Elite meanwhile were involved in a fierce battle with Scholars International in the CIFA Premier League where despite having led for most of the season they gifted Scholars the title after they were held to a 2-2 draw by George Town on the final weekend of the season. The following week Scholars claimed the double after a 1-0 victory over George Town in the FA Cup Final. Earlier in the season Elite had claimed the other major trophy on offer after beating Bodden Town 2-0 in the Digicel Cup final.

CFU CARIBBEAN CUP RECORD

1989 DNE 1991 6 r1 1992-1993 DNQ 1994 7 r1 1995 4 SF (hosts) 1996 DNQ 1997 DNE 1998 6 r1 1999-2010 DNQ 2012 DNE

CAYMAN ISLANDS FOOTBALL ASSOCIATION (CIFA)

Centre for Excellence
Poindexter Road, PO Box 178
Grand Cayman KY1-1104
+1 345 9495775
+1 345 9457673
cifa@candw.ky
www.cifa.ky
FA 1966 CON 1993 FIFA 1992
P Jeffrey Webb
GS Bruce Blake

THE STADIA

2014 FIFA World Cup Stadia	
Truman Boden Stadium	
George Town	7 000
Other Main Stadia	
TE McField SC 'The Annexe'	
George Town	2 500
Ed Bush Stadium	
West Bay	2 500
Haig Bodden Stadium	
Bodden Town	1 500

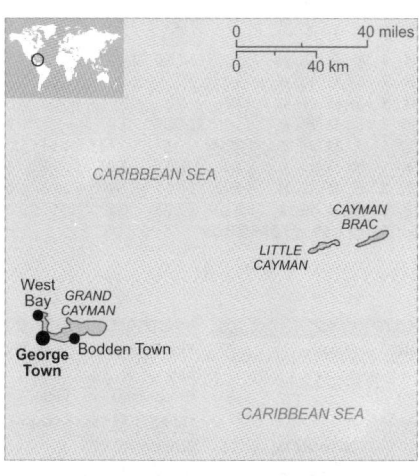

MAJOR CITIES/TOWNS

		Population
1	George Town	35 633
2	West Bay	12 620
3	Bodden Town	7 634
4	East End	1 619
5	North Side	1 313

CAYMAN ISLANDS

Capital	George Town	Population	49 035 (207)	% in cities	100%
GDP per capita	$43 800 (13)	Area km²	264 km² (210)	GMT +/-	-5
Neighbours (km)	Coast 160				

RECENT INTERNATIONAL MATCHES PLAYED BY THE CAYMAN ISLANDS

2008	Opponents	Score	Venue		Scorers	Att.	Referee
3-02	Bermuda	D 1-1	Hamilton	WCq	Allean Grant [87]	2 000	Navarro CAN
30-03	Bermuda	L 1-3	Georgetown	WCq	Marshall Forbes [64p]	3 200	Marrufo USA
27-08	Saint Martin †	W 3-0	Grand Cayman	CCq	Calvin Jefford [55], Jairo Sanchez [65], Nikolai Hill [90]	300	Thomas JAM
30-08	Antigua and Barbuda	D 1-1	Grand Cayman	CCq	O'Neil Taylor [67]	350	Hospedales
31-08	Bermuda	D 0-0	Grand Cayman	CCq		350	Hospedales
11-10	Guadeloupe †	L 1-7	Abymes	CCq	Carson Fagan [86]	4 200	McArthur GUY
13-10	Martinique †	L 0-1	Abymes	CCq		1 000	Matthew SKN
15-10	Grenada	L 2-4	Abymes	CCq	Erickson Brown 2 [32 83]	3 358	Willett ATG
9-11	Jamaica	L 0-2	Grand Cayman	Fr		500	Whittaker CAY
2009							
28-06	Jamaica	L 1-4	Grand Cayman	Fr	Rene Carter [40]	500	Holder CAY
2010							
2-10	Saint Martin †	D 1-1	Bayamon	CCq	Paul Brown [18p]	600	Campbell JAM
4-10	Anguilla	W 4-1	Bayamon	CCq	Mark Ebanks 2 [45p 49], Theron Wood [57], Paul Brwn [59]	500	Davis TRI
6-10	Puerto Rico	L 0-2	Bayamon	CCq		3 800	Campbell JAM
2011							
2-09	Suriname	L 0-1	Paramaribo	WCq		1 000	Skeete BRB
6-09	El Salvador	L 1-4	Georgetown	WCq	Mark Ebanks [73p]	2 200	Rodas GUA
7-10	Suriname	L 0-1	Georgetown	WCq		2 100	Jurisevic USA
11-10	El Salvador	L 0-4	San Salvador	WCq		17 570	Cruz CRC
11-11	Dominican Republic	L 0-4	San Cristobal	WCq		1 000	Guerrero NCA
14-11	Dominican Republic	D 1-1	Georgetown	WCq	Mark Ebanks [72]	1 750	Matthew SKN
2012							

No international matches played in 2012

Fr = Friendly match • CC = Digicel Caribbean Cup • WC = FIFA World Cup • q = qualifier • † Not an official international

CAYMAN ISLANDS 2011-12

CIFA PREMIER LEAGUE

	Pl	W	D	L	F	A	Pts	Scholars	Elite	Bodden Town	George Town	Tigers	Cayman Ath	Roma United	Future
Scholars International	21	14	6	1	49	15	48		2-2 0-0	3-2 1-1	2-1 2-0	0-1	5-2 2-0	4-0	3-1
Elite	21	13	7	1	49	16	46	0-0		4-2 5-1	0-0	3-1 3-1	10-1 1-1	2-0	3-0
Bodden Town	21	13	3	5	56	28	42	1-2	0-2		4-0 2-2	5-0	3-0	4-0 3-1	6-1 3-0
George Town	21	10	5	6	33	27	35	1-3	1-2 2-2	1-2		2-1	1-0	1-0	3-2 5-0
Tigers	21	7	5	9	29	37	26	1-4 0-4	1-2	3-3 0-1	1-1 1-1		1-0 3-1	1-1 3-1	2-1
Cayman Athletic	21	4	5	12	23	45	17	2-2	0-0	1-2 1-5	1-2 1-2	3-2		3-1 3-0	0-2
Roma United	21	3	2	16	14	49	11	0-2 0-5	1-0 0-1	1-3	0-3 1-3	0-3	0-2		2-0 4-2
Future	21	1	5	15	14	50	8	0-0 0-3	1-2 1-5	0-3	0-1	1-3 0-0	0-0 1-1	1-1	

18/09/2011 - 7/05/2012 • Relegation play-off: **Academy** 3-0 Roma United

CIFA FA CUP 2012

Quarter-finals		Semi-finals		Final	
Scholars Int	0 3p				
Elite	0 1p	Scholars Int	2		
Future	1	Academy	1		
Academy	3			Scholars Int	1
Cayman Ath	3			George Town	0
Bodden T	2	Cayman Ath	0	13-05-2012	
Roma Utd	0	George Town	2	Scorer - Mark Ebanks	
George Town	1				

CIFA DIGICEL CAYMAN CUP 2012

First Round		Semi-finals		Final	
Elite	3				
George Town	1	Elite	2 0 4p		
Future	0	Scholars	1 1 2p		
Scholars	2			Elite	2
Roma U	1			Bodden Town	0
Cayman Ath	0	Roma U	1 0	The Annexe, 22-02-2012	
Tigers	1	Bodden T	2 1	Scorers - Alex Belcher [22],	
Bodden T	2			Jose Luis Bush [36]	

CGO – CONGO

FIFA/COCA-COLA WORLD RANKING

'93	'94	'95	'96	'97	'98	'99	'00	'01	'02	'03	'04	'05	'06	'07	'08	'09	'10	'11	'12
103	114	119	100	101	112	94	86	94	97	108	117	110	89	91	68	101	121	133	109

2012													High	Low	Av
Jan	Feb	Mar	Apr	May	Jun	Jul	Aug	Sep	Oct	Nov	Dec				
131	130	101	91	91	83	91	92	83	94	115	109		57	144	102

AC Leopards completed a sensational giant-killing run in the CAF Confederation Cup by winning the competition in November 2012 to become only the second club from the country to win a continental trophy. The provincial team from Dolisie matched the achievement of CARA Brazzaville almost 40 years earlier who won the old-style African Champions Cup in 1974. After a 2-2 draw in the first leg of the final in Bamako, Leopards beat Djoliba of Mali 2-1 in the return in Brazzaville, emerging from virtual obscurity to take the trophy under tutelage of unknown Tunisian-born coach Nasreddine Nabi. That triumph came off the back of a successful year at home where they won the championship in a play-off with Diables Noirs from the capital Brazzaville - who had earlier in the year beaten them in the cup final. French coach Kamel Djabour, who is of Algerian extraction, took over as national team coach after replacing his AJ Auxerre colleague Jean-Guy Wallemme who stood down in October. Under Wallemme the Diables Rouge had made a strong start to the 2014 FIFA World Cup qualifiers after being awarded all three points from their match with Gabon and also by beating Niger. In the 2013 Africa Cup of Nations qualifiers, however, they suffered a 3-5 aggregate defeat at the hands of Uganda.

CAF AFRICA CUP OF NATIONS RECORD

1957-1965 DNE **1968** 7 r1 1970 DNE **1972** 1 Winners **1974** 4 SF 1976 DNQ **1978** 7 r1 1980-1988 DNQ 1990 DNE **1992** 7 QF 1994-1998 DNQ **2000** 14 r1 2002-2013 DNQ

FEDERATION CONGOLAISE DE FOOTBALL (FECOFOOT)

PO Box 1423, Brazzaville

☎ +242 811563

✉ fecofoot@yahoo.fr

FA 1962 CON 1966 FIFA 1962
P Jean Michel Mbono
GS Badji Mombo Wantete

THE STADIA

2014 FIFA World Cup Stadia
Stade Municipal
Pointe Noire — 13 594

Other Main Stadia
Stade Alphonse Massamba Debat
Brazzaville — 27 000
Stade Municipal
Dolisie — 20 000
Stade Omnisport
Owando — 13 037
Stade Felix Eboue
Brazzaville — 5 000

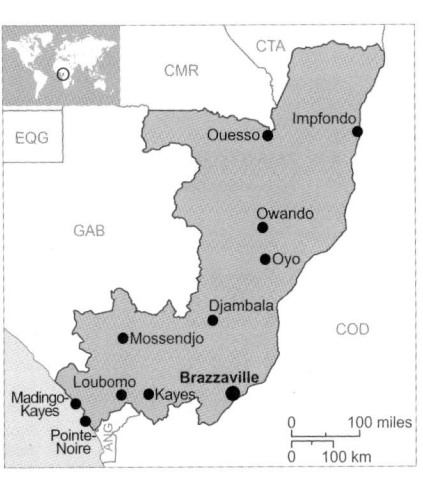

MAJOR CITIES/TOWNS

		Population
1	Brazzaville	1 158 513
2	Pointe Noire	634 995
3	Loubomo	130 080
4	Nkayi	58 559
5	Gamboma	29 357
6	Kinkala	29 248
7	Ouesso	27 142
8	Madingou	23 342
9	Impfondo	20 729
10	Mossendjo	20 414
11	Sibiti	20 096
12	Loandjili	18 488
13	Owando	15 871
14	Djambala	13 570
15	Ngamaba-Mfilou	11 389
16	Makoua	7 427
17	Matsanga	6 246
18	Ewo	5 859
19	Sembé	4 047

REPUBLIQUE DU CONGO • REPUBLIC OF THE CONGO

Capital	Brazzaville	Population	4 012 809 (127)	% in cities	61%
GDP per capita	$3900 (154)	Area km²	342 000 km² (63)	GMT +/-	+1
Neighbours (km)	Angola 201, Cameroon 523, C. African Rep 467, Congo DR 2410, Gabon 1903 • Coast 169				

RECENT INTERNATIONAL MATCHES PLAYED BY CONGO

2009	Opponents	Score	Venue	Comp	Scorers	Att	Referee
27-05	Jordan	D 1-1	Amman	Fr	Epako [47]		
31-05	Bahrain	L 1-3	Manama	Fr	Kapolongo [20]		
12-08	Morocco	D 1-1	Rabat	Fr	Moussilou [18]		
13-10	Korea DPR	D 0-0	Le Mans	Fr			
14-11	Angola	D 1-1	Luanda	Fr	Douniama [91+]		
2010							
11-08	Burkina Faso	L 0-3	Senlis	Fr			
4-09	Sudan	L 0-2	Khartoum	CNq			Kaoma ZAM
10-10	Swaziland	W 3-1	Brazzaville	CNq	Mouko [21p], Sembolo 2 [35] [74]		Ssegonga UGA
2011							
27-03	Ghana	L 0-3	Brazzaville	CNq			Bennett RSA
3-06	Ghana	L 1-3	Kumasi	CNq	Moussilou [75]		
4-09	Sudan	L 0-1	Brazzaville	CNq			
8-10	Swaziland	W 1-0	Lobamba	CNq	Nkolo [47]		
11-11	Sao Tome e Principe	W 5-0	Sao Tome	WCq	Moussilou [1], Douniama [7], Malonga [27], Oniangue [54], Tchilimbou [69]	3 000	Ngbokaye CTA
15-11	Sao Tome e Principe	D 1-1	Pointe Noire	WCq	Nganga [56]	12 000	Mahamat CHA
2012							
29-02	Uganda	W 3-1	Pointe Noire	CNq	Oscar Ewolo [1], Mael Lepicier [77], Matt Moussilou [83]	13 000	Alioum CMR
2-06	Burkina Faso	D 0-0	Ouagadougou	WCq	Congo awarded match 3-0	23 904	El Ahrach MAR
9-06	Niger	W 1-0	Pointe Noire	WCq	Francis Malonga [89]	10 500	Munyemana RWA
16-06	Uganda	L 0-4	Kampala	CNq			
12-10	Egypt	L 0-3	Sharjah	Fr			
14-10	Saudi Arabia	L 2-3	Dammam	Fr	Lys Mouithys [27], Ladislas Douniama [39]		
14-11	Angola	D 1-1	Estoril	Fr	John Delarge [42]		

Fr = Friendly match • CN = African Cup of Nations • CM = CEMAC Cup • WC = FIFA World Cup
q = qualifier • r1 = first round group • sf = semi-final • 3p = third place play-off

CONGO NATIONAL TEAM HISTORICAL RECORDS

Coach: Noel Tosi FRA 2006-07 • Ivica Todorov SRB 2008-10 • Robert Corfu 2010-11 • Jean-Guy Wallemme 2011-

COUPE DU CONGO 2012

Quarter-finals		Semi-finals		Final	
Diables Noirs	3 3				
AS Ponténégrine	0 0	**Diables Noirs**	2 1		
JS Talangai	2 0	St Michel Ouenzé	0 0		
St Michel Ouenzé	3 2			**Diables Noirs** ‡	1
CARA Brazzaville	2 3			AC Léopards Dolisie	0
FC Bilombé	0 0	CARA Brazzaville	0 1	Stade de Kinkala, 15-08-2012	
CNFF	0 1	**AC Léopards Dolisie**	2 3	Scorer - Lorry Kolo for Diables Noirs	
AC Léopards Dolisie	1 6				

‡ Qualified for the CAF Confederation Cup

MEDALS TABLE

		Overall	Lge	Cup	Africa	City/Town
		G S B	G	G S	G S B	
1	Etoile du Congo	18 5	13	5 5		Brazzaville
2	Diables Noirs	13 4	8	5 4		Brazzaville
3	CARA Brazzaville	13 3	9	3 3	1	Brazzaville
4	V. Club Mokanda	6 3	3	3 3		Pointe Noire
5	Inter Club	5 3 2	2	3 3	2	Brazzaville
6	AC Léopards Dolisie	4 1	1	2 1	1	Dolisie
7	Patronage St Anne	3 1	2	1 1		Brazzaville
8	AS Police	3 1	2	1	1	Brazzaville
9	AS Cheminots	3	1	2		Pointe Noire
	Munisport	3	2	1		Pointe Noire
11	St Michel Ouenzé	2	2			Brazzaville

CONGO 2012

CHAMPIONNAT NATIONALE MTN LIGUE 1 GROUP A BRAZZAVILLE

	Pl	W	D	L	F	A	Pts	Diables Noirs	Talangai	Etoile	CARA	St Michel O	Inter Club	St Michel L	Ajax Ouénzé	Police	Cuvette	Kondzo	Tongo	Patronage	Moranzambé
Diables Noirs †	26	19	7	0	46	11	64		1-1	1-0	1-0	1-1	1-1	1-0	3-1	1-0	0-0	3-0	1-0	3-1	1-0
JS Talangai †	26	13	8	5	34	22	47	0-2		2-0	3-0	1-1	1-1	2-1	2-0	1-0	1-0	1-1	0-2	1-0	4-1
Etoile du Congo	26	13	6	7	38	18	45	0-0	0-1		1-0	0-0	1-1	5-0	1-0	5-0	4-0	1-0	1-0	4-1	3-0
CARA Brazzaville	26	12	6	8	33	24	42	1-2	3-2	3-0		2-1	0-1	3-1	1-1	0-1	0-0	1-0	3-1	3-1	3-1
St Michel Ouenzé	26	9	13	4	35	29	40	1-1	1-1	1-1	0-0		1-6	0-0	2-1	3-1	4-1	2-0	2-2	1-1	3-0
Inter Club	26	9	10	7	38	24	37	1-1	3-0	2-2	3-2	1-1		1-2	0-1	4-0	1-1	1-2	0-0	1-1	2-0
St Michel Loukoléla	26	10	7	9	22	23	37	1-2	0-1	0-0	0-0	0-1	1-0		1-0	2-0	1-1	2-0	1-0	1-0	0-0
Ajax Ouénzé	26	9	7	10	20	26	34	0-2	0-2	1-0	0-0	1-1	1-0	1-0		2-1	1-1	3-1	1-1	1-0	2-0	1-0
AS Police	26	8	6	12	22	34	30	1-2	1-0	0-2	0-1	2-1	2-1	1-1	2-1		1-0	0-0	1-1	0-0	1-0
Cuvette	25	7	8	10	21	31	29	0-1	0-2	0-1	2-1	1-0	1-1	1-0	0-1	3-2		1-0	n/p	2-1	3-2
Kondzo	26	5	11	10	22	32	26	1-5	2-2	1-3	1-2	1-1	1-0	1-1	0-0	0-1	0-0		0-0	2-0	2-1
Tongo FC Jambon	25	6	7	12	23	28	25	0-1	2-2	1-0	1-2	1-2	1-2	0-1	4-1	2-1	0-1	1-1		2-0	0-0
Patronage St Anne	26	5	6	15	23	45	21	0-5	0-1	2-1	0-2	1-1	0-1	1-3	2-0	2-1	1-1	1-4	3-0		1-0
AC Moranzambé	26	1	8	17	15	45	11	0-4	0-0	1-2	0-0	2-0	0-3	1-2	0-0	0-1	0-3	1-1	1-1	1-2	3-3

11/02/2012 - 5/11/2012 • † Qualified for the semi-finals

CONGO 2012

CHAMPIONNAT NATIONALE MTN LIGUE 1 GROUP B POINTE NOIRE

	Pl	W	D	L	F	A	Pts	Léopards	Ponténégrine	Munisport	Bilombé	V. Club	La Mancha	Pigeon Vert	Cheminots	Olympic	St Pierre	Nico-Nicoyé	B'gainvillées	ASICO	Olympique
AC Léopards Dolisie †	26	22	1	3	81	11	67		2-0	3-0	3-0	0-3	4-0	4-0	5-0	8-0	3-0	2-0	3-1	8-0	7-0
AS Ponténégrine †	26	16	4	6	58	22	52	0-3		2-0	1-1	2-0	1-0	0-1	1-0	3-0	5-0	1-0	1-0	5-1	7-1
Munisport	26	15	6	5	35	22	51	1-0	1-1		2-1	0-0	2-1	2-0	1-2	1-0	0-0	1-0	2-1	2-0	1-0
FC Bilombé	26	15	4	7	50	20	49	1-2	1-2	3-1		0-1	0-0	1-0	1-0	2-0	3-0	2-0	4-0	5-1	9-0
V. Club Mokanda	26	14	4	8	39	22	46	0-1	0-0	2-0	3-4		1-1	2-0	0-1	2-0	2-0	0-0	0-1	4-1	5-1
La Mancha	26	13	6	7	43	24	45	1-1	2-1	1-2	1-0	0-0		1-4	2-0	4-1	3-0	0-1	5-1	5-0	3-1
Pigeon Vert	26	11	7	8	33	30	40	1-2	2-3	0-0	0-2	3-2	2-1		1-1	3-1	0-1	0-0	2-1	3-3	1-1
AS Cheminots	26	11	7	8	27	30	40	0-4	2-2	1-1	1-1	3-0	0-3	0-2		3-0	0-0	1-0	1-1	4-1	1-0
Olympic Nkayi	26	9	2	15	26	46	29	0-5	3-1	0-0	2-0	1-3	0-1	0-0	3-0		0-1	3-1	2-1	3-1	1-0
US St Pierre	26	7	7	12	14	33	28	0-4	0-3	1-1	0-1	0-3	0-0	0-0	0-0	1-0		1-0	1-0	4-0	0-1
Nico-Nicoyé	26	7	5	14	20	28	26	0-2	1-2	2-4	0-0	2-1	1-1	0-1	0-1	1-0	1-0		1-1	0-1	4-1
JS Bougainvillées	26	4	5	17	21	54	17	0-2	0-6	0-5	0-4	0-1	1-3	0-1	0-1	3-0	1-1	2-2		1-1	2-1
ASICO	26	4	2	20	22	71	14	3-0	1-0	1-4	0-1	1-3	0-1	1-4	1-3	0-3	2-3	0-1	2-0		0-1
Olympique Vision	26	3	2	21	15	71	11	0-3	0-8	0-1	0-3	0-1	0-3	1-2	0-1	1-3	0-0	0-2	2-3	3-0	

11/02/2012 - 11/11/2012 • † Qualified for the semi-finals

CONGO 2012
CHAMPIONNAT NATIONALE PLAY-OFFS

Semi-finals

| AC Léopards Dolisie | 1 | 2 |
| JS Talangai * | 1 | 0 |

| AS Ponténégrine * | 0 | 0 |
| Diables Noirs | 0 | 2 |

Finals

| AC Léopards Dolisie † | 1 4p |
| Diables Noirs | 1 2p |

* Home team in 1st leg

† Qualified for CAF Champions League • Final: 16/12/2012, Pointe Noire.
Scorers - Rudy Ndey [69] for Leopards; Landry Djimbi [48] for Diables Noirs

CHA – CHAD

FIFA/COCA-COLA WORLD RANKING

'93	'94	'95	'96	'97	'98	'99	'00	'01	'02	'03	'04	'05	'06	'07	'08	'09	'10	'11	'12
166	175	180	188	184	178	166	163	176	173	152	168	159	142	141	119	145	141	143	140

2012

Jan	Feb	Mar	Apr	May	Jun	Jul	Aug	Sep	Oct	Nov	Dec	High	Low	Av
142	141	112	115	115	112	123	118	116	125	120	140	112	190	158

Chad were knocked out by Malawi in the first round of qualification for the 2013 Africa Cup of Nations in South Africa and ended the year having played just three internationals. As they had already been eliminated in the preliminary round of the 2014 FIFA World Cup qualifiers in late 2011, the team faced an even bleaker 2013 with no scheduled competitive internationals. A 3-2 home win over Malawi in the first leg of their Nations Cup qualifier was only the second victory for the side in four years as Chad ended 2012 in 140th place in the FIFA/Coca-Cola World Ranking. In club football Gazelle won the Ligue de Ndjamena, which had several false starts before kicking off and was regularly interrupted through the year. Though only a regional league based around the capital, it has for the past three years operated as the de facto national league with very little football activity across the rest of this vast Saharan country. Gazelle finished three points ahead of Foullah Edifice for what was only their second title, having won the last national league to be played back in 2009. Elect Sport won the cup by beating Renaissance on post-match penalties after a 1-1 draw in the final and there was a rare success in the CAF Confederation Cup when Renaissance beat Sahel SC from neighbouring Niger before being eliminated by Mali's CO Bamako.

CAF AFRICA CUP OF NATIONS RECORD
1957-1990 DNE 1992 DNQ 1994 Withdrew 1996-1998 DNE 2000 DNQ 2002 DNE 2004-2008 DNQ 2010 Disqualified 2012-13 DNQ

FEDERATION TCHADIENNE DE FOOTBALL (FTF)

Boite postale 886, N'Djamena

☎ +235 518740

✉ ftfasg@yahoo.fr
🖥 ftfaonline.com

FA 1962 CON 1962 FIFA 1988
P Adoum Younousmi
GS Djibrine Mahamat Dembelle

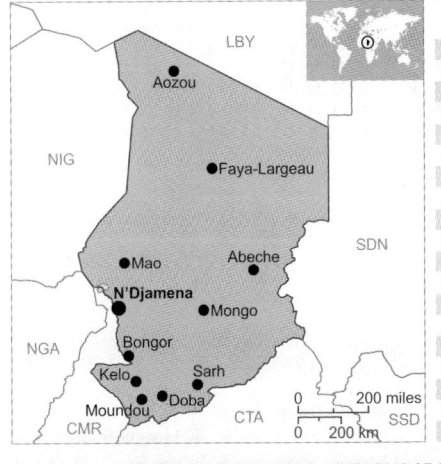

MAJOR CITIES/TOWNS
Population
1 N'Djaména   776 126
2 Moundou   145 486
3 Sarh   110 355
4 Abéché   79 851
5 Kélo   45 780
6 Koumra   39 031
7 Pala   38 173
8 Am Timan   31 089
9 Bongor   29 889
10 Mongo   29 882
11 Doba   26 194
12 Ati   25 912
13 Laï   20 862
14 Oum Hadjer   20 742
15 Bitkine   19 907
16 Mao   19 407
17 Massaguet   19 273
18 Dourbali   19 032
19 Léré   18 440

THE STADIA
2014 FIFA World Cup Stadia
Stade Omnisports Idriss Ouya
N'Djamena   20 000
Other Main Stadia
The Stade Omnisports is the principal stadium in the country

REPUBLIQUE DU CHAD • REPUBLIC OF CHAD

Capital N'Djamena	Population 10 329 208 (79)	% in cities 27%
GDP per capita $1600 (192)	Area km² 1 284 000 km² (21)	GMT +/- +1

Neighbours (km) Cameroon 1094, C. African Rep 1197, Libya 1055, Niger 1175, Nigeria 87, Sudan 1360

RECENT INTERNATIONAL MATCHES PLAYED BY CHAD

2008	Opponents	Score	Venue	Comp	Scorers	Att	Referee
7-06	Mali	L 1-2	N'Djamena	WCq	Kedigui [37]	15 000	Aguidissou BEN
14-06	Congo	W 2-1	N'Djamena	WCq	Kedigui [44p], Syriakata Hassan [48]	8 000	Doue CIV
22-06	Congo	L 0-2	Brazzaville	WCq		8 000	Diouf SEN
24-08	Libya	L 0-3	Tripoli	Fr			
6-09	Sudan	W 2-1	Cairo	WCq	Mbaiam [29], Syriakata Hassan [81]	4 000	Trabelsi TUN
10-09	Sudan	L 1-3	Cairo	WCq	Djime [34]	10 000	Diatta SEN
11-10	Mali	L 1-2	Bamako	WCq	Misdongarde [64]	40 000	Keita GUI
2009							
No international matches played in 2009							
2010							
19-06	Niger	D 1-1	Niamey	Fr	Barthelemy [39]		
1-07	Togo	D 2-2	N'Djamena	CNq	Djimrangar [20], Mbaiam [28]		Benouza ALG
9-07	Botswana	L 0-1	Gaborone	CNq			Seechurn MRI
11-08	Tunisia	L 1-3	N'Djamena	CNq	N'Douassel [72]		Doue CIV
29-08	Ethiopia	L 0-1	Addis Abeba	Fr			
9-10	Malawi	L 2-6	Blantyre	CNq	N'Douassel [26], Mbaiam [81]		Kirwa KEN
17-11	Togo	D 0-0	Lome	CNq			Coulibaly MLI
2011							
8-02	Equatorial Guinea	L 0-2	Malabo	Fr			
26-03	Botswana	L 0-1	N'Djamena	CNq			
5-06	Tunisia	L 0-5	Sousse	CNq			
8-10	Malawi	D 2-2	N'Djamena	CNq	Labo [65], Barthelemy [94+]		
11-11	Tanzania	L 1-2	N'Djamena	WCq	Labo [16]	10 000	Ogunkolade NGA
15-11	Tanzania	W 1-0	Dar es Salaam	WCq	Labo [47]	42 700	Nampiandraza MAD
2012							
29-02	Malawi	W 3-2	N'Djamena	CNq	Mahamat Labbo [38], Leger Djem Nam 2 [45 53]		Doue CIV
31-03	Egypt	L 0-4	Omdurman	Fr			
16-06	Malawi	L 0-2	Blantyre	CNq			Nampiandraza MAD

Fr = Friendly match • CN = African Cup of Nations • WC = FIFA World Cup • q = qualifier

COUPE DE LIGUE DE N'DJAMENA 2012

Quarter-finals	Semi-finals		Final	
Elect-Sport				
	Elect-Sport	2		
	Gazelle	1		
Gazelle			Elect-Sport ‡	1 4p
AS DGSSIE			Renaissance	1 3p
	AS DGSSIE	0	Stade Omnisports,	
	Renaissance	1	N'Djamena, 25-11-2012	
Renaissance				

‡ Qualified for the CAF Confederation Cup

CHI – CHILE

FIFA/COCA-COLA WORLD RANKING

'93	'94	'95	'96	'97	'98	'99	'00	'01	'02	'03	'04	'05	'06	'07	'08	'09	'10	'11	'12
55	47	36	26	16	16	23	19	39	84	80	74	64	41	45	31	15	15	13	26

2012

Jan	Feb	Mar	Apr	May	Jun	Jul	Aug	Sep	Oct	Nov	Dec	High	Low	Av
12	12	14	13	13	11	15	15	14	17	21	26	6	84	37

The Chile national team suffered a drastic loss of form in the second half of 2012 which not only threatened their qualification for the 2014 FIFA World Cup in Brazil but also cost coach Claudio Borghi his job. Consecutive defeats at the hands of Colombia, Ecuador and Argentina saw Chile drop out of the qualification places but the appointment of Jorge Sampaoli was greeted with almost universal acclaim. The Argentine had transformed Universidad de Chile into one of the most attractive teams to watch in South America and one that had won continental as well as domestic honours and the hope was that he could have the same effect on the national team. By winning the 2012 apertura with Sampaoli, 'La U' completed a hat trick of titles for the first time in their history but they failed to make it four league titles in a row when they were beaten by Unión Española in the quarter-finals of the 2012 clausura play-offs. In one of the biggest surprises of recent years the clausura title went to Huachipato from Talcahuano - a city devastated by the huge earthquake and subsequent tsunami of 2010. Known as the Steelers after the local steelworks, Huachipato are the only club from the south ever to have won the championship and are one of just two clubs from outside the central region around Santiago, along with Cobreloa, to have done so.

FIFA WORLD CUP RECORD

1930 5 r1 **1934-1938** DNE **1950** 9 r1 **1954** DNE **1958** DNQ **1962** 3 SF (hosts) **1966** 13 r1 **1970** DNQ **1974** 11 r1
1978 DNQ **1982** 22 r1 **1986-1990** DNQ **1994** DNE **1998** 16 r2 **2002-2006** DNQ **2010** 10 r2

FEDERACION DE FUTBOL DE CHILE (FFCH)

Av. Quilin No. 5635, Comuna
Peñalolén, Casilla No. 3733,
Santiago de Chile
☎ +56 2 8101800
📠 +56 2 2843510
✉ ffch@anfpchile.cl
🖥 www.anfp.cl
FA 1895 CON 1916 FIFA 1913
P Sergio Jadue
GS Nibaldo Jaque

THE STADIA

2014 FIFA World Cup Stadia

Estadio Nacional Santiago	47 000
Estadio Monumental Santiago	47 000

Other Main Stadia

Estadio Municipal Concepcion	35 000
Estadio Santa Laura Santiago	22 000
Estadio German Becker Temuco	18 000

MAJOR CITIES/TOWNS

		Population
1	Santiago	5 145 599
2	Puente Alto	745 752
3	Antofagasta	344 919
4	San Bernardo	298 757
5	Viña del Mar	289 147
6	Valparaíso	268 965
7	Temuco	250 454
8	Rancagua	240 286
9	Talca	223 499
10	Iquique	222 618
11	Concepción	215 097
12	Puerto Montt	198 446
13	Arica	192 278
14	La Serena	189 416
15	Coquimbo	188 995
16	Chillán	155 488
17	Quilpué	153 933
18	Talcahuano	153 532
19	Calama	146 334

REPUBLICA DE CHILE • REPUBLIC OF CHILE

Capital	Santiago	Population	16 601 707 (60)	% in cities	88%
GDP per capita	$14 900 (77)	Area km²	576 102 km² (38)	GMT +/-	-4
Neighbours (km)	Argentina 5308, Bolivia 860, Peru 171 • Coast 6435				

RECENT INTERNATIONAL MATCHES PLAYED BY CHILE

2010	Opponents	Score		Venue	Comp	Scorers	Att	Referee
16-06	Honduras	W	1-0	Nelspruit	WCr1	Beausejour 34	32 664	Maillet SEY
21-06	Switzerland	W	1-0	Port Elizabeth	WCr1	Gonzalez 75	34 872	Al Ghamdi KSA
25-06	Spain	L	1-2	Pretoria	WCr1	Millar 47	41 958	Rodriguez MEX
28-06	Brazil	L	0-3	Johannesburg	WCr2		54 096	Webb ENG
7-09	Ukraine	L	1-2	Kyiv	Fr	Isla 86	10 000	Sevastsyanik BLR
9-10	UAE	W	2-0	Abu Dhabi	Fr	Cereceda 6p, Morales 37	500	Al Ghamdi KSA
12-10	Oman	W	1-0	Muscat	Fr	Morales 21	9 000	Blooshi KUW
17-11	Uruguay	W	2-0	Santiago	Fr	Sanchez 38, Vidal 74	45 017	Torres PAR
2011								
22-01	USA	D	1-1	Carson/LA	Fr	Paredes 53	18 580	Chacon MEX
26-03	Portugal	D	1-1	Leiria	Fr	Fernandez 42	10 694	Blom NED
29-03	Colombia	W	2-0	Den Haag	Fr	Fernandez 7, Beausejour 31	15 000	Vink NED
19-06	Estonia	W	4-0	Santiago	Fr	Fernandez 21, Ponce 42, Suazo 45p, Sanchez 50	20 000	Vazquez URU
23-06	Paraguay	D	0-0	Asuncion	Fr		12 000	Oliveira BRA
4-07	Mexico	W	2-1	Mendoza	CAr1	Paredes 66, Vidal 72	25 000	Soto VEN
8-07	Uruguay	D	1-1	Mendoza	CAr1	Sanchez 64	45 000	Amarilla PAR
12-07	Peru	W	1-0	Mendoza	CAr1	OG 92+	42 000	Fagundes BRA
17-07	Venezuela	L	1-2	San Juan	CAqf	Suazo 69	23 000	Vera ECU
10-08	France	D	1-1	Montpellier	Fr	Cordova 76	30 000	Attwell ENG
2-09	Spain	L	2-3	St Gall	Fr	Isla 11, Vargas 20	14 605	Laperriere SUI
4-09	Mexico	L	0-1	Barcelona	Fr		15 000	Muniz ESP
7-10	Argentina	L	1-4	Buenos Aires	WCq	Fernandez 59	26 161	Roldan COL
11-10	Peru	W	4-2	Santiago	WCq	Ponce 2, Vargas 18, Medel 48, Suazo 63p	39 000	Orosco BOL
11-11	Uruguay	L	0-4	Montevideo	WCq		40 500	Baldassi ARG
15-11	Paraguay	W	2-0	Santiago	WCq	Contreras 28, Campos 86	44 726	Lopes BRA
21-12	Paraguay	W	3-2	La Serena	Fr	Pinto 3 19 62p 74	12 000	Orozco BOL
2012								
15-02	Paraguay	L	0-2	Luque	Fr		15 000	Vuaden BRA
29-02	Ghana	D	1-1	Chester (USA)	Fr	Matias Fernandez 75p	7 000	Bazakos USA
21-03	Peru	W	3-1	Arica	Fr	Esteban Paredes 5, Enzo Andria 43, Eugenio Mena 86	9 000	Quintana PAR
11-04	Peru	W	3-0	Tacna	Fr	Eugenio Mena 46, Felipe Flores 64, Bryan Carrasco 71	20 000	Caceres PAR
2-06	Bolivia	W	2-0	La Paz	WCq	Charles Aranguiz 45, Arturo Vidal 83	34 389	Intriago ECU
9-06	Venezuela	W	2-0	Puerto La Cruz	WCq	Matias Fernandez 85, Charles Aranguiz 91+	35 000	Buitrago COL
15-08	Ecuador	L	0-3	New York	Fr		35 000	Vaughn USA
11-09	Colombia	L	1-3	Santiago	WCq	Matias Fernandez 41	38 000	Carrillo PER
12-10	Ecuador	L	1-3	Quito	WCq	OG 25	32 600	Lopes BRA
16-10	Argentina	L	1-2	Santiago	WCq	Felipe Gutierrez 91+	45 000	Arias PAR
14-11	Serbia	L	1-3	St Gall	Fr	Angelo Henriquez 88	2 116	Kever SUI

Fr = Friendly match • CA = Copa America • WC = FIFA World Cup • q = qualifier • r1 = first round group

CHILE NATIONAL TEAM HISTORICAL RECORDS

Caps
84 - Leonel Sanchez 1955-68 • 73 - Nelson Tapia 1994-2005 • 70 - Alberto Fouilloux 1960-72 & Marcelo Salas 1994-2009 • 69 - Ivan Zamorano 1987-2001 & Fabian Estay 1990-2001 • 67 - Pablo Contreras 1999- & Claudio Bravo 2004- • 63 - Javier Margas 1990-2000 • 62 - Miguel Ramirez 1991-2003 • 61 - Clarence Acuna 1995-2004 • 60 - Humberto Suazo 2005- • 57 - Juan Carlos Letelier 1979-89 • 56 - Gonzalo Jara 2006- • 55 - Pedro Reyes 1994-2001

Goals
37 - Marcelo Salas 1994-2009 • 34 - Ivan Zamorano 1987-2001 • 29 - Carlos Caszely 1969-85 • 23 - Leonel Sanchez 1955-68 • 22 - Jorge Aravena 1983-89 • 21 - Humberto Suazo 2005- • 18 - Juan Carlos Letelier 1979-89 • 17 - Enrique Hormazabal 1950-63 • 14 - Alexis Sanchez 2006- & Matias Fernandez 2005- • 12 - Hugo Eduardo Rubio 1983-91; Jaime Ramirez 1954-66; Raul Toro 1936-41 & Alberto Foulloux 1960-72 • 11 - Pedro Araya 1964-71 & Julio Crisosto 1971-77

Coaches
See Oliver's Almanack 2012 for coaches of Chile pre-1970 • Francisco Hormazabal 1970 • Fernando Riera 1970 • Luis Vera 1971 • Raul Pino 1971-72 • Rudi Gutendorf GER 1972 • Luis Alamos 1973-74 • Pedro Morales 1974-75 • Caupolican Pena 1976-77 • Luis Santibanez 1977-82 • Luis Ibarra 1983 • Isaac Carrasco 1984 • Vicente Cantatore ARG 1984 • Pedro Morales 1985 • Luis Ibarra 1986 • Orlando Aravena 1987 • Manuel Rodriguez 1987 • Orlando Aravena 1988-89 • Arturo Salah 1990-93 • Nelson Acosta 1993 • Mirko Jozic CRO 1994 • Xabier Azkargorta ESP 1995-96 • Nelson Acosta 1996-2000 • Pedro Garcia 2001 • Jorge Garces 2001 • Cesar Vaccia 2002 • Juvenal Olmos 2003-05 • Nelson Acosta 2005-07 • Marcelo Bielsa ARG 2007-11 • Claudio Borghi ARG 2011-12 • Jorge Sampaoli ARG 2013-

CHILE 2012
PRIMERA DIVISION APERTURA

	Pl	W	D	L	F	A	Pts
Universidad de Chile †	17	13	1	3	44	14	40
O'Higgins †	17	11	2	4	31	15	35
Deportes Iquique †	17	10	5	2	30	14	35
Universidad Católica †	17	8	6	3	31	17	30
Unión Española †	17	8	3	6	38	28	27
Colo Colo †	17	7	5	5	22	21	26
Unión La Calera †	17	6	6	5	21	18	24
Cobreloa †	17	7	2	8	23	25	23
Huachipato	17	6	5	6	25	28	23
Univ. de Concepción	17	5	6	6	23	27	21
Santiago Wanderers	17	6	2	9	28	30	20
Audax Italiano	17	5	5	7	24	32	20
Deportes La Serena	17	5	4	8	24	33	19
Rangers Talca	17	5	3	9	17	25	18
Palestino	17	5	3	9	14	26	18
Antofagasta	17	4	5	8	10	20	17
Cobresal	17	3	4	10	17	40	13
Unión San Felipe	17	2	7	8	12	21	13

27/01/2012 - 20/05/2012 • † Qualified for the play-offs
Top scorers (overall): **11** - Emanuel **HERRERA** ARG, Unión Española; Enzo **GUTIERREZ** ARG, O'Higgins & Sebastian **UBILLA**, Santiago Wanderers • **10** - Angelo **HENRIQUEZ**, Univ de Chile • **9** - Esteban **PAREDES**, Colo Colo & Braian **RODRIGUEZ** URU, Huachipato

PENALTIES

	U de Chile		O'Higgins	
			Rojas	✘
✓	Aranguiz			
			Suarez	✘
✘	Diaz			
			Opazo	✘
✓	Ruidiaz			
			Gutierrez	✘

APERTURA 2012 PLAY-OFFS

Quarter-finals		Semi-finals		Final	
Un. de Chile	2 2				
Cobreloa *	0 1	**Un. de Chile**	0 4		
Dep. Iquique	3 1	Colo Colo *	2 0		
Colo Colo *	3 2			**Un. de Chile**	1 2 2p
Un. Española *	3 1			O'Higgins *	2 1 0p
Un. Católica	0 1	Un. Española *	1 1		
U. La Calera *	0 2	**O'Higgins**	0 2		
O'Higgins	1 3	* At home in the first leg			

APERTURA 2012 FINAL

El Teniente, Rancagua, 28-06-2012, Att: 10 000, Ref: Jorge Osorio
O'Higgins 2 Rojas [1], Lopez [72]
Universidad de Chile 1 Marino [29]

O'Higgins - Luis Marin(c) - Yerson Opazo, Nelson Saavedra, Julio Alberto Barroso, Alejandro Lopez - Rodrigo Rojas, Claudio Meneses, Ramon Fernandez (Guillermo Suarez 91+) - Luis Figueroa (Nelson Rebolledo 87), Enzo Gutierrez, Boris Sagredo (Cesar Fuentes 75). Tr: Eduardo Berizzo

U de Chile - Johnny Herrera - Paulo Magalhaes, Osvaldo Gonzalez, Jose Rojas(c), Eugenio Mena - Matias Rodriguez, Marcelo Diaz, Charles Aranguiz, Guillermo Marino• - Angelo Henriquez (Luis Gallegos 65), Junior Fernandes. Tr: Jorge Sampaoli

Estadio Nacional, Santiago, 2-07-2012, Att: 44 198, Ref: Enrique Osses
Universidad de Chile 2 2p Aranguiz [65p], Marino [92+]
O'Higgins 1 0p Fernandez [30p]

U de Chile - Johnny Herrera• - Matias Rodriguez• (Roberto Cereceda 89), Osvaldo Gonzalez, Jose Rojas(c)♦52, Eugenio Mena - Charles Aranguiz•, Marcelo Diaz•, Guillermo Marino - Angelo Henriquez (Raul Ruidiaz 70), Junior Fernandes, Gustavo Lorenzetti (Luis Gallegos 79). Tr: Jorge Sampaoli

O'Higgins - Luis Marin(c) - Yerson Opazo•, Nelson Saavedra•, Julio Alberto Barroso♦51, Alejandro Lopez - Rodrigo Rojas, Claudio Meneses•, Ramon Fernandez (Cesar Fuentes 83) - Luis Figueroa (Guillermo Suarez•77), Enzo Gutierrez•, Boris Sagredo (Nelson Rebolledo 54). Tr: Eduardo Berizzo

CHILE 2012

PRIMERA DIVISION AGGREGATE TABLE

	Pl	W	D	L	F	A	Pts	U de Chile	Iquique	Colo Colo	O'Higgins	Univ Católica	Un Española	Palestino	Rangers	Huachipato	Cobreloa	Audax	Wanderers	Un La Calera	Antofagasta	U Concepción	Cobresal	Un San Felipe	La Serena
Universidad de Chile †	34	22	7	5	76	34	73		1-1	5-0	1-1	0-0	3-2	3-2	2-0	4-0	4-1	2-1	3-0	0-0	4-0	3-1	3-1	2-0	5-2
Deportes Iquique ††	34	19	8	7	54	41	65	0-0		0-1	1-2	3-2	2-4	2-1	2-0	1-0	1-1	1-2	2-1	3-3	2-1	2-0	3-2	4-1	3-1
Colo Colo	34	16	11	7	54	34	55	1-0	0-0		1-0	1-1	3-0	0-1	2-2	3-0	0-1	5-1	3-1	2-1	1-0	1-2	1-2	1-0	0-2
O'Higgins	34	16	7	11	53	42	55	3-0	0-1	1-1		1-2	1-3	5-0	2-2	2-4	1-0	3-1	1-1	2-1	1-0	4-1	1-2	2-1	2-1
Universidad Católica	34	14	11	9	55	40	53	2-1	1-1	0-2	1-0		1-0	1-0	2-0	0-2	5-1	1-0	3-2	1-1	1-0	2-2	5-0	1-1	3-0
Unión Española	34	15	6	13	66	56	51	5-2	1-2	4-2	0-2	2-2		1-0	2-1	1-3	2-1	3-3	2-2	0-0	2-1	4-1	6-1	3-1	5-2
Palestino	34	14	6	14	36	44	48	1-3	0-1	0-3	2-1	1-2	1-3		4-1	2-2	2-1	0-0	2-1	1-0	0-0	1-0	2-1	1-2	1-0
Rangers Talca	34	13	9	12	44	44	48	2-2	5-0	0-2	1-2	1-0	1-0	2-0		2-1	3-0	1-0	2-3	2-0	1-2	1-2	2-0	1-0	2-0
Huachipato †	34	13	9	12	48	49	48	0-3	4-1	0-3	2-1	2-2	2-0	1-1	1-2		0-1	1-1	2-1	1-2	2-0	2-0	1-1	1-0	1-1
Cobreloa	34	13	4	17	46	49	43	0-1	0-1	0-2	0-1	4-3	1-2	1-0	0-1	4-2		1-2	2-4	1-0	3-1	3-1	3-0	2-1	2-2
Audax Italiano	34	11	10	13	53	58	43	0-6	0-1	1-3	5-1	2-0	0-2	1-2	2-0	2-2	2-1		4-1	2-1	1-2	2-2	1-1	0-0	3-2
Santiago Wanderers	34	10	9	15	55	58	39	2-2	2-1	0-1	0-1	2-1	2-2	2-3	2-2	1-1	1-3	4-2		2-0	0-1	3-1	5-2	1-0	1-1
Unión La Calera	34	8	15	11	32	36	39	0-1	1-1	1-1	0-0	1-0	1-0	1-1	2-2	0-2	1-0	1-1	2-1		0-0	1-1	1-1	1-3	3-0
Antofagasta	34	10	7	17	36	49	37	2-4	1-1	1-2	2-3	2-2	1-1	0-1	0-3	1-0	1-2	1-0	2-1	2-1		2-1	2-1	0-0	2-1
Univ. de Concepción	34	8	12	14	40	55	36	0-2	1-1	1-1	1-3	1-1	2-1	2-0	1-0	1-1	3-1	1-1	2-5	0-0	0-2		1-1	1-1	3-1
Cobresal	34	8	11	15	39	64	35	1-2	0-4	2-2	1-0	2-2	2-1	0-1	1-0	0-2	0-3	2-1	1-4	3-1	1-1			1-1	2-2
Unión San Felipe	34	8	10	16	31	42	34	0-1	1-2	1-1	0-1	3-1	1-0	0-0	1-2	0-3	1-3	1-0	0-0	2-1	2-2	0-0			3-0
Deportes La Serena	34	7	10	17	44	66	31	1-3	2-3	1-1	2-2	1-3	2-1	1-1	1-1	2-1	0-0	2-4	3-1	0-1	4-1	1-0	1-1	2-1	

Matches in the shaded boxes were played in the Apertura
† Qualified for Copa Libertadores as Apertura/Clausura winners • †† Qualified for Copa Libertadores on season record
‡ Relegation play-offs: Universidad de Concepción 0-1 1-3 **Everton** • **Cobresal** 1-3 3-0 Barnecha

CHILE 2012
PRIMERA DIVISION CLAUSURA

	Pl	W	D	L	F	A	Pts
Colo Colo †	17	9	6	2	32	14	33
Universidad de Chile †	17	9	6	2	32	20	33
Palestino †	17	9	3	5	22	18	30
Deportes Iquique †	17	9	3	5	24	27	30
Rangers Talca †	17	8	6	3	27	19	30
Huachipato †	17	7	4	6	23	21	25
Unión Española †	17	7	3	7	28	27	24
Audax Italiano †	17	6	5	6	29	26	23
Universidad Católica	17	6	5	6	24	23	23
Cobresal	17	5	7	5	22	24	22
Unión San Felipe	17	6	3	8	19	21	21
Cobreloa	17	6	2	9	23	24	20
Antofagasta	17	6	2	9	26	29	20
O'Higgins	17	5	5	7	22	27	20
Santiago Wanderers	17	4	7	6	27	28	19
Univ. de Concepción	17	3	6	8	17	28	15
Unión La Calera	17	2	9	6	11	18	15
Deportes La Serena	17	2	6	9	20	33	12

7/07/2012 - 14/11/2012 • † Qualified for the play-offs
Top scorers (overall): **12** - Carlos MUNOZ, Colo Colo • **10** - Sebastian SAEZ ARG, Audax Italiano • **9** - Diego CHAVES URU, Palestino & Miguel CUELLAR PAR, Cobresal

PENALTIES

Huachipato		U Española
		Vecchio ✓
✓	Rodriguez	
		Jaime ✗
✗	Villalobos	
		Rubio ✓
✗	Gonzalez	
		Diaz ✗
✓	Cortes	
		Lobos ✗
✗	Aceval	
		Leal ✗
✓	Merlo	

CLAUSURA 2012 PLAY-OFFS

Quarter-finals		Semi-finals		Final	
Huachipato*	1 2				
Palestino	1 1	Huachipato*	1 1		
Dep. Iquique	0 0	Rangers	0 1		
Rangers*	1 1			Huachipato	1 3 3p
Colo Colo	2 4			Un. Española*	3 1 2p
Aud'x Italiano*	0 5	Colo Colo	1 0		
Un. de Chile	0 1	Un. Española*	3 2		
Un. Española*	0 4	* At home in the first leg			

CLAUSURA 2012 FINAL

1st leg. Santa Laura, Santiago, 5-12-2012, Att: 14 663. Ref: Julio Bascunan
Unión Española 3 OG [48], Jaime 2 [60 79]
Huachipato 1 Nunez [10]
Española - Eduardo Lobos - Nicolas Berardo, Jorge Ampuero, Matias Navarrete, Emilio Hernandez• (Braulio Leal 71), Gonzalo Villagra (Patricio Rubio 35), Diego Scotti, Emiliano Vecchio, Dagoberto Currimilla, Mauro Diaz, Sebastian Jaime• (Gonzalo Barriga 88). Tr: Jose Sierra
Huachipato - Nery Veloso - Claudio Munoz, Omar Merlo, Jose Contreras•, Nicolas Nunez (Mauricio Yedro 83), Nicolas Crovetto (Miguel Aceval 63), Gabriel Sandoval (Daniel Gonzalez 63), Lorenzo Reyes, Cesar Cortes, Manuel Villalobos, Braian Rodriguez. Tr: Jorge Pellicer

2nd leg. CAP, Talcahuano, 9-12-2012, Att: 9026, Ref: Claudio Puga
Huachipato 3 3pGonzalez 2 [37 44], Villalobos [89]
Unión Española 1 2pCurrimilla [30]
Huachipato - Nery Veloso - Claudio Munoz, Omar Merlo, Jose Contreras (Juan Carlos Espinoza 75), Daniel Gonzalez•, Nicolas Nunez (Gabriel Sandoval 46), Nicolas Crovetto (Miguel Aceval 58), Lorenzo Reyes, Cesar Cortes, Manuel Villalobos, Braian Rodriguez. Tr: Jorge Pellicer
Española - Eduardo Lobos - Nicolas Berardo, Jorge Ampuero, Rafael Olarra, Emilio Hernandez (Patricio Rubio 69), Braulio Leal, Diego Scotti, Emiliano Vecchio, Dagoberto Currimilla•, Mauro Diaz, Sebastian Jaime•. Tr: Jose Sierra

MEDALS TABLE

		Overall	League	Cup	Sth Am	City
		G S B	G S B	G S	G S B	
1	Colo Colo	40 23 20	29 17 15	10 4	1 2 5	Santiago
2	Universidad de Chile	20 8 18	16 8 13	3	1 5	Santiago
3	Universidad Catolica	14 25 10	10 17 4	4 7	1 6	Santiago
4	Cobreloa	9 13 6	8 8 5	1 3	2 1	Calama
5	Unión Española	8 12 6	6 9 5	2 2	1 1	Santiago
6	Santiago Wanderers	5 5 2	3 3 2	2 2		Valparaíso
7	Everton	5 2	4 2	1		Viña del Mar
8	Audax Italiano	4 10 9	4 8 9	2		Santiago
9	Palestino	4 5 3	2 4 2	2 1	1	Santiago
10	Magallanes	4 5 2	4 4 2	1		Santiago
11	Deportes Iquique	2 1 1	1	2 1		Iquique
12	Huachipato	2 1	2 1			Talcahuano
13	Union San Felipe	2	1	1		San Felipe
14	Santiago Morning	1 3 1	1 2 1	1		Santiago
15	Cobresal	1 2	2	1		El Salvador
16	Deportes La Serena	1 1 2	2	1 1		La Serena
17	Universidad Concepción	1 1	1	1		Concepción
18	Temuco	1 2	1 2			Temuco
19	Luis Cruz Martinez	1	1			Curicó
20	O'Higgins	3 3	1 3	2	1	Rancagua
21	Rangers	3 2	2 2	1		Talca
22	Deportes Concepción	2 1	1	1	1	Concepción

CHILE 2012
PRIMERA B (2) APERTURA
FIRST ROUND

North	Pl	W	D	L	F	A	Pts
Barnechea	6	5	0	1	15	8	15
Everton	6	3	1	2	9	6	10
San Marcos Arica	6	3	1	2	9	7	10
San Luis	6	3	1	2	11	10	10
Coquimbo Unido	6	2	1	3	7	10	7
Santiago Morning	6	1	1	4	6	10	4
Magallanes	6	1	1	4	1	7	4

South	Pl	W	D	L	F	A	Pts
Deportes Concepción	6	4	2	0	13	4	14
Naval Talcahuano	6	3	1	2	10	3	10
Prov. Curicó Unido	6	3	1	2	6	4	10
Puerto Montt	6	2	1	3	8	10	7
Lota Schwager	6	2	1	3	6	10	7
Nublense	6	1	2	3	7	11	5
Unión Temuco	6	1	2	3	4	12	5

4/02/2012 – 18/03/2012

CHILE 2012
PRIMERA B (2) CLAUSURA
FIRST ROUND

North	Pl	W	D	L	F	A	Pts
Magallanes	6	4	1	1	6	3	13
San Marcos Arica	6	4	1	1	6	6	13
San Luis	6	2	2	2	8	10	8
Barnechea	6	2	1	3	7	6	7
Santiago Morning	6	2	1	3	7	8	7
Everton	6	1	3	2	5	3	6
Coquimbo Unido	6	1	1	4	4	7	4

South	Pl	W	D	L	F	A	Pts
Naval Talcahuano	6	4	1	1	11	4	13
Unión Temuco	6	3	2	1	5	4	11
Nublense	6	3	1	2	11	9	10
Deportes Concepción	6	3	1	2	9	9	10
Prov. Curicó Unido	6	2	1	3	7	8	7
Puerto Montt	6	2	0	4	5	8	6
Lota Schwager	6	0	2	4	4	10	2

30/06/2012 – 5/08/2012

CHILE 2012
PRIMERA B (2) APERTURA
FINAL ROUND

	Pl	W	D	L	F	A	Pts
Nublense	13	8	5	0	26	15	29
San Marcos Arica	13	7	5	1	30	14	26
Unión Temuco	13	5	5	3	17	12	20
Everton	13	6	1	6	25	20	19
Barnechea	13	5	3	5	18	18	18
Lota Schwager	13	4	5	4	17	16	17
Magallanes	13	5	2	6	15	20	17
Deportes Concepción	13	4	4	5	16	13	16
Coquimbo Unido	13	4	4	5	19	19	16
San Luis	13	4	4	5	17	21	16
Puerto Montt	13	4	3	6	15	22	15
Santiago Morning	13	3	5	5	18	24	14
Naval Talcahuano	13	2	5	6	15	22	11
Prov. Curicó Unido	13	2	5	6	15	27	11

24/03/2012 – 24/06/2012

PLAY-OFF

Nublense
1-1 2-2 7-6p
Barnechea

Nublense promoted

Barneachea & Evertonl qualified for the play-offs (see Primera A)

CHILE 2012
PRIMERA B (2) CLAUSURA
FINAL ROUND

	Pl	W	D	L	F	A	Pts
Barnechea	13	7	5	1	21	17	26
Coquimbo Unido	13	7	2	4	25	14	23
Everton	13	6	4	3	24	19	22
San Marcos Arica	13	6	4	3	19	15	22
Santiago Morning	13	6	2	5	21	16	20
San Luis	13	5	3	5	17	17	18
Nublense	13	4	5	4	22	21	17
Naval Talcahuano	13	4	5	4	15	19	17
Deportes Concepción	13	4	4	5	14	18	16
Lota Schwager	13	4	3	6	13	16	15
Prov. Curicó Unido	13	3	4	6	12	13	13
Unión Temuco	13	3	4	6	13	20	13
Magallanes	13	1	8	4	4	9	11
Puerto Montt	13	2	5	6	9	15	11

11/09/2011 – 20/11/2011

CHN – CHINA PR

FIFA/COCA-COLA WORLD RANKING

'93	'94	'95	'96	'97	'98	'99	'00	'01	'02	'03	'04	'05	'06	'07	'08	'09	'10	'11	'12
53	40	66	76	55	37	88	75	54	63	86	54	72	84	81	100	93	87	71	88

2012													High	Low	Av
Jan	Feb	Mar	Apr	May	Jun	Jul	Aug	Sep	Oct	Nov	Dec				
74	76	68	66	66	73	68	69	78	85	88	88		37	108	68

Guangzhou Evergrande reclaimed the Chinese Super League and FA Cup titles won in 2011 but did so under the control of World Cup-winning coach Marcello Lippi. Lippi replaced Lee Jang Soo at the southern Chinese club early in the season and guided them to the league title ahead of Jiangsu Sainty before defeating Guizhou Renhe 5-3 on aggregate in the cup final to complete back-to-back doubles. Evergrande's domestic success was matched by a run to the quarter-finals of the AFC Champions League - the first Chinese side to progress to the last eight of the competition since Shanghai Shenhua in 2006. Their campaign was brought to a halt by a narrow defeat at the hands of two-time champions Al Ittihad of Saudi Arabia. The performance of Guangzhou went some way towards alleviating the doom and gloom surrounding the continuing disappointment associated with the national team, who missed out on a place in the final round of qualifying for the 2014 FIFA World Cup finals. Jose Antonio Camacho managed to hold on to his position at the helm of the team despite the poor showing - the third time in a row the Chinese have failed to reach the decisive round of qualifying for the FIFA World Cup - but with a difficult draw for the preliminary rounds of the AFC Asian Cup, the Spaniard's job looked increasingly precarious.

FIFA WORLD CUP RECORD
1930-1954 DNE **1958** DNQ **1962-1978** DNE **1982-1998** DNQ **2002** 31 r1 **2006-2014** DNQ

FOOTBALL ASSOCIATION OF THE PEOPLE'S REPUBLIC OF CHINA (CFA)

Building A, Dong Jiu Da Sha, Xi Zhao Si Street, Chongwen District, Beijing 100061
☎ +86 10 59291030
📠 +86 10 59290309
✉ info.footballchina@gmail.com
🌐 www.fa.org.cn
FA 1924 CON 1974 FIFA 1974
P Yuan Weimin
GS Wei Di

THE STADIA
2014 FIFA World Cup Stadia

University City Stadium Guangzhou	50 000
Tuodong Stadium Kunming	40 000
Shenzhen Bay Sports Center Shenzhen	20 000
Other Main Stadia	
National Stadium 'Bird's Nest' Beijing	80 000
Shanghai Stadium Shanghai	80 000

MAJOR CITIES/TOWNS

		Population
1	Shanghai	15 968 867
2	Beijing	7 817 968
3	Chongqing	4 579 725
4	Xian	4 445 222
5	Wuhan	4 303 340
6	Chengdu	3 916 581
7	Tianjin	3 666 320
8	Shenyang	3 543 444
9	Harbin	3 363 096
10	Nanjing	3 320 712
11	Guangzhou	3 103 466
12	Taiyuan	2 786 596
13	Changchun	2 750 684
14	Shijiazhuang	2 319 694
15	Changsha	2 267 008
16	Jinan	2 191 110
17	Dalian	2 158 193
18	Jilin	2 150 510
19	Nanchang	2 092 603

ZHONGHUA RENMIN GONGHEGUO • PEOPLE'S REPUBLIC OF CHINA

Capital	Beijing	Population	1 338 612 968 (1)	% in cities	43%
GDP per capita	$6000 (133)	Area km^2	9 596 961 km^2 (4)	GMT +/-	+8

Neighbours (km): Afghanistan 76, Bhutan 470, Burma 2185, India 3380, Kazakhstan 1533, Korea DPR 1416, Kyrgyzstan 858, Laos 423, Mongolia 4677, Nepal 1236, Pakistan 523, Russia 3645, Tajikistan 414, Vietnam 1281 • Coast 14 500

RECENT INTERNATIONAL MATCHES PLAYED BY CHINA PR

2010	Opponents	Score	Venue	Comp	Scorers	Att	Referee
6-01	Syria	D 0-0	Zheijang	ACq		29 570	Toma JPN
17-01	Vietnam	W 2-1	Hanoi	ACq	Xu Yang 35, Zhang Linpeng 43	3 000	Abdul Bashir SIN
6-02	Japan	D 0-0	Tokyo	EAC		25 964	Delovski AUS
10-02	Korea Republic	W 3-0	Tokyo	EAC	Yu Hai 5, Gao Lin 27, Deng Zhuoxiang 60	3 629	Ng Kai Lam HKG
14-02	Hong Kong	W 2-0	Tokyo	EAC	Qu Bo 2 44 74p	16 439	Kim Jong Hyeok KOR
4-06	France	W 1-0	Saint-Pierre (REU)	Fr	Deng Zhuoxiang 68	10 043	Proenca POR
26-06	Tajikistan	W 4-0	Kunming	Fr	Yan Xiangchuang 10, Yu Hanchao 2 47 78, Qu Bo 78		
11-08	Bahrain	D 1-1	Nanning	Fr	Hai Yu 10		
3-09	Iran	L 0-2	Zhengzhou	Fr			
7-09	Paraguay	D 1-1	Nanjing	Fr	Gao Lin 33		
8-10	Syria	W 2-1	Kunming	Fr	Zhao Peng 38, Zhang Linpeng 50		
12-10	Uruguay	L 0-4	Wuhan	Fr		50 000	Lee Dong Jun KOR
17-11	Latvia	W 1-0	Kunming	Fr	Xu Yang 89	7 500	Ko Hyung Jin KOR
18-12	Estonia	W 3-0	Zhuhai	Fr	Du Wei 17, Yu Hai 20, Yang Xu 38	8 500	Ko Hyung Jin KOR
22-12	Macedonia FYR	W 1-0	Guangzhou	Fr	Deng Zhuoxiang 90	8 000	
2011							
8-01	Kuwait	W 2-0	Doha	ACr1	Zhang Linpeng 58, Deng Zhuoxiang 67	7 423	Williams AUS
12-01	Qatar	L 0-2	Doha	ACr1		30 778	Kim Dong Jin KOR
16-01	Uzbekistan	D 2-2	Doha	ACr1	Yu Hai 6, Hao Junmin 56	3 529	Al Hilali OMA
25-03	New Zealand	D 1-1	Wuhan	Fr	OG 3		Toma JPN
26-03	Costa Rica	D 2-2	San Jose	Fr	Gao Lin 2 46 90	35 000	Moreno PAN
29-03	Honduras	W 3-0	Wuhan	Fr	Huang Bowen 18, Yang Xu 2 37 86	10 000	Iemoto JPN
5-06	Uzbekistan	W 1-0	Kunming	Fr	Gao Lin 65	40 000	Ko Hyung Jin KOR
8-06	Korea DPR	W 2-0	Guiyang	Fr	Deng Zhuoxiang 38, Gao Lin 41	27 000	
23-07	Laos	W 7-2	Kunming	WCq	Yang Xu 3 45 54 73, Chen Tao 2 58 88, Hao Junmin 2 81 91+	13 500	Delovski AUS
28-07	Laos	W 6-1	Vientiane	WCq	Qu Bo 24, Yu Hanchao 2 36 87, Deng Zhuoxiang 2 67 82, Yang Xu 93+	13 000	Shamsuzzaman BAN
10-08	Jamaica	W 1-0	Hefei	Fr	Zhao Peng 9	60 000	Lee Min Hu KOR
2-09	Singapore	W 2-1	Kunming	WCq	Zheng Zhi 69, Yu Hai 73	17 000	El Haddad LIB
6-09	Jordan	L 1-2	Amman	WCq	Hao Junmin 57	19 000	Irmatov UZB
6-10	UAE	W 2-1	Shenzhen	Fr	Sun Xiang 5, Gao Lin 15	18 652	Singh SIN
11-10	Iraq	L 0-1	Shenzhen	WCq		25 021	Mozaffari IRN
11-11	Iraq	L 0-1	Doha	WCq		5 000	Green AUS
15-11	Singapore	W 4-0	Singapore	WCq	Yu Hai 41, Li Weifeng 56, Zheng Zheng 2 73 81	5 474	Balideh QAT
2012							
29-02	Jordan	W 3-1	Guangzhou	Fr	Hao Junmin 2 43 69, Yu Dabao 88	6 104	Minh Tri Vo VIE
3-06	Spain	L 0-1	Seville	Fr		45 000	Nijhuis NED
8-06	Vietnam	W 3-0	Wuhan	Fr	Gao Lin 2 10 63, Feng Renliang 35		Ko Hyung Jin KOR
15-08	Ghana	D 1-1	Xian	Fr	Gao Lin 57p		Choi Myung Yong KOR
6-09	Sweden	L 0-1	Helsingborg	Fr		9 073	Gestranius FIN
10-09	Brazil	L 0-8	Recife	Fr		29 658	Silvera URU
14-11	New Zealand	D 1-1	Shanghai	Fr	Zhao Peng 32	10 000	Kim Sung Il KOR

Fr = Friendly match • EAC = East Asian Championship • AC = AFC Asian Cup • WC = FIFA World Cup • q = qualifier

CHINA PR NATIONAL TEAM HISTORICAL RECORDS

Caps
114 - Li Weifeng 1998- • 103 - Hao Haidong 1987-2004 • 102 - Fan Zhiyi 1992-2002 • 89 - Li Tie 1997-2007 • 86 - Zhu Bo 1983-93 • 85 - Li Ming 1992-2004 & Ma Mingyu 1996-2002 • 78 - Sun Jihai 1996-2008 • 73 - Qu Bo 2001- • 72 - Xu Yunlong 2000-08 • 71 - Zhao Junzhe 1998-2008 • 69 - Li Jinyu 1997-2008 • 67 - Li Bing 1992-2001 • 66 - Ou Chuliang 1992-2002 • 65 - Jia Xiuquan 1983-92 • 64 - Du Wei 2001- • 63 - Lin Lefeng 1977-85 • 62 - Zhang Enhua 1995-2002 & Zheng Zhi 2002- • 61 - Sun Xiang 2002-

Goals
37 - Hao Haidong 1992-2004 • 27 - Su Maozhen 1992-2002 • 24 - Li Jinyu 1997-2008 • 21 - Ma Lin 1985-90 • 20 - Liu Haiguang 1983-90 • 19 - Li Bing 1992-2001 & Zhao Dayu 1982-86 • 18 - Qu Bo 2000- • 16 - Fan Zhiyi 1992-2002 & Mai Chao 1986-92

Coaches
Li Fenglou 1951-52 • A Joseph HUN 1954-56 • Dai Linjing 1957 • Chen Chengda 1958-62 • Nian Weisi 1963 • Fang Renqiu 1964 • Nian Weisi 1965-73 • Nian Weisi & Ren Bin 1974-76 • Zhang Honggen 1977 • Nian Weisi 1978 • Zhang Honggen 1979 • Nian Weisi 1980 • Su Yongshun 1980-82 • Zhang Honggen 1982 • Zeng Xuelin 1983-85 • Nian Weisi 1985-86 • Gao Fengwen 1986-90 • Xu Genbao 1991-92 • Klaus Schlappner GER 1992-93 • Qi Wusheng 1994-97 • Bobby Houghton ENG 1997-99 • Jin Zhiyang 2000 • Bora Milutinovic SRB 2000-02 • Shen Xiangfu 2002 • Arie Haan NED 2002-04 • Zhu Guanghu 2005-07 • Vladimir Petrovic SRB & Ratomir Dujkovic SRB 2007-08 • Yin Tiesheng 2008-09 • Gao Hongbo 2009-2011 • Jose Camacho ESP 2011-

CHINA PR 2012

CSL (CHINESE SUPER LEAGUE)

	Pl	W	D	L	F	A	Pts	Guangzhou	Jiangsu	Beijing	Guizhou	Dalian Aerbin	Changchun	G'zhou R&F	Tianjin	Shanghai	Liaoning	Hangzhou	Shandong	Qingdao	Dalian Shide	Shanghai	Henan
Guangzhou Ev'grande†	30	17	7	6	51	30	58		5-1	3-2	1-1	2-1	4-0	0-1	0-0	2-2	1-0	3-1	3-2	1-0	3-1	2-1	3-0
Jiangsu Sainty †	30	14	12	4	49	29	54	1-1		0-0	2-0	3-2	1-2	3-1	3-2	2-2	1-0	3-0	3-3	1-0	5-0	1-1	5-1
Beijing Guoan †	30	14	6	10	34	35	48	1-0	0-1		2-1	1-0	0-4	1-0	3-1	3-2	1-1	0-2	2-1	0-0	1-0	1-0	3-0
Guizhou Renhe †	30	12	9	9	44	33	45	2-1	3-1	0-2		2-2	0-0	3-0	1-1	4-2	1-1	5-0	2-1	1-0	2-0	3-1	1-2
Dalian Aerbin	30	11	11	8	51	46	44	0-0	1-1	3-1	2-1		1-2	2-1	1-1	0-0	1-1	1-1	5-2	2-1	3-3	1-1	1-0
Changchun Yatai	30	12	8	10	37	40	44	1-2	0-0	0-1	0-0	1-2		2-1	1-2	2-0	2-1	0-3	1-0	0-0	0-1	1-0	2-2
Guangzhou R&F	30	13	3	14	47	49	42	2-0	1-1	3-1	1-0	1-2	5-1		1-2	1-1	2-1	1-0	4-2	2-3	1-0	3-2	2-1
Tianjin Teda	30	10	10	10	29	30	40	0-1	0-0	2-1	1-2	1-0	0-1	1-2		0-0	1-0	2-0	2-0	0-0	1-1	0-0	1-1
Shanghai Shenhua	30	8	14	8	39	34	38	0-1	1-1	3-1	2-1	2-2	1-3	1-0	0-1		3-0	5-1	0-0	3-0	0-0	0-0	2-1
Liaoning Whowin	30	8	12	10	40	41	36	0-3	0-0	0-0	1-1	5-3	3-3	1-2	2-1	1-1		4-0	1-0	2-0	3-2	3-2	3-1
Hangzhou Greentown	30	9	9	12	34	46	36	2-3	1-2	1-0	1-1	2-2	2-3	2-2	1-2	1-2	2-1		0-0	0-0	1-1	0-0	2-0
Shandong Luneng	30	8	12	10	46	43	36	1-1	0-0	4-0	3-1	3-3	3-0	2-1	2-0	3-3	1-1	1-2		1-1	2-2	3-1	2-0
Qingdao Jonoon	30	10	6	14	26	34	36	2-1	1-0	0-2	0-1	1-3	1-0	3-2	2-1	1-0	3-1	0-0	0-1		1-2	2-1	3-1
Dalian Shide	30	8	10	12	39	49	34	3-1	1-3	0-0	0-3	3-2	1-2	4-1	4-1	0-1	2-2	2-3	1-1	2-1		1-4	0-0
Shanghai Shenxin	30	6	12	12	36	35	30	1-1	0-1	1-2	0-0	3-1	2-2	4-2	0-1	1-1	0-0	0-1	1-1	2-0	1-1		2-0
Henan Jianye	30	7	5	18	28	56	26	1-2	0-3	2-2	3-1	1-2	2-1	3-1	0-2	1-0	1-1	1-3	2-1	1-0	0-1	0-4	

10/03/2012 - 3/11/2012 • † Qualified for the AFC Champions League • Shaanxi moved to Guizhou & Nanchang to Shanghai (as Shenxin)
Top scorers: **23** - Cristian **DANALACHE** ROU, Jiangsu • **19** - Peter **UTAKA** NGA, Dalian Aerbin • **14** - **RAFAEL COELHO** BRA, Guangzhou R&F •
13 - **ANSELMO** BRA, Shanghai Shenxin & Sjoerd **ARS** NED, Tianjin • **12** - **MURIQUI** BRA, Guangzhou Evergrande & Zlatan **MUSLIMOVIC** BIH, Guizhou

MEDALS TABLE

		Overall			League			Cup		Asia			City	DOF	Pro
		G	S	B	G	S	B	G	S	G	S	B			
1	Liaoning Whowin	11	9	6	8	6	5	2	2	1	1	1	Shenyang	1956	1995
2	Dalian Shide	11	6	6	8		5	3	4	2	1		Dalian	1982	1992
3	Beijing Guoan	10	7	14	6	4	13	4	3			1	Beijing	1956	1992
4	Shandong Luneng	8	6	2	4	3	2	4	3				Ji'nan	1956	1993
5	Shanghai Shenhua	7	13	5	4	11	5	3	2				Shanghai	1957	1993
6	August 1st	6	6	5	5	6	5	1					Various	1951-2003	
7	Tianjin Teda	4	7	4	2	6	4	2	1				Tianjin	1957	1993
8	Guangzhou Evergrande	3	3	1	2	2	1	1	1				Guangzhou	1954	1993
9	North East China	2	1		2	1								1951-1956	
10	Guangdong Hongyuan	1	5	1	1	1	1		4				Guiyang	1958-2001	
11	Shenzhen Ruby	1	1	1	1	1						1	Shenzhen	1994	1994
12	Changchun Yatai	1	1		1	1							Changchun	1996	1996

CHINA PR 2012

CHINA LEAGUE ONE (2)

	Pl	W	D	L	F	A	Pts	Shanghai	Wuhan	Fujian	Harbin	Chongqing	Tianjin	Shenzhen	Chongqing FC	Chengdu	Guangdong	Hunan	Shenyang	Yanbian	Beijing 361°	Beijing Baxy	Hohhot
Shanghai East Asia	30	17	8	5	47	25	59		0-1	1-1	3-1	2-0	3-0	3-3	0-0	3-2	2-1	2-0	0-0	2-0	1-0	2-2	1-0
Wuhan Zall	30	16	6	8	40	29	54	0-1		0-0	0-0	1-0	3-0	2-1	2-2	4-2	1-1	2-1	2-0	1-1	2-1	2-2	2-1
Fujian Smart Hero	30	12	10	8	41	32	46	1-1	1-0		1-0	2-3	1-0	1-2	1-0	2-2	4-1	1-0	2-3	1-1	1-1	0-2	4-2
Harbin Yiteng	30	13	6	11	53	43	45	0-3	0-1	0-2		4-3	2-0	4-1	3-3	1-1	0-1	2-1	4-2	4-2	5-1	4-0	1-0
Chongqing Lifan	30	12	9	9	50	45	45	3-1	3-0	1-0	2-2		2-2	2-0	3-1	3-1	2-2	3-0	1-2	2-1	0-0	2-1	1-1
Tianjin Songjiang	30	12	9	9	27	24	45	0-0	0-1	1-1		2-0		1-0	0-0	0-0	1-1	0-3	2-0	2-0	1-0		
Shenzhen Ruby	30	12	6	12	46	41	42	0-1	2-1	1-1	0-1	5-3	1-0		4-2	2-1	2-2	1-1	3-1	4-0	1-2	0-2	3-0
Chongqing FC	30	11	8	11	40	37	41	0-0	3-2	3-0	2-3	4-1	2-0	1-0		4-0	1-0	0-2	1-0	0-0	0-2	0-0	1-1
Chengdu Blades	30	11	8	11	33	41	41	0-1	1-0	1-1	2-1	1-1	0-0	2-1	2-1		2-1	0-1	1-1	1-0	1-0	1-0	1-0
Guangdong S'ray Cave	30	10	8	12	41	46	38	2-2	1-0	1-5	0-0	2-3	1-0	1-1	1-2	2-0		1-2	4-2	2-1	1-2	3-0	2-1
Hunan Billows	30	10	8	12	33	37	38	2-1	1-2	2-1	2-1	2-1	0-0	0-3	1-1	1-2	1-3		1-0	3-1	1-1	1-1	0-0
Shenyang Shenbei	30	9	11	10	36	38	38	1-0	3-2	1-1	2-0	0-1	1-1	2-1	2-0	1-1	2-2			2-2	1-1	1-1	4-0
Yanbian Baekdu	30	10	4	16	39	51	34	0-3	0-1	2-3	1-5	3-2	1-2	1-0	2-0	2-3	1-1	2-1	0-2		2-1	1-0	4-0
Beijing 361°	30	8	8	14	27	41	32	0-3	1-3	0-2	1-2	0-0	1-1	2-0	0-2	0-0	3-1	2-1	1-0	1-2		0-0	1-0
Beijing Baxy	30	8	7	15	34	46	31	1-2	0-1	0-1	2-1	3-0	0-3	0-1	1-2	2-1	0-2	0-3	2-1	2-1	1-3		3-3
Hohhot Dongjin	30	5	12	13	30	42	27	1-3	1-2	0-0	2-2	1-1	0-1	1-1	2-2	1-1	4-0	1-0	2-0	1-3	1-0	2-2	

17/03/2012 - 28/10/2012 • Top scorers: **23** - Babacar **GUEYE** SEN, Shenzhen Ruby • **21** - Johnny **WOODLY** CRC, Fujian • **17** - **WU** Lei, Shanghai EA

PART TWO – THE ASSOCIATIONS

CFA CUP 2012

Third Round

Guangzhou Evergrande	Bye
Chongqing Lifan	0
Henan Jianye *	2
Shenyang Shenbei	2 4p
Shanghai Shenxin *	2 2p
Beijing 361°	1
Dalian Aerbin *	2
Hangzhou Greentown *	3
Shanghai East Asia	0
Jiangsu Sainty *	1 4p
Chengdu Blades	1 5p
Guangzhou R&F *	3
Hunan Billows	2
Liaoning Whowin	Bye
Shandong Luneng *	4
Dongguan Nancheng	0
Tianjin Teda	Bye
Shanghai Shenhua *	0 5p
Shenzhen Ruby	0 4p
Hohhot Dongjin	0
Changchun Yatai *	2
Beijing Guoan	Bye
Guizhou Zhicheng	0
Qingdao Jonoon *	4
Dalian Shide *	8
Yanbian Baekdu	0
Guangdong S'ray Cave	0
Guizhou Renhe *	2

Fourth Round

Guangzhou Evergrande *	2
Henan Jianye	1
Shenyang Shenbei	0
Dalian Aerbin *	2
Hangzhou Greentown *	2
Chengdu Blades	1
Guangzhou R&F	2
Liaoning Whowin *	4
Shandong Luneng	1 4p
Tianjin Teda *	1 2p
Shanghai Shenhua	0 3p
Changchun Yatai *	0 5p
Beijing Guoan *	6
Qingdao Jonoon	0
Dalian Shide	0
Guizhou Renhe *	2

Quarter-finals

Guangzhou Evergrande *	1
Dalian Aerbin	0
Hangzhou Greentown	0
Liaoning Whowin *	1
Shandong Luneng *	1
Changchun Yatai	0
Beijing Guoan *	3
Guizhou Renhe	4

Semi-finals

Guangzhou Evergrande *	1 2
Liaoning Whowin	0 2
Shandong Luneng	1 2
Guizhou Renhe *	1 2

Final

CUP FINAL

Guiyang Olympic Sports Center, 10-11-2012
Att: 45,210. Ref: Alan Miller AUS
Scorers - Jorda [10] for Guizhou; Barrios [49] for Guangzhou

Guizhou - Zhang Lie - Sun Jiha● - (Li Kai 75), Zhang Chenglin, Nano (c), Guo Sheng - Chen Jie (Dino Dulbic● 56), Yang Hao, Li Chunyu● (Rao Weihui● 46), Yu Hai - Zlatan Muslimovic●, Rafa Jorda. Tr: Gao Hongbo
Guangzhou - Li Shuai - Rong Hao (Feng Junyan 68), Zhang Linpeng, Feng Xiaoting, Kim Young Gwon, Sun Xiang - Zhao Xuri (Huang Bowen 77), Zheng Zhi (c) - Dario Conca - Gao Lin●●81, Cleo (Lucas Barrios 46). Tr: Marcello Lippi

Guangzhou Evergrande	1 4
Guizhou Renhe	1 2

CUP FINAL

Tianhe, Guangzhou, 18-11-2012
Att: 39,989. Ref: Kim Sang Woo KOR
Scorers - Barrios 2 [1 66], Zgang Linpeng [44], Conca [92+] for Guangzhou; Jorda [52], Rao Weihui [94+] for Guizhou

Guangzhou - Li Shuai - Zhang Linpeng, Feng Xiaoting, Kim Young Gwon, Sun Xiang - Zhao Xuri● (Rong Hao 78), Qin Sheng●, Zheng Zhi (c) - Dario Conca●, Lucas Barrios (Feng Junyan 88), Muriqui (Cleo 54). Tr: Marcello Lippi
Guizhou - Zhang Lie - Sun Jiha●, Zhang Chenglin, Nano● (c) (Ruben Suarez 56), Guo Sheng● (Rao Weihui 46) - Dino Dulbic●, Chen Jie●, Yang Hao, Yu Hai (Yang Yihu 71) - Zlatan Muslimovic, Rafa Jorda. Tr: Gao Hongbo

* Home team/home team in the 1st leg

CIV – COTE D'IVOIRE

FIFA/COCA-COLA WORLD RANKING

'93	'94	'95	'96	'97	'98	'99	'00	'01	'02	'03	'04	'05	'06	'07	'08	'09	'10	'11	'12
33	25	20	51	52	44	53	51	44	64	70	40	42	18	37	29	16	21	16	14

2012

Jan	Feb	Mar	Apr	May	Jun	Jul	Aug	Sep	Oct	Nov	Dec	High	Low	Av
18	15	15	15	15	16	16	16	16	16	15	14	14	75	36

Cote d'Ivoire faltered once again at the finals of the Africa Cup of Nations, taking to four the number of successive tournaments where they have been installed as clear cut favourites, made an impressive showing in the group stages and then conspired to come unstuck in the knock-out rounds. At the 2013 finals in South Africa it was in the quarter-finals against eventual winners Nigeria, who had been given little hope against the much-vaunted Ivorians, but ended up beating them 2-1 in a thrilling battle in Rustenburg. The tournament certainly marked the last chance for talismanic leader Didier Drogba to win a Nations Cup medal. The captain was even dropped during the tournament by coach Sabri Lamouchi, who had been appointed just eight months earlier. He replaced Francois Zahoui a week before the start of the 2014 FIFA World Cup qualifiers in a startling turn of events that drew much initial criticism but the former France international went unbeaten for 10 matches before losing to Nigeria. The traditional dominance of domestic football by the Abidjan based pair of ASEC Mimosas and Africa Sports came to an end in 2012 as Sewe San Pedro won a first ever championship. It was the first time since 1960 the top trio of ASEC, Africa or Stade Abidjan had failed to win a trophy after Stella Adjame beat Sewe in the cup final.

CAF AFRICA CUP OF NATIONS RECORD

1957-1963 DNE **1965** 3 r1 **1968** 3 SF **1970** 4 SF **1972** DNQ **1974** 7 r1 **1976** DNQ **1978** DNE **1980** 6 r1 **1982** DNE
1984 5 r1 (Hosts) **1986** 3 SF **1988-1990** DNQ **1992** 1 Winners **1994** 3 SF **1996** 11 r1 **1998** 5 QF **2000** 9 r1 **2002** 16 r1
2004 DNQ **2006** 2 F **2008** 4 SF **2010** 5 QF **2012** 2 F **2012** 5 QF

FEDERATION IVOIRIENNE DE FOOTBALL (FIF)

Treichville Avenue 1 - 01
Boîte postale 1202
Abidjan 01 0181462 T
☎ +225 21240027
✆ +225 21259552
✉ fifci@aviso.ci
🌐 www.fif-ci.com
FA 1960 CON 1960 FIFA 1960
P Augustin Diallo
GS Sory Diabate

THE STADIA

2014 FIFA World Cup Stadia

Stade Felix Houphouet-Boigny
Abidjan 40 000

Other Main Stadia

Stade de la paix de Bouaké
Bouaké 35 000
Stade Robert Champroux
Marcory, Abidjan 20 000
Stade Municipal
Abidjan 9 000
Stade Auguste Denise
San Pedro 8 000

MAJOR CITIES/TOWNS

		Population
1	Abidjan	4 011 262
2	Bouaké	641 787
3	Daloa	241 395
4	Yamoussoukro	234 788
5	Korhogo	206 340
6	San-Pédro	163 304
7	Man	160 404
8	Gagnoa	143 830
9	Divo	136 188
10	Anyama	115 325
11	Abengourou	107 433
12	Soubré	101 079
13	Grand Bassam	81 349
14	Dabou	79 815
15	Agboville	76 154
16	Duékoué	70 292
17	Bouaflé	66 302
18	Sinfra	65 169
19	Bondoukou	62 564

REPUBLIQUE DE COTE D'IVOIRE • REPUBLIC OF COTE D'IVOIRE

Capital	Yamoussoukro	Population	20 617 068 (56)	% in cities	49%
GDP per capita	$1700 (191)	Area km²	322 463 km² (68)	GMT +/-	0
Neighbours (km)	Burkina Faso 584, Ghana 668, Guinea 610, Liberia 716, Mali 532 • Coast 515				

RECENT INTERNATIONAL MATCHES PLAYED BY COTE D'IVOIRE

2010	Opponents	Score	Venue	Comp	Scorers	Att	Referee
15-06	Portugal	D 0-0	Port Elizabeth	WCr1		34 850	Nishimura JPN
20-06	Brazil	L 1-3	Johannesburg	WCr1	Drogba [79]	84 445	Lannoy FRA
25-06	Korea DPR	W 3-0	Nelspruit	WCr1	Yaya Toure [14], Romaric [20], Kalou [82]	34 763	Undiano ESP
10-08	Italy	W 1-0	London	Fr	Kolo Toure [55]	11 176	Atkinson ENG
4-09	Rwanda	W 3-0	Abidjan	CNq	Yaya Toure [10], Kalou [19], Eboue [39]		Maillet SEY
9-10	Burundi	W 1-0	Bujumbura	CNq	Romaric [34]		El Raay LBY
17-11	Poland	L 1-3	Poznan	Fr	Gervinho [45]	42 000	Toma JPN
2011							
8-02	Mali	W 1-0	Valence	Fr	Ya Konen [2]		Castro FRA
27-03	Benin	W 2-1	Accra	CNq	Drogba 2 [45] [75]		Kayindi-Ngobi UGA
5-06	Benin	W 6-2	Cotonou	CNq	Ya Konan [13], Drogba 2 [21] [73], Gervinho 2 [30] [79], Bony [86]		Benouza ALG
10-08	Israel	W 4-3	Geneva	Fr	Yaya Toure [44], Ya Konan [45], Kone [67], Drogba [81p]	2 000	Laperriere SUI
3-09	Rwanda	W 5-0	Kigali	CNq	Kalou [33], Bony 2 [42] [43], Ya Konan [68], Gervinho [83]		Grisha EGY
9-10	Burundi	W 2-1	Abidjan	CNq	Kolo Toure [70], Gervinho [91+]		Otogo Castane GAB
12-11	South Africa	D 1-1	Port Elizabeth	Fr	OG [36]		
2012							
13-01	Tunisia	W 2-0	Abu Dhabi	Fr	Kalou [44], Drogba [47p]		Al Junaibi UAE
16-01	Libya	W 1-0	Abu Dhabi	Fr	Kalou [60]		
22-01	Sudan	W 1-0	Malabo	CNr1	Drogba [39]	5 000	Seechurn MRI
26-01	Burkina Faso	W 2-0	Malabo	CNr1	Kalou [16], OG [82]	4 000	Grisha EGY
30-01	Angola	W 2-0	Malabo	CNr1	Eboue [33], Bony [64]	1 500	Jedidi TUN
4-02	Equatorial Guinea	W 3-0	Malabo	CNqf	Drogba 2 [35] [69], Yaya Toure [81]	12 500	Maillet SEY
8-02	Mali	W 1-0	Libreville	CNsf	Gervinho [45]	32 000	Bennett RSA
12-02	Zambia	D 0-0	Libreville	CNf	L 7-8p	40 000	Diatta SEN
29-02	Guinea	D 0-0	Abidjan	Fr			Saba BFA
2-06	Tanzania	W 2-0	Abidjan	WCq	Kalou [10], Drogba [71]	15 000	Jedidi TUN
9-06	Morocco	D 2-2	Marrakech	WCq	Kalou [8], Kolo Toure [60]	36 000	Grisha EGY
15-08	Russia	D 1-1	Moscow	Fr	Gradel [77]	12 500	Cakir TUR
8-09	Senegal	W 4-2	Abidjan	CNq	Kalou 45, Gervinho 65, Drogba 81p, Gradel 85		El Ahrach MAR
13-10	Senegal	W 2-0	Dakar	CNq	Drogba 2 [51] [68p]		Jedidi TUN
14-11	Austria	W 3-0	Linz	Fr	Ya Konan [44], Drogba [61], Traore [76]	13 832	Kralovec CZE
2013							
14-01	Egypt	W 4-2	Abu Dhabi	Fr	Gervinho [38], Traore [40], Gervinho [53], Ya Konan [82]		Hashmi UAE
22-01	Togo	W 2-1	Rustenburg	CNr1	Yaya Toure [8], Gervinho [88]	2 000	Alioum CMR
26-01	Tunisia	W 3-0	Rustenburg	CNr1	Gervinho [21], Yaya Toure [87], Ya Konan [90]	20 000	Seechurn MRI
30-01	Algeria	D 2-2	Rustenburg	CNr1	Drogba [77], Bony [81]	5 000	Otogo Castane GAB
3-02	Nigeria	L 1-2	Rustenburg	CNq	Tiote [50]	25 000	Haimoudi ALG

Fr = Friendly match • CN = African Cup of Nations • WC = FIFA World Cup
q = qualifier • r1 = first round group • qf = quarter-final • sf = semi-final • f = final

COTE D'IVOIRE NATIONAL TEAM HISTORICAL RECORDS

Coach: Henri Michel FRA 2004-06 • Uli Stielike GER 2006-08 • Vahid Halilhodzic BIH 2008-10 • Sven-Goran Eriksson SWE 2010 • Francois Zahoui 2010-12 • Sabri Lamouchi FRA 2012-

COTE D'IVOIRE SQUAD FOR THE 2012 CAF AFRICA CUP OF NATIONS

	Player		Ap	G	Club	Date of Birth		Player		Ap	G	Club	Date of Birth
1	Boubacar Barry	GK	5		Lokeren BEL	30 12 1979	12	Wilfried Bony	FW	1+3	1	Vitesse NED	10 12 1988
2	Benjamin Angoua	DF	0+1		Val'ciennes FRA	28 11 1986	13	Didier Ya Konan	MF	1+2		Hannover GER	25 02 1984
3	Arthur Boka	DF	2+1		Stuttgart GER	2 04 1983	14	Kafoumba Coulibaly	MF	2		Nice FRA	26 10 1985
4	Kolo Toure	DF	6		Man City ENG	19 03 1981	15	Max Gradel	MF	2+3		St-Etienne FRA	30 11 1987
5	Didier Zokora	MF	4		Trabzonspor TUR	14 12 1980	16	Daniel Yeboah	DF			Dijon FRA	13 11 1984
6	Jean-Jacques Gosso	MF	5		Orduspor TUR	15 03 1983	17	Siaka Tiene	DF	4		PSG FRA	22 02 1982
7	Seydou Doumbia	FW	1+1		CSKA M'va RUS	31 12 1987	18	Abdul Kader Keita	MF	0+3		Al Sadd QAT	6 08 1981
8	Salomon Kalou	FW	4+1	1	Chelsea ENG	5 08 1985	19	Yaya Toure	MF	5	1	Man City ENG	13 05 1983
9	Cheick Tiote	MF	4		Newcastle ENG	21 06 1986	20	Igor Lolo	DF	2		Kuban RUS	22 07 1982
10	Gervinho	MF	5	1	Arsenal ENG	27 05 1987	21	Emmanuel Eboue	DF	1+1	1	Galatasaray TUR	4 06 1983
11	Didier Drogba (c)	FW	5+1	3	Chelsea ENG	11 03 1978	22	Sol Bamba	DF	6		Leicester ENG	13 01 1985
							23	Gerard Gnanhouan	GK	0		Avranches FRA	12 02 1979

Tr: Francois Zahoui 21-08-1962

COTE D'IVOIRE 2012

LIGUE 1 MTN — FIRST ROUND GROUPS

Group A

	Pl	W	D	L	F	A	Pts	Séwé	Stella	Bassam	Africa Sports	EFYM	Indenié	Issia Wazi	AFAD	ASEC	JCAT	Denguélé	Bingerville	Ouragahio	SOA
Séwé San Pedro †	12	6	4	2	11	7	22		0-2	2-1	1-1	1-0	1-0	2-1							
Stella Adjamé †	12	3	7	2	9	8	16	0-2		1-1	0-0	1-1	0-0	2-1							
USC Bassam †	12	4	4	4	14	14	16	0-0	1-1		0-0	2-0	0-1	2-1							
Africa Sports	12	3	7	2	9	10	16	1-1	0-0	0-1		1-1	1-1	1-0							
Ecole Yéo Martial	12	4	3	5	11	17	15	1-0	1-0	3-1	0-3		0-1	2-0							
ASI Abengourou ‡	12	3	5	4	8	9	14	0-0	0-1	3-4	1-0	1-1		0-0							
Issia Wazi ‡	12	3	2	7	9	14	11	0-1	1-1	2-1	0-1	2-1	1-0								

Group B

	Pl	W	D	L	F	A	Pts								AFAD	ASEC	JCAT	Denguélé	Bingerville	Ouragahio	SOA
Acad'y Amadou Diallo†	12	6	5	1	18	8	23									0-0	2-1	1-0	4-0	2-2	3-1
ASEC Mimosas †	12	6	4	2	10	5	22								1-0		0-1	2-0	1-0	3-1	0-2
Jeunesse Abidjan †	12	5	4	3	11	8	19								0-0	0-1		0-1	0-0	1-0	1-1
Denguélé Odienné	12	4	3	5	9	9	15								0-0	0-0	1-1		0-1	0-1	3-2
Entente Bingerville	12	4	2	6	8	11	14								1-2	0-0	0-1	1-0		3-0	2-1
ASC Ouragahio ‡	12	3	3	6	11	20	12								2-4	0-0	0-1	0-3	1-0		1-1
SO Armée ‡	12	2	3	7	14	20	9								0-0	1-2	2-4	0-1	1-0	2-3	

2/03/2012 - 20/06/2012 • † Qualified for the championship round • ‡ Relegation play-off

COTE D'IVOIRE 2012

LIGUE 1 MTN — FINAL ROUND

	Pl	W	D	L	F	A	Pts	Séwé	AFAD	ASEC	Bassam	JCAT	Stella
Séwé San Pedro †	10	5	4	1	15	10	19		4-3	2-0	1-1	2-1	2-2
Acad'y Amadou Diallo†	10	5	1	4	16	11	16	0-1		1-0	2-0	4-1	2-0
ASEC Mimosas ‡	10	4	4	2	11	8	16	1-1	1-0		1-1	1-0	0-0
USC Bassam	10	2	7	1	10	9	13	0-0	2-1	1-1		2-0	1-1
Jeunesse Abidjan	10	2	2	6	13	8	2-0	0-0	1-3	0-0		1-0
Stella Adjamé	10	1	4	5	9	16	7	0-2	2-3	1-3	2-2	1-0	

7/07/2012 - 1/09/2012 • † Qualified for the CAF Champions League • ‡ Qualified for the CAF Confederation Cup

RELEGATION PLAY-OFFS

	Pl	W	D	L	F	A	Pts	SOA	ASI	IW	ASCO
SO Armée	3	2	0	1	8	5	6			5-0	3-0
ASI Abengourou	3	1	2	0	5	5	5	3-0			
Issia Wazi	3	1	1	1	4	6	4		1-1		3-0
ASC Ouragahio	3	0	1	2	2	8	1		2-2		

9/07/2012 - 23/07/2012

COUPE NATIONALE 2012

Quarter-finals		Semi-finals		Final	
Stella Adjamé	3				
Jeunesse	0	Stella Adjamé	1 4p		
Bouaké FC	0	ASEC Mimosas	1 1p		
ASEC Mimosas	2			Stella Adjamé ‡	1
SO Armée	2			Séwé San Pedro	0
ES Bafang	1	SO Armée	1		
ASC Ouragahio	0	Séwé San Pedro	3		
Séwé San Pedro	1				

‡ Qualified for the CAF Confederation Cup
Final: Houphouet-Boigny, Abidjan, 6-08-2012. Scorer - Abou Diomandé [18] for Stela

MEDALS TABLE

		Overall		Lge		Cup		Africa		
		G	S	B	G	G	S	G	S	B
1	ASEC Mimosas	42	5	6	24	17	4	1	1	6
2	Africa Sports	34	10	2	17	15	7	2	3	2
3	Stade Abidjan	11	7	1	5	5	7	1		1
4	Stella Adjamé	7	6		3	3	5	1	1	
5	Onze Freres	2			2					
6	SC Gagnon	1	7		1		7			
7	Séwé San Pedro	1	3		1		3			
8	ASC Bouaké	1	2					1	2	
	Jeunesse Abidjan	1	2					1	2	
10	Alliance Bouaké	1	1					1	1	
	Réveil Daloa	1	1					1	1	
	SO Armée	1	1					1	1	
	Issia Wazi	1	1					1	1	
	ASI Abengourou	1	1					1	1	
15	CO Bouaflé	1				1				
	Espoir Man	1				1				

CMR – CAMEROON

FIFA/COCA-COLA WORLD RANKING

'93	'94	'95	'96	'97	'98	'99	'00	'01	'02	'03	'04	'05	'06	'07	'08	'09	'10	'11	'12
23	31	37	56	53	41	58	39	38	16	14	23	23	11	24	14	11	37	50	61

2012													High	Low	Av
Jan	Feb	Mar	Apr	May	Jun	Jul	Aug	Sep	Oct	Nov	Dec				
56	66	66	64	64	64	59	59	61	71	62	61		11	71	31

Cameroon's defeat at the hands of minnows Cape Verde Islands in the qualifiers for the 2013 Africa Cup of Nations in South Africa provided one of the talking points of world football during 2012. The 'Indomitable Lions' missed out on the finals for the second tournament running and have yet to recover from the squad turmoil which scuppered their hopes at the 2010 FIFA World Cup finals. Samuel Eto'o's patriarchal role in the team came under renewed spotlight although a much publicised reconciliation with Barcelona midfielder Alexandre Song promised better times ahead. The start of the 2014 FIFA World Cup qualifiers produced a home win over the Democratic Republic of Congo but was followed a week later by a surprise loss against Libya. September's 2-0 defeat in the Cape Verde Islands saw coach Denis Lavagne fired, ending a brief and bitter tenure where the Frenchman felt undermined by the lack of a firm contract offer. His replacement Jean Paul Akono was the coach when Cameroon won Olympic gold in Sydney in 2000. In club football Union Douala rekindled some of their former glory by winning their first championship since 1990 - and only the second since their heyday in the 1970s. Cotonsport failed to win a trophy for only the second season in a decade after Unisport won the cup, beating New Star 2-0 in the final.

CAF AFRICA CUP OF NATIONS RECORD
1957-1965 DNE **1968** DNQ **1970** 5 r1 **1972** 3 SF (Hosts) **1974** 3 SF **1976** 3 r2 **1978-1980** DNQ **1982** 5 r1
1984 1 Winners **1986** 2 F **1988** 1 Winners **1990** 5 r1 **1992** 4 SF **1994** DNQ **1996** 10 r1 **1998** 8 QF **2000** 1 Winners
2002 1 Winners **2004** 6 QF **2006** 6 QF **2008** 2 F **2010** 7 QF **2012-13** DNQ

FEDERATION
CAMEROUNAISE DE
FOOTBALL (FECAFOOT)
Avenue du 27 aout 1940,
Tsinga-Yaoundé,
Boite Postale 1116, Yaoundé
☎ +237 22210012
📠 +237 22216662
✉ fecafoot@fecafootonline.com
🌐 www.fecafootonline.com
FA 1959 CON 1963 FIFA 1962
P Mohammed Iya
GS Sidiki Tombi a Roko

THE STADIA
2014 FIFA World Cup Stadia
Stade Omnisports Ahmadou-Ahidjo
Yaoundé   38 720
Other Main Stadia
Stade de la Réunification
Douala   30 000
Stade Omnisports Roumdé Adjia
Garoua   22 000
Stade Municipal
Bangangté   20 000
Stade Municipal
Bamenda   10 000

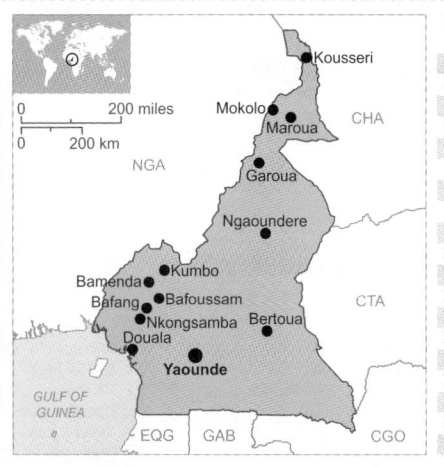

MAJOR CITIES/TOWNS
		Population
1	Douala	2 054 147
2	Yaoundé	1 743 482
3	Garoua	546 060
4	Bamenda	515 593
5	Maroua	415 251
6	Bafoussam	365 017
7	Ngaoundéré	298 016
8	Bertoua	281 139
9	Loum	234 471
10	Kumbo	207 438
11	Edéa	197 861
12	Mbouda	175 986
13	Kumba	173 380
14	Foumban	164 272
15	Djang	140 861
16	Nkongsamba	129 168
17	Ebolowa	123 116
18	Limbe	120 249
19	Guider	116 312

REPUBLIQUE DU CAMEROUN • REPUBLIC OF CAMEROON

Capital	Yaoundé	Population	18 879 301 (58)	% in cities	57%
GDP per capita	$2300 (177)	Area km²	475 440 km² (53)	GMT +/-	+1
Neighbours (km)	Central African Republic 797, Chad 1094, Congo 523, Equatorial Guinea 189, Gabon 298, Nigeria 1690 • Coast 402					

CMR – CAMEROON

RECENT INTERNATIONAL MATCHES PLAYED BY CAMEROON

2009	Opponents	Score	Venue	Comp	Scorers	Att	Referee
11-02	Guinea	W 3-1	Bondoufle	Fr	Geremi [31], Eto'o 2 [58 87]		
28-03	Togo	L 0-1	Accra	WCq		26 450	Abd El Fatah EGY
7-06	Morocco	D 0-0	Yaoundé	WCq		35 000	Seechurn MRI
12-08	Austria	W 2-0	Klagenfurt	Fr	Webo 2 [28 35]	28 800	Olsiak SVK
5-09	Gabon	W 2-0	Libreville	WCq	Emana [65], Eto'o [67]	10 000	Ndinya KEN
9-09	Gabon	W 2-1	Yaoundé	WCq	Makoun [25], Eto'o [64]	38 000	Bennaceur TUN
10-10	Togo	W 3-0	Yaoundé	WCq	Geremi [29], Makoun [46], Emana [54]	36 401	Kaoma ZAM
14-10	Angola	D 0-0	Olhao	Fr			
14-11	Morocco	W 2-0	Fes	WCq	Webo [19], Eto'o [52]	17 000	Bennett RSA
2010							
9-01	Kenya	W 3-1	Nairobi	Fr	Webo [36], Emana [56], Idrissou [58]	6 000	Amwayi KEN
13-01	Gabon	L 0-1	Lubango	CNr1		15 000	Bennett RSA
17-01	Zambia	W 3-2	Lubango	CNr1	Geremi [68], Eto'o [72], Idrissou [86]	15 000	Al Ghamdi KSA
21-01	Tunisia	D 2-2	Lubango	CNr1	Eto'o [47], N'Guemo [64]	19 000	Doue CIV
25-01	Egypt	L 1-3	Benguela	CNqf	Emana [25]	12 000	Damon RSA
3-03	Italy	D 0-0	Monte Carlo	Fr		10 752	Ennjimi FRA
25-05	Georgia	D 0-0	Linz	Fr		3 500	Brugger AUT
29-05	Slovakia	D 1-1	Klagenfurt	Fr	Enoh [84]	10 000	Lechner AUT
1-06	Portugal	L 1-3	Covilha	Fr	Webo [69]	6 125	Weiner GER
5-06	Serbia	L 3-4	Belgrade	Fr	Webo 2 [5 20], Choupo-Moting [67]	30 000	Trattou CYP
14-06	Japan	L 0-1	Bloemfontein	WCr1		30 620	Benquerenca POR
19-06	Denmark	L 1-2	Pretoria	WCr1	Eto'o [10]	38 074	Larrionda URU
24-06	Netherlands	L 1-2	Cape Town	WCr1	Eto'o [65p]	63 093	Pozo CHI
11-08	Poland	W 3-0	Szczecin	Fr	Eto'o 2 [30 52], Aboubakar [86]	17 000	Asumaa FIN
4-09	Mauritius	W 3-1	Bellevue	CNq	Eto'o 2 [39 47], Choupo-Moting [63p]		Damon RSA
9-10	Congo DR	D 1-1	Garoua	CNq	OG [54]		Maillet SEY
2011							
9-02	Macedonia FYR	W 1-0	Skopje	Fr	Mbuta [75]	3 000	Kaluderovic MNE
26-03	Senegal	L 0-1	Dakar	CNq			Saadallah TUN
4-06	Senegal	D 0-0	Yaounde	CNq			Carvalho ANG
7-06	Russia	D 0-0	Salzburg	Fr		3 000	Einwaller AUT
3-09	Mauritius	W 5-0	Yaounde	CNq	Kweuke [54], Mbuta [65], Eto'o [70p], N'Guemo [85], Choupo-Moting [93+]		Bangoura GUI
7-10	Congo DR	W 3-2	Kinshasa	CNq	Eto'o [18], Mbuta [75], Choupo-Moting [79]		
11-10	Equatorial Guinea	D 1-1	Malabo	Fr	Kweuke [13]	20 000	
11-11	Sudan	W 3-1	Marrakech	Fr	Enoh [32], Angbwa [35], Eto'o [82]		
13-11	Morocco	D 1-1	Marrakech	Fr	Eto'o [73]. W 4-2p	20 000	Amalou ALG
14-12	Angola	D 1-1	Cabinda	Fr	Momasso [40]		
2012							
29-02	Guinea-Bissau	W 1-0	Bissau	CNq	Choupo Moting [87]		Gassama GAM
20-05	Egypt	L 1-2	Omdurman	Fr			Adam SUD
2-06	Congo DR	W 1-0	Yaounde	WCq	Choupo Moting [54p]	10 000	Bennett RSA
10-06	Libya	L 1-2	Sfax	WCq	Choupo Moting [15]	1 000	Maerouf ERI
16-06	Guinea-Bissau	W 1-0	Yaounde	CNq	Moukandjo [80]		Bangoura GUI
8-09	Cape Verde Islands	L 0-2	Praia	CNq		10 000	Otogo Castane GAB
14-10	Cape Verde Islands	W 2-1	Yaounde	CNq	Emana [22], Olinga [90]		Grisha EGY
16-10	Colombia	L 0-3	Barranquilla	Fr			Escalante VEN
14-11	Albania	D 0-0	Geneva	Fr		4 500	Studer SUI

Fr = Friendly match • CN = Africa Cup of Nations • WC = FIFA World Cup • q = qualifier

CAMEROON NATIONAL TEAM HISTORICAL RECORDS

Past Coaches: Dominique Colonna FRA 1965-70 • Peter Schnittger FRG 1970-73 • Vladimir Beara YUG 1973-75 • Ivan Ridanovic YUG 1975-80 • Branko Zutic YUG 1980-82 • Jean Vincent 1982 • Claude Le Roy 1985-88 • Valeri Nepomniachi RUS 1988-90 • Philippe Redon FRA 1991-92 • Jules Nyongha 1992-93 • Henri Michel FRA 1994 • Jules Nyongha 1994-96 • Henri Depireux BEL 1996-97 • Jean Manga Onguene 1997-98 • Claude Le Roy FRA 1998 • Pierre Lechantre FRA 1998-00 • Jean-Paul Akono 2000-01 • Pierre Lechantre FRA 2001 • Robert Corfu FRA 2001 • Winfried Schafer GER 2001-04 • Artur Jorge POR 2005-06 • Arie Haan NED 2006-07 • Jules Nyongha 2007 • Otto Pfister GER 2007-09 • Thomas Nkono 2009 • Paul Le Guen FRA 2009-10 • Javier Clemente ESP 2010-11 • Denis Lavagne FRA 2011-12 • Jean-Paul Akono 2012-

CAMEROON 2011-12
MTN ELITE ONE

	Pl	W	D	L	F	A	Pts	Union Douala	Cotonsport	Panthère	YSA	Unisport	New Star	Sable Batie	Canon	Renaissance	Les Astres	Njala Quan	Aigle Royal	Tiko United	Scorpion Bay
Union Douala †	26	17	4	5	38	17	55		1-1	1-2	2-0	0-0	4-1	3-0	2-0	3-1	2-1	2-0	3-1	2-0	1-0
Cotonsport Garoua †	26	15	8	3	33	11	53	0-1		1-0	2-0	2-0	1-0	0-0	2-1	1-0	2-0	2-0	3-0	1-1	3-0
Panthère Bangangté ‡	26	13	6	7	28	16	45	1-0	1-0		4-0	0-3	0-0	1-1	1-0	1-0	1-1	1-0	1-2	2-0	2-0
Young Sports Academy	26	10	10	6	23	26	40	1-2	2-1	1-0		2-1	1-0	0-0	2-1	0-0	0-0	1-1	1-1	1-0	1-0
Unisport Bafang ‡	26	9	12	5	29	22	39	0-0	1-1	0-0	0-0		2-2	1-1	0-0	1-2	3-0	4-2	2-0	2-1	1-0
CNIC UIC Douala	26	9	11	6	40	27	38	1-1	1-1	1-0	3-0	3-1		2-3	5-1	0-0	1-1	1-1	2-0	1-1	5-0
Sable Batie	26	8	10	8	26	26	34	2-0	0-0	1-2	1-2	0-0	0-1		0-1	0-0	0-0	3-0	0-2	3-2	2-1
Canon Yaoundé	26	8	8	10	27	36	32	1-0	1-1	0-1	1-1	2-2	1-3	0-1		1-3	0-2	1-4	2-2	2-1	2-0
Renaissance Ngomoum	26	8	7	11	24	28	31	0-1	1-2	2-1	1-0	1-2	2-1	2-1	1-2		2-2	0-2	1-1	1-0	0-0
Les Astres Douala	26	5	14	7	24	29	29	0-1	0-1	1-1	1-1	0-0	2-2	1-1	1-1	2-2		2-1	1-0	2-1	0-0
Njala Quan Academy	26	7	8	11	23	30	29	1-2	0-0	0-0	0-1	2-0	1-2	0-0	0-2	1-0	1-0		1-0	3-3	1-0
Aigle Royal Dschang	26	5	11	10	22	29	26	1-2	0-1	0-1	2-2	0-0	1-1	1-2	1-1	1-0	3-1	0-0		0-0	2-0
Tiko United	26	4	8	14	21	37	20	1-2	0-2	0-3	1-1	1-2	0-0	2-1	1-1	1-0	1-2	2-0	0-0		1-0
Scorpion Bay	26	3	5	18	14	38	14	1-0	0-2	0-2	1-2	0-1	2-1	2-3	0-1	1-2	1-1	1-1	1-1	3-0	

1/01/2012 – 7/10/2012 • † Qualified for the CAF Champions League • ‡ Qualified for the Confederation Cup

CAMEROON 2011-12
MTN ELITE TWO (2)

	Pl	W	D	L	F	A	Pts
Tonnerre Kalara	26	15	5	6	25	14	50
Douala AC	26	13	9	4	36	19	48
Fovu Baham	26	13	8	5	30	17	47
Botafogo Douala	26	10	12	4	27	21	42
APEJES Mfou	26	11	6	9	26	21	39
National Bamenda	26	9	7	10	29	27	37
Dragon Yaoundé	26	10	5	11	22	22	35
Matelots Douala	26	9	7	10	27	25	34
Achille Yaoundé	26	8	9	9	27	28	33
Université Ngaoundéré	26	8	11	7	26	29	32
Sahel Maroua	26	7	11	8	21	25	32
Caïman Douala	26	6	8	12	18	27	26
Lausanne Yaoundé	26	4	6	16	16	34	18
Santos	26	3	8	15	20	41	17

1/01/2012 – 7/10/2012 •

MEDALS TABLE

		Overall			Lge		Cup		Africa			City
		G	S	B	G	G	S	G	S	B		
1	Canon	25	8	4	10	11	5	4	3	4		Yaoundé
2	Cotonsport	16	3	1	11	5	1		2	1		Garoua
3	Union	13	6	1	5	6	6	2		1		Douala
4	Tonnerre Kalara	10	5	1	5	4	3	1	2	1		Yaoundé
5	Oryx	9	1	1	5	3	1	1		1		Douala
6	Racing Club	5	3		4	1	3					Bafoussam
7	Diamant	4	4	1	1	3	4			1		Yaoundé
8	Lion Club	4				4						Yaoundé
9	Caïman	3	3		3		3					Douala
10	Fovu	3	1		1	2	1					Baham
11	Dynamo	3				3						Douala
12	Unisport	2	3		1	1	3					Bafang
13	Aigle Royal	2	2		2		2					Nkongsamba
14	Léopards	2	1	1	2		1			1		Douala
15	Olympique	2				2						Mvolyé
	Panthère	2				2						Bagante
17	Sable	1	2		1		2					Batié
18	Dihep Nkam	1	1			1	1					Yabassi

COUPE DU CAMEROUN 2012

Round of 16			Quarter-finals			Semi-finals			Final	
Unisport Bafang *	1	2								
Dragon Yaoundé	0	0	**Unisport Bafang**	1	0					
Santos *	0	0	Les Astres Douala *	1	0					
Les Astres Douala	1	3				**Unisport Bafang**	0	5		
Cotonsport Garoua *	1	1				Caïman Douala *	2	1		
Achille Yaoundé	0	0	Cotonsport Garoua	1	1					
Union Douala	0	1	**Caïman Douala** *	0	2					
Caïman Douala *	1	1							**Unisport Bafang** ‡	2
Panthère Bangangté	3	1							New Star Douala	0
Njala Quan Academy *	0	1	**Panthère Bangangté**	0	2					
Canon Yaoundé	1	1	Sable Batie *	1	0					
Sable Batie *	0	2				Panthère Bangangté *	0	1		
Ren'ssance Ngoumou *	1	2				**New Star Douala**	0	2		
Universal Star	1	1	Ren'ssance Ngoumou *	3	0					
Feutcheu Bandjoun	2	0	**New Star Douala**	1	2					
New Star Douala *	1	2								

* Home team in the 1st leg • ‡ Qualified for the Confederation Cup

CUP FINAL

Ahmadou Ahidjo, Yaoundé
23-12-2012
Scorers – Jean Parfait Tchoubia [12],
Raymond Fossouo [33]

COD – CONGO DR

FIFA/COCA-COLA WORLD RANKING

'93	'94	'95	'96	'97	'98	'99	'00	'01	'02	'03	'04	'05	'06	'07	'08	'09	'10	'11	'12
71	68	68	66	76	62	59	70	77	65	56	78	77	66	74	91	107	130	125	107

2012												High	Low	Av
Jan	Feb	Mar	Apr	May	Jun	Jul	Aug	Sep	Oct	Nov	Dec			
116	119	120	119	124	127	114	115	110	103	99	107	51	133	84

The Democratic Republic of Congo failed to get past the first round of the 2013 Africa Cup of Nations finals in South Africa where missed chances and three successive draws cost the talented Leopards a place in the quarter-finals. It also ended coach Claude le Roy's run of having reached the last eight of each of the six previous tournaments he had coached teams at. Qualification for the tournament was relatively straightforward with successive wins over minnows Seychelles and then the 2012 hosts Equatorial Guinea. It also marked the return of Anderlecht striker Dieumerci Mbokani. He became the first Congolese player to win Belgium's player of the year award in some 40 years of its existence, despite decades of exports to the league in the former colonial power. Mbokani was also a scorer at the start of the 2014 FIFA World Cup qualifiers when the Leopards beat Togo 2-0 at home, a week after losing away in Cameroon. TP Mazembe won the Super League albeit with bitter recriminations from Vita Club while Lubumbashi-based Don Bosco, who have close links with Mazembe, were surprise winners over AS Veti de Mataba in the Coupe du Congo. Mazembe, who opened their new stadium at the start of the year, were also CAF Champions League semi-finalists, losing narrowly to Esperance of Tunisia.

CAF AFRICA CUP OF NATIONS RECORD

1957-1963 DNE 1965 5 r1 1968 1 Winners 1970 7 r1 1972 4 SF 1974 1 Winners 1976 7 r1 1978 DNE
1980-1982 DNQ 1984 DNE 1986 DNQ 1988 7 r1 1990 DNQ 1992 6 QF 1994 7 QF 1996 7 QF 1998 3 SF 2000 12 r1 2002 8 QF
2004 15 r1 2006 8 QF 2008-2012 DNQ 2013 10 r1

FEDERATION CONGOLAISE DE FOOTBALL-ASSOCIATION (FECOFA)

31 Avenue de la Justice, c/Gombe, Boite postale 1284, Kinshasa 1
☏ +243 81 9049788
+243 81 3013527
✉ fecofa_sg@yahoo.fr
FA 1919 CON 1973 FIFA 1962
P Constant Omari Selemani
GS Gregoire Badi Elonga

THE STADIA

2014 FIFA World Cup Stadia
Stade des Martyrs
Kinshasa — 80 000

Other Main Stadia
Stade Tata Raphaël
Kinshasa — 50 000
Stade Frédéric Kibassa Maliba
Lubumbashi — 35 000
Stade TP Mazembe
Lubumbashi — 18 500
Stade de la Concorde
Bukavu — 10 000

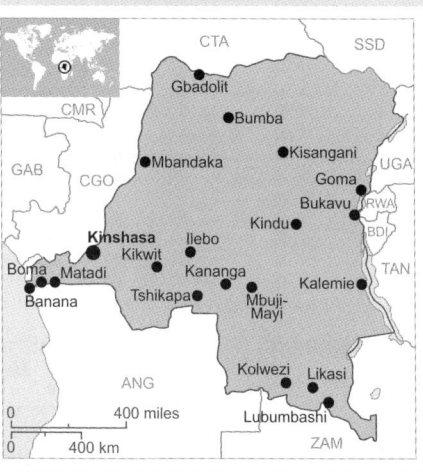

MAJOR CITIES/TOWNS

		Population
1	Kinshasa	9 518 988
2	Lubumbashi	1 713 852
3	Mbuji-Mayi	1 546 705
4	Kolwezi	970 520
5	Kisangani	600 011
6	Boma	527 725
7	Likasi	521 341
8	Kananga	514 070
9	Tshikapa	317 830
10	Bukavu	241 690
11	Mwene-Ditu	218 782
12	Uvira	202 240
13	Kikwit	200 880
14	Mbandaka	199 333
15	Matadi	194 903
16	Gandajika	181 987
17	Kalemie	181 496
18	Butembo	180 721
19	Goma	164 348

REPUBLIQUE DEMOCRATIQUE DU CONGO • DEMOCRATIC REPUBLIC OF THE CONGO

Capital	Kinshasa	Population	68 692 542 (18)	% in cities	34%
GDP per capita	$300 (228)	Area km²	2 344 858 km² (12)	GMT +/-	+1
Neighbours (km)	Angola 2511, Burundi 233, Central African Republic 1577, Congo 2410, Rwanda 217, Sudan 628, Tanzania 459, Uganda 765, Zambia 1930 • Coast 37				

RECENT INTERNATIONAL MATCHES PLAYED BY CONGO DR

2011	Opponents	Score	Venue	Comp	Scorers	Att	Referee
27-03	Mauritius	W 3-0	Kinshasa	CNq	Lua Lua [28p], Matumona [48], Diba Ilunga [61p]		
5-06	Mauritius	W 2-1	Bellevue	CNq	Diba Ilunga [20], Kabangu [45]		Ngosi MWI
10-08	Gambia	L 0-3	Bakau	Fr			
27-08	Angola	W 2-1	Dundo	Fr	Bakongolia [41], Niemba [62]		
3-09	Senegal	L 0-2	Dakar	CNq			Doue CIV
7-10	Cameroon	L 2-3	Kinshasa	CNq	Kaluyituka [11], Kanda [40]		
6-11	Lesotho	W 3-0	Pretoria	Fr	Mputu [30], Kanda [40], Mihayo [82]		
11-11	Swaziland	W 3-1	Lobamba	WCq	Kaluyituka [18], Mputu [22], Bokese [72]	785	Sikazwe ZAM
15-11	Swaziland	W 5-1	Kinshasa	WCq	Mputu 2 [8 49], Kaluyituka 2 [46 61], Diba Ilunga [66]	24 000	Moukoko CGO
2012							
15-01	Oman	D 2-2	Seeb	Fr	Ngoy [47], Angani [78]		
23-02	Tanzania	D 0-0	Dae Es Salaam	Fr			
29-02	Seychelles	W 4-0	Roche Caiman	CNq	Kaluyituka 2 [11 47], Mputu [28], Basilua [90]		Bangoura GUI
2-03	Egypt	D 0-0	Doha	Fr			Al Dosari QAT
2-06	Cameroon	L 0-1	Yaounde	WCq		10 000	Bennett RSA
10-06	Togo	W 2-0	Kinshasa	WCq	Mputu [23], Mbokani [81]	50 000	Farouk EGY
17-06	Seychelles	W 3-0	Kinshasa	CNq	Mbokani [38], Mpeko [45], Kanda [84]		Kayindi Ngobi UGA
9-09	Equatorial Guinea	W 4-0	Kinshasa	CNq	Mbokani 2 [55 79], Kanda [60], OG [74]		Seechurn MRI
14-10	Equatorial Guinea	L 1-2	Malabo	CNq	Mulumbu [43]		Fall SEN
14-11	Burkina Faso	L 0-1	Kinshasa	Fr			
2013							
20-01	Ghana	D 2-2	Port Elizabeth	CNr1	Mputu [53], Mbokani [68p]	7 000	Bennett RSA
24-01	Niger	D 0-0	Port Elizabeth	CNr1		12 000	El Ahrach MAR
28-01	Mali	D 1-1	Durban	CNr1	Mbokani [3p]	8 000	Haimoudi ALG

Fr = Friendly match • CN = CAF African Cup of Nations • WC = FIFA World Cup • q = qualifier

CONGO DR 2012

LINAFOOT SUPER LEAGUE

	Pl	W	D	L	F	A	Pts	Mazembe	Vita	DCMP	S Balende	Molunge	Elima	Muungano	St Eloi	Virunga	Tshinkunku	Makiso	Vutika	Saint-Luc	Nkoy
TP Mazembe †	23	21	1	1	65	6	64		3-0	2-1	4-0	n/p	6-0	5-0	1-0	6-0	5-0	3-0	5-0	3-0	3-0
AS Vita Club †	23	20	2	1	56	12	62	2-2		1-0	2-1	4-1	n/p	3-1	1-0	3-0	4-0	5-0	n/p	3-0	3-0
DC Motema Pembe ‡	23	18	1	4	42	6	55	1-0	0-1		2-0	2-0	n/p	1-0	4-0	2-0	3-0	3-0	1-0	3-1	3-0
SM Sanga Balende	23	11	6	6	33	17	39	0-1	0-0	1-0		4-0	1-0	3-0	1-0	n/p	1-1	n/p	6-0	2-2	3-0
TP Molunge	23	10	4	9	23	25	34	0-2	1-4	0-1	0-1		1-2	n/p	0-0	n/p	1-0	0-1	3-0	1-0	2-0
TC Elima	23	10	3	10	25	28	33	n/p	0-3	0-2	0-2	0-1		1-1	0-0	0-0	3-1	3-1	2-0	3-0	3-0
OC Muungano	23	9	5	9	26	26	32	0-1	0-3	n/p	1-0	0-1	0-2		0-0	2-0	0-0	3-0	3-0	2-1	n/p
St Eloi Lupopo	23	8	7	8	20	15	31	0-3	0-1	0-1	1-1	0-1	1-0	2-0		3-0	0-0	2-0	3-0	n/p	3-0
DC Virunga	23	7	4	12	22	35	25	0-1	0-3	0-3	2-1	0-0	3-0	2-2	1-1		3-0	1-0	3-0	n/p	2-0
US Tshinkunku	23	4	8	11	14	39	20	n/p	0-3	0-3	0-0	1-1	2-0	0-3	n/p	2-1		1-1	2-0	n/p	3-0
CS Makiso	23	5	5	13	15	16	36	18	1-2	n/p	0-1	0-3	1-2	0-0	n/p	2-1	3-0		0-1	3-0	3-0
AS Vutuka	23	4	4	15	9	42	16	0-1	2-3	n/p	0-3	0-2	2-0	0-3	n/p	0-1	0-0	1-0		0-0	n/p
AS Saint-Luc	23	2	8	13	17	40	14	1-3	1-3	0-0	1-1	2-2	0-1	0-2	0-3	2-1	1-1	0-0	1-1		3-0
AC Nkoy	23	4	0	19	10	51	12	0-3	0-1	0-3	n/p	1-2	0-3	1-3	0-1	2-1	3-0	1-0	0-2	2-1	

12/02/2012 - 28/10/2012 • † Qualified for the CAF Champions League • ‡ Qualified for the CAF Confederation Cup

48ÈME COUPE DU CONGO 2012

Semi-finals

CS Don Bosco 4 3
AS Dauphin Noir 0 1

AS Dragons 2 0
AS Veti Matadi 1 2

Finals

CS Don Bosco ‡ 4
AS Veti Matadi 0

‡ Qualified for the CAF Confederation Cup

Final. TPM, Lubumbashi, 26-08-2012. Scorers – Ushindi [13], Darryl Nyandoro [18p], Herve Kamba [70], Reagan Pembele [80]

MEDALS TABLE

	Overall G S B	Lge G	Cup G	Africa G S B	City
1 DC Motema Pembe	26 3	12	5	1 3	Kinshasa
2 TP Mazembe	22 2 3	12	5	5 2 3	Lubumbashi
3 AS Vita Club	22 1 3	12	9	1 1 3	Kinshasa
4 AS Dragons	9 2	4	5	2	Kinshasa
5 St Eloi Lupopo	8 1	6	2	1	Lubumbashi
6 AS Kalamu	4		4		Kinshasa
7 US Bilombe	2	1	1		Bilombe
US Tshinkunku	2	1	1		Kananga

COK – COOK ISLANDS

FIFA/COCA-COLA WORLD RANKING

'93	'94	'95	'96	'97	'98	'99	'00	'01	'02	'03	'04	'05	'06	'07	'08	'09	'10	'11	'12
-	-	-	188	192	173	182	170	179	182	190	190	194	197	200	201	184	188	195	201

2012													High	Low	Av
Jan	Feb	Mar	Apr	May	Jun	Jul	Aug	Sep	Oct	Nov	Dec				
195	197	196	196	196	195	195	196	195	196	198	201		169	202	188

The reorganisation of the OFC Champions League for the 2012-13 campaign gave a major boost to the small Pacific nations like the Cooks Islands thanks to the inclusion of a preliminary round prior to the group stage. Although officially excluded from the tournament for three seasons, the champions of the Cook Islands hadn't taken part since 2006 but Tupapa caused a huge upset when they travelled to Tonga and won the preliminary group. For a nation of just over 10,000 people it was an extraordinary success that had its foundation in the good organisation and youth development of both the football association and the clubs. Thanks in no small part to the FIFA Goal programme, the clubs play at the excellent facilities at CIFA HQ and all compete in leagues and cups for both women and men across age groups. Tupapa drew with Tonga champions Lotoha'apai in their opening game but then beat Samoan champions Kiwi before thrashing American Samoan champions Pago Youth 9-0. That meant a play-off against New Caledonian champions Mont Dore for a place in the group stage, but it was a game too far and they lost 3-1 against vastly more experienced opponents. At home Tupapa completed a hat trick of league titles while their main rivals Nikao Sokattak did the same in the cup after beating Tupapa 3-2 on penalties in the final.

FIFA WORLD CUP RECORD
1930-1994 DNE 1998-2014 DNQ

COOK ISLANDS FOOTBALL ASSOCIATION (CIFA)

Matavera Main Road, PO Box 29, Avarua
☎ +682 28980
📠 +682 28981
✉ cifa@cisoccer.org.ck
🖥 cookislandsfootball.com
FA 1971 CON 1994 FIFA 1994
P Lee Harmon
GS Mii Piri

THE STADIA
2014 FIFA World Cup Stadia
The Cook Islands played their matches at the Toleafoa J.S. Blatter Complex in Apia, Samoa
Other Main Stadia
National Stadium
Avarua, Rarotonga   3 000
CIFA HQ
Matavera, Rarotonga

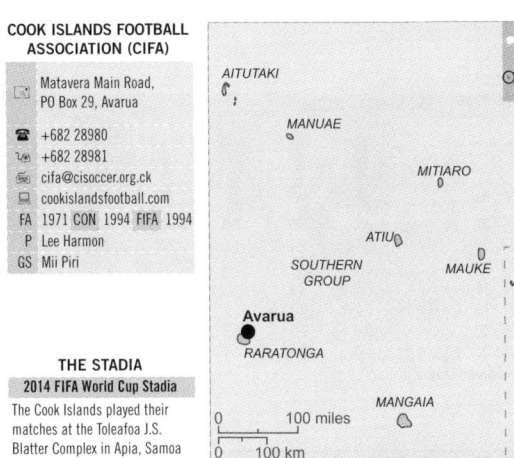

MAJOR CITIES/TOWNS
		Population
1	Avarua	13 273
2	Amuri	329
3	Mangaia	290
4	Atiu	159
5	Omoka	131
6	Mauke	118
7	Mitiaro	78
8	Nassau	49
9	Roto	47
10	Tauhunu	39
11	Rakahanga	32

COOK ISLANDS
Capital	Avarua	Population	11 870 (224)	% in cities	74%
GDP per capita	$9100 (109)	Area km²	236 km² (214)	GMT +/-	-10
Neighbours (km)	Coast 120				

RECENT INTERNATIONAL MATCHES PLAYED BY COOK ISLANDS

2004	Opponents	Score	Venue	Comp	Scorers	Att	Referee
5-05	Samoa	D 0-0	Auckland	Fr			
10-05	Tahiti	L 0-2	Honiara	WCq		12 000	Singh FIJ
12-05	Solomon Islands	L 0-5	Honiara	WCq		14 000	Fred VAN
15-05	Tonga	L 1-2	Honiara	WCq	John Pareanga [59]	15 000	Sosongan PNG
17-05	New Caledonia	L 0-8	Honiara	WCq		400	Singh FIJ
2005							
No international matches played in 2005							
2006							
No international matches played in 2006							
2007							
27-08	Fiji	L 0-4	Apia	WCq		400	Fred VAN
29-08	New Caledonia	L 0-3	Apia	WCq		200	Fox NZL
1-09	Tuvalu †	W 4-1	Apia	WCq	Teariki Mateariki 2 [28 69], Tom Le Mouton [88], Kunda Tom [93+]	200	Hester NZL
3-09	Tahiti	L 0-1	Apia	WCq		100	Aimaasu SAM
2008							
No international matches played in 2008							
2009							
11-06	Tonga	D 1-1	Atele	Fr	Joseph Ngauora [29]		
13-06	Tonga	W 2-1	Atele	Fr	Campbell Best [3], Joseph Ngauora [8]	204	Cross NZL
2010							
No international matches played in 2010							
2011							
27-08	Papua New Guinea	L 0-4	Boulari	PGr1			Billon NCL
30-08	Tahiti	L 0-7	Boulari	PGr1			Oiaka SOL
1-09	Kiribati †	W 3-0	Boulari	PGr1	Taylor Saghabi 2 [27 89], John Pareanga [92+]		Billon NCL
3-09	Fiji	L 1-4	Boulari	PGr1	Joseph Ngauora [41]		Ambassa NCL
22-11	Samoa	L 2-3	Apia	WCq	Campbell Best 2 [35 84]	600	O'Leary NZL
24-11	American Samoa	D 1-1	Apia	WCq	OG [62]	300	George VAN
26-11	Tonga	L 1-2	Apia	WCq	Grover Harmon [35]	200	Ambassa NCL
2012							
No international matches played in 2012							

Fr = Friendly match • WC = FIFA World Cup • q = qualifier • † Not an official international

COOK ISLANDS 2012

RAROTONGA LEAGUE ROUND CUP

	Pl	W	D	L	F	A	Pts	Tupapa	Sokattak	Arorangi	Matavera	Takuvaine	Avatiu	Titikaveka
Tupapa Maraerenga †	12	10	1	1	54	7	**31**		0-2	9-0	2-0	9-0	6-1	3-1
Nikao Sokattak	12	8	0	4	47	14	**24**	1-2		6-1	4-0	2-3	3-2	15-0
Arorangi	12	6	1	5	23	31	**19**	1-1	3-0		5-0	1-3	2-1	5-1
Matavera	12	6	1	5	14	26	**19**	0-9	2-0	3-1		0-1	1-0	2-2
Takuvaine	12	3	3	6	14	37	**12**	0-3	0-2	0-4	1-3		1-1	2-9
Avatiu	12	2	3	7	16	29	**9**	1-6	0-3	2-1	1-2	2-2		0-0
Titikaveka	12	1	3	8	17	48	**6**	0-4	1-9	0-1	0-1	1-1	2-5	

24/08/2012 - 24/11/2012 • † Qualified for the OFC Champions League

CIFA CUP FINAL 2012

CIFA HQ, Rarotonga, 15-12-2012

Nikao Sokattak 1-1 3-2p Tupapa Maraerenga

Scorers - Teariki Mateariki [26] for Sokattak; Rhys Ruka [77] for Tupapa

COL – COLOMBIA

FIFA/COCA-COLA WORLD RANKING

'93	'94	'95	'96	'97	'98	'99	'00	'01	'02	'03	'04	'05	'06	'07	'08	'09	'10	'11	'12
21	17	15	4	10	34	25	15	5	37	39	26	24	34	17	49	39	48	36	5

2012

Jan	Feb	Mar	Apr	May	Jun	Jul	Aug	Sep	Oct	Nov	Dec	High	Low	Av
35	32	31	23	23	20	22	21	22	9	8	5	4	54	24

The years were rolled back in Colombian football during 2012 with the national team regaining the form that had thrilled the world in the 1990s whilst Bogota recaptured some of the glory days at club level that had been missing for more than a quarter of a century. Jose Peckerman's arrival as national team coach saw Colombia storm up the standings in South America's 2014 FIFA World Cup qualifying group, spearheaded on the pitch by Radamel Falcao - the first Colombian to appear in the end of year FIFA/FIFPro World XI. At the halfway stage they stood in third place and hopeful of a place in the finals for the first time since 1998. Colombia had also climbed to fifth in the FIFA/Coca-Cola World Ranking - their highest placing for over a decade. At club level fans of Bogota clubs Santa Fe and Millonarios enjoyed a return to winning ways. Both clubs had dominated Colombian football in the early years of the league after its formation in 1948 but over the past two decades had fallen on hard times. That all changed in 2012 with Santa Fe beating Deportivo Pasto in the apertura final to win their first league title since 1975 while Millonarios won their first championship since 1988 after victory over Independiente Medellin in the clausura final. The season's other trophy winners were Atlético Nacional who beat Deportivo Pasto in the cup final.

FIFA WORLD CUP RECORD
1930-1954 DNE 1958 DNQ **1962** 14 r1 1966-1986 DNQ **1990** 14 r2 **1994** 19 r1 **1998** 21 r1 2002-2010 DNQ

FEDERACION COLOMBIANA DE FUTBOL (COLFUTBOL)

Avenida 32,
No. 16-22 Piso 5°,
Apdo Aéreo 17602, Bogotá
☎ +57 1 2889838
+57 1 2889793
info@colfutbol.org
www.colfutbol.org
FA 1924 CON 1940 FIFA 1936
P Luis Bedoya
GS Celina Sierra

THE STADIA

2014 FIFA World Cup Stadia
Metropolitano Roberto Melendez
Barranquilla   46 788

Other Main Stadia
Estadio Deportivo Cali
Cali   52 000
Estadio General Santander
Cúcuta   42 600
Estadio Atanasio Girardot
Medellín   40 943
Nemesio Camacho 'El Campin'
Bogotá   36 343

MAJOR CITIES/TOWNS

		Population
1	Bogotá	7 240 836
2	Medellín	2 318 002
3	Cali	2 195 218
4	Barranquilla	1 145 015
5	Cartagena	900 111
6	Cúcuta	596 735
7	Soledad	546 854
8	Bucaramanga	519 207
9	Ibagué	494 669
10	Soacha	458 672
11	Santa Marta	429 670
12	Villavicencio	401 559
13	Pereira	387 796
14	Bello	383 740
15	Manizales	363 255
16	Valledupar	332 135
17	Pasto	330 423
18	Buenaventura	315 594
19	Neiva	314 693

REPUBLICA DE COLOMBIA • REPUBLIC OF COLOMBIA;

Capital	Bogotá	Population	45 644 023 (28)	% in cities	74%
GDP per capita	$8800 (114)	Area km²	1 138 914 km² (26)	GMT +/-	-5

Neighbours (km) Brazil 1644, Ecuador 590, Panama 225, Peru 1800, Venezuela • Coast 3208

RECENT INTERNATIONAL MATCHES PLAYED BY COLOMBIA

2009	Opponents	Score	Venue	Comp	Scorers	Att	Referee
7-08	El Salvador	W 2-1	Houston	Fr	Gutierrez 12, Mendoza 87	20 418	Marrufo USA
12-08	Venezuela	L 1-2	New Jersey	Fr	Radamel Falcao 38		Prus USA
5-09	Ecuador	W 2-0	Medellin	WCq	Martinez 82, Gutierrez 94+	42 000	Pezzotta ARG
9-09	Uruguay	L 1-3	Montevideo	WCq	Martinez 63	30 000	Torres PAR
30-09	Mexico	W 2-1	Dallas	Fr	Giovanni Moreno 44, Quintero 79	50 000	Salazar USA
10-10	Chile	L 2-4	Medellin	WCq	Martinez 14, Giovanni Moreno 53	18 000	Rivera PER
14-10	Paraguay	W 2-0	Asuncion	WCq	Ramos 61, Rodallega 80	17 503	De Oliveira BRA
2010							
27-05	South Africa	L 1-2	Johannesburg	Fr	Giovanni Moreno 19p	76 000	Kipngetich KEN
30-05	Nigeria	D 1-1	Milton Keynes	Fr	Valdez 19	BCD	Atkinson ENG
11-08	Bolivia	D 1-1	La Paz	Fr	Bacca 40	4 000	Favale ARG
3-09	Venezuela	W 2-0	Puerto La Cruz	Fr	Cuadrado 17, Dayro Moreno 66	30 000	Moreno PAN
7-09	Mexico	L 0-1	Monterrey	Fr		43 000	Pineda HON
8-10	Ecuador	W 1-0	Harrison	Fr	Radamel Falcao 88	25 000	Chapin USA
12-10	USA	D 0-0	Chester	Fr		8 823	Garcia MEX
17-11	Peru	D 1-1	Bogota	Fr	Luis Nunez 74	6 900	Laverni ARG
2011							
9-02	Spain	L 0-1	Madrid	Fr		70 000	Trutz SVK
26-03	Ecuador	W 2-0	Madrid	Fr	Fredy Guarin 24, Radamel Falcao 74	15 000	Mateu ESP
29-03	Chile	L 0-2	Den Haag	Fr		15 000	Vink NED
2-07	Costa Rica	W 1-0	Jujuy	CAr1	Adrian Ramos 44	23 500	Osses CHI
6-07	Argentina	D 0-0	Cordoba	CAr1		47 000	Fagundes BRA
10-07	Bolivia	W 2-0	Santa Fe	CAr1	Radamel Falcao 2 14 28p	12 000	Chacon MEX
16-07	Peru	L 0-2	Cordoba	CAqf		30 000	Chacon MEX
3-09	Honduras	W 2-0	New York	Fr	Teofilo Gutierrez 2 25p 72	15 000	Gonzalez USA
6-09	Jamaica	W 2-0	Fort Lauderdale	Fr	Teofilo Gutierrez 55, Jackson Martinez 90	8 000	Dellavie USA
11-10	Bolivia	W 2-1	La Paz	WCq	Dorlan Pabon 48, Radamel Falcao 93+	33 155	Amarilla PAR
11-11	Venezuela	D 1-1	Barranquilla	WCq	Fredy Guarin 11	43 953	Ponce ECU
15-11	Argentina	L 1-2	Barranquilla	WCq	Dorlan Pabon 44	49 600	Fagundes BRA
2012							
29-02	Mexico	W 2-0	Miami	Fr	Radamel Falcao 36, Juan Guadrado 59	51 615	Vaughn USA
3-06	Peru	W 1-0	Lima	WCq	James Rodriguez 51	35 724	Pitana ARG
10-06	Ecuador	L 0-1	Quito	WCq		37 353	Seneme BRA
7-09	Uruguay	W 4-0	Barranquilla	WCq	Radamel Falcao 2, Teofilo Gutierrez 2 47 51, Juan Zuniga 90	45 000	Lopes BRA
11-09	Chile	W 3-1	Santiago	WCq	James Rodriguez 58, Radamel Falcao 73, Teofilo Gutierrez 76	38 000	Carrillo PER
12-10	Paraguay	W 2-0	Barranquilla	WCq	Radamel Falcao 2 52 89	45 000	Pezzotta ARG
16-10	Cameroon	W 3-0	Barranquilla	Fr	Jackson Martinez 23, Carlos Bacca 61, Dorlan Pabon 81		Escalante COL
14-11	Brazil	D 1-1	New York	Fr	Cuadrado 43	30 000	Geiger USA

Fr = Friendly match • CA = Copa America • WC = FIFA World Cup • q = qualifier

COLOMBIA NATIONAL TEAM HISTORICAL RECORDS

Caps
111 - Carlos Valderrama 1985-98 • 101 - Leonel Alvarez 1985-97 • 86 - Mario Yepes 1999- • 84 - Freddy Rincon 1990-2001 • 78 - Luis Carlos Perea 1987-94 • 73 - Ivan Cordoba 1997- & Oscar Cordoba 1993-2006 • 68 - Arnoldo Iguaran 1979-93 & Rene Higuita 1987-99 • 67 - Alexis Mendoza 1987-97 & Luis Perea 2003- • 66 - Victor Aristizabal 1993-2003 • 61 - Luis Herrera 1987-96

Goals
25 - Arnoldo Iguaran 1979-93 • 20 - Faustino Asprilla 1993-2001 • 17 - Freddy Rincon 1990-2001 • 15 - Victor Aristizabal 1993-2003 & Radamel Falcao 2007- • 14 - Adolfo Valencia 1992-98 • 13 - Ivan Valenciano 1991-2000 & Anthony de Avila 1983-98 • 12 - Willington Ortiz 1973-85 • 11 - Carlos Valderrama 1985-98 • 9 - Juan Pablo Angel 1996-2006, Edixon Perea 2004-08 & Hernan Herrera 1979-85

Coaches
Alfonso Novoa 1938 • Fernando Paternoster ARG 1938 • Roberto Melendez 1945 • Jose Arana Cruz PER 1946 • Lino Taioli ARG 1947 • Pedro Lopez 1957 • Rafael Orlandi ARG 1957 • Adolfo Pedernera ARG 1961-62 • Gabriel Ochoa Uribe 1963 • Efrain Sanchez 1963 • Antonio Julio De la Hoz 1965 • Cesar Lopez Fretes PAR 1966 • Francisco Zuluaga 1968 • Cesar Lopez Fretes PAR 1970 • Toza Veselinovic YUG 1972-73 • Efrain Sanchez 1975 • Blagoje Vidinic YUG 1976-79 • Carlos Bilardo ARG 1980-81 • Efrain Sanchez 1983-84 • Gabriel Ochoa Uribe 1985 • Francisco Maturana 1987-90 • Luis Garcia 1991 • Humberto Ortiz 1992 • Francisco Maturana 1993-94 • Hernan Dario Gomez 1995-98 • Javier Alvarez 1999 • Luis Garcia 2000-01 • Francisco Maturana 2001 • Reynaldo Rueda 2002 • Francisco Maturana 2002-03 • Reynaldo Rueda 2004-06 • Jorge Pinto 2007-08 • Eduardo Lara 2008-09 • Hernan Dario Gomez 2010-11 8 Leonel Alvarez 2011 • Jose Peckerman ARG 2012-

COLOMBIA 2012
PRIMERA A LIGA POSTEBON I

	Pl	W	D	L	F	A	Pts
Deportes Tolima †	18	10	6	2	28	16	36
Santa Fe †	18	7	8	3	29	19	29
Itagüí Ditaires †	18	8	5	5	25	18	29
Atlético Huila †	18	8	5	5	23	17	29
La Equidad Bogotá †	18	7	7	4	19	16	28
Deportivo Pasto †	18	6	9	3	24	18	27
Boyacá Chico †	18	7	6	5	26	22	27
Deportivo Cali †	18	7	6	5	19	18	27
Patriotas	18	7	6	5	13	17	27
Atlético Junior	18	7	4	7	28	24	25
Envigado	18	5	8	5	23	24	23
At. Nacional Medellín	18	6	4	8	25	20	22
Millonarios	18	4	8	6	22	23	20
Real Cartagena	18	4	8	6	22	31	20
Deportes Quindío	18	3	9	6	20	29	18
Indep. Medellín	18	4	5	9	17	24	17
Once Caldas	18	2	8	8	22	26	14
Cúcuta Deportivo	18	3	2	13	12	35	11

27/01/2012 - 27/05/2012 • † Qualified for the second stage
Top scorers (overall): **13** - Robin Ramirez PAR, Tolima • **11** - Giovanni **HERNANDEZ**, Junior & Humberto **OSORIO**, Millonarios • **10** - Efrain **VIAFARA**, Itagüí • **9** - Diego **CABRERA** BOL, Santa Fe; Edwards **JIMENEZ**, Pasto; Omar **PEREZ** ARG, Santa Fe & Milton **RODRIGUEZ**, Huila

LIGA POSTEBON I SECOND STAGE

Group A

	Pl	W	D	L	F	A	Pts	DP	DC	DT	AH
Deportivo Pasto †	6	3	2	1	7	6	11		1-1	3-1	1-1
Deportivo Cali	6	3	2	1	8	4	11	3-0		1-1	2-1
Deportes Tolima	6	3	1	2	6	5	10	0-1	1-0		2-0
Atlético Huila	6	0	1	5	2	8	1	0-1	0-1	0-1	

Group B

	Pl	W	D	L	F	A	Pts	SF	LEB	BC	ID
Santa Fe †	6	4	2	0	10	6	14		2-1	1-0	2-1
La Equidad Bogotá	6	2	2	2	10	9	8	2-2		3-1	2-1
Boyacá Chico	6	2	1	3	6	8	7	2-2	2-1		0-1
Itagüí Ditaires	6	1	1	4	4	7	4	0-1	1-1	0-1	

14/06/2012 - 8/07/2012 • † Qualified for the final

LIGA POSTEBON I FINAL

Departmental Libertad, Pasto, 11-07-2012, Att: 22 524, Ref: Luis Sanchez
Deportivo Pasto 1 Rendon [25]
Santa Fe 1 Quinonez [44]
Pasto - Jose Cuadrado - Wilson Galeano, Marino Garcia•, Juan Carlos Mosquera, Gilberto Garcia (Mauricio Mina 12) (Victor Zapata 64) - Carlos Giraldo, Rene Rosero (Juan Sebastian Villota 77), Omar Rodriguez•, Kevin Rendon - Oscar Mendez, Edwards Jimenez. Tr: Flavio Torres
Santa Fe - Camilo Vargas - Francisco Meza, German Centurion, Julian Quinones, Sergio Otalvaro•, Juan Daniel Roa• - Omar Perez, Jonathan Copete (Edwin Cardona• 81), Gerardo Bedoya• - Luis Carlos Arias• (Yulian Anchico 85), Diego Cabrera. Tr: Wilson Gutierrez

El Campin, Bogotá, 15-07-2012, Att: 36 500, Ref: Wilmar Roldan
Santa Fe 1 Copete [71]
Deportivo Pasto 0
Santa Fe - Camilo Vargas - Francisco Meza•, Julian Quinones, Sergio Otalvaro, Juan Daniel Roa - Omar Perez, Jonathan Copete (Oscar Rodas 81), Yulian Anchico (Edwin Cardona 70), Daniel Torres• - Luis Carlos Arias, Diego Cabrera (Mario Gomez• 84). Tr: Wilson Gutierrez
Pasto - Jose Cuadrado• - John Jairo Montano, Marino Garcia, Juan Carlos Mosquera, Gilberto Garcia - Carlos Giraldo (Mauricio Mina 76), Rene Rosero•, Omar Rodriguez, Kevin Rendon (Juan Sebastian Villota 75) - Oscar Mendez (Victor Zapata 51), Edwards Jimenez. Tr: Flavio Torres

Santa Fe qualified for the Copa Libertadores

COLOMBIA 2012 PRIMERA A REGULAR SEASON RESULTS

DIMAYOR PRIMERA A	Cali	Cartagena	Chico	Cúcuta	Envigado	Huila	Itagüí	Junior	La Equidad	Medellín	Millonarios	Nacional	Once Caldas	Pasto	Patriotas	Quindío	Santa Fe	Tolima
Deportivo Cali		2-0	2-3	1-0	1-1	3-2	0-1	1-1	3-0	2-0	1-0	3-1	2-1	1-0 0-1	3-0	1-1	2-0	1-3
Real Cartagena	2-2		0-0	0-1	2-3	1-0	3-1	2-1 1-3	0-2	3-2	0-2	1-1	1-2	1-1	2-2	2-1	2-1	1-3
Boyacá Chico	3-1	3-0		5-2	4-1	2-0	1-1	1-1	1-1	1-0	1-1	1-0	1-1	0-1 0-1	2-0	2-0	1-1	
Cúcuta Deportivo	1-2	0-1	2-0		2-1	1-0	0-1	1-0	0-1 1-3	1-2	2-1	1-0	4-1	2-2	0-1	1-0	4-0	0-5
Envigado	0-0	1-0	0-0	2-2		1-1	1-2 0-0	2-1	1-1	1-0	1-1	0-0	2-1	1-2	2-0	3-0	1-1	2-0
Atlético Huila	1-1	1-1	3-0	0-0	1-0		2-3	1-3	0-0	1-0	0-4	0-0	3-2	1-0	3-0	0-1	2-0	3-0 0-0
Itagüí Ditaires	2-0	3-1	1-1	0-0	4-2 1-1	1-0		1-1	3-0	1-1	1-0	1-0	3-0	1-1	4-0	4-0	0-0	2-3
Atlético Junior	1-0	3-1 1-0	3-1	4-0	2-0	4-0	2-1		0-0	1-0	1-3	1-0	2-0	2-0	4-3	1-1	1-1	1-2
La Equidad Bogotá	1-1	1-1	1-1	4-1 3-1	1-0	5-1	1-0	0-0		1-3	0-1	3-2	1-0	2-0	2-1	2-1	0-1	1-0
Indep. Medellín	0-1	5-0	0-3	1-1	2-2	0-0	0-1	2-1	0-1		1-1	1-0 0-3	2-1	1-0	2-0	2-2	1-1	0-1
Millonarios	0-0	1-1	0-1	1-0	2-0	1-1	1-0	2-0	2-0	2-1		2-3	2-1	1-2	0-1	2-1	3-4 2-0	1-1
At. Nacional Medellín	4-0	2-1	4-0	1-1	1-0	1-2	1-1	3-1	0-0	1-2 2-2	0-0		1-0	1-0	1-1	2-0	2-1	0-1
Once Caldas	1-0	2-2	5-2	4-0	1-1	3-1	2-2	2-2	1-1	1-0	0-0	0-2		2-1	1-1	0-0 1-3	2-2	0-1
Deportivo Pasto	1-1 3-0	0-0	2-0	2-1	3-1	3-1	1-1	1-1	3-1	0-0	3-1	0-2	4-1		1-1	3-0	1-1	1-0
Patriotas	1-0	1-1	0-0 1-0	1-1	1-2	1-0	1-0	2-1	0-2	2-1	0-2	0-3	1-0	0-0		2-2	0-0	0-3
Deportes Quindío	2-1	3-2	4-1	1-0	1-0	0-2	2-1	0-0	1-1	1-3	2-2	2-2	1-3 0-1	2-2	1-1		1-0	1-2
Santa Fe	1-0	5-0	1-0	2-0	1-1	4-0	1-0	2-1	1-2	1-1	1-1 1-2	2-2	2-0	2-0	2-1	1-1		2-1
Deportes Tolima	1-1	3-0	2-2	3-0	0-1	1-1 1-1	1-2	2-2	1-1	2-1	0-0	1-0	1-3	1-0	2-1	1-0	2-0 2-1	

Liga Postobon I 2012 results are shown in the shaded boxes • Attendance (incl play-offs): 3,403,548 @ 9,051
Local rivals play each other four times in the regular season. In this instance the Liga Postebon I results are listed first • Real Cartagena relegated with the worst record over three seasons • Cúcuta Deportivo had the second worst record and entered a play-off • Relegation play-off: América Cali 1-4 2-1 **Cúcuta Deportivo**. Cúcuta remain in the Primera A

COLOMBIA 2012
PRIMERA A LIGA POSTEBON II

	Pl	W	D	L	F	A	Pts
Millonarios †	18	11	4	3	25	9	37
La Equidad Bogotá †	18	9	6	3	26	17	33
Atlético Junior †	18	8	8	2	27	15	32
Itagüí Ditaires †	18	8	8	2	23	12	32
At. Nacional Medellín†	18	7	9	2	25	14	30
Deportes Tolima †	18	8	5	5	26	20	29
Indep. Medellín †	18	7	5	6	23	18	26
Deportivo Pasto †	18	7	4	7	22	20	25
Cúcuta Deportivo	18	6	6	6	22	22	24
Santa Fe	18	6	5	7	18	22	23
Deportivo Cali	18	6	4	8	21	22	22
Boyacá Chico	18	5	7	6	19	22	22
Deportes Quindío	18	6	4	8	20	25	22
Envigado	18	5	6	7	15	18	21
Once Caldas	18	6	1	11	19	27	19
Patriotas	18	4	5	9	17	28	17
Real Cartagena	18	3	3	12	15	33	12
Atlético Huila	18	2	6	10	12	31	12

28/07/2012 - 11/11/2012 • † Qualified for the second stage
Top scorers (overall): **9** - Henry **HERNANDEZ**, Cúcuta; Carmelo **VALENCIA**, La Equidad & German **CANO** ARG, Medellín •
8 - Wilberto **COSME**, Millonarios

PENALTIES

Millonarios	Medellín
✓ Rentería	
	Hernandez ✓
✓ Franco	
	Herner ✗[1]
✓ Ortiz	
	Henriquez ✓
✗[2] Vasquez	
	Rojas ✓
✓ Otalvaro	
	Arias ✓
✓ Delgado	
	Correa ✗[2]

[1] = hit bar • [2] = saved

COLOMBIA 2012
PRIMERA B LIGA POSTEBON I (2)

	Pl	W	D	L	F	A	Pts
América Cali †	18	12	2	4	33	15	38
Corporación Tuluá †	18	9	6	3	24	14	33
Deportivo Rionegro †	18	9	5	4	33	19	32
Sucre †	18	8	7	3	22	18	31
Uniautonoma †	18	8	6	4	27	19	30
Universitario Popayán †	18	9	3	6	25	19	30
Unión Magdalena †	18	8	4	6	27	21	28
Real Santander †	18	8	3	7	25	23	27
Fortaleza	18	7	5	6	25	26	26
Valledupar	18	6	6	6	26	28	24
Deportivo Pereira	18	6	5	7	21	23	23
Bogotá FC	18	5	5	8	24	34	20
Academia Bogotá	18	4	7	7	22	22	19
Depor Jamundí	18	5	3	10	23	34	18
Alianza Petrolera	18	3	8	7	19	27	17
Atlético Bucaramanga	18	4	5	9	18	27	17
Barranquilla FC	18	4	4	10	18	28	16
Expreso Rojo	18	3	4	11	8	24	13

28/01/2012 - 26/05/2012 • † Qualified for the second stage

LIGA POSTEBON II SECOND STAGE

Group A

	Pl	W	D	L	F	A	Pts	Mi	DP	AJ	DT
Millonarios †	6	3	1	2	8	6	**10**		1-0	0-0	3-0
Deportivo Pasto	6	3	1	2	8	7	**10**	3-1		1-0	1-1
Atlético Junior	6	2	2	2	5	6	**8**	2-1	1-3		1-1
Deportes Tolima	6	1	2	3	6	8	**5**	1-2	3-0	0-1	

Group B

	Pl	W	D	L	F	A	Pts	IM	AN	ID	LE
Indep. Medellín †	6	3	2	1	4	4	**11**		1-1	0-0	1-0
At. Nacional Medellín	6	3	1	2	6	4	**10**	0-1		1-0	2-0
Itagüí Ditaires	6	2	1	3	4	4	**7**	0-1	2-0		0-1
La Equidad Bogotá	6	2	0	4	5	7	**6**	3-0	0-2	1-2	

17/11/2012 - 9/12/2012 • † Qualified for the final

LIGA POSTEBON II FINAL

Atanasio Girardot, Medellín, 12-12-2012, Att: 44 488, Ref: Juan Ponton
Independiente Medellín 0
Millonarios 0
Medellín - Leandro Castellanos - Daniel Bocanegra, Diego Herner•, Luis Tipton, Jefferson Mena, Jhon Viafara••♦86, Sebastian Hernandez (Andres Correa 81), Amilcar Henriquez, Felipe Pardo, William Zapata (Julian Rojas 69), Andres Mosquera. Tr: Hernan Dario Gomez
Millonarios - Luis Delgado - Roman Torres, Ignacio Ithurralde, Leonard Vasquez, Rafael Robayo, Mayer Candelo• (Jorge Perlaza 90), Jarol Martinez, Harrison Otalvaro (Jose Tancredi 85), Jhonny Ramirez, Wilberto Cosme, Wason Renteria (Omar Vasquez 76). Tr: Hernan Torres

El Campin, Bogotá, 16-12-2012, Att: 36 343, Ref: Luis Sanchez
Millonarios 1 Cosme [45]
Independiente Medellín 1 Zapata [52]
Millonarios - Luis Delgado - Roman Torres, Pedro Franco, Lewis Ochoa, Rafael Robayo (Jorge Perlaza 71), Mayer Candelo (Omar Vasquez 80), Jarol Martinez, Harrison Otalvaro, Jhonny Ramirez (Juan Ortiz• 51), Wilberto Cosme, Wason Renteria. Tr: Hernan Torres
Medellín - Leandro Castellanos - Diego Herner, Daniel Bocanegra (Andres Ortiz 90), Luis Tipton (Andres Correa 69), Jorge Arias•, Jefferson Mena, Julian Rojas, Sebastian Hernandez, Amilcar Henriquez•, Felipe Pardo••♦86, William Zapata (Andres Mosquera 86). Tr: Hernan Dario Gomez

Millonarios qualified for the Copa Libertadores. Deportes Tolima also qualified for the Copa Libertadores as the team with the best overall record in the season

COLOMBIA 2012
PRIMERA B LIGA POSTEBON II (2)

	Pl	W	D	L	F	A	Pts
Deportivo Pereira †	18	13	4	1	37	14	43
Alianza Petrolera †	18	10	4	4	35	18	34
América Cali †	18	10	4	4	31	18	34
Deportivo Rionegro †	18	9	4	5	25	19	31
Universitario Popayán †	18	9	3	6	20	21	30
Corporación Tuluá †	18	8	5	5	27	25	29
Uniautonoma †	18	6	9	3	23	20	27
Atlético Bucaramanga†	18	8	3	7	22	24	27
Valledupar	18	6	7	5	15	12	25
Sucre	18	7	4	7	19	22	25
Bogotá FC	18	7	2	9	22	30	23
Unión Magdalena	18	6	3	9	19	20	21
Depor Jamundí	18	4	7	7	22	25	19
Fortaleza	18	5	4	9	14	18	19
Expreso Rojo	18	4	4	10	12	18	16
Real Santander	18	4	4	10	22	31	16
Barranquilla FC	18	4	3	11	22	37	15
Llaneros	18	3	4	11	11	26	13

21/07/2012 - 14/10/2012 • † Qualified for the second stage

LIGA POSTEBON I SECOND STAGE

Group A

	Pl	W	D	L	F	A	Pts	AC	DR	UP	RS
América Cali †	6	4	2	0	14	6	14		1-1	4-0	5-3
Deportivo Rionegro	6	2	3	1	11	8	9	0-0		3-0	5-2
Universitario Popayán	6	2	0	4	7	9	6	0-1	3-0		4-0
Real Santander	6	1	1	4	10	19	4	2-3	2-2	1-0	

Group B

	Pl	W	D	L	F	A	Pts	UM	Un	Su	CT
Unión Magdalena †	6	3	2	1	9	5	11		2-1	1-0	4-1
Uniautonoma	6	2	2	2	7	7	8	1-1		0-1	1-0
Sucre	6	2	1	3	5	6	7	1-0	1-2		0-0
Corporación Tuluá	6	1	3	2	7	10	6	1-1	2-2	3-2	

31/05/2012 - 23/06/2012 • † Qualified for the final
Final: Union Magdalena 1-1 1-1 4-5p **América Cali**

LIGA POSTEBON II SECOND STAGE

Group A

	Pl	W	D	L	F	A	Pts	DR	Un	DP	CT
Deportivo Rionegro †	6	3	0	3	8	8	9		2-1	3-1	1-0
Uniautonoma	6	3	0	3	11	11	9	2-1		3-0	2-1
Deportivo Pereira	6	2	2	2	7	8	8	2-0	3-1		1-1
Corporación Tuluá	6	2	2	2	8	7	8	2-1	4-2	0-0	

Group B

	Pl	W	D	L	F	A	Pts	AP	AC	UP	AB
Alianza Petrolera †	6	5	0	1	15	6	15		3-0	2-1	2-0
América Cali	6	3	0	3	6	10	9	1-4		2-1	2-1
Universitario Popayán	6	3	0	3	9	11	9	4-3	1-0		1-0
At. Bucaramanga	6	1	0	5	5	8	3	0-1	0-1	4-1	

20/10/2012 - 19/11/2012 • † Qualified for the final
Final: Deportivo Rionegro 0-1 1-3 **Alianza Petrolera**

Primera B Championship Final: **Alianza Petrolera** 2-1 0-1 4-3p América Cali
Alianza Petrolera promoted. **América Cali** remain in the Primera B after losing a play-off against Cúcuta Deportivo

COPA COLOMBIA POSTOBON 2012

Round of 16		Quarter-finals		Semi-finals		Final	
At. Nacional Medellín	2 3						
Santa Fe *	2 0	**At. Nacional Medellín**	2 2				
Itagüí Ditaires *	4 1 3p	Deportes Tolima *	1 1				
Deportes Tolima	1 4 4p			**At. Nacional Medellín**	1 1		
Cúcuta Deportivo *	2 0 4p			Boyacá Chico *	0 0		
Bogotá FC	1 1 3p	Cúcuta Deportivo *	3 1 3p				
Deportivo Cali *	1 0	**Boyacá Chico**	1 3 5p				
Boyacá Chico	1 2					**At. Nacional Medellín**†	0 2
Atlético Bucaramanga*	2 1 4p					Deportivo Pasto *	0 0
Uniautonoma	2 1 2p	**Atlético Bucaramanga***	1 1				
Valledupar *	2 0	América Cali	0 1			CUP FINAL	
América Cali	3 2			Atlético Bucaramanga*	1 0	1st leg. 1-11-2012	
Atlético'Junior *	0 2			**Deportivo Pasto**	0 3	2nd leg. 8-11-2012	
La Equidad Bogotá	0 1	Atlético Junior *	2 0				
Once Caldas *	0 0	**Deportivo Pasto**	3 3			For details see below	
Deportivo Pasto	1 4						

† Qualified for Copa Sudamericana • * Home team in the first leg

1st leg. Departmental Libertad, Pasto, 1-11-2012, Ref: Juan Ponton. **Pasto** - Jose Cuadrado - John Jairo Montano, Juan Carlos Mosquera, Gilberto Garcia, Arbey Diaz - Rene Rosero•, Omar Rodriguez, Kevin Rendon (Ayron Del Valle 46), Jaime Cordoba• (Carlos Giraldo 46) - Oscar Mendez, Edwards Jimenez• (Victor Zapata 67). Tr: Flavio Torres. **Nacional** - Cristian Bonilla - Francisco Najera•, Farid Diaz, Juan Valencia, Oscar Murillo, Stefan Medina - Jherson Cordoba• (Alejandro Bernal 74), Felix Micolta (Wilder Guisao 81), Alexander Mejia, Sebastian Perez - Diego Alvarez (Aviles Hurtado 67). Tr: Juan Carlos Osorio

2nd leg. Atanasio Girardot, Medellin, 8-11-2012, Ref: Hernando Buitrago. Scorers - Uribe [58], Valencia [78] for Nacional. **Nacional** - Cristian Bonilla - Elkin Calle (Alejandro Bernal 46), Farid Diaz, Juan Valencia, Oscar Murillo, Stefan Medina - Macnelly Torres, Jherson Cordoba, Alexander Mejia, Aviles Hurtado (Felix Micolta 83) - Fernando Uribe (Luis Mosquera75). Tr: Juan Carlos Osorio. **Pasto** - Alexis Marquez - Juan Carlos Mosquera•, Gilberto Garcia•, Wilson Galeano, Fausto Obeso - Joselito Vaca (Victor Zapata 60), Rene Rosero (John Jairo Montano 82), Sebastian Villota (Oscar Mendez 46), Omar Rodriguez, Carlos Giraldo - Ayron Del Valle. Tr: Flavio Torres

MEDALS TABLE

		Overall			League			Cup		Sth Am			
		G	S	B	G	S	B	G	S	G	S	B	City
1	Millonarios	16	10	14	14	9	8	1		1	1	6	Bogotá
2	Atlético Nacional	15	11	10	11	9	5	1		3	2	5	Medellín
3	América Cali	14	11	12	13	7	5			1	4	7	Cali
4	Deportivo Cali	9	15	8	8	12	6	1			3	2	Cali
5	Santa Fe	8	5	5	7	3	4	1			2	1	Bogotá
6	Atlético Junior	7	6	3	7	6	2					1	Barranquilla
7	Independiente Medellín	5	8	4	5	8	3					1	Medellín
8	Once Caldas	5	3	1	4	2	1		1	1			Manizales
9	Deportes Tolima	1	5	2	1	5	1					1	Ibagué
10	Deportivo Pasto	1	4		1	2			2				Pasto
11	La Equidad	1	3			3		1					Bogotá
12	Deportes Quindío	1	2	1	1	2	1						Armenia
13	Cúcuta Deportivo	1	1	3	1	1	2						Cúcuta
14	Boyacá Chico	1	1		1					1			Tunja
15	Union Magdalena	1		1	1		1						Santa Marta

COM – COMOROS

FIFA/COCA-COLA WORLD RANKING

'93	'94	'95	'96	'97	'98	'99	'00	'01	'02	'03	'04	'05	'06	'07	'08	'09	'10	'11	'12
-	-	-	-	-	-	-	-	-	-	-	-	-	207	187	198	176	186	187	194

2012

Jan	Feb	Mar	Apr	May	Jun	Jul	Aug	Sep	Oct	Nov	Dec	High	Low	Av
187	188	188	187	187	187	185	193	190	190	196	194	164	207	187

The Comoros Islands did not enter a team in the 2013 Africa Cup of Nations qualifiers, preferring instead to focus on the African Nations Championship - a tournament reserved for African based players, the games in which FIFA have now decided to recognise as full internationals. In December they played Mauritius home and away but lost 2-0 on aggregate in the first round of qualifying. The 2011 club champions Coin Nord also took part in continental competition, entering the 2012 CAF Champions League where they surpassed expectations by winning the first leg of their tie against Coffee FC of Ethiopia before losing 4-2 on aggregate. At home the 2012 championship was won by Djabal from the town of Iconi on the main island of Grande Comore. They finished ahead of Fomboni and Steel Nouvel in November's three-way play-off for the champions of all three islands. Djabal's success in the Grande Comore league was, however, clouded in controversy. Their title was sealed with a 23-0 win over Asim, a result that allowed them to edge out defending champions Coin Nord on goal difference. Coin Nord unsuccessfully protested on the grounds that their match had finished 15 minutes earlier than Djabal's, who then had an advantage in the battle for a better goal difference. Djabal netted 14 goals in the last quarter-hour.

CAF AFRICA CUP OF NATIONS RECORD
1957-2008 DNE 2010-2012 DNQ 2013 DNE

FEDERATION COMORIENNE DE FOOTBALL (FFC)

Boite Postale 798, Moroni

☎ +269 7632666
📠 +269 7738526
✉ fedcom_cenfoot@yahoo.fr

FA 1979 CON 1986 FIFA 2005
P Tourqui Salim
GS Mariyatta Abdou Chacour

THE STADIA

2014 FIFA World Cup Stadia
Stade Said Mohamed Cheikh
Mitsamiouli, Grande Comore 5 000

Other Main Stadia
Stade de Moroni
Moroni, Grande Comore 2 000
Stade El Hadj Ahmed Matoir
Fomboni, Moheli 1 000
Stade de Foot de Hombo
Mutsamudu, Anjouan 1 000

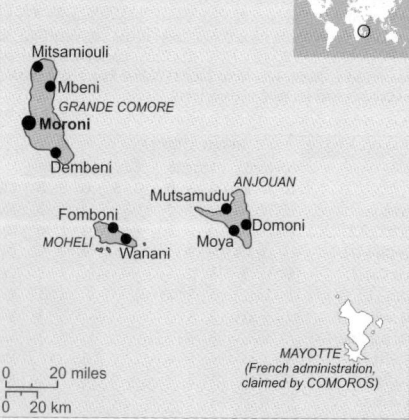

MAJOR CITIES/TOWNS

		Population
1	Moroni	48 192
2	Mutsamudu	24 980
3	Fomboni	16 581
4	Domoni	15 363
5	Tsémbehou	12 232
6	Ongodjou	11 413
7	Sima	10 986
8	Adda Daouéni	10 858
9	Ouani	10 779
10	Mirontsi	10 767
11	Bazmini	8 952
12	Koni Djodjo	8 876
13	Iconi	8 250
14	Moya	8 242
15	Ounkazi	8 024
16	Dindri	7 816
17	Ngandzalé	7 484
18	Mbéni	7 229
19	Mitsamiouli	6 770

UDZIMA WA KOMORI • UNION DE COMORES • UNION OF THE COMOROS

Capital	Moroni	Population	752 438 (161)	% in cities	28%
GDP per capita	$1000 (211)	Area km²	2235 km² (179)	GMT +/-	+3
Neighbours (km)	Coast 340				

RECENT INTERNATIONAL MATCHES PLAYED BY COMOROS

2003	Opponents		Score	Venue	Comp	Scorers	Att	Referee
30-08	Reunion †	L	0-1	Flacq	IOr1		103	Labrosse SEY
2-09	Reunion †	L	0-4	Flacq	IOr1			
4-09	Mauritius †	L	0-5	Curepipe	IOsf		4 500	Labrosse SEY
6-09	Seychelles †	L	0-2	Curepipe	IO3p			
2004								
No international matches played in 2004								
2005								
No international matches played in 2005								
2006								
14-12	Yemen	L	0-2	Sana'a	ARq			
17-12	Djibouti	W	4-2	Sana'a	ARq	Meknesh Bin Daoud [5], Ahmed Seif 2 [33 75], Mohamed Moni [70]		
2007								
14-08	Madagascar	L	0-3	Antananarivo	Fr			
14-10	Madagascar	L	2-6	Antananarivo	WCq	Daoud Midtadi [6], Ibor Bakar [53p]	7 754	Kaoma ZAM
17-11	Madagascar	L	0-4	Moroni	WCq		1 610	Damon RSA
2008								
20-07	Namibia	L	0-3	Secunda	CCr1			Labrosse SEY
22-07	Malawi	L	0-1	Secunda	CCr1			Marange ZIM
24-07	Lesotho	L	0-1	Secunda	CCr1			Labrosse SEY
2009								
18-10	Botswana	D	0-0	Bulawayo	CCr1			Rachide MOZ
20-10	Seychelles	W	2-1	Bulawayo	CCr1	Ahmed Ali [9], Mouigni Mohamed [64]		Rachide MOZ
22-10	Swaziland	L	0-3	Bulawayo	CCr1			Carvalho ANG
2010								
29-08	Madagascar	L	0-1	Mahajanga	Fr			
5-09	Zambia	L	0-4	Lusaka	CNq			Eyob Russom ERI
9-10	Mozambique	L	0-1	Moroni	CNq			Ibada TAN
2011								
28-03	Libya	L	0-3	Bamaoko	CNq			Diatta SEN
5-06	Libya	D	1-1	Mitsamiouli	CNq	Abdoulaide Mze Mbaba [83]		
4-08	Seychelles	D	0-0	Praslin	IOr1		1 800	Dubec REU
6-08	Maldives	D	2-2	Roche Caiman	IOr1	Mchinda Madihali [9], Athoumane Soulaimane [54]	1 000	Dubec REU
9-08	Mauritius	L	0-2	Praslin	IOr1		300	Rassuhi MYT
4-09	Zambia	L	1-2	Mitsamiouli	CNq	Youssouf M'Changama [32]		
8-10	Mozambique	L	0-3	Maputo	CNq			
11-11	Mozambique	L	0-1	Mitsamiouli	WCq		3 000	Jane LES
15-11	Mozambique	L	1-4	Maputo	WCq	Mohamed Youssouf [72]	10 000	Ruzive ZIM
2012								
1-12	Mauritius	L	0-2	Curepipe	Fr			
15-12	Mauritius	D	0-0	Mitsamiouli	Fr			

IO = Indian Ocean Games • CC = COSAFA Castle Cup • AR = Arab Cup • q = qualifier • r1 = first round group
† Not regarded as a full internationals because Comoros was not yet a member of FIFA

COMOROS 2012

	Pl	W	D	L	F	A	Pts	Dj	FC	SN
Djabal	4	2	2	0	6	3	8		0-0	2-1
Fomboni Club	4	1	2	1	6	5	5	2-2		1-3
Steel Nouvel	4	1	0	3	4	8	3	0-2	1-3	

11/11/2012 - 28/11/2012 • † Qualified for the CAF Champions League

COUPE DES COMORES 2012

Semi-finals

Steel Nouvel	1
Fomboni Club	0

Ngazi	0
Enfants de Comores	2

Finals

Steel Nouvel	3
Enfants de Comores	0

Final. Stade de Moroni, Moroni, 26-08-2012
Scorers - Ibrahim Soulaimane [6], Mikidad Daoud 2 [21 87]

CPV – CAPE VERDE ISLANDS

FIFA/COCA-COLA WORLD RANKING

'93	'94	'95	'96	'97	'98	'99	'00	'01	'02	'03	'04	'05	'06	'07	'08	'09	'10	'11	'12
147	161	144	155	171	167	177	156	159	154	143	129	118	78	111	107	97	75	58	69

2012

Jan	Feb	Mar	Apr	May	Jun	Jul	Aug	Sep	Oct	Nov	Dec	High	Low	Av
58	69	62	76	76	77	79	78	65	51	63	69	51	182	130

The Cape Verde Islands had a fairy tale tournament on their debut appearance at the Africa Cup of Nations finals at the start of 2013, reaching the quarter-finals in South Africa to prove their sensational elimination of Cameroon's Indomitable Lions in the qualifiers was no fluke. The island archipelago rose to a high of 51 in the FIFA/Coca-Cola World Ranking in October following the 2-0 first leg victory over Cameroon before holding on for a well earned 3-2 aggregate triumph after the return. They played down their chances at the finals, portraying an image of bewildered schoolboys invited to gate crash an adult party, but proved feisty competitors and went on to finish second behind South Africa in their group after holding the hosts to an embarrassing draw on the opening day of the tournament. There were joyous celebrations, including coach Luis Antunes breaking into song at the post-match press conference, after they reached the quarter-finals where Ghana got some fortuitous calls to finally end the dream run. However, two defeats at the start of their 2014 FIFA World Cup qualifying campaign meant they had little chance of creating more upsets in the immediate future. In club football Sporting Praia won the championship for the 11th time after beating Atletico Sao Nicolau over two legs in the final, while Onze Unidos won the cup.

CAF AFRICA CUP OF NATIONS RECORD
1957-1992 DNE 1994 DNQ 1996-1998 DNQ 2000-2012 DNQ **2013** 7 QF

FEDERACAO CABOVERDIANA DE FUTEBOL (FCF)

 FCF CX, Case postale 234, Praia
☎ +238 2 600847
📠 +238 2 611362
✉ fcf@cvtelecom.cv
🖥 www.fcf.cv
FA 1982 CON 1986 FIFA 1986
P Mario Semedo
GS Jose João Rezende

THE STADIA
2014 FIFA World Cup Stadia
Estadio da Varzea
Praia — 10 000
Other Main Stadia
Estadio Marcelo Leitão
Santa Maria — 8 000
Estadio Municipal Adérito Sena
Mindelo — 5 000

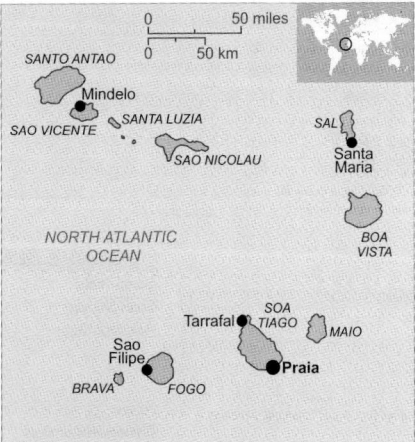

MAJOR CITIES/TOWNS
		Population
1	Praia	128 653
2	Mindelo	76 014
3	Santa Maria	21 195
4	Pedra Badejo	10 237
5	Assomada	8 553
6	São Filipe	8 212
7	Tarrafal	6 974
8	São Miguel	5 888
9	Porto Novo	5 523
10	Ribeira Brava	5 121
11	Ponta do Sol	4 023
12	Vila do Maio	3 264
13	São Domingos	3 220
14	Sal Rei	2 200
15	Pombas	1 799
16	Nova Sintra	1 793
17	Mosteiros	478

REPUBLICA DE CABO VERDE • REPUBLIC OF CAPE VERDE
Capital	Praia	Population	429 474 (171)
GDP per capita	$3800 (156)	Area km²	4033 km² (175)
Neighbours (km)	Coast 965	% in cities	60%
		GMT +/-	-1

RECENT INTERNATIONAL MATCHES PLAYED BY THE CAPE VERDE ISLANDS

2010	Opponents	Score	Venue	Comp	Scorers	Att	Referee
24-05	Portugal	D 0-0	Covilha	Fr		6 000	Gomez ESP
11-08	Senegal	L 0-1	Dakar	Fr			
4-09	Mali	W 1-0	Praia	CNq	Tony Varela 44		Benouza ALG
10-10	Zimbabwe	D 0-0	Harare	CNq			Ndume GAB
16-11	Guinea-Bissau	W 2-1	Lisbon	Fr	Lito 6, Ronny Souto 24		
2011							
9-02	Burkina Faso	W 1-0	Obidos	Fr	Heldon 63		
26-03	Liberia	W 4-2	Praia	CNq	Heldon 2 14 45, Babanco 25, Odair Fortes 53		Ould Ali MTN
5-06	Liberia	L 0-1	Paynesville	CNq			
3-09	Mali	L 0-3	Bamako	CNq			Diatta SEN
8-10	Zimbabwe	W 2-1	Praia	CNq	Valdo 3, Ryan Mendes 13		
2012							
29-02	Madagascar	W 4-0	Antananarivo	CNq	Dady 37, Mendes 38, Tony Varela 2 80 82		Sikazwe ZAM
2-06	Sierra Leone	L 1-2	Freetown	WCq	Marco Soares 93+	25 000	Agbovi GHA
9-06	Tunisia	L 1-2	Praia	WCq	Odair Fortes 26	3 600	Jiyed MAR
16-06	Madagascar	W 3-1	Praia	CNq	Mendes 2 9 81, Djaniny 55		
8-09	Cameroon	W 2-0	Praia	CNq	Ricardo 16, Djaniny 61	10 000	Otogo Castane GAB
14-10	Cameroon	L 1-2	Yaounde	CNq	Heldon 11		Grisha EGY
14-11	Ghana	L 0-1	Lisbon	Fr			
2013							
9-01	Nigeria	D 0-0	Faro	Fr			Miguel POR
19-01	South Africa	D 0-0	Johannesburg	CNr1		50 000	Haimoudi ALG
23-01	Morocco	D 1-1	Durban	CNr1	Platini 36	25 000	Sikazwe ZAM
27-01	Angola	W 2-1	Port Elizabeth	CNr1	Fernando Varela 81, Heldon 91+	20 000	Jedidi TUN
2-02	Ghana	L 0-2	Port Elizabeth	CNqf		8 000	Seechurn MRI

Fr = Friendly match • CN = CAF African Cup of Nations • WC = FIFA World Cup • q = qualifier

CAPE VERDE ISLANDS NATIONAL TEAM HISTORICAL RECORDS

Coach: Carlos Alinho 2003-06 • Ze Rui 2006 • Ricardo Rocha BRA 2007 • Joao de Deus POR 2008-10 • Lucio Antunes 2010-

CAPE VERDE ISLANDS 2011-12
CAMPEONATO NACIONAL

First Round Group Stage

Group A	Pl	W	D	L	F	A	Pts	AF	Ju	Ba	EA	AB
Sporting da Praia	5	3	2	0	15	3	11	2-0	6-1	0-0	2-2	5-0
Académica do Fogo	5	2	2	1	3	3	8		0-0	2-1	0-0	1-0
Juventude	5	2	2	1	8	9	8			1-1	3-1	3-1
Batuque	5	2	2	1	6	3	8				2-0	2-0
Estrela Amadores	5	1	2	2	8	7	5					5-0
Académica da Brava	5	0	0	5	1	16	0					

Group B	Pl	W	D	L	F	A	Pts	APN	Mi	Pa	AB	A83
SC Atlético	5	5	0	0	15	8	15	2-1	1-0	3-1	5-4	4-2
Académica Pt Novo	5	3	1	1	10	6	10		2-0	1-1	3-2	3-1
CS Mindelense	5	2	1	2	10	4	7			4-0	5-0	1-1
Paulense	5	1	2	2	6	9	5				1-1	3-0
Académica Boavista	5	0	2	3	9	16	2					2-2
Académico 83	5	0	2	3	6	13	2					

5/05/2012 - 7/07/2012

Semi-finals

Sporting da Praia	3	3
Académica Pt Novo	0	0

Académica do Fogo	1	1
SC Atlético	2	2

Final

Sporting da Praia	1	0
SC Atlético	1	0

1st leg. 23-06-2012
Estadio Municipal Di Deus, Chazinha

2nd leg. 7-07-2012
Estadio da Vareza, Praia

TACA NACIONAL FINAL
Estádio Marcelo Leitao, Ilha do Sal, 24-08-2012
CD Onze Unidos 2-1 Académica Porto Novo
Scorers - Ze Badiu, Ailton for Onze Unidos; Xaloti for Académica

CRC – COSTA RICA

FIFA/COCA-COLA WORLD RANKING

'93	'94	'95	'96	'97	'98	'99	'00	'01	'02	'03	'04	'05	'06	'07	'08	'09	'10	'11	'12
42	65	78	72	51	67	64	60	30	21	17	27	21	68	70	53	44	69	65	66

2012												High	Low	Av
Jan	Feb	Mar	Apr	May	Jun	Jul	Aug	Sep	Oct	Nov	Dec			
62	63	59	59	59	65	57	62	66	72	64	66	17	93	49

Although they suffered a scare along the way, Costa Rica safely negotiated their first round of 2014 FIFA World Cup qualifying. At one stage El Salvador had threatened to take the second qualifying spot alongside Mexico for the final group stage. A draw at home in their opening group match against El Salvador in San Jose meant the Costa Ricans were on the back foot for much of the four month campaign but salvaged the situation with an excellent 1-0 win in the return in San Salvador to clinch their place in the final hexagonal. At home Herediano were the club with the best record in 2012 and they won the first of the two championships played during the course of the year, beating Santos 6-3 on aggregate in the final. For the best part of seventy years Herediano had been Costa Rica's most successful club but it was their first title since 1993 - a 19 year drought that saw both Saprissa and Alajuelense overtake them in the overall rankings. Herediano then made it through to the final of the championship played in the second half of the year but against Alajuelense they reverted to type, losing 3-2 on aggregate to take their more accustomed role as runners-up. For Alajuelense it took them to a total of 28 titles, just one short of the record held by Deportivo Saprissa.

CONCACAF GOLD CUP RECORD
1991 SF 3p **1993** SF **1996** DNQ **1998** r1 **2000** QF **2002** F r/u **2003** SF 4p **2005** QF **2007** QF **2009** SF **2011** QF

FEDERACION COSTARRICENSE DE FUTBOL (FEDEFUTBOL)

Radial Santa Ana Belen,
500 mts Este del cruce de la Panasonic,
San José 670-1000
☎ +506 25891450
+506 25891457
ejecutivo@fedefutbol.com
www.fedefutbol.org
FA 1921 CON 1962 FIFA 1927
P Eduardo Li
GS Lidia Rojas

THE STADIA
2014 FIFA World Cup Stadia
Estadio Nacional
San José   35 093
Other Main Stadia
Estadio Ricardo Saprissa
San José   23 112
Estadio Alejandro Morera Soto
Alajuela   17 895
Estadio Fello Meza
Cartago   13 500

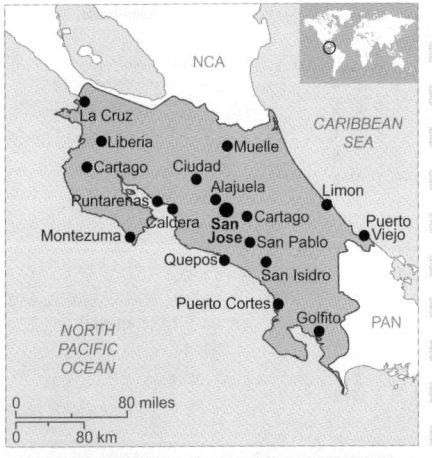

MAJOR CITIES/TOWNS
		Population
1	San José	345 447
2	San Francisco	70 200
3	Limón	66 620
4	Liberia	54 852
5	Alajuela	49 930
6	Paraíso	48 400
7	San Isidro	39 833
8	Desamparados	39 767
9	Curridabat	37 263
10	Puntarenas	37 080
11	San Vicente	35 624
12	San José	33 913
13	Purral	32 125
14	Turrialba	31 987
15	Mercedes	31 713
16	San Rafael Abajo	31 251
17	San Rafael	31 023
18	San Miguel	30 834
19	Aguacaliente	30 547

REPUBLICA DE COSTA RICA • REPUBLIC OF COSTA RICA

Capital	San José	Population	4 253 877 (123)	% in cities	63%
GDP per capita	$11 500 (95)	Area km²	51 100 km² (129)	GMT + / -	-6
Neighbours (km)	Nicaragua 309, Panama 330 • Coast 1290				

RECENT INTERNATIONAL MATCHES PLAYED BY COSTA RICA

2011	Opponents	Score	Venue	Comp	Scorers	Att	Referee
14-01	Honduras	D 1-1	Panama City	UCr1	Victor Nunez [42]	6 000	Garcia MEX
16-01	Guatemala	W 2-0	Panama City	UCr1	Marcos Urena 2 [48 81]	1 500	Moreno PAN
21-01	Panama	D 1-1	Panama City	UCsf	Celso Borges [67], W 4-2p	10 000	Aguilar SLV
23-01	Honduras	L 1-2	Panama City	UCf	Marcos Urena [73]	2 000	Lopez GUA
9-02	Venezuela	D 2-2	Puerto La Cruz	Fr	Bryan Oviedo [7], Marcos Urena [70]	15 000	Gambeta PER
26-03	China PR	D 2-2	San Jose	Fr	Alvaro Saborio [38], Randall Brenes [45]	35 000	Moreno PAN
29-03	Argentina	D 0-0	San Jose	Fr		35 000	Rodriguez.M MEX
5-06	Cuba	W 5-0	Arlington	GCr1	Marco Urena 2 [6 46], Alvaro Saborio [41], Heiner Mora [47], Christian Bolanos [71]	80 108	Moreno PAN
9-06	El Salvador	D 1-1	Charlotte	GCr1	Randall Brenes [95+]	46 012	Marrufo USA
12-06	Mexico	L 1-4	Chicago	GCr1	Marco Urena [69]	62 000	Moreno PAN
18-06	Honduras	D 1-1	New York	GCqf	Dennis Marshall [56], L 2-4p	78 807	Moreno PAN
2-07	Colombia	L 0-1	Jujuy	CAr1		23 500	Osses CHI
7-07	Bolivia	W 2-0	Jujuy	CAr1	Josue Martinez [59], Joel Campbell [78]	23 000	Vera ECU
11-07	Argentina	L 0-3	Cordoba	CAr1		57 000	Rivera PER
10-08	Ecuador	L 0-2	San Jose	Fr		18 000	Aguilar SLV
2-09	USA	W 1-0	Carson	Fr	Rodney Wallace [65]	15 798	Molina HON
6-09	Ecuador	L 0-4	Quito	Fr		6 000	Roldan COL
7-10	Brazil	L 0-1	San Jose	Fr		25 000	Lopez GUA
11-11	Panama	L 0-2	Panama City	Fr		5 000	Garcia MEX
15-11	Spain	D 2-2	San Jose	Fr	Randall Brenes [30], Joel Campbell [41]	25 000	Navarro CAN
11-12	Cuba	D 1-1	Havana	Fr	Kenny Cunningham [90]	10 000	Lopez GUA
22-12	Venezuela	W 2-0	Barquisimeto	Fr	Rodney Wallace [42], Jose Miguel Cubero [54]	33 000	Angela ARU
2012							
29-02	Wales	W 1-0	Cardiff	Fr	Joel Campbell [7]	23 193	Webb ENG
21-03	Jamaica	D 0-0	Kingston	Fr		10 000	Gantar CAN
11-04	Honduras	D 1-1	San Jose	Fr	Olman Vargas [49]	12 000	Geiger USA
25-05	Guatemala	W 3-2	San Jose	Fr	OG [24], Alvaro Sanchez [35], Giancarlo Gonzalez [67]	4 000	Penaloza MEX
1-06	Guatemala	L 0-1	Guatemala City	Fr		2 000	Castro HON
8-06	El Salvador	D 2-2	San Jose	WCq	Alvaro Saborio [10], Joel Campbell [15]	23 701	Lopez GUA
12-06	Guyana	W 4-0	Georgetown	WCq	Alvaro Saborio 3 [20 26 52], Joel Campbell [72]	11 000	Brea CUB
15-08	Peru	L 0-1	San Jose	Fr		9 000	Castro HON
7-09	Mexico	L 0-2	San Jose	WCq		32 500	Moreno PAN
11-09	Mexico	L 0-1	Mexico City	WCq		44 007	Campbell JAM
12-10	El Salvador	W 1-0	San Salvador	WCq	Jose Cubero [31]	35 082	Geiger USA
16-10	Guyana	W 7-0	San Jose	WCq	Randall Brenes 2 [10 48], Cristian Gamboa [14], Alvaro Saborio 2 [51p 77], Cristian Bolanos [61], Celso Borges [70]	27 500	Rodriguez HON
14-11	Bolivia	D 1-1	Santa Cruz	Fr	Joel Campbell [72]	10 000	Henrique BRA

Fr = Friendly match • UC = UNCAF Cup/Copa Centroamericana • GC = CONCACAF Gold Cup • WC = FIFA World Cup
q = qualifier • r1 = first round group • qf = quarter-finals

COSTA RICA NATIONAL TEAM HISTORICAL RECORDS

Caps
135 - Walter Centeno 1995-2009 • 126 - Luis Marin 1993-2006 • 111 - Rolando Fonseca 1992-2008 • 109 - Mauricio Solis 1993-2006 • 99 - Harold Wallace 1995-2009 • 91 - Ronald Gomez 1993-2008 • 89 - Hernan Medford 1987-2002 • 80 - Alvaro Saborio 2002- • 76 - Erick Lonnis 1992-2002 & Wilmer Lopez 1995-2003 • 75 - Oscar Ramirez 1985-97

Goals
47 - Rolando Fonseca 1992-2008 • 45 - Paulo Wanchope 1996-2008 • 30 - Alvaro Saborio 2002- • 27 - Juan Ulloa 1955-70 • 24 - Walter Centeno 1995-2009 & Ronald Gomez 1993-2008 • 23 - Jorge Monge 1954-68 • 18 - Hernan Medford 1987-2002 • 15 - Rafael Madrigal • 14 - Rodolfo Herrera • 12 - Roy Saenz

Coaches
For Costa Rica coaches pre 1990 see Oliver's Almanack 2012 • Bora Milutinovic SRB 1990 • Rolando Villalobos 1991-92 • Hector Nunez URU 1992 • Juan Jose Gamez 1993 • Toribio Rojas 1993-95 • Ignacio Nunez 1995 • Valdeir Viera BRA 1996 • Horacio Cordero ARG 1997 • Juan Hernandez 1997 • Rolando Villalobos 1998 • Francisco Maturana COL 1999 • Marvin Rodriguez 1999-2000 • Gilson Siqueira Nunes BRA 2000 • Alexandre Guimaraes BRA 2001-02 • Rodrigo Kenton 2002 • Steve Sampson USA 2002-04 • Jorge Luis Pinto COL 2004-05 • Alexandre Guimaraes BRA 2005-06 • Hernan Medford 2006-08 • Rodrigo Kenton 2008-09 • Rene Simoes BRA 2009 • Ronald Gonzalez 2009-10 • Ricardo La Volpe ARG 2010-11 • Ronald Brenes 2011 • Jorge Luis Pinto COL 2011-

COSTA RICA 2011-12

PRIMERA DIVISION
TORNEO CLAUSURA VERANO

	Pl	W	D	L	F	A	Pts	P. Zeledón	Santos	Saprissa	Herediano	Alajuelense	Cartaginés	San Carlos	Belén	Puntarenas	Limon	Brujas
AD Pérez Zeledón †	20	11	4	5	38	25	37		3-1	1-0	0-0	2-4	2-3	2-0	2-1	3-2	1-0	4-1
Santos de Guápiles †	20	12	1	7	32	28	37	2-1		0-1	1-0	3-1	3-2	1-3	2-0	1-2	2-1	2-0
Deportivo Saprissa †	20	10	6	4	38	23	36	2-3	3-0		1-3	0-2	4-0	1-1	0-0	3-1	2-2	1-0
CS Herediano †	20	10	4	6	33	20	34	1-1	1-2	0-0		2-3	3-0	2-0	2-1	2-0	3-2	4-0
LD Alajuelense	20	10	3	7	34	25	33	1-1	2-0	1-2	2-0		0-1	1-2	1-1	2-0	3-1	2-0
CS Cartaginés	20	10	3	7	33	30	33	0-2	5-1	1-3	2-1	2-2		0-0	3-2	3-2	3-0	2-0
San Carlos	20	8	5	7	23	25	29	2-1	1-3	3-4	1-0	3-1	1-3		0-3	2-1	0-1	1-0
AD Belén	20	7	7	6	35	28	28	2-1	1-1	2-4	3-3	4-2	1-0	1-1		2-0	7-0	1-0
Puntarenas FC	20	5	3	12	23	35	18	0-3	0-2	1-1	1-2	1-0	2-2	0-0	4-1		3-1	2-1
Limon FC	20	4	4	12	18	37	16	2-2	1-2	1-1	0-2	0-2	1-0	0-1	0-0	2-0		3-2
Brujas FC ‡	20	2	2	16	12	42	8	1-3	0-3	1-5	0-2	0-2	0-1	1-1	2-2	2-1	1-0	

15/01/2012 - 19/05/2012 • † Qualified for the play-off semi-finals • ‡ Relegation play-off
Relegation play-off: Brujas FC 2-2 0-2 **Carmelita**. Brujas FC relegated

CLAUSURA VERANO PLAY-OFFS

Semi-finals

CS Herediano *	1	2
AD Pérez Zeledón	1	0

Deportivo Saprissa *	1	0
Santos de Guápiles ‡	0	1

Finals

CS Herediano *	4	2
Santos de Guápiles	2	1

‡ Qualified on season record
* Home team in 1st leg

CLAUSURA VERANO FINAL 1ST LEG
Eladio Cordero, Heredia, 12-05-2012, Ref: Walter Quesada

CS Herediano	4	Cubero [46], Nunez 2 [70 86], Cancela [76]
Santos	2	

HEREDIANO
Leonel **MOREIRA** - Pablo **SALAZAR**, Cristian **MONTERO**, Whylon **FRANCIS** (Francisco **CALVO** 65) - Jose **CANCELA**, Oscar **ROJAS**, Oscar **GRANADOS** (Minor **DIAZ** 46), Jose **CUBERO**, Ismael **GOMEZ**• (Yosimar **ARIAS** 61) - Jorge **BARBOSA**, Victor **NUNEZ**. Tr: Odir **JACQUES**

SANTOS
Johnny **AGUILAR** - Randall **PORRAS**, Mario **VIQUEZ** (Crisanto **ESQUIVEL** 80), Javier **LOAIZA** - Kevin **FAJARDO**, Juan **MADRIGAL**, Eduardo **TOURBORNE**, Diego **GOMEZ**, Osvaldo **RODRIGUEZ** - Erick **SCOTT** (Maximiliano **ARDETTI** 90), Christhian **LAGOS**• (Jonathan **MOYA** 65). Tr: Eduardo **MENDEZ**

CLAUSURA VERANO FINAL 2ND LEG
Ebal Aguilar, Guápiles, 19-05-2012, Ref: Rafael Vega

Santos	1	Lagos [35]
CS Herediano	2	Cancela [43], Nunez [90]

SANTOS
Mainor **ALVAREZ** - Randall **PORRAS**•, Esteban **MAITLAND**, Maximiliano **ARDETTI**• (Jonathan **MOYA** 68), Javier **LOAIZA**• - Crisanto **ESQUIVEL** (Johan **VENEGAS**• 58), Juan **MADRIGAL**, Eduardo **TOURBORNE**, Osvaldo **RODRIGUEZ**••♦[86] - Erick **SCOTT** (Kenneth **DIXON** 78), Christhian **LAGOS**. Tr: Eduardo **MENDEZ**

HEREDIANO
Leonel **MOREIRA** - Pablo **SALAZAR**, Cristian **MONTERO** (Carlos **HERNANDEZ** 79), Francisco **CALVO**•, Whylon **FRANCIS** - Jose **CANCELA**, Oscar **ROJAS**, Jose **CUBERO** - Jorge **BARBOSA** (Yosimar **ARIAS** 83), Victor **NUNEZ**•, Minor **DIAZ** (Oscar **GRANADOS** 60). Tr: Odir **JACQUES**

COSTA RICA 2011-12
AGGREGATE TABLE

	Pl	W	D	L	F	A	Pts
CS Herediano	40	21	10	9	72	39	73
Deportivo Saprissa	40	19	14	7	72	44	71
LD Alajuelense	40	21	7	12	72	48	70
AD Pérez Zeledón	40	18	9	13	68	54	63
CS Cartaginés	40	17	12	11	64	57	63
Santos de Guápiles	40	18	8	14	58	55	62
San Carlos	40	13	11	16	45	59	50
AD Belén	40	11	14	15	55	57	47
Puntarenas FC	40	12	10	18	50	69	46
Limon FC	40	9	8	23	37	67	35
Brujas FC	40	6	7	27	32	76	25

Relegation play-off: Brujas FC 2-2 0-2 **Carmelita**

COSTA RICA 2012-13

PRIMERA DIVISION — TORNEO APERTURA INVIERNO

	Pl	W	D	L	F	A	Pts	Alajuelense	Saprissa	Herediano	Limon	Santos	Uruguay	P. Zeledón	Belén	Carmelita	Puntarenas	Cartaginés	San Carlos
LD Alajuelense †	22	13	5	4	36	22	44		2-3	0-3	0-0	2-1	2-0	2 1	1-0	2-0	3-1	1-0	1-1
Deportivo Saprissa ‡	22	13	4	5	41	22	43	2-2		2-1	2-0	0-2	2-0	3-1	0-2	2-0	2-1	2-0	2-1
CS Herediano †	22	10	7	5	37	25	37	2-4	2-1		2-0	2-0	2-0	2-1	1-1	0-0	4-1	1-1	1-0
Limon FC †	22	9	6	7	31	30	33	1-0	1-0	3-3		3-2	5-1	2-1	1-1	2-1	0-1	1-2	2-1
Santos de Guápiles	22	9	5	8	39	37	32	0-2	2-2	2-1	3-0		1-1	2-1	3-0	1-2	2-2	3-2	5-1
CS Uruguay	22	9	3	10	25	31	30	1-2	0-4	4-3	0-0	1-0		3-0	0-1	0-1	2-1	1-2	1-1
AD Pérez Zeledón	22	8	4	10	35	31	28	0-1	1-2	2-2	4-3	4-1	2-1		0-1	6-0	1-1	1-0	2-1
AD Belén	22	7	7	8	23	27	28	1-3	1-0	0-0	1-2	3-3	0-2	2-1		1-0	0-0	1-0	2-3
AD Carmelita	22	6	7	9	21	33	25	0-3	1-1	0-0	1-1	2-5	1-2	1-1	2-2		0-1	0-0	4-2
Puntarenas FC	22	5	7	10	22	34	22	2-2	0-0	0-2	2-1	0-0	1-2	0-2	3-2	0-1		1-0	3-3
CS Cartaginés	22	5	6	11	24	25	21	1-1	1-3	2-3	0-1	6-0	0-1	0-0	1-1	1-2	3-1		0-0
San Carlos	22	5	5	12	24	41	20	2-0	1-6	1-0	2-2	0-1	0-2	1-3	1-0	0-2	2-0	0-2	

25/07/2012 - 23/12/2012 • † Qualified for the play-off semi-finals

APERTURA INVIERNO PLAY-OFFS

Semi-finals

LD Alajuelense	1	0
Limon FC *	0	0

Deportivo Saprissa	1	0
CS Herediano *	1	1

Finals

LD Alajuelense	2	1
CS Herediano *	1	1

* Home team in 1st leg

APERTURA INVIERNO FINAL 1ST LEG

Eladio Cordero, Heredia, 17-12-2012, Ref: Ricardo Cerdas

CS Herediano	1	Montero 68
LD Alajuelense	2	Guevara 25, Davis 30

HEREDIANO

Leonel **MOREIRA** - Marvin **OBANDO**, Pablo **SALAZAR**, Cristian **MONTERO**♦89, Mauricio **NUNEZ** - Esteban **RAMIREZ** (Marvin **ANGULO** 46), Oscar **GRANADOS**♦59, Jose **CUBERO** (Ismael **GOMEZ** 56) - Jose **SANCHEZ**, Elias **AGUILAR**, Minor **DIAZ** (Enoc **PEREZ** 46). Tr: Claudio **JARA**

ALAJUELENSE

Patrick **PEMBERTON**• - Elias **PALMA**, Jhonny **ACOSTA**, Cristopher **MENESES**• - Jose **SALVATIERRA**, Alvaro **SANCHEZ** (Anderson **ANDRADE** 56), Jorge **DAVIS**, Allen **GUEVARA** (Juan **GUZMAN** 77), Pablo **GABAS**, Luis **VALLE** - Armando **ALONSO**••♦52. Tr: Oscar **RAMIREZ**

APERTURA INVIERNO FINAL 2ND LEG

Alejandro Soto, Alajuela, 22-12-2012, Ref: Walter Quesada

LD Alajuelense	1	Sanchez 111
CS Herediano	1	Gomez 88p

ALAJUELENSE

Patrick **PEMBERTON** - Christian **OVIEDO** (Juan **GUZMAN**• 58), Elias **PALMA**, Jhonny **ACOSTA**•, Cristopher **MENESES** - Jose **SALVATIERRA**•, Jorge **DAVIS** (Anderson **ANDRADE** 73), Allen **GUEVARA** (Alvaro **SANCHEZ**• 96), Pablo **GABAS**•, Luis **VALLE** - Diego **CALVO**. Tr: Oscar **RAMIREZ**

HEREDIANO

Leonel **MOREIRA** - Marvin **OBANDO**, Pablo **SALAZAR**, Whylon **FRANCIS**•, Jose **GARRO**• - Marvin **ANGULO** (Diego **PAIS** 82), Jose **CUBERO**, Carlos **HERNANDEZ** (Esteban **RAMIREZ** 71) - Elias **AGUILAR** (Ismael **GOMEZ** 56), Yendrick **RUIZ**, Enoc **PEREZ**. Tr: Claudio **JARA**

MEDALS TABLE

		Overall G S B	League G S B	CON'CAF G S B	City
1	Deportivo Saprissa	32 17 8	**29** 15 1	3 2 7	San José
2	Liga Deportiva Alajuelense	30 23 13	28 20 9	2 3 4	Alajuela
3	CS Herediano	22 16 12	22 16 11	1	Heredia
4	CS La Libertad	6 7 4	6 7 4		San José
5	CS Cartaginés	4 10 7	3 10 7	1	Cartago
6	Orión FC	2 6 7	2 6 7		
7	Municipal Puntarenas	1 3 1	1 3 1		Puntarenas
8	CS Uruguay	1 1	1 1		Coronado
9	Universidad de Costa Rica	1 3	1 3		San José
10	Orión FC	1	1		San José
	AD Carmelita	1	1		Alajuela
	Liberia Mia	1	1		Liberia

CRO – CROATIA

FIFA/COCA-COLA WORLD RANKING

'93	'94	'95	'96	'97	'98	'99	'00	'01	'02	'03	'04	'05	'06	'07	'08	'09	'10	'11	'12
122	62	41	24	19	4	9	18	19	32	20	23	20	15	10	7	10	10	8	10

2012

Jan	Feb	Mar	Apr	May	Jun	Jul	Aug	Sep	Oct	Nov	Dec	High	Low	Av
8	9	10	8	8	8	9	9	9	11	10	10	3	125	23

Croatia had the great misfortune to be drawn in the same Euro 2012 group as the eventual finalists Spain and Italy and had luck been on their side, the outcome of the tournament could have been very different. Having beaten the Irish and drawn with Italy, Slaven Bilic's side lost their final group match 1-0 to the Spanish. Ivan Rakitic spurned a glorious chance to give the Croatians a second-half lead and there were strong claims for a penalty near the end, but they were caught on the break two minutes from time and bowed out. After the tournament Bilic stood down and was replaced by Igor Stimac who got the 2014 FIFA World Cup qualifying campaign off to a steady start in a potentially difficult group with fierce rivals Serbia and in-form Belgium. In club football Dinamo Zagreb were once again totally dominant, losing just once all season as they collected yet another league and cup double. Their one defeat came at the hands of Zadar in the league, but they finished 21 points ahead of second placed Hajduk Split whose last championship is becoming something of a distant memory. For Dinamo it was their seventh in a row. In the cup final they faced Osijek but despite being held to a 0-0 draw away in the first leg, they won the return 3-1 to secure their fifth double in just six seasons.

UEFA EUROPEAN CHAMPIONSHIP RECORD

1960-1992 DNE (part of Yugoslavia) **1996** 7 QF **2000** DNQ **2004** 13 r1 **2008** 5 QF **2012** 10 r1

CROATIAN FOOTBALL FEDERATION (HNS)

Rusanova 13,
Zagreb 10 000

+385 1 2361555
+385 1 2441501
info@hns-cff.hr
www.hns-cff.hr

FA 1912 CON 1993 FIFA 1992
P Vlatko Markovic
GS Zorislav Srebric

THE STADIA

2014 FIFA World Cup Stadia

Stadion Maksimir
Zagreb   37 168

Stadion Gradski Vrt
Osijek   20 050

Other Main Stadia

Stadion Poljud
Split   34 448

Stadion Kantrida
Rijeka   10 155

Stadion Aldo Drozina
Pula   9 078

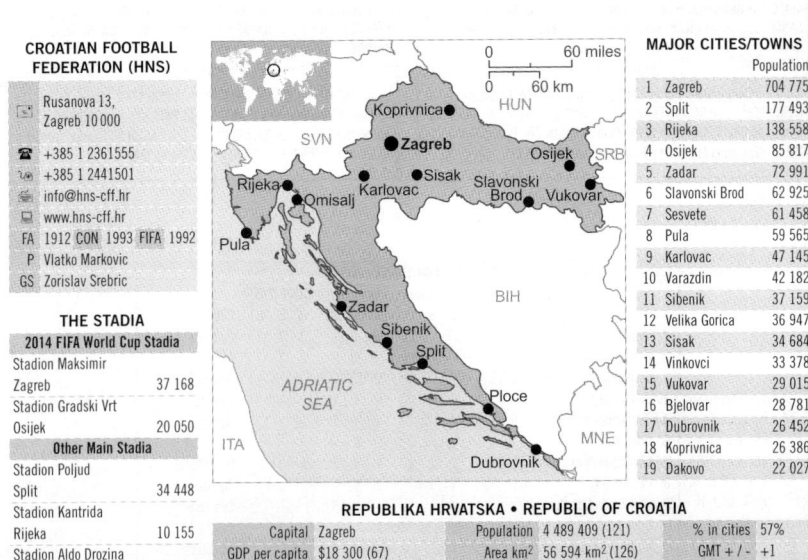

MAJOR CITIES/TOWNS

		Population
1	Zagreb	704 775
2	Split	177 493
3	Rijeka	138 558
4	Osijek	85 817
5	Zadar	72 991
6	Slavonski Brod	62 925
7	Sesvete	61 458
8	Pula	59 565
9	Karlovac	47 145
10	Varazdin	42 182
11	Sibenik	37 159
12	Velika Gorica	36 947
13	Sisak	34 684
14	Vinkovci	33 378
15	Vukovar	29 015
16	Bjelovar	28 781
17	Dubrovnik	26 452
18	Koprivnica	26 386
19	Dakovo	22 027

REPUBLIKA HRVATSKA • REPUBLIC OF CROATIA

Capital Zagreb   Population 4 489 409 (121)   % in cities 57%
GDP per capita $18 300 (67)   Area km² 56 594 km² (126)   GMT +/- +1
Neighbours (km) Bosnia-Herzegovina 932, Hungary 329, Serbia 241, Montenegro 25, Slovenia 455 • Coast 5835

RECENT INTERNATIONAL MATCHES PLAYED BY CROATIA

2009	Opponents	Score	Venue	Comp	Scorers	Att	Referee
11-02	Romania	W 2-1	Bucharest	Fr	Rakitic 28, Kranjcar 75	9 000	Balaj ROU
1-04	Andorra	W 2-0	Andorra La Vella	WCq	Klasnic 15, Eduardo 36	1 100	Trattou CYP
6-06	Ukraine	D 2-2	Zagreb	WCq	Petric 2, Modric 68	32 073	Hauge NOR
12-08	Belarus	W 3-1	Minsk	WCq	Olic 2 22 83, Eduardo 69	21 651	Brych GER
5-09	Belarus	W 1-0	Zagreb	WCq	Rakitic 24	25 628	Plautz AUT
9-09	England	L 1-5	London	WCq	Eduardo 71	87 319	Undiano ESP
8-10	Qatar	W 3-2	Rijeka	Fr	Corluka 7, Klasnic 11, Jelavic 90	5 000	Balaj ROU
14-10	Kazakhstan	W 2-1	Astana	WCq	Vukojevic 10, Kranjcar 93+	10 250	Circhetta SUI
14-11	Liechtenstein	W 5-0	Vinkovci	Fr	Bilic 2 1 48, Srna 10, Eduardo 2 24 46	10 000	Fabian HUN
2010							
19-05	Austria	W 1-0	Klagenfurt	Fr	Bilic 86	20 000	Blom NED
23-05	Wales	W 2-0	Osijek	Fr	Rakitic 45, Gabric 81	15 000	Vincic SVN
26-05	Estonia	D 0-0	Tallinn	Fr		3 000	Svendsen DEN
11-08	Slovakia	D 1-1	Bratislava	Fr	Jelavic 54	6 366	Matejek CZE
3-09	Latvia	W 3-0	Riga	ECq	Petric 43, Olic 51, Srna 82	7 600	Kuipers NED
7-09	Greece	D 0-0	Zagreb	ECq		24 399	Larsen DEN
9-10	Israel	W 2-1	Tel Aviv	ECq	Kranjcar 2 36p 41	33 421	Stark GER
12-10	Norway	W 2-1	Zagreb	Fr	Mandzukic 35, Kranjcar 50	3 000	Skomina SVN
17-11	Malta	W 3-0	Zagreb	ECq	Kranjcar 2 18 42, Kalinic 81	9 000	Gomes POR
2011							
9-02	Czech Republic	W 4-2	Pula	Fr	Eduardo 10, Kalinic 2 13 61, Ilicevic 75	9 500	Orsato ITA
26-03	Georgia	L 0-1	Tbilisi	ECq		55 000	Tagliavento ITA
29-03	France	D 0-0	Paris	Fr		60 000	Kelly IRL
3-06	Georgia	W 2-1	Split	ECq	Mandzukic 76, Kalinic 78	28 000	Johannesson SWE
10-08	Republic of Ireland	D 0-0	Dublin	Fr		20 179	Hagen NOR
2-09	Malta	W 3-1	Ta'Qali	ECq	Vukojevic 11, Badelj 32, Lovren 68	6 150	Chapron FRA
6-09	Israel	W 3-1	Zagreb	ECq	Modric 47, Eduardo 2 55 57	13 688	Velasco ESP
7-10	Greece	L 0-2	Piaeus	ECq		27 200	Webb ENG
11-10	Latvia	W 2-0	Rijeka	ECq	Eduardo 66, Mandzukic 72	8 370	Gautier FRA
11-11	Turkey	W 3-0	Istanbul	ECpo	Olic 2, Mandzukic 32, Corluka 51	42 863	Brych GER
15-11	Turkey	D 0-0	Zagreb	ECpo		26 371	Proenca POR
2012							
29-02	Sweden	L 1-3	Zagreb	Fr	OG 44	10 000	Zganec SVN
25-05	Estonia	W 3-1	Pula	Fr	Corluka 16, Kalinic 20, Vukojevic 81	8 000	Fabian HUN
2-06	Norway	D 1-1	Oslo	Fr	Eduardo 79	14 208	Karasev RUS
10-06	Republic of Ireland	W 3-1	Poznan	ECr1	Mandzukic 2 3 49, Jelavic 43	43 200	Kuipers NED
14-06	Italy	D 1-1	Poznan	ECr1	Mandzukic 72	37 096	Webb ENG
18-06	Spain	L 0-1	Gdansk	ECr1		38 371	Stark GER
15-08	Switzerland	L 2-4	Split	Fr	Eduardo 2 20 64	12 000	Damato ITA
7-09	FYR Macedonia	W 1-0	Zagreb	WCq	Jelavic 69	13 883	Yefet ISR
11-09	Belgium	D 1-1	Brussels	WCq	Perisic 6	39 987	Undiano ESP
12-10	FYR Macedonia	W 2-1	Skopje	WCq	Corluka 33, Rakitic 60	25 230	Rasmussen DEN
16-10	Wales	W 2-0	Osijek	WCq	Mandzukic 27, Eduardo 57	17 500	Tudor ROU

Fr = Friendly match • EC = UEFA EURO 2008/12 • WC = FIFA World Cup • q = qualifier • r1 = first round group • qf = quarter-final

CROATIA NATIONAL TEAM HISTORICAL RECORDS

Caps
100 - Dario Simic 1996-2008 • 99 - Josip Simunic 2001-; Darijo Srna 2002- & Stipe Pletikosa 1999- • 84 - Robert Kovac 1999-2009 • 83 - Niko Kovac 1996-2008 • 81 - Robert Jarni 1990-2002 • 76 - Ivica Olic 2002- & Niko Kranjcar 2004- • 69 - Davor Suker 1990-2002 • 62 - Aljosa Asanovic 1990-2000 & Luka Modric 2006- • 61 - Zvonimir Soldo 1994-2002 • 60 - Vedran Corluka 2006-

Goals
45 - Davor Suker 1990-2002 • 26 - Eduardo da Silva 2004- • 19 - Darijo Srna 2002- • 15 - Goran Vlaovic 1992-2002; Niko Kranjcar 2004- & Ivica Olic 2002- • 14 - Niko Kovac 1996-2008 • 12 - Zvonimir Boban 1990-99; Ivan Klasnic 2004-; Mladen Petric 2001- & Franjo Wolfl 1940-44 • 10 - Bosko Balaban 2000-07; Alen Boksic 1993-2002 & Robert Prosinecki 1993-2002

Coaches
Drazan Jerkovic 1990-91 • Stanko Poklepovic 1992 • Vlatko Markovic 1993 • Miroslav Blazevic 1994-2000 • Mirko Jozic 2000-02 • Otto Baric 2002-04 • Zlatko Kranjcar 2004-06 • Slaven Bilic 2006-12 • Igor Stimac 2012-

CROATIA 2011-12

MAXTV PRVA HNL (1)

	Pl	W	D	L	F	A	Pts	Dinamo	Hajduk	Slaven	Radniki	Cibalia	Zagreb	Lokomotiva	Osijek	Istra	Zadar	Inter	Rijeka	Lucko	Sibenik	Karlovac	Varazdin
Dinamo Zagreb †	30	23	6	1	73	11	75		2-1	2-0	0-0	2-0	1-0	6-0	1-0	4-1	1-1	2-0	2-0	1-0	2-1	5-0	7-0
Hajduk Split ‡	30	16	6	8	50	24	54	1-1		4-1	0-0	1-0	4-0	0-1	3-1	1-1	1-0	1-2	2-1	1-2	2-1	1-0	3-0
Slaven B. Koprivnica ‡	30	14	10	6	41	27	52	0-2	1-1		2-0	0-1	1-0	3-1	2-0	2-2	2-0	3-2	1-0	1-1	1-0	3-0	1-0
Radniki Split	30	14	8	8	43	32	50	0-3	1-1	1-1		1-1	2-0	1-0	2-2	3-1	3-1	1-0	2-0	1-1	2-0	3-1	2-2
Cibalia Vinkovci	30	13	6	11	35	35	45	2-2	0-2	1-4	2-1		0-2	1-0	0-1	1-0	2-0	0-1	2-0	1-3	5-1	2-0	**3-0**
NK Zagreb	30	13	6	11	36	42	45	0-3	2-4	1-1	0-2	1-1		0-0	2-2	2-1	2-0	2-1	2-1	1-0	1-1	3-0	1-0
Lokomotiva Zagreb	30	12	8	10	33	33	44	1-2	1-0	0-0	1-0	1-2	2-3		1-4	0-2	3-0	2-0	0-0	2-2	2-0	2-1	1-0
NK Osijek ‡	30	11	10	9	45	38	43	0-4	2-1	2-0	3-2	1-2	4-0	1-1		2-1	5-0	1-0	1-1	2-0	0-0	0-1	2-2
Istra Pula	30	11	9	10	35	33	42	0-2	0-3	2-1	2-0	3-0	0-1	2-1	0-1		1-1	2-1	0-0	2-0	2-1	2-0	2-1
NK Zadar	30	11	7	12	29	44	40	2-1	1-0	1-3	2-1	1-0	1-0	0-3	2-1	0-0		2-1	4-4	1-0	0-1	2-2	2-0
Inter Zapresic	30	11	5	14	33	33	38	0-0	0-1	0-1	0-3	1-1	3-1	1-1	2-0	1-1	2-0		1-0	1-1	2-0	4-0	**3-0**
NK Rijeka	30	9	11	10	29	29	38	1-1	0-3	1-1	2-0	1-1	0-1	0-0	0-1	1-0			1-0	1-0	**3-0**	1-0
NK Lucko	30	6	13	11	29	36	31	0-4	0-3	1-1	1-2	0-1	0-1	2-2	2-2	0-2	1-1	2-0	1-1		0-0	1-0	**3-0**
NK Sibenik	30	6	9	15	27	40	27	0-3	1-2	1-1	1-2	3-0	2-1	0-1	1-1	0-0	1-1	2-0	2-2	1-1		4-1	1-0
NK Karlovac	30	6	7	17	25	53	24	0-3	1-1	0-0	1-3	2-2	3-3	0-1	2-0	2-1	2-0	0-1	1-2	0-0	1-0		**3-0**
NK Varazdin	24	2	3	19	16	52	8	0-4	**0-3**	**0-3**	1-2	0-1	2-3	0-2	**0-3**	2-2	1-2	3-2	**0-3**	0-2	2-1	0-1	

23/07/2011 - 12/05/2012 • † Qualified for the UEFA Champions League • ‡ Qualified for the Europa League • Matches in bold awarded
Top scorers: **15** - Fatos **BECIRAJ** MNE, Dinamo • **12** - Ante **VUKUSIC**, Hajduk • **10** - Ivan **KRSTANOVIC**, Dinamo & Ivan **SANTINI**, Zadar

CROATIA 2011-12

DRUGA HNL (2)

	Pl	W	D	L	F	A	Pts	Dugopolje	Pomorac	Mosor	Vinogradar	Imotski	Rudes	Gorica	Hrvatski	Radnik	Junak	Solin	Marsonia	Medimurje	HASK	Croatia S'vete
NK Dugopolje	28	17	6	5	50	27	57		2-1	2-2	2-5	1-0	1-0	1-0	5-0	3-0	1-0	3-1	5-0	2-0	1-0	2-0
Pomorac Kostrena	28	18	2	8	63	30	56	1-2		0-1	3-0	5-1	2-1	4-1	3-2	1-0	1-0	2-1	3-1	7-1	3-0	4-0
Mosor Zrnovnica	28	15	7	6	36	16	52	0-2	2-1		3-1	0-0	2-0	1-0	3-0	0-1	0-0	1-2	1-1	4-0	0-0	2-0
Vinogradar Lokosin Dol	28	15	5	8	47	32	50	3-2	4-2	1-0		3-1	2-2	0-2	0-0	4-0	2-0	3-0	1-1	3-0	2-0	3-2
NK Imotski	28	11	9	8	26	21	42	0-1	0-1	0-0	1-0		1-1	1-0	1-0	2-0	1-1	1-0	3-0	1-1	2-1	1-0
Rudes Zagreb	28	11	8	9	42	33	41	1-1	2-1	1-0	2-1	1-3		1-1	2-1	1-0	1-1	0-0	4-0	3-0	3-2	0-1
HNK Gorica	28	10	10	8	27	24	40	3-2	2-0	0-0	0-0	1-0	1-0		0-0	0-0	1-1	0-1	1-0	0-0	2-1	1-1
Hrvatski Dragovoljac	28	10	10	8	36	37	40	4-1	0-6	2-1	1-2	0-0	2-0	2-1		1-1	1-2	2-0	2-0	2-2	2-1	1-1
Radnik Sesvete	28	10	9	9	34	31	39	0-0	2-1	1-2	1-1	0-0	1-1	1-1	0-0		0-2	2-1	5-0	3-0	3-1	1-0
Junak Sinj	28	10	9	9	29	27	39	1-0	0-0	0-1	1-0	0-1	1-2	0-0	2-1	2-4		1-4	1-0	0-0	4-2	2-0
NK Solin	28	10	5	13	35	45	35	0-1	0-2	2-1	2-0	0-0	0-7	2-1	1-1	2-2	1-4		3-1	3-1	1-0	3-1
Marsonia Slav'ski Brod	28	8	6	14	25	50	30	0-0	1-1	0-2	1-2	2-1	4-0	0-0	1-1	1-3	1-0	1-0		2-1	2-1	1-0
Medimurje Cakovec	28	5	7	16	31	60	22	1-1	1-2	1-3	1-2	0-3	3-2	4-1	0-3	1-0	0-0	3-3	5-0		1-2	4-1
HASK Zagreb	28	6	3	19	33	52	21	2-4	2-4	0-0	2-1	1-0	0-2	3-4	1-2	2-1	1-2	3-0	1-1	4-0		1-2
Croatia Sesvete §1	28	4	4	20	23	52	15	2-2	1-2	0-3	0-1	1-1	0-2	**0-3**	0-2	1-2	1-1	1-4	2-3	3-0	3-0	

19/08/2011 - 20/05/2012 • § = points deducted • Match in bold awarded • No teams promoted • Top scorer: **16** - Alen **GUC**, Dugopolje

MEDALS TABLE

		Overall			League			Cup		Europe			
		G	S	B	G	S	B	G	S	G	S	B	City
1	Dinamo Zagreb	26	7	2	**14**	3	2	**12**	4				Zagreb
2	Hajduk Split	11	16	1	6	12	1	5	4				Split
3	NK Rijeka	2	3	2		2	2	2	1				Rijeka
4	NK Zagreb	1	3	3	1	2	3		1				Zagreb
5	Inter Zapresic	1	1			1		1					Zapresic
6	NK Osijek	1	1	6			6	1	1				Osijek
7	Varteks Varazdin		6	3			3		6				Varazdin
8	Slaven Belupo		2	1		1	1		1				Koprivnica
	CROATIAN CLUBS IN YUGOSLAV FOOTBALL												
3	Hajduk Split	18	15	12	9	10	10	9	5		2		
4	Dinamo Zagreb	13	21	7	4	12	6	8	8	1	1	1	
6	Gradanski Zagreb	5	2	3	5	2	3						

HRVATSKOG NOGOMETNOG KUPA 2011-12

First Round

Dinamo Zagreb	5
NK Radoboj *	0
Hrvatski Dragovoljac	1
HASK Zagreb *	2
NK Varazdin	0 4p
Podravac Virje *	0 2p
Rudar Labin *	0
Istra Pula	1
Hajduk Split	5
Jadran Gunja *	1
NK Zadar *	1 8p
NK Karlovac	1 9p
Radniki Split *	5
Segesta Sisak	0
Mladost Petrinja *	1
NK Zagreb	7
Cibalia Vinkovci	3
Fruskogorac *	1
Pomorac Kostrena	1
Rudes Zagreb *	2
Slaven B. Koprivnica	4
Granicar Laze *	0
Konavljanin Citipi	0
Vinogradar Lokosin Dol *	1
NK Rijeka	2
BSK Bijelo Brdo *	1
Inter Zapresic	0
NK Vrbovec *	0
Radnik Sesvete *	2
NK Sibenik	0
NK Opatija *	0
NK Osijek	1

Round of 16

Dinamo Zagreb	4
HASK Zagreb *	0
NK Varazdin *	0
Istra Pula	1
Hajduk Split	3
NK Karlovac	2
Radniki Split	1
NK Zagreb *	2
Cibalia Vinkovci	1
Rudes Zagreb *	0
Slaven B. Koprivnica	1
Vinogradar Lokosin Dol *	2
NK Rijeka *	1
Inter Zapresic	0
Radnik Sesvete	1
NK Osijek *	2

Quarter-finals

Dinamo Zagreb *	1 1 4p
Istra Pula	1 1 3p
Hajduk Split *	1 0 4p
NK Zagreb	0 1 5p
Cibalia Vinkovci *	2 1
Vinogradar Lokosin Dol	1 1
NK Rijeka *	1 0
NK Osijek	2 2

Semi-finals

Dinamo Zagreb *	1 2
NK Zagreb	1 1
Cibalia Vinkovci	0 2
NK Osijek *	3 1

Final

CUP FINAL 1ST LEG

Gradski vrt, Osijek, 2-05-2012
Att: 8000, Ref: Vlado Svilokos
Osijek - Ivan Vargic - Ivan Ibriks, Ivo Smoje● (c), Marko Leskovic, Branko Vrgoc - Hrvoje Kurtovic, Vedran Jugovic● (Domagoj Pusic 80), Tomislav Sorsa, Josip Lukacevic - Anton Maglica (Niksa Petrovic 91+), Antonio Perosevic (Zoran Kurzic 67). Tr: Stanko Mrsic.
Dinamo - Ivan Kelava - Domagoj Vida, Tonel, Josip Simunic (Sime Vrsaljko 80), Josip Pivaric● - Jerko Leko, Milan Badelj (c), Ivan Tomecak, Jorge Sammir● (Mehmed Alispahic 86), Mateo Kovacic - Ivan Krstanovic (Fatos Beqiraj 39). Tr: Ante Cacic

Dinamo Zagreb	0 3
NK Osijek ‡	0 1

CUP FINAL 2ND LEG

Maksimir, Zagreb, 9-05-2012
Att: 10 000, Ref: Ivan Bebek
Scorers - Kovacic [5], Beciraj [63], Ibanez [91+] for Dinamo, Vrsaljko OG [69] for Osijek
Dinamo - Ivan Kelava● - Domagoj Vida, Tonel●, Sime Vrsaljko, Josip Pivaric - Adrian Calello, Jerko Leko, Mateo Kovacic● (Nikola Pokrivac 65), Jorge Sammir (Luis Ibanez 79), Milan Badelj (c) - Fatos Beqiraj. Tr: Ante Cacic
Osijek - Ivan Vargic - Branko Vrgoc●, Marko Leskovic●, Ivan Ibriks, Ivo Smoje (c) - Josip Lukacevic, Hrvoje Kurtovic (Ivan Milicevic 65), Vedran Jugovic●, Zoran Kurzic (Niksa Petrovic 80), Tomislav Sorsa (Domagoj Pusic 65) - Anton Maglica. Tr: Stanko Mrsic

* Home team/home team in the first leg ‡ Qualified for the UEFA Europa League

CTA – CENTRAL AFRICAN REPUBLIC

FIFA/COCA-COLA WORLD RANKING

'93	'94	'95	'96	'97	'98	'99	'00	'01	'02	'03	'04	'05	'06	'07	'08	'09	'10	'11	'12
157	174	180	183	188	192	175	176	182	179	177	180	183	179	182	199	200	111	129	52

2012												High	Low	Av
Jan	Feb	Mar	Apr	May	Jun	Jul	Aug	Sep	Oct	Nov	Dec			
128	128	131	124	123	93	73	71	64	49	52	52	49	202	171

A four week stretch of heady success saw the Central African Republic catapult from one of African football's also-rans to a sensational top 50 place in the FIFA/Coca-Cola Rankings having started the year in 129th place. In June 'Les Fauves' managed to win a first-ever FIFA World Cup qualifier as Foxy Kethevoama scored both goals in a 2-0 win over Botswana in Bangui. Kethevoama, who plays his club soccer in Kazakhstan, netted a goal in each half for a famous win made even more unlikely by the fact coach Jules Accorsi had departed the month before accusing the country's sports ministry of being six months in arrears with his salary. Two weeks later there was an even more sensational result as a 10-man side upset Egypt 3-2 away in the 2013 African Cup of Nations qualifiers, a win that ended Egypt's unbeaten run at home in Nations Cup qualifying - a sequence of 38 matches stretching back to 1965. Egypt were expected to overturn the deficit in Bangui in the return but a 1-1 draw saw the Central African Republic through to the next round. There they won the first leg against Burkina Faso 1-0 in Bangui and looked to be going through to the finals in South Africa on away goals after trailing 2-1 in Ouagadougou, but a goal in the seventh minute of stoppage time by Burkina's Alain Traore saw them lose 3-1 to miss out on the finals.

CAF AFRICA CUP OF NATIONS RECORD
1957-1972 DNE 1974 DNQ 1976-1986 DNE 1988 DNQ 1990-1996 DNE 1998 DNQ 2000 DNE 2002-2004 DNQ 2006-2010 DNE 2012-13 DNQ

FEDERATION CENTRAFRICAINE DE FOOTBALL (RCA)
Avenue de Martyrs, Boite Postale 344, Bangui
☎ +236 70169828
✉ fedefoot60@yahoo.fr

FA 1961 CON 1965 FIFA 1963
P Edouard Patrice Ngaissona
GS Elie Delphin Feidangamo

THE STADIA
2014 FIFA World Cup Stadia
Stade Barthelemy Boganda
Bangui   20 000
Other Main Stadia
The Stade Barthelemy Boganda is the only major stadium in the country although there is a smaller stadium located next to it at the Universite Palais des Sports in Bangui

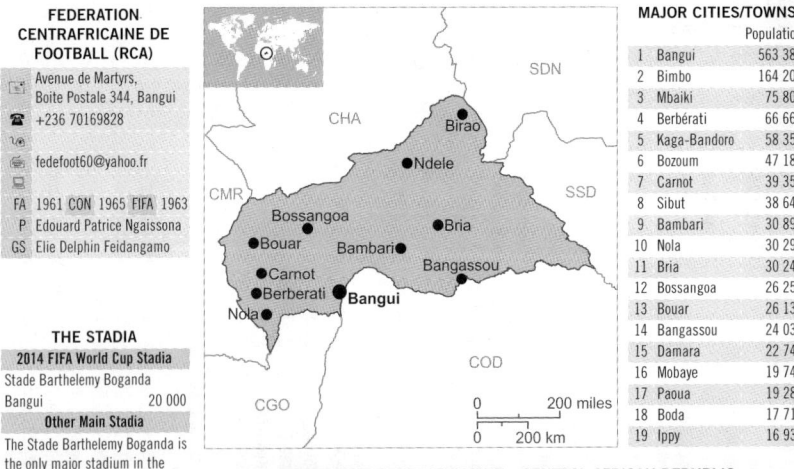

MAJOR CITIES/TOWNS
		Population
1	Bangui	563 383
2	Bimbo	164 208
3	Mbaiki	75 809
4	Berbérati	66 668
5	Kaga-Bandoro	58 353
6	Bozoum	47 187
7	Carnot	39 353
8	Sibut	38 643
9	Bambari	30 894
10	Nola	30 292
11	Bria	30 241
12	Bossangoa	26 259
13	Bouar	26 134
14	Bangassou	24 039
15	Damara	22 749
16	Mobaye	19 742
17	Paoua	19 282
18	Boda	17 719
19	Ippy	16 936

REPUBLIQUE CENTRAFRICAINE • CENTRAL AFRICAN REPUBLIC
Capital Bangui   Population 4 511 488 (120)   % in cities 39%
GDP per capita $700 (221)   Area km² 622 984 km² (44)   GMT +/- +1
Neighbours (km) Cameroon 797, Chad 1197, Congo DR 1577, Congo 467, Sudan 1165

RECENT INTERNATIONAL MATCHES PLAYED BY THE CENTRAL AFRICAN REPUBLIC

2003	Opponents		Score	Venue	Comp	Scorers	Att	Referee
4-05	Congo	L	1-2	Brazzaville	CNq	Igor Makita [84]		
8-06	Congo	D	0-0	Bangui	CNq			Hissene CHA
22-06	Mozambique	L	0-1	Maputo	CNq		15 000	
6-07	Burkina Faso	L	0-3	Bangui	CNq			
7-12	Cameroon	D	2-2	Brazzaville	CMr1	Armel Oroko [10], Sandjo [30]		Mbera GAB
9-12	Cameroon	W	1-0	Brazzaville	CMr1	Sandjo [85]		Mandioukouta CGO
11-12	Gabon	W	2-0	Brazzaville	CMsf			
13-12	Cameroon	L	2-3	Brazzaville	CMf	Armel Oroko [63], Cyr Destin [74]		Bansimba CGO

2004

No international matches played in 2004

2005								
3-02	Gabon	L	0-4	Libreville	CMr1			
5-02	Congo	L	0-1	Libreville	CMr1			

2006								
6-03	Cameroon	L	0-2	Malabo	CMr1			
8-03	Gabon	D	2-2	Malabo	CMr1			

2007								
6-03	Chad	L	2-3	N'Djamena	CMr1	Hilaire Momi [14], Greyanda Fiacre [34]		
8-03	Cameroon	D	0-0	N'Djamena	CMr1			
12-03	Congo	L	1-4	N'Djamena	CMsf	Zinda Romaric [15]		
16-03	Chad	L	0-1	N'Djamena	CM3p			

2008

No international matches played in 2008

2009

No international matches played in 2009

2010								
4-09	Morocco	D	0-0	Rabat	CNq			Coulibaly MLI
10-10	Algeria	W	2-0	Bangui	CNq	Charlie Dopekoulouyen [81], Hilaire Momi [85]		Carvalho ANG

2011								
26-03	Tanzania	L	1-2	Dar es Salaam	CNq	Vianney Mabide [13]		
29-05	Tunisia	L	0-3	Sousse	Fr			
5-06	Tanzania	W	2-1	Bangui	CNq	Hilaire Momi [38], Charlie Dopekoulouyen [89]		
10-08	Malta	L	1-2	Ta'Qali	Fr	Hilaire Momi [25]		Ozkalfa TUR
4-09	Morocco	D	0-0	Bangui	CNq			
7-09	Equatorial Guinea	L	0-3	Malabo	Fr			
9-10	Algeria	L	0-2	Blida	CNq			

2012								
2-06	Botswana	W	2-0	Bangui	WCq	Foxi Kethevoama 2 [19] [49]	20 000	Camille SEY
10-06	Ethiopia	L	0-2	Addis Abeba	WCq		25 000	Raphael MWI
15-06	Egypt	W	3-2	Alexandria	CNq		BCD	Haimoudi ALG
30-06	Egypt	D	1-1	Bangui	CNq	Foxi Kethevoama [33]		Diatta SEN
8-09	Burkina Faso	W	1-0	Bangui	CNq	Vianney Mabidé [22]		Gassama GAM
14-10	Burkina Faso	L	1-3	Ouagadougou	CNq	David Manga [7]		El Ahrach MAR

CN = CAF African Cup of Nations • CM = CEMAC Cup
q = qualifier • r1 = first round group • sf = semi-final • 3p = third place play-off • f = final

CUB – CUBA

FIFA/COCA-COLA WORLD RANKING

'93	'94	'95	'96	'97	'98	'99	'00	'01	'02	'03	'04	'05	'06	'07	'08	'09	'10	'11	'12
159	175	96	68	88	107	77	77	76	71	75	76	75	46	71	79	119	62	115	100

2012

Jan	Feb	Mar	Apr	May	Jun	Jul	Aug	Sep	Oct	Nov	Dec	High	Low	Av
113	116	116	136	136	145	150	149	147	146	141	100	46	175	91

After trooping off the field at the Sir Vivian Richards Stadium in Antigua following their 1-0 defeat at the hands of Martinique in the opening match of the 2012 Caribbean Cup finals, it looked as if Cuba's woeful year was going to get even worse. In the 13 games played to that point the Cubans had won just once, scoring only seven goals - five of which had come in the victory over Suriname, a match that had seen them scrape through to the finals. They had even gone a record breaking eight consecutive games without scoring a goal, a run that coincided with their 2014 FIFA World Cup qualifying campaign. They finished their group in last place, nine points behind third placed Canada. But then something extraordinary happened in Antigua. Ariel Martinez scored two late goals in the next match against French Guiana and when Alianni Urgelles scored a surprise winner against Jamaica, the Cubans found themselves in the semi-finals. Although they had reached the semi-finals in all of the previous six tournaments, the Cubans had never been crowned Caribbean champions but that was about to change for the Walter Benitez coached side. Having been appointed before the start of the qualifiers, Benitez inspired his team to a 1-0 victory over Haiti and then a 1-0 win over Trinidad in the final to get their hands on the elusive trophy at last.

CFU CARIBBEAN CUP RECORD

1989-1991 DNE 1992 4 SF 1993-1994 DNE 1995 3 SF 1996 2 F 1997 DNE 1998 DNQ 1999 2 F
2001 4 SF 2005 2 2007 3 SF 2008 4 SF 2010 3 SF 2012 1 Winners

ASOCIACION DE FUTBOL DE CUBA (AFC)

Estadio Pedro Marrero,
Escuela Nacional de Futbol
- Mario Lopez,
Avenida 41, 44 y 46,
La Habana
☎ +53 7 2076440
+53 7 2043563
futbol@inder.cu
FA 1924 CON 1961 FIFA 1932
P Luis Hernandez
GS Luis Yero

THE STADIA

2014 FIFA World Cup Stadia
Estadio Pedro Marrero
Havana   28 000
Other Main Stadia
Estadio Panamericano
Havana   34 000
Estadio Camilo Cienfuegos
Zuleta   5 000
Estadio Rogelio Palacios
Guantanamo   5 000

MAJOR CITIES/TOWNS

Population
1 Havana   2 133 920
2 Santiago de Cuba   443 585
3 Camagüey   309 818
4 Holguín   291 638
5 Guantánamo   221 373
6 Santa Clara   219 713
7 Las Tunas   165 601
8 Bayamo   162 747
9 Cienfuegos   160 060
10 Pinar del Rio   158 392
11 Matanzas   139 765
12 Ciego de Ávila   121 769
13 Sancti Spíritus   113 739
14 Manzanillo   103 209
15 Cárdenas   97 402
16 Palma Soriano   77 471
17 Mayarí   65 425
18 Moa   64 618
19 Nueva Gerona   60 579

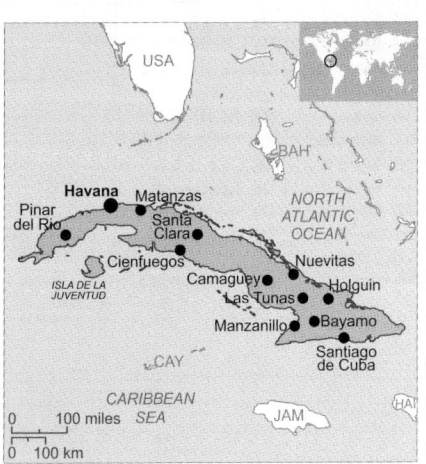

REPUBLICA DE CUBA • REPUBLIC OF CUBA

Capital Havana	Population 11 451 652 (72)	% in cities 76%
GDP per capita $9500 (108)	Area km² 110 860 km² (105)	GMT +/- -5
Neighbours (km)	Coast 3735	

RECENT INTERNATIONAL MATCHES PLAYED BY CUBA

2008 Opponents	Score	Venue	Comp	Scorers	Att	Referee
4-12 Guadeloupe †	W 2-1	Montego Bay	CCr1	Fernandez [8], Linares [74]	2 500	Brizan TRI
6-12 Antigua and Barbuda	W 3-0	Trelawny	CCr1	Marquez [7], Linares [21], Jaime Colome [35]	1 000	Campbell JAM
8-12 Haiti	L 0-1	Montego Bay	CCr1		1 500	Brizan TRI
11-12 Grenada	D 2-2	Kingston	CCsf	Joel Colome [14], Linares [33]. L 5-6p	10 000	Moreno PAN
14-12 Guadeloupe †	D 0-0	Kingston	CC3p	L 4-5p	9 000	Taylor BRB
2009						
No international matches played in 2009						
2010						
26-10 Panama	W 3-0	Pamama City	Fr	Marquez [44], Coroneaux 2 [45 90]	2 116	Moreno PAN
10-11 Dominica	W 4-2	St John's	CCq	Coroneaux [9], Fernandez [20], Joel Colome [27], Hernandez [35]	500	Lancaster GUY
12-11 Suriname	D 3-3	St John's	CCq	Coroneaux [45], Cervantes [65], Ramos [87]	400	Campbell JAM
14-11 Antigua and Barbuda	D 0-0	St John's	CCq		500	Campbell JAM
26-11 Trinidad and Tobago	W 2-0	Fort-de-France	CCr1	Jaime Colome [23], Linares [79]	5 000	Lancaster GUY
28-11 Martinique †	W 1-0	Fort-de-France	CCr1	Marquez [29]	500	Taylor BRB
30-11 Grenada	D 0-0	Fort-de-France	CCr1		2 000	Bogle JAM
3-12 Guadeloupe †	L 1-2	Fort-de-France	CCsf	Fernandez [35]	2 001	Wijngaarde SUR
5-12 Grenada	W 1-0	Fort-de-France	CC3p	Linares [12]	4 000	Lopez GUA
2011						
24-03 El Salvador	L 0-1	Havana	Fr		3 500	Rodriguez PAN
29-03 Panama	L 0-2	Havana	Fr		6 000	Espana GUA
26-05 Nicaragua	D 1-1	Havana	Fr	Hernandez [90]	3 500	Brea CUB
28-05 Nicaragua	W 2-1	Havana	Fr	Hernandez [10], Lahera [17]	2 950	Rubalcaba CUB
5-06 Costa Rica	L 0-5	Arlington	GCr1		80 108	Moreno PAN
9-06 Mexico	L 0-5	Charlotte	GCr1		46 012	Campbell JAM
12-06 El Salvador	L 1-6	Chicago	GCr1	Marquez [83]	62 000	Brizan TRI
11-12 Costa Rica	D 1-1	Havana	Fr	Cordovez [57p]	10 000	Lopez GUA
2012						
22-02 Jamaica	L 0-1	Kingston	Fr		10 000	Moreno PAN
24-02 Jamaica	L 0-3	Montego Bay	Fr		4 000	Moreno PAN
29-02 Bolivia	L 0-1	Cochabamba	Fr		14 494	Caceres PAR
8-06 Canada	L 0-1	Havana	WCq		7 000	Campbell JAM
12-06 Panama	L 0-1	Panama City	WCq		21 000	Geiger USA
7-09 Honduras	L 0-3	Havana	WCq		8 000	Quesada CRC
11-09 Honduras	L 0-1	San Pedro Sula	WCq		12 000	Lopez GUA
12-10 Canada	L 0-3	Toronto	WCq		17 712	Santos PUR
16-10 Panama	D 1-1	Havana	WCq	Alberto Gomez [37]	3 500	Lancaster GUY
14-11 Suriname	W 5-0	Scarborough	CNq	Marcel Hernandez 4 [6 36 62 89], Ariel Martinez [46]	200	Bedeau GRN
16-11 St Vincent/Granadines	D 1-1	Scarborough	CNq	Roberto Linares [48]	300	Taylor BRB
18-11 Trinidad and Tobago	L 0-1	Scarborough	CNq		1 300	Campbell JAM
8-12 Martinique †	L 0-1	St John's	CNr1		100	Wijngaarde SUR
10-12 French Guiana †	W 2-1	St John's	CNr1	Ariel Martinez 2 [74 76]	225	Anderson PUR
12-12 Jamaica	W 1-0	St John's	CNr1	Alianni Urgelles [57]	200	Bonilla SLV
14-12 Haiti	W 1-0	St John's	CNsf	Joel Colome [9]	200	Wijngaarde SUR
16-12 Trinidad and Tobago	W 1-0	St John's	CNf	Marcel Hernandez [113]	750	Legister JAM

Fr = Friendly match • CC = Caribbean Championship • GC = CONCACAF Gold Cup • WC = FIFA World Cup • q = qualifier
r1 = first round group • sf = semi-final • 3p = third place play-off • † Not a full international

CUBA NATIONAL TEAM HISTORICAL RECORDS

Coaches: Jose Tapia 1930-38 • Marcelino Minsal 1947-49 • Frantisek Churda CZE 1963-64 • Karoly Kocza HUN 1966 • Laszlo Mohaczy HUN 1967 • Kim Yong Ha PRK 1970-71 • Sergio Padron 1976 • Tibor Ivanicz 1980-81 • Giovanni Campari ITA 1990-92 • William Bennett 1998 • Miguel Company PER 2000-04 • Armelio Luis 2005 • Reinhold Fanz GER 2006-08 • Raul Gonzalez 2008-12 • Alexander Gonzalez 2012 • Walter Benitez 2012-

CUBA 2012

CAMPEONATO NACIONAL DE FUTBOL

	Pl	W	D	L	F	A	Pts	Villa Clara	Guantánamo	Camagüey	Granma	Cuidad Habana	Ciego de Avila	Cienfuegos	Las Tunas
Villa Clara †	14	10	3	1	21	9	33		2-1	2-0	2-1	2-0	2-0	2-1	1-0
Guantánamo †	14	8	3	3	22	14	27	3-0		1-0	4-1	0-0	1-0	1-1	4-2
Camagüey †	14	7	4	3	19	14	25	0-0	2-1		1-0	0-0	0-3	1-1	4-3
Granma †	14	5	5	4	18	16	20	0-2	3-0	1-1		1-1	2-2	2-0	4-2
Ciudad de La Habana	14	4	5	5	13	15	17	2-2	1-2	1-3	0-0		2-0	3-2	2-1
Ciego de Avila	14	3	3	8	12	19	12	1-2	1-1	1-2	1-2	1-0		0-1	2-1
Cienfuegos	14	2	5	7	10	16	11	0-0	1-2	0-3	0-0	0-1	0-0		0-1
Las Tunas	14	3	0	11	14	26	9	0-2	0-1	0-2	0-1	1-0	3-0	0-3	

4/02/2012 - 11/04/2012 • † Qualified for the semi-finals

CAMPEONATO NACIONAL DE FUTBOL PLAY-OFFS

Semi-finals

Villa Clara	0 2
Granma	0 0

Guantánamo	1 1 2p
Camagüey	1 1 3p

Finals

Villa Clara	3 3
Camagüey	0 2

CAMPEONATO NACIONAL FINAL
1st leg. 21-04-2012
Camagüey 0-3 Villa Clara
Scorers - Roberto Linares 2 43 71, Francisco Salazar 92+

CAMPEONATO NACIONAL FINAL
2nd leg. 28-04-2012
Villa Clara 3-2 Camagüey
Scorers - Arichel Hernández [12], Roberto Linares [33], Yanier Martínez [90] for Villa Clara; Héctor Portel [24], Keyler García 51 for Camagüey

MEDALS TABLE

		Overall	Lge	CON'CAF	City/Town
		G	G	G S B	
1	Villa Clara	12	12		Santa Clara
2	DC Gallego	8	8		Havana
	Real Iberia	8	8		Havana
4	Pinar del Río	7	7	2	Pinar del Río
5	Ciudad de La Habana	6	6		Havana
	Dep. San Francisco	6	6		San Francisco
7	Granjeros	5	5		Granjeros
	Hispano America	5	5		Havana
9	Industriales	4	4		Havana
	La Habana	4	4		Havana
	Cienfuegos	4	4		Cienfuegos
	Ciego de Avila	4	4		Ciego de Avila

CUW – CURACAO

FIFA/COCA-COLA WORLD RANKING

'93	'94	'95	'96	'97	'98	'99	'00	'01	'02	'03	'04	'05	'06	'07	'08	'09	'10	'11	'12
128	*152*	*125*	*142*	*156*	*156*	*167*	*175*	*183*	*177*	*188*	*163*	*168*	*177*	*183*	*152*	*168*	*151*	*151*	177

(Figures in italics are for the Netherlands Antilles)

2012

Jan	Feb	Mar	Apr	May	Jun	Jul	Aug	Sep	Oct	Nov	Dec	High	Low	Av
152	153	154	159	159	160	158	165	161	151	161	177	146	179	159

The transition from playing as the Netherlands Antilles to representing the island of Curaçao alone, has not been as smooth as hoped with the national team losing all four matches played during 2012. Indeed, of the first 15 matches played as Curaçao, only two have been won - both against minnows US Virgin Islands. In the 2012 Caribbean Cup, Curaçao travelled to St Lucia for a preliminary round group also featuring Guyana and St Vincent and they soon found themselves as the whipping boys, losing all three matches without ever threatening to cause an upset. It was all very far removed from the last time the team played under the Curaçao banner. During the 1950s Curaçao were a match for the best that the Caribbean and Central America had to offer, and they finished as runners-up in the now defunct CCCF Championship three times in a row, once behind Haiti and the other two behind Costa Rica. In club football the 2011 champions Hubentut Fortuna entered the CFU Club Championship and scored a satisfying win over Guyana's Milerock in the opening game of their group but those were the only points won as they crashed out at the first stage. Their attempt to retain the championship at home was undone by fielding an ineligible player with the title going instead to Centro Dominguito, 1-0 winners over Undeba in the final.

CFU CARIBBEAN CUP RECORD

1989 4 r1 **1991-1992** DNQ **1993-1994** DNE **1995-1997** DNQ **1998** 7 r1 **1999** DNQ **2001** DNE **2005** withdrew
2007-2010 DNQ as Netherlands Antilles **2012** DNQ as Curaçao

FEDERASHON FUTBOL KORSOU (FFK)

Bonamweg 49, PO Box 341, Willemstad, Curaçao
☎ +599 97365040
📠 +599 97365047
✉ navusoccer@interneeds.net
🌐 www.cura.net/ffk
FA 1921 CON 1961 FIFA 1932
P Rignaal Francisca
GS Franklin Mathilda

MAJOR CITIES/TOWNS

		Population
1	Willemstad	101 096
2	Princess Quarter	16 081
3	Cul De Sac	10 435
4	Cole Bay	8 006
5	**Sint Michiel**	5 323
6	**Montaña Abou**	4 390
7	**Tera Cora**	3 797
8	**Montaña Rey**	3 699
9	**Souax**	3 618
10	**Kralendijk**	3 265
11	**Antriol**	3 157
12	Little Bay	2 881
13	**Groot Piscadera**	2 669
14	**Barber**	2 511
15	**Labadera**	2 441
16	**Soto**	2 059

Bold = Curaçao
Italic = Sint Maarten
<u>Underlined</u> = Bonaire

THE STADIA

2014 FIFA World Cup Stadia
Stadion Ergilio Hato
Willemstad 15 000

Other Main Stadia
Stadion Antoin Maduro
Willemstad 3 500

KORSOU • CURACAO

Capital	Willemstad	Population	142 180 (187)	% in cities	93%
GDP per capita	$15 000 (75)	Area km²	444 km² (199)	GMT +/-	-4
Neighbours (km)	Coast 364 (includes Bonaire, Curaçao, Saba, Sint Eustatius & Sint Maarten)				

RECENT INTERNATIONAL MATCHES PLAYED BY CURACAO

2010	Opponents	Score	Venue	Comp	Scorers	Att	Referee
13-10	Suriname	L 1-2	Paramaribo	CCq	Lacey Pauletta [81]	800	Willet ATG
15-10	Guyana	L 2-3	Paramaribo	CCq	Hujoybert Delando [74p], Kenneth Kunst [84]	750	Matthew SKN
17-10	St Lucia	D 2-2	Paramaribo	CCq	Lisandro Trenidad [30], Bryan Anastatia [89p]	2 800	Willet ATG
29-10	Aruba	W 3-0	Willemstad	Fr	Everon Espacia, Lisandro Trenidad, Giandro Steba		Dimie ANT
31-10	Suriname	D 2-2	Willemstad	Fr	Everon Espacia, Vilyson Lake. L 5-6p		
2011							
20-08	Dominican Republic	L 0-1	San Cristoban	Fr		250	Vasquez DOM
21-08	Dominican Republic	L 0-1	San Cristoban	Fr		300	Hidalgo DOM
2-09	Antigua and Barbuda	L 2-5	St John's	WCq	Rihairo Meulens [9], Richmar Siberie [74]	2 000	Santos PUR
6-09	Haiti	L 2-4	Willemstad	WCq	Orin De Waard [12], Angelo Zimmerman [43]	5 000	Solis CRC
23-09	Suriname	L 0-2	Paramaribo	Fr		2 000	Botland SUR
25-09	Suriname	D 2-2	Paramaribo	Fr	Mirco Colina 2 [27 66]	2 500	Pierau SUR
7-10	Antigua and Barbuda	L 0-1	Willemstad	WCq		2 563	Reyna GUA
11-10	Haiti	D 2-2	Port-au-Prince	WCq	Richmar Siberie [7], Sendley Bito [14]	7 800	Clarke LCA
11-11	US Virgin Islands	W 3-0	Frederikstad	WCq	Richmar Siberie 2 [8 14], Sendley Bito [26]	210	Navarro CAN
15-11	US Virgin Islands	W 6-1	Willemstad	WCq	Shanon Carmelia 2 [33 78], Richmar Siberie 2 [40 86], Everon Espacia [73], Angelo Cijntje [90]	2 000	Legister JAM
4-12	Suriname	L 0-2	Paramaribo	Fr		50	Angela ARU
2012							
13-07	Aruba	L 2-3	Oranjestad	Fr	Jurensly Martina [70], Mirco Colina [72]	300	Pinas SUR
21-10	St Lucia	L 1-5	Gros Islet	CNq	Christopher Isenia [48]	1 650	Willett ATG
23-10	Guyana	L 1-2	Gros Islet	CNq	OG [53]	750	Bogle JAM
25-10	St Vincent/Grenadines	L 0-4	Gros Islet	CNq		852	Vazquez DOM

Fr = Friendly match • CC = Digicel Caribbean Cup • WC = FIFA World Cup • q = qualifier • ‡ Not a full international

CURACAO 2011-12

SEKSHON PAGA FIRST STAGE

	Pl	W	D	L	F	A	Pts	Centro Dominguito	Undeba	Jong Holland	Sithoc	Centro Barber	Victory Boys	Hubentut	VESTA	SUBT
Centro Dominguito †	24	19	5	0	65	17	62		5-0 2-1	0-0	1-1	3-2 1-0	2-0	3-0 0-0	1-0	2-1
Undeba †	23	10	6	7	38	32	36	2-3		2-2 0-1	2-1	2-0 2-0	3-2 3-0	2-4	0-1 1-1	1-1
Jong Holland †	23	7	11	5	29	25	32	1-5 1-1	0-0		1-1	0-2 1-1	0-0	1-3	1-0	3-0
Sithoc † §3	23	10	4	9	44	41	31	0-5 2-5	1-2 0-2	2-1 2-0		1-2	2-2 1-1	1-3	5-0 0-1	4-1
Centro Barber	24	6	8	10	34	36	26	2-2	3-2	2-1	1-2 2-4		0-2 4-0	1-1	4-0	2-2 3-0
Victory Boys	23	6	7	10	34	44	25	1-2 0-4	2-2	0-0 1-2	0-2	1-1		2-2	1-1	2-1 5-2
Hubentut Fortuna §9	20	9	6	5	38	23	24	1-2	2-1 *2-3*	1-1 n/p	3-0 *7-2*	1-0 2-0	2-3 *0-0*		1-0 1-1	5-0
VESTA	24	5	6	13	17	39	21	0-5 1-3	1-2	0-2 1-1	0-1	1-1 1-1	3-2 1-2	0-2		0-2 1-0
SUBT	24	3	5	16	25	67	14	0-2 1-6	2-2 0-3	1-1 0-6	2-6 0-4	4-1	2-4	2-1 1-1	0-2	

4/01/2012 - 18/08/2012 • † Qualified for the Kaya 4 • § = points deducted • Matches in italics declared void • n/p = not played

PLAY-OFF KAYA 4

	Pl	W	D	L	F	A	Pts	Un	Si	JH
Centro Dominguito †	3	2	1	0	9	3	7	3-3	3-0	3-0
Undeba †	3	1	1	1	8	8	4		1-4	4-1
Sithoc	3	1	1	1	4	4	4			0-0
Jong Holland	3	0	1	2	1	7	1			

9/09/2012 - 23/09/2012 • † Qualified for the final

FINAL
Ergilio Hato, Willemstad, 30-09-2012
Centro Dominguito 1-0 Undeba
Scorer - Kenneth Kunst [27] for Central Dominguito

CYP – CYPRUS

FIFA/COCA-COLA WORLD RANKING

'93	'94	'95	'96	'97	'98	'99	'00	'01	'02	'03	'04	'05	'06	'07	'08	'09	'10	'11	'12
72	67	73	78	82	78	63	62	79	80	97	108	96	73	66	94	68	90	127	132

2012

Jan	Feb	Mar	Apr	May	Jun	Jul	Aug	Sep	Oct	Nov	Dec	High	Low	Av
126	127	129	133	133	125	122	123	135	107	127	132	43	135	82

The successful transformation of Cypriot football in recent years was brought into sharp focus with the extraordinary exploits of APOEL Nicosia in the 2011-12 UEFA Champions League where they not only matched their feat of two years earlier by qualifying for the group stage, but then went on to win the group, and then beat Lyon in the first knock-out round before losing to Real Madrid in the quarter-finals. A closer look at AEL Limassol's championship-winning campaign at home gives a clue to the recent development of Cypriot club football. They won their first title since 1968 by effectively signing up a team of foreigners. During the campaign Cypriot players made just 25 appearances for AEL, 16 of those coming from captain Marios Nicolaou. In the cup final between AEL and Omonia there were 14 different countries represented on the pitch, a game in which Omonia denied AEL a first cup triumph since 1989 thanks to a 1-0 win - the winner coming from Brazilian Andre Alves in the first half. There is no doubt that the transformation of club football in Cyprus has been a fantastic experience for the fans but two huge question marks now hang over the future of the game. Firstly where does this leave the national team and secondly just what will be the effect of the banking crisis that hit the nation in early 2013 on club football?

UEFA EUROPEAN CHAMPIONSHIP RECORD
1960-1964 DNE 1968-2012 DNQ

CYPRUS FOOTBALL ASSOCIATION (CFA)

10 Achaion Street,
2413 Engomi, PO Box 25071
Nicosia 1306
☎ +357 22 352341
📠 +357 22 590544
✉ info@cfa.com.cy
🌐 www.cfa.com.cy
FA 1934 CON 1962 FIFA 1948
P Costakis Koutsokoumnis
GS Phivos Vakis

THE STADIA

2014 FIFA World Cup Stadia

Antonis Papadopoulos	
Larnaca	9 319

Other Main Stadia

Neo GSP Stadium	
Nicosia	22 859
Tsirion Stadium	
Limassol	13 152
Zenon Stadium	
Larnaca	13 032
Paphiako Stadium	
Paphos	11 000

MAJOR CITIES/TOWNS

		Population
1	Nicosia	215 551
2	Limassol	169 507
3	Nicosia (T)	53 045
4	Larnaca	52 949
5	Paphos	42 296
6	Famagusta (T)	36 481
7	Girne (T)	29 723
8	Aradippou	16 155
9	Morphou (T)	13 324
10	Paralimni	13 052
11	Gönyeli	12 985
12	Geri	9 446
13	Ypsonas	8 715
14	Lefka (T)	8 456
15	Degirmenlik	8 114
16	Dali	7 008
17	Tseri	6 332
18	Lapta (T)	6 315

(T) = in Turkish controlled zone

KYPRIAKI DIMOKRATIA • REPUBLIC OF CYPRUS

Capital	Nicosia	Population	796 740 (159)	% in cities	70%
GDP per capita	$21 300 (58)	Area km²	9 251 km² (170)	GMT +/-	+2
Neighbours (km)	Coast 648				

RECENT INTERNATIONAL MATCHES PLAYED BY CYPRUS

2008	Opponents	Score	Venue	Comp	Scorers	Att	Referee
6-02	Ukraine	D 1-1	Nicosia	Fr	Alonefitis [19p]	500	
19-05	Greece	L 0-2	Patras	Fr		16 216	MacDonald SCO
20-08	Switzerland	L 1-4	Geneva	Fr	Makridis [35]	14 500	Ceferin SVN
6-09	Italy	L 1-2	Larnaca	WCq	Aloneftis [28]	6 000	Vink NED
11-10	Georgia	D 1-1	Tbilisi	WCq	Konstantinou.M [67]	40 000	Matejak CZE
15-10	Republic of Ireland	L 0-1	Dublin	WCq		55 833	Tudor ROU
19-11	Belarus	W 2-1	Nicosia	Fr	Christofi [29], Avraam [48]		
2009							
10-02	Serbia	L 0-2	Nicosia	Fr			
11-02	Slovakia	W 3-2	Nicosia	Fr	Maragkos [32p], Nicolaou [74], Okkas [82]	300	
28-03	Georgia	W 2-1	Larnaca	WCq	Konstantinou.M [33], Christofi [56]	1 500	Fautrel FRA
1-04	Bulgaria	L 0-2	Sofia	WCq		16 916	Ingvarsson SWE
30-05	Canada	L 0-1	Larnaca	Fr			
6-06	Montenegro	D 2-2	Larnaca	WCq	Konstantinou.M [14], Michail [45p]	3 000	Velasco ESP
12-08	Albania	L 1-6	Tirana	Fr	Charalampidis		Yildirim TUR
5-09	Republic of Ireland	L 1-2	Nicosia	WCq	Ilia [30]	5 191	Einwaller AUT
9-09	Montenegro	D 1-1	Podgorica	WCq	Okkas [63]	4 000	Zimmermann SUI
10-10	Bulgaria	W 4-1	Larnaca	WCq	Charalampidis 2 [11 20], Konstantinou.M [58], Aloneftis [78]	3 700	Allaerts BEL
14-10	Italy	L 2-3	Parma	WCq	Makridis [12], Michail [48]	15 009	Yefet ISR
2010							
3-03	Iceland	D 0-0	Larnaca	Fr			Yordanov.N BUL
11-08	Andorra	W 1-0	Larnaca	Fr	Konstantinou [4]	1 700	Spathas GRE
3-09	Portugal	D 4-4	Guimaraes	ECq	Aloneftis [3], Konstantinou [11], Okkas [57], Avraam [89]	9 100	Clattenburg ENG
8-10	Norway	L 1-2	Larnaca	ECq	Okkas [58]	7 648	Gumienny BEL
12-10	Denmark	L 0-2	Copenhagen	ECq		15 544	Muniz ESP
16-11	Jordan	D 0-0	Amman	Fr		3 500	Ebrahim BHR
2011							
9-02	Romania	D 1-1	Paralimni	Fr	Konstantinou [84]. L 4-5p	2 500	Shvetov UKR
26-03	Iceland	D 0-0	Nicosia	ECq		2 088	Ceferin SVN
29-03	Bulgaria	L 0-1	Larnaca	Fr			Borg MLT
10-08	Moldova	W 3-2	Nicosia	Fr	Avraam 2 [13 51], Dobrasinovic [89]	2 000	Mazic SRB
2-09	Portugal	L 0-4	Nicosia	ECq		15 444	Rocchi ITA
6-09	Iceland	L 0-1	Reykkjavik	ECq		5 267	Jovanetic SRB
7-10	Denmark	L 1-4	Nicosia	ECq	Avraam [45]	2 408	Strahonja CRO
11-10	Norway	L 1-3	Oslo	ECq	Okkas [42]	13 490	Collum SCO
11-11	Scotland	L 1-2	Larnaca	Fr	Christofi [60]	2 000	Levi ISR
2012							
29-02	Serbia	D 0-0	Larnaca	Fr		250	Blom NED
15-08	Bulgaria	L 0-1	Sofia	Fr		400	Lautier MLT
7-09	Albania	L 1-3	Tirana	WCq	Vincent Laban [45]	9 400	Kuchin KAZ
11-09	Iceland	W 1-0	Larnaca	WCq	Konstantinos Makridis [58]	1 600	Delferiere BEL
12-10	Slovenia	L 1-2	Maribor	WCq	Efstathios Aloneftis [83]	7 988	Kruzliak SVK
16-10	Norway	L 1-3	Larnaca	WCq	Efstathios Aloneftis [42]	2 493	Gil POL
14-11	Finland	L 0-3	Nicosia	Fr		300	Balaj Rou

Fr = Friendly match • EC = UEFA EURO 2008/2012 • WC = FIFA World Cup • q = qualifier

CYPRUS NATIONAL TEAM HISTORICAL RECORDS

Caps
106 - Yiannis Okkas 1997- • **86** - Michalis Konstantinou 1998- • **82** - Pambos Pittas 1987-99 • **78** - Nicos Panayiotou 1994-2006 • **70** - Giorgos Theodotou 1996-2008 • **69** - Chrysis Michail 2000- • **68** - Yiannis Yiangoudakis 1980-94 & Kostas Charalambides 2003- • **66** - Marinos Satsias 2000- • **63** - Yiasemakis Yiasoumi 1998-2009 • **60** - Marios Charalambous 1991-2002 & Konstantinos Makridis

Goals
32 - Michalis Konstantinou 1998- • **26** - Yiannis Okkas 1997- • **11** - Kostas Charalambides 2003- • **10** - Marios Agathokleous 1994-2003 & Efstathios Aloneftis 2005- • **8** - Andros Sotiriou 1991-99, Phivos Vrahimis 1977-82; Milenko Spoljaric 1997-2001 & Sinisa Gogic 1994-99

Coaches
Gyula Zsengeller HUN 1958-59 • Argyrios Gavalas GRE 1960-67 • Pambos Avraamidis 1968-69 • Ray Wood ENG 1969-71 • Sima Milovanov YUG 1972 • Pambos Avraamidis 1972-76 • Panikos Krystallis 1976-77 • Kostas Talianos GRE 1977-82 • Vassil Spasov BUL 1982-84 • Panikos Iakovou 1984-91 • Andreas Michaelides 1991-97 • Panikos Georgiou 1997-99 • Stavros Papadopoulos 1999-2001 • Momcilo Vukotic SRB 2001-04 • Angelos Anastasiadis GRE 2004-11 • Nikos Nioplias GRE 2011 -

CYPRUS 2011-12

MARFIN LAIKI A KATEGORIA (1)

	Pl	W	D	L	F	A	Pts	AEL	APOEL	Omonia	Anorthosis	AEK	Apollon	N.Salamina	Alki	Ethnikos	Olympiakos	ENP	Aris	Anagennisi	Ermis
AEL Limassol †	32	20	8	4	37	10	68		0-3	0-0	0-2	0-0	0-1	1-0	2-0	2-0	3-0	1-0	3-2	1-0	0-0	1-0	1-0	2-0
APOEL Nicosia ‡	32	20	6	6	46	19	66	1-0		1-0	1-3	1-2	0-1	1-2	2-0	2-2	2-0	4-1	1-0	1-0	1-1	3-0	2-0	2-0
Omonia Nicosia ‡	32	20	6	6	56	23	66	0-1	1-1		0-0	0-1	1-2	0-0	1-2	3-0	1-0	2-1	3-1	0-0	1-0	2-1	1-0	2-0	2-0
Anorthosis Famagusta‡	32	17	8	7	36	21	59	0-1	1-1	0-1		1-2	2-0	0-4	0-1	1-1	2-0	0-0	2-1	1-0	2-0	2-2	1-0	1-0
AEK Larnaca	32	13	10	9	40	27	49	0-0	2-1	0-0	1-1		6-0	0-1	1-1	2-2	0-3	1-0	0-0	0-2	2-1	1-0	2-0	2-0
Apollon Limassol	32	12	7	13	36	43	43	0-3	1-4	1-0	0-3	1-1	1-0		1-2	1-1	1-0	0-0	1-1	1-1	1-0	2-0	5-2	1-0
Nea Salamis	32	11	10	11	39	47	43	0-3	2-5	0-2	1-1	0-3	1-1	3-2	2-2		5-1	0-0	2-0	2-0	2-0	1-2	1-0	2-0
Alki Larnaca	32	12	6	14	35	45	42	1-2	0-3	2-1	1-3	2-2	0-2	0-2	1-1	0-2	1-1	0		4-2	1-0	0-1	1-0	4-0	2-0
Ethnikos Achnas	32	10	10	12	30	31	40	0-0	0-2	1-4	1-2	1-1	2-3	0-0	2-3			2-0	1-1	0-0	0-0	3-1
Olympiakos Nicosia	32	10	9	13	36	44	39	0-4	1-1	0-2	0-1	1-0	0-2	1-1	2-0	1-2		0-0	2-0	2-0	1-0
ENP Paralimni	32	11	5	16	26	30	38	0-1	0-1	0-3	0-1	1-0	1-0	0-1	2-0	0-1	1-1		4-0	1-1	2-1
Aris Limassol	32	8	8	16	32	44	32	0-1	1-1	0-1	1-0	1-1	2-3	2-0	1-1	2-3	1-0	1-4		2-0	3-0
Anagennisi Dherynia	26	2	5	19	16	45	11	0-1	1-1	1-2	0-2	0-3	1-2	4-1	1-2	0-1	0-2	0-0	1-1		
Ermis Aradippou	26	1	4	21	12	50	7	0-0	0-2	1-4	0-1	0-1	2-2	0-2	1-1	1-3	0-1	0-0	1-5	3-2	

27/08/2011 - 12/05/2012 • † Qualified for the UEFA Champions League • ‡ Qualified for the Europa League
Top scorers: **17** - **FREDDY** ANG, Omonia • **12** - **GONZALO** ESP, AEK & **ARNAL** ESP, Alki • **11** - Esteban **SOLARI** ARG, APOEL & **GELSON** BRA, Aris • **9** - **WENDER** BRA, Ethnikos; **SEMEDO** CPV, ENP & Philip **CHIDI** NGA, Olympiakos • **8** - **VOUHO** CIV, AEL & Christos **CHATZIPANTELIDIS**, Nea Salamis

CYPRUS 2011-12 B KATEGORIA (2)

	Pl	W	D	L	F	A	Pts
Ayia Napa	32	20	7	5	53	20	67
Doxa Katokopia	32	18	8	6	47	26	62
AEP Paphos	32	17	4	11	47	34	55
PAEEK	32	9	9	14	27	43	36
Othellos Athienou	26	9	7	10	30	31	34
Akritas Chloraka	26	9	7	10	37	40	34
Onisilos Sotira	26	9	7	10	23	26	34
Ethnikos Assia	26	9	7	10	29	38	34
APEP Kyperounda	26	9	6	11	26	38	33
Omonia Aradippou	26	7	11	8	40	34	32
Halkanoras Idiliou	26	6	14	6	28	29	32
APOP/Kinyras §12	26	13	4	9	41	23	31
EN Parekklisia	26	7	7	12	21	33	28
Atromitas Yeroskipou§3	26	1	4	21	10	44	4

17/09/2011 - 21/04/2012 • § = points deducted

CYPRUS 2011-12 C KATEGORIA (3)

	Pl	W	D	L	F	A	Pts
AEK Kouklion	26	20	1	5	62	16	61
N&S Erimis	26	16	5	5	42	26	53
AEZ Zakakiou	26	16	4	6	43	28	52
ASIL Lysi	26	13	7	6	56	26	46
Adonis Idaliou	26	12	6	8	43	33	42
ENAD Polis	26	10	8	8	39	33	38
Spartakos Kitiou	26	11	4	11	36	28	37
Digenis Akritas	26	9	6	11	33	35	33
Frenaros FC 2000	26	6	14	6	29	33	32
Elpida Xylofagou	26	8	7	11	26	36	31
PO Ormideia	26	8	6	12	27	33	30
Ahironas Liopetriou	26	8	4	14	32	46	28
Anagennisi Germasoyia	26	5	8	13	21	38	23
Maroniou	26	0	0	26	0	78	0

17/09/2011 - 24/03/2012 • § = points deducted

MEDALS TABLE

		Overall			League			Cup	
		G	S	B	G	S	B	G	S
1	APOEL Nicosia	40	30	15	**21**	20	15	**19**	10
2	Omonia Nicosia	34	21	9	20	15	9	14	6
3	Anorthosis Famagusta	23	16	8	13	10	8	10	6
4	AEL Limassol	13	10	6	7	1	6	6	9
5	Apollon Limassol	9	11	4	3	4	4	6	7
6	EPA Larnaca	7	9	4	2	6	4	5	3
7	Olympiakos Nicosia	4	7	2	3	4	2	1	3
8	Trust AC	4	3		1	2		3	1
9	Pezoporikos Larnaca	3	15	14	2	8	14	1	7
10	Chetin Kaya	3	3	3	1	1	3	2	2
11	NEA Salamis	1	2	4			4	1	2
12	AEK Larnaca	1	2					1	2
13	APOP/Kinyras	1						1	
14	Union Paralimni (ENP)		5	2		1	2		4
15	Alki Larnaca		5	1			1		5
16	Digenis Morphou		2			1			1
17	Aris Limassol		1	1			1		1
18	Ethnikos Achnas		1			1			1

KYPELLO KYPROY 2011-12

First Round		Round of 16		Quarter-finals		Semi-finals		Final	
Omonia Nicosia	Bye	**Omonia Nicosia***	2 8						
Ayia Napa*	2	Nea Salamis	0 1						
Nea Salamis	4			**Omonia Nicosia***	6 3				
Apollon Limassol	Bye	Apollon Limassol*	2 1	Ermis Aradippou	0 0				
APEP Kyperounda*	1	**Ermis Aradippou**	1 3			**Omonia Nicosia***	3 0		
Ermis Aradippou	3					Ethnikos Achnas	0 1		
Olympiakos Nicosia*	3	**Olympiakos Nicosia***	3 2						
Doxa Katokopia	2	Omonia Aradippou	2 0	Olympiakos Nicosia*	0 0				
Omonia Aradippou	Bye			**Ethnikos Achnas**	1 0				
Aris Limassol	3	Aris Limassol	0 0					**Omonia Nicosia ‡**	1
Othellos Athienou*	0	**Ethnikos Achnas***	2 0					AEL Limassol	0
Ethnikos Achnas	Bye								
AEK Larnaca	1	**AEK Larnaca**	5 4	**AEK Larnaca***	1 1				
Halkanoras Idiliou*	0	EN Parekklisia*	0 0	Alki Larnaca	0 2				
Anagennisi Dherynia	1					AEK Larnaca*	0 0		
EN Parekklisia	3	AEP Paphos	0 0			**AEL Limassol**	1 0		
AEP Paphos*	3 5p	**Alki Larnaca***	2 6						
ENP Paralimni	3 4p								
Onisilos Sotira	1								
Alki Larnaca*	4								
Anorthosis Famagusta*	6	**Anorthosis Famagusta**	3 3	**Anorthosis Famagusta**	0 2				
PAEEK	0	APOP/Kinyras*	2 0	**AEL Limassol***	1 1				
Atromitas Yeroskipou*	1 1p								
APOP/Kinyras	1 3p								
APOEL Nicosia*	9	APOEL Nicosia*	0 0						
Akritas Chloraka	1	**AEL Limassol**	1 0						
Ethnikos Assia	0								
AEL Limassol*	2								

* Home team in the first leg • ‡ Qualified for the Europa League

CUP FINAL

GSP Stadium, Nicosia, 16-05-2012
Att: 18 407, Ref: Felix Brych
Scorers - Andre Alves 16 for Omonia
Omonia - Antonis Georgallides - Rasheed Alabi, Dedi Ben Dayan, Christos Karipidis, Yuval Shpungin - Bruno Aguiar (Leandro 66), Veroljub Salatic●, Konstantinos Makridis, Giorgos Efrem, Andreas Avraam (Efstathios Aloneftis 56) - Andre Alves (Dimitris Christofi 84). Tr: Neophytos Larkou
AEL - Matias Degra - Marco Airosa, Edwin Ouon◆30, Dossa Junior - Dede● (Henrique 84), Marios Nicolaou (Silas 75), Gilberto (Edmar Silva 60), Luciano Bebe - Vouho, Chris Dickson, Carlitos. Tr: Pambos Christodoulou

CZE – CZECH REPUBLIC

FIFA/COCA-COLA WORLD RANKING

'93	'94	'95	'96	'97	'98	'99	'00	'01	'02	'03	'04	'05	'06	'07	'08	'09	'10	'11	'12
-	34	14	5	3	8	2	5	14	15	6	4	2	10	6	11	25	30	33	29

2012

Jan	Feb	Mar	Apr	May	Jun	Jul	Aug	Sep	Oct	Nov	Dec	High	Low	Av
31	29	29	26	26	27	18	19	19	22	25	29	2	67	14

The Czech Republic continued their fine run at the finals of the European Championship with their appearance at Euro 2012, where for the third time in five tournaments they progressed beyond the group stage. It didn't look too promising after a heavy defeat at the hands of Russia in their opening match, but Michal Bilek's team fought back with a win over Greece and then a 1-0 victory over Poland which saw them knock out the hosts and finish top of the group. That meant a quarter-final against Portugal but a Cristiano Ronaldo goal 11 minutes from time ended their interest. Success in the FIFA World Cup has been considerably harder to come by for the team and they found themselves in one of the toughest qualifying groups for Brazil alongside Italy, Denmark, Bulgaria and Armenia. In club football there was no silverware for the capital Prague for the second season in a row with Slovan Liberec winning the title while Sigma Olomouc won their first-ever trophy after beating Sparta 1-0 in the cup final. The championship turned into a three-horse race going down to the final match where Slovan faced Viktoria Pilzen in the first-ever winner takes all tie. Defending champions Viktoria needed to win to take the title on the head-to-head rule but they could only draw 0-0 to hand Slovan their third title since first winning it in 2002.

UEFA EUROPEAN CHAMPIONSHIP RECORD
1960 3 SF **1964** r1 **1968-1972** DNQ **1976** 1 Winners **1980** 3 **1984-1992** DNQ (as Czechoslovakia)
1996 2 F **2000** 10 r1 **2004** 3 SF **2008** 11 r1 **2012** 6 QF

FOOTBALL ASSOCIATION OF CZECH REPUBLIC (CMFS)

Diskarska 2431,
PO Box 11,
Praha 6 16017
☎ +420 2 33029111
+420 2 33353107
facr@fotbal.cz
www.fotbal.cz
FA 1901 CON 1954 FIFA 1907
P Miroslav Pelta
GS Rudolf Repka

THE STADIA

2014 FIFA World Cup Stadia
Generali Arena
Prague   19 784
Struncovy Sady
Plzen   11 700

Other Main Stadia
Stadion Eden
Prague   21 000
Na Stínadlech Stadion
Teplice   18 428
Bazaly Stadion
Ostrava   18 020

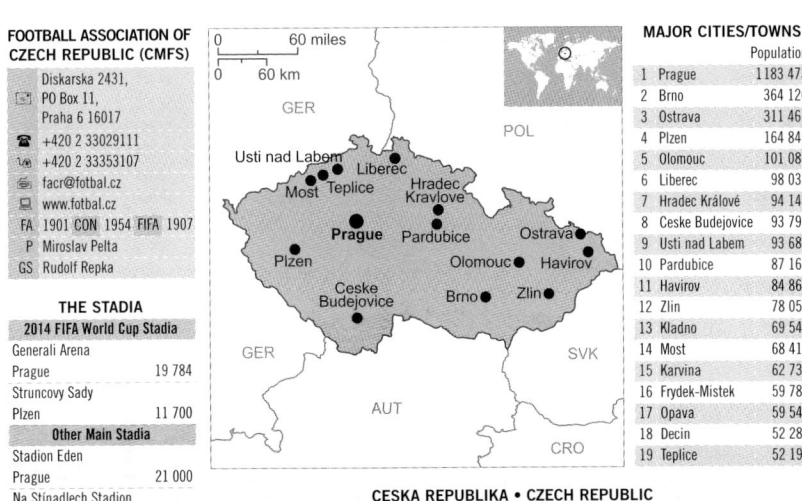

MAJOR CITIES/TOWNS

		Population
1	Prague	1 183 473
2	Brno	364 126
3	Ostrava	311 467
4	Plzen	164 845
5	Olomouc	101 081
6	Liberec	98 035
7	Hradec Králové	94 141
8	Ceske Budejovice	93 791
9	Usti nad Labem	93 680
10	Pardubice	87 164
11	Havirov	84 868
12	Zlin	78 055
13	Kladno	69 544
14	Most	68 416
15	Karvina	62 739
16	Frydek-Mistek	59 780
17	Opava	59 549
18	Decin	52 284
19	Teplice	52 193

CESKA REPUBLIKA • CZECH REPUBLIC

Capital Prague (Praha)	Population 10 211 904 (80)	% in cities 73%
GDP per capita $25 900 (51)	Area km^2 78 867 km^2 (115)	GMT +/- +1
Neighbours (km) Austria 362, Germany 815, Poland 615, Slovakia 197		

RECENT INTERNATIONAL MATCHES PLAYED BY THE CZECH REPUBLIC

2009	Opponents		Score	Venue	Comp	Scorers	Att	Referee
12-08	Belgium	W	3-1	Teplice	Fr	Hubnik [27], Baros [42p], Rozehnal [78]	13 890	Sippel GER
5-09	Slovakia	D	2-2	Bratislava	WCq	Pudil [68], Baros [83]	23 800	Ovrebo NOR
9-09	San Marino	W	7-0	Uherske Hradiste	WCq	Baros 4 [28 44 45 66], Sverkos 2 [47 94+], Necid [86]	8 121	Amirkhanyan ARM
10-10	Poland	W	2-0	Prague	WCq	Necid [51], Plasil [72]	14 010	Larsen DEN
14-10	Northern Ireland	D	0-0	Prague	WCq		8 002	Duhamel FRA
15-11	UAE	D	0-0	Al Ain	Fr	L 2-3p	5 000	Dalkam JOR
18-11	Azerbaijan	L	0-2	Al Ain	Fr			Al Marzouqi UAE
2010								
3-03	Scotland	L	0-1	Glasgow	Fr		26 530	Fautrel FRA
22-05	Turkey	L	1-2	Harrison	Fr	Cerny [81]	16 371	Geiger USA
25-05	USA	W	4-2	East Hartford	Fr	Sivok [44], Polak [58], Fenin [77], Necid [90]	36 218	Morales MEX
11-08	Latvia	W	4-1	Liberec	Fr	Bednar [49], Fenin [54], Pospech [74], Necid [77]	7 456	Dankovsky UKR
7-09	Lithuania	L	0-1	Olomouc	ECq		12 038	Yefet ISR
8-10	Scotland	W	1-0	Prague	ECq	Hubnik [69]	14 922	Bebek CRO
12-10	Liechtenstein	W	2-0	Vaduz	ECq	Necid [12], Vaclav Kadlec [29]	2 555	Sukhina RUS
17-11	Denmark	D	0-0	Aarhus	Fr		9 184	Webb ENG
2011								
9-02	Croatia	L	2-4	Pila	Fr	Sivok [20], Rosicky [45]	9 500	Orsato ITA
25-03	Spain	L	1-2	Granada	ECq	Plasil [29]	16 301	Kassai HUN
29-03	Liechtenstein	W	2-0	Ceske Budejovice	ECq	Baros [3], Michal Kadlec [70]	6 600	Hategan ROU
4-06	Peru	D	0-0	Matsumoto	Fr		7 592	Sato JPN
7-06	Japan	D	0-0	Yokohama	Fr		65 856	Atkinson ENG
10-08	Norway	L	0-3	Oslo	Fr		12 734	Black NIR
3-09	Scotland	D	2-2	Glasgow	ECq	Plasil [78], Michal Kadlec [90p]	51 564	Blom NED
6-09	Ukraine	W	4-0	Prague	Fr	Michal Kadlec 2 [3p 12], Rezek [47], Kolar [51]	7 322	Trutz SVK
7-10	Spain	L	0-2	Prague	ECq		18 800	Tagliavento ITA
11-10	Lithuania	W	4-1	Kaunas	ECq	Michal Kadlec 2 [2p 85p], Rezek 2 [16 45]	4 000	Fernandez ESP
11-11	Montenegro	W	2-0	Prague	ECpo	Pilar [63], Sivok [92+]	14 560	Atkinson ENG
15-11	Montenegro	W	1-0	Podgorica	ECpo	Jiracek [81]	10 100	Rizzoli ITA
2012								
29-02	Republic of Ireland	D	1-1	Dublin	Fr	Baros [50]	37 741	Sousa POR
26-05	Israel	W	2-1	Graz	Fr	Baros [17p], Lafata [94+]	3 400	Trutz SVK
1-06	Hungary	L	1-2	Prague	Fr	Michal Kadlec [24p]	17 102	Probert ENG
8-06	Russia	L	1-4	Wroclaw	ECr1	Pilar [52]	37 348	Webb ENG
12-06	Greece	W	2-1	Wroclaw	ECr1	Jiracek [3], Pilar [6]	53 617	Stark GER
16-06	Poland	W	1-0	Wroclaw	ECr1	Jiracek [72]	44 416	Thomson SCO
21-06	Portugal	L	0-1	Warsaw	ECqf		58 145	Webb ENG
15-08	Ukraine	D	0-0	Lviv	Fr		33 153	Mazic SRB
8-09	Denmark	D	0-0	Copenhagen	WCq		24 004	Stark GER
11-09	Finland	L	0-1	Teplice	Fr		9 053	Siejewicz POL
12-10	Malta	W	3-1	Plzen	WCq	Gebre Selassie [34], Pekhart [52], Rezek [67]	10 358	Salmanov AZE
16-10	Bulgaria	D	0-0	Prague	WCq		16 163	Bezborodov RUS
14-11	Slovakia	W	3-0	Olomouc	Fr	Lafata 2 [3 6], Dockal [72]	11 464	Lechner AUT

Fr = Friendly match • EC = UEFA EURO 2008/2012 • WC = FIFA World Cup • q = qualifier • po = play-off • r1 = first round group

CZECH REPUBLIC NATIONAL TEAM HISTORICAL RECORDS

Caps
118 - Karel Poborsky 1994-2006 • 98 - Petr Cech 2002- • 93 - Milan Baros 2001- • 91 - Jan Koller 1999-2009 & Pavel Nedved 1994-2006 • 88 - Tomas Rosicky 2000- • 81 - Vladimir Smicer 1993-2005 • 80 - Jaroslav Plasil 2004- • 78 - Tomas Ujfalusi 2001-09 • 77 - Marek Jankulovski 2000-09 • 74 - Vratislav Lokvenc 1995-2006 • 69 - Tomas Galasek 1995-2008 • 64 (84) - Jiri Nemec 1994-2001 • 63 (87) - Pavel Kuka 1994-2001 • Figures in brackets include overall total including matches played for Czechoslovakia

Goals
55 - Jan Koller 1999-2009 • 41 - Milan Baros 2001- • 27 - Vladimir Smicer 1993-2005 • 22 (29) - Pavel Kuka 1994-2001 • 20 - Tomas Rosicky 2000- • 18 - Patrick Berger 1994-2001 & Pavel Nedved 1994-2006 • 14 - Vratislav Lokvenc 1995-2006

Coaches
Vaclav Jezek 1993 • Dusan Uhrin 1994-97 • Jozef Chovanec 1998-2001 • Karel Bruckner 2001-08 • Petr Rada 2008-09 • Frantisek Straka 2009 • Ivan Hasek 2009 • Michal Bilek 2009-

CZECH REPUBLIC 2011-12

I. GAMBRINUS LIGA

	Pl	W	D	L	F	A	Pts	Slovan	Sparta	Viktoria P	Mladá	Teplice	Dukla	Slovácko	Jablonec	Pribram	Dynamo CB	Sigma	Slavia	Hradec	Baník	Bohemians	Viktoria Z
Slovan Liberec †	30	20	6	4	68	29	66		1-3	0-0	2-1	0-2	1-2	0-0	2-2	2-0	4-0	1-1	2-1	3-1	3-2	3-0	4-0
Sparta Praha ‡	30	20	4	6	51	25	64	0-3		1-3	0-3	2-2	0-0	1-0	2-1	0-2	3-0	1-0	3-0	1-0	2-0	1-0	4-1
Viktoria Plzen ‡	30	19	6	5	66	33	63	2-2	0-2		3-2	2-0	1-1	1-0	4-2	5-0	4-0	0-4	3-0	5-0	1-1	4-1	4-1
Mladá Boleslav ‡	30	15	5	10	49	34	50	1-4	2-0	0-1		0-1	3-1	1-0	3-0	2-2	3-1	2-3	3-2	1-1	2-1	2-0	2-0
FK Teplice	30	12	10	8	36	30	46	0-1	0-1	3-4	1-3		4-0	2-1	3-2	2-1	0-1	3-1	0-0	0-3	1-1	2-0	0-0
Dukla Praha	30	11	9	10	42	35	42	1-2	1-1	2-4	1-2	0-0		2-0	1-3	2-1	4-2	0-0	0-0	4-0	4-1	2-0	3-0
1.FC Slovácko	30	12	5	13	29	32	41	1-2	0-2	1-3	1-0	0-0	1-0		1-0	2-3	2-0	0-1	1-3	0-3	1-0	3-2	2-1
FK Jablonec	30	11	7	12	54	43	40	0-2	2-4	0-2	0-0	0-1	0-2	1-0		5-1	1-1	2-0	4-0	2-0	4-0	5-0	3-1
1.FK Pribram	30	11	6	13	44	56	39	2-3	0-3	2-1	2-0	0-0	2-2	0-4	4-3		1-2	4-1	0-0	0-0	1-2	3-0	2-1
Dy. Ceské Budejovice	30	9	8	13	30	51	35	0-4	2-4	0-0	1-0	1-1	3-2	2-2	1-5	4-1		1-2	1-0	1-0	0-0	3-1	1-0
Sigma Olomouc §9	30	11	10	9	42	38	34	2-4	0-1	2-3	1-1	1-0	2-1	1-1	1-1	4-4	0-0		1-0	0-2	3-0	4-0	2-1
Slavia Praha	30	8	10	12	28	34	34	1-3	1-1	2-1	1-1	0-0	0-0	0-1	0-0	3-1	2-0	1-0		5-0	0-0	3-1	2-0
Hradec Králové	30	8	7	15	22	38	31	0-3	1-0	0-1	2-0	3-2	0-2	0-1	0-0	0-1	0-0	1-2	1-1		0-1	2-0	1-0
Baník Ostrava	30	7	7	16	31	48	28	1-3	0-2	2-3	1-4	3-4	1-2	0-1	2-2	0-2	1-1	0-0	3-0	1-0		0-1	3-1
Bohemians 1905 Praha	30	6	6	18	20	54	24	1-1	0-4	2-1	0-3	0-0	0-0	1-1	1-2	2-0	2-1	1-1	2-0	0-0	0-1		1-2
Viktoria Zizkov	30	5	4	21	23	55	19	1-4	0-2	0-0	1-2	0-1	1-0	0-1	4-2	1-2	2-0	2-2	1-0	1-1	0-3	0-1	

29/07/2011 – 12/05/2012 • † Qualified for the UEFA Champions League • ‡ Qualified for the Europa League • Attendance: 1,33,701 @ 4,724
Top scorers: **25** – David **LAFATA**, Jablonec • **16** – Marek **BAKOS** SVK, Plzen • **15** – Jiri **STAJNER**, Liberec • **12** – Michal **BREZNANIK** SVK, Liberec

CZECH REPUBLIC 2011-12

DRUHA LIGA (2)

	Pl	W	D	L	F	A	Pts	Usti	Jihlava	Baník	Zbrojovka	Bohemians	Karviná	Varnsdorf	Opava	Most	Zlin	Vlasim	Táborsko	Znojmo	Cáslav	Trinec	Sparta
Usti nad Labem	30	19	4	7	52	35	61		0-0	2-0	2-2	0-1	4-2	1-0	2-1	4-2	3-0	1-0	2-1	1-0	2-0	1-0	2-1
Vysocina Jihlava	30	16	7	7	45	29	55	2-5		1-1	1-0	0-3	1-1	0-1	3-1	3-0	3-3	2-0	4-0	2-0	3-0	3-0	1-0
Baník Sokolov	30	15	7	8	43	31	52	3-2	3-1		2-2	3-0	2-0	0-0	1-0	0-2	2-0	0-1	0-2	2-2	3-1	2-1	2-0
Zbrojovka Brno	30	13	10	7	37	29	49	1-4	0-2	1-0		1-1	4-1	3-1	0-1	2-0	0-0	0-0	2-1	2-0	1-0	0-0	1-1
Bohemians Praha	30	14	6	10	43	31	48	2-0	2-0	3-0	0-1		1-0	1-2	1-2	1-0	0-0	1-1	1-2	4-0	0-0	1-2	3-2
MFK Karviná	30	12	7	11	36	35	43	1-1	1-1	2-1	0-1	2-0		0-1	2-0	2-1	1-0	3-1	1-1	4-1	1-2	2-1	2-1
FK Varnsdorf	30	10	12	8	33	34	42	2-0	4-0	1-3	1-2	1-1	1-1		0-0	2-1	2-0	0-1	3-3	1-1	2-2	1-0	2-5
Slezsky Opava	30	11	8	11	46	36	41	3-1	0-2	2-2	1-4	2-3	3-2	5-0		2-2	0-0	4-1	0-1	0-1	4-0	0-0	1-0
Banik Most	30	11	5	14	31	44	38	0-2	0-0	0-0	1-0	1-0	1-0	0-1	1-4		1-0	2-0	3-0	0-0	3-2	1-4	4-2
Tescoma Zlin	30	9	9	12	28	36	36	2-2	0-1	1-1	0-0	3-0	0-1	0-0	2-0	2-1		2-1	1-2	3-1	1-0	2-0	2-0
Graffin Vlasim	30	9	9	12	36	38	36	0-2	1-3	1-3	1-1	0-1	2-0	1-0	1-1	7-0	1-1		3-1	1-1	1-2	2-2	2-1
MAS Táborsko	30	10	4	16	37	51	341	5-0	0-1	1-2	1-2	2-4	0-2	1-1	1-6	2-0	2-0	0-0		1-0	3-0	2-1	1-3
1.SC Znojmo	30	8	10	12	28	35	34	2-1	1-0	0-1	3-0	0-2	0-0	0-0	0-0	1-0	4-1	0-2	3-1		1-1	0-0	0-1
FC Cáslav	30	8	10	12	27	39	34	1-2	0-0	0-2	1-0	1-1	0-0	0-0	2-1	1-2	3-0	2-1	2-0	1-1		0-0	2-0
Trinec	30	7	9	14	31	41	30	1-2	1-3	1-0	1-2	0-4	2-0	2-2	1-1	0-0	4-1	1-2	2-0	2-1	1-1		0-2
Sparta Praha B	30	8	3	19	37	46	27	0-1	1-2	1-2	2-2	3-1	1-2	0-1	0-1	0-2	0-1	1-1	2-0	1-4	3-0	3-1	

5/08/2011 – 26/05/2012 • Usti nad Labem denied licence for promotion. Banik Sokolov declined promotion • Top scorer: **13** – Jiri **MLIKA**, Sokolov

CZECH REPUBLIC MEDALS TABLE POST 1993

		Overall			League			Cup	
		G	S	B	G	S	B	G	S
1	Sparta Praha	16	10		11	6		5	4
2	Slavia Praha	6	9	2	3	9	2	3	
3	Slovan Liberec	4	2	1	3		1	1	2
4	Baník Ostrava	2	2	3	1		3	1	2
5	Viktoria Zizkov	2	1	2				2	1
6	FK Teplice	2	1	1		1	1	2	
7	Viktoria Plzen	2		1	1		1	1	
8	FK Jablonec	1	4	3		1	3	1	3
9	Sigma Olomouc	1	2	3		1	3	1	1
10	Mladá Boleslav	1	1	1		1	1	1	
11	FC Hradec Králové	1						1	
12	1.FK Drnovice		2	1			1		2
13	1.FC Slovácko		2						2

CLUBS IN CZECHOSLOVAKIAN FOOTBALL 1925–1993

		Overall			League			Cup		Europe		
		G	S	B	G	S	B	G	S	G	S	B
1	Sparta Praha	27	21	8	19	16	7	8	5			1
2	Dukla Praha	19	9	5	11	7	3	8	2			2
4	Slavia Praha	9	11	8	9	9	7		2			
6	Baník Ostrava	6	7	2	3	6	1	3	1			
10	Bohemians Praha	1	2	12	1	1	11		1			1

CLUBS IN CZECH FOOTBALL 1896–1946

		Overall			League			Cup	
		G	S	B	G	S	B	G	S
1	Sparta Praha	25	15		11	3		14	12
2	Slavia Praha	25	13		10	7		15	6
3	Viktoria Zizkov	7	4	3		1	2	7	3

POHAR CMFS 2011-12

Third Round / Round of 16 / Quarter-finals / Semi-finals / Final

Third Round		Round of 16		Quarter-finals		Semi-finals	
Sigma Olomouc	2	**Sigma Olomouc**	4 1				
Vysocina Jihlava *	1	MAS Táborsko *	1 0	**Sigma Olomouc** *	2 2		
HS Kromeriz *	1			Baník Ostrava	1 1		
MAS Táborsko	3	**1.FC Slovácko**	2 0				
1.FC Slovácko	2	1.FC Slovácko *	1 0			**Sigma Olomouc**	0 3
Frydek Mistek *	0	**Baník Ostrava**	1 0			FK Teplice	0 0
Sumperk *	0						
Baník Ostrava	2	**Slovan Liberec**	4 2				
Slovan Liberec *	3	SK Prevysov *	1 1	Slovan Liberec	1 0		
Hradec Králové	1			**FK Teplice** *	1 2		
Slavia Praha	0	**SK Prevysov** *	1 1				
SK Prevysov *	3	**MFK Karviná**	0 1				
MFK Karviná	4	Slezsky Opava	1 3				
Mikulowice *	0	**FK Teplice**					
FK Teplice	4						
FK Jablonec	6	**FK Jablonec**	1 2	**FK Jablonec**	0 5		
TJ Kunice *	4	Dukla Praha	0 3	Dy. Ceské Budejovice *	0 0		
Sokol Tasovice *	0					FK Jablonec	0 2
Dukla Praha	4	**Viktoria Zizkov**	2 0			**Sparta Praha** *	1 3
Viktoria Zizkov	2	Sokol Ovcary *	0 1				
Sokol Ovcary *	0	**Dy. Ceské Budejovice** *	1 1				
Králuv Dvur *	0						
Dy. Ceské Budejovice	2	**Mladá Boleslav**	1 2	Mladá Boleslav *	1 0		
Mladá Boleslav	3	Viktoria Plzen *	1 0	**Sparta Praha**	1 1		
Zbrojovka Brno *	1						
Baník Sokolov *	1	**1.SC Znojmo**	1 0				
Viktoria Plzen	3	Bohemians 1905 Praha	0 1				
1.SC Znojmo	2	**Sparta Praha**	4 3				
Bohemians 1905 Praha	1						
FK Pardubice *	1						
Sparta Praha	3						

* Home team/home team in the first leg • ‡ Qualified for the Europa League

Sigma Olomouc	1
Sparta Praha ‡	0

CUP FINAL

Stadion mesta Plzne, Plzen, 2-05-2012
Att: 7231. Ref: Michal Patak
Scorer - Veprek [46] for Sigma
Sigma - Zdenek Zlamal - Radim Kucera, Ales Skerle - Tomas Janotka, Michal Veprek, Pavel Dreksa - Martin Pospisil, Michal Ordos, Jan Schulmeister (Martin Hala 90), Jan Navratil (Radim Nepozitek 86), Zdenek Klesnil (Adam Varadi 69). Tr: Petr Ulicny
Sparta - Tomas Vaclik - Erich Brabec, Manuel Pamic, Jakub Brabec (Mario Holek 59), Jiri Jarosik - Libor Sionko (Andrej Keric 73), Marek Matejovsky, Josef Husbauer• Peter Grajciar 88), Ladislav Krejci - Leonard Kweuke•, Tomas Prikryl. Tr: Vaclav Jilek

DEN – DENMARK

FIFA/COCA-COLA WORLD RANKING

'93	'94	'95	'96	'97	'98	'99	'00	'01	'02	'03	'04	'05	'06	'07	'08	'09	'10	'11	'12
6	14	9	6	8	19	11	22	18	12	13	14	13	21	31	37	28	28	11	23

2012												High	Low	Av
Jan	Feb	Mar	Apr	May	Jun	Jul	Aug	Sep	Oct	Nov	Dec			
11	10	11	9	10	9	10	10	10	18	22	23	3	38	17

When Denmark were drawn against the Netherlands, Germany and Portugal in their group at the finals of Euro 2012 they were seen as the fall guys up against three potential winners. After beating the Dutch in their opening match, memories of Euro 92 came flooding back and had it not been for late goals conceded in the remaining two matches there might have been a repeat of those heroics. Instead, Denmark were knocked out at the first hurdle, the victory over Holland just one of two during the course of the whole year - the other coming the week before in a pre-tournament friendly against Australia. Drawn in a difficult 2014 FIFA World Cup qualifying group, long-standing coach Morten Olsen faces an uphill battle to qualify for the finals in Brazil after a lack-lustre start to the campaign. In club football there was a major surprise in the league when FC Nordsjælland dethroned perennial champions FC København. Based in the town of Farum to the north of Copenhagen, Nordsjælland had won the cup in 2010 and 2011 and then completed a remarkable treble with the league title in 2012 - not bad for a team formed only in 2003. FC København did finish the season with some silverware after beating Horsens in the cup final, Brazilian midfielder Claudemir scoring the only goal of the game just before half-time.

UEFA EUROPEAN CHAMPIONSHIP RECORD
1960 r1 1964 4 SF 1968-1980 DNQ 1984 3 SF 1988 7 r1 1992 1 Winners 1996 9 r1
2000 16 r1 2004 8 QF 2008 DNQ 2012 11 r1

DANSK BOLDSPIL-UNION (DBU)

DBU Allé 1,
Brøndby 2605

☎ +45 43 262222
📠 +45 43 262245
✉ dbu@dbu.dk
🖥 www.dbu.dk
FA 1889 CON 1954 FIFA 1904
P Allan Hansen
GS Jim Stjerne Hansen

THE STADIA

2014 FIFA World Cup Stadia
| Parken | |
| Copenhagen | 38 009 |

Other Main Stadia
Brøndby Stadion	
Brøndby, Copenhagen	29 000
Blue Water Arena	
Esbjerg	18 000
Fionia Park	
Odense	15 761
Energi Nord Arena	
Aalborg	13 800

MAJOR CITIES/TOWNS

		Population
1	Copenhagen	1 081 788
2	Aarhus	228 723
3	Odense	159 162
4	Aalborg	100 601
5	Esbjerg	70 872
6	Randers	56 134
7	Kolding	55 147
8	Horsens	53 008
9	Vejle	49 901
10	Roskilde	48 219
11	Silkeborg	45 752
12	Herning	44 968
13	Næstved	42 091
14	Greve Strand	40 725
15	Fredericia	37 087
16	Køge	35 860
17	Viborg	35 517
18	Helsingør	35 149
19	Holstebro	32 161

KONGERIGET DANMARK • KINGDOM OF DENMARK

Capital	Copenhagen (København)	Population	5 500 510 (110)	% in cities	87%
GDP per capita	$37 200 (30)	Area km²	43 094 km² (133)	GMT +/-	+1
Neighbours (km)	Germany 68 • Coast 7314				

RECENT INTERNATIONAL MATCHES PLAYED BY DENMARK

2008 Opponents	Score	Venue	Comp	Scorers	Att	Referee
12-08 Chile	L 1-2	Brøndby	Fr	Schone [63]	8 700	Jakobsen ISL
5-09 Portugal	D 1-1	Copenhagen	WCq	Bendtner [43]	37 998	Busacca SUI
9-09 Albania	D 1-1	Tirana	WCq	Bendtner [40]	8 000	Cakir TUR
10-10 Sweden	W 1-0	Copenhagen	WCq	Jakob Poulsen [78]	37 800	Mejuto ESP
14-10 Hungary	L 0-1	Copenhagen	WCq		36 956	Meyer GER
14-11 Korea Republic	D 0-0	Esbjerg	Fr		15 789	Hansson SWE
18-11 USA	W 3-1	Aarhus	Fr	Absalonsen [47], Rieks [52], Bernburg [55]	15 172	Thomson SCO
2010						
3-03 Austria	L 1-2	Vienna	Fr	Bendtner [17]	13 500	Kralovec CZE
27-05 Senegal	W 2-0	Aalborg	Fr	Christian Poulsen [26], Enevoldsen [90]	14 112	Nijhuis NED
1-06 Australia	L 0-1	Roodepoort	Fr		6 000	Bennett RSA
5-06 South Africa	L 0-1	Atteridgeville	Fr		28 000	Mbaga TAN
14-06 Netherlands	L 0-2	Johannesburg	WCr1		83 465	Lannoy FRA
19-06 Cameroon	W 2-1	Pretoria	WCr1	Bendtner [33], Rommedahl [61]	38 074	Larrionda URU
24-06 Japan	L 1-3	Rustenburg	WCr1	Tomasson [81p]	27 967	Damon RSA
11-08 Germany	D 2-2	Copenhagen	Fr	Rommedahl [74], Junker [87]	19 071	Kelly IRL
7-09 Iceland	W 1-0	Copenhagen	ECq	Kahlenberg [91+]	18 908	McDonald SCO
8-10 Portugal	L 1-3	Porto	ECq	OG [79]	27 117	Braamhaar NED
12-10 Cyprus	W 2-0	Copenhagen	ECq	Morten Rasmussen [48], Lorentzen [81]	15 544	Muniz ESP
17-11 Czech Republic	D 0-0	Aarhus	Fr		9 184	Webb ENG
2011						
9-02 England	L 1-2	Copenhagen	Fr	Agger [8]	21 523	Eriksson SWE
26-03 Norway	D 1-1	Oslo	ECq	Rommedahl [27]	24 828	Rocchi ITA
29-03 Slovakia	W 2-1	Trnava	Fr	OG [3], Krohn-Delhi [72]	4 927	Fernandez ESP
4-06 Iceland	W 2-0	Reykjavik	ECq	Schone [60], Eriksen [75]	7 629	Aydinus TUR
10-08 Scotland	L 1-2	Glasgow	Fr	Eriksen [31]	17 582	Borg MLT
6-09 Norway	W 2-0	Copenhagen	ECq	Bendtner 2 [24 44]	37 167	Lannoy FRA
7-10 Cyprus	W 4-1	Nicosia	ECq	Jacobsen [7], Rommedahl 2 [11 22], Krohn-Dehli [20]	2 408	Strahonja CRO
11-10 Portugal	W 2-1	Copenhagen	ECq	Krohn-Dehli [13], Bendtner [63]	37 012	Rizzoli ITA
11-11 Sweden	W 2-0	Copenhagen	Fr	Bendtner [35], Krohn-Delhi [80]	18 057	Moen NOR
15-11 Finland	W 2-1	Esbjerg	Fr	Agger [57], Bendtner [59]	15 100	Jakobsson ISL
2012						
29-02 Russia	L 0-2	Copenhagen	Fr		13 593	Vad HUN
26-05 Brazil	L 1-3	Hamburg	Fr	Bendtner [71]	51 000	Brych GER
2-06 Australia	W 2-0	Copenhagen	Fr	Agger [32p], Bjelland [68]	16 888	Damato ITA
9-06 Netherlands	W 1-0	Kharkov	ECr1	Krohn-Dehli [24]	34 973	Skomina SVN
13-06 Portugal	L 2-3	Lviv	ECr1	Bendtner 2 [41 80]	34 915	Thomson SCO
17-06 Germany	L 1-2	Lviv	ECr1	Krohn-Dehli [24]	32 990	Velasco ESP
15-08 Slovakia	L 1-3	Odense	Fr	Mikkelsen [22]	9 209	Stalhammar SWE
8-09 Czech Republic	D 0-0	Copenhagen	WCq		24 004	Stark GER
12-10 Bulgaria	D 1-1	Sofia	WCq	Bendtner [40]	20 780	Chapron FRA
16-10 Italy	L 1-3	Milan	WCq	Kvist [45]	37 027	Skomina SVN
14-11 Turkey	D 1-1	Istanbul	Fr	Bendtner [65p]	30 000	Brych GER

Fr = Friendly match • EC = UEFA EURO 2012 • WC = FIFA World Cup • q = qualifier • r1 = first round group • qf = quarter-final

DENMARK NATIONAL TEAM HISTORICAL RECORDS

Caps: **129** - Peter Schmeichel 1987-2001 • **121** - Dennis Rommedahl 2000- • **112** - Jon Dahl Tomasson 1997-2010 • **108** - Thomas Helveg 1994-2008 • **103** - Michael Laudrup 1982-98 • **102** - Morten Olsen 1970-89 & Martin Jorgensen 1998-2011 • **101** - Thomas Sorensen 1999- • **92** - Christian Poulsen 2001- • **87** - John Sivebæk 1982-92 • **86** - Jan Heintze 198-2002 • **84** - Lars Olsen 1986-96 • **82** - Brian Laudrup 1987-98 • **80** - Jesper Gronkjær 1999- • **77** - Kim Vilfort 1983-96 • **75** - Per Rontved 1970-82

Goals: **52** - Poul Nielsen 1910-25 & Jon Dahl Tomasson 1997-2010 • **44** - Pauli Jorgensen 1925-39 • **42** - Ole Madsen 1958-69 • **38** - Preben Elkjær-Larsen 1977-88 • **37** - Michael Laudrup 1982-98 • **29** - Henning Enoksen 1958-66 • **22** - Michael Rohde 1915-31; Ebbe Sand 1998-2004 & Nicklas Bendtner 2006- • **21** - Brian Laudrup 1987-98, Flemming Povlsen 1987-94 & Dennis Rommedahl 2000-

Coaches: Charles Willims ENG 1908-10 • Axel Anderson Byrval 1913-5 & 1917-18 • Arne Sorensen 1956-61 • Poul Petersen 1962-66 • Erik Hansen 1967-69 • John Hansen 1969 • Rudi Strittich AUT 1970-75 • Kurt Nielsen 1976-79 • Sepp Piontek GER 1979-90 • Richard Moller Nielsen 1990-96 • Bo Johansson 1996-2000 • Morten Olsen 2000-

DENMARK 2011-12

SUPERLIGAEN

	Pl	W	D	L	F	A	Pts	Nordsjælland	København	Midtjylland	Horsens	AGF	SønderjyskE	AaB	Silkeborg	Brøndby	OB	Lyngby	Køge
FC Nordsjælland †	33	21	5	7	49	22	68		1-0	0-0	1-1 3-0	5-3	1-0 2-0	1-0	2-1 2-1	2-0 1-2	0-0	4-0 0-1	2-0 2-0
FC København †	33	19	9	5	55	26	66	2-0 1-3		2-0 0-0	2-1	1-1 0-0	2-0	2-0 3-0	2-1 2-1	3-1	2-2 1-1	3-0	2-1
FC Midtjylland ‡	33	17	7	9	50	40	58	2-1 1-1	1-0		1-0 4-1	0-2	2-0 1-1	1-3	1-2 2-2	2-1 1-0	2-0	2-1 1-2	2-1
AC Horsens ‡	33	17	6	10	53	37	57	0-2	0-1 2-0	2-1		0-3 3-1	5-0	3-3 1-0	1-1	2-0	4-3 0-1	0-0	3-0 2-1
AGF Aarhus ‡	33	12	12	9	47	40	48	1-0 1-1	0-0	4-2 0-2	1-3		1-3	1-1	0-2	0-0 5-1	2-2 0-0	2-1 2-1	2-0
SønderjyskE	33	11	11	11	48	51	44	1-0	0-2 2-2	1-1	1-3 1-4	3-1 1-1		0-0 5-0	2-4	3-3	0-4	3-1	0-0 2-1
AaB Aalborg	33	11	11	11	48	51	44	1-2 0-2	1-1	1-0 1-2	2-0	2-1 0-2	1-2		3-1	1-0	2-1 2-1	1-2 1-0	1-0
Silkeborg IF	33	11	10	12	51	47	43	1-2	0-0	4-1	1-1 0-1	1-1 2-1	1-1 1-1	1-1 4-2		0-1 2-1	1-3 1-1	3-0	0-1
Brøndby IF	33	9	9	15	35	46	36	0-1	1-2 2-1	0-2	1-4 0-1	0-0	2-2 1-0	2-2 1-1	3-2		1-0	1-0 2-1	5-0 1-1
OB Odense	33	8	10	15	46	50	34	2-0 0-1	1-3	1-4 2-3	0-1	1-2	2-4 1-1	1-2	2-2	2-1 0-0		3-1 4-0	2-1 2-4
Lyngby BK	33	8	4	21	32	61	28	0-2	0-1 1-3	1-2	1-1 1-2	1-1	0-1 0-4	3-2	0-2 2-3	1-0	1-0		3-1 2-2
HB Køge	33	4	7	22	32	71	19	0-2	2-4 0-5	2-3 1-1	2-1	0-2 1-3	1-3	1-4 1-1	3-0 1-3	1-1	1-1	1-4	

16/07/2011 - 23/05/2012 • † Qualified for the UEFA Champions League • ‡ Qualified for the Europa League • Attendance: 1,404,893 @ 7,095
Top scorers: **18** - Dame **N'DOYE** SEN, København • **14** - Nicklas **HELENIUS**, AaB • **13** - **CESAR SANTIN** BRA, København • **11** - Gilberto **MACENA** BRA, Horsens • **10** - Simon **MAKIENOK CHRISTOFFERSEN**, Køge & Christian **HOLST** FRO, Silkeborg

DENMARK 2011-12

1.DIVISION (2)

	Pl	W	D	L	F	A	Pts	Esbjerg	Randers	Vejle	Viborg	Brønshøj	Vestsjælland	Fredericia	Skive	Hobro	Hjørring	AB	Roskilde	Næstved	Blokhus
Esbjerg FB	26	21	3	2	60	19	66		0-2	2-1	4-0	0-0	3-1	4-1	2-1	1-0	3-0	3-0	1-0	5-4	2-1
Randers FC	26	15	4	7	38	22	49	0-0		4-1	1-0	0-1	2-1	0-1	0-3	2-0	1-0	3-1	3-1	2-1	4-0
Vejle BK Kolding	26	12	8	6	58	32	44	0-1	3-0		2-2	4-0	1-1	0-0	3-0	4-0	5-1	2-0	2-2	4-3	5-0
Viborg FF	26	10	10	6	45	34	40	1-2	2-2	1-1		1-1	1-2	0-3	2-2	1-1	4-0	2-2	1-0	2-0	4-2
Brønshøj BK	26	10	10	6	35	34	40	0-0	0-0	2-1	1-3		0-2	0-0	1-1	1-1	2-2	2-1	2-1	2-1	2-1
FC Vestsjælland	26	10	8	8	42	35	38	3-2	1-2	3-1	3-3	3-1		0-2	0-0	0-0	0-3	1-1	0-1	5-1	5-1
FC Fredericia	26	9	8	9	33	30	35	0-1	1-1	2-2	1-2	0-5	3-1		0-1	2-0	0-0	1-1	1-3	2-1	3-0
Skive IK	26	9	7	10	31	41	34	0-4	0-3	3-2	0-0	4-1	0-0	0-2		1-6	1-3	1-1	2-1	1-0	3-1
Hobro IK	26	8	9	9	37	35	33	1-2	1-0	1-4	1-1	4-1	2-2	2-1	2-0		4-0	1-3	1-1	1-0	3-1
FC Hjørring	26	8	7	11	31	42	31	0-4	0-2	1-1	1-2	2-2	1-0	1-4	0-1	0-0		4-0	0-0	3-1	2-2
Akademisk Boldclub	26	7	8	11	32	43	29	0-2	2-3	0-2	1-0	2-2	1-1	2-4	3-2	1-0	1-3		2-1	3-0	2-4
FC Roskilde	26	8	3	15	28	38	27	1-2	1-0	0-3	0-4	0-2	0-2	3-2	0-1	3-2	0-1	0-1		2-0	5-1
Næstved BK	26	6	4	16	32	51	22	2-3	1-0	2-2	0-3	0-2	1-2	1-0	2-2	2-2	2-0	2-1	1-0		1-1
Blokhus FC	26	2	5	19	27	72	11	0-7	0-1	1-2	1-3	0-2	2-3	1-1	2-1	1-1	0-3	2-2	1-2	1-3	

12/08/2011 - 10/06/2012

MEDALS TABLE

		Overall G S B	League G S B	Cup G S	Europe G S B	City
1	KB København	16 19 8	15 15 8	1 4		Copenhagen
2	Brøndby IF	16 11 6	10 9 5	6 2	1	Copenhagen
3	AGF Aarhus	14 8 11	5 5 11	9 3		Aarhus
4	FC København	14 7 2	9 4 2	5 3		Copenhagen
5	B 93 København	11 5 9	10 5 9	1		Copenhagen
6	Vejle BK	11 4 2	5 3 2	6 1		Vejle
7	Akademisk København	10 14 11	9 11 11	1 3		Copenhagen
8	B 1903 København	9 10 8	7 8 8	2 2		Copenhagen
9	Frem København	8 15 9	6 12 9	2 3		Copenhagen
10	OB Odense	8 7 5	3 6 5	5 1		Odense
11	Esbjerg FB	7 9 2	5 3 2	2 6		Esbjerg
12	AaB Aalborg	5 8 3	3 3	2 8		Aalborg
13	Lyngby BK	5 5 3	2 3 3	3 2		Lyngby
14	B 1909 Odense	4 1 1	2	1	2 1	Odense
	Hvidovre IF	4 1 1	3 1 1	1		Copenhagen
16	Randers FC	4 1		1	4	Randers
17	FC Nordsjælland	3 1	1	1 2		Farum

DBU LANDSPOKAL 2011-12

Third Round

FC København	2
FC Vestsjælland*	0
Elite 3000*	0
Brøndby IF	4
FC Midtjylland	6
Jagersborg BK*	0
FC Hjørring*	0
FC Nordsjælland	2
Næsby BK*	2
Næstved BK	1
Randers FC*	4
Silkeborg IF	3
Hobro IK	4
BK Marienlyst*	1
Svebølle BI*	0
SønderjyskE	1
HB Køge	3
Esbjerg FB*	1
FC Svendborg*	1 4p
FC Roskilde	1 5p
AGF Aarhus	2 9p
Hvidovre IF*	2 8p
Ringkøbing IF*	1
Vejle BK Kolding	5
FC Fredericia*	1
OB Odense	0
Nordvest FC*	0
Viborg FF	1
Herlev IF	5
Aars IF*	2
Akademisk Boldklub*	0
AC Horsens	3

Round of 16

FC København	3
Brøndby IF*	0
FC Midtjylland	0
FC Nordsjælland*	1
Næsby BK*	4
Silkeborg IF	3
Hobro IK*	0
SønderjyskE	2
HB Køge	2
FC Roskilde*	1
AGF Aarhus	0
Vejle BK Kolding*	1
FC Fredericia*	1 7p
Viborg FF	1 6p
Herlev IF*	2
AC Horsens	3

Quarter-finals

FC København*	2
FC Nordsjælland	0
Næsby BK*	1
SønderjyskE	5
HB Køge	2
Vejle BK Kolding*	1
FC Fredericia*	1
AC Horsens	2

Semi-finals

FC København*	1 3
SønderjyskE	0 4
HB Køge*	2 0
AC Horsens	2 1

Final

FC København	1
AC Horsens ‡	0

*Home team/home team in the first leg • ‡ Qualified for the Europa League

CUP FINAL

Parken, Copenhagen, 17-05-2012
Att: 21 963. Ref: Lars Christoffersen
Scorer - Claudemir 42 for FC København
København - Kim Christensen - Lars Jacobsen, Kris Stadsgaard, Mathias Jorgensen, Bryan Oviedo - Martin Vingaard, Claudemir•, Christian Grindheim, Pape Pate Diouf (Thomas Kristensen 63) - Mostafa Abdellaoue (Ragnar Sigurdsson 83), Morten Nordstrand (Dame N'Doye 77). Tr: Carsten V. Jensen
Horsens - Frederik Rønnow - Alexander Juel Andersen, Morten Rasmussen, Nabil Aslam, Anders Nøhr (Thomas Kortegaard 80) - Lasse Kryger, Martin Retov, Janus Drachmann, Jeppe Mehl - Martin Spelmann (Niels Lodberg 32), Ken Fagerberg (Andre Bjerregaard 63).
Tr: Johnny Molby

DJI – DJIBOUTI

FIFA/COCA-COLA WORLD RANKING

'93	'94	'95	'96	'97	'98	'99	'00	'01	'02	'03	'04	'05	'06	'07	'08	'09	'10	'11	'12
-	169	177	185	189	191	195	189	193	195	197	201	200	198	173	188	189	191	198

2012

Jan	Feb	Mar	Apr	May	Jun	Jul	Aug	Sep	Oct	Nov	Dec	High	Low	Av
198	198	197	197	197	197	196	198	196	197	202	202	169	202	191

Djibouti finished 2012 as the worst-ranked team in Africa after playing no international football in the year thanks to their failure to enter the annual CECAFA Cup which usually provides them with a regular dose of competitive action. Five successive defeats for their side at the end of 2011 continued the poor performances of one of Africa's smallest states and they ended 2012 in 202nd place in the FIFA/Coca-Cola World Ranking. International competition was restricted to the participation of AS Port in the CECAFA Kagame Inter-Club Cup in Tanzania in July, where they lost all three group games, conceding 13 goals and scoring just once. AS Port retained their league title for a third successive year by edging Guelleh Batal - otherwise known as Garde Republicain - and AS CDE-Colas by two points. But AS Port, coached by Rouffa Mohamed, were not able to replicate their double winning feat of 2011. Instead, cup honours went to Guelleh Batal, who edged AS Ali Sabieh 2-1 in the final. The Super Cup at the end of the year was also won by Guelleh Batal who beat AS Port 2-0 for a second piece of silverware in the space of two months. Djibouti's federation elected a new president in November with Souleiman Hassan Waberi promising a more progressive approach to the development of the game in the Red Sea state.

CAF AFRICA CUP OF NATIONS RECORD
1957-1998 DNE 2000-2002 DNQ 2004-2008 DNE 2010 DNQ 2012-2013 DNE

FEDERATION DJIBOUTIENNE DE FOOTBALL (FDF)

Centre Technique National, Boite postale 2694, Djibouti
☎ +253 353599
📠 +253 353588
✉ fdf_1979@yahoo.fr
🖥 www.fdf.dj
FA 1979 CON 1986 FIFA 1994
P Souleiman Hassan Waberi
GS Hassan Mohamed Kamil

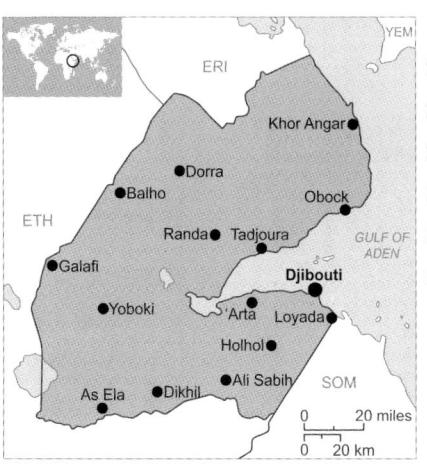

MAJOR CITIES/TOWNS

		Population
1	Djibouti	610 608
2	Ali Sabieh	22 999
3	Dikhil	16 721
4	Arta	11 635
5	Tadjoura	8 740
6	Obock	7 469
7	Ali Adde	5 419
8	Holhol	3 517
9	Yoboki	3 109
10	We'a	3 000
11	Airoli	2 577
12	Dorra	1 465

THE STADIA
2014 FIFA World Cup Stadia
Stade National Hassan Gouled Djibouti 10 000
Other Main Stadia
The Stade National Hassan Gouled is the main stadium in the country

REPUBLIQUE DE DJIBOUTI • JUMHURIYAT JIBUTI • REPUBLIC OF DJIBOUTI

Capital Djibouti	Population 516 055 (168)	% in cities 87%
GDP per capita $2700 (170)	Area km² 23 200 km² (150)	GMT +/- +3
Neighbours (km) Eritrea 109, Ethiopia 349, Somalia 58 • Coast 314		

RECENT INTERNATIONAL MATCHES PLAYED BY DJIBOUTI

2009	Opponents		Score	Venue	Comp	Scorers	Att	Referee
2-01	Burundi	L	0-4	Jinja	CCr1			
4-01	Sudan	D	1-1	Jinja	CCr1	Ahmed Hassan Daher 59		
6-01	Kenya	L	1-5	Jinja	CCr1	Ahmed Hassan Daher 53		
30-11	Ethiopia	L	0-5	Nairobi	CCr1			
2-12	Kenya	L	0-2	Nairobi	CCr1			
4-12	Zambia	L	0-6	Nairobi	CCr1			

2010
No international matches played in 2010

2011

1-11	Somalia	W	1-0	Djibouti	Fr			
11-11	Namibia	L	0-4	Djibouti	WCq		3 000	Bamlak ETH
15-11	Namibia	L	0-4	Windhoek	WCq		2 145	Chirinda MOZ
27-11	Zimbabwe	L	0-2	Dar es Salaam	CCr1			
29-11	Tanzania	L	0-3	Dar es Salaam	CCr1			
2-12	Rwanda	L	2-5	Dar es Salaam	CCr1	Ahmed Hassan Daoud 2 25 34		

2012
No international matches played in 2012

CC = CECAFA Cup • AR = Arab Cup • WC = FIFA World Cup • q = qualifier • r1 = First round group

DJIBOUTI 2011-12

DIVISION 1

	Pl	W	D	L	F	A	Pts	Port	CDE	Guelleh Batal	Tadjourah	Ali Sabieh	SID	Gendarmerie	Dikhil	ONEAD	APEJAS
AS Port	18	12	3	3	52	12	39		2-0	0-0	2-1	1-0	0-1	3-0	3-0	3-0	14-1
AS CDE	18	11	4	3	36	19	37	0-0		2-1	1-3	1-1	1-0	2-2	1-0	2-0	8-1
Guelleh Batal	18	11	4	3	41	17	37	1-2	2-2		0-1	2-1	3-0	3-2	4-1	2-1	5-0
AS Tadjourah	18	11	3	4	39	16	36	1-1	1-3	0-1		1-1	2-1	1-1	3-0	5-0	6-1
AS Ali Sabieh	18	10	5	3	44	13	35	3-0	1-0	1-1	1-2		1-1	3-1	3-0	3-1	1-1
Société Immobilière	18	8	3	7	28	25	27	1-0	2-3	1-1	1-0	0-3		1-0	2-2	2-0	7-1
Gendarmerie Nationale	18	3	4	11	22	35	13	0-5	0-1	1-2	2-3	0-2	3-2		2-1	0-1	5-0
FC Dikhil	18	3	3	12	22	44	12	1-4	1-2	2-3	0-3	0-5	5-3	1-1		1-0	2-2
ONEAD	18	3	2	13	14	47	11	0-7	2-4	0-5	0-2	1-5	0-1	1-1	3-2		2-0
APEJAS	18	1	3	14	14	84	6	2-5	0-3	0-5	0-4	0-9	0-2	3-1	0-3	2-2	

16/12/2011 - 20/04/2012

DJIBOUTI 2011-12 DIVISION 2

	Pl	W	D	L	F	A	Pts
Arhiba	18	12	3	3	54	35	39
EAD	18	11	4	3	62	36	37
Ambouli	18	10	4	4	38	23	34
SDVK	18	8	3	7	45	44	27
L. Mandela	18	8	3	7	36	30	27
Hadji-Dideh	18	6	4	8	42	51	22
Police Nationale	18	6	4	8	41	52	22
ETS Adi	18	6	2	10	54	56	20
Q. 6	18	5	4	9	42	46	19
Kartileh	18	1	3	14	22	63	6

24/10/2011 - 26/03/2012

COUPE DU 27 JUIN FINAL
Stade Hassan Gouled, Djibouti, 19-10-2012
Guelleh Batal 2-1 AS Ali Sabieh

MEDALS TABLE

		Overall G	Lge G	Cup G
1	AS Port	14	6	8
2	CDE (Compagnie Djibouti-Ethiopie)	13	6	7
3	Force Nationale de Securité/Police	10	7	3
4	Balbala	4		4
5	Société Immobilière de Djibouti (SID)	3	2	1
6	AS Ali Sabieh (Djibouti Telecom)	2	1	1
	AS Boreh	2	1	1
	Aéroport	2	1	1
	Guelleh Batal (Garde Republican)	2		2
	Chemin de Fer	2		2
	Gendarmerie Nationale	2	2	
12	Jeunesse Espoir	1		1
	Poste de Djibouti	1		1
	Merill	1	1	

DMA – DOMINICA

FIFA/COCA-COLA WORLD RANKING

'93	'94	'95	'96	'97	'98	'99	'00	'01	'02	'03	'04	'05	'06	'07	'08	'09	'10	'11	'12
-	-	158	138	139	133	149	152	161	174	185	165	172	181	189	191	197	129	171	161

2012														
Jan	Feb	Mar	Apr	May	Jun	Jul	Aug	Sep	Oct	Nov	Dec	High	Low	Av
171	176	174	176	174	173	172	172	174	156	155	161	128	198	164

Harlem United were crowned Premiere Division champions after a winner-takes-all meeting on the final day of the season against the defending champions Bath Estate. The eight team league saw everyone play each other just once to decide the title, leading to a fair amount of criticism about the effect the lack of regular club football was having on the national team. Harlem went into the match knowing that they could afford to lose by a single goal and still take the title on goal difference from Bath but at half-time they found themselves a goal down and reduced to ten men. They hung on and scored an equaliser through Kerry Alleyne 15 minutes from time to secure a record 20th title - their first since 2006 - and deny Bath Estate a fourth consecutive championship. Three months later Bath Estate again found themselves as runners-up after losing 1-0 in the cup final to Northern Bombers. The national team played just three matches during the course of 2012, all of them in the qualifying tournament of the Caribbean Cup. In a group staged in Barbados they beat Aruba 3-2 thanks to two goals from record goalscorer Kurlson Benjamin, who took his total for Dominica to 14, but then lost against the Bajans and the Dominican Republic in close games to crash out at the first hurdle.

CFU CARIBBEAN CUP RECORD

1989 DNQ 1991 DNE 1992-1993 DNQ **1994** 8 r1 1995-1997 DNQ **1998** 8 r1 1999-2012 DNQ

DOMINICA FOOTBALL ASSOCIATION (DFA)

Patrick John Football House, Bath Estate, PO Box 1080, Roseau
+1 767 4487577
+1 767 4487587
domfootball@cwdom.dm
domfootball.com
FA 1970 CON 1994 FIFA 1994
P Glen Etienne
GS Ericson Delgallerie

THE STADIA

2014 FIFA World Cup Stadia
Windsor Park
Roseau 12 000
Other Main Stadia
Bath Estate Football Field
Roseau

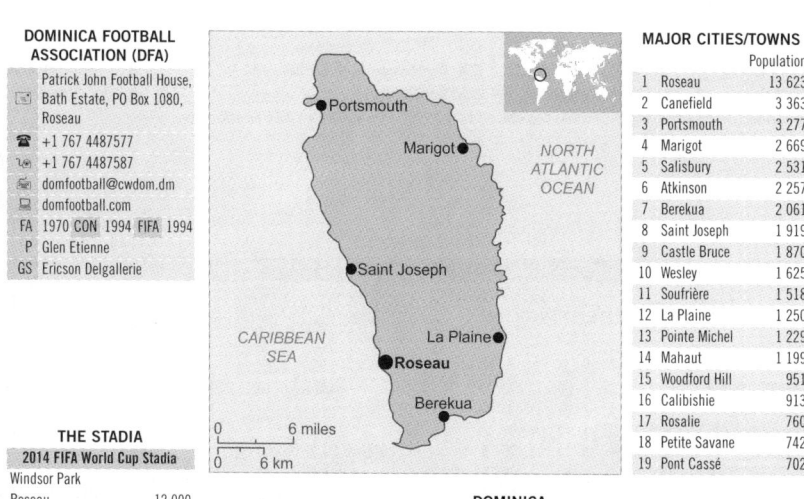

MAJOR CITIES/TOWNS

		Population
1	Roseau	13 623
2	Canefield	3 363
3	Portsmouth	3 277
4	Marigot	2 669
5	Salisbury	2 531
6	Atkinson	2 257
7	Berekua	2 061
8	Saint Joseph	1 919
9	Castle Bruce	1 870
10	Wesley	1 625
11	Soufrière	1 518
12	La Plaine	1 250
13	Pointe Michel	1 229
14	Mahaut	1 199
15	Woodford Hill	951
16	Calibishie	913
17	Rosalie	760
18	Petite Savane	742
19	Pont Cassé	702

DOMINICA

Capital	Roseau	
GDP per capita	$10 000 (106)	
Neighbours (km)	Coast 148	
Population	72 660 (201)	
Area km²	751 km² (188)	
% in cities	74%	
GMT +/-	-4	

RECENT INTERNATIONAL MATCHES PLAYED BY DOMINICA

2005	Opponents	Score	Venue	Comp	Scorers	Att	Referee
30-09	Guyana	L 0-3	Linden	Fr		800	Lancaster GUY
2-10	Guyana	L 0-3	Georgetown	Fr		1 000	Kia SUR
2006							
3-09	Antigua and Barbuda	L 0-1	St John's	Fr		400	Willett ATG
17-09	Barbados	L 0-5	Roseau	Fr		900	Charles DMA
20-09	Martinique †	L 0-4	Abymes	CCq		1 000	Fanus LCA
22-09	Guadeloupe †	L 0-1	Abymes	CCq		1 100	Willett ATG
24-09	Saint Martin †	D 0-0	Abymes	CCq		500	Willett ATG
2007							
No international matches played in 2007							
2008							
6-02	Barbados	D 1-1	Roseau	WCq	Richard Pacquette [21]	4 200	Quesada CRC
26-03	Barbados	L 0-1	Bridgetown	WCq		4 150	Batres GUA
8-08	Guyana	L 0-3	Georgetown	CCq		3 000	Forde BRB
9-08	Surinam	L 1-3	Georgetown	CCq	Prince Austrie [7]	175	Taylor BRB
2009							
5-12	British Virgin Islands	W 4-0	Roseau	Fr	Prince Austrie [8], Kelly Peters [23], Kurlson Benjamin [25], Cheston Benjamin [85]	600	Baptiste DMA
2010							
25-09	Barbados	W 2-0	Bridgetown	Fr	Kurlson Benjamin [24], Mitchell Joseph [38]	625	Taylor BRB
26-09	Barbados	W 3-1	Bridgetown	Fr	Kurlson Benjamin 3 [35,45,74]	580	Skeete DMA
15-10	British Virgin Islands	W 10-0	San Cristobal	CCq	Mitchell Joseph 3 [1,12,13], Chad Bertrand [55], Kurlson Benjamin 5 [47,71,81,84,85], Donald Jervier [87]	200	Santos PUR
17-10	Dominican Republic	W 1-0	San Cristobal	CCq	Elmond Derrick [66]	600	Lebron PUR
10-11	Cuba	L 2-4	St John's	CCq	Kurlson Benjamin 2 [11,87]	500	Lancaster GUY
12-11	Antigua and Barbuda	D 0-0	St John's	CCq		400	Purser JAM
14-11	Suriname	L 0-5	St John's	CCq		500	Lancaster GUY
2011							
2-09	Nicaragua	L 0-2	Roseau	WCq		8 000	Vaughn USA
11-09	St Vincent/Grenadines	L 0-1	Kingstown	Fr		2 500	Cambridge VIN
7-10	Panama	L 0-5	Roseau	WCq		4 000	Wijngaarde SUR
11-11	Nicaragua	L 0-1	Managua	WCq		2 100	Cruz CRC
15-11	Panama	L 0-3	Panama City	WCq		8 000	Vaughn
2012							
23-09	Barbados	L 0-1	Bridgetown	CCq		300	Brizan TRI
25-09	Aruba	W 3-2	Bridgetown	CCq	Chad Bertrand [36], Kurlson Benjamin 2 [45,77]	150	Clarke LCA
27-09	Dominican Republic	L 1-2	Bridgetown	CCq	Lester Langlais [39]	300	Brizan TRI

Fr = Friendly match • CC = Digicel Caribbean Cup • WC = FIFA World Cup • q = qualifier • † Not a full international

DOMINICA 2011-12

DFA LIME PREMIERE DIVISION

	Pl	W	D	L	F	A	Pts	Harlem Utd	Bath Estate	Rollers	Dublanc	Bombers	Kensbro	Aicons	Sagicor
Harlem United	7	5	2	0	12	4	**17**			W 1-0		4-1		4-1	1-0
Bath Estate	7	4	2	1	13	7	**14**	1-1		1-1		2-0	1-2	W	4-1
Wacky Rollers	7	4	1	2	9	7	**13**						2-1	1-4	
Dublanc	6	3	0	3	11	7	**9**	2-4		1-2			5-0	1-0	2-0
Northern Bombers	6	3	0	3	7	9	**9**			0-2	n/n		2-1		
RIC Kensbro	5	1	1	3	4	12	**4**	1-1				0-3		n/n	
Aicons	5	1	0	4	6	8	**3**								n/n
Sagicor Southeast	5	0	0	5	1	9	**0**			0-1		0-1	n/n		

4/12/2011 - 26/02/2012 • n/n = result not known • W = home team won

DOM – DOMINICAN REPUBLIC

FIFA/COCA-COLA WORLD RANKING

'93	'94	'95	'96	'97	'98	'99	'00	'01	'02	'03	'04	'05	'06	'07	'08	'09	'10	'11	'12
153	164	159	130	144	152	155	157	160	149	171	170	174	136	166	185	190	168	131	93

2012													High	Low	Av
Jan	Feb	Mar	Apr	May	Jun	Jul	Aug	Sep	Oct	Nov	Dec				
129	129	135	135	135	133	130	118	103	102	92	93		92	190	156

Football may lag some way behind baseball in the Dominican Republic but it continues to take huge strides forwards with players like Jonathan Fana Frias becoming sporting icons and the national team earning the respect of the more traditional football powers in the Caribbean. As in the previous year, 2012 turned out to be a very successful one with five wins and just two defeats in the nine games played. All of the games were in the 2012 Caribbean Cup - an encouraging sign in itself in that most campaigns in the past had never lasted more than two or three games. For the first time since 1991, and for only the second time ever, the Dominican Republic made it through the preliminaries to qualify for the finals in Antigua. There they had an encouraging start with a 2-1 victory over the hosts - their first ever in the finals - but then lost two close games against Haiti and Trinidad to miss out on a place in the semi-finals. It was an encouraging performance overall and although the majority of the squad were based at clubs in the Dominican Republic, five were at clubs in Europe, notably 18-year old defender Carlos Martinez who has been learning his trade at Barcelona's La Masia and working his way up through the ranks at the club. There can't be a more potent sign of the changing profile of football in the country.

CFU CARIBBEAN CUP RECORD

1989 DNE **1991** 7 r1 1992 DNE 1993-1996 DNQ 1997 DNE 1998-2001 DNQ 2005 withdrew 2007 DNQ 2008 DNE 2010 DNQ **2012** 5 r1

FEDERACION DOMINICANA DE FUTBOL (FEDOFUTBOL)

Centro Olimpico, Ensanche Miraflores, Apartado postal 1953, Santo Domingo
☎ +1 809 5426923
📠 +1 809 3812734
✉ fedofutbol.f@codetel.net.do
🌐 www.fedofutbol.org
FA 1953 CON 1964 FIFA 1958
P Osiris Guzman
GS Felix Ledesma

THE STADIA

2014 FIFA World Cup Stadia
Estadio Panamericano
San Cristóbal   2 800
Other Main Stadia
Estadio Felix Sanchez
Santo Domingo   27 000
Estadio La Barranquita
Santiago   20 000
Estadio Olimpico
La Vega   7 200
Estadio del Colegio Don Bosco
Moca   3 000

MAJOR CITIES/TOWNS
		Population
1	Santo Domingo	2 491 547
2	Santiago	643 162
3	San Pedro	262 142
4	La Romana	240 235
5	San Cristóbal	183 890
6	Higüey	160 651
7	Puerto Plata	134 206
8	San Francisco	131 000
9	La Vega	110 276
10	Barahona	81 960
11	San Juan	80 560
12	Baní	75 621
13	Bonao	75 464
14	Bajos de Haina	73 199
15	Moca	67 171
16	Azua	64 229
17	Boca Chica	60 169
18	Mao	50 093
19	Villa Altagracia	45 930

REPUBLICA DOMINICANA • DOMINICAN REPUBLIC

Capital Santo Domingo Population 9 650 054 (85) % in cities 69%
GDP per capita $8200 (119) Area km² 48 670 km² (131) GMT +/- -4
Neighbours (km) Haiti 360 • Coast 1288

RECENT INTERNATIONAL MATCHES PLAYED BY THE DOMINICAN REPUBLIC

2007 Opponents	Score	Venue	Comp	Scorers	Att	Referee
No international matches played in 2007						
2008						
27-02 Haiti	L 1-2	San Cristobal	Fr		1 300	Minyetty DOM
28-02 Haiti	L 0-2	San Cristobal	Fr		825	Minyetty DOM
26-03 Puerto Rico	L 0-1	Bayamon	WCq		8 000	Morales MEX
8-10 Trinidad and Tobago	L 0-9	Port of Spain	Fr		2 000	
2009						
No international matches played in 2009						
2010						
14-10 British Virgin Islands	W 17-0	San Cristobal	CCq	Darly Batista 5 [4 67 68 72 78], Domingo Peralta 3 [21 43 76], Inoel Navarro 3 [26 47 81], Manuel Reinoso 2 [60 73], Kerwin Severino [63], Erick Obuna 2 [83 90], Gonzalo Frechilla [90]	200	Lebron PUR
17-10 Dominica	L 0-1	San Cristobal	CCq		600	Lebron PUR
2011						
8-07 Anguilla	W 2-0	San Cristobal	WCq	Domingo Peralta [7], Jonathan Fana [42]	1 000	Brizan TRI
10-07 Anguilla	W 4-0	San Cristobal	WCq	Inoel Navarro 2 [18 42], Jhoan Sanchez [27], Jonathan Fana [42]	1 500	Brea CUB
20-08 Curacao	W 1-0	San Cristobal	Fr	Johan Cruz [70]	250	Vasquez DOM
21-08 Curacao	W 1-0	San Cristobal	Fr	Fernando Casanova [28]	300	Hidalgo DOM
2-09 El Salvador	L 2-3	San Salvador	WCq	Johan Cruz [66], Domingo Peralta [89]	25 272	Rodriguez PAN
6-09 Suriname	D 1-1	San Cristobal	WCq	Erick Ozuna [68]	2 300	Castro HON
7-10 El Salvador	L 1-2	San Cristobal	WCq	Erick Ozuna [54]	2 323	Cerdas CRC
11-10 Suriname	W 3-1	Paramaribo	WCq	Jonathan Fana [9], Erick Ozuna 2 [47 76]	1 200	Ward CAN
11-11 Cayman Islands	W 4-0	San Cristobal	WCq	Inoel Navarro [17], Erick Ozuna [38], Kelvin Rodriguez [64], Jack Morillo [79]	1 000	Guerrero NCA
14-11 Cayman Islands	D 1-1	Georgetown	WCq	Cesar Garcia [41]	1 750	Matthew SKN
2012						
23-09 Aruba	D 2-2	Bridgetown	CNq	Erick Ozuna 2 [13 76]	300	Lancaster GUY
25-09 Barbados	W 1-0	Bridgetown	CNq	Pedro Nunez [80]	750	Elskamp SUR
27-09 Dominica	W 2-1	Bridgetown	CNq	Jonathan Fana 2 [66 90]	300	Brizan TRI
23-10 Guadeloupe †	W 2-0	Abymes	CNq	Jonathan Fana 2 [45 90]	1 505	Cambridge VIN
25-10 Martinique †	D 1-1	Abymes	CNq	Domingo Peralta [45]	1 800	Delves VIN
27-10 Puerto Rico	W 3-1	Abymes	CNq	Jonathan Fana 2 [19 70], Gilberto Ulloa [86]	2 891	Cambridge VIN
7-12 Antigua and Barbuda	W 2-1	St John's	CNr1	Cesar Garcia [74], Jonathan Fana [90]	150	Dacosta BAH
9-12 Haiti	L 1-2	St John's	CNr1	Kerbi Rodriguez [12]	800	Bonilla SLV
11-12 Trinidad and Tobago	L 1-2	St John's	CNr1	Kerbi Rodriguez [52]	250	Thomas JAM

Fr = Friendly match • CC = Digicel Caribbean Cup • WC = FIFA World Cup • q = qualifier • † Not a full international

DOMINICAN REPUBLIC 2011-12

LIGA MAYOR (VII)

	Pl	W	D	L	F	A	Pts	Deportivo Pantoja	Bauger	Barcelona	San Cristobal	Universidad OyM
Deportivo Pantoja	12	9	1	2	38	14	**28**		2-1 1-2	2-3 4-1	2-1	5-1 4-1
Bauger	12	8	1	3	20	14	**25**	0-3		1-0	1-0 2-0	1-1
Barcelona	12	7	2	3	34	19	**23**	2-2	4-0 2-3		3-2	5-0 2-2
San Cristobal	11	1	1	9	11	27	**4**	1-3 0-2	0-5	1-4 1-2		4-2
Universidad OyM	11	0	3	8	11	40	**3**	1-8	0-1	1-6	1-1 n/p	

27/11/20012 - 25/03/2012

ECU – ECUADOR

FIFA/COCA-COLA WORLD RANKING

'93	'94	'95	'96	'97	'98	'99	'00	'01	'02	'03	'04	'05	'06	'07	'08	'09	'10	'11	'12
48	55	55	33	28	63	65	54	37	31	37	39	37	30	56	36	37	53	42	13

2012

Jan	Feb	Mar	Apr	May	Jun	Jul	Aug	Sep	Oct	Nov	Dec	High	Low	Av
42	40	39	37	37	36	27	20	17	20	17	13	13	76	44

Ecuador enjoyed a hugely successful year in 2012 with the national team firmly establishing itself in the hunt for a place at the 2014 FIFA World Cup in Brazil. Ecuador finished the year in second place in South America's nine-team group at the halfway stage with the only blemish on their record during the year being a 4-0 defeat in Buenos Aires at the hands of leaders Argentina. A third appearance at the World Cup in just over a decade would be testament to the transformative effect Colombian coaches have had on football in the country since the appointment of Francisco Maturana in 1995. Reinaldo Rueda is the fourth Colombian at the helm since then and is looking to follow in the footsteps of compatriots Hernan Dario Gomez and Luis Suarez by taking Ecuador to the World Cup. In club football the season was dominated by Barcelona from Guayaquil who won their first title since 1997. By winning both the first and second stages of the championship they avoided the need for the end-of-season title play-off. Although the first stage had witnessed a tight finish with just two points separating the top five teams, the second stage was far more clear cut with Barcelona finishing eights points ahead of Emelec. In the crucial Guayaquil 'Clasico del Astillero' between the two at the beginning of November, Barcelona thrashed their rivals 5-0.

FIFA WORLD CUP RECORD
1930-1958 DNE 1962-1998 DNQ **2002** 24 r1 **2006** 12 r2 **2010** DNQ

FEDERACION ECUATORIANA DE FUTBOL (FEF)

Avenida las Aguas y Calle, Alianza, PO Box 09-01-7447, 593 Guayaquil
+593 42 880610
+593 42 880615
fef@gye.satnet.net
www.ecuafutbol.org
FA 1925 CON 1930 FIFA 1926
P Luis Chiriboga
GS Francisco Acosta

THE STADIA

2014 FIFA World Cup Stadia

Estadio Olimpico Atahualpa Quito	40 948

Other Main Stadia

El Monumental Guayaquil	80 624
Estadio Casa Blanca Quito	42 000
Estadio George Capwell Guayaquil	23 000
Estadio Alejandro Serrano Aguilar Cuenca	22 000

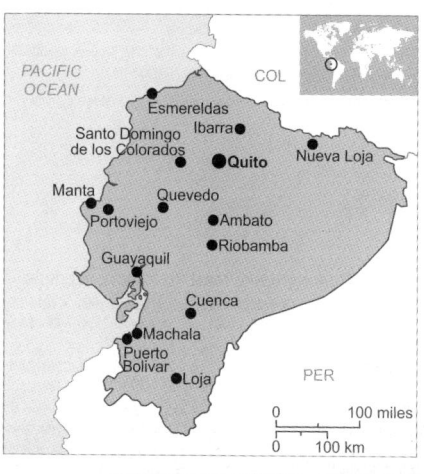

MAJOR CITIES/TOWNS

		Population
1	Guayaquil	2 248 800
2	Quito	1 621 817
3	Cuenca	322 955
4	Machala	247 290
5	Santo Domingo	232 207
6	Manta	210 712
7	Portoviejo	195 941
8	Eloy Alfaro	193 293
9	Ambato	180 048
10	Quevedo	140 945
11	Riobamba	139 778
12	Loja	128 578
13	Ibarra	128 288
14	Milagro	126 831
15	Esmeraldas	112 192
16	Babahoyo	90 016
17	La Libertad	87 417
18	El Carmen	80 270
19	Rosa Zárate	62 813

REPUBLICA DEL ECUADOR • REPUBLIC OF ECUADOR

Capital	Quito	Population	14 573 101 (64)
GDP per capita	$7500 (123)	Area km²	283 561 km² (73)
% in cities	66%	GMT +/-	-5
Neighbours (km)	Colombia 590, Peru 1420 • Coast 2237		

RECENT INTERNATIONAL MATCHES PLAYED BY ECUADOR

2009	Opponents		Score	Venue	Comp	Scorers	Att	Referee
7-05	Mexico	D	0-0	New York	Fr		77 507	Depiero CAN
16-05	Korea Republic	L	0-2	Seoul	Fr		62 209	Wongkamdee THA
4-09	Mexico	W	2-1	Guadalajara	Fr	Cristian Benitez [1], Jaime Ayovi [58]	43 800	Quesada CRC
7-09	Venezuela	L	0-1	Barquisimento	Fr		37 262	Torres PAN
8-10	Colombia	L	0-1	Harrison	Fr		25 000	Chapin USA
12-10	Poland	D	2-2	Montreal	Fr	Cristian Benitez 2 [31 78]	1 000	Navarro CAN
17-11	Venezuela	W	4-1	Quito	Fr	Cristian Benitez 2 [2 4], Walter Ayovi 2 [45p 46]	9 000	Chaibou NGA
2011								
9-02	Honduras	D	1-1	La Ceiba	Fr	Pablo Palacios [13], W 5-4p	15 100	Lopez GUA
26-03	Colombia	L	0-2	Madrid	Fr		15 000	Mateu ESP
29-03	Peru	D	0-0	Den Haag	Fr			Braamhaar NED
20-04	Argentina	D	2-2	Mar Del Plata	Fr	Michael Quinonez [27], Segundo Castillo [68p]	9 000	Silvera URU
28-05	Mexico	D	1-1	Seattle	Fr	Michael Arroyo [37]	50 300	Jurisevic USA
1-06	Canada	D	2-2	Toronto	Fr	Cristian Benitez [62], Michael Arroyo [64]	14 356	Bogle JAM
7-06	Greece	D	1-1	New York	Fr	Frickson Erazo [58]	39 656	Geiger USA
3-07	Paraguay	D	0-0	Santa Fe	CAr1		20 000	Pezzotta ARG
9-07	Venezuela	L	0-1	Salta	CAr1		12 000	Quesada CRC
13-07	Brazil	L	2-4	Cordoba	CAr1	Felipe Caicedo 2 [36 58]	39 000	Silvera URU
10-08	Costa Rica	W	2-0	San Jose	Fr	Cristian Suarez [53], Edison Mendez [66]	18 000	Aguilar SLV
2-09	Jamaica	W	5-2	Quito	Fr	Jaime Ayovi [20], Cristian Suarez [38], Cristian Benitez 2 [45 50], Segundo Castillo [64]	6 000	Buitrago COL
6-09	Costa Rica	W	4-0	Quito	Fr	Cristian Suarez [21], Jaime Ayovi [27], Segundo Castillo [59], Cristian Benitez [75]	6 000	Roldan COL
7-10	Venezuela	W	2-0	Quito	WCq	Jaime Ayovi [15], Cristian Benitez [75]	32 278	Osses CHI
11-10	USA	W	1-0	Harrison, New York	Fr	Jaime Ayovi [79]	20 707	Aguilar SLV
11-11	Paraguay	L	1-2	Asuncion	WCq	Joao Rojas [92+]	11 173	Buitrago COL
15-11	Peru	W	2-0	Quito	WCq	Edison Mendez [69], Cristian Benitez [88]	34 481	Larrionda URU
2012								
29-02	Honduras	W	2-0	Guayaquil	Fr	Cristian Benitez [14], Jaime Ayovi [69]	5 000	Machado COL
2-06	Argentina	L	0-4	Buenos Aires	WCq		50 000	Rivera PER
10-06	Colombia	W	1-0	Quito	WCq	Cristian Benitez [53]	37 353	Seneme BRA
15-08	Chile	W	3-0	New York	Fr	Narciso Mina [10], Jaime Ayovi [14], Jefferson Montero [67]	31 901	Vaughn USA
7-09	Bolivia	W	1-0	Quito	WCq	Felipe Caicedo [73p]	32 213	Soto VEN
11-09	Uruguay	D	1-1	Montevideo	WCq	Felipe Caicedo [7p]	38 000	Amarilla PAR
12-10	Chile	W	3-1	Quito	WCq	Felipe Caicedo 2 [33 56p], Segundo Castillo [92+]	32 600	Lopes BRA
16-10	Venezuela	D	1-1	Puerto La Cruz	WCq	Segundo Castillo [23]	35 076	Pitana ARG

Fr = Friendly match • CA = Copa America • WC = FIFA World Cup • q = qualifier • r1 = first round group

ECUADOR NATIONAL TEAM HISTORICAL RECORDS

Caps: 166 - Ivan Hurtado 1992- • 107 - Alex Aguinaga 1987-2004 • 106 - Edison Mendez 2000- • 101 - Ulises de la Cruz 1995- • 100 - Luis Capurro 1985-2003 • 90 - Giovanny Espinoza 2000- • 89 - Jose Francisco Cevallos 1994- • 86 - Cleber Chala 1994-2004 • 78 - Edwin Tenorio 1998-2007 • 77 - Angel Fernandez 1991-2004 & Walter Ayovi 2001-

Goals: 31 - Agustin Delgado 1994-2006 • 26 - Eduardo Hurtado 1992-2000 • 23 - Alex Aguinaga 1987-2004 • 22 - Christian Benitez 2005- • 17 - Ivan Kaviedes 1998- & Edison Mendez 2000- • 16 - Raul Aviles 1987-2003 • 15 - Ariel Graziani 1997-2000

Coaches: Enrique Lamas CHI 1938 • Ramon Unamuno 1939 • Juan Parodi ARG 1941-42 • Rodolfo Orlandini ARG 1945 • Ramon Unamuno 1947 • Jose Planas ESP 1949 • Gregorio Esperon ARG 1953 • Jose Maria Diaz Granados 1955 • Eduardo Spandre ARG 1957 • Juan Lopez URU 1959-60 • Fausto Montalvan 1963 • Jose Maria Rodriguez URU 1965 • Fausto Montalvan 1966 • Jose Gomes Nogueira BRA 1969 • Ernesto Guerra 1970 • Jorge Lazo 1972 • Roberto Resquin ARG 1973 • Roque Maspoli URU 1975-77 • Hector Morales 1979 • Otto Vieira BRA 1981 • Juan Eduardo Hohberg URU 1981 • Ernesto Guerra 1983 • Antoninho Ferreira BRA 1984-85 • Luis Grimaldi URU 1986-87 • Dusan Draskovic YUG 1988-93 • Carlos Torres Garces 1994 • Carlos Ron 1994 • Francisco Maturana COL 1995-97 • Luis Fernando Suarez COL 1997 • Francisco Maturana COL 1997 • Polo Carrera 1998 • Carlos Sevilla 1999 • Hernan Dario Gomez COL 1999-2004 • Luis Fernando Suarez COL 2004-07 • Sixto Vizuete 2007-10 • Reinaldo Rueda COL 2010-

ECU – ECUADOR

ECUADOR 2012
SERIE A COPA CREDIFE PRIMERA ETAPA

	Pl	W	D	L	F	A	Pts	Barcelona	LDU Loja	Emelec	José Terán	Dep. Cuenca	LDU Quito	Dep. Quito	El Nacional	Manta	Macará	Técnico Univ	Olmedo
Barcelona ‡	22	10	8	4	33	15	38		0-0	1-1	1-1	3-1	1-1	0-0	1-2	4-0	1-3	4-0	4-0
LDU Loja	22	10	8	4	25	18	38	0-0		2-0	0-0	1-0	1-0	1-0	0-0	2-1	2-2	4-1	2-1
Emelec	22	11	4	7	39	23	37	0-1	2-0		1-1	2-1	3-0	2-2	5-0	0-2	3-2	2-1	5-0
Indep. José Terán	22	10	7	5	29	20	37	0-2	1-0	2-1		1-2	2-2	0-0	3-0	0-2	1-0	4-1	3-0
Deportivo Cuenca	22	11	3	8	24	26	36	1-0	1-2	0-3	3-2		0-0	1-4	1-0	2-1	0-2	2-1	1-0
LDU Quito	22	8	10	4	32	22	34	2-2	2-2	2-0	1-1	1-2		0-0	3-2	2-0	3-0	2-1	5-0
Deportivo Quito	22	8	7	7	34	23	31	3-0	4-1	2-1	0-1	1-3	1-1		3-0	1-2	3-0	0-0	2-0
El Nacional	22	8	5	9	24	34	29	0-2	1-3	2-1	1-2	1-2	1-1	2-1		1-1	3-1	0-0	2-1
Manta	22	7	6	9	22	23	27	0-1	1-0	0-0	3-0	0-0	0-1	1-2	1-1		1-1	1-0	3-1
Macará	22	5	6	11	19	33	21	1-0	1-1	0-2	0-2	0-0	0-2	1-0	1-2	1-1		2-0	3-1
Técnico Universitario	22	4	6	12	18	32	18	1-1	0-0	2-3	0-2	0-1	1-1	2-1	1-2	2-1	0-0		1-0
Olmedo	22	4	2	16	14	44	14	0-2	0-1	0-2	0-0	1-0	2-0	4-4	0-1	1-0	2-0	0-3	

3/02/2012 - 8/07/2012 • ‡ Qualified for the Championship final • Attendance: 853,026 @ 6,462

ECUADOR 2012
SERIE A COPA CREDIFE SEGUNDA ETAPA

	Pl	W	D	L	F	A	Pts	Barcelona	Emelec	LDU Quito	José Terán	Técnico Univ	Manta	Macará	LDU Loja	Dep. Cuenca	Dep. Quito	El Nacional	Olmedo
Barcelona ‡	22	13	6	3	42	19	45		5-0	1-0	2-2	0-1	0-0	4-0	1-1	4-1	1-0	3-1	3-1
Emelec	22	11	4	7	28	26	37	1-2		2-2	2-1	2-1	1-0	3-0	3-1	1-0	3-0	2-1	1-0
LDU Quito	22	9	8	5	26	20	35	2-2	1-0		1-0	2-2	1-0	1-2	2-2	0-2	3-0	3-1	0-0
Indep. José Terán	22	9	4	9	22	25	31	1-1	2-0	1-0		1-2	1-0	0-3	2-0	1-0	2-2	1-1	1-0
Técnico Universitario	22	8	7	7	27	34	31	3-2	1-1	0-0	3-0		0-2	1-1	3-0	1-0	0-0	1-3	2-1
Manta	22	8	6	8	27	22	30	1-1	0-2	1-2	0-1	4-0		1-0	1-1	2-0	4-1	1-1	2-1
Macará	22	9	2	11	27	29	29	0-2	0-1	0-2	0-1	2-0	4-2		0-2	2-0	2-1	2-1	1-0
LDU Loja	22	7	6	9	28	29	27	0-1	2-2	1-2	2-1	6-0	1-2	2-1		1-0	0-1	2-2	2-1
Deportivo Cuenca	22	7	6	9	20	23	27	1-2	1-0	3-1	2-1	1-3	1-1	0-0	2-0		0-0	1-0	1-1
Deportivo Quito	22	6	7	9	14	25	25	0-2	0-0	0-0	2-0	0-0	0-1	0-4	0-0	1-1		1-0	2-0
El Nacional	22	5	8	9	24	28	23	2-1	3-0	0-0	0-2	2-2	2-1	2-1	0-1	1-1	0-1		1-1
Olmedo	22	5	6	11	22	27	21	1-2	1-1	0-1	2-0	4-1	1-1	3-2	2-1	0-2	2-0	0-0	

13/07/2012 - 2/12/2012 • ‡ Qualified for the Championship final • Attendance: 812,613 @ 6,203
Top scorers (both stages): **30** - Narciso **MENA**, Barcelona • **20** - Claudio **BIELER**, LDU Quito • **16** - **FABIO RENATO** BRA, LDU Loja • **13** - Marlon **DE JESUS**, Emelec; Carlos Luis **QUINTERO**, Macará & Enner **VALENCIA**, Emelec • **11** - Ariel **NAHUELPAN** ARG, LDU Quito & Daniel **SAMANIEGO**, José Terán

ECUADOR 2012
AGGREGATE TABLE

	Pl	W	D	L	F	A	Pts
Barcelona †	44	23	14	7	75	34	83
Emelec †	44	22	8	14	67	49	74
LDU Quito ‡	44	17	18	9	58	42	69
Indep. José Terán ‡	44	19	11	14	51	45	68
LDU Loja ‡	44	17	14	13	53	47	65
Deportivo Cuenca	44	18	9	17	44	49	63
Manta	44	15	12	17	49	45	57
Deportivo Quito	44	14	14	16	48	48	56
El Nacional	44	13	13	18	48	62	52
Macará	44	14	8	22	46	62	50
Técnico Universitario	44	12	13	19	45	66	49
Olmedo	44	9	8	27	36	71	35

† Qualified for the Copa Libertadores
‡ Qualified for the Copa Sudamericana
Copa Libertadores play-off: LDU Quito 1-2 0-1 **Emelec**
Copa Sudamericana play-off: **LDU Loja** 1-0 1-0 José Terán

MEDALS TABLE

		Overall			League			Sth Am			City
		G	S	B	G	S	B	G	S	B	
1	Barcelona	14	13	10	14	11	5		2	5	Guayaquil
2	El Nacional	13	7	8	13	7	5			3	Quito
3	LDU Quito	12	4	11	10	3	7	2	1	4	Quito
4	Emelec	10	13	13	10	12	11		1	2	Guayaquil
5	Deportivo Quito	5	3	4	5	3	4				Quito
6	Deportivo Cuenca	1	5	1	1	5	1				Cuenca
7	Olmedo	1	1	2	1	1	2				Riobamba
8	Everest	1		1	1		1				Guayaquil
9	9 de Octubre		3	1		3	1				Guayaquil
10	Univ'dad Católica		2	2		2	2				Quito
11	América Quito		2	1		2	1				Quito
	Tecnico Univ'tario		2	1		2	1				Ambato
13	Filanbanco		1	1		1	1				Guayaquil
	Patria Guayaquil		1	1		1	1				Guayaquil
15	Espoli		1			1					Quito
	Valdez		1			1					Milagro
17	Aucas			2			2				Quito

EGY – EGYPT

FIFA/COCA-COLA WORLD RANKING

'93	'94	'95	'96	'97	'98	'99	'00	'01	'02	'03	'04	'05	'06	'07	'08	'09	'10	'11	'12
26	22	23	28	32	28	38	33	41	39	32	34	32	27	39	16	24	9	31	41

2012															
Jan	Feb	Mar	Apr	May	Jun	Jul	Aug	Sep	Oct	Nov	Dec	High	Low	Av
36	61	64	55	57	48	42	40	38	40	40	41	9	64	31

The death of more than 70 spectators in Port Said at a league match between home side Al Masry and Cairo giants Al Ahly in early 2012 led to an immediate suspension of the Egypt league for the rest of the year. It cast a dark shadow over football in the country with an almost immediate impact being felt by the national team, whose surprise loss at home to the Central African Republic in the 2013 Africa Cup of Nations qualifiers turned a routine assignment into an embarrassing defeat, arguably the biggest setback ever suffered by the all-conquering Pharaohs. It was not a great start for Egypt's American coach Bob Bradley although it was preceded by two wins at the start of the 2014 FIFA World Cup qualifiers over Mozambique and, crucially, away in Guinea. But a year of tragedy, during which several attempts to restart the league were stymied, ended on an optimistic note as Al Ahly won the CAF Champions League - despite having to play most of their home ties behind closed doors. They played without regular domestic competition and were forced to seek match fitness at training camps in the Middle East, yet came through a tough group phase before beating Nigeria's Sunshine Stars in the semi-finals. In the first leg of the final they rescued a draw with a late equaliser against holders Esperance before winning the return 2-1 in Tunis.

CAF AFRICA CUP OF NATIONS RECORD

1957 1 winners **1959** 1 winners (hosts) **1962** 2 F **1963** 3 r1 **1965** withdrew **1968** withdrew **1970** 3 SF **1972** DNQ **1974** 3 SF (hosts) **1976** 4 r2 **1978** DNQ **1980** 4 SF **1982** withdrew **1984** 4 SF **1986** 1 winners (hosts) **1988** 5 r1 **1990** 8 r1 **1992** 11 r1 **1994** 6 QF **1996** 7 QF **1998** 1 winners **2000** 5 QF **2002** 5 QF **2004** 9 r1 **2006** 1 winners (hosts) **2008** 1 winners **2010** 1 winners **2012-13** DNQ

EGYPTIAN FOOTBALL ASSOCIATION (EFA)

5 Gabalaya Street, Gezira,
El Borg Post Office, Cairo
☎ +20 2 7351793
+20 2 7367817
efa_football@hotmail.com
www.efa.com.eg
FA 1921 CON 1957 FIFA 1923
P Mohamed Mahmoud Gamal
GS Sarwat Swelam

THE STADIA

2014 FIFA World Cup Stadia
Borg El Arab Stadium
Alexandria 86 000

Other Main Stadia
International Stadium
Cairo 74 100
International Stadium
Suez 45 000
Arab Contractors Stadium
Cairo 35 000
Military Academy Stadium
Cairo 28 500

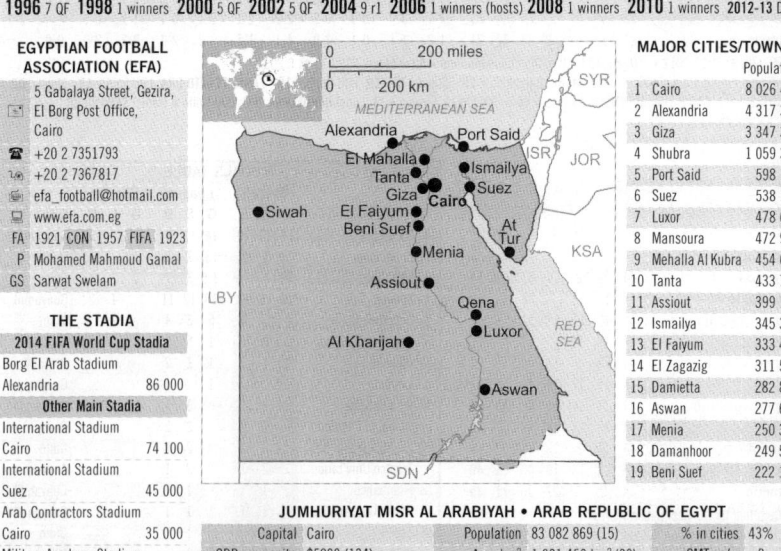

MAJOR CITIES/TOWNS

		Population
1	Cairo	8 026 454
2	Alexandria	4 317 398
3	Giza	3 347 333
4	Shubra	1 059 343
5	Port Said	598 118
6	Suez	538 188
7	Luxor	478 632
8	Mansoura	472 953
9	Mehalla Al Kubra	454 644
10	Tanta	433 779
11	Assiout	399 183
12	Ismailya	345 396
13	El Faiyum	333 466
14	El Zagazig	311 538
15	Damietta	282 800
16	Aswan	277 680
17	Menia	250 322
18	Damanhoor	249 586
19	Beni Suef	222 139

JUMHURIYAT MISR AL ARABIYAH • ARAB REPUBLIC OF EGYPT

Capital Cairo Population 83 082 869 (15) % in cities 43%
GDP per capita $5800 (134) Area km² 1 001 450 km² (30) GMT +/- +2
Neighbours (km) Gaza Strip 11, Israel 266, Libya 1115, Sudan 1273 • Coast 2450

RECENT INTERNATIONAL MATCHES PLAYED BY EGYPT

2010	Opponents	Score	Venue	Comp	Scorers	Att	Referee
12-01	Nigeria	W 3-1	Benguela	CNr1	Moteab [34], Ahmed Hassan [54], Geddo [87]	18 000	Seechurn MRI
16-01	Mozambique	W 2-0	Benguela	CNr1	Khan OG [47], Geddo [81]	16 000	Djaoupe TOG
20-01	Benin	W 2-0	Benguela	CNr1	Al Muhamadi [7], Moteab [23]	12 500	Bennett RSA
25-01	Cameroon	W 3-1	Benguela	CNqf	Ahmed Hassan 2 [37 103], Geddo [92]	12 000	Damon RSA
28-01	Algeria	W 4-0	Benguela	CNsf	Hosny Abd Rabo [39p], Zidan [65], Abdel Shafy [80], Geddo [92+]	25 000	Codjia BEN
31-01	Ghana	W 1-0	Luanda	CNf	Geddo [85]	50 000	Coulibaly MLI
3-03	England	L 1-3	London	Fr	Zidan [23]	80 602	Torres PAR
11-08	Congo DR	W 6-3	Cairo	Fr	Ahmed Ali Kamal 2 [3 34], Ahmed Fathy [41], Aboutrika [44], Ahmed Hassan [49], Geddo [67]		
5-09	Sierra Leone	D 1-1	Cairo	CNq	Mahmoud Fathallah [61]		Diatta SEN
10-10	Niger	L 0-1	Niamey	CNq			Doue CIV
17-11	Australia	W 3-0	Cairo	Fr	El Zaher [29], Geddo [60], Zidan [90p]		Genov BUL
16-12	Qatar	L 1-2	Doha	Fr	Walid Soliman [72]		
2011							
5-01	Tanzania	W 5-1	Cairo	Fr	Hamdy 2 [5 57], Aboutrika [12], OG [24], Ahmed Ali [78]		
8-01	Uganda	W 1-0	Cairo	Fr	Geddo [93+]		
11-01	Burundi	W 3-0	Ismailia	Fr	Geddo [2], Ahmed Ali [11], Hamdy [80]		
14-01	Kenya	W 5-1	Cairo	Fr	Ahmad Belal 3 [13 69 90], Hamdy [21], Gomaa [25]		
17-01	Uganda	W 3-1	Ismailia	Fr	Hamdy 2 [38 70], Geddo [81]		
26-03	South Africa	L 0-1	Johannesburg	CNq			Coulibaly MLI
5-06	South Africa	D 0-0	Cairo	CNq			Jedidi TUN
3-09	Sierra Leone	L 1-2	Freetown	CNq	Marwan Mohsen [44]		
8-10	Niger	W 3-0	Cairo	CNq	Marwan Mohsen 2 [48 71], Mohamed Salah [56]		
14-11	Brazil	L 0-2	Al Rayyan	Fr		18 000	Al Dossari QAT
2012							
27-02	Kenya	W 5-0	Doha	Fr	Mohamed Salah [10], Ahmed Hassan [18p], Abdul Malek [73p], Khairy [83], Abdul Zaher [90]	500	Al Marri QAT
29-02	Niger	W 1-0	Doha	Fr	Hosny Abd Rabo [22p]		Abdou QAT
2-03	Congo DR	D 0-0	Doha	Fr			Al Dosari QAT
29-03	Uganda	W 2-1	Omdurman	Fr	Mohamed Salah [60], Aboutrika [92+]		Abdel Gadir SUD
31-03	Chad	W 4-0	Omdurman	Fr	Mohamed Salah [31], Khairy [44], OG [89], Mekki [91+]		
12-04	Nigeria	W 3-2	Dubai	Fr	Temsah [25], Aboutrika [33p], Mekki [92+]		Alzarooni UAE
15-04	Mauritania	W 3-0	Dubai	Fr	Geddo 2 [24 29], Moteab [39]		
17-04	Iraq	D 0-0	Dubai	Fr			Mohamed UAE
11-05	Lebanon	W 4-1	Tripoli	Fr	Okka [4], Mekki [19], Temsah [44], Khairy [53]	6 000	Ghandour LIB
20-05	Cameroon	W 2-1	Omdurman	Fr	El Mohamady [41], Aboutrika [80p]		Adam SUD
22-05	Togo	W 3-0	Omdurman	Fr	Geddo [26], Mohamed Salah 2 [51 86]		
1-06	Mozambique	W 2-0	Alexandria	WCq	Mahmoud Fathalla [55], Zidan [62]	BCD	Kirwa KEN
10-06	Guinea	W 3-2	Conakry	WCq	Aboutrika 2 [58 66p], Mohamed Salah [93+]	14 000	Alioum CMR
15-06	Central African Rep	L 2-3	Alexandria	CNq	Zidan [9], Mohamed Salah [48]	BCD	Haimoudi ALG
30-06	Central African Rep	D 1-1	Bangui	CNq	Moteab [71]		Diatta SEN
15-08	Oman	D 1-1	Salalah	Fr	Mekki [60]		Abdulnabi BHR
12-10	Congo	W 3-0	Sharjah	Fr	Aboutrika 2 [40 45], Geddo [44]		
16-10	Tunisia	L 0-1	Abu Dhabi	Fr		40 000	
14-11	Georgia	D 0-0	Tbilisi	Fr		4 000	Treimanis LVA

Fr = Friendly match • CN = CAF African Cup of Nations • CC = FIFA Confederations Cup • WC = FIFA World Cup

EGYPT NATIONAL TEAM HISTORICAL RECORDS

Caps: 184 - Ahmed Hassan 1995- • 169 - Hossam Hassan 1985-2006 • 137 - Essam El Hadary 1996- • 125 - Ibrahim Hassan 1985-2004 & Hany Ramzy 1988-2003 • 112 - Abdel Zaher El Sakka 1997-2010 • 106 - Nader El Sayed 1992-2005 • 103 - Wael Gomaa 2001-

Goals: 69 - Hossam Hassan 1985-2006 • 49 - Taher Abouzeid 1984-90 • 39 - Mahmoud Al Khatib 1974-86 • 36 - Mahmoud Aboutrika 2004- • 34 - Emad Moteb 2005- & Magdi Abdelghani 1980-90 • 33 - Ahmed Hassan 1995- • 29 - Amir Zaki 2004- • 20 - Mido 2001-09

Coaches: For Egypt coaches pre 1988 see Oliver's Almanack 2012 • Mahmoud El Gohary 1988-90 • Dietrich Weise GER 1990-91 • Mahmoud El Gohary 1991-93 • Mohamed Sadiq "Shehta" 1993 • Mircea Radulescu ROU 1993-94 • Taha Ismail 1994 • Nol de Ruiter NED 1994-95 • Mohsen Saleh 1995 • Ruud Krul NED 1995-96 • Farouk Gaafar 1996-97 • Mahmoud El-Gohary 1997-99 • Anwar Salama 1999 • Gerard Gili FRA 1999-2000 • Mahmoud El-Gohary 2000 • Mohsen Saleh 2000-03 • Marco Tardelli ITA 2003-04 • Hassan Shehata 2004-11 • Bob Bradley USA 2011-

EGYPT 2011-12

ETISALAT PREMIER LEAGUE

	Pl	W	D	L	F	A	Pts	Haras	Ahly	Zamalek	Masry	Shorta	Ismaily	Misr	ENPPI	El Gouna	Wadi Degla	Telefonad	Jaish	Ittihad	Smouha	Petrojet	Ghazl	Mokawloon	Intag Harby	Dakhleya
Haras Al Hedod	14	12	1	1	25	9	37			2-1	2-0		1-1		1-0									1-0		3-0
Al Ahly †	15	11	3	1	28	12	36	1-0				1-0			1-1			3-0		3-1				2-0		3-1
Zamalek †	14	10	2	2	27	11	32				2-1	1-2											6-1		3-1	2-1
Al Masry	15	7	5	3	17	10	26	3-1						1-0			1-0	1-1	2-0	1-1		1-0			
Ittihad Al Shorta	15	7	5	3	16	10	26	0-1		0-0				0-1		2-0			1-0	2-0	2-0					
Ismaily ‡	14	7	4	3	17	13	25			0-0	1-1			0-0	2-1				1-1		3-1					
Misr Al Maqasah	15	6	6	3	29	19	24	1-2			1-1				2-1			3-0		5-2		2-3	5-1		2-0	
ENPPI ‡	16	7	3	6	28	25	24	2-3	2-1							3-3	3-3		2-2						3-0		3-2
Al Gouna	16	5	7	4	22	18	22					0-0	4-1	1-1				2-1					3-1	2-2	3-0	
Wadi Degla	14	4	7	3	17	15	19	1-2				0-1	3-3			0-0			2-2	2-0						0-0
Telefonad Beni Suef	16	6	1	9	16	21	19		0-2						1-2	1-2		2-1	2-1	2-1	0-0		1-0			
Al Jaish	16	3	8	5	19	21	17	0-1		1-1			1-2	1-1		1-1							3-0	2-1		1-1
Ittihad Al Sakandary	16	3	6	7	14	21	15	0-1	0-2	0-2				3-0		0-0		1-0		3-3						
Smouha	15	3	4	8	15	23	13	1-2		0-1			2-1	3-1		0-1								1-1		2-1
Petrojet	14	1	8	5	12	21	11	0-3	2-2						0-1		1-1		0-0				1-1			
Ghazl Al Mehalla	14	2	5	7	11	29	11		0-2		0-3			2-1		0-0	0-3		0-0		2-2			2-0		
Mokawloon	15	2	4	9	17	24	10	2-3			1-3		2-2	0-1			4-1								0-0	4-1	
Intag Harby	17	1	6	10	8	26	9	1-1			1-1	1-2			0-2			2-3	1-0	1-2	0-0		0-0			
Al Dakhleya	15	1	5	9	12	22	8		2-0		1-2	0-1					0-1		1-1			1-1		0-0		

14/10/2011 - 1/02/2012 • League cancelled due the riot in Port Said after the Al Masry v Al Ahly match which resulted in 72 deaths
† Qualified for the CAF Champions League • ‡ Qualified for the CAF Confederation Cup (The 2010-11 league standings were used)
Top scorers: **7** - Hosny **ABD RABO**, Ismaily • **6** - Ahmed **HASSAN**, Zamalek; Minusu **BUBA** NGA, Al Gouna & Oussou **KONAN** CIV, Misr Al Makasa

MEDALS TABLE

		Overall			League			Cup			Africa			City
		G	S	B	G	S	B	G	S	B	G	S	B	
1	Al Ahly	80	22	5	36	10	2	35	10		10	2	3	Cairo
2	Zamalek	38	42	10	11	30	6	21	11		6	1	4	Cairo
3	Al Tersana	7	8	7	1	4	7	6	4					Cairo
4	Mokawloon	7	3	2		1	1	3	3		3		1	Cairo
5	Ismaily	6	12	20	3	6	16	2	4		1	2	4	Ismailya
6	Al Ittihad	6	4	3			2	6	4				1	Alexandria
7	Olympic	3	3	1	1		1	2	3					Alexandria
8	ENPPI	2	3	2				1	1	2	2		1	Cairo
9	Haras Al Hedod	2		1				1	2					Alexandria
10	Al Masry	1	9	7				5	1	9			2	Port Said
11	Ghazl Al Mehalla	1	7	6	1		5		6		1	1		Al Mehalla
12	Suez	1	3	1				1	1	3				Suez
13	Al Teram	1						1						Alexandria
14	Sekka		6						6					Cairo
15	Mansoura		1	2			1			1			1	Mansoura
16	Aswan		1						1					Aswan
	Baladeyet Mehalla		1						1					Al Mehalla
	Shroeders		1						1					
19	Petrojet			1			1							Suez

ENG – ENGLAND

FIFA/COCA-COLA WORLD RANKING

'93	'94	'95	'96	'97	'98	'99	'00	'01	'02	'03	'04	'05	'06	'07	'08	'09	'10	'11	'12
11	18	21	12	4	9	12	17	10	7	8	8	9	5	12	8	9	6	5	6

2012

Jan	Feb	Mar	Apr	May	Jun	Jul	Aug	Sep	Oct	Nov	Dec	High	Low	Av
5	5	6	7	7	6	4	3	3	5	6	6	3	27	10

The climax to the 2012 Premier League season turned out to be the most thrilling since 1989 with Manchester City scoring twice in injury-time to beat QPR 3-2 in the final game of the season and win the title on goal difference ahead of neighbours Manchester United. Sergio Aguero's winner four minutes into stoppage time saw Arab-backed City claim the league crown for the first time since 1968. Chelsea finished a poor sixth in the table but still sensationally managed to win the European Cup - the first-ever won by a London club - after beating Bayern Munich on penalties in the final after a 1-1 draw. It was a remarkable turn around in their season with coach Roberto Di Matteo also inspiring the team to a 2-1 victory over Liverpool in the FA Cup final, having only taken over from Andre Villas-Boas in March, with the club seemingly in crisis. The England national team faced its own crisis in February with the resignation of coach Fabio Capello and it wasn't until a month before the finals of Euro 2012 that his replacement Roy Hodgson was given the job. England went into the finals with no real expectation but made a positive impression by winning their group ahead of France, hosts Ukraine and Denmark. In their quarter-final, however, they were knocked-out for the sixth time in a major tournament on penalties, this time by Italy.

UEFA EUROPEAN CHAMPIONSHIP RECORD

1960 DNE **1964** r1 **1968** 3 SF **1972** DNQ **1976** DNQ **1980** 5 r1 **1984** DNQ **1988** 8 r1 **1992** 7 r1 **1996** 3 SF (hosts) **2000** 11 r1 **2004** 5 QF **2008** DNQ **2012** 5 QF

THE FOOTBALL ASSOCIATION (FA)

Wembley Stadium,
PO Box 1966,
London SW1P 9EQ
+44 844 9808200
+44 844 9808201
communique@thefa.com
www.TheFA.com
FA 1863 CON 1954 FIFA 1905
P David Bernstein
GS Alex Horne

THE STADIA

2014 FIFA World Cup Stadia
Wembley Stadium
London — 90 000

Other Main Stadia
Old Trafford
Manchester — 75 811
Emirates Stadium
London — 60 361
St James' Park
Newcastle — 52 409
Villa Park
Birmingham — 42 785

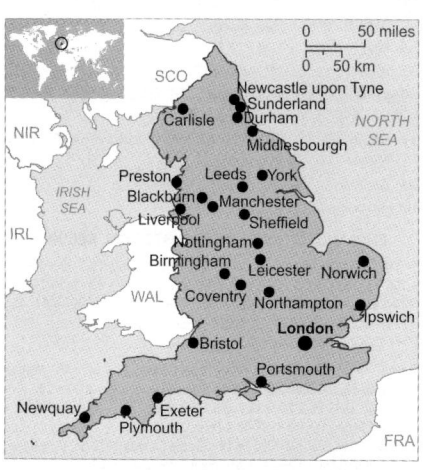

MAJOR CITIES/TOWNS

		Population
1	London	7 683 316
2	Birmingham	945 747
3	Liverpool	454 654
4	Leeds	441 108
5	Sheffield	417 666
6	Manchester	396 309
7	Bristol	374 037
8	Leicester	294 864
9	Bradford	280 407
10	Coventry	271 129
11	Hull	263 227
12	Plymouth	251 916
13	Stoke-on-Trent	248 276
14	Wolverhampton	246 754
15	Derby	244 663
16	Nottingham	237 567
17	Southampton	234 791
18	Portsmouth	201 808
19	Dudley	193 161

ENGLAND (PART OF THE UNITED KINGDOM)

Capital	London	Population	49 138 831 (23)	% in cities	90%
GDP per capita	$43 785 (20)	Area km²	130 439 km² (96)	GMT +/-	0
Neighbours (km)	Scotland 164, Wales 468 • Coast 3200				

RECENT INTERNATIONAL MATCHES PLAYED BY ENGLAND

2009	Opponents		Score	Venue	Comp	Scorers	Att	Referee
12-08	Netherlands	D	2-2	Amsterdam	Fr	Defoe 2 [49][77]	48 000	Rizzoli ITA
5-09	Slovenia	W	2-1	London	Fr	Lampard [31p], Defoe [63]	67 232	Eriksson SWE
9-09	Croatia	W	5-1	London	WCq	Lampard 2 [7p][59], Gerrard 2 [18][67], Rooney [77]	87 319	Undiano ESP
10-10	Ukraine	L	0-1	Dnepropetrovsk	WCq		31 000	Skomina SVN
14-10	Belarus	W	3-0	London	WCq	Crouch 2 [4][76], Wright-Phillips [60]	76 897	Batista POR
14-11	Brazil	L	0-1	Doha	Fr		50 000	Abdou QAT
2010								
3-03	Egypt	W	3-1	London	Fr	Crouch 2 [56][80], Wright-Phillips [75]	80 602	Torres PAR
24-05	Mexico	W	3-1	London	Fr	King [17], Crouch [34], Johnson [47]	88 638	Toma JPN
30-05	Japan	W	2-1	Graz	Fr	Tanaka.MT OG [72], Nakazawa OG [83]	15 326	Eisner AUT
12-06	USA	D	1-1	Rustenburg	WCr1	Gerrard [4]	38 646	Simon BRA
18-06	Algeria	D	0-0	Cape Town	WCr1		64 100	Irmatov UZB
23-06	Slovenia	W	1-0	Port Elizabeth	WCr1	Defoe [23]	36 893	Stark GER
27-06	Germany	L	1-4	Bloemfontein	WCr2	Upson [37]	40 510	Larrionda URU
11-08	Hungary	W	2-1	London	Fr	Gerrard 2 [69][73]	72 024	Lannoy FRA
3-09	Bulgaria	W	4-0	London	ECq	Defoe 3 [3][61][86], Johnson.A [83]	73 426	Kassai HUN
7-09	Switzerland	W	3-1	Basel	ECq	Rooney [10], Johnson.A [69], Bent [88]	37 500	Rizzoli ITA
12-10	Montenegro	D	0-0	London	ECq		73 451	Grafe GER
17-11	France	L	1-2	London	Fr	Crouch [86]	85 495	Larsen DEN
2011								
9-02	Denmark	W	2-1	Copenhagen	Fr	Bent [10], Young [68]	21 523	Eriksson SWE
26-03	Wales	W	2-0	Cardiff	ECq	Lampard [7p], Bent [15]	68 959	Benquerenca POR
29-03	Ghana	D	1-1	London	Fr	Carroll [43]	80 102	Cakir TUR
4-06	Switzerland	D	2-2	London	ECq	Lampard [37p], Young [51]	84 459	Skomina SVN
2-09	Bulgaria	W	3-0	Sofia	ECq	Cahill [13], Rooney 2 [21][45]	27 230	De Bleeckere BEL
6-09	Wales	W	1-0	London	ECq	Young [35]	77 128	Schorgenhofer AUT
7-10	Montenegro	D	2-2	Podgorica	ECq	Young [11], Bent [31]	11 340	Stark GER
12-11	Spain	W	1-0	London	Fr	Lampard [49]	87 189	De Bleeckere BEL
15-11	Sweden	W	1-0	London	Fr	Barry [22]	48 876	Kralovec CZE
2012								
29-02	Netherlands	L	2-3	London	Fr	Cahill 85, Young 91+	76 283	Brych GER
26-05	Norway	W	1-0	Oslo	Fr	Young [9]	21 496	Weiner GER
2-06	Belgium	W	1-0	London	Fr	Welbeck [36]	85 091	Rasmussen DEN
11-06	France	D	1-1	Donetsk	ECr1	Lescott [30]	42 000	Rizzoli ITA
15-06	Sweden	W	3-2	Kyiv	ECr1	Carroll [23], Walcott [64], Welbeck [78]	70 000	Skomina SVN
19-06	Ukraine	W	1-0	Donetsk	ECr1	Rooney [48]	51 504	Kassai HUN
24-06	Italy	D	0-0	Kyiv	ECqf	L 2-4p	56 500	Proenca POR
15-08	Italy	W	2-1	Berne	Fr	Jagielka [27], Defoe [80]	15 000	Kever SUI
7-09	Moldova	W	5-0	Chisinau	WCq	Lampard 2 [4][29], Defoe [32], Milner [74], Baines [83]	10 500	Van Boekel NED
11-09	Ukraine	D	1-1	London	WCq	Lampard [87p]	68 102	Cakir TUR
12-10	San Marino	W	5-0	London	WCq	Rooney 2 [35p][70], Welbeck 2 [37][72], O-Chamberlain [77]	86 645	Mazeika LTU
17-10	Poland	D	1-1	Warsaw	WCq	Rooney [31]	47 000	Rocchi ITA
14-11	Sweden	L	2-4	Stockholm	Fr	Welbeck [35], Caulker [38]	49 967	Moen NOR

Fr = Friendly • EC = UEFA EURO 2012 • WC = FIFA World Cup • q = qualifier

ENGLAND NATIONAL TEAM HISTORICAL RECORDS

Caps

125 - Peter Shilton 1970-90 • **115** - David Beckham 1996-2009 • **108** - Bobby Moore 1962-73 • **106** - Bobby Charlton 1958-70 • **105** - Billy Wright 1946-59 • **100** - Steven Gerrard 2000- • **99** - Ashley Cole 2001- • **93** - Frank Lampard 1999- & Bryan Robson 1980-91 • **89** - Michael Owen 1998-2008 • **86** - Kenny Sansom 1979-88 • **85** - Gary Neville 1995-2007 • **84** - Ray Wilkins 1976-86 • **81** - Rio Ferdinand 1997- • **80** - Gary Lineker 1984-92 • **79** - John Barnes 1983-95 • **78** - Stuart Pearce 1987-99; Wayne Rooney 2003- & John Terry 2003- • **77** - Terry Butcher 1980-90 • **76** - Tom Finney 1946-58 • **75** - David Seaman 1988-2002

Goals

49 - Bobby Charlton 1958-70 • **48** - Gary Lineker 1984-92 • **44** - Jimmy Greaves 1959-67 • **40** - Michael Owen 1998-2008 • **33** - Wayne Rooney 2003- • **30** - Tom Finney 1946-58, Nat Lofthouse 1950-58 & Alan Shearer 1992-2000 • **29** - Vivian Woodward 1903-11 • **28** - Steve Bloomer 1895-1907 • **27** - David Platt 1986-96 & Frank Lampard 1999- • **26** - Bryan Robson 1980-91 • **24** - Geoff Hurst 1966-72 • **23** - Stan Mortensen 1947-53 • **22** - Tommy Lawton 1938-48 & Peter Crouch 2005- • **21** - Mick Channon 1972-77 & Kevin Keegan 1972-82 • **20** - Martin Peters 1966-74 • **19** - Steven Gerrard 2000- • **18** - George Camsell 1929-36, Dixie Dean 1927-32, Roger Hunt 1962-69 & Johnny Haynes 1954-62 • **17** - David Beckham 1996-2009 & Jermain Defoe 2004- • **16** - Tommy Taylor 1953-57 & Tony Woodcock 1978-86

Coaches

Walter Winterbottom 1946-63 • Alf Ramsey 1963-74 • Joe Mercer 1974 • Don Revie 1974-77 • Ron Greenwood 1977-82 • Bobby Robson 1982-90 • Graham Taylor 1990-93 • Terry Venables 1994-96 • Glenn Hoddle 1996-99 • Howard Wilkinson 1999 • Kevin Keegan 1999-2000 • Howard Wilkinson 2000 • Peter Taylor 2000 • Sven-Goran Eriksson SWE 2001-06 • Steve McLaren 2006-07 • Fabio Capello ITA 2008-12 • Roy Hodgson 2012-

ENG – ENGLAND

ENGLAND 2011-12

BARCLAYS PREMIER LEAGUE

	Pl	W	D	L	F	A	Pts	Man City	Man Utd	Arsenal	Spurs	Newcastle	Chelsea	Everton	Liverpool	Fulham	West Brom	Swansea	Norwich	Sunderland	Stoke City	Wigan Ath	Aston Villa	QPR	Bolton W	Blackburn	Wolves
Manchester City †	38	28	5	5	93	29	89		1-0	1-0	3-2	3-1	2-1	2-0	3-0	3-0	4-0	4-0	5-1	3-3	3-0	3-0	4-1	3-2	2-0	3-0	3-1
Manchester United †	38	28	5	5	89	33	89	1-6		8-2	3-0	1-1	3-1	4-4	2-1	1-0	2-0	2-0	2-0	1-0	2-0	5-0	4-0	2-0	3-0	2-3	4-1
Arsenal †	38	21	7	10	74	49	70	1-0	1-2		5-2	2-1	0-0	1-0	0-2	1-1	3-0	1-0	3-3	2-1	3-1	1-2	3-0	1-0	3-0	7-1	1-1
Tottenham Hotspur ‡	38	20	9	9	66	41	69	1-5	1-3	2-1		5-0	1-1	2-0	4-0	2-0	1-0	3-1	1-2	1-0	1-1	3-1	2-0	3-1	3-0	2-0	1-1
Newcastle United ‡	38	19	8	11	56	51	65	0-2	3-0	0-0	2-2		0-3	2-1	2-0	2-1	2-3	0-0	1-0	1-1	3-0	1-0	2-1	1-0	0-2	3-1	2-2
Chelsea †	38	18	10	10	65	46	64	2-1	3-3	3-5	0-0	0-2		3-1	1-2	1-1	2-1	4-1	3-1	1-0	1-0	2-1	1-3	6-1	3-0	2-1	3-0
Everton	38	15	11	12	50	40	56	1-0	0-1	0-1	1-0	3-1	2-0		0-2	4-0	2-0	1-0	1-1	4-0	0-1	3-1	2-2	0-1	1-2	1-1	2-1
Liverpool ‡	38	14	10	14	47	40	52	1-1	1-1	1-2	0-0	3-1	4-1	3-0		0-1	0-0	0-0	1-1	1-1	0-0	1-2	1-1	1-0	3-1	1-1	2-1
Fulham	38	14	10	14	48	51	52	2-2	0-5	2-1	1-3	5-2	1-1	1-3	1-0		1-1	0-3	2-1	1-2	2-1	1-0	0-0	6-0	2-0	1-1	5-0
West Bromwich Albion	38	13	8	17	45	52	47	0-0	1-2	2-3	1-3	1-3	1-0	0-1	0-2	0-0		1-2	1-2	4-0	0-1	1-2	0-0	1-0	2-1	3-0	5-1
Swansea City	38	12	11	15	44	51	47	1-0	0-1	3-2	1-1	0-2	1-1	0-2	1-0	2-0	3-0		2-3	0-0	2-0	0-0	0-0	1-1	1-3	1-3	0-4	4-4
Norwich City	38	12	11	15	52	66	47	1-6	1-2	1-2	0-2	4-2	0-0	2-2	0-3	1-1	0-1	3-1		2-1	1-1	1-1	2-0	2-1	2-0	3-3	2-1
Sunderland	38	11	12	15	45	46	45	1-0	0-1	1-2	0-0	0-1	1-2	1-1	1-1	0-0	2-2	2-0	3-0		4-0	1-2	2-2	3-1	2-2	2-1	1-0
Stoke City	38	11	12	15	36	53	45	1-1	1-1	1-1	2-1	1-3	0-0	1-1	1-0	2-0	1-2	2-0	1-0	0-1		2-2	0-0	2-3	2-2	3-1	2-1
Wigan Athletic	38	11	10	17	42	62	43	0-1	1-0	0-4	1-2	4-0	1-1	1-1	1-0	0-0	2-1	1-0	2-1	1-1	1-4	2-0		0-0	2-0	1-3	3-3	3-2
Aston Villa	38	7	17	14	37	53	38	0-1	0-1	1-2	1-1	1-1	2-4	1-1	0-2	1-0	2-1	0-2	3-2	0-0	1-1	2-0		2-2	1-2	3-1	0-0
Queens Park Rangers	38	10	7	21	43	66	37	2-3	0-2	2-1	1-0	0-0	1-0	1-1	3-2	0-1	1-1	3-0	1-2	2-3	1-0	3-1	1-1		0-4	1-1	1-2
Bolton Wanderers	38	10	6	22	46	77	36	2-3	0-5	0-0	1-4	0-2	1-5	0-2	3-1	0-3	2-2	1-1	1-2	0-2	5-0	1-2	1-2	2-1		2-1	1-1
Blackburn Rovers	38	8	7	23	48	78	31	0-4	0-2	4-3	1-2	0-2	0-1	0-1	2-3	3-1	1-2	4-2	2-0	2-0	1-2	0-1	1-1	3-2	1-2		1-2
Wolverhampton Wand	38	5	10	23	40	82	25	0-2	0-5	0-3	0-2	1-2	1-2	0-0	0-3	2-0	1-5	2-2	2-2	2-1	1-2	3-1	1-2	2-3	0-3	2-3	

13/08/2011 - 13/05/2012 • † Qualified for the UEFA Champions League • ‡ Qualified for the Europa League • Att: 13,148,465. Av: 34,601 (-1.93%)
Top scorers: **30** - Robin **VAN PERSIE** NED, Arsenal • **27** - Wayne **ROONEY**, Man Utd • **23** - Sergio **AGUERO** ARG, Man City • **17** - Clint **DEMPSEY** USA, Fulham • **16** - Emmanuel **ADEBAYOR** TOG, Spurs; Demba **BA** SEN, Newcastle & **YAKUBU** Aiyegbeni NGA, Blackburn • **15** - Grant **HOLT**, Norwich • **14** - Edin **DZEKO** BIH, Man City • **13** - Mario **BALOTELLI** ITA, Man City & Papiss **CISSE** SEN, Newcastle

ENGLAND 2011-12

NPOWER FOOTBALL LEAGUE CHAMPIONSHIP (2)

	Pl	W	D	L	F	A	Pts	Reading	South'pton	West Ham	B'ham City	Blackpool	Cardiff City	Hull City	Leicester	Brighton	Watford	Derby Co	Burnley	Leeds Utd	Ipswich T	Millwall	C Palace	Peter'boro	Nottm For	Bristol City	Barnsley	Portsmouth	Coventry	Doncaster
Reading	46	27	8	11	69	41	89		1-1	3-0	1-0	3-1	1-2	0-0	1-3	1-3	0-0	2-2	2-1	0-2	2-0	1-0	2-2	2-2	3-2	1-0	1-0	1-2	1-0	2-0
Southampton	46	26	10	10	85	46	88	1-3		1-0	4-1	2-2	1-1	3-0	2-1	0-2	3-0	4-0	4-0	2-2	0-3	1-1	1-1	0-2	1-3	2-0	1-2	0-0	2-4	2-0
West Ham United ‡	46	24	14	8	81	48	86	2-4	1-1		3-3	4-0	0-1	1-1	2-1	3-2	6-0	1-3	1-1	2-2	2-0	1-2	1-0	0-1	0-2	1-0	0-1	0-4	3-1	0-1
Birmingham City ‡	46	20	16	10	78	51	76	2-0	0-0	1-1		3-0	1-1	3-0	0-0	2-0	0-0	3-0	2-2	1-1	0-2	1-3	0-3	1-1	1-1	2-2	2-1	1-1	1-0	1-0	2-1
Blackpool ‡	46	20	15	11	79	59	75	3-0	1-4	2-2		1-1	3-0	1-1	3-3	1-0	0-0	1-4	0-1	0-2	1-0	2-1	2-1	2-1	1-1	2-5	1-1	1-1	2-1	2-1
Cardiff City ‡	46	19	18	9	66	53	75	3-1	2-1	0-2	1-0	1-3		2-3	0-3	0-0	1-3	1-1	2-0	0-0	0-1	1-2	2-0	0-2	0-3	1-1	1-0	3-1	5-3	3-2	2-2	2-0
Middlesbrough	46	18	16	12	52	51	70	0-2	2-1	0-2	3-1	2-2	0-2		1-0	0-0	1-0	1-2	0-0	2-0	2-0	0-1	1-0	0-1	1-2	1-1	1-2	0-2	2-1	1-0	0
Hull City	46	19	11	16	47	43	68	1-0	0-2	0-2	2-1	0-2	1-2	2-1		0-3	2-0	1-3	2-3	0-0	2-2	2-0	0-1	1-0	2-1	3-0	3-1	1-0	0-2	0-0	
Leicester City	46	18	12	16	66	55	66	0-2	3-2	1-2	3-1	2-0	1-2	2-2	1		1-0	2-4	0-0	0-0	1-1	1-0	3-3	0-1	1-0	0-1	1-2	1-1	2-1	1-2	1-0	3-0
Brighton & Hove Alb	46	17	15	14	52	52	66	0-1	3-0	0-1	1-1	2-2	2-1	1-0	0-1	0		2-2	2-0	0-1	3-3	3-0	2-1	3-2	0-1	0-2	0-2	0-2	0-2	2-1	2-1	
Watford	46	16	16	14	56	64	64	1-2	0-3	0-4	2-2	0-2	1-1	2-1	1-1	3-2	1-0		0-1	3-2	1-2	1-2	1-0	2-3	2-0	1-2	2-2	1-2	2-0	0-4	0-1	
Derby County	46	18	10	18	50	58	64	0-1	1-1	2-1	2-1	2-1	0-3	0-1	0-2	0-1	0-1	1-2		1-2	1-0	0-3	2-1	1-1	0-2	1-1	2-1	1-1	3-1	1-0	3-0
Burnley	46	17	11	18	61	58	62	0-1	1-1	2-1	3-3	1-1	0-1	3-1	0-2	2-0		1-2	4-0	1-3	1-1	1-1	5-1	1-1	2-0	0-1	1-1	3-0			
Leeds United	46	17	10	19	65	68	61	0-1	0-1	1-1	4-0	5-1	1-0	1-4	1-2	1-2	0-0	2-2	2-1		3-1	2-0	3-2	4-1	3-7	2-1	1-2	1-0	1-1	1-3	2
Ipswich Town	46	17	10	19	69	77	61	2-3	2-5	5-1	1-1	2-2	3-0	1-1	0-1	1-1	2-3	1-1	2-1	0-1	0-2	1	0-3	1-3	2-1	3-3	3-0	1-0	1-0	3-0	2-3
Millwall	46	15	12	19	55	57	57	1-2	2-3	0-0	0-6	2-2	0-0	0-1	3-2	0-2	1-1	1-0	2-0	0-0	0-1	0-4	1-4		0-1	2-2	2-2	0-1	2-0	0-1	0-3	0-3	2
Crystal Palace	46	13	17	16	46	51	56	0-0	0-2	2-2	1-0	1-1	2-0	1-0	0-1	2-1	1-4	0-1	1-2	0-1	1-1	1-1	0-0		1-0	0-3	1-1	0-0	0-1	1-2	
Peterborough Utd	46	13	11	22	67	77	50	3-1	1-3	0-2	1-1	3-1	4-3	1-1	0-1	1-1	1-0	1-2	2-3	2-2	1-2	3-7	1-0	3-2	1		0-1	3-0	3-4	0-3	1-0	1-0	2
Nottingham Forest	46	14	8	24	47	63	50	1-0	0-3	1-4	1-3	0-0	0-1	2-0	1-2	2-1	1-1	1-1	1-2	0-2	0-4	3-2	3-1	0-1	0-1		0-1	0-0	2-0	2-0	1-2
Bristol City	46	12	13	21	44	68	49	2-3	2-0	1-0	2-1	3-1	2-0	1-1	3-2	0-0	2-1	1-3	1-0	3-0	3-1	0-2	2-1	2-2	0-0		2-0	0-0	3-1	2-1	
Barnsley	46	13	9	24	49	74	48	0-4	0-1	0-4	1-3	3-0	1-1	3-2	1-1	1-0	0-0	1-1	2-3	0-4	1-3	3-5	1-3	2-1	1-1	2-2		2-0	2-2	0-2	0
Portsmouth §10	46	13	11	22	50	59	40	1-0	1-1	0-1	4-1	1-0	1-1	3-2	0-1	1-0	2-1	0-1	5-0	0-0	1-0	1-2	1-2	3-3	0-0	0-2	0		2-1	3-1	
Coventry City	46	9	13	24	41	65	40	1-1	2-4	1-2	1-1	2-2	1-3	1-0	1-0	1-2	0-0	0-0	2-1	2-2	1-2	3-0	1-1	1-2	2-1	0-0	1-0	1-0	2-0		0-2
Doncaster Rovers	46	8	12	26	43	80	36	1-1	1-0	0-1	1-3	1-3	0-0	1-3	1-1	2-1	1-1	0-0	1-1	2-1	2-0	3-2	3-0	3-1	0-1	1-0	1-1	2-0	3-4	1-1	

5/08/2011 - 28/04/2012 • ‡ Qualified for the play-offs • Top scorer: **27** - Rickie **LAMBERT**, Southampton • Att: 9,784,100. Av: 17,725 (+1.97%)
Play-off semi-finals: Cardiff City 0-2 0-3 **West Ham** • Blackpool 1-0 2-2 Birmingham City
Play-off final: **West Ham Utd** 2-1 Blackpool. Wembley, 19-05-2012, Att: 78 523, Ref: Webb. Scorers - Carlton Cole [35], Ricardo Vaz Te [87] for West Ham; Tom Ince [48] for Blackpool

ENGLAND 2011-12

NPOWER FOOTBALL LEAGUE ONE (3)

	Pl	W	D	L	F	A	Pts
Charlton Athletic	46	30	11	5	82	36	101
Sheffield Wed'day	46	28	9	9	81	48	93
Sheffield United ‡	46	27	9	10	92	51	90
Huddersfield Town ‡	46	21	18	7	79	47	81
Milton Keynes Dons‡	46	22	14	10	84	47	80
Stevenage ‡	46	18	19	9	69	44	73
Notts County	46	21	10	15	75	63	73
Carlisle United	46	18	15	13	65	66	69
Brentford	46	18	13	15	63	52	67
Colchester United	46	13	20	13	61	66	59
Bournemouth	46	15	13	18	48	52	58
Tranmere Rovers	46	14	14	18	49	53	56
Hartlepool	46	14	14	18	50	55	56
Bury	46	15	11	20	60	79	56
Preston North End	46	13	15	18	54	68	54
Oldham Athletic	46	14	12	20	50	66	54
Yeovil Town	46	14	12	20	59	80	54
Scunthorpe United	46	10	22	14	55	59	52
Walsall	46	10	20	16	51	57	50
Leyton Orient	46	13	11	22	48	75	50
Wycombe Wanderers	46	11	10	25	65	88	43
Chesterfield	46	10	12	24	56	81	42
Exeter City	46	10	12	24	46	75	42
Rochdale	46	8	14	24	47	81	38

6/08/2011 - 5/05/2012 • ‡ Qualified for the play-offs • Top scorer: **36** – Jordan **RHODES**, Huddersfield • Att: 4,070,897. Av: 7375 (-1.92%)
Play-off semi-finals: Milton Keynes Dons 0-2 2-1 **Huddersfield Town** • Stevenage 0-0 1 **Sheffield United**
Final: **Huddersfield Town** 0-0 8-7p Sheffield Utd. Wembley, 26-05-2012, Att: 52 100, Ref: East

ENGLAND 2011-12

NPOWER FOOTBALL LEAGUE TWO (4)

	Pl	W	D	L	F	A	Pts
Swindon Town	46	29	6	11	75	32	93
Shrewsbury Town	46	26	10	10	66	41	88
Crawley Town ‡	46	23	15	8	76	54	84
Southend United ‡	46	25	8	13	77	48	83
Torquay United ‡	46	23	12	11	63	50	81
Cheltenham Town ‡	46	23	8	15	66	50	77
Crewe Alexandra	46	20	12	14	67	59	72
Gillingham	46	20	10	16	79	62	70
Oxford United	46	17	17	12	59	48	68
Rotherham United	46	18	13	15	67	63	67
Aldershot Town	46	19	9	18	54	52	66
Port Vale	46	20	9	17	68	60	59
Bristol Rovers	46	15	12	19	60	70	57
Accrington Stanley	46	14	15	17	64	63	57
Morecambe	46	14	14	18	63	57	56
AFC Wimbledon	46	15	9	22	62	78	54
Burton Albion	46	14	12	20	54	81	54
Bradford City	46	12	14	20	54	59	50
Dagenham & Red.	46	14	8	24	50	72	50
Northampton Town	46	12	12	22	56	79	48
Plymouth Argyle	46	10	16	20	47	64	46
Barnet	46	12	10	24	52	79	46
Hereford United	46	10	14	22	50	70	44
Macclesfield Town	46	8	13	25	39	64	37

6/08/2011 - 5/05/2012 • ‡ Qualified for the play-offs • Top scorers: **18** – Jack **MIDSON**, Wimbledon; Izale **MCLEOD**, Barnet; Adebayo **AKINFENWA**, Northants & Lewis **GRABBAN**, Rotherham • Att: 2,429,939. Av: 4402 (+5.36%)
Play-off semi-finals: **Crewe** 1-0 2-2 Southend • **Cheltenham** 2-0 0-2 1 Torquay United
Play-off final: **Crewe Alex** 2-0 Cheltenham Town. Wembley, 27-05-2012, Att: 24 029, Ref: Pawson. Scorers - Nick Powell [15], Byron Moore [82]

ENGLAND 2011-12

FOOTBALL CONFERENCE BLUE SQUARE PREMIER (5)

	Pl	W	D	L	F	A	Pts
Fleetwood Town	46	31	10	5	102	48	103
Wrexham ‡	46	30	8	8	85	33	98
Mansfield Town ‡	46	25	14	7	87	48	89
York City ‡	46	23	14	9	81	45	83
Luton Town ‡	46	22	15	9	78	42	81
Kidderminster H	46	22	10	14	82	63	76
Southport	46	21	13	12	72	69	76
Gateshead	46	21	11	14	69	62	74
Cambridge United	46	19	14	13	57	41	71
Forest Green Rovers	46	19	13	14	66	45	70
Grimsby Town	46	19	13	14	79	60	70
Braintree Town	46	17	11	18	76	80	62
Barrow	46	17	9	20	62	76	60
Ebbsfleet United	46	14	12	20	69	84	54
Alfreton Town	46	15	9	22	62	86	54
Stockport County	46	12	15	19	58	74	51
Lincoln City	46	13	10	23	56	66	49
Tamworth	46	11	15	20	47	70	48
Newport County	46	11	14	21	53	65	47
AFC Telford United	46	10	16	20	45	65	46
Hayes & Yeading	46	11	8	27	58	90	41
Darlington §10	46	11	13	22	47	73	36
Bath City	46	7	10	29	43	89	31
Kettering Town §3	46	8	9	29	40	100	30

12/08/2011 - 28/04/2012 • ‡ Qualified for the play-offs • § = points deducted • Top scorer: **31** - Jamie **VARDY**, Fleetwood Town
Play-off semi-finals: **York City** 1-1 1-0 Mansfield Town • **Luton Town** 2-0 1-2 Wrexham
Play-off final: **York City** 2-1 Luton Town. Wembley, 20-05-2012, Att: 39 265, Ref: Simpson. Scorers - Ashley Chambers [26], Matty Blair [47] for York; Andre Gray [2] for Luton

ENGLAND 2011-12 FOOTBALL CONFERENCE BLUE SQUARE NORTH (6)

	Pl	W	D	L	F	A	Pts
Hyde	42	27	9	6	90	36	90
Guiseley ‡	42	25	10	7	87	50	85
Halifax Town ‡	42	21	11	10	80	59	74
Gainsborough Tr'ty ‡	42	23	5	14	74	61	74
Nuneaton Town ‡ §6	42	22	12	8	74	41	72
Stalybridge Celtic	42	20	11	11	83	64	71
Worcester City	42	18	11	13	63	58	65
Altrincham	42	17	10	15	90	71	61
Droylsden	42	16	11	15	83	86	59
Bishop's Stortford	42	17	7	18	70	75	58
Boston United	42	15	9	18	60	67	54
Colwyn Bay	42	15	8	19	55	71	53
Workington	42	14	10	18	56	61	52
Gloucester City	42	15	7	20	53	60	52
Harrogate Town	42	14	10	18	59	69	52
Histon	42	12	15	15	67	72	51
Corby Town	42	14	8	20	69	71	50
Vauxhall Motors	42	14	8	20	63	78	50
Solihull Moors	42	13	10	19	44	54	49
Hinckley United	42	13	9	20	75	90	48
Blyth Spartans	42	7	13	22	50	80	34
Eastwood Town	42	4	8	30	37	105	20

13/08/2011 - 28/04/2012 • ‡ Qualified for the play-offs
§ = points deducted
Play-off semis: **Nuneaton Town** 1-1 1-0 Guiseley •
Gainsborough Trinity 2-2 1-0 Halifax Town
Play-off final: Gainsborough Trinity 0-1 **Nuneaton Town**

ENGLAND 2011-12 FOOTBALL CONFERENCE BLUE SQUARE SOUTH (6)

	Pl	W	D	L	F	A	Pts
Woking	42	30	7	5	92	41	97
Dartford ‡	42	26	10	6	89	40	88
Welling United ‡	42	24	9	9	79	47	81
Sutton United ‡	42	20	14	8	68	53	74
Basingstoke Town ‡	42	20	11	11	65	50	71
Chelmsford City	42	18	13	11	67	44	67
Dover Athletic	42	17	15	10	62	49	66
Boreham Wood	42	17	10	15	66	58	61
Tonbridge Angels	42	15	12	15	70	67	57
Salisbury City	42	15	12	15	55	54	57
Dorchester Town	42	16	8	18	58	65	56
Eastleigh	42	15	9	18	57	63	54
Weston-Super-Mare	42	14	9	19	58	71	51
Truro City	42	13	9	20	65	80	48
Staines Town	42	12	10	20	53	64	46
Farnborough §5	42	15	6	21	52	79	46
Bromley	42	10	15	17	52	66	45
Eastbourne Boro	42	12	9	21	54	69	45
Havant & Wat'ville	42	11	11	20	64	75	44
Maidenhead United	42	11	10	21	49	74	43
Hampton & Rich'd	42	10	12	20	53	69	42
Thurrock	42	5	11	26	33	84	26

13/08/2011 - 28/04/2012 • ‡ Qualified for the play-offs
§ = points deducted
Play-off semis: Basingstoke Town 0-1 1-2 **Dartford** •
Sutton United 1-2 0-0 **Welling United**
Play-off final: **Dartford** 1-0 Welling United

PART TWO – THE ASSOCIATIONS

ENGLAND 2011-12
ISTHMIAN LEAGUE
RYMAN PREMIER (7)

	Pl	W	D	L	F	A	Pts
Billericay Town	42	24	13	5	82	38	85
AFC Hornchurch‡	42	26	4	12	68	35	82
Lowestoft Town ‡	42	25	7	10	80	53	82
Wealdstone ‡	42	20	15	7	76	39	75
Bury Town ‡	42	22	9	11	85	55	75
Lewes	42	21	10	11	55	47	73
Hendon	42	21	9	12	69	44	72
Canvey Island	42	22	5	15	66	55	71
Cray Wanderers	42	20	8	14	74	55	68
East Thurrock Utd	42	18	8	16	70	65	62
Kingstonian	42	18	7	17	58	64	61
Met'politan Police	42	18	6	18	63	46	60
Wingate/Finchley	42	16	11	15	63	79	59
Concord Rangers	42	16	9	17	72	66	57
Margate	42	15	9	18	66	65	54
Carshalton Ath	42	14	10	18	48	55	52
Harrow Borough	42	13	8	21	53	70	47
Hastings United	42	13	8	21	43	61	47
Leatherhead	42	11	8	23	46	62	41
Aveley	42	5	12	25	41	88	27
Tooting/Mitcham	42	7	6	29	47	116	27
Horsham	42	3	6	33	38	105	14

20/08/2011 - 7/05/2012 • ‡ Play-offs
Play-off semis: **Hornchurch** 3-1 Bury
Lowestoft 2-1 Wealdstone
Play-off final: **Hornchurch** 2-1 Lowestoft

ENGLAND 2011-12
SOUTHERN LEAGUE
ZAMARETTO PREMIER (7)

	Pl	W	D	L	F	A	Pts
Brackley Town	42	25	10	7	92	48	85
Oxford City ‡	42	22	11	9	68	41	77
AFC Totton ‡	42	21	11	10	81	43	74
Chesham Utd ‡	42	21	10	11	76	53	73
Cambridge City ‡	42	21	9	12	78	52	72
Stourbridge	42	20	12	10	67	45	72
Leamington	42	18	15	9	60	47	69
St Albans City	42	17	11	14	72	77	62
Barwell	42	17	10	15	70	61	61
Bedford Town	42	15	10	17	60	69	55
Chippenham Town	42	14	11	17	55	53	53
Frome Town	42	12	16	14	44	49	52
Bashley	42	13	13	16	58	74	52
Hitchin Town	42	13	12	17	54	57	51
Redditch United	42	14	9	19	45	50	51
Banbury Utd	42	13	10	19	54	61	49
Weymouth	42	13	9	20	54	75	48
Arlesey Town	42	12	11	19	43	60	47
Hemel H'stead T	42	10	14	18	46	66	44
Evesham Utd	42	12	8	22	49	71	44
Swindon S'marine	42	11	11	20	50	86	44
Cirencester Town	42	7	9	26	40	78	30

20/08/2011 - 7/05/2012 • ‡ Play-offs
Play-off semis: **Oxford City** 1-0 Cambridge C
AFC Totton 3-2 Chesham Utd
Play-off final: **Oxford City** 4-2 AFC Totton

ENGLAND 2011-12
NORTHERN LEAGUE
EVO-STIK PREMIER (7)

	Pl	W	D	L	F	A	Pts
Chester	42	31	7	4	102	29	**100**
Northwich Victoria	42	26	8	8	73	43	83
Chorley ‡	42	24	7	11	76	48	79
Bradford Park Av‡	42	24	6	12	77	49	78
Hednesford T ‡	42	21	10	11	67	49	73
FC United of M. ‡	42	21	9	12	83	51	72
Marine	42	19	9	14	56	50	66
Rushall Olympic	42	17	10	15	52	51	61
North Ferriby Utd	42	16	10	16	56	70	58
Nantwich Town	42	15	13	14	65	61	57
Kendal Town	42	15	8	19	78	83	53
Ashton United	42	15	8	19	61	67	53
Buxton	42	15	8	19	64	77	53
Matlock Town	42	12	14	16	52	54	50
Worksop Town	42	13	10	19	56	76	49
Stafford Rangers	42	12	12	18	60	65	48
Whitby Town	42	12	11	19	57	80	47
Stocksbridge PS	42	10	12	20	57	75	42
Frickley Athletic	42	10	12	20	48	69	42
Chasetown	42	10	11	21	50	75	41
MickleoverSports	42	11	10	21	67	85	40
Burscough	42	5	11	26	54	104	26

20/08/2011 - 7/05/2012 • ‡ Play-offs
Play-off semis: **Bradford PA** 2-0 Hednesford
Chorley 0-2 **FC United**
Play-off final: **Bradford PA** 1-0 FC United

MEDALS TABLE

	Overall	League	Cup	LC	Europe	
	G S B	G S B	G S B	G S B	G S B	City/Town
1 Liverpool	41 25 24	18 12 7	7 7 9	**8** 3 3	8 3 5	Liverpool
2 Manchester United	38 28 28	**19** 15 6	**11** 7 9	4 4 4	4 2 9	Manchester
3 Arsenal	27 24 25	13 8 8	10 7 9	2 5 7	2 4 1	London
4 Aston Villa	20 16 17	7 10 2	7 3 10	5 3 5	1	Birmingham
5 Chelsea	18 11 25	4 4 5	7 4 9	4 2 4	3 1 7	London
6 Tottenham Hotspur	17 9 28	2 4 9	8 1 10	4 3 6	3 1 3	London
7 Everton	15 17 21	9 7 7	5 8 12		2 2	Liverpool
8 Newcastle United	11 10 8	4 2 4	6 7 3	1	1 1	Newcastle
9 Manchester City	11 8 11	3 3 4	5 4 2	2 1 4	1 1	Manchester
10 Blackburn Rovers	10 3 18	3 1 3	6 2 10	1	5	Blackburn
11 Wolverhampton Wanderers	9 10 14	3 5 6	4 4 6	2	1	1 1	Wolverhampton
12 Nottingham Forest	9 5 14	1 2 4	2 1 9	4 2	2 1	Nottingham
13 Sunderland	8 8 18	6 5 8	2 2 8		1 2	Sunderland
14 Sheffield Wednesday	8 5 19	4 1 7	3 3 10	1 1 2		Sheffield
15 Leeds United	7 12 13	3 5 2	1 3 4	1 1 3	2 3 4	Leeds
16 West Bromwich Albion	7 9 12	1 2 1	5 5 10	1 2 1		West Bromwich
17 Sheffield United	5 4 8	1 2	4 2 7		1	Sheffield
18 The Wanderers	5		5			London
19 Preston North End	4 11 5	2 6 2	2 5 3			Preston
20 Huddersfield Town	4 7 6	3 3 3	1 4 2		1	Huddersfield
21 Bolton Wanderers	4 5 12		3 4 3 7	2 2		Bolton
22 West Ham United	4 5 10		1	3 2 2	2 6	1 1 1	London
23 Portsmouth	4 3 3	2 1	2 3 2			Portsmouth
24 Leicester City	3 7 5		1 1	4 4	3 2		Leicester
25 Derby County	3 6 16	2 3 4	1 3 9		2	1	Derby
26 Burnley	3 4 14	2 2 5	1 2 5	4		Burnley
27 Ipswich Town	3 2 9	1 2 3	1	2	4	1	Ipswich
28 Birmingham City	2 5 10			2 7	2 1 2	2 1	Birmingham
29 Old Etonians	2 4		2 4			Eton

ENG – ENGLAND

MEDALS TABLE (CONT'D)

		Overall			League			Cup			LC			Europe		City/Town
		G S B		G S B			G S B			G S B			G S B		
30	Norwich City	2 2 5		1			3		2 2 1							Norwich
31	Bury	2 1		2					1							Bury
32	Southampton	1 5 8		1		1 3 7			1 1							Southampton
33	Middlesbrough	1 4 4		1		1 1			1 2 2			1				Middlesbrough
34	Cardiff City	1 4 3		1		1 2 1			1 1				1			Cardiff
35	Blackpool	1 3 2		1 1		1 2			1							Blackpool
	Oxford University	1 3 2				1 3 2										Oxford
37	Queens Park Rangers	1 3 1		1		1			1 1 1							London
38	Royal Engineers	1 3				1 3										Chatham
39	Luton Town	1 2 3				1 3			1 1							Luton
	Stoke City	1 2 3				1 3			1 1							Stoke
41	Charlton Athletic	1 2 1		1 1		1 1										London
42	Notts County	1 1 5		2		1 1 3										Nottingham
43	Barnsley	1 1 1				1 1 1										Barnsley
	Clapham Rovers	1 1 1				1 1 1										London
45	Swindon Town	1 4				2			1 2							Swindon
46	Wimbledon/MK Dons	1 3				1 1			2							London/Milton Keynes
47	Coventry City	1 2				1			2							Coventry
	Old Carthusians	1 2				1 2										London
49	Blackburn Olympic	1 1				1 1										Blackburn
	Oxford United	1 1							1 1							Oxford
51	Bradford City	1				1										Bradford
52	Watford	2 6		1		1 4			2							Watford
53	Fulham	2 5				1 5						1				London
54	Bristol City	2 3		1		1 1			2							Bristol
	Oldham Athletic	2 3		1		3			1							Oldham
56	Queens Park Glasgow	2 2				2 2										Glasgow - SCO
57	Crystal Palace	1 7		1		1 2			4							London
58	Millwall	1 3				1 3										London
59	Tranmere Rovers	1 1							1 1							Birkenhead
60	Brighton & Hove Albion	1				1										Brighton
	London Select XI	1										1				London
	Rochdale	1							1							Rochdale
	Rotherham United	1							1							Rotherham
	Wigan Athletic	1							1							Wigan
65	Plymouth Argyle	3				1			2							Plymouth
	The Swifts	3				3										Slough
	Wycombe Wanderers	3				2			1							Wycombe
68	Grimsby Town	2				2										Grimsby
	Swansea City	2				2										Swansea
70	Cambridge University	1				1										Cambridge
	Carlisle United	1							1							Carlisle
	Chester City	1							1							Chester
	Chesterfield	1				1										Chesterfield
	Crewe Alexandra	1				1										Crewe
	Crystal Palace (am)	1				1										London
	Darwen	1				1										Darwen
	Derby Junction	1				1										Derby
	Glasgow Rangers	1				1										Glasgow
	Hull City	1				1										Hull
	Leyton Orient	1				1										London
	Marlow	1				1										Marlow
	Old Harrovians	1				1										London
	Peterborough United	1							1							Peterborough
	Port Vale	1				1										Stoke
	Reading	1				1										Reading
	Shrewsbury Town	1							1							Shrewsbury
	Shropshire Wanderers	1				1										Shrewsbury
	Stockport County	1							1							Stockport
	Walsall	1							1							Walsall
	York City	1				1										York

FA CUP (SPONSORED BY BUDWEISER) 2011-12

Third Round

Chelsea *	4
Portsmouth	0
Milton Keynes Dons *	1 0
Queens Park Rangers	1 1
Sheffield United *	3
Salisbury City	1
Wolverhampton Wanderers	0 0
Birmingham City *	0 1
Norwich City *	4
Burnley	1
Cardiff City	2
West Bromwich Albion *	4
Swindon Town *	2
Wigan Athletic	1
Nottingham Forest *	0 0
Leicester City	0 4
Bolton Wanderers	2 2
Macclesfield Town *	2 0
Barnsley *	2
Swansea City	4
Southampton	2
Coventry City *	1
Dagenham & Redbridge *	0 0
Millwall	0 5
Stevenage	1
Reading *	0
Doncaster Rovers *	0
Notts County	2
Watford *	4
Bradford City	2
Cheltenham Town	0
Tottenham Hotspur *	3
Everton *	2
Tamworth	0
Charlton Athletic	0
Fulham *	4
Sheffield Wednesday *	1
West Ham United	0
Fleetwood Town *	1
Blackpool	5
Arsenal *	1
Leeds United	0
Bristol Rovers *	1
Aston Villa	3
Middlesbrough *	1
Shrewsbury Town	0
Peterborough United *	0
Sunderland	2
Stoke City	3
Gillingham *	1
Crystal Palace	0
Derby County *	1
Hull City *	3
Ipswich Town	1
Bristol City	0
Crawley Town *	1
Brighton & Hove Albion *	1 1 5p
Wrexham	1 1 4p
Blackburn Rovers	1
Newcastle United *	2
Manchester United	3
Manchester City *	2
Oldham Athletic	1
Liverpool *	5

Fourth Round

Chelsea	1
Queens Park Rangers *	0
Sheffield United *	0
Birmingham City	4
Norwich City *	2
West Bromwich Albion *	1
Swindon Town	0
Leicester City *	2
Bolton Wanderers *	2
Swansea City	1
Southampton	1 2
Millwall *	1 3
Stevenage *	1
Notts County	0
Watford *	0
Tottenham Hotspur	1
Everton *	2
Fulham	1
Sheffield Wednesday	1 0
Blackpool *	1 3
Arsenal *	3
Aston Villa	2
Middlesbrough	1 1
Sunderland *	1 2
Stoke City	2
Derby County *	0
Hull City *	0
Crawley Town	1
Brighton & Hove Albion *	1
Newcastle United	0
Manchester United	1
Liverpool *	2

† First match abandoned after 41 minutes following the collapse of Fabrice Muamba

Fifth Round

Chelsea *	1 2
Birmingham City	1 0
Norwich City *	1
Leicester City	2
Bolton Wanderers	2
Millwall *	0
Stevenage *	0 1
Tottenham Hotspur	0 3
Everton *	2
Blackpool	0
Arsenal	0
Sunderland *	2
Stoke City	2
Crawley Town *	0
Brighton & Hove Albion	1
Liverpool *	6

FA CUP (SPONSORED BY BUDWEISER) 2011-12

Quarter-finals			Semi-finals			Final	
Chelsea *	5						
Leicester City	2						
			Chelsea	5			
			Tottenham Hotspur *	1			
Bolton Wanderers	1	1					
Tottenham Hotspur † *	1	3					
						Chelsea	2
						Liverpool	1
Everton *	1	2					
Sunderland	1	0					
			Everton	1			
			Liverpool	2			
Stoke City	1						
Liverpool *	2						

* Home team
Semi-finals played at Wembley Stadium, London

FA CUP FINAL 2012
Wembley Stadium, London, 5-05-2012, 17:15, Att: 89 102, Ref: Phil Dowd

Chelsea	2	Ramires [11], Didier Drogba [52]
Liverpool	1	Andy Carroll [64]

CHELSEA
Petr CECH - Jose BOSINGWA, Branislav IVANOVIC, John TERRY (c), Ashley COLE - Mikel John OBI•, Frank LAMPARD - RAMIRES (RAUL MEIRELES 75), Juan MATA (Florent MALOUDA 90), Salomon KALOU - Didier DROGBA. Tr: Roberto DI MATTEO

LIVERPOOL
Pepe REINA - Glen JOHNSON, Martin SKRTEL, Daniel AGGER•, Jose ENRIQUE - Jordan HENDERSON, Jay SPEARING (Andy CARROLL 54) - Craig BELLAMY (Dirk KUYT 76), Steven GERRARD (c), Stewart DOWNING - Luis SUAREZ•. Tr: Kenny DALGLISH

CARLING LEAGUE CUP 2011-12

Second Round

Liverpool	3
Exeter City *	1
Sunderland	0
Brighton & Hove Albion *	1
Tottenham Hotspur	Bye
Stoke City	Bye
Everton *	3
Sheffield United	1
Bournemouth *	1
West Bromwich Albion	4
Fulham	Bye
Chelsea	Bye
Arsenal	Bye
Swansea City	1
Shrewsbury Town *	3
Aston Villa *	2
Hereford United	0
Macclesfield Town	1
Bolton Wanderers *	2
Wolverhampton Wanderers	4
Northampton Town *	0
Morecambe	0
Millwall *	2
Birmingham City	Bye
Manchester City	Bye
Crystal Palace *	2
Wigan Athletic	1
Peterborough United *	0
Middlesbrough	2
Preston North End	2
Charlton Athletic *	0
Swindon Town *	1
Southampton	3
Aldershot Town *	2
Carlisle United	0
Queens Park Rangers *	0
Rochdale	2
Leeds United	2
Doncaster Rovers *	1
Manchester United	Bye
Blackburn Rovers *	3
Sheffield Wednesday	1
Bristol Rovers	2
Leyton Orient *	3
Nottingham Forest	4
Wycombe Wanderers *	1
Scunthorpe United *	1
Newcastle United	2
Burnley *	3
Barnet	2
Norwich City *	0
Milton Keynes Dons	4
Leicester City	4
Bury *	2
Huddersfield Town	3
Cardiff City *	5

Third Round

Liverpool	2	
Brighton & Hove Albion *	1	
Tottenham Hotspur	0	6p
Stoke City *	0	7p
Everton *	2	
West Bromwich Albion	1	
Fulham	0	3p
Chelsea *	0	4p
Arsenal *	3	
Shrewsbury Town	1	
Aston Villa *	0	
Bolton Wanderers	2	
Wolverhampton Wanderers *	5	
Millwall	0	
Birmingham City	0	
Manchester City *	2	
Crystal Palace *	2	
Middlesbrough	1	
Preston North End	1	
Southampton *	2	
Aldershot Town *	2	
Rochdale	1	
Leeds United *	0	
Manchester United	3	
Blackburn Rovers *	3	
Leyton Orient	2	
Nottingham Forest *	3	
Newcastle United	4	
Burnley *	2	
Milton Keynes Dons	1	
Leicester City	2	6p
Cardiff City *	2	7p

Fourth Round

Liverpool	2
Stoke City *	1
Everton *	1
Chelsea	2
Arsenal *	2
Bolton Wanderers	1
Wolverhampton Wanderers *	2
Manchester City	5
Crystal Palace *	2
Southampton	0
Aldershot Town *	0
Manchester United	3
Blackburn Rovers *	4
Newcastle United	3
Burnley	0
Cardiff City *	1

* Home team/Home team in the first leg

CARLING LEAGUE CUP 2011–12

Quarter-finals

Liverpool	2
Chelsea *	0

Arsenal *	0
Manchester City	1

Crystal Palace	2
Manchester United *	1

Blackburn Rovers	0
Cardiff City *	2

Semi-finals

Liverpool	1	2
Manchester City *	0	2

Crystal Palace *	1 0	1p
Cardiff City	0 1	3p

Final

Liverpool ‡	2	3p
Cardiff City	2	2p

‡ Qualified for the UEFA Europa League

CARLING LEAGUE CUP FINAL 2012
Wembley Stadium, London, 26-02-2012, 16:00, Att: 89 041, Ref: Mark Clattenburg

Liverpool	2 3p	Martin **SKRTEL** [60], Dirk **KUYT** [108]
Cardiff City	2 2p	Joe **MASON** [19], Ben **TURNER** [118]

LIVERPOOL
Pepe **REINA** - Glen **JOHNSON**, Martin **SKRTEL**, Daniel **AGGER** (Jamie **CARRAGHER** 86), Jose **ENRIQUE** - Steven **GERRARD** (c), Charlie **ADAM** - Jordan **HENDERSON**• (Craig **BELLAMY** 58), Luis **SUAREZ**, Stewart **DOWNING** - Andy **CARROLL** (Dirk **KUYT** 103). Tr: Kenny **DALGLISH**

CARDIFF CITY
Tom **HEATON** - Kevin **MCNAUGHTON** (Darcy **BLAKE** 106), Mark **HUDSON** (c) (Anthony **GERRARD** 99), Ben **TURNER**•, Andrew **TAYLOR** - Don **COWIE**, Peter **WHITTINGHAM**, Aron **GUNNARSSON**, Joe **MASON** (Filip **KISS**• 91) - Kenny **MILLER**, Rudy **GESTEDE**. Tr: Malky **MACKAY**

PENALTIES
(Liverpool 1st): Gerrard ✘[1]; Miller ✘[2]; Adam ✘[3]; Cowie ✓; Kuyt ✓; Gestede ✘[2]; Downing ✓; Whittingham ✓; Johnson ✓; Gerrard ✘[3]; 1 = saved • 2 = hits post • 3 = missed

JOHNSTONE'S PAINT FOOTBALL LEAGUE TROPHY 2011-12

Second Round		Third Round		Quarter-finals (regional semi-finals)		Semi-finals (regional finals)		Final	
Chesterfield	3	**Chesterfield** *	4						
Notts Co *	1	Tranmere Rovers	3						
Accrington Stanley *	0			**Chesterfield**	1 4p				
Tranmere Rovers	1			Preston North End *	1 2p				
Rochdale *	1 3p	Rochdale *	1 2p						
Walsall	1 1p	**Preston North End**	1 4p			**Chesterfield** *	2 1		
Morecambe *	2 6p					Oldham Athletic	1 0		
Preston North End	2 7p								
Bradford City	2 4p	**Bradford City** *	1 6p						
Huddersfield Town *	2 3p	Sheffield United	1 5p						
Rotherham United *	1			Bradford City	0				
Sheffield United	2			**Oldham Athletic** *	2				
Crewe Alexandra *	1	Crewe Alexandra	1						
Macclesfield Town	0	**Oldham Athletic**	3					**Chesterfield**	2
Scunthorpe United *	0							Swindon Town	0
Oldham Athletic	1								
Barnet	3	**Barnet**	2						
Gillingham *	1	Cheltenham Town *	0						
Wycombe Wanderers *	1			**Barnet** *	0 5p				
Cheltenham Town	3			Brentford	0 3p				
Bournemouth *	3	Bournemouth	0			**Barnet** *	1 0		
Yeovil Town	2	**Brentford** *	6			**Swindon Town**	1 1		
Charlton Athletic *	0								
Brentford	3								
Southend United	3	**Southend United**	1						
Dagenham & Redbridge *	1	Oxford United *	0						
Aldershot Town *	1			Southend United *	1				
Oxford United	2			**Swindon Town**	2				
AFC Wimbledon *	2 4p	AFC Wimbledon	1 1p						
Stevenage	2 3p	**Swindon Town** *	1 3p						
Exeter City *	1								
Swindon Town	2								

* Home team/home team in the first leg

TROPHY FINAL

Wembley Stadium, London
25-03-2012, 14:00
Att: 49 602, Ref: Anthony Bates
Scorers - Risser OG [47], Westcarr [94+]
Chesterfield - Tommy Lee - James Hurst - Simon Ford, Josh Thompson, Nathan Smith - Drew Talbot, Mark Allott, Franck Moussa (Mark Randall 81), Alexandre Mendy - Jordan Bowery (Scott Boden 87), Jack Lester (Craig Westcarr 37). Tr: John Sheridan
Swindon - Wes Foderingham - Joe Devera, Oliver Risser (Ronan Murray 62), Alan McCormack, Jay McEvely (Alessandro Cibocchi 77) - Matt Ritchie, Jonathan Smith (John Bostock 72), Simon Ferry, Lee Holmes - Paul Benson, Alan Connell ● - Tr: Paolo Di Canio

ENG – ENGLAND

ARSENAL
2011–12

	13 Newcastle	D	0-0	PL		46 894
	16 Udinese	W	1-0	CLpr	Walcott [4]	58 159
Aug	20 Liverpool	L	0-2	PL 14		60 090
	24 Udinese	W	2-1	CLpr	V. Persie [55], Walcott [69]	26 031
	28 Man Utd	L	2-8	PL 17	Walcott [45], V. Persie [74]	75 448
	10 Swansea	W	1-0	PL 11	Arshavin [40]	60 087
	13 Dortmund	D	1-1	CLgF	V. Persie [42]	65 590
	17 Blackburn	L	3-4	PL 17	Gervinho [10], Arteta [34], Chamakh [85]	22 637
Sep	20 Shrewsbury	W	3-1	LCr3	Gibbs [33], Ox-Chamberlain [58], Benayoun [78]	46 539
	24 Bolton	W	3-0	PL 12	V. Persie 2 [46 71], Song [89]	59 727
	28 Olympiacos	W	2-1	CLgF	Ox-Chamberlain [8], Santos [19]	59 676
	2 Tottenham	L	1-2	PL 15	Ramsey [51]	36 274
	16 Sunderland	W	2-1	PL 10	V. Persie 2 [1 82]	60 078
	19 Marseille	W	1-0	CLgF	Ramsey [92+]	33 258
Oct	23 Stoke	W	3-1	PL 7	Gervinho [27], V. Persie 2 [73 82], Walcott [55]	59 671
	25 Bolton	W	2-1	LCr4	Arshavin [53], Park [56]	56 628
	29 Chelsea	W	5-3	PL 7	V. Persie 3 [36 85 92+], Santos [49], Walcott [55]	41 801
	1 Marseille	D	0-0	CLgF		59 961
	5 West Brom	W	3-0	PL 6	V. Persie [22], Vermaelen [39], Arteta [74]	60 091
Nov	19 Norwich	W	2-1	PL 7	V. Persie 2 [26 59]	26 801
	23 Dortmund	W	2-1	CLgF	V. Persie 2 [49 86]	59 531
	26 Fulham	D	1-1	PL 7	Vermaelen [82]	60 043
	29 Man City	L	0-1	LCqf		60 028
	3 Wigan	W	4-0	PL 5	Arteta [28], Vermaelen [29], Gervinho [61], V. Persie [78]	19 280
	6 Olympiacos	L	1-3	CLgF	Benayoun [57]	30 816
Dec	10 Everton	W	1-0	PL 4	V. Persie [70]	60 062
	18 Man City	L	0-1	PL 5		47 303
	21 Aston Villa	W	2-1	PL	V. Persie [17p], Benayoun [87]	35 618
	27 Wolves	D	1-1	PL	Gervinho [8]	59 686
	31 QPR	W	1-0	PL 4	V. Persie [60]	60 067
	2 Fulham	L	1-2	PL	Koscielny [21]	25 700
	9 Leeds	W	1-0	FAr3	Henry [78]	59 615
Jan	15 Swansea	L	2-3	PL 5	V. Persie [5], Walcott [69]	20 409
	22 Man Utd	L	1-2	PL 5	V. Persie [71]	60 093
	29 Aston Villa	W	3-2	FAr4	V. Persie 2 [54p 61p], Walcott [56]	60 019
	1 Bolton	D	0-0	PL		24 371
	4 Blackburn	W	7-1	PL 6	V. Persie 3 [2 38 62], Arteta [51], Ox-Chamberlain 2 [40 54], Henry [93+]	**59 643**
Feb	11 Sunderland	W	2-1	PL 4	Ramsey [75], Henry [91+]	40 312
	15 Milan	L	0-4	CLr2		64 462
	18 Sunderland	L	0-2	FAr5		26 042
	26 Tottenham	W	5-2	PL 4	Sagna [40], V. Persie [43], Rosicky [51], Walcott 2 [65 68]	60 106
	3 Liverpool	W	2-1	PL 4	V. Persie 2 [31 92+]	44 922
	6 Milan	W	3-0	CLr2	Koscielny [7], Rosicky [26], V. Persie [43p]	59 973
Mar	12 Newcastle	W	2-1	PL	V. Persie [15], Vermaelen [95+]	60 095
	21 Everton	W	1-0	PL	Vermaelen [8]	38 330
	24 Aston Villa	W	3-0	PL 3	Gibbs [16], Walcott [25], Arteta [93+]	60 108
	31 QPR	L	1-2	PL 3	Walcott [37]	18 033
	8 Man City	W	1-0	PL 4	Arteta [87]	60 096
Apr	11 Wolves	W	3-0	PL	V. Persie [9p], Walcott [11], Benayoun [69]	25 815
	16 Wigan	L	1-2	PL	Vermaelen [21]	60 060
	21 Chelsea	D	0-0	PL 3		**60 111**
	28 Stoke	D	1-1	PL	V. Persie [15]	27 502
	5 Norwich	D	3-3	PL 3	Benayoun [2], V. Persie 2 [72 80]	60 092
May	13 West Brom	W	3-2	PL 3	Benayoun [4], Santos [30], Koscielny [54]	26 358
3rd	Att: 1 140 006 • Av: 60 000 (-0.04%) • The Emirates 60 361 (99%)					

KEY
CS = Community Shield • PL = FA Premier League (Barclays Premier League) • FA = FA Cup • LC = Carling League Cup • CL = UEFA Champions League • EL = Europa League
See page 13 for further explanations

ARSENAL LEAGUE APPEARANCES/GOALS 2011–12
Goalkeepers Wojciech Szczesny POL **38**
Defenders Andre Santos BRA **10+5/2** • Johan Djourou SUI **14+4/0** • Kieran Gibbs **15+1/1** • Ignasi Miquel ESP **1+3/0** • Carl Jenkinson **5+4/0** • Laurent Koscielny FRA **33/2** • Per Mertesacker GER **21/0** • Bacary Sagna FRA **20+1/1** • Sebastien Squillaci FRA **0+1/0** • Armand Traore FRA **1/0** • Thomas Vermaelen BEL **28+1/6**
Midfield Mikel Arteta ESP **29/6** • Yossi Benayoun ISR **10+9/4** • Francis Coquelin FRA **6+4/0** • Abou Diaby FRA **0+4/0** • Emmanuel Frimpong GHA **3+3/0** • Henri Lansbury FRA **0+2/0** • Samir Nasri FRA **1/0** • Aaron Ramsey WAL **27+7/2** • Tomas Rosicky CZE **19+9/1** • Alexandre Song CMR **34/1** • Nico Yennaris **0+1/0**
Forwards Andrey Arshavin RUS **8+11/1** • Nicklas Bendtner DEN **0+1/0** • Marouane Chamakh MAR **1+10/1** • Gervinho CIV **19+9/4** • Thierry Henry FRA **0+4/2** • Alex Oxlade-Chamberlain **6+10/2** • Park Chu Young KOR **0+1/0** • Robin van Persie NED **37+1/30** • Theo Walcott **32+3/8**
Coach Arsene Wenger FRA

ASTON VILLA
2011–12

	13 Fulham	D	0-0	PL		25 700
Aug	20 Blackburn	W	3-1	PL 3	Agbonlahor [12], Heskey [25], Bent [67]	32 319
	23 Hereford	W	2-0	LCr2	Lichaj [80], Delfouneso [88]	21 058
	27 Wolves	D	0-0	PL 7		30 776
	10 Everton	D	2-2	PL 8	Petrov [63], Agbonlahor [83]	32 736
Sep	17 Newcastle	D	1-1	PL 6	Agbonlahor [13]	34 248
	20 Bolton	L	0-2	LCr3		22 261
	25 QPR	D	1-1	PL	Bannan [58p]	16 707
	1 Wigan	W	2-0	PL 7	Agbonlahor [36], Bent [62]	30 744
Oct	15 Man City	L	1-4	PL 8	Warnock [65]	47 019
	22 West Brom	L	1-2	PL	Bent [23p]	34 152
	29 Sunderland	D	2-2	PL 9	Petrov [20], Dunne [85]	37 062
Nov	5 Norwich	W	3-2	PL 8	Bent 2 [30 62], Agbonlahor [48]	35 290
	21 Tottenham	L	0-2	PL		35 818
	27 Swansea	D	0-0	PL 8		20 404
	3 Man Utd	L	0-1	PL 9		**40 053**
Dec	10 Bolton	W	2-1	PL 9	Albrighton [33], Petrov [39]	20 285
	18 Liverpool	L	0-2	PL 10		37 460
	21 Arsenal	L	1-2	PL	Albrighton [54]	35 818
	26 Stoke	D	0-0	PL 12		27 739
	31 Chelsea	W	3-1	PL 9	Ireland [28], Petrov [83], Bent [86]	41 332
	2 Swansea	L	0-2	PL		35 642
Jan	7 Bristol Rov	W	3-1	FAr3	Albrighton [35], Agbonlahor [64], Clark [78]	10 883
	14 Everton	D	1-1	PL 13	Bent [56]	31 853
	17 Wolves	W	3-2	PL 11	Bent [11p], Keane 2 [51 84]	27 084
	29 Arsenal	L	2-3	FAr4	Dunne [33], Bent [45]	60 019
	1 QPR	D	2-2	PL	Bent [45], N'Zogbia [79]	32 063
Feb	5 Newcastle	L	1-2	PL 13	Keane [45]	48 569
	12 Man City	L	0-1	PL 15		35 132
	25 Wigan	D	0-0	PL 15		20 601
	3 Blackburn	D	1-1	PL 15	N'Zogbia [24]	20 717
Mar	10 Fulham	W	1-0	PL 15	Weimann [92+]	32 372
	24 Arsenal	L	0-3	PL 15		60 108
	31 Chelsea	L	2-4	PL 15	Collins [77], Lichaj [80]	34 740
	7 Liverpool	D	1-1	PL 15	Herd [10]	44 321
	9 Stoke	D	1-1	PL	Weimann [32]	**30 100**
Apr	15 Man Utd	L	0-4	PL 15		75 138
	22 Sunderland	D	0-0	PL 15		32 557
	24 Bolton	L	1-2	PL	Warnock [61]	32 263
	28 West Brom	D	0-0	PL 15		25 984
May	6 Tottenham	D	1-1	PL 15	Clark [35]	36 008
	13 Norwich	L	0-2	PL 16		26 803
16th	Att: 643 590 • Av: 33 873 (-8.93%) • Villa Park 42 785 (79%)					

VILLA LEAGUE APPEARANCES/GOALS 2011–12

Goalkeepers Shay Given IRL **32** • Brad Guzan USA **6+1**
Defenders Nathan Baker **6+2/0** • Ciaran Clark IRL **13+2/1** • James Collins WAL **31+1/1** • Carlos Cuellar ESP **17+1/0** • Richard Dunne IRL **28/1** • Alan Hutton SCO **29+2/0** • Eric Lichaj USA **9+1/1** • Stephen Warnock **24+1/2** • Luke Young **2/0**
Midfield Marc Albrighton **15+11/2** • Barry Bannan SCO **10+18/1** • Samir Carruthers IRL **0+3/0** • Fabian Delph **10+1/0** • Gary Gardner **5+9/0** • Chris Herd AUS **19/1** • Stephen Ireland IRL **19+5/1** • Jermaine Jenas **1+2/0** • Charles N'Zogbia FRA **24+6/2** • Stilian Petrov BUL **26+1/4**
Forwards Gabriel Agbonlahor **32+1/5** • Darren Bent **21+1/9** • Nathan Delfouneso **1+5/0** • Emile Heskey **18+10/1** • Robbie Keane IRL **5+1/3** • Andreas Weimann AUT **5+9/2**
Coach Alex McLeish SCO (17/06/2011)

BLACKBURN LEAGUE APPEARANCES/GOALS 2011–12

Goalkeepers Mark Bunn **3** • Jake Keane **1** • Paul Robinson **34**
Defenders Scott Dann **27/1** • Gael Givet FRA **21+1/0** • Grant Hanley SCO **19+4/1** • Adam Henley WAL **4+3/0** • Michel Salgado ESP **9/0** • Ryan Nelson NZL **1/0** • Martin Olsson SWE **23+4/0** • Bradley Orr **10+2/0** • Christopher Samba COD **16/2**
Midfield Nick Blackman **0+1/0** • David Dunn **21+5/2** • Brett Emerton AUS **2/0** • Mauro Formica ARG **25+9/4** • Vince Grella AUS **0+1/0** • David Hoilett CAN **34/7** • Jason Lowe **30+2/0** • Josh Morris **0+2/0** • Steven N'Zonzi FRA **31+1/2** • Marcus Olsson SWE **10+2/0** • Morten Pedersen NOR **33/3** • Radosav Petrovic SRB **10+9/0** • Jordan Slew **0+1/0** • Simon Vukcevic MNE **4+3/1** • Yakubu Ayegbeni NGA **29+1/17**
Forwards David Goodwillie SCO **4+16/2** • Anthony Modeste FRA **3+6/0** • Jason Roberts GRN **5+5/0** • Ruben Rochina ESP **9+9/2**
Coach Steve Kean SCO

BLACKBURN ROVERS 2011–12

Aug	13	Wolves	L 1-2	PL	Formica [20]	21 996
	20	Aston Villa	L 1-3	PL 20	Pedersen [52]	32 319
	24	Sheff Wed	W 3-1	LCr2	Rochina 2 [3 4], Goodwillie [7]	8 607
	27	Everton	L 0-1	PL 19		22 826
Sep	11	Fulham	D 1-1	PL	Rochina [32]	24 856
	17	Arsenal	W 4-3	PL 16	Yakubu 2 [25 59], OG 2 [50 68]	22 637
	20	Orient	W 3-2	LCr3	Roberts [44p], Rochina [71], Vukcevic [75]	7 104
	24	Newcastle	L 1-3	PL	Hoilett [37]	46 236
Oct	1	Man City	L 0-4	PL 19		24 760
	15	QPR	D 1-1	PL 20	Samba [24]	16 487
	23	Tottenham	L 1-2	PL 20	Formica [28]	22 786
	26	Newcastle	W 4-3	LCr4	Rochina [5], Yakubu [64], Pedersen [39], Givet [119]	10 682
	29	Norwich	D 3-3	PL 18	Hoilett [45], Yakubu [62], Samba [64]	26 440
Nov	5	Chelsea	L 0-1	PL 19		21 985
	19	Wigan	D 3-3	PL 19	Gomez [7], Caldwell [31], Crusat [88]	17 392
	26	Stoke	L 1-3	PL 20	Rochina [86]	26 686
	29	Cardiff	L 0-2	LCqf		19 436
Dec	3	Swansea	W 4-2	PL 18	Yakubu 4 [20 45 57 82p]	23 080
	11	Sunderland	L 1-2	PL 19	Vukcevic [17]	39 863
	17	West Brom	L 1-2	PL 19	Dann [72]	22 909
	20	Bolton	L 1-2	PL	Yakubu [67]	25 570
	26	Liverpool	D 1-1	PL 20	OG [45]	44 441
	31	Man Utd	W 3-2	PL 19	Yakubu 2 [16p 51], Hanley [80]	75 146
Jan	2	Stoke	L 1-2	PL	Goodwillie [69]	20 615
	7	Newcastle	L 1-2	FAr3	Goodwillie [35]	30 876
	14	Fulham	W 3-1	PL	Pedersen [45], Dunn [46], Formica [79]	**18 003**
	21	Everton	D 1-1	PL 18	Goodwillie [72]	32 464
	1	Newcastle	L 0-2	PL		20 817
Feb	4	Arsenal	L 1-7	PL 19	Pedersen [31]	59 643
	11	QPR	W 3-2	PL 17	Yakubu [15], Nzonzi [23], OG [45]	20 252
	25	Man City	D 0-0	PL 18		46 782
Mar	3	Aston Villa	D 1-1	PL 17	Dunn [85]	20 717
	10	Wolves	W 2-0	PL 16	Hoilett 2 [43 69]	26 121
	20	Sunderland	W 2-0	PL	Hoilett [58], Yakubu [86]	20 056
	24	Bolton	L 1-2	PL 16	Nzonzi [56]	26 901
	2	Man Utd	L 0-2	PL		**26 532**
	7	West Brom	L 0-3	PL 18		23 414
Apr	10	Liverpool	L 2-3	PL	Yakubu 2 [36 61p]	23 571
	14	Swansea	L 0-3	PL 19		18 985
	21	Norwich	W 2-0	PL 18	Formica [41], Hoilett [49]	23 218
	29	Tottenham	L 0-2	PL 19		35 798
May	7	Wigan	L 0-1	PL		26 144
	13	Chelsea	L 1-2	PL 19	Yakubu [60]	40 742

19th Att: 428 474 • Av: 22 551 (-9.79%) • Ewood Park 31 154 (72%)

BOLTON WANDERERS 2011–12

Aug	13	QPR	W 4-0	PL	Cahill [45], OG [67], Klasnic [70], Muamba [79]	15 195
	21	Man City	L 2-3	PL 7	Klasnic [39], Davies.K [63]	24 273
	24	Macc'field	W 2-1	LCr2	Tuncay [56], Petrov [73]	6 777
	27	Liverpool	L 1-3	PL 10	Klasnic [92+]	44 725
Sep	10	Man Utd	L 0-5	PL 13		25 944
	17	Norwich	L 1-2	PL 19	Petrov [64p]	21 223
	20	Aston Villa	W 2-0	LCr3	Eagles [54], Kakuta [77]	22 261
	24	Arsenal	L 0-3	PL 20		59 727
Oct	2	Chelsea	L 1-5	PL 20	Boyata [46]	24 657
	15	Wigan	W 3-1	PL 18	Reo-Coker [4], N'Gog [45], Eagles [92+]	17 261
	22	Sunderland	L 0-2	PL 18		24 349
	25	Aston Villa	L 0-2	LCr4	Muamba [47]	56 628
	29	Swansea	L 1-3	PL 19	OG [73]	19 477
Nov	6	Stoke	W 5-0	PL 18	Davies.K [2], Eagles 2 [23 73], Klasnic 2 [61 81]	**20 028**
	19	West Brom	L 1-2	PL 18	Klasnic [21p]	26 221
	26	Everton	L 0-2	PL 18		24 058
Dec	3	Tottenham	L 0-3	PL 19		35 896
	10	Aston Villa	L 1-2	PL 20	Klasnic [55]	20 285
	17	Fulham	L 0-2	PL 20		25 643
	20	Blackburn	W 2-1	PL	Davies.M [5], Reo-Coker [30]	25 570
	26	Newcastle	L 0-2	PL		26 080
	31	Wolves	D 1-1	PL 20	Ricketts [22]	20 354
Jan	4	Everton	W 2-1	PL	N'Gog [67], Cahill 78	29 561
	7	Macc'field	D 2-2	FAr3	Klasnic [7], Wheater [77]	5 757
	14	Man Utd	L 0-3	PL 19		75 444
	17	Macc'field	W 2-0	FAr3	Davies.K [1], Petrov [26]	9 466
	21	Liverpool	W 3-1	PL 17	Davies.M [4], Reo-Coker [29], Steinsson [50]	26 854
	28	Swansea	W 2-1	FAr4	Pratley [45], Eagles [56]	11 597
Feb	1	Arsenal	D 0-0	PL		24 371
	4	Norwich	L 0-2	PL 18		26 358
	11	Wigan	L 1-2	PL 19	Davies.M [67]	23 450
	18	Millwall	W 2-0	FAr5	Miyaichi [4], N'Gog [58]	11 134
	25	Chelsea	L 0-3	PL 19		40 999
Mar	3	Man City	L 0-2	PL 19		47 219
	10	QPR	W 2-1	PL 17	Pratley [37], Klasnic [86]	21 551
		Tottenham	- 1-1	FAqf	Pratley [6], Abandoned 41'	29 130
	24	Blackburn	W 2-1	PL 17	Wheater 2 [28 35]	**26 901**
	27	Tottenham	L 1-3	FAqf	Davies.K [90]	30 718
	31	Wolves	W 3-2	PL 16	Petrov [63p], Alonso [80], Davies.K [84]	25 215
Apr	7	Fulham	L 0-3	PL 16		21 939
	9	Newcastle	L 0-2	PL		52 264
	21	Swansea	D 1-1	PL 19	Eagles [14]	25 401
	24	Aston Villa	W 2-1	PL	Petrov [49p], N'Gog [63]	32 203
	28	Sunderland	D 2-2	PL 18	Davies.K 2 [26 70]	40 768
May	2	Tottenham	L 1-4	PL	Reo-Coker [51]	22 349
	6	West Brom	D 2-2	PL 18	Petrov [24p], OG [72]	25 662
	13	Stoke	D 2-2	PL 18	Davies.M [39], Davies.K [45]	27 789

18th Att: 449 729 • Av: 23 669 (+3.5%) • Reebok Stadium 28 100 (84%)

BOLTON LEAGUE APPEARANCES/GOALS 2011-12

Goalkeepers Adam Bogdan HUN 20 • Jussi Jaaskelainen FIN 18
Defenders Dedryk Boyata BEL 13+1/1 • Gary Cahill 19/2
Zat Knight 21+4/0 • Marcos Alonso ESP 4+1/1 • Tyrone Mears JAM 1/0
Tim Ream USA 13/0 • Sam Ricketts WAL 20/1 • Joe Riley 2+1/0
Paul Robinson 15+2/0 • Gretar Steinsson ISL 20+3/1
David Wheater 24/2
Midfield Mark Davies 29+6/4 • Chris Eagles 26+8/4
Ricardo Gardner JAM 2+2/0 • Lee Chung Yong KOR 0+2/0
Fabrice Muamba 18+2/1 • Martin Petrov BUL 30+1/4
Darren Pratley 14+11/1 Nigel Reo-Coker 37/4 • Joshua Vela 0+3/0
Forwards Robert Blake 0+1/0 • Kevin Davies 21+10/6
Gael Kakuta FRA 0+4/0 • Ivan Klasnic CRO 16+13/8
Ryo Miyaichi JPN 8+4/0 • David N'Gog FRA 24+9/3
Tuncay Sanli TUR 3+13/0 • Marvin Sordell 0+3/0
Coach Owen Coyle IRL

CHELSEA 2011-12 (CONT'D)

Mar	18 Leicester	W	5-2	FAqf		Cahill [12], Kalou [18], Torres 2 [68 86], Meireles [91+]	38 276
	21 Man City	L	1-2	PL		Cahill [60]	46 324
	24 Tottenham	D	0-0	PL	5		**41 830**
	27 Benfica	W	1-0	CLqf		Kalou [75]	60 830
	31 Aston Villa	W	4-2	PL	5	Sturridge [9], Ivanovic 2 [51 83], Torres [92+]	34 740
Apr	4 Benfica	W	2-1	CLqf		Lampard [21p], Meireles [92+]	37 264
	7 Wigan	W	2-1	PL	5	Ivanovic [62], Mata [93+]	**40 651**
	9 Fulham	D	1-1	PL		Lampard [45p]	25 697
	15 Tottenham	W	5-1	FAsf		Drogba [43], Mata [49], Ramires [77], Lampard [81], Malouda [94+]	85 731
	18 Barcelona	W	1-0	CLsf		Drogba [45]	38 039
	21 Arsenal	D	0-0	PL	6		60 111
	24 Barcelona	D	2-2	CLsf		Ramires [45], Torres [92+]	95 845
	29 QPR	W	6-1	PL	6	Sturridge [1], Terry [13], Torres 3 [19 25 64], Malouda [80]	41 675
May	2 Newcastle	L	0-2	PL			41 559
	5 Liverpool	W	2-1	FAf		Ramires [11], Drogba [52]	89 102
	8 Liverpool	L	1-4	PL		Ramires [50]	40 721
	13 Blackburn	W	2-1	PL	6	Terry [31], Meireles [34]	40 742
	19 Bayern M	D	1-1	CLf		Drogba [88]. W 4-3p	69 901

6th Att: 788 089 • Av: 41 478 (+0.1%) • Stamford Bridge 42 449 (97%)

CHELSEA LEAGUE APPEARANCES/GOALS 2011-12

Goalkeepers Petr Cech CZE 34 • Hilario POR 2 • Ross Turnbull 2
Defenders Alex BRA 3/0 • Ryan Bertrand 6+1/0
Jose Bosingwa POR 24+3/1 • Gary Cahill 9+1/1 • Ashley Cole 31+1/0
David Luiz BRA 18+2/2 • Sam Hutchinson 1+1/0
Branislav Ivanovic SRB 26+3/3 • Paulo Ferreira POR 3+3/0
John Terry 31/6
Midfield Yossi Benayoun ISR 0+1/0 • Michael Essien GHA 10+4/0
Frank Lampard 26+4/11 • Florent Malouda FRA 11+15/2
Juan Mata ESP 29+5/6 • Joshua McEachran 0+2/0
John Mikel NGA 15+7/0 • Oriol Romeu ESP 11+5/0
Ramires BRA 28+2/5 • Raul Meireles POR 23+5/2
Forwards Nicolas Anelka FRA 3+6/1 • Didier Drogba CIV 16+8/5
Fernando Torres ESP 20+12/6 • Salomon Kalou CIV 7+5/1
Romelu Lukaku BEL 1+7/0 • Daniel Sturridge 28+2/11
Coach Andre Villas-Boas POR (22/06/2011) • Roberto Di Matteo ITA (4/03/2012)

CHELSEA 2011-12

	14 Stoke	D	0-0	PL			27 421
Aug	20 West Brom	W	2-1	PL	5	Anelka [53], Malouda [83]	41 091
	27 Norwich	W	3-1	PL	4	Bosingwa [6], Lampard [82p], Mata [101+]	41 765
	10 Sunderland	W	2-1	PL	3	Terry [18], Sturridge [51]	36 699
	13 Leverkusen	W	2-0	CLgE		Luiz [67], Mata [92+]	33 820
	18 Man Utd	L	1-3	PL	3	Torres [46]	75 455
Sep	21 Fulham	D	0-0	LCr3		W 4-3p	37 632
	24 Swansea	W	4-1	PL	3	Torres [29], Ramires 2 [36 76], Drogba [94+]	41 800
	28 Valencia	D	1-1	CLgE		Lampard [56]	33 791
	2 Bolton	W	5-1	PL	3	Sturridge 2 [2 25], Lampard 3 [15 27 59]	24 657
	15 Everton	W	3-1	PL	3	Sturridge [31], Terry [45], Ramires [61]	41 789
Oct	19 Genk	W	5-0	CLgE		Meireles [8], Torres 2 [11 27], Ivanovic [42], Kalou [72]	38 518
	23 QPR	L	0-1	PL	3		18 050
	26 Everton	W	2-1	LCr4		Kalou [38], Sturridge [116]	23 170
	29 Arsenal	L	3-5	PL	3	Lampard [14], Terry [45], Mata [80]	41 801
	1 Genk	D	1-1	CLgE		Ramires [26]	22 584
	5 Blackburn	W	1-0	PL	4	Lampard [51]	21 985
Nov	20 Liverpool	L	1-2	PL	4	Sturridge [55]	41 820
	23 Leverkusen	L	1-2	CLgE		Drogba [48]	29 285
	26 Wolves	W	3-0	PL	5	Terry [7], Sturridge [29], Mata [45]	41 648
	29 Liverpool	L	0-2	LCqf			40 511
	3 Newcastle	W	3-0	PL	4	Drogba [38], Kalou [89], Sturridge [92+]	52 305
	6 Valencia	W	3-0	CLgE		Drogba 2 [3 76], Ramires [22]	41 109
Dec	12 Man City	W	2-1	PL		Meireles [34], Lampard [83p]	41 730
	17 Wigan	D	1-1	PL	4	Sturridge [59]	18 320
	22 Tottenham	D	1-1	PL		Sturridge [23]	36 141
	26 Fulham	D	1-1	PL	4	Mata [47]	41 548
	31 Aston Villa	L	1-3	PL	5	Drogba [23p]	41 332
	2 Wolves	W	2-1	PL		Ramires [54], Lampard [89]	27 289
	8 Portsmouth	W	4-0	FAr3		Mata [48], Ramires 2 [85 87], Lampard [93+]	41 529
Jan	14 Sunderland	W	1-0	PL	4	Lampard [13]	41 696
	21 Norwich	D	0-0	PL	4		26 792
	28 QPR	W	1-0	FAr4		Mata [62p]	15 728
	31 Swansea	D	1-1	PL		OG [93+]	20 526
	5 Man Utd	D	3-3	PL	4	OG [36], Mata [46], Luiz [50]	41 668
	11 Everton	L	0-2	PL	5		33 924
Feb	18 B'ham City	D	1-1	FAr5		Sturridge [60]	36 870
	21 Napoli	L	1-3	CLr2		Mata [27]	52 495
	25 Bolton	W	3-0	PL	4	Luiz [48], Drogba [61], Lampard [79]	40 099
	3 West Brom	L	0-1	PL	5		24 838
	6 B'ham City	W	2-0	FAr5		Mata [54], Meireles [60]	21 822
Mar	10 Stoke	W	1-0	PL	5	Drogba [68]	40 945
	14 Napoli	W	4-1	CLr2		Drogba [29], Terry [47], Lampard [75p], Ivanovic [105]	37 784

EVERTON 2011-12

Aug	20 QPR	L	0-1	PL	18		35 008
	24 Sheff Utd	W	3-1	LCr2		OG [31], Anichebe [37], Arteta [42]	17 173
	27 Blackburn	W	1-0	PL	11	Arteta [92+p]	22 826
	10 Aston Villa	D	2-2	PL	10	Osman [19], Baines [69p]	32 736
Sep	17 Wigan	W	3-1	PL	7	Jagielka [33], Vellios [84], Drenthe [98+]	31 576
	21 West Brom	W	2-1	LCr3		Fellaini [89], Neville [103]	17 647
	24 Man City	L	0-2	PL	10		47 293
	1 Liverpool	L	0-2	PL	13		39 510
	5 Chelsea	L	1-3	PL	15	Vellios [81]	41 789
Oct	23 Fulham	W	3-1	PL	13	Drenthe [3], Saha [90], Rodwell [93+]	25 646
	26 Chelsea	L	1-2	LCr4		Saha [83]	23 170
	29 Man Utd	L	0-1	PL	16		35 494
	5 Newcastle	L	1-2	PL	17	Rodwell [45]	50 671
Nov	19 Wolves	W	2-1	PL	12	Jagielka [44], Baines [83p]	33 953
	26 Bolton	W	2-0	PL	9	Fellaini [49], Vellios [78]	24 058
	4 Stoke	L	0-1	PL	10		33 219
	10 Arsenal	L	0-1	PL	12		60 062
Dec	17 Norwich	D	1-1	PL	14	Osman [81]	31 004
	21 Swansea	W	1-0	PL		Osman [60]	32 004
	26 Sunderland	D	1-1	PL	10	Baines [51p]	43 619

EVERTON 2011-12 (CONT'D)

	Date	Opponent	Res	Score	Comp	Scorers	Att
Jan	1	West Brom	W	1-0	PL	Anichebe [87]	23 038
	4	Bolton	L	1-2	PL	Howard [63]	**29 561**
	7	Tamworth	W	2-0	FAr3	Heitinga [5], Baines [79p]	27 564
	11	Tottenham	L	0-2	PL		36 132
	14	Aston Villa	D	1-1	PL	Anichebe [69]	31 853
	21	Blackburn	D	1-1	PL	Cahill [24]	32 464
	27	Fulham	W	2-1	FAr4	Stracqualursi [27], Fellaini [73]	25 300
	31	Man City	W	1-0	PL	Gibson [60]	29 856
Feb	4	Wigan	D	1-1	PL	Anichebe [83]	18 340
	11	Chelsea	W	2-0	PL	Pienaar [5], Stracqualursi [71]	33 924
	18	Blackpool	W	2-0	FAr5	Drenthe [1], Stracqualursi [7]	38 347
	3	QPR	D	1-1	PL	Drenthe [31]	18 033
	10	Tottenham	W	1-0	PL	Jelavic [22]	34 992
Mar	13	Liverpool	L	0-3	PL		44 921
	17	Sunderland	D	1-1	FAqf	Cahill [23]	38 875
	21	Arsenal	L	0-1	PL		30 330
	24	Swansea	W	2-0	PL	Baines [59], Jelavic [76]	20 509
	27	Sunderland	W	2-0	FAqf	Jelavic [24], OG [57]	43 140
	31	West Brom	W	2-0	PL	OG [18], Anichebe [68]	32 051
	7	Norwich	D	2-2	PL	Jelavic 2 [22 61]	26 554
Apr	9	Sunderland	W	4-0	PL	Gueye [52], Pienaar [75], Osman [76], Anichebe [81]	32 249
	14	Liverpool	L	1-2	FAsf	Jelavic [24]	87 231
	22	Man Utd	D	4-4	PL	Jelavic 2 [33 83], Fellaini [67], Pienaar [85]	75 522
	28	Fulham	W	4-0	PL	Jelavic 2 [7p 40], Fellaini [16], Cahill [60]	31 885
May	1	Stoke	D	1-1	PL	OG [44]	26 500
	6	Wolves	D	0-0	PL		25 466
	13	Newcastle	W	3-1	PL	Pienaar [16], Jelavic [27], Heitanga [65]	**39 517**

7th Att: 631 333 • Av: 33 228 (-7.8%) • Goodison Park 40 157 (82%)

EVERTON LEAGUE APPEARANCES/GOALS 2011-12

Goalkeepers Tim Howard USA 38/1
Defenders Leighton Baines 33/4 • Seamus Coleman IRL 14+4/0 • Sylvain Distin FRA 24+3/0 • Shane Duffy IRL 2+2/0 • Johnny Heitinga NED 29+1/1 • Tony Hibbert 31+1/0 • Phil Jagielka 29+1/2 • Phil Neville 24+3/0
Midfield Mikel Arteta ESP 1+1/1 • Ross Barkley 2+4/0 • Diniyar Bilyaletdinov RUS 7+3/0 • Tim Cahill AUS 27+8/2 • Royston Drenthe NED 10+11/3 • Marouane Fellaini BEL 31+3/3 • Darron Gibson IRL 11/1 • Leon Osman 28+2/4 • Steven Pienaar RSA 14/4 • Jack Rodwell 11+3/2
Forwards Victor Anichebe NGA 5+7/5 • Jose Baxter 0+1/0 • Jermaine Beckford 1+1/0 • Landon Donovan USA 7/0 • Magaye Gueye FRA 3+14/1 Nikica Jelavic CRO 10+3/9 • Connor McAleny 0+2/0 • James McFadden SCO 2+5/0 • Louis Saha FRA 15+3/1 • Denis Stracqualursi ARG 7+14/1 • Apostolos Vellios GRE 2+11/3
Coach David Moyes SCO

FULHAM 2011-12

	Date	Opponent	Res	Score	Comp	Scorers	Att
Jn	30	Runavik	W	3-0	ELp1	Duff [33], Murphy [61p], Johnson [70]	14 910
	7	Runavik	D	0-0	ELp1		1 245
July	14	Crusaders	W	3-1	ELp2	Briggs [39], Zamora [74], Murphy [77p]	2 477
	21	Crusaders	W	4-0	ELp2	Johnson [19], Duff [56], Zamora [66], Sidwell [70]	15 676
	28	RNK Split	D	0-0	ELp3		4 000

FULHAM 2011-12 (CONT'D)

	Date	Opponent	Res	Score	Comp	Scorers	Att
	4	RNK Split	W	2-0	ELp3	Johnson [19], Murphy [57p]	17 087
	13	Aston Villa	D	0-0	PL		**25 700**
Aug	18	Dnipro	W	3-0	ELpo	Hughes [38], Dempsey 2 [43 49]	14 823
	21	Wolves	L	0-2	PL 15		22 657
	25	Dnipro	L	0-1	ELpo		12 750
	28	Newcastle	L	1-2	PL 16	Dempsey [88]	42 684
	11	Blackburn	D	1-1	PL 18	Zamora [38]	24 856
	15	Twente	D	1-1	ELgK	Johnson [19]	14 110
Sep	18	Man City	D	2-2	PL 18	Zamora [55], OG [75]	24 750
	21	Chelsea	D	0-0	LCr3	L 3-4p	37 632
	24	West Brom	D	0-0	PL 17		23 835
	29	Odense	W	2-0	ELgK	Dempsey 2 [36 88]	7 969
	2	QPR	W	6-0	PL 12	Johnson 3 [2 38 59], Murphy [20p], Dempsey [65], Zamora [74]	23 766
Oct	15	Stoke	L	0-2	PL 14		26 890
	20	Wisla	L	0-1	ELgK		16 377
	23	Everton	L	1-3	PL 17	Ruiz [67]	25 646
	29	Wigan	W	2-0	PL 15	Dempsey [41], Dembele [86]	15 796
	3	Wisla	W	4-1	ELgK	Duff [5], Johnson 2 [30 57], Sidwell [79]	20 319
Nov	6	Tottenham	L	1-3	PL 16	OG [57]	25 698
	19	Sunderland	D	0-0	PL 16		37 688
	26	Arsenal	D	1-1	PL 15	OG [65]	60 043
	1	Twente	L	0-1	ELgK		25 250
	5	Liverpool	W	1-0	PL	Dempsey [85]	25 688
	10	Swansea	L	0-2	PL 14		19 296
Dec	14	Odense	D	2-2	ELgK	Dempsey [27], Frei [32]	15 757
	17	Bolton	W	2-0	PL 11	Dempsey [32], Ruiz [34]	25 643
	21	Man Utd	L	0-5	PL		**25 700**
	26	Chelsea	D	1-1	PL 13	Dempsey [56]	41 548
	31	Norwich	D	1-1	PL 13	Sa [7]	26 406
	2	Arsenal	W	2-1	PL	Sidwell [85], Zamora [92+]	**25 700**
	4	Charlton	W	4-0	FAr3	Dempsey 3 [8 61 81p], Duff [87]	20 317
Jan	14	Blackburn	L	1-3	PL 14	Duff [56]	18 003
	21	Newcastle	W	5-2	PL 12	Murphy [52p], Dempsey 3 [59 65 89], Zamora [68p]	25 692
	27	Everton	L	1-2	FAr3	Murphy [14p]	25 300
	1	West Brom	D	1-1	PL	Dempsey [69]	25 689
Feb	4	Man City	L	0-3	PL 14		46 963
	11	Stoke	W	2-1	PL 12	Pogrebnyak [16], OG [28]	**23 555**
	25	QPR	W	1-0	PL 11	Pogrebnyak [7]	18 015
	4	Wolves	W	5-0	PL 8	Pogrebnyak 3 [36 44 61], Dempsey 2 [56 83]	24 034
Mar	10	Aston Villa	L	0-1	PL		32 372
	17	Swansea	L	0-3	PL		25 690
	26	Man Utd	L	0-1	PL		75 570
	31	Norwich	W	2-1	PL 10	Dempsey [2], Duff [13]	**25 700**
	7	Bolton	W	3-0	PL 10	Dempsey 2 [30 45], Diarra [80]	21 939
Apr	9	Chelsea	D	1-1	PL	Dempsey [82]	25 697
	21	Wigan	W	2-1	PL 9	Pogrebnyak [58], Senderos [89]	25 689
	28	Everton	L	0-4	PL 9		31 885
	1	Liverpool	W	1-0	PL	OG [5]	40 106
May	6	Sunderland	W	2-1	PL 8	Dempsey [12], Dembele [35]	25 683
	13	Tottenham	L	0-2	PL 9		36 256

9th Att: 480 576 • Av: 25 293 (+1.0%) • Craven Cottage 25 700 (98%)

FULHAM LEAGUE APPEARANCES/GOALS 2011-12

Goalkeepers Mark Schwarzer AUS 30 • David Stockdale 8
Defenders Chris Baird NIR 13+6/0 • Matthew Briggs 1+1/0 Zdenek Grygera CZE 5/0 • Brede Hangeland NOR 38 Aaron Hughes NIR 18+1/0 • Stephen Kelly IRL 21+3/0 John Arne Riise NOR 35+1/0 • Philippe Senderos SUI 21/1
Midfield Simon Davies WAL 3+3/0 • Clint Dempsey USA 37/17 Mahamadou Diarra MLI 8+3/1 • Damien Duff IRL 23+5/2 • Dickson Etuhu NGA 9+13/0 • Kerim Frei SUI 6+10/0 • Marcel Gecov CZE 0+2/0 • Alexander Kacaniklic SWE 2+2/0 • Pajtim Kasami SUI 3+4/0 Danny Murphy 33+3/3 • Steven Sidwell 12+2/1
Forwards Moussa Dembele BEL 33+3/2 • Andy Johnson 13+7/3 Orlando Sa POR 3+4/1 • Pavel Pogrebnyak RUS 12/6 • Bryan Ruiz CRC 17+10/2 • Marcello Trotta ITA 0+1/0 • Bobby Zamora 14+1/5
Coach Martin Jol NED (7/06/2011)

LIVERPOOL
2011-12

Aug	13	Sunderland	D	1-1	PL	Suarez [12]	45 018
	20	Arsenal	W	2-0	PL	4	OG [78], Suarez [91+]	60 090
	24	Exeter	W	3-1	LCr2	Suarez [23], Rodriguez [55], Carroll [58]	8 290
	27	Bolton	W	3-1	PL	3	Henderson [15], Skrtel [52], Adam [53]	44 725
Sep	10	Stoke	L	0-1	PL	5		27 592
	18	Tottenham	L	0-4	PL	8		36 129
	21	Brighton	W	2-1	LCr3		Bellamy [7], Kuyt [81]	21 897
	24	Wolves	W	2-1	PL	5	OG [11], Suarez [38]	44 922
Oct	1	Everton	W	2-0	PL	5	Carroll [71], Suarez [82]	39 510
	15	Man Utd	D	1-1	PL	5	Gerrard [68]	45 065
	22	Norwich	D	1-1	PL	6	Bellamy [45]	44 931
	26	Stoke	W	2-1	LCr4		Suarez 2 [54 86]	24 934
	29	West Brom	W	2-0	PL	6	Adam [9p], Carroll [45]	25 522
Nov	5	Swansea	D	0-0	PL	6		45 013
	20	Chelsea	W	2-1	PL	6	Rodriguez [33], Johnson [87]	41 820
	27	Man City	D	1-1	PL	6	OG [33]	**45 071**
	29	Chelsea	W	2-0	LCqf		Rodriguez [59], Kelly [63]	40 511
Dec	1	Fulham	L	0-1	PL			25 688
	10	QPR	W	1-0	PL	6	Suarez [47]	45 016
	18	Aston Villa	W	2-0	PL	6	Bellamy [11], Skrtel [15]	37 460
	21	Wigan	D	0-0	PL			19 230
	26	Blackburn	D	1-1	PL	6	Rodriguez [53]	44 441
	30	Newcastle	W	3-1	PL		Bellamy 2 [29 67], Gerrard [78]	44 372
Jan	3	Man City	L	0-3	PL			47 131
	6	Oldham	W	5-1	FAr3		Bellamy [30], Gerrard [45p], Shelvey [68], Carroll [89], Downing [95+]	44 556
	11	Man City	W	1-0	LCsf		Gerrard [13p]	36 017
	14	Stoke	D	0-0	PL	7		44 691
	21	Bolton	L	1-3	PL	7	Bellamy [37]	26 854
	25	Man City	D	2-2	LCsf		Gerrard [40p], Bellamy [74]	44 590
	28	Man Utd	W	2-1	FAr4		Agger [20], Kuyt [88]	43 952
	31	Wolves	W	3-0	PL		Carroll [52], Bellamy [61], Kuyt [78]	27 447
Feb	6	Tottenham	D	0-0	PL			44 461
	11	Man Utd	L	1-2	PL	7	Suarez [80]	74 844
	19	Brighton	W	6-1	FAr5		Skrtel [5], OG 3 [44 71 75], Carroll [56], Suarez [85]	43 940
	26	Cardiff	D	2-2	LCf		Skrtel [60], Kuyt [108], W 3-2p	89 044
Mar	3	Arsenal	L	1-2	PL	7	OG [23]	44 922
	10	Sunderland	L	0-1	PL	7		41 661
	13	Everton	W	3-0	PL		Gerrard 3 [34 51 93+]	44 921
	18	Stoke	W	2-1	FAqf		Suarez [23], Downing [57]	43 962
	21	QPR	L	2-3	PL		Coates [54], Kuyt [72]	18 033
	24	Wigan	L	1-2	PL	7	Suarez [47]	44 431
Apr	1	Newcastle	L	0-2	PL	8		52 363
	7	Aston Villa	D	1-1	PL	8	Suarez [82]	44 321
	10	Blackburn	W	3-2	PL		Rodriguez 2 [13 16], Carroll [91+]	23 571
	14	Everton	W	2-1	FAsf		Suarez [62], Carroll [86]	87 231
	22	West Brom	L	0-1	PL	8		43 660
	28	Norwich	W	3-0	PL	8	Suarez 3 [24 28 82]	26 819
May	1	Fulham	L	0-1	PL			**40 106**
	5	Chelsea	L	1-2	FAf		Carroll [64]	89 102
	8	Chelsea	W	4-1	PL		OG [19], Henderson [25], Agger [28], Shelvey [61]	40 721
	13	Swansea	L	0-1	PL	8		20 605

8th Att: 840 808 • Av: 44 253 (+3.35%) • Anfield 45 276 (97%)

LIVERPOOL LEAGUE APPEARANCES/GOALS 2011-12
Goalkeepers Doni BRA 4 • Brad Jones AUS 0+1 • Pepe Reina ESP 34
Defenders Daniel Agger DEN 24+3/1 • Jamie Carragher 19+2/0
Sebastian Coates URU 4+3/1 • Fabio Aurelio BRA 1+1/0
John Flanagan 5/0 • Glen Johnson 22+1/1 • Jose Enrique ESP 33+2/0
Martin Kelly 7/0 • Martin Skrtel SVK 33+1/2
Midfield Charlie Adam SCO 27+1/2 • Stewart Downing 28+8/0
Steven Gerrard 12+6/5 • Jordan Henderson 31+6/2 • Lucas
Leiva BRA 12/0 • Raul Meireles POR 0+2/0 • Maxi Rodriguez ARG
10+2/4 • Jonjo Shelvey 8+5/1 • Jay Spearing 15+1/0
Forwards Craig Bellamy WAL 12+15/6 • Andy Carroll 21+14/4
Dirk Kuyt NED 22+12/2 • Raheem Sterling 0+3/0
Luis Suarez URU 29+2/11
Coach Kenny Dalglish SCO

MANCHESTER CITY
2011-12

Aug	7	Man Utd	L	2-3	SC		Lescott [38], Dzeko [45]	77 169
	15	Swansea	W	4-0	PL		Dzeko [57], Aguero 2 [68 91+], Silva [71]	46 802
	21	Bolton	W	3-2	PL	1	Silva [26], Barry [37], Dzeko [47]	24 273
	28	Tottenham	W	5-1	PL	2	Dzeko 4 [34 41 55 93+], Aguero [60]	36 150
Sep	10	Wigan	W	3-0	PL	2	Aguero 3 [13 63 69]	46 509
	14	Napoli	D	1-1	CLgA		Kolarov [74]	44 026
	18	Fulham	D	2-2	PL	2	Aguero 2 [18 46]	24 750
	21	B'ham City	W	2-0	LCr3		Hargreaves [17], Balotelli [38]	25 070
	24	Everton	W	2-0	PL	2	Balotelli [68], Milner [89]	47 293
	27	Bayern M	L	0-2	CLgA			66 000
Oct	1	Blackburn	W	4-0	PL	2	Johnson [56], Balotelli [59], Nasri [73], Savic [87]	24 760
	15	Aston Villa	W	4-1	PL	1	Balotelli [28], Johnson [50], Kompany [52], Milner [71]	47 019
	18	Villarreal	W	2-1	CLgA		OG [43], Aguero [93+]	43 326
	23	Man Utd	W	6-1	PL	1	Balotelli 2 [22 60], Aguero [69], Dzeko 2 [90 93+], Silva [91+]	75 487
	26	Wolves	W	5-2	LCr4		Johnson [39], Nasri [39], Dzeko 2 [40 64], OG [50]	12 436
	29	Wolves	W	3-1	PL		Dzeko [52], Kolarov [67], Johnson [91+]	47 142
Nov	2	Villarreal	W	3-0	CLgA		Toure.Y 2 [30 71], Balotelli [45p]	19 358
	5	QPR	W	3-2	PL	1	Dzeko [43], Silva [52], Toure.Y [74]	18 076
	19	Newcastle	W	3-1	PL	1	Balotelli [41p], Richards [44], Aguero [72p]	47 408
	22	Napoli	L	1-2	CLgA		Balotelli [33]	57 575
	27	Liverpool	D	1-1	PL	1	Kompany [31]	45 071
	29	Arsenal	W	1-0	LCqf		Aguero [83]	60 028
Dec	3	Norwich	W	5-1	PL	1	Aguero [2], Nasri [31], Toure.Y [68], Balotelli [88], Johnson [91+]	47 201
	7	Bayern M	W	2-0	CLgA		Silva [36], Toure.Y [52]	46 002
	12	Chelsea	L	1-2	PL		Balotelli [2]	41 730
	18	Arsenal	W	1-0	PL	1	Silva [53]	47 303
	21	Stoke	W	3-0	PL		Aguero 2 [29 54], Johnson [36]	**46 321**
	26	West Brom	D	0-0	PL	1		25 938
Jan	1	Sunderland	L	0-1	PL	1		40 625
	3	Liverpool	W	3-0	PL		Aguero [10], Toure.Y [33], Milner [75p]	47 131
	8	Man Utd	L	2-3	FAr3		Kolarov [47], Aguero [64]	46 808
	11	Liverpool	W	1-0	LCsf		OG [55], Aguero [85]	47 417
	16	Wigan	W	1-0	PL		Dzeko [22]	16 026
	22	Tottenham	W	3-2	PL	1	Nasri [36], Lescott [59], Balotelli [95+]	47 422
	25	Liverpool	D	2-2	LCsf		De Jong [31], Dzeko [67]	44 590
	31	Everton	L	0-1	PL			29 856
Feb	4	Fulham	W	3-0	PL	1	Aguero [10p], OG [30], Dzeko [72]	46 963
	12	Aston Villa	W	1-0	PL	1	Lescott [63]	35 132
	16	Porto	W	2-1	ELr2		OG [55], Aguero [85]	47 417
	22	Porto	W	4-0	ELr2		Aguero [1], Dzeko [76], Silva [84], Pizarro [86]	39 548
	25	Blackburn	W	3-0	PL	1	Balotelli [30], Aguero [52], Dzeko [81]	46 728
Mar	3	Bolton	W	2-0	PL	1	OG [23], Balotelli [69]	47 219
	8	Sporting CL	L	0-1	ELr3			34 371
	11	Swansea	L	0-1	PL	2		20 510
	15	Sporting CL	W	3-2	ELr3		Aguero 2 [60 82], Balotelli [75p]	38 021
	21	Chelsea	W	2-1	PL		Aguero [78p], Nasri [85]	46 324
	24	Stoke	D	1-1	PL		Toure.Y [76]	27 535
Apr	1	Sunderland	D	3-3	PL	2	Balotelli 2 [43p 85], Kolarov [86]	47 007
	8	Arsenal	L	0-1	PL			60 096
	11	West Brom	W	4-0	PL		Aguero 2 [6 54], Tevez [61], Silva [64]	46 746
	14	Norwich	W	6-1	PL	2	Tevez 3 [18 73 80], Aguero 2 [27 75], Johnson [93+]	26 812
	22	Wolves	W	2-0	PL		Aguero [27], Nasri [74]	24 576
	30	Man Utd	W	1-0	PL		Kompany [45]	47 259
May	6	Newcastle	W	2-0	PL	1	Toure.Y 2 [70 89]	52 389
	13	QPR	W	3-2	PL		Zabaleta [39], Dzeko [92+], Aguero [95+]	**48 000**

1st Att: 893 851 • Av: 47 044 (+2.54%) • Etihad Stadium 47 405 (99%)

MAN CITY LEAGUE APPEARANCES/GOALS 2011–12

Goalkeepers Joe Hart 38
Defenders Gael Clichy FRA 28/0 • Aleksandar Kolarov SRB 9+3/2
Vincent Kompany BEL 31/3 • Joleon Lescott 30+1/2
Nedum Onuoha 0+1/0 • Micah Richards 23+6/1
Stefan Savic MNE 5+6/1 • Kolo Toure CIV 8+6/0
Midfield Gareth Barry 31+3/1 • David Silva ESP 33+3/6
Nigel de Jong NED 11+10/0 • Owen Hargreaves 0+1/0
Adam Johnson 10+16/6 • James Milner 17+9/3 • Samir Nasri FRA 26+4/5
David Pizarro CHI 1+4/0 • Abdul Razak CIV 0+1/0
Yaya Toure CIV 31+1/6 • Pablo Zabaleta ARG 18+3/1
Forwards Kun Aguero ARG 31+3/23 • Mario Balotelli ITA 14+9/13
Edin Dzeko BIH 16+14/14 • Carlos Tevez ARG 7+6/4
Coach Roberto Mancini ITA

MANCHESTER UNITED 2011–12

	4	Tottenham	W	3-1	PL		Rooney [45], Young 2 [60 69]	36 034
	8	Ath Bilbao	L	2-3	ELr3		Rooney 2 [22 92+p]	59 265
	11	West Brom	W	2-0	PL	1	Rooney 2 [35 71p]	75 598
Mar	15	Ath Bilbao	L	1-2	ELr3		Rooney [80]	36 958
	18	Wolves	W	5-0	PL		Evans [21], Valencia [43], Welbeck [45], Hernandez 2 [56 61]	27 494
	26	Fulham	W	1-0	PL		Rooney [42]	75 570
	2	Blackburn	W	2-0	PL		Valencia [81], Young [86]	26 532
	8	QPR	W	2-0	PL	1	Rooney [15p], Scholes [68]	75 505
	11	Wigan	L	0-1	PL			18 115
Apr	15	Aston Villa	W	4-0	PL		Rooney 2 [7p 73], Welbeck [43], Nani [93+]	75 138
	22	Everton	D	4-4	PL	1	Rooney 2 [41 69], Welbeck [57], Nani [60]	75 522
	30	Man City	L	0-1	PL			47 259
May	6	Swansea	W	2-0	PL	2	Scholes [28], Young [41]	75 496
	13	Sunderland	W	1-0	PL	2	Rooney [20]	46 452

2nd Att: 1 432 358 • Av: 75 387 (+0.37%) • Old Trafford 75 811 (99%)

MAN UTD LEAGUE APPEARANCES/GOALS 2011–12

Goalkeepers Ben Amos 1 • David De Gea ESP 29
Anders Lindegaard DEN 8
Defenders Jonny Evans NIR 28+1/1 • Patrice Evra FRA 37/0
Fabio BRA 2+3/0 • Rio Ferdinand 29+1/0 • Ezekiel Fryers 0+2/0
Phil Jones 25+4/1 • Rafael BRA 10+2/0 • Chris Smalling 14+5/1
Nemanja Vidic SRB 6/0
Midfield Anderson BRA 8+2/2 • Michael Carrick 27+3/2 • Tom Cleverley 5+5/0 • Darren Fletcher SCO 7+1/1 • Darren Gibson IRL 1/0
Ryan Giggs WAL 14+11/2 • Nani POR 24+5/8 • Park
Ji Sung KOR 10+7/2 • Paul Pogba FRA 0+3/0 • Paul Scholes 14+3/4
Antonio Valencia ECU 22+5/4 • Ashley Young 19+6/6
Forwards Dimitar Berbatov BUL 5+7/7 • Javier Hernandez MEX 18+10/10 • William Keane 0+1/0 • Federico Macheda ITA 0+3/0
Michael Owen • Wayne Rooney 32+2/27 • Danny Welbeck 23+7/9
Coach Alex Ferguson SCO

MANCHESTER UNITED 2011–12

	7	Man City	W	3-2	SC		Smalling [52], Nani 2 [58 93+]	77 169
	14	West Brom	W	2-1	PL		Rooney [13], OG [81]	25 360
Aug	22	Tottenham	W	3-0	PL		Welbeck [61], Anderson [76], Rooney [87]	75 498
	28	Arsenal	W	8-2	PL	1	Welbeck [22], Young 2 [28 91+], Rooney 3 [41 64 82p], Nani [67], Park [70]	75 448
	10	Bolton	W	5-0	PL	1	Hernandez 2 [5 58], Rooney 3 [20 25 68]	25 944
	14	Benfica	D	1-1	CLgC		Giggs [42]	63 822
Sep	18	Chelsea	W	3-1	PL		Smalling [8], Nani [37], Rooney [45]	75 455
	20	Leeds	W	3-0	LCr3		Owen 2 [15 32], Giggs [45]	31 031
	24	Stoke	D	1-1	PL	1	Nani [27]	27 582
	27	Basel	D	3-3	CLgC		Welbeck 2 [16 17], Young [90]	73 115
	1	Norwich	W	2-0	PL	1	Anderson [68], Welbeck [87]	75 514
	15	Liverpool	D	1-1	PL	2	Hernandez [81]	45 065
	18	O. Galati	W	2-0	CLgC		Rooney 2 [64p 92+p]	28 047
Oct	23	Man City	L	1-6	PL	2	Fletcher [81]	75 487
	26	Aldershot	W	3-0	LCr4		Berbatov [15], Owen [41], Valencia [48]	7 044
	29	Everton	W	1-0	PL	2	Hernandez [19]	35 494
	2	O. Galati	W	2-0	CLgC		Valencia [8], OG [88]	74 847
	5	Sunderland	W	1-0	PL	2	OG [45]	75 570
Nov	19	Swansea	W	1-0	PL	2	Hernandez [11]	20 295
	22	Benfica	D	2-2	CLgC		Berbatov [30], Fletcher [59]	74 873
	26	Newcastle	D	1-1	PL	2	Hernandez [49]	75 594
	30	C Palace	W	1-2	LCqf		Macheda [6p]	52 624
	3	Aston Villa	W	1-0	PL	2	Jones [20]	40 053
	7	Basel	L	1-2	CLgC		Jones [89]	36 000
	10	Wolves	W	4-1	PL	2	Nani 2 [17 56], Rooney 2 [27 62]	75 627
Dec	18	QPR	W	2-0	PL	2	Rooney [1], Carrick [56]	18 033
	21	Fulham	W	5-0	PL		Welbeck [5], Nani [28], Giggs [43], Rooney [88], Berbatov [90]	25 700
	26	Wigan	W	5-0	PL	2	Park [8], Berbatov 3 [41 58 78p], Valencia [75]	75 183
	31	Blackburn	L	2-3	PL	2	Berbatov 2 [52 62]	75 146
	4	Newcastle	L	0-3	PL			52 299
	8	Man City	W	3-2	FAr3		Rooney 2 [10 39], Welbeck [30]	46 808
Jan	14	Bolton	W	3-0	PL	2	Scholes [45], Welbeck [74], Carrick [83]	75 444
	22	Arsenal	W	2-1	PL	2	Valencia [45], Welbeck [81]	60 093
	28	Liverpool	L	1-2	FAr4		Park [39]	43 952
	31	Stoke	W	2-0	PL		Hernandez [38p], Berbatov [53p]	74 719
	5	Chelsea	D	3-3	PL	2	Rooney 2 [58p 69p], Hernandez [84]	41 668
Feb	11	Liverpool	W	2-1	PL	2	Rooney 2 [47 50]	74 844
	16	Ajax	W	2-0	ELr2		Young [59], Hernandez [85]	48 966
	23	Ajax	L	1-2	ELr2		Hernandez [6]	67 328
	26	Norwich	W	2-1	PL	2	Scholes [7], Giggs [92+]	26 811

NEWCASTLE UNITED 2011–12

	13	Arsenal	D	0-0	PL			46 894
	20	Sunderland	W	1-0	PL	6	Taylor.R [62]	47 751
Aug	25	Scunthorpe	W	2-1	LCr2		Taylor.R [80], Ameobi.Sa [112]	4 408
	28	Fulham	W	2-1	PL	6	Best 2 [48 66]	**42 684**
	12	QPR	D	0-0	PL			16 211
	17	Aston Villa	D	1-1	PL	4	Best [57]	34 248
Sep	20	Nottm For	W	4-3	LCr3		Lovenkrands 2 [39 60p], Simpson [93], Coloccini [120]	10 208
	24	Blackburn	W	3-1	PL	4	Ba 3 [27 30 54]	46 236
	1	Wolves	W	2-1	PL	4	Ba [17], Gutierrez [38]	26 561
	16	Tottenham	D	2-2	PL	4	Ba [48], Ameobi.Sh [86]	46 420
Oct	22	Wigan	W	1-0	PL	4	Cabaye [81]	48 321
	26	Blackburn	L	3-4	LCr4		Guthrie [90], Cabaye [96+], Lovenkrands [105p]	10 682
	31	Stoke	W	3-1	PL		Ba 3 [12 40 81p]	26 564
	5	Everton	W	2-1	PL	3	OG [12], Taylor.R [29]	50 671
Nov	19	Man City	L	1-3	PL	3	Gosling [89]	47 408
	26	Man Utd	D	1-1	PL	4	Ba [64p]	75 594
	3	Chelsea	L	0-3	PL	6		52 305
	10	Norwich	L	2-4	PL	7	Ba 2 [45 71]	26 816
	17	Swansea	D	0-0	PL	7		51 767
Dec	21	West Brom	L	1-2	PL		Ba 2 [34 81]	51 060
	26	Bolton	W	2-0	PL	7	Ben Arfa [69], Ba [71]	26 080
	30	Liverpool	L	1-3	PL		OG [25]	44 372

ENG – ENGLAND

NEWCASTLE UNITED 2011-12 (CONT'D)

	4	Man Utd	W	3-0	PL		Ba [33], Cabaye [47], OG [90]	52 299
	7	Blackburn	W	2-1	FAr3		Ben Arfa [70], Gutierrez [95+]	30 876
Jan	15	QPR	W	1-0	PL	6	Best [37]	49 865
	21	Fulham	L	2-5	PL	6	Guthrie [43], Ben Arfa [85]	25 692
	28	Brighton	L	0-1	FAr4			21 558
	1	Blackburn	W	2-0	PL		OG [12], Obertan [92+]	20 817
	5	Aston Villa	W	2-1	PL	5	Ba [30], Cisse [71]	48 569
Feb	11	Tottenham	L	0-5	PL	6		36 176
	25	Wolves	D	2-2	PL	6	Cisse [6], Gutierrez [18]	52 287
	4	Sunderland	D	1-1	PL	6	Ameobi.Sh [91+]	52 388
Mar	12	Arsenal	L	1-2	PL		Ben Arfa [14]	60 095
	18	Norwich	W	1-0	PL		Cisse [11]	47 833
	25	West Brom	W	3-1	PL	6	Cisse 2 [6 34], Ben Arfa [12]	25 049
	1	Liverpool	W	2-0	PL	6	Cisse 2 [19 59]	52 363
	6	Swansea	W	2-0	PL		Cisse 2 [5 69]	19 874
Apr	9	Bolton	W	2-0	PL		Ben Arfa [73], Cisse [83]	52 264
	21	Stoke	W	3-0	PL	4	Cabaye 2 [14 57], Cisse [18]	52 162
	28	Wigan	L	0-4	PL	5		22 187
	2	Chelsea	W	2-0	PL		Cisse 2 [19 94+]	41 559
May	6	Man City	L	0-2	PL	5		**52 389**
	13	Everton	L	1-3	PL	5	OG [73]	39 517

5th Att: 948 777 • Av: 49 935 (+4.65%) • St James' Park 52 409 (91%)

NEWCASTLE LEAGUE APPEARANCES/GOALS 2011-12
Goalkeepers Tim Krul NED 38
Defenders Fabricio Coloccini ARG 35/0 • James Perch 13+12/0
Davide Santon ITA 19+5/0 • Danny Simpson 35/0 • Ryan Taylor 23+8/2
Steven Taylor 14/0 • Mike Williamson 21+1/0
Midfield Joey Barton 2/0 • Hatem Ben Arfa FRA 16+10/5
Yohan Cabaye FRA 34/4 • Shane Ferguson NIR 0+7/0
Dan Gosling 1+11/1 • Danny Guthrie 13+3/1 • Jonas Gutierrez ARG
37/2 Sylvain Marveaux FRA 1+6/0 • Cheik Tiote CIV 24/0
Forwards Sammy Ameobi 1+11/0 • Shola Ameobi 8+17/2
Demba Ba SEN 32+2/16 • Leon Best IRL 16+2/4
Papiss Demba Cisse SEN 13+1/13 • Ryan Donaldson
Peter Lovenkrands DEN 2+7/0 • Gabriel Obertan FRA 18+5/1
Alan Smith 0+2/0 • Haris Vuckic SVN 2+2/0
Coach Alan Pardew

NORWICH CITY 2011-12 (CONT'D)

	2	QPR	W	2-1	PL		Pilkington [42], Morison [83]	18 033
Jan	7	Burnley	W	4-1	FAr3		Holt [6], Jackson [12], Surman [60], Morison [73]	22 898
	14	West Brom	W	2-1	PL	9	Surman [43], Morison [79]	24 474
	21	Chelsea	D	0-0	PL	9		26 792
	28	West Brom	W	2-1	FAr4		Holt [35], Jackson [85]	17 434
	1	Sunderland	L	0-3	PL			34 476
	4	Bolton	W	2-0	PL	9	Surman [70], Pilkington [85]	26 358
Feb	11	Swansea	W	3-2	PL	8	Holt 2 [47 63], Pilkington [51]	19 927
	18	Leicester	L	1-2	FAr5		Hoolahan [23]	26 658
	26	Man Utd	L	1-2	PL	8	Holt [83]	26 811
	3	Stoke	L	0-1	PL	11		27 483
	11	Wigan	D	1-1	PL	12	Hoolahan [10]	26 653
Mar	18	Newcastle	L	0-1	PL			47 833
	24	Wolves	W	2-1	PL	11	Holt 2 [26 45p]	26 752
	31	Fulham	L	1-2	PL	12	Wilbraham [77]	25 700
	7	Everton	D	2-2	PL	12	Howson [39], Holt [76]	26 554
	9	Tottenham	W	2-1	PL		Pilkington [13], Bennett [66]	36 126
Apr	14	Man City	L	1-6	PL	11	Surman [51]	26 812
	21	Blackburn	L	0-2	PL	13		23 218
	28	Liverpool	L	0-3	PL	13		**26 819**
May	5	Arsenal	D	3-3	PL	13	Hoolahan [12], Holt [27], Morison [85]	60 092
	13	Aston Villa	W	2-0	PL	12	Holt [8], Jackson [21]	26 803

12th Att: 505 509 • Av: 26 605 (+4.8%) • Carrow Road 27 010 (98%)

NORWICH LEAGUE APPEARANCES/GOALS 2011-12
Goalkeepers Declan Rudd 1+1 • John Ruddy 37
Defenders Daniel Ayala ESP 6+1/0 • Leon Barnett 13+4/1 • Ryan
Bennett 8/0 • Andrew Crofts WAL 13+11/0 • Ritchie De Laet BEL 6/1
Adam Drury 12/0 • Kyle Naughton 29+3/0 • Marc Tierney 17/0
Elliott Ward 12/0 • Zak Whitbread USA 18/0
Midfield Elliott Bennett 22+11/1 • David Fox 23+5/0 • Wesley
Hoolahan IRL 25+8/4 • Jonny Howson 11/1 • Bradley Johnson 25+3/2
Simon Lappin SCO 4/0 • Russell Martin SCO 30+3/2 • Anthony
Pilkington 23+7/8 • Andrew Surman RSA 21+4/4
Forwards Grant Holt 24+12/15 • Simeon Jackson CAN 10+12/3
Chris Martin 3+1/0 • Steve Morison WAL 22+12/9
James Vaughan 1+4/0 • Aaron Wilbraham 2+9/1
Coach Paul Lambert SCO

NORWICH CITY
2011-12

	13	Wigan	D	1-1	PL		Hoolahan [45]	17 454
Aug	21	Stoke	D	1-1	PL	10	De Laet [37]	26 272
	23	MK Dons	L	0-4	LCr2			13 009
	27	Chelsea	L	1-3	PL	14	Holt [63]	41 765
	11	West Brom	L	0-1	PL	17		26 158
Sep	17	Bolton	W	2-1	PL	13	Pilkington [37], Johnson [42]	21 223
	26	Sunderland	W	2-1	PL		Barnett [31], Morison [48]	**26 107**
	1	Man Utd	L	0-2	PL	9		75 514
	15	Swansea	W	3-1	PL	9	Pilkington 2 [1 63], Martin [10]	26 567
Oct	22	Liverpool	D	1-1	PL	8	Holt [60]	44 931
	29	Blackburn	D	3-3	PL	8	Morison [53], Johnson [82], Holt [94+p]	26 440
	5	Aston Villa	L	2-3	PL	9	Bent 2 [30 62], Agbonlahor [48]	35 290
Nov	19	Arsenal	L	1-2	PL	11	Morison [16]	26 801
	26	QPR	W	2-1	PL	10	Martin [15], Holt [73]	26 781
	3	Man City	L	1-5	PL	11	Morison [81]	47 201
	10	Newcastle	W	4-2	PL	10	Hoolahan [39], Holt 2 [59 82], Morison [63]	26 816
Dec	17	Everton	D	1-1	PL	9	Holt [28]	31 004
	20	Wolves	D	2-2	PL		Surman [12], Jackson [76]	27 067
	27	Tottenham	L	0-2	PL			26 807
	31	Fulham	D	1-1	PL	10	Jackson [94+]	26 406

QUEENS PARK RANGERS
2011-12

	13	Bolton	L	0-4	PL			**15 195**
Aug	20	Everton	W	1-0	PL	9	Smith [31]	35 008
	23	Rochdale	L	0-2	LCr2			4 755
	27	Wigan	L	0-2	PL	12		17 225
	12	Newcastle	D	0-0	PL			16 211
Sep	17	Wolves	W	3-0	PL	9	Barton [8], Faurlin [10], Campbell [87]	24 189
	25	Aston Villa	D	1-1	PL	9	OG [93+]	16 707
	2	Fulham	L	0-6	PL	11		23 766
	15	Blackburn	D	1-1	PL	11	Helguson [16]	16 487
Oct	23	Chelsea	W	1-0	PL	10	Helguson [10p]	18 050
	30	Tottenham	L	1-3	PL	12	Bothroyd [62]	36 147
	5	Man City	L	2-3	PL	11	Bothroyd [28], Helguson [69]	**18 076**
Nov	19	Stoke	W	3-2	PL	9	Helguson 2 [22 54], Young [44]	27 618
	26	Norwich	L	1-2	PL	11	Young [59]	26 781
	3	West Brom	D	1-1	PL	12	Helguson [20]	17 290
	10	Liverpool	L	0-1	PL	13		45 016
Dec	18	Man Utd	L	0-2	PL	15		18 033
	21	Sunderland	L	2-3	PL		Helguson [63], Mackie [67]	16 167
	27	Swansea	D	1-1	PL		Mackie [58]	19 530
	31	Arsenal	L	0-1	PL	17		60 067

QUEENS PARK RANGERS 2011–12 (CONT'D)

Jan	2	Norwich	L	1-2	PL	Barton [11]	18 033
	7	MK Dons	D	1-1	FAr3	Helgusson [89]	19 506
	15	Newcastle	L	0-1	PL	18	49 865
	17	MK Dons	W	1-0	FAr3	Gabbidon [73]	10 855
	21	Wigan	W	3-1	PL	16	Helgusson [33p], Buzsaky [45], Smith [81]	16 002
	28	Chelsea	L	0-1	FAr4		15 728
Feb| 1	Aston Villa	D	2-2	PL		Cisse [12], OG [29]	32 063
	4	Wolves	L	1-2	PL	16	Zamora [16]	17 351
	11	Blackburn	L	2-3	PL	16	Mackie 2 [71][92+]	20 252
	25	Fulham	L	0-1	PL	17		18 015
Mar| 3	Everton	D	1-1	PL	16	Zamora [36]	18 033
	10	Bolton	L	1-2	PL	18	Cisse [48]	21 551
	17	Liverpool	W	3-2	PL		Derry [77], Cisse [86], Mackie [91+]	18 033
	24	Sunderland	L	1-3	PL	18	Taiwo [79]	37 128
	31	Arsenal	W	2-1	PL	18	Taarabt [22], Diakite [66]	18 033
Apr| 8	Man Utd	L	0-2	PL	17		75 505
	11	Swansea	W	3-0	PL		Barton [45], Mackie [55], Buzsaky [67]	17 557
	14	West Brom	L	0-1	PL	16		25 521
	21	Tottenham	W	1-0	PL	16	Taarabt [24]	18 021
	29	Chelsea	L	1-6	PL	17	Cisse [84]	41 675
May| 6	Stoke	W	1-0	PL	16	Cisse [89]	17 319
	13	Man City	L	2-3	PL	17	Cisse [48], Mackie [66]	48 000

17th Att: 328 613 • Av: 17 295 (+10.62%) • Loftus Road 18 439 (93%)

QPR LEAGUE APPEARANCES/GOALS 2011–12
Goalkeepers Radek Cerny CZE 5 • Paddy Kenny IRL 33
Defenders Bruno Perone BRA 1/0 • Matthew Connolly 5+1/0 • Anton Ferdinand 31/0 • Daniel Gabbidon WAL 15+2/0 • Fitz Hall 11+3/0 • Michael Harriman IRL 0+1/0 • Clint Hill 19+3/0 • Nedum Onuoha 16/0 • Bradley Orr 2+4/0 • Taye Taiwo NGA 13+2/1 • Armand Traore SEN 18+5/0 • Luke Young 23/2
Midfield Joey Barton 31/3 • Bruno Andrade POR 0+1/0 • Akos Buzsaky HUN 10+8/2 • Shaun Derry 28+1/1 • Samba Diakite MLI 9/1 • Kieron Dyer 1/0 • Hogan Ephraim 0+2/0 • Alejandro Faurlin ARG 20/1 • Jamie Mackie SCO 24+7/7 • Jason Puncheon 0+2/0 • Adel Taarabt MAR 24+3/2 • Shaun Wright-Phillips 24+8/0
Forwards Patrick Agyemang GHA 2/0 • Jay Bothroyd 12+9/2 • DJ Campbell 2+9/1 • Djibril Cisse FRA 7+1/6 • Heidar Helgusson ISL 13+3/8 • Rob Hulse 1+1/0 • Federico Macheda ITA 0+3/0 • Tommy Smith 4+13/2 • Bobby Zamora 14/2
Coach Neil Warnock • Mark Hughes WAL (10/01/2012)

STOKE CITY 2011–12

Jul	28	Hajduk	W	1-0	ELp3	Walters [3]	26 322
	4	Hajduk	W	1-0	ELp3	OG [91+]	33 000
	14	Chelsea	D	0-0	PL		27 421
Aug	18	Thun	W	1-0	ELpo	Pugh [18]	7 850
	21	Norwich	D	1-1	PL	11	Jones [94+]	26 272
	25	Thun	W	4-1	ELpo	Upson [25], Jones 2 [31][72], Whelan [38]	24 148
	28	West Brom	W	1-0	PL	9	Shottom [89]	22 909
Sep| 10	Liverpool	W	1-0	PL	4	Walters [21p]	27 592
	15	Dy Kyiv	D	1-1	ELgE	Jerome [55]	14 500
	18	Sunderland	L	0-4	PL	5		32 296
	20	Tottenham	D	0-0	LCr3	W 7-6p	15 023
	24	Man Utd	D	1-1	PL	7	Crouch [52]	27 582
	29	Besiktas	W	2-1	ELgE	Crouch [15], Walters [78p]	23 551
Oct| 2	Swansea	L	0-2	PL	8		19 523
	15	Fulham	W	2-0	PL	7	Walters [80], Delap [87]	26 890
	20	Maccabi TA	W	3-0	ELgE	Jones [12], Jerome [24], Shotton [32]	22 756
	23	Arsenal	L	1-3	PL	9	Crouch [34]	59 671
	26	Liverpool	L	1-2	LCr4	Jones [44]	24 934
	31	Newcastle	L	1-3	PL		Walters [75p]	26 564

STOKE CITY 2011–12 (CONT'D)

	3	Maccabi TA	W	2-1	ElgE	Whitehead [51], Crouch [64]	10 368
Nov| 6	Bolton	L	0-5	PL	12		20 028
	19	QPR	L	2-3	PL	14	Walters [8], Shawcross [64]	27 618
	26	Blackburn	W	3-1	PL	12	Delap [28], Whelan [58], Crouch [72]	26 686
Dec	1	Dy Kyiv	D	1-1	ELgE	Jones [81]	23 774
	4	Everton	W	1-0	PL	8	Huth [15]	33 219
	11	Tottenham	W	2-1	PL	8	Etherington 2 [13][43]	27 529
	14	Besiktas	L	1-3	ElgE	Fuller [29]	26 118
	17	Wolves	W	2-1	PL	8	OG [58], Crouch [70]	24 684
	21	Man City	L	0-3	PL			46 321
	26	Aston Villa	D	0-0	PL	8		27 739
	31	Wigan	D	2-2	PL	8	Walters [77p], Jerome [84]	26 595
Jan| 2	Blackburn	W	2-1	PL			20 615
	7	Gillingham	W	3-1	FAr3	Walters [34], Jerome [43], Huth [49]	10 360
	14	Liverpool	D	0-0	PL	8		44 691
	17	West Brom	L	1-2	PL	8	Jerome [86]	26 865
	26	Derby Co	W	2-0	FAr4	Jerome [5], Huth [81]	22 247
	31	Man Utd	L	0-2	PL			74 719
Feb| 4	Sunderland	L	0-1	PL	12		27 717
	11	Fulham	L	1-2	PL	13	Shawcross [78]	23 555
	16	Valencia	L	0-1	ELr2		24 185
	19	Crawley	W	2-0	FAr5	Walters [42p], Crouch [53]	4 214
	23	Valencia	L	0-1	ELr2		36 535
	26	Swansea	W	2-0	PL	12	Upson [24], Crouch [39]	26 678
Mar| 3	Norwich	W	1-0	PL	9	Etherington [72]	27 483
	3	Chelsea	L	0-1	PL	13		40 945
	18	Liverpool	L	1-2	FAqf	Crouch [27]	43 962
	21	Tottenham	D	1-1	PL		Jerome [75]	35 172
	24	Man City	D	1-1	PL	12	Crouch [59]	27 535
	31	Wigan	L	0-2	PL	13		19 786
Apr| 7	Wolves	W	2-1	PL	11	Huth [37], Crouch [61]	27 005
	9	Aston Villa	D	1-1	PL		Huth [71]	30 100
	21	Newcastle	L	0-3	PL	14		52 162
	28	Arsenal	D	1-1	PL	14	Crouch [9]	27 502
May| 1	Everton	D	1-1	PL	14	Jerome [69]	26 500
	6	QPR	L	0-1	PL	14		17 319
	13	Bolton	D	2-2	PL	14	Walters 2 [13][77p]	27 789

14th Att: 517 290 • Av: 27 225 (+1.37%) • Britannia Stadium 27 740 (98%)

STOKE LEAGUE APPEARANCES/GOALS 2011–12
Goalkeepers Asmir Begovic BIH 22+1 • Thomas Sorensen DEN 16
Defenders Danny Higginbotham 1+1/0 • Robert Huth GER 31+3/3 • Ryan Shawcross 36/2 • Ryan Shotton 14+9/1 • Matthew Upson 10+4/1 • Andrew Wilkinson 20+5/0 • Marc Wilson IRL 35/0 • Jonathan Woodgate 16+1/0
Midfield Rory Delap IRL 18+8/2 • Salif Diao SEN 2+4/0 • Matthew Etherington 30/3 • Wilson Palacios HON 9+9/0 • Jermaine Pennant 18+9/0 • Danny Pugh 0+3/0 • Glenn Whelan IRL 27+3/1 • Dean Whitehead 24+9/0
Forwards Peter Crouch 31+1/10 • Ricardo Fuller JAM 3+10/0 • Cameron Jerome 7+16/4 • Kenwyne Jones TRI 10+11/1 • Jon Walters IRL 38/7
Coach Tony Pulis WAL

SUNDERLAND 2011–12

Aug	13	Liverpool	D	1-1	PL		Larsson [57]	45 018
	20	Newcastle	L	0-1	PL	13		47 751
	23	Brighton	L	0-1	LCr2			17 090
	27	Swansea	D	0-0	PL	13		19 938
Sep	10	Chelsea	L	1-2	PL	16	Ji Dong Won [91+]	36 699
	18	Stoke	W	4-0	PL	12	Bramble [5], OG [11], Gardner [28], Larsson [58]	32 296
	24	Norwich	L	1-2	PL		Richardson [86]	26 107
Oct	1	West Brom	D	2-2	PL	16	Bendtner [24], Elmohamady [26]	34 815
	16	Arsenal	L	1-2	PL	17	Larsson [31]	60 078
	22	Bolton	W	2-0	PL	14	Sessegnon [82], Bendtner [93+]	24 349
	29	Aston Villa	D	2-2	PL	14	Wickham [38], Sessegnon [89]	37 062

SUNDERLAND 2011-12 (CONT'D)

	Date	Opponent	Res		Comp	Pos	Scorers	Att
Nov	5	Man Utd	L	0-1	PL	15		75 570
	19	Fulham	D	0-0	PL	16		37 688
	26	Wigan	L	1-2	PL	16	Larsson [8]	37 883
Dec	4	Wolves	L	1-2	PL	17	Richardson [52]	25 145
	11	Blackburn	W	2-1	PL	16	Vaughan [84], Larsson [92+]	39 863
	18	Tottenham	L	0-1	PL	16		36 021
	21	QPR	W	3-2	PL		Bendtner [19], Sessegnon [53], Brown [89]	16 167
	26	Everton	D	1-1	PL	14	Colback [26]	43 619
	1	Man City	W	1-0	PL	15	Ji Dong Won [93+]	40 625
Jan	3	Wigan	W	4-1	PL		Gardner [45], McClean [55], Sessegnon [73], Vaughan [80]	15 871
	8	Peter'boro	W	2-0	FAr3		Larsson [48], McClean [58]	8 954
	14	Chelsea	L	0-1	PL	12		41 696
	21	Swansea	W	2-0	PL	10	Sessegnon [14], Gardner [85]	36 904
	29	Midd'boro	D	1-1	FAr4		Campbell [59]	33 275
	1	Norwich	W	3-0	PL		Campbell [21], Sessegnon [28], OG [54]	34 476
Feb	4	Stoke	W	1-0	PL	8	McClean [60]	27 717
	8	Midd'boro	W	2-1	FAr4		Colback [42], Sessegnon [113]	26 707
	11	Arsenal	L	1-2	PL	9	McClean [70]	40 312
	18	Arsenal	W	2-0	FAr5		Richardson [40], OG [77]	26 042
	25	West Brom	L	0-4	PL	9		25 311
	4	Newcastle	D	1-1	PL	12	Bendtner [24p]	52 388
	10	Liverpool	W	1-0	PL	8	Bendtner [56]	41 661
	17	Everton	D	1-1	FAqf		Bardsley [12]	38 875
Mar	20	Blackburn	L	0-2	PL			20 056
	24	QPR	W	3-1	PL	8	Bendtner [41], McClean [70], Sessegnon [76]	37 128
	27	Everton	L	0-2	FAqf			43 140
	31	Man City	D	3-3	PL	9	Larsson 2 [31,55], Bendtner [45]	47 007
	7	Tottenham	D	0-0	PL	9		39 335
Apr	9	Everton	L	0-4	PL			**32 249**
	14	Wolves	D	0-0	PL	9		37 476
	21	Aston Villa	D	0-0	PL	11		32 557
	28	Bolton	D	2-2	PL	11	Bendtner [36], McClean [55]	40 768
May	6	Fulham	L	1-2	PL	11	Bardsley [34]	25 683
	13	Man Utd	L	0-1	PL	13		46 452

13th Att: 742 813 • Av: 39 095 (-2.29%) • Stadium of Light 48 707 (80%)

SWANSEA CITY 2011-12 (CONT'D)

	Date	Opponent	Res		Comp	Pos	Scorers	Att
Oct	2	Stoke	W	2-0	PL	10	Sinclair [9p], Graham [85]	19 523
	15	Norwich	L	1-3	PL	13	Graham [12]	26 567
	22	Wolves	D	2-2	PL	15	Graham [23], Allen [35]	25 216
	29	Bolton	W	3-1	PL		Allen [49], Sinclair [57p], Graham [93+]	19 477
Nov	5	Liverpool	D	0-0	PL	10		45 013
	19	Man Utd	L	0-1	PL	13		20 295
	27	Aston Villa	D	0-0	PL	13		20 404
Dec	3	Blackburn	L	2-4	PL	14	Lita [35], Moore [66]	23 080
	10	Fulham	W	2-0	PL	11	Sinclair [56], Graham [91+]	19 296
	17	Newcastle	D	0-0	PL	12		51 767
	21	Everton	L	0-1	PL			32 004
	27	QPR	D	1-1	PL		Graham [14]	19 530
	31	Tottenham	D	1-1	PL	14	Sinclair [84]	20 393
	2	Aston Villa	W	2-0	PL		Dyer [4], Routledge [47]	35 642
	7	Barnsley	W	4-2	FAr3		Rangel [30], Graham 2 [46,89], Dyer [54]	7 380
Jan	15	Arsenal	W	3-2	PL	10	Sinclair [16p], Dyer [57], Graham [70]	20 409
	21	Sunderland	L	0-2	PL	13		36 904
	28	Bolton	L	1-2	FAr4		Moore [43]	11 597
	31	Chelsea	D	1-1	PL		Sinclair [39]	20 526
Feb	4	West Brom	W	2-1	PL	10	Sigurdsson [55], Graham [59]	24 274
	11	Norwich	L	2-3	PL	11	Graham 2 [23,87p]	19 927
	26	Stoke	L	0-2	PL	14		26 678
	3	Wigan	W	2-0	PL	12	Sigurdsson 2 [45,54]	19 001
Mar	11	Man City	W	1-0	PL	11	Moore [83]	20 510
	17	Fulham	W	3-0	PL		Sigurdsson 2 [36,66], Allen [77]	25 690
	24	Everton	L	0-2	PL	10		20 509
	1	Tottenham	L	1-3	PL	11	Sigurdsson [59]	36 174
	6	Newcastle	L	0-2	PL			19 874
	11	QPR	L	0-3	PL			17 557
Apr	14	Blackburn	W	3-0	PL	12	Sigurdsson [37], Dyer [43], OG [63]	**18 985**
	28	Bolton	D	1-1	PL	12	Sinclair [6]	25 401
	28	Wolves	D	4-4	PL	12	Orlandi [1], Allen [4], Dyer [15], Graham [31]	19 408
May	6	Man Utd	L	0-2	PL	12		75 496
	13	Liverpool	W	1-0	PL	11	Graham [86]	**20 605**

11th Att: 378 978 • Av: 19 946 (+28.63%) • Liberty Stadium 20 520 (97%)

SUNDERLAND LEAGUE APPEARANCES/GOALS 2011-12

Goalkeepers Craig Gordon SCO 1 • Simon Mignolet BEL 29 • Keiren Westwood IRL 8+1
Defenders Phil Bardsley SCO 29+2/1 • Titus Bramble 8/1 • Wayne Bridge 3+5/0 • Wes Brown 20/1 • Ahmed El Mohamadi EGY 7+11/1 Anton Ferdinand 3/0 • Matthew Kilgallon 9+1/0 • Sotirios Kyrgiakos GRE 2+1/0 • John O'Shea IRL 29/0 • Michael Turner 23+1/0
Midfield Lee Cattermole 23/0 • Jack Colback 29+6/1 • Craig Gardner 22+8/3 • Sebastian Larsson SWE 32/7 • David Meyler IRL 1+6/0 • Kieran Richardson 26+3/2 • Stephane Sessegnon BEN 36/7 • David Vaughan WAL 17+5/2
Forwards Nicklas Bendtner DEN 25+3/8 • Frazier Campbell 6+6/1 • Asamoah Gyan GHA 3/0 • Ji Dong Won KOR 2+17/2 • Ryan Noble 0+2/0 James McClean IRL 20+3/5 • Connor Wickham 5+11/1
Coach Steve Bruce • Martin O'Neill NIR (3/12/2011)

SWANSEA LEAGUE APPEARANCES/GOALS 2011-12

Goalkeepers Gerhard Tremmel GER 1 • Michel Vorm NED 37
Defenders Angel Rangel ESP 32+2/0 • Federico Bessone ARG 0+1/0 Steven Caulker 26/0 • Garry Monk 14+2/0 • Vangelis Moras GRE 0+1/0 Alan Tate 1+4/0 • Neil Taylor WAL 35+1/0 • Ashley Williams WAL 37/1
Midfield Kemy Agustien NED 7+6/0 • Joe Allen WAL 31+5/4 Leon Britton 35+1/0 • Nathan Dyer 29+5/5 • Mark Gower 14+6/0 Joshua McEachran 1+3/0 • Andrea Orlandi ESP 2+1/1 Ashley Richards WAL 6+2/0 • Wayne Routledge 17+11/1 Gylfi Sigurdsson ISL 17+1/7
Forwards Stephen Dobbie SCO 2+6/0 • Danny Graham 32+4/12 Leroy Lita 4+12/2 • Luke Moore 3+17/2 • Scott Sinclair 35+3/8
Coach Brendan Rodgers NIR

SWANSEA CITY 2011-12

	Date	Opponent	Res		Comp	Pos	Scorers	Att
Aug	15	Man City	L	0-4	PL			46 802
	20	Wigan	D	0-0	PL	16		19 028
	23	Shrewsbury	L	1-3	LCr2		OG [10]	4 063
	27	Sunderland	D	0-0	PL	15		19 938
Sep	10	Arsenal	L	0-1	PL	19		60 087
	17	West Brom	W	3-0	PL	14	Sinclair [14p], Lita [24], Dyer [49]	20 341
	24	Chelsea	L	1-4	PL	16	Williams [86]	41 800

TOTTENHAM HOTSPUR 2011-12

	Date	Opponent	Res		Comp	Pos	Scorers	Att
Aug	18	Hearts	W	5-0	ULpo		Van der Vaart [5], Defoe [13], Livermore [28], Bale [63], Lennon [78]	16 279
	22	Man Utd	L	0-3	PL			75 498
	25	Hearts	D	0-0	ULpo			24 053
	28	Man City	L	1-5	PL	20	Kaboul [68]	36 150

TOTTENHAM HOTSPUR 2011–12 (CONT'D)

Sep	10	Wolves	W	2-0	PL	14	Adebayor [67], Defoe [80]	25 274
	15	PAOK	D	0-0	ULgA			24 645
	18	Liverpool	W	4-0	PL	11	Modric [7], Defoe [66], Adebayor 2 [68 93+]	36 129
	20	Stoke	D	0-0	LCr3		L 6-7p	15 023
	24	Wigan	W	2-1	PL	6	Van der Vaart [3], Bale [23]	18 788
	29	Shamrock	W	3-1	ULgA		Pavlyuchenko [60], Defoe [62], Dos Santos [66]	24 782
Oct	2	Arsenal	W	2-1	PL	6	Van der Vaart [40], Walker [73]	36 274
	16	Newcastle	D	2-2	PL	6	Van der Vaart [40p], Defoe [68]	46 420
	20	Rubin	W	1-0	ULgA		Pavlyuchenko [33]	24 058
	23	Blackburn	W	2-1	PL	5	Van der Vaart 2 [15 53]	22 786
	30	QPR	W	3-1	PL	5	Bale 2 [20 72], Van der Vaart [33]	36 147
Nov	3	Rubin	L	0-1	ULgA			21 250
	6	Fulham	W	3-1	PL	5	Bale [10], Lennon [45], Defoe [95+]	25 698
	21	Aston Villa	W	2-0	PL	4	Adebayor 2 [14 40]	35 818
	26	West Brom	W	3-1	PL	3	Adebayor 2 [25 93+], Defoe [81]	24 801
	30	PAOK	L	1-2	ULgA		Modric [38p]	26 229
Dec	3	Bolton	W	3-0	PL	3	Bale [7], Lennon [50], Defoe [60]	35 896
	11	Stoke	L	1-2	PL	3	Adebayor [62p]	27 529
	15	Shamrock	W	4-0	ULgA		Pienaar [29], Townsend [38], Defoe [45], Kane [91+]	8 500
	18	Sunderland	W	1-0	PL	3	Pavlyuchenko [61]	36 021
	22	Chelsea	D	1-1	PL		Adebayor [8]	36 141
	27	Norwich	W	2-0	PL		Bale 2 [55 67]	26 807
	31	Swansea	D	1-1	PL	3	Van der Vaart [44]	20 393
Jan	3	West Brom	W	1-0	PL		Defoe [63]	36 062
	7	Cheltenham	W	3-0	FAr3		Defoe [24], Pavlyuchenko [43], Dos Santos [87]	35 672
	11	Everton	W	2-0	PL		Lennon [35], Assou-Ekotto [63]	36 132
	14	Wolves	D	0-0	PL	3	Modric [51]	36 194
	22	Man City	L	2-3	PL	3	Defoe [60], Bale [65]	47 422
	27	Watford	W	1-0	FAr4		Van der Vaart [42]	15 384
	31	Wigan	W	3-1	PL		Bale 2 [29 64], Modric [34]	35 801
Feb	6	Liverpool	D	0-0	PL			44 461
	11	Newcastle	W	5-0	PL	3	Assou-Ekotto [4], Saha 2 [6 20], Kranjcar [34], Adebayor [64]	36 176
	19	Stevenage	D	0-0	FAr5			6 332
	26	Arsenal	L	2-5	PL	3	Saha [4], Adebayor [34p]	60 106
Mar	4	Man Utd	L	1-3	PL	3	Defoe [87]	36 034
	7	Stevenage	W	3-1	FAr5		Defoe 2 [26 75], Adebayor [55p]	35 757
	10	Everton	L	0-1	PL	3		34 992
	21	Stoke	D	1-1	PL		Van der Vaart [93+]	35 172
	24	Chelsea	D	0-0	PL	4		41 830
	27	Bolton	W	3-1	FAqf		Nelsen [74], Bale [77], Saha [93+]	30 718
Apr	1	Swansea	W	3-1	PL	4	Van der Vaart [19], Adebayor 2 [73 86]	36 174
	7	Sunderland	D	0-0	PL	3		39 335
	9	Norwich	L	1-2	PL		Defoe [33]	36 126
	15	Chelsea	L	1-5	FAsf		Bale [56]	85 731
	21	QPR	L	0-1	PL	5		18 021
	29	Blackburn	W	2-0	PL	4	Van der Vaart [22], Walker [75]	35 798
May	2	Bolton	W	4-1	PL		Modric [37], Van der Vaart [60], Adebayor 2 [62 69]	22 349
	6	Aston Villa	D	1-1	PL	4	Adebayor [62p]	36 008
	13	Fulham	W	2-0	PL	4	Adebayor [2], Defoe [63]	36 256

4th Att: 684 501 • Av: 36 026 (-0.9%) • White Hart Lane 36 230 (99%)

SPURS LEAGUE APPEARANCES/GOALS 2011–12
Goalkeepers Brad Friedel USA 38
Defenders Benoit Assou-Ekotto CMR 34/2 • Gareth Bale WAL 36/10
Sebastien Bassong CMR 1+4/0 • Vedran Corluka CRO 1+2/0
Michael Dawson 6+1/0 • William Gallas FRA 15/0
Younes Kaboul FRA 33/1 • Ledley King 21/0 • Ryan Nelsen NZL 0+5/0
Adam Smith 0+1/0 • Kyle Walker 37/2
Midfield Tom Huddlestone 0+2/0 • Niko Kranjcar CRO 9+3/1
Aaron Lennon 19+4/3 • Jake Livermore 7+1/0 • Luka Modric CRO 36/4
Scott Parker 28+1/0 • Steven Pienaar RSA 0+2/0 • Danny Rose 3+8/0
Sandro BRA 17+6/0 • Rafael van der Vaart NED 28+5/11
Forwards Emmanuel Adebayor TOG 32+1/17 • Peter Crouch 1/0
Jermain Defoe 11+14/11 • Giovani Dos Santos MEX 0+7/0
Cameron Lancaster 0+1/0 • Roman Pavlyuchenko RUS 0+5/0
Louis Saha FRA 5+5/3
Coach Harry Redknapp

WEST BROMWICH ALBION 2011–12

Aug	14	Man Utd	L	1-2	PL		Long [37]	25 360
	20	Chelsea	L	1-2	PL	19	Long [4]	41 091
	23	Bournem'th	W	4-1	LCr2		Thomas [7], Fortune 2 [42 78], Cox [53]	6 911
	28	Stoke	L	0-1	PL	18		22 909
Sep	11	Norwich	W	1-0	PL	12	Odemwingie [3]	26 158
	17	Swansea	L	0-3	PL	20		20 341
	21	Everton	L	1-2	LCr3		Brunt [57p]	17 647
	24	Fulham	D	0-0	PL	19		23 835
Oct	1	Sunderland	D	2-2	PL	17	Morrison [4], Long [5]	34 815
	16	Wolves	W	2-0	PL	12	Brunt [8], Odemwingie [75]	24 872
	22	Aston Villa	W	2-1	PL	12	Olsson [45], Scharner [57]	34 152
	29	Liverpool	L	0-2	PL	13		25 522
Nov	5	Arsenal	L	0-3	PL	14		60 091
	19	Bolton	W	2-1	PL	10	Thomas [16], Long [56]	26 221
	26	Tottenham	L	1-3	PL	14	Mulumbu [10]	24 801
Dec	3	QPR	D	1-1	PL	13	Long [81]	17 290
	10	Wigan	L	1-2	PL	15	Reid [33]	25 446
	17	Blackburn	W	2-1	PL	13	Morrison [52], Odemwingie [89]	22 909
	21	Newcastle	W	3-2	PL		Odemwingie [20], McAuley [44], Scharner [85]	51 060
	26	Man City	D	0-0	PL	9		25 938
	1	Everton	L	0-1	PL	11		23 038
Jan	3	Tottenham	L	0-1	PL			36 062
	7	Cardiff	W	4-2	FAr3		Odemwingie [7], Cox 3 [33 61 90]	12 454
	14	Norwich	L	1-2	PL	15	Long [68p]	22 474
	21	Stoke	W	2-1	PL	15	Morrison [35], Dorrans [91+]	26 865
	28	Norwich	L	1-2	FAr4		Fortune [54]	17 434
Feb	1	Fulham	D	1-1	PL		Tchoyi [8]	25 689
	4	Swansea	L	1-2	PL	15	Fortune [54]	24 274
	12	Wolves	W	5-1	PL	14	Odemwingie 3 [34 77 88], Olsson [64], Andrews [85]	27 131
	25	Sunderland	W	4-0	PL	13	Odemwingie 2 [3 48], Morrison [41], Andrews [91+]	25 311
Mar	3	Chelsea	W	1-0	PL	10	McAuley [82]	24 838
	11	Man Utd	L	0-2	PL	14		75 598
	17	Wigan	D	1-1	PL		Scharner [65]	21 379
	25	Newcastle	L	1-3	PL	14	Long [52]	25 049
	31	Everton	L	0-2	PL	14		32 051
Apr	7	Blackburn	W	3-0	PL	13	OG [7], Fortune [69], Ridgewell [85]	23 414
	11	Man City	L	0-4	PL			46 746
	14	QPR	W	1-0	PL	13	Dorrans [22]	25 521
	22	Liverpool	W	1-0	PL	10	Odemwingie [75]	43 660
	28	Aston Villa	D	0-0	PL	10		25 984
May	6	Bolton	D	2-2	PL	10	Brunt [75], Morrison [90]	25 662
	13	Arsenal	L	2-3	PL	10	Long [11], Dorrans [15]	26 358

10th Att: 471 165 • Av: 24 798 (+0.47%) • The Hawthorns 26 360 (94%)

WEST BROM LEAGUE APPEARANCES/GOALS 2011–12
Goalkeepers Ben Foster 37 • Marton Fulop HUN 1
Defenders Craig Dawson 6+2/0 • Gonzalo Jara CHI 1+3/0
Billy Jones 17+1/0 • Gareth McAuley NIR 32/2 • Jonas Olsson SWE 33/2
Steven Reid IRL 21+1/1 • Liam Ridgewell 13/1 • Nicky Shorey 22+3/0
Gabriel Tamas ROU 7+1/0
Midfield Keith Andrews IRL 8+6/2 • Chris Brunt NIR 25+4/2 • Graham
Dorrans SCO 16+15/3 • James Morrison SCO 23+7/5 • Youssuf
Mulumbu COD 34+1/1 • Paul Scharner AUT 18+11/3 • Somen
Tchoyi CMR 6+12/1 • Jerome Thomas 26+3/1 • George Thorne 1+2/0
Forwards Roman Bednar CZE 1/0 • Simon Cox IRL 7+11/0
Marc-Antoine Fortune FRA 12+5/2 • Zoltan Gera HUN 3/0
Shane Long IRL 23+8/8 • Peter Odemwingie NGA 25+5/10
Coach Roy Hodgson

WIGAN ATHLETIC
2011–12

	13	Norwich	D	1-1	PL		Watson [21p]	17 454
Aug	20	Swansea	D	0-0	PL	12		19 028
	27	QPR	W	2-0	PL	8	Di Santo 2 [41 66]	17 225
	10	Man City	L	0-3	PL	9		46 509
Sep	13	C Palace	L	1-2	LCr2		Watson [92+]	/ 649
	17	Everton	L	1-3	PL	15	Di Santo [31]	31 576
	24	Tottenham	L	1-2	PL	15	Diame [50]	18 788
	1	Aston Villa	L	0-2	PL	18		30 744
Oct	15	Bolton	L	1-3	PL	19	Diame [40]	17 261
	22	Newcastle	L	0-1	PL	19		48 321
	29	Fulham	L	0-2	PL	20		**15 796**
	6	Wolves	L	1-3	PL	20	Watson [42]	23 536
Nov	19	Blackburn	D	3-3	PL	20	Gomez [7], Caldwell [31], Crusat [88]	17 392
	26	Sunderland	W	2-1	PL	19	Gomez [44p], Di Santo [93+]	37 883
	3	Arsenal	L	0-4	PL	20		19 280
	10	West Brom	W	2-1	PL	18	Moses [37], Gomez [57p]	25 446
Dec	17	Chelsea	D	1-1	PL	18	Gomez [88]	18 320
	21	Liverpool	D	0-0	PL			19 230
	26	Man Utd	L	0-5	PL	18		75 183
	31	Stoke	D	2-2	PL	18	Moses [45], Watson [87p]	26 595
	3	Sunderland	L	1-4	PL		Rodallega [6]	15 871
	7	Swindon	L	1-2	FAr3		McManaman [35]	13 238
Jan	16	Man City	L	0-1	PL			16 026
	21	QPR	L	1-3	PL	20	Rodallega [66]	16 002
	31	Tottenham	L	1-3	PL		McArthur [80]	35 801
Feb	4	Everton	D	1-1	PL	20	OG [76]	18 340
	11	Bolton	W	2-1	PL	20	Caldwell [43], McArthur [76]	23 450
	25	Aston Villa	D	0-0	PL	20		20 601
	3	Swansea	L	0-2	PL	20		19 001
	11	Norwich	D	1-1	PL	20	Moses [68]	26 653
Mar	17	West Brom	D	1-1	PL		McArthur [54]	21 379
	24	Liverpool	W	2-1	PL	19	Maloney [30p], Caldwell [63]	44 431
	31	Stoke	W	2-0	PL	19	Alcaraz [54], Moses [93+]	19 786
	7	Chelsea	L	1-2	PL	19	Diame [82]	40 651
	11	Man Utd	W	1-0	PL		Maloney [50]	18 115
Apr	16	Arsenal	W	2-1	PL		Di Santo [7], Gomez [8]	60 060
	21	Fulham	L	1-2	PL	17	Boyce [57]	25 689
	28	Newcastle	W	4-0	PL	16	Moses 2 [13 15], Maloney [36], Di Santo [45]	**22 187**
May	7	Blackburn	W	1-0	PL		Alcaraz [87]	26 144
	13	Wolves	W	3-2	PL	15	Di Santo 12, Boyce 2 [14 79]	21 986

15th Att: 354 038 • Av: 18 633 (+10.83%) • DW Stadium 25 133 (74%)

WIGAN LEAGUE APPEARANCES/GOALS 2011–12
Goalkeepers Ali Al Habsi OMA 38
Defenders Antolin Alcaraz PAR 25/2 • Emmerson Boyce BRB 26/3
Gary Caldwell SCO 36/3 • Maynor Figueroa HON 37+1/0
Steve Gohouri CIV 8+2/0 • Piscu ESP 5/0 • Ronnie Stam NED 13+7/0
Patrick van Aanholt 3/0
Midfield Jean Beausejour CHI 16/0 • Albert Crusat ESP 4+11/1
Momo Diame SEN 18+8/3 • David Jones 13+3/0
Jordi Gomez ESP 24+4/5 • Shaun Maloney SCO 8+5/3
James McArthur SCO 18+13/3 • James McCarthy IRL 33/0
Ben Watson 14+7/3
Forwards Franco Di Santo ARG 24+8/7 • Callum McManaman 0+2/0
Victor Moses NGA 36+2/6 • Hugo Rodallega COL 11+12/2
Conor Sammon IRL 8+17/0
Coach Roberto Martinez ESP

WOLVERHAMPTON WANDERERS
2011–12

	13	Blackburn	W	2-1	PL		Fletcher [22], Ward [47]	21 996
Aug	21	Fulham	W	2-0	PL	2	Doyle [42], Jarvis [45]	**22 657**
	23	Northants	W	4-0	LCr2		Ebanks-Blake 2 [31 77], Milijas [37], Vokes [88]	5 512
	27	Aston Villa	D	0-0	PL	5		30 776
	10	Tottenham	L	0-2	PL	7		25 274
	17	QPR	L	0-3	PL	10		24 189
Sep	20	Millwall	W	5-0	LCr3		Edwards [3], Hammill [7], Elokobi [38], Spray [77], Guedioura [88]	7 749
	24	Liverpool	L	1-2	PL	11	Fletcher [49]	44 922
	1	Newcastle	L	1-2	PL	14	Fletcher [88]	26 561
	16	West Brom	L	0-2	PL	16		24 872
Oct	22	Swansea	D	2-2	PL	16	Doyle [84], O'Hara [86]	25 216
	26	Man City	L	2-5	LCr4		Milijas [18], O'Hara [65]	12 436
	29	Man City	L	1-3	PL	17	Hunt [75p]	47 142
	6	Wigan	W	3-1	PL	13	O'Hara [31], Edwards [55], Ward [66]	23 536
Nov	19	Everton	L	1-2	PL	17	Hunt [37p]	33 953
	26	Chelsea	L	0-3	PL	17		41 648
	4	Sunderland	W	2-1	PL	15	Fletcher 2 [73 81]	25 145
	10	Man Utd	L	1-4	PL	17	Fletcher [47]	75 627
Dec	17	Stoke	L	1-2	PL	17	Hunt [17p]	24 684
	20	Norwich	D	2-2	PL		Ebanks-Blake [37], Zubar [82]	27 067
	27	Arsenal	D	1-1	PL		Fletcher [38]	59 686
	31	Bolton	D	1-1	PL	16	Fletcher [49]	20 354
	2	Chelsea	L	1-2	PL		Ward [84]	27 289
	7	B'ham City	D	0-0	FAr3			14 594
Jan	14	Tottenham	D	1-1	PL	16	Fletcher [22]	36 194
	18	B'ham City	L	0-1	FAr3			10 153
	21	Aston Villa	L	2-3	PL	19	Kightly [21], Edwards [31]	27 084
	31	Liverpool	L	0-3	PL			27 447
	4	QPR	W	2-1	PL	17	Jarvis [46], Doyle [71]	17 351
Feb	12	West Brom	L	1-5	PL	18	Fletcher [45]	27 131
	25	Newcastle	D	2-2	PL	16	Jarvis [50], Doyle [66]	52 287
	4	Fulham	L	0-5	PL	18		24 034
	10	Blackburn	L	0-2	PL	19		26 121
Mar	18	Man Utd	L	0-5	PL			**27 494**
	24	Norwich	L	1-2	PL	20	Jarvis [25]	26 752
	31	Bolton	L	1-2	PL	20	Kightly [53], Jarvis [88]	25 215
	7	Stoke	L	1-2	PL	20	Kightly [26]	27 005
	11	Arsenal	L	0-3	PL			25 815
Apr	14	Sunderland	D	0-0	PL	20		36 476
	22	Man City	L	0-2	PL	20		24 576
	28	Swansea	D	4-4	PL	20	Fletcher [28], Jarvis 2 [33 69], Edwards [54]	19 408
May	6	Everton	D	0-0	PL	20		25 466
	13	Wigan	L	2-3	PL	20	Jarvis [9], Fletcher [86]	21 986

20th Att: 487 967 • Av: 25 682 (-7.27%) • Molineux 27 828 (92%)

WOLVES LEAGUE APPEARANCES/GOALS 2011–12
Goalkeepers Dorus de Vries NED 4 • Wayne Hennessey WAL 34
Carl Ikeme NGA 0+1
Defenders Sebastien Bassong CMR 9/0 • Christophe Berra SCO 29+3/0
Jody Craddock 1/0 • Matt Doherty IRL 0+1/0
George Elokobi CMR 3+6/0 • Kevin Foley IRL 11+5/0
Roger Johnson 26/1 • Richard Stearman 28+2/0
Stephen Ward IRL 38/3 • Ronald Zubar GLP 14+1/1
Midfield David Davis 6+1/0 • Dave Edwards WAL 24+2/3
Anthony Forde IRL 3+3/0 • Emmanuel Frimpong 5/0
Johnny Gorman NIR 0+1/0 • Adlene Guedioura ALG 2+8/0
Adam Hammill 3+6/0 • Karl Henry 30+1/0 • Stephen Hunt IRL 16+8/3
Matthew Jarvis 31+6/8 • Eggert Jonsson ISL 2+1/0
Michael Kightly 14+4/3 • Nenad Milijas 6+14/0 • Jamie O'Hara 19/2
Forwards Kevin Doyle IRL 26+7/4 • Sylvain Ebanks-Blake 8+15/1
Steven Fletcher SCO 26+6/12 • Stefan Maierhofer AUT 0+1/0
Sam Vokes 0+4/0
Coach Mick McCarthy IRL • Terry Connor (24/02/2012)

EQG – EQUATORIAL GUINEA

FIFA/COCA-COLA WORLD RANKING

'93	'94	'95	'96	'97	'98	'99	'00	'01	'02	'03	'04	'05	'06	'07	'08	'09	'10	'11	'12
-	-	-	-	-	195	188	187	190	192	160	171	171	109	85	123	135	165	150	79

2012

Jan	Feb	Mar	Apr	May	Jun	Jul	Aug	Sep	Oct	Nov	Dec	High	Low	Av
151	110	108	103	103	114	111	111	107	105	95	79	64	195	153

Equatorial Guinea's quarter-final place at the 2012 Africa Cup of Nations, which they co-hosted with Gabon, did not provide the momentum for progress later in the year. 'Nzalang Nacional' were one of the surprise packages at their own tournament but any hopes that Brazilian coach Gilson Paulo might be able to build on that success quickly disappeared in the 2014 FIFA World Cup qualifiers. Equatorial Guinea lost to Tunisia in their opening Group B match and then dropped home points in a 2-2 draw with Sierra Leone. In the 2013 Nations Cup qualifiers, they lost over two legs to a much stronger Democratic Republic of Congo side. A haul of 72 points ensured that Sony Ela Nguema ended as champions of the Liga Profesional de Futebol de Guinea Ecuatorial. They secured the title in fine style with a 5-1 win over Nzok-Nzomo. The Panther won the national cup, now named after president Obiang Nguema with the final played in his home town of Mongomo. They beat Academica Deportiva Mesi Nkulu with a first half goal from Antonio Ondo. In women's football, Equatorial Guinea hosted and won the African Women's Championship, beating South Africa 4-0 in the final. Their captain Genoveva Anonman, one of a handful of home-born players in their team, finished as the tournament's top scorer with six goals.

CAF AFRICA CUP OF NATIONS RECORD
1957-1988 DNE **1990** DNQ **1992-2000** DNE **2002-2010** DNQ **2012** 7 QF (Hosts) **2013** DNQ

FEDERACION ECUATOGUINEANA DE FUTBOL (FEGUIFUT)

Avenida de Hassan II,
Apartado postal 1017,
Malabo
☎ +240 333 091874
📠 +240 333 091874
✉ fef-sg@yahoo.es
🖥 www.feguifut.net
FA 1960 CON 1986 FIFA 1986
P Domingo Mituy Edjang
GS Inocencio Engon

THE STADIA
2014 FIFA World Cup Stadia
Nuevo Estadio de Malabo
Malabo 15 250
Other Main Stadia
Estadio de Bata
Bata 37 500
Estadio Internacional
Malabo 6 000
Estadio La Libertad
Bata 3 000

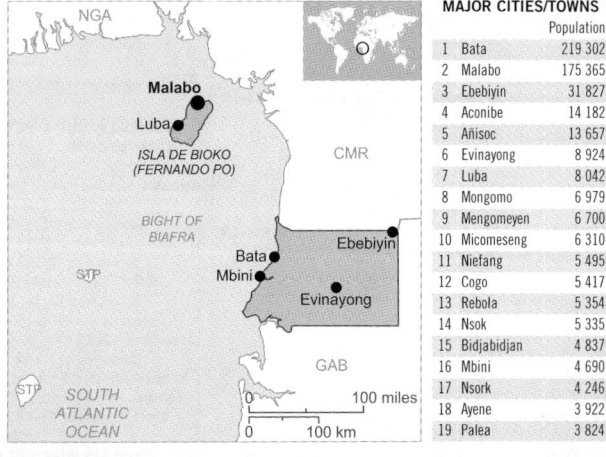

MAJOR CITIES/TOWNS

		Population
1	Bata	219 302
2	Malabo	175 365
3	Ebebiyin	31 827
4	Aconibe	14 182
5	Añisoc	13 657
6	Evinayong	8 924
7	Luba	8 042
8	Mongomo	6 979
9	Mengomeyen	6 700
10	Micomeseng	6 310
11	Niefang	5 495
12	Cogo	5 417
13	Rebola	5 354
14	Nsok	5 335
15	Bidjabidjan	4 837
16	Mbini	4 690
17	Nsork	4 246
18	Ayene	3 922
19	Palea	3 824

REPUBLICA DE GUINEA ECUATORIAL • REPUBLIC OF EQUATORIAL GUINEA

Capital	Malabo	Population	633 441 (165)	% in cities	39%
GDP per capita	$37 300 (29)	Area km²	28 051 km² (145)	GMT +/-	+1
Neighbours (km)	Cameroon 189, Gabon 350 • Coast 296				

RECENT INTERNATIONAL MATCHES PLAYED BY EQUATORIAL GUINEA

2008	Opponents	Score	Venue	Comp	Scorers	Att	Referee
1-06	Sierra Leone	W 2-0	Malabo	WCq	Falcao Carolino [47], Juan Epitie [57]	13 000	Codjia BEN
7-06	South Africa	L 1-4	Atteridgeville	WCq	Juvenal Edjogo [78p]	10 000	Diouf SEN
15-06	Nigeria	L 0-1	Malabo	WCq		15 200	Mendy GAM
21-06	Nigeria	L 0-2	Abuja	WCq		20 000	Ambaya LBY
6-09	Sierra Leone	L 1-2	Freetown	WCq	Rodolfo Bodipo [83p]	22 000	Doue CIV
11-10	South Africa	L 0-1	Malabo	WCq		6 500	Djaoupe TOG
2009							
28-03	Cape Verde Islands	L 0-5	Sal	Fr			
25-04	Mali	L 0-3	Bamoko	Fr			
6-06	Estonia	L 0-3	Tallinn	Fr		2 150	Malzinskas LTU
2010							
11-08	Morocco	L 1-2	Rabat	Fr	Anselmo Eyegue [38]		
12-10	Botswana	L 0-2	Malabo	Fr			
2011							
8-02	Chad	W 2-0	Malabo	Fr	Daniel Ekedo [53p], OG [74]		
29-03	Gambia	W 1-0	Malabo	Fr	Thierry Fidjeu [42]		
3-09	Burkina Faso	L 0-1	Bobo Dioulasso	Fr			
7-09	Central African Rep	W 3-0	Malabo	Fr	Randy [20p], Samuel Itondo 2 [44 83]		
7-10	Gabon	L 0-2	Cannes	Fr			
11-10	Cameroon	D 1-1	Malabo	Fr	Doulla Viera [31]		
11-11	Madagascar	W 2-0	Malabo	WCq	Juvenal [20p], Randy [74p]	10 000	Otogo-Castane GAB
15-11	Madagascar	L 1-2	Antananarivo	WCq	Doulla Viera [24]		
2012							
6-01	South Africa	D 0-0	Bata	Fr			
21-01	Libya	W 1-0	Bata	CNr1	Javier Balboa [87]	35 000	Doue CIV
25-01	Senegal	W 2-1	Bata	CNr1	Randy [61], Kily [93+]	35 000	Abdel Rahman SUD
29-01	Zambia	L 0-1	Malabo	CNr1		44 000	Benouza ALG
4-02	Côte d'Ivoire	L 0-3	Malabo	CNqf		12 500	Maillet SEY
2-06	Tunisia	L 1-3	Monastir	WCq	Randy [34]	10 000	Abid ALG
9-06	Sierra Leone	D 2-2	Malabo	WCq	Juvenal 2 [14 40]	4 000	Cordier CHA
9-09	Congo DR	L 0-4	Kinshasa	CNq			Seechurn MRI
14-10	Congo DR	W 2-1	Malabo	CNq	Javier Balboa [23], Ben Konate [35]		Fall SEN

Fr = Friendly match • CN = CAF African Cup of Nations • CM = CEMAC Cup • WC = FIFA World Cup
q = qualifier • r1 = first round group • qf = quarter-final

COPA DE S.E. EL PRESIDENTE DE LA REPUBLIC FINAL

Bonaire, 19-09-2010
The Panther 1-0 Academica Mesi Nkulu
Scorer - Antonio Ondo

EQUATORIAL GUINEA SQUAD FOR THE 2012 CAF AFRICA CUP OF NATIONS

	Player		Ap	G	Club	Date of Birth
1	Danilo	GK	4		América PE BRA	5 03 1982
2	Dani Evuy	DF	1		Villaviciosa ESP	11 03 1985
3	David Alvarez 'Kily'	DF	3	1	Langreo ESP	5 02 1984
4	Rui	MF	4		Logroñés ESP	28 05 1985
5	Fousseny Kamissoko	DF	4		Al Suwaiq OMA	5 04 1983
6	Juvenal (c)	FW	4		Sabadell ESP	3 04 1979
7	Rolan de la Cruz	MF	0+1		Fortaleza COL	3 10 1984
8	Randy	DF	3	1	Las Palmas ESP	2 06 1987
9	Rodolfo Bodipo	FW	0+1		D.La Coruña ESP	25 10 1977
10	Ivan Bolado	FW	3+1		Cartagena ESP	3 07 1989
11	Javier Balboa	FW	4	1	Beira-Mar POR	13 05 1985
12	Thierry Fidjeu	FW	3+1		Unattached	13 10 1982
13	Juan Maximo Ndong	MF	0		Dep Mongomo	8 11 1992
14	Ben Konate	MF	4		The Panthers	27 12 1986
15	Lawrence Doe	DF	3		Al Shabab OMA	23 05 1978
16	Sipo	DF	0		Badajoz ESP	21 04 1988
17	Narcisse Ekanga	MF	1+2		TP Mazembe COD	30 07 1981
18	Douala Viera Ellong	MF	0+1		Ela Nguema	14 06 1987
19	Raul Fabiani	FW	0+2		Alcoyano ESP	23 02 1984
20	Daniel Ekedo	MF	2+2		San Roque ESP	19 09 1989
21	Achille Pensy	GK	0		The Panthers	5 01 1987
22	Felipe Ovono	GK	0		Ela Nguema	26 07 1993
23	Colin	DF	1		Dep Mongomo	31 12 1987

ERI – ERITREA

FIFA/COCA-COLA WORLD RANKING

'93	'94	'95	'96	'97	'98	'99	'00	'01	'02	'03	'04	'05	'06	'07	'08	'09	'10	'11	'12
-	-	-	-	-	189	169	158	171	157	155	169	169	140	132	162	163	177	190	196

2012

Jan	Feb	Mar	Apr	May	Jun	Jul	Aug	Sep	Oct	Nov	Dec	High	Low	Av
189	190	190	190	190	190	189	187	185	187	192	196	121	196	164

Eritrean football suffered yet another mass defection as 17 players and the team doctor sought asylum in Uganda at the end of the CECAFA Cup in December. The action is likely to lead to a further limitation on the participation of teams from the country in the international arena, which has been increasingly restricted to regional events. Sporting defections have become commonplace in recent years and football, in particular, has been hard hit. Of the squad that took part at the CECAFA championship, just five players and two officials returned home. 15 of the defectors were granted asylum in Uganda while 13 of the players who jumped ship at the end of the 2010 CECAFA Cup in Tanzania have since moved to the USA. Other former Eritrean internationals have been relocated to Australia. Eritrea did not enter the 2013 Africa Cup of Nations qualifiers as their isolation deepened - the third time in a row they have failed to participate in the preliminaries - although they did enter the 2014 FIFA World Cup before being knocked out by Rwanda in late 2011. Unsurprisingly there were no Eritrean clubs in the two annual CAF competitions while the national team also withdrew from the African Nations Championship after being drawn against neighbours Ethiopia, with whom they have had a long-standing border conflict.

CAF AFRICA CUP OF NATIONS RECORD
1957-1998 DNE 2000-2008 DNQ 2010-2013 DNE

ERITREAN NATIONAL FOOTBALL FEDERATION (ENFF)

Sematat Avenue 29-31, PO Box 3665, Asmara
☎ +291 1 120335
+291 1 126821
enff@tse.com.er

FA 1996 CON 1998 FIFA 1998
P Tesfaye Gebreyesus Dsue
GS Mekonen Ghidey Tesfaye

MAJOR CITIES/TOWNS

		Population
1	Asmara	648 530
2	Assab	92 155
3	Keren	74 465
4	Mitsiwa	47 799
5	Addi Ugri	19 096
6	Barentu	17 820
7	Addi K'eyih	15 902
8	Ginda	14 075
9	Edd	13 709
10	Dek'emhare	13 343
11	Ak'ordat	10 784
12	Addi Kwala	8 225
13	Sen'afe	7 311
14	Teseney	4 570

THE STADIA

2014 FIFA World Cup Stadia
Cicero Stadium
Asmara   10 000

Other Main Stadia
Asmara National Stadium
Asmara   20 000

HAGERE ERTRA • STATE OF ERITREA

Capital	Asmara	Population	5 647 168 (109)	% in cities	21%
GDP per capita	$700 (223)	Area km²	117 600 km² (100)	GMT +/-	+3
Neighbours (km)	Djibouti 109, Ethiopia 912, Sudan 605 • Coast 2234				

RECENT INTERNATIONAL MATCHES PLAYED BY ERITREA

2005 Opponents	Score	Venue	Comp	Scorers	Att	Referee
28-11 Zanzibar †	L 0-3	Kigali	CCr1			
30-11 Rwanda	L 2-3	Kigali	CCr1	Suleiman Muhamoul 2		
2-12 Burundi	D 0-0	Kigali	CCr1			
4-12 Tanzania	L 0-1	Kigali	CCr1			
2006						
2-09 Kenya	W 2-1	Nairobi	CNq	Origi OG 15, Shimangus Yednekatchew 67		Lwanja MWI
7-10 Swaziland	D 0-0	Asmara	CNq			Gasingwa RWA
2007						
7-01 Yemen	L 1-4	Sana'a	Fr			
25-03 Angola	L 1-6	Luanda	CNq	Misgina Besirat 73		Evehe CMR
21-05 Sudan	W 1-0	Asmara	Fr	Shimangus Yednekatchew 46		
26-05 Sudan	D 1-1	Asmara	Fr			
2-06 Angola	D 1-1	Asmara	CNq	Hamiday Abdelkadir 15		Marange ZIM
16-06 Kenya	W 1-0	Asmara	CNq	Berhane Arega 80		Abdelrahman SUD
9-09 Swaziland	D 0-0	Manzini	CNq			Ssegonga UGA
30-11 Sudan	L 0-1	Omdurman	Fr			
3-12 Sudan	L 0-1	Omdurman	Fr			
9-12 Rwanda	L 1-2	Dar es Salaam	CCr1	Berhane Arega 38		
11-12 Djibouti	W 3-2	Dar es Salaam	CCr1	Berhane Arega 6, Shimangus Yednekatchew 42, Binam Fissehaye 68		
14-12 Uganda	W 3-2	Dar es Salaam	CCr1	Elmon Yeamekibron 2 53 64, Samuel Ghebrehine 82		
17-12 Burundi	L 1-2	Dar es Salaam	CCqf	Berhane Arega 20		
2008						
No international matches played in 2008						
2009						
1-12 Zimbabwe †	D 0-0	Nairobi	CCr1			
3-12 Rwanda	L 1-2	Nairobi	CCr1	Yosief Tzerezghi 83		
5-12 Somalia	W 3-1	Nairobi	CCr1	Isaias Andberhian 25p, Filmon Tseqay 27, OG 60		
8-12 Tanzania	L 0-4	Nairobi	CCqf			
2010						
No international matches played in 2010						
2011						
19-08 Sudan	L 0-3	Asmara	Fr			
11-11 Rwanda	D 1-1	Asmara	WCq	Tesfalem Tekle 35	6 000	Keita MLI
15-11 Rwanda	L 1-3	Kigali	WCq	Abraham Tedros 89	10 000	Bondo BOT
2012						
26-11 Zanzibar †	D 0-0	Kampala	CCr1			Ogwayo KEN
29-11 Malawi	L 2-3	Kampala	CCr1	Yosieg Ghide 69, Hermon Tecleab 90p		Batte UGA
1-12 Rwanda	L 0-2	Kampala	CCr1			Mujuni TAN

CN = CAF African Cup of Nations • CC = CECAFA Cup • WC = FIFA World Cup • q = qualifier • r1 = first round group • † Not a full international

ESP – SPAIN

FIFA/COCA-COLA WORLD RANKING

'93	'94	'95	'96	'97	'98	'99	'00	'01	'02	'03	'04	'05	'06	'07	'08	'09	'10	'11	'12
5	2	4	8	11	15	4	7	7	3	3	5	5	12	4	1	1	1	1	1

2012

Jan	Feb	Mar	Apr	May	Jun	Jul	Aug	Sep	Oct	Nov	Dec	High	Low	Av
1	1	1	1	1	1	1	1	1	1	1	1	1	25	5

2012 was an extraordinary year for Spanish football - even by comparison with the high standards of recent years. La Roja won a third successive international tournament after beating Italy by a record score of 4-0 in the final of Euro 2012, while at club level Leo Messi scored and incredible 50 league goals for Barcelona - and an incredible 91 over the whole calendar year - yet still didn't win the title which went instead to Real Madrid for whom Cristano Ronaldo scored what would have been a record beating 46 goals. The only dampener on the season were the semi-final defeats suffered by Real and Barca in the UEFA Champions League although Atlético Madrid did make continental success by winning an all-Spanish Europa League final against Athletic Bilbao. Although Spain were not the first national team to win three international titles in a row, they were the first to win a hat trick of European and world titles and by winning Euro 2012 they became the first to successfully defend the European title - all in all a truly remarkable feat in modern football. Criticism that the tiki-taka style perfected by Barcelona and Spain had become over elaborate and boring was blown away in the final with a mesmerising display against Italy who could not cope with the speed, accuracy of passing and penetration of the Spanish.

UEFA EUROPEAN CHAMPIONSHIP RECORD

1960 DNE **1964** 1 Winners (Hosts) 1968 QF 1972 DNQ 1976 QF **1980** 7 r1 **1984** 2 F **1988** 6 r1 1992 DNQ
1996 6 QF 2000 5 QF 2004 1o r1 **2008** 1 Winners **2012** 1 Winners

REAL FEDERACION ESPANOLA DE FUTBOL (RFEF).

Ramon y Cajal s/n,
Apartado postale 385,
28230 Las Rozas, Madrid
☎ +34 91 4959800
📠 +34 91 4959801
✉ rfef@rfef.es
🖥 www.rfef.es
FA 1913 CON 1954 FIFA 1904
P Angel Maria Villar Llona
GS Jorge Perez

THE STADIA
2014 FIFA World Cup Stadia
Vicente Calderon
Madrid 54 851
Other Main Stadia
Camp Nou
Barcelona 99 354
Santiago Bernabeu
Madrid 80 354
Sánchez Pizjuán
Seville 45 500

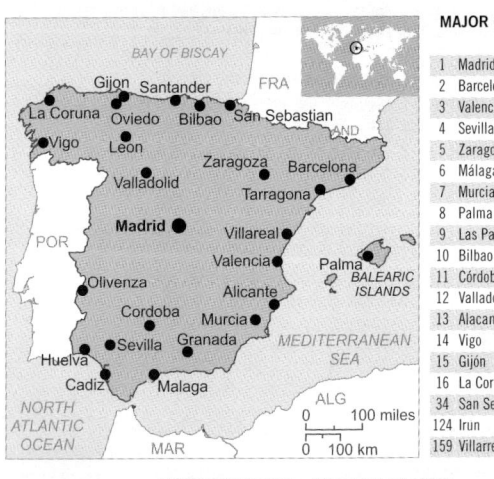

MAJOR CITIES/TOWNS

		Population
1	Madrid	3 119 376
2	Barcelona	1 641 281
3	Valencia	890 020
4	Sevilla	706 146
5	Zaragoza	658 434
6	Málaga	570 055
7	Murcia	440 303
8	Palma	384 097
9	Las Palmas	378 356
10	Bilbao	354 726
11	Córdoba	327 809
12	Valladolid	317 149
13	Alacante	305 523
14	Vigo	294 682
15	Gijon	276 260
16	La Coruña	243 838
34	San Sebastian	184 790
124	Irun	62 743
159	Villarreal	45 214

REINO DE ESPANA • KINGDOM OF SPAIN

Capital Madrid   Population 40 525 002 (32)   % in cities 77%
GDP per capita $34 600 (36)   Area km^2 505 370 km^2 (51)   GMT +/- +1
Neighbours (km) Andorra 63, France 623, Gibraltar 1, Portugal 1214, Morocco 16 • Coast 4964

RECENT INTERNATIONAL MATCHES PLAYED BY SPAIN

2010	Opponents	Score	Venue	Comp	Scorers	Att	Referee
16-06	Switzerland	L 0-1	Durban	WCr1		62 453	Webb ENG
21-06	Honduras	W 2-0	Johannesburg	WCr1	Villa 2 [17,51]	54 386	Nishimura JPN
25-06	Chile	W 2-1	Pretoria	WCr1	Villa [24], Iniesta [37]	41 958	Rodriguez MEX
29-06	Portugal	W 1-0	Cape Town	WCr2	Villa [63]	62 955	Baldassi ARG
3-07	Paraguay	W 1-0	Johannesburg	WCqf	Villa [83]	55 359	Batres GUA
7-07	Germany	W 1-0	Durban	WCsf	Puyol [73]	60 960	Kassai HUN
11-07	Netherlands	W 1-0	Johannesburg	WCf	Iniesta [116]	84 490	Webb ENG
11-08	Mexico	D 1-1	Mexico City	Fr	Silva [90]	105 000	Moreno PAN
3-09	Liechtenstein	W 4-0	Vaduz	ECq	Torres 2 [18,54], Villa [26], Silva [62]	6 100	Yildirim TUR
7-09	Argentina	L 1-4	Buenos Aires	Fr	Llorente [84]	65 600	Ruiz COL
8-10	Lithuania	W 3-1	Salamanca	ECq	Llorente 2 [47,56], Silva [79]	16 800	Rocchi ITA
12-10	Scotland	W 3-2	Glasgow	ECq	Villa [44p], Iniesta [55], Llorente [79]	51 322	Busacca SUI
17-11	Portugal	L 0-4	Lisbon	Fr		38 000	Gautier FRA
2011							
9-02	Colombia	W 1-0	Madrid	Fr	Silva [86]	70 000	Trutz SVK
25-03	Czech Republic	W 2-1	Granada	ECq	Villa 2 [69,72p]	16 301	Kassai HUN
29-03	Lithuania	W 3-1	Kaunas	ECq	Xavi [19], OG [70], Mata [83]	9 180	Duhamel FRA
4-06	USA	W 4-0	Boston	Fr	Cazorla 2 [28,41], Negredo [32], Torres [73]	64 121	Silvera URU
7-06	Venezuela	W 3-0	Puerto La Cruz	Fr	Villa [5], Pedro [20], Xabi Alonso [45]	36 000	Buckley PER
10-08	Italy	L 1-2	Bari	Fr	Xabi Alonso [37p]	50 000	Brych GER
2-09	Chile	W 3-2	St Gall	Fr	Iniesta [55], Fabregas 2 [71,90]	14 605	Laperriere SUI
6-09	Liechtenstein	W 6-0	Logrono	ECq	Negredo 2 [33,37], Xavi [51], Ramos [52], Villa 2 [59,79]	15 660	Lechner AUT
7-10	Czech Republic	W 2-0	Prague	ECq	Mata [7], Xabi Alonso [23]	18 800	Tagliavento ITA
11-10	Scotland	W 3-1	Alicante	ECq	Silva 2 [6,44], Villa [54]	27 559	Johannesson SWE
12-11	England	L 0-1	London	Fr		87 189	De Bleeckere BEL
15-11	Costa Rica	D 2-2	San Jose	Fr	Silva 2 [82,90]	30 000	Navarro CAN
2012							
29-02	Venezuela	W 5-0	Malaga	Fr	Iniesta [37], Silva [40], Soldado 3 [49,54,85]	25 000	Treimanis LVA
26-05	Serbia	W 2-0	St Gall	Fr	Adrian [63], Cazorla [74p]	15 625	Zimmermann SUI
30-05	Korea Republic	W 4-1	Berne	Fr	Torres [11], Xabi Alonso [53p], Cazorla [58], Negredo [82]	10 220	Bieri SUI
3-06	China PR	W 1-0	Seville	Fr	Silva [84]	45 000	Nijhuis NED
10-06	Italy	D 1-1	Gdansk	ECr1	Fabregas [64]	43 615	Kassai HUN
14-06	Republic of Ireland	W 4-0	Gdansk	ECr1	Torres 2 [4,70], Silva [49], Fabregas [83]	36 572	Proenca POR
18-06	Croatia	W 1-0	Gdansk	ECr1	Jesus Navas [88]	38 371	Stark GER
23-06	France	W 2-0	Donetsk	ECqf	Xabi Alonso 2 [19,91+p]	46 145	Rizzoli ITA
27-06	Portugal	D 0-0	Donetsk	ECsf	W 4-2p	51 500	Cakir TUR
1-07	Italy	W 4-0	Kyiv	ECf	Silva [14], Jordi Alba [41], Torres [84], Mata [88]	60 000	Proenca POR
15-08	Puerto Rico	W 2-1	Bayamon	Fr	Cazorla [42], Fabregas [45]	15 000	Escobar PUR
7-09	Saudi Arabia	W 5-0	Pontevedra	Fr	Cazorla [22], Pedro 2 [28,73], Xavi [47], Villa [63p]	11 850	Salmanov AZE
11-09	Georgia	W 1-0	Tbilisi	WCq	Soldado [86]	54 598	Moen NOR
12-10	Belarus	W 4-0	Minsk	WCq	Jordi Alba [12], Pedro 3 [21,69,79]	28 800	Gumienny BEL
16-10	France	D 1-1	Madrid	WCq	Sergio Ramos [25]	46 825	Brych GER
14-11	Panama	W 5-1	Panama City	Fr	Pedro 2 [16,43], Villa [30], Sergio Ramos [82], Susaeta [84]	26 000	Morales MEX

Fr = Friendly match • EC = UEFA EURO 2012 • WC = FIFA World Cup
q = qualifier • r1 = first round group • r2 = second round • qf = quarter-final • sf = semi-final • f = final

SPAIN NATIONAL TEAM HISTORICAL RECORDS

Caps
143 - Iker Casillas 2000- • 126 - Andoni Zubizarreta 1985-98 • 119 - Xavi 2000- • 106 - Xabi Alonso 2003- • 102 - Raul 1996-2006 • 101 - Fernando Torres 2003- • 99 - Carles Puyol 2000- • 98 - Sergio Ramos 2005- • 89 - Fernando Hierro 1989-2002 • 85 - David Villa 2005- • 81 - Jose Antonio Camacho 1975-88 • 77 - Andres Iniesta 2006- • 75 - Cesc Fabregas 2006- & Rafael Gordillo 1978-88 • 69 - Emilio Butragueno 1984-92 ; Carlos Marchena 2002- & David Silva 2006- • 68 - Luis Arconada 1977-85 • 66 - Michel 1985-92 • 62 - Luis Enrique 1991-2002 & Miguel Angel Nadal 1991-2002 • 60 - Victor Munoz 1981-88 & Joan Capdevilla 2002-

Goals
53 - David Villa 2005- • 44 - Raul 1996-2006 • 31 - Fernando Torres 2003- • 29 - Fernando Hierro 1989-2002 • 27 - Fernando Morientes 1998-2007 • 26 - Emilio Butragueno 1984-92 • 23 - Alfredo di Stefano 1957-61 & Julio Salinas 1986-96 • 21 - Michel 1985-92 • 20 - Telmo Zarra 1945-71 • 18 - David Silva 2006- • 17 - Isidro Langara 1932-36 • 16 - Pirri 1966-78 & Luis Regueiro 1927-36

Coaches
For a list of Spain coaches pre 1962 see Oliver's Almanack 2012 • Jose Villalonga 1962-66 • Domingo Balmanya 1966-68 • Luis Molowny 1969 • Ladislao Kubala 1969-80 • Jose Santamaria 1980-82 • Luis Suarez 1988-91 • Vicente Miera 1991-92 • Javier Clemente 1992-98 • Jose Antonio Camacho 1998-2002 • Inaki Saez 2002-04 • Luis Aragones 2004-08 • Vicente del Bosque 2008-

SPAIN 2011-12

LIGA BBVA PRIMERA DIVISION

	Pl	W	D	L	F	A	Pts	Real Madrid	Barcelona	Valencia	Málaga	At. Madrid	Levante	Osasuna	Mallorca	Sevilla	Ath. Bilbao	Getafe	Sociedad	Real Betis	Espanyol	Vallecano	Zaragoza	Granada	Villarreal	Sp. Gijón	Racing
Real Madrid †	38	32	4	2	121	32	**100**		1-3	0-0	1-1	4-1	4-2	7-1	4-1	3-0	4-1	4-2	5-1	4-1	5-0	6-2	3-1	5-1	3-0	3-1	4-0
Barcelona †	38	28	7	3	114	29	91	1-2		5-1	4-1	5-0	5-0	8-0	5-0	0-0	2-0	4-0	2-1	4-2	4-0	4-0	4-0	4-0	5-3	5-0	3-1	3-0
Valencia †	38	17	10	11	59	44	**61**	2-3	2-2		2-0	1-0	1-1	4-0	2-2	1-2	1-1	3-1	0-1	4-2	0-1	2-1	4-1	1-2	1-0	1-0	4-0	4-3
Málaga †	38	17	7	14	54	53	**58**	0-4	1-4	1-0		0-0	1-0	1-1	3-1	2-1	1-0	3-2	1-1	0-2	2-1	4-2	5-1	4-0	2-1	1-0	3-0	4-0
Atlético Madrid ‡	38	15	11	12	53	46	**56**	1-4	1-2	0-0	2-1		3-2	0-0	1-1	0-0	2-1	3-0	1-1	0-2	3-1	3-1	3-1	2-0	3-0	4-0	4-0	
Levante ‡	38	16	7	15	54	50	**55**	1-0	1-2	0-2	3-0	2-0		0-2	0-0	1-0	3-0	1-2	3-2	3-1	3-1	3-5	0-0	3-1	1-0	4-0	1-1	
Osasuna	38	13	15	10	44	61	**54**	1-5	3-2	1-1	1-1	0-1	2-0		2-2	0-0	2-1	0-0	1-0	2-1	2-2	0-0	3-0	2-1	2-1	2-1	0-2	
RCD Mallorca	38	14	10	14	42	46	**52**	1-2	0-2	1-1	0-1	2-1	1-0	1-1		0-0	1-1	1-2	2-1	1-0	1-0	1-0	1-0	0-0	4-0	1-2	2-1	
Sevilla	38	13	11	14	48	47	**50**	2-6	0-2	1-0	2-1	1-1	1-1	2-0	3-1		1-2	3-0	1-0	1-2	0-0	5-2	3-0	1-2	1-2	2-1	2-2	
Athletic Bilbao ‡	38	12	13	13	49	52	**49**	0-3	2-2	0-3	3-0	3-0	3-0	3-1	1-0	1-0		0-0	2-0	2-3	3-3	1-1	2-1	0-1	1-1	1-1	1-1	
Getafe	38	12	11	15	50	51	**47**	0-1	1-0	3-1	1-3	3-2	1-1	2-2	1-3	5-1	0-0		1-0	1-0	1-1	0-1	0-2	1-0	0-0	2-1	1-1	
Real Sociedad	38	12	11	15	46	52	**47**	0-1	2-2	1-0	3-2	0-4	1-3	0-0	1-0	2-0	1-2	0-0		1-1	0-0	4-0	0-3	1-0	1-1	5-1	3-0	
Real Betis	38	13	8	17	47	56	**47**	2-3	2-2	2-1	0-0	2-2	0-1	1-0	1-0	1-1	2-1	1-1	2-3		1-1	0-2	4-3	1-2	3-1	2-0	1-1	
RCD Espanyol	38	12	10	16	46	56	**46**	0-4	1-1	4-0	1-2	4-2	1-2	1-2	1-0	1-1	2-1	1-0	2-2	1-0		5-1	0-2	3-0	0-0	0-0	3-3	1
Rayo Vallecano	38	13	4	21	53	73	**43**	0-1	0-7	1-2	2-0	0-1	1-2	6-0	0-1	2-1	2-3	2-0	4-0	3-0	0-1		0-0	1-0	0-2	1-3	4-2	
Real Zaragoza	38	12	7	19	36	61	**43**	0-6	1-4	0-1	0-0	1-0	1-0	1-1	0-1	0-1	2-1	1-0	2-0	0-2	2-1	1-2		1-0	2-1	2-2	2-1	
Granada	38	12	6	20	35	56	**42**	1-2	0-1	0-1	0-2	1-0	2-1	1-1	2-2	0-3	2-2	1-0	4-1	0-1	2-1	1-2	1-0		1-0	2-1	0-0	
Villarreal	38	9	14	15	39	53	**41**	1-1	0-0	2-2	2-1	0-0	1-0	3-1	1-2	0-0	2-2	2-2	1-2	1-1	1-0	0-0	2-0	2-2	3-1		3-0	1-1
Sporting Gijón	38	10	7	21	42	69	**37**	0-3	0-1	0-1	2-1	1-1	3-2	1-1	2-3	1-0	1-1	2-1	1-2	2-1	1-2	2-1	1-2	2-0	2-3		0-0	
Racing Santander	38	4	15	19	28	63	**27**	0-0	0-0	2-2	1-3	0-0	0-0	2-4	0-3	0-3	1-1	0-2	1-0	0-1	0-0	1-0	1-1	0-1	0-0	1-1	

27/08/2011 - 13/05/2012 • † Qualified for the UEFA Champions League • ‡ Qualified for the Europa League • Attendance: 10,793,170. Av: 28,478
Top scorers: **50** - Lionel **MESSI** ARG, Barcelona • **46** - **CRISTIANO RONALDO** POR, Real Madrid • **24** - Radamel **FALCAO** COL, At. Madrid •
22 - Gonzalo **HIGUAIN** ARG, Real Madrid • **21** - Karim **BENZEMA** FRA, Real Madrid • **17** - Roberto **SOLDADO**, Valencia • **16** - Fernando **LLORENTE**,
Ath. Bilbao & **RUBEN CASTRO**, Betis • **15** - Arouna **KONE** CIV, Levante & **MICHU**, Vallecano • **14** - Alvaro **NEGREDO**, Sevilla • **12** - **MIKU** VEN, Getafe
& Carlos **VELA** MEX, Sociedad

SPAIN 2011-12

SEGUNDA DIVISION A (2)

	Pl	W	D	L	F	A	Pts	Deportivo	Celta Vigo	Valladolid	Alcorcón	Hércules	Córdoba	Almería	Barcelona B	Las Palmas	Numancia	Elche	Villarreal B	Huesca	Xerez	Girona	Guadalajara	Recreativo	Murcia	Sabadell	Cartagena	Alcoyano	Gimnàstic
Deportivo La Coruña	42	29	4	9	76	45	**91**		2-1	1-1	2-1	0-1	2-0	3-1	2-1	3-1	3-1	4-3	1-0	2-2	1-2	1-3	2-4	0-1	0-3	1-2	1-2	1-3	0-2	2-2
Celta Vigo	42	26	7	9	83	37	**85**	2-3		1-1	3-0	0-1	0-0	4-3	4-1	1-2	5-0	1-0	2-2	0-4	0-4	1-2	0-2	0-4	1-1	0-4	1-1	0-4	0-1	0-2
Real Valladolid ‡	42	23	13	6	69	37	**82**	0-0	1-2		1-1	1-1	1-2	0-1	1-1	0-2	1-2	1-2	1-2	1-3	0-2	1-1	0-1	3-1	0-1	3-2	0-2	1-2	0-4	0-2
Alcorcón ‡	42	21	10	11	58	42	**73**	4-0	0-0	2-2		1-0	2-0	1-2	2-3	1-2	2-3	1-1	1-2	0-0	1-1	0-1	0-2	1-3	0-1	0-1	0-2	1-0	1-1	
Hércules ‡	42	22	6	14	62	43	**72**	1-4	1-0	2-2	1-0		0-0	0-2	1-2	1-1	3-1	2-0	2-2	0-2	2-4	2-5	0-0	1-0	1-1	0-2	0-1	1-1		
Córdoba ‡	42	20	11	11	52	43	**71**	0-2	0-2	0-3	1-3	1-1		1-1	1-1	0-1	0-2	1-3	1-2	1-1	0-3	2-0	0-2	1-0	0-2	0-3	0-4	2		
Almería	42	18	16	8	63	43	**70**	2-0	1-0	1-2	0-1	1-2	1-1		1-2	1-2	0-0	2-0	0-2	1-1	1-2	2-4	0-2	2-4	2-3	0-0	0-1	0-3	1	
Barcelona B	42	16	11	15	63	53	**59**	2-3	2-1	1-1	2-3	0-2	0-1	2-0	3-3		2-0	1-0	1-0	2-4	2-2	0-2	2-1	2-2	2-1	0-0	1-4	0-2	1-1	0
Las Palmas	42	16	10	16	58	59	**58**	0-1	3-1	1-0	2-0	0-0	1-2	2-3	1		1-1	1-3	1-1	3-0	0-3	2-3	2-0	0-1	1-3	2-1	2-1	0-1		
Numancia	42	15	12	15	54	52	**57**	0-3	0-2	1-4	0-1	2-1	5-0	1-0	3-0	3-2		3-0	0-1	1-2	1-0	4-1	0-2	1-0	0-2	1-0	0-2	0-0		
Elche	42	17	6	19	56	58	**57**	3-2	0-2	1-2	6-0	0-3	0-0	1-1	3-3	0-1	2-2		3-0	1-2	1-0	1-3	0-2	3-0	3-1	0-1	1-2	1-1	2-1	0
Villarreal B	42	14	10	18	54	64	**52**	0-1	2-3	0-1	0-3	0-1	1-1	2-1	0-0	1-4	0-2	0-2		4-2	3-1	2-3	3-2	0-2	0-3	4-0	0-4	3-3	2	
Huesca	42	14	9	19	49	63	**51**	0-2	1-1	2-0	3-1	2-0	1-1	0-0	1-0	2-0	2-1	0-1	1-1	0		2-1	2-1	2-0	0-2	2-0	0-1	0-3	3-0	0
Xerez	42	13	11	18	50	66	**50**	3-2	3-3	0-4	2-2	1-1	2-0	1-0	6-2	0-1	1-0	2-0	1-0	1-0		2-1	0-2	1-3	1-3	2-1	2-3	0-1	0-0	
Girona	42	12	13	17	58	61	**49**	1-0	0-1	1-1	0-0	1-0	3-1	0-1	1-1	4-2	2-0	1-4	2-1	1-1	5-3		0-0	0-0	1-1	1-0	2-5	1-3	2-2	
Guadalajara	42	14	7	21	50	75	**49**	1-2	0-3	0-3	1-2	1-2	3-1	0-1	2-1	1-1	0-2	4-0	2-2	1-1	2-1	4		0-2	2-1	1-0	2-0	1-1	0	
Recreativo Huelva	42	12	11	19	49	52	**47**	0-1	1-2	1-1	2-1	1-0	0-1	0-0	4-2	1-1	1-0	3-1	1-1	1-1	2-3	0-4	2		0-2	1-1	1-2	3-2		
Real Murcia	42	13	8	21	49	67	**47**	0-0	1-3	2-0	0-0	2-2	6-2	1-0	2-0	2-1	2-2	1-0	2-3	1-0	1-0	1-0	1-0	0-1		2-2	0-3	1-0	2-1	3-2	2-2
Sabadell	42	11	13	18	45	64	**46**	1-0	1-2	1-4	1-0	1-0	3-2	1-0	0-1	1-1	3-0	0-3	1-2	1-2	0-2	3-2	2-1	0-2	2		3-2	2-1	1-0	
Cartagena	42	9	13	20	37	58	**40**	2-1	1-1	0-0	0-2	0-3	0-1	1-0	4-0	0-2	1-1	1-6	2-2	0-0	0-1	1-0	2-3	1-1	2-1	0		1-2	1-3	
Alcoyano	42	9	10	23	46	78	**37**	2-0	0-3	0-1	0-0	5-3	3-2	2-1	4-2	0-1	1-4	0-1	1-0	3-0	1-2	1-0	1-2	1-3	2-1	2-2		0-0		
Gimnàstic Tarragona	42	6	13	23	37	58	**31**	1-2	1-2	0-3	0-2	0-0	1-0	0-1	2-1	1-1	3-1	1-1	0-0	1-1	3-0	1-1	0-1	0-0	1-0	1-2	0-2	5-0	0-0	2-0

26/08/2011 - 3/06/2012 • ‡ Qualified for the play-offs • Villarreal B relegated due to the relegation of Villarreal from the Primera Division
Top scorers: **28** - Leonardo **ULLOA** ARG, Almeria • **23** - Iago **ASPAS**, Celta • **18** - Ferran **COROMINAS**, Girona • Att: 3,221,744. Av: 6989 (-18.4%)
Play-off semi-finals: Cordoba 0-0 0-3 **Real Valladolid**; Hércules 1-1 0-0 **Alcorcón** • Play-off final: Alcorcón 0-1 1-1 **Real Valladolid**. Valladolid
promoted. 1st leg. Santo Domingo, Alcorcón, 13-06-2012, Att: 4700, Ref: Munuera. Scorer - Javi Guerra [29]. 2nd leg. Nuevo Jose Zorrilla, Valladolid,
16-06-2012, Att: 26 500, Ref: Hernandez. Scorers - Javi Guerra [52] for Valladolid; Fernando Sales [44] for Alcorcón

SPAIN 2011-12

SEGUNDA DIVISION B (3) GROUP 1

	Pl	W	D	L	F	A	Pts
Real Madrid Castilla †	38	23	9	6	77	36	78
Tenerife ‡	38	18	10	10	51	32	64
Lugo ‡	38	16	16	6	55	41	64
Albacete ‡	38	18	9	11	56	37	63
Atlético Madrid B	38	15	15	8	58	38	60
Real Oviedo	38	18	6	14	50	43	60
Rayo Vallecano B	38	16	8	14	53	49	56
Getafe B	38	14	11	13	60	63	53
La Roda	38	13	10	15	44	45	49
Sporting de Gijón B	38	11	15	12	42	45	48
Coruxo	38	11	13	14	37	48	46
Leganés	38	10	15	13	50	50	45
Marino Luanco	38	11	12	15	40	53	45
SS Reyes	38	11	11	16	36	47	44
Alcalá	38	9	17	12	40	47	44
Conquese ‡	38	9	17	12	44	41	44
Toledo	38	10	12	16	37	42	42
Montañeros	38	10	10	18	44	63	40
Vecindario	38	10	9	19	37	66	39
Celta Vigo B	38	9	11	18	42	67	38

20/08/2011 - 13/05/2012 • † Championship playoff • ‡ Play-offs

SEGUNDA DIVISION B (3) GROUP 2

	Pl	W	D	L	F	A	Pts
Mirandés †	38	23	13	2	55	22	82
Ponferradina ‡	38	22	8	8	65	34	74
Eibar ‡	38	17	15	6	46	35	66
Amorebieta ‡	38	16	14	8	50	35	62
Logroñés	38	17	9	12	52	38	60
Deportivo Alavés	38	14	17	7	64	39	59
Guijuelo	38	16	10	12	45	44	58
Bilbao Athletic	38	14	13	11	47	39	55
Salamanca	38	14	10	14	50	48	52
Sestao River	38	14	9	15	52	52	51
Zamora	38	12	13	13	41	37	49
Real Sociedad B	38	13	9	16	50	52	48
Osasuna B	38	13	9	16	49	56	48
Real Unión Irún	38	12	12	14	43	48	48
Gimnástica Torrelavega	38	12	10	16	39	50	46
Palencia ‡	38	12	10	16	32	46	46
Arandina	38	9	12	17	38	52	39
Gimnastica Segoviana	38	7	9	22	40	70	30
Lemona	38	6	11	21	26	60	29
Burgos	38	7	7	24	29	63	28

20/08/2011 - 13/05/2012 • † Championship playoff • ‡ Play-offs • Palencia relegated after winning play-off

SPAIN 2011-12

SEGUNDA DIVISION B (3) GROUP 3

	Pl	W	D	L	F	A	Pts	At Baleares	Orihuela	Huracán	Badalona	Llagostera	L'Hospitalet	Lleida	Reus	Olímpic	Sant Andreu	Teruel	Mallorca B	V'cia Mestalla	Ontinyent	Dénia	Zaragoza B	Andorra	Gandía	Manacor	Mahonés
Atlético Baleares †	38	21	9	8	65	39	72		2-1	1-2	3-2	2-0	2-2	0-1	1-0	1-0	0-0	3-0	3-1	3-2	3-0	3-0	3-4	1-1	3-1	3-2	3-0
Orihuela - R ‡	38	18	14	6	50	33	68	1-1		4-1	0-0	0-0	1-2	0-0	1-1	0-3	2-1	1-0	0-0	3-0	0-0	1-0	1-0	2-2	1-0	4-3	4-0
Huracán Valencia ‡	38	18	12	8	48	30	66	1-0	0-1		0-0	0-0	3-1	0-2	2-1	1-0	1-0	2-0	1-2	3-0	1-1	1-1	1-1	3-0	1-1	0-2	2-0
Badalona ‡	38	18	11	9	48	26	65	0-0	1-2	1-1		0-1	2-0	0-0	1-0	1-2	1-1	2-2	1-0	2-3	0-0	1-0	2-1	3-0	1-0	2-0	2-0
Llagostera	38	18	10	10	44	28	64	1-2	1-3	1-1	0-0		0-0	3-1	2-2	0-2	0-0	2-0	4-2	4-2	1-3	1-0	1-0	2-0	3-0	3-0	2-0
L'Hospitalet	38	17	11	10	46	34	62	2-2	1-1	1-0	0-1	1-0		0-0	1-0	1-1	3-2	1-1	1-1	1-1	2-0	1-0	1-0	3-2	2-0	2-0	2-0
Lleida Esportiu	38	16	11	11	50	40	59	0-0	1-2	1-1	1-3	0-0	1-4		1-3	3-0	1-1	2-0	1-0	1-0	2-0	3-2	4-0	0-0	1-1	3-0	2-0
Reus Deportiu	38	15	12	11	43	37	57	1-0	1-1	1-3	2-1	0-1	1-0	0-0		1-0	2-1	1-1	3-1	2-1	1-0	1-0	2-3	2-4	0-0	1-0	2-0
Olímpic Xàtiva	38	15	12	11	41	28	57	3-0	2-1	0-0	2-1	1-0	0-2	1-0	0-0		0-0	1-1	1-0	3-0	0-3	0-2	2-0	3-0	1-1	1-1	2-0
Sant Andreu	38	14	11	13	47	44	53	2-1	0-0	2-5	1-1	0-1	2-1	3-1	2-1	2-1		1-0	1-0	2-4	1-1	1-0	1-0	1-1	1-1	3-2	6-0
Teruel	38	12	16	10	45	43	52	1-2	1-1	1-0	1-0	0-0	1-0	2-1	0-3	0-0	2-1		5-1	1-1	4-0	0-0	1-1	2-1	2-1	2-1	2-0
Mallorca B	38	14	9	15	49	47	51	1-2	1-1	0-1	0-1	2-0	3-1	2-1	0-0	0-1	1-1	1-2		4-3	0-0	1-0	0-0	1-4	0-1	0-4	2-0
Valencia Mestalla	38	13	11	14	52	54	50	3-1	0-1	1-2	1-0	0-2	1-1	3-3	2-2	0-3	3-0	3-2	1-1		3-1	0-0	1-1	0-0	2-0	2-0	3-0
Ontinyent	38	13	10	15	39	44	49	2-3	2-0	0-1	0-1	0-2	1-0	3-0	1-1	0-0	1-0	1-0	2-0	1-2		2-0	2-2	2-1	0-2	3-0	2-0
Dénia	38	13	8	17	39	38	47	0-0	3-0	1-1	0-2	2-0	1-0	0-1	3-1	1-0	1-2	2-2	4-0	1-0	1-1		3-0	0-1	3-2	2-1	4-1
Real Zaragoza B ‡	38	11	11	16	46	60	44	1-5	1-2	0-0	1-3	0-0	1-1	2-3	0-0	2-1	0-1	0-0	1-4	2-3	4-0	1-1		1-0	0-2	1-0	2-1
Andorra	38	11	7	20	40	55	40	1-2	1-2	0-1	0-1	0-1	1-0	2-3	3-2	0-0	1-2	1-1	1-3	0-1	1-0	2-0	1-2		1-1	1-2	3-1
Gandía	38	8	13	17	34	49	37	0-0	0-0	0-3	1-2	1-0	1-0	0-3	0-1	2-1	1-0	2-2	0-2	0-0	0-0	0-0	1-4	6-1		2-1	4-1	2-1
Manacor	38	6	6	26	39	74	24	0-2	1-2	1-2	0-3	0-1	1-2	1-2	0-0	1-1	1-3	2-2	1-1	3-0	1-5	2-0	3-1	1-3	0-2			1-1
Sporting Mahonés	38	5	4	29	13	75	16	0-2	0-3	1-0	0-4	0-3	0-2	1-0	0-1	2-1	1-0	1-1	0-2	1-0	1-2	0-2	0-2	0-2	0-0	0-2	

20/08/2011 - 13/05/2012 • † Championship playoff • ‡ Play-offs • Orihuela & Dénia relegated

SPAIN 2011-12

SEGUNDA DIVISION B (3) GROUP 4

	Pl	W	D	L	F	A	Pts	Cádiz	Linense	Lucena	Real Jaén	Melilla	San Roque	Cacereño	Real Betis B	Villanovense	Sevilla At	Puertollano	Badajoz	Almería B	Ceuta	Ecija	Lorca At	Roquetas	La Unión	Villanueva	Ejido
Cádiz †	38	21	13	4	62	23	76		1-1	4-0	0-0	2-0	1-1	3-1	2-1	3-1	0-0	1-1	3-0	6-1	0-0	2-0	4-1	2-1	0-0	1-0	3-0
Linense ‡	38	21	9	8	57	33	72	0-2		2-0	2-0	0-1	1-0	0-0	1-0	0-3	5-1	3-1	1-0	4-2	1-0	1-0	1-1	2-0	1-1	2-1	2-0
Lucena ‡	38	21	9	8	53	30	72	3-0	0-0		1-0	1-0	2-0	0-1	5-1	1-0	1-0	3-3	4-0	1-2	2-1	2-0	2-1	1-0	1-2	1-1	2-0
Real Jaén ‡	38	19	13	6	48	31	70	1-1	1-1	1-0		0-2	1-0	0-0	0-3	0-0	4-1	2-0	1-2	3-2	2-2	3-0	2-0	3-1	2-1	1-0	2-0
Melilla	38	18	10	10	50	33	64	2-2	1-2	0-1	1-2		2-1	0-0	0-0	1-2	1-1	1-0	1-1	3-3	3-1	1-0	2-2	2-0	3-1	1-1	2-0
San Roque	38	18	7	13	43	35	61	1-0	4-0	1-0	2-0	0-1		2-1	1-2	1-1	2-0	0-2	0-1	2-1	2-1	0-0	3-2	1-0	2-1	0-0	2-0
Cacereño	38	15	16	7	48	33	61	0-0	0-0	1-1	0-0	2-0	0-0		4-0	1-1	1-1	2-2	2-1	2-1	1-1	3-3	0-0	0-3	1-1	0-3	1-0	3-2
Real Betis B	38	18	5	15	58	59	59	1-2	1-0	0-0	1-1	0-1	1-0	1-1		3-1	2-0	1-0	3-1	2-3	3-3	1-4	1-2	1-2	2-1	1-0	2-0
Villanovense	38	17	7	14	53	52	58	0-1	1-4	2-4	0-1	1-4	1-0	1-2	2-1		2-1	1-2	5-2	2-0	1-0	0-0	1-0	0-0	0-2	3-1	3-0
Sevilla Atlético	38	15	10	13	56	45	55	1-0	0-4	1-1	1-1	1-0	5-2	2-0	1-1	2-2		5-0	2-0	0-1	3-2	2-1	1-0	7-2	2-0	2-1	2-0
Puertollano	38	13	12	13	46	49	51	0-1	1-1	1-2	1-1	0-0	2-0	1-0	0-2	5-1	2-1		3-2	1-1	2-1	4-0	2-0	0-1	0-0	1-0	2-0
Badajoz	38	14	8	16	60	58	50	0-0	1-2	1-2	1-3	1-1	1-2	1-1	1-1	3-1	2-1	4-0		1-2	3-4	3-2	0-0	4-0	2-1	3-0	3-1
Almería B	38	13	11	14	50	60	50	0-4	2-4	2-0	0-1	0-1	3-2	2-1	3-2	2-2	1-1	2-1	2-2		1-1	0-0	3-2	1-1	3-0	0-1	0-0
Ceuta	38	13	10	15	47	49	49	0-2	2-1	0-0	1-1	0-1	1-0	1-2	2-3	1-2	0-1	2-1	2-0	1-5	2-0		0-0	1-1	1-0	1-0	3-1	1-1
Ecija	38	11	13	14	33	36	46	0-0	1-0	1-1	0-1	0-1	0-1	0-2	2-3	1-0	1-1	3-0	2-2	0-0	1-0		1-0	0-0	1-0	1-0	5-1
Lorca Atlético ‡	38	10	12	16	39	52	42	1-4	0-3	1-1	1-2	1-0	0-0	1-0	2-3	0-3	1-0	0-2	3-1	1-0	1-1	1-1		1-1	2-0	1-0	4-1
Roquetas	38	11	8	19	34	55	41	1-2	0-3	0-1	4-4	1-1	0-3	2-2	2-1	1-2	1-0	0-3	0-2	0-1	1-2	0-0	1-0		1-0	1-1	2-0
La Unión	38	10	8	20	33	49	38	3-1	2-1	0-3	0-1	1-2	0-1	0-0	2-3	0-1	3-2	0-0	1-0	2-4	0-2	2-1	0-1	1-0		1-1	2-0
Sporting Villanueva	38	2	11	25	16	42	14	0-0	0-1	0-1	0-1	0-0	1-1	1-3	3-0	0-1	0-1	1-1	1-0	0-0	0-1	0-0	0-0	0-1		0-1	
Polideportivo Ejido	38	2	4	32	13	75	7	0-2	0-1	0-2	0-0	0-2	1-1	0-2	0-2	4-1	0-3	0-2	0-2	0-2	0-2	0-2	0-1	0-2	1-2	

20/08/2011 - 13/05/2012 • † Championship playoff • ‡ Play-offs • Puertollano, Badajoz & Cueta relegated

SEGUNDA DIVISION B (3) CHAMPIONSHIP PLAY-OFFS

Semi-finals: **Mirandés** 1-0 2-1 Atlético Baleares • Cádiz 0-3 1-5 **Real Madrid Castilla**

Final: **Real Madrid Castilla** 3-0 3-0 Mirandés • Mirandés and Castilla promoted • Cádiz and At. Baleares join regular play-offs in the second round

SEGUNDA DIVISION B (3) PLAY-OFFS

FIRST ROUND: Albacete 1-1 1-0 Origuela • Badalona 1-1 1-3 **Tenerife** • Amorebieta 1-1 1-2 **Linense** • Real Jaén 2-1 0-2 **Ponferradina** • Huracán Valencia 0-0 0-0 2-4p **Lucena** • **Lugo** 1-0 0-0 Eibar **SECOND ROUND:** Albacete 0-0 0-0 3-4p **Cádiz** • **Lugo** 3-1 0-0 Atlético Baleares • Lucena 2-1 0-3 **Ponferradina** • Linense 0-1 2-3 **Tenerife** • **THIRD ROUND:** Lugo 3-1 1-3 3-2p Cádiz • **Ponferradina** 1-0 2-1 Tenerife • Lugo & Ponferradina promoted • Relegation play-offs: **Real Zaragoza B** 1-0 3-0 Conquense • **Palencia** 2-0 1-1 Lorca Atlético • Conquense & Lorca Atlético relegated

MEDALS TABLE

		Overall G S B	League G S B	Cup G S	Europe G S B	City
1	Real Madrid	61 44 19	**32** 20 7	18 19	11 5 12	Madrid
2	Barcelona	58 38 23	21 23 12	**26** 9	11 6 11	Barcelona
3	Athletic Bilbao	31 22 10	8 7 10	23 13	2	Bilbao
4	Atlético Madrid	21 20 19	9 8 12	9 9	3 3 7	Madrid
5	Valencia	17 18 11	6 6 10	7 9	4 3 1	Valencia
6	Real Zaragoza	8 7 6	1 4	6 5	2 1 2	Zaragoza
7	Sevilla	8 6 4	1 4 4	5 2	2	Sevilla
8	RCD Espanyol	4 7 4	4	4 5	2	Barcelona
9	Real Sociedad	4 7 3	2 3 2	2 4	1	San Sebastián
10	Deportivo La Coruña	3 5 6	1 5 4	2	2	La Coruña
11	Real Betis Balompié	3 2 2	1 2	2 2		Sevilla
12	Real Union Irún	3 1		3 1		Irún
13	RCD Mallorca	1 3 2	2	1 2	1	Palma
14	Arenas Guecho Bilbao	1 3 1	1	1 3		Bilbao
15	Racing Irún	1		1		Irún
16	Sporting Gijón	3 1	1 1	2		Gijón
17	Celta Vigo	3		3		Vigo
18	Las Palmas	2 1	1 1	1		Las Palmas
19	Español Madrid	2		2		Madrid
	Getafe	2		2		Madrid
	Real Valladolid	2		2		Valladolid
22	Villarreal	1 4	1 1		3	Villarreal
23	Racing Santander	1 1	1 1			Santander
24	Deportivo Alavés	1			1	Vitoria
	Basconia	1		1		Basauri
	Castellon	1		1		Castellon
	Castilla	1		1		Madrid
	Elche	1		1		Elche
	España Barcelona	1		1		Barcelona
	Europa	1		1		Barcelona
	Gimnastica Madrid	1		1		Madrid
	Granada	1		1		Granada
	Osasuna	1		1		Pamplona
	Racing Ferrol	1		1		Ferrol
	Recreativo Huelva	1		1		Huelva
	Sabadell	1		1		Sabadell
	Real Vigo Sporting	1		1		Vigo
38	Real Oviedo	3	3			Oviedo
39	Tenerife	1			1	Tenerife

COPA DEL REY 2011-12

Third Elimination Round			Round of 32			Round of 16		
			Barcelona	1	9			
Llagostera *		0	L'Hospitalet *	0	0			
L'Hospitalet		1				**Barcelona** *	4	2
Almería *		1				Osasuna	0	1
Elche		0	Almería *	1	1			
			Osasuna	3	1			
			Málaga	1	2			
			Getafe *	0	2			
						Málaga	2	0
Ponferradina		1				**Real Madrid** *	3	1
Eibar *		0	Ponferradina *	0	1			
			Real Madrid	2	5			
			Levante	1	4			
Alcoyano		1	Deportivo La Coruña *	3	1			
Deportivo La Coruña *		2				**Levante**	1	4
						Alcorcón *	2	0
			Real Zaragoza	1	0			
Numancia		1	**Alcorcón** *	1	2			
Alcorcón *		2						
			Sevilla	1	2			
Andorra *		1	San Roque *	0	1			
San Roque		3				Sevilla	0	2
Cadiz		3				**Valencia** *	1	1
Orihuela *		1	Cádiz *	0	0			
			Valencia	0	4			
Mirandés *		3						
Logroñés		1	**Mirandés** *	1	2			
			Villarreal	1	0			
						Mirandés *	2	1
						Racing Santander	0	1
			Rayo Vallecano	2	4			
			Racing Santander *	3	3			
Córdoba *		1 3p						
Huesca		1 2p	**Córdoba** *	1	1			
			Real Betis	0	2			
						Córdoba *	2	2
Celta Vigo *		4				**RCD Espanyol**	1	4
Real Valladolid		1	Celta Vigo *	0	2			
			RCD Espanyol	0	4			
			RCD Mallorca *	0	2			
			Sporting Gijón	1	0			
						RCD Mallorca	0	6
						Real Sociedad *	2	1
			Granada	1	2			
			Real Sociedad *	4	1			
Albacete *		1						
Alavés		0	**Albacete** *	2	1			
			Atlético Madrid	1	0			
						Albacete *	0	0
						Athletic Bilbao	0	4
			Real Oviedo *	0	0			
			Athletic Bilbao	1	1			

* Home team/home team in the first leg

COPA DEL REY 2011-12

Quarter-finals	Semi-finals	Final

Barcelona	2	2
Real Madrid *	1	2

Barcelona	1	2
Valencia *	1	0

Levante	1	0
Valencia *	4	3

Barcelona	3
Athletic Bilbao ‡	0

Mirandés	2	2
RCD Espanyol *	3	1

Mirandés *	1	2
Athletic Bilbao	2	6

RCD Mallorca	0	0
Athletic Bilbao *	2	1

COPA DEL REY FINAL 2012
Vicente Calderón, Madrid, 25-05-2012, Att: 54 850, Ref: David Borbalan

Barcelona	3	Pedro 2 [3] [25], Messi [20]
Athletic Bilbao	0	

BARCELONA

Jose **PINTO** - Martin **MONTOYA**, Gerard **PIQUE**, Javier **MASCHERANO**, **ADRIANO** - Sergio **BUSQUETS** - **PEDRO** Rodriguez (**THIAGO** Alcantara 87), **XAVI** Hernandez (c)• (Cesc **FABREGAS** 81), Andres **INIESTA**•, **ALEXIS SANCHEZ** (Seydou **KEITA** 72) - Lionel **MESSI**. Tr: Josep **GUARDIOLA**

ATHLETIC

Gorka **IRAIZOZ** - Andoni **IRAOLA** (c)•, Borja **EKIZA**, Fernando **AMOREBIETA**, Jon **AURTENETXE** - **JAVI MARTINEZ**, Oscar **DE MARCOS** (**INIGO PEREZ** 47) - **IBAI GOMEZ**, Markel **SUSAETA**• (**ANDER HERRERA** 46) - Iker **MUNIAIN** - Fernando **LLORENTE** (Gaizka **TOQUERO** 73). Tr: Marcelo **BIELSA**

‡ Qualified for the Europa League

ATHLETIC BILBAO
2011-12

	Date	Opponent	Res	Comp	PD	Scorers	Att
Aug	18	Trabzonspor	D	0-0	ELpo		26 000
	25	Trabzonspor	-	-	ELpo	Trabzonspor withdrew	-
	28	Vallecano	D	1-1	PD	8	Iturraspe[56]	35 000
	11	Espanyol	L	1-2	PD	14	Llorente[62]	21 154
	15	Slovan	W	2-1	ELgF		Susaeta[13], Muniain[40]	6 328
Sep	18	Betis	L	2-3	PD	16	De Marcos[38], Lopez[86p]	40 000
	21	Malaga	L	0-1	PD	18		20 976
	24	Villarreal	D	1-1	PD	19	Gabilondo[44]	37 000
	29	PSG	W	2-0	ELgF		Gabilondo[20], Susaeta[45]	23 487
	2	Sociedad	W	2-1	PD	16	Llorente 2[34 70]	29 000
Oct	17	Osasuna	W	3-1	PD	11	Muniain[30], Gabilondo[38], Javi Martinez[45]	33 000
	20	RB Salzburg	D	2-2	ELgF		Llorente 2[69p 75p]	22 566
	23	Valencia	D	1-1	PD	11	Muniain[72]	27 532
	27	At. Madrid	W	3-0	PD	8	Llorente 2[67 71], Toquero[75]	28 000
	30	Sp. Gijon	W	1-0	PD	9	Susaeta[63]	21 000
	3	RB Salzburg	W	1-0	ELgF		Herrera[37]	10 350
Nov	6	Barcelona	D	2-2	PD	9	Herrera[20], OG[80]	35 000
	20	Sevilla	W	2-1	PD	7	Iraola[5], De Marcos[71]	28 000
	27	Granada	L	0-1	PD	8		30 000
	1	Slovan	W	2-1	ELgF		De Marcos[15]	28 314
	4	Mallorca	D	1-1	PD	9	Amorebieta[45]	12 863
	8	Oviedo	W	1-0	CRr4		De Marcos[11]	15 000
Dec	11	Racing	D	1-1	PD	9	Aurtenetxe[80]	34 000
	14	PSG	L	2-4	ELgF		Aurtenetxe[3], Lopez[55]	37 114
	17	Zaragoza	W	2-1	PD	9	Susaeta[7], Toquero[87]	28 000
	21	Oviedo	W	1-0	CRr4		Herrera[74]	18 000
	3	Albacete	D	0-0	CRr5			12 000
	8	Getafe	D	0-0	PD	9		11 000
	12	Albacete	W	4-0	CRr5		Susaeta[24], Herrera[65], Toquero[78], San Jose[86]	33 000
Jan	15	Levante	W	3-0	PD	5	Amorebieta[11], Llorente[41], San Jose[90]	34 000
	18	Mallorca	W	2-0	CRqf		Llorente[35], Muniain[59]	38 000
	22	Real Madrid	L	1-4	PD	7	Llorente[13]	75 000
	25	Mallorca	L	0-1	CRqf		OG[76]	10 990
	28	Vallecano	W	3-2	PD	6	Llorente 3[16 23 68]	12 450
	31	Mirandes	D	2-1	CRsf		Llorente 2[18 27]	8 000
	4	Espanyol	D	3-3	PD	9	De Marcos[26], Llorente[58], Javi Martinez[65]	30 000
	7	Mirandes	W	6-2	CRsf		Muniain[11], Susaeta[14], Aurtenetxe[22], Llorente 2[71 75], OG[88]	39 000
Feb	11	Betis	L	1-2	PD	9	Javi Martinez[23]	35 000
	16	Lok Moskva	L	1-2	ELr2		Muniain[36]	13 160
	19	Malaga	W	3-0	PD	5	Amorebieta[57], San Jose[60], Toquero[61]	38 000
	23	Lok Moskva	W	1-0	ELr2		Muniain[62]	29 532
	26	Villarreal	D	2-2	PD	5	Llorente[62], Susaeta[66]	18 000
	4	Sociedad	W	2-0	PD	5	Susaeta 2[25 81]	37 000
	8	Man Utd	W	3-2	ELr3		Llorente[44], De Marcos[71], Muniain[90]	59 265
	11	Osasuna	L	1-2	PD	7	Llorente[54]	16 718
	15	Man Utd	W	2-1	ELr3		Llorente[23], De Marcos[66]	36 958
Mar	18	Valencia	L	0-3	PD	8		35 000
	21	At. Madrid	L	1-2	PD	9	Javi Martinez[92+]	30 000
	25	Sp. Gijon	D	1-1	PD	11	De Marcos[76]	35 000
	29	Schalke	W	4-2	ELqf		Llorente 2[21 73], De Marcos[81], Muniain[93+]	53 883
	31	Barcelona	L	0-2	PD	11		88 027
	5	Schalke	D	2-2	ELqf		Ibai[41], Susaeta[55]	37 048
	8	Sevilla	W	1-0	PD	11	Llorente[47]	38 000
	11	Granada	D	2-2	PD	8	Llorente[81], Susaeta[87]	22 500
	15	Mallorca	W	1-0	PD	7	Llorente[19]	25 000
Apr	19	Sporting CP	L	1-2	ELsf		Aurtenetxe[54]	37 286
	22	Racing	W	1-0	PD	6	Toquero[70]	15 000
	26	Sporting CP	W	3-1	ELsf		Susaeta[17], Ibai[45], Llorente[88]	37 598
	29	Zaragoza	D	2-2	PD	7		30 000
	2	Real Madrid	L	0-3	PD	8		39 500
	5	Getafe	D	0-0	PD	9		34 000
May	9	At. Madrid	L	0-3	ELf			52 347
	13	Levante	L	0-3	PD	10		12 000
	25	Barcelona	L	0-3	CRf			54 000

10th Att: 645 500 • Av: 33 974 (-4.5%) • San Mamés 39 750 (85%)

ATHLETIC LEAGUE APPEARANCES/GOALS 2011-12
Goalkeepers Gorka Iraizoz 37 • Raul Fernandez 1
Defenders Fernando Amorebieta VEN 27+1/3 • Jon Aurtenetxe 30+1/1
Borja Ekiza 13+8/0 • Andoni Iraola 32+3/1 • Jonas Ramalho 1+1/0
Mikel San Jose 15+9/2
Midfield Ander Herrera 25+7/1 • David Lopez 4+9/1
Igor Gabilondo 8+8/2 • Carlos Gurpegi 6+1/1 • Igor Martinez 0+2/0
Inigo Perez 14+8/0 • Ander Iturraspe 31+4/1 • Javi Martinez 30+1/4
Markel Susaeta 34+4/6
Forwards Oscar De Marcos 34/4 • Ibai Gomez 7+12/0
Fernando Llorente 24+8/16 • Iker Muniain 30+3/2
Gaizka Toquero 15+20/4
Coach Marcelo Bielsa ARG (7/07/2011)

ATLETICO MADRID
2011-12

	Date	Opponent	Res	Comp	PD	Scorers	Att
Jy	28	Strømsgodset	W	2-1	ELp3		Reyes 2[54 74]	30 056
	4	Strømsgodset	W	2-0	ELp3		Adrian[13], Reyes[93+]	5 807
	18	Guimarães	W	2-0	ELpo		Elias 2[68 73]	27 153
Aug	25	Guimarães	W	4-0	ELpo		Gabi[2p], Adrian 2[18 60], Salvio[81]	10 330
	28	Osasuna	D	0-0	PD	13		28 000
	18	Valencia	L	0-1	PD	15		40 000
	15	Celtic	W	2-0	ELgl		Falcao[3], Diego[68]	28 960
Sep	19	Racing	W	4-0	PD	9	Falcao 3[23 36p 55], Adrian[78]	40 000
	21	Sp. Gijon	W	4-0	PD	8	OG[28], Dominguez[58], Falcao 2[72 80]	38 000
	24	Barcelona	L	0-5	PD	8		83 154
	29	Rennes	D	1-1	ELgl		Juanfran[86]	24 299
	2	Sevilla	D	0-0	PD	8		50 000
	15	Granada	D	0-0	PD	8		21 000
Oct	20	Udinese	L	0-2	ELgl			10 026
	23	Mallorca	D	1-1	PD	9	Falcao[43p]	35 000
	27	Ath. Bilbao	L	0-3	PD	12		28 000
	30	Zaragoza	W	3-1	PD	10	Adrian 2[19 75], Dominguez[31]	40 000
	3	Udinese	W	4-0	ELgl		Adrian 2[7 12], Diego[37], Falcao[67]	18 300
Nov	6	Getafe	L	2-3	PD	11	Falcao[30p], Dominguez[80]	8 000
	20	Levante	W	3-2	PD	9	Pizzi[69], Adrian[75], Diego[83]	27 000
	26	Real Madrid	L	1-4	PD	11	Adrian[15]	78 500
	30	Celtic	W	1-0	ELgl		Turan[30]	10 500
	4	Vallecano	W	3-1	PD	8	Gabi[25], Falcao[74], Salvio[90]	39 000
	8	Albacete	L	1-2	CRr4		Adrian[70]	13 000
	11	Espanyol	L	2-4	PD	10	Falcao[32], Turan[83]	20 823
Dec	15	Rennes	W	3-1	ELgl		Falcao[38p], Dominguez[42], Turan[79]	13 154
	18	Betis	L	0-2	PD	10		40 000
	21	Albacete	L	0-1	CRr4			15 000
	7	Malaga	D	0-0	PD	11		28 000
	15	Villarreal	W	3-0	PD	10	Falcao 2[40 52p], Diego[80]	48 000
Jan	21	Sociedad	W	4-0	PD	8	Falcao 3[3p 83 91+], Adrian[47]	20 000
	30	Osasuna	W	1-0	PD	7	Godin[40]	15 010
	3	Valencia	D	0-0	PD	7		45 000
	11	Racing	D	0-0	PD	6		12 328
Feb	16	Lazio	W	3-1	ELr2		Adrian[25], Falcao 2[37 63]	30 604
	19	Sp. Gijon	D	1-1	PD	6	OG[20]	23 000
	23	Lazio	W	1-0	ELr2		Godin[48]	26 710
	26	Barcelona	L	1-2	PD	9	Falcao[49]	53 000
	3	Sevilla	D	1-1	PD	9	Salvio	45 000
	8	Besiktas	W	3-1	ELr3		Salvio 2[24 27], Adrian[37]	27 431
	11	Granada	W	2-0	PD	8	Miranda[37], Falcao[91+]	45 000
Mar	15	Besiktas	W	3-0	ELr3		Adrian[26], Falcao[83], Salvio[93+]	24 824
	18	Mallorca	L	1-2	PD	10	Falcao[65]	16 857
	21	Ath. Bilbao	W	2-1	PD	8	Falcao 2[50 72]	30 000
	25	Zaragoza	L	0-1	PD	8		30 000
	29	Hannover	W	2-1	ELqf		Falcao[9], Salvio[89]	29 223

ATLETICO MADRID 2011-12 (CONT'D)

Apr	1	Getafe	W	3-0	PD	7	Salvio [24], Diego [62], Falcao [77]	49 000
	5	Hannover	W	2-1	ELqf		Adrian [63], Falcao [87]	44 000
	8	Levante	L	0-2	PD	7		11 400
	11	Real Madrid	L	1-4	PD	9	Falcao [55]	53 000
	15	Vallecano	W	1-0	PD	8	Falcao [64]	10 000
	19	Valencia	W	4-2	ELsf		Falcao 2 [18 78], Miranda [49], Adrian [54]	40 899
	22	Espanyol	W	3-1	PD	5	Godin [9], Turan 2 [59 61]	45 000
	26	Valencia	W	1-0	ELsf		Adrian [60]	43 711
	29	Betis	D	2-2	PD	6	Koke [63], Falcao [94+]	25 000
May	2	Sociedad	D	1-1	PD	6	Gabi [54]	40 000
	5	Malaga	W	2-1	PD	5	Koke [69], Adrian [79]	25 000
	9	Ath. Bilbao	W	3-0	ELf		Falcao 2 [7 34], Diego [85]	52 347
	13	Villarreal	W	1-0	PD	5	Falcao [77]	16 000

5th Att: 770 000 • Av: 40 526 (+0.6%) • Vicente Calderón 54 851 (73%)

ATLETICO LEAGUE APPEARANCES/GOALS 2011-12

Goalkeepers Sergio Asenjo 1+1 • Thibaut Courtois BEL 37
Defenders Antonio Lopez 2/0 • Alvaro Dominguez 22+6/3
Filipe Luis BRA 36/0 • Diego Godin URU 26+1/2 • Miranda BRA 25+2/1
Pedro Martin 0+1/0 • Luis Perea COL 11+8/0 • Silvio POR 8+1/0
Midfield Arda Turan TUR 24+9/3 • Gabi 30+1/2 • Juanfran 23+3/0 • Koke 11+14/2
Fran Merida 0+3/0 • Gabi 30+1/2 • Juanfran 23+3/0 • Koke 11+14/2
Mario Suarez 23+5/0 • Paulo Assuncao BRA 5+4/0
Eduardo Salvio ARG 17+14/3 • Tiago POR 22+2/0
Forwards Adrian Lopez 27+9/7 • Radamel Falcao COL 33+1/24
Pizzi POR 0+11/1 • Jose Antonio Reyes 8+5/0
Coach Gregorio Manzano (8/06/2011) • Diego Simeone (27/12/2011)

BARCELONA 2011-12

Aug	14	Real Madrid	D	2-2	SC		Villa [35], Messi [45]	79 800
	17	Real Madrid	W	3-2	SC		Iniesta [15], Messi 2 [43 88]	92 965
	26	Porto	W	2-0	USC		Messi [39], Fabregas [88]	18 048
	29	Villarreal	W	5-0	PD	2	Thiago [25], Fabregas [45], Sanchez [47], Messi 2 [52 74]	75 097
	2	Sociedad	W	2-2	PD	4	Xavi [10], Fabregas [12]	30 000
	13	Milan	D	2-2	CLgH		Pedro [36], Villa [50]	89 861
Sep	17	Osasuna	W	8-0	PD	3	Messi 3 [5 41 79], Fabregas [13], Villa 2 [34 77], OG [40], Xavi [57]	84 921
	21	Valencia	D	2-2	PD	4	Pedro [13], Fabregas [77]	52 250
	24	At. Madrid	W	5-0	PD	2	Villa 2 [9], OG [5], Messi 3 [26 78 91+]	83 154
	28	BATE	W	5-0	CLgH		OG [19], Pedro [22], Messi 2 [38 56], Villa [90]	29 555
Oct	2	Sp. Gijon	W	1-0	PD	1	Adriano [12]	23 220
	15	Racing	W	3-0	PD	1	Messi 2 [11 68], Xavi [27]	78 000
	19	Vik. Plzen	W	2-0	CLgH		Iniesta [10], Villa [82]	74 375
	22	Sevilla	D	0-0	PD	3		82 743
	25	Granada	W	1-0	PD	2	Xavi [32]	22 000
	29	Mallorca	W	5-0	PD	2	Messi 3 [12p 20 29], Cuenca [49], Alves [91+]	80 153
Nov	1	Vik. Plzen	W	4-0	CLgH		Messi 3 [24 45 92+], Fabregas [72]	20 145
	6	Ath. Bilbao	D	2-2	PD	2	Fabregas [24], Messi [91+]	35 000
	9	L'Hospitalet	W	1-0	CRr4		Iniesta [42]	2 500
	19	Zaragoza	W	4-0	PD	2	Pique [18], Messi [43], Puyol [54], Villa [75]	80 000
	23	Milan	W	3-2	CLgH		OG [14], Messi [31p], Xavi [63]	78 927
	26	Getafe	L	0-1	PD	2		13 000
	29	Vallecano	W	4-0	PD	2	Sanchez 2 [29 41], Villa [43], Messi [50]	53 775
Dec	3	Levante	W	5-0	PD	2	Fabregas 2 [4 33], Cuenca [37], Messi [55], Sanchez [61]	79 361
	6	BATE	W	4-0	CLgH		Sergi [35], Montoya [60], Pedro 2 [63 89p]	37 374
	10	Real Madrid	W	3-1	PD	2	Sanchez [30], Xavi [53], Fabregas [66]	79 900
	15	Al Sadd	W	4-0	CWsf		Adriano 2 [25 43], Keita [64], Maxwell [81]	66 298
	18	Santos	W	4-0	CWf		Messi 2 [17 82], Xavi [24], Fabregas [45]	68 166
	22	L'Hospitalet	W	9-0	CRr4		Pedro [11p], Iniesta [19], Thiago 2 [23 55p], Xavi [36], Tello 2 [43 65], Cuenca 2 [49 81]	56 480

BARCELONA 2011-12 (CONT'D)

	4	Osasuna	W	4-0	CRr5		Fabregas 2 [14 19], Messi 2 [73 91+]	64 124
	8	Espanyol	D	1-1	PD	2	Fabregas [16]	35 122
Jan	12	Osasuna	W	2-1	CRr5		Sanchez [49], Sergi [72]	12 498
	15	Betis	W	4-2	PD	2	Xavi [10], Messi 2 [12 86p], Sanchez [75]	69 889
	18	Real Madrid	W	2-1	CRqf		Puyol [49], Abidal [77]	80 000
	22	Malaga	W	4-1	PD	2	Messi 3 [32 50 81], Sanchez [48]	28 900
	25	Real Madrid	D	2-2	CRqf		Pedro [43], Alves [45]	95 486
	28	Villarreal	D	0-0	PD	2		20 000
	1	Valencia	D	1-1	CRsf		Puyol [36]	51 800
	4	Sociedad	W	2-1	PD	2	Tello [8], Messi [72]	92 000
Feb	8	Valencia	W	2-0	CRsf		Fabregas [16], Xavi [81]	69 476
	11	Osasuna	L	2-3	PD	2	Sanchez [51], Tello [73]	17 284
	14	Leverkusen	W	3-1	CLr2		Messi 2 [41 55], Messi [88]	29 400
	19	Valencia	W	5-1	PD	2	Messi 4 [22 27 76 85], Xavi [91+]	74 240
	24	At. Madrid	W	2-1	PD	2	Alves [36], Messi [81]	53 000
Mar	3	Sp. Gijon	W	3-1	PD	2	Iniesta [42], Keita [79], Xavi [88]	72 442
	7	Leverkusen	W	7-1	CLr2		Messi 5 [25 42 49 58 84], Tello 2 [55 62]	75 632
	11	Racing	W	2-0	PD	2	Messi 2 [28 55p]	18 885
	17	Sevilla	W	2-0	PD	2	Xavi [17], Messi [24]	40 000
	20	Granada	W	5-3	PD	2	Xavi [4], Messi 3 [17 66 85], Tello [82]	62 461
	24	Mallorca	W	2-0	PD	2	Messi [25], Pique [78]	22 284
	28	Milan	D	0-0	CLqf			76 169
	31	Ath. Bilbao	W	2-0	PD	2	Iniesta [40], Messi [58p]	88 027
	3	Milan	W	3-1	CLqf		Messi 2 [11p 41p], Iniesta [53]	94 629
Apr	7	Zaragoza	W	4-1	PD	2	Puyol [36], Messi 2 [39 86p], Pedro [92+]	24 000
	10	Getafe	W	4-0	PD	2	Sanchez 2 [13 73], Messi [44], Pedro [75]	76 041
	14	Levante	W	2-1	PD	2	Messi 2 [64 72p]	25 000
	18	Chelsea	L	0-1	CLsf			38 039
	21	Real Madrid	L	1-2	PD	2	Sanchez [70]	99 252
	24	Chelsea	D	2-2	CLsf		Busquets [35], Iniesta [43]	95 845
	29	Vallecano	W	7-0	PD	2	Messi 2 [16 90], OG [26], Keita [39], Pedro 2 [47 87], Thiago [77]	10 000
May	2	Malaga	W	4-1	PD	2	Puyol [14], Messi 3 [35p 59p 64]	67 854
	5	Espanyol	W	4-0	PD	2	Messi 4 [12 64p 74 79p]	89 044
	8	Betis	D	2-2	PD	2	Busquets [9], Keita [91+]	37 000
	12	Sevilla	D	2-2	PD	2	Busquets 2 [3 25], Messi [20]	54 000
	25	Ath. Bilbao	W	3-0	CRf		Pedro 2 [3 25], Messi [20]	54 000

2nd Att: 1 488 454 • Av: 78 340 (-1.2%) • Camp Nou 99 354 (78%)

BARCELONA LEAGUE APPEARANCES/GOALS 2011-12

Goalkeepers Jose Pinto 3 • Victor Valdes 35
Defenders Eric Abidal FRA 20+2/0 • Adriano BRA 20+6/1
Marc Bartra 0+1/0 • Dani Alves BRA 29+4/2 • Andreu Fontas 1/0
Maxwell 4+3/0 • Martin Montoya 3+4/0 • Marc Muniesa 0+1/0
Gerard Pique 17+5/2 • Carles Puyol 23+3/3
Midfield Ibrahim Afellay NED 1+3/0 • Sergio Busquets 28+3/1
Jonathan dos Santos MEX 1+2/0 • Cesc Fabregas 23+5/9
Andres Iniesta 21+6/2 • Seydou Keita MLI 14+12/3
Javier Mascherano ARG 30+1/0 • Sergi Roberto 1/0 • Thiago 20+7/2
Xavi 26+5/10
Forwards Alexis Sanchez CHI 20+5/11 • David Villa 8+7/5
Isaac Cuenca 11+5/2 • Gerard 0+1/0 • Lionel Messi ARG 36+1/50
Pedro 20+9/5 • Cristian Tello 3+12/3
Coach Josep Guardiola

KEY
SC = Supercopa • USC = UEFA Super Cup •
PD = Primera Division • CR = Copa del Rey •
CL = UEFA Champions League • EL = Europa
League • Shaded matches are home matches
See page 13 for further explanations

REAL BETIS
2011–12

Ag	27	Granada	W	1-0	PD	6	Ruben Castro [88]	18 000
	11	Mallorca	W	1-0	PD	3	Ruben Castro [87]	35 125
	18	Ath. Bilbao	W	3-2	PD	2	Benat [7], Nacho [13], Sevilla [45p]	40 000
Sep	22	Zaragoza	W	4-3	PD	1	Santa Cruz 2 [7 49], Sevilla [12p], Benat [47p]	38 000
	26	Getafe	L	0-1	PD	1		12 000
	2	Levante	L	0-1	PD	7		35 000
	15	Real Madrid	L	1-4	PD	7	Molina [69]	72 000
Oct	23	Vallecano	L	0-2	PD	7		36 000
	27	Espanyol	L	0-1	PD	10		21 810
	30	Racing	L	0-1	PD	12		14 000
	5	Malaga	D	0-0	PD	12		38 000
Nov	19	Villarreal	L	0-1	PD	13		18 000
	27	Sociedad	L	2-3	PD	15	Pereira 2 [81 85]	30 000
	4	Osasuna	L	1-2	PD	17	Ruben Castro [80]	15 701
	10	Valencia	W	2-1	PD	15	Ruben Castro 2 [91+ 93+]	30 000
Dec	13	Cordoba	D	0-1	CRr4			7 300
	18	At. Madrid	W	2-0	PD	11	Pozuelo [55], Santa Cruz [90]	40 000
	21	Cordoba	W	2-1	CRr4		Molina 2 [34 54]	27 000
	8	Sp. Gijon	W	2-0	PD	10	Santa Cruz [23], Molina [92+]	35 000
Jan	15	Barcelona	L	2-4	PD	11	Ruben Castro [32], Santa Cruz [52]	69 889
	21	Sevilla	D	1-1	PD	12	Benat [26]	40 000
	29	Granada	L	1-2	PD	13	Pereira [81]	37 000
	4	Mallorca	L	0-1	PD	16		9 000
Feb	11	Ath. Bilbao	W	2-1	PD	14	Ruben Castro [10], Nelson [91+]	35 000
	20	Zaragoza	W	2-0	PD	12	Ruben Castro 2 [41 68]	20 000
	25	Getafe	D	1-1	PD	12	Molina [51]	42 160
	5	Levante	L	1-3	PD	12	Molina [44]	11 000
	10	Real Madrid	L	2-3	PD	14	Molina [9], Montero [54]	51 300
Mar	17	Vallecano	L	0-3	PD	16		9 216
	22	Espanyol	D	1-1	PD	15	Ruben Castro [79]	35 000
	25	Racing	D	1-1	PD	15	Santa Cruz [17]	34 000
	31	Malaga	W	2-0	PD	15	Ruben Castro [40], Dorado [45]	23 000
	7	Villarreal	W	3-1	PD	13	Santa Cruz [35], Ruben Castro [38], Benat [59]	30 000
Apr	10	Sociedad	D	1-1	PD	14	Ruben Castro [70]	21 000
	15	Osasuna	W	1-0	PD	12	Ruben Castro [34]	37 000
	22	Valencia	L	0-4	PD	13		39 000
	29	At. Madrid	D	2-2	PD	14	Pozuelo [86], Pereira [88]	25 000
	2	Sevilla	W	2-1	PD	11	Benat 2 [43 92+]	45 000
May	5	Sp. Gijon	L	1-2	PD	12	Molina [45]	15 156
	12	Barcelona	L	2-2	PD	13	Ruben Castro 2 [71 74]	37 000

13th Att: 680 585 • Av: 35 820 (+4.4%) • Benito Villamarín 52 745 (67%)

BETIS LEAGUE APPEARANCES/GOALS 2011-12
Goalkeepers Casto 22 • Fabricio 15 • Inaki Goitia 1+1
Defenders Antonio Amaya 9+3/0 • Francisco Chica 14+1/0
Jose Dorado 32+1/1 • Jose Isidoro 10+1/0 • Pedro Mario 12/0
Nelson POR 14/1 • Paulao BRA 17/0 • Dusko Tosic SRB 0+1/0
Ustaritz 6+1/0
Midfield Alex 3+2/0 • Benat 30+5/6 • Jose Canas 17+5/0
Iriney BRA 30+1/0 • Juanma 8+6/0 • Javier Matilla 4+10/0
Momo 0+1/0 • Jefferson Montero ECU 26+6/1 • Nacho 37/0
Salva Sevilla 19+7/2 • Sergio Rodriguez 0+3/0
Forwards Ezequiel 0+4/0 • Jonathan Pereira 14+17/4
Jorge Molina 14+12/6 • Nono 1+1/0 • Alejandro Pozuelo 10+8/2
Ruben Castro 33+1/16 • Roque Santa Cruz PAR 20+13/7
Alvaro Vadillo 2+2/0
Coach Pepe Mel

RCD ESPANYOL
2011–12

Ag	28	Mallorca	L	0-1	PD	18		12 400
	11	Ath. Bilbao	W	2-1	PD	9	Sergio Garcia 2 [25 73]	21 154
Sep	18	Zaragoza	L	1-2	PD	13	Javi Lopez [71]	26 000
	22	Getafe	W	1-0	PD	10	Pandiani [92+]	21 414
	25	Levante	L	1-3	PD	10	Moreno [73]	10 400
	2	Real Madrid	L	0-4	PD	15		34 423
	16	Vallecano	W	1-0	PD	10	Romaric [56]	11 000
Oct	22	Racing	W	1-0	PD	8	Sergio Garcia [59]	16 000
	27	Betis	W	1-0	PD	6	Pandiani [75]	21 810
	30	Malaga	L	1-2	PD	7	Alvaro Vazquez [45]	26 000
	6	Villarreal	D	0-0	PD	7		23 417
Nov	20	Sociedad	D	0-0	PD	8		23 702
	27	Osasuna	L	1-2	PD	9	Alvaro Vazquez [56]	24 052
	3	Valencia	L	1-2	PD	10	Moreno [69]	40 000
	11	At. Madrid	W	4-2	PD	8	Verdu 2 [5 8], Romaric [19], Sergio Garcia [54]	20 823
Dec	13	Celta	D	0-0	CRr4			5 000
	17	Sp. Gijon	W	2-1	PD	8	Thievy [3], Sergio Garcia [84]	23 000
	20	Celta	W	4-2	CRr4		Weiss [31], Alv. Vazquez 2 [49 59], Sergio Garcia [68]	11 410
	5	Córdoba	L	1-2	CRr5		Sergio Garcia [39]	19 300
	8	Barcelona	D	1-1	PD	8	Alvaro Vazquez [86]	35 122
	11	Córdoba	W	2-2	CRr5		Alvaro Vazquez 3 [9 20 88], Didac [35]	22 109
	14	Sevilla	D	0-0	PD	9		31 000
Jan	17	Mirandés	W	3-2	CRqf		Weiss [85], Rui Fonte [87], Verdu [89]	18 408
	21	Granada	W	3-0	PD	5	Baena [26], Verdu [45p], Rui Fonte [81]	26 023
	24	Mirandés	L	1-2	CRqf		OG [46]	5 858
	28	Mallorca	W	1-0	PD	5	Weiss [19]	19 740
	4	Ath. Bilbao	D	3-3	PD	5	Romaric [33], Weiss [48], Albin [90]	30 000
Feb	12	Zaragoza	L	0-2	PD	5		29 310
	18	Getafe	D	1-1	PD	4	Alvaro Vazquez [66]	10 000
	25	Levante	L	1-2	PD	8	Uche [75]	20 000
	4	Real Madrid	L	0-5	PD	11		77 000
	11	Vallecano	W	5-1	PD	9	Uche 3 [3 44 67], Coutinho 2 [9 21]	26 110
Mar	19	Racing	W	3-1	PD	6	Verdu [76], Coutinho [33], Moreno [80]	18 223
	22	Betis	D	1-1	PD	6	Pandiani [93+]	35 000
	25	Malaga	L	1-2	PD	7	Coutinho [23]	26 132
	1	Villarreal	D	0-0	PD	9		17 000
	7	Sociedad	D	2-2	PD	9	OG [45], Weiss [47]	20 110
	10	Osasuna	L	0-2	PD	10		13 210
Apr	15	Valencia	W	4-0	PD	10	Cristian Gomez [26], Verdu [30], Alvaro Vazquez [58], Uche [80]	24 000
	22	At. Madrid	L	1-3	PD	10	Vila [19]	45 000
	28	Sp. Gijon	L	0-3	PD	11		18 000
	1	Granada	L	1-2	PD	13	Vila [54]	21 000
May	5	Barcelona	L	0-4	PD	13		89 044
	13	Sevilla	D	1-1	PD	14	Coutinho [77]	16 627

14th Att: 446 490 • Av: 23 499 (-11.9%) • Cornellà-El Prat 40 500 (58%)

ESPANYOL LEAGUE APPEARANCES/GOALS 2011-12
Goalkeepers Cristian Alvarez ARG 23 • Kiko Casilla 15
Defenders Didac 37/2 • Juan Forlin ARG 26+2/0 • Ernesto Galan 11/0
Jordi Amat 7+2/0 • Hector Moreno MEX 35/3 • Raul Rodriguez 28/0
Midfield Jose Baena 22+10/1 • Coutinho BRA 14+2/5
Cristian Alfonso 0+6/0 • Cristian Gomez 10+9/1 • Jesus Datolo 2+3/0
Javi Lopez 26+3/1 • Javi Marquez 8+1/0 • Luis Garcia 1/0
Paul Quaye GHA 0+1/0 • Romaric CIV 22+6/3 • Joan Verdu 36/5
Victor Sanchez 5+1/0 • Vladimir Weiss SVK 19+9/3
Forwards Juan Albin URU 2+4/1 • Alvaro Vazquez 19+9/5
Bakari 0+1/0 • Walter Pandiani URU 0+16/3 • Rui Fonte POR 7+12/1
Sergio Garcia 21+3/5 • Thievy FRA 11+8/1 • Kalu Uche NGA 11+4/5
Coach Mauricio Pochettino ARG

GETAFE
2011-12

Aug	28	Levante	D	1-1	PD	9 Miku [62]	8 000
	10	Real Madrid	L	2-4	PD	16 Miku 2 [39 73]	76 000
Sep	18	Vallecano	L	0-1	PD	17	12 000
	22	Espanyol	L	0-1	PD	19	21 414
	26	Betis	W	1-0	PD	16 Diego Castro [31]	12 000
	1	Malaga	L	2-3	PD	17 Pedro Leon [55]	28 000
	15	Villarreal	D	0-0	PD	17	13 000
Oct	23	Sociedad	D	0-0	PD	17	25 000
	26	Osasuna	D	2-2	PD	16 Guiza 2 [62 75]	8 000
	29	Valencia	L	1-3	PD	20 Diego Castro [23]	28 000
Nov	6	At. Madrid	W	3-2	PD	14 Barrada [40], Michel [49], Diego Castro [83p]	8 000
	20	Sp. Gijon	L	1-2	PD	16 Miku [35]	22 000
	26	Barcelona	W	1-0	PD	14 Valera [67]	13 000
	5	Sevilla	L	0-3	PD	16	38 000
Dec	11	Granada	W	1-0	PD	13 Casquero [81]	10 000
	13	Malaga	L	0-1	CRr4		5 000
	17	Mallorca	W	2-1	PD	12 Barrada 2 [28 44]	10 000
	21	Malaga	D	2-2	CRr4		6 000
	8	Ath. Bilbao	D	0-0	PD	12	11 000
Jan	14	Zaragoza	D	1-1	PD	13 OG [79]	28 000
	21	Racing	W	2-1	PD	11 Gavilan [26], Miku [83]	10 425
	29	Levante	W	2-1	PD	9 Guiza [32], Diego Castro [82]	9 757
	4	Real Madrid	L	0-1	PD	10	14 000
	12	Vallecano	L	0-2	PD	12	10 000
Feb	18	Espanyol	D	1-1	PD	14 Miku [70p]	10 000
	25	Betis	D	1-1	PD	14 OG [55]	42 160
	3	Malaga	L	1-3	PD	15 Diego Castro [42]	8 000
	12	Villarreal	W	2-1	PD	13 Diego Castro [6], Barrada [72]	18 000
Mar	17	Sociedad	W	1-0	PD	11 OG [82]	7 500
	20	Osasuna	D	0-0	PD	13	14 084
	24	Valencia	W	3-1	PD	10 Pedro Rios [11], Miku [23], OG [30]	8 000
	1	At. Madrid	L	0-3	PD	10	49 000
	7	Sp. Gijon	W	2-0	PD	10 Miku [22], Diego Castro [47]	6 500
Apr	10	Barcelona	L	0-4	PD	11	76 041
	16	Sevilla	W	5-1	PD	9 Miguel Torres [35], Lacen [49], Miku 2 [63 71], Pedro Rios [69]	7 000
	22	Granada	L	0-1	PD	11	21 000
	28	Mallorca	L	1-3	PD	12 Alexis [92+]	5 000
May	1	Racing	D	1-1	PD	10 Miku [59p]	9 500
	5	Ath. Bilbao	D	0-0	PD	11	34 000
	13	Zaragoza	L	0-2	PD	11	9 000

11th   Att: 179 500 • Av: 9 447 (-15.6%) • Coliseum 17 700 (53%)

GETAFE LEAGUE APPEARANCES/GOALS 2011-12
Goalkeepers Jordi Codina 2 • Miguel Moya 36
Defenders Alex Perez 1+1/0 • Alexis 11+1/1 • Alvaro Arroyo 3+1/0
Cata Diaz ARG 36/0 • Alberto Lopo 14+2/0 • Mane 22+1/0
Tsepo Masilela RSA 10+2/0 • Miguel Torres 18+5/1 • Rafa Lopez 9+4/0
Samuel 0+1/0 • Juan Valera 30/1
Midfield Abelaziz Barrada FRA 25+7/4 • Francisco Casquero 19+9/1
Diego Castro 25+6/7 • Jaime Gavilan 13+4/1 • Juan Rodriguez 10+7/0
Medhi Lacen ALG 26+7/1 • Michel 19+3/1 • Pablo Sarabia 10+9/0
Pedro Leon 6+7/1 • Pedro Rios 17+5/2 • Ruben Perez 8+1/0
Forwards Adrian Colunga 0+4/0 • Angel Arizmendi 0+3/0
Daniel Guiza 15+17/3 • Hugo Fraile 0+1/0 • Miku VEN 33+5/12
Coach Luis Garcia Plaza (4/06/2011)

GRANADA
2011-12

Aug	27	Betis	L	0-1	PD	17	18 000
	12	Malaga	L	0-4	PD	20	28 000
Sep	17	Villarreal	W	1-0	PD	15 Uche [56]	21 000
	20	Sociedad	L	0-1	PD	16	23 000
	25	Osasuna	D	1-1	PD	17 Fran Rico [64]	15 000
	1	Valencia	L	0-1	PD	19	36 000
	15	At. Madrid	D	0-0	PD	18	21 000
Oct	22	Sp. Gijon	L	0-2	PD	18	23 000
	25	Barcelona	L	0-1	PD	20	22 000
	31	Sevilla	W	2-1	PD	19 Geijo [79], Mikel Rico [90]	35 000
Nov	6	Racing	D	0-0	PD	19	17 000
	27	Ath. Bilbao	W	1-0	PD	17 Inigo Lopez [32]	30 000
	4	Zaragoza	W	1-0	PD	16 Ighalo [44]	22 000
Dec	7	Mallorca	D	2-2	PD	12 Siqueira [54], Carlos Martins [59]	21 000
	11	Getafe	L	0-1	PD	16	10 000
	13	Sociedad	L	1-4	CRr4	Geijo [72]	18 000
	18	Levante	W	2-1	PD	13 Siqueira [35p], Abel Gomez [45]	22 000
	21	Sociedad	W	2-1	CRr4	Siqueira [19p], Geijo [66]	18 000
	7	Real Madrid	L	1-5	PD	15 Mikel Rocco [22]	78 000
Jan	14	Vallecano	L	1-2	PD	17 Fran Rico [87]	22 500
	21	Espanyol	L	0-3	PD	18	26 023
	29	Betis	W	2-1	PD	16 Ighalo [13], Carlos Martins [40]	37 000
	6	Malaga	W	2-1	PD	14 Ighalo [57], Inigo Lopez [81]	22 500
	12	Villarreal	L	1-3	PD	17 Inigo Lopez [50]	21 000
Feb	19	Sociedad	W	4-1	PD	15 Inigo Lopez [12], Jara [57], Uche 2 [62 87]	22 500
	26	Osasuna	L	1-2	PD	16 Mikel Rico [31]	18 000
	4	Valencia	L	0-1	PD	16	12 000
	11	At. Madrid	L	0-2	PD	16	45 000
Mar	17	Sp. Gijon	W	2-1	PD	15 Carlos Martins [2], Siqueira [24]	22 500
	20	Barcelona	L	3-5	PD	16 Mainz [55], Siqueira 2 [61p 89p]	62 461
	26	Sevilla	L	0-3	PD	17	16 000
	31	Racing	W	1-0	PD	16 Siqueira [89p]	15 960
	8	Mallorca	D	0-0	PD	16	12 762
	14	Ath. Bilbao	D	2-2	PD	16 Jaime Romero [2], Geijo [74]	22 500
Apr	15	Zaragoza	L	0-1	PD	17	24 000
	22	Getafe	W	1-0	PD	16 Jara [18]	21 000
	28	Levante	L	1-3	PD	16 Ighalo [67]	15 000
	1	Espanyol	W	2-1	PD	15 Ighalo 2 [29 35]	21 000
May	5	Real Madrid	L	1-2	PD	15 Jara [5]	22 000
	13	Vallecano	L	0-1	PD	17	10 000

17th   Att: 367 500 • Av: 20 417 (+44.4%) • Nuevo Los Cármenes 22 524

GRANADA LEAGUE APPEARANCES/GOALS 2011-12
Goalkeepers Julio Cesar BRA 16 • Roberto 22
Defenders Borja Gomez 19/0 • David Cortes 8+2/0
Pape Diakhate SEN 10+1/0 • Inigo Lopez 28/4 • Manuel Lucena 2+3/0
Diego Mainz 19+2/1 • Allan Nyom CMR 32/0 • Noe Pamarot FRA 2/0
Midfield Abel Gomez 16+16/1 • Carlos Martins POR 25+4/3
Dani Benitez 26+5/0 • Fran Rico 13+6/2 • Jaime Romero 6+12/1
Mikel Rico 32+4/3 • Moises Hurtado 15+2/0 • Yohan Mollo FRA 2+4/0
Siqueira BRA 35/6 • Hassan Yebda ALG 12+2/0
Forwards Alex Geijo 10+13/2 • Henrique BRA 1+5/0
Odion Ighalo NGA 18+12/6 • Franco Jara ARG 23+8/3
Ikechukwu Uche NGA 26+8/3
Coach Fabri Gonzalez • Abel Resino (23/01/2012)

LEVANTE
2011–12

Ag	28	Getafe	D	1-1	PD	9	Juanlu [77]	8 000
	11	Racing	D	0-0	PD	11		10 500
	18	Real Madrid	W	1-0	PD	8	Kone [68]	18 000
Sep	21	Vallecano	W	2-1	PD	6	Valdo [10], Ballesteros [28]	13 950
	25	Espanyol	W	3-1	PD	3	Ruben Suarez 2 [14p 58p], Barkero [76]	10 400
	2	Betis	W	1-0	PD	2	Juanlu [33]	35 000
	16	Malaga	W	3-0	PD	2	Barkero [14], Juanlu [30], Kone [41]	13 108
Oct	23	Villarreal	W	3-0	PD	1	Juanlu 2 [16 43], Kone [58]	11 000
	26	Sociedad	W	3-2	PD	1	Nano [56], Valdo [61], Ruben Suarez [92+]	12 347
	30	Osasuna	L	0-2	PD	3		16 000
	5	Valencia	L	0-2	PD	4		19 000
Nov	20	At. Madrid	L	2-3	PD	4	Xavi Torres [72], Ruben Suarez [92+]	27 000
	27	Sp. Gijon	W	4-0	PD	4	Barkero [20], Valdo [47], Kone 2 [52 62]	11 287
	3	Barcelona	L	0-5	PD	4		79 361
	10	Sevilla	W	1-0	PD	4	Nano [57]	11 131
Dec	13	Deportivo	L	1-3	CRr4		Aranda [78]	10 000
	18	Granada	L	1-2	PD	4	Kone [60]	22 000
	21	Deportivo	W	4-1	CRr4		El Zhar [4], Ballesteros [38], Ruben Suarez [79], Kone [100]	8 500
	3	Alcorcón	L	1-2	CDr5		Pallardo [23]	2 000
	7	Mallorca	D	0-0	PD	4		10 560
	11	Alcorcón	W	4-0	CDr5		Barkero [23], Roger Marti [45], Iborra [52], Ruben Suarez [66]	10 000
Jan	15	Ath. Bilbao	L	0-3	PD	4		34 000
	19	Valencia	L	1-4	CDqf		Kone [37]	39 000
	22	Zaragoza	D	0-0	PD	4		10 065
	26	Valencia	L	0-3	CDqf			12 100
	29	Getafe	L	1-2	PD	4	Ruben Suarez [90p]	9 757
	5	Racing	D	1-1	PD	4	Kone [23]	7 658
	12	Real Madrid	L	2-4	PD	4	Cabral [5], Kone [63]	67 000
Feb	19	Vallecano	L	3-5	PD	7	Barkero [50p], Ruben Suarez 2 [79 92+]	9 457
	25	Espanyol	W	2-1	PD	4	Valdo [24], Ruben Suarez [89]	20 000
	5	Betis	W	3-1	PD	4	Barkero [34], Xavi Torres [42], Kone [51]	11 000
	10	Malaga	L	0-1	PD	5		28 000
Mar	18	Villarreal	W	1-0	PD	4	Xavi Torres [92+]	12 200
	21	Sociedad	W	3-1	PD	4	Barkero [12p], Kone [45], Xavi Torres [94+]	20 722
	25	Osasuna	L	0-2	PD	5		11 200
	1	Valencia	D	1-1	PD	5	Kone [54]	40 000
	8	At. Madrid	W	2-0	PD	5	Valdo [2], Kone [10]	11 400
	11	Sp. Gijon	L	2-3	PD	5	Valdo [16], Kone [63]	16 000
Apr	14	Barcelona	L	1-2	PD	5	Barkero [23p]	25 000
	21	Sevilla	D	1-1	PD	5	Kone [28]	28 000
	28	Granada	W	3-1	PD	5	Kone [46], Xavi Torres [73], Valdo [84]	15 000
	2	Zaragoza	L	0-1	PD	5		28 000
May	5	Mallorca	L	0-1	PD	7		15 000
	13	Ath. Bilbao	W	3-0	PD	6		12 000

6th Att: 240 570 • Av: 12 662 (-7.6%) • Ciutat de Valencia 25 534 (49%)

LEVANTE LEAGUE APPEARANCES/GOALS 2011-12
Goalkeepers Gustavo Munua URU 37 • Keilor Navas CRC 1
Defenders Sergio Ballesteros 37/1 • Gustavo Cabral ARG 15+1/1
David Navarro 3+1/0 • Asier Del Horno 12+1/0 • Javi Venta 25+1/0
Juanfran 29/0 • Nano 17/2 • Pedro Lopez 17+4/0
Midfield Jose Barkero 30+2/7 • Botelho BRA 10+4/0
Nabil El Zhar MAR 9+13/0 • Francisco Farinos 18+12/1
Jose Higon 0+2/0 • Vicente Iborra 28+5/0 • Juanlu 13+6/5
Miguel Pallardo 0+8/0 • Oscar Serrano 3+3/0 • Valdo CPV 32+2/7
Xavi Torres 32+2/5
Forwards Carlos Aranda 0+10/0 • Abdelkader Ghezzal ALG 9+7/2
Arouna Kone CIV 34/15 • Rafa Jorda 0+2/0 • Roger Marti 0+2/0
Ruben Suarez 7+27/8
Coach Juan Martinez (9/06/2011)

MALAGA
2011–12

Ag	28	Sevilla	L	1-2	PD	15	Santi Cazorla [81]	35 000
	12	Granada	W	4-0	PD	8	Santi Cazorla 2 [5 48], Joaquin 2 [25 73]	28 000
Sep	17	Mallorca	W	1-0	PD	6	Demichelis [39]	13 000
	21	Ath. Bilbao	W	1-0	PD	3	Santi Cazorla [62]	20 976
	25	Zaragoza	D	0-0	PD	6		18 000
	1	Getafe	W	3-2	PD	4	Van Nistelrooy [65], Maresca [88], Julio Baptista [92+]	28 000
Oct	16	Levante	L	0-3	PD	6		13 108
	22	Real Madrid	L	0-4	PD	6		26 000
	26	Vallecano	L	0-2	PD	7		10 000
	30	Espanyol	W	2-1	PD	6	Rondon [5], Apono [73p]	26 000
	5	Betis	D	0-0	PD	6		38 000
Nov	21	Racing	W	3-1	PD	5	Isco [48], OG [65], Seba Fernandez [89]	14 000
	28	Villarreal	W	2-1	PD	5	Toulalan [5], Isco [40]	22 500
	4	Sociedad	L	2-3	PD	6	Rondon [21], Seba Fernandez [59]	24 500
	11	Osasuna	D	1-1	PD	5	Juanmi [70]	20 000
Dec	13	Getafe	W	1-0	CRr4		Juanmi [84]	5 000
	18	Valencia	L	0-1	PD	7		35 000
	21	Getafe	D	2-2	CRr4		Van Nistelrooy [45], Buonanotte [86]	6 000
	3	Real Madrid	L	2-3	CRr5		Sergio Sanchez [10], Demichelis [29]	80 000
	7	At. Madrid	D	0-0	PD	6		28 000
Jan	10	Real Madrid	L	0-1	CRr5			25 000
	15	Sp. Gijon	L	1-2	PD	8	Van Nistelrooy [88]	22 000
	22	Barcelona	L	1-4	PD	10	Rondon [85]	28 900
	29	Sevilla	W	2-1	PD	8	Weligton [8], Seba Fernandez [19]	28 000
	6	Granada	L	1-2	PD	8	Rondon [68]	22 500
	12	Mallorca	W	3-1	PD	7	Seba Fernandez [11], Toulalan [55], Rondon [69]	28 000
Feb	19	Ath. Bilbao	L	0-3	PD	8		38 000
	25	Zaragoza	W	5-1	PD	6	Seba Fernandez [45], OG [67], Demichelis [77], Isco [79], Rondon [88]	26 000
	3	Getafe	W	3-1	PD	4	Eliseu [57], Toulalan [82], Santi Cazorla [92+]	8 000
	10	Levante	W	1-0	PD	4	Rondon [49]	28 000
Mar	18	Real Madrid	D	1-1	PD	5	Santi Cazorla [92+]	75 000
	22	Vallecano	W	4-2	PD	5	Rondon 2 [35 58], Maresca [70], Duda [86]	28 000
	25	Espanyol	W	2-1	PD	4	Van Nistelrooy [75], Demichelis [77]	26 132
	31	Betis	L	0-2	PD	4		23 000
	9	Racing	W	3-0	PD	3	Isco [22], Santi Cazorla [64], Van Nistelrooy [84]	28 000
Apr	12	Villarreal	L	1-2	PD	4	Santi Cazorla [65]	14 000
	15	Sociedad	D	1-1	PD	4	Isco [20]	28 000
	23	Osasuna	D	1-1	PD	4	Santi Cazorla [67]	13.939
	29	Valencia	W	1-0	PD	4	Camacho [27]	22 000
	1	Barcelona	L	1-4	PD	4	Rondon [26]	67 854
May	5	At. Madrid	L	1-2	PD	4	Eliseu [38]	25 000
	13	Sp. Gijon	W	1-0	PD	4	Rondon [49]	

4th Att: 497 376 • Av: 26 177 (+2.8%) • La Rosaleda 28 963 (90%)

MALAGA LEAGUE APPEARANCES/GOALS 2011-12
Goalkeepers Wilfredo Caballero ARG 28 • Carlos Kameni CMR 8+1 •
Ruben Martinez 2+2
Defenders Martin Demichelis ARG 33+2/3 • Jesus Gamez 24+1/0
Joris Mathijsen NED 28/0 • Ignacio Monreal 28+3/0
Sergio Sanchez 16+3/0 • Weligton BRA 19/1
Midfield Apono 2+4/1 • Ignacio Camacho 8+5/1 • Duda POR 14+11/1
Eliseu POR 19+6/2 • Enzo Maresca ITA 9+10/2
Francisco Portillo 1+1/0 • Recio 4+4/0 • Santi Cazorla 38/9
Jeremy Toulalan FRA 25/3
Forwards Diego Buonanotte ARG 4+6/0 • Isco 29+3/5
Joaquin 19+4/2 • Juanmi 2+4/1 • Julio Baptista BRA 4/1
Jose Rondon VEN 29+8/11 • Seba Fernandez URU 15+17/5
Ruud van Nistelrooy NED 10+18/4
Coach Manuel Pellegrini CHI

RCD MALLORCA
2011-12

Aug	28	Espanyol	W	1-0	PD	6	De Guzman [62]	12 400
	11	Betis	L	0-1	PD	10		35 125
Sep	17	Malaga	L	0-1	PD	14		13 000
	20	Villarreal	L	0-2	PD	15		18 000
	25	Sociedad	W	2-1	PD	11	Victor [20], Castro [50]	11 856
	1	Osasuna	D	2-2	PD	10	Hemed 2 [34p 79p]	10 500
	15	Valencia	D	1-1	PD	12	Hemed [90p]	15 000
Oct	23	At. Madrid	D	1-1	PD	12	Hemed [2p]	35 000
	26	Sp. Gijon	L	1-2	PD	13	Castro [16]	9 400
	29	Barcelona	L	0-5	PD	14		80 153
Nov	5	Sevilla	D	0-0	PD	15		11 900
	27	Racing	W	2-1	PD	15	OG [45], Victor [58]	11 672
	4	Ath. Bilbao	D	1-1	PD	12	Alvaro Gimenez [3]	12 863
	7	Granada	D	2-2	PD	-	Victor [23], Hemed [65p]	21 000
Dec	11	Zaragoza	W	1-0	PD	11	Victor [39]	22 000
	13	Sp. Gijon	L	0-1	CRr4			6 400
	17	Getafe	L	1-2	PD	14	Ramis [10]	10 000
	20	Sp. Gijon	W	2-0	CRr4		OG [19], Nsue [70]	6 000
	4	Sociedad	L	0-2	CRr5			23 000
	7	Levante	D	0-0	PD	14		10 560
	10	Sociedad	W	6-1	CRr5		Castro 2 [34 40], Hemed 2 [36 60], Jose Nunes [38], Alfaro [53]	6 500
Jan	14	RealMadrid	L	1-2	PD	16	Hemed [39]	20 000
	18	Ath. Bilbao	L	0-2	CRqf			38 000
	22	Vallecano	W	1-0	PD	14	Ramis [57]	10 000
	25	Ath. Bilbao	L	0-1	CRqf			10 990
	28	Espanyol	L	0-1	PD	15		19 747
	4	Betis	W	1-0	PD	13	Castro [24]	9 000
Feb	12	Malaga	L	1-3	PD	16	Pereira [4]	30 000
	19	Villarreal	W	4-0	PD	13	Victor 2 [41 65], Marti [52], Nunes [68]	14 500
	26	Sociedad	L	0-1	PD	15		25 000
	3	Osasuna	D	1-1	PD	14	Nsue [73]	12 498
	11	Valencia	D	2-2	PD	15	Nsue [56], Victor [64]	35 000
Mar	18	At. Madrid	W	2-1	PD	13	OG [46], Pereira [48]	16 857
	21	Sp. Gijon	W	3-2	PD	12	Nunes [30], OG [46], Alvaro Gimenez [77]	18 000
	24	Barcelona	L	0-2	PD	13		22 284
	2	Sevilla	L	1-3	PD	13	Hemed [74]	35 000
	8	Granada	D	0-0	PD	14		12 762
Apr	12	Racing	W	3-0	PD	12	Nsue [1], Castro [47], Alfaro [53]	10 000
	15	Ath. Bilbao	L	0-1	PD	13		25 000
	21	Zaragoza	W	1-0	PD	12	Victor [33]	13 000
	28	Getafe	W	3-1	PD	10	Victor [30], Alfaro [68], Hemed [78]	5 000
	2	Vallecano	W	1-0	PD	7	Castro [62]	13 000
May	5	Levante	W	1-0	PD	6	Pina [55]	15 000
	13	RealMadrid	L	1-4	PD	8	Castro [52]	79 500

8th Att: 256 992 • Av: 13 526 (-6.0%) • Son Moix 23 142 (58%)

OSASUNA
2011-12

Aug	28	At. Madrid	D	0-0	PD	12		28 000
	11	Sp. Gijon	W	2-1	PD	7	Nino [28], Alvaro Cejudo [30]	15 842
Sep	17	Barcelona	L	0-8	PD	12		84 921
	20	Sevilla	D	0-0	PD	12		14 903
	25	Granada	D	1-1	PD	12	Raul Garcia [29]	15 000
	1	Mallorca	D	2-2	PD	11	Raul Garcia 2 [45 59]	10 500
	17	Ath. Bilbao	L	1-3	PD	15	Nekounam [91+p]	33 000
Oct	23	Zaragoza	W	3-0	PD	10	Raul Garcia [18], Nino [27], Nekounam [30]	17 500
	26	Getafe	D	2-2	PD	11	Balde 2 [6 66]	8 000
	30	Levante	W	2-0	PD	8	Alvaro Cejudo [40], Nino [44]	16 000
Nov	6	RealMadrid	L	1-7	PD	10	Balde [31]	70 000
	20	Vallecano	D	0-0	PD	11		15 270
	27	Espanyol	W	2-1	PD	7	Lamah [44], Nekounam [50]	24 052
	4	Betis	W	2-1	PD	7	Miguel Flano [39], Nekouna [93+]	15 701
	11	Malaga	D	1-1	PD	7	Balde [33]	28 000
Dec	13	Almeria	W	3-1	CRr4		Lekic [16], Nekounam [31p], Annunziata [40]	2 011
	18	Villarreal	W	2-1	PD	5	Balde [75], Sergio [83]	14 241
	21	Almeria	D	1-1	CRr4		Lamah [79]	8 801
	4	Barcelona	L	0-4	CRr5			64 124
	7	Sociedad	D	0-0	PD	5		25 769
Jan	12	Barcelona	L	1-2	CRr5		Lekic [41]	12 498
	15	Racing	L	0-2	PD	6		15 260
	22	Valencia	D	1-1	PD	6	Lolo [92+]	17 359
	30	At. Madrid	L	0-1	PD	10		15 010
	5	Sp. Gijon	D	1-1	PD	9	Lekic [77]	22 000
Feb	11	Barcelona	W	3-2	PD	8	Lekic 2 [5 22], Raul Garcia [56]	17 284
	18	Sevilla	L	0-2	PD	10		34 500
	26	Granada	W	2-1	PD	7	Nekounam [26], Lekic [29]	18 000
	3	Mallorca	D	1-1	PD	7	Alvaro Cejudo [45]	12 498
	11	Ath. Bilbao	W	2-1	PD	6	OG [9], Raul Garcia [30]	16 718
Mar	17	Zaragoza	D	1-1	PD	7	Roversio [87]	22 000
	27	Getafe	D	0-0	PD	7		14 084
	25	Levante	W	2-0	PD	6	Raul Garcia [15], Nino [78]	11 200
	31	RealMadrid	L	1-5	PD	6	Nino [48]	19 600
	7	Vallecano	L	0-6	PD	6		14 000
	10	Espanyol	W	2-0	PD	6	Raul Garcia 2 [53 69]	13 210
Apr	15	Betis	L	0-1	PD	6		37 000
	23	Malaga	D	1-1	PD	8	Nino [53]	13 939
	28	Villarreal	D	1-1	PD	8	Raul Garcia [72]	16 000
	2	Valencia	L	0-4	PD	9		35 000
May	5	Sociedad	W	1-0	PD	8	Balde [14]	17 394
	13	Racing	W	4-2	PD	7	Balde [54], Alvaro Cejudo [68], Raul Garcia [72], Roversio [90]	12 000

7th Att: 297 815 • Av: 15 674 (-5.3%) • Reyno de Navarra 19 800 (79%)

MALLORCA LEAGUE APPEARANCES/GOALS 2011-12
Goalkeepers Dudu Awat ISR 37 • Juan Calatayud 1+2
Defenders Pablo Caceres URU 28+1/0 • Pablo Cendros 20+5/0
Chico 33/0 • Jose Nunes POR 11+3/2 • Kevin 0+1/0
Pablo Mari 0+1/0 • Ivan Ramis 34/2
Midfield Alejandro Alfaro 13+16/2 • Pedro Bigas 12+4/0
Gonzalo Castro URU 30+5/6 • Jonathan de Guzman NED 1/1
Akihiro Ienaga JPN 1+3/0 • Joao Victor BRA 6+4/0 • Jose Marti 24+4/1
Marti Crespi 5+3/0 • Mickael Pereira FRA 26+4/2
Sergio Tejera 7+8/0 • Fernando Tissone ARG 21+6/0
Tomas Pina 24+8/1 • Gianni Zuiverloon NED 6+3/0
Forwards Abdon Prats 0+1/0 • Alvaro Gimenez 9+3/2
Tomer Hemed ISR 18+11/8 • Emilio Nsue 20+10/3
Marvin Ogunjimi BEL 1+6/0 • Victor 30+6/9
Coach Michael Laudrup DEN • Miguel Angel Nadal (27/09/2011)
Joaquin Caparros (3/10/2011)

OSASUNA LEAGUE APPEARANCES/GOALS 2011-12
Goalkeepers Andres Fernandez 37+1 • Asier Riesgo 1
Defenders Damia 24+6/0 • Ion Echaide 1+2/0 • Lolo 16+12/1
Marc Bertran 27+1/0 • Marcos Perez 0+1/0 • Miguel Flano 27+3/1
Jukka Raitala FIN 13+4/0 • Roversio BRA 14+2/2
Ruben Gonzalez 8+3/0 • Eneko Satrustegui 10/0 • Sergio 20/1
Midfield Alvaro Cejudo 28+6/4 • Javier Annunziata 2+4/0
Javier Calleja 1+5/0 • Roland Lamah BEL 23+7/1
Raoul Loe FRA 5+3/0 • Javad Nekounam IRN 28+3/5
Francisco Punal 35/0 • Raul Garcia 30+3/11
David Timor 7+17/0 • Roberto Torres 0+2/0
Forwards Ibrahima Balde SEN 13+9/7 • Kike Sola 6+1/0
Dejan Lekic SRB 9+10/4 • Nino 32+4/6 • Manuel Omwu 1+3/0
Coach Jose Luis Mendilibar

RACING SANTANDER
2011–12

Ag	27	Valencia	L	3-4	PD	14 OG [7], Acosta [14], Adrian [56]	35 000
	11	Levante	D	0-0	PD	13	10 500
Sep	18	At. Madrid	L	0-4	PD	18	40 000
	21	RealMadrid	D	0-0	PD	17	18 870
	25	Sp. Gijon	D	0-0	PD	18	22 000
	1	Vallecano	D	1-1	PD	18 Adrian [59]	10 000
Oct	5	Barcelona	L	0-3	PD	19	78 000
	22	Espanyol	L	0-1	PD	20	16 000
	25	Sevilla	D	2-2	PD	19 Nahuelpan [62], Jairo [69]	38 000
	30	Betis	W	1-0	PD	18 Stuani [62p]	14 000
Nov	6	Granada	D	0-0	PD	18	17 000
	21	Malaga	L	1-3	PD	20 Arana [70]	14 000
	27	Mallorca	L	1-2	PD	20 Nahuelpan [75]	11 672
	3	Villarreal	W	1-0	PD	18 Stuani [27]	16 000
Dec	11	Ath. Bilbao	D	1-1	PD	19 Alvaro [90]	34 000
	13	Vallecano	W	3-2	CRr4	Stuani 2 [6 83], Nahuelpan [90]	5 000
	18	Sociedad	D	0-0	PD	19	9 000
	21	Vallecano	L	3-4	CRr4	Tziolis [7], Stuani 2 [53 74]	8 050
	4	Mirandés	L	0-2	CRr5		5 200
Jan	7	Zaragoza	W	1-0	PD	17 Bernardo [45]	10 000
	10	Mirandés	D	1-1	CRr5	Munitis [35]	9 000
	15	Osasuna	W	2-0	PD	15 Stuani 2 [38p 71p]	15 260
	21	Getafe	L	1-2	PD	16 Stuani [14]	10 425
	29	Valencia	D	2-2	PD	17 Adrian [2], Bernardo [88]	11 494
Feb	4	Levante	D	1-1	PD	18 Arana [61]	7 658
	11	At. Madrid	D	0-0	PD	18	12 328
	18	Real Madrid	L	0-4	PD	18	76 000
	25	Sp. Gijon	D	1-1	PD	18 Stuani [74p]	15 902
Mar	3	Vallecano	L	2-4	PD	18 Torrejon [9], Colsa [28]	11 000
	11	Barcelona	L	0-2	PD	18	18 885
	19	Espanyol	L	1-3	PD	18 Stuani [12]	18 223
	22	Sevilla	L	0-3	PD	18	13 998
	25	Betis	D	1-1	PD	18 Stuani [77]	34 000
	31	Granada	L	0-1	PD	19	15 960
Apr	9	Malaga	L	0-3	PD	20	30 000
	12	Mallorca	L	0-3	PD	20	10 000
	15	Villarreal	D	1-1	PD	20 Acosta [93+]	16 000
	22	Ath. Bilbao	L	0-1	PD	20	15 000
	28	Sociedad	L	0-3	PD	20	20 000
May	1	Getafe	D	1-1	PD	20 Diop [65]	9 500
	5	Zaragoza	L	1-2	PD	20 Christian Fernandez [12]	28 000
	13	Osasuna	L	2-4	PD	20 Stuani [2], Jairo [81]	12 000

20th Att: 254 362 • Av: 13 387 (-14.7%) • El Sardinero 22 271 (60%)

RACING LEAGUE APPEARANCES/GOALS 2011-12
Goalkeepers Mario Fernandez 12+1 • Daniel Sotres 1+1 • Tono 25
Defenders Alvaro Gonzalez 34/1 • Bernardo Espinosa COL 25/2
Borja Garcia 0+1/0 • Christian Fernandez 14+6/1
Domingo Cisma 25+1/0 • Osmar Barba 5+3/0 • Marc Torrejon 27+2/1
Midfield Lautaro Acosta ARG 14+7/2 • Adrian Gonzalez 29+6/3
Manuel Arana 22+6/2 • Gonzalo Colsa 14+4/1
Papa Kouli Diop SEN 33+1/1 • Edu Bedia 7+4/0 • Francis 22/0
Marcos Gullon 9+1/0 • Jairo 14+11/2 • Julian Luque 8+7/0
Pedro Munitis 22+10/0 • Jose Picon 2+1/0 • Enrique Rivero
Quique 4/0 • Oscar Serrano 4+4/0 • Alexandros Tziolis GRE 6+6/0
Forwards Ariel ARG 5+5/2 • Khouma Babacar SEN 4+4/0
Kennedy Bakiricioglu SWE 2+5/0 • Jaime Isuardi 0+2/0
Javi Martinez 0+4/0 • Mamadou Kone 5+1/0
Christian Stuani URU 24+8/9
Coach Hector Cuper ARG (29/06/2011) • Juan Jose Gonzalez
(28/11/2011) • Alvaro Cervera (10/03/2012)

REAL MADRID
2011–12

	14	Barcelona	D	2-2	SC		Ozil [13], Xabi Alonso [54]	79 800
Aug	17	Barcelona	L	2-3	SC		Ronaldo [20], Benzema [82]	92 965
	28	Zaragoza	W	6-0	PD	1	Ronaldo 3 [24 71 87], Marcelo [28], Xabi Alonso [64], Kaka [82]	28 000
	10	Getafe	W	4-2	PD	1	Benzema 2 [14 69], Ronaldo [60p], Higuain [88]	76 000
	14	Din Zagreb	W	1-0	CLgD		Di Maria [53]	27 055
	18	Levante	L	0-1	PD	5		18 000
Sep	21	Racing	D	0-0	PD	7		18 870
	24	Vallecano	W	6-2	PD	5	Ronaldo 3 [39 51p 84p], Higuain [45], Verane [67], Benzema [73]	72 000
	27	Ajax	W	3-0	CLgD		Ronaldo [25], Kaka [41], Benzema [49]	70 320
	2	Espanyol	W	4-0	PD	3	Higuain 3 [17 66 89], Callejon [82]	34 423
	15	Betis	W	4-1	PD	3	Higuain 3 [46 70 73], Kaka [59]	72 000
Oct	18	Lyon	W	4-0	CLgD		Benzema [19], Khedira [47], OG [55], Sergio Ramos [81]	70 028
	22	Malaga	W	4-0	PD	2	Higuain [11], Ronaldo 3 [24 28 38]	26 000
	26	Villarreal	W	3-0	PD	2	Benzema [5], Kaka [11], Di Maria [31]	55 000
	29	Sociedad	W	1-0	PD	1	Higuain [9]	25 289
	2	Lyon	W	2-0	CLgD		Ronaldo 2 [24 69p]	40 099
	6	Osasuna	W	7-1	PD	1	Ronaldo 3 [23 55p 58], Pepe [34], Higuain [40], Benzema 2 [63 81]	70 000
Nov	19	Valencia	W	3-2	PD	1	Benzema [20], Sergio Ramos [72], Ronaldo [79]	45 000
	22	Din Zagreb	W	6-2	CLgD		Benzema 2 [2 66], Calejon 2 [7 49], Higuain [9], Ozil [20]	65 415
	26	At. Madrid	W	4-1	PD	1	Ronaldo 2 [24p 82p], Di Maria [49], Higuain [65]	78 500
	3	Sp. Gijon	W	3-0	PD	1	Di Maria [34], Ronaldo [64], Marcelo [90]	27 000
	7	Ajax	W	3-0	CLgD		Callejon 2 [14 92+], Higuain [41]	51 557
Dec	10	Barcelona	L	1-3	PD	1	Benzema [1]	79 900
	13	Ponf'radina	W	2-0	CRr4		Callejon [29], Ronaldo [74]	8 500
	17	Sevilla	W	6-2	PD	1	Ronaldo 3 [10 41 85p], Callefon [37], Di Maria [66], Altintop [89]	36 400
	20	Ponf'radina	W	5-1	CRr4		Callejon 2 [25 88], Sahin [44], Varane [49], Joselu [79]	52 000
	3	Malaga	W	3-2	CRr5		Khedira [68], Higuain [70], Benzema [78]	83 500
	7	Granada	W	5-1	PD	1	Benzema 2 [19 50], Sergio Ramos [34], Higuain [47], Ronaldo [89]	78 000
Jan	10	Malaga	W	1-0	CRr5		Benzema [72]	25 000
	14	Mallorca	W	2-1	PD	1	Higuain [72], Callejon [84]	20 000
	18	Barcelona	L	1-2	CRqf		Ronaldo [11]	80 000
	22	Ath. Bilbao	W	4-1	PD	1	Marcelo [25], Ronaldo 2 [47p 67p], Callejon [86]	75 000
	25	Barcelona	D	2-2	CRqf		Ronaldo [68], Benzema [72]	95 486
	28	Zaragoza	W	3-1	PD	1	Kaka [32], Ronaldo [49], Ozil [56]	78 000
	4	Getafe	W	1-0	PD	1	Sergio Ramos [18]	14 000
Feb	12	Levante	W	4-2	PD	1	Ronaldo 3 [45p 50 57], Benzema [66]	67 000
	18	Racing	W	4-0	PD	1	Ronaldo [6], Benzema 2 [45 89], Di Maria [73]	76 000
	21	CSKA M'kva	D	1-1	CLr2		Ronaldo [28]	70 000
	26	Vallecano	W	1-0	PD	1	Ronaldo [54]	12 400
	4	Espanyol	W	5-0	PD	1	Ronaldo [23], Khedira [38], Higuain 2 [47 78], Kaka [66]	77 000
	10	Betis	W	3-2	PD	1	Higuain [24], Ronaldo 2 [51 72]	51 300
	14	CSKA M'kva	W	4-1	CLr2		Higuain [26], Ronaldo 2 [55 94+], Benzema [70]	67 743
Mar	18	Malaga	D	1-1	PD	1	Benzema [35]	75 000
	21	Villarreal	D	1-1	PD	1	Ronaldo [62]	21 000
	24	Sociedad	W	5-1	PD	1	Higuain [6], Ronaldo 2 [31 55], Benzema 2 [39 48]	76 000
	27	APOEL	W	3-0	CLqf		Benzema [7], Ronaldo 2 [37 70], Higuain 2 [40 77]	22 385
	31	Osasuna	W	5-1	PD	1	Benzema [7], Ronaldo 2 [37 70], Higuain 2 [40 77]	19 600
Apr	4	APOEL	W	5-2	CLqf		Ronaldo 2 [26 75], Kaka [37], Callejon [80], Di Maria [84]	54 627
	8	Valencia	D	0-0	PD	1		79 000

ESP – SPAIN 325

REAL MADRID 2011-12 (CONT'D)

Apr	11 At. Madrid	W 4-1	PD	1	Ronaldo 3 [25 69 83p], Callejon [87]	53 000
	14 Sp. Gijon	W 3-1	PD	1	Higuain [37], Ronaldo [74], Benzema [82]	72 000
	17 Bayern	L 1-2	CLsf		Ozil [53]	66 000
	21 Barcelona	W 2-1	PD	1	Khedira [17], Ronaldo [73]	99 252
	25 Bayern	W 2-1	CLsf		Ronaldo 2 [6p 14], L 1-3p	71 654
	29 Sevilla	W 3-0	PD	1	Ronaldo [19], Benzema 2 [49 52]	75 000
May	2 Ath. Bilbao	W 3-0	PD	1	Higuain [16], Ozil [20], Ronaldo [50]	39 500
	5 Granada	W 2-1	PD	1	Ronaldo [81p], OG [92+]	22 000
	13 Mallorca	W 4-1	PD	1	Ronaldo [19], Benzema [23], Ozil 2 [49 58]	79 500

1st Att: 1 410 900 • Av: 74 258 (+6.3%) • Bernabéu 80 354 (92%)

REAL LEAGUE APPEARANCES/GOALS 2011-12
Goalkeepers Adan 1 • Iker Casillas 37
Defenders Alvaro Arbeloa 26/0 • Fabio Coentrao POR 12+8/0
Marcelo BRA 31+1/3 • Pepe POR 29/1 • Raul Albiol 5+5/0
Ricardo Carvalho POR 7+1/0 • Sergio Ramos 34/3
Raphael Varane FRA 7+2/1
Midfield Hamit Altintop TUR 1+4/1 • Angel Di Maria ARG 16+7/5
Lassana Diarra FRA 15+2/0 • Esteban Granero 7+10/0
Kaka BRA 17+10/5 • Sami Khedira GER 20+8/2
Mesut Ozil GER 30+5/4 • Nuri Sahin TUR 2+2/0 • Xabi Alonso 35+1/1
Forwards Karim Benzema FRA 26+8/21 • Jose Callejon 5+20/5
Cristiano Ronaldo POR 37+1/46 • Gonzalo Higuain ARG 18+17/22
Jese Rodriguez 0+1/0 • Morata 0+1/0
Coach Jose Mourinho POR

REAL SOCIEDAD 2011-12 (CONT'D)

Mar	4 Ath. Bilbao	L 0-2	PD	13		37 000
	10 Zaragoza	W 3-0	PD	11	Agirretxe 2 [19 40], Vela [22]	23 500
	17 Getafe	L 0-1	PD	14		7 500
	21 Levante	L 1-3	PD	14	Vela [6]	20 722
	24 Real Madrid	L 1-5	PD	14	Xabi Prieto [41]	76 000
Apr	1 Vallecano	W 4-0	PD	14	Agirretxe [6], Zurutuza [31], Griezmann [51], Vela [53]	20 000
	7 Espanyol	D 2-2	PD	15	Vela 2 [12 15]	20 110
	10 Betis	D 1-1	PD	15	Vela [56]	21 000
	15 Malaga	D 1-1	PD	15	Xabi Prieto [49]	28 000
	22 Villarreal	D 1-1	PD	14	Vela [86]	18 000
	28 Racing	W 3-0	PD	13	Griezmann 2 [47 70], Agirretxe [83]	20 000
May	2 At. Madrid	D 1-1	PD	14	Vela [91+]	40 000
	5 Osasuna	L 0-1	PD	14		17 394
	12 Valencia	W 1-0	PD	12	Griezmann [64]	24 000

12th Att: 439 563 • Av: 23 135 (-7.7%) • Anoeta 32 076 (72%)

SOCIEDAD LEAGUE APPEARANCES/GOALS 2011-12
Goalkeepers Claudio Bravo CHI 37 • Enaut Zubikarai 1
Defenders Ion Ansotegi 8+1/0 • Liassine Cadamuro FRA 13+6/0
Carlos Martinez 19+2/0 • Alberto De la Bella 21/0 • Vadim
Demidov NOR 20+3/0 • Inigo Martinez 26/3 • Mikel Gonzalez 25+3/1
Midfield Mikel Aranburu 26+3/2 • Gorka Elustondo 16+1/1
Dani Estrada 25+4/2 • Asier Illarramendi 16+2/0
McDonald Mariga KEN 10+4/0 • Javi Ros • Markel Bergara 9+2/0
Ruben Pardo 2+13/1 • Jeffrey Sarpong NED 1+2/0 • Xabi Prieto 25+9/2
David Zurutuza 30+3/3
Forwards Imanol Agirretxe 27+9/10 • Antoine Griezmann FRA 28+7/7
Diego Ifran URU 4+12/1 • Joseba Llorente 1+16/0 • Carlos Vela MEX
28+7/12
Coach Philippe Montanier FRA (4/06/2011)

REAL SOCIEDAD 2011-12

Ag	27 Sp. Gijon	W 2-1	PD	5	Agirretxe 2 [35 65]	18 000
Sep	10 Barcelona	D 2-2	PD	5	Agirretxe [59], Griezmann [62]	30 000
	17 Sevilla	L 0-1	PD	10		39 000
	20 Granada	W 1-0	PD	9	Estrada [64]	23 000
	25 Mallorca	L 1-2	PD	9	Agirretxe [15]	11 856
Oct	2 Ath. Bilbao	L 1-2	PD	9	Inigo Martinez [61]	29 000
	16 Zaragoza	L 0-2	PD	13		20 000
	23 Getafe	D 0-0	PD	15		25 000
	26 Levante	L 2-3	PD	15	Estrada [4], Inigo Martinez [86]	12 347
	29 Real Madrid	L 0-1	PD	16		25 289
Nov	6 Vallecano	L 0-4	PD	20		10 081
	20 Espanyol	D 0-0	PD	19		23 702
	27 Betis	W 3-2	PD	17	Agirretxe [56], Vela [76], Inigo Martinez [91+]	30 000
Dec	4 Malaga	W 3-2	PD	14	OG [10], Vela [89], Ifran [91+]	24 500
	11 Villarreal	D 1-1	PD	14	Aranburu [52]	16 000
	13 Granada	W 4-1	CRr4		Griezmann [4], Xabi Prieto 2 [7 64], Ifran [90]	18 000
	18 Racing	D 0-0	PD	15		9 000
	21 Granada	L 1-2	CRr4		Agirretxe [83]	18 000
Jan	4 Mallorca	W 2-0	CRr5		Aranburu [17], Agirretxe [54]	23 000
	7 Osasuna	D 0-0	PD	16		25 769
	10 Mallorca	L 1-6	CRr5		Ifran [16]	6 500
	14 Valencia	W 1-0	PD	14	Griezmann [56]	39 000
	21 At. Madrid	L 0-4	PD	15		20 000
	29 Sp. Gijon	W 5-1	PD	12	Zurutuza 2 [23], Elustondo [75], Aranburu [92+], Griezmann [93+]	22 081
Feb	4 Barcelona	L 1-2	PD	15	Vela [73]	92 000
	13 Sevilla	W 2-0	PD	14	Vela [64], Pardo [68]	19 000
	19 Granada	L 1-4	PD	16	Mikel Gonzalez [10]	22 500
	26 Mallorca	W 1-0	PD	13	Agirretxe [79]	25 000

SEVILLA 2011-12

Ag	18 Hannover	L 1-2	ELpo		Kanoute [37]	43 500
	25 Hannover	D 1-1	ELpo		OG [36]	33 026
	28 Malaga	W 2-1	PD		Negredo 2 [2 26]	35 000
Sep	10 Villarreal	D 2-2	PD	6	Negredo [24], Alexis [86]	20 000
	17 Sociedad	W 1-0	PD	4	Kanoute [53]	39 000
	20 Osasuna	D 0-0	PD	5		14 903
	24 Valencia	W 1-0	PD	4	Kanoute [18]	36 000
Oct	2 At. Madrid	D 0-0	PD	6		50 000
	16 Sp. Gijon	W 2-1	PD	5	Manu del Moral [15], Caceres [57]	36 000
	22 Barcelona	D 0-0	PD	4		82 743
	25 Racing	D 2-2	PD	5	Manu del Moral 2 [37 90]	38 000
	31 Granada	L 1-2	PD	5	Manu del Moral [1]	35 000
Nov	5 Mallorca	D 0-0	PD	5		11 900
	20 Ath. Bilbao	L 1-2	PD	6	Jesus Navas [14]	28 000
	27 Zaragoza	W 1-0	PD	6	Negredo [23p]	22 000
Dec	5 Getafe	W 3-0	PD	5	Fazio [33], Manu del Morel [50], Kanoute [90]	38 000
	10 Levante	L 0-1	PD	5		11 131
	13 San Roque	W 1-0	CRr4		Kanoute [11]	2 500
	17 Real Madrid	L 2-6	PD	6	Jesus Navas [69], Negredo [90]	36 400
	20 San Roque	W 2-1	CRr4		Kanoute 2 [53p 60]	10 000
Jan	5 Valencia	L 0-1	CRr5		Escude [62]	38 000
	8 Vallecano	L 1-2	PD	7	Escude [62]	10 146
	11 Valencia	W 2-1	CRr5		Rakitic [70], OG [91+]	25 000
	14 Espanyol	D 0-0	PD	7		31 000
	21 Betis	D 1-1	PD	9	Negredo [41]	40 000
	29 Malaga	L 1-2	PD	11	Luna [15]	30 000

SEVILLA 2011–12 (CONT'D)

Feb	5 Villarreal	L 1-2	PD	11	OG [33]	45 000
	13 Sociedad	L 0-2	PD	13		19 000
	18 Osasuna	W 2-0	PD	11	Medel [16], Trochowski [90]	34 500
	26 Valencia	W 2-1	PD	10	Medel [36], Jesus Navas [70]	45 000
Mar	3 At. Madrid	D 1-1	PD	10	Baba Diawara [54]	45 000
	10 Sp. Gijon	L 0-1	PD	12		20 000
	17 Barcelona	L 0-2	PD	12		40 000
	22 Racing	W 3-0	PD	11	Jesus Navas 34, Manu del Morel 2 [52] [90]	13 998
	26 Granada	W 3-0	PD	9	Negredo [39], Manu del Morel 2 [54] [90]	16 000
Apr	2 Mallorca	W 3-1	PD	8	Negredo [51], Manu del Morel [62], Jesus Navas [68]	35 000
	8 Ath. Bilbao	L 0-1	PD	8		38 000
	12 Zaragoza	W 3-0	PD	7	Fazio [11], Negredo 2 [29] [43]	32 000
	16 Getafe	L 1-5	PD	9	Negredo [19]	7 000
	21 Levante	D 1-1	PD	9	Negredo [21]	28 000
	29 Real Madrid	L 0-3	PD	9		75 000
May	2 Betis	L 1-2	PD	12	Negredo [5]	45 000
	5 Vallecano	W 5-2	PD	10	Baba Diawara 2 [31] [47], Cala [43], Reyes [65], Kanoute [82]	28 000
	13 Espanyol	D 1-1	PD	9	Negredo [45]	16 627

9th Att: 684 900 • Av: 36 047 (+2.9%) • Sánchez Pizjuán 45 500 (79%)

SEVILLA LEAGUE APPEARANCES/GOALS 2011-12
Goalkeepers Javi Varas 25 • Andres Palop 13
Defenders Alexis 1/1 • Cala 7+1/1
Jose Caceres URU 13+1/1 • Coke 24+4/0 • Deivid 3+2/0
Julien Escude FRA 24/1 • Federico Fazio ARG 25+3/2
Fernando Navarro 35/0 • Antonio Luna 11+3/1 • Alberto Moreno 0+1/0
Emir Spahic BIH 22/0
Midfield Emiliano Armenteros 4+9/0 • Jose Campana 2+12/0
Tiberio Guarente ITA 0+3/0 • Jesus Navas 37/5 • Gary Medel CHI 30+1/2 Ivan Rakitic CRO 19+17/0 • Jose Antonio Reyes 15+4/1
Piotr Trochowski GER 27+8/1
Forwards Baba Diawara SEN 2+9/3 • Hiroshi Ibusuki JPN 0+1/0
Frederic Kanoute MLI 12+14/4 • Luis Alberto 0+5/0
Manu del Moral 25+9/10 • Alvaro Negredo 28+2/14
Diego Perotti ARG 13+3/0
Coach Marcelino Garcia Toral (3/06/2011) • Michel (6/02/2012)

SPORTING GIJON 2011–12

Feb	5 Osasuna	D 1-1	PD	19	Carmelo [32]	22 000
	12 Valencia	L 0-4	PD	19		45 000
	19 At. Madrid	D 1-1	PD	19	Eguren [37]	23 000
	25 Racing	D 1-1	PD	19	Barral [43]	15 902
Mar	3 Barcelona	L 1-3	PD	19	Barral [49]	72 442
	10 Sevilla	W 1-0	PD	19	Andre Castro [31]	20 000
	17 Granada	L 1-2	PD	19	Adrian Corlunga [90]	22 500
	21 Mallorca	L 2-3	PD	19	Adrian Corlunga [38], Botia [66]	18 000
	25 Ath. Bilbao	D 1-1	PD	19	Lora [90]	35 000
	31 Zaragoza	L 1-2	PD	20	Eguren [49]	29 538
Apr	7 Getafe	L 0-2	PD	19		6 500
	11 Levante	W 3-2	PD	19	Trejo [22], Lora [74], Sangoy [84]	16 000
	14 Real Madrid	L 1-3	PD	19	De las Cuevas [30p]	72 000
	21 Vallecano	W 2-1	PD	19	Sangoy [18], Bilic [78]	21 000
	28 Espanyol	W 3-0	PD	19	Adrian Corlunga [48], Trejo [70], Bilic [80]	18 000
May	1 Villarreal	L 2-3	PD	19	Lora [39], Galvez [85]	29 000
	5 Betis	W 2-1	PD	19	Sangoy 2 [13p] [55]	15 156
	13 Malaga	L 0-1	PD	19		22 000

19th Att: 414 914 • Av: 21 838 (+0.5%) • El Molinón 29 800 (73%)

SPORTING LEAGUE APPEARANCES/GOALS 2011-12
Goalkeepers Ivan Cuellar 1 • Juan Pablo 37
Defenders Gregory Arnolin FRA 18+3/0 • Alberto Botia 33+1/1
Roberto Canella 30+1/0 • Alejandro Galvez 11+1/2
Alberto Lora 25+2/3 • Alex Menendez 2/0 • Moises Garcia 3/0
Pedro Orfila 10+1/0
Midfield Andre Castro POR 26+3/2 • Ayoze 7+8/0 • Carmelo 6+7/1
Damian Suarez URU 16+3/0 • Miguel De las Cuevas 34+1/3
Sebastian Eguren URU 12+7/2 • Ivan Hernandez 19+1/0
Luis Moran 0+5/0 • Pape Mendy SEN 6+4/0 • Juan Muniz 0+1/0
Nacho Cases 15+6/0 • Ricardo 1+2/0 • Alberto Rivera 21+8/0
Sergio Alvarez 4+2/0
Forwards Adrian Colunga 13+4/3 • David Barral 26+4/9
Mate Bilic CRO 1+19/4 • Nacho Novo 8+3/3
Gaston Sangoy ARG 7+9/4 • Oscar Trejo ARG 26+7/4
Coach Manolo Preciado • Inaki Tejada (31/01/2012) • Javier Clemente (13/02/2012)

SPORTING GIJON 2011–12

Aug	27 Sociedad	L 1-2	PD	16	De las Cuevas [68p]	18 000
Sep	11 Osasuna	L 1-2	PD	19	Barral [75]	15 842
	17 Valencia	L 0-1	PD	20		20 000
	21 At. Madrid	L 0-4	PD	20		38 000
	25 Racing	D 0-0	PD	20		22 000
Oct	2 Barcelona	L 0-1	PD	20		23 220
	16 Sevilla	L 1-2	PD	20	Barral [64]	36 000
	22 Granada	W 2-0	PD	19	Barral [6], Andre Castro [42]	23 000
	26 Mallorca	W 2-1	PD	17	Bilic [49], OG [65]	9 400
	30 Ath. Bilbao	D 1-1	PD	17	Bilic [71]	21 000
Nov	6 Zaragoza	D 2-2	PD	17	Barral 2 [31] [44]	18 161
	20 Getafe	W 2-1	PD	14	Trejo [45], Nacho Novo [89]	22 000
	27 Levante	L 0-4	PD	18		11 287
Dec	3 Real Madrid	L 0-3	PD	18		27 000
	11 Vallecano	W 3-1	PD	18	Barral [10], Nacho Novo 2 [37] [67]	10 100
	13 Mallorca	W 1-0	CRr4		Juan Muniz [84]	6 400
	17 Espanyol	L 1-2	PD	18	Barral [61]	23 000
	20 Mallorca	L 0-2	CRr4			6 000
	8 Betis	L 0-2	PD	19		35 000
Jan	15 Malaga	W 2-1	PD	18	Galvez [36], Trejo [90]	22 000
	23 Villarreal	L 0-3	PD	19		15 000
	29 Sociedad	L 1-5	PD	19	De las Cuevas [46]	22 081

VALENCIA 2011–12

Aug	27 Racing	W 4-3	PD	3	Soldado 3 [2] [88] [90], Rami [58]	35 000
	10 At. Madrid	W 1-0	PD	2	Soldado [52]	40 000
	13 Genk	D 0-0	CLgE			20 248
Sep	17 Sp. Gijon	W 1-0	PD	1	Soldado [30]	20 000
	21 Barcelona	D 2-2	PD	2	OG [12], Pablo Hernandez [23]	52 250
	24 Sevilla	L 0-1	PD	7		36 000
	28 Chelsea	D 1-1	CLgE		Soldado [87p]	33 791
Oct	1 Granada	W 1-0	PD	5	Canales [4]	36 000
	15 Mallorca	D 1-1	PD	6	Rami [38]	15 000
	19 Leverkusen	L 1-2	CLgE		Jonas [24]	26 384
	23 Ath. Bilbao	D 1-1	PD	5	Soldado [89]	27 532
	29 Zaragoza	W 1-0	PD	4	Jordi Alba [82]	18 000
Nov	6 Getafe	W 3-1	PD	4	Feghouli 2 [12] [25], Aduriz [76]	28 000
	1 Leverkusen	W 3-1	CLgE		Jonas [1], Soldado [65], Rami [75]	37 047
	5 Levante	W 2-0	PD	3	OG [31], Tino Costa [50]	19 000
	19 Real Madrid	L 2-3	PD	3	Soldado 2 [75] [83]	45 000
	23 Genk	W 7-0	CLgE		Jonas [10], Soldado 3 [13] [35] [39], Pablo Hernandez [68], Aduriz [70], Tino Costa [81]	35 086
	26 Vallecano	W 3-0	PD	3	Jonas [21], Tino Costa [57]	10 100
	3 Espanyol	W 2-1	PD	3	Tino Costa [6p], Soldado [80]	40 000
Dec	6 Chelsea	L 0-3	CLgE			41 109
	10 Betis	L 1-2	PD	3	OG [66]	35 000
	13 Cádiz	D 0-0	CRr4			6 635
	18 Malaga	W 2-0	PD	3	Soldado 2 [36] [62]	35 000
	22 Cádiz	W 4-0	CRr4		Victor Ruiz [5], Jonas [28], Soldado [41], Ever Banega [68]	20 000

ESP – SPAIN

VALENCIA 2011–12 (CONT'D)

	5	Sevilla	W	1-0	CRr5	Jonas [33]	38 000
	8	Villarreal	D	2-2	PD 3	Feghouli [41], Aduriz [87]	18 000
	11	Sevilla	L	1-2	CRr5	Soldado [67]	25 000
	14	Sociedad	L	0-1	PD 3		39 000
Jan	19	Levante	W	4-1	CRqf	Jonas [24], Soldado [31], Piatti [45], Tino Costa [94+]	39 000
	22	Osasuna	D	1-1	PD 3	Soldado [85]	17 359
	26	Levante	W	3-0	CRqf	Aduriz [25], Piatti 2 [30 85]	12 100
	29	Racing	D	2-2	PD 3	Aduriz 2 [67 79]	11 494
	1	Barcelona	D	1-1	CRsf	Jonas [27]	51 800
	5	At. Madrid	D	0-0	PD 3		45 000
	8	Barcelona	L	0-2	CRsf		90 237
Feb	12	Sp. Gijon	W	4-0	PD 3	Feghouli [33], OG [73], Jonas 2 [91+ 93+]	45 000
	16	Stoke	W	1-0	ELr2	Mehmet Topal [36]	24 185
	19	Barcelona	L	1-5	PD 3	Piatti [9]	74 240
	23	Stoke	W	1-0	ELr2	Jonas [24]	36 535
	26	Sevilla	L	1-2	PD 3	Tino Costa [25]	45 000
	4	Granada	W	1-0	PD 3	Feghouli [32]	12 000
	8	PSV	W	4-2	ELr3	Victor Ruiz [11], OG [13], Soldado [43p], Piatti [56]	25 495
	11	Mallorca	D	2-2	PD 3	Tino Costa [22], Aduriz [41]	35 000
Mar	15	PSV	D	1-1	ELr3	Rami [47]	29 500
	18	Ath. Bilbao	W	3-0	PD 3	Soldado 3 [40 56 84p]	35 000
	21	Zaragoza	L	1-2	PD 3	Pablo Hernandez [5]	39 000
	24	Getafe	L	1-3	PD 3	Soldado [4]	8 000
	29	AZ	L	1-2	ELqf	Mehmet Topal [51]	16 100
	1	Levante	D	1-1	PD 3	Jonas [35]	40 000
	5	AZ	W	2-1	ELqf	Rami 2 [15 17], Jordi Alba [56], Pablo Hernandez [80]	27 738
	8	Real Madrid	D	0-0	PD 4		79 000
	11	Vallecano	W	4-1	PD 3	Jonas 2 [41 77p], Jordi Alba [79], Pablo Hernandez [88]	48 711
Apr	15	Espanyol	L	0-4	PD 3		24 000
	19	At. Madrid	L	2-4	ELsf	Jonas [45], Ricardo Costa [94+]	40 899
	22	Betis	W	4-0	PD 3	Jonas [6], Feghouli [63], Soldado [86], Piatti [88]	39 000
	26	At. Madrid	L	0-1	ELsf		43 711
	29	Malaga	D	0-1	PD 3		22 000
	2	Osasuna	W	4-0	PD 3	Aduriz 2 [77 87], Jonas 2 [83 88]	35 000
May	9	Villarreal	W	1-0	PD 3	Jonas [91+]	35 000
	12	Sociedad	D	0-1	PD 3		24 000

3rd Att: 739 493 • Av: 38 921 (-3.3%) • Mestalla 55 000 (70%)

VALENCIA LEAGUE APPEARANCES/GOALS 2011-12
Goalkeepers Diego Alves BRA 12 • Vicente Guaita 26
Defenders Antonio Barragan 15+3/0 • Juan Bernat 2+5/0
Bruno 11+3/0 • Angel Dealbert 11/0 • Jordi Alba 27+5/2
Hedwiges Maduro NED 4+3/0 • Jeremy Mathieu FRA 27+4/0
Miguel POR 11/0 • Adil Rami FRA 33/2 • Ricardo Costa POR 11+1/0
Victor Ruiz 22/0
Midfield David Albelda 19+2/0 • Ever Banega ARG 13/0
Sergio Canales 6+5/1 • Tino Costa ARG 25+5/5
Sofiane Feghouli ALG 25+5/6 • Mehmet Topal TUR 13+7/0
Pablo Hernandez 19+11/3 • Daniel Parejo 12+4/0
Forwards Paco Alcacer 0+3/0 • Artiz Aduriz 11+18/7
Jonas BRA 23+11/10 • Pablo Piatti ARG 14+16/2
Roberto Soldado 29+3/17
Coach Unai Emery

RAYO VALLECANO 2011–12

Ag	28	Ath. Bilbao	D	1-1	PD	Movilla [62]	35 000
	11	Zaragoza	D	0-0	PD		13 000
Sep	18	Getafe	W	1-0	PD	Michu [4]	12 000
	21	Levante	L	1-2	PD	Tamudo [72p]	13 950
	24	Real Madrid	L	2-6	PD	Michu 2 [1 55]	72 000
	1	Racing	D	1-1	PD	Tamudo [20]	10 000
	16	Espanyol	L	0-1	PD		11 000
Oct	23	Betis	W	2-0	PD	Bangoura [80], Koke [89p]	36 000
	26	Malaga	W	2-0	PD	Pedro Botelho [7], Tamudo [70]	10 000
	29	Villarreal	L	0-2	PD		14 000
	6	Sociedad	W	4-0	PD	Piti [13p], Michu 2 [50 63], Trashorras [73]	10 081
Nov	20	Osasuna	D	0-0	PD		15 270
	26	Valencia	L	1-2	PD	Tamudo [84]	10 100
	29	Barcelona	L	0-4	PD		53 775
	4	At. Madrid	L	1-3	PD	OG [91+]	39 000
	11	Sp. Gijon	L	1-3	PD	Michu [91+]	10 100
Dec	16	Racing	L	2-3	CRr4	Michel [44], Michu [64]	5 000
	21	Racing	W	4-3	CRr4	Piti [33], Michu [36], Delibasic [41], Tamudo [62]	8 050
	8	Sevilla	W	2-1	PD	Michu [45], Tamudo [51]	10 146
Jan	14	Granada	W	2-1	PD	Michu [26], Piti [52]	22 500
	22	Mallorca	L	0-1	PD		10 000
	28	Ath. Bilbao	L	2-3	PD	Michu [11], Arribas [27]	12 450
	5	Zaragoza	W	2-1	PD	Diego Costa [75], Michu [82]	18 000
	12	Getafe	W	2-0	PD	Michu [34], Diego Costa [64]	10 000
Feb	19	Levante	W	5-3	PD	Bangoura 2 [35 70], Diego Costa 2 [62 63], Delibasic [85]	9 457
	26	Real Madrid	L	0-1	PD		12 400
	3	Racing	W	4-2	PD	Michu 2 [45 64], Tamudo [67], Piti [72]	11 000
	11	Espanyol	L	1-5	PD	Tamudo [53]	26 110
Mar	17	Betis	W	3-0	PD	Armenteros [50], Diego Costa [78], Tamudo [91+]	9 216
	22	Malaga	L	2-4	PD	Diego Costa [5p], Trashorras [84p]	30 000
	25	Villarreal	L	0-2	PD		9 652
	1	Sociedad	L	0-4	PD		20 000
	7	Osasuna	W	6-0	PD	Movilla [5], Michu 2 [17 28], Diego Costa [36], Armenteros [57], Tito [79]	14 000
Apr	11	Valencia	L	1-4	PD	Diego Costa [72]	48 711
	15	At. Madrid	L	0-1	PD		10 000
	21	Sp. Gijon	L	1-2	PD	Labaka [51]	21 000
	29	Barcelona	L	0-7	PD		10 000
	2	Mallorca	L	0-1	PD		13 000
May	5	Sevilla	L	2-5	PD	Diego Costa 2 [37p 77]	28 000
	13	Granada	W	1-0	PD	Tamudo [91+]	10 000

15th Att: 207 095 • Av: 10 900 (-8.1%) • Campo de Vallecas 15 489 (70%)

VALLECANO LEAGUE APPEARANCES/GOALS 2011-12
Goalkeepers David Cobeno 14+1 • Dani 11 • Joel 13
Defenders Aitor Nunez 0+1/0 • Alejandro Arribas 34/1
Jose Manuel Casado 32/0 • Jordi Figueras 17/0 • Mikel Labaka 12+1/1
Pedro Botelho 8+3/1 • Jorge Pulido 13+1/0 • Raul Bravo 5+1/0
Rayco 1+5/0 • Rober 2/0 • Tito 36/1
Midfield Alberto Perea 0+1/0 • Emiliano Armenteros ARG 12+1/2
Diego Benito 0+4/0 • Pape Diamanka SEN 2+5/0 • Javi Fuego 31/0
Michel 2+7/0 • Michu 37/15 • Jose Maria Movilla 36+2/2
Rafa Garcia 1+3/0 • Nestor Susaeta 0+2/0
Roberto Trashorras 18+11/2
Forwards Alhassane Bangoura GUI 15+13/3
Andrija Delibasic MNE 5+14/1 • Diego Costa BRA 15+1/10
Koke 0+5/1 • Dani Pacheco 0+11/0 • Piti 29+6/3
Raul Tamudo 17+15/9
Coach Jose Ramon Sandoval

VILLARREAL
2011–12

Aug	17	OB Odense	L	0-1	CLpo		13 002
	23	OB Odense	W	3-0	CLpo	Rossi 2 [50 66], Marchena [82]	18 404
	29	Barcelona	L	0-5	PD	19	75 097
Sep	10	Sevilla	D	2-2	PD	17	Rossi [35p], Marco Ruben [72]	20 000
	14	Bayern M	L	0-2	CLgA		19 168
	17	Granada	L	0-1	PD	19		21 000
	20	Mallorca	W	2-0	PD	13	Rossi [8], Nilmar [52]	18 000
	24	Ath. Bilbao	D	1-1	PD	13	Nilmar [53]	37 000
	27	Napoli	L	0-2	CLgA		46 747
Oct	1	Zaragoza	D	2-2	PD	12	Rossi [41p], Hernan Perez [84]	17 000
	15	Getafe	D	0-0	PD	14		13 000
	18	Man City	L	1-2	CLgA		Cani [4]	43 326
	23	Levante	L	0-3	PD	16		11 000
	26	Real Madrid	L	0-3	PD	18		55 000
	29	Vallecano	W	2-0	PD	13	Bruno Soriano [20], Borja Valero [67]	14 000
Nov	2	Man City	L	0-3	CLgA			19 358
	6	Espanyol	D	0-0	PD	13		23 417
	19	Betis	W	1-0	PD	12	Borja Valero [21]	18 000
	22	Bayern M	L	1-3	CLgA		De Guzman [50]	66 000
	28	Malaga	L	1-2	PD	13	Marco Ruben [16]	22 500
	3	Racing	L	0-1	PD	15		16 000
	7	Napoli	L	0-2	CLgA			15 350
Dec	11	Sociedad	D	1-1	PD	17	Marco Ruben [72]	16 000
	13	Mirandes	D	1-1	CRr4		Borja Valero [84]	4 100
	18	Osasuna	L	1-2	PD	17	Marco Ruben [64]	14 241
	21	Mirandes	L	0-2	CRr4			12 000
	8	Valencia	D	2-2	PD	18	Marco Ruben [14], Gonzalo [18]	18 000
	15	At. Madrid	L	0-3	PD	19		48 000
Jan	23	Sp. Gijon	W	3-0	PD	17	Marco Ruben [57], Borja Valero [59], Bruno Soriano [90]	15 000
	28	Barcelona	D	0-0	PD	18		20 000
	5	Sevilla	W	2-1	PD	17	Borja Valero [22], Camunas [81]	45 000
Feb	12	Granada	W	3-1	PD	15	Marco Ruben [16], Borja Valero [64], OG [73]	21 000
	19	Mallorca	L	0-4	PD	17		14 500
	26	Ath. Bilbao	D	2-2	PD	17	Senna [11], Nilmar [68]	18 000
	4	Zaragoza	L	1-2	PD	17	Martinuccio [16]	15 000
	12	Getafe	L	1-2	PD	17	Nilmar [45p]	18 000
Mar	18	Levante	L	0-1	PD	17		12 200
	21	Real Madrid	L	0-1	PD	17	Senna [83]	21 000
	25	Vallecano	W	2-0	PD	16	Marco Ruben [28], Angel [84]	9 652
	1	Espanyol	D	0-0	PD	17		17 000
	7	Betis	L	1-3	PD	17	Marco Ruben [90p]	30 000
Apr	12	Malaga	W	2-1	PD	17	Senna [83p], Hernan Perez [90]	14 000
	15	Racing	D	1-1	PD	16	Hernan Perez [46]	16 000
	22	Sociedad	D	1-1	PD	17	Senna [42]	18 000
	28	Osasuna	D	1-1	PD	17	Bruno Soriano [44]	16 000
May	1	Sp. Gijon	W	3-2	PD	16	Mario [19], Senna [43p], Hernan Perez [56]	29 000
	5	Valencia	L	0-1	PD	16		35 000
	13	At. Madrid	L	0-1	PD	18		16 000

18th Att: 324 000 • Av: 17 053 (+8.8%) • El Madrigal 25 000 (68%)

VILLARREAL LEAGUE APPEARANCES/GOALS 2011-12
Goalkeepers Cesar Sanchez 1+1 • Diego Lopez 37
Defenders Angel 15+6/1 • Jose Catala 13/0
Gonzalo Rodriguez ARG 24+2/1 • Jaume Costa 6/0 • Joan Oriol 21/0
Florian Lejeune FRA 0+2/0 • Carlos Marchena 9+8/0 • Mario 20+3/1
Mateo Musacchio ARG 29+1/0 • Cristian Zapata COL 28/0
Midfield Borja Valero 36/5 • Bruno Soriano 37/3
Javier Camunas 10+17/1 • Cani 27+2/0
Gonzalo Castellani ARG 1+9/0 • Jonathan de Guzman NED 11+8/0
Moises 0+2/0 • Wakaso Mubarak GHA 1+5/0
Hernan Perez PAR 12+9/4 • Marcos Senna 24+7/5
Forwards Gerard Bordas 0+2/0 • Joselu 3+8/0
Alejandro Martinuccio ARG 5+8/1 • Nilmar BRA 13+8/4
Giuseppe Rossi ITA 9/3 • Marco Ruben ARG 26+5/9
Coach Juan Carlos Garrido • Lotina

REAL ZARAGOZA
2011–12

Ag	28	Real Madrid	L	0-6	PD	20		28 000
	11	Vallecano	D	0-0	PD	18		13 000
	18	Espanyol	W	2-1	PD	11	Luis Garcia 2 [29 90]	26 000
Sep	22	Betis	L	3-4	PD	14	Efrain Juarez [36], Juan Carlos 2 [77 79]	38 000
	25	Malaga	D	0-0	PD	15		18 000
	1	Villarreal	D	2-2	PD	14	Luis Garcia [35], Hernan Perez [84]	17 000
Oct	16	Sociedad	W	2-0	PD	9	Helder Postiga 2 [11 49]	20 000
	23	Osasuna	L	0-3	PD	14		17 500
	26	Valencia	L	0-1	PD	14		18 000
	30	At. Madrid	L	1-3	PD	15	Helder Postiga [79]	40 000
Nov	6	Sp. Gijon	D	2-2	PD	16	OG [28], Helder Postiga [92+]	18 161
	19	Barcelona	L	0-4	PD	18		80 000
	27	Sevilla	L	0-1	PD	19		22 000
Dec	4	Granada	L	0-1	PD	20		22 000
	11	Mallorca	L	0-3	PD	20		22 000
	13	Alcorcón	D	1-1	CRr4		Orti [7]	2 500
	17	Ath. Bilbao	L	1-2	PD	20	Ponzio [22p]	28 000
	21	Alcorcón	L	0-2	CRr4			4 000
Jan	7	Racing	D	0-0	PD	20		10 000
	14	Getafe	D	1-1	PD	20	Lanzaro [39]	28 000
	22	Levante	D	0-0	PD	20		10 065
	28	Real Madrid	L	1-3	PD	20	Lafita [11]	78 000
Feb	5	Vallecano	L	1-2	PD	20	Helder Postiga [33]	18 000
	12	Espanyol	W	2-0	PD	20	Da Silva [55], Juan Carlos [91+]	29 310
	20	Betis	L	0-2	PD	20		20 000
	25	Malaga	L	1-5	PD	20	Aranda [23]	26 000
Mar	4	Villarreal	W	2-1	PD	20	Luis Garcia [85], Abraham [93+]	15 000
	10	Sociedad	L	0-3	PD	20		23 500
	17	Osasuna	D	1-1	PD	20	Helder Postiga [85]	22 000
	21	Valencia	W	2-1	PD	20	Apono 2 [30p 78]	39 000
	25	At. Madrid	W	1-0	PD	20	Apono [95+p]	30 000
	31	Sp. Gijon	W	2-1	PD	18	Helder Postiga [37], Lafita [91+]	29 538
Apr	7	Barcelona	L	1-4	PD	18	Aranda [30]	24 000
	12	Sevilla	L	0-3	PD	18		32 000
	15	Granada	W	2-0	PD	18	Dujmovic [6]	24 000
	21	Mallorca	L	0-1	PD	18		13 000
	29	Ath. Bilbao	W	2-0	PD	18	Oriol [28], Apono [51]	30 000
May	2	Levante	W	1-0	PD	18	Oriol [11]	28 000
	5	Racing	W	2-1	PD	18	Helder Postiga [13], Lafita [78]	28 000
	13	Getafe	W	2-0	PD	16	Apono [58p], Helder Postiga [91+]	9 000

16th Att: 439 161 • Av: 23 114 (-1.5%) • La Romareda 34 596 (66%)

ZARAGOZA LEAGUE APPEARANCES/GOALS 2011-12
Goalkeepers Roberto 38
Defenders Pablo Alvarez ARG 15/0 • Antonio Tomas 3+1/0
Paulo da Silva PAR 27+2/1 • Fernando Meira POR 12/0
Efrain Juarez MEX 15/1 • Maurizio Lanzaro ITA 20+5/1
David Mateos 13+1/0 • Ivan Obradovic SRB 13+4/0
Javier Paredes 32/0 • Adam Pinter HUN 13+3/0
Midfield Abraham Mineiro 17+5/1 • Apono 16+1/5 • Tomislav
Dujmovic CRO 9+3/1 • Juan Carlos 8+16/3 • Angel Lafita 29+8/3
Leonardo Ponzio ARG 16/1 • Ruben Micael POR 23+10/0
Joel Valencia ECU 0+1/0 • Franco Zuculini ARG 11+10/0
Forwards Carlos Aranda 9+4/2 • Pablo Barrera MEX 12+8/1
Braulio 0+2/0 • Helder Postiga POR 29+4/9 • Luis Garcia 27+7/4
Edu Oriol 10+10/2 • Jorge Orti 0+7/0 • Ikechukwu Uche NGA 1/0
Coach Javier Aguirre MEX • Manuel Jimenez (31/12/2011)

EST – ESTONIA

FIFA/COCA-COLA WORLD RANKING

'93	'94	'95	'96	'97	'98	'99	'00	'01	'02	'03	'04	'05	'06	'07	'08	'09	'10	'11	'12
109	119	129	102	100	90	70	67	83	60	68	81	76	106	124	119	102	82	57	86

2012													High	Low	Av
Jan	Feb	Mar	Apr	May	Jun	Jul	Aug	Sep	Oct	Nov	Dec				
52	54	47	53	54	57	56	49	55	69	84	86		47	137	91

Nomme Kalju became the sixth different team to claim the Estonian championship after winning the 2012 title ahead of Levadia and Flora. Based in the wealthy forested suburb of Nomme in the south of the capital Tallinn, Kalju have always had big ambitions. After promotion to the top level in 2007 they announced their intentions by recruiting a number of Brazilian players, but it wasn't until the signing of top Estonian internationals such as Tarmo Neemelo and Kristen Viikmae at the start of 2011 and the hiring of former Levadia coach Igor Prins, that Kalju began to make a significant impact on the pitch. Runners-up in 2011, Kalju went one better in 2012, winning 29 of their 36 matches to finish nine points clear of Levadia, with striker Viikmae securing the title with the winner in a 1-0 victory away to Kuressaare with three games to go. Levadia made up for that disappointment and their trophyless season in 2011 by beating Trans Narva 3-0 in the cup final in May. Once again, Estonia's four representatives in the 2012-13 UEFA club competitions all fell at the first hurdle without winning a game, but Estonia did get its first taste of hosting a major tournament when the UEFA European U-19 Championship was played in Tallinn in July 2012. The Estonians lost all three of their games in a tournament won by Spain.

UEFA EUROPEAN CHAMPIONSHIP RECORD
1960-1992 DNE (Played as part of the Soviet Union) 1996-2012 DNQ

ESTONIAN FOOTBALL ASSOCIATION (EFA)

A. Le Coq Arena,
Asula 4c,
Tallinn 11312
☎ +372 6 279960
📠 +372 6 279969
✉ efa@jalgpall.ee
🖥 www.jalgpall.ee
FA 1921 CON 1992 FIFA 1992
P Aivar Pohlak
GS Anne Rei

THE STADIA
2014 FIFA World Cup Stadia
A. Le Coq Arena
Tallinn — 9 300
Other Main Stadia
Kalevi Keskstaadion
Tallinn — 12 000
Kreenholmi Staadion
Narva — 3 000
Viljandi Linnastaadion
Viljandi — 2 506
Valga Keskstaadion
Valga — 2 500

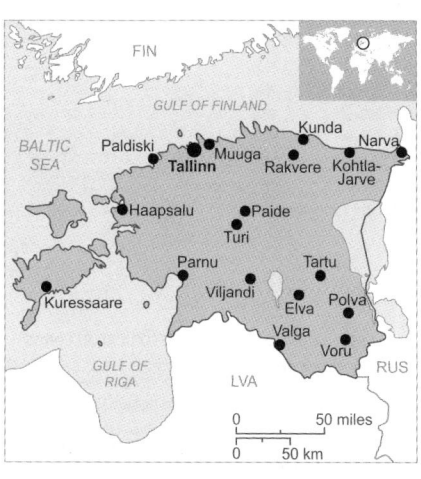

MAJOR CITIES/TOWNS

		Population
1	Tallinn	393 971
2	Tartu	102 285
3	Narva	66 028
4	Kohtla-Järve	44 657
5	Pärnu	43 429
6	Viljandi	20 046
7	Maardu	16 541
8	Rakvere	16 492
9	Sillamäe	16 200
10	Kuressaare	14 951
11	Voru	14 364
12	Valga	13 684
13	Haapsalu	11 605
14	Johvi	11 121
15	Paide	9 826
16	Keila	9 435
17	Kivioli	6 634
18	Polva	6 557
19	Tapa	6 410

ESTI VABARIIK • REPUBLIC OF ESTONIA

Capital Tallinn	Population 1 299 371 (152)	% in cities 69%
GDP per capita $21 400 (57)	Area km² 45 228 km² (132)	GMT +/- +2
Neighbours (km) Latvia 343, Russia 290 • Coast 3794		

RECENT INTERNATIONAL MATCHES PLAYED BY ESTONIA

2010	Opponents	Score	Venue	Comp	Scorers	Att	Referee
3-03	Georgia	L 1-2	Tbilisi	Fr	Purje [83]	40 000	Banari MDA
21-05	Finland	W 2-0	Tallinn	Fr	Oper [5], Post [55]	5 650	Vad HUN
26-05	Croatia	D 0-0	Tallinn	Fr		3 000	Svendsen DEN
19-06	Latvia	D 0-0	Kaunas	BC		300	Mazeika LTU
20-06	Lithuania	L 0-2	Kaunas	BC		600	Sipailo LVA
11-08	Faroe Islands	W 2-1	Tallinn	ECq	Saag [91+], Piiroja [93+]	5 470	Vucemilovic CRO
3-09	Italy	L 1-2	Tallinn	ECq	Zenjov [31]	8 600	Velasco ESP
7-09	Uzbekistan	D 3-3	Tallinn	Fr	Purje [25], Vassiljev 2 [62 71p]	2 055	Jones WAL
8-10	Serbia	W 3-1	Belgrade	ECq	Kink [63], Vassiljev [73], OG [91+]	12 000	Layushkin RUS
12-10	Slovenia	L 0-1	Tallinn	ECq		5 722	Skjerven NOR
17-11	Liechtenstein	D 1-1	Tallinn	Fr	Vassiljev [57p]	1 909	Gvardis RUS
18-12	China PR	L 0-3	Zhuhai	Fr		8 500	Ko Hyung Jin KOR
22-12	Qatar	L 0-2	Doha	Fr			
2011							
25-03	Uruguay	W 2-0	Tallinn	Fr	Vassiljev [61], Zahovaiko [65]	6 817	Munukka FIN
29-03	Serbia	D 1-1	Tallinn	ECq	Vassiljev [84]	5 185	Nijhuis NED
3-06	Italy	L 0-3	Modena	ECq		19 434	Tudor ROU
7-06	Faroe Islands	L 0-2	Toftir	ECq		1 715	Munukka FIN
19-06	Chile	L 0-4	Santiago	Fr		20 000	Vasquez URU
23-06	Uruguay	L 0-3	Rivera	Fr		25 000	Laverni ARG
10-08	Turkey	L 0-3	Istanbul	Fr		20 000	Probert ENG
2-09	Slovenia	W 2-1	Ljubljana	ECq	Vassiljev [29p], Purje [81]	15 480	Studer SUI
6-09	Northern Ireland	W 4-1	Tallinn	ECq	Vunk [28], Kink [32], Zenjov [50], Saag [93+]	8 660	Stalhammar SWE
7-10	Northern Ireland	W 2-1	Belfast	ECq	Vassiljev 2 [77p 84]	12 604	Grafe GER
11-10	Ukraine	L 0-2	Tallinn	Fr		4 501	Malek POL
11-11	Republic of Ireland	L 0-4	Tallinn	ECpo		10 500	Kassai HUN
15-11	Republic of Ireland	D 1-1	Dublin	ECpo	Vassiljev [57]	51 151	Kuipers NED
2012							
29-02	El Salvador	W 2-0	Los Angeles	Fr	Klavan [71], Piiroja [85]	16 800	Salazar USA
25-05	Croatia	L 1-3	Pula	Fr	Vassiljev [83]	8 000	Mihaly HUN
28-05	Ukraine	L 0-4	Kufstein	Fr		1 200	Lechner AUT
1-06	Finland	L 1-2	Tartu	BCsf	Oper [33]	2 470	Direktorenko LVA
3-06	Lithuania	W 1-0	Tartu	BCf	Voskoboinikov [18]	1 094	Kaasik EST
5-06	France	L 0-4	Le Mans	Fr		23 500	Liany ISR
15-08	Poland	W 1-0	Tallinn	Fr	Vassiljev [92+]	5 312	Johnsen NOR
7-09	Romania	L 0-2	Tallinn	WCq		7 936	Mazic SRB
11-09	Turkey	L 0-3	Istanbul	WCq		44 168	Borski POL
12-10	Hungary	L 0-1	Tallinn	WCq		5 661	Liany ISR
16-10	Andorra	W 1-0	Andorra La Vella	WCq	Oper [57]	723	Meckarovski MKD
8-11	Oman	W 2-1	Muscat	Fr	Anier [85], Kams [88]		Albadwawi UAE
14-11	UAE	L 1-2	Abu Dhabi	Fr	Ahjupera [45]		Al Nemari KSA

Fr = Friendly match • EC = UEFA EURO 2012 • BC = Baltic Cup • WC = FIFA World Cup • q = qualifier

ESTONIA NATIONAL TEAM HISTORICAL RECORDS

Caps
157 - Martin Reim 1992-2007 • 143 - Marko Kristal 1992-2005 • 130 - Andres Oper 1995- • 120 - Mart Poom 1992-2009 • 114 - Kristen Viikmae 1997- • 109 - Raio Piiroja 1998- • 103 - Indrek Zelinski 1994-2010 • 94 - Sergei Terehhov 1997-2007 • 91 - Enar Jaager 2002- • 89 - Andrei Stepanov 1999- • 86 - Marek Lemsalu 1992-2007 • 84 - Joel Lindpere 1999- • 83 - Ragnar Klavan 2003-

Goals
38 - Andres Oper 1995- • 27 - Indrek Zelinski 1994-2010 • 21 - Eduard Ellman-Eelma 1921-35 • 18 - Richard Kuremaa 1933-40 • 17 - Arnold Pihlak 1920-31 • 15 - Kristen Viikmae 1997- & Konstantin Vassiljev 2006- • 14 - Georg Siimenson 1932-39 & Martin Reim 1992-2007 • 9 - Friedrich Karm 1920-27 & Marko Kristal 1992-2005

Coaches
Ferenc Konya HUN 1924 • Ferenc Nagy HUN 1925 • Antal Mally HUN 1927 • Fritz Kerr AUT 1930 • Albert Vollrat 1932 • Bernhard Rein 1934 • Antal Mally HUN 1935 • Bernhard Rein 1936-38 • Elmar Saar 1939-40 • Uno Piir 1992-93 • Roman Ubakivi 1994-95 • Aavo Sarap 1995 • Teitur Thordarson ISL 1996-99 • Tarmo Ruutli 1999-2000 • Arno Pijpers NED 2000-04 • Jelle Goes NED 2004-07 • Viggo Jensen DEN 2007 • Tarmo Ruutli 2008-

EST – ESTONIA

ESTONIA 2012
MEISTRILIIGA

	Pl	W	D	L	F	A	Pts	Nomme Kalju	Levadia	Flora	Trans Narva	Sillamäe	Paide LM	Viljandi	Kuressaare	Kalev	Tammeka
Nomme Kalju †	36	29	5	2	106	17	92		0 0 2-2	2-2 2-0	4-1 1-0	5-0 2-2	1-0 1-1	4-0 3-0	2-0 6-1	3-1 7-0	3-0 5-1
Levadia Tallinn ‡	36	25	8	3	85	22	83	1-1 0-1		1-1 5-4	4-0 0-2	1-1 0-2	1-0 4-0	2-0 2-1	5-0 7-0	0-0 4-1	1-0 3-0
Flora Tallinn ‡	36	26	3	7	87	24	81	1-0 1-0	0-1 1-2		2-1 0-1	3-0 4-0	1-0 3-0	5-0 5-0	0-1 2-0	5-0 3-1	4-0 5-1
Trans Narva ‡	36	16	7	13	52	44	55	1-2 0-2	1-2 0-6	1-2 2-2		1-0 0-1	2-0 0-0	3-1 1-1	1-3 2-0	5-1 1-1	2-0 4-0
Sillamäe Kalev	36	15	10	11	51	43	55	0-2 0-2	0-0 1-1	0-2 1-2	2-0 0-3		1-1 1-2	2-0 2-2	0-0 2-1	4-1 3-0	2-0 3-1
Paide Linnameeskond	36	11	9	16	34	52	42	1-3 0-2	1-5 1-2	0-5 0-6	0-0 2-3	1-1 2-0		0-1 0-2	2-1 1-1	1-0 0-0	2-0 4-1
FC Viljandi	36	6	8	22	33	88	26	0-3 1-9	0-3 0-5	0-2 0-2	0-1 2-5	0-3 0-5	0-2 0-2		3-1 6-0	1-1 2-1	3-2 0-0
FC Kuressaare	36	5	11	20	31	80	26	0-1 0-9	0-2 0-1	1-3 0-2	0-0 0-3	2-2 1-2	0-1 1-1	0-0 3-3		3-3 2-1	1-1 3-2
Tallinna Kalev	36	4	9	23	27	87	21	0-5 1-3	1-2 0-6	0-3 1-1	0-0 0-1	1-2 0-3	1-0 0-3	2-1 2-2	2-1 0-3		1-0 1-4
Tammeka Tartu	36	4	8	24	30	79	20	0-4 1-4	0-1 0-3	0-2 0-3	2-3 2-1	0-0 0-3	1-2 1-1	1-1 4-0	0-0 2-2	2-1 1-1	

10/03/2012 - 3/11/2012 • † Qualified for the UEFA Champions League • ‡ Qualified for the Europa League
Relegation play-off: Rakvere Tarvas 1-2 0-1 **Tallinna Kalev** • Top scorers: **23** – Vladislav **IVANOV** RUS, Trans Narva • **22** – Tarmo **NEEMELO**, Nomme Kalju • **17** – Zakaria **BEGLARISHVILI** GEO, Flora • **13** – Juri **JEVDOKIMOV**, Kalju • **12** – Igor **MOROZOV**, Levadia • **11** – Rimo **HUNT**, Levadia • **10** – Aleksandr **ALEKSEEV** RUS, Trans Narva; Andre **FROLOV**, Flora, Artur **RATTEL**, Levadia & Hidetoshi **WAKUI** JPN, Kalju

ESTONIA 2012
ESILIIGA (2)

	Pl	W	D	L	F	A	Pts
Tallinna Infonet	36	26	5	5	94	33	83
Flora Tallinn-2	36	20	9	7	66	32	69
Rakvere Tarvas ‡	36	21	5	10	66	58	68
Tartu SK 10	36	15	9	12	65	58	54
Levadia Tallinn-2	36	15	8	13	77	56	53
Tamme Auto Kivioli	36	12	8	16	78	83	44
FC Puuma Tallinn	36	12	7	17	55	61	43
Tammeka Tartu-2 ‡	36	10	7	19	55	83	37
Pärnu Linnameeskond	36	9	9	18	43	72	36
Lootus Kohtla-Järve	36	6	1	29	40	103	15

11/03/2012 - 3/11/2012 • Promotion/relegation play-offs
Relegation play-off: **Tulevik Viljandi** 1-1 2-1 Tameka Tartu-2
Second teams of the major clubs ineligible for promotion

MEDALS TABLE

	Overall	League	Cup
	G S B	G S B	G S
1 Flora Tallinn	14 10 4	9 6 4	5 4
2 Levadia Tallinn	14 5 2	7 4 2	7 1
3 TVMK Tallinn	3 5 5	1 3 5	2 2
4 Lantana Tallinn	3 4 5	2 1 5	1 3
5 Norma Tallinn	3 2	2 1	1 1
6 Tallinna Sadam	2 2 1	2 1	2
7 Trans Narva	1 5 5	1 5	1 4
8 Nomme Kalju	1 2	1 1	1
9 Levadia II Tallinn	1		1
10 Tulevik Viljandi	3	1	2
11 EP Jõhvi	2	1	1
12 Tammeka Tartu	1		1
Kalev Sillamäe	1		1

ESTONIA 2012
II LIGA EAST/NORTH (3)

	Pl	W	D	L	F	A	Pts
Lokomotiv Johvi	26	20	6	0	79	16	66
Sillamäe Kalev-2	26	15	8	3	82	26	53
Nomme Kalju-2	26	17	2	7	64	34	53
Tallinna Legion	26	14	7	5	63	38	49
Ararat Tallinn	26	12	7	7	58	46	43
Dünamo Tallinn	26	12	5	9	58	46	41
Aiko Kohtla-Järve	26	10	3	13	65	74	33
FC Maardu	26	9	4	13	62	61	31
Ajax Lasnamäe	26	9	4	13	42	42	31
Tallinna Kalev-2	26	8	7	11	45	49	31
Kaitseliit Kalev	26	8	5	13	56	61	29
Tallinna Infonet-2	26	6	3	17	26	59	21
MC Tallinn	26	5	4	17	48	115	19
FC Velldoris	26	2	5	19	29	110	11

6/04/2012 - 21/10/2012

ESTONIA 2012
II LIGA WEST/SOUTH (3)

	Pl	W	D	L	F	A	Pts
Hiiumaa Emmaste	26	19	3	4	114	34	60
Tulevik Viljandi	26	17	5	4	100	32	56
Vändra Vaprus	26	15	6	5	68	39	51
FC Elva	26	15	5	6	65	29	50
Tartu SK 10-2	26	15	1	10	96	50	46
Paide Kumake	26	14	3	9	83	46	45
Pärnu L'meeskond-2	26	12	2	12	78	75	38
Flora Tallinn-3	26	12	1	13	76	77	37
FC Tarvastu	26	11	4	11	69	70	37
Keila JK	26	11	3	12	51	63	36
Sörve JK	26	7	3	16	32	72	24
Türi Ganvix	26	7	0	19	52	122	21
JK Luunja	26	4	2	20	39	126	14
Nomme United	26	3	2	21	25	113	11

6/04/2012 - 21/10/2012
Play-off: **Tulevik Viljandi** 1-1 2-1 Tammeka Tartu-2

EESTI KARIKAS 2011-12

Third Round

Levadia Tallinn *	5
Tallinna Infonet	0
FC Otepää *	0
Tallinna Kalev	7
Paide Kumake	3
Türi Ganvix	2
Ararat Tallinn	1
Flora Tallinn-2 *	2
FC Viljandi	3
Lokomotiv Jõhvi *	0
Keila JK *	2
Rakvere Tarvas	5
Lootus Kohtla-Järve	4 4p
Nõmme Kalju-2 *	4 3p
FC Puuma Tallinn *	1
Flora Tallinn	4
Paide Linnameeskond *	3
Tamme Auto Kivioli *	0
Võru JK	0
Sillamäe Kalev *	8
Saaremaa JK	1
Leisi JK *	0
FC Soccernet	0
Pärnu Linnameeskond *	13
Tammeka Tartu	4
Raasiku Joker *	1
Welco Elekter	1
FC Kuressaare *	2
FC Maardu	2
FC Elva *	1
Navi Vutiselts	0
Trans Narva *	9

Round of 16

Levadia Tallinn *	4
Tallinna Kalev	1
Paide Kumake *	0
Flora Tallinn-2	1
FC Viljandi *	2
Rakvere Tarvas	1
Lootus Kohtla-Järve *	0
Flora Tallinn	9
Paide Linnameeskond *	3 7p
Sillamäe Kalev	3 6p
Saaremaa JK *	1
Pärnu Linnameeskond	4
Tammeka Tartu *	7
FC Kuressaare	0
FC Maardu	0
Trans Narva *	6

Quarter-finals

Levadia Tallinn	2
Flora Tallinn-2 *	0
FC Viljandi	0
Flora Tallinn *	3
Paide Linnameeskond *	4
Pärnu Linnameeskond	0
Tammeka Tartu	1
Trans Narva *	2

Semi-finals

Levadia Tallinn *	0 5p
Flora Tallinn	0 4p
Paide Linnameeskond *	0
Trans Narva	1

Final

Levadia Tallinn ‡	3
Trans Narva	0

CUP FINAL

A. Le Coq Arena, Tallinn, 26-05-2012
Att: 3007, Ref: Roomer Tarajev
Scorers – Podholjuzin [40], Artjunin [65], Morozov [81] for Levadia
Levadia – Roman Smisko – Igor Morozov, Artjom Artjunin, Maksim Podholjuzin, Aleksandr Kulinits, Marek Kaljumae●, Janar Toomet, Andero Pebre (Rino Hunt 46), Igor Subbotin (Andreas Raudsepp 91+), Ilja Antonov● Artur Rattel● (Vitali Leitan 83). Tr: Marko Kristal
Trans – Vladimir Malkov – Stanislav Kitto, Aleksandr Kulik●, Aleksejs Kuplovs-Oginskis●, Erik Grigorjev – Aleksandrs Abramenko, Irie Elysee, Dmitrijs Medeckis● (Sergei Kazakov 70), Maksim Gruznov (Vitaly Kutuzov 68), Vitali Gussev, Aleksandr Alekseev (Vladislav Fjodorov 80). Tr: Sergei Prihhodko

* Home team ● ‡ Qualified for the Europa League

ETH – ETHIOPIA

FIFA/COCA-COLA WORLD RANKING

'93	'94	'95	'96	'97	'98	'99	'00	'01	'02	'03	'04	'05	'06	'07	'08	'09	'10	'11	'12
96	115	105	108	126	145	142	133	155	138	130	151	112	92	105	103	122	124	135	110

2012

Jan	Feb	Mar	Apr	May	Jun	Jul	Aug	Sep	Oct	Nov	Dec	High	Low	Av
133	137	140	138	138	130	119	122	114	118	102	110	86	155	122

Ethiopia returned to the Africa Cup of Nations for the first time in 27 years when they qualified for the 2013 finals in South Africa. The national team was one of the strongest in the early days of the African game, playing in seven straight tournaments between 1957 and 1970 and winning in 1962, but they had not successfully negotiated a qualifying tournament since 1970. They made their way to South Africa by winning both of their ties on goal difference - firstly against Benin and then against Sudan where they came back from a 5-3 defeat to win the home leg 2-0 in Addis Abeba. Ethiopia's performance in South Africa showed the rustiness of the years away and they finished bottom of their group, but not before the feverish support of an estimated 5,000 expatriate supporters in Nelspruit and Rustenburg had left a marked impression on the tournament. Six months earlier, Ethiopia had begun the road to the 2014 FIFA World Cup finals in Brazil with a surprise 1-1 draw in South Africa and that was followed by a 2-0 home win a week later over the Central African Republic. All three goals came from Saladin Said - one of just a handful of foreign-based players in the team - who also scored the decisive goal four months later against the Sudanese in the Cup of Nations qualifier.

CAF AFRICA CUP OF NATIONS RECORD

1957 2 **1959** 3 **1962** 1 Winners (Hosts) **1963** 3 **1965** 6 r1 **1968** 4 SF (Hosts) **1970** 8 r1
1972-1974 DNQ **1976** 5 r1 (Hosts) 1978-1980 DNQ 1982 8 r1 1984 DNQ 1986 DNE 1988 Withdrew 1990 DNQ
1992 Withdrew 1994-1998 DNQ 2000 Withdrew 2002-2008 DNQ 2010 Disqualified 2012 DNQ **2013** 16 r1

ETHIOPIAN FOOTBALL FEDERATION (EFF)

Addis Abeba Stadium,
PO Box 1080,
Addis Abeba
☎ +251 11 5156205
+251 11 5515899
eff1@ethionet.et
www.ethiopianfootball.org
FA 1943 CON 1957 FIFA 1953
P Sahilu Gebremariam
GS Ashenafi Ejigu

THE STADIA

2014 FIFA World Cup Stadia
Addis Abeba Stadium
Addis Abeba   35 000

Other Main Stadia
Abebe Bikila Stadium
Addis Abeba   30 000
Awassa Kenema Stadium
Awassa   25 000
Dire Dawa Stadium
Dire Dawa   18 000
Wonji Stadium
Oromiya   14 000

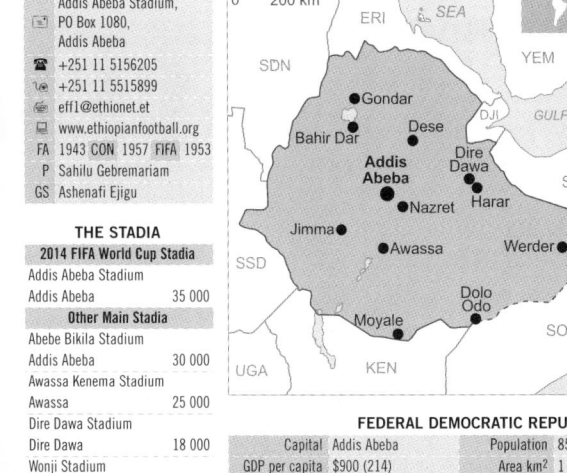

MAJOR CITIES/TOWNS

		Population
1	Addis Abeba	3 230 771
2	Dire Dawa	317 010
3	Nazret	262 462
4	Gondar	223 080
5	Dese	193 705
6	Mek'ele	193 567
7	Bahir Dar	191 804
8	Jimma	182 422
9	Debre Zeyit	150 454
10	Awassa	144 029
11	Harar	137 123
12	Jijiga	112 002
13	Shashemenne	106 938
14	Debre Mark'os	97 983
15	Assela	97 048
16	Nek'emte	97 005
17	Arba Minch	83 299
18	Kembolcha	79 002
19	Gode	77 792

FEDERAL DEMOCRATIC REPUBLIC OF ETHIOPIA

Capital	Addis Abeba	Population	85 237 338 (14)	% in cities	17%
GDP per capita	$900 (214)	Area km²	1 104 300 km² (27)	GMT +/-	+3
Neighbours (km)	Djibouti 349, Eritrea 912, Kenya 861, Somalia 1600, Sudan 1606					

RECENT INTERNATIONAL MATCHES PLAYED BY ETHIOPIA

2011	Opponents	Score	Venue	Comp	Scorers	Att	Referee
27-03	Nigeria	L 0-4	Abuja	CNq			Jedidi TUN
28-05	Sudan	L 1-2	Addis Abeba	Fr	Chala Diriba		
5-06	Nigeria	D 2-2	Addis Abeba	CNq	Saladin Said 2 [45] [50]		
4-09	Guinea	L 0-1	Conakry	CNq			
4-10	Malawi	D 0-0	Addis Abeba	Fr			
8-10	Madagascar	W 4-2	Addis Abeba	CNq	Umed Ukuri [31], Aden Girma [56], Fikru Teferra [59], Shemeles Bekele [73]		
12-11	Somalia	D 0-0	Djibouti	WCq		3 000	Hassan Ourouke DJI
16-11	Somalia	W 5-0	Addis Abeba	WCq	Omod Okwury [5], Shemeles Bekele 2 [62] [65], Getaneh Kebede 2 [87] [92+]	22 000	Kordi TUN
28-11	Sudan	D 1-1	Dar es Salaam	CCr1	Getaneh Kebede [34]		
30-11	Kenya	L 0-2	Dar es Salaam	CCr1			
2-12	Malawi	D 1-1	Dar es Salaam	CCr1	Aden Girma [16p]		
2012							
29-02	Benin	D 0-0	Addis Abeba	CNq			Kirwa KEN
3-06	South Africa	D 1-1	Rustenburg	WCq	Saladin Said [28]	13 611	Nampiandraza MAD
10-06	Central African Rep	W 2-0	Addis Abeba	WCq	Saladin Said 2 [36] [88]	25 000	Raphael MWI
17-06	Benin	D 1-1	Cotonou	CNq	Aden Girma [45]		Gassama GAM
8-09	Sudan	L 3-5	Omdurman	CNq	Getaneh Kebede [15], Aden Girma [68], Tesfaye Seyoum [69]		Alioum CMR
14-10	Sudan	W 2-0	Addis Abeba	CNq	Aden Girma [63], Saladin Said [66]		Diatta SEN
24-11	South Sudan	W 1-0	Kampala	CCr1	Getaneh Kebede [60]		Hakizimana RWA
27-11	Uganda	L 0-1	Kampala	CCr1			El Fadhil SUD
30-11	Kenya	L 1-3	Kampala	CCr1	Elias Mamo [30]		Nkurunziza BDI
4-12	Uganda	L 0-2	Kampala	CCqf			Nkurunziza BDI
30-12	Niger	W 1-0	Addis Abeba	Fr	Getaneh Kebede [39]		
2013							
7-01	Tunisia	D 1-1	Al Wakrah	Fr	Saladin Said [6]		
11-01	Tanzania	W 2-1	Addis Abeba	Fr	Abdus Ibrahim [13], Shemeles Bekele [69]		
21-01	Zambia	D 1-1	Nelspruit	CNr1	Aden Girma [65]	10 000	Otogo Castane GAB
25-01	Burkina Faso	L 0-4	Nelspruit	CNr1		35 000	Camille SEY
29-01	Nigeria	L 0-2	Rustenburg	CNr1		15 000	El Ahrach MAR

Fr = Friendly match • CN = CAF African Cup of Nations • CC = CECAFA Cup • WC = FIFA World Cup • q = qualifier • † Not an official International

ETHIOPIA 2011-12

PREMIER LEAGUE

	Pl	W	D	L	F	A	Pts	Saint George	Dedebit	EEPCO	Awassa City	Muger Cem't	Banks	Sidama Coffee	Arba Minch	Defence	Harar Beer	Eth. Coffee	Adama City	Dire Dawa City	Air Force
Saint George †	26	18	5	2	52	12	59		2-1	2-0	0-0	1-1	1-1	4-2	4-0	2-0	2-1	2-0	7-0	1-0	5-0
Dedebit ‡	26	17	4	5	50	21	55	3-1		0-1	1-0	3-0	1-1	4-0	5-2	0-1	1-0	4-2	0-1	3-1	4-0
EEPCO Mebrat Hail	26	13	7	6	38	24	46	2-1	0-1		4-1	1-1	1-1	1-0	6-0	0-0	3-2	1-0	1-1	2-0	4-0
Awassa City	26	7	14	5	26	23	35	0-0	1-1	1-1		1-0	0-0	1-1	0-0	1-1	0-2	1-3	2-2	2-2	1-0
Muger Cement	26	8	11	7	29	33	35	0-5	1-2	1-3	1-1		0-0	2-1	1-1	1-1	3-1	1-1	3-0	2-1	1-0
Banks	26	7	13	6	31	32	34	0-3	3-3	2-2	1-0	2-0		3-3	3-2	1-1	1-0	1-3	1-1	1-0	1-2
Sidama Coffee	26	7	12	7	26	28	33	0-1	2-2	0-1	2-0	3-2	1-1		0-0	2-1	1-1	2-1	2-1	0-0	1-0
Arba Minch City	26	8	9	9	25	34	33	0-1	1-0	0-1	3-1	0-0	1-0	0-0		3-1	0-0	2-1	1-0	0-1	3-1
Defence Mekelakeya	26	7	11	8	28	32	32	0-0	0-2	1-2	0-0	1-1	2-1	1-1	1-1		2-1	2-4	3-1	3-0	2-1
Harar Beer	26	7	10	9	21	22	31	0-2	0-1	1-0	0-0	0-1	0-0	1-0	1-0	0-0		1-1	0-0	2-0	1-1
Ethiopian Coffee	26	8	7	11	40	44	31	0-3	1-3	3-2	1-1	2-3	1-1	1-2	3-1	1-1	2-2		1-2	3-2	1-1
Adama City	26	7	8	11	20	35	29	0-1	1-2	2-1	1-2	0-0	0-0	3-0	3-2	1-0	0-2	1-0		1-1	1-0
Dire Dawa City	26	5	8	13	22	33	23	1-0	0-1	0-0	1-1	1-2	1-0	0-0	0-0	2-2	1-2	0-1	2-0		4-2
Air Force	26	2	3	21	13	48	9	0-1	0-1	3-2	0-2	0-0	2-3	0-1	1-2	0-1	0-1	0-2	0-2	2-1	

27/11/2011 - 7/07/2012 • † Qualified for the CAF Champions League • ‡ Qualified for the CAF Confederations Cup
Top scorers: 23 - Adane **GIRMA**, Saint George • 20 - Getaneh **KEBEDE**, Dedebit • 16 - Medhane **TADESSE**, Ethiopian Coffee

FIJ – FIJI

FIFA/COCA-COLA WORLD RANKING

'93	'94	'95	'96	'97	'98	'99	'00	'01	'02	'03	'04	'05	'06	'07	'08	'09	'10	'11	'12
107	120	139	157	146	124	135	141	123	140	149	135	135	150	131	106	132	152	161	169

2012

Jan	Feb	Mar	Apr	May	Jun	Jul	Aug	Sep	Oct	Nov	Dec	High	Low	Av
161	159	157	160	160	161	161	155	155	167	167	169	94	170	136

Football in Fiji suffered a double blow in 2012 when the OFC withdrew hosting rights from the country for both the Olympic qualifiers and the 2012 OFC Nations Cup following a legal dispute. Losing the latter was particularly hard on Fiji given that the country had never hosted the showcase regional tournament. Instead, the national team had to travel to the Solomon Islands where they crashed out after the first round of a tournament that also doubled up as the first round of qualifying in Oceania for the 2014 FIFA World Cup. In the three matches played, Fiji failed to win, scoring just one goal and were left wondering how different it could have been had they been the hosts instead. In club football the four trophies on offer during the year were shared between Ba and Suva with the former winning both the league title and the Battle of the Giants while Suva won the FA Cup Tournament and the Inter-District Championship - both at the expense of Ba in the final. There was huge controversy at the last of the four tournaments when Ba walked off in the final of the Inter-District Championship at their own Govind Park stadium after they disputed the winner scored by Suva defender Waisake Navunigasau just two minutes before the end of extra-time. The match was abandoned and the trophy awarded to Suva.

FIFA WORLD CUP RECORD
1930-1978 DNE **1982** DNQ **1986** DNE **1990-2014** DNQ

FIJI FOOTBALL ASSOCIATION (FFA)

Taramati Street,
Vatuwaqa,
PO Box 2514, Suva
☎ +679 3300453
+679 3304642
bobkumar@fijifootball.com.fj
www.fijifootball.com.fj
FA 1938 CON 1966 FIFA 1963
P Rajesh Patel
GS Bob Sant Kumar

THE STADIA
2014 FIFA World Cup Stadia
Fiji played their matches in a group staged at the Lawson Tama Stadium in Honiara, Solomon Islands

Main Stadia
National Stadium		
Suva		30 000
Churchill Park		
Lautoka		18 000
Govind Park		
Ba		13 500

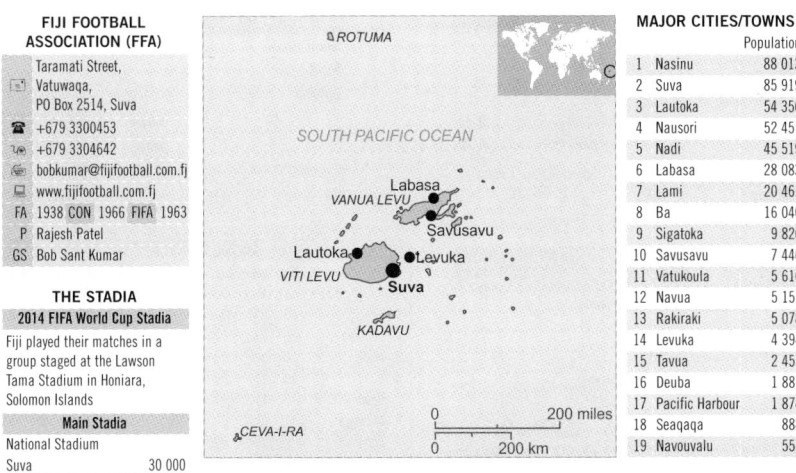

MAJOR CITIES/TOWNS

		Population
1	Nasinu	88 013
2	Suva	85 919
3	Lautoka	54 356
4	Nausori	52 451
5	Nadi	45 519
6	Labasa	28 083
7	Lami	20 461
8	Ba	16 040
9	Sigatoka	9 826
10	Savusavu	7 446
11	Vatukoula	5 616
12	Navua	5 151
13	Rakiraki	5 078
14	Levuka	4 394
15	Tavua	2 457
16	Deuba	1 881
17	Pacific Harbour	1 874
18	Seaqaqa	888
19	Navouvalu	557

MATANITU KO VITI • REPUBLIC OF THE FIJI ISLANDS

Capital	Suva	Population	944 720 (157)	% in cities	52%
GDP per capita	$3 800 (159)	Area km²	18 274 km² (156)	GMT +/-	+12
Neighbours (km)	Coast 1129				

RECENT INTERNATIONAL MATCHES PLAYED BY FIJI

2011	Opponents	Score	Venue	Comp	Scorers	Att	Referee
13-07	Vanuatu	W 2-0	Labasa	Fr	Bolaitoga [13], Naqeleca [90]		
15-07	Vanuatu	L 1-2	Lautoka	Fr	Avinesh [46]		
17-08	Samoa	W 3-0	Navua	Fr	Krishna [29], Kainihewe [33], Dau [88]		
18-08	Samoa	W 5-1	Suva	Fr	Krishna 3 [2 38 51], Tiwa 2 [61 73]		
27-08	Tahiti	W 3-0	Boulari	PGr1	Waqa [28], OG [44], Rokotakala [86]		Kerr NZL
30-08	Kiribati †	W 9-0	Boulari	PGr1	Krishna 3 [17p 56 86], Suwamy [47], Avinesh [52], Dunadamu 2 [63 72], OG [91+], Manuca [92+]		Ambassa NCL
3-09	Cook Islands	W 4-1	Boulari	PGr1	Krishna [24], Kainihewe [35], Dunadamu [57p], Suwamy [69]		Ambassa NCL
5-09	Papua New Guinea	W 2-0	Boulari	PGr1	Suwamy [37], Kainihewe [45]		Billon NCL
7-09	Solomon Islands	L 1-2	Lifou	PGsf	Dunadamu [69]		Jacques TAH
9-09	Tahiti	L 1-2	Boulari	PG3p	Avinesh [58]		Billon NCL
2012							
2-06	New Zealand	L 0-1	Honiara	OCr1		15 000	Ambassa NCL
4-06	Solomon Islands	D 0-0	Honiara	OCr1		12 000	Zitouni TAH
6-06	Papua New Guinea	D 1-1	Honiara	OCr1	Dunadamu [13]	3 000	Zitouni TAH

OC = Oceania Nations Cup • SP = South Pacific Games • WC = FIFA World Cup
q = qualifier • r1 = first round group • sf = semi-final • f = final • † Not a full international

FIJI 2012

NEW WORLD NATIONAL FOOTBALL LEAGUE

	Pl	W	D	L	F	A	Pts	Ba	Nadi	Suva	Lautoka	Rewa	Labasa	Nadroga	Navua	Tavua	Savusavu
Ba †	18	13	3	2	43	11	42		3-2	4-0	1-1	0-1	3-2	12-1	2-0	4-0	2-0
Nadi	18	11	5	2	28	8	38	0-1		1-1	2-0	1-1	3-0	5-1	0-0	5-0	3-1
Suva	18	11	4	3	30	13	37	1-1	0-1		2-1	1-0	2-1	6-0	2-1	3-1	0-0
Lautoka	18	10	3	5	38	17	33	1-2	0-1	2-1		1-0	2-0	1-2	4-0	3-1	5-0
Rewa	18	6	5	7	25	19	23	0-2	0-0	0-3	1-1		5-0	6-0	1-1	2-0	3-0
Labasa	18	5	4	9	20	31	19	1-0	0-1	0-0	1-2	1-1		2-2	2-1	1-1	2-0
Nadroga	18	5	3	10	23	57	18	0-0	0-1	0-3	1-5	3-2	4-3		1-5	4-0	3-1
Navua	18	3	7	8	16	21	16	1-2	0-0	0-1	2-2	0-1	0-1	2-0		1-0	1-1
Tavua	18	4	2	12	12	32	14	0-1	0-1	0-1	0-2	3-0	1-3	2-0	0-0		2-1
Savusavu	18	2	4	12	11	37	10	0-3	0-1	0-3	0-5	2-1	3-0	1-1	1-1	0-1	

2/03/2012 - 23/09//2012 • † Qualified for the OFC Champions League

BATTLE OF THE GIANTS 2012

Semi-finals
Ba 2
Lautoka 0

Finals

Ba	0 4p
Labasa	0 2p

Nadi 0
Labasa 1

Churchill Park, Labasa
29-07-2012

FA CUP TOURNAMENT 2012

Semi-finals
Suva 2
Labasa 0

Finals

Suva	1
Ba	0

Lautoka 0
Ba 1

Govind Park, Ba
20-05-2012
Scorer - Nathan Shivam [3]

INTER-DISTRICT CHAMPIONSHIP 2012

Semi-finals
Suva 1
Lautoka 0

Finals

Suva	1
Ba	0

Navua 1
Ba 2

Govind Park, Ba
13-10-2012, Scorer - Waisake Navunigasau [118]

MEDALS TABLE

		Overall		Lg	ID		BoG		FACT		OFC	
		G	S	G	G	S	G	S	G	S	G	S
1	Ba	63	25	18	22	17	15	6	8	1		1
2	Lautoka	22	17	3	16	9	1	5	2	3		
3	Nadi	20	22	8	6	15	5	4	1	2		1
4	Suva	19	21	2	12	15	3	4	2	2		
5	Rewa	15	11		9	7	5	3	1	1		
6	Nadroga	11	5	3	3	3	3		2	2		
7	Labassa	9	16	2	3	3	1	6	3	7		
8	Navua	5	3		1		1	2	3	1		
9	Tavua	2	3		1			2	1	1		
10	Nasinu	1	6		1	3		2		1		
11	Taileva		1			1						
12	Rakiraki		1			1						

FIN – FINLAND

FIFA/COCA-COLA WORLD RANKING

'93	'94	'95	'96	'97	'98	'99	'00	'01	'02	'03	'04	'05	'06	'07	'08	'09	'10	'11	'12
45	38	44	79	60	55	56	59	46	43	40	43	46	52	36	55	55	83	86	83

2012													High	Low	Av
Jan	Feb	Mar	Apr	May	Jun	Jul	Aug	Sep	Oct	Nov	Dec				
85	79	84	79	79	75	74	72	96	88	91	83		33	96	53

Since bursting onto the Finnish football scene in 2005, FC Honka have gained a reputation as gallant runners-up but that changed in 2012 when they beat the all-powerful HJK Helsinki in the cup semi-final and then claimed their first major trophy after beating KuPS 1-0 in the final. Situated in the west of the Greater Helsinki metropolitan area, Espoo is a city in its own right and has forged a reputation as the hi-tech centre of the country, something that Honka are keen to exploit as they challenge the more traditional clubs in Helsinki and beyond. They had twice won the pre-season League Cup but their big breakthrough came thanks to a first half Antti Makijarvi goal against KuPS who were defeated in the final for the second year running and finished the game with just nine on the pitch. In the league, however, HJK stormed to their fourth straight title although not in the same astonishing fashion as the year before. Their winning margin over Inter Turku was cut from 24 points in 2011 to just six in 2012 but it was enough to see them comfortably home and to become the first team in the history of the league to win four consecutive titles. The national team faced a herculean task in the qualifiers for the 2014 FIFA World Cup and at the end of 2012 found themselves at the bottom of their group with just one point from two home games.

UEFA EUROPEAN CHAMPIONSHIP RECORD
1960-1964 DNE 1968-2012 DNQ

SUOMEN PALLOLIITTO (SPL/FBF)

Urheilukatu 5,
PO Box 191,
00251 Helsinki
☎ +358 9 742151
+358 9 4543352
palloliitto@palloliitto.fi
www.palloliitto.fi
FA 1907 CON 1954 FIFA 1908
P Pertti Alaja
GS Kimmo Lipponen

THE STADIA
2014 FIFA World Cup Stadia

Olympiastadion Helsinki	40 600

Other Main Stadia

Ratina Stadion Tampere	16 850
Lahden Stadion Lahti	14 500
Paavo Nurmen Stadion Turku	13 000
Sonera Stadion Helsinki	10 770

MAJOR CITIES/TOWNS

		Population
1	Helsinki	571 838
2	Espoo	241 741
3	Tampere	210 450
4	Vantaa	194 638
5	Turku	176 346
6	Oulu	132 629
7	Lahti	99 477
8	Kuopio	91 431
9	Jyväskylä	85 362
10	Pori	76 274
11	Lappeenranta	59 213
12	Rovaniemi	58 624
13	Vaasa	58 388
14	Joensuu	57 682
15	Kotka	54 159
16	Hämeenlinna	49 055
17	Mikkeli	48 894
18	Porvoo	48 255
51	Valkeakoski	20 366

SUOMEN TASAVALTA • REPUBLIC OF FINLAND

Capital Helsinki	Population 5 250 275 (113)	% in cities 63%
GDP per capita $37 000 (31)	Area km² 338 145 m² (64)	GMT +/- +2
Neighbours (km) Norway 727, Sweden 614, Russia 1313 • Coast 1250		

RECENT INTERNATIONAL MATCHES PLAYED BY FINLAND

2009	Opponents	Score	Venue	Comp	Scorers	Att	Referee
4-02	Japan	L 1-5	Tokyo	Fr	Porokara [50]	34 532	Huang Junjie CHN
11-02	Portugal	L 0-1	Faro-Loule	Fr		19 834	Bertolini SUI
28-03	Wales	W 2-0	Cardiff	WCq	Johansson [43], Kuqi [91+]	22 604	Iturralde ESP
1-04	Norway	L 2-3	Oslo	Fr	Johansson [39], Alexei Eremenko [91+]	16 239	Styles ENG
6-06	Liechtenstein	W 2-1	Helsinki	WCq	Forssell [33], Johansson [71]	20 319	Kovarik CZE
10-06	Russia	L 0-3	Helsinki	WCq		37 028	Plautz AUT
12-08	Sweden	L 0-1	Stockholm	Fr		15 212	Fautrel FRA
5-09	Azerbaijan	W 2-1	Lenkoran	WCq	Tihinen [74], Johansson [85]	12 000	Trifonos CYP
9-09	Liechtenstein	D 1-1	Vaduz	WCq	Litmanen [74p]	3 132	Panic BIH
10-10	Wales	W 2-1	Helsinki	WCq	Porokara [5], Moisander [77]	14 000	Mazic SRB
14-10	Germany	D 1-1	Hamburg	WCq	Johansson [11]	51 500	Atkinson ENG
2010							
18-01	Korea Republic	L 0-2	Malaga	Fr		270	Fernandez ESP
3-03	Malta	W 2-1	Ta'qali	Fr	Roman Eremenko [66p], Vayrynen [69]	800	Bergonzi ITA
21-05	Estonia	L 0-2	Tallinn	Fr		5 650	Vad HUN
29-05	Poland	D 0-0	Kielce	Fr		14 200	Avram ROU
11-08	Belgium	W 1-0	Turku	Fr	Porokara [13]	7 451	Hamer LUX
3-09	Moldova	L 0-2	Chisinau	ECq		10 300	Malek POL
7-09	Netherlands	L 1-2	Rotterdam	ECq	Forssell [18]	25 000	Nikolaev RUS
12-10	Hungary	L 1-2	Helsinki	ECq	Forssell [86]	18 532	Kelly IRL
17-11	San Marino	W 8-0	Helsinki	ECq	Vayrynen [39], Hamalainen 2 [49 67], Forssell 3 [51 59 78], Litmanen [71p], Porokara [73]	8 192	Matejek POL
2011							
9-02	Belgium	D 1-1	Ghent	Fr	Porokara [90]	12 000	Zimmermann SUI
29-03	Portugal	L 0-2	Aveiro	Fr		13 737	Studer SUI
3-06	San Marino	W 1-0	Serravalle	ECq	Forssell [41]	1 218	Sipailo LVA
7-06	Sweden	L 0-5	Stockholm	ECq		32 128	Gautier FRA
10-08	Latvia	W 2-0	Riga	Fr	Hamalainen [58], Furuholm [88]	5 314	Bezborodov RUS
2-09	Moldova	W 4-1	Helsinki	ECq	Hamalainen 2 [11 43], Forssell [52p], OG [70]	9 056	Kakos GRE
6-09	Netherlands	L 0-2	Helsinki	ECq		21 580	Grafe GER
7-10	Sweden	L 1-2	Helsinki	ECq	Toivio [73]	23 257	Clattenburg ENG
11-10	Hungary	D 0-0	Budapest	ECq		25 169	Undiano ESP
15-11	Denmark	L 1-2	Esbjerg	Fr	Alexei Eremenko [18]	14 132	Jakobsson ISL
2012							
22-01	Trinidad and Tobago	W 3-2	Port of Spain	Fr	Riski [34], Kolehmainen [73], Aaritalo [78]	5 000	Campbell JAM
29-02	Austria	L 1-3	Klagenfurt	Fr	Furuholm [89]	10 200	Valeri ITA
1-06	Estonia	W 2-1	Tartu	BCsf	Kuqi 2 [10 22]	2 470	Direktorenko LVA
3-06	Latvia	D 1-1	Voru	BCf	Kolehmainen [52]. L 5-6p	280	Mazeika LTU
15-08	Northern Ireland	D 3-3	Belfast	Fr	Sparv [22], Puuki [24], Hetemaj [78]	9 575	Liesveld NED
7-09	France	L 0-1	Helsinki	WCq		35 111	Thomson SCO
11-09	Czech Republic	W 1-0	Teplice	Fr	Pukki [43]	9 053	Siejewicz POL
12-10	Georgia	D 1-1	Helsinki	WCq	Hamalainen [62]	12 607	Aranovskiy UKR
14-11	Cyprus	W 3-0	Nicosia	Fr	Pukki [15], Hetemaj [29p], Kolehmainen [85]	300	Balaj ROU

Fr = Friendly match • BC = Baltic Cup • EC = UEFA EURO 2012 • WC = FIFA World Cup • q = qualifier

FINLAND NATIONAL TEAM HISTORICAL RECORDS

Caps: 137 - Jari Litmanen 1989-2010 • 105 - Jonatan Johansson 1996-2010 & Sami Hyypia 1992-2010 • 100 - Ari Hjelm 1983-96 • 98 - Joonas Kolkka 1994-2010 • 84 - Mikael Forssell 1999- & Erkka Petaja 1983-94 • 76 - Arto Tolsa 1964-81 & Hannu Tihinen 1997-2009 • 75 - Toni Kuivasto 1997-2009 • 71 - Mika Nurmela 1992-2007 • 70 - Mika-Matti Paatelainen 1986-2000 & Petri Pasanen 2000-

Goals: 32 - Jari Litmanen 1989-2010 • 28 - Mikael Forssell 1999- • 22 - Jonatan Johansson 1996-2010 • 20 - Ari Hjelm 1983-96 • 18 - Mika-Matti Paatelainen 1986-2000 • 17 - Verner Eklof 1919-27 • 16 - Aulis Koponen 1924-35 & Gunnar Astrom 1923-37 • 14 - Alexei Eremenko 2003- • 13 - William Kanerva 1922-38; Jorma Vaihela 1947-54 & Kai Pahlman 1954-68 • 12 - Kalevi Lehtovirta 1947-59

Past Coaches: Jarl Ohman 1922 • Ferdinand Fabra GER 1936-1937 • Gabor Obitz HUN 1939 • Axel Martensson SWE 1945 • Niilo Tammisalo 1946 • Aatos Lehtonen 1947-1955 • Kurt Weinreich GER 1955-1958 • Aatos Lehtonen 1959-1961 • Olavi Laaksonen 1962-1974 • Martti Kosma 1975 • Aulis Rytkonen 1975-1978 • Esko Malm 1979-1981 • Martti Kuusela 1982-1987 • Jukka Vakkila 1988-1992 • Tommy Lindholm 1993-1994 • Jukka Ikalainen 1994-1996 • Richard Moller Nielsen DEN 1996-1999 • Antti Muurinen 2000-2005 • Jyrki Heliskoski 2005 • Roy Hodgson ENG 2006-2007 • Stuart Baxter SCO 2008-10 • Olli Huttunen 2010-11 • Markku Kanerva 2011 • Mika-Matti Paatelainen 2011-

FINLAND 2012

VEIKKAUSLIIGA (1)

	Pl	W	D	L	F	A	Pts	HJK	Inter	TPS	IFK	Lahti	MYPA	Honka	VPS	JJK	KuPS	Jaro	Haka
HJK Helsinki †	33	19	7	7	63	33	64		2-1 1-1	0-0	3-1 5-1	2-0 2-0	1-1	3-0 1-0	3-3	2-0	2-0 4-1	4-1 0-0	1-0
Inter Turku ‡	33	17	7	9	57	42	58	2-0		3-3 0-0	0-3 1-0	2-0	2-0	2-1	1-1 2-0	2-1 3-2	2-1 1-4	1-1 3-1	4-1
TPS Turku ‡	33	16	6	11	55	33	54	3-1 1-2	4-1		1-1	4-0	0-1 1-0	2-1	1-0 1-0	2-3 1-0	3-0	2-3 1-2	2-0 9-2
IFK Mariehamn	33	13	12	8	50	43	51	2-0	2-1	2-1 1-0		2-0 2-2	0-0 2-2	2-0 0-1	1-0	0-0	3-3	1-1 2-0	2-0 1-0
FC Lahti	33	16	2	15	45	49	50	3-0	0-5 4-3	2-0 1-0	2-0		0-0 3-1	2-1 3-2	1-0	2-1	2-1	0-2	1-0 0-1
MYPA Anjalankoski	33	13	10	10	39	33	49	1-0 1-4	4-0 0-0	1-1	2-1	3-1		0-0	1-0 1-1	0-1 2-1	1-1	2-0	3-1 1-0
Honka Espoo ‡	33	12	7	14	37	38	43	1-0	2-1 3-0	0-2 0-1	2-2		3-2	2-1 1-1		1-1 1-2	0-2 3-0	1-0 2-1	2-0	2-2
VPS Vaasa	33	12	7	14	36	38	43	1-0 1-3	0-2		1-3	1-2 1-3	2-1 1-3	2-0		2-0		2-0	1-1 1-1	1-0 0-1
JJK Jyväskylä	33	12	4	17	54	65	40	0-3 3-6	0-0		2-1	5-2 3-2	2-1 3-1	0-3		0-1	0-2 1-2		1-5	1-1 4-2	1-4 5-0
KuPS Kuopio	33	10	6	17	39	53	36	0-3		0-6	1-1 1-3	2-0	1-2 1-0	1-2 2-0	0-2	0-3 2-1	2-2 2-3		1-0	3-0 1-1
Jaro Pietarsaari	33	8	9	16	28	51	33	2-2	0-1		0-1	0-3 3-3	0-2 2-1	1-0 0-3	0-1 1-0	0-0	0-3	1-0 1-1		1-0
Haka Valkeakoski	33	9	5	19	32	57	32	0-1 2-2	0-2 1-2	1-0	0-2 1-1	0-3		3-1	2-1 1-0	0-1		3-1	0-2	4-1 0-0	

15/04/2012 - 27/10/2012 • † Qualified for the UEFA Champions League • ‡ Qualified for the Europa League
Top scorers: 17 - Irakli **SIRBILADZE** GEO, Inter • 16 - Aleksei **KANGASKOLKKA**, IFK Mariehamn • 15 - Steven **MORRISSEY** JAM, VPS • 14 - Pekka **SIHVOLA**, MYPA • 12 - Tamas **GRUBOROVICS** HUN, JJK; Mika **OJALA**, Inter & Demba **SAVAGE** GAM, HJK

LEAGUE CUP 2012

Quarter-finals		Semi-finals		Final	
TPS Turku	4				
MYPA	0	TPS Turku	2		
Honka Espoo	0	VPS Vaasa	0		
VPS Vaasa	1			TPS Turku	1 4p
Inter Turku	3			HJK Helsinki	1 2p
Jaro Pietarsaari	2	Inter Turku	2 3p		
KuPS Kuopio	1	HJK Helsinki	2 4p		
HJK Helsinki	2	* Home team			

Final: Sonera, Helsinki, 4-04-2012, Att: 2123, Ref: Antamo. Scorers - Juho Lahde [44] for TPS; Joel Pohjanpalo [49] for HJK

MEDALS TABLE

		Overall			League			Cup		LC	
		G	S	B	G	S	B	G	S	G	S
1	HJK Helsinki	40	21	11	25	13	11	11	5	4	3
2	Haka	22	10	10	9	7	10	12	3	1	
3	TPS Turku	12	18	10	8	12	10	3	5	1	1
4	Reipas Lahti	10	9	3	3	6	3	7	3		
5	HPS Helsinki	10	7	2	9	6	2	1	1		
6	Tampere Utd	9	5	3	5	1	3	3	3	1	1
7	KuPS Kuopio	8	11	1	5	9	1	2	2	1	
8	FC Lahti	8	10	1	5	4	1	2	4	1	2
9	HIFK Helsinki	7	8	4	7	7	4		1		
10	KTP Kotka	6	4	2	2		2	4	3		1
11	VPS Vaasa	4	7	1	2	5	1		1	2	1
12	MyPa-47	4	5	3	1	5	3	3			
13	Abo IFK Turku	4	5	1	3	5	1	1			
14	Kronshagen IF	4	2	3	4	1	3				
15	Honka Espoo	3	5			2		1	3	2	
16	Inter Turku	3	3		1	2		1	1	1	
17	IFK Vaasa	3	2	2	3	2	2				
18	AlliansiVantaa	3	2			1		1	1		
19	MP Mikkeli	2	3					3	2		
20	Jazz Pori	2	2	1	2		1		1		1
21	OPS Oulu	2			2						

FINLAND 2012

YKKONEN (2)

	Pl	W	D	L	F	A	Pts	RoPS	SJK	Viikingit	PK-35	OPS	AC Oulu	KooTeePee	JIPPO	Hämeenlinna	HIFK
RoPS Rovaniemi	27	18	5	4	53	20	59		2-0	2-0 0-1	1-1	3-0	1-0 3-2	3-1 3-0	4-0 1-1	3-0	3-1 2-3
SJK Seinäjoki	27	14	5	8	42	29	47	1-3 4-2		3-1	2-1 3-0	0-2 2-3	2-2	0-0	3-1	1-1	3-1 1-0
Viikingit Helsinki	27	14	3	10	36	36	45	1-3	0-2 0-1		0-4 0-4	3-0	1-1	1-0 0-3	1-0	2-1 0-2	2-1 2-1
PK-35 Vantaa	27	13	4	10	54	31	43	0-0 0-1	2-0	0-4		3-0	2-1 0-1	2-1 2-3	5-1 4-3	9-0 3-0	5-1
OPS-jp Oulu	27	10	8	9	34	35	38	0-1 2-0	1-1	1-2 0-1	1-0 1-1		1-1	0-3	2-1 3-0	4-0 2-1	1-1
AC Oulu	27	9	10	8	38	35	37	0-0	3-1 0-2	0-3 3-3	2-1	2-2 1-0		4-1 2-2	1-1 2-0	0-0	3-1
KooTeePee Kotka	27	10	5	12	30	33	35	0-3	0-1 1-0	0-4	1-0	1-1 0-1	0-1		3-0 1-0	0-0 3-0	0-2
JIPPO Joensuu	27	7	7	13	31	44	28	1-1	2-0 0-1	0-2	3-1	3-1	2-3	1-0		3-1 0-0	1-0 5-2
FC Hämeenlinna	27	7	5	15	18	48	22	0-2 0-2	0-2 0-2	3-0	1-2	0-0	1-0 1-3	1-1	1-1		1-3 1-0
HIFK Helsinki	27	5	6	16	29	54	21	1-4	0-4	1-1	0-0 2-1	1-1 3-4	2-2 1-0	0-3 1-2	0-0	0-2	

27/04/2012 - 6/10/2012

SUOMEN CUP 2012

Sixth Round

Honka Espoo	4
FC Hämeenlinna *	0
Jazz Pori	2 2p
Atlantis Helsinki *	2 4p
LPS Laajasalo	3
JPS Jyväskylä *	0
VPS Vaasa	Bye
KooTeePee Kotka *	2
HIFK Helsinki	0
Inter Turku	Bye
Jaro Pietarsaari	2 5p
PS Kemi *	2 4p
HJK Helsinki	Bye
MYPA Anjalankoski	2
MP Mikkeli *	0
Riverball Joensuu *	0
Haka Valkeakoski	4
EIF Ekenäs *	4
FC Kuusysi	1
FC Lahti	0
JIPPO Joensuu *	2
IFK Mariehamn *	4
JJK Jyväskylä	1
JäPS Järvenpää *	0
Gnistan Helsinki	1
TPS Turku	Bye
AC Oulu *	0 7p
KuPS Kuopio	0 8p

Round of 16

Honka Espoo	3
Atlantis Helsinki *	0
LPS Laajasalo *	0
VPS Vaasa	2
KooTeePee Kotka *	2
Inter Turku	1
Jaro Pietarsaari	1
HJK Helsinki *	2
MYPA Anjalankoski	2
Haka Valkeakoski *	1
EIF Ekenäs *	0
JIPPO Joensuu	2
IFK Mariehamn *	1
Gnistan Helsinki *	1
TPS Turku	0 7p
KuPS Kuopio *	0 8p

League Cup semi-finalists given a bye to the round of 16 • * Home team • † Played in Mikkeli • ‡‡ Played in Vantaa • ‡ Qualified for the Europa League

Quarter-finals

Honka Espoo *	2
VPS Vaasa	0
KooTeePee Kotka	0
HJK Helsinki *	3
MYPA Anjalankoski	3
JIPPO Joensuu *	0
IFK Mariehamn	0
KuPS Kuopio *	3

Semi-finals

Honka Espoo ‡‡	1 5p
HJK Helsinki	1 4p
MYPA Anjalankoski	0
KuPS Kuopio ††	1

Final

Honka Espoo ‡	1
KuPS Kuopio	0

CUP FINAL

Sonera, Helsinki, 29-09-2012
Att: 2340, Ref: Mattias Gestranius
Scorer - Antti Makijarvi 23 for Honka
Honka - Tuomas Peltonen - Sampo Koskinen, Tapio Heikkila, Henri Aalto, Lum Rexhepi - Jussi Vasara (Tomi Petrescu 81), Nicholas Otaru, Duarte Tammilehto - Moshtagh Yaghoubi, Tim Vayrynen, Antti Makijarvi. Tr: Mika Lehkosuo
KuPS - Joonas Pontinen - Pyry Karkkainen, Etchu Tabe●●**40**, Atte Hoivala (Ilja Venalainen 57) - Ebrima Sohna, Paul Obiefule●, Sander Puri◆**72**, Ats Purje● (Johann Smith 76), Chris James● - Miikka Ilo (Aleksi Paananen 67), Antti Hynynen●. Tr: Esa Pekonen

FRA − FRANCE

FIFA/COCA-COLA WORLD RANKING

'93	'94	'95	'96	'97	'98	'99	'00	'01	'02	'03	'04	'05	'06	'07	'08	'09	'10	'11	'12
15	19	8	3	6	2	3	2	1	2	2	2	5	4	7	11	7	18	15	17

2012												High	Low	Av
Jan	Feb	Mar	Apr	May	Jun	Jul	Aug	Sep	Oct	Nov	Dec			
15	17	16	16	14	14	14	14	15	13	18	17	1	27	7

There were hopes before Euro 2012 that the French could make a serious impact on the finals in Poland and the Ukraine, but although they did make it through to the quarter-finals, just one win in the four games played saw coach Laurent Blanc stand down after their elimination at the hands of Spain - just two years into his tenure. France were beaten 2-0 in the quarter-finals by the eventual champions in Donetsk and never looked likely to depose a team that they face again in the qualifiers for the 2014 FIFA World Cup in Brazil. Blanc's replacement, Didier Deschamps, got that campaign off to a solid start, including a 1-1 draw with the Spanish in Madrid. At home, the reputation of the French league as one of the most open and competitive leagues in the world may have taken a knock during the seven year domination of Olympique Lyonnais, but the last five years have seen a return to the old ways with Montpellier becoming the fifth different team to claim the championship in that time. What made their triumph all the more remarkable was the fact that it was their first-ever title and was won ahead of the newly-wealthy Paris Saint-Germain, who finished three points behind. There was silverware for Lyon in the French Cup - 1-0 winners over third division Quevilly in the final - and for Marseille who registered a hat trick of League Cup triumphs.

UEFA EUROPEAN CHAMPIONSHIP RECORD
1960 4 SF **1964** QF **1968** QF **1972-1980** DNQ **1984** 1 Winners (Hosts) **1988** DNQ
1992 6 r1 **1996** 4 SF **2000** 1 Winners **2004** 6 QF **2008** 15 r1 **2012** 7 QF

FEDERATION FRANÇAISE DE FOOTBALL (FFF)

87, Boulevard de Grenelle, Paris 75738

☎ +33 1 44317300
📠 +33 1 44317373
✉ webmaster@fff.fr
🖳 fff.fr
FA 1919 CON 1954 FIFA 1904
P Noel Le Graet
GS Brigitte Henriques

THE STADIA
2014 FIFA World Cup Stadia
Stade de France
Saint-Denis, Paris   81 338
Other Main Stadia
Parc des Princes
Paris   47 428
Stade Vélodrome
Marseille   42 000
Stade Félix Bollaert
Lens   41 233
Stade de Gerland
Lyon   41 044

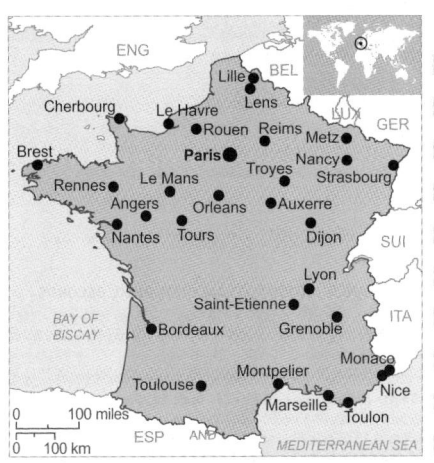

MAJOR CITIES/TOWNS
		Population
1	Paris	2 183 500
2	Marseille	782 687
3	Lyon	485 872
4	Toulouse	453 217
5	Nice	332 817
6	Nantes	280 989
7	Strasbourg	279 152
8	Montpellier	257 712
9	Lille	254 149
10	Bordeaux	239 768
11	Rennes	210 404
12	Reims	203 950
13	Le Havre	181 051
14	Angers	179 574
15	Saint-Etienne	171 257
16	Toulon	169 176
17	Grenoble	160 226
167	Auxerre	42 389
188	Lens	39 493

REPUBLIQUE FRANCAISE • FRENCH REPUBLIC

Capital	Paris	Population	64 057 792 (21)	% in cities	77%
GDP per capita	$33 300 (39)	Area km²	551 500 km² (42)	GMT +/-	+1
Neighbours (km)	Andorra 56, Belgium 620, Germany 451, Italy 488, Luxembourg 73, Monaco 4, Spain 623, Switzerland 573 • Coast 4668				

RECENT INTERNATIONAL MATCHES PLAYED BY FRANCE

2010	Opponents	Score	Venue	Comp	Scorers	Att	Referee
11-06	Uruguay	D 0-0	Cape Town	WCr1		64 100	Nishimura JPN
17-06	Mexico	L 0-2	Polokwane	WCr1		35 370	Al Ghamdi KSA
22-06	South Africa	L 1-2	Bloemfontein	WCr1	Malouda [70]	39 415	Ruiz COL
11-08	Norway	L 1-2	Oslo	Fr	Ben Arfa [48]	15 165	Velasco ESP
3-09	Belarus	L 0-1	Paris	ECq		76 395	Collum SCO
7-09	Bosnia-Herzegovina	W 2-0	Sarajevo	ECq	Benzema [72], Malouda [78]	28 000	Brych GER
9-10	Romania	W 2-0	Paris	ECq	Remy [83], Gourcuff [93+]	79 299	Proenca POR
12-10	Luxembourg	W 2-0	Metz	ECq	Benzema [22], Gourcuff [76]	24 710	Jug SVN
17-11	England	W 2-1	London	Fr	Benzema [16], Valbuena [55]	85 495	Larsen DEN
2011							
9-02	Brazil	W 1-0	Paris	Fr	Benzema [55]	79 712	Stark GER
25-03	Luxembourg	W 2-0	Luxembourg	ECq	Mexes [28], Gourcouf [72]	8 400	Hagen NOR
29-03	Croatia	D 0-0	Paris	Fr		60 000	Kelly IRL
3-06	Belarus	D 1-1	Minsk	ECq	Malouda [22]	26 500	Fernandez ESP
6-06	Ukraine	W 4-1	Donetsk	Fr	Gameiro [58], Martin 2 [87] [90], Kaboul [89]	11 200	Clattenburg ENG
9-06	Poland	W 1-0	Warsaw	Fr	OG [12]	32 000	Kuipers NED
10-08	Chile	D 1-1	Montpellier	Fr	Remy [20]	30 000	Atwell ENG
2-09	Albania	W 2-1	Tirana	ECq	Benzema [11], M'Vila [18]	15 600	Nikolaev RUS
6-09	Romania	D 0-0	Bucharest	ECq		49 137	Webb ENG
7-10	Albania	W 3-0	Paris	ECq	Malouda [11], Remy [38], Reveillere [67]	65 239	Koukoulakis GRE
11-10	Bosnia-Herzegovina	D 1-1	Paris	ECq	Nasri [78p]	78 467	Thomson SCO
11-11	USA	W 1-0	Paris	Fr	Remy [72]	70 018	Koukoulakis GRE
15-11	Belgium	D 0-0	Paris	Fr		52 825	Muniz ESP
2012							
29-02	Germany	W 2-1	Bremen	Fr	Giroud [21], Malouda [69]	37 800	Tagliavento ITA
27-05	Iceland	W 3-2	Valenciennes	Fr	Debuchy [51], Ribery [85], Rami [87]	20 580	Delferiere BEL
31-05	Serbia	W 2-0	Reims	Fr	Ribery [10], Malouda [15]	18 000	Kircher GER
5-06	Estonia	W 4-0	Le Mans	Fr	Ribery [25], Benzema 2 [37] [47], Menez [91+]	23 500	Liany ISR
11-06	England	D 1-1	Donetsk	ECr1	Nasri [39]	42 000	Rizzoli ITA
15-06	Ukraine	W 2-0	Donetsk	ECr1	Menez [53], Cabaye [56]	51 504	Kuipers NED
19-06	Sweden	L 0-2	Kyiv	ECr1		65 000	Proenca POR
23-06	Spain	L 0-2	Donetsk	ECqf		46 145	Rizzoli ITA
15-08	Uruguay	D 0-0	Le Havre	Fr		25 178	Orsato ITA
7-09	Finland	W 1-0	Helsinki	WCq	Diaby [20]	35 111	Thomson SCO
11-09	Belarus	W 3-1	Paris	WCq	Capoue [48], Jallet [68], Ribery [80]	52 552	Gocek TUR
12-10	Japan	L 0-1	Paris	Fr		60 205	Collum SCO
16-10	Spain	D 1-1	Madrid	WCq	Giroud [94+]	46 825	Brych GER
14-11	Italy	W 2-1	Parma	Fr	Valbuena [37], Gomis [67]	19 665	Undiano ESP

Fr = Friendly match • EC = UEFA EURO 2012 • WC = FIFA World Cup
q = qualifier • r1 = first round group • r2 = second round • qf = quarter-final • sf = semi-final • f = final

FRANCE NATIONAL TEAM HISTORICAL RECORDS

Caps
142 - Lilian Thuram 1994-2008 • **123** - Thierry Henry 1997- • **116** - Marcel Desailly 1993-2004 • **108** - Zinedine Zidane 1994-2006 • **107** - Patrick Vieira 1997-2009 • **103** - Didier Deschamps 1989-2000 • **97** - Laurent Blanc 1989-2000 & Bixente Lizarazu 1992-2004 • **92** - Sylvain Wiltord 1999-2006 • **87** - Fabien Barthez 1994-2006 • **84** - William Gallas 2002- • **82** - Manuel Amoros 1982-92 & Youri Djorkaeff 1993-2002 • **80** - Florent Malouda 2004- • **79** - Robert Pires 1996-2004 • **76** - Maxime Bossis 1976-86 • **72** - Michel Platini 1976-87

Goals
51 - Thierry Henry 1997-2010 • **41** - Michel Platini 1976-87 • **34** - David Trezeguet 1998-2008 • **31** - Zinedine Zidane 1994-2006 • **30** - Just Fontaine 1953-60 & Jean-Pierre Papin 1986-95 • **28** - Youri Djorkaeff 1993-2002 • **26** - Sylvain Wiltord 1999-2006 • **22** - Jean Vincent 1953-61 • **21** - Jean Nicolas 1933-38 • **20** - Paul Nicolas 1920-31 & Eric Cantona 1987-95 • **19** - Jean Baratte 1944-52 • **18** - Roger Piantoni 1952-61 & Raymond Kopa 1952-62 • **16** - Larent Blanc 1989-2000 • **15** - Karim Benzema 2007-

Past Coaches
Gaston Barreau 1919-45 • Gabriel Hanot 1945-49 • Paul Baron & Pierre Pibarot 1949-53 • Pierre Pibarot 1953-54 • Jules Bigot & Albert Batteux 1954-56 • Albert Batteux 1956-60 • Albert Batteux & Henri Guerin 1960-64 • Henri Guerin 1964-1966 • Jose Arribas ESP & Jean Snella 1966 • Just Fontaine 1967 • Louis Dugauguez 1967-1968 • Georges Boulogne 1969-1973 • Stefan Kovacs 1973-1975 • Michel Hidalgo 1976-1984 • Henri Michel 1984-1988 • Michel Platini 1988-1992 • Gerard Houllier 1992-1993 • Aime Jacquet 1994-1998 • Roger Lemerre 1998-2002 • Jacques Santini 2002-2004 • Raymond Domenech 2004-2010 • Laurent Blanc 2010-12 • Didier Deschamps 2012-

FRA – FRANCE

FRANCE 2011-12
LIGUE 1 ORANGE

	Pl	W	D	L	F	A	Pts	Montpellier	PSG	Lille	Lyon	Bordeaux	Rennes	St-Etienne	Toulouse	Evian	Marseille	Nancy	Val'ciennes	Nice	Sochaux	Brest	Ajaccio	Lorient	Caen	Dijon	Auxerre
Montpellier-Hérault †	38	25	7	6	68	34	82		0-3	1-0	1-0	1-0	4-0	1-0	1-1	2-2	1-0	2-0	1-0	2-1	1-0	3-0	4-0	3-0	5-3	3-1
Paris Saint-Germain †	38	23	10	5	75	41	79	2-2		0-0	2-0	1-1	3-0	2-0	3-1	3-1	2-1	0-1	2-1	2-1	6-1	1-0	4-1	0-1	4-2	2-0	3-2
Lille OSC †	38	21	11	6	72	39	74	0-1	2-1		3-1	4-5	2-0	3-0	2-1	1-1	3-2	4-1	4-0	4-4	2-2	2-0	4-1	1-1	3-0	2-0	2-2
Olympique Lyonnais ‡	38	19	7	12	64	51	64	2-1	4-4	2-1		3-1	1-2	2-0	3-2	2-1	2-0	3-1	4-3	3-4	2-1	1-1	1-1	3-2	1-2	3-1	2-1
Girondins Bordeaux ‡	38	16	13	9	53	41	61	2-2	1-1	1-1	1-0		2-0	1-2	2-0	0-0	2-1	2-0	2-1	1-2	1-0	1-1	1-1	0-2	0-0	1-1	1-1
Stade Rennais	38	17	9	12	53	44	60	0-2	1-1	1-1	1-1	1-0		1-1	0-0	1-3	2-1	1-1	1-1	3-1	1-0	1-1	3-1	2-0	3-2	5-0	1-1
AS Saint-Etienne	38	16	9	13	49	45	57	1-1	0-1	1-3	0-1	2-3	4-0		1-1	0-2	0-0	1-0	1-2	3-1	1-0	2-1	3-1	4-2	2-0	1-0	1-1
Toulouse FC	38	15	11	12	37	34	56	0-1	1-3	0-0	3-3	2-1	0-0	1-1		2-1	0-0	1-0	2-0	0-0	2-0	0-0	0-2	1-1	1-2	0-1	3-0
Evian-Thonon Gaillard	38	13	11	14	54	55	50	4-2	2-2	2-0	3-1	3-0	0-1	3-1	2-2		2-0	2-2	2-1	1-0	2-3	0-0	1-2	2-1	2-4	0-1	3-1
Olympique Marseille ‡	38	12	12	14	45	41	48	1-3	3-0	2-0	2-0	0-0	0-1	0-0	0-1	2-0		1-0	1-1	0-2	2-1	1-2	0-2	1-1	2-1	1-1	2-3	0-0
AS Nancy-Lorraine	38	11	12	15	38	48	45	1-0	2-1	1-1	2-0	2-2	0-0	3-2	0-3	1-1	1-3		1-1	1-1	0-1	2-1	2-2	2-2	2-1	1-1	1-2	0-0
Valenciennes FC	38	12	7	19	40	50	43	1-0	3-4	0-0	1-0	1-2	1-0	1-2	2-0	0-3	1-1	0		2-0	3-0	0-0	0-1	2-2	0-3	1-4	0-2	1-1
OGC Nice	38	10	12	16	39	46	42	0-1	0-0	1-1	3-3	2-0	0-0	2-1	1-1	1-1	1-1	1-1	2-0		1-1	0-0	3-0	2-0	1-0	1-1	1-0
Sochaux-Montbéliard	38	11	9	18	40	60	42	1-3	0-1	0-1	2-1	0-3	2-6	2-1	3-0	1-1	1-0	0-1	1-2	0		2-1	0-2	1-1	1-1	2-1	1-0	0-0
Stade Brestois	38	8	17	13	31	38	41	2-2	0-1	3-1	1-1	0-2	0-1	2-2	0-0	2-2	2-1	0-0	1-1	0-1	1-0		2-0		1-1	3-1	1-1	1-1	1-0
AC Ajaccio	38	9	14	15	40	61	41	1-3	1-3	2-3	1-1	0-2	1-0	1-1	0-2	1-1	1-1	0-0	0-3	1-1	1-2	1-0				1-1	2-2	1-2	2-1
FC Lorient	38	9	12	17	35	49	39	2-1	1-2	0-1	0-1	1-1	0-2	3-0	0-0	0-1	2-1	2-1	2-1	1-0	1-1	2-1	2-0			0-0	0-0	1-1	
SM Caen	38	9	11	18	39	59	38	1-3	2-2	1-2	1-0	0-0	2-1	4-0	1-2	2-2	1-2	1-2	1-0	1-1	1-1	1-3	0-0	0-0	1-0		3-0	2-1
Dijon FCO	38	9	9	20	38	63	36	1-1	1-2	0-2	1-2	2-0	1-1	5-1	2-1	1-3	1-2	3	0-2	1-2	3-0	0-0	1-0	1-1	2-0	2-0		0-2
AJ Auxerre	38	7	13	18	46	57	34	1-2	1-1	1-0	3-2	4-0	1-0	0-2	0-0	2-2	1-3	2-0	2-1	4-1	4-0	4-1	1-1	1-1	2-2			

6/08/2011 – 20/05/2012 • † Qualified for the UEFA Champions League • ‡ Qualified for the Europa League • Attendance: 7 172 105 @ 18 874

Top scorers: **21** - Olivier **GIROUD**, Montpellier & **NENE** BRA, PSG • **20** - Eden **HAZARD** BEL, Lille • **16** - Pierre Emerick **AUBAMEYANG** GAB, St-Etienne & **LISANDRO LOPEZ** ARG, Lyon • **14** - Bafetimbi **GOMIS**, Lyon & Yoan **GOUFFRAN**, Bordeaux • **13** - Javier **PASTORE** ARG, PSG • **12** - Loic **REMY**, Marseille & Younes **BELHANDA** MAR, Montpellier • **11** - Kevin **GAMEIRO**, PSG • **10** - Jires **KEMBO EKOKO** COD, Rennes; Dennis **OLIECH** KEN, Auxerre & Yannick **SAGBO** CIV, Evian

FRANCE 2011-12
LIGUE 2 ORANGE

	Pl	W	D	L	F	A	Pts	Bastia	Reims	Troyes	Sedan	Clermont	Tours	Guingamp	Monaco	Nantes	Istres	Angers	Lens	Arlés-Avignon	Châteauroux	Le Havre	Laval	Le Mans	Metz	Boulogne	Amiens
SC Bastia	38	21	8	9	61	36	71		1-0	5-1	2-2	1-1	4-1	3-1	1-1	2-1	3-1	3-1	2-2	3-0	2-1	1-0	3-2	1-0	3-0	2-0	2-1
Stade de Reims	38	18	11	9	54	37	65	1-0		1-0	1-2	2-2	2-3	2-1	2-0	3-1	2-1	3-0	1-1	3-2	2-0	2-1	1-1	1-1	3-0	3-2	1-0
ES Troyes AC	38	17	13	8	45	35	64	1-0	1-0		1-1	3-2	2-1	1-1	1-1	2-0	1-1	2-1	2-1	0-0	1-0	1-1	0-3	0-2	1-1	0-2	1-2	0-0
CS Sedan Ardennes	38	15	14	9	56	45	59	2-0	1-0	1-2		1-2	3-0	0-1	2-2	2-0	1-1	2-1	1-0	2-0	2-0	0-3	0-2	1-0	2-1	0-2	1-1	4-3	1
Clermont Foot	38	15	13	10	48	39	58	2-1	1-0	1-1	1-1		0-1	0-1	1-0	0-0	2-2	1-2	2-0	0-0	2-1	2-1	2-0	1-1	0-0	1-1	0-1	2-2	1
Tours FC	38	15	11	12	44	43	56	2-1	1-1	1-0	2-1	0-2		5-1	0-0	2-1	1-2	1-0	0-3	4-1	1-2	0-0	0-0	2-1	1-0	3-1	1-1		
En Avant Guingamp	38	15	10	13	46	43	55	1-1	2-3	0-0	1-3	3-1	0-0		4-0	2-0	1-0	1-0	3-1	1-1	1-0	1-0	1-1	1-0	1-1	1-1			
AS Monaco	38	13	13	12	41	48	52	0-1	1-2	0-2	2-2	0-0	0-0	1-0		2-1	3-2	1-3	2-2	1-0	2-1	1-0	2-1	0-0	2-2	0-2	0-0	1-1	
FC Nantes	38	14	9	15	51	42	51	0-2	2-1	1-1	1-2	1-0	1-0	4-0	3-0		3-1	2-1	1-0	3-0	3-0	1-0	2-3	1-1	0-0	3-3	5-0		
FC Istres	38	13	12	13	46	44	51	1-0	1-1	0-0	1-1	2-2	1-0	2-1	0-1	2-1		0-1	2-1	0-0	3-1	1-1	1-2	1-2	1-0	0-0	2-1		
Angers SCO	38	13	12	13	44	44	51	1-1	0-0	2-3	1-3	0-1	1-0	1-0	1-2	2-0	3-1		1-1	2-0	2-0	1-2	0-0	1-2	0-0	2-1	0-0		
Racing Club Lens	38	12	12	14	42	48	48	1-3	0-2	2-1	4-2	2-1	3-0	0-2	2-2	1-0	1-0	0-0		0-0	2-3	2-0	0-0	1-3	0-2	2-0	1-1		
AC Arlés-Avignon	38	10	18	10	34	41	48	0-0	2-2	0-0	0-0	0-0	2-2	2-1	1-2	1-0	0-1	5-2	2-3		0-0	1-0	1-0	1-0	1-0	1-0	2-1	1-1	
LB Châteauroux	38	14	6	18	38	54	48	0-2	1-1	1-0	2-1	1-1	3-0	2-2	1-2	2-2	0-2	0-1	1-0	1-2			1-0	3-1	1-1	1-1	2-1	1-1		
Le Havre AC	38	11	14	13	38	34	47	2-0	1-1	3-0	0-0	0-0	2-2	1-3	1-2	2-1	1-0	0-0	3-0	0-0	1-3		1-1	1-1	1-1	0-0	1-2		
Stade Lavallois	38	12	11	15	46	50	47	1-0	3-2	0-0	5-1	1-2	1-2	1-0	2-0	0-1	0-1	2-2	2-1	1-1	0-2			2-1	0-0	2-2	3-1		
Le Mans FC	38	11	12	15	39	40	45	3-0	0-1	1-3	1-0	1-0	1-0	0-1	0-0	0-1	0-0	2-2	0-1	1-1	0-1	3-1	1-3			0-1	1-0	3-2	
FC Metz	38	10	12	16	30	44	42	0-1	1-0	2-2	0-2	2-2	1-1	2-1	2-5	0-2	1-3	1-2	1-1	2-0	0-0	2-1	0-2	2-0			
US Boulogne CO	38	7	15	16	40	47	36	0-2	1-0	2-0	0-1	1-1	1-0	0-2	0-0	1-2	2-1	1-1	3-3	0-2	1-1	0-1	1-1	1-3	0-2	0-0	1		0-1
Amiens SFC	38	4	14	20	29	57	26	1-1	0-2	1-0	1-1	0-3	1-1	0-1	1-2	0-2	1-2	1-2	0-3	4-0	0-1	1-0	0-1	1-0	0-0			

29/07/2011 – 18/05/2012 • Attendance: 3,208,671 @ 8,444

Top scorers: **15** - Cedric **FAURE**, Reims • **14** - Kamel **GHILAS** ALG, Reims • **13** - Toifilou **MAOULIDA**, Bastia & Ryan **MENDES** CPV, Le Havre

FRANCE 2011-12

NATIONAL (3)

	Pl	W	D	L	F	A	Pts	Nîmes	Niort	Gazélec	Vannes	Epinal	Rouen	Orléans	Colmar	Fréjus	Créteil	Red Star	Le Poiré	Quevilly	Cherbourg	Luzenac	Paris FC	Beauvais	Martigues	Besançon	Bayonne
Nîmes Olympique	38	18	14	6	65	38	68		3-2	0-0	1-2	1-1	1-2	1-1	2-0	4-1	3-3	3-4	2-0	3-0	0-0	3-2	2-1	1-1	4-1	3-0	1-0
Chamois Niortais FC	38	19	10	9	61	33	67	1-1		2-1	0-0	0-0	3-0	0-1	2-1	2-0	0-2	4-0	1-0	2-0	2-0	4-0	0-2	0-2	3-1	3-0	4-0
Gazélec FC Ajaccio	38	20	8	10	57	32	66	2-1	0-1		2-1	2-1	4-1	1-0	1-0	1-0	0-1	1-1	2-0	0-0	5-0	1-1	1-0	0-0	2-0	2-0	2-0
Vannes Olympique	38	16	14	8	55	38	62	1-1	1-0	3-2		2-1	0-0	2-0	3-1	3-3	4-4	0-0	1-1	1-1	2-0	3-1	1-1	1-1	2-1	2-0	
SAS Epinal	38	17	11	10	61	47	62	2-2	2-1	1-1	2-2		3-2	1-1	3-3	3-0	4-0	5-1	0-2	1-1	0-1	3-3	2-0	2-1	1-0	0-2	2-1	1-1
FC Rouen	38	17	9	12	48	46	60	0-1	2-2	0-1	1-0	0-1		2-1	1-1	4-3	1-0	2-1	2-0	0-2	3-3	2-0	1-0	1-1	2-0	0-0	0-0
US Orléans	38	15	11	12	41	41	56	1-1	1-5	1-0	2-2	1-2	0-0		1-0	0-0	0-1	2-1	2-1	0-1	3-2	2-0	0-0	2-0	0-0	2-0	1-1
SR Colmar	38	15	10	13	54	44	55	0-2	0-2	0-2	0-0	1-0	0-0	2-0		2-1	2-1	0-1	4-1	1-3	0-0	1-1	3-0	4-0	3-0	0-1	0-1
Fréjus Saint-Raphaël	38	15	6	17	50	58	51	2-0	0-0	0-2	1-3	2-1	2-0	3-0	2-3		0-4	2-3	2-5	2-0	1-0	0-0	1-0	3-1	1-0	4-2	2-0
US Créteil-Lusitanos	38	13	11	14	51	50	50	0-2	1-2	2-1	1-1	1-1	1-2	3-3	0-0	3-1		1-0	1-0	2-1	1-0	1-2	2-1	1-1	0-4	0-0	2-4	3-
Red Star Paris	38	15	5	18	44	52	50	1-2	1-2	0-2	2-0	0-3	2-1	1-2	1-0	1-2	2-1		2-0	0-0	1-0	2-3	1-0	0-0	0-2	1-1	1-0	1-2
SJA Le Poiré-sur-Vie	38	14	7	17	41	46	49	0-3	1-0	3-1	2-1	1-2	1-1	1-1	0-2	2-0	0-1	0-2		2-1	1-1	1-1	0-1	0-0	1-0	5-0	1-0	1-1
US Quevilly	38	12	11	15	45	54	47	1-3	0-2	0-3	2-0	0-3	2-3	1-1	4-0	0-1	1-1	1-1	0-1		4-2	2-5	2-2	1-0	1-1	1-1	2-2
AS Cherbourg	38	11	13	14	56	57	46	1-1	1-1	2-4	5-1	1-0	1-0	0-1	1-2	0-2	1-0	0-0	2-1	1-2		4-1	2-0	2-2	1-2	6-2	1-1
US Luzenac	38	11	12	15	47	56	45	0-3	1-1	0-0	2-2	0-2	2-0	0-1	1-1	1-1	1-2	0-1	2-3	1-3	3-2		2-0	0-0	3-3	2-0	1-0
Paris FC	38	12	8	18	39	48	44	0-1	0-1	0-3	2-0	6-0	2-1	1-0	2-4	2-0	1-0	0-4	1-0	2-0	1-3	3-1		0-0	1-2	0-0	2-1
AS Beauvais Oise	38	8	18	12	39	43	42	1-2	2-2	1-0	0-3	4-0	1-1	3-2	3-0	1-1	1-1	4-2	1-2	1-1	1-1	2-0	2-0		0-0	0-0	2-0
FC Martigues	38	9	12	17	43	69	39	1-1	2-1	2-3	1-1	2-1	0-2	0-0	2-1	3-2	2-1	0-1	2-1	1-1	3-3	0-3	0-1	2-3		2-0	1-1
Besançon Racing Club	38	9	11	18	42	64	35	1-1	1-1	1-1	0-2	1-1	4-5	3-2	2-1	3-2	3-2	0-0	2-1	1-2	1-0	2-1	0-1	2-1	1-1		3-2
Aviron Bayonnais	38	7	13	18	38	60	34	2-1	1-1	1-0	0-3	2-1	0-1	0-2	2-2	1-1	0-1	2-1	1-0	2-2	0-0	2-3	2-2	0-2	5-3	1-1	

5/08/2011 - 26/05/2012
Top scorers: 17 - Seydou **KONE**, Nîmes CIV • 14 - Nicolas **BELVITO**, Cherbourg; Abdellah **ASBABOU** MAR, Epinal & Geoffrey **MALFLEURY**, Red Star

		Overall			League			Cup			LC		Europe		
		G	S	B	G	S	B	G	S	B	G	S	G	S	B
1	Olympique Marseille	23	21	7	9	10	5	10	8	3			1	3	2
2	AS Saint-Etienne	16	7	3	10	3	2	6	3					1	1
3	Paris Saint-Germain	14	13	6	2	7	3	8	4	3	1		1	1	3
4	AS Monaco	13	12	14	7	5	10	5	4		1	1	2		4
5	Olympique Lyonnais	13	9	8	7	3	6	5	3		1	3		2	
6	Girondins Bordeaux	12	19	6	6	9	4	3	6	3	3	3		1	2
7	FC Nantes Atlantique	11	13	4	8	7	2	3	5		1	1			
8	Lille OSC	10	11	4	4	7	4	6	4						
9	Stade de Reims	8	6	4	6	3	4	2	1					2	
10	OGC Nice	7	5		4	3		3	1		1				
11	Racing Club Paris	6	4	5	1	2	5	5	2						
12	Racing Club Strasbourg	6	4	3	1	1	3	3	3	2					
13	FC Sochaux-Montbéliard	5	7	5	2	3	4	2	3		1	1			1
14	AJ Auxerre	5	1	6	1		5	4	1						1
15	Red Star 93 Paris	5	1					5	1						
16	FC Sète	4	4	1	2		1	2	4						
17	FC Metz	3	3	1	1	1		2	1	1	1				
18	Racing Club Lens	2	8	3	1	4	2		3	1	1				1
19	CS Sedan Ardennes	2	3	2			2	2	3						
20	Stade Rennais	2	3					2	3						
21	Montpellier HSC	2	2	1	1		1	1	1		1				
	CO Roubaix-Tourcoing	2	2	1	1		1	1	2						
23	CAS Généraux	2						2							
	AS Nancy-Lorraine	2						1		1					
25	SC Bastia	1	4	1			1	1	2		1			1	
26	Toulouse FC	1	1	2	1	2	1								
27	Le Havre AC	1	1				1	1	1						
28	AS Cannes	1	1		1		1								
	En Avant Guingamp	1	1					1	1						
	FC Lorient	1	1					1			1				
	Cercle Athlétique Paris	1	1					1	1						
	SO Montpellier	1	1					1	1						

COUPE DE LA LIGUE 2011-12

Third Round		Fourth Round		Quarter-finals		Semi-finals		Final	
Olympique Marseille	Bye	**Olympique Marseille** *	4						
Evian-Thonon Gaillard	0	Racing Club Lens	0						
Racing Club Lens *	1			**Olympique Marseille**	3				
AJ Auxerre	2	AJ Auxerre *	1	SM Caen *	0				
AS Nancy-Lorraine *	1	**SM Caen**	2						
Stade Brestois	2					**Olympique Marseille** *	2		
SM Caen *	3	**Dijon FCO** *	3			OGC Nice	1		
Dijon FCO *	3	Paris Saint-Germain	2	Dijon FCO	3 3p				
Valenciennes FC	2			**OGC Nice** *	3 5p				
Paris Saint-Germain	Bye	Sochaux-Montbéliard	1					**Olympique Marseille** ‡	1
Sochaux-Montbéliard	Bye	**OGC Nice** *	2					Olympique Lyonnais	0
Toulouse FC *	1	**FC Lorient**	2						
OGC Nice	2	Montpellier-Hérault *	1	**FC Lorient**	1				
FC Lorient	3			Le Mans FC *	0			COUPE DE LA LIGUE FINAL	
En Avant Guingamp *	2	Stade Rennais	Bye					Stade de France, Paris	
Amiens SFC	2 3p	AC Ajaccio	0 1p			**FC Lorient** *	2	14-04-2012. Att: 80'000. Ref: Stephane Lannoy	
Montpellier-Hérault *	2 4p	**Le Mans FC** *	0 4p			**Olympique Lyonnais**	4	Scorer - Brandao [105] for Marseille	
Stade Rennais	Bye	**Lille OSC** *	3					OM - Steve Mandanda (c) - Cesar Azpilicueta,	
AC Ajaccio	0	CS Sedan Ardennes	1	Lille OSC	1			Rod Fanni, Stephane Mbia●, Nicolas	
Le Mans FC *	1	AS Saint-Etienne *	1	**Olympique Lyonnais** *	2			N'Kouloù● - Alou Diarra● (Charles Kabore 82) -	
Lille OSC	Bye	**Olympique Lyonnais**	2					Mathieu Valbuena (Jeremy Morel 118), Benoit	
FC Nantes	0							Cheyrou, Morgan Amalfitano, Andre Ayew - Loic	
CS Sedan Ardennes *	2							Remy● (Brandao 98). Tr: Didier Deschamps	
AS Saint-Etienne *	3							OL - Hugo Lloris - Anthony Reveillere, Samuel	
Girondins Bordeaux	1							Umtiti, Dejan Lovren●●◆[120], Mouhamadou	
Olympique Lyonnais	Bye							Dabo (Aly Cissokho 118) - Jimmy Briand●,	
								Maxime Gonalons, Kim Kallstrom (Alexandre	
								Lacazette [106]), Michel Bastos (Clement	
								Grenier 65) - Bafetimbi Gomis●, Lisandro	
								Lopez (c). Tr: Remi Garde	

* Home team ● Ligue 1 clubs enter in the third round ◆ Qualified for the Europa League ‡ Qualified for the Europa League

COUPE DE FRANCE 2011-12

Round of 64

Olympique Lyonnais	3
Lyon Duchère *	1
US Avranches	1
Vendé Luçon *	2
US Créteil-Lusitanos	3
FC Mulhouse *	1
AS Saint-Etienne *	1 2p
Girondins Bordeaux	1 4p
Dijon FCO	5
FC Versailles *	1
SA Thiers *	1
FC Istres	4
Sablé-sur-Sarthe *	3 4p
CS Sedan Ardennes	3 2p
Saint-Colomban Locminé *	1
Paris Saint-Germain	2
Montpellier-Hérault	4
AS Prix-lès-Mézières *	0
AS Vitré *	1
Tours FC	2
AJ Auxerre	1
FC Chambly *	0
AS Cherbourg *	1
LB Châteauroux	2
JA Drancy *	3 4p
RC Strasbourg	3 2p
US Boulogne CO	0
Limoges FC *	1
ES Troyes AC	4
SM Caen *	2
Toulouse FC	0
Gazélec FC Ajaccio *	1
Stade Rennais *	3
AS Nancy-Lorraine	0
AS Marck *	0
OGC Nice	2
AS Valence *	1 7p
Stade Lavallois	1 6p
FC Metz *	2 3p
Evian-Thonon Gaillard	2 5p
Lille OSC	6
US Chantilly *	0
US Montagnarde	1
AFC Compiègne *	2
SC Bastia *	4
Sochaux-Montbéliard	1
Le Mans FC *	0
Valenciennes FC	2
Olympique Marseille	5
Red Star Paris *	0
FC Lorient	3
Le Havre AC *	4
AC Ajaccio	3
Fréjus Saint-Raphaël *	0
Montceau Bourgogne	1
FC Bourg-Péronnas *	2
US Orléans *	0 5p
Clermont Foot	0 3p
Stade Brestois	0
Chamois Niortais FC *	2
Angers SCO *	4
AS Monaco	3
Tour d'Auvergne Rennes *	0 4p
US Quevilly	0 5p

Round of 32

Olympique Lyonnais	2
Vendé Luçon * ‡‡	0
US Créteil-Lusitanos *	2 3p
Girondins Bordeaux	2 4p
Dijon FCO *	2
FC Istres	1
Sablé-sur-Sarthe * ‡	0
Paris Saint-Germain	4
Montpellier-Hérault	1
Tours FC *	0
AJ Auxerre *	1
LB Châteauroux	2
JA Drancy *	2
Limoges FC *	0
ES Troyes AC	0
Gazélec FC Ajaccio *	1
Stade Rennais	0 5p
OGC Nice *	0 4p
AS Valence *	0
Evian-Thonon Gaillard	2
Lille OSC	1
AFC Compiègne *	0
SC Bastia	1
Valenciennes FC *	3
Olympique Marseille *	3
Le Havre AC	1
AC Ajaccio	2
FC Bourg-Péronnas *	3
US Orléans	2
Chamois Niortais FC *	1
Angers SCO	0
US Quevilly *	1

Round of 16

Olympique Lyonnais *	3
Girondins Bordeaux	1
Dijon FCO *	0
Paris Saint-Germain	1
Montpellier-Hérault	2
LB Châteauroux *	0
JA Drancy	0
Gazélec FC Ajaccio *	2
Stade Rennais *	3
Evian-Thonon Gaillard	2
Lille OSC	1
Valenciennes FC *	2
Olympique Marseille *	3
FC Bourg-Péronnas	1
US Orléans	0
US Quevilly *	2

* Home team • ‡ Played at MMArena, Le Mans • ‡‡ Played at the Stade de la Beaujoire, Nantes

COUPE DE FRANCE 2011–12

Quarter–finals	Semi–finals	Final

Olympique Lyonnais 3
Paris Saint-Germain * 1

Olympique Lyonnais 4
Gazélec FC Ajaccio * 0

Montpellier-Hérault 0
Gazélec FC Ajaccio * 1

Olympique Lyonnais ‡ 1
US Quevilly 0

Stade Rennais 3
Valenciennes FC * 1

Stade Rennais 1
US Quevilly * † 2

Olympique Marseille 2
US Quevilly * † 3

† Played in Caen
‡ Qualified for the Europa League

COUPE DE FRANCE FINAL 2012
Stade de France, Paris, 28-04-2012, Att: 76229, Ref: Herve Piccirillo

Olympique Lyonnais 1 Lisandro Lopez [28]
US Quevilly 0

LYON
Hugo **LLORIS** - Anthony **REVEILLERE**, **CRIS** (c), Dejan **LOVREN** (Bakare **KONE** 18), Aly **CISSOKHO** - Maxime **GONALONS**, Yoann **GOURCUFF** (Clement **GRENIER**• 67), Kim **KALLSTROM**• - Alexandre **LACAZETTE**, Bafetimbi **GOMIS** (Jimmy **BRIAND** 81), Lisandro **LOPEZ**. Tr: Remi **GARDE**

QUEVILLY
Yassine **EL KHARROUBI** - Alexandre **VARDIN**, Frederic **WEIS**, Gregory **BEAUGRARD** (c), Cedric **VANOUKIA** - Zanke **DIARRA** (Abdel **OUAHBI** 77), Matthias **JOUAN** - Anthony **LAUP** (Jean-Christophe **AYINA** 81), Julien **VALERO** (Karim **HEROUAT** 57), Pierrick **CAPELLE** - Joris **COLINET**•. Tr: Regis **BROUARD**

AC AJACCIO
2011–12

Aug	6	Toulouse	L	0-2	L1	19	7 668
	13	Lyon	D	1-1	L1	18 Sammaritano [59]	30 746
	20	Evian	D	1-1	L1	17 Sammaritano [7]	6 886
	27	Auxerre	L	1-4	L1	18 Ilan [83]	8 662
	31	Le Mans	L	0-1	LCr3		6 827
Sep	10	Val'ciennes	W	3-1	L1	15 Sammaritano 2 [47 54], Ilan [58]	5 363
	17	Nice	L	0-3	L1	17	8 242
	21	Montpellier	L	1-3	L1	19 Mostefa [53]	5 670
	25	Brest	D	1-1	L1	19 Socrier [66]	12 142
Oct	1	Dijon	D	1-1	L1	18 Mostefa [18]	12 534
	16	PSG	L	1-3	L1	19 Medjani [24]	8 155
	22	Marseille	L	0-2	L1	20	39 786
	29	Bordeaux	L	0-2	L1	20	5 667
Nov	5	Lorient	L	0-2	L1	20	15 672
	19	Caen	D	2-2	L1	20 Ilan [52p], Andre [91+]	5 125
	26	St-Etienne	L	1-3	L1	20 Diawara [60]	20 059
Dec	3	Lille	L	2-3	L1	20 Kinkela [2], Ilan [37]	5 319
	10	Nancy	D	2-2	L1	20 OG [34], Cavalli [72]	12 440
	18	Rennes	W	1-0	L1	20 Diawara [83]	5 645
	21	Sochaux	W	2-0	L1	20 Andre [65], Mostefa [78]	9 296
	7	Fréjus	W	3-0	CFr9	Diawara [47], Kinkela [70], El Hany [92+]	3 000
Jan	14	Auxerre	W	2-1	L1	20 Eduardo [27], Fousseni [33]	5 522
	21	Bourg-P	L	2-3	CF10	Socrier [46], Mostefa [94+]	8 500
	29	Val'ciennes	W	2-1	L1	15 Eduardo [6], Kinkela [92+]	13 515
Feb	4	Nice	D	1-1	L1	16 Eduardo [58p]	5 742
	11	Montpellier	L	0-3	L1	17		11 647
	18	Brest	D	0-0	L1	17		5 663
	25	Dijon	W	2-1	L1	16 Eduardo [54], Cavalli [55]	5 277
Mar	4	PSG	L	1-4	L1	18 Poulard [42]	44 510
	9	Marseille	L	0-1	L1	19 Andre [89]	7 830
	17	Bordeaux	D	1-1	L1	16 Poulard [92+]	17 946
	24	Lorient	D	1-1	L1	15 Ilan [60]	5 972
Apr	1	Caen	D	0-0	L1	15		13 480
	7	St-Etienne	D	1-1	L1	17 Medjani [78]	6 352
	15	Lille	L	1-4	L1	19 Sammaritano [93+]	16 887
	22	Nancy	D	0-0	L1	17		6 140
	29	Rennes	L	1-3	L1	17 Ilan [89]	17 498
May	2	Sochaux	W	2-1	L1	16 Kinkela [74p], Socrier [85]	8 171
	6	Evian	L	1-2	L1	16 Andre [14]	11 576
	13	Lyon	L	0-1	L1	18 Eduardo [58p]	8 249
	20	Toulouse	W	2-0	L1	16 Cavalli 2 [20 31]	10 892

16th Att: 120 416 • Av: 6 338 (+43.1%) • François Coty 10 660 (59%)

AJACCIO LEAGUE APPEARANCES/GOALS 2011–12
Goalkeepers Thierry Debes 1+1 • Guillermo Ochoa MEX 37
Defenders Samuel Bouhours 25/0 • Fousseni Diawara MLI 21+2/4
Felipe Saad BRA 2+1/0 • Anthony Lippini 19+2/0 • Arnaud Maire 6/0
Carl Medjani ALG 32+3/2 • Jackson Mendy SEN 2+1/0
Yohann Poulard 34/1
Midfield Benjamin Andre 30+3/4 • Fabrice Begeorgi 3/0
Johan Cavalli 29+2/4 • Christian Kinkela COD 11+18/3
Paul Lasne 13+14/0 • Mehdi Mostefa ALG 32+2/3
Leyti N'Diaye SEN 7+1/0 • Jean-Baptiste Pierazzi 32+2/0
Frederic Sammaritano 18+12/5 • Damien Tiberi 18+10/0
Forwards Eduardo BRA 18+1/5 • Andy Delort 2+5/0
Karim El Hany 0+1/0 • Ilan BRA 15+11/6 • Richard Socrier 11+11/2
Coach Olivier Pantaloni

AUXERRE
2011–12

Aug	6	Montpellier	L	1-3	L1	17 Traore [45]	12 198
	14	Marseille	D	2-2	L1	17 Traore [46], Contout [81]	19 342
	20	Bordeaux	D	1-1	L1	16 Traore [66]	20 350
	27	Ajaccio	W	4-1	L1	12 Chafni [34], Traore 2 [75 80], Le Tallec [90]	8 622
	30	Nancy	W	2-1	LCr3	Le Tallec [50], Kossoko [74]	6 086

AUXERRE 2011–12 (CONT'D)

	11	Nancy	D	0-0	L1	10		14 206
Sep	17	Caen	D	1-1	L1	9 Jemaa [32]	8 962
	21	Lorient	D	1-1	L1	11 Oliech [62]	15 661
	25	Sochaux	W	4-1	L1	9 Traore [51], Oliech 3 [52 63 67]	8 437
Oct	1	St-Etienne	D	1-1	L1	9 Sahar [5]	19 338
	15	Lille	L	1-3	L1	10 Oliech [36]	11 175
	23	Rennes	L	0-1	L1	11		9 514
	26	Caen	L	1-2	LCr4	Sahar [29]	7 628
Nov	29	Evian	L	1-3	L1	13 Dudka [71p]	11 060
	6	Toulouse	W	2-0	L1	12 Sanogo [69], Contout [88]	7 238
	20	Val'ciennes	L	1-2	L1	14 Traore [34]	13 383
	27	Lyon	L	0-3	L1	16		12 080
Dec	4	PSG	L	2-3	L1	16 Oliech [59], Dudka [87]	42 035
	10	Nice	W	2-1	L1	13 Oliech [13], Sahar [65]	7 081
	17	Brest	L	0-1	L1	14		13 677
	21	Dijon	D	2-2	L1	15 Le Tallec [80], Jemaa [92+]	14 350
	7	Chambly	W	1-0	CFr9	Dudka [116p]	3 150
Jan	14	Ajaccio	L	1-2	L1	16 Oliech [14]	5 522
	21	Chat'roux	L	1-2	CF10	Dudka [78]	4 641
	28	Nancy	L	1-3	L1	18 Cisse [82]	10 815
Feb	1	Lorient	D	1-1	L1	19 Boly [1]	7 373
	18	Sochaux	D	0-0	L1	18		12 136
	22	Caen	L	1-2	L1	19 Contout [60]	13 928
	25	St-Etienne	D	0-0	L1	19		13 683
Mar	3	Lille	D	2-2	L1	19 Sahar [80], Hengbart [84]	16 971
	11	Rennes	D	1-1	L1	19 Oliech [10]	22 886
	17	Evian	L	0-1	L1	20		17 991
	25	Toulouse	L	0-1	L1	20		30 588
	31	Val'ciennes	W	2-0	L1	20 Chafni [24], Oliech [66]	14 183
Apr	7	Lyon	L	1-2	L1	20 Traore [42]	31 492
	15	PSG	D	1-1	L1	20 Le Tallec [86]	12 010
	21	Nice	L	0-1	L1	20		9 480
	29	Brest	W	4-0	L1	20 Cisse [87], Kapo [17], Traore [78], Contout [39]	14 421
May	3	Dijon	W	2-0	L1	17 Contout [30], Ndinga [86]	14 764
	7	Bordeaux	L	2-4	L1	20 Kapo 2 [67 80]	16 553
	13	Marseille	L	0-3	L1	20		40 810
	20	Montpellier	L	1-2	L1	20 Kapo [20]	16 509

20th Att: 230 338 • Av: 12 123 (+6.8%) • L'Abbé-Deschamps 24 493 (49%)

AUXERRE LEAGUE APPEARANCES/GOALS 2011–12
Goalkeepers Donovan Leon 2 • Olivier Sorin 36
Defenders Jeremy Berthod 14+1/0 • Willy Boly 32+1/1
Adama Coulibaly MLI 8/0 • Stephane Grichting SUI 32+1/0
Cedric Hengbart 27/1 • Cyriaque Rivieyran 3+1/0
Amadou Sidibe MLI 8+4/0
Midfield David Camps 0+2/0 • Kamel Chafni MAR 26+5/2
Edouard Cisse 27+1/2 • Dariusz Dudka POL 33+1/2
Olivier Kapo 11+4/4 • Georges Mandjeck CMR 15/0
Soualiho Meite 1+1/0 • Christopher Missilou CGO 0+1/0
Delvin Ndinga CGO 21+2/1 • Prince Segbefia TOG 10+5/0
Alain Traore BFA 26+1/9
Forwards Roy Contout 16+21/5 • Rudy Haddad 5+5/0
Issam Jemaa TUN 4+3/2 • Jung Jo Guk KOR 0+1/0
Omar Kossoko 4+15/0 • Anthony Le Tallec 12+12/3
Dennis Oliech KEN 29+4/10 • Ben Sahar ISR 13+8/3
Yaya Sanogo 3+4/1
Coach Laurent Fournier (8/06/11) • Jean Guy Wallemme (18/02/12)

KEY
SC = Trophée des Champions (played in Tanger)
• L1 = Ligue 1 • CF = Coupe de France •
LC = Coupe de la Ligue • CL = UEFA Champions
League • EL = Europa League • Matches that
are shaded are home matches
See page 13 for further explanations

GIRONDINS BORDEAUX
2011-12

Aug	7 St-Etienne	L	1-2	L1	14	Jussie 56p	31 609
	13 Lorient	D	1-1	L1	12	Henrique 91+	17 122
	20 Auxerre	D	1-1	L1	15	Gouffran 23	20 350
	27 Val'ciennes	W	2-1	L1	13	Traore 81, Modeste 92+	15 373
	31 St-Etienne	L	1-3	LCr3		Tremoulinas 10	14 647
Sep	10 Evian	D	0-0	L1	1		15 853
	17 Toulouse	L	2-3	L1	13	Diabate 2 19 38	15 457
	20 Lille	D	1-1	L1	13	Diabate 8p	17 927
	24 Lyon	L	1-3	L1	14	Modeste 86p	30 806
	1 Montpellier	D	2-2	L1	14	Diabate 18, Ciani 50	17 713
Oct	15 Nice	L	0-3	L1	18		9 269
	22 Brest	D	1-1	L1	18	Gouffran 52	16 428
	29 Ajaccio	W	2-0	L1	15	Gouffran 2 25 29	5 667
Nov	6 PSG	D	1-1	L1	14	Gouffran 13	29 496
	19 Dijon	L	0-2	L1	18		13 568
	26 Caen	W	2-0	L1	14	Gouffran 59, Modeste 79	17 255
	4 Nancy	W	2-0	L1	12	Plasil 1, Henrique 52	15 404
Dec	10 Marseille	D	0-0	L1	10		40 446
	18 Sochaux	W	1-0	L1	9	Sane 22	23 700
	21 Rennes	L	0-1	L1	10		20 045
	7 St-Etienne	D	1-1	CFr9		Jussie 35, W 4-2p	17 532
Jan	14 Val'ciennes	W	2-1	L1	9	Jussie 7, M-Belay 12	16 274
	21 Créteil	D	2-2	CF10		Ciani 60, M-Belay 91, W 4-3p	11 000
	29 Evian	D	0-0	L1	9		11 543
	4 Toulouse	W	2-0	L1	9	Jussie 1, Obraniak 40	16 485
	8 Lyon	L	1-3	CF11		Jussie 23	7 000
Feb	12 Lille	W	5-4	L1	9	M-Belay 2 2 50, Gouffran 60, Obraniak 2 17 93+	17 256
	19 Lyon	W	1-0	L1	9	Gouffran 41	27 704
	25 Montpellier	L	0-1	L1	9		21 284
Mar	3 Nice	L	1-2	L1	9	Planus 67	18 807
	10 Brest	W	2-0	L1	9	Gouffran 35, Plasil 48	13 100
	17 Ajaccio	D	1-1	L1	8	Diabate 70	17 946
	25 PSG	D	1-1	L1	8	Diabate 77	44 723
	31 Dijon	D	1-1	L1	8	Tremoulinas 72p	20 295
Apr	8 Caen	L	0-1	L1	8		14 936
	15 Nancy	D	2-2	L1	8	Gouffran 17, Tremoulinas 90p	18 098
	21 Marseille	W	2-1	L1	8	Jussie 2 1 29	31 440
	29 Sochaux	W	3-0	L1	8	Jussie 12, M-Belay 63p, Saivet 70	19 352
May	2 Rennes	W	2-0	L1	8	Obraniak 51, N'Guemo 58	19 531
	7 Auxerre	W	4-2	L1	7	Gouffran 2 1 5, Sane 9, Plasil 48	16 553
	13 Lorient	W	1-0	L1	5	Gouffran 92+p	19 320
	20 St-Etienne	W	3-2	L1	5	Diabate 2 23 29, Gouffran 68	22 726

5th Att: 393 537 • Av: 20 712 (-17.1%) • Chaban-Delmas 34 462 (60%)

BORDEAUX LEAGUE APPEARANCES/GOALS 2011–12
Goalkeepers Cedric Carrasso 37 • Abdoulaye Keita 0+1 • Kevin Olimpa 1
Defenders Matthieu Chalme 8/0 • Michael Ciani 30+1/1
Henrique BRA 22+1/2 • Grzegorz Krychowiak 1+1/0
Florian Marange 1+1/0 • Mariano BRA 19/0 • Marc Planus 26+1/1
Ludovic Lamine Sane 30+2/2 • Vujadin Savic SRB 1/0
Benoit Tremoulinas 36/2
Midfield Fahid Ben Khalfallah TUN 7+8/0 • Landry N'Guemo CMR 30+3/1
Ludovic Obraniak POL 17/4 • Jaroslav Plasil CZE 38/3
Gregory Sertic 6+12/0 • Abdou Traore MLI 3+6/1
Forwards David Bellion 4+8/0 • Cheick Diabate MLI 13+13/8
Yoan Gouffran 31+4/14 • Jussie BRA 14+14/6
Nicolas Maurice-Belay 35/4 • Anthony Modeste 4+11/3
Henri Saivet 4+20/1
Coach Francis Gillot (6/06/11)

STADE BRESTOIS
2011-12

Aug	6 Evian	D	2-2	L1	10	Grougi 39, Lesoimier 44	13 910
	13 Val'ciennes	D	0-0	L1	10		19 020
	20 Lyon	D	1-1	L1	13	Lesoimier 12	14 693
	27 Nice	D	0-0	L1	15		7 875
	31 Caen	L	2-3	LCr3		Roux 2 14 79	8 652

STADE BRESTOIS 2011-12

Sep	11 PSG	L	0-1	L1	16		40 134
	17 Montpellier	D	2-2	L1	16	Ben Basat 70, Gentiletti 88	12 548
	21 Dijon	L	0-1	L1	18		12 436
	25 Ajaccio	D	1-1	L1	18	Roux 61	12 142
	2 Marseille	D	1-1	L1	17	Poyet 5	39 598
Oct	15 Caen	D	1-1	L1	16	Grougi 45	12 760
	22 Bordeaux	D	1-1	L1	16	Ben Basat 63	16 428
	29 Lorient	W	3-1	L1	12	Toure 4, Grougi 2 35 43p	14 421
Nov	6 Nancy	L	1-2	L1	15	Lesoimier 85	14 029
	20 Sochaux	W	2-0	L1	13	Grougi 68p, Poyet 80	12 920
	26 Lille	L	0-2	L1	15		16 760
Dec	3 St-Etienne	D	2-2	L1	15	Roux 2 23 27	13 789
	10 Rennes	D	1-1	L1	16	Roux 17	20 275
	17 Auxerre	W	1-0	L1	11	Grougi 34p	13 677
	21 Toulouse	D	0-0	L1	12		22 897
	7 Niort	L	0-2	CFr9			8 322
Jan	14 Nice	W	1-0	L1	11	Ben Basat 6	11 997
	28 PSG	L	0-1	L1	11		14 760
	4 Montpellier	L	0-1	L1	11		11 149
Feb	11 Dijon	D	1-1	L1	14	Gentiletti 93+	13 412
	18 Ajaccio	D	0-0	L1	14		5 633
	26 Marseille	W	1-0	L1	12	Baysse 17	15 096
Mar	4 Caen	D	0-0	L1	12		15 027
	10 Bordeaux	L	0-2	L1	12		13 100
	17 Lorient	L	1-2	L1	13	Ben Basat 11	15 454
	24 Nancy	L	0-1	L1	16		13 970
	31 Sochaux	L	1-2	L1	17	Grougi 3	17 299
Apr	7 Lille	W	3-1	L1	15	Daf 5, Grougi 10p, Alphonse 53	12 917
	15 St-Etienne	L	1-2	L1	17	Jemaa 63	21 028
	21 Rennes	L	0-1	L1	18		14 391
	29 Auxerre	L	0-4	L1	18		14 421
May	2 Toulouse	D	0-0	L1	18		13 183
	6 Lyon	D	1-1	L1	18	Lorenzi 75	31 016
	13 Val'ciennes	W	1-0	L1	16	Grougi 40	13 615
	20 Evian	W	1-0	L1	15	Jemaa 50	11 222

15th Att: 257 318 • Av: 13 543 (-0.1%) • Francis-Le Blé 15 097 (89%)

BREST LEAGUE APPEARANCES/GOALS 2011–12
Goalkeepers Lionel Cappone 1 • Steeve Elana 37
Defenders Paul Baysse 33+1/1 • Ousmane Coulibaly 17+1/0
John Culma COL 20+1/0 • Omar Daf SEN 15+1/1
Santiago Gentiletti ARG 15/2 • Ahmed Kantari MAR 9+3/0
Gregory Lorenzi 14+1/1 • Tripy Makonda 6+2/0 • Johan Martial 24/0
Jonathan Zebina 27+1/0
Midfield Adama Ba 0+8/0 • Yoann Bigne 0+1/0
Oscar Ewolo CGO 15+12/0 • Brahim Ferradj 0+1/0 • Bruno Grougi 34/9
Diallo Guidileye 5+1/0 • Benoit Lesoimier 28+8/3
Mario Licka CZE 17+8/0 • Tomas Micola CZE 0+1/0
Abdoulwhaid Sissoko 5+5/0 • Richard Soumah 1+2/0
Forwards Alexandre Alphonse 9+2/1 • Jonathan Ayite TOG 3+3/0
Eden Ben Basat ISR 26+6/4 • Issam Jemaa TUN 6+4/2
Abel Khaled TUN 3+4/0 • Romain Poyet 23+12/2 • Nolan Roux 18/4
Larsen Toure GUI 7+4/1
Coach Alex Dupont • Corentin Martins ((26/04/12)

SM CAEN
2011-12

Aug	6 Val'ciennes	W	1-0	L1	6	Proment 34	14 085
	13 Sochaux	W	2-1	L1	3	Hamouma 15, Frau 67	12 137
	20 Lille	L	1-2	L1	4	Nivet 90p	16 938
	28 Rennes	L	2-3	L1	10	Heurtaux 58, Bulot 61	19 715
	31 Brest	W	3-2	LCr3		Fajr 35, Hamouma 56, Traore 88	8 652
Sep	10 Toulouse	L	0-1	L1	13		12 575
	17 Auxerre	D	1-1	L1	11	Nivet 45	8 962
	21 Lyon	W	1-0	L1	8	Nivet 45p	16 644
	24 Evian	W	4-2	L1	8	Niang 11, Proment 45, Bulot 69, Traore 72	9 498

SM CAEN 2011–12

	1 Nice	D	1-1	L1	8	Frau [80]	13 234
	15 Brest	D	1-1	L1	8	Heurtaux [85]	12 760
Oct	22 Montpellier	L	1-3	L1	9	Nivet [82p]	14 290
	26 Auxerre	W	2-1	LCr4		Nabab 2 [24 117]	7 628
	29 PSG	L	2-4	L1	10	Heurtaux [12], Vandam [82]	43 812
	6 Dijon	W	3-0	L1	9	Leca [36], Bulot [67], Frau [73]	14 387
Nov	19 Ajaccio	D	2-2	L1	9	Wague [64], Nangis [70]	5 125
	26 Bordeaux	L	0-2	L1	10		17 255
	2 Marseille	L	1-2	L1	10	Frau [23p]	20 470
Dec	10 St-Etienne	L	0-2	L1	12		21 244
	17 Nancy	L	1-2	L1	13	Nivet [60p]	13 528
	21 Lorient	D	0-0	L1	14		15 715
	7 Troyes	L	2-4	CFr9		Hamouma [66], Fajr [76]	2 293
Jan	10 Marseille	L	0-3	LCqf			15 674
	14 Rennes	L	0-2	L1	15		14 785
	28 Toulouse	L	0-1	L1	17		12 023
	1 Lyon	W	2-1	L1	13	Hamouma [13], Nabab [73]	30 692
Feb	18 Evian	D	2-2	L1	12	Frau [45p], Nabab [57]	14 881
	22 Auxerre	W	2-1	L1	14	Traore [71], Nabab [77]	13 928
	25 Nice	L	0-1	L1	13		6 106
	4 Brest	D	0-0	L1	13		15 027
	11 Montpellier	L	0-3	L1	14		14 501
Mar	17 PSG	D	2-2	L1	17	Frau [54], Heurtaux [71]	19 172
	25 Dijon	L	0-2	L1	17		13 477
	1 Ajaccio	D	0-0	L1	18		13 480
	8 Bordeaux	W	1-0	L1	16	Seube [2]	14 936
Apr	18 Marseille	D	1-1	L1	15	Bulot [11]	39 261
	21 St-Etienne	L	1-4	L1	15	Nabab [72]	17 256
	29 Nancy	D	1-1	L1	15	Niang [51]	17 016
	2 Lorient	W	1-0	L1	14	Heurtaux [67]	13 518
May	7 Lille	L	0-3	L1	15		16 941
	13 Sochaux	L	1-3	L1	17	Nivet [58]	17 191
	20 Val'ciennes	L	1-3	L1	18	Nivet [77]	18 024

18th Att: 290 325 • Av: 15 280 (-4.7%) • Michel d'Ornano 22 864 (66%)

CAEN LEAGUE APPEARANCES/GOALS 2011–12

Goalkeepers Alexis Thebaux 38
Defenders Thomas Heurtaux 35+1/5 • Yanick M'Bone CMR 4+3/0
Aurelien Montaroup 15/0 • Nicolas Seube 34+1/1
Jeremy Sorbon 29+1/0 • Jerry Vandam 36/1 • Molla Wague 4+1/0
Midfield Frederic Bulot GAB 35+3/4 • Anthony Deroin 1+4/0
Faycal Fajr 9+4/0 • Romain Hamouma 29+2/2 • Gregory Leca 20+5/1
Damien Marcq 0+3/0 • Benjamin Nivet 13+20/7
Gregory Proment 25+8/2 • Alexandre Raineau 16+3/0
Ibrahima Tandia 0+1/0
Forwards Pierre-Alain Frau 26+6/6 • Livio Nabab 18+4/4
Lenny Nangis 6+5/1 • M'Baye Niang 14+9/2
Kandia Traore CIV 11+22/2
Coach Franck Dumas

DIJON FCO 2011–12

	7 Rennes	L	1-5	L1	20	Jovial [45]	13 754
	13 Toulouse	L	0-2	L1	20		13 356
Aug	20 Lorient	W	2-0	L1	14	Thil [3], Jovial [88]	12 872
	27 Evian	W	1-0	L1	11	Jovial [68]	10 225
	31 Val'ciennes	W	3-2	LCr3		Bautheac [29p], Jovial [40], Guerbert [52]	6 872
	10 Lyon	L	1-2	L1	14	Corgnet [43]	14 325
Sep	17 Val'ciennes	L	0-4	L1	14		13 961
	21 Brest	W	1-0	L1	10	Mandanne [33p]	12 436
	24 Nice	D	1-1	L1	10	Corgnet [14]	8 152
	1 Ajaccio	D	1-1	L1	11	Bautheac [41]	12 534
	18 Montpellier	L	3-5	L1	12	Corgnet 2 [9 11], Guerbert [90]	12 047
Oct	23 PSG	L	0-2	L1	13		44 071
	26 PSG	W	3-2	LCr4		Sankhare [30p], Berenguer [32], Jovial [61p]	10 115
	29 Marseille	L	2-3	L1	17	Jovial [46], Cornet [63]	15 081
Nov	6 Caen	L	0-3	L1	19		14 387
	19 Bordeaux	W	2-0	L1	17	Jovial [69], Cornet [73]	13 568
	26 Nancy	W	2-1	L1	12	Bautheac [18p], Sankhare [83]	15 114

DIJON FCO 2011–12 (CONT'D)

	3 Sochaux	D	0-0	L1	14		13 165
Dec	11 Lille	L	0-2	L1	15		16 726
	17 St-Etienne	L	1-2	L1	17	Bautheac [95+]	14 435
	21 Auxerre	D	2-2	L1	16	Cornet [7], Jovial [33]	14 350
	7 Versailles	W	5-1	CFr9		Thil [38], Diallo [42], Joufreau [50], Bautheac [77], Cornet [82]	4 100
Jan	11 Nice	D	3-3	LCqf		Guerbert [18], Jovial [62], Bautheac [117p], L 3-5p	7 751
	14 Evian	W	3-1	L1	13	Corgnet [42], Jovial 2 [50 56]	12 565
	21 Istres	W	2-1	CFl0		Kakuta [30], Kone [49]	7 103
	28 Lyon	L	1-3	L1	14	Sankhare [61]	35 644
	4 Val'ciennes	L	1-2	L1	17	Thil [92+]	12 054
	11 Brest	D	1-1	L1	16	Kakuta [76]	13 412
Feb	15 PSG	L	0-1	CFl1			9 484
	18 Nice	W	3-0	L1	15	Kakuta [44], Jovial [53], Kone [87]	12 303
	25 Ajaccio	L	1-2	L1	15	Kumordzi [66]	5 277
	3 Montpellier	D	1-1	L1	15	Kakuta [67]	14 016
	11 PSG	L	1-2	L1	18	Paulle [76]	14 446
Mar	17 Marseille	W	2-1	L1	15	Sankhare [24], Kakuta [79p]	40 445
	25 Caen	W	2-0	L1	13	Kone [22], Sankhare [69]	13 477
	31 Bordeaux	D	1-1	L1	13	Guerbert [92+]	20 295
	7 Nancy	L	0-2	L1	15		14 526
Apr	15 Sochaux	L	0-1	L1	16		19 599
	21 Lille	L	0-2	L1	16		14 005
	29 St-Etienne	L	0-1	L1	16		20 753
	3 Auxerre	L	0-2	L1	19		14 764
May	7 Lorient	D	0-0	L1	19		16 966
	13 Toulouse	D	1-1	L1	19	Meite [27]	14 016
	20 Rennes	L	0-5	L1	19		17 601

19th Att: 258 342 • Av: 13 597 (+45.4%) • Gaston Gérard 15 998 (85%)

DIJON LEAGUE APPEARANCES/GOALS 2011–12

Goalkeepers Jean-Daniel Padovani 1 • Baptiste Reynet 37
Defenders Abdoulaye Bamba CIV 21+3/0 • Zie Diabate CIV 12+2/0
Zakaria Diallo 3/0 • Abdoulaye Meite CIV 25/1 • Steven Paulle 17+5/1
Samuel Souprayen 24/0 • Cedric Varrault 24/0
Chaher Zarour 15+2/0
Midfield Hakeem Achour 0+1/0 • Sanaa Altama 11+6/0
Sekou Baradji 1+2/0 • Florin Berenguer 10+6/0
Benjamin Cornet 35+1/8 • Thomas Guerbert 22+11/2
Bennard Kumordzi GHA 16/1 • Lesly Malouda 2+3/0
Damien Marcq 9+5/0 • Daisuke Matsui JPN 2+1/0
Younousse Sankhare 31+2/4
Forwards Eric Bautheac 28+6/3 • Raphael Caceres 0+2/0
Mehdi Courgnaud 4+7/0 • Brice Jovial 22+8/9 • Gael Kakuta 12+2/4
Koro Kone CIV 9+7/2 • Christophe Mandanne REU 2+8/1
Gregory Thil 14+12/2
Coach Patrice Carteron

EVIAN-THONON GAILLARD 2011–12

	6 Brest	D	2-2	L1	9	Sorlin [17], Mmadi [20]	13 910
Aug	14 Nice	W	1-0	L1	7	Khilfa [51]	13 126
	20 Ajaccio	D	1-1	L1	6	Berigaud [75]	6 886
	27 Dijon	L	0-1	L1	14		10 225
	1 Lens	L	0-1	LCr3			13 210
	10 Bordeaux	D	0-0	L1	12		15 853
Sep	18 PSG	D	2-2	L1	10	Leroy [14], Sagbo [20p]	15 162
	21 Marseille	L	0-2	L1	14		39 357
	24 Caen	L	2-4	L1	15	Barbosa 2 [34 39]	9 498
	1 Nancy	D	1-1	L1	15	Mongongu [62p]	15 054
Oct	15 St-Etienne	L	1-2	L1	17	Sagbo [59]	14 798
	5 Lille	D	1-1	L1	13	Khilfa [4]	16 673
	22 Sochaux	D	1-1	L1	14	Angoula [92+]	12 331
	29 Auxerre	W	3-1	L1	14	Sagbo 2 [15 42], Barbosa [68]	11 060
Nov	19 Lorient	W	2-1	L1	12	Sagbo [7p], Wass [59]	10 763
	26 Rennes	L	2-3	L1	13	Barbosa [19], Wass [32]	17 782
	3 Val'ciennes	W	2-1	L1	10	Sorlin [25], Barbosa [33]	9 608
	10 Toulouse	L	1-2	L1	11	Wass [49]	32 842
Dec	17 Lyon	L	1-2	L1	12	Sagbo [49]	35 253
	21 Montpellier	W	4-2	L1	11	Barbosa [52], Khilfa [68], Cambon [71], Djadjedje [75]	12 336

EVIAN-THONON GAILLARD 2011–12 (CONT'D)

Jan	8	Metz	D	2-2	CFr9	Cambon [108], Sagbo [123+], W 5-3p	5 139
Jan	14	Dijon	L	1-3	L1	12 Sagbo [76]	12 565
Jan	21	Valence	W	2-0	CF10	Sagbo [8], Mmadi [90]	1 000
Jan	29	Bordeaux	D	0-0	L1	12	11 543
Feb	4	PSG	L	1-3	L1	13 Cambon [45]	41 624
Feb	7	Rennes	L	2-3	CF11	Berigaud [70p], Govou [73]	6 128
Feb	18	Caen	D	2-2	L1	11 Barbosa [51], Govou [93+]	4 881
Feb	25	Nancy	W	2-0	L1	11 Berigaud 2 [30 32]	10 748
Mar	3	St-Etienne	W	2-0	L1	10 Mongongu [38], Sagbo [91+]	22 254
Mar	6	Marseille	W	2-0	L1	10 Leroy 2 [15 22]	14 920
Mar	10	Sochaux	L	2-3	L1	10 Mongongu [25p], Cambon [71]	10 861
Mar	17	Auxerre	W	2-0	L1	10 Kahlenberg [8], Berigaud [93+]	17 991
Mar	24	Lille	L	0-3	L1	10	12 248
Mar	31	Lorient	W	1-0	L1	10 Djadjedje [19]	14 371
Apr	7	Rennes	L	1-3	L1	10 Leroy [34]	9 672
Apr	15	Val'ciennes	W	3-0	L1	9 Khlifa [29], Berigaud [35], Sagbo [44p]	13 794
Apr	21	Toulouse	W	2-1	L1	9 Angoula [10], OG [75]	10 272
May	1	Montpellier	D	2-2	L1	9 Kahlenberg [44], Berigaud [69]	22 599
May	6	Ajaccio	W	2-1	L1	9 Barbosa [15], Wass [54]	11 576
May	10	Lyon	L	1-3	L1	9 Sagbo [15]	14 973
May	13	Nice	D	1-1	L1	9 OG [13]	10 544
May	20	Brest	L	0-1	L1	9	11 222

9th • Att: 224 612 • Av: 11 822 (+53.1%) • Parc des Sports 15 600 (75%)

EVIAN LEAGUE APPEARANCES/GOALS 2011–12
Goalkeepers Stephan Andersen DEN 29+1 • Bertrand Laquait 7
Quentin Westberg USA 2
Defenders Aldo Angoula 29+1/2 • Cedric Cambon 32+1/3
Brice Dja Djedje CIV 34/2 • Jonathan Mensah GHA 1/0
Cedric Mongongu COD 12+2/3 • Guillaume Rippert 9+2/0
Felipe Saad BRA 0+1/0 • Daniel Wass DEN 27+2/4
Midfield Cedric Barbosa 23+5/8 • Fabrice Ehret 18+1/0
Nicolas Farina 2+12/0 • Thomas Kahlenberg DEN 12+5/2
Guillaume Lacour 3+1/0 • Jerome Leroy 11+8/4
Christian Poulsen DEN 24/0 • Mohammed Rabiu GHA 12+13/0
Olivier Sorlin 32+1/2 • Adrien Thomasson 0+3/0 • Eric Tie Bi 13+12/0
Forwards Youssef Adnane 3+6/0 • Kevin Berigaud 9+10/6
Sidney Govou 11+7/1 • Saber Khelifa TUN 28+3/4
Ali Mmadi COM 5+9/1 • Yannick Sagbo CIV 30+3/10
Coach Bernard Casoni • Pablo Correa URU (2/01/12)

LILLE OSC 2011–12

Jly	27	Marseille	L	4-5	SC		Balmont [9], Hazard [57], Sow [72], Basa [92+]	33 900
Aug	6	Nancy	D	1-1	L1	12 Debuchy [47]	15 060
Aug	14	Montpellier	L	0-1	L1	14	16 304
Aug	20	Caen	W	2-1	L1	10 Pedretti [69], Debuchy [88]	16 938
Aug	28	Marseille	W	3-2	L1	7 Sow 2 [15 75p], Chedjou [66]	17 906
Sep	10	St-Etienne	W	3-1	L1	3 Hazard 2 [55 73], Obraniak [86]	23 061
Sep	14	CSKA M'kva	D	2-2	CLgB	Sow [44], Pedretti [57]	15 274
Sep	17	Sochaux	D	2-2	L1	4 Pedretti [49], Hazard [78]	16 776
Sep	20	Bordeaux	D	1-1	L1	6 Hazard [57]	17 927
Sep	24	Lorient	D	1-1	L1	6 Cole [34]	16 234
Sep	27	Trabzonspor	D	1-1	CLgB	Sow [30]	17 349
Oct	2	Rennes	W	2-0	L1	5 Sow [7], Balmont [32]	16 802
Oct	15	Auxerre	W	3-1	L1	4 Payet [71], Jelen [82], Debuchy [94+p]	11 175
Oct	18	Inter	L	0-1	CLgB		16 996
Oct	23	Lyon	W	3-1	L1	3 Sow [45], Basa [65], Cole [83]	17 247
Oct	26	Sedan	W	3-1	LCr4	Pedretti [34], Cole [39], Jelen [70]	17 016
Oct	30	Val'ciennes	D	0-0	L1	3	21 493
Nov	2	Inter	L	1-2	CLgB	Tulio [83]	24 299
Nov	5	Evian	D	1-1	L1	3 Pedretti [63]	16 673
Nov	20	Toulouse	D	0-0	L1	3	17 653
Nov	22	CSKA M'kva	W	2-0	CLgB	OG [49], Sow [64]	19 100
Nov	26	Brest	W	2-0	L1	3 Payet [11], Sow [88]	16 760
Dec	3	Ajaccio	W	3-2	L1	3 Obraniak [12], Basa [16], Hazard [80p]	5 319
Dec	7	Trabzonspor	D	0-0	CLgB		16 375

LILLE OSC 2011–12 (CONT'D)

Dec	11	Dijon	W	1-0	L1	3 Sow [16], Hazard [58]	16 726
Dec	18	PSG	D	0-0	L1	3	45 195
Dec	21	Nice	D	4-4	L1	3 Chedjou [9], Cole [27], Hazard [76], Balmont [88]	16 847
Jan	7	Chantilly	W	6-0	CFr9	Cole 3 [23 59 67], Hazard [45p], Jelen 2 [56 77]	6 000
Jan	11	Lyon	L	1-2	LCqf	Cole [28]	29 124
Jan	15	Marseille	L	0-2	L1	3	41 279
Jan	21	Compiègne	W	1-0	CF10	Bruno [114]	4 720
Jan	28	St-Etienne	W	3-0	L1	3 Hazard [50p], Roux 2 [86 87]	17 437
Feb	8	Val'ciennes	L	1-2	CF11	Roux [88]	16 229
Feb	12	Bordeaux	L	4-5	L1	3 Rozehnal [8], Hazard [65], Debuchy [75], Roux [90]	17 256
Feb	18	Lorient	W	1-0	L1	3 Debuchy [77]	14 812
Feb	22	Sochaux	W	1-0	L1	3 Roux [76]	15 052
Feb	26	Rennes	D	1-1	L1	3 Chedjou [40]	19 834
Mar	4	Auxerre	D	2-2	L1	3 Hazard 2 [34 63p]	16 971
Mar	10	Lyon	L	1-2	L1	3 Chedjou [45]	33 318
Mar	18	Val'ciennes	W	4-0	L1	3 Hazard [18], OG [57], Chedjou [69], Tulio [83]	17 358
Mar	24	Evian	W	3-0	L1	3 Hazard [36p], Payet [55], Pedretti [67]	12 248
Apr	1	Toulouse	W	2-1	L1	3 Hazard [13p], Payet [32]	17 057
Apr	7	Brest	L	1-3	L1	3 Payet [27]	12 917
Apr	15	Ajaccio	W	4-1	L1	3 OG [16], Cole [75], Bruno [81], Hazard [87p]	16 887
Apr	21	Dijon	W	2-0	L1	3 Mavuba [39], Hazard [45]	14 005
Apr	29	PSG	W	2-1	L1	3 Hazard [71p], Roux [79]	17 262
May	2	Nice	W	1-0	L1	3 Tulio [6]	10 570
May	7	Caen	W	3-0	L1	3 Tulio 2 [26p 36], Payet [60]	16 941
May	13	Montpellier	L	0-1	L1	3	27 649
May	20	Nancy	W	4-1	L1	3 Hazard 3 [10 27 34p], Tulio [24]	17 000

3rd • Att: 322 459 • Av: 16 972 (+3.3%) • Métropole 17 963 (94%)

LILLE LEAGUE APPEARANCES/GOALS 2011–12
Goalkeepers Mickael Landreau 38
Defenders Marko Basa MNE 22/2 • Franck Beria 32/0
Laurent Bonnart 7+4/0 • Mauro Cetto ARG 6+1/0
Aurelien Chedjou CMR 27/5 • Mathieu Debuchy 32/5
Lucas Digne 13+3/0 • David Rozehnal CZE 11+4/1
Pape Souare SEN 2+5/0
Midfield Florent Balmont 30/2 • Joe Cole ENG 20+12/4
Idrissa Gueye SEN 14+11/0 • Eden Hazard BEL 35+3/20
Rio Mavuba 36+2/1 • Ludovic Obraniak POL 5+7/2
Dimitri Payet 23+10/6 • Benoit Pedretti 26+5/4 • Sylvio Rodelin 1+8/0
Forwards Gianni Bruno BEL 0+10/1 • Ireneusz Jelen POL 3+10/1
Nolan Roux 10+7/5 • Moussa Sow SEN 15+3/6 • Tulio BRA 10+5/5
Omar Wade SEN 0+1/0
Coach Rudi Garcia

LORIENT 2011–12

	6	PSG	W	1-0	L1	7	40 048
	13	Bordeaux	D	1-1	L1	8 Jouffre [82]	17 122
Aug	20	Dijon	L	0-2	L1	11	12 872
Aug	27	Nancy	W	2-1	L1	9 Mvuemba [78], M-Paquet [92+]	14 879
Aug	30	Guingamp	W	3-2	LCr3	OG [28], Aliadiere 2 [84 113]	5 448
	10	Sochaux	D	1-1	L1	8 Emeghara [88]	10 031
Sep	17	St-Etienne	W	3-0	L1	6 Aliadiere 2 [11 76], Coutadeur [92+]	14 841
Sep	21	Auxerre	D	1-1	L1	7 Emeghara [23]	15 661
Sep	24	Lille	D	1-1	L1	7 M-Paquet [93+]	16 234
Oct	1	Val'ciennes	W	2-0	L1	6 Campbell [22], Jouffre [68]	15 698
Oct	16	Rennes	L	0-2	L1	7	18 502
Oct	22	Toulouse	D	0-0	L1	7	15 715
Oct	26	Montpellier	W	2-1	LCr4	Emeghara [14], Campbell [69]	4 787
Oct	29	Brest	L	1-3	L1	7 Ecuele [54]	14 421
Nov	6	Ajaccio	W	2-0	L1	7 Jouffre [63], Sunu [82]	15 672
Nov	19	Evian	L	1-2	L1	7 Kone [47]	10 763
Nov	26	Nice	W	1-0	L1	7 Mvuemba [63p]	16 009
Dec	3	Montpellier	L	0-4	L1	9	12 866
Dec	11	Lyon	L	0-1	L1	9	14 998
Dec	17	Marseille	L	1-2	L1	10 Emeghara [77]	40 080
Dec	21	Caen	D	0-0	L1	9	15 715

LORIENT 2011–12 (CONT'D)

	7 Le Havre	L	3-4	CFr9	Coutadeur [16], Romao [18], Mvuemba [61p]	5 241
Jan	11 Le Mans	W	1-0	LCqf	Sunu [70]	7 183
	14 Nancy	D	2-2	L1	10 Coutadeur [63], Campbell [81]	13 500
	28 Sochaux	D	1-1	L1	10 Romao [63]	15 563
	31 Lyon	L	2-4	LCsf	Emeghara [59], M-Paquet [68]	14 610
	11 Auxerre	D	1-1	L1	10 Emeghara [92+]	7 373
Feb	18 Lille	L	0-1	L1	13	14 812
	22 St-Etienne	L	2-4	L1	10 Mvuemba [49], Autret [75]	21 039
	25 Val'ciennes	L	0-2	L1	14	13 969
	4 Rennes	L	0-2	L1	14	15 310
	10 Toulouse	D	1-1	L1	15 Emeghara [61]	13 962
Mar	17 Brest	W	2-1	L1	12 Ecuele [52], M-Paquet [87]	15 454
	24 Ajaccio	D	1-1	L1	14 Bourillon [5]	5 972
	31 Evian	L	0-1	L1	14	14 371
	8 Nice	L	0-2	L1	18	10 001
Apr	15 Montpellier	W	2-1	L1	13 OG [69], Campbell [77]	15 952
	22 Lyon	L	2-3	L1	14 M-Paquet [22], Autret [26]	30 330
	27 Marseille	W	2-1	L1	13 Mvuemba [41p], M-Paquet [53]	15 945
	2 Caen	L	0-1	L1	13	13 518
May	7 Dijon	D	0-0	L1	13	16 966
	13 Bordeaux	L	0-1	L1	14	19 320
	20 PSG	L	1-2	L1	17 M-Paquet [28]	16 529

17th Att: 297 212 • Av: 15 643 (+0.1%) • Stade du Moustoir 18 110 (86%)

LORIENT LEAGUE APPEARANCES/GOALS 2011–12
Goalkeepers Fabien Audard 29 • Florent Chaigneau 2+1
Jeremie Janot 3 • Benjamin Lecomte 4+1
Defenders Maxime Baca 16+8/0 • Gregory Bourillon 20/1
Bruno Ecuele GAB 31+1/2 • Simon Falette 1/0
Lamine Gassama SEN 7+1/0 • Lamine Kone 20+1/1
Wesley Lautoa 5/0 • Arnaud Le Lan 12+2/0
Lucas Mareque ARG 30+1/0 • Pedrinho POR 9+2/0
Midfield Mathias Autret 17+10/2 • Maxime Barthelme 4+5/0
Mathieu Coutadeur 24+6/2 • Sigamary Diarra MLI 2+5/0
Yann Jouffre 25+5/3 • Remi Mulumba 4+4/0 • Arnold Mvuemba 34/4
Gabriel Penalba ARG 0+4/0 • Alaixys Romao TOG 32/1
Forwards Jeremie Aliadiere 15+3/2 • Joel Campbell CRC 11+14/3
Ladislas Douniama CGO 3+3/0 • Sebastian Dubarbier ARG 0+1/0
Innocent Emeghara SUI 13+14/5 • Lynel Kitamba 1+3/0
Kevin Monnet-Paquet 33+2/6 • Julien Quercia 3/0
Fabian Robert 0+1/0 • Gilles Sunu 8+7/1
Coach Christian Gourcuff

OLYMPIQUE LYONNAIS 2011–12

	6 Nice	W	3-1	L1	3	Lopez [10], Gomis [33], Gonalons [74]	14 405
Aug	13 Ajaccio	D	1-1	L1	6 Lopez [83]	30 746
	16 Rubin	W	3-1	CLpo	Gomis [10], OG [40], Briand [71]	35 468
	20 Brest	D	1-1	L1	5 Gomis [69]	14 693
	24 Rubin	D	1-1	CLpo	Kone [87]	20 620
	27 Montpellier	W	2-1	L1	2 Pjanic [49], Pied [83]	31 634
	10 Dijon	W	2-1	L1	2 OG [6], Gomis [54]	14 325
	14 Ajax	D	0-0	CLgD		49 504
Sep	18 Marseille	W	2-0	L1	1 Gomis [17], Bastos [29]	38 010
	21 Caen	L	0-1	L1	3	16 644
	24 Bordeaux	W	3-1	L1	2 Gomis [2 8 33], Bastos [64]	30 806
	27 D. Zagreb	W	2-0	CLgD	Gomis [23], Kone [42]	34 432
	2 PSG	L	0-2	L1	3	44 450
	15 Nancy	W	3-1	L1	3 Bastos [2 26 31p], Gomis [28]	33 825
Oct	18 Real Madrid	L	0-4	CLgD		70 028
	23 Lille	L	1-3	L1	5 Briand [22]	17 247
	26 St-Etienne	W	2-1	LCr4	Briand [40], Bastos [72p]	25 906
	29 St-Etienne	W	2-0	L1	4 Briand [82], Gourcuff [91+]	38 982
	2 Real Madrid	L	0-2	CLgD		40 099
	6 Sochaux	L	1-2	L1	4 Lacazette [14]	15 638
Nov	18 Rennes	L	1-2	L1	5 Ederson [36]	32 193
	22 Ajax	D	0-0	CLgD		35 070
	27 Auxerre	W	3-0	L1	5 Lopez [2 20 68], Bastos [88]	12 080
Dec	4 Toulouse	W	3-2	L1	4 Kone [38], Ederson [52], Lopez [66p]	31 028
	7 D. Zagreb	W	7-1	CLgD	Gomis [4 45 48 52 70], Lopez [64], Gonalons [47], Briand [75]	16 457

OLYMPIQUE LYONNAIS 2011–12 (CONT'D)

	11 Lorient	W	1-0	L1	4 Lacazette [54]	14 998
Dec	17 Evian	W	2-1	L1	4 Briand [35], Lopez [71]	35 253
	21 Val'ciennes	L	0-1	L1	4	16 850
	8 Ly-Duchère	W	3-1	CFr9	Lopez [3 4 30 37]	12 300
	11 Lille	W	2-1	LCqf	Kallstrom [41], Lopez [65]	29 124
	14 Montpellier	L	0-1	L1	4	18 889
Jan	22 Luçon	W	2-0	CF10	Gomis [76], Lopez [90]	15 000
	28 Dijon	W	3-1	L1	4	Briand [8], Gomis [82], Lacazette [90]	35 650
	31 Lorient	W	4-2	LCsf	Lacazette [2 80 122+], Briand [94+], Gomis [102]	14 610
	5 Marseille	D	2-2	L1	4 Gomis [36], OG [45]	41 474
Feb	8 Bordeaux	W	3-1	CF11	Lacazette [36], Gomis [96], Briand [118]	7 000
	11 Caen	L	1-2	L1	4 Lopez [86p]	30 692
	14 APOEL	W	1-0	CLr2	Lacazette [58]	32 010
	19 Bordeaux	L	0-1	L1	6	27 704
	25 PSG	D	4-4	L1	5	Gomis [34], Lopez [36], Bastos [40], Briand [58]	37 347
	3 Nancy	L	0-2	L1	7	17 034
	7 APOEL	L	0-1	CLr2	L 3-4p	22 701
	10 Lille	W	2-1	L1	7 Lacazette [12], Lopez [38]	33 318
	17 St-Etienne	W	1-0	L1	5 Gomis [81]	26 210
Mar	21 PSG	W	3-1	CFqf	Kallstrom [25], Lopez [39], Gomis [92+]	44 000
	24 Sochaux	W	2-1	L1	5 Lovren [4], Gomis [65]	32 730
	1 Rennes	D	1-1	L1	4 Lopez [75]	21 346
	7 Auxerre	W	2-1	L1	4 Lopez [2 29p 72p]	31 492
	10 Gazélec	W	4-0	CFsf	Lacazette [60], Lopez [74], Grenier [80], Gomis [90]	10 163
Apr	14 Marseille	L	0-1	LCf		78 877
	18 Toulouse	L	0-3	L1	4	21 352
	22 Lorient	W	3-2	L1	4 Cris [38], Lopez [77], Gomis [85]	30 330
	28 Quevilly	W	1-0	CFf	Lopez [28]	76 229
	2 Val'ciennes	W	4-1	L1	4	Lopez [2 35 72], Cris [69], Briand [88]	30 890
May	6 Brest	D	1-1	L1	4 Gourcuff [37]	31 016
	10 Evian	W	3-1	L1	4	Kone [23], Briand [68], Lacazette [91+p]	14 973
	13 Ajaccio	D	1-1	L1	4 Gomis [53]	8 249
	20 Nice	L	3-4	L1	4 Lopez [21], Briand [2 26 69]	32 335

4th Att: 629 638 • Av: 33 139 (-6.1%) • Stade de Gerland 41 044 (80%)

LYON LEAGUE APPEARANCES/GOALS 2011–12
Goalkeepers Hugo Lloris 36 • Remy Vercoutre 2+1
Defenders Aly Cissokho 30+1/0 • Cris BRA 20/2
Mouhamadou Dabo 11+4/0 • Timothee Kolodziejczak 1/0
Bakary Kone BFA 25+3/2 • Dejan Lovren CRO 18/1
John Mensah GHA 1/0 • Anthony Reveillere 33/0 • Samuel Umtiti 11+1/0
Midfield Ederson BRA 5+10/2 • Gueida Fofana 10+8/0
Maxime Gonalons 34+1/1 • Yoann Gourcuff 10+3/2
Clement Grenier 13+8/0 • Kim Kallstrom SWE 32/0
Sidy Kone MLI 1+1/0 • Michel Bastos BRA 23+3/6
Miralem Pjanic BIH 1+2/1
Forwards Ishak Belfodil ALG 1+6/0 • Yassine Benzia 0+1/0
Jimmy Briand 30+7/9 • Bafetimbi Gomis 29+7/14
Alexandre Lacazette 15+14/5 • Lisandro Lopez ARG 24+4/16
Harry Novillo 0+1/0 • Jeremy Pied 2+12/1
Coach Remi Garde (21/06/11)

OLYMPIQUE MARSEILLE 2011–12

Jy	27 Lille	W	5-4	SC		Ayew.A [2 71 91+ 95+], Morel [85], Remy [87]	33 900
	6 Sochaux	D	2-2	L1	8 Lucho [38], Remy [74]	41 102
Aug	2 Ajaccio	D	2-2	L1	9 Remy [3], Ayew.A [43]	19 342
	21 St-Etienne	D	0-0	L1	12	41 493
	28 Lille	L	2-3	L1	16 Valbuena [2 57 63]	17 906

OLYMPIQUE MARSEILLE 2011–12 (CONT'D)

Sep| 10	Rennes	L	0-1	L1	17		40 628
	13	Olympiacos	W	1-0	CLgF		Lucho [51]	30 040
	18	Lyon	L	0-2	L1	20		38 010
	21	Evian	W	2-0	L1	15	Remy 2 [25 74]	39 357
	24	Val'ciennes	D	1-1	L1	13	Diawara [16]	21 622
	28	Dortmund	W	3-0	CLgF		Ayew.A 2 [20 69p], Remy [62]	26 142
Oct| 2	Brest	D	1-1	L1	13	Ayew.A [20]	39 598
	15	Toulouse	D	0-0	L1	15		30 082
	19	Arsenal	L	0-1	CLgF			33 258
	22	Ajaccio	W	2-0	L1	12	Ayew.A 2 [30 49]	39 786
	25	Lens	W	4-0	LCr4		Gignac [14], Ayew.J [68], Remy 2 [82 90]	17 972
	29	Dijon	W	3-2	L1	9	Remy [1], Cheyrou [11], Diarra [82]	15 081
Nov| 1	Arsenal	D	0-0	CLgF			59 961
	6	Nice	W	2-0	L1	8	Ayew.J [72], Remy [96+p]	39 716
	19	Montpellier	L	0-1	L1	10		26 241
	23	Olympiacos	L	0-1	CLgF			25 392
	27	PSG	W	3-0	L1	9	Remy [9], Amalfitano [65], Ayew.A [84]	41 512
Dec| 2	Caen	W	2-1	L1	7	Ayew.A [21], Ayew.J [52]	20 470
	6	Dortmund	W	3-2	CLgF		Remy [45], Ayew.A [85], Valbuena [87]	65 000
	10	Bordeaux	D	0-0	L1	8		40 446
	17	Lorient	W	2-1	L1	8	Valbuena [84], Cheyrou [94+]	40 080
	20	Nancy	W	3-1	L1	6	Valbuena [18], Mbia [41], Lucho [91+]	19 304
Jan| 7	Red Star	W	5-0	CFr9		Ayew.J 2 [42 92+], Valbuena [64], Ayew.A [83], Cheyrou [87]	50 892
	10	Caen	W	3-0	LCqf		Valbuena 2 [7 52], Remy [21]	15 674
	15	Lille	W	2-0	L1	6	Remy 2 [61 83]	41 279
	22	Le Havre	W	3-1	CF10		Brandao [64], Amalfitano [104], Remy [120]	12 999
	29	Rennes	W	2-1	L1	5	OG [44], Cheyrou [77]	28 802
Feb| 1	Nice	W	2-1	LCsf		Remy [16], Brandao [57]	12 567
	5	Lyon	D	2-2	L1	5	Cheyrou [16], Brandao [34]	41 474
	15	B-Péronnas	W	3-1	CF11		Brandao 2 [28 45], Ayew.J [54]	8 837
	18	Val'ciennes	D	1-1	L1	5	Diarra [16]	41 055
	22	Inter	W	1-0	CLr2		Ayew.A [93+]	37 646
	26	Brest	L	0-1	L1	8		15 096
Mar| 3	Toulouse	L	0-1	L1	8		40 189
	6	Evian	L	0-2	L1	7		14 920
	9	Ajaccio	L	0-1	L1	8		7 830
	13	Inter	L	1-2	CLr2		Brandao [92+]	63 632
	17	Dijon	L	1-2	L1	9	Remy [11]	40 445
	20	Quevilly	L	2-3	CFqf		Remy 2 [85 113]	19 324
	24	Nice	D	1-1	L1	9	Ayew.A [56]	11 727
	28	Bayern M	L	0-2	CLqf			31 683
Apr| 3	Bayern M	L	0-2	CLqf			66 000
	8	PSG	L	1-2	L1	9	Ayew.A [59]	46 252
	11	Montpellier	L	1-3	L1	9	Mbia [33]	41 519
	14	Lyon	W	1-0	LCf		Brandao [105]	78 877
	18	Caen	D	1-1	L1	10	Remy [26p]	39 261
	21	Bordeaux	L	1-2	L1	10	Ayew.J [56]	31 440
	27	Lorient	L	1-2	L1	11	Valbuena [77]	15 945
May| 2	Nancy	W	1-0	L1	10	Remy [31]	39 430
	7	St-Etienne	D	0-0	L1	10		22 422
	13	Auxerre	W	3-0	L1	10	Fanni [33], Azpilicueta [54], Gignac [90]	40 087
	20	Sochaux	L	0-1	L1	10		18 636

10th Att: 768 457 • Av: 40 445 (-20.9%) • Vélodrome 42 000 (96%)

MONTPELLIER 2011–12

Aug| 6	Auxerre	W	3-1	L1	2	Belhanda [36], Dernis [75], Giroud [91+]	12 198
	14	Lille	W	1-0	L1	2	Giroud [70]	16 304
	21	Rennes	W	4-0	L1	1	Belhanda [31p], Dernis [52], Camara 2 [72 86]	14 021
	27	Lyon	L	1-2	L1	1	Bedimo [91+]	31 634
	31	Amiens	D	2-2	LCr3		Utaka [68], Giroud [76]. W 4-3p	6 179
Sep| 11	Nice	W	1-0	L1	1	Camara [75]	12 168
	17	Brest	D	2-2	L1	2	Giroud 2 [19 41]	12 548
	21	Ajaccio	W	3-1	L1	1	Cabella [3], Estrada [10], Utaka [35]	5 670
	24	PSG	L	0-3	L1	4		24 842
Oct| 1	Bordeaux	D	2-2	L1	2	Belhanda [88p], Hilton [90]	17 713
	15	Dijon	W	5-3	L1	2	Estrada [26], Giroud 3 [50 57p 81], Camara [64]	12 047
	22	Caen	W	3-1	L1	2	Yanga-Mbiwa [14], Utaka [20], Belhanda [79]	14 290
	26	Lorient	L	1-2	LCr4		Giroud [65]	4 787
	29	Nancy	W	2-0	L1	2	Giroud [62], Camara [74]	11 683
Nov| 6	St-Etienne	D	1-1	L1	2	Marveaux [57]	18 788
	19	Marseille	W	1-0	L1	2	OG [62]	26 241
	26	Sochaux	W	3-1	L1	1	Giroud 3 [50 87 89]	11 941
Dec| 3	Lorient	W	4-0	L1	1	Dernis [27], Giroud [47], Utaka [62], Cabella [86]	12 866
	10	Val'ciennes	L	0-1	L1	1		14 078
	17	Toulouse	D	1-1	L1	1	Dernis [7]	16 780
	21	Evian	L	2-4	L1	2	Belhanda [47], Giroud [54]	12 336
Jan| 8	Mézières	W	4-0	CFr9		Cabella 2 [17 40], Estrada [57], Giroud [70]	3 050
	14	Lyon	W	1-0	L1	2	Giroud [62]	18 889
	23	Tours	W	1-0	CF10		Cabella [53]	8 200
	28	Nice	W	1-0	L1	2	Giroud [90]	7 099
Feb| 4	Brest	W	1-0	L1	1	Dernis [41]	11 149
	8	Chateauroux	W	2-0	CF11		Giroud [38], Belhanda [90]	7 713
	11	Ajaccio	W	3-0	L1	2	Belhanda [53p], Cabella [64], Giroud [67]	11 647
	19	PSG	D	2-2	L1	2	Belhanda [45], Utaka [82]	44 398
	25	Bordeaux	W	1-0	L1	1	Utaka [80]	21 284
Mar| 3	Dijon	D	1-1	L1	2	Tinhan [88]	14 016
	11	Caen	W	3-0	L1	2	Ait Fana [51], Camara [83], Giroud [91+p]	14 501
	17	Nancy	L	0-1	L1	2		17 130
	21	Gazélec	L	0-1	CFqf			6 000
	24	St-Etienne	W	1-0	L1	1	Giroud [89]	24 615
	31	Sochaux	W	2-1	L1	1	Belhanda [4], Camara [55]	18 429
Apr| 7	Marseille	W	3-1	L1	1	Belhanda 2 [7p 71], Giroud [49]	41 519
	15	Lorient	W	1-2	L1	1	Giroud [78]	15 952
	21	Val'ciennes	W	1-0	L1	1	Camara [6]	18 731
	27	Toulouse	W	1-0	L1	1	Belhanda [3]	21 251
May| 1	Evian	D	2-2	L1	1	Belhanda [42p], Giroud [84]	22 599
	7	Rennes	W	2-0	L1	1	Camara 2 [26], OG [52]	28 172
	13	Lille	W	1-0	L1	1	Ait Fana [94+]	27 649
	20	Auxerre	W	2-1	L1	1	Utaka 2 [32 76]	16 509

1st Att: 332 339 • Av: 17 492 (+6.1%) • Stade de la Mosson 32 950 (53%)

MARSEILLE LEAGUE APPEARANCES/GOALS 2011–12
Goalkeepers Steve Mandanda 38
Defenders Azpilicueta ESP 27+3/1 • Souleymane Diawara SEN 23/1
Rod Fanni 25+4/1 • Jeremy Morel 31+2/0 • Nicolas N'Koulou CMR 30/0
Jean-Philippe Sabo 1+3/0 • Djimi Traore MLI 7+4/0
Midfield Morgan Amalfitano 28+4/1 • Momar Bangoura 0+2/0
Benoit Cheyrou 27+6/4 • Alou Diarra 28+6/2 • Wesley Jobello 0+1/0
Charles Kabore BFA 16+9/0 • Lucho Gonzalez ARG 14+5/2
Stephane Mbia CMR 14+1/2 • Matthieu Valbuena 27+6/5
Forwards Andre Ayew GHA 23+3/8 • Jordan Ayew GHA 17+17/3
Brandao BRA 9+8/1 • Chris Gadi COD 0+3/0
Andre-Pierre Gignac 6+15/1 • Billel Omrani 0+1/0 • Loic Remy 27+2/12
Coach Didier Deschamps

MONTPELLIER LEAGUE APPEARANCES/GOALS 2011–12
Goalkeepers Geoffrey Jourdren 35 • Laurent Pionnier 3
Defenders Henri Bedimo CMR 36/1 • Garry Bocaly 33+1/0
Abdelhamid El-Kaoutari MAR 3+2/0 • Hilton BRA 34+1/1
Cyril Jeunechamp 4+1/0 • Benjamin Stambouli 13+13/0
Mapou Yanga-Mbiwa 34/1
Midfield Younes Belhanda MAR 26+2/12 • Remy Cabella 16+13/3
Geoffrey Dernis 13+7/5 • Marco Estrada CHI 25+5/1
Joris Marveaux 15+14/1 • Romain Pitau 2+8/0
Jamel Saihi TUN 28+2/0 • Jonathan Tinhan 0+4/0
Forwards Karim Ait Fana MAR 6+5/2
Souleymane Camara SEN 19+14/9 • Olivier Giroud 36/21
Hassan Kabze TUR 0+1/0 • Bengali-Fode Koita 0+4/0
John Utaka NGA 34+1/7
Coach Rene Girard

AS NANCY LORRAINE
2011–12

Aug	6	Lille	D	1-1	L1	13 OG [61]	15 060
	13	St-Etienne	L	0-1	L1	15	22 510
	21	Sochaux	L	1-2	L1	18 Hadji [67p]	15 126
	27	Lorient	L	1-2	L1	19 Bakar [11]	14 879
	30	Auxerre	L	1-2	LCr3	Diakite [55]	6 086
Sep	11	Auxerre	D	0-0	L1	18	14 206
	18	Rennes	D	1-1	L1	19 Andre Luiz [78p]	15 509
	21	Val'ciennes	D	1-1	L1	20 Moukandjo [15]	13 600
	24	Toulouse	L	0-1	L1	20	12 348
Oct	1	Evian	D	1-1	L1	20 Moukandjo [62p]	15 054
	15	Lyon	L	1-3	L1	20 Jung Jo Guk [88]	33 825
	22	Nice	W	1-0	L1	19 Niculae [54]	13 652
	29	Montpellier	L	0-2	L1	19	11 683
Nov	6	Brest	W	2-1	L1	18 Jung Jo Guk [64], Niculae [87]	14 029
	20	PSG	W	1-0	L1	16 Calve [49]	40 199
	26	Dijon	L	1-2	L1	18 Bakar [26]	15 114
Dec	4	Bordeaux	L	0-2	L1	19	15 404
	10	Ajaccio	D	2-2	L1	18 Bakar [10], Niculae [93+]	12 440
	17	Caen	W	2-1	L1	15 Karaboue [3], Sane [56]	13 528
	20	Marseille	L	1-3	L1	18 Lemaitre [37]	19 304
Jan	7	Rennes	L	0-3	CFr9		6 342
	14	Lorient	D	2-2	L1	17 Moukandjo [14], Sane [84]	13 500
	28	Auxerre	W	3-1	L1	13 Mollo [68], Niculae 2 [69 77]	10 815
Feb	4	Rennes	D	0-0	L1	15	12 617
	11	Val'ciennes	L	0-1	L1	15	11 657
	18	Toulouse	L	0-3	L1	16	12 041
	25	Evian	L	0-2	L1	18	10 748
Mar	3	Lyon	W	2-0	L1	17 Puygrenier [66], Bakar [72]	17 049
	10	Nice	D	1-1	L1	17 Niculae [12]	8 405
	17	Montpellier	W	1-0	L1	14 Andre Luiz [63p]	17 130
	24	Brest	W	1-0	L1	12 Traore [18]	13 970
	31	PSG	W	2-1	L1	11 Traore [18], Mollo [89]	18 800
Apr	7	Dijon	W	2-0	L1	11 Traore 2 [6 84]	14 526
	15	Bordeaux	D	2-2	L1	11 Traore [47], Puygrenier [73]	18 098
	22	Ajaccio	D	0-0	L1	11	6 140
	29	Caen	D	1-1	L1	10 Moukandjo [81]	17 016
May	2	Marseille	L	0-1	L1	11	39 430
	7	Sochaux	L	0-1	L1	11	14 059
	13	St-Etienne	W	3-2	L1	11 Moukandjo 2 [6 21], Mollo [43]	17 408
	20	Lille	L	1-4	L1	11 Lemaitre [12]	17 000

11th Att: 291 305 • Av: 15 332 (-5.4%) • Marcel Picot 20 087 (76%)

NANCY LEAGUE APPEARANCES/GOALS 2011–12
Goalkeepers Damien Gregorini 7 • Guy N'Dy Assembe CMR 31
Defenders Andre Luiz BRA 36/2 • Mustapha Bayal SEN 1+1/0
Jonathan Brison 9+1/0 • Jean Calve 7+1/1 • Michael Chretien MAR 4/0
Helder BRA 5+5/0 • Reynald Lemaitre 16+8/2 • Jordan Loties 23+2/0
Thomas Mangani 16+8/0 • Sebastien Puygrenier 18/2
Joel Sami 26+1/0 • Salif Sane 30+2/2
Midfield Pascal Berenguer 2/0 • Alexandre Cuvillier 2+6/0
Samba Diakite MLI 13+2/0 • Massadio Haidara 19/0
Ziri Hammar ALG 0+1/0 • Lossemy Karaboue 36+1/2
Yohan Mollo 18+1/3 • Fouad Rachid COM 1/0
Bakaye Traore MLI 19+3/5 • Distel Zola COD 0+1/0
Forwards Paul Alo'o Efoulou CMR 0+6/0 • Djamel Bakar 25+9/4
Youssouf Hadji MAR 4/1 • Benjamin Jeannot 2+4/0
Jung Jo Guk KOR 3+17/2 • Benjamin Moukandjo CMR 17+10/5
Daniel Niculae ROU 28+3/6
Coach Jean Fernandez (5/06/11)

OGC NICE
2011–12

Aug	6	Lyon	L	1-3	L1	18 Mounier [6]	14 405
	14	Evian	L	0-1	L1	19	13 126
	20	Toulouse	D	1-1	L1	20 Mounier [31]	8 390
	27	Brest	D	0-0	L1	17	7 875
	31	Toulouse	W	2-1	LCr3	Civelli [36], Mounier [47]	6 797

OGC NICE 2011–12 (CONT'D)

Sep	11	Montpellier	L	0-1	L1	19	12 168
	17	Ajaccio	W	3-0	L1	15 Monzon 2 [45p 87p], Civelli [89]	8 242
	21	PSG	L	1-2	L1	17 Monzon [61p]	39 081
	24	Dijon	D	1-1	L1	17 Dja Djedje [91+]	8 152
Oct	1	Caen	D	1-1	L1	16 Mouloungui [89]	13 234
	15	Bordeaux	W	3-0	L1	13 Mouloungui [11], Hellebuyck [35], Clerc [65]	9 269
	22	Nancy	L	0-1	L1	14	13 652
	26	Sochaux	W	2-1	LCr4	Pentecote 2 [39 56]	6 432
	30	Sochaux	W	2-1	L1	16 Mouloungui [30]	8 714
Nov	6	Marseille	L	0-2	L1	17	39 716
	19	St-Etienne	L	0-2	L1	19	8 599
	27	Lorient	L	0-1	L1	19	16 009
Dec	3	Rennes	W	2-0	L1	18 Monzon [15p], Civelli [35]	7 664
	11	Auxerre	L	1-2	L1	19 Mouloungui [21]	7 081
	17	Val'ciennes	W	2-0	L1	18 Mounier 2 [68 93+]	7 358
	21	Lille	D	4-4	L1	17	Civelli [16], Dja Djedje 2 [35 45], Clerc [94+]	16 847
	7	Marck	W	2-0	CFr9	Monzon [52p], Goncalves [92+]	7 000
Jan	11	Dijon	D	3-3	LCqf	Mounier [35], Civelli [78], Monzon [119], W 5-3p	7 751
	14	Brest	L	0-1	L1	18	11 997
	21	Rennes	W	2-0	CF10	L 4-5p	6 088
	28	Montpellier	L	0-1	L1	20	7 099
Feb	1	Marseille	L	1-2	LCsf	Mounier [44]	12 567
	4	Ajaccio	W	2-1	L1	18 Goncalves [85]	5 742
	22	PSG	D	0-0	L1	18	12 332
	18	Dijon	L	0-3	L1	19	12 303
	25	Caen	W	1-0	L1	17 Mounier [50]	6 106
Mar	3	Bordeaux	W	2-1	L1	16 Monzon [18p], Guie Guie [39]	18 807
	10	Nancy	D	1-1	L1	15 Dja Djedje [37]	8 405
	18	Sochaux	L	0-2	L1	18	15 930
	24	Marseille	D	1-1	L1	18 Monzon [76p]	11 727
	31	St-Etienne	W	3-2	L1	16 Mounier 2 [35 56], Clerc [89]	22 035
Apr	8	Lorient	W	2-0	L1	13 Mounier [49], Civelli [57]	10 001
	16	Rennes	L	1-3	L1	14 Clerc [59]	16 722
	21	Auxerre	W	1-0	L1	12 Monzon [36p]	9 480
	29	Val'ciennes	L	0-2	L1	14	13 286
May	2	Lille	L	0-1	L1	15	10 570
	7	Toulouse	D	0-0	L1	14	31 805
	13	Evian	D	1-1	L1	13 Pejcinovic [35]	10 544
	20	Lyon	W	4-3	L1	13	Monzon [31], Coulibaly [37], OG [53], Goncalves [73]	32 335

13th Att: 175 042 • Av: 9 213 (+8.9%) • Stade du Ray 18 696 (49%)

NICE LEAGUE APPEARANCES/GOALS 2011–12
Goalkeepers Raul Fernandez PER 1+1 • David Ospina COL 37
Defenders Renato Civelli ARG 34/4 • Francois Clerc 32/4
Drissa Diakite MLI 12+4/0 • Diacko Fofana 1/0 • Kevin Gomis 12+3/0
Larrys Mabiala COD 8/0 • Kevin Malaga 0+1/0
Luciano Monzon ARG 34/8 • Nemanja Pejcinovic SRB 23/1
Midfield Fabrice Abriel 23+4/0 • Kevin Anin 11+2/0
Alexey Bosetti 0+1/0 • Kafoumba Coulibaly CIV 26+2/1
Didier Digard 29+1/0 • Emerse Fae CIV 3+1/0 • David Hellebuyck 8+4/1
Cyril Hennion 0+3/0 • Camel Meriem 11+9/0
Anthony Mounier 25+4/8 • Lloyd Palun GAB 3+11/0
Julien Sable 16+4/0
Forwards Stephane Bahoken 0+5/0 • Franck Dja Djedje CIV 17+10/4
Esmael Goncalves 7+10/2 • Elliot Grandin 6+6/0
Abraham Guie-Guie CIV 7+14/1 • Eric Mouloungui GAB 23+3/4
Xavier Pentecote 9+1/0 • Mickael Pote 0+1/0
Coach Eric Roy • Rene Marsiglia (15/11/11)

PARIS SAINT-GERMAIN
2011–12

Aug	6	Lorient	L	0-1	L1	15	40 048
	13	Rennes	D	1-1	L1	13 Gameiro [73]	27 927
	18	Differdange	W	4-0	ELpo	Gameiro [17], Bahebeck [71], Ceara [90], Menez [91+]	6 153
	21	Val'ciennes	W	2-1	L1	9 Gameiro [39], Nene [64p]	35 875
	25	Differdange	W	2-0	ELpo	Nene [65], OG [79]	15 194
	28	Toulouse	W	3-1	L1	3	Gameiro [56], Erding [90], Menez [93+]	31 129

PARIS SAINT-GERMAIN 2011-12 (CONT'D)

	6	Lorient	L	0-1	L1	15		40 048
	13	Rennes	D	1-1	L1	13	Gameiro [73]	27 927
Aug	18	Differdange	W	4-0	ELpo		Gameiro [17], Bahebeck [71], Ceara [90], Menez [91+]	6 153
	21	Val'ciennes	W	2-1	L1	9	Gameiro [39], Nene [64p]	35 875
	25	Differdange	W	2-0	ELpo		Nene [65], OG [79]	15 194
	28	Toulouse	W	3-1	L1		Gameiro [56], Erding [90], Menez [93+]	31 129
	11	Brest	W	1-0	L1	4	Pastore [68]	40 134
	15	RB Salzburg	W	3-1	ELgF		Nene [35p], Bodmer [44], Menez [67]	23 039
Sep	18	Evian	D	2-2	L1	5	Pastore [43], Bodmer [80]	15 162
	21	Nice	W	2-1	L1	4	Nene [36p], Gameiro [71p]	39 081
	24	Montpellier	W	3-0	L1	1	Gameiro [39], Pastore 2 [43 80]	24 842
	27	Ath. Bilbao	L	0-2	ElgF			23 487
	2	Lyon	W	1-0	L1	1	Pastore [64], Jallet [90]	44 450
	16	Ajaccio	W	3-1	L1	1	Gameiro 3 [2 50 53]	8 155
	20	Slovan	D	0-0	ElgF			7 238
Oct	23	Dijon	W	2-0	L1	1	Nene 2 [42 90]	44 071
	26	Dijon	L	2-3	LCr4		Bahebeck [16], Erding [20]	10 115
	29	Caen	W	4-2	L1	1	Nene 2 [20p 76p], Menez [55], Pastore [88]	43 812
	3	Slovan	W	1-0	ElgF		Pastore [63]	32 046
Nov	6	Bordeaux	D	1-1	L1	1	Sissoko [10]	29 496
	20	Nancy	L	0-1	L1	1		40 199
	27	Marseille	L	0-3	L1	2		41 512
	1	RB Salzburg	W	0-2	ElgF			8 304
	4	Auxerre	W	3-2	L1	1	Jallet [52], Menez [76], Nene [80p]	42 035
	10	Sochaux	W	1-0	L1	2	Gameiro [20]	16 098
Dec	14	Ath. Bilbao	W	4-2	ElgF		Pastore [21], Bodmer [41], OG [85], Hoarau [90p]	37 114
	18	Lille	D	0-0	L1	2		45 195
	21	St-Etienne	W	1-0	L1		OG [32]	25 136
	8	SC Locmine	W	2-1	CFr9		Pastore [53], Lugano [92+]	18 970
	14	Toulouse	W	3-1	L1	1	Nene 2 [38 68], Pastore [56]	44 669
Jan	20	Sable	W	4-0	CF10		Nene 2 [35p 90], Gameiro 2 [64 74]	25 000
	28	Brest	W	1-0	L1	1	Bisevac [6]	14 760
	4	Evian	W	3-1	L1	1	Nene 2 [47 78p], Gameiro [89]	41 624
Feb	12	Nice	D	0-0	L1	1		12 332
	15	Dijon	W	1-0	CF11		Nene [15]	9 484
	19	Montpellier	D	2-2	L1	1	Alex [41], Hoarau [88]	44 398
	25	Lyon	D	4-4	L1	2	Hoarau 2 [21 94+], Nene [45p], Ceara [73]	37 347
	4	Ajaccio	W	4-1	L1	1	Pastore [27], Menez [29], Hoarau [86], Nene [92+]	44 510
Mar	11	Dijon	W	2-1	L1	1	Tiene [49], Gameiro [91+]	14 446
	17	Caen	D	2-2	L1	1	Pastore [56], Jallet [91+]	19 172
	21	Lyon	L	1-3	CFqf		Nene [19p]	44 000
	25	Bordeaux	D	1-1	L1	2	Hoarau [81]	44 723
	31	Nancy	L	1-2	L1	2	Sissoko [50]	18 800
	8	Marseille	W	2-1	L1	2	Menez [6], Alex [61]	46 252
	15	Auxerre	D	1-1	L1	2	Nene [23]	12 010
Apr	22	Sochaux	W	6-1	L1	2	Pastore [5], Motta [25], Menez [43], Nene 2 [55 59], Armand [92+]	44 366
	29	Lille	L	1-2	L1	2	Pastore [48]	17 262
	2	St-Etienne	W	2-0	L1	2	Nene [21p], Pastore [88]	43 961
May	6	Val'ciennes	W	4-3	L1	2	Nene [15], Maxwell [40], Matuidi [45], Menez [58]	16 914
	13	Rennes	W	3-0	L1	2	Nene 3 [47 58 65p]	45 357
	20	Lorient	W	2-1	L1	2	Pastore [61], Motta [75]	16 529

2nd Att: 814 924 • Av: 42 891 (+46.3%) • Parc des Princes 47 428 (90%)

PSG LEAGUE APPEARANCES/GOALS 2011-12
Goalkeepers Salvatore Sirigu 38
Defenders Alex BRA 15/2 • Sylvain Armand 8+14/1
Milan Bisevac SRB 17+2/1 • Zoumana Camara 17+2/0
Ceara BRA 17+7/1 • Christophe Jallet 26+7/3
Diego Lugano URU 9+3/0 • Maxwell BRA 13+1/1
Mamadou Sakho 20+2/0 • Siaka Tiene CIV 16+7/1
Midfield Mathieu Bodmer 21+10/1 • Clement Chantome 8+7/0
Blaise Matuidi 25+4/1 • Nene BRA 35/21 • Javier Pastore ARG 30+3/13
Mohamed Sissoko MLI 22+3/2 • Thiago Motta ITA 14/2
Forwards Jean-Christophe Bahebeck 0+8/0 • Kevin Gameiro 27+7/11
Guillaume Hoarau 7+13/5 • Jean-Eudes Maurice HAI 0+1/0
Mevlut Erdinc TUR 0+11/0 • Jeremy Menez 33/7
Coach Antoine Kombouare • Carlo Ancelotti (30/12/11)

STADE RENNAIS 2011-12

Jy	28	Rustavi	W	5-2	ULr3		Boukari 2 [17 31], Feret [49], Pitroipa 2 [42 70]	10 312
	4	Rustavi	W	2-0	ULr3		Montano [75], Feret [85]	13 848
	7	Dijon	W	5-1	L1	1	Montano [34], Feret [36], Boukari [50], Mangane [75], Tettey [85]	13 754
	13	PSG	D	1-1	L1	5	Pitroipa [88]	27 927
Aug	18	Cr. Zvezda	W	2-1	ULpo		Pitroipa [41], Montano [75]	51 862
	21	Montpellier	L	0-4	L1	7		14 021
	25	Cr. Zvezda	W	4-0	ULpo		Montano [10], M'Vila [19p], Pajot [85], Kembo-Ekoko [90]	19 364
	28	Caen	W	3-2	L1	5	Boukari [5], Kembo-Ekoko [41], Mangane [45]	19 715
	10	Marseille	W	1-0	L1	6	Kembo-Ekoko [76]	40 628
	15	Udinese	L	1-2	ILgl		Hadji [18]	8 383
	18	Nancy	D	1-1	L1	7	Montano [19]	15 509
Sep	21	Sochaux	W	6-2	L1	4	Montano 2 [22p 71], Kana-Biyik [35], Feret [51], Hadji [69p], Kembo-Ekoko [95+]	10 417
	25	St-Etienne	D	1-1	L1	5	Hadji [41]	18 718
	29	At. Madrid	D	1-1	ILgl		Montano [55]	24 299
	2	Lille	L	0-2	L1	7		16 802
	16	Lorient	W	2-0	L1	5	Kembo-Ekoko [10], Pitroipa [63p]	18 502
Oct	20	Celtic	D	1-1	ILgl		OG [31]	21 825
	23	Auxerre	W	1-0	L1	4	Feret [74]	9 514
	26	Le Mans	D	0-0	LCr4		L 1-4p	11 283
	30	Toulouse	L	0-1	L1	6		15 163
	3	Celtic	L	1-3	ILgl		Mangane [2]	28 578
	6	Val'ciennes	D	1-1	L1	5	Kembo-Ekoko [21]	20 006
Nov	19	Lyon	W	2-1	L1	4	Pitroipa [39], Kembo-Ekoko [53]	32 193
	26	Evian	W	3-2	L1	4	Feret 2 [10 87], Hadji [77]	17 782
	30	Udinese	D	0-0	ILgl			17 428
	3	Nice	D	1-0	L1	5		7 664
	10	Brest	D	1-1	L1	5	Danze [30]	20 275
Dec	15	At. Madrid	L	1-3	ILgl		Mandjeck [86]	13 154
	18	Ajaccio	D	0-1	L1	7		5 645
	21	Bordeaux	W	1-0	L1	5	Kembo-Ekoko [53]	20 045
	7	Nancy	W	3-0	CFr9		Kembo-Ekoko [23], Feret [26], Boukari [43]	6 342
Jan	14	Caen	W	2-0	L1	5	Kembo-Ekoko [22], Montano [65]	14 785
	21	Nice	D	0-0	CF10		W 5-4p	6 088
	29	Marseille	L	1-2	L1	6	Doumbia [14]	28 802
	4	Nancy	D	0-0	L1	6		12 617
Feb	7	Evian	W	3-2	CF11		Kembo-Ekoko [21], Feret [54], Brahimi [68]	6 128
	11	Sochaux	W	1-0	L1	5	Erding [16]	17 177
	19	St-Etienne	L	0-4	L1	7		21 432
	26	Lille	D	1-1	L1	6	Erding [90]	19 834
	4	Lorient	W	2-0	L1	5	Pitroipa [41], Hadji [79]	15 310
Mar	11	Auxerre	D	1-1	L1	5	Brahimi [66]	22 886
	18	Toulouse	L	0-1	L1	7		22 127
	21	Val'ciennes	W	3-1	CFqf		Pitroipa [12], Boye [53], Hadji [87]	14 731
	24	Val'ciennes	L	0-1	L1	7		12 145
	1	Lyon	D	1-1	L1	7	Erding [5]	21 346
	7	Evian	W	3-1	L1	6	Hadji [47], OG [88], Erding [92+]	9 672
	11	Quevilly	L	1-2	CFsf		Feret [8]	21 064
Apr	16	Nice	W	3-1	L1	6	Feret [23], Doumbia [44], Pitroipa [82]	16 722
	21	Brest	W	1-0	L1	5	Feret [45p]	14 391
	29	Ajaccio	W	3-1	L1	5	Feret [27], Boukari [85], Brahimi [91+]	17 498
	2	Bordeaux	L	0-2	L1	5		19 531
May	7	Montpellier	L	0-2	L1	5		28 172
	13	PSG	L	0-3	L1	7		45 357
	20	Dijon	W	5-0	L1	6	Montano [9], Kembo-Ekoko 2 [47p 58], Pitroipa [51], Hadji [82]	17 601

6th Att: 390 644 • Av: 20 560 (-12.2%) • Route de Lorient 31 127 (66%)

RENNES LEAGUE APPEARANCES/GOALS 2011-12
Goalkeepers Benoit Costil 37 • Abdoulaye Diallo 1
Defenders Onyekachi Apam NGA 12/0 • John Boye GHA 14+5/0
Dimitri Foulquier 2/0 • Yassine Jebbour MAR 1/0
Jean-Armel Kana-Biyik 33+1/1 • Kader Mangane SEN 12+1/2
Chris Mavinga 9+5/0 • Kevin Theophile-Catherine 36/0

RENNES LEAGUE APPEARANCES/GOALS 2011–12
(cont'd)
Midfield Abdoulrazak Boukari TOG 7+13/3 • Yacine Brahimi 6+11/2
Stephane Dalmat 0+4/0 • Romain Danze 28+4/1
Cheick Diarra MLI 0+1/0 • Tongo Doumbia MLI 19+6/2
Julien Feret 33+2/8 • Georges Mandjeck CMR 8+4/0 • Yann M'Vila 38/0
Vincent Pajot 15+5/0 • Jonathan Pitroipa BFA 34+2/7
Alexander Tettey NOR 7+12/1
Forwards Abdoul Camara GUI 1+1/0 • Youssouf Hadji MAR 12+11/6
Jires Kembo Ekoko COD 24+8/10 • Mevlut Erdinc TUR 8+4/4
Victor Montano COL 21+8/6
Coach Frederic Antonetti

ST-ETIENNE LEAGUE APPEARANCES/GOALS 2011–12
(cont'd)
Forwards Danijel Aleksic SRB 0+1/0 • Pierre Aubameyang GAB 36/16
Gonzalo Bergessio ARG 2/0 • Lynel Kitambala 9+7/0 • Kevin Mayi 0+1/0
Yoric Ravet 0+1/0 • Idriss Saadi 2+5/0
Florent Sinama-Pongolle 16+7/4
Coach Christophe Galtier

SAINT-ETIENNE
2011–12

Aug	7	Bordeaux	W	2-1	L1	5	OG [18], Aubameyang [31]	31 609
	13	Nancy	W	1-0	L1	4	Marchal [88]	22 510
	21	Marseille	D	0-0	L1	3		41 493
	28	Sochaux	L	1-2	L1	8	Aubameyang [35]	12 183
	31	Bordeaux	W	3-1	LCr3		OG [3], Sako [17], Aubameyang [57]	14 647
Sep	10	Lille	L	1-3	L1	9	OG [8]	23 061
	17	Lorient	L	0-3	L1	12		14 841
	21	Toulouse	D	1-1	L1	12	Boudebouz [89]	18 088
	25	Rennes	D	1-1	L1	11	Aubameyang [56]	18 718
	1	Auxerre	D	1-1	L1	12	Guilavogui [38]	19 338
Oct	15	Evian	W	2-1	L1	9	Batlles [46], Aubameyang [51]	14 798
	22	Val'ciennes	W	1-0	L1	8	Batlles [50]	19 744
	26	Lyon	L	1-2	LCr4		Aubameyang [88]	25 906
	29	Lyon	L	0-2	L1	8		38 982
	6	Montpellier	D	1-1	L1	10	Nicolita [32]	18 788
Nov	19	Nice	W	2-0	L1	8	S-Pongolle [24p], Zouma [39]	8 599
	26	Ajaccio	W	3-1	L1	6	Gradel [7], S-Pongolle [33], Nicolita [84]	20 059
	3	Brest	D	2-2	L1	8	Aubameyang 2 [24] [87]	13 789
Dec	10	Caen	W	2-0	L1	7	Nicolita [10], Sako [74]	21 244
	17	Dijon	W	2-1	L1	5	S-Pongolle [16], Gradel [93+]	14 435
	21	PSG	L	0-1	L1	8		25 136
	7	Bordeaux	D	1-1	CFr9		Guilavogui [95+], L 2-4p	17 532
Jan	14	Sochaux	W	1-0	L1	7	Zouma [77]	20 222
	28	Lille	L	0-3	L1	8		17 437
	12	Toulouse	W	1-0	L1	6	Aubameyang [71]	28 864
Feb	19	Rennes	W	4-0	L1	4	Mignot [24], Batlles [53], Sako [67], Gradel [78]	21 432
	22	Lorient	W	4-2	L1	7	Aubameyang 3 [56] [68] [90], OG [88]	21 039
	25	Auxerre	D	0-0	L1	4		13 683
	3	Evian	L	0-2	L1	5		22 254
Mar	10	Val'ciennes	W	2-1	L1	4	Aubameyang [73], Sako [77]	16 507
	17	Lyon	L	0-1	L1	6		26 210
	24	Montpellier	L	0-1	L1	6		24 615
	31	Nice	L	2-3	L1	6	Gradel [22], Marchal [42]	22 035
	7	Ajaccio	D	1-1	L1	7	S-Pongolle [72]	6 352
	15	Brest	W	2-1	L1	7	Gradel [48p], Sako [72]	21 028
Apr	21	Caen	W	4-1	L1	6	OG [39], Aubameyang 2 [60] [83], Gradel [70]	17 256
	29	Dijon	W	1-0	L1	6	Aubameyang [43]	20 753
	2	PSG	L	0-2	L1	6		43 961
May	7	Marseille	D	0-0	L1	6		22 442
	13	Nancy	L	2-3	L1	6	Aubameyang [39], Batlles [70]	17 408
	20	Bordeaux	L	2-3	L1	7	Guilavogui [19], Aubameyang [49]	22 726

7th Att: 409 129 • Av: 21 533 (-14.2%) • Geoffroy-Guichard 26 747 (80%)

ST-ETIENNE LEAGUE APPEARANCES/GOALS 2011–12
Goalkeepers Stephane Ruffier 38
Defenders Carlos Bocanegra USA 1/0 • Jonathan Brison 3+1/0
Pierrick Cros 0+1/0 • Albin Ebondo 22+3/0 • Faouzi Ghoulam 32/0
Sylvain Marchal 28+1/2 • Jean-Pascal Mignot 25/1
Loris Nery 8+1/0 • Paulao BRA 10/1 • Kurt Zouma 14+7/2
Midfield Alejandro Alonso ARG 2+3/0 • Laurent Batlles 12+24/4
Jeremy Clement 35/0 • Ismael Diomande CIV 1+1/0
Max Gradel CIV 19+10/6 • Josuha Guilavogui 25+4/0
Fabien Lemoine 24+3/0 • Steed Malbranque 0+1/0
Banel Nicolita ROU 16+3/3 • Loic Perrin 10+1/0 • Bakary Sako 28+8/5

SOCHAUX
2011–12

Aug	6	Marseille	D	2-2	L1	11	Martin [58], Nogueira [70]	41 102
	13	Caen	L	1-2	L1	11	Boudebouz [93+]	12 137
	18	Metalist	D	0-0	ULpo			35 886
	21	Nancy	W	2-1	L1	8	Peybernes [53], Privat [64]	15 126
	25	Metalist	L	0-4	ULpo			8 739
	28	St-Etienne	W	2-1	L1	6	Boudebouz 2 [6] [42p]	12 183
Sep	10	Lorient	D	1-1	L1	7	Butin [41]	10 031
	17	Lille	D	2-2	L1	8	Bakambu [70], Privat [86]	16 776
	21	Rennes	L	2-6	L1	9	Butin [24], Maiga [41]	10 417
	25	Auxerre	L	1-4	L1	12	Maiga [2]	8 437
	1	Toulouse	W	3-0	L1	10	Maiga 2 [9] [87], Bakambu [90]	10 142
	16	Val'ciennes	L	0-3	L1	11		13 498
Oct	22	Evian	D	1-1	L1	10	Butin [51]	12 331
	26	Nice	L	1-2	LCr4		Camara [79]	6 432
	30	Nice	D	1-1	L1	11	Boudebouz 35p	8 714
	6	Lyon	W	2-1	L1	10	OG [10], Boudebouz [43p]	15 638
Nov	20	Brest	L	0-2	L1	11		12 920
	26	Montpellier	L	1-3	L1	11	Camara [84]	11 941
	3	Dijon	D	0-0	L1	13		13 165
Dec	10	PSG	L	0-1	L1	14		16 098
	18	Bordeaux	L	0-1	L1	16		23 700
	21	Ajaccio	L	0-2	L1	19		9 296
	7	Bastia	L	1-4	CFr9		Mikari [57]	9 000
Jan	14	St-Etienne	L	0-1	L1	19		20 222
	28	Lorient	D	1-1	L1	19	Bakambu [80]	15 563
	11	Rennes	L	0-1	L1	20		27 015
Feb	18	Auxerre	D	0-0	L1	20		12 136
	22	Lille	L	0-1	L1	20		15 052
	26	Toulouse	L	0-2	L1	20		11 351
	3	Val'ciennes	D	1-1	L1	20	OG [77]	11 069
Mar	10	Evian	W	3-2	L1	20	Butin 2 [30] [66], Nogueira [44]	10 861
	18	Nice	W	2-0	L1	19	Butin [45], Martin [68]	15 930
	24	Lyon	L	1-2	L1	19	Maiga [71]	32 730
	31	Brest	W	2-1	L1	19	Maiga [77], Privat [82]	17 299
Apr	7	Montpellier	L	1-2	L1	19	Maiga [28]	18 429
	15	Dijon	W	1-0	L1	18	Maiga [71]	19 599
	22	PSG	L	1-6	L1	19	Maiga [12]	44 366
	29	Bordeaux	L	0-3	L1	19		19 352
May	2	Ajaccio	L	1-2	L1	20	Privat [58]	8 171
	7	Nancy	W	1-0	L1	17	Roudet [85]	18 223
	13	Caen	W	3-1	L1	15	Privat [26], Poujol [39], Doubai [94+]	17 191
	20	Marseille	W	1-0	L1	14	Boudebouz [55]	18 636

14th Att: 266 483 • Av: 14 025 (+10.9%) • Auguste Bonal 20 005 (63%)

SOCHAUX LEAGUE APPEARANCES/GOALS 2011–12
Goalkeepers Papa Camara SEN 0+1 • Pierrick Cros 7
Teddy Richert 31
Defenders Yaya Banana CMR 13+2/0 • Jeremie Brechet 4+1/0
Sebastien Corchia 28+3/0 • Yassin Mikari TUN 14+5/0
Steven Mouyokolo 4/0 • Damien Perquis POL 18/0
Mathieu Peybernes 22+4/1 • Jerome Roussillon 3+1/0
David Sauget 34+1/0 • Lionel Zouma 2+2/0
Midfield Kevin Anin 14/0 • Ryad Boudebouz ALG 34+2/6
Petrus Boumal CMR 0+1/0 • Carlao BRA 19+2/0
Thierry Doubai CIV 6+4/1 • Joseph Lopy SEN 12+2/0
Marvin Martin 33/2 • Vincent Nogueira 23+5/2 • Loic Poujol 13+6/1
Rafael Dias POR 0+3/0 • Sebastien Roudet 15+8/1
Serdar Gurler TUR 0+1/0
Forwards Cedric Bakambu 9+12/3 • Edouard Butin 22+3/5
Abdoul Camara 10+11/1 • Charlie Davies USA 9+2/0
Modibo Maiga MLI 17+6/9 • Sloan Privat 11+20/5
Coach Mehmed Bazdarevic BIH (10/06/11) • Eric Hely (6/03/12)

TOULOUSE
2011–12

Aug	6	Ajaccio	W	2-0	L1	4	Devaux 45, Machado 73	7 668
	13	Dijon	W	2-0	L1	1	Umut 71, Machado 85p	13 356
	20	Nice	D	1-1	L1	2	Regattin 90	8 390
	28	PSG	L	1-3	L1	4	Capoue 39	31 129
	31	Nice	L	1-2	LCr3		Beauguel 10	6 797
Sep	10	Caen	W	1-0	L1	5	Capoue 93+	12 575
	17	Bordeaux	W	3-2	L1	3	Tabanou 52p, Capoue 59, Riviere 92+	15 457
	21	St-Etienne	D	1-1	L1	5	Tabanou 12	18 088
	24	Nancy	W	1-0	L1	3	Umut 59	12 348
Oct	1	Sochaux	L	0-3	L1	4		10 142
	15	Marseille	D	0-0	L1	6		30 082
	22	Lorient	D	0-0	L1	6		15 715
	30	Rennes	W	1-0	L1	5	Didot 26	15 163
Nov	6	Auxerre	L	0-2	L1	6		7 238
	18	Lille	D	0-0	L1	6		17 653
	26	Val'ciennes	W	2-0	L1	6	Machado 25, Devaux 63	29 234
Dec	4	Lyon	L	2-3	L1	6	Umut 68, Sissoko 75p	31 028
	10	Evian	W	2-1	L1	6	Sissoko 25, Umut 90	32 874
	17	Montpellier	D	1-1	L1	6	Mbengue 40	16 780
	21	Brest	D	0-0	L1	7		28 097
Jan	8	Gazélec	L	0-1	CFr9			4 018
	14	PSG	L	1-3	L1	8	Braaten 88	44 669
	28	Caen	W	1-0	L1	7	Riviere 35	12 023
Feb	4	Bordeaux	L	0-2	L1	8		16 485
	12	St-Etienne	L	0-1	L1	8		28 864
	18	Nancy	W	3-0	L1	8	Sirieix 9, Regattin 20, Riviere 72	12 041
	26	Sochaux	W	2-0	L1	6	Abdennour 9, Riviere 55	11 351
Mar	3	Marseille	W	1-0	L1	6	Abdennour 66	40 189
	10	Lorient	D	1-1	L1	6	OG 51	13 962
	18	Rennes	W	1-0	L1	4	OG 45	22 127
	25	Auxerre	W	1-0	L1	4	Tabanou 38	30 588
Apr	1	Lille	L	1-2	L1	5	Aurier 60	17 057
	7	Val'ciennes	L	0-2	L1	4		13 015
	18	Lyon	W	3-0	L1	5	Sirieix 9, Riviere 22, Umut 91+	21 352
	21	Evian	L	1-2	L1	7	Ben Yedder 72	10 272
	27	Montpellier	L	0-1	L1	7		21 251
May	2	Brest	D	0-0	L1	7		13 183
	7	Nice	D	0-0	L1	8		31 805
	13	Dijon	D	1-1	L1	8	Soukouna 45	14 016
	20	Ajaccio	L	0-2	L1	8		10 892

8th Att: 407 466 • Av: 21 446 (+8.3%) • Municipal 35 575 (60%)

TOULOUSE LEAGUE APPEARANCES/GOALS 2011–12
Goalkeepers Ali Ahamada 38
Defenders Aymen Abdennour TUN 32/2 • Serge Aurier 9+1/1
Daniel Congre 37/0 • Mickael Firmin 4+3/0 • Mohamed Fofana MLI 6/0
Cheikh M'Bengue SEN 30/1 • Pavle Ninkov SRB 25+4/0
Midfield Jean-Daniel Akpa-Akpro 5+7/0 • Wissam Ben Yedder 0+9/1
Daniel Braaten NOR 12+19/1 • Hendrick Cakin 0+1/0
Etienne Capoue 31+2/3 • Antoine Devaux 20+2/2
Etienne Didot 22+1/1 • Paulo Machado POR 19+5/3
Adrien Regattin 14+7/2 • Kevin Rodrigues 0+1/0 • Pantxi Sirieix 13+7/2
Moussa Sissoko 33+2/2 • Franck Tabanou 29+3/3
Forwards Yannick Aguemon 0+2/0 • Xavier Pentecote 0+2/0
Emmanuel Riviere 20+6/5 • Ahmed Soukouna 0+1/0
Amadou Soukouna 2/1 • Umut Bulut TUR 17+14/5
Coach Alain Casanova

VALENCIENNES
2011–12

Aug	6	Caen	L	0-1	L1	16		14 085
	13	Brest	D	0-0	L1	16		19 020
	21	PSG	L	1-2	L1	19	Gomis 45	35 875
	27	Bordeaux	L	1-2	L1	20	Dossevi 27	15 373
	31	Dijon	L	2-3	LCr3		Dossevi 34, Pujol 51	6 872
Sep	10	Ajaccio	L	1-3	L1	20	Danic 36	5 363
	17	Dijon	W	4-0	L1	18	Danic 53, Pujol 2 75 78, Cohade 79	13 961
	21	Nancy	D	1-1	L1	16	Cohade 82	13 600
	24	Marseille	D	1-1	L1	16	Saez 92+	21 622
Oct	1	Lorient	L	0-2	L1	19		15 698
	16	Sochaux	W	3-0	L1	14	Aboubakar 2 43 75, Kadir 71	13 498
	22	St-Etienne	L	0-1	L1	15		19 744
	30	Lille	D	0-0	L1	18		21 493
Nov	6	Rennes	D	1-1	L1	16	Gomis 29	20 006
	20	Auxerre	W	2-1	L1	15	Isimat-Mirin 59, Samassa 80	13 383
	26	Toulouse	L	0-2	L1	17		29 234
Dec	3	Evian	L	1-2	L1	17	Danic 85p	9 608
	10	Montpellier	W	1-0	L1	17	Kadir 46	14 078
	17	Nice	L	0-2	L1	19		7 358
	21	Lyon	W	1-0	L1	13	OG 28	16 850
Jan	6	Le Mans	W	2-0	CFr9		Isimat-Mirin 45, Aboubakar 73	5 791
	14	Bordeaux	L	1-2	L1	14	Kadir 54	16 274
	22	Bastia	W	3-1	CF10		Kadir 2 29 62, Danic 58	12 470
	29	Ajaccio	L	1-2	L1	16	Aboubakar 47	13 515
Feb	4	Dijon	W	2-1	L1	12	Cohade 3, Danic 43	12 054
	8	Lille	W	2-1	CF11		Dossevi 71, Aboubakar 78	16 229
	11	Nancy	W	1-0	L1	11	Samassa 92+	11 657
	18	Marseille	D	1-1	L1	10	Gil 51	41 055
	25	Lorient	W	2-0	L1	10	Samassa 78, Cohade 81	13 969
Mar	3	Sochaux	D	1-1	L1	11	Pujol 69	11 069
	10	St-Etienne	L	1-2	L1	11	Aboubakar 69	16 507
	18	Lille	L	0-4	L1	11		17 358
	24	Rennes	L	1-3	CFqf		Samassa 32	14 731
	24	Rennes	W	1-0	L1	11	Danic 13p	12 135
	31	Auxerre	L	0-2	L1	12		14 183
Apr	7	Toulouse	W	2-0	L1	12	Danic 62, Samassa 89p	13 015
	15	Evian	L	0-3	L1	12		13 794
	21	Montpellier	L	0-1	L1	13		18 731
	29	Nice	W	2-0	L1	12	Kadir 35, OG 54	13 286
May	2	Lyon	L	1-4	L1	12	Cohade 38p	30 890
	8	PSG	L	3-4	L1	12	Aboubakar 8, Gomis 11, Cohade 80	16 914
	13	Brest	L	0-1	L1	12		13 615
	20	Caen	W	3-1	L1	12	Aboubakar 37, Danic 68p, Cohade 87	18 024

12th Att: 292 119 • Av: 15 375 (+31.8%) • Stade du Hainaut 25 172 (61%)

VALENCIENNES LEAGUE APPEARANCES/GOALS 2011–12
Goalkeepers Nicolas Penneteau 38
Defenders Brou Angoua CIV 20/0 • Gaetan Bong CMR 27+1/0
David Ducourtioux 26+4/0 • Gil BRA 23+2/1 • Kenny Lala 0+2/0
Rudy Mater 25+4/0 • Rafael Schmitz BRA 2/0 • Mody Traore 7+7/0
Midfield Pape Camara SEN 8+3/0 • Renaud Cohade 34+1/7
Marco da Silva 0+1/0 • Gael Danic 33+1/7 • Mathieu Dossevi 14+6/1
Dusan Duric SWE 1+4/0 • Remi Gomis 25+4/3
Nicolas Isimat-Mirin 33+1/1 • Foued Kadir ALG 29+5/4
Guillaume Loriot 0+3/0 • Nam Tae Hee KOR 2+11/0
Jose Saez 10+13/1 • Carlos Sanchez COL 20+1/0
Forwards Vincent Aboubakar CMR 25+2/6 • Kama Massampu 0+1/0
Gregory Pujol 8+5/3 • Mamadou Samassa 8+22/4
Coach Daniel Sanchez (8/06/11)

FRO – FAROE ISLANDS

FIFA/COCA-COLA WORLD RANKING

'93	'94	'95	'96	'97	'98	'99	'00	'01	'02	'03	'04	'05	'06	'07	'08	'09	'10	'11	'12
115	133	120	135	117	125	112	117	117	114	126	131	132	181	194	184	117	136	116	153

2012													High	Low	Av
Jan	Feb	Mar	Apr	May	Jun	Jul	Aug	Sep	Oct	Nov	Dec			
114	118	116	118	118	122	155	153	154	158	159	153	104	198	134

Lars Olsen's Faroe Islands national team found itself in one of the toughest 2014 FIFA World Cup qualifying groups after being drawn alongside three teams that had qualified for the finals of Euro 2012. With damage limitation the order of the day, restricting Germany to just three goals in the opening fixture in Hannover was something of a triumph. Sweden were then limited to a 2-1 victory in Torshavn before the Faroes finished the year with a 4-1 defeat at the hands of the Republic of Ireland. The fixture against Austria will bring back memories of their famous victory in 1990 but the best hope for points in the group lies in the matches against Kazakhstan. The 2012 Faroese championship was won by EB/Streymur who in the previous six seasons had finished runners-up five times. It was the second title won by the club following on from their success in 2008 and it came after a tussle with IF Fuglafjørdur with the clubs from the capital well out of the running. IF were hoping for a first championship since 1979 but they needed to win on the final day of the season and rely on EB/Streymur losing - neither of which happened. Earlier in the year EB/Streymur had reached the cup final for a sixth consecutive season but they lost the match on penalties to Vikingur after it had finished 3-3 at the end of extra-time.

UEFA EUROPEAN CHAMPIONSHIP RECORD
1960-1988 DNE 1992-2012 DNQ

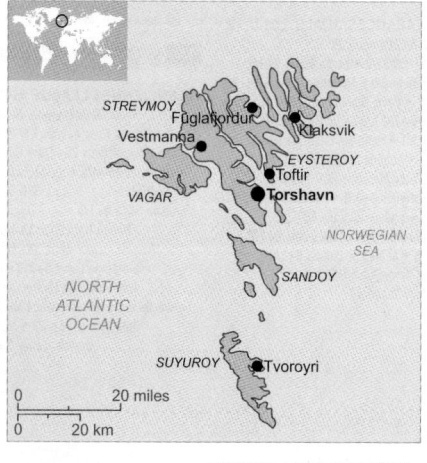

THE FAROE ISLANDS' FOOTBALL ASSOCIATION (FSF)

- Gundadalur, PO Box 3028, 110 Tórshavn
- ☎ +298 351979
- +298 319079
- fsf@football.fo
- www.fsf.fo
- FA 1979 CON 1988 FIFA 1988
- P Christian Andreasen
- GS Virgar Hvidbro

THE STADIA

2014 FIFA World Cup Stadia
Tórsvøllur	
Tórshavn	6 040

Other Main Stadia
Gundadalur	
Tórshavn	8 020
Svangaskard	
Toftir	7 000
KI Stadium	
Klaksvík	3 000
Fuglafjørdur Stadium	
Fuglafjørdur	3 000

MAJOR CITIES/TOWNS

		Population
1	Tórshavn	12 194
2	Klaksvík	4 628
3	Hoyvík	3 200
4	Argir	1 891
5	Fuglafjørður	1 580
6	Vágur	1 406
7	Vestmanna	1 238
8	Tvøroyri	1 213
9	Miðvágur	1 030
10	Sørvágur	988
11	Leirvík	885
12	Saltangará	882
13	Sandavágur	838
14	Strendur	834
15	Kollafjørður	829
16	Toftir	788
17	Skáli	711
18	Hvalba	663
19	Eiði	648

FOROYAR • FAROE ISLANDS

Capital	Tórshavn	Population	48 856 (208)	% in cities	41%
GDP per capita	$31 000 (43)	Area km²	1 393 km² (182)	GMT +/-	0
Neighbours (km)	Coast 1117				

FRO – FAROE ISLANDS

RECENT INTERNATIONAL MATCHES PLAYED BY THE FAROE ISLANDS

2007	Opponents	Score	Venue	Comp	Scorers	Att	Referee
24-03	Ukraine	L 0-2	Toftir	ECq		717	Skomina SVN
28-03	Georgia	L 1-3	Tbilisi	ECq	Rógvi Jacobsen [57]	12 000	Saliy KAZ
2-06	Italy	L 1-2	Tórshavn	ECq	Rógvi Jacobsen [77]	5 800	Malek POL
6-06	Scotland	L 0-2	Toftir	ECq		4 100	Kasnaferis GRE
12-09	Lithuania	L 1-2	Kaunas	ECq	Rógvi Jacobsen [93+]	5 500	Georgiev BUL
13-10	France	L 0-6	Tórshavn	ECq		1 980	Rossi SMR
17-10	Ukraine	L 0-5	Kyiv	ECq		5 000	Jakov ISR
21-11	Italy	L 1-3	Modena	ECq	Rógvi Jacobsen [83]	16 142	Meyer GER
2008							
16-03	Iceland	L 0-3	Kopavogur	Fr		400	Skjerven NOR
4-06	Estonia	L 3-4	Tallinn	Fr	Holst 2 [63 66], Olsen [70]	2 300	Stalhammar SWE
20-08	Portugal	L 0-5	Aveiro	Fr		22 000	Shandor UKR
6-09	Serbia	L 0-2	Belgrade	WCq		9 615	Nikolaev RUS
10-09	Romania	L 0-1	Tórshavn	WCq		805	Strahonja CRO
11-10	Austria	D 1-1	Tórshavn	WCq	Lokin [47]	1 890	Ceferin SVN
15-10	Lithuania	L 0-1	Kaunas	WCq		5 000	Kapitanis CYP
2009							
22-03	Iceland	W 2-1	Kopavogur	Fr	Benjaminsen [22], Antonuisson OG [42]	553	Riley ENG
10-06	Serbia	L 0-2	Tórshavn	WCq		2 896	Levi ISR
12-08	France	L 0-1	Tórshavn	WCq		2 974	Koukoulakis GRE
5-09	Austria	L 1-3	Graz	WCq	Andreas Olsen [82]	12 300	Borg MLT
9-09	Lithuania	W 2-1	Toftir	WCq	Suni Olsen [13], Arnbiorn Hansen [34]	1 942	Vad HUN
10-10	France	L 0-5	Guingamp	WCq		16 755	Malek POL
14-10	Romania	L 1-3	Piatra-Neamt	WCq	Bo [83]	13 000	Gvardis RUS
2010							
21-03	Iceland	L 0-2	Kopavogur	Fr		312	Larsen DEN
4-06	Luxembourg	D 0-0	Hesperange	Fr		713	Bertolini SUI
11-08	Estonia	L 1-2	Tallinn	ECq	Edmundsson [26]	5 470	Vucemilovic CRO
3-09	Serbia	L 0-3	Tórshavn	ECq		1 847	Toussaint LUX
7-09	Italy	L 0-5	Florence	ECq		19 266	Kulbakov BLR
8-10	Slovenia	L 1-5	Ljubljana	ECq	Mouritsen [93+]	15 750	Todorov BUL
12-10	Northern Ireland	D 1-1	Toftir	ECq	Holst [60]	1 921	Zimmermann SUI
16-11	Scotland	L 0-3	Aberdeen	Fr		10 873	Van Boekel NED
2011							
3-06	Slovenia	L 0-2	Toftir	ECq		974	Drachta AUT
7-06	Estonia	W 2-0	Toftir	ECq	Benjaminsen [43p], Hansen.A [47]	1 715	Munukka FIN
10-08	Northern Ireland	L 0-4	Belfast	ECq		13 183	Aleckovic BIH
2-09	Italy	L 0-1	Tórshavn	ECq		5 654	Bognar HUN
6-09	Serbia	L 1-3	Belgrade	ECq	Benjaminsen [37]	7 500	Amirkhanyan ARM
2012							
15-08	Iceland	L 0-2	Reykjavík	Fr		7 256	Kopriwa LUX
7-09	Germany	L 0-3	Hanover	WCq		32 769	Madden SCO
12-10	Sweden	L 1-2	Tórshavn	WCq	Baldvinsson [57]	5 079	Sidiropoulos GRE
16-10	Republic of Ireland	L 1-4	Tórshavn	WCq	Arnbiorn Hansen [69]	4 300	Jemini ALB

Fr = Friendly match • EC = UEFA EURO 2008/2012 • WC = FIFA World Cup • q = qualifier

FAROE ISLANDS NATIONAL TEAM HISTORICAL RECORDS

Caps
83 - Oli Johannesen 1992-2007 • **73** - Jakup Mikkelsen 1995- • **72** - Frodi Benjaminsen 1999- • **65** - Jens Martin Knudsen 1988-2006 • **62** - Julian Johnsson 1995-2006 • **61** - Jakup a Borg 1998-2010 • **57** - John Petersen 1995-2004 • **54** - Allan Morkore 1990-2001 • **53** - Rogvi Jacobsen 1999- • **51** - Ossur Hansen 1992-2002

Goals
10 - Rogvi Jacobsen 1999- • **9** - Todi Jonsson 1991-2005 • **8** - John Petersen 1995-2004 & Uni Arge 1992-2002 • **5** - Frodi Benjaminsen 1999- • **4** - Julian Johnsson 1995-2006, Suni Olsen 2001- & Jan Allan Muller 1988-98

Coaches
Pall Gudlaugsson ISL 1988-93 • Johan Melle Nielsen & Jogvan Nordbud 1993 • Allan Simonsen DEN 1994-2001 • Henrik Larsen DEN 2002-05 • Jogvan Martin Olsen 2006-08 • Hedin Askham 2009 • Brian Kerr 2009-11 • Lars Olsen DEN 2011-

FAROE ISLANDS 2012

MEISTARADEILDIN

	Pl	W	D	L	F	A	Pts	EB	IF	HB	KI	Víkingur	B'36	NSI	TB	B'68	Sudoroy
EB/Streymur Eidi †	27	17	7	3	51	25	58		2-1	2-2 3-2	1-1 1-1	0-1	1-1	1-0 4-0	1-1 3-2	0-0	3-0 4-2
IF Fuglafjørdur ‡	27	16	6	5	55	23	54	1-2 1-1		2-0 0-0	2-0 5-2	1-2	1-1	2-1 3-1	1-1	2-0	3-2
HB Tórshavn ‡	27	13	6	8	56	34	45	0-1	1-4		5-0	1-1 0-0	2-1 2-0	2-4	4-1 3-1	4-0 4-0	6-0
KI Klaksvík	27	13	6	8	59	44	45	1-3	1-0	1-1 1-2		3-3	0-2 3-4	3-2 2-1	0-0 1-1	3-0	5-1 7-1
Víkingur Gøtu/Leirvík ‡	27	12	9	6	43	35	45	2-1 2-3	1-4 0-3	2-2	0-1 4-3		3-2	1-1	1-0	2-0 2-0	4-0 3-1
B'36 Tórshavn	27	10	8	9	42	36	38	1-2 1-4	1-1 0-2	1-0	2-3	3-0 1-1		5-1	2-2	1-2 1-0	1-0 3-1
NSI Runavík	27	9	4	14	36	43	31	1-0	1-2	2-4 2-0	0-2	0-2 1-0	3-1 0-0		2-0 0-1	0-2	0-0 5-1
TB Tvøroyri	27	5	9	13	30	50	24	0-3	1-0 1-2	4-2	1-6	0-2 2-2	1-4 0-0	1-3		3-1 1-4	3-0
B'68 Toftir	27	6	6	15	23	43	24	1-2 0-1	0-2 0-0	1-2	0-2 1-3	1-1	1-1	3-2 1-1	1-1		2-0
FC Sudoroy	27	2	3	22	16	78	9	0-2	0-6 1-4	0-1 0-4	1-4	1-1	0-2	0-2	1-1 1-0	0-1 2-1	

24/03/2012 - 6/10/2012 • † Qualified for the UEFA Champions League • ‡ Qualified for the Europa League
Top scorers: **23** - **CLAYTON** Nascimento BRA, IF • **22** - Pall **KLETTSKARD**, KI • **16** - Arnbjorn **HANSEN**, EB • **14** - Klæmint **OLSEN**, NSI • **12** - Christian **MOURITSEN**, HB • **11** - Kaj Leo í **BARTALSSTOVU**, Víkingur • **9** - Andy **OLSEN**, KI • **8** - Frodi **BENJAMINSEN**, HB; Hjartvard **HANSEN**, EB; Leif **NICLASEN**, EB; Lukasz **CIESLEWICZ** POL, B'36 & Simun **SAMUELSEN**, HB

FAROE ISLANDS 2012
1. DEILD (2)

	Pl	W	D	L	F	A	Pts
07 Vestur	27	22	2	3	68	19	68
AB Argir	27	20	1	6	82	25	61
Skála	27	16	6	5	58	29	54
HB Tórshavn 2	27	14	5	8	53	34	47
KI Klaksvík 2	27	12	2	13	57	58	38
Víkingur Gøtu/Leirvík 2	27	11	3	13	53	52	36
EB/Streymur Eidi 2	27	8	6	13	36	59	30
B'71 Sandur	27	8	3	16	48	72	27
B'68 Toftir 2	27	4	2	21	29	80	14
NSI Runavík 2	27	4	2	21	30	86	14

31/032012 - 22/09/2012

MEDALS TABLE

		Overall			League			Cup	
		G	S	B	G	S	B	G	S
1	HB Tórshavn	47	25	5	21	14	5	26	11
2	KI Klaksvík	22	10	8	17	2	8	5	8
3	B'36 Tórshavn	14	14	6	9	4	6	5	10
4	TB Tvøroyri	12	10		7	5		5	5
5	GI Gøtu	12	6	4	6	3	4	6	3
6	EB/Streymur	6	7		2	5		4	2
7	NSI Runavík	3	5	1	1	1	1	2	4
8	B'68 Toftir	3	2	6	3	1	6		1
9	FC Sudoroy (ex VB)	2	3	2	1		2	1	3
10	B'71 Sandur	2	2	1	1		1	1	2
11	Víkingur Gøtu/Leirvík	2		2			2	2	
12	IF Fuglafjørdur	1	7		1	1			6
13	SI Sørvagur	1			1				
14	Skála		1	1		1	1		
	LIF Leirvík	1						1	
16	Royn Valba	1						1	
	MB Midvágur			1			1		

LØGMANSSTEYPID 2012

Round of 16		Quarter-finals		Semi-finals		Final	
Víkingur Gøtu/Leirvík *	1						
B'36 Tórshavn	0	Víkingur Gøtu/Leirvík	2				
07 Vestur	1	B'68 Toftir *	1				
B'68 Toftir *	2			Víkingur Gøtu/Leirvík *	1 1		
B'71 Sandur	5 5p			FC Sudoroy	0 2		
Undrid FF *	5 3p	B'71 Sandur	1				
Skála	0	FC Sudoroy *	5				
FC Sudoroy *	5					Víkingur Gøtu/Leirvík ‡	3 5p
HB Tórshavn	3					EB/Streymur Eidi	3 4p
TB Tvøroyri *	1	HB Tórshavn	5				
NSI Runavík	2	KI Klaksvík *	3				
KI Klaksvík *	4			HB Tórshavn	1 5		
AB Argir *	5			EB/Streymur Eidi *	2 4		
Giza/Hoyvík	2	AB Argir *	1				
IF Fuglafjørdur *	2	EB/Streymur Eidi	3				
EB/Streymur Eidi	4						

First round: **Undrid FF** 1-0 Royn Hvalba • **Giza/Hoyvík** 3-2 MB Midvágur

‡ Qualified for the Europa League
* Home team/Home team in the first leg

CUP FINAL
Tórsvøllur, Tórshavn, 25-08-2012
Ref: Dagfinn Forna
Scorers - Hans Djurhuus [55], Atli Gregersen [77], Hjartvard Hansen [111] for Víkingur; Jonhard Fredriksburg [31], Levi Hanssen [70], Leif Niclasen [95] for EB

GAB – GABON

FIFA/COCA-COLA WORLD RANKING

'93	'94	'95	'96	'97	'98	'99	'00	'01	'02	'03	'04	'05	'06	'07	'08	'09	'10	'11	'12
60	64	67	46	63	82	74	89	102	121	111	109	104	95	104	62	48	39	77	42

2012													High	Low	Av
Jan	Feb	Mar	Apr	May	Jun	Jul	Aug	Sep	Oct	Nov	Dec				
91	45	43	42	42	49	45	43	44	47	52	42		30	125	79

Gabon did not renew the contract of coach Gernot Rohr after their co-hosting of the Africa Cup of Nations finals with neighbours Equatorial Guinea at the start of 2012. It was harsh on the German-born trainer but a reflection of the deep disappointment that followed their quarter-final elimination on post-match penalties at the hand of Mali. Portuguese trainer Paulo Duarte, previously with Burkina Faso, was appointed in his place but after starting well in the 2014 FIFA World Cup qualifiers with a draw in Niger, Gabon were docked the point won for using ineligible defender Charly Mussono. The Cameroon-born player had been naturalised and used by Gabon at the Nations Cup finals but was found to have competed for Cameroon at the FIFA Beach World Cup, thereby rendering him ineligible to make the nationality switch. A 1-0 win over Burkina Faso followed in the second match to keep alive the hopes of the team. The year ended with a 2-2 draw in a prestige friendly against Portugal in Libreville while Gabon's oil wealth means fans in the capital will also be able to enjoy the 2013 French Super Cup first hand. In club football Mounana from the south of the country won the championship in May, their first ever success in the league, while there was a surprise relegation for FC 105, the most successful club in the country.

CAF AFRICA CUP OF NATIONS RECORD

1957-1970 DNE   1972 DNQ   1974-1976 DNE   1978 DNQ   1980-1982 DNE   1984-1992 DNQ   **1994** 12 r1   **1996** 7 QF
1998 DNQ   2000 15 r1   2002-2008 DNQ   **2010** 10 r1   **2012** 5 QF (Co-hosts)   2013 DNQ

FEDERATION GABONAISE DE FOOTBALL (FGF)

Boite postale 181, Libreville
☎ +241 704985
📠 +241 704992
✉ fegafoot@hotmail.fr
🖥 www.les-pantheres.com
FA 1962 CON 1967 FIFA 1963
P Placide Engandzas
GS Barthelemy Moussadji

THE STADIA

2014 FIFA World Cup Stadia
Stade d'Angondjé
Libreville   40 000

Other Main Stadia
Stade de Franceville
Franceville   25 000
Stade Pierre Claver Divounguy
Port-Gentil   7 000
Stade Gaston Peyrille
Bitam   5 000
Stade Dialogue
Tchibanga   5 000

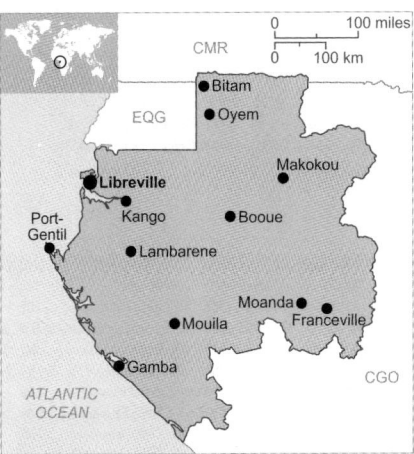

MAJOR CITIES/TOWNS

		Population
1	Libreville	732 885
2	Port-Gentil	138 378
3	Masuku	54 466
4	Oyem	39 132
5	Moanda	38 220
6	Mouila	28 483
7	Lambaréné	26 257
8	Tchibanga	24 547
9	Koulamoutou	20 563
10	Makokou	17 203
11	Bitam	13 053
12	Tsogni	12 621
13	Gamba	12 585
14	Mounana	11 130
15	Ntoum	10 862
16	Nkan	10 808
17	Lastoursville	10 572
18	Okandja	9 070
19	Ndendé	7 860

REPUBLIQUE GABONAISE • GABONESE REPUBLIC

Capital	Libreville	Population	1 514 993 (151)	% in cities	85%
GDP per capita	$14 200 (81)	Area km²	267 667 km² (76)	GMT +/-	+1
Neighbours (km)	Cameroon 298, 1903, Equatorial Guinea 350 • Coast 885				

RECENT INTERNATIONAL MATCHES PLAYED BY GABON

2009	Opponents	Score	Venue	Comp	Scorers	Att	Referee
11-08	Benin	D 1-1	Dieppe	Fr	Pierre Aubameyang [1]		
5-09	Cameroon	L 0-2	Libreville	WCq		10 000	Ndinya KEN
9-09	Cameroon	L 1-2	Yaoundé	WCq	Daniel Cousin [90]	38 000	Bennaceur TUN
10-10	Morocco	W 3-1	Libreville	WCq	OG [43], Eric Mouloungui [65], Daniel Cousin [70]	14 000	Doue CIV
14-11	Togo	L 0-1	Lomé	WCq		10 000	Seechurn MRI
2010							
6-01	Mozambique	W 2-0	Bloemfontein	Fr	Fanuel Massingue [5], Daniel Cousin [76]		
13-01	Cameroon	W 1-0	Lubango	CNr1	Daniel Cousin [17]	15 000	Bennett RSA
17-01	Tunisia	D 0-0	Lubango	CNr1		16 000	Codjia BEN
21-01	Zambia	L 1-2	Benguela	CNr1	Fabrice Do Marcolino [83]	5 000	Benouza ALG
19-05	Togo	W 3-0	Ajaccio	Fr	Pierre Aubameyang [16], OG [27], Fabrice Do Marcolino [80]		
11-08	Algeria	W 2-1	Algiers	Fr	Daniel Cousin [35], Pierre Aubameyang [55]		Rouaissi MAR
6-09	Burkina Faso	D 1-1	Cannes	Fr	Roger Issakounia [52]		
8-10	Oman	L 0-1	Muscat	Fr			
12-10	Saudi Arabia	L 0-1	Istanbul	Fr			
17-11	Senegal	L 1-2	Saint-Gratien	Fr	Pierre Aubameyang [29]		
2011							
9-02	Congo DR	W 2-0	Mantes la Ville	Fr	Stephane N'Guema [24], Daniel Cousin [53p]		
7-06	Gambia	L 0-1	Moanda	Fr			
10-08	Guinea	D 1-1	St Leu La Foret	Fr	Bruno Mbanangoye [41]		
6-09	Niger	W 1-0	Nice	Fr	Bruno Ecuele [44]		
7-10	Equatorial Guinea	W 2-0	Cannes	Fr	Roguy Meye [43], Levy Clement Madinda [59]		
10-11	Brazil	L 0-2	Libreville	Fr			Hlungwani RSA
15-11	Ghana	L 1-2	St Leu La Foret	Fr	Eric Mouloungui [44]		
2012							
9-01	Burkina Faso	D 0-0	Bitam	Fr			
16-01	Sudan	D 0-0	Franceville	Fr			
23-01	Niger	W 2-0	Libreville	CNr1	Pierre Aubameyang [31], Stephane N'Guema [42]	38 000	Maillet SEY
27-01	Morocco	W 3-2	Libreville	CNr1	Pierre Aubameyang [76], Daniel Cousin [79], Bruno Mbanangoye [96+]	35 000	Gassama GAM
31-01	Tunisia	W 1-0	Franceville	CNr1	Pierre Aubameyang [61]	22 000	Doue CIV
5-02	Mali	D 1-1	Libreville	CNqf	Eric Mouloungui [54]. L 4-5p	30 000	Haimoudi ALG
3-06	Niger	D 0-0	Niamey	WCq	Match awarded 3-0 to Niger	20 000	Haimoudi ALG
9-06	Burkina Faso	W 1-0	Libreville	WCq	Remy Ebanega [57]	23 000	Fall SEN
15-06	South Africa	L 0-3	Nelspruit	Fr			
8-09	Togo	D 1-1	Libreville	CNq	Daniel Cousin [69]		Sikazwe ZAM
11-09	Saudi Arabia	W 1-0	Beauvais	Fr	Malick Evouna [75]		
14-10	Togo	L 1-2	Lome	CNq	Pierre Aubameyang [77]		Seechurn MRI
14-11	Portugal	D 2-2	Libreville	Fr	Levy Madinda [33p], Andre Poko [69p]		Lamptey GHA

Fr = Friendly match • CN = CAF African Cup of Nations • CM = CEMAC Cup • WC = FIFA World Cup
q = qualifier • r1 = first round group • sf = semi-final • 3p = third place play-off • f = final

GABON SQUAD FOR THE 2012 CAF AFRICA CUP OF NATIONS

	Player		Ap	G	Club	Date of Birth		Player		Ap	G	Club	Date of Birth
1	Didier Ovono (c)	GK	4		Le Mans FRA	23 01 1983	12	Henri Junior Ndong	DF	0		Bitam	23 08 1992
2	Georges Ambourouet	DF	0+1		Missile	1 05 1986	13	Bruno Zita Mbanangoye	FW	1+3	1	Din. Minsk BLR	15 07 1980
3	Edmond Mouele	DF	4		Mangasport	18 02 1982	14	Levy Madinda	MF	3+1		Celta Vigo ESP	22 06 1992
4	Remy Ebanega	DF	2+1		Bitam	17 11 1989	15	Andre Biyogo Poko	MF	4		Bordeaux FRA	7 03 1993
5	Bruno Ecuele	DF	4		Lorient FRA	16 07 1988	16	Yanne Bidonga	GK	0		Mangasport	20 03 1979
6	Cedric Boussoughou	MF	0		Mangasport	20 07 1991	17	Moise Brou Apanga	DF	2		Brest FRA	4 02 1982
7	Stephane N'Guema	FW	2	1	Bitam	20 11 1984	18	Cedric Moubamba	MF	3		Bitam	14 10 1979
8	Lloyd Palun	MF	1+3		Nice FRA	28 11 1988	19	Rodrigue Moundounga	DF	0		Oly. Béjà TUN	28 08 1982
9	Pierre-E Aubameyang	FW	4	3	St-Etienne FRA	18 06 1989	20	Fabrice Do Marcolino	FW	0+1		Nice FRA	6 10 1984
10	Daniel Cousin	FW	2+2	1	Sapins	7 02 1977	21	Roguy Meye	FW	1		Zalaeg'szeg HUN	7 10 1986
11	Eric Mouloungui	FW	3	1	Laval FRA	14 03 1983	22	Charly Moussono	DF	4		Missile	15 11 1984
							23	Yves Bitseki	GK	0		Bitam	23 04 1983

Tr: Gernot Rohr GER 28-06-1953

GABON 2011-12

CHAMPIONNAT NATIONAL DE D1 (LINAF)

	Pl	W	D	L	F	A	Pts	Mounana	US Bitam	Mangasport	Pélican	Missile	Sapins	US Oyem	Mbilanzambi	CMS	Solidarité	RC Masuku	Sogéa	Stade Mandji	FC 105
CF Mounana †	26	17	6	3	40	20	**57**		3-1	1-0	1-1	0-0	2-0	1-0	1-2	1-1	1-0	3-1	5-2	2-1	2-1
US Bitam ‡	26	14	8	4	30	19	**50**	2-0		0-0	1-0	1-0	1-0	2-0	1-0	1-0	3-2	2-1	1-0	1-0	1-0
Mangasport Moanda	26	13	8	5	40	22	**47**	0-0	3-2		1-1	3-2	2-0	0-0	3-0	2-1	4-1	2-1	1-2	4-0	2-1
AS Pélican	26	12	9	5	27	17	**45**	0-0	0-1	2-0		0-0	1-2	2-0	0-0	0-0	2-0	3-1	0-0	1-0	2-1
Missile FC Libreville	26	13	5	8	42	26	**44**	3-2	1-1	1-0	0-1		2-0	0-1	3-1	3-2	2-1	6-0	2-1	3-1	6-0
Sapins FC	26	12	4	10	34	24	**40**	0-1	1-1	2-1	5-2	2-0		0-0	2-0	5-0	1-2	1-2	1-0	4-1	1-0
US Oyem	26	10	8	8	31	26	**38**	0-1	0-0	1-1	1-0	1-2	0-1		0-0	3-2	1-0	2-1	2-0	1-0	3-1
US Mbilanzambi	26	10	5	11	28	26	**35**	0-2	1-0	1-2	0-1	1-0	1-0	2-3		1-1	2-0	0-1	2-0	1-2	2-2
Cercle Mbéri Sportif	26	7	9	10	31	34	**30**	0-1	1-1	1-1	1-2	2-0	2-1	2-1	1-1		0-0	5-0	1-1	1-0	2-0
Solidarité	26	6	10	10	30	34	**28**	1-2	3-1	0-0	1-1	2-1	0-0	2-2	0-1	0-1		3-3	2-1	1-1	4-0
RC Masuku	26	6	6	14	33	57	**24**	2-2	0-0	1-5	1-1	2-0	0-0	1-6	0-2	3-0	1-2		0-3	1-1	3-1
Sogéa FC	26	5	7	14	25	38	**22**	1-2	2-2	0-1	0-2	0-0	2-0	0-0	3-2	1-1	1-2			2-2	1-2
AS Stade Mandji	26	4	8	14	23	42	**20**	1-2	0-2	1-1	0-1	1-1	1-2	1-1	0-4	1-1	2-2	3-2	1-0		2-0
FC 105 Libreville	26	5	3	18	21	50	**18**	0-2	1-1	0-1	0-1	1-2	0-3	4-2	1-0	2-1	0-0	1-4	1-2	1-0	

8/10/2011 - 27/05/2012 • † Qualified for the CAF Champions League • ‡ Qualified for the CAF Confederation Cup

MEDALS TABLE

		Overall G S B	Lge G	Cup G	Africa G S B	City
1	FC 105	14	9	5		Libreville
2	Mangasport	12	6	6		Moanda
3	US Mbilanzambi (USM)	9	5	4		Libreville
4	AS Sogara	6 1	5	1	1	Port-Gentil
5	Mbilinga	6 1	1	5	1	Port-Gentil
6	US Bitam	5	2	3		Bitam
7	En Avant Estuaire (ex Téléstar)	3		3		Libreville
	Stade Mandji	3	1	2		Port-Gentil
	Vautour Mangoungou	3	2	1		Libreville
10	Aigle Royale	2	2			Libreville
	Olympique Sportif	2	2			Libreville
	Petrosport	2	1	1		Port-Gentil
13	Anges ABC	1	1			Libreville
	Jeunesse AC (JAC)	1	1			Libreville
	AS Police	1	1			Libreville
	AS Solidarité	1	1			Libreville
	Zalang COC	1	1			Libreville
	AO Evizo	1		1		Lambaréné
	Missile FC	1	1			Libreville
	CF Mounana	1	1			Libreville

GAM – GAMBIA

FIFA/COCA-COLA WORLD RANKING

'93	'94	'95	'96	'97	'98	'99	'00	'01	'02	'03	'04	'05	'06	'07	'08	'09	'10	'11	'12
125	117	112	128	132	135	151	155	148	143	138	154	164	134	117	88	116	100	116	141

2012

Jan	Feb	Mar	Apr	May	Jun	Jul	Aug	Sep	Oct	Nov	Dec	High	Low	Av
118	115	123	113	113	108	128	129	129	131	142	141	65	166	129

Gambia gave an early indication that they could turn out to be spoilers in their 2014 FIFA World Cup qualifying group despite being cast as the outsiders amongst the Cote d'Ivoire, Morocco and Tanzania. A draw with the Moroccans in Bakau got their campaign off to a solid start and they then ran Tanzania close in their second qualifier away in Dar-es-Salaam before losing 2-1. Both results came just a week after the demotion of coach Peter Bonsu Johnson and the appointment of his Italian assistant Luciano Mancini, a former coach of Serie C side Grossetto. Johnson had been in charge for the defeat at the hands of Algeria in the Nations Cup qualifier at the start of the year after replacing the Belgian Paul Putt but there was nothing that Mancini could do six months later as Gambia went down 4-1 in the return in Algeria. The administration of the game in the small West African country continued to be run by an ad-hoc committee appointed in the wake of the dismissal of Gambia Football Association office holders in 2011. FIFA extended permission for the mandate of the committee to continue as new structures for the game were being formulated. Real Banjul won the country's first division title by a single point from Armed Forces while Gamtel's convincing 3-0 win over Interior in the GFA Cup final saw them lift the trophy for the third year in a row.

CAF AFRICA CUP OF NATIONS RECORD
1957-1974 DNE 1976 DNQ 1978 DNE 1980-1988 DNQ 1990 DNE 1992 DNQ 1994 DNE 1996 Withdrew 1998-2000 DNE 2002-2013 DNQ

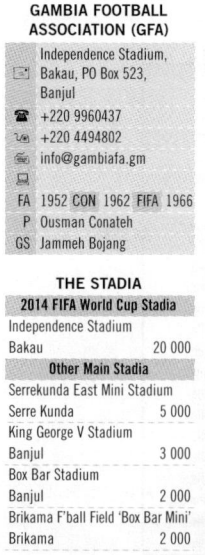

GAMBIA FOOTBALL ASSOCIATION (GFA)
Independence Stadium, Bakau, PO Box 523, Banjul
+220 9960437
+220 4494802
info@gambiafa.gm

FA 1952 CON 1962 FIFA 1966
P   Ousman Conateh
GS Jammeh Bojang

THE STADIA
2014 FIFA World Cup Stadia
Independence Stadium
Bakau   20 000
Other Main Stadia
Serrekunda East Mini Stadium
Serre Kunda   5 000
King George V Stadium
Banjul   3 000
Box Bar Stadium
Banjul   2 000
Brikama F'ball Field 'Box Bar Mini'
Brikama   2 000

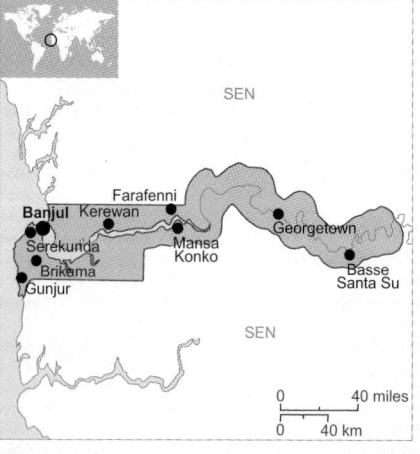

MAJOR CITIES/TOWNS
		Population
1	Serre Kunda	380 416
2	Brikama	93 240
3	Bakau	41 848
4	Banjul	33 422
5	Farafenni	33 305
6	Lamin	32 981
7	Nema Kunku	30 415
8	Brufut	26 724
9	Basse Santa Su	18 414
10	Gunjur	17 520
11	Sukuta	16 832
12	Wellingara	12 744
13	Busumbala	11 189
14	Yundum	10 960
15	Mandinari	10 583
16	Soma	10 211
17	Gambisara	10 102
18	Sabi	8 614
19	Banjulunding	8 505

REPUBLIC OF THE GAMBIA
Capital Banjul
GDP per capita $1300 (202)
Neighbours (km) Senegal 740 • Coast 80
Population 1 782 893 (148)
Area km^2 11 295 km^2 (166)
% in cities 57%
GMT + / - 0

RECENT INTERNATIONAL MATCHES PLAYED BY GAMBIA

2010	Opponents	Score	Venue	Comp	Scorers	Att	Referee
3-01	Angola	D 1-1	Vila Real	Fr	Ebrima Sawaneh [4]		
9-01	Tunisia	W 2-1	Rades/Tunis	Fr	Cherno Samba [57], Sainey Nyassi [85]		
30-05	Mexico	L 1-5	Bayreuth	Fr	Ebrima Sohna [65]		
4-09	Namibia	W 3-1	Banjul	CNq	Sainey Nyassi [10], Momoudou Ceesay [12], Ousman Jallow [34]		Ragab Omar LBY
9-10	Burkina Faso	L 1-3	Ouagadougou	CNq	Momoudou Ceesay [75]		Osman EGY
2011							
9-02	Guinea-Bissau	L 1-3	Lisbon	Fr	Momoudou Ceesay [27]		
29-03	Equatorial Guinea	L 0-1	Malabo	Fr			
7-06	Gabon	W 1-0	Moanda	Fr	Njogu Demba-Nyren [77p]		
24-07	Liberia	L 2-3	Monrovia	Fr	Foday Trawally 2		
10-08	Congo DR	W 3-0	Bakau	Fr	Tijan Jaiteh [19], Demba Savage [24], Momoudou Ceesay [12]		
3-09	Namibia	L 0-1	Windhoek	CNq			
8-10	Burkina Faso	D 1-1	Bakau	CNq	Mamadou Danso [59]		
2012							
29-02	Algeria	L 1-2	Bakau	CNq	Momoudou Ceesay [27]		Coulibaly MLI
2-06	Morocco	D 1-1	Bakau	WCq	Abdou Jammeh [15]	15 000	Alioum CMR
10-06	Tanzania	L 1-2	Dar Es Salaam	WCq	Momoudou Ceesay [8]	20 000	Ruzive ZIM
15-06	Algeria	L 1-4	Blida	CNq	Saihou Gassama [15]		Jedidi TUN

Fr = Friendly match • CN = CAF African Cup of Nations • WC = FIFA World Cup • q = qualifier

GFA CUP 2012

Quarter-finals		Semi-finals		Final	
GAMTEL	0 4p				
Starlight	0 3p	**GAMTEL**	2		
Young Africans	1	Sait Matty	1		
Sait Matty	3			**GAMTEL** ‡	3
Seaview	1			Interior	0
Latrikunda Utd	0	Seaview	0		
Ports Authority	1	**Interior**	2		
Interior	2				

Cup Final: Independence Stadium, Bakau, 22-07-2012
Scorers - Modou Sarr 2 [42 48], Muhammed Jammeh [88] for GAMTEL
‡ Qualified for the CAF Confederation Cup

MEDALS TABLE

		Overall G	Lge G	Cup G	City
1	Wallidan	37	15	22	Banjul
2	Real Banjul	12	9	3	Banjul
3	Ports Authority	7	6	1	Banjul
4	White Phantoms	6		6	
5	GAMTEL	5		5	Banjul
	Hawks	5	2	3	Banjul
7	Augustians	4	2	2	Banjul
	Starlight	4	2	2	Banjul
9	Armed Forces	2	2		Banjul
	Arrance	2		2	
11	Brikama United	1	1		Brikama

GAMBIA 2012

GFA LEAGUE FIRST DIVISION

	Pl	W	D	L	F	A	Pts	Real Banjul	Armed Forces	Ports	Samger	Brikama Utd	Steve Biko	GAMTEL	Y'ng Africans	Bakau Utd	Hawks	Serrekunda	Wallidan
Real Banjul †	22	11	6	5	27	14	39		2-1	1-2	0-0	0-1	2-1	0-0	3-1	0-0	2-0	0-0	2-1
Armed Forces	22	11	5	6	25	17	38	2-0		2-1	0-1	1-1	0-0	0-1	1-1	1-0	2-0	2-0	0-1
Ports Authority	22	8	10	4	24	14	34	0-1	3-0		3-0	1-0	2-2	1-1	0-0	2-2	0-0	0-0	2-0
Samger	22	7	10	5	17	16	31	1-0	0-1	0-0		1-1	4-2	0-0	1-0	1-0	1-3	1-1	2-0
Brikama United	22	7	8	7	23	20	29	0-0	1-2	0-1	1-2		0-3	2-1	0-0	1-1	3-1	4-1	2-0
Steve Biko	22	6	9	7	22	22	27	0-0	1-1	2-2	0-1	0-1		0-0	1-1	1-1	1-1	1-3	2-0
GAMTEL	22	5	12	5	16	18	27	0-3	1-1	1-0	1-1	0-0	0-1		1-1	1-4	0-0	1-1	1-1
Young Africans	22	5	12	5	16	18	27	0-0	2-1	1-3	0-0	0-2	0-1	0-0		3-2	0-0	0-0	2-1
Bakau United	22	7	5	10	16	19	26	1-3	0-2	0-0	1-0	1-1	1-0	0-0			1-0	0-1	1-0
Hawks	22	5	9	8	15	22	24	2-1	1-1	0-1	1-0	1-1	2-1	0-2	0-2	1-0		1-2	0-0
Serrekunda United	22	4	11	7	16	22	23	1-3	0-2	0-0	0-1	0-0	0-1	1-1	0-1	1-1			1-1
Wallidan	22	5	5	12	13	28	20	0-3	0-1	1-0	0-1	2-1	1-0	1-3	0-1	1-0	0-0	1-3	

17/01/2012 - 17/06/2012 • † Qualified for the CAF Champions League

GEO – GEORGIA

FIFA/COCA-COLA WORLD RANKING

'93	'94	'95	'96	'97	'98	'99	'00	'01	'02	'03	'04	'05	'06	'07	'08	'09	'10	'11	'12
-	92	79	95	69	52	66	66	58	90	93	104	104	94	77	108	124	73	73	73

2012													High	Low	Av
Jan	Feb	Mar	Apr	May	Jun	Jul	Aug	Sep	Oct	Nov	Dec			
76	81	74	95	95	95	97	97	86	65	65	73	42	156	84

Georgia joined the growing ranks of European nations to tamper with the structure of the league to try and make it more competitive and to a degree it worked. After the first 22 matches the top eight teams broke away to form a championship group but only took forward their records against those top eight teams. Thus, overnight, Zestafoni had their lead over Metalurgi Rustavi slashed from 21 points to just seven before the second phase began. Metalurgi, who had changed their name from Olimpi at the start of the season, then proceeded to claw back those seven points to finish level with Zestafoni but were denied the title because they had won less games than their rivals over the 36 matches played. Having retained their title by the skin of their teeth, Zestafoni had the chance to complete the double the following week but lost 4-1 to first-time winners Dila Gori in the cup final. With two of the past four world champions in their FIFA World Cup qualifying group, Georgia, Belarus and Finland were only ever going to be cast in the supporting role on the road to the finals in Brazil and after trading home wins with Belarus, Georgia found themselves at the head of the trio at the end of the year. Temuri Ketsbaia's team almost held on for a 0-0 draw against the Spanish in Tbilisi but conceded a goal four minutes from time through Soldado.

UEFA EUROPEAN CHAMPIONSHIP RECORD
1960-1992 DNE (played as part of the Soviet Union) 1996-2012 DNQ

GEORGIAN FOOTBALL FEDERATION (GFF)

76a Chavchavadze Avenue, 0179 Tbilisi

☎ +995 322 912670
📠 +995 322 915995
✉ gff@gff.ge
🌐 www.gff.ge
FA 1990 CON 1992 FIFA 1992
P Domenti Sichinava
GS Revaz Arveladze

THE STADIA
2014 FIFA World Cup Stadia
Boris Paichadze Tbilisi	55 000

Other Main Stadia
Mikheil Meshki Tbilisi	27 223
Evgrapi Shevardnadze Lanchkuti	22 000
Givi Kiladze Kutaisi	19 400
Erosi Mandjgaladze Samtredia	15 000

MAJOR CITIES/TOWNS
		Population
1	Tbilisi	1 137 205
2	Kutaisi	198 403
3	Rustavi	121 786
4	Batumi	121 525
5	Zugdidi	87 407
6	Poti	48 002
7	Gori	47 059
8	Sukhumi	40 366
9	Senaki	30 101
10	Samtredia	30 008
11	Khashuri	29 341
12	Zestafoni	25 599
13	Telavi	20 784
14	Marneuli	18 829
15	Kobuleti	18 302
16	Tskaltubo	18 064
17	Ozurgeti	17 916
18	Akhaltsikhe	17 383
19	Tkvarcheli	16 469

SAK'ART'VELO • GEORGIA
Capital	Tbilisi	Population	4 615 807 (118)	% in cities	53%
GDP per capita	$4700 (142)	Area km²	69 700 km² (120)	GMT +/-	+4
Neighbours (km)	Armenia 164, Azerbaijan 322, Russia 723, Turkey 252 • Coast 310					

RECENT INTERNATIONAL MATCHES PLAYED BY GEORGIA

2008	Opponents	Score	Venue	Comp	Scorers	Att	Referee
20-08	Wales	W 2-1	Swansea	Fr	Kenia [67], Gotsiridze [90]	6 435	Jug SVN
6-09	Republic of Ireland	L 1-2	Mainz	WCq	Kenia [92+]	4 500	Szabo HUN
10-09	Italy	L 0-2	Udine	WCq		27 164	Einwaller AUT
11-10	Cyprus	D 1-1	Tbilisi	WCq	Kobiashvili [73]	40 000	Matejek CZE
15-10	Bulgaria	D 0-0	Tbilisi	WCq		32 250	Kuipers NED
19-11	Romania	L 1-2	Bucharest	Fr	Martsvaladze [11]	2 000	Vassaras GRE
2009							
11-02	Republic of Ireland	L 1-2	Dublin	WCq	Iashvili [1]	45 000	Hyytia FIN
28-03	Cyprus	L 1-2	Larnaca	WCq	Kobiashvili [71p]	1 500	Fautrel FRA
1-04	Montenegro	D 0-0	Tbilisi	WCq		16 000	Malcolm NIR
6-06	Moldova	L 1-2	Tbilisi	Fr	Khizanishvili [85]	8 000	Salyi KAZ
10-06	Albania	D 1-1	Tirana	Fr	Dvalishvili [2]	2 000	Stavrev MKD
12-08	Malta	L 0-2	Ta'Qali	Fr		15 000	Kailis CYP
5-09	Italy	L 0-2	Tbilisi	WCq		32 000	Borski POL
9-09	Iceland	L 1-3	Reykjavík	Fr	Dvalishvili [33]	4 726	Trefoloni ITA
10-10	Montenegro	L 1-2	Podgorica	WCq	Dvalishvili [45]	5 420	Dereli TUR
14-10	Bulgaria	L 2-6	Sofia	WCq	Dvalishvili [34], Kobiashvili [51p]	700	Jakobsson ISL
2010							
3-03	Estonia	W 2-1	Tbilisi	Fr	Kobiashvili [45p], Siradze [90]	40 000	Banari MDA
25-05	Cameroon	D 0-0	Linz	Fr		3 500	Brugger AUT
11-08	Moldova	D 0-0	Chisinau	Fr		3 000	Shvetsov UKR
3-09	Greece	D 1-1	Piraeus	ECq	Iashvili [3]	14 794	Clos ESP
7-09	Israel	D 0-0	Tbilisi	ECq		45 000	Kever SUI
8-10	Malta	W 1-0	Tbilisi	ECq	Siradze [91+]	38 000	Black NIR
12-10	Latvia	D 1-1	Riga	ECq	Siradze [74]	4 330	Neves POR
17-11	Slovenia	W 2-1	Koper	Fr	Guruli [67], Ananidze [68]	4 000	Whitby WAL
2011							
9-02	Armenia	W 2-1	Limassol	Fr	Iashvili [22], Siradze [34]	300	Giannis CYP
26-03	Croatia	W 1-0	Tbilisi	ECq	Kobiashvili [90]	55 000	Tagliavento ITA
29-03	Israel	L 0-1	Tel Aviv	ECq		13 716	Fautrel FRA
3-06	Croatia	L 1-2	Split	ECq	Kankava [17]	28 000	Johannesson SWE
10-08	Poland	L 0-1	Lubin	Fr		12 310	Shandor UKR
2-09	Latvia	L 0-1	Tbilisi	ECq		15 422	Trattou CYP
6-09	Malta	D 1-1	Ta'Qali	ECq	Kankava [15]	5 000	Van Boekel NED
11-10	Greece	L 1-2	Tbilisi	ECq	Targamadze [19]	7 824	Orsato ITA
11-11	Moldova	W 2-0	Tbilisi	Fr	Kobakhidze [36], Ananidze [39p]	4 000	Aliyev AZE
2012							
29-02	Albania	W 2-1	Tbilisi	Fr	Kobakhidze [47], Amisulashvili [88]	18 000	Sidenco MDA
24-05	Turkey	L 1-3	Salzburg	Fr	Targamadze [52]	700	Hameter AUT
15-08	Luxembourg	W 2-1	Oberkorn	Fr	Mchedlidze [2], Amisulashvili [32]	100	Turpin FRA
7-09	Belarus	W 1-0	Tbilisi	WCq	Okriashvili [52]	20 000	Todorov BUL
11-09	Spain	L 0-1	Tbilisi	WCq		54 598	Moen NOR
12-10	Finland	D 1-1	Helsinki	WCq	Kashia [56]	12 607	Aranovskiy UKR
16-10	Belarus	L 0-2	Minsk	WCq		15 300	Schoergenhofer AUT
14-11	Egypt	D 0-0	Tbilisi	Fr		4 000	Treimanis LVA

Fr = Friendly match • EC = UEFA EURO 2012 • WC = FIFA World Cup • q = qualifier

GEORGIA NATIONAL TEAM HISTORICAL RECORDS

Caps: 100 - Levan Kobiashvili 1996- • 85 - Zurab Khizanishvili 1999- • 83 - Kakha Kaladze 1996- • 69 - Giorgi Nemsadze 1992-2004 • 67 - Aleksander Iashvili 1996- • 62 - Gocha Jamarauli 1994-2004 • 60 - Shota Arveladze 1992-2007 • 59 - Levan Tskitishvili 1995-2009 • 55 - Giorgi Demetradze 1996-2007 • 54 - Giorgi Kinkladze 1992-2005 • 52 - Temuri Ketsbaia 1994-2003

Goals: 26 - Shota Arveladze 1992-2007 • 17 - Temuri Ketsbaia 1994-2003 • 15 - Aleksander Iashvili 1996- • 12 - Giorgi Demetradze 1996-2007 & Levan Kobiashvili 1996- • 9 - Mikheil Kavelashvili 1994-2002 • 8 - Giorgi Kinkladze 1992-2005 & David Siradze 2004-

Coaches: Giga Norakidze 1992 • Aleksandr Chivadze 1993-96 • Vladimir Gutsaev 1996 • David Kipiani 1997 • Vladimir Gutsaev 1998-99 • Johan Boskamp 1999 • David Kipiani & Revaz Dzodzuashvili 2000-01 • Aleksandr Chivadze 2001-03 • Ivo Susak 2003 • Merab Jordania 2003 • Gocha Tqhebuchava 2004 • Alain Giresse 2004-05 • Gayoz Darsadze 2005 • Klaus Toppmoller 2006-08 • Hector Cuper 2008-09 • Temuri Ketsbaia 2010-

GEORGIA 2011-12
UMAGLESI LIGA

	Pl	W	D	L	F	A	Pts	Zestafoni	Metalurgi	Torpedo	Dinamo	Dila	Kolkheti	Baia	Merani	WIT	Spartaki	Gagra	Sioni
FC Zestafoni †	28	16	7	5	52	28	55		2-0 2-1	0-1 0-0	5-1 0-1	0-4 2-3	1-1 2-1	1-0 4-1	3-1 3-0	2-0	5-2	4-1	1-0
Metalurgi Rustavi ‡	28	17	4	7	39	28	55	0-0 0-2		2-0 2-1	0-2 2-1	3-1 1-0	0-0 1-0	2-0 4-0	2-1 2-0	0-0	0-0	1-1	1-2
Torpedo Kutaisi ‡	28	14	6	8	33	25	48	1-2 2-1	3-0 0-0		2-1 1-1	2-1 3-2	4-1 3-1	0-0 2-1	2-1 2-0	2-2	2-0	5-2	2-0
Dinamo Tbilisi	28	10	10	8	47	35	40	2-2 1-1	2-3 1-1	2-0 0-1		2-0 0-0	1-1 1-1	5-1 6-1	2-1 2-2	2-0	2-0	3-0	1-0
Dila Gori ‡	28	10	7	11	38	32	37	0-2 2-1	2-3 1-0	1-0 1-1	0-2 1-0		0-0 5-1	0-2 3-1	3-0 4-2	1-1	1-2	1-0	1-0
Kolkheti Poti	28	7	8	13	25	39	29	0-2 0-4	3-1 0-2	0-0 0-1	0-0 0-3	2-1 0-1		0-0 2-1	0-1 4-1	2-0	1-0	2-3	2-1
Baia Zugdidi	28	5	7	16	25	48	22	1-2 1-1	1-2 0-1	1-1 0-2	2-2 1-2	2-0 0-1	1-2 0-2-3		1-0 2-1	0-1	1-3	3-0	3-0
Merani Martvili	28	6	3	19	31	55	21	0-2 4-4	1-2 2-3	1-0 3-0	2-1 1-3	2-2 1-2	0-2 0-1	1-0 2-1		3-0	2-0	1-0	3-0
WIT Georgia Tbilisi	22	6	7	9	23	27	**25**	0-1	0-2	0-1	2-2	4-3	2-1	4-0	0-0		0-0	1-0	4-1
Spartaki Tskhinvali	22	6	6	10	22	32	**24**	1-5	0-1	2-0	1-2	2-2	1-1	1-2	1-2	2-1		2-1	0-0
FC Gagra	22	6	3	13	21	32	**21**	0-1	2-0	0-1	1-2	2-1	1-2	0-1	3-0	1-0	0-0		0-0
Sioni Bolnisi	22	2	6	14	13	37	**12**	1-2	2-2	1-3	0-3	0-3	0-0	2-0	0-0	1-1	1-2	1-3	

6/08/2011 - 20/05/2012 • † Qualified for the UEFA Champions League • ‡ Qualified for the Europa League • Only the matches between the top eight count towards the final standings
Top scorers: **20** - Jaba **DVALI**, Zestafoni • **15** - **XISCO** ESP, Dinamo • **12** - Dimitri **TATANASHVILI**, Metalurgi • **11** - Mate **VATSADZE**, Dila • **10** - Revaz **GOTSIRIDZE**, Torpedo & Shota **GRIGALASHVILI**, Zestafoni • **9** - Giga **JVANIA**, Merani • **8** - Tornike **GORGIASHVILI**, Zestafoni

GEORGIA 2011-12
PROMOTION/RELEGATION (1/2)

	Pl	W	D	L	F	A	Pts
Chikhura Sachkhere	14	8	2	4	25	15	26
Sioni Bolnisi	14	6	6	2	23	13	24
Dinamo Batumi	14	7	3	4	18	13	24
WIT Georgia Tbilisi	14	7	2	5	19	11	23
Guria Lanchkhuti	14	6	5	3	22	21	23
Spartaki Tskhinvali	14	6	3	5	19	16	21
FC Gagra	14	3	4	7	14	21	13
Mertskhali Ozurgeti	14	0	1	13	3	33	1

12/03/2011 - 21/05/2012

MEDALS TABLE

		Overall			League			Cup			Europe		
		G	S	B	G	S	B	G	S	B	G	S	B
1	Dinamo Tbilisi	22	6	5	13	4	5	9	2				
2	Torpedo Kutaisi	5	7	3	3	3	3	2	4				
3	FC Zestafoni	3	4	2	2		2	1	4				
4	Lokomotivi Tbilisi	3	3	1		2	1	3	1				
	WIT Georgia Tbilisi	3	3	1	2	3	1	1					
6	Metalurgi Rustavi	2	2	3	2	1	3		1				
7	Ameri Tbilisi	2	1	1			1	2	1				
8	Dinamo Batumi	1	5	1		1	1	1	4				
9	Sioni Bolnisi	1	2		1	1			1				
	Guria Lanchkhuti	1	2			2		1					
11	FC Gagra	1						1					
	Dila Gori	1						1					
13	Tskhumi Sukhumi		3			1			2				
14	Kolkheti-1913 Poti		2	3		2	3						
15	Gorda Rustavi		1	2			2		1				
16	Margveti Zestafoni		1			1							
	Samgurali		1						1				
	FC Samtredia		1						1				
	Shevardeni 1906		1			1							
20	Alazani Gurdzhaani			1			1						
GEORGIAN CLUBS IN THE SOVIET UNION													
6	Dinamo Tbilisi	4	11	13	2	5	13	2	6	1			1

GEORGIA 2011-12
PIRVELI LIGA GROUP A (2)

	Pl	W	D	L	F	A	Pts
Dinamo Batumi †	18	13	3	2	28	9	42
Mertskhali Ozurgeti †	18	12	2	4	24	17	38
FC Chiatura	18	11	4	3	30	16	37
Chkherimela Kharagauli	18	8	4	6	24	24	28
STU Tbilisi	18	8	2	8	39	42	26
Lokomotivi Tbilisi	18	5	5	8	30	28	20
Kolkheti Khobi	18	5	5	8	18	19	20
Meskheti Akhaltsikhe	18	5	2	11	19	25	17
FC Samtredia	18	3	5	10	15	30	14
Meshakhte Tqibuli	18	2	4	12	16	33	10

23/08/2011 - 8/03/2012 • † Qualified for the play-offs

GEORGIA 2011-12
PIRVELI LIGA GROUP B (2)

	Pl	W	D	L	F	A	Pts
Chikhura Sachkhere †	18	16	1	1	40	6	49
Guria Lanchkhuti †	18	12	3	3	41	15	39
Imereti Khoni	18	9	2	7	31	25	29
Skuri Tsalenjikha	18	8	3	7	25	26	27
Zooveti Tbilisi	18	8	3	7	23	29	27
Norchi Dinamo Tbilisi	18	8	2	8	30	24	26
Samgurali Tskhaltubo	18	6	5	7	27	23	23
Adeli Batumi	18	4	1	13	19	36	13
Sulori Vani	18	2	6	10	11	35	12
Aeti Sukhumi	18	3	2	13	13	41	11

23/08/2011 - 8/03/2012 • † Qualified for the play-offs

SAKARTVELOS TASI 2011-12

First Round

Dila Gori	2	3
Aeti Sukhumi *	0	0
Dinamo Tbilisi	Bye	
Sioni Bolnisi *	1 1	5p
Norchi Dinamo Tbilisi	1 1	4p
Chkherimela Kharagauli	0	1
Baia Zugdidi *	0	3
Merani Martvili *	0	1
Skuri Tsalenjikha	0	0
Zooveti Tbilisi *	0	2
Spartaki Tskhinvali	4	2
Sulori Vani	1	3
FC Samtredia *	1	0
FC Gagra	Bye	
Metalurgi Rustavi	Bye	
Lokomotivi Tbilisi	0	2
Chikhura Sachkhere *	5	2
FC Chiatura	0	2
Guria Lanchkhuti *	0	1
STU Tbilisi	1	0
WIT Georgia Tbilisi *	2	6
Torpedo Kutaisi *	2	6
Meskheti Akhaltsikhe	0	1
Mertskhali Ozurgeti	0	0
Dinamo Batumi *	3	4
Kolkheti Poti	1	1
Kolkheti Khobi *	2	0
FC Zestafoni	Bye	

Second Round

Dila Gori	2	0
Dinamo Tbilisi *	2	0
Sioni Bolnisi	0	1
Baia Zugdidi *	3	2
Merani Martvili *	2	1
Spartaki Tskhinvali	0	1
Sulori Vani *	1	0
FC Gagra	2	4
Metalurgi Rustavi	1	2
Chikhura Sachkhere *	1	0
FC Chiatura *	2	0
WIT Georgia Tbilisi	3	2
Torpedo Kutaisi	2	1
Dinamo Batumi *	0	1
Kolkheti Poti	1	0
FC Zestafoni *	2	0

Quarter-finals

Dila Gori	2	5
Baia Zugdidi *	2	2
Merani Martvili	0	2
FC Gagra *	4	0
Metalurgi Rustavi *	1	2
WIT Georgia Tbilisi	0	1
Torpedo Kutaisi *	1	1
FC Zestafoni	1	2

Semi-finals

Dila Gori	2	0
FC Gagra *	1	1
Metalurgi Rustavi	1	1
FC Zestafoni *	1	0

Final

Dila Gori ‡	4
FC Zestafoni	1

CUP FINAL

Mikheil Meskhi, Tbilisi, 26-05-2012
Att: 10000, Ref: Levan Kvaratskhelia
Scorers - Khojava 3ip, Vatsadze 49 Iluridze 64,
Intskirveli 93+ for Dila;Aptsiauri 14 for Zestafoni

Dila - Marin Skender●- Lasha Salukvadze,
Shota Kashia, Aleksandr Intskirveli, Lasha
Totadze●- Gocha Khojava (Roman Akhalkatsi
80), Zurabi Arziani, Giga Betchvaia, Sandro
Guruli (Georgi Iluridze 61), Georgi Kakhelishvili,
Mate Vatsadze (Revazi Barabadze 88). Tr:
Temur Shalamberidze

Zestafoni - Roin Kvashkvadze - Zaali Eliava,
Edik Sajaia, Teimuraz Ghonghadze◆**30**,
Mamuka Kobakhidze (Abayomi Seun 68), David
Mujiri● (Georgi Oniani 46), Zurab
Menteshashvili, Tornike Gorgiashvili (Levan
Sharikadze 58), Shota Grigalashvili, Tornike
Aptsiauri●, Jaba Dvali●◆**84**. Tr: Giorgi
Tchiabrishvili

* Home team in the first leg ● - ‡ Qualified for the Europa League

GER – GERMANY

FIFA/COCA-COLA WORLD RANKING

'93	'94	'95	'96	'97	'98	'99	'00	'01	'02	'03	'04	'05	'06	'07	'08	'09	'10	'11	'12
1	5	2	2	2	3	5	11	12	4	12	19	16	6	5	2	6	3	3	2

2012

Jan	Feb	Mar	Apr	May	Jun	Jul	Aug	Sep	Oct	Nov	Dec	High	Low	Av
3	2	3	2	2	3	2	2	2	2	2	2	1	22	5

German football re-discovered some of it swagger in 2012 with the national team and Bayern Munich at one stage looking odds on to complete a continental double. In the event, however, Bayern lost at home in the final of the UEFA Champions League while the national team once again saw its title ambitions thwarted by Italy - a nation they have yet to beat in international competition. Their semi-final defeat at Euro 2012 was the third time in four tournaments that they had fallen just short of the final and should the Germans fail to win the World Cup in Brazil, they will beat their longest post-war run without a trophy. At home the Bundesliga continued its resurgence and was rewarded with a television deal worth €2.5bn over four years. The title went to Borussia Dortmund thanks to a fantastic second half of the season, and Jurgen Klopp's young team then beat Bayern 5-2 in the cup final to secure an historic first double for the club. It was their first cup triumph since 1989 and came against a team that had only lost twice before in the final. Bayern had the chance to put their domestic woes behind them a week later when they hosted Chelsea in the UEFA Champions League final, but they failed to secure a fifth European Cup and ended the season with a hat trick of runners-up finishes after losing on penalties to the London team.

UEFA EUROPEAN CHAMPIONSHIP RECORD
1960-1964 DNE **1968** DNQ **1972** 1 Winners **1976** 2 F **1980** 1 Winners **1984** 5 r1 **1988** 3 SF (Hosts) **1992** 2 F **1996** 1 Winners **2000** 14 r1 **2004** 12 r1 **2008** 2 F **2012** 3 SF

DEUTSCHER FUSSBALL-BUND (DFB)

Otto-Fleck-Schneise 6,
Postfach 71 02 65,
Frankfurt 60528
☎ +49 69 67880
📠 +49 69 6788266
✉ info@dfb.de
🌐 www.dfb.de
FA 1900 CON 1954 FIFA 1904
P Wolfgang Niersbach
GS Helmut Sandrock

THE STADIA
2014 FIFA World Cup Stadia

Olympiastadion Berlin	74 064
AWD-Arena Hanover	49 000

Other Main Stadia

Westfalenstadion Dortmund	80 720
Allianz Arena Munich	69 000
Veltins Arena Gelsenkirchen	61 482

MAJOR CITIES/TOWNS

		Population
1	Berlin	3 418 983
2	Hamburg	1 773 537
3	Munich/München	1 360 717
4	Cologne/Köln	1 001 499
5	Frankfurt	653 746
6	Stuttgart	596 337
7	Dortmund	586 344
8	Düsseldorf	582 784
9	Essen	578 549
10	Bremen	549 597
11	Dresden	523 592
12	Hanover	517 553
13	Leipzig	513 810
14	Nuremberg	503 786
15	Duisburg	494 215
26	Gelsenkirchen	262 063
27	Mönch'gladbach	257 896
62	Wolfsburg	121 088
83	Kaiserslautern	97 168

BUNDESREPUBLIK DEUTSCHLAND • FEDERAL REPUBLIC OF GERMANY

Capital	Berlin	Population	82 329 758 (16)	% in cities	74%
GDP per capita	$35 500 (33)	Area km²	357 022 km² (62)	GMT +/-	+1
Neighbours (km)	Austria 784, Belgium 167, Czech Republic 646, Denmark 68, France 451, Luxembourg 138, Netherlands 577, Poland 456, Switzerland 334 • Coast 2389				

RECENT INTERNATIONAL MATCHES PLAYED BY GERMANY

2010	Opponents	Score	Venue	Comp	Scorers	Att	Referee
13-06	Australia	W 4-0	Durban	WCr1	Podolski [8], Klose [26], Muller [68], Cacau [70]	62 660	Rodriguez EX
18-06	Serbia	L 0-1	Port Elizabeth	WCr1		38 294	Undiano ESP
23-06	Ghana	W 1-0	Johannesburg	WCr1	Ozil [60]	83 391	Simon BRA
27-06	England	W 4-1	Bloemfontein	WCr2	Klose [20], Podolski [32], Muller 2 [67 70]	40 510	Larrionda URU
3-07	Argentina	W 4-0	Cape Town	WCqf	Muller [3], Klose 2 [68 89], Friedrich [74]	64 100	Irmatov UZB
7-07	Spain	L 0-1	Durban	WCsf		60 960	Kassai HUN
10-07	Uruguay	W 3-2	Port Elizabeth	WC3p	Muller [19], Jansen [56], Khedira [82]	36 254	Archundia MEX
11-08	Denmark	D 2-2	Copenhagen	Fr	Gomez [19], Helmes [73]	19 071	Kelly IRL
3-09	Belgium	W 1-0	Brussels	ECq	Klose [51]	41 126	Hauge NOR
7-09	Azerbaijan	W 6-1	Cologne	ECq	Westermann [28], Podolski [44], Klose 2 [45 92+], OG [53], Badstuber [86]	43 751	Strombergsson SWE
8-10	Turkey	W 3-0	Berlin	ECq	Klose 2 [42 87], Ozil [79]	74 244	Webb ENG
12-10	Kazakhstan	W 3-0	Astana	ECq	Klose [48], Gomez [76], Podolski [85]	18 000	Tudor ROU
17-11	Sweden	D 0-0	Gothenburg	Fr		21 959	Velasco ESP
2011							
9-02	Italy	D 1-1	Dortmund	Fr	Klose [16]	60 196	Braamhaar NED
26-03	Kazakhstan	W 4-0	Kaiserslautern	ECq	Klose 2 [3 88], Muller.T 2 [25 43]	47 849	Stavrev MKD
29-03	Australia	L 1-2	Monchengladbach	Fr	Gomez [26]	30 152	Lannoy FRA
29-05	Uruguay	W 2-1	Sinsheim	Fr	Gomez [20], Schurrle [35]	25 655	Benquerenca POR
3-06	Austria	W 2-1	Vienna	ECq	Gomez 2 [44 90]	47 500	Busacca SUI
7-06	Azerbaijan	W 3-1	Baku	ECq	Ozil [29], Gomez [40], Schurrle [93+]	30 000	Koukoulakis GRE
10-08	Brazil	W 3-2	Stuttgart	Fr	Schweinster [61p], Gotze [67], Schurrle [80]	54 767	Kassai HUN
2-09	Austria	W 6-2	Gelsenkirchen	ECq	Klose [8], Ozil 2 [23 47], Podolski [28], Schurrle [83], Gotze [88]	53 313	Tagliavento ITA
6-09	Poland	D 2-2	Gdansk	Fr	Kroos [68p], Cacau [96+]	38 000	Orsato ITA
7-10	Turkey	W 3-1	Istanbul	ECq	Gomez [35], Muller.T [66], Schweinsteiger [86p]	49 532	Atkinson ENG
11-10	Belgium	W 3-1	Dusseldorf	ECq	Ozil [30], Schurrle [33], Gomez [48]	48 483	Moen NOR
11-11	Ukraine	D 3-3	Kyiv	Fr	Kroos [38], Rolfes [65], Muller.T [77]	69 720	Velasco ESP
15-11	Netherlands	W 3-0	Hamburg	Fr	Muller.T [15], Klose [26], Ozil [66]	51 500	Cakir TUR
2012							
29-02	France	L 1-2	Bremen	Fr	Cacau [91+]	37 800	Tagliavento ITA
26-05	Switzerland	L 3-5	Basel	Fr	Hummels [45], Schurrle [64], Reus [72]	27 381	Gautier FRA
31-05	Israel	W 2-0	Leipzig	Fr	Gomez [40], Schurrle [82]	43 241	Blom NED
9-06	Portugal	W 1-0	Lviv	ECr1	Gomez [72]		Lannoy FRA
13-06	Netherlands	W 2-1	Kharkov	ECr1	Gomez 2 [24 38]	38 633	Eriksson SWE
17-06	Denmark	W 2-1	Lviv	ECr1	Podolski [19], Bender [80]	32 990	Velasco ESP
22-06	Greece	W 4-2	Gdansk	ECqf	Lahm [39], Khedira [61], Klose [68], Reus [74]	43 000	Skomina SVN
28-06	Italy	L 1-2	Warsaw	ECsf	Ozil [92+p]	58 500	Lannoy FRA
15-08	Argentina	L 1-3	Frankfurt	Fr	Howedes [81]	48 808	Eriksson SWE
7-09	Faroe Islands	W 3-0	Hanover	WCq	Goetze [28], Ozil 2 [54 72]	32 769	Madden SCO
11-09	Austria	W 2-1	Vienna	WCq	Reus [44], Ozil [52p]	47 000	Kuipers NED
12-10	Republic of Ireland	W 6-1	Dublin	WCq	Reus 2 [32 40], Ozil [55p], Klose [58], Kroos 2 [61 83]	49 850	Rizzoli ITA
16-10	Sweden	D 4-4	Berlin	WCq	Klose 2 [8 15], Mertesacker [39], Ozil [55]	72 369	Proenca POR
14-11	Netherlands	D 0-0	Amsterdam	Fr		49 000	Proenca POR

Fr = Friendly match • EC = UEFA EURO 2012 • WC = FIFA World Cup • q = qualifier • r1 = first round group • r2 = second round etc

GERMANY NATIONAL TEAM HISTORICAL RECORDS

Caps
150 - Lothar Matthaus 1980-2000 • 126 - Miroslav Klose 2001- • 108 - Jurgen Klinsmann 1987-98 • 106 - Lukas Podolski 2004- •
105 - Jurgen Kohler 1986-98 • 103 - Franz Beckenbauer 1965-77 • 101 - Thomas Haßler 1988-2000 • 98 - Michael Ballack 1999- •
97 - Bastian Schweinsteiger 2004- • 96 - Berti Vogts 1967-78 • 95 - Sepp Maier 1966-79; Karl-Heinz Rummenigge 1976-86 & Philipp Lahm 2004- • 90 - Rudi Voller 1982-94 • 86 - Andreas Brehme 1984-94 & Oliver Kahn 1995-2006 • 85 - Per Mertesacker 2004-

Goals
68 - Gerd Muller 1966-74 • 67 - Miroslav Klose 2001- • 47 - Jurgen Klinsmann 1987-98 & Rudi Voller 1982-94 • 45 - Karl-Heinz Rummenigge 1976-86 • 44 - Lukas Podolski 2004- • 43 - Uwe Seeler 1954-70 • 42 - Michael Ballack 1999-2010 • 37 - Oliver Bierhoff 1996-2002 • 33 - Fritz Walter 1940-58 • 32 - Klaus Fischer 1977-82 • 30 - Ernst Lehner 1933-42 • 29 - Andreas Moller 1988-99 •
27 - Edmund Conen 1934-42 • 25 - Mario Gomez 2007- • 24 - Richard Hofmann 1927-33

Coaches
Committee 1908-28 • Otto Nerz 1928-36 • Sepp Herberger 1936-64 • Helmut Schon 1964-78 • Jupp Derwall 1978-84 • Franz Beckenbauer 1984-90 • Berti Vogts 1990-98 • Erich Ribbeck 1998-2000 • Rudi Voller 2000-04 • Jurgen Klinsmann 2004-06 • Joachim Low 2006-

GERMANY 2011–12

1. BUNDESLIGA

	Pl	W	D	L	F	A	Pts	Bor. Dortmund	Bayern München	Schalke 04	Gladbach	Bayer Leverkusen	VfB Stuttgart	Hannover 96	VfL Wolfsburg	Werder Bremen	1.FC Nürnberg	TSG Hoffenheim	SC Freiburg	1.FSV Mainz	FC Augsburg	Hamburger SV	Hertha BSC	1.FC Köln	Kaiserslautern
Borussia Dortmund †	34	25	6	3	80	25	81		1-0	2-0	2-0	1-0	4-4	3-1	5-1	1-0	2-0	3-1	4-0	2-1	4-0	3-1	1-2	5-0	1-1
Bayern München †	34	23	4	7	77	22	73	0-1		2-0	0-1	3-0	2-0	2-1	2-0	4-1	1-0	7-0	0-0	2-1	5-0	4-0	3-0	2-0
Schalke 04 †	34	20	4	10	74	44	64	1-2	0-2		1-0	2-0	3-1	3-0	4-0	5-0	4-0	3-1	4-2	1-1	3-1	3-1	4-0	5-1	1-2
B. Mönchengladbach †	34	17	9	8	49	24	60	1-1	3-1	3-0		2-2	1-1	2-1	4-1	5-0	1-0	1-2	0-0	1-0	0-0	1-1	0-0	3-0	1-0
Bayer Leverkusen ‡	34	15	9	10	52	44	54	0-0	2-0	0-1	1-2		2-2	1-0	3-1	1-0	0-3	2-0	0-2	3-2	4-1	2-2	3-3	1-4	3-1
VfB Stuttgart ‡	34	15	8	11	63	46	53	1-1	1-2	3-0	0-3	0-1		3-0	3-2	4-1	1-0	2-0	4-1	4-1	2-1	1-2	5-0	2-0	1-0
Hannover 96 ‡	34	12	12	10	41	45	48	2-1	2-1	2-2	2-1	0-0	4-2		2-0	3-2	1-0	2-1	0-0	1-1	2-2	1-1	1-1	4-1	2-1
VfL Wolfsburg	34	13	5	16	47	60	44	1-3	0-1	2-1	0-0	3-2	1-0	4-1		3-1	2-1	1-2	3-2	2-2	1-2	2-1	2-3	1-0	1-0
Werder Bremen	34	11	9	14	49	58	42	0-2	1-2	2-3	2-2	1-1	2-0	3-0	4-1		0-1	1-1	5-3	0-3	1-1	2-0	2-1	3-2	2-0
1.FC Nürnberg	34	12	6	16	38	49	42	0-2	0-1	1-1	1-0	1-1	4-2	1-2	1-3	1-1		0-2	1-2	3-3	1-0	1-1	2-0	2-1	1-0
TSG Hoffenheim	34	10	11	13	41	47	41	1-0	0-0	1-1	1-0	0-1	1-2	0-0	3-1	1-2	2-3		1-1	1-1	2-2	4-0	1-1	1-1	1-1
SC Freiburg	34	10	10	14	45	61	40	1-4	0-0	2-1	1-0	0-1	1-2	1-1	3-0	2-2	2-2	0-0		1-2	1-0	1-2	2-2	4-1	2-0
1.FSV Mainz	34	9	12	13	47	51	39	1-2	3-2	2-4	0-3	2-0	3-1	1-1	0-0	1-3	2-1	0-4	3-1		0-1	0-0	1-3	4-0	4-0
FC Augsburg	34	8	14	12	36	49	38	0-0	1-2	1-1	1-0	1-4	1-3	0-0	2-0	1-1	0-0	0-0	2-2	2-1		1-0	3-0	2-1	2-2
Hamburger SV	34	8	12	14	35	57	36	1-5	1-1	1-2	0-1	1-1	0-4	1-1	1-3	2-0	2-0	1-3	0-0	1-1		2-2	3-4	1-1
Hertha BSC Berlin ‡‡	34	7	10	17	38	64	31	0-1	0-6	1-2	1-2	3-3	1-0	0-1	1-4	1-0	0-1	3-1	1-2	0-0	2-2	1-2		3-0	1-2
1.FC Köln	34	8	6	20	39	75	30	1-6	1-4	1-4	0-3	0-2	1-1	2-0	0-3	1-1	1-2	2-0	4-0	1-1	3-0	0-1	1-0		1-1
1.FC Kaiserslautern	34	4	11	19	24	54	23	2-5	0-3	1-4	1-2	0-2	0-0	0-0	0-0	0-0	1-2	1-0	3-1	1-1	0-1	1-1	0-1	0-1	

5/08/2011 – 5/05/2012 • † Qualified for the UEFA Champions League • ‡ Qualified for the Europa League
‡‡ Relegation play-off: Hertha BSC Berlin 1-2 2-2 **Fortuna Düsseldorf**. Fortuna promoted in place of Hertha
Top scorers: 29 – Klaas-Jan **HUNTELAAR** NED, Schalke • 26 – Mario **GOMEZ**, Bayern München • 22 – Robert **LEWANDOWSKI** POL, Dortmund •
18 – Claudio **PIZARRO** PER, Werder Bremen; Lukas **PODOLSKI**, Köln & Marco **REUS**, Gladbach • 17 – Martin **HARNIK** AUT, Stuttgart • 16 – Stefan **KIEßLING**, Leverkusen • 15 – **RAUL** ESP, Schalke • 13 – Vedad **IBISEVIC** BIH, Hoffenheim/Stuttgart & Shinji **KAGAWA** JPN, Dortmund

GERMANY 2011–12

2. BUNDESLIGA (2)

	Pl	W	D	L	F	A	Pts	Greuther Fürth	Eint. Frankfurt	For. Düsseldorf	FC St Pauli	SC Paderborn	1860 München	Union Berlin	E. Braunschweig	Dynamo Dresden	MSV Duisburg	VfL Bochum	FC Ingolstadt 04	FSV Frankfurt	Energie Cottbus	Erzgebirge Aue	Karlsruher SC	Al. Aachen	Hansa Rostock
SpVgg Greuther Fürth	34	20	10	4	73	27	70		2-3	1-1	2-1	5-1	2-0	5-0	1-3	1-2	0-2	6-2	3-0	4-0	3-0	2-0	3-0	1-0	3-0
Eintracht Frankfurt	34	20	8	6	76	33	68	0-0		1-1	1-1	0-0	0-2	3-1	2-1	3-0	3-0	3-0	1-1	6-1	1-0	4-0	2-0	4-3	4-1
Fortuna Düsseldorf †	34	16	14	4	64	35	62	2-1	1-1		0-0	2-3	3-1	2-1	1-1	2-1	2-2	2-0	4-1	1-0	4-2	3-1	4-2	0-0	2-0
FC St Pauli	34	18	8	8	59	34	62	2-2	2-0	1-3		5-0	4-2	2-1	0-0	3-1	2-1	0-0	2-1	2-0	0-0	2-3	1-0	3-1	3-0
SC Paderborn 07	34	17	10	7	51	42	61	1-1	1-1		2-2		3-2	1-0	2-2	1-2	0-0	4-1	1-0	3-1	1-0	2-1	0-0	2-1
TSV 1860 München	34	17	6	11	62	46	57	1-4	2-1	2-1	1-1	1-1		3-1	3-0	2-4	2-1	1-3	4-1	4-0	2-0	4-0	2-1	1-2	0-1
1.FC Union Berlin	34	14	6	14	55	58	48	0-4	0-4	0-0	0-2	3-0	0-1		1-0	4-0	1-1	2-1	4-1	4-0	1-0	1-0	2-0	2-0	5-4
Eint. Braunschweig	34	10	15	9	37	34	45	0-0	0-3	1-1	1-0	0-0	3-1	1-2		0-2	0-0	4-0	3-1	0-0	3-1	1-1	0-0	1-1	3-2
1.FC Dynamo Dresden	34	12	9	13	50	52	45	3-1	1-4	2-1	1-0	1-2	0-1	4-0	2-2		2-0	2-1	0-0	2-2	2-1	1-2	5-1	1-1	1-1
MSV Duisburg	34	10	9	15	42	47	39	0-2	2-0	0-2	0-1	0-1	0-3	1-3	3-0		2-1	3-1	1-2	2-2	3-1	1-2	1-3	2-1	2-0	0-0
VfL Bochum	34	10	7	17	41	55	37	1-4	0-2	1-1	1-2	0-4	2-2	4-2	2-0	0-2	2-1		0-1	1-0	0-1	6-0	0-0	1-0	2-1
FC Ingolstadt 04	34	8	13	13	43	58	37	0-0	1-1	1-1	1-0	4-0	0-1	3-3	0-1	4-2	1-1	3-5		1-1	1-0	0-0	2-1	3-3	3-1
FSV Frankfurt	34	7	14	13	43	59	35	1-1	0-4	2-5	3-3	2-2	3-1	1-1	1-1	1-1	0-0	0-2	1-1		0-1	1-2	1-1	2-0	0-0
Energie Cottbus	34	8	11	15	30	49	35	0-2	3-3	1-1	1-4	0-2	0-5	2-1	1-1	1-1	1-1	0-2	1-1			2-0	2-0	1-1	0-1
Erzgebirge Aue	34	8	11	15	31	55	35	1-1	1-2	2-4	2-1	0-2	0-0	1-1	1-1	1-1	2-2	1-1	1-1	4-3	0-0		0-2	1-0	1-0
Karlsruher SC ‡	34	9	6	19	34	60	33	2-2	1-0	0-5	0-2	2-0	1-3	2-0	1-3	2-0	3-2	0-0	3-2	0-4	2-0	2-1		0-2	2-2
Alemannia Aachen	34	6	13	15	30	47	31	0-0	0-3	0-0	2-1	0-3	2-2	1-3	0-2	0-1	2-2	3-1	1-3	0-2	1-1	1-0			0-0
Hansa Rostock	34	5	12	17	34	63	27	2-2	1-5	2-1	1-3	1-2	2-0	2-5	0-0	2-2	4-2	0-0	1-2	0-5	1-1	0-1	1-1	0-0	

15/07/2011 – 6/05/2012
† Promotion play-off (see Bundesliga) • ‡ Relegation play-off: **Jahn Regensburg** 1-1 2-2 Karlsruher SC. Regensburg promoted in place of Karlsruhe
Top scorers: 17 – Alexander **MEIER**, Eintracht Frankfurt; Olivier **OCCEAN** CAN, Greuther Fürth & Nick **PROSCHWITZ**, Paderborn

GERMANY 2011-12

3. FUẞBALL-LIGA (3)

	Pl	W	D	L	F	A	Pts	SV Sandhausen	VfR Aalen	Jahn Regensburg	1.FC Heidenheim	Rot-Weiß Erfurt	W. Burghausen	VfL Osnabrück	Offenbach	Chemnitzer FC	Saarbrücken	VfB Stuttgart-2	Preußen Münster	Arminia Bielefeld	SV Darmstadt 98	Unterhaching	Wiesbabden	SV Babelsberg	Carl Zeiss Jena	RW Oberhausen	Werder Bremen-2
SV Sandhausen	38	19	9	10	57	42	**66**		2-0	2-1	1-2	2-1	3-1	0-0	1-1	0-3	1-1	1-0	2-0	0-0	2-0	3-1	0-0	4-0	1-0	2-1	2-0
VfR Aalen	38	18	10	10	50	42	**64**	2-0		2-1	0-0	2-0	2-0	0-4	2-1	0-2	1-1	2-2	1-0	3-1	1-1	1-0	2-0	1-3	4-1	0-0	2-0
SSV Jahn Regensburg†	38	16	13	9	55	41	**61**	1-1	4-0		1-1	2-2	0-1	0-3	1-3	1-0	4-1	2-0	2-1	2-2	2-1	2-0	2-1	1-1	1-1	0-0	3-2
1.FC Heidenheim	38	16	12	10	48	36	**60**	2-1	3-1	0-0		0-1	1-1	0-2	2-1	3-2	1-1	1-0	4-1	2-1	2-1	3-1	1-1	5-0	0-0	1-0	1-0
Rot-Weiß Erfurt	38	15	14	9	54	41	**59**	4-2	0-1	2-2	2-0		3-3	0-0	0-0	0-0	1-1	3-1	1-1	1-1	0-2	2-2	2-2	3-0	4-0	1-0	
Wacker Burghausen	38	13	18	7	55	47	**57**	0-0	0-0	1-1	2-1	1-1		2-0	2-3	3-0	2-0	1-1	1-0	2-2	1-1	3-1	2-2	1-1	4-2	3-2	3-1
VfL Osnabrück	38	14	13	11	46	35	**55**	2-1	0-0	0-1	0-0	2-3	1-1		1-0	1-0	2-0	0-1	1-0	1-1	4-1	4-1	2-0	1-0	2-2	1-1	1-1
Offenbacher Kickers	38	15	10	13	49	41	**55**	2-0	2-1	2-1	1-0	2-0	2-2	3-0		0-1	2-3	2-0	3-0	0-1	1-1	1-4	0-2	1-1	1-1	1-0	3-0
Chemnitzer FC	38	15	10	13	47	43	**55**	1-3	0-1	0-3	3-0	0-2	2-1	3-1	2-0		1-0	1-1	1-2	1-1	0-0	5-1	1-2	1-1	1-1	1-0	2-0
1.FC Saarbrücken	38	13	15	10	61	51	**54**	2-1	4-2	1-0	0-0	0-2	0-0	2-2	3-1	1-1		0-0	2-2	2-4	4-0	4-2	2-1	2-2	2-1	5-2	2-0
VfB Stuttgart-2	38	12	14	12	44	47	**50**	0-1	2-2	1-0	0-2	2-2	1-3	0-0	2-3	1-0	0-0		1-1	1-1	2-5	1-1	2-1	0-0	3-3	1-3	0-1	1-1	1-0
Preußen Münster	38	12	14	12	40	44	**50**	1-2	1-0	2-0	2-1	3-2	0-0	1-1	0-1	0-2	1-0	1-1		0-0	1-2	1-1	1-1	1-1	1-0	0-0	
Arminia Bielefeld	38	12	14	12	51	57	**50**	1-3	0-1	1-1	0-1	0-0	2-2	1-1	1-1	3-1	0-4	1-2	2-2		3-2	2-1	0-1	1-0	2-1	3-0	1-0
SV Darmstadt 98	38	12	13	13	51	47	**49**	4-1	1-2	1-1	2-1	1-1	2-3	0-1	0-0	2-1	1-0	2-2	2-1	5-1		0-0	0-1	3-1	3-0	1-1	2-0
SpVgg Unterhaching	38	12	8	18	63	59	**44**	2-2	1-1	2-3	1-1	1-3	4-0	1-1	2-0	3-0	3-2	4-0	2-1	5-0	1-0		5-1	1-2	6-0	1-2	0-2
SV Wehen Wiesbabden	38	10	14	14	40	48	**44**	0-4	1-3	1-2	1-2	0-1	0-0	2-1	3-1	2-0	3-2	1-1	3-0	0-0	0-1	0-0		2-2	0-0	1-0	2-1
SV Babelsberg 03	38	11	11	16	44	59	**44**	1-2	2-0	0-0	2-2	3-0	0-2	2-1	0-1	0-0	1-3	1-4	0-2	1-0	1-1	1-2	3-2		0-0	1-0	2-3
Carl Zeiss Jena	38	9	12	17	39	59	**39**	1-2	3-0	1-0	0-1	1-0	1-0	2-0	1-2	1-2	1-1	1-2	1-3	4-3	2-1	2-1	0-1	0-1		0-0	3-1
Rot-Weiß Oberhausen	38	8	14	16	33	47	**38**	4-1	0-0	1-0	2-0	3-0	1-2	0-1	1-1	1-2	2-0	0-2	2-1	2-0	1-1	1-1	0-1	0-1	1-2		1-1
Werder Bremen-2	38	4	10	24	29	70	**22**	0-2	0-4	1-4	2-1	1-1	1-1	0-2	0-4	0-2	2-2	3-1	0-0	2-3	0-4	1-1	1-1	2-2	2-0	0-1	

22/07/2011 - 5/05/2012 • † Promotion play-off (see 2.Bundesliga)
Top scorers: **17** - Marcel **REICHWEIN**, Rot-Weiß Erfurt • **14** - Robert **LECHLEITER**, VfR Aalen & Tobias **SCHWEINSTEIGER**, Jahn Regensburg

GERMANY 2011-12

REGIONALLIGA NORD (4)

	Pl	W	D	L	F	A	Pts	Hallescher FC	Holstein Kiel	RB Leipzig	VfL Wolfsburg-2	TSV Havelse	Hannover 96-2	Berliner AK 07	Hamburger SV-2	ZFC Meuselwitz	VFC Plauen	VfB Lübeck	SV Meppen	Wilhelmshaven	Hertha BSC-2	Energ. Cottbus-2	VfB Germania	FC St Pauli-2	1.FC Magdeburg
Hallescher FC	34	23	08	03	53	15	**77**		1-0	0-0	3-2	3-1	2-1	1-0	2-0	3-1	4-0	0-0	3-0	2-0	2-0	2-0	3-1	5-0	3-0
KSV Holstein Kiel	34	24	03	07	73	31	**75**	0-0		1-0	2-1	1-0	3-0	3-0	3-1	4-2	1-1	4-1	3-1	4-2	6-0	5-2	2-1	4-0	1-0
RB Leipzig	34	22	07	05	71	30	**73**	0-1	2-1		2-2	4-1	4-0	2-1	1-2	0-1	1-1	1-0	3-2	8-2	1-0	1-1	3-2	1-1	1-1
VfL Wolfsburg-2	34	14	09	11	52	41	**51**	1-1	4-1	0-2		1-1	3-0	2-0	1-2	2-1	2-0	1-0	3-0	2-2	2-1	0-1	1-1	2-2	0-0
TSV Havelse	34	14	09	11	54	46	**51**	3-0	1-2	1-1	0-2		2-2	2-1	4-2	0-0	2-1	2-1	0-2	1-1	4-1	4-1	4-2	1-1	3-2	4-0
Hannover 96-2	34	14	08	12	47	48	**50**	0-0	1-3	0-2	3-1	1-1		0-2	3-1	3-0	2-1	3-2	0-0	1-0	5-2	1-0	1-1	3-0	1-1
Berliner AK 07	34	14	05	15	48	47	**47**	0-1	0-3	1-3	4-1	2-0	1-1		1-2	0-1	3-0	0-0	5-1	1-1	1-1	2-1	0-2	2-3	4-2
Hamburger SV-2	34	13	06	15	56	47	**45**	0-1	0-1	1-0	3-1	2-0	2-0	5-0		7-1	1-1	0-2	3-0	0-1	0-1	0-1	2-0	0-0	2-2
ZFC Meuselwitz	34	12	09	13	41	52	**45**	1-0	1-3	1-3	2-1	0-1	5-4	0-1	2-2		2-2	1-0	1-0	3-1	1-1	1-2	0-1	4-1	1-0
VFC Plauen	34	10	13	11	46	50	**43**	0-1	2-1	1-5	1-1	1-1	0-0	1-1	1-0	2-0		1-0	3-2	1-1	4-4	1-2	3-1	4-1	0-0
VfB Lübeck	34	10	08	16	41	47	**38**	0-1	1-0	0-5	0-2	2-3	1-2	1-1	4-2	0-0	0-3		1-1	0-3	1-0	0-0	1-2	5-1	1-0
SV Meppen	34	10	08	16	38	56	**38**	0-2	2-1	0-1	3-1	1-4	1-0	3-1	2-5	1-1	0-1	1-0		2-4	1-0	0-1	1-1	1-0	0-2
SV Wilhelmshaven	34	12	07	15	57	64	**37**	2-0	1-2	1-3	1-4	2-0	0-0	1-2	2-1	2-1	4-1	1-3	2-5		2-1	4-2	1-1	3-2	0-1
Hertha BSC Berlin-2	34	10	07	17	38	58	**37**	0-2	1-0	1-2	1-0	0-3	0-2	1-0	2-2	1-2	1-1	2-1	0-0	2-1		5-0	1-3	2-1	2-0
Energie Cottbus-2	34	09	09	16	39	65	**36**	0-0	0-2	0-1	1-1	2-1	3-2	0-2	4-1	1-3	2-2	3-5	1-1	1-5	1-1		2-1	1-2	1-0
Germania Halberstadt	34	08	10	16	45	53	**34**	0-2	0-3	2-3	0-1	0-1	0-1	1-4	2-2	2-1	0-4	0-0	1-1	3-2	5-0	5-0		4-1	1-2
FC St Pauli-2	34	08	08	18	43	72	**32**	2-2	1-2	1-2	0-3	2-1	3-1	1-3	1-0	3-1	0-2	1-3	2-3	2-2	2-1	3-1	0-0		0-2
1.FC Magdeburg	34	05	14	15	23	43	**29**	0-0	1-1	0-3	0-1	1-1	1-2	0-3	0-1	0-0	0-2	0-0	2-0	0-2	1-1	1-1	2-2		

5/08/2011 - 19/05/2012
Top scorers: **26** - Daniel **FRAHN**, RB Leipzig • **18** - Francky **SEMBOLO** COD, Wilhelmshaven • **17** - Andre **FOMITSCHOW**, Wolfsburg & Jaroslav **LINDNER**, Kiel

GERMANY 2011-12

REGIONALLIGA WEST (4)

	Pl	W	D	L	F	A	Pts
Borussia Dortmund-2	36	24	05	07	84	39	**77**
Sportfreunde Lotte	36	22	10	04	64	31	76
B. Mönchengladbach-2	36	21	06	09	67	45	69
Eintracht Trier	36	19	07	10	57	34	64
Wuppertaler SV	36	16	09	11	68	49	57
1.FC Köln-2	36	15	11	10	59	48	56
Fortuna Köln	36	15	08	13	54	56	53
Rot-Weiß Essen	36	15	07	14	52	57	52
1.FC Kaiserslautern-2	36	13	12	11	56	55	51
SC Verl	36	13	09	14	39	48	46
FC Schalke 04-2	36	13	06	17	55	63	45
1.FSV Mainz 05-2	36	12	07	17	49	47	43
SV Elversberg	36	11	09	16	39	60	42
VfL Bochum-2	36	11	08	17	42	64	41
SC Wiedenbrück	36	10	10	16	44	52	40
SC 07 Idar-Oberstein	36	10	09	17	38	62	39
TuS Koblenz	36	06	13	17	32	51	31
Bayer Leverkusen-2	36	07	10	19	34	57	31
Fortuna Düsseldorf-2	36	05	14	17	39	54	29

5/08/2011 - 19/05/2012

Top scorers: **30** - Christian **KNAPPMANN**, Wuppertaler • **20** - Terrence **BOYD** USA, Dortmund-2 & Andrew **WOOTEN**, Kaiserslautern-2

GERMANY 2011-12

REGIONALLIGA SUD (4)

	Pl	W	D	L	F	A	Pts
Stuttgarter Kickers	34	23	09	02	66	29	**78**
Sonnenhof Großaspach	34	21	06	07	78	40	69
Eintracht Frankfurt-2	34	21	04	09	69	41	67
VfR Wormatia Worms	34	16	10	08	57	48	58
Karlsruher SC-2	34	18	04	12	56	48	58
SpVgg Greuther Fürth-2	34	15	09	10	50	48	54
TSG Hoffenheim-2	34	15	07	12	69	36	52
SC Freiburg-2	34	15	04	15	49	49	49
FC Ingolstadt 04-2	34	15	04	15	46	50	49
1.FC Nürnberg-2	34	11	11	12	59	54	44
KSV Hessen Kassel	34	12	06	16	43	54	42
SV Waldhof Mannheim	34	10	09	15	40	46	39
TSV 1860 München-2	34	10	08	16	28	52	38
Bayern München-2	34	08	10	16	43	54	34
FC Memmingen	34	07	12	15	37	54	33
SC Pfullendorf	34	08	09	17	40	65	33
FSV Frankfurt-2	34	08	04	22	45	70	28
FC Bayern Alzenau	34	06	08	20	39	76	26

5/08/2011 - 19/05/2012

Top scorers: **18** - Karl-Heinz **LAPPE**, Ingolstadt-2 • **17** - Elia **SORIANO** ITA, E. Frankfurt • **16** - Nicolo **MAZZOLA** ITA, & Matthias **MORYS**, Sonnenhof

GER – GERMANY

MEDALS TABLE

		Overall G S B	League G S B	Cup G S B	Europe G S B	City
1	Bayern München	43 17 16	22 9 5	15 3	6 5 11	Munich
2	Schalke 04	13 16 6	7 9 3	5 7	1 3	Gelsenkirchen
3	Borussia Dortmund	13 8 8	8 4 5	3 2	2 2 3	Dortmund
4	1.FC Nürnberg	13 5 1	9 3	4 2	1	Nuremberg
5	Hamburger SV	11 15 6	6 8 2	3 4	2 3 4	Hamburg
6	Werder Bremen	11 12 8	4 7 5	6 4	1 1 3	Bremen
7	B. Mönchengladbach	10 7 8	5 2 5	3 2	2 3 3	Mönchengladbach
8	VfB Stuttgart	8 8 6	5 4 4	3 2	2 2	Stuttgart
9	1.FC Köln	7 15 9	3 8 2	4 6	1 7	Cologne
10	1.FC Kaiserslautern	6 9 4	4 4 2	2 5	2	Kaiserslautern
11	Eintracht Frankfurt	6 4 7	1 1 5	4 2	1 1 2	Frankfurt
12	Lokomotive Leipzig (VfB)	4 2	3 2	1		Leipzig
13	Dresdner SC	4 1	2 1	2		Dresden
14	Fortuna Düsseldorf	3 7 2	1 1 2	2 5	1	Düsseldorf
15	Karlsruher SC	3 3 1	1 1	2 2	1	Karlsruhe
16	TSV München 1860	3 3	1 2	2	1	Munich
17	SpVgg Fürth	3 1	3 1			Fürth
18	Hannover 96	3	2	1		Hanover
19	Bayer 04 Leverkusen	2 8 4	5 3	1 2	1 1 1	Leverkusen
20	Hertha BSC Berlin	2 7 5	2 5 4	2	1	Berlin
21	Viktoria 89 Berlin	2 2	2 2			Berlin
22	Rot-Weiss Essen	2 1	1	1 1		Essen
23	SK Rapid Wien	2	1	1		Vienna - AUT
24	Holstein Kiel	1 2	1 2			Kiel
	Karlsruher FV	1 2	1 2			Karlsruhe
	Kickers Offenbach	1 2		2	1	Offenbach
27	Blau-Weiß Berlin	1 1	1 1			Berlin
	First Vienna	1 1		1	1	Vienna - AUT
	VfL Wolfsburg	1 1		1		Wolfsburg
30	KFC Uerdingen 05	1 2	1	1	1	Krefeld
31	Eint. Braunschweig	1 1	1 1			Braunschweig
32	Freiburger FC	1	1			Freiburg
	Schwarz-Weiss Essen	1		1		Essen
	VfR Mannheim	1	1			Mannheim
35	MSV Duisburg	6 1	2	4	1	Duisburg
36	TSV Alemania Aachen	4	1	3		Aachen
37	1.FC Saarbrücken	2	2			Saarbrücken
	FSV Frankfurt	2	1	1		Frankfurt
	Stuttgarter Kickers	2	1	1		Stuttgart
	VfL Bochum	2		2		Bochum
	1.FC Union Berlin	2	1	1		Berlin
42	Admira Wien	1	1			Vienna - AUT
	Borussia Neunkirchen	1		1		Neunkirchen
	DFC Prag	1	1			Prague - CZE
	Energie Cottbus	1		1		Cottbus
	Fortuna Köln	1		1		Cologne
	Hertha BSC Berlin am	1		1		Berlin
	1.FC Phorzheim	1	1			Pforzheim
	LSV Groß Hamburg	1	1			Hamburg
	Preußen Münster	1	1			Münster
	Waldhof Mannheim	1		1		Mannheim
52	SC Freiburg	1	1			Freiburg

Leading East German Clubs (1948-91)

		G S B	G S B	G S B	G S B	
1	Dynamo Dresden	15 12 8	8 8 6	7 4	1	Dresden
2	Dynamo Berlin	13 10 4	10 4 3	3 6	1	Berlin
3	1.FC Magdeburg	11 2 6	3 2 6	7	1	Magdeburg
4	Viktoria 91 Frankfurt	8 7 1	6 4 1	2 3		Frankfurt/Oder
5	Carl Zeiss Jena	7 13 6	3 9 5	4 3	1 1	Jena
6	Sachsenring Zwickau	5 1 4	2 3	3 1	1	Zwickau
7	Lokomotive Leipzig	4 8 9	3 8	4 4	1 1	Leipzig

DFB POKAL 2011-12

First Round

Borussia Dortmund	3
SV Sandhausen *	0
Bayer Leverkusen	3
1.FC Dynamo Dresden *	4
TSV 1860 München	3
VfL Osnabrück *	2
KSV Hessen Kassel *	0
Fortuna Düsseldorf	3
1.FSV Mainz	2
SVN Zweibrücken *	1
Anker Wismar *	0
Hannover 96	6
MSV Duisburg	2
SV Babelsberg 03 *	0
Energie Cottbus	0
KSV Holstein Kiel *	3
TSG Hoffenheim	3
Germania Windeck *	1
SVN Wiedenbrück *	0
1.FC Köln	3
RB Leipzig	3
VfL Wolfsburg	2
Rot-Weiß Oberhausen *	1
FC Augsburg	2
1.FC Nürnberg	5
Arminia Bielefeld *	1
1.FC Saarbrücken *	1
Erzgebirge Aue	3
SC Paderborn 07	10
Rot-Weiß Ahlen *	0
Eimsbütteler TV *	0
SpVgg Greuther Fürth	10
Borussia Mönchengladbach	3
SSV Jahn Regensburg	1
Werder Bremen	1
1.FC Heidenheim *	2
Karlsruher SC *	3
Alemannia Aachen	1
FC Teningen *	1
Schalke 04	11
1.FC Kaiserslautern	3
BFC Dynamo Berlin *	0
Hallescher FC *	0
Eintracht Frankfurt	2
Rot-Weiß Essen *	2 4p
1.FC Union Berlin	2 3p
ZFC Meuselwitz *	0
Hertha BSC Berlin	4
VfB Stuttgart	2
SV Wehen Wiesbabden *	1
Kickers Emden *	1
FSV Frankfurt	5
Eintracht Trier *	2
FC St Pauli	1
VfB Oldenburg *	1
Hamburger SV	2
VfL Bochum	2 5p
Hansa Rostock *	2 3p
SC Freiburg *	2
SpVgg Unterhaching	3
FC Ingolstadt 04	4
FC Oberneuland *	1
Eintracht Braunschweig *	0
Bayern München	3

Second Round

Borussia Dortmund *	2
1.FC Dynamo Dresden	0
TSV 1860 München	0
Fortuna Düsseldorf *	3
1.FSV Mainz	1
Hannover 96 *	0
MSV Duisburg	0
KSV Holstein Kiel *	2
TSG Hoffenheim *	2
1.FC Köln	1
RB Leipzig *	0
FC Augsburg	1
1.FC Nürnberg	2
Erzgebirge Aue *	1
SC Paderborn 07	0
SpVgg Greuther Fürth *	4
Borussia Mönchengladbach	0 4p
1.FC Heidenheim *	0 3p
Karlsruher SC *	0
Schalke 04	2
1.FC Kaiserslautern	1
Eintracht Frankfurt *	0
Rot-Weiß Essen *	0
Hertha BSC Berlin	3
VfB Stuttgart *	3
FSV Frankfurt	0
Eintracht Trier *	1
Hamburger SV	2
VfL Bochum	4
SpVgg Unterhaching *	1
FC Ingolstadt 04	0
Bayern München *	6

Third Round

Borussia Dortmund	0 5p
Fortuna Düsseldorf *	0 4p
1.FSV Mainz	0
KSV Holstein Kiel *	2
TSG Hoffenheim *	2
FC Augsburg	1
1.FC Nürnberg *	0
SpVgg Greuther Fürth	1
Borussia Mönchengladbach *	3
Schalke 04	1
1.FC Kaiserslautern	1
Hertha BSC Berlin *	3
VfB Stuttgart *	2
Hamburger SV	1
VfL Bochum *	1
Bayern München	2

GER – GERMANY 377

DFB POKAL 2011–12

Quarter-finals	Semi-finals	Final

Borussia Dortmund 4
KSV Holstein Kiel * 0

Borussia Dortmund 1
SpVgg Greuther Fürth * 0

TSG Hoffenheim * 0
SpVgg Greuther Fürth 1

Borussia Dortmund 5
Bayern München 2

Borussia Mönchengladbach 2
Hertha BSC Berlin * 0

Borussia Mönchengladbach * 0 2p
Bayern München 0 4p

VfB Stuttgart * 0
Bayern München 2

* Home team

DFB POKAL FINAL 2012
Olympiastadion, Berlin, 12-05-2012, Att: 74 794, Ref: Peter Gagelmann

Borussia Dortmund 5 Kagawa [3], Hummels [41p], Lewandowski 3 [45 58 81]
Bayern München 2 Robben [25p], Ribery [75]

Roman **WEIDENFELLER**• (Mitchell **LANGERAK** 34) - Lukasz **PISZCZEK**, Neven **SUBOTIC**, Mats **HUMMELS**•, Marcel **SCHMELZER** - Jakub **BLASZCZYKOWSKI** (Ivan **PERISIC** 84), Ilkay **GUNDOGAN**, Sebastian **KEHL** (c), Kevin **GROBKREUTZ** - Shinji **KAGAWA** (Sven **BENDER** 81) - Robert **LEWANDOWSKI**. Tr: Jurgen **KLOPP**

Manuel **NEUER** - Philipp **LAHM** (c), Jerome **BOATENG**, Holger **BADSTUBER**•, David **ALABA** (Diego **CONTENTO** 69) - Arjen **ROBBEN**, **LUIZ GUSTAVO** (Thomas **MULLER** 46), Bastian **SCHWEINSTEIGER**•, Franck **RIBERY** - Toni **KROOS** - Mario **GOMEZ**. Tr: Jupp **HEYNCKES**

378   PART TWO – THE ASSOCIATIONS

FC AUGSBURG
2011–12

Jy	30	RW Ober'en	W 2-1	DPr1	Verhaegh [31], De Roeck [120]	3 786
	6	Freiburg	D 2-2	BL 9	Molders 2 [53 80]	30 403
Aug	14	Kaiser'tern	D 1-1	BL 13	Molders [9]	40 248
	20	Hoffenheim	L 0-2	BL 14		30 004
	27	Nürnberg	L 0-1	BL 16		43 071
	9	Leverkusen	L 1-4	BL 16	Hosogai [5]	30 660
Sep	17	Hertha	D 2-2	BL 17	Hosogai [20], Callsen-Bracker [64]	48 385
	24	Hannover	D 0-0	BL 16		29 113
	1	B Dortmund	L 0-4	BL 17		80 720
	15	Mainz	W 1-0	BL 16	Callsen-Bracker [88p]	30 195
Oct	21	W Bremen	D 1-1	BL 16	Bellinghausen [49]	30 660
	25	RB Leipzig	W 1-0	DPr2	Brinkmann [62]	34 341
	30	Köln	L 0-3	BL 17		48 000
	6	Bayern M	L 1-2	BL 18	Hosogai [59]	30 660
Nov	20	Stuttgart	L 1-2	BL 18	Werner [47]	60 000
	26	Wolfsburg	W 2-0	BL 18	Brinkmann [65], Kapllani [94+]	29 110
	4	Schalke	L 1-3	BL 18	Molders [47]	58 641
Dec	10	Gladbach	W 1-0	BL 17	Callsen-Bracker [51]	30 660
	17	Hamburg	D 1-1	BL 17	Oehrl [60]	48 143
	20	Hoffenheim	L 1-2	DPr3	Oehrl [36]	10 375
	21	Freiburg	L 0-1	BL 18		19 600
Jan	28	Kaiser'tern	D 2-2	BL 17	De Jong [5], Hain [65]	30 028
	4	Hoffenheim	D 2-2	BL 17	Molders [30], Langkamp [71]	22 500
Feb	12	Nürnberg	D 0-0	BL 17		30 660
	18	Leverkusen	L 1-4	BL 17	Koo Ja Cheol [50]	23 368
	25	Hertha	W 3-0	BL 15	Oehrl 2 [61 63], Ndjeng [91+]	29 123
	3	Hannover	D 2-2	BL 16	Bellinghausen [12], Callsen-Bracker [89p]	42 300
Mar	10	B Dortmund	D 0-0	BL 15		30 660
	17	Mainz	W 2-1	BL 15	Koo Ja Cheol [43], Langkamp [51]	30 025
	24	W Bremen	D 2-1	BL 15	Verhaegh [92+]	40 208
	31	Köln	W 2-1	BL 14	Koo Ja Cheol [19], Nando [45p]	30 660
	7	Bayern M	L 1-2	BL 15	Koo Ja Cheol [23]	69 000
	10	Stuttgart	L 1-3	BL 15	Nando [5p]	30 660
Apr	14	Wolfsburg	W 2-1	BL 15	Oehrl [13], Langkamp [88]	25 143
	22	Schalke	L 1-1	BL 15	Langkamp [6]	30 660
	28	Gladbach	D 0-0	BL 15		53 306
My	5	Hamburg	W 1-0	BL 14	Koo Ja Cheol [34]	30 660

14th Att: 514 406 • Av: 30 259 (+32.4%) • SGL Arena 30 660 (98%)

AUGSBURG LEAGUE APPEARANCES/GOALS 2011–12
Goalkeepers Mohamed Amsif MAR 6 • Simon Jentzsch 28
Defenders Jan-Ingwer Callsen-Bracker 25+5/4
Jonas De Roeck BEL 5+4/0 • Sebastian Langkamp 24+2/4
Uwe Mohrle 7+2/0 • Matthias Ostrzolek 11+1/0
Dominik Reinhardt 8+8/0 • Gibril Sankoh SLE 19+1/0
Paul Verhaegh NED 26/1
Midfield Dawda Bah GAM 0+1/0 • Daniel Baier 33/0
Axel Bellinghausen 22+3/2 • Daniel Brinkmann 8+7/1
Lorenzo Davids NED 18+2/0 • Marcel de Jong CAN 12/1
Akaki Gogia 4+8/0 • Hajime Hosogai JPN 31+1/3
Koo Ja Cheol KOR 14+1/5 • Jan Moravek CZE 0+3/0
Marcel Ndjeng CMR 11+8/1 • Andrew Sinkala ZAM 5+7/0
Tobias Werner 13+9/1
Forwards Stephan Hain 3+9/1 • Edmond Kapllani ALB 0+6/1
Patrick Mayer 0+1/0 • Sascha Molders 22+7/5 • Torsten Oehrl 14+2/4
Nando Rafael ANG 5+1/2
Coach Jos Luhukay NED

BAYER LEVERKUSEN
2011–12

Jy	30	Dy Dresden	L 3-4	DPr1	Derdiyok [6], Sam [12], Schurrle [49]	25 959
	7	Mainz	L 0-2	BL 15		32 443
Aug	14	W Bremen	W 1-0	BL 12	Kadlec [85]	30 210
	20	Stuttgart	W 1-0	BL 9	Kießling [28]	53 000
	27	B Dortmund	D 0-0	BL 8		30 210

BAYER LEVERKUSEN 2011–12 (CONT'D)

Sep	9	Augsburg	W 4-1	BL 4	Sam 2 [6 72], Kießling [23], Derdiyok [80]	30 660
	13	Chelsea	L 0-2	CLgE		33 820
	17	Köln	L 1-4	BL 7	Rolfes [70]	30 210
	24	Bayern M	L 0-3	BL 11		69 000
	28	Genk	W 2-0	CLgE	Bender [30], Ballack [91+]	25 138
	1	Wolfsburg	W 3-1	BL 9	Castro [14], Derdiyok [65], Kießling [85]	28 195
Oct	15	Gladbach	D 2-2	BL 8	Reinartz [20], Schurrle [87]	52 858
	19	Valencia	W 2-1	CLgE	Schurrle [52], Sam [56]	26 384
	23	Schalke	L 0-1	BL 9		30 210
	28	Freiburg	W 1-0	BL 8	Ballack [2]	22 300
	1	Valencia	L 1-3	CLgE	Kießling [31]	37 047
	5	Hamburg	D 2-2	BL 8	Schurrle [5], Bender [20]	30 210
Nov	18	Kaiser'tern	W 2-0	BL 7	Ballack [53], Sam [69]	42 245
	23	Chelsea	W 2-1	CLgE	Derdiyok [73], Friedrich [91+]	29 285
	26	Hertha	D 3-3	BL 6	Derdiyok 3 [24 64 79]	44 541
	2	Hoffenheim	W 2-0	BL 6	Derdiyok [10], Sam [79]	25 948
Dec	6	Genk	D 1-1	CLgE	Deriyok [79]	21 187
	10	Hannover	D 0-0	BL 6		44 800
	17	Nürnberg	L 0-3	BL 6		29 239
Jan	22	Mainz	W 3-2	BL 6	OG [10], Friedrich [35], Bender [70]	24 365
	28	W Bremen	D 1-1	BL 6	Reinartz [57]	40 060
	4	Stuttgart	D 2-2	BL 6	Kießling [11], Rolfes [47p]	27 929
	11	B Dortmund	L 0-1	BL 6		80 400
Feb	14	Barcelona	L 1-3	CLr2	Kadlec [52]	29 400
	18	Augsburg	W 4-1	BL 6	Kießling 2 [25 65], Castro [60], Schurrle [70]	23 368
	25	Köln	W 2-0	BL 5	Bender 2 [15 50]	46 500
	3	Bayern M	W 2-0	BL 5	Kießling [79], Bellarabi [90]	30 210
	7	Barcelona	L 1-7	CLr2	Bellarabi [91+]	75 632
Mar	10	Wolfsburg	L 2-3	BL 5	Kießling [3], Derdiyok [91+]	26 112
	17	Gladbach	L 1-2	BL 5	Kießling [75]	30 210
	24	Schalke	L 0-2	BL 5		61 673
	31	Freiburg	L 0-2	BL 7		28 342
	8	Hamburg	D 1-1	BL 6	Schurrle [55]	54 141
	11	Kaiser'tern	W 3-1	BL 6	Kießling [1], Rolfes [57], Reinartz [69]	25 627
Apr	17	Hertha	D 3-3	BL 6	Schurrle [44], Kießling 2 [51 84]	29 704
	21	Hoffenheim	W 1-0	BL 6	Schurrle [79]	28 150
	28	Hannover	W 1-0	BL 5		30 210
My	5	Nürnberg	W 4-1	BL 5	Kießling 3 [6 32 89], Schurrle [77]	48 548

5th Att: 484 397 • Av: 28 494 (-0.6%) • BayArena 30 210 (94%)

LEVERKUSEN LEAGUE APPEARANCES/GOALS 2011–12
Goalkeepers Fabian Giefer 1 • Bernd Leno 33
Defenders Gonzalo Castro 30+1/2 • Vedran Corluka CRO 7/0
Danny da Costa 5+1/0 • Manuel Friedrich 20+4/1
Michal Kadlec CZE 29/1 • Bastian Oczipka 1+8/0
Omer Toprak TUR 26+1/0 • Daniel Schwaab 21+2/0
Midfield Hanno Balitsch 4+4/0 • Michael Ballack 15+3/2
Tranquillo Barnetta SUI 3+4/0 • Karim Bellarabi 0+10/1
Lars Bender 28/4 • Dominik Kohr 0+2/0 • Michael Ortega COL 2+5/0
Stefan Reinartz 26+4/3 • Renato Augusto BRA 16+2/0
Simon Rolfes 22+3/2 • Sidney Sam 16+2/4
Forwards Eren Derdiyok SUI 11+14/7 • Nicolai Jorgensen DEN 0+1/0
Stefan Kießling 28+6/16 • Andre Schurrle 30+1/7 • Samed Yesil 0+1/0
Coach Robin Dutt (1/07/2011) • Sami Hyypia (1/04/2012)

BAYERN MUNCHEN
2011–12

	1	Braun'weig	W 3-0	DPr1	Gomez [9p], Schweinsteiger [39p], Muller [83]	23 645
	7	Gladbach	L 0-1	BL 12		69 000
	13	Wolfsburg	W 1-0	BL 11	Luiz Gustavo [91+]	30 000
Aug	17	Zürich	W 2-0	CLpo	Schweinsteiger [8], Robben [72]	66 000
	20	Hamburg	W 5-0	BL 3	Van Buyten [13], Ribery [41], Robben [34], Gomez [56], Olic [80]	69 000
	23	Zürich	W 1-0	CLpo	Gomez [7]	23 400
	27	Kaiser'tern	W 3-0	BL 1	Gomez 2 [37p 55 69]	49 780
	10	Freiburg	W 7-0	BL 1	Gomez 4 [8 52 55 71p], Ribery 2 [26 41], Petersen [90]	69 000
Sep	14	Villarreal	W 2-0	CLgA	Kroos [7], Rafinha [76]	19 168
	18	Schalke	W 2-0	BL 1	Petersen [21], Muller [75]	61 673

GER – GERMANY

BAYERN MUNCHEN 2011–12 (CONT'D)

Sep	24	Leverkusen	W 3-0	BL	1	Müller [5], Van Buyten [19], Robben [90]	69 000
	27	Man City	W 2-0	CLgA		Gomez 2 [38 45]	66 000
	1	Hoffenheim	D 0-0	BL	1		30 150
	15	Hertha	W 4-0	BL	1	Gomez 2 [5 69p], Ribery [7], Schweinsteiger [13]	69 000
	18	Napoli	D 1-1	CLgA		Kroos [2]	60 074
Oct	23	Hannover	L 1-2	BL	1	Alaba [82]	49 000
	26	Ingolstadt	W 6-0	DPr2		Müller [33], Alaba [49], OG [82], Petersen 2 [53 70], Usami [90]	63 000
	29	Nürnberg	W 4-0	BL	1	Gomez 2 [2 68], Ribery [39], Schweinsteiger [19]	69 000
	2	Napoli	W 3-2	CLgA		Gomez 3 [17 23 42]	66 000
Nov	6	Augsburg	W 2-1	BL	1	Gomez [16], Ribery [28]	30 660
	19	B Dortmund	L 0-1	BL	1		69 000
	22	Villarreal	W 3-1	CLgA		Ribery [3], Gomez [23], Ribery [69]	66 000
	27	Mainz	L 2-3	BL	3	Van Buyten 2 [56 79]	34 000
	3	W Bremen	W 4-1	BL	1	Ribery 2 [22 76], Robben 2 [68p 82p]	69 000
Dec	7	Man City	L 0-2	CLgA			46 002
	11	Stuttgart	W 2-1	BL	1	Gomez 2 [13 57]	60 469
	16	Köln	W 3-0	BL	1	Gomez [48], Alaba [63], Kroos [88]	69 000
	20	Bochum	W 2-1	DPr3		Kroos [52], Robben [91+]	29 299
Jan	20	Gladbach	L 1-3	BL	1	Schweinsteiger [76]	54 047
	28	Wolfsburg	W 2-0	BL	1	Gomez [60], Robben [92+]	69 000
	4	Hamburg	D 1-1	BL	2	Olic [71]	57 000
	8	Stuttgart	W 2-0	DPqf		Ribery [30], Gomez [46]	57 500
Feb	11	Kaiser'tern	W 2-0	BL	2	Gomez [6], Müller [30]	69 000
	18	Freiburg	D 0-0	BL	3		24 000
	22	Basel	L 0-1	CLr2			36 000
	26	Schalke	W 2-0	BL	2	Ribery 2 [36 55]	69 000
	3	Leverkusen	L 0-2	BL	2		30 210
	10	Hoffenheim	W 7-1	BL	2	Gomez 3 [5 35 48], Kroos [18], Robben 2 [12p 29], Ribery [58]	69 000
Mar	13	Basel	W 7-0	CLr2		Robben 2 [11 81], Müller [42], Gomez 4 [44 50 61 67]	66 000
	17	Hertha	W 6-0	BL	2	Müller [9], Robben 3 [12 19p 67p], Gomez [50p], Kroos [51]	74 244
	21	Gladbach	D 0-0	DPsf		W 4-2p	54 049
	24	Hannover	W 2-1	BL	2	Kroos [36], Gomez [68]	69 000
	28	Marseille	W 2-0	CLqf		Gomez [44], Robben [69]	31 683
	31	Nürnberg	W 1-0	BL	2	Robben [69]	48 548
	3	Marseille	W 2-0	CLqf		Olic 2 [13 37]	66 000
Apr	7	Augsburg	W 2-1	BL	2	Gomez 2 [1 60]	69 000
	11	B Dortmund	L 0-1	BL	2		80 720
	14	Mainz	D 0-0	BL	2		69 000
	17	Real Madrid	W 2-1	CLsf		Ribery [17], Gomez [90]	66 000
	21	W Bremen	W 2-1	BL	2	OG [75], Ribery [90]	42 100
	25	Real Madrid	L 1-2	CLsf		Robben [27p], W 3-1p	71 654
	28	Stuttgart	W 2-0	BL	2	Gomez [32], Müller [92+]	69 000
May	5	Köln	W 4-1	BL	2	Müller 2 [34 85], OG [52], Robben [54]	50 000
	12	B Dortmund	L 2-5	DPf		Robben [25p], Ribery [75]	75 708
	19	Chelsea	D 1-1	CLf		Müller [83], L 3-4p	62 500

2nd Att: 1 173 000 • Av: 69 000 (0%) • Allianz Arena 69 000 (100%)

BAYERN LEAGUE APPEARANCES/GOALS 2011-12
Goalkeepers Hans Jorg Butt 1 • Manuel Neuer 33
Defenders Holger Badstuber 32+1/0 • Jerome Boateng 26+1/0
Diego Contento 5+6/0 • Philipp Lahm 31/0 • Rafinha BRA 20+4/0
Daniel Van Buyten BEL 12+1/4
Midfield David Alaba AUT 14+16/2 • Toni Kroos 27+4/4
Luiz Gustavo BRA 18+10/1 • Danijel Pranjic CRO 4+3/0
Franck Ribery FRA 27+5/12 • Arjen Robben NED 18+6/12
Bastian Schweinsteiger 18+4/3 • Anatoliy Tymoshchuk UKR 17+6/4
Takashi Usami JPN 2+1/0
Forwards Mario Gomez 30+3/26 • Thomas Müller 33+1/7
Ivica Olic CRO 4+16/2 • Nils Petersen 2+7/2
Coach Jupp Heynckes (1/07/2011)

BORUSSIA DORTMUND 2011–12

Jul	23	Schalke	D 0-0	SC		L 3-4p	61 673
	30	Sandhausen	W 3-0	DPr1		Lewandowski 2 [10 90], Kagawa [56]	10 231

BORUSSIA DORTMUND 2011–12 (CONT'D)

Aug	5	Hamburg	W 3-1	BL	3	Großkreutz 2 [17 48], Gotze [29]	80 720
	13	Hoffenheim	L 0-1	BL	7		30 150
	20	Nürnberg	W 2-0	BL	6	Lewandowski [50], Großkreutz [80]	78 400
	27	Leverkusen	D 0-0	BL	6		30 210
	10	Hertha	L 1-2	BL	11	Lewandowski [88]	80 720
	13	Arsenal	D 1-1	CLgF		Perisic [88]	65 590
Sep	18	Hannover	L 1-2	BL	11	Kagawa [63]	49 000
	24	Mainz	W 2-1	BL	8	Perisic [63], Piszczek [90]	34 000
	28	Marseille	L 0-3	CLgF			26 142
	1	Augsburg	W 4-0	BL	6	Lewandowski 3 [30 44 78], Gotze [75]	80 720
	14	W Bremen	W 2-0	BL	3	Perisic 42, Owomoyela [71]	42 068
Oct	19	Olympiacos	L 1-3	CLgF		Lewandowski [26]	29 638
	22	Köln	W 5-0	BL	2	Kagawa [7], Schmelzer [25], Lewandowski 2 [44 50], Kehl [66]	80 200
	25	Dy Dresden	W 2-0	DPr2		Lewandowski [31], Gotze [65]	73 100
	29	Stuttgart	D 1-1	BL	3	Piszczek [55]	60 000
	1	Olympiacos	W 1-0	CLgF		Großkreutz [7]	65 590
Nov	5	Wolfsburg	W 5-1	BL	2	Gotze 2 [12 78], Kagawa [45], Bender [61], Lewandowski [66]	80 720
	19	Bayern M	W 1-0	BL	2	Gotze [64]	69 000
	23	Arsenal	L 1-2	CLgF		Kagawa [92+]	59 531
	26	Schalke	W 2-0	BL	1	Lewandowski [16], Santana [61]	80 720
	3	Gladbach	D 1-1	BL	2	Lewandowski [40]	54 057
	6	Marseille	L 2-3	CLgF		Blaszczykowski [23], Hummels [32p]	65 000
Dec	11	Kaiser'tern	D 1-1	BL	2	Kagawa [27]	80 720
	17	Freiburg	W 4-1	BL	2	Lewandowski 2 [7 70], Gundogan [44], Großkreutz [59]	24 000
	20	Fortuna	D 0-0	DPr3		W 5-4p	54 000
Jan	22	Hamburg	W 5-1	BL	2	Großkreutz [16], Kagawa 2 [37 83], Blaszczykowski 2 [58 76p]	57 000
	28	Hoffenheim	W 3-1	BL	2	Kagawa 2 [16 55], Großkreutz [31]	80 500
	3	Nürnberg	W 2-0	BL	1	Kehl [48], Barrios [82]	45 572
Feb	7	H'stein Kiel	W 4-0	DPqf		Lewandowski [11], Kagawa [18], Barrios [80], Perisic [87]	11 522
	11	Leverkusen	W 1-0	BL	1	Kagawa [45]	80 400
	18	Hertha	W 1-0	BL	1	Großkreutz [66]	74 244
	26	Hannover	W 3-1	BL	1	Lewandowski 2 [27 54], Perisic [90]	80 720
	3	Mainz	W 2-1	BL	1	Blaszczykowski [26], Kagawa [77]	80 720
	10	Augsburg	D 0-0	BL	1		30 660
	7	W Bremen	W 1-0	BL	1	Kagawa [8]	80 720
	20	Gr'her Fürth	W 1-0	DPsf		Gundogan [120]	15 500
Mar	25	Köln	W 6-1	BL	1	Piszczek [26], Kagawa 2 [47 80], Lewandowski [52], Gundogan [78], Perisic [84]	50 000
	30	Stuttgart	D 4-4	BL	1	Kagawa [33], Blaszczykowski [49], Hummels [82], Perisic [87]	80 720
	7	Wolfsburg	W 3-1	BL	1	Kagawa 2 [22 90], Gundogan [49]	30 000
Apr	11	Bayern M	W 1-0	BL	1	Lewandowski [77]	80 720
	14	Schalke	W 2-1	BL	1	Piszczek [17], Kehl [63]	61 673
	21	Gladbach	W 2-0	BL	1	Perisic [23], Kagawa [59]	80 720
	28	Kaiser'tern	W 5-2	BL	1	Barrios 3 [18 26 55], Gotze [33], Perisic [76]	49 780
May	5	Freiburg	W 4-0	BL	1	Blaszczykowski 2 [5 39], Lewandowski 2 [20 27]	80 720
	12	Bayern M	W 5-2	DPf		Kagawa [3], Hummels [41p], Lewandowski 3 [45 58 81]	75 708

1st Att: 1 368 860 • Av: 80 521 (+1.7%) • Westfalenstadion 80 720 (99%)

DORTMUND LEAGUE APPEARANCES/GOALS 2011-12
Goalkeepers Mitchell Langerak AUS 2 • Roman Weidenfeller 32
Defenders Felipe Santana BRA 10+3/1 • Mats Hummels 33/1
Chris Lowe 6+1/0 • Patrick Owomoyela 2+9/1
Lukasz Piszczek POL 32/4 • Marcel Schmelzer 28/1
Neven Subotic SRB 25/0
Midfield Sven Bender 21+3/1 • Jakub Blaszczykowski POL 22+7/6
Antonio da Silva BRA 2+3/0 • Mario Gotze 14+3/6
Kevin Großkreutz 26+5/7 • Ilkay Gundogan 22+6/3
Shinji Kagawa JPN 29+2/13 • Sebastian Kehl 21+6/3
Florian Kringe 0+1/0 • Moritz Leitner 2+15/0 • Ivan Perisic CRO 8+20/7
Forwards Lucas Barrios 3+15/4 • Robert Lewandowski POL 34/22
Mohamed Zidan EGY 0+2/0
Coach Jurgen Klopp

BORUSSIA MONCHENGLADBACH
2011–12

Jy	29	Regensburg	W	3-1	DPr1	Stranzl [14], Reus [23], De Camargo [70]	10 388
	7	Bayern M	W	1-0	BL	7 De Camargo [62]	69 000
	13	Stuttgart	D	1-1	BL	4 Daems [67p]	48 322
Aug	19	Wolfsburg	W	4-1	BL	1 Reus 2 [15 67], Daems [32p], Bobadilla [45]	43 224
	28	Schalke	L	0-1	BL	5	61 673
	10	Kaiser'tern	W	1-0	BL	3 Arango [58]	52 083
Sep	17	Hamburg	W	1-0	BL	3 De Camargo [65]	55 797
	24	Nürnberg	W	1-0	BL	3 Daems [75p]	51 117
	1	Freiburg	L	0-1	BL	3	24 000
	15	Leverkusen	D	2-2	BL	2 Reus [65], Hermann [72]	52 858
Oct	22	Hoffenheim	L	0-1	BL	7	30 150
	25	Heidenheim	D	0-0	DPr2	W 4-3p	10 000
	29	Hannover	W	2-1	BL	5 Reus 2 [21 51]	51 036
	5	Hertha	W	2-1	BL	4 Reus 2 [33 55]	60 556
Nov	19	W Bremen	W	5-0	BL	3 Hermann [16], Reus 3 [23 38 51], Arango [53]	53 465
	25	Köln	W	3-0	BL	2 Hanke 2 [20 47], Arango [30]	50 000
	3	B Dortmund	D	1-1	BL	3 Hanke [72]	54 057
Dec	10	Augsburg	L	0-1	BL	4	30 660
	18	Mainz	W	1-0	BL	4 Hermann [5]	49 089
	21	Schalke	W	3-1	DPr3	Arango [18], Reus 2 [56 88]	54 057
	20	Bayern M	W	3-1	BL	4 Reus [11], Herman 2 [41 71]	54 047
Jan	29	Stuttgart	W	3-0	BL	4 Hanke [31], Reus [81], De Camargo [84]	53 600
	4	Wolfsburg	D	0-0	BL	4	30 000
	8	Hertha	W	2-0	DPqf	Daems [101], Wendt [120]	47 465
Feb	11	Schalke	W	3-0	BL	2 Reus [2], Hanke [15], Arango [32]	54 049
	18	Kaiser'tern	W	2-1	BL	2 Hermann [9], Arango [14]	45 661
	24	Hamburg	D	1-1	BL	3 Hanke [45]	54 049
	4	Nürnberg	L	0-1	BL	3	45 675
	10	Freiburg	D	0-0	BL	3	52 207
Mar	17	Leverkusen	W	2-1	BL	3 Reus [7], De Camargo [88]	30 210
	21	Bayern M	D	0-0	DPsf	L 2-4p	54 049
	24	Hoffenheim	L	1-2	BL	4 Reus [38]	52 796
	1	Hannover	L	1-2	BL	4 Nordtveit [78]	49 000
	7	Hertha	D	0-0	BL	4	52 691
	10	W Bremen	D	2-2	BL	4 Hanke 2 [52 66]	42 100
Apr	15	Köln	W	3-0	BL	4 Arango [19], Jantschke [53], Reus [55]	52 990
	21	B Dortmund	L	0-2	BL	4	80 720
	28	Augsburg	D	0-0	BL	4	53 306
My	5	Mainz	W	3-0	BL	4 Reus 2 [31 61], De Camargo [69]	34 000

4th Att: 881 394 • Av: 51 847 (+14.7%) • Borussia-Park 54 057 (95%)

GLADBACH LEAGUE APPEARANCES/GOALS 2011-12
Goalkeepers Marc-Andre ter Stegen 34
Defenders Roel Brouwers NED 17+4/0 • Filip Daems BEL 31/3
Dante BRA 33/0 • Tony Jantschke 31+1/1 • Martin Stranzl AUT 21+1/0
Oscar Wendt SWE 5+9/0 • Matthias Zimmermann 0+1/0
Midfield Juan Arango VEN 34/6 • Tolga Cigerci 1+1/0
Patrick Herrmann 22+5/6 • Julian Korb 0+1/0 • Thorben Marx 7+12/0
Roman Neustadter 33/0 • Havard Nordtveit NOR 27+4/1
Yuki Otsu JPN 0+3/0 • Alexander Ring FIN 1+7/0 • Lucas Rupp 0+3/0
Amin Younes 0+1/0
Forwards Raul Bobadilla ARG 5+10/1 • Igor de Camargo BEL 11+14/5
Mike Hanke 29+2/8 • Joshua King NOR 0+2/0
Mathew Leckie AUT 0+9/0 • Marco Reus 32/18
Coach Lucien Favre SUI

SC FREIBURG
2011–12

Jy	31	Un'haching	L	2-3	DPr1	Makiadi [9], Reisinger [74]	4 100
	6	Augsburg	D	2-2	BL	9 Cisse [47], Makiadi [55]	30 403
	13	Mainz	L	1-2	BL	14 Cisse [90]	20 600
Aug	20	W Bremen	L	3-5	BL	16 Cisse 2 [7 48], Reisinger [84]	39 201
	27	Wolfsburg	W	3-0	BL	13 Barth [30], Jendrisek [40], Makiadi [59]	20 000
	10	Bayern M	L	0-7	BL	14	69 000
Sep	16	Stuttgart	L	1-2	BL	16 Cisse [85]	24 000
	24	Schalke	L	2-4	BL	17 Cisse [2], Jendrisek [83]	60 545
	1	Gladbach	W	1-0	BL	15 Flum [19]	24 000
Oct	16	Hamburg	L	1-2	BL	17 Cisse [46]	24 000
	22	Kaiser'tern	L	0-1	BL	18	40 748
	28	Leverkusen	L	0-1	BL	18	22 300
	5	Nürnberg	W	2-1	BL	17 Rosenthal [34], Cisse [90p]	38 026
Nov	19	Hertha	D	2-2	BL	17 Reisinger 2 [61 90]	21 500
	26	Hoffenheim	D	1-1	BL	17 Dembele [90]	28 250
	3	Hannover	D	1-1	BL	17 Cisse [67]	20 000
Dec	10	Köln	L	0-4	BL	18	44 500
	17	B Dortmund	L	1-4	BL	18 Rosehthal [34]	24 000
	21	Augsburg	W	1-0	BL	17 Ginter [88]	19 600
Jan	29	Mainz	L	1-3	BL	18 Krmas [67]	30 938
	5	W Bremen	D	2-2	BL	18 Makiadi [32], Schmid [70]	22 000
	10	Wolfsburg	L	2-3	BL	18 Flum [11], Caligiuri [38]	23 057
Feb	18	Bayern M	D	0-0	BL	18	24 000
	25	Stuttgart	L	1-4	BL	18 Diagne [27]	46 000
	3	Schalke	W	2-1	BL	17 Freis [18], Caligiuri [66p]	24 000
	10	Gladbach	D	0-0	BL	17	52 207
Mar	17	Hamburg	W	3-1	BL	16 Flum [20], Caligiuri [43], Makiadi [72]	52 414
	24	Kaiser'tern	W	2-0	BL	13 Guede [8], Makiadi [14]	24 000
	31	Leverkusen	W	2-0	BL	13 Schuster [8], Caligiuri [60]	28 342
	7	Nürnberg	D	2-2	BL	13 Caligiuri [53p], Makiadi [79]	24 000
	10	Hertha	W	2-1	BL	13 OG [7], Freis [67]	45 778
Apr	15	Hoffenheim	D	0-0	BL	13	23 500
	22	Hannover	D	0-0	BL	13	48 000
	28	Köln	W	4-1	BL	12 Mujdza [36], Guede [54], Caligiuri [84], Freis [90]	24 000
My	5	B Dortmund	L	0-4	BL	12	80 720

12th Att: 385 500 • Av: 22 676 (-1.7%) • Mage Solar Stadion 24 493 (92%)

FREIBURG LEAGUE APPEARANCES/GOALS 2011-12
Goalkeepers Daniel Batz 1 • Oliver Baumann 33
Defenders Oliver Barth 12/1 • Felix Bastians 16/0
Heiko Butscher 6+2/0 • Fallou Diagne SEN 15/1 • Beg Ferati SUI 3+3/0
Andreas Hinkel 6+1/0 • Immanuel Hohn 6+2/0
Pavel Krmas CZE 18+1/1 • Michael Lumb DEN 4+1/0
Mensur Mujdza BIH 13+1/1 • Oliver Sorg 17/0 • Daniel Williams USA 1/0
Midfield Yacine Abdessadki MAR 8+3/0 • Daniel Caligiuri 18+7/6
Johannes Flum 27+3/3 • Matthias Ginter 11+2/1
Karim Guede SVK 8+2/2 • Cedric Makiadi COD 31+2/6
Maximilian Nicu ROU 2+2/0 • Anton Putsila BLR 15+4/0
Jan Rosenthal 15+3/2 • Jonathan Schmid FRA 22/1
Julian Schuster 19+2/1
Forwards Papiss Demba Cisse SEN 17/9 • Garra Dembele MLI 3+13/1
Sebastian Freis 11+4/3 • Erik Jendrisek SVK 8+11/2
Stefan Reisinger 5+20/3 • Ivan Santini CRO 3+7/0
Coach Christian Streich

KEY
BL = Bundesliga • DP = DFB Pokal
(German Cup) • CL = UEFA Champions
League • EL = Europa League
See page 13 for further explanations

HAMBURGER SV
2011–12

Jy	30	Oldenburg	W	2-1	DPr1	Westermann [26], Petric [72]	15 552
	5	B Dortmund	L	1-3	BL	Tesche [79]	80 720
	13	Hertha	D	2-2	BL	16 Petric [25p], Son Heung Min [61]	52 100
Aug	20	Bayern M	L	0-5	BL	17	69 000
	27	Köln	L	3-4	BL	18 Petric [11p], Rajkovic [59], Son Heung Min [62]	51 289
	10	W Bremen	L	0-2	BL	18	41 600
Sep	17	Gladbach	L	0-1	BL	18	55 797
	23	Stuttgart	W	2-1	BL	18 Bruma [51], Tesche [67]	55 700
	2	Schalke	L	1-2	BL	18 Petric [38]	54 237
	16	Freiburg	W	2-1	BL	18 Son Heung Min [12], Ilicevic [73]	24 000
Oct	22	Wolfsburg	D	1-1	BL	17 Petric [56]	54 378
	25	Eint Trier	W	2-1	DPr2	Berg [62], Aogo [110]	10 300
	30	Kaiser'tern	D	1-1	BL	16 Guerrero [65]	55 348
	5	Leverkusen	L	2-2	BL	16 Westermann [33], Jansen [57]	30 210
Nov	20	Hoffenheim	W	2-0	BL	15 Guerrero [25], Jansen [65]	46 237
	2	Hannover	D	1-1	BL	15 Bruma [64]	49 000
	4	Nürnberg	W	2-0	BL	13 Guerrero [24], Jansen [62]	45 473
Dec	10	Mainz	D	0-0	BL	13	34 000
	17	Augsburg	D	1-1	BL	13 Guerrero [66]	48 143
	21	Stuttgart	L	1-2	DPr3	OG [54]	38 600
Jan	22	B Dortmund	L	1-5	BL	14 Guerrero [86]	57 000
	28	Hertha	W	2-1	BL	11 Jansen [24], Petric [45]	49 168
	4	Bayern M	D	1-1	BL	12 Sala [23]	57 000
Feb	12	Köln	W	1-0	BL	10 Guerrero [88]	46 500
	18	W Bremen	L	1-3	BL	11 Petric [75]	56 553
	24	Gladbach	D	1-1	BL	12 Arslan [56]	54 049
	3	Stuttgart	L	0-4	BL	13	55 263
	11	Schalke	L	1-3	BL	14 Kacar [45]	61 673
Mar	17	Freiburg	L	1-3	BL	14 Ilicevic [75]	52 414
	23	Wolfsburg	L	1-2	BL	16 Berg [47]	30 000
	31	Kaiser'tern	W	1-0	BL	15 Jansen [28]	44 745
	5	Leverkusen	D	1-1	BL	14 Petric [40p]	54 141
	11	Hoffenheim	L	0-4	BL	14	27 000
Apr	14	Hannover	W	1-0	BL	14 Son Heung Min [12]	57 000
	21	Nürnberg	D	1-1	BL	14 Son Heung Min [59]	45 873
	28	Mainz	D	0-0	BL	14	56 537
My	5	Augsburg	L	0-1	BL	15	30 660

15th Att: 908 910 • Av: 53 465 (-1.8%) • Volksparkstadion 57 000 (93%)

HAMBURG LEAGUE APPEARANCES/GOALS 2011-12
Goalkeepers Jaroslav Drobny CZE **32** • Sven Neuhaus **2+1**
Defenders Dennis Aogo **30/0** • Jeffrey Bruma NED **22/2**
Dennis Diekmeier **22+2/0** • Michael Mancienne ENG **14+2/0**
Slobodan Rajkovic SRB **14+2/1** • Heiko Westermann **33/1**
Midfield Anis Ben Hatira TUN **0+1/0** • Romeo Castelen NED **0+2/0**
Gokhan Tore TUR **16+6/0** • Ivo Ilicevic CRO **11+7/2**
Marcell Jansen **26+3/5** • David Jarolim CZE **18+4/0**
Gojko Kacar SRB **14+7/1** • Lam Zhi Gin CHN **4+3/0**
Tomas Rincon VEN **24+3/0** • Jacopo Sala ITA **9+4/1**
Per Skjelbred NOR **5+3/0** • Robert Tesche **11+12/2**
Tolgay Arslan TUR **4+4/1**
Forwards Marcus Berg SWE **9+4/1** • Eljero Elia NED **2+2/0**
Paolo Guerrero PER **20+3/6** • Mladen Petric CRO **21+5/7**
Son Heung Min KOR **11+16/5**
Coach Michael Oenning • Rodolfo Cardoso ARG (19/09/2011) • Frank Arnesen (10/10/2012) • Thorsten Fink (17/10/2011)

HANNOVER 96
2011–12

Jy	31	Wismar	W	6-0	DPr1	Abdellaoue 2 [13 25], Stindl 2 [34 36], Stoppelkamp 2 [71 76]	6 045
	6	Hoffenheim	W	2-1	BL	6 Salihovic [18p], Abdellaoue [30p]	40 315
	13	Nürnberg	W	2-1	BL	2 Abdellaoue [16], Rausch [27p]	37 212
Aug	18	Sevilla	W	2-1	ELpo	Schlaudraff 2 [6 45]	43 500
	21	Hertha	D	1-1	BL	2 Sergio Pinto [33]	41 200
	25	Sevilla	D	1-1	ELpo	Abdellaoue [22]	33 026
	28	Mainz	D	1-1	BL	4 Abdellaoue [30]	40 420
	10	Stuttgart	L	0-3	BL	9	53 000
	15	Standard	D	0-0	ELgB		42 500
Sep	18	B Dortmund	W	2-1	BL	5 Haggui [87], Ya Konan [89]	49 000
	24	Augsburg	D	0-0	BL	6	29 113
	29	Vorskla	W	2-1	ELgB	Abdellaoue [32], Pander [44]	11 000
	2	W Bremen	W	3-2	BL	5 Abdellaoue 3 [2 38 59]	49 000
	16	Köln	L	0-2	BL	7	46 000
Oct	20	København	D	2-2	ELgB	Pander [29], Sergio Pinto [81]	43 100
	23	Bayern M	W	2-1	BL	4 Abdellaoue [22p], Pander [49]	49 000
	26	Mainz	L	0-1	DPr2		30 100
	29	Gladbach	L	1-2	BL	7 Pogatetz [26]	51 036
	3	København	W	2-1	ELgB	Schlaudraff [71], Stindl [74]	27 853
	6	Schalke	D	2-2	BL	6 OG [29], Abdellaoue [59]	49 000
Nov	19	Wolfsburg	L	1-4	BL	8 Schulz [43]	30 000
	26	Hamburg	D	1-1	BL	8 Schlaudraff [79]	49 000
	30	Standard	L	0-2	ELgB		18 104
	3	Freiburg	D	1-1	BL	8 OG [44]	20 000
Dec	10	Leverkusen	D	0-0	BL	8	44 800
	15	Vorskla	W	3-1	ELgB	Rausch [25], Ya Konan [33], Sobiech [78]	42 000
	18	Kaiser'tern	D	1-1	BL	7 Abdellaoue [13]	36 019
	21	Hoffenheim	D	0-0	BL	7	24 800
Jan	27	Nürnberg	W	1-0	BL	7 Abdellaoue [18]	35 400
	4	Hertha	W	1-0	BL	7 Abdellaoue [68]	36 997
	11	Mainz	D	1-1	BL	7 Sobiech [89]	30 173
	16	Brugge	W	2-1	ELr2	Sobiech [73], Schlaudraff [80p]	42 000
Feb	19	Stuttgart	W	4-2	BL	7 Haggui [25], Diouf [32], Pander [46], Stindl [73]	37 800
	23	Brugge	W	1-0	ELr2	Diouf [71]	21 690
	26	B Dortmund	L	1-3	BL	7 Ya Konan [60]	80 720
	3	Augsburg	D	2-2	BL	7 Haggui [33], Diouf [69]	42 300
	8	Standard	D	2-2	ELr3	Stindl [22p], Diouf [56]	17 498
	11	W Bremen	L	0-3	BL	7	41 500
Mar	15	Standard	W	4-0	ELr3	Abdellaoue [4], OG 2 [21 73], Sergio Pinto [93+]	43 000
	18	Köln	W	4-1	BL	7 Stindl [19], Schlaudraff [61p], Diouf 2 [67 83]	45 000
	24	Bayern M	L	1-2	BL	8 Ya Konan [74]	69 000
	29	At Madrid	L	1-2	ELqf	Diouf [38]	29 223
	1	Gladbach	W	2-1	BL	5 Ya Konan [57], Diouf [77]	49 000
	5	At Madrid	L	1-2	ELqf	Diouf [81]	44 000
	8	Schalke	L	0-3	BL	8	61 673
Apr	11	Wolfsburg	W	2-0	BL	7 Diouf [44], Ya Konan [77]	43 800
	14	Hamburg	L	0-1	BL	7	57 000
	21	Freiburg	D	0-0	BL	7	48 000
	28	Leverkusen	L	0-1	BL	7	30 210
My	5	Kaiser'tern	W	2-1	BL	7 OG [38], Ya Konan [71]	49 000

7th Att: 762 035 • Av: 44 826 (+2.1%) • Niedersachsen 49 000 (91%)

HANNOVER LEAGUE APPEARANCES/GOALS 2011-12
Goalkeepers Ron-Robert Zieler **34**
Defenders Christopher Avevor **0+1/0** • Steven Cherundolo USA **22/0**
Mario Eggimann SUI **13+3/0** • Karim Haggui TUN **26+1/3**
Christian Pander **22+7/2** • Emanuel Pogatetz AUT **28+1/1**
Konstantin Rausch **21+12/1** • Christian Schulz **24+3/1**
Midfield Carlitos POR **0+2/0** • Sofian Chahed TUN **12+4/0**
Henning Hauger NOR **1+2/0** • Altin Lala ALB **1+5/0**
Daniel Royer AUT **1+2/0** • Manuel Schmiedebach **28+2/0**
Sergio Pinto **29+1/1** • Lars Stindl **28/2** • Moritz Stoppelkamp **4+17/0**
Forwards Mohammed Abdellaoue NOR **27+1/11**
Mame Diouf SEN **8+2/6** • Jan Schlaudraff **29+2/3**
Artur Sobiech POL **0+12/1** • Didier Ya Konan CIV **16+12/6**
Coach Mirko Slomka

HERTHA BSC BERLIN
2011–12

Jly	31	Meuselwitz	W 4-0	DPr1		Ramos 2 [22][46], Ottl [49], Ebert [56]	7 707
Aug	6	Nürnberg	L 0-1	BL	12		61 118
	13	Hamburg	D 2-2	BL	15	Tunay [43], Mijatovic [88]	52 100
	21	Hannover	D 1-1	BL	13	Lasogga [83]	41 200
	26	Stuttgart	W 1-0	BL	11	Raffael [86]	52 232
Sep	10	B Dortmund	W 2-1	BL	8	Raffael [49], Niemeyer [81]	80 720
	17	Augsburg	D 2-2	BL	10	Lell [46], Tunay [57]	48 385
	25	W Bremen	L 1-2	BL	12	Ramos [3]	40 760
Oct	1	Köln	W 3-0	BL	10	Lasogga 2 [14][26], Raffael [34]	59 491
	15	Bayern M	L 0-4	BL	11		69 000
	22	Mainz	D 0-0	BL	10		47 064
	26	RW Essen	W 3-0	DPr2		Ramos [64], Lasogga [72], Rukavytsya [86]	14 500
	29	Wolfsburg	W 3-2	BL	10	Raffael [27], Kobiashvili [37p], Lasogga [85]	30 000
Nov	5	Gladbach	L 1-2	BL	10	Ramos [18]	60 556
	19	Freiburg	D 2-2	BL	10	Ramos [20], Niemeyer [45]	21 500
	26	Leverkusen	D 3-3	BL	10	Lasogga 2 [7][82], OG [17]	44 541
Dec	3	Kaiser'tern	D 1-1	BL	9	Raffael [15]	36 856
	9	Schalke	L 1-2	BL	11	Ramos [25]	52 382
	17	Hoffenheim	D 1-1	BL	11	Hubnik [90]	25 550
	21	Kaiser'tern	W 3-1	DPr3		Ramos [64], Lasogga [72], Ebert [56]	40 944
Jan	21	Nürnberg	L 0-2	BL	13		39 117
	28	Hamburg	L 1-2	BL	15	Lasogga [81]	49 168
Feb	4	Hannover	L 0-1	BL	15		36 997
	8	Gladbach	L 0-2	DPqf			47 465
	11	Stuttgart	L 0-5	BL	15		45 000
	18	B Dortmund	L 0-1	BL	15		74 244
	25	Augsburg	L 0-3	BL	16		29 123
Mar	3	W Bremen	W 1-0	BL	15	Rukavytsya [63]	52 744
	10	Köln	L 0-1	BL	16		48 000
	17	Bayern M	L 0-6	BL	17		74 244
	24	Mainz	W 3-1	BL	17	Ben Hatira [41], Ramos 2 [52][69]	33 152
	31	Wolfsburg	L 1-4	BL	17	Kobiashvili [13]	46 388
Apr	7	Gladbach	D 0-0	BL	17		52 691
	10	Freiburg	L 1-2	BL	17	Hubnik [81]	45 778
	14	Leverkusen	D 3-3	BL	17	Lasogga [63], Tunay 2 [71][76]	29 704
	21	Kaiser'tern	L 1-2	BL	17	Niemeyer [60]	51 461
	28	Schalke	L 0-4	BL	17		61 673
May	5	Hoffenheim	W 3-1	BL	16	Ben Hatira 2 [14][78], Raffael [90]	51 837
	10	Fortuna	L 1-2	BLpo		Hubnik [19]	68 041
	15	Fortuna	D 2-2	BLpo		Ben Hatira [23], Raffael [85]	51 000

16th Att: 908 630 • Av: 53 449 (+15.8%) • Olympiastadion 74 244 (72%)

HERTHA BSC LEAGUE APPEARANCES/GOALS 2011-12
Goalkeepers Sascha Burchert 0+2 • Thomas Kraft 34
Defenders Felix Bastians 13/0 • Maik Franz 6+1/0
Roman Hubnik CZE 27/2 • Christoph Janker 13+5/0
Christian Lell 28/1 • Andre Mijatovic CRO 18+3/1
Alfredo Morales USA 2+6/0 • Sebastian Neumann 1+1/0
Midfield Anis Ben-Hatira TUN 10+6/3 • Patrick Ebert 21+5/0
Fabian Holland 2/0 • Levan Kobiashvili GEO 31/2
Fabian Lustenberger SUI 4+8/0 • Peter Niemeyer 28+3/3
Andreas Ottl 26/0 • Fanol Perdedaj 6+2/0 • Raffael BRA 30+1/6
Ronny BRA 2+8/0
Forwards Marco Djuricin AUT 0+2/0 • Pierre-Michel Lasogga 19+13/8
Adrian Ramos COL 27+4/6 • Nikita Rukavytsya AUS 16+8/1
Tunay Torun TUR 10+10/4
Coach Markus Babbel • Michael Skibbe (22/12/2011) • Rene Tretschok (13/02/2012) Otto Rehhagel (19/02/2012)

TSG HOFFENHEIM
2011–12

Jly	31	G Windeck	W 3-1	DPr1		Salihovic [51p], Johnson [99], Babel [116]	2 588
Aug	6	Hannover	L 1-2	BL	11	Salihovic [18p]	40 315
	13	B Dortmund	W 1-0	BL	9	Salihovic [9]	30 150
	20	Augsburg	W 2-0	BL	7	Babel 5, Salihovic [75p]	30 004
	27	W Bremen	L 1-2	BL	9	Firmino [36]	28 750
Sep	10	Mainz	W 4-0	BL	5	Firmino [16], Babel 2 [45p][74], OG [85]	31 500
	17	Wolfsburg	W 3-1	BL	4	Babel [20], Firmino 2 [24][85]	26 850
	25	Köln	L 0-2	BL	4		45 500
Oct	1	Bayern M	D 0-0	BL	8		30 150
	15	Stuttgart	L 0-2	BL	9		55 000
	22	Gladbach	W 1-0	BL	8	Ibisevic [56]	30 150
	25	Köln	W 2-1	DPr2		Obasi [41], Musona [50]	16 000
	29	Schalke	L 1-3	BL	9	Ibisevic [63]	60 384
Nov	5	Kaiser'tern	D 1-1	BL	9	Ibisevic [33]	30 150
	20	Hamburg	L 0-2	BL	9		46 237
	26	Freiburg	D 1-1	BL	9	Firmino [24]	28 250
Dec	2	Leverkusen	L 0-2	BL	10		25 948
	10	Nürnberg	W 2-0	BL	9	Ibisevic 2 [39][56]	35 389
	17	Hertha	D 1-1	BL	9	Salihovic [21]	25 550
	20	Augsburg	W 2-1	DPr3		Salihovic [23], Ibisevic [49]	10 375
Jan	21	Hannover	D 0-0	BL	8		24 800
	28	B Dortmund	L 1-3	BL	8	Johnson [63]	80 500
Feb	4	Augsburg	D 2-2	BL	8	Mlapa [37], Salihovic [50p]	22 500
	8	G'ther Fürth	L 0-1	DPqf			14 000
	11	W Bremen	D 1-1	BL	11	Vestergaard [4]	39 176
	17	Mainz	D 1-1	BL	10	OG [9]	24 300
	25	Wolfsburg	W 2-1	BL	9	Firmino [2], Schipplock [84]	23 921
Mar	4	Köln	D 1-1	BL	10	Compper [33]	29 250
	10	Bayern M	L 1-7	BL	12	OG [85]	69 000
	17	Stuttgart	L 1-2	BL	12	Salihovic [74p]	30 150
	24	Gladbach	W 2-1	BL	10	Firmino [77], Vukevic [79]	52 796
Apr	1	Schalke	D 1-1	BL	10	Salihovic [30p]	30 150
	7	Kaiser'tern	W 2-1	BL	10	Salihovic [26p], Vukevic [71]	40 296
	11	Hamburg	W 4-0	BL	9	Vestergaard [17], Salihovic [25p], Johnson [51], Schipplock [59]	27 000
	15	Freiburg	D 0-0	BL	9		23 500
	21	Leverkusen	L 0-1	BL	9		28 150
	29	Nürnberg	L 2-3	BL	11	Beck [22], Braafheid [89]	30 150
May	5	Hertha	L 1-3	BL	11	Compper [85]	51 837

11th Att: 476 450 • Av: 28 026 (-6.5%) • Rhein-Neckar-Arena 30 150 (92%)

HOFFENHEIM LEAGUE APPEARANCES/GOALS 2011-12
Goalkeepers Daniel Haas 1 • Tom Starke 33
Defenders Andreas Beck 31/1 • Edson Braafheid NED 16+5/1
Marvin Compper 30/2 • Andreas Ibertsberger AUT 1/0
Fabian Johnson USA 27+2/2 • Jannik Vestergaard DEN 19+4/2
Isaac Vorsah GHA 20+1/0 • Daniel Williams USA 17+7/0
Midfield Dominik Kaiser 5+4/0 • Roberto Firmino BRA 26+4/7
Sebastian Rudy 27+1/0 • Sejad Salihovic BIH 21+2/9
Gylfi Sigurdsson ISL 7/0 • Tobias Strobl 0+1/0 • Boris Vukcevic 14+4/2
Tobias Weis 11+2/0 • Sandro Wieser LIE 0+1/0
Forwards Ryan Babel NED 28+3/4 • Vedad Ibisevic BIH 7+3/5
Srdan Lakic CRO 4+3/0 • Peniel Mlapa 10+14/1
Knowledge Musona ZIM 2+14/0 • Chinedu Obasi NGA 10+3/0
Sven Schipplock 7+13/2 • Prince Tagoe GHA 0+2/0
Coach Holger Stanislawski (1/07/2011) • Markus Babbel (10/02/2012)

1.FC KAISERSLAUTERN
2011-12

Jy	30	BFCDynamo	W	3-0	DPr1	Ilicevic [18], Tiffert [23], Petsos [50]	10 104
	6	W Bremen	L	0-2	BL	15	41 100
Aug	14	Augsburg	D	1-1	BL	17 Shechter [80]	40 248
	20	Köln	D	1-1	BL	15 Ilicevic [17]	47 200
	27	Bayern M	L	0-3	BL	17	49 780
	10	Gladbach	L	0-1	BL	17	52 083
Sep	17	Mainz	W	3-1	BL	15 OG [24], Shechter [54], Tiffert [73]	43 952
	24	Wolfsburg	L	0-1	BL	15	26 779
	30	Stuttgart	L	0-2	BL	16	46 186
	15	Schalke	W	2-1	BL	14 Tiffert [30p], Kouemaha [72]	61 673
Oct	22	Freiburg	W	1-0	BL	14 Shechter [75]	40 748
	26	E Frankfurt	W	1-0	DPr2	Sukuta-Pasu [119]	46 000
	30	Hamburg	D	1-1	BL	13 De Wit [38]	55 348
	5	Hoffenheim	D	1-1	BL	12 Kouemaha [73]	30 150
Nov	18	Leverkusen	L	0-2	BL	14	42 245
	26	Nürnberg	L	0-1	BL	16	37 266
	3	Hertha	D	1-1	BL	16 OG [6]	36 856
Dec	11	B Dortmund	D	1-1	BL	15 Olcay [60]	80 720
	18	Hannover	D	1-1	BL	16 Nemec [68]	36 019
	21	Hertha	L	1-3	DPr3	Shechter [51]	40 944
Jan	21	W Bremen	D	0-0	BL	16	40 381
	28	Augsburg	D	2-2	BL	16 Dick 2 [25 48]	30 028
	5	Köln	L	0-1	BL	16	38 043
Feb	11	Bayern M	L	0-2	BL	16	69 000
	18	Gladbach	L	1-2	BL	16 Jessen [63]	45 661
	25	Mainz	L	0-4	BL	17	34 000
	3	Wolfsburg	D	0-0	BL	18	34 110
	9	Stuttgart	D	0-0	BL	18	50 100
Mar	18	Schalke	L	1-4	BL	18 Rodnei [3]	49 780
	24	Freiburg	L	0-2	BL	18	24 000
	31	Hamburg	L	0-1	BL	18	44 745
	7	Hoffenheim	L	1-2	BL	18 Bugera [86]	40 296
Apr	1	Leverkusen	L	1-3	BL	18 Derstroff [42]	25 627
	14	Nürnberg	L	0-2	BL	18	42 552
	21	Hertha	W	2-1	BL	18 Kirch [27], Wooten [38]	51 461
	28	B Dortmund	L	2-5	BL	18 OG [16], De Wit [49]	49 780
My	5	Hannover	L	1-2	BL	18 De Wit [7]	49 000

18th Att: 721 382 • Av: 42 434 (-9.3%) • Fritz-Walter 49 780 (85%)

KAISERSLAUTERN LEAGUE APPEARANCES/GOALS 2011-12

Goalkeepers Tobias Sippel 11 • Kevin Trapp 23
Defenders Mathias Abel 20+2/0 • Martin Amedick 13+1/0
Alexander Bugera 20/1 • Florian Dick 32/2 • Dominique Heintz 0+1/0
Leon Jessen DEN 13+2/1 • Willi Orban 1+1/0 • Rodnei BRA 21+1/1
Jan Simunek CZE 6/0 • Anthar Yahia ALG 9+2/0
Midfield Ariel Borysiuk POL 12/0 • Pierre De Wit 24+1/3
Kostas Fortounis GRE 18+10/0 • Ivo Ilicevic CRO 4/1
Oliver Kirch 19+4/1 • Olcay Sahan TUR 23+4/1
Thanos Petsos GRE 9+10/0 • Christian Tiffert 31/2
Gil Vermouth ISR 0+2/0 • Clemens Walch AUT 3+2/0
Steven Zellner 0+1/0
Forwards Julian Derstroff 9+3/1 • Nicolai Jorgensen DEN 1+4/0
Dorge Kouemaha CMR 13+4/2 • Adam Nemec SVK 0+4/1
Itay Shechter ISR 13+10/3 • Richard Sukuta-Pasu 12+12/0
Jakub Swierczok POL 3+3/0 • Sandro Wagner 9+2/0
Andrew Wooten USA 2+5/1
Coach Marco Kurz • Krassimir Balakov BUL (22/03/2012)

1.FC KÖLN
2011-12

Jy	31	Wiedenbrück	W	3-0	DPr1	Novakovic 2 [23 45], Jajalo [78]	12 200
	6	Wolfsburg	L	0-3	BL	17	47 000
	13	Schalke	L	1-5	BL	18 Podolski [12]	61 673
Aug	20	Kaiser'tern	D	1-1	BL	18 Jajalo [19]	47 200
	27	Hamburg	W	4-3	BL	14 Chihi [21], Novakovic [49], Clemens [84], McKenna [88]	51 289
	11	Nürnberg	L	1-2	BL	15 Chihi [39]	43 200
Sep	17	Leverkusen	W	4-1	BL	12 Novakovic [44], Podolski 2 [47 54], Jajalo [90]	30 210
	25	Hoffenheim	W	2-0	BL	10 Jajalo [20], Podolski [64]	45 500
	1	Hertha	L	0-3	BL	12	59 491
	16	Hannover	W	2-0	BL	10 Podolski 2 [24 86]	46 000
Oct	22	B Dortmund	L	0-5	BL	12	80 720
	25	Hoffenheim	L	1-2	DPr2	Jajalo [6]	16 000
	30	Augsburg	W	3-0	BL	11 Podolski 2 [19 24], Peszko [56]	48 000
Nov	5	W Bremen	L	2-3	BL	11 Clemens [3], Podolski [45]	41 500
	25	Gladbach	L	0-3	BL	11	50 000
	3	Stuttgart	D	2-2	BL	11 Podolski 2 [15 88]	56 255
Dec	10	Freiburg	W	4-0	BL	11 Clemens 2 [20 66], Podolski 2 [61 73]	44 500
	13	Mainz	D	1-1	BL	10 Podolski [85]	44 800
	16	Bayern M	L	0-3	BL	10	69 000
	21	Wolfsburg	L	0-1	BL	11	27 057
Jan	28	Schalke	L	1-4	BL	14 Podolski [4]	50 000
	5	Kaiser'tern	W	1-0	BL	9 Roshi [72]	38 043
Feb	12	Hamburg	L	0-1	BL	12	46 500
	18	Nürnberg	L	1-2	BL	14 Novakovic [66]	38 101
	25	Leverkusen	L	0-2	BL	14	46 500
	4	Hoffenheim	D	1-1	BL	14 Podolski [81]	29 250
	10	Hertha	W	1-0	BL	13 Clemens [36]	48 000
Mar	18	Hannover	L	1-4	BL	13 Pezzoni [43]	45 000
	25	B Dortmund	L	1-6	BL	16 Novakovic [13]	50 000
	31	Augsburg	L	1-2	BL	16 Podolski [42p]	30 000
	7	W Bremen	D	1-1	BL	16 Jemal [39]	50 000
Apr	10	Mainz	L	0-4	BL	16	34 000
	15	Gladbach	L	0-3	BL	16	52 990
	21	Stuttgart	D	1-1	BL	16 Peszko [50]	50 000
	28	Freiburg	L	1-4	BL	16 Podolski [47]	24 000
My	5	Bayern M	L	1-4	BL	17 Novakovic [63]	50 000

17th Att: 807 200 • Av: 47 482 (-0.6%) • RheinEnergie 50 000 (94%)

KÖLN LEAGUE APPEARANCES/GOALS 2011-12

Goalkeepers Michael Rensing 32 • Miro Varvodic CRO 2
Defenders Andrezinho BRA 4+3/0 • Miso Brecko SVN 25+2/0
Christian Eichner 25+4/0 • Geromel BRA 27+1/0
Ammar Jemal TUN 13+2/1 • Tomoaki Makino JPN 0+3/0
Kevin McKenna CAN 14+11/1 • Sereno POR 25/0
Midfield Christopher Buchtmann 0+2/0 • Adil Chihi MAR 10/2
Christian Clemens 23+8/5 • Mato Jajalo CRO 25+6/3
Martin Lanig 27+4/0 • Adam Matuszczyk POL 2+7/0
Slawomir Peszko POL 31+1/2 • Kevin Pezzoni 4+8/1
Sascha Riether 33/0 • Odise Roshi ALB 3+17/1 • Mitchell Weiser 0+1/0
Forwards Sebastian Freis 0+4/0 • Mikael Ishak SWE 3+8/0
Milivoje Novakovic SVN 18+2/5 • Lukas Podolski 28+1/18
Chong Tese PRK 0+5/0
Coach Stale Solbakken (1/07/2011) • Frank Schaefer (12/04/2012)

1.FSV MAINZ 05
2011–12

Jly	28	Gaz Metan	D	1-1	ELp3	Bungert [30]	15 759
	31	Zweibrücken	W	2-1	DPr1	Sliskovic [95], Allagui [115]	12 000
Aug	4	Gaz Metan	D	1-1	ELp3	Risse [31], L 3-4p	5 500
	7	Leverkusen	W	2-0	BL 4	Allagui [32], OG [86]	32 443
	13	Freiburg	W	2-1	BL 1	Risse [64], Choupo-Moting [79]	20 600
	21	Schalke	L	2-4	BL 8	Ivanschitz [7], Soto [12]	34 000
	28	Hannover	D	1-1	BL 7	Allagui [2]	40 420
Sep	10	Hoffenheim	L	0-4	BL 12		31 500
	17	Kaiser'tern	L	1-3	BL 13	Choupo-Moting [15]	43 952
	24	B Dortmund	L	1-2	BL 14	Muller [32]	34 000
Oct	1	Nürnberg	D	3-3	BL 14	Bungert [32], Choupo-Moting [45], Ivanschitz [52]	38 107
	15	Augsburg	L	0-1	BL 15		30 195
	22	Hertha	D	0-0	BL 15		47 064
	26	Hannover	W	1-0	DPr2	Ivanschitz [93]	30 100
	29	W Bremen	L	1-3	BL 15	Bungert [23]	34 000
Nov	4	Stuttgart	W	3-1	BL 14	Ujah [2 52 63], Ivanschitz [59p]	34 000
	27	Bayern M	W	3-2	BL 13	Ivanschitz [10], Caligiuri [65], Bungert [74]	34 000
Dec	3	Wolfsburg	D	2-2	BL 12	Ivanschitz [70p], Choupo-Moting [81]	24 321
	10	Hamburg	D	0-0	BL 12		34 000
	13	Köln	D	1-1	BL 12	Allagui [70]	44 800
	18	Gladbach	L	0-1	BL 14		49 089
	21	H'stein Kiel	L	0-2	DPr3		10 649
	22	Leverkusen	L	2-3	BL 15	Polanski [51], Caligiuri [53]	24 365
Jan	29	Freiburg	W	3-1	BL 12	Choupo-Moting 2 [2 17], Polanski [5p]	30 938
Feb	4	Schalke	D	1-1	BL 13	Zidan [15]	60 557
	11	Hannover	D	1-1	BL 13	Zidan [7]	30 173
	17	Hoffenheim	D	1-1	BL 13	Zidan [29]	24 300
	25	Kaiser'tern	W	4-0	BL 11	Zidan [2], Szalai [17], Muller [31], Choupo-Moting [74]	34 000
Mar	3	B Dortmund	L	1-2	BL 12	Zidan [74]	80 720
	10	Nürnberg	W	2-1	BL 11	Muller [1], Zidan [23]	34 000
	17	Augsburg	L	1-2	BL 11	Allagui [36]	30 025
	24	Hertha	L	1-3	BL 12	Choupo-Moting [58]	33 152
	31	W Bremen	W	3-0	BL 11	Szalai [18] Choupo-Moting 2 [48 74]	40 132
Apr	7	Stuttgart	L	1-4	BL 11	Ivanschitz [3p]	55 100
	10	Köln	W	4-0	BL 12	Polanski [19p], Zidan [31], Muller [37], Szalai [54]	34 000
	14	Bayern M	D	0-0	BL 12		69 000
	20	Wolfsburg	D	0-0	BL 12		31 069
	28	Hamburg	D	0-0	BL 13		56 537
My	5	Gladbach	L	0-3	BL 13		34 000

13th Att: 559 470 • Av: 32 910 (+38.7%) • Coface Arena 34 034 (96%)

MAINZ LEAGUE APPEARANCES/GOALS 2011-12
Goalkeepers Heinz Muller 12 • Christian Wetklo 22
Defenders Niko Bungert 27+2/3 • Malik Fathi 15+2/0
Jan Kirchhoff 22+7/0 • Nikolce Noveski MKD 24+2/0
Zdenek Pospech CZE 24+1/0 • Fabian Schonheim 0+1/0
Bo Svensson DEN 7+1/0 • Radoslav Zabavnik SVK 14/0
Midfield Julian Baumgartlinger AUT 14+12/0 • Marco Caligiuri 23+7/2
Andreas Ivanschitz AUT 16+10/6 • Yunus Malli 3+10/0
Nicolai Muller 17+6/4 • Eugen Polanski POL 24+2/3
Marcel Risse 9+1/1 • Elkin Soto COL 31/1 • Zoltan Stieber HUN 5+2/0
Forwards Sami Allagui TUN 13+6/4
Maxim Choupo-Moting CMR 23+11/10 • Mario Gavranovic SUI 1+4/0
Petar Sliskovic CRO 0+1/0 • Adam Szalai HUN 12+3/3
Anthony Ujah NGA 4+8/2 • Deniz Yilmaz TUR 1+1/0
Mohamed Zidan EGY 11+1/7
Coach Thomas Tuchel

1.FC NURNBERG
2011–12

Jly	30	A Bielefeld	W	5-1	DPr1	Feulner 3 [26 35 39], Mak [64], Pekhart [71]	12 705
	6	Hertha	W	1-0	BL 7	Pekhart [80]	61 118
Aug	18	Hannover	L	1-2	BL 9	Pekhart [56]	37 212
	20	B Dortmund	L	0-2	BL 12		78 400
	27	Augsburg	W	1-0	BL 10	Esswein [75]	43 071
	11	Köln	W	2-1	BL 7	Simons 2 [31p 36p]	43 200
Sep	17	W Bremen	D	1-1	BL 8	Wollscheid [62]	43 121
	24	Gladbach	L	0-1	BL 9		51 117
	1	Mainz	D	3-3	BL 11	Feulner [5], Mak [19], Pekhart [82]	38 107
Oct	15	Wolfsburg	L	1-2	BL 13	Eigler [69]	27 112
	22	Stuttgart	D	2-2	BL 13	Simons [10], Wollscheid [71]	46 486
	29	Bayern M	L	0-4	BL 14		69 000
Nov	5	Freiburg	L	1-2	BL 15	Frantz [32]	38 026
	19	Schalke	L	0-4	BL 16		61 673
	26	Kaiser'tern	W	1-0	BL 14	Chandler [13]	37 266
Dec	4	Hamburg	L	0-2	BL 15		45 473
	10	Hoffenheim	L	0-2	BL 16		35 389
	17	Leverkusen	W	3-0	BL 15	Didavi [8], Hegeler [22], Pekhart [73]	29 239
	20	G'ther Fürth	L	0-1	DPr3		48 548
Jan	21	Hertha	W	2-0	BL 12	Esswein [43], Maroh [84]	39 117
	27	Hannover	L	0-1	BL 13		35 400
Feb	3	B Dortmund	L	0-2	BL 14		45 572
	12	Augsburg	D	0-0	BL 14		30 660
	18	Köln	W	2-1	BL 12	Esswein [28], Pekhart [85]	38 101
	25	W Bremen	W	1-0	BL 10	Esswein [65]	40 204
	4	Gladbach	W	1-0	BL 9	Bunjaku [87]	45 675
Mar	10	Mainz	L	1-2	BL 9	Didavi [64]	34 000
	17	Wolfsburg	W	1-3	BL 10	Didavi [9]	39 320
	25	Stuttgart	L	0-1	BL 11		55 800
	31	Bayern M	L	0-1	BL 12		48 548
Apr	7	Freiburg	D	2-2	BL 12	Didavi [8], Pekhart [45]	24 000
	11	Schalke	W	4-1	BL 12	Balitsch [25], Simons [37p], Didavi 2 [45 87]	44 031
	14	Kaiser'tern	W	2-0	BL 11	Didavi [43], Pekhart [73]	42 552
	21	Hamburg	D	1-1	BL 11	Didavi [64]	45 873
	28	Hoffenheim	W	3-2	BL 10	Pekhart 2 [10 72], Didavi [45]	30 150
My	5	Leverkusen	L	0-4	BL 10	Mak [58]	48 548

10th Att: 713 463 • Av: 41 968 (-0.2%) • Frankenstadion 48 548 (86%)

NURNBERG LEAGUE APPEARANCES/GOALS 2011-12
Goalkeepers Patrick Rakovsky 2 • Raphael Schafer 25
Alexander Stephan 7+1
Defenders Timothy Chandler USA 29+1/1 • Timm Klose SUI 13/0
Dominic Maroh 19+2/1 • Per Nilsson SWE 3+2/0 • Javier Pinola 17/0
Marvin Plattenhardt 8+1/0 • Philipp Wollscheid 33/2
Midfield Hanno Balitsch 12/1 • Almog Cohen ISR 12+12/0
Daniel Didavi 18+5/9 • Markus Feulner 23+5/1 • Mike Frantz 7+6/1
Jens Hegeler 19+12/1 • Adam Hlousek CZE 11/0 • Juri Judt 1+1/0
Wilson Kamavuaka CGO 1+4/0 • Markus Mendler 4+3/0
Timmy Simons BEL 34/4 • Julian Wießmeier 1+7/0
Forwards Albert Bunjaku SUI 3+14/1 • Christian Eigler 13+10/1
Alexander Esswein 20+6/4 • Robert Mak SVK 10+7/2
Tomas Pekhart CZE 29+2/9
Coach Dieter Hecking

FC SCHALKE 04
2011–12

	23	B Dortmund	D	0-0	SC	W 4-3p	61 673
Jly	31	Teingen	W	11-1	DPr1	Huntelaar 4 [3 22 40 64], Papadopoulos [7], Raul 2 [13 32], Holtby 2 [58 75], Gavranovic 2 [70 79]	21 000
	6	Stuttgart	L	0-3	BL 17		60 000
Aug	13	Köln	W	5-1	BL 6	Huntelaar 3 [42p 47 84], Holtby [48], Raul [59]	61 673
	18	HJK Helsinki	L	0-2	ELpo		10 504

FC SCHALKE 04 2011-12 (CONT'D)

Aug	21 Mainz	W	4-2	BL	4	Huntelaar [57], Howedes [64], Matip [82], Fuchs [90]	34 000
	25 HJK Helsinki	W	6-1	ELpo		Huntelaar 4 [15p 25 49p 63], Papadopoulos [56], Draxler [82]	52 034
	28 Gladbach	W	1-0	BL	2	Raul [64]	61 673
Sep	11 Wolfsburg	L	1-2	BL	6	Raul [13]	30 000
	15 Steaua	D	0-0	ELgJ			12 390
	18 Bayern M	L	0-2	BL	9		61 673
	24 Freiburg	W	4-2	BL	5	Farfan [33], Huntelaar [62], Holtby [66], Raul [75]	60 545
	29 Mac Haifa	W	3-1	ELgJ		Fuchs 2 [8 66], Marin [82]	49 070
Oct	2 Hamburg	W	4-2	BL	4	Huntelaar 2 [13 73]	54 237
	15 Kaiser'tern	L	1-2	BL	6	Huntelaar [62p]	61 673
	20 AEK L'naca	W	5-0	ELgJ		Holtby [22], Huntelaar 2 [34 88], Matip [40], Draxler [87]	5 344
	23 Leverkusen	W	1-0	BL	3	Farfan [83]	30 210
	26 Karlsruhe	W	2-0	DPr2		Huntelaar [81], Matip [83]	28 916
	29 Hoffenheim	W	3-1	BL	2	Raul [28], Huntelaar 2 [73p 76]	60 384
Nov	3 AEK L'naca	D	0-0	ELgJ			52 077
	6 Hannover	D	2-2	BL	5	Pukki 2 [26 73]	49 000
	19 Nürnberg	W	3-0	BL		Huntelaar 2 [12 65], Raul [38], Holtby [84]	61 673
Dec	26 B Dortmund	L	0-2	BL	5		80 720
	1 Steaua	W	2-1	ELgJ		Papadopoulos [25], Raul [57]	53 123
	4 Augsburg	W	3-1	BL	4	Huntelaar [16], Fuchs [66], Raul [84]	58 641
	9 Hertha	W	2-1	BL	3	Huntelaar [19], Pukki [44]	52 382
	14 Mac Haifa	W	3-0	ELgJ		OG [7], Marica [84], Wiegel [92+]	11 234
	17 W Bremen	W	5-0	BL	3	Raul 3 [16 20 63], Papadopoulos [67], Huntelaar [70]	61 673
Jan	21 Gladbach	L	1-3	DPr3		Draxler [70]	54 057
	21 Stuttgart	W	3-1	BL	3	Matip [3], Papadopoulos [58], Draxler [80]	61 673
	28 Köln	W	4-1	BL	3	Marica 2 [60 72], Huntelaar [78p]	50 000
	4 Mainz	D	1-1	BL	3	Obasi [59]	60 557
	11 Gladbach	L	0-3	BL	4		54 057
	16 Vik Plzen	D	1-1	ELr2			11 435
Feb	19 Wolfsburg	W	4-0	BL	4	Raul [10], Huntelaar 2 [15 72], Matip [49]	60 511
	23 Vik Plzen	W	3-1	ELr2		Huntelaar 3 [8 106 121+]	54 142
	26 Bayern M	L	0-2	BL	4		69 000
	3 Freiburg	L	1-2	BL	4	Pukki [72]	24 000
	8 Twente	L	0-1	ELr3			30 000
Mar	11 Hamburg	W	3-1	BL	3	Pukki [5], Metzelder [26], Huntelaar [33p]	61 673
	15 Twente	W	4-1	ELr3		Huntelaar 3 [29 56p 81], Jones [71]	54 142
	18 Kaiser'tern	W	4-1	BL	4	Holtby [39], Huntelaar [45], Raul [51], Farfan [83]	49 780
	24 Leverkusen	W	2-0	BL	3	Huntelaar 2 [18 86]	61 673
	29 Ath Bilbao	L	2-4	ELqf		Raul 2 [22 59]	53 883
Apr	1 Hoffenheim	D	1-1	BL	3	Huntelaar [80p]	30 150
	5 Ath Bilbao	D	2-2	ELqf		Huntelaar [29], Raul [52]	37 048
	8 Hannover	W	3-0	BL	3	Raul 2 [6 47], Huntelaar [63]	61 673
	11 Nürnberg	L	1-4	BL	3	Holtby [85]	44 031
	14 B Dortmund	L	1-2	BL	3	Farfan [9]	61 673
	22 Augsburg	D	1-1	BL	3	Huntelaar [38]	30 660
My	28 Hertha	W	4-0	BL	3	Huntelaar 2 [32 87], Holtby [73], Raul [84]	61 673
	5 W Bremen	W	3-2	BL	3	Draxler [30], Huntelaar 2 [65 73]	42 100

3rd Att: 1 040 714 • Av: 61 218 (-0.1%) • Veltins-Arena 61 673 (99%)

SCHALKE LEAGUE APPEARANCES/GOALS 2011-12
Goalkeepers Ralf Fahrmann 9 • Timo Hildebrand 5+1
Mathias Schober 0+1 • Lars Unnerstall 20+1
Defenders Sergio Escudero ESP 4+2/0 • Christian Fuchs AUT 29/2
Tim Hoogland 1+2/0 • Benedikt Howedes 21+1/1 • Joel Matip CMR 30/3
Christoph Metzelder 11+5/1 • Kyriakos Papadopoulos GRE 28+1/2
Atsuto Uchida JPN 17+1/0
Midfield Alexander Baumjohann 4+4/0 • Julian Draxler 21+9/2
Marco Hoger 19+8/1 • Lewis Holtby 22+5/6
Jermaine Jones USA 18+2/0 • Jurado ESP 10+8/0 • Peer Kluge 2+1/0
Jan Moravek CZE 2+4/0 • Christoph Moritz 4+4/0
Forwards Edu BRA 0+1/0 • Jefferson Farfan PER 19+4/4
Klaas-Jan Huntelaar NED 32/29 • Ciprian Marica ROU 3+18/2
Chinedu Obasi NGA 6+4/1 • Teemu Pukki FIN 5+14/5 • Raul ESP 32/15
Coach Ralf Rangnick • Huub Stevens NED (27/09/2011)

VFB STUTTGART 2011-12

Jy	29 Wiesbaden	W	2-1	DPr1		Bicakcic [5], Kuzmanovic [51]	11 600
Aug	6 Schalke	W	3-0	BL	1	Cacau [37], Harnik [56], Okazaki [89]	60 000
	13 Gladbach	D	1-1	BL	3	Cacau [71]	48 322
	20 Leverkusen	L	0-1	BL	10		53 000
	26 Hertha	L	0-1	BL	12		52 232
Sep	10 Hannover	W	3-0	BL	10	Okazaki [9], Kuzmanovic [79], Tasci [86]	53 000
	16 Freiburg	W	2-1	BL	6	Harnik 2 [33 73]	24 000
	23 Hamburg	L	1-2	BL	7	Harnik [18]	55 700
Oct	30 Kaiser'tern	W	2-0	BL	7	Cacau [52], Boulahrouz [69]	46 186
	15 Hoffenheim	W	2-0	BL	4	Okazaki [48], Pogrebnyak [77p]	55 000
	22 Nürnberg	D	2-2	BL	5	Kuzmanovic [61p], Maza [84]	46 486
	26 FSV Fr'kfurt	W	3-0	DPr2		Hemlein [4], Cacau [38], Traore [89]	18 270
	29 B Dortmund	D	1-1	BL	6	Tasci [22]	60 000
Nov	4 Mainz	L	1-3	BL	7	Cacau [50]	34 000
	20 Augsburg	W	2-1	BL	6	Harnik 2 [41 51]	60 000
	27 W Bremen	L	0-2	BL	7		40 800
Dec	3 Köln	D	2-2	BL	7	Gentner 2 [29 36]	56 255
	11 Bayern M	L	1-2	BL	7	Gentner [6]	60 469
	17 Wolfsburg	L	0-1	BL	8		25 944
	21 Hamburg	W	2-1	DPr3		Cacau 2 [23 63]	38 600
Jan	21 Schalke	L	1-3	BL	10	Okazaki [87]	61 673
	29 Gladbach	L	0-3	BL	10		53 600
Feb	4 Leverkusen	D	2-2	BL	11	Schieber [23], Harnik [89]	27 929
	8 Bayern M	L	0-2	DPqf			57 500
	11 Hertha	W	5-0	BL	9	Ibisevic [24], Harnik 3 [28 41 58], Okazaki [32]	45 000
	19 Hannover	L	2-4	BL	9	Harnik [75], Okazaki [79]	37 800
	25 Freiburg	W	4-1	BL	8	Harnik 2 [12 83], Okazaki [21], Boulahrouz [63]	46 000
Mar	3 Hamburg	W	4-0	BL	8	Ibisevic [23], Harnik [90], Kuzmanovic 2 [31p 47p]	55 263
	9 Kaiser'tern	D	0-0	BL	8		50 100
	16 Hoffenheim	W	2-1	BL	8	Ibisevic 2 [8 43]	30 150
	25 Nürnberg	W	1-0	BL	7	Cacau [78]	55 000
	30 B Dortmund	D	4-4	BL	6	Ibisevic [71], Schieber 2 [77 79], Gentner [90]	80 720
Apr	7 Mainz	W	4-1	BL	5	Hajnal [8], Ibisevic 2 [49 85], Kuzmanovic [66p]	55 100
	10 Augsburg	W	3-1	BL	5	Tasci [24], Harnik [34], Ibisevic [84]	30 660
	13 W Bremen	W	2-1	BL	5	Gentner [37], Harnik 2 [45 53], Cacau [89]	59 000
	21 Köln	D	1-1	BL	5	Cacau [71]	50 000
	28 Bayern M	L	0-2	BL	6		69 000
My	5 Wolfsburg	W	3-2	BL	6	Cacau [73], Maza [77], Traore [80]	58 500

6th Att: 936 524 • Av: 55 090 (+142%) • Mercedes-Benz 60 441 (91%)

STUTTGART LEAGUE APPEARANCES/GOALS 2011-12
Goalkeepers Sven Ulreich 34
Defenders Arthur Boka CIV 10+3/0 • Khalid Boulahrouz NED 21/2
Stefano Celozzi 2/0 • Matthieu Delpierre FRA 1/0 • Maza MEX 24+2/2
Cristian Molinaro ITA 19+4/0 • Georg Niedermeier 15+2/0
Antonio Rudiger 1/0 • Gotoku Sakai JPN 14/0 • Serdar Tasci 28/3
Midfield Mamadou Bah GUI 0+3/0 • Timo Gebhart 2+10/0
Christian Gentner 16+12/5 • Tamas Hajnal HUN 30+3/1
Raphael Holzhauser AUT 0+2/0 • Zdravko Kuzmanovic SRB 22+4/5
William Kvist DEN 33/0 • Ibrahima Traore GUI 1+11/1
Forwards Cacau 20+13/8 • Martin Harnik AUT 33+1/17
Christoph Hemlein 0+3/0 • Vedad Ibisevic BIH 15/8
Shinji Okazaki JPN 18+8/7 • Pavel Pogrebnyak RUS 5+9/1
Julian Schieber 10+8/3
Coach Bruno Labbadia

WERDER BREMEN 2011–12

Jy	30	Heidenheim	L 1-2	DPr1	Rosenberg [33]	10 000
	6	Kaiser'tern	W 2-0	BL 4	Rosenberg 2 [60 81]	41 100
	14	Leverkusen	L 0-1	BL 8		30 210
Aug	20	Freiburg	W 5-3	BL 6	Fritz [30], Pizarro [34], Hunt [87p], Arnautovic [65], Wesley [90]	39 201
	27	Hoffenheim	W 2-1	BL 3	Arnautovic [38], Rosenberg [83]	28 750
	10	Hamburg	W 2-0	BL 2	Pizarro 2 [52 78]	41 600
Sep	17	Nürnberg	D 1-1	BL 2	Mehmet [24]	43 121
	25	Hertha	W 2-1	BL 2	Pizarro 2 [23 90]	40 760
	2	Hannover	L 2-3	BL 2	Arnautovic [45], Pizarro [83]	49 000
Oct	14	B Dortmund	L 0-2	BL 5		42 068
	21	Augsburg	D 1-1	BL 6	Pizarro [68]	30 660
	29	Mainz	W 3-1	BL 4	Pizarro [29], Hunt [47], Prodl [78]	34 000
	5	Köln	W 3-2	BL 3	Pizarro 3 [49 54p 86]	41 500
Nov	19	Gladbach	L 0-5	BL 5		53 465
	27	Stuttgart	W 2-0	BL 4	Hunt [57], Naldo [67]	40 800
	3	Bayern M	L 1-4	BL 5	Rosenberg [51]	69 000
Dec	10	Wolfsburg	W 4-1	BL 5	Papastathopoulos [18], Pizarro [45], Rosenberg [55], Arnautovic [71]	39 124
	17	Schalke	L 0-5	BL 5		61 673
Jan	21	Kaiser'tern	D 0-0	BL 5		40 381
	28	Leverkusen	L 1-1	BL 5	Pizarro [29]	40 060
	5	Freiburg	D 2-2	BL 5	Pizarro 2 [29 47]	22 000
	11	Hoffenheim	D 1-1	BL 5	Arnautovic [90]	39 176
Feb	18	Hamburg	W 3-1	BL 5	Marin [9], Trybull [45], Arnautovic [Helmes 32, Dejagah]	56 553
	25	Nürnberg	L 0-1	BL 6		40 204
	3	Hertha	L 0-1	BL 6		52 744
Mar	11	Hannover	W 3-0	BL 6	Pizarro [31], Prodl [49], Rosenberg [56]	41 500
	17	B Dortmund	L 0-1	BL 6		80 720
	24	Augsburg	D 1-1	BL 6	Fullkrug [61]	40 208
	31	Mainz	L 0-3	BL 8		40 132
	7	Köln	D 1-1	BL 7	Rosenberg [24]	50 000
Apr	10	Gladbach	D 2-2	BL 8	Rosenberg [18], Naldo [74]	42 100
	13	Stuttgart	L 1-4	BL 8	Rosenberg [25]	59 000
	21	Bayern M	L 1-2	BL 8	Naldo [51]	42 100
	28	Wolfsburg	L 1-3	BL 9	Rosenberg [45]	30 000
My	5	Schalke	L 2-3	BL 9	Pizarro 2 [41p 82]	42 100

9th Att: 693 733 • Av: 40 808 (+7.9%) • Weserstadion 42 100 (96%)

WERDER LEAGUE APPEARANCES/GOALS 2011-12
Goalkeepers Sebastian Mielitz 6+1/0 • Tim Wiese 28
Defenders Francois Affolter SUI 13/0 • Sebastian Boenisch POL 1+3/0
Clemens Fritz 32/1 • Florian Hartherz 10/0 • Per Mertesacker 4/0
Naldo BRA 12+6/3 • Sokratis Papastathopoulos GRE 30/1
Sebastian Prodl AUT 13+3/2 • Lukas Schmitz 20+6/0
Mikael Silvestre FRA 0+1/0 • Andreas Wolf 14+1/0
Midfield Philipp Bargfrede 21+2/0 • Tim Borowski 1/0
Aaron Hunt 18/3 • Aleksandar Ignjovski SRB 22+4/0
Zlatko Junuzovic AUT 15/0 • Felix Kroos 0+1/0 • Marko Marin 16+5/1
Mehmet Ekici TUR 11+10/1 • Aleksandar Stevanovic SRB 2+1/0
Florian Trinks 3+3/0 • Tom Trybull 14+1/1 • Wesley BRA 1+5/1
Forwards Marko Arnautovic AUT 10+9/6 • Niclas Fullkrug 1+10/1
Claudio Pizarro PER 28+1/18 • Markus Rosenberg SWE 26+7/10
Lennart Thy 2+1/0 • Sandro Wagner 0+7/0
Coach Thomas Schaaf

VFL WOLFSBURG 2011–12

Jy	29	RB Leipzig	L 2-3	DPr1	Lakic [25], Salihamidzic [28]	31 212
	6	Köln	W 3-0	BL 1	Helmes 2 [17 90], Schafer [85]	47 000
Aug	13	Bayern M	L 0-1	BL 5		30 000
	19	Gladbach	L 1-4	BL 11	Hasebe [13]	43 224
	27	Freiburg	L 0-3	BL 15		20 000
	11	Schalke	W 2-1	BL 13	Mandzukic 2 [33 82]	30 000
Sep	17	Hoffenheim	L 1-3	BL 14		26 850
	24	Kaiser'tern	W 1-0	BL 13	Dejagah [58]	28 195
	1	Leverkusen	L 1-3	BL 13	Mandzukic [59]	30 000
Oct	15	Nürnberg	W 2-1	BL 12	Mandzukic 2 [24 83p]	27 112
	22	Hamburg	D 1-1	BL 11	Mandzukic [2]	54 278
	29	Hertha	L 2-3	BL 12	Mandzukic [31], Schafer [84]	30 000
	5	B Dortmund	L 1-5	BL 13	Hleb [59]	80 720
Nov	19	Hannover	W 4-1	BL 12	Salihamidzic 2 [22 36], Chris [55], Madlung [74]	30 000
	26	Augsburg	L 0-2	BL 13		29 110
	3	Mainz	D 2-2	BL 14	Mandzukic [10], OG [41]	24 321
Dec	10	W Bremen	L 1-4	BL 14	Schafer [86]	39 124
	17	Stuttgart	W 1-0	BL 12	Polter [74]	25 944
Jan	21	Köln	W 1-0	BL 9	Polter [78]	27 057
	28	Bayern M	L 0-2	BL 9		69 000
	4	Gladbach	D 0-0	BL 10		30 000
Feb	10	Freiburg	W 3-2	BL 8	Jiracek 2 [5 61], Schafer [14]	23 057
	19	Schalke	L 0-4	BL 8		60 511
	25	Hoffenheim	L 1-2	BL 10	Helmes [69p]	23 921
	3	Kaiser'tern	D 0-0	BL 11		34 110
	10	Leverkusen	W 3-2	BL 10	Helmes [32], Dejagah [44], OG [60]	26 112
Mar	17	Nürnberg	W 3-1	BL 9	Mandzukic [15], Helmes 2 [24 54]	39 320
	23	Hamburg	W 2-1	BL 9	Mandzukic [46], Schafer [75]	30 000
	31	Hertha	W 4-1	BL 9	OG [29], Helmes 2 [34 81], Mandzukic [77]	46 388
	7	B Dortmund	L 1-3	BL 9	Mandzukic [61]	30 000
	11	Hannover	L 0-2	BL 10		43 800
Apr	14	Augsburg	L 1-2	BL 10	Helmes [27]	25 143
	20	Mainz	D 0-0	BL 10		31 069
	28	W Bremen	W 3-1	BL 8	Salihamidzic [40], Helmes 2 [66 89]	30 000
My	5	Stuttgart	L 2-3	BL 8	Helmes [28], Russ [60]	58 000

8th Att: 469 446 • Av: 27 614 (-4.5%) • Volkswagen Arena 30 000 (92%)

WOLFSBURG LEAGUE APPEARANCES/GOALS 2011-12
Goalkeepers Diego Benaglio SUI 32 • Marwin Hitz SUI 2
Defenders Hrvoje Cale CRO 0+1/0 • Chris BRA 7+1/1
Felipe Lopes BRA 13/0 • Simon Kjær DEN 3/0 • Robin Knoche 0+3/0
Sotirios Kyrgiakos GRE 7/0 • Alexander Madlung 17+6/1
Patrick Ochs 9+4/0 • Ricardo Rodriguez SUI 17/0 • Marco Russ 21+3/1
Marcel Schafer 34/5 • Michael Schulze 0+2/0 • Bjarne Thoelke 4+2/0
Midfield Maximilian Arnold 0+2/0 • Makoto Hasebe JPN 20+3/1
Thomas Hitzlsperger 2+4/0 • Aliaksandr Hleb BLR 1+3/1
Petr Jiracek CZE 9+4/2 • Josue BRA 26+2/0 • Koo Ja Cheol KOR 7+5/0
Yohandry Orozco VEN 4+1/0 • Jan Polak CZE 13+3/0
Hasan Salihamidzic BIH 10+5/3 • Sebastian Schindzielorz 0+2/0
Ibrahim Sissoko CIV 2/0 • Christian Trasch 29+4/0
Forwards Ashkan Dejagah IRN 24+2/3 • Patrick Helmes 15+1/12
Rasmus Jonsson SWE 3+8/0 • Srdan Lakic CRO 5+5/0
Mario Mandzukic CRO 30+2/12 • Sebastian Polter 1+11/2
Giovanni Sio CIV 1+8/0 • Vieirinha POR 6+3/0
Coach Felix Magath

GHA – GHANA

FIFA/COCA-COLA WORLD RANKING

'93	'94	'95	'96	'97	'98	'99	'00	'01	'02	'03	'04	'05	'06	'07	'08	'09	'10	'11	'12
37	26	29	25	57	48	48	57	59	61	78	77	50	28	43	25	34	16	29	30

2012

Jan	Feb	Mar	Apr	May	Jun	Jul	Aug	Sep	Oct	Nov	Dec	High	Low	Av
26	23	23	22	22	25	33	32	31	31	29	30	14	89	42

Ghana may have reached the semi-finals of the 2013 Africa Cup of Nations in South Africa but a fourth-place finish for a second successive tournament was seen as a failure. Ghana had credible hopes of ending a 30-year drought in the continental championship and finished top of their Port Elizabeth-based opening round group in convincing fashion. They then beat the Cape Verde Islands in the quarter-finals but despite being overwhelming favourites failed to beat Burkina Faso in their semi-final in Nelspruit. The Black Stars went out on post-match penalties after a controversial and drama-laden 1-1 draw. A fourth-place finish at the 2012 finals saw former Yugoslav international Goran Stevanovic pay the price for failing Ghanaian expectations, sacked after just 14 months in charge. His assistant Kwesi Appiah was given his job but faced similar pressure some 12 months later. With key FIFA World Cup qualifiers ahead in 2013 another shake up seemed unlikely. At the end of 2012 Ghana trailed group rivals Zambia after losing to them in Ndola in June having started their campaign with an impressive 7-0 thrashing of Lesotho. In club football Berekum Chelsea reached the group phase of the 2012 CAF Champions League but had their Premier League crown taken away by Asante Kotoko who were emphatic in their dominance of the season.

CAF AFRICA CUP OF NATIONS RECORD

1957-1959 DNE 1962 DNQ **1963** 1 Winners (hosts) **1965** 1 Winners 1968 2 F 1970 2 F 1972-1976 DNQ
1978 1 Winners (hosts) 1980 5 r1 **1982** 1 Winners 1984 6 r1 1986-1990 DNQ 1992 2 F 1994 5 QF 1996 4 SF 1998 11 r1
2000 8 QF (hosts) 2002 7 QF 2004 DNQ 2006 10 r1 2008 3 SF (hosts) 2010 2 F 2012 4 SF 2013 4 SF

GHANA FOOTBALL ASSOCIATION (GFA)

General Secretariat,
South East Ridge,
PO Box AN 19338, Accra
☎ +233 302660380
📠 +233 302668590
✉ info@ghanafa.org
🌐 www.ghanafa.org
FA 1957 CON 1958 FIFA 1958
P Kwesi Nyantakyi
GS Emmanuel Gyimah

THE STADIA

2014 FIFA World Cup Stadia

Baba Yara Stadium	
Kumasi	40 528

Other Main Stadia

Ohene Djan Stadium	
Accra	40 000
Len Clay Stadium	
Obuasi	30 000
Tamale Stadium	
Tamale	21 017
Essipong Stadium	
Sekondi	20 000

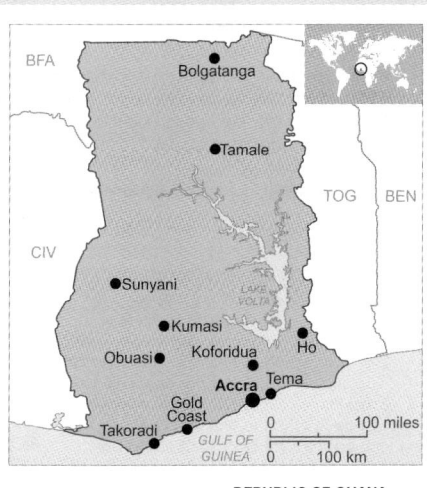

MAJOR CITIES/TOWNS

		Population
1	Accra	2 365 018
2	Kumasi	1 852 449
3	Tamale	447 349
4	Takoradi	308 266
5	Ashiaman	271 850
6	Tema	175 717
7	Cape Coast	175 710
8	Teshie	175 237
9	Sekondi	171 032
10	Obuasi	166 950
11	Madina	133 015
12	Koforidua	109 489
13	Wa	93 394
14	Techiman	87 407
15	Nungua	85 764
16	Tema New Town	84 470
17	Sunyani	81 716
18	Ho	81 532
19	Dome	71 757

REPUBLIC OF GHANA

Capital	Accra	Population	23 832 495 (47)	% in cities	50%
GDP per capita	$1500 (198)	Area km²	238 533 km² (81)	GMT +/-	0
Neighbours (km)	Burkina Faso 549, Cote d'Ivoire 668, Togo 877 • Coast 539				

RECENT INTERNATIONAL MATCHES PLAYED BY GHANA

2011	Opponents	Score	Venue	Comp	Scorers	Att	Referee
8-02	Togo	W 4-1	Antwerp	Fr	Dominic Adiyah [10], Jonathan Mensah [60], OG [69], Samuel Inkoom [83]		
27-03	Congo	W 3-0	Brazzaville	CNq	Prince Tagoe [24], Dominic Adiyah [44], Sulley Muntari [82]		Bennett RSA
29-03	England	D 1-1	London	Fr	Asamoah Gyan [90]	80 102	Cakir TUR
3-06	Congo	W 3-1	Kumasi	CNq	Isaac Vorsah [62], Prince Tagoe [66], Emmanuel Agyemang-Badu [78]		
7-06	Korea Republic	L 1-2	Jeonju	Fr	Asamoah Gyan [63]	41 271	Irmatov UZB
2-09	Swaziland	W 2-0	Accra	CNq	Asamoah Gyan [8], Emmanuel Agyemang-Badu [78]		
5-09	Brazil	L 0-1	London	Fr		25 700	Dean ENG
8-10	Sudan	W 2-0	Khartoum	CNq	Asamoah Gyan [11], John Mensah [20]		
11-10	Nigeria	D 0-0	Watford	Fr		5 000	Clattenburg ENG
15-11	Gabon	W 2-1	St Leu La Foret	Fr	Emmanuel Agyemang-Badu [15], Derek Asamoah [90]		
2012							
24-01	Botswana	W 1-0	Franceville	CNr1	John Mensah [25]	5 000	Diatta SEN
28-01	Mali	W 2-0	Franceville	CNr1	Asamoah Gyan [64], Andre Ayew [71]	7 000	Haimoudi ALG
1-02	Guinea	D 1-1	Franceville	CNr1	Emmanuel Agyemang-Badu [27]	5 500	Bennett RSA
5-02	Tunisia	W 2-1	Franceville	CNqf	John Mensah [9], Andre Ayew [100]	8 000	Alioum CMR
8-02	Zambia	L 0-1	Bata	CNsf		12 000	Benouza ALG
11-02	Mali	L 0-2	Malabo	CN3p		15 000	Grisha EGY
29-02	Chile	D 1-1	Chester	Fr	Richard Mpong [42]	7 000	Bazakos USA
1-06	Lesotho	W 7-0	Kumasi	WCq	Sulley Muntari [15], Dominic Adiyah 2 [24 49], Jordan Ayew 2 [45 89], Christian Atsu [86], Jerry Akaminko [91+]	38 000	Diatta SEN
9-06	Zambia	L 0-1	Ndola	WCq		40 000	Kordi TUN
15-08	China PR	D 1-1	Xian	Fr	Richmond Boakye [80]		Choi Myung Yong KOR
8-09	Malawi	W 2-0	Accra	CNq	Christian Atsu [8], Anthony Annan [51]		Benouza ALG
11-09	Liberia	L 0-2	Monrovia	Fr			Yekeh LBR
13-10	Malawi	W 1-0	Lilongwe	CNq	Afriyie Acquah [3]		Abdel Rahman SUD
14-11	Cape Verde Islands	W 1-0	Lisbon	Fr	Mubarak Wakaso [64]		
2013							
10-01	Egypt	W 3-0	Abu Dhabi	Fr	Emmanuel Agyemang-Badu [18], Richmond Boakye [54], Asamoah Gyan [83]		Mohamed UAE
13-01	Tunisia	W 4-2	Abu Dhabi	Fr	John Boye [63], Mubarak Wakaso [68], Asamoah Gyan [78], Albert Adomah [86]		
20-01	Congo DR	D 2-2	Port Elizabeth	CNr1	Emmanuel Agyemang-Badu [40], Asamoah Gyan [50]	7 000	Bennett RSA
24-01	Mali	W 1-0	Port Elizabeth	CNr1	Mubarak Wakaso [38p]	8 000	Doue CIV
28-01	Niger	W 3-0	Port Elizabeth	CNr1	Asamoah Gyan [6], Christian Atsu [23], John Boye [49]	8 000	Haimoudi ALG
2-02	Cape Verde Islands	W 2-0	Port Elizabeth	CNqf	Mubarak Wakaso 2 [54p 95+]	8 000	Seechurn MRI
6-02	Burkina Faso	D 1-1	Nelspruit	CNsf	Mubarak Wakaso [13p], L 2-3p	35 000	Jedidi TUN
9-02	Mali	L 1-3	Port Elizabeth	CN3p	Asamoah Gyan [82]	6 000	Otogo-Castane GAB

Fr = Friendly match • CN = CAF African Cup of Nations • WC = FIFA World Cup
q = qualifier • r1 = first round group • r2 = second round • qf = quarter-final • sf = semi-final • 3p = third place play-off

GHANA SQUAD FOR THE 2012 CAF AFRICA CUP OF NATIONS

	Player		Ap	G	Club	Date of Birth		Player		Ap	G	Club	Date of Birth
1	Daniel Adjei	GK	0		Liberty Pros	10 11 1989	12	Prince Tagoe	FW	0+4		Bursaspor TUR	9 11 1986
2	Daniel Opare	DF	0		Standard BEL	18 10 1990	13	Jordan Ayew	FW	3+1		Marseille FRA	11 09 1991
3	Asamoah Gyan	FW	5	2	Al Ain UAE	22 11 1985	14	Masahudu Alhassan	DF	3+2		Genoa ITA	1 12 1992
4	John Paintsil	DF	4		Leicester ENG	15 06 1981	15	Isaac Vorsah	DF	2+2		Hoffenheim GER	21 06 1988
5	John Mensah (c)	DF	3	2	Lyon FRA	29 11 1982	16	Adam Larsen Kwarasey	GK	6		Str'godset NOR	12 12 1987
6	Anthony Annan	MF	6		Vitesse NED	21 07 1986	17	Lee Addy	DF	2		Dalian CHN	7 07 1990
7	Samuel Inkoom	DF	5+1		Dnipro UKR	1 06 1989	18	Charles Takyi	MF	0+2		St. Pauli GER	12 11 1984
8	Emmanuel Agyemang	MF	4	1	Udinese ITA	2 12 1990	19	Jonathan Mensah	DF	2+1		Evian FRA	13 07 1990
9	Derek Boateng	DF	1+2		Dnipro UKR	2 05 1983	20	Kwadwo Asamoah	MF	5		Udinese ITA	9 12 1988
10	Andre Ayew	FW	6	2	Marseille FRA	17 12 1989	21	John Boye	DF	5		Rennes FRA	23 04 1987
11	Sulley Muntari	MF	3+2		Inter ITA	27 08 1984	22	Ernest Sowah	GK	0		B'kum Chelsea	31 03 1988
							23	Mohammed Abu	MF	1+1		E. Frankfurt GER	14 11 1991

Tr: Goran Stevanovic SRB 27-11-1966

GHANA 2011-12
GLO PREMIER LEAGUE

	Pl	W	D	L	F	A	Pts	Asante Kotoko	AshantiGold	Hearts of Oak	Medeama	New Edubiase	Aduana Stars	Chelsea	Liberty Pros	All Stars	Ebusua Dwarfs	Tema Youth	Heart of Lions	Arsenal	Wassaman Utd	Bechem Utd	Mighty Jets
Asante Kotoko †	30	18	9	3	43	18	**63**		3-0	2-1	2-1	1-1	0-0	0-0	2-0	2-0	1-0	1-0	2-0	0-0	4-1	4-3	1-0
AshantiGold	30	13	10	7	35	33	49	3-2		1-0	1-1	2-1	1-1	1-1	0-0	2-1	1-1	2-1	0-0	3-2	1-0	1-0	3-0
Hearts of Oak	30	12	11	7	31	20	47	0-0	3-2		2-1	2-0	0-0	0-0	0-1	3-0	0-0	0-0	2-2	4-0	3-0	0-0	2-1
Medeama	30	14	4	12	42	34	46	0-1	3-0	1-1		3-1	2-1	2-1	2-0	1-2	1-0	1-0	4-2	2-1	2-1	3-1	3-0
New Edubiase United	30	14	4	12	36	36	46	1-0	1-0	2-0	1-0		2-1	0-1	2-2	1-0	3-2	4-2	1-0	1-1	2-1	1-0	1-0
Aduana Stars	30	11	12	7	26	17	45	0-0	1-1	0-1	1-0	1-0		3-0	1-1	2-0	0-0	1-0	1-1	1-2	1-0	2-1	1-0
Berekum Chelsea	30	11	12	7	30	23	45	1-0	4-0	2-1	0-1	2-1	1-0		2-1	1-0	1-0	1-0	1-1	3-1	0-0	0-0	1-1
Liberty Professionals	30	11	9	10	38	30	42	1-2	3-1	2-0	2-2	1-1	1-0	1-1		0-0	3-1	1-0	5-1	1-0	1-1	5-0	2-1
All Stars	30	11	9	10	20	20	42	1-0	0-0	0-1	1-0	2-0	1-0	0-0	0-0		1-0	1-0	1-0	1-0	1-1	2-0	0-0
Ebusua Dwarfs	30	9	10	11	23	26	37	0-2	0-2	1-0	1-0	3-1	0-1	0-0	0-3	1-1		2-0	0-0	1-0	1-0	2-0	1-2
Tema Youth	30	9	8	13	32	33	35	1-1	1-1	1-1	3-0	2-1	0-1	3-1	1-0	1-0	0-3		3-0	2-1	1-1	3-0	2-2
Heart of Lions	30	7	13	10	22	30	34	0-0	0-2	0-1	0-0	1-0	0-3	1-0	2-0	1-0	1-1	0-1		3-0	1-0	0-0	0-0
Arsenal Berekum	30	7	9	14	24	39	30	1-1	1-1	0-1	3-2	2-1	0-0	1-0	2-1	1-1	0-1	1-0	0-3		2-1	0-0	0-0
Wassaman United	30	7	8	15	27	43	29	1-3	0-2	0-1	3-2	2-1	1-1	1-4	2-0	0-2	1-1	1-1	1-0	2-1		2-2	2-1
Bechem United	30	6	11	13	25	42	29	2-3	2-0	0-0	1-0	2-3	1-1	1-1	2-1	1-0	1-0	2-1	1-1	1-1	0-1		1-1
Tudu Mighty Jets	30	5	13	12	23	32	28	0-2	0-1	1-1	1-2	0-1	0-0	1-1	1-0	1-1	0-0	2-2	1-1	2-0	1-0	3-0	

9/10/2011 - 27/05/2012 • † Qualified for the CAF Champions League • Top scorer: **21** - Emmanuel **BAFFOUR**, New Edubiase Utd

MEDALS TABLE

		Overall G S B	League G S B	Cup G S	Africa G S B	City
1	Asante Kotoko	32 24 7	22 14 4	8 3	2 7 3	Kumasi
2	Hearts of Oak	30 17 9	19 11 7	9 4	2 2 2	Accra
3	Great Olympics	5 4 6	2 3 5	3 1	1	Accra
4	Real Republicans	5 1	1	4	1	Accra
5	Ashanti Gold	4 9 3	3 6 3	1 2	1	Obuasi
6	Cornerstones	2 6	4	2 2		Kumasi
7	Eleven Wise	2 5 3	1 3 3	1 2		Sekondi
8	Sekondi Hasaacas	2 4 2	1 3 1	1 1	1	Sekondi
9	Cape Coast Dwarfs	2 3 5	1 1 5	1 2		Cape Coast
10	Okwahu United	1 3 2	1 2	1 2		Nkawkaw
11	Ghapoha Tema	1 1		1 1		Tema
12	Aduana Stars	1	1			Dormaa Ahenkro
	Berekum Chelsea	1	1			Berekum
	Nania	1		1		Accra
	New Edubiase United	1		1		
	Voradep Ho	1		1		Ho
17	Real Tamale United	5 3	2 3	3		Tamale

MTN GHANA FA CUP 2012

Round of 16
- New Edubiase Utd — 2
- Heart of Lions — 0
- SP Mirren — 2
- Danbort FC — 3
- Tema Youth — 1
- Liberty Professionals — 0
- Inter Allies — 0 3p
- Wassaman United — 0 4p
- Berekum Chelsea — 0 7p
- Dorma Kyenkyenkye — 0 6p
- Asante Kotoko — 0
- Amidaus Pros — 2
- Hearts of Oak — 4
- Elmina Sharks — 1
- Wa All Stars — 1 3p
- AshantiGold — 1 4p

Quarter-finals
- New Edubiase Utd — 3
- Danbort FC — 0
- Tema Youth — 1
- Wassaman United — 2
- Berekum Chelsea — 1
- Amidaus Pros — 0
- Hearts of Oak — 2 4p
- AshantiGold — 2 5p

Semi-finals
- New Edubiase Utd — 1
- Wassaman United — 0
- Berekum Chelsea — 0
- AshantiGold — 1

Final
- New Edubiase Utd ‡ — 1
- AshantiGold — 0

‡ Qualified for the CAF Confederation Cup

CUP FINAL
Accra Sports Stadium
5-08-2012, Ref: Joseph Lamptey
Scorer - Ibrahim Moro [68] for NEU

GNB – GUINEA-BISSAU

FIFA/COCA-COLA WORLD RANKING

'93	'94	'95	'96	'97	'98	'99	'00	'01	'02	'03	'04	'05	'06	'07	'08	'09	'10	'11	'12
131	122	118	133	148	165	173	177	174	183	186	190	186	191	171	186	194	147	163	174

2012

Jan	Feb	Mar	Apr	May	Jun	Jul	Aug	Sep	Oct	Nov	Dec	High	Low	Av
162	166	168	170	169	169	169	169	171	173	175	174	115	195	166

Guinea-Bissau will take some comfort from the fact that they ran Cameroon close in the qualifiers for the 2013 Africa Cup of Nations, but in the end they were beaten 1-0 in both legs. Those were the only two matches played during the course of 2012 but they still managed to switch coaches between the two ties. Carlos Manuel, who played for Portugal at the 1986 FIFA World Cup finals, was named in place of compatriot Luis Norton de Matos just days before the second leg in June. The two defeats extended to eight, the winless streak of this small former Portuguese colony, whose last win was a 3-1 triumph over Gambia in a friendly international in Portugal in early 2011. Internal conflict within the football federation, which ultimately led to the resignation of president Jose Medina Lobato, led to the suspension of the championship for the year. A sponsorship deal of around 15,000 euros - the first ever in the history of the league - was secured for 2013 tournament which kicked-off in early 2013 with 10 clubs involved. A lack of finance has long hindered football in this West African country so the sponsorship deal, however small, was welcome but it is unlikely to enhance the possibility of the clubs taking part in the CAF club competitions where participation in the past has been intermittent at best.

CAF AFRICA CUP OF NATIONS RECORD
1957-1992 DNE 1994 DNQ 1996 Withdrew 1998-2004 DNE 2006 DNQ 2008 DNE 2010-2013 DNQ

FEDERAÇAO DE FUTEBOL DA GUINE-BISSAU (FFGB)
Alto Bandim (Nova Sede),
Case Postale 375,
1035 Bissau
☎ +245 3206914
📠 +245 3206914
✉ ffgb_bissau@hotmail.com

FA 1974 CON 1986 FIFA 1986
P Manuel Lopes Nascimento
GS Alberto da Silva Dias

MAJOR CITIES/TOWNS
Population
1	Bissau	423 478
2	Bafatá	22 791
3	Gabú	14 561
4	Bissorã	12 027
5	Bolama	9 998
6	Cacheu	9 882
7	Catió	9 342
8	Bubaque	9 229
9	Mansôa	7 414
10	Buba	6 456
11	Canchungo	6 467
12	Farim	6 439
13	Quebo	6 243
14	Quinhámel	2 885
15	Fulacunda	1 321

THE STADIA
2014 FIFA World Cup Stadia
Estádio Lino Correia
Bissau   12 000
Other Main Stadia
Estádio 24 de Setembro
Bissau   20 000

REPUBLICA DA GUINE-BISSAU • REPUBLIC OF GUINEA-BISSAU
Capital Bissau	Population 1 533 964 (150)	% in cities 30%
GDP per capita $600 (224)	Area km² 36 125 km² (137)	GMT +/- 0
Neighbours (km) Guinea 386, Senegal 338 • Coast 350		

RECENT INTERNATIONAL MATCHES PLAYED BY GUINEA-BISSAU

2002 Opponents	Score	Venue	Comp	Scorers	Att	Referee
No international matches played after June 2002						
2003						
10-10 Mali	L 1-2	Bissau	WCq	Dionisio Fernandes 50	22 000	Sowe GAM
14-11 Mali	L 0-2	Bamako	WCq		13 251	Seydou MTN
2004						
No International matches played in 2004						
2005						
18-11 Guinea	D 2-2	Conakry	ACr1	Manuel Fernandes 2 35p 49		
20-11 Sierra Leone	D 1-1	Conakry	ACr1	Agostino Soares 62		
25-11 Senegal †	D 1-1	Conakry	ACsf			
27-11 Mali †	L 0-1	Conakry	AC3p			
2006						
No international matches played in 2006						
2007						
17-10 Sierra Leone	L 0-1	Freetown	WCq		25 000	Mana NGA
17-11 Sierra Leone	D 0-0	Bissau	WCq		12 000	Lamptey GHA
2-12 Sierra Leone	W 2-0	Bissau	ACr1	Emiliano 8, Suleimane 49		
7-12 Cape Verde	D 1-1	Bissau	ACsf	Adilson 7. L 2-3p		
2008						
No international matches played in 2008						
2009						
No international matches played in 2009						
2010						
4-09 Kenya	W 1-0	Bissau	CNq	Dionisio 76		Bennaceur TUN
9-10 Angola	L 0-1	Luanda	CNq			Coulibaly MLI
16-11 Cape Verde Islands	L 1-2	Lisbon	Fr	Cicero 27		
2011						
9-02 Gambia	W 3-1	Lisbon	Fr	Cicero 3 78 90 94+		
26-03 Uganda	L 0-1	Bissau	CNq			
4-06 Uganda	L 0-2	Kampala	CNq			
3-09 Kenya	L 1-2	Nairobi	CNq	Ailton 81		
8-10 Angola	L 0-2	Bissau	CNq			
11-11 Togo	D 1-1	Bissau	WCq	Basile de Carvalho 38	3 000	Diedhiou SEN
15-11 Togo	L 0-1	Lome	WCq		25 000	Mohamadou CMR
2012						
29-02 Cameroon	L 0-1	Bissau	CNq			Gassama GAM
16-06 Cameroon	L 0-1	Yaounde	CNq			Bangoura GUI

AC = Amilcar Cabral Cup • CN = CAF African Cup of Nations • WC = FIFA World Cup
q = qualifier • r1 = first round group • sf = semi-final • 3p = third place play-off • † Not a full international

GRE – GREECE

FIFA/COCA-COLA WORLD RANKING

'93	'94	'95	'96	'97	'98	'99	'00	'01	'02	'03	'04	'05	'06	'07	'08	'09	'10	'11	'12
34	28	34	35	42	53	34	42	57	48	30	18	16	16	11	20	13	11	14	11

2012

Jan	Feb	Mar	Apr	May	Jun	Jul	Aug	Sep	Oct	Nov	Dec	High	Low	Av
14	14	13	14	14	15	12	12	11	10	12	11	8	66	27

The Greek national team made it past the group stage at a European Championship finals for only the second time when they surprisingly ousted group favourites Russia and hosts Poland at the finals of Euro 2012. They got their campaign off to a solid start by holding Poland to a 1-1 draw before a passionate crowd in the opening game of the tournament in Warsaw, but then seemed to have undone all of the good work by losing to a Czech Republic side that had already been thrashed by Russia. Coach Fernando Santos has quickly become a favourite of the Greek fans and a 1-0 win over Russia in the final group game showed just why. In the quarter-finals the Greeks then lost to the more powerful Germans, a tie that symbolised the political crisis sweeping the country at the time with many Greeks blaming the harsh austerity regime at home on Germany. Football offered little respite from the trauma many were experiencing in their daily lives. Attendances in the Super League were down by nearly 25 percent from the previous year although that may have something to do with the dominance of Olympiacos who won their 14th title in 16 seasons. With an average attendance nearly double that of their nearest rivals PAOK, Olympiacos were in another league financially and unsurprisingly they also won the cup to complete a fifth double in eight years.

UEFA EUROPEAN CHAMPIONSHIP RECORD

1960 r1 **1964** DNE **1968-1976** DNQ **1980** 8 r1 **1984-2000** DNQ **2004** 1 Winners **2008** 16 r1 **2012** 7 QF

HELLENIC FOOTBALL FEDERATION (HFF)

Goudi Park,
PO Box 14161,
11510 Athens
☎ +30 210 9306000
📠 +30 210 9359666
✉ epo@epo.gr
🖥 www.epo.gr
FA 1926 CON 1954 FIFA 1927
P George Sarris
GS Pafsanias Papanikolaoy

THE STADIA

2014 FIFA World Cup Stadia
Karaiskaki
Piraeus   33 334

Other Main Stadia
Olympiakó Stádio 'Spiros Louis'
Athens   69 618
Toumba
Thessaloníki   28 701
Pankritio
Irákleio   26 400
AEL Arena
Larissa   16 118

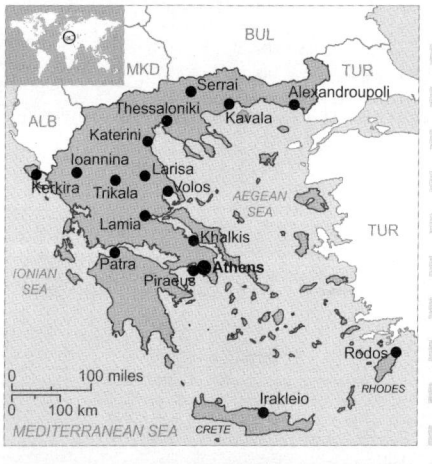

MAJOR CITIES/TOWNS

		Population
1	Athens	752 573
2	Thessaloníki	348 858
3	Piraeus	178 390
4	Pátra	166 815
5	Peristéri	144 911
6	Irákleio	137 291
7	Lárisa	134 138
8	Kallithéa	111 595
9	Glifáda	102 656
10	Níkaia	101 592
11	Kalamariá	96 986
12	Akharnaí	94 771
13	Ilion	86 984
14	Keratsínion	82 775
15	Vólos	82 046
16	Néa Smírni	81 126
17	Ilioúpoli	80 878
18	Khalándrion	80 854
19	Amaroúsion	79 088

ELLINIKI DHIMOKRATIA • HELLENIC REPUBLIC

Capital	Athens	Population	10 737 428 (74)	% in cities	61%
GDP per capita	$32 100 (40)	Area km²	131 957 km² (96)	GMT +/-	+2

Neighbours (km) Albania 282, Bulgaria 494, Turkey 206, Macedonia FYR 246 • Coast 13 676

RECENT INTERNATIONAL MATCHES PLAYED BY GREECE

2010	Opponents	Score	Venue	Comp	Scorers	Att	Referee
3-03	Senegal	L 0-2	Volos	Fr		10 000	Skomina SVN
25-05	Korea DPR	D 2-2	Altach	Fr	Katsouranis [2], Charisteas [48]	3 000	Schorgenhofer AUT
2-06	Paraguay	L 0-2	Winterthur	Fr		5 200	Circhetta SUI
12-06	Korea Republic	L 0-2	Port Elizabeth	WCr1		31 513	Hester NZL
17-06	Nigeria	W 2-1	Bloemfontein	WCr1	Salpingidis [44], Torosidis [71]	31 593	Ruiz COL
22-06	Argentina	L 0-2	Polokwane	WCr1		38 891	Irmatov UZB
11-08	Serbia	W 1-0	Belgrade	Fr	Salpingidis [45]	10 000	Teixeira ESP
3-09	Georgia	D 1-1	Piraeus	ECq	Spiropoulos [72]	14 794	Clos ESP
7-09	Croatia	D 0-0	Zagreb	ECq		24 399	Larsen DEN
8-10	Latvia	W 1-0	Piraeus	ECq	Torosidis [58]	13 520	Damato ITA
12-10	Israel	W 2-1	Piraeus	ECq	Salpingidis [22], Karagounis [63p]	16 935	Hansson SWE
17-11	Austria	W 2-1	Vienna	Fr	Samaras [49], Fotakis [81]	16 200	Kever SUI
2011							
9-02	Canada	W 1-0	Larissa	Fr	Fetfatzidis [63]		Moen NOR
26-03	Malta	W 1-0	Ta'Qali	ECq	Torosidis [92+]	10 605	Weiner GER
29-03	Poland	D 0-0	Larissa	Fr		12 000	Atkinson ENG
4-06	Malta	W 3-1	Piaeus	ECq	Fetfatzidis 2 [7 63], Papadopoulos [26]	14 746	Gil POL
7-06	Ecuador	D 1-1	New York	Fr	Tziolis [16]	39 656	Geiger USA
10-08	Bosnia-Herzegovina	D 0-0	Sarajevo	Fr		12 000	Dabanovic MNE
2-09	Israel	W 1-0	Tel Aviv	ECq	Ninis [60]	13 100	Thomson SCO
6-09	Latvia	D 1-1	Riga	ECq	Papadopoulos [84]	5 415	Todorov BUL
7-10	Croatia	W 2-0	Piraeus	ECq	Samaras [71], Gekas [79]	27 200	Webb ENG
11-10	Georgia	W 2-1	Tbilisi	ECq	Fotakis [79], Charisteas [85]	7 824	Orsato ITA
11-11	Russia	D 1-1	Piraeus	Fr	Katsouranis [60]		Chapron FRA
15-11	Romania	L 1-3	Altach	Fr	Karagounis [34]	800	Gangl AUT
2012							
29-02	Belgium	D 1-1	Heraklion	Fr	Salpingidis [9]	15 000	Stalhammar SWE
26-05	Slovenia	D 1-1	Kufstein	Fr	Torosidis [8]	1 000	Schorgenhofer AUT
31-05	Armenia	W 1-0	Kufstein	Fr	Papadopoulos [24]	600	Harkam AUT
8-06	Poland	D 1-1	Warsaw	ECr1	Salpingidis [51]	56 826	Velasco ESP
12-06	Czech Republic	L 1-2	Wroclaw	ECr1	Gekas [53]	35 213	Lannoy FRA
16-06	Russia	W 1-0	Warsaw	ECr1	Karagounis [45]	58 145	Eriksson SWE
22-06	Germany	L 2-4	Gdansk	ECqf	Samaras [55], Salpingidis [89p]	43 000	Skomina SVN
15-08	Norway	W 3-2	Oslo	Fr	Torosidis [7], Papadopoulos [11], Mitroglou [56]	13 680	Kelly IRL
7-09	Latvia	W 2-1	Riga	WCq	Spiropoulos [57], Gekas [69]	7 956	Bebek CRO
11-09	Lithuania	W 2-0	Piraeus	WCq	Ninis [55], Mitroglou [72]	21 466	Courtney NIR
12-10	Bosnia-Herzegovina	D 0-0	Piraeus	WCq		26 211	Damato ITA
16-10	Slovakia	W 1-0	Bratislava	WCq	Salpingidis [63]	7 494	Collum SCO
14-11	Republic of Ireland	W 1-0	Dublin	Fr	Holevas [29]	16 256	Shmuelevich ISR

Fr = Friendly match • EC = UEFA EURO 2012 • WC = FIFA World Cup • q = qualifier • r1 = First round group

GREECE NATIONAL TEAM HISTORICAL RECORDS

Caps
122 - Giorgos Karagounis 1999- • **120** - Theodoros Zagorakis 1994-2007 • **100** - Kostas Katsouranis 2003- & Angelos Basinas 1999-2009 • **96** - Stratos Apostolakis 1986-98 • **90** - Antonis Nikopolidis 1999-2008 • **88** - Angelos Charisteas 2001- • **78** - Dimitris Saravakos 1982-94 • **77** - Stelios Giannakopoulos 1997-2008 & Tasos Mitropoulos 1978-94 • **76** - Panagiotis Tsalouchidis 1987-95 & Nikos Liberopoulos 1996- • **75** - Nikos Anastopoulos 1977-88 • **72** - Giourkas Seitaridis 2002-

Goals
29 - Nikos Anastopoulos 1977-88 • **25** - Angelos Charisteas 2001- • **23** - Theofanis Gekas 2005- • **22** - Dimitris Saravakos 1982-94 • **21** - Mimis Papaioannou 1963-78 • **18** - Nikos Machlas 1993-2002 • **17** - Demis Nikolaidis 1995-2004 • **16** - Panagiotis Tsalouchidis 1987-95

Coaches
For Greece coaches pre 1960 see Oliver's Almanack 2012 • Paul Barone FRA 1959-60 • Tryfonas Tzanetis 1960-61 • Antonis Migiakis 1961 • Tryfonas Tzanetis 1962-64 • Lakis Petropoulos & Ioannis Magiras 1964-65 • Panos Markovits 1966-67 • Lakis Petropoulos 1967 • Kostas Karapatis 1968 • Dan Georgiadis 1968-69 • Lakis Petropoulos 1969-71 • Bily Bingham NIR 1971-73 • Alketas Panagoulias 1973-76 • Lakis Petropoulos 1976-77 • Alketas Panagoulias 1977-81 • Christos Archontidis 1982-84 • Miltos Papapostolou 1984-88 • Alekos Sofianidis 1988-89 • Antonis Georgiadis 1989-91 • Stefanos Petritsis 1992 • Antonis Georgiadis 1992 • Alketas Panagoulias 1992-94 • Kostas Polychroniou 1994-98 • Anghel Iordanescu ROU 1998-99 • Vassilis Daniil 1999-2001 • Nikos Christidis 2001 • Otto Rehhagel GER 2001-10 • Fernando Santos POR 2010-

GREECE 2011-12

SUPER LEAGUE

	Pl	W	D	L	F	A	Pts	Olympiacos	Panathinaikos	PAOK	Atromitos	AEK	Asteras	Levadiakos	PAS Giannina	Aris	OFI Crete	Xánthi	Panionios	Kérkira	Ergotelis	Panetolikos	Doxa
Olympiacos †	30	23	4	3	68	17	73		1-1	2-1	1-0	2-0	7-2	3-1	2-0	3-0	2-2	2-1	2-0	0-1	3-0	2-0	6-0
Panathinaikos §3	30	22	3	5	54	23	66	0-3		0-2	1-0	3-2	3-1	3-0	3-1	1-0	3-1	3-0	3-0	1-0	4-0	4-0	1-0
PAOK Thessaloníki	30	14	8	8	45	27	50	0-2	1-3		3-1	3-0	2-3	3-1	1-2	0-0	0-0	1-0	1-0	0-0	2-1	3-0	2-0
Atromitos	30	13	11	6	32	26	50	0-2	1-1	0-0		1-0	0-1	1-1	0-0	0-0	2-0	1-0	2-1	3-1	1-0	2-1	2-0
AEK Athens	30	13	9	8	36	30	48	1-1	2-0	0-2	0-0		2-0	2-1	2-1	3-0	1-1	1-1	1-0	1-0	1-0	1-0	0-0
Asteras Tripolis	30	13	6	11	30	34	45	2-0	0-2	1-0	0-0	1-1		0-1	2-1	1-0	2-2	1-1	2-0	0-0	3-0	1-0	1-0
Levadiakos	30	11	6	13	33	42	39	0-4	1-0	4-3	2-2	0-2	0-1		1-1	1-1	0-2	2-0	0-0	4-3	0-1	2-0	1-0
PAS Giannina	30	10	8	12	30	35	38	0-4	0-1	2-2	1-2	2-1	3-1	2-0		0-0	0-0	0-2	0-0	2-1	1-1	1-0	1-0
Aris Thessaloníki §3	30	10	10	10	29	33	37	2-3	3-1	1-1	0-1	1-0	0-3	2-1	1-0		1-0	0-0	4-2	1-1	1-1	0-0	2-0
OFI Crete	30	10	7	13	27	32	37	0-2	0-1	0-2	1-1	3-1	3-0	0-1	0-2	0-1		1-0	0-1	1-0	1-0	1-0	2-0
Xánthi	30	10	6	14	31	35	36	1-0	2-3	0-0	3-0	3-4	0-1	1-1	1-2	0-2	3-1		1-0	1-0	4-2	0-1	1-0
Panionios	30	9	6	15	26	34	33	0-3	1-2	1-2	1-2	0-1	2-0	2-0	0-0	2-1	1-3	1-1		2-0	2-2	1-0	2-0
Kérkira	30	8	8	14	31	44	32	0-4	0-2	0-4	2-2	2-2	0-0	3-2	1-2	1-0	4-1	2-0	0-3		2-1	2-3	3-1
Ergotelis	30	7	8	15	27	44	29	2-3	0-2	2-1	2-2	1-1	2-0	0-1	2-1	1-1	0-1	1-2	1-0	1-0		0-0	2-1
Panetolikos	30	7	7	16	23	37	28	0-1	1-1	1-1	1-1	0-2	1-0	0-2	2-2	5-1	1-0	2-0	0-1	1-1	2-0		0-2
Doxa Dramas	30	4	5	21	11	42	17	0-0	0-1	0-2	0-1	1-1	1-0	0-2	1-2	1-3	0-1	0-2	0-0	0-1	1-1	2-1	

27/08/2011 - 22/04/2012 • † Qualified for the UEFA Champions League • ‡ Qualified for the Europa League • Attendance: 1,186,491 @ 4,985
§ = points deducted • Top scorers: **20** - Kevin **MIRALLAS** BEL, Olympiacos • **16** - Kostas **MITROGLU**, Atromitos • **15** - Sebastian **LETO** ARG, Panathinaikos • **12** - Stefanos **ATHANASIADIS**, PAOK & Rafik **DJEBBOUR** ALG, Olympiacos • **10** - **CHUMBINHO** BRA, OFI Crete/Levadiakos; Njazi **KUQI** FIN, Panionios & Marko **PANTELIC** SRB, Olympiacos • **9** - **LEONARDO** BRA, AEK Athens & Marko **MARKOVSKI** SRB, Xanthi

GREECE 2011-12 FOOTBALL LEAGUE (2)

	Pl	W	D	L	F	A	Pts
Panthrakikos	34	22	7	5	49	16	73
Veria	34	22	6	6	56	19	72
Kallithea †	34	19	7	8	58	32	64
Panachaiki † §5	34	20	6	8	55	33	61
Platanias †	34	17	9	8	41	20	60
Kallonis †	34	15	12	7	46	29	57
Panserraikos	34	16	9	9	39	22	57
Pierikos Katerini	34	16	7	11	41	30	55
Anagennisi Karditsas	34	13	5	16	42	46	44
Larisa	34	11	10	13	38	29	43
Iraklis Psachna	34	10	12	12	29	23	42
Thrasivoulos	34	11	9	14	37	40	42
Anagennisi Epanomis	34	10	9	15	29	44	39
Fokikos	34	8	11	15	27	38	35
Vyzas	34	9	7	18	24	42	34
Agrotikos Asteras	34	9	7	18	24	41	34
Ethnikos Asteras §3	33	5	9	20	14	62	21
Diagoras Rhodos §2	33	1	2	31	3	86	3

28/10/2011 - 23/05/2012 • † Play-offs • § = points deducted

CHAMPIONS/EUROPA LEAGUE PLAY-OFFS

	Pl	W	D	L	F	A	Pts	Pan	AEK	At	PAOK
Panathinaikos §4	6	3	1	2	5	4	14		1-0	1-1	2-0
AEK Athens	6	3	0	3	7	5	9	2-0		3-2	2-0
Atromitos	6	2	2	2	6	6	8	0-1	1-0		1-1
PAOK Thessaloníki	6	2	1	3	3	6	7	1-0	1-0	0-1	

2/05/2012 - 20/05/2012 • § = bonus points • Panathinaikos qualified for the Champions League, Atromitos & PAOK for the Europa League. AEK did not receive a license from UEFA to take part in the Europa League and were replaced by Asteras Tripolis

FOOTBALL LEAGUE PROMOTION PLAY-OFFS

	Pl	W	D	L	F	A	Pts	Pla	Kth	Knis	Pan
Platanias §1	6	3	1	2	7	5	11		0-1	3-0	1-0
Kallithea §2	6	2	2	2	6	5	10	2-0		0-0	2-2
Kallonis	6	2	2	2	5	4	8	0-0	1-0		4-0
Panachaiki §1	6	2	1	3	7	11	8	2-3	2-1	1-0	

13/06/2012 - 30/06/2012 • § = bonus points • Platanias promoted

MEDALS TABLE

		Overall	League	Cup	Europe	
		G S B	G S B	G S B	G S B	City
1	Olympiacos	64 28 10	**39** 17 10	**25** 11		Piraeus
2	Panathinaikos	37 32 19	20 21 17	17 10	1 2	Athens
3	AEK	24 26 16	11 19 15	13 7	1	Athens
4	PAOK	6 17 10	2 5 10	4 12		Thessaloníki
5	Aris	4 11 8	3 3 8	1 8		Thessaloníki
6	Larissa	3 3	1 1	2 2		Larissa
7	Panionios	2 6 3		2 3 2 4		Athens
8	Iraklis	1 7 2		3 2 1 4		Thessaloníki
9	OFI Crete	1 2 2		1 2 1 1		Irákleio
10	Ethnikos	1 2		2 1		Piraeus
11	Kastoria	1		1		Kastoria

KYPELLO ELLADOS 2011-12

Fourth Round

Olympiacos	3
Pierikos Katerini *	1
Levadiakos	1 3p
Thrasivoulos *	1 5p
Panathinaikos	1
Agrotikos Asteras *	0
Kallonis *	2 0 3p
Panionios	3 0 4p
Panserraikos	2
Ergotelis	0
AEP Iraklis *	0
Xánthi	2
Panetolikos	0 10p
Larisa *	0 9p
Panachaiki *	1
OFI Crete	3
Asteras Tripolis	5
Proodeftiki *	0
Diagoras Rhodos *	0
PAS Giannina	1
Doxa Dramas	1
Kallithea *	0
Platanias *	0
Kérkira	3
PAOK Thessaloniki	3
Ethnikos Asteras *	0
Kalamata *	1
AEK Athens	1
Aris Thessaloniki	2
Panthrakikos *	1
Anagennisi Epanomis *	2
Atromitos	3

Fifth Round

Olympiacos *	3
Thrasivoulos	0
Panathinaikos	0 3p
Panionios *	0 4p
Panserraikos	2
Xánthi *	1
Panetolikos *	1
OFI Crete	3
Asteras Tripolis	4
PAS Giannina *	1
Doxa Dramas	0
Kérkira *	2
PAOK Thessaloniki *	2
AEK Athens	0
Aris Thessaloniki	1
Atromitos *	2

Quarter-finals

Olympiacos *	4
Panionios	0
Panserraikos	0
OFI Crete *	3
Asteras Tripolis *	1
Kérkira	0
PAOK Thessaloniki *	1
Atromitos	2

Semi-finals

Olympiacos *	1 0
OFI Crete	0 0
Asteras Tripolis	0 2
Atromitos *	0 2

Final

Olympiacos	2
Atromitos	1

CUP FINAL

Olympic, Athens, 28-04-2012, 20:30
Att: 41,500, Ref: Ilias Spathas
Scorers - Djebbour [29], Fuster [119] for Olympiacos; Iglesias [76] for Atromitos
Olympiacos - Roy Carroll - Vasilis Torosidis (c), Jose Holebas●, Olof Mellberg, Avraam Papadopoulos - Pablo Orbaiz●, Giannis Maniatis (Francois Modesto 103), Jean Makoun (David Fuster 83), Djamel Abdoun (Ioannis Fettatzidis 72) - Rafik Djebbour, Kevin Mirallas. Tr: Ernesto Valverde
Atromitos - Charles Itandje - Ioannis Skondras (c)●, Evangelos Ikonomou●, Wayne Thomas●, Sokratis Fytanidis● - Walter Iglesias● (Francisco Zuela 98), Elini Dimoutsos, Andreas Tatos (Tasos Karamanos 63), Denis Epstein, Brito (Stelios Stakianakis 77) - Kostas Mitroglou. Tr: Giorgos Donis

Superleague clubs enter in the fourth round • * Home team/home team in the first leg

GRN – GRENADA

FIFA/COCA-COLA WORLD RANKING

'93	'94	'95	'96	'97	'98	'99	'00	'01	'02	'03	'04	'05	'06	'07	'08	'09	'10	'11	'12
143	142	141	127	111	117	121	143	133	131	154	144	151	163	176	118	138	94	134	138

2012

Jan	Feb	Mar	Apr	May	Jun	Jul	Aug	Sep	Oct	Nov	Dec	High	Low	Av
132	133	137	144	143	144	142	142	139	134	150	138	88	176	133

Second place at the 2008 Caribbean Cup and a semi-final appearance two years later has raised expectations in Grenada so it was with some disappointment that the national team crashed out of the 2012 tournament at the first hurdle in the qualifiers. Englishman Mike Adams, who had coached Grenada at the 2011 CONCACAF Gold Cup, was replaced in 2012 by local coach Alister Bellotte and his team were spared the first round of qualifying thanks to their excellent recent record in recent years. Instead, their first action was in a second round qualifying group that they hosted in Saint George's and they were very unlucky not to make it through to the finals in Antigua. Grenada finished level on points with French Guiana but were knocked out on goal difference and were left to regret the injury-time equaliser scored by French Guiana in their first match. In club football Hard Rock retained the league title that they had won in 2011 in a close race with Paradise, Grenada Boys and Queens Park Rangers. Hard Rock secured the trophy on the final day of the season with a 3-1 victory over Fontenoy United. The 2012 Waggy T Super Knock Out tournament gave the fans a spectacular end to the season with a thrilling final in which Paradise made up for their league failure by beating champions Hard Rock on penalties after a 4-4 draw.

CFU CARIBBEAN CUP RECORD

1989 2 F **1991** DNE **1992-1994-1996** DNQ **1997** 4 SF **1998** DNQ **1999** 5 r1 **2001-2007** DNQ **2008** 2 F **2010** 4 SF **2012** DNQ

GRENADA FOOTBALL ASSOCIATION (GFA)

National Stadium,
PO Box 326,
St George's
☎ +1 473 4409903
+1 473 4409973
gfa@spiceisle.com
www.grenadafa.com
FA 1924 CON 1969 FIFA 1978
P Cheney Joseph
GS Lester Smith

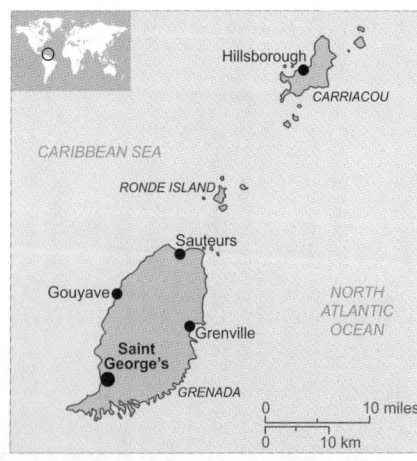

MAJOR CITIES/TOWNS

		Population
1	Saint George's	5 203
2	Gouyave	3 004
3	Grenville	2 379
4	Victoria	2 276
5	Saint Davids	1 315
6	Sauteurs	1 275
7	Hillsborough	789

THE STADIA

2014 FIFA World Cup Stadia
National Stadium
St George's   9 000
Other Main Stadia
Cricket National Stadium
St George's   20 000

GRENADA

Capital Saint George's
GDP per capita $13 200 (85)
Neighbours (km) Coast 121
Population 90 739 (195)
Area km² 344 km² (206)
% in cities 31%
GMT +/- -4

GRN – GRENADA

RECENT INTERNATIONAL MATCHES PLAYED BY GRENADA

2010	Opponents	Score		Venue	Comp	Scorers	Att	Referee
26-11	Martinique	D	1-1	Fort de France	CCr1	Kithson Bain [29]	5 000	Bogle JAM
28-11	Trinidad and Tobago	W	1-0	Fort de France	CCr1	Kithson Bain [69]	500	Cruz CRC
30-11	Cuba	D	0-0	Fort de France	CCr1		2 000	Bogle JAM
3-12	Jamaica	L	1-2	Fort de France	CCsf	Kithson Bain [13]	4 000	Taylor BRB
5-12	Cuba	L	0-1	Fort de France	CC3p		4 000	Lopez GUA
2011								
27-03	St Kitts and Nevis	D	0-0	Basseterre	Fr		1 000	Matthew SKN
2-04	St Kitts and Nevis	L	0-1	St George's	Fr		3 500	Bedeau GRN
27-05	Antigua and Barbuda	D	2-2	St George's	Fr	Clive Murray 2 [3 47]	3 500	Bedeau GRN
29-05	Panama	L	0-2	Panama City	Fr		5 000	Perea PAN
6-06	Jamaica	L	0-4	Carson/LA	GCr1		21 550	Toledo USA
10-06	Honduras	L	1-7	Miami	GCr1	Clive Murray [19]	18 057	Gantar CAN
13-06	Guatemala	L	0-4	Harrison/NY	GCr1		25 000	Toledo USA
2-09	Belize	L	0-3	St George's	WCq		2 600	Rubalcaba CUB
18-09	St Vincent/Grenadines	L	1-2	Kingstown	WCq	Cassim Langaigne [76]	2 500	Ward CAN
7-10	Belize	W	4-1	Belmopan	WCq	Shane Rennie [37], Marcus Julien [37], Lancaster Joseph [50], Clive Murray [80]	1 200	Jarquin NCA
15-10	St Vincent/Grenadines	D	1-1	St George's	WCq	Clive Murray [92+]	2 000	Willett ATG
11-11	Guatemala	L	0-3	Guatemala City	WCq		24 000	Andino HON
15-11	Guatemala	L	1-4	St George's	WCq	Shane Rennie [37p]	200	Angela ARU
2012								
22-02	Guyana	L	1-2	St George's	Fr	Marcus Julien [55]	5 000	Cambridge VIN
14-11	French Guiana	D	1-1	St George's	CNq	Craig Rocastle [33]	1 500	Jauregui CUW
16-11	Guyana	W	2-1	St George's	CNq	Kithson Bain [46], Clive Murray [81]	1 400	Brizan TRI
18-11	Haiti	L	0-2	St George's	CNq		3 000	Brizan TRI

Fr = Friendly match • CC = Digicel Caribbean Cup • WC = FIFA World Cup • q = qualifier • r1 = first round group • sf = semi-final • f = final

GRENADA 2012
PREMIER DIVISION

	Pl	W	D	L	F	A	Pts	Hard Rock	Paradise	GBSS	QPR	Hurricane	Eagles	Fontenoy	Chantimelle	Police	Boca Jun
Hard Rock	18	11	3	4	36	18	36		3-1	1-2	2-2	1-1	2-0	3-1	4-1	5-0	1-0
Lime Paradise	18	11	1	6	31	16	34	2-1		4-0	0-1	0-2	3-0	0-1	3-1	1-1	1-0
Grenada Boys SS	18	10	3	5	39	25	33	0-1	3-1		0-0	1-1	1-1	4-1	4-0	3-0	5-0
Queens Park Rangers	18	8	7	3	26	17	31	1-2	2-1	3-2		3-0	2-2	2-0	1-1	1-1	3-1
Carib Hurricane	18	7	7	4	27	21	28	1-1	0-1	2-3	2-1		2-2	3-0	0-0	1-0	1-0
Eagles Super Strikers	18	8	3	7	33	30	27	3-1	1-3	3-1	0-1	1-5		1-0	0-1	1-0	6-1
Fontenoy United	18	6	4	8	15	24	22	1-3	0-2	0-1	0-0	1-1	2-1		0-0	0-0	1-0
Chantimelle	18	5	5	8	27	32	20	1-2	0-3	5-0	2-0	1-3	3-5	0-2		1-0	3-3
Police	18	3	5	10	16	31	14	0-3	0-2	1-4	0-0	4-1	0-2	3-4	1-1		3-0
Boca Juniors	18	1	2	15	13	49	5	1-0	0-3	1-5	1-3	1-1	2-4	0-1	1-6	1-2	

9/06/2012 - 4/11/2012

GRENADA 2012
FIRST DIVISION

	Pl	W	D	L	F	A	Pts
Happy Hill	18	13	2	3	41	11	41
Ball Dogs	18	12	5	1	32	13	41
Five Stars	18	11	6	1	35	12	39
St John's Sports	18	7	5	6	29	23	26
Morne Jaloux	18	6	5	7	28	18	23
Honved	18	6	5	7	25	20	23
St Andrew's	18	7	2	9	23	29	23
South Stars	18	3	8	7	19	24	17
North Stars	18	3	1	14	14	49	10
Carenage	18	2	1	15	7	54	7

9/06/2012 - 4/11/2012

WAGGY T SUPER KNOCK OUT 2012

Quarter-finals		Semi-finals		Final		
Lime Paradise	3					
Real Ole Men	0	Lime Paradise	2			
Ball Dogs		Hurricane	1			
Hurricane				Lime Paradise	4	6p
GBSS				Hard Rock	4	5p
QPR		GBSS	1			
SGU Knights		**Hard Rock**	3			
Hard Rock						

National Stadium, 8-12-2011. Scorers - Wendell Rennie [7], Jake Rennie [12], Henderson Ettienne [34], Shane Rennie [78] for Paradise; Kimron Redhead 2 [1 6], Shavon John Brown [42], Tyron John [55] for Hard Rock

GUA – GUATEMALA

FIFA/COCA-COLA WORLD RANKING

'93	'94	'95	'96	'97	'98	'99	'00	'01	'02	'03	'04	'05	'06	'07	'08	'09	'10	'11	'12
120	149	145	105	83	73	73	56	67	78	77	71	56	105	106	109	121	118	90	80

2012

Jan	Feb	Mar	Apr	May	Jun	Jul	Aug	Sep	Oct	Nov	Dec	High	Low	Av
89	84	86	82	83	85	88	88	91	81	76	80	50	163	90

The Guatemala national team suffered a torrid time during 2012 and at the start of 2013. They missed out on the final round of 2014 FIFA World Cup qualifying and that was followed by an embarrassing exit from the 2013 Copa Centroamericana at the hands of minnows Belize. Meanwhile it had emerged that two of Guatemala's most capped players had been involved with match fixing. Guillermo Ramirez and Gustavo Cabrera, along with Yoni Flores were banned for life by FIFA in October 2012 for their involvement in fixing the games against Costa Rica in May 2012, Venezuela in June 2011 and a CONCACAF Champions League match between Municipal and Mexico's Santos Laguna in October 2010. In the World Cup qualifiers, a defeat to Jamaica in Kingston in the opening game of the group proved crucial with the Jamaicans finishing a point ahead to qualify for the final phase but there was genuine embarrassment with the first round exit at the Copa Centroamericana in January 2013 and the subsequent defeat to Panama which saw the Guatemalans miss out on the 2013 Gold Cup later in the year. In club football Municipal reached the final of both tournaments played in 2012 but lost to Xelajú in the first and then against fierce rivals Communicaciones in the second.

CONCACAF GOLD CUP RECORD

1991 r1 1993 DNE 1996 4 SF 1998 r1 2000 r1 2002 r1 2003 r1 2005 r1 2007 QF 2009 DNQ 2011 QF

FEDERACION NACIONAL DE FUTBOL DE GUATEMALA (FNFG)

2a. Calle 15-57, Zona 15,
Boulevard Vista Hermosa,
01015 Guatemala City
☎ +502 24227777
📠 +502 24227780
✉ info@fedefutguate.com
🖥 www.fedefutguate.com
FA 1919 CON 1961 FIFA 1946
P Bryan Jimenez
GS Byron Duran

THE STADIA
2014 FIFA World Cup Stadia
Estadio Mateo Flores
Guatemala City 29 950
Other Main Stadia
Estadio Cementos Progreso
Guatemala City 17 000
Estadio Verapáz
Cobán 15 000
Estadio del Ejército
Mixco 12 453

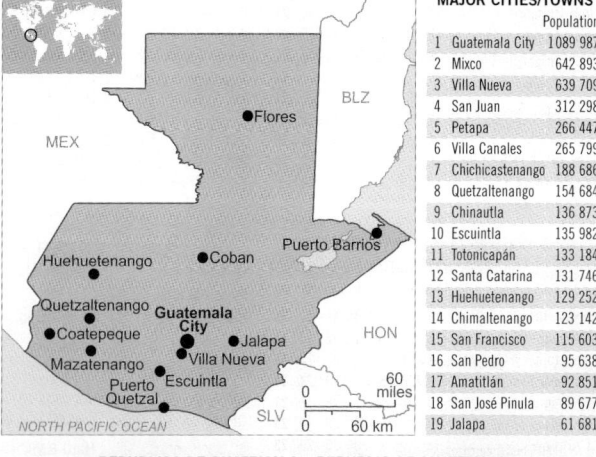

MAJOR CITIES/TOWNS

		Population
1	Guatemala City	1 089 987
2	Mixco	642 893
3	Villa Nueva	639 709
4	San Juan	312 298
5	Petapa	266 447
6	Villa Canales	265 799
7	Chichicastenango	188 686
8	Quetzaltenango	154 684
9	Chinautla	136 873
10	Escuintla	135 982
11	Totonicapán	133 184
12	Santa Catarina	131 746
13	Huehuetenango	129 252
14	Chimaltenango	123 142
15	San Francisco	115 603
16	San Pedro	95 638
17	Amatitlán	92 851
18	San José Pinula	89 677
19	Jalapa	61 681

REPUBLICA DE GUATEMALA • REPUBLIC OF GUATEMALA

Capital Guatemala City	Population 13 276 517 (68)	% in cities 49%
GDP per capita $5300 (136)	Area km² 108 889 km² (106)	GMT +/- -6
Neighbours (km) Belize 266, El Salvador 203, Honduras 256, Mexico 962 • Coast 400		

RECENT INTERNATIONAL MATCHES PLAYED BY GUATEMALA

2011	Opponents		Score	Venue	Comp	Scorers	Att	Referee
16-01	Costa Rica	L	0-2	Panama City	UCr1		1 500	Moreno PAN
18-01	Honduras	L	1-3	Panama City	UCr1	Guillermo Ramirez [24]	10 000	Aguilar SLV
21-01	Nicaragua	W	2-1	Panama City	UCr1	Carlos Ruiz [45], Manuel Leon [66]	5 000	Garcia MEX
28-03	Bolivia	D	1-1	Mazatenango	Fr	Carlos Ruiz [41]	6 154	Aguilar SLV
1-06	Venezuela	L	0-2	Guatemala City	Fr		13 000	Ruano SLV
6-06	Honduras	D	0-0	Carson/LA	GCr1		21 550	Chacon MEX
10-06	Jamaica	L	0-2	Miami	GCr1		18 057	Quesada CRC
13-06	Grenada	W	4-0	Harrison/NY	GCr1	Jose Del Aguila [16], Marco Pappa [22], Carlos Ruiz [54], Carlos Gallardo [59]	25 000	Toledo USA
18-06	Mexico	L	1-2	East Rutherford/NY	GCqf	Carlos Ruiz [5]	78 807	Campbell JAM
2-09	St Vincent/Grenadines	W	4-0	Guatemala City	WCq	Marco Pappa [15], Yony Flores [31], Mario Rodriguez [53], Freddy Garcia [71]	24 000	Andino HON
6-09	Belize	W	2-1	Belmopan	WCq	Gustavo Cabrera [4], Mynor Lopez [75]	3 027	Mejia SLV
7-10	St Vincent/Grenadines	W	3-0	Kingstown	WCq	Mario Rodriguez 2 [44 58], Dwight Pezzarossi [71]	3 000	Brea CUB
11-10	Belize	W	3-1	Guatemala City	WCq	Carlos Gallardo [8p], Mynor Lopez [65], Carlos Ruiz [78p]	21 107	Penaloza MEX
11-11	Grenada	W	3-0	Guatemala City	WCq	Freddy Garcia 2 [1 31], Angelo Padilla [45]	13 710	Brizan TRI
15-11	Grenada	W	4-1	St George's	WCq	Nicko Williams OG [67], Fredy Thompson [77], Guillermo Ramirez [84], Lyndon Joseph OG [90]	200	Angela ARU
2012								
22-02	Paraguay	L	1-2	Asuncion	Fr	Carlos Ruiz [82]	5 138	Lostau ARG
29-02	Guyana	W	2-0	Georgetown	Fr	Mynor Lopez [32], Guillermo Ramirez [90]	3 050	Wijngaarde SUR
25-04	Paraguay	L	0-1	Guatemala City	Fr		10 000	Mejia SLV
25-05	Costa Rica	L	2-3	San Jose	Fr	Carlos Ruiz 2 [4 53]	4 000	Penaloza PAN
1-06	Costa Rica	W	1-0	Guatemala City	Fr	Carlos Ruiz [25]	2 000	Castro HON
8-06	Jamaica	L	1-2	Kingston	WCq	Dwight Pezzarossi [92+]	14 000	Moreno PAN
12-06	USA	D	1-1	Guatemala City	WCq	Marco Papa [81]	18 000	Aguilar SLV
11-08	El Salvador	L	0-1	Carson/LA	Fr		18 500	Vaughn USA
15-08	Paraguay	D	3-3	Washington DC	Fr	Marco Papa [8], Manuel Leon [30], Carlos Ruiz [84]	14 185	Toledo USA
7-09	Antigua and Barbuda	W	3-1	Guatemala City	WCq	Carlos Ruiz 2 [60 79], Dwight Pezzarossi [91+]	8 000	Brea CUB
11-09	Antigua and Barbuda	W	1-0	St John's	WCq	Carlos Ruiz [26]	5 000	Gantar CAN
12-10	Jamaica	W	2-1	Guatemala City	WCq	Carlos Figueroa [15], Carlos Ruiz [85]	20 717	Garcia MEX
16-10	USA	L	1-3	Kansas City	WCq	Carlos Ruiz [5]	16 947	Moreno PAN
14-11	Paraguay	L	1-3	Luque	Fr	Mynor Lopez [87]	10 000	Cortez BRA
2013								
10-01	Panama	L	0-3	Panama City	Fr			Pitty PAN
13-01	Panama	L	0-2	Panama City	Fr			Perea PAN
18-01	Nicaragua	D	1-1	San Jose	UCr1	David Espinoza [67]	200	Aguilar SLV
20-01	Belize	D	0-0	San Jose	UCr1		250	Bonilla SLV
22-01	Costa Rica	D	1-1	San Jose	UCr1	Jose Manuel Contreras [90]	6 760	Rodriguez HON
25-01	Panama	L	1-3	San Jose	UC5p	Minor Lopez [75]	279	Quesada CRC

Fr = Friendly match • UC = UNCAF Cup/Copa Centroamericana • GC = CONCACAF Gold Cup • WC = FIFA World Cup
q = qualifier • r1 = first round group • qf = quarter-final • sf = semi-final • 3p = third place play-off • 5p = 5th place play-off

GUATEMALA NATIONAL TEAM HISTORICAL RECORDS

Caps
106 - Guillermo Ramirez 1997-2012 • **104** - Carlos Ruiz 1998- & Gustavo Cabrera 2001-12 • **90** - Fredy Thompson 2001- • **87** - Juan Carlos Plata 1996-2010 • **83** - Gonzalo Romero 2000- • **82** - Julio Giron 1992-2006 • **80** - Edgar Estrada 1995-2003 • **78** - Mario Rodriguez 2003- • **73** - Fredy Garcia 2000-08 • **72** - Dwight Pezzarossi 2000- • **69** - Erick Miranda 1991-2001 • **66** - Juan Manuel Funes 1985-2000

Goals
55 - Carlos Ruiz 1998- • **35** - Juan Carlos Plata 1996- • **23** - Fredy Garcia 1998- • **15** - Juan Manuel Funes 1985-2000 & Guillermo Ramirez 1997-2012

Coaches
For Guatemala coaches pre 1989 see Oliver's Almanack 2012 • Ruben Amorin URU 1989-90 • Haroldo Cordon 1991 • Miguel Angel Brindisi ARG 1992 • Jorge Roldan 1995 • Juan Ramon Veron ARG 1996 • Horacio Cordero ARG 1996 • Miguel Angel Brindisi ARG 1997-98 • Carlos Bilardo & Eduardo Lujan ARG 1998 • Benjamin Monterroso 1999 • Carlos Miloc URU 2000 • Julio Cesar Cortes URU 2000-03 • Victor Manuel Aguado MEX 2003 • Ramon Maradiaga HON 2004-05 • Hernan Dario Gomez COL 2006-08 • Ramon Maradiaga HON 2008 • Benjamin Monterroso 2008-09 • Ever Almeida PAR 2010-

GUATEMALA 2011-12
LIGA NACIONAL TORNEO CLAUSURA

	Pl	W	D	L	F	A	Pts	Com'ciones	Marquense	Xelajú	Municipal	Suc'péquez	Heredia	Petapa	Mictlán	Malacateco	Peñarol	Zacapa	Retalteca
Comunicaciones †	22	13	3	6	39	23	42		2-0	3-1	2-0	4-3	3-0	1-0	4-1	2-1	2-0	2-2	3-0
Deportivo Marquense †	22	10	8	4	38	18	38	1-0		3-4	3-3	0-0	4-0	3-2	6-0	1-0	2-1	4-0	4-0
Xelajú †	22	8	10	4	27	22	34	1-0	1-1		1-0	1-1	4-0	1-0	2-0	2-0	1-1	0-0	1-1
Municipal †	22	8	7	7	29	25	31	2-1	1-1	1-0		0-0	4-2	0-1	1-2	4-0	1-1	2-1	1-0
Suchitepéquez †	22	8	7	7	33	31	31	2-4	0-0	3-0	3-2		1-0	2-2	1-1	2-0	3-2	4-2	3-1
Deportivo Heredia †	22	9	4	9	30	35	31	2-2	2-0	1-1	1-0	1-1		1-0	2-1	3-1	3-1	6-1	2-1
Deportivo Petapa	22	8	6	8	23	23	30	0-1	0-0	0-0	1-1	2-1	1-0		3-2	1-1	2-0	2-1	2-0
Mictlán	22	9	2	11	25	37	29	1-0	0-0	1-2	0-1	2-1	2-0	1-0		2-1	1-0	3-0	3-0
Malacateco	22	7	6	9	21	30	27	1-1	0-0	0-0	1-0	0-0	2-1	1-1	2-1		1-0	3-3	2-1
Peñarol La Mesilla	22	6	7	9	32	26	25	2-0	0-1	2-2	3-3	4-0	3-0	2-0	5-0	2-0		1-1	2-2
Deportivo Zacapa	22	6	7	9	28	36	25	1-0	2-0	0-1	0-2	1-1	3-1	4-0	2-3	0-0			0-0
Juventud Retalteca	22	4	5	13	20	39	17	1-2	1-4	2-2	1-1	2-0	1-2	1-2	2-1	2-0	1-0	1-2	

14/01/2012 – 29/04/2012 • † Qualified for the play-offs • Top two receive a bye to the semi-finals
Top scorer (Trofeo Juan Carlos Plata): **16** – Henry **HERNANDEZ** COL, Heredia

CLAUSURA 2011-12 PLAY-OFFS

Quarter-finals		Semi-finals		Final	
Xelajú	1 6				
Deportivo Heredia *	2 2	**Xelajú** *	1 1		
		Deportivo Marquense	0 1		
Deportivo Marquense	Bye			**Xelajú** †	0 2
Comunicaciones	Bye			Municipal *	1 1
		Comunicaciones	0 1	Xelajú win on away goals	
Suchitepéquez *	2 0	**Municipal** *	0 2		
Municipal	1 3	† Qualified for the CONCACAF Champions League • * Home team in 1st leg			

CLAUSURA FINAL 2012 1ST LEG
Mateo Flores, Guatemala City, 16-05-2012, Att: 12 662, Ref: Reyna

Municipal	1	Quintanilla [84]
Xelajú	0	

MUNICIPAL
Jaime **PENEDO** - Yony **FLORES**, Jaime **VIDES**♦88, Hamilton **LOPEZ** - Marvin **AVILA**, Eliseo **QUINTANILLA**•, Juan **CASTILLO** (Abner **BONILLA** 61), Saul **PHILLIPS**•, Pedro **SAMAYOA**• (Gonzalo **ROMERO** 68) - Mario **RODRIGUEZ**, Darwin **OLIVA** (Oscar **USAULA** 74). Tr: Javier **DELGADO**

XELAJU
Fernando **PATTERSON** - Fredy **SANTIAGO**, Johny **GIRON**, Nelson **MORALES** (Alexander **CIFUENTES**• 18), Milton **LEAL**• - Franco **SOSA**•, Sergio **MORALES**• (Wilber **CAAL** 81), Julio **ESTACUY**•, Johnny **RUIZ** (Edgar **CHINCHILLA** 72), Kevin **ARRIOLA** - Israel **SILVA**. Tr: Hernan **MEDFORD**

CLAUSURA FINAL 2012 2ND LEG
Camposeco, Quetzaltenango, 20-05-2012, Att: 11 014, Ref: Polanco

Xelajú	2	Israel Silva [7], Caal [78]
Municipal	1	Leon [59]

XELAJU
Fernando **PATTERSON** - Fredy **SANTIAGO** (Cesar **MORALES**• 106), Johny **GIRON**, Alexander **CIFUENTES**, Milton **LEAL** (Edgar **CHINCHILLA** 63) - Franco **SOSA** (Wilber **CAAL** 77), Sergio **MORALES**, Julio **ESTACUY**•, Johnny **RUIZ**•, Kevin **ARRIOLA**• - Israel **SILVA**. Tr: Hernan **MEDFORD**

MUNICIPAL
Jaime **PENEDO**♦3 - Yony **FLORES**, Hamilton **LOPEZ** - Marvin **AVILA**, Eliseo **QUINTANILLA** (Pablo **SOLORZANO** 77), Juan **CASTILLO**•, Manuel **LEON**•, Saul **PHILLIPS**, Kevin **LEMUS** - Mario **RODRIGUEZ** (Evandro **FERREIRA** 88), Darwin **OLIVA** (Cristian **ALVAREZ**• 6). Tr: Javier **DELGADO**

GUATEMALA 2011-12 AGGREGATE TABLE

	Pl	W	D	L	F	A	Pts
Comunicaciones	44	21	14	9	66	43	77
Deportivo Marquense	44	19	17	8	69	38	74
Suchitepéquez	44	22	8	14	67	52	74
Xelajú	44	19	15	10	57	45	72
Deportivo Heredia	44	19	9	16	65	65	66
Municipal	44	16	17	11	66	46	65
Peñarol La Mesilla	44	14	14	16	68	57	56
Malacateco	44	11	16	17	50	72	49
Mictlán	44	14	7	23	48	76	49
Deportivo Petapa	44	11	15	18	47	56	48
Deportivo Zacapa	44	11	13	20	55	79	46
Juventud Retalteca	44	8	13	23	44	72	37

Deportivo Zacapa and Juventud Retalteca relegated

GUA – GUATEMALA

GUATEMALA 2012-13

LIGA NACIONAL
TORNEO APERTURA

	Pl	W	D	L	F	A	Pts	Com'ciones	Municipal	Xelajú	Heredia	Halcones	Malacateco	Suc'péquez	Marquense	Petapa	Mictlán	USAC	Juventud
Comunicaciones †	22	15	5	2	39	16	50		1-0	2-0	3-0	0-0	1-0	4-0	2-0	1-0	2-1	2-0	5-0
Municipal †	22	11	8	3	46	23	41	1-1		2-0	0-0	0-0	1-0	6-1	1-1	3-0	6-2	4-4	5-1
Xelajú †	22	11	3	8	33	28	36	1-2	2-0		1-0	3-2	1-1	1-1	2-1	2-0	2-1	4-0	2-0
Deportivo Heredia †	22	10	5	7	33	24	35	1-0	2-2	2-0		3-0	2-0	2-1	4-0	4-1	2-0	2-1	3-0
Halcones †	22	9	6	7	30	24	33	1-1	2-0	1-0	2-0		4-1	2-2	1-0	4-1	0-0	3-1	3-0
Malacateco †	22	7	7	8	26	25	28	1-2	1-1	2-1	1-1	2-1		1-1	0-0	5-0	1-0	1-1	2-0
Suchitepéquez †	22	7	7	8	36	40	28	4-1	1-3	2-1	2-0	3-1	1-4		0-0	2-0	3-3	4-1	4-2
Deportivo Marquense †	22	6	8	8	24	27	26	2-2	2-2	2-3	2-3	2-1	2-0	2-0		1-1	1-0	3-1	1-0
Deportivo Petapa	22	7	3	12	27	43	24	3-3	1-2	4-1	3-1	2-0	0-3	2-0	1-1		3-0	2-1	2-1
Mictlán	22	6	4	12	22	40	22	0-1	1-1	1-3	2-0	0-1	1-1		1-0	3-1		3-1	2-1
Universidad SC	22	5	6	11	32	38	21	0-1	0-1	2-2	2-2	1-0	4-0	2-1	1-1	2-0	7-0		1-1
Juventud Escuinteca	22	5	4	13	23	43	19	1-2	0-4	1-2	1-1	2-2	0-0	2-1	2-1	3-0	3-0	2-0	

15/07/2012 - 25/11/2012 • † Qualified for the play-offs
Top scorers (Trofeo Juan Carlos Plata): **13** - Robin BETANCOURTH, Hereddia • **12** - LEANDRINHO BARRIOS BRA, Municipal

APERTURA 2012-13 PLAY-OFFS

Quarter-finals			Semi-finals			Final		
Comunicaciones	2	3						
Deportivo Marquense	2	0	**Comunicaciones**	0	2			
Xelajú	0	3	Malacateco	0	1			
Malacateco	5	0				**Comunicaciones** †	3	1
Deportivo Heredia	1	5				Municipal	0	0
Halcones	3	1	Deportivo Heredia	1	2			
Suchitepéquez	1	3	**Municipal**	1	3			
Municipal	1	3	† Qualified for the CONCACAF Champions League • * Home team in 1st leg					

APERTURA FINAL 1ST LEG
Mateo Flores, Guatemala City, 14-12-2012, Att: 13 541, Ref: Leonardo

Municipal 0
Communicaciones 3   Marquez [57], Guerrero [72], Estrada [74]

MUNICIPAL
Jaime PENEDO - Claudio ALBIZURIS, Cristian NORIEGA, Jaime VIDES - Marvin AVILA, Juan CASTILLO (Edgar MENDEZ 73), Santiago LOPEZ (Yosimar ARIAS 62), Saul PHILLIPS (Darwin OLIVA 65), Marco RIVAS, Sergio TRUJILLO - Mario RODRIGUEZ•. Tr: Ramon MARADIAGA

COMMUNICACIONES
Juan PAREDES - Michael UMANA, Joel BENITEZ, Carlos CASTRILLO , Rafael MORALES• - Jose CONTRERAS••♦80, Carlos FIGUEROA (Marcelo GUERRERO• 72), Jairo ARREOLA, Diego ESTRADA• (Bryan ORDONEZ 79), Jean MARQUEZ (Wilfred VELASQUEZ 77) - Dwight PEZZAROSSI. Tr: Ronald GONZALEZ

APERTURA FINAL 2ND LEG
Cementos Progreso, Guatemala City, 17-12-2012, Att: 10 800, Ref: Lopez

Communicaciones 1   Albizuris OG [11]
Municipal 0

COMMUNICACIONES
Juan PAREDES - Michael UMANA, Joel BENITEZ, Carlos CASTRILLO, Rafael MORALES - Jairo ARREOLA (Carlos FIGUEROA 81), Diego ESTRADA (Carlos MEJIA 58), Jean MARQUEZ, Wilfred VELASQUEZ - Dwight PEZZAROSSI (Transito MONTEPEQUE• 63), Marcelo GUERRERO•. Tr: Ronald GONZALEZ

MUNICIPAL
Jaime PENEDO - Claudio ALBIZURIS, Cristian NORIEGA, Jaime VIDES - Marvin AVILA, Santiago LOPEZ (Darwin OLIVA 58), Marco RIVAS, Edgar MENDEZ (Osvar ISAULA• 46), Sergio TRUJILLO• - Mario RODRIGUEZ•, Leandro BARRIOS•. Tr: Ramon MARADIAGA

MEDALS TABLE

		Overall			League			Cup		Cent Am			City
		G	S	B	G	S	B	G	S	G	S	B	
1	Deportivo Municipal	37	22	7	**29**	19	6	**7**	2	1	1	1	Guatemala City
2	Comunicaciones	31	22	10	25	21	7	5		1	2	3	Guatemala City
3	Aurora	10	9	6	8	8	5	2	1			1	Guatemala City
4	Xelajú	7	6	2	6	4	1	1	2			1	Quetzaltenango
5	Deportivo Jalapa	5	1		2			3	1				Jalapa
6	Suchitepéquez	3	6	2	1	5	1	2	1			1	Mazatenango
7	Tip Nac	3	1		3	1							Guatemala City
8	Cobán Imperial	1	6	6	1	3	2		3				Cobán
9	Juventud Retalteca	1	3	2		2	2	1	1				Retalhuleu
10	IRCA	1	2			2	1						
11	Hospicio	1		1	1		1						
	Amatitlan	1		1			1	1					Amatitlán
13	Deportivo Marquense		3			3							San Marcos

GUI – GUINEA

FIFA/COCA-COLA WORLD RANKING

'93	'94	'95	'96	'97	'98	'99	'00	'01	'02	'03	'04	'05	'06	'07	'08	'09	'10	'11	'12
63	66	63	73	65	79	91	80	108	120	101	86	79	23	33	39	73	46	80	60

2012

Jan	Feb	Mar	Apr	May	Jun	Jul	Aug	Sep	Oct	Nov	Dec	High	Low	Av
79	65	65	67	68	67	75	74	69	62	71	60	22	123	72

Between 2004 and 2008 Guinea reached the quarter-finals at three consecutive Africa Cup of Nations and they started with high hopes of repeating that feat at the 2012 finals in Equatorial Guinea and Gabon. Admittedly, they found themselves in a tough group with Ghana and Mali but after falling at the first hurdle questions were being asked about whether they had lost their place amongst the continent's more competitive sides - especially after the disappointing results during the rest of the year where a home defeat at the hands of Egypt in the 2014 FIFA World Cup qualifiers handed the impetus in the group to their North African rivals. 'Syli Nationale' had started the bid for a place in Brazil impressively with an away win in Zimbabwe before losing to the Egyptians. That was followed by the failure to qualify for the 2013 Nations Cup where Guinea lost in the final minutes to Niger. A slender 1-0 lead from the first leg was overturned by Niger who won 2-0 in Niamey to progress to the finals instead. In club football there was a first league championship for Horoya in over a decade after defending champions Fello Star - hoping for a fourth consecutive title - could only finish in third place. In the cup, Sequence created history by becoming the first club to win the trophy three times in a row after beating Ashanti in the final.

CAF AFRICA CUP OF NATIONS RECORD

1957-1962 DNE 1963 Disqualified 1965-1968 DNQ **1970** 6 r1 1972 DNQ **1974** 5 r1 **1976** 2 r2 1978 DNQ **1980** 7 r1 1982-1992 DNQ **1994** 11 r1 1996 DNQ **1998** 9 r1 2000 DNQ 2002 Disqualified **2004** 7 QF **2006** 6 QF **2008** 8 QF 2010 DNQ **2012** 9 r1 2013 DNQ

FEDERATION GUINEENNE DE FOOTBALL (FGF)

- PO Box 3645, Conakry
- +224 62 446944
- +33 13 4296092
- guineefoot59@yahoo.fr
- feguifoot.net
- FA 1960 CON 1962 FIFA 1962
- P Salifou Camara
- GS Ibrahima Barry

THE STADIA

2014 FIFA World Cup Stadia
Stade du 28 septembre
Conakry   25 000

Other Main Stadia
Stade de l'Unité
Conakry   50 000
Stade de Coléah
Conakry   5 000
Stade Saïfoulaye Diallo
Labé   5 000

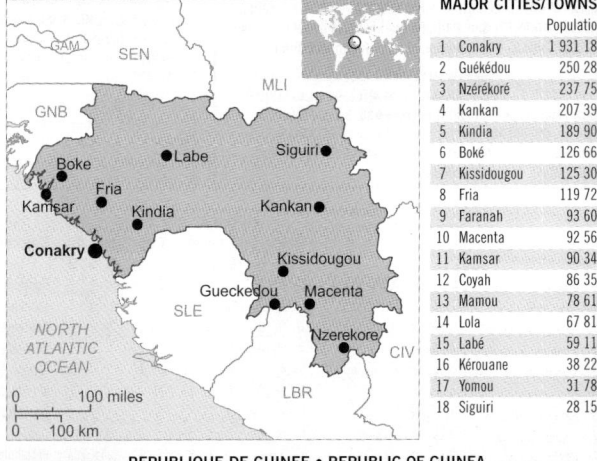

MAJOR CITIES/TOWNS

		Population
1	Conakry	1 931 184
2	Guékédou	250 288
3	Nzérékoré	237 753
4	Kankan	207 390
5	Kindia	189 907
6	Boké	126 668
7	Kissidougou	125 303
8	Fria	119 722
9	Faranah	93 608
10	Macenta	92 569
11	Kamsar	90 341
12	Coyah	86 352
13	Mamou	78 615
14	Lola	67 815
15	Labé	59 110
16	Kérouane	38 224
17	Yomou	31 787
18	Siguiri	28 150

REPUBLIQUE DE GUINEE • REPUBLIC OF GUINEA

Capital	Conakry	Population	10 057 975 (81)	% in cities	34%
GDP per capita	$1100 (208)	Area km²	245 857 km² (78)	GMT +/-	0
Neighbours (km)	Cote d'Ivoire 610, Guinea-Bissau 386, Liberia 563, Mali 858, Senegal 330, Sierra Leone 652, Coast 420				

GUI – GUINEA

RECENT INTERNATIONAL MATCHES PLAYED BY GUINEA

2009 Opponents	Score	Venue	Comp	Scorers	Att	Referee
12-08 Egypt	D 3-3	Cairo	Fr	Souleymane Youla 2 [30] [40], Kaba Diawarra [48]		
5-09 Malawi	L 1-2	Blantyre	WCq	Oumar Kalabane [37]	15 000	Codjia BEN
11-10 Burkina Faso	L 1-2	Accra	WCq	Mamadou Bah [82]	5 000	Ambaya LBY
14-11 Côte d'Ivoire	L 0-3	Abidjan	WCq		28 000	Marange ZIM
2010						
11-08 Mali	W 2-0	Marignane	Fr	Kamil Zayatte [52], Kevin Constant [34]		
5-09 Ethiopia	W 4-1	Addis Abeba	CNq	Ibrahima Yattara [37], Oumar Kalabane [45], Karamoko Cisse [61], Kamil Zayatte [75]		Mnkantjo ZIM
10-10 Nigeria	W 1-0	Conakry	CNq	Kevin Constant [5]		El Ahrach MAR
17-11 Burkina Faso	L 1-2	Mantes-La-Ville	Fr	Karamoko Cisse [10]		
2011						
9-02 Senegal	L 0-3	Dakar	Fr			
27-03 Madagascar	D 1-1	Antananarivo	CNq	Mamadou Bah [80]		Mpanisi ZAM
5-06 Madagascar	W 4-1	Conakry	CNq	Oumar Kalabane [6], Ibrahima Bangoura [17], Abdoulaye Diallo [60], Habib Balde [62]		
10-08 Gabon	D 1-1	St Leu La Foret	Fr	Sadio Diallo [77]		
4-09 Ethiopia	W 1-0	Conakry	CNq	Dianbobo Balde [33]		
6-09 Venezuela	L 1-2	Caracas	Fr	Ibrahima Camara [79p]	14 000	Gambetta PER
8-10 Nigeria	D 2-2	Abuja	CNq	Ibrahima Bangoura [63], Ibrahima Traore [102+]		
11-11 Senegal	L 1-4	Mantes La Ville	Fr	Pascal Feindouno [89p]		
15-11 Burkina Faso	D 1-1	Mantes La Ville	Fr	Ibrahima Conte [90]		
2012						
24-01 Mali	L 0-1	Franceville	CNr1		10 000	Jedidi TUN
28-01 Botswana	W 6-1	Franceville	CNr1	Abdoulaye Diallo 2 [16] [27], Abdoul Camara [41], Ibrahima Traore [45], Mamadou Bah [84], Naby Soumah [86]	4 000	El Ahrach MAR
1-02 Ghana	D 1-1	Franceville	CNr1	Abdoul Camara [45]	5 500	Bennett RSA
29-02 Côte d'Ivoire	D 0-0	Abidjan	Fr			
3-06 Zimbabwe	W 1-0	Harare	WCq	Ibrahima Traore [27]	30 000	Seechurn MRI
10-06 Egypt	L 2-3	Conakry	WCq	Abdoul Camara [20p], Alhassane Bangoura [88]	14 000	Alioum CMR
15-08 Morocco	W 2-1	Rabat	Fr	Mamadou Mara [12], Ismael Bangoura [25]		Diatta SEN
9-09 Niger	W 1-0	Conakry	CNq	Mohamed Yattara [50]		Bennett RSA
14-10 Niger	L 0-2	Niamey	CNq			Gassama GAM
2-12 Sierra Leone	D 0-0	Conakry	Fr			
15-12 Sierra Leone	D 1-1	Freetown	Fr			

Fr = Friendly match • CN = CAF African Cup of Nations • AC = Amilcar Cabral Cup • WC = FIFA World Cup
q = qualifier • r1 = first round group • sf = semi-final • f = final • † = not a full international

GUINEA SQUAD FOR THE 2012 CAF AFRICA CUP OF NATIONS

	Player		Ap	G	Club	Date of Birth		Player		Ap	G	Club	Date of Birth
1	Naby Yattara	GK	3		Arles FRA	12 01 1984	12	Ibrahima Conte	MF	0+1		Gent BEL	3 04 1991
2	Pascal Feindouno	MF	3		Unattached	27 02 1981	13	Morlaye Cisse	DF	0		Gafsa TUN	19 12 1983
3	Ibrahima Bangoura	DF	0		Djoliba MLI	25 07 1987	14	Naby Soumah	MF	0+2		Sfaxien TUN	4 08 1985
4	Mamadou Bah	MF	3	1	Stuttgart GER	25 04 1988	15	Oumar Kalabane	DF	0		Dhafra UAE	8 04 1981
5	Bobo Balde	DF	3		Arles FRA	5 10 1975	16	Abdul Aziz Keita	GK	0		AS Kaloum	16 02 1989
6	Kamil Zayatte (c)	DF	3		Istanbul BB TUR	7 03 1985	17	Thierno Bah	MF	3		Lausanne SUI	5 10 1982
7	Abdoul Camara	FW	2+1	2	Sochaux FRA	20 02 1990	18	Ibrahima Diallo	DF	3		Beveren BEL	26 09 1985
8	Ibrahima Traoré	MF	3	1	Stuttgart GER	21 04 1988	19	Alhassane Bangoura	FW	1+2		Vallecano ESP	30 03 1992
9	Abdoulaye Sadio Diallo	FW	2+1	4	Bastia FRA	28 12 1990	20	Habib Balde	DF	1+1		Univ. Cluj ROU	8 04 1985
10	Ismael Bangoura	DF	3		Al Nasr UAE	2 06 1985	21	Ousmane Barry	FW	0+1		Etoile Sahel TUN	27 09 1991
11	Ibrahima Yattara	MF	0		Al Shabab KSA	3 06 1980	22	Aboubacar Camara	GK	0		Alcoyano ESP	1 06 1993
	Tr: Michel Dussuyer FRA 28-05-1959						23	Lanfia Camara	DF	0		White Star BEL	3 10 1986

GUINEA 2012

CHAMPIONNAT NATIONAL DE LIGUE 1 RIO TINTO

	Pl	W	D	L	F	A	Pts	Horoya	At. Coléah	Fello Star	Kaloum Star	Ashanti GB	Santoba	Satellite	Baté Nafadji	Hafia	ASFAG	Espoir Labé	Baraka Djoma
Horoya AC Conakry †	22	13	8	1	32	9	**47**		1-1	1-1	2-0	1-0	1-0	4-1	2-1	4-0		2-0	4-0
Atlético Coléah	22	13	6	3	26	7	**45**	0-0		0-2	0-0	2-0	2-0	2-0		0-0	1-0	1-0	2-0
Fello Star Labé	22	9	10	3	27	17	**37**	0-0	0-0		1-3	1-2	2-1	3-0	0-0	0-2	1-0	2-2	2-0
AS Kaloum Star	22	9	6	7	19	17	**33**	1-1	1-0	0-0		2-3		2-1	1-0		1-0	0-2	2-0
Ashanti GB Siguiri	22	10	2	10	27	24	**32**	0-1	1-0	0-1	0-1		0-0		3-0	1-0	1-0	5-1	2-1
Santoba FC	22	9	5	8	17	17	**32**	0-0	0-0		2-0	2-3		2-1	0-0	1-0		1-0	2-1
Satellite FC	22	8	5	9	21	23	**29**	0-1		0-1	1-1	2-0	1-1		2-0	1-0	1-1	1-3	1-2
Baté Nafadji	22	7	6	9	17	20	**27**	2-0	1-2	1-1	2-1	4-1	0-1	0-4		1-1	0-1	1-0	
Hafia FC Conakry	22	6	7	9	15	18	**25**	0-1	0-3	2-2	0-0	1-1	0-1	0-0	0-1		1-0	1-0	3-0
ASFAG	22	5	7	10	12	19	**22**	0-2	0-2	0-0	0-0	2-1	1-0	0-1	1-1	0-1		1-1	2-1
Espoir Labé	22	5	5	12	15	24	**20**	1-2	0-2	0-0	1-0	1-0	0-1	0-1	0-1	0-0	0-0		0-1
Baraka Djoma	22	4	1	17	11	44	**13**	0-2	1-4	2-4	1-0	0-3	0-1	0-2	0-1	0-3	1-0	0-2	

25/12/2012 – 19/08/2012 • † Qualified for the CAF Champions League

MEDALS TABLE

		Overall G	Lge G	Cup G	City/Town
1	Hafia FC	19	16	3	Conakry
2	AS Kaloum Star	17	11	6	Conakry
3	Horoya AC	15	11	4	Conakry
4	Fello Star	7	5	2	Labé
5	Satellite FC	4	2	2	Conakry
6	ASFAG	4	1	3	Conakry
7	FC Sequence Dixinn	3		3	Conakry
8	Olympique Kakandé	2		2	Boké
9	AS Baraka Djoma	1		1	Conakry
10	Etoile de Guinée	1		1	Conakry
11	Mankona	1		1	Guéckédou

COUPE NATIONALE 2012

Eighth-finals	Quarter-finals	Semi-finals	Final
Séquence Dixinn			
Espoir Labé	**Séquence Dixinn** 2		
Satellite FC 0 4p	ASFAG 1		
ASFAG 0 5p		**Séquence Dixinn** 0 4p	
Atlético Coleah 1		Hafia FC Conakry 0 3p	
Cl Kamsar 0	Atlético Coleah 1 3p		
Crew Gold 0 6p	**Hafia FC Conakry** 1 4p		**Séquence Dixinn** ‡ 0 3p
Hafia FC Conakry 0 7p			Ashanti GB Siguiri 0 1p
Horoya AC Conakry			
Sanankoro Kérouané	**Horoya AC Conakry** 0 7p		CUP FINAL
Tabounsou Dubréka	Fello Star Labé 0 6p		
Fello Star Labé		Horoya AC Conakry 1 3p	Stade du 1er Mai, Boké
AS Kaloum Star 3		**Ashanti GB Siguiri** 1 4p	2-10-2012
Etoile de Guinée 1	AS Kaloum Star 0		
Sarinka FC Coyah 0	**Ashanti GB Siguiri** 1		
Ashanti GB Siguiri 1		‡ Qualified for CAF Confederation Cup	

GUM – GUAM

FIFA/COCA-COLA WORLD RANKING

'93	'94	'95	'96	'97	'98	'99	'00	'01	'02	'03	'04	'05	'06	'07	'08	'09	'10	'11	'12
-	-	-	188	191	198	200	199	199	200	201	2005	204	198	201	201	184	188	192	181

2012

Jan	Feb	Mar	Apr	May	Jun	Jul	Aug	Sep	Oct	Nov	Dec	High	Low	Av
192	193	193	194	194	194	194	184	185	178	181	181	178	205	196

The Guam national team climbed to a record high of 178 in the FIFA/Coca-Cola World Ranking during 2012 thanks to a couple of impressive performances during a year in which the qualifying tournament for the East Asian Cup provided the focus of their programme. Jason Cunliffe, now Guam's all-time leading goalscorer, impressed for the United States protectorate in the first preliminary round which Guam hosted at the Leo Palace Resort in Yona - a rare taste of international football for fans in the country. Cunliffe was named the Most Valuable Player after finishing as top scorer with four goals in the two games against Macau and Northern Mariana. Wins over the pair ensured Guam progressed to the main qualifying group in Hong Kong, where they met Australia, Korea DPR, Hong Kong and Chinese Taipei. The step up in class, however, proved to be too much for them as Gary White's team suffered heavy losses in three of their four matches. The well earned draw against Chinese Taipei - thanks to a strike by Dylan Naputi - meant that Guam did not go home without something to show for their efforts. In club football there were trophies for Quality Distributors who won the league title and for Guam Shipyard - 4-3 winners over Quality Distributors in the cup final.

FIFA WORLD CUP RECORD
1930-1998 DNE **2002** DNQ **2006-2014** DNE

GUAM FOOTBALL ASSOCIATION (GFA)

PO Box 20008,
96921 Barrigada

☎ +1 671 6374321
📠 +1 671 6374323
✉ info@guamfootball.com
🖥 www.guamfootball.com
FA 1975 CON 1996 FIFA 1996
P Richard Lai
GS Valentino San Gil

THE STADIA
2014 FIFA World Cup Stadia
Guam did not enter the 2014 FIFA World Cup
Other Main Stadia
GFA Field	
Harmon	1 000
Leo Palace Resort Yona	1 000

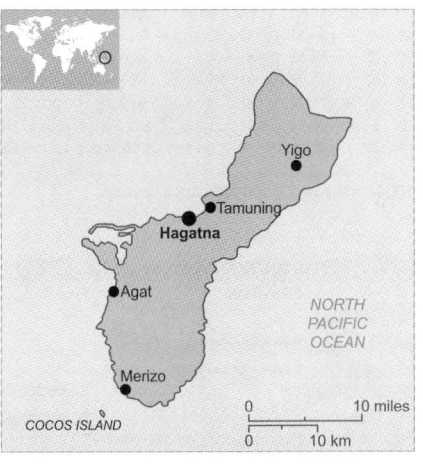

MAJOR CITIES/TOWNS
Population
1	Tamuning	11 809
2	Yigo	10 533
3	Mangilao	10 071
4	Astumbo	6 536
5	Ordot	4 968
6	Barrigada	4 957
7	Agat	4 780
8	Anderson Air Force Base	4 556
9	Mongmong	4 229
10	Agana Heights	3 953
11	Dededo	3 487
12	Talofofo	3 180
13	Chalan Pago	2 977
14	Marbo Annex	2 344
15	Yona	2 330
16	Apra Harbor	2 265
17	Sinajana	2 123
18	Finegayan Station	1 957

GUAHAN • TERRITORY OF GUAM

Capital	Hagatna	Population	178 430 (187)	% in cities	93%
GDP per capita	$15 000 (74)	Area km²	544 km² (195)	GMT +/-	+10
Neighbours (km)	Coast 125				

RECENT INTERNATIONAL MATCHES PLAYED BY GUAM

2009	Opponents	Score		Venue	Comp	Scorers	Att	Referee
11-03	Mongolia	W	1-0	Manenggon Hills	EACq	Christopher Mendiola [9]		Kim Jong Hyeuk KOR
13-03	Northern Mariana Isl †	W	2-1	Manenggon Hills	EACq	Joshua Borja [10], Ian Mariano [68]		Cheng Oi Cho HKG
15-03	Macao	D	2-2	Manenggon Hills	EACq	Joshua Borja [36], Jason Cunliffe [90]		Kim Jong Hyeuk KOR
23-08	Korea DPR	L	2-9	Kaohsiung	EACq	Joshua Borja [1], Jason Cunliffe [20]	2 000	Matsuo JPN
25-08	Chinese Taipei	L	2-4	Kaohsiung	EACq	Joshua Borja 2 [5,26]	7 500	Matsuo JPN
27-08	Hong Kong	L	0-12	Kaohsiung	EACq		1 500	Tojo JPN
2010								
No international matches played in 2010								
2011								
27-08	Solomon Islands	L	0-7	Noumea	PGr1			Varman FIJ
30-08	New Caledonia	L	0-9	Noumea	PGr1			Zitouni TAH
1-09	American Samoa	W	2-0	Noumea	PGr1	Dylan Naputi [49], Elias Merfalen [70]		George VAN
3-09	Vanuatu	L	1-4	Noumea	PGr1	Jason Cunliffe [14]		Kerr NZL
5-09	Tuvalu †	D	1-1	Noumea	PGr1	Jason Cunliffe [18p]		Zitouni TAH
2012								
12-06	Philippines	L	0-3	Bacolod	Fr			
18-07	Northern Mariana Isl †	W	3-1	Yona	EACq	Jason Cunliffe 3 [25,66,90p]	450	Kim Dae Yong KOR
22-07	Macau	W	3-0	Yona	EACq	Jason Cunliffe [15], Marcus Lopez [22], Zachary DeVille [93+]	1 000	Iida JPN
25-09	Philipinnes	L	0-1	Manila	Fr			Phung VIE
27-09	Chinese Taipei	L	0-2	Manila	Fr			Supresencia PHI
29-09	Macau	W	3-0	Manila	Fr	Marcus Lopez 2 [45,55], Dylan Naputi [90]		Villagracia PHI
1-12	Hong Kong	L	1-2	Hong Kong	EACq	Elias Merfalen [56]	3 040	Kim Dae Yong KOR
3-12	Korea DPR	L	0-5	Hong Kong	EACq		4 160	Pechsri THA
5-12	Chinese Taipei	D	1-1	Hong Kong	EACq	Dylan Naputi [67]	989	Kim Dae Yong KOR
7-12	Australia	L	0-9	Hong Kong	EACq		2 315	Wang Zhe CHN

EAC = East Asian Championship • AC = AFC Asian Cup • CC = AFC Challenge Cup
q = qualifier • r1 = first round group • † Not an official international

GUAM 2011-12

BUDWEISER SOCCER LEAGUE DIVISION ONE

	Pl	W	D	L	F	A	Pts	Quality Distributors	Guam Shipyard	Ichiban Espada	Cars Plus	Guahan	Paintco Strykers
Quality Distributors	20	13	4	3	84	25	43		2-1 2-0	2-0 9-0	4-2 9-2	2-0 11-0	4-1 11-0
Guam Shipyard	20	13	2	5	91	25	41	4-2 1-1		3-1 9-2	1-2 2-2	8-0 0-1	3-0 1-0
Ichiban Espada	20	12	1	7	72	54	37	5-4 1-1	1-2 3-2		0-4 1-5	9-0 4-3	6-2 5-3
Cars Plus	20	9	4	7	70	50	31	2-2 0-0	1-2 2-5	0-2 0-4		5-0 4-6	3-3 4-1
Guahan	20	6	0	14	34	128	18	1-8 3-5	1-18 2-9	0-4 0-16	1-10 2-6		5-3 3-2
Paintco Strykers	20	1	1	18	31	100	4	0-4 2-1	0-6 0-14	2-4 3-4	0-6 5-10	2-3 2-3	

7/10/2011 - 18/03/2012
Top scorers: 32 - Jason **CUNLIFFE**, Guam Shipyard & Scott **SPINDEL**, Quality Distributors

BECK'S GFA CUP 2012

Quarter-finals		Semi-finals		Final	
Guam Shipyard	9				
Bank of Guam Crushers	1	**Guam Shipyard**	2		
Rovers FC	1	Ichiban Espada	0		
Ichiban Espada	9			**Guam Shipyard**	4
Cars Plus	7			Quality Distributors	3
Cobras	3	Cars Plus	0		
Coffee Beanery Utd	2	**Quality Distributors**	6		
Quality Distributors	11	3rd Place: Cars Plus 3-2 Ichiban Espada			

Final: GFA Field, Harmon, 8-05-2012. Scorers - Donald Weakley, AJ Pothen, Camden Aguon, Jason Cunliffe for Shipyard; Matt Cruz 2, Scott Spindel for Quality Distributors

GUY – GUYANA

FIFA/COCA-COLA WORLD RANKING

'93	'94	'95	'96	'97	'98	'99	'00	'01	'02	'03	'04	'05	'06	'07	'08	'09	'10	'11	'12
136	154	162	153	168	161	171	183	178	169	182	182	167	100	128	131	127	109	91	124

2012												High	Low	Av
Jan	Feb	Mar	Apr	May	Jun	Jul	Aug	Sep	Oct	Nov	Dec			
92	92	99	99	99	104	109	109	122	122	116	124	86	185	147

In an ideal world Guyana would have qualified for the 2014 FIFA World Cup in neighbouring Brazil and been based in nearby Manaus, the nearest Brazilian city a few hundred kilometers over the border. By winning their first round group in 2011 they moved one step closer to that dream but their limitations were regularly exposed during the course of 2012 as they struggled to keep their head above water against opponents with genuine ambitions of making it through to the finals in Brazil. Against Mexico, Costa Rica and El Salvador they managed to scramble just one point - a 2-2 draw in San Salvador while losing 7-0 to Costa Rica and 5-0 to the Mexicans in the process. In the familiar environment of the 2012 Caribbean Cup, Guyana felt more at home, winning a first round qualifying group. They failed to make it to the finals in Antigua, however, after finishing bottom of a second round group containing Haiti, French Guiana and Grenada - a disappointing end to a difficult year for the team. Club football suffered from the extensive international engagements in 2012 with Alpha United winning a GFA Super League restricted to just nine matches. Both they and Milerock entered the 2012 CFU Caribbean Club Championship but neither made it through a group won by Inter Moengotapoe from Suriname.

CFU CARIBBEAN CUP RECORD

1989 disqualified **1991** 4 SF **1992-2005** DNQ **2007** 5 r1 **2008** DNQ **2010** 8 r1 **2012** DNQ

GUYANA FOOTBALL FEDERATION (GFF)

Lot 17 Dadanawa Street, Section K, Campbellville, PO Box 10727, Georgetown
☎ +592 2 278758
📠 +592 2 252096
✉ gff@networksgy.com
🖥 www.guyanaff.com
FA 1902 CON 1969 FIFA 1968
P Franklin Wilson
GS Noel Adonis

THE STADIA

2014 FIFA World Cup Stadia
National Stadium
Providence 15 000

Other Main Stadia
Bourda Cricket Ground
Georgetown 22 000
Georgetown Football Stadium
Georgetown 2 000
MSC Ground
Linden 1 000

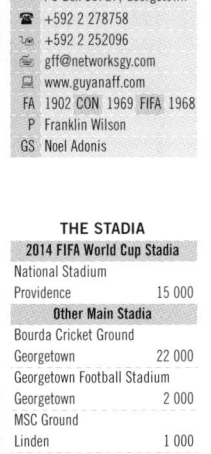

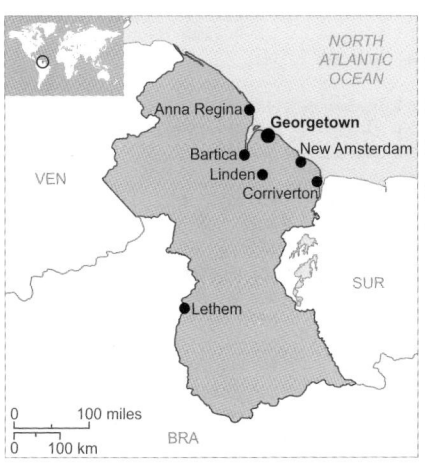

MAJOR CITIES/TOWNS

		Population
1	Georgetown	250 435
2	Linden	42 957
3	New Amsterdam	38 177
4	Bartica	11 958
5	Corriverton	11 758
6	Rosignol	5 874
7	Mahaica	4 997
8	Ituni	4 702
9	Skeldon	4 380
10	Paradise	3 879
11	Vreed en Hoop	3 202
12	Fort Wellington	2 274
13	Mahaicony	2 164
14	Kumaka	1 622
15	Anna Regina	1 454
16	Mabaruma	870
17	Lethem	866

COOPERATIVE REPUBLIC OF GUYANA

Capital	Georgetown	Population	772 298 (160)	% in cities	28%
GDP per capita	$3900 (156)	Area km²	214 969 km² (84)	GMT +/-	-4
Neighbours (km)	Brazil 1606, Suriname 600, Venezuela 743 • Coast 459				

RECENT INTERNATIONAL MATCHES PLAYED BY GUYANA

2008 Opponents	Score	Venue	Comp	Scorers	Att	Referee
8-08 Dominica	W 3-0	Georgetown	CCq	Codrington 2 [20 43], Edmonds [36]	3 000	Forde BRB
10-08 Surinam	D 1-1	Georgetown	CCq	Peters [90]	10 000	Forde BRB
3-09 Trinidad and Tobago	L 0-3	Port of Spain	Fr		1 000	Brizan TRI
21-09 Antigua and Barbuda	L 0-3	St John's	Fr		3 500	Willett ATG
5-11 St Kitts and Nevis	D 1-1	Macoya	CCq	Richardson [35]	750	Cambridge VIN
7-11 Antigua and Barbuda	L 1-2	Macoya	CCq	Jerome [45]	500	Minyetty DOM
9-11 Trinidad and Tobago	D 1-1	Macoya	CCq	Richardson [58p]	1 000	Minyetty DOM
2009						
3-06 Antigua and Barbuda	L 1-2	Paramaribo	Fr	Parks [34]	1 700	Wijngaarde SUR
28-10 Surinam	W 1-0	Paramaribo	Fr	Millington [66]	2 000	Jauregui ANT
30-10 Netherlands Antilles	W 1-0	Paramaribo	Fr	Millington [29]	500	Pinas SUR
1-11 French Guiana †	W 1-0	Paramaribo	Fr	Archer [57]	1 000	Wijngaarde SUR
2010						
26-09 Trinidad and Tobago	D 1-1	Providence	Fr	Dwight Peters [43]	9 000	Lancaster GUY
13-10 St Lucia	W 1-0	Paramaribo	CCq	Christopher Bourne [10]	550	Davis TRI
15-10 Netherlands Antilles	W 3-2	Paramaribo	CCq	Dwight Peters [15], Anthony Abrams [45], Walter Moore [58]	750	Matthew SKN
17-10 Suriname	W 2-0	Paramaribo	CCq	Walter Moore [18p], Devon Millington [90]	2 800	Davis TRI
2-11 Haiti	D 0-0	Marabella	CCq		880	Taylor BRB
4-11 Trinidad and Tobago	L 1-2	Port of Spain	CCq	Shawn Beveney [78]	1 100	Legister JAM
6-11 St Vincent/Grenadines	W 2-0	Port of Spain	CCq	Devon Millington [57], Sean Cameron [81]	850	Taylor BRB
17-11 Guatemala	L 0-3	Kennesaw	Fr		4 124	Okulaja USA
27-11 Guadeloupe	D 1-1	Riviere-Pilote	CCr1	Dwain Jacobs [86]	2 500	Davis TRI
29-11 Antigua and Barbuda	L 0-1	Riviere-Pilote	CCr1		3 000	Wijngaarde SUR
1-12 Jamaica	L 0-4	Riviere-Pilote	CCr1		3 000	Cruz CRC
2011						
20-05 Barbados	W 1-0	Linden	Fr	Chris Bourne [86]	300	Lancaster GUY
22-05 Barbados	W 3-2	Georgetown	Fr	Rishawn Sandiford [28], Colin Nelson [61p], Anani Mohamed [69]	2 500	Young GUY
29-05 Barbados	D 1-1	Bridgetown	Fr	OG [76]	2 055	Taylor BRB
24-08 India	W 2-1	Georgetown	Fr	Vurlon Mills [19], Walter Moore [62]	2 500	Lancaster GUY
2-09 Barbados	W 2-0	Georgetown	WCq	Shawn Beveney [26], Charles Pollard [73]	4 500	St Catherine LCA
6-09 Bermuda	W 2-1	Georgetown	WCq	Vurlon Mills 2 [50 60]	3 500	Geiger USA
7-10 Barbados	W 2-0	Bridgetown	WCq	Anthony Abrams [73], Chris Nurse [87]	2 500	Georges HAI
11-10 Bermuda	D 1-1	Prospect	WCq	Ricky Shakes [81]	2 573	Angela ARU
11-11 Trinidad and Tobago	W 2-1	Georgetown	WCq	Ricky Shakes [10], Leon Cort [81]	18 000	Wijngaarde SUR
15-11 Trinidad and Tobago	L 0-2	Port of Spain	WCq		2 000	Mejia SLV
2012						
19-02 St Vincent/Grenadines	L 0-1	Kingstown	Fr		1 100	Bedaeau GRN
22-02 Grenada	W 2-1	St George's	Fr	Anthony Abrams [72], Walter Moore [90p]	5 000	Cambridge VIN
29-02 Guatemala	L 0-2	Georgetown	Fr		3 050	Wijngaarde SUR
18-05 Jamaica	L 0-1	Montego Bay	Fr		3 500	Marrufo USA
8-06 Mexico	L 1-3	Mexico City	WCq	OG [62]	80 401	Santos PUR
12-06 Costa Rica	L 0-4	Georgetown	WCq		11 000	Brea CUB
15-08 Bolivia	L 0-2	Santa Cruz	Fr		12 000	Caceres PAR
7-09 El Salvador	D 2-2	San Salvador	WCq	Treyon Bobb 2 [16 53]	24 000	Marrufo USA
11-09 El Salvador	L 2-3	Georgetown	WCq	Gregory Richardson [1], Chris Nurse [62]	4 141	Bogle JAM
12-10 Mexico	L 0-5	Houston	WCq		12 115	Lopez GUA
16-10 Costa Rica	L 0-7	San Jose	WCq		27 500	Rodriguez HON
21-10 St Vincent/Grenadines	L 1-2	Gros Islet	CNq	Gregory Richardson [45p]	1 200	Pinas SUR
23-10 Curacao	W 2-1	Gros Islet	CNq	Vurlon Mills [1], Gregory Richardson [42p]	750	Bogle JAM
25-10 St Lucia	W 3-0	Gros Islet	CNq	Vurlon Mills 2 [14 34], Gregory Richardson [37]	2 500	Willett ATG
14-11 Haiti	L 0-1	St George's	CNq		1 000	Skeete BRB
16-11 Grenada	L 1-2	St George's	CNq	Daniel Wilson [48]	1 400	Brizan TRI
18-11 French Guiana †	W 4-3	St George's	CNq	Vurlon Mills [12], Walter Moore [46], Shawn Beveney 2 [58 87p]	1 500	Nunez CUB

Fr = Friendly match • CC = Digicel Caribbean Cup • WC = FIFA World Cup • q = qualifier • † Not a full international

GUYANA 2012

GFF SUPER LEAGUE

	Pl	W	D	L	F	A	Pts	Alpha Utd	Tigers	Dan Amstel	Amelia's Ward	Rosignol Utd	Pele	Milerock	Buxton Utd	Seawall	Victoria Kings
Alpha United	9	8	1	0	32	5	**25**		1-1			2-1	5-2			2-0	
Western Tigers	9	6	1	2	19	7	**19**										
Dan Amstel	10	5	3	2	21	17	**18**	1-5	2-1		1-2	5-4	1-1				5-1
Amelia's Ward United	9	6	0	3	19	17	**18**	0-2	2-4			5-4			2-0	2-0	
Rosignol United	10	5	1	4	25	20	**16**		0-1	2-2			2-0	2-1	3-0	4-3	
Pele	9	4	1	4	14	15	**13**		0-2		6-1				0-1		
Milerock	9	2	2	5	9	21	**8**	0-8	2-1	0-2	0-3		0-1			2-0	
Buxton United	9	2	1	6	7	19	**7**	0-5	0-1	0-1		1-3	1-1			1-0	
Seawall	9	1	2	6	8	16	**5**		0-3	1-1		3-0					
Victoria Kings	9	0	2	7	9	26	**2**	0-2	0-5		0-2	1-3	0-1	3-3	3-4	1-1	

4/03/2012 – 27/06/2012

KASHIF & SHANGHAI CUP 2012-13

First round		Quarter-finals		Semi-finals		Final	
Buxton United	3						
Winners Connection	1	**Buxton United**	1				
Grove Hi-Tech	0	Western Tigers	0				
Western Tigers	7			**Buxton United**	1		
BV/Triumph United	3			Alpha United	0		
Timehri Panthers	1	BV/Triumph United	0				
Rosignol United	1	**Alpha United**	4			**Buxton United**	0 5p
Alpha United	3					Amelia's Ward United	0 4p
Pele	6						
Buxton Stars	0	**Pele**	4			CUP FINAL	
Uitvlugt Warriors	3 1p	Silver Shattas	0				
Silver Shattas	3 4p			Pele	1		
Dan Amstel	2			**Amelia's Ward United**	2	1-01-2013	
Milerock	1	Dan Amstel	0 8p				
Mill Ballers	0	**Amelia's Ward United**	0 9p				
Amelia's Ward United	2			Third place: Alpha United 3-1 Pele			

HAI – HAITI

FIFA/COCA-COLA WORLD RANKING

'93	'94	'95	'96	'97	'98	'99	'00	'01	'02	'03	'04	'05	'06	'07	'08	'09	'10	'11	'12
145	132	153	114	125	109	99	84	82	72	96	95	98	102	69	102	90	90	81	39

2012

Jan	Feb	Mar	Apr	May	Jun	Jul	Aug	Sep	Oct	Nov	Dec	High	Low	Av
80	71	72	72	71	71	62	80	77	60	57	39	39	155	101

Five years after winning the Caribbean Cup for the first time, Haiti came within touching distance of a second title at the end of 2012 following a great campaign during which they firmly established themselves again as one of the top nations in Caribbean football. Cuban coach Israel Cantero was brought in for the campaign in a surprise move that quickly paid dividends. In six qualifying matches, Haiti won five to book their place in the finals in Antigua. There they negotiated the first round with relative ease and then found themselves up against Cantero's Cuban compatriots in the semi-final. A horrible mistake by Haiti goalkeeper Johnny Placide gifted Cuba an early goal and they never recovered although they did finish in third place after beating Martinique in a play-off. In club football there were surprise champions in 2012 with Valencia winning their first-ever title. What made the achievement all the more extraordinary was that Valencia are based in Léogâne, a city located at the epicentre of the 2010 earthquake which damaged 90 per cent of the buildings. Coach Frantz Decembre saw his side finish 14 points ahead of rivals FICA although their withdrawal from the Super 8 tournament won by Tempete at the end of the season put paid to their ambitions of a double.

CFU CARIBBEAN CUP RECORD

1989 DNE **1991** DNQ **1992-1993** DNE **1994** 5 r1 **1995** DNE **1996** 6 r1 **1997** withdrew **1998** 3 SF **1999** 4 SF **2001** 2 F **2005** DNQ **2007** 1 winners **2008** 5 r1 **2010** DNQ **2012** 3 SF

FEDERATION HAITIENNE DE FOOTBALL (FHF)

Stade Sylvio Cator
Rue Oswald Durand,
Port-au-Prince
+509 37018397

info@fhfhaiti.com
www.fhfhaiti.com
FA 1904 CON 1961 FIFA 1933
P Yves Jean Bart
GS Carlo Marcelin

THE STADIA

2014 FIFA World Cup Stadia

Stade Sylvio Cator	
Port-au-Prince	10 500

Other Main Stadia

Parc St Victor	
Cap-Haïtien	7 500
Parc Levelt	
Saint-Marc	5 000
Parc Savil Dessaint	
La Gonave	5 000
Parc Indrich de Four	
Léogâne	2 000

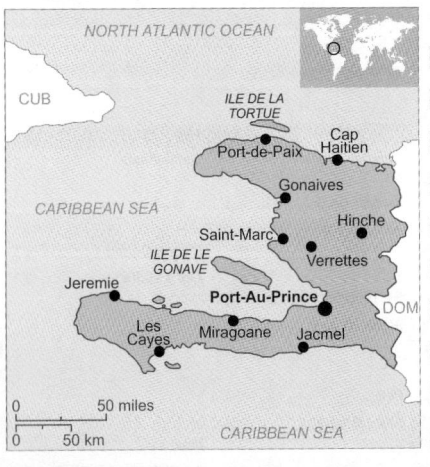

MAJOR CITIES/TOWNS

		Population
1	Port-au-Prince	774 167
2	Carrefour	479 584
3	Delmas	372 549
4	Gonaïves	135 716
5	Pétionville	126 804
6	Cap-Haïtien	125 425
7	Saint-Marc	77 130
8	Verrettes	58 226
9	Les Cayes	51 610
10	Port-de-Paix	38 891
11	Limbe	38 589
12	Jacmel	30 052
13	Jérémie	29 898
14	L'Artibonite	29 483
15	Hinche	28 922
16	Fond-Parisien	21 004
17	Fort-Liberté	20 451
18	Mombin-Crochu	19 146
19	Petit Goâve	16 741

REPUBLIQUE D'HAITI • REPUBLIC OF HAITI

Capital	Port-au-Prince	Population	9 035 536 (88)	% in cities	47%
GDP per capita	$1300 (203)	Area km²	27 750 km² (147)	GMT +/-	-5
Neighbours (km)	Dominican Republic 360 • Coast 1771				

RECENT INTERNATIONAL MATCHES PLAYED BY HAITI

2008 Opponents	Score	Venue	Comp	Scorers	Att	Referee
4-12 Antigua and Barbuda	D 1-1	Montego Bay	CNr1	Sony Norde [53]	2 500	Forde BRB
6-12 Guadeloupe	L 2-3	Trelawny	CNr1	Alexandre Boucicant [45p], Ednelson Raymond [68]	1 000	Taylor BRB
8-12 Cuba	W 1-0	Montego Bay	CNr1	Alexandre Boucicant [37]	1 500	Brizan TRI
2009						
17-01 Guatemala	L 0-1	Fort Pierce	Fr		5 000	Jurisvic USA
11-02 Colombia	L 0-2	Pereira	Fr		20 000	Ruiz COL
31-03 Panama	L 0-4	La Chorrera	Fr		4 500	Amaya PAN
23-05 Jamaica	D 2-2	Fort Lauderdale	Fr	Jean Jerome [39], Leonel Saint-Preux [66]	12 000	Marrufo USA
19-06 Panama	D 1-1	Port-au-Prince	Fr	Philbert Merceus [74]	2 000	Grant HAI
27-06 Syria	L 1-2	Montreal	Fr	Leonel Saint-Preux [29]	4 649	Petrescu CAN
4-07 Honduras	L 0-1	Seattle	GCr1		15 387	Rodriguez MEX
8-07 Grenada	W 2-0	Washington DC	GCr1	Fabrice Noel [13], James Marcelin [79]	26 079	Moreno PAN
11-07 USA	D 2-2	Foxboro	GCr1	Vaniel Sirin [46], Mones Cherry [48]	24 137	Quesada CRC
19-07 Mexico	L 0-4	Dallas	GCqf		85 000	Campbell JAM
2010						
5-05 Argentina	L 0-4	Cutral Co	Fr		16 500	Osses CHI
2-11 Guyana	D 0-0	Marabella	CCq		880	Taylor BRB
4-11 St Vincent/Grenadines	W 3-1	Port of Spain	CCq	Sony Norde [45], Leonel Saint-Preux [62], Ricardo Charles [83]	1 100	Campbell JAM
6-11 Trinidad and Tobago	L 0-4	Port of Spain	CCq		850	Campbell JAM
18-11 Qatar	W 1-0	Doha	Fr	Jean Monuma [53]	5 000	Al Awaji KSA
2011						
9-02 El Salvador	L 0-1	San Salvador	Fr		15 000	Espana GUA
2-09 US Virgin Islands	W 6-0	Port au Prince	WCq	James Marcelin [18], Jean Maurice [27], Pierre Listner [44], Jean Monuma [61], Jean Alexandre 2 [65 78]	12 000	Cruz CRC
6-09 Curacao	W 4-2	Willemstad	WCq	Kevin Lafrance [37], James Marcelin [58], Wilde Guerrier [61], Angelo Zimmerman OG [75]	5 000	Solis CRC
7-10 US Virgin Islands	W 7-0	Frederiksted	WCq	Jean Maurice 3 [5 66 82p], Kim Jaggy [11], Kervens Belfort 2 [57 74p], Reginal Goreux [64]	406	Holder CAY
11-10 Curacao	D 2-2	Port au Prince	WCq	Jean Maurice [25p], Kervens Belfort [60]	7 800	Clarke LCA
11-11 Antigua and Barbuda	L 0-1	St John's	WCq		8 000	Pineda HON
15-11 Antigua and Barbuda	W 2-1	Port au Prince	WCq	Judelin Aveska [60], Kervens Belfort [67]	3 000	Toledo USA
2012						
7-09 Saint-Martin †	W 7-0	Port-au-Prince	CNq	Jean Philippe Peguero 3 [4 40 45], Monuma Constant Junior 2 [22 43], Kevin La France [70], Maurice Jean Eudes [90]	10 000	Morrison JAM
9-09 Bermuda	W 3-1	Port-au-Prince	CNq	Olrish Saurel [30], Maurice Jean Eudes [39], Jean Philippe Peguero [41]	10 500	Skeete BRB
11-09 Puerto Rico	W 2-1	Port-au-Prince	CNq	Jean Philippe Peguero [65p], Maurice Jean Eudes [67]	12 000	Morrison JAM
14-11 Guyana	W 1-0	St George's	CNq	Olrish Saurel [47]	1 000	Skeete BRB
16-11 French Guiana †	L 0-1	St George's	CNq		750	Nunez CUB
18-11 Grenada	W 2-0	St George's	CNq	Jeasony Alcenat [36], OG [58]	3 000	Brizan TRI
7-12 Trinidad and Tobago	D 0-0	St John's	CNr1		150	Legister JAM
9-12 Dominican Republic	W 2-1	St John's	CNr1	Leonel Saint Preaux [10], Jean Philippe Peguero [39]	800	Bonilla SLV
11-12 Antigua and Barbuda	W 1-0	St John's	CNr1	Jean Philippe Peguero [19]	800	Brea CUB
14-12 Cuba	L 0-1	St John's	CNsf		200	Wijngaarde SUR
16-12 Martinique	W 1-0	St John's	CN3p	Leonel Saint Preaux [95]	100	Dacosta BAH

Fr = Friendly match • CC = Digicel Caribbean Cup • GC = CONCACAF Gold Cup • WC = FIFA World Cup
q = qualifier • r1 = first round group stage • sf = semi-final • f = final • † Not a full international

HAITI NATIONAL TEAM HISTORICAL RECORDS

Past Coaches: Ernst Nono Baptiste 1999 • Emmanuel Sanon 1999-2000 • Jorge Castelli ARG 2001-02 • Andres Cruciani ARG 2002-03 • Fernando Clavijo USA 2003-05 • Luis Armelio Garcia CUB 2006-07 • Wagneau Eloi 2008 • Jairo Rios Rendon COL 2009-10 • Edson Tavares BRA 2010-11 • Carlo Marcelin 2011 • Israel Cantero CUB 2012-

SUPER HUIT 2011

Quarter-finals			Semi-finals			Final		
AS Capoise	1	3						
Cavaly Léogâne *	0	0	**AS Capoise** *	0	1			
Valencia Léogâne *	0	0	Baltimore St Marc	0	1			
Baltimore St Marc	0	1				**AS Capoise**	0	5p
Victory FC	1	2				Tempête St Marc	0	4p
America Cayes *	0	0	Victory FC	0	2			
Aigle Noir *	1	3	**Tempête St Marc** *	2	1			
Tempête St Marc	0	1	* Home team in 1st leg					

Played between the eight teams with the best overall record from the 2011 Ouverture and Cloture
Trophée des Champions: Parc Levelt, St Marc, 18-12-2011. Baltimore St Marc 0-0 9-8p Tempête St Marc (played between the Ouverture and Cloture winners).

HAITI 2012

CHAMIONNAT NATIONAL

	Pl	W	D	L	F	A	Pts	Valencia	FICA	Baltimore	Tempête	America	Aigle Noir	Victory	Cavaly	Don Bosco	Mirebalais	Violette	Capoise
Valencia Léogâne †	31	18	10	3	33	8	**64**		0-1	0-0	2-0	3-0	1-0	0-0	2-0	2-0	2-0	3-0	0-0
FICA	32	14	8	10	31	30	**50**	1-2		0-0	1-0	4-1	1-0	3-2	1-0	1-0	1-0	2-0	0-0
Baltimore St Marc	32	12	13	7	26	16	**49**	1-1	1-1		2-1	1-2	3-0	0-0	1-0	0-0	1-0	2-1	1-0
Tempête St Marc	31	13	7	11	29	23	**46**	0-0	1-1	1-0		1-0	2-0	1-0	0-0	2-0	1-1	2-0	2-0
America Cayes	32	11	10	11	24	32	**43**	1-0	2-0	0-0	1-0		1-0	0-0	2-0	1-1	0-0	1-0	2-0
Aigle Noir	32	9	9	14	26	29	**36**	0-0	2-1	1-0	1-0	3-0		1-1	0-1	1-1	1-0	0-0	1-1
Victory FC	32	8	16	8	29	25	**40**	1-2	3-1	0-0	0-0	2-1	1-1		0-1	0-1	1-0	1-1	3-1
Cavaly Léogâne	32	10	10	12	22	28	**40**	0-0	0-1	2-1	0-3	2-2	1-1	0-1		0-0	2-2	2-1	2-1
Don Bosco	32	9	12	11	23	23	**39**	0-1	2-0	1-1	0-0	1-1	1-2	1-0	0-1		0-0	0-1	3-2
AS Mirebalais	32	9	11	12	20	22	**38**	1-0	1-0	0-0	1-0	0-1	2-1	0-0	0-0	0-0		0-1	0-0
Violette AC	32	10	5	17	26	34	**35**	0-1	1-0	0-0	4-0	1-2	1-3	2-0	0-1	0-0	2-1		3-0
AS Capoise	32	7	11	14	18	37	**32**	0-0	0-0	0-2	0-0	1-1	1-2	0-0	2-1	1-0	1-0	1-0	

24/03/2012 - 10/11/2012 • † Qualified for the CFU Club Championship

SUPER HUIT 2012

Quarter-finals			Semi-finals			Final		
Tempête St Marc ‡‡	w/o							
America Cayes								
Cavaly Léogâne	0 0	2p	**Tempête St Marc** ‡	w/o				
Valencia Léogâne	0 0	4p	Valencia Léogâne					
Aigle Noir	0	2				**Tempête St Marc**	2	
Baltimore St Marc	1	0				FICA	0	
Victory SC	0	1	Aigle Noir	0	0	Parc Levelt, St Marc		
FICA	0	5	**FICA**	0	3	16-12-2012		
			* Home team in 1st leg					

Played between the top eight teams from 2012 • ‡‡ Tempete lost the first leg 1-0 before America withdrew •
‡ Valencia walked off in the first leg with Tempête winning 2-1 and were disqualified
Trophée des Champions: **Tempête St Marc** w/o Valencia

HKG – HONG KONG

FIFA/COCA-COLA WORLD RANKING

'93	'94	'95	'96	'97	'98	'99	'00	'01	'02	'03	'04	'05	'06	'07	'08	'09	'10	'11	'12
112	98	111	124	129	136	122	123	137	150	142	133	117	117	125	151	143	146	169	163

2012													High	Low	Av
Jan	Feb	Mar	Apr	May	Jun	Jul	Aug	Sep	Oct	Nov	Dec				
168	163	158	161	161	158	160	154	159	160	172	163		90	172	130

Hong Kong's football administration has been in a state of flux despite government attempts to improve the running of the game in the former British colony. Scottish chief executive Gordon McKie left his post at the Hong Kong Football Association just months after taking over with a remit to overhaul the league and improve the standard of the national team. Head coach Ernie Merrick, appointed during McKie's term in office, resigned from his post in late October as a result of the political fall-out and was replaced by Korean Kim Pan Gon. Kim had taken Hong Kong to the finals of the 2010 East Asia Cup but had little time to make much impact on the team ahead of the qualifying rounds for the 2013 tournament. Hong Kong hosted the five team group and finished third. Only the top team progressed to the finals but there were wins over Guam and Chinese Taipei to celebrate as well as an excellent performance against Australia who were pushed all the way before Brett Emerton scored a late winner to deny Hong Kong a famous result. Kitchee continued to dominate the local league, winning the league title, the League Cup and the Hong Kong FA Cup, defeating TSW Pegasus in the final of both knockout competitions to secure their place in the 2013 AFC Cup. Sun Hei were the other trophy winners with a Senior Shield win over South China.

FIFA WORLD CUP RECORD
1930-1970 DNE 1974-2014 DNQ

THE HONG KONG FOOTBALL ASSOCIATION LTD (HKFA)

- 55 Fat Kwong Street, Homantin, Kowloon
- +852 27129122
- +852 27604303
- hkfa@hkfa.com
- www.hkfa.com

FA 1914 CON 1954 FIFA 1954
P Timothy Tsun Ting Fok
GS Vincent Yuen

THE STADIA

2014 FIFA World Cup Stadia
Siu Sai Wan Sports Ground
Hong Kong — 12 000

Other Main Stadia
Hong Kong Stadium
Hong Kong — 40 000
Mong Kok Stadium
Kowloon — 6 664
Sha Tin Sports Ground
Sha Tin — 5 000
Yuen Long Stadium
Yuen Long — 5 000

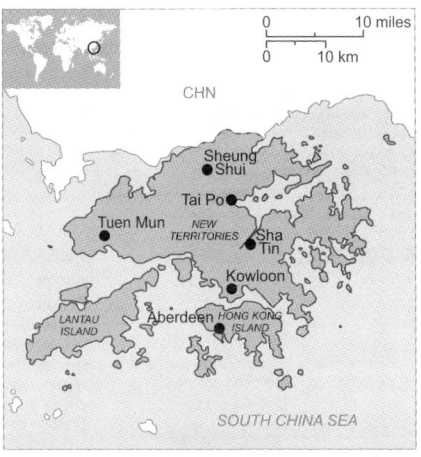

MAJOR CITIES/TOWNS

		Population
1	Sha Tin, NT	628 000
2	Eastern, HKI	616 000
3	Kwun Tong, Kw	562 000
4	Tuen Mun, NT	488 000
5	Kwai Tsing, NT	477 000
6	Yuen Long, NT	449 000
7	Wong Tai Sin, Kw	444 000
8	Kowloon City	381 000
9	Sham Shui Po, Kw	353 000
10	Sai Kung, NT	327 000
11	Tai Po, NT	310 000
12	North, NT	298 000
13	Southern, HKI	290 000
14	Yau Tsim Mong, Kw	282 000
15	Tsuen Wan, NT	275 000
16	Central & Western	261 000

Kw = Kowloon
NT = New Territories
HKI = Hong Kong Island

XIANGGANG TEBIE XINGZHENGQU • HONG KONG SPECIAL ADMINISTRATIVE REGION

Capital Victoria	Population 7 055 071 (100)	% in cities 100%
GDP per capita $43 800 (15)	Area km² 1 104 km² (183)	GMT +/- +8
Neighbours (km) China 30 • Coast 733		

RECENT INTERNATIONAL MATCHES PLAYED BY HONG KONG

2010	Opponents	Score	Venue	Comp	Scorers	Att	Referee
6-01	Bahrain	L 0-4	Manama	ACq		1 550	Balideh QAT
7-02	Korea Republic	L 0-5	Tokyo	EAC		2 728	Sato JPN
11-02	Japan	L 0-3	Tokyo	EAC		16 368	Zhao Liang CHN
14-02	China PR	L 0-2	Tokyo	EAC		16 439	Kim Jong Hyeok KOR
3-03	Yemen	D 0-0	Hong Kong	ACq		1 212	Minh Tri Vo VIE
4-10	India	W 1-0	Pune	Fr	Li Haiqiang [76]	8 000	Patwal IND
9-10	Philippines	W 4-2	Kaohsiung	Fr	Chan Man Fai [5], Xu Deshuai [31], Lo Kwan Yee [84], Ju Yingzhi [91+]	650	Kao Jung Fang TPE
10-10	Macau	W 4-0	Kaohsiung	Fr	Tam Lok Hin [38], Xu Deshuai [52], Lam Hok Hei 2 [72 74]	1 200	Yu Ming Hsun TPE
12-10	Chinese Taipei	D 1-1	Kaohsiung	Fr	Lo Kwan Yee [75p]	3 000	Kao Tsai Hu TPE
17-11	Paraguay	L 0-7	Hong Kong	Fr		6 250	Mohd Salleh MAS
2011							
9-02	Malaysia	L 0-2	Kuala Lumpur	Fr			
3-06	Malaysia	D 1-1	Hong Kong	Fr	Chan Siu Ki [59]	586	
23-07	Saudi Arabia	L 0-3	Dammam	WCq		20 354	Tseytlin UZB
28-07	Saudi Arabia	L 0-5	Hong Kong	WCq		1 402	Minh Tri Vo VIE
30-09	Philippines	D 3-3	Kaohsiung	Fr	Lee Wai Lim [2], Cheng Lai Hin [22], Au Yeung Yiu Chung [86]		
2-10	Macau	W 5-1	Kaohsiung	Fr	Sham Kwok Keung 2 [19 75], Chan Siu Ki [43], Wong Chin Hung 2 [50 81]		
4-10	Chinese Taipei	W 6-0	Kaohsiung	Fr	Chan Siu Ki [15], Kwok Kin Pong [25], Chan Wai Ho [40], Lee Hong Lim 2 [42 68], Lo Kwan Yee [76]		
2012							
29-02	Chinese Taipei	W 5-1	Hong Kong	Fr	Chan Siu Ki 3 [2 5 82], Lee Hong Lim [16], Chan Man Fai [47]	5 187	
1-06	Singapore	W 1-0	Hong Kong	Fr	Lam Ka Wai [36]	4 285	
10-06	Vietnam	L 1-2	Hong Kong	Fr	Au Yeung Yiu Chung [40]	2 983	
15-08	Singapore	L 0-2	Singapore	Fr			
16-10	Malaysia	L 0-3	Hong Kong	Fr		3 267	Kwok Man Liu HKG
14-11	Malaysia	D 1-1	Kuala Lumpur	Fr			
1-12	Guam	W 2-1	Hong Kong	EACq	Chan Siu Ki 2 [2 17]	3 040	Kim Dae Yong KOR
3-12	Australia	L 0-1	Hong Kong	EACq		4 160	Iida JPN
7-12	Chinese Taipei	W 2-0	Hong Kong	EACq	Chan Wai Ho [24], Lee Hong Lim [25]	2 315	Iida JPN
9-12	Korea DPR	L 0-4	Hong Kong	EACq		3 345	Pechsri THA

Fr = Friendly match • EAC = East Asian Championship • AC = AFC Asian Cup • WC = FIFA World Cup • q = qualifier

HONG KONG NATIONAL TEAM HISTORICAL RECORDS

Coaches: Tom Sneddon ENG 1954-56 • Lai Shiu Wing 1958-67 • Chu Wing Keung 1967 • Tang Sum 1968 • Lau Tim 1968 • Hui King Shing 1969-70 • Chan Fai Hung 1970-72 • Ho Ying Fun 1973-75 • Franz van Balkom NED 1976-77 • Chan Yong Chong MAS 1978-79 • Peter McParland ENG 1980 • George Knobel NED 1980 • Lo Tak Kuen 1981 • Kwok Ka Ming 1982-90 • Wong Man Wai 1992 • Chan Hung Ping 1993 • Khoo Luan Khen MAS 1994-95 • Tsang Wai Chung 1996 • Kwok Ka Ming 1997 • Sebastian Araujo BRA 1998 • Chan Hung Ping 1999-2000 • Arie van der Zouwen NED 2000-01 • Casemiro Mior BRA 2002 • Lai Sun Cheung 2003-07 • Lee Kin Wo 2007 • Dejan Antonic SRB & Goran Paulic CRO 2008-09 • Kim Pan Gon KOR 2009 • Liu Chun Fai 2010 • Tsang Wai Chung 2010-11 • Liu Chun Fai 2011-12 • Ernie Merrick SCO 2012 • Kim Pan Gon KOR 2012-

LEAGUE CUP 2011-12

Quarter-finals		Semi-finals		Final	
Kitchee	2				
Tuen Mun	1	**Kitchee**	4		
Tai Po	2	South China	1		
South China	4			**Kitchee**	2
Citizen	1			TSW Pegasus	1
Sun Hei	0	Citizen	1		
Sham Shui Po	1	**TSW Pegasus**	4	Mong Kok Stadium
TSW Pegasus	4			15-04-2012, Att: 3957
				Ref: Ng Kai Lam

1st round: HK Sapling 0-1 **Sham Shui Po** • Biu Chun Rangers 0-0 4-5p **Tuen Mun**

LEAGUE CUP FINAL 2012

Kitchee 2 Yago [35], Lo Kwan Yee [62]
Pegasus 1 Carrijo [90p]

Kitchee - Wang Zhenpeng - Lo Kwan Yee•, Zesh Rehman, Fernando Recio, Dani Cancela - Diaz• (Liu Quankun 51) - Huang Yang - Lam Ka Wai - Chu Siu Kei (c)•, Yago Gonzalez (Jordi Tarres 66), Liang Zicheng (Tsang Kam To• 75). Tr: Josep Gombau
Pegasus - Hisanori Takada - Lee Wai Lun, Ng Wai Chiu, Deng Jinghuang (Lucas 64), Cheung Kin Fung - Eugene Mboma, Lau Nim Yat - Jaimes McKee (Godfred Karikari 46), Itaparica (c)•, Lee Hong Lim (Lau Ka Shing 66) - Leandro Carrijo. Tr: Chan Hiu Ming

HONG KONG 2011-12
COOLPOINT VENTILATION FIRST DIVISION

	Pl	W	D	L	F	A	Pts	Kitchee	Pegasus	South China	Sun Hei	Citizen	Tuen Mun	Rangers	Tai Po	Sapling	Sham Shui Po
Kitchee †	18	13	3	2	44	20	42		3-2	2-2	1-1	3-1	1-0	4-1	4-2	6-0	1-0
TSW Pegasus	18	12	2	4	48	26	38	2-1		2-1	1-2	6-4	3-1	4-1	4-0	4-0	3-0
South China	18	10	6	2	47	17	36	2-0	4-0		0-0	2-2	1-2	3-0	3-0	4-0	1-1
Sun Hei	18	8	4	6	29	22	28	1-2	1-3	2-4		2-3	1-2	1-0	2-1	5-0	5-0
Citizen	18	5	8	5	29	31	23	0-0	2-3	3-3	1-1		1-1	2-2	1-2	0-2	1-0
Tuen Mun	18	5	8	5	26	22	23	0-1	1-1	1-1	1-2	1-2		1-1	3-2	3-0	1-0
Biu Chun Rangers	18	6	4	8	32	38	22	2-6	0-3	2-5	2-0	2-2	1-1		4-1	4-0	2-0
Tai Po	18	6	2	10	24	40	20	2-5	3-1	0-4	0-1	0-0	1-1	1-4		3-0	2-1
Hong Kong Sapling	18	2	4	12	17	53	10	2-3	2-2	0-5	1-1	1-3	1-1	2-3	2-3		2-2
Sham Shui Po	18	1	3	14	9	36	6	0-1	0-4	0-2	0-1	0-1	2-6	2-1	0-1	1-2	

3/09/2011 – 20/05/2012 • † Qualified for the AFC Cup
Top scorers: 11 - **SANDRO** BRA, Rangers & **ITAPARICA** BRA, Pegasus • 10 - **LEANDRO CARRIJO** BRA, Pegasus • 9 - Godfred **KARIKARI**, Pegasus

HONG KONG 2011-12 SECOND DIVISION

	Pl	W	D	L	F	A	Pts
Kam Fung	22	16	2	4	69	24	50
Southern District	22	14	5	3	43	23	47
Hong Kong FC	22	14	4	4	46	23	46
Wanchai	22	12	4	6	35	29	40
Double Flower	22	12	3	7	60	35	39
Happy Valley	22	11	2	9	34	30	35
Shatin	22	7	4	11	41	43	25
Tai Chung	22	7	4	11	35	56	25
Yuen Long	22	6	4	12	26	43	22
Wing Yee	22	6	3	13	36	66	21
Kwun Tong	22	4	4	14	20	43	16
Kwai Tsing	22	2	3	17	25	55	9

3/09/2011 – 15/04/2012

SENIOR SHIELD 2011-12

Quarter-finals		Semi-finals		Final	
Sun Hei	2 2				
Tai Po	1 1	Sun Hei	1 2		
Citizen	2 1	Tuen Mun	0 2		
Tuen Mun	2 2			Sun Hei †	1 5p
TSW Pegasus	5 4			South China	1 3p
Biu Chun Rangers	0 0	TSW Pegasus	2 0	Hong Kong Stadium
Sham Shui Po	1 1	South China	2 1	18-02-2012, Att: 6234
South China	1 2			Ref: Liu Kwok Man

1st round: **Pegasus** 1-1 1-0 Kitchee •
Tuen Mun 3-0 0-0 Hong Kong Sapling
† Qualified for the AFC Cup

Scorers - Dane Milovanovic 52 for Sun Hei; Chan Wai Ho 54 for South China

FA CUP 2011-12

Quarter-finals		Semi-finals		Final	
Kitchee	3				
South China	2	Kitchee	1		
Sun Hei	0	Biu Chun Rangers	0		
Biu Chun Rangers	2			Kitchee	3 5p
Sham Shui Po	2			TSW Pegasus	3 3p
Tai Po	1	Sham Shui Po	1	Hong Kong Stadium
HK Sapling	1	TSW Pegasus	3	26-05-2012, Att: 1990
TSW Pegasus	5			Ref: Ng Chiu Kok

1st round: **HK Sapling** 3-3 5-4p Tuen Mun •
Kitchee 1-0 Citizen

FA CUP FINAL 2012

Kitchee 3 5p Liang Zicheng [32], Lo Kwan Yee [110], Roberto [120]

Pegasus 3 3p Carrijo 2 [67 99], Mckee [109]

Kitchee - Guo Jianqiao - Lo Kwan Yee, Zesh Rehman, Fernando Recio••♦[119], Dani Cancela - Diaz• - Huang Yang, Lam Ka Wai (Tsang Kam To 69) - Chu Siu Kei (c), Yago Gonzalez (Roberto Losada• 42), Liang Zicheng (Chan Man Fai• 81). Tr: Josep Gombau
Pegasus - Hisanori Takada - Lee Wai Lun, Ng Wai Chiu, Lucas•, Poon Yiu Cheuk (Leandro Carrijo 59) - Eugene Mbome, Chan Ming Kong (Lee Hong Lim• 59) - Lau Nim Yat••♦[120], Itaparica (c)•, Cheung Kin Fung (Jaimes McKee 84) - Godfred Karikari•. Tr: Chan Hiu Ming

MEDALS TABLE

	Overall		Lge		FAC		Shield		VC		LC		Asia	
	G	S	G	B	G	B	G	B	G	B	G	B	G	S
1 South China	73	40	31	16	10	4	21	12	8	7	3			1
2 Seiko	29	8	9	3	6	1	8	2	6	2				
3 Eastern	16	9	4	2	3	1	7	2	2	4				
4 Happy Valley	15	38	6	16	2	5	5	9	1	3	1	5		
5 Kitchee	15	13	5	6	1	1	5	5			3	1		
6 Sun Hei	12	8	3	2	3	1	2	4			4	1		
7 Rangers	9	8	1		2	3	4	2	2	2		1		
Sing Tao	9	8	1	4		1	6	2	2	1				
9 Instant-Dict	6	11	2	2	3	2		4	1	3				
10 Bulova	5	4		2	2	1	1	1	2	1				

CUP FINAL PENS

Kitchee			Pegasus
✓	Roberto		
		Itaparica	✓
✓	Chan Man Fai		
		Lee Hong Lim	✗
✓	Rehman		
		Carrijo	✓
✓	Diaz		
		Godfred	✓
✓	Lo Kwan Yee		

HON – HONDURAS

FIFA/COCA-COLA WORLD RANKING

'93	'94	'95	'96	'97	'98	'99	'00	'01	'02	'03	'04	'05	'06	'07	'08	'09	'10	'11	'12
40	53	49	45	73	91	69	46	27	40	49	59	41	56	53	40	37	59	53	58

2012												High	Low	Av
Jan	Feb	Mar	Apr	May	Jun	Jul	Aug	Sep	Oct	Nov	Dec			
51	59	63	61	62	55	63	65	72	66	56	58	20	95	51

Honduras made it through to the final stage of qualifying for the 2014 FIFA World Cup in the CONCACAF region - but only just. Trailing both Canada and Panama by two points going into the last group game they had to beat the Canadians to make it through to the final hexagonal group and they kept their best until last with a resounding 8-1 victory. Their Colombian coach Luis Suarez - who took Ecuador to the 2006 finals - will be out to follow compatriot Reinaldo Rueda by leading Honduras to what would be successive finals. At the start of 2013, however, Honduras failed to win the Copa Centroamericana after losing 1-0 in the final to hosts Costa Rica in the latest clash between the two dominant powers in the region. Striker Jerry Bengtson has given the side more firepower upfront but the lack of depth in the squad remains a concern. In club football Olimpia were once again in dominant form at home winning both tournaments played in 2012 to complete a hat trick of championship wins. It was the eighth straight tournament in which Olimpia had not only qualified for the knockout stage but made it through to the final. In May they beat Marathon 1-0 on aggregate in the final thanks to a Douglas Caetano goal while at the end of the year they won the title in more convincing fashion with a 4-0 aggregate win over Victoria.

CONCACAF GOLD CUP RECORD
1991 F r/u **1993** r1 **1996** r1 **1998** r1 **2000** QF **2002** DNQ **2003** r1 **2005** SF **2007** QF **2009** SF **2011** SF

FEDERACION NACIONAL AUTONOMA DE FUTBOL DE HONDURAS (FENAFUTH)

Colonia Florencia Norte, Edificio Plaza América, Ave. Roble, 1 y 2 Nivel, PO Box 827, 504 Tegucigalpa
☎ +504 22311436
📠 +504 22398826
✉ fenafuth.org@gmail.com
🌐 www.fenafuth.org
FA 1951 CON 1961 FIFA 1951
P Rafael Callejas
GS Alfredo Hawit Banegas

THE STADIA
2014 FIFA World Cup Stadia
Estadio Olimpico
San Pedro Sula   40 000
Other Main Stadia
Estadio Tiburcio Carias Andino
Tegucigalpa   35 000
Estadio Nilmo Edwards
La Ceiba   15 000
Estadio Excélsior
Puerto Cortés   10 000

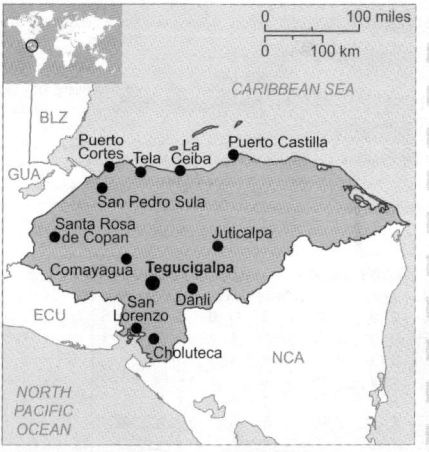

MAJOR CITIES/TOWNS
		Population
1	Tegucigalpa	1 055 298
2	San Pedro Sula	614 912
3	Choloma	206 016
4	La Ceiba	166 835
5	El Progreso	126 396
6	Choluteca	91 193
7	Comayagua	72 802
8	Puerto Cortés	58 914
9	La Lima	57 070
10	Danli	55 169
11	Siguatepeque	53 612
12	Juticalpa	42 523
13	Catacamas	42 370
14	Tocoa	41 028
15	Villanueva	40 235
16	Tela	34 476
17	Olanchito	33 583
18	Santa Rosa	33 479
19	San Lorenzo	27 059

REPUBLICA DE HONDURAS • REPUBLIC OF HONDURAS
Capital Tegucigalpa   Population 7 792 854 (93)   % in cities 48%
GDP per capita $4400 (152)   Area km² 112 090 m² (102)   GMT +/- -6
Neighbours (km) Guatemala 256, El Salvador 342, Nicaragua 922 • Coast 820

RECENT INTERNATIONAL MATCHES PLAYED BY HONDURAS

2010	Opponents	Score	Venue	Comp	Scorers	Att	Referee
16-06	Chile	L 0-1	Nelspruit	WCr1		32 664	Maillet SEY
21-06	Spain	L 0-2	Johannesburg	WCr1		54 386	Nishimura JPN
25-06	Switzerland	D 0-0	Bloemfontein	WCr1		28 042	Baldassi ARG
4-09	El Salvador	D 2-2	Los Angeles	Fr	Oscar Garcia [58], Roger Rojas [86]. W 4-3p	15 000	Stoica USA
7-09	Canada	L 1-2	Montreal	Fr	Erick Norales [34]	7 525	Geiger USA
9-10	New Zealand	D 1-1	Auckland	Fr	Walter Martinez [64]	18 153	O'Leary NZL
12-10	Guatemala	W 2-0	Los Angeles	Fr	Roger Rojas [21], George Welcome [80]	10 000	Hernandez USA
17-11	Panama	L 0-2	Panama City	Fr		3 646	Cruz CRC
18-12	Panama	W 2-1	San Pedro Sula	Fr	Johny Leveron 2 [7 44]	3 000	Rodas GUA
2011							
14-01	Costa Rica	D 1-1	Panama City	UCr1	Ramon Nunez [90]	6 000	Garcia MEX
18-01	Guatemala	W 3-1	Panama City	UCr1	Ramon Nunez [13], Jorge Claros 2 [42 88]	10 000	Aguilar SLV
21-01	El Salvador	W 2-0	Panama City	UCsf	Johnny Leveron [78], Marvin Chavez [90]	5 000	Quesada CRC
23-01	Costa Rica	W 2-1	Panama City	UCf	Walter Martinez [8], Emil Martinez [52]	2 000	Lopez GUA
9-02	Ecuador	D 1-1	La Ceiba	Fr	Carlo Costly [8]. L 4-5p	15 100	Lopez GUA
25-03	Korea Republic	L 0-4	Seoul	Fr		31 224	Sato JPN
29-03	China PR	L 0-3	Wuhan	Fr		10 000	Iemoto JPN
29-05	El Salvador	D 2-2	Houston	Fr	Carlo Costly [44], Jerry Bengtson [49p]	25 380	Villareal USA
6-06	Guatemala	D 0-0	Carson/LA	GCr1		21 550	Chacon MEX
10-06	Grenada	W 7-1	Miami	GCr1	Jerry Bengtson 2 [26 37], Carlo Costly 3 [28 67 71], Walter Martinez [88], Alfredo Mejia [93+]	18 057	Gantar CAN
13-06	Jamaica	L 0-1	Harrison/NY	GCr1		25 000	Aguilar SLV
18-06	Costa Rica	D 1-1	East Rutherford/NY	GCqf	Jerry Bengtson [49]. W 4-2p	78 807	Moreno PAN
22-06	Mexico	L 0-2	Houston	GCsf		70 627	Lopez GUA
10-08	Venezuela	W 2-0	Fort Lauderdale	Fr	Carlo Costly 2 [57 68]	20 000	Vaughn USA
3-09	Colombia	L 0-2	East Rutherford/NY	Fr		15 000	Gonzalez USA
6-09	Paraguay	L 0-3	San Pedro Sula	Fr		20 000	Aguilar SLV
8-10	USA	L 0-1	Miami	Fr		21 170	Campbell JAM
11-10	Jamaica	W 2-1	La Ceiba	Fr	Jerry Bengtson [1], Mario Martinez [54]	18 000	Moreno PAN
14-11	Serbia	W 2-0	San Pedro Sula	Fr	Jerry Bengtson 2 [4 29]	20 000	Rodas GUA
2012							
29-02	Ecuador	L 0-2	Guayaquil	Fr		5 000	Machado COL
11-04	Costa Rica	D 1-1	San Jose	Fr	David Suazo [23]	12 000	Geiger USA
26-05	New Zealand	L 0-1	Dallas	Fr		30 000	Jurisevic USA
2-06	El Salvador	W 3-0	Washington DC	Fr	Victor Bernardez [10], Carlo Costly [50], Allan Lalin [85]	41 780	Salazar USA
8-06	Panama	L 0-2	San Pedro Sula	WCq		28 215	Garcia MEX
12-06	Canada	D 0-0	Toronto	WCq		16 132	Wijngaarde SUR
7-09	Cuba	W 3-0	Havana	WCq	Jerry Bengtson [32], Victor Bernardez [62], Marvin Chavez [93+]	8 000	Quesasa CRC
11-09	Cuba	W 1-0	San Pedro Sula	WCq	Jerry Bengtson [33]	12 000	Lopez GUA
12-10	Panama	D 0-0	Panama City	WCq		27 000	Aguilar SLV
16-10	Canada	W 8-1	San Pedro Sula	WCq	Jerry Bengtson 3 [7 17 83], Carlo Costly 3 [29 49 88], Mario Martinez 2 [33 61]	38 000	Morales MEX
14-11	Peru	D 0-0	Houston	Fr		9 142	Gantar CAN

Fr = Friendly match • UC = UNCAF Cup/Copa Centroamericana • GC = CONCACAF Gold Cup • WC = FIFA World Cup
q = qualifier • r1 = first round group • qf = quarter-final • 5p = fifth place play-off • sf = semi-final • f = final

HONDURAS NATIONAL TEAM HISTORICAL RECORDS

Caps: 137 - Amado Guevara 1994- • 101 - Carlos Pavon 1993- • 98 - Noel Valladares 2000- • 88 - Milton Nunez 1994-2008 • 85 - Danilo Turcios 1999- & Ivan Guerrero 1999- • 84 - Maynor Figueroa 2003- • 83 - Julio Cesar de Leon 1999- • 76 - Wilson Palacios 2003- • 71 - Samuel Caballero 1998-2008

Goals: 58 - Carlos Pavon 1993-2010 • 35 - Wilmer Velasquez 1996-2007 • 34 - Milton Nunez 1994-2008 • 29 - Amado Guevara 1994-2010 • 28 - Nicolas Suazo 1991-98 • 20 - Carlo Costly 2007- • 18 - Saul Martinez 2001-08 • 17 - Eduardo Bennett 1991-2000 • 16 - David Suazo 1999- • 15 - Julio Cesar de Leon 1999- • 13 - Jairo Martinez 1998-

Coaches: Flavio Ortega 1991-92 • Estanislao Malinowski URU 1993-94 • Carlos Carranza 1995-96 • Miguel Company PER 1997-98 • Ramon Maradiaga 1999-02 • Bora Milutinovic SRB 2003-04 • Jose de la Paz Herrera 2005 • Flavio Ortega 2006 • Reinaldo Rueda COL 2006-10 • Juan de Dios Castillo MEX 2010-11 • Luis Fernando Suarez COL 2011-

HONDURAS 2011-12

TORNEO CLAUSURA

	Pl	W	D	L	F	A	Pts	Olimpia	Motagua	Marathón	At. Choloma	Real España	Vida	Victoria	Necaxa	Dep. Savio	Platense
Olimpia †	18	10	5	3	32	14	35		0-0	1-0	2-0	2-2	1-0	1-0	4-0	7-2	2-0
Motagua †	18	7	11	0	22	10	32	0-0		1-1	1-0	2-0	1-1	2-0	2-0	0-0	1-1
Marathón †	18	8	7	3	25	19	31	1-0	0-1		1-1	2-1	2-3	2-1	1-1	1-0	2-2
Atlético Choloma †	18	8	5	5	20	18	29	1-0	0-0	2-3		1-1	2-1	2-1	2-0	2-1	1-0
Real España †	18	7	4	7	28	26	25	1-2	1-1	1-3	3-1		4-0	1-2	2-0	2-1	1-0
Vida †	18	5	9	4	24	25	24	3-3	1-1	2-2	1-1	4-0		1-0	1-0	0-3	0-0
Victoria	18	7	1	10	28	28	22	2-0	1-2	0-1	1-2	2-1	1-2		3-2	5-1	3-2
Necaxa	18	4	4	10	20	25	16	0-0	2-2	0-1	2-0	0-1	0-0	2-3		2-1	5-0
Deportivo Savio	18	4	4	10	25	41	16	2-4	1-4	1-1	0-0	2-5	3-3	2-1	2-1		2-1
Platense	18	1	8	9	14	32	11	0-3	1-1	1-1	0-2	1-1	1-1	2-2	0-3	2-1	

15/01/2012 - 29/04/2012 • † Qualified for the play-offs
Top scorers (including play-offs): 9 - Oscar **TORLACOFF** URU, At. Choloma • 8 - **JOCIMAR NASCIMENTO** BRA, Dep. Savio; Mauricio **COPETE** COL, Victoria & Roger **ROJAS**, Olimpia • 7 - Luis **RAMIREZ**, Marathón; Charles **CORDOBA** COL, Vida & Juan **MEJIA**, Olimpia • 6 - Carlos **DISCUA**, Motagua; Jonathan **HANSEN** ARG, Real España & **DOUGLAS CAETANO** BRA, Olimpia

CLAUSURA 2011-12 PLAY-OFFS

Quarter-finals
Olimpia — Bye
Atlético Choloma 0 1
Real España * 1 2
Motagua — Bye
Vida * 0 1
Marathón 0 2

Semi-finals
Olimpia 1 5
Real España * 0 0
Motagua * 0 0
Marathón 0 2

Final
Olimpia † 0 1
Marathón * 0 0

† Qualified for the CONCACAF Champions League • * Home team in 1st leg

CLAUSURA FINAL 1ST LEG
Olimpico, San Pedro Sula, 12-05-2012, 13 898, Armando Castro

Marathón 0
Olimpia 0

MARATHON
Shane **ORIO** - Mauricio **SABILLON**, Yobani **AVILA**, Romel **MURILLO**, Quiarol **ARZU** (Pastor **MARTINEZ** 46) - David **MEZA**, Alexander **AGUILAR** (Reinieri **MAYORQUIN** 82), Wilmer **FUENTES**, Mario **BERRIOS** - Jerry **PALACIOS** (Mariano **ACEVEDO** 65), Mitchel **BROWN**•. Tr: Ramon **MARADIAGA**

OLIMPIA
Donis **ESCOBER**• - Fabio **DE SOUZA**, Brayan **BECKELES**, Juan **GARCIA**, Johnny **PALACIOS**, Oscar **GARCIA** - Reynaldo **TILGUATH** (Irvin **REYNA** 70), Luis **GARRIDO**, Javier **PORTILLO** (Oscar **BONILLA** 88) - Juan **MEJIA**• (Carlos **MEJIA** 63), Roger **ROJAS**. Tr: Danilo **TOSELLO**

CLAUSURA FINAL 2ND LEG
Tiburcio Andino, Tegucigalpa, 20-05-2012, 26 692, Hector Rodriguez

Olimpia 1 Caetano [47]
Marathón 0

OLIMPIA
Donis **ESCOBER** - Fabio **DE SOUZA**•, Brayan **BECKELES**•, Juan **GARCIA**, Johnny **PALACIOS**, Oscar **GARCIA** - Reynaldo **TILGUATH** (Carlos **MEJIA** 77), Luis **GARRIDO**•, Javier **PORTILLO** - Juan **MEJIA** (Roger **ROJAS** 70), Douglas **CAETANO** (Cristiano **DOS SANTOS** 85). Tr: Danilo **TOSELLO**

MARATHON
Shane **ORIO** - Yobani **AVILA**, Romel **MURILLO**••♦74, Mario **BEATA**, Mauricio **SABILLON** - Alexander **AGUILAR** (Luis **RAMIREZ** 59), David **MEZA**•, Wilmer **FUENTES**, Mario **BERRIOS** (Mariano **ACEVEDO** 79) - Jerry **PALACIOS** (Harrison **ROCHES** 72), Mitchel **BROWN**. Tr: Ramon **MARADIAGA**

HONDURAS 2011-12 AGGREGATE TABLE

	Pl	W	D	L	F	A	Pts
Marathón	36	17	11	8	57	38	62
Olimpia	36	17	10	9	48	25	61
Real España	36	16	11	9	53	39	59
Motagua	36	13	15	8	42	29	54
Vida	36	12	14	10	43	46	50
Atlético Choloma	36	11	14	11	38	45	47
Victoria	36	12	5	19	49	53	41
Deportivo Savio	36	10	10	16	47	66	40
Necaxa	36	10	9	17	36	45	39
Platense	36	7	11	18	28	55	32

Platense relegated but bought the Necaxa franchise to remain at the top level

HONDURAS 2012-13

TORNEO APERTURA

	Pl	W	D	L	F	A	Pts	Olimpia	Victoria	Motagua	Marathón	Choloma	España	Vida	Platense	Savio	Sociedad
Olimpia †	18	11	6	1	32	10	39		3-0	2-0	4-0	4-1	1-0	3-0	1-1	3-1	1-0
Victoria †	18	8	7	3	22	12	31	2-2		2-1	2-0	1-1	3-1	3-0	0-0	2-0	0-0
Motagua †	18	6	8	4	21	15	26	2-2	1-0		4-0	0-0	1-1	0-0	2-0	1-1	2-0
Marathón †	18	6	5	7	21	26	23	1-0	0-0	1-1		1-2	2-2	4-1	2-0	1-0	1-2
Atlético Choloma †	18	5	7	6	29	28	22	0-0	1-1	1-2	2-2		2-2	4-2	5-1	2-1	3-1
Real España †	18	5	6	7	21	22	21	0-0	1-0	1-0	2-3	3-1		2-4	1-1	1-1	1-0
Vida	18	5	6	7	24	35	21	1-3	0-0	2-2	2-2	3-2	0-3		1-0	2-1	2-1
Platense	18	4	8	6	15	22	20	0-1	1-3	0-0	1-0	0-0	1-0	1-1		4-2	3-2
Deportivo Savio	18	5	4	9	16	23	19	1-2	0-1	0-1	1-0	2-1	1-0	2-1	1-1		0-0
Real Sociedad	18	4	5	9	13	21	17	0-0	0-2	2-1	0-1	2-1	1-0	2-2	0-0	0-1	

28/07/2012 - 11/11/2012 • † Qualified for the play-offs (top two qualify for the semi-finals)
Top scorers (including play-offs): **10** - Roger **ROJAS**, Olimpia • **8** - Oscar **TORLACOFF**, Choloma & Aldo **OVIEDO**, Choloma • **7** - Mauricio **COPETE** COL, Victoria & Jonathan **HANSEN** ARG, Real España • **6** - Osnaldo **HERNANDEZ**, Sociedad; Shannon **WELCOME**, Vida; Mitchel **BROWN**, Marathón; Roman **CASTILLO**, Savio; Elmer **ZELAYA**, Vida & Osman **HERNANDEZ**, Choloma

APERTURA 2012-13 PLAY-OFFS

Quarter-finals			Semi-finals			Final		
Olimpia		Bye						
			Olimpia		0 2			
Marathón		0 2	Atlético Choloma *		1 0			
Atlético Choloma *		0 2				**Olimpia** †		0 4
Motagua		4 3				Victoria *		0 0
Real España *		1 2	**Motagua** *		1 2			
			Victoria		1 2			
Victoria		Bye	† Qualified for the CONCACAF Champions League • * Home team in 1st leg					

APERTURA FINAL 1ST LEG
Nilmo Edwards, La Ceiba, 9-12-2012, 13 203, Armando Castro

Victoria 0
Olimpia 0

VICTORIA
Orlin **VALLECILLO** - Jose **VELASQUEZ**, Edder **ARIAS**, Rommel **MURILLO**, Felix **CRISANTO**• (Mario **ROMERO** 53) - Miguel **CASTILLO**, Rigoberto **PADILLA** (Dicktmar **HERNANDEZ** 80), Wilmer **CRISANTO** - Victor **ORTIZ** (Jairo **ROCHEZ** 85), Ruben **LICONA**, Andres **COPETE**•. Tr: Hector **VARGAS**

OLIMPIA
Donis **ESCOBER** - **FABIO DE SOUZA**, Brayan **BECKELES**, Juan **GARCIA**, Luis **GARRIDO**•, Johnny **PALACIOS** - Reynaldo **TILGUATH** (Alexander **LOPEZ** 64), Sebastian **ROSANO**•, Javier **PORTILLO** - DOUGLAS **CAETANO** (Juan **MEJIA** 71), Ramiro **BRUSCHI** (Roger **ROJAS** 65). Tr: Danilo **TOSELLO**

APERTURA FINAL 2ND LEG
Tiburcio Andino, Tegucigalpa, 16-12-2012, Hector Rodriguez

Olimpia 4 Rojas [2], Garcia [13], Portillo [45], Bruschi [85]
Victoria 0

OLIMPIA
Donis **ESCOBER** - **FABIO DE SOUZA**, Brayan **BECKELES**, Juan **GARCIA**, Luis **GARRIDO**, Johnny **PALACIOS**• - Reynaldo **TILGUATH** (Hendry **CORDOVA** 71), Sebastian **ROSANO**, Javier **PORTILLO** - DOUGLAS **CAETANO** (Juan **MEJIA** 80), Roger **ROJAS** (Ramiro **BRUSCHI** 65). Tr: Danilo **TOSELLO**

VICTORIA
Orlin **VALLECILLO** - Jose **VELASQUEZ**, Edder **ARIAS**, Rommel **MURILLO** - Miguel **CASTILLO**•, Hector **CASTELLANOS** (Victor **ORTIZ** 17), Rigoberto **PADILLA**• (Junior **LACAYO**• 67), Wilmer **CRISANTO** - Mario **ROMERO**, Ruben **LICONA** (Felix **CRISANTO** 57), Andres **COPETE**. Tr: Hector **VARGAS**

MEDALS TABLE

		Overall	Lge	Cent Am	City
		G S B	G B	G S B	
1	Olimpia	28 19 1	26 17	2 2 1	Tegucigalpa
2	Motagua	12 9	12 9		Tegucigalpa
3	Real España	10 11 1	10 11	1	San Pedro Sula
4	Marathón	8 13 1	8 12	1	San Pedro Sula
5	Platense	2 3	2 3		Puerto Cortés
	Vida	2 3	2 3		La Ceiba
7	Victoria	1 2	1 2		La Ceiba
8	UNAH	3	2	1	Choluteca
9	At. Morazán	1	1		
	Petrotela	1	1		

HUN – HUNGARY

FIFA/COCA-COLA WORLD RANKING

'93	'94	'95	'96	'97	'98	'99	'00	'01	'02	'03	'04	'05	'06	'07	'08	'09	'10	'11	'12
50	61	62	75	77	46	45	47	66	56	72	64	74	62	50	47	54	42	37	32

2012

Jan	Feb	Mar	Apr	May	Jun	Jul	Aug	Sep	Oct	Nov	Dec	High	Low	Av
37	37	37	36	35	31	31	28	37	49	30	32	27	87	56

After a barren year in 2011 it was back to winning ways for Debrecen in a season which saw them clinch the double for the second time in their history. The Railwaymen went through the entire campaign unbeaten - the first team to do so since 1966 - finishing eight points ahead of defending champions Videoton in a championship notable for the fact that there were no teams from Budapest in the top three for only the second time since the league began in 1901. Debrecen were also unbeaten in the cup although they needed penalties to beat second division champions MTK Hungaria in the final. MTK looked to have secured the trophy against 10-man Debrecen with a goal three minutes from time only to be pegged back by Peter Szakaly's equaliser at the death. David Kalnoki-Kis missed the vital spot-kick to give coach Elemer Kondas his first trophy at Debrecen. The national team made a solid start to the 2014 FIFA World Cup qualifiers, winning three of their first four games, a reflection of how standards have improved recently. Beating the top nations has, however, remained a problem and the heavy loss at home to the Netherlands meant the fight was on with Romania to secure a play-off berth for the finals in Brazil in the attempt to break the nation's longest spell of absence from the finals of a major tournament.

UEFA EUROPEAN CHAMPIONSHIP RECORD
1960 r1 1964 3 SF 1968 QF 1972 4 SF 1976-2012 DNQ

HUNGARIAN FOOTBALL FEDERATION (MLSZ)

Kanai ut. 2.D,
1112 Budapest

☎ +36 1 5779500
📠 +36 1 5779503
✉ mlsz@mlsz.hu
🖥 www.mlsz.hu
FA 1901 CON 1954 FIFA 1906
P Sandor Csanyi
GS Marton Vagi

THE STADIA

2014 FIFA World Cup Stadia

| Stadion Puskás Ferenc Budapest | 56 000 |

Other Main Stadia

Stadion ETO Györ	20 000
Albert Stadion Budapest	18 100
Sóstói Stadion Szekesfehervar	14 300
ZTE Aréna Zalaegerszeg	14 000

MAJOR CITIES/TOWNS

		Population
1	Budapest	1 656 358
2	Debrecen	205 042
3	Miskolc	174 574
4	Szeged	161 725
5	Pécs	155 402
6	Györ	130 391
7	Nyíregyháza	115 113
8	Kecskemét	105 498
9	Székesfehérvár	104 486
10	Szombathely	79 976
11	Szolnok	74 604
12	Tatabánya	71 840
13	Kaposvár	66 332
14	Békéscsaba	64 372
15	Érd	63 547
16	Zalaegerszeg	60 622
17	Veszprém	60 225
18	Sopron	56 219
19	Eger	56 036

MAGYAR KOZTARSASAG • REPUBLIC OF HUNGARY

Capital	Budapest	Population	9 905 596 (82)	% in cities	68%
GDP per capita	$19 800 (63)	Area km²	93 028 km² (109)	GMT +/-	+1
Neighbours (km)	Austria 366, Croatia 329, Romania 443, Serbia 166, Slovakia 676, Slovenia 102, Ukraine 103

RECENT INTERNATIONAL MATCHES PLAYED BY HUNGARY

2009	Opponents	Score	Venue	Comp	Scorers	Att	Referee
12-08	Romania	L 0-1	Budapest	Fr		9 000	Vnuk SVK
5-09	Sweden	L 1-2	Budapest	WCq	Huszti 79p	40 169	Rizzoli ITA
9-09	Portugal	L 0-1	Budapest	WCq		42 000	Lannoy FRA
10-10	Portugal	L 0-3	Lisbon	WCq		50 115	Hamer LUX
14-10	Denmark	W 1-0	Copenhagen	WCq	Buzsaky 35	36 956	Meyer GER
14-11	Belgium	L 0-3	Ghent	Fr		8 000	Piccirillo FRA
2010							
3-03	Russia	D 1-1	Gyor	Fr	Vanczak 39	10 000	Vucemilovic CRO
29-05	Germany	L 0-3	Budapest	Fr		14 000	Larsen DEN
5-06	Netherlands	L 1-6	Amsterdam	Fr	Dzsudzsak 6	45 000	Meyer GER
11-08	England	L 1-2	London	Fr	OG 62	72 024	Lannoy FRA
3-09	Sweden	L 0-2	Stockholm	ECq		32 304	Atkinson ENG
7-09	Moldova	W 2-1	Budapest	ECq	Rudolf 50, Koman 66	9 209	Kovarik CZE
8-10	San Marino	W 8-0	Budapest	ECq	Rudolf 2 11 25, Szalai 3 18 27 48, Koman 60, Dzsudzsak 89, Gera 93+p	10 596	Kaasik EST
12-10	Finland	W 2-1	Helsinki	ECq	Szalai 50, Dzsudzsak 94+	18 532	Kelly IRL
17-11	Lithuania	W 2-0	Szekesfehervar	Fr	Priskin 61, Dzsudzsak 80	4 500	Nijhuis NED
2011							
9-02	Azerbaijan	W 2-0	Dubai	Fr	Rudolf 37, Hajnal 81	500	Al Zarooni UAE
25-03	Netherlands	L 0-4	Budapest	ECq		25 311	Velasco ESP
29-03	Netherlands	L 3-5	Amsterdam	ECq	Rudolf 46, Gera 2 50 75	51 700	Moen NOR
3-06	Luxembourg	W 1-0	Luxembourg	Fr	Szabics 53	1 213	Arnason ISL
7-06	San Marino	W 3-0	Serravalle	ECq	Liptak 40, Szabics 49, Koman 83	1 915	Radovanovic MNE
10-08	Iceland	W 4-0	Budapest	Fr	Koman 32, Rudolf 45, Dzsudzsak 59, Elek 88	12 000	Stark GER
2-09	Sweden	W 2-1	Budapest	ECq	Szabics 44, Rudolf 90	23 500	Skomina SVN
6-09	Moldova	W 2-0	Chisinau	ECq	Vanczak 7, Rudolf 83	10 500	Bebek CRO
11-10	Finland	D 0-0	Budapest	ECq		25 169	Undiano ESP
11-11	Liechtenstein	W 5-0	Budapest	Fr	Priskin 2 10 20, Dzsudzsak 76, Koman 79, Feczesin 89	23 000	Balaj ROU
15-11	Poland	L 1-2	Poznan	Fr	Priskin 78	7 500	Kaasik EST
2012							
29-02	Bulgaria	D 1-1	Gyor	Fr	Szalai 42	15 000	Eriksson SWE
1-06	Czech Republic	W 2-1	Prague	Fr	Dzsudzsak 6, Gyurcso 88	17 102	Probert ENG
15-08	Israel	D 1-1	Budapest	Fr	Dzsudzsak 51	15 000	Kruzliak SVK
7-09	Andorra	W 5-0	Andorra La Vella	WCq	Juhasz 12, Gera 33, Szalai 54, Priskin 68, Koman 82	815	Aleckovic BIH
11-09	Netherlands	L 1-4	Budapest	WCq	Dzsudzsak 7p	22 700	Proenca POR
12-10	Estonia	W 1-0	Tallinn	WCq	Hajnal 46	5 661	Liani ISR
16-10	Turkey	W 3-1	Budapest	WCq	Koman 31, Szalai 50, Gera 57p	21 563	Orsato ITA
14-11	Norway	L 0-2	Budapest	Fr		16 000	Strahonja CRO

Fr = Friendly match • EC = UEFA EURO 2012 • WC = FIFA World Cup • q = qualifier

HUNGARY NATIONAL TEAM HISTORICAL RECORDS

Caps
101 - Jozsek Bozsik 1947-62 • **92** - Laszlo Fazekas 1968-83 • **87** - Gabor Kiraly 1998- • **86** - Gyula Grosics 1947-62 • **85** - Ferenc Puskas 1945-56 • **82** - Imre Garaba 1980-91 • **81** - Sandor Matrai 1956-67 • **77** - Ferenc Sipos 1957-66 & Zoltan Gera 2002- • **76** - Ferenc Bene 1962-79; Mate Fenyvesi 1954-66 & Roland Juhasz 2004- • **75** - Florian Albert 1959-74 & Karoly Sandor 1949-64 • **72** - Lajos Tichy 1955-64 **70** - Jozsef Kiprich 1984-95 & Tibor Nyilasi 1975-85 • **69** - Nandor Hidegkuti 1945-58 • **68** - Imre Schlosser 1906-27; Sandor Kocsis 1948-56

Goals
84 - Ferenc Puskas 1945-56 • **75** - Sandor Kocsis 1948-56 • **59** - Imre Schlosser 1906-27 • **51** - Lajos Tichy 1955-64 • **42** - Gyorgy Sarosi 1931-43 • **39** - Nandor Hidegkuti 1945-58 • **36** - Ferenc Bene 1962-79 • **32** - Gyula Zsengeller 1935-47 & Tibor Nyilasi 1975-85 • **31** - Florian Albert 1959-74 • **29** - Ferenc Deak 1946-49 • **28** - Jozsef Kiprich 1984-95 • **27** - Karoly Sandor 1949-64 • **26** - Jozsef Takacs 1923-33 • **25** - Geza Toldi 1929-40 • **24** - Istvan Avar 1929-35 & Laszlo Fazekas 1968-83 • **23** - Zoltan Gera 2002-

Coaches
For coaches pre 1945 see Oliver's Almanack 2012 • Tibor Gallowich 1945-48 • Gusztav Sebes 1949-56 • Marton Bukovi, Lajos Baroti & Karoly Lakat 1956-57 • Karoly Sos 1957 • Lajos Baroti 1957-66 • Rudolf Illovszky 1966-67 • Karoly Sos 1968-69 • Jozsef Hoffer 1970-71 • Rudolf Illovszky 1971-74 • Jozsef Bozsik 1974 • Ede Moor 1974-75 • Janos Szocs 1975 • Lajos Baroti 1975-78 • Ferenc Kovacs 1978-79 • Karoly Lakat 1979-80 • Kalman Meszoly 1980-83 • Gyorgy Mezey 1983-86 • Imre Komora 1986 • Jozsef Verebes 1987 • Jozsef Garami 1987 • Laszlo Balint 1988 • Gyorgy Mezey 1988 • Bertalan Bicskei 1989 • Kalman Meszoly 1990-91 • Robert Glazer 1991 • Imre Jenei ROU 1992-93 • Ferenc Puskas 1993 • Jozsef Verebes 1993-94 • Kalman Meszoly 1994-95 • Janos Csank 1996-97 • Bertalan Bicskei 1998-01 • Imre Gellei 2001-03 • Lothar Matthaus GER 2004-05 • Peter Bozsik 2006 • Peter Varhidi 2006-08 • Erwin Koeman NED 2008-2010 • Sandor Egervari 2010-

HUNGARY 2011-12

SOPRONI LIGA NB I

	Pl	W	D	L	F	A	Pts	Debrecen	Videoton	Győr	Honvéd	Kecskemét	Paks	Diósgyőr	Haladás	Siófok	Kaposvári	Ferencváros	Pécs	Ujpest	Pápa	Vasas	ZTE
Debreceni VSC †	30	22	8	0	64	18	74		2-1	2-0	1-1	2-1	4-2	5-0	2-0	1-1	3-0	1-0	4-0	3-2	2-2	5-2	5-2
Videoton ‡	30	21	3	6	58	19	66	0-1		2-1	1-0	0-2	4-0	2-0	1-0	7-0	2-0	2-0	4-1	3-0	2-0	4-1	4-1
Győri ETO	30	20	3	7	56	31	63	1-2	1-0		1-3	4-0	4-1	2-0	1-0	4-1	2-1	2-0	3-0	1-0	3-2	3-2	5-1
Budapest Honvéd ‡	30	13	7	10	48	40	46	0-3	1-0	1-2		1-4	2-3	2-1	2-2	3-1	0-0	1-0	1-1	2-0	2-0	4-0	2-0
Kecskeméti TE	30	13	6	11	48	38	45	0-1	0-2	2-0	3-1		0-1	1-0	2-2	3-2	4-0	1-0	1-2	0-0	3-0	1-1	2-0
Paksi SE	30	12	9	9	47	51	45	0-0	1-2	1-2	2-1	3-2		1-1	3-2	1-1	0-0	4-2	4-4	2-0	1-1	2-1	4-2
Diósgyőri VTK	30	13	4	13	42	43	43	0-2	0-2	2-0	2-1	1-2	1-2		1-0	2-1	2-1	2-3	4-0	1-0	2-0	3-2	4-1
Szombathelyi Haladás	30	9	11	10	39	37	38	0-1	2-2	1-1	2-4	2-2	5-0	2-1		2-1	1-1	2-1	1-1	1-1	2-1	3-0	1-0
Bodajk FC Siófok	30	9	9	12	30	41	36	0-0	0-0	0-1	0-0	0-2	2-0	1-0	0-2		3-1	0-2	2-1	2-0	3-1	0-0	2-0
Kaposvári Rákóczi	30	7	14	9	35	42	35	1-1	2-0	0-0	2-2	2-1	4-4	3-2	1-1	2-3		2-2	1-0	2-2	2-0	0-0	3-1
Ferencvárosi TC	30	9	7	14	32	35	34	1-2	0-1	2-2	0-0	3-0	0-0	1-1	1-2	0-0	0-1		0-1	3-0	0-2	1-0	2-0
Pécsi MFC	30	8	10	12	36	50	34	0-0	1-3	3-1	3-4	2-2	1-2	1-2	1-0	1-1	1-1	0-2		0-0	2-1	5-1	2-1
Ujpesti FC	30	8	8	14	34	46	32	1-5	0-2	1-3	2-0	3-1	0-2	1-1	4-1	1-1	3-1	1-1	4-1		0-1	2-0	4-2
Lombard Pápa TFC	30	8	6	16	26	40	30	0-2	2-3	0-2	3-1	1-0	1-0	1-2	1-0	2-0	1-0	1-2	0-0	0-1		0-0	0-1
Vasas SC	30	5	9	16	29	51	22	0-0	0-0	1-2	1-2	2-4	1-0	2-3	0-0	1-0	0-1	2-0	1-2	3-0	1-1		3-2
Zalaegerszegi TE	30	1	10	19	25	65	13	0-2	0-2	0-2	0-4	1-1	1-1	1-1	1-1	1-1	1-1	1-1	2-3	0-0	1-1	1-1	

15/07/2011 - 27/05/2012 • † Qualified for the UEFA Champions League • ‡ Qualified for the UEFA Cup • Attendance: 906,531 @ 3,777
Top scorers: **20** - Adamo **COULIBALY** FRA, Debrecen • **19** - Nemanja **NIKOLIC**, Videoton • **15** - Laszlo **LENCSE**, Kecskemet • **14** - **DANILO** de Oliveira BRA, Honvéd • **13** - Milan **PERIC** SRB, Kaposvár • **12** - **ANDRE ALVES** BRA, Videoton • **11** - Peter **BAJZAT**, Pécs • **10** - Daniel **BODE**, Paks

HUNGARY 2011-12
NB II NYUGATI (WEST)

	Pl	W	D	L	F	A	Pts
MTK Hungária	30	21	6	3	67	20	**69**
Kozármisleny SE	30	17	4	9	50	30	55
Gyirmót SE	30	15	7	8	50	43	52
FC Ajka	30	14	8	8	48	34	50
FC Tatabánya	30	15	6	9	50	34	49
Veszprém FC	30	13	8	9	44	37	47
Szigetszentmiklosi TK	30	12	9	9	52	38	45
Videoton II	30	10	11	9	38	35	41
Bajai LSE	30	10	7	13	46	50	37
Ferencvárosi TC II	30	10	6	14	46	54	36
BKV Előre	30	9	8	13	32	45	35
Paksi SE II	30	7	10	13	27	41	31
Győri ETO II	30	7	9	14	37	49	30
Soproni VSE	30	7	9	14	28	52	**30**
Budaörsi SC	30	8	4	18	25	58	**28**
Dunaújvárosi-Pálhalma	30	7	4	19	37	57	25

20/08/2011 - 3/06/2012

HUNGARY 2011-12
NB II KELETI (EAST)

	Pl	W	D	L	F	A	Pts
Egri FC	30	18	5	7	42	26	**59**
Szolnoki MAV	30	17	4	9	55	32	55
Békéscsabai Elore FC	30	13	12	5	44	30	51
Ceglédi VSE	30	14	5	11	46	43	47
Mezokövesdi SE	30	12	8	10	43	40	44
Orosháza FC	30	11	11	8	47	39	44
Nyíregyháza Spartacus	30	10	13	7	50	47	43
Balmazújvárosi FC	30	12	6	12	52	40	42
Debreceni VSC II	30	11	9	10	42	41	42
Ujpesti FC II	30	11	7	12	46	60	40
Dunakanyar-Vac FC	30	11	5	14	44	48	38
Szeged 2011	30	10	7	13	46	43	37
Kazincbarcika SC	30	10	5	15	32	47	35
Budapest Honvéd II	30	9	7	14	36	44	**34**
Rákospalotai EAC	30	8	7	15	44	61	31
Vecsési FC	30	3	9	18	21	49	17

20/08/2011 - 3/06/2012

MEDALS TABLE

		Overall		League		Cup		Europe		City
		G S B		G S B		G S		G S B		
1	Ferencvárosi TC	49 45 23		28 34 21		20 9		1 2 2		Budapest
2	MTK Hungária FC	35 24 16		23 20 15		12 3		1 1		Budapest
3	Ujpest FC	28 28 20		20 21 18		8 6		1 2		Budapest
4	Budapest-Honvéd FC	20 22 5		13 12 5		7 10				Budapest
5	Debreceni VSC	11 3 3		6 1 3		5 2				Debrecen
6	Vasas SC	10 5 14		6 2 13		4 3		1		Budapest
7	Győri ETO FC	7 5 7		3 2 6		4 3				Győr
8	Csepel SC	4 2		4 2						Budapest
9	Videoton	2 7 3		1 3 3		1 3		1		Székesfehérvár
10	Diósgyőri VTK	2 3 1				1 2 3				Miskolc
11	Budapest TC	2 2 3		2 1 3		1				Budapest
12	Dunakanyar-Vac FC	1 5		1 2		3				Vác
13	Pécsi MFC	1 3 1				1 1		1 2		Pécs
14	Zalaegerszeg TE	1 1 1		1		1				Zalaegerszeg

MAGYAR KUPA 2011-12

Fourth Round

Debreceni VSC *	2	
Ceglédi VSE	0	
Mezőkövesd-Zsóry SE *	2	
Kecskeméti TE	3	
Putnok VSE *	3	
Paksi SE	2	
Rákosmente KSK *	0	
Kaposvári Rákóczi	1	
Bajai LSE *	1	4p
Lombard Pápa TFC	1	3p
Bodajk FC Siófok	1	
Kozármisleny SE	2	
Kaposvári Rákóczi II *	3	
Gyirmót SE	2	
Szigetszentmiklósi TK *	3	3p
Újpesti FC	3	4p
Videoton	2	
FC Tatabánya *	0	
Veszprém FC *	0	
Szombathelyi Haladás	0	
Diósgyőri VTK	4	
BKV Előre	1	
Jánossomorja SE *	2	
Győri ETO	9	
Békéscsabai Előre FC *	3	
Vasas SC	2	
Szolnoki MÁV *	2	
Ferencvárosi TC	5	
Pécsi MFC	3	
Csákvári TK *	2	
Balmazújvárosi FC *	1	
MTK Hungária	2	

Round of 16

Debreceni VSC	2	1
Kecskeméti TE *	1	1
Putnok VSE *	1	0
Kaposvári Rákóczi	1	3
Bajai LSE *	2	0
Kozármisleny SE	0	0
Kaposvári Rákóczi II *	2	0
Újpesti FC	1	2
Videoton *	1	0
Szombathelyi Haladás	0	0
Diósgyőri VTK *	1	1
Győri ETO	1	4
Békéscsabai Előre FC *	0	2
Ferencvárosi TC	0	2
Pécsi MFC	1	1
MTK Hungária *	0	2

Quarter-finals

Debreceni VSC	1	0
Kaposvári Rákóczi *	0	0
Bajai LSE *	1	0
Újpesti FC	3	4
Videoton *	5	1
Győri ETO	1	0
Békéscsabai Előre FC *	0	0
MTK Hungária	3	3

Semi-finals

Debreceni VSC *	2	3
Újpesti FC	1	1
Videoton	3	0
MTK Hungária *	2	2

Final

Debreceni VSC	3	8p
MTK Hungária ‡	3	7p

CUP FINAL

Puskás Ferenc, Budapest, 1-05-2012
Att: 3500. Ref: Zsolt Szabó
Scorers - Selim Bouadla [51], Szakály 2 [55, 89] for DVSC; Könyves [45], Ladányi [62], Zsidai [87] for MTK
DVSC - István Verpecz - Dajan Simac, Norbert Meszáros, Balázs Nikolov◆[60], Mihály Korhut● - Tamás Kulcsár (Zoltán Nagy● [62]), Lucas, László Rezes (Selim Bouadla [46]), Péter Szakály, József Varga, Luis Ramos (Adamo Coulibaly [46]). Tr: Elemér Kondás
MTK - Lajos Hegedűs - Adrián Szekeres, Dániel Vadnai, Dragan Vukmir●, Rafe Wolfe●, Dávid Kálnoki-Kis - József Kanta, László Zsidai, Tibor Ladányi (András Pál [91+]) - Ádám Balajti (Patrick Vass [55]), Norbert Könyves. Tr: József Garami

* Home team in the first leg. ‡ Qualified for the Europa League

IDN – INDONESIA

FIFA/COCA-COLA WORLD RANKING

'93	'94	'95	'96	'97	'98	'99	'00	'01	'02	'03	'04	'05	'06	'07	'08	'09	'10	'11	'12
106	134	130	119	91	87	90	97	87	110	91	91	109	153	133	139	120	127	142	156

2012													High	Low	Av
Jan	Feb	Mar	Apr	May	Jun	Jul	Aug	Sep	Oct	Nov	Dec				
143	146	147	151	151	151	153	159	168	170	165	156		76	170	115

Indonesia may have the fourth largest population in the world but the record of the national team and club sides in international competition is woeful - just two titles won at the South East Asian Games in 1987 and 1991. 2012 did not bring any change to that with the national team starting the year with a 10-0 thrashing at the hands of Bahrain in a 2014 FIFA World Cup qualifier and ending with another humiliating first round exit in the AFF Suzuki Cup. That Indonesia can't even progress in a tournament confined to southeast Asia is a stark reminder of the problems facing the game in the country. The sport has been paralyzed by a long-running battle to control the administration of the game, forcing FIFA to threaten to suspend the federation until such times as the issues are sorted. In the meantime, two rival leagues have been organised in parallel with one another, the Indonesia Super League and the Indonesian Premier League with each claiming to be the legitimate national championship at one time or another. The lack of leadership and battle for control has led to clubs operating on the margins of solvency while players and coaches have gone long periods without payment, leading in extreme cases, to players - such as in the tragic case of Paraguayan Diego Mendieta - passing away due to their inability to afford vital medical care.

FIFA WORLD CUP RECORD
1930-1934 DNE **1938** 15 r1 1950-1954 DNE 1958 DNQ 1962-1970 DNE 1974-2014 DNQ

FOOTBALL ASSOCIATION OF INDONESIA (PSSI)

Gelora Bung Karno,
Pintu X-XI, Senayan,
PO Box 2305, 10023 Jakarta
☎ +62 21 5704762
✉ +62 21 5734386
✉ pssi@pssi.or.id
🖥 www.pssi.or.id
FA 1930 CON 1954 FIFA 1952
P Djohar Arifin Husin
GS Tunjuk Hadiyandra

THE STADIA

2014 FIFA World Cup Stadia
Gelora Bung Karno Stadium
Jakarta 88 083

Other Main Stadia
Gedebage Stadium
Bandung 72 000
Palaran Stadium
Samarinda 60 000
Jakabaring Stadium
Palembang 55 000
Bung Tomo Stadium
Surabaya 50 000

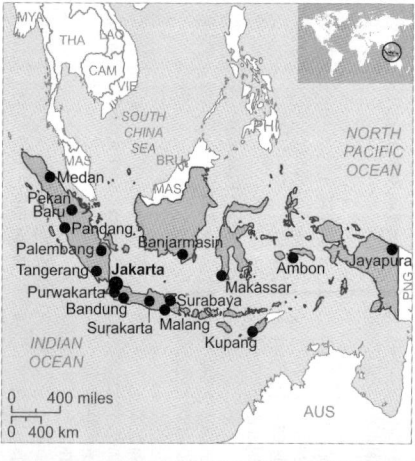

MAJOR CITIES/TOWNS

		Population
1	Jakarta	8 579 263
2	Surabaya	2 336 843
3	Medan	1 772 833
4	Bekasi	1 724 003
5	Bandung	1 601 767
6	Tangerang	1 495 586
7	Depok	1 442 313
8	Makasar	1 440 539
9	Semarang	1 283 279
10	Palembang	1 271 855
11	Padang	960 184
12	BandarLampung	916 561
13	Bogor	834 098
14	Pekan Baru	763 275
15	Malang	755 371
16	Yogyakarta	703 753
17	Banjarmasin	606 631
18	Surakarta	563 208
19	Manado	508 585

REPUBLIK INDONESIA • REPUBLIC OF INDONESIA

Capital	Jakarta	Population	240 271 522 (4)	% in cities	52%
GDP per capita	$3900 (155)	Area km²	1 904 569 km² (16)	GMT +/-	+7
Neighbours (km)	Timor-Leste 228, Malaysia 1782, Papua New Guinea 820 • Coast 54716				

RECENT INTERNATIONAL MATCHES PLAYED BY INDONESIA

2010	Opponents	Score	Venue	Comp	Scorers	Att	Referee
6-01	Oman	L 1-2	Jakarta	ACq	Boaz Salossa 45	45 000	Mohd Salleh MAS
3-03	Australia	L 0-1	Brisbane	ACq		20 422	Ogiya JPN
8-10	Uruguay	L 1-7	Jakarta	Fr	Boaz Salossa 18	25 000	Daud SIN
12-10	Maldives	W 3-0	Bandung	Fr	Oktavianus Maniani 30, Yongki Aribowo 74, Tony Sucipto 90	13 000	Palaniyandi SIN
21-11	Timor-Leste	W 6-0	Palembang	Fr	Muhammad Ridwan 12, Oktavianus Maniani 26, Cristian Gonzales 2 37 46, Bambang Pamungkas 70, Yongki Aribowo 83		
24-11	Chinese Taipei	W 2-0	Palembang	Fr	Cristian Gonzales 10, Firman Utina 18p		Singh SIN
1-12	Malaysia	W 5-1	Jakarta	AFFrl	OG 22, Cristian Gonzales 33, Muhammad Ridwan 52, Arif Suyono 76, Irfan Bachdim 94+	62 000	Vo Min Tri VIE
4-12	Laos	W 6-0	Jakarta	AFFrl	Firman Utina 2 26p 51, Muhammad Ridwan 33, Irfan Bachdim 63, Arif Suyono 77, Oktavianus Maniani 82	70 000	Daud SIN
7-12	Thailand	W 2-1	Jakarta	AFFrl	Bambang Pamungkas 2 82 91+	65 000	Sato JPN
16-12	Philippines	W 1-0	Jakarta	AFFsf	Cristian Gonzales 32	70 000	Moradi IRN
19-12	Philippines	W 1-0	Jakarta	AFFsf	Cristian Gonzales 43	88 000	Ebrahim BHR
26-12	Malaysia	L 0-3	Kuala Lumpur	AFFf		70 000	Toma JPN
29-12	Malaysia	W 2-1	Jakarta	AFFf	Mohammad Nasuha 72, Muhammad Ridwan 88	88 000	Green AUS
2011							
23-07	Turkmenistan	D 1-1	Ashgabat	WCq	Muhammad Ilham 30	7 500	Torky IRN
28-07	Turkmenistan	W 4-3	Jakarta	WCq	Cristian Gonzales 2 9 19, Mohammad Nasuha 43, Muhammad Ridwan 76	88 000	Williams AUS
22-08	Palestine	W 4-1	Surakarta	Fr	Hariono 65, Cristian Gonzales 70, Bambang Pamungkas 2 77 85	25 000	
27-08	Jordan	L 0-1	Amman	Fr			
2-09	Iran	L 0-3	Tehran	WCq		75 800	Toma JPN
6-09	Bahrain	L 0-2	Jakarta	WCq		85 000	Lee Min Hu KOR
7-10	Saudi Arabia	D 0-0	Kuala Lumpur	Fr		150	
11-10	Qatar	L 2-3	Jakarta	WCq	Cristian Gonzales 2 27 35	28 000	Bashir SIN
11-11	Qatar	L 0-4	Doha	WCq		6 500	Basma SYR
15-11	Iran	L 1-4	Jakarta	WCq	Bambang Pamungkas 44	6 000	Tan Hai CHN
2012							
29-02	Bahrain	L 0-10	Manama	WCq		3 000	El Haddad LIB
5-06	Philippines	D 2-2	Manila	Fr	Patrick Wanggai 59, Irfan Bachdim 63		Kuo Jung Fan TPE
10-09	Korea DPR	L 0-2	Jakarta	Fr			
15-09	Vietnam	D 0-0	Surabaya	Fr			
26-09	Brunei Daru Saalam	W 5-0	Bandar S Begawan	Fr	Irfan Bachdim 3 23p 49 72, Hendra Bayauw 63, Vendry Mofu 45		
16-10	Vietnam	D 0-0	Hanoi	Fr			
25-11	Laos	D 2-2	Kuala Lumpur	AFFrl	Raphael Maitamo 43, Vendry Mofu 90		Ng Kai Lam HKG
28-11	Singapore	W 1-0	Kuala Lumpur	AFFrl	Andrik Vermansyah 88		Abdulnabi BHR
1-12	Malaysia	L 0-2	Kuala Lumpur	AFFrl			Kovalenko UZB

Fr = Friendly match • AFF = ASEAN Football Federation Championship • AC = AFC Asian Cup • WC = FIFA World Cup
q = qualifier • rl = first round group • sf = semi-final • f = final

INDONESIA NATIONAL TEAM HISTORICAL RECORDS

Caps
85 - Bambang Pamungkas 1999-

Goals
37 - Bambang Pamungkas 1999- • 31 - Kurniawan Dwi Yulianto 1995-2005 • 16 - Budi Sudarsono 2001- & Rochy Putiray 1991-2004

Past Coaches
Johannes van Mastenbroek NED 1938 • Choo Seng Quee SIN 1951-53 • Antun Pogacnik YUG 1954-64 • EA Mangindaan 1966-70 • Endang Witarsa 1970 • Djamiaat Dalhar 1971-72 • Suwardi Arland 1972-74 • Aang Witarsa 1974-75 • Wiel Coerver NED 1975-76 • Suwardi Arland 1976-78 • Frans Van Balkom NED 1978-79 • Marek Janota 1979-80 • Bernd Fischer GER 1980-81 • Harry Tjong 1981-82 • Sinyo Aliandoe 1982-83 • M. Basri, Iswadi Idris and Abdul Kadir 1983-84 • Bertje Matulapelwa 1985-87 • Anatoli Polosin URS 1987-91 • Ivan Toplak YUG 1991-93 • Romano Matte ITA 1993-95 • Danurwindo 1995-96 • Henk Wullems NED 1996-97 • Rusdy Bahalwan 1998 • Bernard Schumm 1999 • Nandar Iskandar 1999-00 • Benny Dollo 2000-01 • Ivan Kolev BUL 2002-04 • Peter Withe ENG 2004-07 • Ivan Kolev BUL 2007 • Benny Dollo 2008-10 • Alfred Riedl AUT 2010-11 • Wim Rijsbergen NED 2011-12 • Aji Santoso 2012 • Nil Maizar 2012-

INDONESIA 2011–12

DJARUM INDONESIA SUPER LEAGUE (ISL)

	Pl	W	D	L	F	A	Pts	Sriwijaya	Persipura	Persiwa	Persela	Persija	Pelita Jaya	Persiba	Persib	Mitra Kukar	Persifadon	Persisam	Arema	PSPS	Persiram	Gresik United	PSMS	Deltras	PSAP
Sriwijaya Palembang	34	25	4	5	71	31	79		1-0	3-2	3-0	2-1	2-1	5-1	1-0	4-3	5-0	3-1	2-1	2-1	1-0	3-0	2-0	3-1	3-1
Persipura Jayapura	34	20	8	6	65	35	68	2-1		1-1	2-1	0-1	2-1	3-3	4-0	4-2	3-1	3-1	2-1	2-1	3-1	3-1	5-0	2-1	7-1
Persiwa Wamena	34	19	4	11	60	42	61	1-0	0-1		1-0	4-1	4-2	2-0	3-0	3-1	3-0	1-0	1-0	3-0	3-0	4-2	3-1	2-1	4-1
Persela Lamongan	34	15	11	8	58	43	56	1-1	0-0	2-2		2-2	2-2	2-1	3-1	2-1	2-1	1-0	3-1	3-1	5-1	6-2	2-1	1-1	2-0
Persija Jakarta	34	14	10	10	53	36	52	3-0	1-0	1-2	1-1		2-1	4-0	2-2	1-1	0-0	0-0	1-0	4-0	1-2	2-0	1-0	1-0	5-1
Pelita Jaya Karawang	34	15	6	13	68	51	51	1-3	3-2	2-1	1-0	0-2		1-3	1-3	4-0	1-1	3-0	2-1	4-1	2-1	4-0	2-2	3-0	5-2
Persiba Balikpapan	34	14	9	11	60	55	51	2-3	1-2	3-1	0-0	2-2	1-1		2-1	3-1	1-2	3-1	2-1	4-1	5-1	4-2	3-1	4-1	1-1
Persib Bandung	34	14	7	13	49	49	49	1-0	0-1	3-0	1-1	1-0	3-2	2-3		5-0	3-2	0-0	2-0	2-1	3-2	1-0	3-1	3-1	1-1
Mitra Kukar	34	14	5	15	57	56	47	0-1	1-2	6-1	2-0	3-0	1-0	0-0	3-0		0-1	0-1	2-2	3-1	2-1	4-1	3-1	1-0	3-1
Persifadon Dafonsoro	34	13	7	14	57	65	46	2-2	1-1	**0-3**	4-5	3-1	1-1	2-2	2-2	2-1		2-1	2-1	2-1	6-0	3-0	4-1	2-1	4-2
Persisam Putra	34	12	7	15	44	42	43	0-1	3-1	2-0	0-1	1-1	1-4	0-1	2-1	1-2	3-0		2-0	2-1	2-2	4-0	4-2	1-1	3-1
Arema Indonesia	34	10	8	16	45	51	38	1-5	1-2	2-1	0-1	1-1	1-1	3-2	3-1	2-1	5-3	4-0	1-0		2-0	2-2	0-0	2-1	3-1	0-0
PSPS Pekanbaru	34	11	5	18	40	54	38	1-0	2-2	2-0	0-2	0-2	1-1	0-0	0-0	3-1	4-1	2-1	1-0		2-1	3-0	1-1	0-1	3-0
Persiram Raja Ampat	34	10	8	16	45	63	38	1-2	0-0	2-1	2-2	0-6	2-1	1-0	1-2	2-1	5-2	0-0	1-0	1-2		1-1	**3-0**	3-1	4-1
Gresik United	34	11	5	18	36	69	38	1-5	2-1	1-0	3-2	2-0	1-6	0-2	2-0	1-2	3-2	1-1	2-0	0-1	1-0		2-2	2-1	1-0
PSMS Medan	34	9	9	16	43	62	36	0-0	0-0	1-1	4-3	3-3	1-2	4-1	3-2	1-1	1-0	1-0	1-1	3-1	1-0	0-1		1-3	2-1
Delta Raya Sidoarjo	34	9	8	17	34	48	35	0-1	1-1	1-2	1-0	1-0	2-0	2-0	0-0	0-0	0-1	1-3	3-3	1-0	2-2	1-1	0-1		2-1
PSAP Sigli	34	6	9	19	33	66	27	1-1	0-1	0-0	0-0	1-0	0-2	1-1	3-0	2-3	2-1	1-2	1-1	3-2	0-0	1-0	2-1	0-1	

1/12/2011 – 11/07/2012 • Matches in bold awarded
Relegation play-off: **Gresik United** 3-1 PSIM Yogyakarta
Top scorers: 25 - **ALBERTO GONCALVES** BRA, Persipura Jayapura • 22 - Mario **COSTAS** ARG, Persela Lamongan & Keith **GUMBS** SKN, Sriwijaya • 20 - Greg **NWOKOLO**, Pelita Jaya & **SAFEE** Sali MAS, Pelita Jaya • 19 - Boakay Eddie **FODAY** LBR, Persiwa Wamena & Ikpefua Osas **MARVELOUS** NGA, PSMS Medan • 18 - Cristian **GONZALES**, Persisam Putra & **HILTON MOREIRA** BRA, Sriwijaya • 17 - Aldo **BARRETO** PAR, Persiba Balikpapan

INDONESIA 2011–12

INDONESIAN PREMIER LEAGUE (IPL)

	Pl	W	D	L	F	A	Pts	Semen Padang	Persebaya	Arema	Persibo	Persiba	PSM	Persema	Persiraja	Persija	Persijap	Bontang	PSMS
Semen Padang †	22	13	7	2	46	21	46		2-1	3-1	0-0	0-0	3-1	6-2	3-1	1-1	3-0	3-2	3-0
Persebaya 1927	22	12	2	8	31	23	38	0-1		2-1	2-0	0-1	2-0	0-0	2-1	3-3	2-1	1-0	3-0
Arema Indonesia	22	11	4	7	42	26	37	2-1	2-1		2-0	0-1	4-0	4-0	2-1	3-2	2-2	7-0	2-1
Persibo Bojonegoro ‡	22	11	3	8	31	24	36	2-4	1-0	3-1		3-2	1-1	0-0	2-0	1-0	5-0	4-2	1-0
Persiba Bantul	22	10	5	7	27	23	35	1-1	0-1	1-0	2-1		2-0	3-1	1-1	1-0	2-1	1-0	2-2
PSM Makassar	22	9	7	6	29	26	34	1-1	2-0	1-1	2-1	2-1		4-2	3-0	1-1	3-0	2-1	2-1
Persema Malang	22	10	4	8	32	32	34	2-3	2-1	1-0	1-0	3-0	0-0		1-0	0-3	2-1	2-0	4-1
Persiraja Banda Aceh	22	9	5	8	27	30	32	2-2	2-1	1-1	1-0	2-1	2-1	1-0		3-3	2-1	0-0	2-0
Persija Jakarta	22	7	7	8	38	34	28	0-3	0-2	3-3	2-3	0-3	1-0	2-1	3-1		6-1	1-1	1-1
Persijap Jepara	22	4	5	13	18	38	17	1-0	0-1	0-1	1-0	1-0	1-2	1-1	1-2	1-0		2-0	1-1
Bontang	22	4	4	14	21	43	16	0-2	3-4	1-0	2-0	2-0	1-1	2-5	1-2	0-3	1-1		2-0
PSMS Medan	22	2	7	13	17	39	13	1-1	1-2	1-3	0-2	2-2	0-0	0-2	1-0	1-3	1-1	2-0	

26/11/2011 – 17/07/2012 • † Qualified for the AFC Champions League • ‡ Qualified for the AFC Cup
Top scorers: 15 - Ferdinand **SINAGA**, Semen • 13 - Edward **WILSON** LBR, Semen • 11 - M. Nur **ISKANDAR**, Persibo & Emanuel **DE PORRAS** ARG, Persija Jakarta • 10 - Emile **MBAMBA** CMR, Persema Malang; Ilija **SPASOJEVIC** MNE, PSM Makassar & M. **RAHMAT**, PSM Makassar • 8 - Fernando **SOLER** ARG, Persebaya Surabaya • 7 - T.A. **MUSAFRI**, Arema Indonesia • 6 - Fassawa **CAMARA** GUI, Bontang; Samsul **ARIF**, Persibo & Julio **LOPEZ** CHI, Persijap

INDONESIA 2011-12
LIGA INDONESIA PREMIER DIVISION (LPIS) (2) GROUP 1

	Pl	W	D	L	F	A	Pts
Pro Duta ‡	14	11	1	2	19	6	34
PSLS Lhokseumawe	14	11	0	3	22	11	33
Persikabo Bogor	15	8	6	1	18	5	30
PSBL Langsa	15	6	5	4	19	12	23
PSSB Bireuen	15	5	3	7	19	18	18
Persitara Jakarta Utara	15	4	5	6	16	19	17
Persikota Tangerang	15	3	1	11	7	23	10
PS Bengkulu	8	1	3	4	4	12	6
PSP Padang	15	1	2	12	5	26	5

18/12/2011 - 2/06/2012 • ‡ Qualified for the play-offs

INDONESIA 2011-12
LIGA INDONESIA PREMIER DIVISION (LPIS) (2) GROUP 2

	Pl	W	D	L	F	A	Pts
Persepar Palangkaraya‡	18	10	3	5	27	23	33
PSIR Rembang	18	9	3	6	18	16	30
Persik Kediri	18	8	4	6	33	26	28
PSCS Cilacap	18	8	4	6	19	23	28
PSIS Semarang	18	8	3	7	26	18	27
Persipasi Bekasi	18	8	3	7	24	23	27
PSS Sleman	18	7	5	6	29	21	26
Persis Solo	18	6	5	7	26	21	23
Persikab Bandung	18	5	6	7	20	25	21
PPSM Magelang	18	2	2	14	17	43	8

10/12/2011 - 2/06/2012 • ‡ Qualified for the play-offs

INDONESIA 2011-12
LIGA INDONESIA PREMIER DIVISION (LPIS) (2) GROUP 3

	Pl	W	D	L	F	A	Pts
Perseman Manokwari ‡	16	12	3	1	37	9	39
Persbul Buol	16	9	0	7	26	18	27
PSBI Blitar	16	8	3	5	22	23	27
Persipro Bondowoso	16	7	2	7	15	17	23
Persires Bali Devata	15	6	3	6	9	11	21
Madiun Putra	15	5	5	6	14	20	20
Persewangi Banyuwangi	15	5	4	6	15	19	19
Persemalra Langgur	15	5	4	6	10	21	19
Gresik United	15	1	2	12	0	32	5

18/12/2011 - 2/06/2012 • ‡ Qualified for the play-offs

LIGA INDONESIA PREMIER DIVISION (LPIS) GRAND FINAL

	Pl	W	D	L	F	A	Pts	PD	PM
Persepar Palangkaraya	2	1	1	0	1	0	**4**	0-0	1-0
Pro Duta	2	0	2	0	1	1	**2**		1-1
Perseman Manokwari	2	0	1	1	1	2	**1**		

1/07/2012 - 5/07/2012 • All three teams promoted to the IPL

INDONESIA 2011-12
LIGA INDONESIA PREMIER DIVISION (LI) (2) GROUP 1

	Pl	W	D	L	F	A	Pts
Persita Tangerang ‡	20	13	5	2	37	13	44
Persebaya Surabaya ‡	20	12	2	6	34	19	38
Persiku Kudus ‡	20	9	8	3	29	16	35
PSIM Yogyakarta ‡	20	9	6	5	26	20	33
Persitara Jakarta	20	9	3	8	31	23	30
Persip Pekalongan	20	8	3	9	25	24	27
Persis Solo	20	6	5	9	19	26	23
Persih Tembilahan	20	6	4	10	18	27	22
Persitema Temanggung	20	6	2	12	15	32	20
PS Bengkulu	20	5	4	11	15	30	19
PSGL Gayo Lues	20	4	4	12	18	37	16

15/12/2011 - 17/06/2012 • ‡ Qualified for the play-offs

INDONESIA 2011-12
LIGA INDONESIA PREMIER DIVISION (LI) (2) GROUP 2

	Pl	W	D	L	F	A	Pts
Barito Putra ‡	20	13	4	3	41	15	43
Persepam Madura Utd‡	20	11	5	4	26	16	38
West Sumbawa ‡	20	9	6	5	21	18	33
PSBK Blitar	20	9	4	7	24	17	31
PSBS Biak Numfor	20	7	8	5	27	22	29
Perseru Serui	20	8	3	9	24	18	27
Persigo Gorontalo	20	8	3	9	22	37	27
Persid Jember	20	7	2	11	20	23	23
Persekam Metro	20	5	5	10	22	27	20
Perssin Sinjai	20	6	4	10	22	35	16
Mojokerto Putra	20	3	4	13	11	32	13

15/12/2011 - 17/06/2012 • ‡ Qualified for the play-offs

LIGA INDONESIA PREMIER DIVISION (LI) PLAY-OFFS

First round

Group A

	Pl	W	D	L	F	A	Pts	PT	PSBK	PK
Persepam Madura Utd‡	3	2	0	1	3	3	**6**	0-2	2-1	1-0
Persita Tangerang ‡	3	1	2	0	5	3	**5**		1-1	2-2
PSBK Blitar	3	1	1	1	4	3	**4**			2-0
Persiku Kudus	3	0	1	2	2	5	**1**			

Group B

	Pl	W	D	L	F	A	Pts	BP	PS	WS
PSIM Yogyakarta ‡	3	3	0	0	5	2	**9**	1-0	2-1	2-1
Barito Putra ‡	3	1	1	1	6	3	**4**		5-1	1-1
Persebaya Surabaya	3	1	0	2	4	7	**3**			2-0
West Sumbawa	3	0	1	2	2	5	**1**			

25/06/2012 - 8/07/2012 • ‡ Qualified for the semi-finals
Semi-finals: **Barito Putra** 2-0 Persepam; **Persita** 1-0 PSIM
3rd Place play-off: **Persepam** 1-0 PSIM • Final: **Barito Putera** 2-1 Persita
Barito Putera, Persita & Persepam promoted; PSIM to ISL play-off (see ISL)

MEDALS TABLE

		Overall	Lge	Cup	City
		G S	G S	G S	
1	Persija	11 6	11 5	1	Jakarta
2	Persis	8 1	8 1		Solo
3	Persebaya	7 12	7 12		Surabaya
4	Tiga Berlian	7 1	4 1	3	Palembang
5	Persib	6 8	6 8		Bandung
	PSM	6 8	6 8		Makassar
7	PSMS	6 7	6 7		Medan
8	Sriwijaya	5	2	3	Palembang
9	Persipura	4 6	4 3	3	Jayapura
10	Arema	4 3	2 1	2 2	Malang
11	Pelita Jaya	3 5	3 2	3	Karawang
12	Mitra Kukar	3 2	3 1	1	Tenggarong
13	Arseto	2 1	1 1	1	Solo
	PSIS	2 1	2 1		Semarang
	Semen Padang	2 1	1	1 1	Indarung
16	Persik Kediri	2	2		Kediri

PIALA INDONESIA 2012

Second Round

Persibo Bojonegoro	Bye
Persema Malang	Bye
PSM Makassar	1 4
Madiun Putra	1 1
Persipro Probolinggo	0
Arema Indonesia	3
Persiba Bantul	Bye
Persibul Buol	w/o
Perseman Manokwari	
Persis Solo	2 2
Persija Jakarta	1 3
Persipasi Bekasi	
PPSM Sakti Magelang	w/o
Persebaya Surabaya	Bye
Persikab Bandung	0 0
PSLS Lhokseumawe	1 3
PSIS Semarang	4 2
Bontang	0 4
Persijap Jepara	0 0
Persik Kediri	2 1
PSMS Medan	Bye
Persikabo Bogor	0 1
Persiraja Banda Ace	0 3
Pro Duta	0 2
Persitara Jakarta	0 1
Semen Padang	Bye

Round of 16

Persibo Bojonegoro	1 3
Persema Malang*	1 1
PSM Makassar*	2 0
Arema Indonesia	1 1
Persiba Bantul*	2 0
Perseman Manokwari	0 0
Persis Solo*	2 1
PPSM Sakti Magelang	1 3
Persebaya Surabaya	1 3
PSLS Lhokseumawe*	1 0
PSIS Semarang*	1 4
Persik Kediri	1 5
PSMS Medan	2 2
Persiraja Banda Ace*	3 0
Pro Duta	0 0
Semen Padang*	2 3

Quarter-finals

Persibo Bojonegoro*	0 1
Arema Indonesia	0 0
Persiba Bantul	0 3
PPSM Sakti Magelang*	3 1
Persebaya Surabaya	3 3
Persik Kediri*	1 2
PSMS Medan	0 1
Semen Padang*	2 1

Semi-finals

Persibo Bojonegoro	2 3
PPSM Sakti Magelang*	1 1
Persebaya Surabaya*	2 0
Semen Padang	0 3

Final

Persibo Bojonegoro ‡	1
Semen Padang	0

PIALA INDONESIA FINAL

Sultan Agung Stadium, Bantul
14-07-2012
Scorer - Dian Irawan 50 for Persibo
Persibo - Fauzi Toldo - Lexe Anderson (Aries Tuansyah 74), Aang Suparman, Harry Syahputra - Aulia Tri Hartanto (Edy Sibung 84), Mekan Nasirov, Jajang Paliama, Dian Irawan, Gustavo Ortiz - Samsul Arif, M. Nur Iskandar.
Tr: Paulo Camargo
Semen - Jandia Eka Putra - David Pagbe, Abdul Rahman, Hengly Ardiles, Slamet Riyadi - Vendry Mofu (Mustofa Aji 75), Muhammad Rizal, Elie Aiboy (Rudi 87), Esteban Vizcarra - Edward Wilson, Suheri Daud (Arifan Fitra 17).
Tr: Suhatman Imam

* Home team/home team in the first leg • ‡ Qualified for the AFC Cup

IND – INDIA

FIFA/COCA-COLA WORLD RANKING

'93	'94	'95	'96	'97	'98	'99	'00	'01	'02	'03	'04	'05	'06	'07	'08	'09	'10	'11	'12
100	109	121	120	112	110	106	122	121	127	127	132	127	157	143	143	134	142	162	166

2012

Jan	Feb	Mar	Apr	May	Jun	Jul	Aug	Sep	Oct	Nov	Dec	High	Low	Av
158	154	158	165	164	164	163	168	169	168	169	166	94	169	130

Indian athletes returned from the 2012 Olympic Games in London with just six medals - none of which were gold. The two silver and four bronze medals were won in just four sports, an extraordinary statistic for the second most populous nation on earth. Persuading the cricket authorities and cricket fans that football and other sports do not pose a threat to them is the first task but the creation of a multi-sports landscape will not be easy. FIFA has put its full weight behind the development of football in India while the Asian Football Confederation has also committed significant resources to improving the standard of professional football in the country. There was little joy, though, for the national side at the finals of the AFC Challenge Cup in 2012, a title the Indians won in 2008. Tajikistan, the Philippines and eventual champions Korea DPR all beat Savio Medeira's side as India finished bottom of the group. The result cost Medeira his position at the helm of the team and he was replaced by Dutchman Wim Koevermans. Central to any future development will have to be the I-League which in 2012 was won by Dempo for the fifth time in eight seasons. The Goa-based club was beaten in the Federation Cup final by Calcutta's East Bengal to miss out on a first double while the Durand Cup was won by Air India.

FIFA WORLD CUP RECORD
1930-1982 DNE **1986** DNQ **1990** DNE **1994-2014** DNQ

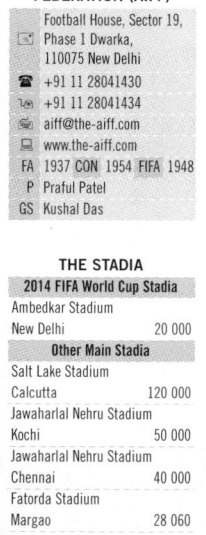

ALL INDIA FOOTBALL FEDERATION (AIFF)

Football House, Sector 19, Phase 1 Dwarka, 110075 New Delhi
☎ +91 11 28041430
📠 +91 11 28041434
✉ aiff@the-aiff.com
🌐 www.the-aiff.com
FA 1937 CON 1954 FIFA 1948
P Praful Patel
GS Kushal Das

THE STADIA
2014 FIFA World Cup Stadia
Ambedkar Stadium
New Delhi   20 000

Other Main Stadia
Salt Lake Stadium
Calcutta   120 000
Jawaharlal Nehru Stadium
Kochi   50 000
Jawaharlal Nehru Stadium
Chennai   40 000
Fatorda Stadium
Margao   28 060

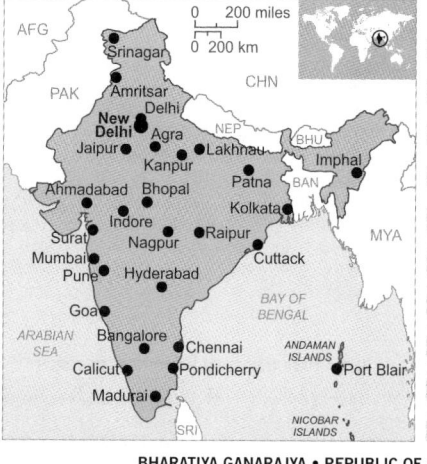

MAJOR CITIES/TOWNS

		Population
1	Mumbai/Bombay	13 922 125
2	Delhi/Dilli	12 259 230
3	Bangalore	5 310 318
4	Calcutta/Kolkata	5 080 519
5	Madras/Chennai	4 590 267
6	Hyderabad	4 025 335
7	Ahmadabad	3 913 793
8	Pune	3 337 481
9	Surat	3 233 988
10	Kanpur	3 144 267
11	Jaipur	3 102 808
12	Lakhnau	2 685 528
13	Nagpur	2 403 239
14	Patna	1 814 012
15	Indore	1 811 513
16	Bhopal	1 752 244
17	Thana	1 739 697
18	Ludhiana	1 701 212
19	Agra	1 638 209

BHARATIYA GANARAJYA • REPUBLIC OF INDIA

Capital	New Delhi	Population	1 166 079 217 (2)	% in cities	29%
GDP per capita	$2900 (167)	Area km²	3 287 263 km² (7)	GMT +/−	+5.5
Neighbours (km)	Bangladesh 4053, Bhutan 605, China 3380, Myanmar 1463, Nepal 1690, Pakistan 2912 • Coast 7000

RECENT INTERNATIONAL MATCHES PLAYED BY INDIA

2010	Opponents	Score	Venue	Comp	Scorers	Att	Referee
4-09	Thailand	L 0-1	Bangkok	Fr			
8-09	Thailand	L 1-2	New Delhi	Fr	Pradeep [60]		
15-09	Namibia	W 2-0	New Delhi	Fr	Wadoo [28], Pereira [54]		Patwal IND
4-10	Hong Kong	L 0-1	Pune	Fr		8 000	Patwal IND
8-10	Vietnam	W 3-1	Pune	Fr	Chetri 3 [25 49 72]		Dinesh IND
13-10	Yemen	L 3-6	Pune	Fr	Pereira [21], Yadav [49], Surkurmar Singh [92+]		Patwal IND
11-11	Iraq	L 0-2	Sharjah	Fr			
14-11	Kuwait	L 1-9	Abu Dhabi	Fr	Rafi [69]		
18-11	UAE	L 0-5	Dubai	Fr			
2011							
10-01	Australia	L 0-4	Doha	ACr1		11 749	Badwawi UAE
14-01	Bahrain	L 2-5	Doha	ACr1	Gouramangi Singh [9], Chetri [52]	11 032	Mohd Salleh MAS
18-01	Korea Republic	L 1-4	Doha	ACr1	Chetri [12p]	11 366	Al Ghamdi KSA
21-03	Chinese Taipei	W 3-0	Petaling Jaya	CCq	Jeje Lalpekhlua [32], Sunil Chetri [76], Jewel Shaikh [88]	50	Abdul Wahab MAS
23-03	Pakistan	W 3-1	Petaling Jaya	CCq	Jeje Lalpekhlua 2 [67 94+], Steven Dias [90]	100	Alrshaidat JOR
25-03	Turkmenistan	D 1-1	Petaling Jaya	CCq	Jeje Lalpekhlua [60]	200	Abdul Wahab MAS
10-07	Maldives	D 1-1	Male	Fr	Sunil Chetri [18]		
23-07	UAE	L 0-3	Al Ain	WCq		3 179	Al Dosari QAT
28-07	UAE	D 2-2	New Delhi	WCq	Jeje Lalpekhlua [74], Gouramangi Moirangthem [92+]	13 000	Bashir SIN
21-08	Trinidad & Tobago	L 0-3	Port of Spain	Fr		6 600	Campbell JAM
24-08	Guyana	L 1-2	Georgetown	Fr	Steven Dias [36]	2 500	Lancaster GUY
13-11	Malaysia	D 1-1	Guwahati	Fr	Syed Nabi [88]	20 000	
16-11	Malaysia	W 3-2	Calcutta	Fr	Sunil Chetri 2 [39 53], Jeje Lalpekhlua [47]	2 500	
29-11	Zambia	L 0-5	Margao	Fr			
3-12	Afghanistan	D 1-1	New Delhi	SAFr1	Sunil Chetri [10]		
5-12	Bhutan	W 5-0	New Delhi	SAFr1	Syed Nabi [29], Clifford Miranda 2 [44 58], Sunil Chetri 2 [69 84]		
7-12	Sri Lanka	W 3-0	New Delhi	SAFr1	Jeje Lalpekhlua [50], Sunil Chetri [70], OG [93+]		
9-12	Maldives	W 3-1	New Delhi	SAFsf	Syed Nabi [24], Sunil Chetri 2 [70p 91+]		
11-12	Afghanistan	W 4-0	New Delhi	SAFf	Sunil Chetri [71p], Clifford Miranda [79], Jeje Lalpekhlua [80], Sushil Singh [95+]		
2012							
23-02	Oman	L 1-5	Seeb	Fr	Joaquim Abranches [64]		
27-02	Azerbaijan	L 0-3	Dubai	Fr		50	Hashmi UAE
9-03	Tajikistan	L 0-2	Kathmandu	CCr1		700	Sabbagh LIB
11-03	Philippines	L 0-2	Kathmandu	CCr1		300	Mahapab THA
13-03	Korea DPR	L 0-4	Kathmandu	CCr1		200	Mahapab THA
22-08	Syria	W 2-1	New Delhi	Fr	Sunil Chetri [45], Anthony Pereira [82]		Tseytlin UZB
25-08	Maldives	W 3-0	New Delhi	Fr	Sunil Chetri 2 [45 70], Syed Rahim Nabi [54]		Hashmi UAE
28-08	Nepal	D 0-0	New Delhi	Fr			Tseytlin UZB
16-10	Singapore	L 0-2	Singapore	Fr		3 448	

Fr = Friendly match • SAF = South Asian Football Federation Cup • CC = AFC Confederation Cup • AC = AFC Asian Cup • WC = FIFA World Cup
q = qualifier • r1 = first round group • qf = quarter-final • sf = semi-final • f = final

INDIA NATIONAL TEAM HISTORICAL RECORDS

Caps: 110 - Shabbir Ali 1974-84 • **107** - Bhaichung Bhutia 1995- • **84** - PK Banerjee 1952-67 • **82** - Mahesh Gawli 1997-2011

Goals: 65 - PK Banerjee 1952-67 • **43** - Bhaichung Bhutia 1995- • **40** - IM Vijayan 1989-2004 • **36** - Sunil Chetri 2005- • **35** - Shabbir Ali 1974-84

Past Coaches: Syed Abdul Rahim 1950-62 • Harry Wright ENG 1963-64 • Pradip Kumar Banerjee 1981-82 • Bob Bootland ENG 1983 • Milovan Ciric YUG 1984 • Barry Ford AUS 1984 • Pradip Kumar Banerjee 1985 • Syed Nayeemuddin 1986 • Amal Dutta 1987 • Jozsef Gelei HUN 1990-91 • Syed Nayeemuddin 1992 • Jiri Pesek CZE 1993-94 • Rustam Akramov UZB 1995-96 • Syed Nayeemuddin 1997-98 • Sukhvinder Singh 1999-02 • Stephen Constantine ENG 2002-05 • Syed Nayeemuddin 2005-06 • Bob Houghton ENG 2006-11 • Armando Colaco 2011 • Savio Medeira 2011-12 • Wim Koevermans 2012-

INDIA 2011-12
ONGC I-LEAGUE

	Pl	W	D	L	F	A	Pts	Dempo	East Bengal	Churchill Bros	Mohun Bagan	Pune	Salgaocar	Prayag Utd	Sporting	Air India	Shillong	Mumbai	Chirag Utd	Pailan Arrows	HAL
Dempo Sports Club	26	18	3	5	59	21	57		0-0	1-2	5-0	0-1	0-0	1-2	3-2	0-2	5-0	4-0	2-1	3-0	3-0
East Bengal †	26	15	6	5	46	22	51	2-1		0-1	1-1	3-1	1-0	0-1	3-0	2-1	2-0	3-1	4-3	4-1	2-0
Churchill Brothers †	26	14	6	6	47	28	48	2-4	1-1		2-3	0-2	0-3	5-2	5-0	2-0	6-0	1-0	4-0	3-2	1-1
Mohun Bagan	26	13	8	5	51	32	47	2-2	1-0	3-0		2-0	0-0	1-2	1-1	3-1	6-1	2-1	2-1	2-0	0-0
Pune	26	13	7	6	44	34	46	1-3	0-0	0-2	2-1		2-0	2-1	2-2	2-2	0-0	3-0	3-1	1-0	3-1
Salgaocar	26	12	8	6	32	19	44	0-1	4-0	1-1	1-1	1-3		1-0	2-1	1-0	2-1	1-0	1-0	4-0	4-0
Prayag United	26	11	9	6	41	29	42	0-3	1-1	1-1	3-2	5-1	0-0		2-2	3-0	1-1	3-0	1-0	2-1	0-0
Sporting Clube Goa	26	11	7	8	53	43	40	1-4	0-1	1-1	2-1	4-2	4-2	2-2		1-3	4-3	5-0	2-0	0-0	7-0
Air India	26	9	5	12	29	37	32	1-3	0-1	0-1	2-2	0-2	3-1	0-0	0-2		0-0	1-4	1-3	2-0	2-1
Shillong Lajong	26	7	7	12	24	44	28	1-2	2-1	0-2	0-0	1-1	0-0	3-5	0-1	0-0		2-1	1-0	1-0	1-0
Mumbai FC	26	7	3	16	31	52	24	0-2	1-4	2-1	1-5	0-0	0-1	3-1	2-1	0-1	2-1		0-2	1-1	4-0
Chirag United	26	6	2	18	28	50	20	1-2	0-2	1-2	1-3	0-3	1-1	2-1	0-3	1-2	3-2	5-2		0-3	0-2
Pailan Arrows	26	2	10	14	17	40	16	0-2	0-0	0-0	1-3	1-1	0-0	0-0	2-3	0-2	0-2	1-1	1-1		1-1
HAL Bangalore	26	1	5	20	19	68	8	0-3	1-8	0-1	2-4	4-6	0-1	0-2	2-2	2-4	0-1	1-5	0-1	1-2	

22/10/2011 - 6/05/2012 • † Qualified for the AFC Cup

Top scorer: **32** - Ranti **MARTINS** NGA, Dempo • **26** - Odafe **ONYEKA** NGA, Mohun Bagan • **18** - Tolgay **OZBEY** AUS, East Bengal • **15** - James **MOGA** SSD, Sporting & Mandjou **KEITA** GUI, Pune • **12** - Ogba **KALU** NGA, Sporting; David **OPARA** NGA, Churchill & Henry **ANTCHOUET** GAB, Churchill

INDIA 2011-12
NATIONAL LEAGUE 2ND DIVISION

	Pl	W	D	L	F	A	Pts
United Sikkim	12	6	4	2	22	17	22
ONGC Mumbai	12	6	4	2	20	9	22
Mohammedan Sporting	12	6	3	3	15	11	21
Kalighat Milan Sangha	12	4	4	4	18	15	16
Royal Wahingdoh	12	5	1	6	14	15	16
Vasco Sports Club	12	3	4	5	18	23	13
Aizawl FC	12	1	2	9	14	31	5

5/03/2012 - 17/04/2012

125TH DURAND CUP 2012

First round group stage

Group A	Pl	W	D	L	F	A	Pts	PA	DU
Air India	2	1	1	0	4	1	4	1-1	3-0
Pailan Arrows	2	0	2	0	3	3	2		2-2
Delhi United	2	0	1	1	2	5	1		

Group B	Pl	W	D	L	F	A	Pts	Sp	OM
Assam Rifles	2	1	1	0	4	3	4	3-2	1-1
Sporting Clube Goa	2	1	0	1	5	4	3		3-1
ONGC Mumbai	2	0	1	1	2	4	1		

Group C	Pl	W	D	L	F	A	Pts	Pu	CRP
SESA Academy	2	1	1	0	4	3	4	1-1	3-2
Pune	2	0	2	0	1	1	2		0-0
Central Reserve Police	2	0	1	1	2	3	1		

Group D	Pl	W	D	L	F	A	Pts	AR	PP
Dodsal Mumbai	2	2	0	0	9	0	6	3-0	6-0
Army Red	2	1	0	1	1	3	3		1-0
Punjab Police	2	0	0	2	0	7	0		

Semi-finals

Air India	2	7p
SESA Academy	2	6p

Assam Rifles	1	5p
Dodsal Mumbai	1	6p

Final

Air India	0	3p
Dodsal Mumbai	0	2p

CUP FINAL
Ambedkar Stadium, New Delhi
1-09-2012, Att: 10 000

Played in New Delhi
16/08/2012 - 1/09/2012

34TH FEDERATION CUP 2012

First round group stage

Group A (Jamshedpur)	Pl	W	D	L	F	A	Pts	PA	SL	Mu
Dempo Sports Club	3	2	1	0	6	1	7	1-1	1-0	4-0
Pailan Arrows	3	1	2	0	5	4	5		2-1	2-2
Shillong Lajong	3	1	0	2	3	4	3			2-1
Mumbai FC	3	0	1	2	3	8	1			

Group B (Siliguri)	Pl	W	D	L	F	A	Pts	MB	AI	MS
Churchill Brothers	3	2	1	0	9	1	7	0-0	4-0	5-1
Mohun Bagan	3	1	1	1	2	3	4		0-2	2-1
Air India	3	1	0	2	2	5	3			0-1
Mohammedan Sporting	3	1	0	2	3	7	3			

Group C (Siliguri)	Pl	W	D	L	F	A	Pts	ONGC	Sp	KMS
East Bengal	3	2	1	0	7	5	7	2-1	1-1	4-3
ONGC Mumbai	3	2	0	1	8	4	6		2-1	5-1
Sporting Clube Goa	3	1	1	1	5	5	4			3-2
Kalighat Milan Sangha	3	0	0	3	6	12	0			

Group D (Jamshedpur)	Pl	W	D	L	F	A	Pts	PU	Pu	US
Salgoacar	3	3	0	0	6	1	9	1-0	2-1	3-0
Prayag United	3	1	1	1	3	2	4		1-1	2-0
Pune	3	1	1	1	3	3	4			1-0
United Sikkim	3	0	0	3	0	6	0			

Semi-finals

East Bengal	1
Churchill Brothers	0
Salgoacar	0
Dempo Sports Club	2

Final

East Bengal	3
Dempo Sports Club	2

19/09/2012 - 30/09/2012

34TH FEDERATION CUP FINAL 2012
Kanchenjunga Stadium, Siliguri, 30-09-2012

East Bengal	3	Lawrence [51], Manandeep Singh [100], Chidi [10]
Dempo SC	2	Mondal [60], Gawli [111]

EAST BENGAL
Abhijit **MONDAL** - Saumik **DEY**, Arnab **MONDAL**, Raju **GAIKWAD**, Thokchom Naoba **SINGH**, Harmanjot **KHABRA** (Lalrindika **RALTE** 91) - Ishfaq **AHMED** (Sanju **PRADHAN** 79), Penn Ikechukwu **ORJI**, Mehtab **HUSSAIN** - Manandeep **SINGH**, Edeh **CHIDI** (Robert **LALTHLAMUANA** 114). Tr: Trevor **MORGAN**

DEMPO
Subhasish **ROYCHOWDHURY** - Creson **ANTAO**, Valeriano **REBELLO**, Peter **CARVALHO**•, Debabrata **ROY**, Mahesh **GAWLI** - Clifford **MIRANDA** (Ryuji **SUEOKA** 79), Anthony **PEREIRA**• (Romeo **FERNANDES** 96), Climax **LAWRENCE** (Godwin **FRANCO** 103) - Joaquim **ABRANCHES**. Tr: Armando **COLACO**

MEDALS TABLE

		Overall			League			FC		D Cup		St	Asia			City	DOF
		G	S	B	G	S	B	G	S	G	S		G	S	B		
1	Mohun Bagan	32	27	2	3	2	1	13	5	16	20	26			1	Kolkata	1889
2	East Bengal FC	26	23	2	3	5	2	8	8	15	10	31				Kolkata	1920
3	JCT Mills	8	8	1	1	1	1	2		5	7	9				Phagwara	1971
4	Salgoacar SC	8	4	2	2	1	2	4	3	2		18				Vasco, Goa	1955
5	Border Security Force	8	3					1	1	7	2	3				Jalandhar	
6	Dempo Sports Club	7	5	1	5	1	1	1	4	1		10				Panjim, Goa	1968
7	Mahindra United	6	6	2	1		2	2	3	3	3	12				Mumbai	1962
8	Churchill Brothers SC	3	7	3	1	5	3			2	2	6				Salcete, Goa	1988
9	Mohammedan Sporting	3	6					2	3	1	3	11				Kolkata	1892
10	Kerala Police	2						2				5				Thiruv'puram	
11	Indian Telephone Ind.	1						1				18				Bangalore	
	Chirag United	1								1						Kolkata	1927
	Air India	1								1		4				Mumbai	1952
14	Sporting Clube de Goa		4	1		1	1		2		1	1				Goa	1999
15	Mafatlal Hills		2						2								
16	Prayag United		1							1							
	Tata Football Academy		1						1							Jamshedpur	1983
	Shillong Lajong		1							1						Shillong	1983
19	Vasco Sports Club			2			2					6				Vasco, Goa	1951

FC = Federation Cup • D Cup = Durand Cup • St = State championship (not included in overall total)

IRL – REPUBLIC OF IRELAND

FIFA/COCA-COLA WORLD RANKING

'93	'94	'95	'96	'97	'98	'99	'00	'01	'02	'03	'04	'05	'06	'07	'08	'09	'10	'11	'12
10	9	28	36	47	56	35	31	17	14	14	12	24	49	35	38	35	36	22	42

2012

Jan	Feb	Mar	Apr	May	Jun	Jul	Aug	Sep	Oct	Nov	Dec	High	Low	Av
23	20	19	18	18	18	26	26	26	28	36	42	6	57	28

Ireland's adventure at the finals of Euro 2012 didn't go to plan and they ended the tournament with the worst record of all the 16 competing nations. Giovanni Trapattoni's team shipped nine goals in the three games they played in Poland and were comprehensively outclassed against the Spanish to whom they lost 4-0. The utilitarian tactics that had served them so well in qualification proved to be wholly inadequate against the top sides. It was Ireland's first appearance at a major finals for a decade but hopes of qualifying for the 2014 FIFA World Cup looked to be on shaky ground after an embarrassing 6-1 defeat to Germany in Dublin at the end of the year. At home, there were celebrations in the north-west of the country after Sligo Rovers won the championship for the first time in 35 years. Englishman Paul Cook had led the renaissance of the club, twice winning the FAI Cup as well as the League Cup, but he left at the start of the season and was replaced by another Englishman, Ian Baraclough. Sligo lost just once before clinching the title with a 3-2 win over St Patrick's in mid-October but they failed in their bid for a hat trick of cup wins. Instead, the final was a repeat of the 2006 final, with Derry City once again beating St Patrick's. This time the score was 3-2, with Rory Patterson scoring the winner in extra-time.

UEFA EUROPEAN CHAMPIONSHIP RECORD
1960 pr 1964 QF 1968-1984 DNQ **1988** 5 r1 1992-2008 DNQ **2012** 16 r1

THE FOOTBALL ASSOCIATION OF IRELAND (FAI)

National Sports Campus, Abbotstown, Dublin 15
☎ +353 1 8999500
+353 1 8999501
info@fai.ie
www.fai.ie
FA 1921 CON 1954 FIFA 1923
P Paddy McCaul
GS John Delaney

THE STADIA
2014 FIFA World Cup Stadia

Aviva Stadium Dublin	51 700

Other Main Stadia

Dalymount Park Dublin	12 000
Hogan Park Limerick	9 000
Turner's Cross Cork	7 485
Tallaght Stadium Dublin	6 500

MAJOR CITIES/TOWNS
Population

1	Dublin	1 064 376
2	Cork	193 328
-	Londonderry	83 652
3	Galway	76 433
4	Waterford	49 094
5	Swords	38 711
6	Limerick	38 439
7	Dundalk	35 867
8	Bray	32 436
9	Drogheda	32 221
10	Navan	29 437
11	Ennis	26 205
12	Kilkenny	23 369
13	Tralee	22 945
14	Naas	21 418
15	Newbridge	20 614
16	Mullingar	20 202
17	Carlow	19 999
18	Sligo	18 926

EIRE • IRELAND

Capital	Dublin	Population	4 203 200 (125)	% in cities	61%
GDP per capita	$45 500 (11)	Area km²	70 273 km² (119)	GMT +/-	0
Neighbours (km)	United Kingdom (Northern Ireland) 360 • Coast 1448				

RECENT INTERNATIONAL MATCHES PLAYED BY THE REPUBLIC OF IRELAND

2009	Opponents	Score	Venue	Comp	Scorers	Att	Referee
12-08	Australia	L 0-3	Limerick	Fr		19 000	Burrull ESP
5-09	Cyprus	W 2-1	Nicosia	WCq	Doyle [5], Keane [83]	5 191	Einwaller AUT
8-09	South Africa	W 1-0	Limerick	Fr	Lawrence [37]	11 300	Thomson SCO
10-10	Italy	D 2-2	Dublin	WCq	Whelan [8], St Ledger [87]	70 640	Hauge NOR
14-10	Montenegro	D 0-0	Dublin	WCq		50 212	Hrinak SVK
14-11	France	L 0-1	Dublin	WCpo		74 103	Brych GER
18-11	France	D 1-1	Paris	WCpo	Keane [33]	79 145	Hansson SWE
2010							
2-03	Brazil	L 0-2	London	Fr		40 082	Dean ENG
25-05	Paraguay	W 2-1	Dublin	Fr	Doyle [7], Lawrence [39]	16 722	Laperriere SUI
28-05	Algeria	W 3-0	Dublin	Fr	Green [31], Keane 2 [51][86]	16 888	Braamhaar NED
11-08	Argentina	L 0-1	Dublin	Fr		45 200	Rasmussen DEN
3-09	Armenia	W 1-0	Yerevan	ECq	Fahey [76]	8 600	Szabo HUN
7-09	Andorra	W 3-1	Dublin	ECq	Kilbane [15], Doyle [41], Keane [54]	40 283	Trattou CYP
8-10	Russia	L 2-3	Dublin	ECq	Keane [72p], Long [78]	50 411	Blom NED
12-10	Slovakia	D 1-1	Zilina	ECq	St Ledger [16]	10 892	Undiano ESP
17-11	Norway	L 1-2	Dublin	Fr	Long [5p]	25 000	Jakobsson ISL
2011							
8-02	Wales	W 3-0	Dublin	Fr	Gibson [60], Duff [66], Fahey [82]	19 783	Courtney NIR
26-03	Macedonia FYR	W 2-1	Dublin	ECq	McGeady [2], Keane [21]	33 200	Vad HUN
29-03	Uruguay	L 2-3	Dublin	Fr	Long [15], Fahey [48p]	20 200	Ennjimi FRA
24-05	Northern Ireland	W 5-0	Dublin	Fr	Ward [24], Keane 2 [37][54p], OG [45], Cox [80]	12 083	Thomson SCO
29-05	Scotland	W 1-0	Dublin	Fr	Keane [23]	17 694	Whitby WAL
4-06	Macedonia FYR	W 2-0	Skopje	ECq	Keane 2 [8][37]	29 500	Meyer GER
7-06	Italy	W 2-0	Liege	Fr	Andrews [36], Cox [90]	21 516	Gumienny BEL
10-08	Croatia	D 0-0	Dublin	Fr		20 179	Hagen NOR
2-09	Slovakia	D 0-0	Dublin	ECq		35 480	Proenca POR
6-09	Russia	D 0-0	Moscow	ECq		49 515	Brych GER
7-10	Andorra	W 2-0	Andorra La Vella	ECq	Doyle [8], McGeady [20]	860	Kovarik CZE
11-10	Armenia	W 2-1	Dublin	ECq	OG [43], Dunne [59]	45 200	Iturralde ESP
11-11	Estonia	W 4-0	Tallinn	ECpo	Andrews [13], Walters [67], Keane 2 [71][88p]	10 500	Kassai HUN
15-11	Estonia	D 1-1	Dublin	ECpo	Ward [32]	51 151	Kuipers NED
2012							
29-02	Czech Republic	D 1-1	Dublin	Fr	Cox [87]	37 741	Sousa POR
26-05	Bosnia-Herzegovina	W 1-0	Dublin	Fr	Long [78]	37 100	Hanni SUI
10-06	Croatia	L 1-3	Poznan	ECr1	St Ledger [19]	43 200	Kuipers NED
14-06	Spain	L 0-4	Gdansk	ECr1		36 572	Proenca POR
18-06	Italy	L 0-2	Poznan	ECr1		44 416	Cakir TUR
15-08	Serbia	D 0-0	Belgrade	Fr		7 800	Tudor ROU
7-09	Kazakhstan	W 2-1	Astana	WCq	Keane [88p], Doyle [90]	12 384	Avram ROU
11-09	Oman	W 4-1	London	Fr	Long [7], Brady [23], Doyle [36], Pearce [85]	6 420	Marriner ENG
12-10	Germany	L 1-6	Dublin	WCq	Keogh [92+]	49 850	Rizzoli ITA
16-10	Faroe Islands	W 4-1	Torshavn	WCq	Wilson [46], Walters [53], OG [73], O'Dea [88]	4 300	Jemini ALB
14-11	Greece	L 0-1	Dublin	Fr		16 256	Shmuelevich ISR

Fr = Friendly match • EC = UEFA EURO 2012 • WC = FIFA World Cup • q = qualifier • po = play-off

REPUBLIC OF IRELAND NATIONAL TEAM HISTORICAL RECORDS

Caps: 125 - Shay Given 1996- • 122 - Robbie Keane 1998- • 110 - Kevin Kilbane 1997- • 102 - Steve Staunton 1988-2002 • 100 - Damien Duff 1998- • 91 - Niall Quinn 1986-2002 • 88 - Tony Cascarino 1986-2000 • 85 - John O'Shea 2001- • 83 - Paul McGrath 1985-97 • 80 - Pat Bonner 1981-96 • 76 - Richard Dunne 2000- • 73 - Ray Houghton 1986-98 • 72 - Kenny Cunningham 1996-2005 & Liam Brady 1975-90 • 71 - Kevin Moran 1980-94 & Frank Stapleton 1977-90 • 70 - Andy Townsend 1989-97 • 69 - John Aldridge 1986-97

Goals: 54 - Robbie Keane 1998- • 21 - Niall Quinn 1986-2002 • 20 - Frank Stapleton 1977-90 • 19 - Don Givens 1969-82; Tony Cascarino 1986-2000 & John Aldridge 1986-97 • 14 - Noel Cantwell 1954-67 • 13 - Jimmy Dunne 1930-39 & Gerry Daly 1973-87 • 12 - Kevin Doyle 2006-

Coaches: Doug Livingstone SCO 1951-53 • Alex Stevenson 1953-55 • Johnny Carey 1955-67 • Noel Cantwell 1967 • Charlie Hurley 1967-69 • Mick Meagan 1969-71 • Liam Tuohy 1971-73 • Sean Thomas 1973 • Johnny Giles 1973-80 • Alan Kelly Snr 1980 • Eoin Hand 1980-85 • Jack Charlton ENG 1986-95 • Mick McCarthy 1996-2002 • Don Givens 2002 • Brian Kerr 2003-05 • Steve Staunton 2006-07 • Don Givens 2007-08 • Giovanni Trapattoni ITA 2008-

IRL – REPUBLIC OF IRELAND 435

REPUBLIC OF IRELAND 2012

EIRCOM LEAGUE OF IRELAND PREMIER DIVISION

	Pl	W	D	L	F	A	Pts	Sligo	Drogheda	St Pat's	Shamrock	Derry	Cork	Bohemians	Shelbourne	UCD	Bray	Dundalk	Monaghan
Sligo Rovers †	30	17	10	3	53	23	61		4-1	1-1 3-2	3-0 0-2	1-1 4-1	2-2	1-0 3-1	3-0	2-1 3-0	1-1	3-0 3-0
Drogheda United ‡	30	17	6	7	51	36	57	1-3 2-1		0-0 0-0	0-1 2-0	2-2 0-2	2-1	1-1	1-0	3-1 2-1	1-0	3-1	0-0 3-2
St Patrick's Athletic ‡	30	15	10	5	44	22	55	0-0	0-2		5-1 2-1	3-0	0-0 1-0	2-1	1-0	2-0 5-0	1-0 0-1	1-2	
Shamrock Rovers	30	14	10	6	56	37	52	1-1	3-1	1-1		1-1 1-3	1-1	2-0 0-1	4-0 2-2	2-2 2-1	0-0	6-0 7-0	
Derry City ‡	30	11	6	13	36	36	39	1-2	0-3	0-2 2-1	0-1		2-0 0-1	1-0 2-0	0-1	0-0 1-2	3-2	1-2 4-0	
Cork City	30	8	12	10	38	36	36	0-1 0-0	2-3 3-2	0-1	1-1 1-2	2-2		1-1	0-0	4-2	1-1 2-0	3-2 3-0	6-0
Bohemians	30	9	9	12	35	38	36	0-0	1-1 1-4	0-0 2-3	4-0	1-2	1-0 1-1		0-2 2-2	1-0	0-0	2-1	1-2
Shelbourne	30	9	8	13	35	43	35	1-1 1-3	1-2	1-1 0-2	2-3	1-0 0-2	1-2 3-2	1-2		1-2	2-1 0-0	4-0	2-1
University College	30	8	7	15	32	48	31	1-0	1-1 1-0	1-1	0-2	0-1	1-0 3-2	1-2 2-2	0-2 1-1		2-3 3-1	1-1	3-2
Bray Wanderers	30	5	10	15	33	54	25	1-2 0-0	2-4 1-3	3-3	2-2 1-3	0-4 0-0	0-3	2-1 1-4	2-3	3-1		1-1	
Dundalk	30	4	8	18	23	63	20	1-2	1-2	0-2 0-1	1-1	1-1	1-1	0-2 2-2	0-0 0-1	2-1 1-2	0-2 2-1		1-2
Monaghan United		Withdrew after 11 matches						0-1	0-4	0-0	1-4						0-1	0-0	

2/03/2012 – 28/10/2012 • † Qualified for the UEFA Champions League • ‡ Qualified for the Europa League • Monaghan's matches were annulled
Top scorers: **22** – Gary **TWIGG** SCO, Shamrock Rovers • **15** – Danny **NORTH** ENG, Sligo Rovers • **14** – Jason **BYRNE**, Bray Wanderers • **13** – Declan **O'BRIEN**, Drogheda Utd & Chris **FAGAN**, St Pat's • **13** – Vincent **SULLIVAN**, Cork City • **11** – Philip **HUGHES**, Shelbourne & David **MCDAID**, Derry City

REPUBLIC OF IRELAND 2012 FIRST DIVISION (2)

	Pl	W	D	L	F	A	Pts
Limerick	28	20	2	6	51	20	62
Waterford United ‡	28	18	4	6	46	29	58
Longford Town ‡	28	15	5	8	42	33	50
Wexford Youths	28	11	6	11	45	40	39
Finn Harps	28	10	6	12	40	43	36
Athlone Town	28	8	5	15	25	41	29
Mervue United	28	6	5	17	34	49	23
Salthill Devon	28	5	5	18	23	51	20

2/03/2012 – 13/10/2012 • ‡ Promotion Play-offs
Longford Town 0-2 1-1 **Waterford United**

MEDALS TABLE

		Overall			League			Cup		LC	
		G	S	B	G	S	B	G	B	G	B
1	Shamrock Rovers	42	29	12	17	14	12	24	9	1	6
2	Shelbourne	21	25	11	13	11	11	7	11	1	3
3	Bohemian FC	21	24	14	11	14	14	7	7	3	3
4	Dundalk	21	19	6	9	10	6	8	5	4	4
5	Derry City	17	10	3	2	4	3	5	4	10	2
6	Cork Athletic	12	8	2	7	2	2	5	6		
7	St. Patrick's Athletic	11	14	3	7	4	3	2	8	2	2
8	Waterford United	10	12	8	6	4	8	2	7	2	1
9	Drumcondra	10	9	4	5	5	4	5	4		
10	Sligo Rovers	9	12	6	3	3	6	4	6	2	3
11	Cork City	7	10	5	2	5	5	2	3	3	2
12	Limerick	7	6	3	2	2	3	2	3	3	1
13	Athlone Town	6	3	3	2	1	3	1		3	2
14	Drogheda United	4	4	4	1	2	4	1	2	2	
15	St. James' Gate	4	3		2	1		2	2		
16	Cork Hibernians	3	3	3	1	1	3	2	2		
17	Galway United	3	3	1		1	1	1	1	2	1
18	Longford Town	3	3					2	2	1	1

LEAGUE OF IRELAND EA SPORTS CUP 2012

Round of 16		Quarter-finals		Semi-finals		Final	
Drogheda United *	1 4p						
Bohemians	1 3p	**Drogheda United** *	1 3p				
Longford Town *	1	Dundalk	1 2p				
Dundalk	2			**Drogheda United** *	2		
Derry City *	4			Sligo Rovers	1		
Finn Harps	0	Derry City	0				
Monaghan United	1	**Sligo Rovers** *	4				
Sligo Rovers *	3					**Drogheda United**	3
Limerick *	3					Shamrock Rovers	1
Cork City	0	**Limerick**	3				
Shelbourne *	1	Bray Wanderers *	1			CUP FINAL	
Bray Wanderers	2			Limerick	1	Tallaght Stadium, Dublin	
St Patrick's Athletic *	2			**Shamrock Rovers** *	4	22-09-2012, Att: 3120, Ref: Connolly	
University College	1	St Patrick's Athletic *	1 2p			Scorers - Declan O'Brien [33], OG [43],	
Salthill Devon *	0	**Shamrock Rovers**	1 4p			Eric Foley [61] for Drogheda; Killian	
Shamrock Rovers	2				* Home team	Brennan [59] for Rovers	

FA OF IRELAND CUP 2012

Second Round

Derry City*	4
Finn Harps	0
Phoenix United	1
University College*	3
Waterford United	0
Everton AFC*	0
Salthill Devon*	0
Mervue United	2
Shamrock Rovers*	1
Limerick	0
Athlone Town	1
Cork City*	6
Cherry Orchard*	2
Longford Town	0
Bray Wanderers*	1 0
Shelbourne	1 1
Dundalk*	4
St Patrick's CY	0
Blarney United*	1
Malahide United	4
Avondale United	3
Kildrum Tigers*	1
Drumkeen United	0
Bohemians*	5
Drogheda United*	6
Mayfield United	1
Douglas Hall*	1 2
Wexford Youths	1 3
Monaghan United	3
Sligo Rovers*	1
Crumlin United*	0
St Patrick's Athletic	3

Round of 16

Derry City	1
University College*	0
Waterford United*	0
Mervue United	4
Shamrock Rovers*	2
Cork City	0
Cherry Orchard	2
Shelbourne*	3
Dundalk	1
Malahide United*	0
Avondale United	0
Bohemians*	1
Drogheda United*	1
Wexford Youths	0
Monaghan United	w-o
St Patrick's Athletic	

Quarter-finals

Derry City*	7
Mervue United	1
Shamrock Rovers	1
Shelbourne*	2
Dundalk	1
Bohemians*	0
Drogheda United	0 1 2p
St Patrick's Athletic*	0 1 3p

Semi-finals

Derry City*	1 3
Shelbourne	1 0
Dundalk*	0
St Patrick's Athletic	3

Final

Derry City ‡	3
St Patrick's Athletic	2

CUP FINAL

Aviva Stadium, Dublin, 4-11-2012
Att: 16 117. Ref: Neil Doyle
Scorers - Greacen [55], Patterson 2 [69p 105] for Derry City; O'Connor [53], Fagan [87] for St Pat's
Derry - Gerard Doherty● - Shane McEleney, Dermot McCaffrey, Simon Madden, Stewart Greacen (Ryan McBride 98) - Barry Molloy - Barry McNamee (Ruaidhri Higgins● 81), Stephen McLaughlin, Patrick McEleney (Rory Patterson● 59) - Kevin Deery, David McDaid. Tr: Declan Devine
St Pat's - Brendan Clarke - Kenny Browne, Ian Bermingham, Conor Kenna, Ger O'Brien (Pat Flynn 105) - Chris Forrester, James Chambers●, Jake Carroll● (John Russell 24), Jake Kelly (Vinny Faherty 45) - Sean O'Connor● Christy Fagan. Tr: Liam Buckley

• * Home team ‡ Qualified for the Europa League

IRN – IRAN

FIFA/COCA-COLA WORLD RANKING

'93	'94	'95	'96	'97	'98	'99	'00	'01	'02	'03	'04	'05	'06	'07	'08	'09	'10	'11	'12
59	75	108	83	46	27	49	37	29	33	28	20	19	38	41	43	64	66	45	59

2012													High	Low	Av
Jan	Feb	Mar	Apr	May	Jun	Jul	Aug	Sep	Oct	Nov	Dec			
44	47	51	51	52	45	50	48	54	58	44	59	15	122	47

While Iran has had a long-held position within the elite of Asian football, the national team has consistently failed to live up to expectations in recent years, falling behind regional leaders Japan, Korea Republic and Australia. Fans in Iran are hopeful that under coach Carlos Queiroz that is about to change and in the qualifiers for the 2014 FIFA World Cup, Queiroz steered his team to the final stage in Asia. However, two crucial defeats - away to Lebanon and at home to Uzbekistan - left the group wide open at the end of 2012 as it reached the halfway stage. In club football Sepahan retained their league title after a three-way tussle with Teraktor-Sazi Tabriz and Esteghlal, a 0-0 draw against Mes Sarcheshme was enough to see them finish a point clear of both their rivals and become the first team to win a hat trick of titles in the history of the league. Two months earlier Esteghlal had beaten first-time finalists Shahin Bushehr on penalties to win the cup for a record breaking sixth time. There was little to celebrate in the 2012 AFC Champions League, however, with both Esteghlal and Persepolis falling in the round of 16. Persepolis lost 3-0 away to Saudi's Al Ittihad while Esteghlal were beaten 2-0 in an all-Iranian tie by Sepahan. Sepahan failed to get beyond the next round, however, knocked out by Saudi Arabia's Al Ahli in the quarter-finals.

FIFA WORLD CUP RECORD

1930-1970 DNE 1974 DNQ **1978** 14 r1 1982-1986 DNE 1990-1994 DNQ **1998** 20 r1 2002 DNQ **2006** 26 r1 2010 DNQ

IR IRAN FOOTBALL FEDERATION (IRIFF)

No. 4. Third St., Seoul Ave., 19958-73591 Tehran
☎ +98 21 88213308
📠 +98 21 88053605
✉ international@ffiri.ir
🖥 www.ffiri.ir
FA 1920 CON 1958 FIFA 1945
P Ali Kafashian
GS Mehdi Mohammad Nabi

THE STADIA

2014 FIFA World Cup Stadia
Azadi Stadium
Tehran   100 000

Other Main Stadia
Yadegar e Emam Stadium
Tabriz   71 000
Ghadir Stadium
Ahvaz   51 000
Shiraz Stadium
Shiraz   50 000
Naghsh e Jahan Stadium
Esfahan   50 000

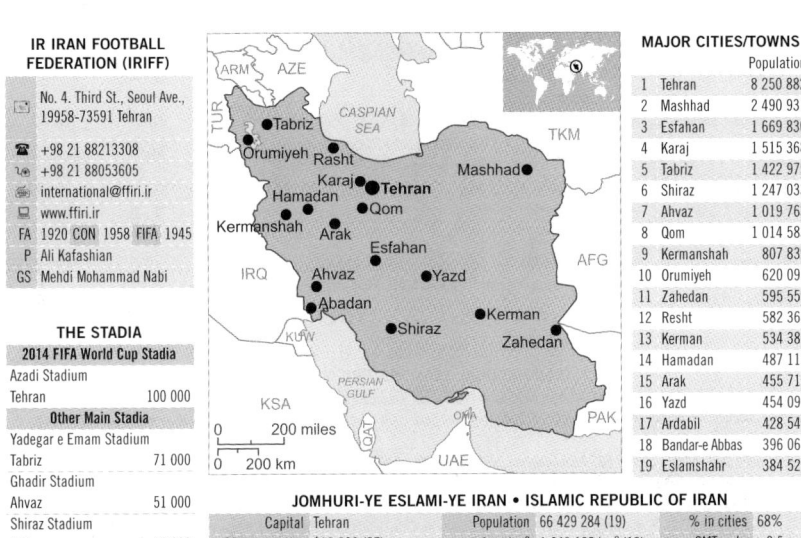

MAJOR CITIES/TOWNS

		Population
1	Tehran	8 250 882
2	Mashhad	2 490 931
3	Esfahan	1 669 830
4	Karaj	1 515 368
5	Tabriz	1 422 975
6	Shiraz	1 247 033
7	Ahvaz	1 019 763
8	Qom	1 014 583
9	Kermanshah	807 839
10	Orumiyeh	620 091
11	Zahedan	595 559
12	Resht	582 368
13	Kerman	534 387
14	Hamadan	487 111
15	Arak	455 713
16	Yazd	454 090
17	Ardabil	428 542
18	Bandar-e Abbas	396 060
19	Eslamshahr	384 521

JOMHURI-YE ESLAMI-YE IRAN • ISLAMIC REPUBLIC OF IRAN

Capital Tehran Population 66 429 284 (19) % in cities 68%
GDP per capita $12 800 (87) Area km² 1 648 195 km² (18) GMT +/- +3.5
Neighbours (km) Afghanistan 936, Armenia 35, Azerbaijan 611, Iraq 1458, Pakistan 909, Turkey 499, Turkmenistan 992 • Coast 2440

RECENT INTERNATIONAL MATCHES PLAYED BY IRAN

2010	Opponents	Score	Venue	Comp	Scorers	Att	Referee
11-08	Armenia	W 3-1	Yerevan	Fr	Aghily 2 [68 90p], Nosrati [71]	3 000	Kvartskhelia GEO
3-09	China PR	W 2-0	Zhengzhou	Fr	Teymourian [38], Gholami [63]	20 000	Kim Jong Hyeok KOR
7-09	Korea Republic	W 1-0	Seoul	Fr	Shojaei [35]	38 642	Mohd Salleh MAS
24-09	Bahrain	W 3-0	Amman	WAr1	Aghili 2 [36 38], Oladi [47]	5 000	Al Ghafari JOR
28-09	Oman	D 2-2	Amman	WAr1	Meydavoudi [15], Teymourian [52]	2 000	Ko Hyung Jin KOR
1-10	Iraq	W 2-1	Amman	WAsf	Hosseini [57], Gholami [82]	10 000	Matsuo JPN
3-10	Kuwait	L 1-2	Amman	WAf	Meydavoudi [95+]	4 000	Al Ghafari JOR
7-10	Brazil	L 0-3	Abu Dhabi	Fr		15 000	Al Marzouqi UAE
28-12	Qatar	D 0-0	Doha	Fr		2 000	Szabo HUN
2011							
2-01	Angola	W 1-0	Al Rayyan	Fr	Nekounam [90]	BCD	
11-01	Iraq	W 2-1	Al Rayyan	ACr1	Rezaei [42], Mobali [84]	10 478	Irmatov UZB
15-01	Korea DPR	W 1-0	Doha	ACr1	Ansarifard [63]	6 488	Shukralla BHR
19-01	UAE	W 3-0	Doha	ACr1	Afshin [67], Nori [83], OG [93+]	5 012	Kim Dong Jin KOR
22-01	Korea Republic	L 0-1	Doha	ACqf		7 111	Irmatov UZB
9-02	Russia	W 1-0	Abu Dhabi	Fr	Khalatbari [90]	5 000	Albadwawi UAE
17-07	Madagascar	W 1-0	Tehran	Fr	Hosseini [18]	10 000	Mombini IRN
23-07	Maldives	W 4-0	Tehran	WCq	Ansari 2 [4 62], Karimi [67], Daghighi [86]	20 195	Mahapab THA
28-07	Maldives	W 1-0	Male	WCq	Khalatbari [45]	9 000	Kim Sang Woo KOR
2-09	Indonesia	W 3-0	Tehran	WCq	Nekounam 2 [53 74], Timotian [87]	75 800	Toma JPN
6-09	Qatar	D 1-1	Doha	WCq	Aghili [46]	8 125	Choi Myung Yong KOR
5-10	Palestine	W 7-0	Tehran	Fr	Ghazi [45], Ansarifard [49], Nekounam [55], Montazeri [59], Nouri [70], Kazemian 2 [58 90]	5 000	Mozaffari IRN
11-10	Bahrain	W 6-0	Tehran	WCq	Hosseini [22], Jabari [34], Aghili [42], Timotian [61], Ansari [75], Rezaei [83]	82 000	Green AUS
11-11	Bahrain	D 1-1	Manama	WCq	Jabari [92+]	18 000	Bashir SIN
15-11	Indonesia	W 4-1	Jakarta	WCq	Midavoodi [7], Jabari [21], Rezaei [25], Nekounam [73]	6 000	Tan Hai
2012							
23-02	Jordan	D 2-2	Dubai	Fr	Ali Karimi [67], Ghazi [92+]	7 000	Mohamed UAE
29-02	Qatar	D 2-2	Tehran	WCq	Dejagah 2 [4 50]	51 300	Irmatov UZB
27-05	Albania	L 0-1	Istanbul	Fr		3 000	Gocek TUR
3-06	Uzbekistan	W 1-0	Tashkent	WCq	Khalatbari [93+]	9 000	Nishimura JPN
12-06	Qatar	D 0-0	Tehran	WCq		100000	Green AUS
15-08	Tunisia	D 2-2	Kecskemet	Fr	Khalatbari [54], Ghazi [60]	200	Fabian HUN
5-09	Jordan	D 0-0	Amman	Fr		3 500	Aljeneibi UAE
11-09	Lebanon	L 0-1	Beirut	WCq		14 000	Tan Hai CHN
16-10	Korea Republic	W 1-0	Tehran	WCq	Nekonam [76]	99 885	Bashir SIN
6-11	Tajikistan	W 6-1	Tehran	Fr	Dehnavi 2 [9 32], Yaghoub Karimi 2 [13 33], Hasanzadeh [50], Abbasfard [89]	30 000	Jahanbazi IRN
14-11	Uzbekistan	L 0-1	Tehran	WCq		43 700	Albadwawi UAE
9-12	Saudi Arabia	D 0-0	Kuwait City	WAr1		1 200	Tojo JPN
12-12	Bahrain	D 0-0	Kuwait City	WAr1		1 000	Al Dosari QAT
15-12	Yemen	W 2-1	Kuwait City	WAr1	Nazari [41], Yaghoub Karimi [53]	500	Sabbagh LIB

Fr = Friendly match • WA = West Asian Federation Championship • AC = AFC Asian Cup • WC = FIFA World Cup • q = qualifier

IRAN NATIONAL TEAM HISTORICAL RECORDS

Caps: 148 - Ali Daei 1993-2006 • 127 - Ali Karimi 1998- • 125 - Javad Nekounam 2000- • 110 - Mehdi Mahdavikia 1996-2009 • 89 - Hossein Kaebi 2002- • 87 - Karim Bagheri 1993-2010 • 82 - Hamid Reza Estili 1990-2000 & Mohammad Nosrati 2002- • 80 - Javad Zarincheh 1987-2000 • 79 - Ahmad Reza Abedzadeh 1987-98

Goals: 109 - Ali Daei 1993-2006 • 50 - Karim Bagheri 1993-2010 • 38 - Ali Karimi 1998- • 34 - Javad Nekounam 2000- • 19 - Gholam Hossein Mazloomi 1969-77 & Farshad Pious 1984-1994 • 18 - Ali Ashgar Modir Roosta 1990-98 • 15 - Vahid Hashemian 1998-2009

Past Coaches: For Iran coaches pre 1989 see Oliver's Almanack 2012 • Ali Parvin 1989-93 • Hassan Habibi 1994-95 • Stanko Poklepovic CRO 1994 • Mayeli Kohan 1996-97 • Valdeir Viera BRA 1997 • Tomislav Ivic CRO 1998 • Jalal Talebi 1998 • Mansour Pourheidari 1998-2000 • Jalal Talebi 2000 • Ademar Braga 2000-01 • Miroslav Blazevic CRO 2001 • Branko Ivankovic CRO 2002 • Homayoun Shahrokhi 2003 • Branko Ivankovic CRO 2003-6 • Amir Ghalenoei 2006-07 • Parviz Mazloomi 2007 • Mansour Ebrahimzadeh 2008 • Ali Daei 2008-09 • Erich Rutemoller GER 2009 • Mayeli Kohan 2009 • Gholam Peyrovani 2009 • Afshin Ghotbi 2009-11 • Carlos Queiroz POR 2011-

IRN – IRAN

IRAN 2011-12

IRAN PRO LEAGUE

	Pl	W	D	L	F	A	Pts	Sepahan	Teraktor-Sazi	Esteghlal	Saba	Naft	Zob Ahan	Damash	Saipa	Sanat Mes	Sanat-Naft	Rah Ahan	Persepolis	Fajr Sepasi	Foolad	Malavan	Shahrdari	Shahin	Mes S'shme
Sepahan †	34	19	10	5	54	27	67		2-1	1-1	1-2	0-1	1-1	3-0	2-1	4-0	2-1	3-2	1-1	1-0	2-0	3-2	1-0	2-0	0-0
Teraktor-Sazi Tabriz †	34	19	9	6	57	32	66	1-0		0-2	2-3	1-2	2-1	3-1	2-2	2-3	1-1	4-1	1-1	4-1	0-0	2-0	2-0	5-1	1-0	0-0
Esteghlal Tehran †	34	19	9	6	58	34	66	1-1	2-3		3-0	3-0	2-2	1-0	1-0	0-1	1-2	1-1	2-3	2-0	2-1	1-0	0-0	3-2	1-0
Saba Qom †	34	12	14	8	40	38	50	0-0	2-2	1-1		0-0	0-1	0-1	3-0	1-1	2-2	2-1	2-2	1-1	1-0	1-0	3-1	1-1	3-1
Naft Tehran	34	13	10	11	36	38	49	0-1	1-1	0-2	2-2		0-1	1-0	2-0	3-2	1-3	2-2	0-3	1-0	1-3	3-1	0-0	2-1	1-0
Zob Ahan	34	9	18	7	29	33	45	0-0	0-1	0-2	2-1	1-1		0-0	1-0	1-3	0-2	2-2	1-1	1-0	0-0	2-2	1-0	1-0
Damash Gilan	34	11	11	12	34	38	44	0-1	2-3	0-1	0-0	1-3	1-1		0-3	1-1	0-0	3-1	2-3	1-0	3-2	0-0	2-1	0-0	2-1
Saipa	34	10	13	11	50	39	43	0-4	0-1	2-2	0-0	0-0	0-1	3-0		4-2	2-2	0-1	0-1	5-0	0-0	1-1	1-2	3-0	3-1
Sanat Mes Kerman	34	11	10	13	35	39	43	3-0	1-0	1-2	0-0	0-1	2-0	2-2	1-0		2-2	0-0	1-0	1-2	1-1	1-0	1-1	3-2	4-1
Sanat-Naft Abadan	34	11	10	13	49	57	43	0-4	3-3	1-2	2-3	2-1	1-1	2-0	0-4	1-0		2-1	4-2	1-1	2-2	1-2	0-2	1-1	2-1
Rah Ahan	34	9	15	10	43	42	42	1-1	0-1	2-2	0-2	2-1	2-2	0-1	2-2	0-2		1-1	1-1	0-0	0-1	2-0	4-1	3-1
Persepolis	34	10	12	12	50	54	42	0-0	0-1	0-2	2-0	0-0	0-0	0-3	2-4	1-1	3-1	3-4		2-3	1-1	1-1	1-2	4-1	2-1
Fajr Sepasi	34	10	11	13	31	38	41	3-2	1-2	2-1	0-0	0-0	0-0	0-1	1-1	1-0	2-0	1-2	1-2		2-1	2-0	2-1	1-0	3-3
Foolad Ahvaz	34	10	10	14	35	37	40	1-2	2-1	1-4	3-0	2-1	0-1	1-1	1-2	0-1	2-0	0-0	1-2	1-0		1-0	0-0	0-0	4-0
Malavan	34	9	12	13	32	33	39	3-4	0-0	4-2	1-0	0-1	3-3	0-1	1-1	0-0	1-2	0-0	2-0	2-0	2-0		1-0	0-0	4-0
Shahrdari Tabriz	34	6	16	12	34	44	34	0-2	0-1	1-2	1-3	2-2	0-0	0-0	1-1	0-1	2-1	2-2	2-2	0-0	1-1	2-0		1-1	1-1
Shahin Bushehr	34	6	15	13	30	43	33	1-1	0-3	1-1	4-0	1-0	1-1	1-1	2-2	1-0	1-1	0-0	2-1	1-0	1-2	0-0	2-3		1-0
Mes Sarcheshme	34	5	9	20	23	54	24	0-0	0-1	0-3	0-1	1-2	0-0	0-4	0-0	2	0	2-1	2-1	2-2	1-0	0-1	0-0	1-2	1-0	

2/08/2011 – 11/05/2012 • † Qualified for the AFC Champions League

Top scorers: **21** – Karim **ANSARIFAD**, Saipa • **20** – Founeke **SY** MLI, Sanat Naft • **18** – Reza **ENAYATI**, Saba Qom • **12** – Ali **KARIMI**, Persepolis • **10** – Mojtaba **JABBARI**, Esteghlal; Mehdi **RAJABZADEH**, Fajr Sepasi; Reza **NOROUZI**, Foolad; Saeed **DAGHIGHI**, Shahrdari & **FLAVIO PAIXAO** POR, Teraktor

IRAN 2011-12
AZADEGAN LEAGUE GROUP A (2)

	Pl	W	D	L	F	A	Pts
Paykan Tehran	26	14	8	4	44	26	50
IranJavan †	26	13	9	4	31	16	48
Shahrdari Bandar Abbas	26	10	8	8	26	27	38
Shahrdari Arak	26	9	10	7	19	17	37
Foolad Yadz	26	9	8	9	25	23	36
AbooMoslem	26	8	10	8	21	18	34
Etka Gorgan	26	9	7	10	21	20	34
Saipa Shomal	26	8	9	9	26	26	33
Gostaresh Foolad	26	7	11	8	25	30	32
Steel Azin Tehran §12	26	10	10	6	29	22	28
Parseh Tehran	26	8	4	14	20	29	28
Mes Rafsanjan	26	6	8	12	22	28	26
Sanat Sari	26	7	5	14	20	34	26
Payam Shiraz	26	5	10	11	15	28	25

14/09/2011 – 18/04/2012 • † Qualified for the play-off
§ = points deducted

Promotion play-off:
Iranjavan
1-1 0-0
Gahar Zagros

Gahar Zagros promoted on away goals

Paykan declared Azadegan champions after Aluminium forfeited the final

IRAN 2011-12
AZADEGAN LEAGUE GROUP B (2)

	Pl	W	D	L	F	A	Pts
Aluminium Hormozgan	26	15	7	4	28	12	52
Gahar Zagros †	26	11	9	6	23	16	42
Machine Sazi	26	11	8	7	32	25	41
Hamedan-Paas	26	10	9	7	29	25	39
Nassaji Mazandaran	26	10	7	9	26	26	37
Esteghlal Khuzestan	26	9	8	9	28	23	35
Shahrdari Yasuj	26	10	5	11	24	27	35
Naft Masjed Soleyman	26	8	10	8	25	26	34
Gol Gohar Sirjan	26	9	6	11	28	28	33
Niroye Zamini Tehran	26	7	11	8	23	24	32
Shirin-Faraz	26	7	11	8	22	27	32
Tarbyat Badani Yazd	26	7	9	10	21	26	30
Sanati Kaveh	26	7	8	11	24	23	29
Bargh Shiraz	26	4	6	16	12	37	18

15/09/2011 – 19/04/2012 • † Qualified for the play-off

MEDALS TABLE

		Overall			League			Cup		Asia			City
		G	S	B	G	S	B	G	S	G	S	B	
1	Esteghlal	15	13	8	7	8	5	**6**	3	2	2	3	Tehran
2	Persepolis	15	9	7	**9**	7	4	5	1	1	1	3	Tehran
3	Sepahan	7	2	2	4	1	2	3				1	Esfahan
4	Pas	6	5	2	5	5	2			1			Tehran
5	Saipa	4		2	3		2	1					Karaj
6	Malavan	3	4	2				2	3	4			Bandar Anzali
7	Zob Ahan	2	5	2		3	2	2	1		1		Esfahan
8	Bahman	1	4			2		1	2				Karaj
9	Moghavemat Sepasi	1	2	1			1	1	2				Shiraz
10	Saba Battery	1	1	1			1	1	1				Qom
11	Bargh	1	1					1	1				Shiraz
12	Foolad	1		2	1		2						Ahvaz
13	Shahin	1						1					Ahvaz

JAAM HAZFI 2011-12

Second Stage - First Round

Esteghlal Tehran*	5
Shirin-Faraz Kermanshah	1
Rah Ahan	1
Mehr Karaj*	3
Zob Ahan*	2
Gostaresh Foolad Tabriz	1
Mes Rafsanjan	1
Persepolis*	2
Foolad Ahvaz*	2
Sepahan	1
Gahar Zagros	1
Sanat-Naft Abadan*	3
Siah Jamegan Khorasan	1
Saipa*	0
Terakator-Sazi Tabriz	0 3p
Shahrdari Yasuj*	0 4p
Sanat Mes Kerman	w-o
Esteghlal Khuzestan	
Etka Gorgan	0
Fajr Sepasi*	1
Mes Sarcheshme	1
Shahrdari Arak*	0 4p
Payam Shiraz	0 5p
Saba Qom*	2
Damash Gilan*	1 5p
Naft Tehran	1 4p
Shahrdari Tabriz*	1
Machine Sazi Tabriz	2
AbooMoslem*	3
Malavan	2
Niroye Zamini Tehran	0
Shahin Bushehr*	3

Round of 16

Esteghlal Tehran	1
Mehr Karaj*	0
Zob Ahan*	2
Persepolis	3
Foolad Ahvaz	2
Sanat-Naft Abadan*	0
Siah Jamegan Khorasan*	1
Shahrdari Yasuj	2
Sanat Mes Kerman*	3
Fajr Sepasi	1
Mes Sarcheshme*	0 4p
Saba Qom	0 5p
Damash Gilan	2
Machine Sazi Tabriz*	1
AbooMoslem*	0
Shahin Bushehr	1

Quarter-finals

Esteghlal Tehran	3
Persepolis*	0
Foolad Ahvaz	1 2p
Shahrdari Yasuj*	1 4p
Sanat Mes Kerman*	1 5p
Saba Qom	1 4p
Damash Gilan*	1
Shahin Bushehr	2

Semi-finals

Esteghlal Tehran*	1
Shahrdari Yasuj	0
Sanat Mes Kerman	0
Shahin Bushehr*	2

Final

Esteghlal Tehran †	0 4p
Shahin Bushehr	0 1p

FINAL PENALTIES

Esteghlal	Shahin
✓ Yousefi	
	Noori ✗
✓ Zandi	
	Shoukouhmagham ✗
✓ Samuel	
	Ansarian ✓
	Jerkovic ✓

HAZFI CUP FINAL

Hafezieh, Shiraz, 15-03-2012
Att: 16 369. Ref: Alireza Faghani
Esteghlal - Mehdi Rahmati - Ali Hamoudi (Goran Jerkovic 112), Pejman Montazeri, Hanif Omranzadeh, Mehdi Amirabadi (c) - Meysam Hosseini (Mohsen Yousefi 91) - Khosro Heydari, Jlloyd Samuel, Ferydoon Zandi, Esmaeil Sharifat (Milad Meydavoudi 91) - Arash Borhani. Tr: Parviz Mazloomi
Shahin - Vahid Talebloo (c) - Mohsen Irannejad, Lek Kcira, Ali Ansarian, Hadi Shakouri (Mehdi Kiani 95) - Morteza Aziz-Mohammadi (Mehrzad Rezaee 82), Mehdi Noori, Amjad Shokouhmagham, Abbas Pourkhosravani - Ivan Petrovic• - Mansour Tanhaei (Babak Latifi 103). Tr: Hamid Derakhshan

* Home team • † Qualified for the AFC Champions League

IRQ – IRAQ

FIFA/COCA-COLA WORLD RANKING

'93	'94	'95	'96	'97	'98	'99	'00	'01	'02	'03	'04	'05	'06	'07	'08	'09	'10	'11	'12
65	88	110	98	68	94	78	79	72	53	43	44	54	83	68	72	88	101	78	92

2012

Jan	Feb	Mar	Apr	May	Jun	Jul	Aug	Sep	Oct	Nov	Dec	High	Low	Av
73	79	76	70	72	74	81	84	78	80	97	92	39	139	78

Iraq's success at international level has come despite the long-standing backdrop of violence and security issues at home with the national team very rarely playing matches within Iraq. However, an extraordinary programme of stadium building is underway that may see the landscape of football in Iraq change for good. The first of those stadia - Sports City in Basra - was opened in early 2013 and will play host to the 2015 Gulf Cup. Other stadia are underway, some of which have looked to European stadium design rather than the utilitarian Chinese inspired bowls so common throughout the region - an exciting development that the authorities hope will transform the image of football in the country. That may be too late for the generation that brought the AFC Asian Cup title to the nation in 2007 but players such as Younus Mahmood and Nashat Akram will be seeking to end their international careers with an appearance at the FIFA World Cup finals in Brazil in 2014. Serbian coach Vladimir Petrovic replaced Zico in early 2013 to take charge of the final push towards the finals. Arbil, meanwhile, successfully defended their league title while also becoming the first Iraqi side to reach the final of the AFC Cup. They hosted the 2012 final against Al Kuwait but saw their hopes of continental glory dashed by the Kuwaitis who won 4-0.

FIFA WORLD CUP RECORD
1930-1970 DNE 1974 DNQ 1978 DNE 1982 DNQ **1986** 23 r1 1990-2010 DNQ

IRAQI FOOTBALL ASSOCIATION (IFA)

Al Shaab Stadium,
PO Box 484,
Baghdad
☎ +964 740 0601245
📠 +44 161 66 27 271
✉ info@ifa.iq
🌐 www.ifa.iq
FA 1948 CON 1971 FIFA 1950
P Najeh Al Obaidi
GS Ahmed Ali Tariq

THE STADIA
2014 FIFA World Cup Stadia
Franso Hariri Stadium
Arbil — 20 000
Other Main Stadia
Basra International Stadium
Basra — 65 000
Al Shabab Stadium
Baghdad — 35 000
Olympic Stadium
Kirkuk — 30 000
Duhok Stadium
Duhok — 30 000

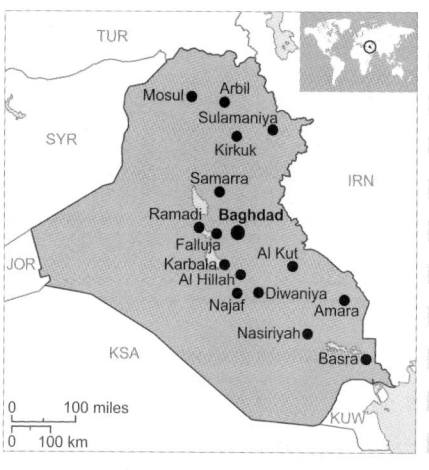

MAJOR CITIES/TOWNS

		Population
1	Baghdad	5 337 684
2	Mosul	2 803 999
3	Basra	1 871 994
4	Arbil	1 190 251
5	Kirkuk	850 787
6	Najaf	828 207
7	Sulamaniya	759 508
8	Al Hillah	528 008
9	Karbala	509 819
10	Amara	465 707
11	Diwaniya	455 473
12	Qubba	421 730
13	Falluja	309 868
14	Ramadi	290 535
15	Al Kut	289 084
16	Nasiriyah	257 091
17	Dahuk	241 033
18	Zakhu	186 129
19	Tall Afar	168 228

AL JUMHURIYAH AL IRAQIYAH • REPUBLIC OF IRAQ

Capital Baghdad Population 28 945 657 (40) % in cities 67%
GDP per capita $3200 (162) Area km² 438 317 km² (58) GMT +/- +3
Neighbours (km) Iran 1458, Jordan 181, Kuwait 240, Saudi Arabia 814, Syria 605, Turkey 352 • Coast 58

RECENT INTERNATIONAL MATCHES PLAYED BY IRAQ

2011	Opponents	Score	Venue	Comp	Scorers	Att	Referee
2-01	China PR	L 2-3	Doha	Fr	Younis Mahmoud 2 [44 50]		
11-01	Iran	L 1-2	Al Rayyan	ACr1	Younis Mahmoud [13]	10 478	Irmatov UZB
15-01	UAE	W 1-0	Al Rayyan	ACr1	Walid Abbas OG [93+]	7 233	Nishimura JPN
19-01	Korea DPR	W 1-0	Al Rayyan	ACr1	Karrar Jassim [22]	4 111	Mohd Salleh MAS
22-01	Australia	L 0-1	Doha	ACqf		7 889	Abdou QAT
26-03	Korea DPR	W 2-0	Sharjah	Fr	Alaa Abdul Zahra 2 [53 71]		
29-03	Kuwait	L 0-1	Sharjah	Fr			
29-06	Syria	L 1-2	Arbil	Fr	Alaa Abdul Zahra [80]		
13-07	Kuwait	L 0-2	Amman	Fr			
16-07	Jordan	D 1-1	Amman	Fr	Mustafa Karim [15], L 4-5p		
23-07	Yemen	W 2-0	Arbil	WCq	Hawar Mohammed [10], Alaa Abdul Zahra [64]	20 000	Kovalenko UZB
28-07	Yemen	D 0-0	Al Ain	WCq		1 500	Basma SYR
19-08	Qatar	W 1-0	Doha	Fr	Salam Shakir [35]		
2-09	Jordan	L 0-2	Arbil	WCq		24 000	Shukralla BHR
6-09	Singapore	W 2-0	Singapore	WCq	Alaa Abdul Zahra [50], Younis Mahmoud [86]	5 505	Tojo JPN
11-10	China PR	W 1-0	Shenzhen	WCq	Younis Mahmoud [45]	25 021	Mozaffari IRN
11-11	China PR	W 1-0	Doha	WCq	Younis Mahmoud [92+]	5 000	Green AUS
15-11	Jordan	W 3-1	Amman	WCq	Nashat Akram 2 [55 81], Qusai Munir [65]	13 000	Albadwawi UAE
13-12	Bahrain	L 0-3	Doha	PGr1			Abdurahaman SUD
16-12	Qatar	D 0-0	Doha	PGr1			Haimoudi ALG
2012							
29-02	Singapore	W 7-1	Doha	WCq	Karrar Jasim [5], Younis Mahmoud 3 [11 61 93+], Hawar Mohammed [22p], Nashat Akram [36p], Mustafa Kareem [48]	950	Al Hilali OMA
17-04	Egypt	D 0-0	Dubai	Fr			Mohamed UAE
23-05	Sierra Leone	W 1-0	Istanbul	Fr	Nashat Akram [4]		
28-05	Botswana	D 1-1	Istanbul	Fr	Karrar Jassim [5]		
3-06	Jordan	D 1-1	Amman	WCq	Nashat Akram [14]	13 000	Kovalenko UZB
12-06	Oman	D 1-1	Doha	WCq	Younis Mahmoud [37p]	1 650	Abdou QAT
24-06	Lebanon	W 1-0	Jeddah	ARr1	Mustafa Karim [89]		Jiyed MAR
30-06	Sudan	D 1-1	Jeddah	ARr1	Mustafa Karim [49], Alaa Abdul Zahra [75]		Albalooshi QAT
3-07	Morocco	L 1-2	Jeddah	ARr1	Salam Shakir [5]		Jedidi TUN
5-07	Saudi Arabia	W 1-0	Jeddah	ARsf	Mustafa Karim [96+p]		Haimoudi ALG
11-09	Japan	L 0-1	Saitama	WCq		60 593	Bashir SIN
11-10	Brazil	L 0-6	Malmo	Fr		14 147	Hansson SWE
16-10	Australia	L 1-2	Doha	WCq	Alaa Abdul Zahra [72]	2 183	Lee Min Hu AUS
14-11	Jordan	W 1-0	Doha	WCq	Hammadi Ahmed [86]	1 755	Tan Hai CHN
3-12	Bahrain	D 0-0	Doha	Fr			
10-12	Jordan	W 1-0	Al Farwaniyah	WAr1	Hammadi Ahmed [62]	1 600	Shaban KUW
13-12	Syria	D 1-1	Kuwait City	WAr1	OG [11]	1 300	Mohamed UAE
18-12	Oman	W 2-0	Al Farwaniyah	WAsf	Amjed Radhi [6], Ahmed Yaseen [39]	500	Mohamed UAE
20-12	Syria	L 0-1	Kuwait City	WAf		5 000	Tojo JPN
30-12	Tunisia	L 1-2	Sharjah	Fr	Younis Mahmoud [87]		Hshmi UAE

Fr = Friendly • WA = West Asian Federation Championship • AC = AFC Asian Cup • GC = Gulf Cup • AR = Arab Cup • WC = FIFA World Cup
q = qualifier • r1 = first round group • qf = quarter-final • sf = semi-final • f = final

IRAQ NATIONAL TEAM HISTORICAL RECORDS

Caps: 126 - Hussein Saeed 1977-90 • 110 - Falah Hassan 1969-86 • 109 - Nashat Akram 2001- • 108 - Hawar Mulla Mohammed 2001 • 105 - Younis Mahmoud 2002- • 100 - Emad Mohammed 2000- • 96 - Laith Hussein 1986-2002 • 95 - Mahdi Karim 2001- • 93 - Ali Rehema 2005-

Goals: 61 - Hussein Saeed 1977-90 • 46 - Younis Mahmoud 2002- • 42 - Ahmed Radhi 1983-97 • 30 - Falah Hassan 1969-86 • 29 - Ali Kadhim 1970-80 • 28 - Emad Mohammed 2000- • 27 - Habib Jafar 1986-2001 • 25 - Laith Hussein 1986-2002 • 24 - Razzaq Farhan 1998-2007

Coaches: For Iraq coaches pre 1999 see Oliver's Almanack 2012 • Najih Humoud 1999 • Adnan Hamad 2000 • Milan Zivadinovic SRB 2000-01 • Adnan Hamad 2001 • Rudolf Belin CRO 2001 • Adnan Hamad 2002 • Bernd Stange GER 2002-04 • Adnan Hamad 2004 • Akram Ahmad Salman 2005-07 • Jorvan Vieira BRA 2007 • Egil Olsen NOR 2007-08 • Adnan Hamad 2008 • Jorvan Vieira BRA 2008-09 • Radhi Shenaishil 2009 • Bora Milutinovic SRB 2009 • Nadhim Shaker 2009-10 • Wolfgang Sidka GER 2010-11 • Zico BRA 2011-

IRAQ 2011-12

PREMIER LEAGUE

	Pl	W	D	L	F	A	Pts	Arbil	Duhok	Quwa AJ	Talaba	Zakho	Baghdad	Shurta	Zawra'a	Najaf	Naft	Mina'a	Kirkuk	Sina'a	Kahrabaa	Karbala	Masafi	Karkh	Taji	Shirqat	Hudod
Arbil †	38	23	14	1	65	22	**83**		2-2	1-1	2-1	2-1	3-3	0-0	1-0	3-1	2-1	3-0	0-0	2-0	3-2	1-0	2-1	1-0	5-0	1-0	1-0
Duhok †	38	21	13	4	56	21	**76**	1-1		0-0	0-1	1-1	2-0	1-1	2-1	2-1	1-1	3-1	1-0	2-0	1-1	1-0	0-0	1-0	1-0	5-0	4-0
Al Quwa Al Jawiya	38	21	11	6	61	23	**74**	0-0	0-1		0-2	3-0	1-0	2-0	1-1	3-0	3-0	2-1	4-0	1-0	2-1	3-2	3-0	4-2	1-0	5-0	3-1
Al Talaba	38	19	11	8	45	29	**68**	1-1	0-0	0-0		2-1	0-3	2-1	2-1	0-0	0-1	1-2	2-0	1-0	3-2	0-0	2-2	0-2	1-1	3-0	2-0
Zakho	38	15	16	7	53	36	**61**	0-0	1-2	1-1	0-0		1-0	3-2	0-0	2-1	0-0	1-0	2-0	2-2	4-1	3-0	3-0	1-1	3-1	1-2	2-0
Baghdad FC	38	16	12	10	41	26	**60**	0-0	0-1	1-0	0-0	2-2		0-0	1-1	2-0	2-1	0-1	1-0	2-2	3-2	2-0	1-0	0-0	1-0	2-0	2-0
Al Shurta	38	16	11	11	45	37	**59**	1-5	0-1	0-0	1-2	2-0	0-1		3-2	3-1	3-0	3-0	0-0	2-1	3-1	2-1	1-0	1-0	1-1	1-0	1-0
Al Zawra'a	38	15	11	12	54	35	**56**	0-0	0-0	1-1	0-1	1-2	1-0	2-1		1-1	1-0	2-1	4-0	1-0	2-1	0-0	0-0	2-1	5-2	2-0	1-0
Al Najaf	38	12	16	10	40	41	**52**	0-4	1-0	0-0	3-1	0-0	2-1	0-0	1-0		0-2	1-1	1-2	0-0	2-1	2-1	0-1	2-1	4-1	3-1	0-0
Al Naft Baghdad	38	12	15	11	39	37	**51**	1-1	1-1	1-2	1-0	1-1	0-0	1-2	1-0	1-2		1-1	3-3	0-0	1-1	1-2	0-0	1-0	3-1	3-0	2-0
Al Mina'a	38	13	11	14	40	44	**50**	1-4	0-3	2-0	2-1	0-0	1-0	1-2	2-1	1-1	0-0		3-3	0-0	2-3	1-0	0-1	2-0	3-0	2-0	3-0
Kirkuk	38	13	10	15	37	46	**49**	1-2	0-2	1-0	1-1	2-1	0-2	4-1	1-0	1-1	0-1	1-0		1-1	1-1	1-1	1-0	1-1	1-0	1-0	4-1
Al Sina'a	38	10	17	11	29	32	**47**	0-1	0-0	2-1	0-1	1-1	0-3	0-0	2-3	0-0	1-0	0-1	0		0-0	0-0	0-0	1-0	1-1	2-1	4-2
Kahrabaa	38	12	10	16	50	55	**46**	0-3	2-0	0-1	1-1	1-3	3-2	2-1	2-1	1-1	1-1	1-2	1-0	0-2		1-1	0-1	4-0	2-2	1-0	2-1
Karbala	38	10	14	14	38	44	**44**	1-0	1-1	0-0	0-3	1-1	1-0	2-2	0-3	1-2	1-2	2-0	3-0	1-1	1-1		2-0	3-1	3-0	2-0	2-1
Masafi Baghdad	38	9	12	17	24	44	**39**	0-4	1-0	2-3	0-1	1-3	0-0	0-0	1-1	1-1	1-3	2-0	1-3	0-1	0-3	0-0		0-1	2-0	2-1	1-0
Karkh	38	8	10	20	32	49	**34**	1-1	1-2	0-4	0-1	1-1	0-1	0-0	3-1	0-2	0-0	1-1	0-1	2-3	1-1	3-0	1-2		2-0	1-0	1-0
Al Taji	38	6	16	16	37	66	**34**	0-0	2-2	0-0	1-2	1-1	0-0	1-0	1-6	0-0	2-2	0-0	2-1	0-0	2-1	0-0	2-0	2-1		3-2	3-3
Shirqat	38	7	5	26	24	67	**26**	0-1	0-6	0-2	0-2	0-2	1-1	0-2	0-0	1-1	0-1	1-1	2-1	1-0	1-2	3-1	0-0	1-2	2-1		2-0
Hudod	38	1	7	30	26	82	**10**	1-2	1-3	0-4	0-2	1-2	0-2	0-2	0-6	2-2	2-1	0-2	0-1	0-1	1-2	2-2	1-1	1-1	4-4	1-2	

29/10/2011 - 20/08/2012 • † Qualified for the AFC Cup
Top scorers: **27** - **HAMMADI AHMAD**, Al Quwa Al Jawiya • **23** - **AMJAD RADHI YOUSIF**, Arbil

MEDALS TABLE

		Overall			League			Cup		Asia			City
		G	S	B	G	S	B	G	S	G	S	B	
1	Al Zawra'a	26	8	2	12	6	2	14	1		1		Baghdad
2	Al Quwa Al Jawia	11	12	10	6	9	10	5	3				Baghdad
3	Al Talaba	7	14	5	5	7	5	2	6		1		Baghdad
4	Al Karkh	5	3	1	3	2	1	2			1		Baghdad
5	Arbil FC	4	2	2	4	1	1			1		1	Arbil
6	Al Jaish	3	6		1	2		2	4				Baghdad
7	Al Shurta	2	9	8	2	3	8		5		1		Baghdad
8	Al Mina'a	1	1	1	1	1	1						Basra
	Duhok	1	1	1	1	1	1						Duhok
10	Al Sina'a	1		3			3	1					Baghdad
11	Salah al Deen	1			1								Tikrit
12	Al Najaf		3	2		3	2						Najaf
13	Al Shabab		3	1			1		3				Baghdad

ISL – ICELAND

FIFA/COCA-COLA WORLD RANKING

'93	'94	'95	'96	'97	'98	'99	'00	'01	'02	'03	'04	'05	'06	'07	'08	'09	'10	'11	'12
47	39	50	60	72	64	43	50	52	58	58	93	94	93	90	83	92	112	104	90

2012

Jan	Feb	Mar	Apr	May	Jun	Jul	Aug	Sep	Oct	Nov	Dec	High	Low	Av
104	103	121	131	131	131	129	130	118	97	96	90	37	131	74

FH Hafnarfjördur have proved to be a model for consistency in Icelandic football by finishing in the top two of the league every season for the past 10 years and in 2012 they reclaimed the title from KR Reykjavík after finishing comfortably ahead of Breidablik. FH have now been champions six times since first winning the league in 2004, with coach Heimir Gudjonsson involved with five of those triumphs - the first two as a player. There were first-time finalists in the Icelandic cup with Stjarnan Gardabær hoping to win a first trophy and build on the worldwide fame they have gained thanks to their original and highly amusing goal celebrations; celebrations which have made the team an internet sensation the world over. They took an early lead but experience prevailed in the end with KR winning 2-1 to secure the trophy for the second season in a row, the winner coming six minutes from the end through Baldur Sigurdsson. In preparation for the 2014 FIFA World Cup qualifying campaign the football association turned to former Sweden coach Lars Lagerback, a decision that paid immediate dividends with a morale-boosting victory at home to Norway and an impressive away win in Albania. Hopes of making an impact in the group were dented, however, after losing 2-0 at home to Switzerland in the final qualifier of the year.

UEFA EUROPEAN CHAMPIONSHIP RECORD
1960 DNE 1964 r1 1968-1972 DNE 1976-2012 DNQ

KNATTSPYRNUSAMBAND ISLANDS (KSI)

Laugardal, Reykjavík 104

☎ +354 5102900
📠 +354 5689793
✉ ksi@ksi.is
🖥 www.ksi.is
FA 1947 CON 1954 FIFA 1947
P Geir Thorsteinsson
GS Thorir Hakonarson

THE STADIA

2014 FIFA World Cup Stadia

Laugardalsvøllur Reykjavík	15 000

Other Main Stadia

Kaplakrikavöllur Hafnarfjördur	7 500
Keflavíkurvöllur Keflavík	6 200
Akranesvöllur Akranes	4 850
Vodafonevöllur Reykjavík	4 200

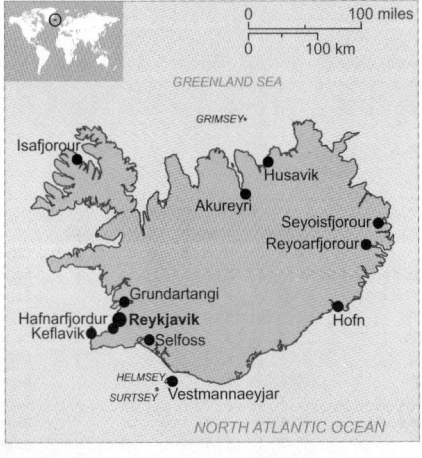

MAJOR CITIES/TOWNS

		Population
1	Reykjavik	118 395
2	Kópavogur	29 586
3	Hafnarfjördur	26 376
4	Akureyri	16 789
5	Garðabær	9 766
6	Keflavík	8 426
7	Selfoss	6 728
8	Akranes	6 374
9	Njarðvík	4 598
10	Seltjarnarnes	4 464
11	Vestmannaeyjar	4 013
12	Reyðarfjörður	3 044
13	Grindavík	2 887
14	Egilsstaðir	2 765
15	Ísafjörður	2 643
16	Sauðárkrókur	2 620
17	Álftanes	2 419
18	Hveragerði	2 399
19	Húsavík	2 318

LYDVELDID ISLAND • REPUBLIC OF ICELAND

Capital Reykjavík	Population 306 694 (178)	% in cities 92%
GDP per capita $42 300 (17)	Area km² 103 000 km² (107)	GMT +/- 0
Neighbours (km) Coast 4970		

RECENT INTERNATIONAL MATCHES PLAYED BY ICELAND

2009	Opponents	Score	Venue	Comp	Scorers	Att	Referee
11-02	Liechtenstein	W 2-0	La Manga	Fr	Smarason [28], Gudjohnsen [47]	150	Reinert FRO
22-03	Faroe Islands	L 1-2	Kopavogur	Fr	Saevarsson [91+]	553	Riley ENG
1-04	Scotland	L 1-2	Glasgow	WCq	Indridi Sigurdsson [54]	42 259	Einwaller AUT
6-06	Netherlands	L 1-2	Reykjavík	WCq	Kristian Sigurdsson [88]	9 635	Dean ENG
10-06	Macedonia FYR	L 0-2	Skopje	WCq		7 000	Ennjimmi FRA
12-08	Slovakia	D 1-1	Reykjavík	Fr	Kristian Sigurdsson [60]	5 099	Christoffersen DEN
5-09	Norway	D 1-1	Reykjavík	WCq	Gudjohnsen [29]	7 321	Tudor ROU
9-09	Georgia	W 3-1	Reykjavík	Fr	Johannsson [14], Skulason [18], Veigar Gunnarsson [55p]	4 726	Trefoloni ITA
13-10	South Africa	W 1-0	Reykjavík	Fr	Veigar Gunnarsson [50]	3 253	Moen NOR
10-11	Iran	L 0-1	Tehran	Fr			Waleed QAT
14-11	Luxembourg	D 1-1	Luxembourg	Fr	Johannsson [63]	913	Van Boekel NED
2010							
3-03	Cyprus	D 0-0	Larnaca	Fr			Yordanov.N BUL
21-03	Faroe Islands	W 2-0	Kopavogur	Fr	Vilhjalmsson [10], Sigthorsson [37]	312	Larsen DEN
24-03	Mexico	D 0-0	Charlotte	Fr		63 227	Geiger USA
29-05	Andorra	W 4-0	Reykjavík	Fr	Helguson 2 [32p 51], Veigar Gunnarsson [87p], Sigthorsson [88]	2 567	Reinert FRO
11-08	Liechtenstein	D 1-1	Reykjavík	Fr	Gislason [20]	3 000	Buttimer IRL
3-09	Norway	L 1-2	Reykjavík	ECq	Helguson [38]	6 137	Banti ITA
7-09	Denmark	L 0-1	Copenhagen	ECq		18 908	McDonald SCO
12-10	Portugal	L 1-3	Reykjavík	ECq	Helguson [17]	9 767	Einwaller AUT
17-11	Israel	L 2-3	Tel Aviv	Fr	Finnbogason [79], Sigthorsson [85]	4 500	Spathas GRE
2011							
26-03	Cyprus	D 0-0	Nicosia	ECq		2 088	Ceferin SVN
4-06	Denmark	L 0-2	Reykjavík	ECq		7 629	Aydinus TUR
10-08	Hungary	L 0-4	Budapest	Fr		12 000	Stark GER
2-09	Norway	L 0-1	Oslo	ECq		22 381	Hategan ROU
6-09	Cyprus	W 1-0	Reykjavík	ECq	Sigthorsson [5]	5 267	Jovanetic SRB
7-10	Portugal	L 3-5	Porto	ECq	Jonasson 2 [48 68], Gylfi Sigurdsson [94+p]	35 715	Nijhuis NED
2012							
24-02	Japan	L 1-3	Osaka	Fr	Smarason [93+p]	42 579	Beath AUS
29-02	Montenegro	L 1-2	Podgorica	Fr	Finnbogason [79]	5 500	Valjic BIH
27-05	France	L 2-3	Valenciennes	Fr	Bjarnason [28], Sigthorsson [34]	20 580	Delferiere BEL
30-05	Sweden	L 2-3	Gothenburg	Fr	Sigthorsson [29], Jonasson [93+]	14 379	Rasmussen DEN
15-08	Faroe Islands	W 2-0	Reykjavík	Fr	Sigthorsson 2 [30 91+]	7 256	Kopriwa LUX
7-09	Norway	W 2-0	Reykjavík	WCq	Arnason [22], Finnbogason [81]	8 352	Gautier FRA
11-09	Cyprus	L 0-1	Larnaca	WCq		1 600	Delferiere BEL
12-10	Albania	W 2-1	Tirana	WCq	Bjarnason [19], Gylfi Sigurdsson [81]	8 200	Asumaa FIN
16-10	Switzerland	L 0-2	Reykjavík	WCq		8 369	Kelly IRL
14-11	Andorra	W 2-0	Andorra La Vella	Fr	Gudmundsson [13], Sigurjonsson [59]	500	Buquet FRA

Fr = Friendly match • EC = UEFA EURO 2012 • WC = FIFA World Cup • q = qualifier

ICELAND NATIONAL TEAM HISTORICAL RECORDS

Caps 104 - Runar Kristinsson 1987-2004 • 89 - Hermann Hreidarsson 1996- • 80 - Gudni Bergsson 1984-2003 • 74 - Brynjar Bjorn Gunnarsson 1997-2009 & Birkir Kristinsson 1988-2004 • 73 - Arnor Gudjohnsen 1979-97 • 72 - Olafur Thordarson 1984-96 • 71 - Arnar Gretarsson 1991-2004 & Arni Gautur Arason 1998- • 70 - Atli Edvaldsson 1976-91 • 69 - Saevar Jonsson 1980-92 & Eidur Gudjohnsen 1996-

Goals 24 - Eidur Gudjohnsen 1996- • 17 - Rikhardur Jonsson 1947-65 • 14 - Rikhardur Dadason 1991-2004 & Arnor Gudjohnsen 1979-97 • 13 - Thordur Gudjonsson 1993-2004 • 12 - Tryggvi Gudmundsson 1997-2008 • 11 - Petur Petursson 1978-90 & Matthias Hallgrimsson 1968-77

Coaches Frederick Steele & Murdo McDougall 1946 • Roland Bergstrom SWE 1947 • Fritz Buchloh GER 1949 • Oli B. Jonsson 1951 • Franz Kohler 1953 • Karl Gudmundsson 1954-56 • Alexander Wier 1957 • Oli B. Jonsson 1958 • Karl Gudmundsson 1959 • Oli B. Jonsson 1960 • Karl Gudmundsson 1961 • Rikhardur Jonsson 1962 • Karl Gudmundsson 1963-66 • Reynir Karlsson 1967 • Walter Pfeiffer 1968 • Rikhardur Jonsson 1969-71 • Duncan McDowell 1972 • Eggert Johannesson 1972 • Henning Enoksen DEN 1973 • Tony Knapp ENG 1974-77 • Juri Ilitchev URS 1978-79 • Gudni Kjartansson 1980-81 • Johannes Atlason 1982-83 • Tony Knapp ENG 1984-85 • Siegfried Held GER 1986-89 • Gudni Kjartansson 1989 • Bo Johansson SWE 1990-91 • Asgeir Eliasson 1991-95 • Logi Olafsson 1996-97 • Gudjon Thordarson 1997-99 • Atli Edvaldsson 2000-03 • Asgeir Sigurvinsson & Logi Olafsson 2003-05 • Eyjolfur Sverrisson 2006-07 • Olafur Johannesson 2007-11 • Lars Lagerback 2011-

ICELAND 2012
URVALSDEILD (1)

	Pl	W	D	L	F	A	Pts	FH	Breidablik	IBV	KR	Stjarnan	IA	Fylkir	Valur	Keflavík	Fram	Selfoss	Grindavík
FH Hafnarfjördur †	22	15	4	3	51	23	49		3-0	2-0	1-3	2-2	2-1	8-0	2-1	3-0	1-0	5-2	1-1
Breidablik ‡	22	10	6	6	32	27	36	0-1		1-0	2-1	2-0	0-1	1-1	1-0	0-4	0-2	1-1	2-0
IBV Vestmannæyjar ‡	22	10	5	7	36	21	35	2-2	0-0		2-0	4-1	0-0	1-1	2-0	0-1	3-2	1-0	2-1
KR Reykjavík ‡	22	10	5	7	39	32	35	2-0	0-4	3-2		2-2	2-0	2-1	2-3	3-0	1-1	3-1	4-1
Stjarnan Gardabær	22	8	10	4	44	38	34	2-2	1-1	1-1	1-1		1-1	2-2	3-2	1-3	4-2	4-2	3-4
IA Akranes	22	9	5	8	32	36	32	2-7	1-1	0-4	3-2	1-2		2-1	1-1	3-2	0-1	4-0	2-1
Fylkir Reykjavík	22	8	7	7	30	39	31	0-1	1-1	0-4	3-2	3-3	0-1		3-1	1-1	1-0	2-0	2-1
Valur Reykjavík	22	9	1	12	34	34	28	3-1	3-4	0-3	0-1	0-2	2-1	1-2		4-0	0-2	3-1	4-1
Keflavík	22	8	3	11	35	38	27	2-4	2-3	1-0	1-1	0-1	2-3	0-2	0-4		5-0	2-2	2-1
Fram Reykjavík	22	8	3	11	31	34	27	0-1	3-2	2-1	1-2	1-1	2-0	4-0	0-1	0-2		0-2	4-3
Selfoss	22	6	3	13	30	44	21	0-1	0-2	2-1	1-0	1-3	1-3	1-2	0-1	2-1	4-2		3-3
Grindavík	22	2	6	14	31	57	12	0-1	2-4	1-3	2-2	1-4	2-2	2-2	2-0	0-4	2-2	0-4	

6/05/2012 - 29/09/2012 • † Qualified for the UEFA Champions League • ‡ Qualified for the Europa League
Top scorers: **12** - Atli **GUDNASON**, FH • **11** - Kristinn Ingi **HALLDORSSON**, Fram • **10** - Ingimundur Niels **OSKARSSON**, Fylkir • **9** - Bjorn Daniel **SVERRISSON**, FH; Christian **OLSEN** DEN, IBV & Gardar **GUNNLAUGSSON**, IA • **8**- Kjartan **FINNBOGASON**, KR & Gardar **JOHANNSSON**, Stjarnan

ICELAND 2012
1.DEILD (2)

	Pl	W	D	L	F	A	Pts
Thór Akureyri	22	16	2	4	40	20	50
Vikingur Olafsvík	22	13	3	6	36	21	42
Thróttur Reykjavík	22	9	6	7	34	26	33
KA Akureyri	22	9	6	7	34	30	33
Haukar Hafnarfjördur	22	9	6	7	23	25	33
Vikingur Reykjavík	22	8	7	7	34	31	31
Fjölnir Reykjavík	22	7	8	7	39	26	29
Tindastoll Saudarkrokur	22	8	3	11	34	42	27
BI/Bolungarvík	22	6	8	8	31	37	26
Leiknir Reykjavík	22	6	7	9	33	36	25
Höttur Egilsstadir	22	5	6	11	30	41	21
IR Reykjavík	22	4	2	16	19	52	14

12/05/2012 - 22/09/2012

DEILDABIKAR (LEAGUE CUP) 2012

Quarter-finals		Semi-finals		Final	
KR Reykjavík	2 5p				
FH Hafnarfjördur	2 4p	**KR Reykjavík**	2		
Keflavík	1	Breidablik	0		
Breidablik	2			**KR Reykjavík**	1
Stjarnan	2			Fram Reykjavík	0
Valur Reykjavík	1	Stjarnan	1	KFK, Reykjavík,	
Thór Akureyri	0	**Fram Reykjavík**	2	28-04-2012, Att: 627	
Fram Reykjavík	4			Scorer - Ragnarsson [57]	

ICELAND 2012
2.DEILD (3)

	Pl	W	D	L	F	A	Pts
Völsungur Húsavík	22	14	4	4	36	21	46
KF Siglufjördur	22	12	7	3	51	23	43
HK Kópavogur	22	13	4	5	43	27	43
KV Reykjavík	22	12	4	6	43	26	40
Afturelding Mosfellsbær	22	13	1	8	50	46	40
Dalvík/Reynir	22	11	3	8	38	25	36
Reynir Sandgerdi	22	9	4	9	35	41	31
Njardvík	22	8	6	8	31	35	30
Hamar Hveragerdi	22	5	6	11	36	41	21
Grótta Seltjarnarnes	22	5	5	12	31	41	20
Fjardabyggd	22	4	3	15	31	48	15
KFR	22	1	3	18	20	71	6

12/05/2012 - 22/09/2012

MEDALS TABLE

		Overall	League	Cup	LC
		G S B	G S B	G S	G S
1	KR Reykjavík	43 33 12	**25** 27 12	**13** 5	**5** 1
2	Valur Reykjavík	31 24 18	20 17 18	9 3	2 4
3	IA Akranes	30 21 13	18 12 13	9 9	3
4	Fram Reykjavík	25 29 16	18 17 16	7 10	2
5	FH Hafnarfjördur	13 11 1	6 7 1	2 3	**5** 1
6	IBV Vestmannæyjar	8 12 10	3 6 10	4 6	1
7	Keflavík IF	8 10 7	4 3 7	4 5	2
8	Vikingur Reykjavík	6 8 8	5 7 8	1 1	
9	Fylkir Reykjavík	2 5 1		2 1 2	3
	Breidablik Kópavogur	2 5 1	1 1 1	1 1	3
11	KA Akureyri	1 3	1	3	
12	Grindavík	1 1 2		2	1 1
13	IBA Akureyri	1 4		4 1	
14	Fjölnir Reykjavík	2		2	
15	Leiftur Olafsfjördur	1 3		3	1
16	Thór Akureyri	1 2		2	1
17	Stjarnan Gardabaer	1		1	
	Thróttur Reykjavík	1			1
	Vídir Gardur	1		1	

BIKARKEPPNI 2012

Third Round

KR Reykjavik	2
IA Akranes *	1
Bl/Bolungarvik	0
Breidablik *	5
Höttur Egilsstadir	4
Augnablik *	1
Vikingur Olafsvik *	0
IBV Vestmannaeyjar	6
Vikingur Reykjavik *	2
Fjölnir Reykjavik	0
FH Hafnarfjördur *	1 2p
Fylkir Reykjavik	1 3p
KA Akureyri *	2
Fjardabyggd	0
Keflavik *	0
Grindavik	1
Thróttur Reykjavik	2
Leiknir Reykjavik *	1
Thor Akureyri *	1
Valur Reykjavik	4
KB Reykjavik	1
KFS *	0
Njardvik	1
Selfoss *	2
Fram Reykjavik	1 4p
Haukar Hafnarfjördur	1 3p
Thróttur Vogar *	1
Afturelding Mosfellsbær	2
Reynir Sandgerdi	3
Dalvik/Reynir *	1
Grótta Seltjarnarnes	1
Stjarnan Gardabær *	4

Round of 16

KR Reykjavik *	3
Breidablik	9
Höttur Egilsstadir	1
IBV Vestmannaeyjar *	6
Vikingur Reykjavik *	2
Fylkir Reykjavik	1
KA Akureyri *	2
Grindavik	3
Thróttur Reykjavik *	2
Valur Reykjavik	1
KB Reykjavik	0
Selfoss *	4
Fram Reykjavik	3
Afturelding Mosfellsbær *	2
Reynir Sandgerdi	0
Stjarnan Gardabær *	1

Quarter-finals

KR Reykjavik	2
IBV Vestmannaeyjar *	1
Vikingur Reykjavik *	0
Grindavik	3
Thróttur Reykjavik *	3
Selfoss	0
Fram Reykjavik	1
Stjarnan Gardabær *	2

Semi-finals

KR Reykjavik	1
Grindavik *	0
Thróttur Reykjavik	0
Stjarnan Gardabær *	3

Final

KR Reykjavik ‡	2
Stjarnan Gardabær	1

CUP FINAL

Laugardalsvöllur, Reykjavik, 18-08-2012
Att: 5080, Ref: Thoroddur Hjaltalin
Scorers - Martin 32, Baldur Sigurdsson 84 for KR; Gardar Johannson 6 for Stjarnan
KR - Hannes Halldorsson - Gudmundur Gunnarsson, Gretar Sigurdarson, Aron Josepsson, Viktor Arnarsson• (Jonas Saevarsson 85) - Bjarni Gudjonsson, Baldur Sigurdsson•, Oskar Hauksson (Emil Atlason 80) - Kjartan Finnbogason•, Gary Martin, Magnus Ludviksson. Tr: Runar Kristinsson
Stjarnan - Arnar Petursson - Johann Laxdal•, Alexander Scholz, Atli Johannsson (Tryggvi Bjarnason 86), Daniel Laxdal• - Mark Doninger, Baldvin Sturluson - Gardar Johannsson - Ellert Hreinsson, Halldor Bjornsson (Gunnar Jonsson 90), Kennie Chopart. Tr: Bjarni Johannsson

* Home team • ‡ Qualified for the Europa League

ISR – ISRAEL

FIFA/COCA-COLA WORLD RANKING

'93	'94	'95	'96	'97	'98	'99	'00	'01	'02	'03	'04	'05	'06	'07	'08	'09	'10	'11	'12
57	42	42	52	61	43	26	41	49	46	51	48	44	44	26	18	26	50	37	78

2012

Jan	Feb	Mar	Apr	May	Jun	Jul	Aug	Sep	Oct	Nov	Dec	High	Low	Av
37	35	38	58	58	81	82	82	75	82	78	78	15	82	42

Not since the title triumph of Maccabi Netanya in 1983 had the Tel Aviv/Haifa/Jersusalem stranglehold on the Israeli championship been broken so it was with some surprise that Ironi from the city of Kiriat Shmona emerged as the 2012 champions - the first title won by the club. Nestled on the border with Lebanon in the shadows of the Golan Heights, Kiriat Shmona was notable for being in the front-line of rocket attacks from across the border and with a population of just 23,000, the city had never made an impact in football. Ironi were only formed in 2000 but have always had lofty ambitions thanks to the backing of Tel Aviv businessman Izzy Sheratzky. They reached the top flight for the first time in 2007, a year after the arrival of head coach Ran Ben-Shimon. Based largely on a homegrown squad that included six Israeli-Arabs and Argentine forward David Solari, Ironi secured the title with a 0-0 draw at home against their closest rivals Hapoel Tel Aviv with five games to spare. Hapoel did, however, make their own piece of history by becoming the first team to win a hat trick of Israeli cups. In a repeat of the 2011 final, Hapoel beat Maccabi Haifa 2-1 thanks to an injury-time goal from Nigerian midfielder Nosa Igiebor to win the trophy for the 15th time overall.

UEFA EUROPEAN CHAMPIONSHIP RECORD
1960-1992 DNE (not a member of UEFA) **1996-2012** DNQ

THE ISRAEL FOOTBALL ASSOCIATION (IFA)
Ramat-Gan Stadium,
299 Aba Hilell Street,
Ramat Gan 52134
☎ +972 3 6171500
✆ +972 3 5702044
✉ karens@football.org.il
🖥 www.football.org.il
FA 1928 CON 1992 FIFA 1929
P Avi Luzon
GS Ori Shilo

THE STADIA
2014 FIFA World Cup Stadia
Ramat Gan National Stadium
Ramat Gan — 41 583
Other Main Stadia
Teddi Malha Stadium
Jerusalem — 21 000
Bloomfield
Tel Aviv — 15 700
Kiryat Eli'ezer Stadium
Haifa — 14 002
HaMoshava Stadium
Petah Tikva — 11 500

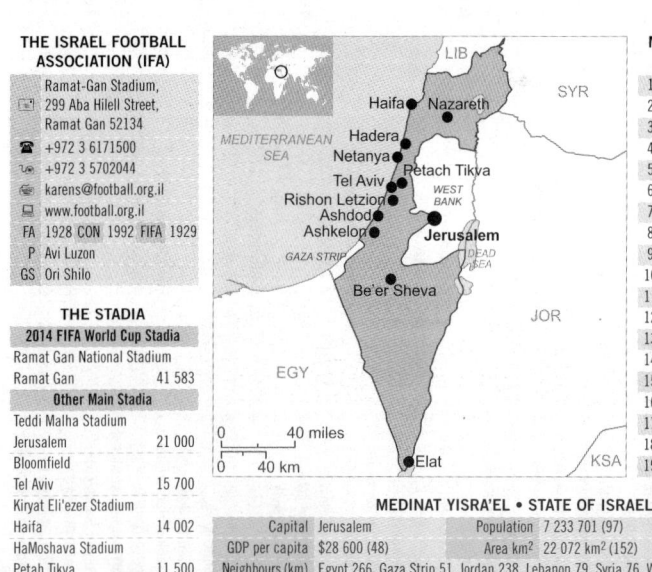

MAJOR CITIES/TOWNS
		Population
1	Jerusalem	759 873
2	Tel Aviv-Jaffa	390 300
3	Haifa	263 208
4	Rishon Letzion	236 411
5	Ashdod	228 564
6	Be'er Sheva	195 695
7	Petah Tikva	184 695
8	Netanya	181 028
9	Holon	164 285
10	Bene Beraq	148 908
11	Ramat Gan	127 354
12	Bat Yam	123 211
13	Ashkelon	112 682
14	Rehoboth	108 710
15	Bet Shemesh	91 318
16	Kfar Saba	83 967
17	Hertzelia	82 971
18	Hadera	79 639
19	Nazareth	69 078

MEDINAT YISRA'EL • STATE OF ISRAEL
Capital	Jerusalem	Population	7 233 701 (97)	% in cities 92%
GDP per capita	$28 600 (48)	Area km²	22 072 km² (152)	GMT +/- +2

Neighbours (km) Egypt 266, Gaza Strip 51, Jordan 238, Lebanon 79, Syria 76, West Bank 307 • Coast 273

ISR – ISRAEL 449

RECENT INTERNATIONAL MATCHES PLAYED BY ISRAEL

2008	Opponents		Score	Venue	Comp	Scorers	Att	Referee
20-08	Finland	L	0-2	Tampere	Fr		4 929	
6-09	Switzerland	D	2-2	Ramat Gan	WCq	Benayoun 73, Sahar 92+	29 600	Hansson SWE
10-09	Moldova	W	2-1	Chisinau	WCq	Golan 39, Saban 45	10 500	Muniz ESP
11-10	Luxembourg	W	3-1	Luxembourg	WCq	Benayoun 2p, Golan 54, Toama 81	3 562	Egorov RUS
15-10	Latvia	D	1-1	Riga	WCq	Benayoun 50	7 100	Hrinak SVK
19-11	Côte d'Ivoire	D	2-2	Tel Aviv	Fr	Barda 18, Golan 24	27 167	
2009								
11-02	Hungary	W	1-0	Tel Aviv	Fr	Benayoun 77	9 500	Borski POL
28-03	Greece	D	1-1	Ramat Gan	WCq	Golan 55	38 000	Rosetti ITA
1-04	Greece	L	1-2	Iraklio	WCq	Barda 58	22 794	Benquerença POR
12-08	Northern Ireland	D	1-1	Belfast	Fr	Barda 27	10 250	Valgeirsson ISL
5-09	Latvia	L	0-1	Ramat Gan	WCq		20 000	Kircher GER
9-09	Luxembourg	W	7-0	Ramat Gan	WCq	Barda 3 9 21 43, Baruchyan 15, Golan 58, Sahar 2 62 84	7 038	Svendsen DEN
10-10	Moldova	W	3-1	Ramat Gan	WCq	Barda 2 22 70, Ben Dayan 65	8 700	Blom NED
14-10	Switzerland	D	0-0	Basel	WCq		38 500	Tudor ROU
2010								
26-05	Uruguay	L	1-4	Montevideo	Fr	Rafaelov 30	60 000	Osses CHI
30-05	Chile	L	0-3	Concepcion	Fr		25 000	Arias PAR
2-09	Malta	W	3-1	Tel Aviv	ECq	Benayoun 3 7 64p 75	17 365	Ennjimi FRA
7-09	Georgia	D	0-0	Tbilisi	ECq		45 000	Kever SUI
9-10	Croatia	L	1-2	Tel Aviv	ECq	Shechter 81	33 421	Stark Ger
12-10	Greece	L	1-2	Piraeus	ECq	OG 59	16 935	Hansson SWE
17-11	Iceland	W	3-2	Tel Aviv	Fr	Damari 2 5 14, Rafaelov 27	4 500	Spathas GRE
2011								
9-02	Serbia	L	0-2	Tel Aviv	Fr		8 000	Nikolaev RUS
26-03	Latvia	W	2-1	Tel Aviv	ECq	Barda 16, Kayal 81	10 801	Mazic SRB
29-03	Georgia	W	1-0	Tel Aviv	ECq	Ben Haim II 59	13 716	Fautrel FRA
4-06	Latvia	W	2-1	Riga	ECq	Benayoun 19, Ben Haim I 43p	6 147	Kelly IRL
10-08	Côte d'Ivoire	L	3-4	Geneva	Fr	Shechter 76, Melikson 2 79 87p	2 000	
2-09	Greece	L	0-1	Tel Aviv	ECq		13 100	Thomson SCO
6-09	Croatia	L	1-3	Zagreb	ECq	Hemed 44	13 688	Velasco ESP
11-10	Malta	W	2-0	Ta'Qali	ECq	Refaelov 11, Gershon 93+	2 164	Duarte POR
2012								
29-02	Ukraine	L	2-3	Petah-Tikva	Fr	Hemed 55p, Sahar 63	4 000	Marciniak POL
26-05	Czech Republic	L	1-2	Graz	Fr	Shechter 45	3 400	Trutz SVN
31-05	Germany	L	0-2	Leipzig	Fr		43 241	Blom NED
15-08	Hungary	D	1-1	Budapest	Fr	Hemed 80	15 000	Kruzliak SVK
7-09	Azerbaijan	D	1-1	Baku	WCq	Natcho 50	22 211	Jug SVN
11-09	Russia	L	0-4	Tel Aviv	WCq		28 131	Clattenburg ENG
12-10	Luxembourg	W	6-0	Luxembourg	WCq	Radi 4, Ben Basat 12, Hemed 3 27 74 91+, Melicsohn 61	2 631	Trattou CYP
16-10	Luxembourg	W	3-0	Tel Aviv	WCq	Hemed 2 13 48, Ben Basat 35	20 400	Lechner AUT
14-11	Belarus	L	1-2	Jerusalem	Fr	Damari 19	8 000	Evans WAL

Fr = Friendly match • EC = UEFA EURO 2012 • WC = FIFA World Cup • q = qualifier

ISRAEL NATIONAL TEAM HISTORICAL RECORDS

Caps: 94 - Arik Benado 1995-2007 • 88 - Alon Harazi 1992-2006 • 87 - Yossi Benayoun 1998- • 85 - Amir Schelach 1992-2001 • 84 - Mordechai Spiegler (57) 1963-77 • 83 - Nir Klinger (76) 1987-97 • 80 - Avi Nimni 1992-2006 • 78 - Tal Banin 1990-2002; Itzhak Shum (53) 1969-81 & Eyal Berkovic 1992-2004 • 74 - Walid Badir 1997-2007 • 72 - Alon Hazan 1990-2000 • 71 - Dudu Aouate 1999-

Goals: 33 - Mordechai Spiegler 1963-77 • 24 - Yehoshua Feigenbaum 1966-77 & Yossi Benayoun 1998- • 23 - Ronen Harazi 1992-99 • 22 - Nahum Stelmach 1956-68 • 21 - Gidi Damti 1971-81 • 18 - Giora Spiegel 1965-80 & Yehoshua Glazer 1949-61

Past Coaches: Egon Pollack AUT 1948 • Lajos Hess 1949 • Vladislav Scali HUN 1950 • Jerry Beit haLevi 1953-54 • Jack Gibbons ENG 1956 • Jerry Beit haLevi 1957 • Moshe Varon 1958 • Gyula Mandi HUN 1959-63 • George Ainsley ENG 1963-64 • Yosef Mirmovich YUG 1964 • Gyula Mandi HUN 1964 • Yosef Mirmovich 1964-65 • Milovan Ciric 1965-68 • Emmanuel Scheffer 1968-70 • Edmond Schmilovich 1970-73 • David Schweitzer 1973-77 • Emmanuel Scheffer 1978-79 • Jack Mansell ENG 1980-81 • Yosef Mirmovich 1983-86 • Miljenko Mihic YUG 1986-88 • Itzhak Schneor & Ya'akov Grundman 1988-92 • Shlomo Scharf 1992-2000 • Richard Moller Nielsen DEN 2000-02 • Avram Grant 2002-06 • Dror Kashtan 2006-10 • Eli Ohana 2010 • Luis Fernandez FRA 2010-11 • Eli Guttman 2011-

Appearances and goals in brackets are totals in games recognised as full internationals by FIFA

ISRAEL 2011-12
LIGAT HA'AL

	Pl	W	D	L	F	A	Pts	Ironi KS	Hapoel TA	Bnei Yehuda	Maccabi N	Maccabi H	Maccabi TA	Ashdod	Bnei Sakhnin	Beitar	Hapoel A	Ironi RH	Hapoel H	Hapoel BS	Maccabi PT	Ironi RL	Hapoel PT
Ironi Kiriat Shmona †	37	21	10	6	48	26	73		1-0	1-0	1-3	1-0	2-1	0-0	0-0	1-0	2-0	4-0	1-0	1-1	1-1	2-0	2-0
Hapoel Tel Aviv ‡ §3	37	16	14	7	63	35	59	2-2		1-1	7-3	3-0	0-1	0-0	0-1	1-0	2-1	0-0	0-0	2-0	4-1	6-0	5-0
Bnei Yehuda Tel Aviv ‡	37	16	11	10	53	36	59	0-1	1-1		1-2	0-0	0-0	1-0	1-1	3-0	4-1	1-1	1-0	5-1	2-2	1-0	5-1
Maccabi Netanya ‡	37	17	8	12	54	48	59	0-1	2-1	1-0		1-4	3-0	1-0	3-1	1-1	1-1	0-2	1-1	2-1	0-1	6-2	1-1
Maccabi Haifa	37	16	10	11	56	44	58	0-3	1-4	1-1	2-1		2-1	1-1	0-0	1-0	5-0	1-3	3-1	4-1	3-1	2-0	2-2
Maccabi Tel Aviv	37	16	7	14	55	43	55	1-1	1-3	0-1	1-1	1-1		4-0	2-0	0-1	2-0	0-1	2-0	4-0	1-0	3-1	1-0
FC Ashdod	37	14	12	11	44	44	54	0-0	2-0	0-0	2-1	1-0	2-1		3-3	3-0	1-1	2-0	3-2	2-0	1-3	2-1	1-1
Bnei Sakhnin §2	37	15	7	15	60	53	50	2-3	0-1	2-1	0-2	1-0	2-1	0-1		3-0	2-1	3-0	0-1	4-3	3-0	1-0	3-0
Beitar Jerusalem §2	37	15	7	15	32	44	50	1-0	1-1	1-2	2-1	1-4	0-0	1-0	0-3		3-1	0-1	1-0	0-1	0-0	1-1	1-2
Hapoel Acre	37	13	9	15	51	46	48	1-2	0-2	0-1	1-2	0-1	3-0	2-2	2-1	1-1		2-0	1-0	2-0	0-0	2-2	3-1
Ironi Ramat Hasharon	37	11	13	13	37	45	46	1-1	1-1	2-1	0-1	0-0	3-1	1-1	0-1	2-0	1-1		2-0	3-3	0-1	1-2	0-0
Hapoel Haifa	37	11	11	15	41	43	44	0-1	0-0	0-2	1-1	1-1	2-0	2-1	2-2	1-3	2-0	1-0		0-2	1-1	3-2	2-2
Hapoel Be'er Sheva	37	12	7	18	39	61	43	0-3	1-1	3-1	1-2	1-1	1-4	2-1	0-2	0-1	2-1	1-3	2-0		0-0	2-1	1-0
Maccabi Petah Tikva §3	37	11	10	16	39	57	40	0-2	1-0	0-0	1-0	1-4	2-1	2-3	1-3	2-3	0-4	2-3	2-1	1-2		2-2	1-1
Ironi Rishon Letzion	37	6	9	22	39	70	27	1-1	1-2	0-1	0-0	4-2	0-2	2-1	4-2	2-0	0-3	1-1	1-1	0-1	2-2		0-0
Hapoel Petah Tikva §9	37	8	11	18	36	55	26	1-1	1-2-3	0-1	3-1	3-1	1-3	0-1	1-2	0-1	1-0	2-1	2-0	1-0	0-1	0-1	

20/08/2011 - 12/05/2012 • † Qualified for the UEFA Champions League • ‡ Qualified for the Europa League • § = points deducted
Top scorers: **20** - Achmad **SABA'A**, Maccabi Netanya • **17** - Omer **DAMARI**, Hapoel Tel Aviv • **16** - Pedro **GALVAN** ARG, Bnei Yehuda • **14** - Kostadin **HAZUROV** BUL, Bnei Sakhnin & Viam **AMASHA**, Maccabi Haifa • **13** - Yuval **AVIDOR**, Ironi Kiryat Shmona/Hapoel Haifa; Shimon **ABUHAZEIRA**, Ironi Kiryat Shmona; Toto **TAMUZ**, Hapoel Tel Aviv; Maharan **RADI**, Bnei Sakhnin & Eliran **ATAR**, Maccabi Tel Aviv

ISRAEL 2011-12 LIGA LEUMIT (2)

	Pl	W	D	L	F	A	Pts
Hapoel Ramat Gan †	35	21	6	8	54	26	37
Hapoel Bnei Lod †	35	20	9	6	56	35	37
Maccabi Hertzelia	35	16	13	6	42	24	37
Maccabi Akhi Nazareth	35	16	7	12	43	47	31
Hapoel Ranana	35	14	9	12	37	30	27
Hapoel Jerusalem	35	13	8	14	44	40	25
Hapoel Kfar Saba	33	12	10	11	42	34	26
Beitar Tel Aviv Ramla	33	12	10	11	48	43	25
Hapoel Ashkelon	33	11	12	10	42	43	25
Maccabi Om El Fahem	33	12	9	12	30	36	23
Sektzia Nes Tziona	35	10	14	11	50	48	25
Hapoel Nazareth Illit	35	11	8	16	34	47	25
Hakoah Ramat Gan	35	10	11	14	34	50	25
Ironi Bat Yam	35	9	10	16	34	43	21
Maccabi Be'er Sheva	35	7	8	20	39	58	17
Hapoel Herzelia	35	6	8	21	25	51	16

19/08/2011 - 11/05/2012 • † Qualified for promotion play-off
Promotion play-off: Hapoel Ramat Gan 2-0 Hapoel Bnei Lod

CHAMPIONSHIP PLAY-OFFS

	Ironi	HTA	BY	MN	MH	MTA	Ash	BS
Ironi Kiriat Shmona		0-0	0-1		0-1		1-0	
Hapoel Tel Aviv			3-3	1-3		0-0		3-1
Bnei Yehuda Tel Aviv				1-0	2-1	4-3		
Maccabi Netanya	1-3				1-0			3-2
Maccabi Haifa			1-1			2-1	3-0	
Maccabi Tel Aviv	3-2			1-0				5-2
FC Ashdod		0-2	2-1	0-2		1-1		
Bnei Sakhnin	5-0		0-3		0-2		1-2	

RELEGATION PLAY-OFFS

	BJ	HA	IRH	HH	HBS	MPT	IRL	HPT
Beitar Jerusalem		1-0		0-0		3-1		2-0
Hapoel Acre			2-0	0-0			1-2	2-3
Ironi Ramat Hasharon	0-1				0-0		5-2	2-1
Hapoel Haifa			1-1		2-1		2-0	2-1
Hapoel Be'er Sheva	3-1	1-3				1-0		
Maccabi Petah Tikva			0-0	2-1			2-1	
Ironi Rishon Letzion	1-2	1-2			0-1			
Hapoel Petah Tikva						1-1	0-1	2-0

MEDALS TABLE

		Overall			League			Cup			Asia/Eur			City
		G	S	B	G	S	B	G	S	B	G	S	B	
1	Maccabi Tel Aviv	42	20	9	18	9	9	22	11		2			Tel Aviv
2	Hapoel Tel Aviv	28	22	6	12	13	6	15	8		1	1		Tel Aviv
3	Maccabi Haifa	17	16	5	12	6	5	5	10					Haifa
4	Beitar Jerusalem	13	9	5	6	6	5	7	3					Jerusalem
5	Hapoel Petah Tikva	8	15	4	6	9	4	2	6					Petach Tikva
6	Maccabi Netanya	6	6	4	5	4	4	1	2					Netanya
7	Hapoel Haifa	4	7	8	1	2	8	3	5					Haifa
8	Hakoah Ramat Gan	4	1	1	2			2	1					Ramat Gan
9	Hapoel Kfar Saba	4			1			3						Kfar Saba
10	Bnei Yehuda Tel Aviv	3	7	3	1	3	3	2	4					Tel Aviv
11	Hapoel Beer Sheva	3	2	5	2		5	1	2					Beer Sheva
12	Maccabi Petach Tikva	2	5	1				3	1		2	2		Petach Tikva

G'VIAA H'AMEDINA (STATE CUP) 2011-12

Eighth Round

Hapoel Tel Aviv*	3		
Maccabi Yavne	0		
Beitar Jerusalem	0 3p		
Hapoel Bnei Lod*	0 4p		
Ironi Kiriat Shmona	1		
Hapoel Haifa	0		
Sektzia Nes Tziona*	1		
Maccabi Netanya	2		
Maccabi Hertzelia	1		
Givat Olga*	0		
Bnei Yehuda Tel Aviv	3 1p		
Hapoel Be'er Sheva*	3 4p		
Beitar Kfar Saba	2		
Ironi Rishon Letzion*	0		
Hapoel Acre	1		
Ironi Ramat Hasharon*	3		
FC Ashdod	3		
Hapoel Petah Tikva*	0		
Hapoel Atula	2		
Maccabi Om El Fahem*	3		
Hapoel Jerusalem*	1		
Maccabi Tel Aviv	0		
Bnei Sakhnin	0		
Maccabi Petah Tikva*	2		
Hapoel Nazareth Illit*	4		
Hapoel Asi Gilboa	2		
Kfar Kasem	2		
Hapoel Ramat Gan*	3		
Hapoel Kfar Saba	2 4p		
Beitar Tel Aviv Ramla	2 2p		
Maccabi Be'er Sheva*	1 0 3p		
Maccabi Haifa	2 0 4p		

Round of 16

Hapoel Tel Aviv	3	
Hapoel Bnei Lod*	1	
Ironi Kiriat Shmona	1	
Maccabi Netanya	2	
Maccabi Hertzelia	1 5p	
Hapoel Be'er Sheva*	1 4p	
Beitar Kfar Saba*	0	
Ironi Ramat Hasharon	1	
FC Ashdod	3	
Maccabi Om El Fahem	1	
Hapoel Jerusalem*	0	
Maccabi Petah Tikva	1	
Hapoel Nazareth Illit *	4	
Hapoel Ramat Gan	2	
Hapoel Kfar Saba*	0 3p	
Maccabi Haifa	0 4p	

Quarter-finals

Hapoel Tel Aviv	1
Maccabi Netanya*	0
Maccabi Hertzelia	0
Ironi Ramat Hasharon *	1
FC Ashdod	3
Maccabi Petah Tikva*	1
Hapoel Nazareth Illit	0
Maccabi Haifa *	2

Semi-finals

Hapoel Tel Aviv	3
Ironi Ramat Hasharon	0
FC Ashdod	1
Maccabi Haifa	2

Final

Hapoel Tel Aviv ‡	2
Maccabi Haifa	1

CUP FINAL

National Stadium, Ramat Gan, 15-05-2012
Att: 37 000, Ref: Alon Yefet
Scorers - Oremus [58], Igiebor [92+] for Hapoel; Yampolsky [62] for Maccabi
Hapoel - Apoula Edel - Nael Khotaba, Marko Suler, Walid Badir, Igal Antebi - Avihai Yadin, Roy Gordana (Bevan Fransman 90), Eiroi Cohen (Toto Tamuz 70), Mirko Oremus (Salim Tuaama 85), Emmanuel Igiebor - Omer Damari. Tr: Nitzan Shirazi
Maccabi - Nir Davidovich - Eyal Meshumar, Edin Cocalic (Sari Falach 89), Jurica Buljat, Taleb Tawatha - Seydou Yahaya, Gustavo Boccoli, Idan Vered, Muhammad Ghdir (Bamidele Yampolski 60) - Yaniv Katan (Alon Turgeman 79), Viam Amasha. Tr: Elisha Levi

Premier League clubs enter in the eighth round • * Home team • Semi-finals played at Ramat Gan • ‡ Qualified for the Europa League

ITA – ITALY

FIFA/COCA-COLA WORLD RANKING

'93	'94	'95	'96	'97	'98	'99	'00	'01	'02	'03	'04	'05	'06	'07	'08	'09	'10	'11	'12
2	4	3	10	9	7	14	4	6	13	10	10	12	2	3	4	4	14	9	4

2012

Jan	Feb	Mar	Apr	May	Jun	Jul	Aug	Sep	Oct	Nov	Dec	High	Low	Av
9	8	9	12	12	12	6	6	6	8	5	4	1	16	7

A crisis in Italian club football once again proved to be all the motivation the national team needed to put in an outstanding performance at an international tournament as the Azzurri defied expectations to reach the final of Euro 2012. Having beaten the English on penalties in the quarter-finals, Italy maintained their extraordinary record of never having lost to Germany in international competition, beating them 2-1 in the semi-final. In the final, however, they simply weren't a match for a majestic Spanish team who ran out 4-0 winners in Kyiv. Before the tournament, coach Cesare Prandelli had even offered to pull out of the finals in the wake of yet another corruption scandal at club level. Having just led Juventus to the title, coach Antonio Conte was banned for 10 months after failing to report attempts to influence the outcome of a match in the 2010-11 season while coach of Siena. The Scommessopoli scandal went much deeper though, revealing widespread corruption and match-fixing in the Italian game. It prompted prime minister Mario Monti to call for football in the country to be suspended for three years to eradicate the problems and make a fresh start. On the field, Juventus, undefeated in the league, lost just one game all season, to Napoli in the cup final, a win that secured Napoli their first trophy since the days of Maradona.

UEFA EUROPEAN CHAMPIONSHIP RECORD

1960 DNE 1964 r2 **1968** 1 Winners 1972 QF 1976 DNQ **1980** 4 3p/o 1984 DNQ **1988** 4 SF 1992 DNQ
1996 10 r1 **2000** 2 F **2004** 9 r1 **2008** 8 QF **2012** 2 F

FEDERAZIONE ITALIANA GIUOCO CALCIO (FIGC)

Via Gregorio Allegri 14,
Roma 00198

☎ +39 06 84912542
📠 +39 06 84912620
✉ international@figc.it
🖥 www.figc.it
FA 1898 CON 1954 FIFA 1905
P Giancarlo Abete
GS Antonello Valentini

THE STADIA
2014 FIFA World Cup Stadia
Giuseppe Meazza 'San Siro'
Milan   80 074
Stadio Alberto Braglia
Modena   20 507
Other Main Stadia
Stadio Olimpico
Rome   72 698
Stadio San Paolo
Naples   60 240
Juventus Stadium
Turin   41 137

MAJOR CITIES/TOWNS

		Population
1	Rome	2 491 807
2	Milan	1 324 927
3	Naples	959 303
4	Turin	862 469
5	Palermo	647 870
6	Genoa	585 060
7	Florence	378 158
8	Bologna	371 940
9	Bari	304 594
10	Catania	289 838
11	Venice	265 493
12	Verona	263 899
13	Messina	236 530
14	Padova	215 258
15	Trieste	198 389
16	Brescia	195 448
17	Taranto	190 548
18	Parma	186 566
49	Udine	97 669

REPUBBLICA ITALIANA • ITALIAN REPUBLIC

Capital	Rome	Population	58 126 212 (23)	% in cities	68%
GDP per capita	$31 400 (41)	Area km^2	301 340 km^2 (71)	GMT + / -	+1
Neighbours (km)	Austria 430, France 488, San Marino 39, Slovenia 199, Switzerland 740 • Coast 7600

RECENT INTERNATIONAL MATCHES PLAYED BY ITALY

2010	Opponents	Score	Venue	Comp	Scorers	Att	Referee
3-03	Cameroon	D 0-0	Monte Carlo	Fr		10 752	Ennjimi FRA
3-06	Mexico	L 1-2	Brussels	Fr	Bonucci [89]	30 000	Verbist BEL
5-06	Switzerland	D 1-1	Geneva	Fr	Quagliarella [14]	30 000	Piccirillo FRA
14-06	Paraguay	D 1-1	Cape Town	WCr1	De Rossi [63]	62 869	Archundia MEX
20-06	New Zealand	D 1-1	Nelspruit	WCr1	Iaquinta [29p]	38 229	Batres GUA
24-06	Slovakia	L 2-3	Johannesburg	WCr1	Di Natale [81], Quagliarella [92+]	53 412	Webb ENG
10-08	Cote d'Ivoire	L 0-1	London	Fr		11 176	Atkinson ENG
3-09	Estonia	W 2-1	Tallinn	ECq	Cassano [60], Bonucci [63]	8 600	Velasco ESP
7-09	Faroe Islands	W 5-0	Florence	ECq	Gilardino [11], De Rossi [22], Cassano [27], Quagliarella [81], Pirlo [90]	19 266	Kulbakov BLR
8-10	Northern Ireland	D 0-0	Belfast	ECq		15 200	Chapron FRA
12-10	Serbia	W 3-0	Genoa	ECq	Match abanondoned after six minutes at 0-0	28 000	Thomson SCO
17-11	Romania	D 1-1	Klagenfurt	Fr	OG [82]	14 000	Einwaller AUT
2011							
9-02	Germany	D 1-1	Dortmund	Fr	Rossi [81]	60 196	Braamhaar NED
25-03	Slovenia	W 1-0	Ljubljana	ECq	Thiago Motta [73]	15 790	Brych GER
29-03	Ukraine	W 2-0	Kyiv	Fr	Rossi [27], Matri [81]	18 000	Nikolaev RUS
3-06	Estonia	W 3-0	Modena	ECq	Rossi [21], Cassano [39], Pazzini [68]	19 434	Tudor ROU
7-06	Republic of Ireland	L 0-2	Liege	Fr		21 516	Gumienny BEL
10-08	Spain	W 2-1	Bari	Fr	Montolivo [11], Aquilani [84]	50 000	Brych GER
2-09	Faroe Islands	W 1-0	Torshavn	ECq	Cassano [11]	5 654	Bognar HUN
6-09	Slovenia	W 1-0	Florence	ECq	Pazzini [85]	18 000	Moen NOR
7-10	Serbia	D 1-1	Belgrade	ECq	Marchisio [2]	35 000	Proenca POR
11-10	Northern Ireland	W 3-0	Pescara	ECq	Cassano 2 [21 53], OG [74]	19 480	Mateu ESP
11-11	Poland	W 2-0	Wroclaw	Fr	Balotelli [30], Pazzini [60]	42 771	Duhamel FRA
15-11	Uruguay	L 0-1	Rome	Fr		42 000	Duarte POR
2012							
29-02	USA	L 0-1	Genoa	Fr		15 000	Aydinus TUR
1-06	Russia	L 0-3	Zurich	Fr		20 000	Hanni SUI
10-06	Spain	D 1-1	Gdansk	ECr1	Di Natale [61]	43 615	Kassai HUN
14-06	Croatia	D 1-1	Poznan	ECr1	Pirlo [39]	37 096	Webb ENG
18-06	Republic of Ireland	W 2-0	Poznan	ECr1	Cassano [36], Balotelli [90]	44 416	Cakir TUR
24-06	England	D 0-0	Kyiv	ECqf	W 4-2p	56 500	Proenca POR
28-06	Germany	W 2-1	Warsaw	ECsf	Balotelli 2 [20 36]	58 500	Lannoy FRA
1-07	Spain	L 0-4	Kyiv	ECf		60 000	Proenca POR
15-08	England	L 1-2	Berne	Fr	De Rossi [15]	15 000	Kever SUI
7-09	Bulgaria	D 2-2	Sofia	WCq	Osvaldo 2 [36 40]	12 993	Atkinson ENG
11-09	Malta	W 2-0	Modena	WCq	Destro [5], Peluso [92+]	18 000	Munukka FIN
12-10	Armenia	W 3-1	Yerevan	WCq	Pirlo [11p], De Rossi [64], Osvaldo [82]	25 000	Strahonja CRO
16-10	Denmark	W 3-1	Milan	WCq	Montolivo [34], De Rossi [37], Balotelli [54]	37 027	Skomina SVN
14-11	France	L 1-2	Parma	Fr	El Shaarawy [35]	19 665	Undiano ESP

Fr = Friendly match • EC = UEFA EURO 2012 • WC = FIFA World Cup • q = qualifier • r1 = first round group • qf = quarter-finals

ITALY NATIONAL TEAM HISTORICAL RECORDS

Caps
136 - Fabio Cannavaro 1997- • 126 - Paolo Maldini 1988-2002 • 123 - Gianluigi Buffon 1997- • 112 - Dino Zoff 1968-83 • 98 - Gianluca Zambrotta 1999- • 94 - Giacinto Facchetti 1963-77 & Andrea Pirlo 2002- • 91 - Alessandro Del Piero 1995-2008 • 82 - Daniele De Rossi 2004- • 81 - Franco Baresi 1982-94, Giuseppe Bergomi 1982-98; Marco Tardelli 1976-85 • 79 - Demetrio Albertini 1991-2002 • 78 - Alessandro Nesta 1996-2006 & Gaetano Scirea 1975-86

Goals
35 - Luigi Riva 1965-74 • 33 - Giuseppe Meazza 1930-39 • 30 - Silvio Piola 1935-52 • 27 - Roberto Baggio 1988-2004 & Alessandro Del Piero 1995-2008 • 25 - Adolfo Baloncieri 1920-30; Filippo Inzaghi 1997-2007 & Alessandro Altobelli • 23 - Christian Vieri 1997-2005 & Francesco Graziani 1975-83 • 22 - Alessandro Mazzola 1963-74 • 20 - Paolo Rossi 1977-86 • 19 - Roberto Bettega 1975-83

Coaches
For Italy coaches pre 1960 see Oliver's Almanack 2012 • Giuseppe Viani 1960 • Giovanni Ferrari 1960-61 • Giovanni Ferrari & Paolo Mazza 1962 • Edmondo Fabbri 1962-66 • Helenio Herrera & Ferruccio Valcareggi 1966-67 • Ferruccio Valcareggi 1967-74 • Fulvio Bernardini 1974-75 • Fulvio Bernardini & Enzo Bearzot 1975-77 • Enzo Bearzot 1977-86 • Azeglio Vicini 1986-91 • Arrigo Sacchi 1991-96 • Cesare Maldini 1997-98 • Dino Zoff 1998-2000 • Giovanni Trapattoni 2000-04 • Marcello Lippi 2004-06 • Roberto Donadoni 2006-08 • Marcello Lippi 2008-10 • Cesare Prandelli 2010-

ITALY 2011-12

SERIE A

	Pl	W	D	L	F	A	Pts
Juventus †	38	23	15	0	68	20	84
Milan †	38	24	8	6	74	33	80
Udinese †	38	18	10	10	52	35	64
Lazio ‡	38	18	8	12	56	47	62
Napoli ‡	38	16	13	9	66	46	61
Internazionale ‡	38	17	7	14	58	55	58
Roma	38	16	8	14	60	54	56
Parma	38	15	11	12	54	53	56
Bologna	38	13	12	13	41	43	51
Chievo Verona	38	12	13	13	35	45	49
Catania	38	11	15	12	47	52	48
Atalanta §6	38	13	13	12	41	43	46
Fiorentina	38	11	13	14	37	43	46
Siena	38	11	11	16	45	45	44
Cagliari	38	10	13	15	37	46	43
Palermo	38	11	10	17	52	62	43
Genoa	38	11	9	18	50	69	42
Lecce	38	8	12	18	40	56	36
Novara	38	7	11	20	35	65	32
Cesena	38	4	10	24	24	60	22

9/09/2011 - 13/05/2012 • † Qualified for the UEFA Champions League • ‡ Qualified for the UEFA Europa League • Attendance: 8,547,308 @ 22,493
§ Points deducted • Lecce relegated to the Lega Pro Prima Divisione
Top scorers: 28 - Zlatan **IBRAHIMOVIC** SWE, Milan • 24 - Diego **MILITO** ARG, Inter • 23 - Edinson **CAVANI** URU, Napoli & Antonio **DI NATALE**, Udinese • 19 - Rodrigo **PALACIO** ARG, Genoa • 16 - German **DENIS** ARG, Atalanta & Fabrizio **MICCOLI**, Palermo • 15 - Sebastian **GIOVINCO**, Parma
• 14 - Stevan **JOVETIC** MNE, Fiorentina • 12 - Miroslav **KLOSE** GER, Lazio & Mattia **DESTRO**, Siena

ITALY 2011-12

SERIE B (2)

	Pl	W	D	L	F	A	Pts
Pescara	42	26	5	11	90	55	83
Torino	42	24	11	7	57	28	83
Sassuolo ‡	42	22	14	6	57	33	80
Verona ‡	42	23	9	10	60	41	78
Varese ‡	42	20	11	11	57	41	71
Sampdoria ‡	42	17	16	9	53	34	67
Padova	42	18	9	15	56	58	63
Brescia	42	15	12	15	48	50	57
Juve Stabia §4	42	16	13	13	53	49	57
Reggina	42	14	13	15	63	59	55
Crotone §2	42	13	15	14	60	58	52
Modena	42	12	16	14	50	58	52
Bari §6	42	14	14	14	47	48	50
Grosseto	42	11	16	15	47	60	49
Ascoli §7	42	15	11	16	47	50	49
Cittadella	42	13	9	20	51	64	48
Livorno	42	12	12	18	49	49	48
Empoli ‡	42	12	11	19	48	59	47
Vicenza ‡	42	10	14	18	43	61	44
Nocerina	42	10	10	22	52	71	40
Gubbio	42	7	11	24	37	69	32
Albinoleffe	42	6	12	24	39	69	30

25/08/2011 - 26/05/2012 • ‡ = promotion/relegation play-off • § = points deducted • Att: 2 848 760 @ 6166
Top scorer: **28** - Ciro **IMMOBILE**, Pescara
Play-off semis: **Sampdoria** 2-1 1-1 Sassuolo; **Varese** 2-0 1-1 Verona • Play-off final: **Sampdoria** 3-2 1-0 Varese • Sampdoria promoted
Relegation play-off: Vicenza 0-0 2-3 **Empoli** • Vicenza avoided relegation due to the demotion of Lecce to the Lega Pro Prima Divisione

ITALY 2011-12

LEGA PRO PRIMA DIVISIONE GROUP A (3)

	Pl	W	D	L	F	A	Pts	Ternana	Taranto	Carpi	Sorrento	Pro Vercelli	Benevento	Pisa	Lumezzane	Reggiana	Avellino	Foggia	Tritium	Como	Viareggio	SPAL	Pavia	Monza	Foligno
Ternana	34	17	14	3	40	19	65		1-1	2-1	0-0	1-0	2-0	1-0	1-0	2-0	2-1	1-1	2-0	2-1	1-0	0-1	2-2	1-1	2-1
Taranto ‡ §7 R¹	34	19	13	2	41	16	63	0-1		1-1	1-0	0-0	1-1	0-0	1-0	1-0	2-0	2-1	2-0	3-1	2-0	1-0	2-1	2-1	1-0
Carpi ‡	34	17	10	7	46	26	61	1-1	0-2		1-0	2-1	1-1	2-2	3-0	3-1	0-0	3-2	4-0	1-0	3-0	1-0	2-1	2-0	1-0
Sorrento ‡ §2	34	16	12	6	43	26	58	0-0	0-0			2-1	2-0	1-1	1-2	2-1	2-0	2-0	2-0	2-0	2-0	1-1	2-2	0-0	1-0
Pro Vercelli ‡	34	15	12	7	40	19	57	0-0	0-0	0-0	0-0		4-0		3-0	0-0	1-0	2-0	4-1	0-0	2-0	2-0	1-0	0-1	1-1	0-1
Benevento §2	34	17	7	10	46	34	56	0-2	2-1	0-1	1-0	1-1		2-0	3-0	2-2	2-2	0-1	1-0	1-0	5-1	2-0	2-0	1-0	1-0
Pisa	34	11	13	10	37	35	46	1-1	2-2	2-1	2-2	1-4	2-0		0-2	2-1	3-0	1-1	0-2	1-0	2-0	1-2	1-0	2-2	1-0
Lumezzane	34	12	7	15	28	35	43	0-0	0-3	1-1	0-1	0-1	0-2	1-1		1-0	2-1	2-0	1-0	2-2	1-0	0-0	1-2	0-0	3-0
Reggiana §2	34	12	7	15	36	42	41	0-2	0-1	1-1	1-1	1-1	0-2	1-1	0-1		1-0	0-2	3-1	2-4	1-1	3-0	2-1	1-2	2-1
Avellino	34	11	7	16	39	46	40	1-3	1-2	1-0	0-1	2-1	1-1	1-0	2-1	2-0		4-0	1-2	3-3	2-0	2-1	1-1	1-2	2-0
Foggia §4 R¹	34	11	9	14	33	38	38	3-1	0-1	1-2	1-1	1-1	1-2	1-0	1-0	0-2	1-1		0-1	1-2	1-1	1-0	1-2	1-0	2-0
Tritium	34	9	10	15	26	40	37	2-0	1-1	0-1	0-0	1-2	2-1	0-0	0-0	0-1	1-0	1-1		1-1	0-2	1-1	1-1	1-3	0-1
Como §3	34	10	9	15	39	47	36	0-0	1-1	1-0	2-2	1-0	2-1	1-2	2-1	1-2	1-0	0-0	1-2		1-2	0-2	2-1	0-1	2-2
Viareggio ‡	34	10	6	18	31	47	36	0-3	0-0	0-3	2-2	0-1	2-1	2-0	4-0	2-1	0-1	0-2	0-1	1-2		2-0	1-3	1-1	1-0
SPAL ‡ §8	34	11	9	14	32	36	34	0-0	0-0	2-2	0-1	1-1	0-2	1-1	0-2	0-1	3-1	1-2	2-1	2-1	1-0		4-0	0-0	3-2
Pavia ‡	34	7	12	15	37	50	33	0-0	0-2	0-0	0-2	1-2	1-2	1-1	0-2	1-1	2-3	0-2	2-2	2-1	1-2	1-0		0-0	3-0
Monza ‡	34	7	12	15	27	42	33	0-2	0-0	0-1	0-3	0-1	1-2	0-2	0-1	0-2	1-1	2-1	1-1	1-1	0-3	3-1	2-2		2-1
Foligno §4	34	6	7	21	24	47	21	1-1	1-2	1-0	2-1	0-0	2-2	0-2	1-2	1-1	1-0	0-1	1-0	1-2	1-1	0-1	2-2	1-0	

4/09/2011 - 6/05/2012 • ‡ Entered play-offs • § Points deducted • R¹ Relegated due to bankruptcy, financial or match fixing issues
Promotion play-off semi-finals: **Pro Vercelli** 2-1 0-0 Taranto; Sorrento 0-1 1-0 **Carpi** (Carpi qualified on higher league position)
Promotion play-off final: **Pro Vercelli** 0-0 3-1 Carpi • Pro Vercelli promoted
Relegation play-offs: Monza 0-1 1-4 **Viareggio**; **Pavia** 0-0 2-0 SPAL • SPAL and Monza relegated

LEGA PRO CHAMPIONSHIP

Ternana 0-0 1-2 **Spezia**

Spezia are Lega Pro Prima Divisione Champions

ITALY 2011-12

LEGA PRO PRIMA DIVISIONE GROUP B (3)

	Pl	W	D	L	F	A	Pts	Spezia	Trapani	Siracusa	Virtus L'ciano	Cremonese	Barletta	Südtirol	Carrarese	Frosinone	Portogruaro	Pergocrema	Andria BAT	FeralpiSalò	Prato	Triestina	Latina	Piacenza	Bassano V'tus
Spezia	34	17	11	6	48	29	62		2-0	1-1	1-0	0-0	1-1	2-1	1-1	2-1	0-2	2-0	0-0	3-0	1-0	1-1	3-0	3-0	3-0
Trapani ‡	34	17	9	8	57	42	60	1-0		1-2	1-3	0-0	1-1	1-0	1-0	2-2	1-5	0-0	1-1	2-0	2-1	3-2	2-0	3-0	3-3
Siracusa ‡ §5 R¹	34	18	9	7	46	31	58	3-1	3-1		1-0	0-0	2-0	1-3	3-1	1-0	1-0	1-2	2-0	1-0	3-0	2-0	0-0	3-0	2-2
Virtus Lanciano ‡	34	15	9	10	40	35	54	0-0	0-0	1-1		2-1	2-1	1-1	0-0	0-1	0-0	2-1	1-2	0-3	2-1	2-1	1-2	1-0
Cremonese ‡ §6	34	15	10	9	47	30	49	3-2	2-4	3-1	2-0		2-2	1-1	1-0	0-0	0-1	0-0	2-1	1-1	1-0	0-0	1-1	2-0	0-1	4-2
Barletta §1	34	12	13	9	43	38	48	0-1	0-2	3-2	2-2	1-0		1-1	2-0	1-0	1-1	2-0	2-2	0-1	3-1	1-1	1-1	2-1	1-0
Südtirol	34	11	13	10	39	34	46	1-2	1-1	0-0	1-0	2-0	3-2		1-1	1-0	2-0	0-1	1-1	2-0	2-2	1-1	2-0	1-2	0-0
Carrarese	34	11	12	11	43	39	45	2-1	3-0	1-1	1-3	2-1	0-0	1-1		0-1	2-0	4-1	3-1	0-0	0-0	3-0	2-0	2-2	1-0
Frosinone	34	13	6	15	40	41	45	3-2	1-2	0-1	2-1	0-1	2-1	1-2	1-0		2-1	5-1	1-0	1-1	3-1	2-1	1-1	2-0	1-2
Portogruaro	34	10	12	12	41	45	42	1-1	2-2	0-1	2-3	0-4	1-1	1-0	3-1	1-0		0-1	1-1	0-0	2-2	3-1	1-1	2-2	1-1
Pergocrema §5 R¹	34	12	9	13	33	46	40	1-2	0-5	2-0	0-2	1-3	0-2	2-1	2-2	3-0	1-4		0-0	1-0	0-0	0-0	1-1	0-2	2-0
Andria BAT	34	9	13	12	33	37	38	1-2	0-5	1-2	0-1	1-1	2-0	2-2	5-0	1-2		1-1		1-0	2-1	1-0	0-1	1-0	1-1
FeralpiSalò	34	9	11	14	26	37	38	1-1	1-2	1-2	1-1	1-0	1-0	0-0	2-2	0-2	0-3	0-0		0-1	2-0	2-1	0-1	0-0
Prato ‡	34	8	11	15	36	44	35	2-2	1-2	0-1	0-1	0-0	1-2	2-3	1-1	1-0	1-1	2-0	2-1	2-3		5-0	2-1	0-3	0-2
Triestina ‡	34	9	8	17	43	55	35	1-2	2-1	4-0	3-0	1-0	1-2	1-2	2-3	1-2	1-0	3-2	1-1	1-0	0-2		2-2	1-3	2-2
Latina ‡	34	8	11	15	37	45	35	1-2	3-0	1-1	1-3	1-1	1-1	2-1	1-0	2-0	4-1	1-2	5-2	0-1	0-1	0-2		2-2	0-1
Piacenza ‡ §9	34	10	13	11	41	49	34	0-1	0-1	1-1	3-1	1-3	2-2	0-0	0-3	1-1	0-0	0-0	0-0	2-2	4-3	0-3	1-1		3-2
Bassano Virtus	34	7	11	16	29	48	32	0-0	0-7	1-2	0-1	1-3	0-1	0-0	1-0	2-1	1-0	0-1	0-2	1-2	0-0	2-0	0-1	2-2	

4/09/2011 - 6/05/2012 • ‡ Entered play-offs • § Points deducted • R¹ Relegated due to bankruptcy, financial or match fixing issues
Promotion play-off semi-finals: Cremonese 1-1 1-1 **Trapani** (Trapani qualified on higher league position); **Virtus Lanciano** 1-0 2-2 Siracusa
Promotion play-off final: **Virtus Lanciano** 1-1 3-1 Trapani • Virtus Lanciano promoted
Relegation play-offs: Piacenza 1-0 0-1 **Prato** (Trapani won on higher league position); **Latina** 2-0 2-2 Triestina • Piacenza and Triestina relegated

ITALY 2011-12

LEGA PRO SECONDA DIVISIONE GROUP A (4)

	Pl	W	D	L	F	A	Pts
Treviso §2	38	19	12	7	59	33	67
San Marino	38	19	9	10	65	41	66
Cuneo ‡	38	19	8	11	60	47	65
Casale ‡	38	17	11	10	50	32	62
Virtus Entella ‡	38	17	10	11	61	37	61
Rimini ‡	38	17	10	11	43	40	61
Pro Patria §11	38	19	14	5	58	36	60
Santarcangelo	38	16	6	16	46	42	54
Poggibonsi	38	15	9	14	50	49	54
Borgo a Buggiano	38	14	9	15	46	46	51
Alessandria §3	38	13	13	12	45	45	49
Renate	38	11	15	12	40	44	48
Savona §7	38	13	14	11	47	41	463
Bellaria Igea	38	10	15	13	39	45	45
Giacomense	38	10	15	13	46	53	45
Mantova ‡	38	10	14	14	44	49	44
Lecco ‡	38	9	10	19	34	66	37
Montichiari §5	38	9	13	16	48	59	35
Sambonifacese	38	6	8	24	37	80	26
Valenzana	38	5	9	24	28	63	24

4/09/2011 - 6/05/2012 • ‡ Entered play-offs • § Points deducted
Promotion play-off semi-finals: Rimini 0-0 0-1 **Cuneo**; **Virtus Entella** 3-2 2-2 Casale
Final: Virtus Entella 1-1 2-5 **Cunea** • Cunea and Virtus Entella promoted
Relegation play-offs: Lecco 1-1 1-2 **Mantova** • Lecco relegated. Mantova play-off against Vibonse. Vibonese 0-0 0-4 **Mantova**. Vibonese relegated

ITALY 2011-12

LEGA PRO SECONDA DIVISIONE GROUP B (4)

	Pl	W	D	L	F	A	Pts
Perugia	40	26	9	5	65	29	87
Catanzaro	40	23	14	3	66	29	83
Vigor Lamezia ‡	40	23	11	6	57	27	80
Chieti ‡	40	20	9	11	55	38	69
Aprilia ‡	40	18	11	11	60	44	65
Paganese ‡	40	17	14	9	47	37	65
Gavorrano	40	16	14	10	69	54	62
L'Aquila	40	15	15	10	38	31	60
Arzanese	40	14	13	13	50	55	55
Fano §4	40	16	10	14	48	48	54
Aversa Normanna §1	40	12	12	16	31	37	47
Fondi	40	11	12	17	41	49	45
Campobasso §1	40	11	12	17	38	47	44
Giulianova §2 R[1]	40	12	10	18	39	51	44
Milazzo	40	9	17	14	44	46	44
Melfi §3	40	11	13	16	46	50	43
Vibonese §1 ‡	40	9	15	16	41	51	41
Neapolis Mugnano §2 ‡	40	10	12	18	42	59	40
Isola Liri §2	40	8	10	22	39	62	32
Ebolitana §3	40	7	13	20	34	62	31
Celano	40	7	4	29	31	75	25

4/09/2011 - 6/05/2012 • ‡ Entered play-offs • § Points deducted • R[1] Relegated due to bankruptcy, financial or match fixing issues
Promotion play-off semi-finals: **Paganese** 1-0 1-0 Vigor Lamezia; Aprilia 2-2 1-1 **Chieti**
Final: **Paganese** 2-0 0-0 Chieti • Paganese promoted
Relegation play-offs: Neapolis Mugnano 0-1 0-2 Vibonese. Neapolis relegated. Vibonese play-off against Mantova (see group A) • Vibonese relegated

MEDALS TABLE

		Overall			League			Cup			Europe			City
		G	S	B	G	S	B	G	S	B	G	S	B	
1	Juventus	43	33	19	28	20	13	9	5		6	8	6	Turin
2	Milan	32	25	22	18	14	18	5	6		9	5	4	Milan
3	Internazionale	31	23	22	18	14	14	7	6		6	3	8	Milan
4	Torino	13	17	7	8	9	6	5	7			1	1	Turin
5	Roma	13	20	7	3	11	5	9	7		1	2	2	Rome
6	Genoa 1893	10	5	2	9	4	1	1	1				1	Genoa
7	Fiorentina	9	11	7	2	5	5	6	3		1	3	2	Florence
8	Bologna	9	4	5	7	4	3	2					2	Bologna
9	Lazio	8	8	5	2	6	4	5	1		1	1	1	Rome
10	Napoli	7	8	8	2	4	7	4	4		1		1	Naples
11	Pro Vercelli	7	1		7	1								Vercelli
12	Sampdoria	6	6	4	1	1	3	4	3		1	2	1	Genoa
13	Parma	6	4	3		1	2	3	2		3	1	1	Parma
14	Hellas-Verona	1	3		1				3					Verona
15	Atalanta	1	2	1				1	2				1	Bergamo
	Venezia	1	2	1				1	1		1	1		Venice
	Vicenza	1	2	1		2		1					1	Vicenza
18	Cagliari	1	1	1	1	1							1	Cagliari
19	Casale	1			1									Casale Monferrato
	Novese	1			1									Novi Ligure
	Vado	1						1						Vado Ligure
22	Palermo		3						3					Palermo
23	Udinese		2	2		1	2		1					Udine
24	US Milanese		2	1		2	1							Milan
25	Alba		2			2								Rome
	Livorno		2			2								Livorno
27	Alessandria		1	1			1		1					Alessandria
	Padova		1	1			1		1					Padua
29	Ancona		1						1					Ancona
	Catanzaro		1						1					Catanzaro
	Fortitudo		1			1								Rome
	Novara		1						1					Novarra
	Perugia		1			1								Perugia
	Pisa		1			1								Pisa
	Savoia		1			1								Torre Annunziata
	SPAL Ferrara		1						1					Ferrara
37	Modena			1			1							Modena

COPPA ITALIA 2011-12

Third Round			Fourth Round			Round of 16		
						Napoli *	2	
						Cesena	1	
Gubbio *	4							
Atalanta	3		Gubbio	0				
Ascoli *	0		**Cesena** *	3				
Cesena	1							
Genoa *	4							
Nocerina	3		**Genoa** *	3				
Avellino	0		Bari	2				
Bari *	4					Genoa	1	
						Internazionale *	2	
						Chievo Verona	2	
						Udinese *	1	
Modena *	2							
Reggina	1		Modena	0				
Livorno	0		**Chievo Verona** *	3				
Chievo Verona *	1							
Siena *	1							
Torino	0		**Siena**	2				
Albinoleffe	1		Cagliari *	1				
Cagliari *	5					Palermo *	4 0p	
						Siena	4 3p	
						Milan *	2	
						Novara	1	
Catania *	2							
Brescia	1		Catania *	2				
Triestina	0		**Novara**	3				
Novara *	4							
Verona	3 4p							
Sassuolo *	3 2p		**Verona**	2				
Grosseto	1		Parma *	0				
Parma *	4					Verona	2	
						Lazio *	3	
						Roma *	3	
						Fiorentina	0	
Empoli *	2							
Sampdoria	1		Empoli	1				
Cittadella	1		**Fiorentina** *	2				
Fiorentina *	2							
Bologna *	2							
Padova	1		**Bologna** *	4				
Lecce *	0		Crotone	2				
Crotone	2					Bologna	1	
						Juventus *	2	

Clubs playing in Europe enter in the round of 16

COPPA ITALIA 2011-12

Quarter-finals — Semi-finals — Final

Napoli *	2
Internazionale	0

Napoli	1 2
Siena *	2 0

Chievo Verona *	0
Siena	1

Napoli ‡	2
Juventus	0

Milan *	3
Lazio	1

Milan *	1 2
Juventus	2 2

Roma	0
Juventus *	3

‡ Qualified for the UEFA Europa League
* Home team/Home team in the first leg

COPPA ITALIA FINAL 2012

Stadio Olimpico, Rome, 20-05-2012, Att: 70 000, Ref: Christian Brighi

Napoli	2	Cavani [62p], Hamsik [83]
Juventus	0	

NAPOLI
Morgan **DE SANCTIS**• - Salvatore **ARONICA**, Hugo **CAMPAGNARO**, Paolo **CANNAVARO** (c)•, Juan Camilo **ZUNIGA** - Blerim **DZEMAILI**• - Christian **MAGGIO**, Gokhan **INLER**, Ezequiel **LAVEZZI** (Goran **PANDEV** 73) - Marek **HAMSIK** (Andrea **DOSSENA** 86), Edinson **CAVANI** (Miguel **BRITOS** 93+). Tr: Walter **MAZZARRI**

JUVENTUS
Marco **STORARI**• - Stephan **LICHTSTEINER** (Mirko **VUCINIC** 68), Andrea **BARZAGLI**, Leonardo **BONUCCI**, Martin **CACERES** - Claudio **MARCHISIO**• - Andrea **PIRLO**, Marcelo **ESTIGARRIBIA** - Arturo **VIDAL** - Alessandro **DEL PIERO** (c) (Simone **PEPE** 68), Marco **BORRIELLO**• (Fabio **QUAGLIARELLA** 72♦**90**). Tr: Antonio **CONTE**

ATALANTA
2011–12

Ag	21	Gubbio	L 3-4	ICr3	Moralez [30], Tiribocchi [40], Gabbiadini [78]	3 556
Sep	11	Genoa	D 2-2	SA 20	Moralez 2 [8 43]	19 917
	18	Palermo	W 1-0	SA 20	Denis [34]	12 368
	21	Lecce	W 2-1	SA 17	Denis 2 [3p 56]	8 090
	25	Novara	W 2-1	SA 14	Schelotto [34], Cigarini [59]	13 910
Oct	1	Roma	L 1-3	SA 16	Denis [48]	36 200
	16	Udinese	D 0-0	SA 15		14 444
	23	Parma	W 2-1	SA 15	Moralez 2 [55 58]	13 003
	26	Inter	D 1-1	SA 12	Denis [44]	19 613
	30	Bologna	L 1-3	SA 15	Denis [7]	17 870
Nov	6	Cagliari	W 1-0	SA 12	Denis [80]	11 604
	20	Siena	D 2-2	SA 13	Denis 2 [15p 53]	8 526
	26	Napoli	D 1-1	SA 13	Denis [64]	17 827
	4	Chievo	D 0-0	SA 13		8 000
Dec	11	Catania	D 1-1	SA 13	Tiribocchi [71]	13 716
	17	Fiorentina	D 2-2	SA 14	Masiello [81], Denis [86]	15 812
	21	Cesena	W 4-1	SA 11	Denis [17p], Marilungo 2 [18 44], Peluso [71]	16 081
Jan	8	Milan	L 0-2	SA 13		22 172
	15	Lazio	L 0-2	SA 15		27 438
	21	Juventus	L 0-2	SA 15		22 335
	29	Cesena	W 1-0	SA 13	OG [76]	15 315
Feb	5	Palermo	L 1-2	SA 14	Moralez [56]	15 302
	12	Lecce	D 0-0	SA 15		11 877
	15	Genoa	W 1-0	SA 13	Marilungo [78]	16 000
	19	Novara	D 0-0	SA 13		9 000
	26	Roma	W 4-1	SA 11	Marilungo [10], Denis 3 [19 47 66]	16 000
Mar	4	Udinese	D 0-0	SA 11		16 000
	11	Parma	D 1-1	SA 12	Manfredini [5]	14 210
	18	Inter	D 0-0	SA 12		38 610
	25	Bologna	W 2-0	SA 9	Gabbiadini [50], Tiribocchi [90]	13 600
Apr	1	Cagliari	L 0-2	SA 11		10 000
	7	Siena	L 1-2	SA 13	Schelotto [9]	15 000
	11	Napoli	W 3-1	SA 12	Bonaventura [10], Bellini [58], Carmona [68]	35 519
	21	Catania	L 0-2	SA 14		14 446
	24	Chievo	W 1-0	SA 11	Moralez [72]	15 045
	29	Fiorentina	W 2-0	SA 10	Denis [11], Bonaventura [51]	14 714
May	2	Milan	L 0-2	SA 11		38 204
	6	Lazio	L 0-2	SA 11		16 293
	13	Juventus	L 1-3	SA 12	OG [83]	40 944

12th Att: 297 309 • Av: 15 648 (-15.1%) • At.Azzurri d'Italia 26 393 (59%)

ATALANTA LEAGUE APPEARANCES/GOALS 2011-12
Goalkeepers Andrea Consigli 35 • Giorgio Frezzolini 2+2 • Ciro Polito 1
Defenders Gianpaolo Bellini 12+8/1 • Daniele Capelli 9+2/0
Michele Ferri 8+5/0 • Stefano Lucchini 24+2/0
Thomas Manfredini 25+1/1 • Andrea Masiello 17/1
Federico Peluso 33/1 • Guglielmo Stendardo 15+1/0
Midfield Adriano BRA 1+6/0 • Giacomo Bonaventura 20+9/2
Matteo Brighi 8+3/0 • Carlos Carmona CHI 24+4/1
Alessandro Carrozza 3+9/0 • Fabio Caserta 0+1/0
Riccardo Cazzola 5+7/0 • Luca Cigarini 30+2/1 • Nadir Minotti 0+3/0
Maximiliano Moralez ARG 31+3/6 • Massimo Mutarelli 0+1/0
Simone Padoin 18+1/0 • Leonardo Pettinari 0+1/0
Cristian Raimondi 10+3/0 • Ezequiel Schelotto 33+4/2
Forwards German Denis ARG 32+1/16 • Manolo Gabbiadini 8+15/1
Guido Marilungo 9+9/4 • Simone Tiribocchi 5+8/2
Coach Stefano Colantuono

BOLOGNA
2011–12

Ag	21	Padova	W 2-1	ICr3	Portanova [68], Della Rocca [94+]	7 308
	11	Fiorentina	L 0-2	SA 17		20 040
Sep	18	Lecce	L 0-2	SA 19		15 353
	21	Juventus	D 1-1	SA 19	Portanova [52]	35 679
	24	Inter	L 1-3	SA 19	Diamanti [66p]	22 473
	2	Udinese	L 0-2	SA 20		16 338
Oct	16	Novara	W 2-0	SA 18	Ramirez [45], Acquafresca [64]	10 033
	23	Lazio	L 0-2	SA 18		17 851
	26	Chievo	W 1-0	SA 17	Acquafresca [53]	8 300
	30	Atalanta	W 3-1	SA 14	Di Vaio [45p], Ramirez [48], Loria [68]	17 870
Nov	5	Palermo	L 1-3	SA 16	Ramirez [87]	18 507
	20	Cesena	L 0-1	SA 17		20 397
	23	Crotone	W 4-2	ICr4	Diamanti [11p], Gimenez [48], Vantaggiato [48], Paponi [65]	1 432
Dec	27	Cagliari	D 1-1	SA 17	Di Vaio [75]	8 000
	4	Siena	W 1-0	SA 17	Di Vaio [28]	18 316
	8	Juventus	L 1-2	ICr5	Raggi [94+]	25 000
	11	Milan	D 2-2	SA 16	Di Vaio [11], Diamanti [73]	25 736
	18	Genoa	L 1-2	SA 16	Ramirez [51]	19 278
	2	Roma	L 0-2	SA 17		17 855
Jan	8	Catania	W 2-0	SA 17	Cherubin [50], Di Vaio [90]	14 572
	16	Napoli	D 1-1	SA 16	Acquafresca [14]	42 956
	22	Parma	D 0-0	SA 16		15 141
	29	Roma	D 1-1	SA 16	Di Vaio [57]	34 073
Feb	5	Lecce	D 0-0	SA 16		5 962
	17	Inter	W 3-0	SA 16	Di Vaio 2 [37 38], Acquafresca [85]	20 043
	21	Fiorentina	W 2-0	SA	Diamanti [30], Ramirez [43]	19 000
	26	Udinese	L 1-3	SA 15	Kone [81]	16 209
Mar	4	Novara	W 1-0	SA	Acquafresca [83]	19 000
	7	Juventus	D 1-1	SA 13	Di Vaio [17]	19 000
	11	Lazio	W 3-1	SA 9	Portanova [11], Diamanti [28], Krhin [69]	25 000
	18	Chievo	D 2-2	SA 9	Di Vaio [59], Diamanti [81]	17 446
	25	Atalanta	L 0-2	SA 10		13 600
Apr	1	Palermo	L 1-3	SA 13	Sorensen [50]	19 440
	7	Cesena	D 0-0	SA 14		16 497
	15	Cagliari	W 1-0	SA 12	Diamanti [54]	15 124
	22	Milan	L 0-2	SA 12	Ramirez [26]	51 725
	25	Siena	D 1-1	SA 13	Diamanti [69]	10 000
May	29	Genoa	W 3-2	SA 11	Portanova [24], Ramirez [38], Garics [67]	23 510
	2	Catania	W 1-0	SA 9	Ramirez [79]	14 000
	6	Napoli	W 2-0	SA 9	Diamanti [17], Rubin [64]	26 647
	13	Parma	L 0-1	SA 9		16 922

9th Att: 360 940 • Av: 18 997 (-4.4%) • Renato Dall'Ara 39 444 (48%)

BOLOGNA LEAGUE APPEARANCES/GOALS 2011-12
Goalkeepers Federico Agliardi 9+1 • Jean-Francois Gillet BEL 29
Defenders Mikael Antonsson SWE 22+2/0 • Nicolo Cherubin 14+7/1
Crespo ESP 3+4/0 • Gyorgy Garics AUT 12+6/1 • Simone Loria 7+2/1
Archimede Morleo 25+4/0 • Daniele Portanova 34/3
Andrea Raggi 31/0 • Matteo Rubin 9+1/1 • Frederik Sorensen 1+1/1
Midfield Federico Casarini 8+3/0 • Panagiotis Kone GRE 18+13/1
Rene Krhin SVN 4+3/1 • Gaby Mudingayi BEL 33+1/0
Diego Perez URU 27+1/0 • Nico Pulzetti 16+9/0
Gaston Ramirez URU 28+5/8 • Saphir Sliti Taider FRA 9+5/0
Forwards Robert Acquafresca 17+15/5 • Ishak Belfodil ALG 1+7/0
Alessandro Diamanti 27+3/8 • Marco Di Vaio 32+5/10
Henry Gimenez URU 2+12/0 • Daniele Paponi 0+1/0
Daniele Vantaggiato 0+2/0
Coach Pierpaolo Bisoli (26/05/2011) • Stefano Pioli ((4/10/2011)

KEY
SC = Supercoppa (played in Beijing) • SA =
Serie A • IC = Coppa Italia • CL = UEFA
Champions League • EL = Europa League
See page 13 for further explanations

CAGLIARI
2011–12

Ag	21	AlbinoLeffe	W 5-1	ICr3	Nene [36p], Larrivey 3 [40 51 69], Conti [50]	10 000
Sep	11	Roma	W 2-1	SA 6	Conti [68], El Kabir [90]	45 000
	17	Novara	W 2-1	SA 4	Thiago Ribeiro [38], Larrivey [86]	10 050

CAGLIARI 2011-12 (CONT'D)

Ag	21	AlbinoLeffe	W 5-1	ICr3	Nene [36p], Larrivey 3 [40 51 69], Conti [50]		10 000
	11	Roma	W 2-1	SA	6	Conti [68], El Kabir [90]	45 000
	17	Novara	W 2-1	SA	4	Thiago Ribeiro [38], Larrivey [86]	10 050
Sep	21	Palermo	L 2-3	SA	7	Conti [84], Nainggolan [90]	18 965
	25	Udinese	D 0-0	SA	8		10 000
	2	Lecce	W 2-0	SA	5	Thiago Ribeiro [10], Biondini [40]	2 892
	16	Siena	D 0-0	SA	3		11 000
Oct	23	Napoli	D 0-0	SA	4		11 000
	26	Cesena	D 1-1	SA	6	Nene [20p]	14 482
	30	Lazio	L 0-3	SA	8		12 500
	6	Atalanta	L 0-1	SA	10		11 604
	19	Inter	L 1-2	SA	15	Larrivey [88]	45 289
Nov	24	Siena	L 1-2	ICr4		Rui Sampaio [84]	2 000
	27	Bologna	D 1-1	SA	14	Conti [81p]	8 000
	4	Catania	W 1-0	SA	7	Ibarbo [85]	14 818
Dec	11	Parma	D 0-0	SA	9		7 100
	17	Chievo	L 0-2	SA	12		7 000
	20	Milan	L 0-2	SA	15		20 000
	8	Genoa	W 3-0	SA	10	Larrivey [13p], Ibarbo [56], OG [72]	6 000
	15	Juventus	D 1-1	SA	13	Cossu [48]	38 293
Jan	22	Fiorentina	D 0-0	SA	11		6 000
	29	Milan	L 0-3	SA	14		40 242
	1	Roma	W 4-2	SA	12	Thiago Ribeiro 2 [7 49], Pinilla [41], Ekdal [90]	9 500
Feb	5	Novara	D 0-0	SA	11		8 952
	11	Palermo	W 2-1	SA	9	Pinilla [56], Dessena [81]	6 000
	19	Udinese	D 0-0	SA	9		13 000
	26	Lecce	L 1-2	SA	12	Larrivey [50p]	6 000
	4	Siena	L 0-3	SA	15		8 529
	9	Napoli	L 1-3	SA	17	Larrivey 3 [38 77 90]	40 022
Mar	18	Cesena	W 3-0	SA	14	Pinilla 3 [14 45p 56p]	9 500
	25	Lazio	L 0-1	SA	13		29 290
	1	Atalanta	W 2-0	SA	12	Conti [11], Pinilla [55]	10 000
	7	Inter	D 2-2	SA	12	Astori [5], Pinilla [61]	19 000
Apr	11	Bologna	L 0-1	SA	14		15 124
	21	Parma	L 0-3	SA	16		14 271
	24	Catania	W 3-0	SA	15	Thiago Ribeiro [21], Pinilla [79], Ibarbo [90]	8 000
	28	Chievo	D 0-0	SA	15		9 500
May	2	Genoa	L 1-2	SA	15	Ariaudo [13]	BCD
	6	Juventus	L 0-2	SA	16		9 500
	13	Fiorentina	D 0-0	SA	15		17 787

15th Att: 188 650 • Av: 9929 (-19.8%) • Sant'Elia 23 486 (42%)

CAGLIARI LEAGUE APPEARANCES/GOALS 2011-12

Goalkeepers Michael Agazzi 36 • Vlada Avramov SRB 2+1
Defenders Alessandro Agostini 35/0 • Lorenzo Ariaudo 16+8/1
Davide Astori 28/1 • Michele Canini 34/0
Sebastian Eriksson SWE 0+1/0 • Simone Gozzi 0+2/0
Nicola Murru 0+2/0 • Gabriele Perico 5+10/0 • Francesco Pisano 34/0
Midfield Davide Biondini 13+2/1 • Paolo Ceppelini URU 1+4/0
Daniele Conti 30+2/4 • Andrea Cossu 31+1/1 • Daniele Dessena 12/1
Albin Ekdal SWE 23+7/1 • Segundo Ibarbo COL 14+24/3
Radja Nainggolan BEL 37/1 • Rui Sampaio POR 0+6/0
Forwards Moestafa El Kabir NED 1+6/1
Joaquin Larrivey ARG 13+14/7 • Nene BRA 11+7/1
Mauricio Pinilla CHI 14/8 • Thiago Ribeiro BRA 28+7/5
Coach Massimo Ficcadenti (16/08/2011) • Davide Ballardini (9/11/2011) • Massimo Ficcadenti (11/03/2012)

CATANIA 2011-12

Ag	21	Brescia	W 2-1	ICr3		Maxi Lopez [38], Gomez [91+]	5 000
	11	Siena	D 0-0	SA	12		13 223
Sep	18	Cesena	W 1-0	SA	6	Maxi Lopez [45p]	12 237
	22	Genoa	L 0-3	SA	11		21 649
	25	Juventus	D 1-1	SA	13	Bergessio [21]	20 839

CATANIA 2011-12 (CONT'D)

	2	Novara	D 3-3	SA	11	Legrottaglie [14], Lodi [56], Gomez [90]	10 632
Oct	15	Inter	W 2-1	SA	8	Almiron [47], Lodi [50p]	19 504
	22	Fiorentina	D 2-2	SA	9	Delvecchio [43], Maxi Lopez [82]	18 783
	26	Lazio	D 1-1	SA	10	Bergessio [63]	26 951
	29	Napoli	W 2-1	SA	6	Marchese [25], Bergessio [48]	10 000
	6	Milan	L 0-4	SA	8		44 091
Nov	20	Chievo	L 1-2	SA	12	Almiron [78]	14 248
	6	Lecce	W 1-0	SA	8	Barrientos [90]	5 962
	29	Novara	L 2-3	ICr4		Lanzafame [3], Maxi Lopez [70]	3 500
	4	Cagliari	L 0-1	SA	9		14 818
	11	Atalanta	D 1-1	SA	11	Legrottaglie [18]	13 716
Dec	18	Palermo	W 2-0	SA	9	Lodi [32], Maxi Lopez [61p]	16 471
	21	Parma	D 3-3	SA	8	Almiron [22], Lodi [74p], Catellani [85]	10 800
	8	Bologna	L 0-2	SA	8		14 572
Jan	22	Udinese	L 1-2	SA	10	Lodi [90]	16 064
	28	Parma	D 1-1	SA	14	Bergessio [33]	13 098
	8	Roma	D 1-1	SA	15	Legrottaglie [24]	14 000
	12	Genoa	W 4-0	SA	9	Lodi [6p], Barrientos 2 [49 52], Bergessio [62]	12 606
Feb	2	Juventus	L 1-3	SA	14	Barrientos [4]	31 000
	22	Siena	W 1-0	SA	14	Lodi [23p]	10 000
	26	Novara	W 3-1	SA	10	Bergessio [30], Marchese [47], Gomez [55]	13 250
	4	Inter	D 2-2	SA	8	Gomez [20], Izco [38]	47 000
	7	Cesena	D 0-0	SA	8		14 490
	11	Fiorentina	W 1-0	SA	7	Lodi [58p]	16 308
Mar	18	Lazio	W 1-0	SA	7	Legrottaglie [80]	17 406
	25	Napoli	D 2-2	SA	7	Spolli [75], Lanzafame [85]	51 055
	31	Milan	D 1-1	SA	8	Spolli [57]	20 253
	7	Chievo	L 2-3	SA	10	OG [32], Almiron [85]	7 000
	14	Lecce	L 1-2	SA	8	Bergessio [52]	16 570
Apr	21	Atalanta	W 2-0	SA	8	Gomez [31], Seymour [85]	14 446
	24	Cagliari	L 0-3	SA	8		8 000
	28	Palermo	D 1-1	SA	8	Legrottaglie [25]	18 462
	2	Bologna	L 0-1	SA	10		14 000
May	5	Roma	D 2-2	SA	10	Lodi [58p], Marchese [67]	32 585
	13	Udinese	L 0-2	SA	11		16 359

11th Att: 289 636 • Av: 15 244 (+17%) • Angelo Massimino 23 420 (65%)

CATANIA LEAGUE APPEARANCES/GOALS 2011-12

Goalkeepers Mariano Andujar ARG 16 • Andrea Campagnolo 4
Juan Carrizo ARG 14 • Tomas Kosicky SVK 2+1 • Pietro Terracciano 2
Defenders Pablo Alvarez 7/0 • Giuseppe Bellusci 30+2/0
Luca Calapai 0+1/0 • Ciro Capuano 5+2/0 • Nicola Legrottaglie 31/5
Giovanni Marchese 32+1/3 • Marco Motta 12+1/0
Alessandro Potenza 9/0 • Nicolas Spolli ARG 29+2/2
Wellington Tom BRA 0+1/0
Midfield Sergio Almiron ARG 31+1/4 • Pablo Barrientos ARG 20+5/4
Marco Biagianti 8+6/0 • Gennaro Delvecchio 7+6/1
Alejandro Gomez ARG 33+1/4 • Mariano Izco ARG 25/1
Pablo Ledesma 1+2/0 • Cristian Llama ARG 2+13/0
Francesco Lodi 35+2/9 • Adrian Ricchiuti ARG 9+11/0
Fabio Sciacca 2+5/0 • Felipe Seymour CHI 5+8/1
Forwards Gonzalo Bergessio ARG 30+4/7 • Andrea Catellani 4+17/1
Osariemen Ebagua NGA 0+3/0 • Davide Lanzafame 4+7/1
Maxi Lopez ARG 9+5/3 • David Suazo HON 0+6/0
Coach Vincenzo Montella (9/06/2011)

CESENA 2011-12

Ag	21	Ascoli	W 1-0	ICr3		Bogdani [119]	1 439
	10	Napoli	L 1-3	SA	16	Guana [24]	20 942
	18	Catania	L 0-1	SA	18		12 237
Sep	21	Lazio	L 1-2	SA	20	Mutu [15]	16 347
	24	Milan	L 0-1	SA	20		39 225
	2	Chievo	D 0-0	SA	19		14 875
	16	Fiorentina	D 0-0	SA	20		16 308
Oct	23	Siena	L 0-2	SA	20		8 935
	26	Cagliari	D 1-1	SA	20	Candreva [45p]	14 482
	30	Parma	L 0-2	SA	20		12 480

CESENA 2011-12 (CONT'D)

	6 Lecce	L	0-1	SA	20	15 182
	20 Bologna	W	1-0	SA	20 Parolo [84]	20 397
Nov	27 Genoa	W	2-0	SA	19 Mutu 2 [70p 80]	15 977
	30 Gubbio	W	3-0	ICr4	Bogdani [11p], Benalouane [68], Candreva [90]	1 704
	4 Juventus	L	0-2	SA	19	38 217
Dec	10 Palermo	W	1-0	SA	18 Mutu [63]	18 474
	18 Inter	L	0-3	SA	18	20 183
	21 Atalanta	L	1-4	SA	19 Candreva [12]	16 081
	4 Udinese	L	1-0	SA	19 Eder [39]	16 651
	12 Napoli	L	1-2	ICr5	Popescu [20]	28 082
Jan	15 Novara	W	3-1	SA	18 Mutu 2 [20 39p], OG [45]	15 087
	21 Roma	L	1-5	SA	19 Eder [59]	32 347
	29 Atalanta	L	0-1	SA	19	15 315
	1 Napoli	D	0-0	SA	19	25 297
Feb	9 Lazio	L	2-3	SA	19 Mutu [14], Iaquinta [35p]	23 129
	19 Milan	L	1-3	SA	19 Pudil [65]	20 021
	26 Chievo	L	0-1	SA	20	11 000
	4 Fiorentina	L	0-2	SA	20	26 834
	7 Catania	D	0-0	SA	19	14 490
Mar	11 Siena	L	0-2	SA	20	15 360
	18 Cagliari	L	0-3	SA	20	9 500
	25 Parma	D	2-2	SA	20 Santana [46], Del Nero [53]	14 919
	1 Lecce	D	0-0	SA	20	6 950
	7 Bologna	L	0-1	SA	20	16 497
Apr	11 Genoa	D	1-1	SA	20 Mutu [76]	19 822
	22 Palermo	D	2-2	SA	20 Santana [26], Rennella [28]	13 932
	25 Juventus	L	0-1	SA	20 Borriello [80]	23 343
	29 Inter	L	1-2	SA	20 Ceccarelli [57]	45 802
May	2 Udinese	L	0-1	SA	20	13 650
	6 Novara	L	0-3	SA	20	8 224
	13 Roma	L	2-3	SA	20 Del Nero [9], Santana [90]	14 883

20th Att: 311 793 • Av: 16 410 (-0.4%) • Dino Manuzzi 23 860 (68%)

CESENA LEAGUE APPEARANCES/GOALS 2011-12
Goalkeepers Francesco Antonioli 30 • Nicola Ravaglia 8
Defenders Leonardo Arrigoni 0+1/0 • Yohan Benalouane FRA 8+3/0
Gianluca Comotto 28/0 • Maurizio Lauro 20/0
Vangelis Moras GRE 14+1/0 • Daniel Pudil CZE 7/1 • Luca Ricci 0+2/0
Guillermo Rodriguez URU 28/0 • Marco Rossi 14+7/0
Steve von Bergen SUI 27/0
Midfield Tommaso Arrigoni 8+4/0 • Antonio Candreva 15+3/2
Luca Ceccarelli 19+6/1 • Giuseppe Colucci 18+4/0
Damjan Djokovic SRB 3+12/0 • Roberto Guana 27+4/1
David Meza PAR 0+2/0 • Marco Parolo 30+1/1
Rafael Martinho BRA 14+4/0 • Mario Santana ARG 15+1/3
Francesco Urso 0+1/0
Forwards Erjon Bogdani ALB 3+11/0 • Simone Del Nero 5+6/2
Eder BRA 14+3/2 • Mattia Filippi 0+4/0
Abdelkader Ghezzal ALG 10+3/0 • Vincenzo Iaquinta 6+1/1
Marko Livaja CRO 0+3/0 • Nicolo Lolli 0+1/0
Dominique Malonga FRA 7+6/0 • Jorge Martinez URU 4+9/0
Adrian Mutu ROU 28/8 • Vincenzo Rennella 8+7/1
Coach Marco Giampaolo (4/06/2011) • Daniele Arrigoni (1/11/2011)
Mario Beretta (21/02/2012)

CHIEVO VERONA 2011-12

	21 Livorno	W	1-0	ICr3	Cesar [12]	1 000
Ag	11 Novara	D	2-2	SA	7 Pellissier [5], Thereau [24]	7 000
Sep	18 Parma	L	1-2	SA	11 Paloschi [79]	11 189
	21 Napoli	W	1-0	SA	10 Moscardelli [72]	9 000
	25 Genoa	W	2-1	SA	6 Pellissier [74], Moscardelli [90]	8 490
	2 Cesena	D	0-0	SA	8	14 875
Oct	16 Juventus	D	0-0	SA	7	22 000
	23 Inter	L	0-1	SA	13	48 058
	26 Bologna	L	0-1	SA	15	8 300
	30 Siena	L	1-4	SA	16 Moscardelli [75]	13 000
Nov	6 Fiorentina	W	1-0	SA	14 Rigoni [66]	8 250
	20 Catania	W	2-1	SA	9 Pellissier [45p], Sammarco [73]	14 248
	23 Modena	W	3-0	ICr4	Uribe 2 [34 45], Paloschi [49]	150
	27 Milan	L	0-4	SA	11	40 891

CHIEVO VERONA 2011-12 (CONT'D)

	4 Atalanta	D	0-0	SA	12	8 000
Dec	11 Udinese	L	1-2	SA	15 Paloschi [83]	16 062
	17 Cagliari	W	2-0	SA	11 Thereau [35], Sardo [57]	7 000
	21 Lazio	D	0-0	SA	12	26 217
	8 Roma	L	0-2	SA	14	38 054
	11 Udinese	W	2-1	ICr5	Sammarco [9], Thereau [91+]	5 200
Jan	15 Palermo	W	1-0	SA	9 Sammarco [50]	6 500
	22 Lecce	D	2-2	SA	9 Paloschi 2 [3 24]	6 543
	25 Siena	L	0-1	ICqf		3 000
	29 Lazio	L	0-3	SA	12	8 000
	2 Novara	W	2-1	SA	10 Pellissier [33], Thereau [78]	8 516
Feb	5 Parma	L	1-2	SA	13 Thereau [50]	7 500
	13 Napoli	L	0-2	SA	15	22 397
	19 Genoa	W	1-0	SA	11 Thereau [30]	21 000
	26 Cesena	W	1-0	SA	10 Moscardelli [78]	11 000
	3 Juventus	D	1-1	SA	10 Drame [76]	30 027
Mar	9 Inter	L	0-2	SA	11	19 000
	18 Bologna	D	2-2	SA	11 Andreolli [27], Thereau [69]	17 446
	25 Siena	D	1-1	SA	11 Acerbi [9]	6 500
	1 Fiorentina	W	2-1	SA	9 Pellissier [24], Rigoni [88]	19 791
Apr	7 Catania	W	3-2	SA	9 Bradley [6], Pellissier [20p], Paloschi [50]	7 000
	10 Milan	L	0-1	SA	9	19 984
	21 Udinese	D	0-0	SA	9	8 000
	24 Atalanta	L	0-1	SA	12	15 045
	28 Cagliari	L	0-0	SA	12	9 500
May	1 Roma	D	0-0	SA	12	7 500
	6 Palermo	D	4-4	SA	12 Pellissier 2 [28p 72], Uribe [30], Luciano [46]	22 627
	13 Lecce	W	1-0	SA	10 Vacek [78]	8 000

10th Att: 187 024 • Av: 9843 (-25.5%) • Bentegodi 39 211 (25%)

CHIEVO LEAGUE APPEARANCES/GOALS 2011-12
Goalkeepers Christian Puggioni 1 • Stefano Sorrentino 37
Defenders Francesco Acerbi 14+3/1 • Marco Andreolli 22+1/1
Bostjan Cesar SVN 24+5/0 • Dario Dainelli 4+2/0
Boukary Drame SEN 17+1/1 • Nicholas Frey FRA 24+3/0
Bojan Jokic SVN 20/0 • Davide Mandelli 4+3/0
Santiago Morero ARG 8+1/0 • Gennaro Sardo 15+6/1
Midfield Michael Bradley USA 34+1/1 • Rinaldo Cruzado PER 13+7/0
Nikola Gulan SRB 0+1/0 • Perparim Hetemaj FIN 19+13/0
Luciano BRA 22+3/1 • Luca Rigoni 22+3/2 • Paolo Sammarco 19+9/2
Kamil Vacek CZE 10+10/1
Forwards Francesco Grandolfo 0+2/0 • Davide Moscardelli BEL 5+20/4
Alberto Paloschi 20+12/5 • Sergio Pellissier 35/8
Cyril Thereau FRA 27+5/6 • Fernando Uribe COL 2+3/1
Coach Domenico Di Carlo (9/06/2011)

FIORENTINA 2011-12

Ag	21 Cittadella	W	2-1	ICr3	Gilardino [11], Cerci [47]	6 000
	11 Bologna	W	2-0	SA	3 Gilardino [20], Cerci [47]	20 040
Sep	18 Udinese	L	0-2	SA	8	16 125
	21 Parma	W	3-0	SA	5 Jovetic 2 [46 81], Cerci [61]	20 436
	24 Napoli	D	0-0	SA	5	40 653
	2 Lazio	L	1-2	SA	9 Cerci [8]	24 000
	16 Cesena	D	0-0	SA	10	16 308
Oct	23 Catania	D	2-2	SA	10 Jovetic 2 [20 62]	18 783
	25 Juventus	L	1-2	SA	13 Jovetic [58]	35 517
	30 Genoa	W	1-0	SA	12 Lazzari [41]	19 312
	6 Chievo	L	0-1	SA	13	8 250
Nov	19 Milan	D	0-0	SA	14	33 295
	24 Empoli	W	2-1	ICr4	Cerci 2 [28 37]	47 282
	27 Palermo	L	0-2	SA	16	19 536
	4 Roma	W	3-0	SA	10 Jovetic [17p], Gamberini [44], Silva [86]	21 863
Dec	10 Inter	L	0-2	SA	14	39 917
	17 Atalanta	D	2-2	SA	15 Gilardino [9], Jovetic [88]	15 812
	20 Siena	D	0-0	SA	14	9 117

FIORENTINA 2011-12 (CONT'D)

Jan	8 Novara	W	3-0	SA	9	Jovetic 2 [20p 49], Montolivo [49]	10 984
	11 Roma	L	0-3	lCr5			16 320
	15 Lecce	L	0-1	SA	12		18 474
	22 Cagliari	D	0-0	SA	13		6 000
	29 Siena	W	2-1	SA	10	Jovetic [4], Natali [63]	16 784
Feb	5 Udinese	W	3-2	SA	11	Jovetic 2 [39p 84p], Cassani [56]	16 684
	17 Napoli	L	0-3	SA			20 042
	21 Bologna	L	0-2	SA			19 000
	26 Lazio	L	0-1	SA			32 000
Mar	4 Cesena	W	2-0	SA	15	OG [61], Nastasic [74]	26 834
	7 Parma	D	2-2	SA	12	Nastastic [60], Cerci [71]	13 000
	11 Catania	D	0-1	SA	14		16 308
	17 Juventus	L	0-5	SA	15		36 387
	25 Genoa	D	2-2	SA	15	Montolivo [31], Natali [70]	17 200
Apr	1 Chievo	L	1-2	SA	17	Ljajic [71]	19 791
	7 Milan	W	2-1	SA	17	Jovetic [47], Amauri [89]	58 646
	14 Palermo	D	0-0	SA	16		20 037
	22 Inter	D	0-0	SA	15		23 567
	25 Roma	W	2-1	SA	16	Jovetic [2], Lazzari [90]	36 287
	29 Atalanta	L	0-2	SA	16		14 714
May	2 Novara	D	2-2	SA	16	Montolivo 2 [48p 71]	18 132
	5 Lecce	W	1-0	SA	13	Cerci [35]	12 693
	13 Cagliari	D	0-0	SA	13		17 787

13th Att: 408 060 • Av: 21 477 (-5.7%) • Artemio Franchi 47 282 (45%)

FIORENTINA LEAGUE APPEARANCES/GOALS 2011-12
Goalkeepers Artur Boruc POL 36 • Neto BRA 2
Defenders Michele Camporese 6+1/0 • Mattia Cassani 24+2/1
Lorenzo De Silvestri 15+7/0 • Felipe BRA 2+1/0
Alessandro Gamberini 29/1 • Matija Nastasic SRB 21+4/2
Cesare Natali 35/2 • Manuel Pasqual 32/0 • Romulo BRA 4+6/0
Midfield Valon Behrami SUI 31/0 • Stevan Jovetic MNE 27/14
Houssine Kharja MAR 10+9/0 • Andrea Lazzari 26+7/2
Adem Ljajic SRB 9+6/1 • Marco Marchionni 3+5/0
Riccardo Montolivo 30/4 • Gianni Munari 5+6/0
Ruben Olivera URU 5+4/0 • Amidu Salifu GHA 6+8/0
Juan Vargas PER 18+6/0
Forwards Maxwell Acosty GHA 0+5/0 • Amauri 11+2/1
Khouma Babacar SEN 0+1/0 • Alessio Cerci 18+5/5
Alberto Gilardino 9+3/2 • Tanque Silva URU 3+9/1
Coach Sinisa Mihajlovic SRB • Delio Rossi (7/11/2011) • Vincenzo Guerini (3/05/2012)

GENOA 2011-12

Ag	20 Nocerina	W	4-3	lCr3		Palacio 2 [13 49], Pratto [15], Kaladze [90]	10 572
	11 Atalanta	D	2-2	SA	8	Veloso [6], Mesto [55]	19 917
Sep	18 Lazio	W	2-1	SA	5	Palacio [54], Kucka [72]	32 164
	21 Catania	W	3-0	SA	1	Palacio 2 [29 34], Constant [79]	21 649
	25 Chievo	L	1-2	SA	3	Palacio [48]	8 490
Oct	2 Parma	L	1-3	SA	10	Palacio [90p]	12 627
	16 Lecce	D	0-0	SA	11		20 101
	22 Juventus	D	2-2	SA	12	Rossi [31], Caracciolo [85]	35 618
	26 Roma	W	2-1	SA	8	Jankovic [38], Kucka [89]	21 235
	30 Fiorentina	L	0-1	SA	11		19 312
Nov	20 Novara	W	1-0	SA	8	Veloso [86]	20 336
	24 Bari	W	3-2	lCr4		Birsa [37p], Jorquera [90], Pratto [115]	6 299
	27 Cesena	L	0-2	SA	9		15 977
Dec	2 Milan	L	0-2	SA			22 864
	10 Siena	W	2-0	SA	9	Rossi [57], Palacio [90]	9 190
	13 Inter	L	0-1	SA	14		23 708
	18 Bologna	W	2-1	SA	8	Rossi [39], Pratto [85]	19 278
	21 Napoli	L	1-6	SA	10	Jorquera [27]	43 141
	8 Cagliari	L	0-3	SA	12		6 000
Jan	15 Udinese	W	3-2	SA	8	Granqvist [49], Jankovic [51], Palacio [71]	19 860
	19 Inter	L	1-2	lCr5		Birsa [92+]	12 823
	22 Palermo	L	3-5	SA	10	Palacio 2 [14 59p], Jankovic [89]	15 658
	29 Napoli	W	3-2	SA	9	Palacio 2 [31 70], Gilardino [36]	22 418

GENOA 2011-12 (CONT'D)

	5 Lazio	W	3-2	SA	9	Palacio [10], Jankovic 2 [25 46]	19 089
	12 Catania	L	0-4	SA	9		12 606
Feb	15 Atalanta	L	0-1	SA	10		16 000
	19 Chievo	L	0-1	SA	12		21 000
	25 Parma	D	2-2	SA	13	Palacio 2 [78 90]	21 000
	4 Lecce	D	2-2	SA	14	Sculli 2 [21 85]	10 000
Mar	11 Juventus	D	0-0	SA	13		27 527
	19 Roma	L	0-1	SA	13		31 460
	25 Fiorentina	D	2-2	SA	14	Belluschi [20], Palacio [89]	17 200
	1 Inter	L	4-5	SA	16	Moretti [45], Palacio [59p], Gilardino 2 [80p 90p]	42 322
Apr	7 Novara	D	1-1	SA	17	Palacio [7]	10 066
	11 Cesena	D	1-1	SA	17	Rossi [41]	19 822
	22 Siena	L	1-4	SA	17	OG [79]	20 078
	25 Milan	L	0-1	SA	17		48 295
	29 Bologna	L	2-3	SA	17	Palacio [59], Jorquera [77]	23 510
May	2 Cagliari	W	2-1	SA	17	Palacio [12], Jankovic [76]	BCD
	6 Udinese	L	0-2	SA	17		19 471
	13 Palermo	W	2-0	SA	17	Gilardino [52], Sculli [70]	BCD

17th Att: 357 080 • Av: 18 794 (-20.8%) • Luigi Ferraris 36 685 (51%)

GENOA LEAGUE APPEARANCES/GOALS 2011-12
Goalkeepers Sebastien Frey FRA 38
Defenders Masahudu Alhassan GHA 2+2/0 • Luca Antonelli 8+3/0
Cesare Bovo 5+3/0 • Dario Dainelli 12+1/0
Andreas Granqvist SWE 26+2/1 • Kakha Kaladze GEO 26+1/0
Alberto Marchiori 6+1/0 • Emiliano Moretti 8+1/1
Roger Carvalho BRA 6+3/0 • Mario Sampirisi 1+3/0
Midfield Fernando Belluschi ARG 9+5/1 • Davide Biondini 19+1/0
Valter Birsa SVN 4+5/0 • Kevin Constant GUI 17+4/1
Bosko Jankovic SRB 18+12/6 • Cristobal Jorquera CHI 4+18/2
Juraj Kucka SVK 20+6/2 • Alexander Merkel GER 10+3/0
Giandomenico Mesto 29+2/1 • Miguel Veloso POR 25+4/2
Marco Rossi 30/4 • Felipe Seymour CHI 6+6/0
Forwards Andrea Caracciolo 8+4/1 • Alberto Gilardino 14/4
Rodrigo Palacio ARG 32/19 • Lucas Pratto ARG 4+10/1
Giuseppe Sculli 16+1/3 • Ze Eduardo BRA 3+6/0
Coach Alberto Malesani (19/06/2011) • Pasquale Marino (22/12/2011)
• Alberto Malesani (2/04/2012) • Luigi De Canio (22/04/2012)

INTERNAZIONALE 2011-12

Ag	6 Milan	L	1-2	SC		Sneijder [22]	70 000
	11 Palermo	L	3-4	SA	14	Milito 2 [33 51p], Forlan [90]	20 795
	14 Trabzonspor	L	0-1	CLgB			24 444
Sep	17 Roma	D	0-0	SA	11		47 944
	20 Novara	L	1-3	SA	18	Cambiasso [89]	15 596
	24 Bologna	W	3-1	SA	16	Pazzini [39], Milito [81p], Lucio [87]	22 473
	27 CSKA M'kva	W	3-2	CLgB		Lucio [6], Pazzini [23], Zarate [79]	35 000
	1 Napoli	L	0-3	SA	17		64 824
	15 Catania	L	1-2	SA	17	Cambiasso [6]	19 504
Oct	18 Lille	W	1-0	CLgB		Pazzini [21]	16 996
	23 Chievo	W	1-0	SA	16	Thiago Motta [34]	48 058
	26 Atalanta	D	1-1	SA	16	Sneijder [32]	19 613
	29 Juventus	L	1-2	SA	17	Maicon [2]	75 000
	2 Lille	W	2-1	CLgB		Samuel [18], Milito [65]	24 299
Nov	19 Cagliari	W	2-1	SA	17	Thiago Motta [54], Coutinho [60]	45 289
	22 Trabzonspor	D	1-1	CLgB		Alvarez [18]	21 611
	27 Siena	W	1-0	SA	16	Castaignos [90]	13 587
	3 Udinese	L	0-1	SA	15		42 122
	7 CSKA M'kva	L	1-2	CLgB		Cambiasso [51]	23 295
	10 Fiorentina	W	2-0	SA	16	Pazzini [41], Nagatomo [49]	39 917
Dec	17 Genoa	W	1-0	SA	7	Nagatomo [67]	23 708
	18 Cesena	W	1-0	SA		Ranocchia [63]	20 183
	21 Lecce	W	4-1	SA	5	Pazzini [34], Milito [49], Cambiasso [73], Alvarez [81]	39 602
	7 Parma	W	5-0	SA	5	Milito 2 [13 41], Thiago Motta [18], Pazzini [56], Faraoni [78]	47 326
	15 Milan	W	1-0	SA	5	Milito [54]	79 522
Jan	19 Genoa	W	2-1	lCr5		Maicon [2], Poli [50]	12 823
	22 Lazio	W	2-1	SA	4	Milito [44], Pazzini [63]	57 893
	25 Napoli	L	0-1	lCqf			27 265
	29 Lecce	L	0-1	SA	5		14 078

INTERNAZIONALE 2011–12 (CONT'D)

	1 Palermo	D	4-4	SA	5	Milito 4 [22 55p 61 69]	18 320
	5 Roma	L	0-4	SA	7		33 445
Feb	12 Novara	L	0-1	SA	5		21 703
	17 Bologna	L	0-3	SA	1		20 043
	22 Marseille	L	0-1	CLr2			37 646
	26 Napoli	L	0-1	SA	7		45 000
	4 Catania	D	2-2	SA	7	Forlan [71], Milito [80]	47 000
Mar	9 Chievo	W	2-0	SA	8	Samuel [87], Milito [90]	19 000
	13 Marseille	W	2-1	CLr2		Milito [75], Pazzini [96+p]	63 632
	18 Atalanta	D	0-0	SA	8		38 610
	25 Juventus	L	0-2	SA	8		38 536
	1 Genoa	W	5-4	SA	7	Milito 3 [13 27 85p], Samuel [38], Zarate [74]	42 322
Apr	7 Cagliari	D	2-2	SA	7	Milito [6], Cambiasso [64]	19 000
	11 Siena	W	2-1	SA	7	Milito 2 [42 81p]	46 327
	22 Fiorentina	D	0-0	SA	7		23 567
	25 Udinese	W	3-1	SA	5	Sneijder 2 [10 28], Alvarez [37]	24 219
	29 Cesena	W	2-1	SA	5	OG [59], Zarate [72]	45 802
	2 Parma	L	1-3	SA	6	Sneijder [13]	14 817
May	6 Milan	W	4-2	SA	6	Milito 3 [14 53p 79p], Maicon [87]	79 522
	13 Lazio	L	1-3	SA	6	Milito [45p]	45 051

6th Att: 867 624 • Av: 45 664 (-23.3%) • San Siro 80 074 (57%)

INTER LEAGUE APPEARANCES/GOALS 2011-12
Goalkeepers Luca Castellazzi 5+2 • Julio Cesar BRA 33
Defenders Cristian Chivu ROU 13+1/0 • Ivan Cordoba COL 1+4/0
Davide Faraoni 7+7/1 • Jonathan BRA 2+2/0 • Juan BRA 0+1/0
Lucio BRA 34/1 • Maicon BRA 24/2 • Yuto Nagatomo JPN 30+5/2
Andrea Ranocchia 11+1/1 • Walter Samuel ARG 27/2
Javier Zanetti ARG 34/0
Midfield Ricardo Alvarez ARG 15+6/2
Esteban Cambiasso ARG 35+2/4 • Coutinho BRA 4+1/1
Fredy Guarin COL 5+1/0 • Sulley Ali Muntari GHA 1+3/0
Joel Obi NGA 11+16/0 • Angelo Palombo 2+1/0 • Andrea Poli 9+9/0
Wesley Sneijder NED 15+5/4 • Dejan Stankovic SRB 14+5/0
Thiago Motta 10/3
Forwards Luc Castaignos NED 1+5/1 • Diego Forlan URU 14+4/2
Samuele Longo 0+1/0 • Diego Milito ARG 29+4/24
Giampaolo Pazzini 22+11/5 • Mauro Zarate ARG 10+12/2
Coach Gian Piero Gasperini (24/06/2011) • Claudio Ranieri (21/09/2011) • Andrea Stramaccioni (26/03/2012)

JUVENTUS 2011–12 (CONT'D)

	5 Siena	D	0-0	SA	1		35 226
	8 Milan	W	2-1	ICsf		Caceres 2 [53 83]	31 384
Feb	15 Parma	D	0-0	SA	1		13 000
	18 Catania	W	3-1	SA	2	Pirlo [22], Chiellini [74], Quagliarella [81]	31 000
	25 Milan	D	1-1	SA	2	Matri [83]	79 208
Mar	3 Chievo	D	1-1	SA	2	De Ceglie [18]	39 027
	7 Bologna	D	1-1	SA	2	Vucinic [58]	19 000
	11 Genoa	D	0-0	SA	2		27 527
	17 Fiorentina	W	5-0	SA	2	Vucinic [15], Vidal [28], Marchisio [55], Pirlo [67], Padoin [72]	36 387
	20 Milan	D	2-2	ICsf		Del Piero [28], Vucinic [96]	41 000
	25 Inter	W	2-0	SA	2	Caceres [57], Del Piero [71]	38 536
	1 Napoli	W	3-0	SA	2	Bonucci [54], Vidal [75], Quagliarella [83]	38 644
Apr	7 Palermo	W	2-0	SA	1	Bonucci [56], Quagliarella [69]	28 941
	11 Lazio	W	2-1	SA	1	Pepe [30], Del Piero [82]	38 346
	22 Roma	W	4-0	SA	1	Vidal 2 [4 8], Pirlo [29], Marchisio [52]	38 686
	25 Cesena	W	1-0	SA	1	Borriello [80]	23 343
	29 Novara	W	4-0	SA	1	Vucinic 2 [16 64], Borriello [40], Vidal [50]	17 649
	2 Lecce	D	1-1	SA	1	Marchisio [8]	38 573
May	6 Cagliari	W	2-0	SA	1	Vucinic [6], OG [74]	9 500
	13 Atalanta	D	3-1	SA	1	Marrone [10], Del Piero [28], Barzagli [90p]	40 944
	20 Napoli	L	0-2	ICf			70 000

1st Att: 713 827 • Av: 37 570 (+69.3%) • Juventus Stadium 41 137 (91%)

JUVENTUS LEAGUE APPEARANCES/GOALS 2011-12
Goalkeepers Gianluigi Buffon 35 • Marco Storari 3
Defenders Andrea Barzagli 34+1/1 • Leonardo Bonucci 28+4/3
Martin Caceres URU 6+5/1 • Giorgio Chiellini 34/2 • Fabio Grosso 2/0
Stephan Lichtsteiner SUI 34+1/2
Midfield Paolo De Ceglie 16+5/1 • Marcelo Estigarribia PAR 9+5/1
Milos Krasic SRB 4+3/1 • Claudio Marchisio 35+1/9
Luca Marrone 1+2/1 • Simone Padoin 3+3/1 • Simone Pepe 25+6/6
Michele Pazienza 1+7/0 • Andrea Pirlo 37/3 • Arturo Vidal CHI 30+3/7
Forwards Marco Borriello 6+7/2 • Alessandro Del Piero 4+19/3
Eljero Elia NED 1+3/0 • Emanuele Giaccherini 9+14/1
Alessandro Matri 23+8/10 • Fabio Quagliarella 9+14/4
Mirko Vucinic MNE 29+3/8
Coach Antonio Conte (31/05/2011)

JUVENTUS 2011–12

	11 Parma	W	4-1	SA		Lichtsteiner [16], Pepe [58], Vidal [73], Marchisio [83]	41 000
Sep	18 Siena	W	1-0	SA	2	Matri [54]	15 265
	21 Bologna	D	1-1	SA	2	Vucinic [29]	35 679
	25 Catania	D	1-1	SA	1	Krasic [49]	20 839
	2 Milan	W	2-0	SA	1	Marchisio 2 [87 90]	37 281
Oct	16 Chievo	D	0-0	SA	1		22 000
	22 Genoa	D	2-2	SA	3	Matri 2 [6 58]	35 618
	25 Fiorentina	W	2-1	SA	1	Bonucci [13], Matri [65]	35 517
	29 Inter	W	2-1	SA	1	Vucinic [11], Marchisio [32]	75 000
Nov	20 Palermo	W	3-0	SA	1	Pepe [20], Matri [48], Marchisio [65]	36 489
	26 Lazio	W	1-0	SA	1	Pepe [34]	57 148
	29 Napoli	D	3-3	SA	1	Matri [48], Estigarribia [72], Pepe [79]	57 402
	4 Cesena	W	2-0	SA	1	Marchisio [72], Vidal [83p]	38 217
Dec	8 Bologna	W	2-1	ICr5		Giaccherini [90], Marchisio [103]	25 000
	12 Roma	D	1-1	SA	1	Chiellini [61]	49 547
	18 Novara	W	2-0	SA	1	Pepe [4], Quagliarella [75]	38 318
	21 Udinese	D	0-0	SA	2		28 588
	8 Lecce	W	1-0	SA	2	Matri [27]	23 298
	15 Cagliari	D	1-1	SA	1	Vucinic [7]	38 293
Jan	21 Atalanta	W	2-0	SA	1	Lichtsteiner [55], Giaccherini [82]	22 335
	24 Roma	W	3-0	ICqf		Giaccherini [6], Del Piero [30], OG [90]	38 498
	28 Udinese	W	2-1	SA	1	Matri 2 [42 62]	38 433

LAZIO 2011–12

	18 Rabotnicki	W	6-0	ELpo		Hernanes [19], Mauri [39], Cisse 2 [51 65], Rocchi [87], Klose [90]	24 532
Aug	25 Rabotnicki	W	3-1	ELpo		Rocchi 2 [23 77], Hernanes [74]	7 100
	11 Milan	D	2-2	SA	9	Klose [12], Cisse [21]	55 000
	15 Vaslui	D	2-2	ELgD		Cisse [35p], Sculli [71]	13 913
Sep	18 Genoa	L	1-2	SA	11	Sculli [11]	32 164
	21 Cesena	W	2-1	SA	9	Hernanes [48p], Klose [54]	16 347
	25 Palermo	D	0-0	SA	10		29 934
	29 Sporting CP	L	1-2	ELgD		Klose [40]	33 725
	2 Fiorentina	W	2-1	SA	7	Hernanes [28], Klose [83]	24 000
	16 Roma	W	2-1	SA	4	Hernanes [51p], Klose [90]	51 265
Oct	20 FC Zürich	D	1-1	ELgD		Sculli [22]	10 800
	23 Bologna	W	2-0	SA	2	OG [23], Lulic [48]	17 851
	26 Catania	D	1-1	SA	3	Klose [17]	26 951
	30 Cagliari	W	3-0	SA	3	Lulic [39], Klose [44], Rocchi [89]	12 500
	3 FC Zürich	W	1-0	ELgD		Brocchi [62]	13 414
Nov	6 Parma	W	1-0	SA	2	Sculli [85]	29 564
	19 Napoli	D	0-0	SA	2		46 524
	26 Juventus	L	0-1	SA	4		57 148

LAZIO 2011-12 (CONT'D)

	1	Vaslui	D	0-0	ElgD		7 000
	5	Novara	W	3-0	SA	4 Biava [17], Rocchi 2 [24 73]	26 334
Dec	10	Lecce	W	3-2	SA	4 Klose 2 [28 87], Cana [48]	6 846
	14	Sporting CP	W	2-0	ElgD	Kozak [42], Sculli [55]	8 295
	18	Udinese	D	2-2	SA	4 Lulic [43], OG [51]	31 884
	21	Chievo	D	0-0	SA	4	26 217
	7	Siena	L	0-4	SA	4	10 270
Jan	10	Verona	W	3-2	ICr5	Andre Dias [44], Rocchi [58], Hernanes [91+]	10 000
	15	Atalanta	W	2-0	SA	4 Hernanes [20p], Klose [90]	27 438
	22	Inter	L	1-2	SA	5 Rocchi [30]	57 893
	26	Milan	L	1-3	ICqf	Cisse [5]	1 920
	29	Chievo	W	3-0	SA	4 Hernanes [21], Klose 2 [88 89]	8 000
	1	Milan	W	2-0	SA	4 Hernanes [76], Rocchi [85]	29 208
	5	Genoa	L	2-3	SA	4 Ledesma [54p], Gonzalez [90]	19 089
Feb	9	Cesena	W	3-2	SA	3 Hernanes [53], Lulic [61], Kozak [63]	23 129
	16	At. Madrid	L	1-3	ELr2	Klose [19]	30 604
	19	Palermo	L	1-5	SA	4 Kozak [85]	21 000
	23	At. Madrid	L	0-1	ELr2		26 700
	26	Fiorentina	W	1-0	SA	4 Klose [36]	32 000
	4	Roma	W	2-1	SA	3 Hernanes [10p], Mauri [61]	37 000
	11	Bologna	L	1-3	SA	3 OG [56]	25 000
Mar	18	Catania	L	0-1	SA	3	17 406
	25	Cagliari	W	1-0	SA	3 Diakite [88]	29 290
	31	Parma	L	1-3	SA	3 Scaloni [37]	13 115
	7	Napoli	W	3-1	SA	3 Candreva [9], Mauri [68], Ledesma [81p]	38 410
Apr	11	Juventus	L	1-2	SA	3 Mauri [45]	38 346
	22	Lecce	D	1-1	SA	3 Matuzalem [82]	30 513
	25	Novara	L	1-2	SA	3 Candreva [37]	9 946
	29	Udinese	L	0-2	SA	6	19 760
	2	Siena	D	1-1	SA	5 Ledesma [62p]	26 194
May	6	Atalanta	W	2-0	SA	4 Kozak [35], Cana [90]	16 293
	13	Inter	W	3-1	SA	4 Kozak [59], Candreva [63], Mauri [90]	45 051

4th Att: 617 694 • Av: 32 510 (+11.7%) • Olimpico 72 698 (44%)

LAZIO LEAGUE APPEARANCES/GOALS 2011-12
Goalkeepers Albano Bizzarri ARG 7 • Juan Carrizo ARG 0+2
Federico Marchetti 31
Defenders Andre Dias BRA 22+1/0 • Giuseppe Biava 25+1/1
Luis Cavanda BEL 1/0 • Mobido Diakite FRA 19+6/1
Garrido ESP 10+1/0 • Abdoulay Konko MAR 25+1/0
Stefan Radu ROU 21/0 • Marius Stankevicius LTU 9+2/0
Luciano Zauri 6+2/0
Midfield Cristian Brocchi 12+3/0 • Lorik Cana ALB 8+7/2
Antonio Candreva 10+5/3 • Alvaro Gonzalez URU 23+8/1
Hernanes BRA 27+4/8 • Cristian Ledesma 36+1/3
Senad Lulic BIH 23+4/4 • Matuzalem BRA 12+9/1
Stefano Mauri 14+2/4 • Ogenyi Onazi NGA 0+1/0
Lionel Scaloni ARG 11+8/1 • Enrico Zampa 0+1/0
Forwards Emiliano Alfaro URU 1+7/0 • Djibril Cisse FRA 13+5/1
Simone Del Nero 0+2/0 • Miroslav Klose GER 26+1/12
Libor Kozak CZE 4+13/4 • Tommaso Rocchi 17+3/5
Antonio Rozzi 0+3/0 • Giuseppe Sculli 5+6/2
Coach Edoardo Reja

LECCE
2011-12

Ag	21	Crotone	L	0-2	ICr3		8 168
	11	Udinese	L	0-2	SA	18	10 000
Sep	18	Bologna	W	2-0	SA	8 Giacomazzi [37], Grossmuller [59]	15 353
	21	Atalanta	L	1-2	SA	18 Mesbah [26]	8 090
	25	Siena	L	0-3	SA	17	8 469
	2	Cagliari	L	0-2	SA	18	2 892
	16	Genoa	D	0-0	SA	19	20 101
Oct	23	Milan	L	3-4	SA	19 Giacomazzi [4], Oddo [30p], Grossmuller [37]	13 295
	27	Palermo	L	0-2	SA	19	19 730
	30	Novara	D	1-1	SA	19 Strasser [32]	6 223

LECCE 2011-12 (CONT'D)

	6	Cesena	W	1-0	SA	18 Cuadrado [56]	15 182
Nov	20	Roma	L	1-2	SA	18 Bertolacci [61]	30 768
	26	Catania	L	0-1	SA	20	5 962
	3	Napoli	L	2-4	SA	20 Muriel [54], Corvia [90]	39 544
	10	Lazio	L	2-3	SA	20 Di Michele [12p], Ferrario [59]	6 846
Dec	18	Parma	D	3-3	SA	20 Di Michele 2 [58 61], Cuadrado [77]	12 161
	21	Inter	L	1-4	SA	20 Muriel [20]	39 602
	8	Juventus	L	0-1	SA	20	23 298
Jan	15	Fiorentina	W	1-0	SA	19 Di Michele [66p]	18 474
	22	Chievo	D	2-2	SA	18 Esposito [30], Di Michele [90]	6 543
	29	Inter	W	1-0	SA	18 Giacomazzi [40]	14 078
	1	Udinese	L	1-2	SA	18 Di Michele [26]	15 818
	5	Bologna	D	0-0	SA	18	5 962
Feb	12	Atalanta	D	0-0	SA	18	11 877
	19	Siena	W	4-1	SA	18 Muriel [32], Di Michele [68p], Cuadrado [82], Brivio [90]	8 000
	26	Cagliari	W	2-1	SA	18 Muriel [44], Bertolacci [62]	6 000
	4	Genoa	D	2-2	SA	18 Muriel [61], Brivio [81]	10 000
	11	Milan	L	0-2	SA	18	54 329
Mar	18	Palermo	D	1-1	SA	18 Di Michele [6p]	8 477
	25	Novara	D	0-0	SA	18	9 943
	1	Cesena	D	0-0	SA	18	6 950
	7	Roma	W	4-2	SA	18 Muriel 2 [22 49], Di Michele 2 [44 56p]	12 600
Apr	11	Catania	W	2-1	SA	18 Corvia [88], Di Michele [90]	16 570
	22	Lazio	D	1-1	SA	18 Bojinov [90]	30 513
	25	Napoli	L	0-2	SA	18	18 113
	29	Parma	L	1-2	SA	18 Tomovic [83]	10 293
	2	Juventus	D	1-1	SA	18 Bertolacci [85]	38 573
May	5	Fiorentina	L	0-1	SA	18	12 693
	13	Chievo	L	0-1	SA	18	8 000

18th Att: 190 315 • Av: 10 017 (+6.9%) • Via del Mare 33 876 (29%)

LECCE LEAGUE APPEARANCES/GOALS 2011-12
Goalkeepers Massimiliano Benassi 29 • Ugo Gabrieli 1+1
Julio Sergio BRA 8+2 • Davide Petrachi 0+1
Defenders Davide Brivio 23+3/2 • Morris Carrozzieri 12/0
Juan Cuadrado COL 32+1/3 • Andrea Esposito 25+2/1
Stefano Ferrario 9/1 • Leonardo Miglionico URU 13+1/0
Massimo Oddo 26+1/1 • Nenad Tomovic SRB 31+2/1
Midfield Andrea Bertolacci 13+15/3 • Manuele Blasi 14+2/0
Gennaro Delvecchio 15+1/0 • Luca Di Matteo 2+5/0
Guillermo Giacomazzi URU 31+2/3 • Manuel Giandonato 2+6/0
Carlos Grossmuller URU 11+3/2 • Djamel Mesbah ALG 12/1
Chris Obodo NGA 16+7/0 • Ruben Olivera URU 10+2/0
Ignacio Piatti ARG 5+6/0 • Rodney Strasser SLE 9+3/1
Forwards Valeri Bojinov BUL 3+7/1 • Daniele Corvia 6+16/2
David Di Michele 28+1/11 • Luis Muriel COL 25+4/7
Edward Ofere NGA 1+6/0 • Christian Pasquato 5+6/0
Haris Seferovic SUI 1+4/0
Coach Eusebio Di Francesco (27/06/2011) • Serse Cosmi (4/12/2011)

MILAN
2011-12

Ag	6	Inter	W	2-1	SC		Ibrahimovic [61], Boateng [69]	70 000
	9	Lazio	D	2-2	SA	10 Ibrahimovic [29], Cassano [33]	55 000
	13	Barcelona	D	2-2	CLgH	Pato [1], Thiago Silva [92+]	89 861
Sep	18	Napoli	L	1-3	SA	17 Aquilani [12]	51 025
	21	Udinese	D	1-1	SA	16 El Shaarawy [63]	37 592
	24	Cesena	W	1-0	SA	12 Seedorf [5]	39 225
	28	Vik Plzen	W	2-0	CLgH	Ibrahimovic [53p], Cassano [66]	66 859
	2	Juventus	L	0-2	SA	15	37 281
	15	Palermo	W	3-0	SA	13 Nocerino [40], Robinho [55], Cassano [64]	44 992
Oct	19	BATE	W	2-0	CLgH	Ibrahimovic [33], Boateng [70]	66 040
	23	Lecce	W	4-3	SA	7 Boateng 3 [49 55 63], Yepes [83]	13 295
	26	Parma	W	4-1	SA	5 Nocerino 3 [30 32 91+], Ibrahimovic [73]	35 753
	29	Roma	W	3-2	SA	4 Ibrahimovic 2 [17 78], Nesta [30]	45 000
	1	BATE	D	1-1	CLgH	Ibrahimovic [22]	29 100
Nov	6	Catania	W	4-0	SA	4 Ibrahimovic [7p], Robinho [24], OG [69], Zambrotta [72]	44 091

MILAN 2011–12 (CONT'D)

Nov	19 Fiorentina	D 0-0	SA	3		33 295
	23 Barcelona	L 2-3	CLgH		Ibrahimovic [20], Boateng [54]	78 927
	27 Chievo	W 4-0	SA	2	Thiago Silva [8], Ibrahimovic 2 [16 44p], Pato [33]	40 891
Dec	2 Genoa	W 2-0	SA	2	Ibrahimovic [56p], Nocerino [79]	22 864
	6 Vik Plzen	D 2-2	CLgH		Pato [47], Robinho [48]	19 854
	11 Bologna	D 2-2	SA	3	Seedorf [16], Ibrahimovic [72p]	25 736
	17 Siena	W 2-0	SA	2	Nocerino [54], Ibrahimovic [64p]	41 759
	20 Cagliari	W 2-0	SA	1	OG [4], Ibrahimovic [61]	20 000
	8 Atalanta	W 2-0	SA	1	Ibrahimovic [22p], Boateng [82]	22 172
	15 Inter	L 0-1	SA	2		79 522
	18 Novara	W 2-1	ICr5		El Shaarawy [24], Pato [100]	1 920
Jan	22 Novara	W 3-0	SA	2	Ibrahimovic 2 [57 90], Robinho [74]	16 068
	26 Lazio	W 3-1	ICqf		Robinho [15], Seedorf [18], Ibrahimovic [84]	1 920
	29 Cagliari	W 3-0	SA	2	Ibrahimovic [32], Nocerino [39], Ambrosini [75]	40 242
Feb	1 Lazio	L 0-2	SA	2		29 208
	5 Napoli	D 0-0	SA	2		44 011
	8 Juventus	L 1-2	ICsf		El Shaarawy [62]	31 384
	11 Udinese	W 2-1	SA	1	Maxi Lopez [77], El Shaarawy [85]	22 370
	15 Arsenal	W 4-0	CLr2		Boateng [15], Robinho 2 [38 49], Ibrahimovic [79p]	64 462
	19 Cesena	W 3-1	SA	1	Muntari [29], Emanuelson [31], Robinho [55]	20 021
	25 Juventus	D 1-1	SA	1	Nocerino [14]	79 208
Mar	3 Palermo	W 4-0	SA	1	Ibrahimovic 3 [21 31 35], Thiago Silva [58]	20 000
	6 Arsenal	L 0-3	CLr2			59 973
	11 Lecce	W 2-0	SA	1	Nocerino [7], Ibrahimovic [65]	54 329
	17 Parma	W 2-0	SA	1	Ibrahimovic [17p], Emanuelson [55]	19 481
	20 Juventus	D 2-2	ICsf		Mesbah [51], Maxi Lopez [81]	41 000
	24 Roma	W 2-1	SA	1	Ibrahimovic 2 [53p 83]	59 133
	28 Barcelona	D 0-0	CLqf			76 169
	31 Catania	D 1-1	SA	1	Robinho [34]	20 253
Apr	3 Barcelona	L 1-3	CLqf		Nocerino [32]	94 629
	7 Fiorentina	L 1-2	SA	2	Ibrahimovic [31p]	58 646
	10 Chievo	W 1-0	SA	2	Muntari [8]	19 984
	22 Bologna	D 1-1	SA	2	Ibrahimovic [90]	51 725
	25 Genoa	W 1-0	SA	2	Boateng [86]	48 295
May	29 Siena	W 4-1	SA	2	Cassano [26], Nocerino [90], Ibrahimovic 2 [29 94+]	14 665
	2 Atalanta	W 2-0	SA	2	Muntari [9], Robinho [93+]	38 204
	6 Inter	L 2-4	SA	2	Ibrahimovic 2 [44p 46]	79 522
	13 Novara	W 2-1	SA	2	Flamini [56], Inzaghi [82]	45 211

2nd Att: 937 829 • Av: 49 359 (-8.5%) • San Siro 80 074 (56%)

MILAN LEAGUE APPEARANCES/GOALS 2011-12
Goalkeepers Christian Abbiati 31 • Marco Amelia 7+2
Defenders Luca Antonini 17+3/0 • Daniele Bonera 17+3/0
Mattia De Sciglio 2+1/0 • Philippe Mexes FRA 13+1/0
Alessandro Nesta 16+1/1 • Taye Taiwo NGA 4/0 • Thiago Silva BRA 27/2
Mario Yepes COL 10+1/1 • Gianluca Zambrotta 10+2/1
Midfield Ignazio Abate 29/0 • Massimo Ambrosini 17+5/1
Alberto Aquilani 14+9/1 • Kevin Prince Boateng GHA 15+4/5
Stephan El Shaarawy 6+16/2 • Urby Emanuelson NED 17+13/2
Mathieu Flamini FRA 0+2/1 • Gennaro Gattuso 4+2/0
Alexander Merkel GER 0+1/0 • Djamel Mesbah ALG 7+1/0
Sulley Ali Muntari GHA 13/3 • Antonio Nocerino 33+2/10
Clarence Seedorf NED 14+4/2 • Rodney Strasser SLE 0+1/0
Mark van Bommel NED 22+3/0
Forwards Antonio Cassano 11+5/3 • Zlatan Ibrahimovic SWE 32/28
Filippo Inzaghi 0+7/1 • Maxi Lopez ARG 2+6/1 • Pato BRA 7+4/1
Robinho BRA 21+7/6
Coach Massimiliano Allegri

NAPOLI 2011–12

Sep	10 Cesena	W 3-1	SA	2	Lavezzi [3], Campagnaro [67], Hamsik [87]	20 942
	14 Man City	D 1-1	CLgA		Cavani [69]	44 026

NAPOLI 2011–12 (CONT'D)

Sep	18 Milan	W 3-1	SA	1	Cavani 3 [14 36 51]	51 025
	21 Chievo	L 0-1	SA	4		9 000
	24 Fiorentina	D 0-0	SA	4		40 653
	27 Villarreal	W 2-0	CLgA		Hamsik [15], Cavani [17p]	46 747
Oct	1 Inter	W 3-0	SA	3	Campagnaro [43], Maggio [57], Hamsik [75]	64 824
	15 Parma	L 1-2	SA	5	Mascara [76]	41 042
	18 Bayern M	D 1-1	CLgA		OG [39]	60 074
	23 Cagliari	D 0-0	SA	5		11 000
	26 Udinese	W 2-0	SA	4	Lavezzi [20], Maggio [44]	35 565
	29 Catania	L 1-2	SA	5	Cavani [1]	10 000
Nov	2 Bayern M	L 2-3	CLgA		Fernandez 2 [45 79]	66 000
	19 Lazio	D 0-0	SA	6		46 524
	22 Man City	W 2-1	CLgA		Cavani 2 [17 49]	57 575
	26 Atalanta	D 1-1	SA	7	Cavani [90]	17 827
	29 Juventus	D 3-3	SA	6	Hamsik [22], Pandev 2 [40 68]	57 402
Dec	3 Lecce	W 4-2	SA	5	Lavezzi [26], Cavani 2 [33 82], Dzemaili [41]	39 544
	7 Villarreal	W 2-0	CLgA		Inler [65], Hamsik [76]	15 350
	11 Novara	W 3-1	SA	5	Dzemaili [84]	16 328
	18 Roma	L 1-3	SA	6	Hamsik [82]	38 048
	21 Genoa	W 6-1	SA	6	Cavani 2 [12 24], Hamsik [17], Pandev [45], Gargano [49], Zuniga [80]	43 141
Jan	8 Palermo	W 3-1	SA	4	Pandev [35], Cavani [54], Hamsik [60]	22 110
	12 Cesena	D 1-1	ICr5		Cavani [65], Pandev [86]	28 082
	16 Bologna	D 1-1	SA	6	Cavani [71p]	42 956
	22 Siena	D 1-1	SA	7	Pandev [86]	14 643
	25 Inter	W 2-0	ICqf		Cavani 2 [50 93+]	27 265
	29 Genoa	L 2-3	SA	7	Cavani [81], Lavezzi [82]	22 418
Feb	1 Cesena	D 0-0	SA	7		25 297
	5 Milan	D 0-0	SA	7		44 011
	9 Siena	L 1-2	ICsf		OG [86]	4 616
	13 Chievo	W 2-0	SA	5	Britos [15], Cavani [38p]	22 397
	17 Fiorentina	W 3-0	SA	6	Cavani 2 [3 54], Lavezzi [90]	20 042
	21 Chelsea	W 3-1	CLr2		Lavezzi 2 [39 65], Cavani [45]	52 495
	26 Inter	W 1-0	SA	5	Lavezzi [59]	45 000
Mar	4 Parma	W 2-1	SA	5	Cavani [40], Lavezzi [86]	13 000
	9 Cagliari	W 6-3	SA	4	Hamsik [1], Maggio [19], Lavezzi [56p], Cavani 2 [70], OG [30], Gargano [70], Maggio [84]	40 022
	14 Chelsea	L 1-4	CLr2		Inler [55]	37 784
	18 Udinese	D 2-2	SA	4	Cavani 2 [81 85]	21 661
	21 Siena	W 2-0	ICsf		OG [11], Cavani [32]	56 418
	25 Catania	D 2-2	SA	4	Dzemaili [60], Cavani [67]	51 055
Apr	1 Juventus	L 0-3	SA	4		38 644
	7 Lazio	L 1-3	SA	5	Pandev [34]	38 048
	11 Atalanta	L 1-3	SA	6	Lavezzi [13]	35 519
	14 Novara	W 2-0	SA	5	Cavani [21], Cannavaro [37]	31 675
	25 Lecce	W 2-0	SA	4	Hamsik [5], Cavani [51]	18 113
	28 Roma	D 2-2	SA	3	Zuniga [49], Cavani [57]	29 643
May	1 Palermo	W 2-0	SA	3	Cavani [16p], Hamsik [35]	41 397
	6 Bologna	L 0-2	SA	5		26 647
	13 Siena	W 2-1	SA	5	Dossena 2 [3 34]	43 582
	20 Juventus	W 2-0	ICf		Cavani [63p], Hamsik [83]	70 000

5th Att: 771 844 • Av: 40 623 (-10.9%) • San Paolo 60 240 (67%)

NAPOLI LEAGUE APPEARANCES/GOALS 2011-12
Goalkeepers Morgan De Sanctis 37 • Antonio Rosati 1
Defenders Salvatore Aronica 29+2/0 • Miguel Britos ARG 9+2/1
Hugo Campagnaro ARG 30+1/2 • Paolo Cannavaro 31+1/2
Andrea Dossena 24+9/2 • Federico Fernandez ARG 9+7/0
Ignacio Fideleff ARG 4/0 • Gianluca Grava 3+3/0
Christian Maggio 27+6/3 • Juan Zuniga COL 22+9/2
Midfield Blerim Dzemaili SUI 21+7/3 • Walter Gargano URU 30+3/2
Marek Hamsik SVK 30+7/9 • Gokhan Inler SUI 29+7/0
Mario Santana ARG 4+4/0
Forwards Massimiliano Ammendola 0+1/0
Edinson Cavani URU 32+3/23 • Cristian Chavez ARG 0+2/0
Ezequiel Lavezzi ARG 25+5/9 • Cristiano Lucarelli 0+3/0
Giuseppe Mascara 2+5/1 • Goran Pandev MKD 19+11/6
Eduardo Vargas CHI 0+10/0
Coach Walter Mazzarri

NOVARA
2011-12

Ag	21 Triestina	W 4-0	ICr2	OG [10], Pinardi [57], Meggiorini [74], Gemiti [78]	3 457
Sep	11 Chievo	D 2-2	SA	11 Marianini [27], Paci [86]	7 000
	17 Cagliari	L 1-2	SA	11 Morimoto [88]	10 050
	20 Inter	W 3-1	SA	8 Meggiorini [38], Rigoni 2 [86p 90]	15 596
	25 Atalanta	L 1-2	SA	15 Porcari [89]	13 910
Oct	2 Catania	D 3-3	SA	13 Rigoni [45p], Morimoto [66], Jeda [85]	10 632
	16 Bologna	L 0-2	SA	16	10 033
	23 Udinese	L 0-3	SA	17	15 988
	26 Siena	D 1-1	SA	18 Gemiti [80]	8 384
	30 Lecce	D 1-1	SA	18 Rigoni [44p]	6 223
Nov	5 Roma	L 0-2	SA	19	12 513
	20 Genoa	L 0-1	SA	19	20 336
	26 Parma	W 2-1	SA	18 Rubino [70], Rigoni [78]	8 964
	29 Catania	W 3-2	ICr4	Granoche [68], Meggiorini 2 [78 90]	3 500
Dec	5 Lazio	L 0-3	SA	18	26 334
	11 Napoli	D 1-1	SA	19 Radovanovic [70]	16 328
	18 Juventus	L 0-2	SA	19	38 318
	21 Palermo	D 2-2	SA	18 Mazzarani [77], Rigoni [85]	8 392
	8 Fiorentina	L 0-3	SA	18	10 984
Jan	15 Cesena	L 1-3	SA	20 Morimoto [89]	15 087
	18 Milan	L 1-2	ICr5	Radovanovic [89]	1 920
	22 Milan	L 0-3	SA	20	16 068
	29 Palermo	L 0-2	SA	20	16 224
Feb	2 Chievo	L 1-2	SA	20 Mascara [79]	8 516
	5 Cagliari	D 0-0	SA	20	8 952
	12 Inter	W 1-0	SA	20 Caracciolo [56]	21 703
	19 Atalanta	D 0-0	SA	19	9 000
	26 Catania	L 1-3	SA	19 Rubino [84]	13 250
Mar	4 Bologna	L 0-1	SA	20	19 000
	11 Udinese	W 1-0	SA	19 Jeda [16]	8 708
	18 Siena	W 2-0	SA	19 Rigoni [72], Porcari [81]	9 891
	25 Lecce	D 0-0	SA	19	9 943
Apr	1 Roma	L 2-5	SA	19 Caracciolo [17], Morimoto [78]	38 237
	7 Genoa	D 1-1	SA	19 Mascara [68]	10 066
	11 Parma	L 0-2	SA	19	11 682
	21 Napoli	L 0-2	SA	19	31 675
	25 Lazio	W 2-1	SA	19 OG [35], Mascara [79]	9 946
	29 Juventus	L 0-4	SA	19	17 649
May	2 Fiorentina	D 2-2	SA	19 Jeda [14], Rigoni [30p]	18 132
	6 Cesena	W 3-0	SA	19 Rigoni 3 [28p 68p 86]	8 224
	13 Milan	L 1-2	SA	19 Garcia [20]	45 211

19th Att: 208 898 • Av: 10 995 (+109.5%) • Silvio Piola 17 876 (61%)

NOVARA LEAGUE APPEARANCES/GOALS 2011-12
Goalkeepers Achille Coser 2 • Alberto Fontana 12+3
Samir Ujkani ALB 24
Defenders Matteo Centurioni 20+2/0 • Jean Coubronne FRA 0+1/0
Hernan Dellafiore ARG 15+2/0 • Gabriel Silva BRA 1+2/0
Santiago Garcia ARG 21/1 • Carlos Labrin CHI 0+1/0
Andrea Lisuzzo 21/0 • Carlalberto Ludi 8+2/0
Michel Morganella SUI 28+3/0 • Massimo Paci 22+4/1
Leandro Rinaudo 5/0
Midfield Giuseppe Gemiti GER 32+2/1 • Luigi Giorgi 3+7/0
Daniel Jensen DEN 3+3/0 • Francesco Marianini 10+3/1
Andrea Mazzarani 10+10/1 • Simone Pesce 16+5/0
Alex Pinardi 6+4/0 • Filippo Porcari 32+3/2
Ivan Radovanovic SRB 17+11/1 • Marco Rigoni 35/11
Raffaele Rubino 7+12/2
Forwards Andrea Caracciolo 17+2/2 • Pablo Granoche URU 4+7/0
Jeda BRA 15+9/3 • Mattia Maggio GER 0+1/0
Giuseppe Mascara 13+2/3 • Riccardo Meggiorini 11+2/1
Takayuki Morimoto JPN 8+10/4
Coach Attilio Tesse • Emiliano Mondonico (30/01/2012)
Attilio Tesse (6/03/2012)

PALERMO
2011-12

Jy	28 Thun	D 2-2	ELp3		Ilicic [13], Miccoli [92+]	28 760
Ag	4 Thun	D 1-1	ELp3		Gonzalez [49]	7 227
	11 Inter	W 4-3	SA	5	Miccoli 2 [48 86], Hernandez [54], Pinilla [88]	20 795
Sep	18 Atalanta	L 0-1	SA	7		12 368
	21 Cagliari	W 3-2	SA	6	Zahavy [1], Bertolo [15], Miccoli [1]	18 965
	25 Lazio	D 0-0	SA	7		29 934
	2 Siena	W 2-0	SA	4	Migliaccio [19], Hernandez [93+p]	20 461
	15 Milan	L 0-3	SA	6		44 992
Oct	23 Roma	L 0-1	SA	8		35 738
	27 Lecce	W 2-0	SA	7	Pinilla [28p], Hernandez [77]	19 730
	30 Udinese	L 0-1	SA	9		13 000
Nov	5 Bologna	W 3-1	SA	5	Zahavy [13], Silvestre [52], Ilicic [74]	18 507
	20 Juventus	L 0-3	SA	6		36 489
	27 Fiorentina	W 2-0	SA	5	Miccoli [22], Ilicic [73]	19 536
	4 Parma	D 0-0	SA	6		11 793
	10 Cesena	L 0-1	SA	6		18 474
Dec	13 Siena	D 4-4	ICr5		Ilicic 3 [39p 46 91+p], Bertolo [98], L 0-3p	6 489
	18 Catania	L 0-2	SA	10		16 471
	21 Novara	D 2-2	SA	9	OG [20], Bertolo [73]	8 392
	8 Napoli	L 1-3	SA	11	Miccoli [89]	22 110
	15 Chievo	L 0-1	SA	14		6 500
Jan	22 Genoa	W 5-3	SA	8	Budan [26], Silvestre [37], Mantovani [42], Miccoli [75], Migliaccio [84]	15 658
	29 Novara	W 2-0	SA	8	Budan 2 [41 72]	16 224
	1 Inter	D 4-4	SA	8	Matovani [17], Miccoli 3 [52 66 85]	18 320
	5 Atalanta	W 2-1	SA	8	Miccoli [29p], Budan [49]	15 302
	11 Cagliari	L 1-2	SA	8	Hernandez [83p]	6 000
Feb	19 Lazio	W 5-1	SA	8	Barreto [10], Donati [20], Silvestre [42], Budan [47], Miccoli [52]	21 000
	26 Siena	L 1-4	SA	8	Budan [12]	8 604
	3 Milan	L 0-4	SA	9		20 000
	10 Roma	L 0-1	SA	10		16 451
Mar	18 Lecce	D 1-1	SA	10	Munoz [15]	8 477
	24 Udinese	D 1-1	SA	12	Miccoli [31]	17 918
	1 Bologna	W 3-1	SA	10	Budan [69], Hernandez [76], Ilicic [86]	19 440
	7 Juventus	L 0-2	SA	11		28 941
Apr	11 Fiorentina	D 0-0	SA	10		20 037
	22 Cesena	D 2-2	SA	11	Bertolo [20], Silvestre [45]	13 932
	25 Parma	L 1-2	SA	14	Hernandez [6]	14 365
	28 Catania	D 1-1	SA	14	Miccoli [47]	18 462
	1 Napoli	L 0-2	SA	14		41 397
May	6 Chievo	D 4-4	SA	15	Miccoli 3 [10 19 74], Silvestre [89]	22 677
	13 Genoa	L 0-2	SA	16		BCD

16th Att: 365 526 • Av: 19 238 (-22.5%) • Renzo Barbera 37 242 (51%)

PALERMO LEAGUE APPEARANCES/GOALS 2011-12
Goalkeepers Francesco Benussi 7 • Giacomo Brichetto 0+1
Alexandros Tzorvas GRE 11 • Emiliano Viviano 20
Defenders Matias Aguirregaray URU 5+7/0
Federico Balzaretti 26+1/0 • Mauro Cetto ARG 6+1/0
Carlos Labrin CHI 9/0 • Andrea Mantovani 22+2/2
Milan Milanovic SRB 4+1/0 • Ezequiel Munoz ARG 18+1/1
Eros Pisano 27+1/0 • Matias Silvestre ARG 29/5
Midfield Afriyie Acquah GHA 10+10/0 • Edgar Alvarez HON 4+4/0
Armin Bacinovic SVN 7+6/0 • Edgar Barreto PAR 33+1/1
Nicolas Bertolo ARG 18+10/3 • Francesco Della Rocca 12+9/0
Massimo Donati 18/1 • Josip Ilicic SVN 25+8/3
Ignacio Lores URU 1+5/0 • Giulio Migliaccio 29+1/2
Franco Vazquez ARG 4+10/0
Forwards Igor Budan CRO 14+8/7 • Abel Hernandez URU 16+4/6
Agon Mehmeti SWE 1+2/0 • Fabrizio Miccoli 24+4/16
Mauricio Pinilla CHI 7+6/2 • Eran Zahavy ISR 11+9/2
Coach Stefano Pioli (2/06/2011) • Devis Mangia (31/08/2011) •
Bortolo Mutti (19/12/2011)

PARMA
2011–12

Aug	21	Grosseto	W	4-1	ICr3	Giovinco 2 [44 57], Crespo 2 [73 90]	3 352
	11	Juventus	L	1-4	SA	19 Giovinco [90p]	41 000
Sep	18	Chievo	W	2-1	SA	10 Giovinco 2 [24 90]	11 189
	21	Fiorentina	L	0-3	SA	13	20 436
	25	Roma	L	0-1	SA	18	12 822
	2	Genoa	W	3-1	SA	12 Giovinco 2 [29 42p], Morrone [50]	12 627
	15	Napoli	W	2-1	SA	9 Gobbi [58], Modesto [83]	41 042
Oct	23	Atalanta	L	1-2	SA	14 Valdes [80]	13 003
	26	Milan	L	1-4	SA	15 Giovinco [78]	35 753
	30	Cesena	W	2-0	SA	12 Paletta [41], Lucarelli [71]	12 480
	6	Lazio	L	0-1	SA	15	29 564
Nov	20	Udinese	W	2-0	SA	10 Biabiany [58], Giovinco [76p]	14 128
	26	Novara	L	1-2	SA	10 OG [29]	8 964
	29	H Verona	L	0-2	ICr4		3 719
	4	Palermo	D	0-0	SA	11	11 793
	11	Cagliari	D	0-0	SA	12	7 100
Dec	18	Lecce	D	3-3	SA	13 Floccari [18p], Pelle [86], Galloppa [90]	12 161
	21	Catania	D	3-3	SA	13 Modesto [5], Biabiany [23], Floccari [44]	10 800
	7	Inter	L	0-5	SA	15	47 326
Jan	15	Siena	W	3-1	SA	11 Biabiany [24], Valiani [66], Giovinco [90]	11 570
	22	Bologna	D	0-0	SA	12	15 141
	28	Catania	D	1-1	SA	11 Modesto [43]	13 098
	5	Chievo	W	2-1	SA		Giovinco [46], OG [69]	7 500
Feb	15	Juventus	D	0-0	SA			13 000
	19	Roma	L	0-1	SA			29 433
	25	Genoa	D	2-2	SA		Gobbi [6], Floccari [53]	21 000
	4	Napoli	L	1-2	SA	14 Zaccardo [77]	13 000
	7	Fiorentina	D	2-2	SA	16 Okaka [28], Giovinco [87p]	13 000
Mar	11	Atalanta	D	1-1	SA	16 Paletta [55]	14 210
	17	Milan	L	0-2	SA	17		19 481
	25	Cesena	D	2-2	SA	17 Floccari [40], Paletta [61]	14 919
	31	Lazio	W	3-1	SA	15 Mariga [6], Floccari 2 [12 71]	13 115
	7	Udinese	L	1-3	SA	16 Lucarelli [84]	17 831
	11	Novara	W	2-0	SA	15 Giovinco [27], Jonathan [40]	11 682
Apr	21	Cagliari	W	3-0	SA	13 Giovinco [29], Floccari [73p], Okaka [90p]	14 271
	25	Palermo	W	2-1	SA	9 Okaka [55], Biabiany [70]	14 365
	29	Lecce	W	2-1	SA	9 Giovinco [67], Paletta [78]	10 293
May	2	Inter	W	3-1	SA	8 Marques [53], Giovinco [67], Biabiany [82]	14 817
	6	Siena	W	2-0	SA	8 Giovinco [67], Floccari [90]	8 640
	13	Bologna	W	1-0	SA	8 Biabiany [37]	16 922

8th Att: 251 861 • Av: 13 256 (-8.9%) • Ennio Tardini 27 906 (47%)

PARMA LEAGUE APPEARANCES/GOALS 2011-12
Goalkeepers Antonio Mirante 29 • Nicola Pavarini 9+1
Defenders Brandao POR 2/0 • Rolf Feltscher VEN 2+2/0
Stefano Ferrario 4/0 • Jonathan BRA 9+3/1
Alessandro Lucarelli 33+1/2 • Francesco Modesto 20+5/3
Nwankwo Obiora NGA 1/0 • Gabriel Paletta ARG 33/4
Matteo Rubin 1+1/0 • Fabiano Santacroce 5+7/0
Cristian Zaccardo 35/1
Midfield Manuele Blasi 0+6/0 • Daniele Galloppa 28+2/1
Massimo Gobbi 26/2 • Abderrazzak Jadid MAR 5/0
MacDonald Mariga KEN 11/1 • Fernando Marques ESP 1+3/1
Stefano Morrone 24+6/1 • Gianluca Musacci 7+8/0
Danilo Pereira POR 0+5/0 • Jaime Valdes CHI 14+6/1
Francesco Valiani 17+9/1 • Ze Eduardo BRA 1+3/0
Forwards Jonathan Biabiany FRA 27+1/6 • Hernan Crespo ARG 0+4/0
Sergio Floccari 24+4/8 • Sebastian Giovinco 36/15
Stefano Okaka 4+10/3 • Raffaele Palladino 1+4/0
Graziano Pelle 7+4/1
Coach Franco Colomba • Roberto Donadoni (9/01/2012)

ROMA
2011–12

Aug	18	Slovan	L	0-1	ELpo		10 548
	25	Slovan	D	1-1	ELpo	Perrotta [11]	47 302
	11	Cagliari	L	1-2	SA	15 De Rossi [90]	45 000
Sep	17	Inter	D	0-0	SA	15	47 944
	22	Siena	D	1-1	SA	14 Osvaldo [25]	34 896
	25	Parma	W	1-0	SA	11 Osvaldo [50]	12 822
	1	Atalanta	W	3-1	SA	6 Krkic [20], Osvaldo [31], Fabio Simplicio [81]	36 200
Oct	16	Lazio	L	1-2	SA	12 Osvaldo [5]	51 265
	23	Palermo	W	1-0	SA	6 Lamela [8]	35 738
	26	Genoa	L	1-2	SA	9 Borini [82]	21 235
	29	Milan	L	2-3	SA	13 Burdisso [28], Krkic [87]	40 075
Nov	5	Novara	W	2-0	SA	7 Krkic [73], Osvaldo [76]	12 513
	20	Lecce	W	2-1	SA	5 Pjanic [25], Gago [54]	30 768
	25	Udinese	L	0-2	SA	7	18 310
	4	Fiorentina	L	0-3	SA	8	21 863
Dec	12	Juventus	D	1-1	SA	10 De Rossi [5]	49 547
	18	Napoli	W	3-1	SA	7 OG [3], Osvaldo [59], Fabio Simplicio [90]	38 048
	21	Bologna	W	2-0	SA	7 Taddei [17], Osvaldo [40]	17 855
	8	Chievo	W	2-0	SA	7 Totti 2 [34p 78p]	38 054
	11	Fiorentina	W	3-0	ICr5	Lamela 2 [53 66], Borini [75]	16 320
Jan	21	Cesena	W	5-1	SA	7 Totti 2 [1 8], Borini [9], Juan [62], Pjanic [70]	32 347
	24	Juventus	L	0-3	ICqf		38 498
	29	Bologna	D	1-1	SA	6 Pjanic [62]	34 073
	1	Cagliari	L	2-4	SA	6 Juan [13], Borini [34]	9 500
	5	Inter	W	4-0	SA	6 Juan [13], Borini 2 [41 49], Krkic [89]	33 445
Feb	8	Catania	D	1-1	SA	6 De Rossi [28]	14 000
	13	Siena	L	0-1	SA	6	9 288
	19	Parma	W	1-0	SA	5 Borini [26]	29 433
	26	Atalanta	L	1-4	SA	6 Borini [36]	16 000
	4	Lazio	L	1-2	SA	6 Borini [16]	37 000
	10	Palermo	W	1-0	SA	6 Borini [3]	16 451
Mar	19	Genoa	W	1-0	SA	6 Osvaldo [3]	31 460
	24	Milan	L	1-2	SA	6 Osvaldo [44]	59 133
	1	Novara	W	5-2	SA	6 Marquinho [25], Osvaldo [34], Fabio Simplicio [55], Krkic [61], Lamela [50]	38 237
	7	Lecce	L	2-4	SA	6 Krkic [88], Lamela [90]	12 600
Apr	11	Udinese	W	3-1	SA	5 Osvaldo [8], Totti [86], Marquinho [90]	29 672
	22	Juventus	L	0-4	SA	6	38 686
	25	Fiorentina	L	1-2	SA	7 Totti [71]	36 287
	28	Napoli	D	2-2	SA	7 Marquinho [41], F. Simplicio [88]	29 643
	1	Chievo	D	0-0	SA	7	7 500
May	5	Catania	D	2-2	SA	7 Totti 2 [52 77]	32 585
	13	Cesena	W	3-2	SA	7 Krkic [27], Lamela [32], De Rossi [49]	14 883

7th Att: 679 385 • Av: 35 757 (+3.4%) • Olimpico 72 698 (49%)

ROMA LEAGUE APPEARANCES/GOALS 2011-12
Goalkeepers Gianluca Curci 2+1 • Bogdan Lobont ROU 7+2
Maarten Stekelenburg NED 29
Defenders Nicolas Burdisso ARG 8+2/1 • Marco Cassetti 3+4/0
Cicinho BRA 1+1/0 • Gabriel Heinze ARG 27+3/0
Jose Angel ESP 24+3/0 • Juan BRA 16/3 • Simon Kjær DEN 20+2/0
Midfield Daniele De Rossi 32/4 • Fabio Simplicio BRA 9+10/4
Fernando Gago ARG 24+6/1 • Leandro Greco 9+10/0
Erik Lamela ARG 23+6/4 • Marquinho BRA 10+5/3
Simone Perrotta 8+11/0 • David Pizarro CHI 5+2/0
Miralem Pjanic BIH 29+1/3 • Aleandro Rosi 21/0 • Taddei BRA 24/1
Federico Viviani 2+4/0
Forwards Fabio Borini 20+4/9 • Marco Borriello 2+5/0
Gianluca Caprari 0+1/0 • Bojan Krkic ESP 13+20/7
Pablo Osvaldo 24+2/11 • Giammario Piscitella 0+2/0
Gadji Tallo CIV 0+3/0 • Francesco Totti 26+1/8
Coach Luis Enrique ESP (10/06/2011)

SIENA
2011–12

Aug	21 Torino	W	1-0	ICr3	Calaio [80p]	1 007
	11 Catania	D	0-0	SA	13	13 223
Sep	18 Juventus	L	0-1	SA	16	15 265
	22 Roma	D	1-1	SA	15	Vitiello [88]	34 896
	25 Lecce	W	3-0	SA	9	Destro [6], Calaio 2 [53 70]	8 469
	2 Palermo	L	0-2	SA	14		20 461
	16 Cagliari	D	0-0	SA	14		11 000
Oct	23 Cesena	W	2-0	SA	11	Gonzalez [9], Calaio [53]	8 935
	26 Novara	D	1-1	SA	11	Calaio [17]	8 384
	30 Chievo	W	4-1	SA	7	Destro 2 [25 57], D'Agostino [61], Calaio [90]	13 000
	6 Udinese	L	1-2	SA	9	Bolzoni [77]	16 033
Nov	20 Atalanta	D	2-2	SA	11	D'Agostini [44p], Gazzi [87]	8 526
	24 Cagliari	W	2-1	ICr4		Gonzalez [17], Angelo [52]	2 000
	27 Inter	L	0-1	SA	12		13 587
	4 Bologna	L	0-1	SA	15		18 316
	10 Genoa	L	0-2	SA	17		9 190
Dec	13 Palermo	D	4-4	ICr5		Reginaldo 2 [21 59], Gonzalez [40], Angelo [100]. W 3-0p	6 489
	17 Milan	L	0-2	SA	17		41 759
	20 Fiorentina	D	0-0	SA	16		9 117
	7 Lazio	W	4-0	SA	16	Destro 2 [11 81], Calaio 2 [35p 45p]	10 270
Jan	15 Parma	L	1-3	SA	17	Grossi [79]	11 570
	22 Napoli	D	1-1	SA	17	Calaio [67]	14 643
	25 Chievo	W	1-0	ICqf		Destro [54]	3 000
	29 Fiorentina	L	1-2	SA	17	Calaio [89p]	16 784
	5 Juventus	D	0-0	SA	17		35 226
	9 Napoli	W	2-1	ICsf		Reginaldo [42], D'Agostino [66]	4 616
	13 Roma	W	1-0	SA		Calaio [51p]	9 288
Feb	19 Lecce	L	1-4	SA		Del Grosso [25]	8 000
	22 Catania	L	0-1	SA	17		10 000
	26 Palermo	W	4-1	SA		Terzi [23p], Bogdani [34], Rossettini [46], Brienza [58]	8 604
	4 Cagliari	W	3-0	SA	10	Bogdani [41], Calaio [80], Del Grosso [82]	8 529
Mar	11 Cesena	W	2-0	SA	15	Brienza [75], Bogdani [81]	15 360
	18 Novara	L	0-2	SA	16		9 891
	21 Napoli	L	0-2	ICsf			56 418
	25 Chievo	D	1-1	SA	10	Destro [51]	6 500
	1 Udinese	W	1-0	SA	10	Destro [70]	9 094
	7 Atalanta	W	2-1	SA	10	Larrondo [13p], Destro [90]	15 500
	11 Inter	L	1-2	SA	13	D'Agostino [6]	46 327
Apr	22 Genoa	W	4-1	SA	10	Brienza 2 [17 37], Destro [19], Giorgi [49]	20 078
	25 Bologna	D	1-1	SA	10	Destro [52]	9 011
	29 Milan	L	1-4	SA	13	Bogdani [83]	14 665
	2 Lazio	D	1-1	SA	13	Destro [26]	26 194
May	6 Parma	L	0-2	SA	14		8 640
	13 Napoli	L	1-2	SA	14	Destro [6]	43 582

14th Att: 198 724 • Av: 10 459 (+43.1%) • Artemio Franchi 15 373 (68%)

SIENA LEAGUE APPEARANCES/GOALS 2011-12
Goalkeepers Zeljko Brkic SRB 18 • Simone Farelli 1
Gianluca Pegolo 19
Defenders Angelo BRA 7+6/0 • Nicola Belmonte 1+1/0
Matteo Contini 12+4/0 • Cristiano Del Grosso 31+1/2
Emanuele Pesoli 7+2/0 • Luca Rossettini 30+1/1 • Andrea Rossi 7+3/0
Claudio Terzi 33+2/1 • Roberto Vitiello 33/1
Midfield Francesco Bolzoni 8+8/1 • Franco Brienza 34+2/4
Paul Codrea ROU 0+1/0 • Gaetano D'Agostino 19+5/3
Alessandro Gazzi 31+2/1 • Luigi Giorgi 12+1/1 • Paolo Grossi 9+8/1
Daniele Mannini 12+9/0 • Francesco Parravicini 1+8/0
Alessio Sestu 1+4/0 • Simone Vergassola 23+6/0
Forwards Erjon Bogdani ALB 4+7/4 • Emanuele Calaio 24+1/11
Mattia Destro 26+4/12 • Pablo Gonzalez ARG 5+11/1
Marcelo Larrondo ARG 6+8/1 • Reginaldo BRA 4+9/0
Coach Giuseppe Sannino (6/06/2011)

UDINESE
2011–12

Aug	16 Arsenal	L	0-1	CLpo		58 159
	24 Arsenal	L	1-2	CLpo	Di Natale [39]	26 031
	11 Lecce	W	2-0	SA	4	Basta [2], Di Natale [16]	10 000
	15 Rennes	W	2-1	ELgl		Di Natale [39], Armero [83]	8 383
Sep	18 Fiorentina	W	2-0	SA	3	Di Natale [8p], Isla [29]	16 125
	21 Milan	D	1-1	SA	3	Di Natale [29]	37 592
	25 Cagliari	D	0-0	SA	2		10 000
	29 Celtic	D	1-1	ELgl	Abdi [88p]	28 476
	2 Bologna	W	2-0	SA	2	Benatia [29], Di Natale [72p]	16 338
	16 Atalanta	D	0-0	SA	2		14 444
Oct	20 At Madrid	W	2-0	ELgl		Benatia [88], Flores [94+]	10 026
	23 Novara	W	3-0	SA	1	Di Natale 2 [33 49], Domizzi [39]	15 988
	26 Napoli	L	0-2	SA	2		35 565
	30 Palermo	W	1-0	SA	2	Di Natale [38]	13 000
	3 At Madrid	L	0-4	ELgl			18 300
	6 Siena	W	2-1	SA	2	Basta [2], Di Natale [64]	16 033
Nov	20 Parma	L	0-2	SA	4		14 128
	25 Roma	W	2-0	SA	3	Di Natale [79], Isla [89]	18 310
	30 Rennes	D	0-0	ELgl			17 428
	3 Inter	W	1-0	SA	3	Isla [73]	42 122
	11 Chievo	W	2-1	SA	2	Di Natale [68], Basta [79]	16 062
Dec	15 Celtic	D	1-1	ELgl	Di Natale [45]	8 644
	18 Lazio	D	2-2	SA	3	Flores [27], Pinzi [74]	31 884
	21 Juventus	D	0-0	SA	3		28 588
	8 Cesena	W	4-1	SA	3	Di Natale 2 [1 82], Asamoah [54], Basta [75]	16 651
Jan	11 Chievo	L	1-2	ICr5	Di Natale [84]	5 200
	15 Genoa	L	2-3	SA	3	Ferronetti [14], Di Natale [75p]	19 860
	22 Catania	W	2-1	SA	3	Armero [20], Di Natale [53]	16 064
	28 Juventus	L	1-2	SA	3	Flores [56]	38 433
	1 Lecce	W	2-1	SA	3	Pazienza [2], Di Natale [36]	15 818
	5 Fiorentina	L	2-3	SA	3	Di Natale [14], Torje [89]	16 684
Feb	8 Milan	L	1-2	SA	4	Di Natale [19]	22 370
	16 PAOK	D	0-0	ELr2			11 641
	19 Cagliari	D	0-0	SA	3		13 000
	23 PAOK	W	3-0	ELr2		Larangeira [6], Flores [15], Domizzi [51p]	22 400
	26 Bologna	W	3-1	SA	3	Di Natale [38p], Basta [56], Flores [84]	16 209
	4 Atalanta	D	0-0	SA	4		16 000
	8 AZ	L	0-2	ELr3			12 579
	11 Novara	W	0-1	SA	5		8 708
Mar	15 AZ	W	2-1	ELr3	Di Natale 2 [3p 15]	13 300
	18 Napoli	D	2-2	SA	5	Pinzi [28], Di Natale [52]	21 661
	24 Palermo	D	1-1	SA	5	Torje [85]	17 918
	1 Siena	L	0-1	SA	5		9 094
	7 Parma	W	3-1	SA	4	Asamoah 2 [45 90], Di Natale [56]	17 831
Apr	11 Roma	L	1-3	SA	4	Fernandes [43]	29 672
	21 Chievo	D	0-0	SA	4		8 000
	25 Inter	L	1-3	SA	6	Danilo [6]	24 219
	29 Lazio	W	2-0	SA	4	Di Natale [69], Pereyra [90]	19 760
	2 Cesena	W	1-0	SA	4	Fabbrini [4]	13 650
May	6 Genoa	W	2-0	SA	3	Di Natale [30], Flores [66]	19 471
	13 Catania	W	2-0	SA	3	Di Natale [19], Fabbrini [58]	16 359

3rd Att: 343 289 • Av: 18 068 (+7.1%) • Friuli 41 652 (43%)

UDINESE LEAGUE APPEARANCES/GOALS 2011-12
Goalkeepers Samir Handanovic SVN 38
Defenders Mehdi Benatia FRA 27/1 • Andrea Coda 6+1/0
Danilo BRA 37/1 • Maurizio Domizzi 30+1/1
Damiano Ferronetti 11+4/1 • Mauricio Isla CHI 21/3
Neuton BRA 1+3/0 • Giovanni Pasquale 13+8/0
Midfield Almen Abdi SUI 9+14/0 • Emmanuel Agyemang GHA 6+4/0
Pablo Armero COL 25+3/1 • Kwadwo Asamoah GHA 31/3
Dusan Basta SRB 31/5 • Cristian Battocchio 0+4/0
Thierry Doubai CIV 0+1/0 • Joel Ekstrand SWE 5+6/0
Gelson Fernandes SUI 12+4/1 • Michele Pazienza 12+3/1
Roberto Pereyra ARG 7+4/1 • Giampiero Pinzi 27+1/2
Gabriel Torje ROU 12+9/2
Forwards Barreto BRA 2+5/0 • Antonio Di Natale 35+1/23
Diego Fabbrini 8+6/2 • Antonio Floro Flores 12+14/4
Coach Francesco Guidolin (24/05/10)

JAM – JAMAICA

FIFA/COCA-COLA WORLD RANKING

'93	'94	'95	'96	'97	'98	'99	'00	'01	'02	'03	'04	'05	'06	'07	'08	'09	'10	'11	'12
80	96	56	32	39	33	41	48	53	51	46	49	42	57	97	65	81	58	54	56

2012													
Jan	Feb	Mar	Apr	May	Jun	Jul	Aug	Sep	Oct	Nov	Dec	High	Low	Av
52	50	54	56	51	60	63	66	60	57	50	56	27	116	58

Having won the Caribbean Cup in 2008 and 2010 Jamaica were aiming to claim a hat trick of titles at the 2012 finals but they came away from Antigua without a win in what was their worst-ever performance at the finals. A 0-0 draw against Martinique was the best Theodore Whitmore's side could manage alongside defeats at the hands of both French Guiana and the tournament winners Cuba. Six weeks previously, however, the Jamaicans had exceeded all expectations by reaching the final hexagonal in the CONCACAF qualifiers for the 2014 FIFA World Cup. Their home form proved to be the key in their first-round qualifying group with wins over Guatemala, the USA and Antigua as they finished second behind the Americans and ahead of Guatemala on goal difference. At home Portmore United won a record-equalling fifth championship in a tight race with Boys Town. The two met in the penultimate round, a match won 2-1 by Boys Town, but Portmore secured the point needed on the final day of the season at home to Waterhouse. A dispute between the football authorities and a local cable TV company meant that the popular JFF Flow Champions Cup wasn't organised for the 2011-12 season while once again Jamaican clubs were absent from the CFU Caribbean Club Championship.

CFU CARIBBEAN CUP RECORD

1989 DNQ **1991** 1 winners (hosts) **1992** 2 F **1993** 2 F (hosts) **1994** DNQ **1995** 5 r1 (co-hosts) **1996** 5 r1 **1997** 3 SF
1998 1 winners (co-hosts) **1999** 3 SF **2001** 5 r1 **2005** 1 winners **2007** DNQ **2008** 1 winners (hosts) **2010** 1 winners **2012** 8 r1

JAMAICA FOOTBALL FEDERATION (JFF)

20 St Lucia Crescent,
Kingston 5

☎ +1 876 9298036
+1 876 9290438
jamff@hotmail.com

FA 1910 CON 1961 FIFA 1962
P Horace Burrell
GS Raymond Grant

THE STADIA

2014 FIFA World Cup Stadia
National Stadium (part of the Independence Park complex)
Kingston   35 000
Other Main Stadia
Greenfield Stadium
Trelawny   25 000
Catherine Hall Sports Complex
Montego Bay   9 000
Harbour View Stadium
Kingston   7 000

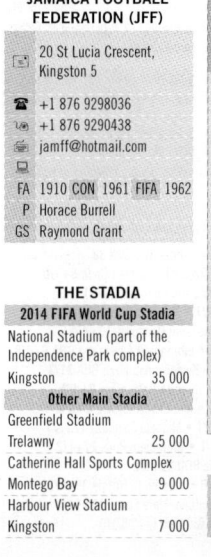

MAJOR CITIES/TOWNS

		Population
1	Kingston	578 356
2	Spanish Town	158 458
3	Portmore	105 238
4	Montego Bay	80 650
5	Mandeville	48 300
6	May Pen	44 345
7	Old Harbour	28 079
8	Linstead	22 292
9	Savanna la Mar	19 408
10	Half Way Tree	18 198
11	Port Antonio	14 392
12	Bog Walk	13 889
13	Ewarton	13 807
14	Saint Ann's Bay	13 671
15	Constant Spring	12 585
16	Morant Bay	10 200
17	Hayes	9 798
18	Ocho Rios	9 554
19	Old Harbour Bay	8 537

JAMAICA

Capital	Kingston	Population	2 825 928 (138)
GDP per capita	$8600 (115)	Area km²	10 991 km² (167)
Neighbours (km)	Coast 1022	% in cities	53%
		GMT +/-	-5

RECENT INTERNATIONAL MATCHES PLAYED BY JAMAICA

2010	Opponents		Score	Venue	Comp	Scorers	Att	Referee
31-01	Canada	W	1-0	Kingston	Fr	Shelton [67]	18 000	Hospedales TRI
10-02	Argentina	L	1-2	Mar Del Plata	Fr	Johnson [46]	20 000	Rivera PER
28-04	South Africa	L	0-2	Offenbach	Fr		562	Sippel GER
11-08	Trinidad and Tobago	W	3-1	Macoya	Fr	Richards [7], Austin [30p], Bryan [52]	4 500	Taylor BRB
5-09	Costa Rica	W	1-0	Kingston	Fr	Johnson [66]	15 000	Brizan TRI
7-09	Peru	L	1-2	Fort Lauderdale	Fr	Cummings [18]	5 217	Vaughn USA
10-10	Trinidad and Tobago	W	1-0	Kingston	Fr	Richards [19p]	7 000	Archundia MEX
17-11	Costa Rica	D	0-0	Fort Lauderdale	Fr		4 000	Renso USA
27-11	Antigua and Barbuda	W	3-1	Riviere-Pilote	CCr1	Shelton 2 [14 37], Richards [40]	3 000	Wijngaarde SUR
29-11	Guadeloupe †	W	2-0	Riviere-Pilote	CCr1	Francis [53], Johnson [93+]	3 000	Lopez GUA
1-12	Guyana	W	4-0	Riviere-Pilote	CCr1	Richards [42], Morgan 2 [49 75], Vernan [90]	3 000	Cruc CRC
3-12	Grenada	W	2-1	Fort de France	CCsf	Richards [7], Smith [96]	4 000	Taylor BRB
5-12	Guadeloupe †	D	1-1	Riviere-Pilote	CCf	Cummings [32]. W 5-4p	4 000	Wijngaarde SUR
2011								
25-03	Venezuela	L	0-2	Montego Bay	Fr		6 000	Wijngaarde SUR
29-03	El Salvador	W	3-2	San Salvador	Fr	Dane Richards 2 [24 26], Omar Cummings [53]	15 000	Rodas GUA
6-06	Grenada	W	4-0	Carson	GCr1	Luton Shelton [21], Ryan Johnson [39], Demar Phillips [79] Omar Daley [84]	21 550	Toledo USA
10-06	Guatemala	W	2-0	Miami	GCr1	Demar Phillips 2 [65 77]	18 057	Quesada CRC
13-06	Honduras	W	1-0	Harrison	GCr1	Ryan Johnson [35]	25 000	Aguilar SLV
19-06	USA	L	0-2	Washington DC	GCqf		45 424	Rodriguez.M MEX
10-08	China PR	L	0-1	Hefei	Fr		60 000	Lee Min Hu KOR
2-09	Ecuador	L	2-5	Quito	Fr	Omar Cummings [55], Demar Phillips [66]	6 000	Buitriago COL
6-09	Colombia	L	0-2	Fort Lauderdale	Fr		8 000	Dellavie USA
11-10	Honduras	L	1-2	La Ceiba	Fr	Demar Phillips [45]	18 000	Moreno PAN
2012								
22-02	Cuba	W	1-0	Kingston	Fr	Jorginho James [87]	10 000	Moreno PAN
24-02	Cuba	W	3-0	Montego Bay	Fr	Ryan Johnson [35], Jevaugh Watson [37], Mitchily Waul [83]	4 000	Moreno PAN
29-02	New Zealand	W	3-2	Auckland	Fr	Xavian Virgo [39], Tremaine Stewart [53], Navian Boyd [77]	15 379	Huata TAH
21-03	Costa Rica	D	0-0	Kingston	Fr		10 000	Gantar CAN
18-05	Guyana	W	1-0	Montego Bay	Fr	Jeremie Lynch 61	3 500	Marrufo USA
27-05	Panama	L	0-1	Kingston	Fr		13 000	Morales MEX
1-06	Panama	L	1-2	Panama City	Fr	Dane Richards [43]	8 642	Cerdas CRC
8-06	Guatemala	W	2-1	Kingston	WCq	Demar Phillips [40], Ryan Johnson [46]	14 000	Moreno PAN
12-06	Antigua and Barbuda	D	0-0	St John's	WCq		8 500	Lancaster GUY
15-08	El Salvador	W	2-0	Washington DC	Fr		14 185	Gantar CAN
7-09	USA	W	2-1	Kingston	WCq	Rodolph Austin [24], Luton Shelton [61]	25 000	Rodriguez.M MEX
11-09	USA	L	0-1	Columbus	WCq		23 881	Pineda HON
12-10	Guatemala	L	1-2	Guatemala City	WCq	Luton Shelton [60p]	20 717	Garcia MEX
16-10	Antigua and Barbuda	W	4-1	Kingston	WCq	Demar Phillips [16], Nyron Nosworthy [18], Dane Richards 2 [77 88]	8 000	Quesada CRC
8-12	French Guiana	L	1-2	St John's	CNr1	Tremaine Stewart [22]	100	Vazquez DOM
10-12	Martinique	D	0-0	St John's	CNr1		225	Johnson GUY
12-12	Cuba	L	0-1	St John's	CNr1		200	Bonilla SLV

Fr = Friendly match • CC = Digicel Caribbean Cup • GC = CONCACAF Gold Cup • WC = FIFA World Cup
q = qualifier • r1 = first round group • qf = quarter-final • † Not a full international

JAMAICA NATIONAL TEAM HISTORICAL RECORDS

Caps: 118 - Ian Goodison 1996- • **110** - Theodore Whitmore 1993-2005 • **109** - Ricardo Gardner 1997-2009 • **107** - Durrant Brown 1984-1998

Goals: 35 - Luton Shelton 2004- • **28** - Paul Young 1993-98 • **27** - Onandi Lowe 1994-2004 • **24** - Theodore Whitmore 1993-2005 • **19** - Walter Boyd 1991-2001

Past Coaches: Geoffrey Maxwell 1989-90 • Carl Brown 1990-94 • Rene Simoes BRA 1994-2000 • Sebastiao Lazaroni BRA 2000 • Clovis De Oliveira BRA 2000-01 • Carl Brown 2001-04 • Sebastiao Lazaroni BRA 2004 • Wendell Downswell 2004-06 • Carl Brown 2006 • Bora Milutinovic 2006-07 • Theodore Whitmore 2007-08 • Rene Simoes BRA 2008 • Theodore Whitmore 2008 • John Barnes ENG 2008-09 • Theodore Whitmore 2009-

JAMAICA 2011-12

DIGICEL PREMIER LEAGUE

	Pl	W	D	L	F	A	Pts	Portmore U	Boys' Town	Waterhouse	Humble L	Tivoli G'ns	Harbour V	Montego B	Arnett G'ns	Sporting	Highgate U	Village U	Reno
Portmore United	38	19	10	9	48	37	67		1-0 2-4	1-0 1-1	1-0 0-3	2-0 1-1	0-0 0-1	2-1 1-0		1-1	2-1 1-0	0-0 1-0	2-0	4-1
Boys' Town	38	18	12	8	44	34	66	1-0 2-1		1-2 1-0	2-2 0-0	2-2 2-1	0-0 2-0	1-1		2-0	2-2	1-0	2-1 0-0	3-1 0
Waterhouse	38	16	12	10	42	32	60	1-2 1-2	1-2 0-0		1-0 3-0	2-0 0-0	1-1 2-0	1-0 1-1		0-2	2-0 2-0	3-2 1-0	4-1	2-1
Humble Lions	38	15	12	11	41	33	57	1-2 1-2	0-0 3-0	0-1 1-1		0-0 1-0	2-0 0-1	1-3		0-0 0-0	1-2 0-1	3-0	2-3	0-0 1-0
Tivoli Gardens	38	14	14	10	42	33	56	1-0 1-2	3-1 1-2	1-1 3-0	3-1 0-1		1-2 2-1	2-1 2-2		0-2	1-1 2-0	1-1 2-0	0-1	1-0
Harbour View	38	12	17	9	35	31	53	2-1 1-1	0-0 2-0	1-1 1-1	1-1 2-0	0-0 1-0		0-0		1-3	2-0	1-1	2-0 0-0	2-0 3-1
Montego Bay United	38	14	12	12	48	34	54	3-3	3-0 0-0	3-1	0-0 1-2	1-1	0-2 1-1			1-0 1-1	1-1 3-0	6-0 0-1	1-0 2-0	2-3 2-0
Arnett Gardens	38	14	11	13	31	39	53	1-0 2-3	1-2 0-1	1-0 2-1	1-5	1-2 1-2	0-0 1-0	1-2 1-2			0-1 1-0	0-1 1-1	3-1 2-1	2-0
Sporting Central Acad.	38	10	13	15	33	48	43	1-2	0-3 1-0	1-1	0-2	0-2	1-1 1-2	1-0 1-0	3-1 1-1			0-0 1-0	1-0 0-1	1-1 5-5
Highgate United	38	9	13	16	30	43	40	0-1	2-2 0-1	0-1	0-1 0-1	1-3	2-2 3-0	1-0 2-0	0-0 0-0	0-2 2-2			2-1 1-2	2-1 0-2 1
Village United	38	7	11	20	28	45	32	2-0 2-2	0-1	0-0 0-1	1-2 0-0	0-0 0-0	0-0	0-1 0-1	1-2 1-1	1-2 2-0	1-0 2-1			0-1 0-1
Reno	38	5	13	20	28	51	28	0-0 0-2	0-0	0-1 0-1	2-3	0-0 0-0	0-2	0-0 0-2	1-1 2-0	0-1 1-1	1-0	1-3 2-1	1-1	

11/09/2011 - 7/05/2012 • Top scorer: **14** - Jermaine **ANDERSON**, Waterhouse

MEDALS TABLE

		Overall			League		Cup		City/Town
		G	S	B	G	S	G	S	
1	Portmore United (ex Hazard Utd)	9	6		**5**	3	**4**	3	Portmore
2	Tivoli Gardens	8	6		**5**	4	3	2	Kingston
3	Harbour View	7	7		3	5	**4**	2	Kingston
4	Boys' Town	5	6		3	5	2	1	Kingston
5	Reno	5	3		3	3	2		Savannah del Mar
6	Santos	5	1		**5**	1			Kingston
7	Waterhouse	4	3		2	2	2	1	Kingston
8	Arnett Gardens	3	5		3	4		1	Kingston
9	Seba United	3	4		2	4	1		Montego Bay
10	Wadadah	2	2		2			2	Montego Bay
11	Violet Kickers	2	1		2			1	Montego Bay
12	Olympic Gardens	2				2			Kingston
13	Cavalier	1	3		1	3			Kingston
14	Jamaica Defence Force	1			1				Kingston
	Naggo's Head	1			1		2		Portmore
16	Black Lions		1			1			
	Constant Spring		1			1			Constant Spring
	Humble Lions		1					1	Clarendon
	Rivoli United		1					1	Spanish Town
	St George's		1			1			
	Thunderbolts		1			1			
	Village United		1					1	Falmouth

JOR – JORDAN

FIFA/COCA-COLA WORLD RANKING

'93	'94	'95	'96	'97	'98	'99	'00	'01	'02	'03	'04	'05	'06	'07	'08	'09	'10	'11	'12
87	113	143	146	124	126	115	105	99	77	47	40	86	95	120	124	111	104	82	94

2012

Jan	Feb	Mar	Apr	May	Jun	Jul	Aug	Sep	Oct	Nov	Dec	High	Low	Av
81	82	83	81	81	83	84	83	87	78	90	94	37	152	99

Adnan Hamed's national team enjoyed another successful year in 2012 during which they kept alive Jordan's hopes of qualifying for the FIFA World Cup finals for the first time. Their campaign in the final phase of qualifying for Brazil 2014 had started poorly, drawing at home with Iraq before losing 6-0 to Japan after the harsh sending off of Abdallah Deeb. That was followed, however, with a surprise 2-1 victory over Australia in Amman in September, a result that threw the race for second place behind runaway leaders Japan wide open. In club football Al Faysali won back the league title from Al Wihdat in an exciting season that needed a championship play-off after both Faysali and Al Ramtha finished the season level on 51 points. Al Wihdat had tried their best to deny fierce rivals Faysali the championship but a 0-0 draw on the final day of the season between the two saw Faysali through to a play-off against Al Ramtha who had beaten Al Jazeera 1-0. In the play-off Faysali beat Ramtha 3-0 to deny their opponents a first championship since 1982. Victory in the JFA Cup, thanks to a 1-0 win over Mansheyat Bani Hasan in the final, ensured Al Faysali completed the league-and-cup double. Al Wihdat, meanwhile, had to satisfy themselves with a run to the quarter-finals of the AFC Cup, where they lost to eventual champions Al Kuwait.

FIFA WORLD CUP RECORD
1930-1982 DNE **1986-2010** DNQ

JORDAN FOOTBALL ASSOCIATIOM (JFA)

Al-Hussein Youth City,
PO Box 962024,
Amman 11196
+962 6 5657662
+962 6 5657660
info@jfa.com.jo
www.jfa.com.jo
FA 1949 CON 1970 FIFA 1958
P HRH Prince Ali Bin Al Hussein
GS Khalil Al Salem

THE STADIA

2014 FIFA World Cup Stadia
International Stadium
Amman 20 000
Al-Qwaismeh 'King Abdullah Int'
Amman 18 000

Other Main Stadia
Prince Mohammed Stadium
Al Zarqa 17 000
Al Hasan Stadium
Irbit 15 000

MAJOR CITIES/TOWNS

		Population
1	Amman	1 155 710
2	Al Zarqa	460 007
3	Russeifa	309 152
4	Irbit	302 061
5	Quaismeh	198 777
6	Khelda	179 928
7	Wadi Essier	159 554
8	Khraibet Essooq	133 849
9	Aqaba	99 265
10	Ramtha	92 461
11	Salt	91 385
12	Madaba	86 372
13	Jbaiha	85 732
14	Swaileh	72 705
15	Al Muqabalayn	70 421
16	Mshairfet Ras	60 013
17	Mafraq	58 447
18	Sahab	55 562
19	Um Qsair	54 341

AL MAMLAKAH AL URDUNIYAH AL HASHIMIYA • HASHEMITE KINGDOM OF JORDAN

Capital Amman	Population 6 342 948 (104)	% in cities 78%
GDP per capita $5200 (139)	Area km² 89 342 km² (111)	GMT +/- +2

Neighbours (km) Iraq 181, Israel 238, Saudi Arabia 744, Syria 375, West Bank 97

RECENT INTERNATIONAL MATCHES PLAYED BY JORDAN

2010	Opponents	Score	Venue	Comp	Scorers	Att	Referee
24-09	Syria	D 1-1	Amman	WAr1	Amer Deeb [13]	18 000	
28-09	Kuwait	D 2-2	Amman	WAr1	Hasan Mahmoud 2 [38 51]	18 000	
16-11	Cyprus	D 0-0	Amman	Fr		3 500	Ebrahim BHR
28-12	Bahrain	L 1-2	Dubai	Fr	Baha Suleiman [60]		
2011							
2-01	Uzbekistan	D 2-2	Sharjah	Fr	Amer Deeb [33], Odai Al Saify [75]		Hashmi UAE
9-01	Japan	D 1-1	Doha	ACr1	Hasan Mahmoud [45]	6 255	Abdul Bashir SIN
13-01	Saudi Arabia	W 1-0	Al Rayyan	ACr1	Baha Suleiman [42]	17 349	Albadwawi UAE
17-01	Syria	W 2-1	Doha	ACr1	Ali Dyab OG [30], Odai Alsaify [59]	9 849	Abdou QAT
21-01	Uzbekistan	L 1-2	Doha	ACqf	Bashar Yaseen [58]	16 073	Abdul Bashir SIN
26-03	Kuwait	D 1-1	Sharjah	Fr	Hasan Mahmoud [23p]		
29-03	Korea DPR	D 1-1	Sharjah	Fr	Hasan Mahmoud [29]		
5-07	Syria	L 1-3	Istanbul	Fr	Amer Deeb [10]		
8-07	Yemen	W 4-0	Istanbul	Fr	Ahmad Ibrahim [62], Hasan Mahmoud [65], Shadi Abu Hashhash [90], Abdallah Salim [92+]		
13-07	Saudi Arabia	D 1-1	Amman	Fr	Hasan Mahmoud [9]. L 3-4p		
16-07	Iraq	D 1-1	Amman	Fr	Mohammed Al Dumeiri [5]. W 5-4p		
23-07	Nepal	W 9-0	Amman	WCq	Hasan Mahmoud 4 [7 72 83 90], Amer Khalil 2 [20 57], Ahmad Ibrahim 2 [20 62], Abdallah Salim [24]	17 000	Jahanbazi IRN
28-07	Nepal	D 1-1	Kathmandu	WCq	Saeed Almurjan [53]	20 000	Fan Qi CHN
22-08	Tunisia	D 3-3	Amman	Fr	Abdallah Salim 2 [20 52], Ahmad Hayel [47]		
27-08	Indonesia	W 1-0	Amman	Fr	Abdallah Salim [55]		
2-09	Iraq	W 2-0	Arbil	WCq	Hasan Mahmoud [43], Abdallah Salim [47]	24 000	Shukralla BHR
6-09	China PR	W 2-1	Amman	WCq	Baha Suleiman [49], Amer Khalil [56]	19 000	Irmatov UZB
6-10	Thailand	D 0-0	Bangkok	Fr			
11-10	Singapore	W 3-0	Singapore	WCq	Abdallah Salim [11], Anas Bani Yaseen [54], Ahmad Ibrahim [64]	3 799	Choi Myung Yong KOR
11-11	Singapore	W 2-0	Amman	WCq	Ahmad Ibrahim [15], Amer Khalil [65]	19 000	Williams AUS
15-11	Iraq	L 1-3	Amman	WCq	Hasan Mahmoud [17]	13 000	Albadwawi UAE
2012							
23-02	Iran	D 2-2	Dubai	Fr	Ahmad Ibrahim [39], Abdallah Salim [55p]	7 000	Mohamed UAE
29-02	China PR	L 1-3	Guangzhou	WCq	Basem Othman [85]	6 104	Minh Tri Vo VIE
18-05	Lebanon	W 2-1	Saida	Fr	Hamza Al Dardour 2 [7 77]	3 500	Taweel SYR
3-06	Iraq	D 1-1	Amman	WCq	Ahmad Ibrahim [43]	13 000	Kovalenko UZB
8-06	Japan	L 0-6	Saitama	WCq		60 874	Kim Dong Jin KOR
13-08	Uzbekistan	L 0-1	Amman	Fr			Tufaylieh SYR
15-08	Uzbekistan	W 2-0	Amman	Fr	Ahmad Ibrahim [57], Hasan Mahmoud [68p]		Taweel SYR
5-09	Iran	D 0-0	Amman	Fr		3 500	Aljeneibi UAE
11-09	Australia	W 2-1	Amman	WCq	Hasan Mahmoud [50p], Amer Khalil [73]	16 000	Balideh QAT
8-10	Qatar	D 1-1	Doha	Fr	Hasan Abdel Fattah [66]		
16-10	Oman	L 1-2	Muscat	WCq	Thaer Bawab [90]	26 000	Shukralla BHR
8-11	Bahrain	L 0-3	Manama	Fr			
14-11	Iraq	L 0-1	Doha	WCq		1 755	Tan Hai CHN
10-12	Iraq	L 0-1	Al Farwaniyah	WAr1		1 600	Shaban KUW
16-12	Syria	L 1-2	Kuwait City	WAr1	Khalil Bani Ateyah [22]	3 000	Ko Hyung Jin KOR

Fr = Friendly match • WA = West Asian Federation Championship • AC = AFC Asian Cup • WC = FIFA World Cup
q = qualifier • r1 = first round group

JORDAN NATIONAL TEAM HISTORICAL RECORDS

Past Coaches: Mohammad Awad 1985-2000 • Branko Smiljanic SRB 2000-02 • Mahmoud El Gohary EGY 2002-07 • Nelo Vingada POR 2007-09 • Adnan Hamad IRQ 2009-

JORDAN 2011-12
PROFESSIONAL LEAGUE

	Pl	W	D	L	F	A	Pts	Al Faysali	Al Ramtha	Al Wihdat	Al Buq'aa	Al Arabi	Al Jazeera	Shabab	That Ras	Mansheyat	Al Yarmouk	Al Jaleel	Kfarsoum
Al Faysali ‡	22	16	3	3	50	17	51		1-0	0-0	3-2	3-2	1-1	1-0	3-1	1-0	4-0	6-1	3-1
Al Ramtha ‡	22	15	6	1	45	15	51	1-0		0-0	2-2	3-2	1-0	2-0	4-0	3-0	2-0	1-0	2-1
Al Wihdat	22	11	7	4	34	18	40	0-0	1-1		2-0	2-0	1-1	3-1	3-0	1-2	3-1	2-0	4-2
Al Buq'aa	22	10	6	6	30	26	36	0-2	1-1	2-2		2-0	1-2	1-0	2-1	2-1	0-0	1-1	1-4
Al Arabi	22	7	7	8	28	32	28	0-7	2-2	2-1	2-0		3-0	2-2	1-1	0-0	2-1	0-0	2-1
Al Jazeera	22	7	6	9	26	31	27	1-2	0-1	3-0	1-2	1-0		0-2	1-1	1-2	3-2	1-1	1-2
Shabab Al Ordon	22	6	8	8	24	25	26	0-1	1-1	2-1	1-1	3-2	0-2		0-0	5-2	0-0	1-1	1-0
That Ras	22	5	9	8	31	36	24	3-0	1-2	1-1	0-1	1-1	5-1	3-1		3-2	1-1	2-2	2-1
Mansheyat Bani Hasan	22	6	6	10	30	36	24	2-1	0-5	0-1	0-3	0-0	2-2	1-1	1-1		1-2	4-0	7-1
Al Yarmouk	22	5	6	11	19	35	21	0-2	1-3	0-1	0-2	2-1	0-1	1-0	1-1	2-2		0-0	1-0
Al Jaleel	22	3	9	10	22	38	18	2-3	0-2	0-3	0-2	0-2	1-1	0-0	3-1	1-0	3-4		5-1
Kfarsoum	22	4	1	17	26	56	13	0-6	2-6	0-2	1-2	0-2	1-2	0-3	4-2	0-1	3-0	1-1	

5/08/2011 - 3/05/2012 • ‡ Qualified for the AFC Cup • Championship play-off: **Al Faysali** 3-0 Al Ramtha

JORDAN 2011-12
FIRST DIVISION (2)

Group A

	Pl	W	D	L	F	A	Pts
Al Ahli †	12	7	3	2	21	12	24
Al Sareeh †	12	6	4	2	20	11	22
Al Salt	12	6	4	2	25	17	22
Blama	12	6	3	3	21	20	21
Ain Karem	12	4	3	5	16	14	15
Al Qouqazy	12	3	0	9	16	25	9
Al Badiah Al Wosta	12	1	1	10	8	28	4

Group B

	Pl	W	D	L	F	A	Pts
Al Ittihad Al Ramtha †	12	6	6	0	26	5	24
Shabab Al Hussein †	12	6	5	1	21	8	23
Al Sheikh Hussein	12	6	2	4	16	13	20
Ittihad Al Zarqa	12	5	3	4	12	13	18
Al Hussein	12	4	4	4	15	12	16
Shehan	12	2	3	7	10	25	9
Al Tora	12	1	1	10	12	36	4

Final Round

	Pl	W	D	L	F	A	Pts
Shabab Al Hussein	3	2	0	1	7	4	6
Al Sareeh	3	2	0	1	6	5	6
Al Ahli	3	2	0	1	7	5	60
Al Ittihad Al Ramtha	3	0	0	3	3	9	

5/09/2011 - 31/12/2011 • † Qualified for final round

MEDALS TABLE

	Overall G S B	Lge G	Cup G S	FAS G S	Asia G S B	City
1 Al Faysali	58 11	32	17 5	7 5	2 1	Amman
2 Al Wihdat	28 10 3	12	9 4	7 6	3	Amman
3 Al Ramtha	9 10 1	2	2 9	5 1	1	Irbid
4 Al Ahli	8 1	8	1			Amman
5 Al Jazeera	6 2	3	1 1	2 1		Amman
6 Shabab Al Ordon	5 3	1	2 2	1 1	1	Zarqa
7 Al Hussein	3 12		5	3 7		Irbid
8 Amman	3 1	1		2 1		Amman
9 Al Arabi	1 2		1 1	1		Irbid
10 Jordan	1	1				Amman
Kfarsoum	1			1		
Al Yarmouk	1			1		Irbid
13 Al Buq'aa	3		1	2		Amman
Shabab Al Hussein	3		1	2		Amman
15 Mansheyat	2		2			B.Hasan
16 Al Jalil	1			1		
Al Qadisiya	1			1		

JFA CUP 2011-12

First Round		Quarter-finals		Semi-finals		Final	
Al Faysali	2						
Al Ramtha *	1	**Al Faysali** *	2 2				
Ain Karem	0	Al Wihdat	1 3				
Al Wihdat *	5			**Al Faysali**	1 3		
Kfarsoum	2			Shabab Al Ordon *	0 2		
Shabab Al Hussein *	0	Kfarsoum *	2 1				
That Ras *	3	**Shabab Al Ordon**	1 3				
Shabab Al Ordon	7					**Al Faysali**	1
Al Jazeera	1					Mansheyat B. Hasan	0
Al Jaleel *	0	**Al Jazeera** *	1 1				
Al Sareeh *	0	Al Arabi	0 2			CUP FINAL	
Al Arabi	1			Al Jazeera	1 2		
Al Yarmouk	2 5p			**Mansheyat B. Hasan** *	1 2	Amman International, Amman	
Al Buq'aa *	2 4p	Al Yarmouk	0 3			29-04-2012	
Al Tora *	1	**Mansheyat B. Hasan** *	1 2			Scorer - Ibrahim Al Zwahrh [6]	
Mansheyat B. Hasan	6			* Home team/home team in the first leg			

JPN – JAPAN

FIFA/COCA-COLA WORLD RANKING

'93	'94	'95	'96	'97	'98	'99	'00	'01	'02	'03	'04	'05	'06	'07	'08	'09	'10	'11	'12
43	36	31	21	14	20	57	38	34	22	29	17	15	47	34	35	43	29	19	22

2012

Jan	Feb	Mar	Apr	May	Jun	Jul	Aug	Sep	Oct	Nov	Dec	High	Low	Av
19	30	33	30	30	23	20	22	23	23	24	22	9	62	31

Sanfrecce Hiroshima underlined the unpredictability that has made the J.League one of Asia's most entertaining domestic championships by claiming their first ever title. Led by the goals of national team striker Hisato Sato, Sanfrecce became the seventh of the original ten J.League members to win the title in what was the competition's 20th season. Defending champions Kashiwa Reysol, coached by the Brazilian Nelsinho Baptista, struggled in the league with AFC Champions League commitments hampering their progress. They resurrected their season in the second half of the year, however, and ended up winning the Emperor's Cup after beating Gamba Osaka 1-0 in the final on New Year's Day. For Gamba Osaka it was the final act of a traumatic season that saw them relegated to the second division for the first time - just four years after being crowned Asian champions. Alberto Zaccheroni's national team, meanwhile, stood on the verge of qualifying for the 2014 FIFA World Cup finals after going unbeaten through the first five games of the final round of Asian qualifying. That went some way towards making up for the disappointment of the defeat at the hands of South Korea in the bronze medal play-off at the 2012 London Olympics. There was a silver medal for the women's team after they reached their final, before losing 2-1 to the USA.

FIFA WORLD CUP RECORD

1930-1950 DNE   1954 DNQ   1958 DNE   1962 DNQ   1966 DNE   1970-1994 DNQ   **1998** 31 r1   **2002** 9 r2 (hosts)   **2006** 28 r1   **2010** 9 r2

JAPAN FOOTBALL ASSOCIATION (JFA)

JFA House, Football Ave., Bunkyo-ku, Tokyo 113-8311

☎ +81 3 38302004
📠 +81 3 38302005
✉ inter_national@info.jfa.jp
🌐 www.jfa.or.jp
FA 1921 CON 1954 FIFA 1929
P Kuniya Daini
GS Michihiro Tanaka

THE STADIA

2014 FIFA World Cup Stadia

Saitama Stadium 2002 Saitama	63 700
Osaka Nagai Stadium Osaka	50 000
Toyota Stadium Toyota	45 000

Other Main Stadia

International Stadium Yokohama	72 370
National Olympic Stadium Tokyo	57 363

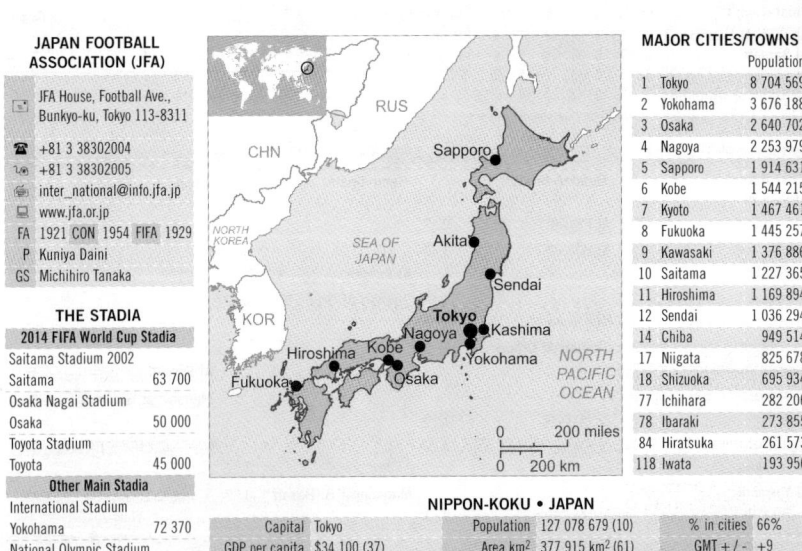

MAJOR CITIES/TOWNS

		Population
1	Tokyo	8 704 569
2	Yokohama	3 676 188
3	Osaka	2 640 702
4	Nagoya	2 253 979
5	Sapporo	1 914 631
6	Kobe	1 544 215
7	Kyoto	1 467 461
8	Fukuoka	1 445 616
9	Kawasaki	1 376 886
10	Saitama	1 227 365
11	Hiroshima	1 169 894
12	Sendai	1 036 294
14	Chiba	949 514
17	Niigata	825 678
18	Shizuoka	695 934
77	Ichihara	282 206
78	Ibaraki	273 855
84	Hiratsuka	261 573
118	Iwata	193 956

NIPPON-KOKU • JAPAN

Capital	Tokyo	Population	127 078 679 (10)	% in cities	66%
GDP per capita	$34 100 (37)	Area km²	377 915 km² (61)	GMT +/-	+9
Neighbours (km)	Coast 29 751				

RECENT INTERNATIONAL MATCHES PLAYED BY JAPAN

2010	Opponents	Score	Venue	Comp	Scorers	Att	Referee
14-06	Cameroon	W 1-0	Bloemfontein	WCr1	Honda [39]	30 620	Benquerenca POR
19-06	Netherlands	L 0-1	Durban	WCr1		62 010	Baldassi ARG
24-06	Denmark	W 3-1	Rustenburg	WCr1	Honda [17], Endo [30], Okazaki [87]	27 967	Damon RSA
29-06	Paraguay	D 0-0	Pretoria	WCr2	L 3-5p	36 742	De Bleeckere BEL
4-09	Paraguay	W 1-0	Yokohama	Fr	Kagawa [70]	65 157	Rodriguez.M MEX
7-09	Guatemala	W 2-1	Osaka	Fr	Morimoto 2 [12 20]	44 541	Archundia MEX
8-10	Argentina	W 1-0	Saitama	Fr	Okazaki [19]	57 735	Gil POL
12-10	Korea Republic	D 0-0	Seoul	Fr		62 503	Irmatov UZB
2011							
9-01	Jordan	D 1-1	Doha	ACr1	Yoshida [92+]	6 255	Abdul Bashir SIN
13-01	Syria	W 2-1	Doha	ACr1	Hasebe [35], Honda [82p]	10 453	Torky IRN
17-01	Saudi Arabia	W 5-0	Al Rayyan	ACr1	Okazaki 3 [8 13 80], Maeda 2 [19 51]	2 022	Irmatov UZB
21-01	Qatar	W 3-2	Doha	ACqf	Kagawa 2 [29 71], Inoha [90]	19 479	Mohd Salleh MAS
25-01	Korea Republic	D 2-2	Doha	ACsf	Maeda [36], Hosogai [97]. W 3-0p	16 171	Al Ghamdi KSA
29-01	Australia	W 1-0	Doha	ACf	Lee [109]	37 174	Irmatov UZB
1-06	Peru	D 0-0	Niigata	Fr		39 048	Webb ENG
7-06	Czech Republic	D 0-0	Yokohama	Fr		65 856	Atkinson ENG
10-08	Korea Republic	W 3-0	Sapporo	Fr	Kagawa 2 [34 54], Honda [52]	38 263	Irmatov UZB
2-09	Korea DPR	W 1-0	Saitama	WCq	Yoshida [94+]	62 000	Albadwawi UAE
6-09	Uzbekistan	D 1-1	Tashkent	WCq	Okazaki [65]	32 000	Al Ghamdi KSA
7-10	Vietnam	W 1-0	Kobe	Fr	Lee [24]	27 522	Mahapab THA
11-10	Tajikistan	W 8-0	Osaka	WCq	Havenaar 2 [11 47], Okazaki 2 [19 74], Komano [35], Kagawa 2 [41 68], Nakamura.K [56]	44 688	Williams AUS
11-11	Tajikistan	W 4-0	Dushanbe	WCq	Konno [36], Okazaki 2 [61 92+], Maeda [82]	18 000	Kim Dong Jin KOR
15-11	Korea DPR	L 0-1	Pyongyang	WCq		50 000	Shukralla BHR
2012							
24-02	Iceland	W 3-1	Osaka	Fr	Maeda [2], Fujimoto [53], Mkino [79]	42 579	Beath AUS
29-02	Uzbekistan	L 0-1	Toyota	WCq		42 720	Balideh QAT
23-05	Azerbaijan	W 2-0	Shizuoka	Fr	Kagawa [43], Okazaki [58]	30 276	Bashir SIN
3-06	Oman	W 3-0	Saitama	WCq	Honda [11], Maeda [51], Okazaki [54]	63 551	Irmatov UZB
8-06	Jordan	W 6-0	Saitama	WCq	Maeda [18], Honda 3 [22 31 53p], Kagawa [35], Kurihara [89]	60 874	Kim Dong Jin KOR
12-06	Australia	D 1-1	Brisbane	WCq	Kurihara [65]	40 189	Al Ghamdi KSA
15-08	Venezuela	D 1-1	Sapporo	Fr	Endo [14]	39 396	Lee Min Hu KOR
6-09	UAE	W 1-0	Niigata	Fr	Havenaar [69]	42 020	Ma Ning CHN
11-09	Iraq	W 1-0	Saitama	WCq	Maeda [25]	60 593	Bashir SIN
12-10	France	W 1-0	Paris	Fr	Kagawa [88]	60 205	Collum SCO
16-10	Brazil	L 0-4	Wroclaw	Fr		36 000	Borski POL
14-11	Oman	W 2-1	Muscat	WCq	Kiyotake [20], Okazaki [90]	28 360	Balideh QAT

Fr = Friendly match • EAF - East Asian Federation Cup • AC = AFC Asian Cup • WC = FIFA World Cup • q = qualifier

JAPAN NATIONAL TEAM HISTORICAL RECORDS

Caps
124 - Yasuhito Endo 2002- • 122 - Masami Ihara 1988-99 • 116 - Yoshikatsu Kawaguchi 1997- • 110 - Yuji Nakazawa 1999- • 98 - Shunsuke Nakamura 2000-10 • 89 - Kazuyoshi Miura 1990-2000 • 82 - Junichi Inamoto 2000-10 & Alessandro dos Santos 2002-06 • 78 - Satoshi Tsunami 1980-95 • 77 - Seigo Narazaki 1998-2010 • 72 - Keiji Tamada 2004- & Yuichi Komano 2005-

Goals
55 - Kunishige Kamamoto 1964-77 & Kazuyoshi Miura 1990-2000 • 31 - Shiji Okazaki 2008- • 28 - Takuya Takagi 1992-97 • 24 - Shunsuke Nakamura 2000-10 & Hirome Hara 1978-88 • 23 - Naohiro Takahara 2000-08 • 21 - Masashi Nakayama 1990-2003

Coaches
Hirokazu Ninomiya 1951 • Shigemaru Takenokoshi 1951-56 • Hidetoki Takahashi 1957 • Taizo Kawamoto 1958 • Shigemaru Takenokoshi 1958-59 • Dettmar Cramer (Technical Director) 1960-64 • Hidetoki Takahashi 1960-62 • Ken Naganuma 1962-70 • Shunichiro Okano 1970-72 • Ken Naganuma 1972-76 • Hiroshi Ninomiya 1976-78 • Yukio Shimomura 1979-80 • Masashi Watanabe 1980 • Saburo Kawabuchi 1980-1981 • Takaji Mori 1981-1986 • Yoshinobu Ishii 1986-1987 • Kenzo Yokoyama 1988-1992 • Hans Ooft 1992-1993 • Falcão 1993-94 • Shu Kamo 1995-1997 • Takeshi Okada 1997-1998 • Philippe Troussier 1998-2002 • Zico 2002-2006 • Ivica Osim 2006-2007 • Takeshi Okada 2007-2010 • Alberto Zaccheroni 2010-

JAPAN 2012

J.LEAGUE DIVISION 1

	Pl	W	D	L	F	A	Pts	Sanfrecce	Vegalta	Urawa Reds	Marinos	Sagan Tosu	Kashiwa	Nagoya	Kawasaki	Shimizu	FC Tokyo	Kashima	Jubilo	Omiya	Cerezo	Albirex	Vissel	Gamba	Consadole
Sanfrecce Hiroshima †	34	19	7	8	63	34	64		2-1	1-0	1-3	4-1	1-2	1-1	3-0	1-2	0-1	2-0	2-0	0-0	4-1	0-1	3-2	4-1	3-0
Vegalta Sendai †	34	15	12	7	59	43	57	2-2		3-2	2-2	1-1	0-0	4-0	2-1	0-1	4-0	1-0	2-2	4-1	1-1	0-1	2-1	2-1	4-1
Urawa Reds †	34	15	10	9	47	42	55	0-0	1-2		4-3	1-0	2-0	1-1	1-0	2-2	2-1	2-0	1-1	0-0	1-1	2-0	0-5	1-2	
Yokohama F-Marinos	34	13	14	7	44	33	53	0-0	0-2	1-2		1-0	1-2	1-1	2-2	3-0	1-0	0-0	4-0	1-1	1-3	2-1	3-1	0-0	2-1
Sagan Tosu	34	15	8	11	48	39	53	1-0	1-1	3-1	1-0		3-1	1-3	0-1	1-1	2-0	3-2	1-1	0-0	1-0	3-0	4-1	1-0	
Kashiwa Reysol	34	15	7	12	57	52	52	2-5	2-3	1-2	3-3	1-1		1-2	1-0	2-1	1-1	1-1	0-3	1-4	4-1	2-0	1-0	2-2	3-1
Nagoya Grampus	34	15	7	12	46	47	52	1-2	0-0	1-2	1-1	1-1	0-1		2-3	1-0	1-0	1-2	2-0	0-0	0-1	2-1	5-1	0-5	3-1
Kawasaki Frontale	34	14	8	12	51	50	50	1-4	3-2	4-2	0-0	1-2	0-2	0-1		2-1	0-1	2-2	4-3	4-1	0-1	1-0	1-2	2-3	1-0
Shimizu S-Pulse	34	14	7	13	39	40	49	2-1	3-1	0-2	0-0	1-1	3-5	3-2	0-0		1-1	3-0	3-2	0-0	1-0	1-1	1-0	1-0	
FC Tokyo	34	14	6	14	47	44	48	0-1	6-2	1-1	3-1	3-2	0-1	3-2	1-2	0-1		1-2	2-1	0-1	2-0	0-2	0-1	3-2	5-0
Kashima Antlers	34	12	10	12	50	43	46	2-2	3-3	1-3	1-2	0-0	2-0	2-3	0-1	1-2	5-1		2-1	1-0	3-2	0-1	1-0	5-0	7-0
Jubilo Iwata	34	13	7	14	57	53	46	1-1	1-1	2-2	1-0	2-1	1-0	0-2	2-2	0-1	3-1	3-0		4-0	4-3	0-0	1-3	2-1	4-1
Omiya Ardija	34	11	11	12	38	45	44	1-2	1-3	2-0	0-0	1-0	2-4	1-1	1-2	1-0	1-0	0-0	2-1		0-3	1-1	2-2	1-0	2-1
Cerezo Osaka	34	11	9	14	47	53	42	1-4	1-2	1-1	2-2	1-0	3-2	1-2	0-2	2-2	3-2	1-1	0-1	3-2	1-3		0-1	1-2	2-1	4-0
Albirex Niigata	34	10	10	14	29	34	40	0-2	0-1	0-0	0-0	0-0	2-1	1-1	5-0	0-1	0-1	0-2	1-1	1-6	1-2	0-1		0-0	1-1	4-1
Vissel Kobe	34	11	6	17	41	50	39	0-1	0-1	1-0	1-2	0-0	3-1	0-1	3-3	0-1	0-2	1-2	1-2	3-0	2-3	1-0		1-2	
Gamba Osaka	34	9	11	14	67	65	38	1-1	1-1	1-2	1-2	2-3	2-6	2-2	3-2	3-1	2-2	2-2	1-2	3-1	2-2	1-1	2-3		7-2
Consadole Sapporo	34	4	2	28	25	88	14	1-3	2-1	1-2	0-2	2-3	0-2	2-1	2-3	0-2	0-0	0-0	0-5	1-0	0-1	2-4	0-4		

10/03/2012 - 1/12/2012 • † Qualified for the AFC Champions League • Att: 5 365 310 @ 17 534
Top scorers: **22** - Hisato **SATO**, Sanfrecce • **19** - Yohei **TOYODA**, Sagan Tosu • **14** - Shingo **AKAMINE**, Vegalta & **LEANDRO** BRA, Gamba • **13** - Masato **KUDO**, Kashiwa; Ryoichi **MAEDA**, Jubilo; Genki **OMAE**, Shimizu & **WILSON** BRA, Vegalta • **11** - Yoichiro **KAKITANI**, Cerezo; Shinzo **KOROKI**, Kashima & Akihiro **SATO**, Gamba • **10** - **RENATINHO** BRA, Kawasaki; **LEANDRO DOMINGUES** BRA, Kashiwa; **MARQUINHOS** BRA, Marinos & Kensuke **NAGAI**, Nagoya

JAPAN 2012

J.LEAGUE DIVISION 2

	Pl	W	D	L	F	A	Pts	Ventforet	Shonan	Kyoto Sanga	Yokohama FC	JEF United	Oita Trinita	Tokyo Verdy	Fagiano	Giravanz	Montedio	Tochigi	Matsumoto	Mito H'hock	Rosso	Tokushima	Ehime	Thespa	Avispa	Kataller	Gainare	FC Gifu	Machida
Ventforet Kofu	42	24	14	4	63	35	86		2-2	0-3	2-1	0-3	1-1	0-1	2-0	0-2	1-2	1-1	0-2	0-0	2-2	1-1	1-4	1-1	1-0	1-1	0-1
Shonan Bellmare	42	20	15	7	66	43	75	1-1		2-1	3-2	1-1	1-1	1-1	2-1	0-0	2-1	1-0	2-0	0-0	0-2	0-3	1-1	0-1	0-2	1-2	0-0	
Kyoto Sanga ‡	42	23	5	14	61	45	74	0-0	1-2		2-1	2-0	1-2	1-0	1-1	0-2	2-1	0-0	4-1	2-0	2-1	2-1	0-1	1-0	1-3	2-0	1-3	1-3	1-2-1
Yokohama FC ‡	42	22	7	13	62	45	73	0-2	1-0	2-1		0-1	0-1	0-0	1-1	2-1	2-1	3-1	2-1	2-0	1-0	0-0	0-3	0-1	1-3	0-3	1-3	2-2	4
JEF United Chiba ‡	42	21	9	12	61	33	72	0-1	1-1	1-3	2-3		0-0	1-2	2-2	0-0	0-3	2-0	0-0	2-0	3-0	4-0	3-0	1-0	2-0	1-1	1-3	1-0	1-0	1
Oita Trinita ‡	42	21	8	13	59	40	71	1-2	1-4	2-0	1-0	2-2		2-1	1-0	0-0	1-3	0-0	1-2	0-1	0-0	0-0	1-0	2-3	1-0	1-3	2-0	2-2	2-1
Tokyo Verdy	42	20	6	16	65	46	66	1-3	1-2	0-1	2-1	3-1		0-1	0-2	0-2	4	1-2	2-0	0-2	2-1	0-0	1-0	1-0	3-0	1-1	0-1	1-1	0-4	1-1
Fagiano Okayama	42	17	14	11	41	34	65	1-1	3	1-1	1-1	2-0	1-0	0-2		1-1	2-1	1-2	1-0	0-3	2-0	0-0	1-1	2-1	2-1	1-1	2-0	0-1	2-1
Giravanz Kitakyushu	42	19	7	16	53	47	64	2-3	3-3	2-2	0-1	2-1	2-0	2-1	5-0		0-1	1-0	1-1	0-2	0-1	2-2	0-0	1-4	2-1	0-1	0-2	1-1	
Montedio Yamagata	42	16	13	13	51	49	61	2-1	1-2	1-0	0-1	0-2	3-2	1-1	2-1	0		2-1	1-0	0-0	0-1	2-1	0-2	2-1	0-3	1-1	0-5	1-2	1-3	1
Tochigi SC	42	17	9	16	50	49	60	1-2	1-1	1-1	2-3	4-2	1-1	0-3	3-2	0-1	2-1		3-2	1-0	2-0	1-1	1-0	0-2	0-0	0-0	1-1	1-1	0
Matsumoto Yamaga	42	15	14	13	46	43	59	1-1	1-1	0-0	2-1	0-0	0-3	2-3	0-1	0-1	0-2		2-1	0-0	1-1	1-0	2-2	2-0	3-7	1-1	0-3	0
Mito Hollyhock	42	15	11	16	47	49	56	1-3	1-1	3-1	1-3	1-2	1-0	2-0	0-0	3-1	2-2	3-3	1-0	0		2-0	2-1	0-2	1-4	2-1	0-2	0-1	1-1	1
Rosso Kumamoto	42	15	10	17	40	48	55	0-0	3-3	0-1	0-1	1-0	2-1	0-0	0-0	2-2	2-1	3-0	0-3	2-1		0-3	0-1	1-1	3-3	0-2	3-0	1-0
Tokushima Vortis	42	13	12	17	45	49	51	0-2	0-0	2-4	1-2	0-3	0-4	2-1	1-1	2-2	1-2	0-0	1-1	2-1	2-1		3-0	0-0	0-4	4-3	0-3	0-3	0-1	0
Ehime FC	42	12	14	16	47	46	50	0-0	2-1	2-1	1-0	1-2	2-1	2-3	1-1	0-2	2-2	1-3	0-1	1-0	0-0	1-2		3-1	4-2	0-1	0-0	0-0	2-0
Thespa Kusatsu	42	12	11	19	31	45	47	1-2	1-3	1-0	1-0	2-0	0-1	1-0	0-0	0-2	3-1	1-1	2-0	0-0	0-0	0-0	1-0		1-0	0-1	1-2	1-1	1
Avispa Fukuoka	42	9	14	19	53	68	41	2-3	3-1	2-0	1-0	0-0	1-1	3-1	1-1	0-1	1-1	1-2	2-1	1-2	1-1	3-1	1-0	0-3		3-2	4-0	0-0	1-1
Kataller Toyama	42	9	11	22	38	59	38	1-1	0-2	1-0	0-2	0-2	3-1	4-1	1-2	1-1	2-1	1-2	3-1	2-3	1-0	0-2	1-1	1-1	3-1		2-1	1-0	1-1
Gainare Tottori	42	11	5	26	33	78	38	0-0	1-2	2-1	2-5	2-1	1-0	0-0	2-0	2-1	2-2	1-2	1-0	2-1	0-3	1-4	2-0	2-1	1-1	0		1-0	0-3
FC Gifu	42	7	14	21	27	55	35	0-3	3-3	2-0	1-0	2-0	0-0	2-1	0-0	0-0	1-0	0-1	0-2	2-0	0-1	0-0	0-0	3-2	2-2	2		1-0	
Machida Zelvia	42	7	11	24	34	67	32	0-1	0-3	1-2	0-4	1-6	1-3	1-2	2-2	0-1	0-0	0-3	0-1	0-1	0-2	4-0	2-0	1-3	2-0	3-0	1-0		

4/03/2012 - 11/11/2012 • ‡ Qualified for the promotion play-offs
Play-off semi-finals: Kyoto Sanga 0-4 **Oita Trinita** • Yokohama FC 0-4 **JEF United Chiba**
Play-off final: **Oita Trinita** 1-0 JEF United Chiba. Oita Bank Dome, 23-11-2012, Att: 27 433, Ref: Nishimura. Scorer - Takeniri Hayashi [86] for Oita
Top scorers: **32** - **DAVI** BRA, Ventforet • **18** - Takuma **ABE**, Verdy & Kengo **KAWAMATA**, Fagiano • **15** - Yoshihito **FUJITA**, JEF United Chiba

JAPAN 2012

JAPAN FOOTBALL LEAGUE (JFL) (3)

	Pl	W	D	L	F	A	Pts	V-Varen	Nagano	Sagawa S	Kamatamare	Honda	YSCC	Sagawa P	MIO	FC Ryukyu	Yokogawa	Fujieda	Sony Sendai	Blaublitz	Zweigen	Hoyo	Honda Lock	Tochigi
V-Varen Nagasaki	32	20	7	5	57	24	**67**		2-2	2-2	4-2	2-0	2-1	0-0	1-1	4-1	1-0	3-1	1-0	1-0	2-0	4-0	1-1	2-2
Nagano Parceiro	32	17	7	8	57	34	58	1-0		2-2	0-1	5-0	0-1	2-1	3-1	1-0	5-0	4-0	1-1	1-0	2-2	1-2	2-0	3-1
Sagawa Shiga - R	32	16	9	7	61	37	**57**	2-0	0-1		2-1	4-0	1-4	4-0	4-0	4-3	1-2	1-1	3-1	0-1	0-0	2-1	2-3	3-0
Kamatamare Sanuki	32	15	8	9	49	29	53	0-1	0-2	0-1		1-0	2-0	1-0	0-1	1-1	1-2	1-2	0-0	3-0	1-1	1-0	6-0	0-0
Honda FC	32	16	5	11	55	39	53	1-0	4-0	2-2	3-1		6-0	2-0	0-1	4-1	1-0	2-1	2-0	1-0	1-1	0-1	0-2	1-3
Yokohama SCC	32	15	4	13	58	50	49	0-3	1-2	1-3	1-2	0-2		1-2	3-0	2-0	1-2	4-1	2-0	4-1	1-2	3-3	4-1	2-0
Sagawa Printing	32	12	9	11	43	43	45	1-1	1-0	1-0	2-4	0-0	1-1		1-1	2-2	1-1	2-0	0-2	1-1	1-2	6-2	0-1	4-1
MIO Biwako Kusatsu	32	11	10	11	53	52	43	1-4	3-3	2-2	1-1	3-1	2-2	1-2		2-2	1-1	1-0	0-3	0-1	3-1	1-0	1-2	2-4
FC Ryukyu	32	12	7	13	58	62	43	1-0	0-2	2-1	2-2	1-2	3-4	4-0	4-1		1-3	1-2	1-1	0-1	3-2	3-2	1-0	4-2
Yokogawa Musashino	32	11	8	13	35	50	41	1-0	1-1	1-1	0-3	0-7	1-2	2-0	1-2	2-2		1-3	1-0	2-0	1-2	0-4	0-1	2-1
Fujieda MYFC	32	11	7	14	39	48	40	1-2	1-0	2-4	0-0	0-2	4-1	2-5	1-7	3-0	0-1		3-0	2-0	0-0	0-0	1-1	2-2
Sony Sendai	32	9	12	11	27	29	39	0-1	1-2	0-0	0-0	0-1	0-0	0-1	2-0	1-1	1-0	1-1		3-2	0-0	0-1	1-1	1-0
Blaublitz Akita	32	9	10	13	33	41	37	1-2	1-2	1-2	1-2	1-0	0-1	3-3	0-0	1-0	1-1	0-0	2-2		2-1	1-1	1-0	1-1
Zweigen Kanazawa	32	8	12	12	33	41	36	0-1	2-2	0-1	1-1	2-1	0-4	0-1	2-2	2-3	2-1	1-3	0-0	1-2		0-0	2-0	0-0
Hoyo Oita	32	9	8	15	40	57	35	0-2	3-1	0-3	0-6	1-1	1-2	1-0	0-5	4-5	2-2	0-2	1-1	0-4	0-3		1-1	1-0
Honda Lock	32	7	7	18	28	56	28	0-4	1-0	1-1	1-2	0-3	0-1	0-1	1-4	2-3	2-3	1-0	0-1	1-1	2-0	0-2		2-4
Tochigi Uva ‡	32	4	10	18	36	70	22	1-4	1-4	2-3	0-3	3-3	1-6	1-3	0-3	1-1	0-0	0-1	2-4	3-1	1-1	0-0	2-1	

11/03/2012 - 18/11/2012 • ‡ Relegation play-off • Sagawa Shiga withdrew from the JFL at the end of the season
Relegation play-off: Norbritz Hokkaido 2-1 0-1 1-4p **Tochigi Uva**. Tochigi remain in the JFL

MEDALS TABLE

		Overall			J.League			JSL			EC		JLC		Asia			City	Former name	DoF
		G	S	B	G	S	B	G	S	B	G	S	G	S	G	S	B			
1	Tokyo Verdy	16	8	1	2	1		5	3		5	3	3	1	1		1	Tokyo	Yomiuri	1969
2	Kashima Antlers	16	7	3	7	2	2				4	2	5	3			1	Ibaraki	Sumitomo	1947
3	Yokohama F.Marinos	14	8	2	3	2	1	2	4		6	1	1		2	1	1	Yokohama	Nissan	1972
4	Urawa Reds	13	15	7	1	3	1	4	6	5	6	3	1	3		1		1	Saitama	Mitsubishi	1950
5	Sanfrecce Hiroshima	9	13	2	1	1		5	1	1	3	10		1			1	Hiroshima	Toyo Kogyo/Mazda	1938
6	Jubilo Iwata	9	10	3	3	3		1		3	2	2	2	3	1	2		Iwata	Yamaha	1970
7	JEF United	9	4	6			2	2	1	4	4	2	2	1	1				Ichihara	Furukawa	1946
8	Cerezo Osaka	7	12	2			1	4	4	1	3	8						Osaka	Yanmar	1957
9	Shonan Bellmare	7	5	3				3	1	3	3	4			1			Hiratsuka	Fujita	1968
10	Kashiwa Reysol	6	4	7	1		2	1	1	5	3	3	1					Kashiwa	Hitachi	1940
11	Gamba Osaka	6	4	6	1	1	6				3	2	1	1	1			Osaka	Matsushita	1980
12	Shimizu S-Pulse	3	9	3		1	2				1	4	1	4	1		1	Shimizu		1991
13	Nagoya Grampus	3	4	3	1	2	2				2	1			1	1		Nagoya	Toyota	1939
14	Yokohama Flugels	3	2	3			1	1	1		2	1			1		1	Yokohama	All Nippon	1964-98
15	FC Tokyo	3									1		2					Tokyo	Tokyo Gas	1935
16	Yawata/Nippon Steel	1	5	2				2	2		1	3						Kitakyushu		1950-99
17	Nippon Kokan	1	4					3			1	1						Kawasaki		1912-94
18	Kyoto Sanga	1	1								1	1						Kyoto	Kyoto Shiko	1922
19	Oita Trinita	1											1					Oita		1994
20	Kawasaki Frontale		6			3								3				Kawasaki	Fujitsu	1955
21	Vegalta Sendai		1			1												Sendai		1988
22	Honda			2					2									Hamamatsu		1971

The creation of the J.League saw all of the company teams change their names as listed above • In 1998 Yokohama Marinos merged with Yokohama Flugels (previously All Nippon Airways) to form Yokohama F.Marinos. Disgruntled Flugels' fans then formed Yokohama FC in protest
JSL = Japan Soccer League (1965-92) • EC = Emperor's Cup • JLC = J.League Cup • Keio University are the Emperor's Cup record holders with 9

EMPEROR'S CUP 2012

Second Round

Kashiwa Reysol *	3
Kashiwa Reysol U-18	0
Ehime FC	0
Shonan Bellmare *	1
Nagano Parceiro	1 5p
Consadole Sapporo *	1 3p
FC Tokyo *	0
Yokogawa Musashino	1
Kawasaki Frontale *	2
Tokuyama University	0
Fagiano Okayama Next	1
Tokushima Vortis *	5
Avispa Fukuoka *	4
Fukuoka University	2
Blaublitz Akita	0
Omiya Ardija *	2
Nagoya Grampus *	2
FC Kariya	0
Kataller Toyama	0
Fagiano Okayama *	2
Vegalta Sendai *	1
Sony Sendai	0
FC Gifu	3
Rosso Kumamoto *	4
Urawa Reds *	2
Volca Kagoshima	1
Sagan Tosu *	0
Kamatamare Sanuki	1
Yokohama FC	1
Tochigi SC *	0
Yokohama SCC	2
Yokohama F-Marinos *	4
Kashima Antlers *	7
University of Tsukuba	1
Thespa Kusatsu	1
Gainare Tottori *	2
Kyoto Sanga	3
Matsumoto Yamaga *	1
Suzuka Rampole	0
Jubilo Iwata *	7
Fukushima United	0 4p
Ventforet Kofu *	0 3p
Saurcos Fukui	1
Albirex Niigata *	2
Sagawa Shiga	2
Vissel Kobe *	1
V-Varen Nagasaki	0
JEF United Chiba *	1
Cerezo Osaka *	4
Nara Club	0
Tonan Maebashi	0
Montedio Yamagata *	3
Tokyo Verdy *	3
Hoyo Oita	0
Arterivo Wakayama	0
Shimizu S-Pulse *	5
Machida Zelvia *	1 5p
Giravanz Kitakyushu	1 4p
Sanfrecce Hiroshima *	1
FC Imabari	2
Mito Hollyhock	2 5p
Oita Trinita *	2 3p
Kansai University	0
Gamba Osaka *	3

Third Round

Kashiwa Reysol *	2
Shonan Bellmare	1
Nagano Parceiro *	0 9p
Yokogawa Musashino	0 10p
Kawasaki Frontale *	3
Tokushima Vortis	2
Avispa Fukuoka	1
Omiya Ardija *	3
Nagoya Grampus	3
Fagiano Okayama *	2
Vegalta Sendai *	1
Rosso Kumamoto	2
Urawa Reds	2
Kamatamare Sanuki *	1
Yokohama FC	1
Yokohama F-Marinos *	2
Kashima Antlers *	2
Gainare Tottori	1
Kyoto Sanga	1 3p
Jubilo Iwata *	1 5p
Fukushima United	1
Albirex Niigata *	0
Sagawa Shiga *	1 6p
JEF United Chiba	1 7p
Cerezo Osaka *	2
Montedio Yamagata	1
Tokyo Verdy	0
Shimizu S-Pulse *	1
Machida Zelvia	5
FC Imabari *	2
Mito Hollyhock	0
Gamba Osaka *	1

Fourth Round

Kashiwa Reysol *	1
Yokogawa Musashino	0
Kawasaki Frontale	3
Omiya Ardija *	4
Nagoya Grampus *	5
Rosso Kumamoto	2
Urawa Reds *	0
Yokohama F-Marinos	2
Kashima Antlers *	3
Jubilo Iwata	1
Fukushima United	0
JEF United Chiba *	5
Cerezo Osaka *	4
Shimizu S-Pulse	0
Machida Zelvia	2
Gamba Osaka *	3

J.League clubs join in the second round • * Home team

JPN – JAPAN

EMPEROR'S CUP 2012

Quarter-finals **Semi-finals** **Final**

Kashiwa Reysol 3
Omiya Ardija * 2

         Kashiwa Reysol ‡ 1
         Yokohama F-Marinos 0

Nagoya Grampus * 0 6p
Yokohama F-Marinos 0 7p

                  Kashiwa Reysol † 1
                  Gamba Osaka 0

Kashima Antlers 1
JEF United Chiba * 0

         Kashima Antlers 0
         Gamba Osaka †† 1

92ND EMERPOR'S CUP FINAL 2012

National Stadium, Tokyo, 1-01-2013, Att: 46 480, Ref: Toshimitsu Yoshida

Kashiwa Reysol	1	Watanabe 35
Gamba Osaka	0	

KASHIWA

Takanori **SUGENO**● - Daisuke **NASU**, Tatsuya **MASUSHIMA**, Wataru **HASHIMOTO**, Hirofumi **WATANABE** - **JORGE WAGNER**●, Hidekazu **OTANI**● (Ryoichi **KURISAWA** 67), Koki **MIZUNO** (Junya **TANAKA** 32), **LEANDRO DOMINGUES** - Masakatsu **SAWA**, Akimi **BARADA**. Tr: Nelson **BAPTISTA**

GAMBA

Yohei **TAKEDA** - Akira **KAJI**, Yasuyuki **KONNO**, Keisuke **IWASHITA**, Daiki **NIWA** (Takuya **TAKEI** 85), Hiroke **FUJIHARU** - Yasuhito **ENDO**, Takahiro **FUTAGAWA** (Hayato **SASAKI** 69), Tomokazu **MYOJIN**, Shu **KURATA** (Akihiro **IENAGA**● 55) - **LEANDRO**. Tr: Masanobu **MATSUNAMI**

Cerezo Osaka * 1
Gamba Osaka 2

‡ Played at National Stadium, Tokyo
†† Played at Ecopa Stadium, Fukuroi, Shizuoka
† Qualified for the AFC Champions League

J.LEAGUE YAMAZAKI NABISCO CUP 2012

First Round Groups

Group A

	Pl	W	D	L	F	A	Pts	CO	VS	JI	UR	ST	SH	KF
Cerezo Osaka	6	4	0	2	15	7	12				5-0	2-1	3-2	
Vegalta Sendai	6	4	0	2	11	5	12	1-0				2-0		1-0
Jubilo Iwata	6	4	0	2	10	11	12	2-1			4-3		1-0	
Urawa Reds	6	3	0	3	12	10	9	1-4	1-0			3-0		
Sagan Tosu	6	3	0	3	8	16	9			3-2	2-1			2-1
Sanfrecce Hiroshima	6	3	1	0	4	8	4		1-3				5-1	1-1
Kawasaki Frontale	6	1	1	4	7	11	4		3-1	0-1	0-3			

Group B

	Pl	W	D	L	F	A	Pts	SS	KA	AN	YM	OA	CS	VK
Shimizu S-Pulse	6	5	0	1	12	4	15			1-0	1-0	3-1		2-0
Kashima Antlers	6	5	0	1	10	5	15	2-1				1-0		1-0
Albirex Niigata	6	3	1	2	6	5	10		0-1			4-3		
Yokohama F-Marinos	6	1	2	3	7	9	5		3-2	0-0			1-2	
Omiya Ardija	6	1	2	3	7	10	5				1-1		1-2	1-0
Consadole Sapporo	6	1	2	3	6	11	5	0-4	1-2	0-1				
Vissel Kobe	6	1	1	4	6	10	4	1-2			3-2	2-2		

Gamba Osaka, Kashiwa Reysol, FC Tokyo and Nagoya Grampus qualified directly for the knock-out stage due to AFC Champions League commitments

Quarter-finals

Kashima Antlers*	2	3
Cerezo Osaka	1	0

Gamba Osaka*	1	1
Kashiwa Reysol	3	2

FC Tokyo	2	2
Vegalta Sendai*	2	0

Nagoya Grampus	1	3
Shimizu S-Pulse*	0	4

Semi-finals

Kashima Antlers*	3	2
Kashiwa Reysol	2	2

FC Tokyo*	2	0
Shimizu S-Pulse	1	3

Final

Kashima Antlers	2
Shimizu S-Pulse	1

CUP FINAL

National Stadium, Tokyo, 3-11-2012
Att: 45 228. Ref: Masaaki Iemoto
Scorers - Shibasaki 2 [73p 93] for Kashima;
Omae [77] for Shimizu

Kashima - Hitoshi Sogahata● - Daiki Iwamasa,
Daigo Nishi, Gen Shoji● (Toru Araiba 83) - Mitsuo
Ogasawara, Takeshi Aoki●, Yasushi Endo, Takuya
Honda (Chikashi Masuda 70), Gaku Shibasaki -
Yuya Osako●, Shinzo Koroki● (Junior Dutra● 46).
Tr: Jorginho
Shimizu - Akihiro Hayashi - Calvin Jong-a-Pin●,
Yasuhiro Hiraoka, Yutaka Yoshida, Taisuke
Muramatsu, Lee Ki Jee - Yosuke Kawai●, Kohei
Hattanda - Genki Omae, Kim Hyun Sung●,
Toshiyuki Takagi. Tr: Afshin Ghotbi

* Home team in the first leg

KAZ – KAZAKHSTAN

FIFA/COCA-COLA WORLD RANKING

'93	'94	'95	'96	'97	'98	'99	'00	'01	'02	'03	'04	'05	'06	'07	'08	'09	'10	'11	'12
-	153	163	156	107	102	123	120	98	117	136	147	137	135	112	137	125	138	138	142

2012

Jan	Feb	Mar	Apr	May	Jun	Jul	Aug	Sep	Oct	Nov	Dec	High	Low	Av
139	138	142	137	137	141	147	145	142	147	140	142	98	166	129

Shakhter Karagandy retained their league title ahead of a resurgent Irtysh Pavlodar with a 3-0 win over Kaiser on the penultimate weekend, enough to see them claim the trophy for only the second time. Victor Kumykov's team lost over a quarter of their 26 matches during the campaign - as many as Ordabasy halfway down the table - but by managing to convert many potential draws into wins, Shakhter could afford the luxury of losing to Irtysh on the final weekend and still finish two points clear of their rivals. For Irtysh, who have achieved little since dominating the league a decade previously, there was the further disappointment of losing the cup final to FC Astana, who claimed their second trophy in just three short years of existence. Astana had won the cup in 2010 when known as Lokomtiv Astana, but had been unable to take part in European competition because they had not been playing for three years - the minimum requirement for a UEFA License. The national team made a stuttering start to their 2014 FIFA World Cup qualifiers in a very difficult group, but there were encouraging signs in their home matches. Austria were held to a draw while against the Republic of Ireland a famous victory looked to be on the cards with Kazakhstan winning 1-0 with just two minutes left, but they were denied even a draw after two late goals from the Irish.

UEFA EUROPEAN CHAMPIONSHIP RECORD
1960-1992 DNE (Played as part of the Soviet Union) **1996-2004** DNE (as a member of the AFC) **2008-2012** DNQ

FOOTBALL FEDERATION OF KAZAKHSTAN (FSK)

- 29 Syganak Street, 14th floor, Astana 010000
- ☎ +7 172 790780
- +7 172 790788
- info@kff.kz
- www.kff.kz
- FA 1914 CON 2002 FIFA 1994
- P Adilbek Jaxybekov
- GS Sayan Khamitzhanov

THE STADIA

2014 FIFA World Cup Stadia	
Astana Arena Astana	30 500
Other Main Stadia	
Almaty Centralny Almaty	25 057
Shakhter Stadion Karagandy	19 000
Kazhimukan Shymkent	17 000
Aktobe Centralny Aktobe	13 500

MAJOR CITIES/TOWNS

		Population
1	Almaty	1 351 521
2	Astana	708 794
3	Shymkent	461 798
4	Karagandy	427 906
5	Taraz	406 262
6	Pavlodar	358 262
7	Oskemen	347 925
8	Semey	314 013
9	Aktobe	289 179
10	Uralsk	260 504
11	Kostanay	252 115
12	Petropavl	206 991
13	Akmechet	186 007
14	Aktau	182 799
15	Temirtau	179 035
16	Ekibastuz	160 492
17	Atyrau	160 008
18	Kokshetau	133 561
19	Rudni	126 839

QAZAQSTAN RESPUBLIKASY • REPUBLIC OF KAZAKHSTAN

Capital Astana	Population 15 399 437 (62)	% in cities 58%
GDP per capita $11 500 (96)	Area km² 2 724 900 km² (9)	GMT +/- +4 +5
Neighbours (km) China 1533, Kyrgyzstan 1224, Russia 6846, Turkmenistan 379, Uzbekistan 2203		

RECENT INTERNATIONAL MATCHES PLAYED BY KAZAKHSTAN

2008	Opponents		Score	Venue	Comp	Scorers	Att	Referee
3-02	Azerbaijan	D	0-0	Antalya	Fr			Kamil TUR
6-02	Moldova	L	0-1	Antalya	Fr		300	Lehner AUT
26-03	Armenia	L	0-1	Pernis	Fr			Vink NED
23-05	Russia	L	0-6	Moscow	Fr		10 000	
27-05	Montenegro	L	0-3	Podgorica	Fr		9 000	Tusin LUX
20-08	Andorra	W	3-0	Almaty	WCq	Ostapenko 2 [14 30], Uzdenov [44]	7 700	Banari MDA
6-09	Croatia	L	0-3	Zagreb	WCq		17 424	Johannesson SWE
10-09	Ukraine	L	1-3	Almaty	WCq	Ostapenko [68]	17 000	Brych GER
11-10	England	L	1-5	London	WCq	Kukeyev [68]		
2009								
11-02	Estonia	W	2-0	Antalya	Fr	Baltiyev 2 [33 82]	200	Gocek TUR
1-04	Belarus	L	1-5	Almaty	WCq	Abdulin [10]	19 000	Jech CZE
6-06	England	L	0-4	Almaty	WCq		24 000	Jakobsson ISL
10-06	Ukraine	L	1-2	Kyiv	WCq	Nusserbayev [18]	11 500	Paixao POR
9-09	Andorra	W	3-1	Andorra La Vella	WCq	Khizhnichenko 2 [14 35], Baltiyev [29]	510	Toussaint LUX
10-10	Belarus	L	0-4	Brest	WCq		9 530	Ennjimmi FRA
14-10	Croatia	L	1-2	Astana	WCq	Khizhnichenko [26]	10 250	Circhetta SUI
2010								
3-03	Moldova	L	0-1	Antalya	Fr		500	Bezborodov RUS
11-08	Oman	W	3-1	Astana	Fr	Karpovich [20], Zhumaskaliev [43], OG [62]		Irmatov UZB
3-09	Turkey	L	0-3	Astana	ECq		15 800	Vad HUN
7-09	Austria	L	0-2	Salzburg	ECq		22 500	Strahonja CRO
8-10	Belgium	L	0-2	Astana	ECq		8 500	Borski POL
12-10	Germany	L	0-3	Astana	ECq		18 000	Tudor ROU
2011								
9-02	Belarus	D	1-1	Antalya	Fr	Ostapenko [88]	1 500	Banari MDA
26-03	Germany	L	0-4	Kaiserslautern	ECq		47 849	Stavrev MKD
3-06	Azerbaijan	W	2-1	Astana	ECq	Gridin 2 [57 68]	10 000	Norris SCO
10-08	Syria	D	1-1	Astana	Fr	Kukeev [70]	13 500	Egorov RUS
2-09	Turkey	L	1-2	Istanbul	ECq	Konysbayev [55]	47 756	Turpin FRA
6-09	Azerbaijan	L	2-3	Baku	ECq	Ostapenko [20], Yevstigneyev.V [77]	9 112	Hermansen DEN
7-10	Belgium	L	1-4	Brussels	ECq	Nurdauletov [86p]	29 758	Mazic SRB
11-10	Austria	D	0-0	Astana	ECq		11 000	Kaasik EST
2012								
29-02	Latvia	D	0-0	Antalya	Fr		100	Banari MDA
1-06	Kyrgyzstan	W	5-2	Almaty	Fr	Logvinenko [4], Tazhimbetov 3 [13 32 90], Nurdauletov [57p]	14 000	Talibdjanov UZB
5-06	Armenia	L	0-3	Yerevan	Fr		7 500	Kvaratskhelia GEO
7-09	Republic of Ireland	L	1-2	Astana	WCq	Nurdauletov [37]	12 384	Avram ROU
11-09	Sweden	L	0-2	Malmo	WCq		20 414	Boiko UKR
12-10	Austria	D	0-0	Astana	WCq		12 900	Bognar HUN
16-10	Austria	L	0-4	Vienna	WCq		43 000	Kehlet DEN

Fr = Friendly match • EC = UEFA EURO 2012 • WC = FIFA World Cup • q = qualifier • BCD = behind closed doors

KAZAKHSTAN NATIONAL TEAM HISTORICAL RECORDS

Caps: 73 - Ruslan Baltiyev 1997-2009 • 59 - Samat Smakov 2000-11 • 54 - Nurbol Zhumaskaliyev 2001- • 51 - Andrey Karpovich 2000- • 38 - David Loriya 2000-11 • 36 - Sergei Ostapenko 2007- • 35 - Alexandr Kuchma 2000- & Farkhadbek Irismetov 2004- • 34 - Alexandr Familtsev 1997-2006 • 32 - Dmitry Byakov 2000-08 • 29 - Maxim Zhalmagambetov 2004-08

Goals: 13 - Ruslan Baltiyev 1997-2009 • 12 - Viktor Zubarev 1997-2002 • 8 - Dmitry Byakov 2000-08 • 6 - Igor Avdeyev 1996-2005; Oleg Litvinenko 1997-2006; Nurbol Zhumaskaliyev 2001- & Sergei Ostapenko 2007-

Past Coaches: Bakhtiar Baiseitov 1992 • Baurzhan Baimukhammedov 1994 • Serik Berdalin 1995-97 • Sergei Gorokhovadatskiy 1998 • Voit Talgaev 2000 • Vladimir Fomichev 2000 • Vakhid Masudov 2001-02 • Leonid Pakhomov RUS 2003-04 • Sergey Timofeev 2004-05 • Arno Pijpers NED 2006-08 • Bernd Storck GER 2008-10 • Miroslav Beranek CZE 2011-

KAZAKHSTAN 2012

	Pl	W	D	L	F	A	Pts	Shakhter	Irtysh	Aktobe	Taraz	Astana	Tobol	Ordabasy	Akzhayuk	Kaisar	Kairat	Atyrau	Zhetysu	Sunkar	Okzhetpes
Shakhter Karagandy †	26	17	2	7	48	15	53		0-1	2-0	1-0	0-1	3-0	1-1	3-1	3-0	4-1	4-0	5-1	2-0	4-0
Irtysh Pavlodar ‡	26	15	6	5	46	20	51	1-0		1-2	1-1	3-0	4-1	3-0	3-1	1-1	1-0	0-0	3-0	4-0	3-0
FK Aktobe ‡	26	15	5	6	44	22	50	1-0	1-0		4-1	2-1	0-1	0-0	3-4	2-0	1-1	1-0	4-0	2-1	5-2
FK Taraz	26	14	4	8	32	30	46	1-1	3-2	1-0		1-1	1-0	2-1	3-2	1-0	2-1	0-1	1-3	1-0	2-0
FC Astana ‡	26	13	7	6	34	24	46	1-0	2-2	1-0	0-2		1-1	1-0	2-1	3-0	2-1	5-0	1-0	0-0	1-4
Tobol Kostanay	26	13	6	7	42	27	45	3-1	2-2	2-2	0-1	3-2		1-0	6-0	2-0	4-0	1-0	2-1	4-0	3-1
Ordabasy Shymkent	26	10	9	7	29	24	39	0-1	2-1	1-1	1-3	0-0	2-0		2-0	1-0	0-0	1-1	4-1	3-1	1-1
Akzhayuk Uralsk	26	10	4	12	34	39	34	0-1	0-1	1-0	3-0	0-1	2-1	1-1		0-0	1-2	3-1	2-2	1-1	2-1
Kaisar Kyzylorda	26	8	6	12	21	33	30	1-0	2-0	0-2	1-2	0-1	1-2	2-1	1-2		1-1	1-0	1-0	2-1	1-0
Kairat Almaty	26	7	8	11	23	34	29	0-1	0-0	0-3	2-1	0-2	1-0	1-1	2-1	1-1		1-1	1-0	1-3	3-0
FK Atyrau	26	7	6	13	16	32	27	0-2	0-2	0-2	0-0	1-0	1-1	2-3	0-1	0-1	2-0		2-1	1-0	1-0
Zhetysu Taldykorgan	26	6	5	15	27	45	23	1-5	1-2	1-1	2-0	1-1	1-1	0-1	1-2	5-2	2-1	1-0		1-1	1-0
Sunkar Kaskelen	26	5	8	13	16	31	23	0-2	0-1	0-1	0-1	1-1	0-0	0-0	1-0	0-0	0-2	0-0	1-0		3-1
Okzhetpes Kokshetau	26	3	2	21	20	56	11	0-2	1-4	1-4	3-1	1-3	0-1	1-2	0-3	2-2	1-1	1-2	1-0	0-2	

9/03/2012 - 28/10/2012 • † Qualified for the UEFA Champions League • ‡ Qualified for the Europa League
Top scorers: **14** - Ulugbek **BAKAEV** UZB, Irtysh • **10** - Tanat **NUSERBAEV**, Astana & Ihar **ZYANKOVICH** BLR, Akzhayuk

KAZAKHSTAN 2012 PERVAIA (2)

	Pl	W	D	L	F	A	Pts
Ilie-Saulet	30	17	10	3	52	20	61
Vostock Oskemen	30	16	9	5	40	21	57
FK Astana 64	30	16	9	5	38	17	57
Bayterek Astana	30	14	11	5	39	19	53
Kyran Shymkent	30	14	6	10	51	38	48
Spartak Semey	30	14	4	12	38	45	46
Bolat-AMT Temirtau	30	12	10	8	30	23	46
Kaspiy Aktau	30	12	7	11	39	31	43
Ak Bulak Talgar	30	11	8	11	34	29	41
Lashin Taraz	30	11	8	11	33	28	41
Kyzylzhar Pet'pavlovsk	30	11	7	12	36	43	40
Ekibastuzetc	30	11	4	15	45	43	37
Sport Academy	30	9	9	12	37	41	36
Aktobe-Zhas	30	8	2	20	31	62	26
CSKA Almaty	30	4	6	20	18	55	18
BIIK Shymkent	30	3	4	23	20	66	13

27/04/2012 - 19/10/2012

MEDALS TABLE

		Overall			League			Cup		City
		G	S	B	G	S	B	G	S	
1	Kairat Almaty	7	2	3		2	3	5	2	Almaty
2	Irtysh Pavlodar	6	7	5	5	4	5	1	3	Pavlodar
3	FK Astana	6	2	1	3		1	3	2	Astana
4	FK Aktobe	5	3	2	4	2	2	1	1	Aktobe
5	FK Semey	4		1	3		1	1		Semey
6	Tobol Kostanay	2	6	3	1	4	3	1	2	Kostanay
7	FK Taraz	2	4		1	2		1	2	Taraz
8	Shakhter Karagandy	2	2	3	2		3			Oskemen
9	FC Astana	2	1			1		2		Atyrau
10	Ordabasy Shymkent	1	3	1		1	1	1	2	Kyzylorda
11	Vostock Oskemen	1	2					1	2	Almaty
	FK Atyrau	1	2			2			1	Astana
13	Kaisar Kyzylorda	1	1					1	1	Almaty
	FK Almaty	1	1					1	1	Petropavl
15	Dostyk Almaty	1						1		Shymkent
16	Yesil-Bogatyr Petropavl		3	1		2	1		1	Karagandy
17	Ekibastuzetc		2			2				Ekibastuz
18	Zhetysu Taldykorgan		1			1				Taldykorgan
19	Gornyak Khromtau			1			1			Khromtau

KUBOK KAZAKHSTANA 2012

First round		Quarter-finals		Semi-finals		Final	
FC Astana	1 2						
Ak Bulak Talgar *	1 0	**FC Astana**	0 4				
Kairat Almaty	0 1	Kaisar Kyzylorda *	1 1				
Kaisar Kyzylorda *	2 0			**FC Astana**	1 2		
Zhetysu Taldykorgan *	1 2			Shakhter Karagandy *	2 0		
FK Taraz	1 0	Zhetysu Taldykorgan *	1 0				
CSKA Almaty *	0 0	**Shakhter Karagandy**	1 1				
Shakhter Karagandy	4 3					**FC Astana** ‡	2
FK Aktobe *	5 2					Irtysh Pavlodar	0
Lashin Taraz	0 0	**FK Aktobe** *	0 1				
Akzhayuk Uralsk *	1 0	Ordabasy Shymkent	0 0			**CUP FINAL**	
Ordabasy Shymkent	2 5			FK Aktobe	0 3	Astana Arena, Astana, 11-11-2012,	
Tobol Kostanay	3 0			**Irtysh Pavlodar** *	5 1	Att: 11 500, Ref: Slambelov	
Okzhetpes Kokshetau *	1 1	Tobol Kostanay	0 1			Scorers - Kairat Nurdauletov [5], Tanat	
Sport Academy *	1 0	**Irtysh Pavlodar** *	3 0			Nuserbaev [82] for Astana	
Irtysh Pavlodar	4 4	* Home team/Home team in first leg • ‡ Qualified for the Europa League					

KEN – KENYA

FIFA/COCA-COLA WORLD RANKING

'93	'94	'95	'96	'97	'98	'99	'00	'01	'02	'03	'04	'05	'06	'07	'08	'09	'10	'11	'12
74	83	107	112	89	93	103	108	104	81	72	74	89	127	110	68	98	120	120	134

2012

Jan	Feb	Mar	Apr	May	Jun	Jul	Aug	Sep	Oct	Nov	Dec	High	Low	Av
121	123	113	117	117	111	125	126	125	128	130	134	68	137	100

Kenya ended a disappointing year with defeat in the final of the CECAFA Cup after being beaten by their old nemesis Uganda in Kampala, where they gave up a last minute goal to go down 2-1. The Harambee Stars had earlier in the year again failed to qualify for the Africa Cup of Nations and made a poor start to the 2014 FIFA World Cup qualifiers. Togo knocked Kenya out of the Nations Cup on the away goals rule while a home draw with Malawi and a loss away in Namibia represented setbacks in the bid to get to Brazil despite a strong side that included Victor Wanyama, McDonald Mariga and Denis Oliech, all making names for themselves in European club football. It cost coach Francis Kimanzi his job and led to the surprise appointment of the taciturn former France manager Henri Michel, whose command of English is limited. His tenure lasted just three months up to December when he made the decision to leave before the CECAFA tournament, turning the job over to his assistant James Nandwa. An exciting finish to the league saw Tusker retain their championship ahead of Gor Mahia whose efforts to win a first title since 1995 had created much excitement at the end of the campaign. There was double cup success for Gor Mahia, however, when they lifted both the President's Cup and the newly created Top 8 Cup.

CAF AFRICA CUP OF NATIONS RECORD

1957-1959 DNE 1962-1970 DNQ **1972** 6 r1 1974-1982 DNQ 1984 DNE 1986 DNQ
1988 8 r1 **1990** 7 r1 **1992** 12 r1 1994 DNQ 1996 DNE 1998-2002 DNQ **2004** 13 r1 2006-2013 DNQ

FOOTBALL KENYA LTD

Nyayo Sports Complex
Kasarani,
PO Box 12705-00400 NRB,
Nairobi
☎ +254 20 2644630
📠 +254 20 2644632
✉ info@fk.co.ke
🖥 www.fkf.co.ke
FA 1960 CON 1968 FIFA 1960
P Sam Nyamweya
GS Michael Esakwa

THE STADIA

2014 FIFA World Cup Stadia
Nyayo National Stadium
Nairobi   60 000
Moi International Sports Centre
Nairobi   30 000
Other Main Stadia
Nairobi City Stadium
Nairobi   15 000
Municipal Stadium
Mombasa   10 000
Afraha Stadium
Nakuru   8 200

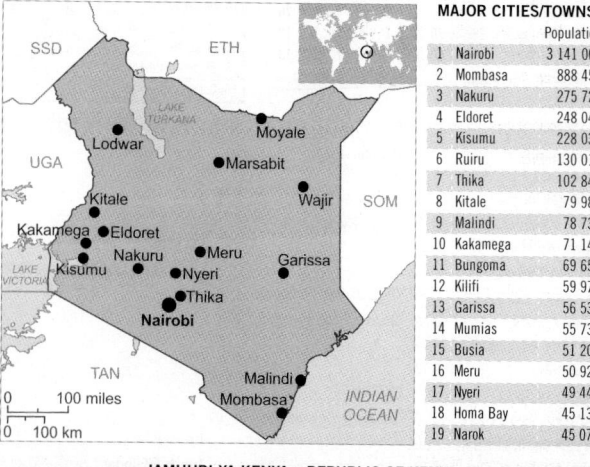

MAJOR CITIES/TOWNS

		Population
1	Nairobi	3 141 065
2	Mombasa	888 454
3	Nakuru	275 723
4	Eldoret	248 042
5	Kisumu	228 032
6	Ruiru	130 016
7	Thika	102 847
8	Kitale	79 984
9	Malindi	78 731
10	Kakamega	71 140
11	Bungoma	69 658
12	Kilifi	59 976
13	Garissa	56 533
14	Mumias	55 737
15	Busia	51 204
16	Meru	50 921
17	Nyeri	49 442
18	Homa Bay	45 139
19	Narok	45 078

JAMHURI YA KENYA • REPUBLIC OF KENYA

Capital	Nairobi	Population	39 002 772 (33)	% in cities	22%
GDP per capita	$1600 (193)	Area km²	580 367 km² (48)	GMT +/-	+3
Neighbours (km)	Ethiopia 861, Somalia 682, Sudan 232, Tanzania 769, Uganda 933 • Coast 536				

RECENT INTERNATIONAL MATCHES PLAYED BY KENYA

2010	Opponents	Score	Venue	Comp	Scorers	Att	Referee
9-01	Cameroon	L 1-3	Nairobi	Fr	Situma [8]		
15-01	Yemen	L 1-3	Sana'a	Fr	Julius Owino [11p]		
11-08	Tanzania	D 1-1	Dar es Salaam	Fr	McDonald Mariga [13]		
18-08	Ethiopia	W 3-0	Addis Abeba	Fr	Allan Wanga 2 [13 55], Levy Muaka [70]		
4-09	Guinea-Bissau	L 0-1	Bissau	CNq			Bennaceur TUN
9-10	Uganda	D 0-0	Nairobi	CNq			Diatta SEN
23-11	Tanzania	L 0-1	Dar es Salaam	Fr			
29-11	Malawi	L 2-3	Dar es Salaam	CCr1	John Baraza [34], Fred Ajwang [45]		
2-12	Ethiopia	L 1-2	Dar es Salaam	CCr1	Fred Ajwang [85]		
5-12	Uganda	L 0-2	Dar es Salaam	CCr1			
2011							
5-01	Sudan	W 1-0	Cairo	Fr	Collins Okoth [17p]		
8-01	Congo DR	L 0-1	Cairo	Fr			
14-01	Egypt	L 1-5	Cairo	Fr	Kevin Opondo [67]		
17-01	Congo DR	L 0-1	Ismailia	Fr			
9-02	South Africa	L 0-2	Rustenburg	Fr			
26-03	Angola	W 2-1	Nairobi	CNq	Jamal Mohammed [53], McDonald Mariga [87]		
29-03	Nigeria	L 0-3	Abuja	Fr			
5-06	Angola	L 0-1	Luanda	CNq			Maillet SEY
25-06	Sudan	L 1-2	Nairobi	Fr	Dennis Oliech [10]		
10-08	Botswana	L 0-1	Gaborone	Fr			
3-09	Guinea-Bissau	W 2-1	Nairobi	CNq	Mike Baraza [58], Dennis Oliech [93+]		
8-10	Uganda	D 0-0	Kampala	CNq			
11-11	Seychelles	W 3-0	Roche Caiman	WCq	Pascal Ochieng [41], Dennis Oliech 2 [75 81]	2 000	Batte UGA
15-11	Seychelles	W 4-0	Nairobi	WCq	Brian Mandela [19], Dennis Oliech [36], Titus Mulama [45], Victor Wanyama [74]	5 000	Gomes RSA
28-11	Malawi	L 0-2	Dar es Salaam	CCr1			
30-11	Ethiopia	W 2-0	Dar es Salaam	CCr1	Bob Mugalia [13], Victor Ochieng [44]		
3-12	Sudan	L 0-1	Dar es Salaam	CCr1			
2012							
27-02	Egypt	L 0-5	Doha	Fr			
29-02	Togo	W 2-1	Nairobi	CNq	James Situma [24], Allan Wanga [66]		Seechurn MRI
2-06	Malawi	D 0-0	Nairobi	WCq		14 000	Otogo-Castane GAB
9-06	Namibia	L 0-1	Windhoek	WCq		12 000	Bondo BOT
17-06	Togo	L 0-1	Lome	CNq			Alioum CMR
12-07	Botswana	W 3-1	Nairobi	Fr	Clifton Miheso [47], Raphael Mungai 2 [53 69]		
16-10	South Africa	L 1-2	Nairobi	Fr	Dennis Oliech [73p]		
24-11	Uganda	L 0-1	Kampala	CCr1			Nkurunziza BDI
27-11	South Sudan	W 2-0	Kampala	CCr1	Duncan Ochieng [13], Clifton Miheso [66]		Mujuni TAN
30-11	Ethiopia	W 3-1	Kampala	CCr1	Rama Salim [19], Clifton Miheso [26], Duncan Ochieng [72]		Nkurunziza BDI
4-12	Malawi	W 1-0	Kampala	CCqf	Mike Baraza [58]		Mujuni TAN
6-12	Zanzibar	D 2-2	Kampala	CCsf	OG [30]. W 4-2p		Nkurunziza BDI
8-12	Uganda	L 1-2	Kampala	CCf	Edwin Lavatsa [87]		Nkurunziza BDI
16-12	Burundi	L 0-1	Bujumbura	Fr			

Fr = Friendly match • CN = CAF African Cup of Nations • CC = CECAFA Cup • WC = FIFA World Cup • q = qualifier • r1 = first round group

KENYA NATIONAL TEAM HISTORICAL RECORDS

Coaches: Ray Bachelor ENG 1961 • Jack Gibbons ENG 1966 • Elijah Lidonde 1967 • Eckhard Krautzun GER 1971 • Jonathan Niva 1972 • Ray Wood ENG 1975 • Grzegorz Polakow 1979 • Stephen Yongo 1979 • Marshall Mulwa 1980-83 • Bernhard Zgoll 1984 • Reinhard Fabisch GER 1987 • Christopher Makokha 1988 • Mohammed Kheri 1988-90 • Gerry Saurer 1992 • Mohammed Kheri 1995 • Vojo Gardasevic MNE 1996 • Reinhard Fabisch GER 1997 • Abdul Majid 1998 • Christian Chukwu NGA 1998-99 • James Siang'a 1999-00 • Reinhard Fabisch GER 2001-02 • Joe Kadenge 2002 • Jacob 'Ghost' Mulee 2003-04 • Twahir Muhiddin 2004-05 • Mohammed Kheri 2005 • Bernard Lama FRA 2006 • Tom Olaba 2006 • Jacob 'Ghost' Mulee 2007-08 • Francis Kimanzi 2008-09 • Antoine Hey GER 2009 • Twahir Muhiddin 2009-10 • Jacob 'Ghost' Mulee 2010 • Zedekiah Otieno 2010-11 • Francis Kimanzi 2011-12 • Henri Michel FRA 2012 • Fames Nandwa 1012 • Adel Amrouche ALG 2013-

KENYA 2012

PREMIER LEAGUE

	Pl	W	D	L	F	A	Pts	Tusker	Gor Mahia	AFC Leopards	Sofapaka	Thika United	Ulinzi Stars	Chemelil	Mathare Utd	W'tern Stima	KCB	Sony Sugar	Karuturi	City Stars	Muhoroni Yth	Oserian	Rangers
Tusker FC †	30	17	9	4	39	14	**60**		2-0	0-0	0-1	2-1	0-0	2-0	2-2	2-0	0-0	1-0	2-2	2-1	1-0	3-1	2-0
Gor Mahia	30	17	8	5	37	18	**59**	1-0		0-0	1-0	1-1	1-0	1-0	1-1	0-0	3-1	1-0	1-0	2-1	0-1	1-1	1-1
AFC Leopards	30	17	6	7	45	27	**57**	0-2	1-2		1-0	5-0	2-1	1-0	4-2	2-1	0-2	1-1	1-1	1-0	2-1	2-0	6-2
Sofapaka	30	13	9	8	34	24	**48**	0-0	0-0	2-1		0-1	3-2	1-1	2-0	1-2	2-1	2-2	2-1	2-0	2-2	0-0	2-1
Thika United	30	12	10	8	36	33	**46**	0-0	0-2	1-2	1-4		2-2	0-0	2-1	0-0	1-1	1-0	1-0	0-1	1-0	1-1	4-0
Ulinzi Stars	30	13	6	11	35	29	**45**	0-2	1-0	0-2	1-0	1-1		2-1	0-1	1-0	1-2	2-1	2-1	2-1	2-0	2-0	3-1
Chemelil Sugar	30	9	14	7	18	17	**41**	1-1	0-1	1-0	1-0	0-0	1-0		1-0	0-1	1-0	2-0	0-0	0-0	0-0	1-1	1-1
Mathare United	30	10	11	9	36	36	**41**	1-0	2-2	0-2	2-0	1-2	2-2	2-2		0-0	3-1	1-1	1-0	2-1	1-0	1-1	1-1
Western Stima	30	11	7	12	27	25	**40**	1-0	1-2	2-1	1-2	1-1	1-0	2-1	0-1		0-1	2-1	3-0	0-1	1-0	3-0	2-3
Kenya Com'cial Bank	30	11	6	13	35	31	**39**	0-2	2-3	1-2	2-1	2-3	2-1	0-0	0-1	0-2		0-1	1-2	4-0	3-0	3-0	3-1
Sony Sugar	30	11	5	14	26	26	**38**	0-1	0-0	0-1	0-1	3-0	1-0	0-1	3-1	2-0	1-0		0-0	1-1	1-0	1-0	3-1
Karuturi Sports	30	7	11	12	18	26	**32**	0-2	1-0	1-1	0-0	0-1	0-0	2-0	1-3	1-1	1-1	1-0		0-0	1-0	0-1	0-0
Nairobi City Stars	30	6	11	13	16	32	**29**	0-3	0-4	3-0	0-0	3-2	0-0	0-0	1-1	0-0	1-0	0-1	0-0		1-2	1-0	0-0
Muhoroni Youth	30	7	6	17	19	34	**27**	0-1	0-4	1-2	0-2	0-1	1-2	0-1	1-1	0-0	1-0	1-2	1-0	2-1		1-0	0-0
Oserian	30	5	9	16	15	33	**24**	0-0	1-0	1-3	0-0	0-1	0-2	0-1	2-1	0-0	0-0	1-2	1-0	1-0	0-0		3-0
Rangers	30	4	12	14	22	53	**24**	2-4	1-2	0-0	0-2	0-6	0-3	0-0	1-1	2-1	0-0	1-0	0-0	0-0	0-1	2-2	

10/03/2012 – 28/10/2012 • † Qualified for the CAF Champions League

KPL TOP 8 CUP 2012

Quarter-finals
- Gor Mahia — w/o
- AFC Leopards
- Rangers — 2
- **Tusker FC** — 3
- **Sony Sugar** — 1
- Sofapaka — 0
- Chemelil Sugar — 2 1p
- **Ulinzi Stars** — 2 2p

Semi-finals
- **Gor Mahia** — 1 3
- Tusker FC — 0 0
- Sony Sugar — 1 1
- **Ulinzi Stars** — 1 2

Final
- **Gor Mahia** — 2
- Ulinzi Stars — 0

Final: Moi International, Nairobi, 19-08-2012.
Scorers – RamaSalim [93], Itubu Imbem [104] for Gor

MEDALS TABLE

		Overall G	Lge G	Cup G
1	Gor Mahia	22	12	9
2	AFC Leopards	19	12	7
3	Tusker (ex Breweries)	13	10	3
4	Luo Union	5	2	3
5	Ulinzi Stars	4	4	
6	Mathare United	3	1	2
7	Sofapaka	2	1	1

Gor Mahia have also won the African Cup Winners Cup

FKF PRESIDENT'S CUP 2012

Round of 16
- **Gor Mahia** — 1 5p
- Western Stima — 1 4p
- Kakamega Homeboyz — 1
- **Muhoroni Youth** — 2
- **Karuturi Sports** — 0 4p
- Nairobi Stima — 0 3p
- Congo JMJ United — 1
- **AFC Leopards** — 3
- **Tusker FC** — 13
- Wamo — 0
- Nzoia United — 0
- **Talanta** — 2
- **Kenya Revenue Auth'y** — 2
- Wazito — 1
- Mahakama — 2
- **Sofapaka** — 4

Quarter-finals
- **Gor Mahia** — 0 4p
- Muhoroni Youth — 0 2p
- Karuturi Sports — 1
- **AFC Leopards** — 3
- **Tusker FC** — 2
- Talanta — 0
- Kenya Revenue Auth'y — 1
- **Sofapaka** — 2

Semi-finals
- **Gor Mahia** — 2
- AFC Leopards — 1
- Tusker FC — 0
- **Sofapaka** — 1

Final
- Gor Mahia ‡ — 0 3p
- Sofapaka — 0 0p

CUP FINAL

Nyayo National, Nairobi
20-11-2012, Ref: Kirwa

‡ Qualified for the CAF Confederation Cup

KGZ – KYRGYZSTAN

FIFA/COCA-COLA WORLD RANKING

'93	'94	'95	'96	'97	'98	'99	'00	'01	'02	'03	'04	'05	'06	'07	'08	'09	'10	'11	'12
-	166	172	168	140	151	159	174	164	171	157	150	157	139	139	158	159	174	191	199

2012

Jan	Feb	Mar	Apr	May	Jun	Jul	Aug	Sep	Oct	Nov	Dec	High	Low	Av
191	192	192	195	195	196	196	196	197	198	200	199	119	200	160

Dordoi Bishkek won their eighth championship in nine years as their stranglehold over honours in Kyrgyzstan continued. Dordoi finished 16 points ahead of Bishkek rivals Alga in second place with the rest of the field even further behind. Unsurprisingly, the two also met in the cup final where Dordoi maintained their one hundred percent record with a 6-1 victory over Alga. It was Dordoi's sixth triumph in nine years and they are steadily closing in on Alga's record total of nine cup wins. Dordoi were not able to transfer their domestic dominance to the continental stage when they represented Kyrgyzstan in the 2012 AFC President's Cup. It is a tournament in which they have an astonishing record, having reached the final on a record six occasions and winning the title twice - in 2006 and 2007. Sergei Dvoryankov's side progressed through the qualifying round with few problems, finishing on top of their group ahead of Phnom Penh Crown from Cambodia, Nepal Police Club and Yeedzin of Bhutan to advance to the finals. There, though, the challenge proved to be too much. An opening 2-0 loss at the hands of Turkmenistan's Esteghlal - the eventual winners of the tournament - effectively eliminated Dordoi after a win over Phnom Penh Crown was not enough to rescue their hopes of a place in the semi-finals.

FIFA WORLD CUP RECORD
1930-1994 DNE   1998-2014 DNQ

FOOTBALL FEDERATION OF KYRGYZ REPUBLIC (FFKR)

Mederova Street 1 "B", PO Box 1484, Bishkek 720082
☎ +996 312 518342
+996 312 518342
media@ffkr.kg
www.ffkr.kg
FA 1992 CON 1994 FIFA 1994
P Semetey Sultanov
GS Asylbek Kadraliev

THE STADIA
2014 FIFA World Cup Stadia
Spartak Stadion
Bishkek   23 000
Other Main Stadia
Suyumbayev Stadion
Osh   12 000
Dynamo Stadion
Bishkek   10 000
Tsentralnyi Stadion
Kara-Su   6 000
Abdysh-Ata Stadion
Kant   3 000

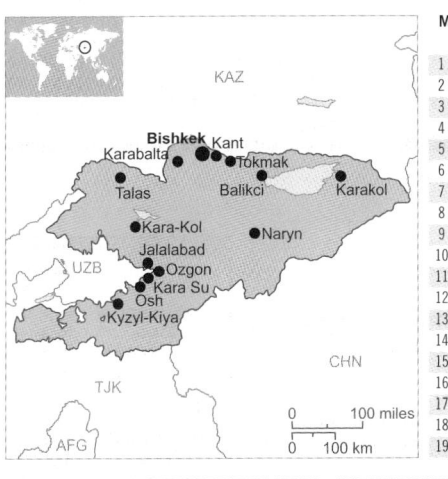

MAJOR CITIES/TOWNS
Population
1 Bishkek   930 377
2 Osh   235 861
3 Jalalabad   78 739
4 Karakol   68 589
5 Tokmak   60 371
6 Karabalta   55 215
7 Balikci   44 084
8 Ozgön   39 667
9 Naryn   39 409
10 Talas   34 404
11 Kizil-Kiya   28 061
12 Bazarkurgon   27 991
13 Tashkömür   22 310
14 Gulcha   22 034
15 Colponata   19 884
16 Karakol   19 008
17 Toktogul   18 918
18 Kant   18 290
19 Kara-Su   16 727

KYRGYZ RESPUBLIKASY • KYRGYZ REPUBLIC

Capital Bishkek	Population 5 431 747 (112)	% in cities 36%
GDP per capita $2200 (184)	Area km² 199 951 km² (86)	GMT +/- +6
Neighbours (km) China 858, Kazakhstan 1224, Tajikistan 870, Uzbekistan 1099		

RECENT INTERNATIONAL MATCHES PLAYED BY KYRGYZSTAN

2010	Opponents	Score	Venue	Comp	Scorers	Att	Referee
17-02	India †	W 2-1	Colombo	CCr1	Ildar Amirov [15], Anton Zemlianuhin [32]	800	Shukralla BHR
19-02	Korea DPR	L 0-4	Colombo	CCr1		300	El Haddad LIB
21-02	Turkmenistan	L 0-1	Colombo	CCr1		100	El Haddad LIB
2011							
21-03	Tajikistan	L 0-1	Male	CCq		4 000	Mohamed UAE
23-03	Maldives	L 1-2	Male	CCq	OG [87]	9 000	Al Awaji KSA
25-03	Cambodia	W 4-3	Male	CCq	Aziz Sydykov [5], Rustem Usanov [45], Cholponbek Esenkul uulu 2 [80][85]	1 000	Zhao Liang CHN
23-07	Uzbekistan	L 0-4	Tashkent	WCq		20 257	Balideh QAT
28-07	Uzbekistan	L 0-3	Bishkek	WCq		14 700	Abdulnabi BHR
2012							
1-06	Kazakhstan	L 2-5	Almaty	Fr	Azamat Baimatov [27], Kaiumzhan Sharipov [36]	14 000	Talibdjanov UZB

Fr = Friendly match • CC = AFC Challenge Cup • WC = FIFA World Cup • † Not a full international
q = qualifier • r1 = first round group • qf = quarter-final • sf = semi-final

KYRGYZSTAN NATIONAL TEAM HISTORICAL RECORDS

Caps: 38 - Vyacheslav Amin 2000-09 & Ruslan Sydykov 1997-2009 • 37 - Vadim Kharchenko 2003- • 30 - Vladimir Salo 1994-2004 • 29 - Zakir Djalilov • 27 - Valeriy Berezovskii & Ruslan Djamshidov 1999- • 26 - Igor Kudrenko 2001-08 • 25 - Marat Djumakeev 1992-2001

Goals: 4 - Mirlan Murzaev 2009- • 3 - Sergey Chikishev 2003-04; Sergey Kutsov 1996-2001; Farhad Khaytbaev 1994-2000; Zamirbek Zhumagulov 1992-2003; Ruslan Djamshidov 1999- ; Cholponbek Esenkul uulu 2007- ; Anton Zemlianuhin 2007-

Coaches: Meklis Koshaliyev 1992-96 • Evgeniy Novikov 1997-2001 • Nematzhan Zakirov 2003-05 • Boris Podkorytov 2006 • Nematzhan Zakirov 2007-08 • Anarbek Ormombekov 2009-11 • Marat Djumakeev 2011-12 • Sergey Dvoryankov RUS 2012-

KYRGYZSTAN 2012

PREMIER LEAGUE

	Pl	W	D	L	F	A	Pts	Dordoi	Alga	Alay	Dinamo	Abdish-Ata	Ala-Too	Khimik	FC-95
Dordoi Bishkek †	28	24	2	2	89	17	74		0-2 2-1	2-0 4-2	2-1 5-2	5-2 4-0	6-0 1-0	7-1 3-0	7-0 4-0
Alga Bishkek	28	18	4	6	61	26	58	0-4 0-2		0-0 1-1	2-1 0-0	0-0 2-1	2-0 3-1	7-2 3-0	6-1 3-0
Alay Osh	28	14	7	7	45	27	49	0-3 1-1	2-1 0-3		1-2 2-0	1-0 1-0	2-0 2-1	1-1 3-0	4-0 3-0
Dinamo Bishkek	28	14	6	8	51	35	48	3-3 0-3	0-3 2-1	1-1 2-1		0-0 1-1	2-1 3-4	3-0 3-0	1-0 4-0
Abdish-Ata Kant	28	13	8	7	51	21	47	0-2 1-0	3-1 0-2	3-0 0-0	1-1 3-0		3-0 0-0	8-0 3-0	7-0 6-0
Ala-Too Naryn	28	9	3	16	39	50	30	1-4 0-5	2-3 0-2	0-4 0-0	0-2 0-2	0-0 0-1-2		7-0 3-0	4-0 2-0
Khimik Karabalta	28	2	1	25	14	94	7	0-3 0-3	1-2 0-3	0-5 0-3	1-2 0-3	0-3 0-3	1-2 0-3		4-1 0-3
FC-95 Bishkek	28	2	1	25	13	93	7	0-3 0-1	1-7 0-1	1-2 1-3	0-7 0-3	0-1 0-0	1-2 0-5	1-3 3-0	

14/04/2012 - 13/11/2012 • † Qualified for the AFC President's Cup
Top scorers: **17** - Kayumjan **SHARIPOV**, Dordoi • **16** - Sergey **KALEUTIN**, Abdish-Ata/Dordoi & Azamat **BAYMATOV**, Dordoi

KYRGYZSTAN CUP 2012

Semi-finals	Finals		
Dordoi Bishkek			
	Dordoi Bishkek	6	
	Alga Bishkek	1	
Alga Bishkek			

MEDALS TABLE

		Overall			League			Cup		Asia		
		G	S	B	G	S	B	G	S	G	S	B
1	Dordoi-Dynamo	16	5	3	8	1	3	6		2	4	
2	Alga Bishkek	14	9		5	7		9	2			
3	Abdish-Ata Kant	3	4	2		4	2	3				
4	Dinamo Bishkek	3	2		3	1			1			
5	Kant-Oil		2			2						
6	Zhashtyk Kara-Su	1	9	5	1	2	5		7			
7	Neftchi Kochkorata	1	3		1	1			2			
8	AiK Bishkek	1	2	2		2	2	1				
9	Semetey Kyzyl-Kiya	1	2	1	1	1	1		1			
10	Metallurg Kadamjay	1	1		1			1				
11	Ak-Maral Tokmak	1						1	1			
12	Alay Osh		6	6				6	6			

KOR – KOREA REPUBLIC

FIFA/COCA-COLA WORLD RANKING

'93	'94	'95	'96	'97	'98	'99	'00	'01	'02	'03	'04	'05	'06	'07	'08	'09	'10	'11	'12
41	35	46	44	27	17	51	40	42	20	22	22	29	51	42	42	52	40	32	35

2012

Jan	Feb	Mar	Apr	May	Jun	Jul	Aug	Sep	Oct	Nov	Dec	High	Low	Av
30	34	30	31	31	35	28	29	27	25	32	35	17	62	36

Ulsan Hyundai continued Korea Republic's domination of the AFC Champions League, defeating Al Ahli from Saudi Arabia in the 2012 final to become the third K-League side in four seasons to be crowned continental champions. The win ensured the Koreans dominated at the AFC Awards in Kuala Lumpur at the end of the year as Lee Keun Ho, whose performances for Ulsan had sparked the club's success, was named the AFC Player of the Year, the first Korean to win the award since it was inaugurated in 1994. At home the K-League title was claimed by run-away champions FC Seoul who dominated the competition in it's new split-season format, claiming the crown ahead of Jeonbuk Hyundai Motors. The season's other winners were Pohang Steelers who beat Gyeongnam 1-0 in the FA Cup final. Ulsan's coach Kim Ho Gon was named AFC Coach of the Year ahead of compatriot Hong Myung Bo, the former national team defender who had steered the Koreans to the bronze medal at the Olympic Games in London. The national side made a strong start towards qualifying for the 2014 FIFA World Cup with wins over Qatar and Lebanon, but their progress stalled with a draw against Uzbekistan and defeat at the hands of a 10-man Iran in Tehran before securing a last-gasp 2-1 win over Qatar in Seoul.

FIFA WORLD CUP RECORD

1930-1950 DNE **1954** 15 r1 **1958** DNE **1962** DNQ **1966** DNE **1970-1982** DNQ
1986 20 r1 **1990** 22 r1 **1994** 20 r1 **1998** 30 r1 **2002** 4 SF (co-hosts) **2006** 17 r1 **2010** 15 r2

KOREA FOOTBALL ASSOCIATION (KFA)

1-131 Sinmunno, 2-ga,
Jongno-Gu,
110-062 Seoul
☎ +82 2 7377538
📠 +82 2 7352755
✉ kfainfo@kfa.or.kr
🖥 www.kfa.or.kr
FA 1928 CON 1954 FIFA 1948
P Chung Mong Gyu
GS An Gi Heon

THE STADIA

2014 FIFA World Cup Stadia

Seoul World Cup Stadium	
Seoul	66 806
Suwon World Cup Stadium	
Suwon	43 959
Goyang Stadium	
Goyang	42 055

Other Main Stadia

Daegu Stadium	
Daegu	66 422
Busan Asiad Stadium	
Busan	56 000

MAJOR CITIES/TOWNS

		Population
1	Seoul	9 660 532
2	Busan	3 351 991
3	Incheon	2 533 513
4	Daegu	2 413 599
5	Goyang	1 518 319
6	Daejeon	1 437 093
7	Suwon	1 374 548
8	Gwangju	1 360 225
9	Seongnam	1 023 219
10	Ulsan	957 963
12	Bucheon	810 980
13	Jeonju	720 987
15	Anyang	623 289
16	Jeongju	619 781
18	Changwon	518 370
19	Kimhae	417 161
35	Gimpo	220 543
48	Gwangyang	138 012
63	Seogwipo	92 056

TAEHAN-MIN'GUK • REPUBLIC OF KOREA

Capital	Seoul	Population	48 508 972 (25)	% in cities	81%
GDP per capita	$27 700 (50)	Area km²	99 720 km² (108)	GMT +/-	+9
Neighbours (km)	Korea DPR 238 • Coast 2413				

RECENT INTERNATIONAL MATCHES PLAYED BY KOREA REPUBLIC

2010	Opponents	Score	Venue	Comp	Scorers	Att	Referee
12-06	Greece	W 2-0	Port Elizabeth	WCr1	Lee Jung Soo [7], Park Ji Sung [52]	31 513	Hester NZL
17-06	Argentina	L 1-4	Johannesburg	WCr1	Lee Chung Yong [45]	82 174	De Bleeckere BEL
22-06	Nigeria	D 2-2	Durban	WCr1	Lee Jung Soo [38], Park Chu Young [49]	61 874	Benquerencia POR
26-06	Uruguay	L 1-2	Port Elizabeth	WCr2	Lee Chung Yong [68]	30 597	Stark GER
11-08	Nigeria	W 2-1	Suwon	Fr	Yoon Bit Garam [17], Choi Hyo Jin [44]	40 331	Nishimura JPN
7-09	Iran	L 0-1	Seoul	Fr		38 642	Mohd Salleh MAS
12-10	Japan	D 0-0	Seoul	Fr		62 503	Irmatov UZB
30-12	Syria	W 1-0	Abu Dhabi	Fr	Ji Dong Won [83]	500	Al Marzouqi UAE
2011							
10-01	Bahrain	W 2-1	Doha	ACr1	Koo Ja Cheol 2 [40 52]	6 669	Al Hilali OMA
14-01	Australia	D 1-1	Doha	ACr1	Koo Ja Cheol [24]	15 526	Abdou QAT
18-01	India	W 4-1	Doha	ACr1	Ji Dong Won 2 [6 23], Koo Ja Cheol [9], Son Heung Min [81]	11 366	Al Ghamdi KSA
22-01	Iran	W 1-0	Doha	ACqf	Yoon Bit Garam [105]	7 111	Irmatov UZB
25-01	Japan	D 2-2	Doha	ACsf	Li Sung Yueng [23p], Hwang Jae Won [120]. L 0-3p	16 171	Al Ghamdi
28-01	Uzbekistan	W 3-2	Doha	AC3p	Koo Ja Cheol [18], Ji Dong Won 2 [28 39]	8 199	Abdul Bashir SIN
9-02	Turkey	D 0-0	Trabzon	Fr		20 000	Boyko UKR
25-03	Honduras	W 4-0	Seoul	Fr	Lee Jung Soo [28], Kim Jung Woo [44], Park Chu Young [83], Lee Keun Ho [90]	31 224	Sato JPN
3-06	Serbia	W 2-1	Seoul	Fr	Park Chu Young [10], Kim Young Kwon [54]	40 000	Albadwawi UAE
7-06	Ghana	W 2-1	Jeonju	Fr	Ji Dong Won [10], Koo Ja Cheol [90]	41 271	Irmatov UZB
10-08	Japan	L 0-3	Sapporo	Fr		38 263	Irmatov UZB
2-09	Lebanon	W 6-0	Goyang	WCq	Park Chu Young 3 [8 45 67], Ji Dong Woon 2 [66 85], Kim Jung Woo [82]	37 655	Abdul Bashir SIN
6-09	Kuwait	D 1-1	Kuwait City	WCq	Park Chu Young [9]	20 000	Torky IRN
7-10	Poland	D 2-2	Seoul	Fr	Park Chu Young 2 [66 76]	40 000	Shukralla BHR
11-10	UAE	W 2-1	Suwon	WCq	Park Chu Young [55], OG [64]	28 689	Tan Hai CHN
11-11	UAE	W 2-0	Dubai	WCq	Lee Keun Ho [88], Park Chu Young [93+]	8 272	Irmatov UZB
15-11	Lebanon	L 1-2	Beirut	WCq	Koo Ja Cheol [20]	35 000	Al Ghamdi KSA
2012							
25-02	Uzbekistan	W 4-2	Jeonju	Fr	Lee Dong Gook 2 [19 45], Kim Chi Woo 2 [46 91+]	28 931	Mahapab THA
29-02	Kuwait	W 2-0	Seoul	WCq	Lee Dong Gook [65], Lee Keun Ho [71]	46 551	Nishimura JPN
30-05	Spain	L 1-4	Berne	Fr		10 220	Bieri SUI
8-06	Qatar	W 4-1	Doha	WCq	Lee Keun Ho 2 [26 80], Kwak Tae Hwi [55], Kim Shin Wook [64]	10 730	Albadwawi UAE
12-06	Lebanon	W 3-0	Goyang	WCq	Kim Bo Kyung 2 [30 48], Koo Ja Cheol [90]	36 756	Toma JPN
15-08	Zambia	W 2-1	Anyang	Fr	Lee Keun Ho 2 [17 48]	16 606	Shukralla BHR
11-09	Uzbekistan	D 2-2	Tashkent	WCq	OG [44], Lee Dong Gook [57]	33 000	Williams AUS
16-10	Iran	L 0-1	Tehran	WCq		43 700	Albadwawi UAE
14-11	Australia	L 1-2	Hwaseong	Fr	Lee Dong Gook [12]	15 000	Wang Zhe CHN

Fr = Friendly match • AC = AFC Asian Cup • EAC = East Asian Championship • WC = FIFA World Cup
q = qualifier • r1 = first round group • qf = quarter-final • sf = semi-final • 3p = third place play-off

KOREA REPUBLIC NATIONAL TEAM HISTORICAL RECORDS

Caps
136 - Hong Myung Bo 1990-2002 • **131** - Lee Woon Jae 1994-2010 • **127** - Lee Young Pyo 1999- • **120** - Yoo Sang Chul 1994-2005 • **119** - Cha Bum Kun 1972-86 • **104** - Kim Tae Young 1992-2004 • **102** - Hwang Seon Hong 1993-2002 • **100** - Park Ji Sung 2000- • **97** - Kim Nam Il 1998- • **95** - Lee Dong Gook 1998- ; Choi Soon Hoo 1980-91 & Ha Seok Joo 1991-2001 • **92** - Cho Young Jeung 1975-86 & Park Sung Hwa 1974-84 • **89** - Choi Jong Duk 1975-86 & Seo Jung Won 1990-2001 • **88** - Park Kyung Hoon 1981-90 • **84** - Huh Jung Moo 1974-86

Goals
55 - Cha Bum Kun 1972-86 • **50** - Hwang Seon Hong 1993-2002 • **30** - Lee Dong Gook 1998- & Choi Soon Hoo 1980-91 • **29** - Huh Jung Moo 1974-86 & Kim Do Hoon 1994-2003 • **27** - Choi Yong Soo 1995-2003 & Lee Tae Hoo 1980-91 • **24** - Lee Young Moo 1974-82 & Park Sung Hwa 1974-84 • **23** - Ha Seok Joo 1991-2001 & Park Chu Young 2005- • **22** - Chung Hae Won 1980-90

Coaches
For coaches prior to 1984 see Oliver's Almanack of World Football 2011 • Mun Jeong-Sik 1984-85 • Kim Jung-Nam 1985-86 • Park Jong-Hwan 1986-88 • Kim Jung-Nam 1988 • Lee Hoi-Taek 1988-90 • Lee Cha-Man 1990 • Park Jong-Hwan 1990-91 • Ko Jae-Wook 1991 • Kim Ho 1992-94 • Anatoliy Byshovets RUS 1994-95 • Park Jong-Hwan 1995 • Huh Jung-Moo 1995 • Jeong Byeong-Tak 1995 • Ko Jae-Wook 1995 • Park Jong-Hwan 1996-97 • Cha Bum-Kun 1997-98 • Kim Pyung-Seok 1998 • Huh Jung-Moo 1998-2000 • Guus Hiddink NED 2001-02 • Kim Ho-Gon 2002 • Humberto Coelho POR 2003-04 • Park Seong-Hwa 2004 • Jo Bonfrere NED 2004-05 • Dick Advocaat NED 2005-06 • Pim Verbeek NED 2006-07 • Huh Jung-Moo 2007-10 • Cho Kwang-Rae 2010-11 • Choi Kang Hee 2011-

KOREA REPUBLIC 2012

HYUNDAI OILBANK K-LEAGUE

	Pl	W	D	L	F	A	Pts	Seoul	Jeonbuk	Pohang	Suwon	Ulsan	Jeju	Busan	Gyeongnam	Incheon	Daegu	Chunnam	Seongnam	Daejeon	Gangwon	Gwangju	Sangju
FC Seoul †	44	29	9	6	76	42	96		2-1	2-1	0-2	1-1	1-1	6-0	2-1	3-1	2-0	2-0	1-0	2-0	3-2	3-2	2-0
Jeonbuk Hyundai Motors †	44	22	13	9	82	49	79	0-0		2-0	3-0	2-1	3-3	0-0	5-3	1-2	2-3	1-1	3-2	0-1	2-1	5-2	2-0
Pohang Steelers †	44	23	8	13	72	47	77	1-0	1-0		5-0	0-1	2-3	2-2	0-1	2-1	4-2	1-0	3-1	0-0	1-2	1-0	0-1
Suwon Samsung Bluewings †	44	20	13	11	61	51	73	2-0	0-3	2-0		2-1	1-1	1-0	0-3	3-1	1-0	3-2	2-1	2-2	3-0	4-1	3-1
Ulsan Hyundai	44	18	14	12	60	52	68	2-2	1-1	3-1	3-2		2-2	2-1	2-2	0-1	1-1	1-0	3-0	2-0	1-2	2-1	2-2
Jeju United	44	16	15	13	71	56	63	3-3	1-3	0-1	2-1	0-0		5-2	3-1	3-1	2-0	6-0	1-2	4-1	4-2	0-2	2-1
Busan I'Park	44	13	14	17	40	51	53	0-0	0-0	0-0	0-0	1-0	1-1		1-0	1-2	2-0	0-0	1-0	3-1	1-0	1-2	0-0
Gyeongnam FC	44	14	8	22	50	60	50	0-1	0-2	0-1	0-0	3-2	3-1	2-0		0-0	4-1	0-1	2-0	3-0	0-2	2-1	2-3
Incheon United	44	17	16	11	46	40	67	3-2	3-3	1-1	0-2	0-1	0-0	0-0	0-0		1-0	1-0	0-0	2-1	2-0	1-1	1-0
Daegu FC	44	16	13	15	55	56	61	1-1	1-5	1-0	0-0	1-0	2-0	2-1	2-3	1-0		1-0	1-2	1-1	2-0	1-1	2-1
Chunnam Dragons	44	13	14	17	47	60	53	0-3	2-3	3-4	1-1	0-1	1-0	2-3	3-1	0-0	0-3		0-1	3-1	0-0	2-2	0-0
Seongnam Ilhwa Chunma	44	14	10	20	47	56	52	2-3	0-0	0-2	1-1	0-1	1-1	0-1	2-0	1-0	0-0	1-1		0-3	1-2	4-2	1-1
Daejeon Citizen	44	13	11	20	46	67	50	0-2	0-1	0-1	2-1	0-0	0-3	0-1	1-1	0-2	2-2	0-1	0-1		0-3	2-1	2-2
Gangwon FC	44	14	7	23	57	68	49	1-2	0-1	1-2	1-4	1-2	1-1	1-2	0-3	2-1	2-0	3-4	1-2	0-2		0-0	0-3
Gwangju FC	44	10	15	19	57	67	45	1-2	0-3	1-1	2-2	0-1	3-2	0-2	0-1	0-0	2-2	6-0	1-2	1-2	1-1		1-0
Sangju Sangmu Phoenix	44	7	6	31	29	74	27	0-1	0-3	1-2	0-3	3-4	2-1	1-2	1-0	1-0	1-1	1-2	0-3	1-2	2-1	0-1	

3/03/2012 - 2/12/2012 • † Qualified for the AFC Champions League

Top scorers: **31** - Dejan **DAMJANOVIC** MNE, Seoul • **26** - **LEE** Dong Gook, Jeonbuk • **18** - **JAIR** BRA, Jeju & Mauricio **MOLINA** COL, Seoul • **16** - Kevin **ORIS** BEL, Daejeon & **KIM** Eun Jung, Gangwon • **15** - Ianis **ZICU** ROU, Gangwon & **ENINHO** BRA, Jeonbuk • **14** - **SANTOS** BRA, Jeju • **13** - **MARANHAO** BRA, Ulsan & **KIM** Shin Wook, Ulsan

CHAMPIONSHIP PLAY-OFFS

	Seoul	Jeonbuk	Pohang	Suwon	Ulsan	Jeju	Busan	Gy'gnam
Seoul		1-0	3-2	1-1	3-1	1-0	2-1	1-0
Jeonbuk	1-1		0-3	3-1	3-3	0-0	3-0	2-1
Pohang	5-0	3-2		3-0	3-1	1-1	0-2	3-3
Suwon	1-0	1-1	1-2		0-0	2-1	2-1	2-1
Ulsan	1-2	1-3	0-1	0-0		0-0	2-2	3-1
Jeju	1-2	0-1	2-1	2-1	2-2		2-1	2-0
Busan	0-2	2-2	1-1	0-1	0-1	1-2		0-0
Gyeongnam	0-3	2-1	0-4	0-0	1-2	0-0	1-0	

RELEGATION PLAY-OFFS

	Incheon	Daegu	Ch'nnam	S'gnam	Daejeon	G'gwon	Gwangju	Sangju
Incheon		2-1	0-0	0-0	1-0	2-1	3-2	2-0
Daegu	2-2		0-1	1-0	4-1	2-2	2-0	2-0
Chunnam	0-0	2-2		2-0	3-1	0-0	1-1	2-0
Seongnam	1-2	0-2	2-2		1-2	0-1	3-4	2-0
Daejeon	1-1	1-0	1-0	1-1		5-3	1-1	2-0
Gangwon	2-1	3-0	2-3	0-1	5-1		1-0	2-0
Gwangju	1-1	1-1	1-0	2-3	1-1	1-1		2-0
Sangju	0-2	0-2	0-2	0-2	0-2	0-2	0-2	

KOREA REPUBLIC 2012
KOREA NATIONAL LEAGUE (2) OVERALL STANDINGS

	Pl	W	D	L	F	A	Pts
Goyang Kookmin Bank†	26	15	10	1	51	20	55
Ulsan Mipo Dolphins †	26	15	4	7	61	30	49
Gangneung City †	26	14	5	7	32	21	47
Changwon City †	26	14	4	8	36	30	46
Incheon Korail †	26	12	6	8	39	30	42
Yongin City †	26	12	6	8	37	35	42
Busan Kyotong	26	11	8	7	28	23	41
Mokpo City	26	10	6	10	28	37	36
Suwon City	26	9	7	10	29	32	34
Ansan Hallelujah	26	8	8	10	25	34	32
Gimhae City	26	6	10	10	26	34	28
Chungju Hummel	26	5	6	15	20	34	21
Cheonan City	26	6	1	19	25	45	19
Daejeon HNP	26	3	3	20	22	54	12

10/03/2012 - 17/11/2012 • † Qualified for play-offs
Play-offs first round: Gangneung City 0-0 2-4p **Yongin City**
Changwon City 0-2 **Incheon Korail**
Play-off second round: Yongin City 1-3 **Incheon Korail**
Play-off semi-finals: Ulsan Mipo 1-2 **Incheon Korail**
Play-off final: **Incheon Korail** 1-0 3-2 Goyang Kookmin Bank
Incheon Korail are the 2012 National Champions

MEDALS TABLE

		Overall			League			Cup			LC			Asia		
		G	S	B	G	S	B	G	S	B	G	S	B	G	S	B
1	Suwon S. Bluewings	15	6	4	4	2	3	3	3	6				2	1	1
2	Seongnam I. Chunma	14	11	1	7	3		2	3		3	3		2	2	1
3	Pohang Steelers	12	9	5	4	4	4	3	3		2	2	1	3		
4	Busan I'Park	9	9	7	4	3	2	1	1	3	5	4		1		1
5	Ulsan Hyundai	8	10	7	2	6	4		1		5	3	1	1		2
6	FC Seoul	8	10	1	5	5			1		2	4	1	1		
7	Jeonbuk Hyundai	6	5	2	2	1			3	1		1	1	1	2	1
8	Jeju United	4	7	4	1	4	4			1	3	2				
9	Chunnam Dragons	3	6	1		1	1	3	1		3			1		
10	Daejeon Citizen	1	1					1	1			1				
11	Gimpo Halleluyah	1				1										
12	Gyeongnam FC		2	1							2			1		
13	Incheon United	1				1						1				
	Ulsan Mipo Dolphins	1									1					

HANA BANK KOREAN FA CUP 2012

First Round		Second Round		Quarter-finals		Semi-finals		Final	
Pohang Steelers *	4	**Pohang Steelers** *	3						
Cheongju Jijki	0	Gwangju FC	1						
Chungju Hummel *	2			**Pohang Steelers** *	3				
Gwangju FC	4			Jeonbuk Hyundai Motors	2				
Chunnam Dragons *	1	Chunnam Dragons	0						
Changwon City	0	**Jeonbuk Hyundai Motors** *	1			**Pohang Steelers** *	2		
Cheonan City	0					Jeju United	1		
Jeonbuk Hyundai Motors *	3								
Daejeon Citizen *	2	**Daejeon Citizen** *	2 4p						
Gyeongju Citizen	1	Sangju Sangmu Phoenix	2 2p						
Ulsan Mipo Dolphins	1			**Daejeon Citizen** *	1				
Sangju Sangmu Phoenix *	2			**Jeju United**	2				
Daegu FC *	3	Daegu FC	0						
Korean Police	1	**Jeju United** *	2					**Pohang Steelers** †	1
Incheon Korail	1							Gyeongnam FC	0
Jeju United *	2								
Ulsan Hyundai *	1	**Ulsan Hyundai**	2					CUP FINAL	
Daejeon HNP	0	Seongnam Ilhwa Chunma *	1						
Suwon City	5			**Ulsan Hyundai** *	6			Steelyard, Pohang, 20-10-2012	
Seongnam Ilhwa Chunma *	5			Goyang Kookmin Bank	1			Scorer - Park Seong Ho [120] for Pohang	
Incheon United *	3	Incheon United *	2 3p					**Pohang** - Shin Hwa Yong - Kim Gwang Seok, Kim Won Il, Kim Dae Ho (Ryu Chang Hyun 86) - Hwang Ji Soo, Park Hee Chul (Shin Kwang Hoon 30), Shin Jin Ho. Lee Myeong Ju - Park Seong Ho, No Byung Jun (Ko Mu Yeol 83), Derek Asamoah (Kim Jin Ryong 115). Tr: Hwang Sun Hong	
Gimhae City	0	**Goyang Kookmin Bank**	2 4p			**Ulsan Hyundai** *	0		
Busan I'Park *	0					**Gyeongnam FC**	3		
Goyang Kookmin Bank	1								
Suwon Samsung Bluewings *	5	**Suwon Samsung Bluewings**	2						
Gangneung City	2	FC Seoul *	0						
Mokpo City	0			Suwon Samsung Bluewings	1 2p			**Gyeongnam** - Kim Byung Ji - Kang Min Hyuk, Luke DeVere, Yoon Shin Young, Lee Jae Myung, Yu Ho Jun (Choi Hyun Yeon 65), Caique, Yun Il Lok (Lee Jae An 107), Kim In Han, Choi Young Jun, Jeong Da Hooeon. Tr: Choi Jin Han	
FC Seoul *	3			**Gyeongnam FC** *	1 4p				
Gangwon FC *	1	Gangwon FC	0						
Korea University	0	**Gyeongnam FC** *	1						
Busan Kyotong *	2 4p								
Gyeongnam FC	2 5p								

* Home team • † Qualified for the AFC Champions League

KSA – SAUDI ARABIA

FIFA/COCA-COLA WORLD RANKING

'93	'94	'95	'96	'97	'98	'99	'00	'01	'02	'03	'04	'05	'06	'07	'08	'09	'10	'11	'12
38	27	54	37	33	30	39	36	31	38	26	28	33	64	61	48	63	81	96	126

2012

Jan	Feb	Mar	Apr	May	Jun	Jul	Aug	Sep	Oct	Nov	Dec	High	Low	Av
87	89	88	89	89	92	101	104	105	113	112	126	21	126	48

Saudi Arabia's proud record amongst Asia's leading nations has counted for little in recent seasons as the national team continues to struggle. Since the disappointment of missing out on a place at the 2010 FIFA World Cup in South Africa, results have if anything got worse. Most distressingly for football fans in the kingdom was the national side's inability to progress to the final phase of qualifying for the 2014 FIFA World Cup, a performance that - along with poor results at both the 2012 Gulf Cup and the 2012 West Asian Championship - cost Frank Rijkaard his job as team coach. Softening the blow somewhat, were the performances of Saudi clubs in the 2012 AFC Champions League. For the first time two Saudi clubs met in the semi-finals as Jeddah duo Al Ahli and Al Ittihad went head-to-head for a place in the final. Al Ahli prevailed, only to lose out to Korea Republic's Ulsan Hyundai in the title decider - the seventh year in succession that Saudi clubs have failed to land Asia's top club prize. At home Al Shabab were crowned champions ahead of Al Ahli and Al Hilal in a close three-way tussle. There was consolation for the two who missed out, however, with Al Hilal beating Al Ittifaq 2-1 to win the Crown Prince Cup while Ali Alhi won the end of season's Champions Cup final 4-1 against Al Nasr.

FIFA WORLD CUP RECORD

1930-1974 DNE   1978-1990 DNQ   **1994** 12 r2   **1998** 28 r1   **2002** 32 r1   **2006** 28 r1   2010-2014 DNQ

SAUDI ARABIAN FOOTBALL FEDERATION (SAFF)

Al Mather Quarter, Prince Faisal Bin Fahad Street, PO Box 5844, Riyadh 11432
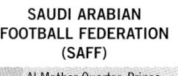
☎ +966 1 4822240
📠 +966 1 4821215
✉ info@football-saudi.com
🌐 www.thesaff.com.sa
FA 1959 CON 1972 FIFA 1959
P Ahmed Eid Al Harbi
GS Abdullah Al Sehli

THE STADIA

2014 FIFA World Cup Stadia
King Fahd International Stadium
Riyadh   67 000
Prince Mohammed Bin Fahad
Dammam   35 000
Other Main Stadia
Prince Abdullah Al Faisal
Jeddah   24 000
King Fahd Stadium
Taif   17 000

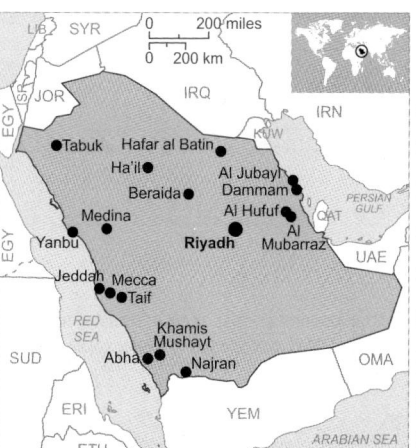

MAJOR CITIES/TOWNS

		Population
1	Riyadh	4 742 038
2	Jeddah	3 160 961
3	Mecca	1 453 533
4	Medina	1 071 218
5	Dammam	877 397
6	Taif	572 428
7	Tabuk	518 752
8	Khamis Mushayt	454 896
9	Beraida	449 216
10	Al Hufuf	316 219
11	Al Mubarraz	315 668
12	Najran	311 267
13	Ha'il	310 949
14	Al Jubayl	309 997
15	Hafar Al Batin	282 858
16	Yanbu	256 126
17	Abha	252 126
18	Al Kharj	226 227
19	Taqbah	225 599

AL MAMLAKAH AL ARABIYAH AS SUUDIYAH • KINGDOM OF SAUDI ARABIA

Capital Riyadh	Population 28 686 633 (41)	% in cities 82%
GDP per capita $20 500 (60)	Area km² 2 149 690 km² (14)	GMT +/− +3

Neighbours (km) Iraq 814, Jordan 744, Kuwait 222, Oman 676, Qatar 60, UAE 457, Yemen 1458 • Coast 2640

RECENT INTERNATIONAL MATCHES PLAYED BY SAUDI ARABIA

2010	Opponents	Score	Venue	Comp	Scorers	Att	Referee
22-11	Yemen	W 4-0	Aden	GCr1	Osama Al Harbi [4], Mohammad Al Shalhoub [58], Mohanad Aseri [71p], Mishal Al Saeed [90]		Al Marzouqi UAE
25-11	Kuwait	D 0-0	Abyan	GCr1			Ogiya JPN
28-11	Qatar	D 1-1	Aden	GCr1	OG [89]		Al Marzouqi UAE
2-12	UAE	W 1-0	Aden	GCsf	Ahmad Abbas [55]		Ogiya JPN
5-12	Kuwait	L 0-1	Aden	GCf			Al Harrasi OMA
28-12	Iraq	L 0-1	Dammam	Fr			
31-12	Bahrain	W 1-0	Manama	Fr	Osama Hawsawi [66]		
2011							
4-01	Angola	D 0-0	Dammam	Fr			
9-01	Syria	L 1-2	Al Rayyan	ACr1	Taisser Al Jassam [60]	15 768	Kim Dong Jin KOR
13-01	Jordan	L 0-1	Al Rayyan	ACr1		17 349	Albadwawi UAE
17-01	Japan	L 0-5	Al Rayyan	ACr1		2 022	Irmatov UZB
13-07	Jordan	D 1-1	Amman	Fr	Nassir Al Shamrani [94+]. W 4-3p		
16-07	Kuwait	L 0-1	Amman	Fr			
23-07	Hong Kong	W 3-0	Dammam	WCq	Nassir Al Shamrani 2 [45 47], Osama Al Harbi [45]	20 354	Tseytlin UZB
28-07	Hong Kong	W 5-0	Hong Kong	WCq	Hassan Fallatah [34], Mohammed Noor [71p], Nassir Al Shamrani [73], Mohammed Al Sahlawi [79], Osama Hawsawi [93+]	1 402	Minh Tri Vo VIE
2-09	Oman	D 0-0	Seeb	WCq		14 000	Abdou QAT
6-09	Australia	L 1-3	Dammam	WCq	Nassir Al Shamrani [66]	15 000	Nishimura JPN
7-10	Indonesia	D 0-0	Kuala Lumpur	Fr			
11-10	Thailand	D 0-0	Bangkok	WCq		42 000	Irmatov UZB
11-11	Thailand	W 3-0	Riyadh	WCq	Naif Hazazi [59], Ahmed Al Fraidi [80], Mohammed Noor [89p]	32 500	Liu Kwok Man HKG
15-11	Oman	D 0-0	Riyadh	WCq		62 740	Torky IRN
2012							
29-02	Australia	L 2-4	Melbourne	WCq	Salem Aldawsari [19], Nassir Al Shamrani [45]	24 240	Kim Dong Jin KOR
22-06	Kuwait	W 4-0	Taif	ARr1	Moh'd Al Sahlawi 2 [22 93+], Essa Al Mehyani 2 [51 56]		Grisha EGY
28-06	Palestine	D 2-2	Taif	ARr1	Abdullah Suhail [9], Khaled Al Zylaeei [85]		Abdel Rahman SUD
5-07	Iraq	L 0-1	Jeddah	AR3p			Abdel Rahman SUD
7-09	Spain	L 0-5	Pontevedra	Fr		11 850	Salmanov AZE
11-09	Gabon	L 0-1	Beauvais	Fr			
14-10	Congo	W 3-2	Dammam	Fr	Osama Al Harbi [77], Rabea Sefiani [88], Mansoor Al Harbi [95+p]		
14-11	Argentina	D 0-0	Riyadh	Fr		51 000	Abdulnabi BHR
9-12	Iran	D 0-0	Kuwait City	WAr1		1 200	Tojo JPN
12-12	Yemen	W 1-0	Al Farwaniyah	WAr1	Abdullah Otayf [39]	1 000	Tufaylieh SYR
15-12	Bahrain	L 0-1	Al Farwaniyah	WAr1		200	Al Ghafari JOR

Fr = Friendly match • AC = AFC Asian Cup • GC = Gulf Cup • WC = FIFA World Cup • q = qualifier • r1 = first round group • sf = semi-final • f = final

SAUDI ARABIA NATIONAL TEAM HISTORICAL RECORDS

Caps
178 - Mohammed Al Deayea 1990-2006 • **161** - Sami Al Jaber 1992-2006 • **139** - Majed Abdullah 1978-94 • **138** - Mohammed Al Khilaiwi 1990-2001 • **126** - Majed Abdullah 1978-94 • **122** - Abdullah Zubromawi 1993-2002 • **109** - Yasser Al Kahtani 2002- • **108** - Hussein Al Sulaimani 1996-2009

Goals
118 - Majed Abdullah 1978-94

Coaches
For Saudi coaches pre 1993 see Oliver's Almanack 2012 • Leo Beenhakker NED 1993-94 • Mohammed Al Kharashy 1994 • Ivo Wortmann BRA 1994 • Jorge Solari ARG 1994 • Mohammed Al Kharashy 1995 • Ze Mario BRA 1995-96 • Nelo Vingada POR 1996-97 • Otto Pfister GER 1998 • Carlos Alberto Parreira BRA 1998 • Mohammed Al Kharashy 1998 • Otto Pfister GER 1999 • Milan Macala CZE 1999-2000 • Nasser Al Johar 2000 • Slobodan Santrac SRB 2001 • Nasser Al Johar 2001-02 • Gerard van der Lem NED 2002-04 • Nasser Al Johar 2004 • Gabriel Calderon ARG 2004-05 • Marcos Paqueta BRA 2006-07 • Helio dos Anjos BRA 2007-08 • Nasser Al Johar 2008-09 • Jose Peseiro POR 2009-11 • Nasser Al Johar 2011 • Rogerio Lourenco BRA 2011 • Frank Rijkaard 2011-13 • Juan Ramon Lopez Caro ESP 2013-

SAUDI ARABIA 2011-12

ZAIN SAUDI PREMIER LEAGUE

	Pl	W	D	L	F	A	Pts	Shabab	Ahli	Hilal	Ittifaq	Ittihad	Fat'h	Nasr	Faysali	Najran	Ra'ed	Hajr	Taawun	Qadisiya	Ansar
Al Shabab †	26	19	7	0	50	16	64		1-1	0-0	1-0	2-2	1-0	2-2	1-1	4-0	3-2	6-1	1-0	1-0	3-0
Al Ahli †	26	19	5	2	60	22	62	1-1		1-0	0-0	0-1	3-3	2-0	2-0	4-0	1-0	4-3	4-2	2-1	5-1
Al Hilal †	26	18	6	2	58	22	60	0-2	4-0		3-3	1-1	3-2	1-0	2-1	2-1	2-0	3-1	1-1	3-0	6-1
Al Ittifaq †	26	13	8	5	41	26	47	0-0	0-4	2-2		1-0	1-0	2-0	1-2	3-3	1-1	0-5	5-1	3-2	1-1
Al Ittihad	26	10	7	9	49	35	37	0-2	1-3	0-2	0-1		1-2	1-1	4-2	2-2	1-1	7-0	5-3	1-0	3-2
Al Fat'h	26	10	7	9	37	41	37	0-1	2-2	0-5	2-1	3-2		0-1	2-1	2-2	0-0	1-0	0-0	1-6	3-0
Al Nasr	26	10	5	11	39	37	35	1-2	1-3	0-3	1-3	1-3	1-2		1-1	3-2	1-0	0-0	5-0	3-2	4-1
Al Faysali	26	7	9	10	36	41	30	1-3	0-1	0-2	1-4	0-1	1-0	1-1		4-1	2-1	2-2	1-1	2-2	2-1
Najran	26	7	9	10	34	49	30	1-4	0-2	0-2	0-3	1-1	0-0	2-1	1-1		3-1	1-1	1-1	2-2	2-1
Al Ra'ed	26	8	4	14	28	39	28	1-2	1-5	1-1	1-2	2-0	1-2	1-4	1-4	0-1		1-2	2-0	1-0	3-2
Hajr	26	6	7	13	23	45	25	0-1	0-2	1-2	1-0	0-0	2-4	0-3	1-1	1-0	0-2		2-1	1-0	1-0
Al Taawun	26	4	7	15	28	52	19	1-2	0-2	0-1	1-0	2-1	3-3	1-2	1-2	1-4	0-2	2-1		2-2	2-0
Al Qadisiya	26	4	6	16	34	52	18	1-2	0-3	4-5	1-0	0-8	1-2	2-1	2-2	0-2	0-1	1-1	1-1		2-1
Al Ansar	26	3	1	22	19	60	10	0-2	0-1	0-2	0-2	1-3	2-1	0-2	2-1	1-2	0-1	0-2	2-1	0-3	

9/09/2011 - 18/04/2012 • † Qualified for the AFC Champions League

Top scorers: **21** - **VICTOR SIMOES** BRA, Ahli & Nasser **AL SHAMRANI**, Shabab • **15** - Amad **AL HOSNI** OMA, Ahli & Mohammed **AL SAHLAWI**, Nasr • **12** - Hadj **BOUGUECHE** ALG, Qadisiya/Nasr; Youssef **EL ARABI** MAR, Hilal & Bader **AL KHARASHI**, Faysali

SAUDI ARABIA 2011-12
FIRST DIVISION (2)

	Pl	W	D	L	F	A	Pts
Al Sho'ala	30	15	10	5	48	34	55
Al Wahda	30	15	9	6	59	37	54
Al Nahda	30	14	10	6	39	24	52
Abha	30	14	7	9	36	28	49
Al Hazm	30	13	9	8	39	28	48
Al Ta'ee	30	12	11	7	42	26	47
Al Jeel	30	12	11	7	32	28	47
Al Khaleej	30	12	7	11	41	41	43
Hitteen	30	10	8	12	53	52	38
Al Urooba	30	10	7	13	24	38	37
Al Watani	30	10	6	14	31	45	36
Al Riyadh	30	7	13	10	27	23	34
Al Baten	30	8	10	12	39	50	34
Ohod	30	7	7	16	30	42	28
Dhemk	30	6	8	16	33	51	26
Al Suqoor	30	6	5	19	28	54	23

14/09/2011 - 3/05/2012

MEDALS TABLE

		Overall		Lge		Cup		CC		Asia			City
		G	S	B	G S	G S		G	S	B	
1	Al Hilal	33	20	3	13 10	16 7		1	4	2	3	Riyadh
2	Al Ittihad	22	19	4	8 7	10 8	1 3	3	1			Jeddah
3	Al Ahli	17	15		2 6	13 7	**2**			2		Jeddah
4	Al Nasr	14	14		6 5	7 6		1	1	2		Riyadh
5	Al Shabab	12	12	1	6 5	3 6	**2**	1	1	1		Riyadh
6	Al Ittifaq	4	9	1	2 2	2 7					1	Dammam
7	Al Wahda	2	6			2 6						Mecca
8	Al Qadisiya	2	1			1 1		1				Khobar
9	Al Riyadh	1	5			1 4						Riyadh
10	Al Ta'ee	1				1						Ha'il
	Al Taawun	1				1						Beraida

SAUDI ARABIA 2011-12
SECOND DIVISION GROUP A (3)

	Pl	W	D	L	F	A	Pts
Al Najma	18	11	2	5	36	16	35
Al Kawkab ‡	18	9	5	4	26	16	32
Al Adalh	18	7	9	2	25	15	30
Al Arabi	18	8	5	5	18	18	29
Al Safa	18	6	7	5	22	22	25
Al Uyoon	18	6	6	6	24	25	24
Al Taraji	18	6	4	8	22	29	22
Najd	18	5	5	8	25	27	20
Ukhdood	18	3	5	10	19	25	14
Al Nakheal	18	2	6	10	15	39	12

28/09/2011 - 5/04/2012 • ‡ Promotion play-off

3rd place promotion play-off
Al Kawkab 2-0 2-0 Al Rabi'a
Kawkab promoted

SAUDI ARABIA 2011-12
SECOND DIVISION GROUP B (3)

	Pl	W	D	L	F	A	Pts
Sudoos	18	14	3	1	41	13	45
Al Rabi'a ‡	18	10	5	3	40	22	35
Al Draih	18	8	3	7	28	22	27
Al Jabalain	18	7	3	8	27	23	24
Al Ramh	18	7	3	8	33	33	24
Hamada	18	5	6	7	27	30	21
Faiha'a	18	6	3	9	23	36	21
Al Ameade	18	5	5	8	27	39	20
Al Taqdom	18	4	7	7	22	31	19
Al Slam	18	3	4	11	17	36	0

28/09/2011 - 5/04/2012 • ‡ Promotion play-off

SECOND DIVISION FINAL
Al Najma 1-2 1-2 **Sudoos**

CROWN PRINCE CUP 2011-12

First Round		Quarter-finals		Semi-finals		Final	
Al Hilal	6						
Al Sho'ala *	1	Al Hilal *	4				
Al Fat'h *	0 7p	Al Nasr	1				
Al Nasr	0 8p			Al Hilal *	2		
Al Faysali	2			Al Ittihad	0		
Al Ta'ee *	1	Al Faysali	0				
Al Ra'ed	0	Al Ittihad *	1				
Al Ittihad *	4					Al Hilal	2
Al Ahli	3					Al Ittifaq	1
Hajr *	0	Al Ahli	1				
Al Qadisiya	1	Al Shabab *	0				
Al Shabab *	2			Al Ahli *	1		
Najran	2			Al Ittifaq	2		
Al Taawun *	1	Najran	0				
Al Ansar	0	Al Ittifaq *	3				
Al Ittifaq *	2	* Home team					

CROWN PRINCE CUP FINAL 2012
King Fahd International, Riyadh, 10-02-2012, Ref: Rizzoli ITA

Al Hilal	2	Wilhelmsson [9], Nawaf Al Abid [21]
Al Ittifaq	1	Yahya Al Shehri [35]

AL HILAL
Khaled **SHARAHILI** - Osama **HAWSAWI**, Majed **AL MARSHADI**●, Sultan **AL BISHI**● - Christian **WILHELMSSON** (Ahmed **AL FRAIDI** 25), Mohammad **AL SHALHOUB** (Mohammed **AL QARNI** 79), Adil **HERMACH**●, Nawaf **AL ABID**●, Salman **AL FARAJ**, Salem **AL DAWSARI** - **YOO** Byung Soo●♦88. Tr: Ivan **HASEK**

AL ITTIFAQ
Faiz **AL SOBEA** - Hassan **MUDHAFAR** (Ahmad Walpi **AQQASH** 36) (Abdulmutalib **AL TRAIDI** 80), **CARLOS**, Sayyaf **AL BISHI** - Bruno **LAZARONI**, Yahya **AL SHEHRI**, Yahya **ATEEN**●, Waleed **MOJAMMAMI** - Yousef **AL SALEM**, Sebastian **TAGLIABUE** (Zamil **AL SULIM** 56), Hamad **AL HAMAD**. Tr: Branko **IVANKOVIC**

CHAMPIONS CUP 2012

Quarter-finals		Semi-finals		Final	
Al Ahli *	5 3				
Al Faysali	1 0	Al Ahli	1 2		
Al Ittihad *	2 1	Al Hilal *	0 2		
Al Hilal	2 1				
Al Fat'h	2 3			Al Ahli	4
Al Ittifaq *	1 2	Al Fat'h *	0 1	Al Nasr	1
Al Shabab *	1 1	Al Nasr	2 0		
Al Nasr	2 2				

3rd place play-off: Fat'h 3-0 Hilal ● * Home team in 1st leg

CHAMPIONS CUP FINAL 2012
Prince Abdullah, Jeddah, 18-05-2011, Ref: Banti ITA

Al Ahli	4	Emad Al Hosani [36], Abdulrahim Jaizawi 2 [46 77], Kamil Al Mousa [74]
Al Nasr	1	Vinicius Reche [82]

AL AHLI
Abdullah **AL MAIOUF** - Kamil **AL MOUSA**, Mansour **AL HARBI**, Kamel **AL MOR** - Taisir **AL JASSIM**, Jairo **PALOMINO**, Motaz **AL MUSA** (Mohammed **MASSAD** 88), Marcelo **CAMACHO**●, Abdulrahim **JAIZAWI** (Yasir **AL FAHMI** 87) - **VICTOR SIMOES**, Emad **AL HOSANI** (Waleed **RASHID** 71). Tr: Karel **JAROLIM**

AL NASR
Abdullah **AL ENAZI** - Hussein **ABDUL GHANI**, Mohamed **EID**, Shaya Ali **SHARAHLI** (Abdulaziz **BIN SARAN** 64), Khaled **AL GHAMDI**, Omar **HAWSAWI** - Khaled **AZIZ**, Khaled **AL ZEALAIY** (Ibrahim **GHALEB** 81), Saud **HAMOUD** (**VINICIUS RECHE** 46) - Hadj **BOUGUECHE**●●♦72, Mohammad **AL SAHLAWI**. Tr: Francisco **MATURANA**

KUW – KUWAIT

FIFA/COCA-COLA WORLD RANKING

'93	'94	'95	'96	'97	'98	'99	'00	'01	'02	'03	'04	'05	'06	'07	'08	'09	'10	'11	'12
64	54	84	62	44	24	82	74	74	83	48	54	72	78	119	127	104	102	99	117

2012													High	Low	Av
Jan	Feb	Mar	Apr	May	Jun	Jul	Aug	Sep	Oct	Nov	Dec				
95	91	94	87	86	87	93	96	100	112	110	117		24	128	78

Al Kuwait strengthened the nation's claims for at least one berth in the AFC Champions League with another triumph in the AFC Cup, the second time in four seasons that they had won the Asian Football Confederation's second tier club competition. Kuwaiti clubs have not secured enough points on the governing body's criteria to have representation in the premier club competition, but Al Kuwait's 3-0 victory over Arbil in the 2012 final - 12 months after losing the previous final against Uzbekistan's Nasaf - further enhanced claims that the country should be competing for the continental title. While Al Kuwait were picking up silverware at Asian level, Al Qadisiya were dominating at home, winning the Kuwait Premier League and the Emir Cup while also reaching the final of the Crown Prince Cup where they lost to Al Arabi. Al Kuwait did win one domestic honour after beating Kazma 4-3 to claim the Federation Cup. The national team failed to build on the successes of two years previously when they had won the West Asian Championship and the Gulf Cup. At the end of 2012 Kuwait hosted an expanded West Asian Championship but crashed out early after losing to Oman in the key game of their group. At the beginning of 2012 they had missed out on the final phase of Asia's qualifying tournament for the 2014 FIFA World Cup.

FIFA WORLD CUP RECORD
1930-1970 DNE   1974-1978 DNQ   **1982** 21 r1   1986-2014 DNQ

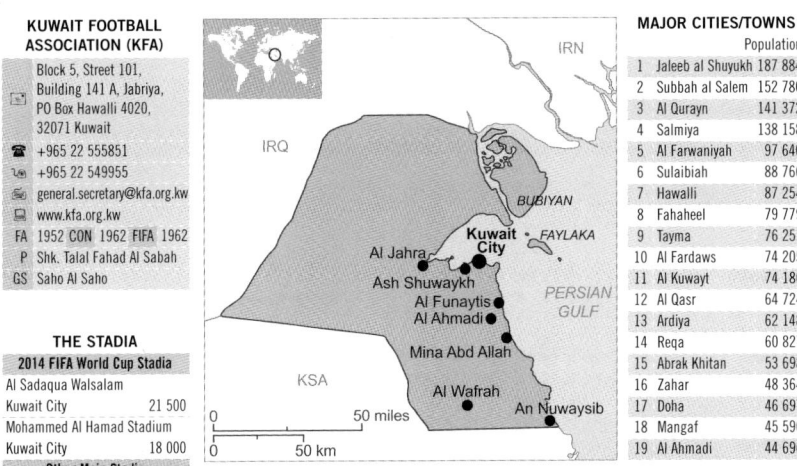

KUWAIT FOOTBALL ASSOCIATION (KFA)

Block 5, Street 101, Building 141 A, Jabriya, PO Box Hawalli 4020, 32071 Kuwait
☎ +965 22 555851
📠 +965 22 549955
✉ general.secretary@kfa.org.kw
🖥 www.kfa.org.kw
FA 1952   CON 1962   FIFA 1962
P Shk. Talal Fahad Al Sabah
GS Saho Al Saho

THE STADIA
2014 FIFA World Cup Stadia
Al Sadaqua Walsalam Kuwait City	21 500
Mohammed Al Hamad Stadium Kuwait City	18 000

Other Main Stadia
Jaber Al Ahmad International Kuwait City	65 000
Al Sabah	
Al Farwaniyah	14 000

MAJOR CITIES/TOWNS
		Population
1	Jaleeb al Shuyukh	187 884
2	Subbah al Salem	152 780
3	Al Qurayn	141 372
4	Salmiya	138 158
5	Al Farwaniyah	97 640
6	Sulaibiah	88 766
7	Hawalli	87 254
8	Fahaheel	79 779
9	Tayma	76 251
10	Al Fardaws	74 205
11	Al Kuwayt	74 180
12	Al Qasr	64 724
13	Ardiya	62 148
14	Reqa	60 827
15	Abrak Khitan	53 698
16	Zahar	48 364
17	Doha	46 697
18	Mangaf	45 590
19	Al Ahmadi	44 696

DAWLAT AL KUWAYT • STATE OF KUWAIT

Capital Kuwait City	Population 2 691 158 (139)	% in cities 98%
GDP per capita $57 500 (6)	Area km² 17 818 km² (157)	GMT +/- +3
Neighbours (km) Iraq 240, Saudi Arabia 222 • Coast 499		

RECENT INTERNATIONAL MATCHES PLAYED BY KUWAIT

2010	Opponents	Score	Venue	Comp	Scorers	Att	Referee
2-07	Lebanon	W 6-0	Beirut	Fr	Musaed Neda 2 [23 33], Yousef Al Sulaiman 2 [54 68], Waleed Jumah 2 [62 78]		
6-07	Oman	D 1-1	Beirut	Fr	Yousef Al Sulaiman [45]		
13-07	Iraq	W 2-0	Amman	Fr	Fahad Awadh [66], Hussain Fadel [84]		
16-07	Saudi Arabia	W 1-0	Amman	Fr	Bader Al Mutwa [70]		
23-07	Philippines	W 3-0	Kuwait City	WCq	Yousef Naser [17], Mesaed Al Enezi [68], Fahad Al Ebrahim [85]	20 000	Abu Loum JOR
28-07	Philippines	W 2-1	Manila	WCq	Yousef Naser [63], Waleed Jumah [85]	13 000	Liu Kwok Man HKG
10-08	Korea DPR	D 0-0	Kuwait City	Fr			
27-08	Oman	L 0-1	Muscat	Fr			
2-09	UAE	W 3-2	Al Ain	WCq	Yousef Naser 2 [7 65], Bader Al Mutwa [51]	8 715	Basma SYR
6-09	Korea Republic	D 1-1	Kuwait City	WCq	Hussain Ali [54]	20 000	Torky IRN
11-10	Lebanon	D 2-2	Beirut	WCq	Mesaed Al Enezi [51], OG [89]	32 000	Toma JPN
4-11	Bahrain	L 0-1	Kuwait City	Fr			
11-11	Lebanon	L 0-1	Kuwait City	WCq		17 500	Kovalenko UZB
15-11	UAE	W 2-1	Kuwait City	WCq	Fahad Al Enezi [50], OG [68]	10 000	Al Hilali OMA
22-12	Palestine	W 3-0	Doha	PG3p	Hussain Al Moussawi [92], Fahad Al Rashidi [94], Bader Al Mutwa [119]		
2012							
17-01	Uzbekistan	W 1-0	Kuwait City	Fr	Bader Al Mutwa [87]		
17-02	Korea DPR	D 1-1	Changsha	Fr	Fahad Al Rashidi [85]		
29-02	Korea Republic	L 0-2	Seoul	WCq		46 551	Nishimura JPN
22-06	Saudi Arabia	L 0-4	Taif	ARr1			Grisha EGY
25-06	Palestine	W 2-0	Taif	ARr1	Abdulhadi Khamis [27], Ahmad Ali Rashidi [92+]		Hashmi UAE
7-09	Uzbekistan	L 0-3	Tashkent	Fr		30 000	Irmatov UZB
11-09	UAE	L 0-3	Dubai	Fr			
16-10	Philippines	W 2-1	Kuwait City	Fr	Bader Al Mutwa [36], Mesaed Neda [70p]		
14-11	Bahrain	D 1-1	Kuwait City	Fr	Abdulrahman Bani [33]		
8-12	Palestine	W 2-1	Kuwait City	WAr1	Yousef Al Sulaiman [2], Bader Al Mutwa [6p]	1 500	Adday IRQ
11-12	Oman	L 0-2	Kuwait City	WAr1		1 400	Al Ghafari JOR
14-12	Lebanon	W 2-1	Kuwait City	WAr1	Yousef Al Sulaiman [8], Abdulhadi Khamis [79]	4 000	Adday IRQ

Fr = Friendly match • AC = AFC Asian Cup • GC = Gulf Cup • PG = Pan Arab Games • WC = FIFA World Cup • q = qualifier

KUWAIT NATIONAL TEAM HISTORICAL RECORDS

Caps: 133 - Bashar Abdulaziz 1996-2007 • 118 - Bader Al Mutwa 2003- • 111 - Waleed Jumah 2002- • 109 - Wael Sulaiman Al Habashi 1986-96 • 108 - Nohayer Al Shammari • 107 - Jamal Mubarak 1994-2004 • 102 - Jarah Al Ataiqi 2001-

Goals: 75 - Bashar Abdulaziz 1996-2008 • 38 - Bader Al Mutwa 2003-

Coaches: Milan Macala CZE 1996-99 • Dusan Uhrin CZE 1999-2001 • Berti Vogts GER 2001-02 • Radojko Avramovic SRB 2002-03 • Paulo Cesar Carpegiani BRA 2003-04 • Mohammed Ibrahem 2004 • Slobodan Pavkovic SRB 2005 • Mohammed Ibrahem 2005 • Mihai Stoichita ROU 2005-06 • Saleh Zakaria 2006-07 • Rodion Gacanin CRO 2007-08 • Mohammed Ibrahim 2008-09 • Goran Tufegdzic SRB 2009-

FEDERATION CUP 2011-12

Group 1	Pl	W	D	L	F	A	Pts	Sh	Ku	Qa	Ja	Ta	Ar	Na
Al Shabab	6	3	2	1	8	9	11							
Al Kuwait	6	2	4	0	8	2	10	0-0			3-0	3-0		0-0
Al Qadisiya	6	2	3	1	9	8	9	3-3	1-1			1-1		2-1
Jahra	6	3	0	3	6	7	9	1-2		2-1		0-1		
Al Tadamon	6	2	1	3	9	9	7	5-1						
Al Arabi	6	2	1	3	6	8	7	0-1	1-1	0-1	0-2	2-1		
Al Nasr	6	1	1	4	5	8	4	0-1			0-1	2-1	2-3	

Group 2	Pl	W	D	L	F	A	Pts	Sa	Ka	Kh	Ya	Fe	So	Sa
Salmiya	6	4	2	0	12	5	14		1-1		1-1			
Kazma	6	4	1	1	18	5	13			7-0	0-2		4-0	
Khitan	6	4	0	2	9	13	12	2-4			1-0			1-0
Al Yarmouk	6	2	1	3	7	7	7							
Fehayheel	6	2	1	3	7	8	7	0-1	2-4	0-1	3-1		1-0	1-1
Solaybeekhat	6	2	0	4	8	12	6	1-3		2-4	2-0			
Al Sahel	6	0	1	5	1	12	1	0-2	0-2		0-3		0-3	

Semi-finals

Al Kuwait	0	4
Salmiya	0	1

Al Shabab	1	0
Kazma	4	10

Final

Al Kuwait	4
Kazma	3

CUP FINAL

Sabah Al Salem, Kuwait City
18-12-2011

5/09/2011 - 18/12/2011

KUWAIT 2011-12

PREMIER LEAGUE

	Pl	W	D	L	F	A	Pts	Qadisiya	Al Kuwait	Arabi	Salmiya	Jahra	Kazma	Nasr	Shabab
Al Qadisiya	21	16	3	2	40	10	51		2-0 0-2	1-3 4-2	3-0	1-1	1-0 1-0	6-0 1-0	3-0
Al Kuwait	21	11	7	3	29	19	40	0-1		0-0 0-1	1-0 1-1	3-1 3-2	2-1 2-2	1-1	1-1
Al Arabi	21	9	6	6	27	20	33	0-1	1-1		2-1	0-1 0-0	0-1 6-1	2-1 2-1	2-0 1-1
Salmiya	21	7	4	10	26	34	25	0-2 0-3	1-3	2-0 3-1		2-2	2-2	2-1	1-2
Jahra	21	4	12	5	25	30	24	0-2 1-1	2-2	0-0	2-0 1-3		1-1	2-1 0-3	2-2
Kazma	21	5	7	9	31	38	22	0-3	1-2	1-1	3-0 0-1	1-1 2-3		2-3 4-2	1-0
Al Nasr	21	4	5	12	23	35	17	0-0	0-1 0-1	0-1	0-2 2-1	1-1	3-3		1-2 2-0
Al Shabab	21	2	8	11	20	35	14	0-2 1-2	0-1 1-2	0-2		1-2 2-2	1-1 1-1	2-3 2-2	1-1

30/12/2011 - 1/06/2012 • ‡ Qualified for the AFC Cup • Relegation play-off: Yarmouk 1-1 0-5 **Nasr**

KUWAIT 2011-12 FIRST DIVISION (2)

	Pl	W	D	L	F	A	Pts
Solaybeekhat	20	12	4	4	38	30	40
Al Yarmouk ‡	20	11	6	3	32	15	39
Khitan	20	8	3	9	25	23	27
Fehayheel	20	8	1	11	29	35	25
Al Tadamon	20	6	5	9	24	29	23
Al Sahel	20	4	3	13	22	38	15

30/12/2011 - 25/05/2012 • ‡ promotion play-off

MEDALS TABLE

	Overall	League	EC	CPC	FC	Asia
	G S B	G S B	G S B	G S	G S	G S B
1 Al Qadisiya	38 17 5	15 7 4	14 7	6 2	3	1 1
2 Al Arabi	37 17 5	16 3 5	15 11	6 2	1	
3 Al Kuwait	28 21 3	10 6 3	9 9	5 4	2 1	2 1
4 Kazma	12 16 5	4 4 5	7 9	1 1	2	
5 Salmiya	7 11 5	4 5 5	2 6	1		
6 Al Yarmouk	2 2		2 1			
7 Al Jahra	1 2	1	2			
8 Al Fahaheel	1		1			

CROWN PRINCE CUP 2011-12

Group 1	Pl	W	D	L	F	A	Pts	Qa	Ar	Na	Ka	Ja	Kh	Ta
Al Qadisiya	6	6	0	0	16	1	18				1-0	4-0	3-0	
Al Arabi	6	4	1	1	12	5	13	0-2				3-1		5-1
Al Nasr	6	3	0	3	8	10	9	0-2 0-2			3-1			
Kazma	6	2	2	2	9	8	8	1-4	1-1	4-0				
Jahra	6	2	1	3	5	7	7			1-0			0-0	2-0
Khitan	6	0	3	3	4	12	3		0-1	1-4	2-2			
Al Tadamon	6	0	1	5	2	13	1			0-1	0-1	1-1		

Group 2	Pl	W	D	L	F	A	Pts	Ya	Sa	Sh	Ku	Sa	Fe	So
Al Yarmouk	6	3	3	0	9	3	12		1-0					2-0
Salmiya	6	3	2	1	7	5	11	2-2		0-1				2-1
Al Shabab	6	3	2	1	9	5	11	1-1	1-2		0-0	1-0		
Al Kuwait	6	3	1	2	13	6	10			0-1		5-0	4-1	
Al Sahel	6	2	2	2	5	10	8	0-3 0-0					2-0	
Fehayheel	6	0	2	4	4	10	2	0-0 0-1			2-3			
Solaybeekhat	6	0	2	4	7	15	2		2-5 3-3			1-1		

Semi-finals
Al Arabi 4 1
Al Yarmouk 0 0

Salmiya 1 0
Al Qadisiya 4 1

19/08/2011 - 27/12/2011

Final
Al Arabi 0 4p
Al Qadisiya 0 1p

CUP FINAL
Al Arabi 1
Al Qadisiya 0
Sabah Al Salem, Kuwait City
27-12-2011

EMIR CUP 2011-12

First Round		Quarter-finals		Semi-finals		Final	
Al Qadisiya	Bye						
		Al Qadisiya	0 4				
Khitan	0 3	Al Kuwait	1 0				
Al Kuwait	1 5			**Al Qadisiya**	1 4		
Salmiya	3 1			Solaybeekhat	0 1		
Al Sahel	1 0	Salmiya	0 2				
Al Nasr	2 0	**Solaybeekhat**	2 1			**Al Qadisiya**	1
Solaybeekhat	2 2					Kazma	0
Jahra	3 1						
Al Tadamon	1 1	**Jahra**	1 0 6p				
Al Yarmouk	0 1	Al Shabab	0 1 5p				
Al Shabab	0 3			Jahra	1 0 5p		
Al Arabi	2 1			**Kazma**	0 1 6p	### CUP FINAL	
Fehayheel	0 0	Al Arabi	2 0			Sabah Al Salem, Kuwait City	
		Kazma	1 2			13-03-2012	
Kazma	Bye						

LAO – LAOS

FIFA/COCA-COLA WORLD RANKING

'93	'94	'95	'96	'97	'98	'99	'00	'01	'02	'03	'04	'05	'06	'07	'08	'09	'10	'11	'12
146	160	152	147	143	144	156	165	162	170	167	162	170	151	176	169	178	169	174	171

2012													High	Low	Av
Jan	Feb	Mar	Apr	May	Jun	Jul	Aug	Sep	Oct	Nov	Dec		High	Low	Av
174	171	173	175	173	172	190	194	193	193	179	171		134	194	164

After years of seclusion following the communist revolution of 1975, Laos is slowly opening up to the rest of the world. Its national football team has been at the forefront of the change in recent years and with it have come some surprising results. After qualifying for the finals of the 2010 AFF Suzuki Cup - southeast Asia's keenly contested regional competition - Laos made it to the finals of the 2012 tournament by finishing second in the qualifying competition. Wins over Cambodia and Brunei saw them finish second behind Myanmar to make it through to the finals in Malaysia. Laos had threatened an upset at the 2010 event following their surprise draw with regional powerhouse Thailand in their opening game, and in the 2012 edition there was to be a repeat performance, only this time it was Indonesia who were held to a 2-2 draw in Kuala Lumpur. Defeat against Malaysia was followed by a narrow 4-3 loss to eventual champions Singapore, a result that eliminated Laos from the competition but will have provided additional encouragement to the authorities in Vientiane that football in the country is on the correct path. There are also plans for the league champions to enter the AFC President's Cup from 2014 onwards - a move that would enable clubs like 2012 champions Police to benefit from a higher continental profile.

FIFA WORLD CUP RECORD
1930-1998 DNE 2002-2006 DNQ 2010 DNE 2014 DNQ

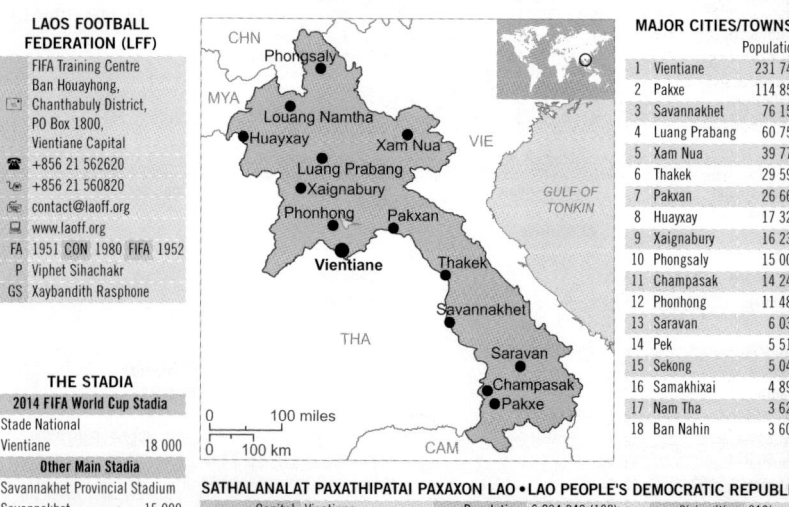

LAOS FOOTBALL FEDERATION (LFF)

FIFA Training Centre
Ban Houayhong,
Chanthabuly District,
PO Box 1800,
Vientiane Capital
☎ +856 21 562620
+856 21 560820
contact@laoff.org
www.laoff.org
FA 1951 CON 1980 FIFA 1952
P Viphet Sihachakr
GS Xaybandith Rasphone

THE STADIA
2014 FIFA World Cup Stadia
Stade National
Vientiane   18 000
Other Main Stadia
Savannakhet Provincial Stadium
Savannakhet   15 000
Luang Prabang Stadium
Luang Prabang   10 000

MAJOR CITIES/TOWNS

		Population
1	Vientiane	231 742
2	Pakxe	114 852
3	Savannakhet	76 150
4	Luang Prabang	60 750
5	Xam Nua	39 775
6	Thakek	29 598
7	Pakxan	26 668
8	Huayxay	17 325
9	Xaignabury	16 238
10	Phongsaly	15 005
11	Champasak	14 241
12	Phonhong	11 484
13	Saravan	6 039
14	Pek	5 513
15	Sekong	5 042
16	Samakhixai	4 898
17	Nam Tha	3 623
18	Ban Nahin	3 607

SATHALANALAT PAXATHIPATAI PAXAXON LAO • LAO PEOPLE'S DEMOCRATIC REPUBLIC

Capital Vientiane   Population 6 834 942 (102)   % in cities 31%
GDP per capita $2100 (186)   Area km² 236 800 km² (83)   GMT +/- +7
Neighbours (km) Cambodia 541, China 423, Myanmar 235, Thailand 1754, Vietnam 2130

RECENT INTERNATIONAL MATCHES PLAYED BY LAOS

2007	Opponents	Score		Venue	Comp	Scorers	Att	Referee
13-01	Indonesia	L	1-3	Singapore	AFFr1	Xaysongkham [13]		
15-01	Singapore	L	0-11	Singapore	AFFr1		5 224	U Hla Tint MYA
17-01	Vietnam	L	0-9	Singapore	AFFr1		1 005	
22-08	Lesotho	L	1-3	Petaling Jaya	Fr	Visay Phaphouvanin		
25-08	Myanmar	L	0-1	Kuala Lumpur	Fr			
2008								
17-10	Cambodia	L	2-3	Phnom Penh	AFFq	Luanglath [30], Leupvisay [30]		
21-10	Philippines	W	2-1	Phnom Penh	AFFq	Luanglath [56], Phaphouvanin [59]		
23-10	Brunei Darussalam	W	3-2	Phnom Penh	AFFq	Phaphouvanin [8], Singto [89], Saynakhonevieng [93+]		
25-10	Timor-Leste	W	2-1	Phnom Penh	AFFq	Singto [7], Phaphouvanin [50]		
6-12	Malaysia	L	0-3	Phuket	AFFr1		5 000	Nitrorejo IDN
8-12	Thailand	L	0-6	Phuket	AFFr1		10 000	Hadimin BRU
10-12	Vietnam	L	0-4	Phuket	AFFr1			Cho Win MYA
2009								
No international matches played in 2009								
2010								
22-10	Cambodia	D	0-0	Vientiane	AFFq			Abdul Wahab MAS
24-10	Philippines	D	2-2	Vientiane	AFFq	Soukaphone [29], Kanyala [41]		Pechsri THA
26-10	Timor-Leste	W	6-1	Vientiane	AFFq	Kovanh [11], Soukaphone [17], Lamnao [47p], Konekham [59], Kanyala [61], Ketsada [78]		Phung Dinh Dung VIE
1-12	Thailand	D	2-2	Jakarta	AFFr1	Inthammavong [54], Sysomvang [82]		Sato JPN
4-12	Indonesia	L	0-6	Jakarta	AFFr1		70 000	Daud SIN
7-12	Malaysia	L	1-5	Palembang	AFFr1	Lamnao [8]		Vo Minh Tri VIE
2011								
10-02	Chinese Taipei	L	2-5	Kaohsiung	CCq	Ketsada [65], Phattana [73]	1 000	Ng Chiu Kok HKG
16-02	Chinese Taipei	D	1-1	Vientiane	CCq	Vongchiengkham [82]	15 300	Abdul Wahab MAS
29-06	Cambodia	L	2-4	Phnom Penh	WCq	Phomsouvanh 2 [10 61]	25 000	Jahanbazi IRN
3-07	Cambodia	W	6-2	Vientiane	WCq	Singto 2 [19 55], Sayavutthi [34], Syphasay [46], Phaphouvanin [94], Sysomvang [112]	9 000	Sato JPN
23-07	China PR	L	2-7	Kunming	WCq	Vongchiengkham [5], Phaphouvanin [31]	13 500	Delovski AUS
28-07	China PR	L	1-6	Vientiane	WCq	Phaphouvanin [47]	13 000	Shamsuzzaman BAN
2012								
7-10	Cambodia	W	1-0	Yangon	AFFq	Phaphouvanin [40]	100	Alzaabi UAE
9-10	Timor-Leste	L	1-3	Yangon	AFFq	Phaphouvanin [77]		Aslam MDV
11-10	Brunei-Darussalam	W	3-1	Yangon	AFFq	Namthavixay [35], Sayavutthi [51p], Sysomvang [83p]		Shamsuzzaman BAN
13-10	Myanmar	D	0-0	Yangon	AFFq			Alzaabi UAE
26-10	Vietnam	L	0-4	Ho Chi Minh City	Fr			Ramachandran MAS
28-10	Turkmenistan	L	2-4	Ho Chi Minh City	Fr	Liththideth [57], Saysana [83]		Vo Quang Vinh VIE
25-11	Indonesia	D	2-2	Kuala Lumpur	AFFr1	Sayautthi [30p], Liththideth [80]		Ng Kai Lam HKG
28-11	Malaysia	L	1-4	Kuala Lumpur	AFFr1	Sihavong [39]		Fan Qi CHN
1-12	Singapore	L	3-4	Kuala Lumpur	AFFr1	Sayautthi 2 [21 81p], Liththideth [40]		Ng Kai Lam HKG

AFF = ASEAN Football Federation Championship • AC = AFC Asian Cup 2004 • WC = FIFA World Cup • q = qualifier • r1 = first round group

LAOS 2011 LAO LEAGUE

	Pl	W	D	L	F	A	Pts
Yotha (MPWT)	18	16	2	0			50
Bank	18	12	2	4			38
Ezra	18	11	4	3			37
Army	18	11	4	3			37
Vientiane	18	9	2	7			29
Police	18	7	4	7			25
Lao-American College	18	6	4	8			22
Eastern Star	18	4	1	13			13
Lao Lanexang	18	1	1	16			4
Friends Development	18	1	0	17			3

LAOS 2012 LAO LEAGUE

	Pl	W	D	L	F	A	Pts
Police	18	14	2	2	70	13	44
Yotha	18	14	1	3	82	17	43
Vientiane	18	11	5	2	82	20	38
Army	18	11	3	4	71	29	36
Ezra	18	9	4	5	72	25	31
Lao Airlines	18	7	3	8	38	33	24
Lao-American College	18	6	0	12	37	38	18
Friends Development	18	5	0	13	16	76	15
Lao Lanexang	18	2	1	15	16	152	7
Eastern Star	18	1	1	16	14	97	4

LBR – LIBERIA

FIFA/COCA-COLA WORLD RANKING

'93	'94	'95	'96	'97	'98	'99	'00	'01	'02	'03	'04	'05	'06	'07	'08	'09	'10	'11	'12
123	127	87	94	94	108	105	95	73	88	110	123	135	115	145	139	161	160	123	112

2012												High	Low	Av
Jan	Feb	Mar	Apr	May	Jun	Jul	Aug	Sep	Oct	Nov	Dec			
123	125	125	112	112	124	120	117	111	98	114	112	66	164	114

Liberia's national team continued to struggle to produce results in 2012 but faced added turmoil when coach Kaetu Smith sacked his captain and suspended other key players. Skipper Anthony Laffor, Francis Doe and Dioh Williams were kicked out of the squad for disciplinary reasons in June after the country had started its qualifying campaign for the 2014 FIFA World Cup. Liberia lost their opening match against Senegal in Dakar and then drew at home to Angola. The trio were absent from the Africa Cup of Nations match the following week where a 0-0 draw in Windhoek saw Liberia make it through to the final round of qualifying for the finals in South Africa and a tie against Nigeria. Smith had been appointed earlier in the year but was fired in December after Liberia suffered a heavy defeat at the hands of the Nigerians. After holding the Super Eagles to a 2-2 draw at home, the 'Lone Star' were thrashed 6-1 away in Calabar in the return. In club football second division Barrack Young Controllers II won cup honours by beating Watanga in the final - the second lower league team to win the FA Cup in four years. LISCR FC became the only club to win the Premier League in successive years in a campaign which saw Liberia's second oldest club Mighty Barrolle relegated for the first time.

CAF AFRICA CUP OF NATIONS RECORD

1957-1965 DNE 1968 DNQ 1970-1974 DNE 1976 DNQ 1978-1980 DNE 1982 DNQ 1984 DNE 1986-1990 DNQ
1992 DNE 1994 DNQ **1996** 9 r1 1998-2000 DNQ **2002** 10 r1 2004-2013 DNQ

LIBERIA FOOTBALL ASSOCIATION (LFA)

Professional Building,
Benson Street
PO Box 10-1066, Monrovia
☎ +231 776 892693
✉ lbrfootballassoc@yahoo.com
🌐 www.liberiansoccer.com
FA 1936 CON 1962 FIFA 1962
P Musa Bility
GS Alphonso Armah

THE STADIA

2014 FIFA World Cup Stadia

Antoinette Tubman Stadium		
Monrovia		10 000

Other Main Stadia

Samuel Doe Sports Complex		
Monrovia		30 000
Nancy Doe Sports Stadium		
Kakata		9 500
Doris Williams Stadium		
Buchanan		3 000
Harbel Stadium		
Harbel		2 000

MAJOR CITIES/TOWNS

		Population
1	Monrovia	1 172 090
2	Bensonville	28 970
3	Gbarnga	21 355
4	Buchanan	15 674
5	Harper	15 547
6	Yekepa	10 891
7	Zwedru	10 874
8	Ganta	7 447
9	Robertsport	5 039
10	Tubmanburg	1 314

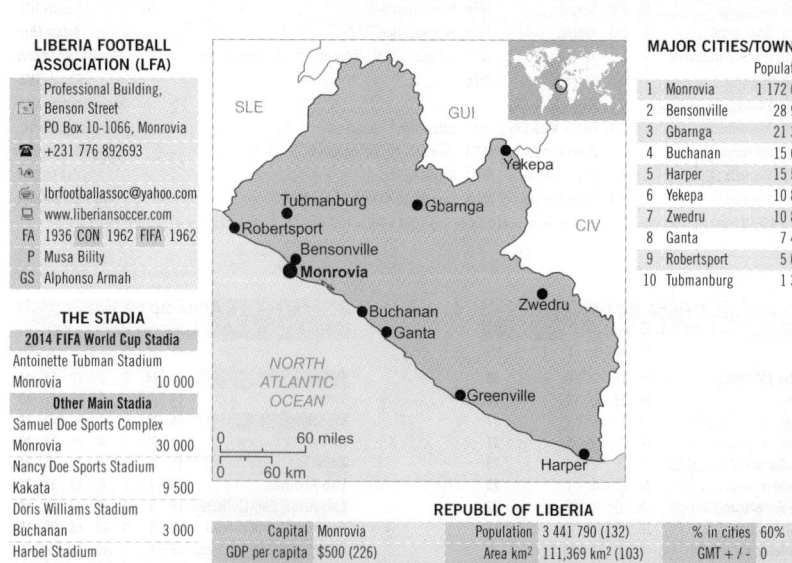

REPUBLIC OF LIBERIA

Capital	Monrovia	Population	3 441 790 (132)	% in cities	60%
GDP per capita	$500 (226)	Area km²	111,369 km² (103)	GMT +/-	0
Neighbours (km)	Guinea 563, Cote d'Ivoire 716, Sierra Leone 306 • Coast 579				

RECENT INTERNATIONAL MATCHES PLAYED BY LIBERIA

2008	Opponents	Score	Venue	Comp	Scorers	Att	Referee
1-06	Gambia	D 1-1	Monrovia	WCq	Makor 82	35 000	Keita GUI
6-06	Algeria	L 0-3	Blida	WCq		40 000	Lemghambodj MTN
15-06	Senegal	D 2-2	Monrovia	WCq	Williams 74, Makor 85	18 000	Djaoupe TOG
21-06	Senegal	L 1-3	Dakar	WCq	Williams 89	40 000	Chaibou NIG
6-09	Gambia	L 0-3	Banjul	WCq		10 000	Ambaya LBY
11-10	Algeria	D 0-0	Monrovia	WCq		2 000	Ahmed Auda EGY
2009							
No international matches played in 2009							
2010							
5-09	Zimbabwe	D 1-1	Paynesville	CNq	Sekou Oliseh 68		Codjia BEN
9-10	Mali	L 1-2	Bamako	CNq	Theo Weeks 42		Djaoupe TOG
2011							
26-03	Cape Verde Islands	L 2-4	Praia	CNq	Patrick Wleh 38, Alseny Keita 85		Lemghaifry MTN
5-06	Cape Verde Islands	W 1-0	Paynesville	CNq	Francis Doe 31		
24-07	Gambia	W 3-2	Monrovia	Fr	James Roberts 3, Vatalis Sieh 58, Marcus Marcauley		
10-08	Angola	D 0-0	Monrovia	Fr			
14-08	Niger	D 0-0	Monrovia	Fr			
4-09	Zimbabwe	L 0-3	Harare	CNq			
8-10	Mali	D 2-2	Paynesville	CNq	Dioh Williams 2, Patrick Wleh 90		
2012							
15-02	Nigeria	L 0-2	Monrovia	Fr			
29-02	Namibia	W 1-0	Monrovia	CNq	Dioh Williams 67		Otogo Castane GAB
2-06	Senegal	L 1-3	Dakar	WCq	Francis Forkey 15	15 000	Doue CIV
10-06	Angola	D 0-0	Monrovia	WCq		15 000	Lemghaifry MTN
16-06	Namibia	D 0-0	Windhoek	CNq			Sikazwe ZAM
4-09	Malawi	W 1-0	Monrovia	Fr	Zah Krangar 88		Neewon LBR
8-09	Nigeria	D 2-2	Paynesville	CNq	Tonia Tisdell 8, Sekou Oliseh 66		Coulibaly MLI
11-09	Ghana	W 2-0	Monrovia	Fr	Zah Krangar 2 6 9		Yekeh LBR
9-10	Niger	L 3-4	Niamey	Fr	Marcus Macaulay 23, Ansu Toure 53, Zah Krangar 55		Hama NIG
13-10	Nigeria	L 1-6	Calabar	CNq	Patrick Wleh 79		Bennett RSA
2-12	Mauritania	L 0-1	Paynesville	Fr			
15-12	Mauritania	L 1-2	Nouakchott	Fr			

CN = CAF African Cup of Nations • WC = FIFA World Cup • q = qualifier

LIBERIA NATIONAL TEAM HISTORICAL RECORDS

Coach: George Weah & Dominic Vava 2000-02 • Kadalah Kromah 2002-04 • Joseph Sayon 2004-06 • Shawky El Din EGY 2006 • Joe Nagbe 2006-08 • Antoine Hey GER 2008-09 • Bertalan Bicskei HUN 2010-11 • Roberto Landi ITA 2011-12 • Thomas Kojo 2012 • Kaetu Smith 2012

LIBERIA 2012 PREMIER DIVISION

	Pl	W	D	L	Pts
LISCR †	30	17	10	3	**61**
Nimba United	30	16	10	4	**58**
LPRC Oliers	30	14	12	4	**54**
Barrack Young Controllers	30	14	12	4	**54**
MC Breweries	30	15	8	7	**53**
Jubilee FC	29	14	7	8	**49**
Fatu FC	30	11	8	11	**41**
Watanga FC	30	9	13	8	**40**
Invincible Eleven	29	10	9	10	**39**
Mighty Blue Angels	30	9	10	11	**37**
Mighty Barrolle	30	8	10	12	**34**
Utd Soccer Ambassador	30	9	5	16	**32**
NPA Anchors	29	5	11	13	**26**
Green Pastures	29	6	7	16	**25**
UMC Roots	30	4	9	17	**21**
Devereux FC	30	5	3	22	**18**

† Qualified for the CAF Champions League

LFA CELLCOM CUP 2012

Semi-finals
Barrack Youth Controllers-II 2
Mighty Blue Angels 0

Small Town FC 1
Watanga FC 4

Finals
Barrack Youth Controllers-II ‡ 1
Watanga FC 0

7-10-2012
Scorer - Ezekiel Doe 49

‡ Qualified for the CAF Confederation Cup

LBY – LIBYA

FIFA/COCA-COLA WORLD RANKING

'93	'94	'95	'96	'97	'98	'99	'00	'01	'02	'03	'04	'05	'06	'07	'08	'09	'10	'11	'12
152	167	175	184	147	147	131	116	116	104	83	61	80	99	95	82	115	72	63	54

2012													High	Low	Av
Jan	Feb	Mar	Apr	May	Jun	Jul	Aug	Sep	Oct	Nov	Dec				
63	53	55	46	46	42	39	38	36	53	59	54		36	187	110

The fragile security situation in Libya continued to keep a restart of the league on hold after its suspension in March 2011 when the struggle to depose president Gaddafi began. His downfall coincided with Libya's fairy tale qualification for the 2012 Africa Cup of Nations where they beat Senegal and held champions-elect Zambia to a draw - despite not getting past the first round. Coach Marqos Paqueta did not have his contact renewed after the tournament and was replaced by Abdul-Hafeedh Arbeesh who took charge of the opening 2014 FIFA World Cup qualifiers. Libya started their campaign to reach Brazil with a draw in Togo and then beat Cameroon 2-1 in Sfax, across the border in Tunisia where they had been forced to move the game. In the 2013 Nations Cup qualifiers Libya hosted Algeria in Casablanca, Morocco, losing 1-0 in the first leg. The second leg in Blida was fraught with tension, highlighted by a halt to the proceedings in the second half as the Libyans threatened to walk off as the Algerian crowd chanted the word "rats" over and over again, a reference to the derogatory term that Gaddafi used to describe his opponents when the revolution against his regime first began. Libya lost 2-0. No Libyan clubs took part in African club competitions in 2012 but it was agreed they would compete again in 2013.

CAF AFRICA CUP OF NATIONS RECORD
1957-1965 DNE 1968 DNQ 1970 DNE 1972 DNQ 1974-1980 DNE **1982** 2 F (hosts)
1984-1986 DNQ 1988-1998 DNE 2000-2004 DNQ **2006** 14 r1 2008-2010 DNQ **2012** 10 r1 2013 DNQ

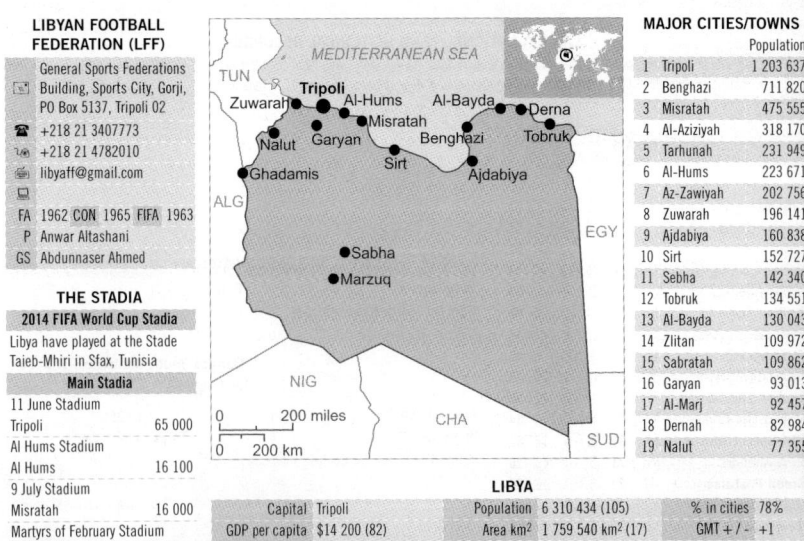

LIBYAN FOOTBALL FEDERATION (LFF)
General Sports Federations Building, Sports City, Gorji, PO Box 5137, Tripoli 02
☎ +218 21 3407773
📠 +218 21 4782010
✉ libyaff@gmail.com

FA 1962 CON 1965 FIFA 1963
P Anwar Altashani
GS Abdunnaser Ahmed

THE STADIA
2014 FIFA World Cup Stadia
Libya have played at the Stade Taieb-Mhiri in Sfax, Tunisia

Main Stadia
11 June Stadium
Tripoli   65 000
Al Hums Stadium
Al Hums   16 100
9 July Stadium
Misratah   16 000
Martyrs of February Stadium
Benghazi   10 550

MAJOR CITIES/TOWNS
		Population
1	Tripoli	1 203 637
2	Benghazi	711 820
3	Misratah	475 555
4	Al-Aziziyah	318 020
5	Tarhunah	231 949
6	Al-Hums	223 671
7	Az-Zawiyah	202 756
8	Zuwarah	196 141
9	Ajdabiya	160 838
10	Sirt	152 727
11	Sebha	142 340
12	Tobruk	134 551
13	Al-Bayda	130 043
14	Zlitan	109 972
15	Sabratah	109 862
16	Garyan	93 013
17	Al-Marj	92 457
18	Dernah	82 984
19	Nalut	77 355

LIBYA
Capital Tripoli   Population 6 310 434 (105)   % in cities 78%
GDP per capita $14 200 (82)   Area km² 1 759 540 km² (17)   GMT +/- +1
Neighbours (km) Algeria 982, Chad 1055, Egypt 1115, Niger 354, Sudan 383, Tunisia 459 • Coast 1770

LBY - LIBYA

RECENT INTERNATIONAL MATCHES PLAYED BY LIBYA

2008 Opponents	Score	Venue	Comp	Scorers	Att	Referee
1-06 Ghana	L 0-3	Kumasi	WCq		27 908	Maillet SEY
7-06 Gabon	W 1-0	Tripoli	WCq	Brou OG [5]	30 000	Chaibou NIG
15-06 Lesotho	W 1-0	Bloemfontein	WCq	Ahmed Saad Osman [85]	3 500	Marange ZIM
20-06 Lesotho	W 4-0	Tripoli	WCq	Osama Salah [3], Omar Dawood [50], Younus Al Shibani [68], Hesham Shaban [80]	30 000	Trabelsi TUN
20-08 Senegal	D 0-0	Tripoli	Fr			
24-08 Chad	W 3-0	Tripoli	Fr	Omar Dawood [19], Mohamed Esnani [77], Nader Kara [80]		
28-08 Niger	W 6-2	Tripoli	Fr	Mohamed El Mughrby 2 [34 76], Ahmed Masli [44], Mohamed Zubya [87]		
5-09 Ghana	W 1-0	Tripoli	WCq	Ahmed Saad Osman [86]	45 000	Coulibaly MLI
11-10 Gabon	L 0-1	Libreville	WCq		26 000	Bennett RSA
2009						
11-02 Uruguay	L 2-3	Tripoli	Fr	Mohamed Esnani [31], Osama Salah [57]		
5-10 Kuwait	D 1-1	Cairo	Fr	Ahmed Kerwaa [88]		
2010						
6-01 Benin	L 0-1	Cotonou	Fr			
3-03 Mali	W 2-1	Tripoli	Fr	Mohamed El Mughrby [35p], Khalid Al Deelawi [81]		
5-09 Mozambique	D 0-0	Maputo	CNq			Bangoura GUI
10-10 Zambia	W 1-0	Tripoli	CNq	Ahmed Saad Osman [36]		Gassama GAM
17-11 Niger	D 1-1	Tripoli	Fr	Mohamed Al-Ghandour [69]. W 4-1p		
2011						
9-02 Benin	W 3-2	Tripoli	Fr	Ahmed Zuway [4], Abdullah Al Sharif [16], Ahmed Saad Osman [35]		
28-03 Comoros	W 3-0	Bamako	CNq	Walid Al Khatroushi [20], Ahmed Abdelkader [70], Djamal Mohamed [82]		Diatta SEN
5-06 Comoros	D 1-1	Mitsamiouli	CNq	Ihaab Boussefi [43]		
3-09 Mozambique	W 1-0	Cairo	CNq	Rabie Ellafi [28]		
8-10 Zambia	D 0-0	Chingola	CNq			
15-11 Belarus	D 1-1	Dubai	Fr	Ahmed Saad Osman [32]	250	Mohamed UAE
2012						
16-01 Côte d'Ivoire	L 0-1	Abu Dhabi	Fr			
21-01 Equatorial Guinea	L 0-1	Bata	CNr1		35 000	Doue CIV
25-01 Zambia	D 2-2	Bata	CNr1	Ahmed Saad Osman 2 [4 47]	1 500	Coulibaly MLI
29-01 Senegal	W 2-1	Bata	CNr1	Ihaab Boussefi 2 [6 84]	10 000	Seechurn MRI
3-06 Togo	D 1-1	Lome	WCq	Ahmed Zuway [16]	15 000	Coulibaly MLI
10-06 Cameroon	W 2-1	Sfax	WCq	Ahmed Zuway [6], Hamd Ahniash [93+]	1 000	Maeruf ERI
26-08 Sudan	W 3-0	Tunis	Fr	Ihab Al Boussifi, Faisal Al Badri, Walid Al Sabai		
9-09 Algeria	L 0-1	Casablanca	CNq			Diatta SEN
14-10 Algeria	L 0-2	Blida	CNq		15 000	Bangoura GUI

Fr = Friendly match • CN = CAF African Cup of Nations • WC = FIFA World Cup • q = qualifier • r1 = first round

LIBYA SQUAD FOR THE 2012 CAF AFRICA CUP OF NATIONS

	Player		Ap	G	Club	Date of Birth
1	Samir Aboud (c)	GK	3		Al Ittihad	29 09 1972
2	Abubaker Rabea	DF	2+1		Club Africain TUN	1 12 1990
3	Abdulaziz Belreesh	DF	2+1		Al Ittihad	12 07 1990
4	Ahmed Al Alwani	MF	0		Al Medina	19 08 1981
5	Younus Al Shibani	DF	3		Khouribga MAR	27 06 1981
6	Mohamed Esnani	MF	3		US Monastir TUN	13 05 1984
7	Osama Chtiba	DF	0		Nejmeh LIB	27 09 1988
8	Abdallah Sharif	MF	0+3		Al Medina	30 03 1985
9	Mohamed Al Ghanodi	FW	0		Al Ahly Tripoli	22 11 1992
10	Ahmed Saad Osman	FW	3	2	Club Africain TUN	7 08 1979
11	Mohamed El Mughrby	DF	2		Khouribga MAR	19 04 1985
12	Guma Mousa	GK	0		Al Ahly Tripoli	1 12 1978
13	Mohamed Mounir	DF	0		FK Jagodina SRB	8 04 1992
14	Ali Salama	DF	3		Oly. Béjà TUN	18 09 1987
15	Marwan Mabrouk	MF	1+1		Al Ittihad	15 12 1989
16	Abubakr Al Abaidy	MF	2+1		Al Nasr	27 10 1981
17	Walid Mhadeb	MF	2		Al Ittihad	6 11 1985
18	Faisal Al Badri	MF	0		Al Ahly Benghazi	4 06 1990
19	Ahmed Zuway	FW	3		CA Bizertin TUN	28 12 1982
20	Ihaab Boussefi	FW	1+2	2	Al Ittihad	23 06 1985
21	Moataz Ben Amer	MF	0		Al Ahly Benghazi	2 02 1981
22	Muhamad Nashnoush	GK	0		Al Ittihad	15 06 1988
23	Djamal Mahamat	MF	3		Braga POR	26 04 1983

Tr: Marcos Paqueta

LCA – ST LUCIA

FIFA/COCA-COLA WORLD RANKING

'93	'94	'95	'96	'97	'98	'99	'00	'01	'02	'03	'04	'05	'06	'07	'08	'09	'10	'11	'12
139	157	114	134	142	139	152	135	130	112	130	114	128	160	180	176	186	181	185	149

2012												High	Low	Av
Jan	Feb	Mar	Apr	May	Jun	Jul	Aug	Sep	Oct	Nov	Dec			
185	186	185	188	188	188	186	187	184	185	147	149	108	192	146

There was perhaps no more unlucky nation than St Lucia in the 2012 Caribbean Cup after they fell at the first hurdle in the qualifiers for the finals in Antigua. Having won just two international matches in the previous seven years, Francis Lastic's side won two matches in the space of two days in a qualifying group they hosted at the Beausejour Cricket Ground in Gros Islet. An impressive 5-1 victory over Curacao was followed by a hard fought 1-0 win over neighbours and fierce rivals St Vincent. Although a difficult tie against Guyana lay ahead in their final match, St Lucia looked odds on to claim one of the two places that would take them through to the second qualifying round. Their hopes were shattered, however, as results conspired against them. St Lucia made a disastrous start against Guyana and found themselves 3-0 down at half-time. With St Vincent winning comfortably against Curacao all three teams looked set to finish on six points. With head-to-head results then counting, St Lucia needed to score twice in the second half to make it through at the expense of St Vincent but they failed to get on the scoresheet and were out. In club football VSADC retained their league title in 2012 while the annual Blackheart/Kashif & Shanghai Football Tournament was won by Dennery who beat Soufriere 1-0 in the final.

CFU CARIBBEAN CUP RECORD
1989 DNQ **1991** 3 SF 1992 DNQ **1993** 7 r1 1994 DNE **1995** 8 r1 1996-2007 DNQ 2008 DNE 2010-2012 DNQ

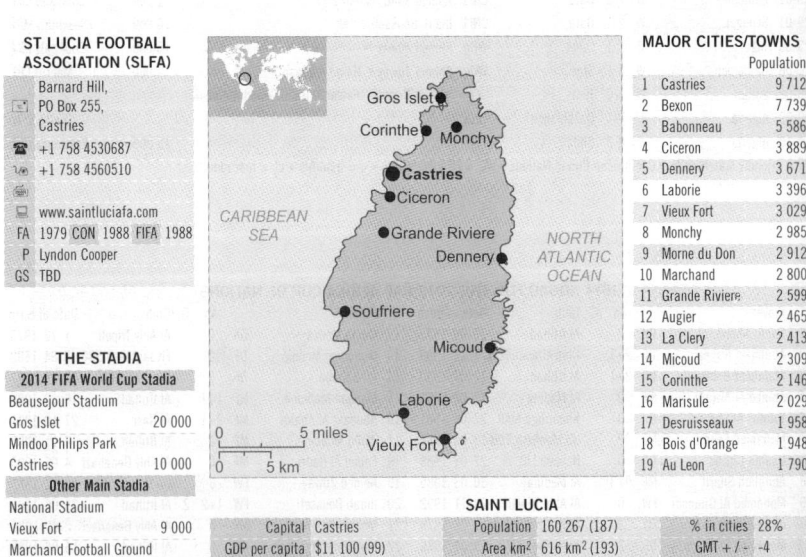

ST LUCIA FOOTBALL ASSOCIATION (SLFA)
Barnard Hill,
PO Box 255,
Castries
☎ +1 758 4530687
+1 758 4560510
www.saintluciafa.com
FA 1979 CON 1988 FIFA 1988
P Lyndon Cooper
GS TBD

THE STADIA
2014 FIFA World Cup Stadia
Beausejour Stadium
Gros Islet   20 000
Mindoo Philips Park
Castries   10 000
Other Main Stadia
National Stadium
Vieux Fort   9 000
Marchand Football Ground
Castries   3 500

MAJOR CITIES/TOWNS
		Population
1	Castries	9 712
2	Bexon	7 739
3	Babonneau	5 586
4	Ciceron	3 889
5	Dennery	3 671
6	Laborie	3 396
7	Vieux Fort	3 029
8	Monchy	2 985
9	Morne du Don	2 912
10	Marchand	2 800
11	Grande Riviere	2 599
12	Augier	2 465
13	La Clery	2 413
14	Micoud	2 309
15	Corinthe	2 146
16	Marisule	2 029
17	Desruisseaux	1 958
18	Bois d'Orange	1 948
19	Au Leon	1 790

SAINT LUCIA
Capital Castries
GDP per capita $11 100 (99)
Neighbours (km) Coast 158
Population 160 267 (187)
Area km² 616 km² (193)
% in cities 28%
GMT +/- -4

RECENT INTERNATIONAL MATCHES PLAYED BY ST LUCIA

2006	Opponents		Score	Venue	Comp	Scorers	Att	Referee
27-09	Jamaica	L	0-4	Kingston	CCq		4 000	Tamayo CUB
29-09	Haiti	L	1-7	Kingston	CCq	Germal Valcin 90p	3 000	Callendar BRB
1-10	St Vincent/Grenadines	L	0-8	Kingston	CCq		3 000	Tamayo CUB
2007								
No international matches played in 2007								
2008								
6-02	Turks and Caicos Isl	L	1-2	Providenciales	WCq	Nyhime Gilbert 92+	2 200	Whittaker CAY
26-03	Turks and Caicos Isl	W	2-0	Vieux Fort	WCq	Kenwin McPhee 28, Titus Elva 85	1 200	Forde BRB
18-05	Antigua and Barbuda	L	1-6	St John's	Fr	Barnet Bledman 91+	4 000	Willett ATG
14-06	Guatemala	L	0-6	Guatemala City	WCq		24 600	Archundia MEX
21-06	Guatemala	L	1-3	Los Angeles	WCq	Kenwin McPhee 45	12 000	Wijngaarde SUR
2009								
No international matches played in 2009								
2010								
10-09	St Vincent/Grenadines	L	1-5	Vieux Fort	Fr	Jamil Joseph 10	400	St Catherine LCA
21-09	Trinidad and Tobago	L	0-3	St John's	Fr		205	St Catherine LCA
23-09	Antigua and Barbuda	L	0-5	St John's	Fr		500	Willett ATG
13-10	Guyana	L	0-1	Paramaribo	CCq		550	Davis TRI
15-10	Suriname	L	1-2	Paramaribo	CCq	Zacchaeus Polius 77	750	Baptiste DMA
17-10	Netherlands Antilles	D	2-2	Paramaribo	CCq	Zacchaeus Polius 2 7 35	2 800	Willet ATG
2011								
8-07	Aruba	L	2-4	Oranjestad	WCq	Kevin Edward 20, Cliff Magnam Valcin 46	300	Foster CAY
12-07	Aruba	W	4-2	Castries	WCq	Jamil Joseph 3 14 29 74, Kurt Frederick 74. W 5-4p	500	Lancaster GUY
21-08	Barbados	L	0-4	Bridgetown	Fr		3 500	Skeete BRB
2-09	Canada	L	1-4	Toronto	WCq	Tremain Paul 7	11 500	Marrufo USA
6-09	St Kitts and Nevis	L	2-4	Gros Islet	WCq	Zaine Pierre 65, Cliff Magnam Valcin 84	2 005	Thomas JAM
7-10	Canada	L	0-7	Gros Islet	WCq	Match awarded to Canada	1 005	Vidal PAN
11-10	St Kitts and Nevis	D	1-1	Basseterre	WCq	Cliff Magnam Valcin 74	1 000	Skeete BRB
11-11	Puerto Rico	L	0-4	Bayamon	WCq	Match awarded to Puerto Rico	350	Holder BRB
14-11	Puerto Rico	L	0-3	Mayaguez	WCq		1 050	Willett ATG
2012								
21-10	Curacao	W	5-1	Gros Islet	CCq	Tremain Paul 14, Magnam Valcin 44, Charles Eden 51, Tafari Charlemagne 86, Kurt Frederick 90	1 650	Willett ATG
23-10	St Vincent/Grenadines	W	1-0	Gros Islet	CCq	Tremain Paul 69	1 652	Vazquez DOM
25-10	Guyana	L	0-3	Gros Islet	CCq		2 500	Willett ATG

Fr = Friendly match • CC = Digicel Caribbean Cup • WC = FIFA World Cup • q = qualifier

BLACKHEART/KASHIF & SHANGHAI FOOTBALL TOURNAMENT 2012

First Round		Quarter-finals		Semi-finals		Final	
Dennery	2						
Labories	0	**Dennery**	4				
Marchand	0	Micoud	2				
Micoud	1			**Dennery**	1		
Vieux Fort South	1			Gros Islet	0		
Desruisseaux	0	Vieux Fort South	1				
Anse-la-Raye	1	**Gros Islet**	5				
Gros Islet	7					**Dennery**	1
Canaries	2					Soufrière	0
Roseau Valley	1	**Canaries**	3				
South Castries	1	Vieux Fort North	0			CUP FINAL	
Vieux Fort North	4			Canaries	1		
Mon Repos	3			**Soufrière**	2	9-06-2012	
Central Castries	1	Mon Repos	0			Scorer - Levi Gilbert 115 for Dennery	
Mabouya Valley	1	**Soufrière**	3	3rd place: Gros Islet 4-0 Canaries			
Soufrière	2						

LES – LESOTHO

FIFA/COCA-COLA WORLD RANKING

'93	'94	'95	'96	'97	'98	'99	'00	'01	'02	'03	'04	'05	'06	'07	'08	'09	'10	'11	'12
138	135	149	162	149	140	154	136	126	132	120	144	145	160	154	161	150	170	147	159

2012

Jan	Feb	Mar	Apr	May	Jun	Jul	Aug	Sep	Oct	Nov	Dec	High	Low	Av
153	161	160	163	163	170	166	167	157	158	158	159	120	185	146

Lesotho suffered several disappointing setbacks in 2012, a year in which the national team managed just a solitary win in the ten international matches played. Defeat at the hands of Sao Tome e Principe at the start of the year in the preliminary round of the 2013 Africa Cup of Nations qualifiers was a severe and unexpected blow for the Basotho side and was followed by a 7-0 drubbing by Ghana in Kumasi at the start of the 2014 FIFA World Cup qualifiers. Coach Lesley Notsi's decision to try and rebuild the side with a nucleus of the team that had qualified for the 2011 African Youth Championship was largely abandoned as the reality of the gap between age-group football and the rigours of the international game was made forcefully apparent. Losing to Sao Tome meant Lesotho lost out on the potential of two more rounds of qualification and much-needed international exposure. Instead they were left to play friendlies against serial opponents Botswana and Swaziland. A dispute in the league caused further problems in this small mountain kingdom although the Premier League did continue to enjoy sponsorship where there is the potential of a television deal in the near future. The league was won by Lesotho Correctional Services who beat Lesotho Defence Force XI into second place.

CAF AFRICA CUP OF NATIONS RECORD
1957-1974 DNQ 1976-1978 DNE 1980-1982 DNQ 1984-1992 DNE 1994 DNQ
1996 Withdrew 1998 DNE 2000-2010 DNQ 2012 DNE 2013 DNQ

LESOTHO FOOTBALL ASSOCIATION (FAL)

Bambatha Tsita Sports Arena Old Polo Ground, PO Box 1879, 100 Maseru
☎ +266 22311879
+266 22310586
fal@leo.co.ls
www.lesothofootball.com
FA 1932 CON 1964 FIFA 1964
P Salemane Phafane
GS Mokhosi Mohapi

THE STADIA

2014 FIFA World Cup Stadia
Setsoto National Stadium
Maseru — 20 000

Other Main Stadia
Pitso Ground
Maseru — 3 000
TSL Ground
Hlotse — 1 000
Bantu Stadium
Mafeteng — 1 000

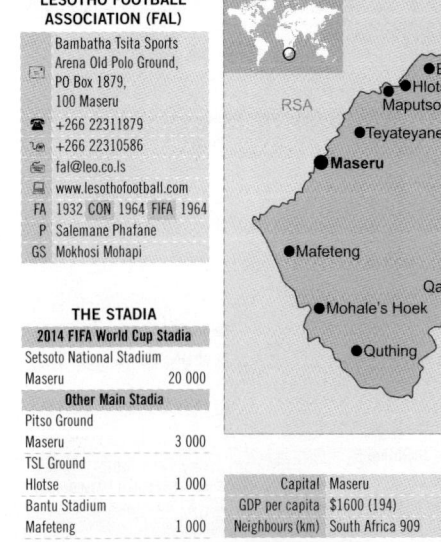

MAJOR CITIES/TOWNS
Population
1 Maseru — 247 237
2 Hlotse — 44 148
3 Mafeteng — 39 876
4 Teyateyaneng — 26 554
5 Maputsoa — 23 037
6 Mohale's Hoek — 21 869
7 Qacha's Nek — 16 606
8 Quthing — 6 453
9 Mokhotlong — 5 980
10 Butha Buthe — 5 868
11 Thaba-Tseka — 4 767

KINGDOM OF LESOTHO

Capital	Maseru	Population	2 130 819 (142)	% in cities	25%
GDP per capita	$1600 (194)	Area km²	30 355 km² (141)	GMT +/-	+2
Neighbours (km)	South Africa 909				

LES – LESOTHO

RECENT INTERNATIONAL MATCHES PLAYED BY LESOTHO

2008 Opponents	Score	Venue	Comp	Scorers	Att	Referee
20-07 Malawi	L 0-1	Secunda	CCr1			Seechurn MRI
22-07 Namibia	D 1-1	Secunda	CCr1	Thabane Rankara [80]		Seechurn MRI
24-07 Comoros	W 1-0	Secunda	CCr1	Moli Lesesa [50]		Labrosse SEY
30-08 Botswana	L 0-1	Gaborone	Fr			
7-09 Gabon	L 0-3	Bloemfontein	WCq		1 500	Abd El Fatah
11-10 Ghana	L 0-3	Sekondi	WCq		20 000	Rahman SUD
2009						
1-04 Botswana	D 0-0	Maseru	Fr			
19-06 Swaziland	D 1-1	Manzini	Fr	Thapelo Tale [72]		
21-06 Swaziland	D 1-1	Lobamba	Fr	Thapelo Mokhele [41]		
12-08 Zimbabwe	D 1-1	Bulawayo	Fr	Thabo Motsweli [31p]		
11-09 Malaysia	L 0-5	Kuala Lumpur	Fr			
19-10 Zimbabwe	D 2-2	Harare	CCr1	Thabiso Maile 2 [50p 90p]		Ramocha BOT
21-10 Mauritius	W 1-0	Harare	CCr1	Mophane Boakang [88]		Ngosi MWI
2010						
No international matches played in 2010						
2011						
20-08 Swaziland	D 0-0	Maseru	Fr			
22-08 Swaziland	L 0-1	Maseru	Fr			
30-08 Botswana	W 2-1	Gaborone	Fr			
31-10 Namibia	D 0-0	Windhoek	Fr			
6-11 Congo DR	L 0-3	Pretoria	Fr			
11-11 Burundi	W 1-0	Maseru	WCq	Lehlomela Ramabele [82]	5 000	Shikongo NAM
15-11 Burundi	D 2-2	Bujumbura	WCq	Thapelo Tale [16], Bokang Mothoana [22]	7 200	Raphael MWI
21-12 Botswana	L 0-3	Rustenburg	Fr			
2012						
15-01 Sao Tome e Principe	L 0-1	Sao Tome	CNq			
22-01 Sao Tome e Principe	D 0-0	Maseru	CNq			
23-05 Botswana	L 0-3	Gaborone	Fr			
1-06 Ghana	L 0-7	Kumasi	WCq		38 000	Diatta SEN
10-06 Sudan	D 0-0	Maseru	WCq		4 000	Shikongo NAM
17-07 Zimbabwe	L 3-5	Molepolole	Fr	Jeremea Kamela [10], Thabiso Maile [25p], Katleho Moleko [62]		
18-07 Botswana	D 0-0	Molepolole	Fr			
12-10 Swaziland	W 2-1	Maseru	Fr	Thabiso Maile, Tsepo Lekhooana		
14-10 Swaziland	L 0-1	Maseru	Fr			
11-11 Swaziland	D 0-0	Manzini	Fr			

Fr = Friendly match • CN = CAF African Cup of Nations • CC = COSAFA Castle Cup • WC = FIFA World Cup • q = qualifier • r1 = first round group

LESOTHO 2011-12

BUDDIE PREMIER LEAGUE

	Pl	W	D	L	F	A	Pts	LCS Maseru	LDF Maseru	Bantu United	Matlama	LMPS Maseru	Lioli	Celtics	Linare	Likhopo	Joy	Maduma	Majantja
LCS Maseru †	22	13	5	4	39	18	**44**		2-0	1-0	1-2	2-0	2-0	1-0	2-1	3-0	2-1	5-1	3-2
LDF Maseru	22	10	8	4	26	17	**38**	2-1		2-2	2-0	1-2	1-0	3-0	0-0	2-0	2-1	1-0	0-0
Bantu United	22	8	11	3	25	16	**35**	0-0	2-2		2-1	3-0	0-1	1-1	1-1	0-0	2-0	0-1	1-1
Matlama	22	10	4	8	27	27	**34**	1-1	0-0	0-2		3-1	1-2	1-0	2-1	0-2	1-2	3-2	1-0
LMPS Maseru	22	7	9	6	21	25	**30**	2-1	1-1	1-1	1-1		1-0	1-2	0-0	0-0	1-0	1-1	1-1
Lioli	22	7	9	6	18	15	**30**	1-1	0-1	0-0	0-2	1-2		0-0	2-0	1-0	0-0	1-0	1-1
Mpharane Celtics	22	6	9	7	26	30	**27**	1-4	2-1	1-2	2-4	1-1	1-1		2-0	1-0	1-1	2-2	2-1
Linare	22	7	5	10	22	30	**26**	0-2	3-2	0-1	2-0	2-1	0-3	1-3		0-0	2-3	3-2	1-0
Likhopo	22	5	9	8	14	17	**24**	1-0	1-1	1-1	0-1	0-1	0-0	1-0	0-2		3-1	2-2	3-0
Joy	22	5	9	8	20	23	**24**	0-2	0-1	1-1	0-0	2-0	0-0	2-2	1-2	0-0		2-0	0-0
Maduma	22	4	8	10	27	35	**20**	2-2	0-0	1-2	3-1	2-3	2-2	2-2	2-0	1-0	1-1		0-1
Majantja	22	2	10	10	11	23	**16**	1-1	0-1	0-1	1-2	0-0	0-2	0-0	1-1	0-0	0-2	1-0	

27/08/2011 - 6/05/2012 • † Qualified for the CAF Champions League

LIB – LEBANON

FIFA/COCA-COLA WORLD RANKING

'93	'94	'95	'96	'97	'98	'99	'00	'01	'02	'03	'04	'05	'06	'07	'08	'09	'10	'11	'12
108	129	134	97	90	85	111	110	93	119	115	105	125	126	134	150	148	154	111	127

2012															
Jan	Feb	Mar	Apr	May	Jun	Jul	Aug	Sep	Oct	Nov	Dec	High	Low	Av
112	114	124	128	129	143	144	127	124	109	112	127	85	178	120

There was an exciting climax to the Lebanese championship when the top two met on the final day of the season. At the Saida International Stadium Mohammad Zain Tahhan secured an historic first title for Safa with the only goal of the game in a 1-0 victory over Nijmeh who need to win to prise the title away from their opponents. In a match marred by clashes between the two sets of supporters, Safa held on for their first major trophy since winning the Cup in 1986. For Nijmeh there was double disappointment when five days later they lost in the cup final to Al Ansar. Played behind closed doors due to the violence at the league decider, Nijmeh looked to have claimed the trophy but conceded an equaliser three minutes into injury-time at the end. In extra-time they then fell behind to a Mohammad Hammoud penalty which gave Ansar the cup for the 13th time in just 25 years. The national team progressed to the final phase of Asian qualifying for the 2014 FIFA World Cup finals in Brazil but Theo Bucker's side found the step up in the quality of opposition hard to live with although a 1-0 win over Iran gave a much needed boost to morale. The Lebanese game has, however, been badly tarnished by allegations of widespread match fixing and in February 2013 the federation banned 24 players - for their involvement.

FIFA WORLD CUP RECORD
1930-1990 DNE **1994-2010** DNQ

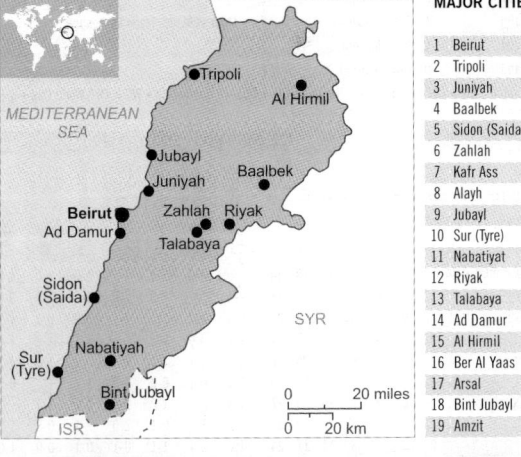

LEBANESE FOOTBALL ASSOCIATION (FLFA)

Verdun Street - Bristol,
Radwan Center,
PO Box 4732, Beirut
☎ +961 1 745745
+961 1 349529
libanfa@cyberia.net.lb

FA 1933 CON 1964 FIFA 1935
P Hachem Haydar
GS Jihad El Chohof

THE STADIA

2014 FIFA World Cup Stadia

Camille Chamoun Sports City	
Beirut	47 799

Other Main Stadia

Saida International Stadium	
Saida	22 600
International Olympic Stadium	
Tripoli	22 400
Municipal Stadium	
Beirut	18 000
Sur Stadium	
Sur	6 500

MAJOR CITIES/TOWNS

		Population
1	Beirut	2 006 452
2	Tripoli	190 793
3	Juniyah	99 581
4	Baalbek	81 842
5	Sidon (Saida)	58 364
6	Zahlah	53 627
7	Kafr Ass	50 478
8	Alayh	45 074
9	Jubayl	44 807
10	Sur (Tyre)	41 824
11	Nabatiyat	35 333
12	Riyak	29 648
13	Talabaya	28 046
14	Ad Damur	27 216
15	Al Hirmil	23 834
16	Ber Al Yaas	23 338
17	Arsal	17 081
18	Bint Jubayl	16 686
19	Amzit	15 629

AL JUMHURIYAH AL LUBNANIYAH • LEBANESE REPUBLIC

Capital	Beirut	Population	4 017 095 (126)	% in cities	87%
GDP per capita	$11 100 (98)	Area km²	10 400 km² (169)	GMT +/-	+2
Neighbours (km)	Israel 79, Syria 375 • Coast 225				

LIB – LEBANON

RECENT INTERNATIONAL MATCHES PLAYED BY LEBANON

2009	Opponents	Score	Venue	Comp	Scorers	Att	Referee
14-01	Vietnam	L 1-3	Hanoi	ACq	Akram Moghrabi [73]	13 000	Toma JPN
21-01	Thailand	L 1-2	Phuket	Fr	Mahmoud El Ali [50]	15 000	Veerapool THA
23-01	Korea DPR	W 1-0	Phuket	Fr	Abbas Atwi [2p]		
28-01	Syria	L 0-2	Saida	ACq		300	Balideh QAT
1-04	Namibia	D 1-1	Saida	Fr	Zakaria Shararah [72]		Mansour LIB
19-08	India	W 1-0	New Dehli	Fr	Ali Al Saadi [4]		Abdul Hannan BAN
22-08	Sri Lanka	L 3-4	New Dehli	Fr	Akram Moghrabi 9, Ali Al Saadi 45, Korhani [97+p]		Rowan IND
25-08	Kyrgyzstan	D 1-1	New Dehli	Fr	Abbas Atwi [56]		Abdul Hannan BAN
27-08	Syria	L 0-1	New Dehli	Fr			Rowan IND
14-11	China PR	L 0-2	Beirut	ACq		2 000	Albadwawi UAE
22-11	China PR	L 0-1	Zheijang	ACq		21 520	Breeze AUS
2010							
6-01	Vietnam	D 1-1	Saida	ACq	Mahmoud El Ali [19]	50	Kovalenko UZB
3-03	Syria	L 0-4	Damascus	ACq		16 000	Kim Dong Jin KOR
2011							
2-07	Kuwait	L 0-6	Beirut	Fr		BCD	El Haddad LIB
9-07	Oman	L 0-1	Beirut	Fr			Ayad LIB
17-07	UAE	L 2-6	Al Ain	Fr	Mahmoud El Ali 2 [29 67]		Ali BHR
23-07	Bangladesh	W 4-0	Beirut	WCq	Hassan Maatouk 16, Mahmoud El Ali [27], Ali Al Saadi [55], Tarek El Ali [64]	2 000	Auda IRQ
28-07	Bangladesh	L 0-2	Dhaka	WCq		11 000	Aonrak THA
17-08	Syria	L 2-3	Saida	Fr	Hassan Maatouk [18], Mohammad Ghaddar [71]	200	Ghandour LIB
2-09	Korea Republic	L 0-6	Goyang	WCq		37 655	Abdul Bashir SIN
6-09	UAE	W 3-1	Beirut	WCq	Mohammad Ghaddar [37p], Akram Moghrabi [52], Roda Antar [83]	4 000	Faghani IRN
11-10	Kuwait	D 2-2	Beirut	WCq	Hassan Maatouk 2 [15 86p]	32 000	Toma JPN
11-11	Kuwait	W 1-0	Kuwait City	WCq	Mahmoud El Ali [57]	17 500	Kovalenko UZB
15-11	Korea Republic	W 2-1	Beirut	WCq	Ali Al Saadi [4], Abbas Ali Atwi [32]	35 000	Al Ghamdi KSA
2012							
29-02	UAE	L 2-4	Abu Dhabi	WCq	Mahmoud El Ali [23], Hassan Maatouk [45]	10 000	Green AUS
11-05	Egypt	L 1-4	Tripoli	Fr	Ahmad Zreik [30p]	6 000	Ghandour LIB
18-05	Jordan	L 1-2	Saida	Fr	Ali Al Saadi [88]	3 500	Taweel SYR
27-05	Oman	D 1-1	Muscat	Fr	Mohammad Ghaddar [23]		Shaban KUW
3-06	Qatar	L 0-1	Beirut	WCq		40 000	Shukralla BHR
8-06	Uzbekistan	D 1-1	Beirut	WCq	Ali Al Saadi [34]	13 000	Al Hilali OMA
12-06	Korea Republic	L 0-3	Goyang	WCq		36 756	Toma JPN
24-06	Iraq	L 0-1	Jeddah	ARr1			Jiyed MAR
27-06	Sudan	L 0-2	Jeddah	ARr1			Jaber JOR
6-09	Australia	L 0-3	Beirut	Fr		5 000	Nikolaides CYP
11-09	Iran	W 1-0	Beirut	WCq	Rodar Antar [27]	14 000	Tan Hai CHN
16-10	Yemen	W 2-1	Saida	Fr	Mohamed Haidar [12], Fayez Shamsin [63]		Jaber JOR
14-11	Qatar	L 0-1	Doha	WCq		12 870	Al Ghamdi KSA
8-12	Oman	W 1-0	Al Farwaniyah	WArl	Adnan Haidar [11]	2 000	Mohamed UAE
11-12	Palestine	L 0-1	Al Farwaniyah	WArl		2 000	Ko Hyung Jin KOR
14-12	Kuwait	L 1-2	Kuwait City	WArl	Abbas Ali Atwi [61p]	4 000	Adday IRQ

Fr = Friendly match • WA = West Asian Cup • AR = Arab Cup • AC = AFC Asian Cup • WC = FIFA World Cup • q = qualifier
r1 = first round group

LEBANON NATIONAL TEAM HISTORICAL RECORDS

Coaches: Joseph Nalbandian 1958-69 • Joseph Abou Murad 1971-73 • Adnan Meckdache 1974-76 • Joseph Abou Murad 1976-78 • Adnan Meckdache 1987-92 • Adnan Al Shargi 1993 • Terry Yorath WAL 1995-97 • Dietmar Werner GER 1998 • Mahmoud Saad EGY 1998-2000 • Josip Skoblar CRO 2000 • Theo Bucker GER 2000-01 • Richard Tardi 2002 • Mohammad Qwid SYR 2004-05 • Adnan Al Shargi 2005 • Emile Rustom 2005-06 • Adnan Meckdache 2006-08 • Emile Rustom 2009-11 • Theo Bucker 2011-

LEBANON 2011-12

PREMIER LEAGUE

	Pl	W	D	L	F	A	Pts	Safa	Nijmeh	Ahed	Ansar	Akhaa	Shabab	Tripoli	Racing	Salam Sur	Tadamon	Mabarra	Ahly
Safa ‡	22	17	4	1	50	15	55		0-1	2-0	2-2	2-1	3-0	2-1	0-0	3-1	5-2	2-0	5-0
Al Nijmeh	22	16	3	3	37	16	51	0-1		1-1	2-0	2-1	1-0	2-1	1-0	2-1	3-1	3-0	2-2
Al Ahed	22	14	6	2	40	17	48	1-1	3-0		2-2	3-0	1-0	2-2	1-1	3-1	3-1	2-0	2-1
Al Ansar	22	13	5	4	38	18	44	1-3	0-0	1-0		1-2	2-3	2-0	1-0	3-1	0-1	3-2	4-2
Al Akhaa Al Ahli Aley	22	8	4	10	28	32	28	0-1	1-0	1-5	0-1		1-1	3-1	0-1	1-0	0-0	4-2	4-1
Shabab Al Sahel	22	7	6	9	25	26	27	0-2	0-2	0-2	0-1	4-1		1-3	1-1	1-3	1-0	0-0	3-0
Tripoli SC	22	5	9	8	26	26	24	0-0	1-2	0-0	2-2	1-0	0-1		2-0	2-3	0-0	0-0	5-2
Racing Club Beirut	22	5	8	9	18	25	23	2-3	0-3	0-3	0-2	0-1	1-1	1-1		0-0	1-1	1-0	2-0
Salam Sur	22	5	6	11	28	38	21	2-3	1-2	1-2	1-3	2-2	0-2	0-0	2-1		0-0	1-0	2-1
Al Tadamon Sur	22	3	11	8	14	26	20	1-3	0-3	1-2	0-0	1-0	1-1	0-0	1-1	1-1		1-1	0-0
Al Mabarra	22	3	4	15	21	44	13	1-3	2-4	0-2	0-1	2-2	0-4	1-3	1-4	3-2	0-2		4-0
Al Ahly Saida	22	2	4	16	18	53	10	0-4	0-1	0-2	1-3	1-2	3-1	1-1	2-1	1-1	3-3	1-0	

22/10/2011 – 4/05/2012 • ‡ Qualified for AFC Cup
Top scorers: **12** – Mohamad **HAIDAR**, Safa • **11** – Hassan **CHAITO**, Al Ahed • **10** – Oliseh **DIALLI** MLI, Shabab & Ngo **SAMUEL** NGA, Safa

ELITE CUP 2012

Semi-finals		Finals	
Safa	1		
Al Ansar	0		
		Safa	2
		Al Ahed	0
Al Nijmeh	1		
Al Ahed	2		

Sports City, Beirut
17-09-2012

MEDALS TABLE

		Overall			Lge	Cup			Asia			
		G	S	B	G	G	S		G	S	B	City
1	Al Ansar	26	3		**13**	13	3					Beirut
2	Al Nijmeh	12	7	2	7	5	6		1	2		Beirut
3	Homenetmen	10	3		7	3	3					Beirut
4	Al Nahda	9	1		5	4	1					
5	Al Ahed	7	2		3	4	2					Beirut
6	Homenmen	4	4		4		4					Beirut
7	Safa SC	3	8		1	2	7		1			Beirut
8	Racing Club	3	2		3		2					Beirut
9	Shabiba Al Mazra	3	1		1	2	1					Beirut
	Sika	3	1		3		1					Beirut
11	American University	3			3							Beirut
12	Tripoli SC (Olympic)	2	1		1	1	1					Tripoli
	Helmi Sport	2	1			2	1					
14	Shabab Al Sahel	1	2			1	2					Beirut
15	Al Tadamon Sur	1	1			1	1					Tyre
	Al Mabarra	1	1			1	1					
17	Al Bourj	1				1						

FA CUP 2011-12

Round of 16		Quarter-finals		Semi-finals		Final	
Al Ansar *	2						
Salam Sur	1	**Al Ansar**	6				
Homenetmen		Al Ahly Saida *	1				
Al Ahly Saida *	2			**Al Ansar**	3		
Racing Club Beirut *	2			Safa	1		
Al Akhaa Al Ahli Aley	0	Racing Club Beirut *	1				
Tripoli SC	0	**Safa**	2				
Safa *	1					**Al Ansar** ‡	2
Shabab Al Sahel *	2					Al Nijmeh	1
Shabab Al Ghazieh	0	**Shabab Al Sahel**	0				
Al Ershad	0	Al Tadamon Sur *	1				
Al Tadamon Sur *	1			Shabab Al Sahel	1		
Al Ahed	1			**Al Nijmeh**	2		
Al Mabarra *	0	Al Ahed	2				
Al Khoyol	0	**Al Nijmeh** *	3				
Al Nijmeh *	2						

* Home team • ‡ Qualified for AFC Cup

CUP FINAL
Saida International, Saida
9-05-2012, Att: BCD
Scorers – Mohammad Atwi [93+], Mohammad Hammoud [105p] for Ansar; Hasan Mohammad [68] for Nijmeh

LIE – LIECHTENSTEIN

FIFA/COCA-COLA WORLD RANKING

'93	'94	'95	'96	'97	'98	'99	'00	'01	'02	'03	'04	'05	'06	'07	'08	'09	'10	'11	'12
160	156	157	154	158	159	125	147	150	147	148	142	122	158	122	149	154	148	132	154

2012													High	Low	Av
Jan	Feb	Mar	Apr	May	Jun	Jul	Aug	Sep	Oct	Nov	Dec				
130	124	137	129	128	148	149	148	149	155	157	154		118	165	145

The longest cup winning streak in history came to an end in May 2012 when Eschen/Mauren beat Vaduz on penalties in the cup final after the match had finished 2-2. Aiming for a 15th straight triumph, which would have also seen them equal the world record total of 41 wins overall held by Northern Ireland's Linfield, Vaduz looked to have done just that only for Eren Dulundu to equalise for Eschen/Mauren four minutes into injury-time at the end. Franz Burgmeier and Mariano Tripodi then missed from the spot for Vaduz as Eschen/Mauren clinched the trophy for the first time since 1987. In the intervening years Eschen/Mauren had been on the losing side in eleven finals to Vaduz, so their triumph was sweet revenge indeed and a notable success for their German coach Uwe Wegmann. There was also disappointment for Vaduz in the Swiss Challenge League after an indifferent campaign saw them finish mid-table, although they did score notable victories over Vojvodina Novi Sad and Hapoel Tel Aviv in the Europa League before being knocked out by the latter on aggregate. The national team got off to an awful start in their 2014 FIFA World Cup qualifiers with an 8-1 defeat at home to Bosnia-Herzegovina and they then proceeded to lose their next three games 2-0 to end the year firmly rooted to the bottom of the group.

UEFA EUROPEAN CHAMPIONSHIP RECORD
1960-1992 DNE **1996-2012** DNQ

LIECHTENSTEINER FUSSBALLVERBAND (LFV)

Landstrasse 149, 9494 Schaan
☎ +423 2374747
+423 2374748
info@lfv.li
www.lfv.li
FA 1934 CON 1992 FIFA 1976
P Matthias Voigt
GS Roland Ospelt

THE STADIA

2014 FIFA World Cup Stadia	
Rheinpark Stadion Vaduz	7 789
Other Main Stadia	
Eschen Sportpark Eschen	6 000
Blumenau Stadion Triesen	1 000
Sportplatz Stadion Balzers	1 000
Rheinwiese Stadion Schaan	1 000

MAJOR CITIES/TOWNS

		Population
1	Schaan	5 747
2	Vaduz	5 070
3	Triesen	4 674
4	Balzers	4 450
5	Eschen	4 141
6	Mauren	3 718
7	Triesenberg	2 566
8	Ruggell	1 920
9	Gamprin	1 463
10	Schellenberg	1 032
11	Planken	387

FUERSTENTUM LIECHTENSTEIN • PRINCIPALITY OF LIECHTENSTEIN

Capital	Vaduz	Population	34 761 (210)	% in cities	14%
GDP per capita	$118 000 (1)	Area km²	160 km² (218)	GMT +/-	+1
Neighbours (km)	Austria 34, Switzerland 41				

RECENT INTERNATIONAL MATCHES PLAYED BY LIECHTENSTEIN

2009	Opponents	Score	Venue	Comp	Scorers	Att	Referee
12-08	Portugal	L 0-3	Vaduz	Fr		5 525	Bertolini SUI
5-09	Russia	L 0-3	St Petersburg	WCq		21 000	Constantin ROU
9-09	Finland	D 1-1	Vaduz	WCq	Michele Polverino 75	3 132	Panic BIH
10-10	Azerbaijan	L 0-2	Vaduz	WCq		1 635	Radovanovic NME
14-10	Wales	L 0-2	Vaduz	WCq		1 858	Kaldma EST
14-11	Croatia	L 0-5	Vinkovci	Fr		10 000	Fabian HUN
2010							
11-08	Iceland	D 1-1	Reykjavik	Fr	Michael Stocklasa 70	3 000	Buttimer IRL
3-09	Spain	L 0-4	Vaduz	ECq		6 100	Yildirim TUR
7-09	Scotland	L 1-2	Glasgow	ECq	Mario Frick 47	37 050	Shvestov UKR
12-10	Czech Republic	L 0-2	Vaduz	ECq		2 555	Sukhina RUS
17-11	Estonia	D 1-1	Tallinn	Fr	Mario Frick 35	1 909	Gvardis RUS
2011							
9-02	San Marino	W 1-0	Serravalle	Fr	Michele Polverino 57	147	Banti ITA
29-03	Czech Republic	L 0-2	Ceske Budejovice	ECq		6 600	Hategan ROU
3-06	Lithuania	W 2-0	Vaduz	ECq	Philippe Erne 7, Michele Polverino 36	1 886	Kuchin KAZ
10-08	Switzerland	L 1-2	Vaduz	Fr	Marco Ritzberger 51	5 444	Eisner AUT
2-09	Lithuania	D 0-0	Kaunas	ECq		3 500	Johnsen NOR
6-09	Spain	L 0-6	Logrono	ECq		15 660	Lechner AUT
8-10	Scotland	L 0-1	Vaduz	ECq		5 636	Hagen NOR
11-11	Hungary	L 0-5	Budapest	Fr		23 000	Balaj ROU
2012							
29-02	Malta	L 1-2	Ta'Qali	Fr	Martin Buchel 48	2 300	Whitby WAL
14-08	Andorra	W 1-0	Vaduz	Fr	Nicolas Hasler 45	847	Klossner SUI
7-09	Bosnia-Herzegovina	L 1-8	Vaduz	WCq	Mathias Christen 60	5 900	Borg MLT
11-09	Slovakia	L 0-2	Bratislava	WCq		4 326	Evans WAL
12-10	Lithuania	L 0-2	Vaduz	WCq		1 112	Vincic SVN
16-10	Latvia	L 0-2	Riga	WCq		3 500	Kovacs ROU
14-11	Malta	L 0-1	Vaduz	Fr		550	Hanni SUI

Fr = Friendly match • EC = UEFA EURO 2012 • WC = FIFA World Cup • q = qualifier

LIECHTENSTEIN NATIONAL TEAM HISTORICAL RECORDS

Caps: 106 - Mario Frick 1993- • 104 - Martin Stocklasa 1996- • 95 - Peter Jehle 1998- • 86 - Thomas Beck 1998- • 78 - Daniel Hasler 1993-2007 • 75 - Franz Burgmeier 2001- • 73 - Martin Telser 1996-2007 • 72 - Ronny Buchel 1998-2010 • 70 - Michael Stocklasa 1998-

Goals: 16 - Mario Frick 1993- • 7 - Franz Burgmeier 2001- • 5 - Martin Stocklasa 1996- & Thomas Beck 1998- • 3 - Michele Polverino 2007- • 2 - Michael Stocklasa 1998- ; Fabio D'Elia 2001- & Benjamin Fischer 2005-

Coaches: Dietrich Weise GER 1994-96 • Alfred Riedl AUT 1997-98 • Ralf Loose GER 1998-2003 • Walter Hormann AUT 2003-04 • Martin Andermatt SUI 2004-06 • Hans-Peter Zaug SUI 2006-12 • Rene Pauritsch AUR 2012-

LIECHTENSTEINER CUP 2011-12

Second Preliminary round		Quarter-finals		Semi-finals		Final	
USV Eschen/Mauren	Bye						
		USV Eschen/Mauren	4				
Schaan Azurri	2	FC Triesen	0				
FC Triesen	4			USV Eschen/Mauren	2		
FC Schaan	2			FC Balzers	1		
FC Ruggell	1	FC Schaan	2				
		FC Balzers	4				
FC Balzers	Bye					USV Eschen/Mauren ‡	2 4p
FC Triesenberg	Bye					FC Vaduz	2 2p
		FC Triesenberg	2				
FC Balzers-2	2	USV Eschen/Mauren-2	0				
USV Eschen/Mauren-2	3			FC Triesenberg	1		
FC Triesen-2	3			**FC Vaduz**	3		
FC Triesenberg-2	0	FC Triesen-2	0				
		FC Vaduz	17				
FC Vaduz	Bye						

CUP FINAL

Rheinparkstadion, Vaduz
16-05-2012, Att: 960, Ref: Reisch
Scorers - Manojlovic 68p, Dulundu 94+ for Eschen/Mauren; Cerrone 41p, Sara 55 for Vaduz

‡ Qualified for the Europa League

LTU – LITHUANIA

FIFA/COCA-COLA WORLD RANKING

'93	'94	'95	'96	'97	'98	'99	'00	'01	'02	'03	'04	'05	'06	'07	'08	'09	'10	'11	'12
85	59	43	48	45	54	50	85	97	100	101	100	100	69	59	51	62	55	92	116

2012

Jan	Feb	Mar	Apr	May	Jun	Jul	Aug	Sep	Oct	Nov	Dec	High	Low	Av
93	93	91	89	89	88	90	85	116	110	119	116	37	119	73

After a decade in the doldrums, the revival of Zalgiris continued as the club from the capital Vilnius - the only Lithuanian side to make an impact in the Soviet era - fell just short of what would have been their first double since 1991. In May they beat holders Ekranas 3-1 on penalties in the cup final - a first trophy since 2003 - but they failed to land the title in a close race with Ekranas, finishing a point behind their rivals who won eight of their last nine matches to hold Zalgiris at bay. For Ekranas, it meant a fifth consecutive championship. One more and they will equal the record of six set by FBK Kaunas between 1999 and 2004 as well as overtaking Kaunas as the most successful Lithuanian club in the post Soviet era. Arturas Rimkevicius provided the individual performance of the season; the Siauliai striker scoring 35 goals in just 29 games to establish a new league record. He played only a bit part, however, in what proved to be a disappointing start to the national team's qualifying campaign for the 2014 FIFA World Cup in Brazil. A solitary victory over Liechtenstein in their first four games left Lithuania with a mountain to climb by the end of the year in a group in which they would have at least hoped to cause an upset or two and challenge for a place in the play-offs.

UEFA EUROPEAN CHAMPIONSHIP RECORD
1960-1992 DNE (Played as part of the Soviet Union) **1996-2012** DNQ

LITHUANIAN FOOTBALL FEDERATION (LFF)

Stadiono g. 2,
02106 Vilnius

☎ +370 52638741
📠 +370 52638740
✉ info@lff.lt
🖥 www.lff.lt
FA 1922 CON 1992 FIFA 1992
P Julius Kvedaras
GS Edvinas Eimontas

THE STADIA

2014 FIFA World Cup Stadia
LFF Stadium
Vilnius 5 500

Other Main Stadia
Zalgiris Stadium
Vilnius 15 030
S. Darius & S. Girenas Stadium
Kaunas 8 248
Suduva Stadium
Marijampole 6 250
Aukstaitija Stadium
Panevezys 4 000

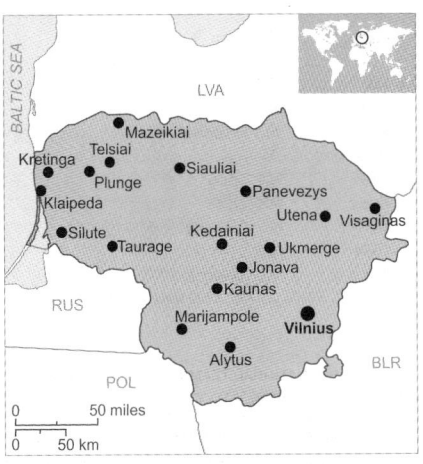

MAJOR CITIES/TOWNS

		Population
1	Vilnius	543 859
2	Kaunas	352 440
3	Klaipeda	183 436
4	Siauliai	127 105
5	Panevézys	113 230
6	Alytus	68 263
7	Marijampolé	46 998
8	Mazeikiai	40 525
9	Jonava	34 203
10	Utena	32 592
11	Kédainiai	31 000
12	Telsiai	29 868
13	Visaginas	28 061
14	Tauragé	27 754
15	Ukmerge	27 426
16	Plungé	23 145
17	Kretinga	21 548
18	Siluté	20 903
19	Radviliskis	19 454

LIETUVOS RESPUBLIKA • REPUBLIC OF LITHUANIA

Capital	Vilnius	Population 3 555 179 (130)	% in cities 67%
GDP per capita	$17 800 (69)	Area km² 65 300 km² (122)	GMT +/- +2
Neighbours (km)	Belarus 680, Latvia 576, Poland 91, Russia 227 • Coast 90		

RECENT INTERNATIONAL MATCHES PLAYED BY LITHUANIA

2008	Opponents	Score	Venue	Comp	Scorers	Att	Referee
20-08	Moldova	W 3-0	Vilnius	Fr	Poskus 2 [23 54], Danilevicius [61]	2 000	Kaasik EST
6-09	Romania	W 3-0	Cluj	WCq	Stankevicius [31], Mikoliunas [69], Kalonas [86]	14 000	Kelly IRL
10-09	Austria	W 2-0	Marijampole	WCq	Danilevicius 2 [52 58]	4 500	Tagliavento ITA
11-10	Serbia	L 0-3	Belgrade	WCq		22 000	Mejuto ESP
15-10	Faroe Islands	W 1-0	Kaunas	WCq	Danilevicius [20]	5 000	Kapitanis CYP
19-11	Moldova	D 1-1	Tallinn	Fr	Savenas [72p]	100	Tohver EST
22-11	Estonia	D 1-1	Kuressaare	Fr	Kavaliauskas [35]	1 000	Nieminen FIN
2009							
7-02	Poland	D 1-1	Faro-Loule	Fr	Klimavicius [26]	150	Gomes POR
11-02	Andorra	W 3-1	Albufeira	Fr	Velicka [44], Boar [53], Kavaliauskas [83]		Xistra POR
28-03	France	L 0-1	Kaunas	WCq		8 700	Braamhaar NED
1-04	France	L 0-1	Paris	WCq		79 543	Webb ENG
6-06	Romania	L 0-1	Marijampole	WCq		5 850	Eriksson SWE
12-08	Luxembourg	W 1-0	Luxembourg	Fr	Danilevicius [40]	1 000	Black NIR
9-09	Faroe Islands	L 1-2	Toftir	WCq	Danilevicius [22p]	1 942	Vad HUN
10-10	Austria	L 1-2	Innsbruck	WCq	Stankevicius [66]	14 200	Gumienny BEL
14-10	Serbia	W 2-1	Marijampole	WCq	Kalonas [20p], Stankevicius [68p]	2 000	Guenov BUL
2010							
25-05	Ukraine	L 0-4	Kharkov	Fr		42 000	Sukhina RUS
18-06	Latvia	D 0-0	Kaunas	BC		1 000	Kaasik EST
20-06	Estonia	W 2-0	Kaunas	BC	Savenas [31p], Rimkevicius [90]	600	Sipailo LVA
11-08	Belarus	L 0-2	Kaunas	Fr		3 500	Satchi MDA
3-09	Scotland	D 0-0	Kaunas	ECq		5 248	Cakir TUR
7-09	Czech Republic	W 1-0	Olomouc	ECq	Sernas [27]	12 038	Yefet ISR
8-10	Spain	L 1-3	Salamanca	ECq	Sernas [54]	16 800	Rocchi ITA
17-11	Hungary	L 0-2	Szekesfehervar	Fr		4 500	Nijhuis NED
2011							
25-03	Poland	W 2-0	Kaunas	Fr	Mikoliunas [18], Cesnauskis [29]	5 000	Treimanis LVA
29-03	Spain	L 1-3	Kaunas	ECq	Stankevicius [57]	9 180	Duhamel FRA
3-06	Liechtenstein	L 0-2	Vaduz	ECq		1 886	Kuchin KAZ
7-06	Norway	L 0-1	Oslo	Fr		12 945	Attwell ENG
10-08	Armenia	W 3-0	Kaunas	Fr	Klimavicius [8], Cesnauskis [75], Beniusis [78]		Sipailo LVA
2-09	Liechtenstein	D 0-0	Kaunas	ECq		3 500	Johnsen NOR
6-09	Scotland	L 0-1	Glasgow	ECq		34 071	Jakobsson ISL
11-10	Czech Republic	L 1-4	Kaunas	ECq	Sernas [68p]	4 000	Fernandez ESP
2012							
1-06	Latvia	L 0-5	Voru	BCsf		125	Gestranius FIN
3-06	Estonia	L 0-1	Tartu	BC3p		1 094	Kaasik EST
7-06	Belarus	D 1-1	Minsk	Fr	Radavicius [43]	2 000	Satschi MDA
15-08	FYR Macedonia	L 0-1	Skopje	Fr		7 000	Ozkahya TUR
7-09	Slovakia	D 1-1	Vilnius	WCq	Zaliukas [18]	4 000	Clos Gomez ESP
11-09	Greece	L 0-2	Piraeus	WCq		21 466	Courtney NIR
12-10	Liechtenstein	W 2-0	Vaduz	WCq	Cesnauskis 2 [50 74]	1 112	Vincic SVN
16-10	Bosnia-Herzegovina	L 0-3	Zenica	WCq		11 920	Zelinka CZE
14-11	Armenia	L 2-4	Yerevan	Fr	Rimkevicius 2 [66 82p]	10 500	Silagava GEO

Fr = Friendly match • EC = UEFA EURO 2012 • BC = Baltic Cup • WC = FIFA World Cup • q = qualifier

LITHUANIA NATIONAL TEAM HISTORICAL RECORDS

Caps: 84 - Andrius Skerla 1996- • 81 - Deividas Semberas 1996- • 71 - Tomas Danilevicius 1998- • 65 - Aurelijus Skarbalius 1991-2005 • 63 - Zydrunas Karcemarskas 2002- • 62 - Marius Stankevicius 2001- • 61 - Gintaras Stauce 1992-2004 • 56 - Edgaras Jankauskas 1995-2008; Andrius Tereskinas 1991-2000 & Tomas Zvirgzdauskas 1998-2008 • 55 - Saulius Mikoliunas 2004- • 52 - Deividas Cesnauskis 2001-

Goals: 19 - Tomas Danilevicius 1998- • 12 - Antanas Lingis 1928-38 • 10 - Edgaras Jankauskas 1995-2008 & Robertas Poskus 1999- • 9 - Virginijus Baltusnikas 1990-98 • 8 - Jaroslavas Citavicius 1926-33; Valdas Ivanauskas 1992-2000 & Darius Maciulevicius 1991-2005

Coaches: Benjaminas Zelkevicius 1990-91 • Algimantas Liubinskas 1992-94 • Benjaminas Zelkevicius 1995-97 • Kestutis Latoza 1998-99 • Robertas Tautkus 1999 • Stasys Stankus 1999-2000 • Julius Kvedaras 2000 • Benjaminas Zelkevicius 2000-03 • Algimantas Liubinskas 2003-08 • Jose Couceiro POR 2008-09 • Raimondas Zutautas 2010-11 • Csaba Laszlo HUN 2012-

LITHUANIA 2012

A LYGA

	Pl	W	D	L	F	A	Pts	Ekranas	Zalgiris	Suduva	Kruoja	Siauliai	Banga	Dainava	Atlantas	Tauras	REO
Ekranas Panevezys †	36	27	7	2	83	25	88		1-0 0-0	2-0 2-2	1-0 2-0	2-2 3-0	3-0 2-0	3-2 3-0	2-0 6-2	5-0 5-0	6-1 3-0
Zalgiris Vilnius ‡	36	27	6	3	80	22	87	0-0 2-1		4-0 2-2	0-2 2-1	2-0 4-1	2-0 2-0	4-0 3-0	7-0 3-1	2-0 5-0	0-1 3-0
Suduva Marijampole ‡	36	21	7	8	77	37	70	3-1 2-3	0-0 1-2		0-1 1-1	4-1 1-0	3-1 3-0	3-1 3-2	6-0 2-0	1-0 4-1	0-0 3-0
Kruoja Pakruojis	36	20	5	11	56	31	65	1-1 0-2	0-1 0-1	2-1 2-1		0-4 1-0	1-0 2-2	1-0 2-3	1-5 0-0	1-0 3-1	2-1 3-0
KFK Siauliai	36	17	4	15	79	57	55	0-1 3-4	2-2 2-4	3-3 1-0	2-1 1-0		1-2 0-1	4-2 3-3	5-1 6-0	7-3 7-2	2-0 3-0
Banga Gargzdai	36	13	8	15	43	41	47	1-1 0-2	1-2 0-0	0-1 0-0	1-1 1-0	0-1 2-1		2-1 5-0	0-1 1-0	1-0 4-0	2-2 2-1
Dainava Alytus	36	9	5	22	42	71	32	0-1 2-2	1-3 1-2	2-4 0-3	0-0 1-2	1-0 0-2	0-0 0-4		1-0 1-2	3-1 2-0	3-2 2-0
Atlantas Klaipeda	36	7	6	23	33	92	27	0-3 1-2	0-1 3-4	0-4 1-5	0-1 2-1	0-3 1-2	1-1 2-2	0-0 2-1		0-5 4-1	0-0 4-2
Tauras Taurage	36	7	2	27	35	97	23	1-2 0-2	0-2 0-4	1-4 1-0	0-4 1-0	0-4 3-2	1-3 2-4	1-3 0-0	1-1		2-0 3-0
FK REO Vilnius	36	5	4	27	26	81	19	0-1 0-3	1-2 0-3	0-2 0-3	2-2 0-3	3-1 3-5	1-0 0-3	1-0 0-3	3-0 0-3	0-1 2-3	

10/03/2012 - 11/11/2012 • † Qualified for the UEFA Champions League • ‡ Qualified for the Europa League
Top scorers: **35** - Arturas **RIMKEVICIUS**, Siauliai • **20** - **RAFAEL LEDESMA** BRA, Suduva • **17** - Arsenij **BUINICKIJ**, Ekranas • **16** - Calum **ELLIOT** SCO, Zalgiris • **15** - Serhiy **ZHYHALOV** UKR, Kruoja • **12** - Kamil **BILINSKI** POL, Zalgiris • **11** - Giorgi **ALAVERDASHVILI** GEO, Banga; Tino **LAGATOR** CRO, Atlantas; Povilas **LUKSYS**, Suduva & Ramunas **RADAVICIUS**, Zalgiris • **10** - Santiago **CESANELLI** ARG, Siauliai & Vitalijus **KAVALIAUSKAS**, Ekranas

LITHUANIA 2012 LFF 1 LYGA (2)

	Pl	W	D	L	F	A	Pts
Lietava Jonava	27	19	5	3	68	18	62
Nevezis Kedainiai	27	18	4	5	65	23	58
Granitas Vilnius	27	15	7	5	56	33	52
FK Trakai	27	14	6	7	57	29	48
Polonija Vilnius	27	12	1	14	50	48	37
NFA Kaunas	27	10	3	14	66	61	33
FK Silute	27	8	8	11	39	33	32
FK Palanga	27	8	6	13	38	55	30
Venta Kursenai	27	8	1	18	44	70	25
Lifosa Kedainiai	27	1	3	23	15	128	6

31/03/2012 - 27/10/2012

MEDALS TABLE

		Overall G S B	League G S B	Cup G S
1	FBK Kaunas	12 4 1	8 2 1	4 2
2	Ekranas Panevezys	11 7 4	7 3 4	4 4
3	Zalgiris Vilnius	9 15 3	3 10 3	6 5
4	Kareda Siauliai	4 2	2 2	2
5	Inkaras Kaunas	3 2 1	2 1	1 2
6	Atlantas Klaipeda	2 3 3	2 3	2 1
7	Suduva Marijampole	2 3 4	2 4	2 1
8	Sirijus Klaipeda	2 1 1	1 1	1 1
9	Neris Vilnius	1 1	1 1	
10	ROMAR Mazeikiai	1	1 1	
11	Vetra Vilnius	5 3	1 3	4
12	Panerys Vilnius	1 1	1 1	
13	Banga Gargzdai	1		
	Tauras Siauliai	1		1
	Tauras Taurage	1		1

LFF TAURE 2011-12

Round of 16		Quarter-finals		Semi-finals		Final	
Zalgiris Vilnius	1						
KFK Siauliai *	0	Zalgiris Vilnius *	0 5p				
Polonija	1	Banga Gargzdai	0 4p				
Banga Gargzdai *	9			Zalgiris Vilnius *	1 1		
FBK Kaunas *	5			Suduva Marijampole	0 2		
Jambo Klaipeda	0	FBK Kaunas *	0				
Atlantas Klaipeda	0	Suduva Marijampole	3				
Suduva Marijampole *	9					Zalgiris Vilnius ‡	0 3p
FK Reo LT Vilnius	2					Ekranas Panevezys	0 1p
Tauras Taurage *	1	FK Reo LT Vilnius	7				
Glestum Klaipeda	1	Lifosa Kedainiai *	1			CUP FINAL	
Lifosa Kedainiai *	5			FK Reo LT Vilnius *	0 0		
Kruoja Pakruojis *	1 5p			Ekranas Panevezys	2 2	Suduva Stadium, Marijampole	
FK Mazeikiai	1 4p	Kruoja Pakruojis *	1			20-05-2012	
Nevezis Kedainiai	0	Ekranas Panevezys	2				
Ekranas Panevezys *	2						

* Home team in the first leg
‡ Qualified for the Europa League

LUX – LUXEMBOURG

FIFA/COCA-COLA WORLD RANKING

'93	'94	'95	'96	'97	'98	'99	'00	'01	'02	'03	'04	'05	'06	'07	'08	'09	'10	'11	'12
111	128	100	123	138	143	124	139	142	148	153	155	150	186	149	121	128	134	128	148

2012

Jan	Feb	Mar	Apr	May	Jun	Jul	Aug	Sep	Oct	Nov	Dec	High	Low	Av
127	133	127	119	119	121	110	110	106	142	144	148	93	195	137

Although Grevenmacher led the league table for a significant part of the season, the race for honours turned into a duel between F91 Dudelange and Jeunesse d'Esch. Dudelange had made a poor start to the season and in October replaced coach Dan Theis with the Belgian Didier Philippe and it paid handsome dividends with the club winning a fourth double in seven seasons. Grevenmacher were unbeaten until the end of February but then lost four of six games to hand the initiative to their rivals with Dudelange clinching the title on the penultimate weekend of the season ahead of Jeunesse. The two then met in the cup final, a game which went to extra-time before goals from Aurelien Joachim and Amodou Abdullei sealed a 4-2 victory for Dudelange - the 15th trophy won by the club in just 13 seasons. The national team continued its recent improvement, starting the year with victory over Macedonia in a friendly and then earning a draw in Belfast against Northern Ireland in a 2014 FIFA World Cup qualifier. Earlier, Luxembourg had lost narrowly at home to Portugal but the year ended with two heavy defeats against Israel to leave them in familiar territory at the bottom of the table. That was accompanied by a sharp fall in the FIFA/Coca-Cola World Ranking from 106th - their best position since May 1996 - to 148th.

UEFA EUROPEAN CHAMPIONSHIP RECORD
1960 DNE **1964** QF **1968-2012** DNQ

FEDERATION LUXEMBOURGEOISE DE FOOTBALL (FLF)

PO Box 5, Mondercange 3901
☎ +352 4886651
📠 +352 48866582
✉ flf@football.lu
🌐 www.football.lu
FA 1908 CON 1954 FIFA 1910
P Paul Philipp
GS Joel Wolff

THE STADIA

2014 FIFA World Cup Stadia
Stade Josy-Barthel
Luxembourg   8 100

Other Main Stadia
Stade du Thillenberg
Differdange   7 150
Stade de la Frontière
Esch sur Alzette   5 090
Stade Henri Dunant
Beggen   4 830
Stade Jos Nosbaum
Dudelange   4 500

MAJOR CITIES/TOWNS

		Population
1	Luxemburg	75 375
2	Esch-sur-Alzette	28 950
3	Dudelange	18 473
4	Schifflange	8 364
5	Bettembourg	7 627
6	Pétange	7 371
7	Ettelbruck	6 466
8	Diekirch	6 343
9	Strassen	6 026
10	Bertrange	5 634
11	Fousbann	5 509
12	Belvaux	5 449
13	Differdange	5 431
14	Soleuvre	5 116
15	Mamer	5 066
16	Wiltz	5 021
17	Echternach	4 901
18	Rodange	4 803
19	Obercorn	4 786

GRAND DUCHE DE LUXEMBOURG

Capital Luxembourg   Population 491 775 (169)   % in cities 82%
GDP per capita $81 200 (3)   Area km² 2 586 km² (178)   GMT +/- +1
Neighbours (km) Belgium 148, France 73, Germany 138

RECENT INTERNATIONAL MATCHES PLAYED BY LUXEMBOURG

2008	Opponents	Score	Venue	Comp	Scorers	Att	Referee
6-09	Greece	L 0-3	Luxembourg	WCq		4 596	Hermansen DEN
10-09	Switzerland	W 2-1	Zurich	WCq	Jeff Strasser [27], Fons Leweck [87]	20 500	Filipovic SRB
11-10	Israel	L 1-3	Luxembourg	WCq	Rene Peters [14]	3 562	Egorov RUS
15-10	Moldova	D 0-0	Luxembourg	WCq		2 157	Borski POL
19-11	Belgium	D 1-1	Luxembourg	Fr	Mario Mutsch [47]		Riley ENG
2009							
28-03	Latvia	L 0-4	Luxembourg	WCq		2 516	Whitby WAL
1-04	Latvia	L 0-2	Riga	WCq		6 700	Aydinus TUR
12-08	Lithuania	L 0-1	Luxembourg	Fr		1 000	Black NIR
5-09	Moldova	D 0-0	Chisinau	WCq		7 820	Mazeika LTU
9-09	Israel	L 0-7	Ramat Gan	WCq		7 038	Svendsen DEN
10-10	Switzerland	L 0-3	Luxembourg	WCq		8 031	Iturralde ESP
14-10	Greece	L 1-2	Athens	WCq	Papadopoulos OG [90]	13 932	Ceferin SVN
14-11	Iceland	D 1-1	Luxembourg	Fr	Kim Kintziger [75]	913	Van Boekel NED
2010							
3-03	Azerbaijan	L 1-2	Luxembourg	Fr	Jeff Strasser [33]	874	Kari FIN
4-06	Faroe Islands	D 0-0	Hesperange	Fr		713	Bertolini SUI
11-08	Wales	L 1-5	Llanelli	Fr	Joel Kitenge [44]	4 904	Gestranius FIN
3-09	Bosnia-Herzegovina	L 0-3	Luxembourg	ECq		7 327	Banari MDA
7-09	Albania	L 0-1	Tirana	ECq		10 000	Trutz SVK
8-10	Belarus	D 0-0	Luxembourg	ECq		1 857	Stavrev MKD
12-10	France	L 0-2	Metz	ECq		24 710	Jug SVN
17-11	Algeria	D 0-0	Luxembourg	Fr		7 033	Sippel GER
2011							
9-02	Slovakia	W 2-1	Luxembourg	Fr	Daniel Da Mota 2 [60] [81]		Thual FRA
25-03	France	L 0-2	Luxembourg	ECq		8 400	Hagen NOR
29-03	Romania	L 1-3	Piatra-Neamt	ECq	Lars Gerson [22]	13 500	Gocek TUR
3-06	Hungary	L 0-1	Luxembourg	Fr		1 213	Arnason ISL
7-06	Belarus	L 0-2	Minsk	ECq		9 500	Salmanov AZE
10-08	Portugal	L 0-5	Faro	Fr			Mateu ESP
2-09	Romania	L 0-2	Luxembourg	ECq		2 812	Karasev RUS
6-09	Albania	W 2-1	Luxembourg	ECq	Gilles Bettmer [27], Aurelien Joachim [78]	2 132	Kari FIN
7-10	Bosnia-Herzegovina	L 0-5	Zenica	ECq		12 000	Evans WAL
15-11	Switzerland	L 0-1	Luxembourg	Fr		852	Delferiere BEL
2012							
29-02	FYR Macedonia	W 2-1	Luxembourg	Fr	Maurice Deville 2 [55] [90]	787	Crangle NIR
2-06	Malta	L 0-2	Luxembourg	Fr		1 054	Hameter AUT
15-08	Georgia	L 1-2	Oberkorn	Fr	Aurelien Joachim [84p]	1 000	Turpin FRA
7-09	Portugal	L 1-2	Luxembourg	WCq	Daniel Da Mota [13]	8 125	Tohver EST
11-09	Northern Ireland	D 1-1	Belfast	WCq	Daniel Da Mota [86]	10 674	Glodovic SRB
12-10	Israel	L 0-6	Luxembourg	WCq		2 631	Trattou CYP
16-10	Israel	L 0-3	Tel Aviv	WCq		20 400	Lechner AUT
14-11	Scotland	L 1-2	Luxembourg	Fr	Lars Gerson [47]	2 521	Zimmermann SUI

Fr = Friendly match • EC = UEFA EURO 2008/2012 • WC = FIFA World Cup • q = qualifier

LUXEMBOURG NATIONAL TEAM HISTORICAL RECORDS

Caps
98 - Jeff Strasser 1993-2010 • 88 - Carlo Weis 1978-98 & Rene Peters 2000- • 82 - Eric Hoffmann 2002- • 77 - Francois Konter 1955-69 • 73 - Roby Langers 1980-98 • 69 - Manuel Cardoni 1993-2004 • 67 - Ernest Brenner 1955-65 • 64 - Marcel Bossi 1980-93 & Jeff Saibene 1986-2001 • 63 - Gilbert Dresch 1975-87 • 62 - Mario Mutsch 2005- • 58 - Jean-Paul Girres 1980-92 • 58 - Jonathan Joubert 2006- • 57 - Fernand Brosius 1956-66 • 56 - Nicolas Kettel 1946-59 • 55 - Guy Hellers 1982-97; Luc Holtz 1991-2002 & Jeannot Moes 1971-83

Goals
16 - Leon Mart 1936-45 • 15 - Gustave Kemp 1937-45 • 14 - Camille Libar 1938-47 • 13 - Nicolas Kettel 1946-59 • 12 - Francois Muller 1949-54 • 11 - Leon Letsch 1947-62 • (Totals include all matches and not just full internationals)

Coaches
Ernst Melchior 1969-72 • Louis Pilot 1978-84 • Paul Philipp 1985-2001 • Allan Simonsen 2001-04 • Guy Hellers 2004-10 • Luc Holz 2010-

LUXEMBOURG 2011-12
BGL LIGUE DIVISION NATIONALE

	Pl	W	D	L	F	A	Pts	Dudelange	Jeunesse	Grevenmacher	Differdange	Käerjeng	Fola Esch	RM Hamm	Pétange	Progrès	Racing Union	Kayl Tetange	Swift	Rumelange	Hostert
F91 Dudelange †	26	16	6	4	67	20	54		3-3	1-1	1-1	4-1	1-0	1-0	10-0	5-0	0-1	2-0	2-1	2-0	3-0
Jeunesse d'Esch ‡	26	15	6	5	56	37	51	2-1		1-2	1-2	0-0	2-0	2-3	2-0	2-1	2-2	4-3	2-1	1-0	3-2
CS Grevenmacher ‡	26	14	7	5	50	27	49	0-2	1-2		2-1	2-0	2-1	2-2	2-0	1-2	2-1	0-2	2-0	2-1	4-0
FC Differdange 03 ‡	26	13	9	4	64	26	48	3-1	0-3	0-0		5-0	2-2	2-2	2-1	2-3	2-2	4-1	6-1	6-1	3-0
UN Käerjeng 97	26	12	7	7	37	35	43	0-0	3-0	2-1	1-1		2-3	3-0	3-2	0-0	3-2	1-2	1-0	2-1	3-0
Fola Esch	26	10	8	8	41	30	38	1-1	1-3	1-2	1-1	4-0		2-0	0-1	1-1	0-0	4-1	4-1	0-0	3-1
RM Hamm Benfica	26	12	2	12	54	47	38	1-4	2-4	1-3	1-2	2-3	2-0		0-4	2-0	4-0	1-0	8-2	9-1	3-1
CS Pétange	26	10	6	10	29	37	36	0-0	3-0	2-2	0-0	0-2	2-1	2-0		0-1	1-1	2-0	0-3	0-0	3-0
Progrès Niedercorn	26	9	6	11	32	35	33	1-2	1-1	0-1	1-0	0-0	0-1	0-2	1-2		1-2	2-0	1-0	4-2	0-2
Racing Union	26	7	11	8	40	41	32	2-0	1-3	1-1	1-0	1-2	2-2	3-0	0-0	3-3		3-3	1-3	3-1	3-3
Union Kayl Tetange	26	8	5	13	39	51	29	1-3	1-3	3-3	2-6	0-0	0-3	3-2	1-2	1-1	2-0		2-0	1-0	5-0
Swift Hesperange	26	7	5	14	34	53	26	0-3	1-1	1-1	0-3	3-3	1-2	1-2	3-1	1-0	1-0	1-1		3-0	1-3
US Rumelange	26	5	4	17	27	71	19	0-6	1-5	0-5	0-7	2-0	1-1	1-3	3-0	2-1	0-3	4-1	3-3		3-2
US Hostert	26	2	2	22	22	82	8	1-9	1-6	0-6	0-2	2-2	1-1	0-1	2-5	2-2	0-3	1-2	1-0		

5/08/2011 - 13/05/2012 • † Qualified for the UEFA Champions League • ‡ Qualified for the Europa League
Relegation play-off: Swift 2-6 **FC Wiltz** • Top scorer: **23** - Omar **ER RAFIK** MAR, Differdange • **21** - Sanel **IBRAHIMOVIC** BIH, RM Hamm • **20** - Daniel **HUSS**, Grevenmacher • **19** - Aurelien **JOACHIM**, Dudelange • **16** - Stefano **BENSI**, Dudelange • **15** - Tony **LOPES** FRA, Union Kayl Tetange

LUXEMBOURG 2011-12
DIVISION HONOUR (2)

	Pl	W	D	L	F	A	Pts
Jeunesse Canach	26	18	3	5	57	19	57
Etzella Ettelbruck	26	18	2	6	76	26	56
FC Wiltz 71	26	16	4	6	67	37	52
US Mondorf-les-Bains	26	11	7	8	36	41	40
Victoria Rosport	26	11	6	9	60	48	39
FF Norden 02	26	10	7	9	37	36	37
FC Mondercange	26	11	2	13	50	50	35
FC Mamer 32	26	9	7	10	31	40	34
UNA Strassen	26	8	9	9	42	44	33
FC 72 Erpeldange	26	9	6	11	43	47	33
CS Obercorn †	26	8	5	13	43	48	29
Young Boys Diekirch †	26	7	5	14	26	61	26
Muhlenbach-Sandzak	26	4	7	15	23	55	19
Koeppchen W'dange	26	5	4	17	25	64	19

5/08/2011 - 13/05/2012
† Relegation play-off: Young Boys 2-2 4-2p Steinfort
Obercorn 1-0 Atert Bissen

LUXEMBOURG 2011-12
1. DIVISION SERIE 1 (3)

	Pl	W	D	L	F	A	Pts
Alliance Aischdall	26	17	4	5	67	36	55
Atert Bissen †	26	16	6	4	64	32	54
Minerva Lintgen	26	16	4	6	63	33	52
Marisca Mersch	26	14	5	7	54	35	47
Pratzerthal-Redange	26	12	6	8	54	43	42
FC Lorentzweiler	26	12	3	11	44	47	39
Orania Vianden	26	11	5	10	41	41	38
US Feulen	26	11	2	13	47	55	35
Sporting Mertzig	26	8	7	11	42	50	31
Green Boys	26	6	9	11	32	42	27
Daring Echternach	26	8	3	15	40	57	27
Jeunesse Schieren	26	7	5	14	29	41	26
FC Kehlen	26	7	4	15	35	57	25
Résidence Walferdange	26	3	5	18	18	61	14

5/08/2011 - 13/05/2012 • † Promotion play-off

MEDALS TABLE

		Overall			League			Cup	
		G	S	B	G	S	B	G	S
1	Jeunesse Esch/Alzette	40	25	15	**28**	13	15	12	12
2	Red Boys Differdange	21	19	14	6	10	14	15	9
3	AC Spora Luxembourg	19	18	10	11	10	10	8	8
4	Union Luxembourg	16	18	12	6	8	12	10	10
5	F91 Dudelange	15	8		10	4		5	4
6	Stade Dudelange	14	13	6	10	6	6	4	7
7	Avenir Beggen	13	9	3	6	5	3	7	4
8	Fola Esch/Alzette	8	9	4	5	8	4	3	1
9	Progres Niedercorn	7	8	8	3	5	8	4	3
10	CS Grevenmacher	5	12	5	1	7	5	4	5
11	US Hollerich	5	3	2	5	3	2		
12	Aris Bonnevoie	4	6	2	3	1	2	1	5
13	US Rumelange	2	5	1				3	1	2	2
14	Sporting Club Luxembourg	2	3	2	2	3	2		
15	The National Schifflange	2	3		1	2		1	1
16	Alliance Dudelange	2	2					2	1
17	FC Differdange 03	2	1	1				1	1	2
18	Racing Club Luxembourg	2		3				1	3	1

LUXEMBOURG 2011-12
1. DIVISION SERIE 2 (3)

	Pl	W	D	L	F	A	Pts
US Sandweiler	26	20	2	4	79	21	62
Sporting Steinfort †	26	16	5	5	47	28	53
US Esch	26	14	4	8	49	34	46
Avenir Beggen	26	12	3	11	48	31	39
Jeunesse Junglinster	26	12	2	12	43	41	38
Flaxweiler Beyren	26	10	8	8	47	46	38
Berdenia Berbourg	26	9	10	7	41	38	37
The Belval Belvaux	26	11	3	12	35	40	36
Yellow Boys Weiler	26	8	9	9	28	30	33
FC CeBra	26	9	4	13	38	56	31
FC Munsbach	26	6	10	10	38	46	28
ES Clemency	26	7	5	14	25	49	26
Un. Mertet/Wasserbillig	26	5	10	11	34	55	25
FC Schifflange	26	4	3	19	25	62	15

5/08/2011 - 13/05/2012 • † Promotion play-off

COUPE DE LUXEMBOURG 2011-12

Fifth Round

F91 Dudelange	4
Minerva Lintgen *	1
Sporting Bertrange *	1
RM Hamm Benfica	2
UN Käerjeng 97	2
Mamer 32 *	1
Un. Mertert/Wasserbillig *	1
Union Kayl Tetange	3
US Mondorf-les-Bains *	2
US Rumelange	1
UNA Strassen *	1
CS Pétange	5
ES Clemency *	2
Progrès Niedercorn	1
Young Boys Diekirch *	0
Fola Esch	2
FC Differdange 03	6
Victoria Rosport *	0
CS Obercorn *	1
Luna Obercorn	0
Racing Union	8
FC Rodange 91 *	0
FC Wiltz 71 *	1
CS Grevenmacher	4
Etzella Ettelbruck *	2
The Belval Belvaux	0
Flaxweiler Beyren *	3
Swift Hesperange	4
US Hostert	4
Jeunesse Junglinster *	2
US Sandweiler *	1
Jeunesse d'Esch	4

Round of 16

F91 Dudelange	5
RM Hamm Benfica	1
UN Käerjeng 97 *	0
Union Kayl Tetange	2
US Mondorf-les-Bains *	3 (4p)
CS Pétange	3 (1p)
ES Clemency *	0
Fola Esch	3
FC Differdange 03	2
CS Obercorn *	0
Racing Union *	2
CS Grevenmacher	3
Etzella Ettelbruck *	2
Swift Hesperange	1
US Hostert	0
Jeunesse d'Esch *	4

Quarter-finals

F91 Dudelange *	4
Union Kayl Tetange	2
US Mondorf-les-Bains	0
Fola Esch *	3
FC Differdange 03 *	2
CS Grevenmacher	1
Etzella Ettelbruck	2 (0p)
Jeunesse d'Esch *	2 (3p)

Semi-finals

F91 Dudelange *	1 (5p)
Fola Esch	1 (4p)
FC Differdange 03 *	1
Jeunesse d'Esch	2

Final

F91 Dudelange	4
Jeunesse d'Esch	2

CUP FINAL

Josy Barthel, Luxembourg, 26-05-2012
Att: 2847, Ref: Christian Holtgen
Scorers - Joachim 2 32 105, Benzouien 50, Abdullei 120 for F91; Gomez 2 3, Benajiba 65 for JE
F91 - Jonathan Joubert - Julien Tournut, Jean-Philippe Caillet, Bryan Melisse◆113, Sofian Benzouien (Lehit Zeghdane 90), Ben Payal, Yasin Karaca (Amodou Abdullei 68), Jean-Sebastien Legros◆83, Stefano Bensi (Michael Wiggers 68), Aurelien Joachim, Daniel Da Mota. Tr: Didier Philippe
Jeunesse - Marc Oberweis - Ricardo Delgado (Clayton De Sousa 77), Adrien Portier, Eric Hoffmann, Dzenid Ramdedovic (Rene Peters 45), Dan Collette - Khalid Benichou (Miceli 65), Yassine Benajiba - Dieumerci Ndongala◆113, Frankie Quere, Daniel Gomez. Tr: Sebastien Grandjean

* Home team

LVA – LATVIA

FIFA/COCA-COLA WORLD RANKING

'93	'94	'95	'96	'97	'98	'99	'00	'01	'02	'03	'04	'05	'06	'07	'08	'09	'10	'11	'12
86	69	60	82	75	77	62	92	106	79	51	65	69	90	86	67	45	78	68	106

2012

Jan	Feb	Mar	Apr	May	Jun	Jul	Aug	Sep	Oct	Nov	Dec	High	Low	Av
70	74	78	74	74	76	72	70	94	118	108	106	45	118	75

Since their formation in 2001 as FK Ditton, Daugava, from Latvia's second city Daugavpils, have had a turbulent history. They won the cup in 2008 as Dinaburg but financial problems and then involvement in a match fixing scandal saw the club re-emerge as Daugava. With the federation eager to see Daugavpils represented in the Virsliga, Daugava were invited back and in 2012 they won the title for the first time. Coached by Moldavian Ivan Tabanov, who was brought in after a 6-1 defeat at the hands of Jurmala early in the campaign, Daugava were involved in a tight race between the top four, finishing four points ahead of the Marians Pahars-coached Skonto Riga. Earlier in the season Skonto had beaten Metalurgs on penalties in the cup final after a 1-1 draw to end their ten year wait to lift the cup again. It was only the second trophy won by Skonto since their record winning run of 13 successive championships came to an end in 2004 and they look on track to establish themselves once again as a driving force in the Latvian game. The national team made a poor start to their 2014 FIFA World Cup qualifying campaign in a group in which they had realistic hopes of causing an upset or two. A solitary victory over Liechtenstein was all that kept them of the bottom of the standings at the end of the year.

UEFA EUROPEAN CHAMPIONSHIP RECORD
1960-1992 DNE (Played as part of the Soviet Union) **1996-2000** DNQ **2004** 14 r1 **2008-2012** DNQ

LATVIAN FOOTBALL FEDERATION (LFF)
Olympic Sports Center,
Grostonas Street 6b,
1013 Riga
☎ +371 67292988
+371 67315604
futbols@lff.lv
www.lff.lv
FA 1921 CON 1992 FIFA 1992
P Guntis Indriksons
GS Janis Mezeckis

THE STADIA
2014 FIFA World Cup Stadia
Skonto Stadions
Riga 8 207

Other Main Stadia
Daugava Stadions
Liepaja 5 083
Daugava Stadions
Riga 5 008
Celtnieks Stadions
Daugavpils 5 000
Olimpiskais Centrs
Ventspils 3 085

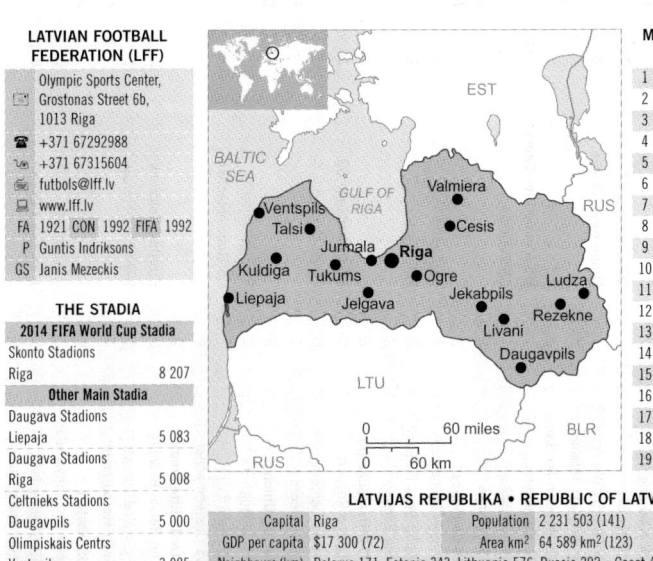

MAJOR CITIES/TOWNS
		Population
1	Riga	711 789
2	Daugavpils	105 520
3	Liepaja	84 492
4	Jelgava	66 120
5	Jurmala	55 061
6	Ventspils	43 098
7	Rezekne	35 680
8	Valmiera	27 339
9	Jekabspils	26 713
10	Ogre	26 167
11	Tukums	19 904
12	Salaspils	18 084
13	Cesis	17 844
14	Kuldiga	12 892
15	Olaine	12 719
16	Saldus	12 353
17	Dobele	11 104
18	Talsi	11 059
19	Sigulda	10 760

LATVIJAS REPUBLIKA • REPUBLIC OF LATVIA
Capital Riga Population 2 231 503 (141) % in cities 68%
GDP per capita $17 300 (72) Area km² 64 589 km² (123) GMT +/- +2
Neighbours (km) Belarus 171, Estonia 343, Lithuania 576, Russia 292 • Coast 498

LVA – LATVIA

RECENT INTERNATIONAL MATCHES PLAYED BY LATVIA

2008	Opponents	Score	Venue	Comp	Scorers	Att	Referee
20-08	Romania	L 0-1	Urziceni	Fr		10 000	Ovrebo NOR
6-09	Moldova	W 2-1	Tiraspol	WCq	Karlsons.G [8], Astafjevs [22]	4 300	Courtney NIR
10-09	Greece	L 0-2	Riga	WCq		8 600	Chapron FRA
11-10	Switzerland	L 1-2	St Gall	WCq	Ivanovs [71]	18 026	Batista POR
15-10	Israel	D 1-1	Riga	WCq	Kolesnicenko [89]	7 100	Hrinak SVK
12-11	Estonia	D 1-1	Tallinn	Fr	Grebis [75]	2 000	Sandmoen NOR
2009							
11-02	Armenia	D 0-0	Limassol	Fr		150	
28-03	Luxembourg	W 4-0	Luxembourg	WCq	Karlsons [24], Cauna [48], Visnakovs [72], Pereplotkins [86]	2 516	Whitby WAL
1-04	Luxembourg	W 2-0	Riga	WCq	Zigajevs [43], Verpakovskis [75]	6 700	Aydinus TUR
12-08	Bulgaria	L 0-1	Sofia	Fr		2 000	Pamporidis GRE
5-09	Israel	W 1-0	Ramat Gan	WCq	Gorkss [59]	20 000	Kircher GER
9-09	Switzerland	D 2-2	Riga	WCq	Cauna [62], Astafjevs [75]	8 600	Kralovec CZE
10-10	Greece	L 2-5	Athens	WCq	Verpakovskis 2 [12 40]	18 981	Ovrebo NOR
14-10	Moldova	W 3-2	Riga	WCq	Rubins 2 [32 44], Grebis [76]	3 800	Hyytia FIN
14-11	Honduras	L 1-2	Tegucigalpa	Fr	Kolesnicenko [45p]		Quesada CRC
2010							
22-01	Korea Republic	L 0-1	Malaga	Fr		150	Velasco ESP
5-06	Ghana	L 0-1	Milton Keynes	Fr		8 108	Clattenburg ENG
18-06	Lithuania	D 0-0	Kaunas	BC		1 000	Kaasik EST
19-06	Estonia	D 0-0	Kaunas	BC		300	Mazeika LTU
11-08	Czech Republic	L 1-4	Liberec	Fr	Cauna [90]	7 456	Dankovsky UKR
3-09	Croatia	L 0-3	Riga	ECq		7 600	Kuipers NED
7-09	Malta	W 2-0	Ta'Qali	ECq	Gorkss [43], Verpakovskis [85]	6 255	Asumaa FIN
8-10	Greece	L 0-1	Piraeus	ECq		13 520	Damato ITA
12-10	Georgia	D 1-1	Riga	ECq	Cauna [91+]	4 330	Neves POR
17-11	China PR	L 0-1	Kunming	Fr		7 500	Ko Hyung Jin KOR
2011							
26-03	Israel	L 1-2	Tel Aviv	ECq	Gorkss [62]	10 801	Mazic SRB
4-06	Israel	L 1-2	Riga	ECq	Cauna [62p]	6 147	Kelly IRL
7-06	Austria	L 1-3	Graz	Fr	Mihadjuks [49]	8 500	Evans WAL
10-08	Finland	L 0-2	Riga	Fr		5 314	Bezborodov RUS
2-09	Georgia	W 1-0	Tbilisi	ECq	Cauna [64]	15 422	Trattou CYP
6-09	Greece	D 1-1	Riga	ECq	Cauna [19]	5 415	Todorov BUL
7-10	Malta	W 2-0	Riga	ECq	Visnakovs.A [33], Rudnevs [83]	4 315	Trutz SVK
11-10	Croatia	L 0-2	Rijeka	ECq		8 370	Gautier FRA
2012							
29-02	Kazakhstan	D 0-0	Antalya	Fr		100	Banari MDA
22-05	Poland	L 0-1	Klagenfurt	Fr		200	Lechner AUT
1-06	Lithuania	W 5-0	Voru	BCsf	Cauna [13p], Gauracs 2 [17 48], Visnakovs [36], Smirnovs [81]	125	Gestranius FIN
3-06	Finland	D 1-1	Voru	BCf	Gauracs [54]. W 6-5p	280	Mazeika LTU
15-08	Montenegro	L 0-2	Podgorica	Fr		4 500	Grujic SRB
7-09	Greece	L 1-2	Riga	WCq	Cauna [41p]	7 956	Bebek CRO
11-09	Bosnia-Herzegovina	L 1-4	Zenica	WCq	Gorkss [5]	11 900	Aytekin GER
12-10	Slovakia	L 1-2	Bratislava	WCq	Verpakovskis [84p]	4 012	Makkelie NED
16-10	Liechtenstein	W 2-0	Riga	WCq	Kamess [29], Gauracs [77]	3 500	Kovacs ROU

Fr = Friendly match • EC = UEFA EURO 2012 • BC = Baltic Cup • WC = FIFA World Cup • q = qualifier

LATVIA NATIONAL TEAM HISTORICAL RECORDS

Caps
167 - Vitalijs Astafjevs 1992-2010 • **117** - Andrejs Rubins 1998- • **108** - Juris Laizans 1998- • **106** - Imants Bleidelis 1995-07 • **105** - Mihails Zemlinskis 1992-2005 • **100** - Igors Stepanovs 1995- • **95** - Maris Verpakovskis 1999- • **86** - Aleksandrs Kolinko 1997- • **81** - Andrejs Stolcers 1994-2005 • **75** - Marian Pahars 1996-2007 • **73** - Vitas Rimkus 1995-2008 • **70** - Oleg Blagonadezdins 1992-2004

Goals
29 - Maris Verpakovskis 1999- • **24** - Eriks Petersons 1929-39 • **16** - Vitalijs Astafjevs 1992-2010 • **15** - Marian Pahars 1996-2007 & Juris Laizans 1998- • **14** - Alberts Seibelis 1925-39 • **13** - Ilja Vestermans 1935-38 • **12** - Mihails Zemlinskis 1992-2005

Coaches
Janis Gilis 1992-97 • Revaz Dzodzuashvili GEO 1998-99 • Gary Johnson ENG 1999-2001 • Aleksandrs Starkovs 2001-04 • Jurijs Andrejevs 2004-07 • Aleksandrs Starkovs 2007-

LATVIA 2012

VIRSLIGA

	Pl	W	D	L	F	A	Pts	Daugava D	Skonto	Ventspils	Metalurgs	Spartaks	Jurmala	Jelgava	Metta	Daugava R	Gulbene
Daugava Daugavpils †	36	23	9	4	64	25	78		1-1	0-0	3-0	0-0	0-0	0-0	1-0	3-2	2-0	2-0	2-0	0-0	2-0	1-0	3-1	3-0	3-0	1-0
Skonto Riga ‡	36	21	11	4	58	22	74	3-0 0-0		1-0 1-0 0-1 3-1 1-0 0-0 1-0 1-0 2-3 2-0 5-0 5-0 1-0 1-1 4-1 3-1
FK Ventspils ‡	36	23	5	8	63	22	74	1-2 1-0 0-0 1-0		0-3 1-0 3-2 2-0 1-1 2-1 0-1 0-0 1-0 4-0 2-0 5-0 3-0 4-0
Liepajas Metalurgs ‡	36	21	7	8	60	33	70	2-0 1-3 0-1 1-0 0-0 1-0		1-2 2-1 2-0 3-2 1-1 2-0 3-2 4-1 1-0 4-0 0-1 3-1
FK Spartaks Jurmala	36	13	10	13	61	56	49	2-2 0-3 2-2 0-1 2-0 0-3 2-2 0-3		0-0 4-2 2-0 1-1 3-1 3-4 2-2 2-2 3-1 2-2
FC Jurmala	36	10	9	17	47	49	39	6-1 2-4 3-3 0-0 1-2 0-1 0-2 0-2 0-1 0-3		0-0 3-1 0-0 3-0 1-1 2-3 2-2 4-0
FK Jelgava	36	7	10	19	32	56	31	1-2 0-2 1-2 1-1 0-2 0-1 0-2 1-2 1-3 3-2 0-2 1-3		1-4 1-1 3-4 2-2 0-1 0-0
FS Metta	36	7	8	21	39	82	29	1-1 0-5 1-2 1-2 1-6 0-2 4-1 1-0 2-1 3-3 0-2 0-3 1-1 1-3		0-3 4-3 0-0 1-1
Daugava Riga	36	5	12	19	42	79	27	0-4 0-3 1-1 1-3 1-4 0-4 1-3 3-3 1-2 2-5 1-1 1-2 1-0 1-2 1-0 1-1		2-2 1-1
FB Gulbene	36	5	9	22	28	70	24	0-2 1-3 0-1 0-4 0-5 1-2 1-1 1-3 0-3 0-1 2-0 0-1 1-2 0-1 5-1 0-3 0-0 2-1	

24/03/2012 - 10/11/2012 • † Qualified for the UEFA Champions League • ‡ Qualified for the Europa League
Relegation play-off: **Daugava Riga** 1-0 3-1 BFC Daugava
Top scorer: 18 - Mamuka **GHONGHADZE** GEO, Daugava Daugavpils • 15 - Yosuke **SAITO** JPN, Gulbene/Ventspils • 12 - David **CORTES** COL, Spartaks & Daniel **TURKOVS**, Ventspils • 11 - Antons **JEMELINS**, Spartaks; Tadas **LABUKAS** LTU, Skonto & Velerijs **SABALA**, Skonto

LATVIA 2012 PIRMALIGA (2)

	Pl	W	D	L	F	A	Pts
Liepajas Metalurgs-2	25	21	4	0	92	20	67
Ilukstes NSS	26	18	3	5	87	38	57
Skonto Riga-2	26	17	5	4	56	32	56
Daugava Daugavpils-2	26	15	7	4	49	20	52
Rigas Futbola Skola	26	16	3	7	62	33	51
FK Ventspils-2	26	15	3	8	57	37	48
SFK Varaviksne	26	11	7	8	47	45	40
FK Valmiera	26	8	3	15	39	53	27
FK Spartaks Jurmala-2	26	7	5	14	48	71	26
FK Rezekne/BJSS	25	8	1	16	49	57	25
FS Metta-2	26	7	3	16	33	52	24
FK Auda	26	6	3	17	36	51	21
FK Tukums	26	4	1	21	28	116	13
FK Jelgava-2	26	3	2	21	29	87	11

23/04/2012 - 11/11/2012

MEDALS TABLE

		Overall			League			Cup		City
		G	S	B	G	S	B	G	S	
1	Skonto Riga	23	8	3	15	2	3	8	6	Riga
2	FK Ventspils	9	6	6	4	5	6	5	1	Ventspils
3	Liepajas Metalurgs	3	14	4	2	8	4	1	6	Liepaja
4	FK Jelgava	3	2	2		2	2	3		Jelgava
5	Daugava Daugavpils	2		1			1	1		Daugavpils
6	Dinaburg Daugavpils	1	3	2		1	2	1	2	Daugavpils
7	Olimpija Riga	1	1			1		1		Riga
8	FK Riga	1		1			1	1		Riga
9	Daugava Riga		5			3			2	Riga
10	VEF/DAG/Olimpija/FK		2	3			3		2	Riga/Liepaja
11	FK Jurmala		1						1	Jurmala
	Olimps Riga		1						1	Riga

LATVIJAS KAUSS 2011-12

Round of 16		Quarter-finals		Semi-finals		Final	
Skonto Riga	2						
Rigas Futbola Skola *	0	**Skonto Riga**	1				
Mett/LU *	0	FC Jurmala *	0				
FC Jurmala	3			**Skonto Riga**	1		
FK Jurmala VV	4			FB Gulbene *	0		
FK Tukums *	0	FK Jurmala VV *	1				
FK Valmiera *	1	**FB Gulbene**	3				
FB Gulbene	3					**Skonto Riga**	1 4p
FK Jelgava	3					Liepajas Metalurgs ‡	1 3p
Olimps/RFS Riga	1	**FK Jelgava** *	2				
FK Spartaks *	1	FK Ventspils	1				
FK Ventspils	2			FK Jelgava *	1		
Daugava Daugavpils	11			**Liepajas Metalurgs**	4		
FK Kvarcs/Madona *	0	Daugava Daugavpils	0				
SFK Varaviksne *	1	**Liepajas Metalurgs** *	1				
Liepajas Metalurgs	3						

* Home team • ‡ Qualified for the Europa League

CUP FINAL

Skonto, Riga, 12-05-2012
Att: 2731, Ref: Direktorenk
Scorers - Sabala [55] for Skonto;
Kamess [75] for Metalurgs

MAC – MACAU

FIFA/COCA-COLA WORLD RANKING

'93	'94	'95	'96	'97	'98	'99	'00	'01	'02	'03	'04	'05	'06	'07	'08	'09	'10	'11	'12
166	175	180	172	157	174	176	180	180	188	184	188	192	185	190	196	187	193	197	198

2012

Jan	Feb	Mar	Apr	May	Jun	Jul	Aug	Sep	Oct	Nov	Dec	High	Low	Av
197	196	199	198	198	198	199	201	200	199	199	198	156	201	182

Macau's struggles at international level continued in 2012 as the former Portuguese colony could only manage a solitary win in the qualifying tournament of the 2013 East Asian Cup. At a preliminary round group in Guam, Macau finished second behind the hosts after losing 3-0 in the key match between the two after both had beaten minnows Northern Mariana. Macau's 5-1 victory over Northern Mariana was their only win in five matches played in 2012 but as their opponents are not affiliated to FIFA it does not count towards the official record. That was also bad news for Chan Kin Seng whose rare hat trick for the national team does not count either. Second place meant that Macao failed to progress to the main qualifying group later in the year as the team slipped to its lowest ever position of 201 in the FIFA/Coca-Cola World Ranking the following month. The only other matches played by Leung Sui Wing's team during 2012 were in the Philippines Peace Cup, a four-team tournament staged in Manila where Macau managed to move up the rankings thanks to a hard fought draw with Chinese Taipei before suffering two more defeats at the hands of Guam and the hosts. In club football Windsor Arch Ka I were involved in a close tussle with Monte Carlo for the league title before claiming the trophy with a 3-1 victory over Police on the final day.

FIFA WORLD CUP RECORD
1930-1978 DNE 1982-1986 DNQ 1990 DNE 1994-2014 DNQ

MACAU FOOTBALL ASSOCIATION (AFM)

Avenida Wai Leong Taipa, University of Science and Technology, Football Field, Block I, Taipa, Macau
☎ +853 28830287
📠 +853 28830409
✉ macaufa@macau.ctm.net
🖥 www.macaufa.com
FA 1939 CON 1976 FIFA 1976
P Vitor Lup Kwan Cheung
GS Kam Vai Choi

THE STADIA

2014 FIFA World Cup Stadia
Estádio Campo Desportivo
Macau   15 490

Other Main Stadia
Campo Desportivo   1 700
Macau
Campo de Futebol da UTCM
Macau   1 684

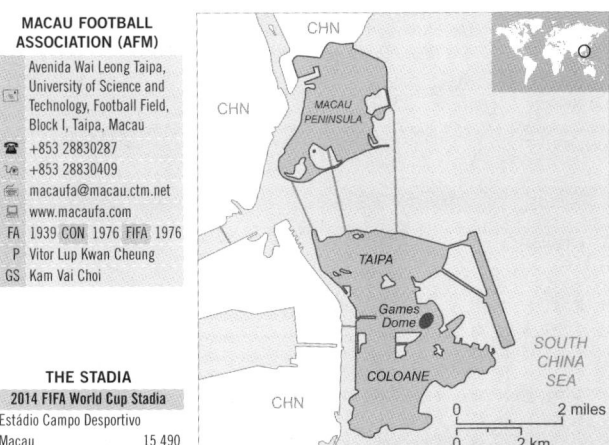

MAJOR CITIES/TOWNS
Population
1 Macau   559 846

AOMEN TEBIE XINGZHENGQU • MACAU SPECIAL ADMINISTRATIVE REGION

Capital Macau	Population 559 846 (167)	% in cities 100%
GDP per capita $30 000 (45)	Area km² 28 km² (235)	GMT +/- +8
Neighbours (km) China 0.3 • Coast 41		

RECENT INTERNATIONAL MATCHES PLAYED BY MACAU

2007	Opponents	Score	Venue	Comp	Scorers	Att	Referee
17-06	Mongolia	D 0-0	Macau	EAq		300	Matsuo JPN
21-06	Korea DPR	L 1-7	Macau	EAq	Chan Kin Seng [46]	300	Wan Daxue CHN
24-06	Chinese Taipei	L 2-7	Macau	EAq	De Sousa [48], Leong Chong In [78]	200	Kim Eui Soo KOR
8-10	Thailand	L 1-6	Bangkok	WCq	Chan Kin Seng [23]	11 254	Chynybekov KGZ
15-10	Thailand	L 1-7	Macau	WCq	Chan Kin Seng [92+]	500	Recho SYR
2008							
25-05	Nepal	L 2-3	Phnom Penh	CCq	Che Chi Man [29p], Chan Kin Seng [59]	2 000	Vo Minh Tri VIE
28-05	Cambodia	L 1-3	Phnom Penh	CCq	Che Chi Man [65]	3 000	Kurbanov TKM
19-11	Hong Kong	L 1-9	Macau	Fr			
2009							
11-03	Northern Mariana Is †	W 6-1	Manenggon Hills	EAq	Chan Kin Seng 2 [13 24], Ho Man Hou 2 [33 90], Leong Chong In [40], Loi Wai Hong [62]		Sato JPN
13-03	Mongolia	L 1-2	Manenggon Hills	EAq	Ho Man Hou [79]		Fan Qi CHN
15-03	Guam	D 2-2	Manenggon Hills	EAq	Chan Kin Seng 2 [10 51]	1 400	Kim Jong Hyeuk KOR
7-04	Mongolia	W 2-0	Macau	CCq	Chan Kin Seng [22], Leong Chong In [24]	500	Perera SRI
14-04	Mongolia	L 1-3	Ulaan-Baatar	CCq	Chan Kin Seng [39]	3 000	Yu Ming Hsun TPE
16-04	Myanmar	L 0-4	Dhaka	CCq		3 600	Mashentsev KGZ
28-04	Cambodia	L 1-2	Dhaka	CCq	Che Chi Man [75]	6 000	Saleem MDV
30-04	Bangladesh	L 0-3	Dhaka	CCq		8 700	Mashentsev KGZ
2010							
9-10	Chinese Taipei	L 1-7	Kaohsiung	Fr	Leong Ka Hang [82]	1 000	
10-10	Hong Kong	L 0-4	Kaohsiung	Fr		1 200	Yu Ming Hsun TPE
12-10	Philippines	L 0-5	Kaohsiung	Fr		700	Yu Ming Hsun TPE
2011							
9-02	Cambodia	L 1-3	Phnom Penh	CCq	Leong Ka Hang [80]	2 000	Win Cho MYA
16-02	Cambodia	W 3-2	Macau	CCq	Vernon Wong [62], Leong Ka Hang [73], Alves Vinicio [75]	100	Perea SRI
29-06	Vietnam	L 0-6	Ho Chi Minh City	WCq		20 000	Mashentsev KGZ
3-07	Vietnam	L 1-7	Macau	WCq	Leong Ka Hang [59]	500	Auda IRQ
30-09	Chinese Taipei	L 0-3	Kaohsiung	Fr			
2-10	Hong Kong	L 1-5	Kaohsiung	Fr	Leong Ka Hang [82]		
4-10	Philippines	L 0-2	Kaohsiung	Fr			
2012							
20-07	Northern Mariana Is †	W 5-1	Yona	EAq	Chan Kin Seng 3 [27 55 59], Ho Man Hou [40], Vernon Wong [62]	150	Iida JPN
22-07	Guam	L 0-3	Yona	EAq		1 000	Iida JPN
25-09	Chinese Taipei	D 2-2	Manila	Fr	Ricardo Torrao [45], Chan Kin Seng [57]		Villagracia PHI
27-09	Philippines	L 0-5	Manila	Fr			Vo Quang Vinh VIE
29-09	Guam	L 0-3	Manila	Fr			Villagracia PHI

Fr = Friendly match • EA = East Asian Championship • AC = AFC Asian Cup • CC = AFC Challenge Cup • WC = FIFA World Cup
q = qualifier • † not an official international

MACAU 2012

CAMPEONATO 1° DIVISAO LIGA DE ELITE

	Pl	W	D	L	F	A	Pts	Ka I	Monte Carlo	Benfica	Porto	Lam Pak	Kuan Tai	Lam Ieng	Policia	U-23	Hong Ngai
Windsor Arch Ka I	18	14	3	1	59	12	45		0-0	2-1	2-2	2-0	5-1	3-0	3-1	4-1	6-0
Monte Carlo	18	13	4	1	45	18	43	1-0		2-1	2-1	3-3	3-1	4-3	2-2	3-0	2-1
Benfica de Macau	18	11	2	5	35	15	35	1-3	1-3		2-1	3-0	2-0	0-0	3-1	2-0	5-0
FC Porto de Macau	18	9	3	6	36	21	30	1-2	2-0	0-3		1-0	1-0	2-1	2-0	3-0	4-1
Lam Pak	18	8	4	6	41	32	28	0-1	1-1	1-0	3-3		1-2	3-1	2-0	2-1	6-0
Kuan Tai	18	8	2	8	32	32	26	1-1	0-3	2-4	2-0	2-3		1-0	2-0	4-2	4-1
Lam Ieng	18	5	3	10	30	39	18	1-3	1-4	0-3	0-0	9-7	1-2		2-2	2-1	4-1
Policia	18	5	2	11	17	30	17	1-6	0-1	0-1	3-0	0-3	2-1	1-0		3-0	2-0
Macau U-23	18	4	3	11	25	40	15	0-6	1-2	0-0	2-1	2-2	3-3	2-3	1-0		4-0
Hong Ngai	18	0	0	18	5	86	0	0-10	0-8	0-3	0-11	1-4	0-4	0-2	0-2	0-5	

6/01/2012 - 10/06/2012

MAD – MADAGASCAR

FIFA/COCA-COLA WORLD RANKING

'93	'94	'95	'96	'97	'98	'99	'00	'01	'02	'03	'04	'05	'06	'07	'08	'09	'10	'11	'12
89	111	132	140	163	150	134	114	122	101	118	147	149	184	149	135	158	155	160	179

| 2012 ||||||||||||| High | Low | Av |
Jan	Feb	Mar	Apr	May	Jun	Jul	Aug	Sep	Oct	Nov	Dec				
160	158	163	166	166	163	167	165	163	171	173	179		81	188	137

Madagascar continued a disappointing drop down the FIFA/Coca-Cola World Ranking after playing just two internationals in 2012 and losing both. They finished the year just shy of their all-time low in 179th place. A 7-1 aggregate defeat at the hands of the Cape Verde Islands in the first round of the 2013 Africa Cup of Nations qualifiers represented a major setback, notably a record 4-0 home loss to the islanders from the other side of the African continent. There was also a heavy defeat for Japan's Acteul in the first round of the CAF Champions League against Power Dynamos of Zimbabwe, where they were eliminated 8-1 on aggregate. But Tana FC proved more competitive in the CAF Confederation Cup, where they lost only on post-match penalties to InterClube of Angola in the second round. AS Adema won a third championship in the last decade by edging Tana FC in the 2012 championship play-offs. Adema's success provided some compensation for coach Auguste Raux, who had been in charge of the national team's debacle against the Cape Verde. TCO Boeny from Mahajanga denied Adama a double when they won the cup thanks to an early goal in the final from Toky after taking advantage of a defensive mix-up. It was the first trophy for a club from the city of Mahajanga since Sotema won championship in back in 1992.

CAF AFRICA CUP OF NATIONS RECORD

1957-1970 DNE 1972-1974 DNQ 1976-1978 DNE 1980-1988 DNQ 1990 DNE 1992 DNQ 1994 DNE 1996 Withdrew 1998 DNE 2000-2013 DNQ

FEDERATION MALAGASY DE FOOTBALL (FMF)

26 rue de Russie, Isoraka,
PO Box 4409,
101 Antananarivo
☎ +261 20 2268374
+261 20 2268373
fmf@blueline.mg

FA 1961 CON 1963 FIFA 1964
P Ahmad
GS Stanislas Rakotomalala

THE STADIA

2014 FIFA World Cup Stadia
Stade Municipal de Mahamasina
Antananarivo 22 000

Other Main Stadia
Stade Barikadimy
Toamasina 20 000
Stade Olympique d'Emyrne
Antananarivo 15 000
Stade Rabemananjara
Mahajanga 10 000
Stade Municipal Maitre Kira
Toliara 5 000

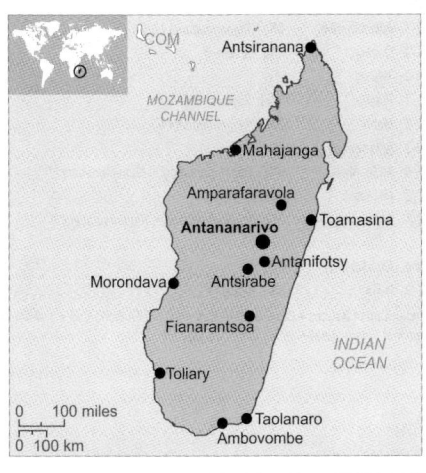

MAJOR CITIES/TOWNS

		Population
1	Antananarivo	1 612 632
2	Toamasina	219 669
3	Antsirabé	192 499
4	Fianarantsoa	179 302
5	Mahajanga	162 807
6	Toliary	120 790
7	Antsiranana	86 421
8	Antanifotsy	75 485
9	Ambovombe	70 740
10	Amparafaravola	55 578
11	Taolanaro	47 791
12	Ambatondrazaka	46 532
13	Mananara	44 455
14	Soavinandriana	43 237
15	Mahanoro	43 021
16	Soanierana Ivongo	42 364
17	Faratsiho	40 148
18	Vavatenina	39 824
19	Morondava	38 963

REPUBLIQUE DE MADAGASCAR • REPUBLIC OF MADAGASCAR

Capital	Antananarivo	Population	20 653 556 (55)	% in cities	29%
GDP per capita	$1000 (212)	Area km²	587 041 km² (46)	GMT +/-	+3
Neighbours (km)	Coast 4828				

RECENT INTERNATIONAL MATCHES PLAYED BY MADAGASCAR

2006	Opponents	Score	Venue	Comp	Scorers	Att	Referee
2-09	Gabon	L 0-4	Libreville	CNq			Diatta SEN
2007							
25-03	Côte d'Ivoire	L 0-3	Antananarivo	CNq			Maillet SEY
28-04	Zimbabwe	L 0-1	Maputo	CCr1			Faduco MOZ
29-04	Seychelles	W 5-0	Maputo	CCr1	Voavy 3 [11 14 69], Ramiadamanana [62], Andriatsima [84]		Mpopo LES
3-06	Côte d'Ivoire	L 0-5	Bouaké	CNq			Louzaya CGO
17-06	Gabon	L 0-2	Antananarivo	CNq			Mlangeni SWZ
29-07	Congo DR	D 0-0	Antananarivo	Fr			
14-08	Comoros	W 3-0	Antananarivo	Fr	Voavy 2 [70 89], Ramiadamanana 90		
14-10	Comoros	W 6-2	Antananarivo	WCq	Andriatsima 4 [30 40 49p 57], Rakotomandimby [65], Tsaralaza [79]	7 754	Kaoma ZAM
17-11	Comoros	W 4-0	Moroni	WCq	Nomenjanahary 2 [37 51], Rakotomandimby [61], Robson [73]	1 610	Damon RSA
2008							
9-03	Mauritius	W 2-1	Curepipe	Fr	Rabemananjara 2 [77 81]		
31-05	Botswana	D 0-0	Gaborone	WCq		11 087	Kaoma ZAM
8-06	Côte d'Ivoire	D 0-0	Antananarivo	WCq			Labrosse SEY
15-06	Mozambique	D 1-1	Antananarivo	WCq	Mamihasindrahona [91p]	15 501	Ebrahim RSA
22-06	Mozambique	L 0-3	Maputo	WCq		20 000	Maillet SEY
19-07	Swaziland	D 1-1	Witbank	CCr1	Robson [65]		Nhlapo RSA
21-07	Seychelles	D 1-1	Witbank	CCr1	Rabenandrasana [23]		Kaoma ZAM
23-07	Mauritius	W 2-1	Witbank	CCr1	Rabenandrasana [52], Rabemananjara [63]		Marange ZIM
30-07	Mozambique	L 1-2	Thulamahashe	CCsf	Rabemananjara		Marange ZIM
3-08	Zambia	L 0-2	Thulamahashe	CC3p			
7-09	Botswana	W 1-0	Antananarivo	WCq	Rabemananjara [24]	20 000	Seechurn MRI
11-10	Côte d'Ivoire	L 0-3	Abidjan	WCq		24 000	Benouza ALG
2009							
19-09	South Africa	L 0-1	Kimberley	Fr			
2010							
29-08	Comoros	W 1-0	Mahajanga	Fr			
5-09	Nigeria	L 0-2	Calabar	CNq			Jedidi TUN
10-10	Ethiopia	L 0-1	Antananarivo	CNq			Ngosi MWI
2011							
27-03	Guinea	D 1-1	Antananarivo	CNq	Rajoarimanana [17]		
5-06	Guinea	L 1-4	Conakry	CNq	Arsene [24]		
17-07	Iran	L 0-1	Tehran	Fr			
4-08	Mayotte †	D 1-1	Praslin	IOGr1	Rajoarimanana [36]	1 800	Camille SEY
6-08	Reunion †	L 1-2	Mahe	IOGr1	Rajoarimanana [22]	1 000	Seechurn MRI
4-09	Nigeria	L 0-2	Antananarivo	CNq			
8-10	Ethiopia	L 2-4	Addis Abeba	CNq	Razafimandimby [3], Nomenjanahary [57]		
11-11	Equatorial Guinea	L 0-2	Malabo	WCq		10 000	Otogo-Castane GAB
15-11	Equatorial Guinea	W 2-1	Antananarivo	WCq	Rajoarimanana [54], Ramanamahefa [90]	5 000	Nunkoo MRI
2012							
29-02	Cape Verde Islands	L 0-4	Antananarivo	CNq			Sikazwe ZAM
16-06	Cape Verde Islands	L 1-3	Praia	CNq	Voavy [83]		

Fr = Friendly match • CN = CAF African Cup of Nations • CC = COSAFA Cup • WC = FIFA World Cup • † Not a full international
q = qualifier • r1 = first round group • sf = semi-final • 3p = third place play-off

MADAGASCAR 2012 THB CHAMPIONS LEAGUE FIRST STAGE

Group A - Ambanja	Pl	W	D	L	F	A	Pts
COSFA Analamanga ‡	5	4	0/1	0	6	0	13
TCO Boeny ‡	5	1	4/0	0	3	2	11
FC Amazone ‡	5	2	1/0	2	5	3	8
FC Maeva	4	1	0/1	2	1	3	4
FC Motul Bealanana	4	1	0/1	2	2	6	4
JSA Antalaha	5	0	0/2	3	0	3	2

Group B - Toamasina	Pl	W	D	L	F	A	Pts
Tana FC ‡	5	5	0/0	0	7	1	15
CNaPS Sport Itasy ‡	5	3	1/0	1	9	2	11
Toamasina FC ‡	5	2	1/1	1	3	1	9
Voromaherin Alaotra	5	2	0/1	2	6	3	7
Andry Tsiroanomandidy	5	1	0/0	4	2	9	3
Hery Fenerive	5	0	0/0	5	2	13	0

Group C - Antsirabe	Pl	W	D	L	F	A	Pts
Adema Antananarivo ‡	4	4	0/0	0	14	2	12
FC Jirama ‡	4	3	0/0	1	15	2	9
FC Vakinankaratra ‡	4	2	0/0	2	1	5	6
Sporting Miandrivazo	4	1	0/0	3	5	15	3
FC Zanaboay	4	0	0/0	4	2	13	0
AJSM Maintirano				Withdrew			

Group D - Manakara	Pl	W	D	L	F	A	Pts
Tiavo Tem ‡	5	3	0/0	1	9	3	9
AS Comato ‡	5	3	0/0	1	11	5	9
FC2A Amboasary ‡	5	2	0/1	1	2	3	7
FCA Ilakaka	5	0	1/0	2	3	5	2
TMT Vangaindrano	5	0	0/0	3	0	9	0
Espoir Ambovombe				Withdrew			

10/08/2012 - 19/08/2012 • ‡ Qualified for the second stage

MADAGASCAR 2012 THB CHAMPIONS LEAGUE SECOND STAGE

Group A - Fianarantsoa	Pl	W	D	L	F	A	Pts
Adema Antananarivo ‡	5	3	1/1	0	7	1	12
CNaPS Sport Itasy ‡	5	3	1/1	0	9	3	12
Tiavo Tem	5	2	1/0	2	7	5	8
Toamasina FC	5	1	1/1	2	5	5	6
FC Vakinankaratra	5	1	1/1	2	3	5	6
FC Amazone	5	0	0/1	4	1	13	1

Group B - Mahajanga	Pl	W	D	L	F	A	Pts
Tana FC ‡	5	4	1/0	0	17	3	14
COSFA Analamanga ‡	5	4	0/0	1	10	4	12
TCO Boeny	5	1	1/2	1	3	3	7
FC2A Amboasary	5	1	1/0	3	4	11	5
FC Jirama	5	1	0/2	2	8	14	5
AS Comato	5	0	1/0	4	3	10	2

14/09/2012 - 23/09/2012 • ‡ Qualified for the final stage

MADAGASCAR 2012 THB CHAMPIONS LEAGUE FINAL STAGE (POULE DES AS)

Final Stage	Pl	W	D	L	F	A	Pts	Ad	Ta	CSI	CA
Adema Antananarivo †	3	3	2	1	7	5	11		2-1	1-1	1-0
Tana FC	3	3	1	2	9	9	10	2-1		2-1	0-3
CNaPS Sport Itasy	3	1	3	2	4	5	6	0-1	1-1		0-0
COSFA Analamanga	3	1	2	3	5	6	5	1-1	1-3	0-1	

10/10/2012 - 18/11/2012 • † Qualified for the CAF Champions League
Matches in bold played in Mahajanga. All other matches in Antananarivo

TELMA COUPE DE MADAGASCAR 2012

Round of 16		Quarter-finals		Semi-finals		Final	
TCO Boeny	4						
FC Varatraza	2	**TCO Boeny**	1				
COSFA Analamanga	0	FC Tiavo Vatovavy	0	**TCO Boeny**	0 6p		
FC Tiavo	1			CNaPS Sport Itasy	0 5p		
Voromahery Alaotra	2						
FC Toamasina	0	Voromahery Alaotra	0				
JSMS Diana	1	**CNaPS Sport Itasy**	1			**TCO Boeny** ‡	1
CNaPS Sport Itasy	9					Adema Antananarivo	0
Tana FC	3						
3FB Ambatondrazaka	0	**Tana FC**	2			CUP FINAL	
AS Comato	0	FC Real V7V	1	Tana FC	0	Stade Alexandre Rabemananjara,	
FC Real V7V	3			**Adema Antananarivo**	2	25-11-2012	
FCE Atsinanana	2					Scorer - Toky 12 for TCO	
IFC Analamanga	1	FCE Atsinanana	2 6p				
United Vakinankaratra	0	**Adema Antananarivo**	2 7p				
Adema Antananarivo	2			‡ Qualified for the CAF Confederation Cup			

MAR – MOROCCO

FIFA/COCA-COLA WORLD RANKING

'93	'94	'95	'96	'97	'98	'99	'00	'01	'02	'03	'04	'05	'06	'07	'08	'09	'10	'11	'12
30	33	38	27	15	13	24	28	36	35	38	33	36	39	39	41	67	79	61	74

2012

Jan	Feb	Mar	Apr	May	Jun	Jul	Aug	Sep	Oct	Nov	Dec	High	Low	Av
61	62	61	62	60	70	71	68	68	75	72	74	10	95	38

Morocco drew all three matches at the 2013 Africa Cup of Nations in South Africa to exit at the group stage yet again. Not since the 2004 tournament, when they reached the final, has the team made it through to the knock-out stage. New coach Rachid Taoussi had made a number of changes after taking over from Eric Gerets in September and it was a squad of some promise on paper. However, as had been the case at the 2012 Nations Cup finals, they failed to deliver on the pitch after letting a lead over their hosts slip in the decisive group game. Under Gerets, the Moroccans had made a poor start in the 2014 FIFA World Cup qualifiers after he had predicted his team, boosted by a plethora of French-born players, would have a credible chance of going to Brazil. They drew away at tiny Gambia and then at home to Cote d'Ivoire in June to leave their chances hanging by a thread. In club football the 2012 championship went down to the wire with a winner-takes-all tie between the top two on the last day of the season. Maghreb Tetouan travelled to Rabat with a one point lead over their hosts FUS and secured a first-ever championship thanks to a Abdelkarim Benhania goal in a 1-0 victory. Six months later Raja Casablanca completed a frustrating year for clubs from the capital when they beat FAR Rabat in the cup final on penalties.

CAF AFRICA CUP OF NATIONS RECORD

1957-1962 DNQ 1963 DNQ 1965-1968 DNE 1970 DNQ **1972** 5 r1 1974 DNE **1976** 1 Winners **1978** 6 r1
1980 SF 3 (hosts) 1982-1984 DNQ **1986** 4 SF **1988** 4 SF 1990 DNQ **1992** 9 r1 1994-1996 DNQ **1998** 7 QF
2000 9 r1 **2002** 9 r1 **2004** 2 F **2006** 13 r1 **2008** 11 r1 2010 DNQ **2012** 12 r1 **2013** 10 r1 **2015** Qualified (hosts)

FEDERATION ROYALE MAROCAINE DE FOOTBALL (FRMF)

51 Bis, Avenue Ibn Sina,
Agdal, Case Postale 51,
10 000 Rabat
☎ +212 537 672706
📠 +212 537 671070
✉ contact@frmf.ma
🌐 www.frmf.ma
FA 1955 CON 1966 FIFA 1960
P Ali Fassi Fihri
GS Tarik Najem

THE STADIA

2014 FIFA World Cup Stadia
Stade de Marrakech
Marrakesh　　　　　45 240
Other Main Stadia
Stade Mohammed V
Casablanca　　　　　67 000
Stade Moulay Abdellah
Rabat　　　　　52 000
Complexe Sportif de Fès
Fès　　　　　45 000

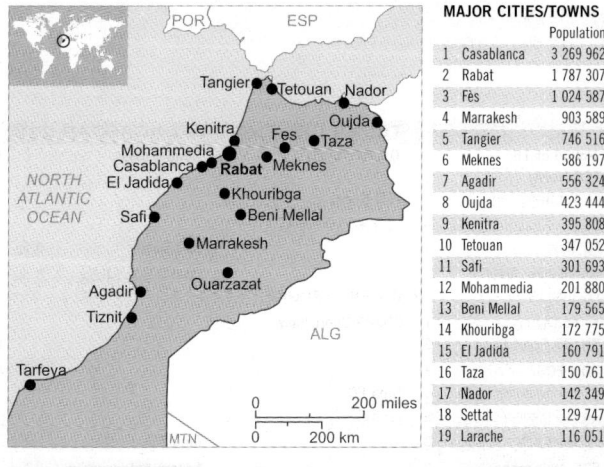

MAJOR CITIES/TOWNS

		Population
1	Casablanca	3 269 962
2	Rabat	1 787 307
3	Fès	1 024 587
4	Marrakesh	903 589
5	Tangier	746 516
6	Meknes	586 197
7	Agadir	556 324
8	Oujda	423 444
9	Kenitra	395 808
10	Tetouan	347 052
11	Safi	301 693
12	Mohammedia	201 880
13	Beni Mellal	179 565
14	Khouribga	172 775
15	El Jadida	160 791
16	Taza	150 761
17	Nador	142 349
18	Settat	129 747
19	Larache	116 051

AL MAMLAKAH AL MAGHRIBIYAH • KINGDOM OF MOROCCO

Capital Rabat	Population 34 859 364 (35)	% in cities 56%
GDP per capita $4500 (148)	Area km^2 446 550 km^2 (57)	GMT +/- 0
Neighbours (km) Algeria 1559, Western Sahara 443, Spain 16 • Coast 1835		

RECENT INTERNATIONAL MATCHES PLAYED BY MOROCCO

2011	Opponents		Score	Venue	Comp	Scorers	Att	Referee
9-02	Niger	W	3-0	Marrakech	Fr	Moubarek Boussoufa 2 [16 82p], El Bakkali [91+]		Ilboudo BFA
27-03	Algeria	L	0-1	Annaba	CNq			Seechurn MRI
4-06	Algeria	W	4-0	Marrakech	CNq	Mehdi Benatia [27], Marouane Chamakh [39], Youssef Hadji [60], Oussama Assaidi [69]		Doue CIV
10-08	Senegal	W	2-0	Dakar	Fr	Houssine Kharja [10], Youssef El Arabi [25]		Gassama GAM
4-09	Central African Rep	D	0-0	Bangui	CNq			Jedidi TUN
9-10	Tanzania	W	3-1	Marrakech	CNq	Marouane Chamakh [20], Adel Taarabt [69], Moubarek Boussoufa [89]	38 000	Gassama GAM
11-11	Uganda	L	0-1	Marrakech	Fr			Keita GUI
13-11	Cameroon	D	1-1	Marrakech	Fr	Nordin Amrabat [90]. L 2-4p	20 000	
2012								
23-01	Tunisia	L	1-2	Libreville	CNr1	Houssine Kharja [86]	18 000	Bennett RSA
27-01	Gabon	L	2-3	Libreville	CNr1	Houssine Kharja 2 [24 90p]	22 000	Doue CIV
31-01	Niger	W	1-0	Libreville	CNr1	Younes Belhanda [78]	4 000	Nampiandraza MAD
29-02	Burkina Faso	W	2-0	Marrakech	Fr	Moubarek Boussoufa [18], Youssef El Arabi [64]		Lemghaifry MTN
25-05	Senegal	L	0-1	Marrakech	Fr			Jaouadi TUN
2-06	Gambia	D	1-1	Bakau	WCq	Houssine Kharja [76]	15 000	Alioum CMR
9-06	Côte d'Ivoire	D	2-2	Marrakech	WCq	Houssine Kharja [42], Hamza Abourazzouk [89]	36 000	Grisha EGY
23-06	Bahrain	W	4-0	Jeddah	ARr1	Brahim El Bahri [17], Yassine Salhi [78], OG [83], Abdessalam Benjelloun [90]		Albalooshi QAT
26-06	Libya †	D	0-0	Jeddah	ARr1			Haimoudi ALG
29-06	Yemen	W	4-0	Jeddah	ARr1	Yassine Salhi 4 [10p 48 58 63p]		Al Amri KSA
3-07	Iraq	W	2-1	Jeddah	ARsf	Oussama El Gharib [23], Yassine Salhi [78]		Haimoudi ALG
6-07	Libya †	D	1-1	Jeddah	ARf	Brahim El Bahri [5]. W 3-1p		Jedidi TUN
15-08	Guinea	L	1-2	Rabat	Fr	Yassine Salhi [92+]		Diatta SEN
9-09	Mozambique	L	0-2	Maputo	CNq			Kirwa KEN
13-10	Mozambique	W	4-0	Marrakech	CNq	Abdel Barrada [38], Houssine Kharja [64p], Youssef El Arabi [85], Nordin Amrabat [93+]		Alioum CMR
14-11	Togo	L	0-1	Casablanca	Fr			
2013								
8-01	Zambia	D	0-0	Johannesburg	Fr			Gomes RSA
12-01	Namibia	W	2-1	Johannesburg	Fr	Mounir El Hamdaoui [2], Youssef Kaddioui [80]		
19-01	Angola	D	0-0	Johannesburg	CNr1		4 600	Diatta SEN
23-01	Cape Verde Islands	D	1-1	Durban	CNr1	Youssef El Arabi [78]	15 470	Sikazwe ZAM
27-01	South Africa	D	2-2	Durban	CNr1	Issam El Adoua [10], Abdelilha Hafidi [82]	45 000	Gassama GAM

Fr = Friendly match • CN = CAF Africa Cup of Nations • AR = Arab Championship • WC = FIFA World Cup
q = qualifier • r1 = first round group • qf = quarter-final • sf = semi-final • f = final

MOROCCO NATIONAL TEAM HISTORICAL RECORDS

Gl Cp
115 - Noureddine Naybet 1990-2006
42 - Ahmed Faras 1965-79

Coaches
For Morocco coaches pre 1990 see Oliver's Almanack 2012 • Werner Olk GER 1990-92 • Abdelkhalek Louzani 1992 • Abdellah Ajri Blinda 1993-94 • Mohammed Lamari 1994 • Gilson Nunez BRA 1995 • Henri Michel FRA 1995-2000 • Henryk Kasperczak POL 2000 • Mustapha Madih 2001 • Humberto Coelho POR 2002 • Badou Zaki 2002-05 • Philippe Troussier FRA 2005 • Mohamed Fakhir 2005-07 • Henri Michel FRA 2007-08 • Roger Lemerre FRA 2008-09 • Hassan Moumen 2009-10 • Eric Gerets BEL 2010-12 • Rachid Taoussi 2012-

MOROCCO SQUAD FOR THE 2012 CAF AFRICA CUP OF NATIONS

	Player		Ap	G	Club	Date of Birth		Player		Ap	G	Club	Date of Birth
1	Nadir Lamyaghri	GK	2		Wydad	13 02 1976	12	Mohamed Amsif	GK	1		Augsburg GER	7 02 1989
2	Michael Chretien	DF	2		Bursaspor TUR	10 07 1984	13	Houssine Kharja (c)	MF	3	3	Fiorentina ITA	9 11 1982
3	Badr El Kaddouri	DF	3		Celtic SCO	31 01 1981	14	Mbark Boussoufa	MF	2		Anzhi RUS	15 08 1984
4	Ahmed Kantari	DF	2		Brest FRA	28 06 1985	15	Abdelhamid El Kaoutari	DF	1		Montpellier FRA	17 03 1990
5	Mehdi Benatia	DF	2		Udinese ITA	17 04 1987	16	Jamal Alioui	DF	1+1		Al Khritiyat QAT	2 06 1982
6	Adil Hermach	MF	1+1		Al Hilal KSA	27 06 1986	17	Marouane Chamakh	FW	2		Arsenal ENG	10 01 1984
7	Adel Taarabt	MF	0+2		QPR ENG	24 05 1989	18	Abdelfettah Boukhriss	DF	1		FUS Rabat	22 10 1986
8	Karim El Ahmadi	MF	1		Feyenoord NED	27 01 1985	19	Mehdi Carcela	MF	1+1		Anzhi RUS	1 07 1989
9	Youssef El Arabi	FW	1+1		Al Hilal KSA	3 02 1987	20	Youssouf Hadji	FW	2+1		Rennes FRA	25 02 1980
10	Younes Belhanda	MF	3	1	Montpellier FRA	25 02 1990	21	Nordin Amrabat	MF	1+2		Kayserispor TUR	31 03 1987
11	Oussama Assaidi	MF	1		Heerenveen NED	15 08 1988	22	Issam Badda	GK	0		FUS Rabat	10 05 1983
							23	Mustapha Lamrani	DF	1		MAS Fès	2 03 1980

Tr: Eric Gerets BEL 18-05-1954

MOROCCO 2011-12

CHAMPIONNAT DU GNF1

	Pl	W	D	L	F	A	Pts	MAT	FUS	WAC	RCA	DHJ	MAS	FAR	OCS	OCK	CODM	KAC	HUSA	CRH	WAF	JSM	IZK
MA Tétouan †	30	17	10	3	41	13	61		0-0	2-0	1-2	3-0	1-0	3-0	3-1	2-0	1-0	0-0	2-2	1-1	2-0	1-0	2-0
FUS Rabat †	30	16	9	5	32	16	57	0-1		0-0	2-0	1-0	2-1	0-0	1-2	1-0	2-1	2-1	1-0	1-0	2-1	2-0	3-0
Wydad Casablanca ‡	30	13	12	5	32	18	51	1-0	2-0		0-0	0-1	1-1	2-0	2-1	3-0	1-0	1-1	3-1	1-0	2-2	2-0	2-0
Raja Casablanca	30	14	9	7	34	24	51	0-2	1-0	0-1		2-1	1-1	3-1	2-1	2-1	1-0	5-2	2-0	0-0	2-0	1-0	1-0
Difaa El Jadida	30	13	9	8	32	24	48	0-1	1-1	1-0	3-1		2-0	2-1	2-1	1-0	2-1	0-0	0-1	1-1	3-0	0-1	1-0
Maghreb Fès	30	10	11	9	35	26	41	1-1	1-1	1-1	1-1	1-0		2-1	5-1	1-2	0-0	3-0	2-0	1-0	0-0	0-1	1-2
FAR Rabat	30	10	11	9	32	29	41	0-1	1-2	2-2	0-0	2-3	2-1		2-1	1-1	1-0	3-1	2-0	0-0	1-0	3-1	0-1
Olympique Safi	30	9	9	12	34	43	36	0-0	0-0	2-1	2-1	3-3	0-2	1-1		0-2	2-0	1-1	0-0	1-0	2-0	2-2	2-0
Olympique Khouribga	30	8	11	11	27	32	35	1-3	0-2	1-1	1-1	0-2	1-1	1-1	1-1		2-1	0-1	0-1	2-1	0-1	2-0	0-0
COD Meknès	30	10	6	14	19	26	36	0-0	1-0	0-0	0-1	1-1	0-3	0-0	1-0	1-1		1-0	1-0	2-1	1-0	2-1	2-1
Kénitra AC	30	7	14	9	29	40	35	1-1	1-1	1-1	1-0	2-2	1-1	0-3	2-1	2-4	1-0		0-1	1-1	2-1	1-1	1-0
HUS Agadir	30	8	11	11	22	31	35	0-0	1-2	1-0	0-0	0-0	2-1	0-0	1-1	0-0	0-1	2-2		0-0	3-0	1-1	1-0
CR Hoceima	30	8	9	13	31	27	33	3-1	0-0	0-0	0-0	2-1	1-2	0-2	5-1	0-2	1-0	0-1	5-0		4-0	1-0	3-1
Wydad Fès	30	7	9	14	26	39	30	0-0	0-1	0-1	2-0	0-1	0-1	1-1	3-1	1-1	1-0	1-1	3-2	2-1		3-0	1-1
JS Massira	30	7	7	16	24	42	28	0-3	0-2	0-0	1-4	0-0	1-0	0-1	0-1	0-0	1-0	1-2	3-1	2-1	2-0		3-2
IZ Khemisset	30	5	9	16	12	32	24	0-3	0-0	0-1	0-0	1-1	0-0	0-0	0-2	0-1	1-0	0-1	0-1	1-0	0-0	1-0	

19/08/2011 - 28/05/2012 • † Qualified for the CAF Champions League • ‡ Qualified for the CAF Confederation Cup
Top scorers: **17** - Karl Max **DANY** CHA, Difaa • **15** - Abderrazak **HAMDALLAH**, Olympique Safi & Aziz **JOUNAID**, FAR Rabat

MOROCCO 2011-12

CHAMPIONNAT DU GNF2 (2)

	Pl	W	D	L	F	A	Pts	RBM	RSB	TAS	USM	KACM	ASS	USMAM	RAC	CAYB	MCO	CKT	IRT	RB	UST	CCH	SM
Raja Beni Mellal	30	12	12	6	25	15	48		1-0	1-2	3-0	1-0	0-0	2-0	0-0	2-0	1-0	0-1	0-0	2-0	0-1	0-0	0-0
RS Berkane	30	13	8	9	29	27	47	1-1		1-0	0-2	1-0	1-0	0-2	0-0	1-1	2-0	1-0	1-0	1-1	1-0	0-0	1-0
TAS Casablanca	30	11	15	4	32	27	46	3-1	1-0		0-3	0-2	3-1	1-1	2-2	1-1	2-2	1-0	2-1	2-1	1-1	1-0	1-0
US Mohammedia	30	11	10	9	38	27	43	0-0	3-1	1-1		1-1	0-0	0-1	2-0	2-1	0-0	3-0	2-0	1-0	0-0	3-1	5-0
Kawkab Marrakech	30	10	12	8	29	19	42	0-1	1-1	0-0	3-2		1-0	6-0	1-1	1-1	2-0	2-1	0-0	4-0	0-0	1-0	2-1
AS Salé	30	9	14	7	32	24	41	1-1	3-1	0-0	2-0	0-0		1-1	1-1	3-0	3-2	0-1	0-1	5-3	0-1	1-0	0-0
Union Aït Melloul	30	10	10	10	37	40	40	0-1	2-0	2-2	2-2	1-0	0-1		1-1	3-0	2-0	3-1	1-0	1-1	1-0	2-3	1-1
Racing Casablanca	30	8	15	7	27	24	39	0-1	1-2	2-2	1-0	0-1	0-0	4-1		2-2	1-0	1-0	1-1	1-1	0-0	1-0	2-0
CAY Berrechid	30	9	12	9	33	34	39	0-1	2-3	0-0	2-0	1-0	2-1	2-1	0-0		2-0	0-0	4-1	2-1	1-0	3-3	0-0
Mouloudia Oujda	30	10	9	11	26	31	39	1-0	1-1	0-0	0-1	0-0	0-2	2-1	1-3	2-1		1-0	1-1	1-2	0-2	2-1	1-0
Chabab Kasba Tadla	30	8	11	11	22	27	35	0-0	0-1	1-2	0-0	0-0	0-0	2-3	2-0	2-1	0-0		1-1	0-0	1-1	2-2	2-1
IR Tanger	30	6	16	8	21	26	34	1-1	0-3	0-0	2-1	2-0	1-1	3-1	0-0	0-0	1-1	1-2		1-1	1-0	0-0	0-1
Rachad Bernoussi	30	6	15	9	26	33	33	1-1	2-1	1-1	1-1	2-0	2-2	1-0	1-2	2-1	0-0	0-0	0-1		1-0	0-0	2-1
TUS Temara	30	5	17	8	15	20	32	1-0	1-1	0-0	0-1	0-0	1-3	2-1	0-0	0-0	1-0	1-1	0-0	0-0		1-1	2-2
Chabab Houara	30	6	13	11	22	32	31	2-2	0-2	0-0	2-1	1-1	1-1	1-1	0-1	1-0	0-1	1-0	1-2	0-0	1-0	0-0	2-1
Stade Marocain	30	6	11	13	26	34	29	0-1	2-0	0-1	2-2	1-0	0-1	1-1	1-0	2-2	2-3	2-0	1-1	0-0	1-1	3-0	

17/09/2011 - 27/05/2012

MEDALS TABLE

			Overall			League			Cup			Africa		
			G	S	B	G	S	B	G	S	B	G	S	B
1	FAR Rabat	FAR	25	12	7	**12**	5	5	**11**	5		2	2	2
2	Wydad Casablanca	WAC	23	15	11	**12**	7	9	9	6		2	2	2
3	Raja Casablanca	RCA	21	12	10	10	7	9	7	4		4	1	1
4	Kawkab Marrakech	KACM	9	8	3	2	6	3	6	2		1		
5	Maghreb Fès	MAS	8	11	2	4	3	2	3	8		1		
6	FUS Rabat	FUS	6	5	1		3	1	5	2		1		
7	KAC Kénitra	KAC	5	5	1	4	2	1	1	3				
8	Mouloudia Oujda	MCO	5	2	3	1	1	3	4	1				
9	Olympic Casablanca	OC	3	1		1	1		2					
10	Olympique Khouribga	OCK	2	6	3	1	2	3	1	4				
11	Rennaisance Settat	RSS	2	5	3	1	2	3	1	3				
12	Chabab Mohammedia	SCCM	2	2	1	1		1	1	2				
	COD Meknès	CODM	2	2	1		1	1	1	2				
14	Hassania Agadir	HUSA	2	2		2				2				
15	Racing Casablanca	RAC	1	2			2		1					
16	Maghreb Tetouan	MAT	1		1	1					1			

COUPE DU TRONE 2012

Second Round

Raja Casablanca	2			
Olympique Safi	0			
CAY Berrechid	1			
HUS Agadir	2			
Wydad Fès	1 4p			
Chabab Mrirt	1 3p			
Rapide Oued Zem	0			
Kawkab Marrakech	5			
Raja Beni Mellal	2			
JS Massira	1			
US Mohammedia	0			
Maghreb Fès	1			
Olympique Khouribga	2			
Renaissance Zmamra	1			
Chabab Mohammedia	1			
Wydad Casablanca	3			
AS Salé	6			
USK Sidi Kacem	0			
Maghreb Tetouan	2			
CA Khenifra	3			
Amal Souk Sebt	1			
Difaa El Jadida	0			
FUS Rabat	1			
Mouloudia Oujda	3			
CR Hoceima	1 5p			
Kasr Lakbir	1 3p			
Kénitra AC	1			
COD Meknès	0			
TAS Casablanca	3			
Rachad Bernoussi	0			
IZ Khemisset	0			
FAR Rabat	2			

Round of 16

Raja Casablanca *	2
HUS Agadir	1
Wydad Fès *	1 2p
Kawkab Marrakech	1 4p
Raja Beni Mellal *	2
Maghreb Fès	1
Olympique Khouribga *	0
Wydad Casablanca	1
AS Salé *	0 3p
CA Khenifra	0 1p
Amal Souk Sebt	0
Mouloudia Oujda *	1
CR Hoceima *	1
COD Meknès	0
TAS Casablanca *	2
FAR Rabat	3

Quarter-finals

Raja Casablanca	1
Kawkab Marrakech *	0
Raja Beni Mellal *	0
Wydad Casablanca	1
AS Salé *	1
Mouloudia Oujda	0
CR Hoceima *	1
FAR Rabat	2

Semi-finals

Raja Casablanca ‡‡	3
Wydad Casablanca	1
AS Salé	2 3p
FAR Rabat ‡‡	2 4p

Final

Raja Casablanca	0 5p
FAR Rabat ‡	0 4p

CUP FINAL

Moulay Abdallah, Rabat
18-11-2012, Att: 60 000
Raja - Khalid Al Askari - Rachid Soulaimani, Amine Erbati, Adil El Kerrouchi; Mohamed Oulhaj, Vivian Mabidi, Koko Kodji, Adil Echadli (Chems-Eddine Chtibi 65), Abdelilah El Hafidi (Hamza Bourazzouk 105), Mohcine Metouali, Mohcine Yajour (Yassine Salhi 70). Tr: Mohamed Fakhir
FAR - Ali Aït Lguerrouni - Younes Hammal, Hicham El Fatihi, Yassine El Kourdi, Mohamed Saïdi, Abderrahim Chakir, Youssef El Kaddioui, Salaheddin Akkal (Adil El Meskini 78), Mohammed Amine Bekkali, Moustapha Lemrani, Ayoub Bourhim (Mehdi Neghmi 90). Tr: Rachid Taoussi

†† Played in Rabat • ‡‡ Played in Casablanca • * Home team • ‡ Qualified for the CAF Confederation Cup

MAS – MALAYSIA

FIFA/COCA-COLA WORLD RANKING

'93	'94	'95	'96	'97	'98	'99	'00	'01	'02	'03	'04	'05	'06	'07	'08	'09	'10	'11	'12
79	89	106	96	87	113	117	107	111	128	116	120	123	152	159	156	160	144	148	158

2012

Jan	Feb	Mar	Apr	May	Jun	Jul	Aug	Sep	Oct	Nov	Dec	High	Low	Av
148	150	152	156	153	154	157	157	156	162	163	158	75	170	123

Malaysia were knocked off their position at the summit of southeast Asian football as K. Rajagopal's side made a disappointing attempt to defend the AFF Suzuki Cup title they had won in 2010. That win had prompted an upswing in interest in the national side's fortunes after years of disinterest amongst Malaysians, many of whom unrealistically expect the Tigers to be competing on level terms with the best in Asia. The Malaysians qualified from the group stage of the 2012 tournament despite an opening loss to bitter rivals Singapore, but a draw in the first leg of the semi-final against Thailand was followed by a 2-0 loss in Bangkok that saw them eliminated. In club football Kelantan's dominance of the domestic scene was absolute as the northern state side claimed the treble of the Malaysia Super League, the FA Cup and the prestigious Malaysia Cup. Kelantan finished ten points clear of Singapore Lions XII in what was the first time a team from Singapore had competed in the top flight of Malaysian football since Singapore won the Malaysia Cup in 1994. Lions XII - a squad made up predominantly of players under the age of 23 from Singapore plus several foreigners - also reached the semi-finals of the Malaysia Cup, where they lost out to Malaysia Premier League winners ATM FA.

FIFA WORLD CUP RECORD
1930-1970 DNE **1974-2014** DNQ

FOOTBALL ASSOCIATION OF MALAYSIA (FAM)

- 3rd Floor Wisma FAM, Jalan SS5A/9, Kelana Jaya, Petaling Jaya 47301
- ☎ +60 3 78733100
- +60 3 78757984
- gensecfam@gmail.com
- www.fam.org.my
- FA 1933 CON 1954 FIFA 1956
- P HRH Tengku Abdullah
- GS Azzuddin Bin Ahmad

THE STADIA

2014 FIFA World Cup Stadia
National Stadium Bukit Jalil
Kuala Lumpur 100 200

Other Main Stadia
Shah Alam Stadium
Kuala Lumpur 69 372
Sultan Mizan Stadium
Terengganu 50 000
Negeri Pulau Pinang
Penang 40 000
Sarawak Stadium
Kuching 40 000

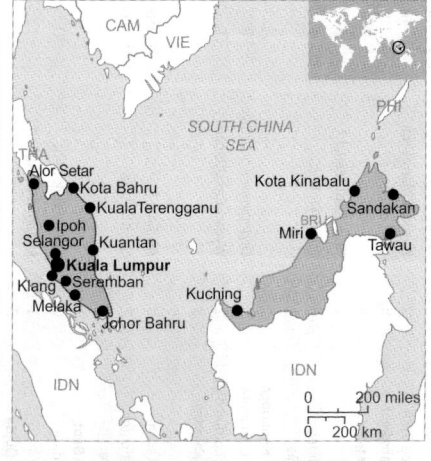

MAJOR CITIES/TOWNS
Population

1	Kuala Lumpur	1 468 984
2	Subang Jaya	1 321 672
3	Klang	1 055 207
4	Johor Bahru	895 509
5	Ampang Jaya	756 309
6	Ipoh	702 464
7	Kuching	658 562
8	Shah Alam	617 149
9	Kota Kinabalu	579 304
10	Petaling Jaya	543 415
11	Batu Sembilan	515 961
12	Sandakan	479 121
13	Kajang-Sungai	428 131
14	Seremban	419 536
15	Kuantan	407 778
17	Kuala Terengganu	286 433
18	Kota Bahru	277 301
20	Selangor	265 297
25	Alor Setar	213 624

MALAYSIA

Capital Kuala Lumpur Population 25 715 819 (46) % in cities 70%
GDP per capita $15 200 (75) Area km² 329 847 km² (66) GMT +/- +8
Neighbours (km) Brunei 381, Indonesia 1782, Thailand 506 • Coast 4675

MAS – MALAYSIA

RECENT INTERNATIONAL MATCHES PLAYED BY MALAYSIA

2010	Opponents	Score	Venue	Comp	Scorers	Att	Referee
6-01	UAE	L 0-1	Dubai	ACq		3 500	Basma SYR
27-02	Yemen	W 1-0	Kuala Lumpur	Fr	Baddrol Bin Bakhtiar [55]		
3-09	Oman	L 0-3	Doha	Fr			
1-12	Indonesia	L 1-5	Jakarta	AFFr1	Norshahrul Talaha [18]	62 000	Vo Min Tri VIE
4-12	Thailand	D 0-0	Jakarta	AFFr1			Win Cho MYA
7-12	Laos	W 5-1	Palembang	AFFr1	Amri Yahyah 2 [4 40], Mohd Zainal [73], Norshahrul Talaha [77], Mahalli Jasuli [90]		Vo Min Tri VIE
15-12	Vietnam	W 2-0	Kuala Lumpur	AFFsf	Safee Sali 2 [60 79]	45 000	Sun Baojie CHN
18-12	Vietnam	D 0-0	Hanoi	AFFsf		40 000	Kim Sang Woo KOR
26-12	Indonesia	W 3-0	Kuala Lumpur	AFFf	Safee Sali 2 [61 73], Ashaari Shamsuddin [68]	70 000	Toma JPN
29-12	Indonesia	L 1-2	Jakarta	AFFf		80 000	Green AUS
2011							
9-02	Hong Kong	W 2-0	Kuala Lumpur	Fr	Safiq Bin Rahim [43], Amirul Hadi Zainal [90]		
3-06	Hong Kong	D 1-1	Hong Kong	Fr	Hadi Bin Yahaya [65]		
18-06	Myanmar	W 2-0	Kota Bahru	Fr	Amirul Hadi Zainal [28], Baddrol Bin Bakhtiar [55]		
29-06	Chinese Taipei	W 2-1	Kuala Lumpur	WCq	Safiq Bin Rahim [29], Mohamad Abd Radzak [54]	45 000	Mahapab THA
3-07	Chinese Taipei	L 2-3	Taipei	WCq	Mohamad Abd Radzak [8], Safiq Bin Rahim [40]	16 768	Minh Tri Vo VIE
23-07	Singapore	L 3-5	Singapore	WCq	Safee Sali 2 [1 71], Hadi Bin Yahaya [70]	6 000	Shukralla BHR
28-07	Singapore	D 1-1	Kuala Lumpur	WCq	Safee Sali [57]	90 000	Takayama JPN
7-10	Australia	L 0-5	Canberra	Fr			
13-11	India	D 1-1	Guwahati	Fr	Safiq Bin Rahim [44]		
16-11	India	L 2-3	Calcutta	Fr	Safee Sali 2 [45 60]		
2012							
29-02	Philippines	D 1-1	Manilla	Fr	Shakir Bin Shaari [91+]		
28-04	Sri Lanka	W 6-0	Kuala Lumpur	Fr	Wan Bin Wan Noor 2 [25 26], Hawzan Bakri 3 [73 83 90], Azammuddin Mohd Akil [86]		
1-06	Philippines	D 0-0	Kuala Lumpur	Fr			
8-06	Singapore	D 2-2	Singapore	Fr	Azammuddin Mohd Akil [43], Safiq Bin Rahim [60]		
12-06	Singapore	W 2-0	Kuala Lumpur	Fr	Shakir Bin Shaari [19], Safiq Bin Rahim [62]		
11-09	Vietnam	L 0-2	Kuala Lumpur	Fr			
16-10	Hong Kong	W 3-0	Hong Kong	Fr	Safee Sali [59], Safiq Bin Rahim [82], Ahmad Bin Saarani [92+]		
3-11	Vietnam	L 0-1	Hanoi	Fr			
7-11	Thailand	L 0-2	Bangkok	Fr			
14-11	Hong Kong	D 1-1	Kuala Lumpur	Fr	Safee Sali [59]		
20-11	Bangladesh	D 1-1	Kuala Lumpur	Fr	Mohd Bin Zambri [23]		
25-11	Singapore	L 0-3	Kuala Lumpur	AFFr1			Kovalenko UZB
28-11	Laos	W 4-1	Kuala Lumpur	AFFr1	Safiq Bin Rahim [16], Safee Sali [67], Wan Bin Wan Noor [76], Mohd Bin Zambri [80]		Fan Qi CHN
1-12	Indonesia	W 2-0	Kuala Lumpur	AFFr1	Azammuddin Mohd Akil [27], Mahalli Bin Jasuli [30]		Kovalenko UZB
9-12	Thailand	D 1-1	Kuala Lumpur	AFFsf	Norshahrul Talaha [49]		Torki IRN
13-12	Thailand	L 0-2	Bangkok	AFFsf			Lee Min Hu KOR

Fr = Friendly match • AFF = ASEAN Football Federation Championship • AC = AFC Asian Cup • WC = FIFA World Cup
q = qualifier • r1 = first round group • sf = semi-final • 3p = third place play-off • † not a full international

MALAYSIA NATIONAL TEAM HISTORICAL RECORDS

Coaches: For Malaysia coaches pre 1990 see Oliver's Almanack 2012 • Ahmad Shafie 1990 • Rahim Abdullah 1991 • Ken Worden AUS 1992-93 • Claude Le Roy FRA 1994-95 • Hatem Souisi TUN 1995 • Wan Jamak Wan Hassan 1996-97 • Hatem Souisi 1998 • Abdul Rahman Ibrahim 1998-2000 • Allan Harris 2001-04 • K. Rajagopal1 2004 • Bertalan Bicskei HUN 2004-05 • Norizan Bakar 2005-07 • Bhaskaran Sathianathan 2007-09 • Krishnasamy Rajagobal 2009-

MALAYSIA 2012

MALAYSIAN SUPER LEAGUE (MSL)

	Pl	W	D	L	F	A	Pts	Kelantan	Singapore	Selangor	Perak	Terengganu	Negeri	PKNS	T-Team	Johor	Felda Utd	Sarawak	Kedah	Sabah	KLFA
Kelantan FA ‡	26	18	6	2	53	18	60		3-0	1-0	6-0	2-1	2-1	1-1	1-1	2-1	5-1	3-1	2-1	2-0	3-0
Singapore Lions XII	26	15	5	6	48	23	50	1-2		1-1	2-1	0-1	3-1	5-0	2-1	0-1	3-1	3-0	3-3	9-0	2-1
Selangor FA ‡	26	12	7	7	40	26	43	2-1	1-1		1-0	6-1	1-3	1-0	5-0	2-0	2-1	0-0	1-1	3-2	3-0
Perak FA	26	13	3	10	40	43	42	0-2	1-2	2-0		1-0	2-1	1-2	3-2	2-1	2-1	2-1	1-2	2-2	2-1
Terengganu FA	26	11	8	7	41	33	41	2-2	0-1	3-0	2-2		1-0	1-1	2-1	0-0	3-0	2-2	1-1	6-3	2-1
Negeri Sembilan FA	26	10	7	9	41	38	37	2-3	2-4	2-2	3-1	1-1		1-1	2-1	2-1	1-0	3-1	2-1	2-2	1-1
PKNS FC	26	8	11	7	35	35	35	0-3	1-0	2-0	2-2	2-2	2-1		2-1	1-2	0-1	1-4	0-0	2-2	1-1
PBDKT T-Team FC	26	10	5	11	35	36	35	1-2	2-1	1-2	2-0	0-3	1-1	1-4		1-1	0-1	1-0	3-0	0-0	2-1
Johor FC	26	10	5	11	29	31	35	0-0	0-1	1-1	0-1	2-0	0-2	3-2	1-3		1-1	1-2	2-1	2-1	1-0
Felda United FC	26	11	2	13	25	31	35	1-0	0-2	1-0	1-2	2-1	1-0	0-0	0-3	0-1		0-1	2-0	2-0	1-0
Sarawak FA †	26	8	6	12	28	32	30	1-1	0-1	0-1	1-2	0-1	2-2	0-0	0-1	3-1	2-1		0-2	1-0	2-0
Kedah FA †	26	7	7	12	27	38	28	0-3	0-0	1-0	3-0	2-1	0-2	1-3	1-1	1-3	1-2	0-2		2-2	2-1
Sabah FA †	26	7	7	12	33	52	28	0-0	0-1	1-1	1-3	1-3	3-1	0-4	1-2	2-1	1-0	2-1	1-0		2-0
Kuala Lumpur FA	26	0	5	21	14	53	5	0-1	0-0	0-4	2-5	0-1	1-2	1-1	0-3	0-2	0-4	1-1	0-2	1-4	

10/01/2012 - 14/07/2012 • ‡ Qualified for the AFC Cup • † Relegation play-off
Top scorers: **15** - Jean-Emmanuel **EFFA OWONA** CMR, Negeri & Francis **DOE** LBR, Terengganu • **13** - Michal **KUBALA** SVK, Perak
Relegation play-offs: Semis: **Pahang FA** 1-0 Sarawak FA; **Kedah FA** 1-0 Sabah FA • Final: **Pahang FA** 2-2 3-2p Kedah FA. Pahang promoted

MALAYSIA 2012 PREMIER LEAGUE (2)

	Pl	W	D	L	F	A	Pts
ATM FA	22	17	3	2	73	20	54
Pahang FA †	22	14	4	4	60	29	46
Sime Darby FC	22	14	3	5	54	19	45
Johor FA	22	12	5	5	47	23	41
PDRM FA	22	11	5	6	50	38	38
USM FC	22	11	3	8	41	35	36
Pos Malaysia FC †	22	8	6	8	32	31	30
Harimau Muda B	22	7	3	12	33	37	24
Muar Mun'al Council †	22	6	3	13	36	67	21
Betaria FA	22	6	2	14	23	59	20
Perlis FA	22	4	3	15	38	68	15
MJB FC	22	1	2	19	18	79	5

9/01/2012 - 13/07/2012 • † Promotion/relegation play-off
Shahzan Muda 1-5 **Pos Malaysia**; **Muar MC** 3-0 Betaria FC

MEDALS TABLE

	Overall			League			MCup		FAC		Asia		
	G	S	B	G	S	B	G	S	G	S	G	S	B
1 Selangor FA	43	20	2	6	2	2	32	15	5	2	1		
2 FA of Singapore	26	19		2			24	19					
3 Perak FA	11	15	3	2	1	3	7	11	2	3			
4 Kedah FA	10	10	1	3	3	1	4	6	3	1			
5 Penang FA	8	13		3	2		4	9	1	2			
6 Pahang FA	8	7		5	2		2	4	1	1			
7 Kuala Lumpur FA	8	2		2			3	1	3	1			
8 Negri Sembilan FA	6	4	3	1	1	3	3	3	2				
9 Kelantan FA	5	6	1	2	1	1	2	3	1	2			
10 Terengganu FA	3	9	1		3	1	1	4	2	2			
11 Johor FA	4	1		1			2	1	1				
12 Perlis FA	3	5	2	1	1	2	2	1		3			
13 Sabah FA	2	6	2	1		2	3	1	3				

MALAYSIA CUP 2012

First Round Groups

Group A	Pl	W	D	L	F	A	Pts	SL	Jo	Jo	PK
S'pore Lions XII	6	2	3	1	4	2	9		0-0	1-0	3-1
Johor FC	6	2	3	1	6	6	9	0-0		1-3	2-1
Johor FA	6	2	2	2	7	5	8	0-0	1-2		2-0
PKNS FC	6	1	2	3	5	9	5	1-0	1-1	1-1	

Group B								Ke	AT	Ke	Te
Kelantan FA	6	3	2	1	13	8	11		4-3	2-1	6-1
ATM FA	6	2	2	1	12	8	11	1-1		2-2	2-1
Kedah FA	6	1	3	2	6	8	6	0-0	0-2		2-1
Terengganu FA	6	1	1	4	6	13	4	2-0	0-2	1-1	

Group C								NS	FU	Pe	SD
Negeri S'bilan	6	2	4	0	8	3	10		1-1	0-0	4-0
Felda United	6	1	4	1	13	12	7	1-1		2-2	2-3
Perak FA	6	1	3	2	7	9	6	0-1	2-4		2-1
Sime Darby	6	1	3	2	9	13	6	1-1	3-3	1-1	

Group D								Se	Pa	Sa	TT
Selangor FA	6	4	1	1	12	6	13		2-2	2-0	2-1
Pahang FA	6	3	1	2	17	13	10	1-4		6-0	3-2
Sarawak FA	6	2	1	3	10	13	7	2-1	2-3		6-1
PBDKT T-Team	6	1	1	4	7	14	4	0-1	3-2	0-0	

Quarter-finals

Kelantan FA	2	2
Felda United *	1	2

Johor FC *	1	1
Selangor FA	3	2

S'pore Lions XII	1	2
Pahang FA *	2	0

Negeri S'bilan	2	1
ATM FA *	3	3

* Home team in the 1st leg

Semi-finals

Kelantan FA *	1	2
Selangor FA	0	0

S'pore Lions XII	114p
ATM FA	115p

Final

Kelantan FA	3
ATM FA	2

CUP FINAL
Shah Alam, Selangor
20-10-2012
Scorers - Norshahrul
Idlan Talaha 2 [44] [50], Indra
Putra Mahayuddin [96] for
Kelantan;
Rezal Yahya [49], Marlon
James [62] for ATM

MALAYSIA FA CUP 2012

First Round

Kelantan FA*	2		
Sarawak FA	1		
Muar Municipal Council	0		
Kuala Lumpur FA*	3		
Preah Khan Reach CAM*	2		
Penang FA	1		
MBJB FC	0		
SPA FC*	3		
PBDKT T-Team FC	2		
Johor FA*	0		
Felda United FC*	0		
Pahang FA	1		
Perlis FA*	3		
SDMS Kepala Batas FC	0		
PKNS FC	1 2p		
Kedah FA*	1 4p		
Terengganu FA*	4		
PDRM FA	0		
ATM FA	0		
Perak FA*	1		
Betaria FC*	4		
Malacca FA	0		
UiTM FC*	0		
Singapore LionsXII	2		
Singapore LionsXII*	3		
Johor FC	2		
Negeri Sembilan FA*	1 2 5p		
Johor FC*	2 4p		
Shahzan Muda FC*	0		
Selangor FA	4		
USM FC	2		
Pos Malaysia FC*	1		
Sabah FA	0		
Sime Darby FC*	2		

Round of 16

Kelantan FA*		
Kuala Lumpur FA		
Preah Khan Reach*	0	
SPA FC	1	
PBDKT T-Team FC*		
Pahang FA		
Perlis FA	2	
Kedah FA*	3	
Terengganu FA*	1	
Perak FA	0	
Betaria FC	0	
Singapore LionsXII	2	
Johor FC*	2 5p	
Selangor FA	2 4p	
USM FC*	0	
Sime Darby FC	2	

Quarter-finals

Kelantan FA	3	2
SPA FC*	0	0
PBDKT T-Team FC	0	1
Kedah FA*	0	2
Terengganu FA*	1	0
Singapore LionsXII	0	0
Johor FC	2	1
Sime Darby FC*	3	2

Semi-finals

Kelantan FA*	1	2
Kedah FA	1	2
Terengganu FA*	1	0
Sime Darby FC	2	0

Final

Kelantan FA	1
Sime Darby FC	0

CUP FINAL

National Stadium, Bukit Jalil, Kuala Lumpur 19-05-2012. Att: 85000. Ref: Suhaizi Shukri
Scorer - Ghaddar [59p] for Kelantan
Kelantan - Khairul Fahmi - Daudsu Jamaluddin (Farisham Ismail 82), Obinna Nwaneri, Zairul Fitree - Fahmi 40), Obinna Nwaneri, Zairul Fitree - Suppiah Chanturu (Azwan Roya 62), Shakir Shaari, Badri Radzi (c), Indra Putra - Mohammed Ghaddar, Norshahrul Idlan Talaha. Tr: Bojan Hodak
Sime Darby - Redzuan Harun - Shazian Alias, Es Lizuan Zahid(c), Fairuz Abdul Aziz, Muhd Arif Ismail - Faiz Mohd Isa, Mohd Nor Ismail, Leandro (Razali Umar Kandasamy 55), Azmirul Azmi (Shukor 79), Shoufiq Kusaini - Ronaldinho. Tr: Ismail Zakaria

* Home team/home team in the first leg

MDA – MOLDOVA

FIFA/COCA-COLA WORLD RANKING

'93	'94	'95	'96	'97	'98	'99	'00	'01	'02	'03	'04	'05	'06	'07	'08	'09	'10	'11	'12
-	118	109	117	131	116	93	94	103	111	106	114	107	86	52	97	94	84	136	128

2012

Jan	Feb	Mar	Apr	May	Jun	Jul	Aug	Sep	Oct	Nov	Dec	High	Low	Av
135	142	143	142	142	140	139	137	141	145	132	128	37	149	104

It was back to business as usual for Sheriff in 2012, a year after Dacia had ended their run of ten consecutive titles. Once again the two clubs were involved in an intense struggle, with Sheriff finishing four points ahead of their rivals from the capital. Of the 11 championships now won by Sheriff, only one - their first in 2001 - had provided a tighter finish with Dacia proving that their title in 2011 was not a flash in the pan. However, the failure to retain their league crown cost coach Igor Dobrovolskiy his job. New boss Igor Negrescu then saw Dacia team crash out in the semi-final of the cup at the hands of Milsami Orhei, a club founded just seven years previously. In the final Milsami then beat CSCA Rapid to claim their first-ever trophy after winning the cup on penalties in front of their home crowd in Orhei following a goalless draw. The Moldavian national team had a wretched time in 2012 which was only tempered by a 2-0 victory over San Marino at the end of the year in the 2014 FIFA World Cup qualifiers. That win came on the back of a run of eight games in which the team had failed to score a single goal and the stark fact for coach Ion Caras is that since their excellent qualifying campaign for Euro 2008, Moldova have won just four competitive internationals - three against San Marino and one against Finland.

UEFA EUROPEAN CHAMPIONSHIP RECORD
1960-1992 DNE (Played as part of the Soviet Union) **1996-2012** DNQ

FOOTBALL ASSOCIATION OF MOLDOVA (FMF)

Federatia Moldoveneasca de Fotbal, Str. Tricolorului 39, 2012 Chisinau
☎ +373 22 210413
📠 +373 22 210432
✉ fmf@fmf.md
🖥 www.fmf.md
FA 1990 CON 1992 FIFA 1994
P Pavel Cebanu
GS Nicolai Cebotari

THE STADIA
2014 FIFA World Cup Stadia
Stadionul Zimbru
Chisinau   10 400
Other Main Stadia
Bolshaja Sportivnaja Arena
Tiraspol   14 300
Malaya Arena
Tiraspol   9 300
Stadionul Orasenesc
Balti   5 953
Stadionul Dinamo
Bender   5 061

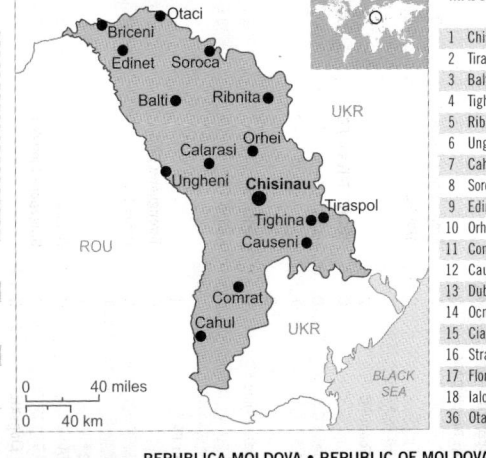

MAJOR CITIES/TOWNS

		Population
1	Chisinau	586 151
2	Tiraspol	143 977
3	Balti	100 176
4	Tighina	98 001
5	Ribnita	50 345
6	Ungheni	31 344
7	Cahul	30 487
8	Soroca	23 484
9	Edinet	21 944
10	Orhei	21 878
11	Comrat	20 750
12	Causeni	20 433
13	Dubasari	20 199
14	Ocnita	18 556
15	Ciadir Lunga	17 523
16	Straseni	17 459
17	Floresti	15 324
18	Ialoveni	14 311
36	Otaci	8 400

REPUBLICA MOLDOVA • REPUBLIC OF MOLDOVA

Capital Chisinau   Population 4 320 748 (122)   % in cities 42%
GDP per capita $2500 (172)   Area km² 33 851 km² (139)   GMT +/- +2
Neighbours (km) Romania 450, Ukraine 940

RECENT INTERNATIONAL MATCHES PLAYED BY MOLDOVA

2008	Opponents	Score	Venue	Comp	Scorers	Att	Referee
20-08	Lithuania	L 0-3	Vilnius	Fr		2 000	Kaasik EST
6-09	Latvia	L 1-2	Tiraspol	WCq	Alexeev [76]	4 300	Courtney NIR
10-09	Israel	L 1-2	Chisinau	WCq	Picusciac [1]	10 500	Muniz ESP
11-10	Greece	L 0-3	Piraeus	WCq		13 684	Berntsen NOR
15-10	Luxembourg	D 0-0	Luxembourg	WCq		2 157	Borski POL
18-11	Estonia	L 0-1	Tallinn	Fr		1 500	Larsen DEN
19-11	Lithuania	D 1-1	Tallinn	Fr	Bugalov [65]	100	Tohver EST
2009							
11-02	Macedonia FYR	D 1-1	Antalya	Fr	Andronic [60]	600	Salyi KAZ
28-03	Switzerland	L 0-2	Chisinau	WCq		10 500	McDonald SCO
1-04	Switzerland	L 0-2	Geneva	WCq		20 100	Rocchi ITA
6-06	Georgia	W 2-1	Tbilisi	Fr	Sofroni [7], Golovatenco [57]	8 000	Salyi KAZ
10-06	Belarus	D 2-2	Borisov	Fr	Calincov [77], Andronic [82]	2 000	Mazeika LTU
12-08	Armenia	W 4-1	Yerevan	Fr	Golovatenco 2 [34 64], Andronic [82], Epureanu [90p]	1 000	Silagava GEO
5-09	Luxembourg	D 0-0	Chisinau	WCq		7 820	Mazeika LTU
9-09	Greece	D 1-1	Chisinau	WCq	Andronic [90]	9 870	Stalhammar SWE
10-10	Israel	L 1-3	Ramat Gan	WCq	Calincov [92+]	8 700	Blom NED
14-10	Latvia	L 2-3	Riga	WCq	Ovseannicov [25], Sofroni [90]	3 800	Hyytia FIN
2010							
3-03	Kazakhstan	W 1-0	Antalya	Fr	Epureanu [65]	500	Bezborodov RUS
26-05	Azerbaijan	D 1-1	Seekirchen	Fr	Cojocari [81]	200	Lechner AUT
29-05	UAE	L 2-3	Anif	Fr	Tigirlas [14], Bulgaru [80]	200	Schorgenhofer AUT
11-08	Georgia	D 0-0	Chisinau	Fr		3 000	Shvestov UKR
3-09	Finland	W 2-0	Chisinau	ECq	Suvorov [69], Doros [74]	10 300	Malek POL
7-09	Hungary	L 1-2	Budapest	ECq	Suvorov [79]	9 209	Kovarik CZE
8-10	Netherlands	L 0-1	Chisinau	ECq		10 500	Meyer GER
12-10	San Marino	W 2-0	Serravalle	ECq	Josan [20], Doros [86p]	714	Courtney NIR
2011							
6-02	Poland	L 0-1	Vila Real	Fr		250	Dos Anjos POR
9-02	Andorra	W 2-1	Lagos	Fr	Picusceac [66], Bugaev [90]		Lopes POR
29-03	Sweden	L 1-2	Stockholm	ECq	Suvorov [92+]	25 544	Kircher GER
3-06	Sweden	L 1-4	Chisinau	ECq	Bugaev [61]	10 500	Marriner ENG
10-08	Cyprus	L 2-3	Nicosia	Fr	Armas [23], Ovsyannikov [45]	2 000	Mazic SRB
2-09	Finland	L 1-4	Helsinki	ECq	Alexeev [85]	9 056	Kakos GRE
6-09	Hungary	L 0-2	Chisinau	ECq		10 500	Bebek CRO
7-10	Netherlands	L 0-1	Rotterdam	ECq		47 226	Jug SV
11-10	San Marino	W 4-0	Chisinau	ECq	Zmeu [30], OG [62], Suvorov [66], Andronic.G [87]	6 534	Reinert FRO
11-11	Georgia	L 0-2	Tbilisi	Fr			Aliyev AZE
2012							
29-02	Belarus	D 0-0	Antalya	Fr		100	Mazieka LTU
23-05	Venezuela	L 0-4	Puerto Ordaz	Fr		20 000	Gambetta PER
26-05	El Salvador	L 0-2	Dallas	Fr		35 000	Ward USA
15-08	Albania	D 0-0	Tirana	Fr		6 000	Yildirim TUR
7-09	England	L 0-5	Chisinau	WCq		10 500	Van Boekel NED
11-09	Poland	L 0-2	Wroclaw	WCq		26 145	Spathas GRE
12-10	Ukraine	D 0-0	Chisinau	WCq		12 500	Turpin FRA
16-10	San Marino	W 2-0	Serravalle	WCq	Dadu [72], Epureanu [78]	736	Panayi CYP

Fr = Friendly match • EC = UEFA EURO 2012 • WC = FIFA World Cup • q = qualifier

MOLDOVA NATIONAL TEAM HISTORICAL RECORDS

Caps 74 - Radu Rebeja 1991-2008 • 69 - Serghey Clescenco 1991-2006 • 56 - Ion Testemitanu 1991-2007 • 55 - Valeriu Catinsus 1999-2009 • 52 - Serghei Rogaciov 1996-2007 • 48 - Alexandru Epureanu 2006- • 46 - Serghei Epureanu 1996-2006 & Serghei Stroenco 1992-2007

Goals 11 - Serghey Clescenco 1991-2006 • 9 - Serghei Rogaciov 1996-2007 • 8 - Iurie Miteranu 1992-2006; Igor Bugaiov 2007- & Serghei Dadu 2002- • 6 - Viorel Frunza 2002-08 • 5 - Ion Testemitanu 1991-2007 & Alexandr Suvorov 2007-

Coaches Ion Caras 1991-92 • Eugen Piunovschi 1992 • Ion Caras 1992-97 • Ivan Daniliant 1998-99 • Alexandru Matiura 1999-2001, Alexandru Spiridon 2001 • Viktor Pasulko UKR 2002-06 • Anatol Teslev 2006-07 • Igor Dobrovolski RUS 2007-09 • Gavril Balint Rou 2010-11 • Ion Caras 2012-

MOLDOVA 2011-12

PREMIER LEAGUE

	Pl	W	D	L	F	A	Pts	Sheriff	Dacia	Zimbru	Milsami	Olimpia	Tiraspol	Iskra-Stal	Nistru	Academia	Sfintul	CSCA Rapid	Costuleni
Sheriff Tiraspol †	33	25	6	2	75	18	81		0-0 0-0	2-1	2-1	0-0 6-0	3-1	5-1 2-1	4-0 3-0	1-1	5-0 5-0	2-0	4-0 4-1
Dacia Chisinau ‡	33	24	5	4	63	17	77	0-0		2-0 4-0	2-0 2-1	3-1	1-1 0-0	1-2	1-0	3-1 3-0	2-0	3-0 2-0	1-0 3-0
Zimbru Chisinau ‡	33	17	10	6	47	24	61	0-1 1-0	3-1		2-0	2-0 1-1	2-2	4-1 1-0	3-0 3-0	1-1	2-0 2-0	0-0	0-0 1-0
Milsami Orhei ‡	33	14	5	14	41	37	47	0-2 0-1	0-1	1-1 1-0		0-0 2-2	1-0	0-1	1-2 0-2	3-2	0-1 3-0	3-1	5-1 2-1
Olimpia Balti	33	10	15	8	26	27	45	1-2	0-1 1-0	0-0	0-1		1-0 0-0	2-1 0-0	0-3	1-0 1-0	1-2	4-0 3-0	0-0 2-0
FC Tiraspol	33	10	12	11	36	32	42	2-3 0-3	0-2	0-0 1-0	0-0 4-1	0-0		0-1	2-0 2-3	0-0	1-1 1-1	0-1	3-1
Iskra-Stal Rîbnita	33	11	7	15	41	48	40	1-2	1-4 0-2	0-3	0-1 0-2	1-1	3-1 0-2		0-0	1-1 1-1	3-0	4-0 1-2	3-0 1-1
Nistru Otaci	33	10	9	14	30	41	39	0-3	1-3 1-3	2-2	2-1	0-1 1-1	1-1	1-2 1-0		0-1 0-0	2-0	2-0 3-0	0-0
Academia Chisinau	33	6	13	14	32	48	31	1-2 2-0	0-3	0-2 1-2	2-5 1-0	1-1	0-2 1-1	1-3	0-0		2-2	1-1 3-1	1-0
Sfintul G. Suruceni	33	7	9	17	23	55	30	2-2	0-6 3-1	0-3	0-1	0-1 0-0	1-0	2-2 0-1	2-2 1-0	0-2 2-0		0-0	2-1
CSCA Rapid Ghidighici	33	6	8	19	20	52	26	1-2 0-2	1-2	1-2 2-3	1-1 0-1	0-0	0-1 0-2	2-1	0-0	3-2	0-0 1-0		0-0
FC Costuleni	33	3	11	19	19	54	20	0-2	0-1	0-0	1-3	0-0	0-4 1-2	3-3	0-0 0-1	1-1 2-2	1-1 0-1	2-1 0-0	

23/07/2011 - 23/05/2012 • † Qualified for the UEFA Champions League • ‡ Qualified for the Europa League
Top scorers: **18** - Benjamin **BALIMA** BFA, Sheriff • **14** - Aleksandar **PESIC** SRB, Sheriff & Oleg **MOLLA**, Zimbru • **12** - Vasily **PAVLOV** RUS, Dacia • **11** - Maxim **MIHALIOV**, Dacia & Ghenadie **ORBU**, Dacia • **9** - Henrique **LUVANNOR** BRA, Sheriff; Constantin **IAVORSCHI** & Eric **SACKEY** GHA, Zimbru • **8** - Milos **KRKOTIC** MNE, Dacia & Radu **CATAN**, Zimbru

MOLDOVA 2011-12 DIVIZIA A (2)

	Pl	W	D	L	F	A	Pts
Sheriff-2 Tiraspol	30	21	6	3	75	27	69
Speranta Crihana	30	20	6	4	52	23	66
Dacia-2 Chisinau	30	19	5	6	65	28	62
Intersport-Aroma	30	16	5	9	54	41	53
Saxan Ceadîr-Lunga	30	14	8	8	49	25	50
Zimbru-2 Chisinau	30	15	4	11	54	37	49
Dinamo Auto Tiraspol	30	13	7	10	52	32	46
Olimpia-2 Balti	30	12	6	12	37	35	42
Gagauziya Comrat	30	11	6	13	43	54	39
CSCA Rapid-2	30	11	6	13	31	45	39
Lokomotiva Balti	30	11	5	14	42	59	38
Tighina Bender	30	10	5	15	43	53	35
Lilcora Chisinau	30	6	8	16	36	56	26
Milsami-2 Orhei	30	7	5	18	31	60	26
MIPAN-Voran Chisinau	30	6	5	19	27	62	23
Sfintul-2 G. Suruceni	30	2	5	23	22	76	11

12/08/2011 - 30/05/2012 • Reserve teams ineligible for promotion

MEDALS TABLE

		Overall			League			Cup			City
		G	S	B	G	S	B	G	S	B	
1	Sheriff Tiraspol	18	3		11	2		7	1		Tiraspol
2	Zimbru Chisinau	13	7	3	8	5	3	5	2		Chisinau
3	Tiligul-Tiras	3	8	3		6	3	3	2		Tiraspol
4	FC Tiraspol	3	3	4	1	1	4	2	2		Tiraspol
5	Nistru Otaci	1	11	3		3	3	1	8		Otaci
6	Dacia Chisnau	1	6	1	1	3	1		3		Chisinau
7	Iskra-Stal Ribnita	1	1	1		1	1	1			Ribnita
8	Bugeac Comrat	1						1	1		Comrat
	Milsami Orhei		1					1	1		Orhei
10	Olimpia Balti		1	2			2			1	Balti
11	CSCA Rapid		1							1	Ghidghici
	Dinamo Chisinau		1							1	Chisinau
13	Codru Calarasi			1			1				Calarasi
	Moldova Boroseni			1			1				Boroseni

CUPA MOLDOVEI 2011-12

Round of 16			Quarter-finals			Semi-finals			Final		
Milsami Orhei	5										
Gagauziya Comrat *	1		**Milsami Orhei** *	2							
Tighina Bender	0		Olimpia Balti	1							
Olimpia Balti *	5					**Milsami Orhei** *	5				
FC Tiraspol *	6					Dacia Chisinau	4				
Saxan Ceadîr-Lunga	0		FC Tiraspol	0							
Sfintul G. Suruceni *	2		**Dacia Chisinau** *	1					**Milsami Orhei** ‡	0	5p
Dacia Chisinau	6								CSCA Rapid	0	3p
Sheriff Tiraspol	10										
Lokomotiv *	0		**Sheriff Tiraspol**	1					CUP FINAL		
Lilcora Chisinau	0		Zimbru Chisinau *	0							
Zimbru Chisinau *	2					Sheriff Tiraspol	1	2p			
Nistru Otaci	1					**CSCA Rapid** *	1	4p	Complexul Sportiv Raional, Orhei		
Iskra-Stal Rîbnita *	0		Nistru Otaci	1					27-05-2012, Ref: Sidenco		
Academia Chisinau	1		**CSCA Rapid** *	2							
CSCA Rapid *	2					* Home team • ‡ Qualified for the Europa League					

MDV – MALDIVES

FIFA/COCA-COLA WORLD RANKING

'93	'94	'95	'96	'97	'98	'99	'00	'01	'02	'03	'04	'05	'06	'07	'08	'09	'10	'11	'12
148	162	169	176	160	166	143	154	147	152	141	139	133	158	151	154	137	162	173	159

2012

Jan	Feb	Mar	Apr	May	Jun	Jul	Aug	Sep	Oct	Nov	Dec	High	Low	Av
173	175	174	164	164	165	164	161	159	160	160	159	126	183	154

New Radiant cruised to the 2012 Dhivehi League title after going through the campaign unbeaten and finishing a comfortable 11 points ahead of Maziya. It was the second time that they had won the league following on from their success in 2006, but it was the previously unheralded Maziya who surprised everyone, not only by finishing as runners-up in the league but also by winning the FA Cup. Their 2-1 victory over Eagles in the final saw them claim a first trophy since the club's creation in 1996 and they joined New Radiant in qualifying for the 2013 AFC Cup. Two weeks after having claimed the league title, New Radiant added the President's Cup to their season's honours by defeating Victory in the final on penalties. Their hopes of a clean sweep of trophies, however, had ended in the quarter-finals of the FA Cup when they lost to Eagles. Both New Radiant and Maziya will be hoping to fare better than compatriots Victory and VB had done in the 2012 edition of the AFC Cup. Victory were unable to progress beyond the preliminary rounds, losing to Al Tilal from Yemen, while VB struggled in the tournament proper, picking up only a point in a difficult group that also featured Al Ittifaq from Saudi Arabia, eventual champions Al Kuwait and Lebanon's Al Ahed.

FIFA WORLD CUP RECORD
1930-1994 DNE **1998-2014** DNQ

FOOTBALL ASSOCIATION OF MALDIVES (FAM)

FAM House,
Ujaalaahingun,
Male 20388
☎ +960 3317006
+960 3317005
media@famaldives.com
www.famaldives.com
FA 1982 CON 1986 FIFA 1986
P Ali Azim
GS Shah Ismail

MAJOR CITIES/TOWNS

		Population
1	Malé	118 202
2	Hithadhoo	9 472
3	Fuvammulah	7 683
4	Kulhudhuffushi	7 257
5	Thinadhoo	4 286
6	Ugoofaaru	4 035
7	Naifaru	3 676
8	Hinnavaru	2 941
9	Gamu	2 670
10	Feydhoo	2 660
11	Ihavandhoo	2 633
12	Eydhafushi	2 438
13	Dhidhdhoo	2 424
14	Hoarafushi	2 199
15	Maafushi	2 160
16	Alifushi	2 089
17	Maradhoo	2 039
18	Funadhoo	1 988
19	Meedhoo	1 888

THE STADIA

2014 FIFA World Cup Stadia
Galolhu National Stadium
Male 11 850

Other Main Stadia
The Galolhu National Stadium is the only stadium in the Maldives

DHIVEHI RAAJJEYGE JUMHOORIYYAA • REPUBLIC OF MALDIVES

Capital Male	Population 396 334 (174)	% in cities 38%
GDP per capita $4500 (149)	Area km² 298 km² (209)	GMT +/- +5
Neighbours (km) Coast 644		

RECENT INTERNATIONAL MATCHES PLAYED BY THE MALDIVES

2008	Opponents	Score	Venue	Comp	Scorers	Att	Referee
9-04	Lebanon	L 0-4	Beirut	ACq			
23-04	Lebanon	L 1-2	Male	ACq	Shamveel Qasim [22]		
3-06	Pakistan	W 3-0	Male	SAFr1	Mohamed Shifan [45], Ahmed Thariq [48], Akram OG [90]		
5-06	Nepal	W 4-1	Male	SAFr1	Ismail Mohamed 2 [10 47], Ibrahim Fazeel 2 [51 62]		
7-06	India	L 0-1	Male	SAFr1			
11-06	Sri Lanka	W 1-0	Colombo	SAFsf	Ibrahim Fazeel [70]		
14-06	India	W 1-0	Colombo	SAFf	Mukhtar Naseer [87]		
2009							
28-03	Sri Lanka	D 1-1	Colombo	Fr	Ibrahim Fazeel [19]		
14-04	Turkmenistan	L 1-3	Male	CCq	Ibrahim Fazeel [61p]	9 000	Al Ghafary JOR
16-04	Philippines	W 3-2	Male	CCq	Ibrahim Fazeel [26p], Ali Ashfaq [45], Mukhthar Naseer [82]	9 000	Faghani IRN
18-04	Bhutan	W 5-0	Male	CCq	Ali Ashfaq 2 [4 36], Ibrahim Fazeel [45p 47], Mohamed Umair [80]	9 000	Lazeem IRQ
5-12	Nepal	D 1-1	Dhaka	SAFr1	Ahmed Thariq [61]		
7-12	Afghanistan	W 3-1	Dhaka	SAFr1	Ahmed Thariq [52], Ali Ashfaq 2 [69 89]		
9-12	India †	W 2-0	Dhaka	SAFr1	Ahmed Thariq [15], Ibrahim Fazeel [82]		
11-12	Sri Lanka	W 5-1	Dhaka	SAFsf	Ahmed Thariq [21], Ibrahim Fazeel 2 [63 85p], Ali Ashfaq [76], Ali Ashad [87]		
13-12	India †	D 0-0	Dhaka	SAFf	L 1-3p		
2010							
12-10	Indonesia	L 0-3	Bandung	Fr			
2011							
21-03	Cambodia	W 4-0	Male	CCq	Mukhthar Naseer [2], Ali Ashfaq 3 [41 84 88]	8 000	Zhao Liang CHN
23-03	Kyrgyzstan	W 2-1	Male	CCq	Ali Ashadh [5], Shamveel Qasim [79]	9 000	Al Awaji KSA
25-03	Tajikistan	D 0-0	Male	CCq		9 000	Mohamed UAE
7-06	Singapore	L 0-4	Singapore	Fr			
10-07	India	D 1-1	Male	Fr	Mukhthar Naseer		
23-07	Iran	L 0-4	Tehran	WCq		20 195	Mahapab THA
28-07	Iran	L 0-1	Male	WCq		9 000	Kim Sang Woo KOR
4-08	Mauritius	D 1-1	Praslin	IOGr1	Mohamed Arif [32]	1 800	Rakotonjanahary MAD
6-08	Comoros	D 2-2	Roche Caiman	IOGr1	Ahmed Thariq [4], Ibrahim Fazeel [45p]	1 000	Dubec REU
9-08	Seychelles	L 1-5	Roche Caiman	IOGr1	Shamveel Qasim [26]	5 500	Rakotonjanahary MAD
22-11	Seychelles	W 3-0	Male	Fr	Ahmed Thariq 2 [13 45], Ali Ashfaq [78]		
24-11	Seychelles	W 2-1	Male	Fr	Ibrahim Fazeel 2 [85 92+p]		
2-12	Nepal	D 1-1	New Delhi	SAFr1	Ali Ashfaq [45]		Singh SIN
4-12	Pakistan	D 0-0	New Delhi	SAFr1			Robesh SRI
6-12	Bangladesh	W 3-1	New Delhi	SAFr1	Ahmed Thariq 2 [6 17], Ali Ashfaq [70]		Tufaylieh SYR
9-12	India	L 1-3	New Delhi	SAFsf	Shamveel Qasim [60]		Faizullin KGZ
2012							
24-02	Thailand	L 0-3	Chiang Mai	Fr			
8-03	Turkmenistan	L 1-3	Kathmandu	CCr1	Hassan Adhuham [20]	1 000	Almarzouq KUW
10-03	Nepal	W 1-0	Kathmandu	CCr1	Mohamed Rasheed [51]	15 000	Mashentsev KGZ
12-03	Palestine	L 0-2	Kathmandu	CCr1		300	Jin Jang Chol KOR
23-08	Nepal	W 2-1	New Delhi	Fr	Assadhulla Abdulla [6], Ismail Easa [77]		Kumar IND
25-08	India	L 0-3	New Delhi	Fr			Hashmi UAE
27-08	Syria	W 2-1	New Delhi	Fr	Ali Ashfaq [59], Ahmed Rasheed [93+]		Kumar IND

Fr = Friendly match • SAF = South Asian Football Federation Cup • CC = AFC Challenge Cup • AC = AFC Asian Cup • WC = FIFA World Cup
q = qualifier • r1 = first round group • sf = semi-final • f = final • † Not a full international

MALDIVES NATIONAL TEAM HISTORICAL RECORDS

Coach: Yordan Stoikov BUL 1999 • Victor Stanculescu ROU 1999-2000 • Jozef Jankech SVK 2001-03 • Manuel Gomes POR 2004 • Yordan Stoikov BUL 2005-06 • Jozef Jankech SVK 2007-08 • Teoman Yamanlar TUR 2008-09 • Istvan Urbanyi HUN 2009-10 • Andres Cruciani ARG 2010-11 • Istvan Urbanyi HUN 2011-

MALDIVES 2012

DHIRAAGU DHIVEHI LEAGUE

	Pl	W	D	L	F	A	Pts	New Radiant	Maziya	Victory	VB Addu	Eagles	AYL	Vyansa	Valencia
New Radiant †	19	15	4	0	48	9	49		1-0 2-1	5-1 3-1	4-0 0-0	1-1 2-0	3-0 5-1	0-0	3-0
Maziya S&RC	19	12	2	5	43	23	38	1-5		2-3 0-1	2-1 4-2	2-1 2-0	2-1 6-1	1-1	3-0
Victory	19	10	4	5	46	30	34	0-0	2-3		2-1 5-2	1-1 5-0	0-4 4-2	3-0	5-1
VB Addu	19	7	4	8	47	45	25	1-5	1-5	2-1		6-3 6-3	1-1 0-1	0-0	2-2
Eagles	19	5	6	8	26	39	21	0-1	0-0	1-1	1-4		2-1 5-2	1-0	1-0
All Youth Linkage	19	4	3	12	21	45	15	1-2	0-2	1-1	1-6	0-0		0-5	0-1
Vyansa	14	2	3	9	10	25	9	0-1	1-3	0-2	0-6	2-3	0-3		0-2
Valencia	14	2	2	10	17	42	8	1-5	0-4	2-8	5-6	3-3	0-1	0-1	

18/04/2012 - 4/10/2012 • Top four qualify for the President's Cup • † Qualified for the AFC Cup
Round One matches are listed as the first or only result in the top right section of the grid. Round two matches are listed in the bottom left section of the grid. Round Three matches are the second of the two results listed in the top right section of the grid

PRESIDENT'S CUP 2012

Preliminary round		Semi-final		Final	
		New Radiant	2		
		Victory	1		
				New Radiant	0 2p
Maziya	6			Victory	0 1p
VB Addu	2	Maziya	2		
		Victory	3		

Final: Galolhu, Malé, 15-10-2012. Penalties: (Victory first) Akram ✘[1]; Oppo ✓; Umair ✓; Kudus ✘[2]; Shafiu ✘[3]; Ahmed Abdullah ✘[1]; Fasir ✘[2]; Niyaz ✓; Rilwan ✘[2]
(1 = saved • 2 = over crossbar • 3 = hit post)

FA CUP 2012

Quarter-finals		Semi-finals		Final	
Maziya S&RC	1				
Vyansa	0	**Maziya S&RC**	2		
Valencia	2	Victory	1		
Victory	4			**Maziya S&RC**	2
All Youth Linkage	2 4p			Eagles	1
VB Addu	2 2p	All Youth Linkage	1		
New Radiant	0	**Eagles**	2		
Eagles	1	Third place: AYL 4-3 Victory			

Final: Galolhu, Malé, 23-10-2012. Scorers - OG [23], Ahmed Rasheed [58] for Maziya; Moosa Rameez [26] for Eagles

MEDALS TABLE

		Overall			Lge	PC	FAC		CW	Asia			Town
		G	S	B	G	G	G	S	G	G	S	B	
1	Victory SC	30	3		2	21	4	3	3				Malé
2	New Radiant SC	24	7	1	2	8	10	7	4		1		Malé
3	Club Valencia	20	8		5	5	4	8	6				Malé
4	VB Addu	12	3		3	3	6	3					Malé
5	Hurriyya	1	2		1			2					Malé
6	Maziya S&RC	1	1				1	1					
7	Eagles		1					1					

VB Addu were previously Club Lagoons, Island FC and VB Sports • LGE = Dhivehi League • PC = President's Cup (also known historically as the National Championship) • FAC = FAC Cup • CW = Cup Winners Cup

MEX – MEXICO

FIFA/COCA-COLA WORLD RANKING

'93	'94	'95	'96	'97	'98	'99	'00	'01	'02	'03	'04	'05	'06	'07	'08	'09	'10	'11	'12
16	15	12	11	5	10	10	12	9	8	7	7	5	20	15	26	17	27	21	

2012

Jan	Feb	Mar	Apr	May	Jun	Jul	Aug	Sep	Oct	Nov	Dec	High	Low	Av
21	21	22	20	20	19	19	18	21	19	14	15	4	33	13

2012 will long be remembered as a breakthrough year for football in Mexico following the epic gold medal success in the football tournament of the London Olympic Games. It was Mexico's first ever medal in football at the Olympics and came thanks to a 2-1 victory over Brazil at Wembley. Oribe Peralta was the hero of the day scoring both goals in the final. The senior national team got its qualifying campaign for the 2014 FIFA World Cup off to the perfect start after winning all six matches in its first round of group games and the Mexicans have not been beaten by a rival CONCACAF nation in a competitive international since mid-2009. At club level, Monterrey successfully defended their CONCACAF Champions League title by beating Santos Laguna in the final but there was consolation for Santos when they then beat Monterrey in the clausura final to claim their fifth Mexican title. The real story of the season, however, was the stunning success of Tijuana in winning the 2012 apertura at the end of the year - just five years after being formed. Given Tijuana's location just across the border from San Diego in the USA, it has meant that Mexico's drug wars have taken a fearsome toll on the city but 'Los Xolos' have risen above the chaos and are helping to give the city back some of its lost sense of pride.

CONCACAF GOLD CUP RECORD
1991 SF **1993** Winners **1996** Winners **1998** Winners **2000** QF **2002** QF
2003 Winners **2005** QF **2007** F **2009** Winners **2011** Winners

FEDERACION MEXICANA DE FUTBOL ASOCIACION, A.C. (FMF)

Colima No. 373, Colonia Roma, 06700 Mexico D.F.
☎ +52 55 52073274
📠 +52 55 52410191
✉ fccerrilla@femexfut.org.mx
🖥 www.femexfut.org.mx
FA 1927 CON 1961 FIFA 1929
P Justino Compean
GS Fernando Cerrilla

THE STADIA

2014 FIFA World Cup Stadia
Estadio Azteca
Mexico City — 105 064
Nuevo Estadio Corona
Torreon — 30 000

Other Main Stadia
Olimpico Universitario
Mexico City — 72 449
Estadio Jalisco
Guadalajara — 63 163
Estadio Omnilife
Zapopan, Guadalajara — 45 500

MAJOR CITIES/TOWNS

		Population
1	Mexico City	8 587 132
2	Ecatepec	1 956 531
3	Guadalajara	1 605 520
4	Tijuana	1 595 681
5	Juárez	1 585 034
6	Puebla	1 483 341
7	Nezahualcóyotl	1 216 077
8	León	1 197 771
9	Monterrey	1 113 114
10	Zapopan	1 060 417
11	Naucalpan	846 554
12	Guadalupe	767 167
13	Mérida	760 249
14	Chihuahua	750 039
15	San Luis Potosí	718 137
17	Aguascalientes	712 682
19	Cancún	700 394
30	Toluca	571 143
33	Torreon	540 078

ESTADOS UNIDOS MEXICANOS • UNITED MEXICAN STATES

Capital	Mexico City	Population	111 211 789 (11)	% in cities	77%
GDP per capita	$14 300 (79)	Area km²	1 964 375 km² (15)	GMT +/-	-6
Neighbours (km)	Belize 250, Guatemala 962, US 3141 • Coast 9330		

MEX – MEXICO

RECENT INTERNATIONAL MATCHES PLAYED BY MEXICO

2010	Opponents	Score		Venue	Comp	Scorers	Att	Referee
11-06	South Africa	D	1-1	Johannesburg	WCr1	Rafael Marquez [79]	84 490	Irmatov UZB
17-06	France	W	2-0	Polokwane	WCr1	Hernandez [64], Blanco [79p]	35 370	Al Ghamdi KSA
22-06	Uruguay	L	0-1	Rustenburg	WCr1		33 425	Kassai HUN
27-06	Argentina	L	1-3	Johannesburg	WCr2	Hernandez [71]	84 377	Rosetti ITA
11-08	Spain	D	1-1	Mexico City	Fr	Hernandez [10]	100 000	Moreno PAN
4-09	Ecuador	L	1-2	Guadalajara	Fr	OG [40]	43 800	Quesada CRC
7-09	Colombia	W	1-0	Monterrey	Fr	Hernandez [89]	43 000	Pineda HON
12-10	Venezuela	D	2-2	Juarez	Fr	Hernandez [33], Dos Santos [60]	20 000	Aguilar SLV
2011								
9-02	Bosnia-Herzegovina	W	2-0	Atlanta	Fr	OG [48], Pacheco [54]	45 000	Marrufo USA
26-03	Paraguay	W	3-1	Oakland	Fr	Hernandez.J 2 [6 34], Guardado [28]		Ward CAN
29-03	Venezuela	D	1-1	San Diego	Fr	De Nigris [62]		Salazar USA
28-05	Ecuador	D	1-1	Seattle	Fr	Torres [7]	50 305	Jurisevic USA
1-06	New Zealand	W	3-0	Denver	Fr	Dos Santos 2 [22 30], De Nigris [43]	45 401	Vaughn USA
5-06	El Salvador	W	5-0	Arlington	GCr1	Juarez [55], De Nigris [58], Hernandez.J 3 [60 67 95+p]	80 108	Wijngaarde SUR
9-06	Cuba	W	5-0	Charlotte	GCr1	Hernandez.J 2 [36 76], Dos Santos 2 [63 68], De Nigris [65]	46 012	Campbell JAM
12-06	Costa Rica	W	4-1	Chicago	GCr1	Marquez [16], Guardado 2 [19 25], Barrera [38]	62 000	Moreno PAN
18-06	Guatemala	W	2-1	New York	GCqf	De Nigris [48], Hernandez.J [66]	78 807	Campbell JAM
22-06	Honduras	W	2-0	Houston	GCsf	De Nigris [92], Hernandez.J [99]	70 627	Lopez GUA
25-06	USA	W	4-2	Pasadena	GCf	Barrera 2 [29 50], Guardado [36], Dos Santos [76]	93 420	Aguilar SLV
4-07	Chile	L	1-2	Mendoza	CAr1	Araujo [40]	25 000	Soto VEN
8-07	Peru	L	0-1	Mindozo	CAr1		10 000	Pezzotta ARG
12-07	Uruguay	L	0-1	La Plata	CAr1		36 000	Orozco BOL
10-08	USA	D	1-1	Philadelphia	Fr	Peralta [17]	30 132	Bogle JAM
2-09	Poland	D	1-1	Warsaw	Fr	Hernandez.J [35]	18 000	Deaconu ROU
4-09	Chile	W	1-0	Barcelona	Fr	Guardado [79]	7 210	Muniz ESP
11-10	Brazil	L	1-2	Torreon	Fr	OG [10]	30 000	Mejia SLV
11-11	Serbia	W	2-0	Queretaro	Fr	Salcido [3], Hernandez.J [89p]	34 000	Lopez GUA
2012								
25-01	Venezuela	W	3-1	Houston	Fr	Salcido [68], Marquez Lugo [89], Peralta [90]	40 128	Jurisevic USA
29-02	Colombia	L	0-2	Miami	Fr		51 615	Vaughn USA
27-05	Wales	W	2-0	New York/NJ	Fr	De Nigris 2 [42 88]	35 518	Salazar USA
31-05	Bosnia-Herzegovina	W	2-1	Chicago	Fr	Dos Santos [6], Hernandez.J [90]	51 240	Vaughn USA
3-06	Brazil	W	2-0	Arlington	Fr	Dos Santos [22], Hernandez.J [32p]	84 519	Petrescu CAN
8-06	Guyana	W	3-1	Mexico City	WCq	Salcido [10], Dos Santos [15], OG [51]	80 401	Santos PUR
12-06	El Salvador	W	2-1	San Salvador	WCq	Zavala [60], Moreno [82]	29 712	Pineda HON
15-08	USA	L	0-1	Mexico City	Fr		52 151	Quesada CRC
7-09	Costa Rica	W	2-0	San Jose	WCq	Salcido [44], Zavala [52]	32 500	Moreno PAN
11-09	Costa Rica	W	1-0	Mexico City	WCq	Hernandez.J [61]	44 007	Campbell JAM
12-10	Guyana	W	5-0	Houston	WCq		12 115	Lopez GUA
16-10	El Salvador	W	2-0	Torreon	WCq	Peralta [64], Hernandez.J [85]	26 333	Perea PAN

Fr = Friendly match • GC = CONCACAF Gold Cup • CA = Copa America • CC = FIFA Confederations Cup • WC = FIFA World Cup
q = qualifier • r1 = first round group • r2 = second round • qf = quarter-final • sf = semi-final • f = final

MEXICO NATIONAL TEAM HISTORICAL RECORDS

Caps
177 - Claudio Suarez 1992-2006 • 145 - Pavel Pardo 1996-2009 • 134 - Gerardo Torrado 1999- • 129 - Jorge Campos 1991-2003 • 119 - Ramon Ramirez 1991-2000 • 118 - Cuauhtemoc Blanco 1995- • 111 - Rafael Marquez 1997- • 108 - Alberto Garcia-Aspe 1988-2002 • 106 - Carlos Salcido 2004- • 99 - Oswaldo Sanchez 1996-2011 • 90 - Carlos Hermosillo 1984-97 • 89 - Jared Borgetti 1997-2008 • 88 - Andres Guardado 2005- • 85 - Luis Hernandez 1995-2002 • 84 - Zague 1988-2002; Salvador Carmona 1996-2005 & Duilio Davino 1996-2006 • 82 - Gustavo Pena 1961-74 • 81 - Miguel Espana 1984-94 • 80 - Ricardo Osorio 2003-

Goals
46 - Jared Borgetti 1997-2008 • 39 - Cuauhtemoc Blanco 1995- 2010 • 35 - Carlos Hermosillo 1984-97 & Luis Hernandez 1995-2002 • 31 - Enrique Borja 1966-75 • 30 - Zague 1988-2001 • 29 - Luis Flores 1983-93; Luis Garcia 1991-98 & Hugo Sanchez 1977-98 • 28 - Benjamin Galindo 1983-97 • 27 - Javier Hernandez 2009- • 21 - Francisco Fonseca 2004-08 & Alberto Garcia-Aspe 1988-2002 • 19 - Javier Fragoso 1965-70 • 16 - Isidoro Diaz 1960-70 & Ricardo Pelaez 1989-99

Coaches
For Mexico coaches prior to 1983 see Oliver's Almanack of World Football 2011 • Bora Milutinovic YUG 1983-86 • Mario Velarde 1987-89 • Alberto Guerra 1989 • Manuel Lapuente 1990-91 • Cesar Luis Menotti ARG 1991-92 • Miguel Mejia Baron 1993-95 • Bora Milutinovic YUG 1995-97 • Manuel Lapuente 1997-2000 • Mario Carrillo 1999 • Gustavo Vargas 1999 • Enrique Meza 2000-01 • Javier Aguirre 2001-02 • Ricardo La Volpe ARG 2002-06 • Hugo Sanchez 2006-08 • Jesus Ramirez 2008 • Sven-Goran Eriksson SWE 2008-09 • Javier Aguirre 2009-10 • Enrique Meza 2010 • Efrain Flores 2010 • Jose Manuel de la Torre 2010-

MEXICO 2011–12
PRIMERA DIVISION NACIONAL (CLAUSURA)

	Pl	W	D	L	F	A	Pts
Santos Laguna †	17	11	3	3	33	18	36
Monterrey †	17	9	5	3	32	15	32
América †	17	9	5	3	30	18	32
Morelia †	17	9	4	4	25	18	31
Tigres UANL †	17	9	4	4	22	16	31
Pachuca †	17	7	7	3	24	17	28
Tijuana †	17	7	7	3	18	11	28
Jaguares de Chiapas †	17	8	3	6	26	20	27
Cruz Azul	17	6	7	4	29	21	25
Atlas	17	4	8	5	7	13	20
Toluca	17	6	4	7	24	27	22
Puebla	17	5	4	8	19	23	19
Atlante	17	4	4	9	20	31	16
Pumas UNAM	17	3	7	7	13	18	16
Guadalajara	17	4	3	10	12	21	15
San Luis	17	3	3	11	15	30	12
Querétaro	17	2	6	9	14	30	12
Estudiantes Tecos	17	2	6	9	12	28	12

7/01/2012 – 29/04/2012 • † Qualified for the play-offs
Top scorers (inc play-offs): **14** - Ivan **ALONSO** URU, Toluca & Christian **BENITEZ** ECU, América • **9** - Aldo **DE NIGRIS**, Monterrey; Oribe **PERALTA**, Santos & Miguel **SABAH**, Morelia • **8** - Lucas **LOBOS** ARG, UANL; Luis Gabriel **REY** COL, Jaguares; Jackson **MARTINEZ** COL, Jaguares & Emanuel **VILLA** ARG, Cruz Azul • **7** - Jose **SAND** ARG, Tijuana & Humberto **SUAZO** CHI, Monterrey

MEXICO 2012–13
PRIMERA DIVISION NACIONAL (APERTURA)

	Pl	W	D	L	F	A	Pts
Toluca	17	10	4	3	28	17	34
Tijuana	17	9	7	1	23	15	34
León	17	10	3	4	34	17	33
América	17	8	7	2	28	15	31
Morelia	17	6	9	2	25	16	27
Cruz Azul	17	6	8	3	22	15	26
Monterrey	17	5	8	4	23	23	23
Guadalajara	17	6	5	6	17	17	23
Santos Laguna	17	6	5	6	22	26	23
Pumas UNAM	17	7	2	8	18	23	23
Jaguares de Chiapas	17	6	4	7	23	24	22
Tigres UANL	17	5	6	6	23	18	21
Pachuca	17	5	6	6	13	20	21
Atlante	17	5	5	7	23	28	20
San Luis	17	3	6	8	14	24	15
Puebla	17	3	4	10	16	26	13
Atlas	17	1	9	7	16	27	12
Querétaro	17	1	4	12	11	30	7

20/07/2012 – 1/11/2012 • † Qualified for the play-offs
Top scorers (inc play-offs): **11** - Christian **BENITEZ** ECU, América & Esteban **PAREDES** CHI, Atlante • **8** - Nelson **MAZ** URU, León; Luis Gabriel **REY** COL, Jaguares; Duvier **RIASCOS** COL, Tijuana & Miguel **SABAH**, Morelia • **7** - Mariano **PAVONE** MEX, Cruz Azul & Carlos **QUINTERO** COL, Santos Laguna

CLAUSURA 2011–12 PLAY-OFFS

Quarter-finals
Santos 4 2
Jaguares * 3 1
Morelia 0 1
Tigres UANL * 1 4
América 3 0
Pachuca * 1 1
Tijuana * 1 2
Monterrey 2 2

Semi-finals
Santos † 1 2
Tigres UANL * 1 2
América * 0 0
Monterrey 0 2

Final
Santos 1 2
Monterrey 1 1

* Home team in 1st leg • † Qualified on overall record

CLAUSURA 2011–12 FINAL
Tecnológico, Monterrey, 17-05-2012, Att: 33 000, Ref: Mauricio Morales
Monterrey 1 Suazo [94+p]
Santos Laguna 1 Peralta [69]
Monterrey - Jonathan Orozco - Severo Meza, Hiram Mier, Jose Basanta, Darvin Chavez - Cesar Delgado (Angel Reyna 68), Jesus Zavala (Neri Cardozo 68), Luis Ernesto Perez, Walter Ayovi (Abraham Carreno 73) - Aldo de Nigris, Humberto Suazo. Tr: Victor Vucetich
Santos - Oswaldo Sanchez• - Jorge Estrada•, Felipe Baloy•, Aaron Galindo, Osmar Mares - Daniel Luduena• (Santiago Hoyos 76), Rodolfo Salinas, Marc Crosas•, Christian Suarez (Candido Ramirez 71) - Carlos Quintero• (Jaime Toledo 87), Oribe Peralta. Tr: Benjamin Galindo

Nuevo Estadio Corona, Torreón, 20-05-2012, Att: 30 000, Ref: Roberto Garcia
Santos Laguna 2 Ludena [5], Peralta [64]
Monterrey 1 De Nigris [78]
Santos - Oswaldo Sanchez - Jorge Estrada, Felipe Baloy, Aaron Galindo, Osmar Mares (Cesar Ibanez 45) - Carlos Quintero•, Marc Crosas, Rodolfo Salinas, Christian Suarez (Candido Ramirez 55) - Daniel Luduena - Oribe Peralta (Juan Pablo Rodriguez 71). Tr: Benjamin Galindo
Monterrey - Jonathan Orozco - Severo Meza, Hiram Mier, Jose Basanta, Darvin Chavez (Neri Cardozo 52) - Angel Reyna, Jesus Zavala (Cesar Delgado 52), Luis Ernesto Perez (Abraham Carreno 69), Walter Ayovi - Aldo de Nigris•, Humberto Suazo•. Tr: Victor Vucetich

APERTURA 2012–13 PLAY-OFFS

Quarter-finals
Tijuana 1 1
Monterrey * 0 1
Cruz Azul * 2 0
León * 1 3
América 2 1
Morelia * 0 2
Guadalajara * 1 1
Toluca 2 3

Semi-finals
Tijuana 0 3
León * 2 0
América * 0 2
Toluca 2 1

Final
Tijuana * 2 2
Toluca 1 0

* Home team in 1st leg • † Qualified on overall record

APERTURA 2012–13 FINAL
1st leg. Estadio Caliente, Tijuana, 29-11-2012, Att: 21 000, Ref: Roberto Garcia
Tijuana 2 Martinez [24], Aguilar [40]
Toluca 1 Benitez [26]
Tijuana - Cirilo Saucedo - Edgar Castillo, Javier Gandolfi, Pablo Aguilar, Juan Nunez, Fernando Arce•, Fidel Martinez (Raul Enriquez 79), Joe Corona (Leandro Augusto 73), Cristian Pellerano•, Alfredo Moreno (Richard Ruiz 55), Duvier Riascos. Tr: Antonio Mohamed
Toluca - Alfredo Talavera• - Diego Novaretti, Marvin Cabrera, Edgar Duenas, Wilson Mathias, Carlos Rodriguez, Lucas Silva, Zinha• (Juan Cacho 71), Antonio Rios (Edy Brambila 46), Edgar Benitez (Isaac Brizuela 82), Luis Tejada. Tr: Enrique Meza

2nd leg. Nemesio Diez, Toluca, 2-12-2012, Att: 26 000, Ref: Francisco Chacon
Toluca 0
Tijuana 2 Ruiz [69], Riascos [71]
Toluca - Alfredo Talavera - Diego Novaretti•, Edgar Duenas (Juan Cacho 65), Wilson Mathias, Carlos Rodriguez, Lucas Silva, Zinha, Antonio Rios (Edy Brambila 46), Carlos Esquivel•, Edgar Benitez, Luis Tejada (Isaac Brizuela 77). Tr: Enrique Meza
Tijuana - Cirilo Saucedo - Edgar Castillo, Javier Gandolfi, Pablo Aguilar, Juan Nunez, Fernando Arce, Fidel Martinez, Joe Corona (Joshua Abrego 67), Cristian Pellerano, Alfredo Moreno (Richard Ruiz 46), Duvier Riascos• (Jorge Hernandez 75). Tr: Antonio Mohamed

MEX – MEXICO

MEXICO 2011-12

PRIMERA DIVISION NACIONAL RESULTS AND RELEGATION TABLE

	Pl	Pts	Av	Monterrey	Cruz Azul	Santos Laguna	Morelia	Tigres UANL	América	Toluca	Pachuca	Pumas UNAM	Guadalajara	Tijuana	Jaguares	Puebla	San Luis	Atlante	Querétaro	Atlas	Estudiantes
Monterrey	102	180	1.7647		1-2	2-0	2-0	2-0	0-3	0-0	1-1	1-1	2-0	4-2	2-1	2-1	3-0	3-2	4-1	2-0	4-0
Cruz Azul	102	177	1.7353	4-3		0-1	0-1	1-1	3-1	0-0	1-1	1-1	1-1	2-1	2-0	2-0	3-1	2-1	1-2	2-1	5-2
Santos Laguna	102	171	1.6765	1-1	1-0		0-2	3-0	1-1	3-2	0-0	2-1	1-1	1-3	1-0	3-1	5-2	3-0	2-0	3-0	1-1
Morelia	102	167	1.6373	0-0	2-0	3-1		2-0	3-1	1-2	2-2	0-1	1-2	1-1	1-0	0-0	2-0	1-1	4-2	0-0	0-2
Tigres UANL	102	159	1.5588	0-0	1-1	2-1	4-1		2-2	2-2	5-0	4-1	2-1	1-0	1-1	1-2	1-0	1-0	1-0	0-0	2-1
América	102	155	1.5196	2-3	2-2	3-1	1-1	0-1		1-1	1-0	2-1	1-3	1-1	2-0	2-3	2-2	0-1	2-1	5-2	1-2
Toluca	102	150	1.4706	1-1	0-3	1-3	2-1	2-1	1-1		3-4	0-2	0-0	1-1	3-1	4-3	2-1	2-1	0-1	0-0	3-1
Pachuca	102	146	1.4314	4-0	1-0	1-4	1-2	1-1	2-0	3-0		0-0	3-1	1-0	1-0	3-1	1-1	3-2	1-1	4-2	2-0
Pumas UNAM	102	146	1.4314	2-1	1-2	1-1	3-0	0-2	1-0	4-1	0-1		0-0	1-1	0-3	0-2	2-0	1-0	1-1	1-4	0-0
Guadalajara	102	143	1.402	2-1	2-1	2-1	1-2	1-0	0-1	2-0	2-2	0-0		0-2	2-1	1-4	0-0	0-1	0-1	0-1	5-2
Tijuana	34	46	1.3529	1-0	0-0	1-3	1-2	1-1	1-1	1-1	3-2	1-1	0-1		2-0	1-1	0-0	2-1	1-1	2-0	0-2
Jaguares	102	130	1.2745	1-4	1-1	3-2	1-0	2-2	5-3	1-1	3-2	4-0	3-1	0-0		0-1	3-1	1-1	3-0	1-1	1-0
Puebla	102	123	1.2059	3-3	1-1	1-2	1-2	0-1	2-3	2-1	2-2	2-1	1-2	1-1	1-2		0-1	1-2	1-0	0-0	2-1
San Luis	102	118	1.1569	1-0	1-1	0-1	2-3	0-2	1-3	5-1	0-0	1-0	2-0	0-1	2-3	2-1		2-3	2-1	0-1	2-1
Atlante	102	117	1.1471	0-3	2-2	1-2	4-4	1-0	0-4	0-2	0-1	1-2	0-2	1-1	2-2	5-1	1-1		1-3	0-0	2-1
Querétaro	102	112	1.098	2-1	1-0	1-3	0-3	0-0	0-2	2-2	2-1	4-0	0-0	0-2	1-2	0-1	2-2	2-3		2-1	3-0
Atlas	102	110	1.0784	1-0	0-0	1-3	1-1	0-1	1-1	0-0	0-0	1-1	2-2	0-3	0-1	1-1	2-3	3-0			0-2
Estudiantes Tecos	102	101	0.9902	2-3	0-2	5-2	1-2	0-1	1-1	1-2	2-1	1-2	1-0	0-2	0-2	1-1	0-2	1-1	0-2	1-1	

The relegation averages are worked out over three years. This table lists the results of the 2010-11 season – the Apertura played in the second half of 2010 and the Clausura in the first half of 2011. For details of the Apertura see Oliver's Almanack of World Football 2012. The Apertura results are in the shaded boxes

MEDALS TABLE

		Overall G S B	League G S B	Cup G S	CON'CAF G S B	Sth Am	City
1	Club América	25 14 9	14 10 5	6 3	5 1	1 3	Mexico City
2	Real Club España	20 5 4	15 5 4	5			
3	Necaxa	16 8 9	7 7 7	7	2 1 1	1	Aguascalientes
4	Cruz Azul	15 14 1	8 9	2 2	5 2 1	1	Mexico City
5	CD Guadalajara	14 17 9	11 9 4	2 5	1 2 1	1 4	Guadalajara
6	CD Toluca	14 9 5	10 6 2	2 1	2 2 2	1	Toluca
7	CF Pachuca	14 7 6	7 7 5	2	4 1	1	Pachuca
8	UNAM Pumas	11 8 2	7 6	1	3 1 2	1	Mexico City
9	Asturias	11 4 3	3 4 3	8			
10	CF Atlante	10 13 3	5 8 3	3 4	2 1		Mexico City
11	León	10 10 6	5 5 4	5 4	1 2		León
12	Reforma	8 3 2	6 3 2	2			
13	CF Monterrey	7 6 5	4 4 2	1 2	2 3		Monterrey
14	Puebla FC	7 4 3	2 2 3	4 2	1		Puebla
15	Santos Laguna	5 6 2	5 5		1 1	1	Torreón
16	CF Atlas	5 4 4	1 3 4	4 1			Guadalajara
17	Tigres UANL	5 4 1	3 3	2 1	1		Monterrey
18	CD Zacatepec	4 3 1	2 1 1	2 2			Zacatepec
19	UAG Tecos	3 6	1 4	1 2	1		Zapopan
20	CD Veracruz	3 3 3	2 3	1 3			Veracruz
21	Club Mexico	3 1 1	1 1 1	2			
22	Marte FC	3 1	3 1				Xochitepec
23	Tampico Madero	2 4	1 2	1 2			Tampico Madero
24	British Club	2 3 5	1 3 5	1			
25	Moctezuma	2 3		3 2			
26	Oro Jalisco	1 6	1 5	1			
	Monarcas Morelia	1 6	1 3	1	2		Morelia
28	Rovers	1 1 1	1 1	1			
29	Mexico Cricket Club	1	1				
	Orizaba	1	1				
	Tijuana	1	1				Tijuana

MKD – FYR MACEDONIA

FIFA/COCA-COLA WORLD RANKING

'93	'94	'95	'96	'97	'98	'99	'00	'01	'02	'03	'04	'05	'06	'07	'08	'09	'10	'11	'12
-	90	94	86	92	59	68	76	89	85	92	92	87	54	58	56	65	76	103	81

2012

Jan	Feb	Mar	Apr	May	Jun	Jul	Aug	Sep	Oct	Nov	Dec	High	Low	Av
103	101	102	98	98	101	103	102	97	104	83	81	46	147	80

After the best part of a decade in the doldrums 2012 saw a welcome return to form for Vardar Skopje. Macedonia's most decorated club won the championship with relative ease for what was only their second trophy since last winning the league in 2003. What made the triumph all the more remarkable was the fact that Vardar had only just escaped relegation at the end of the previous season. That was a shock to the system that saw new backers arrive at the club along with coach Ilco Gjorgioski, a title winner with Makedonija Skopje in 2009. Vardar lost just once all season, finishing nine points ahead of Metalurg. Renova were the season's other trophy winners after beating Rabotnicki 3-1 in the cup final. The 2010 champions had knocked out Vardar in the semi-final on away goals, after the two had drawn both of their matches, with the victory in the final seeing them win the trophy for the first time in their history. After a disappointing year in charge of the Macedonian national team, John Toshack was replaced as coach by Cedomir Janevski prior to the 2014 FIFA World Cup qualifying campaign. An encouraging draw away to Scotland and an excellent win at home over Serbia was tempered by two defeats at the hands of Croatia who, along with Belgium, look set to leave the rest of the group trailing in their wake.

UEFA EUROPEAN CHAMPIONSHIP RECORD
1960-1992 DNE (Played as part of Yugoslavia) **1996-2012** DNQ

FOOTBALL FEDERATION OF MACEDONIA (FFM)

Osma Udarna brigada 31-A,
PO Box 84,
1000 Skopje
☎ +389 23 129291
📠 +389 23 165448
✉ ffm@ffm.com.mk
🌐 www.ffm.com.mk
FA 1908 CON 1994 FIFA 1994
P Ilcho Gjorgjioski
GS Dimitar Zisovski

THE STADIA
2014 FIFA World Cup Stadia
Philip II of Macedonia Arena
Skopje   32 580
Other Main Stadia
Stadion Goce Delcev
Prilep   15 000
Gradski Stadion
Stip   10 000
Gradski Stadion
Tetovo   9 760
Milano Arena
Kumanovo   7 000

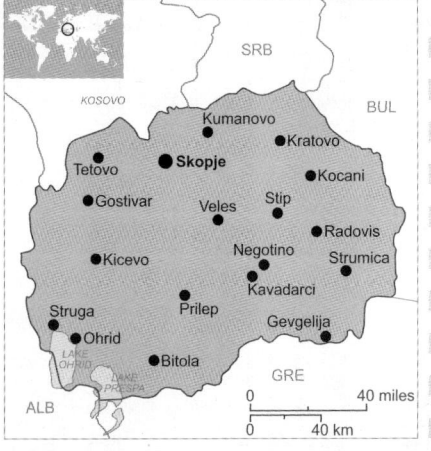

MAJOR CITIES/TOWNS

		Population
1	Skopje	480 678
2	Kumanovo	114 283
3	Bitola	85 622
4	Tetovo	75 045
5	Prilep	73 648
6	Veles	57 623
7	Ohrid	55 021
8	Gostivar	52 406
9	Stip	48 425
10	Strumica	45 591
11	Kavadarci	38 944
12	Struga	37 656
13	Kocani	34 668
14	Kicevo	32 161
15	Lipkovo	29 259
16	Saraj	26 726
17	Zelino	26 586
18	Radovis	25 387
47	Kratavo	9 906

REPUBLIKA MAKEDONIJA • REPUBLIC OF MACEDONIA

Capital	Skopje	Population	2 066 718 (144)	% in cities	67%
GDP per capita	$9100 (111)	Area km²	25 713 km² (149)	GMT +/-	+1

Neighbours (km) Albania 151, Bulgaria 148, Greece 246, Kosovo 159, Serbia 62

RECENT INTERNATIONAL MATCHES PLAYED BY FYR MACEDONIA

2009	Opponents		Score	Venue	Comp	Scorers	Att	Referee
11-02	Moldova	D	1-1	Antalya	Fr	Pandev [54]	600	Saliy KAZ
1-04	Netherlands	L	0-4	Amsterdam	WCq		47 750	Rasmussen DEN
6-06	Norway	D	0-0	Skopje	WCq		7 000	Tagliavento ITA
10-06	Iceland	W	2-0	Skopje	WCq	Stojkov [9], Ivanovski [85]	7 000	Ennjimmi FRA
12-08	Spain	L	2-3	Skopje	Fr	Pandev 2 [8 33]	25 000	Vink NED
5-09	Scotland	L	0-2	Glasgow	WCq		50 214	Stark GER
9-09	Norway	L	1-2	Oslo	WCq	Grncarov [79]	14 766	Paixao POR
11-10	Qatar	W	2-1	Skopje	Fr	Pandev 2 [25 40]	5 000	Georgiev BUL
14-11	Canada	W	3-0	Strumica	Fr	Sedloski [48], Pandev 2 [61p 90p]	6 000	Genov BUL
18-11	Iran	D	1-1	Tehran	Fr	Pandev [49]	3 000	Moradi IRN
2010								
3-03	Montenegro	W	2-1	Skopje	Fr	Naumoski [27], Pandev [31]	7 000	Janku ALB
29-05	Azerbaijan	W	3-1	Villach	Fr	Trickovski [8], Despotovski [66], Djurovski [88]	100	Drabek AUT
2-06	Romania	W	1-0	Bischofshofen	Fr	Sikov [28]	1 000	Krassnitzer AUT
11-08	Malta	D	1-1	Ta'Qali	Fr	Trickovski [36]	2 500	Rossi SMR
3-09	Slovakia	L	0-1	Bratislava	ECq		5 980	Circhetta SUI
7-09	Armenia	D	2-2	Skopje	ECq	Gjurovski [42], Naumoski [96+p]	9 000	Berntsen NOR
8-10	Andorra	W	2-0	Andorra La Vella	ECq	Naumoski [42], Sikov [60]	550	Mazeika LTU
12-10	Russia	L	0-1	Skopje	ECq		10 500	Johannesson SWE
17-11	Albania	D	0-0	Korce	Fr		12 000	Gocek TUR
22-12	China PR	L	0-1	Guangzhou	Fr		8 000	Kim Jong Hyeok KOR
2011								
9-02	Cameroon	L	0-1	Skopje	Fr		3 000	Kalugjerovic MNE
26-03	Republic of Ireland	L	1-2	Dublin	ECq	Trickovski [45]	33 200	Vad HUN
4-06	Republic of Ireland	L	0-2	Skopje	ECq		29 500	Meyer GER
10-08	Azerbaijan	W	1-0	Baku	Fr	Pandev [57]	1 000	Kulbakov BLR
2-09	Russia	L	0-1	Moscow	ECq		31 028	Yildirim TUR
6-09	Andorra	W	1-0	Skopje	ECq	Ivanovski [59]	5 000	Whitby WAL
7-10	Armenia	L	1-4	Yerevan	ECq	Sikov [86]	14 403	Schorgenhofer AUT
11-10	Slovakia	D	1-1	Skopje	ECq	Noveski [79]	4 100	Chapron FRA
15-11	Albania	D	0-0	Prilep	Fr		4 500	Vincic SVN
2012								
29-02	Luxembourg	L	1-2	Luxembourg	Fr	Hasani [24]	787	Crangle NIR
26-05	Portugal	D	0-0	Leira	Fr		19 323	Kelly IRL
29-05	Angola	D	0-0	Lisbon	Fr		200	Proenca POR
15-08	Lithuania	W	1-0	Skopje	Fr	Pandev [54]	7 000	Ozkahya TUR
7-09	Croatia	L	0-1	Zagreb	WCq		13 883	Yefet ISR
11-09	Scotland	D	1-1	Glasgow	WCq	Noveski [11]	32 430	Karasev RUS
12-10	Croatia	L	1-2	Skopje	WCq	Ibraimi [16]	25 230	Rasmussen DEN
16-10	Serbia	W	1-0	Skopje	WCq	Ibraimi [59p]	26 181	Nijhuis NED
14-11	Slovenia	W	3-2	Skopje	Fr	Tasevski [26], Jahovic [41], Ibraimi [51]	3 000	Grujic SRB
14-12	Poland	L	1-4	Antalya	Fr	Blazevski [87]	100	Gocek TUR

Fr = Friendly match • EC = UEFA EURO 2012 • WC = FIFA World Cup • q = qualifier

FYR MACEDONIA NATIONAL TEAM HISTORICAL RECORDS

Caps: 100 - Goce Sedloski 1996-2010 • 83 - Velice Sumulikoski 2002- • 73 - Artim Sakiri 1996-2006 • 70 - Igor Mitreski 2001- • 68 - Goran Pandev 2001- • 59 - Petar Milosevski 1998-2009 • 55 - Nikolce Noveski 2004- • 50 - Vlatko Grozdanoski 2001- • 48 - Georgi Hristov 1995-2003 • 46 - Ilco Naumoski 2003- • 44 - Toni Micevski 1993-2002 • 43 - Goran Maznov 2001- & Vlade Lazarevski 2003-

Goals: 25 - Goran Pandev 2001- • 16 - Georgi Hristov 1995-2003 • 15 - Artim Sakiri 1996-2009 • 10 - Goran Maznov 2001- • 9 - Ilco Naumoski 2003- • 8 - Goce Sedloski 1996- & Sasa Ciric 1996-2003

Past Coaches: Andon Doncevski 1993-95 • Gjoko Hadzievski 1996-99 • Dragan Kanatlarovski 1999-2001 • Gjore Jovanovski 2001-02 • Nikola Ilievski 2002-03 • Dragan Kanatlarovski 2003-05 • Slobodan Santrac SRB 2005 • Boban Babunski 2005-06 • Srecko Katanec SVN 2006-09 • Mirsad Jonuz 2009-11 • John Toshack 2011-12 • Cedomir Janevski 2012-

FYR MACEDONIA 2011-12

PRVATA FUDBALSKA LIGA

	Pl	W	D	L	F	A	Pts	Vardar	Metalurg	Shkendija	Renova	Bregalnica	Sileks	Napredok	Rabotnicki	Turnovo	Teteks	Ohrid	11 Oktomvri
Vardar Skopje †	33	22	10	1	50	15	**76**		1-0 2-1	2-0	0-0 1-1	3-0 2-1	2-1	5-1	1-0 2-2	3-0 0-0	1-0	2-0 4-0	2-0
Metalurg Skopje ‡	33	19	10	4	53	16	**67**	1-1		0-0 1-0	2-1	1-0 2-1	3-0 1-0	2-0 1-1	0-0	1-0	2-0 5-0	6-0	0-0 3-0
Shkendija Tetovo ‡	33	20	6	7	53	28	**66**	0-1 1-0	2-0		2-2 4-0	1-0 3-2	2-1	3-0	2-0 1-0	2-0 2-1	0-0	2-0 1-0	3-0
Renova Cepciste ‡	33	13	13	7	56	38	**52**	0-0	1-1 1-0	0-2		0-0 2-2	2-0 1-0	4-0 5-0	3-1	0-0	2-2 0-0	2-0	1-1 3-2
Bregalnica Stip	33	13	6	14	51	46	**45**	2-3	1-1	2-3	3-2		3-1	0-1 3-2	3-2	0-1 2-1	2-0 1-1	2-3 1-2	0-2 0-4 1
Sileks Kratovo	33	13	3	17	42	51	**42**	1-1 1-2	1-1	1-4 1-4	2-1	2-1 2-1		2-1	2-1 1-0	3-2 0-1	4-0	1-0 5-2	2-0
Napredok Kicevo	33	12	6	15	37	51	**42**	0-1 0-0	0-4	0-0 3-0	1-1	0-1	1-0 3-0		1-1	1-0	4-0 2-1	3-0	1-0 2-0
Rabotnicki Skopje	33	11	8	14	49	45	**41**	1-2	0-1 0-3	3-1	5-1 3-1	2-1 1-3	2-0	4-0 4-1		1-1	1-1 0-0	1-2 3-2	1-0
Turnovo ‡‡	33	10	8	15	34	42	**38**	1-2	1-2 1-1	2-1	0-1 0-1	2-2	2-1	0-2 2-1	1-0 5-4		0-2 2-1	1-2	1-0
Teteks ‡‡	33	8	11	14	23	48	**35**	0-0 0-0	0-2	2-0 0-2	1-5	3-1	1-1 2-1	1-0	1-1	0-3		1-1 0-0	1-0 2-0
Ohrid 2004	33	6	8	19	26	62	**26**	0-2	0-0 1-4	1-2	2-2 1-7	0-0	2-0	3-1 1-2	0-1 0-2	0-0 1-1	1-0		1-1
11 Oktomvri Prilep	33	3	7	23	26	58	**16**	0-1 0-1	0-1	2-2 1-1	0-3	0-1	1-2 1-3	2-2	2-3	2-0 1-2	4-0	0-3 3-1	

30/07/2011 - 23/05/2012 • † Qualified for the UEFA Champions League • ‡ Qualified for the Europa League • ‡‡ Relegation play-off
Relegation play-offs: **Teteks** 0-0 5-4p Skopje • **Turnovo** 1-0 Gorno Lisice
Top scorers: **25** - Filip **IVANOVSKI**, Vardar • **17** - Borce **MANEVSKI**, Rabotnicki • **14** - Boban **JANCEVSKI**, Renova; Muharem **BAJRAMI**, Renova & Angel **NACEV**, Sileks • **13** - Blagoja **GESOSKI**, 11 Oktomvri • **11** - Genc **HYSENI**, Bregalnica & Cvetan **CURLINOV**, Metalurg • **10** - Baze **ILLJOSKI**, Metalurg

FYR MACEDONIA 2011-12
VTORA LIGA (2)

	Pl	W	D	L	F	A	Pts
Pelister Bitola	30	19	4	7	42	23	**61**
Drita Bogovinje	30	16	10	4	49	19	**58**
Gorno Lisice ‡‡	30	17	5	8	60	30	**56**
Skopje ‡‡	30	17	5	8	50	26	**56**
Miravci	30	16	6	8	45	23	**54**
Makedonija GP Skopje	30	14	6	10	48	31	**48**
Tikves Kavadarci	30	13	6	11	45	41	**45**
Rufeja Miletino	30	14	5	11	48	35	**47**
Lokomotiva Skopje	30	14	4	12	35	31	**46**
Rinija Gostivar	30	11	8	11	39	34	**41**
Pobeda Prilep	30	12	5	13	36	38	**41**
Korab Debar	30	11	3	16	34	45	**36**
Vlazrimi Kicevo	30	7	8	15	28	68	**29**
Osogovo Kocani	30	6	4	20	29	63	**22**
Belasica Strumica	30	4	6	20	27	56	**18**
Ohrid Lote	30	6	1	23	22	74	**19**

7/08/2011 - 22/05/2012 • ‡‡ Promotion play-off

MEDALS TABLE

		Overall			League			Cup		
		G	S	B	G	S	B	G	S	City
1	Vardar Skopje	11	3	3	6	2	3	5	1	Skopje
2	Sloga Jugomagnat	6	7	2	3	2	2	3	5	Skopje
3	Sileks Kratovo	5	6		3	5		2	1	Kratovo
4	Rabotnicki Skopje	5	4	1	3	2	1	2	2	Skopje
5	Pobeda Prilep	3	4	4	2	2	4	1	2	Prilep
6	Makedonija Skopje	2	2	2	1	1	2	1	1	Skopje
7	Renova Cepciste	2			1		2	1		Tetovo
8	Pelister Bitola	1	2	1			1	1	2	Bitola
	Metalurg Skopje	1	2	1		2	1	1		Skopje
10	Cementarnica Skopje	1	1	1			1	1	1	Skopje
	Shkendija Tetovo	1	1	1	1		1			Tetovo
12	Teteks	1	1					1	1	Tetovo
13	Baskimi Kumanovo	1						1		Kumanovo
14	Milano Kumanovo		3			2			1	Kumanovo
15	Belasica Strumica		2			2				Strumica
16	Madzari Skopje		1						1	Skopje
	Napredok Kicevo		1						1	Kicevo
18	Balkan Skopje			1			1			Skopje
	Balkan Stokokomerc			1			1			Skopje

KUP NA MAKEDONIJA 2011-12

First Round

Renova Cepciste	4
Karoman Struga *	0
Ljuboten *	1
Rinija Gostivar	2
Sileks Kratovo	7
Vasilevo *	1
Treska *	0 3p
Teteks	0 5p
11 Oktomvri Prilep	w-o
Karbinci	
Madzari Solidarnost *	2 1p
Skopje	2 3p
Tikves Kavadarci	w-o
Prespa	
Gorno Lisice *	0
Vardar Skopje *	6 1
Turnovo	2
Pobeda Prilep *	1
Rudar Probistip *	1 1
Pelister Bitola	0 1
Shkendija Tetovo	7
Ohrid Lote *	0
Babi Stip *	0
Bregalnica Stip	3
Napredok Kicevo	0 5p
Lokomotiva Skopje *	0 4p
Drita Bogovinje *	2
Miravci	3
Metalurg Skopje	1
Rufeja Miletino *	0
Mogila *	0
Rabotnicki Skopje	3

Round of 16

Renova Cepciste *	0 5
Rinija Gostivar	1 1
Sileks Kratovo *	2 0
Teteks	2 0
11 Oktomvri Prilep *	4 0
Skopje	0 2
Tikves Kavadarci	1 0
Vardar Skopje *	6 1
Turnovo *	1 1
Pelister Bitola	0 1
Shkendija Tetovo *	2 0 0p
Bregalnica Stip	0 2 3p
Napredok Kicevo *	3 3
Miravci	1 2
Metalurg Skopje	0 0 3p
Rabotnicki Skopje *	0 0 5p

Quarter-finals

Renova Cepciste *	6 3
Teteks	0 2
11 Oktomvri Prilep	0 2
Vardar Skopje *	2 1
Turnovo *	3 0
Bregalnica Stip	1 0
Napredok Kicevo	1 0
Rabotnicki Skopje *	4 3

Semi-finals

Renova Cepciste	1 0
Vardar Skopje *	1 0
Turnovo	1 1
Rabotnicki Skopje *	1 3

Final

Renova Cepciste ‡	3
Rabotnicki Skopje	1

CUP FINAL
Gradski, Stip, 2-05-2012
Att: 1000, Ref: Goran Spirkorski
Scorers - Bajrami 12, Simovski 65, Gafuri 90 for Renova; Manevski 52 for Rabotnicki
Renova - Suat Zendeli - Bilal Velija (Saimir Fetai 90), Dusan Simovski (Ersen Asani 69), Metodija Stepanovski, Sasko Ristov - Muarem Bajrami, Goran Siljanovski, Argient Gafuri, Fisnik Nuhiu - Boban Jancevski Ismail Ismaili 57), Marjan Aridonov. Tr: Vlatko Kostov
Rabotnicki - Damjan Siskovski - Vladica Brdarovski, Aleksandar Vasilev, Milos Zivkovic - Filip Despotovski, Blaze Todorovski, Darko Velkovski (Hristijan Denkovski 78) - Borce Manevski (c), Darko Velkoski, Viktor Angelov (Bosko Stupic 46), Aleksandar Pandovski (Bojan Gjorgjievski 11). Tr: Robert Pevnik

* Home team in the first leg   ‡ Qualified for the Europa League

MLI – MALI

FIFA/COCA-COLA WORLD RANKING

'93	'94	'95	'96	'97	'98	'99	'00	'01	'02	'03	'04	'05	'06	'07	'08	'09	'10	'11	'12
70	52	52	67	80	70	72	98	112	73	54	51	63	36	46	45	47	67	67	25

2012

Jan	Feb	Mar	Apr	May	Jun	Jul	Aug	Sep	Oct	Nov	Dec	High	Low	Av
69	44	42	39	39	43	40	39	32	27	28	25	25	117	62

Mali won the bronze medal for the second time in a row at the Africa Cup of Nations finals after beating Ghana in the 2013 third place play-off match in South Africa - just as they had done twelve months previously in Malabo. It represented a triumph for coach Patrice Carteron who had only taken over in July in the wake of Alain Giresse's departure. But it was a much more remarkable achievement in the context of the civil strife in Mali, following the military coup in March. The instability was enough to prompt Giresse to quit and also to force FIFA to move their 2014 FIFA World Cup qualifier against Algeria in June to neighbouring Burkina Faso. Mali still won 2-1 under caretaker coach Amadou Pathe Diallo having lost their opening match away to Benin. Djoliba were runners-up in the CAF Confederation Cup, winning their group over AC Leopards but then losing to the Congolese club in the final 3-4 on aggregate. Djoliba thus failed to match the achievement of fellow Bamako-based club Stade Malien three years previously but they did beat them into second place for the league title, finishing six points clear at the top. US Bougounio became the first-ever second division side to win the Coupe du Mali, beating Onze Createurs from Niarela 2-1 in what was the first final not to involve one of the big three clubs from Bamako.

CAF AFRICA CUP OF NATIONS RECORD

1957-1963 DNE 1965-1970 DNQ **1972** 2 F 1974-1976 DNQ 1978 Disqualified 1980 DNE 1982-1986 DNQ 1988 DNE 1990-1992 DNQ **1994** 4 SF 1996-2000 DNQ **2002** 4 SF **2004** 4 SF **2006** DNQ **2008** 10 r1 **2010** 9 r1 **2012** 3 SF **2013** 3 SF

FEDERATION MALIENNE DE FOOTBALL (FMF)

Avenue du Mali, Hamdallaye
ACI 2000, PO Box 1020,
00000 Bamako
☎ +223 20238844
+223 20224254
malifoot@afribone.net.ml

FA 1960 CON 1963 FIFA 1962
P Hammadoun Kola Cisse
GS Boubacar Thiam

THE STADIA

2014 FIFA World Cup Stadia
Stade du 26 Mars
Bamoko   55 000

Due to political instability, Mali played their qualifier v Algeria in Ouagadougou, Burkina Faso

Other Main Stadia
Stade Modibo Keita
Bamako   35 000
Stade Omnisports
Sikasso   20 000

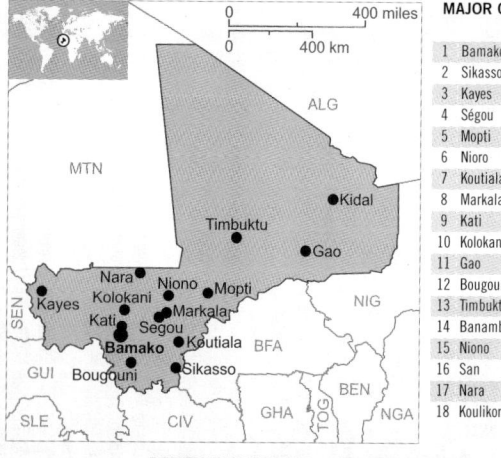

MAJOR CITIES/TOWNS

		Population
1	Bamako	1 728 444
2	Sikasso	192 400
3	Kayes	133 101
4	Ségou	104 987
5	Mopti	103 428
6	Nioro	92 387
7	Koutiala	79 502
8	Markala	76 914
9	Kati	51 105
10	Kolokani	48 679
11	Gao	46 608
12	Bougouni	36 527
13	Timbuktu	35 638
14	Banamba	31 817
15	Niono	30 838
16	San	30 028
17	Nara	28 822
18	Koulikoro	28 222

REPUBLIQUE DE MALI • REPUBLIC OF MALI

Capital	Bamako	Population	12 666 987 (70)	% in cities	32%
GDP per capita	$1100 (209)	Area km²	1 240 192 km² (24)	GMT +/-	0
Neighbours (km)	Algeria 1376, Burkina Faso 1000, Guinea 858, Cote d'Ivoire 532, Mauritania 2237, Niger 821, Senegal 419				

RECENT INTERNATIONAL MATCHES PLAYED BY MALI

2010	Opponents	Score	Venue	Comp	Scorers	Att	Referee
2-01	Qatar	D 0-0	Doha	Fr			Vad HUN
4-01	Egypt	L 0-1	Dubai	Fr			
10-01	Angola	D 4-4	Luanda	CNr1	Seydou Keita 2 [79 93+], Kanoute [88], Yattabare [94+]	45 000	Abd El Fatah EGY
14-01	Algeria	L 0-1	Luanda	CNr1		4 000	Ssegonga UGA
18-01	Malawi	W 3-1	Cabinda	CNr1	Kanoute [1], Seydou Keita [3], Bagayoko [85]	21 000	Seechurn MRI
3-03	Libya	L 1-2	Tripoli	Fr	Bakary Coulibaly [15]		
11-08	Guinea	L 0-2	Marignane	Fr			Bouzalmat FRA
4-09	Cape Verde Islands	L 0-1	Praia	CNq			Benouza ALG
9-10	Liberia	W 2-1	Bamako	CNq	Abdou Traore [2], OG [51]		Djaoupe TOG
17-11	Congo DR	W 3-1	Evreux	Fr	Maiga [48], Abdou Traore [54], Ndiaye [75p]	130	Duhamel FRA
2011							
8-02	Côte d'Ivoire	L 0-1	Valence	Fr			Castro FRA
26-03	Zimbabwe	W 1-0	Bamako	CNq	Cheick Diabate [24]		Gassama GAM
5-06	Zimbabwe	L 1-2	Harare	CNq	Mahamane Traore [49]		Bennett RSA
10-08	Tunisia	L 2-4	Monastir	Fr	Modibo Maiga [45], Cheick Diabate [56]		Keita GUI
3-09	Cape Verde Islands	W 3-0	Bamako	CNq	Cheick Diabate 2 [27 30], Mahamane Traore [50]		Diatta SEN
8-10	Liberia	D 2-2	Paynesville	CNq	Cheick Diabate [16], Cedric Kante [87]		Cordier CHA
11-11	Burkina Faso	D 1-1	St Leu La Foret	Fr	Seydou Keita [47]		
2012							
24-01	Guinea	W 1-0	Franceville	CNr1	Bakaye Traore [30]	10 000	Jedidi TUN
28-01	Ghana	L 0-2	Franceville	CNr1		7 000	Haimoudi ALG
1-02	Botswana	W 2-1	Libreville	CNr1	Garra Dembele [56], Seydou Keita [74]	20 000	Abdul Rahman SUD
5-02	Gabon	D 1-1	Libreville	CNqf	Cheick Diabate [85], W 5-4p	30 000	Haimoudi ALG
8-02	Côte d'Ivoire	L 0-1	Libreville	CNsf		32 000	Bennett RSA
11-02	Ghana	W 2-0	Malabo	CN3p	Cheick Diabate 2 [23 80]	15 000	Grisha EGY
3-06	Benin	L 0-1	Cotonou	WCq		20 000	Sikazwe ZAM
10-06	Algeria	W 2-1	Ouagadougou	WCq	Mamadou Ndiaye [30], Modibo Maiga [81]	5 847	Bennett RSA
8-09	Botswana	W 3-0	Bamoko	CNq	Cheick Diabate [27p], Mamadou Ndiaye [59], Modibo Maiga [77]		Jedidi TUN
13-10	Botswana	W 4-1	Lobatse	CNq	Cheick Diabate [29], Modibo Maiga [55], Mamadou Samassa [70], Kalilou Traore [79]		Nampiandraza MAD
2013							
20-01	Niger	W 1-0	Port Elizabeth	CNr1	Seydou Keita [84]	20 000	Jedidi TUN
24-01	Ghana	L 0-1	Port Elizabeth	CNr1		8 000	Doue CIV
28-01	Congo DR	D 1-1	Durban	CNr1	Mamadou Samassa [14]	8 000	Haimoudi ALG
2-02	South Africa	D 1-1	Durban	CNqf	Seydou Keita [58]. W 3-1p	45 000	Alioum CMR
6-02	Nigeria	L 1-4	Durban	CNsf	Cheikh Diarra [74]	54 000	Gassama GAM
9-02	Ghana	W 3-1	Port Elizabeth	CN3p	Mamadou Samassa [21], Seydou Keita [48], Sigamary Diarra [94+]	6 000	Otogo-Castane

Fr = Friendly match • CN = CAF African Cup of Nations • WC = FIFA World Cup • q = qualifier

MALI SQUAD FOR THE 2012 CAF AFRICA CUP OF NATIONS

	Player		Ap	G	Club	Date of Birth
1	Oumar Sissoko	GK	2		Metz FRA	13 09 1987
2	Abdoulaye Maiga	DF	1		USM Alger ALG	20 12 1988
3	Adama Tamboura	DF	6		Metz FRA	18 05 1985
4	Ousmane Berthe	DF	4		J. Cosmos RSA	5 02 1982
5	Cedric Kante (c)	DF	6		Pan'naikos GRE	6 07 1979
6	Mustapha Yatabare	FW	1+4		Guingamp FRA	26 01 1986
7	Abdou Traore	MF	4		Bordeaux FRA	17 01 1988
8	Souleymane Keita	MF	0+1		Sivasspor TUR	24 11 1986
9	Cheick Diabate	FW	4+2	3	Bordeaux FRA	25 04 1988
10	Modibo Maiga	FW	4		Sochaux FRA	3 09 1987
11	Garra Dembele	FW	2+3	1	Freiburg GER	21 02 1986
12	Seydou Keita	MF	6	1	Barcelona ESP	16 01 1980
13	Idrissa Coulibaly	DF	0+1		Espérance TUN	19 12 1987
14	Drissa Diakite	DF	5		Nice FRA	18 02 1985
15	Bakaye Traore	MF	6	1	Nancy FRA	6 03 1985
16	Soumbeila Diakite	GK	4		Stade Malien	25 08 1984
17	Mahamane Traore	MF	0+1		Metz FRA	31 08 1988
18	Samba Sow	MF	4+2		Lens FRA	29 04 1989
19	Sidi Kone	MF	0		Lyon FRA	6 06 1992
20	Samba Diakite	MF	5		Nancy FRA	24 01 1989
21	Mahamadou N'Diaye	DF	1		Guimarães POR	21 07 1990
22	Almamy Sogoba	GK	0		Real Bamako	5 07 1988
23	Ousmane Coulibaly	DF	1+2		Brest FRA	9 07 1989

Tr: Alain Giresse FRA 2-09-1952

MALI 2012

PREMIERE DIVISION

	Pl	W	D	L	F	A	Pts	Djoliba	Stade Malien	Bakaridjan	ASKO	Jeanne d'Arc	CSD	COB	ASOM	AS Bamako	Réal Bamako	Onze Cr'teurs	Nianan	CSK	Sigui Kayes	Stade Sikasso	AS Police
Djoliba †	30	22	8	0	46	9	74		2-0	3-1	3-2	3-0	5-0	2-0	0-0	1-1	1-1	0-0	4-1	1-1	3-0	2-1	1-0
Stade Malien †	30	20	6	4	74	23	66	0-0		2-0	1-2	0-2	3-0	2-3	2-2	5-0	3-0	3-2	2-0	4-0	5-0	3-0	2-0
Bakaridjan Ségou	30	15	7	8	31	20	52	0-0	0-0		2-0	1-0	4-1	1-0	0-1	1-2	1-0	2-0	1-0	0-1	1-0	2-0	0-0
AS Korofina Bamako	30	13	7	10	35	28	46	0-1	2-0	0-0		0-1	2-2	1-0	3-0	2-0	1-0	4-1	3-2	0-1	0-2	0-1	3-2
Jeanne d'Arc	30	14	4	12	32	29	46	0-1	2-4	0-2	1-2		0-1	1-0	0-0	2-0	0-2	2-0	3-2	0-0	4-1	4-0	2-1
Duguwolofila Koulikoro	30	13	6	11	37	32	45	0-1	0-0	0-1	1-0	4-1		1-2	0-1	0-0	2-1	3-1	2-0	2-0	0-1	3-1	1-1
Club Olympique	29	12	6	11	31	26	42	0-1	0-2	0-0	2-2	1-0	1-0		2-0	0-2	1-1	1-0	2-0	0-1	0-0	5-0	2-1
Olympique Missira	30	11	9	10	36	36	42	0-2	0-5	1-2	0-1	0-0	0-3	0-0		3-1	3-2	2-6	6-0	1-1	1-2	1-1	5-0
AS Bamako	30	12	6	12	36	40	42	0-2	0-2	3-1	0-0	0-1	2-1	3-2	1-2		1-3	1-1	1-1	0-1	4-0	2-0	0-2
Réal Bamako	30	10	9	11	33	28	39	0-1	2-2	0-1	1-0	1-0	0-0	1-0	0-1	0-1		1-3	2-1	4-0	3-0	0-0	2-0
Onze Créateurs ‡	30	8	9	13	28	43	33	1-2	1-1	0-0	1-2	0-1	1-4	1-3	0-3	5-1	1-0		1-1	0-1	3-1	3-0	2-1
Nianan Koulikoro	30	8	8	14	30	43	32	0-0	1-2	1-0	1-1	2-0	0-1	2-1	1-0	0-2	1-1	1-1		2-0	1-0	1-2	5-1
Centre Salif Keita	30	7	10	13	16	41	31	0-1	0-6	1-1	0-2	1-2	0-1	0-1	0-0	0-0	2-2	1-1	2-1		0-0	0-0	0-4
Sigui Kayes	30	6	8	16	18	46	26	0-1	0-5	2-1	0-0	0-0	0-2	0-3	0-0	2-3	1-1	0-0	0-1	3-0		1-2	2-0
Stade Sikasso	29	6	6	17	19	42	24	0-1	1-2	0-1	0-0	0-2	2-1	0-3	0-1	0-3	0-2	0-1	2-0	0-1	0-0		4-0
AS Police Bamako	30	4	7	19	29	55	19	0-1	3-4	2-4	0-2	0-1	1-2	1-1	1-2	0-2	0-0	1-1	1-1	2-1	2-0	2-2	

1/12/2011 - 4/09/2012 • † Qualified for the CAF Champions League • ‡ Qualified for the CAF Confederation Cup

MEDALS TABLE

		Overall G S B	Lge G	Cup G S	Africa G S B	City
1	Djoliba AC	41 11 3	22	19 10	1 3	Bamako
2	Stade Malien	35 10	17	17 9	1 1	Bamako
3	Real Bamako	15 8	5	10 7	1	Bamako
4	Cercle Olympique	3 2		3 2		Bamako
5	AS Bamako	1 1		1 1		Bamako
6	AS Sigui Kayes	1		1		Kayes
	US Bougouni	1		1		
8	Avenir Ségou	4		4		Ségou
9	AS Nianan Koulikoro	3		3		Koulikoro
10	Kayésienne	2		2		Kayes
	USFAS Bamako	2		2		Bamako

COUPE DU MALI 2012

Round of 16
- US Bougouni 4
- Al Farouk Timbuktu 0
- Debo Mopti 2
- Nianan Koulikoro 3
- Bakaridjan Ségou 0 3p
- Jeanne d'Arc 0 2p
- Sigui Kayes 0
- Club Olympique 4
- Djoliba 5
- Atar Club Kidal 1
- AS Bamako 0
- Réal Bamako 1
- Mamahira Kati 3
- AS Sahel Gao 0
- Centre Salif Keita 1
- Onze Créateurs 2

Quarter-finals
- US Bougouni 1
- Nianan Koulikoro 0
- Bakaridjan Ségou 1 4p
- Club Olympique 1 5p
- Djoliba 3
- Réal Bamako 2
- Mamahira Kati 2
- Onze Créateurs 3

Semi-finals
- US Bougouni 1 4p
- Club Olympique 1 3p
- Djoliba 0
- Onze Créateurs 1

Final
- US Bougouni ‡ 2
- Onze Créateurs ‡ 1

‡ Qualified for the CAF Confederation Cup

CUP FINAL
Modibo Keita, Bamako
25-08-2012
Scorers - Boubacar Camara [49], Youssouf Camara [54] for USB; Hamidou Sinayoko [14p] for OC

MLT – MALTA

FIFA/COCA-COLA WORLD RANKING

'93	'94	'95	'96	'97	'98	'99	'00	'01	'02	'03	'04	'05	'06	'07	'08	'09	'10	'11	'12
83	78	90	122	133	130	116	119	131	122	129	134	118	119	136	147	146	164	156	146

2012												High	Low	Av
Jan	Feb	Mar	Apr	May	Jun	Jul	Aug	Sep	Oct	Nov	Dec			
156	159	148	150	150	147	145	143	139	153	150	146	66	173	125

38-year-old Gilbert Agius was persuaded to play on for another season for champions Valletta and was rewarded with yet another league title - his eighth overall - although the club couldn't repeat their unbeaten campaign of the previous season, losing twice to runners-up Hibernians on the way to reclaiming their title. Had Valletta not lost their final league game to Hibernians the six point gap between the two at the top would have been greater. There was huge consolation for Hibernians after they claimed the cup for the third time in the past seven seasons. In the final they beat Qormi 3-1 with their Brazilian midfielder Jackson scoring twice but it was heartbreaking for Qormi who two years after their first appearance in the final, found themselves on the losing side again. The Malta national team experienced a curious year in 2012 after winning four of the seven matches played - the first time since 1966 that they had finished the year with a positive record. The problem for new coach Pietro Ghedin was that the three matches lost were all 2014 FIFA World Cup qualifiers and the four matches won were all friendlies against fellow minnows Liechtenstein, Luxembourg and San Marino. The Italian, in his second spell in charge, faces a tough challenge to find even a point in what is a very strong group.

UEFA EUROPEAN CHAMPIONSHIP RECORD
1960 DNE **1964** r1 **1968** DNE **1972-2012** DNQ

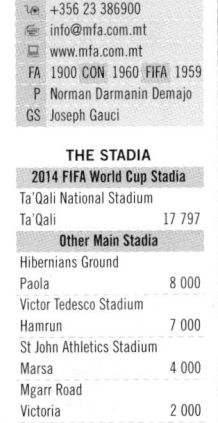

MALTA FOOTBALL ASSOCIATION (MFA)

Millenium Stand, Floor 2, National Stadium, Ta'Qali, ATD 400
☎ +356 23 386000
📠 +356 23 386900
✉ info@mfa.com.mt
🌐 www.mfa.com.mt
FA 1900 CON 1960 FIFA 1959
P Norman Darmanin Demajo
GS Joseph Gauci

THE STADIA
2014 FIFA World Cup Stadia
Ta'Qali National Stadium
Ta'Qali — 17 797

Other Main Stadia
Hibernians Ground
Paola — 8 000
Victor Tedesco Stadium
Hamrun — 7 000
St John Athletics Stadium
Marsa — 4 000
Mgarr Road
Victoria — 2 000

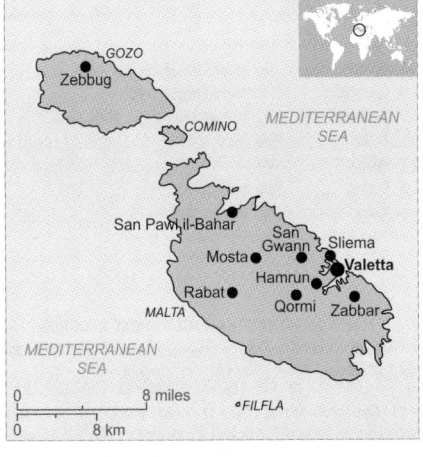

MAJOR CITIES/TOWNS

		Population
1	Birkirkara	20 737
2	Mosta	19 152
3	St Paul's Bay	16 507
4	Qormi	15 743
5	Zabbar	14 519
6	San Gwann	12 741
7	Naxxar	12 704
8	Sliema	12 595
9	Marsascala	11 335
10	Zebbug	11 335
11	Fgura	11 196
12	Zejtun	11 129
13	Rabat	10 684
14	Attard	10 523
15	Zurrieq	10 002
16	Birzebugia	9 057
17	Hamrun	8 665
18	Paola	8 330
38	Marsaxlokk	3 302

REPUBBLIKA TA' MALTA • REPUBLIC OF MALTA

Capital	Valletta	Population	405 165 (173)
GDP per capita	$24 600 (52)	Area km²	316 km² (207)
Neighbours (km)	Coast 196	% in cities	94%
		GMT +/−	+1

RECENT INTERNATIONAL MATCHES PLAYED BY MALTA

2008	Opponents	Score	Venue	Comp	Scorers	Att	Referee
20-08	Estonia	L 1-2	Tallinn	Fr	Ian Azzopardi [9]	2 700	Gilewski POL
6-09	Portugal	L 0-4	Ta'Qali	WCq		11 000	Blom NED
10-09	Albania	L 0-3	Tirana	WCq		7 400	Schoergenhofer AUT
11-10	Denmark	L 0-3	Copenhagen	WCq		33 124	Paniashvili GEO
15-10	Hungary	L 0-1	Ta'Qali	WCq		4 797	Valgeirsson ISL
19-11	Iceland	L 0-1	Corradino	Fr		500	De Marco ITA
2009							
11-02	Albania	D 0-0	Ta'Qali	WCq		2 041	Deaconu ROU
28-03	Denmark	L 0-3	Ta'Qali	WCq		6 235	Mikulski POL
1-04	Hungary	L 0-3	Budapest	WCq		34 400	Sukhina RUS
5-06	Czech Republic	L 0-1	Jablonec	Fr		6 019	Fautrel FRA
10-06	Sweden	L 0-4	Gothenburg	WCq		25 271	Murray SCO
12-08	Georgia	W 2-0	Ta'Qali	Fr	Michael Mifsud 2 [64 73]	15 000	Kailis CYP
4-09	Cape Verde Islands	L 0-2	Ta'Qali	Fr		1 000	Banti ITA
9-09	Sweden	L 0-1	Ta'Qali	WCq		4 705	McCourt NIR
10-10	Angola	L 1-2	Vila Real	Fr	Andrew Cohen [13]	150	Almeida POR
14-10	Portugal	L 0-4	Guimaraes	WCq		29 350	Kelly IRL
18-11	Bulgaria	L 1-4	Paola	Fr	Michael Mifsud [46]	2 000	Nijhuis NED
2010							
3-03	Finland	L 1-2	Ta'Qali	Fr	Michael Mifsud [17]	1 050	Bergonzi ITA
13-05	Germany	L 0-3	Aachen	Fr		27 000	Hamer LUX
11-08	FYR Macedonia	D 1-1	Ta'Qali	Fr	Michael Mifsud [47]	2 500	Rossi ITA
2-09	Israel	L 1-3	Tel Aviv	ECq	Jamie Pace [38]	17 365	Ennjimi FRA
7-09	Latvia	L 0-2	Ta'Qali	ECq		6 255	Asumaa FIN
8-10	Georgia	L 0-1	Tbilisi	ECq		38 000	Black NIR
17-11	Croatia	L 0-3	Zagreb	ECq		9 000	Gomes POR
2011							
9-02	Switzerland	D 0-0	Ta'Qali	Fr		3 000	Stamatis CYP
26-03	Greece	L 0-1	Ta'Qali	ECq		10 605	Weiner GER
4-06	Greece	L 1-3	Piraeus	ECq	Michael Mifsud [54]	14 746	Gil POL
10-08	Central African Rep	W 2-1	Ta'Qali	Fr	Michael Mifsud 2 [2p 44]		Ozkalfa TUR
2-09	Croatia	L 1-3	Ta'Qali	ECq	Michael Mifsud [38]	6 150	Chapron FRA
6-09	Georgia	D 1-1	Ta'Qali	ECq	Michael Mifsud [25]	5 000	Van Boekel NED
7-10	Latvia	L 0-2	Riga	ECq		4 315	Trutz SVK
11-10	Israel	L 0-2	Ta'Qali	ECq		2 164	Paixao POR
2012							
29-02	Liechtenstein	W 2-1	Ta'Qali	Fr	Michael Mifsud 2 [54 63]	2 300	Whitby WAL
2-06	Luxembourg	W 2-0	Luxembourg	Fr	Michael Mifsud 2 [20 80]	1 054	Hameter AUT
14-08	San Marino	W 3-2	Serravalle	Fr	Michael Mifsud 2 [13 85], Andrei Agius [22]		Tagliavento ITA
7-09	Armenia	L 0-1	Ta'Qali	WCq		3 517	Eisner AUT
11-09	Italy	L 0-2	Modena	WCq		18 000	Munukka FIN
12-10	Czech Republic	L 1-3	Plzen	WCq	Roderick Briffa [38]	10 358	Salmanov AZE
14-11	Liechtenstein	W 1-0	Vaduz	Fr	Jonathan Caruana [38]	550	Hanni SUI

Fr = Friendly match • EC = UEFA EURO 2012 • WC = FIFA World Cup • q = qualifier

MALTA NATIONAL TEAM HISTORICAL RECORDS

Caps
121 - David Carabott 1987-2005 • 120 - Gilbert Agius 1993- • 111 - Carmel Busuttil 1982-2001 • 103 - Joe Brincat 1988-2004 • 95 - John Buttigieg 1984-2000 • 92 - Michael Mifsud 2000- • 91 - Brian Said 1996-2009 • 90 - Silvio Vella 1988-2000 • 74 - Michael Degiorgio 1981-92 • 72 - Luke Dimech 1999- • 70 - Hubert Suda 1988-2003 • 69 - Jeffrey Chetcuti 1994-2005

Goals
36 - Michael Mifsud 2000- • 23 - Carmel Busuttil 1982-2001 • 12 - David Carabott 1987-2005 • 8 - Gilbert Agius 1993- & Hubert Suda 1988-2003 • 6 - Kristian Laferla 1986-98; Raymond Xuereb 1971-85; Joe Brincat 1988-2004 & George Mallia 1999-

Coaches
Joe A. Griffiths 1957-61 • Carm Borg 1961-64 • Janos Bedl HUN 1966 • Tony Formosa 1966 • Joseph Attard 1969 • Saviour Cuschieri 1970 • Victor Scerri 1973 • Terrenzio Polverini ITA 1974-76 • John Calleja 1976-78 • Victor Scerri 1978-83 • Guentcho Dobrev BUL 1984-87 • Horst Heese GER 1988-91 • Pippo Psaila 1991-93 • Pietro Ghedin ITA 1993-95 • Robert Gatt 1996 • Milorad Kosanovic YUG 1996-97 • Josif Ilic YUG 1997-2001 • Sigfried Held GER 2001-03 • Horst Heese GER 2003-06 • Dusan Fitzel CZE 2006-09 • John Buttigieg 2009-11 • Robert Gatt 2012 • Pietro Ghedin ITA 2012-

MALTA 2011-12

PREMIER LEAGUE

	Pl	W	D	L	F	A	Pts	Valletta	Hibernians	Birkirkara	Floriana	Sliema W	Balzan Yth	Qormi	Mosta	Tarxien	Hamrun	Mqabba	Marsaxlokk
Valletta (28) †	32	25	5	2	75	24	54		0-2 1-2	1-1 1-1	1-2 0-1	1-3 0-2	0-1 0-1	3-1	1-0	4-2	4-0	2-1	5-2
Hibernians (26) ‡	32	22	6	4	74	26	46	1-1 2-3		5-0 0-1	1-1 1-0	1-1 2-1	3-1 3-0	4-0	2-1	2-0	5-0	4-1	2-1
Birkirkara (18) ‡	32	17	4	11	55	37	38	1-4 0-2	0-3 2-0		0-1 3-1	0-1 1-1	2-1 3-0	2-0	0-0	2-3	3-1	1-0	1-0
Floriana (21) ‡	32	16	6	10	46	32	29	0-1 0-1	0-0 0-2	0-3 2-1		0-1 1-4	3-1 3-1	2-1	1-2	1-0	4-2	2-0	4-0
Sliema Wanderers (18)	32	9	14	9	43	50	23	0-0 0-2	3-3 1-3	1-0 1-4	0-0 1-3		1-1 1-1	3-3	2-0	3-0	1-1	1-1	2-2
Balzan Youth (16)	32	9	6	17	36	64	15	0-2 2-7	3-2 1-4	0-4 0-5	2-2 0-3	2-1 3-3		2-0	1-1	1-0	**2-0**	1-2	3-1
Qormi (15)	32	15	2	15	54	48	33	1-4	0-2	2-0	1-1	1-3	3-0		4-1 1-4	4-1 1-0	3-0 6-0	0-1 2-1	3-1 5-1
Mosta (12)	32	10	8	14	45	47	27	0-3	0-2	1-3	2-3	3-2	1-0	1-0 2-0			2-1 0-2	0-1 2-2	3-0 2-2 0-0 5-0
Tarxien Rainbows (9)	32	11	3	18	45	54	27	1-4	1-2	1-3	1-2	1-1	1-2	2-0 1-2	1-0 2-1		1-1 1-2	3-2 1-0	2-4 2-4
Hamrun Spartans (10)	32	9	7	16	47	71	25	0-2	1-1	0-4	0-1	4-2	1-2	2-3 1-0	2-2 1-1	3-1 0-3		0-2 0-0	6-2 3-1
Mqabba (10)	32	9	7	16	40	55	24	2-4	1-6	2-2	0-1	0-2	2-2	1-4 0-1	1-1 1-0	1-1 0-5	2-3 4-1		1-0 3-0
Marsaxlokk (6) §4	32	5	2	25	34	88	8	0-2	0-2	1-2	0-4	0-2	0-1	1-2 1-0	5-2 1-5	2-2 0-2	5-3 1-6	0-2 0-4	

19/08/2011 - 12/05/2012 • † Qualified for the UEFA Champions League • ‡ Qualified for the Europa League • Points taken forward for the final round in brackets • § = points deducted • Match in bold awarded

Top scorers: **34** - Obinna **OBIEFULE** NGA, Marsaxlokk/Mosta • **23** - **EDISON** BRA, Hibernians • **19** - **JORGINHO** BRA, Qormi • **17** - **ANDERSON RIBEIRO** BRA, Hamrun • **15** - **MOISES** Avila **PEREZ** ESP, Birkirkara & Bojan **MAMIC** SRB, Mqabba • **13** - Clayton **FAILLA**, Hibernians & **PEDRINHO** BRA, Balzan • **12** - **DENNI** BRA, Valletta & **WILLIAM** BRA, Valletta

MALTA 2011-12

PREMIER LEAGUE

	Pl	W	D	L	F	A	Pts	Melita	Rabat Ajax	Pietà H	Zejtun	Vittoriosa	Naxxar	Lija Ath	St Andrews	Birzebbuga	Dingli	St Patrick	St George's
Melita	22	14	5	3	46	23	47		1-0	3-1	5-0	1-1	1-1	4-3	4-2	2-1	4-0	2-1	2-1
Rabat Ajax	22	14	3	5	26	12	45	3-0		0-1	2-3	3-1	0-2	1-0	1-0	0-0	2-0	1-2	0-0
Pietà Hotspurs	22	12	2	8	27	19	38	1-0	0-1		0-1	0-2	4-0	2-0	2-0	4-3	1-0	2-1	0-2
Zejtun Corinthians	22	11	3	8	29	21	36	0-1	0-1	0-0		0-2	0-1	1-0	2-0	1-0	1-0	4-0	5-1
Vittoriosa Stars	22	9	7	6	38	25	34	1-4	1-1	1-3	0-0		1-1	4-0	2-1	5-1	0-1	4-1	4-2
Naxxar Lions	22	9	6	7	32	32	33	2-2	1-2	1-3	2-1	0-3		0-0	1-4	4-2	1-1	1-1	5-0
Lija Athletic	22	8	5	9	26	25	29	1-1	0-1	1-0	0-0	0-0	0-1		3-1	2-3	1-1	0-1	4-1
St Andrews	22	8	3	11	24	30	27	0-0	0-1	1-0	1-2	0-1	2-1	2-1		1-0	1-1	0-1	0-1
Birzebbuga St Peter's	22	7	2	13	31	40	23	3-2	0-2	1-2	3-1	2-1	1-3	0-1	2-2		1-2	0-1	2-1
Dingli Swallows	22	6	4	12	16	30	22	0-3	0-1	0-1	0-2	1-3	0-2	0-2	2-1	2-1		3-0	0-2
St Patrick	22	5	4	13	18	37	19	1-2	0-1	1-0	1-3	1-4	1-2	1-3	1-2	1-3	0-0		1-3
St George's	22	5	4	13	19	39	19	0-2	0-2	0-0	1-4	0-0	2-0	1-2	1-2	0-2	0-2	0-0	

9/09/2011 - 14/05/2012

MALTA 2011-12
SECOND DIVISION (3)

	Pl	W	D	L	F	A	Pts
Gzira United	26	18	6	2	58	16	60
Gudja United	26	16	6	4	57	20	54
Mellieha	26	16	6	4	51	27	52
Gharghur	26	13	5	8	57	37	44
Zebbug Rangers	26	11	10	5	47	30	43
San Gwann	26	10	9	7	43	35	39
Msida St Joseph	26	11	3	12	42	29	36
Kirkop United	26	11	2	13	44	52	35
St Venera	26	9	6	11	27	45	33
Zurrieq	26	8	5	13	26	40	29
Siggiewi	26	7	6	13	31	51	27
Attard	26	7	4	15	30	56	25
Senglea Athletic	26	4	3	19	34	71	15
Luqa St Andrew's	26	4	3	19	24	62	15

9/09/2011 - 14/05/2012

MEDALS TABLE

		Overall			League			Cup		
		G	S	B	G	S	B	G	S	City
1	Sliema Wanderers	46	50	19	**26**	31	19	**20**	19	Sliema
2	Floriana	44	24	13	25	12	13	19	12	Floriana
3	Valletta	33	29	20	21	16	20	12	13	Valletta
4	Hibernians	19	20	9	10	10	9	9	10	Paola
5	Hamrun Spartans	13	13	13	7	10	13	6	3	Hamrun
6	Birkirkara	7	9	7	3	6	7	4	3	Birkirkara
7	Rabat Ajax	3	2	1	2	1	1	1	1	Rabat
8	St. Georges	1	6	5	1	4	5		2	Cospicua
9	Zurrieq	1	2	2			2	1	2	Zurrieq
10	Marsaxlokk	1	2	1	1	1	1		1	Marsaxlokk
	Melita St. Julians	1	2	1		1	1	1	1	Melita
12	Gzira United	1		1				1	1	Gzira
13	KOMR Militia	1			1					

FA TROPHY 2011-12

Second Round

Hibernians	5
Pembroke Athleta	3
Kirkop United	0
Rabat Ajax	3
Balzan Youth	2
Zejtun Corinthians	1
Luqa St Andrew's	1
Floriana	6
St George's	2
Gharghur	0
Victoria Hotspurs	0
Lija Athletic	6
Birkirkara	4
Vittoriosa Stars	0
Dingli Swallows	1
Hamrun Spartans	3
Valletta	2
St Patrick	0
Mqabba	2
Sliema Wanderers	4
Xewkija Tigers	3
Senglea Athletic	0
Msida St Joseph	0
Mosta	1
Pietà Hotspurs	3
Tarxien Rainbows	0
San Gwann	3
Marsaxlokk	5
Mellieha	0 4p
Siggiewi	0 3p
Gzira United	0
Qormi	1

Round of 16

Hibernians	5
Rabat Ajax	0
Balzan Youth	0
Floriana	1
St George's	1 5p
Lija Athletic	1 4p
Birkirkara	2
Hamrun Spartans	3
Valletta	5
Sliema Wanderers	2
Xewkija Tigers	1
Mosta	3
Pietà Hotspurs	5
Marsaxlokk	1
Mellieha	0
Qormi	5

Quarter-finals

Hibernians	1
Floriana	0
St George's	
Hamrun Spartans	
Valletta	3
Mosta	1
Pietà Hotspurs	0
Qormi	1

Semi-finals

Hibernians	2
Hamrun Spartans	1
Valletta	3
Qormi	4

Final

Hibernians ‡	3
Qormi	1

CUP FINAL

National, Ta' Qali, 27-05-2012
Att: 7000, Ref: Marco Borg
Scorers - Clayton Failla 36p Jackson 2 43 47 for Hibernians; Farrugia 95+ for Qormi
Hibernians - Mario Muscat - Jason Vandelannoite, Jonathan Pearson● (Steve Pisani 76), Edward Herrera, Ryan Camilleri - Rodolfo Soares, Clayton Failla, Jackson Lima (Marcelo Dias 83), Bjorn Kristensen - Andrew Cohen, Tarabai● (Johann Bezzina 92+).
Tr: Mark Miller
Qormi - Matthew Farrugia - Jonathan Bondin (Luke Sciberras 80), Roderick Sammut, Kris Thackray, Vincent Kouadio (Stephen Wellman 65) - Triston Caruana● - Matthew Bartolo, Joseph Chetcuti (Kenneth Sciciuna 54), Joseph Farrugia, Abubakar Bello Osagie, Jorge Pereira.
Tr: Stephen Azzopardi

‡ Qualified for the Europa League

MNE – MONTENEGRO

FIFA/COCA-COLA WORLD RANKING

'93	'94	'95	'96	'97	'98	'99	'00	'01	'02	'03	'04	'05	'06	'07	'08	'09	'10	'11	'12
-	-	-	-	-	-	-	-	-	-	-	-	-	-	172	112	74	25	51	31

2012

Jan	Feb	Mar	Apr	May	Jun	Jul	Aug	Sep	Oct	Nov	Dec	High	Low	Av
50	51	44	54	55	50	50	50	48	44	34	31	16	199	85

Buducnost from the capital Podgorica finally threw off their reputation as gallant runners-up after winning the 2012 championship ahead of Rudar. Four times in the league and twice in the cup they had finished second but despite losing their lead to Rudar in March - having led from the start of the season - they fought back in convincing fashion by winning their next ten matches. They eventually claimed the title for the second time in their history after a 1-1 draw at home to Rudar. Three days earlier, Rudar had been on the end of a shock result in the cup final, losing 2-1 to second division champions Celik - the first second division team to win the trophy. Rudar had been hoping for a hat trick of cup wins but despite dominating for much of the game could not recover from the two first-half goals scored by Celik, a team representing Niksic, Montenegro's second largest city. After a terrible time in 2011, the national team turned things around in convincing fashion in 2012, going through the year unbeaten and leading their 2014 FIFA World Cup qualifying group ahead of England, Poland and the Ukraine. Montenegro have made a big splash since playing their first international in 2007 and they will harbour genuine hopes of making a first appearance at a major finals by qualifying for Brazil although their group looks to be amongst the toughest.

UEFA EUROPEAN CHAMPIONSHIP RECORD
1960-2004 DNE (Played as Yugoslavia) 2008 DNE 2012 DNQ

FOOTBALL ASSOCIATION OF MONTENEGRO (FAM)

Fudbalski savez Crne Gore,
Ulica 19. Decembar 13,
PO Box 275,
81000 Podgorica
☎ +382 20 445600
📠 +382 20 445660
✉ info@fscg.me
🖥 www.fscg.me
FA 1931 CON 2007 FIFA 2007
P Dejan Savicevic
GS Momir Djurdjevac

THE STADIA

2014 FIFA World Cup Stadia
Stadion pod Goricom
Podgorica 13 000

Other Main Stadia
Stadion Gradski
Berane 11 000
Stadion Kraj Bistrice
Niksic 10 800
Stadion pod Golubinjom
Pljevlja 10 000

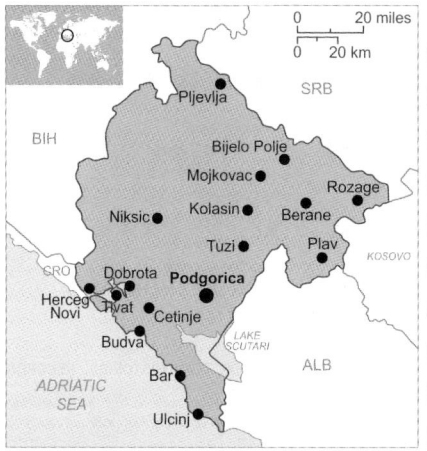

MAJOR CITIES/TOWNS

		Population
1	Podgorica	145 192
2	Niksic	58 712
3	Pljevlja	21 354
4	Bijelo Polje	15 357
5	Bar	15 112
6	Cetinje	14 569
7	Herceg Novi	13 361
8	Budva	13 093
9	Berane	11 498
10	Ulcinj	11 056
11	Tivat	10 056
12	Rozaje	9 130
13	Dobrota	8 533
14	Danilovgrad	5 574
15	Tuzi	4 564
16	Bijela	4 102
17	Mojkovac	3 938
18	Skaljari	3 874
19	Igalo	3 785

CRNA GORA • MONTENEGRO

Capital	Podgorica	Population	672 180 (164)	% in cities	60%
GDP per capita	$10 100 (104)	Area km²	13 812 km² (161)	GMT +/-	+1
Neighbours (km)	Albania 172, Bosnia-Herzegovina 225, Croatia 25, Kosovo 79, Serbia 124 • Coast 293					

INTERNATIONAL MATCHES PLAYED BY MONTENEGRO

2008	Opponents	Score		Venue	Comp	Scorers	Att	Referee
26-03	Norway	W	3-1	Podgorica	Fr	Burzanovic [7], Boskovic [37], Dalovic [59]	9 000	Stavrev MKD
27-05	Kazakhstan	W	3-0	Podgorica	Fr	Dalovic 2 [15 45], Drincic [21]	9 000	Tusin LUX
31-05	Romania	L	0-4	Bucharest	Fr		8 000	Tudor ROU
20-08	Hungary	D	3-3	Budapest	Fr	Jovetic 2 [45p 68], Vukevic [51]	4 913	Havrilla SVK
6-09	Bulgaria	D	2-2	Podgorica	WCq	Vucinic [61], Jovetic [82p]	9 000	Oriekhov UKR
10-09	Republic of Ireland	D	0-0	Podgorica	WCq		12 000	Kaldma EST
15-10	Italy	L	1-2	Lecce	WCq	Vucinic [19]	20 162	Proenca POR
19-11	Macedonia FYR	W	2-1	Podgorica	Fr	Dzudovic [24], Jovetic [33p]	5 000	Panic BIH
2009								
28-03	Italy	L	0-2	Podgorica	WCq		10 500	Atkinson ENG
1-04	Georgia	D	0-0	Tbilisi	WCq		16 000	Malcolm NIR
6-06	Cyprus	D	2-2	Larnaca	WCq	Damjanovic 2 [65 77]	3 000	Velasco ESP
12-08	Wales	W	2-1	Podgorica	Fr	Jovetic [31p], Dalovic [45]	5 000	Mazic SRB
5-09	Bulgaria	L	1-4	Sofia	WCq	Jovetic [9]	7 543	Asumaa FIN
9-09	Cyprus	D	1-1	Podgorica	WCq	Vucinic [56p]	4 000	Zimmermann SUI
10-10	Georgia	W	2-1	Podgorica	WCq	Batak [14], Delibasic [78]	5 420	Dereli TUR
14-10	Republic of Ireland	D	0-0	Dublin	WCq		50 212	Hrinal SVK
18-11	Belarus	W	1-0	Podgorica	Fr	Vucinic [80]	5 000	Stavrev MKD
2010								
3-03	FYR Macedonia	L	1-2	Skopje	Fr	Basa [62]	7 000	Janku ALB
25-05	Albania	L	0-1	Podgorica	Fr		7 000	Strahonja CRO
29-05	Norway	L	1-2	Oslo	Fr	Vucinic [82]	13 132	Eriksson SWE
11-08	Northern Ireland	W	2-0	Podgorica	Fr	Dalovic 2 [43 59]	5 000	Jovanetic SRB
3-09	Wales	W	1-0	Podgorica	ECq	Vucinic [30]	7 442	Kakos GRE
7-09	Bulgaria	W	1-0	Sofia	ECq	Zverotic [36]	9 470	Bezborodov RUS
8-10	Switzerland	W	1-0	Podgorica	ECq	Vucinic [68]	10 750	Iturralde ESP
12-10	England	D	0-0	London	ECq		73 451	Grafe GER
17-11	Azerbaijan	W	2-0	Podgorica	Fr	Pejovic [62], Beciraj [74]	3 000	Stavrev MKD
2011								
25-03	Uzbekistan	W	1-0	Podgorica	Fr	Vukevic [90]	6 000	Glodovic SRB
4-06	Bulgaria	D	1-1	Podgorica	ECq	Djalovic [53]	11 500	Yefet ISR
10-08	Albania	L	2-3	Tirana	Fr	Savic 2 [40 49]	5 500	Genov BUL
2-09	Wales	L	1-2	Cardiff	ECq	Jovetic [71]	8 194	Banti ITA
7-10	England	D	2-2	Podgorica	ECq	Zverotic [45], Delibasic [91+]	11 340	Stark GER
11-10	Switzerland	L	0-2	Basel	ECq		19 997	Benquerenca POR
11-11	Czech Republic	L	0-2	Prague	ECpo		14 560	Atkinson ENG
15-11	Czech Republic	L	0-1	Podgorica	ECpo		11 000	Rizzoli ITA
2012								
29-02	Iceland	W	2-1	Podgorica	Fr	Jovetic 2 [56 88]	5 500	Valjic BIH
25-05	Belgium	D	2-2	Brussels	Fr	Vucinic [5], Drincic [76]	21 110	Turpin FRA
15-08	Latvia	W	2-0	Podgorica	Fr	Jovanovic [36], Kasalica [76]	4 500	Grujic SRB
7-09	Poland	D	2-2	Podgorica	WCq	Drincic [27], Vucinic [45]	11 420	Jakobsson ISL
11-09	San Marino	W	6-0	Serravalle	WCq	Djordjevic [24], Beciraj 2 [26 51], Zverotic [69], Delibasic 2 [78 82]	1 947	Doyle IRL
16-10	Ukraine	W	1-0	Kyiv	WCq	Damjanovic [45]	50 597	Koukoulakis GRE
14-11	San Marino	W	3-0	Podgorica	WCq	Delibasic 2 [14 31], Zverotic [68]	7 158	Szabo HUN

Fr = Friendly match • EC = UEFA EURO 2012 • WC = FIFA World Cup • q = qualifier

MONTENEGRO NATIONAL TEAM HISTORICAL RECORDS

Caps
40 - Simon Vukcevic 2007- • **34** - Elsad Zverotic 2008- • **32** - Milan Jovanovic 2007- • **31** - Mirko Vucinic 2007- & Savo Pavicevic 2007- • **30** - Vladimir Bozovic 2007- & Milorad Petkovic 2007- • **28** - Nikola Drincic 2007- • **27** - Mladen Bozovic 2007-

Goals
13 - Mirko Vucinic 2007- • **10** - Stevan Jovetic 2007- • **7** - Radomir Dalovic 2007- • **6** - Andrija Delibasic 2009-

Coaches
Zoran Filipovic 2007-10 • Zlatko Kranjcar 2010-11 • Branko Brnovic 2011-

MONTENEGRO 2011-12

PRVA CRNOGORSKA LIGA

	Pl	W	D	L	F	A	Pts	Buducnost	Rudar	Zeta	Mogren	Petrovac	Lovcen	Mladost	Sutjeska	Grbalj	Decic	Berane	Bokelj
Buducnost Podgorica †	33	25	5	3	82	27	80		0-2 1-1	5-0 2-2	1-2		5-1	4-0 0-3	3-1 6-0	2-0 3-0	3-1	5-0 3-1	3-1	1-1
Rudar Pljevlja ‡	33	23	8	2	60	20	77	2-2		1-0	2-0 4-1	2-1 0-0	1-1 1-2	3-0		0-0	3-0 1-0	1-0	1-0 3-1	4-1 6-2
Zeta Golubovci ‡	33	17	9	7	55	40	60	0-2	4-1 0-3		0-0	1-0 2-0	3-0 3-2	2-1		0-0	0-0 3-1	1-0	2-3 4-2	1-1 3-0
Mogren Budva	33	15	9	9	54	37	54	1-2 1-3	1-1	2-2 2-3		1-1	2-0 1-2	1-1 2-1	1-2 1-1	2-1	0-1	5-1 3-0	2-0	2-1
OFK Petrovac	33	13	9	11	36	39	48	1-1 1-4	0-2	1-2	1-2 0-1		3-2 1-0	0-0 1-0	0-0 1-1	2-1	1-0 1-3	2-1	2-0	
Lovcen Cetinje	33	10	10	13	34	42	40	0-2	1-3	0-0	0-1	0-2		0-2	2-0 1-0	0-0 2-0	0-0 3-1	1-1 2-0	2-1 1-1
Mladost Podgorica	33	10	7	16	32	45	37	0-1	0-2 0-1	0-4 0-0	1-1	0-1	2-2 1-3			2-2	2-0 4-1	1-0	0-2 4-1	1-0 2-0
Sutjeska Niksic	33	9	9	15	29	36	36	2-3	0-1 0-3	0-1 4-2	0-0	2-0	0-0	0-0 2-0			0-3	1-2 2-0	0-1	1-0 2-0
Grbalj Radanovici	33	9	7	17	28	49	34	1-3 0-4	0-1	0-1	1-1 1-0	0-3 1-1	0-0	1-2	2-0 0-4		2-0 2-1	1-0	2-1
Decic Tuzi	33	10	4	19	34	51	34	1-3	1-2 0-0	1-3 2-2	1-1	2-3	3-0	1-0 2-0	1-0	3-1		3-0 1-0	0-1 1-0
FK Berane	33	8	5	20	32	54	28	0-1 0-1	0-0	2-3	2-4 1-3	2-2 1-2	2-1	0-1	1-1 2-0	1-3 1-1	2-0		1-0
Bokelj Kotor	33	5	6	22	21	57	21	0-1 1-2	1-2	2-1	0-3 0-5	0-0 0-1	1-1	0-3	0-2	1-0 1-1	1-3	2-0 0-1	

6/08/2011 - 30/05/2012 • † Qualified for the UEFA Champions League • ‡ Qualified for the Europa League
Relegation play-offs: Decic 0-0 0-2 **Jedinstvo** • Berane 1-2 0-3 **Mornar**
Top scorers: **22** - Admir **ADROVIC**, Buducnost • **21** - Zarko **KORAC**, Zeta • **18** - Ivica **JOVANIVIC** SRB, Rudar • **17** - Dragan **BOSKOVIC**, Buducnost • **14** - Srdan **RADONJIC**, Buducnost & Nikola **VUJOVIC**, Mogren • **12** - Nenad **JOVANOVIC** SRB, Petrovac • **10** - Djordje **SUSNJAR** SRB, Sutjeska & Luka **DORDEVIC**, Mogren • **9** - Igor **IVANOVIC**, Rudar; Nenad **STOJANOVIC** SRB, Rudar & Bozo **MARKOVIC**, Sutjeska

MONTENEGRO 2011-12

DRUGA LIGA (2)

	Pl	W	D	L	F	A	Pts	Celik	Mornar	Jedinstvo	Zabjelo	Bratstvo	OSK Igalo	Jezero	OFK Bar	Iskra	Ibar	Kom	Petnjica
Celik Niksic	33	25	5	3	72	14	80		1-0	1-0 1-1	3-2 2-0	2-0	2-0	4-0	4-1 5-1	3-0 5-0	3-1 4-0	3-0	3-0 5-0
Mornar Bar ‡	33	19	7	7	55	26	64	0-0 3-1		2-0	2-0 2-0	2-1	2-0	1-0	2-0 4-1	2-3 4-0	1-0 3-0	2-2	1-1 5-1
Jedinstvo Bijelo Polje ‡	33	18	7	8	50	23	61	1-0	0-0 1-2		3-0	2-0 3-1	0-0 2-0	2-1 3-0	1-0	4-0	0-0	1-0 1-2	3-0 3-0
Zabjelo Podgorica	33	15	5	13	47	46	50	1-2	5-1	3-2 2-1		0-0 1-1	1-0 2-0	3-1 1-0	0-2	2-1	1-1	3-0 0-2	1-0 5-0
Bratstvo Cijevna	33	14	6	13	44	40	48	0-1 1-0	2-1 0-2	1-0	3-1		0-0	2-1	3-6 1-0	0-0 0-1	2-0 4-0	1-2	2-1 3-2
OSK Igalo	33	12	8	13	25	27	44	0-1 0-0	0-3 2-0	0-0	2-0	1-0 1-1		0-0	1-0	2-1 2-0	0-1 0-0	1-0	1-0
Jezero Plav	33	11	9	13	26	35	42	0-1 0-0	1-0 1-0	1-1	2-0	1-1 3-2	0-1 1-0		1-0	0-1 0-0	1-2	1-0	1-1
OFK Bar	33	12	4	17	44	54	40	0-3	0-0	1-2 3-3	2-0 1-1	2-0	2-0 2-5	4-0 0-1		2-1	1-0	2-0 3-2	1-2 2-0
Iskra Bugojno	33	11	6	16	31	47	39	1-4	0-1	1-2 1-0	0-1 1-1	0-3	1-0	0-1	1-1 5-1		1-0 1-0	0-1 3-3	1-0
Ibar Rozaje	33	10	8	15	35	42	38	1-2	1-1	0-1 0-3	1-2 7-2	1-2	0-1	1-1 1-0	4-0 1-0	1-0		2-2	4-1
Kom Podgorica	33	9	10	14	35	47	37	0-0 0-1	1-1 1-4	0-3	1-3	0-3 2-1	0-0 2-1	1-1 1-2	1-0	1-1	0-0 2-2		0-1
FK Petnjica	33	3	3	27	15	78	12	0-5	0-1	0-1	0-3	1-3	1-0 2-4	0-2 1-1	0-3	0-2 0-3	0-1 0-2	0-3 0-3	

14/08/2011 - 30/05/2012 • ‡ Promotion play-off

MEDALS TABLE

		Overall	League	Cup	
		G S B	G S B	G S	City
1	Rudar Pljevlja	4 2 1	1 1 1	3 1	Pljevlja
2	Mogren Budva	3 1 2	2 2	1 1	Budva
3	Buducnost Podgorica	2 6	2 4	2	Podgorica
4	Zeta Golubovci	1 1 1	1 1 1		Golubovci
5	OFK Petrovac	1		1	Petrovac
	Celik Niksic	1		1	Niksic
7	Sutjeska Niksic	1 1		1	Niksic
8	Lovcen Cetinje			1	Cetinje
9	Grbalj Radanovici	1	1		Radanovici

KUPA CRNE GORE 2011–12

First Round

Celik Niksic	2
Blue Star*	0
Drezga Piperi*	1
Lovcen Cetinje	3
Buducnost Podgorica	3
Kom Podgorica*	0
Otrant Ulcinj*	0
Bokelj Kotor	4
Zeta Golubovci	2
Polimlje Murino*	1
Zabjelo Podgorica*	0
Sutjeska Niksic	2
Arsenal Tivat*	2
FK Petnjica	1
Decic Tuzi	0
Jedinstvo Bijelo Polje*	2
OFK Petrovac*	2
Iskra Bugojino	0
OFK Bar	0
Brskovo Mojkovac*	1
Bratstvo Cijevna*	3
Jezero Plav	1
Ibar Rozaje*	0
Mladost Podgorica	2
Mogren Budva	Bye
FK Berane	2
Mornar Bar*	4
Grbalj Radanovici	2 4p
OSK Igalo*	2 2p
Rudar Pljevlja	Bye

Round of 16

Celik Niksic	1 1
Lovcen Cetinje*	0 0
Buducnost Podgorica	0 2
Bokelj Kotor*	3 0
Zeta Golubovci	0 3
Sutjeska Niksic*	2 0
Arsenal Tivat	0 1
Jedinstvo Bijelo Polje*	3 4
OFK Petrovac*	0 2
Brskovo Mojkovac	0 0
Bratstvo Cijevna	0 4
Mladost Podgorica*	2 3
Mogren Budva*	2 2
Mornar Bar	0 0
Grbalj Radanovici	1 1
Rudar Pljevlja*	1 3

Quarter-finals

Celik Niksic	1 1
Bokelj Kotor*	0 1
Zeta Golubovci	0 2
Jedinstvo Bijelo Polje*	1 2
OFK Petrovac*	0 3
Mladost Podgorica	0 1
Mogren Budva*	1 0
Rudar Pljevlja	4 0

Semi-finals

Celik Niksic	0 3
Jedinstvo Bijelo Polje*	1 0
OFK Petrovac	0 1
Rudar Pljevlja*	2 1

Final

Celik Niksic ‡	2
Rudar Pljevlja	1

CUP FINAL

Pod Goricom, Podgorica, 23-05-2012
Att: 6000, Ref: Zeljko Radunovic
Scorers - Dubljevic [10] Bojic [34] for Celik;
Jovanovic [47] for Rudar
Celik - Zoran Banovic - Veselin Bojic● - Ilija Radovic - Aleksandar Dubljevic●, Ilija Bulatovic - Boris Bulajic●, Zijad Adrovic - Darko Zoric (Milovan Nikolic 82), Ivan Ivanovic, Ljubia Vukelja● (Bojan Brnovic 90), Vasilije Jovovic (Elmir Kudluzovic 71). Tr: Slavoljub Bubanja
Rudar - Milan Mijatovic - Igor Radusinovic● (Ermin Alic 46), Vladan Adzic, Igor Ivanovic●, Milos Popovic● - Edi Rustemovic 64) - Miroje Jovanovic, Nedeljko Vlahovic (Milienko Neric 76), Predrag Brnovic, Andrija Kaluderovic - Nenad Stojanovic, Ivica Jovanovic. Tr: Dragan Radojicic

* Home team in the first leg • ‡ Qualified for the Europa League

MNG – MONGOLIA

FIFA/COCA-COLA WORLD RANKING

'93	'94	'95	'96	'97	'98	'99	'00	'01	'02	'03	'04	'05	'06	'07	'08	'09	'10	'11	'12
-	-	-	-	-	196	198	196	187	193	179	185	179	181	178	192	171	182	168	179

2012													High	Low	Av
Jan	Feb	Mar	Apr	May	Jun	Jul	Aug	Sep	Oct	Nov	Dec			
169	170	171	177	177	176	184	183	182	185	186	179	160	200	184

Erchim, the Super Cup winners in 2011, became the first club from Mongolia to play in the AFC President's Cup after teams from the country were granted entry into the lower tier continental club competition. Despite drawing their opening game with India's Khan Research Labs at the first round group, staged in Lahore in Pakistan, Erchim missed out on progressing to the next round after finishing bottom of their three-team group following a 1-0 defeat at the hands of defending champions Taiwan Power Company. It proved to be the only international action of the year after the national team was prevented from entering the preliminary round of the 2013 East Asian Cup due to a ban handed down to the Mongolia Football Federation by the East Asian Football Federation in early 2011. Fresh from their outing at the 2012 AFC President's Cup, Erchim made sure of their participation at the 2013 tournament after dominating the competition at home. In the league they finished three points ahead of Khoromkhon in the 12-match season and then went on to retain the cup by beating Khasiin Khulguud on penalties after the final had ended in a 1-1 draw. Having done the double, they then had to face Khasiin Khulguud again in the 2012 Super Cup for a place in the AFC President's Cup, a match they emphatically won 7-2.

FIFA WORLD CUP RECORD
1930-1998 DNE **2002-2014** DNQ

MONGOLIA FOOTBALL FEDERATION (MFF)

PO Box 259,
210646 Ulaan-Baatar

☎ +976 11 345968
📠 +976 11 345966
✉ mongolianff@the-mff.mn
🌐 the-mff.mn
FA 1959 CON 1998 FIFA 1998
P Ganbold Buyannemekh
GS Terbaatar Dambiijav

THE STADIA
2014 FIFA World Cup Stadia
Football Center MFF
Ulaan Baatar 3 500
Other Main Stadia
National Sports Stadium
Ulaan Baatar 20 000

MAJOR CITIES/TOWNS

		Population
1	Ulaan Baatar	922 127
2	Erdenet	90 353
3	Darchan	78 254
4	Choybalsan	46 525
5	Saynshand	31 784
6	Olgiy	31 747
7	Moron	29 536
8	Ulaan Gom	29 529
9	Hovd	29 486
10	Uliastay	27 657
11	Suche Baatar	25 906
12	Bayanhongor	24 148
13	Arvaiheer	21 929
14	Dzuunharaa	19 949
15	Tsetserleg	19 675
16	Altay	19 344
17	Dzuunmod	19 024
18	Bulgan	18 239
19	Nalajh	17 311

MOGOL ULS • MONGOLIA

Capital	Ulaan-Baatar	Population	3 041 142 (136)	% in cities	57%
GDP per capita	$3200 (163)	Area km²	1 564 116 km² (19)	GMT +/-	+8
Neighbours (km)	China 4677, Russia 3543					

RECENT INTERNATIONAL MATCHES PLAYED BY MONGOLIA

2005	Opponents	Score	Venue	Comp	Scorers	Att	Referee
5-03	Hong Kong	L 0-6	Taipei	EAq			
7-03	Korea DPR	L 0-6	Taipei	EAq			
9-03	Guam	W 4-1	Taipei	EAq	Tugsbayer 2 [31] [34], Bayarzorig [46], Buman-Uchral [81]		
13-03	Chinese Taipei	D 0-0	Taipei	EAq			
2006							
No international matches played in 2006							
2007							
17-06	Macau	D 0-0	Macau	EAq		300	Matsuo JPN
19-06	Korea DPR	L 0-7	Macau	EAq		300	Ogiya JPN
23-06	Guam	W 5-2	Macau	EAq	OG [24], Davaa 2 [37] [42], Bayasgalan [46], Batchuluun [75]	100	Wan Daxue CHN
21-10	Korea DPR	L 1-4	Ulaan-Baatar	WCq	Selenge [93+]	4 870	Takayama JPN
28-10	Korea DPR	L 1-5	Pyongyang	WCq	Lumbengarav Donorov [41]	5 000	Gosh BAN
2008							
No international matches played in 2008							
2009							
11-03	Guam	L 0-1	Manenggon Hills	EAq			Kim Jong Hyeuk KOR
13-03	Macau	W 2-1	Manenggon Hills	EAq	Norjmoo Tsedenbal [67], Lumbengarav Donorov [69]		Fan Qi CHN
15-03	Northern Marianas†	W 4-1	Manenggon Hills	EAq	Lumbengarav Donorov [16], Badrakhzaya Sukhbaatar [42], Norjmoo Tsedenbal [71], Ariunbold Batsaikhan [90]	700	Sato JPN
7-04	Macau	L 0-2	Macau	CCq		500	Perera SRI
14-04	Macau	W 3-1	Ulaan-Baatar	CCq	Munkhbaatar Altankhuu [55], OG [77], Lumbengarav Donorov [89]	3 000	Yu Ming Hsun TPE
2010							
No international matches played in 2010							
2011							
9-02	Philippines	L 0-2	Bacolod	CCq		20 000	Yu Ming Hsun TPE
15-03	Philippines	W 2-1	Ulaan-Baatar	CCq	Lumbengarav Donorov [22], Garidmagnai Bayasgalan [35]	3 000	Ko Hyung Jin KOR
29-06	Myanmar	W 1-0	Ulaan-Baatar	WCq	Tsend-Ayush Khurelbaatar [48]	3 500	Kim Jong Hyeok KOR
3-07	Myanmar	L 0-2	Yangon	WCq		18 000	Liu Kwok Man HKG
2012							
No international matches played in 2012							

EA = EAFF East Asian Championship • AC = AFC Asian Cup • CC = AFC Challenge Cup • WC = FIFA World Cup • q = qualifier

MONGOLIA 2012

NIISLEL LIG FIRST STAGE

	Pl	W	D	L	F	A	Pts	Erchim	Khoromkhon	U'baatar Univ	Khasiin	Khangarid	Ulaanbaatar	Selenge Press	Mazaalai
Erchim †	12	8	3	1	35	11	27		1-1	3-3	2-0	3-3	3-1	7-1	
Khoromkhon	12	7	3	2	25	14	24	1-0		2-3	1-1	3-3	0-1	5-2	5-1
Ulaanbaatar University	12	7	2	3	38	25	23	2-2	1-2		4-1	1-2	4-0	7-1	
Khasiin Khulguud	12	5	1	6	29	24	16	0-2	1-3	2-3		4-2	1-2	3-0	1-2
Khangarid	12	5	1	6	21	23	16	1-2	0-1	3-2	1-2		1-0	4-2	4-2
FC Ulaanbaatar	12	4	0	8	17	32	12	1-6	1-3	4-6	0-4	0-1		3-2	
Selenge Press	12	1	0	11	18	54	3	0-3	0-3	4-1	4-10	1-4	1-4		1-1
Mazaalai	7	1	2	4	7	20	5	0-4		0-4			1-1		

30/06/2012 - 19/08/2012 • † Qualified for the AFC President's Cup • Mazaalai withdrew after seven matches. All their results were annulled

---

MFF CUP FINAL 2012
Erchim Football Pitch, Thermal Power Plant 4, 15-09-2012
Erchim 1-1 5-4p Khasiin Khulguud

MOZ – MOZAMBIQUE

FIFA/COCA-COLA WORLD RANKING

'93	'94	'95	'96	'97	'98	'99	'00	'01	'02	'03	'04	'05	'06	'07	'08	'09	'10	'11	'12
104	94	76	85	67	80	101	112	128	125	127	126	130	128	75	95	72	96	105	112

2012

Jan	Feb	Mar	Apr	May	Jun	Jul	Aug	Sep	Oct	Nov	Dec	High	Low	Av
105	102	104	106	110	117	107	107	109	99	110	112	66	134	103

Mozambique stood on the brink of a place at the 2013 Africa Cup of Nations finals in neighbouring South Africa but surrendered a two-goal lead against the much-fancied Morocco, to go out in the final round of qualifiers. Their 4-0 loss in the second leg quashed their hopes although they claimed to be hard done by with several controversial decisions in Marrakech, including a home penalty and the sending off of their captain Miro. It put a further dampener on a year that also saw the Mambas start their 2014 FIFA World Cup campaign with just a single point from their first two games after an expected defeat away to Egypt and then the disappointment of dropping points at home in a draw with neighbours Zimbabwe. Maxaquene, the Maputo-based club affiliated with the national airline TAM, won the MocamBola for the first time in nine years and fifth time overall, finishing three points ahead of Ferrovario Beira. A goal from Telinho, later transferred to Naval 1° de Maio in Portugal, gave Liga Muculmana a first cup success after two successive league titles in 2010 and 2011. The former champions, who had former Sporting Lisbon player Litos as their coach for the second half of the season, beat Costa do Sol 1-0 in the final played at the Estadio Nacional de Zimpeto.

CAF AFRICA CUP OF NATIONS RECORD

1957-1980 DNE 1982-1984 DNQ **1986** 8 r1 1988-1994 DNQ **1996** 14 r1 **1998** 16 r1 2000-2008 DNQ **2010** 15 r1 2012-2013 DNQ

FEDERACAO MOCAMBICANA DE FUTEBOL (FMF)

Av. Samora Machel, Número 11, PO Box 1467, 1467 Maputo
☎ +258 21 300366
+258 21 300367
fmfbol@tvcabo.co.mz
www.fmf.co.mz
FA 1976 CON 1978 FIFA 1980
P Feizal Sidat
GS Filipe Johane

THE STADIA

2014 FIFA World Cup Stadia
Estádio Nacional do Zimpeto
Maputo 42 000
Other Main Stadia
Estádio da Machava
Maputo 45 000
Estádio do Maxaquene
Maputo 15 000
Estádio do Costa do Sol
Maputo 10 000

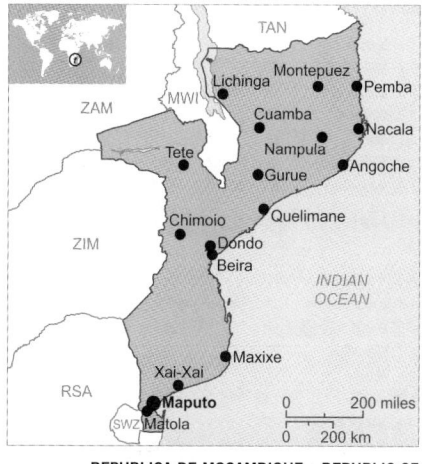

MAJOR CITIES/TOWNS

		Population
1	Maputo	1 120 245
2	Matola	729 469
3	Nampula	515 320
4	Beira	441 957
5	Chimoio	253 259
6	Nacala	217 479
7	Quelimane	200 788
8	Tete	164 201
9	Lichinga	155 277
10	Pemba	153 900
11	Garue	127 074
12	Gurué	119 598
13	Xai-Xai	118 667
14	Maxixe	107 292
15	Cuamba	98 719
16	Angoche	84 356
17	Dondo	78 639
18	Montepuez	77 515

REPUBLICA DE MOCAMBIQUE • REPUBLIC OF MOZAMBIQUE

Capital	Maputo	Population	21 669 278 (52)	% in cities	37%
GDP per capita	$900 (215)	Area km²	799 380 km² (35)	GMT +/-	+2
Neighbours (km)	Malawi 1569, South Africa 491, Swaziland 105, Tanzania 756, Zambia 419, Zimbabwe 1231 • Coast 2470				

RECENT INTERNATIONAL MATCHES PLAYED BY MOZAMBIQUE

2008	Opponents	Score	Venue	Comp	Scorers	Att	Referee
1-06	Côte d'Ivoire	L 0-1	Abidjan	WCq		20 000	Auda EGY
8-06	Botswana	L 1-2	Maputo	WCq	Miro [60]	30 000	Faudze SWZ
15-06	Madagascar	D 1-1	Antananarivo	WCq	Dario [33]	15 501	Ebrahim RSA
22-06	Madagascar	W 3-0	Maputo	WCq	Tico-Tico [23], Carlitos [52], Domingues [64]	20 000	Maillett SEY
27-07	Botswana	W 2-0	Secunda	CCqf	Momed Hagi [18], Txuma [89]		Katjimune NAM
30-07	Madagascar	W 2-1	Thulamahashe	CCsf	Tico-Tico [19], Momed Hagi [66]		Marange ZIM
20-08	Swaziland	W 3-0	Maputo	Fr	Dario 2 [4 12], Domingues [35]		
7-09	Côte d'Ivoire	D 1-1	Maputo	WCq	Miro [56]	35 000	El Achiri MAR
11-10	Botswana	W 1-0	Gaborone	WCq	Genito [6]	2 000	Seck SEN
19-11	Tanzania	L 0-1	Dar es Salaam	Fr			
2009							
11-02	Malawi	W 2-0	Maputo	Fr	Dario [31], Domingues [90]		
29-03	Nigeria	D 0-0	Maputo	WCq		35 000	Eyob ERI
6-06	Tunisia	L 0-2	Rades/Tunis	WCq		30 000	Djaoupe TOG
20-06	Kenya	L 1-2	Nairobi	WCq	Domingues [49]	15 000	Keita GUI
12-08	Swaziland	W 1-0	Maputo	Fr	Miro [39]		
6-09	Kenya	W 1-0	Maputo	WCq	Tico-Tico [66]	35 000	Coulibaly MLI
11-10	Nigeria	L 0-1	Abuja	WCq		13 000	Abdel Rahman SUD
25-10	Malawi	W 1-0	Harare	CCqf	Josemar [35]		Ramocha BOT
29-10	Zambia	L 0-2	Bulawayo	CCsf			Ramocha BOT
14-11	Tunisia	W 1-0	Maputo	WCq	Dario [83]	30 000	Doue CIV
19-12	Malawi	L 0-1	Tete	Fr			
28-12	Zambia	L 0-1	Johannesburg	Fr			
2010							
6-01	Gabon	L 0-2	Bloemfontein	Fr			
12-01	Benin	D 2-2	Benguela	CNr1	Miro [29], Fumo [54]	15 000	Abdel Rahman SUD
16-01	Egypt	L 0-2	Benguela	CNr1		16 000	Djaoupe TOG
20-01	Nigeria	L 0-3	Lubango	CNr1		10 000	Coulibaly MLI
3-03	Botswana	L 0-1	Maputo	Fr			
8-06	Portugal	L 0-3	Johannesburg	Fr		34 000	Dyer RSA
11-08	Swaziland	W 2-1	Maputo	Fr	Domingues [9p], Miro [51]		
5-09	Libya	D 0-0	Maputo	CNq			Bangoura GUI
9-10	Comoros	W 1-0	Moroni	CNq	Josemar [90]		Ibada TAN
2011							
9-02	Botswana	D 1-1	Maputo	Fr	Miro [58]		
27-03	Zambia	L 0-2	Maputo	CNq			
23-04	Tanzania	W 2-0	Maputo	Fr	Jerry Sitoe 2 [17 48]		
4-06	Zambia	L 0-3	Chingola	CNq			
3-09	Libya	L 0-1	Cairo	CNq			Omar EGY
8-10	Comoros	W 3-0	Maputo	CNq	Maninho [6], Dario [18p], Domingues [40]		
11-11	Comoros	W 1-0	Mitsamiouli	WCq	Miro [54p]	3 000	Jane LES
15-11	Comoros	W 4-1	Maputo	WCq	Domingues [26], Jerry Sitoe [45], Whiskey [59], Clesio Bauque [84]	10 000	Ruzive ZIM
2012							
22-02	Namibia	L 0-3	Windhoek	Fr			
29-02	Tanzania	D 1-1	Dar es Salaam	CNq	Clesio Bauque [19]		Farouk EGY
26-05	Namibia	D 0-0	Wuerzburg	Fr			
1-06	Egypt	L 0-2	Alexandria	WCq		BCD	Kirwa KEN
10-06	Zimbabwe	D 0-0	Maputo	WCq		26 000	Kalyango UGA
17-06	Tanzania	D 1-1	Maputo	CNq	Jerry Sitoe [10]. W 7-6p		Bennett RSA
23-06	Vietnam	L 0-1	Ho Chi Minh City	Fr			
9-09	Morocco	W 2-0	Maputo	CNq	Almiro Lobo [75], Domingues [93+]		Kirwa KEN
11-09	South Africa	L 0-2	Nelspruit	Fr			
13-10	Morocco	L 0-4	Marrakech	CNq		40 000	Alioum CMR
2-12	Seychelles	W 4-0	Maputo	Fr			
15-12	Seychelles	W 2-1	Roche Caiman	Fr			

Fr = Friendly match • CN = CAF African Cup of Nations • CC = COSAFA Cup • WC = FIFA World Cup • q = qualifier

MOZ – MOZAMBIQUE

MOZAMBIQUE 2012

CAMPEONATO NACIONAL DA 1ª DIVISAO

	Pl	W	D	L	F	A	Pts	Maxaquene	Ferroviário B	Costa do Sol	Ferroviário M	Vilankulo	L Muçulmana	Chibuto	HCB Songo	Ferroviário	Têxtil Púnguè	Chingale Tete	Desportivo	Incomáti	Ferroviário P
Maxaquene †	26	13	11	2	26	11	50		1-1	1-1	2-1	1-0	2-1	1-0	1-0	2-1	1-0	0-0	0-1	0-0	0-0
Ferroviário Beira	26	12	11	3	31	17	47	1-1		1-0	0-0	1-0	2-0	3-0	1-1	2-0	3-0	0-0	0-0	0-0	4-1
Costa do Sol	26	10	12	4	34	23	42	0-0	3-4		3-1	0-0	2-1	1-0	1-0	0-0	4-0	4-0	2-2	2-2	1-1
Ferroviário Maputo	26	12	6	8	25	20	42	0-2	0-1	1-1		1-0	0-1	4-1	0-0	1-0	2-1	3-2	1-0	2-0	1-0
Vilankulo	26	10	10	6	18	10	40	0-0	0-0	0-0	0-0		1-0	2-0	0-0	3-0	1-0	1-0	3-0	1-0	1-0
Liga Muçulmana	26	10	8	8	29	19	38	0-0	1-2	1-1	1-2	0-0		0-0	1-0	1-0	4-0	5-0	0-0	2-0	3-3
Chibuto	26	10	7	9	24	21	37	0-2	0-0	1-2	0-0	3-0	1-0		1-0	5-1	2-1	1-1	2-0	1-0	1-0
HCB Songo	26	9	7	10	19	17	34	0-1	2-0	1-0	1-0	1-0	1-2	0-1		1-1	4-0	0-0	0-1	2-0	1-0
Ferroviário Nampula	26	9	6	11	18	24	33	1-1	1-2	0-0	2-0	0-0	0-1	0-1	3-0		0-1	1-0	1-0	1-0	2-0
Têxtil Púnguè	26	9	5	12	19	30	32	0-0	1-0	1-1	0-0	2-1	1-0	1-0	0-0	0-1		2-0	2-1	1-0	4-0
Chingale Tete	26	6	13	7	16	22	31	1-2	0-0	4-1	1-0	0-0	0-0	0-0	1-1	0-0	1-0		1-0	1-0	2-0
Desportivo Maputo	26	6	7	13	18	29	25	1-3	1-1	1-2	1-2	0-1	1-1	2-1	0-1	1-0	1-0	0-0		1-0	2-1
Incomáti Xinavane	26	6	7	13	17	23	25	1-0	4-0	0-1	0-2	1-1	0-1	0-0	2-1	1-0	2-0	1-1	1-1		2-0
Ferroviário Pemba	26	2	6	18	10	38	12	0-2	0-2	0-1	0-1	0-2	0-3	0-0	0-1	0-1	1-1	0-0	2-1	1-0	

17/03/2012 - 18/11/2012 • † Qualified for the CAF Champions League

MEDALS TABLE

		Overall	Lge	Cup	City/Town
		G	G	G S	
1	Costa do Sol	20	9	11 4	Maputo
2	Ferroviário Maputo	14	9	5 4	Maputo
3	Maxaquene	14	5	9 3	Maputo
4	Desportivo Maputo	8	6	2 1	Maputo
5	Liga Muçulmana	3	2	1	Maputo
	Matchedje	3	2	1 1	Maputo
7	Ferroviário Nampula	2	1	1 1	Nampula
8	Têxtil Púnguè	1	1	3	Beira
	Textáfrica Chimoio	1	1	3	Chimoio
	Palmeiras Beira	1		1 3	Beira
	Ferroviário Beira	1		1 2	Beira
	Clube de Gaza	1		1 1	Xai-Xai
	Atlético Muçulmano	1		1	Matola
14	Chingale Tete			2	Tete

TACA NACIONAL 2012

Fase Interprovincial		Fase Nacional Quarter-finals		Semi-finals		Final	
Liga Muçulmana	1						
Aguias Especiais	0	Liga Muçulmana	1				
Mandimba	1	Ferroviário Pemba	0				
Ferroviário Pemba	2			Liga Muçulmana	1		
Chibuto	1			Incomáti Xinavane	0		
AD Maxixe	0	Chibuto	1				
Maxaquene	0	**Incomáti Xinavane**	2				
Incomáti Xinavane	1					Liga Muçulmana ‡	1
Ferroviário Beira	3					Costa do Sol	0
Têxtil Púnguè	0	**Ferroviário Beira**	1				
Chingale Tete	0	Ferroviário Quelimane	0			**CUP FINAL**	
Ferroviário Quelimane	1			Ferroviário Beira	0	Estadio Nacional de Zimpeto, Maputo, 25-11-2012 Ref: Samuel Chirindza Scorer - Telinho [75] for Liga Muçulmana	
HCB Songo	1			Costa do Sol	1		
Textáfrica Chimoio	0	HCB Songo	1				
Ferroviário Maputo	0 2p	**Costa do Sol**	2				
Costa do Sol	0 4p			‡ Qualified for the CAF Confederation Cup			

Cup Final line-ups: **Liga Muçulmana** - Caio - Miro, Cantona, Chico, Aguiar - Mustafa, Momed Hagi, Muandro (Italo), Cantona, Zicco (Mayunda) - Josimar, Sonito (Telinho) • **Costa do Sol** - Gervasio - Ze Inacio, Gildo (Eboh), Sanito, Dito - Manuelito I, Alvarito (Parkim), Manuelito II, Ruben - Reginaldo, Themba (David)

MRI – MAURITIUS

FIFA/COCA-COLA WORLD RANKING

'93	'94	'95	'96	'97	'98	'99	'00	'01	'02	'03	'04	'05	'06	'07	'08	'09	'10	'11	'12
133	146	154	150	151	148	118	118	124	126	123	140	143	138	158	170	181	191	194	202

2012

Jan	Feb	Mar	Apr	May	Jun	Jul	Aug	Sep	Oct	Nov	Dec	High	Low	Av
194	195	195	192	192	192	193	194	200	201	203	202	116	203	148

Failure to enter both the 2014 FIFA World Cup qualifiers and the 2013 Africa Cup of Nations qualifiers was a disappointing blow for football fans on the Indian Ocean island as the national team slipped to an all-time low of 203rd in the FIFA/Coca-Cola World Ranking in November 2012. Just two matches at the end of the year against the nearby Comoros Islands in the African Nations Championship - now regarded as full internationals by FIFA - represented the sum total of participation for Mauritius in the international arena, with their clubs having decided not to enter the 2013 CAF club competitions. It was a change of tack for Mauritian football which has a good record of participation but which in 2012 was heavily constrained by budgetary issues and political machinations. Pamplemousse dethroned AS Port Louis 2000 for the Premier League title but had to wait until the last day of the season when they beat Savanne 1-0 before making sure. A dramatic penalty shootout decided the outcome of the Republic Cup in the first part of the year with Savanne edging AS Riviere Rampart 11-10 in the shootout after a 1-1 draw. Both teams took 15 kicks each with ASRR goalkeeper Nicholas Doro both hero and villain as he made four saves but still contrived to miss the deciding kick and hand the trophy to opponents Savanne.

CAF AFRICA CUP OF NATIONS RECORD

1957-1965 DNE 1968-1972 DNQ **1974** 8 r1 1976-1986 DNQ 1988 DNE 1990-2012 DNQ 2013 DNE

MAURITIUS FOOTBALL ASSOCIATION (MFA)

Football House, Trianon

☎ +230 4652200
📠 +230 4547911
✉ asg.mfa@intnet.mu
🌐 www.mfa.mu
FA 1952 CON 1962 FIFA 1962
P Dinnanathlall Persunnoo
GS Pathak Ballgobin

THE STADIA

2014 FIFA World Cup Stadia
Mauritius did not enter the 2014 FIFA World Cup qualifiers

Other Main Stadia
Stade Anjalay Belle Vue	18 000
Stade George V Curepipe	6 200
Stade Germain Comarmond Bambous	6 000
Stade Auguste Vollaire Flacq	4 000

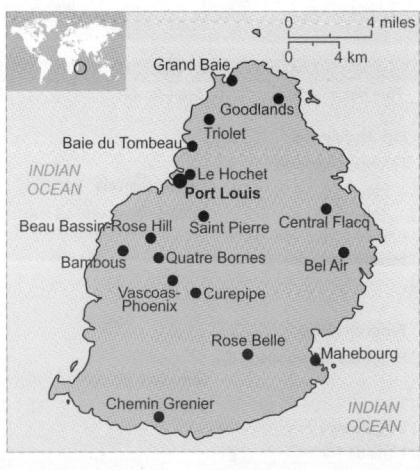

MAJOR CITIES/TOWNS

		Population
1	Port Louis	155 603
2	Beau Bassin-Rose Hill	110 360
3	Vascoas-Phoenix	106 316
4	Curepipe	83 849
5	Quatre Bornes	80 624
6	Triolet	23 588
7	Goodlands	21 078
8	Central Flacq	17 914
9	Bel Air	17 874
10	Mahébourg	17 147
11	Saint Pierre	16 382
12	Le Hochet	15 403
13	Bambous	13 674
14	Baie du Tombeau	13 330
15	Rose Belle	12 697
16	Chemin Grenier	12 364
17	Riviere du Rempart	11 769
18	Grand Baie	11 605

REPUBLIC OF MAURITIUS

Capital	Port Louis	Population	1 284 264 (153)	% in cities	42%
GDP per capita	$12 100 (91)	Area km²	2040 km² (180)	GMT +/-	+4
Neighbours (km)	Coast 177				

MRI – MAURITIUS

RECENT INTERNATIONAL MATCHES PLAYED BY MAURITIUS

2006	Opponents	Score	Venue	Comp	Scorers	Att	Referee
3-09	Tunisia	D 0-0	Curepipe	CNq			Ncobo RSA
7-10	Seychelles	L 1-2	Roche Caiman	CNq	Kervin Godon 53		Raolimanana MAD
2007							
21-03	Côte d'Ivoire	L 0-3	Bellevue	Fr			
25-03	Sudan	L 1-2	Curepipe	CNq	Ricardo Naboth 61		Mwanza ZAM
26-05	Swaziland	D 0-0	Mbabane	CCr1	W 6-5p		Labrosse SEY
27-05	South Africa	L 0-2	Mbabane	CCr1			Mufeti NAM
2-06	Sudan	L 0-3	Omdurman	CNq			Lwanja MWI
16-06	Tunisia	L 0-2	Rades/Tunis	CNq			Benouza ALG
14-08	Seychelles	W 3-0	Antananarivo	Fr	Giovanni Jeannot 2 24 64, Kersley Appou 40		
9-09	Seychelles	D 1-1	Curepipe	CNq	Christopher Perle 62		Mwandike TAN
2008							
9-03	Madagascar	L 1-2	Curepipe	Fr	Wesley Marquette 68		
31-05	Tanzania	D 1-1	Dar es Salaam	WCq	Wesley Marquette 39	35 000	Marange ZIM
8-06	Cameroon	L 0-3	Curepipe	WCq		2 400	Martins ANG
15-06	Cape Verde Islands	L 0-1	Curepipe	WCq		1 400	Kaoma ZAM
22-06	Cape Verde Islands	L 1-3	Praia	WCq	Andy Sophie 67	2 850	Coulibaly MLI
19-07	Seychelles	L 0-7	Witbank	CCr1			Kaoma ZAM
21-07	Swaziland	D 1-1	Witbank	CCr1	Johan Marmitte 35		Nhlapo RSA
23-07	Madagascar	L 1-2	Witbank	CCr1	Wesley Marquette 34		Marange ZIM
6-09	Tanzania	L 1-4	Curepipe	WCq	Wesley Marquette 13	103	Ndinya KEN
11-10	Cameroon	L 0-5	Yaounde	WCq		12 000	Lemghambodj MTN
2009							
2-10	Egypt	L 0-4	Cairo	Fr			
17-10	Zimbabwe	L 0-3	Harare	CCr1			Ebrahim RSA
21-10	Lesotho	L 0-1	Harare	CCr1			Ngosi MWI
2010							
4-09	Cameroon	L 1-3	Bellevue	CNq	Jonathan Bru 45p		Damon RSA
9-10	Senegal	L 0-7	Dakar	CNq			Bennett RSA
2011							
27-03	Congo DR	L 0-3	Kinshasa	CNq			Solomon NGA
5-06	Congo DR	L 1-2	Bellevue	CNq	Jonathan Bru 11p		Kalyoto MWI
4-08	Maldives	D 1-1	Praslin	IOGr1	Fabrice Pithia 9	1 800	Rakotonjanahary MAD
6-08	Seychelles	L 1-2	Roche Caiman	IOGr1	Fabrice Pithia 77	6 500	Rassuhi MAY
9-08	Comoros	W 2-0	Praslin	IOGr1	Fabrice Pithia 35, Gurty Calambe 87	300	Rassuhi MAY
11-08	Mayotte †	D 0-0	Roche Caiman	IOGsf	W 5-4p	2 500	Adelaid COM
13-08	Seychelles	D 1-1	Roche Caiman	IOGf	Jerry Louis 62, L 3-4p	10 000	Dubec REU
3-09	Cameroon	L 0-5	Yaounde	CNq			Bangoura GUI
9-10	Senegal	L 0-2	Bellevue	CNq			
2012							
1-12	Comoros	W 2-0	Curepipe	Fr	Gurty Calambe 59, Fabrice Pithia 72		
15-12	Comoros	D 0-0	Mitsamiouli	Fr			

Fr = Friendly match • CN = CAF African Cup of Nations • CC = COSAFA Cup • IOG = Indian Ocean Games • WC = FIFA World Cup
q = qualifier • r1 = first round group • † Not an official international

MAURITIUS NATIONAL TEAM HISTORICAL RECORDS

Coaches: Harry Brophy ENG 1957-59 • Joseph Le Roy 1959-63 • Danny McLennan SCO 1963-64 • Mohammad Anwar Elahee 1970-88 • Helmut Kosmehl GER 1976-88 • Mohammad Anwar Elahee 1994-96 • Rudi Gutendorf GER 1997 • Ashok Chundunsing 1998 • Rajen Dorasami & France L'Aiguille 1998-02 • Patrick Parizon FRA 2002-03 • Akbar Patel 2003 • Elvis Antoine & Rajesh Gunesh 2003-05 • Sarjoo Gowreesunkur 2006 • Rajen Dorasami & France L'Aiguille 2006 • Akbar Patel 2007 • Ashok Chundunsing 2007-08 • Benjamin Theodore 2008-09 • Marc Collat FRA 2009 • Akbar Patel 2009-

MAURITIUS 2012

BARCLAYS PREMIER LEAGUE

	Pl	W	D	L	F	A	Pts	Pamplemousses	ASPL 2000	Cercle	Petite Rivière	ASRR	ASVP	Savanne	CSSC	Entente	PAS Mates
Pamplemousses SC	18	12	2	4	41	20	**38**		2-1	1-0	3-1	3-0	0-2	5-1	6-1	3-2	2-0
AS Port-Louis 2000	18	11	2	5	31	17	35	2-1		0-1	0-5	2-0	0-1	0-0	0-1	2-0	5-3	0-0
Cercle de Joachim	18	10	4	4	32	19	34	1-1	0-1		1-0	2-1	1-1	3-2	2-0	3-0	3-0
Petite Rivière Noire	18	9	4	5	30	20	31	3-1	2-1	2-2		0-0	0-0	5-0	3-2	2-1	0-1
AS Rivière Rempart	18	9	3	6	31	21	30	2-2	0-3	3-0	1-3		4-1	2-1	0-1	6-0	1-0
AS Vacoas-Phoenix	18	6	6	6	15	18	24	0-1	0-0	1-3	0-1	2-1		0-1	1-0	3-1	0-0
Savanne SC	18	7	2	9	24	34	23	0-1	0-4	3-1	2-2	0-2	3-0		1-1	2-1	2-0
Curepipe Starlight	18	6	1	11	25	33	19	3-0	1-2	1-2	0-2	0-2	1-2	3-1		1-2	5-4
Entente Boulet Rouge	18	3	3	12	21	48	**12**	0-5	0-5	2-3	3-2	2-2	1-1	1-3	1-2		1-0
Pointe-aux-Sables	18	2	3	13	11	31	9	1-4	1-2	0-0	0-2	1-3	0-1	3-1	0-3	0-0	

24/11/2011 – 27/05/2012

REPUBLIC CUP 2012

Round of 16		Quarter–finals		Semi–finals		Final	
Savanne SC	2 15p						
AS Port-Louis 2000	2 14p	**Savanne SC**	4				
Faucon Flacq SC	2	Entente Boulet Rouge*	2				
Entente Boulet Rouge	3			**Savanne SC**	2		
Petite Rivière Noire	2			Curepipe Starlight *	1		
US Highlands	1	Petite Rivière Noire *	0				
Cercle de Joachim		**Curepipe Starlight**	3				
Curepipe Starlight						Savanne SC	1 11p
Pamplemousses SC	5					AS Rivière Rempart	1 10p
Chamarel SC *	0	**Pamplemousses SC** *	2				
Etoile de l'Ouest	0	Pointe-aux-Sables	0				
Pointe-aux-Sables	3			Pamplemousses SC	0		
AS Vacoas-Phoenix	1			**AS Rivière Rempart** *	1		
Black Horns	0	AS Vacoas-Phoenix	1				
AS Quatre-Bornes		**AS Rivière Rempart** *	2				
AS Rivière Rempart		* Home team					

REPUBLIC CUP FINAL 2012
Stade Anjalay, Beele Vue, 1-05-2012

Savanne SC	1 11p	Stephane Nabab [56]
AS Rivière-du-Rempart	1 10p	Thierry Francois [85]

SAVANNE

Fabrice DEBOUCHERVILLE - Yannick DIG DIG, Steward ST LOUIS●(Wasley LABOUCHERIE 104), Kelly MARIVA (c)◆115, Samuel HANGEL - Stephan NABAB, Steve COCO (90), Damien BAULUCK (Curty DESSALES 67), Guillano CHIFFONE, Kersley LOUIS - Jonathan Tetteh●. Tr: PRAKASH PARMANUND

RIVIERE-DU-REMPART

Nicholas DORO (c) - Raffic MADRON, Shanawaze ALLYBOCCUS, Perianen AYASSAMY, Jeremie SAKAC - Jonathan EDOUARD●, Thierry FRANCOIS, Vidiadeo BOODHUN (Hemmansing EMRITH 105), Jean-Marc MARIE● - Tony FRANCOIS (Evans MIMI 65), Sewram GOBIN. Tr: Tony FRANCOIS

MSR – MONTSERRAT

FIFA/COCA-COLA WORLD RANKING

'93	'94	'95	'96	'97	'98	'99	'00	'01	'02	'03	'04	'05	'06	'07	'08	'09	'10	'11	'12
-	-	-	-	-	-	201	202	203	203	204	202	202	198	201	201	203	203	206	174

2012

Jan	Feb	Mar	Apr	May	Jun	Jul	Aug	Sep	Oct	Nov	Dec	High	Low	Av
206	205	205	205	205	206	205	206	206	181	183	174	174	206	201

It's amazing what a game or two can do for your standing in world football as Montserrat found out when they climbed from last place to the dizzy heights of 174 in the FIFA/Coca-Cola World Ranking. Given that the team has always been the barometer of just how bad things can get, this was extraordinary progress indeed and came about as a result of their 2012 Caribbean Cup campaign. Coach Kenny Dyer took his team to Martinique for a qualifying group that along with the hosts included Guyana and the British Virgin Islands. Made up largely of English players of Montserrat descent playing amateur football in the UK, they got off to the worst possible start - a 7-1 mauling at the hands of Suriname. They then lost 5-0 to Martinique which left the match against the BVI for the wooden spoon. Montserrat had lost the two previous meetings between the two but with the BVI quickly taking over Montserrat's role as the worst team in the world, there was genuine hope that they could end their 22-match losing streak stretching back to 1995. Not only did Montserrat do that but they did it in magnificent style, thrashing BVI 7-0 - their first-ever victory in an official international since joining FIFA in 1996. It was an historic moment that even the talismanic Kenny Dyer will be pushed to better in the future.

CFU CARIBBEAN CUP RECORD

1989 DNE 1991-1992 DNQ 1993 DNE 1994-1995 DNQ 1996-1998 DNE 1999-2005 DNQ 2007-2008 DNE 2010-2012 DNQ

MONTSERRAT FOOTBALL ASSOCIATION INC. (MFA)

PO Box 505, Blakes
☎ +1 664 4951043
+1 664 4912719
mfainc@candw.ms

FA 1994 CON 1996 FIFA 1996
P Vincent Cassell
GS Tandica Hughes

MAJOR CITIES/TOWNS

		Population
1	Brades	1 305
2	Saint Peter's	794
3	Saint John's-Old Norwood	728
4	Salem	552
5	Blakes Estate	492
6	Davy Hill	427
7	Olveston	381
8	Happy Hill	359
9	Woodlands	315
10	Gerald's	269
11	Plymouth	0

THE STADIA

2014 FIFA World Cup Stadia
Montserrat played their home qualifier at the Ato Boldon Stadium in Couva, Trinidad

Stadia in Montserrat
MFA Complex
Blakes Estate

MONTSERRAT

Capital	Plymouth	Population	5 097 (228)	% in cities	14%
GDP per capita	$3400 (160)	Area km²	102 km² (225)	GMT +/-	-4
Neighbours (km)	Coast 40				

INTERNATIONAL MATCHES PLAYED BY MONTSERRAT

1991	Opponents	Score	Venue	Comp	Scorers	Att	Referee
10-05	St Lucia	L 0-3	Vieux Fort	CCq			
14-05	Anguilla	D 1-1	Vieux Fort	CCq			
1992							
15-04	Antigua and Barbuda	L 0-5	Basseterre	CCq			
17-04	St Kitts and Nevis	L 0-10	Basseterre	CCq			
1993							
No international matches played in 1993							
1994							
23-02	St Kitts and Nevis	L 1-9	Basseterre	CCq			
25-02	Antigua and Barbuda	L 0-8	Basseterre	CCq			
1995							
26-03	Anguilla	W 3-2	Plymouth	CCq	Ian Edwards, Julian Wade, Everton Morris		
2-04	Anguilla	W 1-0	The Valley	CCq	Curt Webb		
1-05	St Vincent/Grenadines	L 0-9	Kingstown	CCq			
7-05	St Vincent/Grenadines	L 0-11	Plymouth	CCq			
1996-1998							
No international matches played in 1996, 1997 & 1998							
1999							
5-02	British Virgin Islands	L 1-3	Road Town	CCq	Curt Webb		
7-02	British Virgin Islands	L 0-3	Road Town	CCq			
2000							
15-03	Dominican Republic	L 0-3	San Cristobal	WCq		2 000	
19-03	Dominican Republic	L 1-3	Port of Spain	WCq	Wayne Dyer [88]	50	
2001							
6-02	Saint-Martin †	L 1-3	Marigot	CCq			
8-02	Anguilla	L 1-4	Marigot	CCq	Joseph Morris [53]		
2002							
30-06	Bhutan	L 0-4	Thimphu	Fr		25 000	
2003							
No international matches played in 2003							
2004							
29-02	Bermuda	L 0-13	Hamilton	WCq		3 000	Kennedy USA
21-03	Bermuda	L 0-7	Plymouth	WCq		250	Charles DMA
31-10	St Kitts and Nevis	L 1-6	Basseterre	CCq	Curt Adams [81]		Bedeau GRN
2-11	Antigua and Barbuda	L 4-5	Basseterre	CCq	Tesfaye Bramble [36], Ruel Fox [41], Junior Mendes [50], Vladimir Farrell [61]		Phillip GRN
4-11	St Lucia	L 0-3	Basseterre	CCq	Not played. St Lucia awarded the match 3-0		
2005-2007							
No international matches played in 2005, 2006 & 2007							
2008							
26-03	Surinam	L 1-7	Macoya	WCq	Vladimir Farrell [48]	100	Aguilar SLV
2009							
No international matches played in 2009							
2010							
6-10	St Vincent/Grenadines	L 0-7	Kingstown	CCq		5 000	Pinas PUR
8-10	Barbados	L 0-5	Kingstown	CCq		350	Pinas PUR
10-10	St Kitts And Nevis	L 0-4	Kingstown	CCq		1 100	Elskamp SUR
2011							
15-06	Belize	L 2-5	Couva	WCq	Jay Lee Hodgson 2 [44,86]	100	Willett ATG
17-07	Belize	L 1-3	San Pedro Sula	WCq	Jay Lee Hodgson [58]	150	Reyna GUA
2012							
5-09	Suriname	L 1-7	Le Lamentin	CCq	Kendell Allen [48]	188	Angela ARU
7-09	Martinique †	L 0-5	Riviere-Pilote	CCq		400	Da Costa BAH
9-09	British Virgin Islands	W 7-0	Fort de France	CCq	OG [33], Marlon Campbell 2 [35,45], Darryl Roach [49], Bradley Woods [53], Ellis Remy 2 [71,87]	120	Anderson PUR

Fr = Friendly match • CC = Digicel Caribbean Cup • WC = FIFA World Cup • q = qualifier • † Not an official international. All matches played before Montserrat joined FIFA in 1996 are not considered as full internationals by FIFA

MTN – MAURITANIA

FIFA/COCA-COLA WORLD RANKING

'93	'94	'95	'96	'97	'98	'99	'00	'01	'02	'03	'04	'05	'06	'07	'08	'09	'10	'11	'12
144	137	85	113	135	142	160	161	177	180	165	175	178	133	130	158	169	180	204	206

2012

Jan	Feb	Mar	Apr	May	Jun	Jul	Aug	Sep	Oct	Nov	Dec	High	Low	Av
204	203	203	202	201	203	202	203	204	205	206	206	85	204	152

Mauritania returned to the international arena in 2012 with three matches, ending almost two years without any action for the national team. French coach Patrice Neveu spent the previous year attempting to build a team in a country whose last participation in competitive action was back in 2008 in the qualifiers for the 2010 FIFA World Cup in South Africa where they lost all six of their group matches. Since then Mauritania have skipped the preliminaries of three continental championships and did not enter the 2014 FIFA World Cup. A win in Liberia in December represented a first-ever away success for the country which has been playing international football - albeit irregularly - since 1964. The two matches against Liberia were in the preliminary round of the African Nations Championship which FIFA now regards as full internationals. Club silverware in the North African country went to ASC Tevragh Zeina and ASAC Concorde. Tevragh Zeina edged FC Nouadhibou by a single point to win the league in June and a week later the team, coached by Birama Gaye, completed the double by beating Concorde 1-0 in the cup final. Concorde's 2-1 win over Tevragh Zeina in November at the start of the new season in the Super Cup extracted a measure of revenge.

CAF AFRICA CUP OF NATIONS RECORD
1957-1978 DNE 1980-1982 DNQ 1984 DNE 1986 DNQ 1988-1990 DNE 1992 DNQ
1994 DNE 1996-1998 DNQ 2000 DNE 2002-2010 DNQ 2012-2013 DNE

FEDERATION DE FOOTBALL DE LA REPUBLIQUE ISLAMIQUE DE MAURITANIE (FFM)

Route de l'Espoir,
BP 566,
Nouakchott
☎ +222 35 241860
+222 35 241861
✉ dmassa59@yahoo.fr
🖥 www.ffrim.org
FA 1961 CON 1968 FIFA 1964
P Ahmed Yahya
GS Massa Momoye Diarra

THE STADIA

2014 FIFA World Cup Stadia
Mauritania did not enter the 2014 FIFA World Cup qualifiers

Main Stadia
Stade Olympique Nouakchott	40 000
Stade Nouadhibou Nouadhibou	5 000
Stade d'Atar Atar	2 000

MAJOR CITIES/TOWNS

		Population
1	Nouakchott	798 725
2	Nouadhibou	83 277
3	Kifah	80 612
4	Rusu	72 400
5	Kayhaydi	54 593
6	Zuwarat	50 949
7	an-Na'mah	41 583
8	Bu Tilimit	37 812
9	Silibabi	33 084
10	Atar	31 958
11	Buqah	27 859
12	Tinbadgah	27 562
13	Guérou	27 031
14	Magta' Lahjar	26 026
15	Alak	25 140
16	Ayun	24 991
17	Tintane	19 118
18	Tijiqjah	18 375
19	Adel Bagrou	16 004

AL JUMHURIYAH AL ISLAMIYAH AL MURITANIYAH • ISLAMIC REPUBLIC OF MAURITANIA

Capital Nouakchott	Population 3 129 486 (135)	% in cities 41%
GDP per capita $2100 (187)	Area km² 1 030 700 km² (29)	GMT +/- 0
Neighbours (km) Algeria 463, Mali 2237, Senegal 813, Western Sahara 1561 • Coast 754

RECENT INTERNATIONAL MATCHES PLAYED BY MAURITANIA

2008	Opponents	Score	Venue	Comp	Scorers	Att	Referee
31-05	Rwanda	L 0-3	Kigali	WCq		12 000	Doue CIV
7-06	Morocco	L 1-4	Nouakchott	WCq	Ahmed Teguedi [82p]	9 500	Lamptey GHA
13-06	Ethiopia	L 0-1	Nouakchott	WCq		5 000	Ambaya EGY
22-06	Ethiopia	L 1-6	Addis Abeba	WCq	Voulani Ely [44]	13 000	Lwanja MWI
6-09	Rwanda	L 0-1	Nouackchott	WCq		1 000	Bennaceur TUN
11-10	Morocco	L 1-4	Rabat	WCq	Ahmed Teguedi [67]	1 472	Aboubacar CIV
2009							
No international matches played in 2009							
2010							
11-08	Palestine	D 0-0	Nouakchott	Fr			
2011							
No international matches played in 2011							
2012							
15-04	Egypt	L 0-3	Dubai	Fr			
2-12	Liberia	W 1-0	Paynesville	Fr	Yacoub Fall [20p]		
15-12	Liberia	W 2-1	Nouakchott	Fr	Yacoub Deyna, Al Mamy Traore [82p]		

Fr = Friendly match • CN = CAF African Cup of Nations • AR = Arab Cup • WC = FIFA World Cup • q = qualifier • r1 = first round group

MAURITANIA 2011-12

CHAMPIONNAT NATIONAL

	Pl	W	D	L	F	A	Pts	Tevragh Zeina	Nouadhibou	Concorde	Cansado	Tidjikja	Kédia	Armée	ACS Ksar	Imraguens	Police	ZemZem	Trarza	Entente	Lasa
ASC Tevragh Zeina	26	19	2	5	57	21	59		4-1	0-1	2-3	4-1	4-1	2-1	1-0	3-0	3-0	2-1	3-1	3-0	3-1
FC Nouadhibou	26	18	4	4	45	17	58	0-1		3-1	1-0	0-0	2-0	2-0	1-1	3-0	3-1	2-0	2-0	1-0	1-2
ASAC Concorde	26	15	8	3	56	21	53	3-0	1-0		1-0	1-1	2-0	6-1	4-1	2-3	2-2	4-1	3-0	4-0	2-0
CF Cansado	26	15	6	5	44	18	51	2-0	1-2	0-0		1-0	2-0	1-0	0-0	1-1	3-0	0-0	4-1	2-1	3-0
ASC Tidjikja	26	12	9	5	42	26	45	0-0	1-2	2-0	0-2		4-1	1-3	4-1	2-1	5-0	2-2	0-0	3-1	2-2
ASC Kédia Zouératt	26	11	7	8	18	22	40	0-0	1-1	0-0	1-0	0-1		0-1	1-0	0-0	0-0	0-0	1-0	1-0	1-0
ASC Armée	26	9	6	11	30	45	33	2-1	0-4	1-4	0-4	0-2	1-2		1-3	3-1	1-3	1-0	1-1	0-0	0-0
ACS Ksar	26	5	10	11	27	34	25	2-3	1-3	1-1	1-0	1-1	0-2	0-0		0-1	3-3	0-0	4-1	0-1	2-0
Imraguens	26	6	7	13	25	38	25	0-3	0-1	1-1	1-2	1-3	0-1	1-2	3-3		0-1	1-1	2-0	1-1	2-1
ASC Police	26	5	10	11	29	48	25	1-3	0-2	0-2	1-5	2-3	1-1	2-3	0-0	1-1		0-0	0-1	2-2	1-1
Nasr ZemZem	26	3	13	10	24	41	22	0-7	2-3	0-1	2-2	1-1	1-2	1-1	2-1	1-0	2-3		0-0	1-1	1-3
Legwareb Trarza Rosso	26	5	7	14	18	35	22	0-1	0-3	2-2	1-1	1-2	1-0	0-2	0-0	0-1	0-1	1-2		0-0	5-0
Entente Sebkha	26	3	9	14	21	43	18	0-2	0-2	2-2	1-2	0-0	1-2	2-2	0-2	1-0	2-4	2-2	0-1		1-0
UC Lasa	26	4	6	16	20	47	18	0-2	0-0	0-6	1-3	0-1	0-1	2-3	1-0	1-3	0-0	1-1	0-1	4-2	

28/10/2011 - 30/06/2012

COUPE NATIONALE DU PRESIDENT DE LA REPUBLIQUE 2012

Eighth-finals		Quarter-finals		Semi-finals		Final	
ASC Tevragh Zeina	3						
ASC Police	0	**ASC Tevragh Zeina**	2				
Entente Sebkha	2	Nasr ZemZem	0				
Nasr ZemZem	4			**ASC Tevragh Zeina**	1		
Imraguens	2 2p			Assaba FC Kiffa	0		
ASC Gendrim	2 1p	Imraguens	0				
UC Lasa	0 2p	**Assaba FC Kiffa**	1				
Assaba FC Kiffa	0 4p					**ASC Tevragh Zeina**	1
ASC Kédia Zouératt	0 4p					ASAC Concorde	0
ASC Garde Nationale	0 3p	**ASC Kédia Zouératt**	1				
ASC Tidjikja	0 11p	ASC Armée	0			CUP FINAL	
ASC Armée	0 10p			ASC Kédia Zouératt	0		
FC Nouadhibou	2			**ASAC Concorde**	3	Olympique, Nouakchott	
Nasr Dar Naim	0	FC Nouadhibou	1 2p			6-07-2012	
ASC Adrar	1	**ASAC Concorde**	1 4p			Scorer - Ely Cheikh Ould Foullany	
ASAC Concorde	8						

MWI – MALAWI

FIFA/COCA-COLA WORLD RANKING

'93	'94	'95	'96	'97	'98	'99	'00	'01	'02	'03	'04	'05	'06	'07	'08	'09	'10	'11	'12
67	82	89	88	97	89	114	113	120	95	105	109	106	104	138	104	99	86	94	111

2012												High	Low	Av
Jan	Feb	Mar	Apr	May	Jun	Jul	Aug	Sep	Oct	Nov	Dec			
99	98	96	102	102	107	93	90	90	96	101	111	67	138	99

There was huge disappointment in Malawi at missing out on the 2013 Africa Cup of Nations finals in South Africa, where a sizeable chunk of the national team play their club football. The Flames beat Chad in the first preliminary round - revenge of sorts against a team whose late equaliser in Ndjamena in 2011 deprived the Malawians of a place at the 2012 finals in Equatorial Guinea and Gabon - but their campaign then faltered against the might of Ghana, who won both home and away over two legs to advance to the finals instead. In the 2014 FIFA World Cup qualifiers, a John Banda injury time equaliser against Nigeria in June rescued a point for Malawi to keep the group wide open, especially after they then picked up a key away point in Kenya. Malawi were guest competitors at the end of year CECAFA Cup in Uganda where the Kenyans eliminated them in the quarter-finals. In club football Silver Strikers won league honours in early 2012 by a single point from Escom United while Wanderers prevented them from securing a double with a 2-1 victory in the FAM cup final. In the third cup tournament, the Presidential Cup, new wonderkid Gabadinho Mhango scored in every round - the first player ever to do so - as Bullets, known as the people's team, won their first trophy for seven years after beating Moyale Barracks 1-0 in the final.

CAF AFRICA CUP OF NATIONS RECORD
1957-1974 DNE 1976-1982 DNQ **1984** 7 r1 1986-2008 DNQ **2010** 12 r1 2012-2013 DNQ

FOOTBALL ASSOCIATION OF MALAWI (FAM)
Cimwembe Technical Centre,
Off Cimwembe Road
PO Box 51657, Limbe
☎ +265 1 987201
📠 +265 1 875109
✉ generalsecretary@fam.mw
🌐 www.fam.mw
FA 1966 CON 1968 FIFA 1967
P Walter Nyamilandu
GS Suzgo Nyirenda

THE STADIA

2014 FIFA World Cup Stadia	
Kamuzu Stadium Blantyre	40 000

Other Main Stadia	
Civo Stadium Lilongwe	40 000
Silver Stadium Lilongwe	20 000
Mzuzu Stadium Mzuzu	10 000
Balaka Stadium Balaka	5 000

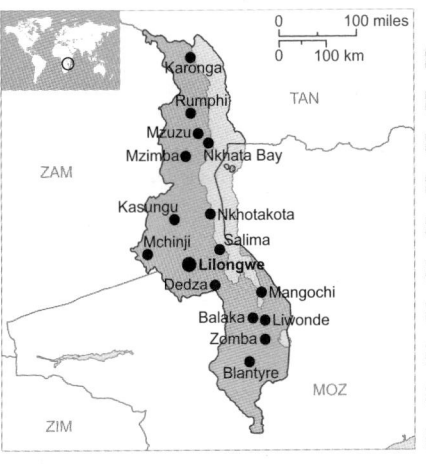

MAJOR CITIES/TOWNS

		Population
1	Lilongwe	922 894
2	Blantyre	760 064
3	Mzuzu	187 151
4	Zomba	105 264
5	Kasungu	64 433
6	Mangochi	54 509
7	Karonga	44 112
8	Salima	42 651
9	Nkhotakota	34 741
10	Liwonde	31 218
11	Rumphi	29 803
12	Nsanje	28 246
13	Mzimba	27 778
14	Mchinji	27 135
15	Balaka	25 169
16	Mulanje	21 890
17	Luchenza	16 350
18	Dedza	15 681
19	Nkhata Bay	15 294

DZIKO LA MALAWI • REPUBLIC OF MALAWI

Capital	Lilongwe	Population	14 268 711 (66)	% in cities	19%
GDP per capita	$800 (220)	Area km²	118 484 km² (99)	GMT +/-	+2
Neighbours (km)	Mozambique 1569, Tanzania 475, Zambia 837				

RECENT INTERNATIONAL MATCHES PLAYED BY MALAWI

2009	Opponents	Score	Venue	Comp	Scorers	Att	Referee
5-09	Guinea	W 2-1	Blantyre	WCq	Msowoya 2 [46 59]	15 000	Codjia BEN
10-10	Côte d'Ivoire	D 1-1	Blantyre	WCq	Ngwira [64]	25 000	El Achiri MAR
25-10	Mozambique	L 0-1	Harare	CCqf			Ramocha BOT
14-11	Burkina Faso	L 0-1	Ouagadougou	WCq		20 000	Abd El Fatah EGY
19-12	Mozambique	W 1-0	Tete	Fr	Nyirenda [88]		
29-12	Egypt	D 1-1	Cairo	Fr	Msowoya [87]		
2010							
5-01	Ghana	D 0-0	Manzini	Fr			
11-01	Algeria	W 3-0	Luanda	CNr1	Mwafulirwa [17], Kafoteka [35], Banda [48]	1 000	Diatta SEN
14-01	Angola	L 0-2	Luanda	CNr1		48 500	Doue CIV
18-01	Mali	L 1-3	Luanda	CNr1	Mwafulirwa [58]	21 000	Seechurn MRI
3-03	Zimbabwe	L 1-2	Harare	Fr	Makandawire [13]		
12-05	Yemen	L 0-1	Sana'a	Fr			
9-07	Togo	D 1-1	Lome	CNq	Mwakasungula [18]		Bennett RSA
11-08	Botswana	D 1-1	Blantyre	CNq	Banda [75]		Carvalho ANG
4-09	Tunisia	D 2-2	Rades/Tunis	CNq	Msowoya [45], Kanyenda [82p]		Lamptey GHA
9-10	Chad	W 6-2	Blantyre	CNq	Zakazaka [13], Kanyenda 2 [21 52], Msowoya 2 [68 79], Ngambi [85]		Kirwa KEN
17-11	Rwanda	W 2-1	Blantyre	Fr	Banda [56], Nyirenda [76]		
29-11	Kenya	W 3-2	Dar es Salaam	CFr1	Nyirenda [1], Banda 2 [26 81]		
2-12	Uganda	D 1-1	Dar es Salaam	CFr1	Nyirenda [2]		
4-12	Ethiopia	D 1-1	Dar es Salaam	CFr1	Kabichi [27]		
2011							
9-02	Namibia	W 2-1	Windhoek	Fr	Wadabwa [41], Harawa [82]		
26-03	Togo	W 1-0	Blantyre	CNq	Chavula [18]		
29-05	Swaziland	D 1-1	Manzini	Fr	Nyondo [56]		
5-06	Botswana	D 0-0	Lobatse	CNq			
6-07	Namibia	L 0-1	Mzuzu	Fr			
3-09	Tunisia	D 0-0	Blantyre	CNq			
4-10	Ethiopia	D 0-0	Addis Abeba	Fr			
8-10	Chad	D 2-2	N'Djamena	CNq	Ngambi [35], Nyirenda [81]		
28-11	Kenya	W 2-0	Dar es Salaam	CFr1	Banda [23], Kamwendo [66p]		
30-11	Sudan	D 0-0	Dar es Salaam	CFr1			
2-12	Ethiopia	D 1-1	Dar es Salaam	CFr1	Kabichi [27]		
6-12	Tanzania	L 0-1	Dar es Salaam	CFqf			
2012							
29-02	Chad	L 2-3	N'Djamena	CNq	Atusaye Nyondo 2 [42 67]		Doue CIV
26-05	Tanzania	D 0-0	Dar es Salaam	Fr			
2-06	Kenya	D 0-0	Nairobi	WCq		14 000	Otogo-Castane GAM
9-06	Nigeria	D 1-1	Blantyre	WCq	John Banda [93+]	25 000	Seechurn MRI
16-06	Chad	W 2-0	Blantyre	CNq	John Banda [31], Joseph Kamwendo [73]		Nampiandraza MAD
6-07	Zambia	W 1-0	Blantyre	Fr	Joseph Kamwendo [84]		
4-09	Liberia	L 0-1	Monrovia	Fr			Neewon LBR
8-09	Ghana	L 0-2	Accra	CNq			Benouza ALG
13-10	Ghana	L 0-1	Lilongwe	CNq			Abdel Rahman SUD
26-11	Rwanda	L 0-2	Kampala	CFr1			Kalyango UGA
29-11	Eritrea	W 3-2	Kampala	CFr1	Chiukepo Msowoya 2 [3 67], Miciam Mhone [11]		Batte UGA
1-12	Zanzibar	W 2-0	Kampala	CFr1	Ndaziona Chatsalira [3], Chiukepo Msowoya [6]		El Fadhil SUD
4-12	Kenya	L 0-1	Kampala	CFqf			Mujuni TAN
22-12	South Africa	L 1-3	Durban	Fr	Joseph Kamwendo [48p]		Rachide MOZ

Fr = Friendly match • CN = CAF African Cup of Nations • CC = COSAFA Cup • CF = CECAFA Cup • WC = FIFA World Cup
q = qualifier • r1 = first round group • qf = quarter-final • sf = semi-final • f = final

MALAWI NATIONAL TEAM HISTORICAL RECORDS

Coaches: Young Chimodzi 2000 • Kim Splidsboel DEN 2001-02 • Alan Gillett ENG 2003 • Edington Ngonamo 2003-04 • John Kaputa 2004, Yassin Osman 2004-05 • Michael Hennigan ENG 2005 • Burkhard Ziese GER 2006 • Kinnah Phiri 2006-07 • Stephen Constantine ENG 2007-08 • Kinnah Phiri 2008-

MALAWI 2011-12

SUPER LEAGUE

	Pl	W	D	L	F	A	Pts	Strikers	Escom	Wanderers	CIVO	Moyale	EPAC	Blantyre U	Eagles	Lions	Tigers	Bullets	MAFCO	Cobbe	Zomba	Em'gweni U
Silver Strikers	28	14	6	8	60	28	48		1-3	0-1	2-1	4-1	3-2	3-1	4-1	0-0	1-1	0-1	3-0	4-0	8-0	9-0
Escom United	28	14	5	9	38	26	47	0-1		0-0	2-1	2-1	1-1	1-2	3-1	1-1	1-2	1-1	2-1	2-0	2-0	2-0
MTL Wanderers	28	12	9	7	29	19	45	1-0	2-1		0-1	0-1	1-1	3-0	0-1	1-2	2-1	0-0	0-0	2-0	0-0	
CIVO United	28	13	5	10	36	28	44	2-2	1-0	2-1		3-1	1-0	3-1	1-2	2-2	0-1	0-1	1-2	1-0	2-1	1-0
Moyale Barracks	28	13	4	11	51	34	43	1-1	1-0	2-1	0-1		1-0	1-1	3-1	3-0	0-0	1-2	5-1	4-0	1-0	5-0
EPAC United	28	13	4	11	41	32	43	3-2	4-1	1-1	2-4	1-0		2-2	1-0	0-1	0-1	2-1	1-1	4-0	2-0	5-1
Blantyre United	28	11	9	8	40	33	42	2-0	0-2	0-2	0-0	2-1	0-1		0-1	1-1	2-1	2-2	2-0	2-0	4-1	4-1
Blue Eagles	28	12	6	10	30	32	42	2-0	1-0	1-1	0-1	1-1	1-0	1-0		1-0	0-1	1-1	1-1	2-0	1-0	1-0
Red Lions	28	10	11	7	30	24	41	0-1	0-2	0-0	0-0	3-2	3-1	0-1	1-1		3-1	1-1	0-1	2-0	2-1	0-0
Azam Tigers	28	12	4	12	41	39	40	1-2	1-2	1-2	1-0	3-6	2-1	3-2	4-1	0-3		1-2	0-0	2-3	3-1	4-1
Bullets	28	10	10	8	29	28	40	1-1	1-2	1-2	1-3	3-0	1-0	1-2	1-0	1-1	0-3		0-0	2-1	0-0	1-0
MAFCO	28	10	9	9	20	31	39	0-3	0-0	1-0	1-0	0-3	0-0	0-0	0-2	1-2	1-0	1-1		1-1	2-0	1-0
Cobbe Barracks	28	7	6	15	27	47	27	2-0	0-2	0-1	2-4	3-2	3-0	2-2	2-2	0-2	0-0	0-1	1-2		2-1	2-0
Zomba United	28	6	4	18	21	51	22	1-1	0-2	1-3	2-1	1-0	1-2	2-2	1-0	1-1	3-2	1-0	0-1	0-1		2-1
Embangweni United	28	5	4	19	17	58	19	0-4	2-1	1-2	1-0	0-4	0-1	0-2	2-4	1-0	1-0	0-0	0-1	2-2	3-0	

9/07/2011 - 28/01/2012 • § = points deducted

FAM STANDARD BANK CUP 2011

Quarter-finals		Semi-finals		Final	
Blue Eagles	4 6				
MAFCO	1 0	**Blue Eagles**	0 4p		
Silver Strikers	1 1	CIVO United	0 3p		
CIVO United	2 2			**Blue Eagles**	2
Red Lions	3 1			Moyale Barracks	1
ESCOM United	2 1	Red Lions	1	Lilongwe, 11-12-2011
MTL Wanderers	0 0	**Moyale Barracks**	3	Scorers -Innocent Bokosi [26],
Moyale Barracks	3 1			John Banda for Eagles; Andy Simukonda [5] for Moyale

FAM STANDARD BANK CUP 2012

Quarter-finals		Semi-finals		Final	
MTL Wanderers	1 2				
Escom United	1 1	**MTL Wanderers**	1 5p		
EPAC United	0 0	Bullets	1 4p		
Bullets	1 0			**MTL Wanderers**	2
CIVO United	1 0			Silver Strikers	0
Moyale Barracks	1 0	CIVO United	1	Lilongwe, 6-10-2012
Blue Eagles	1 1	**Silver Strikers**	4	Scorers - Victor Mpinganjira [41], Moses Chavula [85] for Wanderers
Silver Strikers	3 1				

MEDALS TABLE

	Overall G	Lge G	Cup G	City/Town
1 Bullets	46	11	35	Blantyre
2 Wanderers	25	4	21	Blantyre
3 Silver Strikers	17	4	13	Lilongwe
4 MDC United	9	1	8	Blantyre
5 Tigers	7	1	6	Blantyre
6 CIVO United	5	1	4	Lilongwe
7 Moyale Barracks	3		3	Mzuzu
Red Lions	3		3	Zomba
Sucoma	3		3	Chikwawa
MITCO	3		3	Lilongwe
Michuru Castles	3		3	Blantyre
Escom United	3	2	1	Blantyre
13 Blue Eagles	1		1	Lilongwe

The Cup column is an amalgamation of all the different cup tournaments played from 1967 onwards

PRESIDENTIAL CUP 2012

Round of 16		Quarter–finals		Semi–finals		Final	
Bullets	3						
Silver Strikers	1	**Bullets**	4				
EPAC United	1	Bvumbwe Research	0				
Bvumbwe Research	4			**Bullets**	2 5p		
MAFCO	2			Escom United	2 4p		
Blantyre United	1	MAFCO	1				
Embangweni United	0	**Escom United**	2			**Bullets**	1
Escom United	2					Moyale Barracks	0
Red Lions	2						
CIVO United	0	**Red Lions**	1			CUP FINAL	
Kasungu Police	2	Super Eagles	0			Civo Stadium, Lilongwe 1-09-2012
Super Eagles	5			Red Lions	2	Scorer - Gabadinho Mhango [3] for Bullets
Chikhwawa United	1			**Moyale Barracks**	3	
Blue Eagles	0	Chikhwawa United	1				
Azam Tigers	0	**Moyale Barracks**	3				
Moyale Barracks	1						

MYA – MYANMAR

FIFA/COCA-COLA WORLD RANKING

'93	'94	'95	'96	'97	'98	'99	'00	'01	'02	'03	'04	'05	'06	'07	'08	'09	'10	'11	'12
110	124	115	104	114	115	126	124	151	162	140	144	147	154	157	156	140	149	172	162

2012

Jan	Feb	Mar	Apr	May	Jun	Jul	Aug	Sep	Oct	Nov	Dec	High	Low	Av
172	174	177	173	175	174	180	184	183	184	156	162	97	184	139

After decades of isolation, Myanmar is opening up to the rest of the world following the release from house arrest of opposition leader Aung San Suu Kyi in November 2010, and football is at the forefront of this trend. With a population of nearly 50 million there is the potential for the game to regain some of the prestige it enjoyed throughout Asia in the 1960s although as results in 2012 showed there is some way to go. The first task is to make their presence felt in southeast Asia and in October the national team comfortably won a preliminary round group for the 2012 AFF Suzuki Cup - Park Sung Hwa's team securing their place in the 2012 finals with three comfortable wins. Their performance in the finals, however, was not so impressive as once again they bowed out after the first-round group stage following a draw with Vietnam and defeats at the hands of Thailand and the Philippines. Meanwhile, clubs from Myanmar were given entry to the AFC Cup for the first time in 2012, a reflection of the progress the league has made and the cosmopolitan make up of the clubs which feature players from all over the world. Yangon United retained the league title they first won in 2011 thanks to the goals of Brazilian Cezar Augusto - one of the seven foreigners in the top eight of the scoring charts. At the top of the list was Serbia's Sasa Ramkovic with 20 goals.

FIFA WORLD CUP RECORD
1930-2006 DNE **2010-2014** DNQ

MYANMAR FOOTBALL FEDERATION (MFF)

National Football Training Centre, Waizayanta Road, Thuwunna, Thingankyun, Township, PO Box 11070, Yangon
☎ +951 561539
📠 +951 570000
✉ mffnftc@myanmar.com.mm
🖥 www.themff.org
FA 1947 CON 1954 FIFA 1957
P Zaw Zaw
GS Aung Tin

THE STADIA
2014 FIFA World Cup Stadia
Thuwanna YTC Stadium
Yangon   32 000
Other Main Stadia
Bogyoke Aung San Stadium
Yangon   40 000
Zabuthiri Stadium
Naypyidaw   32 000
Zayyarthiri Stadium
Naypyidaw   30 000

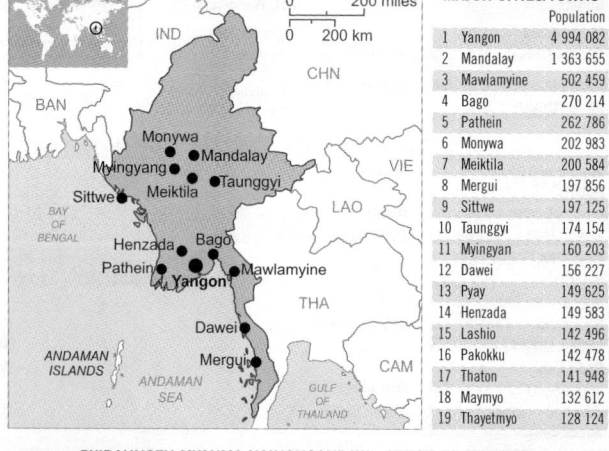

MAJOR CITIES/TOWNS

		Population
1	Yangon	4 994 082
2	Mandalay	1 363 655
3	Mawlamyine	502 459
4	Bago	270 214
5	Pathein	262 786
6	Monywa	202 983
7	Meiktila	200 584
8	Mergui	197 856
9	Sittwe	197 125
10	Taunggyi	174 154
11	Myingyan	160 203
12	Dawei	156 227
13	Pyay	149 625
14	Henzada	149 583
15	Lashio	142 496
16	Pakokku	142 478
17	Thaton	141 948
18	Maymyo	132 612
19	Thayetmyo	128 124

PYIDAUNGZU MYANMA NAINGNGANDAW • UNION OF MYANMAR

Capital	Yangon	Population	48 137 741 (26)	% in cities	33%
GDP per capita	$1200 (206)	Area km^2	676 578 km^2 (40)	GMT +/-	+6.5

Neighbours (km) Bangladesh 193, China 2185, India 1463, Laos 235, Thailand 1800 • Coast 1930

RECENT INTERNATIONAL MATCHES PLAYED BY MYANMAR

2010	Opponents	Score	Venue	Comp	Scorers	Att	Referee
16-02	Sri Lanka	W 4-0	Colombo	CCr1	Thi Ha Kyaw [39], Paing Yan [71], Pai Soe [81], Min Tun Myo [87]	3 000	Faghani IRN
18-02	Bangladesh	W 2-1	Colombo	CCr1	Tun Win Tun [16], Pai Soe [32]	500	Al Yarimi YEM
20-02	Tajikistan	L 0-3	Colombo	CCr1		100	Shukralla BHR
24-02	Korea DPR	L 0-5	Colombo	CCsf		400	Al Yarimi YEM
27-02	Tajikistan	L 0-1	Colombo	CC3p		300	El Haddad LIB
2-12	Vietnam	L 1-7	Hanoi	AFFr1	Kyaw Moe Aung [16]	40 000	Patwal IND
5-12	Singapore	L 1-2	Hanoi	AFFr1	Khin Maung Lwin [13]		Tao Ranchang CHN
8-12	Philippines	D 0-0	Nam Dinh	AFFr1			Patwal IND
2011							
21-03	Philippines	D 1-1	Yangon	CCq	Khin Maung Lwin [93+]	5 000	
23-03	Bangladesh	L 0-2	Yangon	CCq		3 000	
25-03	Palestine	L 1-3	Yangon	CCq	Zaw Htat Aung [25p]	1 500	Abdulhusin BHR
18-06	Malaysia	L 0-2	Kota Bahru	Fr			
29-06	Mongolia	L 0-1	Ulaan-Baatar	WCq		3 500	Kim Jong Hyeok KOR
3-07	Mongolia	W 2-0	Yangon	WCq	Paing Soe [62], Mai Aih Naing [88]	18 000	Liu Kwok Man HKG
14-07	Thailand	L 0-1	Buriram	Fr			
15-07	Thailand	D 1-1	Buriram	Fr	Paing Soe [63]		
23-07	Oman	L 0-2	Seeb	WCq	Awarded 3-0 to Oman	6 300	Sabbagh LIB
28-07	Oman	L 0-2	Yangon	WCq	Abandoned 45 mins. Awarded 3-0 to Oman	30 000	Sato JPN
2012							
11-09	Singapore	D 1-1	Yangon	Fr	David Htan [80]		
5-10	Brunei Darussalam	W 1-0	Yangon	AFFq	Yan Aung Win [84]	2 552	Aslam MDV
7-10	Timor-Leste	W 2-1	Yangon	AFFq	Kyi Lin 2 [38 74]	4 117	Shamsuzzaman BAN
11-10	Cambodia	W 3-0	Yangon	AFFq	Kyi Lin [60], Kaung Si Thu 2 [66 92+]	3 112	Al Yarimi YEM
13-10	Laos	D 0-0	Yangon	AFFq		6 234	Alzaabi UAE
24-11	Vietnam	D 1-1	Bangkok	AFFr1	Kyi Lin [53p]		El Haddad LIB
27-11	Thailand	L 0-4	Bangkok	AFFr1			Abdul Baki OMA
30-11	Philippines	L 0-2	Bangkok	AFFr1			Abdul Baki OMA

Fr = Friendly match • AFF = AFF Championship • CC = AFC Challenge Cup • q = qualifier • r1 = 1st round group

MYANMAR NATIONAL TEAM HISTORICAL RECORDS

Coaches: Sein Hlaing 1964-79 • Bert Trautmann GER 1972-74 • Ratomir Dujkovic SRB 1996-97 • David Booth ENG 2000-03 • Ivan Kolev BUL 2004-05 • Sann Win 2006-07 • Marcos Falopa BRA 2007-08 • Tim Myint Aung 2009 • Drago Mamic CRO 2009-10 • Tim Myint Aung 2010 • Milan Zivadinovic SRB 2011 • Sann Win 2011 • Park Sung Hwa KOR 2011-

MYANMAR 2012

MNL GRAND ROYAL LEAGUE	Pl	W	D	L	F	A	Pts	Yangon Utd	Kanbawza	Yadanarbon	Zeyar SM	Ayeyawady	Magway	Nay Pyi Taw	Manaw Myay	Hantharwady	Rakhapura	Sth Myanmar	Zwekapin	Mawyawadi	Chin United
Yangon United †	26	18	6	2	69	17	60		2-2	2-2	1-0	4-0	2-1	1-1	2-1	2-0	5-0	4-1	3-0	5-0	6-0
Kanbawza	26	18	5	3	64	25	59	1-0		3-1	1-1	2-1	1-0	1-2	2-2	2-0	3-2	2-0	2-0	6-0	4-0
Yadanarbon	26	16	8	2	57	22	56	1-1	2-2		4-1	2-3	1-0	2-0	4-0	2-0	5-1	1-0	2-0	1-0	1-0
Zeyar Shwe Myay	26	16	3	7	51	26	51	0-1	2-1	1-1		1-0	3-0	2-1	3-1	2-0	3-1	3-0	3-0	7-1	4-1
Ayeyawady United	26	13	7	6	45	31	46	1-1	0-1	1-1	2-1		0-2	2-1	2-1	0-1	3-1	1-0	1-0	4-1	3-2
Magway	26	8	8	6	39	21	43	1-2	1-2	1-1	1-0	0-0		4-0	1-2	1-0	0-0	4-1	1-1	1-1	4-1
Nay Pyi Taw	26	12	6	8	38	25	42	0-0	2-0	0-0	2-1	2-2	1-2		1-0	1-0	0-0	0-1	3-0	3-0	2-1
Manaw Myay	26	10	6	10	32	32	36	2-1	1-2	0-2	0-1	1-1	0-0	1-0		0-0	1-2	0-3	1-0	1-0	3-1
Hantharwady United	26	9	7	10	28	30	34	1-2	3-3	3-5	0-1	1-1	0-1	2-1	1-1		2-1	2-1	2-0	2-0	1-1
Rakhapura United	26	7	7	12	40	48	28	1-3	1-4	2-2	5-3	1-4	1-1	2-2	1-3	1-1		2-0	0-1	0-0	4-1
Southern Myanmar	26	6	3	17	24	49	21	0-2	0-3	0-3	1-4	1-3	0-1	0-2	0-4	1-1	0-3		2-1	4-0	3-1
Zwekapin United	26	5	3	18	16	51	18	1-6	0-6	1-3	0-2	3-3	0-1	1-4	0-2	0-1	1-0	1-1		0-1	2-0
Mawyawadi	26	1	6	19	8	74	8	0-5	2-6	0-4	0-0	0-3	0-5	0-4	1-1	0-1	0-4	0-3	0-1		1-3
Chin United	26	1	3	22	17	77	6	0-6	0-2	0-4	1-3	0-4	1-5	0-3	1-3	0-3	0-4	1-1	1-2	0-0	

7/01/2012 - 9/09/2012 • † Qualified for the AFC President's Cup

Top scorer: **20** - Sasa **RAMKOVIC** SRB, Zeyar Shwe Myay • **16** - Adama **KONE** CIV, Yadanarbon & **NUNEZ** BRA, Kanbawza • **15** - **LEANDRO** BRA, Nay Pyi Taw; Lassina **KONE** CIV, Magway & **CEZAR AUGUSTO** BRA, Yangon United • **13** - Soe Min **OO**, Kanbawza & Molo **HILAIRE** CIV, Manaw Myay

NAM – NAMIBIA

FIFA/COCA-COLA WORLD RANKING

'93	'94	'95	'96	'97	'98	'99	'00	'01	'02	'03	'04	'05	'06	'07	'08	'09	'10	'11	'12
156	123	116	103	86	69	80	87	101	123	144	158	161	116	114	115	113	138	121	121

2012

Jan	Feb	Mar	Apr	May	Jun	Jul	Aug	Sep	Oct	Nov	Dec	High	Low	Av
122	120	132	121	120	134	117	113	115	108	117	121	68	167	118

National team coach Bernard Kaanjuka's determination to try and build a new side based on the promising youth players in the country produced mixed results which ultimately lead to a change of heart. Namibia's decline from a team which spent the last four years of the 1990s in the top 100 of the FIFA/Coca Cola World Ranking, to a side battling to stay competitive, continued to provoke much soul searching. Kaanjuka remained determined, despite mediocre results, to build a side with the potential to grow but eventually had to persuade veteran striker Henrico Botes out of international retirement to lead the national team's forward line. Namibia were eliminated by Liberia in the first round of the 2013 Africa Cup of Nations qualifiers but there were encouraging performances in the first two weeks in June in the 2014 FIFA World Cup qualifiers. The 'Brave Warriors' narrowly lost in Nigeria but then beat Kenya with Botes scoring the winner in Windhoek. Clubs from the capital Windhoek continue to dominate the domestic competitions with Black Africa runaway winners of the Premier League for a second successive year, beating Civics and African Stars into second and third place respectively. Black Africa had the satisfaction of securing the title in a derby match with arch rivals Orlando Pirates.

CAF AFRICA CUP OF NATIONS RECORD
1957-1994 DNE 1996 DNQ **1998** 14 r1 2000-2006 DNQ **2008** 14 r1 2010-2013 DNQ

NAMIBIA FOOTBALL ASSOCIATION (NFA)
Richard Kamumuka Street, Soccer House, Katutura, PO Box 1345, Windhoek 9000
☎ +264 61 265691
📠 +264 61 265693
✉ info@nfa.org.na
🌐 www.nfa.org.na
FA 1990 CON 1990 FIFA 1992
P John Muinjo
GS Barry Rukoro

THE STADIA
2014 FIFA World Cup Stadia
Sam Nujoma Stadium
Windhoek   10 300
Other Main Stadia
Independence Stadium
Windhoek   25 000
Oshakati Independence Stadium
Oshakati   8 000
Kuisebmund Stadium
Walvis Bay   4 000
Khomasdal Stadium
Windhoek   2 000

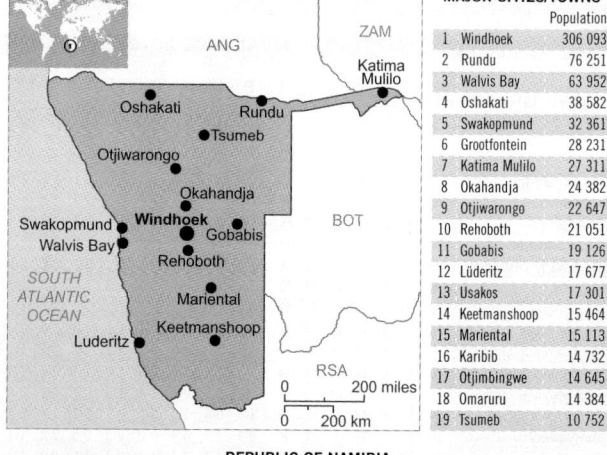

MAJOR CITIES/TOWNS

		Population
1	Windhoek	306 093
2	Rundu	76 251
3	Walvis Bay	63 952
4	Oshakati	38 582
5	Swakopmund	32 361
6	Grootfontein	28 231
7	Katima Mulilo	27 311
8	Okahandja	24 382
9	Otjiwarongo	22 647
10	Rehoboth	21 051
11	Gobabis	19 126
12	Lüderitz	17 677
13	Usakos	17 301
14	Keetmanshoop	15 464
15	Mariental	15 113
16	Karibib	14 732
17	Otjimbingwe	14 645
18	Omaruru	14 384
19	Tsumeb	10 752

REPUBLIC OF NAMIBIA

Capital	Windhoek	Population	2 108 665 (143)	% in cities	37%
GDP per capita	$6400 (129)	Area km²	824 292 km² (34)	GMT +/-	+1

Neighbours (km) Angola 1376, Botswana 1360, South Africa 967, Zambia 233 • Coast 1572

RECENT INTERNATIONAL MATCHES PLAYED BY NAMIBIA

2009	Opponents	Score		Venue	Comp	Scorers	Att	Referee
21-03	Botswana	D	0-0	Keetmanshoop	Fr			
1-04	Lebanon	D	1-1	Saida	Fr	Rudolph Bester [70]		
4-04	Angola	D	0-0	Dundo	Fr			
6-06	Congo DR	W	4-0	Windhoek	Fr	Quinton Jacobs [34], Rudolph Bester [49], Heinrich Isaacks 2 [73 84]		
5-09	Swaziland	D	1-1	Windhoek	Fr	Rudolph Bester [28]		
25-10	Zambia	L	0-1	Harare	CCqf			Ebrahim RSA
2010								
3-03	South Africa	D	1-1	Durban	Fr	Rudolph Bester [42]	35 000	Nguluwe MWI
21-03	Botswana	D	0-0	Windhoek	Fr			
4-09	Gambia	L	1-3	Banjul	CNq	Wilko Risser [90]		Ragab LBY
15-09	India	L	0-2	New Delhi	Fr			
2011								
9-02	Malawi	L	1-2	Windhoek	Fr	Wilko Risser [35]		
16-03	Botswana	D	1-1	Maun	Fr	Eslin Kamuhanga [33]		
26-03	Burkina Faso	L	0-4	Ouagadougou	CNq			Cordier CHA
4-06	Burkina Faso	L	1-4	Windhoek	CNq	Tangeni Shipahu [83]		
6-07	Malawi	W	1-0	Mzuzu	Fr	Sydney Urikhob [85]		
3-09	Gambia	W	1-0	Windhoek	CNq	Tangeni Shipahu [83]		
31-10	Lesotho	D	0-0	Windhoek	Fr			
11-11	Djibouti	W	4-0	Djibouti	WCq	Rudolf Bester 2 [13 52], Lazarus Kaimbi [50], Sydney Urikhob [88]	3 000	Bamlak ETH
15-11	Djibouti	W	4-0	Windhoek	WCq	Heinrich Isaacks [17], Lazarus Kaimbi 2 [34 58], Sydney Urikhob [88]	2 145	Chirinda MOZ
22-12	Angola	D	0-0	Lubango	Fr			
2012								
14-01	Zambia	D	0-0	Johannesburg	Fr			
22-02	Mozambique	W	3-0	Windhoek	Fr	Sydney Urikhob [45], Benson Shilongo 2 [64 85]		
29-02	Liberia	L	0-1	Monrovia	CNq			Otogo Castane GAB
26-05	Mozambique	D	0-0	Wuerzburg	Fr			
3-06	Nigeria	L	0-1	Calabar	WCq		10 000	Adel SUD
9-06	Kenya	W	1-0	Windhoek	WCq	Henrico Botes [75]	12 000	Bondo BOT
16-06	Liberia	D	0-0	Windhoek	CNq			Sikazwe ZAM
14-11	Rwanda	D	2-2	Kigali	Fr	Henrico Botes [73], Petrus Shitembi [93+]		Batte UGA

Fr = Friendly match • CN = CAF African Cup of Nations • CC = COSAFA Cup • WC = FIFA World Cup • q = qualifier • rl = first round group

NAMIBIA 2011-12

MTC PREMIER LEAGUE

	Pl	W	D	L	F	A	Pts	Black Africa	Civics	African Stars	Blue Waters	SK Windhoek	Tigers	Ramblers	Mighty Gunners	Orlando Pirates	Eleven Arrows	United Stars	Hotspurs
Black Africa	22	17	4	1	42	12	55		2-0	1-0	1-1	2-2	2-0	2-0	0-0	1-0	3-0	2-0	2-1
Civics	22	11	5	6	30	17	38	0-1		3-0	1-1	2-0	0-0	1-0	0-1	2-1	2-0	2-2	1-0
African Stars	22	10	5	7	26	17	35	1-2	0-1		2-0	0-1	0-0	0-0	2-1	2-0	3-1	1-0	1-1
Blue Waters	22	8	10	4	27	21	34	2-2	1-1	1-0		1-1	0-3	0-0	2-1	2-1	2-1	0-0	5-0
SK Windhoek	22	8	9	5	19	14	33	0-1	1-0	1-1	0-0		1-1	1-0	0-0	1-2	1-0	2-0	1-0
United Africa Tigers	22	7	11	4	23	21	32	0-3	2-1	1-1	2-1	0-0		1-1	1-1	1-1	2-0	1-0	2-0
Ramblers	22	8	5	9	23	24	29	1-0	2-3	0-3	1-0	0-2	0-0		3-0	3-1	2-0	0-1	4-2
Mighty Gunners	22	7	6	9	27	30	27	1-2	0-2	3-1	1-1	2-0	2-3	0-0		1-1	0-3	2-0	2-3
Orlando Pirates	22	6	6	10	26	25	24	1-2	1-0	0-1	0-0	0-1	1-1	3-0	1-3		3-0	2-0	1-1
Eleven Arrows	22	5	5	12	18	31	20	0-2	1-0	0-0	1-1	0-0	2-0	2-1	2-3	0-0		2-0	0-1
United Stars	22	4	5	13	15	36	17	1-6	1-2	0-4	1-2	1-0	2-2	0-1	1-0	0-2	2-0		1-1
Hotspurs	22	3	5	14	23	51	14	1-3	0-5	0-2	1-3	0-3	2-0	1-3	2-3	1-4	3-3	2-2	

16/09/2011 - 19/05/2012

NCA – NICARAGUA

FIFA/COCA-COLA WORLD RANKING

'93	'94	'95	'96	'97	'98	'99	'00	'01	'02	'03	'04	'05	'06	'07	'08	'09	'10	'11	'12
155	168	174	179	182	188	193	191	188	186	173	158	152	168	161	181	133	158	154	145

2012

Jan	Feb	Mar	Apr	May	Jun	Jul	Aug	Sep	Oct	Nov	Dec	High	Low	Av
145	144	144	146	146	141	141	139	144	138	136	145	132	193	168

The one thing that the Nicaragua national team can usually rely on when they take part in the Copa Centroamericana is that they will either beat Belize or draw with them and make it through to the fifth place play-off. That ensures a crack at qualifying for the Gold Cup finals which in 2009 they succeeded in doing after beating Guatemala. At the 2013 finals at the start of the year in Costa Rica, however, the Nicaraguans contrived to lose to Belize and were on the first bus home. That was a huge disappointment given the work going on behind the scenes to improve the infrastructure of football in a country dominated by baseball. In April 2011 FIFA President Sepp Blatter opened the first phase of the new National Stadium for football in the south of Managua and for the first time games in the championship are now largely played in football specific stadia - a big improvement to the basic facilities that the game previously shared with baseball such as in the Estadio Nacional Dennis Martinez. In the 2011-12 championship Real Esteli made it six titles in a row after winning both the apertura and clausura finals which meant that they were declared overall champions without the need for a play-off. Of the 12 finals played in those six years, Esteli have failed to qualify for just two of them.

CONCACAF GOLD CUP RECORD
1991-2007 DNQ **2009** r1 **2011-2013** DNQ

FEDERACION NICARAGUENSE DE FUTBOL (FENIFUT)

Porton Principal del Hospital Bautista 1 c. abajo, 1 c. al sur y 1/2 c. abajo, Apartado Postal 976, Managua
☎ +505 22227035
+505 22227885
✉ fenifut@yahoo.com
🖥 www.fenifut.org.ni
FA 1931 CON 1968 FIFA 1950
P Rolando Lopez
GS Florencio Leiva

THE STADIA
2014 FIFA World Cup Stadia
Estadio Nacional de Futbol Managua — 11 000
Other Main Stadia
Estadio Nacional Dennis Martinez Managua — 30 100
Estadio Cacique Diriangén Diriamba — 8 500
Estadio Olímpico del IND Managua — 8 000

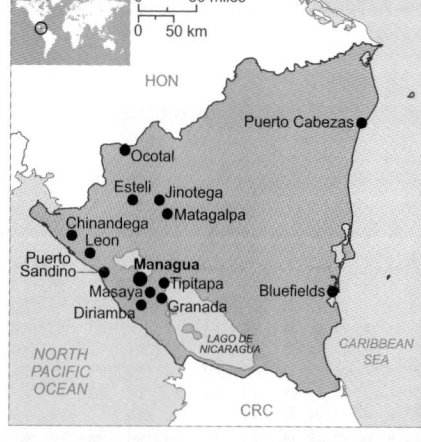

MAJOR CITIES/TOWNS

		Population
1	Managua	925 313
2	León	144 179
3	Estelí	97 488
4	Chinandega	93 996
5	Tipitapa	93 080
6	Masaya	93 053
7	Matagalpa	89 132
8	Granada	81 674
9	Ciudad Sandino	75 610
10	Puerto Cabezas	48 491
11	Jinotega	45 580
12	Juigalpa	44 686
13	El Viejo	41 110
14	Bluefields	40 297
15	Ocotal	38 148
16	Diriamba	36 827
17	Chichigalpa	36 186
18	Jinotepe	33 604
19	Mateare	32 114

REPUBLICA DE NICARAGUA • REPUBLIC OF NICARAGUA

Capital Managua Population 5 891 199 (108) % in cities 57%
GDP per capita $2900 (165) Area km² 130 370 km² (97) GMT +/- -6
Neighbours (km) Costa Rica 309, Honduras 922 • Coast 910

RECENT INTERNATIONAL MATCHES PLAYED BY NICARAGUA

2006	Opponents	Score		Venue	Comp	Scorers	Att	Referee
No international matches played in 2006								
2007								
8-02	Guatemala	L	0-1	San Salvador	UCr1		10 000	Pineda HON
10-02	El Salvador	L	1-2	San Salvador	UCr1	Samuel Wilson [53]	20 000	Arredondo MEX
12-02	Belize	W	4-2	San Salvador	UCr1	Emilio Palacios 3 [12 20 68], Milton Bustos [28]	5 000	Quesada CRC
15-02	Honduras	L	1-9	San Salvador	UC5p	Samuel Wilson [31]	3 000	Aguilar SLV
2008								
6-02	Netherlands Antilles	L	0-1	Diriamba	WCq		7 000	Lopez GUA
26-03	Netherlands Antilles	L	0-2	Willemstad	WCq		9 000	Wijngaarde SUR
2009								
22-01	El Salvador	D	1-1	Tegucigalpa	UCr1	Marlon Medina [85]	20 000	Batres GUA
24-01	Honduras	L	1-4	Tegucigalpa	UCr1	Armando Reyes [30]	20 000	Batres GUA
26-01	Belize	D	1-1	Tegucigalpa	UCr1	Juan Barrera [66]	8 000	Moncada HON
29-01	Guatemala	W	2-0	Tegucigalpa	UC5p	Samuel Wilson 2 [39 85]	150	Moncada HON
5-07	Mexico	L	0-2	Oakland	GCr1		32 700	Ward CAN
9-07	Guadeloupe	L	0-2	Houston	GCr1		47 713	Moncada HON
12-07	Panama	L	0-4	Phoenix	GCr1		23 876	Pineda HON
2010								
4-09	Guatemala	L	0-5	Fort Lauderdale	Fr		5 000	Vaughn USA
2011								
14-01	El Salvador	L	0-2	Panama City	UCr1		2 000	Quesada CRC
16-01	Panama	L	0-2	Panama City	UCr1		7 747	Lopez GUA
18-01	Belize	D	1-1	Panama City	UCr1	Denis Espinoza [10p]	10 000	Brea CUB
21-01	Guatemala	L	1-2	Panama City	UC5p	Felix Rodriguez [24]	5 000	Garcia MEX
26-05	Cuba	D	1-1	Havana	Fr	Raul Leguias [44p]	3 500	Brea CUB
28-05	Cuba	L	1-2	Havana	Fr	OG [89]	2 950	Rubalcaba CUB
2-09	Dominica	W	2-0	Roseau	WCq	Raul Leguias [1], Felix Rodriguez [36]	3 000	Legister JAM
6-09	Panama	L	1-2	Managua	WCq	OG [18]	10 521	Reyna GUA
11-10	Panama	L	1-5	Panama City	WCq	Daniel Reyes [88]	10 846	Ventura SLV
11-11	Dominica	W	1-0	Managua	WCq	Raul Leguias [57]	2 100	Cruz CRC
2012								
24-02	Puerto Rico	W	1-0	Managua	Fr	Ricardo Vega [90]	2 000	Jarquin NCA
26-02	Puerto Rico	W	4-1	Managua	Fr	Ricardo Vega [41], Axel Villanueva 2 [73 78], Felix Zeledon [90]	2 300	Davilla NCA
1-06	Puerto Rico	L	1-3	Bayamon	Fr	Juan Barrera [90]	1 277	Anderson PUR
3-06	Puerto Rico	D	1-1	Bayamon	Fr	Ulises Pavon [79]	994	Santos PUR
2013								
18-01	Guatemala	D	1-1	San Jose	UCr1	Josue Quijano [41]	200	Aguilar SLV
20-01	Costa Rica	L	0-2	San Jose	UCr1		5 980	Moreno PAN
22-01	Belize	L	1-2	San Jose	UCr1	Elvis Figueroa [85]	750	Aguilar SLV

Fr = Friendly match • UC = UNCAF Cup/Copa Centroamericana • GC = CONCACAF Gold Cup • WC = FIFA World Cup • q = qualifier
r1 = first round group • 5p = fifth place play-off

NICARAGUA 2011-12

XXVIII CAMPEONATO NACIONAL PRIMERA DIVISION TORNEO CLAUSURA

	Pl	W	D	L	F	A	Pts	Real Estelí	Walter Ferreti	Diriangén	Managua	Ocotal	Juventus	Real Madriz	Chinandega
Real Estelí †	14	10	2	2	27	8	32		1-1	3-0	1-1	5-1	1-0	3-0	3-1
Dep. Walter Ferreti †	14	6	3	5	17	12	21	1-2		2-1	1-2	0-1	0-0	1-2	3-1
Diriangén †	14	5	6	3	15	12	21	1-0	0-0		2-2	2-0	1-0	3-0	0-0
Managua †	14	5	6	3	19	17	21	0-1	0-3	1-1		0-2	1-0	3-0	4-1
Deportivo Ocotal	14	6	2	6	22	24	20	0-2	0-1	3-1	3-1		3-3	1-3	4-0
Juventus Managua	14	4	3	7	19	22	15	0-2	0-2	1-3	2-2	4-1		2-1	0-1
Real Madriz	14	4	3	7	18	23	15	0-2	2-1	0-0	1-1	0-1	2-3		5-0
VCP Chinandega	14	1	5	8	11	30	8	1-2	0-1	0-0	0-0	2-2	2-4	2-2	

21/01/2012 - 4/04/2012 • † Qualified for the Clausura play-offs • Xilotepelt and América relegated
See Oliver's Almanack 2012 for 2011-12 Apertura details

CLAUSURA SEMI-FINALS

	Pl	W	D	L	F	A	Pts	RE	Di	Ma	WF
Real Estelí †	6	4	2	0	9	3	14		3-0	1-1	2-1
Diriangén †	6	4	0	2	12	5	12	0-1		3-0	1-0
Managua	6	2	1	3	6	11	7	0-1	0-3		2-1
Dep. Walter Ferreti	6	0	1	5	6	13	1	1-1	1-4	2-3	

14/04/2012 - 6/05/2012 • † Qualified for the Clausura final

CLAUSURA FINAL

Olímpico del IND, Managua, 13-05-2012
Diriangén 0-3 Real Estelí

Scorers - Marlon Medina [5], Felix Rodriguez 2 [35 57] for Real Estelí

Estadio Nacional, Managua
Real Estelí 3-1 Diriangén

Scorers - Rudel Calero [7], Samuel Wilson 2 [12 53] for Real Estelí; Eulises Pavon [43] for Diriangén

NICARAGUA 2011-12 AGGREGATE TABLE

	Pl	W	D	L	F	A	Pts
Real Estelí	28	20	5	3	48	16	65
Managua	28	13	7	8	41	32	46
Dep. Walter Ferreti	28	13	5	10	45	30	44
Diriangén	28	11	10	7	34	28	43
VCP Chinandega	28	8	7	13	27	45	31
Deportivo Ocotal	28	8	5	15	39	55	29
Juventus Managua	28	7	7	14	41	51	28
Real Madriz	28	7	4	17	38	56	25

Real Estelí both both the 2011-12 Apertura and Clausura so were automatically declared champions

MEDALS TABLE

		Overall G	Lge G	City/Town
1	Diriangén	25	25	Diriamba
2	Real Estelí	1	11	Estelí
3	Santa Cecilia	5	5	Diriamba
4	UCA Managua	4	4	Managua
5	Aduana	3	3	Managua
6	América	3	3	Managua

NICARAGUA 2012-13

XXIX CAMPEONATO NACIONAL PRIMERA DIVISION TORNEO APERTURA

	Pl	W	D	L	F	A	Pts	Real Estelí	Managua	Walter Ferreti	Juventus	Diriangén	Ocotal	Chinandega	Xilotepelt
Real Estelí †	14	7	5	2	22	12	26		1-1	1-1	1-2	2-0	2-2	4-2	2-0
Managua †	14	6	4	4	16	11	22	0-2		2-1	1-2	2-0	0-1	2-1	3-0
Dep. Walter Ferreti †	14	6	2	6	15	11	20	2-1	0-1		0-1	3-0	3-0	1-0	1-0
Juventus Managua †	14	5	5	4	13	14	20	0-0	2-2	0-1		0-2	1-0	2-1	0-0
Diriangén	14	6	1	7	14	16	19	0-2	0-0	1-0	2-1		2-1	5-1	1-0
Deportivo Ocotal	14	3	7	4	12	16	16	0-0	0-0	1-1	1-1	1-0		0-0	3-0
VCP Chinandega	14	4	3	7	16	22	15	1-2	1-0	2-1	3-1	1-0	0-0		2-2
Xilotepelt	14	4	3	7	12	18	15	1-2	0-2	1-0	0-0	2-1	5-1	1-0	

22/07/2012 - 7/10/2012 • † Qualified for the Apertura play-offs

APERTURA SEMI-FINALS

	Pl	W	D	L	F	A	Pts	RE	WF	Ma	JM
Real Estelí †	6	3	3	0	10	5	12		1-1	2-1	1-1
Dep. Walter Ferreti †	6	2	3	1	5	5	9	0-2		1-0	1-0
Managua	6	2	2	2	6	6	8	1-1	0-0		2-1
Juventus Managua	6	0	2	4	6	11	2	1-3	2-2	1-2	

21/10/2012 - 2/12/2012 • † Qualified for the Apertura final

APERTURA FINAL

1st leg. Olímpico del IND, Managua, 9-12-2012
Walter Ferreti 0-0 Real Estelí

2nd leg. Independencia, Estelí, 16-12-2012
Real Estelí 4-0 Walter Ferreti

Scorers - Rudel Calero 2 [35 60], Manuel Rosas 2 [77p 80] for Estelí

NCL – NEW CALEDONIA

FIFA/COCA-COLA WORLD RANKING

'93	'94	'95	'96	'97	'98	'99	'00	'01	'02	'03	'04	'05	'06	'07	'08	'09	'10	'11	'12
-	-	-	-	-	-	-	-	-	-	-	186	187	176	118	130	147	156	166	108

2012

Jan	Feb	Mar	Apr	May	Jun	Jul	Aug	Sep	Oct	Nov	Dec	High	Low	Av
166	163	162	154	155	155	143	141	128	113	104	108	95	188	154

The New Caledonia national team enjoyed a very good year in 2012 and but for two significant defeats it would have been an exceptional one. With the first round of the OFC Nations Cup also acting as the first round of qualifying for the 2014 FIFA World Cup there was plenty at stake as the eight teams gathered in Honaria, the capital of the Solomon Islands, for the tournament. By finishing as group runners-up to an inspired Tahiti team, New Caledonia made it through to the final four of World Cup qualifying to be played later in the year and also to the semi-finals of the Nations Cup. In the semi-final they faced a New Zealand team out to win a record fifth continental title but a fantastic performance saw New Caledonia win 2-0 - their first-ever victory over the Kiwis. With one hand seemingly on the trophy and a trip to Brazil for the Confederations Cup on the cards, they stumbled and lost 1-0 to Tahiti in the final. The second key defeat came three months later at home to New Zealand in the final round of World Cup qualifying - the only points dropped in their first four games, but with just the group winners qualifying for the Asia-Oceania play-off it looked to be a key defeat. At home Magenta came within a penalty shoot out of the league and cup double but having reclaimed their league title after a two year gap they then lost in the cup final to Lossi.

FIFA WORLD CUP RECORD
1930-2002 DNE 2006-2010 DNQ

FEDERATION CALEDONIENNE DE FOOTBALL (FCF)

7 bis, rue Suffren, Quartier Latin, BP 560, Nouméa 99845
☎ +687 272383
📠 +687 263249
✉ fedcalfoot@canl.nc
🖥 www.fedcalfoot.com
FA 1928 CON FIFA 2004
P Edmond Bowen
GS Olivier Dokunengo

THE STADIA

2014 FIFA World Cup Stadia	
Stade Numa-Daly Magenta Nouméa	9 646
Other Main Stadia	
Stade Boewa Boulari Bay	
Stade Rivière Salée Nouméa	3 000
Stade de Hnassé We, Lifou	1 680
Stade Edouard-Pentecost Thio	1 000

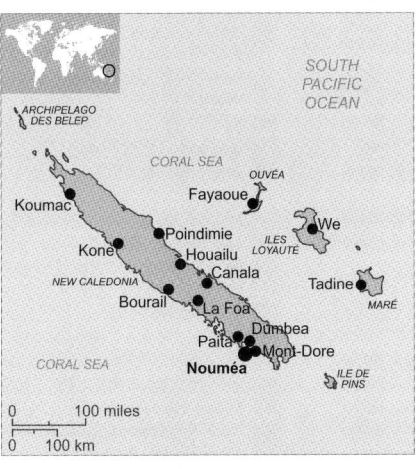

MAJOR CITIES/TOWNS

		Population
1	Nouméa	100 479
2	Mont-Doré	26 549
3	Dumbéa	22 400
4	Païta	15 206
5	Wé	10 549
6	Tadine	7 807
7	Poindimié	5 131
8	Bourail	5 003
9	Koné	4 845
10	Houaïlu	4 664
11	Fayaoué	4 612
12	Canala	3 633
13	Koumac	3 278
14	La Foa	3 141
15	Hienghène	2 862
16	Thio	2 783
17	Ponerihouen	2 778
18	Poya	2 697
19	Voh	2 419

NOUVELLE-CALEDONIE • NEW CALEDONIA

Capital	Nouméa	Population	227 436 (181)	% in cities	65%
GDP per capita	$15 000 (76)	Area km²	18 575 km² (155)	GMT +/-	+11
Neighbours (km)	Coast 2254				

RECENT INTERNATIONAL MATCHES PLAYED BY NEW CALEDONIA

2006	Opponents	Score	Venue	Comp	Scorers	Att	Referee
No international matches played in 2006							
2007							
17-07	Vanuatu	W 5-3	Noumea	Fr	Mapou [40], Toto 2 [47 62], Hmae.J [56], Wajoka [69p]		
19-07	Vanuatu	L 0-2	Noumea	Fr			
25-08	Tahiti	W 1-0	Apia	WCq	Wajoka [9p]	400	Hester NZL
27-08	Tuvalu †	W 1-0	Apia	WCq	Kabeu [52]	250	Sogo SOL
29-08	Cook Islands	W 3-0	Apia	WCq	Kabeu 3 [35 51 85]	200	Fox NZL
3-09	Fiji	D 1-1	Apia	WCq	Wajoka [44]	1 000	Fred VAN
5-09	Solomon Islands	W 3-2	Apia	WCq	Kabeu [37], Toto [54], Mercier [94+]	600	Minan PNG
7-09	Fiji	W 1-0	Apia	WCq	Hmae.J [61]	400	Hester NZL
17-11	Fiji	D 3-3	Ba	WCq	Djamali [67], Kaudre [83], Hmae.M [88]	1 500	O'Leary NZL
21-11	Fiji	W 4-0	Noumea	WCq	Wajoka [28p], Hmae.M 2 [30 55], Mapou [59]		Breeze AUS
2008							
14-06	Vanuatu	D 1-1	Port Vila	WCq	Djamali [73]	4 000	Varman FIJ
21-06	Vanuatu	W 3-0	Noumea	WCq	Wajoka [36], Hmae.M [60], Diaike [87]	2 700	Hester NZL
6-09	New Zealand	L 1-3	Noumea	WCq	Hmae.M [55]	2 589	Varman FIJ
10-09	New Zealand	L 0-3	Auckland	WCq		8 000	Hauata TAH
24-09	Tahiti	W 1-0	Paris	Fr	Hmae.M [91+]		
27-09	Guadeloupe †	L 0-4	Paris	Fr			Alain GYF
30-09	Martinique †	D 1-1	Paris	Fr	Lolohea		Alain GYF
3-10	Mayotte	W 3-2	Paris	Fr	Wajoka 2 [53 87p], Kai [58]		Touraine GLP
2009							
No international matches played in 2009							
2010							
23-09	Guadeloupe †	D 1-1	Paris	Fr	Hmae.M		Prevot FRA
26-09	Martinique †	L 0-4	Paris	Fr			Tetauira FRA
29-09	Tahiti	D 1-1	Paris	Fr	Watrone [6]. L 3-5p		Fouquet FRA
2011							
24-01	Vanuatu	D 0-0	Port Vila	Fr			
3-04	Tahiti	W 3-1	Papeete	Fr	Kabeu 3 [29 81 86]		
7-04	Tahiti	L 0-1	Papeete	Fr			
27-08	Vanuatu	W 5-0	Noumea	PGr1	Gope-Fenepej 3 [5 31 63], Bako [43], Lolohea [51]		Achari FIJ
30-08	Guam	W 9-0	Noumea	PGr1	Kai 5 [12 26 40 47 91+], Boawe [70], Kaneu [73], Wakanumune [83], Hmae.M [85]		Zitouni TAH
1-09	Tuvalu †	W 8-0	Noumea	PGr1	Gorendiawe [15], Kabeu 2 [26 35], Gope-Fenepej [38], Haeko [50], Lolohea [61], Hmae.M 2 [67 85]		Kerr NZL
3-09	American Samoa	W 8-0	Noumea	PGr1	Kai 4 [10 38 44 66], Haeko [50], Qaeze [55], Vendegou [72], Hmae.M [89]		Varman FIJ
5-09	Solomon Islands	L 1-2	Noumea	PGr1	Kai [74]		Kerr NZL
7-09	Tahiti	W 3-1	Kone	PGsf	Gope-Fenepej 2 [89 108], Hmae [115]		Varman FIJ
9-09	Solomon Islands	W 2-0	Noumea	PGf	Gope-Fenepej [9], Bako [11]		Kerr NZL
2012							
1-06	Vanuatu	W 5-2	Honiara	OCr1	Kai 3 [32 58 78], Gope-Fenepej [66], Kayara.R [89]	6 000	O'Leary NZL
3-06	Tahiti	L 3-4	Honiara	OCr1	Bako [76], Haeko [83], Kauma [89]	3 500	Kerr NZL
5-06	Samoa	W 9-0	Honiara	OCr1	Kayara.R [10], Haeko 5 [11 45 71 89 91+], Kabeu [22], Ixoee [25p], Gnipate [44]	1 000	Oiaka SOL
8-06	New Zealand	W 2-0	Honiara	OCsf	Kai [60], Gope-Fenepej [93+]	10 000	Hauata TAH
10-06	Tahiti	L 0-1	Honiara	OCf		10 000	O'Leary NZL
7-09	New Zealand	L 0-2	Noumea	WCq		6 000	Hauata TAH
11-09	Tahiti	W 4-0	Papeete	WCq	OG [59], Kai [60], Gope-Fenepej 2 [63 90]	574	Achari FIJ
12-10	Solomon Islands	W 6-2	Honiara	WCq	Kayara.R [8], Gope-Fenepej 3 [45 81 91+], OG [77], Haeko [89]	8 000	O'Leary NZL
16-10	Solomon Islands	W 5-0	Noumea	WCq	Gope-Fenepej [4], Kayara.R [8], Kabeu [30], Lolohea 2 [42 80]	4 000	Zitouni TAH

Fr = Friendly match • OC = OFC Oceania Nations Cup • PG = Pacific Games • WC = FIFA World Cup
q = qualifier • r1 = first round group • sf = semi-final • f = final • † Not a full international

NEW CALEDONIA 2012

GRAND TERRE SUPER LIGUE COCA-COLA

	Pl	W	D	L	F	A	Pts	Magenta	Hienghène	Lössi	Gaïtcha	Mont-Dore	Qanono	Thio Sport	Kunié	Tiga Sport	Baco	Mouli
AS Magenta †	20	13	4	3	42	32	63		2-2	2-1	2-1	2-1	1-1	2-2	2-3	3-2	4-3	5-4
Hienghène Sports	20	10	7	3	64	32	57	1-1		0-4	1-1	1-2	4-0	4-3	0-2	9-1	3-3	5-1
AS Lössi	20	11	3	6	60	42	56	2-0	2-4		4-1	0-2	1-3	4-4	0-2	4-2	8-2	3-2
Gaïtcha FCN	20	10	2	8	52	33	52	1-2	2-2	5-2		1-0	1-2	2-0	7-0	2-3	4-2	6-2
AS Mont-Dore	20	9	3	8	36	29	50	1-2	1-1	1-2	1-3		1-1	0-1	3-1	2-1	1-2	1-1
AS Qanono	20	8	6	6	43	38	49	4-0	1-2	1-1	0-2	0-3		4-4	3-2	1-1	2-0	4-3
AS Thio Sport	20	8	5	7	55	54	49	1-2	0-5	1-5	3-2	3-1	2-1		3-4	2-4	3-2	3-1
AS Kunié	20	9	1	10	32	47	47	0-1	1-4	1-3	1-0	0-3	1-6	2-2		2-1	2-1	3-1
Tiga Sport	20	6	4	10	40	49	42	0-3	3-3	1-4	0-1	2-4	1-1	3-3	3-1		1-0	1-2
JS Baco	20	4	2	14	49	79	34	1-3	1-8	5-5	2-7	2-4	5-4	5-10	4-1	1-4		6-2
Mouli Sport	20	3	1	16	39	77	29	1-3	1-5	3-5	4-3	3-4	3-4	1-5	0-3	1-6	3-2	

15/02/2012 - 15/12/2012 • † Qualified for the OFC Champions League

COUPE DE CALEDONIE 2012

Round of 16		Quarter-finals		Semi-finals		Final	
AS Lössi	7						
JS Maré	3	**AS Lössi**	9				
AS Kunie	0	FC Belep	0				
FC Belep	2			**AS Lössi**	2		
Hienghène Sports				AS Qanono	1		
ES Maréenne		Hienghène Sports	5				
AS Wet	0	**AS Qanono**	6				
AS Qanono	1					**AS Lössi**	1 3p
JS Baco						AS Magenta	1 2p
Tiga Sport		**JS Baco**	2 4p				
AS Grand Nord		Gaïtcha FCN	2 3p			CUP FINAL	
Gaïtcha FCN				JS Baco	1		
AS Mont-Dore	2			**AS Magenta**	2	Stade Numa-Daly, Nouméa	
AS Thio Sport	1	AS Mont-Dore	1			3-11-2012	
Mouli Sport	2	**AS Magenta**	5			Scorers - Michel Wassin [61] for Lossi;	
AS Magenta	8					Noel Kaudre [92+] for Magenta	

Cup Final line-ups: **Lossi** - Hne - Luepak, B. Hmaloko, Kauma, J-Ch. Wajoka - Tain (F. Forest 79), Wamowe - Wassin (Poulawa 78), L. Wahnyamalla (c), J-J. Wahnyamalla (L. Wahnawe 74) - Aucher. Tr: Thierry Sardo • **Magenta** - St. Ixoee - J. Dokunengo, Wadriako, J-P. Wakanumune, L. Wakanumune - Kaudre (c), Jewine (Mawea 70) - Gnipate, Xalite (W. Waheo 65), V. Waheo (Yekawene 65) - Poatinda. Tr : Kevin Coma

NED – NETHERLANDS

FIFA/COCA-COLA WORLD RANKING

'93	'94	'95	'96	'97	'98	'99	'00	'01	'02	'03	'04	'05	'06	'07	'08	'09	'10	'11	'12
7	6	6	9	22	11	19	8	8	6	4	6	3	7	9	3	3	2	2	8

2012

Jan	Feb	Mar	Apr	May	Jun	Jul	Aug	Sep	Oct	Nov	Dec	High	Low	Av
2	3	2	4	4	4	8	8	8	6	7	8	1	25	7

The Dutch national team may on occasion miss out on the final tournament of the FIFA World Cup or the European Championship, but it is rare that they have a complete disaster when they do qualify. The finals of Euro 2012 were an exception. Although they were drawn in the most difficult group, the 2010 FIFA World Cup finalists were tipped by many as potential winners. As in South Africa they kicked off their campaign against Denmark, but this time they lost 1-0 despite dominating the game, a result that left them chasing the group. A defeat at the hands of Germany did not end their campaign but in the final group game against Portugal, despite taking the lead they couldn't find a second goal which would have taken them through and lost 2-1. Louis van Gaal was appointed coach after the finals and with four wins in four in the 2014 FIFA World Cup qualifiers, spirits were restored. At home, Ajax retained their league title - the first time they had managed that since 1996. Coach Frank de Boer inspired his team to win their last 14 matches of the campaign to finish six points ahead of a rejuvenated Feyenoord team as the big three of Ajax, Feyenoord and PSV filled the top three places for the first time since 2004. PSV were the cup winners, beating first-time finalists Heracles Almelo 3-0 for their first trophy in four seasons.

UEFA EUROPEAN CHAMPIONSHIP RECORD

1960 DNE 1964 r2 1968-1972 DNQ **1976** 3 SF **1980** 5 r1 1984 DNQ **1988** 1 Winners **1992** 3 SF
1996 8 QF **2000** 3 SF (co-hosts) **2004** 4 SF **2008** 6 QF **2012** Qualified

KONINKLIJKE NEDERLANDSE VOETBALBOND (KNVB)

Woudenbergseweg 56-58, PO Box 515, Am Zeist 3700
☎ +31 343 499201
📠 +31 343 499189
✉ concern@knvb.nl
🖥 www.knvb.nl
FA 1889 CON 1954 FIFA 1904
P Michael Van Praag
GS Bert van Oostveen

THE STADIA

2014 FIFA World Cup Stadia
Amsterdam Arena
Amsterdam — 53 052
Stadion Feyenoord 'De Kuip'
Rotterdam — 51 577

Other Main Stadia
Philips Stadion
Eindhoven — 35 000
De Grolsche Veste
Enschede — 30 026
Abe Lenstra Stadion
Heerenveen — 26 100

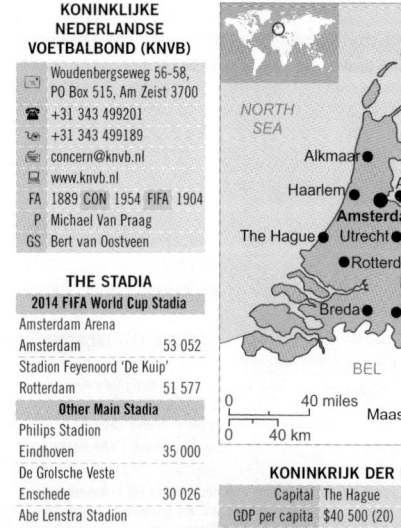

MAJOR CITIES/TOWNS

		Population
1	Amsterdam	755 207
2	Rotterdam	590 113
3	s-Gravenhage	489 410
4	Utrecht	296 046
5	Eindhoven	217 469
6	Tilburg	203 927
7	Almere	199 542
8	Groningen	185 514
9	Breda	174 899
10	Nijmegen	161 502
11	Enschede	157 312
12	Apeldoorn	155 307
13	Haarlemmermeer	154 177
14	Haarlem	149 660
17	Arnhem	140 223
18	s-Hertogenbosch	139 133
19	Maastricht	123 550
28	Alkmaar	99 599
70	Kerkrade	48 974

KONINKRIJK DER NEDERLANDEN • KINGDOM OF THE NETHERLANDS

Capital	The Hague	Population	16 715 999 (59)
GDP per capita	$40 500 (20)	Area km^2	41 543 km^2 (134)
Neighbours (km)	Belgium 450, Germany 577 • Coast 451	% in cities	82%
		GMT +/-	+1

NED – NETHERLANDS

RECENT INTERNATIONAL MATCHES PLAYED BY THE NETHERLANDS

2010	Opponents	Score	Venue	Comp	Scorers	Att	Referee
14-06	Denmark	W 2-0	Johannesburg	WCr1	Agger OG [46], Kuyt [85]	83 465	Lannoy FRA
19-06	Japan	W 1-0	Durban	WCr1	Sneijder [53]	62 010	Baldassi ARG
24-06	Cameroon	W 2-1	Cape Town	WCr1	Van Persie [36], Huntelaar [83]	63 093	Pozo CHI
28-06	Slovakia	W 2-1	Durban	WCr2	Robben [18], Sneijder [84]	61 962	Undiano ESP
2-07	Brazil	W 2-1	Port Elizabeth	WCqf	Sneijder 2 [53 68]	40 186	Nishimura JPN
6-07	Uruguay	W 3-2	Cape Town	WCsf	Van Bronckhorst [18], Sneijder [70], Robben [73]	62 479	Irmatov UZB
11-07	Spain	L 0-1	Johannesburg	WCf		84 490	Webb ENG
11-08	Ukraine	D 1-1	Donetsk	Fr	Lens [73]	18 051	Skomina SVN
3-09	San Marino	W 5-0	Serravalle	ECq	Kuyt [16p], Huntelaar 3 [38 48 66], Van Nistelrooy [90]	4 127	Evans WAL
7-09	Finland	W 2-1	Rotterdam	ECq	Huntelaar 2 [7 16p]	25 000	Nikolaev RUS
8-10	Moldova	W 1-0	Chisinau	ECq	Huntelaar [37]	10 500	Meyer GER
12-10	Sweden	W 4-1	Amsterdam	ECq	Huntelaar 2 [4 55], Afellay 2 [37 59]	46 000	Lannoy FRA
17-11	Turkey	W 1-0	Amsterdam	Fr	Huntelaar [52]	35 500	Kassai HUN
2011							
9-02	Austria	W 3-1	Eindhoven	Fr	Sneijder [28], Huntellar [48], Kuyt [70p]	33 000	Brych GER
25-03	Hungary	W 4-0	Budapest	ECq	Van der Vaart [8], Afellay [45], Kuyt [54], Van Persie [62]	25 311	Velasco ESP
29-03	Hungary	W 5-3	Amsterdam	ECq	Van Persie [13], Sneijder [61], Van Nistelrooy [73], Kuyt 2 [78 81]	51 700	Moen NOR
4-06	Brazil	D 0-0	Goiania	Fr		36 449	Amarilla PAR
8-06	Uruguay	D 1-1	Montevideo	Fr	Kuyt [90], L 3-4p	55 000	Pitana ARG
2-09	San Marino	W 11-0	Eindhoven	ECq	Van Persie 4 [7 65 67 79], Sneijder 2 [12 87], Heitinga [17], Kuyt [49], Huntelaar 2 [56 77], Wijnaldum [90]	35 000	Liany ISR
6-09	Finland	W 2-0	Helsinki	ECq	Strootman [29], De Jong [93+]	21 580	Grafe GER
7-10	Moldova	W 1-0	Rotterdam	ECq	Huntelaar [40]	47 226	Jug SVN
11-10	Sweden	L 2-3	Stockholm	ECq	Huntelaar [23], Kuyt [50]	33 066	Cakir TUR
11-11	Switzerland	D 0-0	Amsterdam	Fr		50 000	Eriksson SWE
15-11	Germany	L 0-3	Hamburg	Fr		51 500	Cakir TUR
2012							
29-02	England	W 3-2	London	Fr	Robben 2 [57 92+], Huntelaar [58]	76 283	Brych GER
26-05	Bulgaria	L 1-2	Amsterdam	Fr	Van Persie [45]	45 000	Teixeira ESP
30-05	Slovakia	W 2-0	Rotterdam	Fr	OG [8], Van der Vaart [75]	51 177	Bezborodov RUS
2-06	Northern Ireland	W 6-0	Amsterdam	Fr	Van Persie 2 [11 29], Sneijder [15], Afellay 2 [37 51], Vlaar [78]	50 000	Schorgenhofer AUT
9-06	Denmark	L 0-1	Kharkov	ECr1		34 973	Skomina SVN
13-06	Germany	L 1-2	Kharkov	ECr1	Van Persie [73]	38 633	Eriksson SWE
17-06	Portugal	L 1-2	Kharkov	ECr1	Van der Vaart [11]	38 633	Rizzoli ITA
15-08	Belgium	L 2-4	Brussels	Fr		50 000	Atkinson ENG
7-09	Turkey	W 2-0	Amsterdam	WCq	Van Persie [17], Narsingh [93+]	49 500	Velasco ESP
11-09	Hungary	W 4-1	Budapest	WCq	Lens 2 [3 53], Martins [19], Huntelaar [75]	22 700	Proenca POR
12-10	Andorra	W 3-0	Rotterdam	WCq	Van der Vaart [7], Huntelaar [15], Schaken [50]	43 000	Kulbakou BLR
16-10	Romania	W 4-1	Bucharest	WCq	Lens [9], Martins [29], Van der Vaart [45p], Van Persie [86]	53 329	Thomson SCO
14-11	Germany	D 0-0	Amsterdam	Fr		49 000	Proenca POR

Fr = Friendly match • EC = UEFA EURO 2012 • WC = FIFA World Cup • q = qualifier • r1 = first round group • qf = quarter-final

NETHERLANDS NATIONAL TEAM HISTORICAL RECORDS

Caps: 130 - Edwin van der Sar 1995-2008 • 112 - Frank de Boer 1990-2004 • 106 - Giovanni van Bronckhorst 1996-2010 • 103 - Rafael van der Vaart 2001- • 101 - Phillip Cocu 1996-2006 • 92 - Dirk Kuyt 2004- • 90 - Wesley Sneijder 2003- • 87 - Clarence Seedorf 1994-2008 • 86 - Marc Overmars 1993-2004 • 85 - John Heitinga 2004- • 84 - Aron Winter 1987-2000 & Joris Mathijsen 2004- • 83 - Ruud Krol 1969-83 • 79 - Patrick Kluivert 1994-2004; Dennis Bergkamp & Mark van Bommel 2000- • 78 - Ronald Koeman 1983-94 • 74 - Edgar Davids 1994-2005 • 73 - Hans van Breukelen 1980-92 & Frank Rijkaard 1981-94 • 72 - Michael Reiziger 1994-2004 • 71 - Robin van Persie 2004

Goals: 40 - Patrick Kluivert 1994-2004 • 37 - Dennis Bergkamp 1990-2000 • 35 - Faas Wilkes 1946-61 & Ruud van Nistelrooy 1998- • 34 - Klaas-Jan Huntelaar 2006- • 33 - Abe Lenstra 1940-59 & Johan Cruijff 1966-77 • 31 - Robin van Persie 2005- • 28 - Beb Bakhuys 1928-37 • 26 - Kick Smit 1935-46 • 24 - Marco van Basten 1983-92; Dirk Kuyt 2004- & Wesley Sneijder 2003-

Coaches: For coaches prior to 1966 see Oliver's Almanack of World Football 2011 • Georg Kessler GER 1966-70 • Frantisek Fadrhonc CZE 1970-74 • Rinus Michels 1974 • George Knobel 1974-76 • Jan Zwartkruis 1976-77 • Ernst Happel AUT 1977-78 • Jan Zwartkruis 1978-81 • Kees Rijvers 1981-84 • Rinus Michels 1984-85 • Leo Beenhakker 1985-86 • Rinus Michels 1986-88 • Thijs Libregts 1988-90 • Leo Beenhakker 1990 • Rinus Michels 1990-92 • Dick Advocaat 1992-95 • Guus Hiddink 1995-98 • Frank Rijkaard 1998-2000 • Louis van Gaal 2000-02 • Dick Advocaat 2002-04 • Marco van Basten 2004-08 • Bert van Marwijk 2008-12 • Louis van Gaal 2012-

NETHERLANDS 2011-12

EREDIVISIE

	Pl	W	D	L	F	A	Pts	Ajax	Feyenoord	PSV	AZ	Heerenveen	Twente	Vitesse	NEC	RKC	Roda	Utrecht	Heracles	NAC	Groningen	ADO	VVV	Graafschap	Excelsior
Ajax †	34	23	7	4	93	36	76		1-1	2-0	2-2	5-1	1-1	4-1	4-1	3-0	4-1	0-2	6-0	2-2	2-0	4-0	2-0	3-1	4-1
Feyenoord †	34	21	7	6	70	37	70	4-2		2-0	1-0	2-2	3-2	3-2	3-1	0-1	1-1	3-0	1-1	4-1	3-1	1-0	0-3	4-0	4-0 3-0
PSV Eindhoven ‡	34	21	6	7	87	47	69	2-2	3-2		3-2	5-1	2-6	3-1	2-1	1-0	7-1	1-0	4-1	1-0	6-1	5-0	2-0	4-1	6-1
AZ Alkmaar ‡	34	19	8	7	64	35	65	1-1	2-1	3-1		3-3	2-2	4-0	4-0	1-0	1-0	2-0	3-1	0-0	1-0	3-0	2-1	4-0	2-0
SC Heerenveen ‡	34	18	10	6	79	59	64	0-5	2-3	1-5	5-1		1-5	1-1	2-2	1-1	4-3	2-0	1-1	1-0	3-0	4-0	4-1	1-1	4-2
FC Twente Enschede ‡	34	17	9	8	82	46	60	1-2	0-2	2-2	2-0	3-4		0-0	2-0	5-0	2-0	1-0	2-3	2-2	4-1	5-2	4-1	4-0	2-2
Vitesse Arnhem ‡	34	15	8	11	48	43	53	1-3	0-4	1-1	2-2	1-1	1-4		0-1	4-0	5-0	2-1	2-0	1-0	0-0	1-0	4-0	2-0	3-2
NEC Nijmegen	34	13	6	15	42	45	45	0-3	0-2	0-2	1-1	2-4	3-1	0-1		1-1	2-3	2-1	1-2	4-0	2-0	2-0	2-0	2-0	
RKC Waalwijk	34	13	6	15	40	49	45	0-1	1-2	2-1	1-2	0-1	0-4	1-0	2-2		5-2	0-2	2-2	2-1	1-1	5-0	4-0	3-0	
Roda JC Kerkrade	34	14	2	18	55	70	44	0-4	0-0	1-3	2-0	1-2	2-1	3-1	1-0	0-2		1-3	3-1	4-3	2-1	4-1	3-1	0-2	7-0
FC Utrecht	34	11	10	13	55	58	43	6-4	2-2	1-1	3-0	1-4	2-6	2-2	0-0	3-0	3-1		2-2	1-3	3-1	1-1	4-2	2-2	3-2
Heracles Almelo	34	11	7	16	52	62	40	0-2	3-1	1-1	0-1	2-4	1-1	0-1	1-2	1-1	2-1	3-1		2-1	2-1	0-0	2-2	4-0	3-1 1-2
NAC Breda	34	10	8	16	45	54	38	0-2	1-3	3-1	2-1	2-2	0-1	1-0	1-1	3-2	0-3	1-0	1-2		2-2	4-0	3-1	1-1	2-0
FC Groningen	34	10	7	17	41	61	37	1-0	6-0	3-0	0-3	1-3	1-1	3-3	0-3	0-1	1-0	2-1	1-1		4-2	2-1	1-1	2-0	
ADO Den Haag	34	8	8	18	38	67	32	0-2	1-2	0-3	0-6	0-0	1-1	1-0	1-0	0-1	1-3	2-2	2-0	3-0	3-0		2-0	3-5	1-1
VVV Venlo ‡‡	34	9	4	21	42	78	31	2-2	2-1	3-3	1-3	0-3	4-2	1-3	0-2	4-1	2-0	0-0	3-1	2-1	2-0	2-1		1-2	0-0
De Graafschap ‡‡	34	6	6	22	36	74	24	1-4	0-3	1-3	0-2	0-2	1-2	0-1	1-0	1-3	1-2	3-0	2-3	1-3	2-0	3-1	1-4		2-2
Excelsior Rotterdam	34	4	7	23	28	76	19	1-4	0-2	1-3	0-0	0-5	0-1	0-2	0-2	1-2	1-2	2-3	0-2	3-0	0-1	1-1	3-1	1-1	

5/08/2011 – 6/05/2012 • † Qualified for the UEFA Champions League • ‡ Qualified for the Europa League • Attendance: 5,978,689 @ 19,538
‡‡ Relegation play-off

Top scorers: 32 - Bas **DOST**, Heerenveen • 25 - Luk **DE JONG**, Twente & Sanharib **MALKI** SYR, Roda • 21 - Dries **MERTENS** BEL, PSV • 20 - John **GUIDETTI** SWE, Feyenoord • 18 - Ola **TOIVONEN** SWE, PSV • 15 - Jozy **ALTIDORE** USA, AZ Alkmaar • 14 - Tim **MATAVZ** SVN, Groningen/PSV • 13 - Siem **DE JONG**, Ajax • 12 - Glynor **PLET**, Heracles/Twente & Wilfred **BONY** CIV, Vitesse

Europa League play-off semi-finals: **NEC** 3-2 0-2 Vitesse; **RKC Waalwijk** 1-1 1-0 FC Twente • Final: RKC Waalwijk 1-3 1-2 **Vitesse** • Vitesse qualified for the Europa League, as did Twente who despite losing in the play-off qualified on the UEFA Fair Play ranking

NETHERLANDS 2011-12

EERSTE DIVISIE

	Pl	W	D	L	F	A	Pts	Zwolle	Sparta	Eindhoven	Helmond	Willem II	Den Bosch	Cambuur	Maastricht	Go Ahead	Dordrecht	Fortuna	Volendam	Almere	Oss	Telstar	Veendam	AGOVV	Emmen
FC Zwolle	34	22	6	6	68	34	72		2-0	0-0	2-3	1-0	1-0	3-0	1-1	0-0	5-0	4-2	3-1	3-2	2-1	7-3	2-0	3-0	1-0
Sparta Rotterdam †	34	19	8	7	59	32	65	2-0		2-2	0-3	2-1	2-0	2-0	0-0	4-1	2-0	1-0	0-0	2-1	2-2	1-0	2-1	4-1	1-1
FC Eindhoven †	34	18	9	7	52	33	63	2-2	0-2		0-0	2-3	2-2	1-1	4-1	1-0	4-3	2-0	0-2	2-0	3-1	2-0	3-2	3-0	
Helmond Sport †	34	18	8	8	62	50	62	3-1	3-2	0-1		0-7	1-0	1-3	2-2	5-1	2-1	2-2	1-0	2-0	2-1	3-2	3-2	1-0	0-1
Willem II Tilburg †	34	17	7	10	67	41	58	3-1	1-1	1-1	3-3		0-3	0-0	2-1	1-1	1-1	1-1	1-1	2-0	1-1	0-3	3-1	5-0	5-0
FC Den Bosch †	34	16	9	9	57	32	57	2-2	0-1	0-2	0-0	1-0		1-1	3-0	1-1	0-0	1-1	1-2	2-0	1-0	3-2	3-0	4-0	5-1
Cambuur-Leeuwarden†	34	16	8	10	68	44	56	3-0	1-2	0-1	2-2	0-2	1-0		5-1	1-1	4-0	3-1	4-1	3-0	4-2	3-1	5-1	2-0	2-1
MVV Maastricht †	34	14	9	11	59	55	51	1-3	1-1	1-0	3-3	3-1	1-4	2-0		1-2	1-1	3-1	3-0	3-2	3-1	1-0	2-1	2-2	6-0
Go Ahead Eagles †	34	14	8	12	65	56	50	0-1	1-2	1-3	2-3	1-3	1-1	4-1	2-1		4-2	2-1	5-0	2-2	7-2	1-0	2-2	3-1	1-0
FC Dordrecht	34	13	11	10	56	62	50	1-2	3-2	2-2	3-2	2-3	4-3	2-1	3-3	3-1		2-2	0-0	2-2	7-2	1-0	2-2	3-1	1-0
Fortuna Sittard	34	13	9	12	62	51	48	0-1	1-0	0-1	0-1	3-1	2-2	0-0	2-0	1-1	1-2		3-2	0-0	2-1	2-5	1-0	5-1	4-1
FC Volendam	34	14	6	14	57	55	48	0-1	0-3	1-4	0-2	1-4	1-3	1-2	0-2	1-4	2-1	3-2		3-1	3-1	1-2	4-1	3-2	6-1 3-1
Almere City	34	11	7	16	52	62	40	0-3	1-1	1-2	2-1	1-4	1-3	1-1	0-2	1-2	0-2	5-3	1-4		2-1	3-0	0-4	4-1	2-0
FC Oss	34	10	5	19	56	76	35	1-0	1-5	1-0	3-1	1-1	0-2	3-2	0-2	5-3	3-3	1-3	3-4		5-3	1-3	4-4	1-0	1-1
Telstar	34	9	5	20	45	70	32	0-3	0-2	1-1	0-0	1-0	0-0	2-5	2-3	0-2	2-1	2-2	3-1	2-1		1-1	1-3	2-1	
BV Veendam	34	8	4	10	20	42	67	22	0-4	0-6	0-0	0-3	2-1	2-3	2-4	1-1	3-2	1-2	0-4	1-2	0-4	2-2	1-0	1-1	1-2	1-1		4-0	3-0
AGOVV Apeldoorn	34	5	4	25	36	94	19	0-1	1-2	1-3	1-2	1-3	1-2	0-4	0-6	0-0	0-3	2-1	2-3	2-4	1-1	3-1	2-2	3-1		0-1
FC Emmen §6	34	6	5	23	24	73	17	1-2	1-1	0-0	1-1	1-1	2-1	2-1	1-3	2-1	1-1	0-0	0-4	0-4	2-1	2-3	1-0	2-0	1-0	

5/08/2011 – 27/04/2012 • § = points deducted • † Qualified for Nacompetitie • Attendance: 1,269,267 @ 4,148
Top scorers: 20 - Jack **TUYP**, Volendam • 18 - Nassir **MAACHI**, Zwolle & Erik **QUEKEL**, Helmond • 16 - **CECILIO LOPES** CPV, Dordrecht

NED – NETHERLANDS

NACOMPETITIE 2012

			Willem II Tilburg *	2 1				
FC Den Bosch		1 2	Sparta Rotterdam	1 1	Willem II Tilburg		0 2	
Go Ahead Eagles *		1 0	De Graafschap	0 1	FC Den Bosch *		0 1	
			FC Den Bosch *	0 1				
			Helmond Sport *	1 2				
MVV Maastricht *		0 1	FC Eindhoven	0 0	Helmond Sport *		1 2	
Cambuur-Leeuwarden		2 0	Cambuur-Leeuwarden *	0 3	VVV Venlo		2 2	
			VVV Venlo	0 4				

* Home team in 1st leg • VVV Venlo remain in the Eredivisie, De Graafschap relegated to the Eerstedivisie, ADO Den Haag promoted to the Eredivisie

MEDALS TABLE

		Overall G S B	League G S B	Cup G S	Europe G S B	Town/City
1	Ajax	55 30 14	31 21 11	18 5	6 3 3	Amsterdam
2	PSV Eindhoven	32 20 19	21 13 15	9 7	2 4	Eindhoven
3	Feyenoord	28 24 16	14 20 12	11 4	3 4	Rotterdam
4	HVV Den Haag	9 3	8	1 3		The Hague
5	Sparta Rotterdam	9 2 5	6 5	3 2		Rotterdam
6	HBS Den Haag	5 5	3	2 5		The Hague
7	AZ Alkmaar	5 4 6	2 2 5	3 1	1 1	Alkmaar
8	Willem II Tilburg	5 2 5	3 1 5	2 1		Tilburg
9	Quick Den Haag	5	1	4		The Hague
10	Twente Enschede	4 8 9	1 3 7	3 4	1 2	Enschede
11	ADO Den Haag	4 6 4	2 4	2 6		The Hague
	Go Ahead Eagles	4 6 4	4 5 4	1		Deventer
13	RCH Heemstede	4	2	2		Haarlem
14	Roda JC Kerkrade	3 6	1 2	2 4		Kerkrade
15	Haarlem	3 3 1	1	2 3		Haarlem
16	FC Utrecht	3 2 1	1	3 2		Utrecht
17	RAP Amsterdam	3 1	2	1 1		Amsterdam
18	HFC Haarlem	3		3		Haarlem
19	NAC Breda	2 7 3	1 4 3	1 3		Breda
20	Fortuna Sittard	2 3 1	1 1	2 2		Sittard
21	VOC Rotterdam	2 3	1	2 2		Rotterdam
22	Heracles Almelo	2 2 1	2 1 1	1		Almelo
23	FC Eindhoven	2 2	1 2	1		Eindhoven
	FC Dordrecht	2 2		2 2		Dordrecht
25	Wageningen	2		2		Wageningen
26	SC Heerenveen	1 5 1	3 1	1 2		Heerenveen

NETHERLANDS 2011-12 TOPKLASE ZATERDAG (3)

	Pl	W	D	L	F	A	Pts
SV Spakenburg	30	20	5	5	84	44	65
Rijnsburgse Boys	30	19	7	4	76	36	64
VV Katwijk	30	15	10	5	78	41	55
VV Noordwijk	30	16	7	7	66	43	55
GVVV Veenendaal	30	16	5	9	70	56	53
IJsselmeervogels	30	15	3	12	67	50	48
SC Genemuiden	30	14	5	11	60	55	47
Excelsior '31 Rijssen	28	14	3	11	39	47	45
HHC Hardenberg	30	14	3	13	48	59	45
VV Capelle	30	11	9	10	47	46	42
FC Lisse	30	10	8	12	48	56	38
BVV Barendrecht	30	9	9	12	39	40	30
Harkemase Boys	30	7	4	19	39	61	25
SV Zwaluwen Wierden	30	7	4	19	36	72	25
VV Montfort	30	4	8	18	34	73	18
ARC	30	2	4	24	36	88	10

20/08/2011 - 12/05/2012

NETHERLANDS 2011-12 TOPKLASE ZONDAG (3)

	Pl	W	D	L	F	A	Pts
Achilles '29	30	23	2	5	72	26	71
VV Haaglandia	30	20	2	8	82	50	62
WKE Emmen	30	16	5	9	52	49	53
De Treffers	30	14	8	8	59	41	50
HSC '21 Haaksbergen	30	13	10	7	61	40	49
EVV Echt	30	13	8	9	50	43	47
FC Lienden	30	14	4	12	49	40	46
HVV Hollandia	30	14	4	12	45	39	46
HBS Den Haag	30	14	2	14	55	62	44
Amsterdamsche FC	30	10	8	12	57	55	38
JVC Cuijk	30	10	7	13	44	49	37
VVSB Noordwijkerhout	30	10	7	13	37	41	37
UNA Zeelst	30	9	5	16	48	62	32
FC Hilversum	30	8	7	15	35	60	31
Argon Mijdrecht	30	6	7	17	38	63	25
Quick '20 Oldenzaal	30	2	2	26	23	87	8

20/08/2011 - 13/05/2012

KNVB BEKER 2011-12

Second Round

PSV Eindhoven	8
VVSB Noordwijkerhout *	0
HBS Den Haag *	2
FC Lisse	3
SC Genemuiden *	3
HSC '21 Haaksbergen	1
VV Zwaluwen *	1
FC Twente Enschede	8
Achilles '29 *	1 3p
Telstar	1 2p
ARC *	0
MVV Maastricht	8
FC Volendam	3
UNA Zeelst *	1
Fortuna Sittard *	2
NEC Nijmegen	4
Vitesse Arnhem *	0 5p
NAC Breda	0 4p
SVV Scheveningen *	1
ADO Den Haag	3
Almere City	2
Argon Mijdrecht *	0
FC Emmen	1
FC Eindhoven *	3
FC Oss	5
EVV Echt *	1
WKE Emmen *	1
FC Den Bosch	2
Harkemase Boys *	4
Willem II Tilburg	2
VVV Venlo *	0
SC Heerenveen	2
AZ Alkmaar *	4
FC Groningen	2
IJsselmeervogels *	0
FC Dordrecht	1
Roda JC Kerkrade	6
VV Bennekom *	1
VV Noordwijk *	1
Ajax	3
Sparta Rotterdam	6
VV Montfoort *	1
VV Staphorst	2
Sparta Nijkerk *	4
Excelsior Rotterdam	5
Excelsior '31 Rijssen *	0
Zwaluwen '30 *	1
GVVV Veenendaal	2
RKC Waalwijk	3
BVV Barendrecht *	0
Cambuur-Leeuwarden *	0
FC Zwolle	1
Feyenoord *	4
AGOVV Apeldoorn	0
Helmond Sport	1
Go Ahead Eagles *	3
De Graafschap *	1 4p
FC Utrecht	1 3p
HHC Hardenberg	2
De Treffers *	3
VV Berkum *	2
BV Veendam	0
JVC Cuijk *	0
Heracles Almelo	1

Third Round

PSV Eindhoven *	3
FC Lisse	0
SC Genemuiden	3
FC Twente Enschede *	4
Achilles '29 *	1
MVV Maastricht	0
FC Volendam	0
NEC Nijmegen *	1
Vitesse Arnhem *	2
ADO Den Haag	1
Almere City *	1
FC Eindhoven	2
FC Oss *	3
FC Den Bosch	1
Harkemase Boys	1
SC Heerenveen *	6
AZ Alkmaar	3
FC Dordrecht *	2
Roda JC Kerkrade *	2
Ajax	4
Sparta Rotterdam *	4
Sparta Nijkerk	0
Excelsior Rotterdam *	0
GVVV Veenendaal	3
RKC Waalwijk	1
FC Zwolle *	0
Feyenoord	1
Go Ahead Eagles *	2
De Graafschap	5
De Treffers *	1
VV Berkum	0
Heracles Almelo *	4

Fourth Round

PSV Eindhoven	2
FC Twente Enschede *	1
Achilles '29	0
NEC Nijmegen *	3
Vitesse Arnhem	2
FC Eindhoven *	1
FC Oss	1
SC Heerenveen *	11
AZ Alkmaar	3
Ajax *	2
Sparta Rotterdam *	1 4p
GVVV Veenendaal	1 5p
RKC Waalwijk *	3
Go Ahead Eagles	2
De Graafschap	0
Heracles Almelo *	4

* Home team • Professional clubs join in the second round

KNVB BEKER 2011-12

Quarter-finals — **Semi-finals** — **Final**

PSV Eindhoven *	3
NEC Nijmegan	2

PSV Eindhoven	3
SC Heerenveen *	1

Vitesse Arnhem *	1
SC Heerenveen	2

PSV Eindhoven ‡	3
Heracles Almelo	0

AZ Alkmaar *	2
GVVV Veenendaal	1

AZ Alkmaar *	2
Heracles Almelo	4

RKC Waalwijk	0
Heracles Almelo *	3

‡ Qualified for the Europa League

KNVB BEKER FINAL 2012

De Kuip, Rotterdam, 8-04-2012, Att: 50 000, Ref: Pol van Boekel

PSV Eindhoven	3	Toivonen [31], Mertens [56], Lens [63]
Heracles Almelo	0	

PSV EINDHOVEN

Przemyslaw **TYTON** - Erik **PIETERS**•, Wilfred **BOUMA**, **MARCELO**, Atiba **HUTCHINSON** - Kevin **STROOTMAN**, Zakaria **LABYAD**• (Orlando **ENGELAAR** 75) - Jeremain **LENS** (Tim **MATAVZ** 80), Ola **TOIVONEN**•, Georginio **WIJNALDUM**, Dries **MERTENS** (Memphis **DEPAY** 86). Tr: Phillip **COCU**

HERACLES

Remko **PASVEER** - Antoine **VAN DER LINDEN**, Mark **LOOMS**, Tim **BREUKERS**, Ben **RIENSTRA**• - Kwame **QUANSAH**, Willie **OVERTOOM** (Ninos **GOURIYE** 71), Lerin **DUARTE** (Marko **VEJINOVIC** 66), **EVERTON**, Darl **DOUGLAS** (Thomas **BRUNS** 66), Samuel **ARMENTEROS**. Tr: Peter **BOSZ**

NEP – NEPAL

FIFA/COCA-COLA WORLD RANKING

'93	'94	'95	'96	'97	'98	'99	'00	'01	'02	'03	'04	'05	'06	'07	'08	'09	'10	'11	'12
124	138	147	151	155	176	157	166	156	165	165	177	175	170	186	174	152	172	153	171

2012

Jan	Feb	Mar	Apr	May	Jun	Jul	Aug	Sep	Oct	Nov	Dec	High	Low	Av
153	152	153	149	149	149	155	162	166	165	169	171	124	188	161

Nepal played host to the finals of the AFC Challenge Cup in March 2012, the first time the Himalayan nation had hosted one of the Asian Football Confederation's major competitions. The AFC Challenge Cup brings together the leading national sides amongst the lower tier of countries within the confederation's ranking system, with a place in the finals of the AFC Asian Cup at stake for the winners. Despite hosting the tournament, Nepal failed to take advantage and bowed out at the end of the group phase. The national team lost all three of their matches - against Palestine, the Maldives and Turkmenistan - much to the disappointment of the large crowds that flocked to watch the side play in Kathmandu's Dashrath Stadium. In club football Nepal Police Club, champions in 2011, retained their position as the country's leading club, claiming the National League title two points ahead of Yeti Himalayan Sherpa. Earlier in the year Police Club's involvement in the 2012 edition of the AFC President's Cup ended with early elimination after they failed to progress from a group won by Dordoi Bishkek. A new league season kicked-off in November 2012 with the league restructured again, moving away from the national set up that had been used earlier in the year and reverting to a league focused on Kathmandu.

FIFA WORLD CUP RECORD
1930-1982 DNE 1986-1990 DNQ 1994 DNE 1998-2002 DNQ 2006 DNE 2010-2014 DNQ

ALL-NEPAL FOOTBALL ASSOCIATION (ANFA)
ANFA House, Satobato,
Lalitpur-17, PO Box 12582, Kathmandu
☎ +977 1 5201060
+977 1 4424314
anfanepal@gmail.com

FA 1951 CON 1971 FIFA 1970
P Ganesh Thapa
GS Dhirendra Pradhan

THE STADIA
2014 FIFA World Cup Stadia
Dashrath Rangasala Stadium
Kathmandu   25 000
Other Main Stadia
Narayani Stadium
Birganj   15 000
Saheed Stadium
Biratnagar   10 000
Nepal Police Club Stadium
Kathmandu   8 000
Pokhara Rangasala
Pokhara   5 000

MAJOR CITIES/TOWNS
Population
1 Kathmandu   949 486
2 Pokhara   225 369
3 Lalitpur   210 317
4 Biratnagar   203 018
5 Birganj   161 059
6 Bharatpur   130 696
7 Dhangadhi   129 387
8 Dharan   125 969
9 Janakpur   122 427
10 Butwal   113 658
11 Hetauda   107 859
12 Mahendranagar   98 233
13 Bhaktapur   82 896
14 Siddharthanagar 77 978
15 Triyuga   73 977
16 Nepalganj   66 648
17 Madhyapur Thimi 64 350
18 Gulariya   62 489
19 Mechinagar   60 736

FEDERAL DEMOCRATIC REPUBLIC OF NEPAL

Capital	Kathmandu	Population	28 563 377 (42)	% in cities	17%
GDP per capita	$1100 (210)	Area km²	147 181 km² (93)	GMT +/-	+5.75
Neighbours (km)	China 1236, India 1690				

NEP – NEPAL

RECENT INTERNATIONAL MATCHES PLAYED BY NEPAL

2008 Opponents	Score	Venue	Comp	Scorers	Att	Referee
15-10 Malaysia	L 0-4	Petaling Jaya	Fr			
17-10 Afghanistan	D 2-2	Petaling Jaya	Fr	Anil Gurung [63], Bijay Gurung [78]		
2009						
26-03 Palestine	D 0-0	Kathmandu	CCq		12 000	El Haddad LIB
28-03 Kyrgyzstam	D 1-1	Kathmandu	CCq	Biraj Maharjan [2]	15 000	Jahanbazi IRN
29-11 Bhutan	W 2-1	Calcutta	Fr	Anil Gurung [70], Bijay Gurung [80]		
5-12 Maldives	D 1-1	Dhaka	SAFr1	Ju Manu Rai [68]		
7-12 India †	L 0-1	Dhaka	SAFr1			
9-12 Afghanistan	W 3-0	Dhaka	SAFr1	Anil Gurung 2 [55 73], Bijay Gurung [56]		
2010						
No international matches played in 2010						
2011						
17-03 Bhutan	W 1-0	Pokhara	Fr	Santosh Shahukhala [29]		
19-03 Bhutan	W 2-1	Pokhara	Fr	Bikash Chhetri [24], Bharat Khawas [75]		
7-04 Afghanistan	W 1-0	Kathmandu	CCq	Bharat Khawas [27]	9 100	Abdul Baki OMA
9-04 Korea DPR	L 0-1	Kathmandu	CCq		22 000	Alabbasi BHR
11-04 Sri Lanka	D 0-0	Kathmandu	CCq		13 500	Adday IRQ
29-06 Timor-Leste	W 2-1	Kathmandu	WCq	Anil Gurung [15p], Jumanu Rai [70]	9 000	Sabbagh LIB
2-07 Timor-Leste	W 5-0	Kathmandu	WCq	Anil Gurung [4p], Bhola Silwal [56], Jumanu Rai [59], Jagajeet Shrestha [89], Sujal Shrestha [90]	15 000	Lee Min Hu KOR
23-07 Jordan	L 0-9	Amman	WCq		17 000	Jahanbazi IRN
28-07 Jordan	D 1-1	Kathmandu	WCq	Bharat Khawas [80]	20 000	Fan Qi CHN
11-10 Philippines	L 0-4	Manila	Fr			
2-12 Maldives	D 1-1	New Delhi	SAFr1	Sandip Rai [51]		Singh SIN
4-12 Bangladesh	W 1-0	New Delhi	SAFr1	Sagar Thapa [95+]		Kumar IND
6-12 Pakistan	D 1-1	New Delhi	SAFr1	Bharat Khawas [37]		Noor Mohamed MAS
9-12 Afghanistan	L 0-1	New Delhi	SAFsf			Tufaylieh SYR
2012						
8-03 Palestine	L 0-2	Kathmandu	CCr1		12 300	Sato JPN
10-03 Maldives	L 0-1	Kathmandu	CCr1		15 000	Mashentsev KGZ
12-03 Turkmenistan	L 0-3	Kathmandu	CCr1		2 400	Sabbagh LIB
23-08 Maldives	L 1-2	New Delhi	Fr	Jumanu Rai [94+]		Kumar IND
28-08 India	D 0-0	New Delhi	Fr			Seytlin UZB
30-08 Syria	L 0-2	New Delhi	Fr			Arumughan IND
20-09 Bangladesh	D 1-1	Kathmandu	Fr	Bhola Silwal [60]		Pandey NEP

Fr = Friendly match • SAF = South Asian Football Federation Cup • CC = AFC Challenge Cup • AC = AFC Asian Cup
q = qualifier • r1 = first round group • qf = quarter-final • sf = semi-final

NEPAL 2012

MARTYR'S MEMORIAL RED BULL ANFA A DIVISION

	Pl	W	D	L	F	A	Pts	Police Club	Sherpa	Manang	Jawalakhel	Army	Three Star	Ranipokhari	New Road	Sangam	Mitra Milan
Nepal Police Club †	9	6	3	0	14	3	21		3-0	0-0	1-1	2-0	0-0	2-1	1-0	4-1	1-0
Yeti Himalayan Sherpa	9	6	1	2	14	8	19			1-0	3-1	2-1	0-1	0-0	2-1	4-1	2-0
Manang Marsyangdi	9	5	2	2	17	6	17				2-0	1-0	1-1	1-0	1-2	5-0	6-2
Jawalakhel Youth Club	9	5	1	3	11	9	16					1-0	1-0	1-0	0-1	4-1	2-1
Nepal Army Club	9	4	1	4	15	9	13						0-0	2-0	2-0	5-1	6-2
Three Star Club	9	3	4	2	11	6	13							0-1	2-2	1-0	6-1
Ranipokhari Corner	9	4	1	4	11	8	13								1-0	5-1	3-1
New Road Team	9	3	2	4	7	8	11									1-0	0-0
Sangam Club	9	1	0	8	8	30	3										3-1
Mitra Milan	9	0	1	8	8	29	1										

30/12/2011 - 22/01/2012 • † Qualified for the AFC President's Cup

NGA – NIGERIA

FIFA/COCA-COLA WORLD RANKING

'93	'94	'95	'96	'97	'98	'99	'00	'01	'02	'03	'04	'05	'06	'07	'08	'09	'10	'11	'12
18	12	27	63	71	65	76	52	40	29	35	21	24	9	20	19	22	32	43	52

2012													High	Low	Av
Jan	Feb	Mar	Apr	May	Jun	Jul	Aug	Sep	Oct	Nov	Dec				
45	56	57	60	63	60	58	58	58	63	57	52		5	82	36

Nigeria were winners of the 2013 Africa Cup of Nations in South Africa, securing a third continental title against all expectations - even those of their own coach Stephen Keshi. He went into the tournament cautioning that his young side were a work in progress and was using the finals to start building a squad that could challenge for FIFA World Cup honours in Russia in 2018. Thanks to two late penalties against Ethiopia, Nigeria made it through to the last eight where they came to life under the midfield generalship of John Obi Mikel, the attacking play of Victor Moses and the finishing of Emmanuel Emenike to go on and beat the Cote d'Ivoire, Mali and then Burkina Faso in the final - the winning goal in a 1-0 victory scored by Sunday Mba. In club football Kano Pillars won the Nigerian Premier League in a season mired by controversy. Ocean Boys were thrown out of the League after failing to turn up to their matches having been relegated. All of their results were declared null and void which meant Kano Pillars won the championship. However, after winning six points against Ocean Boys, Enugu Rangers claimed the title would have been theirs had the results been allowed to stand. In the Federation Cup final Heartland beat Lobi Stars 2-1, a result that gave Heartland keeper Chijoke Ejoigu a record sixth cup winners medal.

CAF AFRICA CUP OF NATIONS RECORD

1957-1962 DNE **1963** 6 r1 1965 DNE 1968 DNQ 1970 DNE 1972-1974 DNQ **1976** 3 r2 **1978** 3 SF **1980** 1 Winners (hosts)
1982 6 r1 **1984** 2 F 1986 DNQ **1988** 2 F **1990** 2 F **1992** 3 SF **1994** 1 Winners 1996 withdrew 1998 DNE **2000** 2 F (co-hosts)
2002 3 SF **2004** 3 SF **2006** 3 SF **2008** 7 QF **2010** 3 SF **2012** DNQ **2013** 1 Winners

NIGERIA FOOTBALL FEDERATION (NFF)

Plot 2033, Olusegun, Obasanjo Way, Zone 7, PO Box 5101 Garki, Abuja
☎ +234 9 5237326
nigeria_fa@yahoo.com
www.nigeriaff.com
FA 1945 CON 1959 FIFA 1959
P Aminu Maigari
GS Musa Adamu

THE STADIA

2014 FIFA World Cup Stadia
UJ Esuene Stadium
Calabar — 25 000

Other Main Stadia
Abuja Stadium
Abuja — 60 000
Surulere Stadium
Lagos — 55 000
Liberty Stadium
Ibadan — 35 000
Sani Abacha Stadium
Kano — 25 000

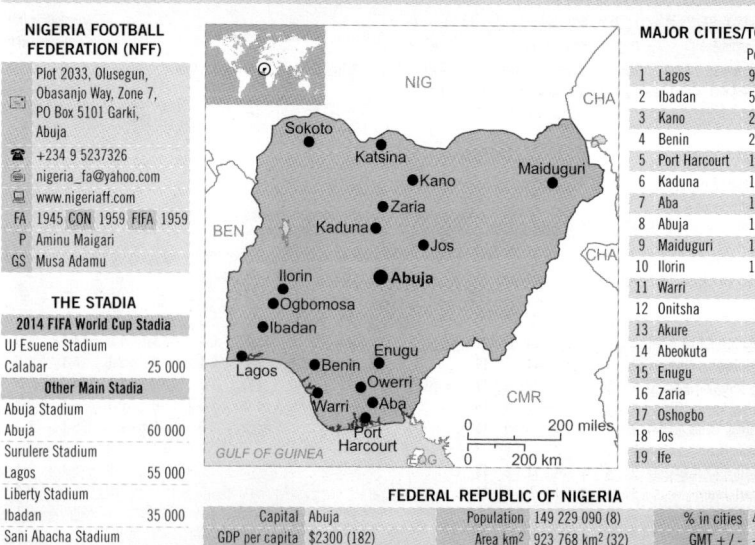

MAJOR CITIES/TOWNS

		Population
1	Lagos	9 733 876
2	Ibadan	5 003 747
3	Kano	2 359 248
4	Benin	2 324 188
5	Port Harcourt	1 999 375
6	Kaduna	1 994 242
7	Aba	1 529 729
8	Abuja	1 243 152
9	Maiduguri	1 096 414
10	Ilorin	1 050 031
11	Warri	893 929
12	Onitsha	871 554
13	Akure	804 104
14	Abeokuta	771 585
15	Enugu	698 136
16	Zaria	667 446
17	Oshogbo	647 652
18	Jos	619 122
19	Ife	599 924

FEDERAL REPUBLIC OF NIGERIA

Capital Abuja   Population 149 229 090 (8)   % in cities 48%
GDP per capita $2300 (182)   Area km² 923 768 km² (32)   GMT +/- +1
Neighbours (km) Benin 773, Cameroon 1690, Chad 87, Niger 1497 • Coast 853

NGA – NIGERIA

RECENT INTERNATIONAL MATCHES PLAYED BY NIGERIA

2010	Opponents	Score	Venue	Comp	Scorers	Att	Referee
12-06	Argentina	L 0-1	Johannesburg	WCr1		55 686	Stark GER
17-06	Greece	L 1-2	Bloemfontein	WCr1	Kalu Uche [16]	31 593	Ruiz COL
22-06	Korea Republic	D 2-2	Durban	WCr1	Kalu Uche [12], Yakubu [69p]	61 874	Benquerenca POR
11-08	Korea Republic	L 1-2	Suwon	Fr	Odemwingie [26]	40 331	Nishimura JPN
5-09	Madagascar	W 2-0	Calabar	CNq	Martins [19], Eneramo [45]		Jedidi TUN
10-10	Guinea	L 0-1	Conakry	CNq			El Ahrach MAR
2011							
9-02	Sierra Leone	W 2-1	Lagos	Fr	Taye Taiwo [15p], Ekigho Ehiosun [45]		
27-03	Ethiopia	W 4-0	Abuja	CNq	Peter Utaka 2 [2 53], Ikechukwu Uche 2 [77 90]		Jedidi TUN
29-03	Kenya	W 3-0	Abuja	Fr	Ikechukwu Uche [2], Victor Obinna 2 [73p 76]		
1-06	Argentina	W 4-1	Abuja	Fr	Ikechukwu Uche 2 [14 40], Victor Obinna [25p], Emmanuel Emenike [52]	30 000	Chaibou NIG
5-06	Ethiopia	D 2-2	Addis Abeba	CNq	Ikechukwu Uche [27], Joseph Yobo [86]		
4-09	Madagascar	W 2-0	Antananarivo	CNq	Joseph Yobo [68], Victor Obinna [72]		Kirwa KEN
6-09	Argentina	L 1-3	Dhaka	Fr	Chidu Obasi [47]	36 000	Shamsuzzaman BAN
8-10	Guinea	D 2-2	Abuja	CNq	Obinna [63], Ikechukwu Uche [77]		
11-10	Ghana	D 0-0	Watford	Fr			
12-11	Botswana	D 0-0	Benin City	Fr			
15-11	Zambia	W 2-0	Kaduna	Fr	Kalu Uche [9], Ikechukwu Uche [90]		
2012							
11-02	Angola	D 0-0	Abuja	Fr			
15-02	Liberia	W 2-0	Monrovia	Fr			
29-02	Rwanda	D 0-0	Kigali	CNq			Bennett RSA
12-04	Egypt	L 2-3	Dubai	Fr	Sunday Mba [13], Uche Kalu [43]		Alzarooni UAE
23-05	Peru	L 0-1	Lima	Fr		30 000	Espinel ECU
3-06	Namibia	W 1-0	Calabar	WCq	Ikechukwu Uche [80]	10 000	Abdel SUD
9-06	Malawi	D 1-1	Blantyre	WCq	Azubuike Egwuekwe [89]	25 000	Seechurn MRI
16-06	Rwanda	W 2-0	Calabar	CNq	Ikechukwu Uche [9], Ahmed Musa [56]		Doue CIV
8-09	Liberia	D 2-2	Paynesville	CNq	Nosa Igiebor [14], Ikechukwu Uche [16]		Coulibaly MLI
13-10	Liberia	W 6-1	Calabar	CNq	Efe Ambrose [2], Ahmed Musa [42], Victor Moses 2 [47 85], John Obi Mikel [51p], Ikechukwu Uche [71]		Bennett RSA
14-11	Venezuela	W 3-1	Miami	Fr	Brown Ideye [49], Nosa Igiebor [53], Ogenyi Omazi [94+]	13 500	Vaughn USA
2013							
9-01	Cape Verde Islands	D 0-0	Faro	Fr			Miguel POR
21-01	Burkina Faso	D 1-1	Nelspruit	CNr1	Emmanuel Emenike [22]	8 500	Benouza ALG
25-01	Zambia	D 1-1	Nelspruit	CNr1	Emmanuel Emenike [57]	25 000	Grisha EGY
29-01	Ethiopia	W 2-0	Rustenburg	CNr1	Victor Moses 2 [80p 90p]	15 000	El Ahrach MAR
3-02	Côte d'Ivoire	W 2-1	Rustenburg	CNqf	Emmanuel Emenike [43], Sunday Mba [78]	25 000	Haimoudi ALG
6-02	Mali	W 4-1	Durban	CNsf	Elderson Echiejile [25], Brown Ideye [30], Emmanuel Emenike [44], Ahmed Musa [58]	54 000	Gassama GAM
10-02	Burkina Faso	W 1-0	Johannesburg	CNf	Sunday Mba [40]	85 000	Haimoudi ALD

Fr = Friendly match • CN = CAF African Cup of Nations • WC = FIFA World Cup • q = qualifier • r1 = first round group

NIGERIA NATIONAL TEAM HISTORICAL RECORDS

Caps: 95 - Joseph Yobo 2001- • 86 - Nwankwo Kanu 1995-2010 & Muda Lawal 1975-85 • 77 - Vincent Enyeama 2002- • 73 - Jay-Jay Okocha 1993-2006 • 63 - Sunday Oliseh 1993-2002 • 62 - Finidi George 1991-2002 • 61 - Peter Rufai 1981-98 • 60 - Aloy Atuegbu 1974-81 • 59 - Henry Nwosu 1980-91 • 58 - Rashidi Yekini 1984-98 • 57 - Stephen Keshi 1981-94 & Yakubu Aiyegbeni 2000-

Goals: 37 - Rashidi Yekini 1986-98 • 23 - Segun Odegbami 1976-81 • 21 - Yakubu Aiyegbeni 2000- • 18 - Obafemi Martins 2004- & Ikechukwu Uche 2007- • 16 - Sunday Oyarekhua 1969-76 & Samson Siasia 1989-98 • 15 - Thompson Usiyen 1976-81 • 14 - Jay-Jay Okocha 1993-2006 & Julius Aghahowa 1999-2005 • 12 - Nwankwo Kanu 1995-2010; Daniel Amokachi 1990-99; Asuquo Ekpe 1960-65; Kenneth Olayombo 1966-76 & Muda Lawal 1976-84

Coaches: For coaches pre 1989 see Oliver's Almanack 2012 • Clemens Westerhof NED 1989-94 • Shaibu Amodu 1994-95 • Jo Bonfere NED 1995-96 • Shaibu Amodu 1996-97 • Philippe Troussier FRA 1997-98 • Monday Sinclar 1997-98 • Bora Milutinovic SRB 1998 • Thijs Libregts NED 1999 • Jo Bonfrere NED 1999-2001 • Shaibu Amodu 2001-02 • Adegboyega Onigbinde 2002 • Christian Chukwu 2002-05 • Augustine Eguavoen 2005-07 • Berti Vogts GFR 2007-08 • James Peters 2008 • Shaibu Amodu 2008-10 • Lars Lagerback SWE 2010 • Augustine Eguavoen 2010 • Samson Siasia 2010-11 • Stephen Keshi 2011-

NIGERIA 2012

NIGERIAN PREMIER LEAGUE

	Pl	W	D	L	F	A	Pts	Kano Pillars	Enugu Rangers	Lobi Stars	Enyimba	Sunshine Stars	Kwara United	Sharks	Heartland	Gombe United	Wikki Tourists	Dolphin	Akwa United	Shooting Stars	Kaduna United	Warri Wolves	ABS	Niger Tornadoes	Jigawa G. Stars	Rising Stars	Ocean Boys
Kano Pillars †	36	17	10	9	46	26	61		2-0	1-0	2-0	1-0	2-0	4-0	1-1	0-0	4-0	2-1	1-0	3-0	2-1	1-0	2-1	1-0	0-3	2-1	*3-0*
Enugu Rangers †	36	17	7	12	45	27	58	3-1		1-0	1-0	3-0	2-0	3-0	1-1	3-0	1-0	2-0	2-1	3-2	3-0	0-0	1-0	3-0	5-0	3-1	*4-0*
Lobi Stars ‡	36	18	3	15	38	30	57	1-0	3-0		2-0	1-0	2-1	2-0	1-0	2-0	2-0	2-0	1-0	1-1	1-0	2-1	2-0	2-0	1-0	2-1	*3-0*
Enyimba	36	16	6	14	38	30	54	2-2	2-0	0-0		2-1	2-0	2-0	1-0	3-1	3-0	1-0	1-1	1-0	2-0	2-0	2-0	3-0	1-0	1-0	*2-0*
Sunshine Stars	36	15	7	14	41	35	52	2-1	2-0	2-0	0-0		1-1	3-2	1-0	2-0	4-1	1-0	1-0	0-0	2-0	1-1	2-1	2-1	3-0	3-3	*2-1*
Kwara United	36	16	4	16	35	36	52	1-0	0-0	1-0	1-0	1-0		2-0	1-0	2-0	1-2	1-1	2-1	1-0	2-0	3-1	1-0	0-1	2-2	4-2	*2-0*
Sharks	36	16	4	16	43	46	52	0-0	1-0	2-0	1-0	1-0	1-0		2-0	5-2	2-3	3-3	1-0	0-2	1-1	0-1	1-0	1-2	2-0	4-0	*3-1*
Heartland ‡	36	14	9	13	32	30	51	1-1	1-0	2-0	2-3	1-1	1-0	0-1		2-1	2-0	1-0	1-0	1-0	1-0	3-1	2-1	2-1	1-0	2-0	*1-0*
Gombe United	36	15	6	15	40	45	51	1-0	2-1	2-0	3-1	1-0	0-2	5-0	2-2		1-0	1-0	1-0	2-1	1-1	1-0	1-1	3-1	1-0	2-1	*3-1*
Wikki Tourists	36	16	3	17	33	46	51	1-0	1-1	2-1	1-1	1-0	1-0	1-0	1-0	3-1		2-1	1-0	2-1	2-1	1-0	0-0	2-0	2-1	3-0	
Dolphin	36	15	5	16	37	39	50	1-0	1-0	0-2	1-1	1-0	4-1	1-0	1-1	2-1	3-0		2-1	0-0	3-0	1-0	2-0	2-1	2-1	2-0	*3-0*
Akwa United	36	15	5	16	27	31	50	0-1	1-1	2-1	2-1	1-0	1-0	1-0	0-0	3-1	1-0	3-2		1-0	1-0	2-1	2-1	2-0	1-0	1-0	*3-0*
Shooting Stars	36	14	7	15	31	34	49	2-1	1-0	1-0	1-0	1-1	1-0	2-1	2-0	0-0	2-0	1-0	2-0		2-1	1-1	2-1	3-1	1-0	0-0	*1-0*
Kaduna United	36	15	4	17	37	42	49	2-0	1-0	3-1	1-0	1-0	2-1	2-1	2-0	0-0	1-3	0-1	1-2	0-2		2-1	1-2	1-0	2-1	1-0	*2-0*
Warri Wolves	36	13	9	14	32	29	48	0-0	1-0	2-1	1-0	1-2	2-0	4-1	0-0	2-0	2-1	1-1	1-0	1-0	1-0		1-0	2-0	2-0	0-0	*2-1*
Bukola Babes ABS	36	14	6	16	42	40	48	2-2	0-1	2-1	3-0	4-1	0-0	1-3	1-1	1-0	2-1	2-0	2-0	2-0	3-1	0-0		3-2	3-0	1-0	
Niger Tornadoes	36	14	6	16	38	42	48	1-1	1-1	1-1	1-0	2-0	3-1	1-0	1-0	2-0	1-0	4-0	2-0	1-0	4-1	1-0	1-1		2-0	1-0	*3-0*
Jigawa Golden Stars	36	14	6	16	29	42	48	0-0	1-0	1-0	1-0	1-0	0-1	2-1	2-0	0-0	2-1	3-1	1-0	2-0	0-0	2-1	2-0	1-0		0-0	
Rising Stars	36	10	9	17	23	37	39	1-1	0-0	1-0	1-0	0-3	1-0	0-0	1-0	2-1	1-0	1-0	0-1	0-0	1-0	2-2	1-0	2-1	1-0		*2-0*
Ocean Boys								*1-0*	*0-1*	*1-2*	*0-0*	*0-3*	*2-1*	*2-0*	*0-0*	*2-1*	*1-1*	*0-0*	*1-1*	*1-2*		*0-0*	*1-1*	*1-0*	*3-0*	*0-3*	

7/01/2012 - 7/09/2012 • † Qualified for the CAF Champions League • ‡ Qualified for the CAF Confederation Cup
Ocean Boys were disqualified on September 5th 2012 and their record expunged. Match in bold awarded after Ocean Boys refused to play

MEDALS TABLE

		Overall			Lge			Cup			Africa			
		G	S	B	G	G	S	G	S	B	G	S	B	City
1	Shooting Stars	15	4	1	5	8	2	2	2	1				Ibadan
2	Enugu Rangers	11	8	4	5	5	7	1	1	4				Enugu
3	Enyimba	10	2	2	6	2	2	2		2				Aba
4	Heartland (ex Iwuanyanwu)	8	4	3	5	3	2				2	3		Owerri
5	Dolphin (ex Eagle Cement)	7	1		3	4			1					Port Harcourt
	Lagos Railways	7	1			7	1							Lagos
7	Bendel Insurance	6	3	2	2	3	2	1	1	2				Benin City
8	BCC Lions	6	2			4	1	1	1					Gboko
9	Stationery Stores	5	3	1	1	4	2		1	1				Lagos
10	Julius Berger	4	3		2	2	1	2						Lagos
11	Port Harcourt FC	3	3			3	3							Port Harcourt
12	Kano Pillars	3	2	1	2	1	2			1				Kano
13	Leventis United	3	1		1	2			1					Ibadan
14	Lagos ECN	3				3								Lagos
15	Abiola Babes	2	2	1		2	2			1				Mashood
16	Lobi Stars	2	2		1	1	2							Makurdi
17	El Kanemi Warriors	2	1	1		2	1			1				Maiduguri
18	Ocean Boys	2			1	1								Yenagoa
	Nigerian Ports Authority	2				2								Warri
20	Plateau United	1	10			1	10							Jos
21	Mighty Jets	1	2		1		2							Jos
22	Niger Tornados	1	1			1	1							Minna
	Lagos UAC	1	1			1	1							Lagos
	Racca Rovers	1	1		1		1							Kano
25	Bayelsa United	1		1	1					1				
26	Calabar	1				1								Calabar
	Kaduna United	1				1								
	Lagos PAN Bank	1				1								Lagos
	New Nigeria Bank	1			1									Benin City
	Police	1				1								Abuja
	Udoji United	1			1									Awka
	Wikki Tourists	1				1								Bauchi

FEDERATION CUP 2012

Second Round

Lobi Stars	1
Niger Tornados	0
Kogi United	0
Enyimba	1
Samba	1
Canaan	0
Spotlite Senior	1 3p
Warri Wolves	1 4p
Kano Pillars	2
Kaduna United	0
PBS FC	0
Crown	1
El Kanemi	1
Abia Warriors	0
Akpabio Boys	1
Kwara United	2
Prime FC	5
Gamji	1
First Bank	1
Sharks	3
Enugu Rangers	2
JUTH	0
Akwa United	1
Dynamite Force	2
Heartland	2
Unicem Rovers	1
Ranchers Bees	0
Plateau United	2
Gombe United	1
Fame FC	0
Sunshine Stars	0
Nasarawa United	3

Third round groups

Group A in Bauchi

	Pl	W	D	L	F	A	Pts	En	Sa
Lobi Stars	2	2	0	0	2	0	**6**	1-0	1-0
Enyimba	2	1	0	1	3	2	**3**		3-1
Samba	2	0	0	2	1	4	**0**		
Warri Wolves				Withdrew					

Group B in Lagos

	Pl	W	D	L	F	A	Pts	Cr	EK	KU
Kano Pillars	3	2	1	0	5	2	**7**	1-1	2-0	2-1
Crown	3	1	2	0	4	3	**5**		0-0	3-2
El Kanemi	3	1	1	1	2	4	**4**			1-0
Kwara United	3	0	0	3	3	6	**0**			

Group C in Ibadan

	Pl	W	D	L	F	A	Pts	Sh	ER	DF
Prime FC	3	2	1	0	4	2	**7**	1-1	1-0	2-1
Sharks	3	1	2	0	5	4	**5**		3-2	1-1
Enugu Rangers	3	1	0	2	3	4	**3**			1-0
Dynamite Force	3	0	1	2	2	4	**1**			

Group D in Port Harcourt

	Pl	W	D	L	F	A	Pts	PU	GU	NU
Heartland	3	1	2	0	2	1	**5**	1-0	0-0	1-1
Plateau United	3	1	1	1	3	2	**4**		1-1	2-0
Gombe United	3	0	3	0	1	1	**3**			0-0
Nasarawa United	3	0	2	1	1	3	**2**			

3rd Place: **Prime FC** 1-1 3-1p Kano Pillars • * Home team in the first leg • ‡ Qualified for the CAF Confederation Cup

Quarter-finals

Heartland	2
Crown	0
Enyimba	0
Prime FC	2
Kano Pillars	3
Plateau Utd	2
Sharks	1
Lobi Stars	3

Semi-finals

Heartland	0 3p
Prime FC	0 0p
Kano Pillars	0 4p
Lobi Stars	0 5p

Final

Heartland ‡	2
Lobi Stars	1

CUP FINAL

Teslim Balogun, Lagos
26-08-2012
Scorers - Osas Jolly 30', Brendan Ogbu 92+ for Heartland;
Ezekiel Bassey 6 for Lobi

NIG – NIGER

FIFA/COCA-COLA WORLD RANKING

'93	'94	'95	'96	'97	'98	'99	'00	'01	'02	'03	'04	'05	'06	'07	'08	'09	'10	'11	'12
81	70	93	129	150	154	164	182	191	184	164	173	177	147	155	143	163	94	97	105

2012

Jan	Feb	Mar	Apr	May	Jun	Jul	Aug	Sep	Oct	Nov	Dec	High	Low	Av
98	111	114	123	122	122	114	115	126	137	107	105	68	196	144

Niger's national team 'Mena' wrote another piece of footballing history for the arid Saharan nation at the 2013 Africa Cup of Nations finals in South Africa with their first point at the finals following a 0-0 draw against the Democratic Republic of Congo in Port Elizabeth. It was not enough to save the side from finishing bottom of the Group C standings but reflected the continuing rise of a country whose FIFA/Coca-Cola World Ranking has catapulted from 163rd at the start of the decade to regular appearances in the top 100. Niger qualified for their second successive Nations Cup with a hard fought win over Guinea, a surprise result that was again based on their strength at home where the Stade General Seyni Kountche has become a veritable fortress. They had lost by a single goal in Conakry in the first game in charge for coach Gernot Rohr, who took over from charismatic Frenchman Rolland Courbis after Niger had won just a single point from their first two 2014 FIFA World Cup qualifiers. Niger turned around the deficit against Guinea to win 2-0 in the second leg in Niamey with both goals coming in a dramatic last quarter-hour. It meant a return to the Nations Cup finals for a country whose self belief has grown considerably after their remarkable feat in knocking out both Egypt and South Africa in the 2012 qualifiers.

CAF AFRICA CUP OF NATIONS RECORD

1957-1968 DNE 1970-1972 DNQ 1974 DNE 1976 DNQ 1978-1982 DNE 1984 DNQ 1986-1990 DNE 1992-1994 DNQ
1996 Withdrew 1998 DNE 2000-2010 DNQ 2012 15 r1 2013 15 r1

FEDERATION NIGERIENNE DE FOOTBALL (FENIFOOT)

Avenue Francois Mitterand, BP 10299, Niamey
+227 20724575
info@fenifut.net
www.fenifoot.net
FA 1967 CON 1967 FIFA 1967
P Hamidou Djibrilla
GS Ibrahim Elh Tiemogo

THE STADIA

2014 FIFA World Cup Stadia

| Stade General Seyni Kountche | |
| Niamey | 30 000 |

Other Main Stadia

Stade de Zinder	
Zinder	10 000
Stade de Maradi	
Maradi	10 000
Stade de Tahoua	
Tahoua	10 000
Stade d'Arlit	
Arlit	7 000

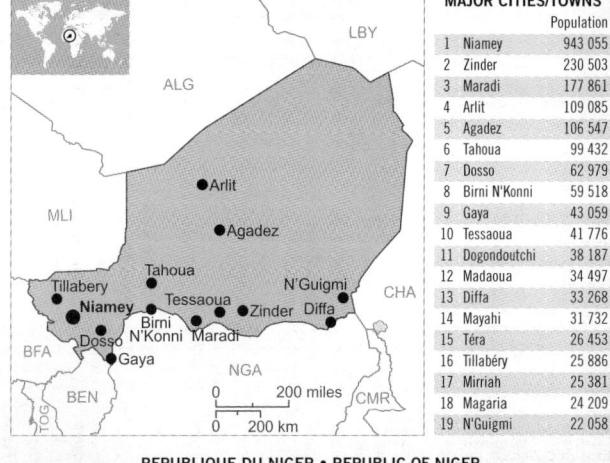

MAJOR CITIES/TOWNS

		Population
1	Niamey	943 055
2	Zinder	230 503
3	Maradi	177 861
4	Arlit	109 085
5	Agadez	106 547
6	Tahoua	99 432
7	Dosso	62 979
8	Birni N'Konni	59 518
9	Gaya	43 059
10	Tessaoua	41 776
11	Dogondoutchi	38 187
12	Madaoua	34 497
13	Diffa	33 268
14	Mayahi	31 732
15	Téra	26 453
16	Tillabéry	25 886
17	Mirriah	25 381
18	Magaria	24 209
19	N'Guigmi	22 058

REPUBLIQUE DU NIGER • REPUBLIC OF NIGER

Capital	Niamey	Population	15 306 252 (63)	% in cities	16%
GDP per capita	$700 (222)	Area km²	1 267 000 km² (22)	GMT +/−	+1
Neighbours (km)	Algeria 956, Benin 266, Burkina Faso 628, Chad 1175, Libya 354, Mali 821, Nigeria 1497				

NIG – NIGER

RECENT INTERNATIONAL MATCHES PLAYED BY NIGER

2012	Opponents	Score	Venue	Comp	Scorers	Att	Referee
23-01	Gabon	L 0-2	Libreville	CNr1		38 000	Maillet SEY
27-01	Tunisia	L 1-2	Libreville	CNr1	William N'Gounou [9]	20 000	Sikazwe ZAM
31-01	Morocco	L 0-1	Libreville	CNr1		4 000	Nampiandraza MAD
29-02	Egypt	L 0-1	Doha	Fr			Abdou QAT
26-05	Algeria	L 0-3	Blida				
3-06	Gabon	D 0-0	Niamey	WCq	Match awarded 3-0 to Niger	20 000	Haimoudi ALG
9-06	Congo	L 0-1	Pointe Noire	WCq		10 500	Munyemana RWA
9-09	Guinea	L 0-1	Conakry	CNq			Bennett RSA
9-10	Liberia	W 4-3	Niamey	Fr	Daouda Kamilou 2 [14] [26], Karim Konate [80], Moussa Maazou [85]		
14-10	Guinea	W 2-0	Niamey	CNq	Chikoto Mohamed [75], Issoufou Boubacar Garba [85]		Gassama GAM
30-12	Ethiopia	L 0-1	Addis Abeba	Fr			
2013							
20-01	Mali	L 0-1	Port Elizabeth	CNr1		20 000	Jedidi TUN
24-01	Congo DR	D 0-0	Port Elizabeth	CNr1		12 000	El Ahrach MAR
28-01	Ghana	L 0-3	Port Elizabeth	CNr1		10 000	Diatta SEN

Fr = Friendly match • CN = CAF African Cup of Nations • WC = FIFA World Cup • q = qualifier

NIGER SQUAD FOR THE 2012 CAF AFRICA CUP OF NATIONS

	Player		Ap	G	Club	Date of Birth		Player		Ap	G	Club	Date of Birth
1	Saminou Rabo	GK	0		Sahel	23 08 1981	12	Djibril Moussa Souna	DF	0		AS GNN	7 05 1992
2	Moussa Maazou	FW	3		Waregem BEL	25 08 1988	13	Mohamed Chicoto	DF	3		Plat. Stars RSA	28 02 1989
3	Abdoul Karim Lancina	MF	3		Cotonsport CMR	20 05 1987	14	Issoufou Boubacar	MF	3		Phuket THA	2 02 1990
4	Amadou Kader	DF	1		Olympic	5 04 1989	15	Sulliman Mazadou	DF	1		Marignane FRA	11 04 1985
5	Jimmy Bulus	DF	2+1		Hussein Dey ALG	22 10 1986	16	Kassaly Daouda	GK	3		Cotonsport CMR	19 08 1983
6	Idrissa Laouali	MF	1+1		AS-FAN	9 11 1983	17	William N'Gounou	MF	2	1	Limhamn SWE	31 07 1983
7	Idrissa Seydou	FW	0		Cotonsport CMR	24 12 1988	18	Kofi Dankowa	DF	2		ES Zarzis TUN	19 09 1994
8	Olivier Bonnes	MF	2		Lille FRA	7 02 1990	19	Issiaka Koudize	DF	0+1		AS GNN	18 10 1990
9	Daouda Kamilou	FW	0+2		CS Sfaxien TUN	29 12 1987	20	Amadou Moutari	MF	0+1		Akokana	19 01 1994
10	Talatou Boubacar	MF	1		O. Pirates RSA	3 12 1987	21	Yacouba Seydou Ali	MF	2+1		Africa Sports CIV	6 04 1992
11	Issoufou Alhassane	FW	1+2		Raja MAR	1 01 1981	22	Losseny Doumbia	GK	0		DCMP COD	5 04 1992
							23	Mohamed Soumaila	DF	3		Olympic	30 10 1994

Tr: Harouna Gabde

COUPE NATIONALE 2012 FINAL
Stade Regional, Zinder, 3-08-2012
Sahel SC Niamey 2-1 Urana FC

NIGER 2011-12

LIGUE 1 ORANGE

	Pl	W	D	L	F	A	Pts	Olympic	Akokana	Douane	Urana	ASN	ASGNN	Sahel	AS-FAN	Dan Kassawa	Alkali	Jangorzo	Espoir	Zumunta	Police
Olympic FC †	26	12	11	3	28	15	47		4-2	0-0	1-1	0-2	2-1	1-0	1-1	4-1	1-0	0-0	3-1	3-0	1-0
Akokana Arlit	26	13	8	5	35	20	47	0-0		0-0	2-0	1-0	1-0	0-0	1-0	0-0	0-0	1-0	1-1	7-0	4-3
AS Douane	26	12	8	6	27	10	44	0-1	2-1		0-1	0-0	0-1	0-0	4-0	1-0	4-0	3-2	0-0	1-0	0-0
Urana FC	26	10	10	6	25	25	40	0-0	0-0	2-0		2-1	0-0	1-1	1-0	0-0	1-0	0-0	1-0	2-0	4-4
ASN NIGELEC	25	9	10	6	33	22	37	2-2	2-1	0-1	2-1		0-0	0-2	1-1	2-1	0-1	3-1	n/p	3-0	2-1
AS Garde Nationale	25	10	7	8	26	24	37	0-0	1-2	0-3	4-1	1-1		0-2	2-1	0-1	1-0	0-0	3-0	0-0	1-0
Sahel SC Niamey ‡	25	9	9	7	25	16	36	1-1	1-2	1-0	1-1	1-1	1-2		0-1	0-0	1-0	3-2	1-0	0-1	0-1
AS-FAN Niamey	25	7	9	9	19	21	30	0-0	3-1	0-3	0-1	1-0	4-0	n/p		1-0	1-1	1-1	3-1	0-0	0-0
Dan Kassawa Maradi	25	7	9	9	22	22	30	2-0	0-0	0-1	4-1	1-1	1-1	0-2	1-1		4-0	n/p	1-1	2-1	1-0
Alkali Nassara Zinder	25	8	5	12	13	25	29	0-1	1-0	0-1	1-0	0-2	n/p	0-3	0-0	2-1		0-1	1-1	1-1	2-1
Jangorzo Maradi	25	7	7	11	17	26	28	1-0	0-3	0-1	2-0	0-0	3-2	1-0	1-0	0-0	1-0		1-0	1-0	0-1
Espoir FC Zinder	25	6	8	11	16	28	26	0-0	1-0	2-0	0-5	2-1	0-0	1-0	1-1	0-1	0-0			2-2	2-1
Zumunta AC Niamey	25	4	9	12	12	32	21	0-0	1-2	0-3	0-0	1-1	1-2	0-0	1-0	2-0	0-1	0-0	0-1		n/p
AS Police	25	4	8	13	22	34	20	0-1	1-2	0-0	1-1	2-2	1-2	0-4	0-0	0-2	4-2	1-0	0-1		

21/12/2011 - 31/07/2012 • † Qualified for the CAF Champions League • ‡ Qualified for the CAF Confederation Cup

NIR – NORTHERN IRELAND

FIFA/COCA-COLA WORLD RANKING

'93	'94	'95	'96	'97	'98	'99	'00	'01	'02	'03	'04	'05	'06	'07	'08	'09	'10	'11	'12
39	45	45	64	93	86	84	93	88	103	122	107	103	48	32	52	40	43	88	96

2012

Jan	Feb	Mar	Apr	May	Jun	Jul	Aug	Sep	Oct	Nov	Dec	High	Low	Av
87	86	87	100	100	103	102	101	129	117	100	96	27	129	73

David Jeffrey steered Linfield to yet another league and cup double as the club continued its complete domination of club football in Northern Ireland. It was Linfield's sixth double in just seven seasons and since taking over in 1997 Jeffrey has won 22 major trophies - nine in the league, seven in the Irish Cup and six in the Irish League Cup. If all the minor trophies are included his total is 30, just one short of Linfield's most successful manager Roy Coyle who spent 15 years with the club between 1975 and 1990. The one trophy that eluded Linfield during the season was the League Cup which was won by Crusaders, 1-0 winners over Coleraine in the final. Crusaders were out to win a cup double when they qualified for the final of the Irish Cup but lost 4-1 at Windsor Park to hosts Linfield. National team coach Michael O'Neill had a torrid start to his tenure with his side shipping nine goals in his first two games and by the end of the year he had yet to win a match. In their 2014 FIFA World Cup qualifying campaign, Northern Ireland lost to Russia in Moscow in the opening game which was then followed by three draws. In the first two, against Luxembourg and Portugal they were denied victory by late equalisers although it took a goal six minutes into injury-time to rescue a point in the third, at home to Azerbaijan.

UEFA EUROPEAN CHAMPIONSHIP RECORD
1960 DNE **1964** r2 **1968-2012** DNQ

IRISH FOOTBALL ASSOCIATION (IFA)

20 Windsor Avenue,
Belfast, BT9 6EG,
United Kingdom
☎ +44 28 90669458
📠 +44 28 90667620
✉ info@irishfa.com
🌐 www.irishfa.com
FA 1880 CON 1954 FIFA 1911
P Jim Shaw
GS Patrick Nelson

THE STADIA
2014 FIFA World Cup Stadia
Windsor Park
Belfast 12 950

Other Main Stadia
New Grosvenor Stadium
Lisburn 8 000
Solitude
Belfast 6 224
The Oval
Belfast 5 056
Mourneview Park
Lurgan 5 000

MAJOR CITIES/TOWNS
Population
1 Belfast 260 735
2 Londonderry 89 915
3 Lisburn 83 172
4 Newtownabbey 65 869
5 Bangor 62 364
6 Craigavon 61 920
7 Castlereagh 57 093
8 Newtownards 29 583
9 Carrickfergus 29 535
10 Ballymena 29 438
11 Newry 28 146
12 Coleraine 24 321
13 Omagh 22 507
14 Antrim 22 064
15 Larne 18 777
16 Banbridge 18 012
17 Enniskillen 15 592
18 Armagh 15 126
19 Strabane 15 060

NORTHERN IRELAND (PART OF THE UNITED KINGDOM)

Capital Belfast	Population 1 716 942 (149)	% in cities 90%
GDP per capita $36 700 (32)	Area km² 14 120 km² (160)	GMT +/- 0
Neighbours (km) Republic of Ireland 360 • Coast 539		

RECENT INTERNATIONAL MATCHES PLAYED BY NORTHERN IRELAND

2008	Opponents	Score	Venue	Comp	Scorers	Att	Referee
20-08	Scotland	D 0-0	Glasgow	Fr		28 072	Vollquartz DEN
6-09	Slovakia	L 1-2	Bratislava	WCq	Durica OG [81]	5 445	Ivanov.N RUS
10-09	Czech Republic	D 0-0	Belfast	WCq		12 882	Bebek CRO
11-10	Slovenia	L 0-2	Maribor	WCq		12 385	Iturralde ESP
15-10	San Marino	W 4-0	Belfast	WCq	Healy [31], McCann [43], Lafferty [56], Davis [75]	12 957	Kari FIN
19-11	Hungary	L 0-2	Belfast	Fr		6 251	Schoergenhofer AUT
2009							
11-02	San Marino	W 3-0	Serravalle	WCq	McAuley [7], McCann [33], Brunt [63]	1 942	Stankovic SRB
28-03	Poland	W 3-2	Belfast	WCq	Feeney [10], Evans [47], Zewlakow.M OG [62]	13 357	Hansson SWE
1-04	Slovenia	W 1-0	Belfast	WCq	Feeney [73]	13 243	Yefet ISR
6-06	Italy	L 0-3	Pisa	Fr		16 583	Blom NED
12-08	Israel	D 1-1	Belfast	Fr	McCann [19]	10 250	Valgeirsson ISL
5-09	Poland	D 1-1	Chorzow	WCq	Lafferty [38]	38 914	Mejuto ESP
9-09	Slovakia	L 0-2	Belfast	WCq		13 019	Kuipers NED
14-10	Czech Republic	D 0-0	Prague	WCq		8 002	Duhamel FRA
14-11	Serbia	L 0-1	Belfast	Fr		13 500	Toussaint LUX
2010							
3-03	Albania	L 0-1	Tirana	Fr		7 500	Pilav BIH
26-05	Turkey	L 0-2	New Britain	Fr		4 000	Vaughn USA
30-05	Chile	L 0-1	Chillan	Fr		12 000	Prudente URU
11-08	Montenegro	L 0-2	Podgorica	Fr		5 000	Jovanetic SRB
3-09	Slovenia	W 1-0	Maribor	ECq	Evans [70]	12 000	Balaj ROU
8-10	Italy	D 0-0	Belfast	ECq		15 200	Chapron FRA
12-10	Faroe Islands	D 1-1	Toftir	ECq	Lafferty [76]	1 921	Zimmermann SUI
17-11	Morocco	D 1-1	Belfast	Fr	Patterson [86p]	15 000	Hagen NOR
2011							
9-02	Scotland	L 0-3	Dublin	NC		18 742	Connolly IRL
25-03	Serbia	L 1-2	Belgrade	ECq	McAuley [40]	BCD	Gumienny BEL
29-03	Slovenia	D 0-0	Belfast	ECq		14 200	Kuipers NED
24-05	Republic of Ireland	L 0-5	Dublin	NC		15 083	Thomson SCO
27-05	Wales	L 0-2	Dublin	NC		529	Kelly IRL
10-08	Faroe Islands	W 4-0	Belfast	ECq	Hughes [5], Davis [66], McCourt 2 [71 88]	13 183	Aleckovic BIH
2-09	Serbia	L 0-1	Belfast	ECq		15 148	Einwaller AUT
6-09	Estonia	L 1-4	Tallinn	ECq	OG [40]	8 660	Stalhammar SWE
7-10	Estonia	L 1-2	Belfast	ECq	Davis [22]	12 604	Grafe GER
11-10	Italy	L 0-3	Pescara	ECq		19 480	Mateu ESP
2012							
29-02	Norway	L 0-3	Belfast	Fr		9 759	Jones WAL
2-06	Netherlands	L 0-6	Amsterdam	Fr		50 000	Schorgenhofer AUT
15-08	Finland	D 3-3	Belfast	Fr	Ferguson [7], Lafferty [19], Paterson [84p]	9 575	Liesveld NED
7-09	Russia	L 0-2	Moscow	WCq		14 300	Mateu Lahoz ESP
11-09	Luxembourg	D 1-1	Belfast	WCq	Shiels [14]	10 674	Glodovic SRB
16-10	Portugal	D 1-1	Porto	WCq	McGinn [30]	48 711	Kinhoffer GER
14-11	Azerbaijan	D 1-1	Belfast	WCq	Healy [96+]	12 372	Shvetsov UKR

Fr = Friendly match • EC = UEFA EURO 2012 • WC = FIFA World Cup • NC = Nations Cup • q = qualifier

NORTHERN IRELAND NATIONAL TEAM HISTORICAL RECORDS

Caps: 119 - Pat Jennings 1964-86 • 94 - David Healy 2000- • 91 - Mal Donaghy 1980-94 • 88 - Sammy McIlroy 1972-87 • 87 - Maik Taylor 1999- • 86 - Keith Gillespie 1996-2008 • 84 - Aaron Hughes 1998- • 73 - Jimmy Nicholl 1976-86 • 71 - Michael Hughes 1992-2004 • 67 - David McCreery 1976-90 • 66 - Nigel Worthington • 64 - Martin O'Neill 1972-85 • 63 - Gerry Armstrong 1977-86

Goals: 36 - David Healy 2000- • 13 - Billy Gillespie 1913-32 & Colin Clarke 1986-93 • 12 - Joe Bambrick 1928-40; Gerry Armstrong 1977-86; Jimmy Quinn 1985-96 & Iain Dowie 1990-2000 • 11 - Olphie Stanfield 1887-97 • 10 - Billy Bingham 1951-64; Jimmy McIlroy 1952-66; Peter McParland 1954-62 & Johnny Crossan 1960-68

Coaches: Peter Doherty 1951-62 • Bertie Peacock 1962-67 • Billy Bingham 1967-71 • Terry Neill 1971-75 • Dave Clements 1975-76 • Danny Blanchflower 1976-79 • Billy Bingham 1980-94 • Bryan Hamilton 1994-98 • Lawrie McMenemy ENG 1998-99 • Sammy McIlroy 2000-03 • Lawrie Sanchez 2004-07 • Nigel Worthington 2007-11 • Michael O'Neill 2012-

NORTHERN IRELAND 2011-12
IFA JJB SPORTS PREMIERSHIP

	Pl	W	D	L	F	A	Pts	Linfield	Portadown	Cliftonville	Coleraine	Crusaders	Glentoran	Ballymena	Donegal	Swifts	Glenavon	Distillery	Carrick R
Linfield †	38	27	4	7	79	29	85		2-0 2-1	4-1 2-1	1-1 0-0	0-2 0-5	0-1 0-2	1-0	5-0 4-0	1-0 3-0	1-0 2-0	1-1	3-0 4-1
Portadown ‡	38	22	5	11	72	47	71	2-0 1-1		1-2 3-3	1-1 2-0	1-3 1-2	2-1 0-1	2-1	5-2 2-1	2-1	1-0	5-1	3-0
Cliftonville ‡	38	21	6	11	83	62	69	4-2 1-3	0-2 2-3		1-2 1-1	2-1 1-1	2-1 3-0	3-4	2-3	4-1 2-1	5-3 4-3	3-1	1-0 2-1
Coleraine	38	18	12	8	61	38	66	1-3 1-0	4-3 4-1	1-1 1-0		0-0 1-0	1-1 1-1	1-0 2-0	2-0 0-1	3-2	1-1 3-1	2-3	4-0
Crusaders ‡	38	18	10	10	63	47	64	0-1 1-1	0-3 0-1	2-2 3-2	1-1 2-1		1-2 2-0	3-2 2-2	1-2	2-0	2-0 1-0	1-1 2-2	5-1 3-1
Glentoran	38	16	9	13	67	52	57	2-0 1-0	0-2 2-2	0-1 1-0	1-1 3-3	2-2 0-4		2-4 1-2	1-2	2-1	2-0	3-3 1-3	6-1
Ballymena United	38	14	8	16	66	71	50	1-2 1-2	2-4 1-2	3-7 0-1	1-5	0-3	0-3		2-0 2-2	1-1 1-1	3-3 2-2	1-0 2-2	0-2 3-0
Donegal Celtic	38	12	5	21	44	80	41	1-5	1-0	1-3 0-2	0-1	0-2 1-1	0-4 0-1	2-3 0-3			0-2 3-1	2-1 1-1	2-2 2-1	1-2 3-5
Dungannon Swifts	38	8	11	19	42	71	35	1-4	0-3 2-0	1-4	0-0 1-2	0-2 1-2	0-5 2-1	1-1 2-4	2-2 2-1		1-1 1-5	0-2 3-2	3-1 0-0
Glenavon	38	8	10	20	60	71	34	1-2	0-2 0-2	1-2	1-0	3-2	1-3 1-0	3-0 0-2	0-1 4-0	1-1 2-2		5-2 2-3	1-2 3-2
Lisburn Distillery	38	8	8	22	56	84	32	2-3 0-3	0-2 0-2	1-2 1-2	1-3 3-1	1-2	0-5	1-4 2-3	0-2 3-0	1-2 0-2	2-1 3-3		2-3 3-1
Carrick Rangers	38	7	10	21	50	91	31	0-4	2-2 3-1	3-3	0-2 0-4	1-2	3-3 2-2	0-2 1-3	1-2 2-3	1-1 0-0	2-2 4-4	0-2 1	

6/08/2011 - 28/04/2012 • † Qualified for the UEFA Champions League • ‡ Qualified for the Europa League
Relegation play-off: Lisburn Distillery 0-0 3-2 Newry City
Top scorers: **27** - Gary MCCUTCHEON SCO, Ballymena • **24** - Matthew TIPTON WAL, Portadown • **22** - Gary LIGGETT, Distillery • **20** - Curtis ALLEN, Coleraine • **17** - Kevin BRANIFF, Portadown • **16** - Chris SCANNELL, Cliftonville

NORTHERN IRELAND 2011-12
IFA CHAMPIONSHIP (2)

	Pl	W	D	L	F	A	Pts
Ballinamallard United	26	20	3	3	62	24	63
Newry City	26	15	6	5	51	22	51
Institute	26	13	4	9	37	34	43
Bangor	26	12	6	8	45	34	42
Ards	26	11	6	9	39	31	39
Limavady United	26	12	2	12	48	43	38
Loughgall	26	11	5	10	45	41	38
Dergview	26	8	10	8	38	37	34
HW Welders	26	10	4	12	30	35	34
Larne	26	9	5	12	37	47	32
Tobermore United	26	8	7	11	34	44	31
Warrenpoint Town	26	7	7	12	34	37	28
Banbridge Town	26	5	4	17	30	70	19
Glebe Rangers	26	3	7	16	25	56	16

6/08/2011 - 28/04/2012

MEDALS TABLE

		Overall			League			Cup		LC	
		G	S	B	G	S	B	G	B	G	B
1	Linfield	102	43	14	51	20	14	42	20	9	3
2	Glentoran	50	48	25	23	24	25	20	19	7	5
3	Belfast Celtic	22	8	8	14	4	8	8	4		
4	Lisburn Distillery	19	15	9	6	8	9	12	7	1	
5	Cliftonville	12	18	7	3	6	7	8	10	1	2
6	Glenavon	9	21	6	3	10	6	5	10	1	1
7	Portadown	9	19	7	4	10	7	3	7	2	2
8	Crusaders	9	9	4	4	3	4	3	3	2	3
9	Coleraine	7	20	9	1	9	9	5	6	1	5
10	Ballymena United	6	10	5		2	5	6	8		
11	Ards	6	4	8	1	1	8	4	2	1	1
12	Derry City †	4	10	3	1	7	3	3	3		
13	Shelbourne Dublin †	3	4	1		1	1	3	3		
14	Queen's Island	3	3		1	3		2			
15	Bangor	2	3	2				1	2	1	2
16	Bohemians Dublin †	1	5							1	5
17	Ulster FC	1	3			1		1	2		
18	Carrick Rangers	1	2							1	2

CIS INSURANCE LEAGUE CUP 2011-12

Round of 16		Quarter-finals		Semi-finals		Final	
Crusaders	4						
Lisburn Distillery *	2	**Crusaders**	7				
Limavady United	1	Carrick Rangers *	0				
Carrick Rangers *	3			**Crusaders**	1		
Dergview	1			Ballymena United *	0		
Donegal Celtic *	0	Dergview *	2				
Bangor *	0	**Ballymena United**	6				
Ballymena United	2					**Crusaders**	1
Cliftonville *	5					Coleraine	0
Dungannon Swifts	0	**Cliftonville**	2				
Linfield *	0 5p	Glenavon *	1			CUP FINAL	
Glenavon	0 6p			Cliftonville *	1		
Glentoran *	2			**Coleraine**	2	Ballymena Showgrounds, Ballymena	
Portadown	1	Glentoran *	1			28-02-2012, Ref: Turkington	
Newry City *	0	**Coleraine**	2			Scorer - Morrow [34] for Crusaders	
Coleraine	3						

* Home team

JJB SPORTS IRISH CUP 2011-12

Fifth Round

Linfield *	7	
Ballyclare Comrades	1	
Killymoon Rangers *	1	
Carrick Rangers	3	
NewBuildings United *	4	
Dunmurry Recreation	1	
Loughgall	2 1	
Coagh United *	2 2	
Ballymena United	2	
Lisburn Distillery *	1	
Dergview *	0	
Derriaghy Cricket Club	1	
Ballymoney United	4	
Bangor *	2	
Banbridge Town *	0	
Newry City	1	
Dungannon Swifts *	3	
Larne	1	
Glentoran *	0	
Newington Youth Club	1	
Cliftonville *	2	
Ards	0	
Institute *	1 0	
Donegal Celtic	1 1	
Coleraine *	3	
Larne Tech Old Boys	2	
Dundela *	0	
Ballinamallard United	3	
Glenavon *	2	
Portadown	1	
Warrenpoint Town	0	
Crusaders *	3	

Round of 16

Linfield *	5
Carrick Rangers	1
NewBuildings United	1 1
Coagh United *	1 4
Ballymena United *	3
Derriaghy Cricket Club	1
Ballymoney United *	1
Newry City	6
Dungannon Swifts *	3
Newington Youth Club	0
Cliftonville	0
Donegal Celtic *	1
Coleraine *	3
Ballinamallard United	0
Coleraine *	0
Crusaders	2
Glenavon *	0
Crusaders	4

Quarter-finals

Linfield *	4
Coagh United	0
Ballymena United ‡‡	2
Newry City *	1
Dungannon Swifts	1 1
Donegal Celtic *	1 0
Coleraine *	0
Crusaders	2

‡‡ Ballymena disqualified for fielding an ineligible player

Semi-finals

Linfield ††	7
Newry City	0
Dungannon Swifts	0
Crusaders †	1

Final

Linfield	4
Crusaders ‡	1

CUP FINAL

Windsor Park, Belfast, 5-05-2012
Att: 6000, Ref: Raymond Crangle
Scorers - McAllister 2 [28 41], Carvill [60] Mulgrew [83] for Linfield; Coates [56] for Distillery
Linfield - Alan Blayney (c) - Jim Ervin, William Murphy, Albert Watson, Damien Curran - Philip Lowry, Jamie Mulgrew● (Billie Joe Burns 89), Robert Garrett● (Chris Casement 71), Michael Carvill● - Peter Thompson, Mark McAllister (Daryl Fordyce 92). Tr: David Jeffrey
Crusaders - Sean O'Neill - Gareth McKeown● (Paul Leeman 45), David Magowan, Colin Coates● (c), Stephen McBride (Aidan Watson 81) - Declan Caddell●, David McMaster (Jordan Owens 45), Chris Morrow, Stuart Dallas - Timmy Adamson, David Rainey. Tr: Stephen Baxter

* Home team in the first leg • † Played at Mourneview Park, Lurgan • †† Played at The Oval, Belfast • ‡ Qualified for the Europa League

NOR – NORWAY

FIFA/COCA-COLA WORLD RANKING

'93	'94	'95	'96	'97	'98	'99	'00	'01	'02	'03	'04	'05	'06	'07	'08	'09	'10	'11	'12
4	8	10	14	13	14	7	14	26	26	42	35	38	50	29	59	32	12	25	24

2012

Jan	Feb	Mar	Apr	May	Jun	Jul	Aug	Sep	Oct	Nov	Dec	High	Low	Av
24	24	24	24	24	26	24	25	34	26	26	24	2	59	23

Before 2009 the county of Møre og Romsdal on the north coast of western Norway was considered a relative backwater of Norwegian football. Over the course of four seasons, however, that has changed for good thanks to the exploits of Molde and Aalesund which culminated in 2011 with Molde winning their first-ever title and Aalesund winning the cup. In 2012 the area once again scooped both trophies with Ole Gunnar Solskjær's Molde retaining the championship but it was the exploits of tiny Hødd in the cup that captured the imagination of the nation. Situated in the small town of Ulsteinvik, 23 kilometers to the southwest of Aalesund, Hødd only just escaped relegation to the third level on goal difference but against Tippeligaen side Tromsø in the final, they rode their luck to win the trophy on penalties - an extraordinary achievement for a town of just over 5000 inhabitants. The national team got off to the worst possible start in the qualifiers for the 2014 FIFA World Cup when they lost 2-0 to Iceland in Reykjavík but ended the year tucked in behind group leaders Switzerland against whom they earned a draw in Berne. Egil Olsen's team will be hoping to qualify for what would only be their fourth appearance at the World Cup finals from a group that on paper should be very winnable.

UEFA EUROPEAN CHAMPIONSHIP RECORD
1960 r1 1964 r1 1968-1996 DNQ **2000** r1 2004-2012 DNQ

NORGES FOTBALLFORBUND (NFF)

Ullevaal Stadion, 0840 Oslo

☎ +47 21029300
📠 +47 21029301
✉ nff@fotball.no
🖥 www.fotball.no
FA 1902 CON 1954 FIFA 1908
P Yngve Hallen
GS Kjetil Siem

THE STADIA

2014 FIFA World Cup Stadia
Ullevaal Stadion
Oslo   25 572

Other Main Stadia
Lerkendal Stadion
Trondheim   21 166
Brann Stadion
Bergen   17 824
Viking Stadion
Stavanger   16 100
Sør Arena
Kristiansand   14 300

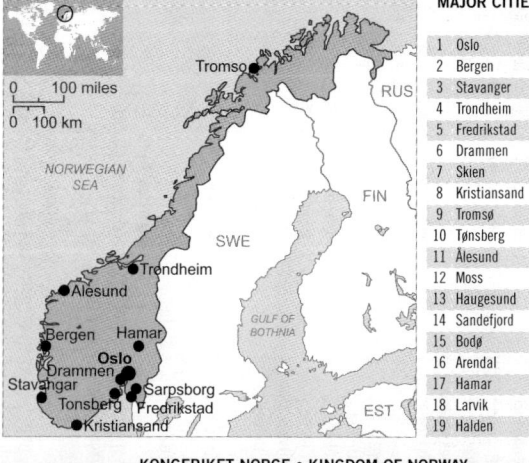

MAJOR CITIES/TOWNS

		Population
1	Oslo	864 838
2	Bergen	226 463
3	Stavanger	188 869
4	Trondheim	157 917
5	Fredrikstad	101 164
6	Drammen	95 109
7	Skien	86 436
8	Kristiansand	67 281
9	Tromsø	54 774
10	Tønsberg	47 130
11	Ålesund	46 380
12	Moss	45 491
13	Haugesund	41 980
14	Sandefjord	40 809
15	Bodø	37 008
16	Arendal	31 858
17	Hamar	30 081
18	Larvik	23 604
19	Halden	22 665

KONGERIKET NORGE • KINGDOM OF NORWAY

Capital Oslo   Population 4 660 539 (116)   % in cities 77%
GDP per capita $59 500 (5)   Area km² 323 802 km² (67)   GMT +/- +1
Neighbours (km) Finland 727, Sweden 1619, Russia 196 • Coast 25 148

RECENT INTERNATIONAL MATCHES PLAYED BY NORWAY

2009	Opponents	Score	Venue	Comp	Scorers	Att	Referee
11-02	Germany	W 1-0	Dusseldorf	Fr	Grindheim [63]	42 000	Messner AUT
28-03	South Africa	L 1-2	Rustenburg	Fr	Pedersen [27]	30 000	Fleischer GHA
1-04	Finland	W 3-2	Oslo	Fr	Riise.JA [56], Hoiland [90], Pedersen [92+]	16 239	Styles ENG
6-06	Macedonia FYR	D 0-0	Skopje	WCq		7 000	Tagliavento ITA
10-06	Netherlands	L 0-2	Rotterdam	WCq		45 600	Baskakov RUS
12-08	Scotland	W 4-0	Oslo	WCq	Riise.JA [35], Pedersen 2 [45 90], Huseklepp [60]	24 493	Hamer LUX
5-09	Iceland	D 1-1	Reykjavik	WCq	Riise.JA [11]	7 321	Tudor ROU
9-09	Macedonia FYR	W 2-1	Oslo	WCq	Helstad [2], Riise.JA [25]	14 766	Paixao POR
10-10	South Africa	W 1-0	Oslo	Fr	Waehler [48]	13 504	Collum SCO
14-11	Switzerland	W 1-0	Geneva	Fr	Carew [48p]	16 000	Whitby WAL
2010							
3-03	Slovakia	W 1-0	Zilina	Fr	Moldskred [67]	9 756	Nijhuis NED
29-05	Montenegro	W 2-1	Oslo	Fr	Grindheim [44], Pedersen [89]	13 132	Eriksson SWE
2-06	Ukraine	L 0-1	Oslo	Fr		10 178	Blom NED
11-08	France	W 2-1	Oslo	Fr	Huseklepp 2 [51 71]	15 165	Velasco ESP
3-09	Iceland	W 2-1	Reykjavík	ECq	Hangeland [58], Abdellaoue [75]	6 137	Banti ITA
7-09	Portugal	W 1-0	Oslo	ECq	Huseklepp [21]	24 535	Duhamel FRA
8-10	Cyprus	W 2-1	Larnaca	ECq	Riise.JA [2], Carew [42]	7 648	Gumienny BEL
12-10	Croatia	L 1-2	Zagreb	Fr	Abdellaoue [21]	3 000	Skomina SVN
17-11	Republic of Ireland	W 2-1	Dublin	Fr	Pedersen [34], Huseklepp [86]	25 000	Jakobsson ISL
2011							
9-02	Poland	L 0-1	Faro	Fr		500	Dos Anjos POR
26-03	Denmark	D 1-1	Oslo	ECq	Huseklepp [81]	24 828	Rocchi ITA
4-06	Portugal	L 0-1	Lisbon	ECq		47 829	Cakir TUR
7-06	Lithuania	W 1-0	Oslo	Fr	Pedersen [84]	12 945	Attwell ENG
10-08	Czech Republic	W 3-0	Oslo	Fr	Abdellaoue 2 [23 89p], Riise.JA [72]	12 734	Black NIR
2-09	Iceland	W 1-0	Oslo	ECq	Abdellaoue [88p]	22 381	Hategin ROU
6-09	Denmark	L 0-2	Copenhagen	ECq		37 167	Lannoy FRA
11-10	Cyprus	W 3-1	Oslo	ECq	Pedersen [25], Carew [34], Hogli [65]	13 490	Collum SCO
12-11	Wales	L 1-4	Cardiff	Fr	Huseklepp [61]	12 600	Grubelnik AUT
2012							
18-01	Thailand	W 1-0	Bangkok	Fr	Reginiussen [84]	6 000	Yamamoto JPN
29-02	Northern Ireland	W 3-0	Belfast	Fr	Nordveit [55], El Younoussi [88], Ruud [92+]	9 759	Jones WAL
26-05	England	L 0-1	Oslo	Fr		21 496	Weiner GER
2-06	Croatia	D 1-1	Oslo	Fr	El Younoussi [92+]	14 208	Karasyov RUS
15-08	Greece	L 2-3	Oslo	Fr	Hangeland [13], Riise.JA [75]	13 680	Kelly IRL
7-09	Iceland	L 0-2	Reykjavík	WCq		8 352	Gautier FRA
11-09	Slovenia	W 2-1	Oslo	WCq	Waehler [16], Henriksen [26], Riise.JA [93+]	11 168	Aydinus TUR
12-10	Switzerland	D 1-1	Berne	WCq	Hangeland [81]	30 712	Fernandez ESP
16-10	Cyprus	W 3-1	Larnaca	WCq	Hangeland [45], El Younoussi [81p], King [83]	2 493	Gil POL
14-11	Hungary	W 2-0	Budapest	Fr	Nielsen [39], Abdellaoue [79]	16 000	Strahonja CRO

Fr = Friendly match • EC = UEFA EURO 2012 • WC = FIFA World Cup • q = qualifier

NORWAY NATIONAL TEAM HISTORICAL RECORDS

Caps
109 - John Arne Riise 2000- • 104 - Thorbjorn Svenssen 1947-62 • 100 - Henning Berg 1992-2004 • 97 - Erik Thorstvedt 1982-96 • 91 - John Carew 1998- • 86 - Oyvind Leonhardsen 1990-2003 • 83 - Kjetil Rekdal 1987-2000 • 82 - Brede Hangeland 2002- • 79 - Steffen Iversen 1998- • 78 - Erik Mykland 1990-2000 • 77 - Svein Grondalen 1973-84 • 76 - Tore Andre Flo 1995-2004

Goals
33 - Jorgen Juve 1928-37 • 26 - Einar Gundersen 1917-28 • 25 - Harald Hennum 1949-60 • 24 - John Carew 1998- • 23 - Ole Gunnar Solskjær 1995-2007 & Tore Andre Flo 1995-2004 • 22 - Gunnar Thoresen 1946-59 • 21 - Steffen Iversen 1998-2011 • 20 - Jan Age Fjortoft 1986-96 • 19 - Odd Iversen 1967-79; Olav Nilsen 1962-71 & Oyvind Leonhardsen 1990-2003

Coaches
Willibald Hahn AUT 1953-55 • Ron Lewin ENG 1956-57 • Edmund Majowsky 1958 • Ragnar Larsen 1958 • Kristian Henriksen 1959 • Wilhelm Kment AUT 1960-62 • Ragnar Larsen 1962-66 • Wilhelm Kment AUT 1967-69 • Oivind Johannessen 1970-71 • George Curtis ENG 1972-74 • Kjell Schou-Andreassen & Nils Arne Eggen 1975-77 • Tor Roste Fossen 1978-87 • Tord Grip SWE 1987-88 • Ingvar Stadheim 1988-90 • Egil Olsen 1990-98 • Nils Johan Semb 1998-2003 • Age Hareide 2003-08 • Egil Olsen 2009-

NORWAY 2012

TIPPELIGAEN

	Pl	W	D	L	F	A	Pts	Molde	Strømsg'set	Rosenborg	Tromsø	Viking	Brann	Haugesund	Vålerenga	Lillestrøm	Odd	Aalesund	Sogndal	Hønefoss	Sandnes	Fredrikstad	Stabæk
Molde FK †	30	19	5	6	51	31	62		2-1	2-0	3-2	1-2	2-1	1-0	2-0	3-2	3-1	2-1	2-1	1-0	3-2	2-0	4-3
IF Strømsgodset ‡	30	17	7	6	62	40	58	1-1		2-1	2-0	1-0	2-0	3-3	3-2	3-3	1-0	4-0	3-0	4-0	2-1	5-0	3-1
Rosenborg BK ‡	30	15	10	5	53	26	55	1-0	3-3		3-0	1-1	3-1	5-2	3-0	1-1	0-0	3-0	0-0	0-1	2-0	0-1	3-1
Tromsø IL	30	14	7	9	45	32	49	1-1	4-0	1-1		5-1	2-0	2-0	3-1	5-1	0-1	1-0	1-1	0-0	1-1	1-0	3-0
Viking FK	30	14	7	9	41	36	49	1-0	3-2	1-4	0-1		2-1	0-2	2-1	1-2	1-0	1-1	2-1	2-1	5-0	3-0	1-0
SK Brann	30	13	3	14	57	50	42	4-1	1-2	2-1	0-2	0-0		3-2	1-2	2-3	6-2	2-1	5-0	3-2	3-1	2-0	2-1
SK Haugesund	30	11	9	10	46	40	42	2-0	2-3	0-1	1-1	1-0	2-1		4-2	1-1	0-1	4-2	0-0	1-1	3-2	1-0	4-1
Vålerenga IF	30	12	5	13	42	44	41	1-2	1-1	0-0	1-0	1-0	1-1	2-1		1-2	3-1	0-0	0-2	3-2	4-0	3-2	1-2
Lillestrøm SK	30	9	12	9	46	47	39	1-1	0-1	2-2	4-2	0-0	3-4	0-0	1-1		1-1	0-0	1-0	2-2	1-3	1-2	6-0
Odd Grenland	30	11	7	12	40	43	39§	0-0	2-1	0-1	2-2	1-4	1-0	2-1	2-3	2-0		3-0	0-4	4-0	2-2	1-1	1-2
Aalesunds SK	30	9	11	10	40	41	38	0-1	3-1	2-2	0-0	1-1	2-0	2-2	3-1	2-1	2-1		2-2	2-0	3-1	3-0	3-1
Sogndal IL	30	8	10	12	29	37	34	2-1	1-1	0-3	1-0	1-2	2-0	1-1	1-0	1-0	0-1	1-1		0-0	0-0	1-3	3-1
Hønefoss BK	30	7	12	11	30	42	33	1-1	1-1	1-4	0-1	2-2	2-1	3-2	1-0	0-0	1-4	3-1	0-0		1-1	1-1	0-0
Sandnes Ulf	30	8	8	14	44	56	32	0-2	2-1	1-1	5-1	2-2	3-3	0-2	0-2	0-1	0-0	1-1	3-1	1-0		5-1	2-1
Fredrikstad FK	30	9	3	18	42	59	30	0-2	2-3	1-2	2-0	3-0	3-4	0-0	1-2	3-4	4-2	1-3	2-1	0-2	3-4		5-1
Stabæk Fotball	30	5	2	23	25	69	17	0-5	1-2	0-2	0-1	0-1	0-4	0-2	1-3	4-1	0-2	0-0	2-1	0-2	2-1	0-1	

23/03/2012 - 18/11/2012 • † Qualified for the UEFA Champions League • ‡ Qualified for the Europa League
Relegation play-off: Ullensaker/Kisa 0-4 1-3 **Sandnes Ulf**. Sandnes remain in the Tippeligaen • Top scorers: **14** - Peter **KOVACS** HUN, Strømsgodset & Zdenek **ONDRASEK** CZE, Tromsø • **13** - Davy Claude **AGNAN** CIV, Molde • **12** - Nikola **DURDIC** SRB, Haugesund

MEDALS TABLE

		Overall G S B	League G S B	Cup G S	City
1	Rosenborg BK	31 10 3	22 5 3	9 5	Trondheim
2	Fredrikstad FK	20 16 1	9 9 1	11 7	Fredrikstad
3	Viking SK	13 7 8	8 2 8	5 5	Stavanger
4	Odd Grenland	12 10	2	12 8	Skien
5	Lillestrøm SK	10 16 3	5 8 3	5 8	Lillestrøm
6	SFK Lyn	10 10 4	2 4 4	8 6	Oslo
7	SK Brann	9 13 3	3 5 3	6 8	Bergen
8	FK Skeid	9 8 1	1 5 1	8 3	Oslo
9	Vålerenga IF	9 5 3	5 3 3	4 2	Oslo
10	FK Sarpsborg	6 6 2		2 6 6	Sarpsborg
11	IF Stromsgodset	6 3 3	1 1 3	5 2	Drammen
12	Molde FK	4 9 3	2 6 3	2 3	Molde

NORWAY 2012

ADECCOLIGAEN (2)

	Pl	W	D	L	F	A	Pts	Start	Sarpsborg	Sandefjord	Mjøndalen	Bodø-Glimt	Ullensaker	Ranheim	HamKam	Kongsvinger	Bryne	Strømmen	Hødd	Tromsdalen	Bærum	Notodden	Alta
IK Start	30	20	6	4	71	35	66		3-4	1-0	3-1	3-0	2-0	2-2	3-1	3-0	3-1	3-1	2-1	3-3	4-0	7-0	4-0
Sarpsborg 08	30	19	6	5	73	43	63	4-4		0-3	3-1	1-1	2-1	2-2	4-1	1-2	2-2	4-0	2-2	2-0	1-0	3-2	6-0
Sandefjord Fotball ‡	30	16	7	7	44	29	55	1-1	1-2		1-1	2-1	2-0	3-0	2-1	0-0	1-0	1-0	1-2	0-0	3-3	2-2
Mjøndalen IF ‡	30	16	7	7	52	43	55	3-0	0-2	0-3		2-1	2-1	2-1	4-2	2-1	1-1	3-2	2-1	3-0	2-1	2-2	4-0
FK Bodø-Glimt ‡	30	13	9	8	59	36	48	5-0	2-3	4-0	2-2		1-0	0-3	3-1	1-1	4-1	0-0	4-0	3-2	3-1	6-0	1-0
Ullensaker/Kisa IL ‡	30	14	2	14	45	39	44	0-3	2-1	1-1	5-0	0-3		1-0	0-1	0-1	1-2	1-1	3-1	2-1	5-2	2-0	3-0
Ranheim Fotball	30	11	10	9	55	40	43	1-1	1-2	1-2	1-2	1-1	3-0		1-1	7-0	0-0	1-2	1-1	4-1	3-1	3-2	2-1
Hamarkameratene §2	30	13	6	11	51	49	43	1-2	3-5	2-3	1-1	0-0	2-1	2-1		0-5	1-1	2-3	2-0	7-2	3-1	1-0	3-0
Kongsvinger IL	30	12	3	15	44	48	39	0-1	1-3	2-0	0-2	1-2	1-0	2-2	0-3		1-2	2-1	2-1	2-0	6-2	3-1	4-0
Bryne FK	30	10	8	12	41	53	38	0-3	4-3	0-1	2-2	2-1	0-2	0-1	0-1	2-1		3-1	1-0	4-2	3-1	2-1	1-1
Strømmen IF	30	10	7	13	39	51	37	1-2	1-2	2-1	1-1	2-2	1-1	1-0	0-1	2-1	3-1		1-1	4-2	5-0	1-2	2-1
IL Hødd	30	10	5	15	43	52	35	0-0	2-1	1-0	3-0	2-1	1-3	1-3	5-0	0-2	0-1	4-1		4-3	2-0	2-1	1-1
Tromsdalen UIL	30	10	5	15	51	62	35	1-2	0-0	0-3	2-0	3-0	1-2	1-3	1-2	1-2	2-1	5-1	3-0	3-2		2-3	1-0	1-1
Bærum SK	30	5	7	18	49	73	22	2-3	2-4	1-3	0-3	3-3	1-3	2-2	1-2	4-1	5-4	0-0	1-2	1-2		6-0	1-1
Notodden FK	30	6	4	20	38	71	22	2-1	0-1	0-0	1-3	0-0	0-4	1-2	2-3	0-3	3-1	3-0	2-2	1-5	2-2		4-1
Alta IF §1	30	4	10	16	30	61	21	0-2	1-3	0-1	0-1	1-1	1-3	1-1	0-0	1-1	3-2	2-3	5-0	3-2	3-3	1-0	

9/04/2012 - 11/11/2012 • § = points deducted • ‡ Promotion play-offs • Play-off semi-finals: Sandefjord 3-4 **Ullensaker/Kisa**; Mjøndalen 1-2 **Bodø/Glimt** • Final: **Ullensaker/Kisa** 2-0 Bodø/Glimt. Ullensaker qualified to meet Sandnes • Top scorer: **20** - Martin Wiig, Sarpsborg

NM SAS BRAATHENS CUPEN 2012

Third Round

IL Hødd *	2
Sarpsborg 08	1
Stabæk Fotball	1
Asker Fotball *	2
Odd Grenland	3
Raufoss IL *	2
Egersunds IK	0
SK Haugesund *	8
IF Strømsgodset *	3
Notodden FK	2
Hønefoss BK	2 1p
Mjøndalen IF *	2 3p
Viking FK	2
Åsane Fotball	0
Nest-Sotra Fotball *	0
SK Brann	3
Molde FK *	3
Hamarkameratene	2
Rosenborg BK *	4
Kvik Halden	3
Aalesunds SK *	4
Byåsen Toppfotball3	0
Vålerenga IF	1
Sandefjord Fotball *	3
FK Bodø-Glimt	2 4p
Alta IF *	2 5p
Ullensaker/Kisa IL *	0
Lillestrøm SK	3
IK Start	1
Kongsvinger IL *	0
Tromsdalen UIL	0
Tromsø IL *	4

Round of 16

IL Hødd *	
Asker Fotball	
Odd Grenland *	
SK Haugesund	
IF Strømsgodset	
Mjøndalen IF *	
Viking FK *	
SK Brann	
Molde FK *	
Rosenborg BK	
Aalesunds SK	1
Sandefjord Fotball *	2
FK Bodø-Glimt *	4
Lillestrøm SK	0
IK Start *	1 1p
Tromsø IL	1 4p

Quarter-finals

IL Hødd	2 5p
SK Haugesund *	2 4p
IF Strømsgodset	3
SK Brann *	4
Molde FK *	2
Sandefjord Fotball	1
FK Bodø-Glimt	0
Tromsø IL *	1

Semi-finals

IL Hødd *	3
SK Brann	1
Molde FK	1
Tromsø IL *	2

Final

IL Hødd ‡	1 4p
Tromsø IL	1 2p

PENALTIES

	Hødd		Tromsø
✓	Latifu		Arst ✓
✓	Nilsen		Drage ✓
✓	Helland		Johansen ✗
✗	Sandal		Ciss ✗
✓	Rekdal		

CUP FINAL

Ullevaal, Oslo, 25-11-2012
Att: 24,217, Ref: Kjetil Sælen
Scorers - Sellin 62 for Hødd; Ciss 87 for Tromsø
Hødd - Ørjan Nyland - Akeem Latifu, Fredrik Klock (c), Steffen Moltu, Victor Grodås - Fredrik Aursnes (Bendik Torset 120), Erik Sandal, Sivert Nilsen - Vegard Heltne● (Andreas Rekdal 85), Kjell Sellin (Espen Standal 96), Pål Andre Helland. Tr: Lars Arne Nilsen
Tromsø - Benny Lekstrøm - Hans Norbye, Fredrik Bjørck, Saliou Ciss●, Ruben Kristiansen - Thomas Bendiksen (Magnus Andersen 81), Kara Mbodj (Remi Johansen 67), Ruben Jenssen (c), Thomas Drage - Aleksandar Prijovic (Ole Martin Årst 54), Zdenek Ondrašek. Tr: Per-Mathias Høgmo

* Home team • ‡ Qualified for the Europa League

NZL – NEW ZEALAND

FIFA/COCA-COLA WORLD RANKING

'93	'94	'95	'96	'97	'98	'99	'00	'01	'02	'03	'04	'05	'06	'07	'08	'09	'10	'11	'12
77	99	102	132	120	103	100	91	84	49	88	95	120	131	95	86	82	63	119	91

2012

Jan	Feb	Mar	Apr	May	Jun	Jul	Aug	Sep	Oct	Nov	Dec	High	Low	Av
118	120	119	130	130	100	95	95	95	92	93	91	47	156	96

New Zealand failed in their attempt to become champions of Oceania for a record breaking fifth time after a surprise 2-1 defeat at the hands of New Caledonia in the semi-finals of the 2012 OFC Nations Cup in the Solomon Islands. It was the first time that the Kiwis had lost to their opponents but they more than made up for it with a convincing win three months later when the two met again in a 2014 FIFA World Cup qualifier. That was the first game in the final round of qualifying in Oceania and it set them on the path to wins in each of their next three games to finish the year with maximum points. The Kiwis will be aiming to finish top of the group and once again secure an inter-continental play-off against the fifth placed team in Asia for a berth in Brazil. In club football Auckland United won the OFC Champions League title in 2012 to qualify again for the FIFA Club World Cup. Once there, however, they were the first team to leave, beaten 1-0 in a preliminary round tie by hosts Sanfrecce Horoshima of Japan. At home they were beaten in the semi-finals of the championship play-offs by Team Wellington who in turn lost to Waitakere in the final. Fijian striker Roy Krishna was the star for Waitakere in the 4-1 victory in the final securing a hat trick of titles for the Neil Emblen coached team.

FIFA WORLD CUP RECORD
1930-1966 DNE 1970-1978 DNQ **1982** 23 r1 1986-2006 DNQ **2010** 22 r1

NEW ZEALAND FOOTBALL (NZF)

- North Harbour Stadium, Stadium Drive, PO Box 301, 043 Albany, Auckland
- +64 9 4140175
- +64 9 4140176
- tracy.brady@nzfootball.co.nz
- www.nzfootball.co.nz
- FA 1891 CON 1966 FIFA 1948
- P Frank Van Hattum
- GS Grant Mckavanagh

THE STADIA

2014 FIFA World Cup Stadia

North Harbour Stadium Auckland	25 000
AMI Stadium Christchurch	18 000

Other Main Stadia

Westpac Stadium Wellington	36 000
Forsyth Barr Stadium Dunedin	30 500
Waikato Stadium Hamilton	25 800

MAJOR CITIES/TOWNS

		Population
1	Auckland	415 400
2	Manukau	400 208
3	Christchurch	373 178
4	North Shore	295 695
5	Waitakere	202 786
6	Wellington	186 122
7	Hamilton	163 757
8	Tauranga	117 085
9	Dunedin	111 855
10	Lower Hutt	97 568
11	Palmerston North	77 177
12	Hastings	63 259
13	Napier	56 891
14	Rotorua	54 070
15	Whangarei	50 272
16	New Plymouth	49 619
17	Porirua	48 761
18	Invercargill	46 320
19	Nelson	43 571

NEW ZEALAND

Capital	Wellington	Population	4 213 418 (124)
GDP per capita	$27 900 (49)	Area km²	267 710 km² (75)
Neighbours (km)	Coast 15 134	% in cities	87%
		GMT +/-	+12

NZL – NEW ZEALAND

RECENT INTERNATIONAL MATCHES PLAYED BY NEW ZEALAND

2008	Opponents		Score	Venue	Comp	Scorers	Att	Referee
6-09	New Caledonia	W	3-1	Noumea	WCq	Sigmund [16], Smeltz 2 [66 76]	2 589	Varman FIJ
10-09	New Caledonia	W	3-0	Auckland	WCq	Smeltz 2 [49 76], Christie [69]	8 000	Hauata TAH
19-11	Fiji	L	0-2	Lautoka	WCq		4 500	Fred VAN
2009								
28-03	Thailand	L	1-3	Bangkok	Fr	Elliott [14]		
3-06	Tanzania	L	1-2	Dar es Salaam	Fr	Smeltz [10p]		
6-06	Botswana	D	0-0	Gaborone	Fr			
10-06	Italy	L	3-4	Atteridgeville	Fr	Smeltz [13], Killen 2 [42 57p]	2 000	Bennett RSA
14-06	Spain	L	0-5	Rustenburg	CCr1		21 649	Codjia BEN
17-06	South Africa	L	0-2	Rustenburg	CCr1		36 598	Archundia MEX
20-06	Iraq	D	0-0	Johannesburg	CCr1		23 295	Webb ENG
9-09	Jordan	W	3-1	Amman	Fr	Smeltz 2 [17p 65], Fallon [45]		
10-10	Bahrain	D	0-0	Manama	WCq		37 000	Kassai HUN
14-11	Bahrain	W	1-0	Wellington	WCq	Fallon [45]	36 500	Larrionda URU
2010								
3-03	Mexico	L	0-2	Pasadena	Fr		90 526	Marrufo USA
24-05	Australia	L	1-2	Melbourne	Fr	Killen [16]	55 659	Salazar USA
29-05	Serbia	W	1-0	Klagenfurt	Fr	Smeltz [22]	14 000	Drachta AUT
4-06	Slovenia	L	1-3	Maribor	Fr	Fallon [20]	10 965	Kakkos GRE
15-06	Slovakia	D	1-1	Rustenburg	WCr1	Reid [93+]	23 871	Damon RSA
20-06	Italy	D	1-1	Nelspruit	WCr1	Smeltz [7]	38 229	Batres GUA
24-06	Paraguay	D	0-0	Polokwane	WCr1		34 850	Nishimura JPN
9-10	Honduras	D	1-1	Auckland	Fr	Wood [45]	18 153	O'Leary NZL
12-10	Paraguay	L	0-2	Wellington	Fr		16 477	Cross NZL
2011								
25-03	China PR	D	1-1	Wuhan	Fr	McGlinchey [53]		Toma JPN
1-06	Mexico	L	0-3	Denver	Fr		45 401	Vaughn USA
5-06	Australia	L	0-3	Adelaide	Fr		21 281	Tojo JPN
2012								
29-02	Jamaica	L	2-3	Auckland	Fr	Wood [55], Killen [89]	15 379	Hauata TAH
23-05	El Salvador	D	2-2	Houston	Fr	Hogg [28], Barbarouses [64]	18 000	Vaughn USA
26-05	Honduras	W	1-0	Dallas	Fr	Smeltz [45]	30 000	Jurisevic USA
2-06	Fiji	W	1-0	Honiara	OCr1	Tommy Smith [11]	15 000	A-Ambassa NCL
4-06	Papua New Guinea	W	2-1	Honiara	OCr1	Smeltz [2], Wood [52]	3 000	George VAN
6-06	Solomon Islands	D	1-1	Honiara	OCr1	Wood [13]	18 000	Hauata TAH
8-06	New Caledonia	L	0-2	Honiara	OCsf		10 000	Hauata TAH
10-06	Solomon Islands	W	4-3	Honiara	OC3p	Wood 3 [10 24 29], Smeltz [90]	15 000	Zitouni TAH
7-09	New Caledonia	W	2-0	Noumea	WCq	Smeltz [11], Wood [39]	6 000	Hauata TAH
11-09	Solomon Islands	W	6-1	Auckland	WCq	Smeltz [12], Barbarouses [25], Killen [53], Lochhead [69], Wood [80], Rojas [83]	7 931	Billon NCL
12-10	Tahiti	W	2-0	Papeete	WCq	Smeltz [24], Sigmund [82]	600	George VAN
16-10	Tahiti	W	3-0	Christchurch	WCq	McGlinchey 2 [2 93+], Killen [89]	10 751	Oiaka SOL
14-11	China PR	D	1-1	Shanghai	Fr	Wood [44]	10 000	

Fr = Friendly match • OC = OFC Oceania Nations Cup • CC = FIFA Confederations Cup • WC = FIFA World Cup

NEW ZEALAND NATIONAL TEAM HISTORICAL RECORDS

Caps: **85** - Ivan Vicelich 1995- • **69** - Simon Elliott 1995- • **64** - Vaughn Coveny 1992-2007 • **61** - Ricki Herbert 1980-89 • **60** - Chris Jackson 1995-2003 • **59** - Brian Turner 1967-82

Goals: **28** - Vaughn Coveny 1992-2007 • **23** - Shane Smeltz 2003- • **22** - Steve Sumner 1976-88 • **21** - Brian Turner 1967-82 • **16** - Jock Newall 1951-52 & Keith Nelson 1977-83 • **15** - Grant Turner 1980-88 • **14** - Chris Killen 2000-

Coaches: Matthew Robinson AUS 1947-56 • Ken Armstrong ENG 1957-64 • Lou Brocic YUG 1965-66 • Juan Schwanner CHI 1967-68 • Lou Brocic YUG 1969 • Barrie Truman 1970-76 • Wally Hughes 1977-78 • John Adshead ENG 1979-82 • Allan Jones 1983-84 • Kevin Fallon 1985-88 • John Adshead ENG 1989 • Ian Marshall SCO 1990-93 • Bobby Clark SCO 1994-95 • Keith Pritchett SCO 1996-97 • Joe McGrath IRL 1997-98 • Ken Dugdale 1998-2002 • Mick Waitt ENG 2002-04 • Ricki Herbert 2005-

NEW ZEALAND 2011-12

NEW ZEALAND FOOTBALL CHAMPIONSHIP ASB PREMIERSHIP

	Pl	W	D	L	F	A	Pts	Auckland	Canterbury	Waitakere	Wellington	Hawkes Bay	Otago	Waikato	YoungHeart
Auckland City †	14	11	3	0	43	11	36		3-0	3-1	4-2	3-2	3-0	0-0	5-0
Canterbury United	14	9	2	3	38	12	29	1-1		2-1	1-0	7-0	3-0	5-0	9-1
Waitakere United †	14	9	0	5	44	17	27	1-3	1-2		3-1	3-0	5-0	4-0	6-1
Team Wellington	14	8	2	4	33	18	26	1-1	1-1	1-2		3-1	2-0	3-0	2-0
Hawkes Bay United	14	6	1	7	28	35	19	1-3	3-0	1-0	2-6		4-2	3-2	2-2
Otago United	14	3	2	9	15	37	11	1-3	1-0	0-6	1-2	2-0		0-2	2-2
Waikato	14	2	3	9	17	39	9	1-5	0-3	1-4	2-3	2-4	3-3		1-1
YoungHeart Manawatu	14	0	3	11	12	61	3	0-6	0-4	2-7	0-6	0-5	2-3	1-3	

22/10/2011 - 8/04/2012 • Top four qualified for the play-offs • † Qualified for OFC Champions League
Play-off Semi-finals: Waitakere United 0-1 5-2 **Canterbury United; Team Wellington** 1-0 3-1 **Auckland City**
Grand Final: Waitakere United 4-1 **Team Wellington. Waitakere United** are the 2012 NZFC champions
Top scorers: **12** - George **SLEFENDORFAS** PNG, Canterbury United • **9** - Aaron **CLAPHAM**, Canterbury United & Allan **PEARCE**, Waitakere United •
8 - Emiliano **TADE** ARG, Auckland City; Manel **EXPOSITO** ESP, Auckland City; Louis **FENTON**, Team Wellington & Russell **KAMO**, Canterbury United •
7 - Roy **KRISHNA** FIJ, Waitakere United & Ryan **DE VRIES** RSA, Waitakere United • **6** - Sam **MARGETTS**, Hawke's Bay & Hamish **WATSON**, Hawke's Bay

CHAMPIONSHIP FINAL 2012

Trusts Stadium, Auckland, 28-04-2012

Waitakere United 4 Krishna 2 [45 89], Pearce [77], Butler [84]
Team Wellington 1 Fa'arodo [85]

WAITAKERE
Danny ROBINSON - Aaron SCOTT, Tim MYERS, Matt CUNNEEN, Martin BULLOCK (Ross MCKENZIE 94+), Chris BALE•, Allan PEARCE, Roy KRISHNA, Jake BUTLER (c), Ryan DE VRIES (Rory TURNER 87), Sean LOVEMORE (Jordan VALE 91+). Tr: Neil EMBLEN

WELLINGTON
Phil IMRAY - Michael EAGAR, Johnny RAJ, Darren CHERITON, Wiremu PATRICK (Ethan GALBRAITH 56), Patrick FLEMING (Michael FIFII 81), Dakota LUCAS, Henry FA'ARODO, James MUSA•, Luke ROWE, Justin GULLEY (Dominic ROWE 86). Tr: Matt CALCOTT

MEDALS TABLE OVERALL (1923-)

		Ov'rall		Lge		Cup		OFC	
		G	S	G	S	G	S	G	S
1	Uni - Mt Wellington	13	13	6	7	7	5		
2	Christchurch United	12	5	6	2	6	3		
3	Napier City Rovers	8	5	4	3	4	2		
4	Waitakere City	8	3	5	1	3	2		
5	Auckland City	8	1	4	1			4	
6	North Shore United	7	9	2	3	5	6		
7	Central United	7	3	2	1	5	2		
8	Miramar Rangers	6	5	2	4	4	1		
9	Eastern Suburbs	6	4	1	1	5	3		
	Waitakere United	6	4	4	3			2	1
11	Waterside	4	1			4	1		
12	Western	3	5			3	5		
13	Western Suburbs	3	2			3	2		
14	Manurewa	3		1		2			
	Petone	3				3			
	Wellington United	3		3					
17	Northern	2	6			2	6		
18	Gisborne City	2	5	1	3	1	2		
19	Blockhouse Bay	2	2	1	1	1	1		
20	Marist	2	1			2	1		
21	Ponsonby	2				2			
	Seatoun	2				2			

MEDALS TABLE (NZFC CLUBS)

		Overall		Lge		OFC		City/Town
		G	S	G	S	G	S	
1	Auckland City	8	1	4	1	4		Auckland
2	Waitakere United	6	4	4	3	2	1	Waitakere
3	Canterbury United	2		2				Christchurch
4	Team Wellington	2		2				Wellington

CHATHAM CUP 2012

Round of 16		Quarter-finals		Semi-finals		Final	
Central United	3						
Three Kings United *	2	**Central United** *	2				
Melville United *	0	Eastern Suburbs	0				
Eastern Suburbs	1			**Central United**	6		
Dunedin Technical *	1			Miramar Rangers *	0		
Western	0	Dunedin Technical	1				
Stop Out	0	**Miramar Rangers** *	5				
Miramar Rangers *	4					**Central United**	6
Caversham *	4					Lower Hutt City	1
Cashmere Technical	2	**Caversham** *	3				
Papatoetoe	1 3p	Manukau City	1			CUP FINAL	
Manukau City *	1 4p			Caversham *	0	Newton Park, Wellington	
Birkenhead United *	4			**Lower Hutt City**	4	25-08-2012, Ref: Conger	
Hamilton Wanderers	1	Birkenhead United *	2			Scorers - Emiliano Tade [19], David	
Napier City Rovers	0	**Lower Hutt City**	3			Mulligan [23], Daniel Koprivcic 2 [45 71],	
Lower Hutt City *	2			* Home team		Ivan Vicelich [60], Jason Hicks [86] for Central; Hamish Price [92+] for LHC	

OMA – OMAN

FIFA/COCA-COLA WORLD RANKING

'93	'94	'95	'96	'97	'98	'99	'00	'01	'02	'03	'04	'05	'06	'07	'08	'09	'10	'11	'12
97	71	98	91	81	58	92	106	91	96	62	56	91	72	84	96	79	99	85	95

2012															
Jan	Feb	Mar	Apr	May	Jun	Jul	Aug	Sep	Oct	Nov	Dec	High	Low	Av
90	95	92	93	92	97	96	92	93	95	86	95	50	117	87

Oman's hopes of appearing at a first-ever FIFA World Cup finals remained intact at the end of 2012 thanks to their home form, with Paul Le Guen's side picking up points in Muscat against big hitters Australia and Iraq in the final phase of Asia's qualifying for the 2014 finals in Brazil. The Omanis, who saw off four-time qualifiers Saudi Arabia to reach the last round, had only made it so far on one previous occasion - in the 2002 World Cup. Japan were the only nation to beat them in the qualifiers during the course of 2012 with Le Guen's side losing both home and away to Alberto Zaccheroni's AFC Asian Cup holders. Oman also reached the semi-finals of the West Asian Championship at the end of the year, losing to Iraq in the last four before defeating Bahrain to take third place in the regional competition. In club football Fanja secured the league title by defeating Al Shabab on penalties in a championship play-off after both clubs finished level on 43 points at the end of the 22-game season. Victory secured Fanja a place in the 2013 AFC Cup alongside Dhofar, winners of the Sultan Qaboos Cup in December 2011, whose success came too late for them to be admitted into the 2012 edition of the competition. Traditionally played in the second half of the year, the 2012 Sultan Qaboos Cup was extended in order to finish in mid-2013.

FIFA WORLD CUP RECORD
1930-1986 DNE **1990-2010** DNQ

OMAN FOOTBALL ASSOCIATION (OFA)

Seeb Sports Complex,
PO Box 3462,
Ruwi 112
☎ +968 24 533004
+968 24 543023
info@ofa.om
www.ofa.om
FA 1978 CON 1979 FIFA 1980
P Khalid Hamad Al Busaidi
GS Hazza Al Saadi

THE STADIA

2014 FIFA World Cup Stadia

Sultan Qaboos Sports Complex	
Muscat	39 000
Seeb Stadium	
Seeb	12 000

Other Main Stadia

Regional Sports Complex	
Sohar	19 000
Sur Youth Complex	
Sur	15 000
Ibri Youth Complex	
Ibri	15 000

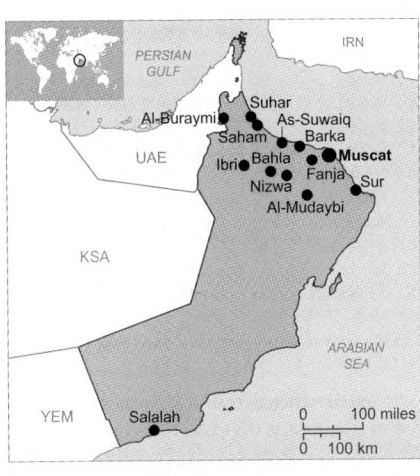

MAJOR CITIES/TOWNS

		Population
1	Muscat	1 152 254
2	Salalah	197 169
3	As-Suwaiq	133 894
4	Suhar	129 737
5	Ibri	122 960
6	Saham	109 763
7	Barka	106 378
8	Ar-Rustaq	101 132
9	Al-Buraymi	96 920
10	Sur	89 863
11	Nizwa	88 021

The Muscat metroplolitan area consists of:

Seeb	299 416
Matrah	229 266
Bawshar	199 505
Qurayyat	54 219
Al Amarat	47 411
Muscat	25 690

SALTANAT UMAN • SULTANATE OF OMAN

Capital Muscat	Population 3 418 085 (133)	% in cities 72%
GDP per capita $20 200 (61)	Area km² 309 500 km² (70)	GMT +/- +4
Neighbours (km) Saudi Arabia 676, UAE 410, Yemen 288 • Coast 2092		

RECENT INTERNATIONAL MATCHES PLAYED BY OMAN

2010	Opponents	Score	Venue	Comp	Scorers	Att	Referee
26-09	Bahrain	L 0-2	Amman	WAr1		500	
28-09	Iran	D 2-2	Amman	WAr1	Osma Hadid [40], Yacoob Abdul Karim [45]	3 000	
8-10	Gabon	W 1-0	Muscat	Fr	Hassan Rabia [9]		
12-10	Chile	L 0-1	Muscat	Fr		9 000	Blooshi KUW
17-11	Belarus	L 0-4	Muscat	Fr		1 000	Al Amri KSA
23-11	Bahrain	D 1-1	Aden	GCr1	Amad Ali [37]		Al Enezi KUW
26-11	UAE	D 0-0	Aden	GCr1			Shaaban EGY
29-11	Iraq	D 0-0	Abyan	GCr1			Younis EGY
2011							
29-03	Tunisia	W 2-1	Seeb	Fr	Ahmed Mubarak 2 [10p 85p]		
6-07	Kuwait	D 1-1	Beirut	Fr	Hassan Rabia [30]		
9-07	Lebanon	W 1-0	Beirut	Fr	Hamood Al Sadi [86]		
15-07	Syria	D 1-1	Seeb	Fr	Qasim Said [61]		
23-07	Myanmar	W 2-0	Seeb	WCq	Amad Ali [22], Ismail Al Ajmi [79]. Match awarded 3-0 to Oman	6 300	Sabbagh LIB
28-07	Myanmar	W 2-0	Yangon	WCq	Amad Ali [22], Ahmed Mubarak [39p]. Match abandoned and awarded to Oman	30 000	Sato JPN
10-08	Bahrain	D 1-1	Dubai	Fr	Ahmed Hadid [25]. Abandoned 65'. Result stood		
27-08	Kuwait	W 1-0	Muscat	Fr	Hussain Al Hadhri [64]		
2-09	Saudi Arabia	D 0-0	Seeb	WCq		14 000	Abdou QAT
6-09	Thailand	L 0-3	Bangkok	WCq		19 000	Kim Dong Jin KOR
11-10	Australia	L 0-3	Sydney	WCq		24 732	Kovalenko UZB
4-11	Qatar	D 0-0	Doha	Fr			
11-11	Australia	W 1-0	Muscat	WCq	Amad Ali [18]	4 500	Abdulnabi BHR
15-11	Saudi Arabia	D 0-0	Riyadh	WCq		62 740	Torky IRN
2012							
15-01	Congo DR	D 2-2	Seeb	Fr	Jaber Al Owaisi [7], Hassan Mudhafar [57]		
23-02	India	W 5-1	Seeb	Fr	Mohammed Al Ghassani [5], Ismail Al Ajmi 2 [7 58], Hassan Al Housni [87], Abdul Al Mukhaini [90]		
29-02	Thailand	W 2-0	Muscat	WCq	Hussain Al Hadhri [8], Abdulaziz Al Muqbali [92+]	22 000	Toma JPN
27-05	Lebanon	D 1-1	Muscat	Fr	Waleed Al Saadi [54]		Shaban KUW
3-06	Japan	L 0-3	Saitama	WCq		63 551	Irmatov UZB
8-06	Australia	D 0-0	Muscat	WCq		11 000	Faghani IRN
12-06	Iraq	D 1-1	Doha	WCq	Mohammed Al Balushi [8]	1 650	Abdou QAT
15-08	Egypt	D 1-1	Salalah	Fr	Abdulaziz Al Muqbali [91]		Abdulnabi BHR
11-09	Republic of Ireland	L 1-4	London	Fr	Eid Al Farsi [72]	6 420	Marriner ENG
28-09	Yemen	W 2-1	Muscat	Fr	Qasim Said [73], Abdullah Saleh [85]		
16-10	Jordan	W 2-1	Muscat	WCq	Ahmed Mubarak [62], Juma Al Maashari [87]	26 000	Shukralla BHR
8-11	Estonia	L 1-2	Muscat	Fr	Abdulaziz Al Muqbali [17]		Albadwawi UAE
14-11	Japan	L 1-2	Muscat	WCq	Ahmed Mubarak [77]	28 360	Balideh QAT
8-12	Lebanon	L 0-1	Al Farwaniyah	WAr1		2 000	Mohamed UAE
11-12	Kuwait	W 2-0	Kuwait City	WAr1	Qasim Hardan 2 [36 45]	1 400	Al Ghafari JOR
14-12	Palestine	W 2-1	Al Farwaniyah	WAr1	Mohamed Al Seyabi [5], Qasim Hardan [33]	500	Tojo JPN
18-12	Iraq	L 0-2	Al Farwaniyah	WAsf		500	Mohamed UAE
19-12	Benin	W 2-0	Sur	Fr	Juma Darwish [5], Younis Al Mashaifi [85p]		
20-12	Bahrain	W 1-0	Al Farwaniyah	WA3p	Qasim Hardan [68]	100	Al Dosari QAT
29-12	Togo	L 0-1	Sohar	Fr			

Fr = Friendly match • GC = Gulf Cup • WA = West Asian Championship • AC = AFC Asian Cup • WC = FIFA World Cup
q = qualifier • r1 = first round group • sf = semi-final • f = final

OMAN NATIONAL TEAM HISTORICAL RECORDS

Past Coaches: Mamadoh Al Khafaji EGY 1974-76 • George Smith ENG 1979 • Hamed El Dhiab TUN 1980-82 • Mansaf El Meliti TUN 1982 • Paulo Heiki BRA 1984 • Antonio Clemente BRA 1986 • Jorge Vitorio BRA 1986-88 • Karl-Heinz Heddergott GER 1988-89 • Bernd Patzke GER 1990-92 • Heshmat Mohajerani IRN 1992-94 • Rashid Jaber Al Yafi'i 1995-96 • Mahmoud El Gohary EGY 1996 • Jozef Venglos SVK 1996-97 • Ian Porterfield SCO 1997 • Valdeir Vieira BRA 1998-99 • Carlos Alberto Torres BRA 2000-01 • Milan Macala CZE 2001 • Bernd Stange GER 2001 • Rashid Jaber Al Yafi'i 2002 • Milan Macala CZE 2003-05 • Srecko Juricic CRO 2005-06 • Hamad Al Azani 2006 • Milan Macala CZE 2006-07 • Gabriel Calderon ARG 2007-08 • Julio Cesar Ribas URU 2008 • Hamad Al Azani 2008 • Claude Le Roy FRA 2008-11 • Paul Le Guen FRA 2011-

OMAN 2011-12
OFA OMAN MOBILE ELITE LEAGUE

	Pl	W	D	L	F	A	Pts	Fanja	Shabab	Urooba	Tali'aa	Dhofar	Oman Club	Suwaiq	Sur	Nahda	Hilal	Masnaah	Ahli
Fanja ‡	22	12	7	3	31	19	43		0-1	1-0	1-1	2-0	2-1	1-1	2-1	3-1	0-0	2-1	2-1
Al Shabab	22	13	4	5	28	19	43	2-2		0-2	2-2	0-2	1-0	2-1	0-1	2-0	1-0	0-1	0-2
Al Urooba	22	10	10	2	28	16	40	1-0	0-0		1-0	0-0	2-1	1-1	1-1	4-2	1-2	1-1	3-1
Al Tali'aa	22	9	5	8	23	22	32	0-1	0-2	0-0		2-0	0-0	1-0	1-0	1-0	1-0	2-1	2-1
Dhofar	22	8	7	7	19	18	31	0-0	1-1	0-0	3-0		0-2	1-2	0-2	0-1	1-1	2-1	1-0
Oman Club	22	9	3	10	24	25	30	1-0	0-2	0-1	2-1	0-1		1-0	1-2	3-2	1-1	1-0	1-0
Al Suwaiq	22	7	7	8	30	22	28	2-2	0-1	0-1	2-1	0-1	0-0		3-0	1-1	4-0	2-1	4-1
Sur	22	7	7	8	20	23	28	0-0	1-2	0-2	0-1	1-1	2-1	1-0		0-0	1-1	2-1	2-2
Al Nahda	22	8	3	11	27	33	27	1-2	1-2	1-2	3-2	0-1	2-1	1-0	1-0		1-1	4-3	1-1
Al Hilal Salalah	22	6	7	9	22	35	25	2-3	0-1	2-2	0-3	1-0	2-1	2-2	1-0	2-1		1-5	2-1
Al Masnaah	22	6	4	12	35	39	22	2-3	0-2	1-1	3-2	2-2	3-4	0-3	1-1	1-2	3-0		2-1
Al Ahli Sidab	22	3	4	15	24	40	13	0-2	3-4	2-2	0-0	0-2	1-2	2-2	1-2	2-1	2-1	1-2	

25/09/2011 - 19/05/2012 • ‡ Qualified for the AFC Cup • Relegation play-off: **Al Seeb** 1-1 3-2 Al Hilal Salalah • The league was extended to 14 teams for the 2012-13 season so Al Hilal Salalah and Al Masnaah remained in the Elite League

CHAMPIONSHIP PLAY-OFF
Sultan Qaboos, Muscat, 21-05-2012
Fanja 3-3 7-6p Al Shabab

Scorers - Mohammed Mubarak [42], Cisse Elie [105], Ameen al Majri [123+] for Fanja; Hassan Rabee'a [18], Younus Ojana 2 [92] [110] for Shabab

OMAN 2011-12 FIRST DIVISION (2)

	Pl	W	D	L	F	A	Pts
Saham	26	17	4	5	53	22	55
Al Nasr Salalah	26	14	8	4	42	15	50
Seeb	26	15	3	8	35	26	48
Al Ittihad	26	13	6	7	45	31	45
Al Salam	26	10	11	5	34	25	41
Muscat	26	11	6	9	40	37	39
Bashayer	26	11	4	11	42	34	37
Sohar	26	9	6	11	36	39	33
Majees	26	7	10	9	35	45	31
Khaboora	26	8	6	12	30	44	30
Al Mudhaibi	26	6	8	12	20	34	26
Mirbat	26	6	7	13	25	41	25
Yankel	26	5	6	15	32	54	21
Busher	26	6	3	17	26	48	21

5/10/2011 - 21/05/2012

MEDALS TABLE

		Overall G S B	Lge G	Cup G	Asia G S B	City
1	Dhofar	17	9	8		Salalah
2	Fanja	16	8	8		Fanja
3	Al Nasr	9	5	4		Salalah
4	Al Ahli	6	1	5		Sidab
	Al Urooba	6	3	3		Sur
6	Sur	5	2	3		Sur
7	Muscat	4	3	1		Muscat
8	Oman Club	3 1	1	2	1	Muscat
9	Seeb	3		3		Seeb
	Al Suwaiq	3	2	1		Al Suwaiq
11	Al Nahda	2 1	2		1	Al Buraimi
12	Al Tali'aa	1		1		Sur
	Saham	1		1		Saham

PAK – PAKISTAN

FIFA/COCA-COLA WORLD RANKING

'93	'94	'95	'96	'97	'98	'99	'00	'01	'02	'03	'04	'05	'06	'07	'08	'09	'10	'11	'12
142	158	160	173	153	168	179	190	181	178	168	177	158	164	163	165	156	171	179	189

2012												High	Low	Av
Jan	Feb	Mar	Apr	May	Jun	Jul	Aug	Sep	Oct	Nov	Dec			
179	181	181	182	181	181	178	176	177	177	180	189	141	192	169

Defending champions Khan Research Labs cruised to another Pakistan league title in 2012 as they continued to establish themselves as the pre-eminent club in the country. They finished a comfortable nine points ahead of Karachi Electric and lost just one game all season in the ninth edition of the Pakistan Premier Football League. It was their third title in four years and, just as they had done in 2011, KRL beat Karachi Electric in the final of the Challenge Cup to complete the league and cup double, although victory on this occasion was only secured in a penalty shootout. KRL entered the 2012 AFC President's Cup and hosted a first round group containing Taiwan Power Company and Mongolian champions Erchim from which they qualified for the final tournament in Tajikistan. There they were once again drawn with Taiwan Power Company along with Shabab Al Amari from Palestine. A 3-1 loss against the Taiwanese made life difficult for KRL and a 5-1 reversal against the Palestinians ended the club's involvement in the competition. KRL's participation in the AFC President's Cup was one of the few instances of international exposure for Pakistani football in 2012 as the national team from this cricket mad country was all but dormant, playing just once during the 12 months.

FIFA WORLD CUP RECORD
1930-1986 DNE **1990-2014** DNQ

PAKISTAN FOOTBALL FEDERATION (PFF)

PFF Football House,
Nashar Park, Ferozepur
Road, Lahore 54600
☎ +92 42 99230821
📠 +92 42 99230823
✉ mail@pff.com.pk
🌐 www.pff.com.pk
FA 1948 CON 1954 FIFA 1948
P Makhdoom Saleh Hayat
GS Ahmed Yar Khan Lodhi

THE STADIA

2014 FIFA World Cup Stadia
Punjab Stadium
Lahore — 10 000

Other Main Stadia
Jinnah Sport Stadium
Islamabad — 48 800
People's Football Stadium
Karachi — 40 000
Football Stadium
Hyderabad — 25 000
Benazir Sports Complex
Karachi — 15 000

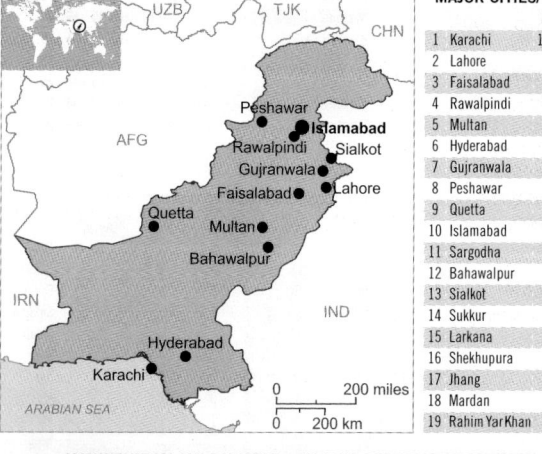

MAJOR CITIES/TOWNS

		Population
1	Karachi	12 827 927
2	Lahore	6 936 563
3	Faisalabad	2 793 721
4	Rawalpindi	1 933 933
5	Multan	1 566 932
6	Hyderabad	1 536 398
7	Gujranwala	1 526 168
8	Peshawar	1 390 874
9	Quetta	859 973
10	Islamabad	673 766
11	Sargodha	586 922
12	Bahawalpur	530 438
13	Sialkot	502 721
14	Sukkur	476 776
15	Larkana	435 817
16	Shekhupura	411 834
17	Jhang	365 198
18	Mardan	340 898
19	Rahim YarKhan	340 810

JAMHURYAT ISLAMI PAKISTAN • ISLAMIC REPUBLIC OF PAKISTAN

Capital	Islamabad	Population	176 242 949 (6)	% in cities	36%
GDP per capita	$2500 (173)	Area km²	796 095 km² (36)	GMT +/-	+5
Neighbours (km)	Afghanistan 2430, China 523, India 2912, Iran 909 • Coast 1046				

RECENT INTERNATIONAL MATCHES PLAYED BY PAKISTAN

2006	Opponents	Score	Venue	Comp	Scorers	Att	Referee
18-02	Palestine	L 0-3	Manama	Fr			
22-02	Jordan	L 0-3	Amman	ACq			Basma SYR
1-03	United Arab Emirates	L 1-4	Karachi	ACq	Muhammad Essa [60]	10 000	Tongkhan THA
2-04	Kyrgyzstan	W 1-0	Dhaka	CCr1	Muhammad Essa [59]	2 500	Shamsuzzaman BAN
4-04	Tajikistan	L 0-2	Dhaka	CCr1		5 000	Tan Hai CHN
6-04	Macau	D 2-2	Dhaka	CCr1	Adeel [12], Muhammad Essa [43]	1 000	Shamsuzzaman BAN
16-08	Oman	L 1-4	Quetta	ACq	Muhammad Essa [79p]	4 000	Torky IRN
6-09	Oman	L 0-5	Muscat	ACq		10 000	Nema IRQ
11-10	Jordan	L 0-3	Lahore	ACq		4 000	Orzuev TJK
15-11	UAE	L 2-3	Abu Dhabi	ACq	Naveed Akram [22], Tanveer Ahmed [67]	6 000	Sarkar IND
2007							
22-10	Iraq	L 0-7	Lahore	WCq		2 500	Chynybekov KGZ
28-10	Iraq	D 0-0	Damascus	WCq		8 000	Al Fadhli KUW
2008							
25-03	Nepal	L 1-2	Pokhara	Fr	Muhammad Essa [21]		
27-03	Nepal	W 2-0	Pokhara	Fr	Muhammad Qasim [46], Muhammad Rasool [90]		
2-04	Chinese Taipei	W 2-1	Taipei	CCq	Muhammad Essa [13], Michael Masih [34]	800	Iemoto JPN
4-04	Sri Lanka	L 1-7	Taipei	CCq	Adnan Farooq Ahmed [17]	300	Kovalenko UZB
6-04	Guam	W 9-2	Taipei	CCq	Jamshed Anwar 2 [9 18], Farooq Shah [28], Muhammad Qasim 3 [44 72 82], Ahmed Tanveer [62], Zahid Hameed [65p], Abdul Rehman [85]	200	Auda Lazim IRQ
3-06	Maldives	L 0-3	Male	SAFr1			
5-06	India	L 1-2	Male	SAFr1	Adnan Farooq Ahmed [88]		
7-06	Nepal	L 1-4	Male	SAFr1	Samar Ishaq [54]		
10-10	Malaysia	L 1-4	Kuala Lumpur	Fr	Arif Mehmood [86]		
2009							
4-04	Chinese Taipei	D 1-1	Colombo	CCq	Adnan Ahmed [53]	400	Tseytlin UZB
6-04	Brunei Darussalam	W 6-0	Colombo	CCq	Safiullah Khan 4 [19 61 68 78], Pathan Khan [31], Adnan Ahmed [84]	200	Orzuev TJK
8-04	Sri Lanka	D 2-2	Colombo	CCq	Safiullah Khan [82], Atif Bashir [84]	3 000	Tseytlin UZB
4-12	Sri Lanka	L 0-1	Dhaka	SAFr1			
6-12	Bangladesh	D 0-0	Dhaka	SAFr1			
8-12	Bhutan	W 7-0	Dhaka	SAFr1	Muhammad Essa 2 [21 54], Reis Ashraf [23], Arif Mehmood 3 [28 35 66], Shabir Khan [45]		
2010							
No international matches played in 2010							
2011							
21-03	Turkmenistan	L 0-3	Petaling Jaya	CCq		150	Bakhshizadeh IRN
23-03	India	L 1-3	Petaling Jaya	CCq	Arif Mehmood [32]	100	Alrshaidat JOR
25-03	Chinese Taipei	W 2-0	Petaling Jaya	CCq	Arif Mehmood [26], Atif Bashir [67]	50	Alrshaidat JOR
29-06	Bangladesh	L 0-3	Dhaka	WCq		5 326	Abu Loum JOR
3-07	Bangladesh	D 0-0	Lahore	WCq		3 500	Abdulnabi BHR
2-12	Bangladesh	D 0-0	New Delhi	SAFr1			Faizullin KGZ
4-12	Maldives	D 0-0	New Delhi	SAFr1			Robesh SRI
6-12	Nepal	D 1-1	New Delhi	SAFr1	Samar Ishaq [49p]		Noor Mohamed MAS
2012							
19-11	Singapore	L 0-4	Singapore	Fr			

Fr = Friendly match • SAF = South Asian Federation Cup • AC = AFC Asian Cup • CC = AFC Challenge Cup • WC = FIFA World Cup
q = qualifier • r1 = first round group • sf = semi-final • 3p = third place play-off

PAKISTAN NATIONAL TEAM HISTORICAL RECORDS

Coaches: Dave Burns ENG 2000-01 • John Layton 2001-02 • Joseph Herel SVK 2002-03 • Tariq Lutfi 2003-05 • Salman Sharida BHR 2005-07 • Akhtar Mohiuddin 2007-08 • Shahzad Anwar 2008 • George Kottan AUT 2009-10 • Tariq Lutfi 2011 • Zavisa Milosavljevic SRB 2011-

PAKISTAN 2012

NATIONAL FOOTBALL LEAGUE PREMIER LEAGUE

	Pl	W	D	L	F	A	Pts	KRL	KESC	Muslim SC	Army	PAF	NBP	Navy	PIA	Afghan	Baloch	WAPDA	KPT	HBL	ZTBL	PMC	Wohaib
Khan Research Labs †	30	21	8	1	65	15	71		2-2	4-1	0-0	2-1	1-0	2-1	1-1	4-0	4-0	1-0	3-1	4-0	1-1	3-0	5-1
Karachi Electric SC	30	18	8	4	60	27	62	0-3		3-0	2-1	1-0	1-1	1-0	1-1	2-0	5-0	1-0	0-1	2-0	4-0	5-1	5-0
Muslim SC	30	18	8	4	47	22	62	1-0	2-0		0-0	3-0	1-0	3-0	2-0	1-1	1-1	3-0	2-1	1-1	1-0	4-0	3-0
Pakistan Army	30	17	7	6	36	14	58	0-1	1-2	2-0		0-1	1-1	1-0	2-0	1-0	2-0	2-1	4-1	1-0	1-0	3-0	2-0
Pakistan Air Force	30	15	8	7	46	27	53	1-2	1-0	2-2	0-1		3-1	1-0	3-0	2-1	5-0	2-2	0-0	5-0	1-1	1-0	1-1	3-0
Nat. Bank of Pakistan	30	11	11	8	34	26	44	0-0	1-1	0-0	1-0	1-2		0-3	1-3	3-0	2-0	0-1	2-0	2-2	2-1	0-1	3-0	
Pakistan Navy	30	9	10	11	31	32	37	1-1	0-3	0-0	0-2	0-1	0-3		1-1	3-0	4-0	0-0	3-0	0-0	2-0	2-1	4-0	
Pakistan Int. Airlines	30	8	12	10	28	27	36	0-0	2-2	0-1	0-1	0-2	1-1	1-1		1-0	1-0	3-1	0-1	0-0	2-1	3-0	4-0	
Afghan FC	30	10	5	15	28	38	35	0-2	0-2	1-2	1-1	3-0	0-0	3-0	1-0		0-1	3-0	1-0	2-1	1-3	0-1	3-0	
Baloch Nushki	30	8	10	12	28	37	34	0-0	1-2	0-0	0-0	3-0	4-1	3-0	0-0	3-0		3-0	0-0	2-0	1-1	1-1	3-0	
WAPDA	30	7	11	12	36	44	32	1-4	3-4	1-3	0-0	0-2	1-1	1-1	1-1	1-1	3-0		1-1	1-2	4-1	1-0	3-1	
Karachi Port Trust	30	8	8	14	34	44	32	1-2	4-6	3-2	0-0	2-2	0-1	1-2	1-0	2-0	1-1	1-1			1-3	1-2	5-0	2-0
Habib Bank Ltd	30	7	11	12	28	38	32	1-2	1-0	0-0	0-1	2-0	0-1	1-1	1-3	0-2	1-3	1-1	2-2	1-1		1-0	0-0	6-0
Zaraj Taraqiati Bank Ltd	30	6	9	15	22	39	27	0-3	0-1	1-2	0-3	1-1	0-1	1-1	1-0	0-1	1-0	0-3	2-0	0-0		0-0	3-0	
PMC Club Faisalabad	30	4	13	13	19	45	25	0-4	1-1	0-1	1-1	0-0	1-2	0-1	1-1	1-1	0-0	1-1	3-0	0-1	1-1			2-2
Wohaib FC	30	1	5	24	8	75	8	0-4	1-1	1-4	0-2	0-3	0-2	1-1	0-0	0-1	1-0	0-2	0-2	0-1	0-0	0-1	

5/09/2012 - 15/01/2013 • † Qualified for the AFC Presidents Cup
Top scorer: **35** - Karim **ULLAH**, Khan Research Labs • **25** - Muhammad **RASOOL**, KESC • **16** - Ansar **ABBAS**, Army • **13** - **MUHAMMAD**, KPT

MEDALS TABLE

			All		Lge		Cup	
			G	S	G	S	G	S
1	Pakistan Int. Airlines	PIA	10	6	9	5	1	1
2	WAPDA		8	8	8	5		3
3	Punjab		8	1	8	1		
4	Khan Research Labs	KRL	7	5	3	2	4	3
5	Allied Bank Limited	ABL	7	3	3	2	4	1
6	Pakistan Army		6	8	4	7	2	1
7	Karachi		6	5	6	5		
8	Crescent Textile Mills		4		2		2	
9	Balochistan		3	1	3	1		
10	Pakistan Railways		2	9	2	9		
11	Habib Bank Limited	HBL	2	3	1	3	1	
12	Sindh		2	2	2	2		

NATIONAL FOOTBALL CHALLENGE CUP 2012

First Round Groups

Group A	Pl	W	D	L	F	A	Pts		Na	NY
WAPDA	2	2	0	0	6	0	6		3-0	3-0
Navy	2	1	0	1	2	3	3			2-0
Nat Youth B	2	0	0	2	0	5	0			
ASM			Withdrew							

Group B									KPT	PS	GPA
KESC	3	2	1	0	7	3	7		3-1	2-0	2-2
KPT	3	2	0	1	8	4	6			3-0	4-1
Pakistan Steel	3	1	0	2	4	5	3				4-0
GPA	3	0	1	2	3	10	1				

Group C									NY	NB	Po
KRL	3	2	1	0	7	3	7		2-1	2-2	3-0
Nat Youth A	3	1	1	1	3	3	4			0-0	2-1
NBP	3	0	3	0	3	3	3				1-1
Police	3	0	1	2	2	6	1				

Group D									PW	PAF	Ra
Army	3	2	1	0	6	1	7		4-0	1-1	1-0
PPWD	3	2	0	1	4	5	6			2-0	2-1
PAF	3	1	1	1	2	3	4				1-0
Railways	3	0	0	3	1	4	0				

Quarter-finals

KRL	3
KPT	0

Army	0 3p
Navy	0 4p

WAPDA	3
PPWD	2

Nat Youth A	1
KESC	3

Semi-finals

KRL	1
Navy	0

WAPDA	0
KESC	3

3rd place: **WAPDA** 2-2 4-1p Navy

Final

KRL	0 3p
KESC	0 1p

CUP FINAL

KPT Stadium, Karachi
24-03-2012

PAN – PANAMA

FIFA/COCA-COLA WORLD RANKING

'93	'94	'95	'96	'97	'98	'99	'00	'01	'02	'03	'04	'05	'06	'07	'08	'09	'10	'11	'12
132	140	126	101	119	131	138	121	109	129	125	100	78	81	67	88	70	64	49	51

2012													High	Low	Av
Jan	Feb	Mar	Apr	May	Jun	Jul	Aug	Sep	Oct	Nov	Dec				
47	49	50	52	52	46	48	54	50	43	46	51		43	150	100

Since the expansion of the FIFA World Cup finals to 32 teams CONCACAF has whittled its entrants down to a final group of six from which half are guaranteed a place in the finals. The Panamanians have made it to the hexagonal just once - in 2006 - when they finished bottom. In the 2014 FIFA World Cup qualifiers, Panama made it through once again and with a potential fourth place in Brazil at stake via a play-off with the winners from Oceania there was real hope at the end of 2012 that Julio Dely Valdez and his team could make history. To round off a successful year fans were treated to a visit from the world and European champions Spain in December, a match they lost 5-1 - the result showing the task that would lie ahead should the Panamanians make it to the finals in Brazil. Club football in Panama has yet to follow the lead of the national team in making its presence felt in the region and once again there was little progress in the CONCACAF Champions League with both Tauro and Chorillo finishing bottom of their groups and without a point in the 2012-13 tournament. At home, Tauro beat Chepo in the clausura final in June to increase their record haul of titles to nine whilst Arab Unido beat the unfortunate Chepo - a club set up in 1999 to develop young talent - in the apertura final at the end of the year.

CONCACAF GOLD CUP RECORD

1991 DNQ **1993** r1 1996 DNQ 1998 DNQ 2000 DNE 2002 DNQ 2003 DNQ **2005** F r/u **2007** QF **2009** QF **2011** SF

FEDERACION PANAMENA DE FUTBOL (FEPAFUT)

Urbanizacion Chanis,
Calle 153, Edif. Christine PB,
Apartado postal 0827-00391
Zona 8, Panama
☎ +507 2333896
📠 +507 2330582
✉ info@fepafut.com
🌐 www.fepafut.com
FA 1937 CON 1961 FIFA 1938
P Pedro Chaluja
GS Jorge Aued

THE STADIA
2014 FIFA World Cup Stadia
Estadio Rommel Fernandez
Panama City　32 000
Other Main Stadia
Estadio Agustin Muquita Sanchez
La Chorrera　8 000
Estadio Armando Dely Valdes
Colon　4 000
Estadio Municipal
Balboa　2 000

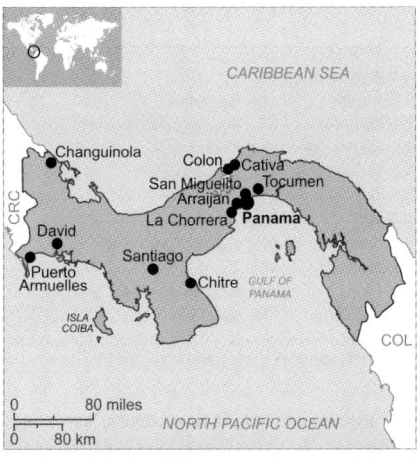

MAJOR CITIES/TOWNS

		Population
1	Panama	425 557
2	San Miguelito	366 201
3	Arraiján	102 355
4	Tocumen	100 800
5	Las Cumbres	93 590
6	David	93 351
7	Colón	87 838
8	La Chorrera	70 297
9	Pacora	63 218
10	Santiago	52 432
11	Chitré	50 122
12	Vista Alegre	47 570
13	Chilibre	38 179
14	Cativá	35 471
15	Nuevo Arraiján	26 861
16	Changuinola	25 496
17	Alcalde Díaz	22 390
18	La Cabima	22 081
19	Puerto Armuelles	20 648

REPUBLICA DE PANAMA • REPUBLIC OF PANAMA

Capital	Panama City	Population	3 360 474 (134)	% in cities	73%
GDP per capita	$11 800 (94)	Area km²	75 420 km² (117)	GMT +/-	-5
Neighbours (km)	Colombia 225, Costa Rica 330 • Coast 2490					

RECENT INTERNATIONAL MATCHES PLAYED BY PANAMA

2010	Opponents		Score	Venue	Comp	Scorers	Att	Referee
20-01	Chile	L	1-2	Coquimbo	Fr	Roberto Brown [87]	15 000	Vasquez URU
3-03	Venezuela	W	2-1	Barquisimeto	Fr	Roman Torres [9], Blas Perez [51]	37 000	Buitrago COL
11-08	Venezuela	W	3-1	Panama City	Fr	Luis Tejada [75], Blas Perez [88], Edwin Aguilar [90]	2 000	Quesada CRC
3-09	Costa Rica	D	2-2	Panama City	Fr	Luis Tejada 2 [27 38]	23 005	Delgadillo MEX
7-09	Trinidad and Tobago	W	3-0	Panama City	Fr	Edwin Aguilar [13], Luis Tejada [75], Gavilan Gomez [87]	6 645	Cruz CRC
8-10	El Salvador	W	1-0	Panama City	Fr	Blas Perez [61]	16 175	Ruiz COL
12-10	Peru	W	1-0	Panama City	Fr	Gabriel Torres [76]	8 528	Cerdas CRC
26-10	Cuba	L	0-3	Panama City	Fr		2 116	Moreno PAN
17-11	Honduras	W	2-0	Panama City	Fr	Luis Tejada [25], Aramis Haywood [52]	3 646	Cruz CRC
18-12	Honduras	L	1-2	San Pedro Sula	Fr	Edwin Aguilar [40]	3 000	Rodas GUA
2011								
14-01	Belize	W	2-0	Panama City	UCr1	Edwin Aguilar [21], Roberto Brown [28]	10 000	Pineda HON
16-01	Nicaragua	W	2-0	Panama City	UCr1	Armando Cooper [16], Luis Renteria [80]	7 747	Lopez GUA
18-01	El Salvador	W	2-0	Panama City	UCr1	Edwin Aguilar [24], Armando Cooper [78]	10 000	Garcia MEX
21-01	Costa Rica	D	1-1	Panama City	UCsf	Blas Perez [76]. L 2-4p	10 000	Aguilar SLV
23-01	El Salvador	D	0-0	Panama City	UC3p	W 5-4p	2 000	Pineda HON
8-02	Peru	L	0-1	Moquegua	Fr		8 000	Ubriaco URU
25-03	Bolivia	W	2-0	Panama City	Fr	Gabriel Gomez [19], Luis Renteria [83]	4 000	Lopez GUA
29-03	Cuba	W	2-0	Havana	Fr	Luis Renteria [37], Alberto Quintero [80]	6 000	Espana GUA
29-05	Grenada	W	2-0	Panama City	Fr	Gabriel Gomez [2], Alberto Quintero [46]	5 000	Perea PAN
7-06	Guadeloupe †	W	3-2	Detroit	GCr1	Blas Perez [29], Luis Tejada [31], Gabriel Gomez [57p]	28 209	Mejia SLV
11-06	USA	W	2-1	Tampa	GCr1	OG [19], Gabriel Gomez [36]	27 731	Rodriguez.M MEX
14-06	Canada	D	1-1	Kansas City	GCr1	Luis Tejada [91+]	20 109	Lopez GUA
19-06	El Salvador	D	1-1	Washington DC	GCqf	Luis Tejada [90]. W 5-3p	45 424	Quesada CRC
22-06	USA	L	0-1	Houston	GCsf		70 627	Wijngaarde SUR
10-08	Bolivia	W	3-1	Santa Cruz	Fr	Luis Tejada 2 [67 76p], Armando Cooper [90]	10 000	Carrillo PER
2-09	Paraguay	L	0-2	Panama City	Fr		11 000	Pineda HON
6-09	Nicaragua	W	2-1	Managua	WCq	Luis Tejada [7], Blas Perez [50]	10 521	Reyna GUA
7-10	Dominica	W	5-0	Roseau	WCq	Amir Waithe 2 [26 89], Luis Tejada [34], Blas Perez [57], Ricardo Buitrago [62]	4 000	Wijngaarde SUR
11-10	Nicaragua	W	5-1	Panama City	WCq	Luis Tejada 2 [27 64], Blas Perez 3 [48 51 87]	10 846	Ventura SLV
11-11	Costa Rica	W	2-0	Panama City	Fr	Gabriel Gomez [26p], Blas Perez [28]	5 000	Garcia MEX
15-11	Dominica	W	3-0	Panama City	WCq	Rolando Blackburn [6], Ricardo Buitrago [20], Blas Perez [84]	8 000	Vaughn USA
2012								
25-01	USA	L	0-1	Panama City	Fr		15 000	Chacon MEX
29-02	Paraguay	L	0-1	Asuncion	Fr		10 000	Polic CHI
27-05	Jamaica	W	1-0	Kingston	Fr	Luis Renteria [18]	13 000	Morales MEX
1-06	Jamaica	W	2-1	Panama City	Fr	Blaz Perez [34], Luis Renteria [76]	8 642	Cerdas CRC
8-06	Honduras	W	2-0	San Pedro Sula	WCq	Blas Perez 2 [65 80]	28 215	Garcia MEX
12-06	Cuba	W	1-0	Panama City	WCq	Nelson Barahona [57]	21 000	Geiger USA
15-08	Portugal	L	0-2	Faro	Fr		24 181	Fernandez ESP
7-09	Canada	L	0-1	Toronto	WCq		17 586	Solis CRC
11-09	Canada	W	2-0	Panama City	WCq	Rolando Blackburn [22], Blas Perez [57]	20 000	Bonilla SLV
12-10	Honduras	D	0-0	Panama City	WCq		27 000	Aguilar SLV
16-10	Cuba	D	1-1	Havana	WCq	Nelson Barahona [77]	3 500	Lancaster GUY
14-11	Spain	L	1-5	Panama City	Fr	Gabriel Gomez [87p]	26 000	Morales MEX

Fr = Friendly match • UC = UNCAF Cup/Copa Centroamericana • GC = CONCACAF Gold Cup • WC = FIFA World Cup • † Not a full international
q = qualifier • r1 = first round group • qf = quarter-final • sf = semi-final • 3p = third place play-off • f = final

PANAMA NATIONAL TEAM HISTORICAL RECORDS

Coaches: Romeo Parravicini URU 1938 • Rogelio Diaz 1952 • Renato Panay CHI 1976 • Omar Muraco ARG 1978 • Edgardo Bone Baldi URU 1979 • Luis Borghini URU 1980 • Ruben Cardenas 1980 • Orlando Munoz 1984 • Carlos Cavagnaro ARG 1984 • Juan Colecchio ARG 1986-88 • Gustavo de Simone URU 1992 • Orlando Munoz 1996 • Cesar Maturana COL 1996 • Oscar Aristizabel COL 1999 • Miguel Mansilla URU 2000 • Leopoldo Lee 2000 • Ezequiel Fernandez 2000 • Mihai Stoichita ROU 2001 • Carlos Alberto Daluz BRA 2002-03 • Jose Eugenio Hernandez COL 2004-05 • Julio Dely Valdes & Jorge Dely Valdes 2006 • Victor Rene Mendieta 2006 • Alexandre Guimaraes CRC 2006-08 • Gary Stempel ENG 2008-09 • Julio Dely Valdes 2010-

PANAMA 2011-12

LIGA PROFESIONAL DE FUTBOL CLAUSURA

	Pl	W	D	L	F	A	Pts	San Miguelito	Arabe Unido	Chepo	Tauro	Chorrillo	San Francisco	Chiriquí	Alianza	Colón C-3	Plaza Amador
SportingSan Miguelito†	18	9	6	3	23	15	33		1-0	0-0	1-0	3-1	3-1	1-1	1-3	1-2	1-0
Arabe Unido †	18	9	5	4	21	13	32	0-0		2-1	1-0	1-0	2-1	1-1	3-1	1-0	1-1
Chepo †	18	8	7	3	24	13	31	2-2	2-1		2-1	1-1	1-0	2-0	5-0	2-1	2-0
Tauro †	18	6	8	4	20	16	26	0-0	1-0	0-0		1-1	0-2	1-1	1-1	2-0	1-1
Municipal Chorrillo	18	5	10	3	23	20	25	1-1	1-1	0-0	1-1		3-1	0-2	3-1	3-1	2-1
San Francisco	18	5	7	6	17	18	22	0-1	1-0	1-0	1-1	1-1		1-1	1-0	1-1	3-1
Atlético Chiriquí	18	4	8	6	14	17	20	0-1	0-2	1-0	0-1	1-2	0-0		0-2	0-0	0-0
Alianza	18	5	5	8	21	28	20	1-3	0-2	1-2	4-2	1-1	1-1	1-1		2-0	1-0
Colón C-3	18	3	6	9	14	25	15	1-0	1-1	1-1	0-3	2-2	0-1	0-1	1-1		2-1
Plaza Amador	18	2	6	10	16	28	12	2-3	1-2	1-1	1-3	0-0	1-1	2-4	1-0	2-1	

21/01/2012 - 22/05/2012 • † Qualified for the play-offs
Play-off final details: Rommel Fernández, Panama City, 22-05-2011, Att: 8000, Ref: Roberto Moreno. Scorers - Leonel Parris [20], Luis Rentería [79] for Tauro; Cristian Bangueras [86] for Chepo
Colón C-3 relegated • Top scorers: **14** - Luis **RENTERIA**, Tauro • **8** - Miguel **LASSO**, Colón • **7** - Jose Luis **GONZALEZ**, Chepo & Cesar **MEDINA**, Alianza

CLAUSURA 2011-12 PLAY-OFFS

Semi-finals

			Finals	
Tauro	1	1		
Sp. San Miguelito	0	0	**Tauro** †	2
Arabe Unido	0	0	Chepo	1
Chepo	1	0		

† Qualified for the CONCACAF Champions League • * Home team in first leg • **Tauro** are the Clausura champions

APERTURA 2012-13 PLAY-OFFS

Semi-finals

			Finals	
Arabe Unido	3	2		
Plaza Amador	1	0	**Arabe Unido** †	4
Rio Abajo	0	1	Chepo	1
Chepo	2	1		

† Qualified for the CONCACAF Champions League • * Home team in first leg • **Arabe Unido** are the Apertura champions

MEDALS TABLE

		Overall		Lge		City/Town
		G	S	G	S	
1	Tauro FC	9	8	9	8	Panama City
2	San Francisco FC	7	6	7	6	La Chorrera
3	Deportivo Arabe Unido	7	3	7	3	Colon
4	CD Plaza Amador	5	3	5	3	Panama City
5	Chorrillo FC	1	2	1	2	Panama City
	AFC Euro Kickers	1	2	1	2	Panama City
7	Panama Viejo FC	1		1		Panama City
8	Chepo		2		2	
9	Sporting Colon		1		1	Colon
	Projusa		1		1	

PANAMA 2012-13

LIGA PROFESIONAL DE FUTBOL APERTURA

	Pl	W	D	L	F	A	Pts	Rio Abajo	Arabe Unido	Plaza Amador	Chepo	Chorrillo	Tauro	San Miguelito	San Francisco	Alianza	Chiriquí
Rio Abajo †	18	9	5	4	28	20	32		1-2	0-1	1-0	0-0	0-0	1-1	2-1	2-0	3-0
Arabe Unido †	18	8	8	2	25	20	32	2-5		2-2	1-1	0-0	3-2	1-0	2-0	0-1	1-1
Plaza Amador †	18	8	2	8	22	23	26	0-1	2-2		0-1	2-2	3-2	1-1	1-0	1-0	1-1
Chepo †	18	5	10	3	22	18	25	3-3	2-2	5-1		1-1	2-2	2-1	0-0	0-1	1-0
Municipal Chorrillo	18	5	10	3	22	19	25	0-1	1-1	1-1	1-1		0-3	0-0	4-1	3-1	2-1
Tauro	18	5	6	7	25	27	21	3-4	1-0	2-2	2-0	0-0		1-2	1-4	1-0	1-0
Sporting San Miguelito	18	4	8	6	14	17	20	1-0	0-1	1-0	1-1	0-1	2-2		0-1	1-3	0-0
San Francisco	18	4	6	8	20	22	18	4-0	0-1	1-2	0-0	2-2	2-0	1-2		1-3	0-0
Alianza	18	4	6	8	21	24	18	1-1	1-1	0-1	1-2	2-3	2-2	0-0	1-1		2-2
Atlético Chiriquí	18	2	9	7	14	23	15	1-3	1-2	1-1	0-0	2-1	1-0	1-1	1-1	1-3	

21/07/2012 - 2/12/2012 • † Qualified for the play-offs
Play-off final details: Rommel Fernández, Panama City, 2-12-2012. Scorers - Orlando Rodriguez 2 [24,25], Abdiel Arroyo [42], Jose Gonzalez [60] for Arabe Unido; Ricardo Romero [29] for Chepo
Top scorers: **10** - Jorman **AGUILAR**, Rio Abajo & Edwin **AGUILAR**, Tauro • **8** - Antony **BASILE**, Rio Abajo & Bernardo **PALMA**, Chepo

PAR – PARAGUAY

FIFA/COCA-COLA WORLD RANKING

'93	'94	'95	'96	'97	'98	'99	'00	'01	'02	'03	'04	'05	'06	'07	'08	'09	'10	'11	'12
61	87	64	38	29	25	17	10	13	18	22	30	30	35	21	17	29	24	24	37

2012

Jan	Feb	Mar	Apr	May	Jun	Jul	Aug	Sep	Oct	Nov	Dec	High	Low	Av
27	27	25	25	25	22	25	27	29	38	35	37	8	103	30

Although Paraguay won six and drew one of the 11 games they played in 2012, their four defeats all came in FIFA World Cup qualifiers which left a place at the finals in neighbouring Brazil in doubt. At the halfway stage of South America's nine-team group, the Paraguayans were in last place and left hoping that better results in the second half of the campaign would see them through to a fifth consecutive finals. After losing to Bolivia at altitude in La Paz, coach Francisco Arce was replaced by the Uruguayan Gerardo Pelusso who had just taken Olimpia to their first title in a decade. His first three matches in charge saw three defeats before a crucial 1-0 victory over Peru in October at least kept the team within touching distance of a qualifying spot. At home, Pelusso had taken Olimpia to within striking distance of consecutive championships when they lead Cerro Porteño by a point going into the final day clash between the two. However, in a bad tempered game which saw three players sent off, including two from Olimpia, Cerro, coached by the Uruguayan Jorge Fossati, won 2-1. Another Uruguayan coach, Ruben Israel, then led Libertad to the clausura title at the end of the year after a tight contest with long-time leaders Guarani.

FIFA WORLD CUP RECORD

1930 9 r1 **1934-1938** DNE **1950** 11 r1 **1954** DNQ **1958** 12 r1 **1962-1982** DNQ **1986** 13 r2
1990-1994 DNQ **1998** 14 r2 **2002** 16 r2 **2006** 18 r1 **2010** 8 QF

ASOCIACION PARAGUAYA DE FUTBOL (APF)

Estadio de los Defensores
del Chaco, Calle Mayor
Martinez 1393, Asuncion
☎ +595 21 480120
📠 +595 21 480124
✉ secretaria_general@apf.org.py
🖥 www.apf.org.py
FA 1906 CON 1921 FIFA 1925
P Juan Angel Napout
GS Wigberto Duarte

THE STADIA

2014 FIFA World Cup Stadia
Defensores del Chaco
Asuncion 36 000

Other Main Stadia
General Pablo Rojas
Asuncion 32 910
Estadio Antonio Oddone Sarubbi
Ciudad del Este 28 000
Estadio Feliciano Cáceres
Luque 25 000
Estadio Manuel Ferreira
Asuncion 20 000

MAJOR CITIES/TOWNS

		Population
1	Asunción	539 795
2	Ciudad del Este	338 885
3	Luque	293 267
4	Capiatá	291 591
5	San Lorenzo	283 280
6	Limpio	150 879
7	Ñemby	146 409
8	Lambaré	143 479
9	Fernando de la Mora	136 121
10	Itauguá	106 406
11	San Antonio	103 593
12	Mariano Roque Alonso	88 618
13	Villa Elisa	88 459
14	Encarnación	87 581
15	Pedro Juan Caballero	76 816
16	Hernandariaz	73 115
17	Presidente Franco	68 493
18	Caaguazú	65 263
19	Coronel Oviedo	59 757

REPUBLICA DEL PARAGUAY • REPUBLIC OF PARAGUAY

Capital	Asunción	Population	6 995 655 (101)	% in cities	60%
GDP per capita	$4200 (153)	Area km²	406 752 km² (59)	GMT +/-	-4
Neighbours (km)	Argentina 1880, Bolivia 750, Brazil 1365				

RECENT INTERNATIONAL MATCHES PLAYED BY PARAGUAY

2010	Opponents		Score	Venue	Comp	Scorers	Att	Referee
14-06	Italy	D	1-1	Cape Town	WCr1	Antolin Alcaraz [39]	62 869	Archundia MEX
20-06	Slovakia	W	2-0	Bloemfontein	WCr1	Enrique Vera [27], Cristian Riveros [86]	26 643	Maillet SEY
24-06	New Zealand	D	0-0	Polokwane	WCr1		34 850	Nishimura JPN
29-06	Japan	D	0-0	Pretoria	WCr2	W 5-3p	36 742	De Bleeckere BEL
3-07	Spain	L	0-1	Johannesburg	WCqf		55 359	Batres GUA
11-08	Costa Rica	W	2-0	Asuncion	Fr	Vera [8], Riveros [73]	22 000	Beligoy ARG
4-09	Japan	L	0-1	Yokohama	Fr		65 157	Rodriguez MEX
7-09	China PR	D	1-1	Nanjing	Fr	Barrios [8]	30 000	Wang Di CHN
9-10	Australia	L	0-1	Sydney	Fr		25 210	Nishimura JPN
12-10	New Zealand	W	2-0	Wellington	Fr	Valdez [22p], Martinez [28]	16 477	Cross NZL
17-11	Hong Kong	W	7-0	Hong Kong	Fr	Roque Santa Cruz 2 [4 32], Edgar Barreto [30], Jose Ortigoza 2 [46 54], Marcos Riveros [75], Cristian Riveros [90]	6 250	Mohd Salleh MAS
2011								
26-03	Mexico	L	1-3	Oakland	Fr	Cristian Riveros [87]	48 110	Ward CAN
29-03	USA	W	1-0	Nashville	Fr	Oscar Cardozo [18]	29 059	Benigno HON
25-05	Argentina	L	2-4	Resistencia	Fr	Pablo Zeballos [14], Elvis Marecos [55]	24 000	Silvera URU
4-06	Bolivia	W	2-0	Santa Cruz	Fr	Lucas Barrios [34], Federico Santander [73]	27 000	Garay PER
7-06	Bolivia	D	0-0	Ciudad del Este	Fr		15 000	Lopes BRA
11-06	Romania	W	2-0	Asuncion	Fr	Nelson Valdez [2], Roque Santa Cruz [29]	8 000	Larrionda URU
23-06	Chile	D	0-0	Asuncion	Fr		12 000	Oliveira BRA
3-07	Ecuador	D	0-0	Santa Fe	CAr1		20 000	Pezzotta ARG
9-07	Brazil	D	2-2	Cordoba	CAr1	Roque Santa Cruz [54], Nelson Valdez [66]	57 000	Roldan COL
13-07	Venezuela	D	3-3	Salta	CAr1	Antolin Alcaraz [32], Lucas Barrios [62], C. Riveros [85]	18 000	Osses CHI
17-07	Brazil	D	0-0	La Plata	CAqf	W 2-0p	36 000	Pezzotta ARG
20-07	Venezuela	D	0-0	Mendoza	CAsf	W 5-3p	8 000	Chacon MEX
24-07	Uruguay	L	0-3	Buenos Aires	CAf		57 921	Fagundes BRA
2-09	Panama	W	2-0	Panama City	Fr	Oscar Cardoza [7], Robin Ramirez [10]	11 000	Pineda HON
6-09	Honduras	W	3-0	San Pedro Sula	Fr	Nestor Camacho [30], Oscar Cardozo 2 [86 90]	20 000	Aguilar SLV
7-10	Peru	L	0-2	Lima	WCq		39 600	Pezzotta ARG
11-10	Uruguay	D	1-1	Asuncion	WCq	Richard Ortiz [92+]	12 922	Seneme BRA
11-11	Ecuador	W	2-1	Asuncion	WCq	Cristian Riveros [47], Dario Veron [57]	11 173	Buitrago COL
15-11	Chile	L	0-2	Santiago	WCq		44 726	Lopes BRA
21-12	Chile	L	2-3	La Serena	Fr	Edgar Benitez [51p], Julio Manzur [56]	12 000	Orozco BOL
2012								
15-02	Chile	W	2-0	Luque	Fr	Edgar Benitez [45], Jose Ortigoza [70]	5 606	Vuaden BRA
22-02	Guatemala	W	2-1	Asuncion	Fr	Edgar Benitez [33], Ariel Bogado [70p]	5 138	Lostau ARG
29-02	Panama	W	1-0	Asuncion	Fr	Jonathan Santana [88]	10 000	Polic CHI
25-04	Guatemala	W	1-0	Guatemala City	Fr	Ricardo Mazacotte [6]	10 000	Mejia SLV
9-06	Bolivia	L	1-3	La Paz	WCq	Cristian Riveros [81]	17 320	Silvera URU
15-08	Guatemala	D	3-3	Washington DC	Fr	Oscar Cardozo [1], Jonathan Fabbro [63], Hernan Perez [64]	14 185	Toledo USA
7-09	Argentina	L	1-3	Cordoba	WCq	Jonathan Fabbro [17]	51 000	Seneme BRA
11-09	Venezuela	L	0-2	Asuncion	WCq		13 680	Osses CHI
12-10	Colombia	L	0-2	Barranquilla	WCq		45 000	Pezzotta ARG
16-10	Peru	W	1-0	Asuncion	WCq	Pablo Aguilar [52]	10 114	Lunati ARG
14-11	Guatemala	W	3-1	Luque	Fr	Luis Caballero [3f], Pablo Aguilar 2 [58 90]	10 000	Cortez BRA

Fr = Friendly match • CA = Copa America • WC = FIFA World Cup • q = qualifier • r1 = 1st round • qf = quarter-final

PARAGUAY NATIONAL TEAM HISTORICAL RECORDS

Caps
110 - Carlos Gamarra 1993-2006 • 108 - Paulo Da Silva 2000- • 100 - Denis Caniza 1996-2010 • 98 - Roberto Acuna 1993-2011 • 95 - Justo Villar 1999- • 92 - Roque Santa Cruz 1999- • 85 - Celso Ayala 1993-2003 • 83 - Cristian Riveros 2005- • 82 - Jose Cardozo 1991-2006 • 78 - Roberto Fernandez 1976-89 & Carlos Bonet 2002- • 77 - Juan Torales 1979-89 • 74 - Jose Luis Chilavert 1989-2003; Carlos Paredes 1998-2008 & Estanislao Struway 1991-2002 • 70 - Julio Cesar Enciso 1995-2004

Goals
25 - Jose Cardozo 1991-2006 & Roque Santa Cruz 1999- • 15 - Cristian Riveros 2005- • 13 - Saturnino Arrua 1969-80 & Julio Cesar Romero 1979-86 • 12 - Carlos Gamarra 1993-2006; Gerardo Rivas 1921-26 & Nelson Valdez 2004- • 11 - Miguel Angel Benitez 1996-99

Coaches
For coaches pre 1993 see Oliver's Almanack 2012 • Alicio Solalinde 1993-94 • Laszlo Kubala ESP 1995 • Paulo Cesar Carpegiani BRA 1996-98 • Ever Almeida 1998-99 • Sergio Markarian URU 1999-2001 • Cesare Maldini ITA 2001-02 • Anibal Ruiz URU 2002-06 • Raul Amarilla 2006-07 • Gerardo Martino ARG 2007-11 • Francisco Arce 2011-12 • Gerardo Pelusso URU 2012-

PARAGUAY 2012
DIVISION PROFESIONAL APERTURA

	Pl	W	D	L	F	A	Pts	Cerro Porteño	Olimpia	Libertad	Sol	Nacional	Guaraní	C. Porteño PF	Sp. Luqueño	Independiente	Carapegua	Rubio Nu	Tacuary
Cerro Porteño †	22	16	1	5	40	23	49		0-1	1-0	2-0	2-1	1-0	1-0	3-0	1-2	5-3	1-0	2-0
Olimpia	22	14	5	3	30	20	47	1-2		2-1	1-0	2-1	2-0	3-3	2-1	1-1	1-0	3-2	2-1
Libertad	22	13	5	4	40	19	44	2-1	0-1		0-1	1-0	2-2	2-0	1-0	1-1	1-0	1-1	2-1
Sol de América	22	11	2	9	38	27	35	2-2	0-1	0-3		3-2	0-1	4-1	2-3	1-2	2-0	1-0	2-0
Nacional	22	10	3	9	40	32	33	2-0	0-0	1-2	2-1		1-1	2-1	2-1	5-0	0-2	3-1	2-0
Guaraní	22	8	6	8	28	25	30	0-1	0-1	2-3	2-1	1-3		0-0	3-1	3-1	1-0	2-1	4-0
Cerro Porteño PF	22	7	6	9	26	29	27	1-2	0-0	0-2	1-1	5-0	2-1		0-1	1-1	3-1	1-0	2-1
Sportivo Luqueño	22	6	8	8	23	30	26	2-0	2-1	0-4	0-2	2-1	2-2	3-0		1-3	1-1	1-1	1-1
Independiente	22	6	7	9	28	42	25	1-4	3-0	1-4	2-4	2-5	0-1	1-1	1-1		1-0	1-1	2-1
Deportivo Carapegua	22	4	8	10	23	29	20	1-2	1-2	2-2	0-2	2-1	0-0	1-2	0-0	3-0		2-1	1-1
Rubio Nu	22	5	3	14	24	40	18	2-3	2-3	1-5	0-3	3-3	2-1	1-2	0-0	2-1			1-0
Tacuary	22	1	8	13	15	39	11	2-4	0-0	1-1	2-6	0-3	1-1	1-0	0-0	1-1	0-1	1-1	

5/02/2012 - 8/07/2012 • † Qualified for the Copa Libertadores
Top scorers: **13** - Jose Maria **ORTIGOZA**, Sol • **8** - Eduardo **ECHEVERRIA**, Carapeguá; Rogerio **LEICHTWEIS**, Cerro & Enzo **PRONO**, Sol • **7** - Jorge **AYALA**, Carapeguá; Ariel **BOGADO**, Nacional; Luis **CABALLERO**, Olimpia; Guido **DI VIANNI** ARG, Luqueño & Santiago **SALCEDO**, Cerro

PARAGUAY 2012 DIVISION INTERMEDIA (2)

	Pl	W	D	L	F	A	Pts
General Díaz	30	18	6	6	48	22	60
Deportivo Capiatá	30	17	7	6	61	37	58
Deportivo Santaní	30	15	9	6	46	27	54
Sportivo San Lorenzo	30	14	6	10	40	35	48
Sportivo Trinidense	30	13	7	10	34	33	46
Sport Colombia	30	12	8	10	48	33	44
3 de Febrero	30	12	6	12	48	41	42
General Caballero	30	12	6	12	31	33	42
River Plate	30	11	8	11	38	45	41
2 de Mayo	30	11	7	12	36	37	40
Resistencia	30	10	10	10	43	45	40
Fernando de la Mora	30	10	6	14	31	40	36
Paranaense	30	8	10	12	31	39	34
Atlético Colegiales	30	7	12	11	22	29	33
Sportivo Iteño	30	4	11	15	35	60	23
29 de Setiembre	30	4	5	21	28	64	17

16/03/2012 - 14/10/2012

MEDALS TABLE

		Overall			Lge		Sth Am			City
		G	S	B	G	S	G	S	B	
1	Olimpia	43	25	8	39	21	4	4	8	Asunción
2	Cerro Porteño	29	28	7	29	28			7	Asunción
3	Libertad	16	20	2	16	20			2	Asunción
4	Guaraní	10	12	1	10	12			1	Asunción
5	Nacional	8	10		8	10				Asunción
6	Sol de América	2	12		2	12				Vila Elisa
7	Sportivo Luqueño	2	4		2	4				Luque
8	Presidente Hayes	1			1					Tacumbu
9	Atlántida		3			3				Asunción
	River Plate		3			3				Asunción
11	12 de Octubre		1			1				Itaugua
12	Atlético Colegiales		1						1	Asunción

PARAGUAY 2011
DIVISION PROFESIONAL CLAUSURA

	Pl	W	D	L	F	A	Pts	Libertad	Nacional	Guaraní	Cerro Porteño	Sp. Luqueño	Olimpia	C. Porteño PF	Carapegua	Sol	Tacuary	Rubio Nu	Independiente
Libertad † ‡	22	13	8	1	44	16	47		1-0	0-0	1-0	2-0	1-1	3-0	2-1	1-1	2-2	3-0	3-0
Nacional ‡	22	14	2	6	36	16	44	1-2		1-2	0-1	0-0	4-1	3-0	2-0	1-0	2-0	2-0	5-1
Guaraní ‡	22	13	4	5	28	19	43	0-2	0-1		2-1	1-0	2-1	1-0	2-1	3-2	2-0	2-0	3-1
Cerro Porteño	22	10	7	5	39	21	37	3-3	1-1	1-2		1-1	4-1	2-2	1-0	2-3	5-1	3-0	2-0
Sportivo Luqueño	22	9	6	7	23	24	33	0-2	1-2	1-1	0-0		2-1	1-2	3-1	1-0	2-0	1-0	1-0
Olimpia †	22	8	8	6	33	31	32	2-2	1-0	0-1	0-0	2-0		0-0	3-0	1-0	2-2	3-2	3-1
Cerro Porteño PF	22	7	5	10	19	31	26	0-1	2-3	1-0	0-5	0-1	2-2		1-0	0-1	2-0	1-0	1-1
Sportivo Carapegua	22	7	4	11	30	34	25	2-0	1-3	1-2	1-1	5-1	4-1	1-2		1-1	0-4	2-1	2-0
Sol de América	22	4	10	8	22	29	22	0-0	2-0	1-1	2-1	2-2	1-1	0-2	1-3		3-1	1-1	1-1
Tacuary	22	6	4	12	31	39	22	1-1	0-1	2-0	0-2	1-2	2-3	4-0	2-2	2-1		1-2	3-2
Rubio Nu	22	4	6	12	18	38	18	2-7	0-1	1-0	1-2	1-1	0-3	0-0	1-1	0-0	3-1		1-0
Independiente	22	1	6	15	14	44	9	0-5	0-3	1-1	0-1	0-1	1-1	2-1	0-1	1-1	0-2	2-2	

28/07/2012 - 16/12/2012 • † Qualified for the Copa Libertadores • ‡ Qualified for the Copa Sudamericana
Tacuary & Independiente relegated on three season average • Top scorers: **13** - Diego **CENTURION**, Guaraní & Ariel **NUNEZ**, Libertad • **12** - Nicholas **MARTINEZ**, Tacuary • **10** - Pablo **VELAZQUEZ**, Libertad • **9** - Roberto **NANNI** ARG, Cerro Porteño & **RODRIGO TEIXEIRA** BRA, Nacional

PER – PERU

FIFA/COCA-COLA WORLD RANKING

'93	'94	'95	'96	'97	'98	'99	'00	'01	'02	'03	'04	'05	'06	'07	'08	'09	'10	'11	'12
73	72	69	54	38	72	42	45	43	82	74	66	66	70	63	75	68	68	35	46

| 2012 ||||||||||||| High | Low | Av |
Jan	Feb	Mar	Apr	May	Jun	Jul	Aug	Sep	Oct	Nov	Dec			
34	33	34	34	36	37	32	47	51	37	44	46	25	91	59

Peru's performance in the first half of South America's mammoth 2014 FIFA World Cup qualifying group did little to suggest that they would end their 30-year absence from the finals. At the halfway stage they stood one place off the bottom having won just two of their first nine matches, at home to Venezuela and Paraguay. Coach Sergio Makarian can call on some notable European-based players such as Genoa's Juan Manuel Vargas and Claudio Pizarro of Bayern Munich along with Paolo Guerrero of Club World Cup champions Corinthians - scorer of the winner in the final against Chelsea - but strength in depth remains a problem. At home the team of the season proved to be newly-promoted Real Garcilaso from the Andean city of Cusco who outshone their city rivals Cienciano by qualifying for the championship final. There was a return to the system where the league split into two groups after the first thirty matches with the winners of each facing off in the final. There Real Garcilaso met Sporting Cristal whose form was the one bright spark for football in Lima in an otherwise poor year for the capital. Experience told for Sporting Cristal with 1-0 victories at home and away with Junior Ross scoring both goals as his team won the title for the first time since 2005.

FIFA WORLD CUP RECORD

1930 10 r1 **1934** DNE **1938** DNQ **1950-1954** DNE **1958-1966** DNQ **1970** 7 QF **1974** DNQ **1978** 8 r2 **1982** 20 r1 **1986-2010** DNQ

FEDERACION PERUANA DE FUTBOL (FPF)

Av. Aviación 2085,
San Luis,
Lima 30
☎ +51 1 2258236
+51 1 2258240
fepefutbol@fpf.org.pe
www.fpf.com.pe
FA 1922 CON 1926 FIFA 1926
P Manuel Burga
GS Javier Quintana

THE STADIA

2014 FIFA World Cup Stadia	
Estadio Nacional Lima	40 000
Other Main Stadia	
Estadio Monumental Lima	80 093
Estadio Mansiche Trujillo	25 036
Estadio Max Augustin Iquitos	25 000
Estadio Joel Gutierrez Tacna	21 000

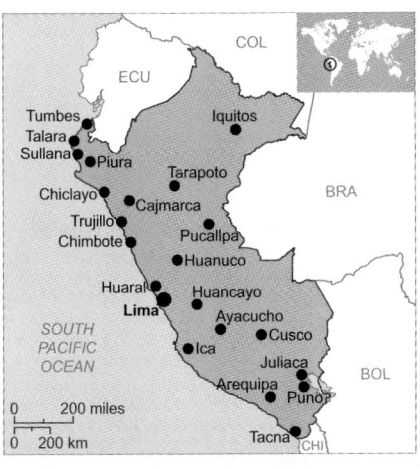

MAJOR CITIES/TOWNS

		Population
1	Lima	7 902 851
2	Arequipa	904 931
3	Trujillo	825 143
4	Chiclayo	524 630
5	Piura	387 948
6	Iquitos	385 986
7	Cusco	353 686
8	Chimbote	326 455
9	Huancayo	324 188
10	Sullana	287 685
11	Pucallpa	276 304
12	Tacna	247 855
13	Ica	238 383
14	Juliaca	234 660
15	Ayacucho	182 291
16	Huánuco	152 865
17	Chincha Alta	151 228
18	Cajamarca	142 210
25	Huaral	85 423

REPUBLICA DEL PERU • REPUBLIC OF PERU

Capital Lima	Population 29 546 963 (39)	% in cities 71%
GDP per capita $8500 (116)	Area km² 1 285 216 km² (20)	GMT + / - -5
Neighbours (km) Bolivia 1075, Brazil 2995, Chile 171, Colombia 1800, Ecuador 1420 • Coast 2414		

RECENT INTERNATIONAL MATCHES PLAYED BY PERU

2010	Opponents	Score	Venue	Comp	Scorers	Att	Referee
4-09	Canada	W 2-0	Toronto	Fr	Jose Carlos Fernandez [68], Jean Tragodara [72]	10 619	Jurisevic USA
7-09	Jamaica	W 2-1	Fort Lauderdale	Fr	OG [4], Jose Carlos Fernandez [85]	5 217	Vaughn USA
8-10	Costa Rica	W 2-0	Lima	Fr	Luis Ramirez [3], Hernan Rengifo [5]	15 000	Ponce ECU
12-10	Panama	L 0-1	Panama City	Fr		8 528	Cerdas CRC
17-11	Colombia	D 1-1	Bogota	Fr	Luis Ramirez [32]	6 900	Laverni ARG
2011							
8-02	Panama	W 1-0	Moquegua	Fr	Orlando Contreras [40]	8 000	Ubriaco URU
29-03	Ecuador	D 0-0	Den Haag	Fr			Braamhaar NED
1-06	Japan	D 0-0	Niigata	Fr		39 048	Webb ENG
4-06	Czech Republic	D 0-0	Matsumoto	Fr		7 592	Sato JPN
4-07	Uruguay	D 1-1	Mendoza	CAr1	Paolo Guerrero [23]	25 000	Roldan COL
8-07	Mexico	W 1-0	Mendoza	CAr1	Paolo Guerrero [82]	10 000	Pezzotta ARG
12-07	Chile	L 0-1	Mendoza	CAr1		42 000	Fagundes BRA
16-07	Colombia	W 2-0	Cordoba	CAqf	Carlos Lobaton [101], Juan Vargas [111]	30 000	Chacon MEX
19-07	Uruguay	L 0-2	La Plata	CAsf		25 000	Orosco BOL
23-07	Venezuela	W 4-1	La Plata	CA3p	William Chiroque [41], Paolo Guerrero 3 [63 89 92+]	20 000	Roldan COL
2-09	Bolivia	D 2-2	Lima	Fr	Rinaldo Cruzado [36], Claudio Pizarro [81p]	35 000	Soto VEN
5-09	Bolivia	D 0-0	La Paz	Fr		16 670	Arias PAR
7-10	Paraguay	W 2-0	Lima	WCq	Paolo Guerrero 2 [46 71]	39 600	Pezzotta ARG
11-10	Chile	L 2-4	Santiago	WCq	Claudio Pizarro [49], Jefferson Farfan [60]	39 000	Orosco BOL
15-11	Ecuador	L 0-2	Quito	WCq		34 481	Larrionda URU
2012							
29-02	Tunisia	D 1-1	Tunis	Fr	Claudio Pizarro [45p]	5 000	Fleischer GHA
21-03	Chile	L 1-3	Arica	Fr	John Galliquio [21]		Quintana PAR
11-04	Chile	L 0-3	Tacna	Fr			Caceres PAR
23-05	Nigeria	W 1-0	Lima	Fr	Paolo Guerrero [35]	30 000	Espinel ECU
3-06	Colombia	L 0-1	Lima	WCq		35 724	Pitana ARG
10-06	Uruguay	L 2-4	Montevideo	WCq	OG [40], Paolo Guerrero [47]	55 000	Pedro BRA
15-08	Costa Rica	W 1-0	San Jose	Fr	Andre Carrillo [8]	9 000	Castro HON
7-09	Venezuela	W 2-1	Lima	WCq	Jefferson Farfan 2 [47 59]	34 703	Vazquez URU
11-09	Argentina	D 1-1	Lima	WCq	Carlos Zambrano [21]	34 111	Roldan COL
12-10	Bolivia	D 1-1	La Paz	WCq	Juan Carlos Marino [21]	36 500	Vera ECU
16-10	Paraguay	L 0-1	Asuncion	WCq		10 114	Lunati ARG
14-11	Honduras	D 0-0	Houston	Fr		9 142	Gantar CAN

Fr = Friendly match • CA = Copa América • WC = FIFA World Cup • q = qualifier

PERU NATIONAL TEAM HISTORICAL RECORDS

Caps: 128 - Roberto Palacios 1992-2009 • 104 - Hector Chumpitaz 1965-81 • 100 - Jorge Soto PER 1992-2005 • 97 - Juan Jose Jayo 1994-2008 • 95 - Nolberto Solano 1994-2009 • 89 - Ruben Diaz 1972-85 • 84 - Juan Reynoso • 83 - Percy Olivares 1987-2001 • 82 - Jose Velasquez 1972-85 • 81 - Teofilo Cubillas 1968-82 • 75 - Jose Soto 1992-2003 • 74 - Jose Del Solar 1986-2001 • 67 - Juan Carlos Oblitas 1973-85

Goals: 26 - Teofilo Cubillas 1968-82 • 24 - Teodoro Fernandez 1935-47 • 20 - Nolberto Solano 1994-2009 • 19 - Roberto Palacios 1992-2009 & Paolo Guerrero 2004- • 18 - Hugo Sotil 1970-79 • 17 - Oswaldo Ramirez 1969-82 & Claudio Pizarro 1999- • 16 - Franco Navarro 1980-89 • 15 - Pedro Leon 1963-73 & Jefferson Farfan 2003- • 14 - Oscar Gomez Sanchez 1953-59 • 13 - Jorge Alcalde 1935-39

Coaches: Pedro Olivieri URU 1927 • Julio Borrelli URU 1929 • Francisco Bru ESP 1930-33 • Telmo Carbajo 1934-35 • Alberto Denegri 1936-37 • Jack Greenwell ENG 1938-39 • Domingo Arrillaga ESP 1940-41 • Angel Fernandez ARG 1942-45 • Jose Arana 1946-47 • Arturo Fernandez 1948-50 • Alfonso Huapaya 1951-52 • William Cook ENG 1953 • Angel Fernandez ARG 1953 • Juan Valdivieso 1954-55 • Arturo Fernandez 1956 • Gyorgy Orth HUN 1957-59 • Jorge de Almeyda BRA 1963 • Dan Georgiadis GRE 1964-65 • Marcos Calderon 1965-67 • Didi BRA 1968-70 • Lajos Baroti HUN 1971-72 • Roberto Scarone URU 1972-73 • Marcos Calderon 1975-79 • Jose Chiarella 1979 • Tim BRA 1980-82 • Juan Jose Tan 1983 • Moises Barack 1984-85 • Roberto Challe 1985-87 • Fernando Cuellar 1987 • Marcos Calderon 1987 • Pepe BRA 1988-89 • Miguel Company 1991 • Vladimir Popovic YUG 1992-93 • Miguel Company 1994-95 • Juan Carlos Oblitas 1996-99 • Francisco Maturana COL 1999-2000 • Julio Cesar Uribe 2000-02 • Paulo Autuori BRA 2003-05 • Freddy Ternero 2005-06 • Franco Navarro 2006 • Julio Cesar Uribe 2007 • Jose del Solar 2007-10 • Sergio Markarian URU 2010-

PERU 2012

PRIMERA DIVISION — FIRST STAGE

Liguilla A

	Pl	W	D	L	F	A	Pts	Sp Cristal	Sp Huancayo	Inti Gas	Un San Martin	José Gálvez	Cienciano	Universitario	Cobresol	Real Garcilaso	César Vallejo	Juan Aurich	FBC Melgar	Un Comercio	León	Alianza	Sport Boys
Sporting Cristal ‡	44	25	11	8	93	44	86		2-2 1-1 0-2 0-4 0-4 1-3 1-4 0-2 0-4 0-3 3-1 1-1 1-2 1-6 0-1							3-0	2-2	5-1	3-1	2-0	1-0	1-1	3-1
Sport Huancayo	44	18	9	17	52	51	63	1-1 3-1		2-2 2-1 1-2 1-0 1-0 1-2 0-2 0-2 0-1 1-3 0-3 0-1-1						0-2	2-0	1-0	1-0	2-1	2-1	3-1	1-2
Inti Gas Deportes	44	17	11	16	43	45	62	2-1 1-1 0-0 1-3			2-1 1-0 1-0-2 1-1 0-0 1-1 0-1 0-2 1-2 0					2-2	0-2	2-0	2-1	0-0	1-0	3-0	4-1
Univ. San Martin	44	16	12	16	49	52	61	2-1 1-1 1-1 2-2 0-2 0-1-1				2-3 1-1 3-2 1-0 0-1 0-1 2-0 1-0				0-0	0-0	5-1	0-0	1-0	0-1	0-0	3-1
José Gálvez	44	17	10	17	48	54	61	0-2 3-1 1-0 0-1 1-0 3-1 1-1 1-2					2-0 0-3 1-1 4-0 4-0			2-2	0-1	3-1	0-0	2-1	1-0	0-2	1-1
Cienciano	44	16	9	19	58	59	57	2-1 1-2 2-2 1-1 1-2 0-0 2-0 2-2 3-1 2-0						2-3 3-0 4-0 2-0		2-0	2-0	0-1	2-0	0-0	2-3	3-2	2-1
Universitario	44	15	13	16	52	58	57	0-2 0-3 3-1 0-1 3-1 0-0 1-2 2-1 0-0 3-0 1-1 1-1							3-2 4-0	2-1	1-1	3-1	3-0	1-3	2-1	2-1	1-1
Cobresol	44	6	8	30	33	82	22	1-0 0-2 0-2 4-0 1-2 0-0 1-2 1-2 1-1 1-0 0-2 1-2 1-1 3-0								1-1	0-2	2-2	0-2	0-3	1-1	0-0	0-1

Liguilla B

	Pl	W	D	L	F	A	Pts	Real Garcilaso	Univ. César Vallejo	Juan Aurich	FBC Melgar	Unión Comercio	León de Huanuco	Alianza Lima	Sport Boys
Real Garcilaso ‡	44	24	10	10	63	35	82		3-0 2-0 1-0 3-0 3-0 1-0 2-1 2-0					1-0 1-1 1-0 3-1 2-0 3-0 1-0 3-0 1-0 2-1 2-1 3-0 1-1 3-0		
Univ. César Vallejo	44	21	11	12	57	44	74	2-3		1-1 0-2 4-0 1-0 2-0 3-1 2-1 0-1				0-0 1-1 2-4 1-1 1-0 3-1 2-0 2-1 1-0 2-0 0-0 0-2 2-1 0	
Juan Aurich	44	20	9	15	56	54	71	1-0	3-0		2-1 0-0 1-2 3-0 1-0	1-2	0-0 3-2 2-1 3-1	3-1 2-0 2-2 2-1 1-1 1-1 0-2 1-1 1	
FBC Melgar	44	18	12	14	56	44	66	1-2	1-0	1-0		3-0 2-1 3-0 3-1	2-1 0-0 1-0 0-2 4-0 1-1 1-0		3-0 3-0 1-0 2-0 3-0 2-0 1-1 5-1
Unión Comercio	44	16	9	19	51	61	57	1-1	2-0	1-0	2-0		0-3 2-0 2-3	2-1 0-1 2-1 0-1 1-2 3-0 1-0 3-2 1-1	2-3 2-0 0-0 2-1 2-1 2-1
León de Huanuco	44	13	15	16	54	47	54	2-3	1-0	1-0	2-2	0-0	4-1 0-0	3-0 2-2 0-2 1-1 2-0 3-3 2-0 0-0 1-1 1-7 1-0 0	0-0 1-2 2-0 3-0
Alianza Lima	44	14	15	15	50	51	53	1-1	3-1	1-1	1-1	2-0	1-1	1-0	2-2 2-0 2-0 2-2 0-2 0-3 2-1 0-0 0-0 3-2 1-1 2-2 1-2	2-1 4-0
Sport Boys	44	6	16	22	36	70	32	0-5	2-0	0-0	0-1	0-1	1-1	1-1	1-0	0-0 3-1 3-0 1-1 0-1 1-2 1-1 1-1 1-0 0-1 1-0 1-0 4

19/02/2012 – 25/11/2012 • ‡ Qualified for the championship final • Stage One played over two rounds between all 16 teams. Teams are then split into two groups of eight with points taken forward to the second stage

Top scorers: **27** – Andy **Pando**, Real Garcilaso • **20** – Miguel **Ximenez** URU, Universitario • **18** – Roberto **Jimenez**, Univ. César Vallejo • **16** – Henan **Rengifo**, Cristal; Carlos **Orejuela**, Sport Boys & Junior **Ross**, Cristal

CHAMPIONSHIP FINAL 2012

1st leg. Estadio Inca, Cusco, 2-12-2012, Att: 29 132, Ref: Victor Rivera

Real Garcilaso 0
Sporting Cristal 1 Ross [34]

Real – Diego Carranza – Jhoel Herrera (Jose Granda 46), Eduardo Uribe•, Jaime Huerta, Fernando Allocco• – Diego Santillan•, Edson Uribe• (Christian Vildoso 85), Fabio Ramos•, Carlos Flores (Ricardo Uribe 71) – Andy Pando, Ramon Rodriguez (c). Tr: Freddy Garcia
Sporting – Erick Delgado• (c) – Walter Vilchez, Marcos Delgado, Nicolas Ayr•, Yoshimar Yotun (Jesus Alvarez 38) – Carlos Lobaton• (Oscar Vilchez 88), Luis Advincula•, Jorge Cazulo – Hernan Rengifo (Juan Marino 75), Junior Ross, Irven Avila. Tr: Roberto Mosquera

CHAMPIONSHIP FINAL 2012

2nd leg. Nacional, Lima, 9-12-2012, Att: 38 660, Ref: Victor Carrillo

Sporting Cristal 1 Ross [24]
Real Garcilaso 0

Sporting – Erick Delgado (c) – Walter Vilchez, Jesus Alvarez, Nicolas Ayr, Juan Marino• – Carlos Lobaton (Hernan Rengifo 71♦89), Renzo Sheput (Oscar Vilchez 58), Luis Advincula•, Jorge Cazulo• – Junior Ross (Marcos Delgado 79), Irven Avila. Tr: Roberto Mosquera
Real – Juan Goyoneche – Emiliano Ciucci, Eduardo Uribe•, Jaime Huerta ♦92+, Fernando Allocco – Diego Santillan•, Jose Granda (Victor Rossel 82), Edson Uribe, Fabio Ramos•, Carlos Flores• (Ricardo Uribe 72) – Ramon Rodriguez (c). Tr: Freddy Garcia

COPA PERU 2012

Semi-finals

UTC Cajamarca *	7	0
Alianza Cristiana	0	0

* Home team in 1st leg

Sport Victoria	0	3
Alfonso Ugarte *	4	1

Finals

UTC Cajamarca *	2	2
Alfonso Ugarte	0	3

Cajamarca promoted to the Primera Division

PERU 2012 — SEGUNDA DIVISION (2)

	Pl	W	D	L	F	A	Pts
Pacífico	18	10	6	2	33	14	36
Deportivo Coopsol	18	11	2	5	32	17	35
Los Caimanes	18	9	6	3	29	14	33
Sport Ancash §4	18	11	2	5	39	23	31
Alianza Huánuco	18	9	4	5	34	19	31
Atlético Mineiro	18	9	2	7	25	20	29
Coronel Bolognesi §8	18	6	1	11	19	33	11
Atlético Torino §14	18	7	2	9	19	24	9
Alianza Unicachi §6	18	4	1	13	11	36	7
Hijos de Acosvinchos §8	18	0	0	18	1	51	-8

12/05/2012 – 16/09/2012 • § = points deducted • Alianza Unicachi and Hijos withdrew with all remaining matches awarded 3-0 to their opponents

MEDALS TABLE

		Overall			League			Sth Am			City
		G	S	B	G	S	B	G	S	B	
1	Universitario	25	14	18	**25**	13	14		1	4	Lima
2	Alianza Lima	20	19	12	20	19	9			3	Lima
3	Sporting Cristal	16	16	6	16	15	6		1		Lima
4	Sport Boys	6	7	5	6	7	5				Callao
5	Deportivo Municipal	4	7	6	4	7	6				Lima
6	Univ San Martin	3			3						Lima
7	Atlético Chalaco	2	5	4	2	5	4				Callao
8	Mariscal Sucre	2	2	2	2	2	2				Lima
9	Unión Huaral	2	1		2	1					Huaral
10	Cienciano	1	4			4		1			Cusco
11	Juan Aurich	1	1	3	1	1	3				Chiclayo

PHI – PHILIPPINES

FIFA/COCA-COLA WORLD RANKING

'93	'94	'95	'96	'97	'98	'99	'00	'01	'02	'03	'04	'05	'06	'07	'08	'09	'10	'11	'12
163	171	166	166	175	175	181	179	175	181	189	188	191	171	179	160	167	150	159	147

2012												High	Low	Av
Jan	Feb	Mar	Apr	May	Jun	Jul	Aug	Sep	Oct	Nov	Dec			
157	156	156	148	148	149	152	150	150	147	143	147	143	195	172

Since the national team reached the semi-finals of the 2010 AFF Suzuki Cup, football in the Philippines has quickly risen to prominence in the basketball-mad southeast Asian nation. The Azkals - which means Street Dogs in Tagalog - qualified automatically for the finals of the 2012 tournament following their exploits of two years previously and the Filipinos managed a repeat performance, defeating Vietnam and Myanmar on their way to the last four. Such have been the improvements in football in the Philippines since 2010, including government backing to enhance the infrastructure to support the game, the Azkals were able to host their semi-final meeting with Singapore at Manila's Rizal Memorial Stadium, where they drew 0-0. However, a narrow 1-0 loss in the return in Singapore saw the Philippines eliminated. The national team's success has seen an upsurge in interest around the United Football League, which was formed in 2009. National team striker Phil Younghusband scored 23 goals in the 18-game season won by Global but he was extraordinarily prolific in the Cup, scoring 25 times in just seven matches, including five hat-tricks - two of which were double hat-tricks. The only match in which he didn't score was during the final between his club Loyola, and the Air Force team which was lost 2-0.

FIFA WORLD CUP RECORD
1930-1994 DNE **1998-2002** DNQ **2006-2010** DNE **2014** DNQ

PHILIPPINE FOOTBALL FEDERATION (PFF)
- No 27 Danny Floro, Corner Capt Henry Javiers Sts., Oranbo, 1600 Pasig City
- ☎ +63 2 5712870
- +63 2 5712872
- philippine.football.federation@gmail.com
- www.the-pff.com
- FA 1907 CON 1954 FIFA 1930
- P Mariano Araneta
- GS Edwin Gastanes

THE STADIA
2014 FIFA World Cup Stadia
Rizal Memorial
Manila — 30 000

Other Main Stadia
Pana-ad Stadium
Bacolod — 20 000
Amoranto Sports Complex
Quezon City — 15 000
Cebu City Sports Complex
Cebu — 10 000

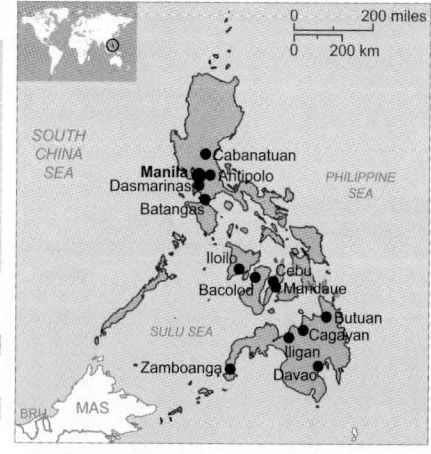

MAJOR CITIES/TOWNS
		Population
1	Manila	11 165 131
2	Davao	1 627 171
3	Cebu	821 499
4	Zamboanga	762 624
5	Dasmariñas	711 476
6	Dadiangas	657 891
7	Antipolo	628 923
8	Calamba	560 456
9	Cagayan	545 873
10	Bacolod	484 099
11	Bacoor	469 925
12	Iloilo	421 924
13	San Jose	397 951
14	Mandaue	394 174
15	Batangas	388 989
16	Cainta	370 873
17	Iligan	367 763
18	Cabanatuan	357 768
19	Butuan	354 151

REPUBLIKA NG PILIPINAS • REPUBLIC OF THE PHILIPPINES
Capital	Manila	Population	97 976 603 (12)	% in cities	65%
GDP per capita	$3300 (161)	Area km^2	300 000 km^2 (72)	GMT +/-	+8
Neighbours (km)	Coast 36 289				

PHI – PHILIPPINES

RECENT INTERNATIONAL MATCHES PLAYED BY THE PHILIPPINES

2010	Opponents	Score	Venue	Comp	Scorers	Att	Referee
22-10	Timor-Leste	W 5-0	Vientiane	AFFq	Ian Araneta 3 [27 41 57], Phil Younghusband [30p], Anton Del Rosario [32]		Leow SIN
24-10	Laos	D 2-2	Vientiane	AFFq	Phil Younghusband [76p], James Younghusband [94+]	2 000	Pechsri THA
26-10	Cambodia	D 0-0	Vientiane	AFFq			Abdul Wahab MAS
2-12	Singapore	D 1-1	Hanoi	AFFr1	Chris Greatwich [93+]		Mahapab THA
5-12	Vietnam	W 2-0	Hanoi	AFFr1	Chris Greatwich [38], Phil Younghusband [79]	40 000	Napitupulu IDN
8-12	Myanmar	D 0-0	Nam Dinh	AFFr1			Patwal IND
16-12	Indonesia	L 0-1	Jakarta	AFFsf		70 000	Moradi IRN
19-12	Indonesia	L 0-1	Jakarta	AFFsf		88 000	Ebrahim BHR
2011							
9-02	Mongolia	W 2-0	Bacolod	CCq	Emilio Caligdong [43], Phil Younghusband [94+]	20 000	Yu Ming Hsun TPE
15-03	Mongolia	L 1-2	Ulaan Baatar	CCq	James Younghusband [4]	3 000	Ko Hyung Jin KOR
21-03	Myanmar	D 1-1	Yangon	CCq	James Younghusband [76p]	5 000	
23-03	Palestine	D 0-0	Yangon	CCq		500	Adday IRQ
25-03	Bangladesh	W 3-0	Yangon	CCq	Ian Araneta [41], Angel Guirado 2 [55 80]	200	Kim Jong Hyeok KOR
29-06	Sri Lanka	D 1-1	Colombo	WCq	Nathaniel Burkey [50]	4 000	Shamsuzzaman BAN
3-07	Sri Lanka	W 4-0	Manila	WCq	Emilio Caligdong [20], Phil Younghusband 2 [43 57p], Angel Guirado [50]	12 500	Kim Sang Woo KOR
23-07	Kuwait	L 0-3	Kuwait City	WCq		20 000	Abu Loum JOR
28-07	Kuwait	L 1-2	Manila	WCq	Stephan Schrock [45]	13 000	Liu Kwok Man HKG
30-09	Hong Kong	D 3-3	Kaohsiung	Fr	Phil Younghusband [31p], Emilio Caligdong 2 [44 61]		
2-10	Chinese Taipei	D 0-0	Kaohsiung	Fr			
4-10	Macau	W 2-0	Kaohsiung	Fr	Emilio Caligdong 2 [58 87]		
7-10	Singapore	L 0-2	Singapore	Fr			
11-10	Nepal	W 4-0	Manila	Fr	Phil Younghusband 2 [43 57p], James Younghusband [30], Matt Hartman [88]		
2012							
29-02	Malaysia	D 1-1	Manilla	Fr	Denis Wolf [34]		
9-03	Korea DPR	L 0-2	Kathmandu	CCr1		1 500	Patwal IND
11-03	India	W 2-0	Kathmandu	CCr1	Phil Younghusband 2 [10 73]	300	Mahapab THA
13-03	Tajikistan	W 2-1	Kathmandu	CCr1	Phil Younghusband [54], Angel Guirado [80]	800	Sato JPN
16-03	Turkmenistan	L 1-2	Kathmandu	CCsf	Phil Younghusband [25]	500	Ko Hyung Jin KOR
19-03	Palestine	W 4-3	Kathmandu	CC3p	Phil Younghusband 2 [4 25p], Angel Guirado [42], Juan Guirado [69]		Sabbagh LIB
1-06	Malaysia	D 0-0	Kuala Lumpur	Fr			
5-06	Indonesia	D 2-2	Manila	Fr	James Younghusband [57], Phil Younghusband [84]		Kuo Jung Fan TPE
12-06	Guam	W 3-0	Bacolod	Fr	Angel Guirado 2 [7 45], Carli de Murga [11]		
7-09	Singapore	W 2-0	Singapore	Fr	Emilio Caligdong [8], Phil Younghusband [49]		
25-09	Guam	W 1-0	Manila	Fr	Patrick Reichelt [81]		Phung Dinh Dung VIE
27-09	Macau	W 5-0	Manila	Fr	Denis Wolf 3 [22 45 64], Carli de Murga [49], Patrick Reichelt [69]		Vo Quang Vinh VIE
29-09	Chinese Taipei	W 3-1	Manila	Fr	Denis Wolf [10], Emelio Caligdong [34], OJ Porteria [43]		Phung Dinh Dung VIE
12-10	Bahrain	D 0-0	Manama	Fr			
16-10	Kuwait	L 1-2	Kuwait City	Fr	Phil Younghusband [60p]		
15-11	Singapore	W 1-0	Cebu	Fr	Marwin Angeles [56]		
24-11	Thailand	L 1-2	Bangkok	AFFr1	Paul Mulders [77]		Sato JPN
27-11	Vietnam	W 1-0	Bangkok	AFFr1	Emelio Caligdong [86]		Ma Ning CHN
30-11	Myanmar	W 2-0	Bangkok	AFFr1	Phil Younghusband [47], Angel Guirado [94+]		Abdul Baki OMA
8-12	Singapore	D 0-0	Manila	AFFsf			Al Hilali OMA
12-12	Singapore	L 0-1	Singapore	AFFsf			Tan Hai CHN

Fr = Friendly match • AFF = ASEAN Football Federation Championship • CC = AFC Challenge Cup • q = qualifier • r1 = 1st round

PHILIPPINES NATIONAL TEAM HISTORICAL RECORDS

Past Coaches: Alan Rogers ENG 1962-63 • Danny McLennan SCO 1963 • Carlos Cavagnaro ARG 1989 • Eckhard Krautzun GER 1991-92 • Noel Casilao 1993-96 • Juan Cutillas ESP 1996-2000 • Rodolfo Alicante 2000 • Masataka Imai JPN 2001 • Sugao Kambe JPN 2002-03 • Aris Caslib 2004-07 • Norman Fegidero 2008 • Juan Cutillas ESP 2008-09 • Aris Caslib 2009 • Des Bulpin ENG 2009-10 • Simon McMenemy ENG 2010 • Michael Weiss GER 2011-

PHILIPPINES 2012

UNITED FOOTBALL LEAGUE DIVISION ONE

	Pl	W	D	L	F	A	Pts	Global	Kaya	Loyola	Stallions	Air Force	Pasargad	Nomads	Archers	Army	Navy
Global	18	13	3	2	49	17	42		1-1	1-1	1-0	5-3	4-0	1-1	1-0	1-2	3-2
Kaya	18	13	3	2	30	17	42	1-5		2-2	1-1	3-1	3-0	2-1	2-1	1-0	1-0
Loyola	18	11	4	3	66	29	37	4-3	2-0		3-0	3-3	3-4	5-0	3-2	4-0	14-0
Stallions	18	8	5	5	37	20	29	1-3	0-1	4-1		2-1	0-0	2-2	5-2	3-0	7-0
Philippine Air Force	18	7	4	7	31	35	25	0-4	0-1	2-1	1-4		2-0	3-2	1-1	2-2	2-1
Pasargad	18	7	3	8	30	31	24	0-2	1-2	0-1	1-0	3-2		2-3	1-1	6-3	1-2
Manila Nomads	18	4	7	7	27	38	19	1-5	1-3	2-2	2-2	0-3	0-1		1-1	1-1	1-0
Green Archers	18	3	5	10	30	34	14	0-1	0-2	2-3	1-4	0-1	1-1	1-2		3-1	5-0
Philippine Army	18	3	4	11	23	48	13	0-3	0-2	1-2	0-0	2-2	2-3	1-4	2-7		3-2
Philippine Navy	18	1	2	15	15	69	5	0-5	1-2	1-10	0-6	1-2	0-6	1-1	2-2	2-3	

14/01/2012 – 30/06/2012
Top scorers: **23** - Phil **YOUNGHUSBAND**, Loyola • **13** - Izzeldin **ELHABBIB** SDN, Global • **12** - Mark **HARTMANN**, Loyola & Tating **PASILAN**, Green Archers • **11** - James **YOUNGHUSBAND**, Loyola & Ian **ARANETA**, Air Force

PHILIPPINES 2012

UNITED FOOTBALL LEAGUE DIVISION TWO (2)

	Pl	W	D	L	F	A	Pts	Pachanga	Diliman	Cebu	Agila	Union	Forza	Socceroos	Laos	Dolphins	All-Japan	Lions	S. Garden
Pachanga	22	21	1	0	123	8	64		2-1	1-0	4-0	8-0	8-1	8-0	4-0	1-0	7-0	13-0	13-0
Diliman	22	18	2	2	82	25	56	2-2		1-1	4-1	3-1	5-0	3-2	3-1	2-1	10-0	5-0	5-1
Cebu Queen City Utd	22	14	5	3	83	29	47	0-4	4-1		1-2	4-1	8-2	6-1	6-1	0-0	5-2	4-4	3-2
Agila	22	12	1	9	48	49	37	0-4	4-9	0-0		1-6	4-3	5-0	2-1	0-1	2-1	3-0	8-2
Union International	22	8	5	9	46	60	29	1-4	1-5	4-4	1-0		4-1	0-6	1-6	0-0	1-0	2-2	4-1
Forza	22	9	2	11	50	71	29	0-3	0-2	1-6	4-1	1-3		6-1	0-2	4-3	1-1	3-0	5-4
Team Socceroo	22	8	4	10	51	61	28	0-8	2-4	3-4	1-3	2-2	0-1		0-0	1-1	3-1	5-1	6-2
Laos	22	8	3	11	36	45	27	1-4	1-6	0-2	1-3	2-1	3-3	0-1		1-1	0-1	2-1	3-1
Dolphins United	22	4	9	9	28	35	21	2-3	0-2	1-5	2-0	2-2	2-4	3-3	0-2		0-0	1-1	0-1
Manila All-Japan	22	5	4	13	30	60	19	0-7	0-1	1-1	1-3	2-3	9-6	1-2	2-0	2-2		2-0	1-5
Manila Lions	22	3	2	17	17	77	11	0-2	0-6	0-7	0-1	3-1	1-2	1-7	1-5	0-2	1-0		1-3
Sunken Garden Utd	22	3	0	19	35	109	9	0-13	1-2	0-12	3-5	3-7	1-2	1-5	2-4	1-4	0-3	1-3	

14/01/2012 – 24/06/2012 • Top scorers: **34** - Freddy **GONZALES**, Pachanga • **21** - Isaac **AGYIE** GHA, Forza • **20** - Dan **VILLARICO**, Cebu

UNITED FOOTBALL LEAGUE CUP 2011-12

Round of 16		Quarter-finals		Semi-finals		Final	
Philippine Air Force	15						
Manhur	3	**Philippine Air Force**	3				
Manila Lions	0	Green Archers	1				
Green Archers	3			**Philippine Air Force**	2		
Pachanga	0 4p			Global	0		
Philippine Navy	0 2p	Pachanga	0				
Philippine Army	0	**Global**	1			**Philippine Air Force**	2
Global	3					Loyola	0
Kaya	2						
Team Socceroo	0	**Kaya**	3				
Pasargad	0	Manila Nomads	0				
Manilla Nomads	1			Kaya	4		
Stallions	2			Loyola	5		
Diliman	1	Stallions	1				
Sunken Garden Utd	0	**Loyola**	2				
Loyola	14						

3rd place: Global 2-1 Kaya

CUP FINAL
Rizal Memorial, Manila
10-12-2011
Scorers - Ian Araneta [40], Yanti Barsales [89] for Air Force

PLE – PALESTINE

FIFA/COCA-COLA WORLD RANKING

'93	'94	'95	'96	'97	'98	'99	'00	'01	'02	'03	'04	'05	'06	'07	'08	'09	'10	'11	'12
-	-	-	-	-	184	170	171	145	151	139	126	137	128	165	179	173	177	158	152

| 2012 ||||||||||||| High | Low | Av |
Jan	Feb	Mar	Apr	May	Jun	Jul	Aug	Sep	Oct	Nov	Dec				
162	162	160	153	154	153	154	152	151	149	149	152		115	191	155

Palestine qualified for the finals of the 2012 AFC Challenge Cup in Nepal and impressed by reaching the semi-finals. Under current coach Jamal Mahmoud the side has undergone a significant transformation and he has overseen a steady rise up the rankings and an improvement in performances. Wins over Nepal and the Maldives ensured Palestine progressed to the semi-finals although a 0-0 draw with Turkmenistan meant that Mahmoud's side finished their group in second place. That meant a tough game against the defending champions Korea DPR which was lost 2-0. In the third place play-off with the Philippines a double strike by Abdelhamid Abuhabib and a goal from Fahed Attal were not enough as Palestine went down 4-3. An early exit at the Arab Cup was also followed by elimination from the West Asian Championship at the group stage, but not before registering a 1-0 win over Lebanon thanks to Iyad Gharqoud's goal. The 2011 West Bank Premier League champions Markaz Shabab Al Amari also made a positive impression at the 2012 AFC President's Cup in Pakistan, finishing as runners-up after losing 2-1 in the final to Esteghlal of Tajikistan in what was the first appearance in the final of an Asian competition by a Palestinian team. They failed to retain their title at home which was won by Jerusalem's Hilal.

FIFA WORLD CUP RECORD
1930-1998 DNE **2002-2014** DNQ

PALESTINE FOOTBALL ASSOCIATION (PFA)
PO Box 4373, Ramallah-Al Bireh
☎ +972 2 2959102
📠 +972 2 2959101
✉ international.dept.pfa@gmail.com
🌐 www.pfa.com
FA 1928 CON 1998 FIFA 1998
P Jibril Al Rajoub
GS Abdelmajeed Hijjeh

THE STADIA
2014 FIFA World Cup Stadia
Faysal Al-Husseini Stadium
Al Ram — 12 500
Other Main Stadia
Jericho International
Jericho — 15 000
Palestine Stadium
Gaza — 10 000
Al Khader Stadium
Al Khader — 6 000
Municipal Stadium
Nablus — 4 000

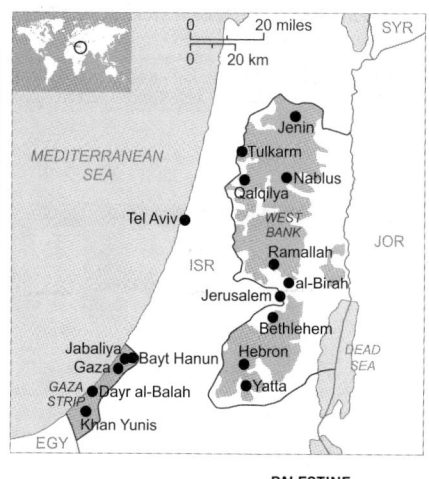

MAJOR CITIES/TOWNS
		Population
1	Gaza	674 309
2	Jabaliya	251 324
3	Khan Yunis	250 817
4	Hebron	229 258
5	Nablus	182 734
6	Rafah	181 619
7	al-Nusayrat	89 954
8	Dayr al-Balah	86 229
9	Bayt Lahya	85 096
10	Tulkarm	62 006
11	Qalqilya	61 903
12	Yatta	59 240
13	al-Birah	54 954
14	al-Burayj	50 681
15	Jenin	48 813
16	Bayt Hanun	46 028
17	Bani Suhalyah	45 651
18	Bethlehem	41 176
19	Ramallah	35 439

PALESTINE
Capital Ramallah | Population 3 636 195 (130) | % in cities 72%
GDP per capita $2900 (164) | Area km² 6 200 km² (171) | GMT +/- +2
Neighbours (km) For the West Bank and Gaza: Israel 358, Jordan 97, Egypt 11 • Coast 40

RECENT INTERNATIONAL MATCHES PLAYED BY PALESTINE

2011	Opponents	Score	Venue	Comp	Scorers	Att	Referee
9-02	Tanzania	L 0-1	Dar es Salaam	Fr			
21-03	Bangladesh	W 2-0	Yangon	CCq	Murad Eleyan 2 [46] [65]	1 000	
23-03	Philippines	D 0-0	Yangon	CCq		500	Adday IRQ
25-03	Mayanmar	W 3-1	Yangon	CCq	Murad Eleyan 3 [39] [90], Ahmed Mahajna [71]	1 500	Abdulhusin BHR
29-06	Afghanistan	W 2-0	Tursunzade	WCq	Murad Eleyan [22], Ismail Alamour [88]	5 000	Al Ghafari JOR
3-07	Afghanistan	D 1-1	Al Ram	WCq	Hussam Wadi [12]	9 000	Al Dosari QAT
23-07	Thailand	L 0-1	Buriram	WCq		17 000	Lee Min Hu KOR
28-07	Thailand	D 2-2	Al Ram	WCq	Murad Eleyan 2 [5] [90]	11 500	Abbas BHR
22-08	Indonesia	L 1-4	Surakarta	Fr	Sulaiman Obaid [49]		
5-10	Iran	L 0-7	Tehran	Fr			
6-12	Bahrain	W 1-0	Al Muharraq	Fr	Ali Khatib [66]		
17-12	Sudan	W 2-0	Al Rayyan	Fr	Ali Khatib [39], Ismail Alamour [62]		
20-12	Bahrain	L 1-3	Doha	Fr	Ashraf Alfawaghra [40p]		
22-12	Kuwait	L 0-3	Doha	Fr			
2012							
24-02	UAE	L 0-3	Abu Dhabi	Fr			
8-03	Nepal	W 2-0	Kathmandu	CCr1	Alaa Atya [4], Fahed Attal [65]	12 300	Sato JPN
10-03	Turkmenistan	D 0-0	Kathmandu	CCr1		1 000	Ko Hyung Jin KOR
12-03	Maldives	W 2-0	Kathmandu	CCr1	Husam Wadi [59], Ashraf Alfawaghra [94+]	300	Mashentsev KGZ
16-03	Korea DPR	L 0-2	Kathmandu	CCsf		3 000	Almarzouqi KUW
19-03	Philippines	L 3-4	Kathmandu	CC3p	Abdelhamid Abuhabib 2 [21] [67], Fahed Attal [78]	1 000	Sabbagh LIB
28-05	Qatar	D 0-0	Doha	Fr			
18-06	Yemen	W 2-1	Sana'a	Fr	Ashraf Numan [36], Ismail Amour [92+]		
25-06	Kuwait	L 0-2	Taif	ARr1			Hashmi UAE
28-06	Saudi Arabia	D 2-2	Taif	ARr1	Husam Abusaleh [45p], Ismail Alamour [73]		Abdel Rahman SUD
17-11	Syria	D 1-1	Amman	Fr	Mousa Abu Jazar [53]		
20-11	Syria	W 2-1	Zarqa	Fr	Iyad Gharqoud [6], Husam Abusaleh [18p]		
29-11	Bahrain	L 0-2	Al Wakrah	Fr			
8-12	Kuwait	L 1-2	Kuwait City	WAr1	Ashraf Alfawaghra [45]	1 500	Adday IRQ
11-12	Lebanon	W 1-0	Al Farwaniyah	WAr1	Iyad Gharqoud [74]	2 000	Ko Hyung Jin KOR
14-12	Oman	L 1-2	Al Farwaniyah	WAr1	Imad Zatara [40]	500	Tojo JPN

Fr = Friendly match • AC = AFC Asian Cup • CC = AFC Challenge Cup • WA = West Asian Championship • WC = FIFA World Cup • q = qualifier

PALESTINE NATIONAL TEAM HISTORICAL RECORDS

Past Coaches: Ricardo Carugati ARG 1998 • Ricardo Carugati ARG & Azmi Nassar 1999 • Azmi Nassar 2000 • Mansour Hamid El Bouri EGY 2000 • Mustafa Abdel Ghali Yacoub EGY 2001 • Andrzej Wisniewski POL 2002 • Nicola Hadwa Shahwan 2002-04 • Alfred Riedl AUT 2004 • Ghassan Balawi 2004 • Tamas Viczko HUN 2004 • Azmi Nassar 2005-07 • Nelson Dekmak 2007 • Naeem Swerky 2008 • Izzat Hamza 2008-09 • Jamal Daraghmeh 2009 • Mousa Bezaz ALG 2009-11 • Abdel-Nasser Barakat 2011 • Jamal Mahmoud 2011-

PALESTINE 2011-12

PREMIER LEAGUE

	Pl	W	D	L	F	A	Pts	Hilal J	Shabab K	Shabab T	W. Al-Neiss	S. Al Amari	Markaz B	Jabal	Al-Bireh	Thagafi	Markaz T
Hilal Jerusalem †	18	14	3	1	43	10	45		1-0	3-1	5-1	3-0	2-1	4-0	2-0	3-2	6-0
Shabab Al Khaleel	18	11	4	3	27	10	37	2-1		0-1	1-0	2-1	0-1	0-0	1-1	2-0	3-0
Shabab Al-Thahriyeh	18	10	4	4	36	16	34	1-2	0-1		2-2	2-1	1-1	2-0	3-1	5-0	2-1
Wadi Al-Neiss	18	8	6	4	33	21	30	1-2	0-1	1-0		5-1	3-3	1-2	2-2	3-1	4-1
Shabab Al Amari	18	9	0	9	32	30	27	1-4	1-2	0-1	1-2		3-0	2-3	1-0	5-2	3-0
Markaz Balata	18	6	6	6	22	26	24	0-4	1-1	1-1	1-2	0-2		2-0	1-0	0-0	2-1
Jabal Mukabar	18	5	4	9	17	30	19	0-0	0-5	0-4	0-3	1-2	1-1		1-0	4-0	3-0
Al-Bireh	18	4	4	10	15	25	16	0-2	1-2	0-4	0-0	0-1	1-2	1-1		1-0	4-1
Thagafi Tulkarm	18	4	3	11	20	37	15	0-3	1-1	1-1	0-1	1-2	2-0	2-1	1-2		4-1
Markaz Tulkarm	18	1	2	15	15	55	5	0-0	0-3	1-5	2-2	2-5	2-5	1-0	0-1	2-3	

2/09/2011 - 21/04/2012 • † Qualified for the AFC President's Cup

PNG – PAPUA NEW GUINEA

FIFA/COCA-COLA WORLD RANKING

'93	'94	'95	'96	'97	'98	'99	'00	'01	'02	'03	'04	'05	'06	'07	'08	'09	'10	'11	'12
-	-	-	169	167	172	183	192	196	167	172	161	166	178	183	201	203	203	193	188

2012												High	Low	Av
Jan	Feb	Mar	Apr	May	Jun	Jul	Aug	Sep	Oct	Nov	Dec			
193	194	194	193	193	193	187	186	193	193	195	188	160	203	182

Hekari United's OFC Champions League success in 2010 and subsequent appearance at the FIFA Club World Cup may have given Papua New Guinea a brief spell in the footballing spotlight but it is very much back to business as usual with the national team ensconced near the bottom of the FIFA/Coca-Cola World Ranking and Hekari struggling to rediscover the magic formula that worked so well for them in 2010. At the 2012 OFC Nations Cup in the Solomon Islands the national team was drawn in a tough group containing the hosts as well as the tournament favourites New Zealand. With the group games also doubling up as 2014 FIFA World Cup qualifiers there was much at stake but PNG lost to both of their rivals by the odd goal before drawing the final match with Fiji, results that saw them finish bottom of the group and exit both tournaments. Frank Farina's side were never outclassed but with no fixtures planned for the forseeable future, taking the team to the next level will be hard especially after the departure of Farina in November 2012 to take over as coach of A-League side Sydney FC. Once again Hekari United remained unchallenged in club football at home, winning their sixth straight championship after beating Eastern Stars 3-0 in the play-off final.

FIFA WORLD CUP RECORD
1930-1994 DNE **1998** DNQ **2002** DNE **2006** DNQ **2010** DNE **2014** DNQ

PAPUA NEW GUINEA FOOTBALL ASSOCIATION (PNGFA)

- PO Box 957, Lae 411, Morobe Province
- +675 4306390
- +675 4751399
- pngfa@yahoo.com
- www.pngfootball.com.pg
- FA 1962 CON 1966 FIFA 1963
- P David Chung
- GS Dimirit Mileng

THE STADIA
2014 FIFA World Cup Stadia
PNG played their qualifiers in Honiara, Solomon Islands as part of the 2012 OFC Nations Cup

Other Main Stadia
PMRL Stadium Port Moresby	15 000
Hubert Murray Stadium Port Moresby	15 000
Lloyd Robson Oval Port Moresby	10 000

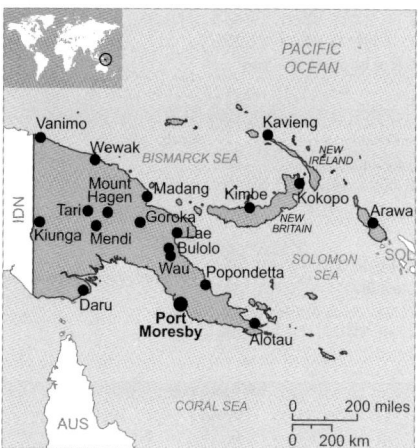

MAJOR CITIES/TOWNS

		Population
1	Port Moresby	307 643
2	Lae	72 967
3	Arawa	39 741
4	Mount Hagen	39 003
5	Popondetta	37 793
6	Mendi	37 163
7	Kokopo	32 957
8	Madang	26 897
9	Kimbe	22 811
10	Bulolo	19 106
11	Goroka	18 192
12	Daru	17 288
13	Kavieng	17 248
14	Wewak	16 698
15	Wau	16 350
16	Kiunga	14 879
17	Alotau	13 928
18	Tari	12 457
19	Vanimo	12 129

PAPUANIUGINI • PAPUA NEW GUINEA

Capital	Port Moresby	Population	6 057 263 (106)	% in cities	12%
GDP per capita	$2300 (181)	Area km²	462 840 km² (54)	GMT +/-	+10
Neighbours (km)	Indonesia 820 • Coast 5152				

RECENT INTERNATIONAL MATCHES PLAYED BY PAPUA NEW GUINEA

2007	Opponents	Score	Venue	Comp	Scorers	Att	Referee
13-07	Solomon Islands	L 1-2	Honiara	Fr	Davani		
2008							
No international matches played in 2008							
2009							
No international matches played in 2009							
2010							
No international matches played in 2010							
2011							
27-08	Cook Islands	W 4-0	Boulari	PGr1	Hans 2 [18 50], Muta.D [55], Lepani [85]		Billon NCL
1-09	Tahiti	D 1-1	Boulari	PGr1	Muta.C [15]		Achari FIJ
3-09	Kiribati †	W 17-1	Boulari	PGr1	Kini 3 [13 79 85], Lepani 4 [15 16 54 68], Foster [16], Hans 2 [21 45p], Moka 3 [24 28 41], Yasasa 2 [73 74], Bondaluke [76], Wasi [92+]		Oiaka SOL
5-09	Fiji	L 0-2	Boulari	PGr1			Billon NCL
2012							
2-06	Solomon Islands	L 0-1	Honiara	OCr1		15 000	Hauata TAH
4-06	New Zealand	L 1-2	Honiara	OCr1	Hans [89p]	3 000	George VAN
6-06	Fiji	D 1-1	Honiara	OCr1	Kema Jack [85]	3 000	Zitouni TAH

Fr = Friendly match • PG = Pacific Games • WC = FIFA World Cup • † Not a full international

PAPUA NEW GUINEA 2011-12

NATIONAL SOCCER LEAGUE

	Pl	W	D	L	F	A	Pts	Hekari	Eastern	PNG Utd	Gigira	Tukoko	Bulolo	Souths
Hekari United †	16	13	2	1	56	9	41		3-1	1-2 n/p	3-0	1-0 5-0	3-0	6-1
Eastern Stars †	17	8	7	2	35	16	31	0-0 1-1		1-1	0-0	5-2	0-0 4-2	7-0 3-0
PNG United †	15	7	4	4	23	18	25	0-3	0-1 n/p		0-1 3-1	1-1 n/p	2-0	2-1
Gigira Laitepo Morobe	17	7	1	9	20	31	22	0-4 0-3	2-0 0-5	1-3		2-3 n/p	3-1	2-1 n/p
Tukoko University †	17	5	3	9	26	39	18	0-5	0-1 3-3	2-2	3-1		1-3 0-2	1-2 4-2
Bulolo United	18	5	2	11	25	41	17	0-4 2-9	1-2	0-1 2-2	0-3 0-1	0-3		5-1
Petro Souths	16	3	1	12	19	50	10	2-5 n/p	1-1	0-2 3-2	0-2	3-1	2-4 0-3	

15/10/2011 - 31/03/2012 • † Qualified for the play-off semi-finals

PLAY-OFFS

Semi-finals

Hekari United	3
Tukoko University	1

Finals

Hekari United †	3
Eastern Stars	0

PNG United	0
Eastern Stars	1

† Qualified for OFC Champions League

Final: Lloyd Robson Oval, Port Moresby, 2-04-2012
3rd place: PNG United 2-2 3-2p Tukoko University

MEDALS TABLE

		Overall		Lge		OFC	Town
		G	S	G	S	G S	
1	Hekari United	6		6		1	Port Moresby
2	Gelle Hills United		2		2		Port Moresby
3	Eastern Stars		2		2		Milne Bay
4	Gigira Rapatona Morobe		1		1		Lae
5	Rapatona Tigers		1		1		Port Moresby

POL – POLAND

FIFA/COCA-COLA WORLD RANKING

'93	'94	'95	'96	'97	'98	'99	'00	'01	'02	'03	'04	'05	'06	'07	'08	'09	'10	'11	'12
28	29	33	53	48	31	32	43	33	34	25	25	22	24	22	34	58	73	66	55

2012

Jan	Feb	Mar	Apr	May	Jun	Jul	Aug	Sep	Oct	Nov	Dec	High	Low	Av
68	70	75	65	65	62	54	54	56	54	54	55	16	75	37

The finals of Euro 2012 were a triumph for co-hosts Poland with a summer of fine football that will live long in the collective memory but for the Polish national team it is a tournament that supporters will want to forget quickly. It got off to the best possible start when star striker Robert Lewandowski scored an early goal against Greece but it was mainly downhill from then on. The Greeks pulled a goal back to draw the game and that was also the result of the second match against Russia. That left a winner-takes-all tie against the Czech Republic, but much to the disappointment of the passionate crowd they lost 1-0 and finished bottom of their group and were out. Coach Franciszek Smuda stepped down and was replaced by Waldemar Fornalik for a very tricky 2014 2014 FIFA World Cup qualifying group. The legacy effect of hosting the finals was very quickly apparent even before the finals kicked-off with Slask Wroclaw winning their first title since 1977. Playing in the magnificent new Municipal Stadium, Slask won away to Wisla Kraków on the final day of the season on which three other clubs - Ruch, Legia and Lech - were also in contention. A second half goal from their Slovenian defender Rok Elsner secured the title for Slask while the cup went to Legia who beat Ruch Chorzów 3-0 in the final in Kielce.

UEFA EUROPEAN CHAMPIONSHIP RECORD
1960 r1   **1964** r1   **1968-2004** DNQ   **2008** 14 r1   **2012** 13 r1 (co-hosts)

POLISH FOOTBALL ASSOCIATION (PZPN)

Bitwy Warszawskiej 1920 r.7, 02-366 Warsaw
+48 22 5512300
+48 22 5512240
pzpn@pzpn.pl
www.pzpn.pl
FA 1919 CON 1954 FIFA 1923
P Zbigniew Boniek
GS Maciej Sawicki

THE STADIA
2014 FIFA World Cup Stadia

Stadion Narodowy
Warsaw — 58 500
Stadion Miejski
Wroclaw — 43 308

Other Main Stadia

PGE Arena
Gdansk — 43 615
Stadion Miejski
Poznan — 43 269
Stadion im. Henryka Reymana
Kraków — 33 326
Pepsi Arena
Warsaw — 31 103

MAJOR CITIES/TOWNS

#	City	Population
1	Warsaw	1 707 566
2	Kraków	755 192
3	Lódz	743 898
4	Wroclaw	631 154
5	Poznan	557 972
6	Gdánsk	453 404
7	Szczecin	405 539
8	Bydgoszcz	357 833
9	Lublin	350 387
10	Katowice	308 170
11	Bialystok	296 227
12	Gdynia	249 946
13	Czestochowa	241 063
14	Radom	223 424
15	Sosnowiec	219 551
16	Torun	204 891
17	Kielce	204 550
18	Zabrze	187 349
36	Chorzów	111 794

RZECZPOSPOLITA POLSKA • REPUBLIC OF POLAND

Capital: Warsaw   Population: 38 482 919 (34)   % in cities: 61%
GDP per capita: $17 800 (69)   Area km²: 312 685 km² (69)   GMT +/-: +1
Neighbours (km): Belarus 605, Czech Republic 615, Germany 456, Lithuania 91, Russia 432, Slovakia 420, Ukraine 428 • Coast 440

RECENT INTERNATIONAL MATCHES PLAYED BY POLAND

2010	Opponents	Score	Venue	Comp	Scorers	Att	Referee
20-01	Thailand	W 3-1	Nak'n Ratchasima	Fr	Glik [43], Malecki [52], Robak [87]	20 000	Mbaga TAN
23-01	Singapore	W 6-1	Nak'n Ratchasima	Fr	Lewandowski.R 2 [26p 37], Iwanski [45p], Brozek.Pi [69], OG [80], Nowak.T [88p]		Amwayi KEN
3-03	Bulgaria	W 2-0	Warsaw	Fr	Blaszczykowski [42], Lewandowski.R [62]	6 800	Kever SUI
29-05	Finland	D 0-0	Kielce	Fr		14 200	Avram ROU
2-06	Serbia	D 0-0	Kufstein	Fr		2 000	Drabek AUT
8-06	Spain	L 0-6	Murcia	Fr		30 000	Koukoulakis GRE
11-08	Cameroon	L 0-3	Szczecin	Fr		17 000	Asumaa FIN
4-09	Ukraine	D 1-1	Lodz	Fr	Jelen [41]	6 500	Irmatov UZB
7-09	Australia	L 1-2	Krakow	Fr	Lewandowski.R [18]	17 000	Bebek CRO
9-10	USA	D 2-2	Chicago	Fr	Matuszczyk [29], Blaszczykowski [72]	31 696	Depiero CAN
12-10	Ecuador	D 2-2	Montreal	Fr	Smolarek [60], Obraniak [70]	1 000	Navarro CAN
17-11	Cote d'Ivoire	W 3-1	Poznan	Fr	Lewandowski.R 2 [19 80], Obraniak [65]	42 000	Toma JPN
10-12	Bosnia-Herzegovina	D 2-2	Antalya	Fr	Pawel Brozek 2 [7 52]	100	Ogretmenoglu TUR
2011							
6-02	Moldova	W 1-0	Vila Real	Fr	Plizga [15]	250	Dos Anjos POR
9-02	Norway	W 1-0	Faro	Fr	Lewandowski.R [18]	500	Dos Anjos POR
25-03	Lithuania	L 0-2	Kaunas	Fr		5 000	Treimanis LVA
29-03	Greece	D 0-0	Larissa	Fr		12 000	Atkinson ENG
5-06	Argentina	W 2-1	Warsaw	Fr	Mierzejewski [26], Pawel Brozek [67]	12 000	Grafe GER
9-06	France	L 0-1	Warsaw	Fr		32 000	Kuipers NED
10-08	Georgia	W 1-0	Lubin	Fr	Blaszczykowski [35]	12 310	Shandor UKR
2-09	Mexico	D 1-1	Warsaw	Fr	Pawel Brozek [27]	18 000	Deaconu ROU
6-09	Germany	D 2-2	Gdansk	Fr	Lewandowski.R [55], Blaszczykowski [90p]	38 000	Orsato ITA
7-10	Korea Republic	D 2-2	Seoul	Fr	Lewandowski.R [29], Blaszczykowski [83]	40 000	Shukralla BHR
11-10	Belarus	W 2-0	Wiesbaden	Fr	Blaszczykowski [31], Lewandowski.R [69]	5 116	Sippel GER
11-11	Italy	L 0-2	Wroclaw	Fr		42 771	Duhamel FRA
15-11	Hungary	W 2-1	Poznan	Fr	Pawel Brozek [37], OG [85]	7 500	Kaasik EST
2012							
29-02	Portugal	D 0-0	Warsaw	Fr		53 179	Yefet ISR
22-05	Latvia	W 1-0	Klagengurt	Fr	Sobiech [82]	200	Lechner AUT
26-05	Slovakia	W 1-0	Klagenfurt	Fr	Perquis [30]	2 100	Eisner AUT
2-06	Andorra	W 4-0	Warsaw	Fr	Obraniak [13], Lewandowski.R [37], Blaszczykowski [39p], Wasilewski [77p]	26 000	Delferiere BEL
8-06	Greece	D 1-1	Warsaw	ECr1	Lewandowski.R [17]	56 826	Velasco ESP
12-06	Russia	D 1-1	Warsaw	ECr1	Blaszczykowski [57]	53 617	Stark GER
16-06	Czech Republic	L 0-1	Wroclaw	ECr1		44 416	Thomson SCO
15-08	Estonia	L 0-1	Tallinn	Fr		5 312	Johnsen NOR
7-09	Montenegro	D 2-2	Podorica	WCq	Blaszczykowski [6], Mierzejewski [55]	11 420	Jakobsson ISL
11-09	Moldova	W 2-0	Wroclaw	WCq	Blaszczykowski [33], Wawrzyniak [81]	26 145	Spathas GRE
12-10	South Africa	W 1-0	Warsaw	Fr	Komorowski [82]	42 026	Prihoda CZE
17-10	England	D 1-1	Warsaw	WCq	Glik [70]	47 000	Rocchi ITA
14-11	Uruguay	L 1-3	Gdansk	Fr	Obraniak [64]	39 460	Collum SCO
14-12	FYR Macedonia	W 4-1	Antalya	Fr	Milik [12], Pawlowski [23], Jedrzejczyk [63], Sobota [79]	100	Gocek TUR

Fr = Friendly match • EC = UEFA EURO 2008 • WC = FIFA World Cup • q = qualifier • r1 = first round group

POLAND NATIONAL TEAM HISTORICAL RECORDS

Caps: 102 - Michal Zewlakow 1998- • 100 - Grzegorz Lato 1971-84 • 97 - Kazimierz Deyna 1968-78 • 96 - Jacek Bak 1993-2008 & Jacek Krzynowek 1999-2009 • 91 - Wladislaw Zmuda 1973-86 • 82 - Antoni Szymanowski 1970-80 • 80 - Zbigniew Boniek 1976-88 • 75 - Wlodzimierz Lubanski 1963-80 • 74 - Tomasz Waldoch 1991-2002 • 72 - Maciej Zurawski 1998-2008 • 70 - Piotr Swierczewski 1992-2003

Goals: 48 - Wlodzimierz Lubanski 1963-80 • 45 - Grzegorz Lato 1971-84 • 41 - Kazimierz Deyna 1968-78 • 39 - Ernst Pol 1955-65 • 32 - Andrzej Szarmach 1973-82 • 27 - Gerard Cieslik 1947-58 • 24 - Zbigniew Boniek 1976-88 • 21 - Ernest Willimowski 1934-39 • 20 - Dariusz Dziekanowski 1981-90 & Euzebiusz Smolarek 2002- • 19 - Roman Kosecki 1988-95 • 18 - Lucjan Brychczy 1954-69

Coaches: For coaches pre 1976 see Oliver's Almanack 2012 • Jacek Gmoch 1976-78 • Ryszard Kulesza 1978-80 • Antoni Piechniczek 1981-86 • Wojciech Lazarek 1986-89 • Andrzej Strejlau 1989-93 • Leslaw Cmikiewicz 1993 • Henryk Apostel 1994-95 • Wladyslaw Stachurski 1996 • Antoni Piechniczek 1996-97 • Krzysztof Pawlak 1997 • Janusz Wojcik 1997-99 • Jerzy Engel 2000-02 • Zbigniew Boniek 2002 • Pawel Janas 2003-06 • Leo Beenhakker 2006-09 • Stefan Majewski 2009 • Franciszek Smuda 2009-12 • Waldemar Fornalik 2012-

POLAND 2011-12

LIGA POLSKA
ORANGE EKSTRAKLASA

	Pl	W	D	L	F	A	Pts	Slask	Ruch	Legia	Lech	Korona	Polonia	Wisla	Górnik	Zaglebie	Jagiellonia	Widzew	Podbeskidzie	Lechia	GKS	LKS	Cracovia
Slask Wroclaw †	30	17	5	8	47	31	56		1-1	0-4	3-1	1-2	4-0	0-1	1-1	2-1	3-1	1-2	1-0	1-0	1-0	4-0	3-0
Ruch Chorzów ‡	30	16	7	7	44	28	55	0-1		0-1	3-0	4-1	0-1	1-0	0-0	2-1	1-0	3-1	2-2	1-2	2-1	2-2	2-0
Legia Warszawa ‡	30	15	8	7	42	17	53	1-2	2-0		0-1	1-0	0-0	2-0	3-1	3-0	1-1	2-0	1-2	3-0	1-1	2-0	0-0
Lech Poznan ‡	30	15	7	8	42	22	52	2-0	3-0	0-0		1-0	1-0	0-1	1-0	3-2	4-1	0-1	1-0	2-1	0-1	4-0	3-1
Korona Kielce	30	13	9	8	34	29	48	2-1	2-2	1-0	2-2		3-0	0-0	0-2	2-0	0-2	2-0	1-0	2-2	0-2	0-0	
Polonia Warszawa	30	13	6	11	33	32	45	3-0	0-1	2-1	1-0	0-0		1-1	1-1	0-4	4-1	1-2	2-2	1-0	2-1	2-0	2-1
Wisla Krakow	30	12	7	11	29	26	43	0-1	3-2	0-0	0-0	0-1	0-1		0-1	1-0	3-1	1-0	0-1	0-1	2-0	3-2	1-0
Górnik Zabrze	30	11	9	10	36	30	42	0-2	1-2	2-0	2-1	2-0	1-0	2-0		4-1	2-0	1-1	3-0	2-2	1-0	0-0	0-1
Zaglebie Lubin	30	11	7	12	36	42	40	1-5	1-1	0-4	1-1	3-1	1-0	2-2	2-1		2-1	1-0	0-0	0-1	1-1	2-1	1-1
Jagiellonia Bialystok	30	11	6	13	35	45	39	0-2	0-1	0-0	2-0	1-1	3-2	1-0	2-1	3-1		4-1	0-2	1-0	2-1	2-1	
Widzew Lodz	30	9	12	9	25	26	39	2-2	1-2	1-1	0-0	0-0	1-0	1-1	2-0	0-0	4-2		0-1	0-1	1-0	0-1	1-0
Podbeskidzie	30	9	8	13	26	39	35	1-1	0-1	0-1	0-0	2-3	1-1	1-3	1-1	1-0	2-2	0-0		1-0	1-0	0-1	1-0
Lechia Gdansk	30	7	10	13	21	30	31	1-1	1-0	1-0	0-0	0-0	1-3	0-2	2-1	0-1	0-1	0-0	2-3		0-0	0-0	1-1
GKS Belchatow	30	7	10	13	34	36	31	3-0	1-1	0-2	0-3	0-2	2-1	2-2	1-1	2-1	2-0	0-0	6-0	1-3		3-0	2-2
LKS Lodz	30	5	9	16	23	53	24	1-2	0-4	1-3	0-5	0-2	0-2	1-2	1-1	1-2	1-1	1-1	2-1	0-0	1-1		2-2
Cracovia	30	4	10	16	20	41	22	0-1	0-2	1-3	0-3	1-2	0-0	1-0	1-3	0-2	0-0	0-0	3-1	1-1	2-1	0-1	

29/07/2011 - 6/05/2012 • † Qualified for the UEFA Champions League • ‡ Qualified for the Europa League • Attendance: 2,121,248 @ 8,839
Top scorers: **22** - Artjoms **RUDNEVS** LVA, Lech Poznan • **15** - Tomasz **FRANKOWSKI**, Jagiellonia • **12** - Arkadiusz **PIECH**, Ruch Chorzów

MEDALS TABLE

		Overall			League			Cup		Europe		
		G	S	B	G	S	B	G	S	G	S	B
1	Legia Warszawa	23	17	16	8	11	14	15	6		2	
2	Górnik Zabrze	20	12	7	14	4	7	6	7		1	
3	Wisla Kraków	18	18	9	14	12	9	4	6			
4	Ruch Chorzów	16	12	8	13	6	8	3	6			
5	Lech Poznan	11	2	4	6		4	5	2			
6	Widzew Lódz	5	7	4	4	7	3	1				1
7	Cracovia	5	2		5	2						
8	Zaglebie Sosnowiec	4	5	2		4	2	4	1			
9	Slask Wroclaw	4	3	1	2	3	1	2				
10	Pogon Lwow	4	3		4	3						
	Polonia Warszawa	4	3		2	3		2				
12	GKS Katowice	3	9	4		4	4	3	5			
13	LKS Lódz	3	2	2	2	1	2	1	1			

POLAND 2011-12

I LIGA POLSKA

	Pl	W	D	L	F	A	Pts	Piast	Pogon	Zawisza	Kolejarz	LKS	Górnik	Arka	Flota	Ruch	Warta	Olimpia	Sandecja	GKS	Dolcan	Polonia	Wisla	Polkowice	Olimpia
Piast Gliwice	34	19	7	8	57	40	64		2-1	3-0	2-0	1-1	2-2	2-2	3-2	0-1	3-0	1-0	2-1	3-0	3-2	3-1	2-1	1-1	1-0
Pogon Szczecin	34	18	7	9	54	30	61	2-1		1-0	1-2	0-2	4-0	3-1	1-0	5-1	2-1	1-1	1-0	1-0	2-3	3-0	3-0	3-2	3-1
Zawisza Bydgoszcz	34	16	11	7	47	39	59	1-1	2-1		1-1	2-3	3-2	3-0	2-2	2-1	0-0	4-3	1-1	2-0	3-1	1-1	2-1	1-0	0-0
Kolejarz Stróze	34	16	9	9	40	34	57	0-1	1-1	0-0		0-3	1-2	1-1	0-0	0-2	3-2	0-0	2-0	2-3	2-0	3-1	2-2
LKS Nieciecza	34	15	11	8	42	26	56	2-3	1-1	0-0	1-2		0-0	2-1	2-3	0-0	2-2	2-0	0-0	2-0	2-1	1-0	1-0	2-0	3-0
Górnik Leczna	34	15	9	10	50	37	54	2-0	0-1	4-2	3-0	0-0		2-1	5-2	0-2	1-1	2-0	0-2	2-0	1-1	2-1	2-1	3-0	2-0
Arka Gdynia	34	13	12	9	50	41	51	2-2	0-2	5-2	0-1	1-0	2-2		1-1	1-3	0-0	1-1	2-0	1-1	3-1	4-0	1-0	2-1	3-1
Flota Swinoujscie	34	12	13	9	46	43	49	0-0	1-0	1-2	0-2	1-0	1-1	0-1		5-1	0-0	0-0	0-4	0-0	1-2	0-0	2-2	3-0	2-1
Ruch Radzionków	34	13	9	12	46	51	48	1-2	1-1	4-1	1-1	1-0	0-1	2-3	2-2		2-0	1-1	1-1	2-2	1-0	0-0	1-0	4-4	4-1
Warta Poznan	34	12	10	12	44	36	46	1-3	1-2	0-1	0-1	2-2	2-0	1-1	4-2	1-0		1-2	1-2	2-2	3-0	2-0	1-2	1-0	2-0
Olimpia Grudziadz	34	10	13	11	46	41	43	2-0	0-0	0-1	4-1	1-1	0-0	0-0	1-2	4-0	2-1		1-1	1-1	0-2	3-1	3-3	3-2	3-0
Sandecja Nowy Sacz	34	10	10	14	42	46	40	4-0	1-0	0-1	1-1	2-0	1-4	3-0	1-1	1-2	0-3	1-1		0-0	1-2	2-3	1-1	1-1	2-0
GKS Katowice	34	9	12	13	33	38	39	3-2	0-2	0-1	0-1	0-1	1-0	0-0	0-0	1-2	0-3	1-0	2-0		3-1	2-0	0-1	5-0	1-1
Dolcan Zabki	34	10	9	15	40	53	39	3-1	2-1	1-0	1-2	1-0	0-0	1-1	2-2	2-0	0-2	0-3	1-2	0-0		0-0	1-2	1-2	2-2
Polonia Bytom	34	9	9	16	37	51	36	0-2	0-3	1-1	0-1	0-0	1-1	1-3	1-2	1-2	0-1	4-1	2-1	4-2	1-1		2-0	1-1	3-2
Wisla Plock	34	9	8	17	39	50	35	1-0	1-0	2-1	0-2	1-3	3-1	0-2	0-2	2-0	3-3	1-1	6-1	0-2	1-2	0-2		1-0	1-1
KS Polkowice	34	7	9	18	40	64	30	0-2	1-1	1-1	1-0	0-2	1-4	0-1	3-2	3-1	0-0	3-2	0-0	1-2	3-2	0-2	2-2		3-1
Olimpia Elblag	34	4	10	20	33	66	22	1-3	2-1	0-3	0-2	0-1	1-0	1-4	1-3	1-2	0-2	0-0	0-0	2-2	4-1	2-1	1-1	3-4	

22/07/2011 - 27/05/2012 • Top scorer: **18** - Wojciech **KEDZIORA**, Piast

PUCHAR POLSKI 2011-12

Second Round

Legia Warszawa	4	
Rozwój Katowice *	1	
OKS 1945 Olsztyn *	0	
Widzew Lodz	1	
Górnik Zabrze	1	
Dolcan Zabki *	0	
Korona Kielce	0	
Gryf Orlex Wejherowo *	1	
Slask Wroclaw	3	
Okocimski KS Brzesko *	1	
GKS Belchatow	0	
Podbeskidzie *	3	
Polonia Warszawa	4	
Ruch Radzionków *	0	
Olimpia Elblag *	0 1p	
Arka Gdynia	0 3p	
Wisla Krakow	4	
Flota Swinoujscie *	2	
Lechia Gdansk	0	
Limanovia Limanowa *	1	
Polonia Bytom	1 5p	
Puszcza Niepolomice *	1 4p	
Chrobry Glogów *	0	
Lech Poznan	3	
Ruch Zdzieszowice *	3	
Jagiellonia Bialystok	1	
Zaglebie Lubin	2	
MKS Kluczbork *	3	
Cracovia	1	
Piast Gliwice *	0	
LKS Lodz *	0	
Ruch Chorzow	1	

Third Round

Legia Warszawa *	3	
Widzew Lodz	0	
Górnik Zabrze	0	
Gryf Orlex Wejherowo *	1	
Slask Wroclaw	1	
Podbeskidzie *	0	
Polonia Warszawa	1	
Arka Gdynia *	3	
Wisla Krakow	2	
Limanovia Limanowa *	1	
Polonia Bytom *	1	
Lech Poznan	3	
Ruch Zdzieszowice *		
MKS Kluczbork		
Cracovia	1	
Ruch Chorzów *	2	

Quarter-finals

Legia Warszawa	3	1
Gryf Orlex Wejherowo *	0	1
Slask Wroclaw	0	3
Arka Gdynia *	2	1
Wisla Krakow	1	1
Lech Poznan *	0	0
Ruch Zdzieszowice *	1	1
Ruch Chorzów	4	2

Semi-finals

Legia Warszawa	2	2
Arka Gdynia *	1	1
Wisla Krakow	1	3	5p
Ruch Chorzów *	3	1	6p

Final

Legia Warszawa ‡	3
Ruch Chorzów	0

CUP FINAL

Arena Kielc, Kielce, 24-04-2012
Att: 10,100. Ref: Hubert Siejewicz
Scorers – Ljuboja [8], Radovic [41], Zyro [55] for Legia
Legia – Dusan Kuciak – Artur Jedrzejczyk, Jakub Wawrzyniak (Tomasz Kielbowicz 70), Inaki Astiz, Michael Zewlakow (c) (Rafal Wolski 86) – Miroslav Radovic, Ivica Vrdoljak●, Janusz Gol, Michal Zyro (Jakub Rzezniczak 82) – Danijel Ljuboja●, Michal Kucharczyk●. Tr: Maciej Skorza
Ruch – Michal Peskovic – Piotr Stawarczyk, Rafal Grodzicki, Marek Szyndrowski (Wojciech Gryb 46), Lukasz Burliga●, Marcin Malinowski (Pawel Lisowski 32), Lukasz Janoszka, Marek Zienczuk, Gabor Straka, Andrzej Niedzielan (Pawel Abbott 57), Maciej Jankowski. Tr: Waldemar Fornalik

* Home team/home team in the 1st leg · ‡ Qualified for the Europa League

POR – PORTUGAL

FIFA/COCA-COLA WORLD RANKING

'93	'94	'95	'96	'97	'98	'99	'00	'01	'02	'03	'04	'05	'06	'07	'08	'09	'10	'11	'12
20	20	16	13	30	36	15	6	4	11	17	9	10	8	8	11	5	8	7	7

2012

Jan	Feb	Mar	Apr	May	Jun	Jul	Aug	Sep	Oct	Nov	Dec	High	Low	Av
7	6	7	5	5	10	5	5	4	3	4	7	3	43	12

Portugal suffered the heartbreak of defeat on penalties for the first time at an international tournament when they lost to Spain in the semi-finals of Euro 2012. The match in Donetsk saw the Portuguese match their opponents throughout but neither side could score and it was Joao Moutinho and Bruno Alves who missed during the shoot-out to send the Spanish through. Portugal had qualified from the most difficult first round group, a task made more tricky when they lost their opener to Germany, but inspired by Cristiano Ronaldo they won their next three games to make it to the semi-finals and maintain their record of having reached the knock-out stage of every European Championship for which they have qualified. At home, FC Porto retained their league title although not in the same emphatic form that had seen them win the treble the season before. They lost just once - to Gil Vicente - but failed to get past the last 32 of the cup where they lost to Academica Coimbra. Inspired by the victory, Academica then made it all the way to final where they beat Sporting 1-0, a fourth-minute goal by Marinho winning the first trophy for the club since 1939. Having earlier lost to Athletic Bilbao in the semi-final of the Europa League, Sporting were the only one of the 'Big Three' to miss out on a trophy after Benfica claimed the League Cup.

UEFA EUROPEAN CHAMPIONSHIP RECORD
1960 QF 1964 r1 1968-1980 DNQ **1984** SF 1988-1992 DNQ **1996** QF **2000** SF **2004** 2 F (Hosts) **2008** 7 QF **2012** 4 SF

FEDERACAO PORTUGUESA DE FUTEBOL (FPF)
Rua Alexandre Herculano, no.58, Apartado 24013, 1250-012 Lisbon
☎ +351 21 3252700
📠 +351 21 3252780
✉ ceo@fpf.pt
🌐 www.fpf.pt
FA 1914 CON 1954 FIFA 1923
P Fernando Gomes Da Silva
GS Tiago Craveiro

THE STADIA
2014 FIFA World Cup Stadia
Estádio do Dragão
Porto — 50 399
Estádio AXA
Braga — 30 286

Other Main Stadia
Estádio da Luz
Lisbon — 65 647
Estádio José Alvalade
Lisbon — 50 049

MAJOR CITIES/TOWNS
		Population
1	Lisbon	482 678
2	Porto	237 448
3	Amadora	181 377
4	Braga	130 300
5	Setúbal	121 668
6	Queluz	120 811
7	Coimbra	110 764
8	Cacém	109 120
9	Funchal	93 938
10	Mem Martins	89 121
11	Rio de Mouro	65 237
12	Corroios	59 395
13	Aveiro	57 459
14	Odivelas	55 544
15	Amora	55 047
16	Rio Tinto	53 068
17	Leiria	50 087
18	Guimarães	43 062
19	Faro	42 301

REPUBLICA PORTUGUESA • PORTUGUESE REPUBLIC
Capital	Lisbon	Population	10 707 924 (75)	% in cities	59%
GDP per capita	$22 200 (54)	Area km²	92 090 km² (110)	GMT +/-	0
Neighbours (km)	Spain 1214 • Coast 1793				

RECENT INTERNATIONAL MATCHES PLAYED BY PORTUGAL

2010	Opponents	Score	Venue	Comp	Scorers	Att	Referee
15-06	Côte d'Ivoire	D 0-0	Port Elizabeth	WCr1		37 034	Larrionda URU
21-06	Korea DPR	W 7-0	Cape Town	WCr1	Raul Meireles 29, Simao 53, Hugo Almeida 56, Tiago 2 60 89, Liedson 81, Cristiano Ronaldo 87	63 644	Pozo CHI
25-06	Brazil	D 0-0	Durban	WCr1		62 712	Archundia MEX
29-06	Spain	L 0-1	Cape Town	WCr2		62 955	Baldassi ARG
3-09	Cyprus	D 4-4	Guimaraes	ECq	Hugo Almeida 8, Raul Meireles 29, Danny 50, Manuel Fernandes 60	9 100	Clattenburg ENG
7-09	Norway	L 0-1	Oslo	ECq		24 535	Duhamel FRA
8-10	Denmark	W 3-1	Porto	ECq	Nani 2 29 30, Cristiano Ronaldo 85	27 117	Braamhaar NED
12-10	Iceland	W 3-1	Reykjavik	ECq	Cristiano Ronaldo 3, Raul Meireles 27, Postiga 72	9 767	Einwaller AUT
17-11	Spain	W 4-0	Lisbon	Fr	Carlos Martins 45, Postiga 2 49 68, Hugo Almeida 90	38 000	Gautier FRA
2011							
9-02	Argentina	L 1-2	Geneva	Fr	Cristiano Ronaldo 21	30 000	Busacca SUI
26-03	Chile	D 1-1	Leiria	Fr	Varela 16	10 694	Blom NED
29-03	Finland	W 2-0	Aveiro	Fr	Ruben Micael 2 10 71	13 737	Studer SUI
4-06	Norway	W 1-0	Lisbon	ECq	Helder Postiga 53	47 829	Cakir TUR
10-08	Luxembourg	W 5-0	Faro	Fr	Helder Postiga 26, Cristiano Ronaldo 44, Fabio Coentrao 47, Hugo Almeida 2 59 73		Mateu ESP
2-09	Cyprus	W 4-0	Nicosia	ECq	Cristiano Ronaldo 2 35p 82, Hugo Almeida 84, Danny 92+	15 444	Rocchi ITA
7-10	Iceland	W 5-3	Porto	ECq	Nani 2 13 21, Helder Postiga 44, Joao Moutinho 81, Eliseu 87	35 715	Nijhuis NED
11-10	Denmark	L 1-2	Copenhagen	ECq	Cristiano Ronaldo 92+	37 012	Rizzoli ITA
11-11	Bosnia-Herzegovina	D 0-0	Zenica	ECpo		15 292	Webb ENG
15-11	Bosnia-Herzegovina	W 6-2	Lisbon	ECpo	Cristiano Ronaldo 2 8 53, Nani 24, Helder Postiga 2 72 82, Miguel Veloso 80	47 728	Stark GER
2012							
29-02	Poland	D 0-0	Warsaw	Fr		53 179	Yefet ISR
26-05	FYR Macedonia	D 0-0	Leiria	Fr		19 323	Kelly IRL
2-06	Turkey	L 1-3	Lisbon	Fr	Nani 57	62 000	Studer Sui
9-06	Germany	L 0-1	Lviv	ECr1			Lannoy FRA
13-06	Denmark	W 3-2	Lviv	ECr1	Pepe 24, Helder Postiga 36, Varela 87	34 915	Thomson SCO
17-06	Netherlands	W 2-1	Kharkov	ECr1	Cristiano Ronaldo 2 28 74	38 633	Rizzoli ITA
21-06	Czech Republic	W 1-0	Warsaw	ECqf	Cristiano Ronaldo 79	58 145	Webb ENG
27-06	Spain	D 0-0	Donetsk	ECsf	L 2-4p	51 500	Cakir TUR
15-08	Panama	W 2-0	Faro	Fr	Nelson Oliveira 30, Cristiano Ronaldo 51	24 181	Fernandez ESP
7-09	Luxembourg	W 2-1	Luxembourg	WCq	Cristiano Ronaldo 28, Helder Postiga 54	8 125	Tohver EST
11-09	Azerbaijan	W 3-0	Braga	WCq	Varela 63, Helder Postiga 85, Bruno Alves 88	29 971	Marciniak POL
12-10	Russia	L 0-1	Moscow	WCq		54 212	Kassai HUN
16-10	Northern Ireland	D 1-1	Porto	WCq	Helder Postiga 79	48 711	Kinhoffer GER
14-11	Gabon	D 2-2	Libreville	Fr	Pizzi 35p, Hugo Almeida 60		Lamptey GHA

Fr = Friendly match • EC = UEFA EURO 2012 • WC = FIFA World Cup • q = qualifier • r1 = first round group • qf = quarter-final

PORTUGAL NATIONAL TEAM HISTORICAL RECORDS

Caps: **127** - Luis Figo 1991-2006 • **110** - Fernando Couto 1990-2004 • **101** - Cristiano Ronaldo 2003- • **94** - Rui Costa 1993-2004 • **88** - Pauleta 1997-2006 • **85** - Simao 1998- • **81** - Joao Pinto 1991-2002 • **80** - Vitor Baia 1990-2002 • **79** - Ricardo 2001-08 & Nuno Gomes 1996- • **75** - Ricardo Carvalho 2003- • **73** - Deco 2003- • **70** - Joao Pinto 1983-96 • **66** - Nene 1971-84

Goals: **47** - Pauleta 1997-2006 • **41** - Eusebio 1961-73 • **38** - Cristiano Ronaldo 2003- • **32** - Luis Figo 1991-2006 • **29** - Nuno Gomes 1996- • **26** - Rui Costa 1993-2004 • **24** - Helder Postiga 2003- • **23** - Joao Pinto 1991-2002 • **22** - Nene 1971-84 & Simao 1998-

Coaches: Committee 1921-23 • Ribeiro dos Reis 1925-26 • Candido de Oliveira 1926-29, 1935-45, 1952 • Maia Loureiro 1929 • Laurindo Grijo 1930 • Tavares da Silva 1931, 1945-47, 1951, 1955-57 • Salvador do Carmo 1932-33, 1950, 1953-54 • Virgilio Paula 1947-48 • Armando Sampaio 1949 • Jose Maria Antunes 1957-60, 1962-64 • Armando Ferreira 1961 • Fernando Peyroteo 1961 • Armando Ferreira 1962-64 • Manuel da Luz Afonso 1964-66 • Jose Gomes da Silva 1967 • Jose Maria Antunes 1968-69 • Jose Gomes da Silva 1970-71 • Jose Augusto 1972-73 • Jose Maria Pedroto 1974-76 • Juca 1977-78 • Mario Wilson 1978-80 • Juca 1980-82 • Otto Gloria 1982-83 • Fernando Cabrita 1983-84 • Jose Augusto Torres 1984-86 • Rui Seabra 1986-87 • Juca 1987-89 • Artur Jorge 1990-91 • Carlos Queiroz 1991-93 • Nelo Vingada 1994 • Antonio Oliveira 1994-96 • Artur Jorge 1996-97 • Humberto Coelho 1997-2000 • Antonio Oliveira 2000-02 • Agostinho Oliveira 2002 • Luiz Felipe Scolari 2003-08 • Carlos Queiroz 2008-10 • Paulo Bento 2010-

PORTUGAL 2011-12

LIGA ZON SAGRES

	Pl	W	D	L	F	A	Pts	Porto	Benfica	Braga	Sporting CP	Marítimo	Guimarães	Nacional	Olhanense	Gil Vicente	Paços	Setúbal	Beira-Mar	Académica	Rio Ave	Feirense	Leiria
FC Porto †	30	23	6	1	69	19	**75**		2-2	3-2	2-0	2-0	3-1	5-0	2-0	3-1	3-0	3-0	3-0	1-1	2-0	2-0	4-0
SL Benfica †	30	21	6	3	66	27	**69**	2-3		2-1	1-0	4-1	2-1	4-1	2-1	4-1	4-1	3-1	4-1	5-1	3-1	1-0
Sporting Braga †	30	19	5	6	59	29	**62**	0-1	1-1		2-1	2-0	4-0	2-0	1-2	3-1	5-2	3-0	1-0	2-1	2-1	3-0	2-1
Sporting CP ‡	30	18	5	7	47	26	**59**	0-0	1-0	3-2		2-3	5-0	1-0	1-1	6-1	1-0	3-0	2-0	2-1	1-0	1-0	3-1
CS Marítimo ‡	30	14	8	8	41	38	**50**	0-2	0-1	1-2	2-0		2-1	2-4	2-1	3-2	1-1	1-0	0-0	3-2	2-1	2-1	1-0
Vitória SC Guimarães	30	14	3	13	40	40	**45**	0-1	1-0	1-1	0-1	1-0		1-0	2-2	1-1	3-1	3-0	0-3	1-2	2-1	1-0	3-2
CD Nacional	30	13	5	12	48	50	**44**	0-2	0-2	1-3	2-3	2-2	1-4		1-0	3-1	1-0	1-1	2-1	4-1	2-1	2-0	2-2
SC Olhanense	30	9	12	9	36	38	**39**	0-0	0-0	3-4	0-0	0-0	1-0	4-4		0-0	1-2	2-2	2-1	0-2	0-2	1-2	2-1
Gil Vicente FC	30	8	10	12	31	42	**34**	3-1	2-2	0-3	2-0	0-0	3-1	0-3	1-1		1-2	0-1	0-0	2-0	0-0	3-1	2-1
Paços de Ferreira	30	8	7	15	35	53	**31**	1-1	1-2	1-1	2-3	1-1	1-5	0-2	1-1	1-2		2-1	0-3	2-0	2-2	3-1	2-1
Vitória FC Setúbal	30	8	6	16	24	49	**30**	1-3	1-3	0-1	1-0	1-1	1-0	0-3	2-3	0-0	2-1		1-0	1-1	2-1	1-1	1-0
SC Beira-Mar	30	8	5	17	26	38	**29**	1-2	0-1	1-2	0-0	1-2	0-1	0-3	1-2	1-0	2-0	2-3		2-1	0-0	2-1	0-1
Académica Coimbra ‡	30	7	8	15	27	38	**29**	0-3	0-0	0-0	1-1	0-1	0-2	4-0	0-1	0-2	0-1	1-0	0-1		1-0	4-0	0-0
Rio Ave FC	30	7	7	16	33	42	**28**	2-5	2-2	0-0	2-3	1-3	0-1	2-1	0-1	2-0	1-0	3-0	4-0	0-0		2-2	2-0
CD Feirense	30	5	9	16	27	49	**24**	0-0	1-2	1-4	0-2	2-2	1-3	0-0	1-1	0-0	0-0	1-0	1-3	1-1	2-0		2-1
União de Leiria	30	5	4	21	25	56	**19**	2-5	0-4	1-0	0-1	1-3	1-0	2-3	1-3	0-0	2-4	2-0	0-0	1-2	1-0	0-4	

12/08/2011 - 12/05/2012 • † Qualified for the UEFA Champions League • ‡ Qualified for the UEFA Cup • Attendance: 1,531,517 @ 9,282
Top scorers: **20** - Oscar **CARDOZO** PAR, Benfica & **LIMA** BRA, Braga • **16** - **HULK** BRA, Porto • **14** - Ricky **VAN WOLFSWINKEL** NED, Sporting CP • **13** - James **RODRIGUEZ** COL, Porto • **11** - **JOAO TOMAS**, Rio Ave; **EDGAR** BRA, Guimarães & **NOLITO** ESP, Benfica • **10** - **BABA DIAWARA** SEN, Marítimo; **CLAUDEMIR** BRA, Nacional; **BRUNO CESAR** BRA, Benfica; Lorenzo **MELGAREJO** PAR, Paços & Mario **RONDON** VEN, Nacional

PORTUGAL 2011-12

LIGA DE HONRA (2)

	Pl	W	D	L	F	A	Pts	Estoril-Praia	Moreirense	Aves	Naval	Belenenses	Oliveirense	Trofense	Penafiel	Atlético CP	União	Leixões	Santa Clara	Arouca	Freamunde	Covilhã	Portimonense
GD Estoril-Praia	30	16	9	5	40	20	**57**		1-0	1-0	2-0	1-0	0-0	0-2	1-1	5-0	1-0	1-1	0-0	2-2	3-0	0-0	1-0
Moreirense FC	30	15	7	8	47	32	**52**	2-1		1-1	1-1	3-2	1-0	4-1	3-1	4-1	2-0	0-1	2-0	0-2	0-0	1-1	2-0
Desportivo Aves	30	12	14	4	38	23	**50**	2-0	0-0		1-1	3-1	1-0	3-1	2-0	3-1	1-1	1-3	2-2	2-0	0-0	1-0	1-1
Naval 1° de Maio	30	12	10	8	40	33	**46**	0-3	1-2	1-1		0-1	1-1	2-1	1-0	2-2	2-0	0-1	5-1	0-0	1-1	2-1	2-0
Os Belenenses	30	10	11	9	34	32	**41**	2-2	1-0	0-0	0-1		2-1	1-3	2-0	0-0	1-1	1-0	2-1	3-0	1-0	0-0	1-1
UD Oliveirense	30	10	9	11	39	38	**39**	0-1	2-3	1-1	3-2	3-2		5-0	2-2	2-1	1-0	2-4	1-0	2-2	2-0	2-0	1-1
CD Trofense	30	11	6	13	36	45	**39**	0-1	2-1	1-0	1-2	1-0	0-0		2-2	1-0	1-0	0-2	2-1	1-1	4-0	2-2	3-1
SC Penafiel	30	10	8	12	33	36	**38**	3-1	1-0	0-1	0-0	2-2	1-0	2-0		1-0	3-1	0-1	1-1	2-1	1-0	0-1	0-3
Atlético CP	30	9	10	11	27	37	**37**	1-0	2-3	0-0	1-0	0-2	2-0	3-0	1-1		1-1	1-0	0-0	1-0	2-2	0-0	0-1
CF União Madeira	30	9	10	11	35	40	**37**	0-0	0-3	3-2	1-3	2-2	2-1	0-1	2-3	1-1		3-1	2-0	2-2	2-2	1-1	2-1
Leixões SC	30	11	7	12	32	34	**37**	0-1	2-1	0-0	0-2	0-1	1-1	2-3	2-1	0-1	1-0		1-2	0-2	2-2	1-0	1-1
GD Santa Clara	30	8	10	12	29	38	**34**	1-2	2-2	0-2	2-2	1-1	2-1	1-0	1-1	1-2	0-1	2-0		0-0	1-0	1-0	2-1
FC Arouca	30	7	13	10	32	36	**34**	1-4	3-1	2-2	1-2	2-0	3-3	2-0	0-2	2-0	0-0	1-1	1-0		0-0	1-1	1-2
SC Freamunde	30	7	13	10	35	40	**34**	2-2	1-1	1-2	1-1	2-1	3-0	3-1	1-0	2-2	2-0	2-1	1-2	2-0		2-2	2-0
Sporting Covilhã	30	7	11	12	22	29	**32**	0-1	1-2	0-2	0-2	0-0	0-1	1-0	0-1	0-2	2-2	1-0	1-1	1-1	2-1		2-0
Portimonense SC	30	8	8	14	35	42	**32**	0-2	1-2	1-1	2-1	2-3	0-1	2-2	3-2	0-1	1-2	2-1	2-2	0-0	2-0	2-1	

20/08/2011 - 13/05/2012 • Top scorers: **19** - **Joeano** BRA, Arouca • **14** - **Manoel** BRA, Panafiel • **12** - **Pires**, Aves & **Lica**, Estoril-Praia • **10** - **Bruno Moreira**, Moreirense; **Bock**, Freamunde & **Adriano Louzada** BRA, Oliveirense • **9** - **Fabio Espinho**, Moreirense; **Guima**, Oliveirense & **Reguila**, Trofense

PORTUGAL 2011-12
II DIVISAO NORTE (3)

	Pl	W	D	L	F	A	Pts
Varzim SC †	30	20	8	2	48	12	**68**
AD Fafe	30	16	6	8	46	29	54
GD Chaves	30	15	9	6	41	26	54
SC Mirandela	30	14	10	6	55	32	52
FC Tirsense	30	11	11	8	39	29	44
AD Os Limianos	30	11	11	8	34	25	44
GD Ribeirão	30	10	14	6	39	31	44
CD Ribeira Brava	30	12	6	12	33	37	42
FC Famalicão	30	10	9	11	29	32	39
Macedo de Cavaleiros	30	10	9	11	43	48	39
FC Vizela	30	9	11	10	40	42	38
CS Marítimo B	30	10	8	12	41	45	38
AD Camacha	30	8	10	12	29	36	**34**
AD Lousada	30	8	8	14	30	45	**32**
Merelinense FC	30	3	7	20	33	68	**16**
AD Oliveirense	30	1	7	22	14	57	**10**

4/09/2011 - 29/04/2012 • † Play-offs

PORTUGAL 2011-12
II DIVISAO CENTRO (3)

	Pl	W	D	L	F	A	Pts
CD Tondela †	30	19	6	5	49	22	**63**
Sporting Espinho	30	19	5	6	50	32	62
CD Operário	30	15	7	8	34	26	52
Boavista FC	30	15	5	10	43	31	50
Amarante FC	30	13	10	7	48	30	49
São João de Ver	30	15	4	11	43	46	49
Gondomar SC	30	13	5	12	27	31	44
CD Cinfães	30	12	7	11	35	40	43
SC Coimbrões	30	9	15	6	30	31	42
Anadia FC	30	11	7	12	45	42	40
Padroense FC	30	11	6	13	47	50	39
Aliados Lordelo	30	10	7	13	41	40	37
Oliveira do Bairro	30	7	7	16	34	50	**28**
SC Angrense	30	5	8	17	36	49	**23**
USC Paredes	30	6	5	19	30	50	**23**
FC Madalena	30	5	6	19	32	54	**21**

4/09/2011 - 29/04/2012 • † Play-offs

PORTUGAL 2011-12
II DIVISAO SUL (3)

	Pl	W	D	L	F	A	Pts
CD Fátima †	30	18	6	6	50	30	60
Oriental Lisboa	30	16	8	6	49	17	56
SCU Torreense	30	15	11	4	47	27	56
AD Carregado	30	15	8	7	57	38	53
CD Pinhalnovense	30	16	5	9	47	32	53
CD Mafra	30	10	16	4	33	22	46
Louletano DC	30	13	7	10	28	33	46
Sertanense FC	30	11	10	9	37	32	43
Estrela Vendas Novas	30	11	5	14	35	34	38
GD Tourizense	30	8	11	11	30	34	35
1° Dezembro	30	8	10	12	28	29	34
Juventude SC Evora	30	9	5	16	29	42	32
GDR Monsanto	30	6	11	13	28	41	**29**
Atlético Reguengos	30	5	11	14	31	53	**26**
Moura AC	30	6	7	17	28	57	**25**
Caldas SC	30	3	9	18	17	53	**18**

4/09/2011 - 29/04/2012 • † Play-offs

PORTUGAL 2011-12
II DIVISAO CHAMPIONSHIP/PROMOTION PLAY-OFFS (3)

	Pl	W	D	L	F	A	Pts	Varzim	Tondela	Fátima
Varzim SC	4	3	1	0	10	2	**10**		3-1	4-1
CD Tondela	4	1	2	1	5	6	**5**	0-0		1-1
CD Fátima	4	0	1	3	4	11	1	0-3	2-3	

13/05/2012 - 10/06/2012

MEDALS TABLE

		Overall	League	Cup	Europe
		G S B	G S B	G S	G S B
1	SL Benfica	61 42 19	32 26 15	27 10	2 6 4
2	FC Porto	50 39 12	26 24 11	20 14	4 1 1
3	Sporting Clube Portugal	38 37 29	18 19 26	19 17	1 1 3
4	OS Belenenses	7 11 14	1 3 14	6 8	
5	Boavista FC	6 4 2	1 3 1	5 1	1
6	Vitória FC Setúbal	3 9 3		1 3	3 8
7	Académica de Coimbra	2 5	1	2 4	
8	Sporting Clube Braga	1 5 1	1 1	1 3	1
9	Atlético Clube Portugal	1 3 2	2	1 3	
10	CS Maritimo	1 2		1 2	
11	SC Olhanense	1 1		1 1	
	Leixoes SC	1 1		1 1	
	SC Beira Mar	1 1		1 1	
14	CF Estrella Amadora	1		1	
15	Vitória SC Guimaraes	5 4	4	5	
16	FC Barreirense	2		2	
17	Campomaiorense	1		1	
	GD Estoril Praia	1		1	
	SC Farense	1		1	
	GD Chaves	1		1	
	FC Paços de Ferreira	1		1	
	FC Rio Ave	1		1	
	Sporting Clube Covilha	1		1	
	SC Uniao Torriense	1		1	
	União Leiria	1		1	
26	GD Fabril		1	1	

TACA DA LIGA BWIN CUP 2011-12

First Round Group Stage

Group A
	Pl	W	D	L	F	A	Pts	Be	Pe	Tr	Le
Os Belenenses	3	2	1	0	8	4	7		3-1	5-3	
SC Penafiel	3	0	3	0	2	2	3	0-0			1-1
CD Trofense	3	0	2	1	1	3	2		1-1		1-1
Leixões SC	3	0	2	1	5	7	2			1-1	

Group B
	Pl	W	D	L	F	A	Pts	SC	Na	SC	Ar
GD Santa Clara	3	2	1	0	3	1	7		1-0		1-1
Naval 1° de Maio	3	2	0	1	4	2	6			2-1	2-0
Sporting Covilhã	3	1	0	2	2	3	3	0-1			1-0
FC Arouca	3	0	1	2	1	4	1			0-1	

Group C
	Pl	W	D	L	F	A	Pts	Mo	Po	Fr	At
Moreirense FC	3	2	1	0	6	4	7				2-1
Portimonense	3	1	1	1	6	6	4	2-3			1-1
SC Freamunde	3	1	1	1	4	4	4	1-1	2-3		
Atlético CP	3	0	1	2	2	4	1			0-1	

Group D
	Pl	W	D	L	F	A	Pts	EP	UM	DA	Ol
GD Estoril-Praia	3	2	0	1	5	3	6		2-0	1-0	
União Madeira	3	1	1	1	1	1	4	4-3		3-2	
Desportivo Aves	3	1	1	1	2	4	4		0-0		
UD Oliveirense	3	1	0	2	2	3	3		2-1	0-1	

Second Round

Gil Vicente FC	1	2
Os Belenenses*	2	0

CS Marítimo	3	2
União Madeira*	2	0

SC Beira-Mar	2	1
Moreirense FC*	2	2

União de Leiria	1	1
GD Santa Clara*	3	0

SC Penafiel*	1	1
Académica C'bra	1	0

CD Feirense	0	2	4p
Portimonense*	1	1	5p

Vitória Setúbal	2	2
Naval 1° Maio*	1	2

SC Olhanense	3	0
GD Estoril-Praia*	4	0

Third Round Group Stage

Group A
	Pl	W	D	L	F	A	Pts	GV	Mo	Sp	RA
Gil Vicente FC	3	2	1	0	4	2	7		2-1		1-0
Moreirense FC	3	1	1	1	3	3	4			1-0	
Sporting CP	3	0	2	1	2	3	2	0-1	1-1		
Rio Ave FC	3	0	2	1	2	3	2		1-1		1-1

Group B
	Pl	W	D	L	F	A	Pts	Be	Ma	SC	VG
SL Benfica	3	3	0	0	9	1	9		3-0	2-0	
CS Marítimo	3	2	0	1	4	3	6			2-0	
GD Santa Clara	3	1	0	2	1	4	3				1-0
Vitória Guimarães	3	0	0	3	1	7	0		1-4	0-2	

Group C
	Pl	W	D	L	F	A	Pts	SB	Na	Pe	Po
Sporting Braga	3	3	0	0	5	1	9			2-0	1-0
CD Nacional	3	1	1	1	3	4	4	1-2			0-0
SC Penafiel	3	1	0	2	2	4	3		1-2		
Portimonense SC	3	0	1	2	2	1	1			0-1	

Group D
	Pl	W	D	L	F	A	Pts	Po	PF	VS	EP
FC Porto	3	3	0	0	5	1	9		2-0	1-0	
Paços de Ferreira	3	2	0	1	3	2	6			1-2	
Vitória Setúbal	3	1	0	2	3	4	3				3-1
GD Estoril-Praia	3	0	0	3	1	5	0		0-1		

Semi-finals

SL Benfica	3
FC Porto	2

Sporting Braga	2	2p
Gil Vicente FC	2	4p

Final

SL Benfica	2
Gil Vicente FC	1

CUP FINAL

Estadio EFAPEL, Coimbra
14-04-2012. Att: 23 452. Ref: Neves
Scorers - Rodrigo [31], Saviola [83] for
Benfica; Ze Luis [79] for Gil Vicente
Benfica - Eduardo - Ezequiel Garay,
Maxi Pereira, Joan Capdevila, Jardel -
Pablo Aimar (Oscar Cardozo 62), Axel
Witsel, Nemanja Matic, Bruno
Cesar●, Nelson Oliveira (Nicolas
Gaitan● 46), Rodrigo (Javier
Saviola● 82). Tr: Jorge Jesus
Gil Vicente - Adriano Facchini -
Cesar Peixoto, Rodrigo Galo,
Halisson, Claudio●, Junior Caicara -
Andre Cunha, Luis Manuel●
(Ze Luis 56), Richard (Joao Vilela 76)
- Luis Carlos (Guilherme 67), Hugo
Vieira. Tr: Paulo Alves

Sporting CP, Rio Ave, SL Benfica, Vitória Guimaraes, Sporting Braga, CD Nacional, FC Porto and Paços de Ferreira all received a bye to the third round group stage. • * Home team in the 1st leg

TACA DE PORTUGAL 2011-12

Round of 64

Académica Coimbra *	1
Oriental Lisboa	0
CA Pêro Pinheiro *	0
FC Porto	8
Santa Maria FC *	1 3p
GDR Monsanto	1 1p
SCM Aljustrelense	0
Leixões SC *	1
CD Ribeira Brava	2
Portosantense *	0
Sporting Lamego *	1
Sporting Covilha	4
Vitória SC Guimarães *	2
Moura AC	1
FC Infesta *	0
Desportivo Aves	4
SC Olhanense	3
FC Pampilhosa *	0
União de Leiria	1
GD Alcochetense *	2
SC Penafiel *	3
Merelinense FC	2
AC Vila Meã	1
GD Estoril-Praia *	3
SC Mirandela *	1
Vitória FC Setúbal	0
GD Joane *	0
Gondomar SC	1
CD Tondela	3
Anadia FC *	2
Sporting Pombal *	1
UD Oliveirense	7
CD Nacional	1
CD Feirense *	0
GD Chaves	0
Paços de Ferreira *	1
São João de Ver	1 4p
Sporting Espinho *	1 2p
UD Sampedrense	1
FC Tirsense *	3
SCU Torreense *	1
Gil Vicente FC	0
UD Sousense	2
Rio Ave FC *	5
AD Lousada *	1
SC Coimbrões	0
AD Pontassolense	1
Moreirense FC *	3
CS Marítimo	1
SC Beira-Mar *	0
Esperança de Lagos	0
Juventud SC Evora *	2
Naval 1° de Maio	1 4p
Macedo de Cavaleiros *	1 2p
Portimonense SC *	0
SL Benfica	2
Os Belenenses	2
CD Trofense *	1
AD Fafe	2 1p
FC Vizela *	2 3p
Sporting Braga	3
1° Dezembro *	1
FC Famalicão	0
Sporting CP	2

Round of 32

Académica Coimbra *	3
FC Porto	0
Santa Maria FC	0
Leixões SC *	1
CD Ribeira Brava *	0 5p
Sporting Covilha	0 4p
Vitória SC Guimarães	0 2p
Desportivo Aves *	0 3p
SC Olhanense	0 4p
GD Alcochetense *	0 2p
SC Penafiel	1
GD Estoril-Praia *	2
SC Mirandela *	1 5p
Gondomar SC	1 4p
CD Tondela *	0
UD Oliveirense	1
CD Nacional	2 5p
Paços de Ferreira *	2 4p
São João de Ver *	0
FC Tirsense	3
SCU Torreense	3
Rio Ave FC *	2
AD Lousada	1
Moreirense FC *	7
CS Marítimo	1
Juventud SC Evora *	0
Naval 1° de Maio *	0
SL Benfica	1
Os Belenenses *	2
FC Vizela	0
Sporting Braga	0
Sporting CP *	2

Round of 16

Académica Coimbra	5
Leixões SC *	2
CD Ribeira Brava	1
Desportivo Aves *	2
SC Olhanense	2 4p
GD Estoril-Praia *	2 2p
SC Mirandela *	1 4p
UD Oliveirense	1 5p
CD Nacional	0 4p
FC Tirsense *	0 3p
SCU Torreense	1
Moreirense FC *	2
CS Marítimo *	2
SL Benfica	1
Os Belenenses	0
Sporting CP *	2

POR – PORTUGAL

TACA DE PORTUGAL 2011-12

Quarter-finals **Semi-finals** **Final**

Académica Coimbra 3
Desportivo Aves 2

Académica Coimbra * 1 2
UD Oliveirense 0 2

SC Olhanense 1
UD Oliveirense 2

Académica Coimbra ‡ 1
Sporting CP 0

CD Nacional 2 6p
Moreirense FC 2 5p

CD Nacional 2 1
Sporting CP * 2 3

TACA DE PORTUGAL 2012
Estadio Nacional, Lisbon, 20-05-2012, Att: 37 522, Ref: Paulo Baptista
Académica Coimbra 1 Marinho [4]
Sporting CP 0

ACADEMICA

RICARDO - CEDRIC Soares●, Abdoulaye BA, JOAO REAL, HELDER CABRAL - DIOGO MELO (c)● (DANILO 80) - ADRIEN SILVA, DAVID SIMAO● (FLAVIO Ferreira 69) - MARINHO (RUI MIGUEL 91+), EDINHO, DIOGO VALENTE. Tr: PEDRO EMANUEL

SPORTING

RUI PATRICIO - JOAO PEREIRA●, ANDERSON POLGA (c), Oguchi ONYEWU, Emiliano INSUA● (ANDRE MARTINS 69) - Stijn SCHAARS● - ELIAS● (Marat IZMAILOV 46), MATIAS FERNANDEZ (JEFFREN Suarez 77) - Andre CARRILLO, Ricky VAN WOLFSWINKEL, DIEGO CAPEL. Tr: Ricardo SA PINTO

CS Marítimo 0
Sporting CP 3

* Home team/home team in the 1st leg
‡ Qualified for the Europa League

PRK – KOREA DPR

FIFA/COCA-COLA WORLD RANKING

'93	'94	'95	'96	'97	'98	'99	'00	'01	'02	'03	'04	'05	'06	'07	'08	'09	'10	'11	'12
62	84	117	144	166	158	172	142	136	124	117	95	82	113	115	113	86	108	110	99

2012												High	Low	Av
Jan	Feb	Mar	Apr	May	Jun	Jul	Aug	Sep	Oct	Nov	Dec			
107	106	111	86	86	89	89	91	81	86	81	99	57	181	118

Korea DPR's status as 'the best of the rest' in Asian football was reinforced at the finals of the AFC Challenge Cup in Nepal in March 2012 as the reclusive nation retained the title they won in 2010. A perfect record in the group stage, thanks to wins over the Philippines, Tajikistan and India, took the North Koreans into the semi-finals of the competition without conceding a goal. Pak Kwang Ryong's brace in the 2-0 win over Palestine in the semi-finals then set up a repeat of the 2010 final with Turkmenistan where a Jang Song Hyok penalty with just three minutes remaining secured the title. Victory means the North Koreans join Japan, Korea Republic and hosts Australia in qualifying for the finals of the AFC Asian Cup in 2015, but with back-to-back wins they have been excluded from competing in the 2014 AFC Challenge Cup. In the twelve games played in 2012 North Korea won nine and drew three but the year ended in disappointment. At the qualifying group for the finals of the 2013 East Asian Cup held in Hong Kong they were knocked-out on goal difference by Australia. The Socceroos 8-0 win over Chinese Taipei in their final match ensured Holger Osieck's side took the one place available in the tournament proper, to be staged in neighbouring South Korea in mid-2013.

FIFA WORLD CUP RECORD

1930-1962 DNE 1966 8 QF 1970 DNE 1974 DNQ 1978 DNE 1982-1994 DNQ 1998-2002 DNE 2006 DNQ 2010 32 r1 2014 DNQ

DPR KOREA FOOTBALL ASSOCIATION (PRK)

Kumsongdong, Kwangbok Street, Mangyongdae Dist., PO Box 818, Pyongyang
☎ +850 2 3814334
Fax +850 2 3814434
✉ chukku-prkfa@hotmail.com

FA 1945 CON 1974 FIFA 1958
P Kim Jong Su
GS Kim Jong Man

THE STADIA

2014 FIFA World Cup Stadia
Kim Il Sung Stadium
Pyongyang 70 000
Yanggakdo Stadium
Pyongyang 30 000

Other Main Stadia
Hamhung Stadium
Hamhung 35 000
Nampo Stadium
Nampo 30 000
Seosan Stadium
Pyongyang 25 000

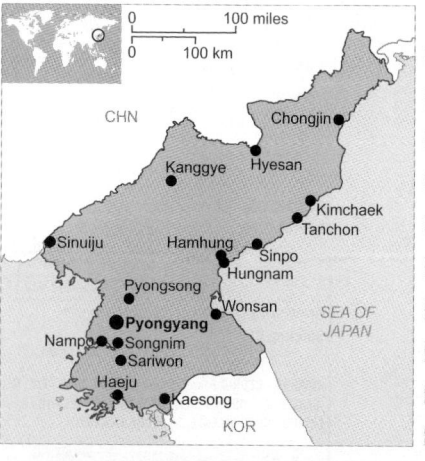

MAJOR CITIES/TOWNS

		Population
1	Pyongyang	3 198 937
2	Hamhung	580 914
3	Nampo	467 044
4	Hungnam	359 613
5	Kaesong	351 503
6	Wonsan	340 174
7	Chongjin	329 382
8	Sinuiju	285 903
9	Haeju	227 231
10	Kanggye	207 807
11	Kimchaek	197 552
12	Sariwon	161 058
13	Songnim	158 441
14	Pyongsong	123 489
15	Hyesan	98 212
16	Sinpo	79 415
17	Hongwon	73 696
18	Chongpyong	72 384
19	Tanchon	71 457

DEMOCRATIC PEOPLE'S REPUBLIC OF KOREA

Capital Pyongyang   Population 22 665 345 (50)   % in cities 63%
GDP per capita $1800 (189)   Area km² 120 538 km² (98)   GMT +/- +9
Neighbours (km) China 1416, Korea Republic 238, Russia 19 • Coast 2495

PRK – KOREA DPR

RECENT INTERNATIONAL MATCHES PLAYED BY KOREA DPR

2010	Opponents	Score	Venue	Comp	Scorers	Att	Referee
24-02	Myanmar	W 5-0	Colombo	CCsf	Choe Myong Ho [6], Choe Chol Man 2 [12 73], Pak Song Chol [13], Kim Seong Yong [85]	400	Al Yarimi YEM
27-02	Turkmenistan	D 1-1	Colombo	CCf	Ryang Yong Gi [75], W 5-4p	3 000	Faghani IRN
6-03	Venezuela	L 1-2	Puerto La Cruz	Fr		10 000	Buitrago COL
17-03	Mexico	L 1-2	Torreon	Fr	Choe Kum Chol [56]	30 000	Moreno PAN
22-04	South Africa	D 0-0	Taunusstein-Wehen	Fr		628	Brych GER
15-05	Paraguay	L 0-1	Nyon	Fr		1 000	Bertolini SUI
25-05	Greece	D 2-2	Altach	Fr	Jong Tae Se 2 [24 51]	3 000	Schorgenhofer AUT
6-06	Nigeria	L 1-3	Johannesburg	Fr	Cha Jong Hyok [64]	20 000	
15-06	Brazil	L 1-2	Johannesburg	WCr1	Ji Yun Nam [89]	54 331	Kassai HUN
21-06	Portugal	L 0-7	Cape Town	WCr1		63 644	Pozo CHI
25-06	Côte d'Ivoire	L 0-3	Nelspruit	WCr1		34 763	Undiano ESP
24-09	Vietnam	D 0-0	Hanoi	Fr			
2-11	Singapore	W 2-1	Hanoi	Fr	Ri Kwang Chon [80], Hong Yong Jo [90]		
6-11	Vietnam	W 2-0	Hanoi	Fr	Myong Cha Hyon [55], Ri Jin Hyok [67]		
10-11	Yemen	D 1-1	Aden	Fr	Ri Chol Myong [2]		
24-12	Kuwait	L 1-2	6th October City	Fr	Ri Chol Myong [33]		
27-12	Kuwait	D 2-2	6th October City	Fr			
31-12	Qatar	W 1-0	Doha	Fr	Ryang Yong Gi [70p]		
2011							
4-01	Bahrain	W 1-0	Riffa	Fr	An Chol Hyok [59]		
11-01	UAE	D 0-0	Doha	ACr1		3 639	Mohd Salleh MAS
15-01	Iran	L 0-1	Doha	ACr1		6 488	Shukralla BHR
19-01	Iraq	L 0-1	Al Rayyan	ACr1		4 111	Mohd Salleh MAS
26-03	Iraq	L 0-2	Sharjah	Fr			
29-03	Jordan	D 1-1	Sharjah	Fr	Pak Song Chol [32]		
7-04	Sri Lanka	W 4-0	Kathmandu	CCq	Choe Kum Chol 2 [2 47], Ri Chol Myong [5], Pak Nam Chol [21]	2 000	Almarzouq KUW
9-04	Nepal	W 1-0	Kathmandu	CCq	Jong Il Gwan [31]	22 000	Alabbasi BHR
11-04	Afghanistan	W 2-0	Kathmandu	CCq	Choe Kum Chol [45], Ri Chol Myong [68]	1 000	Abdul Baki OMA
8-06	China PR	L 0-2	Guiyang	Fr		27 000	
10-08	Kuwait	D 0-0	Kuwait City	Fr			
2-09	Japan	L 0-1	Saitama	WCq		62 000	Albadwawi UAE
6-09	Tajikistan	W 1-0	Pyongyang	WCq	Pak Nam Chol [14]	28 000	Minh Tri Vo VIE
11-10	Uzbekistan	L 0-1	Pyongyang	WCq		29 000	Faghani IRN
11-11	Uzbekistan	L 0-1	Tashkent	WCq		27 525	El Haddad LIB
15-11	Japan	W 1-0	Pyongyang	WCq	Pak Nam Chol [50]	50 000	Shukralla BHR
2012							
17-02	Kuwait	D 1-1	Changsha	Fr			
29-02	Tajikistan	D 1-1	Khujand City	Fr	Jang Song Hyok [53p]		
9-03	Philippines	W 2-0	Kathmandu	CCr1	Pak Nam Chol [58], Jang Kuk Chol [70]	1 500	Patwal IND
11-03	Tijikistan	W 2-0	Kathmandu	CCr1	Pak Nam Chol [4], Jang Kuk Chol [86]	1 000	Almarzouq KUW
13-03	India	W 4-0	Kathmandu	CCr1	Jon Kwang Ik [3], Ri Kwang Hyok [34], Pak Nam Chol [59], Ri Chol Myong [70]	200	Mahapab THA
16-03	Palestine	W 2-0	Kathmandu	CCsf	Pak Kwang Ryong 2 [42 68]	3 000	Almarzouq KUW
19-03	Turkmenistan	W 2-1	Kathmandu	CCf	Jong Il Gwan [36], Jang Song Hyok [87p]	9 000	Sato JPN
10-09	Indonesia	W 2-0	Jakarta	Fr	Pak Song Chol [67], Jong Il Gwan [77]		
1-12	Chinese Taipei	W 6-1	Hong Kong	EAq	An Il Bom [28], Pak Song Chol [34], Ri Kwang Hyok [42], Pak Nam Chol I [65], Ri Myong Jun 2 [67 89]	3 040	Wang Zhe CHN
3-12	Guam	W 5-0	Hong Kong	EAq	An Il Bom [26], Ri Myong Jun 2 [34 59], Pak Chol I [82], Jong Il Gwan [87]	4 160	Pechsri THA
5-12	Australia	D 1-1	Hong Kong	EAq	An Yong Hak [64]	989	Kim Dae Yong KOR
9-12	Hong Kong	W 4-0	Hong Kong	EAq	Pak Nam Chol II [27], Ryang Yong Gi [33], Pak Nam Chol I [36], Pak Sang Chol I [85]	3 345	Pechsri THA

Fr = Friendly match • CC = AFC Challenge Cup • EA = East Asian Championship • WC = FIFA World Cup • q = qualifier

PUR – PUERTO RICO

FIFA/COCA-COLA WORLD RANKING

'93	'94	'95	'96	'97	'98	'99	'00	'01	'02	'03	'04	'05	'06	'07	'08	'09	'10	'11	'12
105	112	128	149	169	182	186	195	195	198	200	194	195	195	196	142	165	133	108	132

2012												High	Low	Av
Jan	Feb	Mar	Apr	May	Jun	Jul	Aug	Sep	Oct	Nov	Dec			
108	113	134	138	138	137	140	138	137	129	130	132	97	202	166

It's not often that the world champions pitch up in Puerto Rico to play a game of football but fans in the country were treated to watching their national team take on a full strength Spanish team on their own doorstep. It was Spain's first game after their Euro 2012 championship heroics and there was probably nothing better to bring them down to earth than taking the field in the Juan Ramon Loubriel Stadium, an old baseball arena in Bayamon in the western outskirts of the capital San Juan. It was the first time that the Puerto Ricans had played a European team - in fact they had never played opponents from outside of the Americas - and they put up a sterling performance, restricting the Spaniards to a 2-1 victory with Marc Cintron scoring their goal. 2012 saw a $7million renovation project start on the stadium, known affectionately as La Meca due to the pivotal role it has played in the huge increase in the popularity of football in recent years. The major beneficiaries of that will be Puerto Rico Islanders who enjoyed another good season in the NASL although they failed in their bid to win a hat trick of Caribbean Club Championship titles after losing to Trinidad's W Connection in the semi-finals. In the local Puerto Rico Soccer League the title was won for the first time by Bayamon who went through the season unbeaten.

CFU CARIBBEAN CUP RECORD

1989 DNE 1991 DNQ 1992 DNE **1993** 5 r1 1994-1995 DNQ 1996-1997 DNE 1998-2005 DNQ 2007-2008 DNE 2010-2012 DNQ

FEDERACION PUERTORRIQUENA DE FUTBOL (FPF)

Calle Los Angeles Final,
Parque de Santurce,
Apartado postal 367567,
San Juan PR 00936

☎ +1 787 7652895
📠 +1 787 7672288
✉ info@fedefutbolpr.com
🖥 www.fedefutbolpr.com
FA 1940 CON 1962 FIFA 1960
P Eric Labrador
GS Dariel Collazo

THE STADIA

2014 FIFA World Cup Stadia
Juan Ramon Loubriel Stadium
Bayamon, San Juan   10 500
Mayagüez Athletics Stadium
Mayagüez   12 000

Other Main Stadia
Estadio Hiram Bithorn
San Juan   18 264
Estadio Sixto Escobar
San Juan   9 400

MAJOR CITIES/TOWNS

		Population
1	San Juan	407 386
2	Bayamón	197 009
3	Carolina	167 303
4	Ponce	145 676
5	Caguas	82 148
6	Guaynabo	80 952
7	Mayagüez	72 042
8	Trujillo Alto	54 862
9	Arecibo	47 550
10	Fajardo	33 717
11	Vega Baja	28 930
12	Levittown	28 563
13	Cataño	25 486
14	Guayama	20 749
15	Yauco	20 280
16	Humacao	19 561
17	Candelaria	17 348
18	Cayey	17 263
19	Manati	15 448

COMMONWEALTH OF PUERTO RICO

Capital San Juan
GDP per capita $17 800 (70)
Neighbours (km) Coast 501
Population 3 971 020 (128)
Area km² 13 790 km² (162)
% in cities 98%
GMT +/- -4

RECENT INTERNATIONAL MATCHES PLAYED BY PUERTO RICO

2008	Opponents	Score	Venue	Comp	Scorers	Att	Referee
16-01	Bermuda	W 2-0	Hamilton	Fr	Taylor Graham [47], Andres Cabrero [67]	500	Mauchette BER
18-01	Bermuda	W 1-0	Hamilton	Fr	Noah Delgado [13]	325	Raynor BER
26-01	Trinidad and Tobago	D 2-2	Bayamon	Fr	Kupono Low [15], Christopher Megaloudis [33]	4 500	Santos PUR
26-03	Dominican Republic	W 1-0	Bayamon	WCq	Petter Villegas [96p]	8 000	Morales MEX
4-06	Honduras	L 0-4	San Pedro Sula	WCq		20 000	Campbell JAM
14-06	Honduras	D 2-2	Bayamon	WCq	Christopher Megaloudis [31], Petter Villegas [41]	5 000	Lopez GUA
2009							
No international matches played in 2009							
2010							
2-10	Anguilla	W 3-1	Bayamon	CCq	Joshua Hansen [28], Christopher Megaloudis 2 [32 81]	2 050	Thomas JAM
4-10	Saint Martin †	W 2-0	Bayamon	CCq	John Krause [26], Cristian Arrieta [80]	1 800	Legister JAM
6-10	Cayman Islands	W 2-0	Bayamon	CCq	Christopher Megaloudis [26], Gadiel Figueroa [89]	3 800	Campbell JAM
22-10	Grenada	L 1-3	St George's	CCq	Isaac Nieves [81]	600	Wijngaarde SUR
24-10	Guadeloupe †	L 2-3	St George's	CCq	Christopher Megaloudis [65], Peter Villegas [74]	200	Baptiste DMA
26-10	St Kitts and Nevis	L 0-1	St George's	CCq		500	Morrison JAM
2011							
2-09	St Kitts and Nevis	D 0-0	Basseterre	WCq		2 500	Arellano MEX
6-09	Canada	L 0-3	Bayamon	WCq		4 000	Wijngaarde SUR
7-10	St Kitts and Nevis	D 1-1	Bayamon	WCq	Andres Cabrero [37]	2 500	Brizan TRI
11-10	Canada	D 0-0	Toronto	WCq		12 178	Lancaster GUY
11-11	St Lucia	W 4-0	Bayamon	WCq	Cristian Arrieta [4], Hector Ramos 2 [14 46], Andres Carero [54]	350	Holder CAY
15-11	St Lucia	W 3-0	Mayaguez	WCq	Hector Ramos 2 [13 85], Joseph Marrero [87]	1 050	Willet ATG
2012							
24-02	Nicaragua	L 0-1	Managua	Fr		2 000	Jarquin NCA
26-02	Nicaragua	L 1-4	Managua	Fr	Cristian Arrieta [10]	2 300	Davilla NCA
1-06	Nicaragua	W 3-1	Bayamon	Fr	Cristian Arrieta [39], Andres Cabrero [62], Joshua Hansen [83]	1 277	Anderson PUR
3-06	Nicaragua	D 1-1	Bayamon	Fr	Joshua Hansen [61]	994	Santos PUR
15-08	Spain	L 1-2	Bayamon	Fr	Marc Cintron [65]	10 500	Santos PUR
7-09	Bermuda	W 2-1	Port-au-Prince	CCq	Joseph Marrero [68], Hector Ramos [90]	2 000	Taylor BRB
9-09	Saint Martin	W 9-0	Port-au-Prince	CCq	Hector Ramos 4 [14 43 46 81], Tyler Wilson [25], Cristian Arrieta [45], Joseph Marrero 2 [69 83], Alex Oikkonen [76]	2 000	Royal JAM
11-09	Haiti	L 0-2	Port-au-Prince	CCq	Noah Delgado [73]	12 000	Morrison JAM
23-10	Martinique †	L 1-2	Les Abymes	CCq	Hector Ramos [55]	100	Baptiste DMA
25-10	Guadeloupe †	L 1-4	Baie-Mauault	CCq	Hector Ramos [83]	1 800	Leslie DMA
27-10	Dominican Republic	L 1-3	Les Abymes	CCq	Marco Velez [80]	2 891	Cambridge VIN

Fr = Friendly match • CC = Digicel Caribbean Cup • WC = FIFA World Cup • q = qualifier • † Not an official internatiuonal

PUERTO RICO 2012

PUERTO RICO SOCCER LEAGUE

	Pl	W	D	L	F	A	Pts	Bayamón	Sevilla	Atléticos	Universitarios	Guayama	Criollos	Fraigcomar	EFBR
Bayamón	13	12	1	0	70	10	37		5-1	2-0	7-1	10-1	4-0	11-1	8-0
Sevilla	14	11	1	2	47	21	34	0-4		4-0	4-0	6-5	5-0	4-0	3-1
Atléticos	13	7	0	6	24	27	21	n/p	0-3		1-3	3-1	1-0	5-2	2-1
Universitarios	14	5	2	7	21	32	17	2-3	2-5	1-3		3-0	0-1	1-1	2-1
Guayama	14	4	3	7	31	43	15	1-2	1-2	1-3	4-0		2-2	1-1	4-2
Criollos	14	3	5	6	20	27	14	2-2	1-2	4-1	2-2	1-2		1-2	3-1
Fraigcomar	14	3	3	8	22	45	12	1-4	1-6	5-2	0-1	6-7	1-1		1-0
EFBR	14	1	3	10	12	42	6	0-8	2-2	0-3	0-3	1-1	2-2	1-0	

20/04/2012 - 18/09/2012

QAT – QATAR

FIFA/COCA-COLA WORLD RANKING

'93	'94	'95	'96	'97	'98	'99	'00	'01	'02	'03	'04	'05	'06	'07	'08	'09	'10	'11	'12
54	60	83	69	70	60	107	102	80	62	65	66	95	58	87	84	86	112	93	98

2012												High	Low	Av
Jan	Feb	Mar	Apr	May	Jun	Jul	Aug	Sep	Oct	Nov	Dec			
97	96	88	84	84	91	98	98	92	101	104	98	51	113	79

The pressure is mounting on the Qatar national team to qualify for the 2014 FIFA World Cup finals ahead of hosting the tournament in 2022 in the knowledge that there has never been a host nation that had not appeared in the finals prior to staging them. The Qataris made it through to the final round of qualifying in Asia at the start of 2012 but they were in for a bumpy ride for the rest of the year. Qatar have gone close to making it to the finals before when, in 1997, they narrowly missed out on a place in France after losing out to Saudi Arabia in their final qualifying match but the road to Brazil looked to be much trickier. Coached by the Brazilian Paulo Autuori, Qatar lost key games at home to Korea Republic and Uzbekistan although a pair of victories over Lebanon saw them keep in touch with the possibility of a play-off. The erratic form saw Autuori lose his job and he was replaced by Fahad Thani at the start of 2013. In club football much attention has been focused on the Qatari involvement with PSG in France but the Qatar Stars League continues to grow in stature and was won in 2012 by Lekhwia who retained the title they had first won the year before. Al Gharafa secured the Emir's Cup with a penalty shoot-out victory over Al Sadd - who also lost in the final of the two other cup competitions, both of which were won by Al Rayyan.

FIFA WORLD CUP RECORD
1930-1974 DNE **1978-2010** DNQ

QATAR FOOTBALL ASSOCIATION (QFA)

28th Floor, Al Bidda Tower,
Corniche Street, West Bay,
PO Box 5333, Doha
☎ +974 44754444
📠 +974 44754300
✉ info@qfa.com.qa
🖥 www.qfa.com.qa
FA 1960 CON 1972 FIFA 1970
P Shk Hamad Al Thani
GS Saoud Al Mohannadi

THE STADIA

2014 FIFA World Cup Stadia
Jassim Bin Hamad Stadium
Doha — 15 000

Other Main Stadia
Khalifa International
Doha — 40 000
Al Ghafara Stadium
Doha — 27 000
Ahmed Bin Ali Stadium
Al Rayyan — 21 282
Al Wakra Stadium
Al Wakra — 20 000

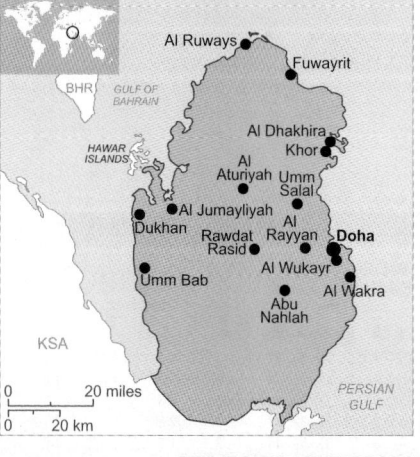

MAJOR CITIES/TOWNS
Population

1	Doha	410 494
2	Al Rayyan	367 026
3	Umm Salal	39 905
4	Al Wakra	31 922
5	Khor	27 260
6	Al Dhakhira	21 268
7	Al Shahniya	15 540
8	Musayid	12 080
9	Dukhan	9 408
10	Al Hisah	6 456
11	Al Wukayr	5 952
12	Rawdat Rasid	4 532
13	Al Ruways	4 119
14	Abu Nahlah	3 335
15	Umm Bab	3 085
16	Al Guwariyah	2 784
17	Al Jumayliyah	2 283
18	Al Kiranah	1 727
19	Fuwayrit	1 663

DAWLAT QATAR • STATE OF QATAR

Capital Doha
GDP per capita $111 000 (2)
Neighbours (km) Saudi Arabia 60 • Coast 563
Population 833 285 (158)
Area km² 11 586 km² (165)
% in cities 96%
GMT +/- +3

RECENT INTERNATIONAL MATCHES PLAYED BY QATAR

2010	Opponents	Score	Venue	Comp	Scorers	Att	Referee
10-08	Bosnia-Herzegovina	D 1-1	Sarajevo	Fr	Wesam Rizik 58p	18 000	Vuckov CRO
3-09	Bahrain	D 1-1	Doha	Fr	Majdi Siddiq 41		
7-09	Oman	D 1-1	Doha	Fr	Fabio Cesar 68		
12-10	Iraq	L 1-2	Doha	Fr	Magid Hassan 33		
18-11	Haiti	L 0-1	Doha	Fr			
22-11	Kuwait	L 0-1	Aden	GCr1			Al Rashid OMA
25-11	Yemen	W 2-1	Abyan	GCr1	Jaralla Al Marri 2 35 55		Abid Iddan IRQ
28-11	Saudi Arabia	D 1-1	Aden	GCr1	Ibrahim Al Ghanim 84		Al Marzouqi UAE
16-12	Egypt	W 2-1	Doha	Fr	Soria 21, OG 43		
22-12	Estonia	W 2-0	Doha	Fr	Soria 2 37 78		
28-12	Iran	D 0-0	Doha	Fr			
31-12	Korea DPR	L 0-1	Doha	Fr			
2011							
7-01	Uzbekistan	L 0-2	Doha	ACr1		37 143	Nishimura JPN
12-01	China PR	W 2-0	Doha	ACr1	Yusef Ahmed 2 27 45	30 778	Kim Dong Jin KOR
16-01	Kuwait	W 3-0	Doha	ACr1	Bilal Mohammed 12, Mohamed El Sayed 16, Fabio Cesar 86	28 339	Abdul Bashir SIN
21-01	Japan	L 2-3	Doha	ACqf	Soria 13, Fabio Cesar 63	19 479	Mohd Salleh MAS
29-03	Russia	D 1-1	Doha	Fr	Kasola Mohammed 4		
23-07	Vietnam	W 3-0	Doha	WCq	Kasola Mohammed 6, Meshal Budawood 51, Yusef Ali 67	6 786	Albadwawi UAE
28-07	Vietnam	L 1-2	Hanoi	WCq	Yusef Ali 17	20 000	Green AUS
19-08	Iraq	L 0-1	Doha	Fr			
25-08	UAE	L 1-3	Al Ain	Fr	Junior Marcone 88		
2-09	Bahrain	D 0-0	Manama	WCq		5 000	Alzarooni UAE
6-09	Iran	D 1-1	Doha	WCq	Mohamed El Sayed 56	8 125	Choi Myung Yong KOR
11-10	Indonesia	W 3-2	Jakarta	WCq	Abdulaziz Al Sulaiti 14, Khalfan Al Khalfan 32, Mohammed Razak 30	28 000	Bashir SIN
4-11	Oman	D 0-0	Doha	Fr			
11-11	Indonesia	W 4-0	Doha	WCq	Mohammed Razak 30, Khalfan Al Khalfan 2 34p 63, Andres Quintana 92+	6 500	Basma SYR
15-11	Bahrain	D 0-0	Doha	WCq		10 509	Nishimura JPN
10-12	Bahrain	D 2-2	Doha	Fr	Jaralla Al Marri 17, Mohammed Razak 34		
16-12	Iraq	D 0-0	Doha	Fr			
2012							
29-02	Iran	D 2-2	Tehran	WCq	Khalfan Al Khalfan 9, Kasola Mohammed 86	51 300	Irmatov UZB
22-05	Albania	L 1-2	Madrid	Fr		100	Carballo ESP
28-05	Palestine	D 0-0	Doha	Fr			
3-06	Lebanon	W 1-0	Beirut	WCq	Andres Quintana 64	40 000	Shukralla BHR
8-06	Korea Republic	L 1-4	Doha	WCq	Yusef Ali 22	10 730	Albadwawi UAE
12-06	Iran	D 0-0	Tehran	WCq		100 000	Green AUS
6-09	Tajikistan	L 1-2	Ingolstadt	Fr	Andres Quintana 75		Weiner GER
8-10	Jordan	D 1-1	Doha	Fr	Magid Mohamed 67		
16-10	Uzbekistan	L 0-1	Doha	WCq		11 260	Tan Hai CHN
14-11	Lebanon	W 1-0	Doha	WCq	Andres Quintana 75	12 870	Al Ghamdi KSA

Fr = Friendly match • AC = AFC Asian Cup • GC = Gulf Cup • WC = FIFA World Cup

QATAR NATIONAL TEAM HISTORICAL RECORDS

Past Coaches: Mohammed Hassan Kheiri 1969-72 • Helmi Hussein Mahmoud 1974 • Frank Wignall ENG 1975-76 • Hassan Othman 1979 • Evaristo de Macedo BRA 1980-86 • Procopio Cardoso BRA 1987-88 • Anatoly Prokopenko URS 1988 • Cabralzinho BRA 1989 • Dino Sani BRA 1989-90 • Evaristo de Macedo BRA 1992 • Ivo Wortmann BRA 1992 • Sebastiao Lapola BRA 1992-93 • Abdul Mallalah 1993 • Dave Mackay SCO 1994-95 • Jorgen Larsen DEN 1995-96 • Jo Bonfrere NED 1996-97 • Dzemal Hadziabdic YUG 1997 • Ze Mario BRA 1998 • Luiz Gonzaga Milioli 1998 • Dzemal Hadziabdic YUG 2000-01 • Paulo Luiz Campos BRA 2001 • Pierre Lechantre FRA 2002-03 • Philippe Troussier FRA 2003-04 • Dzemaludin Musovic BIH 2004-07 • Jorge Fossati URU 2007-08 • Bruno Metsu FRA 2008-11 • Milovan Rajevac SRB 2011 • Sebastiao Lazaroni BRA 2011 • Paulo Autuori BRA 2012-13 • Fahad Thani 2013-

QATAR 2011–12

QATAR STARS LEAGUE

	Pl	W	D	L	F	A	Pts	Lekhwia	Jaish	Rayyan	Sadd	Khor	Gharafa	Wakra	Khritiyat	Arabi	Qatar SC	Umm Salal	Ahli
Lekhwia †	22	12	7	3	36	16	43		1-1	2-1	0-1	4-0	2-0	1-2	1-1	3-0	3-0	3-1	1-0
Al Jaish †	22	12	5	5	48	24	41	2-3		3-2	2-1	0-2	4-1	4-0	1-1	1-0	3-2	0-0	1-3
Al Rayyan †	22	10	9	3	49	26	39	3-1	4-4		2-1	0-1	1-1	1-0	2-2	3-0	2-2	0-0	3-0
Al Sadd	22	10	6	6	35	24	36	1-2	1-1	0-0		3-1	0-0	3-1	1-1	4-1	3-3	4-1	1-0
Khor	22	9	5	8	30	29	32	0-2	0-2	0-0	1-1		2-1	2-3	1-2	2-2	0-0	2-0	0-1
Al Gharafa †	22	8	7	7	26	27	31	0-0	1-0	1-5	3-1	0-2		2-1	0-0	1-1	2-0	0-1	2-2
Al Wakra	22	8	4	10	30	37	28	0-1	1-6	1-3	0-2	1-1	1-0		2-1	0-1	5-1	3-0	2-2
Al Khritiyat	22	5	10	7	23	34	25	1-1	0-6	1-4	0-1	1-3	2-3	0-0		0-0	2-1	2-1	2-1
Al Arabi	22	4	12	6	19	28	24	1-1	0-3	1-1	1-0	2-3	0-0	3-2	0-0		0-0	0-0	2-0
Qatar SC	22	6	6	10	32	46	24	0-0	1-2	2-8	1-0	2-1	0-2	1-2	3-0	3-3		2-1	1-0
Umm Salal	22	4	8	10	20	32	20	0-0	1-0	1-1	1-3	1-2	1-2	0-0	1-1	1-1	4-3		3-0
Al Ahli	22	3	3	16	23	49	12	0-4	0-2	2-3	2-3	1-3	1-4	2-3	1-4	0-0	3-4	3-1	

16/09/2011 – 13/04/2012 • † Qualified for AFC Champions League • Top scorers: **18** - **ADRIANO** BRA, Jaish • **17** - **RODRIGO TABATA** BRA, Rayyan • **15** - **AFONSO AVES** BRA, Rayyan • **12** - Moumouni **DAGANO** BFA, Khor & Alain **KALUYITUKA** COD, Ahli • **10** - **CABORE** BRA, Umm Salal & **WAGNER RIBEIRO** BRA, Jaish • **9** - Said **BOUTAHAR** NED, Wakra; Yahia **KEBE** BFA, Khritiyat & Sebastian **SORIA** QAT, Qatar SC
Relegation play-off: **Umm Salal** 1-0 Maitheer

QATAR 2011–12 2ND DIVISION

	Pl	W	D	L	F	A	Pts
Al Siliya	14	9	1	4	33	16	28
Maitheer	14	7	2	5	24	22	23
Al Shamal	14	6	3	5	25	24	21
Markheya	14	5	1	8	16	27	16
Mseimeer	14	3	6	5	17	18	15
Shahaniya	14	3	5	6	14	22	14

17/11/2011 – 2/04/2012

CROWN PRINCE CUP 2012

Semi-finals
Al Rayyan	3
Al Jaish	2
Lekhwia	2
Al Sadd	4

Finals
Al Rayyan	1 5p
Al Sadd	1 4p

Played at the end of the season between the top four teams of the Qatar Stars League

MEDALS TABLE

	Overall			Lge	Cup		CP	SJ	QS	Asia		
	G	S	B	G	G	S				G	S	B
1 Al Sadd	44	7	1	12	12	7	5	12	1	2		1
2 Al Arabi	22	4	1	7	8	3	1	6			1	1
3 Al Gharafa	21	4		7	7	4	3	3	1			
4 Al Rayyan	19	9	1	7	5	9	4	3				1
5 Qatar SC	13	3		3	3	3	3	4				
6 Al Wakra	8	6		2		6	1	4	1			
7 Al Oruba	5			5								
8 Al Ahli	4	5			4	5						
9 Umm Salal	3	1	1		1	1		2				1
10 Al Maref	3			3								
11 Khor	2	2					2	1	1			
12 Lekhwia	2			2								

Name changes: Al Gharafa were called Al Ittihad • Kor were previously Al Taawun • Lekhwia were previously Al Shorta • Al Oruba merged with Qatar SC to form Esteqlal but reverted to Qatar SC in 1981 • Cup = Emir Cup • CP = Crown Prince Cup • SJ = Sheikh Jassim Cup • QS = Qatar Stars Cup

EMIR'S CUP 2011–12

Round of 16		Quarter-finals		Semi-finals		Final	
Al Gharafa	2						
Al Arabi	0	Al Gharafa	2				
		Lekhwia	1				
Lekhwia	Bye			Al Gharafa	1 4p		
Al Rayyan	Bye			Al Khritiyat	1 3p		
		Al Rayyan	1 1p				
		Al Khritiyat	1 3p				
Al Ahli	2					Al Gharafa †	0 4p
Al Khritiyat	4					Al Sadd	0 3p
Al Jaish	Bye						
		Al Jaish	1 4p				
Qatar SC	1	Khor	1 2p				
Khor	2			Al Jaish	0		
Al Wakra	1 4p			Al Sadd	3		
Umm Salal	1 3p	Al Wakra	0				
		Al Sadd	2				
Al Sadd	Bye			† Qualified for AFC Champions League			

CUP FINAL

Khalifa International, Doha
12-05-2012

SHEIKH JASSIM CUP 2012-13

First Round Groups

Group A

	Pl	W	D	L	F	A	Pts	Gh	Sh	Le
Al Arabi	3	3	0	0	10	4	9	4-2	2-0	4-2
Al Gharafa	3	1	1	1	7	7	4		4-2	1-1
Al Shamal	3	1	0	2	4	7	3			2-1
Lekhwia	3	0	1	2	4	7	1			

Group B

	Pl	W	D	L	F	A	Pts	US	Kh	Ma	Sh
Al Rayyan	4	3	1	0	6	1	10	1-0	2-1	0-0	3-0
Umm Salal	4	3	0	1	7	2	9		2-0	2-1	3-0
Al Khritiyat	4	1	1	2	4	5	4			2-0	1-1
Markheya	4	1	1	2	4	6	4				3-2
Shahaniya	4	0	1	3	3	10	1				

Group C

	Pl	W	D	L	F	A	Pts	Wa	Qa	Ms	Si
Al Sadd	4	3	1	0	8	3	10	1-1	3-2	2-0	2-0
Al Wakra	4	2	2	0	6	3	8		2-1	1-1	2-0
Qatar SC	4	2	0	2	6	5	6			2-0	1-0
Mseimeer	4	0	2	2	3	7	2				2-2
Al Siliya	4	0	1	3	2	7	1				

Group D

	Pl	W	D	L	F	A	Pts	Kh	Ma	Ah
Al Jaish	3	3	0	0	12	1	9	3-0	6-0	3-1
Khor	3	1	1	1	5	5	4		2-2	3-0
Maitheer	3	0	2	1	5	11	2			3-3
Al Ahli	3	0	1	2	4	9	1			

Semi-finals

Al Rayyan	1
Al Jaish	0

Al Arabi	0
Al Sadd	3

Final

Al Rayyan	1
Al Sadd	0

CUP FINAL

Khalifa International, Doha
14-08-2012
Scorer - Jaralla Al Marri [49]

25/07/2012 - 14/08/2012

QATAR STARS CUP 2011-12

First Round Groups

Group A

	Pl	W	D	L	F	A	Pts	Kh	Ra	Sa	Qa	Ah
Lekhwia	5	4	0	1	15	7	12	1-3	3-1	5-1	3-1	3-1
Al Khritiyat	5	3	1	1	12	6	10		2-2	4-0	2-3	1-0
Al Rayyan	5	2	2	1	12	6	8			0-0	5-1	4-0
Al Sadd	5	2	1	2	5	11	7				1-0	3-2
Qatar SC	5	2	0	3	7	12	6					2-1
Al Ahli	5	0	0	5	4	13	0					

Group B

	Pl	W	D	L	F	A	Pts	Wa	Ar	Ja	Gh	Kh
Umm Salal	5	3	1	1	6	4	10	1-1	2-1	2-1	1-0	2-1
Al Wakra	5	2	2	1	7	6	8		1-1	2-1	0-2	3-1
Al Arabi	5	2	1	2	3	3	7			1-0	0-1	0-1
Al Jaish	5	2	0	3	9	7	6				4-2	3-0
Al Gharafa	5	2	0	3	6	7	6					1-2
Khor	5	2	0	3	5	9	6					

Semi-finals

Al Wakra	3
Lekhwia	2

Umm Salal	2
Al Khritiyat	3

Final

Al Wakra	0	10p
Al Khritiyat	0	9p

CUP FINAL

Jassim Bin Hamad, Doha
2-03-2012

7/10/2011 - 2/03/2012

ROU – ROMANIA

FIFA/COCA-COLA WORLD RANKING

'93	'94	'95	'96	'97	'98	'99	'00	'01	'02	'03	'04	'05	'06	'07	'08	'09	'10	'11	'12
13	11	11	16	7	12	8	13	15	24	27	29	27	19	13	21	36	56	56	33

2012

Jan	Feb	Mar	Apr	May	Jun	Jul	Aug	Sep	Oct	Nov	Dec	High	Low	Av
55	52	53	45	45	52	52	51	57	46	37	33	3	57	22

With the railwaymen of Cluj winning the title for the third time in five seasons, 2012 proved to be yet another miserable year in the league for clubs from Bucharest. Not since the 1920s have clubs from the capital experienced such a poor run in the championship as the established order continues to be challenged by provincial clubs with wealthy backers. Dinamo Bucharest had led for much of the season but their collapse saw Cluj claim the title on the penultimate weekend with a 3-2 victory over neighbours Universitatea. There was some consolation for Dinamo with a 1-0 victory over neighbours Rapid in the cup final in what was their first trophy since 2007. Despite Romania losing its automatic UEFA Champions League place, Cluj ensured Romanian representation at the group stage for the sixth consecutive season by making it through the qualifying rounds and they were desperately unlucky to be knocked out by Galatasaray on their head-to-head record. The national team had the best possible start to their 2014 FIFA World Cup qualifying campaign with three straight wins - including a crucial win over Turkey in Istanbul - but hopes of automatic qualification for Brazil were dealt a blow with a 4-1 defeat at home to the Netherlands, a result that left the team with the prospect of a tussle with Hungary for a play-off spot.

UEFA EUROPEAN CHAMPIONSHIP RECORD

1960 QF 1964 r1 1968 DNQ 1972 QF 1976-1980 DNQ **1984** r1 1988-1992 DNQ **1996** r1 **2000** QF 2004 DNQ **2008** r1 2012 DNQ

ROMANIAN FOOTBALL FEDERATION (FRF)

Federatia Romana de Fotbal, House of Football, Str. Serg. Serbanica Vasile 12, 022186 Bucharest
☎ +40 21 3029150
📠 +40 21 3029192
✉ frf@frf.ro
🌐 www.frf.ro
FA 1909 CON 1954 FIFA 1923
P Mircea Sandu
GS Adalbert Kassai

THE STADIA
2014 FIFA World Cup Stadia
Arena Nationala
Bucharest   55 600
Other Main Stadia
Stadionul Dan Paltinisanu
Timisoara   32 972
Cluj Arena
Cluj-Napoca   30 201
Stadionul Steaua
Bucharest   28 365

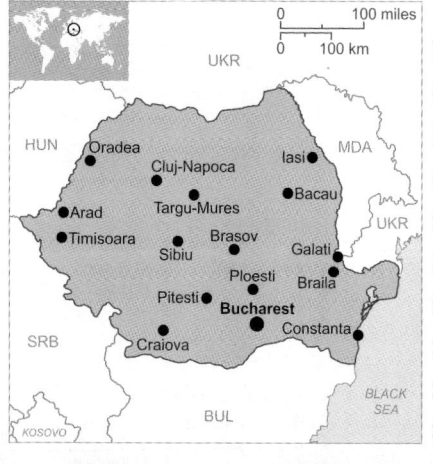

MAJOR CITIES/TOWNS
Population
1 Bucharest   1 920 121
2 Cluj-Napoca   300 257
3 Constanta   299 384
4 Craiova   296 717
5 Galati   296 550
6 Iasi   289 745
7 Timisoara   286 728
8 Brasov   278 817
9 Ploiesti   233 987
10 Braila   219 759
11 Oradea   204 882
12 Bacau   184 639
13 Pitesti   173 082
14 Arad   162 798
15 Sibiu   152 389
16 Baia Mare   143 812
17 Targu-Mure   143 426
18 Buzau   140 003
19 Botosani   119 073

ROMANIA

Capital	Bucharest	Population	22 215 421 (51)	% in cities	54%
GDP per capita	$12 200 (90)	Area km²	238 391 km² (82)	GMT +/-	+2

Neighbours (km) Bulgaria 608, Hungary 443, Moldova 450, Serbia 476, Ukraine 531 • Coast 225

RECENT INTERNATIONAL MATCHES PLAYED BY ROMANIA

2009	Opponents	Score	Venue	Comp	Scorers	Att	Referee
12-08	Hungary	W 1-0	Budapest	Fr	Ghioane [42]	9 000	Vnuk SVK
5-09	France	D 1-1	Paris	WCq	Escude OG [55]	78 209	Bebek CRO
9-09	Austria	D 1-1	Bucharest	WCq	Bucur [54]	7 505	Atkinson ENG
10-10	Serbia	L 0-5	Belgrade	WCq		39 839	Kapitanis CYP
14-10	Faroe Islands	W 3-1	Piatra-Neamt	WCq	Apostal [16], Bucur [65], Mazilu [87]	13 000	Gvardis RUS
14-11	Poland	W 1-0	Warsaw	Fr	Niculae [59]	8 000	Mashiah ISR
2010							
29-05	Ukraine	L 2-3	Lviv	Fr	Tamas [54], Niculae [63]	22 000	Kralovec CZE
2-06	Macedonia FYR	L 0-1	Bischofshofen	Fr		1 000	Krassnitzer AUT
5-06	Honduras	W 3-0	St Velt An Der Glan	Fr	Niculae [20], Florescu [45], Radoi [76p]	700	Grobelnik AUT
11-08	Turkey	L 0-2	Istanbul	Fr		15 000	Mazic SRB
3-09	Albania	D 1-1	Piatra-Neamt	ECq	Stancu [80]	13 400	Schorgenhofer AUT
7-09	Belarus	D 0-0	Minsk	ECq		26 354	Kralovec CZE
9-10	France	L 0-2	Paris	ECq		79 299	Proenca POR
17-11	Italy	D 1-1	Klagenfurt	Fr	Marica [34]	14 000	Einwaller AUT
2011							
8-02	Ukraine	D 2-2	Paralimni	Fr	Alexa 2 [33 44], L 2-4p	1 000	Johannesson SWE
9-02	Cyprus	D 1-1	Paralimni	Fr	Torje [56], W 5-4p	2 500	Shvetov UKR
26-03	Bosnia-Herzegovina	L 1-2	Zenica	ECq	Marica [29]	13 000	Teixeira ESP
29-03	Luxembourg	W 3-1	Piatra-Neamt	ECq	Mutu 2 [24 68], Zicu [78]	13 500	Gocek TUR
3-06	Bosnia-Herzegovina	W 3-0	Bucharest	ECq	Mutu [37], Marica 2 [41 55]	8 200	Eriksson SWE
7-06	Brazil	L 0-1	Sao Paulo	Fr		30 059	Pezzotta ARG
11-06	Paraguay	L 0-2	Asuncion	Fr		8 000	Larrionda URU
10-08	San Marino	W 1-0	Serravalle	Fr	Herea [72]	3 000	Rocchi ITA
2-09	Luxembourg	W 2-0	Luxembourg	ECq	Torje 2 [34 45]	2 812	Karasev RUS
6-09	France	D 0-0	Bucharest	ECq		49 137	Webb ENG
7-10	Belarus	D 2-2	Bucharest	ECq	Mutu 2 [19 51p]	29 486	Kelly IRL
11-10	Albania	D 1-1	Tirana	ECq	Luchin [77]	3 000	Mazeika LTU
11-11	Belgium	L 1-2	Liege	Fr	Niculae [67]	15 000	Ennjimi FRA
15-11	Greece	W 3-1	Altach	Fr	Torje [17], Tanase [61], Chipciu [81]	8 00	Gangl AUT
2012							
27-01	Turkmenistan	W 4-0	Belek	Fr	Niculae 2 [3 90p], Tanase 2 [46 51]	50	Baliyan ARM
29-02	Uruguay	D 1-1	Bucharest	Fr	Stancu [50]	20 000	Kassai HUN
30-05	Switzerland	W 1-0	Lucerne	Fr	Grozav [56]	11 850	Moen NOR
5-06	Austria	D 0-0	Innsbruck	Fr		12 500	Makkelie NED
15-08	Slovenia	L 3-4	Ljubljana	Fr	Papp [56], Torje [58p], Grozav [80]	5 000	Aleckovic BIH
7-09	Estonia	W 2-0	Tallinn	WCq	Torje [56], Marica [76]	7 936	Mazic SRB
11-09	Andorra	W 4-0	Bucharest	WCq	Torje [29], Lazar [44], Gaman [90], Maxim [93+]	24 630	Radovanovic MNE
12-10	Turkey	W 1-0	Istanbul	WCq	Grozav [45]	46 203	Webb ENG
16-10	Netherlands	L 1-4	Bucharest	WCq	Marica [40]	53 329	Thomson SCO
14-11	Belgium	W 2-1	Bucharest	Fr	Maxim [32], Torje [66p]	4 000	Bergonzi ITA

Fr = Friendly match • EC = UEFA EURO 2008/2012 • WC = FIFA World Cup • q = qualifier • r1 = first round group

ROMANIA NATIONAL TEAM HISTORICAL RECORDS

Caps: **134** - Dorinel Munteanu 1991-2007 • **124** - Gheorghe Hagi 1983-2000 • **115** - Gheorghe Popescu 1988-2003 • **102** - Ladislau Boloni 1975-88 • **95** - Dan Petrescu 1989-2000 • **91** - Bogdan Stelea 1988-2005 • **90** - Michael Klein 1981-91 • **86** - Razvan Rat 2002- • **84** - Marius Lacatus 1984-98 • **83** - Mircea Rednic 1981-91 • **78** - Bogdan Lobont 1998- • **77** - Silviu Lung 1979-93

Goals: **35** - Gheorghe Hagi 1983-2000 • **34** - Adrian Mutu 2000- • **31** - Iuliu Bodola 1931-39 • **26** - Anghel Iordanescu 1971-81 • **25** - Viorel Moldovan 1993-2005 & Ladislau Boloni 1975-88 • **22** - Rodion Camataru 1978-90 • **21** - Dudu Georgescu 1973-80 & Florin Raducioiu 1988-96 • **20** - Stefan Dobay 1930-39 & Ilie Dumitrescu 1989-98 • **19** - Ioan Ganea 1998-2006

Coaches: Valentin Stanescu 1973-75 • Cornel Dragusin 1975 • Stefan Kovacs 1976-79 • Florin Halagian 1979 • Constantin Cernaianu 1979 • Stefan Kovacs 1980 • Valentin Stanescu 1980-1981 • Mircea Lucescu 1981-86 • Emerich Jenei 1986-90 • Gheorghe Constantin 1990 • Mircea Radulescu 1990-92 • Cornel Dinu 1992-93 • Anghel Iordanescu 1993-98 • Victor Piturca 1998-99 • Emerich Jenei 2000 • Ladislau Boloni 2000-01 • Gheorghe Hagi 2001-02 • Anghel Iordanescu 2002-04 • Victor Piturca 2005-09 • Razvan Lucescu 2009-11 • Victor Piturca 2011-

ROMANIA 2011-12

LIGA I BURGER

	Pl	W	D	L	F	A	Pts	CFR Cluj	Vaslui	Steaua	Rapid	Dinamo	Otelul	Pandurii	Universitatea	Concordia	Brasov	Ceahlaul	Astra	Gaz Metan	Petrolul	Târgu Mures	Vointa	Sportul	Mioveni
CFR 1907 Cluj †	34	21	8	5	63	31	71		2-0	1-1	0-5	2-3	2-0	2-0	3-1	2-4	1-0	2-1	2-0	0-2	1-1	1-0	2-1	6-1	3-0
SC Vaslui †	34	22	4	8	58	29	70	1-1		0-0	2-3	3-1	1-0	3-2	1-0	4-0	0-1	1-2	2-1	4-0	0-0	4-0	2-0	1-0	3-0
Steaua Bucuresti ‡	34	19	9	6	47	26	66	1-1	0-1		0-0	3-2	2-1	1-2	2-1	2-1	1-0	1-0	2-1	0-0	2-1	2-0	1-0	4-1	4-0
Rapid Bucuresti ‡	34	18	10	6	54	29	64	1-1	3-0	1-1		0-0	1-0	2-2	1-1	2-0	1-1	1-2	3-2	5-3	2-0	1-1	3-0	2-0	4-0
Dinamo Bucuresti ‡	34	18	8	8	57	32	62	0-1	0-1	1-3	0-0		2-1	2-0	2-2	2-0	0-0	3-2	3-0	2-0	1-3	1-0	1-0	1-3	4-1
Otelul Galati	34	15	7	12	34	29	52	0-4	1-2	1-2	2-0	1-1		2-1	2-0	0-0	1-0	0-0	1-1	1-0	1-0	0-0	3-0	1-0	0-0
Pandurii Târgu Jiu	34	12	11	11	47	40	47	2-0	1-2	1-1	3-0	2-2	0-1		1-0	5-2	2-1	1-1	1-2	1-0	1-0	2-0	0-0	1-1	5-1
Universitatea Cluj	34	11	14	9	46	37	47	2-3	0-1	0-1	2-0	0-0	1-1	0-1		1-1	1-0	1-0	3-1	3-0	3-2	3-1	3-1	1-1	2-2
Concordia Chiajna	34	13	6	15	42	52	45	0-4	0-3	0-2	1-0	1-3	1-0	3-1	0-0		2-1	2-0	1-0	0-0	0-2	4-1	2-0	1-2	3-1
FC Brasov	34	13	6	15	39	34	45	1-2	1-2	1-2	1-0	2-0	0-2	2-1	1-1	2-3		1-1	2-0	2-1	1-0	2-1	3-0	1-0	4-0
Ceahlaul Piatra Neamt	34	11	9	14	36	46	42	0-2	1-3	1-0	1-2	0-5	0-2	1-1	1-1	0-0	1-0		1-2	2-0	2-1	1-1	2-1	1-2	2-0
Astra Ploesti	34	11	8	15	36	43	41	0-1	1-0	2-1	0-1	0-0	3-1	2-0	0-0	0-2	1-4	0-0		2-0	1-1	0-2	0-1	2-2	3-1
Gaz Metan Medias	34	11	8	15	39	54	41	1-1	1-1	1-3	0-2	2-2	0-5	1-0	3-2	2-5	1-0	1-1	3-1		0-0	0-1	2-1	3-0	3-1	1-1
Petrolul Ploiesti	34	10	9	15	42	45	39	1-1	1-2	**0-3**	0-1	1-5	2-1	0-0	2-2	3-4	2-0	0-1	3-1	4-0		0-1	4-1	0-3	3-1
FCM Târgu Mures	34	8	11	15	33	47	35	0-2	2-3	1-0	0-2	0-1	1-2	2-3	1-1	3-0	0-0	4-3	2-2	1-0	1-2		0-0	2-1	2-0
Vointa Sibiu	34	8	8	18	24	45	32	0-1	3-0	1-1	0-1	0-1	0-1	0-0	0-0	1-0	2-1	1-2	1-0	0-2	1-1	1-1		1-0	3-1
Sportul Studentesc	34	6	12	16	33	55	30	1-1	1-0	0-0	0-2	0-2	0-2	0-0	2-4	2-2	2-1	1-1	0-4	1-2	1-1	1-2	2-2		0-0
CS Mioveni	34	2	6	26	20	77	12	0-5	0-5	0-1	1-2	0-1	1-2	0-2	0-1	1-3	0-1	1-2	0-1	4-2	0-0	0-0	1-2	2-1	

22/07/2011 - 19/05/2012 • † Qualified for the UEFA Champions League • ‡ Qualified for the Europa League • Attendance: 1,508,383 @ 4,962
Top scorers: **27** - **WESLEY** BRA, Vaslui • **19** - Marius **NICULAE**, Dinamo • **13** - Ionel **DANCIULESCU**, Dinamo & Raul **RUSESCU**, Steaua • **12** - Ovidiu **HEREA**, Rapid; Hamza **YOUNES** TUN, Petrolul & Pantelis **KAPETANOS** GRE, Cluj • **11** - Daniel **OPRITA**, Petrolul

ROMANIA 2011-12
LIGA II SERIA I (2)

	Pl	W	D	L	F	A	Pts
Studentesc Iasi	30	19	4	7	51	26	61
Viitorul Constanta	30	17	10	3	55	18	61
Delta Tulcea	30	17	8	5	55	28	59
Sageata Navodari	30	14	7	9	47	33	49
FC Botosani	30	13	9	8	42	31	48
CF Braila	30	15	3	12	47	40	48
FCM Bacau	30	13	6	11	43	31	45
Farul Constanta	30	11	11	8	45	42	44
Callatis Mangalia	30	13	4	13	43	41	43
Dunarea Galati	30	11	7	12	38	40	40
Astra Giurgiu	30	10	6	14	35	48	36
CS Otopeni	30	10	5	15	37	44	35
Dinamo Bucuresti-2	30	8	10	12	32	35	34
FC Snagov ‡	30	6	6	18	29	60	24
Gloria Buzau	30	6	5	19	26	62	23
Victoria Branesti ‡	30	4	3	23	17	64	15

19/08/2011 - 4/06/2011 • † Play-off

Politehnica Timisoara not promoted
‡ Teams withdrew at the halfway stage. All remaining matches awarded 3-0 to their opponents

ROMANIA 2011-12
LIGA II SERIA II (2)

	Pl	W	D	L	F	A	Pts
Politehnica Timisoara	30	19	8	3	54	19	65
Gloria Bistrita	30	19	8	3	60	29	65
Gaz Metan Severin	30	18	5	7	50	25	59
UTA Arad	30	14	9	7	41	20	51
Alro Slatina	30	14	8	8	41	22	50
Luceafarul Oradea	30	13	8	9	34	27	47
Chindia Târgoviste	30	11	11	8	34	24	44
Bihor Oradea	30	12	8	10	40	35	44
Unirea Alba Iulia	30	10	11	9	34	26	41
Arges Pitesti	30	10	9	11	34	47	39
FCMU Baia Mare	30	10	5	15	38	50	35
Râmnicu Vâlcea	30	9	8	13	34	38	35
Olt Slatina	30	9	7	14	30	35	34
Juventus Bucuresti	30	4	8	18	24	44	20
Muresul Deva	30	6	2	22	20	72	20
Ariesul Turda ‡	30	2	5	23	10	65	11

19/08/2011 - 4/06/2011 • † Play-off

MEDALS TABLE

		Overall			League			Cup			Europe		
		G	S	B	G	S	B	G	S	B	G	S	B
1	Steaua Bucuresti	46	21	10	23	13	8	22	7		1	1	2
2	Dinamo Bucuresti	32	32	11	19	20	9	13	12				2
3	Rapid Bucuresti	16	20	8	3	14	8	13	6				
4	Universitatea Craiova	10	10	8	4	5	7	6	5				1
5	UT Arad	8	3	1	6	1	1	2	2				
6	Venus Bucuresti	8	1	1	8		1		1				
7	Petrolul Ploiesti	6	4	2	4	3	2	2	1				
	Ripensia Timisoara	6	4	2	4	2	2	2	2				
9	Chinezul Timisoara	6	1		6				1				
10	CFR 1907 Cluj	6		1	3		1	3					
11	Politehnica Timisoara	2	7	5		1	5	2	6				
12	FC Arges Pitesti	2	3	4	2	2	4		1				
13	FC Bihor Oradea	2	3	1	1	2	1	1	1				

CUPA ROMANIEI 2011-12

Sixth Round

Dinamo Bucuresti*	1
Luceafarul Oradea	0
CS Mioveni	2 1p
Gaz Metan Severin*	2 4p
Astra Ploiesti*	1
CFR 1907 Cluj	0
Concordia Chiajna	0
Petrolul Ploiesti	1
FC Timisoara*	2
Ceahlaiul Piatra Neamt	0
Sanatatea Cluj	0
Steaua Bucuresti*	4
Astra Giurgiu-2*	1
Universitatea Cluj	0
CF Braila*	0
Gaz Metan Medias	1
SC Vaslui*	8
Vointa Livezile	0
Sportul Studentesc	0
Dunarea Galati*	1
FCM Targu Mures*	1
Viitorul Constanta	0
Oltchim Râmnicu Vâlcea	1
Otelul Galati*	2
Pandurii Târgu Jiu*	0 3p
CS Visina Noua	0 2p
FCM Bacau	0
FC Brasov	2
CS Otopeni	0 4p
Vointa Sibiu*	0 3p
Juventus Bucuresti	1
Rapid Bucuresti*	4

Round of 16

Dinamo Bucuresti*	5
Gaz Metan Severin	0
Astra Ploiesti*	0
Petrolul Ploiesti	1
FC Timisoara*	2
Steaua Bucuresti	0
Astra Giurgiu-2	0
Gaz Metan Medias*	1
SC Vaslui*	4
Dunarea Galati	1
FCM Târgu Mures	1
Otelul Galati*	2
Pandurii Târgu Jiu*	3
FC Brasov	2
CS Otopeni	0
Rapid Bucuresti*	5

Quarter-finals

Dinamo Bucuresti*	2
Petrolul Ploiesti	1
FC Timisoara*	0
Gaz Metan Medias	1
SC Vaslui	3
Otelul Galati*	2
Pandurii Târgu Jiu	0
Rapid Bucuresti*	2

Semi-finals

Dinamo Bucuresti*	1	1
Gaz Metan Medias	0	2
SC Vaslui*	0	2
Rapid Bucuresti	1	3

Final

Dinamo Bucuresti ‡	1
Rapid Bucuresti	0

CUP FINAL

Arena Nationala, Bucharest, 23-05-2012
Att: 40 000, Ref: Daniele Orsato (ITA)
Scorer - Scarlatache 58 for Dinamo
Dinamo - Kristijan Naumovski● - Srdjan Luchin, Dragos Grigore, Cosmin Moti, Adrian Scarlatache - Djakaridja Kone, Laurentiu Rus - Alexandru Curtean, Marius Alexe (Cristian Pulhac 67), Marius Niculae (c) ● (George Tucudean 81), Ionel Danciulescu (Catalin Munteanu 71). Tr: Dario Bonetti
Rapid - Danut Coman - Mihai Roman, Marcos Antonio (c), Cristian Oros●, Vladimir Bozovic - Dan Alexa (Alexandru Ionita 79) - Filipe Teixeira, Nicolae Grigore - Romeo Surdu (Stefan Grigore● 59), Ovidiu Herea (Daniel Pancu 74), Ciprian Deac. Tr: Razvan Lucescu

Liga 1 teams enter in the sixth round • * Home team/home team in the 1st leg • ‡ Qualified for the Europa League

RSA – SOUTH AFRICA

FIFA/COCA-COLA WORLD RANKING

'93	'94	'95	'96	'97	'98	'99	'00	'01	'02	'03	'04	'05	'06	'07	'08	'09	'10	'11	'12
95	56	40	19	31	26	30	20	35	30	36	38	49	67	77	76	85	51	52	87

2012

Jan	Feb	Mar	Apr	May	Jun	Jul	Aug	Sep	Oct	Nov	Dec	High	Low	Av
56	58	60	71	67	68	68	67	74	76	84	87	16	109	48

Hopes of a revival for the South Africa national team rested firmly on home advantage at the 2013 Africa Cup of Nations finals and so the penalty shoot-out defeat at the hands of Mali in the quarter-finals was greeted with huge disappointment. Bafana Bafana have been in the doldrums for several years and the situation was further exacerbated by a poor start to their 2014 FIFA World Cup qualifiers which saw coach Pitso Mosimane fired after a 1-1 home draw with Ethiopia. Steve Komphela was caretaker the next week for a 1-1 draw in Botswana before Gordon Igesund was appointed in July to try and turn matters around. South Africa produced an astonishing display of nerves in the opening game of the Nations Cup in January 2013 where they were held to a draw by the tiny Cape Verde Islands. They still finished top of the group after beating Angola and grabbing a late equaliser against Morocco before bowing out against Mali in Durban. Orlando Pirates retained their championship as the Premier Soccer League began a five year television contract worth some 100-million Euros - by far the biggest on the continent and among the top 10 in the world for any football league. SuperSport United, Moroka Swallows and Bloemfontein Celtic won the three cup trophies on offer during 2012.

CAF AFRICA CUP OF NATIONS RECORD
1957-1992 DNE 1994 DNQ **1996** 1 Winners (Hosts) **1998** 2 F **2000** 3 SF **2002** 6 QF
2004 1 r1 **2006** 16 r1 **2008** 13 r1 2010-2012 DNQ **2013** 6 QF (Hosts)

SOUTH AFRICAN FOOTBALL ASSOCIATION (SAFA)

76 Nasrec Road, Nasrec Extension 3, PO Box 910, Johannesburg 2190
☎ +27 11 5672010
+27 11 4943013
ceo@safa.net
www.safa.net
FA 1991 CON 1992 FIFA 1992
P Kirsten Nematandani
GS Dennis Mumble

THE STADIA
2014 FIFA World Cup Stadia
Royal Bafokeng Stadium
Rustenburg 42 000
Other Main Stadia
FNB Stadium Soccer City
Johannesburg 94 736
Cape Town Stadium
Cape Town 55 000
Moses Mabhida Stadium
Durban 54 000
Nelson Mandela Stadium
Port Elizabeth 48 459

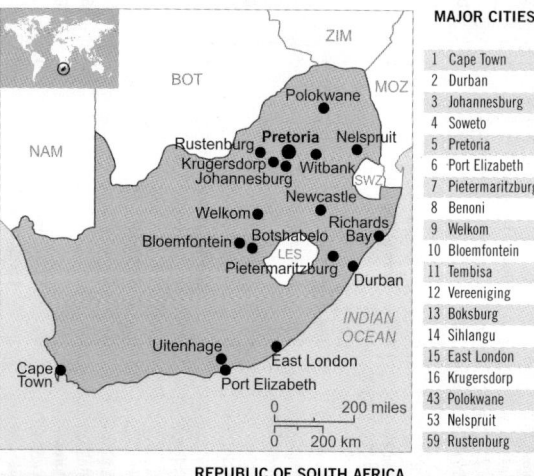

MAJOR CITIES/TOWNS
		Population
1	Cape Town	3 569 359
2	Durban	3 409 081
3	Johannesburg	2 023 456
4	Soweto	1 755 247
5	Pretoria	1 679 164
6	Port Elizabeth	1 146 350
7	Pietermaritzburg	891 607
8	Benoni	654 509
9	Welkom	584 719
10	Bloemfontein	583 253
11	Tembisa	573 022
12	Vereeniging	473 975
13	Boksburg	473 121
14	Sihlangu	463 706
15	East London	453 207
16	Krugersdorp	422 884
43	Polokwane	136 107
53	Nelspruit	116 705
59	Rustenburg	108 483

REPUBLIC OF SOUTH AFRICA

Capital	Pretoria	Population	49 052 489 (24)	% in cities	61%
GDP per capita	$10 100 (105)	Area km²	1 219 090 km² (25)	GMT +/-	+2
Neighbours (km)	\multicolumn{5}{l}{Botswana 1840, Lesotho 909, Mozambique 491, Namibia 967, Swaziland 430, Zimbabwe 225 • Coast 2798}

RECENT INTERNATIONAL MATCHES PLAYED BY SOUTH AFRICA

2010	Opponents		Score	Venue	Comp	Scorers	Att	Referee
11-06	Mexico	D	1-1	Johannesburg	WCr1	Siphiwe Tshabalala [55]	84 490	Irmatov UZB
16-06	Uruguay	L	0-3	Pretoria	WCr1		42 658	Busacca SUI
22-06	France	W	2-1	Bloemfontein	WCr1	Bongani Khumalo [20], Katlego Mphela [37]	39 415	Ruiz COL
11-08	Ghana	W	1-0	Johannesburg	Fr	Katlego Mphela [42]	47 000	
4-09	Niger	W	2-0	Nelspruit	CNq	Katlego Mphela [12], Bernard Parker [45]	40 000	Abdel Rahman SUD
10-10	Sierra Leone	D	0-0	Freetown	CNq		60 000	Lemghaifry MTN
17-11	USA	L	0-1	Cape Town	Fr		52 000	Kirwa KEN
2011								
9-02	Kenya	W	2-0	Rustenburg	Fr	Davide Somma [2], Steven Pienaar [45]	15 000	Ruzive ZIM
26-03	Egypt	W	1-0	Johannesburg	CNq	Katlego Mphela [93+]	55 000	Coulibaly MLI
14-05	Tanzania	W	1-0	Dar es Salaam	Fr	Siyabonga Sangweni [44]	5 000	Ssesonga UGA
5-06	Egypt	D	0-0	Cairo	CNq		25 000	Jedidi TUN
10-08	Burkina Faso	W	3-0	Johannesburg	Fr	Katlego Mphela 2 [14 51], Siphiwe Tshabalala [19]	10 000	
4-09	Niger	L	1-2	Niamey	CNq	Andile Jali [71]		Haimoudi ALG
8-10	Sierra Leone	D	0-0	Nelspruit	CNq			Ngosi MWI
12-11	Côte d'Ivoire	D	1-1	Port Elizabeth	Fr	Katlego Mphela [53]	28 000	
15-11	Zimbabwe	L	1-2	Harare	Fr	Bradley Grobler [28]		
2012								
6-01	Equatorial Guinea	D	0-0	Bata	Fr			Otogo-Castane GAB
29-02	Senegal	D	0-0	Durban	Fr			Ruzive ZIM
3-06	Ethiopia	D	1-1	Rustenburg	WCq	Katlego Mphela [77]	13 611	Nampiandraza MAD
9-06	Botswana	D	1-1	Gaborone	WCq	Morgan Gould [14]	7 500	Keita MLI
15-06	Gabon	W	3-0	Nelspruit	Fr	Siphiwe Tshabalala [42], Tokelo Rantie [68], Mzikayise Mashaba [75]		Makhobalo LES
7-09	Brazil	L	0-1	Sao Paulo	Fr		51 500	Pittana ARG
11-09	Mozambique	W	2-0	Nelspruit	Fr	Bernard Parker 2 [7 88]		Fakude SWZ
12-10	Poland	L	0-1	Warsaw	Fr		42 026	Prihoda CZE
16-10	Kenya	W	2-1	Nairobi	Fr	Tokelo Rantie [20], OG [76]		Mbaga TAN
14-11	Zambia	L	0-1	Johannesburg	Fr		17 000	Nhleko SWZ
22-12	Malawi	W	3-1	Durban	Fr	Lehlehonolo Majoro [6], Siphiwe Tshabalala [10], May Mahlangu [74]		Rachide MOZ
2013								
12-01	Algeria	D	0-0	Johannesburg	Fr		14 558	Koto LES
19-01	Cape Verde Islands	D	0-0	Johannesburg	CNr1		63 450	Haimoudi ALG
23-01	Angola	W	2-0	Durban	CNr1	Siyabonga Sangweni [30], Lehlehonolo Majoro [62]	45 890	Coulibaly MLI
27-01	Morocco	D	2-2	Durban	CNr1	May Mahlangu [71], Siyabonga Sangweni [86]	45 000	Gassama GAM
2-02	Mali	D	1-1	Durban	CNqf	Tokelo Rantie [31]. L 1-3p	45 000	Alioum CMR

Fr = Friendly match • CN = CAF African Cup of Nations • CC = COSAFA Cup • CF = FIFA Confederations Cup • WC = FIFA World Cup
q = qualifier • r1 = first round group • sf = semi-final • 3p = 3rd place play-off

SOUTH AFRICA NATIONAL TEAM HISTORICAL RECORDS

Caps: 107 - Aaron Mokoena 1999- • 82 - Siyabonga Nomvete 1999- • 79 - Benni McCarthy 1997- • 74 - Shaun Bartlett 1995-2005 & Siphiwe Tshabalala 2006- • 73 - John Moshoeu 1992-2004 & Delron Buckley 1999-2008 • 70 - Lucas Radebe 1992-2003 • 67 - Andre Arendse 1995-2004 & Sibusiso Zuma 1998-2008 • 62 - Mark Fish 1993-2004 • 58 - Phil Masinga 1992-2001 & MacBeth Sibaya 2001-

Goals: 31 - Benni McCarthy 1997- • 29 - Shaun Bartlett 1995-2005 • 23 - Katlego Mphela 2005- • 18 - Phil Masinga 1992-2001 • 16 - Siyabonga Nomvete 1999- • 13 - Sibusiso Zuma 1998-2008 • 12 - Bernard Parker 2007- • 10 - Teko Modise 2007- & Delron Buckley 1999-2008

Coaches: Stanley Tshabalala 1992 • Ephraim Mashaba 1992 • Augusto Palacios PER 1992-94 • Clive Barker 1994-97 • Jomo Sono 1998 • Philippe Troussier FRA 1998 • Trott Moloto 1998-2000 • Carlos Queiroz POR 2000-02 • Jomo Sono 2002 • Ephraim Mashaba 2002-03 • April Phumo 2004 • Stuart Baxter SCO 2004-05 • Ted Dumitru ROU 2005-06 • Pitso Mosimane 2006 • Carlos Alberto Parreira BRA 2007-08 • Joel Santana BRA 2008-09 • Carlos Alberto Parreira BRA 2009-10 • Pitso Mosimane 2010-12 • Steve Komphela 2012 • Gordon Igesund 2012-

SOUTH AFRICA 2011-12

PREMIER SOCCER LEAGUE — THE ABSA PREMIERSHIP

	Pl	W	D	L	F	A	Pts	Pirates	Swallows	SuperSport	Sundowns	Chiefs	Free State	AmaZulu	Celtic	Ajax	Platinum S	Maritzburg	Wits	Arrows	Leopards	Santos	Cosmos
Orlando Pirates †	30	17	7	6	39	26	58		1-1	3-0	0-0	3-2	3-1	0-0	2-1	1-0	1-0	1-0	0-0	2-0	1-0	1-0	2-1
Moroka Swallows	30	15	11	4	48	34	56	0-0		1-1	2-2	0-2	2-1	1-1	0-0	3-2	2-1	2-2	3-0	3-2	4-1	3-2	2-0
SuperSport United	30	15	9	6	39	23	54	1-2	0-0		1-3	2-0	1-1	0-1	0-1	2-1	2-0	7-0	2-1	2-1	3-0	1-0	0-0
Mamelodi Sundowns	30	14	10	6	44	23	52	0-0	4-0	0-1		0-1	1-0	0-0	2-1	2-3	1-2	1-0	1-1	0-0	5-1	3-1	0-0
Kaizer Chiefs	30	14	8	8	35	23	50	2-1	3-0	1-2	2-0		2-1	0-0	2-0	2-0	1-0	0-1	2-1	1-2	0-1	0-0	2-1
Free State Stars	30	14	6	10	38	31	48	1-0	0-1	1-1	0-2	1-2		2-1	2-1	0-0	0-0	4-1	0-0	3-1	2-2	2-0	1-0
AmaZulu	30	10	11	9	32	24	41	0-1	0-1	1-2	0-1	0-0	0-1		2-0	4-0	1-2	0-0	2-0	1-0	0-1	2-2	0-0
Bloemfontein Celtic	30	11	8	11	36	33	41	1-0	1-1	1-2	0-0	0-0	1-0	1-1		4-2	0-1	1-1	0-0	3-2	2-0	2-0	3-1
Ajax Cape Town	30	11	7	12	42	49	40	1-1	2-2	0-0	0-3	2-1	3-1	2-4	2-0		3-2	1-1	0-2	4-1	4-3	1-1	1-1
Platinum Stars	30	10	6	14	37	39	36	3-4	0-0	0-0	0-0	1-2	0-1	0-1	2-1	2-0		1-1	0-2	1-0	2-2	4-1	4-1
Maritzburg United	30	7	13	10	26	38	34	2-1	0-1	0-0	0-0	0-2	1-1	2-0	0-2	2-1			2-2	2-0	1-1	1-1	0-1	3-1
Bidvest Wits	30	7	12	11	31	38	33	3-1	1-3	0-1	2-3	1-1	1-3	3-1	1-3	1-1	2-1	0-0		2-2	0-0	1-0	0-1
Golden Arrows	30	9	5	16	40	48	32	2-4	2-0	1-2	1-1	0-0	2-0	1-2	0-3	0-1	3-1	4-1	1-1		4-2	1-3	3-1
Black Leopards	30	7	8	15	36	58	29	0-2	2-5	1-0	1-2	0-2	1-3	1-4	2-2	3-1	2-3	0-0	1-2	2-0		2-1	1-1
Santos	30	7	6	17	34	48	27	3-0	1-3	0-1	2-5	2-1	0-1	1-2	0-1	1-1	1-2	2-1	3-1	1-2	1-1		1-0
Jomo Cosmos	30	2	13	15	24	46	19	1-2	0-2	2-2	0-2	1-1	2-2	0-0	1-2	1-2	2-1	1-1	0-0	0-2	2-2	2-2	

12/08/2011 - 19/05/2012 • † Qualified for the CAF Champions League
Top scorers: **20** - Siyabonga **NOMVETHE**, Swallows • **12** - Eleazar **ROGERS**, Santos • **11** - Edward **MANQELE**, Free State • **10** - Lehlohonolo **MAJORO**, Kaizer Chiefs; David **MATHEBULA**, Swallows; Benni **MCCARTHY**, Pirates & Katlego **MPHELA**, Sundowns

SOUTH AFRICA 2011-12

PSL PLAY-OFF TOURNAMENT

	Pl	W	D	L	F	A	Pts	Chippa	Santos	Thanda
Chippa United	4	2	2	0	8	4	8		4-3	1-1
Santos	4	1	1	2	5	6	4	0-0		1-2
Thanda Royal Zulu	4	1	1	2	3	6	4	0-3	0-1	

23/05/2012 - 30/06/2012 • Chippa United promoted, Santos relegated

SOUTH AFRICA 2011-12

NATIONAL FIRST DIVISION (2)

	Pl	W	D	L	F	A	Pts	Tuks	Chippa Utd	Thanda	Rovers	FC AK	Warriors	Vasco	Cape Town	United FC	Polokwane	Sivutsa	Spurs	Black Aces	Dynamos	Atlie	Carara Kicks
University of Pretoria	30	15	10	5	45	25	55		0-2	0-1	3-0	0-0	1-0	2-0	2-0	4-1	1-1	4-0	3-1	1-1	3-0	2-0	1-1
Chippa United †	30	14	9	7	46	29	51	0-0		3-0	2-0	1-1	0-2	1-0	0-1	3-1	1-1	0-2	1-0	2-0	3-1	1-0	1-0
Thanda Royal Zulu †	30	13	11	6	34	28	50	1-1	2-1		1-0	1-0	2-2	4-1	2-1	2-2	2-1	0-0	0-0	1-0	0-0	0-2	
Blackburn Rovers	30	14	7	9	44	37	49	1-1	1-1	0-1		1-1	0-1	2-1	2-0	0-2	0-1	4-2	2-1	2-2	1-0	1-0	1-0
FC AK Johannesburg	30	12	9	9	45	43	45	0-0	0-4	1-0	1-2		2-1	3-2	3-1	1-2	1-1	5-1	0-0	2-1	0-0	1-0	4-0
African Warriors	30	11	10	9	43	36	43	1-2	1-1	3-0	1-1	4-0		1-2	2-2	1-0	2-1	2-1	0-0	3-2	3-1	1-0	1-2
Vasco da Gama	30	12	7	11	51	45	43	1-2	2-2	1-1	3-4	3-0	4-2		1-3	2-2	3-1	3-1	4-0	2-2	3-1	1-1	3-1
FC Cape Town	30	10	9	11	38	36	39	2-2	1-1	0-1	1-0	1-2	1-1	0-1		2-0	5-2	3-0	2-1	0-1	3-1	2-3	0-0
United FC	30	10	9	11	46	45	39	0-0	2-2	0-3	1-2	2-0	4-2	0-0	5-3		0-2	2-2	2-3	3-2	2-1	4-1	3-0
Polokwane City	30	8	11	11	32	40	35	0-0	2-2	0-0	2-3	1-4	0-0	0-1	1-3	0-0		1-1	1-0	3-1	1-3	1-1	2-1
Sivutsa Stars	30	9	7	14	39	47	34	1-2	3-1	2-1	0-3	2-0	2-3	3-2	1-0	2-2	0-0		0-1	3-0	1-0	5-0	1-1
Witbank Spurs	30	9	7	14	32	42	34	1-2	0-1	4-1	3-3	3-4	3-2	2-0	0-0	0-3	0-0	1-0		0-1	0-0	1-0	2-3
Mpuma'ga Black Aces	30	7	12	11	33	41	33	3-2	2-2	1-1	1-3	1-1	1-0	0-1	0-1	1-1	2-1	0-0	1-2		0-2	1-1	3-0
Dynamos Giyani	30	9	5	16	37	49	32	1-2	2-3	0-2	2-1	4-3	0-0	2-1	1-1	2-1	0-1	1-0	3-0	1-2		1-2	2-2
Atlie	30	6	10	14	24	42	28	1-2	1-5	1-1	0-2	1-2	0-0	0-0	0-0	2-0	1-1	0-1	1-0	0-3			2-2
Carara Kicks §18	30	9	11	10	42	46	20	1-0	1-0	1-1	2-2	3-3	1-1	2-3	0-1	0-0	2-0	2-1	3-2	1-1	7-2	1-3	

12/08/2011 - 19/05/2012 • † Qualified for the PSL Play-off Tournament • § = points deducted

RSA – SOUTH AFRICA

MTN 8 CUP 2012

First Round
Moroka Swallows *	2
AmaZulu	0
Kaizer Chiefs	1
Mamelodi Sundowns *	4
Orlando Pirates *	1
Bloemfontein Celtic	0
Free State Stars	1
SuperSport United *	2

Semi-finals
Moroka Swallows	3	3
Mamelodi Sundowns *	3	2
Orlando Pirates	0	0
SuperSport United *	0	3

* Home team/home in 1st leg

Final
Moroka Swallows	2
SuperSport United	1

Orlando Stadium, Johannesburg
22-09-2012, Att: 20 000, Ref: Mfiki
Scorers - Nergadze [18], Chenene [86] for Swallows; Cale [5] for United

TELKOM KNOCK-OUT LEAGUE CUP 2011-12

First Round
Bloemfontein Celtic	2
Chippa United	1
Black Leopards	0
Orlando Pirates	2
Bidvest Wits	3
Kaizer Chiefs	2
Golden Arrows	1
Free State Stars	3
SuperSport United	1 4p
Ajax Cape Town	1 3p
Moroka Swallows	0 3p
Maritzburg United	0 4p
AmaZulu	3
Platinum Stars	1
University of Pretoria	0
Mamelodi Sundowns	1

Quarter-finals
Bloemfontein Celtic	3	5p
Orlando Pirates	3	3p
Bidvest Wits	0	3p
Free State Stars	0	4p
SuperSport United	2	
Maritzburg United	0	
AmaZulu	0	
Mamelodi Sundowns	2	

* Home team • ‡ Played in Polokwane • ‡‡ Played in Durban

Semi-finals
Bloemfontein Celtic	3
Free State Stars	2
SuperSport United	0
Mamelodi Sundowns	1

Final
Bloemfontein Celtic	1
Mamelodi Sundowns	0

CUP FINAL
Moses Mabhida, Durban
1-12-2012, Att: 20 000
Scorer - Joel Mogorosi [47]

MEDALS TABLE

		Overall G S B	League G S B	Cup G S	T8	LCup	Africa G S B	City
1	Kaizer Chiefs	50 20 5	10 6 5	12 5	14 6	13 3	1	Johannesburg
2	Orlando Pirates	28 22 8	9 5 6	7 7	10 4	1 6	1 2	Johannesburg
3	Mamelodi Sundowns	16 18 3	8 3 3	3 5	3 5	2 4	1	Pretoria
4	Moroka Swallows	8 10 1	2 1	5 1	3 5	2		Johannesburg
5	SuperSport United	7 8 2	3 2 2	3 1	1 3	2		Pretoria
6	Bidvest Wits	6 6 2	2	2 1	2 3	2 2		Johannesburg
7	Jomo Cosmos	5 8 1	1 1	1 4	1 1	2 2	1	Johannesburg
8	Bush Bucks	4 2 1	1 1 1			3 1		Umtata
9	Santos	4 1 1	1 1	2	1	1		Cape Town
10	Ajax Cape Town	3 8	3	1 1	2	2 2		Cape Town
11	Bloemfontein Celtic	3 1	1	1	1	1		Bloemfontein
12	AmaZulu	2 7 2	1 2	6	1 1	1		Durban
13	Arcadia	2 2 1	1		1 2	1		Pretoria
14	Witbank Aces	2 2		1 1	1 1			Witbank
15	Cape Town Spurs	2 1	1 1	1				Cape Town
16	Durban City	2	2					Durban
17	Highlands Park	1 4	1	1	1	2		Johannesburg
18	QwaQwa Stars	1 3		1	1	1 1		QwaQwa
19	Rangers	1 2	1 1		1			Johannesburg
	Silver Stars	1 2	1			1 1		Rustenburg
21	Manning Rangers	1 1	1	1				Durban
	Dynamos	1 1			1	1		Johannesburg
23	Golden Arrows	1			1			Durban
	Lusitano	1	1					
	Vaal Professionals	1		1				Vereeneging
26	Hellenic	2 1	1 1			1		Cape Town
27	African Wanderers	2		2				
28	Free State Stars	1 1	1			1		QwaQwa

NEDBANK FA CUP 2011-12

First Round

SuperSport United	1 4p
Batau FC *	1 2p
Vardos *	1
United FC	3
Platinum Stars *	5
The Dolphins	0
African Warriors *	1
Jomo Cosmos	2
Santos *	1
Pretoria University	0
Polokwane City	0
Roses United *	2
Witbank Spurs	1 3p
Mpuma'ga Black Aces *	1 2p
Ajax Cape Town	3 3p
AmaZulu *	3 4p
Free State Stars *	4
Sivutsa Stars	1
Ethekwini Coastal *	0
Orlando Pirates	1
Black Leopards *	2
Blackburn Rovers	0
Cape Town All Stars	0
Kaizer Chiefs *	3
Maritzburg United *	1
Bloemfontein Celtic	0
NW Shining Stars	0
Golden Arrows *	5
Bidvest Wits	1
Moroka Swallows *	0
Powerlines *	0
Mamelodi Sundowns	24

Second Round

SuperSport United	
United FC *	
Platinum Stars	1 3p
Jomo Cosmos *	1 4p
Santos	
Roses United *	
Witbank Spurs	0
AmaZulu *	1
Free State Stars	2
Orlando Pirates *	1
Black Leopards *	0
Kaizer Chiefs	4
Maritzburg United	1
Golden Arrows *	0
Bidvest Wits *	0
Mamelodi Sundowns	2

Quarter-finals

SuperSport United ††	1
Jomo Cosmos	0
Santos	0
AmaZulu *	1
Free State Stars	1
Kaizer Chiefs ††	0
Maritzburg United	0
Mamelodi Sundowns †	2

Semi-finals

SuperSport United ††	3
AmaZulu	0
Free State Stars	0
Mamelodi Sundowns †	2

Final

SuperSport United ‡	2
Mamelodi Sundowns	0

* Home team • † played at Lucas Moripe, Pretoria • †† played at Peter Mokaba, Polokwane
‡ Qualified for the CAF Confederation Cup

CUP FINAL

Orlando Stadium, Johannesburg
26-05-2012, Ref: Gabriel Sekopo
Scorers - September [40] Erasmus 71 for United
SuperSport - Ronwen Williams - Thabo September●, Morgan Gould, Tebogo Langerman, Davis Nkausu - Sameehg Doutie, Moffat Mdluli (Ashley Hartog 58), Edwin Gyimah - Sibusiso Zuma● (Mabhuti Khenyeza 80), Kermit Erasmus (Mogogi Gabonamong 74), Thabiso Nkoana. Tr: Gavin Hunt
Sundowns - Wayne Sandilands - Clayton Daniels●**19**, Punch Masenamela, Siyanda Xulu, Method Mwanjali - Teko Modise, Surprise Moriri (Esrom Nyandoro 65), Lebohang Mokoena, Domingues (Katlego Mphela 67), Hlompho Kekana - Nyasha Mushekwi. Tr: Johann Neeskens

RUS – RUSSIA

FIFA/COCA-COLA WORLD RANKING

'93	'94	'95	'96	'97	'98	'99	'00	'01	'02	'03	'04	'05	'06	'07	'08	'09	'10	'11	'12
14	13	5	7	12	40	18	21	21	23	24	32	34	22	23	9	12	13	12	9

2012												High	Low	Av
Jan	Feb	Mar	Apr	May	Jun	Jul	Aug	Sep	Oct	Nov	Dec			
13	13	12	11	11	13	13	11	13	12	9	9	3	40	19

After losing to Iran in a relatively meaningless friendly in February 2011, the Russian national team played 22 matches to the end of 2012 and lost just once. Unfortunately for them it was the one that mattered most - a 1-0 defeat at the hands of Greece in the finals of Euro 2012 and it sent them crashing out of the tournament after the first round group stage. The Russians had begun the tournament in fine style, beating the Czech Republic 4-1 to set themselves up as potential winners. They then held hosts Poland to a draw in the charged atmosphere of the National Stadium in Warsaw before facing what looked on paper to be the easiest of the group ties against the Greeks. It was a goal from Georgios Karagounis that sent them home early but there are signs that new coach Fabio Capello's side are stepping up to the mark in preparation for the 2018 FIFA World Cup which they will host and they set off at a blistering pace in the 2014 qualifiers, racing ahead of the group by the end of the year. At home, the mammoth transitional league season came to an end after 14 months and was won by Zenit St Petersburg who retained their title 18 months on from the last. There were first time winners in the cup after Rubin Kazan beat Dinamo 1-0 in the final to add to the club's two league titles won in 2008 and 2009.

UEFA EUROPEAN CHAMPIONSHIP RECORD

1960 1 winners **1964** 2 F **1968** 4 SF **1972** 2 F **1976-1984** DNQ **1988** 2 F (as the Soviet Union) **1992** 8 r1 (as the CIS)
1996 14 r1 **2000** DNQ **2004** 10 r1 **2008** 3 SF **2012** 9 r1

FOOTBALL UNION OF RUSSIA (RFU)

House of Football,
Ulitsa Narodnaya 7,
115 172 Moscow
☎ +7 495 9261300
info@rfs.ru
www.rfs.ru
FA 1912 CON 1992 FIFA 1992
P Nikolai Tolstykh
GS TBD

THE STADIA

2014 FIFA World Cup Stadia

Luzhniki Moscow	89 318
Lokomotiv Moscow	28 800

Other Main Stadia

SKA SKVO Stadion Rostov-na-Donu	33 000
Tsentralnyi Kazan	28 500
Petrovskiy Saint Petersburg	21 405

MAJOR CITIES/TOWNS

		Population
1	Moscow	10 494 522
2	Saint Petersburg	4 523 802
3	Novosibirsk	1 380 638
4	Yekaterinburg	1 305 070
5	Nizhniy Novgorod	1 263 758
6	Omsk	1 128 973
7	Samara	1 122 068
8	Kazan	1 118 623
9	Chelyabinsk	1 090 454
10	Rostov-na-Donu	1 048 157
11	Ufa	1 021 381
12	Perm	986 851
13	Volgograd	979 720
14	Krasnoyarsk	929 136
15	Voronezh	844 448
16	Saratov	835 418
17	Tolyatti	709 482
18	Krasnodar	702 427
56	Vladikavkaz	313 354

ROSSIYSKAYA FEDERATSIYA • RUSSIAN FEDERATION

Capital	Moscow	Population	140 041 247 (9)	% in cities	73%
GDP per capita	$16 100 (71)	Area km²	17 098 242 km² (1)	GMT +/-	+2 to +12

Neighbours (km): Azerbaijan 284, Belarus 959, China 3645, Estonia 290, Finland 1313, Georgia 723, Kazakhstan 6846, Korea DPR 17, Latvia 270, Lithuania 227, Mongolia 3441, Norway 196, Poland 432, Ukraine 1576 • Coast 37 653

RECENT INTERNATIONAL MATCHES PLAYED BY RUSSIA

2009	Opponents	Score	Venue	Comp	Scorers	Att	Referee
28-03	Azerbaijan	W 2-0	Moscow	WCq	Pavlyuchenko [32], Zyrianov [71]	62 000	Gumienny BEL
1-04	Liechtenstein	W 1-0	Vaduz	WCq	Zyrianov [38]	5 679	McKeon IRL
10-06	Finland	W 3-0	Helsinki	WCq	Kerzhakov 2 [27 53]	37 028	Plautz AUT
12-08	Argentina	L 2-3	Moscow	Fr	Semshov [17], Pavlyuchenko [78]	28 800	De Bleeckere BEL
5-09	Liechtenstein	W 3-0	St Petersburg	WCq	Berezutsky.V [17], Pavlyuchenko 2 [40p 45p]	21 000	Constantin ROU
9-09	Wales	W 3-1	Cardiff	WCq	Semshov [36], Ignashevich [71], Pavlyuchenko [91+]	14 505	De Sousa POR
10-10	Germany	L 0-1	Moscow	WCq		72 100	Busacca SUI
14-10	Azerbaijan	D 1-1	Baku	WCq	Arshavin [13]	17 000	Webb ENG
14-11	Slovenia	W 2-1	Moscow	WCpo	Bilyaletdinov 2 [40 52]	71 600	Larsen DEN
18-11	Slovenia	L 0-1	Maribor	WCpo		12 510	Hauge NOR
2010							
3-03	Hungary	D 1-1	Gyor	Fr	Bilyaletdinov [59]	10 000	Vucemilovic CRO
11-08	Bulgaria	W 1-0	St Petersburg	Fr	Shirokov [6]	8 200	Rizzoli ITA
3-09	Andorra	W 2-0	Andorra La Vella	ECq	Pogrebnyak 2 [14 64p]	1 100	Borg MLT
7-09	Slovakia	L 0-1	Moscow	ECq		27 052	De Bleeckere BEL
8-10	Republic of Ireland	W 3-2	Dublin	ECq	Kerzakhov [11], Dzagoev [29], Shirokov [50]	50 411	Blom NED
12-10	Macedonia FYR	W 1-0	Skopje	ECq	Kerzhakov [8]	10 500	Johannesson SWE
17-11	Belgium	L 0-2	Voronezh	Fr		31 743	Kaasik EST
2011							
9-02	Iran	L 0-1	Abu Dhabi	Fr		5 000	Albadwawi UAE
26-03	Armenia	D 0-0	Yerevan	ECq		14 800	Thomson SCO
29-03	Qatar	D 1-1	Doha	Fr	Pavlyuchenko [34]	9 000	Al Awaji KSA
4-06	Armenia	W 3-1	St Petersburg	ECq	Pavlyuchenko 3 [26 59 73p]	18 000	Lannoy FRA
7-06	Cameroon	D 0-0	Salzburg	Fr		3 000	Einwaller AUT
10-08	Serbia	W 1-0	Moscow	Fr	Pogrebnyak [53]	27 000	Hategan ROU
2-09	FYR Macedonia	W 1-0	Moscow	ECq	Semshov [41]	31 028	Yildirim TUR
6-09	Republic of Ireland	D 0-0	Moscow	ECq		49 515	Brych GER
7-10	Slovakia	W 1-0	Zilina	ECq	Dzagoev [71]	10 087	Eriksson SWE
11-10	Andorra	W 6-0	Moscow	ECq	Dzagoev 2 [5 44], Ignashevich [26], Pavlyuchenko [30], Glushakov [59], Bilyaletdinov [78]	38 790	Hacmon ISR
11-11	Greece	D 1-1	Piraeus	Fr	Shirokov [2]		Chapron FRA
2012							
29-02	Denmark	W 2-0	Copenhagen	Fr	Shirokov [4], Arshavin [45]	13 593	Vad HUN
25-05	Uruguay	D 1-1	Moscow	Fr	Kerzhakov [50]	18 000	Blom NED
29-05	Lithuania †	D 0-0	Nyon	Fr		500	Bergonzi ITA
1-06	Italy	W 3-0	Zurich	Fr	Kerzhakov [60], Shirokov 2 [75 89]	20 000	Hanni SUI
8-06	Czech Republic	W 4-1	Wroclaw	ECr1	Dzagoev 2 [15 79], Shirokov [24], Pavlyuchenko [82]	41 000	Webb ENG
12-06	Poland	D 1-1	Warsaw	ECr1	Dzagoev [37]	55 920	Stark GER
16-06	Greece	L 0-1	Warsaw	ECr1		55 614	Eriksson SWE
15-08	Côte d'Ivoire	D 1-1	Moscow	Fr	Dzagoev [55]	12 500	Cakir TUR
7-09	Northern Ireland	W 2-0	Moscow	WCq	Faizulin [30], Shirokov [78p]	14 300	Mateu Lahoz ESP
11-09	Israel	W 4-0	Tel Aviv	WCq	Kerzhakov 2 [7 64], Kokorin [18], Faizulin [78]	28 131	Clattenburg ENG
12-10	Portugal	W 1-0	Moscow	WCq	Kerzhakov [6]	54 212	Kassai HUN
16-10	Azerbaijan	W 1-0	Moscow	WCq	Shirokov [84p]	15 033	Stavrev MKD
14-11	USA	D 2-2	Krasnodar	Fr	Smolov [9], Shirokov [84p]	28 200	Rizzoli ITA

Fr = Friendly match • EC = UEFA EURO 2008/2012 • WC = FIFA World Cup • q = qualifier
r1 = first round group • qf = quarter-final • sf = semi-final • † Not a full international

RUSSIA NATIONAL TEAM HISTORICAL RECORDS

Caps
113 - Viktor Onopko 1992-2004 • 84 - Sergei Ignashevich 2002- • 75 - Andrei Arshavin 2002- • 73 - Aleksandr Anyukov 2004- • 72 - Valeri Karpin 1992-2003 • 71 - Vladimir Beschastnykh 1992-2003 • 69 - Aleksandr Kerzhakov 2002- • 68 - Vasili Berezutskiy 2003- • 65 - Sergei Semak 1997- • 57 - Igor Akinfeev 2004- & Igor Semshov 2002-

Goals
26 - Vladimir Beschastnykh 1992-2003 • 22 - Aleksandr Kerzhakov 2002- • 21 - Roman Pavlyuchenko 2003- • 17 - Valeri Karpin 1992-2003 & Andrei Arshavin 2002- • 15 - Dmitri Sychev 2002- • 12 - Igor Kolyvanov 1992-98 • 11 - Roman Shirokov 2008- • 10 - Sergei Kiryakov 1992-98 & Aleksandr Mostovoi 1992-2004 • 9 - Igor Simutenkov 1994-98

Coaches
Pavel Sadyrin 1992-94 • Oleg Romantsev 1994-96 • Boris Ignatyev 1996-98 • Anatoli Byshovets 1998 • Oleg Romantsev 1999-2002 • Valeri Gazzaev 2002-03 • Georgi Yartsev 2003-05 • Yuri Semin 2005 • Aleksandr Borodyuk 2006 • Guus Hiddink 2006-10 • Dick Advocaat 2010-12 • Fabio Capello ITA 2012-

RUSSIA 2011-12

PREMIER LEAGUE

	Pl	W	D	L	F	A	Pts	Zenit	Spartak	CSKA	Dinamo	Anzhi	Rubin	Lokomotiv	Kuban	Krasnodar	Amkar	Terek	Krylya	Rostov	Volga	Tom	Spartak N
Zenit St Petersburg †	44	24	16	4	85	40	88		2-3	2-0	2-1	0-0	1-1	2-1	1-1								
Spartak Moskva †	44	21	12	11	69	47	75	1-2		1-2	1-1	0-3	2-0	2-0	2-0								
CSKA Moskva ‡	44	19	16	9	72	47	73	2-2	2-1		1-1	0-0	1-2	0-2	0-0								
Dinamo Moskva ‡	44	20	12	12	66	50	72	1-5	1-3	1-0		0-1	1-1	2-2	2-1								
Anzhi Makhachkala ‡	44	19	13	12	54	42	70	0-2	0-0	2-1	0-1		3-1	3-1	2-0								
Rubin Kazan ‡	44	17	17	10	55	41	68	2-2	1-1	3-1	2-0	1-0		0-0	1-1								
Lokomotiv Moskva	44	18	12	14	59	48	66	0-1	0-2	0-3	0-2	1-0	0-0		2-0								
Kuban Krasnodar	44	15	16	13	50	45	61	2-2	1-1	1-1	1-1	2-2	1-0	1-1									
FK Krasnodar	44	16	13	15	58	61	61										0-1	1-3	0-2	1-0	2-1	3-1	3-2
Amkar Perm	44	14	13	17	40	51	55									2-2		2-0	2-1	1-0	4-1	0-0	1-0
Terek Groznyi	44	14	10	20	45	62	52									0-1	3-1		0-0	1-0	1-3	1-0	2-0
Krylya Sovetov Samara	44	12	15	17	33	50	51									1-1	2-1	1-1		2-1	1-0	1-0	1-0
FK Rostov	44	12	12	20	45	61	48									1-1	1-1	1-1	1-0		1-0	3-1	2-1
Volga Nizhniy Novgorod	44	12	5	27	37	60	41									1-2	1-2	1-3	0-0	2-0		2-0	1-0
Tom Tomsk	44	8	13	23	30	70	37									0-0	0-0	3-0	0-0	2-1	1-0		1-1
Spartak Nalchik	44	7	13	24	39	60	34									3-3	1-2	3-0	0-0	2-2	3-0	0-2	

12/03/2011 - 13/05/2012 • † Qualified for the UEFA Champions League • ‡ Qualified for the Europa League
Results from the first two rounds are listed in Oliver's Almanack of World Football 2012
Top scorers: 28 - Seydou **DOUMBIA** CIV, CSKA • 23 - Aleksandr **KERZHAKOV**, Zenit • 18 - Lacina **TRAORE** CIV, Kuban • 14 - Yura **MOVSISYAN** ARM, Krasnodar • 13 - Emmanuel **EMENIKE** NGA, Spartak; Kevin **KURANYI** GER, Dinamo & Samuel **ETO'O** CMR, Anzhi • 12 - Igor **SEMSHOV**, Dinamo & Danko **LAZOVIC** SRB, Zenit • 11 - Andriy **VORONIN** UKR, Dinamo; Denis **GLUSHAKOV**, Lokomotiv, Roman **ADAMOV**, Rostov & Artyom **DZYUBA**, Spartak M

RUSSIA 2011-12

FIRST DIVISION (2)

	Pl	W	D	L	F	A	Pts	Mordovia	Alania	Nizhniy	Shinnik	Dinamo	Ural	SIBIR	Torpedo M	KamAZ	Yenisey	SKA-Energiya	Torpedo V	Khimki	Volgar	Baltika	Gazovik	Luch-Energiya	Chernomorets	Fakel	Sochi
Mordovia Saransk	52	29	13	10	91	56	100		2-0	3-1	2-0	3-1	2-2	0-2	2-0												
Alania Vladikavkaz	52	28	13	11	66	39	97	2-4		1-0	0-0	2-0	1-2	1-1	1-0												
FC Nizhniy Novgorod - R	52	29	7	16	76	58	94	0-2	2-0		1-0	3-1	1-1	4-3	3-2												
Shinnik Yaroslavl	52	25	10	17	70	56	85	2-0	1-1	1-1		0-2	2-1	1-2	1-0												
Dinamo Bryansk - R	52	22	12	18	62	57	78	1-0	1-2	1-2	0-1		2-1	1-0	1-1												
Ural Yekaterinburg	52	19	21	12	71	52	78	1-1	2-2	0-2	0-1	0-0		1-1	2-0												
SIBIR Novosibirsk	52	19	19	14	76	57	76	2-1	1-1	2-0	3-1	1-0	0-0	0-1	1-1												
Torpedo Moskva	52	17	17	18	63	53	68	0-0	0-1	3-0	1-1	2-3	2-6	1-1													
KamAZ Chelny - R	48	19	10	19	53	46	67										2-1	0-1		0-1	0-0		2-0				
Yenisey Krasnoyarsk	48	17	15	16	53	53	66									1-1		2-1		1-1	0-0	2-1					
SKA Khabarovsk	48	16	14	18	57	66	62									2-0			1-1	2-1	0-1	0-0					
Torpedo Vladimir - R	48	17	10	21	62	73	61									3-0				5-2	1-1	1-1		2-1			
FK Khimki	48	16	11	21	54	74	59									1-0	0-0	0-2			1-1		1-3				
Volgar Astrakhan	48	15	14	19	44	57	59									1-1		3-1	0-1		0-1				2-1		
Baltika Kaliningrad	48	14	17	17	42	54	59									0-1			3-0	1-0			2-1	1-1	1-0	2-0	
Gazovik Orenburg	48	14	17	17	54	52	59										2-0	1-0	3-0	1-0				2-0			
Luch Vladivostock	48	11	21	16	37	39	54										1-2		1-2	0-0		0-0			2-1		
Ch'morets Novorossiysk	48	14	10	24	40	45	52									1-0		1-2	3-0	1-0	0-0						
Fakel Voronez	48	9	13	26	34	59	40										1-0	2-1				0-2	0-1	0-0			
Zhemchuzhina Sochi	38	8	2	28	22	81	26																				

4/04/2011 - 27/05/2012 • Results from the first two rounds are listed in Oliver's Almanack of World Football 2012
Nizhniy-Novgorod, Dinamo Bryansk, KamAZ Chelny & Torpedo Vladimir all relegated for financial reasons
Top scorers: 31 - Ruslan **MUKHAMETSHIN**, Mordovia • 22 - Dmitri **GOLUBOV**, Baltika/Dinamo Bryansk • 20 - Dmitri **AKIMOV**, SIBIR

KUBOK ROSSII 2011-12

Fourth Round

Rubin Kazan	Bye
SIBIR Novosibirsk *	0
Ural Yekaterinburg	1
Metalurg Novokuznetsk *	2
FK Chelyabinsk	0
Amkar Perm	Bye
Luch Vladivostock	2
Radian-Baikal Irkutsk *	1
Krylya Sovetov Samara	Bye
Yenisey Krasnoyarsk *	1
SKA Khabarovsk	0
Lokomotiv Moskva	Bye
Fakel Voronez	2
FAYUR Beslan *	1
FK Krasnodar	Bye
CSKA Moskva	Bye
Alania Vladikavkaz *	0
Volgar Astrakhan	1
Tom Tomsk	Bye
Chernomorets Novorossiysk *	1 4p
Metallurg Stary Oskol	1 5p
Zhemchuzhina Sochi	4
Torpedo Armavir *	3
FK Rostov	Bye
Volga Nizhniy Novgorod	Bye
Baltika Kaliningrad	1
Shinnik Yaroslavl *	2
FC Istra *	2
Volga Tver	1
Spartak Moskva	Bye
Torpedo Vladimir	3
Rusichi Oryol *	1
Spartak Nalchik	Bye
FC Nizhniy Novgorod	1
Tekstilshchik Ivanovo *	0
Terek Groznyi	Bye
Zenit St Petersburg	Bye
Vityaz Podolsk *	0
FK Khimki	2
Kuban Krasnodar	Bye
Torpedo Moskva	0
Dinamo Bryansk *	2
Anzhi Makhachkala	Bye
Gazovik Orenburg	1 7p
Volga Ulyanovsk *	1 8p
Mordovia Saransk	2
KamAZ Chelny *	1
Dinamo Moskva	Bye

Fifth Round

Rubin Kazan	0 6p
Ural Yekaterinburg *	0 5p
Metalurg Novokuznetsk *	0
Amkar Perm	1
Luch Vladivostock *	1
Krylya Sovetov Samara	0
Yenisey Krasnoyarsk *	0
Lokomotiv Moskva	2
Fakel Voronez *	2
FK Krasnodar	1
CSKA Moskva	0
Volgar Astrakhan *	1
Tom Tomsk	1
Metallurg Stary Oskol *	0
Zhemchuzhina Sochi *	1
FK Rostov	2
Volga Nizhniy Novgorod	1
Shinnik Yaroslavl *	0
FC Istra *	0
Spartak Moskva	1
Torpedo Vladimir *	3
Spartak Nalchik	0
FC Nizhniy Novgorod *	0
Terek Groznyi	2
Zenit St Petersburg	3
FK Khimki *	2
Kuban Krasnodar	1
Dinamo Bryansk *	3
Anzhi Makhachkala	3
Volga Ulyanovsk *	0
Mordovia Saransk *	0
Dinamo Moskva	5

The 16 Premier League teams enter in the fifth round and are drawn away to the 16 qualifiers

Sixth Round

Rubin Kazan	2
Amkar Perm *	0
Luch Vladivostock	0
Lokomotiv Moskva *	1
Fakel Voronez *	2
Volgar Astrakhan	0
Tom Tomsk	1
FK Rostov *	3
Volga Nizhniy Novgorod	1 6p
Spartak Moskva *	1 5p
Torpedo Vladimir	0
Terek Groznyi *	2
Zenit St Petersburg *	2
Dinamo Bryansk	0
Anzhi Makhachkala	0
Dinamo Moskva *	1

KUBOK ROSSII 2011-12

Quarter-finals	Semi-finals	Final

Rubin Kazan †	4
Lokomotiv Moskva	0

Rubin Kazan *	2
FK Rostov	0

Fakel Voronez	0 3p
FK Rostov *	0 4p

Rubin Kazan ‡	1
Dinamo Moskva	0

Volga Nizhniy Novgorod *	2
Terek Groznyi	1

Volga Nizhniy Novgorod	1
Dinamo Moskva *	2

Zenit St Petersburg *	0
Dinamo Moskva	1

KUBOK ROSSI FINAL 2012
Tsentralnyi, Yekaterinburg, 9-05-2012, Att: 27 000, Ref: Mikhail Vilkov

Rubin Kazan	1	Eremenko [78]
Dinamo Moskva	0	

RUBIN

Sergey Ryzhikov - Oleg Kuzmin, Cristian Ansaldi, Cesar Navas•, Roman Sharonov• - Aleksandr Ryazantsev, Roman Eremenko•, Gokdeniz Karadeniz (Pyotr Bystrov 90), Bibras Natkho - Nelson Haedo Valdez (Sergei Davydov 90), Vladimir Dyadyun (Salvatore Bocchetti 87). Tr: Kurban Berdyev

DINAMO

Anton Shunin - Igor Shitov (Alexandru Epureanu 63), Leandro Fernandez, Vladimir Granat, Vladimir Rykov - Balazs Dzsudzsak, Zvjezdan Misimovic (Aleksandr Kokorin 82), Aleksandr Samedov, Igor Semshov• - Andriy Voronin (c), Kevin Kuranyi. Tr: Sergei Silkin

* Home team
† Played at Akhmat Arena, Grosny
‡ Qualified for the Europa League

RWA – RWANDA

FIFA/COCA-COLA WORLD RANKING

'93	'94	'95	'96	'97	'98	'99	'00	'01	'02	'03	'04	'05	'06	'07	'08	'09	'10	'11	'12
-	-	168	159	172	107	146	128	144	130	109	99	89	121	99	78	102	132	106	134

2012												High	Low	Av
Jan	Feb	Mar	Apr	May	Jun	Jul	Aug	Sep	Oct	Nov	Dec			
110	108	105	105	105	119	125	125	120	124	122	134	78	178	127

Rwanda remain one of the more ambitious nations in African football but those aims were not matched by results on the pitch in 2012 with just two wins to their name. The national side, 'Amavubi', had a busy year under Serbia coach Milutin 'Micho' Sredojevic but they had tough draws in the qualifiers for both the 2014 FIFA World Cup and the 2013 Africa Cup of Nations. In the Nations Cup, Rwanda had the misfortune to be drawn against Nigeria and went out after a creditable home draw and respectable 0-2 defeat away in the second leg. Prospects in the FIFA World Cup were tempered by a poor start which saw a 4-0 defeat in Algeria followed by a 0-0 draw at home to Benin, and with Mali also in the group, hopes were not high for the rest of the campaign. In truth regional CECAFA-organised tournaments offer the best prospects of success for football in Rwanda, but there was disappointment with a quarter-final exit at the CECAFA Cup in Uganda, where they lost 2-0 to Tanzania, and when APR FC fell to Tanzania's Young Africans in the semi-finals of the CECAFA Kagame Inter-Club Cup - a tournament that they won in 2010. The army club did, however, retain their league title at home and completed the double for the third year running with Police FC finishing as runners-up in both the league and the cup.

CAF AFRICA CUP OF NATIONS RECORD
1957-1980 DNE 1982-1984 DNQ 1986-1998 DNE 2000-2002 DNQ **2004** 9 r1 2006-2012 DNQ

FEDERATION RWANDAISE DE FOOTBALL (FERWAFA)

Boite Postale 2000, Kigali

☎ +250 518525
📠 +250 518523
✉ ferwafa@yahoo.fr
🖥 www.ferwafa.rw
FA 1972 CON 1976 FIFA 1978
P Celestin Ntagungira
GS Michel Gasingwa

THE STADIA
2014 FIFA World Cup Stadia
Stade Amahoro
Kigali   30 000
Other Main Stadia
Stade Regional Nyamirambo
Kigali   22 000
Stade Huye
Butare   15 000
Stade Umuganda
Gisenyi   5 000

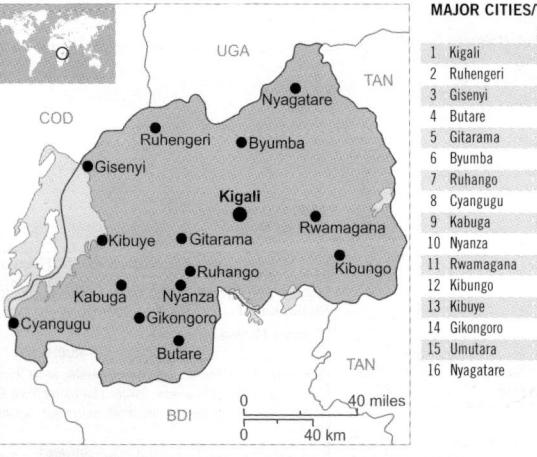

MAJOR CITIES/TOWNS
		Population
1	Kigali	965 398
2	Ruhengeri	110 717
3	Gisenyi	106 335
4	Butare	103 312
5	Gitarama	88 031
6	Byumba	74 143
7	Ruhango	70 086
8	Cyangugu	68 031
9	Kabuga	56 973
10	Nyanza	55 806
11	Rwamagana	52 599
12	Kibungo	48 564
13	Kibuye	48 097
14	Gikongoro	34 757
15	Umutara	8 918
16	Nyagatare	3 759

REPUBLIKA Y'U RWANDA • REPUBLIC OF RWANDA
Capital	Kigali	Population	10 473 282 (77)	% in cities	18%
GDP per capita	$900 (218)	Area km²	26 338 km² (148)	GMT +/-	+2
Neighbours (km)	Burundi 290, Congo DR 217, Tanzania 217, Uganda 169				

RECENT INTERNATIONAL MATCHES PLAYED BY RWANDA

2009	Opponents		Score	Venue	Comp	Scorers	Att	Referee
28-03	Algeria	D	0-0	Kigali	WCq		22 000	Codjia BEN
30-05	Malawi	L	0-2	Blantyre	Fr			
6-06	Zambia	L	0-1	Chililabombwe	WCq		28 000	Seck SEN
5-07	Egypt	L	0-3	Cairo	WCq		18 000	Imiere NGA
12-08	Tanzania	L	1-2	Kigali	Fr	Mwiseneza [68]		
5-09	Egypt	L	0-1	Kigali	WCq		20 000	Lamptey GHA
11-10	Algeria	L	1-3	Blida	WCq	Mutesa [19]	22 000	Keita GUI
14-11	Zambia	D	0-0	Kigali	WCq		18 000	Ambaya LBY
29-11	Somalia	W	1-0	Nairobi	CCr1	Mwalimu OG [4]		
3-12	Eritrea	W	2-1	Nairobi	CCr1	Ndayishimiye [20], Wolday OG [45]		
5-12	Zimbabwe †	W	1-0	Nairobi	CCr1	Ndayishimiye [20]		
8-12	Zimbabwe †	W	4-1	Nairobi	CCqf	Ndayishimiye [30], Ndamuhanga 2 [67 76], Niyonzima [90]		
10-12	Tanzania	W	2-1	Nairobi	CCsf	Ndayishimiye [68], Mafisango [77]		
13-12	Uganda	L	0-2	Nairobi	CCf			
2010								
7-01	Côte d'Ivoire	L	0-2	Dar es Salaam	Fr			
4-09	Côte d'Ivoire	L	0-3	Abidjan	CNq			Maillet SEY
9-10	Benin	L	0-3	Kigali	CNq			Haimoudi ALG
17-11	Malawi	L	1-2	Blantyre	Fr	Birori [8]		
1-12	Sudan	D	0-0	Dar es Salaam	CCr1			
3-12	Zanzibar	D	0-0	Dar es Salaam	CCr1			
8-12	Tanzania	L	0-1	Dar es Salaam	CCqf			
2011								
26-03	Burundi	W	3-1	Kigali	CNq	Jean-Claude Iranzi [34], Elias Uzamukunda 45p, Eric Gasana [88]		
5-06	Burundi	L	1-3	Bujumbura	CNq	Labama Kamana [48]		
3-09	Côte d'Ivoire	L	0-5	Kigali	CNq			
9-10	Benin	W	1-0	Cotonou	CNq	Medie Kagere [6]		
11-11	Eritrea	D	1-1	Asmara	WCq	Elias Uzamukunda [58]	6 000	Keita MLI
15-11	Eritrea	W	3-1	Kigali	WCq	Olivier Karekezi [4], Jean-Claude Iranzi [70], Labama Kamana [79]	10 000	Bondo BOT
26-11	Tanzania	W	1-0	Dar es Salaam	CCr1	Olivier Karekezi [22]		
29-11	Zimbabwe	W	2-0	Dar es Salaam	CCr1	Medie Kagere 2 [24 82]		
2-12	Djibouti	W	5-2	Dar es Salaam	CCr1	Labama Kamana [3], Jean-Baptiste Mugiraneza [57], Olivier Karekezi 3 [78 80 86]		
5-12	Zanzibar †	W	2-1	Dar es Salaam	CCqf	Jean-Baptiste Mugiraneza [39], Medie Kagere [88]		
8-12	Sudan	W	2-1	Dar es Salaam	CCsf	Jean-Claude Iranzi [6], Olivier Karekezi [78]		
10-12	Uganda	D	2-2	Dar es Salaam	CCf	Medie Kagere 2 [51 79]. L 2-3p		
2012								
29-02	Nigeria	D	0-0	Kigali	CNq			Bennett RSA
27-05	Tunisia	L	1-5	Monastir	Fr	Dady Birori [57]		Errahmani MAR
2-06	Algeria	L	0-4	Blida	WCq		20 000	Gassama GAM
10-06	Benin	D	1-1	Kigali	WCq	Labama Kamana [86]	15 000	Bamlak ETH
16-06	Nigeria	L	0-2	Calabar	CNq			Doue CIV
14-11	Namibia	D	2-2	Kigali	Fr	Jimmy Mbaraga [58], Elias Uzamukunda [67]		Batte UGA
26-11	Malawi	W	2-0	Kampala	CCr1	Jean-Baptiste Mugiraneza [37], Haruna Niyonzima [79]		Kalyango UGA
29-11	Zanzibar †	L	1-2	Kampala	CCr1	Dady Birori [80]		Kalyango UGA
1-12	Eritrea	W	2-0	Kampala	CCr1	Dady Birori [16], Tumaine Ntamuhanga [77]		Mujuni TAN
3-12	Tanzania	L	0-2	Kampala	CCqf			El Fadhil SUD

Fr = Friendly match • CN = CAF African Cup of Nations • CC = CECAFA Cup • WC = FIFA World Cup
q = qualifier • r1 = first round group • sf = semi-final • f = final • † Not a full international

RWANDA NATIONAL TEAM HISTORICAL RECORDS

Past Coaches: Rudi Gutendorf GER 1999-2000 • Ratomir Dujkovic SRB 2001-04 • Roger Palmgren SWE 2004-05 • Michael Nees GER 2006-07 • Josip Kuze CRO 2007-08 • Raul Shungu COD 2008 • Branco Tucak CRO 2008-09 • Eric Nhsimiyimana 2009-10 • Sellas Tetteh GHA 2010-11 • Milutin Sredojevic 2011-

RWANDA 2011-12
PRIMUS NATIONAL FOOTBALL LEAGUE PREMIER DIVISION

	Pl	W	D	L	F	A	Pts	APR	Police	Mukura	Rayon	Kiyovu	Isonga	Marines	Etincelles	Jeunesse	AS Kigali	Amagaju	Nyanza	Espoir
APR FC †	24	16	4	4	51	22	52		2-3	0-1	3-2	4-1	2-1	7-1	1-1	3-1	2-0	2-0	4-2	1-0
Police FC Kibungo ‡	24	15	5	4	37	15	50	0-0		0-1	2-2	2-1	2-0	1-0	1-1	3-0	3-0	4-0	1-0	3-0
Mukura Victory	24	14	7	3	33	14	49	1-0	0-0		0-0	3-0	2-1	2-2	0-0	2-1	1-1	1-0	5-0	2-1
Rayon Sport	24	13	7	4	41	21	46	2-2	3-1	3-1		0-1	1-3	2-0	3-0	1-0	4-1	2-0	2-0	1-0
Kiyovu Sport	24	11	5	8	27	27	38	0-3	0-0	1-0	1-1		1-1	1-2	1-2	3-2	1-0	3-1	2-1	2-1
Isonga	24	8	8	8	23	27	32	2-1	0-3	1-0	0-2	0-0		0-1	1-0	1-0	**0-3**	1-1	3-1	2-1
Marines FC Gisenyi	24	8	6	10	22	30	30	1-2	1-0	1-1	1-1	0-2	1-1		0-2	0-0	1-0	0-0	2-0	3-0
Etincelles Gisenyi	24	7	7	10	23	28	28	1-3	0-1	1-2	1-1	1-1	0-0	2-2		1-2	1-2	1-0	1-0	1-0
La Jeunesse	24	7	4	13	23	33	25	0-3	0-2	1-1	2-1	0-1	1-1	2-0	3-1		3-1	1-1	0-0	2-0
AS Kigali	24	7	5	12	22	33	26	0-2	1-2	0-3	0-1	1-0	1-1	1-0	1-1	3-1		1-2	0-1	2-1
Amagaju Nyamagabe	24	6	7	11	17	27	25	1-1	0-1	0-0	0-1	1-0	1-0	0-1	2-1	2-0	1-0		0-2	0-0
Nyanza Huye	24	6	5	13	18	31	23	0-1	2-0	1-2	1-1	1-3	0-1	1-1	1-0	0-2	0-1	0-0		1-1
Espoir FC Cyangugu	24	1	4	19	16	45	7	1-2	1-2	0-2	1-4	1-2	0-0	0-3	1-3	1-2	1-1	4-3	0-1	

16/09/2011 - 17/05/2012 • † Qualified for the CAF Champions League • ‡ Qualified for the Confederation Cup • Match in bold awarded

RWANDA 2011-12
SECOND DIVISION GROUP A (2)

	Pl	W	D	L	F	A	Pts
Muhanga Gitarama †	18	12	6	0	33	9	42
Espérance Kigali †	18	9	6	3	25	18	33
Gasabo United †	18	9	2	7	26	23	29
Intare Butare †	18	7	7	4	33	14	28
ASPOR Kigali	18	6	6	6	41	22	24
Stella Maris Gisenyi	18	6	5	7	22	22	23
Unity FC	18	5	7	6	17	22	22
Bugesera Nyamata	18	4	6	8	18	31	18
Zèbres FC Byumba	18	5	2	11	12	30	17
Kirehe FC	18	2	3	13	13	53	9

16/09/2011 - 21/04/2012 • † Qualified for the play-offs

RWANDA 2011-12
SECOND DIVISION GROUP B (2)

	Pl	W	D	L	F	A	Pts
Musanze Huye †	16	11	3	2	36	6	36
Rwamagana City †	16	11	3	2	24	7	36
SEC Academy Kigali †	16	10	3	3	22	7	33
Interforce Kigali †	16	9	1	6	19	20	28
Etoile de l'Est Kibungo	16	7	6	3	26	16	27
UNR Kigali	16	5	0	11	12	23	15
SORWATHE Kinikira	16	3	3	10	11	26	12
Pépinière Kinikira	16	3	1	12	12	38	10
United Stars	16	3	2	11	13	30	8

16/09/2011 - 21/04/2012 • † Qualified for the play-offs

SECOND DIVISION PLAY-OFFS

Quarter-finals
Musanze 1 1
Intare 1 0

SEC Academy 2 0
Espérance 2 1

Gasabo Utd 0 2
Rwamagana 0 2

Interforce 0 0
Muhanga 1 2

Semi-finals
Musanze 0 2
Espérance 0 0

Gasabo Utd 1 0
Muhanga 1 3

Final
Musanze 2 5p
Muhanga 2 4p

Final: 19-05-2012
Both finalists promoted

MEDALS TABLE

		Overall G	Lge G	Cup G	City
1	APR FC	24	13	11	Kigali
2	Rayon Sport	15	6	9	Kigali
3	Panthères Noires	9	5	4	Kigali
4	AS Kiyovu Sport	5	3	2	Kigali
5	Mukura Victory	4		4	Butare

COUPE AMAHORO 2012

Round of 16		Quarter-finals		Semi-finals		Final	
APR FC *	9						
Bugesera Nyamata	0	APR FC	3 2				
Unity FC *	1	SEC Academy *	1 1				
SEC Academy	3			APR FC *	3 1		
Kiyovu Sport *	3			Rayon Sport	1 0		
ASPOR Kigali	1	Kiyovu Sport *	0 2				
La Jeunesse	2	Rayon Sport	1 2				
Rayon Sport *	5					APR FC	2
AS Kigali *						Police FC Kibungo	1
Interforce Kigali		AS Kigali	0 3				
Etincelles Gisenyi	2 4p	Mukura Victory *	0 0				
Mukura Victory *	2 5p			AS Kigali	0 2		
Marines FC Gisenyi *				Police FC Kibungo *	0 2		
Amagaju Nyamagabe		Marines FC Gisenyi *	1 1				
Nyanza Huye	0	Police FC Kibungo	5 4				
Police FC Kibungo *	2						

CUP FINAL
Amahoro, Kigali
4-07-2012

* Home team in the 1st leg • 3rd place: Rayon Sport 2-2 5-4p AS Kigali

SAM – SAMOA

FIFA/COCA-COLA WORLD RANKING

'93	'94	'95	'96	'97	'98	'99	'00	'01	'02	'03	'04	'05	'06	'07	'08	'09	'10	'11	'12
-	-	-	177	183	164	180	173	172	163	176	179	182	187	146	176	182	185	149	173

2012

Jan	Feb	Mar	Apr	May	Jun	Jul	Aug	Sep	Oct	Nov	Dec	High	Low	Av
150	151	150	155	156	173	173	164	164	165	173		146	204	175

Safely negotiating a preliminary round of 2014 FIFA World Cup qualifying at the end 2011 meant that the Samoan national team not only progressed to the next round but also booked a place at the finals of the 2012 OFC Nations Cup, the first round of which had been decided would double up as a World Cup qualifying round. They travelled to the Solomon Islands for the Nations Cup with no great expectations but were handed a very nasty shock when they got there. Samoa opened their campaign with a 10-1 thrashing at the hands of Tahiti and although two days later managed to keep the score down to 5-0 against Vanuatu, any hope of further improvement was dashed when New Caledonia put nine past them in the final group game. It was an embarrassing outing for the team that did nothing to help the image of football in this rugby-league-mad country. It certainly had nothing to do with the football infrastructure in the country which has been the beneficiary of the FIFA Goal projects and which is now turning its attention to developing the game in Savai'i the western of the two main islands in Samoa. At club level the 2011 champions Kiwi entered the 2012-13 OFC Champions League but failed to get past a preliminary round held in Tonga, although they did manage a win against American Samoan champions Pago Youth.

FIFA WORLD CUP RECORD
1930-1994 DNE 1998-2014 DNQ

FOOTBALL FEDERATION SAMOA (FFS)

PO Box 1682, Apia
☎ +685 29993
+685 27895
tpetana@footballsamoa.ws
www.footballsamoa.ws
FA 1968 CON 1984 FIFA 1986
P Toetu Petana
GS Sarai Bareman

THE STADIA
2014 FIFA World Cup Stadia
Toleafoa J.S. Blatter Complex
Apia 3 500

Other Main Stadia
Apia Park
Apia 15 000

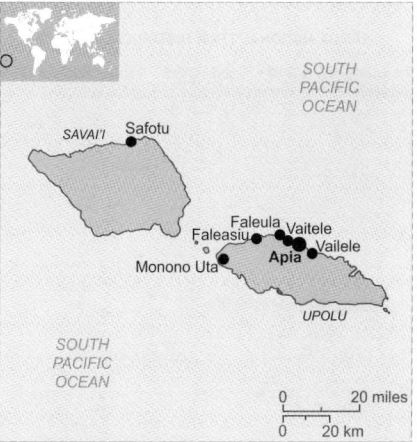

MAJOR CITIES/TOWNS

		Population
1	Apia	36 679
2	Vaitele	7 061
3	Faleasiu	3 780
4	Vailele	3 188
5	Leauvaa	3 145
6	Vaiusu	2 303
7	Faleula	2 197
8	Laulii	2 070
9	Malie	2 004
10	Siusega	1 951
11	Nofoalii	1 823
12	Afega	1 789
13	Fasitoouta	1 765
14	Solosolo	1 686
15	Fagalii	1 650
16	Nuu	1 504
17	Safotu	1 473
18	Manono Uta	1 420
19	Fasitoo Tai	1 371

MALO SA'OLOTO TUTO'ATASI O SAMOA • INDEPENDENT STATE OF SAMOA

Capital	Apia	Population	219 998 (184)	% in cities	23%
GDP per capita	$4700 (143)	Area km²	2831 km² (177)	GMT +/-	-11
Neighbours (km)	Coast 403				

RECENT INTERNATIONAL MATCHES PLAYED BY SAMOA

2004	Opponents	Score	Venue	Comp	Scorers	Att	Referee
5-05	Cook Islands	D 0-0	Auckland	Fr			Afu SOL
10-05	American Samoa	W 4-0	Apia	WCq	Bryce [12], Fasavalu 2 [30 53], Michael [66]	500	Afu SOL
15-05	Vanuatu	L 0-3	Apia	WCq		650	Breeze AUS
17-05	Fiji	L 0-4	Apia	WCq		450	Diomis AUS
19-05	Papua New Guinea	L 1-4	Apia	WCq	Michael [69]	300	Diomis AUS
2005							
No international matches played in 2005							
2006							
No international matches played in 2006							
2007							
25-08	Vanuatu	L 0-4	Apia	WCq		300	Jacques TAH
27-08	America Samoa	W 7-0	Apia	WCq	Tumua 2 [24 51], Faaiuaso [29], Cahill 2 [43p 67], Fonotti [61], Michael [76]	2 800	Minan PNG
29-08	Tonga	W 2-1	Apia	WCq	Faaiuaso [45], Taylor [83]	1 850	Sosongan PNG
3-09	Solomon Islands	L 0-3	Apia	WCq		200	Hester NZL
2008							
No international matches played in 2008							
2009							
No international matches played in 2009							
2010							
No international matches played in 2010							
2011							
17-08	Fiji	L 0-3	Navua	Fr			
18-08	Fiji	L 1-5	Suva	Fr	Albert Bell [53]		
22-11	Cook Islands	W 3-2	Apia	WCq	Luki Gosche 2 [19 36], Albert Bell [91+]	600	O'Leary NZL
24-11	Tonga	D 1-1	Apia	WCq	Shaun Easthope [43p]	180	Jacques TAH
26-11	American Samoa	W 1-0	Apia	WCq	Silao Malo [89]	800	O'Leary NZL
2012							
1-06	Tahiti	L 1-10	Honuara	OCr1	Silao Malo [69]	3 000	Oiaka SOL
3-06	Vanuatu	L 0-5	Honuara	OCr1		2 200	Saohu SOL
5-06	New Caledonia	L 0-9	Honuara	OCr1		1 000	Oiaka SOL

Fr = Friendly match • WC = FIFA World Cup • q = qualifier

SAMOA NATIONAL TEAM HISTORICAL RECORDS

Coaches
Rowan Naylor 1996-01 • Pedro Smerdon ARG 2001-02 • Alexander Balson & Grant Bedford 2002-03 • Rudi Guttendorf GER 2003-04 • David Brand ENG 2004-07 • Pailasi Saumani 2007-11 • Tunoa Lui ASA 2011-12 • Jez Teague 2012-

SCO – SCOTLAND

FIFA/COCA-COLA WORLD RANKING

'93	'94	'95	'96	'97	'98	'99	'00	'01	'02	'03	'04	'05	'06	'07	'08	'09	'10	'11	'12
24	32	26	29	37	38	20	25	50	59	54	86	60	25	14	33	46	52	47	72

2012

Jan	Feb	Mar	Apr	May	Jun	Jul	Aug	Sep	Oct	Nov	Dec	High	Low	Av
48	48	51	48	48	41	49	46	47	56	70	72	13	88	40

Rarely before has Scottish football experienced a year like 2012. Much of the football may have been unremarkable but it was the spectacular collapse of Rangers which grabbed all the headlines. Forced at first into administration, the club was then liquidated with its assets and SFA membership handed over to a new company which was forced to step down to the fourth tier of Scottish league football. It was a dramatic turn of events for a club that had played every season in the top flight since the league began in 1890 and had only once finished outside of the top five - a sixth place finish in 1926. The uncertainty surrounding Rangers may have helped inspire Celtic to regain the league title after four years and there were unfamiliar names on the two knock-out trophies with Kilmarnock beating Celtic 1-0 in the League Cup final - their first trophy for 15 years - while the Scottish Cup saw the first Edinburgh derby in the final since 1896 with Hearts thrashing Hibernian 5-1. Celtic ended the year on a high by not only inflicting a rare defeat on Barcelona but also by qualifying for the knock-out rounds of the UEFA Champions League, but there was little joy for the national team. After a poor start to the 2014 FIFA World Cup qualifiers with just two points from four games, manager Craig Levein was replaced by Gordon Strachan.

UEFA EUROPEAN CHAMPIONSHIP RECORD
1960-1964 DNE 1968-1988 DNQ **1992** r1 **1996** r1 2000-2012 DNQ

THE SCOTTISH FOOTBALL ASSOCIATION (SFA)

Hampden Park,
Glasgow G42 9AY,
United Kingdom
☎ +44 141 6166000
✆ +44 141 6166001
✉ info@scottishfa.co.uk
🌐 www.scottishfa.co.uk
FA 1873 CON 1954 FIFA 1910
P Campbell Ogilvie
GS Stewart Regan

THE STADIA

2014 FIFA World Cup Stadia
Hampden Park
Glasgow 52 063

Other Main Stadia
Celtic Park 'Parkhead'
Glasgow 60 355
Ibrox
Glasgow 51 082
Pittodrie Stadium
Aberdeen 22 199
Tynecastle Stadium
Edinburgh 17 420

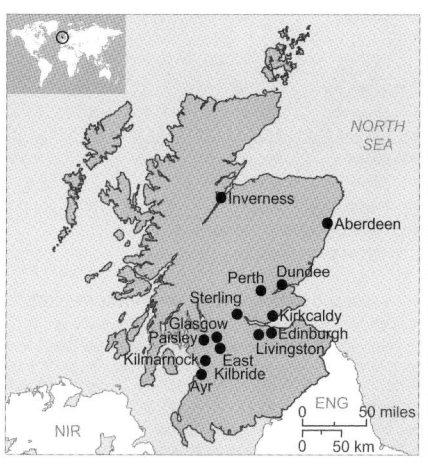

MAJOR CITIES/TOWNS

		Population
1	Glasgow	578 725
2	Edinburgh	449 058
3	Aberdeen	166 927
4	Dundee	141 616
5	East Kilbride	74 604
6	Paisley	71 730
7	Livingston	58 968
8	Cumbernauld	54 003
9	Dunfermline	51 456
10	Hamilton	47 979
11	Kirkcaldy	47 649
12	Ayr	45 899
13	Kilmarnock	45 163
14	Perth	44 201
15	Greenock	42 695
16	Coatbridge	41 454
17	Inverness	41 111
18	Glenrothes	38 862
19	Airdrie	35 309

SCOTLAND (PART OF THE UNITED KINGDOM)

Capital Edinburgh	Population 5 057 400 (114)	% in cities 89%
GDP per capita $39 680 (20)	Area km² 77 000 km² (117)	GMT +/- 0
Neighbours (km) England 164 • Coast 9911		

RECENT INTERNATIONAL MATCHES PLAYED BY SCOTLAND

2008	Opponents	Score		Venue	Comp	Scorers	Att	Referee
26-03	Croatia	D	1-1	Glasgow	Fr	Miller.K [31]	28 821	Hauge NOR
30-05	Czech Republic	L	1-3	Prague	Fr	Clarkson [85]	11 314	Braamhaar NED
20-08	Northern Ireland	D	0-0	Glasgow	Fr		28 072	Vollquartz DEN
6-09	Macedonia FYR	L	0-1	Skopje	WCq		9 000	Kralovec CZE
10-09	Iceland	W	2-1	Reykjavik	WCq	Broadfoot [19], McFadden [59]	9 767	Gumienny BEL
11-10	Norway	D	0-0	Glasgow	WCq		50 205	Busacca SUI
19-11	Argentina	L	0-1	Glasgow	Fr		32 492	Brych GER
2009								
28-03	Netherlands	L	0-3	Amsterdam	WCq		50 000	Duhamel FRA
1-04	Iceland	W	2-1	Glasgow	WCq	McCormack [39], Fletcher.S [65]	42 259	Einwaller AUT
12-08	Norway	L	0-4	Oslo	WCq		24 493	Hamer LUX
5-09	Macedonia FYR	W	2-0	Glasgow	WCq	Brown [56], McFadden [80]	50 214	Stark GER
9-09	Netherlands	L	0-1	Glasgow	WCq		51 230	Larsen DEN
10-10	Japan	L	0-2	Yokohama	Fr		61 285	Kim KOR
14-11	Wales	L	0-3	Cardiff	Fr		13 844	Zimmermann SUI
2010								
3-03	Czech Republic	W	1-0	Glasgow	Fr	Brown [62]	26 530	Fautrel FRA
11-08	Sweden	L	0-3	Stockholm	Fr		25 249	Rocchi ITA
3-09	Lithuania	D	0-0	Kaunas	ECq		5 248	Cakir TUR
7-09	Liechtenstein	W	2-1	Glasgow	ECq	Miller.K [63], McManus [97+]	37 050	Shvetsov UKR
8-10	Czech Republic	L	0-1	Prague	ECq		14 922	Bebek CRO
12-10	Spain	L	2-3	Glasgow	ECq	Naismith.S [58], OG [66]	51 322	Busacca SUI
16-11	Faroe Islands	W	3-0	Aberdeen	Fr	Wilson [24], Commons [31], Mackie [45]	10 873	Van Boekel NED
2011								
9-02	Northern Ireland	W	3-0	Dublin	Fr	Miller [19], McArthur [32], Commons [51]	18 742	Connolly IRL
27-03	Brazil	L	0-2	London	Fr		53 087	Webb ENG
25-05	Wales	W	3-1	Dublin	Fr	Morrison [56], Miller.K [65], Berra [71]	6 036	Crangle NIR
29-05	Republic of Ireland	L	0-1	Dublin	Fr		17 694	Whitby WAL
10-08	Denmark	W	2-1	Glasgow	Fr	OG [22], Snodgrass [44]	17 582	Borg MLT
3-09	Czech Republic	D	2-2	Glasgow	ECq	Miller.K [45], Fletcher.D [82]	51 564	Blom NED
6-09	Lithuania	W	1-0	Glasgow	ECq	Naismith.S [50]	34 071	Jakobsson ISL
8-10	Liechtenstein	W	1-0	Vaduz	ECq	Mackail-Smith [32]	5 636	Hagen NOR
11-10	Spain	L	1-3	Alicante	ECq	Goodwillie [66p]	27 559	Johannesson SWE
11-11	Cyprus	W	2-1	Larnaca	Fr	Miller.K [23], Mackie [57]	2 000	Levi ISR
2012								
29-02	Slovenia	D	1-1	Koper	Fr	Berra [40]	4 190	Stavrev MKD
26-05	USA	L	1-5	Jacksonville	Fr	OG [15]	44 438	Bonilla SLV
15-08	Australia	W	3-1	Edinburgh	Fr	Rhodes [29], OG [63], McCormack [76]	11 110	Hagen NOR
8-09	Serbia	D	0-0	Glasgow	WCq		47 369	Eriksson SWE
11-09	FYR Macedonia	D	1-1	Glasgow	WCq		32 430	Karasev RUS
12-10	Wales	L	1-2	Cardiff	WCq	Morrison [27]	23 249	Meyer GER
16-10	Belgium	L	0-2	Brussels	WCq		44 132	Hagen NOR
14-11	Luxembourg	W	2-1	Luxembourg	Fr	Rhodes 2 [11 23]	2 521	Zimmermann SUI

Fr = Friendly match • EC = UEFA EURO 2012 • WC = FIFA World Cup • q = qualifier

SCOTLAND NATIONAL TEAM HISTORICAL RECORDS

Caps: 102 - Kenny Dalglish 1971-86 • 91 - Jim Leighton 1982-98 • 77 - Alex McLeish 1980-93 • 76 - Paul McStay 1983-97 • 72 - Tom Boyd 1990-2001 • 69 - David Weir 1997-2010 • 67 - Christian Dailly 1997-2008 • 65 - Kenny Miller 2001- & Willie Miller 1975-89 • 62 - Danny McGrain 1973-82 • 61 - Darren Fletcher 2003- ; Richard Gough 1983-93 & Ally McCoist 1985-98 • 58 - John Collins 1988-2000 • 57 - Roy Aitken 1980-92 & Gary McAllister 1990-99 • 55 - Denis Law 1959-74 & Maurice Malpas 1984-93 • 54 - Billy Bremner 1965-76 & Graeme Souness 1976-86 • 53 - Gary Caldwell 2002- ; Kevin Gallacher 1988-2001; Alan Rough 1976-86 & George Young 1946-57

Goals: 30 - Kenny Dalglish 1971-86 & Denis Law 1959-74 • 23 - Hughie Gallacher 1924-35 • 22 - Lawrie Reilly 1948-57 • 19 - Ally McCoist 1985-98 • 16 - Kenny Miller 2001- • 15 - Robert Hamilton 1899-1911 & James McFadden 2002- • 14 - Mo Johnston 1984-91

Coaches: Committee 1872-54 • Andy Beattie 1954 • Committee 1954-58 • Dawson Walker 1958 • Matt Busby 1958 • Andy Beattie 1959-60 • Ian McColl 1960-65 • Jock Stein 1965-66 • John Prentice 1966 • Malcolm MacDonald 1966-67 • Bobby Brown 1967-71 • Tommy Docherty 1971-72 • Willie Ormond 1973-77 • Ally MacLeod 1977-78 • Jock Stein 1978-85 • Alex Ferguson 1985-86 • Andy Roxburgh 1986-93 • Craig Brown 1993-2002 • Berti Vogts GER 2002-04 • Tommy Burns 2004 • Walter Smith 2004-07 • Alex McLeish 2007 • George Burley 2008-09 • Craig Levein 2009-12 • Billy Stark 2012 • Gordon Strachan 2013-

SCOTLAND 2011-12

CLYDESDALE BANK PREMIER LEAGUE

	Pl	W	D	L	F	A	Pts	Celtic	Rangers	Motherwell	Dundee Utd	Hearts	St Johnstone	Kilmarnock	St Mirren	Aberdeen	Inverness CT	Hibernian	Dunfermline
Celtic †	38	30	3	5	84	21	**93**		1-0 3-0	4-0 1-0	5-1 2-1	1-0 5-0	0-1 2-0	2-1	5-0	2-1	2-0 1-0	0-0	2-1 2-0
Rangers - R	38	26	5	7	77	28	**73**	4-2 3-2		3-0 0-0	3-1 5-0	1-1 1-2	0-0 **4-0**	2-0 0-1	1-1 3-1	2-0 1-1	2-1	1-0 4-0	2-1
Motherwell †	38	18	8	12	49	44	**62**	1-2 0-3	0-3 1-2		0-0 0-2	1-0 3-0	0-3 3-2	0-0	1-1	1-0 1-0	3-0 0-1	**4-3**	3-1
Dundee United ‡	38	16	11	11	62	50	**59**	0-1 1-0	0-1 2-1	1-3 1-1		1-0 2-2	0-0 **2-0**	1-1 4-0	1-1 0-0	1-2	3-1 3-0	3-1	0-1 3-0
Heart of Midlothian ‡	38	15	7	16	45	43	**52**	2-0 0-4	0-2 0-3	2-0 0-1	0-1 0-2		1-2 2-0	0-1	2-0 5-2	3-0 3-0	2-1	2-0 2-0	4-0
St Johnstone ‡	38	14	8	16	43	50	**50**	0-2 **0-1**	0-2 1-2	0-3 1-5	3-3 1-5	2-0 2-1		2-0	0-1	1-2	2-0 0-0	3-1	0-1 3-1
Kilmarnock	38	11	14	13	44	61	**47**	3-3 0-6	1-0	0-0 2-0	1-1	0-0 1-1	1-2 0-0		2-1 0-2	2-0 1-1	3-6 4-3	4-1 1-3	3-2 0-3
St Mirren	38	9	16	13	39	51	**43**	0-2 0-2	2-1	0-1 0-0	2-2	0-0 0-3	3-0 4-2			1-0 1-1	1-2 0-2	1-2 3-1	0-2 1-4
Aberdeen	38	9	14	15	36	44	**41**	0-1 1-1	1-2		1-2	3-1 3-1	0-0	0-0 0-2	2-0 0-2		2-1 0-1	1-0 1-2	4-0 1-0
Inverness Caley Thistle	38	10	9	19	42	60	**39**	0-2	0-2 1-4	2-3		2-3	1-1 1-0	0-1	2-1 1-2	1-0 2-1 0-2		0-1 2-3	3-1 1-0 0-
Hibernian	38	8	9	21	40	67	**33**	0-2 0-5	0-2	0-1 1-1	3-3 0-2	1-3	3-2 2-3	1-1 0-1	1-2 0-0	0-0 0-0	1-1 **0-2**		0-1 4-0
Dunfermline Athletic	38	5	10	23	40	82	**25**	0-3	0-4 1-4	2-4 0-2	1-4	0-2 1-2	0-3	1-1 1-2	0-0 1-1	3-3 3-0	3-3 1-1	2-2 2-3	

23/07/2011 – 13/05/2012 • † Qualified for the UEFA Champions League • ‡ Qualified for the Europa League • Attendance: 1,739,901 @ 10,057
Matches in bold are away matches • Rangers were deducted 10 points and later relegated to the Third Division
Top scorers: **24** - Gary **HOOPER** ENG, Celtic • **19** - Jon **DALY** IRL, Dundee United • **14** - Michael **HIGDON** ENG, Motherwell & **FRAN SANDAZA**, ESP, St Johnstone & Nikica **JELAVIC** CRO, Rangers • **13** - Steven **THOMPSON**, St Mirren • **12** - Gary **O'CONNOR**, Hibernian; Dean **SHIELS** NIR, Kilmarnock; Rudolf **SKACEL** CZE, Hearts; Anthony **STOKES** IRL, Celtic & Sone **ALUKO** NGA, Rangers

SCOTLAND 2011-12

IRN-BRU FIRST DIVISION (2)

	Pl	W	D	L	F	A	Pts	Ross County	Dundee	Falkirk	Hamilton	Livingston	Partick	Raith	Morton	Ayr United	QotS
Ross County	36	22	13	1	72	32	**79**		1-1 3-0	3-1 2-1	1-0 5-1	1-1 3-0	2-2 3-0	4-2 1-1	0-0 2-2	4-0 1-1	2-0 2-1
Dundee	36	15	10	11	53	43	**55**	1-2 1-1		4-2 3-1	0-1 2-2	3-0 1-0	0-1 0-3	1-0 1-1	0-1 0-1	1-1 1-4	2-1 1-1
Falkirk	36	13	13	10	53	48	**52**	1-1 1-1	2-1 1-1		0-0 3-0	4-3 2-5	2-1 1-1	2-0 2-3	1-0 0-2	0-0 3-2	1-0 3-0
Hamilton Academical	36	14	7	15	55	56	**49**	5-1 0-2	1-6 3-1	0-1 0-1		1-1 0-1	1-0 2-2	2-2 2-1	1-2 4-3	2-3 3-2	3-1 3-0
Livingston	36	13	9	14	56	54	**48**	0-3 1-3	4-2 2-3	1-1 1-2	1-0 0-4		2-1 3-1	1-1 4-0	1-1 0-0	1-2 0-1	2-2 2-2
Partick Thistle	36	12	11	13	50	39	**47**	0-1 0-1	0-1 0-0	2-2 1-1	1-1 2-0	2-1 2-3		0-1 1-1	5-0 0-0	4-0 4-2	1-1
Raith Rovers	36	11	11	14	46	49	**44**	0-1 1-1	0-1 0-1	1-0 2-2	3-2 2-1	0-1 0-3	2-0 2-1		1-1 5-0	0-1 2-2	0-2 3-1
Greenock Morton	36	10	12	14	40	55	**42**	0-2 1-1	1-2 0-2	3-2 0-0	0-2 1-2	2-1 1-3	1-2 1-0	1-1 1-3		4-1 3-1	2-2 2-2
Ayr United †	36	9	11	16	44	67	**38**	2-3 1-3	1-3 3-2	2-2 1-0	1-2 2-0	0-3 1-0	0-1 3-2	1-1 0-1	0-0		1-0 1-1
Queen of the South	36	8	8	18	38	64	**32**	0-0 3-5	0-0 1-1	1-5 0-0	1-0 1-2	0-2 0-4	0-0 0-5	1-3 1-0	4-1 2-1	4-1 2-1	

6/08/2011 – 5/05/2012 • † Play-off (see second division)
Top scorers: **19** - Colin **MCMENAMIN**, Ross County • **18** - Farid **EL ALAGUI** MAR, Falkirk • **13** - Kris **DOOLAN**, Partick & Michael **GARDYNE**, Ross Co

SCOTLAND 2011-12

IRN-BRU SECOND DIVISION (3)

	Pl	W	D	L	F	A	Pts	Cowdenbeath	Arbroath	Dumbarton	Airdrie United	Stenhousemuir	East Fife	Forfar Athletic	Brechin City	Albion Rovers	Stirling Albion
Cowdenbeath	36	20	11	5	68	29	**71**		0-0 2-3	0-0 4-1	2-0 0-0	2-0 0-0	3-2 4-0	3-1 2-0	3-1 2-0	1-2 0-1	3-0 2-0 4-1
Arbroath †	36	17	12	7	76	51	**63**	1-1 1-1		4-3 2-0	3-1 2-2	1-0 0-0	3-0 2-2	4-1 0-1	1-1 2-3	6-2 6-1	4-2 2-0
Dumbarton †	36	17	7	12	61	61	**58**	0-4 0-2	3-4 3-2		1-1 2-1	3-0 0-2	3-0 0-4	1-1 1-0	1-0 4-2	2-1 1-0	1-5 4-1
Airdrie United †	36	14	10	12	68	60	**52**	1-5 1-1	3-3 2-0	3-0 2-3		5-2 0-3	1-3 2-0	4-4 3-3	2-3 4-1	4-0 1-0	1-1 4-1
Stenhousemuir	36	15	6	15	54	49	**51**	3-1 0-2	2-0 1-3	3-1 1-2	1-1 0-3		2-1 1-0	2-3 1-2	1-2 1-3	3-0 1-2	4-0 4-0
East Fife	36	14	6	16	55	57	**48**	0-2 0-6	1-2 2-0	0-2 0-1	0-2 1-3	1-1		4-3 4-0	1-1 2-2	2-0 1-3	1-1
Forfar Athletic	36	11	9	16	59	72	**42**	2-2 1-0	1-1 2-4	0-2 2-3	3-2 2-3	2-3 1-2	3-2 1-4		0-0 4-1	0-2 4-0	2-2 4-3
Brechin City	36	10	11	15	47	62	**41**	1-0 2-2	2-3 1-1	3-3 2-2	1-1 1-1	2-0 1-0	0-2 1-3	2-1 0-1		1-4 2-1	1-3 1-2
Albion Rovers †	36	10	7	19	43	66	**37**	3-3 1-0	1-0 1-1	3-1 1-1	7-2 0-1	1-1 1-0	0-3 1-1	1-0 2-2	1-2 0-1		0-1 1-2
Stirling Albion	36	7	9	20	46	70	**34**	1-0 2-2	0-1 1-1	0-1 1-1	1-2 1-4	0-2 2-2	3-1 1-0	0-1 2-4	2-2 1-5	0-2 3-2	

6/08/2011 – 5/05/2012 • † Play-off • Top scorer: **21** - Steven **DORIS**, Arbroath
Play-off semis: **Dumbarton** 2-1 0-0 Arbroath; **Airdrie United** 0-0 3-1 Ayr United • Final: **Dumbarton** 2-1 4-1 Airdrie United (Both promoted)

SCOTLAND 2011-12

IRN-BRU THIRD DIVISION (4)

	Pl	W	D	L	F	A	Pts	Alloa Ath	Queen's Park	Stranraer	Elgin City	Peterhead	Annan Ath	Berwick R	Montrose	Clyde	East Stirling
Alloa Athletic	36	23	8	5	70	39	**77**		1-0 4-0	1-0 3-1	3-0 8-1	2-1 2-3	1-0 1-1	1-1 0-1	4-2 2-0	2-2 1-0	1-1 5-1
Queen's Park †	36	19	6	11	70	48	**63**	1-3 1-2		2-0 3-2	6-0 1-3	1-1 0-1	0-0 2-0	1-1 2-2	3-1 5-0	3-0 3-0	2-0 5-1
Stranraer †	36	17	7	12	77	57	**58**	2-3 0-4	2-3 2-3		1-0 5-2	2-1 0-3	4-2 4-2	2-1 1-3	4-4 3-1	0-0 1-0	6-0 4-1
Elgin City †	36	16	9	11	68	60	**57**	5-0 3-0	2-0 1-1	1-1 1-2		6-1 6-1	3-0 1-2	4-1 4-0	3-1 2-1	0-3 1-1	2-0 3-1
Peterhead	36	15	6	15	51	53	**51**	1-1 0-1	1-1 2-1	1-3 1-1	1-3 3-0		2-3 3-2	1-0 1-2	2-3 2-1	0-0 1-1	1-0 2-0
Annan Athletic	36	13	10	13	53	53	**49**	2-0 1-2	5-2 2-3	0-3 1-3	1-1 1-1	2-0 0-3		2-2 1-1	2-1 1-2	1-0 1-0	3-0 2-2
Berwick Rangers	36	12	12	12	61	58	**48**	2-2 5-0	2-0 1-4	2-2 1-0	1-1 3-3	2-1 0-1	0-1 1-3		1-2 2-2	0-2 3-0	4-2 0-2
Montrose	36	11	5	20	58	75	**38**	1-1 0-2	0-1 3-1	0-6 1-3	3-0 2-3	2-1 1-3	2-3 1-1	3-5 1-1		4-0 5-0	2-1 3-1
Clyde	36	8	11	17	35	50	**35**	0-1 1-1	0-2 1-2	1-1 2-1	1-2 0-2	2-0 0-1	0-0 1-1	1-4 2-2	1-0 1-2		7-1 3-0
East Stirlingshire	36	6	6	24	38	88	**24**	0-1 1-3	1-3 1-2	1-3 2-2	1-1 2-2	0-2 6-3	1-0 0-4	1-3 2-1	1-0 3-1	1-1 0-1	

6/08/2011 - 5/05/2012 • † Play-off • Top scorer: **22** - Martin **BOYLE**, Montrose
Play-off semis: Elgin City 1-0 0-2 **Albion Rovers**; Stranraer 3-1 2-0 Queen's Park • Final: Stranraer 2-0 1-3 3-5p **Albion Rovers** (Stranraer promoted)

MEDALS TABLE

		Overall			League			Cup			LC			Europe			Town/City
		G	S	B	G	S	B	G	S	B	G	S	B	G	S	B	
1	Rangers	115	57	19	**54**	30	17	33	17		**27**	7		1	3	2	Glasgow
2	Celtic	93	66	21	43	31	17	**35**	18		14	15		1	2	4	Glasgow
3	Aberdeen	17	28	9	4	13	8	7	8		5	7		1		1	Aberdeen
4	Heart of Midlothian	16	22	17	4	14	17	8	6		4	2					Edinburgh
5	Queen's Park	10	2					10	2								Glasgow
6	Hibernian	9	22	15	4	6	13	2	10		3	6				2	Edinburgh
7	Kilmarnock	5	14	4	1	4	3	3	5		1	5				1	Kilmarnock
8	Dundee United	5	12	9	1		8	2	7		2	4		1	1		Dundee
9	Dundee	5	11	3	1	4	1	1	4		3	3				2	Dundee
10	Motherwell	4	12	8	1	5	8	2	5		1	2					Motherwell
11	East Fife	4	2	2			2	1	2		3						Methil
12	St. Mirren	3	5	2			2	3	3			2					Paisley
	Third Lanark	3	5	2	1		2	2	4			1					Glasgow
14	Dumbarton	3	5		2			1	5								Dumbarton
15	Vale of Levan	3	4					3	4								Alexandria
16	Clyde	3	3	3			3	3	3								Cumbernauld
17	Dunfermline Athletic	2	6	3			2	2	3			3				1	Dunfermline
18	Falkirk	2	5	1	2	1		2	2			1					Falkirk
19	Partick Thistle	2	4	3			3	1	1		1	3					Glasgow
20	Renton	2	3					2	3								Renton
21	Airdrie United	1	7	1				4	1		1	3					Airdrie
22	Morton	1	3	2	1	2		1	1			1					Greenock
23	Raith Rovers	1	2	1				1			1	1		1	1		Kirkcaldy
24	St. Bernard's	1		1				1		1							Edinburgh
	Livingston	1						1			1						Livingston
26	St. Johnstone		2	2				2				2					Perth
27	Hamilton Academical		2						2								Hamilton
28	Albion Rovers		1						1								Coatbridge
	Ayr United		1									1					Ayr
	Cambuslang		1						1								Cambuslang
	Clydesdale		1						1								Glasgow
	Gretna		1						1								Gretna
	Queen of the South		1						1								Dumfries
	Ross County		1						1								Dingwall
	Thornliebank		1						1								Glasgow

CO-OPERATIVE INSURANCE SCOTTISH LEAGUE CUP 2011-12

Second Round

Kilmarnock	Bye
Forfar Athletic	0
Queen of the South	3
Aberdeen	1
Dundee	0
Dunfermline Athletic	1
East Fife	2
St Mirren	4
Greenock Morton	3
Livingston	0
St Johnstone	3
Heart of Midlothian	Bye
Inverness Caley Thistle	0
Ayr United	1
Falkirk	3
Stenhousemuir	2
Rangers	Bye
Airdrie United	2
Raith Rovers	0
Dundee United	Bye
Hibernian	5
Berwick Rangers	0
Clyde	0
Motherwell	4
Ross County	2
Hamilton Academical	1
Celtic	Bye

Third Round

Kilmarnock *	5	
Queen of the South	0	
Aberdeen *	3	3p
East Fife	3	4p
St Mirren	2	
St Johnstone *	0	
Heart of Midlothian	1	1p
Ayr United *	1	4p
Falkirk *	3	
Rangers	2	
Airdrie United *	0	
Dundee United	2	
Hibernian	2	7p
Motherwell *	2	6p
Ross County *	0	
Celtic	2	

Quarter-finals

Kilmarnock *	2	
East Fife	0	
St Mirren *	0	
Ayr United	1	
Falkirk	2	5p
Dundee United *	2	4p
Hibernian *	1	
Celtic	4	

Semi-finals

Kilmarnock †	1
Ayr United	0
Falkirk	1
Celtic †	3

Final

Kilmarnock	1
Celtic	0

* Home team • † Both semi-finals played at Hampden Park, Glasgow

Premier League clubs enter in the second round while those in European competition enter in the third round

LEAGUE CUP FINAL

Hampden Park, Glasgow, 18-03-2012
Att: 49 572. Ref: William Collum
Scorer - Van Tornhout [84] for Kilmarnock
Kilmarnock - Cammy Bell - James Fowler (c), Mahamadou Sissoko (Zdenek Kroca 86), Michael Nelson, Ben Gordon - Liam Kelly●, Danny Buijs (Lee Johnson● 20), Gary Harkins (Dieter Van Tornhout 73), Garry Hay - Dean Shiels - Paul Heffernan. Tr: Kenny Shiels
Celtic - Fraser Forster - Adam Matthews, Thomas Rogne (Ki Sung Yueng 56), Kelvin Wilson, Charlie Mulgrew - James Forrest, Victor Wanyama, Scott Brown (c), Joe Ledley (Kris Commons 86) - Anthony Stokes●, Gary Hooper (Georgios Samaras 80). Tr: Neil Lennon

ACTIVE NATION SCOTTISH CUP 2011–12

Third Round

Vale of Leithen	1
Auchinleck Talbot *	3
Brechin City *	3
Dumbarton	0
Ross County *	4
Albion Rovers	0
Annan Athletic	0
Stenhousemuir *	4
Gala Fairydean	0
Airdrie United *	11
Arbroath	1
Kieth *	0
Peterhead	4
Inverurie Loco Works *	2
Stranraer *	1 0
Forfar Athletic	1 3
Partick Thistle	1 4
Culter *	1 0
Greenock Morton *	5
Deveronvale	1
Queen's Park	1 3
Elgin City *	1 1
Ayr United *	2 2
Montrose	2 1
Irvine Meadow *	0
Livingston	6
East Fife *	5
East Stirlingshire	0
Stirling Albion *	1
Dundee	2
Cowdenbeath	3
Bo'ness United *	0

Fourth Round

Heart of Midlothian *	1
Auchinleck Talbot	0
Brechin City	1
St Johnstone *	2
Ross County *	7
Stenhousemuir	0
Hamilton Academical	0 0
St Mirren *	0 1
Dundee United	6
Airdrie United *	2
Arbroath *	0
Rangers	4
Inverness Caley Thistle *	1 3
Dunfermline Athletic	1 1
Peterhead *	0
Celtic	3
Aberdeen	4
Forfar Athletic *	0
Partick Thistle *	0
Queen of the South	1
Greenock Morton	2
Raith Rovers *	1
Queen's Park	0
Motherwell *	4
Ayr United	2
Livingston *	1
East Fife	0
Falkirk *	2
Kilmarnock	1 2
Dundee *	1 1
Cowdenbeath *	2
Hibernian	3

Fifth Round

Heart of Midlothian *	1 2
St Johnstone	1 1
Ross County	1 1
St Mirren *	1 2
Dundee United	2
Rangers *	0
Inverness Caley Thistle *	0
Celtic	2
Aberdeen *	1 2
Queen of the South	1 1
Greenock Morton	0
Motherwell *	6
Ayr United *	2
Falkirk	1
Kilmarnock	0
Hibernian *	1

* Home team

ACTIVE NATION SCOTTISH CUP 2011-12

Quarter-finals | **Semi-finals** | **Final**

| Heart of Midlothian * | 2 | 2 |
| St Mirren | 2 | 0 |

| Heart of Midlothian | 2 |
| Celtic | 1 |

| Dundee United * | 0 |
| Celtic | 4 |

| Heart of Midlothian ‡ | 5 |
| Hibernian | 1 |

| Aberdeen | 2 |
| Motherwell * | 1 |

| Aberdeen | 1 |
| Hibernian | 2 |

| Ayr United * | 0 |
| Hibernian | 2 |

Top 16 teams from the previous season enter in the fourth round. Clubs positioned 17-32 enter in the third round
Both semi-finals played at Hampden Park
‡ Qualified for the Europa League

SCOTTISH FA CUP FINAL 2012
Hampden Park, Glasgow, 19-05-2012, Att: 51 041, Ref: Craig Thomson

| Heart of Midlothian | 5 | Barr [15], Skacel 2 [27][75], Grainger [48p], McGowan [50] |
| Hibernian | 1 | McPake [41] |

HEARTS

Jamie **MACDONALD** - Ryan **MCGOWAN**, Andy **WEBSTER**, Marius **ZALIUKAS**, Danny **GRAINGER** - **SUSO SANTANA** (Craig **BEATTIE** 76), Ian **BLACK** (Scott **ROBINSON** 86), Darren **BARR**, Rudi **SKACEL**, Andrew **DRIVER** (Mehdi **TAOUIL** 84) - Stephen **ELLIOTT**. Tr: **PAULO SERGIO**

HIBS

Mark **BROWN** - Matt **DOHERTY**•, Paul **HANLON**, James **MCPAKE**, Pa **KUJABI**••♦47, Jorge **CLAROS** (Ivan **SPROULE** 42), Tom **SOARES** (George **FRANCOMB** 76), Lewis **STEVENSON**, Isaiah **OSBOURNE** - Garry **O'CONNOR** (Eoin **DOYLE** 54), Leigh **GRIFFITHS**. Tr: Pat **FENLON**

SDN – SUDAN

FIFA/COCA-COLA WORLD RANKING

'93	'94	'95	'96	'97	'98	'99	'00	'01	'02	'03	'04	'05	'06	'07	'08	'09	'10	'11	'12
119	116	86	74	108	114	132	132	118	106	103	114	92	120	92	93	108	92	113	101

2012

Jan	Feb	Mar	Apr	May	Jun	Jul	Aug	Sep	Oct	Nov	Dec	High	Low	Av
120	111	110	113	113	101	105	104	103	100	102	101	74	137	108

Sudan's progress to the quarter-finals of the 2012 Africa Cup of Nations at the start of the year, allied with strong performances at club level in recent continental club competitions, pointed to the rise of a new powerhouse in the African game. But those expectations hit a roadblock in 2012 as the North African country, who were stripped of FIFA World Cup points for using an ineligible player, failed to qualify for the 2013 Nations Cup and, despite having three teams in the last eight of the CAF Confederation Cup, did not get a club to the final. FIFA stripped Sudan of three points and reversed a 2-0 win over Zambia at the start of the 2014 FIFA World Cup qualifiers after the Sudanese used suspended Saif Ali in the match. The 2013 Nations Cup qualifiers produced a thrilling match with neighbours and long-standing rivals Ethiopia. A 5-3 win for Sudan in the first leg suggested a fragile defence and so it proved in the final minutes of the return leg in Addis where Ethiopia won 2-0 to advance to the tournament in South Africa on the away goals rule. In the 2012 CAF Confederation Cup, Sudan set a new standard by having three clubs in the same group with Al Ahly Shendi, Al Hilal and Al Merreikh all competing for a semi-final place. Merreikh won the group with Hilal second but both lost their semi-final ties.

CAF AFRICA CUP OF NATIONS RECORD

1957 3 **1959** 2 F **1962** DNQ **1963** 2 F **1965-1968** DNQ **1970** 1 Winners **1972** 7 r1 **1974** DNQ **1976** 6 r1 **1978** DNE **1980** DNQ **1982** DNE **1984** DNQ **1986** DNE **1988-1996** DNQ **1998** Withdrew **2000** DNE **2002-2006** DNQ **2008** 16 r1 **2010** DNQ **2012** 8 QF **2013** DNQ

SUDAN FOOTBALL ASSOCIATION (SFA)

Baladia Street,
PO Box 437,
11111 Khartoum
☎ +249 183 560088
📠 +249 183 776633
✉ ballafoot@hotmail.com
🖥 www.sudanfootball.com
FA 1936 CON 1957 FIFA 1948
P Mutasim Sirelkhatim
GS Magdi Shams El Din

THE STADIA

2014 FIFA World Cup Stadia

Al Hilal Stadium	
Omdurman	35 000

Other Main Stadia

Al Merreikh Stadium	
Omdurman	42 000
Khartoum Stadium	
Khartoum	15 000
Wad Madani Stadium	
Wad Madani	15 000
Port Sudan Stadium	
Port Sudan	7 000

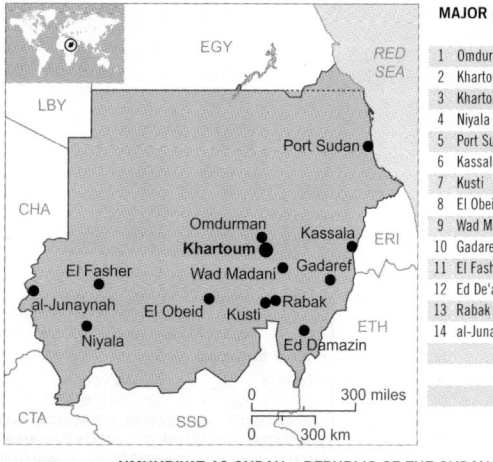

MAJOR CITIES/TOWNS

		Population
1	Omdurman	2 482 917
2	Khartoum	2 316 348
3	Khartoum North	898 224
4	Niyala	531 022
5	Port Sudan	513 792
6	Kassala	474 115
7	Kusti	438 387
8	El Obeid	435 643
9	Wad Madani	368 021
10	Gadaref	366 606
11	El Fasher	286 277
12	Ed De'aein	225 503
13	Rabak	192 136
14	al-Junaynah	186 483

UMHURIYAT AS-SUDAN • REPUBLIC OF THE SUDAN

Capital	Khartoum	Population	34 206 710 (37)	% in cities	40%
GDP per capita	$3000 (170)	Area km²	1 861 484 km² (16)	GMT +/-	+3
Neighbours (km)	Central African Republic 175, Chad 1360, Egypt 1273, Eritrea 605, Ethiopia 769, Libya 383, South Sudan 2184, Uganda 435 • Coast 853				

RECENT INTERNATIONAL MATCHES PLAYED BY SUDAN

2011	Opponents		Score	Venue	Comp	Scorers	Att	Referee
5-01	Kenya	L	0-1	Cairo	Fr			
11-01	Congo DR	L	1-2	Cairo	Fr	Mudathir El Tahir 71		
16-01	Tanzania	W	2-0	Cairo	Fr	Hytham Karar 52, Alaeldin Yousif 61		
27-03	Swaziland	W	3-0	Omdurman	CNq	Mohamed Bashir 2 2 63, Mudathir El Tahir 71		
28-05	Ethiopia	W	2-1	Addis Abeba	Fr	Bakri Abdel Kader 2		
5-06	Swaziland	W	2-1	Manzini	CNq	Badr Eldin Galag 64, Alaeldin Yousif 88		
25-06	Kenya	W	2-1	Nairobi	Fr	Mohamed Mussa 5, Bakri Abdel Kader 27		
19-08	Eritrea	W	3-0	Asmara	Fr			
26-08	Bahrain	L	0-1	Manama	Fr			
4-09	Congo	W	1-0	Brazzaville	CNq	Bakri Abdel Kader 77		
8-10	Ghana	L	0-2	Khartoum	CNq			
11-11	Cameroon	L	1-3	Marrakech	Fr	Mohamed Tahir 74p		
13-11	Uganda	D	0-0	Marrakech	Fr	L 2-3p		
28-11	Ethiopia	D	1-1	Dar es Salaam	CCr1	Mohamed Tahir 8		
30-11	Malawi	D	0-0	Dar es Salaam	CCr1			
3-12	Kenya	W	1-0	Dar es Salaam	CCr1	Muawia Bashir 25		
5-12	Burundi	W	2-0	Dar es Salaam	CCqf	Amir Rabei Abdelnabi 41, Mohamed Mussa 60		
8-12	Rwanda	L	1-2	Dar es Salaam	CCsf	Ramadan Alagab 68		
10-12	Tanzania	W	1-0	Dar es Salaam	CC3p	Mohamed Eldin 84		
17-12	Palestine	L	0-2	Al Rayyan	Fr			
2012								
9-01	Tunisia	L	0-3	Sharjah	Fr			
12-01	Senegal	L	0-1	Dakar	Fr			
16-01	Gabon	D	0-0	Franceville	Fr			
22-01	Côte d'Ivoire	L	0-1	Malabo	CNr1		5 000	Seechurn MRI
26-01	Angola	D	2-2	Malabo	CNr1	Mohamed Bashir 2 32 74	2 500	Lemghaifry MTN
30-01	Burkina Faso	W	2-1	Bata	CNr1	Mudathir El Tahir 2 33 79	132	Otogo-Castane GAB
4-02	Zambia	L	0-3	Bata	CNqf		200	Gassama GAM
2-06	Zambia	(W 2-0) L 0-3		Khartoum	WCq	Muhannad Tahir 53, Saif Masawi 73. Match awarded 3-0 to Zambia	18 000	Bangoura GUI
10-06	Lesotho	D	0-0	Maseru	WCq		4 000	Shikongo NAM
27-06	Lebanon	W	2-0	Jeddah	ARr1	Ankba 55, Muawia Bashir 83		Jaber JOR
30-06	Iraq	D	1-1	Jeddah	ARr1	Ahmed Adil Hamad 9		Jedidi TUN
26-08	Libya	L	0-3	Tunis	Fr			
8-09	Ethiopia	W	5-3	Omdurman	CNq	Mudathir El Tahir 8, Mohamed Bashir 17, Musaab Maaz 36, Muhannad Tahir 2 85p 90p		Alioum CMR
14-10	Ethiopia	L	0-2	Addis Abeba	CNq			Diatta SEN
25-11	Tanzania	L	0-2	Kampala	CCr1			Batte UGA
28-11	Somalia	W	1-0	Kampala	CCr1	Farid Mohammed 85		Maeruf ERI
1-12	Burundi	L	0-1	Kampala	CCr1			Batte UGA

Fr = Friendly match • CN = CAF African Cup of Nations • CC = CECAFA Cup • WC = FIFA World Cup • † Not a full international
q = qualifier • r1 = first round group • sf = semi-final • f = final

SUDAN SQUAD FOR THE 2012 CAF AFRICA CUP OF NATIONS

	Player		Ap	G	Club	Date of Birth		Player		Ap	G	Club	Date of Birth
1	Mohamed Rihan	GK	0		Al Hilal	1 01 1979	12	Bader Galag	MF	0+3		Al Merreikh	4 10 1981
2	Mohamed Eldin	FW	0		Al Nil Hasahesa	19 03 1985	13	Amer Kamal	DF	1+2		Al Merreikh	13 09 1987
3	Muawia Bashir	DF	4		Al Ittihad	17 04 1986	14	Balla Jabir	DF	2		Al Merreikh	12 09 1985
4	Najem Abdullah	DF	4		Al Merreikh	17 11 1987	15	Ahmed Al Basha	DF	1		Al Merreikh	2 01 1982
5	Alaeldin Yousif	MF	4		Al Hilal	3 01 1982	16	El Muez Mahgoub	GK	1		Al Hilal	14 08 1978
6	Mosaab Omer	DF	0+1		Al Merreikh	4 06 1984	17	Mudathir El Tahir	FW	4	2	Al Hilal	23 07 1988
7	Ramadan Agab	FW	0+3		Al Mawrada	20 02 1986	18	Khalifa Ahmed	DF	2		Al Hilal	23 11 1983
8	Haitham Mustafa (c)	MF	4		Al Hilal	19 07 1977	19	Mohamed Bashir	MF	4	2	Al Hilal	23 05 1987
9	Saif Masawi	MF	3		Al Hilal	30 11 1979	20	Mohamed Musa	MF	0		Al Nsoor	7 08 1990
10	Muhannad Tahir	FW	3+1		Al Hilal	3 12 1984	21	Akram El Hadi Salem	GK	3		Al Merreikh	27 02 1987
11	Faisal Agab	MF	0		Al Merreikh	24 08 1978	22	Abdelrahman Karongo	FW	0		Al Merreikh	28 11 1978
Tr: Mohamed Abdalla							23	Hamid Nazar	MF	4		Al Hilal	3 10 1988

SUDAN 2012

PREMIER LEAGUE

	Pl	W	D	L	F	A	Pts	Hilal O	Merreikh	Ahli S	Khartoum-3	Nsoor	Ahli K	Nil	Amal	Hilal K	Mawrada	Ahli WM	Hilal PS	Rabta	Jazeerat
Al Hilal Omdurman †	26	22	4	0	62	12	**70**		1-0	4-1	2-2	2-0	2-1	3-0	3-0	3-1	2-1	3-1	2-1	3-1	4-0
Al Merreikh †	26	21	2	3	73	15	**65**	1-1		0-1	3-2	5-1	2-0	3-0	0-1	2-0	3-0	2-1	3-0	6-0	6-1
Al Ahli Shendi ‡	26	11	8	7	29	23	**41**	0-0	0-2		1-0	2-0	3-1	0-0	1-0	1-1	4-1	3-2	2-0	1-0	1-1
Khartoum-3 ‡	26	12	4	10	33	36	**40**	0-4	0-7	2-1		0-2	1-1	0-2	4-1	3-0	0-1	1-0	2-1	1-0	4-2
Al Nsoor	26	10	4	12	27	32	**34**	0-1	1-3	1-1	1-2		1-3	1-1	1-2	1-0	2-0	1-1	3-0	0-2	2-1
Al Ahli Khartoum	26	8	9	9	31	36	**33**	1-5	1-3	1-1	0-0	1-0		1-1	0-0	1-3	2-0	3-1	2-0	2-1	0-1
Al Nil Hasahisa	26	7	12	7	22	29	**33**	0-2	0-5	1-2	1-1	1-0	0-0		1-0	1-0	3-2	2-0	1-1	0-0	1-1
Al Amal Atbara	26	9	6	11	20	28	**33**	0-0	0-3	0-0	0-1	0-1	3-1	1-0		1-2	2-1	1-1	2-0	2-0	3-1
Al Hilal Kadugli	26	9	5	12	26	30	**32**	0-1	0-2	1-1	0-1	1-0	3-2	0-0	0-0		1-0	1-0	3-3	3-1	2-0
Al Mawrada Omdurman	26	8	5	13	28	38	**29**	0-2	2-3	1-0	2-1	1-2	1-1	1-1	3-0	1-0		0-1	2-1	1-1	2-1
Al Ahli Wad Medani	26	7	6	13	23	33	**27**	1-3	1-2	0-1	0-2	0-2	1-1	2-1	1-0	1-0	1-1		4-0	1-0	1-1
Al Hilal Port Sudan	26	7	6	13	28	43	**27**	0-3	0-3	1-0	2-1	1-2	0-0	2-2	3-0	1-3	1-1	2-0		3-0	2-1
Al Rabta Kosti	26	6	8	12	19	36	**26**	0-3	1-1	2-1	1-0	0-0	2-3	1-1	0-1	2-1	1-0	0-0	1-1		2-1
Jazeerat Al-Feel	26	3	5	18	19	49	**14**	0-3	0-3	1-0	1-2	1-2	1-2	0-1	0-0	1-0	2-3	0-1	0-2	0-0	

29/02/2012 - 19/11/2012 • † Qualified for the CAF Champions League • ‡ Qualified for the CAF Confederations Cup

MEDALS TABLE

		Overall	Lge	Cup	Africa			City
		G	G	G	G	S	B	
1	Al Merreikh	40	18	21	1	1	3	Omdurman
2	Al Hilal	35	27	8		2	6	Omdurman
3	Al Mawrada	6	1	5			1	Omdurman
4	Burri	1	1					Khartoum
	Al Hilal	1	1					Port Sudan
	Al Ahly	1		1				Wad Medani
	Al Ittihad	1		1				Wad Medani
	Hay Al Arab	1		1				Port Sudan
	Al Nil	1		1				Khartoum

SUDAN CUP 2012

Quarter-finals	Semi-finals		Final		
Al Merreikh					
	Al Merreikh	7			
	Al Nil Hasahisa	0			
Al Nil Hasahisa			**Al Merreikh**	0	3p
Al Ahli Wad Medani			Al Hilal Omdurman	0	1p
	Al Ahli Wad Medani	0			
	Al Hilal Omdurman	5			
Al Hilal Omdurman					

SEN – SENEGAL

FIFA/COCA-COLA WORLD RANKING

'93	'94	'95	'96	'97	'98	'99	'00	'01	'02	'03	'04	'05	'06	'07	'08	'09	'10	'11	'12
56	50	47	58	85	95	79	88	65	27	33	31	30	41	38	50	89	70	44	77

2012											
Jan	Feb	Mar	Apr	May	Jun	Jul	Aug	Sep	Oct	Nov	Dec
43	68	70	77	77	63	61	61	62	68	75	77

High	Low	Av
26	95	56

A year that promised potential glory turned into a nightmare for the West African nation after an embarrassingly early exit at the 2012 Africa Cup of Nations finals followed by the failure to qualify for the 2013 edition. A riot in Dakar midway through the second half of the 2013 Nations Cup qualifier against Cote d'Ivoire brought the tie to a premature halt and led to a one year ban on Senegal hosting international matches. The team were also officially booted out of the Nations Cup although they had been comprehensively outplayed by the Ivorians over the two legs. Senegal did manage to get their 2014 FIFA World Cup qualifying campaign off to a decent start with four points from their first two matches while the U-23 team impressed at the London Olympics where they reached the quarter-finals before an extra-time defeat at the hands of Mexico. In club football Casa Sport were crowned champions for the first time after beating Diambars 1-0 on the final day of the season to overtake their opponents and win the title by a point. It meant that for a second successive year there were debut champions following US Ouakam's success in 2011. ASC HLM from Dakar won the 52nd edition of the cup, beating fellow second division club Renaissance Dakar 4-3 on post-match penalties after a goalless draw in the final.

CAF AFRICA CUP OF NATIONS RECORD

1957-1963 DNE 1965 3 r1 1968 5 r1 1970-1978 DNQ 1980 DNE 1982-1984 DNQ 1986 5 r1 1988 DNQ 1990 4 SF 1992 5 QF (Hosts)
1994 8 QF 1996-1998 DNQ 2000 7 QF 2002 2 F 2004 5 QF 2006 4 SF 2008 12 r1 2010 DNQ 2012 13 r1 2013 DNQ

FEDERATION SENEGALAISE DE FOOTBALL (FSF)

VDN-Ouest-Foire en face du CICES, Boite Postale 13021, Dakar
☎ +221 33 8692828
📠 +221 33 8200592
✉ fsf@senegalfoot.sn
🖥 www.senegalfoot.sn
FA 1960 CON 1963 FIFA 1962
P Augustin Senghor
GS Victor Cisse

THE STADIA

2014 FIFA World Cup Stadia
Stade Léopold Sédar Senghor
Dakar   60 000
Other Main Stadia
Stade Demba Diop
Dakar   15 000
Stade Aline Sitoe Diatta
Ziguinchor   10 000
Stade Maniang Soumaré
Thiès   8 000

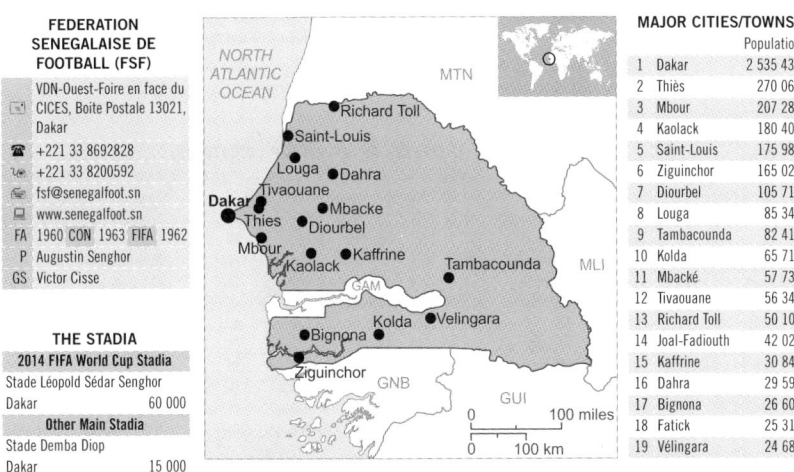

MAJOR CITIES/TOWNS

		Population
1	Dakar	2 535 431
2	Thiès	270 065
3	Mbour	207 286
4	Kaolack	180 409
5	Saint-Louis	175 988
6	Ziguinchor	165 027
7	Diourbel	105 713
8	Louga	85 344
9	Tambacounda	82 412
10	Kolda	65 714
11	Mbacké	57 731
12	Tivaouane	56 345
13	Richard Toll	50 102
14	Joal-Fadiouth	42 024
15	Kaffrine	30 846
16	Dahra	29 590
17	Bignona	26 603
18	Fatick	25 318
19	Vélingara	24 687

REPUBLIQUE DU SENEGAL • REPUBLIC OF SENEGAL

Capital	Dakar	Population	13 711 597 (67)	% in cities	42%
GDP per capita	$1600 (141)	Area km²	196 722 km² (87)	GMT +/-	0
Neighbours (km)	Gambia 740, Guinea 330, Guinea-Bissau 338, Mali 419, Mauritania 813 • Coast 531				

RECENT INTERNATIONAL MATCHES PLAYED BY SENEGAL

2009	Opponents	Score	Venue	Comp	Scorers	Att	Referee
28-03	Oman	L 0-2	Muscat	Fr			
1-04	Iran	D 1-1	Tehran	Fr	Papiss Cisse [77]		
12-08	Congo DR	W 2-1	Blois	Fr	Papiss Cisse 2 [66 69]		
5-09	Angola	D 1-1	Portimao	Fr	Mamadou Niang [54]		
14-10	Korea Republic	L 0-2	Seoul	Fr		31 574	Tan Hai CHN
2010							
3-03	Greece	W 2-0	Volos	Fr	Mamadou Niang [71], Guirane N'Daw [80]	10 000	Skomina SVN
10-05	Mexico	L 0-1	Chicago	Fr		60 610	Salazar USA
27-05	Denmark	L 0-2	Aalborg	Fr		14 112	Nijhuis NED
11-08	Cape Verde Islands	W 1-0	Dakar	Fr	Mame Biram Diouf [46]		
5-09	Congo DR	W 4-2	Kinshasa	CNq	Moussa Sow [6], Mamadou Niang 3 [12 22 57p]		Haimoudi ALG
9-10	Mauritius	W 7-0	Dakar	CNq	Papiss Cisse 3 [8 38 76], Mamadou Niang 2 [22 62], Moussa Sow [47], OG [90]		Bennett RSA
17-11	Gabon	W 2-1	Sannois St Gratien	Fr	Papiss Cisse [37], Issiar Dia [57]		
2011							
9-02	Guinea	W 3-0	Dakar	Fr	Papiss Cisse [19], Moussa Sow [60], Dame N'Doye [85]		
26-03	Cameroon	W 1-0	Dakar	CNq	Demba Ba [92+]		
4-06	Cameroon	D 0-0	Yaounde	CNq			
10-08	Morocco	L 0-2	Dakar	Fr			
3-09	Congo DR	W 2-0	Dakar	CNq	Moussa Sow 2 [33 53]		
9-10	Mauritius	W 2-0	Bellevue	CNq	Dame N'Doye [9], Papiss Cisse [26]		
11-11	Guinea	W 4-1	Mantes la Villes	Fr	Guirane N'Daw [12], Souleymane Camara [26], Deme N'Deaye [30p], Mame Biram Diouf [71]		
2012							
12-01	Sudan	W 1-0	Dakar	Fr	Demba Ba [23]		
21-01	Zambia	L 1-2	Bata	CNr1	Dame N'Doye [73]	17 500	Alioum CMR
25-01	Equatorial Guinea	L 1-2	Bata	CNr1	Moussa Sow [89]	35 000	Abdel Rahman SUD
29-01	Libya	L 1-2	Bata	CNr1	Deme N'Diaye [10]	10 000	Seechurn MRI
29-02	South Africa	D 0-0	Durban	Fr			Ruzive ZIM
25-05	Morocco	W 1-0	Marrakech	Fr	Moussa Konate [11]		Jaouadi TUN
2-06	Liberia	W 3-1	Dakar	WCq	Ibrahima Balde [33], Dame N'Doye [71], Sadio Mane [83]	15 000	Doue CIV
9-06	Uganda	D 1-1	Kampala	WCq	Papiss Cisse [37]	30 000	Benouza ALG
8-09	Côte d'Ivoire	L 2-4	Abidjan	CNq	Dame N'Doye [35], Papiss Cisse [60]		El Ahrach MAR
13-10	Côte d'Ivoire	L 0-2	Dakar	CNq			Jedidi TUN

Fr = Friendly match • CN = CAF African Cup of Nations • WC = FIFA World Cup • q = qualifier • r1 = first round group • qf = quarter-final

SENEGAL SQUAD FOR THE 2012 CAF AFRICA CUP OF NATIONS

	Player		Ap	G	Club	Date of Birth		Player		Ap	G	Club	Date of Birth
1	Bouna Coundoul	GK	2		None	4 03 1982	12	Moustapha Bayal Sall	DF	0		Saint-Etienne	30 11 1985
2	Remi Gomis	MF	2		Valenciennes	14 02 1984	13	Jacques Faty	DF	1		Sivasspor	25 02 1984
3	Ludovic Sane	DF	1		Bordeaux	22 03 1987	14	Deme N'Diaye	MF	1+1	1	Arles-Avignon	6 02 1985
4	Pape Diakhate	DF	1		Granada	21 06 1984	15	Papiss Demba Cisse	FW	1+2		Newcastle Utd	3 06 1985
5	Souleymane Diawara	DF	3		Marseille	24 12 1978	16	Khadim N'Diaye	GK	1		ASC Linguère	30 11 1984
6	Kader Mangane	DF	3		Rennes	23 03 1983	17	Omar Daf	DF	1		Brest	12 02 1977
7	Moussa Sow	FW	1+2	1	Lille	19 01 1986	18	Guirane N'Daw	MF	1		Birmingham City	24 04 1984
8	Mamadou Niang (c)	FW	2+1		Al Sadd	13 10 1979	19	Demba Ba	FW	3		Newcastle Utd	25 05 1985
9	Souleymane Camara	FW	1		Montpellier	22 12 1982	20	Armand Traore	DF	0		QPR	8 10 1989
10	Issiar Dia	MF	1+2		Fenerbahçe	8 06 1987	21	Mohamed Diame	MF	3		Wigan Athletic	14 06 1987
11	Dame N'Doye	FW	1+1	1	København	21 02 1985	22	Cheikh M'Bengue	DF	3		Toulouse	23 07 1988
	Coach: Amara Traore, 25-09-1965						23	Pape Latyr N'Diaye	GK	0		US Ouakam	4 04 1985

SENEGAL NATIONAL TEAM HISTORICAL RECORDS

Coaches: Peter Schnittger GER 1999-2000 • Bruno Metsu FRA 2000-02 • Guy Stephan FRA 2002-05 • Abdoulaye Sarr 2005-06 • Henryk Kasperczak POL 2006-08 • Lamine N'Diaye 2008 • Amara Traore 2009-12 • Joseph Koto 2012 • Alain Giresse 2013-

SENEGAL 2012

CHAMPIONNAT NATIONAL

POULE A

	Pl	W	D	L	F	A	Pts	Diambars	Ouakem	DUC	CSS RT	La Linguère	Guédiawaye	Gorée	Yakaar
Diambars Saly †	14	8	2	4	18	8	**26**		0-0	0-1	0-1	1-0	3-0	1-0	3-0
US Ouakem †	14	6	7	1	18	7	**25**	1-1		3-0	1-1	0-1	3-1	1-1	3-0
DUC Dakar	14	7	3	4	10	9	**24**	1-0	0-0		2-0	1-0	1-0	0-2	1-0
CSS Richard Toll	14	5	6	3	11	10	**21**	0-1	0-1	1-1		0-0	1-1	1-1	1-0
ASC La Linguère	14	4	6	4	12	12	**18**	0-1	0-0	2-1	0-0		3-2	1-1	0-0
Guédiawaye FC Dakar	14	4	3	7	10	17	**15**	2-0	0-2	0-0	0-1	0-2		1-0	1-0
US Gorée	14	3	5	6	14	17	**14**	1-4	1-2	1-0	2-3	4-2	0-1		0-0
ASC Yakaar	14	0	6	8	4	17	**6**	1-3	1-1	0-1	0-1	1-1	1-1	0-0	

POULE B

	Pl	W	D	L	F	A	Pts	Niary Tally	Casa Sport	Diaraf	Pikine	Douanes	T Kounda	Yeggo	Dahra
ASC Niary Tally Dakar †	14	8	4	2	13	7	**28**		1-0	2-0	1-0	1-0	1-0	1-0	3-0
Casa Sport †	14	7	4	3	15	6	**25**	3-0		1-0	3-0	0-1	2-1	0-1	2-0
ASC Diaraf	14	7	4	3	17	8	**25**	0-0	1-2		4-1	2-0	0-0	2-0	1-0
AS Pikine	14	6	4	4	13	12	**22**	2-0	0-0	1-2		2-0	1-0	1-0	1-0
AS Douanes	14	3	6	5	6	8	**15**	0-0	0-0	0-0	0-0		0-0	1-0	3-0
Touré Kounda	14	2	8	4	5	7	**14**	0-0	1-1	0-1	1-1	1-0		0-0	0-0
ASC Yeggo Dakar	14	2	5	7	6	14	**11**	1-1	0-1	1-4	1-1	0-0	0-1		1-1
ASC Dahra	14	1	5	8	4	17	**8**	1-2	0-0	0-0	0-2	2-1	0-0	0-1	

24/12/2011 - 20/05/2012 • † Qualified for the championship play-offs

SENEGAL 2012

CHAMPIONNAT NATIONAL PLAY-OFFS

	Pl	W	D	L	F	A	Pts	Casa Sport	Diambars	Niary Tally	Ouakem
Casa Sport †	6	3	2	1	5	2	**11**		0-2	2-0	0-0
Diambars Saly	6	3	1	2	6	4	**10**	0-1		0-0	1-0
ASC Niary Tally Dakar	6	2	1	3	6	7	**7**	0-2	2-3		1-0
US Ouakem	6	1	2	3	1	5	**5**	0-0	1-0	0-3	

17/06/2012 - 2/09/2012 • † Qualified for the CAF Champions League

MEDALS TABLE

		All	Lge	Cup
		G	G	G
1	ASC Diaraf	25	**11**	**14**
2	Jeanne d'Arc	16	10	6
3	AS Douanes	11	5	6
4	US Gorée	7	3	4
5	ASC La Linguère	5	1	4
	SUNEOR	5	4	1
7	ASF Police	4	1	3
	ASEC Ndiambour	4	3	1
	Port Autonome	4	3	1
	US Ouakem	4	1	3
11	ASFA Dakar	3	3	
	Casa Sport	3	1	2
13	Olympique Thiès	2	2	
	Espoir Saint-Louis	2	1	1
15	Saltigues	1		1
	AS Saint-Louisienne	1		1
	Touré Kounda	1		1
	ASC HLM	1		1

COUPE NATIONALE 2012

Round of 16

ASC HLM Dakar	0 5p
Almamy St Louis	0 4p
Olympique Sport	1
ASC Diaraf	2
US Gorée	2 4p
ASFA	2 3p
Zig Inter	0
UCST Port Autonome	2
Walidane Thiès	0 4p
SUNEOR	0 2p
Cambérène	
Casa Sport	W-O
ETICS Mboro	1 3p
Guédiawaye FC Dakar	1 2p
AS Saloum Kaolack	
Renaissance Dakar	W-O

Quarter-finals

ASC HLM Dakar	2
ASC Diaraf	0
US Gorée	1
UCST Port Autonome	2
Walidane Thiès	0 4p
Casa Sport	0 1p
ETICS Mboro	0
Renaissance Dakar	2

Semi-finals

ASC HLM Dakar	0 8p
UCST Port Autonome	0 7p
Walidane Thiès	0
Renaissance Dakar	1

Final

ASC HLM Dakar ‡	0 4p
Renaissance Dakar	0 3p

‡ Qualified for the CAF Confederation Cup

CUP FINAL

Demba Diop, Dakar, 22-09-2012

SEY – SEYCHELLES

FIFA/COCA-COLA WORLD RANKING

'93	'94	'95	'96	'97	'98	'99	'00	'01	'02	'03	'04	'05	'06	'07	'08	'09	'10	'11	'12
157	175	176	175	181	181	192	188	192	185	163	173	176	130	163	166	178	196	188	196

2012

Jan	Feb	Mar	Apr	May	Jun	Jul	Aug	Sep	Oct	Nov	Dec	High	Low	Av
188	189	189	189	189	189	187	189	190	190	194	196	129	199	175

Seychelles had little chance in the 2013 Africa Cup of Nations qualifiers after being drawn against a more powerful Congo DR team and were easily beaten 7-0 on aggregate. Having already been eliminated in late 2011 from the FIFA World Cup qualifiers, it left the country bereft of competitive action which saw them slip down the FIFA/Coca-Cola World Ranking to 196th place, close to their all-time low of 199. There were also no entrants in the two annual CAF club competitions - a reflection of tougher economic times. In club football Côte d'Or made history by winning the Airtel League Cup, the first team from the island of Praslin - the second largest in the Seychelles - to win a major trophy. The league, however, was won by St Michel United who continued their dominance of the domestic arena, taking an 11th title by finishing two points ahead of La Passe from the smaller island of La Digue. Anse Reunion were the season's other winners when they won the FA Cup by beating Cote d'Or 3-2 in the final. Seychelles' biggest contribution to world football in the year was arguably the work of its officials. Seychelles Football Federation president Suketu Patel retained his presidency of the regional COSAFA body while referee Eddy Maillet retired to take over as the head of refereeing for the Cairo-based CAF.

CAF AFRICA CUP OF NATIONS RECORD
1957-1988 DNE 1990 DNQ 1992-1996 DNE 1998 DNQ 2000-2002 DNE 2004-2010 DNQ 2012 DNE 2013 DNQ

SEYCHELLES FOOTBALL FEDERATION (SFF)

Maison Football,
Roche Caiman,
PO Box 843, Mahe
☎ +248 601161
📠 +248 601163
✉ sff@seychelles.net
🖥 www.sff.sc
FA 1979 CON 1986 FIFA 1986
P Elvis Chetty
GS Jemmy Adela

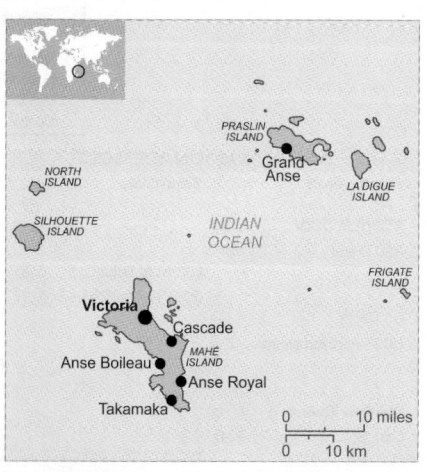

MAJOR CITIES/TOWNS

		Population
1	Victoria	25 500
2	Anse Royal	3 700
3	Cascade	2 400
4	Takamaka	2 200
5	Anse Boileau	2 000

THE STADIA

2014 FIFA World Cup Stadia
Stade Linite
Roche Caiman, Victoria 10 000

Other Main Stadia
People's Stadium
Roche Caiman, Victoria 7 000
Praslin Stadium
Praslin

REPUBLIC OF SEYCHELLES

Capital	Victoria	Population	87 476 (197)	% in cities	54%
GDP per capita	$21 000 (59)	Area km²	455 km² (198)	GMT +/-	+4
Neighbours (km)	Coast 491				

RECENT INTERNATIONAL MATCHES PLAYED BY THE SEYCHELLES

2006 Opponents	Score	Venue	Comp	Scorers	Att	Referee
22-07 Namibia	D 1-1	Katutura	CCr1	Wilnes Brutus [18], W 4-2p		Simisse MRI
23-07 Zambia	L 0-2	Katutura	CCr1			Ngobo RSA
3-09 Sudan	L 0-3	Khartoum	CNq			Kidane ERI
7-10 Mauritius	W 2-1	Roche Caiman	CNq	Wilnes Brutus 2 [23 81]		Raolimanana MAD
2007						
24-03 Tunisia	L 0-3	Victoria	CNq			Ssegonga UGA
28-04 Mozambique	L 0-2	Maputo	CCr1			Mpopo LES
29-04 Madagascar	L 0-5	Maputo	CCr1			Mpopo LES
2-06 Tunisia	L 0-4	Rades/Tunis	CNq			Diatta SEN
16-06 Sudan	L 0-2	Roche Caiman	CNq			Dlamini SWZ
14-08 Mauritius	L 0-3	Antananarivo	Fr			
9-09 Mauritius	D 1-1	Curepipe	CNq	Godfrey Denis [43p]		Mwandike TAN
2008						
1-06 Burundi	L 0-1	Bujumbura	WCq		4 000	Imiere NGA
7-06 Tunisia	L 0-2	Victoria	WCq		2 033	Faduco MOZ
14-06 Burkina Faso	L 2-3	Victoria	WCq	Philip Zialor [47], Don Annacoura [53]	1 000	Seechurn MRI
21-06 Burkina Faso	L 1-4	Ouagadougou	WCq	Bernard St Ange [44]	12 500	Lamptey GHA
19-07 Mauritius	W 7-0	Witbank	CCr1	Colin Laporte [14], Philip Zialor 4 [35 51 59 88], Don Annacoura [66], Trevor Poiret [87]		Kaoma ZAM
21-07 Madagascar	D 1-1	Witbank	CCr1	Godfrey Denis [48]		Kaoma ZAM
23-07 Swaziland	L 0-1	Witbank	CCr1			Katjimune NAM
6-09 Burundi	L 1-2	Victoria	WCq	Philip Zialor [63]	3 000	Djaoupe TOG
11-10 Tunisia	L 0-5	Tunis/Rades	WCq		10 000	Diatta SEN
2009						
18-10 Swaziland	L 1-2	Bulawayo	CCr1	Nelson Laurence [8]		Carvalho ANG
20-10 Comoros	L 1-2	Bulawayo	CCr1	Don Anacoura [54]		Rachide MOZ
22-10 Botswana	L 0-2	Bulawayo	CCr1			Seechurn MRI
2010						
No international matches played in 2010						
2011						
4-08 Comoros	D 0-0	Praslin	IOGr1		1 800	Dubec REU
6-08 Mauritius	W 2-1	Roche Caiman	IOGr1	Nelson Laurence [1], Archille Henriette [28]	6 500	Rassuhi MAY
9-08 Maldives	W 5-1	Roche Caiman	IOGr1	Nelson Laurence [16], Don Anacoura [23], Archille Henriette [62], Alpha Balde 2 [75 80]	5 500	Rakotonjanahary MAD
11-08 Reunion	W 2-1	Roche Caiman	IOGsf	Alex Nibourette [77], Karl Hall [118]	6 500	Ali Saleem MDV
13-08 Mauritius	D 1-1	Roche Caiman	IOGf	W 4-3p. Kevin Betsy [16]	10 000	Dubec REU
11-11 Kenya	L 0-3	Roche Caiman	WCq		2 000	Batte UGA
15-11 Kenya	L 0-4	Nairobi	WCq		5 000	Gomes RSA
22-11 Maldives	L 0-3	Male	Fr			
24-11 Maldives	L 1-2	Male	Fr	Leroy Coralie [49]		
2012						
29-02 Congo DR	L 0-4	Roche Caiman	CNq			Bangoura GUI
17-06 Congo DR	L 0-3	Kinshasa	CNq			Kayindi-Ngobi UGA
2-12 Mozambique	L 0-4	Maputo	Fr			
15-12 Mozambique	L 1-2	Roche Caiman	Fr			

Fr = Friendly match • CN = CAN African Cup of Nations • IOG = Indian Ocean Games • CC = COSAFA Castle Cup • WC = FIFA World Cup
q = qualifier • r1 = first round group

SEYCHELLES 2012

BARCLAYS LEAGUE DIVISION ONE

	Pl	W	D	L	F	A	Pts	St Michel	La Passe	Côte d'Or	Anse	Dynamo	St Louis	St Roch	St Francis	Light Stars	Quincy
St Michel United †	18	12	6	0	74	21	**42**		2-2	0-0	4-1	2-2	0-0	6-0	7-1	7-1	10-1
La Passe	18	12	4	2	47	17	**40**	2-2		0-0	0-1	2-1	2-1	1-2	2-1	3-1	3-0
Côte d'Or	18	11	4	3	36	16	**37**	1-1	0-1		4-2	1-1	3-2	3-2	2-1	2-0	5-0
Anse Reunion	18	11	2	5	30	22	**35**	2-3	0-2	2-1		4-2	2-0	2-0	1-0	1-0	1-0
Northern Dynamo	18	6	5	7	26	29	**23**	0-4	0-1	0-2	1-1		0-1	2-1	2-1	3-2	2-1
St Louis Suns United	18	6	4	8	30	26	**22**	1-4	1-2	1-2	2-0	2-2		0-1	1-0	5-1	5-0
St Roch United	18	5	5	8	18	32	**20**	1-5	1-1	2-0	0-0	1-3	1-5		3-1	0-0	1-1
St Francis	18	4	2	12	24	41	**14**	2-8	1-3	0-2	2-1	1-1	4-3	1-0		0-0	5-0
Light Stars	18	3	3	12	21	44	**12**	2-3	1-8	0-1	0-2	0-3	2-2	1-2	2-1		1-0
Quincy	18	1	3	14	14	72	**6**	1-13	0-7	1-5	2-5	0-3	1-1	1-1	3-2	1-5	

14/03/2012 - 9/11/2012 • † Qualified for the CAF Champions League
Relegation play-off: Lightstars 6-1 SPDF

AIRTEL LEAGUE CUP 2012

Semi-finals
Côte d'Or	2
La Passe	1

Anse Reunion	0
St Michel United	2

Final
Côte d'Or	1
St Michel United	0

Stade Linite, Victoria
27-08-2012

Scorer - Patrick Ramsamimanana [76] for Côte d'Or

MEDALS TABLE

		Overall	League	Cup	LC	City
		G S B	G S B	G S	G S	
1	St Michel United	24 7	11 5	8	5 2	Anse aux Pins
2	Red Star	8 6 4	2 2 4	4 3	2 1	Anse aux Pins
3	La Passe	5 8 4	4 4 4	3	1 3	La Passe
4	St Louis Suns Utd †	4 10 4	1 3 4	3 4	3	Victoria
5	Anse Reunion	4 5 3	1 1 3	2 3	1 1	Anse Reunion
6	Côte d'Or	1 1 2		2	1 1	Praslin
7	Seychelles MB	1 1		1	1	Victoria
8	Light Stars	2			1 1	Grand Anse
9	Ascot	1		1		

LAND MARINE FA CUP 2012

Round of 16
Anse Reunion	3 4p
St Roch United	3 2p
St Louis Suns United	1
St Michel United	3
The Lions	4
Beginners	0
Northern Dynamo	2
St Francis	3
La Passe	
Light Stars	
Tigers	7
Mont Buxton	0
Foresters	
Côte d'Or	

Quarter-finals
Anse Reunion	2
St Michel United	1
The Lions	2
St Francis	3
La Passe	6
Light Stars	0
Tigers	0
Côte d'Or	6

Semi-finals
Anse Reunion	5
St Francis	1
La Passe	1
Côte d'Or	2

All matches played at Stade Linite
‡ Qualified for the CAF Confederation Cup

Final
Anse Reunion ‡	3
Côte d'Or	2

CUP FINAL
Stade Linite, Victoria
17-11-2012
Scorer - Sezou [30], Yelvanny Rose [45], Nickerro Marie [48] for Anse; Mazinot [26], Dean Suzette [70] for Côte d'Or

SIN – SINGAPORE

FIFA/COCA-COLA WORLD RANKING

'93	'94	'95	'96	'97	'98	'99	'00	'01	'02	'03	'04	'05	'06	'07	'08	'09	'10	'11	'12
75	95	104	92	103	81	104	101	115	118	106	112	92	111	126	132	110	140	145	154

2012													
Jan	Feb	Mar	Apr	May	Jun	Jul	Aug	Sep	Oct	Nov	Dec	High	Low	Av
147	148	150	158	158	157	158	162	161	162	163	154	73	163	112

Following on from their triumphs in 1998, 2004 and 2007, Singapore's extraordinary success in the AFF Suzuki Cup continued in 2012 when they beat Thailand in the final to secure the trophy for a record-breaking fourth time. Singapore may be the smallest nation in southeast Asia, with a population of under 5 million, but Raddy Avramovic's Lions continue to punch well above their weight. The Serb, who took over as national team coach in 2003 and led Singapore to the 2004 and 2007 titles, announced before the finals that he would step down from his post, marking the end of a hugely successful era. The AFF Suzuki Cup remains the most important competition for the ASEAN nations, none of whom have realistic ambitions in either the FIFA World Cup or AFC Asian Cup, and that was evident by the 87,410 who watched the first leg of the semi-final between Malaysia and Thailand. In the final, Singapore beat the Thais 3-1 in the first leg at home before hanging on in the second to win 3-2 on aggregate. In club football Tampines Rovers won the S-League crown ahead of DPMM Brunei, who won the S-League Cup, while Singapore Armed Forces - who have been rebranded as the Warriors for the 2013 season - secured the Singapore Cup by defeating Tampines 2-1 in the final thanks to an injury-time winner from Erwan Gunawan.

FIFA WORLD CUP RECORD
1930-1974 DNE **1978-2014** DNQ

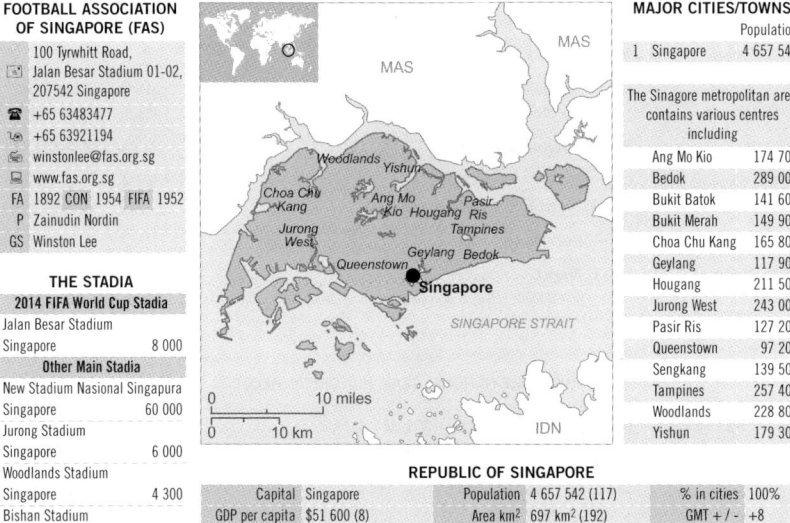

FOOTBALL ASSOCIATION OF SINGAPORE (FAS)

100 Tyrwhitt Road,
Jalan Besar Stadium 01-02,
207542 Singapore
☎ +65 63483477
📠 +65 63921194
✉ winstonlee@fas.org.sg
🌐 www.fas.org.sg
FA 1892 CON 1954 FIFA 1952
P Zainudin Nordin
GS Winston Lee

THE STADIA

2014 FIFA World Cup Stadia
Jalan Besar Stadium
Singapore 8 000

Other Main Stadia
New Stadium Nasional Singapura
Singapore 60 000
Jurong Stadium
Singapore 6 000
Woodlands Stadium
Singapore 4 300
Bishan Stadium
Singapore 4 200

REPUBLIC OF SINGAPORE

Capital	Singapore	Population	4 657 542 (117)	% in cities	100%
GDP per capita	$51 600 (8)	Area km²	697 km² (192)	GMT +/-	+8
Neighbours (km)	Coast 193				

MAJOR CITIES/TOWNS

		Population
1	Singapore	4 657 542

The Sinagore metropolitan area contains various centres including

Ang Mo Kio	174 700
Bedok	289 000
Bukit Batok	141 600
Bukit Merah	149 900
Choa Chu Kang	165 800
Geylang	117 900
Hougang	211 500
Jurong West	243 000
Pasir Ris	127 200
Queenstown	97 200
Sengkang	139 500
Tampines	257 400
Woodlands	228 800
Yishun	179 300

RECENT INTERNATIONAL MATCHES PLAYED BY SINGAPORE

2010	Opponents	Score	Venue	Comp	Scorers	Att	Referee
6-01	Iran	L 1-3	Singapore	ACq	Noh Alam Shah [31]	7 356	Sun Baojie CHN
17-01	Thailand	L 0-1	Nakhon Ratch'ma	Fr		20 000	Mbaga TAN
20-01	Denmark	L 1-5	Nakhon Ratch'ma	Fr	Fazrul Shahul [84]		
23-01	Poland	L 1-6	Nakhon Ratch'ma	Fr	Jiayi Shi [39]		Amwayi KEN
3-03	Jordan	L 1-2	Amman	ACq	Noh Alam Shah [48]	17 000	Abdou QAT
11-08	Thailand	L 0-1	Nonthaburi	Fr			Aonrak THA
2-11	Korea DPR	L 1-2	Hanoi	Fr	Aleksandar Duric [41]		
4-11	Vietnam	D 1-1	Hanoi	Fr	Jiayi Shi [24]		
2-12	Philippines	D 1-1	Hanoi	AFFr1	Aleksandar Duric [65]		Mahapab THA
5-12	Myanmar	W 2-1	Hanoi	AFFr1	Aleksandar Duric [62], Casnir [94+]		Tao Ranchang CHN
8-12	Vietnam	L 0-1	Hanoi	AFFr1		40 000	Mahapab THA
2011							
7-06	Maldives	W 4-0	Singapore	Fr	Li Qiu 2 [13p 19], Jiayi Shi [30], Aleksandar Duric [49]		
18-07	Chinese Taipei	W 3-2	Singapore	Fr	Aleksandar Duric 2 [17 54], Fazrul Shahul [83]		
23-07	Malaysia	W 5-3	Singapore	WCq	Aleksandar Duric 2 [8 81], Li Qiu [22], Mustafic Fahrudin [44], Jiayi Shi [45]	6 000	Shukralla BHR
28-07	Malaysia	D 1-1	Kuala Lumpur	WCq	Jiayi Shi [71]	90 000	Takayama JPN
24-08	Thailand	D 0-0	Bangkok	Fr			
2-09	China PR	L 1-2	Kunming	WCq	Aleksandar Duric [33]	17 000	El Haddad LIB
6-09	Iraq	L 0-2	Singapore	WCq		5 505	Tojo JPN
7-10	Philippines	W 2-0	Singapore	Fr	Shaiful Esah [51], Aleksandar Duric [65]		
11-10	Jordan	L 0-3	Singapore	WCq		3 799	Choi Myung Yong KOR
11-11	Jordan	L 0-2	Amman	WCq		19 000	Williams AUS
15-11	China PR	L 0-4	Singapore	WCq		5 474	Balideh QAT
2012							
24-02	Azerbaijan	D 2-2	Dubai	Fr	Shahril Bin Ishak [71p], Mustafic Fahrudin [93+]	50	Banihammad UAE
29-02	Iraq	L 1-7	Doha	WCq	Mohammad Abdul [27]	950	Al Hilali OMA
1-06	Hong Kong	L 0-1	Hong Kong	Fr		4 285	
8-06	Malaysia	D 2-2	Singapore	Fr	Shahdan Bin Sulaiman [88], Li Qui [95+]		
12-06	Malaysia	L 0-2	Kuala Lumpur	Fr			
15-08	Hong Kong	W 2-0	Singapore	Fr	Aleksandar Duric 2 [6 21]		
7-09	Philippines	L 0-2	Singapore	Fr			
11-09	Myanmar	D 1-1	Yangon	Fr	Agu Casmir [53]		
16-10	India	W 2-0	Singapore	Fr	Khairul Amri [42], Fazrul Shahul [50]		
15-11	Philippines	L 0-1	Cebu	Fr			
19-11	Pakistan	W 4-0	Singapore	Fr	Jiayi Shi [2], Khairul Amri [29], Shahril Bin Ishak [77], Aleksandar Duric [88]		
25-11	Malaysia	W 3-0	Kuala Lumpur	AFFr1	Shahril Bin Ishak 2 [32 38], Aleksandar Duric [75]	51 478	Kovalenko UZB
28-11	Indonesia	L 0-1	Kuala Lumpur	AFFr1		12 676	Abdulnabi BHR
1-12	Laos	W 4-3	Kuala Lumpur	AFFr1	Shahril Bin Ishak 2 [45 53], Khairul Amri [63], Fazrul Shahul [65]	579	Ng Kai Lam HKG
8-12	Philippines	D 0-0	Manila	AFFsf		15 534	Al Hilali
12-12	Philippines	W 1-0	Singapore	AFFsf	Khairul Amri [63]	7 613	Tan Hai CHN
19-12	Thailand	W 3-1	Singapore	AFFf	Mustafic Fahrudin [10p], Khairul Amri [62], Baihakki Bin Khaizan [91+]	7 613	Toma JPN
22-12	Thailand	L 0-1	Bangkok	AFFf		23 158	Irmatov UZB

Fr = Friendly match • AC = AFC Asian Cup • AFF = ASEAN Football Federation Championship • WC = FIFA World Cup
q = qualifier • r1 = first round group • sf = semi-final • f = final

SINGAPORE NATIONAL TEAM HISTORICAL RECORDS

Caps: **128** - Daniel Bennett 2002- • **121** - Aide Iskandar 1995-2007 • **115** - Shunmugham Subramani 1996-2007 • **110** - Shahril Bin Ishak 2003- • **108** - Indra Sahdan Daud 1997-2010 • **100** - Nasri Nasir 1990-2004

Goals: **52** - Fandi Ahmad 1978-97

Coaches: Hussein Aljunied 1984-86 • Seak Poh Leong 1986-88 • Jita Singh 1988-89 • Robin Chan 1990-92 • Milous Kvacek CZE 1992 • PN Sivaji 1992-94 • Ken Worden ENG 1994 • Douglas Moore ENG 1994-96 • Barry Whitbread ENG 1996-98 • Vincent Subramaniam 1998-2000 • Jan Poulsen DEN 2000-02 • Radojko Avramovic SRB 2003-12 • Varadaraju Sundramoorthy 2013-

SIN – SINGAPORE

SINGAPORE 2012

S.LEAGUE

	Pl	W	D	L	F	A	Pts	Tampines	DPMM	Albirex	Harimau M	Home Utd	Balestier	SAF	Hougang U	Gombak U	Young Lions	Geylang U	Tanjong PU	Woodlands
Tampines Rovers ‡	24	16	4	4	49	24	52		1-0	3-4	1-0	2-0	3-1	0-1	1-1	3-2	2-1	2-1	2-1	4-0
DPMM Brunei	24	15	3	6	49	27	48	2-2		2-1	1-2	3-2	0-2	1-2	5-1	1-1	1-0	4-1	3-2	3-0
Albirex Niigata	24	12	7	5	37	26	43	1-0	2-0		1-0	0-0	1-2	3-2	2-3	1-0	2-2	1-1	4-1	2-0
Harimau Muda	24	13	3	8	37	23	42	2-3	1-1	0-0		0-3	2-0	4-1	3-1	1-2	3-1	3-1	3-0	2-1
Home United	24	11	7	6	43	29	40	0-2	1-0	4-2	2-1		0-0	0-3	1-1	1-1	3-1	7-3	3-1	3-1
Balestier Khalsa	24	11	6	7	23	20	39	1-0	1-3	1-0	2-0	1-0		1-0	0-3	1-1	2-0	0-0	1-1	2-0
S'pore Armed Forces	24	9	5	10	43	41	32	2-3	1-2	3-4	1-2	3-3	0-0		1-0	6-1	4-3	2-2	0-1	2-1
Hougang United	24	7	8	9	31	33	29	1-1	1-3	1-2	0-0	1-2	0-1	2-2		0-0	0-2	2-0	1-1	2-2
Gombak United	24	7	8	9	23	29	29	1-1	0-3	0-0	0-2	1-2	1-0	0-1	2-1		1-0	2-0	0-0	0-0
Young Lions	24	6	5	13	25	37	23	0-3	1-3	1-1	1-0	0-0	1-1	2-1	0-3	1-0		0-2	1-1	0-1
Geylang United	24	5	6	13	28	50	21	1-5	1-3	0-0	0-2	1-7	3-1	3-0	1-2	3-2	2-0		0-0	1-1
Tanjong Pagar United	24	5	5	14	17	41	20	1-2	0-3	0-2	0-2	1-0	1-0	1-3	0-1	0-3	0-5	1-0		2-3
Woodlands Wellington	24	3	5	16	19	44	14	0-3	1-2	0-1	0-2	0-0	0-2	2-2	1-3	1-2	1-2	3-1	0-1	

9/02/2012 – 4/11/2012 • ‡ Qualified for the AFC Cup

Top scorers: **20** – Frederic **MENDY** FRA, Home Utd • **14** – Jozef **KAPLAN** CZE, Geyland Utd & Mislav **KAROGLAN** BIH, SAF • **13** – Shahrazen **SAID** BRU, DPMM • **12** – Jordan **WEBB** CAN, Hougang Utd; Yasuhiro **YAMAKOSHI** JPN, Albirex & Aleksandar **DURIC**, Tampines • **10** – Shotaro **IHATA** JPN, Home Utd • **9** – Fazrul **NAWAZ**, SAF & Shimpei **SAKURADA** JPN, SAF • **8** – Sead **HADZIBULIC** BIH, Tampines

SINGAPORE LEAGUE CUP 2012

Quarter-finals	Semi-finals	Final
DPMM Brunei 1 4p		
Home United 1 2p	DPMM Brunei 2	
Hougang United 0	S'pore A. Forces 0	
S'pore A. Forces 1		**DPMM Brunei** 2
Tampines Rov 3 6p		Geylang United 0
Albirex Niigata 3 5p	Tampines Rov 0	Jalan Basar, 10-08-2012
Gombak United 0	**Geylang United** 2	Att: 1874, Ref: Sukhbir Singh, Scorers -
Geylang United 1		Shahrazen Said 36, Azwan Bin Muhamad Saleh 76

First round played in four groups of three teams

MEDALS TABLE

		All G	Lge G	Cup G	LC G
1	Singapore Armed Forces	20	11	8	
2	Geylang United	18	11	7	
3	Tampines Rovers	10	7	3	
4	Tanjong Pagar United	9	2	7	
	Home United	9	3	6	
6	Farrer Park United	4	1	3	
7	Toa Payoh United	2		2	
	Etoile FC	2	1		1
	DPMM Brunei	2			2
10	Perth Kangaroos	1	1		
	Bangkok Glass	1		1	
	Balestier United	1		1	
	Jurong Town	1		1	
	Woodlands Wellington	1			1
	Gombak United	1			1
	Albirex Niigata	1			1

RHB SINGAPORE CUP 2012

First round	Quarter-finals	Semi-finals	Final
S'pore Armed Forces 1 6p			
Balestier Khalsa 1 5p	**S'pore Armed Forces** 2 3		
DPMM Brunei 0	Home United 1 3		
Home United 1		**S'pore Armed Forces** 1 1	
Hougang United 1 4p		Gombak United 0 0	
Tanjong Pagar United 1 3p	Hougang United 2 0		
Harimau Muda 0	**Gombak United** 1 2		
Gombak United 3			**S'pore Armed Forces** ‡ 2
Loyola Meralco Sparks 2			Tampines Rovers 1
Geylang United 1	**Loyola Meralco Sparks** 3 2		
Woodlands Wellington 1	Kanbawza 1 2		**CUP FINAL**
Kanbawza 2		Loyola Meralco Sparks 0 0	Jalan Besar, Singapore
Albirex Niigata 1		**Tampines Rovers** 2 3	28-10-2012, Ref: Muhd Taqi
Yotha 0	Albirex Niigata 1 0		Scorers - Shimpei Sakurada 78,
Phnom Penh Crown 3	**Tampines Rovers** 2 2	3rd place: **Gombak Utd** 4-0 Sparks	Erwan Gunawan 92+ for SAF; Jantan OG 25 for Tampines
Tampines Rovers 4		* Home Team in the first leg • ‡ Qualified for the AFC Cup	

SKN – ST KITTS AND NEVIS

FIFA/COCA-COLA WORLD RANKING

'93	'94	'95	'96	'97	'98	'99	'00	'01	'02	'03	'04	'05	'06	'07	'08	'09	'10	'11	'12
166	175	150	121	127	132	137	146	129	109	134	118	129	143	160	152	156	121	116	123

2012

Jan	Feb	Mar	Apr	May	Jun	Jul	Aug	Sep	Oct	Nov	Dec	High	Low	Av
114	117	109	111	111	114	112	113	113	122	106	123	106	176	134

For the second time in three tournaments Warner Park in Basseterre was chosen to host a qualifying group in the Caribbean Cup with Trinidad, French Guiana and Anguilla travelling to the capital of St Kitts in October 2012. Minnows Anguilla were dispatched with relative ease in the first game with West Brom Midfielder Romaine Sawyers scoring his first goal for St Kitts and MLS-based Atiba Harris scoring his first since 2006. It was always going to be a big task to get past the other two, however, and in the second game St Kitts went down to their eleventh defeat in twelve matches against Trinidad. That was followed by a 3-0 defeat at the hands of French Guiana as their quest for a first appearance at the finals since 2001 continues. In club football, Conaree United made a gallant attempt to upset the odds and win a first league title. They made it through to the final but came up against Newtown United, the most successful and popular team in the country. Both matches at a packed Warner Park were lost 2-0 as Newtown claimed their fifth SKNFA Premier League title and their 16th championship overall. They couldn't repeat their double success of 2010, however, after going down 2-1 to St Paul's United in the cup final with Javeim Blanchette the two goal hero for St Pauls.

CFU CARIBBEAN CUP RECORD

1989-1992 DNQ **1993** 4 SF 1994-1995 DNQ **1996** 8 r1 **1997** 2 F (Hosts) 1998 DNQ **1999** 8 r1 **2001** 6 r1 2005-20122012 DNQ

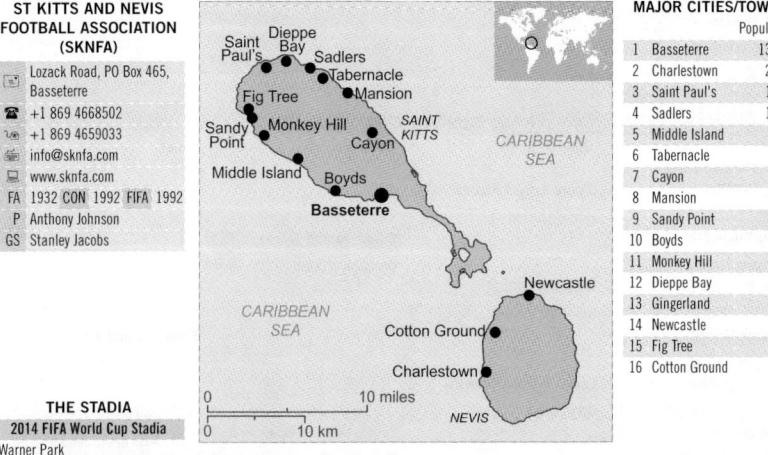

ST KITTS AND NEVIS FOOTBALL ASSOCIATION (SKNFA)

Lozack Road, PO Box 465, Basseterre
☎ +1 869 4668502
✆ +1 869 4659033
✉ info@sknfa.com
🖥 www.sknfa.com
FA 1932 CON 1992 FIFA 1992
P Anthony Johnson
GS Stanley Jacobs

MAJOR CITIES/TOWNS

		Population
1	Basseterre	13 243
2	Charlestown	2 093
3	Saint Paul's	1 319
4	Sadlers	1 037
5	Middle Island	905
6	Tabernacle	830
7	Cayon	806
8	Mansion	798
9	Sandy Point	758
10	Boyds	749
11	Monkey Hill	728
12	Dieppe Bay	622
13	Gingerland	572
14	Newcastle	570
15	Fig Tree	490
16	Cotton Ground	422

THE STADIA

2014 FIFA World Cup Stadia
Warner Park
Basseterre 10 000
Other Main Stadia
Warner Park is the only major sporting facility

FEDERATION OF SAINT KITTS AND NEVIS

Capital Basseterre
GDP per capita $19 100 (65)
Neighbours (km) Coast 135
Population 40 131 (209)
Area km^2 261 km^2 (211)
% in cities 32%
GMT + / - -4

RECENT INTERNATIONAL MATCHES PLAYED BY ST KITTS AND NEVIS

2006	Opponents		Score	Venue	Comp	Scorers	Att	Referee
20-09	Barbabdos	D	1-1	St John's	CCq	Atiba Harris [60]	300	Campbell JAM
22-09	Anguilla	W	6-1	St John's	CCq	George Isaac 2 [14 68], Ian Lake 3 [30 46 79], Jevon Francis [81]	500	Phillips GRN
24-09	Antigua and Barbuda	L	0-1	St John's	CCq		2 800	Wijngaarde SUR
2007								
18-11	Antigua and Barbuda	W	3-0	Basseterre	Fr	Jevon Francis [36], Christian OG [43], Aiden Nurse [44]	3 000	Matthew SKN
1-12	Antigua and Barbuda	L	0-2	St John's	Fr		3 800	Willett ATG
14-12	Bermuda	W	2-1	Hamilton	Fr	Jevon Francis [25], Ian Lake [38]	800	Mauchette BER
16-12	Bermuda	L	2-4	Hamilton	Fr	Imran Ponteen [44], Stedro Charles	1 500	Raynor BER
2008								
6-02	Belize	L	1-3	Guatemala City	WCq	Gerard Williams [13]	500	Stennet JAM
26-03	Belize	D	1-1	Basseterre	WCq	Orlando Mitchum [84]	2 000	Brizan TRI
8-06	Antigua and Barbuda	L	0-2	St John's	Fr		4 000	Willett ATG
24-09	British Virgin Islands	W	4-0	Basseterre	CCq	Jevon Francis [15], Zevon Archibald [21], Venton James OG [52], Ian Lake [77]	500	Charles DMA
28-09	Barbados	L	1-3	Basseterre	CCq	George Isaac [13]	500	Charles DMA
5-11	Guyana	D	1-1	Macoya	CCq	Ian Lake [29]	750	Cambridge VIN
7-11	Trinidad and Tobago	L	1-3	Macoya	CCq	Jevon Francis [86]		Wijngaarde SUR
9-11	Antigua and Barbuda	L	3-4	Macoya	CCq	Jevon Francis 3 [57 70 80]	1 000	Wijngaarde SUR
2009								
12-07	Trinidad and Tobago	L	2-3	Basseterre	Fr	Ian Lake [48], Gerard Williams [62]	3 100	Matthew SKN
16-08	Jamaica	L	0-1	Basseterre	Fr		5 000	Willett ATG
5-09	St Vincent/Grenadines	W	3-0	Kingstown	Fr	Stephen Clarke [50], Tishan Hanley [55], Alexis Saddler [81]	3 500	Cambridge VIN
20-09	St Vincent/Grenadines	D	1-1	Basseterre	Fr	Shashi Isaac [10]	1 600	Matthew SKN
2010								
28-08	Antigua and Barbuda	D	1-1	Basseterre	Fr	Ian Lake [30]	500	Matthew SKN
6-10	Barbados	D	1-1	Kingstown	CCq	George Isaac [62]	250	Elskamp SUR
8-10	St Vincent/Grenadines	D	1-1	Kingstown	CCq	Jevon Francis [40]	1 600	Jauregui ANT
10-10	Montserrat	W	4-0	Kingstown	CCq	Alexis Saddler 2 [18 31], Keith Gumbs [21], Ian Lake [90]	1 100	Elskamp SUR
22-10	Guadeloupe	L	1-2	St George's	CCq	Jevon Francis [83p]	300	Taylor BRB
24-10	Grenada	L	0-2	St George's	CCq		500	Morrison JAM
26-10	Puerto Rico	W	1-0	St George's	CCq	Jevon Francis [90]	500	Morrison JAM
2011								
27-03	Grenada	D	0-0	Basseterre	Fr		1 000	Matthew SKN
2-04	Grenada	W	1-0	St George's	Fr	Alexis Saddler [66]	3 500	Bedeau GRN
2-09	Puerto Rico	D	0-0	Basseterre	WCq		2 500	Arellano MEX
6-09	St Lucia	W	4-2	Gros Islet	WCq	Ian Lake [7], Jevon Francis [12], Orlando Mitchum [15], Devaughn Elliott [44]	2 005	Thomas JAM
7-10	Puerto Rico	D	1-1	Bayamon	WCq	Ian Lake [59]	2 500	Brizan TRI
11-10	St Lucia	D	1-1	Basseterre	WCq	Ian Lake [83]	1 000	Skeete BRB
11-11	Canada	D	0-0	Basseterre	WCq		4 000	Bonilla SLV
15-11	Canada	L	0-4	Toronto	WCq		10 235	Cerdas CRC
2012								
3-03	Antigua and Barbuda	W	1-0	Basseterre	Fr	Tiran Hanley [25]	2 000	Willett ATG
10-10	Anguilla	W	2-0	Basseterre	CNq	Romaine Sawyers [15], Atiba Harris [20]	700	Johnson GUY
12-10	Trinidad and Tobago	L	0-1	Basseterre	CNq		1 700	Rubalcaba CUB
14-10	French Guiana	L	0-3	Basseterre	CNq		200	Brea CUB

Fr = Friendly match • CC = Digicel Caribbean Cup • WC = FIFA World Cup • q = qualifier

ST KITTS AND NEVIS NATIONAL TEAM HISTORICAL RECORDS

Coaches: Ces Podd 1999-2002 • Elvis Browne 2002-04 • Lenny Lake 2004-07 • Lester Morris 2008-09 • Clinton Percival 2010-12 • Jeffrey Hazel 2012

ST KITTS 2011-12

SKNFA DIGICEL SUPER LEAGUE FIRST STAGE

	Pl	W	D	L	F	A	Pts	St Pauls	Conaree	Newtown	Hotspurs	Superstars	St Peters	St Thomas	Cayon	Mantab
St Pauls United †	24	16	4	4	50	17	52		1-2	1-0 3-1	3-1 2-0	2-1	1-0 1-2	3-0 3-1	5-0 0-1	4-0
Conaree United †	24	14	6	4	49	30	48	1-1 0-0		2-3	3-1 2-2	1-4 3-2	2-1	3-2 3-1	4-2	3-1 2-1
Newtown United †	24	13	4	7	45	29	43	1-1	0-1 0-2		1-1	0-3	2-1 1-2	1-0	2-1 2-2	3-0
Garden Hotspurs †	24	12	6	6	42	30	42	2-0	2-0	3-2 1-2		1-4 1-4	1-0	2-2 0-1	3-1	2-2
Village Superstars	24	9	5	10	41	34	32	0-0 0-3	3-1	0-1 2-3	0-2 1-2		2-3	1-1 1-0	1-1 3-3	2-1 3-0
St Peters Strikers	24	7	5	12	33	46	26	2-3	0-5 0-4	1-4	0-1 1-2	2-2 2-4		2-2	1-1 1-1	3-2 3-0
Cayon	24	5	7	12	26	41	22	1-4	1-1	1-1 1-3	2-2	1-0	1-2 1-2		2-0 1-1	0-1 1-5
St Thomas Strikers	24	4	9	11	22	40	21	0-1	0-2 0-0	0-2	1-6 0-0	1-0	2-1	0-1		3-0
Mantab United	24	3	4	17	19	60	13	0-3 1-5	2-2	0-8 0-2	0-3 0-2	0-2	1-1	0-2	1-1	

15/10/2011 - 24/05/2012 • † Qualified for play-offs

SKNFA DIGICEL SUPER LEAGUE SUPER FOUR PLAY-OFFS

	Pl	W	D	L	F	A	Pts	Conaree	Newtown	St Pauls	Hotspurs
Conaree United †	3	2	1	0	5	1	7		0-0		3-0
Newtown United †	3	1	2	0	2	1	5			1-1	
St Pauls United	3	1	0	2	5	3	3	1-2	0-1		4-0
Garden Hotspurs	3	0	1	2	1	8	1				

2/06/2012 - 9/06/2012 • † Qualified for the final

SKNFA DIGICEL SUPER LEAGUE FINAL

Champions	Score	Runners-up
Newtown United	2-0 2-0	Conaree United

1st leg. 13-06-2012. Warner Park, Basseterre, Scorers - Ian Lake [25], Shashi Isaac [57] for Newtown • 2nd leg. 16-06-2012, Warner Park, Basseterre. Scorers - Alexis Saddler [4], Ian Lake [80] for Newtown

MEDALS TABLE

	Overall G	Lge G	Cup G	Town
1 Newtown United	18	16	2	Basseterre
2 Village Superstars	9	6	3	Basseterre
3 Garden Hotspurs	4	4		Basseterre
4 St Pauls United	3	2	1	Basseterre
5 Cayon Rockets	2	1	1	Cayon

SKNFA CUP 2012

Round of 16		Quarter-finals		Semi-finals	Final	
St Pauls United	0 3p					
Conaree	0 1p	**St Pauls United**	0 4p			
SPD United	1 1p	Garden Hotspurs	0 2p			
Garden Hotspurs	1 4p			**St Pauls United**		
Newton Ground	2			Village Superstars		
National U-16	1	Newton Ground	0			
Lodge Patriots	0	**Village Superstars**	5			
Village Superstars	3				**St Pauls United**	2
St Thomas Strikers	1 5p				Newtown United	1
Mantab	1 4p	**St Thomas Strikers**	0 4p			
Challengers United	0	Cayon	0 3p			
Cayon	3			St Thomas Strikers		
St Peters Strikers	2			**Newtown United**		
St Peters Juniors	0	St Peters Strikers	1 4p			
Trafalgar Southstars	0	**Newtown United**	1 5p			
Newtown United	4					

CUP FINAL

Warner Park, Basseterre
19-05-2012
Scorers - Javeim Blanchette 2 [46 78] for St Pauls; Zevon Archibald [81] for Newtown

SLE – SIERRA LEONE

FIFA/COCA-COLA WORLD RANKING

'93	'94	'95	'96	'97	'98	'99	'00	'01	'02	'03	'04	'05	'06	'07	'08	'09	'10	'11	'12
76	76	58	84	84	111	120	129	138	133	146	160	163	148	156	116	138	125	60	62

2012

Jan	Feb	Mar	Apr	May	Jun	Jul	Aug	Sep	Oct	Nov	Dec	High	Low	Av
60	64	73	63	61	59	65	57	59	67	61	62	51	172	116

Sierra Leone came within a whisker of qualifying for the 2013 Africa Cup of Nations in South Africa but were held off by errant shooting and some good goalkeeping in their decisive tie against Tunisia in October 2012. The Leone Stars, coached by the Swede Lars-Olaf Mattsson and with an increasingly impressive-looking squad, had been held 2-2 at home by the more fancied Tunisians in the first leg of their final round qualifying tie. But in the return match it was Sierra Leone who dominated proceedings and with a little more fortune would have snatched an unexpected away win and a place in South Africa. They will have to console themselves with the hope of extracting some revenge on the North Africans as they also share the same 2014 FIFA World Cup qualifying group, although the Tunisians will be favourites to claim top spot. Sierra Leone started their campaign by beating the Cape Verde Islands at home and then drawing away against Equatorial Guinea. Domestic league honours went to Diamond Stars, the first provincial side ever to win the country's Premier League title. From Kono, the mineral-rich area of the country from where their name is derived, Diamond Stars were coached by former Sierra Leone international Lamin Bangura.

CAF AFRICA CUP OF NATIONS RECORD

1957-1972 DNE 1974 DNQ 1976 DNE 1978 DNQ 1980 DNE 1982-1984 DNQ 1986 DNE 1988 DNQ
1990 DNE 1992 DNQ **1994** 10 r1 **1996** 12 r1 1998 DNE 2000 Disqualified 2002-2013 DNQ

SIERRA LEONE FOOTBALL ASSOCIATION (SLFA)

21 Battery Street, Kingtom,
PO Box 672, Freetown
☎ +232 22 240071
✉ starssierra@yahoo.com
🌐 slfa.1hwy.com
FA 1967 CON 1967 FIFA 1967
P Alie Forna
GS Abdul Rahman Swaray

THE STADIA

2014 FIFA World Cup Stadia
National Stadium
Freetown   30 000

Other Main Stadia
Bo Stadium
Bo   25 000
Koidu-Sefadu Sports Stadium
Koidu Town   10 500
Wusum Sports Stadium
Makeni   10 000
Kenema Town Field
Kenema

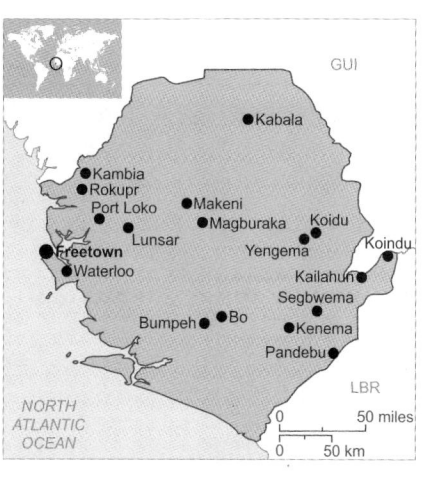

MAJOR CITIES/TOWNS

		Population
1	Freetown	827 985
2	Bo	206 769
3	Kenema	164 125
4	Makeni	99 549
5	Koidu	91 042
6	Lunsar	23 609
7	Port Loko	22 397
8	Pandebu	19 378
9	Kabala	18 616
10	Waterloo	17 469
11	Kailahun	17 210
12	Magburaka	15 770
13	Segbwema	15 714
14	Koindu	15 659
15	Bumpeh	14 825
16	Yengema	13 225
17	Kambia	12 282
18	Goderich	12 178
19	Rokupr	12 166

REPUBLIC OF SIERRA LEONE

Capital	Freetown	Population	6 440 053 (103)	% in cities	38%
GDP per capita	$900 (217)	Area km^2	71 740 km^2 (118)	GMT +/-	0
Neighbours (km)	Guinea 652, Liberia 306 • Coast 402				

RECENT INTERNATIONAL MATCHES PLAYED BY SIERRA LEONE

2010	Opponents	Score	Venue	Comp	Scorers	Att	Referee
5-09	Egypt	D 1-1	Cairo	CNq	Mustapha Bangura [56]		Diatta SEN
10-10	South Africa	D 0-0	Freetown	CNq			Lemghaifry MTN
2011							
9-02	Nigeria	L 1-2	Lagos	Fr	Mohamed Kabia [89]		
27-03	Niger	L 1-3	Niamey	CNq	Mohamed Bangura [11]		
4-06	Niger	W 1-0	Freetown	CNq	Teteh Bangura [50]		
3-09	Egypt	W 2-1	Freetown	CNq	Sheriff Suma [14], Mohamed Bangura [89p]		
8-10	South Africa	D 0-0	Nelspruit	CNq			
2012							
14-01	Angola	L 1-3	Cabinda	Fr	Desmond Wellington [16]	13 000	Dos Santos ANG
29-02	Sao Tome e Principe	L 1-2	Sao Tome	CNq	Alhadji Kamara [55]		Raphael MWI
23-05	Iraq	L 0-1	Istanbul	Fr		200	Ozkahya TUR
2-06	Cape Verde Islands	W 2-1	Freetown	WCq	Mohamed Kamara [11], Sheriff Suma [26]	25 000	Agbovi GHA
9-06	Equatorial Guinea	D 2-2	Malabo	WCq	Samuel Barclay [22], Ibrahim Bangura [25]	4 000	Cordier CHA
16-06	Sao Tome e Principe	W 4-2	Freetown	CNq	Kei Kamara 2 [17 33], Teteh Bangura 2 [21 40]		Lemghaifry MTN
8-09	Tunisia	D 2-2	Freetown	CNq	Sheriff Suma [8], Alhassan Kamara [85]		Abdel Rahman SDN
13-10	Tunisia	D 0-0	Monastir	CNq			Lemghaifry MTN
2-12	Guinea	D 0-0	Conakry	Fr			B Ouerdraogo BFA
15-12	Guinea	D 1-1	Freetown	Fr	Seray Jah [90]		Gueye SEN

Fr = Friendly match • CN = CAF African Cup of Nations • AC = Amilcar Cabral Cup • WC = FIFA World Cup • q = qualifier

SIERRA LEONE NATIONAL TEAM HISTORICAL RECORDS

Coach: Dusan Drasovic MNE 2000 • Christian Cole 2001 • Jose Antonio Nogueira BRA 2003 • John Sherington 2003-06 • Andy Gray ENG 2006 • James Peters 2006-07 • Mohamed Kanu 2007-09 • Daniel Koroma 2009-10 • Christian Cole 2010-11 • Lars-Olof Mattsson SWE 2011-

MEDALS TABLE

		Overall G	Lge G	Cup G	City
1	Mighty Blackpool	14	10	4	Freetown
	East End Lions	14	11	3	Freetown
3	Ports Authority	9	7	2	Freetown
4	Kallon FC (inc Fisheries)	5	4	1	Freetown
5	Real Republicans	4	3	1	Freetown
6	Old Edwardians	3	1	2	Freetown
7	Bai Bureh Warriors	2		2	Port Loko
	Diamond Stars	2	1	1	Kono
	Kamboi Eagles	2		2	Kenema
10	Freetown United	1	1		Freetown
	Wusum Stars	1		1	Bombali

SIERRA LEONE 2012

AFRICELL PREMIER LEAGUE

	Pl	W	D	L	F	A	Pts	Diamond Stars	Kallon FC	East End Lions	Johansen	Kamboi Eagles	Blackpool	Edwardians	Ports Authority	Bo Rangers	Central Parade	Gem Stars	Freetown City	Wusum Stars	Kissy All Stars
Diamond Stars †	26	16	2	8	33	18	50		1-0	0-0	1-0	1-0	1-0	1-2	0-1	1-0	1-0	1-0	2-1	3-0	3-0
Kallon FC	26	13	8	5	27	16	47	1-0		1-0	1-1	1-0	0-0	2-0	0-1	1-0	1-1	0-0	2-0	2-0	2-1
East End Lions	26	10	11	5	28	17	41	1-0	2-2		1-0	3-0	0-1	1-0	1-1	0-0	1-0	1-2	1-2	1-0	1-1
FC Johansen ‡	26	10	11	5	22	17	41	1-0	0-0	2-2		2-1	2-2	1-0	0-0	1-0	2-2	0-0	1-0	1-0	2-1
Kamboi Eagles	26	10	10	6	22	15	40	2-0	2-0	0-0	1-0		2-0	0-1	0-0	1-1	0-0	1-0	0-0	2-0	1-1
Mighty Blackpool	26	8	12	6	21	18	36	2-1	1-1	0-0	1-2	2-0		3-1	0-0	0-1	0-0	1-1	1-0	1-0	1-0
Old Edwardians	26	11	3	12	21	25	36	0-3	1-2	0-0	1-0	0-3	0-0		1-0	2-3	0-1	1-0	2-0	3-0	1-1
Ports Authority	26	8	11	7	20	22	35	1-1	1-3	2-2	0-0	1-1	2-1	0-1		1-1	1-0	1-0	0-2	1-0	1-1
Bo Rangers	26	8	10	8	18	22	34	1-2	0-0	0-4	0-0	0-0	0-1	1-0	0-1		2-1	1-0	0-2	2-1	0-0
Central Parade	26	8	8	10	20	22	32	1-4	1-0	1-0	0-0	0-1	1-1	0-1	2-0	0-1		2-0	0-1	0-0	1-1
Gem Stars	26	7	8	11	19	21	29	0-1	0-1	1-1	1-1	1-1	1-1	2-1	2-0	0-1	1-2		1-0	1-0	1-0
Freetown City	26	7	5	14	19	26	26	1-2	2-1	0-1	0-1	0-1	0-0	0-1	0-0	2-2	1-2	2-1		3-0	0-1
Wusum Stars	26	6	4	16	17	35	22	2-1	1-2	1-3	1-2	0-0	1-0	1-0	2-1	1-1	2-1	0-3	3-0		1-1
Kissy All Stars	26	2	13	11	14	27	19	1-2	0-1	0-1	0-0	1-2	1-1	0-1	1-4	0-0	0-0	0-0	0-0	1-0	

14/12/2011 - 22/07/2012 • † Qualified for the CAF Champions League • ‡ Qualified for the CAF Confederation Cup

SLV – EL SALVADOR

FIFA/COCA-COLA WORLD RANKING

'93	'94	'95	'96	'97	'98	'99	'00	'01	'02	'03	'04	'05	'06	'07	'08	'09	'10	'11	'12
66	80	82	65	64	92	96	83	86	94	95	106	124	156	134	111	78	117	69	103

2012													High	Low	Av
Jan	Feb	Mar	Apr	May	Jun	Jul	Aug	Sep	Oct	Nov	Dec		High	Low	Av
64	54	58	49	49	55	67	64	67	78	94	103		49	169	93

After posting a perfect record in their first round qualifying group for the 2014 FIFA World Cup, El Salvador's campaign hit the buffers in their second round group in which they finished some way behind Mexico and Costa Rica. After the team broke through into the top 50 of the FIFA/Coca-Cola World Ranking for the first time ever in April 2012, on the back of a year of excellent results, there had been real hope of making the final round hexagonal. By the end of the year, however, the Salvadorians were not even in the top 100 and were out of the World Cup. A draw away in Costa Rica in the first match was as good as it got but after failing to beat Guyana at home the game was up. In club football Isidro-Metapan proved to be the team of the year after reaching the final of both championships in 2012. They had finished top in the regular season of both tournaments but lost the first of the two finals to Aguila. At the end of the year Isidro-Metapan met Alianza in the final and, for the second time in three years, beat them on penalties after the match had finished all square at 1-1. At the end of 2011 Isidro-Metapan had become the first club from El Salvador since 2004 to reach the knock-out stage of the CONCACAF Champions League but despite beating Mexico's UNAM 2-1 in the first leg they then lost the second 8-0.

CONCACAF GOLD CUP RECORD

1991 DNQ 1993 DNQ **1996** r1 **1998** r1 2000 DNQ **2002** QF **2003** QF 2005 DNQ **2007** r1 **2009** r1 **2011** QF

FEDERACION SALVADORENA DE FUTBOL (FESFUT)

Avenida José Matias Delgado,
Frente al Centro Español,
Colonia Escalón, Zona 10,
1029 San Salvador
☎ +503 22096200
📠 +503 22637528
✉ jvaliente@fesfut.org.sv
🌐 www.fesfut.org.sv
FA 1935 CON 1961 FIFA 1938
P Carlos Mendez
GS Juan Valiente

THE STADIA

2014 FIFA World Cup Stadia
Estadio Cuscatlán
San Salvador 39 043
Other Main Stadia
Estadio Jorge Magico Gonzalez
San Salvador 35 000
Estadio Oscar Alberto Quinteño
Santa Ana 15 000
Estadio Juan Francisco Barraza
San Miguel 10 000

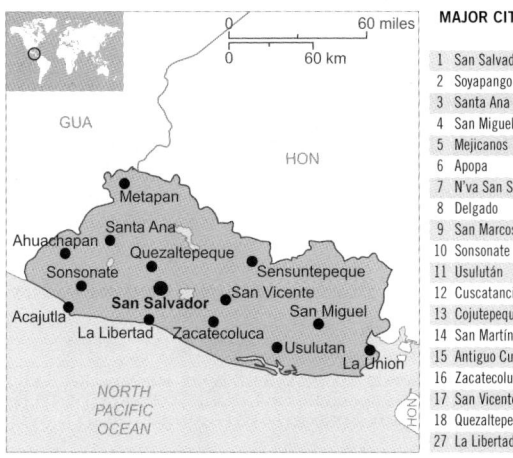

MAJOR CITIES/TOWNS

		Population
1	San Salvador	550 828
2	Soyapango	402 198
3	Santa Ana	189 014
4	San Miguel	174 467
5	Mejicanos	165 652
6	Apopa	136 818
7	N'va San Salvador	131 971
8	Delgado	87 335
9	San Marcos	66 623
10	Sonsonate	63 729
11	Usulután	55 041
12	Cuscatancingo	54 124
13	Cojutepeque	51 348
14	San Martín	48 015
15	Antiguo Cuscatlán	44 829
16	Zacatecoluca	42 234
17	San Vicente	39 742
18	Quezaltepeque	38 348
27	La Libertad	22 890

REPUBLICA DE EL SALVADOR • REPUBLIC OF EL SALVADOR

Capital San Salvador	Population 7 185 218 (99)	% in cities 61%
GDP per capita $6200 (131)	Area km² 21 041 km² (153)	GMT +/- -6
Neighbours (km) Guatemala 203, Honduras 342 • Coast 307		

RECENT INTERNATIONAL MATCHES PLAYED BY EL SALVADOR

2010	Opponents	Score	Venue	Comp	Scorers	Att	Referee
24-02	USA	L 1-2	Tampa	Fr	Rudis Corrales [59]	21 737	Petrescu CAN
3-03	Guatemala	L 1-2	Los Angeles	Fr	Eliseo Quintanilla [89]	10 000	Salazar USA
4-09	Honduras	D 2-2	Los Angeles	Fr	Rodolfo Zelaya 2 [42 90], L 3-4p	15 000	Stoica USA
8-10	Panama	L 0-1	Panama City	Fr		16 175	Ruiz COL
12-10	Costa Rica	L 1-2	Quesada	Fr	Rafael Burgos [53]	4 000	Rodriguez PAN
2011							
14-01	Nicaragua	W 2-1	Panama City	UCr1	Jaime Alas [71], Rafael Burgos [76]	2 000	Quesada CRC
16-01	Belize	W 5-2	Panama City	UCr1	Osael Romero [15], Rafael Burgos 2 [25 46], Jaime Alas [54], Deris Umanzor [59]	1 500	Cerdas CRC
18-01	Panama	L 0-2	Panama City	UCr1		10 000	Garcia MEX
21-01	Honduras	L 0-2	Panama City	UCsf		5 000	Quesada CRC
23-01	Panama	D 0-0	Panama City	UC3p	L 4-5p	2 000	Pineda HON
9-02	Haiti	W 1-0	San Salvador	Fr	Rafael Burgos [14]	15 000	Espana GUA
24-03	Cuba	W 1-0	Havana	Fr	Denis Alas [74]	3 500	Rodriguez PAN
29-03	Jamaica	L 2-3	San Salvador	Fr	Jaime Alas [41], Mark Blanco [90]	15 000	Rodas GUA
29-05	Honduras	D 2-2	Houston	Fr	Rodolfo Zelaya [73], Rudis Corrales [77]	25 380	Villareal USA
5-06	Mexico	L 0-5	Arlington/Dallas	GCr1		80 108	Wijngaarde SUR
9-06	Costa Rica	D 1-1	Charlotte	GCr1	Rodolfo Zelaya [45]	46 012	Marrufo USA
12-06	Cuba	W 6-1	Chicago	GCr1	Rodolfo Zelaya 2 [13 71], William Romero [29], Lester Blanco [69], Arturo Alvarez [84], Eliseo Quintanilla [94+]	62 000	Brizan TRI
19-06	Panama	D 1-1	Washington DC	GCqf	Rodolfo Zelaya [78p], L 3-5p	45 424	Quesada CRC
7-08	Venezuela	W 2-1	Washington DC	Fr			
2-09	Dominican Republic	W 3-2	San Salvador	WCq	Rodolfo Zelaya 2 [54 77], Cristian Bautista [63]	25 272	Rodriguez PAN
6-09	Cayman Islands	W 4-1	Georgetown	WCq	Cristian Bautista [49], Luis Anaya 2 [62 80], Moises Garcia [93+]	2 200	Rodas GUA
7-10	Dominican Republic	W 2-1	San Cristobal	WCq	Osael Romero [37p], Mark Blanco [67]	2 323	Cerdas CRC
11-10	Cayman Islands	W 4-0	San Salvador	WCq	Victor Turcios [6], Steve Purdy [13], Jaime Alas [45], Herbert Sosa [88p]	17 570	Cruz CRC
11-11	Suriname	W 3-1	Paramaribo	WCq	Mark Blanco 2 [21 58], Edwin Sanchez [78]	500	Brea CUB
15-11	Suriname	W 4-0	San Salvador	WCq	Osael Romero 2 [33 62], Rafael Burgos 2 [76 83]	9 659	Santos PUR
2012							
29-02	Estonia	L 0-2	Los Angeles	Fr		16 800	Salazar USA
23-05	New Zealand	D 2-2	Houston	Fr	Rafael Burgos [13], OG [56]	18 000	Vaughn USA
26-05	Moldova	W 2-0	Dallas	Fr		35 000	Ward CAN
2-06	Honduras	L 0-3	Washington DC	Fr		41 780	Salazar USA
8-06	Costa Rica	D 2-2	San Jose	WCq	Jose Gutierrez [23], Osael Romero [53]	23 701	Lopez GUA
12-06	Mexico	L 1-2	San Salvador	WCq	Alfredo Pacheco [64]	29 712	Pineda HON
11-08	Guatemala	W 1-0	Carson/LA	Fr	Nelson Bonilla [28]	18 500	Vaughn USA
15-08	Jamaica	L 0-2	Washington DC	Fr		14 185	Gantar CAN
7-09	Guyana	D 2-2	San Salvador	WCq	Jose Gutierrez [3], Osael Romero [28]	24 000	Marrufo USA
11-09	Guyana	W 3-2	Georgetown	WCq	Osael Romero [13], Jaime Alas [51], Rafael Burgos [77]	4 141	Bogle JAM
12-10	Costa Rica	L 0-1	San Salvador	WCq		35 082	Geiger USA
16-10	Mexico	L 0-2	Torreon	WCq		26 333	Perea PAN

Fr = Friendly match • UC = UNCAF Cup/Copa Centroamericana • GC = CONCACAF Gold Cup • WC = FIFA World Cup • q = qualifier

EL SALVADOR NATIONAL TEAM HISTORICAL RECORDS

Caps
89 - Luis Guevara Mora 1979-96 • **87** - Alfredo Pacheco 2002- • **83** - Marvin Gonzalez 2002- • **81** - Denis Alas 2001- • **78** - Rudis Corrales 1999- • **77** - Ramon Sanchez 2001- • **74** - Guillermo Rivera 1988-2002 • **73** - Jorge Rodriguez 1991-2004 • **71** - Eliseo Quintanilla 2007-

Goals
39 - Raul Diaz Arce 1991-2000 • **22** - Jose Maria Rivas 1979-89 • **21** - Jorge Gonzalez 1976-98 • **17** - Luis Ramirez Zapata 1971-89 & Rudis Corrales 1999- • **16** - Osael Romero 2007; Norberto Huezo 1973-87; Miguel Cruz 1935-43 • **15** - Eliseo Quinanilla 2007- • **13** - Rodolfo Zelaya 2008- ; Juan Francisco Barraza 1953-69 & Ever Hernandez 1976-85 • **12** - Rafael Corado 1943-55 & Gustavo Marroquin 1927-30

Coaches
For El Salvador coaches pre 1991 see Oliver's Almanack 2012 • Oscar Emigdio Benitez 1991 • Jorge Aude URU 1991-92 • Anibal Ruiz URU 1992 • Jorge Vieira BRA 1993-94 • Jose Omar Pastoriza ARG 1995-96 • Armando Contreras 1996-97 • Milovan Doric YUG 1997-98 • Kiril Dojcinovski YUG 1998 • Marinho Peres BRA 1998 • Oscar Emigdio Benitez 1999-2000 • Carlos Recinos 2000-02 • Juan Ramon Paredes 2002-04 • Armando Contreras 2004 • Carlos Cavagnaro ARG 2005 • Miguel Aguilar 2005-06 • Carlos de los Cobos MEX 2006-09 • Jose Luis Rugamas 2010-11 • Ruben Israel URU 2011-12 • Juan Castillo MEX 2012 • Augustin Castillo PER 2012-

EL SALVADOR 2011-12

PRIMERA DIVISION PROFESIONAL CAMPEONATO CLAUSURA

	Pl	W	D	L	F	A	Pts	I-Metapán	Aguila	LA Firpo	FAS	Municipal	Juventud	UES	At. Marte	Alianza	V. Hermosa
CD Isidro-Metapán †	18	10	8	0	34	15	38		4-1	2-1	1-1	1-0	4-1	1-0	1-1	3-0	3-1
CD Aguila †	18	9	2	7	28	18	29	0-1		1-0	2-0	1-0	2-2	1-3	5-0	2-0	5-0
Luis Angel Firpo †	18	7	7	4	30	23	28	2-4	1-1		3-0	1-0	1-0	2-1	0-0	4-4	2-1
Deportivo FAS †	18	6	9	3	24	23	27	1-1	2-0	2-2		2-1	1-0	4-1	1-1	3-0	1-1
Once Municipal	18	7	6	5	25	13	27	0-0	1-0	0-0	5-0		2-1	4-1	0-0	2-1	3-0
Juv'tud Independiente	18	6	7	5	31	24	25	1-1	2-1	0-0	1-1	2-2		5-0	4-2	3-0	2-0
Univ'dad El Salvador	18	5	4	9	24	36	19	1-1	1-0	3-4	1-1	1-1	2-2		0-2	2-1	0-2
Atlético Marte	18	4	5	9	17	29	17	0-2	0-2	0-4	0-1	1-0	1-2	2-1		2-3	4-1
Alianza	18	3	6	9	25	40	15	2-2	1-3	3-3	2-2	1-1	2-1	2-4	1-0		1-2
Vista Hermosa	18	3	6	9	17	34	15	2-2	0-1	1-0	1-1	0-3	2-2	1-2	1-1	1-1	

8/01/2012 - 15/04/2012 • † Qualified for the play-offs

Top scorers: **12** - Nicolas **MUNOZ** PAN, Aguila & Anel **CANALES** PAN, LA Firpo • **10** - Juan Carlos **REYES** URU, Juventud • **7** - Alexander **CAMPOS**, Municipal; Sean **FRASER** JAM, Alianza; Christian **BAUTISTA**, Metapán; Cesar **LARIOS**, UES; Alex **ARAZO**, Juventud & Marvin **MONTERROSA**, Metapán

CLAUSURA PLAY-OFFS

Semi-finals — **Finals**

CD Aguila 4 1
Luis Angel Firpo * 0 2 — CD Aguila 2

Deportivo FAS * 2 0 — CD Isidro-Metapán 1
CD Isidro-Metapán 0 3

* At home in the first leg

CHAMPIONSHIP FINAL CLAUSURA 2012

Cuscatalan, San Salvador, 6-05-2012, Att: 18 506, Ref: Joel Aguilar

CD Aguila 2 Osael Romero [38p], Munoz [70]
CD Isidro-Metapán 1 Ramon Sanchez [78]

Aguila - Benji **VILLALOBOS**• - Luis **ANAYA**, Mardoqueo **HENRIQUEZ**, Glauber **DA SILVA** (Henry **ROMERO**• 17), Deris **UMANZOR** - Darwin **BONILLA** (Rolando **TORRES** 80), Isaac **ZELAYA**, Osael **ROMERO**, Ronald **TORRES** - Irza **SANTOS**• (Irving **FLORES** 59), Nicolas **MUNOZ**. Tr: Victor **COREAS**
I-Metapán - Miguel **MONTES**• - Ricardo **ALVARADO** (Julio **MARTINEZ** 54), Alexander **ESCOBAR**, Milton **MOLINA**, Alfredo **PACHECO**• - Omar **MEJIA**, Marvin **MONTERROSA** (Christian **BAUTISTA** 54), Ramon **SANCHEZ**•, Edwin **SANCHEZ** - Lester **BLANCO**, Allan **KARDECK**• (Leonardo **DA SILVA** 67). Tr: Edwin **PORTILLO**

EL SALVADOR 2012-13

PRIMERA DIVISION PROFESIONAL TORNEO APERTURA

	Pl	W	D	L	F	A	Pts	I-Metapán	Alianza	FAS	Aguila	LA Firpo	A. Marte	Santa Tecla	UES	Juventud	Municipal
CD Isidro-Metapán †	18	11	3	4	37	25	36		1-0	2-1	3-2	1-0	1-0	1-1	1-2	1-1	5-0
Alianza †	18	10	4	4	36	19	34	0-2		3-2	0-2	1-1	2-1	7-1	1-1	2-0	2-0
Deportivo FAS †	18	9	6	3	27	15	33	4-1	2-1		0-0	1-1	2-0	4-1	0-0	1-0	1-0
CD Aguila †	18	9	4	5	29	19	31	1-2	0-3	1-1		3-2	1-3	0-0	2-1	3-0	3-0
Luis Angel Firpo	18	7	4	7	26	24	25	4-2	0-2	1-0	0-1		0-2	2-0	3-2	2-3	4-2
Atlético Marte	18	7	2	9	28	25	23	4-1	0-2	1-2	0-1	2-1		3-2	1-1	2-3	5-1
Santa Tecla	18	5	6	7	24	33	21	2-2	2-2	2-2	1-3	0-1	0-0		3-0	1-0	4-0
Univ'dad El Salvador	18	4	8	6	20	26	20	1-4	3-3	0-0	1-0	0-0	1-0	0-1		2-2	2-1
Juv'tud Independiente	18	4	7	7	27	34	19	1-4	0-3	0-1	2-2	1-1	4-3	5-1	1-1		3-3
Once Municipal	18	1	2	15	16	50	5	1-3	1-2	1-3	0-4	1-3	0-1	1-2	3-2	1-1	

14/07/2012 - 25/11/2012 • † Qualified for the play-offs

Top scorers (inc play-offs): **14** - Nicolas **MUNOZ** PAN, Isidro-Metapán • **13** - Sean **FRASER** JAM, Alianza • **9** - Cesar **LARIOS**, UES

APERTURA PLAY-OFFS

Semi-finals — **Finals**

CD Isidro-Metapán 2 3
CD Aguila * 1 2 — CD Isidro-Metapán 1 5p

Deportivo FAS * 1 0 — Alianza 1 4p
Alianza 1 0

* At home in the first leg

FINAL PENALTIES
Alianza first; Isidro-Metapán second
Castillo ✓; Pacheco ✓; Albarran ✗[1]; Martinez ✗[1]; Torres ✓;
Sanchez ✓; Veliz ✓; Munoz ✓; Flores ✓; Quintanilla ✓;
Montes ✗[1]; Molina ✓ (1 = saved)

CHAMPIONSHIP FINAL APERTURA 2012

Cuscatalan, San Salvador, 16-12-2012, Att: 20 359, Ref: Joel Aguilar

CD Isidro-Metapán 1 5p Munoz [106]
Alianza 1 4p Fraser [110]

I-Metapán - Fidel **MONDRAGON** - Luis **PERLA**• (Julio **MARTINEZ** 90), Milton **MOLINA**, Ernesto **AQUINO**, Alfredo **PACHECO** - Paolo **SUAREZ**•, Omar **MEJIA**•, Ramon **SANCHEZ**•, Jose **PERAZA** (Eliseo **QUINTANILLA** 46) - Cristian **BAUTISTA** (Jorge **RAMIREZ** 73), Nicolas **MUNOZ**. Tr: Edwin **PORTILLO**
Alianza - Miguel **MONTES** - Danny **TORRES**•, Jonathan **BARRIOS**••♦90, Ramon **MARTINEZ**, Carlos **AREVALO** - Rudy **VALENCIA**, Roberto **MARADIAGA** (Arturo **ALBARRAN** 21), Elman **RIVAS**• (Emerson **VELIZ** 72), Christian **CASTILLO** - Rodolfo **ZELAYA** (Odir **FLORES** 97), Sean **FRASER**•. Tr: Ramiro **CEPEDA**

EL SALVADOR 2011-12
PRIMERA DIVISION
AGGREGATE TABLE

	Pl	W	D	L	F	A	Pts
CD Isidro-Metapán	36	21	11	4	66	36	74
Deportivo FAS	36	15	14	7	48	40	59
CD Aguila	36	17	7	12	62	43	58
Once Municipal	36	15	12	9	54	32	57
Luis Angel Firpo	36	15	12	9	61	50	57
Juv'tud Independiente	36	11	9	16	49	54	42
Atlético Marte	36	10	10	16	38	50	40
Alianza	36	9	12	15	43	57	39
Univ'dad El Salvador	36	7	12	17	39	65	33
Vista Hermosa	36	4	13	19	28	59	25

MEDALS TABLE

		Overall			Lge		Cup		Cent Am			Town/City
		G	S	B	G	B	G	S	G	S	B	
1	Deportivo FAS	18	18		17	18			1			Santa Ana
2	CD Aguila	17	10		15	9	1	1	1			San Miguel
3	Alianza FC	10	10	2	9	10			1		2	San Salvador
4	CD Luis Angel Firpo	9	11		9	10	1					Usulután
5	CD Atlético Marte	8	1		8					1		San Salvador
6	AD Isidro Metapán	7	2		7	2						Metapán
7	Once Municipal	3	5		2	5	1					Ahuachapán
8	Hércules	3			3							San Salvador
9	Juventud Olimpica	2	5		2	5						Sonsonate
10	CD Dragon	2	2		2	2						San Miguel
11	CD 33	2			2							San Salvador
	Quequeisque	2			2							La Libertad
13	Chacarita Juniors (Chinamega)	1	1		1	1						San Miguel
	CD Santiagueño	1	1		1	1						Santiago de Maria
	CD Atlético Balboa	1	1			1	1					La Unión
	Libertad FC	1	1		1	1						San Salvador
	San Salvador FC	1	1		1	1						San Salvador
18	CD Platense Municipal	1			1							Zacatecoluca
	CD Vista Hermosa	1			1							Gotera
20	Independiente Nacional		3			2	1					San Vicente
21	Atlante		2			2						
	Excelsior		2			2						Santa Ana
	Municipal Limeño		2			2						Santa Rosa de Lima
	Chalatenango (ex Alacranes)		2			2						Chalatenango
25	Cojutepeque		1			1						Cojutepeque
	El Transito		1			1						La Libertad
	Ferrocarril		1			1						Sonsonate
	Leones		1			1						San Salvador
	Maya		1			1						Quezaltepeque
	Nequepio		1			1						Cuscatlán
	Universidad		1			1						

SMR – SAN MARINO

FIFA/COCA-COLA WORLD RANKING

'93	'94	'95	'96	'97	'98	'99	'00	'01	'02	'03	'04	'05	'06	'07	'08	'09	'10	'11	'12
121	131	951	165	173	179	150	168	158	160	162	164	155	194	197	201	203	203	206	2007

2012

Jan	Feb	Mar	Apr	May	Jun	Jul	Aug	Sep	Oct	Nov	Dec	High	Low	Av
206	205	205	205	205	206	205	206	206	207	207	207	118	207	171

By losing to Montenegro in November 2012, San Marino became the first nation to lose 50 consecutive international matches and there is little to suggest that this sequence will end any time soon. They did, however, manage to score twice in a 3-2 defeat in a friendly against Malta in August, a game in which they managed to take the lead for only the third time in their 118-game history - the others being against Liechtenstein in 2004 and against England in 1993. It was a match that also saw Manuel Marani become only the second player to score more than one goal for the national team, following in the footsteps of Andy Selva. There were no goals to celebrate in the four 2014 FIFA World Cup qualifiers played in 2012, stretching their run of competitive internationals without a goal to 22. At home there was a first league title for Tre Penne who came through the world's most complicated championship-deciding mechanism to defeat Libertas 1-0 in the final, having previously lost to them in an earlier knock-out round. Tre Penne had lost in the final in both 2010 and 2011 and it was a late strike by Matteo Valli that proved third time lucky for them. La Fiorita were the season's other winners, beating Pennarossa 3-2 in the Coppa Titano final to secure their first trophy since 1990 and their first cup triumph since 1986.

UEFA EUROPEAN CHAMPIONSHIP RECORD
1960-1988 DNE **1992-2012** DNQ

FEDERAZIONE SAMMARINESE GIUOCO CALCIO (FSGC)

Strada di Montecchio 17, 47890 San Marino
+378 054 9990515
+378 054 9992348
fsgc@omniway.sm
www.fsgc.sm
FA 1931 CON 1988 FIFA 1988
P Giorgio Crescentini
GS Luciano Casadei

MAJOR CITIES/TOWNS

		Population
1	Serravalle	9 894
2	Borgo Maggiore	6 058
3	San Marino	4 433
4	Domagnano	2 872
5	Fiorentino	2 250
6	Acquaviva	1 914
7	Murata	1 580
8	Faetano	1 175
9	Chiesanuova	1 042
10	Montegiardino	837

THE STADIA
2014 FIFA World Cup Stadia
Stadio Olimpico
Serravalle   7 000
Other Main Stadia
The Stadio Olimpico is the only stadium in San Marino

REPUBBLICA DI SAN MARINO • REPUBLIC OF SAN MARINO

Capital	San Marino	Population	30 324 (212)	% in cities	94%
GDP per capita	$41 900 (19)	Area km²	61 km² (228)	GMT +/−	+1
Neighbours (km)	Italy 39				

RECENT INTERNATIONAL MATCHES PLAYED BY SAN MARINO

2006	Opponents	Score	Venue	Comp	Scorers	Att	Referee
16-08	Albania	L 0-3	Serravalle	Fr		700	Zammit MLT
6-09	Germany	L 0-13	Serravalle	ECq		5 090	Dereli TUR
7-10	Czech Republic	L 0-7	Liberec	ECq		9 514	Aliyev AZE
15-11	Republic of Ireland	L 0-5	Dublin	ECq		34 018	Isaksen FRO
2007							
7-02	Republic of Ireland	L 1-2	Serravalle	ECq	Manuel Marani [86]	3 294	Rasmussen DEN
28-03	Wales	L 0-3	Cardiff	ECq		18 752	Tchagharyan ARM
2-06	Germany	L 0-6	Nuremberg	ECq		43 967	Asumaa FIN
22-08	Cyprus	L 0-1	Serravalle	ECq		552	Janku ALB
8-09	Czech Republic	L 0-3	Serravalle	ECq		3 412	Filipovic SRB
12-09	Cyprus	L 0-3	Nicosia	ECq		1 000	Kulbakov BLR
13-10	Slovakia	L 0-7	Dubnica n. Vahom	ECq		2 576	Wilmes LUX
17-10	Wales	L 1-2	Serravalle	ECq	Andy Selva [73]	1 182	Zammit MLT
21-11	Slovakia	L 0-5	Serravalle	ECq		538	Sipailo LVA
2008							
10-09	Poland	L 0-2	Serravalle	WCq		2 374	Zografos GRE
11-10	Slovakia	L 1-3	Serravalle	WCq	Andy Selva [45]	1 037	Kever SUI
15-10	Northern Ireland	L 0-4	Belfast	WCq		12 957	Kari FIN
19-11	Czech Republic	L 0-3	Serravalle	WCq		1 318	Kaasik EST
2009							
11-02	Northern Ireland	L 0-3	Serravalle	WCq		1 942	Stankovic SRB
1-04	Poland	L 0-10	Kielce	WCq		15 200	Kulbakou BLR
6-06	Slovakia	L 0-7	Bratislava	WCq		6 652	Efong Nzolo BEL
12-08	Slovenia	L 0-5	Maribor	WCq		4 400	Meckarovski MKD
9-09	Czech Republic	L 0-7	Uherske Hradiste	WCq		8 121	Amirkhanyan ARM
14-10	Slovenia	L 0-3	Serravalle	WCq		1 745	Szabo HUN
2010							
3-09	Netherlands	L 0-5	Serravalle	ECq		4 127	Evans WAL
7-09	Sweden	L 0-6	Malmo	ECq		21 083	McKeon IRL
8-10	Hungary	L 0-8	Budapest	ECq		10 596	Kaasik EST
12-10	Moldova	L 0-2	Serravalle	ECq		714	Courtney NIR
17-11	Finland	L 0-8	Helsinki	ECq		8 192	Matejek CZE
2011							
9-02	Liechtenstein	L 0-1	Serravalle	Fr		147	Banti ITA
3-06	Finland	L 0-1	Serravalle	ECq		1 218	Sipailo LVA
7-06	Hungary	L 0-3	Serravalle	ECq		1 915	Radovanovic MNE
10-08	Romania	L 0-1	Serravalle	Fr		3 000	Rocchi ITA
2-09	Netherlands	L 0-11	Eindhoven	ECq		35 000	Liany ISR
6-09	Sweden	L 0-5	Serravalle	ECq		2 946	McLean SCO
11-10	Moldova	L 0-4	Chisinau	ECq		6 534	Reinert FRO
2012							
14-08	Malta	L 2-3	Serravalle	Fr	Manuel Marani [7], Danilo Rinaldi [93+p]		Tagliavento ITA
11-09	Montenegro	L 0-6	Serravalle	WCq		1 947	Doyle IRL
12-10	England	L 0-5	London	WCq		86 645	Mazeika LTU
16-10	Moldova	L 0-2	Serravalle	WCq		736	Panayi CYP
14-11	Montenegro	L 0-3	Podgorica	WCq		7 158	Szabo HUN

Fr = Friendly match • EC = UEFA EURO 2008/2012 • WC = FIFA World Cup • q = qualifier

SAN MARINO NATIONAL TEAM HISTORICAL RECORDS

Caps: **69** - Damiano Vannucci 1996- • **59** - Andy Selva 1998- • **58** - Simone Bacchiocchi 1997- • **48** - Mirco Gennari 1992-2003 • **47** - Paolo Montagna 1995- • **44** - Ivan Matteoni 1990-2003

Goals: **8** - Andy Selva 1998- • **2** - Manuel Mariani 2003-

Coaches: Giorgio Leoni 1990-95 • Massimo Bonini 1996-98 • Giampaolo Mazza 1998-

SAN MARINO 2011-12

CAMPIONATO SAMMARINESE DI CALCIO

Group A

	Pl	W	D	L	F	A	Pts	Libertas	Cosmos	Faetano	Pennarossa	Murata	S. Giovanni	Cailungo	Domagnano	Tre Fiori	La Fiorita	Tre Penne	Virtus	Fiorentino	Juvenes/D	Folgore
Libertas †	21	10	9	2	37	24	39		1-1	2-2	1-0	3-1	2-1	2-1	2-0	2-2		0-3	1-0		2-2	
Cosmos †	21	10	5	6	29	23	35	1-1		1-0	2-1	1-3	1-0	1-0	2-2	1-1	1-2	1-2	1-0	3-0	2-4	
Faetano †	21	10	3	8	32	34	33	2-1	0-4		2-0	1-2	2-1	0-2	2-0		2-0				1-2	
Pennarossa	21	9	3	9	25	28	30	1-3	1-0	2-3			1-0	1-1	4-2	1-0			0-1	1-2		
Murata	21	9	3	9	30	32	30	2-2	3-1	1-1	0-1		1-2	1-2	1-0	0-4			1-2		3-2	1-0
San Giovanni	21	5	7	9	32	29	22	2-2	1-2	1-2	1-2	1-3		1-1	6-0			2-0	0-1	2-1		2-3
Cailungo	21	4	7	10	21	29	19	0-1	1-2	2-2	1-2	0-1	1-1		1-1	0-2		0-1	2-1			3-2
Domagnano	21	2	3	16	11	45	9	0-3	0-1	0-5	2-1	0-5	0-3	2-0			0-2			0-1	1-1	1-2

Group B

	Pl	W	D	L	F	A	Pts															
Tre Fiori †	20	15	4	1	44	14	49			4-1	1-1		0-0		3-1		3-0	3-1	2-3	2-1	3-1	2-0
La Fiorita †	20	12	5	3	42	20	41	0-0		4-0	3-0	2-2	1-1		1-2			1-0	2-1	1-1	2-2	3-1
Tre Penne †	20	11	3	6	37	24	36			2-0		1-1			2-1	1-2	1-3		2-2	6-2	0-0	2-0
Virtus	20	9	3	8	25	25	30			0-2	0-1				1-0	0-2	2-5	3-1		2-1	2-0	2-0
Fiorentino	20	8	3	9	30	33	27	0-3		7-0		4-0		1-1		0-2	0-7	2-3	0-0		1-0	1-0
Juvenes/Dogana	20	3	9	8	23	31	18				1-1		2-2	0-0		0-1	1-2	0-4	2-2	0-1		1-1
Folgore/Falciano	20	2	3	15	14	41	9	3-3	0-0	0-2	1-3					0-3	0-1	1-4	0-1	0-4	0-2	

17/09/2011 - 20/04/2012 • † Qualified for the play-offs • Top scorers (inc play-offs): 11 - Cristian **MENIN**, Cosmos & Simon **PARMA**, La Fiorita

PLAY-OFFS WINNERS BRACKET

Libertas	Bye				
		Libertas	1	5p	
		Tre Fiori	1	3p	
Tre Fiori	Bye			Libertas	1 3p
Faetano	1 4p			Tre Penne	1 2p
La Fiorita	1 2p	Faetano	1		
Cosmos	1	Tre Penne	2		
Tre Penne	4	Losing teams drop down to the losers bracket			

FINAL

Olimpico, Serravalle
29-05-2012, Ref: Casanova
Scorer - Valli [79] for Tre Penne

Tre Penne †	1
Libertas ‡	0

† Qualified for the UEFA Champions League • ‡ Qualified for the Europa League

PLAY-OFFS LOSERS BRACKET

Teams losing in the losers bracket are eliminated having lost twice overall

				Tre Penne	2
				Tre Fiori	1
			Tre Fiori	0 6p	Tre Penne qualify to meet Libertas in
			Cosmos	0 5p	the final • Tre Fiori qualified for the
	Cosmos	2			Europa League
	Faetano	1			
Cosmos	1				
La Fiorita	0				

COPPA TITANO 2011-12

Quarter–finals		Semi–finals		Final	
La Fiorita	4				
Juvenes/Dogana	0	La Fiorita	1		
Cosmos	0	Libertas	0		
Libertas	3			La Fiorita	3
Murata	2 7p			Pennarossa	2
Tre Penne	2 6p	Murata	0	Olimpico, 2-05-2012
Folgore	1	Pennarossa	2	Scorers - Bollini.G [42], Parma [45], Fucili [88] for Fiorita; Rosti [51], Conti [94+] for Pennarossa
Pennarossa	2				

MEDALS TABLE

		Overall	Lge	Cup
		G	G	G
1	Tre Fiori	13	7	6
2	Domagnano	12	4	8
3	Libertas	11	1	10
4	Faetano	6	3	3
	Murata	6	3	3
	Tre Penne	6	1	5
7	Cosmos	5	1	4
	Juvenes	5		5
9	La Fiorita	4	2	2
10	Folgore Falciano	3	3	
	Pennarossa	3	1	2
12	Dogana	2		2
	Juvenes/Dogana	2		2
14	Fiorentino	1	1	

SOL – SOLOMON ISLANDS

FIFA/COCA-COLA WORLD RANKING

'93	'94	'95	'96	'97	'98	'99	'00	'01	'02	'03	'04	'05	'06	'07	'08	'09	'10	'11	'12
149	163	170	171	130	128	144	130	134	142	156	130	140	160	123	163	172	177	180	150

2012												High	Low	Av
Jan	Feb	Mar	Apr	May	Jun	Jul	Aug	Sep	Oct	Nov	Dec			
180	182	182	184	183	183	174	159	153	141	150	150	120	184	150

The Solomon Islands were given the hosting rights for the 2012 OFC Nations Cup after the event was taken away from Fiji but they could not make the most of home advantage and failed to win the title for the first time. A 1-0 win in their opening match at the Lawson Tama Stadium in the capital Honiara was the only match won by the team in the five played at the tournament. Draws against Fiji and New Zealand saw them through to the semi-finals and with their fans dreaming of an appearance at the 2013 FIFA Confederations Cup in Brazil they were brought down to earth by surprise package Tahiti who beat them 1-0 to deny the Solomons a place in the final. They then lost 4-3 to New Zealand in the third-place play-off but it was enough to see them through to the final round of qualiying for the 2014 FIFA World Cup. The Solomon Islands gained revenge over Tahiti in the opening match of the group but then lost the following three games to rule out any hopes of making it to the finals in Brazil. In club football Solomon Warriors won both the Telekom S-League and the knock-out S-League Championship which saw them qualify automatically for the 2012-13 OFC Champions League where they will hope to improve on the performance of Koloale who finished bottom of their group in the 2011-12 tournament.

FIFA WORLD CUP RECORD
1930-1990 DNE **1994-2014** DNQ

SOLOMON ISLANDS FOOTBALL FEDERATION (SIFF)

Allan Boso Complex,
Ranadi Highway,
PO Box 854,
Honiara
☎ +677 26496
📠 +677 26497
✉ malufurai@yahoo.com.au
🌐 www.siff.com.sb
FA 1978 CON 1988 FIFA 1988
P Martin Alufurai
GS Neil Poloso

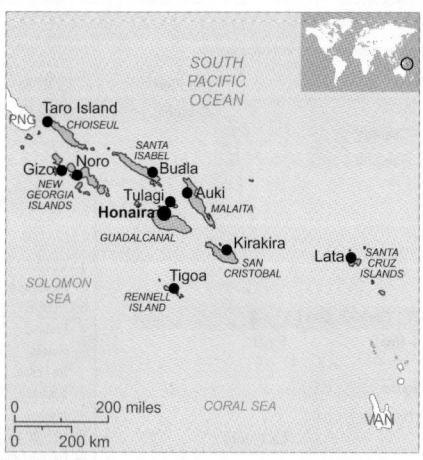

MAJOR CITIES/TOWNS

		Population
1	Honiara	66 824
2	Gizo	6 608
3	Auki	4 455
4	Noro	3 482
5	Buala	2 909
6	Tulagi	1 687
7	Kirakira	1 247
8	Lata	616
9	Taro Island	556
10	Tigoa	243

THE STADIA
2014 FIFA World Cup Stadia
Lawson Tama Stadium
Honiara 10 000
Other Main Stadia
Lawson Tama is the only major stadium used for football

SOLOMON ISLANDS

Capital	Honiara	Population	595 613 (166)	% in cities	18%
GDP per capita	$2700 (169)	Area km²	28 896 km² (143)	GMT +/-	+11
Neighbours (km)	Coast 5313				

RECENT INTERNATIONAL MATCHES PLAYED BY THE SOLOMON ISLANDS

2011	Opponents	Score	Venue	Comp	Scorers	Att	Referee
7-07	Vanuatu	W 2-1	Honiara	Fr	Lui [61], Totori [64]		
9-07	Vanuatu	D 0-0	Honiara	Fr			
27-07	Vanuatu	D 0-0	Port Vila	Fr			
30-07	Vanuatu	L 0-2	Port Vila	Fr			
27-08	Guam	W 7-0	Noumea	PGr1	Fa'arado 2 [11, 22], Totori 3 [24, 41p, 89], Nawo [72], Paia [86]		Varman FIJ
30-08	American Samoa	W 4-0	Noumea	PGr1	Totori [8], Bule [14], Lui 2 [28, 34]		Jacques TAH
1-09	Vanuatu	L 0-1	Noumea	PGr1			Zitouni TAH
3-09	Tuvalu †	W 6-1	Noumea	PGr1	Totori 2 [15, 41p], Lui [23], Naka 2 [37, 46], Faisi [91+]		Jacques TAH
5-09	New Caledonia	W 2-1	Noumea	PGr1	Nawo [66], Naka [79]		Kerr NZL
7-09	Fiji	W 2-1	Lifou	PGsf	Nawo [77], Fa'arodo [93p]		Jacques TAH
9-09	New Caledonia	L 0-2	Noumea	PGf			Kerr NZL
2012							
2-06	Papua New Guinea	W 1-0	Honiara	OCr1	Totori [5]	15 000	Hauata TAH
4-06	Fiji	D 0-0	Honiara	OCr1		12 000	Zitouni TAH
6-06	New Zealand	D 1-1	Honiara	OCr1	Totori [56]	18 000	Hauata TAH
8-06	Tahiti	L 0-1	Honiara	OCsf		15 000	O'Leary NZL
10-06	New Zealand	L 3-4	Honiara	OC3p	Teleda [48], Totori 2 [54, 87]	10 000	O'Leary NZL
7-09	Tahiti	W 2-0	Honiara	WCq	Faarodo [17], Teleda [60]	22 000	Cross NZL
11-09	New Zealand	L 1-6	Auckland	WCq	Faarodo [51]	7 931	Billon NCL
12-10	New Caledonia	L 2-6	Honiara	WCq	Tanito [33], Nawo [59]	8 000	O'Leary NZL
16-10	New Caledonia	L 0-5	Noumea	WCq		4 000	Zitouni TAH

Fr = Friendly match • OC = OFC Oceania Nations Cup • SP = South Pacific Games • WC = FIFA World Cup
q = qualifier • r1 = first round group • f = final • † Not a full international

SOLOMON ISLANDS NATIONAL TEAM HISTORICAL RECORDS

Past Coaches: Edward Ngara 1995-96 • Wilson Maelaua 1996 • Alexander Napa 1998 • George Cowie SCO 2000-03 • Alan Gillett ENG 2004-05 • Airton Andrioli BRA • Jacob Moli 2010-

SOLOMON ISLANDS 2012

TELEKOM S-LEAGUE

	Pl	W	D	L	F	A	Pts	Warriors	Western Utd	Koloale	Kakamora	Malaita	Kossa	Hana	Marist Fire
Solomon Warriors †	14	11	1	2	41	11	34		0-1	2-1	3-0	3-0	5-2	3-0	4-0
Western United	14	10	1	3	33	22	31	0-2		0-2	4-2	1-0	4-2	3-1	2-1
Koloale	14	8	3	3	54	20	27	3-3	4-1		2-3	3-1	7-1	5-0	1-1
Real Kakamora	14	7	0	7	22	29	21	0-1	1-2	0-6		1-0	2-3	2-1	3-2
Malaita Kingz	14	4	3	7	19	23	15	2-1	1-3	2-2	2-1		1-3	1-0	5-0
Kossa	14	4	2	8	29	41	14	0-2	2-4	4-2	0-1	3-3		1-4	4-1
Hana	14	3	2	9	22	44	11	0-3	2-6	2-8	3-5	1-1	3-2		3-2
Marist Fire	14	1	4	9	16	46	7	2-9	2-2	2-2	0-8	0-1	1-0	2-2	

23/10/2011 - 25/04/2012 • † Qualified for the OFC Champions League play-off

S-LEAGUE CHAMPIONSHIP 2012

Quarter-finals		Semi-finals		Final	
Solomon Warriors	11 7				
Marist Fire	2 2	**Solomon Warriors**	4		
Koloale	1 3	Kossa	2		
Kossa	4 0			**Solomon Warriors** †	2
Real Kakamora	4 1			Western United	0
Malaita Kingz	0 4	Real Kakamora	1	Lawson Tama, Honiara	
Hana	0 1	**Western United**	3	12-08-2012	
Western United	8 2	† Qualified for the OFC Champions League play-off			

SOM – SOMALIA

FIFA/COCA-COLA WORLD RANKING

'93	'94	'95	'96	'97	'98	'99	'00	'01	'02	'03	'04	'05	'06	'07	'08	'09	'10	'11	'12
-	159	165	178	187	190	197	194	197	190	191	193	184	193	195	200	170	182	189	195

2012

Jan	Feb	Mar	Apr	May	Jun	Jul	Aug	Sep	Oct	Nov	Dec	High	Low	Av
190	191	191	191	191	191	191	190	187	188	193	195	158	203	186

The continuing violence in Somalia took a heavy toll in April 2012 when the Somali Football Federation president Said Mohamed Nur and the head of the country's Olympic Committee, Aden Yabarow Wiish, were both killed in a blast during a ceremony to mark the first anniversary of the launch of Somalia's national television station. It was a huge blow to the burgeoning football federation, which had burst to life again under Nur's dynamism and appetite for work. The year was punctuated by further tragedy, notably the death of several sports media members in a targeted campaign by religious zealots. But the year ended with much hope as FIFA completed the installation of an artificial pitch at the Banadir Stadium in Mogadishu, the traditional home of football in the country. Football officials also continued their attempts to wrestle back control of the larger Mogadishu Stadium, for years now a base for the military intervention forces in the country. It is now occupied by peacekeepers from the African Union but there is the hope it could be used for football again soon. Somalia kept up its determination to continue playing in international competition with participation in the CECACAF Cup where they were heavily beaten. The team lost all three group games and conceded 13 goals in the process.

CAF AFRICA CUP OF NATIONS RECORD
1957-1972 DNE **1976** DNQ **1976** DNE **1978** DNQ **1980-1982** DNE **1984-2010** DNQ **2012-2013** DNE

SOMALI FOOTBALL FEDERATION (SFF)

DHL Mogadishu, BN 03040 Mogadishu

☎ +252 1 216199
📠 +252 1 600601
✉ sofofed@hotmail.com
🌐 www.somsoccer.com
FA 1951 CON 1968 FIFA 1960
P Alisaid Ghuled
GS Abdiqani Said Arab

THE STADIA
2014 FIFA World Cup Stadia
Somalia played their home match in the 2014 FIFA World Cup at the Stade Gouled in Djibouti

Other Main Stadia
Banadir Stadium		
Mogadishu		15 000
Mogadishu Stadium		
Mogadishu		35 000

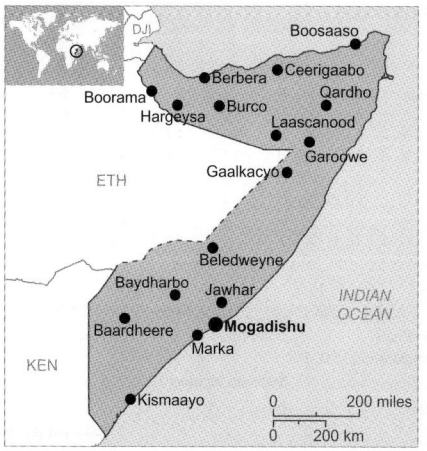

MAJOR CITIES/TOWNS

		Population
1	Mogadishu	1 663 223
2	Hargeysa	443 539
3	Burco	153 988
4	Beledweyne	109 935
5	Boosaaso	109 825
6	Baydhabo	90 138
7	Gaalkacyo	86 680
8	Berbera	72 343
9	Boorama	70 004
10	Kismaayo	68 042
11	Laascaanood	41 259
12	Jawhar	38 421
13	Garoowe	34 251
14	Baardheere	33 518
15	Qardho	28 116
16	Ceerigaabo	25 696
17	Dhusa Harreb	22 746
18	Marka	22 012
19	Wanlaweyn	19 949

JAMHUURIYADA DEMUQRAADIGA SOOMAALIYEED • SOMALIA

Capital	Mogadishu	Population	9 832 017 (83)	% in cities	37%
GDP per capita	$600 (225)	Area km^2	637 657 km^2 (43)	GMT +/-	+3
Neighbours (km)	Djibouti 58, Ethiopia 1600, Kenya 682 • Coast 3025				

SOM – SOMALIA

RECENT INTERNATIONAL MATCHES PLAYED BY SOMALIA

2006	Opponents		Score	Venue	Comp	Scorers	Att	Referee
27-11	Rwanda	L	0-3	Addis Abeba	CCr1			
30-11	Sudan	L	0-3	Addis Abeba	CCr1			
3-12	Uganda	L	0-2	Addis Abeba	CCr1			
21-12	Sudan	L	1-6	Beirut	ARr1	Mohammed Abdulaziz 93+		
24-12	Lebanon	L	0-4	Beirut	ARr1			
27-12	Mauritania	L	2-8	Beirut	ARr1	Abdulaziz Ali 2 26 67		
2007								
16-11	Djibouti	L	0-1	Djibouti	WCq		10 000	Abdul Rahman SUD
10-12	Burundi	L	0-1	Dar es Salaam	CCr1			
12-12	Tanzania	L	0-1	Dar es Salaam	CCr1			
14-12	Kenya	L	0-2	Dar es Salaam	CCr1			
2008								
23-12	Djibouti	W	3-2	Djibouti	Fr	Isse Midnimo, Ali Baashi, Ismail Yusuf		
2009								
1-01	Zanzibar †	L	0-2	Kampala	CCr1			
3-01	Tanzania	W	1-0	Kampala	CCr1	Abshir Cisse 14		
5-01	Rwanda	L	0-3	Kampala	CCr1			
7-01	Uganda	L	0-4	Kampala	CCr1			
29-11	Rwanda	L	0-1	Nairobi	CCr1			
3-12	Zimbabwe †	L	0-2	Nairobi	CCr1			
5-12	Eritrea	L	1-3	Nairobi	CCr1	Mohamed Hassan 70		
2010								
28-11	Burundi	L	0-2	Dar es Salaam	CCr1			
30-11	Tanzania	L	0-3	Dar es Salaam	CCr1			
3-12	Zambia	L	0-6	Dar es Salaam	CCr1			
2011								
1-11	Djibouti	L	0-1	Djibouti	Fr			
12-11	Ethiopia	D	0-0	Djibouti	WCq		3 000	Hassan Ourouke DJI
16-11	Ethiopia	L	0-5	Addis Abeba	WCq		22 000	Kordi TUN
25-11	Burundi	L	1-4	Dar es Salaam	CCr1	Khaled Ali 92+		
28-11	Uganda	L	0-4	Chamazi	CCr1			
1-12	Zanzibar	L	0-3	Dar es Salaam	CCr1			
2012								
25-11	Burundi	L	1-5	Kampala	CCr1	Mohamed Hassan 51p		Kalyango UGA
28-11	Sudan	L	0-1	Kampala	CCr1			Maeruf ERI
1-12	Tanzania	L	0-7	Kampala	CCr1			Kalema UGA

Fr = Friendly match • CC = CECAFA Cup • AR = Arab Cup • WC = FIFA World Cup
q = qualifier • r1 = first round group • † Not a full international

SOMALIA 2012

SFF FIRST DIVISION

	Pl	W	D	L	F	A	Pts	Elman	Heegan	Jeenyo	Banadir	Ports	Sahafi Hotel	Horseed	Badbaado
Elman	13	9	2	2	31	15	29		1-3	1-2	1-1	4-0	2-1	2-0	3-1
Heegan	13	7	4	2	21	14	25	0-3		0-1	3-2	1-1	2-0	1-0	3-1
LLPP Jeenyo	12	5	7	0	17	8	22	1-1	0-0		n/p	n/p	1-1	0-0	4-0
Banadir Telecom	13	3	7	3	17	14	16	1-2	1-1	1-1		1-2	1-0	1-1	2-2
Ports	12	3	5	4	18	20	14	2-3	2-4	1-1	1-1		0-0	n/p	5-1
Sahafi Hotel	13	2	7	4	7	10	13	n/p	0-1	1-1	0-0	0-0		1-1	2-1
Horseed	12	2	5	5	10	15	11	1-3	2-2	1-2	0-2	2-1	0-0		2-0
Badbaado	12	0	1	11	11	36	1	2-5	n/p	1-3	0-3	2-3	0-1	n/p	

4/06/2012 - 25/10/2012

SRB – SERBIA

FIFA/COCA-COLA WORLD RANKING

'93	'94	'95	'96	'97	'98	'99	'00	'01	'02	'03	'04	'05	'06	'07	'08	'09	'10	'11	'12
-	-	-	-	-	-	-	-	-	-	-	-	47	33	27	30	19	23	27	38

2012

Jan	Feb	Mar	Apr	May	Jun	Jul	Aug	Sep	Oct	Nov	Dec	High	Low	Av
27	25	26	32	32	34	37	35	42	33	42	38	13	47	27

Partizan made it five in a row as they cruised to the 2012 league title, winning 26 of their 30 matches during a campaign in which they lost just twice. They finished 12 points ahead of their fierce rivals Red Star but couldn't get past them in the cup when the two met in the semi-finals. Both matches ended in draws with Red Star qualifying for the final thanks to away goals. There they met the already-relegated Borac Cacak who were appearing in their first final and there were no surprises when Red Star won 2-0 to lift the trophy for the 11th time since the break up of Yugoslavia and the 24th time overall. Serbia's stock on the international stage plummeted in 2012 with clubs and the national team posting poor results. Partizan were dumped out of the UEFA Champions League by AEL Limassol of Cyprus while the national team clocked up six games without a win. That sequence was broken by a 6-1 victory over Wales in a 2014 FIFA World Cup qualifier in September 2012 but was followed by a 3-0 defeat at the hands of Belgium in Belgrade which seriously undermined Serbia's hopes of a third consecutive appearance in the finals. Coach Sinisa Mihajlovic, appointed in April 2012, faced the difficult task of inspiring his team to a better second half of the campaign, especially in the crucial games against neighbours Croatia.

UEFA EUROPEAN CHAMPIONSHIP RECORD

1960 2 F **1964** r2 **1968** 2 F **1972** QF **1976** 4 SF (Hosts) **1980** DNQ **1984** 8 r1 **1988** DNQ **1992** Qualified but then suspended
1996 DNE **2000** 8 QF (as Yugoslavia) **2004** DNQ (as Serbia and Montenegro) **2008-2012** DNQ (as Serbia)

FOOTBALL ASSOCIATION OF SERBIA (FSS)

Fudbalski savez Srbije,
Terazije 35, PO Box 263,
11000 Belgrade
+381 11 3234253
+381 11 3233433
office@fss.rs
www.fss.rs
FA 1919 CON 1954 FIFA 1923
P Tomislav Karadzic
GS Zoran Lakovic

THE STADIA

2014 FIFA World Cup Stadia
Stadion Crvena Zvezda
Belgrade 55 538
Karadorde
Novi Sad 19 500

Other Main Stadia
Stadion Partizan
Belgrade 32 710
Stadion Kraj Stare Zelezare
Smederevo 16 656
Gradski Stadion
Subotica 13 000

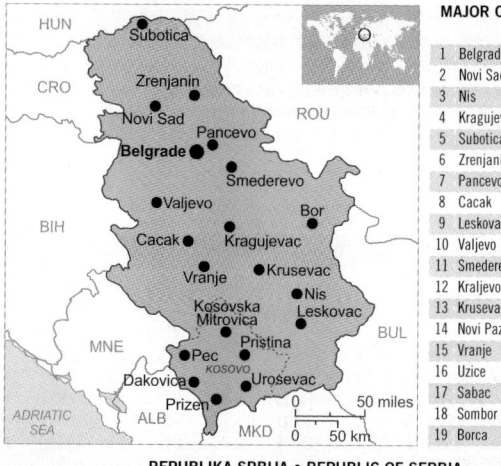

MAJOR CITIES/TOWNS

		Population
1	Belgrade	1 101 752
2	Novi Sad	198 867
3	Nis	172 842
4	Kragujevac	145 292
5	Subotica	99 460
6	Zrenjanin	78 801
7	Pancevo	78 307
8	Cacak	76 488
9	Leskovac	63 455
10	Valjevo	62 754
11	Smederevo	62 473
12	Kraljevo	57 914
13	Krusevac	56 956
14	Novi Pazar	56 873
15	Vranje	56 821
16	Uzice	55 981
17	Sabac	55 124
18	Sombor	52 546
19	Borca	42 841

REPUBLIKA SRBIJA • REPUBLIC OF SERBIA

Capital	Belgrade (Beograd)	Population	7 379 339 (95)	% in cities	52%
GDP per capita	$10 400 (104)	Area km²	77 474 km² (116)	GMT +/-	+1
Neighbours (km)	Bosnia-Herzegovina 302, Bulgaria 318, Croatia 241, Hungary 151, Kosovo 352, Macedonia 62, Montenegro 124, Romania 476				

INTERNATIONAL MATCHES PLAYED BY SERBIA

2010	Opponents	Score	Venue	Comp	Scorers	Att	Referee
7-04	Japan	W 3-0	Osaka	Fr	Mrda 2 [15 23], Tomic [60]	46 270	Choi Myung Yong KOR
29-05	New Zealand	L 0-1	Klagenfurt	Fr		14 000	Drachta AUT
2-06	Poland	D 0-0	Kufstein	Fr		2 000	Drabek AUT
5-06	Cameroon	W 4-3	Belgrade	Fr	Krasic [16], Stankovic [25], Milijas [44p], Pantelic [45]	30 000	Trattou CYP
13-06	Ghana	L 0-1	Pretoria	WCr1		38 833	Baldassi ARG
18-06	Germany	W 1-0	Port Elizabeth	WCr1	Jovanovic [38]	38 294	Undiano ESP
23-06	Australia	L 1-2	Nelspruit	WCr1	Pantelic [84]	37 836	Larrionda URU
11-08	Greece	L 0-1	Belgrade	Fr		10 000	Teixeira ESP
3-09	Faroe Islands	W 3-0	Torshavn	ECq	Lazovic [14], Stankovic [18], Zigic [91+]	1 847	Toussaint LUX
7-09	Slovenia	D 1-1	Belgrade	ECq	Zigic [86]	24 028	Benquerenca POR
8-10	Estonia	L 1-3	Belgrade	ECq	Zigic [60]	12 000	Layushkin RUS
12-10	Italy	L 0-3	Genoa	ECq	Match awarded to Italy. Abandoned after 6'	28 000	Thomson SCO
17-11	Bulgaria	W 1-0	Sofia	Fr	Zigic [80]	1 500	Avram ROU
2011							
9-02	Israel	W 2-0	Tel Aviv	Fr	Tosic [23], Trivunovic [77]	8 000	Nikolaev RUS
25-03	Northern Ireland	W 2-1	Belgrade	ECq	Pantelic [65], Tosic [74]	BCD	Gumienny BEL
29-03	Estonia	D 1-1	Tallinn	ECq	Pantelic [38]	5 185	Nijhuis NED
3-06	Korea Republic	L 1-2	Seoul	Fr	Petrovic [87]	40 000	Albadwawi UAE
7-06	Australia	D 0-0	Melbourne	Fr		28 149	Tojo JPN
10-08	Russia	L 0-1	Moscow	Fr		27 000	Hategan ROU
2-09	Northern Ireland	W 1-0	Belfast	ECq	Pantelic [67]	15 148	Einwaller AUT
6-09	Faroe Islands	W 3-1	Belgrade	ECq	Jovanovic [6], Tosic [22], Kuzmanovic [69]	7 500	Amirkhanyan ARM
7-10	Italy	D 1-1	Belgrade	ECq	Ivanovic [26]	35 000	Proenca POR
11-10	Slovenia	L 0-1	Maribor	ECq		9 848	De Bleeckere BEL
11-11	Mexico	L 0-2	Queretaro	Fr		34 000	Lopez GUA
14-11	Honduras	L 0-2	Honduras	Fr		20 000	Rodas GUA
2012							
28-02	Armenia	W 2-0	Limassol	Fr	Kumanovic [15], Ivanovic [29]	100	Trattos CYP
29-02	Cyprus	D 0-0	Larnaca	Fr		250	Blom NED
26-05	Spain	L 0-2	St Gall	Fr		15 625	Zimmerman SUI
31-05	France	L 0-2	Reims	Fr		18 000	Kircher GER
5-06	Sweden	L 1-2	Solna	Fr	Subotic [27]	20 691	Brych GER
15-08	Republic of Ireland	D 0-0	Belgrade	Fr		7 800	Tudor ROU
8-09	Scotland	D 0-0	Glasgow	WCq		47 369	Eriksson SWE
11-09	Wales	W 6-1	Novi Sad	WCq	Kolarov [16], Tosic [24], Durcic [37], Tadic [55], Ivanovic [80], Sulejmani [90]	10 660	Gomes POR
12-10	Belgium	L 0-3	Belgrade	WCq		21 650	Kralovec CZE
16-10	FYR Macedonia	L 0-1	Skopje	WCq		26 181	Nijhuis NED
14-11	Chile	W 3-1	St Gall	Fr		1 800	Kever SUI

Fr = Friendly match • EC = UEFA EURO 2012 • WC = FIFA World Cup • q = qualifier

SERBIA NATIONAL TEAM HISTORICAL RECORDS

Caps
102 - Savo Milosevic 1994-2008 & Dejan Stankovic 1998- • 84 - Dragan Stojkovic 1983-2001 • 73 - Predrag Mijatovic 1989-2003 • 64 - Slavisa Jokanovic 1991-2002 • 63 - Sinisa Mihajlovic 1991-2003 • 59 - Mladen Krstajic 1999-2008 & Zoran Mirkovic 1995-2003 • 58 - Darko Kovacevic 1994-2004 & Branislav Ivanovic 2005- • 57 - Nikola Zigic 2004- • 56 - Dejan Savicevic 1986-1999
The lists for caps and goals only includes players who have represented Serbia but does include their caps or goals for Yugoslavia if any. The leading cap winner for Yugoslavia was Dragan Dzajic with 85 while the leader goalscorer was Stejpan Bobek with 38

Goals
37 - Savo Milosevic 1994-2008 • 28 - Predrag Mijatovic 1989-2003 • 20 - Nikola Zigic 2004- • 19 - Dejan Savicevic 1986-2003 • 17 - Mateja Kezman 2000-2006 • 15 - Dragan Stojkovic 1983-2001 & Dejan Stankovic 1998- • 11 - Danko Lazovic 2002- & Milan Jovanovic 2007- • 10 - Slavisa Jokanovic 1991-2002; Darko Kovacevic 1994-2004 & Marko Pantelic 2003-

Coaches
Slobodan Santrac 1994-98 • Milan Zivadinovic 1998-99 • Vujadin Boskov 1999-2000 • Ilija Petkovic 2000-01 • Milovan Doric 2001 • Vujadin Boskov, Ivan Curkovic & Dejan Savicevic 2001 • Dejan Savicevic 2001-03 • Ilija Petkovic 2003-06 • Javier Clemente ESP 2006-07 • Miroslav Dukic 2007-08 • Radomir Antic 2008-10 • Vladimir Petrovic 2010-11 • Radovan Curcic 2011-12 • Sinisa Mihajlovic 2012-

SERBIA 2011-12
JELEN SUPERLIGA

	Pl	W	D	L	F	A	Pts	Partizan	Red Star	Vojvodina	Jagodina	Sloboda	Radnicki	Spartak	OFK	Javor	Rad	Hajduk	BSK	Smederevo	Novi Pazar	Borac	Metalac
Partizan Beograd †	30	26	2	2	67	12	**80**		0-1	4-1	4-0	0-0	3-0	2-0	3-0	2-1	1-0	2-0	2-0	3-1	5-0	5-1	1-0
Crvena Zvezda ‡	30	21	5	4	57	18	**68**	0-2		0-2	1-0	1-0	1-1	1-0	3-1	2-0	3-1	3-0	2-0	4-0	3-1	2-0	5-0
Vojvodina Novi Sad ‡	30	14	10	6	44	26	**52**	1-2	2-1		0-0	2-0	1-1	1-1	2-0	1-1	0-2	4-0	2-0	2-0	3-0	3-1	0-0
Jagodina ‡	30	14	9	7	34	20	**51**	0-1	1-3	1-1		1-1	1-0	3-0	2-0	1-0	1-1	0-1	2-0	3-0	1-0	0-0	0-2
Sloboda Uzice	30	15	6	9	42	35	**51**	2-1	1-1	2-2	1-2		2-2	2-0	1-2	1-0	0-2	4-2	0-1	2-1	3-0	2-1	4-1
Radnicki Kragujevac	30	11	14	5	38	27	**47**	0-1	0-0	0-0	0-0	2-1		1-1	1-1	2-0	4-2	0-0	1-1	3-0	3-1	2-0	3-2
Spartak Subotica	30	11	10	9	31	31	**43**	1-2	2-0	5-1	0-4	0-0	0-0		1-1	1-0	0-0	1-1	1-0	4-1	1-0	2-1	0-0
OFK Beograd	30	12	4	14	34	36	**40**	1-2	1-1	1-0	2-0	0-1	1-3	2-3		2-3	2-1	2-3	0-1	1-0	3-0	2-0	2-0
Javor Ivanjica	30	11	6	13	28	32	**39**	0-2	1-3	0-0	0-0	3-1	2-4	1-0	0-0		1-0	2-1	2-0	0-1	1-0	0-2	1-1
Rad Beograd	30	10	7	13	33	31	**37**	1-4	1-2	1-1	1-2	1-2	2-1	1-2	1-0	0-1		3-0	1-1	2-0	0-0	2-1	3-0
Hajduk Kula	30	9	6	15	28	44	**33**	0-2	0-1	1-0	0-2	1-2	0-0	3-1	1-2	1-4	1-0		3-0	3-1	1-0	2-1	0-0
BSK Borca	30	7	9	14	18	39	**30**	0-1	1-4	0-4	0-4	0-2	0-0	2-0	1-0	1-1	1-0	0-0		0-1	2-2	0-0	0-0
FC Smederevo	30	9	2	19	22	42	**29**	0-2	0-1	2-0	1-2	1-2	1-2	1-1	1-0	0-1	0-1	0-0	3-0		2-1	2-0	0-1	1-0
Novi Pazar	30	6	10	14	21	41	**28**	1-1	0-0	1-2	0-0	4-0	0-0	0-2	2-1	1-0	0-3	2-1	1-1	1-0		0-0	1-1
Borac Cacak	30	4	7	19	16	45	**19**	0-4	0-3	0-2	0-0	1-2	3-1	0-1	0-2	1-0	0-0	0-0	0-2	0-1	0-2		0-0
Metalac G. Milanovic	30	2	9	19	14	48	**15**	0-3	0-5	0-3	0-1	0-1	0-1	0-0	0-1	1-2	0-1	1-3	1-2	0-1	1-1	3-2	

13/08/2011 - 20/05/2012 • † Qualified for the UEFA Champions League • ‡ Qualified for the Europa League
Top scorers: **19** - Darko **SPALEVIC**, Radnicki • **13** - Zvonimir **VUKIC**, Partizan • **12** - Savo **KOVACEVIC**, Sloboda • **11** - **CADU** BRA, Crvena Zvezda; Lamine **DIARRA** SEN, Partizan & Nemanja **TOMIC**, Partizan • **10** - Milan **BUBALO**, Hajduk

SERBIA 2011-12
PRVA LIGA TELEKOM SRBIJA (2)

	Pl	W	D	L	F	A	Pts
Radnicki Nis	34	20	7	7	52	28	**67**
Donji Srem	34	16	13	5	34	15	**61**
Mladost Lucani	34	13	14	7	42	27	**53**
Bezanija Novi Beograd	34	11	19	4	33	15	**52**
Indjija	34	14	10	10	35	32	**52**
Napredak Krusevac	34	13	12	9	39	29	**51**
Sloga Kraljevo	34	14	8	12	33	33	**50**
Teleoptik Zemun	34	12	13	9	45	26	**49**
Proleter Novi Sad	34	14	7	13	33	34	**49**
RFK Novi Sad	34	11	10	13	37	42	**43**
Mladenovac	34	11	10	13	46	52	**43**
Kolubara Lazarevac	34	12	7	15	35	43	**43**
Cukaricki Stankom	34	10	11	13	31	39	**41**
Banat Zrenjanin	34	9	14	11	34	41	**41**
Radnicki Sombor	34	11	8	15	25	33	**41**
Mladi R'nik Pozarevac	34	9	9	16	29	38	**36**
Sindelic Nis	34	7	10	17	34	50	**31**
Srem Sremska Mitrovica	34	4	8	22	27	67	**20**

13/08/2011 - 6/06/2012 •

MEDALS TABLE

	Overall	League	Cup	
	G S B	G S B	G S	City/Town
1 Partizan	20 10 1	**13** 7 1	7 3	Belgrade
2 Crvena Zvezda	19 16 2	7 12 2	**12** 4	Belgrade
3 Obilic	1 3 2	1 1 2	2	Belgrade
4 FK Smederevo	1 1 1		1 1 1	Smederevo
5 Zeleznik	1		1 1	Belgrade
6 Vojvodina	5 10	1 10		Novi Sad
7 OFK Beograd	1 2		2	Belgrade
8 Borac Cacak	1			Cacak
Spartak Subotica	1		1	Subotica
Napredak Krusevac	1			Krusevac
Buducnost Dvor	1		1	Banatski Dvor
FK Zemun	1			Belgrade
Sevojno	1			Sevojno
14 Vozdovac Beograd	1		1	Belgrade
Zeta Golubovci	1		1	Podgorica

From 1992, the season after Croatian clubs left the Yugoslav league

SERBIAN CLUBS IN YUGOSLAVIA UNTIL 1991

	Overall	League	Cup	Europe
	G S B	G S B	G S	G S B
1 Crvena Zvedza (Red Star)	31 17 11	**18** 8 7	**12** 8	1 1 4
2 Partizan Beograd	16 14 8	11 9 8	5 4	1
5 OFK Beograd	9 6 5	5 6 4	4	1
8 Vojvodina Novi Sad	2 4 1	2 3 1	1	
10 Yugoslavija Beograd	2 3 3	2 3 3		
17 Nasa Krila Zemun	2		2	
20 FK Radnicki	1 2		2	1
23 FK Bor	1		1	
Spartak Subotica	1		1	
Trepca Mitrovica	1		1	
29 Radnicki Nis		3	2	1
30 Belgrade Select XI	1			1
Vozdovac Beograd	1	1		

LAV KUP SRBIJE 2011-12

First Round

Crvena Zvezda	2
Mladost Lucani *	1
BSK Borca	0
Banat Zrenjanin *	2
Sloboda Uzice *	1 4p
Teleoptik Zemun	1 2p
BASK Beograd	0
FC Smederevo *	1
OFK Beograd	5
Radnicki Nis *	0
Hajduk Kula *	0
Kolubara Lazarevac	1
Metalac G. Milanovic *	3
Srem Sremska Mitrovica	0
Novi Pazar *	0
Partizan Beograd	3
Vojvodina Novi Sad	1
Donji Srem *	0
Sumadija Jagnjilo *	2 5p
Indjija	2 6p
Jagodina	2
Sindelic Nis *	1
RFK Novi Sad	0
Javor Ivanjica *	1
Spartak Subotica	2
Napredak Krusevac *	0
Rad Beograd	0 2p
Radnicki Kragujevac *	0 4p
Proleter Novi Sad	0 5p
Cukaricki Stankom *	0 3p
Radnicki Sombor	1
Borac Cacak *	4

Round of 16

Crvena Zvezda *	1
Banat Zrenjanin	0
Sloboda Uzice *	1 2p
FC Smederevo	1 4p
OFK Beograd *	
Kolubara Lazarevac	
Metalac G. Milanovic	1
Partizan Beograd *	3
Vojvodina Novi Sad	2
Indjija *	1
Jagodina *	1 2p
Javor Ivanjica	1 4p
Spartak Subotica *	1 5p
Radnicki Kragujevac	1 4p
Proleter Novi Sad *	0 1p
Borac Cacak	0 4p

Quarter-finals

Crvena Zvezda *	4
FC Smederevo	0
OFK Beograd *	0
Partizan Beograd	2
Vojvodina Novi Sad *	1
Javor Ivanjica	0
Spartak Subotica	0 2p
Borac Cacak *	0 4p

Semi-finals

Crvena Zvezda *	2 2
Partizan Beograd	0 0
Vojvodina Novi Sad	0 0
Borac Cacak *	0 1

Final

Crvena Zvezda	2
Borac Cacak	0

CUP FINAL

Mladost, Krusevac, 16-05-2012
Att: 11 000, Ref: Milorad Mazic
Scorers - Evandro [40], Borja [85] for Partizan
Red Star - Boban Bajkovic - Nikola Mikic, Nikola Maksimovic, Dusko Tosic, Filip Mladenovic - Srdan Mijailovic - Luka Milivojevic● (Cadu 80), Evandro Goebel - Darko Lazovic, Cristian Borja● (Marko Vesovic 89), Filip Kasalica (Luka Milunovic 78). Tr: Robert Prosinecki
Borac - Nikola Milojevic - Bogdan Milicic●, Aleksandar Ignjatovic●, Sinisa Radanovic, Stevan Reljic - Vasilije Prodanovic● - Stefan Spirovski (William Alves 58), Marko Mugosa (Marko Zocevic 70), Filip Kneznevic, Marko Pavicevic, Jovan Radivojevic (Milos Zivanovic 82). Tr: Slavko Vojicic

* Home team/home team in the 1st leg

SRI – SRI LANKA

FIFA/COCA-COLA WORLD RANKING

'93	'94	'95	'96	'97	'98	'99	'00	'01	'02	'03	'04	'05	'06	'07	'08	'09	'10	'11	'12
126	139	135	126	136	134	153	149	143	139	135	140	144	145	167	163	151	163	180	190

2012

Jan	Feb	Mar	Apr	May	Jun	Jul	Aug	Sep	Oct	Nov	Dec	High	Low	Av
180	182	186	181	184	184	181	179	179	180	182	190	122	190	149

2012 proved to be a rather barren year for Sri Lankan football with both the national team and the clubs suffering from a lack of organised competition. The withdrawal of 2011-12 league champions Ratnam from the qualifying rounds of the AFC President's Cup highlighted the lack of activity internationally but after the finish of the league at the end of February 2012, a new season had yet to get underway by the end of the year. That meant the only competitive action for Sri Lankan clubs came in the Holcim FA Cup. It was won by the Navy team who beat the Army in the final after a penalty shootout following a 1-1 draw. With cricket dominating the sporting landscape, as it does throughout South Asia, the profile of football in Sri Lanka is limited. The national team barely featured at all in the sporting consciousness in 2012 - a 6-0 loss to Malaysia in a friendly in Kuala Lumpur was the only international played and went almost unnoticed. The country's under-22 team did enter the newly created AFC U-22 Asian Cup, taking part in a qualifying group in Saudi Arabia in the middle of the year but they struggled against some of the continent's more advanced federations. Draws against Pakistan and Palestine were the high points in a group that saw the Sri Lankan youngsters lose heavily to Saudi Arabia, Syria and Kyrgyzstan.

FIFA WORLD CUP RECORD
1930-1990 DNE 1994-2014 DNQ

FOOTBALL FEDERATION OF SRI LANKA (FFSL)

100/9 Independence Avenue, Colombo 07

☎ +94 11 2686120
📠 +94 11 2682471
✉ ffsl@srilankafootball.com
🖥 www.srilankafootball.com
FA 1939 CON 1958 FIFA 1950
P Sarath Weerasekera
GS Upali Hewage

THE STADIA
2014 FIFA World Cup Stadia
Sugathadasa Stadium
Colombo 25 000

Other Main Stadia
Kalutara Stadium
Kalutara 15 000
CR & FC Grounds
Colombo 500

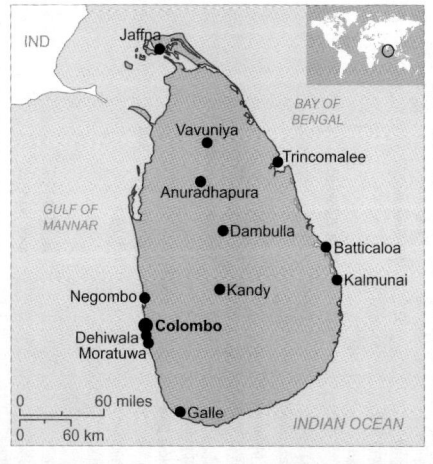

MAJOR CITIES/TOWNS
		Population
1	Colombo	682 046
2	Dehiwala	232 220
3	Moratuwa	202 021
4	Negombo	142 451
5	Trincomalee	131 954
6	Kotte	125 914
7	Kandy	119 186
8	Kalmunai	103 879
9	Vavuniya	101 143
10	Jaffna	98 193
11	Galle	97 209
12	Batticaloa	95 489
13	Katunayaka	90 231
14	Battaramulla	84 200
15	Dambulla	75 290
16	Daluguma	74 129
17	Maharagama	74 117
18	Kotikawatta	71 879
19	Anuradhapura	66 951

SHRI LAMKA • SRI LANKA

Capital	Colombo	Population	21 324 791 (53)	% in cities	15%
GDP per capita	$4400 (150)	Area km²	65 610 km² (121)	GMT +/-	+5.5
Neighbours (km)	Coast 1340				

RECENT INTERNATIONAL MATCHES PLAYED BY SRI LANKA

2009	Opponents	Score		Venue	Comp	Scorers	Att	Referee
28-03	Maldives	D	1-1	Colombo	Fr	Channa Edribandanage [37]		
4-04	Brunei Darussalam	W	5-1	Colombo	CCq	Kasun Weerarathna 4 [23 53 67 73], Moh'd Asmeer [32]	700	Zhao Liang CHN
6-04	Chinese Taipei	W	2-1	Colombo	CCq	Kasun Weerarathna [35], Rohana Ruwan Dinesh [39]	1 400	Al Zahrani KSA
8-04	Pakistan	D	2-2	Colombo	CCq	Rohana Ruwan Dinesh [2], Sanjeev Shanmugarajah [88]	3 000	Tseytlin UZB
22-08	Lebanon	W	4-3	New Delhi	Fr	Moh'd Izzadeen 3 [6 80 88], Chathura Weerasinghe [83]		Rowan IND
24-08	Syria	L	0-4	New Delhi	Fr			Singh IND
26-08	India	L	1-3	New Delhi	Fr	Rohana Ruwan Dinesh [62]		Ali Adil MDV
28-08	Kyrgyzstan	L	1-4	New Delhi	Fr	Chathura Weerasinghe [53]		Singh IND
4-12	Pakistan	W	1-0	Dhaka	SAFr1	Chathura Gunarathna [23]		
6-12	Bhutan	W	6-0	Dhaka	SAFr1	Channa Ediri 2 [7 25], Kasun Weerarathna 3 [39 66 78], Chathura Gunarathna [90]		
8-12	Bangladesh	L	1-2	Dhaka	SAFr1	Channa Ediri [42]		
11-12	Maldives	L	1-5	Dhaka	SAFsf	Channa Ediri [62]		
2010								
16-02	Myanmar	L	0-4	Colombo	CCr1		3 000	Faghani IRN
18-02	Tajikistan	L	1-3	Colombo	CCr1	Philip Dalpethado [78]	1 000	Tan Hai CHN
20-02	Bangladesh	W	3-0	Colombo	CCr1	Mohamed Kaiz [7], Chathura Gunarathna [43], Sanjeev Shanmugarajah [79]	600	Mahapab THA
2011								
27-03	Tajikistan	D	2-2	Colombo	Fr	Kaiz Shafraz [12p], Mohamed Zain [80]		
29-03	Tajikistan	L	0-2	Colombo	Fr			
7-04	Korea DPR	L	0-4	Kathmandu	CCq		2 000	Almarzouq KUW
9-04	Afghanistan	L	0-1	Kathmandu	CCq		1 800	Adday IRQ
11-04	Nepal	D	0-0	Kathmandu	CCq		13 500	Adday IRQ
29-06	Philippines	D	1-1	Colombo	WCq	Chathura Wellala [43]	4 000	Shamsuzzaman BAN
3-07	Philippines	L	0-4	Manila	WCq		12 500	Kim Sang Woo KOR
3-12	Bhutan	W	3-0	New Delhi	SAFr1	Mohamed Zain [29], Nipuna Bandara 2 [35 65]		Tufaylieh SYR
5-12	Afghanistan	L	1-3	New Delhi	SAFr1	Mohamed Zain [17]		Faizullin KGZ
7-12	India	L	0-3	New Delhi	SAFr1			Faizullin KGZ
2012								
28-04	Malaysia	L	0-6	Kuala Lumpur	Fr			

Fr = Friendly match • SAF = South Asian Federation Cup • CC = AFC Challenge Cup • WC = FIFA World Cup • q = qualifier

HOLCIM FA CUP 2012

Round of 16		Quarter–finals		Semi–finals		Final	
Navy	4						
Kalutara Park	0	**Navy**	1				
Blue Star	0 2p	Air Force	0				
Air Force	0 4p			**Navy**	1		
Java Lane	0			Ratnam	0		
Don Bosco	2	Don Bosco	1				
Matara City	0	**Ratnam**	3				
Ratnam	4					**Navy**	1 5p
Renown	3					Army	1 4p
Nandimithra	1	**Renown**	2				
SLTB	1	New Youngs	0				
New Youngs	3			Renown	1 2p		
Police	2			**Army**	1 4p		
Old Bens	0	Police	0				
Kurunegala Pelicans	0	**Army**	1				
Army	1						

CUP FINAL

Jayatillake Stadium, Nawalapitiya
18-08-2012, Ref: Dilan Perera
Scorers - Jeewantha Dhammika Ratnayake [75] for Navy; Izzadeen [24] for Army

SSD – SOUTH SUDAN

FIFA/COCA-COLA WORLD RANKING

'93	'94	'95	'96	'97	'98	'99	'00	'01	'02	'03	'04	'05	'06	'07	'08	'09	'10	'11	'12
-	-	-	-	-	-	-	-	-	-	-	-	-	-	-	-	-	-	-	199

2012

Jan	Feb	Mar	Apr	May	Jun	Jul	Aug	Sep	Oct	Nov	Dec	High	Low	Av
							199	197	198	200	199	197	200	199

The raising of the flag of the newly independent South Sudan at the Confederation of African Football Congress in Libreville in February 2012 and an emotive speech from its sports minister, proved a moving start to membership of the world footballing family for the youngest nation on the globe. It came before the first elections for the country's football association and at a time when CAF believed it would be years before structures and teams were up and running. Within months, however, the first officials had been elected and by the end of the year South Sudan's national team, the Antelopes, had made their competitive debut at the CECAFA Cup in Kampala, Uganda, having employed the Serbian Zoran Djordjevic as their first coach. July 2012 had seen South Sudan host neighbours Uganda at home in Juba in their first-ever international which was staged on the first anniversary of independence. Among the first team members was James Moja Joseph who had been a long standing member of the Sudan national side but threw in his lot in with the newly independent breakaway state. Another sign of the country's unexpectedly quick progression to normality was the entry of El Nasir Juba into the 2013 CAF Confederation Cup after winning September's cup final.

FIFA WORLD CUP RECORD
1930-2014 DNE

SOUTH SUDAN FOOTBALL ASSOCIATION

Juba National Stadium
Hai Himra Talata
Juba
☎ +211 955 333395
✉ chaburgoc@yahoo.com

FA 2011 CON 2012 FIFA 2012
P Chabur Alei
GS Sestilio Lerib

THE STADIA
2014 FIFA World Cup Stadia
Juba Stadium
Juba   22 000

Other Main Stadia
Gbudue Stadium
Yambio   10 000
Wau Stadium
Wau   5 000

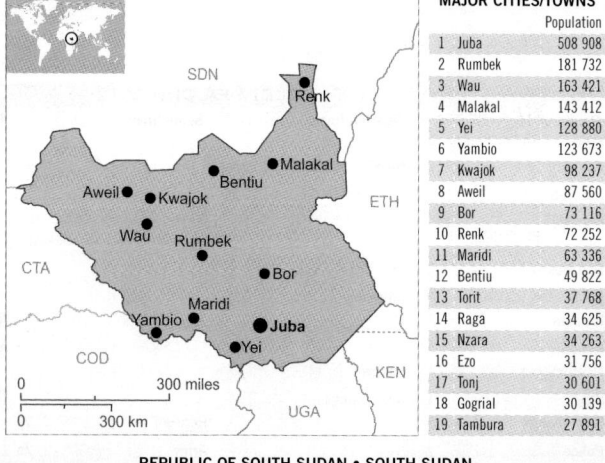

MAJOR CITIES/TOWNS

		Population
1	Juba	508 908
2	Rumbek	181 732
3	Wau	163 421
4	Malakal	143 412
5	Yei	128 880
6	Yambio	123 673
7	Kwajok	98 237
8	Aweil	87 560
9	Bor	73 716
10	Renk	72 252
11	Maridi	63 336
12	Bentiu	49 822
13	Torit	37 768
14	Raga	34 625
15	Nzara	34 263
16	Ezo	31 756
17	Tonj	30 601
18	Gogrial	30 139
19	Tambura	27 891

REPUBLIC OF SOUTH SUDAN • SOUTH SUDAN

Capital	Juba	Population	10 625 176 (80)
GDP per capita	$900 (219)	Area km^2	644 329 km^2 (42)
		% in cities	22%
		GMT +/-	+3

Neighbours (km) Central African Rep 989, Congo DR 639, Ethiopia 934, Kenya 232, Sudan 2184, Uganda 435

RECENT INTERNATIONAL MATCHES PLAYED BY SOUTH SUDAN

	Opponents	Score	Venue	Comp	Scorers	Att	Referee
	No international matches played before 2012						
2012							
10-07	Uganda	D 2-2	Juba	Fr	Richard Justin [13p], James Moga [42]	22 000	Onyango KEN
24-11	Ethiopia	L 0-1	Kampala	CCr1			Hakizimana RWA
27-11	Kenya	L 0-2	Kampala	CCr1			Mujuni TAN
30-11	Uganda	L 0-4	Kampala	CCr1			Hakizimana RWA

Fr = Friendly match • CC = CECAFA Cup

SOUTH SUDAN NATIONAL CUP 2012

Eighth-finals		Semi-finals		Final	
El Nasir Juba	3 1				
Borokano Tariti	2 1				
		El Nasir Juba	2		
		Akwachi Dit Rumbek	0		
Akwachi Dit Rumbek					
				El Nasir Juba ‡	2
				El Meriekh Renk	1
El Meriekh Awail	0 2				
Nahda Bentiu	0 1			**CUP FINAL**	
		El Meriekh Awail		Juba Stadium, Juba	
		El Meriekh Renk		12-09-2012, Att: 21 000	
El Meriekh Renk				Scorers - Adnan Nan [33] for Nasir; Kun James Garawick [50] for Meriekh	

‡ Qualified for the CAF Confederation Cup

STP – SAO TOME E PRINCIPE

FIFA/COCA-COLA WORLD RANKING

'93	'94	'95	'96	'97	'98	'99	'00	'01	'02	'03	'04	'05	'06	'07	'08	'09	'10	'11	'12
-	-	-	-	-	194	187	181	186	191	192	195	197	198	-	-	-	-	196	119

2012

Jan	Feb	Mar	Apr	May	Jun	Jul	Aug	Sep	Oct	Nov	Dec	High	Low	Av
196	168	115	116	116	118	132	131	133	132	133	119	115	200	185

Sao Tome began the year with an historic triumph over Lesotho in a 2013 Africa Cup of Nations preliminary round tie, winning at home by a single goal and then drawing away in the return a week later to progress 1-0 on aggregate. It set up a meeting with Sierra Leone in the next round where again they won the home tie but then lost 4-2 away in Freetown in June to go out 4-5 on aggregate. The two wins and a draw catapulted Sao Tome up the FIFA/Coca-Cola World Ranking from 196 at the start of the year to a highest-ever position of 115th in the space of two months - an extraordinary rise of 84 places. It came at the end of an eight-year hiatus from the international game, although the 'Seleccao de Falcao e Papagaio', as the team is known, did not play again for the rest of the year which negated much of the work achieved by coach Gustave Clemente. Sporting Club Principe won the national championship for a second successive year under coach Valdir Veiga and they were also victorious in the national cup over Guadalupe, where Artur scored in what was a first cup success for the club. That brought to four the total number of trophies won in 2012 as they had already won the Principe league and cup double. Their sister club Sporting Praia won the prestigious Sao Tome championship while Guadalupe won the Sao Tome cup.

CAF AFRICA CUP OF NATIONS RECORD
1957-1998 DNE 2000-2002 DNQ 2004 DNE 2006 DNQ 2008-2012 DNE 2013 DNQ

FEDERACAO SANTOMENSE DE FUTEBOL (FSF)

Rua Ex-João de Deus
Casa postale 440,
São Tomé
☎ +239 222 6558
📠 +239 222 4231
✉ fsfstp@hotmail.com
🖥 www.fsf.st
FA 1975 CON 1986 FIFA 1986
P Idalecio Pachire
GS Leonel Vagente

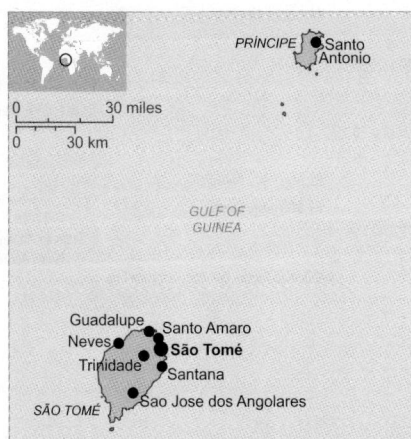

MAJOR CITIES/TOWNS

		Population
1	São Tomé	64 007
2	Trindade	7 993
3	Santo Amaro	7 926
4	Neves	7 261
5	Santana	7 167
6	São José dos Angolares	2 344
7	Guadalupe	2 069
8	Santo António	1 299

THE STADIA

2014 FIFA World Cup Stadia
Estadio Nacional 12 de Julho
São Tomé   15 000

Other Main Stadia
Estádio 13 de Junho
San António do Príncipe   1 000

REPUBLICA DEMOCRATICA DE SAO TOME E PRINCIPE

Capital São Tomé   Population 212 679 (186)   % in cities 61%
GDP per capita $1300 (205) Area km² 964 km² (184)   GMT +/- 0
Neighbours (km) Coast 209

RECENT INTERNATIONAL MATCHES PLAYED BY SAO TOME E PRINCIPE

2003	Opponents	Score		Venue	Comp	Scorers	Att	Referee
11-10	Libya	L	0-1	São Tomé	WCq		4 000	Yameogo JPN
12-11	Equatorial Guinea	L	1-3	Malabo	Fr			
16-11	Libya	L	0-8	Benghazi	WCq		20 000	Guirat TUN
2004								
No international matches played in 2004								
2005								
No international matches played in 2005								
2006								
No international matches played in 2006								
2007								
No international matches played in 2007								
2008								
No international matches played in 2008								
2009								
No international matches played in 2009								
2010								
No international matches played in 2010								
2011								
11-11	Congo	L	0-5	São Tomé	WCq		3 000	Ngbokaye CTA
15-11	Congo	D	1-1	Pointe Noire	WCq	Orgando dos Santos [50]	12 000	Mahamat CHA
2012								
15-01	Lesotho	W	1-0	Sao Tome	CNq	Jair Nunes [3p]		
22-01	Lesotho	D	0-0	Maseru	CNq			
29-02	Sierra Leone	W	2-1	Sao Tome	CNq	Jair Nunes [65p], Jorge dos Santos [86]		Raphael MWI
16-06	Sierra Leone	L	2-4	Freetown	CNq	Jair Nunes [2], Jose da Silva [47]		Lemghaifry MTN

Fr = Friendly match • CN = CAF African Cup of Nations • WC = FIFA World Cup • q = qualifier

SAO TOME E PRINCIPE 2012

SAO TOME CHAMPIONSHIP

	Pl	W	D	L	F	A	Pts	Sporting	UDRA	Barrios	Cruz	Vitória	Oque	UDESCAI	Aliança	Agrosport	6° Setembro
Sporting Club Praia	18	15	0	3	38	18	**45**		2-1	1-0	2-1	1-0	3-0	6-0	3-0	3-1	2-1
UDRA	18	12	1	5	34	21	37	6-2		1-2	1-0	1-0	2-4	1-0	2-1	1-0	3-1
Barrios Unidos CG	18	10	3	5	31	21	33	1-0	3-1		2-2	1-2	3-1	2-1	2-0	4-1	2-2
Cruz Vermelha	18	6	6	6	24	22	24	0-1	0-2	1-0		0-0	1-0	1-1	3-2	5-1	3-2
Vitória FC Riboque	18	7	3	8	21	24	24	3-4	2-0	0-1	2-2		0-1	1-0	3-2	1-2	2-0
Oque d'El Rei	18	4	7	7	24	31	19	0-2	1-3	3-2	0-0	1-1		0-0	3-2	1-2	2-2
UDESCAI Agua Ize	18	4	7	7	13	21	19	1-0	1-2	1-1	1-1	2-1	0-0		0-0	2-1	1-1
Aliança Nacional	18	5	3	10	26	35	18	1-2	**0-3**	1-0	1-2	1-0	2-2	1-0		4-0	2-6
Agrosport Monte Café	18	5	3	10	25	39	17	1-2	2-2	3-4	1-0	2-3	1-1	2-1	2-2		3-1
DM 6 de Setembro	18	4	3	11	29	39	15	1-2	0-2	0-1	3-2	**0-3**	5-4	0-1	2-4	2-0	

21/04/2012 - 21/10/2012 • Matches in bold awarded

CAMPEONATO NACIONAL 2012
Estádio 13 de Junho, San António do Príncipe, 3-11-2012
Sporting Príncipe 3-1 Sporting Club Praia
Scorers - Remy Lima 2 [85] [118], Rany [119] for Sporting Príncipe; Jair [89p] for Sporting Club Praia

TACA NACIONAL FINAL 2012
Estádio Nacional 12 de Julho, São Tomé, 17-11-2012
Sporting Príncipe 1-0 Guadalupe
Scorer - Artur [67] for Sporting Príncipe

Sporting Club Príncipe won the Príncipe championship and the Príncipe Cup Final. Guadalupe won the São Tomé Cup Final 1-0 against Oque d'El Rei

SUI – SWITZERLAND

FIFA/COCA-COLA WORLD RANKING

'93	'94	'95	'96	'97	'98	'99	'00	'01	'02	'03	'04	'05	'06	'07	'08	'09	'10	'11	'12
12	7	18	47	62	83	47	58	63	44	44	51	35	17	44	24	18	22	17	12

2012

Jan	Feb	Mar	Apr	May	Jun	Jul	Aug	Sep	Oct	Nov	Dec	High	Low	Av
16	16	18	18	18	21	21	23	20	15	16	12	3	83	37

It was a season to remember for FC Basel as they cruised to a third league and cup double in five years and also sensationally beat Manchester United in a crucial UEFA Champions League group game to qualify for the next stage and send the English champions crashing out - the first Swiss team to make it to knock-out rounds. There they beat Bayern Munich 1-0 at home in the first leg, but were then on the end of a 7-0 thrashing in the return. At home, Basel had been in imperious form despite changing coaches early in the season when Heiko Vogel came in for Thorsten Fink. The talents of Bayern Munich-bound playmaker Xherdan Shaqiri and the goals of veteran forward Alexander Frei saw Basel finish 20 points clear of Luzern in second place, clinching the championship with five rounds to spare. Luzern were their opponents in the cup final although this time the difference was less marked after Basel claimed the trophy on penalties after a 1-1 draw. The Swiss national team made a confident start to the 2014 FIFA World Cup qualifiers which saw them lead the group at the end of the year. Ottmar Hitzfeld's team landed in what looks amongst the least challenging groups on paper so there would be huge disappointment for his rapidly-developing team if they were not to make it through to a third consecutive World Cup finals.

UEFA EUROPEAN CHAMPIONSHIP RECORD
1960 DNE 1964 r1 1968-1992 DNQ **1996** r1 2000 DNQ **2004** r1 2008 r1 (co-hosts) 2012 DNQ

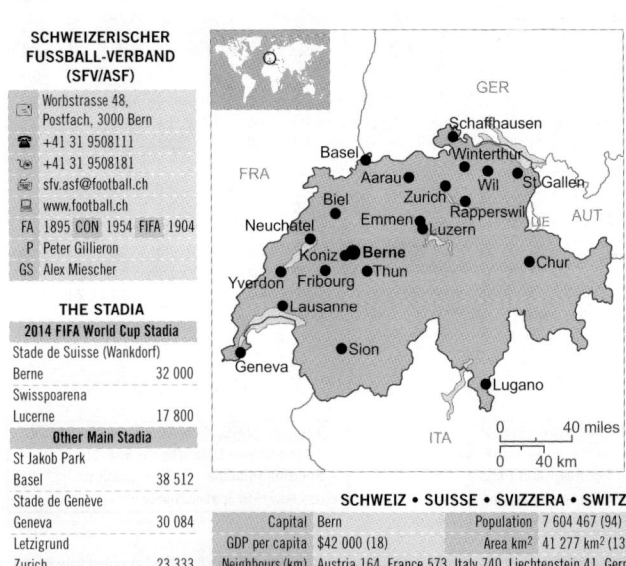

SCHWEIZERISCHER FUSSBALL-VERBAND (SFV/ASF)

- Worbstrasse 48, Postfach, 3000 Bern
- +41 31 9508111
- +41 31 9508181
- sfv.asf@football.ch
- www.football.ch
- FA 1895 CON 1954 FIFA 1904
- P Peter Gilliéron
- GS Alex Miescher

THE STADIA
2014 FIFA World Cup Stadia

Stade de Suisse (Wankdorf) Berne	32 000
Swissporarena Lucerne	17 800

Other Main Stadia

St Jakob Park Basel	38 512
Stade de Genève Geneva	30 084
Letzigrund Zurich	23 333

MAJOR CITIES/TOWNS

		Population
1	Zürich	353 485
2	Geneva	179 019
3	Basel	160 663
4	Berne	121 242
5	Lausanne	118 606
6	Winterthur	96 851
7	Saint Gall	69 713
8	Luzern	57 913
9	Lugano	55 907
10	Biel	49 089
11	Thun	41 754
12	Köniz	37 644
13	La Chaux-de-Fonds	36 853
14	Schaffhausen	33 519
15	Fribourg	33 293
16	Neuchâtel	32 390
17	Chur	32 251
18	Uster	31 296
62	Grenchen	16 060

SCHWEIZ • SUISSE • SVIZZERA • SWITZERLAND

Capital	Bern	Population	7 604 467 (94)	% in cities	73%
GDP per capita	$42 000 (18)	Area km²	41 277 km² (135)	GMT +/-	+1
Neighbours (km)	Austria 164, France 573, Italy 740, Liechtenstein 41, Germany 334				

RECENT INTERNATIONAL MATCHES PLAYED BY SWITZERLAND

2009	Opponents	Score	Venue	Comp	Scorers	Att	Referee
11-02	Bulgaria	D 1-1	Geneva	Fr	Huggel [45]	9 500	Duarte POR
28-03	Moldova	W 2-0	Chisinau	WCq	Frei [32], Fernandes [92+]	10 500	McDonald SCO
1-04	Moldova	W 2-0	Geneva	WCq	N'Kufo [20], Frei [52]	20 100	Rocchi ITA
12-08	Italy	D 0-0	Basel	Fr		31 500	Kircher GER
5-09	Greece	W 2-0	Basel	WCq	Grichting [84], Padalino [87]	38 500	De Bleeckere BEL
9-09	Latvia	D 2-2	Riga	WCq	Frei [43], Derdiyok [80]	8 600	Kralovec CZE
10-10	Luxembourg	W 3-0	Luxembourg	WCq	Senderos 2 [6 8], Huggel [22]	8 031	Iturralde ESP
14-10	Israel	D 0-0	Basel	WCq		38 500	Tudor ROU
14-11	Norway	L 0-1	Geneva	Fr		16 000	Whitby WAL
2010							
3-03	Uruguay	L 1-3	St Gall	Fr	Gokhan Inler [29p]	12 500	Rizzoli ITA
1-06	Costa Rica	L 0-1	Sion	Fr		11 300	Buttimer IRL
5-06	Italy	D 1-1	Geneva	Fr	Gokhan Inler [10]	30 000	Piccirillo FRA
16-06	Spain	W 1-0	Durban	WCr1	Fernandes [52]	62 453	Webb ENG
21-06	Chile	L 0-1	Port Elizabeth	WCr1		34 872	Al Ghamdi KSA
25-06	Honduras	D 0-0	Bloemfontein	WCr1		28 042	Baldassi ARG
11-08	Austria	W 1-0	Klagenfurt	Fr	Costanzo [73]	18 000	Rubinos ESP
3-09	Australia	D 0-0	St Gall	Fr		14 660	Einwaller AUT
7-09	England	L 1-3	Basel	ECq	Shaqiri [71]	37 500	Rizzoli ITA
8-10	Montenegro	L 0-1	Podgorica	ECq		10 750	Iturralde ESP
12-10	Wales	W 4-1	Basel	ECq	Stocker 2 [8 89], Streller [21], Gokhan Inler [82p]	26 000	Hamer LUX
17-11	Ukraine	D 2-2	Geneva	Fr	Frei 2 [40 62]	11 100	Gumienny BEL
2011							
9-02	Malta	D 0-0	Ta'Qali	Fr		3 000	Stamatis CYP
26-03	Bulgaria	D 0-0	Sofia	ECq		9 600	Collum SCO
4-06	England	D 2-2	London	ECq	Barnetta 2 [32 35]	84 459	Skomina SVN
10-08	Liechtenstein	W 2-1	Vaduz	Fr	Derdiyok [15], OG [34]	5 444	Eisner AUT
6-09	Bulgaria	W 3-1	Basel	ECq	Shaqiri 3 [45 62 90]	16 880	Kralovec CZE
7-10	Wales	L 0-2	Swansea	ECq		12 317	Kuipers NED
11-10	Montenegro	W 2-0	Basel	ECq	Derdiyok [51], Lichtsteiner [65]	19 997	Benquerenca POR
11-11	Netherlands	D 0-0	Amsterdam	Fr		50 000	Eriksson SWE
15-11	Luxembourg	W 1-0	Luxembourg	Fr	Xhaka [9]	852	Delferiere BEL
2012							
29-02	Argentina	L 1-3	Berne	Fr	Shaqiri [50]	30 250	Meyer GER
26-05	Germany	W 5-3	Basel	Fr	Derdiyok 3 [21 23 50], Lichtsteiner [67], Mehmedi [76]	27 381	Gautier FRA
30-05	Romania	L 0-1	Lucerne	Fr		11 850	Moen NOR
15-08	Croatia	W 4-2	Split	Fr	Xhaka [12], Barnetta [37], Gavranovic 2 [51 81]	12 000	Damato ITA
7-09	Slovenia	W 2-0	Ljubljana	WCq	Xhaka [20], Inler [51]	13 213	Tagliavento ITA
11-09	Albania	W 2-0	Lucerne	WCq	Shaqiri [23], Inler [68p]	16 500	Hategan ROU
12-10	Norway	D 1-1	Berne	WCq	Gavranovic [79]	30 712	Fernandez ESP
16-10	Iceland	W 2-0	Reykjavik	WCq	Barnetta [66], Gavranovic [79]	8 369	Kelly IRL
14-11	Tunisia	W 2-1	Sousse	Fr	Derdiyok [39], Shaqiri [95+]	1 500	Fleischer GHA

Fr = Friendly match • EC = UEFA EURO 2012 • WC = FIFA World Cup • q = qualifier • po = play-off

SWITZERLAND NATIONAL TEAM HISTORICAL RECORDS

Caps
118 - Heinz Hermann 1978-91 • 112 - Alain Geiger 1980-96 • 103 - Stephane Chapuisat 1989-2004 • 94 - Johann Vogel 1995-2007 • 87 - Hakan Yakin 2000-11 • 84 - Alexander Frei 2001-11 • 81 - Patrick Muller 1998-2008 • 80 - Severino Minelli 1930-43 • 79 - Andre Egli 1979-94 & Ciriaco Sforza 1991-2001 • 75 - Raphael Wicky 1996-2007 • 72 - Stephane Henchoz 1993-2005 • 71 - Alfred Bickel 1936-54

Goals
42 - Alexander Frei 2001-11 • 34 - Max Abegglen 1922-37 & Kubilay Turkyilmaz 1988-2001 • 29 - Andre Abegglen 1927-43 & Jacques Fatton 1946-55 • 26 - Adrian Knupp 1989-96 • 23 - Josef Hugi 1951-61 • 22 - Charles Antenen 1948-62 • 21 - Lauro Amado 1935-48 & Stephane Chapuisat 1989-2004 • 20 - Hakan Yakin 2000- • 19 - Robert Ballaman • 15 - Alfred Bickel 1936-54 & Heinz Hermann 1978-91

Coaches
Karl Rappan AUT 1960-63 • Alfredo Foni ITA 1964-67 • Erwin Ballabio 1967-69 • Louis Maurer 1970-71 • Rene Hussy 1973-76 • Miroslav Blazevic YUG 1976-77 • Roger Vonlanthen 1977-79 • Leo Walker 1979-80 • Paul Wolfisberg 1981-85 • Daniel Jeandupeux 1986-89 • Uli Stielike GER 1989-91 • Roy Hodgson ENG 1992-95 • Artur Jorge POR 1996 • Rolf Fringer AUT 1996-97 • Gilbert Gress FRA 1998-99 • Enzo Trossero ENG 2000-01 • Jakob Kuhn 2001-08 • Ottmar Hitzfeld GER 2008-

SWITZERLAND 2011–12

AXPO SUPER LEAGUE

	Pl	W	D	L	F	A	Pts	Basel	Luzern	Young Boys	Servette	Thun	Zürich	Lausanne	Neuchâtel	Grasshoppers	Sion
FC Basel †	34	22	8	4	78	33	74		1-0 3-1	1-0 1-2	3-0 5-0	2-1 2-1	1-2 1-0	6-0 3-1	2-0	4-1 6-3	3-3 0-0
FC Luzern ‡	34	14	12	8	46	32	54	3-1 1-1		1-1 2-0	1-2 3-1	0-0 0-1	3-1 1-1	2-0 3-2	1-2	2-1 1-0	2-0 0-0
BSC Young Boys ‡	34	13	12	9	52	38	51	1-1 2-2	1-0 2-2		1-1 3-1	0-2 4-0	2-3 1-0	4-1 1-3	4-1	0-1 2-2	1-1 3-0
Servette FC ‡	34	14	6	14	45	53	48	0-4 2-1	0-2 2-1	1-0 2-1		1-2 0-2	0-1 1-1	4-2 0-0	2-1	3-4 3-1	0-2 2-2
FC Thun	34	11	10	13	38	41	43	1-1 2-3	3-1 1-1	1-1 2-2	3-0 1-0		0-2 2-4	5-2 2-0	0-0	3-0 0-0	0-3 1-1
FC Zürich	34	11	8	15	43	44	41	0-1 1-5	1-1 0-0	1-2 2-2	2-3 0-1	0-0 1-1		4-1 2-0	0-2	6-0 2-0	1-1 0-1
Lausanne-Sport	34	8	6	20	29	61	30	2-3 0-2	0-1 0-0	0-3 0-0	0-0 3-1	1-0 1-0	2-1 0-1		1-3	2-1 2-1	0-2 1-0
Neuchâtel Xamax - R	18	7	5	6	22	22	26	1-1	0-3	0-0	0-0	4-0	3-1	2-2		2-0	0-3
Grasshopper-Club	34	7	5	22	32	66	26	2-2 0-2	0-1 2-2	0-3 2-0	1-4 0-3	1-0 2-4	3-1 0-0	3-0 0-1	2-0 0-0		2-1 0-2
FC Sion ††	34	15	8	11	40	35	17	0-1 0-3	1-1 1-3	1-2 0-1	0-4 0-1	2-0 1-0	1-0 2-1	1-0 1-0	2-0	2-0 3-2	

16/07/2011 – 23/05/2012 • † Qualified for the UEFA Champions League • ‡ Qualified for the Europa League • †† Relegation play-off
Relegation play-off: **Sion** 3-0 0-1 Aarau • Neuchâtel relegated in January 2012. Their results from the first half of the season stood
Top scorers: **24** - Alexander **FREI**, Basel • **13** - Marco **STRELLER**, Basel • **9** - Emmanuel **MAYUKA** ZAM, Yound Boys; Vilmos **VANCZAK** HUN, Sion; Xherdan **SHAQIRI**, Basel & Matias **VITKIEVIEZ**, Servette/Yound Boys • **8** - Goran **KARANOVIC**, Servette; Matt **MOUSSILOU** CGO, Lausanne; Christian **SCHNEUWLY**, Thun; Ishmael **YARTEY** GHA, Servette & Steven **ZUBER**, Grasshoppers

SWITZERLAND 2011–12

CHALLENGE LEAGUE (2)

	Pl	W	D	L	F	A	Pts	St Gallen	Aarau	Bellinzona	Winterthur	Lugano	Wil	Chiasso	Vaduz	Locarno	Biel-Bienne	Wohlen	Nyon	Etoile	Delémont	Kriens	Brühl
FC St Gallen	30	19	7	4	67	31	64		1-2	1-1	1-1	1-0	3-2	0-1	4-2	5-0	4-1	0-0	2-2	2-1	6-0	3-2	3-1
FC Aarau †	30	18	5	7	64	34	59	2-2		2-3	2-1	1-0	1-2	1-4	2-1	4-1	1-3	2-0	2-1	7-0	5-0	3-1	1-0
AC Bellinzona	30	18	5	7	49	21	59	0-1	0-1		2-0	3-1	0-1	0-0	2-1	2-0	5-2	5-0	2-0	1-2	2-0	1-3	1-0
FC Winterthur	30	15	8	7	44	29	53	0-1	1-2	1-0		1-2	1-4	0-0	2-0	0-0	2-1	1-2	2-1	0-0	0-0	4-1	2-1
AC Lugano	30	14	7	9	44	38	49	3-1	3-1	2-0	1-2		0-3	1-1	2-0	1-1	1-3	0-2	2-1	2-0	3-1	2-0	3-1
FC Wil 1900	30	12	10	8	59	41	46	2-2	3-2	1-1	1-1	1-1		1-1	1-2	1-2	2-1	3-1	2-0	6-1	1-1	3-0	
FC Chiasso	30	11	12	7	34	23	45	1-1	0-0	1-0	1-1	1-1	2-1		3-0	1-2	0-4	1-0	1-0	0-1	4-0	2-1	3-0
FC Vaduz	30	13	6	11	54	45	45	1-2	3-2	0-0	2-2	1-1	3-2	1-0		2-0	3-3	1-1	3-4	3-1	3-0	3-0	1-0
FC Locarno	30	12	9	9	47	44	45	0-2	1-1	0-3	1-1	1-1	2-1	1-1	2-1		2-0	2-0	2-2	3-0	3-0	1-3	2-1
FC Biel-Bienne	30	12	7	11	55	54	43	3-2	2-3	0-0	1-2	1-2	0-4	2-1	3-5	1-1		0-0	0-2	0-0	4-1	4-1	3-0
FC Wohlen	30	9	9	12	39	44	36	1-2	1-3	0-1	2-3	0-1	2-2	1-1	2-1	5-2	2-2		4-2	0-0	1-1	3-0	1-1
Stade Nyonnais	30	8	10	12	41	49	34	0-3	2-2	1-2	0-2	3-2	2-2	0-0	1-0	1-1	0-0	0-1		1-1	1-0	3-0	2-2
Etoile Carouge	30	8	6	16	25	56	30	1-5	0-2	1-3	0-2	3-0	1-1	2-1	0-4	1-5	3-2	1-3	0-1		2-0	2-1	0-2
SR Delémont	30	4	8	18	24	60	20	0-2	2-2	1-3	0-1	0-1	4-0	0-0	1-1	2-1	1-2	0-1	2-2	0-1		1-1	3-0
SC Kriens	30	4	5	21	37	66	17	0-2	0-2	0-1	0-2	2-1	0-4	2-3	2-4	4-1	3-4	1-1	2-0		7-1		
SC Brühl	30	4	4	22	30	78	16	1-3	0-3	1-4	0-5	3-4	1-1	0-2	2-3	0-6	1-4	3-2	3-1	1-2	1-1	2-0	

22/07/2011 – 23/05/2012 • † Promotion play-off (see Super League) • Top scorer: **19** - Armando **SADIKU** ALB, Locarno

MEDALS TABLE

		Overall	League	Cup	Europe	City
		G S B	G S B	G S	G S B	
1	Grasshopper-Club	45 32 14	27 19 13	18 13	1	Zürich
2	FC Basel	26 12 5	15 6 5	11 6		Basel
3	Servette FC	24 28 12	17 16 12	7 12		Geneva
4	FC Zürich	19 10 9	12 9 7	7 1	2	Zürich
5	BSC Young Boys	17 23 12	11 16 11	6 7	1	Berne
6	Lausanne-Sport	16 16 9	7 8 8	9 8	1	Lausanne
7	FC Sion	14 2 6	2 2 6	12		Sion
8	FC La Chaux-de-Fonds	9 4 7	3 3 7	6 1		La Chaux-de-Fonds
9	AC Lugano	6 9 10	3 5 10	3 4		Lugano
10	FC Aarau	4 3 3	3 1 3	1 2		Aarau
11	Neuchâtel Xamax FC	3 9 9	3 3 9	6		Neuchâtel
12	FC Luzern	3 6 1	1 2 1	2 4		Luzern
13	FC Winterthur	3 4 1	3 2 1	2		Wintherthur
14	FC St Gallen	3 3 3	2	3	1 3	St Gallen

SCHWEIZER CUP / COUPE DE SUISSE 2011-12

Second Round

FC Basel	5
FC Schötz*	1
FC Locarno*	1 4p
FC Wil 1900	1 5
AC Bellinzona	1
ES FC Malley*	0
FC Schattdorf*	0
Lausanne-Sport	5
FC St Gallen*	4
FC Thun	0
FC Aarau*	1
FC Zürich	3
BSC Young Boys	4
SC Freienbach*	0
SC Brühl	0
FC Winterthur*	2
FC Sion	2
Stade Nyonnais	1
FC Breitenrain*	1
FC Tuggen	2
Servette FC	3
Yverdon-Sport*	0
AC Lugano*	0
FC Biel-Bienne	1
Grasshopper-Club	1
FC Chiasso*	0
Neuchâtel Xamax	2
SC Kriens*	2
FC Wohlen	5
SC Cham*	1
FC Grand-Lancy*	1
FC Luzern	3

Round of 16

FC Basel	3
FC Wil 1900*	2
AC Bellinzona*	0
Lausanne-Sport	4
FC St Gallen*	4
FC Zürich	2
BSC Young Boys	1 2p
FC Winterthur*	1 3p
FC Sion	2
FC Tuggen*	1
Servette FC	0
FC Biel-Bienne*	3
Grasshopper-Club	2 5p
SC Kriens*	2 3p
FC Wohlen*	1
FC Luzern	2

Quarter-finals

FC Basel*	5
Lausanne-Sport	2
FC St Gallen	2 4p
FC Winterthur*	2 5p
FC Sion	3
FC Biel-Bienne*	1
Grasshopper-Club	0
FC Luzern*	3

Semi-finals

FC Basel	2
FC Winterthur*	1
FC Sion*	0
FC Luzern	1

Final

FC Basel	1 4p
FC Luzern	1 2p

PENALTIES

	Basel		Luzern
✓	Yapi Yapo		
			Renggli ✓
✓	Streller		
			Ohayon ✗1
✓	Zoua		
			Gygax ✓
✓	Shaqiri		
			Stahel ✗1

1 = saved

CUP FINAL

Stade de Suisse, Berne, 16-05-2012
Att: 30 100, Ref: Daniel Wermelinger
Scorers: Huggel 56 for Basel; Puljic 67 for Luzern

Basel - Yann Sommer - Markus Steinhofer, David Abraham, Aleksandar Dragovic (Radoslav Kovac 72), Park Joo Ho - Xherdan Shaqiri, Benjamin Huggel (Gilles Yapi Yapo 97), Granit Xhaka, Valentin Stocker Jacques Zoua 74) - Alexander Frei, Marco Streller. Tr: Heiko Vogel

Luzern - David Zibung - Sally Sarr, Florian Stahel, Tomislav Puljic, Claudio Lustenberger - Alain Wiss, Michel Renggli - Adrian Winter, Xavier Hochstrasser (Daniel Gygax 60), Nelson Ferreira (Moshe Ohayon 104) - Dario Lezcano (Jahmir Hyka 95). Tr: Murat Yakin

* Home team

SUR – SURINAME

FIFA/COCA-COLA WORLD RANKING

'93	'94	'95	'96	'97	'98	'99	'00	'01	'02	'03	'04	'05	'06	'07	'08	'09	'10	'11	'12
117	104	124	131	145	160	162	164	141	141	158	149	152	122	153	129	144	115	125	114

2012

Jan	Feb	Mar	Apr	May	Jun	Jul	Aug	Sep	Oct	Nov	Dec	High	Low	Av
125	126	130	133	133	128	132	135	138	130	125	114	84	168	136

The Suriname national team failed in its bid to qualify for the finals of the Caribbean Cup for the first time since 2001 after being outgunned by both Trinidad and eventual champions Cuba in a second round group staged in Trinidad. The team had travelled to Martinique in the first round and had made it through comfortably thanks to expected wins over minnows Montserrat and the British Virgin Islands and a 2-2 draw with the hosts. Two rounds of qualifying for the Caribbean Cup were introduced in 2005 and for the past four tournaments the Surinamese have had little trouble negotiating the first round but have come unstuck each time in the second. The same fate befell the 2011 Suriname club champions Inter Moengotapoe in the 2012 CFU Club Championship. In a first round group they won all three matches against opponents from Guyana and Curacao to make it through to the second stage but then lost 3-0 against USA-based Antigua Barracuda, 6-0 to Trinidad's W Connection and 8-2 to Victory from Haiti. There was also disappointment at home as Inter lost their domestic crown in a new-look championship that had discarded the play-offs. Robinhood, the most successful club in the country, re-claimed the title after a seven year gap although there was consolation for Inter after a 5-2 win over Excelsior in the cup final.

CFU CARIBBEAN CUP RECORD

1989 DNE 1991 DNQ **1992** 6 r1 1993 Withdrew **1994** 4 SF 1995 DNQ **1996** 4 SF 1997 DNE 1998-1999 DNQ **2001** 7 r1 2005-2012 DNQ

SURINAAMSE VOETBAL BOND (SVB)

Letitia Vriesdelaan 7,
PO Box 1223,
Paramaribo
☎ +597 473112
+597 425100
svb@sr.net
www.svb.sr
FA 1920 CON 1964 FIFA 1929
P Louis Giskus
GS Antonius Stienstra

THE STADIA

2014 FIFA World Cup Stadia

Andre Kamperveen Stadion Paramaribo	6 000

Other Main Stadia

Flora Stadion Paramaribo	3 500
Ronnie Brunswijkstadion Moengo	3 000
Eddie Blackman Stadion Livorno	1 250
Stadion Meerzorg Meerzorg	300

MAJOR CITIES/TOWNS

		Population
1	Paramaribo	236 398
2	Lelydorp	19 281
3	Nieuw Nickerie	13 470
4	Moengo	7 179
5	Meerzorg	6 781
6	Nieuw Amsterdam	5 118
7	Marienburg	4 592
8	Wageningen	4 248
9	Albina	4 045
10	Groningen	3 435
11	Brownsweg	3 018
12	Brokopondo	2 594
13	Onverwacht	2 259
14	Totness	1 706

REPUBLIEK SURINAME • REPUBLIC OF SURINAME

Capital	Paramaribo	Population 481 267 (170)	% in cities 75%
GDP per capita	$8900 (113)	Area km² 163 820 km² (91)	GMT + / - -3
Neighbours (km)	Brazil 593, French Guiana 510, Guyana 600 • Coast 386		

SUR – SURINAME

RECENT INTERNATIONAL MATCHES PLAYED BY SURINAME

2008	Opponents		Score	Venue	Comp	Scorers	Att	Referee
9-08	Dominica	W	3-1	Georgetown	CCq	Marlon Felter [18], Clifton Sandvliet [54], Ferdinand Jap-a-Joe [81]	175	Taylor BRB
10-08	Guyana	D	1-1	Georgetown	CCq	Vangellino Sastromedjo [22]	10 000	Forde BRB
20-08	Haiti	D	2-2	Port-au-Prince	WCq	Wensley Christoph 2 [33 45]	7 800	Navarro CAN
6-09	Costa Rica	L	0-7	San Jose	WCq		11 000	Dipiero CAN
10-09	El Salvador	L	0-2	Paramaribo	WCq		3 400	Archundia MEX
11-10	Costa Rica	L	1-4	Paramaribo	WCq	Clifton Sandvliet [48]	3 000	Campbell JAM
15-10	El Salvador	L	0-3	San Salvador	WCq		20 000	Batres GUA
23-10	Barbados	L	2-3	Havana	CCq	Clifton Sandvliet [33], Sergio Aroepa [42]	100	Morrison JAM
25-10	Netherlands Antilles	W	2-1	Havana	CCq	Cleven Wanabo 2 [70 76]	1 000	Holder CAY
27-10	Cuba	L	0-6	Havana	CCq		1 000	Holder CAY
19-11	Haiti	D	1-1	Paramaribo	WCq	Wensley Christoph [40]	800	Rodriguez MEX
2009								
28-10	Guyana	L	0-1	Paramaribo	Fr		2 000	Jaurequi ANT
30-10	French Guiana †	W	4-0	Paramaribo	Fr	Roche Emanuelson, Milton Pinas 3	2 000	
1-11	Netherlands Antilles	D	1-1	Paramaribo	Fr	Valies [9]	2 500	
2010								
13-10	Netherlands Antilles	W	2-1	Paramaribo	CCq	Ives Vlijter [31], Ronny Aloema [90p]	800	Willet ATG
15-10	St Lucia	W	2-1	Paramaribo	CCq	Stefano Rijssel [14], Ives Vlijter [38p]	750	Baptiste DMA
17-10	Guyana	L	0-2	Paramaribo	CCq		2 800	Davis TRI
31-10	Netherlands Antilles	D	2-2	Willemstad	Fr	OG [20], Roche Emanuelson [36], W 6-5p		
10-11	Antigua and Barbuda	L	1-2	St John's	CCq	Roche Emanuelson [34]	2 000	Morrison JAM
12-11	Cuba	D	3-3	St John's	CCq	Wensley Christoph [8], Stefano Rijssel [50], Derrik Garden [80]	400	Campbell JAM
14-11	Dominica	W	5-0	St John's	CCq	Naldo Kwasie [45], Ives Vlijter [45p], Emilio Limon [56], Roche Emanuelson [75], Stefano Rijssel [88p]	500	Lancaster GUY
2011								
2-09	Cayman Islands	W	1-0	Paramaribo	WCq	Friso Mando [11p]	1 000	Skeete BRB
6-09	Dominican Republic	D	1-1	San Cristobal	WCq	Friso Mando [25p]	2 300	Castro HON
23-09	Curacao	W	2-0	Paramaribo	Fr	Stefano Rijssel [25], Milton Pinas [60]	2 000	Botland SUR
25-09	Curacao	D	2-2	Paramaribo	Fr	Evani Esperance [14], Giovanni Drenthe [61]	2 500	Pierau SUR
7-10	Cayman Islands	W	1-0	Georgetown	WCq	Giovanni Drenthe [57]	2 100	Jurisebic USA
11-10	Dominican Republic	L	1-3	Paramaribo	WCq	Naldo Kwasie [81]	1 200	Ward CAN
11-11	El Salvador	L	1-3	Paramaribo	WCq	Evani Esperance [81]	500	Brea CUB
15-11	El Salvador	L	0-4	San Salvador	WCq		9 659	Santos PUR
2-12	Aruba	D	0-0	Paramaribo	Fr	L 3-5p	150	Jauregui ANT
4-12	Curacao	W	2-0	Paramaribo	Fr	Stefano Baneti [46], Emilio Limon [76]	50	Angela ARU
2012								
15-07	Aruba	L	0-1	Oranjestad	Fr		650	Jauregui CUW
5-09	Montserrat	W	7-1	La Lamentin	CCq	Giovanni Waal 2 [3 11], Romano Sordam [16], Jurmen Eugene Vallei [39], Giovanni Drenthe [45], Stefano Rijssel 2 [85 90]	188	Angela ARU
7-09	British Virgin Islands	W	4-0	Riviere-Pilote	CCq	Stefano Rijssel 2 [35 42], Giovanni Drenthe [36], Donovan Loswijk [81]	200	Anderson PUR
9-09	Martinique	D	2-2	Fort de France	CCq	Ronny Aloema [25], Donovan Loswijk [90p]	241	Angela ARU
14-11	Cuba	L	0-5	Scarborough	CCq		200	Bedeau GRN
16-11	Trinidad and Tobago	L	0-3	Scarborough	CCq		950	Georges HAI
18-11	St Vincent/Grenadines	W	1-0	Scarborough	CCq	Ronny Aloema [25]	200	Georges HAI

Fr = Friendly match • CC = Digicel Caribbean Cup • WC = FIFA World Cup • q = qualifier • † Not a full international

SURINAME NATIONAL TEAM HISTORICAL RECORDS

Coaches: Ronald Kolf 2000-01 • Edgardo Baldi URU 2003-04 • Kenneth Jaliens 2006-07 • Wensley Bundel 2008-10 • Kees Zwamborn NED 2010 • Ricardo Winter 2010 • Kenneth Jaliens 2011-12 • Ricardo Winter 2012

SURINAME 2011-12

HOOFDKLASSE

	Pl	W	D	L	F	A	Pts	Robinhood	Inter	WBC	Leo Victor	Transvaal	Boskamp	Notch	Excelsior	Voorwarts	Kamal
Robinhood	27	19	4	4	75	29	**61**		2-2 2-2	3-3	2-1 1-0	5-2 0-1	5-0 5-0	4-1 0-2	4-1	3-0	2-0
Inter Moengotapoe	27	13	11	3	56	32	**50**	1-2		3-2	3-1 2-1	1-1	2-1	1-1 1-1	1-1	4-0 1-1	1-1 7-0
Walking Boyz Co	27	15	3	9	55	44	**48**	1-2 0-3	0-2 2-1		3-0	1-1	1-3	2-1 3-1	2-4 1-2	3-1	1-0 1-0
Leo Victor	27	14	4	9	49	40	**46**	4-3	2-2	3-3 4-1		1-0	3-3	2-1 3-1	1-5 1-2	4-3 4-0	2-0
Transvaal	27	11	9	7	38	28	**42**	2-3	2-3 1-1	1-2 1-2	0-0 1-0		3-1	2-2	0-0 3-1	0-1	1-0 1-0
Boskamp	27	9	4	14	49	62	**31**	0-1	0-0 4-1	1-7 4-2	1-4 1-4	1-0 1-3 1-2		5-0	2-1	2-3 2-0	1-2
Notch Moengo	27	8	6	13	37	56	**30**	0-0	1-4	1-2	1-3	0-4 0-0	5-2 4-3		4-1	1-2	1-0 1-0
Excelsior	27	8	5	14	41	58	**29**	2-6 0-2	2-3 0-3	1-4	0-1	1-1	1-2 1-1	1-2 3		0-3	3-1
Voorwarts †	27	8	3	16	38	54	**27**	1-3 1-4	1-2	0-1 1-3	0-1	1-1 0-2	3-2	1-2 5-1	5-2 1-2		1-2 2-1
Kamal Dewaker	27	4	3	20	19	54	**15**	0-7 2-1	0-2	0-2	0-1 1-2	0-2	1-4 2-2	3-0	2-3 0-2	1-1	

8/12/2011 - 29/07/2012 • † Relegation play-off: **Randjiet Boys** 1-0 1-1 Voorwarts

SURINAME 2010-11
EERSTE KLASSE

	Pl	W	D	L	F	A	Pts
SNL	22	16	3	3	60	21	**51**
Randjiet Boys †	22	13	5	4	57	37	**44**
Takdier Boys	22	13	4	5	57	26	**43**
Boma Star	22	12	4	6	62	46	**40**
Acoconut	22	10	3	9	50	50	**33**
Inter Rica	22	9	5	8	46	35	**32**
Tammenga	22	9	5	8	54	53	**32**
De Ster	22	7	5	10	41	36	**26**
Santos	22	7	2	13	43	57	**23**
Real Saramacca †	22	6	4	12	40	57	**22**
FCS Nacional	22	4	3	15	30	78	**15**
The Brothers	22	4	1	17	25	69	**13**

27/11/2011 - 7/07/2012 • † Play-off
Relegation play-off: **Botopasie** 6-3 4-3 Real Saramacca

MEDALS TABLE

		Overall	Lge	Cup	CON'CAF
		G	G	G	G S B
1	Robinhood	28	23	5	5 3
2	Transvaal	24	19	3	2 3
3	Voorwaarts	6	6		
	Leo Victor	6	5	1	
5	Inter Moengotapoe	5	4	1	
6	Walking Boyz Co	4	3	1	
	Cicerone	4	4		
8	Ajax	2	2		
	Arsenal	2	2		
	MVV	2	2		
	FCS Nacional	2	1	1	

SVB BEKER 2011-12

Quarter-finals

Inter Moengotapoe	w/o
Notch Moengo	
Walking Boyz Co	0 p
Robinhood	0 p
Leo Victor	6
FCS Nacional	0
SNL	1 p
Voorwarts	1 p
Santos	Bye
Acoconut	1
Excelsior	4

Semi-finals

	Pl	W	D	L	F	A	Pts	RH	LV
Inter Moengotapoe	2	2	0	0	7	1	**6**	2-1	5-0
Robinhood	2	1	0	1	3	3	**3**		2-1
Leo Victor	2	0	0	2	1	7	**0**		

	Pl	W	D	L	F	A	Pts	Sa	Vo
Excelsior	2	2	0	0	9	5	**6**	4-3	5-2
Santos	1	0	0	1	3	4	**0**		n/p
Voorwarts	1	0	0	1	2	5	**0**		

Final

Inter Moengotapoe	5
Excelsior	2

CUP FINAL

Andre Kamperveen, Paramaribo
12-08-2012

SVK – SLOVAKIA

FIFA/COCA-COLA WORLD RANKING

'93	'94	'95	'96	'97	'98	'99	'00	'01	'02	'03	'04	'05	'06	'07	'08	'09	'10	'11	'12
150	43	35	30	34	32	21	24	47	55	50	53	45	37	53	44	33	20	40	47

2012

Jan	Feb	Mar	Apr	May	Jun	Jul	Aug	Sep	Oct	Nov	Dec	High	Low	Av
39	38	35	35	34	39	44	42	45	48	43	47	16	150	40

MSK Zilina wrote themselves into the record books in 2012 after a fine campaign in which they equalled Slovan's record of six league titles as well as winning the cup for the first time. Given that Zilina had been the losing side in five previous cup finals, their 3-2 win over Senica was particularly satisfying for their fans with the extra-time winner coming from their Peruvian midfielder Jean Deza. He was also on the scoresheet 12 days later when they completed the double with a final-day victory over Dunajska Streda, a result that saw Zilina finish two points ahead of Spartak Trnava and eight ahead of defending champions Slovan. In April it looked as if Zilina were about to buckle under the pressure but Dutchman Frans Adelaar was brought in as coach to calm nerves and take them to their historic double. The view that the thrilling exploits of the Slovak national team at the 2010 FIFA World Cup in South Africa would come to be seen as an extravagant one-off grew as the team blew hot and cold in the qualifiers for the 2014 finals in Brazil. Under new coaches Michal Hipp and Stanislav Griga, Slovakia made a promising start to one of the least challenging European groups but then lost at home to Greece and with Bosnia seemingly in fine form the Slovaks will have to step up a gear if they are to challenge for a place in the finals.

UEFA EUROPEAN CHAMPIONSHIP RECORD

1960 3 SF **1964** r1 **1968-1972** DNQ **1976** 1 Winners **1980** 3 **1984-1992** DNQ (as Czechoslovakia) **1996-2012** DNQ

SLOVAK FOOTBALL ASSOCIATION (SFZ)

Trnavska cesta 100,
821 01 Bratislava

☎ +421 2 48206000
📠 +421 2 48206099
✉ office@futbalsfz.sk
🖥 www.futbalsfz.sk
FA 1993 CON 1994 FIFA 1907
P Jan Kovacik
GS Jozef Kliment

THE STADIA
2014 FIFA World Cup Stadia
Stadion Pasienky
Bratislava 13 000
Other Main Stadia
Tehelné Polé
Bratislava 30 087
Antona Malatinsky Stadion
Trnava 18 448
DAC Stadion
Dunajska Streda 16 490
Pod Dubnon Stadion
Zilina 11 181

MAJOR CITIES/TOWNS
Population
1 Bratislava 423 415
2 Kosice 234 125
3 Presov 91 169
4 Zilina 85 488
5 Nitra 83 983
6 Banska Bystrica 80 291
7 Trnava 68 024
8 Martin 58 867
9 Trencin 56 221
10 Poprad 54 756
11 Prievidza 50 548
12 Zvolen 42 879
13 Povazska Bystrica 42 019
14 Nove Zamky 40 818
15 Michalovce 39 944
16 Spisska Nova Ves 39 242
22 Ruzomberok 29 717
44 Puchov 18 520
50 Senec 15 919

SLOVENSKA REPUBLIKA • SLOVAK REPUBLIC

Capital Bratislava	Population 5 463 046 (111)	% in cities 56%
GDP per capita $22 000 (55)	Area km² 49 035 km² (130)	GMT +/- +1

Neighbours (km) Austria 91, Czech Republic 197, Hungary 676, Poland 420, Ukraine 90

RECENT INTERNATIONAL MATCHES PLAYED BY SLOVAKIA

2009	Opponents	Score	Venue	Comp	Scorers	Att	Referee
12-08	Iceland	D 1-1	Reykjavik	Fr	Vittek 35	5 099	Christoffersen DEN
5-09	Czech Republic	D 2-2	Bratislava	WCq	Sestak 59, Hamsik 73p	23 800	Ovrebo NOR
9-09	Northern Ireland	W 2-0	Belfast	WCq	Sestak 15, Holosko 67	13 019	Kuipers NED
10-10	Slovenia	L 0-2	Bratislava	WCq		23 800	Stark GER
14-10	Poland	W 1-0	Chorzow	WCq	Gancarczyk OG 3	5 000	Eriksson SWE
14-11	USA	W 1-0	Bratislava	Fr	Hamsik 26p	7 200	Messner AUT
17-11	Chile	L 1-2	Zilina	Fr	Sestak 17	11 072	Vad HUN
2010							
3-03	Norway	L 0-1	Zilina	Fr		9 756	Nijhuis NED
29-05	Cameroon	D 1-1	Klagenfurt	Fr	Kopunek 6	10 000	Lechner AUT
5-06	Costa Rica	W 3-0	Bratislava	Fr	OG 16, Vittek 47, Sestak 88p	12 000	Messner AUT
15-06	New Zealand	D 1-1	Rustenburg	WCr1	Vittek 50	23 871	Damon RSA
20-06	Paraguay	L 0-2	Bloemfontein	WCr1		26 643	Maillet SEY
24-06	Italy	W 3-2	Johannesburg	WCr1	Vittek 2 25 73, Kopunek 89	53 412	Webb ENG
28-06	Netherlands	L 1-2	Durban	WCr2	Vittek 94+	61 962	Undiano ESP
11-08	Croatia	D 1-1	Bratislava	Fr	Stoch 50	6 366	Matejek CZE
3-09	FYR Macedonia	W 1-0	Bratislava	ECq	Holosko 91+	5 980	Circhetta SUI
7-09	Russia	W 1-0	Moscow	ECq	Stoch 27	27 052	De Bleeckere BEL
8-10	Armenia	L 1-3	Yerevan	ECq	Weiss 37	8 500	Orsato ITA
12-10	Republic of Ireland	D 1-1	Zilinia	ECq	Durica 36	10 892	Undiano ESP
17-11	Bosnia-Hercegovina	L 2-3	Bratislava	Fr	Sebo 3, Grajciar 63	7 822	Mikulski POL
2011							
9-02	Luxembourg	L 1-2	Luxembourg	Fr	Jendrisek 55	862	Thual FRA
26-03	Andorra	W 1-0	Adorra La Vella	ECq	Sebo 21	850	Masiah ISR
29-03	Denmark	L 1-2	Trnava	Fr	Holosko 32	4 927	Fernandez ESP
4-06	Andorra	W 1-0	Bratislava	ECq	Karhan 63	4 300	Jemini ALB
10-08	Austria	W 2-1	Klagenfurt	Fr	Kucka 21, Jez 30	13 000	Ceferin SVN
2-09	Republic of Ireland	D 0-0	Dublin	ECq		35 480	Proenca POR
6-09	Armenia	L 0-4	Zilina	ECq		7 238	Borski POL
7-10	Russia	L 0-1	Zilina	ECq		10 087	Eriksson SWE
11-10	FYR Macedonia	D 1-1	Skopje	ECq	Piroska 54	4 100	Chapron FRA
2012							
29-02	Turkey	W 2-1	Bursa	Fr	Weiss 24, Stoch 39	13 000	Kinhofer GER
26-05	Poland	L 0-1	Klagenfurt	Fr		2 100	Eisner AUT
30-05	Netherlands	L 0-2	Rotterdam	Fr		51 177	Bezborodov RUS
15-08	Denmark	W 3-1	Odense	Fr	Jakubko 63, Hamsik 72, Guldan 83	9 209	Stalhammar SWE
7-09	Lithuania	D 1-1	Vilnius	WCq	Sapara 41	4 000	Clos Gomez ESP
11-09	Liechtenstein	W 2-0	Bratislava	WCq	Sapara 37, Jakubko 79	4 326	Evans WAL
12-10	Latvia	W 2-1	Bratislava	WCq	Hamsik 5p, Sapara 9	4 012	Makkelie NED
16-10	Greece	L 0-1	Bratislava	WCq		7 494	Collum SCO
14-11	Czech Republic	L 0-3	Olomouc	Fr		11 464	Lechner AUT

Fr = Friendly match • EC = UEFA EURO 2012 • WC = FIFA World Cup • q = qualifier

SLOVAKIA NATIONAL TEAM HISTORICAL RECORDS

Caps: **107** - Miroslav Karhan 1995- • **79** - Robert Vittek 2001- • **60** - Marek Hamsik 2007- & Filip Holosko 2005- • **58** - Martin Skrtel 2004- ; Szilard Nemeth 1996-2006 & Radoslav Zabavnik 2003- • **54** - Stanislav Varga 1997-2006 • **53** - Jan Durica 2004- • **52** - Robert Tomaschek 1994-2001 • **51** - Marek Cech 2004-

Goals: **23** - Robert Vittek 2001- • **22** - Szilard Nemeth 1996-2006 • **14** - Marek Mintal 2002-09 & Miroslav Karhan 1995- • **12** - Peter Dubovsky 1994-2000 • **11** - Stanislav Sestak 2004- • **10** - Marek Hamsik 2007- • **9** - Tibor Jancula 1995-2001 & Lubomir Reiter 2001-05

Coaches: Jozef Venglos 1993-95 • Jozef Jankech 1995-98 • Dusan Radolsky 1998 • Josef Adamec 1999-2001 • Ladislav Jurkemik 2002-03 • Dusan Galis 2004-06 • Jan Kocian 2006-08 • Vladimir Weiss 2008-12 • Michal Hipp 2012 • Michal Hipp & Stanislav Griga 2012-

SLOVAKIA 2011-12

SUPER LIGA

	Pl	W	D	L	F	A	Pts	Zilina	Spartak	Slovan	Senica	Trencin	Ruzomberok	Zlaté Moravce	Nitra	Dukla	Tatran	Kosice	DAC
MSK Zilina †	33	19	10	4	52	27	**67**		0-1 1-0	2-1 3-0	3-1	0-0 2-2	2-1	2-2 1-0	2-0 2-0	3-1	1-0	1-1 1-0	2-0
Spartak Trnava ‡	33	19	8	6	44	22	**65**	1-1		2-0	1-1 1-0	1-0 2-2	0-2 3-0	1-0	1-2	3-1 2-1	2-0 0-0 1-0	1-0	2-1 3-0
Slovan Bratislava ‡	33	16	11	6	48	35	**59**	2-1	2-1 0-0		3-2 2-2	3-1 2-2	2-0	0-0 3-0	0-0 2-1	3-2	2-0	2-1 1-1	3-1
FK Senica ‡	33	15	12	6	47	23	**57**	1-2 1-1	1-1	2-2		4-0 4-0	2-1 2-0	1-0	3-1	0-0 0-0	3-0 0-0	0-1	3-0 5-1
AS Trencín	33	12	12	9	51	49	**48**	3-3	4-2	2-2	0-1		1-1 2-1	3-1	0-0 5-2	2-2	4-0 2-0	4-1 1-1	1-0 2-1
MFK Ruzomberok	33	11	11	11	39	34	**44**	1-2 0-1	0-0	1-0 0-0	0-1	1-1		4-0	0-0 1-1	2-0 2-0	1-1	1-1 2-0	3-1
ViOn Zlaté Moravce	33	11	8	14	34	43	**41**	1-1	0-1 0-2	1-1	0-0 1-3	3-0 2-3	1-0 3-5		1-1	1-0	1-2 1-2	3-2	2-1 3-2
FC Nitra	33	9	12	12	33	39	**39**	0-2	1-3 0-2	0-1	0-0 1-0	0-0	2-3	0-1 1-0		2-2	2-2 0-1	1-1	2-0 3-0
Dukla Banska Bystrica	33	9	10	14	37	44	**37**	1-3 2-1	0-3	1-2 1-1	1-1	2-0 1-2	2-0	0-1 0-0	1-2 1-1		2-0	4-0 0-0	1-0
Tatran Presov	33	7	12	14	23	35	**33**	0-0 1-1	2-0	0-1 2-1	0-1	1-0	1-1 1-1	0-1	1-1	0-1 2-2		0-1	0-2 4-0
MFK Kosice	33	6	11	16	25	40	**29**	1-2	1-1 0-1	0-1	0-1 0-0	1-2	1-1	1-1 0-1	0-2 1-2	3-1	1-0 0-0		3-0
DAC Dunajská Streda	33	5	1	27	21	63	**16**	2-1 0-2	0-1	1-0 2-3	0-1	2-0	0-2 0-1	0-2	0-2	1-3 1-2	0-0	0-1 2-0	

15/07/2011 - 20/05/2012 • † Qualified for the UEFA Champions League • ‡ Qualified for the Europa League

Top scorers: **18** - Pavol **MASARYK**, Ruzomberok • **15** - Juraj **HALENAR**, Slovan • **11** - Lester **PELTIER** TRI, Trencin • **10** - Martin **JAKUBKO**, Dukla & Robert **PICH**, Zilina • **9** - Tomas **MAJTAN**, Zilina & Martin **VYSKOCIL** CZE, Spartak Trnava • **9** - John **DELARGE** CMR, Dunajska & David **PETRIS** ARG, Trencin

SLOVAKIA 2011-12
II LIGA (2)

	Pl	W	D	L	F	A	Pts
Spartak Myjava	33	20	11	2	64	16	**71**
Sport Podbrezova	33	18	11	4	53	19	**65**
MFK Dolny Kubin	33	15	6	12	43	42	**51**
SFM Senec	33	13	11	9	41	33	**50**
Rimavska Sobota	33	13	9	11	42	42	**48**
Zemplin Michalovce	33	13	7	13	41	46	**46**
MFK Ruzomberok B	33	12	9	12	42	39	**45**
MFK Dubnica	33	10	13	10	32	31	**43**
Bodva Moldava	33	9	15	9	30	35	**42**
Tatran Lip'sky Mikulas	33	10	5	18	34	48	**35**
LAFC Lucenec	33	6	6	21	26	65	**24**
FC Petrzalka 1898	33	4	7	22	22	54	**19**

23/07/2011 - 27/05/2012

MEDALS TABLE

		Overall	League	Cup	City
		G S B	G S B	G S	
1	Slovan Bratislava	11 3 4	6 2 4	5 1	Bratislava
2	MSK Zilina	7 4 1	6 3 1	1 1	Zilina
3	Inter Bratislava	5 2 3	2 2 3	3	Bratislava
4	Artmedia Petrzalka	4 5	2 3	2 2	Bratislava
5	MFK Kosice	3 5 1	2 3 1	1 2	Kosice
6	MFK Ruzomberok	2 1 2	1	2	1 1	Ruzomberok
7	Spartak Trnava	1 7 4		3 4	1 4	Trnava
8	Dukla Banská Bystrica	1 2 2		1 2	1 1	Banská Bystrica
9	Matador Púchov	1 2		1	1 1	Púchov
10	FC Senec	1 1			1 1	Senec
11	1.HFC Humenné	1			1	Humenné
	ViOn Zlaté Moravce	1			1	Zlaté Moravce
13	FK Senica	2		1		1	Senica
	Tatran Presov	2			2	Presov
15	DAC Dunajská Streda	1 1		1	1	Dunajská Streda
16	Trans Licartovce	1			1	
17	FC Nitra	1			1	Nitra

MEDALS TABLE FOR SLOVAK CLUBS IN CZECHOSLOVAKIAN FOOTBALL

		Overall	League	Cup	Europe
		G S B	G S B	G S	G S B
3	Slovan Bratislava	14 16 3	8 10 3	5 6	1
5	Spartak Trnava	9 2 2	5 1 1	4 1	1
7	Lokomotíva Kosice	2 1 2		2	2 1	
8	TJ Internacional	1 6 5	1 3 5	3	
9	1.FC Kosice	1 4 2		1 2	1 3	
14	DAC Dunajská Streda	1 1		1	1	
17	Tatran Presov	4 1		2 1	2	
18	Jednota Trencin	2 1		1 1	1	
20	FC Nitra	1 1		1 1		
22	SK Zilina	1		1		
	Dukla Banská Bystrica	1		1		

SLOVENSKY POHAR 2011-12

Second Round

MSK Zilina	5
FK Spisska Nova Ves*	0
Lokomotiva Zvolen*	1
FK Poprad	2
LAFC Lucenec*	4
SK Kremnicka	0
Sport Podbrezova	2
Tatran Presov*	4
Spartak Trnava	3
FK Puchov*	0
STK Samorin	0
FKS Nemsova*	2
Sokol Dolna Zdana*	2 5p
MFK Ruzomberok	2 4p
Zemplin Michalovce*	1 3p
Dukla Banska Bystrica	1 4p
ViOn Zlaté Moravce	4
OTJ Moravany*	1
DAC Dunajská Streda*	0
Spartak Myjava	1
FC Nitra	3
MFK Vrbové*	0
MFK Dolny Kubin	1
MFK Kosice*	4
Slovan Bratislava	1 4p
PSC Pezinok*	0 2p
FC Petrzalka 1898*	0
AS Trencin	3
Banik Ruzina*	w/o
Slovan Giraltovce	
Povazska Bystrica*	1
FK Senica	2

Third Round

MSK Zilina	0 4p
FK Poprad*	0 3p
LAFC Lucenec	0
Tatran Presov*	4
Spartak Trnava	2
FKS Nemsova*	0
Sokol Dolna Zdana*	0
Dukla Banska Bystrica	2
ViOn Zlaté Moravce*	3
Spartak Myjava	0
FC Nitra	1
MFK Kosice*	2
Slovan Bratislava	1 4p
AS Trencin*	1 2p
Banik Ruzina*	0
FK Senica	3

Quarter-finals

MSK Zilina*	2 1 5p
Tatran Presov	1 2 4p
Spartak Trnava*	1 1
Dukla Banska Bystrica	2 1
ViOn Zlaté Moravce*	2 1
MFK Kosice*	2 0
Slovan Bratislava	0 2 2p
FK Senica*	2 0 4p

Semi-finals

MSK Zilina*	1 0
Dukla Banska Bystrica	0 0
ViOn Zlaté Moravce*	1 0
FK Senica	1 3

Final

MSK Zilina	3
FK Senica	2

FINAL

Mestsky, Bardejov, 8-05-2012
Att: 3000. Ref: Lubomir Samotnny
Scorers - Majtan 7, Barcik 49, Deza 104 for Zilina. Kona 2 11 73 for Senica
Zilina - Martin Krnac - Ernest Mabouka (Stanislav Angelovic 46), Jozef Piacek, Vladimir Leitner●, Ricardo Nunes - Viktor Pecovsky - Peter Sulek (Roman Gergel 78), Miroslav Barcik (c)●, Robert Pich - Tomas Majtan, Jan Novak (Jean Deza 81). Tr: Frans Adelaar
Senica - Petr Bolek (c) - Juraj Krizko, Petr Pavlik (Bolinha 110), Nicolas Gorosito, Pedro Leal - Stef Wijlaars, Tomas Strnad - Tomas Kona - Martin Durica● (Jaroslav Cerny 101), Rolando Blackburn (Lamine Diarrassouba 71), Jaroslav Divis. Tr: Stanislav Griga

* Home team/home team in the 1st leg

SVN – SLOVENIA

FIFA/COCA-COLA WORLD RANKING

'93	'94	'95	'96	'97	'98	'99	'00	'01	'02	'03	'04	'05	'06	'07	'08	'09	'10	'11	'12
134	81	71	77	95	88	40	35	25	36	31	42	68	77	83	57	31	17	26	49

2012

Jan	Feb	Mar	Apr	May	Jun	Jul	Aug	Sep	Oct	Nov	Dec	High	Low	Av
25	27	28	28	28	30	34	33	24	35	49	49	15	134	56

Maribor made a successful defence of a league title for the first time in almost a decade, finishing 20 points ahead of Olimpija from the capital Ljubljana with what was a record haul of 85 points. Darko Milanic's side won 26 of their 36 matches to seal their tenth championship and then went on to claim their first double since 1999. It was Maribor's fifth appearance in the cup final in six seasons and it took a penalty shoot-out against Celje to get their hands on the trophy after twice having come from behind in a 2-2 draw. Slovenian clubs have become a successful breeding ground for players who, the moment they make their mark, move on. In 2012 that included Maribor's star players Etien Velikonja (Cardiff) and Dalibor Volas (Sheriff) as well as the league's top scorer Dare Vrsic (FK Austria) and as a result the new national team coach Slavisa Stojanovic has at his disposal a wide range of players gaining experience across Europe. Slovenia were drawn in a 2014 FIFA World Cup qualifying group which didn't contain a single finalist from Euro 2012, but despite this they had a disastrous opening, losing against their main rivals Switzerland and Norway as well as against Albania, leaving any hopes of making it to the finals in Brazil hanging by a thread. At the end of the year they were joint bottom of the group with Cyprus.

UEFA EUROPEAN CHAMPIONSHIP RECORD
1960-1992 DNE (played as part of Yugoslavia) 1996 DNQ **2000** r1 2004-2012 DNQ

FOOTBALL ASSOCIATION OF SLOVENIA (NZS)

Nogometna Zveza Slovenije, Cerinova 4, PO Box 3986, 1001 Ljubljana
+386 1 5300400
+386 1 5300410
fas@nzs.si
www.nzs.si
FA 1920 CON 1992 FIFA 1992
P Aleksander Ceferin
GS Ales Zavrl

THE STADIA
2014 FIFA World Cup Stadia
Sportni Park Stozice Ljubljana 16 135
Ljudski VRT Stadion Maribor 12 437
Other Main Stadia
Arena Petrol Celje 13 400
Fazanerija Stadion Murska Sobota 5 500

MAJOR CITIES/TOWNS

		Population
1	Ljubljana	194 727
2	Maribor	88 349
3	Celje	36 723
4	Kranj	34 782
5	Velenje	26 857
6	Koper	24 725
7	Novo mesto	22 941
8	Ptuj	19 014
9	Trbovlje	15 637
10	Kamnik	13 698
11	Jesenice	13 433
12	Domzale	12 465
13	Nova Gorica	12 407
14	Skofja Loka	12 254
15	Murska Sobota	12 135
16	Izola	11 403
17	Kocevje	9 111
18	Postojna	8 867
27	Adajdovscina	6 972

REPUBLIKA SLOVENIJA • REPUBLIC OF SLOVENIA

Capital Ljubljana   Population 2 005 692 (145)   % in cities 48%
GDP per capita $29 600 (47)   Area km^2 20 273 km^2 (154)   GMT +/- +1
Neighbours (km) Austria 330, Croatia 455, Hungary 102, Italy 199 • Coast 46

RECENT INTERNATIONAL MATCHES PLAYED BY SLOVENIA

2009	Opponents	Score	Venue	Comp	Scorers	Att	Referee
11-02	Belgium	L 0-2	Genk	Fr		13 135	Kever SUI
28-03	Czech Republic	D 0-0	Maribor	WCq		12 500	Proenca POR
1-04	Northern Ireland	L 0-1	Belfast	WCq		13 243	Yefet ISR
12-08	San Marino	W 5-0	Maribor	WCq	Koren 2 [19][74], Radosavljevic [39], Kirm [54], Ljubijankic [93+]	4 400	Meckarovski MKD
5-09	England	L 1-2	London	Fr	Ljubijankic [85]	67 232	Eriksson SWE
9-09	Poland	W 3-0	Maribor	WCq	Dedic [13], Novakovic [44], Birsa [62]	10 226	Collum SCO
10-10	Slovakia	W 2-0	Bratislava	WCq	Birsa [56], Pecnik [93+]	23 800	Stark GER
14-10	San Marino	W 3-0	Serravalle	WCq	Novakovic [24], Stevanovic [68], Suler [81]	1 745	Szabo HUN
14-11	Russia	L 1-2	Moscow	WCpo	Pecnik [88]	71 600	Larsen DEN
18-11	Russia	W 1-0	Maribor	WCpo	Dedic [44]	12 510	Hauge NOR
2010							
3-03	Qatar	W 4-1	Maribor	Fr	Novakovic [14], Cesar [30], Kirm [34], Jokic [67]	4 900	Van Boekel NED
4-06	New Zealand	W 3-1	Maribor	Fr	Novakovic 2 [7][30], Kirm [44]	10 965	Kakkos GRE
13-06	Algeria	W 1-0	Polokwane	WCr1	Koren [79]	30 325	Batres GUA
18-06	USA	D 2-2	Johannesburg	WCr1	Birsa [13], Ljubijankic [42]	45 573	Coulibaly MLI
23-06	England	L 0-1	Port Elizabeth	WCr1		36 893	Stark GER
11-08	Australia	W 2-0	Ljubljana	Fr	Dedic [78], Ljubijankic [90]	16 135	Tagliavento ITA
3-09	Northern Ireland	L 0-1	Maribor	ECq		12 000	Balaj ROU
7-09	Serbia	D 1-1	Belgrade	ECq	Novakovic [63]	24 028	Benquerenca POR
8-10	Faeroe Islands	W 5-1	Ljubljana	ECq	Matavz 3 [25][36][65], Novakovic [72p], Dedic [84]	15 750	Todorov BUL
12-10	Estonia	W 1-0	Tallinn	ECq	OG [67]	5 722	Skjerven NOR
17-11	Georgia	L 1-2	Koper	Fr	Cesat [51]	4 000	Whitby WAL
2011							
9-02	Albania	W 2-1	Tirana	Fr	Novakovic [25], Dedic [90p]		Koukoulakis GRE
25-03	Italy	L 0-1	Ljubljana	ECq		15 790	Brych GER
29-03	Northern Ireland	D 0-0	Belfast	ECq		14 200	Kuipers NED
3-06	Faroe Islands	W 2-0	Toftir	ECq	Matavz [29], OG [47]	974	Drachta AUT
10-08	Belgium	D 0-0	Ljubljana	Fr		12 230	Strahonja CRO
2-09	Estonia	L 1-2	Ljubljana	ECq	Matavz [78]	15 480	Studer SUI
6-09	Italy	L 0-1	Florence	ECq		18 000	Moen NOR
11-10	Serbia	W 1-0	Maribor	ECq	Vrsic [45]	9 848	De Bleeckere BEL
15-11	USA	L 2-3	Ljubljana	Fr	Matavz 2 [26][60]	8 140	Schorgenhofer AUT
2012							
29-02	Scotland	D 1-1	Koper	Fr	Kirm [33]	4 190	Stavrev MKD
26-05	Greece	D 1-1	Kufstein	Fr	Kurtic [87]	1 000	Schorgenhofer AUT
15-08	Romania	W 4-3	Ljubljana	Fr	Cesar [4], Dedic 2 [51p][60], Kirm [70]	5 000	Aleckovic BIH
7-09	Switzerland	L 0-2	Ljubljana	WCq		13 213	Tagliavento ITA
11-09	Norway	L 1-2	Oslo	WCq	OG [17]	11 168	Aydinus TUR
12-10	Cyprus	W 2-1	Maribor	WCq	Matavz 2 [38][61]	7 988	Kruzliak SVK
16-10	Albania	L 0-1	Tirana	WCq		9 000	Hansson SWE
14-11	FYR Macedonia	L 2-3	Skopje	Fr	Pecnik 2 [49][63]	3 000	Grujic SRB

Fr = Friendly match • EC = UEFA EURO 2012 • WC = FIFA World Cup • q = qualifier • po = play-off

SLOVENIA NATIONAL TEAM HISTORICAL RECORDS

Caps: 80 -Zlatko Zahovic 1992-2004 • 74 - Milenko Acimovic 1998-2007 & Ales Ceh 1992-2002 • 71 - Dzoni Novak 1992-2002 • 66 - Marinko Galic 1994-2002 & Bostjan Cesar 2003- • 65 - Mladen Rudonja 1994-2003 & Aleksander Knavs 1998-2006 • 64 - Amir Karic 1996-2004 • 63 - Miran Pavlin 1994-2004 • 61 - Robert Koren 2003- • 60 - Samir Handanovic 2004-

Goals: 35 - Zlatko Zahovic 1992-2004 • 19 - Milvoje Novakovic 2006- • 16 - Saso Udovic 1993-2000 • 14 - Ermin Siljak 1994-2005 • 13 - Milenko Acimovic 1998-2007 • 10 - Primoz Gliha 1993-98 • 9 - Tim Matavz 2009- • 8 - Milan Osterc 1997-2002 & Zlatko Edic 2004-

Coaches: Bojan Prasnikar 1991-93 • Zdenko Verdenik 1994-97 • Bojan Prasnikar 1998 • Srecko Katanec 1998-2002 • Bojan Prasnikar 2002-04 • Branko Oblak 2004-06 • Matjaz Kek 2007-11 • Slavisa Stojanovic 2011-12 • Srecko Katanec 2013-

SLOVENIA 2011-12

PRVA LIGA

	Pl	W	D	L	F	A	Pts	Maribor	Olimpija	Mura	Koper	Gorica	Rudar	Domzale	Celje	Triglav	Nafta
NK Maribor †	36	26	7	3	88	35	**85**		2-2 3-2	6-0 3-1	2-1 1-1	2-1 2-1	2-1 1-0	0-0 2-1	5-2 3-1	2-0 8-0	0-2 6-0
Olimpija Ljubljana ‡	36	19	8	9	60	38	**65**	4-1 1-2		3-1 3-1	3-1 0-1	2-1 1-2	3-1 2-1	3-1 2-0	0-3 0-0	1-0 0-0	1-1 1-0
Mura Murska Sobota ‡	36	18	5	13	52	46	**59**	1-3 1-3	4-2 1-0		1-0 1-0	1-0 0-1	0-0 1-0	1-1 3-4	4-0 3-0	0-1 2-0	0-2 2-0
FC Koper	36	16	10	10	48	35	**58**	2-2 2-2	1-1 2-0	0-0 3-1		0-4 0-0	1-1 3-1	2-1 2-1	1-2 0-0	3-0 0-1	4-1 2-0
ND Gorica	36	14	11	11	49	37	**53**	1-1 0-0	2-1 2-3	1-1 1-2	4-1 0-1		2-2 4-1	0-3 0-0	2-0 1-1	0-0 1-1	2-1 3-1
Rudar Velenje	36	11	10	15	55	54	**43**	0-3 0-2	2-2 0-3	1-0 1-2	0-1 0-1	1-0 1-0		0-2 6-0	3-3 1-1	5-0 3-0	2-4 5-2
Domzale	36	11	7	18	39	52	**40**	1-4 0-2	0-1 0-1	2-1 1-2	1-1 1-0	0-3 1-2	2-3 1-1		1-0 0-2	2-0 0-1	2-1 0-0
NK Celje ‡	36	9	10	17	44	56	**37**	2-3 1-2	0-0 1-2	0-1 1-3	2-0 0-4	1-2 0-0	2-3 1-1	3-0 0-2		1-2 3-0	1-1 1-1
Triglav 2000 Kranj	36	9	6	21	42	67	**33**	0-2 2-1	0-1 0-2	1-2 0-3	0-3 0-2	0-2 2-0	0-0 1-5	0-4 1-1	0-1 4-3		2-1 1-1
Nafta Lendava	36	5	10	21	34	71	**25**	1-2 0-3	1-1 0-6	2-2 0-3	0-0 1-2	2-3 1-1	1-2 1-1	2-1 0-2	0-2 1-3	1-0 1-2	

16/07/2011 - 20/05/2012 • † Qualified for the UEFA Champions League • ‡ Qualified for the Europa League
Relegation play-off: Triglav 0-2 0-4 **Roltek Dob**
Top scorers: **22** - Dare **VRSIC**, Olimpija • **20** - Nusmir **FAJIC** BIH, Mura • **17** - Vito **PLUT**, Gorica & Dalibor **VOLAS**, Maribor • **16** - Roman **BEZJAK**, Celje • **14** - Etien **VELIKONJA**, Maribor • **10** - Goran **GALESIC** BIH, Gorica; Luka **MAJCEN**, Rudar; Dejan **MEZGA** CRO, Maribor & **MARCOS TAVARES** BRA, Maribor

SLOVENIA 2011-12 2.SNL (2)

	Pl	W	D	L	F	A	Pts
Aluminij Kidricevo	27	21	5	1	54	12	**68**
Roltek Dob ‡	27	13	9	5	42	33	**48**
Garmin Sencur	27	12	7	8	46	35	**43**
Interblock Ljubljana	27	10	8	9	33	30	**38**
NK Radomlje	27	10	2	15	36	42	**32**
NK Krsko	27	7	10	10	24	27	**31**
Simer Sampion Celje	27	7	7	13	38	40	**28**
Dravinja Kostroj	27	8	4	15	25	49	**28**
Bela Krajina Crnomelj	27	6	10	11	31	40	**28**
Smartno 1928	27	7	6	14	33	54	**27**

6/08/2011 - 19/05/2012 • ‡ Play-off (see Prva Liga)

MEDALS TABLE

		Overall			League			Cup		
		G	S	B	G	S	B	G	S	City
1	NK Maribor	17	7	3	10	4	3	7	3	Maribor
2	Olimpija Ljubljana	8	7	1	4	4	1	4	3	Ljubljana
3	ND Gorica	6	5	5	4	4	5	2	1	Nova Gorica
4	NK Domzale	3	4		2	3		1	1	Domzale
5	FC Koper	3	2	3	1	1	3	2	1	Koper
6	Interblock Ljubljana	2						2		Ljubljana
7	NK Celje	1	6	1		1	1	1	5	Celje
8	Mura Murska Sobota	1	3	3		2	3	1	1	Murska Sobota
9	Rudar Velenje	1		3			3	1		Velenje
10	Primorje Ajdovscina	5	1		2	1			3	Ajdovscina
11	Korotan Prevalje	1							1	Prevalje
	Aluminij Kidricevo	1							1	Kidricevo
	NK Dravograd	1							1	Dravograd
14	Izola Belvedur		1			1				Izola

SLOVENIA 2011-12 3.SNL WEST (3)

	Pl	W	D	L	F	A	Pts
NK Krka	26	19	1	6	77	31	**58**
NK Ankaran Hrvatini	26	15	2	9	57	33	**47**
Jadran Dekani	26	13	5	8	41	32	**44**
NK Tolmin	26	12	4	19	44	41	**40**
NK Ivanca Gorica	26	12	4	10	44	38	**40**
NK Zagorje	26	11	6	9	36	44	**39**
MNK Izola	26	10	6	10	45	49	**36**
Zarica Kranj	26	10	5	11	53	57	**35**
NK Brda	26	9	8	9	37	46	**35**
Calcit Kamnik	26	10	5	11	37	39	**35**
Adria Miren	26	7	8	11	32	41	**29**
Ilirska Bistrica	26	9	1	16	40	43	**28**
Jesenice	26	5	8	13	26	49	**23**
Svoboda Ljubljana	26	5	7	14	23	49	**22**

20/08/2011 - 9/06/2012

SLOVENIA 2011-12 3.SNL EAST (3)

	Pl	W	D	L	F	A	Pts
NK Zavrc	26	23	1	2	93	23	**70**
Koroska Dravograd	26	10	12	4	36	26	**42**
NK Stojnci	26	12	4	10	43	42	**40**
Carda Martjanci	26	11	6	9	45	43	**39**
NK Zrece	26	10	8	8	33	34	**38**
Tromejnik G. Kalamar	26	12	2	12	42	46	**38**
Tehnostroj Verzej	26	11	4	11	42	35	**37**
Kovinar Store	26	10	6	10	39	40	**36**
NK Odranci	26	10	2	14	39	48	**32**
NK Grad	26	9	4	13	43	51	**31**
NK Malecnik	26	7	9	10	39	46	**30**
NK Rakican	26	8	4	14	38	65	**28**
Aha Emmi Bistrica	26	8	2	16	29	50	**26**
Paloma Sladki	26	7	4	15	36	48	**25**

20/08/2011 - 9/06/2012

734　　　　　　　　　　　　　　　　　　　　　　　　　　PART TWO – THE ASSOCIATIONS

POKAL HERVIS 2011-12

First Round		Round of 16		Quarter-finals		Semi-finals		Final	
NK Maribor	Bye	**NK Maribor**	2						
Adria Miren	Bye	Adria Miren*	0						
				NK Maribor	3 1				
Domzale	Bye	Domzale	0	NK Zavrc*	3 0				
Marles Hise*	0	**NK Zavrc***	5						
NK Zavrc	6					**NK Maribor**	4 4		
ND Gorica	5	**ND Gorica**	2			Rudar Velenje*	2 2		
NK Hotiza*	0	NK Tolmin*	1	ND Gorica	1 1				
NK Krka*	3 11p			**Rudar Velenje***	2 1				
NK Tolmin	3 12p								
NK Sentjur	Bye	NK Sentjur*	0						
Ilirska Bistrica*	1	**Rudar Velenje**	10						
Rudar Velenje	2								
Garmin Sencur	6	**Garmin Sencur**	1						
Portoroz Piran*	1	Nafta Lendava	0						
NK Krsko*	0			**Garmin Sencur***	0 2				
Nafta Lendava	2	Olimpija Ljubljana	0	FC Koper	0 2				
Olimpija Ljubljana	Bye	**FC Koper***	2			**Garmin Sencur***	1 1 7p		
FC Koper	Bye					**NK Celje**	1 1 8p		
Interblock Ljubljana	2	**Interblock Ljubljana**	7						
NK Malecnik*	1	NK Odranci*	0						
Tehnostroj Verzej*	2			Interblock Ljubljana*	2 0				
NK Odranci	3			**NK Celje**	0 7				
Triglav 2000 Kranj	2	Triglav 2000 Kranj*	0						
NK Britof*	1	**NK Celje**	1						
NK Grad*	1								
NK Celje	3								

PENALTIES

	Maribor		Celje	
	Cvjanovic	✗	Verbic	✗
	Rajcevic	✓	Gobec	✓
	Volas	✓	Bezjak	✗
	Mejac	✗	Romih	✓
	Tavares	✓	Centrih	✗

NK Maribor　　2 3p
NK Celje ‡　　　2 2p

FINAL

Stozice, Ljubljana, 23-05-2012
Att: 3000, Ref: Matej Jug
Scorers - Volas 46, Crnic 99 for Maribor;
Romih 36, Verbic 92 for Celje
Maribor - Marko Pridigar - Ales Mejac, Dejan Mezza (Marcos Tavares 67), Agim Ibraimi●●◆116, Etien Velikonja (Matic Crnic 91), Goran Cvijanovic●, Aleksander Rajcevic, Mitja Viler●, Robert Beric (Dalibor Volas● 46), Arghus, Ales Mertelj, Tr. Darko Milanic
Celje - Amel Mujcinovic - Sasa Kovjenic (Benjamin Verbic 57), Alen Romih●, Roman Bezjak, Sasa Bakaric, Bekim Kapic●, Stefan Ristovski●, Sebastjan Gobec●, Matej Centrih, Mario Mocic (Tadej Kotnik● 100), Klemen Medved● (Jure Skafar 48); Tr: Damjani Romih

* Home team/home team in the 1st leg ● ‡ Qualified for the Europa League

SWE – SWEDEN

FIFA/COCA-COLA WORLD RANKING

'93	'94	'95	'96	'97	'98	'99	'00	'01	'02	'03	'04	'05	'06	'07	'08	'09	'10	'11	'12
9	3	13	17	18	18	16	23	16	25	19	13	14	24	32	42	33	18	20

2012

Jan	Feb	Mar	Apr	May	Jun	Jul	Aug	Sep	Oct	Nov	Dec	High	Low	Av
17	18	17	17	17	17	17	17	18	21	23	20	2	43	19

Sweden were perhaps the unluckiest side to exit from the finals of Euro 2012 at the group stage after three spirited performances in Kyiv. Indeed they led in all three matches and had it not been for defensive errors they would have gone further. Against hosts Ukraine in their opening match they were undone by two second-half Andriy Shevchenko goals and in a pulsating game against England they came from a goal down to lead 2-1 only to lose 3-2. By the time of their victory over France it was too late to salvage the situation. The spirit of the team shone through again in their 2014 FIFA World Cup qualifier against Germany in Berlin where the Swedes found themselves 4-0 down after 55 minutes but staged a truly remarkable recovery with Rasmus Elm's injury-time goal securing a stunning 4-4 draw. Equally remarkable was the four-goal display by Zlatan Ibrahimovic against England which marked the opening of the new Friends Arena in Stockholm. It was the first time any player had scored four goals against the English, the last of which was a stunning overhead kick from well outside the area. At home, Elfsborg won a close race in the championship, finishing two points ahead of Gothenburg club Hacken, which, due to the change in timing for the cup, was the only trophy on offer during 2012.

UEFA EUROPEAN CHAMPIONSHIP RECORD

1960 DNE 1964 QF 1968-1988 DNQ **1992** 4 SF (Hosts) **1996** DNQ **2000** 14 r1 **2004** 7 QF **2008** 9 r1 **2012** 13 r1

SVENSKA FOTBOLLFORBUNDET (SVFF)

PO Box 1216,
SE-17 123 Solna
☎ +46 8 7350900
+46 8 7350901
svff@svenskfotboll.se
www.svenskfotboll.se
FA 1904 CON 1954 FIFA 1904
P Karl-Erik Nilsson
GS Mikael Santoft

THE STADIA

2014 FIFA World Cup Stadia
Swedbank Stadion
Malmö 24 000

Other Main Stadia
Friends Arena
Stockholm 54 329
Nya Ullevi
Göteborg 43 200
Borås Arena
Borås 16 894
Nya Arena
Norrköping 16 700

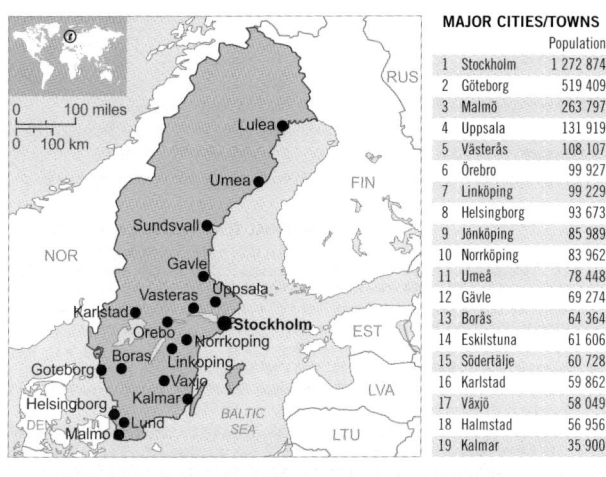

MAJOR CITIES/TOWNS

		Population
1	Stockholm	1 272 874
2	Göteborg	519 409
3	Malmö	263 797
4	Uppsala	131 919
5	Västerås	108 107
6	Örebro	99 927
7	Linköping	99 229
8	Helsingborg	93 673
9	Jönköping	85 989
10	Norrköping	83 962
11	Umeå	78 448
12	Gävle	69 274
13	Borås	64 364
14	Eskilstuna	61 606
15	Södertälje	60 728
16	Karlstad	59 862
17	Växjö	58 049
18	Halmstad	56 956
19	Kalmar	35 900

KONUNGARIKET SVERIGE • KINGDOM OF SWEDEN

Capital	Stockholm	Population	9 059 651 (87)	% in cities	85%
GDP per capita	$38 200 (25)	Area km²	450 295 km² (55)	GMT +/-	+1
Neighbours (km)	Finland 614, Norway 1619 • Coast 3218				

RECENT INTERNATIONAL MATCHES PLAYED BY SWEDEN

2010	Opponents	Score	Venue	Comp	Scorers	Att	Referee
20-01	Oman	W 1-0	Muscat	Fr	Svensson [35]	1 000	Shukralla BHR
23-01	Syria	D 1-1	Damascus	Fr	Ranegie [87]	10 000	Najm LIB
3-03	Wales	W 1-0	Swansea	Fr	Elmander [44]	8 258	Black NIR
29-05	Bosnia-Herzegovina	W 4-2	Stockholm	Fr	Toivonen [44], Olsson 2 [68 82], Berg [90]	22 589	Grafe GER
2-06	Belarus	W 1-0	Minsk	Fr	Wilhelmsson [48]	12 000	Nikolaev RUS
11-08	Scotland	W 3-0	Stockholm	Fr	Ibrahimovic [4], Bajrami [39], Toivonen [56]	25 249	Rocchi ITA
3-09	Hungary	W 2-0	Stockholm	ECq	Wernbloom 2 [51 73]	32 304	Atkinson ENG
7-09	San Marino	W 6-0	Malmo	ECq	Ibrahimovic 2 [7 77], OG 2 [11 26], Granqvist [51], Berg [92+]	21 083	McKeon IRL
12-10	Netherlands	L 1-4	Amsterdam	ECq	Granqvist [69]	46 000	Lannoy FRA
17-11	Germany	D 0-0	Gothenburg	Fr		21 959	Velasco ESP
2011							
19-01	Botswana	W 2-1	Cape Town	Fr	Gerndt [30], Svensson [74]	2 000	Hlungwani RSA
22-01	South Africa	D 1-1	Nelspruit	Fr	Hysen [30]		
8-02	Cyprus	W 2-0	Nicosia	Fr	Hysen [26], Berg [45]	2 000	Tudor ROU
9-02	Ukraine	D 1-1	Nicosia	Fr	Elmander [7], L 4-5p	2 000	Trattou CYP
29-03	Moldova	W 2-1	Stockholm	ECq	Lustig [30], Larsson.S [82]	25 544	Kircher GER
3-06	Moldova	W 4-1	Chisinau	ECq	Toivonen [11], Elmander 2 [30 58], Gerndt [88]	10 500	Marriner ENG
7-06	Finland	W 5-0	Stockholm	ECq	Kallstrom [11], Ibrahimovic 3 [31 35 53], Bajrami [83]	32 128	Gautier FRA
10-08	Ukraine	W 1-0	Kharkov	Fr	Hysen [90]		Tagliavento ITA
2-09	Hungary	L 1-2	Budapest	ECq	Wilhelmsson [60]	23 500	Skomina SVN
6-09	San Marino	W 5-0	Serravalle	ECq	Kallstrom [64], Wilhelmsson 2 [70 93+], Olsson.M [81], Hysen [89]	2 946	McLean SCO
7-10	Finland	W 2-1	Helsinki	ECq	Larsson.S [8], Olsson.M [52]	23 257	Clattenburg ENG
11-10	Netherlands	W 3-2	Stockholm	ECq	Kallstrom [14], Larsson.S [52p], Toivonen [53]	30 066	Cakir TUR
11-11	Denmark	L 0-2	Copenhagen	Fr		18 057	Moen NOR
15-11	England	L 0-1	London	Fr		48 876	Kralovec CZE
2012							
18-01	Bahrain	W 2-0	Doha	Fr	Hysen [58p], Hiljemark [81]	100	Al Dosari QAT
29-02	Croatia	W 3-1	Zagreb	Fr	Ibrahimovic [13p], Larsson.S 2 [46 69]	10 000	Zganec SVN
30-05	Iceland	W 3-2	Gothenburg	Fr	Ibrahimovic [2], Toivonen [15], Wilhelmsson [81]	14 379	Rasmussen DEN
5-06	Serbia	W 2-1	Stockholm	Fr	Toivonen [23], Ibrahimovic [52p]	20 691	Brych GER
11-06	Ukraine	L 1-2	Kyiv	ECr1	Ibrahimovic [52]	64 290	Cakir TUR
15-06	England	L 2-3	Kyiv	ECr1	OG [49], Mellberg [59]	64 640	Skomina SVN
19-06	France	W 2-0	Kyiv	ECr1	Ibrahimovic [54], Larsson [91+]	63 010	Proenca POR
15-08	Brazil	L 0-3	Stockholm	Fr		32 781	Kassai HUN
6-09	China PR	W 1-0	Helsingborg	Fr	Elmander [47]	9 073	Gestranius FIN
11-09	Kazakhstan	W 2-0	Malmo	WCq	Elm [37], Berg [94+]	20 414	Boiko UKR
12-10	Faroe Islands	W 2-1	Torshavn	WCq	Kacaniklic [65], Ibrahimovic [75]	5 079	Sidiropoulos GRE
16-10	Germany	D 4-4	Berlin	WCq	Ibrahimovic [62], Lustig [64], Elmander [76], Elm [93+]	72 369	Proenca POR
14-11	England	W 4-2	Stockholm	Fr	Ibrahimovic 4 [20 78 84 91+]	49 967	Moen NOR

Fr = Friendly match • EC = UEFA EURO 2012 • WC = FIFA World Cup • q = qualifier • r1 = first round group • r2 = second round

SWEDEN NATIONAL TEAM HISTORICAL RECORDS

Caps
143 - Thomas Ravelli 1981-97 • 132 - Anders Svensson 1999- • 117 - Olof Mellberg 2000- • 116 - Roland Nilsson 1986-2000 • 115 - Bjorn Nordqvist 1963-78 • 109 - Niclas Alexandersson 1993-2008 • 106 - Henrik Larsson 1993-2009 • 102 - Andreas Isaksson 2002- 98 - Kim Kallstrom 2001- • 96 - Patrik Andersson 1991-2002 • 94 - Orvar Bergmark 1951-65 • 86 - Teddy Lucic 1995-2006 • 85 - Zlatan Ibrahimovic 2001- • 83 - Kennet Andersson 1990-2000 • 79 - Christian Wilhelmsson 2001- • 77 - Ronnie Hellstrom 1968-80 • 76 - Tobias Linderoth 1999-2008 • 75 - Joachim Bjorklund 1991-2000; Fredrik Ljungberg 1998-2008 & Jonas Thern 1987-97

Goals
49 - Sven Rydell 1923-32 • 43 - Gunnar Nordahl 1942-48 • 39 - Zlatan Ibrahimovic 2001- • 37 - Henrik Larsson 1993-2009 • 32 - Gunnar Gren 1940-58 • 31 - Kennet Andersson 1990-2000 • 29 - Marcus Allback 1999-2008 & Martin Dahlin 1991-2000 • 27 - Agne Simonsson 1957-67 • 26 - Tomas Brolin 1990-95 • 23 - Per Kaufeldt 1922-29 • 22 - Karl Gustafsson 1908-18 • 21 - Albin Dahl 1920-30 • 20 - Sven Jonasson 1934-40; Erik Persson 1932-39 & Nils-Ake Sandell 1952-56

Coaches
Ludvig Kornerup 1908 • Wilhelm Friberg 1909-11 • John Ohlson 1912 • Ruben Gelbord 1912-13 • Hugo Leevin 1914-15 • Frey Svenson 1916 • Anton Johanson 1917-20 • John Pettersson 1921-24 • Jozsef Nagy HUN 1924-27 • John Pettersson 1927-34 • Jozsef Nagy HUN 1934 • John Pettersson 1934-36 • Carl Linde 1937 • Jozsef Nagy HUN 1938 • Gustaf Carlsson 1938-42 • Selection Committee 1942 • Rudolf Kock 1943-46 • George Raynor ENG 1946-54 • Rudolf Kock 1954-56 • George Raynor ENG 1956-58 • Eric Person 1958-61 • George Raynor ENG 1961 • Lennart Nyman 1962-65 • Orvar Bergmark 1966-70 • Georg Ericson 1971-79 • Lars Arnesson 1980-85 • Olle Nordin 1986-90 • Nils Andersson 1990 • Tommy Svensson 1991-97 • Tommy Soderberg 1998-99 • Tommy Soderberg & Lars Lagerback 2000-04 • Lars Lagerback 2004-09 • Erik Hamren 2009-

SWEDEN 2012

ALLSVENSKAN

	Pl	W	D	L	F	A	Pts	Elfsborg	Hacken	Malmö	AIK	Norrköping	Helsingborg	IFK Göteborg	Atvidaberg	Djurgården	Kalmar	Gefle	Mjällby	Syrianska	Sundsvall	Orebro	GAIS
IF Elfsborg †	30	18	5	7	48	29	59		2-0	4-1	1-0	2-0	2-1	1-0	1-1	2-1	3-0	2-0	0-0	1-0	0-0	1-0	2-1
BK Hacken Göteborg ‡	30	17	6	7	67	36	57	4-2		5-0	1-1	6-0	2-2	1-2	5-2	1-1	1-2	3-0	4-2	5-1	1-2	2-1	3-1
Malmö FF ‡	30	16	8	6	49	33	56	1-0	0-0		4-0	2-0	3-0	1-2	2-1	3-1	2-0	0-0	1-1	2-0	2-0	1-1	2-0
AIK Stockholm	30	15	10	5	41	27	55	1-1	3-1	2-0		5-2	2-1	1-1	1-0	1-1	1-2	0-1	0-0	1-1	1-1	3-0	1-0
IFK Norrköping	30	15	7	8	50	43	52	2-1	1-2	3-2	2-2		1-0	0-0	2-2	1-1	2-1	0-1	2-1	1-4	2-2	3-0	7-2
Helsingborgs IF	30	13	11	6	52	33	50	2-1	3-2	1-1	0-0	1-2		2-0	3-0	1-1	7-2	4-1	1-1	1-0	4-0	1-1	1-1
IFK Göteborg	30	9	12	9	36	41	39	2-1	1-1	2-2	0-1	1-2	1-1		2-1	1-0	1-1	1-1	4-2	1-0	2-0	2-2	0-0
Atvidabergs FF	30	9	10	11	48	48	37	5-1	0-3	0-1	2-0	1-1	1-2	1-2		2-1	3-0	6-1	0-0	1-0	2-2	1-1	2-1
Djurgårdens IF	30	8	13	9	37	40	37	0-0	0-3	2-3	0-3	1-1	3-1	3-2	1-1		1-1	1-1	0-1	1-1	1-0	2-1	3-0
Kalmar FF	30	10	7	13	36	45	37	2-1	3-1	1-2	1-2	0-2	1-1	3-0	2-0	2-2		0-1	1-2	3-0	1-1	1-2	2-2
Gefle IF	30	9	9	12	26	37	36	1-2	0-2	0-2	0-1	0-2	2-2	5-0	1-2	0-1	0-0		1-0	1-1	0-0	2-1	0-0	
Mjällby AIF	30	8	10	12	33	39	34	2-3	1-2	0-2	0-1	0-2	0-2	1-1	2-0	4-3	1-0	0-0		0-2	1-0	0-0	4-0
Syrianska FC	30	9	7	14	35	45	34	1-4	1-2	0-2	0-1	1-2	1-3	2-1	2-2	1-1	3-0	1-0	2-1		1-1	2-2	2-0
GIF Sundsvall	30	6	11	13	35	46	29	0-3	1-2	1-1	2-3	0-4	0-1	3-3	3-3	0-1	0-1	0-1	3-1	4-0		3-1	2-0
Orebro SK	30	5	9	16	32	46	24	0-2	1-2	2-1	2-2	0-1	0-0	1-0	3-4	2-3	0-1	1-2	0-1	0-1	2-2		4-0
GAIS Göteborg	30	1	9	20	24	61	12	1-2	0-0	2-3	0-1	2-0	1-3	1-1	2-2	0-0	1-2	2-3	2-2	1-4	1-2	0-1	

31/03/2012 - 4/11/2012 • † Qualified for the UEFA Champions League • ‡ Qualified for the Europa League • Attendance: 1,730,197 @ 7,209
Relegation play-off: **Halmstads BK** 3-0 3-4 GIF Sundsvall
Top scorers: 23 - Waris **MAJEED** GHA, Hacken • 17 - Gunnar **THORVALDSSON** ISL, Norrköping • 15 - Viktor **PRODELL**, Atvidaberg • 14 - Abiola **DAUDA** NGA, Kalmar • 13 - Par **ERICSSON**, Mjällby & Erton **FEJZULLAHU**, Mjällby • 12 - Alfred **FINNBOGASSON** ISL, Helsingborg & Rene **MAKONDELE** COD, Hacken

MEDALS TABLE

		Overall G S B	League G S B	Cup G S	Europe G S B	City
1	Malmö FF	30 19 7	16 15 7	14 3	1	Malmö
2	IFK Göteborg	25 16 14	18 10 13	5 6	2 1	Gothenburg
3	AIK Stockholm	19 20 9	11 13 9	8 7		Solna, Stockholm
4	IFK Norrköping	18 14 4	12 10 4	6 4		Norrköping
5	Djurgårdens IF	15 14 8	11 11 8	4 3		Stockholm
6	Örgryte IS Göteborg	15 6 5	14 5 5	1 1		Gothenburg
7	Helsingborgs IF	12 12 8	7 10 8	5 2		Helsingborg
8	IF Elfsborg	8 9 5	6 6 5	2 3		Borås
9	GAIS Göteborg	7 5 3	6 4 3	1 1		Gothenburg
10	Östers IF Växjö	5 7 4	4 3 4	1 4		Växjö

SWEDEN 2012

SUPERETTAN (2)

	Pl	W	D	L	F	A	Pts	Osters	Brommapojkarna	Halmstad	Hammarby	Ljungskile	Landskrona	Jönköpings	Assyriska	Angelholm	Brage	Varberg	Degerfors	Falkenberg	Värnamo	Trelleborg	Umeå
Osters IF Växjö	30	20	6	4	57	28	66		4-1	2-1	0-0	0-0	0-1	2-1	1-0	2-1	1-0	1-0	2-0	4-1	1-1	2-1	5-1
IF Brommapojkarna	30	20	1	9	61	39	61	3-1		0-3	2-1	0-1	2-0	3-2	4-2	4-0	4-1	5-1	1-0	1-0	2-4	2-0	2-1
Halmstads BK	30	18	2	10	58	33	56	3-2	2-0		2-0	1-0	1-1	3-2	3-1	0-0	4-0	3-1	2-0	1-1	2-3	3-1	3-0
Hammarby IF	30	13	10	7	40	33	49	0-2	3-1	1-0		0-1	0-0	2-2	0-2	2-1	3-1	1-1	4-2	2-2	1-0	0-0	1-0
Ljungskile SK	30	11	9	10	36	36	42	0-1	3-1	0-0	0-1		2-0	1-0	3-1	1-1	1-1	2-2	3-3	2-1	3-2	1-0	2-0
Landskrona BoIS	30	12	5	13	35	43	41	1-2	1-2	3-3	4-1	2-1		3-2	3-2	1-0	2-1	0-0	2-1	0-1	0-3	2-1	
Jönköpings Sodra	30	10	10	10	52	47	40	3-3	3-2	1-1	1-1	4-1	2-0		2-0	2-2	0-1	1-1	2-2	2-1	1-0	2-0	3-3
Assyriska FF	30	11	6	13	44	49	39	1-0	0-2	2-1	1-1	2-0	2-1	4-1		1-4	3-1	0-0	0-0	0-0	3-0	2-5	1-1
Angelholms FF	30	10	9	11	40	46	39	0-2	0-2	0-2	1-1	3-1	2-1	2-2	3-1		0-1	3-2	2-0	1-3	1-0	1-4	1-0
IK Brage	30	10	9	11	35	45	39	0-1	1-2	2-1	0-2	1-1	1-0	2-1	1-1		4-4	1-1	1-0	1-1	3-1	0-0	
Varbergs BoIS	30	8	13	9	49	52	37	2-4	2-2	2-2	2-2	3-1	3-0	4-1	1-2	1-3	2-2		1-0	1-0	1-1	2-2	2-1
Degerfors IF	30	9	8	13	46	53	35	2-2	0-2	2-2	1-3	2-1	2-0	1-3	4-2	1-1	3-2	3-1		2-3	6-1	2-1	1-2
Falkenbergs FF	30	8	10	12	45	47	34	1-1	3-1	3-1	1-3	1-1	1-2	1-1	1-1	2-2	1-2	1-1	4-1		3-2	2-0	1-1
IFK Värnamo	30	8	6	16	47	54	30	1-2	0-1	2-5	0-1	2-2	1-1	1-5	1-2	4-0	3-0	0-1	2-3	3-4		3-0	5-0
Trelleborgs IF	30	8	5	17	40	55	29	2-3	0-4	1-2	1-1	1-0	0-1	0-1	3-2	1-1	1-1	2-2	0-2	3-1	1-2		4-2
Umeå FC	30	6	5	19	34	61	23	0-4	1-3	0-4	0-1	0-1	3-1	1-0	1-3	1-3	1-2	1-2	2-3	0-1	2-1	1-1 5-1	

6/04/2012 - 3/11/2012 • Top scorers: **18** - Pablo Pinones **ARCE**, Brommapojkarna • **17** - Robin **SIMOVIC**, Angelholms
Relegation play-offs: BK Forward 0-0 1-2 **Falkenbergs** FF; Lunds BK 0-2 2-2 **IFK Värnamo**. All four clubs remain at the same level

SWZ – SWAZILAND

FIFA/COCA-COLA WORLD RANKING

'93	'94	'95	'96	'97	'98	'99	'00	'01	'02	'03	'04	'05	'06	'07	'08	'09	'10	'11	'12
99	125	148	160	165	149	127	137	132	116	114	126	134	148	148	138	135	160	180	178

2012													High	Low	Av
Jan	Feb	Mar	Apr	May	Jun	Jul	Aug	Sep	Oct	Nov	Dec				
180	179	179	179	179	179	182	181	190	190	185	178		92	190	139

An absence of any meaningful games, a lack of players gaining experience abroad and the surprising decision not to enter the 2013 Africa Cup of Nations qualifiers saw the Swazi national team lapse into something of a slump. After the promise of the mid-2000s when the small Southern African kingdom punched above its weight, Swaziland dropped down to their lowest-ever position of 190 in the FIFA Coca-Cola World Ranking in September and October. Their decision to forego entry into the preliminaries for the Nations Cup reflected tighter times as the National Football Association of Swaziland found state support for international assignments harder to procure. The paucity of real talent in the team is reflected by the fact that all their key players are home-based as the best Swazi talent usually goes next door to the professional ranks in South Africa. The Swazi Premier League may not be of the highest standard but it is well organised and competitive. The 2012 title was won by Mbabane Swallows who beat Manzini Wanderers 1-0 on the final day of the season to finish two points ahead of Royal Leopards. Defending champions Green Mamba had a disappointing season in the league but beat Mbabane Highlanders 3-1 in the cup final to claim the trophy for the first time since 2004.

CAF AFRICA CUP OF NATIONS RECORD
1957-1984 DNE 1986 DNQ 1988 DNE 1990-1992 DNQ 1994-1998 DNE 2000-2012 DNQ 2013 DNE

NATIONAL FOOTBALL ASSOCIATION OF SWAZILAND (NFAS)

Sigwaca House, Plot 582,
Sheffield Road, PO Box 641,
H100 Mbabane
☎ +268 24046852
📠 +268 24046206
✉ info@nfas.org.sz
🖥 www.nfas.org.sz
FA 1968 CON 1976 FIFA 1978
P Adam Mthethwa
GS Frederick Mngomezulu

THE STADIA
2014 FIFA World Cup Stadia
Somhlolo National Stadium
Lobamba 20 000
Other Main Stadia
Mavuso Sports Centre
Manzini 5 000
Trade Fair Ground
Manzini 5 000
Simunye Park
Simunye

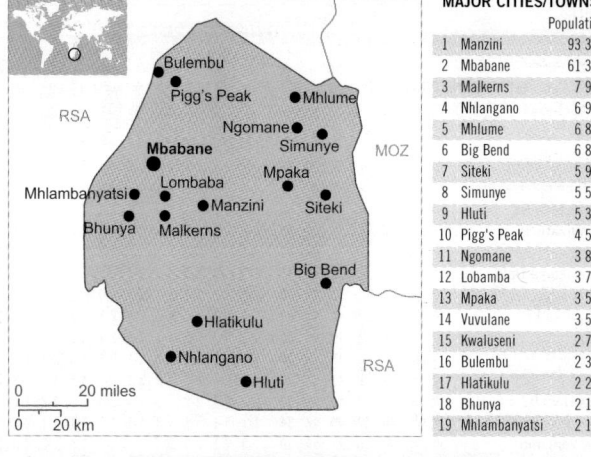

MAJOR CITIES/TOWNS
		Population
1	Manzini	93 374
2	Mbabane	61 391
3	Malkerns	7 902
4	Nhlangano	6 991
5	Mhlume	6 876
6	Big Bend	6 835
7	Siteki	5 910
8	Simunye	5 520
9	Hluti	5 387
10	Pigg's Peak	4 548
11	Ngomane	3 824
12	Lobamba	3 736
13	Mpaka	3 571
14	Vuvulane	3 522
15	Kwaluseni	2 784
16	Bulembu	2 321
17	Hlatikulu	2 271
18	Bhunya	2 187
19	Mhlambanyatsi	2 167

UMBUSO WESWATINI • KINGDOM OF SWAZILAND
Capital	Mbabane	Population	1 123 913 (156)	% in cities	25%
GDP per capita	$4400 (151)	Area km²	17 364 km² (158)	GMT +/-	+1
Neighbours (km)	Mozambique 105, South Africa 430				

SWZ - SWAZILAND

RECENT INTERNATIONAL MATCHES PLAYED BY SWAZILAND

2007	Opponents	Score		Venue	Comp	Scorers	Att	Referee
25-03	Kenya	L	0-2	Nairobi	CNq			Seechurn MRI
26-05	Mauritius	D	0-0	Mbabane	CCr1	L 5-6p		Labrosse SEY
27-05	Malawi	W	1-0	Mbabane	CCr1	Mphile Tsabedze [85]		Labrosse SEY
3-06	Kenya	D	0-0	Mbabane	CNq			Katjimune NAM
17-06	Angola	L	0-3	Luanda	CNq			Marange ZIM
9-09	Eritrea	D	0-0	Manzini	CNq			Ssegonga UGA
18-11	Malawi	L	0-3	Manzini	Fr			
2008								
9-02	Botswana	L	1-4	Mbabane	Fr	Tony Tsabedze [77]		
10-02	Lesotho	D	2-2	Mbabane	Fr	Barry Steenkamp [48], Baiano Kunene [58]. L 1-4p		
23-05	Lesotho	D	1-1	Mbabane	Fr	Felix Badenhorst [20]		
8-06	Togo	W	2-1	Mbabane	WCq	Siza Dlamini [55], Collen Salelwako [73]	5 819	Niyongabo BDI
15-06	Zambia	D	0-0	Mbabane	WCq		7 462	Kotey GHA
21-06	Zambia	L	0-1	Chililabombwe	WCq		14 458	Marange ZIM
19-07	Madagascar	D	1-1	Witbank	CCr1	Phinda Dlamini [39]		Nhlapo RSA
21-07	Mauritius	D	1-1	Witbank	CCr1	Gcina Mazibuko [51]		Nhlapo RSA
23-07	Seychelles	W	1-0	Witbank	CCr1	Mfanzile Dlamini [89]		Katjimune NAM
20-08	Mozambique	L	0-3	Maputo	Fr			
11-10	Togo	L	0-6	Accra	WCq		8 000	Evehe CMR
2009								
19-06	Lesotho	D	1-1	Manzini	Fr	Mxolisi Mthethwa [74]		
21-06	Lesotho	D	1-1	Lobamba	Fr	Mfanafuthi Bhembe [83]		
6-07	Malawi	L	1-3	Blantyre	Fr	Thokozani Mkhulisi [77p]		
12-08	Mozambique	L	0-1	Maputo	Fr			
5-09	Namibia	D	1-1	Windhoek	Fr	Mxolisi Mthethwa [38]		
18-10	Seychelles	W	2-1	Bulawayo	CCr1	Mathokoza Twala [72], Mfanzile Dlamini [74]		Carvalho ANG
20-10	Botswana	L	0-1	Bulawayo	CCr1			Seechurn MRI
22-10	Comoros	W	3-0	Bulawayo	CCr1	Mathokoza Twala [37], Mxolisi Mthethwa [46], Mfanzile Dlamini [67]		Carvalho ANG
2010								
11-08	Mozambique	L	1-2	Maputo	Fr	Siza Dlamini [29]		
5-09	Ghana	L	0-3	Lobamba	CNq			Seechurn MRI
10-10	Congo	L	1-3	Brazzaville	CNq	Darren Christie [37]		Ssegonga UGA
27-10	Botswana	L	0-2	Lobatse	Fr			
2011								
9-02	Zambia	L	0-4	Manzini	Fr			
27-03	Sudan	L	0-3	Omdurman	CNq			
25-05	Botswana	D	0-0	Manzini	Fr			
29-05	Malawi	D	1-1	Manzini	Fr	Sidumo Shongwe [69]		
5-06	Sudan	L	1-2	Manzini	CNq	Manqoba Kunene [80]		
31-07	Botswana	L	0-2	Pretoria	Fr			
20-08	Lesotho	D	0-0	Maseru	Fr			
22-08	Lesotho	W	1-0	Maseru	Fr	Mbuso Gina [30]		
2-09	Ghana	L	0-2	Accra	CNq			
8-10	Congo	L	0-1	Lobamba	CNq			
11-11	Congo DR	L	1-3	Lobamba	WCq	Sidumo Shongwe [63]	785	Sikazwe ZAM
15-11	Congo DR	L	1-5	Kinshasa	WCq	Sidumo Shongwe [63]	24 000	Moukoko CGO
2012								
12-10	Lesotho	L	1-2	Maseru	Fr	Wonder Nhleko		
14-10	Lesotho	W	1-0	Maseru	Fr	Zweli Nxumalo [46]		
11-11	Lesotho	D	0-0	Manzini	Fr			

Fr = Friendly match • CN = CAF African Cup of Nations • CC = COSAFA Castle Cup • WC = FIFA World Cup • q = qualifier • r1 = first round group

SWAZILAND NATIONAL TEAM HISTORICAL RECORDS

Coaches: Jan Van Winckel BEL 2006 • Ayman El Yamani EGY 2006-07 • Martin Chabangu 2007 • Raoul Savoy SUI 2007-08 • Ephraim Mashaba RSA 2008-10 • Musa Zwane 2010-11 • Obed Mlotsa 2011 • Caleb Ngwenya 2011-12 • Valere Billen BEL 2012

SWAZILAND 2011-12

MTN PREMIER LEAGUE

	Pl	W	D	L	F	A	Pts	Swallows	Leopards	Sundowns	Highlanders	Wanderers	Chiefs	Pirates	Green Mamba	Buffaloes	Red Lions	Callies	Hellenic
Mbabane Swallows †	22	15	2	5	46	27	47		0-1	4-2	1-2	0-1	1-4	1-0	4-2	3-2	2-2	3-2	4-0
Royal Leopards	22	14	3	5	48	19	45	1-2		2-1	1-0	2-1	6-2	1-1	1-3	4-2	5-0	7-0	6-0
Manzini Sundowns	22	13	2	7	34	22	41	1-3	2-0		3-0	1-1	2-0	0-1	0-4	1-0	3-1	3-0	1-0
Mbabane Highlanders	22	12	4	6	29	21	40	1-2	1-0	0-3		1-0	1-4	0-0	3-0	2-0	4-1	2-0	0-0
Manzini Wanderers	22	11	5	6	33	20	38	0-1	1-2	2-1	2-1		1-1	2-0	0-1	2-1	5-0	4-1	1-2
Malanti Chiefs	22	10	6	6	47	35	36	2-2	2-2	2-3	0-1	2-1		1-2	2-2	2-2	2-1	3-1	2-1
Moneni Pirates	22	11	2	9	22	19	35	1-0	0-1	0-1	0-0	1-2	1-4		2-0	1-2	3-2	1-0	2-0
Green Mamba	22	10	4	8	29	27	34	0-1	1-3	0-2	1-1	0-2	0-3	1-0		1-0	1-0	3-0	0-0
Young Buffaloes	22	4	9	9	22	33	21	1-4	1-1	0-0	0-2	1-1	1-1	0-3	1-1		0-0	2-0	1-0
Masibini Red Lions	22	3	5	14	24	51	14	1-4	0-2	1-3	1-2	1-1	3-2	1-2	1-3	2-2		2-1	1-0
Tambankulu Callies	22	3	3	16	14	44	12	0-2	0-0	1-0	1-2	0-0	1-3	0-1	0-1	0-1	2-1		2-2
Hellenic FC	22	1	5	16	15	45	8	1-2	0-2	0-1	1-3	2-3	0-3	0-1	1-4	2-2	2-2	1-2	

10/09/2011 - 6/05/2012 • † Qualified for the CAF Champions League

MEDALS TABLE

		Overall G	Lge G	Cup G	City/Town
1	Mbabane Highlanders	19	12	7	Mbabane
2	Manzini Wanderers	7	6	1	Manzini
3	Mbabane Swallows	6	4	2	Mbabane
4	Eleven Men in Flight	5	2	3	Siteki
	Manzini Sundowns	5	2	3	Manzini
6	Royal Leopards	5	3	2	Simunye
7	Green Mamba	3	1	2	Matsapha
8	Mhlambanyatsi Rovers	2	1	1	Mhlambanyatsi
	Bulembu Young Aces	2		2	Bulembu
	Moneni Pirates	2		2	Manzini
11	Peacemakers	1	1		Mhlume
	Young Buffaloes	1	1		Matsapha
	Hub Sundowns	1		1	
	Malanti Chiefs	1		1	Pigg's Peak
	Mhlume United	1		1	Mhlume

SWAZI BANK CUP FINAL

Somhlolo National Stadium, Mbabane, 1-04-2012, Att: 18 000

Green Mamba 0 Tembe [42], Welile [45], Muntu [60]
Highlanders 1 Ndebele [68]

GREEN MAMBA
Mpendulo **DLAMINI** - Siphiwo **GAMEDZE**, Roger **BAHIYA**, Sabelo **SHILUBANE**, Ntobeko **MTHIMKHULU**, Mandla **MKHWANAZI**, Phumlani **NGWENYA**, Muzi **DLAMINI**, Muntu **MAMBA** (Musa **NGWENYA**), Lungelo **TEMBE**, Welile **MASEKO**

HIGHLANDERS
Sebenele **MALAZA** - Sipho **SIBANDZE**, Sabelo **GAMEDZE**, Thembumenzi **MAYISELA**, Mlungisi **NGUBANE**, Dumsani **MDLULI** (Hloniphani **NDEBELE**), Mfanafikile **NDZIMANDZE** (Sandile **NDWANDWE**), Vuyani **MAZIBUKO**, Msimisi **NCANYWA**, Muzi **DLAMINI**, Xolani **SIBANDZE**

SWAZI BANK CUP 2012

Round of 16		Quarter-finals		Semi-finals		Final	
Green Mamba	2						
Moneni Pirates	1	**Green Mamba**	2				
Manzini Wanderers	0	Young Buffaloes	0				
Young Buffaloes	1			**Green Mamba**	2		
Mbabane Swallows	2			Black Swallows	1		
Midas City	0	Mbabane Swallows	1 1				
Malanti Chiefs	0	**Black Swallows** †	2 3				
Black Swallows	3					**Green Mamba**	3
Masibini Red Lions						Mbabane Highlanders‡	1
Tambankulu Callies	0	**Masibini Red Lions**	3				
Mhlambanyatsi Rovers	0	Royal Leopards	1			CUP FINAL	
Royal Leopards	1			Masibini Red Lions	0	Somhlolo, Mbabane	
Manzini Sundowns	2			**Mbabane Highlanders**	4	1-04-2012, Att: 18 000	
Zwicle	0	Manzini Sundowns	0			Scorers - Tembe [42], Welile [45],	
Malkerns	1	**Mbabane Highlanders**	2			Muntu [60] for Mambas; Ndebele [68] for Highlanders	
Mbabane Highlanders	2	† First match annulled • ‡ Qualified for the CAF Confederation Cup					

SYR – SYRIA

FIFA/COCA-COLA WORLD RANKING

'93	'94	'95	'96	'97	'98	'99	'00	'01	'02	'03	'04	'05	'06	'07	'08	'09	'10	'11	'12
82	105	136	115	98	84	109	100	90	91	85	85	98	112	107	105	91	107	114	144

2012													High	Low	Av
Jan	Feb	Mar	Apr	May	Jun	Jul	Aug	Sep	Oct	Nov	Dec			
117	122	126	126	126	126	132	147	148	150	148	144	78	150	103

Two years of civil war have had a major impact on football in Syria with FIFA ordering the country not to host visiting teams due to security concerns. As a result the Syrian national side has adopted a nomadic existence playing its home games in the likes of Iran and Jordan. Several leading players have spoken out against the regime, including top striker Firas Al Khatib, who retired from representing Syria in 2012 before moving to China to sign for Shanghai Shenhua. Al Khatib's hometown of Homs was particularly badly affected by the conflict, with 25-year-old Al Wathba player Yousef Sulaiman killed in an attack on a hotel ahead of a league match with Al Nawair. Despite the upheaval, the national side - coached by Hossam Al Sayed - claimed the West Asian Championship for the first time ever, defeating Bahrain in the semi-finals on penalties after emerging from the group stages ahead of Iraq and Jordan. A 1-0 win over the Iraqis in the final, courtesy of a goal from Ahmed Al Salih, secured the title for the Syrians. The domestic league has been reconfigured for the 2013 season with all matches using Damascus as a centralised venue and the league divided into two groups of nine teams. Al Shorta emerged as the 2012 champions while Al Wahda were declared cup winners after the three other semi-finalists withdrew.

FIFA WORLD CUP RECORD
1930-1954 DNE 1958 DNQ 1962-1970 DN E 1974 DNQ 1978 DNE 1982-2014 DNQ

SYRIAN FOOTBALL ASSOCIATION (SFA)

Al Faihaa Sports Complex,
PO Box 421,
Damascus
+963 11 4330451
+963 11 3331511
syrianfa@hotmail.com

FA 1936 CON 1970 FIFA 1937
P Salah Edeen Ramadan
GS Toufik Sarhan

THE STADIA

2014 FIFA World Cup Stadia
Match played at King Abdullah International in Amman, Jordan

Main Stadia
Aleppo International Aleppo	75 000
Khaled bin Walid Homs	38 000
Abbasiyyin Stadium Damascus	25 000
Al As'ad Stadium Latakia	22 000

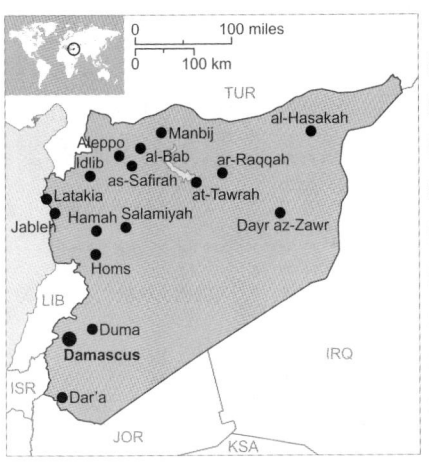

MAJOR CITIES/TOWNS

		Population
1	Aleppo	1 693 803
2	Damascus	1 614 297
3	Homs	869 718
4	Hamah	530 994
5	Latakia	366 566
6	Dayr az-Zawr	283 434
7	ar-Raqqah	196 529
8	al-Bab	159 784
9	Idlib	157 427
10	Duma	123 494
11	as-Safirah	117 831
12	Salamiyah	110 042
13	al-Hajar al-Aswad	105 060
14	Tartus	96 401
15	at-Tawrah	95 496
16	al-Qamisl	89 873
17	Ma'arrat-al-Numan	87 742
18	al-Hasakah	82 097
19	Jableh	78 163

AL JUMHURIYAH AL ARABIYAH AS SURIYAH • SYRIAN ARAB REPUBLIC

Capital	Damascus	Population	20 178 485 (57)	% in cities	54%
GDP per capita	$4600 (146)	Area km^2	185 180 km^2 (88)	GMT +/-	+2

Neighbours (km) Iraq 605, Israel 76, Jordan 375, Lebanon 375, Turkey 822 • Coast 193

RECENT INTERNATIONAL MATCHES PLAYED BY SYRIA

2011	Opponents	Score	Venue	Comp	Scorers	Att	Referee
2-01	UAE	L 0-2	Al Ain	Fr		2 400	Abdul BAKI OMA
9-01	Saudi Arabia	W 2-1	Al Rayyan	ACr1	Abdelrazaq Al Hussain 2 [38] [63]	15 768	Kim Dong Jin KOR
13-01	Japan	L 1-2	Doha	ACr1	Firas Al Khatib [76p]	10 453	Torky IRN
17-01	Jordan	L 1-2	Doha	ACr1	Mohamed Al Zeno [15]	9 849	Abdou QAT
29-06	Iraq	W 2-1	Arbil	Fr	Abdelrazaq Al Hussain [15], Nadim Sabagh [75]		
5-07	Jordan	W 3-1	Istanbul	Fr	Feras Ismail [25], Abdelrazaq Al Hussain [40], Maher Al Sayed [88]		
15-07	Oman	D 1-1	Seeb	Fr	Feras Ismail [85]		
23-07	Tajikistan	L 0-3	Amman	WCq	Orig W 2-1. George Mourad 45, Raja Rafe [77]	2 500	Al Ghafari JOR
28-07	Tajikistan	L 0-3	Tursunzade	WCq	Orig W 4-0. Raja Rafe 2 [6] [35], Nadim Sabagh [53], OG [86]		Mashentsev KGZ
10-08	Kazakhstan	D 1-1	Astana	WCq	Nadim Sabagh [63]		
17-08	Lebanon	W 3-2	Saida	Fr	Burhan Sahyouni [23], Maher Al Sayed [79], Nadim Sabagh [53]		
2012							
22-08	India	L 1-2	New Delhi	Fr	Alaa Al Shbli [92+]		Tseytlin UZB
27-08	Maldives	L 1-2	New Delhi	Fr	Alaa Al Shbli [81]		Santosh IND
30-08	Nepal	W 2-0	New Delhi	Fr	Hani Al Taiar [9], Ali Ghalioum [49]		Arumughan IND
17-11	Palestine	D 1-1	Amman	Fr	Ahmad Al Doni [60]		
20-11	Palestine	L 1-2	Zarqa	Fr	Ahmad Al Doni [70]		
13-12	Iraq	D 1-1	Kuwait City	WAr1	Ahmad Al Doni [48]	1 300	Mohamed UAE
16-12	Jordan	W 2-1	Kuwait City	WAr1	Ahmad Al Doni 2 [62] [82]	3 000	Ko Hyung Jin KOR
18-12	Bahrain	D 1-1	Kuwait City	WAsf	Ahmad Al Doni [72], W 3-2p	6 000	Shaban KUW
20-12	Iraq	W 1-0	Kuwait City	WAf	Ahmad Al Salih [74]	5 000	Tojo JPN

Fr = Friendly match • WA = West Asian Championship • AC = AFC Asian Cup • WC = FIFA World Cup
q = qualifier • r1 = first round group • sf = semi-final • 3p = third place play-off • f = final

SYRIA NATIONAL TEAM HISTORICAL RECORDS

Coaches: Jalal Talebi IRN 2001-02 • Janusz Wojcik 2003 • Ahmed Rifaat EGY 2003-04 • Miloslav Radenovic SRB 2005-06 • Fajr Ibrahim 2006-08 • Mohamed Qwayed 2008 • Fajr Ibrahim 2008-10 • Ayman Hakeem 2010 • Ratomir Dujkovic SRB 2010 • Tita Valeriu ROU 2010-11 • Claude Le Roy FRA 2011 • Nizar Mahrous 2011 • Marwan Khoury 2012 • Hossam Al Sayed 2012-

SYRIA 2011-12

PREMIER DIVISION	Pl	W	D	L	F	A	Pts	Shorta	Jaish	Wahda	Taliya	Majd	Baniyas	Wathba	Karama	Hurriya	Foutoua	Ittihad	Jazira	Hottin	Nwair	Teshrin
Al Shorta †	10	7	2	1	15	8	23		2-1 3-0 0-0	1-3	2-2	1-1 n/p							2-0			5-1
Al Jaish	9	3	4	2	15	8	13	0-1		0-0	1-0 0-0 0-0	6-0	0-1		2-1							
Al Wahda	10	3	4	3	7	9	13	2-0	0-2		n/p	1-3	9-1		0-1			1-2		2-0		
Al Taliya	9	3	3	3	12	10	12	1-2 1-0 0-0	0-0			0-0	2-2	0-1						2-1		
Al Majd	10	2	4	4	10	14	10	0-1	2-2	0-2	1-3 1-1			1-0	1-1		2-2		1-0			
Baniyas Refinery	10	1	3	6	9	15	6	0-1	3-3 0-0 0-1	0-2	2-0					2-3						1-1
Al Wathba		Withdrew after 1st round						1-5									1-0	0-1		2-1		
Al Karama		Withdrew after 1st round						1-4												0-0		0-0	1-0
Al Hurriya	12	7	2	3	22	8	**23**			1-1	0-2						1-2 0-1	1-1	4-1	3-0	1-0	5-0
Al Foutoua	12	4	6	2	17	7	**18**		1-2			2-2				0-0		3-0	0-0 0-5-1	1-1	9-2	
Al Ittihad	12	3	8	1	13	8	**17**	1-3					2-2		1-2	0-0			0-1 3-1	2-2	1-1	4-0
Al Jazira	12	4	5	3	17	19	**17**			1-1			0-1			2-1	1-1	3-2		1-1	1-1 2-7 2-2	
Hottin	12	3	6	3	16	21	**15**	0-1							1-0 2-1	3-2	1-2	1-1			2-1	2-2
Al Nwair	12	4	3	5	6	9	**15**						0-4			0-2	1-0	0-1 1-3	0-1	1-2		1-0
Teshrin	12	2	4	6	8	23	**10**		0-2							0-2	0-2 1-1 1-2 4-2	0-0	2-1 1-0		

9/10/2011 - 27/05/2012 • † Qualified for the AFC Cup • Tournament played in two stages. Final standings include only the matches played in the second round of championship and relegations groups. Matches in shaded boxes played in the first round except where there are two results in the same box. The second of these were played in the championship or relegation round.

TAH – TAHITI

FIFA/COCA-COLA WORLD RANKING

'93	'94	'95	'96	'97	'98	'99	'00	'01	'02	'03	'04	'05	'06	'07	'08	'09	'10	'11	'12
141	148	156	158	161	123	139	131	127	115	133	124	141	173	162	188	194	184	184	139

2012

Jan	Feb	Mar	Apr	May	Jun	Jul	Aug	Sep	Oct	Nov	Dec	High	Low	Av
184	184	183	179	179	179	138	136	119	127	139	139	111	195	151

2012 proved to be a sensational year for football in Tahiti with the national team becoming the champions of Oceania - the first nation other than New Zealand or Australia to do so - while club side Tefana came within a whisker of making it an unlikely double before losing narrowly in the final of the OFC Champions League to New Zealand's Auckland City. Tahiti's OFC Nations Cup success was unexpected but followed the impressive performances of the youth team in reaching the finals of the 2009 FIFA U-20 World Cup in Egypt and the beach soccer team which won the nation's first match at a FIFA tournament in the 2011 finals at Ravenna. Tahiti started the OFC Nations Cup with an impressive 10-0 win over Samoa and finished top of their group. In the semi-finals they held on to an early lead to beat hosts Solomon Islands before beating New Caledonia - victors over New Zealand in the semi-finals - 1-0 in the final, an early goal from Steevy Chong Hue creating history for the Tahitians. In the OFC Champions League, Tefana had surprisingly topped their group ahead of New Zealand's Waitakere United, but despite coming away from the away leg with a respectable 2-1 defeat against Auckland City in the final, they could not overturn the deficit in Fa'aa, losing to a solitary goal to go down 3-1 on aggregate.

FIFA WORLD CUP RECORD
1930-1990 DNE   1994-2010 DNQ

FEDERATION TAHITIENNE DE FOOTBALL (FTF)

Rue Coppenrath,
Stade de Fautaua,
BP 50358, Pirae 98716
☎ +689 540954
📠 +689 419629
✉ lara@ftf.pf
🖥 www.ftf.pf
FA 1989 CON 1990 FIFA 1990
P   Henry Ariiotima
GS Marc Ploton

THE STADIA

2014 FIFA World Cup Stadia	
Stade Pater	
Papeete	10 000
Other Main Stadia	
Stade Hamuta	
Papeete	10 000
Stade Louis Ganivet	
Fa'aa	5 000
Place To'ata	
Papeete	1 500

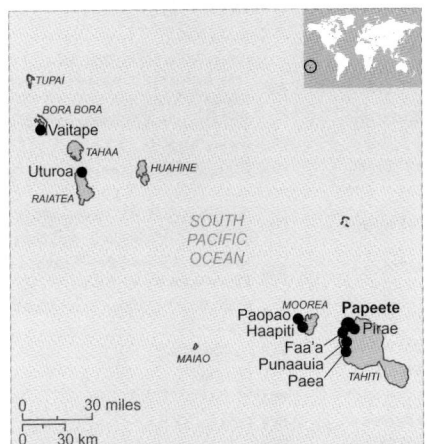

MAJOR CITIES/TOWNS

		Population
1	Faa'a (T)	30 448
2	Punaauia (T)	26 286
3	Papeete (T)	25 980
4	Mahina (T)	14 845
5	Pirae (T)	14 489
6	Paea (T)	12 139
7	Papara (T)	11 121
8	Arue (T)	9 543
9	Afaahiti (T)	5 720
10	Vaitape (BB)	5 182
11	Mataiea (T)	4 580
12	Paopao (M)	4 448
13	Papeari (T)	4 385
14	Haapiti (M)	4 264
15	Uturoa (R)	3 863
	(T) = Tahiti	
	(BB) = Bora Bora	
	(M) = Moorea	
	(R) = Raiatea	

POLYNESIE FRANCAISE • FRENCH POLYNESIA

Capital	Papete	Population	287 032 (179)	% in cities	52%
GDP per capita	$18 000 (68)	Area km^2	4167 km^2 (174)	GMT +/-	-10
Neighbours (km)	Coast 2525				

RECENT INTERNATIONAL MATCHES PLAYED BY TAHITI

2004	Opponents	Score	Venue	Comp	Scorers	Att	Referee
10-05	Cook Islands	W 2-0	Honiara	WCq	Axel Tematauа [2], Rino Moretta [80]	12 000	Singh FIJ
12-05	New Caledonia	D 0-0	Honiara	WCq		14 000	Rakaroi FIJ
17-05	Tonga	W 2-0	Honiara	WCq	Gabriel Wajoka [1], Axel Tematauа [78]	400	Sosongan PNG
19-05	Solomon Islands	D 1-1	Honiara	WCq	Vincent Simon [30]	18 000	Rakaroi FIJ
29-05	Fiji	D 0-0	Adelaide	WCq		3 000	Farina ITA
31-05	Australia	L 0-9	Adelaide	WCq		1 200	Attison VAN
2-06	Solomon Islands	L 0-4	Adelaide	WCq		50	Rakaroi FIJ
4-06	New Zealand	L 0-10	Adelaide	WCq		200	Shield AUS
6-06	Vanuatu	W 2-1	Adelaide	WCq	Axel Tematauа [40], Gabriel Wajoka [89]	300	Rakaroi FIJ

2005
No international matches played in 2005

2006
No international matches played in 2006

2007

25-08	New Caledonia	L 0-1	Apia	WCq		400	Hester NZL
29-08	Tuvalu †	D 1-1	Apia	WCq	Axel Williams [45]	100	Lengeta SOL
1-09	Fiji	L 0-4	Apia	WCq		200	Fox NZL
3-09	Cook Islands	W 1-0	Apia	WCq	Temarii Tinorua [64]	100	Aimaasu SAM

2008

24-09	New Caledonia	L 0-1	Paris	Fr			
27-09	Martinique †	L 0-1	Paris	Fr			
30-09	Guadeloupe †	L 0-1	Paris	Fr			

2009
No international matches played in 2009

2010

23-09	Martinique †	L 1-4	Paris	Fr	Li Fung Kee [27]		Panot FRA
26-09	Guadeloupe †	D 1-1	Paris	Fr	Lorenzo Tehau [57]. W 4-2p		Fouquet FRA
29-09	New Caledonia	D 1-1	Paris	Fr	Axel Williams [30]. W 5-3p		Fouquet FRA

2011

3-04	New Caledonia	L 1-3	Papeete	Fr	Sebastien Labayen [61p]		
7-04	New Caledonia	W 1-0	Papeete	Fr	Rochette [72]		
27-08	Fiji	L 0-3	Boulari	PGr1			Kerr NZL
30-08	Cook Islands	W 7-0	Boulari	PGr1	Taufa Neuffer [48], Stanley Atani [59], OG [69], Chong Hue 2 [73 91+], Hiroana Poroiae 2 [82p 89]		Oiaka SOL
1-09	Papua New Guinea	D 1-1	Boulari	PGr1	Stanley Atani [23]		Achari FIJ
5-09	Kiribati	W 17-1	Boulari	PGr1	Hiroana Poroiae 2 [16 44p], Chong Hue 4 [19 28 33 46], Efrain Araneda [21], Billy Mataitai [53], Teheivarii Ludivion [57], Teaonui Tehau 6 [73 79 85 88 90 91+], Stephane Faatiarau [83p], Stanley Atani [86]		Oiaka SOL
7-09	New Caledonia	L 1-3	Kone	PGsf	Hiroana Poroiae [52]		Varman FIJ
9-09	Fiji	W 2-1	Boulari	PG3p	Stanley Atani [5], Lorenzo Tehau [65]		Billon NCL

2012

1-06	Samoa	W 10-1	Honiara	OCr1	Lorenzo Tehau 4 [8 82 84 85], Jonathan Tehau 2 [16 78], Alvin Tehau 2 [18 40], Teaonui Tehau [54], Chong Hue [61]	3 000	Oiaka SOL
3-06	New Caledonia	W 4-3	Honiara	OCr1	Alvin Tehau [19], Nicolas Vallar [28p], Lorenzo Tehau [34], Roihau Degage [86]	3 500	Kerr NZL
5-06	Vanuatu	W 4-1	Honiara	OCr1	Nicolas Vallar [14p], Jonathan Tehau [37], Alvin Tehau [57], Teaonui Tehau [86]	1 000	O'Leary NZL
8-06	Solomon Islands	W 1-0	Honiara	OCsf	Jonathan Tehau [15]	15 000	O'Leary NZL
10-06	New Caledonia	W 1-0	Honiara	OCf	Chong Hue [10]	10 000	O'Leary NZL
7-09	Solomon Islands	L 0-2	Honiara	WCq		22 000	Cross NZL
11-09	New Caledonia	L 0-4	Papeete	WCq		574	Achari FIJ
12-10	New Zealand	L 0-2	Papeete	WCq		600	George VAN
16-10	New Zealand	L 0-3	Christchurch	WCq		10 751	Oiaka SOL

Fr = Friendly match • OC = OFC Oceania Cup • SP = South Pacific Games • WC = FIFA World Cup
q = qualifier • r1 = first roundgroup • sf = semi-final • 3p = third place play-off • † Not a full international

TAHITI 2011-12

DIVISION FEDERALE — STAGE ONE

	Pl	W	D	L	F	A	Pts	Dragon	Tefana	Manu Ura	Tamarii Faa'a	Central	Pirae	Roniu	Tamarii P'ruu	Tahiti U-20	Vénus	Vaiete
AS Dragon †	10	9	0	1	36	7	39					0-2	7-0		5-0		3-2	7-0
AS Tefana †	10	7	2	1	39	6	35	1-2				5-0	5-0			8-0	2-2	
AS Manu Ura †	10	6	3	1	24	13	31	0-2	1-1		1-1			4-2	2-1		4-1	7-2
AS Tamarii Faa'a †	10	5	3	2	28	17	30		0-1			3-1	1-1	4-5			7-2	5-3
AS Central Sport †	10	4	1	5	17	25	25			0-1				4-3	2-0			1-4
AS Pirae †	10	4	2	4	19	20	24	1-2			2-3	0-3			1-1	2-0		
AS Roniu †	10	4	0	6	27	36	24		1-5				3-5				5-3	
AS Tamarii Punaruu	10	2	2	6	12	22	22	1-3	0-6		1-3			3-0				
Tahiti U-20	10	3	2	5	20	31	21	0-5		1-1	2-2	0-4		2-5	3-2			10-1
AS Vénus	10	1	3	6	20	30	18					2-2	0-3		1-1	1-2		6-1
AS Vaiete	10	1	0	9	15	50	13		0-5					2-4	1-3	1-2		

1/10/2011 - 18/12/2011 • † Qualified for play-offs • Top six split off for a Championship play-off along with the champions of Temanava, while the bottom four join the top four of the second division in a relegation/promotion play-off group • Four points for a win, two points for a draw and one point for a defeat

CHAMPIONSHIP PLAY-OFF

	Pl	W	D	L	F	A	Pts	Dragon	Tamarii	Manu	Tefana	Central	Pirae	Mamarii	Roniu
AS Dragon †	14	11	3	0	42	9	52		1-0	3-0	0-0	4-1	5-3	2-1	6-0
AS Tamarii Faa'a	14	9	2	3	25	20	43	2-2		2-0	1-0	3-2	3-2	3-2	4-1
AS Manu Ura	14	8	3	3	29	15	41	0-0	1-0		1-1	5-3	3-0	4-1	3-0
AS Tefana	14	6	6	2	24	13	38	2-3	0-0	2-1		3-0	2-2	5-1	3-0
AS Central Sport	14	3	3	8	27	36	26	0-5	0-1	0-0	1-1		1-2	5-2	3-1
AS Pirae	14	3	3	8	21	35	26	0-4	2-3	1-3	1-1	2-5		2-1	0-1
AS Mamarii Tapuhute	14	3	2	9	23	39	25	0-5	6-0	0-5	2-3	4-3	2-2		1-0
AS Roniu	14	1	2	11	10	34	19	0-2	1-3	2-3	0-1	3-3	1-2	0-0	

14/01/2012 - 20/04/2012 • † Qualified for the OFC Champions League • Bonus points in brackets

RELEGATION/PROMOTION PLAY-OFF

	Pl	W	D	L	F	A	Pts	Venus	Vaiete	Olympic	Tamarii	Excelsior	Aorai	Vairao
AS Vénus	12	7	4	1	26	16	37		1-1	0-0	1-2	1-0	2-1	4-2
AS Vaiete	12	4	6	2	27	22	30	1-1		1-0	1-2	5-5	5-3	1-1
Olympic Mahina	12	5	2	5	20	17	29	2-4	3-3		0-1	2-3	3-0	2-0
AS Tamarii Punaruu	12	4	4	4	18	20	28	1-3	1-1	1-2		3-2	2-2	1-2
AS Excelsior	12	4	2	6	23	26	26	2-4	2-3	0-2	2-2		1-0	3-2
AS Aorai	12	4	2	6	20	23	26	2-2	2-1	2-3	3-1	1-3		3-0
AS Vairao	12	3	2	7	14	24	23	2-3	1-4	2-1	1-1	1-0	0-1	

16/01/2012 - 30/04/2012 • Top four play the 2012-13 season in the Division Federal

MEDALS TABLE

		Overall G	Lge G	Cup G	Town
1	AS Central Sport	38	20	18	Papeete
2	AS Venus	15	9	6	Mahina
	AS Pirae	15	7	8	Pirae
	AS Fei Pi	15	7	8	Papeete
5	AS Excelsior	11	7	4	Papeete
6	AS Tefana	8	3	5	Faa'a
	AS Jeunes Tahitiens	8	3	5	Papeete
8	AS Manu Ura	7	5	2	Papeete
9	AS Dragon	4	1	3	Papeete
10	AS PTT	3	1	2	Papeete
	AS Tamarii Punaruu	3	1	2	Papeete
12	AS Arue	2	1	1	Arue
13	CAICT	1		1	
	Marine	1		1	
	AS Temanava	1		1	Moorea
	AS Vaiete	1		1	Papeete

TAN – TANZANIA

FIFA/COCA-COLA WORLD RANKING

'93	'94	'95	'96	'97	'98	'99	'00	'01	'02	'03	'04	'05	'06	'07	'08	'09	'10	'11	'12
98	74	70	89	96	118	128	140	149	153	159	172	165	110	89	99	106	116	137	130

2012

Jan	Feb	Mar	Apr	May	Jun	Jul	Aug	Sep	Oct	Nov	Dec	High	Low	Av
137	139	141	145	145	139	127	128	132	132	134	130	65	175	122

Tanzania achieved success again at regional level in the CECAFA Kagame Inter-Club Cup on home soil in July when Young Africans beat fellow Dar-es-Salaam club Azam 2-0 in the final. For Yanga, as they are known, it was a second successive East African title after beating another home side, arch rivals Simba, in the 2011 final. Newcomers Azam continued their climb to prominence having only won a place in the top flight of Tanzanian football in 2008. In the Premier League it was Simba who took the honours after they finished six points ahead of Azam to reclaim the championship they had last won in 2010. In the 2012 CECAFA Cup, Tanzania's mainland team lost to Zanzibar in the third-place play-off of a tournament hosted by Uganda, having lost to the Ugandans in the semi-finals for the second year running. The Taifa Stars have been paired in a tough 2014 FIFA World Cup qualifying group with Cote d'Ivoire and Morocco - both past qualifiers for the finals - and they lost to the Ivorians in the opening match. They did, however, beat Gambia in the next match to revive their hopes. Kim Poulsen took over from compatriot Jan Poulsen as national coach when he was promoted from the under-20 side to replace his Danish namesake who was sacked in May, two months before the expiry of his two-year contract.

CAF AFRICA CUP OF NATIONS RECORD

1957-1965 DNE 1968 Withdrew 1970-1978 DNQ **1980** 8 r1 1982 DNE 1984 DNQ
1986 Withdrew 1988-1992 DNQ 1994 Withdrew 1996-2002 DNQ 2004 Withdrew 2006-2013 DNQ

THE FOOTBALL ASSOCIATION OF TANZANIA (FAT)

Karume Memorial Stadium, Uhuru/Shaurimoyo Moyo Road, Ilala, PO Box 1574, Dar-es-Salaam
☎ +255 755 264181
📠 +255 22 2861815
✉ info@tff.or.tz
🌐 www.tff.or.tz
FA 1930 CON 1960 FIFA 1964
P Leodegar Tenga
GS Angetile Osiah

THE STADIA

2014 FIFA World Cup Stadia
Benjamin Mkapa
Dar es Salaam ... 60 000
Other Main Stadia
CCM Kirumba Stadium
Mwanza ... 35 000
Sheikh Amri Abeid Memorial
Arusha ... 20 000
Uhuru Stadium
Dar es Salaam ... 20 000

MAJOR CITIES/TOWNS

		Population
1	Dar es Salaam	3 092 430
2	Mwanza	553 342
3	Zanzibar	473 666
4	Arusha	422 478
5	Mbeya	306 794
6	Morogoro	270 103
7	Tanga	240 027
8	Kigoma	176 371
9	Dodoma	174 467
10	Tabora	157 974
11	Moshi	155 237
12	Kasulu	139 205
13	Musoma	134 493
14	Songea	132 805
15	Kazilamihunda	130 879
16	Uvinza	123 799
17	Iringa	110 216
18	Turiani	90 129

JAMHURI YA MUUNGANO WA TANZANIA • UNITED REPUBLIC OF TANZANIA

Capital	Dodoma	Population	41 048 532 (30)	% in cities	25%
GDP per capita	$1400 (201)	Area km²	947 300 km² (31)	GMT +/-	+3
Neighbours (km)	Burundi 451, Congo DR 459, Kenya 769, Malawi 475, Mozambique 756, Rwanda 217, Uganda 396, Zambia 338 • Coast 1424				

RECENT INTERNATIONAL MATCHES PLAYED BY TANZANIA

2011	Opponents	Score	Venue	Comp	Scorers	Att	Referee
5-01	Egypt	L 1-5	Cairo	Fr	Rashid Gumbo 82		
8-01	Burundi	D 1-1	Cairo	Fr	Shadrack Nsajigwa 76p		
11-01	Uganda	D 1-1	Cairo	Fr	Yudah Mugalu 64		
16-01	Sudan	L 0-2	Cairo	Fr			
9-02	Palestine	W 1-0	Dar es Salaam	Fr	Mrisho Ngassa 63		
26-03	Central African Rep	W 2-1	Dar es Salaam	CNq	Shaban Nditi 49, Mbwana Samata 91+		
23-04	Mozambique	L 0-2	Maputo	Fr			
14-05	South Africa	L 0-1	Dar es Salaam	Fr			
5-06	Central African Rep	L 1-2	Bangui	CNq	Shaban Nditi 76		
3-09	Algeria	D 1-1	Dar es Salaam	CNq	Mbwana Samata 22		
9-10	Morocco	L 1-3	Marrakech	CNq	Abdi Kassim Sadala 40		
11-11	Chad	W 2-1	N'Djamena	WCq	Mrisho Ngassa 11, Bakari Hamadi 80	10 000	Ogunkolade NGA
15-11	Chad	L 0-1	Dar es Salaam	WCq		42 700	Nampiandraza MAD
26-11	Rwanda	L 0-1	Dar es Salaam	CCr1			
29-11	Djibouti	W 3-0	Dar es Salaam	CCr1	Thomas Ulimwengu 2, Mwinyi Kazimoto 37, Rashid Yusuf 85		
3-12	Zimbabwe	L 1-2	Dar es Salaam	CCr1	Mwinyi Kazimoto 88p		
6-12	Malawi	W 1-0	Dar es Salaam	CCqf	Nurdin Bakari 37		
8-12	Uganda	L 1-3	Dar es Salaam	CCsf	Mrisho Ngassa 17		
10-12	Sudan	L 0-1	Dar es Salaam	CC3p			
2012							
23-02	Congo DR	D 0-0	Dar es Salaam	Fr			
29-02	Mozambique	D 1-1	Dar es Salaam	CNq	Mwinyi Kazimoto 38		Farouk EGY
26-05	Malawi	D 0-0	Dar es Salaam	Fr			
2-06	Côte d'Ivoire	L 0-2	Abidjan	WCq		15 000	Jedidi TUN
10-06	Gambia	W 2-1	Dar es Salaam	WCq	Shomari Kapombe 61, Erasto Nyoni 85	20 000	Ruzive ZIM
17-06	Mozambique	D 1-1	Maputo	CNq	Aggrey Morris 89, L 6-7p		Bennett RSA
15-08	Botswana	D 3-3	Molepole	Fr	Erasto Nyoni 17, Mwinyi Kazimoto 31, Mrisho Ngasa 84		
25-11	Sudan	W 2-0	Kampala	CCr1	John Bocco 2 14 29		Batte UGA
28-11	Burundi	L 0-1	Kampala	CCr1			Kalema UGA
1-12	Somalia	W 7-0	Kampala	CCr1	Mrisho Ngassa 5 1 23 44 73 75, John Bocco 2 26 42		Kalema UGA
3-12	Rwanda	W 2-0	Kampala	CCqf	Amri Kiemba 34, John Bocco 54		El Fadhil SDN
6-12	Uganda	L 0-3	Kampala	CCsf			El Fadhil SDN
8-12	Zanzibar †	D 1-1	Kampala	CC3p	Mwinyi Kazimoto 19, L 5-6p		Batte UGA

Fr = Friendly match • CN = CAF African Cup of Nations • CC = CECAFA Cup • WC = FIFA World Cup
q = qualifier • r1 = first round group • sf = semi-final • f = final • † Not a full international

TANZANIA 2011-12

PREMIER LEAGUE (LIGI KUU TANZANIA BARA)

	Pl	W	D	L	F	A	Pts	Simba	Azzam Utd	Yanga	Mtibwa Sugar	Coastal Union	JKT Oljoro	Kagera Sugar	Ruvu Stars	Shooting Stars	African Lyon	Toto Africa	Villa Squad	Moro Utd	Polisi Dodoma
Simba SC †	26	19	5	2	47	12	62		2-0	5-0	1-0	2-1	2-0	3-1	2-0	2-0	4-0	0-0	1-0	3-0	1-0
Azzam United ‡	26	17	5	4	40	15	56	0-0		1-0	1-2	3-0	3-0	2-1	4-1	1-0	0-1	3-1	4-1	1-0	3-1
Young Africans	26	15	4	7	41	30	49	1-0	1-3		3-1	5-0	1-0	1-0	0-1	1-0	1-0	4-2	3-2	1-1	3-1
Mtibwa Sugar	26	12	6	8	34	25	42	1-2	1-0	0-0		0-1	0-1	1-0	1-1	2-1	2-2	2-1	2-1	3-1	4-0
Coastal Union	26	12	3	11	27	28	39	0-1	0-1	3-0	1-1		1-0	1-1	2-0	1-0	1-0	6-1	1-2	1-0	
JKT Oljoro	26	9	8	9	20	25	35	0-2	1-1	1-4	1-0	1-0		0-1	0-1	0-1	0-0	1-1	1-0	1-0	1-0
Kagera Sugar	26	7	11	8	26	27	32	1-1	0-0	1-0	0-2	1-0	1-2		0-1	0-0	1-1	1-0	1-1	2-2	2-0
JKT Ruvu Stars	26	7	11	8	27	34	32	0-3	0-2	1-3	3-2	3-0	0-0	2-2		2-2	1-1	0-0	0-0	2-2	0-1
Ruvu Shooting Stars	26	7	10	9	24	24	31	0-1	0-0	1-1	3-1	2-1	1-1	1-1	1-1		2-0	2-0	1-2	1-0	0-0
African Lyon	26	6	9	11	23	30	27	0-2	1-2	1-2	0-0	0-1	2-2	0-1	2-0	0-1		1-1	3-1	2-1	2-0
Toto Africa	26	5	11	10	24	31	26	3-3	1-1	3-2	0-2	0-0	0-2	1-1	0-0	1-0	3-0		3-0	0-0	2-1
Villa Squad	26	7	5	14	29	46	26	1-0	0-0	0-1	0-2	4-2	1-2	2-4	1-2	2-2	0-0	2-0		1-1	2-1
Moro United	26	3	10	13	28	46	19	3-3	0-1	2-2	0-1	0-2	2-2	2-2	1-3	1-0	0-3	2-1	1-2		2-5
Polisi Dodoma	26	3	8	15	20	37	17	0-1	0-1	0-1	1-1	0-1	0-0	1-0	2-2	2-2	1-1	0-0	1-2	2-2	

20/08/2011 - 6/05/2012 • † Qualified for the CAF Champions League • ‡ Qualified for the CAF Confederation Cup

TCA – TURKS AND CAICOS ISLANDS

FIFA/COCA-COLA WORLD RANKING

'93	'94	'95	'96	'97	'98	'99	'00	'01	'02	'03	'04	'05	'06	'07	'08	'09	'10	'11	'12
-	-	-	-	-	-	196	200	200	202	203	203	203	169	181	168	177	187	200	207

2012														
Jan	Feb	Mar	Apr	May	Jun	Jul	Aug	Sep	Oct	Nov	Dec	High	Low	Av
200	205	205	205	205	206	205	206	206	207	207	207	158	207	192

The TCIFA passed up the chance to enter the 2012 Caribbean Cup which meant that for the third tournament running the national team was unable to test itself at the top level of Caribbean football. It also left the team without any games until the next edition in 2014 or, failing that, the qualifiers for the 2018 FIFA World Cup in Russia. Inevitably the team plunged down the FIFA/Coca-Cola World Ranking, reaching the bottom in October 2012 alongside Bhutan and San Marino. There was some disruption to sporting activity in Providenciales with a legal dispute affecting the National Stadium while unpaid water bills meant facilities had to be closed when supplies were cut off but a championship was played and was won by newcomers Cheshire Hall. Coached by Oliver Smith they finished the season unbeaten after winning seven of the eight games and only dropping points against runners-up SWA Sharks - the oldest club in the league. The only other match Cheshire Hall didn't win during the season was a group game against Sharks in the President's Cup but they qualified for the final ahead of their rivals on goal difference thanks to a 13-0 thrashing of HAB. In the final they met Pedagogue and at the TCIFA National Academy, a match they won 4-2 thanks to a Samuel Narcius hat trick to complete the league and cup double.

CFU CARIBBEAN CUP RECORD
1989-1998 DNE 1999 DNQ 2001-2005 DNE 2007 DNQ 2008-2012 DNE

TURKS AND CAICOS ISLANDS FOOTBALL ASSOCIATION (TCIFA)

TCIFA National Academy,
PO Box 626,
Providenciales
☎ +1 649 9415532
+1 649 9415554
tcifa@tciway.tc
www.football.tc
FA 1996 CON 1998 FIFA 1998
P Christopher Bryan
GS Sonia Bien-Aime

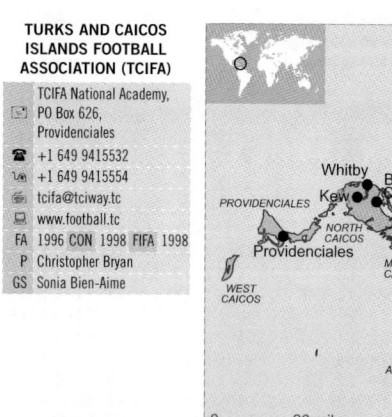

MAJOR TOWNS

Grand Turk
Cockburn Town (3 691)
Salt Cay
Balfour Town
Providenciales
Providenciales
North Caicos
Bottle Creek
Kew
Whitby
Sandy Point
Middle Caicos
Conch Bar
Lorimers
Bambarra
Turks Islands
Balfour Town

THE STADIA
2014 FIFA World Cup Stadia
TCIFA National Academy
Providenciales
Other Main Stadia
National Stadium
Providenciales   3 000

TURKS AND CAICOS ISLANDS

Capital	Cockburn Town	Population	22 942 (216)
GDP per capita	$11 500 (97)	Area km²	948 km² (185)
Neighbours (km)	Coast 389	% in cities	92%
		GMT +/-	-5

TCA – TURKS AND CAICOS ISLANDS

RECENT INTERNATIONAL MATCHES PLAYED BY TURKS AND CAICOS

2004	Opponents	Score	Venue	Comp	Scorers	Att	Referee
18-02	Haiti	L 0-5	Miami †	WCq		3 000	Stott USA
21-02	Haiti	L 0-2	Hialeah †	WCq		3 000	Valenzuela USA
2005							
No international matches played in 2005							
2006							
2-09	Cuba	L 0-6	Havana	CCq		2 000	Campbell JAM
4-09	Cayman Islands	W 2-0	Havana	CCq	Gavin Glinton [14], Maxime Fleuriot [72]	100	Stennett JAM
6-09	Bahamas	L 2-3	Havana	CCq	Gavin Glinton 2 [51 72]	120	Campbell JAM
2007							
No international matches played in 2007							
2008							
6-02	St Lucia	W 2-1	Providenciales	WCq	David Lowery [31], Gavin Glinton [74]	2 200	Whittaker CAY
26-03	St Lucia	L 0-2	Vieux Fort	WCq		1 200	Forde BRB
2009							
No international matches played in 2009							
2010							
No international matches played in 2010							
2011							
2-07	Bahamas	L 0-4	Providenciales	WCq		1 021	Cruz CRC
9-07	Bahamas	L 0-6	Nassau	WCq		1 600	Santos PUR
2012							
No international matches played in 2012							

CC = Digicel Caribbean Cup • WC = FIFA World Cup • q = qualifier • † Both matches played in the USA

TURKS AND CAICOS ISLANDS NATIONAL TEAM HISTORICAL RECORDS

Coach: Luigino Pacetto ITA 1999 • Charlie Cook 2000-03 • Paul Crosbie SCO 2003-04 • Matthew Green ENG 2006-08 • Gary Brough 2011-

TURKS AND CAICOS ISLANDS 2011-12

WIV PROVO PREMIER LEAGUE

	Pl	W	D	L	F	A	Pts	Cheshire Hall	SWA Sharks	AFC Academy	Pedagogue	HAB
Cheshire Hall	8	7	1	0	34	8	**22**		1-0	6-3	3-0	5-1
SWA Sharks	8	5	1	2	19	10	**16**	2-2		3-1	2-0	3-0
AFC Academy	8	2	2	4	15	23	**8**	0-3	3-1		1-1	3-2
Pedagogue	8	2	1	5	20	25	**7**	0-7	3-5	6-3		1-4
HAB	8	1	1	6	10	32	**4**	2-7	0-3	1-1	0-9	

21/01/2012 - 7/04/2012 •

Top scorers: 11 - Samuel **NARCIUS**, Cheshire Hall & Fred **DORVIL**, AFC Academy • 7 - Dukens **DORISCA**, HAB • 6 - Stevens **DERILIEN**, SWA Sharks

PRESIDENT'S CUP 2012

Group Stage

	Pl	W	D	L	F	A	Pts	CH	SWA	AFC	HAB
Pedagogue †	2	2	0	0	9	5	6			4-3	5-2
Cheshire Hall †	2	1	1	0	15	2	4		2-2		13-0
SWA Sharks	2	1	1	0	4	3	4			2-1	
AFC Academy	2	0	0	2	4	6	0				
HAB	2	0	0	2	2	18	0				

† Qualified for the final
Played 14/04/2012 - 5/05/2012

Final

Cheshire Hall	4
Pedagogue	2

CUP FINAL
TCIFA National Academy
5-05-2012, Scorers - Samuel Narcius 3,
David Archer for Cheshire Hall;
Alex Cranston, Marknique Williams pen
for Pedagogue

TGA – TONGA

FIFA/COCA-COLA WORLD RANKING

'93	'94	'95	'96	'97	'98	'99	'00	'01	'02	'03	'04	'05	'06	'07	'08	'09	'10	'11	'12
-	-	-	164	174	163	178	185	173	175	180	183	185	188	170	188	188	188	176	185

2012

Jan	Feb	Mar	Apr	May	Jun	Jul	Aug	Sep	Oct	Nov	Dec	High	Low	Av
176	177	176	178	177	176	175	174	172	174	177	185	163	202	180

The start of the Tongan 2012 Major League season was delayed due to the mourning period for the late King George Tupou V, but when it did get underway in September it had expanded to 22 teams in the men's section and nine in the women's, along with 16 youth teams - a reflection of the growing popularity of football in the country and a tribute to the excellent facilities players and officials can now enjoy due to the FIFA Goal programme. Earlier in the year the senior men's league had been won, yet again, by Lotoha'apai United who then played host to a preliminary round of the 2012-13 OFC Champions League at the Loto-Tonga Centre to the south of the capital Nuku'alofa across the Fanga'uta Lagoon. It was a rare experience for football fans to watch a senior international football event and there was plenty of drama as teams from four of the weakest OFC nations battled it out for a place in the group stage of the tournament. Having already notched up a first-ever win in the tournament, Lotoha'apai United went into their final game against Samoa's Kiwi knowing that a solid win would likely see them through, a match they duly won 2-1. What they didn't count on, however, was rivals Tupapa from the Cook Islands winning their game 9-0 against Pago Youth from American Samoa, a result which saw the Tongans knocked out on goal difference.

FIFA WORLD CUP RECORD
1930-1994 DNE **1998-2014** DNQ

TONGA FOOTBALL ASSOCIATION (FTF)

Loto Tonga Soko Center,
Off Valungafulu Road -
'Atele, PO Box 852,
Nuku'alofa
☎ +676 30233
📠 +676 30240
✉ tfa@kalianet.to
🖥 www.tongafootball.to
FA 1965 CON 1994 FIFA 1994
P Lord Veehala
GS Lui Aho

THE STADIA
2014 FIFA World Cup Stadia
Tonga played their qualifiers in a group at the Toleafoa J.S. Blatter Complex in Apia, Samoa
Other Main Stadia
Teufaiva Sports Stadium
Niku'alofa   10 000
Loto-Tonga Centre
'Atele   500

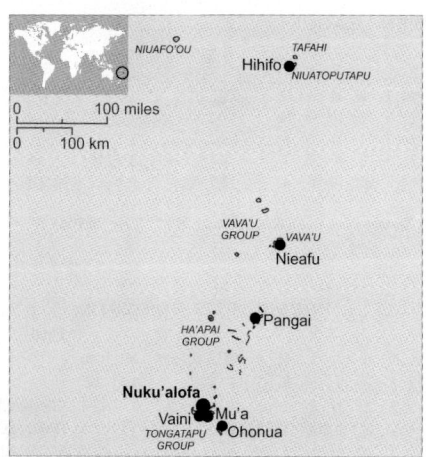

MAJOR CITIES/TOWNS
		Population
1	Nuku'alofa	24 184
2	Mu'a	5 140
3	Neiafu	3 969
4	Haveloloto	3 518
5	Vaini	3 064
6	Tofoa-Koloua	2 610
7	Pangai	1 591
8	Ohonua	1 252
9	Hihifo	671

PULE'ANGA TONGA • KINGDOM OF TONGA

Capital	Nuku'alofa	Population	120 898 (188)	% in cities	25%
GDP per capita	$4600 (145)	Area km^2	747 km^2 (189)	GMT +/-	+13
Neighbours (km)	Coast 419				

RECENT INTERNATIONAL MATCHES PLAYED BY TONGA

2002	Opponents	Score	Venue	Comp	Scorers	Att	Referee
No international matches played in 2002 after June							
2003							
1-07	Papua New Guinea	D 2-2	Suva	SPr1	Unaloto-Ki-Atenoa Feao 2 [62] [75]	3 000	Singh FIJ
3-07	New Caledonia	L 0-4	Suva	SPr1		700	Shah FIJ
5-07	Micronesia †	W 7-0	Nausori	SPr1	Ipeni Fonua [5], Maamaloa Tevi [15], Mark Uhatahi 2 [22] [36], Unaloto-Ki-Atenoa Feao 2 [34] [55], Kilifi Uele [72]	1 000	Moli SOL
7-07	Tahiti	L 0-4	Lautoka	SPr1		3 000	Shah FIJ
2004							
10-05	Solomon Islands	L 0-6	Honiara	WCq		12 385	Attison VAN
15-05	Cook Islands	W 2-1	Honiara	WCq	Mark Uhatahi [46], Viliami Vaitaki [61]	15 000	Sosongan PNG
17-05	Tahiti	L 0-2	Honiara	WCq		400	Sosongan PNG
19-05	New Caledonia	L 0-8	Honiara	WCq		14 000	Fred VAN
2005							
No international matches played in 2005							
2006							
No international matches played in 2006							
2007							
27-08	Solomon Islands	L 0-4	Apia	WCq		350	Aimaasu SAM
29-08	Samoa	L 1-2	Apia	WCq	Unaloto-Ki-Atenoa Feao [54]	1 850	Sosongan PNG
1-09	American Samoa	W 4-0	Apia	WCq	Lafaele Moala [38], Pio Palu 2 [56] [63], Kaisani Uhatahi [86]	200	Minan PNG
3-09	Vanuatu	L 1-4	Apia	WCq	Malakai Savieti [50]	50	Minan PNG
2008							
No international matches played in 2008							
2009							
11-06	Cook Islands	D 1-1	Atele	Fr	Mark Uhatahi [35]		
13-06	Cook Islands	L 1-2	Atele	Fr	Mark Uhatahi [48]		
2010							
No international matches played in 2010							
2011							
22-11	American Samoa	L 1-2	Apia	WCq	Unaloto-Ki-Atenoa Feao [88]	150	Achari FIJ
24-11	Samoa	D 1-1	Apia	WCq	Lokoua Taufahema [81]	180	Jacques TAH
26-11	Cook Islands	W 2-1	Apia	WCq	Timote Maamaloa [26], Kinitoni Falatau [90]	200	Ambassa NCL
2012							
No international matches played in 2012							

Fr = Friendly match • SP = South Pacific Games • WC = FIFA World Cup • q = qualifier • r1 = first round group • † Not a full international

THA – THAILAND

FIFA/COCA-COLA WORLD RANKING

'93	'94	'95	'96	'97	'98	'99	'00	'01	'02	'03	'04	'05	'06	'07	'08	'09	'10	'11	'12
69	85	77	57	54	45	60	61	61	66	60	79	111	137	121	126	105	121	122	136

2012														
Jan	Feb	Mar	Apr	May	Jun	Jul	Aug	Sep	Oct	Nov	Dec	High	Low	Av
124	130	139	141	141	136	135	133	131	139	152	136	43	152	86

Thailand's status as the pre-eminent football nation in southeast Asia was undermined when the national team was beaten in the final of the 2012 AFF Suzuki Cup by Singapore, a defeat that saw Singapore overtake the Thais to become the most successful nation in the history of the regional tournament. The loss heaped pressure on their German coach Winfried Schafer's who took over in 2011 from former England midfielder Bryan Robson and Thailand have now not won the hotly contested tournament since 2002. In club football the Thai Premier League continued to grow in status and was won in 2012 by Muangthong United who reclaimed the title from 2011 champions Buriram United. Buriram did, however, claim a cup double after winning both the FA Cup and League Cup. They and Muangthong have established themselves as the powerhouses of the club game in the country and both qualified to take part in the 2013 AFC Champions League, with Muangthong securing an automatic berth in the group stages and Buriram taking a spot in the qualifying rounds. Buriram will be keen to build on their debut in the continental club competition in 2012 when they secured wins over Chinese champions Guangzhou Evergrande and J.League champions Kashiwa Reysol, only to miss out narrowly on a place in the knock-out phase.

FIFA WORLD CUP RECORD
1930-1970 DNE 1974-2014 DNQ

THE FOOTBALL ASSOCIATION OF THAILAND (FAT)

National Stadium, Gate 3, Rama 1 Road, Patumwan, 10330 Bangkok
☎ +66 2 2164691
+66 2 2154494
secretariat@fat.or.th
www.fat.or.th
FA 1916 CON 1957 FIFA 1925
P Worawi Makudi
GS Ong-Arj Kosinkar

THE STADIA

2014 FIFA World Cup Stadia
Rajamangala National Stadium
Bangkok   65 000
Suphachalasai
Bangkok   30 000
I-Mobile Stadium 'Thunder Castle'
Buriram   24 000

Other Main Stadia
700th Anniversary Stadium
Chiang Mai   25 000

MAJOR CITIES/TOWNS

		Population
1	Bangkok	5 802 832
2	Samut Prakan	446 375
3	Nonthaburi	396 669
4	Udon Thani	228 738
5	Chon Buri	202 292
6	Nakhon Ratchasima	201 685
7	Hat Yai	199 062
8	Phra Pradaeng	196 644
9	Pak Kret	193 071
10	Si Racha	184 893
11	Chiang Mai	184 887
12	Thanyaburi	171 301
13	Khlong Luang	155 444
14	Khon Kaen	140 520
15	Lampang	138 088
16	Nakhon Pathom	128 097
17	Surat Thani	127 309
18	Rayong	126 773
19	Nakhon Si Thammarat	117 441

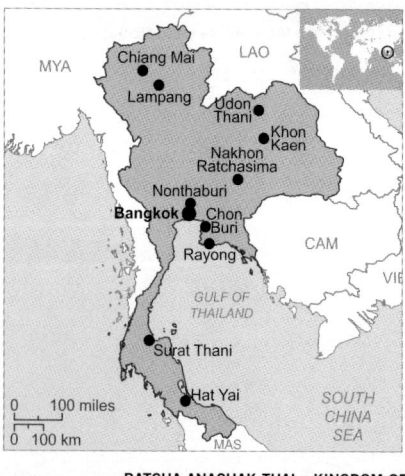

RATCHA ANACHAK THAI • KINGDOM OF THAILAND

Capital Bangkok   Population 65 905 410 (20)   % in cities 33%
GDP per capita $8400 (118)   Area km^2 513 120 km^2 (50)   GMT +/- +7
Neighbours (km) Myanmar 1800, Cambodia 803, Laos 1754, Malaysia 506 • Coast 3219

THA - THAILAND

RECENT INTERNATIONAL MATCHES PLAYED BY THAILAND

2009	Opponents	Score	Venue	Comp	Scorers	Att	Referee
14-01	Jordan	D 0-0	Amman	ACq		5 000	Racho SYR
21-01	Lebanon	W 2-1	Phuket	Fr	Teerasil Dangda [12], Suchao Nutnum [22]		
28-01	Iran	D 0-0	Bangkok	ACq		10 000	Kovalenko UZB
5-02	Saudi Arabia	L 1-2	Sendai	Fr	Teerasil Dangda [89]		
28-03	New Zealand	W 3-1	Bangkok	Fr	Teerasil Dangda 2 [12 74], Tawan Sripan [21]		
8-11	Syria	D 1-1	Bangkok	Fr	Teeratep Winothai [59]		
14-11	Singapore	W 3-1	Singapore	ACq	Sutee Suksomkit 2 [12p 81], Therdsak Chaiman [76]	22 183	Takayama JPN
18-11	Singapore	L 0-1	Bangkok	ACq		30 000	Balideh QAT
29-12	Zimbabwe	W 3-0	Bangkok	Fr	Sutinun Phukhom 2 [27 81], Kirati Keawsombut [84]		
2010							
6-01	Jordan	D 0-0	Bangkok	ACq		15 000	Williams AUS
17-01	Singapore	W 1-0	N'hon Ratchasima	Fr	Sutee Suksomkit [59]		Mbaga TAN
20-01	Poland	L 1-3	N'hon Ratchasima	Fr	Therdsak Chaiman [90p]	20 000	Mbaga TAN
23-01	Denmark	L 0-3	N'hon Ratchasima	Fr			
3-03	Iran	L 0-1	Tehran	ACq		17 000	Balideh QAT
16-05	South Africa	L 0-4	Nelspruit	Fr		30 000	Kipngetich KEN
11-08	Singapore	W 1-0	Nonthaburi	Fr	Sarayoot Chaikamdee [28]		Aonrak THA
4-09	India	W 1-0	Bangkok	Fr	Sarayoot Chaikamdee [72]		Mahapab THA
8-09	India	W 2-1	New Delhi	Fr	Teeratep Winothai [48], Keerati Keawsombut [64]		
1-12	Laos	D 2-2	Jakarta	AFFr1	Sarayoot Chaikamdee 2 [67 91+]		Sato JPN
4-12	Malaysia	D 0-0	Jakarta	AFFr1			Win Cho MYA
7-12	Indonesia	L 1-2	Jakarta	AFFr1	Sukha Suree [68]	65 000	Sato JPN
2011							
14-07	Myanmar	W 1-0	Buriram	Fr	Teerasil Dangda [2]		
15-07	Myanmar	D 1-1	Buriram	Fr	Jakkapan Pornsai [17p]		
23-07	Palestine	W 1-0	Buriram	WCq	Jakkaphan Kaewprom [18]	17 000	Lee Min Hu KOR
28-07	Palestine	D 2-2	Al Ram	WCq	Datsakorn Thonglao 2 [34 93+]	11 500	Abbas BHR
24-08	Singapore	D 0-0	Bangkok	Fr			
2-09	Australia	L 1-2	Brisbane	WCq	Teerasil Dangda [15]	24 540	Balideh QAT
6-09	Oman	W 3-0	Bangkok	WCq	Sompong Soleb [35], Teerasil Dangda [41], OG [91+]	19 000	Kim Dong Jin KOR
6-10	Jordan	D 0-0	Bangkok	Fr			
11-10	Saudi Arabia	D 0-0	Bangkok	WCq		42 000	Irmatov UZB
11-11	Saudi Arabia	L 0-3	Riyadh	WCq		32 500	Liu Kwok Man HKG
15-11	Australia	L 0-1	Bangkok	WCq		19 400	Mozaffari IRN
2012							
18-01	Norway	L 0-1	Bangkok	Fr		6 000	Yamamoto JPN
24-02	Maldives	W 3-0	Chiang Mai	Fr	Chatree Chimtalay		
29-02	Oman	L 0-2	Muscat	WCq		22 000	Toma JPN
7-11	Malaysia	W 2-0	Bangkok	Fr	Prayad Boonya [26], Arthit Sunthornphit [80]		
14-11	Bhutan	W 5-0	Bangkok	Fr	Apipoo Suntornpanavej 3 [5 6 29], Napat Thamrongsupakorn [36], Rattana Phectaporn [50]		
17-11	Bangladesh	W 5-0	Bangkok	Fr	Phichitpong Choeichiu [5], Teerasil Dangda 3 [12 20 52], Napat Thamrongsupakorn [74]		
24-11	Philippines	W 2-1	Bangkok	AFFr1	Jakkapan Pornsai [39], Anucha Kitpongsri [41]	9 503	Sato JPN
27-11	Myanmar	W 4-0	Bangkok	AFFr1	Teerasil Dangda 3 [20 82 89], Apipoo Suntornpanavej [59]	12 797	Abdul BAki OMA
30-11	Vietnam	W 3-1	Bangkok	AFFr1	Kirati Keawsombut 2 [21 65], OG [82]	13 196	Sato JPN
9-12	Malaysia	D 1-1	Kuala Lumpur	AFFsf	Teerasil Dangda [79]	87 410	Torki IRN
13-12	Malaysia	W 2-0	Bangkok	AFFsf	Teerasil Dangda [60], Theerathon Butmathan [65]	19 566	Lee Min Hu KOR
19-12	Singapore	L 1-3	Singapore	AFFf	Adul Lahsoh [65]	7 613	Toma JPN
22-12	Singapore	W 1-0	Bangkok	AFFf	Kirati Keawsombut [45]	23 158	Irmatov UZB

Fr = Friendly match • AFF = ASEAN Football Federation Championship • AC = AFC Asian Cup • WC = FIFA World Cup • q = qualifier • r1 = 1st round

THAILAND NATIONAL TEAM HISTORICAL RECORDS

Coaches: Burkhard Ziese GER 1985-86 • Carlos Roberto de Carvalho BRA 1989-91 • Peter Stubbe GER 1992-94 • Worawit Sumpachanyasathit 1994 • Chatchai Paholpat 1994-95 • Arj-han Srongngamsub 1996 • Thawatchai Sartjakul 1996 • Dettmar Cramer GER 1997 • Withaya Laohakul 1997-98 • Peter Withe ENG 1998-2002 • Carlos Roberto de Carvalho BRA 2003-04 • Chatchai Paholpat 2004-04 • Siegfried Held GER 2004-05 • Charnwit Polcheewin 2005-08 • Peter Reid ENG 2008-09 • Bryan Robson ENG 2009-11 • Winfried Schafer GER 2011-

THAILAND 2012

SPONSOR THAI PREMIER LEAGUE

	Pl	W	D	L	F	A	Pts	Muangthong	Chonburi	BEC Tero	Buriram Utd	Osotspa	Esan Utd	Samut	B'kok Glass	Chiangrai Utd	Army Utd	Police Utd	TOT-CAT	Wuachon Utd	Chainat	Pattaya Utd	Thai Port	BBCU	TTM
Muangthong United †	34	25	9	0	78	31	84		2-0	2-1	1-1	2-1	3-0	1-0	2-2	2-0	2-1	3-1	2-1	2-0	1-0	3-2	5-1	2-0	3-0
Chonburi	34	21	7	6	65	33	70	2-2		3-0	4-2	3-1	5-1	1-2	1-1	2-1	3-1	1-0	2-0	1-0	4-3	2-1	4-0	4-1	1-0
BEC Tero Sasana	34	16	9	9	53	43	57	2-2	1-2		0-0	0-4	0-1	1-0	3-0	3-2	0-0	2-2	2-1	2-1	4-2	3-1	0-2	1-1	7-1
Buriram United	34	14	12	8	60	40	54	1-1	3-4	0-1		4-2	2-2	0-0	3-2	3-1	1-1	2-2	2-1	0-0	7-2	1-1	1-0	3-0	1-0
Osotspa Saraburi	34	16	4	14	55	48	52	1-2	3-1	2-3	2-1		2-1	0-1	1-3	4-1	1-0	2-0	2-1	1-2	2-1	4-2	1-0	1-0	4-3
Esan United	34	11	14	9	41	42	47	1-1	2-1	4-0	1-1	2-1		2-1	1-0	3-3	1-1	1-1	1-1	2-3	3-3	0-1	2-1	1-0	2-1
Samut Songkhram	34	12	10	12	37	39	46	1-2	1-0	1-1	0-3	1-0	0-0		3-2	0-0	1-0	1-0	4-0	4-4	2-3	2-0	1-0	2-0	0-0
Bangkok Glass	34	10	15	9	53	39	45	1-2	0-0	1-1	1-2	1-0	0-0	4-1		4-1	0-0	2-0	0-0	2-0	5-3	1-1	4-0	5-2	2-2
Chiangrai United	34	11	11	12	40	47	44	1-1	0-0	0-1	2-1	4-3	2-1	1-0	1-0		0-1	1-0	0-1	1-1	1-1	2-1	1-1	2-0	3-2
Army United	34	10	13	11	34	38	43	1-2	0-0	1-0	1-3	3-3	1-3	1-0	1-0	0-0		1-1	2-1	1-3	1-1	2-0	1-0	1-1	2-2
Police United	34	10	12	12	37	38	42	1-2	1-2	0-2	0-0	1-0	0-1	3-1	1-1	1-0	0-1		1-1	2-0	4-2	1-0	1-0	1-1	1-0
TOT–CAT	34	10	12	12	43	46	42	1-1	1-1	1-1	0-1	1-3	3-1	3-0	3-2	1-0	0-2	1-2		3-3	1-1	3-1	1-1	3-2	1-0
Wuachon United	34	9	14	11	46	54	41	1-4	1-4	1-2	2-1	1-0	1-1	1-3	2-1	1-5	2-2	2-0	3-2		2-4	0-0	0-0	2-2	2-0
Chainat	34	9	12	13	59	72	39	4-4	0-3	2-1	0-3	2-2	1-1	1-1	2-2	1-2	1-0	1-3	2-2	1-1		4-2	2-0	1-3	0-1
Pattaya United	34	9	10	15	35	47	37	0-1	0-2	1-0	1-0	0-0	2-2	0-0	0-0	2-2	1-1	1-1	1-3	1-0	0-2		1-0	2-2	2-2
Thai Port	34	8	9	17	32	48	33	1-2	1-2	0-2	2-1	0-0	1-2	0-0	2-0	1-1	0-1	0-0	0-2	2-2	2-4		3-2	1-0	
BBCU	34	4	13	17	32	63	25	1-8	0-0	2-2	1-4	0-0	1-0	2-2	0-0	1-2	1-1	1-1	3-2	1-1	0-1	0-2	1-3		1-1
TTM Changmai	34	2	12	20	25	57	18	0-3	0-1	0-1	0-2	1-2	0-0	0-1	0-0	0-0	2-2	0-2	0-1	2-2	2-3	1-2	0-1	2-5	

17/03/2012 – 28/10/2012 • † Qualified for the AFC Champions League
Buriram PEA renamed Buriram United; Buriram FC renamed Wuachon United; Sisaket renamed Esan United; TTM Phichit moved to Changmai
Top scorers: 24 – **CLEITON SILVA** BRA, BEC Tero Sasana & Teerasil **DANGDA**, Muangthong Utd • 15 – Tana **CHANABUT**, Polive Utd • 14 – Mario **GUROVSKI** MKD, Muangthong Utd & **PIPOB** On-Mo, Chonburi • 13 – Phuwadol **SUWANNACHART**, Chainat • 12 – Frank **ACHEAMPONG** GHA, Buriram Utd & Ludovic **TAKAM** CMR, Pattaya Utd • 11 – Samuel **AJAYI** NGA, Bangkok Glass & Bireme **DIOUF** CIV, Samut Songkhram

THAILAND 2012

YAMAHA LEAGUE-1 (2)

	Pl	W	D	L	F	A	Pts	Ratchaburi	Suphanburi	Bangkok Utd	Sriracha	PTT Rayong	Krabi	Siam Navy	Ratchasima	Air Force Utd	Bangkok FC	Khon Kaen	Saraburi	FC Phuket	Songkhla	Phattalung	JW Rangsit	Raj Pracha	Chanthaburi
Ratchaburi	34	24	6	4	85	31	78		0-0	1-2	1-1	5-3	4-0	4-2	1-1	3-1	2-1	4-0	4-0	3-0	3-0	1-1	3-1	6-2	2-1
Suphanburi	34	23	6	5	58	17	75	1-2		3-0	2-0	3-0	1-0	2-0	4-0	2-1	3-0	2-1	1-0	2-0	3-1	0-0	1-2	1-0	4-0
Bangkok United	34	23	5	6	57	29	74	0-1	2-1		0-0	0-1	0-1	1-0	2-0	0-0	2-1	2-0	1-0	2-1	3-1	2-4	2-0	3-1	2-1
Sriracha	34	21	4	9	70	41	67	2-3	0-2	4-0		0-2	1-0	1-1	3-1	2-1	4-1	2-0	2-0	4-2	4-0	5-1	3-1	3-1	3-0
PTT Rayong	34	19	5	10	61	33	62	1-0	1-1	0-1	1-2		1-0	2-1	0-1	0-0	2-0	2-1	3-0	6-0	2-2	0-2	2-0	1-1	5-0
Krabi	34	17	6	11	49	28	57	1-0	0-1	0-2	2-2	1-1		1-2	1-0	3-1	2-1	2-0	2-0	0-0	0-0	0-4	1-0	1-4	6-0
Siam Navy	34	13	11	10	54	42	50	0-3	2-4	2-2	1-2	2-2	0-0		2-2	2-0	1-1	4-0	2-1	2-0	2-2	2-1	2-1	0-0	2-0
Nakhon Ratchasima	34	12	11	11	42	46	47	0-3	1-0	0-2	2-0	2-5	0-0	2-1		2-1	2-2	2-1	1-1	0-1	2-3	2-2	0-0	2-2	5-0
Air Force United	34	12	8	14	45	45	44	0-0	0-0	2-3	2-4	1-0	0-2	1-1	3-1		0-0	1-0	1-0	3-0	0-1	1-2	4-1	4-2	3-1
Bangkok FC	34	11	9	14	62	56	42	1-3	0-1	2-0	1-2	0-1	2-2	1-1		3-0	3-3	0-1	1-1	4-2	5-0	4-1	2-1		
Khon Kaen	34	12	6	16	36	50	42	1-0	2-1	0-0	0-3	1-0	1-3	1-1	0-1	1-1	2-2		2-1	1-1	0-0	0-0	1-0	2-0	1-0
Saraburi	34	11	8	15	49	53	41	1-1	0-1	1-2	3-0	1-2	3-1	2-1	1-0	1-1	3-3	1-2		5-1	3-3	1-0	2-2	2-1	5-2
FC Phuket	34	10	10	14	41	47	40	0-0	0-0	0-3	0-1	0-1	0-1	1-0	1-1	3-3	2-1	5-2	0-1		1-0	0-0	5-0	1-1	8-1
Songkhla	34	9	10	15	38	51	37	1-2	0-0	0-3	2-3	1-0	0-2	2-3	2-0	2-3	3-3	2-1	2-1	0-1		0-0	3-1	2-1	2-0
Phattalung	34	7	13	14	37	58	34	3-3	0-0	1-4	2-1	1-4	1-0	1-1	0-3	0-1	2-3	3-2	1-2	1-1	1-0		2-2	1-1	2-2
JW Rangsit	34	8	7	19	36	65	31	0-2	1-3	0-3	1-2	3-1	0-3	1-4	1-1	2-0	3-2	0-2	0-1	0-0	3-1	1-1		1-0	4-0
Raj Pracha	34	6	7	21	33	66	25	1-3	0-4	0-1	3-0	2-1	0-4	0-3	0-0	0-1	0-2	1-1	1-4	1-0	1-2	1-0			4-0
Chanthaburi	34	0	4	30	21	115	4	1-9	1-3	0-3	1-5	1-5	1-3	0-4	2-2	0-7	1-4	1-2	0-1	0-0	0-0	2-2	2-3		

17/03/2012 - 27/10/2012
Top scorers: 22 – Lee **TUCK** ENG, Bangkok FC • 19 – **DOUGLAS** BRA, Ratchaburi • 18 – Anuwat **NAKKASEAM**, Sriracha & Kouassi Yao **HERMANN** CIV, Air Force Utd • 17 – Romain **GASMI** FRA, Bangkok Utd • 16 – Promphong **KRANSUMRONG**, Nakhon Ratchasima & Suphakorn **NAKNOI**, Saraburi

THAICOM FA CUP 2012

Round of 16		Quarter-finals		Semi-finals		Final	
Buriram United	7						
Ratchaburi	1	**Buriram United**	3				
Samut Songkhram	1	BEC Tero Sasana	0				
BEC Tero Sasana	3			**Buriram United**	2		
Ayutthaya	2			Bangkok Glass	0		
Thai Port	1	Ayutthaya	1				
Chainat	0	**Bangkok Glass**	2				
Bangkok Glass	1					**Buriram United** †	2
Chiangrai United	2 5p					Army United	1
Police United	2 4p	**Chiangrai United**	3				
Songkhla	0	Suphanburi	1			CUP FINAL	
Suphanburi	1			Chiangrai United	1	Suphachalasai, Bangkok	
Muangthong United	2			**Army United**	2	4-11-2012. Ref: Toshida JPN	
Nakhon Ratchasima	0	Muangthong United	2			Scorer - Goran Jerkovic 2 [36][62] for	
PTT Rayong	0 1p	**Army United**	3			Buriram; Isarapong Lilakorn [81] for Army	
Army United	0 3p			* Home team • † Qualified for the AFC Champions League			

MEDALS TABLE

		All	PL	FAC	LC	Cup	Asia	
		G	G	G	G	G	G	City
1	Air Force United	16	2	3		11		Rangsit
2	Bangkok Bank	11	1	3		7		Bangkok
3	Thai Port	10		1	1	8		Bangkok
4	Raj Pracha	9		5		4		Nakhon Pathom
5	Thai Farmers Bank	7		1		4	2	Bangkok
6	Buriram PEA	5	2	1	2			Buriram
7	Krung Thai Bank	4	2			2		Bangkok
8	Raj Vithi	4				4		Bangkok
9	Muangthong United	3	3					Nonthaburi
10	Vajiravudh College	3				3		Bangkok
11	BEC Tero Sasana	2	2					Bangkok
12	Chonburi	2	1	1				Chonburi
13	Muangthong Utd	2	1	1				Bangkok

PL = Thai Premier League • FAC = FA Cup • Cup = Yai Cup & Khor Royal Cup • LC = League Cup

THAI LEAGUE CUP 2012

Round of 16		Quarter-finals		Semi-finals		Final	
Buriram United	1						
Samut Prakan United*	0	**Buriram United** *	1 2				
Suphanburi *	1	BEC Tero Sasana	1 2				
BEC Tero Sasana	3			**Buriram United**	3 1		
Chonburi	2			Bangkok Glass *	2 0		
Customs United *	0	Chonburi	0 1				
Chiangrai United	1	**Bangkok Glass** *	1 1				
Bangkok Glass *	3					**Buriram United**	4
TOT–CAT *	3					Ratchaburi	1
TTM Changmai	0	**TOT–CAT**	2 2			CUP FINAL	
Thai Port *	0	Muangthong United *	1 2			Suphachalasai, Bangkok	
Muangthong United	2			TOT–CAT	0 2	10-11-2012	
Wuachon United	1			**Ratchaburi** *	1 2	Scorers - Yves Ekwalla [36], Goran Jerkovic 2 [44][88], Osmar Barba [63] for Buriram; OG [65] for Ratchaburi	
Pattani *	0	Wuachon United	0 1				
Pattaya United	0	**Ratchaburi** *	2 0				
Ratchaburi *	1			* Home team in the 1st leg			

TJK – TAJIKISTAN

FIFA/COCA-COLA WORLD RANKING

'93	'94	'95	'96	'97	'98	'99	'00	'01	'02	'03	'04	'05	'06	'07	'08	'09	'10	'11	'12
-	155	164	163	118	120	119	134	154	168	137	136	141	124	137	146	165	145	139	136

2012

Jan	Feb	Mar	Apr	May	Jun	Jul	Aug	Sep	Oct	Nov	Dec	High	Low	Av
140	140	145	131	131	129	124	140	142	136	137	136	114	180	142

Esteghlal reasserted Tajikistan's status as the dominant nation in the AFC President's Cup by winning the 2012 tournament on home soil at the end of September. Compatriots Regar TadAZ had won three of the first five championships but no Tajik side had claimed the title since 2009. After qualifying comfortably for the finals, the Dushanbe-based club played host and, after seeing off the challenge of former winners Dordoi Bishkek in the group stage, Esteghlal met Palestine's Shabab Al Amari in the final. Two goals in eight second half minutes from Davronjon Ergashev and Dilshod Vasiev secured the title for Esteghlal. They were not quite so successful at home, however, after failing to retain their league title later on in the year - which went to first-time winners Ravshan Kulob - and they also lost to Regar TadAZ on penalties in the cup final. Tajikistan's national team qualified for the finals of the 2012 AFC Challenge Cup but were unable to make much of an impression and were eliminated at the end of the group stage. A win over India in their opening game gave Kemal Alispahic's side hope but losses at the hands of Korea DPR and the Philippines ended their chances. That led to the departure of Bosnian Alispahic and the appointment of Nikola Kavazovic, the Serbian dividing his duties between the national team and Esteghlal.

FIFA WORLD CUP RECORD
1930-1994 DNE **1998-2014** DNQ

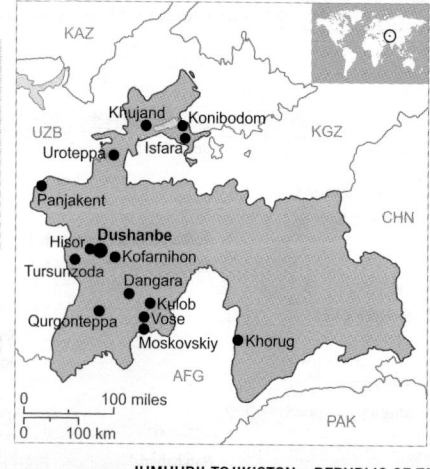

TAJIKISTAN FOOTBALL FEDERATION (TFF)

14/3 Ayni Street,
734 025 Dushanbe

☎ +992 44 6208181
📠 +992 44 6208282
✉ tajikfootball@yahoo.com
🖥 www.fft.tj
FA 1936 CON 1994 FIFA 1994
P Rustam Emomali
GS Firdavs Fayzullaev

THE STADIA

2014 FIFA World Cup Stadia
Central (Pamir) Stadium
Dushanbe 30 000
20 Years of Idependence Stadium
Khujand 25 000
Metallurg
Tursunzade 20 000
Other Main Stadia
Central Stadium
Qurgonteppa 10 000

MAJOR CITIES/TOWNS

		Population
1	Dushanbe	703 969
2	Khujand	147 483
3	Kulob	85 467
4	Qurgonteppa	64 709
5	Konibodom	57 792
6	Uroteppa	56 874
7	Kofarnihon	45 693
8	Tursunzoda	40 435
9	Isfara	40 073
10	Panjakent	38 575
11	Khorug	32 470
12	Boshkengash	27 495
13	Hisor	27 200
14	Dangara	26 435
15	Farkhor	25 145
16	Vose	25 145
17	Moskovskiy	22 631
18	Chkalovsk	21 634
19	Tugalan	21 373

JUMHURII TOJIKISTON • REPUBLIC OF TAJIKISTAN

Capital	Dushanbe	Population	7 349 145 (96)	% in cities	26%
GDP per capita	$1800 (190)	Area km²	143 100 km² (95)	GMT +/-	+5
Neighbours (km)	Afghanistan 1206, China 414, Kyrgyzstan 870, Uzbekistan 1161				

RECENT INTERNATIONAL MATCHES PLAYED BY TAJIKISTAN

2011	Opponents	Score	Venue	Comp	Scorers	Att	Referee
21-03	Kyrgyzstan	W 1-0	Male	CCq	OG [88]	4 000	Mohamed UAE
23-03	Cambodia	W 3-0	Male	CCq	Davronov [2], Ergashev [83], Rabimov [89]	550	Patwal IND
25-03	Maldives	D 0-0	Male	CCq		9 000	Mohamed UAE
27-03	Sri Lanka	D 2-2	Colombo	Fr	Rabimov [56], Vasiev [73]		
29-03	Sri Lanka	W 2-0	Colombo	Fr	Ergashev [21], Vasiev [23]		
23-07	Syria	W 3-0	Amman	WCq	Originally L 1-2. Saidov [47]	2 500	Al Ghafari JOR
28-07	Syria	W 3-0	Tursunzade	WCq	Originally L 0-4	9 000	Mashentsev KGZ
2-09	Uzbekistan	L 0-1	Tursunzade	WCq		15 000	Tan Hai CHN
6-09	Korea DPR	L 0-1	Pyongyang	WCq		28 000	Minh Tri Vo VIE
11-10	Japan	L 0-8	Osaka	WCq		44 688	Williams AUS
11-11	Japan	L 0-4	Dushanbe	WCq		18 000	Kim Dong Jin KOR
15-11	Uzbekistan	L 0-3	Tashkent	WCq		5 325	Alzarooni UAE
2012							
29-02	Korea DPR	D 1-1	Khujand	WCq	Khamrakulov [61]	35 000	Al Dosari QAT
9-03	India	W 2-0	Kathmandu	CCr1	Khamrakulov [61], Davronov [66]	700	Sabbagh LIB
11-03	Korea DPR	L 0-2	Kathmandu	CCr1		1 000	Almarzouq KUW
13-03	Philippines	L 1-2	Kathmandu	CCr1		800	Sato JPN
6-09	Qatar	W 2-1	Ingolstadt	Fr	Ergashev [65], Vasiev [74]		Weiner GER
6-11	Iran	L 1-6	Tehran	Fr	Savankulov [67]	30 000	Jahanbazi IRN

Fr = Friendly match • AC = AFC Asian Cup • CC = AFC Challenge Cup • WC = FIFA World Cup
q = qualifier • r1 = first round group • qf = quarter-final • sf = semi-final • f = final

TAJIKISTAN NATIONAL TEAM HISTORICAL RECORDS

Goals: 16 - Yusuf Rabiev 2003- & Numonjon Hakimov 2003- • 10 - Tokhirjon Muminov 1993-2000 • 7 - Djomikhon Mukhidinov 2003- • 6 - Alier Ashurmamadov 1992-2005 & Chukhrat Djabarov 1997-2000

Past Coaches: Sharif Nazarov 1992-94 • Vladimir Gulyamkhaydarov 1994-95 • Abdulla Muradov 1996 • Sharif Nazarov 2003 • Zoir Babaev 2004 • Sharif Nazarov 2004-06 • Makhmadjon Khabibulloev 2007 • Pulod Kodirov 2008-11 • Alimzhon Rafikov 2011-12 • Kemal Alispahic BIH 2012 • Nikola Kavazovic 2012-

MEDALS TABLE

		Overall			League			Cup			Asia			City
		G	S	B	G	S	B	G	S	B	G	S	B	
1	Regar TadAZ	16	10	1	7	7		6	3		3		1	Tursunzoda
2	Vakhsh	5	4	5	3	1	4	2	2			1	1	Qurgonteppa
3	Esteghlal	5	2	1	2		1	2	2		1			Dushanbe
4	Varzob	5	1		3			2	1					Dushanbe
5	FK Hujand	3	6	4		3	4	3	3					Khujand
6	SKA Pamir	3	3	1	2	2	1	1	1					Dushanbe
7	Sitora	3	1	1	2	1	1	1						Dushanbe
8	Parvoz	2	2	3		2	3	2						B. Gafurov
9	Ravshan	2	2	2	1		2	1	2					Kulob

TAJIKISTAN CUP FINAL 2012
Dushanbe, 5-10-2012
Regar TadAZ 1-1 6-5p Esteghlal Dushanbe

TAJIKISTAN 2012

VYSSHAYA LIGA

	Pl	W	D	L	F	A	Pts	Ravshan	Regar	Esteghlal	Xayr	Parvoz	Vakhsh	SKA Pamir	Hujand	Istaravshan	Energetik	Hosilot	Guardia	Zarafshon
Ravshan Kulob †	24	20	2	2	51	10	62		0-0	1-0	4-0	1-0	3-0	1-0	3-0	5-0	2-0	2-1	3-0	2-0
Regar TadAZ	24	19	4	1	77	16	61	1-0		0-0	5-2	4-1	1-0	2-0	2-0	5-1	3-1	9-1	11-0	12-0
Esteghlal Dushanbe	24	16	5	3	76	13	53	1-2	1-2		1-1	1-0	1-0	4-1	10-0	4-0	1-1	4-1	7-0	6-0
Xayr Vahdat	24	16	4	4	45	27	52	1-2	1-0	1-1		2-0	1-0	2-0	2-0	4-1	4-1	2-1	2-1	3-0
Parvoz B'jon Gafurov	24	10	4	10	47	36	34	2-2	1-2	0-3	5-2		0-1	2-1	2-3	2-2	2-1	6-1	1-0	6-0
Vakhsh Qurghonteppa	24	9	4	11	31	24	31	0-1	1-1	0-1	1-2	3-4		0-1	0-0	1-1	1-1	3-0	4-1	4-0
SKA Pamir Dushanbe	24	8	6	10	26	25	30	0-1	0-2	1-1	0-0	0-0	0-3		3-1	1-1	1-0	3-0	4-0	5-0
FK Hujand	24	8	6	10	29	44	30	0-1	0-3	0-1	0-2	1-1	1-0	0-0		2-2	2-1	1-0	4-1	5-2
FK Istaravshan	24	8	4	12	33	44	28	3-1	1-2	0-2	1-2	1-0	2-1	1-0	1-2		0-0	0-1	1-0	4-1
Energetik Dushanbe	24	7	6	11	35	34	27	1-2	0-1	0-5	1-1	2-1	0-1	2-0	2-2	3-2		4-0	2-0	8-0
Hosilot Farkhor	24	4	2	18	18	64	14	0-5	1-2	0-5	0-2	1-2	0-2	1-3	1-0	2-1	1-1		0-1	1-1
Guardia Dushanbe	24	4	0	20	18	72	12	0-4	0-3	1-6	1-3	0-3	0-2	0-1	3-0	2-4	0-1	4-2		0-3
Zarafshon Pendjikent	24	1	3	20	21	98	6	0-3	1-4	1-10	1-3	2-6	2-3	1-1	1-2	1-3	2-2	1-2	1-3	

7/04/2012 - 29/11/2012 • † Qualified for the AFC President's Cup • Top scorer: **24** - Dilshod **VASIEV**, Esteghlal

TKM – TURKMENISTAN

FIFA/COCA-COLA WORLD RANKING

'93	'94	'95	'96	'97	'98	'99	'00	'01	'02	'03	'04	'05	'06	'07	'08	'09	'10	'11	'12
-	108	133	141	134	122	129	125	114	134	99	98	116	155	127	148	141	135	146	129

2012

Jan	Feb	Mar	Apr	May	Jun	Jul	Aug	Sep	Oct	Nov	Dec	High	Low	Av
146	149	166	142	144	138	137	123	127	125	129	129	86	174	130

Turkmenistan went close to a first continental title in 2012 but lost in the final of the AFC Challenge Cup to Korea DPR - just as they had done two years previously in the 2010 final in Sri Lanka. But while the 2010 defeat came via a penalty shootout, the 2012 loss in Kathmandu, Nepal was in regular time against a very strong North Korean side that having won the title twice in a row will not be given an entry for the next tournament in 2014 where Turkmenistan hope it will be third time lucky. Yazguly Hojageldiyev's side advanced from the group phase of the competition with wins over the Maldives and Nepal either side of a draw with Palestine. A 2-1 win over tournament dark horses the Philippines set up a repeat of the 2010 final, only for Turkmenistan to suffer a 2-1 defeat. Balkan Balkanabat, meanwhile, successfully defended their league title at home, finishing a point ahead of Merv Mary before claiming the Turkmenistan Cup as well with a 2-1 victory over HTTU Ashgabat in the final. However, Balkan were unable to make a significant impact on the 2012 AFC President's Cup after being drawn in a tough qualifying group with Esteghlal of Tajikistan and Palestine's Shabab Al Amari. Balkan finished bottom of the three-team group, behind the two teams who would go on to contest the final.

FIFA WORLD CUP RECORD
1930-1994 DNE 1998-2014 DNQ

FOOTBALL ASSOCIATION OF TURKMENISTAN (FFT)

Sportcomplex Kopetdag
245 A. Niyazova Street,
Stadium Kopetdag,
744 001 Ashgabat
☎ +993 12 363433
+993 12 363433
nfct@online.tm

FA 1992 CON 1994 FIFA 1994
P Sapardurdy Toylyyew
GS Meret Satylov

THE STADIA
2014 FIFA World Cup Stadia
Olympic Stadium
Ashgabat 30 000
Other Main Stadia
Kopetdag Stadium
Ashgabat 26 000
Ashgabat Stadium
Ashgabat 20 000
Dashoguz Stadium
Dashoguz 12 000

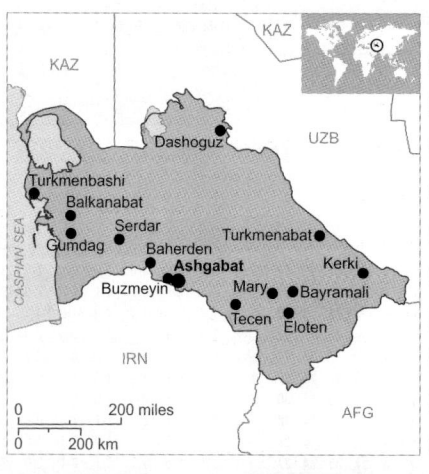

MAJOR CITIES/TOWNS
		Population
1	Ashgabat	921 503
2	Turkmenabat	252 866
3	Dashoguz	227 184
4	Mary	123 904
5	Balkanabat	89 785
6	Serdar	89 582
7	Bayramali	88 486
8	Tecen	77 024
9	Türkmenbashi	70 962
10	Govurdak	64 845
11	Büzmeyin	42 269
12	Kerki	38 350
13	Elöten	37 705
14	Köhne Urgenç	34 677
15	Annau	29 606
16	Khazar	28 095
17	Yilanli	26 901
18	Gumdag	26 831
19	Gazojak	25 043

TURKMENISTAN
Capital Ashgabat Population 4 884 887 (114) % in cities 49%
GDP per capita $6500 (128) Area km² 488 100 km² (52) GMT +/- +5
Neighbours (km) Afghanistan 744, Iran 992, Kazakhstan 379, Uzbekistan 1621 • Caspian Sea 1768

RECENT INTERNATIONAL MATCHES PLAYED BY TURKMENISTAN

2007	Opponents		Score	Venue	Comp	Scorers	Att	Referee
11-10	Cambodia	W	1-0	Phnom Penh	WCq	Karadanov [85]	3 000	Gosh BAN
28-10	Cambodia	W	4-1	Ashgabat	WCq	Nasyrov [41], Gevorkyan 2 [50 66], Karadanov [74]	5 000	Saidov UZB
10-11	Hong Kong	D	0-0	Hong Kong	WCq		2 823	Mujghef JOR
18-11	Hong Kong	W	3-0	Ashgabat	WCq	Nasyrov [42], Bayramov [53], Mirzoev [80]	30 000	Al Hilali OMA
2008								
6-02	Korea Republic	L	0-4	Seoul	WCq		25 738	Najm LIB
26-03	Jordan	L	0-2	Ashgabat	WCq		20 000	Tongkhan THA
18-05	Oman	L	1-2	Nizwa	Fr	Saparov [53]		
2-06	Korea DPR	D	0-0	Ashgabat	WCq		20 000	Al Ghamdi KSA
7-06	Korea DPR	L	0-1	Pyongyang	WCq		25 000	Al Saeedi UAE
14-06	Korea Republic	L	1-3	Ashgabat	WCq	Ovekov [77p]	11 000	Takayama JPN
22-06	Jordan	L	0-2	Amman	WCq		150	Williams AUS
30-07	Tajikistan	D	0-0	Hyderabad	CCr1		150	Kovalenko UZB
1-08	Afghanistan	W	5-0	Hyderabad	CCr1	Ovekov 4 [1 41 77 80], Krendelev [23]	100	Saleem MDV
3-08	India	L	1-2	Hyderabad	CCr1	Orazmamedov [84]	1 000	Jasim UAE
3-10	Mynamar	W	2-1	Ho Chi Minh	Fr			
5-10	Vietnam	W	3-2	Ho Chi Minh	Fr			
2009								
18-01	Syria	L	1-5	Kuwait City	Fr	Bablin [12]		
20-01	Kuwait	L	0-2	Kuwait City	Fr			
14-04	Maldives	W	3-1	Male	CCq	Nasyrov [42], Shamuradov [49], Mirzoyev [68p]	9 000	Al Ghafary JOR
16-04	Bhutan	W	7-0	Male	CCq	Atayev 3 [13 67 79], Chonkayev [16], Urazov [47], Mingazov [62], Mirzoyev [93+]	300	Perera SRI
18-04	Philippines	W	5-0	Male	CCq	OG [26], Shamuradov 2 [54 63], Nasyrov [58], Urazov [65]	400	Al Ghafary JOR
20-10	Vietnam	L	0-1	Ho Chi Minh	Fr			
22-10	Singapore	L	2-4	Ho Chi Minh	Fr	Shamuradov [14p], Ovekov [84]		
2010								
17-02	Korea DPR	D	1-1	Colombo	CCr1	Karadanov [36]	400	Mahapab THA
19-02	India	W	1-0	Colombo	CCr1	Karadanov [24p]	450	Matsuo JPN
21-02	Kyrgyzstan	W	1-0	Colombo	CCr1	Nurmuradov [70]	100	El Haddad LIB
24-02	Tajikistan	W	2-0	Colombo	CCsf	Amanov [33], Urazov [42]	300	Faghani IRN
27-02	Korea DPR	D	1-1	Colombo	CCf	Shamuradov [33]. L 4-5p	3 000	Faghani IRN
2011								
21-03	Pakistan	W	3-0	Petaling Jaya	CCq	Urazov [6], Amanov [46], Karadanov [86]	150	Bakhshizadeh IRN
23-03	Chinese Taipei	W	2-0	Petaling Jaya	CCq	Shamuradov [73], Hangeldiyev [76]	100	Serazitdinov UZB
25-03	India	D	1-1	Petaling Jaya	CCq	Conkayev [52p]	200	Abdul Wahab MAS
23-07	Indonesia	D	1-1	Ashgabat	WCq	Krendelev [12]	7 500	Torki IRN
28-07	Indonesia	L	3-4	Jakarta	WCq	Amanov [72], Shamuradov [84], Conkayev [87p]	88 000	Williams AUS
2012								
27-01	Romania	L	0-4	Belek	Fr		50	Baliyan ARM
8-03	Maldives	W	3-1	Kathmandu	CCr1	Mingazov [33], Conkayev [78], Amanov [85]	1 000	Almarzouq KUW
10-03	Palestine	D	0-0	Kathmandu	CCr1		1 000	Ko Hyung Jin KOR
12-03	Nepal	W	3-0	Kathmandu	CCr1	Tagayev [7], OG [79], Hangeldiyev [89]	2 400	Sabbagh LIB
16-03	Philippines	W	2-1	Kathmandu	CCsf	Amanov [80], Conkayev [86]	500	Ko Hyung Jin KOR
19-03	Korea DPR	L	1-2	Kathmandu	CCf	Shamuradov [2]	9 000	Sato JPN
24-10	Vietnam	W	1-0	Ho Chinh City	Fr	Bayramov [56]	20 000	Mat Karim MAS
28-10	Laos	W	4-2	Ho Chinh City	Fr	Boliyan [17], Jumanazarov [30], Abylov [47], Muhadov [64]		Vo Quang Vinh VIE

Fr = Friendly match • AC = AFC Asian Cup • CC = AFC Challenge Cup • WC = FIFA World Cup • q = qualifier • r1 = first round group

TURKMENISTAN NATIONAL TEAM HISTORICAL RECORDS

Coaches: Bayram Durdiev 1992-96 • Elguja Gugushvili GEO 1996-97 • Tacmirat Agamiradov 1997-98 • Viktor Pozhechevsky UKR 1998-99 • Gurban Berdiev 1999 • Rowsen Muhadov 1999-2000 • Tacmirat Agamiradov 2000-01 • Vladimir Bessonov UKR 2002-03 • Rahim Gurbanmammedov 2003-04 • Boris Grigoryants 2005 • Amangylyc Gocumov 2005-06 • Rahim Gurbanmammedov 2007-09 • Boris Grigoryants 2009-10 • Yazguly Hojageldiyev 2010-

TURKMENISTAN 2012

YOKARY LIGA

	Pl	W	D	L	F	A	Pts	Balkan	Merv	HTTU	Ahal	Sagadam	Altyn	Talyp	Lebap	Ashgabat
Balkan Balkanabat †	32	23	4	5	66	19	**73**		0-1 7-0	0-0 2-0	0-0 2-5	7-0 1-0	3-3 1-0	4-0 2-1	0-0 0-0	2-1 7-0
Merv Mary	32	21	9	2	58	26	**72**	2-1 1-1		3-0 0-0	2-0 2-0	1-0 0-0	2-1 3-0	2-1 4-0	0-0 2-1	4-0 5-2
HTTU Ashgabat	32	15	11	6	48	20	**56**	0-0 0-1	2-1 1-1		0-0 4-0	4-0 2-1	0-1 4-1	2-0 3-0	2-1 6-1	0-0 3-0
FC Ahal	32	15	5	12	59	45	**50**	1-0 1-3	0-2 3-4	1-1 2-1		2-2 0-2	0-0 2-2	1-0 3-0	4-0 2-1	2-4 4-2
Sagadam Turkmenbasy	32	14	5	13	43	39	**47**	0-1 0-2	1-1 1-2	0-1 1-0	2-0 2-1		2-1 1-0	4-0 3-0	2-2 3-1	2-1 3-0
Altyn Asyr	32	13	7	12	46	39	**46**	0-0 0-4	1-1 0-2	0-0 1-1	0-2 2-1	1-0 2-1		4-1 1-0	2-0 3-0	6-0 2-0
Talyp Sporty Ashgabat	32	6	4	22	23	70	**22**	0-1 0-5	1-1 1-3	1-1 0-3	0-6 0-2	0-3 1-3	3-2 2-2		1-0 2-1	1-0 0-0
Lebap Türkmenabat	32	6	3	23	30	69	**21**	2-1 0-1	0-2 1-1	1-3 0-0	2-4 0-2	2-1 0-1	2-3 1-0	2-3 0-0		3-2 0-0
FK Ashgabat	32	5	4	23	28	80	**19**	0-3 1-4	0-1 0-2	0-4 0-0	3-4 0-4	1-1 2-1	0-3 0-2	0-3 2-1	1-3 0-0	

10/04/2012 - 10/11/2012 • † Qualified for the AFC President's Cup • Top scorer: **23** - Aleksandr **BOLIYAN**, Sagadam

MEDALS TABLE

		Overall G S B	League G S B	Cup G S	Asia G S B	City
1	Kopetdag Ashgabat	12 6	6 3	6 3		Ashgabat
2	Balkan Balkanabat	8 8 6	4 5 6	4 3		Balkanabat
3	Nisa Ashgabat	5 8 1	4 5 1	1 3		Ashgabat
4	HTTU Ashgabat	5 5 2	3 3 1	2 2	1	Ashgabat
5	Merv Mary	2 4 3	1 3	2 3		Mary
6	FK Ashgabat	2 1 4	2 2	1	2	Ashgabat
7	Sagadam Turkmenbasy	2 1 1	1 1	1 1		Turkmenbasy
8	Altyn Asyr	1 2	1	1 1		Asyr
9	FK Dasoguz	1 1		1 1		Dasoguz
10	Garagam Türkmenabad	1 1		1 1		Türkmenabad

TURKMENISTAN CUP 2012

Quarter-finals	Semi-finals		Final	
Balkan Balkanabat				
Bezirgen	**Balkan Balkanabat**	1 3		
Talyp Sporty Ashgabat	Sagadam Turkmenbasy	1 0		
Sagadam Turkmenbasy			**Balkan Balkanabat**	2
Merv Mary			HTTU Ashgabat	1
Altyn Asyr	Merv Mary	0 0 3p		
Gallaçy	**HTTU Ashgabat**	0 0 4p	Ashgabat Stadium, 5-12-2012	
HTTU Ashgabat	* Home team in the first leg			

TLS – TIMOR-LESTE

FIFA/COCA-COLA WORLD RANKING

'93	'94	'95	'96	'97	'98	'99	'00	'01	'02	'03	'04	'05	'06	'07	'08	'09	'10	'11	'12
-	-	-	-	-	-	-	-	-	-	-	-	-	198	201	197	200	201	205	182

2012

Jan	Feb	Mar	Apr	May	Jun	Jul	Aug	Sep	Oct	Nov	Dec	High	Low	Av
205	204	204	204	204	205	204	205	205	206	187	182	182	206	199

Timor-Leste's short football history reached a significant milestone in 2012 when the national team secured its first-ever wins in international football during the qualifying rounds for the 2012 AFF Suzuki Cup in Myanmar late in the year. The maiden victory was achieved in some style as Emerson Alcantara's team handed Cambodia a 5-1 thrashing in the Myanmar capital Yangon with Murilo de Almeida and Adelino Trinidade both scoring twice. Alan Leandro claimed the fifth from the penalty spot in the landmark game. The win got Timor-Leste dreaming of a place in the ournament proper and, even after a defeat at the hands of Myanmar, a second victory - this time a 3-1 win over Laos - left them with a strong chance of progressing ahead of their final group game against minnows Brunei. However, a 2-1 loss shattered the hopes of the national side known as 'The Rising Sun' but the tournament did mark a breakthrough for football in the country. It also saw the team rise up the FIFA/Coca-Cola World Ranking to a highest ever position of 182nd by the end of the year. Up until that first win Timor-Leste had been ranked joint last after having lost 21 of their previous 22 matches with just a single draw against Cambodia in 2008 to break the losing sequence.

FIFA WORLD CUP RECORD
1930-2006 DNE 2010-2014 DNQ

FEDERACAO FUTEBOL TIMOR-LESTE (FFTL)

Campo Democracia Ave,
Bairo Formosa,
PO Box 406
Dili
☎ +670 3310670
📠 +670 3310671
✉ federacao_futebol@yahoo.com

FA 2002 CON 2002 FIFA 2005
P Francisco Lay
GS Armandio Sarmento

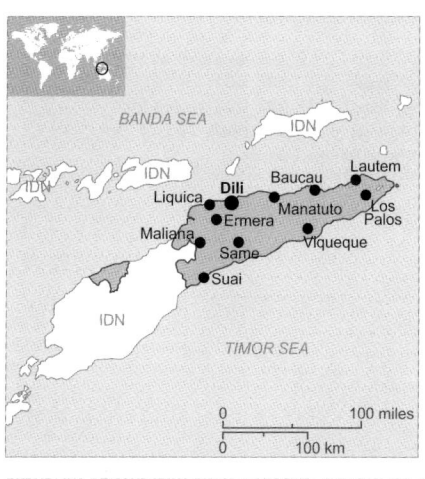

MAJOR CITIES/TOWNS

		Population
1	Dili	174 096
2	Dare	20 327
3	Los Palos	17 598
4	Baucau	15 307
5	Ermera	13 768
6	Maliana	12 016
7	Suai	6 729
8	Aubá	6 085
9	Viqueque	5 545
10	Liquiça	4 998
11	Oecussi	4 789
12	Metinaro	4 583
13	Bazartete	3 499
14	Lolotoi	3 440
15	Lautem	3 233
16	Ainaro	3 172
17	Same	2 328
18	Manatuto	1 979
19	Aileu	1 962

THE STADIA
2014 FIFA World Cup Stadia
Timor-Leste played both matches against Nepal in Kathmandu

Main Stadia
Estádio do Dili
Dili   5 000

REPUBLIKA DEMOKRATIKA TIMOR LOROSA'E • DEMOCRATIC REPUBLIC OF TIMOR-LESTE

Capital	Dili	Population	1 131 612 (155)	% in cities	27%
GDP per capita	$2300 (180)	Area km²	14 874 km² (159)	GMT +/-	+9
Neighbours (km)	Indonesia 228 • Coast 706				

RECENT INTERNATIONAL MATCHES PLAYED BY TIMOR-LESTE

2002 Opponents	Score	Venue	Comp	Scorers	Att	Referee
No international matches played before 2003						
2003						
21-03 Sri Lanka	L 2-3	Colombo	ACq			
23-03 Chinese Taipei	L 0-3	Colombo	ACq			
2004						
8-12 Malaysia	L 0-5	Kuala Lumpur	AFFr1			
12-12 Thailand	L 0-8	Kuala Lumpur	AFFr1			
14-12 Philippines	L 1-2	Kuala Lumpur	AFFr1	Anai [14]		
16-12 Myanmar	L 1-3	Kuala Lumpur	AFFr1	Simon Diamantino [15p]		
2005						
No international matches played in 2005						
2006						
12-11 Brunei	L 2-3	Bacolod	AFFq	Adelio Maria Costa [33], Anatacio Belo [77]		
14-11 Philippines	L 0-7	Bacolod	AFFq			
16-11 Laos	L 2-3	Bacolod	AFFq	Antonio Ximenes [82], Adelio Maria Costa [89]		
20-11 Cambodia	L 1-4	Bacolod	AFFq	Adelio Maria Costa [63]		
2007						
21-10 Hong Kong	L 2-3	Gianyar	WCq	Emilio Da Silva 2 [41 69]	1 500	Shaharul MAS
28-10 Hong Kong	L 1-8	Hong Kong	WCq	Emilio Da Silva	1 542	Torky IRN
2008						
17-10 Philippines	L 0-1	Phnom Penh	AFFq		15 000	
19-10 Cambodia	D 2-2	Phnom Penh	AFFq	Anggisu Barbosa [45], Joao Perreira [67p]	12 000	
21-10 Brunei Darussalam	L 1-4	Phnom Penh	AFFq	Rosito Soares [80]		
25-10 Laos	L 1-2	Phnom Penh	AFFq	Alfredo Esteves [44]		
2009						
No international matches played in 2009						
2010						
22-10 Philippines	L 0-5	Vientiane	AFFq			Leow SIN
24-10 Cambodia	L 2-4	Vientiane	AFFq	Chiquito Do Carmo [5], Anggisu Barbosa [85]		Phung Dinh Dung VIE
26-10 Laos	L 1-6	Vientiane	AFFq	Chiquito Do Carmo [9]		
21-11 Indonesia	L 0-6	Palembang	Fr			
2011						
29-06 Nepal	L 1-2	Kathmandu	WCq	Joao Perreira [47]	9 000	Sabbagh LIB
2-07 Nepal	L 0-5	Kathmandu	WCq		15 000	Lee Min Hu KOR
2012						
5-10 Cambodia	W 5-1	Yangon	AFFq	Murilo 2 [39 44], Ade 2 [57 73], Alan [87p]	897	Al Yarimi YEM
7-10 Myanmar	L 1-2	Yangon	AFFq	Alan [55]	4 117	Shamsuzzaman BAN
9-10 Laos	W 3-1	Yangon	AFFq	Murilo [43p], Ade [51], Alan [83]	753	Aslam MDV
13-10 Brunei Darussalem	L 1-2	Yangon	AFFq	Pinto [79]	2 423	Takayama JPN

AC = AFC Asian Cup • AFF = ASEAN Football Federation Championship
q = qualifier • r1 = first round group • Matches played before September 2005 are not full internationals

TOG – TOGO

FIFA/COCA-COLA WORLD RANKING

'93	'94	'95	'96	'97	'98	'99	'00	'01	'02	'03	'04	'05	'06	'07	'08	'09	'10	'11	'12
113	86	92	87	78	68	87	81	71	86	94	89	56	60	72	86	71	103	101	71

2012

Jan	Feb	Mar	Apr	May	Jun	Jul	Aug	Sep	Oct	Nov	Dec	High	Low	Av
100	94	97	88	88	98	98	99	99	93	73	71	46	123	82

Togo put in their best ever performance at the finals of the Africa Cup of Nations when they reached the quarter-finals of the 2013 tournament in South Africa. It was the first time they had reached the knock-out rounds after seven failed attempts. Their 1-1 draw with Tunisia in Nelspruit ensured the point they needed to finish second behind the Cote d'Ivoire in Group D to qualify for a quarter-final against Burkina Faso. That match went to extra-time before Burkina Faso scored through a Jonathan Pitroipa goal to knock out the Togolese. Once again, however, Emmanuel Adebayor caused a stir with his questionable commitment to the team, exacerbated this time by a turbulent relationship with coach Didier Six. Adebayor twice had meetings with Togo president Faure Gnassingbe in an effort to persuade him back after he sat out two 2014 FIFA World Cup qualifying matches in June 2012 where Libya held them at home in Lome before the Togolese lost away to Congo DR. It was not until days before the Nations Cup kick-off that Adebayor joined up with the side, providing a talismanic contribution to the team. Despite the quarter-final placing Adebayor was heavily critical of Six, who had originally left him out of the 23-man squad when he failed initially to commit to travel to South Africa.

CAF AFRICA CUP OF NATIONS RECORD

1957-1965 DNQ 1968-1970 DNQ **1972** 7 r1 1974 DNE 1976-1982 DNQ **1984** 8 r1 1986-1988 DNQ 1990 DNE 1992 DNQ 1994 Withdrew 1996 DNQ **1998** 12 r1 **2000** 9 r1 **2002** 12 r1 2004 DNQ **2006** 15 r1 2008 DNQ 2010 Withdrew 2012 DNQ **2013** 8 QF

FEDERATION TOGOLAISE DE FOOTBALL (FTF)

Route de Kégué,
Boite postale 05,
Lome
☎ +228 22412535
📠 +228 22258639
✉ ftftogo@gmail.com

FA 1960 CON 1963 FIFA 1962
P Gabriel Ameyi
GS Delali Klussey

THE STADIA

2014 FIFA World Cup Stadia
Stade de Kegue
Lomé   30 000
Other Main Stadia
Stade Général Eyadéma
Lomé   15 000
Stade Municipal
Sokodé   10 000
Stade Municipal
Kara   10 000

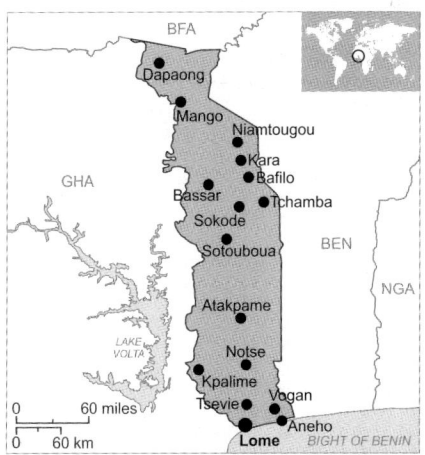

MAJOR CITIES/TOWNS

		Population
1	Lomé	1 565 121
2	Sokodé	112 522
3	Kara	107 889
4	Atakpamé	80 463
5	Kpalimé	77 681
6	Dapaong	54 495
7	Tsévié	50 778
8	Notsé	37 221
9	Aného	27 000
10	Bassar	25 937
11	Mango	25 601
12	Niamtougou	25 599
13	Tchamba	22 485
14	Sotouboua	22 162
15	Vogan	21 523
16	Bafilo	19 851
17	Tabligbo	19 668
18	Badou	13 986
19	Kandé	9 989

REPUBLIQUE TOGOLAISE • TOGOLESE REPUBLIC

Capital	Lomé	Population	6 019 877 (107)	% in cities	42%
GDP per capita	$900 (216)	Area km²	56 785 km² (125)	GMT +/-	0
Neighbours (km)	Benin 644, Burkina Faso 126, Ghana 877 • Coast 56				

RECENT INTERNATIONAL MATCHES PLAYED BY TOGO

2010	Opponents	Score	Venue	Comp	Scorers	Att	Referee
19-05	Gabon	L 0-3	Ajaccio	Fr			
1-07	Chad	D 2-2	N'Djamena	CNq	Sapol Mani [25], Backer Aloenouvo [68]		Benouza ALG
9-07	Malawi	D 1-1	Lomé	CNq	Backer Aloenouvo [75]		Bennett RSA
11-08	Saudi Arabia	L 0-1	Riyadh	Fr			
4-09	Botswana	L 1-2	Gaborone	CNq	Serge Gakpe [44]		Kagabo RWA
10-10	Tunisia	L 1-2	Lomé	CNq	Sapol Mani [40]		Abdul Rahman SUD
17-11	Chad	D 0-0	Lomé	CNq			Coulibaly MLI
2011							
8-02	Ghana	L 1-4	Antwerp	Fr	Komlan Amewou [50p]		
26-03	Malawi	L 0-1	Blantyre	CNq			
10-08	Niger	D 3-3	Niamey	Fr	Komlan Amewou [2], Kondo Arimiyaou [43], Backer Aloenouvo [60]		
4-09	Botswana	W 1-0	Lome	CNq	Kondo Arimiyaou [23]		
8-10	Tunisia	L 0-2	Rades	CNq			
11-11	Guinea-Bissau	D 1-1	Bissau	WCq	Serge Gakpe [32]	3 000	Diedhiou SEN
15-11	Guinea-Bissau	W 1-0	Lome	WCq	OG [3]	25 000	Mohamadou CMR
2012							
29-02	Kenya	L 1-2	Nairobi	CNq	Razak Boukari [42]		Seechurn MRI
22-05	Egypt	L 0-3	Omdurman	Fr			
3-06	Libya	D 1-1	Lome	WCq	Kalen Damessi [8]	15 000	Coulibaly MLI
10-06	Congo DR	L 0-2	Kinshasa	WCq		50 000	Farouk EGY
17-06	Kenya	W 1-0	Lome	CNq	Serge Gakpe [59]		Alioum CMR
8-09	Gabon	D 1-1	Libreville	CNq	Emmanuel Adebayor [82]		Sikazwe ZAM
14-10	Gabon	W 2-1	Lome	CNq	Dove Wome [36], Emmanuel Adebayor [57]		Seechurn MRI
14-11	Morocco	W 1-0	Casablanca	Fr	Emmanuel Adebayor [75]		
1-12	Burkina Faso	L 1-2	Ouagadougou	Fr	Placca Fessou [80]		
16-12	Burkina Faso	L 0-1	Lome	Fr			
29-12	Oman	W 1-0	Sohar	Fr	Dove Wome [83]		
2013							
22-01	Côte d'Ivoire	L 1-2	Rustenburg	CNr1	Jonathan Ayite [45]	2 000	Alioum CMR
26-01	Algeria	W 2-0	Rustenburg	CNr1	Emmanuel Adebayor [31], Dove Wome [93+]	35 000	Nampiandraza MAD
30-01	Tunisia	D 1-1	Nelspruit	CNr1	Serge Gakpe [13]	7 500	Bennett RSA
3-02	Burkina Faso	L 0-1	Nelspruit	CNqf		27 000	Diatta SEN

Fr = Friendly match • CN = CAF African Cup of Nations • WC = FIFA World Cup • q = qualifier • r1 = first round group

TOGO 2012

PREMIER LEAGUE

	Pl	W	D	L	F	A	Pts	Dynamic	Maranatha	Unisport	Gomido	ASKO Kara	Douanes	Koroki	Sèmassi	Foadan	Togo Port	Agaza	Kotoko	Abou Ossé	Tchaoudjo	Okiti	Sara Sport
Dynamic Togolais †	30	15	8	7	36	21	53		6-2	1-0	0-0	0-0	0-1	2-1	1-0	1-0	0-0	2-1	1-0	2-0	1-0	4-0	1-0
Maranatha Fiokpo	29	12	9	8	31	26	45	1-2		1-0	0-0	1-0	1-0	3-1	2-0	0-1	1-1	3-0	1-1	3-0	1-1	0-1	3-1
Unisport Sokodé	30	12	9	9	29	28	45	2-1	1-0		0-0	1-1	1-0	4-0	1-0	1-0	3-2	1-0	0-0	1-0	1-0		2-0
Gomido	30	10	12	8	32	24	42	1-1	1-2	1-0		0-0	3-0	1-0	0-0	2-1	0-0	2-1	1-1	5-0	0-0	1-0	4-0
ASKO Kara	30	9	15	6	23	21	42	0-0	1-1	2-0			1-0	0-1	1-1	2-0	2-1	1-0	1-1	0-0	3-1	0-0	0-0
AS Douanes ‡	30	12	5	13	27	24	41	1-0	1-2	0-0	1-0	2-0		0-1	0-1	3-1	1-0	0-0	0-0	0-0	0-1	4-1	4-1
US Koroki Tchamba	30	11	8	11	28	35	41	1-1	1-0	2-2	1-0	0-2	1-1		0-0	1-0	2-0	2-1	0-0	2-1	4-0	1-1	2-0
Sèmassi Sokodé	29	10	10	9	31	24	40	2-2	n/p	2-2	2-2	3-1	2-1	3-0		0-0	1-1	1-2	2-1	1-1	0-0	1-0	3-0
Foadan	30	11	7	12	26	20	40	1-0	0-0	3-0	1-2	3-0	2-0	0-0	3-0		1-1	1-0	2-0	2-0	1-0	1-0	3-0
Togo Port	30	10	10	10	30	25	40	2-0	2-0	3-1	0-1	0-0	1-0	4-1	0-2	0-0		0-2	1-1	4-1	0-0	3-0	2-0
Agaza Lomé	30	11	6	13	41	33	39	1-2	4-1	1-1	1-1	1-2	2-3	3-0	0-1	3-0	1-1		0-0	3-3	1-0	1-0	0-0
Kotoko Lavié	30	8	14	8	23	21	38	0-2	0-0	2-1	0-0	0-0	0-1	1-1	1-0	0-0	2-0	1-0		2-0	0-0	2-1	3-0
Abou Ossé Anié	30	11	5	14	26	42	38	1-0	0-2	3-1	2-1	2-3	0-1	1-0	1-0	1-0	1-0	2-0	1-1		3-2	2-0	1-1
Tchaoudjo AC Sokodé	30	9	10	11	25	28	37	1-1	0-0	3-0	3-2	0-1	0-0	0-3	0-0	1-2	2-2	1-0	1-0			3-0	1-0
Okiti Badou	30	10	7	13	23	29	37	1-0	0-0	0-0	0-0	4-1	0-0	1-0	1-0	1-0	0-1	3-1	3-0	3-0	0-0		1-2
Sara Sport Bafilo	30	6	9	15	15	45	27	1-0	1-1	1-1	1-0	0-0	0-2	1-2	0-0	1-0	2-0	0-4	0-3	2-1	0-0	0-0	

22/10/2011 - 21/10/2012 • † Qualified for the CAF Champions League • ‡ Qualified for the CAF Confederation Cup
Etoile Filante withdrew after five games following a bus accident on their way to a game against Sèmassi. They were not relegated

TPE – CHINESE TAIPEI

FIFA/COCA-COLA WORLD RANKING

'93	'94	'95	'96	'97	'98	'99	'00	'01	'02	'03	'04	'05	'06	'07	'08	'09	'10	'11	'12
161	170	178	174	154	169	174	162	170	166	150	155	156	166	169	167	162	153	167	169

2012

Jan	Feb	Mar	Apr	May	Jun	Jul	Aug	Sep	Oct	Nov	Dec	High	Low	Av
167	166	168	169	168	167	176	175	176	176	176	169	144	180	164

Taiwan Power Company had become the first team from Chinese Taipei to taste success at continental level when they won the AFC President's Cup competition in 2011 but the club from Taipei - who are also known as Kaohsiung Taipower - were unable to perform a repeat of that historic achievement in 2012. After qualifying for the finals once again, thanks to wins over KRL from Pakistan and Mongolia's Erchim, Taipower missed out on a place in the final to Palestinian side Shabab Al Amari, who eliminated them on goal difference in a second round group staged in Dushanbe after the two had drawn 1-1. There were struggles for the national team in the qualifying group for the 2013 EAFF East Asian Cup finals where they drew with Guam but lost to Australia, Korea DPR and hosts Hong Kong to finish joint bottom of the standings. Chinese Taipei's only win of 2012 came against Guam in a friendly tournament in Manila in the Philippines. Kaohsiung Taipower will represent the island state in the 2013 AFC President's Cup after claiming the league crown ahead of Taipei City Tatung. Both clubs finished the 12-match season level on points, but Taipower won the title on goal-difference to claim the trophy for the third year running and the 17th time in the past 25 years.

FIFA WORLD CUP RECORD
1930-1954 DNE 1954 DNQ 1958-1974 DNE 1978-2014 DNQ

CHINESE TAIPEI FOOTBALL ASSOCIATION (CTFA)

Room 210, 2F,
55 Chang Chi Street,
Tatung District,
Taipei 10363
☎ +886 2 25961185
📠 +886 2 25951594
✉ ctfa7155@ms59.hinet.net
🖥 www.ctfa.com.tw
FA 1924 CON 1954 FIFA 1954
P Lu Kun Shan
GS Chris Wang

THE STADIA

2014 FIFA World Cup Stadia
Municipal Stadium
Taipei City   20 000

Other Main Stadia
Kaohsiung National Stadium
Kaohsiung   40 000
Chungcheng Stadium
Kaohsiung   30 000
Taiwan Provincial Stadium
Taichung   28 000

MAJOR CITIES/TOWNS
		Population
1	Taipei	2 655 423
2	Kaohsiung	1 525 999
3	Taizhong	1 078 348
4	Tainan	772 279
5	Banqiao	547 444
6	Zhonghe	414 984
7	Taoyuan	405 289
8	Xinzhu	401 991
9	Xinzhuang	400 647
10	Jilong	389 737
11	Sanchong	380 859
12	Zhongli	367 943
13	Fengshan	343 332
14	Xindian	293 572
15	Jiayi	274 657
16	Zhanghua	239 716
17	Tucheng	237 795
18	Yonghe	236 448
19	Pingdong	217 819

CHINESE TAIPEI

Capital	Taipei	Population	22 974 347 (49)	% in cities	69%
GDP per capita	$31 100 (42)	Area km²	35 980 km² (138)	GMT +/-	+8
Neighbours (km)	Coast 1566				

RECENT INTERNATIONAL MATCHES PLAYED BY CHINESE TAIPEI

2009	Opponents	Score	Venue	Comp	Scorers	Att	Referee
4-04	Pakistan	D 1-1	Colombo	CCq	Chang Han [21]	400	Tseytlin UZB
6-04	Sri Lanka	L 1-2	Colombo	CCq	Huang Wei Yi [80]	1 400	Al Zahrani KSA
8-04	Brunei Darussalam	W 5-0	Colombo	CCq	Chen Po Liang 3 [11 13 58], Huang Wei Yi [30], Kuo Chun Yi [80]	1 000	Al Zahrani KSA
23-08	Hong Kong	L 0-4	Kaohsiung	EAq		12 000	Tojo JPN
25-08	Guam	W 4-2	Kaohsiung	EAq	Chen Po Liang 2 [45 68], Chang Han [61], Lo Chih En [75]	7 500	Matsuo JPN
27-08	Korea DPR	L 1-2	Kaohsiung	EAq	Chang Han [49]	10 000	Matsuo JPN
2010							
16-01	Philippines	D 0-0	Kaohsiung	Fr			
9-10	Macau	W 7-1	Kaohsiung	Fr	Lin Cheng Yi [16], Lo Chih En [43], Lo Chih An [45], Chen Po Hao 2 [46 77], Chang Han [55], Chen Po Liang [67]	1 000	San Hua Nien TPE
10-10	Philippines	D 1-1	Kaohsiung	Fr	Lo Chih An [48]	890	Kao Tsai Hu TPE
12-10	Hong Kong	D 1-1	Kaohsiung	Fr	Lo Chih An [40]	3 000	Kao Tsai Hu TPE
24-11	Indonesia	L 0-2	Palembang	Fr			Singh SIN
2011							
10-02	Laos	W 5-2	Kaohsiung	CCq	Lin Cheng Yi [10], Chang Han 2 [22 56], Chen Po Liang [44], Lo Chih An [49]	1 000	Ng Chiu Kok HKG
16-02	Laos	D 1-1	Vientiane	CCq	Chen Po Liang [65]	15 300	Abdul Wahab MAS
21-03	India	L 0-3	Petaling Jaya	CCq		50	Abdul Wahab MAS
23-03	Turkmenistan	L 0-2	Petaling Jaya	CCq		100	Serazitdinov UZB
25-03	Pakistan	L 0-2	Petaling Jaya	CCq		50	Alrshaidat JOR
29-06	Malaysia	L 1-2	Kuala Lumpur	WCq	Chen Po Liang [76]	45 000	Mahapab THA
3-07	Malaysia	W 3-2	Taipei	WCq	Chang Han [31], Chen Po Liang [44p], Chen Tsan Yuan [75p]	16 768	Minh Tri Vn VIF
18-07	Singapore	L 2-3	Singapore	Fr	Lo Chih An [48], Chiang Shih Lu [62]		
30-09	Macau	W 3-0	Kaohsiung	Fr	Huang Chiu Yi [11], Chen Po Liang [31], Wu Chin Hung [45]		
2-10	Philippines	D 0-0	Kaohsiung	Fr			
4-10	Hong Kong	L 0-6	Kaohsiung	Fr		5 210	
2012							
29-02	Hong Kong	L 1-5	Hong Kong	Fr	Kuo Yin Hung [45]	5 187	
25-09	Macau	D 2-2	Manila	Fr	Lo Chih En [11], Yang Chao Hsun [89p]		Villagracia PHI
27-09	Guam	W 2-0	Manila	Fr	Lo Chih An [11], OG [45]		Supresencia PHI
29-09	Philippines	L 1-3	Manila	Fr	Chang Han [51]		Phung Dinh Dung VIE
1-12	Korea DPR	L 1-6	Hong Kong	EAq	Chen Hao Wei [79]	3 040	Wang Zhe CHN
5-12	Guam	D 1-1	Hong Kong	EAq	Lo Chih An [92+]	989	Kim Dae Yong KOR
7-12	Hong Kong	L 0-2	Hong Kong	EAq		2 315	Iida JPN
9-12	Australia	L 0-8	Hong Kong	EAq		3 345	Kim Dae Yong KOR

Fr = Friendly match • EA = East Asian Championship • AC = AFC Asian Cup • CC = AFC Challenge Cup • WC = FIFA World Cup • q = qualifier

CHINESE TAIPEI NATIONAL TEAM HISTORICAL RECORDS

Coaches: Lee Wai Tong 1954-58 • Law Pak 1977-81 • Chiang Chia 1981-85 • Lo Chih Tsung 1985-88 • Huang Jen Cheng 1988-93 • Chiang Mu Tsai 1994-2000 • Huang Jen Cheng 2000-01 • Lee Po Houng 2001-05 • Dido BRA 2005 • Toshiaki Imai JPN 2005-07 • Chen Sing An 2008-09 • Lo Chih Tsung 2009-11 • Lee Tae Ho KOR 2001 • Chen Kuei Jen 2012 • Chiang Mu Tsai 2012 • Chen Kuei Jen 2013-

CHINESE TAIPEI 2012

CITY A-LEAGUE

	Pl	W	D	L	F	A	Pts	Taipower	Tatung	NSTC	NTCPE	Ming Chuan	Tainan	I-Shou
Kaohsiung Taipower ‡	12	8	3	1	32	5	27		0-1	2-0	2-0	3-0	1-0	8-0
Taipei City Tatung	12	9	0	3	30	14	27	0-2		1-0	4-3	2-1	2-1	1-2
NSTC	12	7	1	4	23	22	22	1-1	0-4		5-3	2-1	3-2	1-0
NTCPE	12	5	2	5	28	23	17	2-2	1-0	1-3		2-3	2-0	6-1
Ming Chuan University	12	5	1	6	30	31	16	0-6	2-7	5-0	1-5		1-1	7-1
Tainan City	12	1	3	8	13	23	6	1-1	0-4	2-3	1-2	1-3		1-1
I-Shou University	12	1	2	9	9	47	5	0-4	2-4	0-5	1-1	1-6	0-3	

2/06/2012 - 17/11/2012 • ‡ Qualified for the AFC President's Cup

TRI – TRINIDAD AND TOBAGO

FIFA/COCA-COLA WORLD RANKING

'93	'94	'95	'96	'97	'98	'99	'00	'01	'02	'03	'04	'05	'06	'07	'08	'09	'10	'11	'12
88	91	57	41	56	51	44	29	32	47	70	63	50	91	81	77	82	89	76	68

2012

Jan	Feb	Mar	Apr	May	Jun	Jul	Aug	Sep	Oct	Nov	Dec	High	Low	Av
78	85	82	83	82	82	80	80	82	77	79	68	25	106	63

In the first 12 years of the Caribbean Championship, Trinidad and Tobago won the title a record eight times but in the eleven years since the last of those titles in 2001 they have yet to win it again. There may have been fewer tournaments played since 2001 but after losing in the final of the 2012 edition in Antigua to Cuba, the Soca Warriors have now gone five championships without being crowned as kings of the Caribbean. Their displays in Antigua were less than impressive with just one win in the five matches played. They squeezed through the group stage thanks to a face-saving 2-1 win over the Dominican Republic but needed an injury-time equaliser and penalties to knock out Martinique in the semis. With the traditionally more pro baseball Spanish speaking nations in the north of the Caribbean starting to flex their football muscles, the Trinidadians have found themselves with more competition on their hands than their usual rivals Jamaica and it was Cuba who beat them in the final to claim the title for the first time. There was, however, success for Trinidadian clubs in the CFU Club Championship with Caledonia AIA winning the title for the first time after beating compatriots W Connection 4-3 on penalties. The two clubs also shared the domestic honours with the cup going to Caledonia and the league title to W Connection.

CFU CARIBBEAN CUP RECORD

1989 1 Winners **1991** 2 F **1992** Winners (Hosts) **1993** 3 SF **1994** 1 Winners (Hosts) **1995** 1 Winners
1996 1 Winners (Hosts) **1997** 1 Winners **1998** 2 F (Co-hosts) **1999** 1 Winners (Hosts)
2001 1 Winners (Hosts) **2005** 3 **2007** 2 F (Hosts) **2008** 5 r1 **2010** 6 r1 **2012** 2 F

TRINIDAD AND TOBAGO FOOTBALL FEDERATION (TTFF)

6 Ana Street, Woodbrook, PO Box 400, Port of Spain
☎ +1 868 6239500
📠 +1 868 6258150
✉ ttff1908@yahoo.com
🌐 www.ttffonline.com
FA 1908 CON 1964 FIFA 1963
P Raymond Tim Kee
GS Richard Groden

THE STADIA

2014 FIFA World Cup Stadia
Hasely Crawford Stadium
Port of Spain — 27 000

Other Main Stadia
Larry Gomes Stadium
Malabar — 10 000
Manny Ramjohn Stadium
Marabella — 10 000
Marvin Lee Stadium
Tunapuna — 8 000
Dwight Yorke Stadium
Scarborough — 7 500

MAJOR CITIES/TOWNS

		Population
1	Chaguanas	76 136
2	San Juan	58 815
3	San Fernando	57 032
4	Port of Spain	50 044
5	Arima	37 332
6	Marabella	26 624
7	Tunapuna	18 826
8	Point Fortin	18 748
9	Sangre Grande	17 156
10	Tacarigua	15 973
11	Arouca	12 779
12	Princes Town	10 969
13	Siparia	8 355
14	Couva	5 316
15	Peñal	5 058
16	Saint Joseph	4 979
17	Scarborough	4 734
18	Mucurapo	4 542
19	Tabaquite	3 402

REPUBLIC OF TRINIDAD AND TOBAGO

Capital	Port of Spain	Population	1 229 953 (154)	% in cities	13%
GDP per capita	$23 600 (53)	Area km²	5 128 km² (173)	GMT +/-	-4
Neighbours (km)	Coast 362				

RECENT INTERNATIONAL MATCHES PLAYED BY TRINIDAD AND TOBAGO

2010	Opponents	Score	Venue	Comp	Scorers	Att	Referee
5-05	Chile	L 0-2	Iquique	Fr		10 000	Antequera BRA
21-07	Antigua and Barbuda	W 4-1	Macoya	Fr	Kevon Carter 2 [10 30], Kerry Baptiste [18], Devorn Jorsling [67]	1 700	Brizan TRI
11-08	Jamaica	L 1-3	Macoya	Fr	Devorn Jorsling [28]	4 500	Taylor BRB
7-09	Panama	L 0-3	Panama City	Fr		6 645	Cruz CRC
10-09	Belize	D 0-0	Belmopan	Fr		5 000	Mejia SLV
19-09	Antigua and Barbuda	W 1-0	St John's	Fr	Devorn Jorsling [70]	500	Willett ATG
21-09	St Lucia	W 3-0	St John's	Fr	Devorn Jorsling [22], Jamal Gay [53], Hughton Hector [86]	205	St Catherine LCA
26-09	Guyana	D 1-1	Providence	Fr	Devorn Jorsling [35]	9 000	Lancaster GUY
10-10	Jamaica	L 0-1	Kingston	Fr		7 000	Archundia MEX
2-11	St Vincent/Grenadines	W 6-2	Marabella	CCq	Devorn Jorsling 3 [2 35 59], Kerry Baptiste 2 [57 67], Hughton Hector [90]	1 100	Peterkin JAM
4-11	Guyana	W 2-1	Marabella	CCq	Lester Peltier [34], Devorn Jorsling [42]	1 100	Legister JAM
6-11	Haiti	W 4-0	Marabella	CCq	Hughton Hector 2 [4 33], Devon Jorsling [8], Kerry Baptiste [29]	850	Campbell JAM
26-11	Cuba	L 0-2	Fort de France	CCr1		5 000	Lancaster GUY
28-11	Grenada	L 0-1	Fort de France	CCr1		500	Cruz CRC
30-11	Martinique	W 1-0	Fort de France	CCr1	Hughton Hector [47]	2 000	Taylor BRB
2011							
21-08	India	W 3-0	Port of Spain	Fr	Stern John [19p], Darryl Roberts 2 [46 84]	6 600	Campbell JAM
2-09	Bermuda	W 1-0	Port of Spain	WCq	Kenwyne Jones [45]	6 000	Perea PAN
6-09	Barbados	W 2-0	Bridgetown	WCq	Keon Daniel [17], Darryl Roberts [67]	775	Bonilla SLV
7-10	Bermuda	L 1-2	Prospect	WCq	Kevin Molino [82]	2 243	Solis CRC
11-10	Barbados	W 4-0	Port of Spain	WCq	Lester Peltier 3 [6 55 63], Hughtun Hector [90]	3 000	Bogle JAM
11-11	Guyana	L 1-2	Georgetown	WCq	Kenwyne Jones [45 93+]	18 000	Wijngaarde SUR
15-11	Guyana	W 3-0	Port of Spain	WCq	Originally 2-0. Kenwyne Jones [59], Lester Peltier [69]	2 000	Mejia SLV
2012							
22-01	Finland	L 2-3	Port of Spain	Fr	Mekeil Williams [33], Kevin Molino [66]	5 000	Campbell JAM
29-02	Antigua and Barbuda	W 4-0	St John's	Fr	Devorn Jorsling 3 [57 67 75], Willis Plaza [80]	2 500	Baptiste DMA
15-08	Canada	L 0-2	Fort Lauderdale	Fr		BCD	Marrufo USA
10-10	French Guiana †	W 4-1	Basseterre	CCq	Hughton Hector [26], Jamal Gay [35], Keon Daniel [72], Willis Plaza [82]	400	Brea CUB
12-10	St Kitts and Nevis	W 1-0	Basseterre	CCq	Kevon Carter [51]	1 700	Rubalcaba CUB
14-10	Anguilla	W 10-0	Basseterre	CCq	Jamal Gaye 4 [7 21 32 38], Keon Daniel 3 [11 35 40], Willis Plaza 2 [53 63], Sylvester Tessdale [71]	40	Johnson GUY
14-11	St Vincent/Grenadines	D 1-1	Scarborough	CCq	Atullah Guerra [67]	1 300	Campbell JAM
16-11	Suriname	W 3-0	Scarborough	CCq	Seon Power [35], Richard Roy [50], Aubrey David [88]	950	Georges HAI
18-11	Cuba	W 1-0	Scarborough	CCq	Devorn Jorsling [3]	800	Campbell JAM
7-12	Haiti	D 0-0	St John's	CCr1		150	Legister JAM
9-12	Antigua and Barbuda	L 0-2	St John's	CCr1		2 000	Rubalcaba CUB
11-12	Dominican Republic	W 2-1	St John's	CCr1	Kevon Carter [14], Kevin Molino [70]	250	Thomas JAM
14-12	Martinique	D 1-1	St John's	CCsf	Richard Roy [90]. W 5-4p	200	Bonilla SLV
16-12	Cuba	L 0-1	St John's	CCf		750	Legister JAM

Fr = Friendly match • CC = Digicel Caribbean Cup • GC = CONCACAF Gold Cup • WC = FIFA World Cup
q = qualifier • r1 = first round group • † Not a full international

TRINIDAD AND TOBAGO NATIONAL TEAM HISTORICAL RECORDS

Caps: 113 - Angus Eve 1994-2005 • 108 - Stern John 1995-2009 • 101 - Marvin Andrews 1996-2009 • 89 - Dennis Lawrence 2000-10 & Densill Theobald 2002- • 83 - Carlos Edwards 1999- • 81 - Russell Latapy 1988-2009 • 79 - Clayton Ince 1997-2010 • 74 - Arnold Dwarika 1993-2008 • 72 - Dwight Yorke 1989-2009 & Keyeno Thomas 1998-2009 • 70 - Avery John 1996-2009

Goals: 70 - Stern John 1995- • 34 - Angus Eve 1994-2005 • 29 - Russell Latapy 1988-2009 • 28 - Arnold Dwarika 1993-2008 • 23 - Cornell Glen 2002- • 22 - Nigel Pierre 1998-2008 • 21 - Leonson Lewis 1988-96 • 19 - Dwight Yorke 1989-2009 • 17 - Devorn Jorsling 2007-

Coaches: Bertille St. Clair 1997-2000 • Ian Porterfield SCO 2000-01 • Rene Simoes BRA 2001-02 • Hannibal Najjar 2002-03 • Zoran Vranes SRB 2003 • Stuart Charles Fevrier LCA 2003-04 • Bertille St. Clair 2004-05 • Leo Beenhakker NED 2005-06 • Wim Rijsbergen NED 2006-07 • Francisco Maturana COL 2008-09 • Russell Latapy 2009-11 • Otto Pfister GER 2011-12 • Hutson Charles 2012-

TRI – TRINIDAD AND TOBAGO

TRINIDAD AND TOBAGO 2011-12

DIGICEL PRO LEAGUE

	Pl	W	D	L	F	A	Pts	W Connection	T&TEC	Caledonia AIA	Defence Force	San Juan	Police	NE Stars	St Anne's
W Connection	21	13	1	7	32	20	**40**		1-0	1-2 2-1	0-1	0-2	1-2 8-1	2-1	2-1 3-1
T&TEC Sports Club	21	11	6	4	36	19	**39**	2-0 1-1		2-0	3-1 3-0	1-0 2-1	1-4	0-0	3-0
Caledonia AIA	21	12	2	7	34	28	**38**	0-2	1-0 3-2		1-2	3-1	1-1	0-1 3-2	1-0 2-0
Defence Force	21	9	5	7	32	28	**32**	0-1 2-0	1-1	2-3 2-3		1-1 3-0	1-1 0-0	1-1	4-1
San Juan Jabloteh	21	7	6	8	29	30	**27**	2-0 0-1	1-1	1-1 1-2	2-1		1-0	1-1 0-2	3-3 2-2
Police	21	5	6	10	30	47	**21**	0-1	1-6 1-2	1-3 3-2	4-2	1-3 2-4		2-3 2-1	0-0
North East Stars	21	5	5	11	21	27	**20**	0-1 1-4	1-2 1-1	0-1	0-1 1-2	1-2	0-0		1-2 2-0
St Ann's Rangers	21	4	5	12	24	39	**17**	0-1	1-1 0-2	2-1	1-3 1-2	2-1	2-2 5-2	0-1	

9/09/2011 - 3/03/2012

Top scorers: **15** - Richard **ROY**, Defence • **11** - Willis **PLAZA**, San Juan • **10** - Sylvester **TEESDALE**, T&TEC • **9** - Devon **MODESTE**, St Anne's • **8** - Devorn **JORSLING**, Caledonia • **7** - Jerrel **BRITTO**, W Connection; Jamal **GAY**, Caledonia & Ataullah **GUERRA**, Caledonia

FIRST CITIZENS BANK CUP 2012

Quarter-finals		Semi-finals		Final	
Caledonia AIA	2				
T&TEC SC	0	**Caledonia AIA**	1		
Police	0 0p	W Connection	0		
W Connection	0 3p			**Caledonia AIA**	2
St Ann's Rangers	2			Defence Force	1
North East Stars	1	St Ann's Rangers	1	5-10-2012	
Central	0	**Defence Force**	2	Scorers - Jamal Gay [22], Trayon Bobb [49] for CAIA; Richard Roy [28] for Defence	
Defence Force	3				

MEDALS TABLE

		All	P	L	Cp	FC	C
		G	G	G	G	G	G
1	Defence Force	31	4	17	6	2	2
2	Maple Club	20		13	7		
3	Casuals	15		11	4		
4	Shamrock	13		9	4		
	W Connection	13	4		3	6	
6	Malvern Utd	9		2	7		
7	SJ Jabloteh	8	4		2	2	
8	Joe Public	7	3		3	1	
	Everton	7		3	4		
	Colts	7		4	3		
11	Police	6		3	3		
	Sporting Club	6		5	1		
	UB Oilfields	6			6		
14	Utd Petrotin	5			5		
15	Caledonia AIA	4			2	2	
	Notre Dame	4		3	1		
17	NE Stars	2	1		1		
18	Queen's Park	1		1			

P = Pro League (since 1996) • L = League (pre 1996) • Cp = FA Trophy • FC = First Citizens Bank Cup • C = CONCACAF Champions League

FA TROPHY 2011-12

Eighth-finals		Quarter-finals		Semi-finals		Final	
Caledonia AIA	1 4p						
North East Stars	1 3p	**Caledonia AIA**	2				
St Ann's Rangers	1	Joe Public	0				
Joe Public	3			**Caledonia AIA**	1		
Scarborough High	0 3p			W Connection	0		
Caroni Samba	0 1p	Scarborough High	0				
San Juan Jabloteh	0	**W Connection**	5				
W Connection	1					**Caledonia AIA**	1
WASA	2					Defence Force	0
Club Sando	1	**WASA**	3				
Harlem Strikers	0	OJ Soldado	1			**CUP FINAL**	
OJ Soldado	2			WASA	1		
St Francois Nationals	2			**Defence Force**	3	25-03-2012	
Clint Marcelle School	1	St Francois Nationals	0			Scorer - Devorn Jorsling [81] for Caledonia	
Police	2	**Defence Force**	5				
Defence Force	3						

TUN – TUNISIA

FIFA/COCA-COLA WORLD RANKING

'93	'94	'95	'96	'97	'98	'99	'00	'01	'02	'03	'04	'05	'06	'07	'08	'09	'10	'11	'12
32	30	22	23	23	21	31	26	28	41	45	35	28	32	47	46	53	45	59	45

2012													High	Low	Av
Jan	Feb	Mar	Apr	May	Jun	Jul	Aug	Sep	Oct	Nov	Dec				
59	56	56	57	56	46	43	41	41	45	46	45		19	65	36

Tunisia turned in another timid showing at the 2013 Africa Cup of Nations in South Africa, costing coach Sami Trabelsi his job after they failed to beat Togo in their last Group D game that saw them eliminated at the first hurdle. The performances reflected a generally poor 2012 for the national side, who although winning both opening 2014 FIFA World Cup qualifiers, were exceedingly fortunate to reach the Nations Cup finals in South Africa. They sneaked through on the away goals rule over Sierra Leone, having survived several close calls in the second leg at home. In club football Esperance Tunis reached the 2012 CAF Champions League final - their third in a row - but were unable to retain the title they won in 2011 despite holding Al Ahly of Egypt to a draw in the first leg away in Alexandria. They were thoroughly outplayed in the return in front of a restricted crowd at the re-named Stade Olympique de Rades and lost 2-1. Domestic football remained cloistered largely behind closed doors as post-Arab Spring security fears continued to hit hard at the club's income with limited numbers of tickets allowed to be sold for international matches. Esperance won a 24th title in an prolonged season that finished late in October and then offered just a few week's respite before the new campaign got underway.

CAF AFRICA CUP OF NATIONS RECORD
1957-1957 DNE 1962 3 SF 1963 5 r1 1965 2 F (Hosts) 1968 DNQ 1970-1974 DNE 1976 DNQ 1978 4 SF
1980 DNE 1982 7 r1 1984-1992 DNQ 1994 9 r1 (Hosts) 1996 2 F 1998 6 QF
2000 4 SF 2002 11 r1 2004 1 Winners (Hosts) 2006 7 QF 2008 5 QF 2010 11 r1 2012 6 QF

FEDERATION TUNISIENNE DE FOOTBALL (FTF)
Stade annexe d'El Menzah, Cité Olympique, Tunis 1003
☎ +216 71 793760
📠 +216 71 783843
✉ directeur@ftf.org.tn
🌐 www.ftf.org.tn
FA 1956 CON 1960 FIFA 1960
P Wadii El Jery
GS Ridha Kraiem

THE STADIA
2014 FIFA World Cup Stadia
Mustapha Ben Jannet
Monastir   20 000

Other Main Stadia
Stade Olympique de Rades
Rades, Tunis   60 000
Stade El Menzah
Tunis   45 000
Stade Olympique
Sousse   28 000
Stade Taïeb-Mhiri
Sfax   22 000

MAJOR CITIES/TOWNS
		Population
1	Tunis	741 427
2	Sfax	284 027
3	Ariana	277 114
4	At Tadaman	198 854
5	Sousse	195 100
6	Kairouan	124 505
7	Gabès	123 600
8	Bizerte	118 714
9	El Mourouj	91 693
10	Gafsa	89 492
11	Kasserine	81 443
12	Monastir	80 847
13	Ben Arous	78 601
14	La Marsa	78 585
15	Zarzis	73 142
16	Hammamet	66 065
17	Masakin	65 603
18	Tatouine	65 436
19	Béja	56 517

AL JUMHURIYAH AT TUNISIYAH • TUNISIAN REPUBLIC
Capital	Tunis	Population	10 486 339 (76)	% in cities	67%
GDP per capita	$7900 (122)	Area km²	163 610 km² (92)	GMT +/-	+1
Neighbours (km)	Algeria 965, Libya 459 • Coast 1148

RECENT INTERNATIONAL MATCHES PLAYED BY TUNISIA

2011 Opponents		Score	Venue	Comp	Scorers	Att	Referee
29-03 Oman	L	1-2	Seeb	Fr	Sami Allagui [63]		
29-05 Central African Rep	W	3-0	Sousse	Fr	Oussama Darragi 2 [32p 50], Lamjed Chehoudi [45]		
5-06 Chad	W	5-0	Sousse	CNq	Issam Jemaa 3 [22 44 53], Aymen Abdennour [35], Oussama Darragi [47]		
10-08 Mali	W	4-2	Monastir	Fr	Sami Allagui 2 [19 50], Ammar Jemal [29p], Issam Jemaa [83]		
22-08 Jordan	D	3-3	Amman	Fr	Ammar Jemal 2 [30p 80p], Lamjed Chehoudi [33]		
3-09 Malawi	D	0-0	Blantyre	CNq			
8-10 Togo	W	2-0	Rades	CNq	Walid Hichri [19], Saber Khelifa [79]		
12-11 Algeria	L	0-1	Algiers	Fr			
2012							
9-01 Sudan	W	3-0	Sharjah	Fr	Saber Khelifa [12], Zouheir Dhaouadi [60], Amine Chermiti [83]		
13-01 Côte d'Ivoire	L	0-2	Abu Dhabi	Fr			
23-01 Morocco	W	2-1	Libreville	CNr1	Khaled Korbi [34], Youssef Msakni [76]	18 000	Bennett RSA
27-01 Niger	W	2-1	Libreville	CNr1	Youssef Msakni [4], Issam Jemaa [90]	20 000	Sikazwe ZAM
31-01 Gabon	L	0-1	Franceville	CNr1		22 000	Doue CIV
5-02 Ghana	L	1-2	Franceville	CNqf	Saber Khelifa [41]	8 000	Alioum CMR
29-02 Peru	D	1-1	Tunis	Fr	Wissem Ben Yahia [45]	5 000	Fleischer GHA
27-05 Rwanda	W	5-1	Monastir	Fr	Amar Jemal [17p], Hamadi Harbaoui 2 [50 53], Issam Jemaa [68], Jamel Saihi [77]		
2-06 Equatorial Guinea	W	3-1	Monastir	WCq	Issam Jemaa [51], Hamadi Harbaoui [56], Chedi Hammami [86]	10 000	Abid ALG
9-06 Cape Verde Islands	W	2-1	Praia	WCq	Saber Khalifa [14], Issam Jemaa [46]	3 600	Yiyed MAR
15-08 Iran	D	2-2	Kecskemet	Fr	Amar Jemal [55], Issam Jemaa [83]		
8-09 Sierra Leone	D	2-2	Freetown	CNq	Fatah Gharbi [65], Youssef Msakni [87]		Abdel Rahman SUD
13-10 Sierra Leone	D	0-0	Monastir	CNq			Lemghaifry MTN
16-10 Egypt	W	1-0	Abu Dhabi	Fr	Zouheir Dhaouadi [19]	40 000	
14-11 Switzerland	L	1-2	Sousse	Fr	Hamadi Harbaoui [59]	1 500	Fleischer GHA
30-12 Iraq	W	2-1	Sharjah	Fr	Issam Jemaa [47], Fakhereedine Ben Youssef [58]		Hashmi UAE
2013							
7-01 Ethiopia	D	1-1	Al Wakrah	Fr	Oussama Darragi [4p]		
10-01 Gabon	D	1-1	Abu Dhabi	Fr	Saber Khlifa [15]		
13-01 Ghana	L	2-4	Abu Dhabi	Fr	Issam Jemaa 2 [19 52]		
22-01 Algeria	W	1-0	Rustenburg	CCr1	Youssef Msakni [91+]	10 000	Gassama GAM
26-01 Côte d'Ivoire	L	0-3	Rustenburg	CCr1		20 000	Seechurn MRI
30-01 Togo	D	1-1	Nelspruit	CCr1	Khaled Mouelhi [30p]	7 500	Bennett RSA

Fr = Friendly match • CN = CAF African Cup of Nations • WC = FIFA World Cup • q = qualifier • r1 = first round group • qf = quarter-final

TUNISIA NATIONAL TEAM HISTORICAL RECORDS

Coaches: For coaches pre 1989 see Oliver's Almanack 2012 • Mrad Moujab 1989-93 • Youssef Zouaoui 1993-94 • Faouzi Benzarti 1994 • Henryk Kasperczak POL 1994-98 • Francesco Scoglio ITA 1998-01 • Eckhard Krautzun GER 2001 • Henri Michel FRA 2001-02 • Ammar Souayah 2002 • Youssef Zouaoui 2002 • Roger Lemerre FRA 2002-08 • Humberto Coelho POR 2008-09 • Faouzi Benzarti 2009-10 • Sami Trabelsi 2010 • Bertrand Marchand FRA 2010 • Faouzi Benzarti 2010-2011 • Ammar Souayah 2011 • Sami Trabelsi 2011-13

TUNISIA SQUAD FOR THE 2012 CAF AFRICA CUP OF NATIONS

	Player		Ap	G	Club	Date of Birth		Player		Ap	G	Club	Date of Birth
1	Moez Ben Chrifia	GK	0		Espérance	24 06 1991	12	Khalil Chemmam	DF	2		Espérance	24 07 1987
2	Bilel Ifa	DF	4		Club Africain	9 03 1990	13	Wissem Ben Yahia	MF	1		Mersin IY TUR	9 09 1984
3	Karim Haggui (c)	DF	3		Hannover GER	20 01 1984	14	Mejdi Traoui	MF	3		Espérance	13 12 1983
4	Adel Chedli	MF	0		Etoile du Sahel	16 09 1976	15	Zouheir Dhaouadi	FW	3		Club Africain	1 01 1988
5	Ammar Jemal	DF	2		1.FC Köln GER	20 04 1987	16	Aymen Mathlouthi	GK	3		Etoile du Sahel	14 09 1984
6	Hocine Ragued	MF	2+1		Karabükspor TUR	11 02 1983	17	Issam Jemaa	FW	1+2	1	Auxerre FRA	28 01 1984
7	Youssef Msakni	MF	3+1	2	Espérance	28 10 1990	18	Anis Boussaidi	DF	1+1		Rostov RUS	10 04 1981
8	Khaled Korbi	FW	2	1	Espérance	16 12 1985	19	Saber Khelifa	FW	3	1	Evian FRA	14 12 1986
9	Yassine Chikhaoui	FW	2+1		Zürich SUI	22 09 1986	20	Aymen Abdennour	DF	4		Toulouse FRA	6 08 1989
10	Oussama Darragi	MF	0+3		Espérance	3 04 1987	21	Jamel Saihi	MF	2		Montpellier FRA	27 01 1987
11	Sami Allagui	FW	1+2		Mainz GER	28 05 1986	22	Rami Jridi	GK	1		Stade Tunisien	15 09 1984
	Tr: Sami Trabelsi 4-02-1968						23	Amine Chermiti	FW	1+1		Zürich SUI	26 12 1987

TUNISIA 2011-12
LIGUE NATIONALE A

	Pl	W	D	L	F	A	Pts	Espérance	Bizertin	Sfaxien	Etoile	Marsa	Club Africain	Monastir	Olympique	Stade	Gafsa	H-Sousse	Kairouan	Espérance Z	Hammam Lif	Gabés	Béni Khalled
Espérance Tunis †	30	22	3	5	61	22	**69**		0-1	1-0	1-0	1-0	3-2	3-0	3-1	2-1	1-0	7-0	2-0	5-0	4-0	4-1	1-0
CA Bizertin †	30	20	5	5	54	25	**65**	2-1		2-2	1-0	1-2	2-1	2-0	2-1	1-1	4-1	2-1	3-0	2-0	1-0	2-1	5-2
CS Sfaxien ‡	30	15	11	4	48	26	**56**	2-1	1-0		1-1	1-1	2-1	2-2	0-0	2-1	3-0	1-0	3-0	5-1	2-1	4-0	2-1
Etoile du Sahel ‡	30	13	10	7	33	22	**49**	0-2	1-0	3-1		0-1	0-1	0-0	2-0	1-0	1-0	3-1	2-1	2-1	0-0	2-2	0-0
AS Marsa	30	12	11	7	39	28	**47**	1-2	1-1	2-2	0-0		0-0	2-0	2-1	0-0	1-0	0-0	1-0	1-0	5-2	2-0	3-1
Club Africain	30	10	12	8	36	30	**42**	1-2	2-2	1-1	0-0	1-1		1-1	0-0	4-0	2-1	1-0	2-1	0-0	2-0	0-0	3-0
US Monastir	30	7	15	8	31	34	**36**	1-1	0-2	1-1	2-0	2-1	1-0		1-0	0-0	1-0	1-1	2-2	2-2	2-1	1-0	5-0
Olympique Béjà	30	8	10	12	31	35	**36**	3-1	0-0	1-2	1-2	1-0	0-1	0-0		1-1	1-0	1-1	2-5	1-1	2-0	1-0	1-0
Stade Tunisien	30	9	9	12	30	37	**36**	3-1	1-2	1-0	1-0	0-1		1-1	1-3		1-1	0-2	1-0	3-1	1-1	2-1	1-1
EGS Gafsa	30	9	9	12	27	38	**36**	1-1	2-1	0-0	0-2	3-2	2-2	1-1	2-1	1-0		1-0	0-0	2-1	1-0	1-0	4-2
ES Hammam-Sousse	30	8	11	11	29	37	**35**	0-2	1-3	1-1	0-0	1-1	1-1	0-0	1-1	4-1	2-1		0-0	2-1	1-0	0-0	1-1	3-2
JS Kairouan	30	8	9	13	29	38	**33**	0-2	1-0	0-1	2-2	0-0	1-2	5-2	2-1	1-1	0-0	1-0		1-1	1-0	2-1	1-0
Espérance Zarzis	30	7	9	14	35	51	**31**	2-2	0-1	1-3	2-3	1-1	2-2	3-2	1-2	3-2	2-1	1-0	2-0		1-1	1-1	1-2
CS Hammam Lif	30	8	7	15	28	46	**31**	0-2	1-4	2-1	0-4	2-4	1-1	1-0	2-1	1-0	4-1	1-1	2-1	1-2		2-0	1-0
AS Gabés	30	4	10	16	24	45	**22**	0-2	0-3	0-0	1-2	1-2	3-2	2-1	1-1	2-2	0-1	0-0	1-2	2-0	1-1	1-1		0-0
ES Béni Khalled	30	4	9	17	24	44	**21**	0-1	1-2	0-1	0-0	1-1	0-1	0-0	0-1	1-1	1-3	0-2	2-1	1-1	1-2	1-1	2-0	

4/11/2011 - 3/10/2012 • † Qualified for the CAF Champions League • ‡ Qualified for the CAF Confederation Cup
Top scorers: **17** - Youssef **MSAKNI**, Espérance • **15** - Joseph Yannick **N'DJENG** CMR, Espérance • **13** - Ahmed **ZUWAY** LBY, Bizertin & Didier **LEBRI** CIV, Marsa • **11** - Nour **HADHRIA**, Bizertin & Maher **AMEUR**, Espérance Zarzis • **9** - Ezechiel **NDOUASSEL** CHA, Club Africain & Chedi **HAMMEMI**, Sfax

TUNISIA 2011-12
LIGUE NATIONAL B (2)

	Pl	W	D	L	F	A	Pts
Olympique Kef	30	15	8	7	37	29	**53**
Stade Gabésien	30	13	11	6	38	24	**50**
US Ben Guerdane	30	13	10	7	34	25	**49**
CS Korba	30	13	9	8	37	24	**48**
CS Masakin	30	12	10	8	31	24	**46**
SC Moknine	30	11	9	10	44	47	**42**
Grombalia Sports	30	10	11	9	34	33	**41**
AS Kasserine	30	11	6	13	28	32	**39**
CS Hilalien	30	10	8	12	28	32	**38**
Jendouba Sport	30	8	13	9	29	28	**37**
AS Djerba	30	8	13	9	30	33	**37**
LPTA Tozeur	30	10	6	14	26	26	**36**
EA Mateur	30	8	11	11	26	30	**35**
CO Transports	30	11	2	17	26	42	**35**
Stade Nabeulien	30	8	9	13	30	39	**33**
Kalaâ Sport	30	6	10	14	27	37	**28**

4/11/2011 - 30/06/2012

MEDALS TABLE

			Overall			League			Cup			Africa			City
			G	S	B	G	S	B	G	S		G	S	B	
1	Espérance Sportive de Tunis	EST	41	21	12	24	10	9	13	6		4	5	3	Tunis
2	Club Africain	CA	22	35	14	10	20	12	11	12		1	3	2	Tunis
3	Etoile Sportive du Sahel	ESS	21	30	15	8	16	15	7	9		6	5		Sousse
4	Club Sportif Sfaxien	CSS	14	8	8	7	1	7	4	5		3	2	1	Sfax
5	Stade Tunisien	ST	10	8	6	4	3	6	6	5					Tunis
6	Avenir Sportif de la Marsa	ASM	5	8	2		1	2	5	7					Marsa, Tunis
7	Club Athlétique Bizertin	CAB	4	4	2	1	3	1	2	1		1		1	Bizerte
8	Club Sportif de Hammam Lif	CSHL	3	1	2	1			2	1				1	Hammam Lif
9	Olympique de Béjà	OB	2	2					2	2					Béja
10	Jeunesse Sportive Kairouan	JSK	1	2		1	1			1					Kairouan
	Sfax Railways Sport	SRS	1	2		1				2					Sfax
12	Club Olympique Transports	COT	1	1	2		1	2	1						Tunis
13	Espérance Sportive de Zarzis	ESZ	1						1						Zarzis

TUR – TURKEY

FIFA/COCA-COLA WORLD RANKING

'93	'94	'95	'96	'97	'98	'99	'00	'01	'02	'03	'04	'05	'06	'07	'08	'09	'10	'11	'12
52	48	30	31	43	57	29	30	23	9	8	14	11	26	16	10	41	31	28	40

2012												
Jan	Feb	Mar	Apr	May	Jun	Jul	Aug	Sep	Oct	Nov	Dec		High	Low	Av
29	25	32	33	33	33	29	30	35	36	38	40		5	67	28

The return of Fatih Terim as coach of Galatasaray inspired the club to a first championship success in four seasons, although thanks to the revised format of the tournament they nearly threw it away at the end. Having finished nine points clear of rivals Fenerbahçe after the normal 34-game season, Gala's lead was cut to just five after the points were halved for the extra six matches played between the top four. Going into the final game of the play-offs, away to Fenerbahçe, their lead was down to just one point but they managed to hold on for a 0-0 draw to win their 18th title, joining Fenerbahçe at the top of the all-time list. Four days later Fenerbahçe managed to salvage their season with a 4-0 win over Bursaspor in the Turkish cup final. Remarkably, it was the club's first cup triumph since 1983 during which time they had been losing finalists seven times. After the failure to qualify for the finals of Euro 2012, Dutchman Guus Hiddink was replaced by Abdullah Avci as the Turkish national team coach but despite a fine run of wins in mid-year Turkey got off to a nightmare start in their 2014 FIFA World Cup qualifying group. They lost to their main group rivals Romania, Hungary and the Netherlands, results that left the team well off the pace at the end of the year and in need of some inspiring performances in the remaining fixtures.

UEFA EUROPEAN CHAMPIONSHIP RECORD
1960 r1 **1964** r1 **1968-1992** DNQ **1996** r1 **2000** QF **2004** DNQ **2008** SF **2012** DNQ

TURKIYE FUTBOL FEDERASYONU (TFF)
Istinye Mahallesi Darüssafaka Caddesi, No 45, Kat 2 Sariyer, 34460 Istanbul
☎ +90 212 3622222
📠 +90 212 3234968
✉ intdept@tff.org
🖥 www.tff.org
FA 1923 CON 1962 FIFA 1923
P Yildirim Demiroren
GS Emre Alkin

THE STADIA
2014 FIFA World Cup Stadia
Sükrü Saracoglu
Istanbul — 50 509
Other Main Stadia
Atatürk Olimpiyat Stadi
Istanbul — 76 092
Türk Telecom Arena
Istanbul — 52 647
Kadir Has Stadi
Kayseri — 40 458
Hüseyin Avni Aker Stadi
Trabzon — 22 749

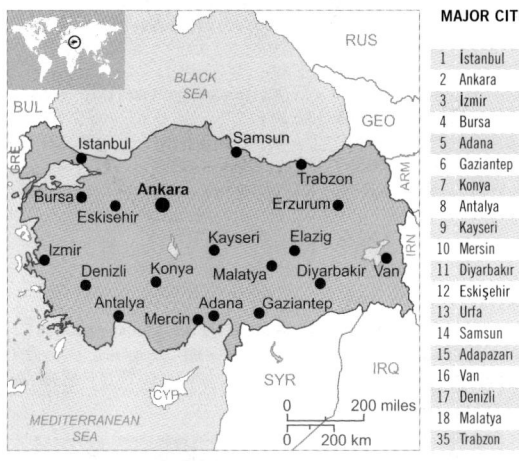

MAJOR CITIES/TOWNS
		Population
1	İstanbul	12 175 592
2	Ankara	4 082 184
3	İzmir	2 815 046
4	Bursa	1 567 756
5	Adana	1 491 066
6	Gaziantep	1 388 004
7	Konya	950 645
8	Antalya	809 437
9	Kayseri	796 291
10	Mersin	629 224
11	Diyarbakır	610 117
12	Eskişehir	599 987
13	Urfa	494 598
14	Samsun	461 369
15	Adapazan	427 885
16	Van	354 771
17	Denizli	351 097
18	Malatya	346 064
35	Trabzon	197 510

TURKIYE CUMHURIYETI • REPUBLIC OF TURKEY
Capital	Ankara	Population	76 805 524 (17)	% in cities	69%
GDP per capita	$11 200 (100)	Area km²	783 562 km² (37)	GMT +/-	+2
Neighbours (km)	Armenia 268, Azerbaijan 9, Bulgaria 240, Georgia 252, Greece 206, Iran 499, Iraq 352, Syria 822 • Coast 7200				

RECENT INTERNATIONAL MATCHES PLAYED BY TURKEY

2009	Opponents	Score	Venue	Comp	Scorers	Att	Referee
12-08	Ukraine	W 3-0	Kyiv	Fr	Tuncay Sanli [58], Servet Cetin [63], Hamit Altintop [65]		Ceferin SVN
5-09	Estonia	W 4-2	Kayseri	WCq	Tuncay Sanli 2 [27,72], Sercan Yildirim [37], Arda Turan [62]	28 569	Skjerven NOR
9-09	Bosnia-Herzegovina	D 1-1	Zenica	WCq	Emre Belozoglu [4]	14 000	Benquerença POR
10-10	Belgium	L 0-2	Brussels	WCq		30 131	Trefoloni ITA
14-10	Armenia	W 2-0	Bursa	WCq	Halil Altintop [16], Servet Cetin [28]	16 200	Hansson SWE
2010							
3-03	Honduras	W 2-0	Istanbul	Fr	Emre Gungor [41], Hamit Altintop [55]	17 000	Olsiak SVK
22-05	Czech Republic	W 2-1	Harrison	Fr	Arda Turan [31], Nihat Kahveci [48]	16 371	Geiger USA
26-05	Northern Ireland	W 2-0	New Britain	Fr	Sercan Yildirim [48], Semih Senturk [72]	4 000	Vaughn USA
29-05	USA	L 1-2	Philadelphia	Fr	Arda Turan [27]	55 407	Petrescu CAN
11-08	Romania	W 2-0	Istanbul	Fr	Emre Belozoglu [4]	15 000	Mazic SRB
3-09	Kazakhstan	W 3-0	Astana	ECq	Arda Turan [24], Hamit Altintop [26], Nihat Kahveci [76]	15 800	Vad HUN
7-09	Belgium	W 3-2	Istanbul	ECq	Hamit Altintop [48], Semih Senturk [66], Arda Turan [78]	43 538	Skomina SVN
8-10	Germany	L 0-3	Berlin	ECq		74 244	Webb ENG
12-10	Azerbaijan	L 0-1	Baku	ECq		29 500	Deaconu ROU
17-11	Netherlands	L 0-1	Amsterdam	Fr		35 500	Kassai HUN
2011							
9-02	Korea Republic	D 0-0	Trabzon	Fr		20 000	Boyko UKR
29-03	Austria	W 2-0	Istanbul	ECq	Arda Turan [28], Gokhan Gonul [78]	40 420	Kralovec AUT
3-06	Belgium	D 1-1	Brussels	ECq	Burak Yilmaz [22]	44 145	Rizzoli ITA
10-08	Estonia	W 3-0	Istanbul	Fr	Emre Belozoglu [8p], Kazim-Richards 2 [28,35]	20 000	Probert ENG
2-09	Kazakhstan	W 2-1	Istanbul	ECq	Burak Yilmaz [31], Arda Turan [96+]	47 756	Turpin FRA
6-09	Austria	D 0-0	Vienna	ECq		47 500	Undiano ESP
7-10	Germany	L 1-3	Istanbul	ECq	Hakan Balta [79]	49 532	Atkinson ENG
11-10	Azerbaijan	W 1-0	Istanbul	ECq	Burak Yilmaz [60]	32 174	Rasmussen DEN
11-11	Croatia	L 0-3	Istanbul	ECpo		47 000	Brych GER
15-11	Croatia	D 0-0	Zagreb	ECpo		34 000	Proenca POR
2012							
29-02	Slovakia	L 1-2	Bursa	Fr	Omer Toprak [85]	13 000	Kinhofer GER
24-05	Georgia	W 3-1	Salzburg	Fr	Hamit Altintop [12], Nuri Sahin [40], Selcuk Inan [82p]	700	Hameter AUT
26-05	Finland †	L 2-3	Salzburg	Fr	Burak Yilmaz 2 [21,55]	1 000	Schuttengruber AUT
29-05	Bulgaria	W 2-0	Salzburg	Fr	Omer Toprak [22], Burak Yilmaz [91+]	2 000	Grobelnik AUT
2-06	Portugal	W 3-1	Lisbon	Fr	Umut Bulut 2 [35,52], OG [88]	62 000	Studer SUI
5-06	Ukraine	W 2-0	Ingolstadt	Fr	Caner Erkin [30], Mustafa Pektemek [70]	14 000	Weiner GER
15-08	Austria	L 0-2	Vienna	Fr		23 500	Valasek SVK
7-09	Netherlands	L 0-2	Amsterdam	WCq		49 500	Velasco ESP
11-09	Estonia	W 3-0	Istanbul	WCq	Emre Belozoglu [44], Umut Bulut [60], Selcuk Inan [75]	44 168	Borski POL
12-10	Romania	L 0-1	Istanbul	WCq		46 203	Webb ENG
16-10	Hungary	L 1-3	Budapest	WCq	Mevlut Erdinc [22]	21 563	Orsato ENG
14-11	Denmark	D 1-1	Istanbul	Fr	Mevlut Erdinc [69]	30 000	Brych GER

Fr = Friendly match • EC = UEFA EURO 2012 • WC = FIFA World Cup • q = qualifier • r1 = first round group • † Not a full international

TURKEY NATIONAL TEAM HISTORICAL RECORDS

Caps
120 - Rustu Recber 1994-2012 • 112 - Hakan Sukur 1992-2008 • 102 - Bulent Korkmaz 1990-2005 • 94 - Tugay Kerimoglu 1990-2007 • 90 - Alpay Ozlan 1995-2005 • 89 - Emre Belozoglu 2000- • 80 - Tuncay Sanli 2002- • 77 - Hamit Altintop 2004- • 76 - Ogun Temizkanoglu 1990-2002 • 71 - Abdullah Ercan 1992-2003 • 70 - Oguz Cetin 1988-98 • 69 - Nihat Kahveci 2000- • 64 - Fatih Akyel 1997-2004 • 61 - Arda Turan 2006- • 60 - Arif Erdem 1994-2003

Goals
51 - Hakan Sukur 1992-2008 • 22 - Tuncay Sanli 2002- • 21 - Lefter Kucukandonyadis 1948-61 • 19 - Nihat Kahveci 2000- ; Metin Oktay 1956-65 & Cemil Turan 1969-79 • 15 - Zeki-Riza Sporel 1923-32 • 12 - Arda Turan 2006-

Coaches
For coaches prior to 1980 see Oliver's Almanack of World Football 2011 • Ozkan Sumer 1980-81 • Fethi Demircan 1981 • Coskun Ozarı 1982-84 • Candan Tarhan 1984 • Yılmaz Gokdel 1984-85 • Kalman Meszoly HUN 1985 • Coskun Ozarı 1985-86 • Mustafa Denizli 1987 • Tınaz Tırpan 1988-89 • Fatih Terim 1990 • Sepp Piontek GER 1990-93 • Fatih Terim 1993-96 • Mustafa Denizli 1996-2000 • Senol Gunes 2000-04 • Unal Karaman 2004 • Ersun Yanal 2004-05 • Fatih Terim 2005-09 • Oguz Cetin 2010 • Guus Hiddink NED 2010-11 • Abdullah Avci 2011-

TURKEY 2011-12

TURKCELL SUPER LIG

	Pl	W	D	L	F	A	Pts	Galatasaray	Fenerbahçe	Trabzonspor	Besiktas	Eskisehirspor	Istanbul BB	Sivasspor	Bursaspor	Gençlerbirligi	Gaziantepspor	Kayserispor	Karabükspor	Mersin IY	Orduspor	Antalyaspor	Samsunspor	Manisaspor	Ankaragücü
Galatasaray †	34	23	8	3	69	24	77		3-1	1-1	3-2	2-0	4-1	2-1	2-1	2-0	2-4	1-0	5-1	0-0	2-0	1-1	3-1	1-0	4-0
Fenerbahçe †	34	20	8	6	61	34	68	2-2		1-0	2-0	1-0	4-2	4-2	1-0	6-1	3-1	4-0	1-0	2-1	1-0	2-0	0-0	1-1	4-2
Trabzonspor †	34	15	11	8	60	39	56	0-3	1-1		0-1	4-1	0-1	2-1	2-1	1-2	4-0	2-1	3-1	2-3	4-1	2-2	4-0	2-1	3-2
Besiktas †	34	15	10	9	50	39	55	0-0	2-2	1-2		2-0	1-1	3-1	3-1	3-2	3-2	0-2	1-0	0-1	2-1	1-0	0-1	4-1	3-1
Eskisehirspor ‡	34	14	8	12	42	41	50	0-0	2-1	0-2	2-1		3-1	1-1	1-1	0-0	0-2	1-0	1-2	2-0	0-1	1-0	1-0	0-2	3-2
Istanbul BB ‡	34	14	8	12	48	49	50	2-0	3-2	0-2	2-2	2-2		1-1	0-0	1-0	3-1	1-0	2-2	0-0	1-1	4-0	3-0	3-2	3-0
Sivasspor ‡	34	13	11	10	57	54	50	0-4	2-0	2-2	1-1	0-4	0-1		3-0	1-1	0-0	1-1	2-0	1-0	1-1	2-1	3-2	2-2	3-0
Bursaspor ‡	34	13	10	11	44	35	49	1-0	0-2	1-1	1-2	0-1	2-1	1-2		4-0	0-2	3-0	3-0	1-0	0-0	0-0	1-0	0-0	2-1
Gençlerbirligi	34	13	10	11	49	48	49	0-1	0-0	1-1	4-2	2-1	4-0	3-3	2-2		1-0	1-0	2-1	1-2	3-1	3-0	1-1	3-0	1-1
Gaziantepspor	34	13	9	12	39	33	48	1-2	1-3	0-1	0-0	0-1	5-0	2-1	2-2	3-0		1-2	3-0	1-0	1-0	1-0	1-0	1-1	1-0
Kayserispor	34	13	5	16	42	39	44	0-2	0-1	3-3	1-0	2-2	1-0	6-2	0-2	2-3	1-1		2-0	2-2	1-0	0-1	2-0	2-0	3-0
Karabükspor	34	13	5	16	44	56	44	1-1	2-1	2-1	1-1	1-2	2-0	2-1	3-1	2-1	0-0	1-0		3-5	1-2	2-1	2-1	2-1	3-2
Mersin Idman Yurdu	34	12	6	16	34	45	42	1-3	1-2	1-1	0-1	0-0	2-0	1-5	1-3	2-1	2-0	1-2	0-2		1-0	0-2	1-0	0-0	1-2
Orduspor	34	10	12	12	28	34	42	0-2	1-1	0-0	1-1	2-1	1-0	1-2	1-1	0-0	0-0	1-0	3-2	0-1		3-2	0-0	1-0	2-0
Antalyaspor	34	10	9	15	32	42	39	0-0	0-0	2-1	1-2	0-0	2-1	2-2	1-3	2-2	1-0	1-2	1-2	1-1	1-2		0-2	2-1	1-0
Samsunspor	34	9	9	16	36	47	36	2-4	3-1	1-1	1-1	3-1	2-4	1-2	0-3	3-2	0-0	0-1	0-0	2-0	2-0	1-0		1-2	2-2
Manisaspor	34	8	8	18	31	52	32	0-4	1-2	1-1	1-4	2-3	0-2	1-3	1-3	0-1	0-2	1-0	2-1	2-0	0-0	1-0	1-1		2-0
MKE Ankaragücü	34	2	5	27	22	77	11	0-3	0-2	0-4	0-0	2-5	1-2	1-2	0-0	0-1	0-0	0-5	2-1	1-2	0-2	0-3	0-1		

9/09/2011 - 8/04/2012 • † Qualified for the Championship group • ‡ Qualified for the Europa League group • Half of the points total taken forward
Top scorers (both stages): **33** - **BURAK** Yilmaz, Trabzonspor • **15** - Diomansy **KAMARA** SEN, Eskisehirspor; Herve **TUM** CMR, Gençlerbirligi; Michael **ENERAMO** NGA, Sivasspor & Pierre **WEBO** CMR, Istanbul BB • **14** - **ALEX** BRA, Fenerbahçe; **TITA** BRA Antalyaspor & **DOKA MADUREIRA** BRA, Istanbul BB • **13** - Pablo **BATALLA** ARG, Bursapor; **NACATI** Ates, Antalyaspor/Galatasaray & **SELCUK** Inan, Galatasaray

SUPERLIG PLAY-OFFS

Championship

	Pl	W	D	L	F	A	Pts	Ga	Fe	Tr	Be
Galatasaray †	6	2	3	1	9	6	48		1-2	0-0	2-2
Fenerbahçe †	6	4	1	1	9	4	47	0-0		2-0	2-1
Trabzonspor †	6	1	2	3	5	10	33	2-4	1-3		1-0
Besiktas	6	1	2	3	5	8	33	0-2	1-0	1-1	

Europa League

								Bu	Es	Is	Si
Bursaspor ‡	6	4	0	2	12	10	37		3-2	3-2	2-0
Eskisehirspor ‡	6	3	2	1	12	7	36	2-0		3-1	1-1
Istanbul BB	6	2	1	3	11	14	32	0-4	1-1		4-2
Sivasspor	6	1	4	9	13	29	4-0	1-3	1-2		

14/04/2012 - 12/05/2012 • † Qualified for the UEFA Champions League
• ‡ Qualified for the Europa League

SPOR TOTO CUP FINAL
Istanbul, 17-05-2012

Orduspor 1-3 **Gaziantepspor**

Played at the end of the season between the teams placed 9-16 in the Super Lig. Played in two groups of four with the winners of each group qualifying for the final

MEDALS TABLE

		Overall			League			Cup		Europe			City
		G	S	B	G	S	B	G	S	G	S	B	
1	Galatasaray	33	14	17	**18**	9	16	**14**	5	1		1	Istanbul
2	Fenerbahçe	23	27	6	**18**	18	6	5	9				Istanbul
3	Besiktas	20	20	8	11	14	8	9	6				Istanbul
4	Trabzonspor	14	13	7	6	8	7	8	5				Trabzon
5	Altay	2	5	2				2	5				Izmir
6	Gençlerbirligi	2	3	2				2	3				Ankara
7	Bursaspor	2	4	1	1			1	4				Bursa
8	MKE Ankaragücü	2	3					2	3				Ankara
9	Göztepe	2	1	2			1	2	1			1	Izmir
10	Kocaelispor	2		1				1	2				Izmit
11	Eskisehirspor	1	5	2		3	2	1	2				Eskisehir
12	Kayserispor	1						1					Kayseri
	Sakaryaspor	1						1					Sakarya
14	Samsunspor		1	2			2		1				Samsun
15	Boluspor		1	1				1	1				Bolu

TURKEY 2011-12

PTT 1.LIG (2)

	Pl	W	D	L	F	A	Pts	Akhisar	Elazigspor	C. Rizespor	Kasimpasa	Konyaspor	Adanaspor	Boluspor	K. Erciyesspor	Kartalspor	Denizlispor	T. Linyitspor	Bucaspor	Göztepe Izmir	Gaziantep BB	Karsiyaka	Giresunspor	Sakaryaspor	Güngörenspor
Akhisar Belediyespor	34	17	12	5	46	28	**63**		0-0	3-0	2-2	1-1	1-1	0-0	2-0	0-0	3-3	1-0	0-1	1-0	1-1	3-0	1-1	2-0	0-0
Elazigspor	34	18	7	9	45	30	**61**	1-0		0-2	2-1	1-0	1-0	2-0	0-0	1-0	2-0	3-0	2-1	3-0	0-1	0-2	3-0	3-0	3-2
Caykur Rizespor †	34	16	11	7	52	44	**59**	1-2	3-5		4-2	2-2	1-1	2-2	0-2	2-1	3-1	2-1	0-0	2-3	0-0	2-1	1-1	1-0	0-0
Kasimpasa †	34	16	11	7	50	39	**59**	1-2	0-1	1-2		3-1	1-1	1-1	1-0	1-1	2-0	0-1	3-1	2-1	2-1	2-1	2-2	3-2	2-1
Konyaspor †	34	16	11	7	35	25	**59**	0-0	4-1	1-3	0-0		0-2	1-1	1-0	0-0	1-0	0-1	1-0	2-1	1-0	1-0	1-1	1-0	2-1
Adanaspor †	34	14	11	9	46	32	**53**	0-1	2-0	0-2	0-0	0-0		0-0	2-1	2-1	2-2	1-0	4-0	4-3	3-0	0-1	2-1	2-2	2-0
Boluspor	34	13	12	9	40	33	**51**	2-1	2-2	1-4	0-1	1-2	0-0		1-2	1-0	2-3	1-0	0-0	0-1	1-0	2-0	2-1	0-0
Kayseri Erciyesspor	34	12	10	12	43	39	**46**	2-3	1-1	4-0	2-2	0-0	2-1	1-2		0-0	1-1	1-2	1-3	4-2	2-1	1-1	1-0	2-0
Kartalspor	34	11	12	11	37	32	**45**	0-1	1-0	1-2	1-1	3-2	0-2	1-1	1-2		3-1	1-1	1-0	2-0	2-1	2-0	3-1	1-1	2-2
Denizlispor	34	11	12	11	51	46	**45**	2-3	0-1	1-1	0-3	1-2	3-1	2-0	1-1	1-1		1-3	1-2	2-1	0-0	0-0	6-1	4-0	3-1
Tavsanli Linyitspor	34	12	7	15	42	39	**43**	1-2	1-0	1-2	0-1	1-1	1-1	1-1	3-0	1-1	1-2		3-1	0-1	4-2	0-4	2-0	1-0	2-1
Bucaspor	34	12	7	15	45	53	**43**	1-3	2-1	0-1	3-3	0-0	2-2	0-2	1-1	0-2	5-2	2-7		1-2	2-1	2-0	2-1	3-0	2-1
Göztepe Izmir	34	11	8	15	36	43	**41**	0-0	1-1	0-1	1-1	1-2	1-0	1-0	0-1	2-1	0-2	1-1	0-0	1-2		0-1	1-1	1-1	1-1	3-1
Gaziantep BB	34	9	13	12	36	37	**40**	1-1	1-2	3-0	4-1	0-1	2-1	0-0	1-3	2-0	0-0	1-1	2-1	2-4		0-0	0-0	5-1	0-0
Karsiyaka	34	10	9	15	31	37	**39**	2-0	0-1	2-4	0-1	1-0	0-2	1-3	0-1	2-1	1-1	2-1	0-0	1-0	0-0		2-1	1-0	0-0
Giresunspor	34	8	15	11	39	48	**39**	3-1	0-0	1-1	0-0	0-0	0-0	1-1	2-1	1-0	0-3	0-0	3-0	0-0	2-2	3-2		1-3	6-2
Sakaryaspor	34	4	9	21	31	66	**21**	1-3	3-3	0-0	1-2	0-2	2-3	2-7	2-1	0-2	0-0	1-0	1-2	0-1	0-0	1-1	1-2		2-2
Güngörenspor	34	2	11	21	24	58	**17**	0-1	0-0	0-1	1-2	0-2	2-3	2-7	0-1	2-0	0-2	2-1	1-5	1-1	2-0	1-3	2-3	2-3	

9/09/2011 - 13/05/2012 • † Qualified for the promotion play-offs • Top scorer: **18** - Severin Brice **BIKOKO** CMR, Caykur Rizespor

PROMOTION PLAY-OFFS (2)

Semi-finals

Kasimpasa	2	4
Konyaspor *	0	0

Caykur Rizespor	1	0
Adanaspor *	3	1

Final

Kasimpasa	3
Adanaspor	2

* Home team in the 1st leg

TURKEY 2011-12
SPOR-TOTO 2.LIG BEYAZ (3)

	Pl	W	D	L	F	A	Pts
Sanliurfaspor	32	23	6	3	63	20	**75**
Balikesirspor †	32	20	8	4	73	32	**68**
Bozüyükspor †	32	20	5	7	58	33	**65**
Polatli Bugsasspor †	32	15	11	6	49	29	**56**
Turgutluspor †	32	16	6	10	56	33	**54**
Tepecikspor	32	14	10	8	44	39	**52**
Altay Izmir	32	15	6	11	48	31	**51**
Gaziosmanpasa	32	14	4	14	44	40	**46**
Iskenderun DC	32	14	4	14	45	42	**46**
Konya Sekerspor	32	13	5	14	45	40	**44**
Ofspor	32	11	10	11	45	41	**43**
Pendikspor	32	8	16	8	36	31	**40**
Yeni Malatyaspor	32	9	9	14	45	43	**36**
Tokatspor	32	8	4	20	27	57	**28**
Diyarbakirspor	32	6	7	19	27	56	**25**
Corumspor	32	2	10	20	19	57	**16**
Kocaelispor	32	2	3	27	30	130	**9**

11/09/2011 - 20/05/2012 • † Promotion play-offs

TURKEY 2011-12
SPOR-TOTO 2.LIG KIRMIZI (3)

	Pl	W	D	L	F	A	Pts
1461 Trabzon	32	17	11	4	50	23	**62**
Bandirmaspor †	32	16	8	8	37	22	**56**
Adana Demirspor †	32	16	7	9	46	31	**55**
Fethiyespor †	32	15	9	8	54	38	**54**
Kizilcahamamspor †	32	15	8	9	48	34	**53**
Körfez FK	32	13	13	6	39	26	**52**
Denizli Belediyespor	32	12	9	11	39	32	**45**
Kirklarelispor	32	11	11	10	34	26	**44**
Eyüpspor	32	11	11	10	34	35	**44**
Sariyer	32	12	7	13	39	37	**43**
Cankiri Belediyespor	32	11	9	12	40	41	**42**
Alanyaspor	32	9	15	8	26	28	**42**
Unyespor	32	9	13	10	32	32	**40**
Beypazari Sekerspor	32	10	9	13	37	45	**39**
Altinordu	32	9	11	12	31	33	**38**
Adiyamanspor	32	4	8	20	23	51	**20**
Mardinspor	32	1	3	28	11	86	**6**

11/09/2011 - 20/05/2012 • † Promotion play-offs

PROMOTION PLAY-OFFS (3)

Quarter-finals

Adana Demirspor	1
Balikesirspor	0

Bandirmaspor	1
Polatli Bugsasspor	2

Bozüyükspor	1
Kizilcahamamspor	0

Turgutluspor	0
Fethiyespor	1

Semi-finals

Adana Demirspor	0	9p
Polatli Bugsasspor	0	8p

Bozüyükspor	2	3p
Fethiyespor	2	4p

Final

Adana Demirspor	2
Fethiyespor	1

All matches played in Denizli

TURKIYE KUPASI 2011-12

Third Round

Fenerbahçe *	4
Konya Sekerspor	1
Orduspor	0 2p
Samsunspor *	0 4p
Istanbul BB	2
Adanaspor *	1
Akhisar Belediyespor *	0
Kayserispor	1
Boluspor *	3
Gençlerbirligi	2
Gaziantep BB	1
Besiktas *	2
Caykur Rizespor *	3
Gaziantepspor	2
Unyespor	0
Karabükspor	1
Eskisehirspor *	3
Eyüpspor *	2
MKE Ankaragücü	2
Kasimpasa	6
Trabzonspor *	2
Güngörenspor	0
Gaziosmanpasa *	1
Antalyaspor	2
Sivasspor	3
Mersin Idman Yurdu *	1
Adana Demirspor	1
Galatasaray *	4
Polatli Bugsasspor *	2
Manisaspor	1
Sanliurfaspor	1
Bursaspor *	4

Round of 16

Fenerbahçe *	3
Samsunspor	0
Istanbul BB	0
Kayserispor *	1
Boluspor *	1
Besiktas	0
Caykur Rizespor *	0
Karabükspor	1
Eskisehirspor *	3
Kasimpasa	0
Trabzonspor	1
Antalyaspor *	2
Sivasspor	1
Galatasaray *	0
Polatli Bugsasspor *	0
Bursaspor	2

Quarter-finals

Fenerbahçe †‡	2 5p
Kayserispor	2 4p
Boluspor	0
Karabükspor †‡	1
Eskisehirspor ‡‡	3
Antalyaspor	0
Sivasspor	1
Bursaspor ‡‡	4

Semi-finals

Fenerbahçe †‡	2
Karabükspor	0
Eskisehirspor ††	0
Bursaspor ††	3

Final

Fenerbahçe	4
Bursaspor ‡	0

†† Played at Atatürk, Izmir
‡‡ Played at 19 Mayis, Ankara
‡‡ Played at Sukru Saracoglu, Istanbul

CUP FINAL
19 Mayis, Ankara, 16-05-2012
Att: 19 500, Ref: Bulent Yildirim
Scorers - Caner [2], Baroni [45], Semi [58], Alex [77] for Fenerbahçe
Fenerbahçe - Volkan Demirel - Gokhan Gonul (Orhan Sam 58), Bekir Irtegun, Joseph Yobo (Serdat Kesimal 30), Reto Ziegler - Caner Erkin, Emre Belozoglu●, Cristian Baroni●, Mehmet Topuz - Semi Senturk, Alex (Moussa Sow 81). Tr: Aykut Kocaman
Bursaspor - Scott Carson - Michael Chretien●, Ibrahim Ozturk, Serdar Aziz, Gokcek Vederson● - Alfred N'Diaye (Turgay Bahadir 63), Adem Kocak (Musa Cagiran● 56), Ozan Ipek, Stanislav Sestak (Okan Deniz 71), Pablo Batalla - Sebastian Pinto●. Tr: Ertugrul Saglam

Super Lig teams joined in the third round • * Home team in the first leg • ‡ Qualified for the Europa League

UAE – UNITED ARAB EMIRATES

FIFA/COCA-COLA WORLD RANKING

'93	'94	'95	'96	'97	'98	'99	'00	'01	'02	'03	'04	'05	'06	'07	'08	'09	'10	'11	'12
51	46	75	60	50	42	54	64	60	89	75	82	85	87	100	110	112	105	130	96

2012

Jan	Feb	Mar	Apr	May	Jun	Jul	Aug	Sep	Oct	Nov	Dec		High	Low	Av
138	132	122	121	120	119	116	121	120	116	109	96		42	138	81

Football in the United Arab Emirates continued to make steady progress although the failure of the national team to make the final round of qualifying for the 2014 FIFA World Cup in Brazil was a big disappointment for the Gulf state. Local coach Mahdi Ali was appointed to take charge of the national team midway through 2012 with the team already eliminated from the World Cup and he also took the U-23 team to the Olympic in London for what was a first appearance in the games. Great emphasis and hope is being placed on youth for the future especially the much-coveted talents of Al Ain midfielder Omar Abdulrahman. Abdulrahman was a key component of the team that played in London and although the UAE failed to progress from the group stage, the 21-year-old is seen as the leader of a generation that, it is hoped, can go some way towards emulating the country's greatest achievements, two of which were qualifying for the 1990 FIFA World Cup in Italy and reaching the final of the AFC Asian Cup in 1996. Abdulrahman was also part of the Al Ain team that claimed a first championship since 2004 after finishing well clear of Al Nasr in second place. The cup was won by Abu Dhabi's Al Jazira who beat Bani-Yas 3-1 in a final played in Al Jazira's extraordinary redeveloped stadium in the capital.

FIFA WORLD CUP RECORD
1930-1982 DNE **1986** DNQ **1990** 24 r1 **1994-2014** DNQ

UAE FOOTBALL ASSOCIATION (UAEFA)

Zayed Athletic City,
PO Box 961,
Abu Dhabi
✆ +971 2 4445600
✉ +971 2 4448558
✉ info@uaefa.ae
🌐 www.uaefa.ae
FA 1971 CON 1974 FIFA 1972
P Yousuf Al Serkal
GS Yousuf Abdullah

THE STADIA
2014 FIFA World Cup Stadia
Al Rashid Stadium
Dubai   18 000
Sheikh Khalifa International
Al Ain   16 000
Tahnoun Bin Mohamed 'Al Qatara'
Al Ain   15 187
Al Wahda Stadium 'Al Nahyan'
Abu Dhabi   11 842
Other Main Stadia
Mohammed Bin Zayed 'Al Jazira'
Abu Dhabi   42 056

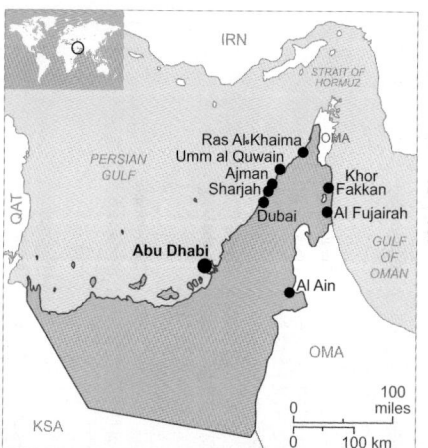

MAJOR CITIES/TOWNS

		Population
1	Dubai	1 770 533
2	Abu Dhabi	896 751
3	Sharjah	845 617
4	Al Ain	651 904
5	Ajman	372 923
6	Ras Al Khaima	171 903
7	Al Fujairah	107 940
8	Umm al Quwain	69 936
9	Khor Fakkan	49 635

AL IMARAT AL ARABIYAH AL MUTTAHIDAH • UNITED ARAB EMIRATES

Capital Abu Dhabi   Population 4 798 491 (115)   % in cities 78%
GDP per capita $44 600 (12)   Area km^2 83 600 km^2 (114)   GMT +/- +4
Neighbours (km) Oman 410, Saudi Arabia 457 • Coast 1318

RECENT INTERNATIONAL MATCHES PLAYED BY THE UNITED ARAB EMIRATES

2010	Opponents	Score	Venue	Comp	Scorers	Att	Referee
6-01	Malaysia	W 1-0	Dubai	ACq	Ahmed Khalil [93+]	3 500	Basma SYR
3-03	Uzbekistan	W 1-0	Tashkent	ACq	Sultan Al Menhali [93+]	20 000	Shamsuzzaman BAN
29-05	Moldova	W 3-2	Anif	Fr	Fares Juma [26], Mohamed Al Shehhi [31], Ahmed Khalil [89]	200	Schorgenhofer AUT
5-06	Algeria	L 0-1	Fürth	Fr		12 500	Grafe GER
7-09	Kuwait	W 3-0	Abu Dhabi	Fr	Ahmed Khalil [22], Ismael Matar [42], Saeed Al Kuthairi [91+]		
9-10	Chile	L 0-2	Abu Dhabi	Fr		500	Al Ghamdi KSA
12-10	Angola	L 0-2	Abu Dhabi	Fr			
18-11	India	W 5-0	Dubai	Fr	Saeed Al Kas [15], Amir Mubarak [35], Ali Al Wehaibi 2 [61 73], Ahmed Jumaa [72]		
23-11	Iraq	D 0-0	Aden	GCr1			Al Qatani KSA
26-11	Oman	D 0-0	Aden	GCr1			Shaaban EGY
29-11	Bahrain	W 3-1	Aden	GCr1	Subait Khater [4], Fares Juma [8], Ahmed Juma [64]		Al Marry BHR
2-12	Saudi Arabia	L 0-1	Aden	GCsf			Ogiya JPN
2011							
2-01	Syria	W 2-0	Al Ain	Fr	Saeed Al Kathiri [63], Theyab Awana [89]	2 400	Abdul Baki OMA
5-01	Australia	D 0-0	Al Ain	Fr			Shaban KUW
11-01	Korea DPR	D 0-0	Doha	ACr1		3 639	Mohd Salleh MAS
15-01	Iraq	L 0-1	Al Rayyan	ACr1		7 233	Nishimura JPN
19-01	Iran	L 0-3	Doha	ACr1		5 012	Kim Dong Jin KOR
17-07	Lebanon	W 6-2	Al Ain	Fr	Ahmed Khalil 3 [9 18 54], Mohamed Al Shehhi [22], Hamdan Al Kamali [41], Theyab Awana [79p]		
23-07	India	W 3-0	Al Ain	WCq	Hamdan Al Kamali [21p], Mohamed Al Shehhi [29p], Ismail Al Hammadi [81]	3 179	Al Dosari QAT
28-07	India	D 2-2	New Delhi	WCq	Mohamed Al Shehhi [40], Ali Al Wehaibi [72]	13 000	Bashir SIN
25-08	Qatar	W 3-1	Al Ain	Fr	Hamdan Al Kamali [24p], Ahmed Khalil 2 [50 68]		
2-09	Kuwait	L 2-3	Al Ain	WCq	Ismail Al Hammadi [84], Ahmed Khalil [89]	8 715	Basma SYR
6-09	Lebanon	L 1-3	Beirut	WCq	Mahmoud Al Hammadi [16]	4 000	Faghani IRN
6-10	China PR	L 1-2	Shenzhen	Fr	Eisa Al Marzouqi [86]		
11-10	Korea Republic	L 1-2	Suwon	WCq	Ismael Matar [92+]	28 689	Tan Hai CHN
11-11	Korea Republic	L 0-2	Dubai	WCq		8 272	Irmatov UZB
15-11	Kuwait	L 1-2	Kuwait City	WCq	Ismael Matar [19]	10 000	Al Hilali OMA
2012							
29-01	Uzbekistan	W 1-0	Dubai	Fr	Ismael Matar [72]		
24-02	Palestine	W 3-0	Abu Dhabi	Fr	Essa Shirook [4], Yousuf Jaber [12p], Majed Nasser [89p]		
29-02	Lebanon	W 4-2	Abu Dhabi	WCq	Basheer Saedd 2 [20 78], Ali Al Wehaibi [38], Ismael Matar [69]	10 000	Green AUS
6-09	Japan	L 0-1	Niigata	Fr		42 000	Na Ning CHN
11-09	Kuwait	W 3-0	Dubai	Fr	Saeed Al Kathiri [36], Habib Fardan [76], Walid Abbas [85]		Arafah JOR
12-10	Uzbekistan	D 2-2	Dubai	Fr	Ismael Matar [28], Saeed Al Kathiri [62]		
16-10	Bahrain	W 6-2	Dubai	Fr	Ali Al Wehaibi 4 [19 39 53 56], Hamdan Al Kamali [50p], Rashid Al Hosani [87]		
14-11	Estonia	W 2-1	Abu Dhabi	Fr	Hamdan Al Kamali [31p], Ali Ahmed Al Hajeri [70]		Al Nemari KSA
25-12	Yemen	W 2-0	Doha	Fr	Amer Abdulrahman [61], Omar Abdulrahman [82]		

Fr = Friendly match • AC = AFC Asian Cup • GC = Gulf Cup • WC = FIFA World Cup • q = qualifier • r1 = first round group • sf = semi-final

UAE NATIONAL TEAM HISTORICAL RECORDS

Caps: 161 - Adnan Al Talyani 1984-97 • **120** - Subait Al Junaibi 1999- • **115** - Abdulraheem Jumaa 1998-2009 • **112** - Zuhair Bakheet 1988-2002 • **111** - Abdulsalam Jumaa 1997-2010 • **107** - Ismael Matar 2003- • **106** - Mushin Musabah 1985-99 • **102** - Mohamed Omar 1996-2009

Goals: 53 - Adnan Al Talyani 1984-97 • **28** - Ismael Matar 2003-

Coaches: Mohammed Sheita EGY 1972-73 • Jumaa Gharib 1973 • Mohammed Sheita EGY 1973-74 • Mimi El Sherbini EGY 1975 • Jumaa Gharib 1975-76 • Dimitri Tadic YUG 1976 • Don Revie ENG 1977-80 • Heshmat Mohajerani IRN 1980-84 • Carlos Alberto Parreira BRA 1984-88 • Mario Zagallo BRA 1988-90 • Bernhard Blaut POL 1990 • Valery Lobanovsky UKR 1990-92 • Antoni Piechniczek POL 1992-95 • Tomislav Ivic CRO 1995-96 • Lori Sandri BRA 1997 • Milan Macala CZE 1997 • Lori Sandri BRA 1998 • Carlos Queiroz POR 1998-99 • Srecko Juricic CRO 1999 • Dr Abdullah Masfar 2000 • Henri Michel FRA 2000-01 • Abdullah Saqr 2001 • Tini Ruijs NED 2001 • Jo Bonfrere NED 2001-02 • Roy Hodgson ENG 2002-04 • Aad De Mos NED 2004-05 • Dick Advocaat NED Aug 2005 • Bruno Metsu FRA 2006-08 • Dominique Bathenay FRA 2008-09 • Srecko Katanec SVN 2009-11 • Abdullah Masfar 2011-12 • Mahdi Ali 2012-

UNITED ARAB EMIRATES 2011-12
PRO LEAGUE

	Pl	W	D	L	F	A	Pts	Ain	Nasr	Shabab	Jazeera	Ahli	Wahda	Ajman	Wasl	Bani-Yas	Dubai	Emirates	Sharjah
Al Ain †	22	17	4	1	52	16	**55**		2-0	3-1	2-0	1-0	1-0	4-0	2-0	3-0	2-1	4-0	2-1
Al Nasr †	22	11	8	3	49	33	41	2-0		2-1	2-2	4-0	0-1	1-1	1-1	2-1	0-1	5-3	3-2
Al Shabab ‡	22	10	8	4	39	27	38	1-1	2-2		3-2	2-0	2-1	4-4	2-0	1-1	1-1	1-0	5-1
Al Jazira	22	11	2	9	47	38	35	1-3	1-5	2-0		4-0	4-2	1-0	1-0	3-1	0-2	4-1	5-0
Al Ahli Dubai	22	10	4	8	45	42	34	0-2	3-3	2-3	2-1		2-2	2-0	1-2	6-4	5-2	2-0	2-2
Al Wahda	22	8	9	5	32	30	33	2-2	1-1	0-0	3-2	3-3		1-0	2-1	2-1	1-1	2-2	1-0
Ajman	22	9	4	9	36	35	31	1-4	1-2	0-1	3-4	0-1	3-1		1-1	1-1	3-0	1-0	2-1
Al Wasl	22	7	5	10	32	40	26	2-2	2-2	2-2	0-1	2-6	0-2	2-4		1-0	1-2	4-1	3-0
Bani-Yas	22	6	6	10	34	39	24	2-2	2-2	0-1	2-1	1-3	2-2	1-2	1-2		2-0	4-1	2-2
Dubai Club	22	5	5	12	29	40	20	0-2	1-2	1-1	2-4	1-2	0-0	1-3	5-2	1-2		2-4	3-0
Emirates Club ‡	22	5	2	15	28	56	17	1-4	1-3	1-5	3-2	2-1	2-1	1-3	1-2	0-2	2-1		1-2
Sharjah ‡	22	2	5	15	26	53	11	1-4	4-5	1-0	2-2	1-2	1-2	1-3	1-2	1-2	1-2	1-1	

15/10/2011 - 27/05/2012 • † Qualified for the AFC Champions League • ‡ Relegation play-offs
Top scorers: **22** - Asamoah GYAN GHA, Al Ain • **16** - GRAFITE BRA, Al Ahli & Andre SENGHOR SEN, Bani-Yas • **14** - RICARDO OLIVEIRA BRA, Al Jazeera • **13** - Luis JIMENEZ CHI, Al Ahli & Juan Manuel OLIVEIRA URU, Al Wasl • **11** - CIEL BRA, Al Shabab

UNITED ARAB EMIRATES 2011-12 SECOND DIVISION

GROUP A

	Pl	W	D	L	F	A	Pts
Al Ittihad Kalba	21	13	4	4	53	28	43
Dibba Al Fujeira	21	12	4	5	46	28	40
Al Sha'ab ‡	21	10	5	6	42	38	35
Dhafra ‡	21	10	4	7	52	47	34
Al Khaleej	21	7	6	8	35	33	27
Al Ahli Fujeira	21	6	8	7	33	30	26
Masafi	21	5	7	9	23	34	22
Al Urooba	21	1	2	18	16	62	5

GROUP B

	Pl	W	D	L	F	A	Pts
Hatta	21	16	1	4	47	16	49
Thaid	21	12	7	2	42	20	43
Dibba Al Hisn	21	10	6	5	34	31	36
Al Arabi	21	8	10	3	34	25	34
Al Taawon	21	5	7	9	21	23	22
Masfut	21	5	4	12	31	40	19
Al Jazira Al Hamra	21	3	6	12	26	46	15
Ramms	21	2	5	14	22	56	11

24/11/2011 - 12/05/2012 • ‡ Play-offs

RELEGATION/PROMOTION PLAY-OFFS

	Pl	W	D	L	F	A	Pts	Dh	AS	Sh	EC
Dhafra	3	2	0	1	8	4	**6**				5-1
Al Sha'ab	3	2	0	1	5	4	**6**	3-2		0-1	
Sharjah	3	2	0	1	3	3	**6**		0-1		2-1
Emirates Club	3	0	0	3	2	9	**0**		1-2		

4/09/2012 - 14/09/2012 • Dhafra & Al Sha'ab promoted

MEDALS TABLE

		Overall			Lge	Cup	Asia			
		G	S	B	G	G	G	S	B	City
1	Al Ain	16	1	1	**10**	5	1	1	1	Al Ain
2	Sharjah	13			5	**8**				Sharjah
3	Al Ahli	12			5	7				Dubai
4	Al Wasl	9	1		7	2			1	Dubai
5	Al Shabab	7		1	3	4			1	Dubai
6	Al Nasr	6			3	3				Dubai
7	Al Wahda	5	1		4	1				Abu Dhabi
8	Al Jazira	3			1	2				Abu Dhabi
9	Al Sha'ab	1	1			1		1		Sharjah
10	Ajman	1				1				Ajman
	Bani Yas	1				1				Abu Dhabi
	Emirates Club	1				1				Ras Al Khaima

PRESIDENT'S CUP 2011-12

Round of 16		Quarter-finals		Semi-finals		Final	
Al Jazira	4						
Al Shabab	2	Al Jazira	6				
Dibba Al Hisn	0	Ajman	2				
Ajman	1			Al Jazira	4		
Al Ittihad Kalba	3			Sharjah	1		
Dhafra	2	Al Ittihad Kalba	0				
Al Khaleej	1	Sharjah	3				
Sharjah	2					Al Jazira †	3
Al Wahda	4					Bani-Yas	1
Dubai Club	0	Al Wahda	3				
Al Ahli Dubai	0	Al Wasl	2				
Al Wasl	4			Al Wahda	1		
Al Ain	4			Bani-Yas	3		
Emirates Club	2	Al Ain	0				
Al Nasr	0	Bani-Yas	1				
Bani-Yas	1						

† Qualified for the AFC Champions League

CUP FINAL
Sheikh Zayed, Abu Dhabi
23-04-2012
Scorers - Lucas Neill [6], Ricardo Oliveira [72], Ahmed Mobarak [90] for Jazeera; Nawaf Mubarak [47] for Bani-Yas

UGA – UGANDA

FIFA/COCA-COLA WORLD RANKING

'93	'94	'95	'96	'97	'98	'99	'00	'01	'02	'03	'04	'05	'06	'07	'08	'09	'10	'11	'12
94	93	74	81	109	105	108	103	119	102	103	109	101	103	76	71	75	80	89	84

2012

Jan	Feb	Mar	Apr	May	Jun	Jul	Aug	Sep	Oct	Nov	Dec	High	Low	Av
82	87	88	92	93	94	85	88	88	90	86	84	63	121	95

Uganda won the regional CECAFA Cup in 2012 but suffered heartbreak in their bid to qualify for the 2013 Africa Cup of Nations finals in South Africa. The national team had missed out on a place in the 2012 finals in Gabon and Equatorial Guinea after failing to win their final home qualifier against neighbours Kenya, but for the 2013 finals they were only a penalty shoot-out away from making the trip to South Africa. Under Scottish coach Bobby Williamson 'the Cranes' had impressed in the first round of qualifying after hammering Congo 4-0 to overturn a 3-1 defeat from the first leg but they showed real quality in the second qualifying round against defending champions Zambia. Uganda lost the first leg in Ndola by a single goal but were level on aggregate inside the first half-hour of the return in Kampala. Only some miraculous saves from Kennedy Mweene kept the Ugandans at bay in the game and the Zambian goalkeeper was the hero again in the shoot-out as the Cranes suffered another massive disappointment. In the CECAFA Cup Uganda used home advantage to swarm through the field and beat Kenya 2-1 in the final to take their fourth title in five years although it wasn't enough for Williamson to keep his job. In club football Bunamwayo Wakiso finished runners-up in the league to Express and in the cup to Uganda Revenue Authority.

CAF AFRICA CUP OF NATIONS RECORD

1957-1959 DNE **1962** 4 SF **1963** DNE **1965** DNQ **1968** 7 r1 1970-1972 DNQ
1974 6 r1 **1976** 8 r1 **1978** 2 F 1980-1982 DNE 1984-1988 DNQ 1990 DNE 1992-2013 DNQ

FEDERATION OF UGANDA FOOTBALL ASSOCIATIONS (FUFA)

FUFA House, Plot No. 879,
Kyadondo Block 8,
Mengo Wakaliga Road,
PO Box 22518, Kampala
☎ +256 41 4272702
📠 +256 41 4272702
✉ fufaf@yahoo.com
🌐 www.fufa.co.ug
FA 1924 CON 1959 FIFA 1959
P Lawrence Mulindwa
GS Edgar Watson Suubi

THE STADIA

2014 FIFA World Cup Stadia
Mandela National 'Namboole'
Kampala 45 202

Other Main Stadia
Nakivubo Stadium
Kampala 15 000
Bunamwaya Stadium
Wakiso Town 5 000
Kakindu Municipal Stadium
Jinja 1 000

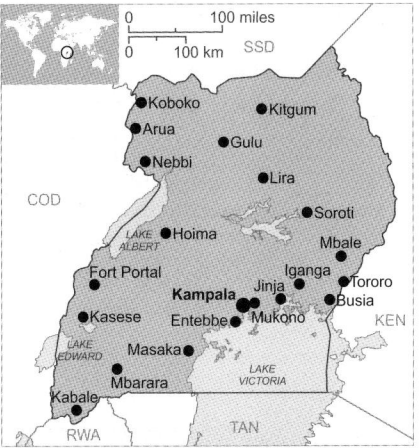

MAJOR CITIES/TOWNS

		Population
1	Kampala	1 560 080
2	Gulu	208 268
3	Lira	174 630
4	Mukono	111 058
5	Jinja	101 604
6	Mbarara	93 969
7	Kasese	91 906
8	Mbale	84 215
9	Kitgum	83 233
10	Njeru	75 380
11	Arua	71 226
12	Masaka	70 273
13	Entebbe	70 052
14	Koboko	59 430
15	Kabale	58 269
16	Iganga	56 074
17	Tororo	55 366
18	Hoima	52 670
19	Mityana	50 612

REPUBLIC OF UGANDA

Capital	Kampala	Population	32 369 558 (38)	% in cities	13%
GDP per capita	$1300 (204)	Area km²	241 038 km² (80)	GMT +/-	+3

Neighbours (km) Congo DR 765, Kenya 933, Rwanda 169, Sudan 435, Tanzania 396

RECENT INTERNATIONAL MATCHES PLAYED BY UGANDA

2010	Opponents	Score	Venue	Comp	Scorers	Att	Referee
29-11	Ethiopia	W 2-1	Dar es Salaam	CCr1	Simeon Masaba [35p], Henry Kisseka [46]		
2-12	Malawi	D 1-1	Dar es Salaam	CCr1	Emmanuel Okwi [80]		
5-12	Kenya	W 2-0	Dar es Salaam	CCr1	Emmanuel Okwi [81], Andrew Mwesigwa [92+p]		
8-12	Zanzibar †	D 2-2	Dar es Salaam	CCqf	Mike Serumaga [13], Emmanuel Okwi [47p]. W 5-3p		
10-12	Tanzania	D 0-0	Dar es Salaam	CCsf	L 4-5p		
12-12	Ethiopia	W 4-3	Dar es Salaam	CC3p	Henry Kisseka [5], Emmanuel Okwi [48], Tony Mawejje [53], Sula Matovu [72]		
2011							
5-01	Burundi	W 3-1	Cairo	Fr	Manko Kaweesa [33], Noah Ssemakula [55], Owen Kasule [89]		
8-01	Egypt	L 0-1	Cairo	Fr			
11-01	Tanzania	D 1-1	Cairo	Fr	Athuman Machupa [24]		
14-01	Congo DR	W 1-0	Cairo	Fr	Habib Kavuma [23]		
17-01	Egypt	L 1-3	Ismailia	Fr	Ceasar Okhuti [84p]		
26-03	Guinea-Bissau	W 1-0	Bissau	CNq	David Obua [22]		
4-06	Guinea-Bissau	W 2-0	Kampala	CNq	Godfrey Walusimbi [43], Geofrey Massa [62]		
4-09	Angola	L 0-2	Luanda	CNq			
8-10	Kenya	D 0-0	Kampala	CNq			
11-11	Morocco	W 1-0	Marrakech	Fr	Mike Serumaga [47]		
13-11	Sudan	D 0-0	Marrakech	Fr	W 3-2p		
25-11	Zanzibar †	W 2-1	Dar es Salaam	CCr1	Dan Wagaluka [40], Mike Serumaga [77]		
28-11	Somalia	W 4-0	Chamazi	CCr1	Dan Wagaluka [48], Emmanuel Okwi 3 [61 76 90]		
1-12	Burundi	L 0-1	Dar es Salaam	CCr1			
6-12	Zimbabwe	W 1-0	Dar es Salaam	CCqf	Hamis Kizza [15]		
8-12	Tanzania	W 3-1	Dar es Salaam	CCsf	Andrew Mwesigwa 56, Emmanuel Okwi 102, Isaac Isinde [112p]		
10-12	Rwanda	D 2-2	Dar es Salaam	CCf	Isaac Isinde [77], Karekezi OG [80]. W 3-2p		
2012							
29-02	Congo	L 1-3	Pointe Noire	CNq	Mike Serumaga [77]	13 000	Alioum CMR
29-03	Egypt	L 1-2	Omdurman	Fr	Fabian Kizito [35]		Abdel Kadir SUD
3-06	Angola	D 1-1	Luanda	WCq	Emmanuel Okwi [88]	48 000	Grisha EGY
9-06	Senegal	D 1-1	Kampala	WCq	Godfrey Walusimbi [87]	30 000	Benouza ALG
16-06	Congo	W 4-0	Kampala	CNq	Andrew Mwesigwa [33], Godfrey Walusimbi [51p], Geofrey Massa [63], Emmanuel Okwi [86]		El Ahrach MAR
10-07	South Sudan	D 2-2	Juba	Fr	Caesar Okhuti [7], Julius Ogwang [33]	22 000	Onyango KEN
26-08	Botswana	D 0-0	Gaborone	Fr			
8-09	Zambia	L 0-1	Ndola	CNq			Doue CIV
13-10	Zambia	W 1-0	Kampala	CNq	Geofrey Massa [27]. L 8-9p		Haimoudi ALG
24-11	Kenya	W 1-0	Kampala	CCr1	Fabian Kizito [60]		Nkurunziza BDI
27-11	Ethiopia	W 1-0	Kampala	CCr1	Brian Umony [9]		El Fadhil SDN
30-11	South Sudan	W 4-0	Kampala	CCr1	Brian Umony 2 [24 40], Robert Ssentongo [47], Hamis Kizza [79]		Hakizimana RWA
4-12	Ethiopia	W 2-0	Kampala	CCqf	Fabian Kizito [4], Robert Ssentongo [60]		Nkurunziza BDI
6-12	Tanzania	W 3-0	Kampala	CCsf	Emmanuel Okwi [12], Robert Ssentongo 2 [52 72]		El Fadhil SDN
8-12	Kenya	W 2-1	Kampala	CCf	Robert Ssentongo [28], Fabian Kizito [90]		Nkurunziza BDI

Fr = Friendly match • CN = CAF African Cup of Nations • CC = CECAFA Cup • WC = FIFA World Cup
q = qualifier • r1 = first round group • qf = quarter-final • sf = semifinal • 3p = third place play-off • f = final • † Not a full international

UGANDA NATIONAL TEAM HISTORICAL RECORDS

Coaches: Burkhard Pape GDR 1968-1972 • David Otti 1973-1974 • Otto Westerhoff 1974-1975 • Peter Okee 1976-1981 • Bidandi Ssali 1982 • Peter Okee 1983 • George Mukasa 1984-1985 • Barnabas Mwesiga 1986-1988 • Robert Kiberu 1988-1989 • Polly Ouma 1989-1995 • Timothy Ayieko 1995-1996 • Asuman Lubowa 1996-1999 • Paul Hasule 1999 • Harrison Okagbue NGA 1999-2001 • Paul Hasule 2001-2003 • Pedro Pasculli ARG 2003 • Leo Adraa 2003-2004 • Mike Mutebi 2004 • Muhammed Abbas EGY 2004-2006 • Csaba Laszlo HUN 2006-2008 • Bobby Williamson SCO 2008-

UGANDA 2011-12

ECOBANK SUPER LEAGUE

	Pl	W	D	L	F	A	Pts	Express	Bunamwaya	URA	Simba	Villa	Proline	KCC	MLC	Water	Maroons	Victors	Police	BIDCO	Hoima	UTODA	Fire Masters
Express RE Kampala †	28	15	9	4	39	21	54		1-1	2-2	3-0	0-0	0-0	0-0	2-1	0-0	3-2	3-0	1-0	2-0	1-0	4-1
Bunamwaya Wakiso	28	15	8	5	46	18	53	1-1		1-0	0-1	2-0	3-0	2-1		1-1	1-0	1-1	1-0	3-0	4-0	1-1
URA Kampala	28	14	9	5	40	23	51	1-1	2-1		1-1		2-2	2-1	1-0	0-0	1-0	1-1	1-1	4-1	1-0	3-0
Simba	28	13	7	8	26	21	46	3-0	1-1	1-0		1-0	1-0	0-1	3-1	2-0	0-0	1-1	2-0	0-0	0-0	2-1
SC Villa Kampala	28	12	9	7	25	20	45	0-2	1-4	1-1	1-0		0-1	2-0	1-0	1-0	0-0	4-2	0-0	0-0	1-0	1-0
Proline Buikwe	28	11	11	6	30	16	44	1-0	0-1	1-0	1-2	0-0		2-1	0-0	3-0	1-0	1-0	0-0	0-1	8-1	0-0
Kampala City Council	28	12	8	8	32	22	44	2-0	0-1	1-1	3-0	0-0	2-0		1-0	1-2	1-0	0-0	0-0	1-1	3-1	4-1
Masaka Local Council	28	11	5	12	21	24	38	0-1	2-0	2-0	0-1	1-0	0-2	0-1		0-1	1-0	1-0	0-0	2-1	3-1	1-0
Water	28	7	13	8	18	27	34	0-1	2-1	0-3	2-1	1-1	0-0	2-1	0-0		0-2	1-1	0-1	1-0	2-1	1-1
Maroons Kampala	28	8	9	11	25	25	33	2-0	0-0	0-2	1-0	1-2	1-1	1-1	3-0			1-1	3-3	0-1	2-3	1-0
Victors Jinja	28	7	12	9	21	22	33	0-1	1-0	2-1	0-0	0-0	0-0	0-0	0-1	1-1	0-0		2-1	2-0	2-0	1-0
Uganda Police Kampala	28	6	13	9	23	30	31	1-3	0-5	0-2	2-0	0-2	0-0	0-1	3-1	0-0	0-0	1-0		1-1	2-2	4-1
BIDCO	28	7	10	11	21	31	31	1-2	2-2	1-2	1-0	0-1	0-0	2-2	0-1	0-0	0-1	1-0			1-0	2-1
Hoima	28	5	5	18	22	48	20	0-0	0-2	1-2	0-1	1-2	0-2	0-1	0-0	0-0	2-1	1-0	1-2	2-3		3-1
Kampala UTODA	28	0	6	22	16	57	**6**	2-5	0-3	0-1	1-2	0-3	1-4	1-2	1-2	1-1	0-1	0-3	0-0	0-0	1-2	
Fire Masters				Withdrew																			

909/2011 - 10/06/2012 • † Qualified for the CAF Champions League

MEDALS TABLE

		Overall G S B	Lge G S	Cup G S	Africa G S B	City
1	SC Villa	24 5	16 8 3		2	Kampala
2	Kampala City Council	16 5 1	8 8 5		1	Kampala
3	Express FC	16 4 1	6 10 4		1	Kampala
4	Uganda Revenue Authority - URA	6 2	4 2 2			Kampala
5	Simba SC	4 4	2 2 3		1	Lugazi
6	Coffee SC	2 2	2 2			
7	Mbale Heroes	2 1	2 1			Mbale
8	Prisons FC	2	2			Kampala
	Victors	2	2			Jinja
10	Nile Breweries	1 4	1 4			Jinja
11	Uganda Commercial Bank	1 3	1 3			Kampala
12	Bunamwaya	1 1	1	1		Wakiso
	Police FC	1 1	1	1		Jinja
	Uganda Electricity Board - Umeme	1 1			1 1	Jinja
15	Coffee United	1	1			Kakira
	Nsambya	1		1		Kampala

BELL UGANDA CUP 2012

Round of 16		Quarter-finals		Semi-finals		Final	
URA Kampala	6						
Luwero United	2	**URA Kampala**	w-o				
Old Timers	1	SC Villa Kampala					
SC Villa Kampala	5			**URA Kampala**	2 1		
Water	3			Masaka Local Council	0 0		
CRO	0	Water	0 2p				
Victors Jinja	0	**Masaka Local Council**	0 3p			**URA Kampala** ‡	1
Masaka Local Council	1					Bunamwaya Wakiso	0
Maroons Kampala	2						
Aurum Roses	0	**Maroons Kampala**	1 3p			CUP FINAL	
Jinja MC		Kireka United	1 0p				
Kireka United				Maroons Kampala	0 0		
Uganda Police				**Bunamwaya Wakiso**	1 2	Pece Stadium, Gulu	
Boroboro Tigers		Uganda Police	2			12-05-2012	
Masindi	1	**Bunamwaya Wakiso**	4			Scorer - Robert Ssentongo for URA	
Bunamwaya Wakiso	3			‡ Qualified for the CAF Confederation Cup			

UKR – UKRAINE

FIFA/COCA-COLA WORLD RANKING

'93	'94	'95	'96	'97	'98	'99	'00	'01	'02	'03	'04	'05	'06	'07	'08	'09	'10	'11	'12
90	77	71	59	49	47	27	34	45	45	60	57	40	13	30	15	22	34	55	47

2012

Jan	Feb	Mar	Apr	May	Jun	Jul	Aug	Sep	Oct	Nov	Dec	High	Low	Av
54	59	49	49	50	52	46	45	39	42	55	47	11	132	45

Ukraine had not always been the most popular of hosts for a European championship finals with construction delays causing tensions with UEFA while political problems led to many leaders from other countries boycotting matches in Ukraine during the tournament. However, after falling behind to Sweden in their opening match in Kyiv, Andriy Shevchenko sensationally turned the match around in the second half with two quick goals and for four days Ukrainian football was on top of the world. The euphoria didn't last, however, as the team lost to both France and England to exit at the first stage. While the national team may be in a transitional stage, club football should be poised to flourish with the finals prompting the construction of new stadia even in non-host cities such as in Odessa and Dnipropetrovsk. Donetsk has certainly been a major beneficiary of the Euro 2012 legacy, even before the tournament was staged. The Donbass Arena has been the launchpad for Shakhter to challenge the best in Europe and the 2012-13 UEFA Champions League saw them qualify for the knock-out rounds at the expense of holders Chelsea. Earlier in the year they had completed their third league and cup double in five years, finishing four points ahead of Dynamo in the league and beating Metalurh 2-1 in the first all-Donetsk cup final.

UEFA EUROPEAN CHAMPIONSHIP RECORD
1960-1992 DNE (Played as part of the Soviet Union) 1996-2008 DNQ **2012** 11 r1 (Co-hosts)

FOOTBALL FEDERATION OF UKRAINE (FFU)

Provulok Laboratornyi 7-A,
PO Box 55,
01133 Kyiv
☎ +380 44 5210521
📠 +380 44 5210550
✉ info@ffu.org.ua
🖥 www.ffu.org.ua
FA 1991 CON 1992 FIFA 1992
P Anatoliy Konkov
GS Maksym Bondarev

THE STADIA

2014 FIFA World Cup Stadia

Stadion NSK Olimpiyskiy	
Kyiv	70 050

Other Main Stadia

Donbass Arena	
Donetsk	52 187
Stadion Metalist	
Kharkiv	40 003
Arena Lviv	
Lviv	34 915
Stadion Chernomorets	
Odesa	32 164

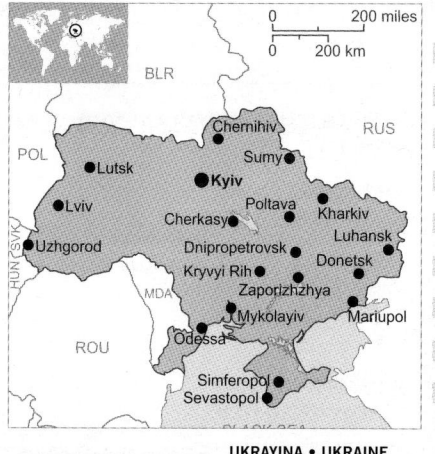

MAJOR CITIES/TOWNS

		Population
1	Kyiv	2 304 511
2	Kharkiv	1 461 234
3	Dnipropetrovsk	1 046 608
4	Odessa	992 669
5	Donetsk	989 569
6	Zaporizhzhya	787 865
7	Lviv	735 417
8	Kryvyi Rih	722 303
9	Mykolayiv	507 710
10	Mariupol	476 263
11	Luhansk	446 411
12	Makiyivka	365 536
13	Vinnytsia	365 227
14	Simferopol	341 281
15	Sevastopol	338 743
16	Kherson	312 536
17	Poltava	305 067
18	Chernihiv	299 989

UKRAYINA • UKRAINE

Capital	Kyiv	Population	45 700 395 (27)	% in cities	68%
GDP per capita	$7400 (124)	Area km²	603 550 km² (45)	GMT +/-	+2
Neighbours (km)	Belarus 891, Hungary 103, Moldova 940, Poland 428, Romania 538, Russia 1576, Slovakia 90 • Coast 2782				

RECENT INTERNATIONAL MATCHES PLAYED BY UKRAINE

2009	Opponents	Score	Venue	Comp	Scorers	Att	Referee
12-08	Turkey	L 0-3	Kyiv	Fr			Ceferin SVN
5-09	Andorra	W 5-0	Kyiv	WCq	Yarmolenko [18], Milevskiy 2 [45 92+p], Shevchenko [72p], Seleznov [94+p]	14 870	Sipailo LVA
9-09	Belarus	D 0-0	Minsk	WCq		21 727	Kassai HUN
10-10	England	W 1-0	Dnepropetrovsk	WCq	Nazarenko [30]	31 000	Skomina SVN
14-10	Andorra	W 6-0	Andorra La Vella	WCq	Shevchenko [22], Gusev [61], Lima.IOG [69], Rakits Kyy [80], Seleznov [81], Yarmolenko [83]	820	Thomson SCO
14-11	Greece	D 0-0	Athens	WCpo		39 045	Duhamel FRA
18-11	Greece	L 0-1	Donetsk	WCpo		31 643	Benquerença POR
2010							
25-05	Lithuania	W 4-0	Kharkov	Fr	Aliev 2 [10 17], Shevchenko 2 [68p 78]	42 000	Sukhina RUS
29-05	Romania	W 3-2	Lviv	Fr	Aliev [15], Konoplyanka [75], OG [78]	22 000	Kralovec CZE
2-06	Norway	W 1-0	Oslo	Fr	Zozulya [78]	10 178	Blom NED
11-08	Netherlands	D 1-1	Donetsk	Fr	Aliev [75]	18 051	Skomina SVN
4-09	Poland	D 1-1	Lodz	Fr	Seleznev [90]	6 500	Irmatov UZB
7-09	Chile	W 2-1	Kyiv	Fr	Rakitskiy [36], Aliev [52]	10 000	Sevastsyanik BLR
8-10	Canada	D 2-2	Kyiv	Fr	Milevskiy [59], Tymoshchuk [80]	10 000	Mikulski
11-10	Brazil	L 0-2	Derby	Fr		13 088	Atkinson ENG
17-11	Switzerland	D 2-2	Geneva	Fr	Aliev [48], Konoplyanka [75]	11 100	Gumienny BEL
2011							
8-02	Romania	D 2-2	Paralimni	Fr	Rakitskiy [23], Milevskiy [31]. W 4-2p	1 000	Johannesson SWE
9-02	Sweden	D 1-1	Nicosia	Fr	Devic [20p]. 5-4p	2 000	Tudor ROU
29-03	Italy	L 0-2	Kyiv	Fr		18 000	Nikolaev RUS
1-06	Uzbekistan	W 2-0	Kyiv	Fr	Tymoshchuk [54], Voronin [60]		Ozkahya TUR
6-06	France	L 1-4	Donetsk	Fr	Tymoshchuk [53]	11 200	Clattenburg ENG
10-08	Sweden	L 0-1	Kharkov	Fr			Tagliavento ITA
2-09	Uruguay	L 2-3	Kharkov	Fr	Yarmolenko [1], Konoplyanka [44]	30 000	Kuipers NED
6-09	Czech Republic	L 0-4	Prague	Fr		7 322	Trutz SVK
7-10	Bulgaria	W 3-0	Kyiv	Fr	Selin [15], Shevchenko [40], Yarmolenko [82]		Kralovec CZE
11-10	Estonia	W 2-0	Tallinn	Fr	Gusev [45], Aliev [68]	4 501	Malek POL
11-11	Germany	D 3-3	Kyiv	Fr	Yarmolenko [28], Konoplyanka [37], Nazarenko [45]	69 720	Velasco ESP
15-11	Austria	W 2-1	Lviv	Fr	Milevskiy [18], Devic [90]	31 879	Moen NOR
2012							
29-02	Israel	W 3-2	Petah-Tikva	Fr	Gusev [17p], Konoplyanka [45], Yarmolenko [61]	4 000	Marciniak POL
28-05	Estonia	W 4-0	Kufstein	Fr	Yarmolenko [9], Gusev [35], Voronin [41], Milevskiy [50]	1 200	Lechner AUT
1-06	Austria	L 2-3	Innsbruck	Fr	Gusev 2 [56 65]	13 000	Zwayer GER
5-06	Turkey	L 0-2	Ingolstadt	Fr		14 000	Weiner GER
11-06	Sweden	W 2-1	Kyiv	ECr1	Shevchenko 2 [55 62]	64 290	Cakir TUR
15-06	France	L 0-2	Donetsk	ECr1		48 000	Kuipers NED
19-06	England	L 0-1	Donetsk	ECr1		48 700	Kassai HUN
15-08	Czech Republic	D 0-0	Lviv	Fr		33 153	Mazic SRB
11-09	England	D 1-1	London	WCq	Konoplyanka [39]	68 102	Cakir TUR
12-10	Moldova	D 0-0	Chisinau	WCq		12 500	Turpin FRA
16-10	Montenegro	L 0-1	Kyiv	WCq		50 597	Koukoulakis GRE
14-11	Bulgaria	W 1-0	Sofia	Fr	Kucher [34]	1 000	Mazic SRB

Fr = Friendly match • EC = UEFA Euro 2012 • WC = FIFA World Cup • q = qualifier • r1 = first round group • po = play-off

UKRAINE NATIONAL TEAM HISTORICAL RECORDS

Caps
125 - Anatoliy Tymoschuk 2000- • 111 - Andriy Shevchenko 1995- • 92 - Olexandr Shovkovskiy 1994-2012 • 79 - Oleh Gusev 2003- • 75 - Serhiy Rebrov 1992-2006 • 74 - Andriy Voronin 2002- • 71 - Andriy Gusin 1993-2006 • 68 - Andriy Vorobei 2000-08 • 67 - Andriy Nesmachnyi 2000- • 65 - Ruslan Rotan 2003- • 63 - Vladyslav Vashchuk 1996-2007 • 58 - Olexandr Holovko 1995-2004

Goals
48 - Andriy Shevchenko 1995- • 15 - Serhiy Rebrov 1992-2006 • 12 - Serhiy Nazarenko 2003- & Oleh Gusev 2003- • 9 - Andriy Yarmolenko 2009-; Andriy Vorobei 2000-08 & Andriy Gusin 1993-2006 • 8 - Andriy Voronin 2002- ; Artem Milevskiy 2006 & Tymerlan Guseynov 1993-97

Coaches
Viktor Prokopenko 1992 • Nikolay Pavlov 1992 • Oleh Bazilevich 1993-94 • Nikolay Pavlov 1994 • Jozsef Szabo 1994 • Anatoliy Konkov 1995 • Jozsef Szabo 1996-99 • Valery Lobanovsky 2000-01 • Leonid Buryak 2002-03 • Oleh Blokhin 2003-07 • Olexiy Mykhailychenko 2008-09 • Myron Markevych 2010 • Yuriy Kalitvintsev 2010-11 • Oleh Blokhin 2011-12 • Andriy Bal 2012 • Oleksandr Zavarov 2012 • Mykhaylo Fomenko 2013-

UKRAINE 2011-12

VYSCHA LIHA

	Pl	W	D	L	F	A	Pts	Shakhtar	Dynamo Kyiv	Metalist	Dnipro	Arsenal	Tavriya	Metalurh D	Vorskla	Chernomorets	Kryvbas	Illychivets	Volyn	Zorja	Karpaty	Obolon	Oleksandrija
Shakhtar Donetsk †	30	25	4	1	80	18	79		2-0	1-2	1-1	5-0	3-1	2-0	1-0	4-0	2-0	3-0	5-1	4-1	2-1	4-0	3-0
Dynamo Kyiv †	30	23	6	1	56	12	75	0-0		1-1	2-0	1-0	1-1	1-0	3-0	3-1	1-0	3-1	2-1	6-1	2-0	4-0	4-0
Metalist Kharkiv ‡	30	16	11	3	54	32	59	1-2	1-2		1-0	0-0	2-0	2-0	2-2	1-0	1-1	0-0	3-1	3-2	3-1	1-0	2-1
Dnipro Dnipropetrovsk‡	30	15	7	8	50	35	52	1-3	0-4	2-2		1-0	2-1	1-0	1-1	1-0	0-2	3-0	1-2	3-1	2-0	2-2	5-1
Arsenal Kyiv ‡	30	14	9	7	44	27	51	1-1	0-2	4-2	3-3		2-3	1-0	2-0	0-1	2-0	0-0	3-0	1-1	3-2	4-1	0-0
Tavriya Simferopol	30	12	9	9	43	36	45	1-3	0-0	0-0	0-2	1-1		1-1	0-2	2-0	1-2	3-2	1-0	3-1	1-1	0-0	4-1
Metalurh Donetsk ‡	30	12	6	12	35	34	42	0-2	0-0	0-1	0-3	1-1	1-3		6-3	3-0	1-0	0-0	0-3	3-0	2-1	2-0	3-1
Vorskla Poltava	30	9	10	11	38	43	37	0-2	1-2	2-2	0-0	0-2	3-2	4-2		3-1	2-1	3-1	3-1	2-2	1-1	0-1	0-1
Chernomorets Odessa	30	10	7	13	32	42	37	2-2	1-2	3-3	1-1	0-3	1-0	0-1	2-1		1-2	1-0	0-0	2-3	2-2	1-0	2-1
Kryvbas Kryvyi Rih	30	9	6	15	22	38	33	0-4	0-3	0-1	0-2	0-2	0-3	1-2	0-0	1-0		2-0	1-0	2-1	1-1	1-0	1-2
Illychivets Mariupil	30	8	8	14	28	42	32	0-1	0-1	0-1	3-2	0-0	0-2	2-1	4-1	1-1	1-3		1-2	1-1	1-0	2-1	2-0
Volyn Lutsk	30	7	6	17	25	43	27	1-2	0-1	0-3	1-2	1-0	2-2	0-2	0-0	0-2	0-0	0-1		2-2	0-2	1-1	3-1
Zorja Luhansk	30	6	8	16	34	58	26	1-5	0-0	1-5	2-0	0-3	0-1	1-0	0-0	0-2	2-0	2-2	0-2		5-1	1-2	2-0
Karpaty Lviv	30	5	8	17	27	51	23	0-5	0-1	1-2	0-2	0-3	2-3	0-2	0-2	1-1	2-0	3-0	1-0	2-1		0-0	1-1
Obolon Kyiv	30	4	9	17	17	42	21	0-2	0-1	3-3	1-4	0-1	1-3	0-1	1-0	0-1	0-0	0-0	1-0	0-0	2-0		1-1
FK Oleksandrija	30	4	8	18	24	58	20	2-3	1-3	1-3	1-5	1-2	0-0	0-0	1-1	1-3	1-1	1-2	0-1	1-0	1-1	1-0	

8/07/2011 - 10/05/2012 • † Qualified for the UEFA Champions League • ‡ Qualified for the Europa League • Attendance: 2,710,874 @ 11,295
Top scorers: 14 - Yevhen **SELEZNEV**, Shakhtar & **MAICON** BRA, Volyn • 12 - Ideye **BROWN** NGA, Dynamo; Andriy **YARMOLENKO**, Dynamo & **LUIZ ADRIANO** BRA, Shakhtar • 11 - Anton **SHINDER**, Tavriya & Marko **DEVIC**, Metalist

MEDALS TABLE

		Overall			League			Cup		Europe		
		G	S	B	G	S	B	G	S	G	S	B
1	Dynamo Kyiv	22	11	2	13	8		9	3			2
2	Shakhtar Donetsk	16	14		7	10		8	4	1		
3	Chernomorets Odessa	2	2	3		2	3	2				
4	Tavriya Simferopol	2	1			1		1	1			
5	Vorskla Poltava	1		1			1	1				
6	Dnipro Dnipropetrovsk		4	4		1	4		3			
7	Metalurh Donetsk		2	3				3		2		
8	Karpaty Lviv		2	1				1		2		
9	CSCA Kyiv		2						2			
10	Metallist Kharkiv		1	6				6		1		

Ukrainian Clubs in the Soviet era

		Overall			League			Cup		Europe		
		G	S	B	G	S	B	G	S	G	S	B
1	Dynamo Kyiv	24	13	5	**13**	11	3	9	2	2	2	
7	Shakhtar	4	6	2		2	2	4	4			
9	Dnipro	3	2	2	2	2	2	1				
13	Zorya	1	2		1			2				
15	Metallist	1	1							1	1	
16	Karpaty	1						1				
21	Chernomorets			1			1					

UKRAINE 2011-12

PERSHA LIHA (2)

	Pl	W	D	L	F	A	Pts	Zakarpattya	Metalurh	Sevastopol	Arsenal	Krymteplytsja	Bukovyna	Stal	Dynamo	Helios	Naftovyk	Zirka	Olimpik	Nyva	Tytan	MFK	Enerhetyk	FK Lviv
Zakarpattya Uzhgorod	34	27	3	4	67	16	84		1-0	1-0	5-0	4-0	2-0	1-0	1-0	2-0	1-0	2-0	4-1	2-0	3-1	6-0	3-0	2-1	4-0
Metalurh Zaporizhya	34	24	4	6	77	32	76	1-1		1-0	5-2	4-0	3-2	3-0	2-1	4-2	2-1	4-1	3-2	1-0	5-1	3-0	1-0	4-0	4-0
FC Sevastopol	34	23	7	4	60	22	76	2-1	2-1		1-1	1-1	0-0	2-1	1-0	0-3	2-1	3-1	2-0	0-0	5-1	2-0	1-0	3-0	2-1	4-0
Arsenal Bila Tserkva	34	18	8	8	51	39	62	0-0	2-1	0-1		0-0	1-0	3-2	1-0	1-1	0-2	2-1	1-0	2-2	1-0	2-0	0-1	5-0	1-2	2-0
Krymteplytsja	34	17	9	8	50	38	60	1-0	0-0	0-2	1-2		0-1	4-1	0-0	4-3	3-2	2-0	3-0	2-0	2-1	4-0	2-1	2-2	2-1
Bukovyna Chernivtsi	34	15	12	7	38	29	57	2-2	3-2	1-1	0-0	0-1		1-0	2-1	1-0	0-0	3-2	1-0	1-1	3-1	1-0	1-0	2-0	0-0
Stal Alchevsk	34	14	8	12	51	50	50	3-2	1-1	0-0	3-2	2-3	2-2		0-2	0-0	3-0	1-1	2-0	0-0	2-2	2-1	2-2	3-0	2-0
Dynamo Kyiv-2	34	15	5	14	42	39	50	0-2	1-0	2-3	0-2	0-2	3-0	1-3		2-1	1-2	2-2	2-1	0-0	2-0	0-0	1-0	3-1	5-0
Helios Kharkiv	34	13	9	12	54	46	48	2-3	0-1	3-2	2-2	2-2	0-2	4-0	1-2		0-0	3-2	2-1	2-1	2-1		4-2	3-0	2-0
Naftovyk-Ukrnafta	34	12	8	14	49	43	44	0-2	1-1	3-1	1-2	1-1	1-1	3-4	3-0	1-2		5-1	0-1	0-4	1-1	3-1	3-0	**3-0**	2-1
Zirka Kirovohrad	34	13	5	16	53	49	44	0-1	4-0	0-1	3-0	0-1	1-0	0-1	3-2	2-1	1-1		2-0	3-0	4-1	2-3	2-1	4-1	4-1
Olimpik Donetsk	34	11	7	16	38	44	40	0-1	1-2	1-4	2-2	1-0	0-1	0-1	1-2	1-1		0-1	1-1		0-0	3-0	1-0	0-0	3-2	4-0
Nyva Vinnytsia	34	7	11	16	21	39	32	0-1	1-4	0-0	0-2	0-0	0-2	**0-3**	1-2	1-0	0-1	1-1		0-1	0-0	0-1	4-1	1-1	
Tytan Armyansk	34	9	5	20	33	59	32	0-2	0-2	0-2	0-2	1-2	2-1	1-0	0-0	1-4	0-2	3-1	0-1		1-0	0-0	3-0	2-0	
FC Odessa	34	7	10	17	37	51	31	0-1	0-1	1-3	1-0	1-1	1-2	4-0	1-3	1-1	1-3	1-1	0-1	5-2		3-0	2-2	2-3	
MFK Mykolajiv §3	34	9	4	21	33	51	28	0-1	1-2	0-1	1-2	3-2	1-2	1-2	2-2	0-3	1-1	2-0	0-2		1-0				1-1
Enerhetyk Burshtyn	34	5	4	25	26	75	19	1-3	0-4	1-5	2-3	0-2	0-0	3-0	**0-3**	0-3	0-2	1-0	1-3	2-0	0-0	0-2	0-1	1-2	1-0
FK Lviv §3	34	6	3	25	21	79	18	1-0	1-5	0-2	1-4	1-0	1-2	2-3	0-1	1-3	0-2	1-0	0-4	1-1	1-3	1-4	2-1	**3-0**	

16/07/2011 - 30/05/2012 • Top scorer: **19** - Oleksandr **KOSYRIN**, Odessa/Zakarpattia • Relegation play-off: MFK Mykolajiv 4-3 Avanhard Kramatorsk

KUBOK UKRAINY 2011-12

First Round

Shakhtar Donetsk	2	
Shakhtar Sverdlovsk *	0	
Kremin Kremenchuk *	2	
Dynamo Kyiv	3	
Vorskla Poltava	2	
MFK Mykolajiv *	0	
Zakarpattya Uzhgorod	0	
Metalurh Zaporizhya *	3	
Arsenal Kyiv *	5	
FK Oleksandrija	0	
Obolon Kyiv	1	
Bukovyna Chernivtsi *	2	
Dnipro Dnipropetrovsk	1	
Tytan Armyansk *	0	
Illychivets Mariupil	1	
Volyn Lutsk *	7	
Karpaty Lviv	1	
FC Poltava *	0	
Berehvdyek Berehove *	0	
Metalist Kharkiv	3	
Stal Dniprodzerzhinsk *	2	
FC Sevastopol	1	
Enerhetyk Burshtyn *	0	
Chernomorets Odessa	4	
Zorja Luhansk	2	
Slovkhlib Slovyansk *	0	
Zirka Kirovohrad	1 2p	
FC Sumy *	1 3p	
Kryvbas Kryvyi Rih	3	
Arsenal Bila Tserkva *	2	
Tavriya Simferopol	0	
Metalurh Donetsk *	4	

Second Round

Shakhtar Donetsk	3	
Dynamo Kyiv *	2	
Vorskla Poltava	0	
Metalurh Zaporizhya *	3	
Arsenal Kyiv	2	
Bukovyna Chernivtsi *	0	
Dnipro Dnipropetrovsk	2	
Volyn Lutsk *	3	
Karpaty Lviv *	1	
Metalist Kharkiv	0	
Stal Dniprodzerzhinsk *	0	
Chernomorets Odessa	1	
Zorja Luhansk	3	
FC Sumy *	1	
Kryvbas Kryvyi Rih	0	
Metalurh Donetsk *	2	

Quarter-finals

Shakhtar Donetsk	1	
Metalurh Zaporizhya *	0	
Arsenal Kyiv *	0	
Volyn Lutsk	1	
Karpaty Lviv *	2	
Chernomorets Odessa	1	
Zorja Luhansk *	0	
Metalurh Donetsk	1	

Semi-finals

Shakhtar Donetsk	4	
Volyn Lutsk *	3	
Karpaty Lviv	0 6p	
Metalurh Donetsk *	0 7p	

Final

Shakhtar Donetsk	2	
Metalurh Donetsk ‡	1	

CUP FINAL

Olimpiysky NSC, Kyiv, 6-05-2012
Att: 47 314, Ref: Anatoliy Abdula
Scorers - Texeira 23, Kucher 104 for Shakhtar; Morozyuk 69 for Metalurh
Shakhtar - Andriy Pyatov - Dario Sma (c), Yaroslav Rakitsky, Oleksandr Kucher, Razvan Rat - Fernandinho●, Oleksiy Gai (Taras Stepanenko 107), Alex Teixeira, Willian - Henrikh Mkhitaryan● (Douglas Costa 62), Adriano (Yevhen Seleznyov 106). Tr: Mircea Lucescu
Metalurh - Olexandr Bandura - Mykola Morozyuk, Vyacheslav Checher (c), Olexandr Volovyk, China - Karlen Mkrtchyan●, Dorde Lazic, Ze Soares● (Oleh Mishchenko 114), Velizar Dimitrov (Danilo 90) - Gevorg Ghazaryan● (Gregory Nelson 73), Dramane Traore. Tr: Volodymyr Pyatenko

* Home team ● ‡ Qualified for the Europa League

URU – URUGUAY

FIFA/COCA-COLA WORLD RANKING

'93	'94	'95	'96	'97	'98	'99	'00	'01	'02	'03	'04	'05	'06	'07	'08	'09	'10	'11	'12
17	37	32	43	40	76	46	32	22	28	21	16	18	29	28	23	20	7	4	16

2012

Jan	Feb	Mar	Apr	May	Jun	Jul	Aug	Sep	Oct	Nov	Dec	High	Low	Av
4	4	4	3	3	2	3	4	5	7	11	16	2	76	26

The Uruguay national team had a poor 2012 after winning just two of the ten matches played during the year although bizarrely they rose to a highest position of second in the FIFA/Coca-Cola World Ranking in June before falling back to 16th in December. The South American champions experienced heavy defeats at the end of the year in Argentina and, more damagingly, in Colombia. The 4-0 reverse in Barranquilla saw the Colombians establish their credentials once again as a force to be reckoned with on the continent but with Ecuador and Venezuela also mounting strong campaigns it won't be an easy passage to the finals. With players of genuine international class in just about every position it would be a major surprise and disappointment if the Uruguayans didn't qualify for Brazil - the scene for their second World Cup triumph in 1950. In club football Nacional beat Defensor Sporting in the 2012 championship final for the second year running. Before a capacity crowd at the Centenario, former Inter player Alvaro Recoba scored the only goal of the game as Nacional secured the 44th title in their history. In the 2012 Copa Libertadores there were no repeats of Peñarol's heroics of the previous year with all three Uruguayan representatives - Nacional, Defensor and Peñarol - bowing out at the group stage.

FIFA WORLD CUP RECORD

1930 1 Winners (hosts) **1934-1938** DNE **1950** 1 Winners **1954** 4 SF **1958** DNQ **1962** 13 r1 **1966** 7 QF **1970** 4 SF **1974** 13 r1 **1978-1982** DNQ **1986** 16 r2 **1990** 16 r2 **1994-1998** DNQ **2002** 26 r1 **2006** DNQ **2010** 4 SF

ASOCIACION URUGUAYA DE FUTBOL (AUF)

Guayabo 1531,
11200 Montevideo

☎ +59 82 4004814
+59 82 4090550
presidencia@auf.org.uy
www.auf.org.uy
FA 1900 CON 1916 FIFA 1923
P Sebastian Bauza
GS Fernando Caceres

THE STADIA

2014 FIFA World Cup Stadia
Estadio Centenario
Montevideo 65 235

Other Main Stadia
Parque Central
Montevideo 25 000
Estadio Atilio Paiva Olivera
Rivera 25 000
Parque Artigas
Paysandu 25 000
Estadio Domingo Burgeño
Maldonado 20 000

MAJOR CITIES/TOWNS

		Population
1	Montevideo	1 328 600
2	Salto	106 286
3	Ciudad de la Costa	101 047
4	Paysandú	77 767
5	Las Piedras	77 484
6	Rivera	69 744
7	Maldonado	63 061
8	Tacuarembó	54 263
9	Melo	53 852
10	Mercedes	44 307
11	Artigas	44 275
12	Minas	39 200
13	San José	39 100
14	Durazno	35 432
15	Florida	33 522
16	San Carlos	28 608
17	Treinta y Tres	27 017
18	Pando	26 869
19	Rocha	26 820

REPUBLICA ORIENTAL DEL URUGUAY • ORIENTAL REPUBLIC OF URUGUAY

Capital Montevideo   Population 3 494 382 (131)   % in cities 92%
GDP per capita $12 400 (89)   Area km² 176 215 km² (90)   GMT +/- -3
Neighbours (km) Argentina 580, Brazil 1068 • Coast 660

RECENT INTERNATIONAL MATCHES PLAYED BY URUGUAY

2010	Opponents	Score	Venue	Comp	Scorers	Att	Referee
3-03	Switzerland	W 3-1	St Gall	Fr	Forlan [35], Suarez [50], Cavani [87]	12 500	Rizzoli ITA
26-05	Israel	W 4-1	Montevideo	Fr	Forlan [15], Alvaro Pereira [37], Abreu 2 [75 81]	60 000	Osses CHI
11-06	France	D 0-0	Cape Town	WCr1		64 100	Nishimura JPN
16-06	South Africa	W 3-0	Pretoria	WCr1	Forlan 2 [24 80p], Alvaro Pereira [95+]	42 658	Busacca SUI
22-06	Mexico	W 1-0	Rustenburg	WCr1	Suarez [43]	33 425	Kassai HUN
26-06	Korea Republic	W 2-1	Port Elizabeth	WCr2	Suarez 2 [8 80]	30 597	Stark GER
2-07	Ghana	D 1-1	Johannesburg	WCqf	Forlan [55]. W 4-2p	84 017	Benquerenca POR
6-07	Netherlands	L 2-3	Cape Town	WCsf	Forlan [41], Maxi Pereira [92+]	62 479	Irmatov UZB
10-07	Germany	L 2-3	Port Elizabeth	WC3p	Cavani [28], Forlan [51]	36 254	Archundia MEX
11-08	Angola	W 2-0	Lisbon	Fr	Cavani [84], Hernandez [90]	1 500	Miguel POR
8-10	Indonesia	W 7-1	Jakarta	Fr	Cavani 3 [35 80 83], Suarez 3 [43 54 69p], Eguren [58]	25 000	Daud SIN
12-10	China PR	W 4-0	Wuhan	Fr	OG [70], Cavani [78], Rodriguez [81], Fernandez [84]	50 000	Lee Dong Jun KOR
17-11	Chile	L 0-2	Santiago	Fr		45 000	Torres PAR
2011							
25-03	Estonia	L 0-2	Tallinn	Fr		6 817	Munukka FIN
29-03	Republic of Ireland	W 3-2	Dublin	Fr	Lugano [12], Cavani [22], Hernandez [40]	20 200	Ennjimi FRA
29-05	Germany	L 1-2	Sinsheim	Fr	Gargano [48]	25 655	Benquerenca POR
8-06	Netherlands	D 1-1	Montevideo	Fr	Suarez [82]. W 4-3p	55 000	Pitana ARG
23-06	Estonia	W 3-0	Rivera	Fr	Caceres [12], OG [55], Lodeiro [72]	25 000	Laverni ARG
4-07	Peru	D 1-1	Mendoza	CAr1	Suarez [45]	25 000	Roldan COL
8-07	Chile	D 1-1	Mendoza	CAr1	Alvaro Pereira [53]	45 000	Amarilla PAR
12-07	Mexico	W 1-0	La Plata	CAr1	Alvaro Pereira [14]	36 000	Orozco BOL
16-07	Argentina	D 1-1	Santa Fe	CAqf	Perez [6]. W 5-4p	47 000	Amarilla PAR
19-07	Peru	W 2-0	La Plata	CAsf	Suarez 2 [52 57]	25 000	Orozco BRA
24-07	Paraguay	W 3-0	Buenos Aires	CAf	Suarez [11], Forlan 2 [41 89]	57 921	Fagundes BRA
2-09	Ukraine	W 3-2	Kharkov	Fr	Gonzalez [43], Lugano [61], Hernandez [87]	30 000	Kuipers NED
7-10	Bolivia	W 4-2	Montevideo	WCq	Suarez [3], Lugano 2 [25 71], Cavani [34]	25 500	Carrillo PER
11-10	Paraguay	D 1-1	Asuncion	WCq	Forlan [68]	12 922	Seneme BRA
11-11	Chile	W 4-0	Montevideo	WCq	Suarez 4 [42 45 67 73]	40 500	Baldassi ARG
15-11	Italy	W 1-0	Rome	Fr	Fernandez [3]	42 000	Duarte POR
2012							
29-02	Romania	D 1-1	Bucharest	Fr	Cavani [2]	20 000	Kassai HUN
25-05	Russia	D 1-1	Moscow	Fr	Suarez [48]	18 000	Blom NED
2-06	Venezuela	D 1-1	Montevideo	WCq	Forlan [38]	57 000	Arias PAR
10-06	Peru	W 4-2	Montevideo	WCq	Suarez [15], Maxi Pereira [29], Rodriguez [62], Eguren [93+]	55 000	Pedro BRA
15-08	France	D 0-0	Le Havre	Fr		25 178	Orsato ITA
7-09	Colombia	L 0-4	Barranquilla	WCq		45 000	Lopes BRA
11-09	Ecuador	D 1-1	Montevideo	WCq	Cavani [66]	38 000	Amarilla PAR
12-10	Argentina	L 0-3	Mendoza	WCq		31 997	Pedro BRA
16-10	Bolivia	L 1-4	La Paz	WCq	Suarez [80]	25 402	Rivera PER
14-11	Poland	W 3-1	Gdansk	Fr	OG [21], Cavani [34], Suarez [66]	39 460	Collum SCO

Fr = Friendly match • CA = Copa America • WC = FIFA World Cup
q = qualifier • po = play-off • r1 = first round group • qf = quarter-final • sf = semi-final • 3p = third place play-off

URUGUAY NATIONAL TEAM HISTORICAL RECORDS

Caps 94 - Diego Forlan 2002- • 81 - Diego Perez 2001- • 79 - Rodolfo Rodriguez 1976-86 • 77 - Diego Lugano 2003- • 74 - Fabian Carini 1999-2009 • 73 - Maxi Pereira 2005- • 72 - Enzo Francescoli 1982-97 • 70 - Sebastian Abreu 1996- • 69 - Alvaro Recoba 1995-2007 • 68 - Angel Romano 1911-27; Pablo Garcia 1997-2008 & Diego Lugano 2003- • 65 - Carlos Aguilera 1982-97 • 62 - Diego Godin 2005-

Goals 33 - Diego Forlan 2002- • 31 - Hector Scarone 1917-30 • 30 - Luis Suarez 2007- • 28 - Angel Romano 1911-27 • 27 - Oscar Miguez 1950-58 • 26 - Sebastian Abreu 1996- • 24 - Pedro Petrone 1924-30 • 23 - Carlos Aguilera 1983-97 • 22 - Fernando Morena 1971-83 • 20 - Jose Piendibene 1909-23 • 19 - Severino Varela 1935-42 • 18 - Hector Castro 1926-35 & Carlos Scarone 1909-21

Coaches For coaches pre 1969 see Oliver's Almanack 2011 • Juan Hohberg 1969-70 • Hugo Bagnulo 1970-73 • Roberto Porta 1974-74 • Juan Alberto Schiaffino 1974-75 • Jose Maria Rodriguez 1975-77 • Juan Hohberg 1977 • Raul Bentancor 1977-79 • Roque Maspoli 1979-82 • Omar Borras 1982-87 • Roberto Fleitas 1987-88 • Oscar Tabarez 1988-90 • Luis Cubilla 1990-93 • Ildo Maneiro 1993-94 • Hector Nunez 1994-96 • Juan Ahuntchain 1996-97 • Roque Maspoli 1997-98 • Victor Pua 1998-2000 • Daniel Passarella 2000-01 • Victor Pua 2001-03 • Juan Ramon Carrasco 2003-04 • Jorge Fossati 2004-06 • Juan Ferrin 2006 • Oscar Tabarez 2006-

URUGUAY 2011-12

PRIMERA DIVISION PROFESSIONAL TABLA ANUAL

	Pl	W	D	L	F	A	Pts	Rel	Nacional	Peñarol	Defensor	Cerro Largo	Liverpool	Danubio	River Plate	Wanderers	Cerro	Racing	El Tanque	Rampla Jun	Bella Vista	Fénix	Cerrito	Rentistas
Nacional †	30	20	7	3	68	31	67	130		2-1	2-2	4-0	4-3	3-1	3-2	2-0	3-0	3-2	3-0	1-1	3-1	0-0	6-1	3-0
Peñarol †	30	19	5	6	71	30	62	114	2-3		1-0	4-2	0-1	2-1	1-0	1-2	3-1	4-2	2-0	4-1	4-1	2-1	1-0	4-1
Defensor †	30	19	5	6	54	27	62	120	2-2	0-0		2-1	4-2	0-1	0-2	2-1	2-3	5-1	3-0	2-0	2-1	1-1	1-0	
Cerro Largo ‡	30	16	6	8	46	34	54	108	4-2	0-0	0-3		1-0	1-0	0-3	3-0	1-0	2-2	3-0	3-2	1-0	2-0	2-1	1-0
Liverpool ‡	30	17	2	11	48	39	53	93	0-1	3-0	2-3	2-1		1-2	1-2	1-2	2-1	2-1	1-0	0-1	2-0	5-4	3-1	2-1
Danubio ‡	30	13	11	6	37	26	52	93	1-1	3-2	0-1	1-1	0-0		0-0	1-0	1-0	1-1	2-1	3-2	4-1	4-0	1-0	1-1
River Plate	30	14	8	8	50	40	50	85	3-3	0-4	2-1	2-1	1-3	1-1		2-2	3-3	2-1	4-0	2-1	1-2	2-1	2-2	2-0
Wanderers	30	13	5	12	49	50	44	82	1-3	1-5	0-2	3-2	0-1	1-1	0-3		3-1	3-0	1-3	2-0	4-0	2-1	3-1	3-0
Cerro	30	10	6	14	35	37	36	78	0-0	0-0	2-3	0-1	2-1	1-2	2-0	1-0		2-3	1-0	0-0	0-2	1-1	3-1	3-0
Racing CM	30	9	8	13	41	53	34	73	1-0	2-2	0-3	1-3	1-1	0-1	4-2	3-2	1-0		3-0	1-3	0-1	0-0	0-0	3-1
El Tanque Sisley	30	9	4	17	29	48	31	72	0-1	0-2	2-2	0-3	0-1	1-1	1-1	3-2	2-0	3-0		1-3	1-2	0-2	3-2	2-0	
Rampla Juniors	30	9	4	17	34	55	31	**62**	0-2	1-7	0-2	0-3	0-2	0-0	2-1	1-3	0-1	4-3	2-1		1-0	0-4	1-3	4-0
Bella Vista	30	9	3	18	28	46	30	74	1-0	0-3	0-1	1-2	1-2	2-1	0-1	2-2	0-0	0-1	1-2	3-1		0-0	0-1	1-0
Fénix	30	5	10	15	33	46	25	70	0-2	2-2	0-1	1-1	1-2	1-1	1-2	3-3	0-3	2-3	0-2	0-1	2-1		3-1	1-1
Cerrito	30	5	9	16	24	52	24	**48**	0-3	0-5	0-2	0-0	1-2	1-0	0-0	1-2	1-4	0-0	0-1	0-0	3-2	1-1		1-0
Rentistas	30	4	7	19	19	51	19	**38**	2-3	0-3	0-2	1-1	3-0	0-1	0-2	1-1	1-0	1-1	0-0	0-3	2-1	2-0	1-1	

13/08/2011 - 3/06/2012 • † Qualified for the Copa Libertadores • ‡ Qualified for the Copa Sudamericana
Apertura matches are in the shaded boxes • Relegation calculated over two seasons (promoted clubs have season total doubled)
Championship play-offs: Nacional qualified for the final as the overall leading points scorer. The winners of the Apertura (Nacional) and Clausura (Defensor) played off for the right to meet Nacional in the final • **Nacional** 1-0 Defensor. Nacional won the championship as they had already qualified for the final (details below).
Top scorers: 17 - Richard **Porta** AUS, Nacional • 16 - Marcelo **Zalayeta**, Peñarol • 15 - Rino **Lucas**, Cerro Largo • 13 - Diego **Vera**, Liverpool •
12 - Gonzalo **Mastriani**, Cerro; Pablo **Olivera**, River Plate & Sebastian **Taborda**, River Plate • 11 - Nicolas **Olivera**, Defensor

URUGUAY 2011-12 TORNEO APERTURA

	Pl	W	D	L	F	A	Pts
Nacional †	15	9	5	1	30	11	32
Danubio	15	8	5	2	19	8	31
Peñarol	15	9	3	3	30	12	30
River Plate	15	8	4	3	22	17	28
Cerro Largo	15	8	3	4	18	16	27
Defensor	15	7	3	5	23	16	24
Cerro	15	7	3	5	17	12	24
Liverpool	15	6	1	8	17	18	19
El Tanque Sisley	15	5	3	7	15	23	18
Wanderers	15	5	2	8	23	25	17
Racing CM	15	4	6	5	20	23	171
Rampla Juniors	15	5	1	9	16	22	16
Fénix	15	4	4	7	15	22	16
Rentistas	15	4	2	9	10	21	14
Cerrito	15	3	4	8	10	23	13
Bella Vista	15	3	1	11	9	25	10

13/08/2011 - 4/12/2011 • † Qualified for play-off

URUGUAY 2011-12 TORNEO CLAUSURA

	Pl	W	D	L	F	A	Pts
Defensor †	15	12	2	1	31	11	38
Nacional	15	11	2	2	38	20	35
Liverpool	15	11	1	3	31	21	34
Peñarol	15	10	2	3	41	18	32
Cerro Largo	15	8	3	4	28	18	27
Wanderers	15	7	3	5	26	25	24
River Plate	15	6	4	5	28	23	22
Danubio	15	5	6	4	18	18	21
Bella Vista	15	6	2	7	19	21	20
Racing CM	15	5	2	8	21	30	17
Rampla Juniors	15	4	3	8	18	33	15
El Tanque Sisley	15	4	1	10	14	25	13
Cerro	15	3	3	9	18	25	12
Cerrito	15	2	5	8	14	29	11
Fénix	15	1	6	8	18	25	9
Rentistas	15	0	5	10	9	30	5

18/02/2012 - 3/06/2012 • † Qualified for play-off

CHAMPIONSHIP FINAL 2012
Centenario, Montevideo, 16-06-2012, Att: 60 000, Ref: Dario Ubriaco

Nacional	1	Recoba [41]
Defensor	0	

NACIONAL
Jorge **BAVA**• - Christian **NUNEZ**, Andres **SCOTTI**•, Alexis **ROLIN**•, Diego **PLACENTE**• (Darwin **TORRES** 72) - Matias **CABRERA** (Israel **DAMONTE**• 61), Facundo **PIRIZ**•, Maximiliano **CALZADA** - Alvaro **RECOBA** (c) - Tabare **VIUDEZ**• (Vicente **SANCHEZ** 14), Richard **PORTA**. Tr: Marcelo **GALLARDO**

DEFENSOR
Yonathan **IRRAZABAL** - Pablo **PINTOS**•, Ramon **ARIAS**, Nestor **MOIRAGHI**, Robert **HERRERA**• (Diego Manuel **RODRIGUEZ** 60) - Diego Martin **RODRIGUEZ**, Diego **FERREIRA**, Diego **ROLAN** 75) - Federico **PINTOS**, Matias **BRITOS** - Nicolas **OLIVERA** (c)•, Ignacio **RISSO** (Juan **AMADO** 60).
Tr: Gustavo **DIAZ**

URUGUAY 2010-11
SEGUNDA DIVISION PROFESIONAL (2)

	Pl	W	D	L	F	A	Pts
Central Español	24	16	6	2	47	18	**54**
Juventud Las Piedras	24	12	7	5	37	22	**43**
Progreso †	24	12	6	6	36	31	**42**
Tacuarembó †	24	9	10	5	28	22	37
Huracán †	24	9	8	7	27	32	35
Miramar Misiones †	24	10	4	10	38	31	34
Boston River †	24	7	12	5	28	23	33
Atenas †	24	8	8	8	30	31	32
Sud América †	24	6	9	9	23	24	27
Plaza Colonia †	24	7	6	11	28	39	27
Maldonado	24	6	8	10	27	30	26
Rocha	24	5	4	15	28	51	21
Villa Teresa	24	2	6	16	19	42	11

1/10/2011 - 26/05/2012 • † Qualified for play-off

PROMOTION PLAY-OFFS

Quarter-finals
- Progreso 3 1
- Plaza Colonia 1 0
- Boston River 0 0
- Miramar 0 4
- Tacuarembó 0 2
- Sud América 0 1
- Atenas 1 0
- Huracán 1 1

Semi-finals
- Progreso 1 0
- Miramar 0 0
- Tacuarembó 2 1 4p
- Huracán 2 1 5p
- 2/06/2012 - 30/06/2012

Final
- Progreso 3 0 3p
- Huracán 1 2 2p

Progreso Promoted

MEDALS TABLE

		Overall	League	Sth Am
		G S B	G S B	G S B
1	CA Peñarol	53 47 18	**48** 40 5	5 7 13
2	Club Nacional de Football	47 45 22	44 41 12	3 4 10
3	Montevideo Wanderers FC	4 6 14	4 6 14	
4	Defensor Sporting	4 8 8	4 8 8	
5	River Plate FC	4 1 1	4 1 1	
6	Danubio FC	3 4 5	3 4 4	1
7	Rampla Juniors FC	1 5 14	1 5 14	
8	CA Bella Vista	1 1 2	1 1 2	
9	Central Español FC	1 4	1 4	
10	CA Progreso	1	1	
11	CA Cerro	1 6	1 6	
12	Universal	1 4	1 4	
13	CA River Plate	1 2	1 2	
14	Albion	1 1	1 1	
15	Rocha FC	1	1	
16	CA Fénix	3	3	
	Liverpool FC	3	3	

COPA CELESTE OLIMPICA 2012

First Round
- River Plate 1 7p
- Fénix 1 6p
- Cerro Largo 0 0p
- Rampla Juniors 0 3p
- Bella Vista 3
- Nacional 2
- Liverpool 3 5p
- El Tanque Sisley 3 6p
- Wanderers 2 6p
- Cerro 2 5p
- Danubio 0
- Cerrito 1
- Racing CM 1 5p
- Defensor 1 4p
- Rentistas 0
- Peñarol 3

Quarter-finals
- River Plate 3
- Rampla Juniors 0
- Bella Vista 0 3p
- El Tanque Sisley 0 4p
- Wanderers 0 5p
- Cerrito 0 3p
- Racing CM 0
- Peñarol 3

Semi-finals
- River Plate 1 3p
- El Tanque Sisley 1 1p
- Wanderers 0 2p
- Peñarol 0 4p

Final
- River Plate 2
- Peñarol 1

CUP FINAL

Estadio Atilio Paiva Olivera, Rivera
12-02-2012, Ref: Fernando Cabrera
Scorers - Maureen Franco 2 [7] [44] for River; Alejandro Siles [24] for Peñarol

USA – UNITED STATES OF AMERICA

FIFA/COCA-COLA WORLD RANKING

'93	'94	'95	'96	'97	'98	'99	'00	'01	'02	'03	'04	'05	'06	'07	'08	'09	'10	'11	'12
22	23	19	18	26	23	22	16	24	10	11	11	8	31	19	22	14	18	34	28

2012

Jan	Feb	Mar	Apr	May	Jun	Jul	Aug	Sep	Oct	Nov	Dec	High	Low	Av
33	31	27	29	29	28	36	36	33	32	27	28	4	36	19

David Beckham signed off his MLS career in some style by helping LA Galaxy to a record equalling fourth title after overcoming Houston Dynamo in the final for the second year running. Beckham was given a standing ovation as he was substituted just before the end of a game Galaxy won 3-1 thanks to a goal from Omar Gonzalez and two penalties converted by Landon Donovan and Robbie Keane. In the Lamar Hunt US Open Cup Seattle Sounders went through a fourth consecutive campaign unbeaten but failed to win the trophy when they lost to Sporting Kansas City on penalties in the final. Kansas looked to have wrapped up the title with a penalty just minutes from time only for Seattle to equalise two minutes later but three consecutive missed penalties in the shoot out - the last by Eddie Johnson - saw Kansas secure their first trophy since winning the 2004 Open Cup as Kansas City Wizards. The lack of progress in challenging Mexican clubs in the CONCACAF Champions League continues to be a source of frustration for American soccer with both Galaxy and Seattle failing to make it past the quarter-finals of the 2011-12 tournament. In the 2014 FIFA World Cup qualifiers the USA safely negotiated their first round qualifying group - despite losing away to Jamaica - to make it through to the final hexagonal.

CONCACAF GOLD CUP RECORD
1991 Winners **1993** 2 F **1996** 3 SF **1998** 2 F **2000** QF
2002 Winners **2003** 3 SF **2005** Winners **2007** Winners **2009** 2 F **2011** 2 F

US SOCCER FEDERATION (USSF)

US Soccer House,
1801 S. Prairie Avenue,
Chicago IL 60616
☎ +1 312 8081300
+1 312 8081301
communications@ussoccer.org
www.ussoccer.com
FA 1913 CON 1961 FIFA 1914
P Sunil Gulati
GS Dan Flynn

THE STADIA
2014 FIFA World Cup Stadia
Raymond James Stadium
Tampa   65 647
Crew Stadium
Columbus   22 555
Livestrong Sporting Park
Kansas   18 500
Other Main Stadia
Rose Bowl
Pasadena   92 109
The Home Depot Center
Carson, Los Angeles   27 000

MAJOR CITIES/TOWNS
		Population
1	New York	8 459 053
2	Los Angeles	3 878 732
3	Chicago	2 878 957
4	Houston	2 307 889
5	Phoenix	1 635 801
6	Philadelphia	1 445 991
7	San Antonio	1 402 014
8	San Diego	1 309 752
9	Dallas	1 304 933
10	San Jose	977 894
11	Detroit	901 163
12	Jacksonville	822 422
13	San Francisco	817 244
14	Indianapolis	803 933
15	Austin	792 779
16	Columbus	768 665
17	Fort Worth	751 151
18	Charlotte	723 518
19	Memphis	662 997

UNITED STATES OF AMERICA
Capital Washington DC   Population 307 212 123 (3)   % in cities 82%
GDP per capita $47 500 (10)   Area km² 9 826 675 km² (3)   GMT + / - -5 to -11
Neighbours (km) Canada 8893, Mexico 3141 • Coast 19 924

RECENT INTERNATIONAL MATCHES PLAYED BY THE USA

2010	Opponents	Score		Venue	Comp	Scorers	Att	Referee
12-06	England	D	1-1	Rustenburg	WCr1	Dempsey [40]	38 646	Simon BRA
18-06	Slovenia	D	2-2	Johannesburg	WCr1	Donovan [48], Bradley [82]	45 573	Coulibaly MLI
23-06	Algeria	W	1-0	Pretoria	WCr1	Donovan [91+]	35 827	De Bleeckere BEL
26-06	Ghana	L	1-2	Rustenburg	WCr2	Donovan [62p]	34 976	Kassai HUN
10-08	Brazil	L	0-2	New Jersey	Fr		77 223	Brizan TRI
9-10	Poland	D	2-2	Chicago	Fr	Altidore [13], Onyewu [52]	31 696	Depiero CAN
12-10	Colombia	D	0-0	Chester	Fr		8 823	Garcia MEX
17-11	South Africa	W	1-0	Cape Town	Fr	Agudelo [85]	52 000	Kirwa KEN
2011								
22-01	Chile	D	1-1	Carson/LA	Fr	Bunbury [75]	18 580	Chacon MEX
26-03	Argentina	D	1-1	New Jersey	Fr	Agudelo [59]	78 936	Garcia MEX
29-03	Paraguay	L	0-1	Nashville	Fr		29 059	Benigno HON
4-06	Spain	L	0-4	Foxboro/Boston	Fr		64 121	Silvera URU
7-06	Canada	W	2-0	Detroit	GCr1	Altidore [15], Dempsey [62]	28 209	Lopez GUA
11-06	Panama	L	1-2	Tampa	GCr1	Goodson [66]	27 731	Rodriguez.M MEX
14-06	Guadeloupe	W	1-0	Kansas City	GCr1	Altidore [9]	20 109	Solis CRC
19-06	Jamaica	W	2-0	Washington DC	GCqf	Jones [49], Dempsey [79]	45 424	Rodriguez.M MEX
22-06	Panama	W	1-0	Houston	GCsf	Dempsey [77]	70 627	Wijngaarde SUR
25-06	Mexico	L	2-4	Pasadena	GCf	Bradley [8], Donovan [23]	93 420	Aguilar SLV
10-08	Mexico	D	1-1	Philadelphia	Fr	Rogers [73]	30 132	Bogle JAM
2-09	Costa Rica	L	0-1	Carson/LA	Fr		15 798	Molina HON
6-09	Belgium	L	0-1	Brussels	Fr		21 946	Collum SCO
8-10	Honduras	W	1-0	Miami	Fr	Dempsey [36]	21 170	Campbell JAM
11-10	Ecuador	L	0-1	Harrison/NY	Fr		20 707	Aguilar SLV
11-11	France	L	0-1	Paris	Fr		70 018	Koukoulakis GRE
15-11	Slovenia	W	3-2	Ljubljana	Fr	Buddle [9], Dempsey [41], Altidore [43p]	8 140	Schorgenhofer AUT
2012								
21-01	Venezuela	W	1-0	Glendale	Fr	Clarke [90]	22 403	Garcia MEX
25-01	Panama	W	1-0	Panama City	Fr	Zusi [9]	15 000	Chacon MEX
29-02	Italy	W	1-0	Genoa	Fr	Dempsey [55]	15 000	Aydinus TUR
26-05	Scotland	W	5-1	Jacksonville	Fr	Donovan 3 [3 60 65], Bradley [11], Jones [70]	44 438	Bonilla SLV
30-05	Brazil	L	1-4	Washington DC	Fr	Gomez [45]	67 619	Calderon CRC
3-06	Canada	D	0-0	Toronto	Fr		15 247	Morales MEX
8-06	Antigua and Barbuda	W	3-1	Tampa	WCq	Bocanegra [8], Dempsey [44p], Gomez [72]	23 971	Cruz CRC
12-06	Guatemala	D	1-1	Guatemala City	WCq	Dempsey [39]	18 000	Aguilar SLV
15-08	Mexico	W	1-0	Mexico City	Fr	Orozco Fiscal [79]	52 151	Quesada CRC
7-09	Jamaica	L	1-2	Kingston	WCq	Dempsey [1]	25 000	Rodriguez MEX
11-09	Jamaica	W	1-0	Columbus	WCq	Gomez [55]	23 881	Pineda HON
12-10	Antigua and Barbuda	W	2-1	St John's	WCq	Johnson 2 [20 90]	7 000	Brizan TRI
16-10	Guatemala	W	3-1	Kansas City	WCq	Bocanegra [10], Dempsey 2 [18 36]	16 947	Moreno PAN
14-11	Russia	D	2-2	Krasnodar	Fr	Bradley [76], Diskerud [90]	28 200	Rizzoli ITA

Fr = Friendly match • GC = CONCACAF Gold Cup • CC = FIFA Confederations Cup • WC = FIFA World Cup
q = qualifier • r1 = first round group • qf = quarter-final • sf = semi-final • f = final

USA NATIONAL TEAM HISTORICAL RECORDS

Caps
164 - Cobi Jones 1992-2004 • 142 - Landon Donovan 2000- • 134 - Jeff Agoos 1988-2003 • 127 - Marcelo Balboa 1988-2000 • 112 - Claudio Reyna 1994-2006 • 110 - Paul Caligiuri 1984-97 • 108 - Carlos Bocanegra 2001- • 106 - Eric Wynalda 1990-2000 • 101 - Kasey Keller 1990-2007 • 100 - Earnie Stewart 1990-2004; Tony Meola 1988-2006; Joe-Max Moore 1992-2002 • 97 - DaMarcus Beasley 2001- • 96 - Alexi Lalas 1990-98 • 95 - Brian McBride 1993-2006 • 92 - Clint Dempsey 2004- • 90 - John Harkes 1987-2000

Goals
49 - Landon Donovan 2000- • 34 - Eric Wynalda 1990-2000 • 31 - Clint Dempsey 2004- • 30 - Brian McBride 1993-2006 • 24 - Joe-Max Moore 1992-2002 • 21 - Bruce Murray 1985-93 • 17 - DaMarcus Beasley 2001- & Earnie Stewart 1990-2004 • 15 - Cobi Jones 1992-2004

Coaches
For coaches pre 1968 see Oliver's Almanack 2012 • Phil Woosnam 1968 • Gordon Jago 1969 • Bob Kehoe 1971-72 • Max Wosniak 1973 • Eugene Chyzowych 1973 • Gordon Bradley 1973 • Dettmar Cramer 1974 • Al Miller 1975 • Manny Schellscheidt 1975 • Walter Chyzowych 1976-80 • Bob Gansler 1982 • Alkis Panagoulias 1983-85 • Lothar Osiander 1986-88 • Bob Gansler 1989-91 • John Kowalski 1991 • Bora Milutinovic 1991-95 • Steve Sampson 1995-98 • Bruce Arena 1998-2006 • Bob Bradley 2006-11 • Jurgen Klinsmann 2011-

USA 2012
MLS EASTERN CONFERENCE

	Pl	W	D	L	F	A	Pts
Sporting Kansas City ‡	34	18	7	9	42	27	63
DC United ‡	34	17	10	7	53	43	58
New York Red Bulls ‡	34	16	9	9	57	46	57
Chicago Fire ‡	34	17	11	6	46	41	57
Houston Dynamo ‡	34	14	9	11	48	41	53
Columbus Crew	34	15	12	7	44	44	52
Montreal Impact	34	12	16	6	45	51	42
Philadelphia Union	34	10	18	6	37	45	36
New England Revs	34	9	17	8	39	44	35
Toronto FC	34	5	21	8	36	62	23

10/03/2012 - 29/10/2012 • ‡ Qualified for the play-offs

USA 2012
MLS WESTERN CONFERENCE

	Pl	W	D	L	F	A	Pts
San Jose Earthquakes ‡	34	19	6	9	72	43	66
Real Salt Lake ‡	34	17	11	6	46	35	57
Seattle Sounders ‡	34	15	8	11	51	33	56
Los Angeles Galaxy ‡	34	16	12	6	59	47	54
Vancouver Whitecaps ‡	34	11	13	10	35	41	43
FC Dallas	34	9	13	12	42	47	39
Colorado Rapids	34	11	19	4	44	50	37
Portland Timbers	34	8	16	10	34	56	34
Chivas USA	34	7	18	9	24	58	30

10/03/2012 - 29/10/2012 • ‡ Qualified for the play-offs

MLS REGULAR SEASON OVERALL STANDINGS AND RESULTS

MLS REGULAR SEASON	Pts	San Jose	Kansas	DC United	New York	Salt Lake	Chicago	Seattle	LA Galaxy	Houston	Columbus	Vancouver	Montreal	Dallas	Colorado	Ph'delphia	NE Revs	Portland	Chivas	Toronto
San Jose †	66		5-3		3-1 5-0	1-1		2-1	4-3 2-2	0-1		1-1	3-1		2-1 3-3	4-1		1-0	2-2	1-1 4-0
Kansas	63	2-1		2-1	1-0	0-1 2-0		1-0	0-0 1-1	1-2		0-2	2-1		2-1	3-0 0-0				2-0 2-1
DC United	58		0-1		4-1 2-2		4-2	0-0		3-2	1-0 3-2		1-1 3-0	4-1	2-0	1-1	3-2 2-1		1-0	3-1	
New York	57	2-2	0-2 0-0	3-2			1-0 0-2	2-2		1-0 2-0	3-1		5-2		4-1	2-0	1-0	3-2	1-1	4-1
Salt Lake	57	1-2		1-0	2-0			0-0	2-3		2-1 0-0	1-0	3-2 1-2 2-0 2-0		2-1	3-0 2-1	0-1	3-2
Chicago	57		2-1	1-1	3-1	0-0		1-2	0-2	1-1 3-1 2-1 2-1	1-0	3-1	2-1		1-0 1-3	2-1		2-1	
Seattle	56	0-1 1-2	1-1		0-1 0-0				2-0 4-0	0-2	0-2			3-1	1-0 2-1	1-0		3-0	2-1	3-1
LA Galaxy	54	2-3		3-1		0-1 1-3 1-2	1-0			3-0 2-0		1-1 2-0	2-0	1-2		1-3	3-1 1-0	3-1	4-2
Houston	53		2-1	1-0 4-0	2-0	1-0	0-0		2-1		2-2		3-0 0-1	2-1	2-1 3-1	2-0	0-0			3-3 1-1
Columbus	52		0-2 1-1	1-0	1-4	2-0	2-1		1-1	2-2		0-1	2-0 2-1	2-1		3-2	4-3		1-0	2-1 2-1	
Vancouver	43	2-1 2-1	1-3		0-0	1-1	2-1		2-2 0-0	2-2	3-1			2-0	1-0 0-2 1-0 2-2			0-1	4-0	
Montreal	42	3-1	1-3 0-0	3-0	1-2 3-1		1-1	4-1	1-1	4-2	2-1				2-0	2-1 0-1	2-0			2-1 0-3
Dallas	39	0-0			2-1	1-1		0-2 1-1	0-1		1-0	2-1			0-2 3-2	1-1	2-0	1-1 5-0 0-2 2-2	1-1
Colorado	37	1-2 1-4	2-2			1-0	2-0	1-2	1-2 1-1	2-0	2-0	0-1	3-2	1-2				3-0 3-0 4-0 1-1		
Ph'delphia	36	1-2	4-0	0-1 0-1 2-3 0-3	0-0		1-3			3-1	1-0 1-2	0-0	2-1		1-2		2-1 1-0			3-0
NE Revs	35		0-1	1-2	2-0 1-1		2-0 1-0	2-2		2-2	0-0 2-0	4-1	0-1		2-1	0-0		1-0	3-3	0-1
Portland	34	2-1 1-1	1-0	1-1		2-3	2-1	2-1 1-1	3-5		0-0	1-1 2-1		1-1	1-0	3-1			1-2 0-1	
Chivas	30	0-2	0-1		0-3 0-4	1-2	1-1 2-6 1-0 0-4	0-1		0-1 0-0	2-1	1-1	0-2	0-1		1-0				
Toronto	23	0-3	0-1	0-2 0-1	1-1		2-3 1-2			4-0		0-2	1-0	3-2	0-0		2-1	1-0 1-1	2-2	2-2	

† Qualified for the CONCACAF Champions League • Attendance (inc play-offs): 6,408,107 @ 18,958
Top scorers: 27 - Chris **WONDOLOWSKI**, San Jose • 18 - Kenny **COOPER**, New York • 17 - Alvaro **SABORIO** CRC, Salt Lake • 16 - Robbie **KEANE** IRL, LA Galaxy • 15 - Thierry **HENRY** FRA, New York • 14 - Eddie **JOHNSON**, Seattle • 13 - Alan **GORDON**, San Jose & Fredy **MONTERO** COL, Seattle • 12 - Will **BRUIN**, Houston & Chris **PONTIUS**, DC United • 11 - Kei **KAMARA** SLE, Kansas & Saer **SENE** FRA, New England

MLS PLAY-OFFS 2012

Conference Semis			Conference Finals			MLS Cup Final		
LA Galaxy *	0	3						
San Jose	1	1	LA Galaxy *	3	1			
Salt Lake	0	0	Seattle	0	2			
Seattle *	0	1				LA Galaxy	3	
DC United *	1	1				Houston	1	
New York RB	1	0	DC United	1	1			
Sp. Kansas City	0	1	Houston *	3	1			
Houston *	2	0						

* Home team in the 1st leg
East preliminary knock-out: Chicago Fire 1-2 **Houston Dynamo**
West preliminary knock-out: **LA Galaxy** 2-1 Vancouver Whitecaps

MLS CUP 2012

Home Depot Center, Carson, Los Angeles, 1-12-2012,
Att: 30 510, Ref: Silviu Petrescu

LA Galaxy	3	Gonzalez [60], Donovan [65p], Keane [94+p]
Houston Dynamo	1	Carr [44]

LA GALAXY
Josh **SAUNDERS** - Sean **FRANKLIN**, Omar **GONZALEZ**, Tommy **MEYER**, Todd **DUNIVANT** - Christian **WILHELMSSON** (Edson **BUDDLE** 74), **JUNINHO** (Michael **STEPHENS** 76), David **BECKHAM** (Marcelo **SARVAS** 89), Mike **MAGEE** - Robbie **KEANE**, Landon **DONOVAN**• (c). Tr: Bruce **ARENA**

HOUSTON DYNAMO
Tally **HALL**• - Kofi **SARKODIE** (Brian **CHING** 77), Bobby **BOSWELL**•, Jermaine **TAYLOR**, Corey **ASHE** - Oscar Boniek **GARCIA**, Ricardo **CLARK**, Adam **MOFFAT** (Giles **BARNES** 71), Brad **DAVIS** (c) - Calen **CARR** (Macoumba **KANDJI** 59), Will **BRUIN**. Tr: Dominic **KINNEAR**

USA 2012 NASL (2)

	Pl	W	D	L	F	A	Pts
San Antonio Scorpions	28	13	8	7	46	27	47
Tampa Bay Rowdies ‡	28	12	9	7	37	30	45
Puerto Rico Islanders ‡	28	11	8	9	32	30	41
Carolina RailHawks ‡	28	10	10	8	44	46	40
Ft Lauderdale Strikers ‡	28	9	9	10	40	46	36
NSC Minnesota Stars ‡	28	8	11	9	34	33	35
Atlanta Silverbacks	28	7	9	12	35	46	30
FC Edmonton	28	5	10	13	26	36	25

8/04/2012 - 24/09/2012 • ‡ Qualified for the play-offs
Top scorers: **20** - Pablo **CAMPOS** BRA, San Antonio • **15** - Nick **ZIMMERMAN**, Carolina • **11** - Mark **ANDERSON** ENG, Fort Lauderdale • **10** - Matt **HORTH**, Atlanta

NASL PLAY-OFFS

Quarter-finals		Semi-finals		Final	
		Tampa Bay	2 3		
Ft Lauderdale	1	Carolina	1 3		
Carolina	3			Tampa Bay	0 3 3p
				Minnesota	2 1 2p
		San Antonio	0 1		
Puerto Rico	1	Minnesota	0 2		
Minnesota	2				

Final 1st leg. NSC, Blaine, 20-10-2012, Att: 4642, Ref: Terry. Scorers - Amani Walker [67], Martin Nunez [90] for Minnesota
2nd leg. Progress Energy Park, St Petersburg, 27-10-2012, Att: 6208, Ref: Mariscal. Scorers - Carl Cort [25], Keith Savage [51], Dan Antoniuk [86] for Tampa Bay; Lucas Rodriguez [52] for Minnesota

USA 2012 USL PRO (3)

	Pl	W	D	L	F	A	Pts
Orlando City ‡	24	17	6	1	50	18	57
Rochester Rhinos ‡	24	12	5	7	27	23	41
Charleston Battery ‡	24	12	2	10	36	26	38
Richmond Kickers ‡	24	11	5	8	31	27	38
Wilmington H'heads ‡	24	10	7	7	34	32	37
Harrisburg City Isl's ‡	24	10	7	7	34	29	37
Charlotte Eagles	24	11	3	10	34	26	36
Los Angeles Blues	24	9	3	12	26	29	30
Dayton Dutch Lions	24	4	10	10	20	29	22
Pittsburgh Riverhounds	24	4	5	15	20	39	17
Antigua Barracuda	24	5	1	18	16	50	16

7/04/2012 - 20/08/2012 • ‡ Qualified for the play-offs
Top scorers: **11** - Dennis **CHIN**, Orlando • **10** - Nicki **PATERSON** SCO, Charleston • **9** - Corey **HERZOG**, Wilmington & Matt **LUZUNARIS**, Orlando • **8** - Andriy **BUDNYY** UKR, Wilmington

USL PRO PLAY-OFFS

Quarter-finals		Semi-finals		Final	
Charleston *	2				
Harrisburg	1	Charleston	1 4p		
		Rochester *	1 3p		
				Charleston *	1
		Orlando City *	3	Wilmington	0
Richmond *	2	Wilmington	4		
Wilmington	3	* Home team			

Final: Blackbaud, Charleston, 8-09-2012, Att: 4963, Ref: Sibiga. Scorer - Michael Azira [74], for Charleston

MEDALS TABLE

		Overall	Lge	Cup	CON'CAF	City
		G S B	G S	G S	G S B	
1	Los Angeles Galaxy	7 7	4 4	2 2	1 1	Carson/Los Angeles
2	DC United	7 3 6	4 1	2 2	1 6	Washington
3	Chicago Fire	5 4 2	1 2	4 2	2	Bridgeview/Chicago
4	Sporting Kansas City	3 1 1	1 1	2	1	Kansas City
5	Seattle Sounders	3 1		3 1		Seattle
6	Columbus Crew	2 2	1	1 2		Columbus
7	Houston Dynamo	2 2 2	2 2		2	Houston
8	San Jose Earthquakes	2	2			Santa Clara/San Jose
9	New England Revolution	1 5	4	1 1		Foxboro/Boston
10	FC Dallas	1 3	1	1 2		Frisco/Dallas
11	Colorado Rapids	1 2	1 1	1		Commerce City/Denver
12	Rochester Raging Rhinos	1 1		1 1		Rochester
13	Real Salt Lake	1 1	1		1	Sandy/Salt Lake
14	New York Red Bulls	2	1	1		New York
15	Charleston Battery	1		1		Charleston
	Miami Fusion	1		1		Fort Lauderdale
17	Toronto FC	1			1	Toronto

The record holders for the US Open Cup are Bethlehem Steel and Maccabi Los Angeles with five titles. Along with Chicago Fire, three other clubs have won it four times - Greek American, Philadelphia Ukrainians and Fall River Marksmen. New York Pancyprian-Freedoms have won it three times.

LAMAR HUNT US OPEN CUP 2012

Third Round		Fourth Round		Quarter-finals		Semi-finals		Final	
Sporting Kansas City*	3	**Sporting Kansas City***	2						
Orlando City	2	Colorado Rapids	0						
Tampa Bay Rowdies*	1			**Sporting Kansas City***	3				
Colorado Rapids	3			Dayton Dutch Lions	0				
Michigan Bucks*	2	**Michigan Bucks***	1						
Chicago Fire	1	**Dayton Dutch Lions**	2			**Sporting Kansas City**	2		
Columbus Crew	1					Philadelphia Union*	0		
Dayton Dutch Lions	2								
Harrisburg City Islanders*	3 4p	**Harrisburg City Islanders***	3						
New England Revs	3 3p	New York Red Bulls	1						
Charleston Battery	0			**Harrisburg City Islanders**	2				
New York Red Bulls	3			**Philadelphia Union***	5				
DC United	2	DC United*	1						
Richmond Kickers	1	**Philadelphia Union**	2						
Rochester Rhinos	0							**Sporting Kansas City** †	1 3p
Philadelphia Union*	3							Seattle Sounders	1 2p
Chivas USA	2	**Chivas USA**	2						
Ventura County Fusion*	0	Carolina RailHawks*	1						
Los Angeles Galaxy	1			**Chivas USA***	2				
Carolina RailHawks	2			Charlotte Eagles	1				
San Antonio Scorpions*	1	San Antonio Scorpions*	1						
Houston Dynamo	0	**Charlotte Eagles**	2						
FC Dallas*	1					Chivas USA	1		
Charlotte Eagles	2					**Seattle Sounders***	4		
San Jose Earthquakes*	2	**San Jose Earthquakes***	1						
Fort Lauderdale Strikers	1	Minnesota Stars	0						
Real Salt Lake	1			San Jose Earthquakes*	0				
Minnesota Stars	3			**Seattle Sounders**	1				
CAL FC	1	CAL FC	0						
Portland Timbers*	0	**Seattle Sounders***	5						
Atlanta Silverbacks	1								
Seattle Sounders*	5								

MLS teams enter in the third round • * Home team • † Qualified for the CONCACAF Champions League

PENALTIES

	Kansas		Seattle
✓	Kamara		
		✓	Evans
✗2	Espinoza		
		✓	Burch
✓	Besler		
		✗1	Alonso
✗1	Zusi		
		✗2	Tiffert
✓	Nagamura		
		✗1	Johnson

1 = missed   2 = saved

CUP FINAL

Livestrong Sporting Park, Kansas City
8-08-2012, Att. 18 873, Ref: Ricardo Salazar
Scorers - Kamara 84o for Kansas;
Scott 86 for Seattle
Kansas - Jimmy Nielsen (c) - Chance Myers, Lawrence Olum, Matt Besler, Seth Sinovic (Michael Harrington 100) - Julio Cesar, Paulo Nagamura - Kei Kamara, Graham Zusi, Roger Espinoza - Teal Bunbury (C. J. Sapong 89). Tr: Peter Vermes
Seattle - Michael Gspurning - Zach Scott●, Patrick Ianni●◆118, Jhon Kennedy Hurtado, Leonardo Gonzalez - Mauro Rosales (c)●, Osvaldo Alonso●, Andy Rose (Brad Evans 59), Alex Caskey (Christian Tiffert 69) - Fredy Montero (Marc Burch 106), Eddie Johnson. Tr: Sigi Schmid

UZB – UZBEKISTAN

FIFA/COCA-COLA WORLD RANKING

'93	'94	'95	'96	'97	'98	'99	'00	'01	'02	'03	'04	'05	'06	'07	'08	'09	'10	'11	'12
-	78	97	109	79	66	55	71	62	98	81	47	59	45	64	72	76	109	75	67

2012												High	Low	Av
Jan	Feb	Mar	Apr	May	Jun	Jul	Aug	Sep	Oct	Nov	Dec			
67	77	67	69	70	66	65	63	70	70	69	67	45	119	75

Uzbekistan's status as the most successful of the former Soviet republics to have joined the Asian Football Confederation was enhanced during 2012 as Mirdjalal Kasimov led the national team to a strong position in the 2014 FIFA World Cup qualifiers as well as taking Bunyodkor to a semi-final in the AFC Champions League. Kasimov, widely regarded as the Uzbekistan's greatest ever player, took over as national team boss from Vadim Abramov in June after Uzbekistan kicked-off the final phase of Asia's World Cup qualifying with a defeat at the hands of Iran. Following Kasimov's return to the national team - he was previously in charge from 2008 to 2010 - Uzbekistan drew with Lebanon and Korea Republic before beating Qatar and Iran, results that put the Uzbeks in a commanding position to qualify for the finals in Brazil. Kasimov has had to juggle national team and club commitments and in 2012 Bunyodkor relinquished their four year grip on the league title to fierce rivals Pakhtakor who finished two points above them in the final standings after a close run race between the two. Bunyodkor did, however, win the Uzbek cup for the third time in five seasons. They beat Pakhtakor in the semi-finals before beating the 2011 AFC Cup winners Nasaf Karshi 3-0 in the final.

FIFA WORLD CUP RECORD
1930-1994 DNE 1998-2010 DNQ

UZBEKISTAN FOOTBALL FEDERATION (UFF)

O'zbekiston Futbol Federatsiyasi,
Uzbekistanskaya 98/A,
100 011 Tashkent
☎ +998 71 2441684
📠 +998 71 2441683
✉ info@the-uff.com
🌐 www.the-uff.com
FA 1946 CON 1994 FIFA 1994
P Mirabror Usmanov
GS Sardor Rakhmatullaev

THE STADIA
2014 FIFA World Cup Stadia

Pakhtakor Markaziy Stadium	
Tashkent	35 000
JAR Stadium	
Tashkent	8 460

Other Main Stadia

Bunyodkor Stadium	
Tashkent	34 000
Metalourg Stadium	
Bekabad	15 000

MAJOR CITIES/TOWNS

		Population
1	Tashkent	2 130 904
2	Namangan	434 388
3	Andijan	370 833
4	Samarkand	349 613
5	Nukus	241 652
6	Karshi	232 654
7	Bukhara	232 574
8	Kukon	207 664
9	Fergana	169 403
10	Margilan	166 868
11	Navoiy	160 302
12	Jizak	149 055
13	Termiz	145 070
14	Urganch	142 347
15	Chirchik	127 966
16	Angren	123 190
17	Olmalik	108 887
18	Denov	108 127
19	Khujayli	107 338

OZBEKISTON RESPUBLIKASI • REPUBLIC OF UZBEKISTAN

Capital	Tashkent	Population	27 606 007 (44)	% in cities	%
GDP per capita	$2600 (171)	Area km²	447 400 km² (56)	GMT +/-	+5
Neighbours (km)	Afghanistan 137, Kazakhstan 2203, Kyrgyzstan 1099, Tajikistan 1161, Turkmenistan 1621				

RECENT INTERNATIONAL MATCHES PLAYED BY UZBEKISTAN

2009	Opponents	Score	Venue	Comp	Scorers	Att	Referee
6-06	Japan	L 0-1	Tashkent	WCq		34 000	Basma SYR
17-06	Bahrain	L 0-1	Manama	WCq		14 100	Moradi IRN
5-09	Iran	D 0-0	Tashkent	Fr		9 500	Irmatov UZB
14-11	Malaysia	W 3-1	Tashkent	ACq	Djeparov [46], Geynrikh 2 [57 65]	5 000	Moradi IRN
18-11	Malaysia	W 3-1	Kuala Lumpur	ACq	Gafurov [32], Nasimov [58], Kapadze [73]	2 000	Tan Hai CHN
2010							
3-03	UAE	L 0-1	Tashkent	ACq		20 000	Shamsuzzaman BAN
25-05	Armenia	L 1-3	Yerevan	Fr	Geynrikh [70]	20 000	Kvaratskhelia GEO
11-08	Albania	L 0-1	Durres	Fr		8 000	Radovanovic MNE
7-09	Estonia	D 3-3	Tallinn	Fr	Shatskikh [40], Geynrikh [55], Salomov [86]	2 055	Jones WAL
9-10	Saudi Arabia	L 0-4	Jeddah	Fr			
12-10	Bahrain	W 4-2	Manama	Fr	Haydarov [5], Navkarov [12], Ahmedov [44], Shatskikh [45]		
25-12	Bahrain	D 1-1	Dubai	Fr	Geynrikh [15]		
2011							
2-01	Jordan	D 2-2	Sharjah	Fr	Hasanov [70], Navkarov [77]		
7-01	Qatar	W 2-0	Doha	ACr1	Ahmedov [59], Djeparov [77]	37 143	Nishimura JPN
12-01	Kuwait	W 2-1	Doha	ACr1	Shatskikh [41], Djeparov [65]	3 481	Shukralla BHR
16-01	China PR	D 2-2	Doha	ACr1	Ahmedov [30], Geynrikh [46]	3 529	Al Hilali OMA
21-01	Jordan	W 2-1	Doha	ACqf	Bakaev 2 [47 49]	16 073	Abdul Bashir SIN
25-01	Australia	L 0-6	Doha	ACsf		24 826	Albadwawi UAE
28-01	Korea Republic	L 2-3	Doha	AC3p	Geynrikh 2 [45p 53]	8 199	Abdul Bashir SIN
25-03	Montenegro	L 0-1	Podgorica	Fr		6 000	Glodovic SRB
1-06	Ukraine	L 0-2	Kyiv	Fr			Ozkahya TUR
5-06	China PR	L 0-1	Kuming	Fr		40 000	Ko Hyung Jin KOR
23-07	Kyrgyzstan	W 4-0	Tashkent	WCq	Geynrikh [28], Bikmaev [48], Djeparov [55], Bakaev [92+]	20 257	Balideh QAT
28-07	Kyrgyzstan	W 3-0	Bishkek	WCq	Karpenko [47], Nasimov 2 [65 90]	14 700	Abdulnabi BHR
2-09	Tajikistan	W 1-0	Tursunzade	WCq	Shatskikh [72]	15 000	Tan Hai CHN
6-09	Japan	D 1-1	Tashkent	WCq	Djeparov [8]	32 000	Al Ghamdi KSA
11-10	Korea DPR	W 1-0	Pyongyang	WCq	Geynrikh [26]	29 000	Faghani IRN
11-11	Korea DPR	W 1-0	Tashkent	WCq	Kapadze [48]	27 525	El Haddad LIB
15-11	Tajikistan	W 3-0	Tashkent	WCq	Tursunov [35], Ahmedov [60], Geynrikh [70]	5 325	Alzarooni UAE
2012							
17-01	Kuwait	L 0-1	Kuwait City	Fr			
29-01	UAE	L 0-1	Dubai	Fr			Al Rawahi OMA
25-02	Korea Republic	L 2-4	Jeonju	Fr	Rahimov [79], Andreev [83p]	28 931	Mahapab THA
29-02	Japan	W 1-0	Toyota	WCq	Shadrin [53]	42 720	Balideh QAT
3-06	Iran	L 0-1	Tashkent	WCq		9 000	Nishimura JPN
8-06	Lebanon	D 1-1	Beirut	WCq	Khasanov [12]	13 000	Al Hilali OMA
13-08	Jordan	W 1-0	Amman	Fr			Tufaylieh SYR
15-08	Jordan	L 0-2	Amman	Fr			Taweel SYR
7-09	Kuwait	W 3-0	Tashkent	Fr	Tursunov [17], Geynrikh 2 [45 49]	30 000	Irmatov UZB
11-09	Korea Republic	D 2-2	Tashkent	WCq	OG [13], Tursunov [59]	33 000	Williams AUS
12-10	UAE	D 2-2	Dubai	Fr	Tursonov [45], Djeparov [67p]		
16-10	Qatar	W 1-0	Doha	WCq	Tursonov [13]	11 260	Tan Hai CHN
14-11	Iran	W 1-0	Tehran	WCq	Bakaev [71]	43 700	Albadwawi UAE

Fr = Friendly match • AC = AFC Asian Cup • WC = FIFA World Cup
q = qualifier • po = play-off • r1 = first round group • qf = quarter-final • po = play-off

UZBEKISTAN NATIONAL TEAM HISTORICAL RECORDS

Caps 89 - Timur Kapadze 2002- • 80 - Server Djeparov 2002- • 68 - Alexander Geynrikh 2002- • 67 - Mirdjalal Kasimov 1992-2005 • 64 - Andrei Fedorov 1994-2006 & Ignaty Nesterov 2002- • 63 - Nikolai Shirshov 1996-2005 & Asror Alikulov 1999-2008 • 59 - Maksim Shatskikh 1999- • 58 - Victor Karpenko 2003- • 54 - Bahtiyor Ashurmatov 1997-2008 • 52 - Fevzi Davletov 1994-2005

Goals 34 - Maksim Shatskikh 1999- • 31 - Mirdjalal Kasimov 1992-2005 • 26 - Alexander Geynrikh 2002- • 20 - Igor Shkvyrin 1992-2000 • 17 - Server Djeparov 2002- • 15 - Jafar Irismetov 1997-2007 • 13 - Nikolai Shirshov 1996-2005

Coaches Makhmud Rahimov 1999-2002 • Viktor Borisov 2000 • Pavel Sadyrin RUS 2000 • Yuri Sarkisyan 2000-04 • Hans-Jurgen Gede GER 2004 • Ravshan Haydarov 2004-05 • Bob Houghton ENG 2005 • Valeri Nepomniachi RUS 2006 • Rauf Inileyev 2007-08 • Mirdjalal Kasimov 2008-10 • Vadim Abramov 2010-12 • Mirdjalal Kasimov 2012-

UZB – UZBEKISTAN

UZBEKISTAN 2012
O'ZBEKISTON CHEMPIONATI OLIY LIGA

	Pl	W	D	L	F	A	Pts	Pakhtakor	Bunyodkor	Lokomotiv	Nasaf	Shurton	Neftchi	Bukhara	Olmalik	Dinamo	Metallurg	Kizilgum	Navbahor	Mashal	Andijan
Pakhtakor Tashkent †	26	18	5	3	51	16	59		1-1	2-1	0-0	0-0	3-0	4-1	0-0	2-0	5-0	4-0	2-1	3-0	1-0
Bunyodkor Tashkent †	26	17	6	3	42	16	57	2-0		1-1	0-0	3-0	2-1	1-0	2-0	2-1	3-1	3-0	1-0	1-0	0-0
Lokomotiv Tashkent †	26	14	7	5	43	22	49	1-1	3-1		0-1	4-1	1-1	2-1	4-2	3-1	5-1	0-1	3-0	1-0	1-1
Nasaf Karshi	26	14	7	5	37	20	49	0-2	0-0	0-2		2-1	1-2	3-0	4-2	2-1	1-0	2-0	1-1	3-0	4-0
Shurton Guzor	26	12	4	10	38	33	40	3-1	0-1	2-1	2-3		2-0	0-1	1-1	1-0	1-2	2-0	4-0	1-0	6-1
Neftchi Fergana	26	10	7	9	36	29	37	3-1	1-2	1-1	0-0	1-1		3-1	4-2	1-0	4-0	3-1	3-0	3-0	2-0
FK Bukhara	26	10	5	11	24	31	35	0-1	0-4	1-1	1-0	0-1	1-1		0-1	2-0	2-0	1-0	2-1	1-1	1-0
Olmalik FK	26	9	4	13	39	46	31	0-3	2-1	1-0	0-1	2-3	0-0	1-3		1-2	3-2	2-2	1-0	4-0	3-2
Samarkand Dinamo	26	9	2	15	27	29	29	0-1	0-1	0-1	0-2	1-0	2-0	0-1	0-1		3-2	3-0	2-0	2-0	3-0
Metallurg Bekobod	26	8	5	13	32	46	29	1-2	1-3	0-1	1-0	4-0	1-1	2-0	4-3	2-1		1-0	0-0	2-1	1-1
Kizilgum Zarafshon	26	6	9	11	22	41	27	0-4	2-2	1-1	1-1	2-0	2-1	1-0	2-1	1-1	0-0		1-1	1-1	1-2
Navbahor Namangan	26	6	8	12	19	34	26	0-1	2-1	0-2	1-2	1-1	1-0	1-1	3-1	1-1	1-0	0-0		2-2	1-0
Mashal Muborak	26	6	5	15	20	43	23	0-3	0-2	1-2	0-0	1-3	3-0	1-1	2-1	2-0	2-1	0-2	2-0		1-0
FK Andijan	26	4	4	18	28	52	16	2-4	0-2	0-1	3-4	1-2	0-1	1-2	1-4	0-3	3-3	5-1	0-1	4-0	

15/03/2012 - 21/11/2012 • † Qualified for the AFC Champions League
Top scorers: **19** - Anvar **BERDIEV**, Neftchi • **14** - Igor **TARAN**, Shurtan • **13** - Temurkhuja **ABDUKHOLIKOV**, Pakhtakor & Vladimir **SHISHELOV**, Andijan/Nasaf • **12** - Zaynitdin **TADJIYEV**, Lokomotiv • **11** - Ruzimboy **AHMEDOV**, Dinamo • **9** - Zakhid **ABDULLAYEV**, Metallurg; Arturas **FOMENKA** LTU, Lokomotiv & Artur **GEWORKYAN** TKM, Nasaf • **8** - Shakzodbek **NURMATOV**, Metallurg

UZBEKISTAN 2012 BIRINCHI LIGA (2)

	Pl	W	D	L	F	A	Pts
Sogdiana Jizak	30	22	1	7	71	40	67
Guliston	30	20	5	5	69	41	65
NBU Osiyo Tashkent	30	16	8	6	50	33	56
Yangiyer	30	16	5	9	56	28	53
Nasaf Karshi-2	30	15	3	12	68	47	48
Yuzhanin	30	14	5	11	40	35	47
Horezm Urganch	30	13	6	11	41	35	45
Oktepa	30	15	0	15	67	62	45
Kokand 1912	30	12	8	10	45	43	44
Xiva	30	11	3	16	40	51	36
Neftchi Hamza	30	10	4	16	45	61	34
Registan	30	10	3	17	41	48	33
Dinamo Gallakor	30	10	2	18	39	62	32
FK Bukhara-2	30	9	4	17	39	61	31
Kosonsoy Zakovat	30	8	3	19	37	62	27
Chust-Pakhtakor	30	7	4	19	23	62	25

9/08/2012 - 29/10/2012

MEDALS TABLE

	Overall			League			Cup		Asia		
	G	S	B	G	S	B	G	S	G	S	B
1 Pakhtakor Tashkent	20	7	3	9	5	1	11	2			2
2 Neftchi Fergana	7	14	2	5	9	1	2	5			1
3 Bunyodkor Tashkent	7	4	2	4	2		3	2			2
4 Navbahor Namangan	4	1	8	1		8	3	1			
5 Dustlik Tashkent	3			2			1				
6 Nasaf Karshi	1	4	6				1	6	3	1	
7 MHSK Tashkent	1	2	1	1	1	1		1			
8 Mashal Muborak		2	1				1	1			
9 Nurafshon Bukhara			1				1				
Samarkand Dinamo			1								1
Shurton Guzor			1								1
Temirulchi Kukon			1								1
13 Traktor Tashkent			1					1			
FK Yangier			1					1			
15 Kizilgum Zarafshon		1						1			
Sogdiana Jizak		1						1			

UZBEKISTAN CUP 2012

Second Round			Quarter-finals			Semi-finals			Final	
Bunyodkor Tashkent	2	1								
Shurton Guzor	0	0	**Bunyodkor Tashkent** *	3	0					
Kizilgum Zarafshon	1	0	Mashal Muborak	0	0					
Mashal Muborak *	2	2				**Bunyodkor Tashkent** *	1	3		
FK Andijan *	3	1				Pakhtakor Tashkent	1	1		
Olmalik FK	1	2	FK Andijan *	1	0					
Navbahor Namangan *	1	1	**Pakhtakor Tashkent**	2	2					
Pakhtakor Tashkent	2	1							**Bunyodkor Tashkent**	3
FK Bukhara	2	0							Nasaf Karshi	0
Samarkand Dinamo *	1	0	**FK Bukhara** *	2	0	7p				
Neftchi Fergana	1	3	Lokomotiv Tashkent	0	2	6p				
Lokomotiv Tashkent *	2	2				FK Bukhara	0	3		
Metallurg Bekobod *	3	3				**Nasaf Karshi** *	2	3		
Sogdiana Jizak	1	2	Metallurg Bekobod *	2	2					
Guliston	1	0	**Nasaf Karshi**	1	4					
Nasaf Karshi *	6	2				* Home team/Home team in the first leg				

CUP FINAL
Pakhtakor, Tashkent, 30-11-2012
Att: 5270, Ref: Irmatov
Scorers - Shavkat Salomov [10], Kamoliddin Murzoev [34], Victor Karpenko [45] for Bunyodkor

VAN – VANUATU

FIFA/COCA-COLA WORLD RANKING

'93	'94	'95	'96	'97	'98	'99	'00	'01	'02	'03	'04	'05	'06	'07	'08	'09	'10	'11	'12
164	172	179	180	186	177	184	167	168	156	160	143	146	167	140	141	155	167	174	165

2012

Jan	Feb	Mar	Apr	May	Jun	Jul	Aug	Sep	Oct	Nov	Dec	High	Low	Av
174	173	172	172	172	171	168	156	167	172	174	165	131	188	164

2012 saw the Vanuatu national team back in FIFA World Cup qualifying action thanks to their performance at the 2011 Pacific Games which meant they qualified for the 2012 OFC Nations Cup in the Solomon Islands, a tournament that doubled up as a first round of qualifying for Brazil. With the team capable of upsetting the odds there were high hopes of a top two finish in the group which would not only see them through to the semi-finals of the Nations Cup but also to the last four of World Cup qualifying in Oceania. They were never really in the running, however, and although they could have overtaken Tahiti in the final game they needed to win by a substantial margin to qualify on goal difference and in the event bowed out after losing 4-1. At home Amicale made it a hat trick of championships after a close battle with Tafea in the Port Vila league early in 2012 and they went on to claim the national title as well in mid-year. By the end of the year Amicale had claimed a fourth consecutive Port Vila title, this time after a close battle with Erakor Golden Star with the once invincible Tafea finishing back in third place. That was the first time Tafea had finished outside of the top two since their record-breaking run of 15 consecutive titles began way back in 1993.

FIFA WORLD CUP RECORD
1930-1990 DNE 1994-2010 DNQ

VANUATU FOOTBALL FEDERATION (VFF)

VFF House, Anabrou,
PO Box 266,
Port Vila
☎ +678 27239
📠 +678 25236
✉ lambertmatlock@yahoo.com
🌐 www.vanuafoot.vu
FA 1934 CON 1988 FIFA 1988
P Lambert Maltock
GS TBC

THE STADIA
2014 FIFA World Cup Stadia
Vanuatu played their matches at the Lawson Tama stadium in Honiara in the Solomon Islands

Main Stadia	
Korman Stadium	
Port Vila	2 000

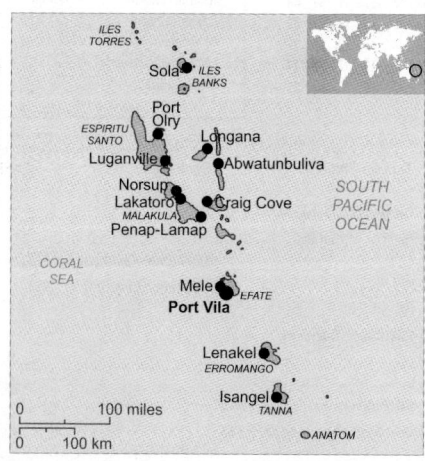

MAJOR CITIES/TOWNS

		Population
1	Port Vila	47 510
2	Luganville	13 800
3	Port Olry	2 897
4	Mele	2 484
5	Norsup	2 374
6	Isangel	1 695
7	Lenakel	1 473
8	Palikulo	1 450
9	Litslits	1 346
10	Lakatoro	1 247
11	Penap-Lamap	1 236
12	Leviamp	1 180
13	Hog Harbour	1 174
14	Abwatunbuliva	1 071
15	Sola	1 065
16	Craig Cove	1 063
17	Longana	648

RIPABLIK BLONG VANUATU • REPUBLIC OF VANUATU

Capital	Port Vila	Population	218 519 (185)	% in cities	25%
GDP per capita	$4600 (144)	Area km²	12 189 km² (163)	GMT +/-	+11
Neighbours (km)	Coast 2528				

RECENT INTERNATIONAL MATCHES PLAYED BY VANUATU

2011	Opponents	Score	Venue	Comp	Scorers	Att	Referee
24-01	New Caledonia	D 0-0	Port Vila	Fr			
7-07	Solomon Islands	L 1-2	Honiara	Fr	Michel [89]		
9-07	Solomon Islands	D 0-0	Honiara	Fr			
13-07	Fiji	L 0-2	Labasa	Fr			
15-07	Fiji	W 2-1	Lautoka	Fr	August [7], Tasso [21]		
27-07	Solomon Islands	D 0-0	Port Vila	Fr			
30-07	Solomon Islands	W 2-0	Port Vila	Fr	August [52], Tangis [76]		
27-08	New Caledonia	L 0-5	Noumea	PGr1			Achari FIJ
30-08	Tuvalu †	W 5-1	Noumea	PGr1	Kaltak.J 4 [8 38 45 80], Yelou [49p]		Varman FIJ
1-09	Solomon Islands	W 1-0	Noumea	PGr1	Kaltak.J [92+]		Zitouni TAH
3-09	Guam	W 4-1	Noumea	PGr1	Tangis [50], Tasso [53], Kaltak.J [75], Tari [82]		Kerr NZL
5-09	American Samoa	W 8-0	Noumea	PGr1	Michel 2 [8 22], Garae [43], Kaltak.J 3 [62 70 78], Kaltak.M [64], Aala [73]		Achari FIJ
2012							
1-06	New Caledonia	L 2-5	Honiara	OCr1	Tasso [52], Naprapol [61]	7 000	O'Leary NZL
3-06	Samoa	W 5-0	Honiara	OCr1	Naprapol [29], Kaltack.B [45], Malas [47], Tasso [74], Vava [93+]	2 200	O'Leary NZL
5-06	Tahiti	L 1-4	Honiara	OCr1	Tasso [95+]	1 000	O'Leary NZL

Fr = Friendly match • WC = FIFA World Cup • PG = Pacific Games • † Not a full international

VANUATU 2011–12
PVFA LIK PREMIA DIVISEN

	Pl	W	D	L	F	A	Pts	Amicale	Tafea	Shepherds	Tupuji	Seveners	Spirit 08	Ifira	Teouma
Amicale ‡	14	12	1	1	50	4	37		1-2	1-0	5-0	2-0	4-1	2-0	6-1
Tafea ‡	14	11	0	3	35	8	33	0-1		0-2	4-0	3-1	2-1	4-0	2-1
Shepherds United ‡	14	7	2	5	25	24	23	0-8	0-2		2-2	3-0	1-3	2-1	2-0
Tupuji Imere ‡	14	5	3	6	14	27	18	0-7	0-1	1-1		1-2	2-1	0-1	2-0
Seveners United ‡	14	4	4	6	15	24	16	0-3	1-0	3-6	2-2		0-0	3-1	1-1
Spirit 08	14	4	3	7	18	20	15	0-0	0-3	2-1	0-1	0-1		2-2	4-0
Ifira Black Bird	14	3	1	10	13	40	10	0-6	0-7	**1-3**	1-2	1-0	0-3		2-6
Teouma Academy	14	2	2	10	13	36	8	0-4	0-5	0-2	0-1	1-1	3-1	0-3	

29/09/2011 - 12/04/2012 • ‡ Qualified for the National Soccer League

VANUATU 2012 NATIONAL SOCCER LEAGUE

	Pl	W	D	L	F	A	Pts
Amicale †	8	6	1	1	20	3	19
Tafea	8	4	3	1	16	6	15
Shepherds United	8	2	3	3	9	17	9
Tupuji Imere	8	2	2	4	6	10	8
Seveners United	8	1	1	6	5	20	4

† Qualified for the OFC Champions League

MEDALS TABLE

	Overall G	Lge G	Nat G	Cup
1 Tafea	17	15		2
2 Amicale	7	4	3	
3 Port Vila Sharks	1			1
4 Pango Green Bird	1	1		

VANUATU 2011–12
PVFA LIK PREMIA DIVISEN

	Pl	W	D	L	F	A	Pts	Amicale	Tafea	Shepherds	Tupuji	Seveners	Spirit 08	Ifira	Teouma
Amicale ‡	14	12	1	1	50	4	37		1-2	1-0	5-0	2-0	4-1	2-0	6-1
Tafea ‡	14	11	0	3	35	8	33	0-1		0-2	4-0	3-1	2-1	4-0	2-1
Shepherds United ‡	14	7	2	5	25	24	23	0-8	0-2		2-2	3-0	1-3	2-1	2-0
Tupuji Imere ‡	14	5	3	6	14	27	18	0-7	0-1	1-1		1-2	2-1	0-1	2-0
Seveners United ‡	14	4	4	6	15	24	16	0-3	1-0	3-6	2-2		0-0	3-1	1-1
Spirit 08	14	4	3	7	18	20	15	0-0	0-3	2-1	0-1	0-1		2-2	4-0
Ifira Black Bird	14	3	1	10	13	40	10	0-6	0-7	**1-3**	1-2	1-0	0-3		2-6
Teouma Academy	14	2	2	10	13	36	8	0-4	0-5	0-2	0-1	1-1	3-1	0-3	

29/09/2011 - 12/04/2012 • ‡ Qualified for the National Soccer League

VEN – VENEZUELA

FIFA/COCA-COLA WORLD RANKING

'93	'94	'95	'96	'97	'98	'99	'00	'01	'02	'03	'04	'05	'06	'07	'08	'09	'10	'11	'12
93	110	127	111	115	129	110	111	81	69	57	62	67	73	62	65	50	60	39	57

2012

Jan	Feb	Mar	Apr	May	Jun	Jul	Aug	Sep	Oct	Nov	Dec	High	Low	Av
41	46	46	43	43	40	47	52	52	39	48	57	39	129	83

With five potential places in the 2014 FIFA World Cup up for grabs for the nine South American hopefuls, there was a genuine belief in Venezuela that this tournament could mark a breakthrough for the national team and at the end of 2012 'La Vinotinto' stood in fourth place with half of the games played in group. Consistency does however remain a problem for coach Cesar Farias. The team is capable of beating leaders Argentina one day but then losing to lowly Peru the next and that could prove to be their downfall as they seek to secure a place in the finals in neighbouring Brazil. At home, there was no need for the season finale championship play-off when for the first time in seven seasons the apertura and clausura were both won by the same team. Deportivo Lara lost just once all season on their way to the 2012 title, a 1-0 defeat at Deportivo Anzoategui which also ended a record-breaking run of 28 games without defeat in the league. It was the first time since 1965 that a team from Barquisimeto - Venezuela's fourth largest city - had won the title although the Lara that won the title that year are not related to the 2012 champions - who were formed in 2009. Deportivo Anzoategui were the season's other winners, beating Estudiantes de Merida 2-1 on aggregate in the cup final to win the trophy for the second time.

COPA AMERICA RECORD

1916-1963 DNE **1967** 5/6 **1975** 10/10 r1 **1979** 10/10 r1 **1983** 10/10 r1 **1987** 10/10 r1 **1989** 10/10 r1 **1991** 10/10 r1 **1993** 11/12 r1 **1995** 12/12 r1 **1997** 12/12 r1 **1999** 12/12 r1 **2001** 11/12 r1 **2004** 11/12 r1 **2007** 6/12 QF (Hosts) **2011** 4/12 SF

FEDERACION VENEZOLANA DE FUTBOL (FVF)

Avda. Santos Erminy, 1a Calle las Delicias Torre Mega II, Sabana Grande, Caracas 1050
☎ +58 212 7624472
📠 +58 212 7620596
✉ sec_presidencia_fvf@cantv.net

FA 1926 CON 1965 FIFA 1952
P Rafael Esquivel
GS Serafin Boutureira

THE STADIA

2014 FIFA World Cup Stadia
Polideportivo de Pueblo Nuevo
San Cristobal — 42 500
General Jose Antonio Anzoategui
Puerto La Cruz — 41 000

Other Main Stadia
Estadio Monumental
Maturin — 52 000
Estadio Metropolitano de Futbol
Barquisimeto — 40 312

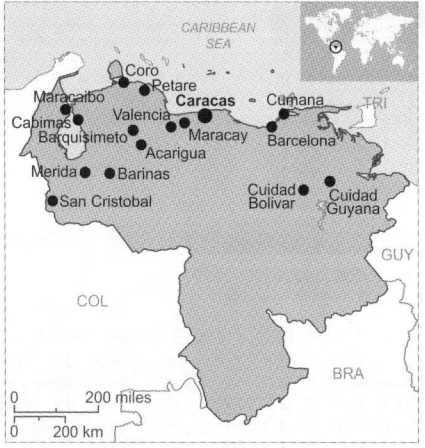

MAJOR CITIES/TOWNS

		Population
1	Maracaibo	2 637 443
2	Caracas	1 966 466
3	Valencia	1 855 268
4	Barquisimeto	1 157 843
5	Ciudad Guayana	1 019 336
6	Maracay	628 194
7	Barcelona	621 131
8	Maturín	593 285
9	Petare	568 325
10	Ciudad Bolívar	480 077
11	Turmero	455 679
12	Barinas	428 395
13	Puerto la Cruz	372 800
14	San Cristóbal	364 743
15	Cabimas	351 804
16	Cumaná	333 364
17	Santa Teresa	313 960
18	Mérida	311 314
19	Acarigua	222 321

REPUBLICA BOLIVARIANA DE VENEZUELA • BOLIVARIAN REPUBLIC OF VENEZUELA

Capital Caracas   Population 26 814 843 (45)   % in cities 93%
GDP per capita $13 500 (84)   Area km² 912 050 km² (33)   GMT +/- -4
Neighbours (km) Brazil 2200, Colombia 2050, Guyana 743 • Coast 2800

VEN – VENEZUELA

RECENT INTERNATIONAL MATCHES PLAYED BY VENEZUELA

2010	Opponents	Score	Venue	Comp	Scorers	Att	Referee
11-08	Panama	L 1-3	Panama City	Fr	Vizcarrondo [70]	2 000	Quesada CRC
3-09	Colombia	L 0-2	Puerto La Cruz	Fr		30 000	Moreno PAN
7-09	Ecuador	W 1-0	Barquisimeto	Fr	Fedor [86]	37 262	Torres PAN
7-10	Bolivia	W 3-1	Santa Cruz	Fr	Chourio 2 [10 37], Vizcarrondo [28]	35 000	Chaibou NIG
12-10	Mexico	D 2-2	Juarez	Fr	Arango 2 [6 40]	20 000	Aguilar SLV
17-11	Ecuador	L 1-4	Quito	Fr	Maldonado [49p]	9 000	Chaibou NIG
2011							
9-02	Costa Rica	D 2-2	Puerto La Cruz	Fr	Rondon 2 [24 81]	15 000	Gambeta PER
16-03	Argentina	L 1-4	San Juan	Fr	Arismendi [29]	25 000	Puga CHI
25-03	Jamaica	W 2-0	Montego Bay	Fr	Fedor [64], Moreno [67]	6 000	Wijngaarde SUR
29-03	Mexico	D 1-1	San Diego	Fr	Vizcarrondo [73]	60 808	Salazar USA
1-06	Guatemala	W 2-0	Guatemala City	Fr	Fedor [26], Perozo [67]	13 000	Ruano SLV
7-06	Spain	L 0-3	Puerto La Cruz	Fr		36 000	Buckley PER
3-07	Brazil	D 0-0	La Plata	CAr1		35 000	Orozco BOL
9-07	Ecuador	W 1-0	Salta	CAr1	Cesar Gonzalez [62]	12 000	Quesada CRC
13-07	Paraguay	D 3-3	Salta	CAr1	Rondon [5], Fedor [89], Perozo [92+]	18 000	Osses CHI
17-07	Chile	W 2-1	San Juan	CAqf	Vizcarrondo [34], Cuchero [80]	23 000	Vera ECU
20-07	Paraguay	D 0-0	Mendoza	CAsf	L 3-5p	8 000	Chacon MEX
23-07	Peru	L 1-4	La Plata	CA3p	Arango [77]	20 000	Roldan COL
7-08	El Salvador	L 1-2	Washington DC	Fr	Aristeguieta [29]	25 000	Toledo USA
10-08	Honduras	L 0-2	Fort Lauderdale	Fr		20 000	Vaughn USA
2-09	Argentina	L 0-1	Calcutta	Fr		90 000	Rowan IND
6-09	Guinea	W 2-1	Caracas	Fr	Maldonado 2 [25p 39p]	14 000	Gambetta PER
7-10	Ecuador	L 0-2	Quito	WCq		32 278	Osses CHI
11-10	Argentina	W 1-0	Puerto La Cruz	WCq	Amorebieta [62]	35 600	Silvera URU
11-11	Colombia	D 1-1	Barranquilla	WCq	Feltscher [78]	43 953	Ponce ECU
15-11	Bolivia	W 1-0	San Cristobal	WCq	Vizcarrondo [25]	33 351	Buckley PER
22-12	Costa Rica	L 0-2	Barquisimeto	Fr		33 000	Angela USA
2012							
21-01	USA	L 0-1	Glendale	Fr		22 403	Garcia MEX
25-01	Mexico	L 1-3	Houston	Fr	Greco [51]	40 128	Jurisevic USA
29-02	Spain	L 0-5	Malaga	Fr		25 000	Treimanis LVA
23-05	Moldova	W 4-0	Puerto Ordaz	Fr	Seijas [45], Rondon 2 [50 72], Vizcarrondo [54]	20 000	Gambetta PER
2-06	Uruguay	D 1-1	Montevideo	WCq	Rondon [84]	57 000	Arias PAR
9-06	Chile	L 0-2	Puerto La Cruz	WCq		35 000	Buitrago COL
15-08	Japan	D 1-1	Sapporo	Fr	Miku [62]	39 396	Lee Min Hu KOR
7-09	Peru	L 1-2	Lima	WCq	Arango [42]	34 703	Vazquez URU
11-09	Paraguay	W 2-0	Asuncion	WCq	Rondon 2 [45 67]	13 680	Osses CHI
16-10	Ecuador	D 1-1	Puerto La Cruz	WCq	Arango [5]	35 076	Pitana ARG
14-11	Nigeria	L 1-3	Miami	Fr	Feltscher [70]	13 500	Vaughn USA

Fr = Friendly match • CA = Copa América • WC = FIFA World Cup • q = qualifier

VENEZUELA NATIONAL TEAM HISTORICAL RECORDS

Caps 115 - Jose Manuel Rey 1997- • 110 - Juan Arango 1999- • 91 - Jorge Rojas 1999-2009 • 85 - Miguel Mea Vitali 1999- • 77 - Gabriel Urdaneta 1996-2005 & Luis Vallenilla 1996-2007 • 66 - Renny Vega 1999- • 65 - Ruberth Moran 1996-2007 & Giancarlo Maldonado 2003- • 64 - Leopoldo Jimenez 1999-2005 & Ricardo Paez 2000-07 • 58 - Leonel Vielma 2000-07 • 57 - Rafael Dudamel 1993-2007

Goals 22 - Giancarlo Maldonado 2003- • 21 - Juan Arango 1999- • 14 - Ruberth Moran 1996-2007 • 11 - Jose Manuel Rey 1997- & Daniel Arismendi 2006- • 10 - Jose Rondon 2008- & Miku 2006- • 9 - Gabriel Urdaneta 1996-2005 & Nicolas Fedor 2006-

Coaches Vittorio Godigna ITA 1938 • Alvaro Cartea 1947-48 • Orlando Fantoni BRA 1956 • Rafael Franco ARG 1965-69 • Gregorio Gomez ARG 1969-72 • Walter Roque 1975 • Dan Georgiadis GRE 1975-77 • Jose Hernandez 1979 • Walter Roque 1979-85 • Rafael Santana 1987 • Luis Mendoza 1989 • Carlos Moreno ARG 1989 • Victor Pignanelli 1991 • Ratomir Dujkovic SRB 1992-95 • Lino Alonso 1995 • Rafael Santana 1996 • Eduardo Borrero COL 1997 • Omar Pastoriza ARG 1999-2001 • Richard Paez 2001-07 • Cesar Farias 2007-

VENEZUELA 2011-12
PRIMERA DIVISION
TORNEO APERTURA 2011

	Pl	W	D	L	F	A	Pts
Deportivo Lara †	17	12	5	0	39	12	41
Caracas FC	17	11	3	3	27	13	36
Deportivo Petare	17	10	5	2	28	15	35
Deportivo Anzoátegui	17	9	3	5	16	11	30
Mineros de Guayana	17	8	4	5	21	21	28
Zulia FC	17	7	6	4	28	20	27
Yaracuyanos FC	17	6	6	5	24	17	24
Zamora FC	17	5	8	4	23	19	23
Aragua FC	17	5	8	4	15	19	23
Monagas SC	17	6	3	8	20	23	21
Trujillanos FC	17	5	5	7	22	21	20
Real Esppor	17	5	5	7	18	23	20
Deportivo Táchira	17	5	5	7	14	21	20
Atlético El Vigía	17	4	5	8	17	25	17
Tucanes de Amazonas	17	3	4	10	21	30	13
Llaneros Guanare	17	2	7	8	18	28	13
Estudiantes Mérida	17	1	8	8	15	37	11
Carabobo FC §1	17	1	6	10	17	27	8

8/08/2011-18/12/2011 • † Qualified for the final

VENEZUELA 2011-12
PRIMERA DIVISION
TORNEO CLAUSURA 2012

	Pl	W	D	L	F	A	Pts
Deportivo Lara	17	13	3	1	32	12	42
Mineros de Guayana	17	9	7	1	29	14	34
Deportivo Anzoátegui	17	9	5	3	21	10	32
Caracas FC	17	8	4	5	23	20	28
Llaneros Guanare	17	7	5	5	17	14	26
Zamora FC	17	7	4	6	23	23	25
Zulia FC	17	8	1	8	13	13	25
Trujillanos FC	17	5	8	4	17	16	23
Aragua FC	17	5	6	6	16	17	21
Carabobo FC	17	5	6	6	14	15	21
Deportivo Táchira	17	5	5	7	18	19	20
Monagas SC	17	5	5	7	14	15	20
Yaracuyanos FC	17	5	5	7	18	20	20
Estudiantes Mérida	17	4	7	6	17	19	19
Real Esppor	17	4	6	7	9	14	18
Deportivo Petare	17	3	7	7	16	22	16
Atlético El Vigía	17	4	4	9	11	24	16
Tucanes de Amazonas	17	2	2	13	15	36	8

14/01/2012-13/05/2012 • † Qualified for the final

Deportivo Lara won both the Apertura and Clausura and so were declared champions

VENEZUELA 2011-12
AGGREGATE TABLE

	Pl	W	D	L	F	A	Pts	Dep. Lara	Caracas	Dep. Anzoátegui	Mineros	Zulia	Dep. Petare	Zamora	Yaracuyanos	Aragua	Trujillanos	Monagas	Dep. Táchira	Llaneros	Real Esppor	Atlético El Vigía	Estudiantes	Carabobo	Tucanes
Deportivo Lara † ‡	34	25	8	1	71	24	83		0-0	0-0	5-1	1-0	2-1	4-0	1-0	1-1	1-1	2-1	3-1	1-0	4-0	3-0	3-1	2-0	6-1
Caracas FC †	34	19	7	8	50	33	64	2-3		0-0	4-0	2-1	1-4	1-0	2-0	2-1	1-0	2-1	1-1	1-0	2-0	2-1	2-1	2-1	3-0
Deportivo Anzoátegui †	34	18	8	8	37	21	62	1-0	1-0		0-1	3-2	1-3	1-0	2-1	0-1	2-1	2-0	2-1	1-0	0-0	2-1	3-1	0-0	6-1
Mineros de Guayana †	34	17	10	7	50	37	61	0-1	1-1	2-0		0-2	0-1	3-1	1-1	2-2	2-0	3-1	2-0	2-1	1-0	4-1	1-0	2-0	1-1
Zulia FC	34	16	6	12	42	33	54	1-2	2-0	1-0	1-0		0-1	1-0	2-0	1-3	1-0	1-0	1-1	3-3	1-1	1-0	1-0	3-1	3-2
Deportivo Petare	34	13	12	9	44	37	51	3-4	1-0	0-1	2-4	1-2		2-2	1-0	1-0	2-2	1-1	1-0	0-0	0-0	0-0	1-1	2-1	1-0
Zamora FC	34	12	12	10	46	41	48	1-3	0-0	1-0	1-2	1-1	1-2		1-2	2-2	3-1	1-0	1-1	0-0	4-0	3-0	3-2	2-1	2-2
Yaracuyanos FC	34	11	11	12	42	37	44	0-2	3-3	1-0	2-2	1-2	0-2	0-0		1-0	0-0	1-0	2-0	4-0	1-2	2-0	5-1	3-2	2-3
Aragua FC	34	10	14	10	31	36	44	1-1	0-0	0-2	1-0	1-4	0-0	2-1	0-3		2-0	0-2	1-0	2-1	1-1	3-2	0-0	0-0	1-1
Trujillanos FC	34	10	13	11	39	37	43	1-3	2-1	0-0	1-1	1-0	0-0	1-3	2-2	2-1		2-0	1-1	4-0	0-2	3-0	2-0	1-1	2-0
Monagas SC	34	11	8	15	34	37	41	0-2	2-0	1-1	0-1	1-0	2-0	0-0	0-0	1-1		3-0	1-1	1-0	2-1	3-2	2-0	3-2
Deportivo Táchira	34	10	10	14	32	40	40	1-1	2-1	0-2	1-2	1-0	3-3	0-0	1-1	2-0	2-0	1-0		3-1	0-1	0-0	3-0	2-1	1-0
Llaneros Guanare	34	9	12	13	35	42	39	1-2	1-2	0-1	1-1	1-0	1-0	2-2	2-1	0-0	1-1	1-1	3-0		2-0	2-0	1-1	1-0	2-1
Real Esppor	34	9	11	14	27	37	38	0-0	0-1	1-1	0-1	1-0	0-3	1-2	2-0	1-1	1-1	2-0	2-0	3-2		0-0	0-0	0-2	3-1
Atlético El Vigía	34	8	9	17	28	49	33	0-2	2-3	1-0	1-2	1-1	2-1	1-2	1-1	2-1	0-2	0-0	2-1	1-0		1-1	1-0	1-1
Estudiantes Mérida	34	5	15	14	32	56	30	1-2	0-2	0-0	1-1	2-2	1-1	1-1	1-0	1-1	1-0	0-0	2-1	1-2	0-5	1-0		2-2	2-0
Carabobo FC §1	34	6	12	16	31	42	29	2-3	1-2	0-1	2-2	0-1	2-0	0-0	1-1	1-1	1-2	1-0	0-0	2-0	1-1	2-2		1-0
Tucanes de Amazonas	34	5	6	23	36	66	21	1-1	1-4	0-1	1-2	0-2	1-3	0-1	0-1	1-3	3-1	1-2	1-1	2-0	1-1	2-0	1-5	1-0	

8/08/2011 - 13/05/2012 • † Qualified for the Copa Libertadores • ‡ Qualified for the Copa Sudamericana • Attendance: 1,631,472 @ 5,366
Apertura matches in shaded boxes • § = points deducted
Top scorers: **20** - Rafael **CASTELLIN**, Deportivo Lara • **14** - Richard **BLANCO**, Deportivo Petare • **13** - Heiber **DIAZ**, Carabobo • **12** - Victor **RENTERIA** COL, Tucanes • **11** - Alexander **RONDON**, Aragua & Fernando **ARISTEGUIETA**, Caracas

COPA VENEZUELA 2012

Round of 16

Deportivo Anzoátegui	2 2 6p
Aragua FC *	2 2 5p
Deportivo Petare *	1 0
Atlético Venezuela	2 2
Caracas FC	0 0 4p
Mineros de Guayana *	0 0 3p
Angostura FC *	1 0
Real Esppor	3 6
Zamora FC	1 3
Yaracuyanos FC *	1 1
Deportivo Táchira	0 1
Trujillanos FC *	0 1
SC Guaraní *	0 2
Atlético El Vigía	1 1
Deportivo Lara *	1 2
Estudiantes Mérida	2 5

Quarter-finals

Deportivo Anzoátegui *	3 0
Atlético Venezuela	1 1
Caracas FC *	0 1 2p
Real Esppor	1 0 3p
Zamora FC	2 2
Trujillanos FC *	1 1
SC Guaraní *	0 2
Estudiantes Mérida	1 4

Semi-finals

Deportivo Anzoátegui	0 3
Real Esppor *	0 1
Zamora FC *	2 0
Estudiantes Mérida	3 1

Final

Deportivo Anzoátegui *	1 1
Estudiantes Mérida	1 0

CUP FINAL
1st leg. 21-11-2012
2nd leg. 29-11-2012

* Home team in the 1st leg • ‡ Qualified for the Copa Sudamericana

COPA VENEZUELA FINAL 2012
Estadio José Antonio Anzoátegui, Puerto La Cruz
21-011-2012, Att: 2250, Ref: Maron Escalante

Deportivo Anzoátegui 1 Fuenmayor [52]
Estudiantes Mérida 1 Marquez [77]

Anzoátegui - Leonardo Morales - Carlos Lopez, Carlos Rivero•, Carlos Salazar, Juan Fuenmayor - Rolando Escobar (Robert Hernandez 89), Robert Garces, Evelio Hernandez, David Zalzman (Jose Boggio 68) - Jose Reyes, Gelmin Rivas (Jeremias Caggiano 89). Tr: Daniel Farias
Estudiantes - Angel Hernandez - Carlos De Castro, Elvis Martinez, Francisco Pineda, Henry Plazas - Christian Flores (Jesus Quintero 78), Yorwin Lobo, Nicolas Nunez (Javier Guillen 87), Anyelo Rodriguez• - Nicolas Marquez (Francisco La Mantia 90), Pierre Pluchino. Tr: Jose Vera

COPA VENEZUELA FINAL 2012
Estadio Metropolitano, Mérida
28-11-2012, Att: 30 258, Ref: Jesus Valenzuela

Estudiantes Mérida 0
Deportivo Anzoátegui 1 Evelio Hernandez [17p]

Estudiantes - Angel Hernandez - Carlos De Castro, Elvis Martinez, Francisco Pineda (Javier Guillen 77), Henry Plazas - Christian Flores, Yorwin Lobo, Nicolas Nunez, Anyelo Rodriguez• - Nicolas Marquez•, Pierre Pluchino. Tr: Jose Vera
Anzoátegui - Leonardo Morales - Carlos Lopez•, Carlos Rivero, Carlos Salazar, Juan Fuenmayor - Francisco Flores, Evelio Hernandez•, Robert Hernandez (Rolando Escobar 63), Jose Boggio - Jose Reyes• (Manuel Cuarez 77), Gelmin Rivas (Jeremias Caggiano 69). Tr: Daniel Farias

MEDALS TABLE

		Overall	Lge	Cup	Sth Am	
		G S B	G B	G B	G S B	City
1	Caracas FC	16 5 1	11 3	5 2	1	Caracas
2	Deportivo Galicia	9 6	4 5	5 1		Caracas
3	Deportivo Tachira	8 9	7 8	1 1		San Cristobal
4	Deportivo Petare (ex Italia)	8 8	5 7	3 1		Caracas
5	Portuguesa FC	8 4 1	5 3	3 1	1	Acarígua
6	Unión SC	7 3	7 3			Caracas
7	Dos Caminos SC	6 8	6 7	1		Caracas
8	Deportivo Portugués	6 3	4 2	2 1		Caracas
9	CS Maritimo	6 1	4 1	2		Caracas
10	Estudiantes Merida	5 10	2 7	3 3		Merida
11	Centro Atlético	4 7	4 7			Caracas
12	Loyola SC	4 5	4 5			Caracas
13	Universidad de Los Andes	4 2 1	3 1	1 1	1	Merida
14	Deportivo Venezuela	4	4			Caracas
15	Valencia	3 5	1 2	2 3		Valencia
16	Unión Deportivo Canarias	3 3	1	2 3		Caracas
	Universidad Central	3 3	3 3			Caracas
18	Mineros de Guayana	3 1	1 1	2		Puerto Ordaz
19	Trujillanos	2 5		2 2 3		Valera
20	La Salle	2 4	2 4			Caracas
	Deportivo Español	2 4	2 3	1		Caracas
22	Zamora FC	2 2		1 2 1		Barinas
23	América	2 1	2 1			
24	Deportivo Anzoátegui	2		2		Puerto La Cruz
25	Minervén	1 5	1 3	2		Puerto Ordaz
26	Litoral	1 4	1 4			
	Unión Atlético Maracaibo	1 4	1 3	1		Maracaibo

VGB – BRITISH VIRGIN ISLANDS

FIFA/COCA-COLA WORLD RANKING

'93	'94	'95	'96	'97	'98	'99	'00	'01	'02	'03	'04	'05	'06	'07	'08	'09	'10	'11	'12
-	-	-	-	180	187	161	172	163	161	175	165	171	190	192	180	191	176	199	191

2012

	Jan	Feb	Mar	Apr	May	Jun	Jul	Aug	Sep	Oct	Nov	Dec		High	Low	Av
	198	198	197	199	199	200	199	191	189	195	197	191		160	200	176

A 1-0 victory in a friendly match against Anguilla spared the British Virgin Islands the indignity of ending the year at the bottom of the FIFA/Coca-Cola World Ranking but it barely rescued the reputation of a team that clearly struggles even amongst the smallest islands of the Caribbean. For the third time in three years the BVI shipped double figures in a Caribbean Cup qualifier. This time it was against Martinique who won 16-0 at home in Lamentin, with 11 of the goals coming in the second half. Coach Avondale Williams will be thankful that the result will not go down in the official record thanks to Martinique not being members of FIFA. That was scant consolation, however, for the disaster that occurred in the final of the three group matches - a 7-0 thrashing at the hands of Montserrat. Perhaps the result should not have been unexpected but to lose so heavily to a team traditionally regarded as the weakest in world football was very embarrassing for the BVI. As one of the few nations not to have benefitted from the FIFA Goal programme, perhaps it is time that the BVIFA asked for some assistance. In club football, Islanders secured a league and cup double in May 2012, relegating One Love United to the runners-up spot in both tournaments although they did get their revenge in the final of the 2012 Terry Evans Knock-Out Cup later on in the year.

FIFA WORLD CUP RECORD
1930-1998 DNE **2002-2014** DNQ

BRITISH VIRGIN ISLANDS FOOTBALL ASSOCIATION (BVIFA)

	Botanic Station, Road Town, PO Box 4269, Tortola VG 1110
☎	+1 284 4945655
📠	+1 284 4948968
@	bvifa@surfbvi.com
🖥	bvifootballassociation.com
FA	1974 CON 1996 FIFA 1996
P	Andrew Bickerton
GS	Alfred Reid

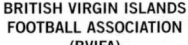

MAJOR TOWNS

Tortola
Road Town (9 467)
Virgin Gorda
Spanish Town
Anegada
The Settlement
Jost Van Dyke
Great Harbour

THE STADIA

2014 FIFA World Cup Stadia
AO Shirley Recreational Field
Road Town, Tortola   3 000

Other Main Stadia
There are no other stadia in the British Virgin Islands

BRITISH VIRGIN ISLANDS

Capital	Road Town	Population	24 491 (215)	% in cities 40%
GDP per capita	$38 500 (23)	Area km²	151 km² (219)	GMT +/- -4
Neighbours (km)	Coast 80		

RECENT INTERNATIONAL MATCHES PLAYED BY THE BRITISH VIRGIN ISLANDS

2008	Opponents	Score	Venue	Comp	Scorers	Att	Referee
26-03	Bahamas	D 1-1	Nassau	WCq	Rohan Lennon [68]	450	Moreno PAN
30-03	Bahamas	D 2-2	Nassau	WCq	Avondale Williams 2 [72 90p]	940	Suazo DOM
24-09	St Kitts and Nevis	L 0-4	Basseterre	CCq		500	Charles DMA
26-09	Barbados	L 1-2	Basseterre	CCq	Rohan Lennon [23]	150	Baptiste DMA
2009							
5-12	Dominica	L 0-4	Roseau	Fr		600	Baptiste DMA
2010							
25-09	Anguilla	W 2-1	Saint-Martin	Fr	Henroy Mitchell 2 [5 8]	100	
14-10	Dominican Republic	L 0-17	San Cristobal	CCq		200	Lebron PUR
15-10	Dominica	L 0-10	San Cristobal	CCq		200	Santos PUR
2011							
3-07	US Virgin Islands	L 0-2	Charlotte Amalie	WCq		350	Navarro CAN
10-07	US Virgin Islands	L 1-2	Tortola	WCq	Trevor Peters [38]	600	Morrison JAM
2012							
7-07	Anguilla	W 1-0	Road Town	Fr	Carlos Septus [60]	150	Willett ATG
5-09	Martinique †	L 0-16	Le Lamentin	CCq		800	Santos PUR
7-09	Suriname	L 0-4	Riviere-Pilote	CCq		200	Anderson PUR
9-09	Montserrat	L 0-7	Fort-de-France	CCq		120	Anderson PUR

Fr = Friendly match • CC = Digicel Caribbean Cup • WC = FIFA World Cup • q = qualifier • † Not a full international

BRITISH VIRGIN ISLANDS 2012

BVIFA FOOTBALL LEAGUE

	Pl	W	D	L	F	A	Pts	Islanders	One Love	Sugar Boys	Wolues	Lucian Stars	VG United	VG Ballstars	Old Madrid	Panthers	Haitian Stars
Islanders	18	17	0	1			51		4-0	3-1		2-0	3-0	14-0	8-1	5-0	3-0
One Love United	17	11	4	2			37	3-2		4-3	0-0		1-1	2-1	5-0		7-0
Sugar Boys	17	11	2	4			35	0-4			1-0		2-3	3-2		1-0	8-1
Wolues	17	9	3	5			30	1-4	1-1			5-2	1-1	6-1	3-0	4-1	5-1
St Lucian Stars	17	7	0	10			21	1-5	0-2	0-4	1-2				12-1	3-0	10-0
Virgin Gorda United	18	6	2	10			20		2-4	0-2	0-2	6-0		2-6		3-0	7-1
Virgin Gorda Ballstars	18	5	3	10			18		1-2	4-5		0-2	3-1		1-1		3-0
Old Madrid	18	5	3	10			18			1-6	2-0	5-1	0-2	0-0			5-0
HBA Panthers	18	5	2	11			17	0-3	0-3	1-0	1-2	3-4	3-0	2-2	1-0		11-1
Haitian Stars	18	0	1	17			1	1-3		0-6	0-2			1-3			

27/11/2011 - 13/05/2012

HEINEKEN CHALLENGE CUP 2012

Semi-finals		Finals	
Islanders	1 5p		
Sugar Boys	1 4p		
		Islanders	4
		One Love United	0
Wolues	0		19-05-2012
One Love United	3		

WENDOL WILLIAMS KNOCK-OUT CUP 2011

Quarter-finals		Semi-finals		Final	
Virgin Gorda Ballstars					
One Love United		**Virgin Gorda Ballstars**			
Wolues					
Islanders		Islanders		**Virgin Gorda Ballstars**	4
Virgin Gorda United	3			HBA Panthers	0
Haitian Stars	0	Virgin Gorda United			
Old Madrid	2 2p	**HBA Panthers**		16-10-2011	
HBA Panthers	2 4p				

VIE – VIETNAM

FIFA/COCA-COLA WORLD RANKING

'93	'94	'95	'96	'97	'98	'99	'00	'01	'02	'03	'04	'05	'06	'07	'08	'09	'10	'11	'12
135	151	122	99	104	98	102	99	105	108	98	103	120	172	142	155	123	137	99	131

2012

Jan	Feb	Mar	Apr	May	Jun	Jul	Aug	Sep	Oct	Nov	Dec	High	Low	Av
101	100	98	97	97	98	120	146	146	140	138	131	84	172	118

Phan Thanh Hung's Vietnam national team were desperately disappointing at the 2012 AFF Suzuki Cup after failing to progress beyond the group stage for the first time since 2004 and for only the second time ever. A draw with Myanmar in their opening game in Bangkok was followed by defeats at the hands of the Philippines and Thailand, which means the Vietnamese will have to go through the indignity of attempting to qualify for the finals via the preliminary rounds for the next tournament in 2014. It's a far cry from five years ago when football in the country seemed to be on the threshold of a breakthrough with a quarter-final appearance in the 2007 AFC Asian Cup and victory in the 2008 AFF Suzuki Cup. Vietnamese clubs also find themselves relegated to the second tier AFC Cup after a short spell in the Champions League and both Song Nam Nghe An and Navibank Saigon failed to get beyond the group stage of the 2012 tournament. At home Da Nang won a very closely-fought race in the league to win the championship for a second time after leapfrogging both Saigon FC and Hanoi T&T who held each other to a draw on the final day of the season. The two also met in the cup final ten days later when Saigon FC beat their rivals from Hanoi in convincing fashion with a 4-1 victory to secure their first-ever trophy.

FIFA WORLD CUP RECORD
1930-1970 DNE 1974 DNQ 1978-1990 DNE 1994-2014 DNQ

VIETNAM FOOTBALL FEDERATION (VFF)

National Youth Football Training Centre,
Le Quang Dao Str, My Dinh,
Tu Liem, 844 Hanoi
☎ +84 4 37344456
📠 +84 4 38233119
✉ vietnamff@gmail.com
🖥 www.vff.org.vn
FA 1962 CON 1954 FIFA 1964
P Nguyen Trong Hy
GS Le Bang Ngo

THE STADIA

2014 FIFA World Cup Stadia	
My Dinh National Stadium Hanoi	40 192
Other Main Stadia	
San Chi Lang Da Nang	28 000
Lach Tray Hai Phong	26 000
Thong Nhat Ho Chi Minh City	25 000

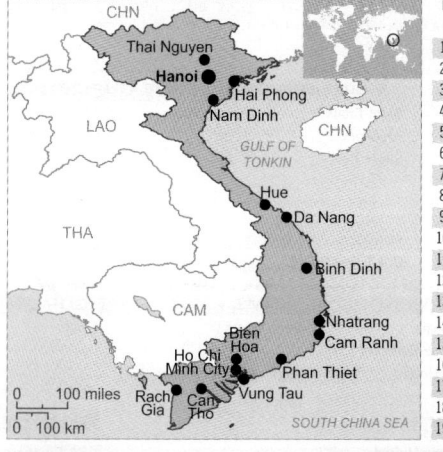

MAJOR CITIES/TOWNS

		Population
1	Ho Chi Minh City	3 873 661
2	Hanoi	1 491 404
3	Hai Phong	635 820
4	Da Nang	490 700
5	Bien Hoa	446 476
6	Hue	305 721
7	Nhatrang	304 167
8	Can Tho	270 754
9	Rach Gia	267 561
10	Vung Tau	235 642
11	Binh Dinh	224 336
12	Nam Dinh	200 516
13	Phan Thiet	169 992
14	Long Xuyen	164 659
15	Buon Ma Thuot	160 360
16	Cam Ranh	155 748
17	Ha Long	155 006
18	Cam Pha	154 894
19	Thai Nguyen	138 555

CONG HOA XA HOI CHU NGHIA VIET NAM • SOCIALIST REPUBLIC OF VIETNAM

Capital	Hanoi	Population	86 967 524 (13)	% in cities	28%
GDP per capita	$2800 (168)	Area km²	331 210 km² (65)	GMT +/-	+7

Neighbours (km) Cambodia 1228, China 1281, Laos 2130 • Coast 3444

VIE – VIETNAM

RECENT INTERNATIONAL MATCHES PLAYED BY VIETNAM

2009	Opponents	Score	Venue	Comp	Scorers	Att	Referee
14-01	Lebanon	W 3-1	Hanoi	ACq	Nguyen Minh Phuong [11], Le Cong Vinh [30], Nguyen Vu Phong [69]	13 000	Toma JPN
21-01	China PR	L 1-6	Zheijang	ACq		15 300	Kim Dong Jin KOR
31-05	Kuwait	W 1-0	Kuwait City	Fr	Nguyen Trong Hoang [36]		
20-10	Turkmenistan	W 1-0	Ho Chi Minh City	Fr	Nguyen Quang Hai [58]		
24-10	Singapore	D 2-2	Ho Chi Minh City	Fr	Nguyen Quang Hai [18], Vu Nhu Thanh [85p]		
14-11	Syria	L 0-1	Hanoi	ACq		30 000	Williams AUS
18-11	Syria	D 0-0	Aleppo	ACq		19 000	Al Hilali OMA
2010							
6-01	Lebanon	D 1-1	Saida	ACq	Pham Thanh Luong [39]	50	Kovalenko UZB
17-01	China PR	L 1-2	Hanoi	ACq	Le Cong Vinh [76p]	3 000	Abdul Bashir SIN
24-09	Korea DPR	D 0-0	Hanoi	Fr			
8-10	India	L 1-3	Pune	Fr	Vu Nhu Thanh [62]		
12-10	Kuwait	L 1-3	Kuwait City	Fr	Nguyen Minh Phuong [57]		
4-11	Singapore	D 1-1	Hanoi	Fr	Phan Van Tai Em [76]		
6-11	Korea DPR	L 0-2	Hanoi	Fr			
2-12	Myanmar	W 7-1	Hanoi	AFFr1	Nguyen Minh Phuong [30], Nguyen Anh Duc 2 [13 56], Le Tan Tai [51], Nguyen Trong Hoang 2 [13 56], Nguyen Vu Phong [94+]	40 000	Patwal IND
5-12	Philippines	L 0-2	Hanoi	AFFr1		40 000	Napitupulu IDN
8-12	Singapore	W 1-0	Hanoi	AFFr1	Nguyen Vu Phong [32]	40 000	Mahaprab THA
15-12	Malaysia	L 0-2	Kuala Lumpur	AFFsf		45 000	Sun Baojie CHN
18-12	Malaysia	D 0-0	Hanoi	AFFsf		40 000	Kim Sang Woo KOR
2011							
29-06	Macau	W 6-0	Ho Chi Minh City	WCq	Le Cong Vinh 3 [20 36 42], Phan Thanh Phan [62], Nguyen Ngoc Thanh [67], Nguyen Van Quyet [89]	20 000	Mashentsev KGZ
3-07	Macau	W 7-1	Macau	WCq	Huynh Quang Thanh 2 [2 86], Nguyen Quang Hai [23], Le Cong Vinh 4 [29 42 74 82]	500	Auda IRQ
23-07	Qatar	L 0-3	Doha	WCq		6 786	Albadwawi UAE
28-07	Qatar	W 2-1	Hanoi	WCq	Nguyen Trong Hoang [50], Nguyen Quang Hai [23]	20 000	Green AUS
7-10	Japan	L 0-1	Kobe	Fr		27 522	Mahapab THA
2012							
8-06	China PR	L 0-3	Wuhan	Fr			Ko Hyung Jin KOR
10-06	Hong Kong	W 2-1	Hong Kong	Fr	Nguyen Trong Hoang [71], Nguyen Quang Hai [74]	2 983	
23-06	Mozambique	W 1-0	Ho Chi Minh City	Fr	OG [62]		
11-09	Malaysia	W 2-0	Kuala Lumpur	Fr	Le Cong Vinh [32], Huynh Thanh Quang [49]		
15-09	Indonesia	D 0-0	Surabaya	Fr			
16-10	Indonesia	D 0-0	Hanoi	Fr			
24-10	Turkmenistan	L 0-1	Ho Chi Minh City	Fr		20 000	Mat Karim MAS
26-10	Laos	W 4-0	Ho Chi Minh City	Fr	Nguyen Quang Hai 2 [17 37p], Nguyen Trong Hoang [77], Huynh Quoc Anh [80]		Ramachandran MAS
3-11	Malaysia	W 1-0	Hanoi	Fr	Nguyen Trong Hoang [74]		Vo Minh Tri VIE
24-11	Myanmar	D 1-1	Bangkok	AFFr1	Tan Tai Le [34]	2 312	El Haddad LIB
27-11	Philippines	L 0-1	Bangkok	AFFr1		6 801	Ma Ning CHN
30-11	Thailand	L 1-3	Bangkok	AFFr1	Nguyen Van Quyet [72]	13 196	Sato JPN

Fr = Friendly match • AFF = ASEAN Football Federation Championship • AC = AFC Asian Cup • WC = FIFA World Cup
q = qualifier • r1 = first round group • sf = semi-final • 3p = third place play-off

VIETNAM NATIONAL TEAM HISTORICAL RECORDS

Caps
73 - Nguyen Minh Phuong 2002-10

Goals
31 - Le Cong Vinh 2004- • **30** - Le Huynh Duc 1995-2004

Coaches
Tran Duy Long 1995 • Edson Tavares BRA 1995 • Karl-Heinz Weigang GER 1995-97 • Colin Murphy ENG 1997 • Alfred Riedl AUT 1998-2001 • Henrique Calisto 2002 • Alfred Riedl AUT 2003 • Edson Tavares BRA 2004 • Tran Van Khanh 2004 • Alfred Riedl AUT 2006-07 • Henrique Calisto POR 2008-11 • Mai Duc Chung 2011 • Falko Gotz 2011 • Phan Thanh Hung 2012 • Hoang Van Phuc 2013-

EXIMBANK V-LEAGUE — VIETNAM 2012

	Pl	W	D	L	F	A	Pts	Da Nang	T&T Hanoi	Saigon FC	SLNA	HAGL	Binh Duong	Navibank	Ninh Binh	Hanoi	Khanh Hoa	Than Hoa	Kien Giang	Dong Thap	Hai Phong
Da Nang †	26	14	6	6	47	31	48		2-0	2-1	1-1	4-1	1-0	0-0	3-0	2-1	3-2	1-0	2-2	0-1	2-1
T&T Hanoi	26	13	8	5	43	35	47	2-1		1-0	2-6	1-3	1-0	3-1	2-3	3-1	1-1	3-2	2-1	1-1	2-1
Saigon FC †	26	12	10	4	43	23	46	2-1	0-0		2-2	1-1	0-1	1-1	4-1	2-0	2-1	0-0	1-0	3-1	4-0
Song Lam Nghe An	26	9	14	3	44	30	41	0-4	2-2	1-1		2-0	1-1	1-1	5-3	2-0	3-1	0-0	2-2	0-0	5-2
Hoang Anh Gia Lai	26	11	6	9	33	33	39	2-0	0-0	0-3	2-2		2-0	0-2	2-1	2-1	0-0	2-0	3-0	1-0	3-1
Binh Duong	26	10	6	10	32	31	36	1-2	1-3	1-1	0-0	1-2		1-1	3-1	3-1	0-2	4-1	2-0	1-0	5-3
Navibank Saigon	26	8	11	7	32	30	35	3-1	2-0	2-2	1-1	0-0	0-1		1-2	4-1	1-0	2-0	3-1	0-0	2-2
Ninh Binh	26	10	3	13	40	49	33	1-3	2-2	2-0	0-2	2-1	1-2	1-2		2-3	3-1	1-0	4-1	2-2	2-0
Hanoi FC	26	9	5	12	46	47	32	3-3	0-1	0-1	0-0	3-2	4-1	1-1	1-2		4-1	3-1	1-3	2-1	5-0
Khanh Hoa	26	9	5	12	33	34	32	1-2	1-1	2-2	1-0	3-0	1-1	3-0	4-0	1-2		0-1	1-0	1-0	1-0
Than Hoa	26	9	5	12	32	36	32	0-0	2-4	1-1	2-0	2-1	2-1	2-0	1-0	3-5	1-2		2-1	4-0	3-0
Kien Giang	26	9	5	12	30	39	32	2-1	1-1	0-2	0-3	2-3	1-0	2-0	0-0	2-1	1-0	0-0		0-2	1-0
Dong Thap	26	7	9	10	32	38	30	3-3	1-3	0-4	0-1	0-0	0-0	3-1	4-1	2-2	3-1	3-2	1-3		3-0
Hai Phong	26	3	5	18	27	59	14	2-3	0-2	2-3	2-2	2-0	0-1	1-1	0-3	1-1	3-1	2-0	1-3	1-1	

31/12/2011 - 19/08/2012 • † Qualified for the AFC Cup

Top scorers: **17** - Timothy **ANJEMBE** NGA, Hanoi • **16** - Gaston **MERLO** ARG, Da Nang • **14** - Samson **KAYODE** NGA, T&T Hanoi; Christian **AMOUGOU** CMR, Saigon; **KESLEY ALVES** BRA/VIE, Saigon & Felix **AJALA** NGA, Dong Thap • **12** - **NGUYEN** Van Quyet, T&T Hanoi & Moussa **SANOGO** CIV, Ninh Binh

VIETNAM 2011 SECOND DIVISION

	Pl	W	D	L	F	A	Pts
Dong Tam Long An	26	15	4	7	36	26	49
T&T Hanoi II	26	15	3	8	35	+5	48
Dong Nai	26	11	7	8	40	+10	40
Than Quang Ninh	26	10	9	7	37	+9	39
Can Tho	26	10	9	7	37	+7	39
Binh Dinh	26	9	11	6	40	+6	38
Da Nang II	26	10	7	9	42	+3	37
Lam Dong	26	9	6	11	28	-8	33
An Giang	26	8	8	10	30	+1	32
Quang Nam	26	7	10	9	27	-5	31
Hanoi FC II	26	8	5	13	34	+0	29
Binh Duong II	26	7	8	11	27	-10	29
Tay Ninh	26	8	5	13	28	-10	29
Ho Chi Minh City	26	5	8	13	36	-18	23

30/12/2011 - 19/08/2012

MEDALS TABLE

	Overall			League			Cup		Asia		
	G	S	B	G	S	B	G	S	G	S	B
1 Cang Saigon	6	3	3	4		3	2	3			
2 The Cong Hanoi	5	5	6	5	2	6		3			
3 Song Lam Nghe An	5	4	2	3	3	2	2	1			
4 Cong An Thanh Pho	3	5	2	1	3	2	2	2			
5 Dong Tam Long An	3	4	1	2	3	1	1	1			
6 Binh Duong	3	3	2	2	2	1	1	1			1
Hai Quan	3	3	2	1	2	2	2	1			
8 Da Nang	3	1	1	2	1	1	1				
9 Quang Nam Da Nang	2	2	1	1	2						1
10 Hoang Anh Gia Lai	2	1	1	2		1		1			
Binh Dinh	2	1	1			1	2	1			
12 Hanoi ACB	2	1		1			1	1			
13 Dong Thap	2		1	2		1					
14 Hai Phong	1	4	2		3	2	1	1			
15 Cong An Hanoi	1	3	2	1	1	2		2			
16 Hanoi T&T	1	3		1	2		1				
17 Nam Dinh	1	2	1		2	1	1	1			
18 Saigon FC	1		1				1	1			

VIETNAM CUP 2012

Round of 16		Quarter-finals		Semi-finals		Final	
Saigon FC *	3						
Khanh Hoa	2	Saigon FC *	3				
Can Tho *	1	Than Hoa	1				
Than Hoa	3			Saigon FC	3		
Ninh Binh *	2			Song Lam Nghe An *	1		
Hanoi FC	1	Ninh Binh	3 4p				
Dong Thap	1	Song Lam Nghe An *	3 5p				
Song Lam Nghe An *	2					Saigon FC †	4
Da Nang	1 3p					T&T Hanoi	1
Lam Dong *	1 1p	Da Nang *	3				
Hoang Anh Gia Lai	1	Kien Giang	0				
Kien Giang *	2			Da Nang	0		
Binh Dinh	4			T&T Hanoi *	1		
Navibank Saigon *	3	Binh Dinh *	1				
Hai Phong	0	T&T Hanoi	3				
T&T Hanoi *	2						

* Home team • † Qualified for the AFC Cup

CUP FINAL

Thong Nhat Stadium, Ho Chi Minh
29-08-2012, 12 000, Vo Quang Vinh
Scorers - Kesley Alves [11], Carlos [35], Hai Anh [76], Rogerio [91+] for Saigon; Marronkle [52] for T&T Hanoi

VIN – ST VINCENT AND THE GRENADINES

FIFA/COCA-COLA WORLD RANKING

'93	'94	'95	'96	'97	'98	'99	'00	'01	'02	'03	'04	'05	'06	'07	'08	'09	'10	'11	'12
129	144	95	93	122	138	141	127	125	144	169	137	130	85	101	133	152	142	144	125

2012

Jan	Feb	Mar	Apr	May	Jun	Jul	Aug	Sep	Oct	Nov	Dec	High	Low	Av
144	145	146	147	146	147	146	145	143	136	143	126	125	73	170	132

Vincey Heat continued to make their presence felt in international football in the Caribbean after making it through to the second round of qualifying for the 2012 Caribbean Cup - the fourth time in five tournaments that they have made it through the first stage. A strong programme of friendlies gave the team plenty of preparation for their first round group in St Lucia and they were rewarded with excellent victories over both Guyana and Curacao with Myron Samuel and Cornelius Stewart scoring five goals between them. For their second round group they travelled to Tobago and looked to be on the verge of making it through to the finals in Antigua after having held both hosts Trinidad and Cuba to commendable draws. That meant a win in their third match against Suriname - potentially the weakest of their three opponents - would see them through to the finals for only the second time in sixteen years. Instead Vincey Heat lost 1-0, a result that allowed Trinidad and Cuba to progress and eventually contest the final itself. In club football Avenues United won the National Club Championship in 2012 to complete a hat trick of titles although the club game continues to struggle to get national attention with local leagues, spread around the 32 islands and Cays, remaining the main focus of the game.

CFU CARIBBEAN CUP RECORD

1989 6 r1 **1991** DNE **1992** 8 r1 **1993** 6 r1 **1994** DNQ **1995** 2 F **1996** 7 r1 **1997-2005** DNQ **2007** 7 r1 **2008-2012** DNQ

SAINT VINCENT AND THE GRENADINES FOOTBALL FEDERATION (SVGFF)

Nichols Building (2nd Floor), Bentinck Square, Victoria Park, PO Box 1278, Kingstown
☎ +1 784 4561092
📠 +1 784 4572913
✉ svgfootball@vincysurf.com
🌐 www.svgff.com
FA 1979 CON 1988 FIFA 1988
P Venold Coombs
GS Trevor Huggins

THE STADIA
2014 FIFA World Cup Stadia
Arnos Vale Sporting Complex
Kingstown 18 000
Other Main Stadia
Victoria Park
Kingstown 3 500

MAJOR CITIES/TOWNS
		Population
1	Kingstown	16 532
2	Georgetown	1 443
3	Byera	1 173
4	Biabou	902
5	Port Elizabeth	766
6	Chateaubelair	631
7	Calliaqua	608
8	Hamilton	575
9	Dovers	479

SAINT VINCENT AND THE GRENADINES

Capital	Kingstown	Population	104 574 (192)	% in cities	47%
GDP per capita	$10 200 (103)	Area km²	389 km² (202)	GMT +/-	-4
Neighbours (km)	Coast 84				

RECENT INTERNATIONAL MATCHES PLAYED BY ST VINCENT AND THE GRENADINES

2008	Opponents		Score	Venue	Comp	Scorers	Att	Referee
13-01	Guyana	L	0-1	Blairmont	Fr		1 300	James GUY
27-01	Guyana	D	2-2	Kingstown	Fr	Randolph Williams [6], George Emerald [80]	2 000	Cambridge VIN
10-02	Grenada	L	1-2	Kingstown	Fr	Alwyn Guy [49]	1 000	Cambridge VIN
13-03	Barbados	L	0-2	Kingstown	Fr		1 050	Cambridge VIN
3-06	Jamaica	L	1-5	Kingston	Fr	Marlon James [56]	20 000	Whittaker CAY
7-06	Cuba	L	0-1	Havana	Fr		400	Duran CUB
15-06	Canada	L	0-3	Kingstown	WCq		5 000	Batres GUA
20-06	Canada	L	1-4	Montreal	WCq	Marlon James [75]	11 500	Aguilar SLV
15-09	Martinique †	L	0-3	Fort de France	CCq		250	George LCA
17-09	Anguilla	W	3-1	Fort de France	CCq	Theon Gordon [35], Darren Hammlet [39], Myron Samuel [80]	100	Fanus LCA
2009								
5-09	St Kitts and Nevis	L	0-3	Kingstown	Fr		3 500	Cambridge VIN
20-09	St Kitts and Nevis	D	1-1	Basseterre	Fr	Wendell Cuffy [47]	1 600	Matthew SKN
2010								
10-09	St Lucia	W	5-1	Vieux Fort	Fr	Norrel George [19], Myron Samuel 2 [21 43], Romano Snagg [57], Wendell Cuffy [72]	400	St Catherine LCA
17-09	Grenada	L	0-1	Kingstown	Fr		350	Gurley VIN
19-09	Grenada	D	0-0	Kingstown	Fr		350	Cambridhe VIN
6-10	Montserrat	W	7-0	Kingstown	CCq	Shandel Samuel 3 [25p 26 66], Damon Francis [56], Cornelius Stewart [63], Chad Balcombe [70], Romano Snagg [89]	5 000	Pinas SUR
8-10	St Kitts and Nevis	D	1-1	Kingstown	CCq	Keith James [73]	1 600	Jauregui ANT
10-10	Barbados	D	0-0	Kingstown	CCq		5 420	Jauregui ANT
2-11	Trinidad and Tobago	L	2-6	Marabella	CCq	Shandel Samuel [28], Cornelius Stewart [45]	1 100	Peterkin JAM
4-11	Haiti	L	1-3	Port of Spain	CCq	Shandel Samuel [64]	1 100	Campbell JAM
6-11	Guyana	L	0-2	Port of Spain	CCq		850	Taylor BRB
2011								
27-05	Barbados	D	0-0	Bridgetown	Fr		3 500	Skeete BRB
26-08	Antigua and Barbuda	L	0-1	St John's	Fr		2 000	Willett ATG
28-08	Antigua and Barbuda	D	2-2	St John's	Fr	Reginald Richardson [21], Shandel Samuel [54p]	2 500	Charles ATG
2-09	Guatemala	L	0-4	Guatemala City	WCq		24 000	Andino HON
11-09	Dominica	W	1-0	Kingstown	Fr	Akeeno Hazelwood [21]	2 500	Cambridge VIN
18-09	Grenada	W	2-1	Kingstown	WCq	Myron Samuel [22], Cornelius Stewart [72]	2 500	Ward CAN
7-10	Guatemala	L	0-3	Kingstown	WCq		3 000	Brea CUB
15-10	Grenada	D	1-1	St George's	WCq	Myron Samuel [22]	2 000	Willett ATG
11-11	Belize	D	1-1	Belmopan	WCq	Cornelius Stewart [11]	300	Skeete BRB
15-11	Belize	L	0-2	Kingstown	WCq		500	Thomas JAM
2012								
19-02	Guyana	W	1-0	Kingstown	Fr	Wendell Cuffy [7]	1 100	Bedeau GRN
30-03	Antigua and Barbuda	W	1-0	Kingstown	Fr	Shandel Samuel [54]	300	Clarke LCA
1-04	Antigua and Barbuda	L	1-2	Kingstown	Fr	Shandel Samuel [56p]	250	Brizan TRI
1-09	Barbados	W	2-0	Kingstown	Fr	Myron Samuel [9], Cornelius Stewart [87]	200	Delves VIN
2-09	Barbados	D	1-1	Kingstown	Fr	Cornelius Stewart [7]	500	Cambridge VIN
21-10	Guyana	W	2-1	Gros Islet	CCq	Myron Samuel [30], Cornelius Stewart [79]	1 200	Pinas SUR
23-10	St Lucia	L	0-1	Gros Islet	CCq		1 652	Vazquez DOM
25-10	Curacao	W	4-0	Gros Islet	CCq	Cornelius Stewart 2 [8 76], Dorren Hamlet [58], Myron Samuel [78]	852	Vazquez DOM
14-11	Trinidad and Tobago	D	1-1	Scarborough	CCq	Myron Samuel [24]	800	Campbell JAM
16-11	Cuba	D	1-1	Scarborough	CCq	Cornelius Stewart [8]	300	Taylor BRB
18-11	Suriname	L	0-1	Scarborough	CCq		200	Georges HAI

Fr = Friendly match • CC = Digicel Caribbean Cup • WC = FIFA World Cup • q = qualifier • r1 = first round group • † Not a full international

ST VINCENT AND THE GRENADINES NATIONAL TEAM HISTORICAL RECORDS

Past Coaches: Jorge Ramos BRA 1992 • Lenny Taylor JAM 1995-96 • Bertile St Clair ATG 1996 • Lenny Taylor JAM 2000-01 • Elvis Brown JAM 2002 • Adrian Shaw ENG 2003 • Zoran Vranes SRB 2004-07 • Roger Gurley 2008 • Stewart Hall 2009 • Samuel Carrington 2010 • Colwyn Rowe ENG 2011 • Cornelius Huggins 2012-

VIR – US VIRGIN ISLANDS

FIFA/COCA-COLA WORLD RANKING

'93	'94	'95	'96	'97	'98	'99	'00	'01	'02	'03	'04	'05	'06	'07	'08	'09	'10	'11	'12
-	-	-	-	-	-	194	198	198	197	199	196	196	198	201	195	199	200	178	186

2012												High	Low	Av
Jan	Feb	Mar	Apr	May	Jun	Jul	Aug	Sep	Oct	Nov	Dec			
178	180	180	183	182	182	177	178	178	179	190	186	149	202	194

The US Virgin Islands declined to enter the 2012 Caribbean Cup, a decision which left the national team without any fixtures for the year and unable to build on the valuable experience gained in 2011 which had seen eight FIFA World Cup qualifiers played, including the two historic wins over neighbours British Virgin Islands. It was also a decision that saw the team head back down the FIFA Coca-Cola World Ranking from an unprecedented high of 149 in mid-2011 to more familiar territory at the end of 2012. The World Cup experience did, however, give football a higher profile in the country and fans were treated to a full season of club football on both Saint Croix and Saint Thomas along with the return, after an absence of two years, of the Association Club Championship. The Saint Croix title was won by Helenites and along with Rovers they qualified for the play-offs for the national title. They were joined by Saint Thomas champions New Vibes along with runners-up Togetherness in the four-team tournament at the Lionel Roberts Stadium in Charlotte Amalie. Fittingly, both champions met in the final and they produced a thriller with Helenites and New Vibes drawing 3-3. Player of the tournament Jonah Lesmond was the hero with a hat trick as his side went on to claim the title 5-4 on penalties.

CFU CARIBBEAN CUP RECORD
1989-1998 DNE **1999-2007** DNQ **2008-2012** DNE

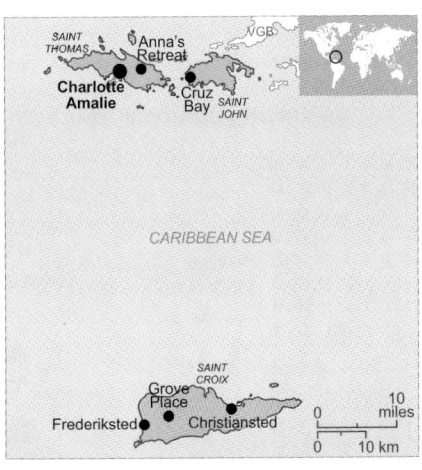

U.S.V.I. SOCCER FEDERATION INC. (USVISA)
498D Strawberry,
PO Box 2346,
00851 Christiansted,
St Croix
☎ +1 340 7199707
📠 +1 340 7199709
✉ usvisoccer@gmail.com
FA 1992 CON 1998 FIFA 1998
P Hillaren Frederick
GS Chantel Bird

MAJOR TOWNS
Saint Thomas
Charlotte Amalie (17 420)
Anna's Retreat (7 369)
Saint John
Cruz Bay (3 059)
Saint Croix
Frederiksted (3 036)
Grove Place (2 911)
Christiansted (2 691)

THE STADIA
2014 FIFA World Cup Stadia
Lionel Roberts Stadium	
Charlotte Amalie	9 000
Paul E. Joseph Stadium	
Frederiksted	5 000
Other Main Stadia
| Football Park | |
| Christiansted | 2 100 |

UNITED STATES VIRGIN ISLANDS
Capital	Charlotte Amalie	Population	109 825 (190)	% in cities	95%
GDP per capita	$14 500 (78)	Area km²	1910 km² (181)	GMT +/-	-4
Neighbours (km)	Coast 188				

RECENT INTERNATIONAL MATCHES PLAYED BY THE US VIRGIN ISLANDS

2004	Opponents	Score		Venue	Comp	Scorers	Att	Referee
30-01	British Virgin Islands	L	0-5	Road Town	Fr		350	Charles DMA
31-01	Dominica	L	0-5	Road Town	Fr		550	Matthew SKN
18-02	St Kitts and Nevis	L	0-4	Charlotte Amalie	WCq		225	Brizan TRI
31-03	St Kitts and Nevis	L	0-7	Basseterre	WCq		800	Recinos SLV
25-09	British Virgin Islands	L	1-2	Road Town	Fr	Shane Challenger 65	300	Frederick VIR
24-11	Haiti	L	0-11	Kingston	CCq		250	Piper TRI
26-11	Jamaica	L	1-11	Kingston	CCq	Victor Lauro 72	4 200	Piper TRI
28-11	St Martin †	D	0-0	Kingston	CCq		200	Brizan TRI

2005

No international matches played in 2005

2006

| 27-09 | Bermuda | L | 0-6 | Charlotte Amalie | CCq | | 150 | Small BRB |
| 1-10 | Dominican Republic | L | 1-6 | Charlotte Amalie | CCq | Bryce Pierre 7 | 250 | Davis TRI |

2007

No international matches played in 2007

2008

14-03	British Virgin Islands	D	0-0	Road Town	Fr		300	
15-03	British Virgin Islands	D	1-1	Road Town	Fr		350	
26-03	Grenada	L	0-10	St George's	WCq		3 000	James GUY

2009

No international matches played in 2009

2010

No international matches played in 2010

2011

19-06	Anguilla	D	0-0	The Valley	Fr		550	Burton AIA
3-07	British Virgin Islands	W	2-0	Charlotte Amalie	WCq	Alderman Lesmond 7, Reid Klopp 57	350	Navarro CAN
10-07	British Virgin Islands	W	2-1	Tortola	WCq	Dwayne Thomas 2, Reid Klopp 93+	600	Morrison JAM
2-09	Haiti	L	0-6	Port au Prince	WCq		12 000	Cruz CRC
6-09	Antigua and Barbuda	L	1-8	Frederiksted	WCq	Jamie Browne 49	250	Lancaster GUY
7-10	Haiti	L	0-7	Frederiksted	WCq		406	Holder CAY
11-10	Antigua and Barbuda	L	0-10	St John's	WCq		1 500	Matthew SKN
11-11	Curaçao	L	0-3	Frederiksted	WCq		210	Navarro CAN
15-11	Curaçao	L	1-6	Willemstad	WCq	Keithroy Cornelius 51	2 000	Legister JAM

2012

No international matches played in 2012

Fr = Friendly match • CC = Digicel Caribbean Cup • WC = FIFA World Cup • q = qualifier • † Not a full international

US VIRGIN ISLANDS 2011-12

Saint Croix Championship

Group A	Pl	W	D	L	F	A	Pts
Helenites ‡	18	15	3	0	66	6	48
Rovers ‡	18	13	2	3	56	11	41
Unique	18	10	3	5	62	43	33
Prankton	18	6	4	8	37	45	22
Skills	18	5	2	11	32	61	17
Freewill Baptist	18	3	2	13	32	68	11
Chelsea	18	2	2	14	17	66	8

Saint Thomas Championship

Group B	Pl	W	D	L	F	A	Pts
New Vibes ‡	12	8	0	4			24
Togetherness ‡	12	6	3	3			21
Raymix	12	4	3	5			15
UWS	12	4	2	6			14
Laraza	12	3	2	7			11

6/08/2011 - 26/02/2012 • ‡ Qualified for the Play-offs • 3rd place: Togetherness 3-2 Rovers

Final

| Helenites | 2 |
| Togetherness | 0 |

| Rovers | 0 |
| New Vibes | 2 |

| Helenites | 3 5p |
| New Vibes | 3 4p |

CUP FINAL

Lionel Roberts Stadium
26-02-2012
Scorers - Jonah Lesmond 3 for Helenites;
Marlon Wilton, Brian Charley, Carlos Claxton for New Vibes

WAL – WALES

FIFA/COCA-COLA WORLD RANKING

'93	'94	'95	'96	'97	'98	'99	'00	'01	'02	'03	'04	'05	'06	'07	'08	'09	'10	'11	'12
29	41	61	80	102	97	98	109	100	52	66	68	71	73	57	60	77	112	48	82

2012													High	Low	Av
Jan	Feb	Mar	Apr	May	Jun	Jul	Aug	Sep	Oct	Nov	Dec				
49	42	48	41	41	38	38	37	45	57	66	82		27	117	73

The New Saints powered their way to the league and cup double in 2012 after an exciting end to the season which saw them beat defending champions Bangor City 5-0 in a winner-takes-all championship decider on the final day of the season, their Kiwi striker Greg Draper scoring hat trick. Two weeks later they faced Cefn Druids in the cup final where their opponents were making their first appearance for 108 years but once again Draper was on target as TNS won 2-0 to win the cup without conceding a goal. In-between those two matches Afan Lido beat Newtown on penalties to secure the league cup - their first trophy since winning the first two editions of the tournament in the early 1990s. Across the border in England, Swansea City impressed on their return to the top flight, finishing 11th in the Premier League while Cardiff City fell just short in joining them after losing in the play-offs to West Ham. Earlier in the season they had become the first Welsh team to make it to the final of the League Cup but were cruelly denied after losing a penalty shoot-out to Liverpool following a 2-2 draw at Wembley. New Wales coach Chris Coleman knew it was not going to be easy following on from Gary Speed but he experienced a difficult first year in the job, losing six of the seven matches played.

UEFA EUROPEAN CHAMPIONSHIP RECORD
1960 DNE 1964 r1 1968-1972 DNQ 1976 QF 1980-2012 DNQ

THE FOOTBALL ASSOCIATION OF WALES, LTD (FAW)

11/12 Neptune Court,
Vanguard Way,
Cardiff CF24 5PJ
☎ +44 29 20435830
📠 +44 29 20496953
✉ info@faw.co.uk
🌐 www.faw.org.uk
FA 1876 CON 1954 FIFA 1910
P Trefor Hughes
GS Jonathan Ford

THE STADIA

2014 FIFA World Cup Stadia	
City Stadium Cardiff	26 828
Other Main Stadia	
Millennium Stadium Cardiff	74 500
Liberty Stadium Swansea	20 532
Racecourse Ground Wrexham	15 891

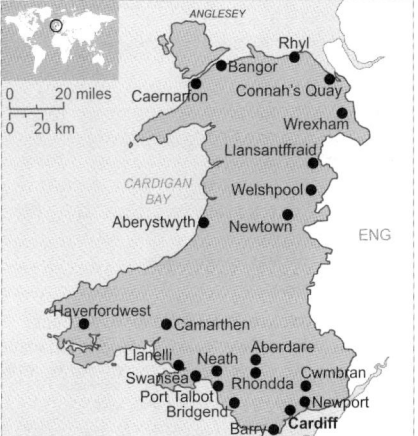

MAJOR CITIES/TOWNS

		Population
1	Cardiff	316 794
2	Swansea	173 870
3	Newport	120 052
4	Rhondda	60 062
5	Barry	53 457
6	Cwmbran	49 608
7	Llanelli	48 890
8	Neath	46 961
9	Wrexham	45 541
10	Bridgend	44 292
11	Pontypool	36 308
12	Port Talbot	34 926
13	Aberdare	34 611
14	Colwyn Bay	31 789
15	Pontypridd	31 614
16	Merthyr Tydfil	29 946
17	Rhyl	26 767
18	Aberystwyth	21 877
188	Llansantffraid	1 889

WALES (PART OF THE UNITED KINGDOM)

Capital	Cardiff	Population	3 004 600 (137)	% in cities	89%
GDP per capita	$30 546 (45)	Area km²	20 779 km² (154)	GMT +/-	0
Neighbours (km)	England 468 • Coast 627				

RECENT INTERNATIONAL MATCHES PLAYED BY WALES

2008	Opponents	Score	Venue	Comp	Scorers	Att	Referee
20-08	Georgia	L 1-2	Swansea	Fr	Koumas [17]	6 435	Jug SVN
6-09	Azerbaijan	W 1-0	Cardiff	WCq	Vokes [83]	17 106	Stavrev MKD
10-09	Russia	L 1-2	Moscow	WCq	Ledley [67]	28 000	Skomina SVN
11-10	Liechtenstein	W 2-0	Cardiff	WCq	Edwards [42], Frick OG [80]	13 356	Vejlgaard DEN
15-10	Germany	L 0-1	Mönchengladbach	WCq		44 500	Duhamel FRA
19-11	Denmark	W 1-0	Brøndby	Fr	Bellamy [77]	10 271	Weiner GER
2009							
11-02	Poland	L 0-1	Vila Real	Fr		487	Paixao POR
28-03	Finland	L 0-2	Cardiff	WCq		22 604	Iturralde ESP
1-04	Germany	L 0-2	Cardiff	WCq		26 064	Hauge NOR
29-05	Estonia	W 1-0	Llanelli	Fr	Earnshaw [26p]	4 071	Thorisson ISL
6-06	Azerbaijan	W 1-0	Baku	WCq	Edwards [42]	25 000	Strombergsson SWE
12-08	Montenegro	L 1-2	Podgorica	Fr	Vokes [47]	5 000	Mazic SRB
9-09	Russia	L 1-3	Cardiff	WCq	Collins [53]	14 505	De Sousa POR
10-10	Finland	L 1-2	Helsinki	WCq	Bellamy [17]	14 000	Mazic SRB
14-10	Liechtenstein	W 2-0	Vaduz	WCq	Vaughan [16], Ramsey [80]	1 858	Kaldma EST
14-11	Scotland	W 3-0	Cardiff	Fr	Edwards [17], Church [32], Ramsey [35]	13 844	Zimmermann SUI
2010							
3-03	Sweden	L 0-1	Swansea	Fr		8 258	Black NIR
23-05	Croatia	L 0-2	Osijek	Fr		15 000	Vincic SVN
11-08	Luxembourg	W 5-1	Llanelli	Fr	Cotterill [35], Ledley [47p], King [55], Williams [78], Bellamy [82]	4 904	Gestranius FIN
3-09	Montenegro	L 0-1	Podgorica	ECq		7 442	Kakos GRE
8-10	Bulgaria	L 0-1	Cardiff	ECq		14 061	Eriksson SWE
12-10	Switzerland	L 1-4	Basel	ECq	Bale [13]	26 000	Hamer LUX
2011							
8-02	Republic of Ireland	L 0-3	Dublin	Fr		19 783	Courtney NIR
26-03	England	L 0-2	Cardiff	ECq		68 959	Benquerenca POR
25-05	Scotland	L 1-3	Dublin	Fr	Earnshaw [36]	6 036	Thomson SCO
27-05	Northern Ireland	W 2-0	Dublin	Fr	Ramsey [36], Earnshaw [71]	529	Kelly IRL
10-08	Australia	L 1-2	Cardiff	Fr	Blake [83]	6 378	Tohver EST
2-09	Montenegro	W 2-1	Cardiff	ECq	Morison [29], Ramsey [50]	8 194	Banti ITA
6-09	England	L 0-1	London	ECq		77 128	Schorgenhofer AUT
7-10	Switzerland	W 2-0	Swansea	ECq	Ramsey [60p], Bale [71]	12 317	Kuipers NED
11-10	Bulgaria	W 1-0	Sofia	ECq	Bale [45]	11 340	Gil POL
12-11	Norway	W 4-1	Cardiff	Fr	Bale [11], Bellamy [16], Vokes 2 [88 89]	12 600	Grubelnik AUT
2012							
29-02	Costa Rica	L 0-1	Cardiff	Fr		23 193	Webb ENG
27-05	Mexico	L 0-2	New York	Fr		35 518	Salazar USA
15-08	Bosnia-Herzegovina	L 0-2	Llanelli	Fr		6 253	Borg MLT
7-09	Belgium	L 0-2	Cardiff	WCq		16 557	Johannesson SWE
11-09	Serbia	L 1-6	Novi Sad	WCq	Bale [31]	10 660	Gomes POR
12-10	Scotland	W 2-1	Cardiff	WCq	Bale 2 [80 87p]	23 249	Meyer GER
16-10	Croatia	L 0-2	Osijek	WCq		17 500	Tudor ROU

Fr = Friendly match • EC = UEFA EURO 2012 • WC = FIFA World Cup • q = qualifier

WALES NATIONAL TEAM HISTORICAL RECORDS

Caps 92 - Neville Southall 1982-98 • 85 - Gary Speed 1990-2004 • 75 - Dean Saunders 1986-2001 • 73 - Peter Nicholas 1979-91 & Ian Rush 1980-96 • 72 - Mark Hughes 1984-99 & Joey Jones 1975-86 • 70 - Craig Bellamy 1998- • 68 - Ivor Allchurch 1950-66 • 66 - Brian Flynn 1974-84 • 65 - Andy Melville 1989-2004 • 64 - Ryan Giggs 1991-2007 • 62 - David Phillips 1984-98 • 59 - Barry Horne 1988-96, Cliff Jones 1954-70, Kevin Ratcliffe 1981-93; Terry Yorath 1970-81 & Robert Earnshaw 2002-

Goals 28 - Ian Rush 1980-96 • 23 - Ivor Allchurch 1950-66 & Trevor Ford 1947-57 • 22 - Dean Saunders 1986-2001 • 19 - Craig Bellamy 1998- • 16 - Robert Earnshaw 2002-; Mark Hughes 1984-99 & Cliff Jones 1954-70 • 15 - John Charles 1950-65 • 14 - John Hartson 1997-2005 • 12 - John Toshack 1969-80; Ryan Giggs 1991-2007; Dai Astley 1931-39 & Billy Lewis 1885-1898 • 11 - Billy Meredith 1895-1920

Coaches Committee 1876-1954 • Wally Barnes 1954-55 • Jimmy Murphy 1956-64 • Trevor Morris 1964 • Dave Bowen 1964-74 • Mike Smith ENG 1974-79 • Mike England 1979-87 • David Williams 1988 • Terry Yorath 1988-93 • John Toshack 1994 • Mike Smith ENG 1994-95 • Bobby Gould ENG 1995-99 • Mark Hughes 1999-2004 • John Toshack 2004-10 • Brian Flynn 2010 • Gary Speed 2010-11 • Chris Coleman 2012-

WAL – WALES

WALES 2011-12

LEAGUE OF WALES

	Pl	W	D	L	F	A	Pts	New Saints	Bangor	Neath	Llanelli	Bala	Prestatyn	Airbus UK	Aberystwyth	Port Talbot	Afan Lido	Carmarthen	Newtown
The New Saints †	32	23	5	4	75	31	**74**		3-4 5-0	3-0 1-2	4-2 1-1	1-1 3-2	2-1 2-1	3-1	3-2	3-2	3-0	4-0	5-0
Bangor City ‡	32	22	3	7	72	46	**69**	0-3 1-3		2-1 1-3	3-2 2-2	2-1 4-2	5-3 2-1	2-1	1-1	3-1	4-1	4-0	4-0
Neath - R	32	18	8	6	60	36	**62**	1-1 0-1	2-0 1-3		2-0 1-5	4-0 2-0	3-1 1-0	3-0	4-2	3-2	2-1	1-0	5-0
Llanelli ‡	32	18	5	9	63	36	**59**	0-1 0-2	2-1 0-1	0-1 1-2		3-1 1-2	3-2 3-2	1-1	2-0	2-0	4-1	2-0	9-2
Bala Town	32	14	7	11	48	41	**49**	2-2 0-1	1-2 0-1	0-0 2-2	2-4 0-1		1-1 3-0	1-0	3-0	2-0	3-1	2-0	2-2
Prestatyn Town	32	8	4	20	41	63	**28**	0-2 0-4	0-5 0-4	1-2 1-3	2-3 0-2	1-2 0-1		2-2	1-0	2-1	3-1	6-1	2-1
Airbus UK Broughton	32	10	9	13	48	50	**39**	1-2	2-4	2-2	1-1	1-2	2-1		1-1 3-2	1-1 2-2	3-1 1-1	3-1 0-1	3-2 3-1
Aberystwyth Town §1	32	8	10	14	44	50	**33**	1-1	0-2	1-1	1-2	0-4	1-3	1-2 2-0		0-2 1-1	1-1 1-1	4-1 2-2	4-1 3-2
Port Talbot Town	32	8	9	15	39	51	**33**	2-1	1-2	1-2	0-1	2-2	0-0	2-1 2-1	0-4 2-1		2-2 1-2	2-0 0-1	3-1 1-1
Afan Lido	32	7	11	14	40	53	**32**	3-1	0-0	1-0	0-0	0-1	0-1	0-0 1-2	0-0 0-2	1-2 2-2		1-0 5-1	3-2 1-6
Carmarthen Town	32	7	11	14	40	53	**32**	0-1	1-2	2-2	0-3	0-1	2-1	3-1 1-0	2-1 0-3	2-0 1-0	2-5 3-2		0-1 3-2
Newtown §3	32	7	5	20	44	82	**23**	1-3	2-1	0-4	0-2	0-2	1-2	1-3 0-4	1-2 1-1	2-0 2-2	2-1 1-1	4-2 2-1	

12/08/2011 - 21/04/2012 • † Qualified for the UEFA Champions League • ‡ Qualified for the Europa League • § = points deducted
Top scorers: **24** - Rhys **GRIFFITHS**, Llanelli • **22** - Greg **DRAPER** NZL, New Saints • **16** - Les **DAVIES**, Bangor • **15** - Luke **BOWEN**, Neath

WALES 2011-12
WELSH LEAGUE DIVISION 1 (2)

	Pl	W	D	L	F	A	Pts
Cambrian & Clydach V	30	16	10	4	78	25	58
Taff's Well	30	16	4	10	60	42	52
Haverfordwest County	30	15	7	8	58	43	52
Bryntirion Athletic	30	16	3	11	52	43	51
AFC Porth	30	13	9	8	54	36	48
Barry Town	30	12	10	8	48	37	46
Goytre United	30	12	8	10	71	55	44
Bridgend Town	30	13	5	12	50	41	44
Ton Pentre	30	9	16	5	48	40	43
Pontardawe Town	30	11	9	10	48	53	42
West End	30	11	5	14	53	62	38
Cwmbran Celtic	30	12	2	16	32	54	38
Aberaman Athletic	30	8	9	13	46	55	33
Cwmaman Institute	30	7	8	15	36	59	29
Cardiff Corinthians	30	6	10	14	50	67	28
Caerau	30	4	3	23	37	109	15

12/08/2011 - 12/05/2012

WALES 2011-12
CYMRU ALLIANCE (2)

	Pl	W	D	L	F	A	Pts
Connah's Quay	30	21	5	4	89	23	68
Rhyl	30	19	5	6	80	22	62
Buckley Town	30	19	4	7	67	43	61
Porthmadog	30	19	5	6	68	41	59
Penrhyncoch	30	17	4	9	56	44	55
Cefn Druids	30	17	3	10	58	42	54
Caersws	30	17	1	12	49	68	52
Llandudno	30	14	7	9	55	40	49
Flint Town United	30	13	7	10	59	47	46
Conwy United	30	10	7	13	59	65	37
Guilsfield	30	10	4	16	41	58	34
Ruthin Town	30	6	7	17	28	60	25
Penycae	30	7	4	19	30	76	25
Llanrhaeadr	30	3	9	18	40	77	18
Llangefni Town	30	4	2	24	32	96	14
Rhos Aelwyd	30	2	7	21	29	76	13

12/08/2011 - 21/04/2012

LEAGUE CUP 2011-12

Quarter-finals
| Afan Lido | 2 | 0 |
| Port Talbot * | 0 | 0 |

| Llanelli * | 0 | 2 |
| **Neath** | 0 | 4 |

| **New Saints *** | 2 | 1 |
| Airbus UK | 1 | 0 |

| Bangor City * | 1 | 1 |
| **Newtown** | 1 | 5 |

Semi-finals
| **Afan Lido** | 1 | 2 |
| Neath * | 0 | 1 |

| New Saints * | 3 | 0 |
| **Newtown** | 1 | 2 |

* Home team

Final
| **Afan Lido** | 1 | 3p |
| Newtown | 1 | 2p |

Park Avenue, Aberystwyth
28-04-2012, 301, Morgan
Scorers: Jones [42] for AL; Rushton [90] for Newtown

MEDALS TABLE

		Overall	League	Cup	LC	PC
		G S B	G S B	G S	G S	G S
1	Wrexham	28 25		23 22		5 3
2	Cardiff City	23 12 1		22 10		1 2
3	Barry Town	18 3	7 1	6 1	4 1	1
4	The New Saints	15 7 1	6 5 1	3 2	5	1
5	Swansea City	12 10		10 8		2 2
6	Bangor City	11 16 3	3 1 3	8 9	6	
7	Rhyl	8 11 2	2 2 2	4 4	2 4	
8	NEWI Cefn Druids	8 6		8 6		
9	Shrewsbury Town	6 3		6 3		
10	Chirk	5 1		5 1		
11	Chester City	3 10		3 10		
12	Llanelli AFC	3 7 1	1 3 1	1 2	1 1	1
13	Merthyr Tydfil	3 3		3 3		
14	Afan Lido	3 2	1	1	3	
15	Oswestry Town	3 1		3 1		
	Caersws	3 1			3 1	
17	Wellington Town	3		3		
18	Newtown	2 7	2	2 4	1	
19	Newport County	2 4		1 2		1 2
20	Carmarthen Town	2 3 1		1	1 2	1 1
21	Crewe Alexandra	2		2		
22	Cwmbran Town	1 5 2	1 1 2	3	1	
23	UWIC Inter Cardiff	1 4	4	1		
24	Hereford United	1 3		1 3		
25	Connah's Quay	1 2		1 2		
26	Ebbw Vale	1 1 2		2	1	1
27	Aberystwyth Town	1 1 1		1	1 1	

WELSH CUP 2011-12

Third Round

The New Saints*	6
Bryntirion Athletic	0
Barry Town	2
Newport County	3
Flint Town United*	3
Newport Civil Service	0
West End	0
Neath*	4
Llanelli	4
Bangor City*	2
Newtown*	1
Rhyl	2
Buckley Town*	4
Taff's Well	3
Merthyr Saints*	0
Bala Town	6
Airbus UK Broughton	
Wrexham*	
Port Talbot Town*	0
Afan Lido	1
AFC Porth*	0 4p
Cambrian & Clydach Vale	0 3p
Bridgend Town	1
Carmarthen Town*	2
Aberystwyth Town*	6
FC Cefn	1
Caersws*	1
Llandudno	1
Prestatyn Town*	6
Goytre United	2
Connah's Quay*	1
Cefn Druids	2

Fourth Round

The New Saints*	4
Newport County	0
Flint Town United*	1
Neath	3
Llanelli	3 5p
Rhyl*	3 4p
Buckley Town*	2
Bala Town	4
Airbus UK Broughton	2 5p
Afan Lido*	2 4p
AFC Porth	1
Carmarthen Town*	3
Aberystwyth Town*	1 5p
Llandudno	1 4p
Prestatyn Town*	0
Cefn Druids	1

Quarter-finals

The New Saints	1
Neath	0
Llanelli	1 4p
Bala Town	1 5p
Airbus UK Broughton	3
Carmarthen Town	1
Aberystwyth Town	0
Cefn Druids	1

Semi-finals

The New Saints	4
Bala Town*	0
Airbus UK Broughton	1
Cefn Druids ††	4

Final

The New Saints	2
Cefn Druids ‡	0

CUP FINAL

Nanporth Stadium, Bangor, 5-05-2012
Att: 731, Ref: Kevin Parry
Scorers - Draper [14], Darlington [15] for TNS
TNS - Paul Harrison - Simon Spender, Chris Marriott, Phil Baker, Steve Evans - Christian Seargeant, Craig Jones, Aeron Edwards (Scott Ruscoe 84) - Ryan Fraughan (Tom Roberts 68), Greg Draper (Nicky Ward 77), Alex Darlington. Tr: Carl Darlington & Craig Harrison
Cefn Druids - Chris Mullock - Mark Harris, Adam Hesp, Marc Griffiths - Joe Price, Tom McElmeel, George Hughes, Warren Duckett, Kieron Quinn (Jack Edwards 88) - Andrew Swarbrick (Paul Speed 91+), Tony Cann. Tr: Huw Griffiths

* Home team • †† Played at Belle Vue, Rhyl • ‡ Qualified for the Europa League

YEM – YEMEN

FIFA/COCA-COLA WORLD RANKING

'93	'94	'95	'96	'97	'98	'99	'00	'01	'02	'03	'04	'05	'06	'07	'08	'09	'10	'11	'12
91	103	123	139	128	146	158	160	135	145	132	124	139	141	144	145	130	126	151	164

2012

Jan	Feb	Mar	Apr	May	Jun	Jul	Aug	Sep	Oct	Nov	Dec	High	Low	Av
149	147	148	156	157	159	148	151	152	157	162	164	90	164	135

Al Sha'ab Ibb claimed the Yemen Premier League title in 2012 after finishing ahead of local rivals Al Ittihad Ibb on goal difference in an exciting climax to the championship. Defending champions Al Urooba led the table going into the final games but they were beaten 1-0 by Ittihad - a result that in the end was not good enough for either team with Sha'ab securing a 2-1 victory over Al Tilal. Al Ahly Taizz secured qualification for the 2013 AFC Cup alongside Sha'ab by defeating their local rivals Taliat Taizz 1-0 in the President's Cup final. The national team took part in both the Arab Nations Cup and West Asian Championship in 2012 but the victory over Bahrain in the group stages of the former - thanks to goals from Akram Al Selwi and Mohammed Barioes - was the only win secured during a disappointing 2012 as Yemen were eliminated from both tournaments after the group stage. Defeats at the hands of Bahrain and Saudi Arabia ensured Amine Al Sunaini's side would not advance to the next phase of the West Asian tournament with Essam Al Worafi's goal in the 2-1 loss to Iran in their final group game the only consolation. Yemen's attempt to progress to the finals of the AFC Asian Cup for the first time will see the country face off against Bahrain, Qatar and Malaysia in the qualifiers for Australia 2015.

FIFA WORLD CUP RECORD
1930-1982 DNE 1986-1990 DNQ (as North Yemen) 1930-1982 DNE 1986-1990 DNQ (as South Yemen) 1994-2014 DNQ

YEMEN FOOTBALL ASSOCIATION (YFF)

Quarter of Sport Al Jeraf, (Stadium Ali Mushen), PO Box 908 Sanaa, Al Thawra City
☎ +967 1 310923
📠 +967 1 431953
✉ yemenfootball@yahoo.com
🌐 www.yemenfa.org
FA 1962 CON 1972 FIFA 1980
P Ahmed Al Esi
GS Hamid Al Shaibani

THE STADIA
2014 FIFA World Cup Stadia
Yemen played their home match at the Khalifa Bin Zayed Stadium in Al Ain, UAE

Other Main Stadia
Althawra Sports City
Sana'a — 30 000
May 22 Stadium
Aden — 30 000

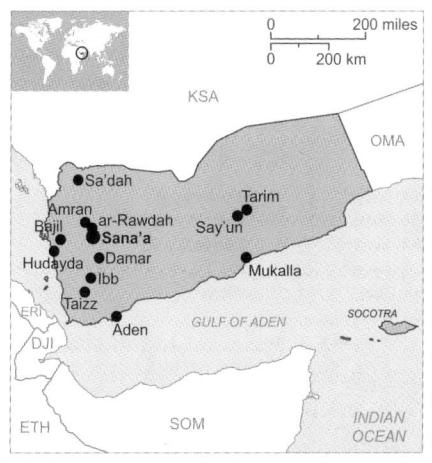

MAJOR CITIES/TOWNS
		Population
1	Sana'a	2 079 766
2	Aden	692 931
3	Taizz	556 541
4	Hudayda	471 208
5	Ibb	295 125
6	Mukalla	210 222
7	ar-Rawdah	192 249
8	Damar	179 607
9	Amran	87 181
10	Bajil	64 510
11	Sa'dah	62 755
12	Yerim	60 692
13	Shahir	57 008
14	Say'un	56 101
15	Tarim	55 678
16	Rada	55 272
17	Bayt al-Faqih	46 004
18	Al Qa'idah	44 297
19	Hajja	40 365

AL JUMHURIYAH AL YAMANIYAH • REPUBLIC OF YEMEN

Capital Sana'a | Population 23 822 783 (48) | % in cities 31%
GDP per capita $2500 (175) | Area km² 527 968 km² (49) | GMT +/- +3
Neighbours (km) Oman 288, Saudi Arabia 1458 • Coast 1906

RECENT INTERNATIONAL MATCHES PLAYED BY YEMEN

2008	Opponents	Score	Venue	Comp	Scorers	Att	Referee
26-01	Bahrain	L 1-2	Manama	Fr	Abdullah Yaslam [67]		
4-04	Tanzania	W 2-1	Sana'a	Fr	Abdullah Yaslam 2 [2 50]		
25-04	Indonesia	L 0-1	Bandung	Fr			
3-05	Oman	D 0-0	Muscat	Fr			
22-05	Sudan	D 1-1	Sana'a	Fr	Muaz Assaj [47]		
2009							
5-01	UAE	L 1-3	Muscat	GCr1	Ali Al Nono [90]		
8-01	Saudi Arabia	L 0-6	Muscat	GCr1			
11-01	Qatar	L 1-2	Muscat	GCr1	Ali Al Nono [30p]		
20-01	Japan	L 1-2	Kumamoto	ACq	Zaher Al Fadhli [47]	32 000	Tan Hai CHN
28-01	Hong Kong	W 1-0	Sana'a	ACq	Akram Al Selwi [51]	10 000	Al Hilali OMA
8-11	Tanzania	D 1-1	Sana'a	Fr	Ali Mubarak [78]		
11-11	Tanzania	W 2-1	Sana'a	Fr	Tamer Hanash [13p], Akram Al Worafi [37]		
18-11	Bahrain	L 0-4	Manama	ACq		1 000	Basma SYR
30-12	Tajikistan	W 2-1	Sana'a	Fr	Khaled Baleid [71], Ali Al Nono [85]		
2010							
2-01	Tajikistan	L 0-1	Sana'a	Fr			
6-01	Japan	L 2-3	Sana'a	ACq	Basem Al Aqel [13], Salem Abbod [39]	10 000	Albadwawi UAE
15-01	Kenya	W 3-1	Sana'a	Fr	Ali Al Nono [45], Ala Al Sasi 2 [48 50]		
20-01	Bahrain	W 3-0	Sana'a	ACq	Ali Al Nono 2 [5 25], Mohammed Al Abidi [86]	7 000	Torky IRN
27-02	Malaysia	L 0-1	Kuala Lumpur	Fr			
3-03	Hong Kong	D 0-0	Hong Kong	ACq		1 212	Minh Tri Vo VIE
12-05	Malawi	W 1-0	Sana'a	Fr			
18-05	Oman	L 0-1	Sana'a	Fr			
7-09	Syria	W 2-1	Sana'a	Fr	Ali Al Nono 2 [18p 55]		
18-09	Zambia	L 0-1	Sana'a	Fr			
25-09	Iraq	L 1-2	Amman	WAr1	Ali Al Nono [10]		
27-09	Palestine	W 3-1	Amman	WAr1	Ali Al Nono 2 [43p 83], Haitham Thabit [63]		
1-10	Kuwait	D 1-1	Amman	WAsf	Ali Al Nono [55]. L 3-4p		
13-10	India	W 6-3	Pune	Fr	Haitham Thabit [9], Khaled Baleid [28], Akram Al Worafi [61], Ala Al Sasi 2 [77 88], Yasser Basuhai [93+]		
7-11	Uganda	D 2-2	Sana'a	Fr	Ali Al Nono 2 [9 11]		
10-11	Korea DPR	D 1-1	Sana'a	Fr	Akram Al Worafi [42]		
22-11	Saudi Arabia	L 0-4	Aden	GCr1			Al Marzouqi UAE
25-11	Qatar	L 1-2	Zinjibar	GCr1	Akram Al Worafi [17]		Abid IRQ
28-11	Kuwait	L 0-3	Zinjibar	GCr1			Abbas BHR
2011							
8-07	Jordan	L 0-4	Istanbul	Fr			
23-07	Iraq	L 0-2	Arbil	WCq		20 000	Kovalenko UZB
28-07	Iraq	D 0-0	Al Ain	WCq		1 500	Basma SYR
2012							
18-06	Palestine	L 1-2	Sana'a	Fr	Mohamed Msaad		
26-06	Bahrain	W 2-0	Jeddah	ARr1	Akram Al Selwi 53p,		Jedidi TUN
29-06	Morocco	L 0-4	Jeddah	ARr1	Mohamed Ba Rowis [65]		Al Amri KSA
28-09	Oman	L 1-2	Muscat	Fr			
16-10	Lebanon	L 1-2	Saida	Fr	Al Saadi [3]		Jaber JOR
9-12	Bahrain	L 0-1	Al Farwaniyah	WAr1		150	Sabbagh LIB
12-12	Saudi Arabia	L 0-1	Al Farwaniyah	WAr1		1 000	Tufaylieh SYR
15-12	Iran	L 1-2	Kuwait City	WAr1	Essam Al Worafi [45]	500	Sabbagh LIB
25-12	UAE	L 0-2	Doha				

Fr = Friendly match • GC = Gulf Cup • AC = AFC Asian Cup • WC = FIFA World Cup • q = qualifier • r1 = first round group

YEMEN NATIONAL TEAM HISTORICAL RECORDS

Coach: Milan Zivadinovic SRB 2003-04 • Rabah Saadane ALG 2004-05 • Mohsen Saleh 2007-09 • Hamza Al Jamal 2009 • Sami Hasan Al Nash 2009 • Srecko Jurcic CRO 2009-10 • Amine Al Sunaini 2010-

YEMEN 2012

PREMIER LEAGUE

	Pl	W	D	L	F	A	Pts	Sha'ab I	Ittihad	Urooba	Ahly S	Hilal H	Sha'ab H	Taliat	Shula	Wahda A	Tilal	Shabab	Sha'ab S	Ahly T	Najm
Al Sha'ab Ibb ‡	26	13	9	4	39	20	48		1-0	1-1	3-1	2-1	1-0	2-0	1-0	2-1	2-1	6-0	0-0	1-0	3-0
Al Ittihad Ibb	26	14	6	6	28	20	48	1-1		1-0	1-1	1-0	0-0	1-0	2-0	3-1	2-0	1-0	1-0	1-0	2-1
Al Urooba	26	13	7	6	38	20	46	2-1	0-1		1-2	4-1	2-3	2-0	1-1	1-2	1-0	2-1	1-0	3-0	2-1
Al Ahly Sana'a	26	12	7	7	34	29	43	0-1	1-0	0-0		0-1	3-0	2-0	3-0	4-2	0-0	4-2	1-0	2-1	3-0
Al Hilal Hudayda	26	11	7	8	31	30	40	1-1	2-1	0-3	5-1		2-2	1-2	0-0	1-1	2-1	0-1	1-0	2-1	1-2
Al Sha'ab Hadramaut	26	11	5	10	31	30	38	1-0	1-0	1-1	1-1	0-1		1-0	1-0	1-2	1-0	2-1	3-0	4-1	0-1
Taliat Taizz	26	11	4	11	27	22	37	2-2	0-1	0-0	0-0	0-0	3-1		2-0	2-0	2-0	1-0	3-0	2-0	1-0
Shula Aden	26	9	9	8	29	19	36	3-0	0-0	1-0	2-0	0-1	1-2	2-0		0-1	1-1	2-1	4-0	1-1	4-0
Al Wahda Aden	26	10	4	12	31	34	34	0-0	1-1	1-1	5-0	1-2	3-2	2-1	0-3		0-1	3-2	0-1	1-0	2-0
Al Tilal Aden	26	8	9	9	20	26	33	0-0	2-2	0-0	1-2	0-3	2-1	1-0	1-1	1-0		2-1	0-0	2-0	1-1
Al Shabab Al Baydaa	26	9	4	13	27	38	31	2-1	1-0	1-3	2-1	4-0	1-2	0-4	0-0	1-0	0-0		1-0	1-3	2-0
Al Sha'ab Sana'a	26	7	5	14	16	28	26	1-1	1-2	1-2	0-0	1-1	2-0	2-0	0-2	1-0	1-2	0-1		3-1	1-0
Al Ahly Taizz	26	5	8	13	25	35	23	2-2	4-0	0-2	1-1	1-1	1-0	1-2	0-0	3-0	0-1	1-1	1-0		1-1
Najm Sba	26	4	6	16	41	18	0-4	2-3	0-3	0-1	0-1	1-1	1-0	0-1	0-2	3-0	0-0	0-1	1-1	

28/12/2011 - 16/07/2012 • ‡ Qualified for the AFC Cup
Championship play-off: **Al Sha'ab Ibb** 3-2 Al Ittihad Ibb
Play-off details: Ali Muhesen Stadium, Sana'a, 25-07-2012. Scorers - Gaems 2 [15 53], Radwan [50] for Sha'ab; Jelani [6], Al Gerani [29] for Ittihad
Top scorers: 14 - Shaaban **NAGGAR**, Al Urooba • 12 - Ali **AL NONO**, Al Ahli Sana'a & Emad **MANSOUR**, Taliat Taizz

MEDALS TABLE

		Overall G	Lge G	Cup G S	City
1	Al Ahly	9	6	3	Sana'a
2	Al Sha'ab	5	3	2 1	Ibb
3	Al Hilal	4	2	2 2	Hudayda
	Al Tilal	4	2	2 2	Aden
5	Al Wahda	4	4		Sana'a
6	Al Sha'ab Hadramaut	2		2 3	Mukalla
7	Al Saqr	2	2		Taizz
8	Al Ahli	1		1	Hudayda
	Al Ahly	1		1	Taizz
	Al Ittihad	1		1	Ibb
	Al Urooba	1	1		Zabid
12	Al Shula			2	Aden
13	Al Rasheed			1	Taizz
	Al Shabab			1	Al Baydaa
	Al Tadamun			1	Shabwa
	Tailat			1	Taizz

PRESIDENTS CUP 2012

Round of 16		Quarter–finals		Semi–finals		Final	
Al Ahly Taizz	2						
Shula Aden	1	**Al Ahly Taizz**	2				
Al Tadamun Shabwa	0	Al Nasr Aden	1				
Al Nasr Aden	1			Al Ahly Taizz	0 9p		
Al Ahly Sana'a	5			Al Tilal Aden	0 8p		
Khanfar	0	Al Ahly Sana'a	1				
Al Shrth	1	**Al Tilal Aden**	2				
Al Tilal Aden	7					Al Ahly Taizz ‡	1
Al Hilal Hudayda	1					Taliat Taizz	0
Al Sha'ab Hadramaut	0	**Al Hilal Hudayda**	1 3p				
Seuon	0	May 22 Sana'a	1 0p			CUP FINAL	
May 22 Sana'a	3			Al Hilal Hudayda	0		
Al Fateh	3			**Taliat Taizz**	1	Ali Muhesen, Sana'a	
Najm Sba	0	Al Fateh	0			26-11-2012	
Al Nasir Al Talla	1	**Taliat Taizz**	2				
Taliat Taizz	4			‡ Qualified for the AFC Cup			

ZAM – ZAMBIA

FIFA/COCA-COLA WORLD RANKING

'93	'94	'95	'96	'97	'98	'99	'00	'01	'02	'03	'04	'05	'06	'07	'08	'09	'10	'11	'12
27	21	25	20	21	29	36	49	64	67	68	70	58	62	65	72	84	76	79	34

2012

Jan	Feb	Mar	Apr	May	Jun	Jul	Aug	Sep	Oct	Nov	Dec	High	Low	Av
71	43	41	40	40	43	41	44	42	41	39	34	15	102	52

Zambia followed their 2012 Africa Cup of Nations success with two vital victories at the start of their FIFA World Cup qualifying campaign to make 2012 a truly memorable year for the southern African country. Basking in the glow of their unexpected success in Equatorial Guinea and Gabon, Zambia beat Ghana 1-0 in a World Cup qualifier as they opened a new stadium in Ndola named after former president Levy Mwanawasa. It had been completed by Chinese builders in 2011 but the opening had been delayed after problems with the pitch. The win over Ghana came one week after Zambia had lost their opening group game in Sudan but that result was overturned into a 3-0 win after their opponents were found to have fielded a suspended player. The Zambians rode their luck to qualify for the 2013 Africa Cup of Nations in South Africa after beating Uganda on penalties, but the defence of their title ended ignominiously after they drew all three matches and failed to get past the first round. At just two days shy of a year, it was the shortest ever reign as African champions. At home, the league went down to the wire with Zanaco beating Nkana 3-1 to claim the title ahead of Power Dynamos who lost away to Red Arrows. The following week NAPSA Stars beat Power Dynamos in the cup final to complete a miserable six days for the Kitwe-based Club.

CAF AFRICA CUP OF NATIONS RECORD

1957-1968 DNE 1970-1972 DNQ **1974** 2 F 1976 DNQ **1978** 5 r1 1980 DNQ **1982** 3 SF 1984 DNQ
1986 7 r1 1988 DNE **1990** 3 SF **1992** 7 QF **1994** 2 F **1996** 3 SF **1998** 10 r1 **2000** 13 r1
2002 14 r1 2004 DNQ **2006** 11 r1 **2008** 9 r1 **2010** 7 QF **2012** 1 Winners **2013** 12 r1

FOOTBALL ASSOCIATION OF ZAMBIA (FAZ)

Football House, Alick Nkhata Road, Long Acres, PO Box 34751, Lusaka
☎ +260 211 250940
+260 211 250946
faz@zamnet.zm
www.fazfootball.com
FA 1929 CON 1964 FIFA 1964
P Kalusha Bwalya
GS George Kasengele

THE STADIA

2014 FIFA World Cup Stadia
New Ndola Stadium
Ndola 40 000

Other Main Stadia
Independence Stadium
Lusaka 25 000
Arthur Davies Stadium
Kitwe 15 000
Konkola Stadium
Chililabombwe 15 000
Nchanga Stadium
Chingola 15 000

MAJOR CITIES/TOWNS

		Population
1	Lusaka	1 460 566
2	Kitwe	526 937
3	Ndola	495 004
4	Kabwe	215 015
5	Chingola	178 092
6	Mufulira	141 056
7	Livingstone	133 936
8	Luanshya	132 117
9	Kasama	111 588
10	Chipata	109 344
11	Kalulushi	100 712
12	Mazabuka	95 723
13	Chililabombwe	71 876
14	Mongu	69 379
15	Choma	59 151
16	Kapiri Mposhi	56 860
17	Kansanshi	51 986
18	Kafue	47 838

REPUBLIC OF ZAMBIA

Capital Lusaka
GDP per capita $1500 (200)
Neighbours (km) Angola 1110, Congo DR 1930, Malawi 837, Mozambique 419, Namibia 233, Tanzania 338, Zimbabwe 797
Population 11 862 740 (71)
Area km^2 752 618 km^2 (39)
% in cities 35%
GMT +/- +2

RECENT INTERNATIONAL MATCHES PLAYED BY ZAMBIA

2011	Opponents	Score	Venue	Comp	Scorers	Att	Referee
9-02	Swaziland	W 4-0	Manzini	Fr	James Chamanga [15], Collins Mbesuma [47], Isaac Chansa [60], Cifford Mulenga [92+]		
27-03	Mozambique	W 2-0	Maputo	CNq	James Chamanga [15], Emmanuel Mayuka [90]		
4-06	Mozambique	W 3-0	Chingola	CNq	Chris Katongo 2 [47 68], Collins Mbesuma [86]		
10-08	Zimbabwe	L 0-2	Harare	Fr			
4-09	Comoros	W 2-1	Mitsamiouli	CNq	Felix Katongo [23], Emmanuel Mayuka [87]		
8-10	Libya	D 0-0	Chingola	CNq			
15-11	Nigeria	L 0-2	Kaduna	Fr			
29-11	India	W 5-0	Margao	Fr	Jimmy Chisenga [14], Joseph Sitali [56], Bruce Musakanya 3 [69 72 90]		
18-12	Angola	L 0-1	Dundo	Fr			
2012							
14-01	Namibia	D 0-0	Johannesburg	Fr			
21-01	Senegal	W 2-1	Bata	CNr1	Emmanuel Mayuka [12], Rainford Kalaba [20]	17 500	Alioum CMR
25-01	Libya	D 2-2	Bata	CNr1	Emmanuel Mayuka [29], Chris Katongo [54]	1 500	Coulibaly MLI
29-01	Equatorial Guinea	W 1-0	Malabo	CNr1	Chris Katongo [67]	44 000	Benouza ALG
4-02	Sudan	W 3-0	Bata	CNqf	Stopila Sunzu [15], Chris Katongo [66], James Chamanga [86]	200	Gassama GAM
8-02	Ghana	W 1-0	Bata	CNsf	Emmanuel Mayuka [78]	8 000	Alioum CMR
12-02	Côte d'Ivoire	D 0-0	Libreville	CNf	W 8-7p	40 000	Diatta SEN
16-05	Angola	D 0-0	Luanda	Fr			
2-06	Sudan	L 0-2	Khartoum	WCq	Awarded 3-0 to Zambia	18 000	Bangoura GUI
9-06	Ghana	W 1-0	Ndola	WCq	Chris Katongo [66]	40 000	Kordi TUN
6-07	Malawi	L 0-1	Blantyre	Fr			
15-08	Korea Republic	L 1-2	Anyang	Fr	Emmanuel Mayuka [29]	18 200	Shukralla BHR
8-09	Uganda	W 1-0	Ndola	CNq	Chris Katongo [20]		Doue CIV
13-10	Uganda	L 0-1	Kampala	CNq	W 9-8p		Haimoudi ALG
14-11	South Africa	W 1-0	Johannesburg	Fr	Collins Mbesuma [64]		Nhleko SWZ
2013							
8-01	Morocco	D 0-0	Johannesburg	Fr			Gomes RSA
21-01	Ethiopia	D 1-1	Nelspruit	CNr1	Collins Mbesuma [45]	10 000	Otogo-Castane GAB
25-01	Nigeria	D 1-1	Nelspruit	CNr1	Kennedy Mweene [85p]	25 000	Grisha EGY
29-01	Burkina Faso	D 0-0	Nelspruit	CNr1		8 000	Alioum CMR

Fr = Friendly match • CC = COSAFA Cup • CE = CECAFA Cup • CN = CAF African Cup of Nations • WC = FIFA World Cup • BCD = Behind closed doors
q = qualifier • r1 = first round group • qf = quarter-final • sf = semi-final • f = final • † Not an official international

ZAMBIA NATIONAL TEAM HISTORICAL RECORDS

Coaches: Jochen Figge GER 1992-93 • Godfrey Chitalu 1993 • Ian Porterfield SCO 1993-94 • Roald Poulsen DEN 1994-96 • George Mungwa 1996-97 • Obby Kapita 1997 • Burkhard Ziese GER 1997-98 • Ben Bamfuchile 1998-2001 • Jan Brouwer NED 2001 • Roald Poulsen DEN 2002 • Kalusha Bwalya 2003-06 • Patrick Phiri 2006-08 • Herve Renard FRA 2008-10 • Dario Bonetti ITA 2010-11 • Herve Renard FRA 2011-

ZAMBIA SQUAD FOR THE 2012 CAF AFRICA CUP OF NATIONS

	Player		Ap	G	Club	Date of Birth		Player		Ap	G	Club	Date of Birth
1	Kalililo Kakonje	GK	0		TP Mazembe COD	1 01 1985	12	James Chamanga	FW	1+3	1	Dalian CHN	2 02 1980
2	Francis Kasonde	DF	3+2		TP Mazembe COD	1 09 1986	13	Stophira Sunzu	DF	6	1	TP Mazembe COD	22 06 1989
3	Chisamba Lungu	MF	5+1		Ural Y'burg RUS	31 01 1991	14	Noah Chivuta	MF	0+1		Free State RSA	25 12 1983
4	Joseph Musonda	DF	6		G. Arrows RSA	30 05 1977	15	Chintu Kampamba	DF	0		Bidvest Wits RSA	28 12 1980
5	Hijani Himoonde	DF	6		TP Mazembe COD	15 06 1985	16	Kennedy Mweene	GK	6		Free State RSA	11 12 1984
6	Davies Nkausu	DF	4+1		Supersport RSA	1 01 1986	17	Rainford Kalaba	MF	6	1	TP Mazembe COD	14 08 1986
7	Clifford Mulenga	MF	0+1		Bloemf'tein RSA	5 08 1987	18	Evans Kangwa	FW	0		Nkana	21 06 1994
8	Isaac Chansa	MF	6		O. Pirates RSA	23 03 1984	19	Nathan Sinkala	MF	6		Green Buffaloes	23 04 1991
9	Collins Mbesuma	FW	0+1		G. Arrows RSA	3 02 1984	20	Emmanuel Mayuka	FW	5+1	3	Young Boys SUI	21 11 1990
10	Felix Katongo	MF	0+2		Green Buffaloes	18 04 1984	21	Jonas Sakuwaha	MF	0+1		El Merreikh SUD	22 07 1983
11	Chris Katongo (c)	FW	6	3	Henan CHN	31 08 1982	22	Joshua Titima	GK	0		Power Dynamos	20 10 1992
							23	Nyambe Mulenga	DF	0+2		Zesco United	27 08 1987

Tr: Herve Renard FRA 30-09-1968

ZAMBIA 2012

KONKOLA COPPER MINES PREMIER LEAGUE

	Pl	W	D	L	F	A	Pts	Zanaco	Dynamos	ZESCO	Red Arrows	Konkola	Nchanga	Buffaloes	Forest Rang	Roan United	NAPSA Stars	Nkana	Konkola MP	Green Eagles	Nat Assembly	Nakambala	Indeni
Zanaco †	30	17	10	3	33	14	**61**		0-0	2-1	0-1	2-0	1-0	1-1	1-1	2-2	1-0	0-0	2-0	1-0	1-0	3-0	1-0
Power Dynamos ‡	30	16	8	6	44	20	**56**	3-0		2-1	1-0	3-0	0-2	1-1	1-1	1-1	2-1	2-0	3-0	0-0	2-0	3-1	5-1
ZESCO United	30	15	9	6	41	20	**54**	1-0	0-1		0-0	0-1	2-0	2-0	1-1	1-1	1-1	1-0	1-1	2-1	1-2	4-0	3-0
Red Arrows	30	11	14	5	35	18	**47**	0-1	1-0	0-0		1-1	2-0	3-1	2-0	1-1	4-2	3-1	0-0	0-0	1-1	0-1	4-1
Konkola Blades	30	12	9	9	27	29	**45**	1-1	1-1	1-2	0-0		1-0	0-0	3-1	2-1	0-0	0-0	2-2	2-1	1-0	0-1	2-1
Nchanga Rangers	30	13	5	12	30	27	**44**	0-1	1-0	0-2	0-0	1-0		1-0	2-1	3-0	0-1	1-1	2-2	0-1	3-1	1-0	2-1
Green Buffaloes	30	11	10	9	28	28	**43**	0-1	0-1	1-0	0-0	2-0	2-1		0-1	1-1	1-2	3-1	2-1	1-0	2-1	1-1	1-0
Forest Rangers	30	9	11	10	30	29	**38**	0-0	0-0	0-0	0-0	0-0	1-1	0-2		4-0		2-3	2-1	3-1	0-2	0-1	2-1	1-0
Roan United	30	8	14	8	32	36	**38**	0-3	3-0	1-1	2-1	2-1	1-2	1-1	2-1			2-2	0-3	0-1	0-0	2-1	1-0	1-0
NAPSA Stars	30	10	7	13	33	38	**37**	0-1	2-1	2-3	0-3	0-1	2-1	0-0	0-0	2-1		2-1	3-1	0-0	2-1	2-0	1-2
Nkana	30	7	14	9	35	39	**35**	1-3	1-5	2-2	1-1	3-0	1-1	1-0	1-1	1-3			3-0	2-1	1-0	1-1	1-0
Konkola Mine Police	30	8	11	11	26	34	**35**	0-0	0-0	0-3	0-0	1-2	1-0	0-2	1-1	1-1	0-0		1-1	2-0	1-2	3-2	3-0
Green Eagles	30	6	13	11	14	21	**31**	0-0	0-1	0-2	1-1	1-0	0-1	1-1	1-0	0-0	1-2	1-1		0-0	0-0	1-0
National Assembly	30	7	8	15	22	34	**29**	1-1	0-2	0-1	2-1	1-1	1-1	1-1	1-2	1-0	1-0	0-1	1-0		1-0	1-2
Nakambala Leopards	30	6	8	16	19	38	**26**	1-1	2-1	0-2	0-2	1-0	0-1	0-0	0-1	1-1	1-1	1-0	0-1	2-1			1-0
Indeni	30	6	5	19	23	47	**23**	0-1	0-2	0-1	1-3	1-2	2-1	1-1	1-3	0-0	2-1	4-2	0-1	1-1	1-0	1-1	

24/03/2012 – 11/11/2012 • † Qualified for the CAF Champions League • ‡ Qualified for the CAF Confederation Cup

BARCLAYS CUP 2012

Quarter-finals
- NAPSA Stars 1
- Red Arrows 0
- Konkola Blades 0
- ZESCO United 1
- Zanaco 2 8p
- Lime 2 7p
- Kabwe Warriors 0
- Power Dynamos 1

Semi-finals
- NAPSA Stars 0
- ZESCO United 1
- Zanaco 0
- Power Dynamos 1

Semis played at Woodlands, Lusaka

Final
- NAPSA Stars 4 4p
- Power Dynamos 4 2p

Final: Levy Mwanawasa Stadium, Ndola, 17-11-2012. Scorers - Chabusha Malumani [44], Vincent Mangamu [93+], Spencer Ngalande 2 [91] [104], for NAPSA; Graven Chitalu 2 [9] [82], Emmanuel Chimpinde [95], Felix Nyaende [100p] for PD

MEDALS TABLE

		Overall			Lg	C	T8	LC	BC	Africa			City
		G	S	B	G	G	G	G	G	G	S	B	
1	Mufulira Wanderers	27		3	9	**9**	**9**					3	Mufulira
2	Nkana	24	1	5	**11**	6	7				1	5	Kitwe
3	Kabwe Warriors	19			5	5	8	1					Kabwe
4	Power Dynamos	18	1		6	6	2	1	2	1	1		Kitwe
5	Green Buffaloes	12			6	1	5						Lusaka
	Zanaco	12			6	1	3	2					Lusaka
7	Roan United	8			1	4	3						Luanshya
	ZESCO United	8			3	1		1	**3**				Ndola
9	Nchanga Rangers	6	1		2	1	3					1	Chingola
10	City of Lusaka	5			1	2	2						Lusaka
11	Red Arrows	3			1	1	1						Lusaka
	Konkola Blades	3				3							Chililabombwe
13	Mufulira Blackpool	2			2								Mufulira
	Ndola United	2			1	1							Ndola
	Kitwe United	2					2						Kitwe
16	Chambishi	1					1						Kitwe
	Forest Rangers	1					1						Ndola
	Lusaka Celtic	1				1							Lusaka
	Lusaka Dynamos	1				1							Lusaka
	NAPSA Stars	1							1				Lusaka
	Strike Rovers	1			1								Ndola
	Vitafoam United	1				1							Ndola
	Zamsure	1				1							Lusaka

C = Castle/Independence/Mosi Cup • T8 = Top 8 Cup • LC = League Cup (2001-07) • BC = Barclays Cup

ZIM – ZIMBABWE

FIFA/COCA-COLA WORLD RANKING

'93	'94	'95	'96	'97	'98	'99	'00	'01	'02	'03	'04	'05	'06	'07	'08	'09	'10	'11	'12
46	51	59	71	74	74	67	68	68	57	53	60	53	76	87	97	109	119	98	101

2012

Jan	Feb	Mar	Apr	May	Jun	Jul	Aug	Sep	Oct	Nov	Dec	High	Low	Av
102	99	106	104	104	106	100	106	98	89	98	101	40	131	73

Football in Zimbabwe was overshadowed in 2012 by the 'Asiagate' match-fixing revelations which resulted in life bans for 15 players, coaches, officials and journalists and a lengthy list of suspensions - almost all later lifted - followed by an extensive commission of inquiry headed by a retired judge. The affair had an impact on the national team with the 'Brave Warriors', weakened by the suspension of another 70 footballers, missing out on the 2013 Africa Cup of Nations finals in neighbouring South Africa. It was a close run thing, though. Zimbabwe led Angola 3-1 after the first leg at home in Harare but that lead evaporated in no time in the return leg one month later in Luanda when Angola scored twice in the opening six minutes to win 2-0 and advance on away goals. The defeat prompted the resignation of coach Rahman Gumbo who had also overseen the disappointing start to the 2014 FIFA World Cup qualifiers with the 1-0 defeat at home to Guinea in their opening Group G match. The country's best-supported club Dynamos won the league and cup double for a second successive season by edging traditional rivals Highlanders in the championship race even though the Bulawayo-based side lost only one league game all season. In the cup final Rodrick Mutuma scored both goals as Dynamos beat Monomotapa 2-0.

CAF AFRICA CUP OF NATIONS RECORD
1957-1980 DNE **1982-2002** DNQ **2004** 12 r1 **2006** 12 r1 **2008-2013** DNQ

ZIMBABWE FOOTBALL ASSOCIATION (ZIFA)

53 Livingstone Avenue, Causeway, PO Box CY 114, Harare
☎ +263 4 798627
📠 +263 4 798626
✉ zifa@africaonline.co.zw
🌐 www.zifa.org.zw
FA 1965 CON 1965 FIFA 1965
P Cuthbert Dube
GS Jonathan Mashingaidze

THE STADIA
2014 FIFA World Cup Stadia
National Stadium
Harare   60 000

Other Main Stadia
Rufaro Stadium
Harare   35 000
Barbourfields
Bulawayo   32 000
Sakubva Stadium
Mutare   10 000
Ascot Stadium
Gweru   5 000

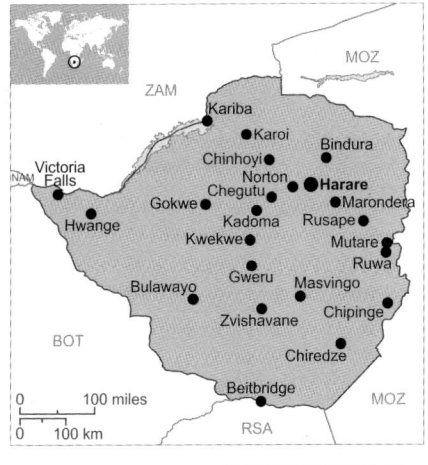

MAJOR CITIES/TOWNS
Popul.

1	Harare	1 727 713
2	Bulawayo	748 883
3	Chitungwiza	357 280
4	Mutare	185 238
5	Gweru	141 793
6	Epworth	140 645
7	Kwekwe	99 561
8	Kadoma	77 485
9	Masvingo	72 132
10	Norton	67 177
11	Marondera	63 717
12	Chinhoyi	61 289
13	Chegutu	46 359
14	Bindura	42 488
15	Zvishavane	34 851
16	Ruwa	34 693
17	Redcliff	34 601
18	Hwange	34 177
19	Beitbridge	33 763

REPUBLIC OF ZIMBABWE

Capital	Harare	Population	11 392 629 (73)	% in cities	37%
GDP per capita	$200 (229)	Area km²	390 757 km² (60)	GMT +/-	+2
Neighbours (km)	Botswana 813, Mozambique 1231, South Africa 225, Zambia 797

RECENT INTERNATIONAL MATCHES PLAYED BY ZIMBABWE

2008	Opponents		Score	Venue	Comp	Scorers	Att	Referee
20-08	Botswana	W	1-0	Harare	Fr	Edward Sadomba [30]		
7-09	Guinea	D	0-0	Harare	WCq		23 000	Evehe CMR
10-09	Oman	L	2-3	Muscat	Fr	Pride Tafirenyika [15], Justice Majabvi [67]		
11-10	Namibia	L	2-4	Windhoek	WCq	Esrom Nyandoro [58], Cuthbert Malajila [85]	4 000	Coulibaly MLI
2009								
11-02	Tanzania	D	0-0	Dar es Salaam	Fr			
23-03	Bahrain	L	2-5	Manama	Fr	Ashley Rambanapasi [86p], Tito Marfumo [91+]		
13-05	Jordan	L	0-2	Amman	Fr			
12-08	Lesotho	D	1-1	Bulawayo	Fr	Guthrie Zhokinyu [80]		
17-10	Mauritius	W	3-0	Harare	CCr1	Cuthbert Malajila 2 [48 57], Method Mwanjale [87]		Ebrahim RSA
19-10	Lesotho	D	2-2	Harare	CCr1	Cuthbert Malajila [6], Sello OG [62]		Ramocha BOT
26-10	Botswana	W	1-0	Bulawayo	CCqf	Mthulisi Maphosa [88]		Carvalho ANG
28-10	South Africa †	D	1-1	Harare	CCsf	Phillip Marufu [54], W 3-2p		Seechurn MRI
1-11	Zambia	W	3-1	Harare	CCf	Nyasha Mushekwi 2 [26 35], Cuthbert Malajila [45]		Carvalho ANG
1-12	Eritrea †	D	0-0	Nairobi	CFr1			
3-12	Somalia †	W	2-0	Nairobi	CFr1	Tapiwa Mangezi [30], Guthrie Zhokinyi [46]		
5-12	Rwanda †	L	0-1	Nairobi	CFr1			
8-12	Rwanda †	L	1-4	Nairobi	CFqf	Lionel Mtizwa [8]		
29-12	Thailand	L	0-3	Bangkok	Fr			
2010								
27-01	South Africa	L	0-3	Durban	Fr		35 000	Nhleko SWZ
3-03	Malawi	W	2-1	Harare	Fr	OG [17], Tafadzwa Rusike [25]		
2-06	Brazil	L	0-3	Harare	Fr		30 000	Martins ANG
4-08	Botswana	L	0-2	Selibe-Phikwe	Fr			
5-09	Liberia	D	1-1	Paynesville	CNq	Knowledge Musona [30]		Codjia BEN
10-10	Cape Verde Islands	D	0-0	Harare	CNq			Ndume GAB
2011								
26-03	Mali	L	0-1	Bamako	CNq			
5-06	Mali	W	2-1	Harare	CNq	Knowledge Musona 2 [45 90p]		
10-08	Zambia	W	2-0	Harare	Fr	Willard Katsande [45], Khama Billiat [47]		
4-09	Liberia	W	3-0	Harare	CNq	Willard Katsande [16], Ovidy Karuru [45], Khama Billiat [85]		
8-10	Cape Verde Islands	L	1-2	Praia	CNq	Knowledge Musona [68]		
15-11	South Africa	W	2-1	Harare	Fr	Knowledge Musona 2 [52 66]		
27-11	Djibouti	W	2-0	Dar es Salaam	CFr1	Donald Ngoma [9], Qadr Amin [73]		
29-11	Rwanda	L	0-2	Dar es Salaam	CFr1			
3-12	Tanzania	W	2-1	Dar es Salaam	CFr1	Donald Ngoma [1], OG [11]		
6-12	Uganda	L	0-1	Dar es Salaam	CFqf			
2012								
7-01	Botswana	D	0-0	Gaborone	Fr			
29-02	Burundi	L	1-2	Bujumbura	CNq	Knowledge Musona [60]		Abdel Rahman SDN
3-06	Guinea	L	0-1	Harare	WCq		30 000	Seechurn MRI
10-06	Mozambique	D	0-0	Maputo	WCq		26 000	Kalyango UGA
17-06	Burundi	W	1-0	Harare	CNq	Knowledge Musona [36]		Otogo-Castane GAB
16-07	Botswana	L	0-1	Molepolole	Fr			
17-07	Lesotho	W	5-3	Molepolole	Fr	Ronald Chitiyo [23], Nelson Mazivisa 2 [40 44], Rodwell Chinyengetere [50], Charles Sibanda [73]		
9-09	Angola	W	3-1	Harare	CNq	OG [4], Khama Billiat [21], Archieford Gutu [35]		Nampiandraza MAD
14-10	Angola	L	0-2	Luanda	CNq			Kirwa KEN

Fr = Friendly match • CN = CAF African Cup of Nations • CC = COSAFA Cup • CF = CECAFA Cup • WC = FIFA World Cup
q = qualifier • r1 = first round group • qf = quarter-final • sf = semi-final • f = final • † Not a full international

ZIMBABWE 2012

NATIONAL PREMIER SOCCER LEAGUE

	Pl	W	D	L	F	A	Pts	Dynamos	Highlanders	Chicken Inn	Monomatapa	Shabanie	Buffaloes	Platinum	Motor Action	Harare City	CAPS United	Hwange	Black Mambas	Gunners	Blue Rangers	Hardbody	Quelaton
Dynamos †	30	21	6	3	58	15	**69**		1-1	2-1	0-1	4-1	3-0	2-0	1-0	0-1	1-0	4-2	4-1	4-0	6-0	3-0	2-0
Highlanders	30	20	9	1	49	15	**69**	1-1		0-0	3-0	1-0	1-0	1-0	2-1	1-1	1-0	1-0	1-0	1-0	4-0	5-3	7-1
Chicken Inn	30	13	11	6	39	23	**50**	1-0	0-0		2-1	2-1	0-1	1-1	1-0	1-0	2-2	2-1	1-0	0-0	5-1	3-2	2-0
Monomatapa United	30	15	5	10	42	33	**50**	1-2	3-0	1-0		1-2	1-0	2-0	3-1	1-1	1-0	3-0	3-2	0-2	1-0	4-2	1-0
Shabanie Mine	30	12	10	8	35	30	**46**	0-0	0-2	1-1	2-1		2-2	0-0	0-2	1-0	0-0	2-1	1-1	2-0	2-1	1-0	1-0
Buffaloes	30	11	11	8	25	24	**44**	0-2	1-1	1-1	1-3	2-1		1-1	1-0	0-0	0-0	1-1	1-0	2-2	1-0	0-1	1-0
FC Platinum	30	12	7	11	40	39	**43**	1-2	1-3	1-1	0-3	2-2	1-0		2-0	0-1	0-2	1-0	2-4	2-1	2-1	3-1	2-0
Motor Action	30	12	6	12	35	28	**42**	0-0	0-0	1-1	0-1	1-1	1-1	3-0		0-0	0-3	2-1	2-2	0-1	3-2	1-0	2-0
Harare City	30	9	13	8	24	24	**40**	0-1	0-0	1-1	2-1	1-0	0-1	1-4	2-1		0-0	2-1	1-0	2-1	0-2	3-0	0-1
CAPS United	30	10	9	11	28	30	**39**	0-3	0-2	0-3	0-0	2-0	1-1	3-1	0-2	1-1		1-2	1-1	2-1	2-0	2-1	1-0
Hwange	30	10	6	14	49	47	**36**	0-2	0-1	1-1	5-1	1-4	1-0	1-1	2-0	0-0	3-2		2-1	0-3	7-1	5-1	4-3
Black Mambas	30	9	7	14	34	42	**34**	0-3	1-3	1-1	1-1	0-1	0-1	1-3	0-3	1-1	0-2	0-0		2-0	1-2	2-1	3-1
Gunners	30	10	4	16	27	36	**34**	1-2	0-1	2-0	1-0	0-2	0-1	1-3	0-1	1-0	2-0	1-1	0-2		1-0	2-1	1-0
Blue Rangers	30	6	7	17	30	64	**25**	1-1	0-2	0-3	1-1	1-1	0-2	1-2	0-5	1-1	0-1	2-2	2-2	3-2		3-2	3-1
Hardbody	30	6	6	18	26	48	**24**	1-1	0-2	1-0	0-0	1-1	0-2	0-0	2-0	1-1	0-1	2-0	0-1	1-1	0-1		1-0
Quelaton	30	3	5	22	15	58	**11**	0-1	1-1	0-3	3-2	0-3	0-0	0-4	0-3	1-1	1-1	0-5	0-1	1-0	1-1	0-1	

31/03/2012 - 18/11/2012 • † Qualified for the CAF Champions League

UHURU CUP 2012

Semi-finals		Finals	
Dynamos	0 4p		
Gunners	0 3p	**Dynamos**	2
Bantu Rovers	0	Highlanders	0
Highlanders	2	18-04-2012	

MEDALS TABLE

		All	Lg	C	IT	LC	S8	
		G	G	G	G	G		City
1	Dynamos	41	20	11	7	2	1	Harare
2	CAPS United	23	4	9	4	5	1	Harare
3	Highlanders	16	7	2	6	1		Bulawayo
4	Zimbabwe Saints	6	2	3	1			Bulawayo
5	Black Rhinos	5	2	1	2			Mutare
	Black Aces	5	2	2		1		Harare
7	Masvingo Utd	4		2	2			Masvingo
8	Hwange	3		3				Hwange
	Arcadia United	3	1	2				Harare
	Bulawayo Rov	3	2	1				Bulawayo
	Motor Action	3	1		1		1	Mutare

Lg = League • C = Castle/Unity/CBZ/Mbada Cup • IT = Independence Trophy/Uhuru Cup • LC = League Cup • S8 = Super Eight

MBADA DIAMONDS CUP 2012

Round of 16		Quarter-finals		Semi-finals		Final	
Dynamos	1 4p						
Quelaton	1 2p	**Dynamos**	3				
Chicken Inn	2	Gunners	0				
Gunners	3			**Dynamos**	3		
Buffaloes	2			CAPS United	0		
Black Mambas	1	Buffaloes	0				
Motor Action	0	**CAPS United**	2				
CAPS United	1					**Dynamos**	2
FC Platinum	3					Monomatapa United	0
Harare City	0	**FC Platinum**	1				
Hwange	0	Shabanie Mine	0			CUP FINAL	
Shabanie Mine	1			FC Platinum	0	National Stadium, Harare	
Highlanders	2			**Monomatapa United**	1	24-11-2012	
Blue Rangers	1	Highlanders	2			Scorer - Roderick Mutuma 2 [65] [74] for Dynamos	
Hardbody	2	**Monomatapa United**	3				
Monomatapa United	3						

PART THREE

THE CONTINENTAL CONFEDERATIONS

PART THREE

THE CONTINENTAL CONFEDERATIONS

AFC
ASIAN FOOTBALL CONFEDERATION

AFC MEMBER ASSOCIATIONS (46)

AFG - Afghanistan • AUS - Australia • BHR - Bahrain • BAN - Bangladesh • BHU - Bhutan • BRU - Brunei Darussalam • CAM - Cambodia
CHN - China PR • TPE - Chinese Taipei • GUM - Guam • HKG - Hong Kong • IND - India • IDN - Indonesia • IRN - Iran • IRQ - Iraq
JPN - Japan • JOR - Jordan • PRK - Korea DPR • KOR - Korea Republic • KUW - Kuwait • KGZ - Kyrgyzstan • LAO - Laos • LIB - Lebanon
MAC - Macau • MAS - Malaysia • MDV - Maldives • MGL - Mongolia • MYA - Myanmar • NEP - Nepal • OMA - Oman • PAK - Pakistan
PLE - Palestine • PHI - Philippines • QAT - Qatar • KSA - Saudi Arabia • SIN - Singapore • SRI - Sri Lanka • SYR - Syria • TJK - Tajikistan
THA - Thailand • TLS - Timor Leste • TKM - Turkmenistan • UAE - United Arab Emirates • UZB - Uzbekistan • VIE - Vietnam • YEM - Yemen

AFC PROVISIONAL ASSOCIATE MEMBER ASSOCIATION (1)
MNI - Northern Mariana Islands • Not affiliated to FIFA

After securing world titles in both 2010 and 2011 Asian football was hoping to make it three years on the trot with success at one of the six FIFA tournaments played in 2012. It didn't happen but the performances of the Asian representatives were very encouraging and only a penalty shoot-out defeat at the hands of France denied Korea DPR in the final of the FIFA U-17 Women's World Cup in Azerbaijan. At the London Olympics there was a silver medal for the Japanese women who lost 2-1 to the USA in the women's final while both Japan and South Korea reached the semi-finals in the men's tournament. Defeats at the hands of Mexico and Brazil respectively, saw them square up against each each in the bronze medal play-off, a match the Koreans won 2-0 to take their first ever Olympic football medal. The start of the year saw North Korea sucessfully defend their AFC Challenge Cup crown at the finals in Nepal where they beat Turkmenistan 2-1 in the final. 2012 also saw two major regional tournaments staged with the West Asian Championship attracting its strongest ever field of 11 entrants. The title was won for the first time by Syria, a nation deprived of any regular football as a result of the ongoing civil war. The year ended with the AFF Suzuki Cup for ASEAN nations which was won for a record fourth time by Singapore who beat Thailand 3-2 on aggregate in the final. In club football South Korea's excellent record in the AFC Champions League continued with Ulsan Hyundai winning their first title - the sixth different Korean club to be crowned Asian champions. They faced Al Ahli from Jeddah in the final which was played on their home ground in Ulsan, a match they comfortably won 3-0. There was success for Arab clubs in the AFC Cup where Al Kuwait beat Iraq's Arbil 4-0 in the final while Tajikistan's Esteghlal Dushanbe beat Shabab Al Am'ari from Palestine 2-1 in the AFC President's Cup final.

Asian Football Confederation (AFC)
AFC House, Jalan 1/155B, Bukit Jalil, 57000 Kuala Lumpur, Malaysia
Tel +60 3 89943388   Fax +60 3 89946168
media@the-afc.com
www.the-afc.com
Acting President: Zhang Jilong CHN
General Secretary: Alex Soosay MAS
AFC Formed: 1954

AFC EXECUTIVE COMMITTEE

Acting President: Zhang Jilong CHN	Vice-President: Tengku Abdullah Ahmad Shah MAS	Vice-President: Yousuf Al Serkal UAE
Vice-President: Moya Dodd AUS		Vice-President: Ganesh Thapa NEP
FIFA Vice-President: Prince Ali Bin Al Hussein JOR	FIFA ExCo Member: Worawi Makudi THA	FIFA ExCo Member: Vernon Manilal Fernando SRI

MEMBERS OF THE EXECUTIVE COMMITTEE

Dr Hafez Al Medlej KSA	Richard Lai GUM	Zaw Zaw MYA
Mahfuza Akhter Kiron BAN	Shk. Ali Bin Khalifa Al Khalifa BHR	Praful Patel IND
Kohzo Tashima JPN	Ganbold Buyannemekh MGL	Ali Azim MDV
Sayyid Khalid Hamed Al Busaidi OMA	Makhdoom Syed Faisal Saleh Hayat PAK	Winston Lee SIN
Tran Quoc Tuan VIE	Co-opted: Susan Shalabi Molano PLE	General-Secretary: Alex Soosay MAS

832   PART THREE – THE CONTINENTAL CONFEDERATIONS

MAP OF AFC MEMBER NATIONS

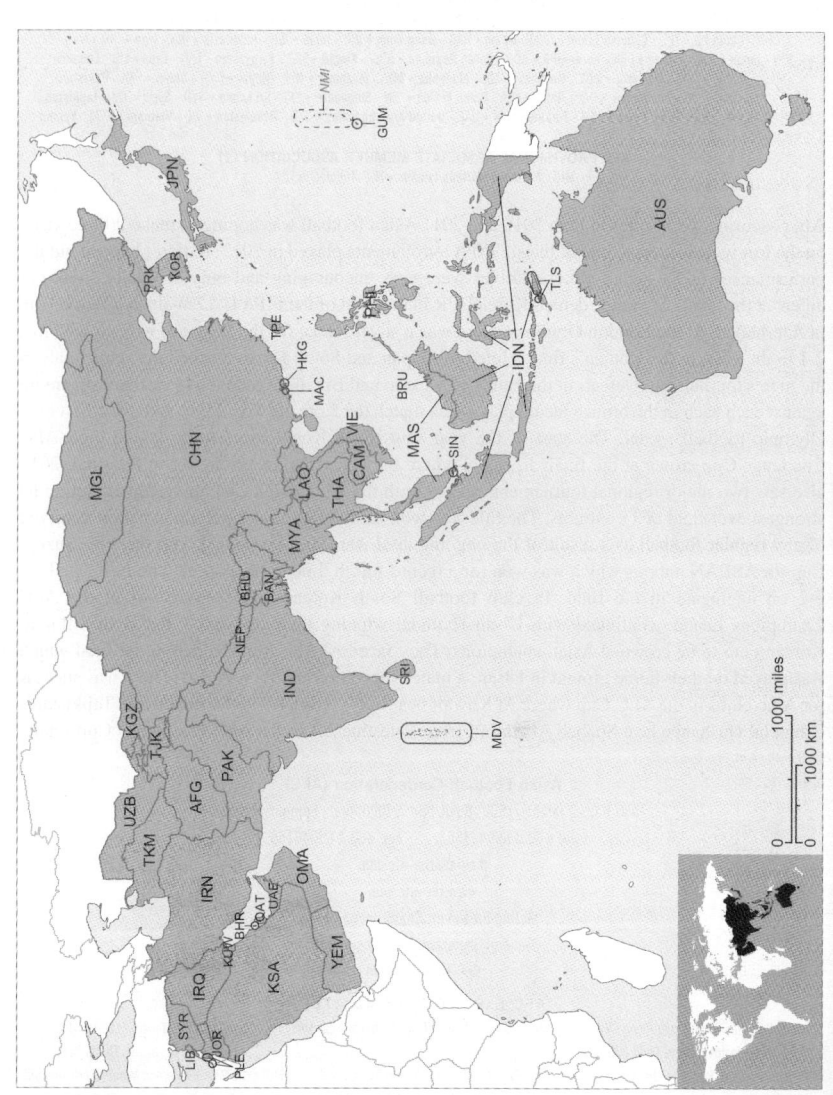

ASIAN TOURNAMENTS

ASIAN NATIONAL TEAM TOURNAMENTS

AFC ASIAN CUP

Year	Host Country	Winners	Score	Runners-up	Venue
1956	Hong Kong	Korea Republic	2-1	Israel	Government Stadium, Hong Kong
1960	Korea Republic	Korea Republic	3-0	Israel	Hyochang Park, Seoul
1964	Israel	Israel	2-0	India	Bloomfield, Jaffa
1968	Iran	Iran	3-1	Burma	Amjadieh, Tehran
1972	Thailand	Iran	2-1	Korea Republic	Suphachalasai, Bangkok
1976	Iran	Iran	1-0	Kuwait	Azadi, Tehran
1980	Kuwait	Kuwait	3-0	Korea Republic	Kuwait City
1984	Singapore	Saudi Arabia	2-0	China PR	National Stadium, Singapore
1988	Qatar	Saudi Arabia	0-0 4-3p	Korea Republic	Khalifa, Doha
1992	Japan	Japan	1-0	Saudi Arabia	Main Stadium, Hiroshima
1996	UAE	Saudi Arabia	0-0 4-2p	United Arab Emirates	Zayed, Abu Dhabi
2000	Lebanon	Japan	1-0	Saudi Arabia	Camille Chamoun, Beirut
2004	China PR	Japan	3-1	China PR	Workers' Stadium, Beijing
2007	ASEAN co-hosts	Iraq	1-0	Saudi Arabia	Gelora Bung Karno, Jakarta
2011	Qatar	Japan	1-0	Australia	Khalifa International, Doha

From 1956 to 1968 the tournament was played as a league. The result listed is that between the winners and runners-up.

AFC ASIAN CUP MEDALS TABLE

	Country	G	S	B	F	SF
1	Japan	4			4	5
2	Saudi Arabia	3	3		6	6
3	Iran	3		4	2	7
4	Korea Republic	2	3	4	3	6
5	Israel	1	2	1		
6	Kuwait	1	1	1	2	4
7	Iraq	1			1	2
8	China PR		2	2	2	6
9	Utd Arab Emirates		1		1	2
10	Australia		1		1	1
11	India		1			
	Myanmar		1			
13	Thailand			1		1
	Chinese Taipei			1		
	Hong Kong			1		
16	Bahrain					1
	Cambodia					1
	Korea DPR					1
	Uzbekistan					1
		15	15	14	22	44

KEY
G = Gold (winners) • **S** = Silver (runners-up) • **B** = Bronze (semi-finalists) • **F** = appearances in the final • **SF** = appearances in the semi-final

AFC CHALLENGE CUP

Year	Host Country	Winners	Score	Runners-up	Venue
2006	Bangladesh	Tajikistan	4-0	Sri Lanka	Bangabandhu, Dhaka
2008	India	India	4-1	Tajikistan	Ambedkar, Delhi
2010	Sri Lanka	Korea DPR	1-1 5-4p	Turkmenistan	Sugathadasa, Colombo
2012	Nepal	Korea DPR	2-1	Turkmenistan	Dasarath Rangasala, Kathmandu

AFC CHALLENGE CUP MEDALS TABLE

	Country	G	S	B	F	SF
1	Korea DPR	2		1	2	3
2	Tajikistan	1	1	1	2	3
3	India	1			1	1
4	Turkmenistan		2		2	2
5	Sri Lanka		1		1	1
6	Kyrgyzstan			1		1
	Nepal			1		1
	Philippines			1		1
		4	4	5	8	13

GULF CUP OF NATIONS

Year	Host Country	Winners	Score	Runners-up	Venue
1970	Bahrain	Kuwait	3-1†	Bahrain	Isa Town
1972	Saudi Arabia	Kuwait	2-2†	Saudi Arabia	Riyadh
1974	Kuwait	Kuwait	4-0	Saudi Arabia	Kuwait City
1976	Qatar	Kuwait	4-2‡	Iraq	Doha
1979	Iraq	Iraq	3-1†	Kuwait	Al Shabab, Baghdad
1982	UAE	Kuwait	2-0†	Bahrain	Abu Dhabi
1984	Oman	Iraq	1-1 4-3p‡	Qatar	Police Stadium, Muscat
1986	Bahrain	Kuwait	1-0†	UAE	Manama
1988	Saudi Arabia	Iraq	0-0†	UAE	King Fahd International, Riyadh
1990	Kuwait	Kuwait	2-0†	Qatar	Al Sadaqua Walsalam, Kuwait City
1992	Qatar	Qatar		Bahrain/Saudi Arabia	Doha
1994	UAE	Saudi Arabia	1-1†	UAE	Abu Dhabi
1996	Oman	Kuwait	2-1†	Qatar	Muscat
1998	Bahrain	Kuwait	1-2†	Saudi Arabia	Manama
2002	Saudi Arabia	Saudi Arabia	3-1†	Qatar	Riyadh
2003	Kuwait	Saudi Arabia	1-0†	Bahrain	Al Sadaqua Walsalam, Kuwait City
2004	Qatar	Qatar	1-1 6-5p	Oman	Doha
2007	UAE	UAE	1-0	Oman	Zayed Sports City, Abu Dhabi
2009	Oman	Oman	0-0 6-5p	Saudi Arabia	Sultan Qaboos, Muscat
2010	Yemen	Kuwait	1-0	Saudi Arabia	May 22, Aden
2013	Bahrain	UAE	2-1	Iraq	National Stadium, Riffa

† Played on a league basis. The result listed is between the top two teams • ‡ Play-off after top two finished level

GULF CUP OF NATIONS MEDALS TABLE

	Country	G	S	B
1	Kuwait	10	1	3
2	Saudi Arabia	3	6	7
3	Iraq	3	2	1
4	Qatar	2	4	3
5	UAE	2	3	5
6	Oman	1	2	
7	Bahrain		4	4
		21	22	23

SOUTH ASIAN FOOTBALL FEDERATION CUP

Year	Host Country	Winners	Score	Runners-up	Venue
1993	Pakistan	India	2-0	Sri Lanka	Lahore
1995	Sri Lanka	Sri Lanka	1-0	India	Colombo
1997	Nepal	India	5-1	Maldives	Dasharath Rangashala, Kathmandu

SOUTH ASIAN FOOTBALL FEDERATION CUP (CONT'D)

Year	Host Country	Winners	Score	Runners-up	Venue
1999	Goa	India	2-0	Bangladesh	Margao
2003	Bangladesh	Bangladesh	1-1 5-3p	Maldives	Bangabandu, Dhaka
2005	Pakistan	India	2-0	Bangladesh	Karachi
2008	Sri Lanka/Maldives	Maldives	1-0	India	Sugathadhasa, Colombo
2009	Bangladesh	India	0-0 3-1p	Maldives	Bangabandu, Dhaka
2011	India	India	4-0	Afghanistan	Jawaharlal Nehru, New Delhi

SOUTH ASIAN FOOTBALL FEDERATION CUP MEDALS TABLE

	Country	G	S	B
1	India	6	2	1
2	Maldives	1	3	3
3	Bangladesh	1	2	2
4	Sri Lanka	1	1	2
5	Afghanistan		1	
6	Nepal			2
	Pakistan			2
8	Bhutan			1
		9	9	13

ASEAN CHAMPIONSHIP

Year	Host Country	Winners	Score	Runners-up	Venue
1996		Thailand	1-0	Malaysia	
1998	Vietnam	Singapore	1-0	Vietnam	Hanoi Stadium, Hanoi
2000	Thailand	Thailand	4-1	Indonesia	Bangkok
2002	Indonesia/Sin'pore	Thailand	2-2 4-2p	Indonesia	Gelora Senayan, Jakarta
2004	Malaysia/Vietnam	Singapore	3-1 2-1	Indonesia	Jakarta, Singapore
2007	Singapore/Th'land	Singapore	2-1 1-1	Thailand	Singapore, Bangkok
2008	Indonesia/Th'land	Vietnam	2-1 1-1	Thailand	Bangkok, Hanoi
2010	Indonesia/Vietnam	Malaysia	3-0 1-2	Indonesia	Kuala Lumpur, Jakarta
2012	Malaysia/Thailand	Singapore	3-1 0-1	Thailand	Singapore/Bangkok

ASEAN CHAMPIONSHIP MEDALS TABLE

	Country	G	S	B
1	Singapore	4		1
2	Thailand	3	3	
3	Malaysia	1	1	4
	Vietnam	1	1	4
5	Indonesia		4	2
6	Philippines			2
		9	9	13

WEST ASIAN FOOTBALL FEDERATION CHAMPIONSHIP

Year	Host Country	Winners	Score	Runners-up	Venue
2000	Jordan	Iran	1-0	Syria	Malek Abdullah, Amman
2002	Syria	Iraq	3-2	Jordan	Al Abbassiyyine, Damascus
2004	Iran	Iran	4-1	Syria	Tehran
2007	Jordan	Iran	2-1	Iraq	International, Amman
2008	Iran	Iran	2-1	Jordan	Tehran
2010	Jordan	Kuwait	2-1	Iran	King Abdullah, Amman
2012	Kuwait	Syria	1-0	Iraq	Al Sadaqua Walsalam, Kuwait City

WEST ASIAN FOOTBALL CHAMPIONSHIP MEDALS TABLE

	Country	G	S	B
1	Iran	4	1	1
2	Iraq	1	2	2
	Syria	1	2	2
4	Kuwait	1		
5	Jordan		2	2
	Oman			1
	Qatar			1
	Yemen			1
		7	7	10

EAST ASIAN CHAMPIONSHIP

Year	Host Country	Winners	Score	Runners-up	Venue
2003	Japan	Korea Republic	0-0	Japan	International, Yokohama
2005	Korea Republic	China PR	2-2	Japan	World Cup Stadium, Daejeon
2008	China PR	Korea Republic	1-1	Japan	Sports Centre, Chongqing
2010	Japan	China PR	3-0	Korea Republic	Ajinomoto & National, Tokyo

Tournament played as a league. The result listed is that between the winners and runners-up

EAST ASIAN CHAMPIONSHIP MEDALS TABLE

	Country	G	S	B
1	Korea Republic	2	1	
2	China PR	2		2
3	Japan		3	1
4	Korea DPR			1
		4	4	4

FOOTBALL TOURNAMENT OF THE ASIAN GAMES

Year	Host Country	Winners	Score	Runners-up	Venue
1951	India	India	1-0	Iran	New Delhi
1954	Philippines	Chinese Taipei	5-2	Korea Republic	Manilla
1958	Japan	Chinese Taipei	3-2	Korea Republic	Tokyo
1962	Indonesia	India	2-1	Korea Republic	Djakarta
1966	Thailand	Burma	1-0	Iran	Bangkok
1970	Thailand	Burma/KoreaRepublic	0-0		Bangkok
1974	Iran	Iran	1-0	Israel	Tehran
1978	Thailand	Korea Rep/Korea DPR	0-0		Bangkok
1982	India	Iraq	1-0	Kuwait	New Dehli
1986	Korea Republic	Korea Republic	2-0	Saudi Arabia	Seoul
1990	China PR	Iran	0-0 4-1p	Korea DPR	Beijing
1994	Japan	Uzbekistan	4-2	China PR	Hiroshima
1998	Thailand	Iran	2-0	Kuwait	Bangkok
2002	Korea Republic	Iran	2-1	Japan	Busan
2006	Qatar	Qatar	1-0	Iraq	Doha
2010	China PR	Japan	1-0	UAE	Guangzhou

FOOTBALL TOURNAMENT OF THE ASIAN GAMES MEDALS TABLE

	Country	G	S	B
1	Iran	4	2	1
2	Korea Republic	3	3	3
3	India	2		1
	Myanmar	2		1

FOOTBALL TOURNAMENT OF THE ASIAN GAMES MEDALS TABLE (CONT'D)

	Country	G	S	B
5	Chinese Taipei	2		
6	Japan	1	1	2
7	Iraq	1	1	
	Korea DPR	1	1	
9	Qatar	1		
	Uzbekistan	1		
11	Kuwait		2	2
	China PR		1	2
13	Saudi Arabia		1	1
14	Israel		1	
	UAE		1	
16	Malaysia			2
17	Indonesia			1
		18	14	16

FOOTBALL TOURNAMENT OF THE SOUTH EAST ASIAN GAMES

Year	Host Country	Winners	Score	Runners-up	Venue
1959	Thailand	Vietnam	3-1	Thailand	Bangkok
1961	Burma	Malaysia	2-0	Burma	Rangoon
1965	Malaysia	Burma	2-2†	Thailand	Kuala Lumpur
1967	Thailand	Burma	2-1	South Vietnam	Bangkok
1969	Burma	Burma	3-0	Thailand	Rangoon
1971	Malaysia	Burma	2-1	Malaysia	Kuala Lumpur
1973	Singapore	Burma	2-1	South Vietnam	Singapore
1975	Thailand	Thailand	2-1	Malaysia	Bangkok
1977	Malaysia	Malaysia	2-0	Thailand	Kuala Lumpur
1979	Indonesia	Malaysia	1-0	Indonesia	Jakarta
1981	Philippines	Thailand	2-1	Malaysia	Manila
1983	Singapore	Thailand	2-1	Singapore	Singapore
1985	Thailand	Thailand	2-0	Singpaore	Bangkok
1987	Indonesia	Indonesia	1-0	Malaysia	Jakarta
1989	Malaysia	Malaysia	3-1	Singapore	Merdeka, Kuala Lumpur
1991	Philippines	Indonesia	0-0 4-3p	Thailand	Manila
1993	Singapore	Thailand	4-3	Myanmar	Singapore
1995	Thailand	Thailand	4-0	Vietnam	Chiang Mai
1997	Indonesia	Thailand	1-1 4-2p	Indonesia	Jakarta
1999	Brunei	Thailand	2-0	Vietnam	Bandar Seri Begawan
2001	Malaysia	Thailand	1-0	Malaysia	Kuala Lumpur
2003	Vietnam	Thailand	2-1	Vietnam	Hanoi
2005	Philippines	Thailand	3-0	Vietnam	Manila
2007	Thailand	Thailand	2-0	Myanmar	Korat
2009	Laos	Malaysia	1-0	Vietnam	Vientiane
2011	Indonesia	Malaysia	1-1 4-3p	Indonesia	Jakarta

† Gold medal shared • Until 2001 the SEA Games featured full national teams but is now a U-23 event

FOOTBALL TOURNAMENT OF THE SEA GAMES MEDALS TABLE

	Country	G	S	B
1	Thailand	13	4	5
2	Malaysia	6	5	7
3	Myanmar	5	3	4
4	Indonesia	2	3	3
5	Vietnam	1	7	4
6	Singapore		3	6
	Laos			1
		27	25	30

FOOTBALL TOURNAMENT OF THE SOUTH ASIAN GAMES

Year	Host Country	Winners	Score	Runners-up	Venue
1984	Nepal	Nepal	4-2	Bangladesh	Dasharath Rangashala, Kathmandu
1985	Bangladesh	India	1-1 4-1p	Bangladesh	Dhaka
1987	India	India	1-0	Nepal	Salt Lake, Calcutta
1989	Pakistan	Pakistan	1-0	Bangladesh	Islamabad
1991	Sri Lanka	Pakistan	2-0	Maldives	Colombo
1993	Bangladesh	Nepal	2-2 4-3p	India	Dhaka
1995	India	India	1-0	Bangladesh	Madras
1999	Nepal	Bangladesh	1-0	Nepal	Dasharath Rangashala, Kathmandu
2004	Pakistan	Pakistan	1-0	India	Jinnah Stadium, Islamabad
2006	Sri Lanka	Pakistan	1-0	Sri Lanka	Colombo
2010	Bangladesh	Bangladesh	4-0	Afghanistan	Bangabandhu, Dhaka

FOOTBALL TOURNAMENT OF THE SOUTH ASIAN GAMES MEDALS TABLE

	Country	G	S	B
1	Pakistan	4		1
2	India	3	2	2
3	Bangladesh	2	4	1
4	Nepal	2	2	2
5	Sri Lanka		1	3
6	Maldives		1	2
7	Afghanistan		1	
		11	11	11

FOOTBALL TOURNAMENT OF THE EAST ASIAN GAMES

Year	Host Country	Winners	Score	Runners-up	Venue
1993	China PR	Korea Republic	1-1†	Korea DPR	Shanghai
1997	Korea Republic	Korea Republic	0-1†	Japan	Pusan
2001	Japan	Japan	2-1	Australia	Nagai, Osaka
2005	Macao	China PR	1-0	Korea DPR	Macau Stadium, Macau
2009	Hong Kong	Hong Kong	1-1 4-2p	Japan	Hong Kong

† Played on a league basis. The result listed is between the top two teams, both of which occurred in the last round of games • U-23 event

EAST ASIAN CHAMPIONSHIP MEDALS TABLE

	Country	G	S	B
1	Korea Republic	2		2
2	Japan	1	2	1
3	China PR	1		2
4	Hong Kong	1		
5	Korea DPR		2	
6	Australia		1	
		5	5	5

ASIAN CLUB TOURNAMENTS

AFC CHAMPIONS LEAGUE

Year	Winners	Country	Score	Country	Runners-up
1967	Hapoel Tel Aviv	ISR	2-1	MAS	Selangor
1968	Maccabi Tel Aviv	ISR	1-0	KOR	Yangzee
1970	Taj Club	IRN	2-1	ISR	Hapoel Tel Aviv
1971	Maccabi Tel Aviv	ISR	W-O	IRQ	Police Club

AFC CHAMPIONS LEAGUE (CONT'D)

Year	Winners	Country	Score	Country	Runners-up
1986	Daewoo Royals	KOR	3-1	KSA	Al Ahly
1987	Furukawa	JPN	4-3	KSA	Al Hilal
1988	Yomiuri	JPN	W-0	KSA	Al Hilal
1989	Al Saad	QAT	2-3 1-0	IRQ	Al Rasheed
1990	Liaoning	CHN	2-1 1-1	JPN	Nissan
1991	Esteghlal SC	IRN	2-1	CHN	Liaoning
1992	Al Hilal	KSA	1-1 4-3p	IRN	Esteghlal SC
1993	Pas	IRN	1-0	KSA	Al Shabab
1994	Thai Farmers Bank	THA	2-1	OMA	Omani Club
1995	Thai Farmers Bank	THA	1-0	QAT	Al Arabi
1996	Ilhwa Chunma	KOR	1-0	KSA	Al Nasr
1997	Pohang Steelers	KOR	2-1	KOR	Ilhwa Chunma
1998	Pohang Steelers	KOR	0-0 6-5p	CHN	Dalian
1999	Jubilo Iwata	JPN	2-1	IRN	Esteghlal SC
2000	Al Hilal	KSA	3-2	JPN	Jubilo Iwata
2001	Suwon Samsung Bluewings	KOR	1-0	JPN	Jubilo Iwata
2002	Suwon Samsung Bluewings	KOR	0-0 4-2p	KOR	Anyang LG Cheetahs
2003	Al Ain	UAE	2-0 0-1	THA	BEC Tero Sasana
2004	Al Ittihad	KSA	1-3 5-0	KOR	Seongnam Ilhwa Chunma
2005	Al Ittihad	KSA	1-1 4-2	UAE	Al Ain
2006	Jeonbuk Hyundai Motors	KOR	2-0 1-2	SYR	Al Karama
2007	Urawa Reds	JPN	1-1 2-0	IRN	Sepahan
2008	Gamba Osaka	JPN	3-0 2-0	AUS	Adelaide United
2009	Pohang Steelers	KOR	2-1	KSA	Al Ittihad
2010	Seongnam Ilhwa Chunma	KOR	3-1	IRN	Zob Ahan
2011	Al Sadd	QAT	2-2 4-2p	KOR	Jeonbuk Hyundai Motors
2012	Ulsan Hyundai	KOR	3-0	KSA	Al Ahli

AFC CHAMPIONS LEAGUE MEDALS TABLE

	Country	G	S	B	F	SF
1	Korea Republic	10	5	6	15	24
2	Japan	5	3	4	8	13
3	Saudi Arabia	4	7	5	11	16
4	Iran	3	4	5	7	14
5	Israel	3	1		4	4
6	Qatar	2	1	2	3	5
7	Thailand	2	1	1	3	4
8	China PR	1	2	3	3	8
9	UAE	1	1	3	2	6
10	Iraq		2		2	4
11	Syria		1	1	1	2
12	Australia		1		1	1
	Malaysia		1		1	1
	Oman		1		1	1
15	Uzbekistan			5		6
16	Indonesia			1		3
17	Lebanon			1		1
	Korea DPR			1		1
	Kuwait			1		
20	India					1
	Kazakhstan					1
		31	31	37	62	117

AFC CHAMPIONS LEAGUE MEDALS TABLE – CLUBS

	Club		G	S	B
1	Pohang Steelers	KOR	3		
2	Esteghlal	IRN	2	2	3
3	Al Hilal	KSA	2	2	2
4	Seongnam Ilhwa Chunma	KOR	2	2	1
5	Al Ittihad	KSA	2	1	2
6	Suwon Samsung Bluewings	KOR	2		1
	Thai Farmers Bank	THA	2		1
8	Maccabi Tel Aviv	ISR	2		
9	Al Saad	QAT	2		
10	Jubilo Iwata	JPN	1	2	
11	Al Ain	UAE	1	1	1
	Liaoning	CHN	1	1	1
	Jeonbuk Hyundai Motors	KOR	1	1	1
14	Hapoel Tel Aviv	ISR	1	1	
15	Busan I'Park	KOR	1		1
	Urawa Reds	JPN	1		1
	Tokyo Verdy	JPN	1		1
	Ulsan Hyundai	KOR	1		1
19	Gamba Osaka	JPN	1		
	JEF United	JPN	1		
	Pass	IRN	1		
22	Al Ahli	KSA		2	
23	Dalian	CHN		1	1
	Al Shabab	KSA		1	1
25	Adelaide United	AUS		1	
	Al Arabi	QAT		1	
	Al Karama	SYR		1	

AFC CHAMPIONS LEAGUE MEDALS TABLE (CONT'D)

	Club		G	S	B
	Al Nasr	KSA		1	
	Al Rasheed	IRQ		1	
	Anyang LG Cheetahs	KOR		1	
	BEC Tero Sasana	THA		1	
	Omani Club	OMA		1	
	Police	IRQ		1	
	Selangor	MAS		1	
	Sepahan	IRN		1	
	Yangzee	KOR		1	
	Yokohama Marinos	JPN		1	
	Zob Ahan	IRN		1	
39	Pirouzi	IRN			3
40	Bunyodkor Tashkent	UZB			2
	Pakhtakor Tashkent	UZB			2
42	Al Qadisiya	KUW			1
	Al Rayyan	QAT			1
	Al Wasl	UAE			1
	April 25th	PRK			1
	Homenetmen	LIB			1
	Nagoya Grampus	JPN			1
	Neftchi Fergana	UZB			1
	Sanfrecce Hiroshima	JPN			1
	Shenzhen	CHN			1
	Tiga Berlian	IDN			1
	Tungsten Mining	KOR			1
	Umm Salal	QAT			1
	Al Wahda	UAE			1
			31	31	39

ASIAN CUP WINNERS' CUP

Year	Winners	Country	Score	Country	Runners-up
1991	Pirouzi	IRN	0-0 1-0	BHR	Al Muharraq
1992	Nissan	JPN	1-1 5-0	KSA	Al Nasr
1993	Nissan	JPN	1-1 1-0	IRN	Pirouzi
1994	Al-Qadisiyah	KSA	4-2 2-0	HKG	South China
1995	Yokohama Flugels	JPN	2-1	UAE	Al Shaab
1996	Bellmare Hiratsuka	JPN	2-1	IRQ	Al Talaba
1997	Al Hilal	KSA	3-1	JPN	Nagoya Grampus Eight
1998	Al Nasr	KSA	1-0	KOR	Suwon Samsung Bluewings
1999	Al Ittihad	KSA	3-2	KOR	Chunnam Dragons
2000	Shimizu S-Pulse	JPN	1-0	IRQ	Al Zawra
2001	Al Shabab	KSA	4-2	CHN	Dalian Shide
2002	Al Hilal	KSA	2-1	KOR	Chonbuk Hyundai Motors

CUP WINNERS CUP MEDALS TABLE

	Country	G	S	B	F	SF
1	Saudi Arabia	6	1	3	7	10
2	Japan	5	1	4	6	10
3	Iran	1	1		2	4
4	Korea Republic		3	1	3	4
5	Iraq		2		2	3
6	China PR		1	1	1	3
7	United Arab Emirates		1	1	1	2
8	Bahrain		1		1	1
	Hong Kong		1		1	1
10	Qatar			2		2
11	Thailand			1		2

CUP WINNERS CUP MEDALS TABLE (CONT'D)

	Country	G	S	B	F	SF
12	Indonesia			1		1
	Jordan				1	1
	Vietnam			1		1
15	Uzbekistan					1
	Kuwait					1
	Turkmenistan					1
		12	12	16	24	48

ASIAN CUP WINNERS CUP MEDALS TABLE – CLUBS

	Club		G	S	B
1	Yokohama Marinos (Nissan)	JPN	2		1
2	Al Hilal	KSA	2		1
3	Pirouzi	IRN	1	1	
	Al Nasr	KSA	1	1	
5	Al Ittihad	KSA	1		2
6	Yokohama Flugels	JPN	1		1
	Shimizu S-Pulse	JPN	1		1
8	Al Qadisiyah	KSA	1		
	Bellmare Hiratsuka	JPN	1		
	Al Shabab	KSA	1		
11	Al Shaab	UAE		1	
	Al Talaba	IRQ		1	
	Al Zawra	IRQ		1	
	Chunnam Dragons	KOR		1	
	Jeonbuk Hyundai Motors	KOR		1	
	Dalian	CHN		1	

ASIAN CUP WINNERS CUP MEDALS TABLE (CONT'D)

	Club		G	S	B
	Muharraq	BHR		1	
	Nagoya Grampus Eight	JPN		1	
	South China	HKG		1	
	Suwon Samsung Bluewings	KOR		1	
21	Al Shabab	UAE			1
	Al Ramtha	JOR			1
	Bangkok Bank	THA			1
	Pupuk Kaltim	IDN			1
	Quang Nam Danang	VIE			1
	Al Arabi	QAT			1
	Al Sadd	QAT			1
	Ulsan Hyundai	KOR			1
	Beijing Guoan	CHN			1
	Kashima Antlers	JPN			1
			12	12	16

AFC CUP

Year	Winners	Country	Score	Country	Runners-up
2004	Al Jaish	SYR	3-2 0-1	SYR	Al Wahda
2005	Al Faysali	JOR	1-0 3-2	LIB	Al Nejmeh
2006	Al Faysali	JOR	3-0 2-4	BHR	Muharraq
2007	Shabab Al Ordun	JOR	1-0 1-1	JOR	Al Faysali
2008	Muharraq	BHR	5-1 5-4	LIB	Safa
2009	Al Kuwait	KUW	2-1	SYR	Al Karama
2010	Al Ittihad Aleppo	SYR	1-1 4-2p	KUW	Al Qadisiya
2011	Nasaf Karshi	UZB	2-1	KUW	Al Kuwait
2012	Al Kuwait	KUW	4-0	IRQ	Arbil

AFC CUP MEDALS TABLE

	Country	G	S	B	F	SF
1	Jordan	3	1	3	4	7
2	Syria	2	2		4	4
3	Bahrain	1	1	1	2	3
4	Kuwait	2	2		4	4
5	Uzbekistan	1			1	1
6	Lebanon		2	2	2	4
7	Singapore			2		2
	Hong Kong			2		2

AFC CUP MEDALS TABLE (CONT'D)

	Country	G	S	B	F	SF
9	Maldives			1		1
	India			1		1
	Iraq		1	1	1	2
	Oman			1		1
	Saudi Arabia			1		1
	Thailand			2		2
				1		1
		8	8	16	16	32

AFC CUP MEDALS TABLE – CLUBS

	Club		G	S	B
1	Al Faysali	JOR	2	1	
	Al Kuwait	KUW	2	1	
3	Muharraq	BHR	1	1	
4	Al Ittihad Aleppo	SYR	1		
	Al Jaish	SYR	1		
	Al Shabab Al Ordun	JOR	1		
	Nasaf Karshi	UZB	1		
8	Al Nijmeh	LIB		1	2
9	Arbil	IRQ		1	1
10	Al Karama	SYR		1	
	Al Qadisiya	KUW		1	
	Safa	LIB		1	
	Al Wahda	SYR		1	
14	Al Wihdat	JOR			3

AFC CUP MEDALS TABLE (CONT'D)

	Club		G	S	B
15	Binh Duong	VIE			1
	Chonburi	THA			1
	Dempo SC	IND			1
	Geylang United	SIN			1
	Home United	SIN			1
	Al Ittifaq	KSA			1
	Muangthong United	THA			1
	Al Nahda	OMA			1
	New Radiant	MDV			1
	Riffa	BHR			1
	South China	HGK			1
	Sun Hei	HKG			1
			9	9	18

AFC PRESIDENT'S CUP

Year	Winners	Country	Score	Country	Runners-up
2005	Regar TadAZ	TJK	3-0	KGZ	Dordoi-Dynamo
2006	Dordoi-Dynamo	KGZ	2-1	TJK	Vakhsh Qurgonteppa
2007	Dordoi-Dynamo	KGZ	2-1	NEP	Mahendra Police Club
2008	Regar TadAZ	TJK	1-1 4-3p	KGZ	Dordoi-Dynamo
2009	Regar TadAZ	TJK	2-0	KGZ	Dordoi-Dynamo
2010	Yadanabon	MYA	1-0	KGZ	Dordoi-Dynamo
2011	Kaohsiung Taipower	TPE	3-2	CAM	Phnom Penh Crown
2012	Esteghlal Dushanbe	TJK	2-1	PLE	Shabab Al Am'ari

AFC PRESIDENT'S CUP MEDALS TABLE

	Country	G	S	B	F	SF
1	Tajikistan	4	1	2	5	6
2	Kyrgyzstan	2	4		6	6
3	Chinese Taipei	1		1	1	1
4	Myanmar	1			1	1
5	Nepal		1	2	1	3
6	Cambodia		1	1	1	1
7	Palestine		1		1	
8	Turkmenistan			3		3
9	Sri Lanka			2		2
	Pakistan			1		1
		8	8	12	16	24

AFC PRESIDENT'S CUP MEDALS TABLE

	Club		G	S	B
1	Regar TadAZ	TJK	3		1
2	Dordoi-Dynamo	KGZ	2	4	
3	Esteghlal Dushanbe	TJK	1		
	Kaohsiung Taipower	TPE	1		
	Yadanabon	MYA	1		
6	Nepal Police Club	NEP		1	1
	Vakhsh Qurgonteppa	TJK		1	1
8	Phnom Penh Crown	CAM		1	
	Shabab Al Am'ari	PLE		1	
10	FK Ashgabat	TKM			2
11	Blue Star Club	SRI			1
	HTTU Ashgabat	TKM			1
	Khmera	CAM			1
	Ratnam SC	SRI			1
	Tatung	TPE			1
	Three Star Club	NEP			1
	WAPDA	PAK			1
			8	8	12

ASIAN YOUTH TOURNAMENTS

AFC U-19 CHAMPIONSHIP

Year	Host Country	Winners	Score	Runners-up	Venue
1959	Malaysia	Korea Republic	2-1	Malaysia	Kuala Lumpur
1960	Malaysia	Korea Republic	4-0	Malaysia	Kuala Lumpur
1961	Thailand	Burma	0-0†	Indonesia	Bangkok
1962	Thailand	Thailand	2-1	Korea Republic	Bangkok
1963	Malaysia	Burma	2-2†	Korea Republic	Penang
1964	Vietnam	Burma	0-0†	Israel	Saigon
1965	Japan	Israel	5-0	Burma	Tokyo
1966	Philippines	Burma	1-1	Israel	Manila
1967	Thailand	Israel	3-0	Indonesia	Bangkok
1968	Korea Republic	Burma	4-0	Malaysia	Seoul
1969	Thailand	Burma	2-2†	Thailand	Bangkok
1970	Philippines	Burma	3-0	India	Manila
1971	Japan	Israel	1-0	Korea Republic	Tokyo
1972	Thailand	Israel	1-0	Korea Republic	Bangkok
1973	Iran	Iran	2-0	Japan	Tehran
1974	Thailand	Iran	2-2†	India	Bangkok
1975	Kuwait	Iran	0-0†	Iraq	Kuwait City
1976	Thailand	Iran	0-0†	Korea DPR	Bangkok
1977	Iran	Iraq	4-3	Iran	Tehran
1978	Bangladesh	Iraq	1-1†	Korea Republic	Dhaka
1980	Thailand	Korea Republic	4-1‡	Qatar	Bangkok
1982	Thailand	Korea Republic	1-1‡	China PR	Bangkok
1984	UAE	China PR	2-2‡	Saudi Arabia	Abu Dhabi
1986	Saudi Arabia	Saudi Arabia	2-0	Bahrain	Riyadh
1988	Qatar	Iraq	1-1 5-4p	Syria	Doha
1990	Indonesia	Korea Republic	0-0 4-3p	Korea DPR	Jakarta
1992	UAE	Saudi Arabia	2-0	Korea Republic	Dubai
1994	Indonesia	Syria	2-1	Japan	Jakarta
1996	Korea Republic	Korea Republic	3-0	China PR	Suwon

AFC U-19 CHAMPIONSHIP (CONT'D)

Year	Host Country	Winners	Score	Runners-up	Venue
1998	Thailand	Korea Republic	2-1	Japan	Chiang Mai
2000	Iran	Iraq	2-1	Japan	Tehran
2002	Qatar	Korea Republic	1-0	Japan	Doha
2004	Malaysia	Korea Republic	2-0	China PR	Kuala Lumpur
2006	India	Korea DPR	1-1 5-3p	Japan	Kolkata
2008	Saudi Arabia	UAE	2-1	Uzbekistan	Damman
2010	China PR	Korea DPR	3-2	Australia	Zibo
2012	UAE	Korea Republic	1-1 4-1p	Iraq	Ras al-Khaimah

† Title shared between both finalists • ‡ Played on a league system so the match indicated was not a final

AFC U-19 MEDALS TABLE

	Country	G	S	B
1	Korea Republic	12	4	4
2	Myanmar	7	1	2
3	Israel	6		1
4	Iraq	5	1	1
5	Iran	5	1	1
6	Korea DPR	3	1	3
7	Saudi Arabia	2	1	2
8	Thailand	2		4
9	China PR	1	3	2
10	Indonesia	1	2	1
11	Syria	1	1	1
12	India	1	1	
13	UAE	1		2
14	Japan		6	4
15	Malaysia		3	1
16	Qatar		1	1
	Bahrain		1	1
	Uzbekistan		1	1
19	Australia		1	
20	Kuwait			2
21	Hong Kong			1
	Vietnam			1
		47	29	36

AFC U-16 CHAMPIONSHIP

Year	Host Country	Winners	Score	Runners-up	Venue
1984	Qatar	Saudi Arabia	4-3	Qatar	Doha
1986	Qatar	Korea Republic	0-0 5-4p	Qatar	Doha
1988	Thailand	Saudi Arabia	2-0	Bahrain	Bangkok
1990	UAE	Qatar	2-0	UAE	Dubai
1992	Saudi Arabia	China PR	2-2 8-7p	Qatar	Riyadh
1994	Qatar	Japan	1-0	Qatar	Doha
1996	Thailand	Oman	1-0	Thailand	Bangkok
1998	Qatar	Thailand	1-1 3-2p	Qatar	Doha
2000	Vietnam SR	Oman	1-0	Iran	Danang
2002	UAE	Korea Republic	1-1 5-3p	Yemen	Abu Dhabi
2004	Japan	China PR	1-0	Korea DPR	Shizuoka
2006	Singapore	Japan	4-2	Korea DPR	Singapore
2008	Uzbekistan	Iran	2-1	Korea Republic	Tashkent
2010	Uzbekistan	Korea DPR	2-0	Uzbekistan	Tashkent
2012	Iran	Uzbekistan	1-1 3-1p	Japan	Tehran

AFC U-16 MEDALS TABLE

	Country	G	S	B
1	Japan	2	1	1
2	Korea Republic	2	1	
3	China PR	2		3
4	Saudi Arabia	2		2
5	Oman	2		1
6	Qatar	1	5	1
7	Korea DPR	1	2	
8	Iran	1	1	
	Thailand	1	1	
	Uzbekistan	1	1	
11	Bahrain		1	2
12	UAE		1	
	Yemen		1	
14	Iraq			1
	Tajikistan			1
		15	15	12

ASIAN WOMEN'S TOURNAMENTS

AFC WOMEN'S ASIAN CUP

Year	Host Country	Winners	Score	Runners-up	Venue
1975	Hong Kong	New Zealand	3-1	Thailand	Government Stadium, Hong Kong
1977	Chinese Taipei	Chinese Taipei	3-1	Thailand	Municipal Stadium, Taipei
1979	India	Chinese Taipei	2-0	India	Calicut
1981	Hong Kong	Chinese Taipei	5-0	Thailand	Government Stadium, Hong Kong
1983	Thailand	Thailand	3-0	India	Bangkok
1986	Hong Kong	China PR	2-0	Japan	Mong Kok, Hong Kong
1989	Hong Kong	China PR	1-0	Chinese Taipei	Mong Kok, Hong Kong
1991	Japan	China PR	5-0	Japan	Fukuoka
1993	Malaysia	China PR	3-0	Korea DPR	Kuching
1995	Malaysia	China PR	2-0	Japan	
1997	China PR	China PR	2-0	Korea DPR	Guangdong
1999	Philippines	China PR	3-0	Chinese Taipei	Bacolod City
2001	Chinese Taipei	Korea DPR	2-0	Japan	Yunlin County Stadium, Dounan
2003	Thailand	Korea DPR	2-1	China PR	Rajamangala, Bangkok
2006	Australia	China PR	2-2 4-2p	Australia	Hindmarsh Stadium, Adelaide
2008	Vietnam	Korea DPR	2-1	China PR	Thong Nhat, Ho Chi Minh City
2010	China PR	Australia	1-1 5-4p	Korea DPR	Chengdu Sports Center, Cengdu

AFC WOMEN'S ASIAN CUP MEDALS TABLE

	Country	G	S	B
1	China PR	8	2	1
2	Korea DPR	3	3	2
3	Chinese Taipei	3	2	2
4	Thailand	1	3	1
5	Australia	1	1	1
6	New Zealand	1		
7	Japan		4	5
8	India		2	1
9	Hong Kong			1
	Korea Republic			1
	Singapore			1
	Malaysia			1
		18	14	16

WOMEN'S FOOTBALL TOURNAMENT OF THE ASIAN GAMES

Year	Host Country	Winners	Score	Runners-up	Venue
1990	China PR	China PR	5-0	Japan	Beijing
1994	Japan	China PR	2-0	Japan	Hiroshima
1998	Thailand	China PR	1-0	Korea DPR	Bangkok
2002	Korea Republic	Korea DPR	0-0	China PR	Busan
2006	Qatar	Korea DPR	0-0 4-2p	Japan	Doha
2010	China PR	Australia	1-1 5-4p	Korea DPR	Chengdu

In 1990, 1994 and 2002 the tournament was played as a league. The result listed is that between the winners and runners-up

WOMEN'S FOOTBALL TOURNAMENT OF THE ASIAN GAMES MEDALS TABLE

	Country	G	S	B
1	China PR	3	1	1
2	Korea DPR	2	2	1
3	Japan	1	3	2
4	Chinese Taipei			1
	Korea Republic			1

AFC U-19 WOMEN'S CHAMPIONSHIP

Year	Host Country	Winners	Score	Runners-up	Venue
2002	India	Japan	2-1	Chinese Taipei	
2006	Malaysia	China PR	1-0	Korea DPR	
2007	China PR	Korea DPR	1-0	Japan	Sports Centre, Chongqing
2009	China PR	Japan	2-1	Korea Republic	Hankou Sports Stadium, Wuhan
2011	Vietnam	Japan	2-1	Korea DPR	Thong Nhat, Ho Chi Minh City

AFC U-19 WOMEN'S CHAMPIONSHIP MEDALS TABLE

	Country	G	S	B
1	Japan	3	1	
2	Korea DPR	1	2	2
3	China PR	1	1	3
4	Korea Republic	1	1	
5	Chinese Taipei		1	
6	Australia			1
		6	6	6

AFC U-16 WOMEN'S CHAMPIONSHIP

Year	Host Country	Winners	Score	Runners-up	Venue
2005	Korea Republic	Japan	1-1 3-1p	China PR	Namhae
2007	Malaysia	Korea DPR	3-0	Japan	MPPJ Stadium, Petaling Jaya
2009	Thailand	Korea Republic	4-0	Korea DPR	Supachalasai, Bangkok
2011	China PR	Japan	1-0	Korea DPR	Jiangning Sports Center, Nanjing

In 2011 the U-19 and U-16 tournaments were played as a league. The result listed is that between the winners and runners-up

AFC U-16 WOMEN'S CHAMPIONSHIP MEDALS TABLE

	Country	G	S	B
1	Japan	2	1	1
2	Korea DPR	1	2	
3	Korea Republic	1		1
4	China PR		1	1
5	Thailand			1
		4	4	4

NATIONAL TEAM TOURNAMENTS IN ASIA 2012

AFC CHALLENGE CUP NEPAL 2012

Qualifying groups

Group A	Pts
Palestine	7
Philippines	5
Bangladesh	3
Myanmar	1

Group B	Pts
India	7
Turkmenistan	7
Pakistan	3
Chinese Taipei	0

Group C	Pts
Maldives	7
Tajikistan	7
Kyrgyzstan	3
Cambodia	0

Group D	Pts
Korea DPR	9
Nepal	4
Afghanistan	3
Sri Lanka	1

First round groups

Group A	Pts
Turkmenistan	7
Palestine	7
Maldives	3
Nepal	0

Group B	Pts
Korea DPR	9
Philippines	6
Tajikistan	3
India	0

Semi-finals

Korea DPR	2
Palestine	0

Philippines	1
Turkmenistan	2

Final

Korea DPR	2
Turkmenistan	1

3rd Place Play-off

Philippines	4
Palestine	3

Finals held in Kathmandu, Nepal from 8-03-2012 to 19-03-2012

Preliminary Round

Bhutan 0-3 0-2 **Afghanistan** • **Philippines** 2-0 1-2 Mongolia • **Chinese Taipei** 5-2 1-1 Laos • **Cambodia** 3-1 2-3 Macau

PRELIMINARY ROUND

TAU DEVI LAL, PANCHKULA
23-03-2011, Att: 200, Ref: Mahapab THA

Bhutan	0
Afghanistan	3

AFG - Walizada 3 [2 36 80]

BHU: LEKI - P. RINCHEN, PEMA (c) (Kinley TENZIN 68), Jigme TENZIN, Kelzang DORJI (Dawa GYELTSHEN 58) - Passang TSHERING, NIM, NAWANG, Chimi DORJI• - (Sonam TENZIN 31) - Karma Shedrup TSHERING, CHENCHO. Tr: Hiroki MATSUYAMA

AFG: Mansur FAQIRYAR - Maqaddar QAZIZADA• (Ali Ahmad YARZADA 84), Zohib ISLAM, Zakria REZAI, Djelaluddin SHARITYAR - Maqsood HASHEMI (Masiullah BARAKZAI 62), Israfeel KOHISTANI (c), Wahid NADEEM, Arian HAREZ - Mohammad WALIZADA, Mohammad MASHRIQI (Hashmatullah BARAKZAI 66). Tr: Yosuf KARGAR

TAU DEVI LAL, PANCHKULA
25-03-2011, Att: 2000, Ref: Mombeni IRN

Afghanistan	2
Bhutan	0

AFG - Nadeem [61], Kohistani [65]

AFG: Mansur FAQIRYAR (Hamidullah YOUSUFZAI 75) - Maqaddar QAZIZADA•, Zohib ISLAM (FAISAL 72), Ali Ahmad YARZADA, Djelaluddin SHARITYAR (c) - Maqsood HASHEMI•, Israfeel KOHISTANI, Nadeem WAHID, Arian HAREZ• - Mohammad WALIZADA, Mohammad MASHRIQI (Hashmatullah BARAKZAI 48). Tr: Yosuf KARGAR

BHU: LEKI (Hari GURUNG 77) - P. RINCHEN, PEMA (c), Jigme TENZIN, Dawa GYELTSHEN - NIM, NAWANG (Passang TSHERING 67), Thinley DORJI - Tshering WANGDI, Karma Shedrup TSHERING, CHENCHO. Tr: Hiroki MATSUYAMA

PANAAD, BACOLOD CITY
9-02-2011, Att: 20 000, Ref: Yu Ming Hsun TPE

Philippines
Mongolia

PHI - Caligdong [43], Phil Younghusband [94+]

PHI: Neil ETHERIDGE - Robert GIER, Anton DEL ROSARIO (Jason SABIO 70), Alexander BORROMEO (c) - Roel GENER (Simon GREATWICH 46), James YOUNGHUSBAND, Philip YOUNGHUSBAND•, Jason DE JONG (Peter JAUGAN 89), Ray JONSSON - Emelio CALIGDONG, Ian ARANETA. Tr: Hans WEISS

MGL: Ganbayar TSEVEENSUREN - Ochbayar OLZVOI (Ganbat BEKHBAT 92+), D LUMBENGARAV (c), TS ENKHJARGAL - B GARIDMAGNAI, Chinzorig AMGALAN, Zorigt BATTULGA (Tsatsral JARGAL 64), P ALTANTULGA••◆25, Norjmoo TSEDENBAL, TS TUMENJARGAL (Batchuluun ANAR 82) - Tugsbayar GANBAATAR•. Tr: S ERDENEBAT

MFF, ULAANBAATAR
15-03-2011, Att: 3000, Ref: Ko Hyung Jin KOR

Mongolia 2
Philippines 1

MGL - Lumbengarev [22], Garidmagnai [35]
PHI - James Younghusband [4]

MGL: Ganbayar TSEVEENSUREN - Ochbayar OLZVOI, D LUMBENGARAV (c)•, Selenge ODKHUU, TS ENKHJARGAL - B GARIDMAGNAI, Chinzorig AMGALAN, TS TUMENJARGAL (A ERDENEBAYAR 89), Ganzorig ERDENE-OCHIR (Zorigt BATTULGA 63), Norjmoo TSEDENBAL - Tugsbayar GANBAATAR (Batchuluun ANAR 80). Tr: S ERDENEBAT

PHI: Eduard SACAPANO - Anton DEL ROSARIO, Alexander BORROMEO (c)•, Jason SABIO - Roel GENER, James YOUNGHUSBAND•, Simon GREATWICH•, Philip YOUNGHUSBAND (Yanti BARSALES 68), Ray JONSSON - Emelio CALIGDONG, Ian ARANETA. Tr: Hans WEISS

NATIONAL, KAOHSIUNG CITY
10-02-2011, Att: 1000, Ref: Ng Chiu Kok HKG

Chinese Taipei 5
Laos 2

TPE - Lin Cheng Yi [10], Chang Han 2 [22 56], Chen Po Liang [44], Lo Chi An [49]
LAO - Thongkhen [65], Syvilay [73]

TPE: LIN Po Cheng - CHEN Shan Fu, CHANG Yung Hsien, LIN Cheng Yi, CHEN Yu Lin (c) - TSAI Hsien Tang, CHAN Che Yuan (WU Chun Ching 60), LO Chih An (LIU Chi Chao 79) (WU Wai Ho 93+), CHEN Po Liang - CHANG Han, LO Chih En. Tr: LO Chih Tsung

LAO: Sengathit SOMVANG - Saynakhonevieng PHOMMAPANYA•, Khamla PINKEO, Khampoumy HANEVILAY - Kanlaya SYSOMVANG•, Khotsaya DAO (Soukaphone VONGCHIENGKHAM 52), Manolom PHOMSOUVANH (Keoviengphet LITHIDETH 76), Khonekham INTHAMMAVONG (Phattana SYVILAY 46) - Kitsada THONGKHEN (c), Lamnao SINGTO•, Khampheng SAYAVUTTHI. Tr: Bounlap KHENKITISACK

NATIONAL, VIENTIANE
16-02-2011, Att: 15 300, Ref: Ab. Wahab MAS

Laos 1
Chinese Taipei 1

LAO - Vongchiengkam [82] • TPE - Chen Po Liang [65]

LAO: Sourasay KEOSOUVANDENG - Saynakhonevieng PHOMMAPANYA•, KOVANH NAMTHAVIXAY, Khampoumy HANEVILAY (Phattana SYVILAY 64) - Kanlaya SYSOMVANG•, Keoviengphet LITHIDETH, Manolom PHOMSOUVANH (Khonekham INTHAMMAVONG 72••◆86) - Kitsada THONGKHEN (c), Lamnao SINGTO• (Visay PHAPHOUVANIN 56), Soukaphone VONGCHIENGKHAM, Khampheng SAYAVUTTHI. Tr: Bounlap KHENKITISACK

TPE: LIN Po Cheng (CHUNG Kuang Tien 50) - CHEN Shan Fu, CHANG Yung Hsien, LIN Cheng Yi, CHEN Yu Lin (c) - TSAI Hsien Tang•, CHAN Che Yuan (WU Chun Ching 87), LO Chih An•, CHEN Po Liang• - CHANG Han, LO Chih En•. Tr: LO Chih Tsung

NATIONAL OLYMPIC, PHNOM PENH
9-02-2011, Att: 2000, Ref: Win Cho MYA

Cambodia 3
Macau 1

CAM - Nasa 2 [48 53], Laboravy [59] • MAC - Leong Ka Hang [80]

CAM: Ouk MIC (c) - Lay RAKSMEY•, Tieng TINY, San NARITH, Say PISETH - Khuon LABORAVY (Chan RITHY 69), Chhun SOTHEARATH, Prak MONY OUDOM (Keo SOKNGON 61), Sun SOPANHA - Kouch SOKUMPHEAK, Samel NASA (Srey VEASNA 78). Tr: LEE Tae Hoon

MAC: LEONG Chon Kit - HO Wai Tong, MONTEIRO Soares, KWOK Siu Tin, KONG Cheng Hou, LAO Pak Kin - Geofredo DE SOUSA (C), CHE Chi Man, CHEANG Cheng, HO Man Hou (ALVES VINICIO 66) - LEONG Chong In (LEONG Ka Hang 52). Tr: LEUNG Sui Wing

MACAU STADIUM, MACAU
16-02-2011, Att: 100, Ref: Perera SRI

Macau 3
Cambodia 2

MAC - Wong Vernon [62], Leong Ka Hang [73], Alves Vinicio [75] • CAM - Borey [45], Nasa [107]

MAC: LEONG Chon Kit - LAM Ka Pou, HO Wai Tong, KWOK Siu Tin (HO Man Hou• 71), KONG Cheng Hou•, LAO Pak Kin - Geofredo DE SOUSA (C), CHE Chi Man, CHEANG Cheng (LEONG Ka Hang 46), WONG Vernon - LEONG Chong In (ALVES VINICIO 55). Tr: LEUNG Sui Wing

CAM: Ouk MIC (c) - Lay RAKSMEY (San NARITH• 38), Tieng TINY•, Touch PACHARONG, Say PISETH - Khuon LABORAVY, Chan RITHY, Chhun SOTHEARATH, Sun SOPANHA (Keo SOKNGON• 72) - Khim BOREY• (Samel NASA 61), Kouch SOKUMPHEAK. Tr: LEE Tae Hoon

QUALIFYING GROUP A

		Pl	W	D	L	F	A	Pts	PHI	BAN	MYA
Palestine	PLE	3	2	1	0	5	1	**7**	0-0	2-0	3-1
Philippines	PHI	3	1	2	0	4	1	**5**		3-0	1-1
Bangladesh	BAN	3	1	0	2	2	5	**3**			2-0
Myanmar	MYA	3	0	1	2	2	6	**1**			

THUWUNNA YTC, YANGON
21-03-2011, Att: 5000, Ref: Kim Jong Hyeok KOR

Myanmar 1
Philippines 1

MYA - Khin Maung Lwin [93+] • PHI - James Younghusband [76p]

MYA: Kyaw Zin HTET◆73 - Aye SAN (Naing Zayar TUN 75), Han Win AUNG (Soe Min OO 58), Zaw Min TUN, Yan Aung WIN, Nyar Na LWIN - Khin Maung LWIN, Myo Min TUN (c), Paing SOE, Yaza Win THEIN (Min Min TUN 70) - Yan PAING. Tr: Milan ZIVADINOVIC

PHI: Neil ETHERIDGE - Robert GIER, Anton DEL ROSARIO, Alexander BORROMEO (c) - Roel GENER, James YOUNGHUSBAND, Angel GUIRADO, Simon GREATWICH, (Yannick TUASON 61), Ian ARANETA (Yanti BARSALES 46) (William ESPINOSA 77). Tr: Hans WEISS

THUWUNNA YTC, YANGON
21-03-2011, Att: 1000, Ref: Abdulhusin BHR

Palestine 2
Bangladesh 0

PLE - Eleyan 2 [46 65]

PLE: Abdallah ALSIDAWI (c) - Samer HELSI, Khaled MAHDI, Ahmed MAHAJNA, Abdallatif ALBAHDARI - Hisham SALHI (Husam ABUSALAH 88), Murad ELEYAN, Ismail ALAMOUR•, Ashraf ALFAWAGHRA (Atef ABUBELAL 66), Hussam WADI (Sulaiman OBAID 16), Khader ABUHAMMAD. Tr: Mousa BEZAZ

BAN: Mamun KHAN - Atiqur MESHU (Yeamin MUNNA 85), Karim RAZAUL, Mohamed MINTU SHEIKH, Mohamed LINKON - Zahid HOSSAIN, Miah MAMUN, Mohamed HASSAN UZZAL (Hossain RONY 75), Ahmed SHAKIL (Mithun CHOWDHURY 67), Mohamed RAJU• - Hassan AMELI (c). Tr: Robert RUBCIC

THUWUNNA YTC, YANGON
23-03-2011, Att: 500, Ref: Adday IRQ

Philippines 0
Palestine 0

PHI: Neil ETHERIDGE - Robert GIER, Anton DEL ROSARIO •, Alexander BORROMEO (c) - James YOUNGHUSBAND•, Angel GUIRADO, Simon GREATWICH• (Yannick TUASON 62) (Roel GENER 82), Ray JONSSON, Jerry LUCENA - Emelio CALIGDONG, Ian ARANETA (Yanti BARSALES 59). Tr: Hans WEISS

PLE: Abdallah ALSIDAWI - Samer HELSI, Khaled MAHDI, Ahmed MAHAJNA, Abdallatif ALBAHDARI - Murad ELEYAN, Sulaiman OBAID, Ismail ALAMOUR (Mohammed JEBREEN 78), Ashraf ALFAWAGHRA (Atef ABUBELAL 68), Hussam WADI, Khader ABUHAMMAD (Hisham SALHI 87). Tr: Mousa BEZAZ

AFC CHALLENGE CUP 2012 NEPAL

THUWUNNA YTC, YANGON
23-03-2011, Att: 3000, Ref: Apisit THA

Bangladesh	2
Myanmar	0

BAN - Shakil Ahmed [10], Komol [88]

BAN: Mamun KHAN•, Mohamed Islam NAZIR•, Mohamed Mintu SHEIKH•, Mohamed Razaul KARIM•, Atiqur MESHU - Mohamed Islam MAMUN, Shakil AHMED (Mithun CHOWDHURY 79), Mohamded Zahid HOSSAIN• (Uttam BONIK 86), Mohamed Hassan UZZAL (Abdul Mazumder KOMOL 67), Mohamed Khan RAJU• - Mohamed Hasan AMELI. Tr: Robert RUBCIC

MYA: Naing Zayar TUN - Aye SAN• (Myo Min TUN 65), Moe WIN, Zaw Min TUN, Yan Aung WIN - Khin Maung LWIN•, Ye Zaw Htet AUNG, Pai SOE, Min Min TUN - Yan PAING (Soe Min OO 46), Soe Myat THU (Yazar Win THEIN 72). Tr: Milan ZIVADINOVIC

THUWUNNA YTC, YANGON
25-03-2011, Att: 1500, Ref: Abdulhusin BHR

Myanmar	1
Palestine	3

MYA - Zaw Htet Aung [25p] • PLE - Murad Eleyan 2 [39 90], Ahmed Harbi [71]

MYA: Kyaw Zin HTET - Shwe Hlaing WIN, Han Win AUNG (Aye SAN 69), Zaw Min TUN•, Yan Aung WIN - Khin Maung LWIN (Yazar Win THEIN 77), Zaw Htet AUNG, Myo Min TUN (Soe Myat THU 83•), Pai SOE•, Hla Aye HTWE• - Ye Soe Min OO. Tr: Milan ZIVADINOVIC

PLE: Mohammed SHBAIR• - Abdallatif AL BAHDARI•, Samer HIJAZI, Ahmed HARBI (Hussam ABUSALAH 75), Khaled MAHDI, Hussam WADI, Khader YOUSSEF, Ashraf ALFAWAGHRA• (Atef ABU BILAL 75), Ismail AL AMOUR• (Mohammed JEBREEN 85), Sulaiman OBAID•, Murad ALYAN. Tr: Mousa BEZAZ

THUWUNNA YTC, YANGON
25-03-2011, Att: 200, Ref: Kim Jong Hyeok KOR

Bangladesh	0
Philippines	3

PHI - Araneta [41], Angel Guirado 2 [55 80]

BAN: Mamun KHAN• - Mohamed Islam NAZIR, Mohamed Mintu SHEIKH•, Mohamed Razaul KARIM•, Atiqur MESHU (Mithun CHOWDHURY 46) - Mohamed LINKON, Mohamed Islam MAMUN, Shakil AHMED (Yeamin Chowdhury MUNNA 91•), Mohamed Zahid HOSSAIN, Mohamed Hassan UZZAL (Abdul Mazumder KOMOL 46) - Mohamed Hasan AMELI. Tr: Robert RUBCIC

PHI: Neil ETHERIDGE - Anton DEL ROSARIO, Alexander BORROMEO, Jerry LUCENA, Ray JONSSON - James YOUNGHUSBAND (Yannick TUASON 91•), Jason SABIO, Ian ARANETA - Emelio CALIGDONG (Roel GENER 77), Yanti BARSALES (Simon GREATWICH 83), Angel GUIRADO. Tr: Hans WEISS

QUALIFYING GROUP B

		Pl	W	D	L	F	A	Pts	TKM	PAK	TPE
India	IND	3	2	1	0	7	2	7	1-1	3-1	3-0
Turkmenistan	TKM	3	2	1	0	6	1	7		3-0	2-0
Pakistan	PAK	3	1	0	2	3	6	3			2-0
Chinese Taipei	TPE	3	0	0	3	0	7	0			

MBPJ STADIUM, PETALING JAYA
21-03-2011, Att: 150, Ref: Zadeh IRN

Turkmenistan	3
Pakistan	0

TKM - Urazov [6], Amanov [46], Garadanov [86]

TKM: Rahmanberdi ALYHANOV - Hemayat KOMEKOV•, Gochguly GOCHGULYYEV, Maksim BELYH, Nazar CHOLIYEV, David SARKISOV• (Azat GARAJAYEV 73) - Bahtiyar HOJAAHMEDOV•, Dowran ALLANAZAROV - Mammedaly GARADANOV, Didargylyc URAZOV (Guvanc HANGELDIYEV 38), Arslanmyrat AMANOV (Gahyrmanberdi CONKAYEV 79). Tr: Yazguly HOJAGELDIYEV

PAK: Muhammad OMER (Amir GUL 78) - Zeshan REHMAN, Samar ISHAQ, Atif BASHIR, Adnan Farooq AHMED, Abdul AZIZ (Kaleem ULLAH 29), Muhammad ADIL, Faisal IQBAL, Arif MEHMOOD, Muhammad Rizwan ASIF• (Mehmood KHAN 63), Muhammad QASIM. Tr: Tariq LUTFI

MBPJ STADIUM, PETALING JAYA
21-03-2011, Att: 50, Ref: Abdul Wahab MAS

India	3
Chinese Taipei	0

Ind - Lalpekhlua [32], Chhetri [76], Shaikh [88]

IND: Subrata PAL - Syed Rahim NABI, Rakesh MASIH (Shilton D'SILVA 87), Nanjangud MANJU (Joaquim ABRANCHES 70), Govin SINGH, Raju GAIKWAD, Jagpreet SINGH, Steven DIAS (Jewel RAJA 88), Gouramangi SINGH, Sunil CHHETRI, Jeje LALPEKHLUA. Tr: Robert HOUGHTON

TPE: LIN Po Cheng - CHEN Yu Lin, CHANG Yung Hsien, TSAI Hsien Tang•, LIN Cheng Yi, CHEN Shan Fu, CHEN Yuan, CHANG Han (LIU Chi Chao 91•), LO CHIH An, LO Chih En. Tr: LO Chih Tsung

MBPJ STADIUM, PETALING JAYA
23-03-2011, Att: 100, Ref: Alrshaidat JOR

Pakistan	1
India	3

PAK - Mehmood Arif [32]
IND - Lalpekhlua 2 [67 94+], Fias [90]

PAK: Amir GUL - Zeshan REHMAN, Samar ISHAQ•, Atif BASHIR, Manzoor AHMED, Adnan Farooq AHMED, Muhammad ADIL, Faisal IQBAL (Muhammad Rizwan ASIF 74), Syed Arif HUSSAIN, Arif MEHMOOD (Imran NIAZI 86•), Muhammad QASIM (Kaleem ULLAH 61). Tr: Tariq LUTFI

IND: Subrata PAL - Syed Rahim NABI, Rakesh MASIH, Nanjangud MANJU, Govin SINGH (Denzil FRANCO 46), Anwar ALI, Jagpreet SINGH (Shilton D'SILVA 66) (Steven DIAS 93+), Gouramangi SINGH, Sunil CHHETRI, Jeje LALPEKHLUA. Tr: Robert HOUGHTON

MBPJ STADIUM, PETALING JAYA
23-03-2011, Att: 100, Ref: Serazitdinov UZB

Chinese Taipei	0
Turkmenistan	2

TKM - Shamuradov [73], Hangeldiyev [76]

TPE: LIN Po Cheng• - CHEN Yu Lin, CHANG Yung Hsien•, TSAI Hsien Tang, LIN Cheng Yi (CHIANG Ming Han 59), CHEN Shan Fu, CHEN Po Liang (CHANG Han 51), CHAN Che Yuan, LO Chih An, LO Chih En, WU Chun Ching. Tr: LO Chih Tsung

TKM: Rahmanberdi ALYHANOV - Gochguly GOCHGULYYEV•, Begli ANNAGELDIYEV•, Nazar CHOLIYEV•, Azat GARAJAYEV (Gahyrmanberdi CONKAYEV 69), Shohrat SOYUNOV (Maksim BELYH 46), Bahtiyar HOJAAHMEDOV, Guvanc HANGELDIYEV, Berdy SHAMURADOV (Mammedaly GARADANOV 75), Arslanmyrat AMANOV, Aleksandr BOLIYAN•. Tr: Yazguly HOJAGELDIYEV

MBPJ STADIUM, PETALING JAYA
25-03-2011, Att: 200, Ref: Abdul Wahab MAS

Turkmenistan	1
India	1

TKM - Conkayev [52] • IND - Lalpekhlua [60]

TKM: Mamed ORAZMUHAMEDOV - Begli ANNAGELDIYEV, Guvanc REJEPOV, David SARKISOV•, Shohrat SOYUNOV - Hemayat KOMEKOV, Maksim BELYH, Mihail MUHAMMEDOV (Guvanc HANGELDIYEV 46•), Dowran ALLANAZAROV (Gahyrmanberdi CONKAYEV 46) - Amir GURBANI (Arslanmyrat AMANOV 69), Mammedaly GARADANOV. Tr: Yazguly HOJAGELDIYEV

IND: Subrata PAL - Syed Rahim NABI, Nallappan MOHANRAJ, Anwar ALI, Denzil FRANCO, Raju GAIKWAD, Joaquim ABRANCHES, Jewel RAJA, Shilton D'SILVA•, Jeje LALPEKHLUA, Chinadorai SABEETH (Gurpreet Singh SANDHU 55). Tr: Robert HOUGHTON

MBPJ STADIUM, PETALING JAYA
25-03-2011, Att: 50, Ref: Alrshaidat JOR

Chinese Taipei	0
Pakistan	2

PAK - Mehmood Arif [26], Atif Bashir [67]

TPE: CHUNG Kuang Tien - CHEN Yu Lin, TSAI Hsien Tang, LIN Cheng Yi (CHEN Yi Wei 71), CHEN Shan Fu, CHAN Che Yuan, WU Pai Ho, CHANG Han (CHEN Hao Wei 55), LO Chih An, LO Chih En, WU Chun Ching. Tr: LO Chih Tsung

PAK: Amir GUL - Zeshan REHMAN, Samar ISHAQ, Atif BASHIR, Manzoor AHMED, Alamgir KHAN, Adnan Farooq AHMED, Muhammad ADIL, Faisal IQBAL, Arif MEHMOOD (Muhammad QASIM 69•), Muhammad Rizwan ASIF (Jadeed Khan PATHAN 38), Kaleem ULLAH. Tr: Tariq LUTFI

QUALIFYING GROUP C

		Pl	W	D	L	F	A	Pts	TJK	KGZ	CAM
Maldives	MDV	3	2	1	0	6	1	7	0-0	2-1	4-0
Tajikistan	TJK	3	2	1	0	4	0	7		1-0	3-0
Kyrgyzstan	KGZ	3	1	0	2	5	6	3			4-3
Cambodia	CAM	3	0	0	3	3	11	0			

NATIONAL STADIUM, MALE
21-03-2011, Att: 4000, Ref: Mohamed UAE

Tajikistan	1
Kyrgyzstan	0

TJK - OG 88

TJK: Alisher **DODOV** - Davronjon **ERGASHEV**, Eradzsh **RADZHABOV**•, Sohib **SAVANKULOV**, Akmal **SABUROV**, Dilshod **VASIEV** (Asatullo **NURULLOEV** 84), Ibrahim **RABIMOV** (Farkhod **TOKHIROV** 72), Fatkhullo **FATKHULLOEV**, Nuriddin **DAVRONOV**, Davronjon **TUKHTASUNOV** (Kamil **SAIDO** 90), Makhmadali **SADYKOV**. Tr: Pulod **KHODIROV**

KGZ: Vladislav **VOLKOV** - Ruslan **SYDYKOV**•, Azamat **BAIMATOV**, Faruh **ABITOV** (Talant **SAMSALIEV** 74), Davron **ASKAROV** (Almazbek **MIRZALIEV** 90), Kursanbek **SHERATOV**•, Aziz **SYDYKOV**, Vadim **KHARCHENKO**, Anatolii **VLASICHEV**, Evgeniy **MALININ**, Ildar **AMIROV** (Esenkul **UULU** 77). Tr: Anarbek **ORMOMBEKOV**

NATIONAL STADIUM, MALE
21-03-2011, Att: 8000, Ref: Zhao Liang CHN

Maldives	4
Cambodia	0

MDV - Shamveel Qasim 2, Ali Ashfaq 3 41 84 88

MDV: Imran **MOHAMED** - Akram **ABDUL GHANI**•, Assad **ABDUL GHANI**, Mohamed **UMAIR**•, Ahmed **SAEED**, Mohamed **ARIF**, Ali **ASHFAQ**, Hussain Niyaz **MOHAMED** (Ismail **MOHAMED** 54), Mukhthaar **NASEER** (Shamveel **QASIM** 80), Ibrahim **FAZEEL** (Mohamed **SIFAN** 88), Ali **ASHADH**•. Tr: Diego **CRUCIANI**

CAM: Ouk **MIC** - Sun **SOPANHA**, Lay **RAKSMEY**, Tieng **TINY**•, Touch **PACHARONG**, Say **PISETH**•, Chhun **SOTHEARATH**, Prak **UDOM** (Chan **RITHY** 76), Kouch **SOKUMPHEAK**, Khuon **LABORAVY** (Chhin **CHHOEUN** 46), Sam **EL NASA** (Sok **PHENG** 44). Tr: **LEE** Tae Hoon

NATIONAL STADIUM, MALE
23-03-2011, Att: 9000, Ref: Al Awaji KSA

Kyrgyzstan	1
Maldives	2

KGZ - OG 87 • **MDV** - Ali Ashadh 5, Shamveel Qasim 79

KGZ: Vladislav **VOLKOV** - Ruslan **SYDYKOV**• (Rustem **USANOV** 82), Azamat **BAIMATOV**••♦76, Faruh **ABITOV**• (Talant **SAMSALIEV** 70), Davron **ASKAROV**, Kursanbek **SHERATOV**, Aziz **SYDYKOV**, Vadim **KHARCHENKO** (Esenkul **UULU** 67), Anatolii **VLASICHEV**, Evgeniy **MALININ**, Ildar **AMIROV**. Tr: Anarbek **ORMOMBEKOV**

MDV: Imran **MOHAMED** - Akram **ABDUL GHANI**, Assad **ABDUL GHANI**, Mohamed **UMAIR**•, Ahmed **SAEED**, Ismail **MOHAMED** (Shamveel **QASIM** 67), Mohamed **ARIF**, Ali **ASHFAQ**•, Mukhthaar **NASEER**• (Ahmed **RASHEED** 76), Ibrahim **FAZEEL** (Thasneem **MOHAMED** 89), Ali **ASHADH**. Tr: Diego **CRUCIANI**

NATIONAL STADIUM, MALE
23-03-2011, Att: 550, Ref: Patwal IND

Cambodia	0
Tajikistan	3

TJK - Davronov 2, Ergashev 83, Rabimov 89

CAM: Peng **BUNCHAY** - Tieng **TINY**, Pheak **RADY**•, Touch **PACHARONG**•, Sok **RITHY**•, Chan **RITHY**, Chhun **SOTHEARATH** (Sun **SOPANHA** 67), Pung **SOKSANA** (Sok **PHENG** 56), Soun **VEASNA**, Kouch **SOKUMPHEAK** (Chhin **CHHOEUN** 77), Khuon **LABORAVY**. Tr: **LEE** Tae Hoon

TJK: Alisher **DODOV** - Davronjon **ERGASHEV**, Eradzsh **RADZHABOV**•, Sohib **SAVANKULOV**, Akmal **SABUROV**, Dilshod **VASIEV**, Fatkhullo **FATKHULLOEV** (Asatullo **NURULLOEV** 87), Nuriddin **DAVRONOV**, Davronjon **TUKHTASUNOV** (Ibrahim **RABIMOV** 66), Kamil **SAIDOV** (Farkhod **TOKHIROV** 46), Makhmadali **SADYKOV**. Tr: Pulod **KHODIROV**

NATIONAL STADIUM, MALE
25-03-2011, Att: 9000, Ref: Mohamed UAE

Tajikistan	0
Maldives	0

TJK: Alisher **TUYCHIEV** - Davronjon **ERGASHEV**, Asatullo **NURULLOEV** (Dilshod **VASIEV** 59), Sohib **SAVANKULOV**•, Furug **QODIROV**, Akmal **SABUROV**, Nizom **RAKHIMOV** (Fatkhullo **FATKHULLOEV** 67), Ibrahim **RABIMOV**, Nuriddin **DAVRONOV**, Davronjon **TUKHTASUNOV**• (Farkhod **TOKHIROV** 84), Makhmadali **SADYKOV**. Tr: Pulod **KHODIROV**

MDV: Imran **MOHAMED** (Mohamed **FAISAL** 87) - Akram **ABDUL GHANI**, Assad **ABDUL GHANI**, Mohamed **UMAIR**, Ahmed **SAEED**, Ismail **MOHAMED** (Shamveel **QASIM** 64), Mohamed **ARIF**•, Ali **ASHFAQ**•, Mukhthaar **NASEER**, Ibrahim **FAZEEL** (Mohamed **SIFAN** 72), Ali **ASHADH**. Tr: Diego **CRUCIANI**

NATIONAL STADIUM, MALE
25-03-2011, Att: 1000, Ref: Zhao Liang CHN

Cambodia	3
Kyrgyzstan	4

CAM - Kouch Sokumpheak 2 39 49, Sok Rithy 89 • **KGZ** - Sydykov 5, Usanov 45, Uulu 2 80 85

CAM: Ouk **MIC** - Sun **SOPANHA**• (Soun **VEASNA** 75), Tieng **TINY**, Pheak **RADY**, Touch **PACHARONG** (Thong **UDOM** 85), Chan **RITHY**•, Chhun **SOTHEARATH**, Prak **UDOM**, Kouch **SOKUMPHEAK**, Sam **EL NASA**, Sok **PHENG** (Khuon **LABORAVY** 48). Tr: **LEE** TAE Hoon

KGZ: Valery **KASHUBA** - Talant **SAMSALIEV**, Faruh **ABITOV**, Davron **ASKAROV**, Rustem **USANOV**, Kursanbek **SHERATOV**, Aziz **SYDYKOV**, Artem **MULADJANOV** (Ildar **AMIROV** 53), Anatolii **VLASICHEV**, Evgeniy **MALININ**•, Almazbek **MIRZALIEV**• (Esenkul **UULU** 42). Tr: Anarbek **ORMOMBEKOV**

QUALIFYING GROUP D

		Pl	W	D	L	F	A	Pts	NEP	AFG	SRI
Korea DPR	PRK	3	3	0	0	7	0	9	1-0	2-0	4-0
Nepal	NEP	3	1	1	1	1	4	4		1-0	0-0
Afghanistan	AFG	3	1	0	2	1	3	3			1-0
Sri Lanka	SRI	3	0	1	2	0	5	1			

HALCHOWK, KATHMANDU
7-04-2011, Att: 2000, Ref: Almarzouq KUW

Korea DPR	4
Sri Lanka	0

PRK - Choe Kum Chol 2 2 47, Ri Chol Myong 5, Pak Nam Chol 21

PRK: KIM Myong Gil - RI Kwang Chon•, RI Kwang Hyok, PAK Nam Chol, KANG Kuk Chol (JONG Il Gwan 23), PAK Nam Chol (PAK Song Chol 57), KIM Kuk Jin, PAK Song Chol, RI Chol Myong, JON Kwang Ik, CHOE Kum Chol (CHOE Myong Ho 57•). Tr: YUN Jong Su

SRI: Viraj ASANKA (Manjula Kumara FERNANDO 22) - Well RUWANTHILAKE (Sumeda WEWALAGE 61), Rathnayake WARAKAGODA, Sembukuti Tharaka SILVA, Widana KRISHANTHA, Liyana Suranda BANDARA, Mohamed Nagoor MEERA, Mohamed Mohamed ZAIN, Pasqualhandi PUSHPAKUMARA, Shanmugarajah SANJEEV, Mohammed KAIZ (Philip Costa PATABANDIGE 80•). Tr: JUNG Jang

DASHRATH, KATHMANDU
7-04-2011, Att: 9100, Ref: Abdul Baki OMA

Afghanistan	0
Nepal	1

NEP - Bharat Khawas 27

AFG: Mansur FAQIRYAR - Djeladudin SHARITYAR, Zohib AMIRI, Zakria REZAI, Abassin ALIKHIL, Harez Arian HABIB, Sayed MAQSOOD (Masihullah BARAKZAI 70), Israfeel KOHISTANI•, Nadeem WAHEED (Yusef MASHRIQI 47), Sidiq WALIZADA (Hashmatullah BARAKZAI 87), Mustafa HADID. Tr: Mohammad KARGAR

NEP: Kiran CHEMZONG - Biraj MAHARJAN, Sagar THAPA, Rabin SHRESTHA (Deepak BHUSAL 85), Nirajan KHADKA, Sandeep RAI, Raju TAMANG (Bhola SILWAL 75), Rohit CHAND•, Anil GURUNG, Ju RAI, Bharat KHAWAS• (Santosh SHAHUKHALA 60). Tr: Graham ROBERTS

DASHRATH, KATHMANDU
9-04-2011, Att: 22 000, Ref: Alabbasi BHR

Nepal	0
Korea DPR	1

PRK - Jong Il Gwan 31

NEP: Kiran CHEMZONG - Biraj MAHARJAN, Sagar THAPA, Rabin SHRESTHA, Sagar THAPA, Rabin SHRESTHA, Bikash CHHETRI, Nirajan KHADKA, Sandeep RAI, Raju TAMANG (Ju Rai 46), Bhola SILWAL, Bharat KHAWAS (Santosh SHAHUKHALA 46), Ganesh LAWATI. Tr: Graham ROBERTS

PRK: KIM Myong Gil - RI Kwang Chon, RI Kwang Hyok, PAK Nam Chol (KIM Song Gi 51), PAK Nam Chol, KIM Kuk Jin (AN Byong Jun 40), PAK Song Chol, RI Chol Myong, JON Kwang Ik•, CHOE Kum Chol• (PAK Song Chol 61), JONG Il Gwan. Tr: YUN Jong Su

AFC CHALLENGE CUP 2012 NEPAL

HALCHOWK, KATHMANDU		
9-04-2011, Att: 1800, Ref: Adday IRQ		
Sri Lanka		0
Afghanistan		1

AFG - Mustafa Hadid [82]

SRI: Manjula Kumara **FERNANDO** - Rathnayake **WARAKAGODA**, Lankesara **KUMARA**●, Sembukuti Tharaka **SILVA** (Shafrath Mohamed **NAZAR** 61), Widana **KRISHANTHA**, Liyana Suranda **BANDARA**, Sumeda **WEWALAGE**, Mohamed Nagoor **MEERA** (Mohamed **IZZADEEN** 77), Mohamed Mohamed **ZAIN**, Pasqualhandi **PUSHPAKUMARA**, Mohammed **KAIZ** (Philip Costa **PATABANDIGE** 83). Tr: **JUNG** Jang

AFG: Mansur **FAQIRYAR** - Djelaludin **SHARITYAR**, Muqadar **QAZIZADAH**, Zohib Islam **AMIRI**●, Zakria **REZAI**, Abassin **ALIKHIL** (Qays **SHAYESTEH** 51), Harez Arian **HABIB**, Israfeel **KOHISTANI**, Sidiq **WALIZADA** (Hashmatullah **BARAKZAI** 73), Mustafa **HADID**, Yusef **MASHRIQI** (Sayed **MAQSOOD** 59). Tr: Mohammad **KARGAR**

DASHRATH, KATHMANDU		
11-04-2011, Att: 13 500, Ref: Adday IRQ		
Nepal		0
Sri Lanka		0

NEP: Kiran **CHEMZONG** - Biraj **MAHARJAN**, Sagar **THAPA**, Deepak **BHUSAL**, Nirajan **KHADKA** (Raju **TAMANG** 60), Sandeep **RAI**, Rohit **CHAND**, Bhola **SILWAL**, Anil **GURUNG** (Rabin Shrestha 71), Ju **RAI**, Bharat **KHAWAS** (Santosh **SHAHUKHALA** 54). Tr: Graham **ROBERTS**

SRI: Manjula Kumara **FERNANDO** - Well **RUWANTHILAKE**●, Rathnayake **WARAKAGODA**, Lankesara **KUMARA**●, Widana **KRISHANTHA**, Liyana Suranda **BANDARA**, Tuwan **RIZNI**● (Mohamed Nagoor **MEERA** 46), Mohamed Mohamed **ZAIN** (Pasqualhandi **PUSHPAKUMARA** 69), Mohamed **IZZADEEN**, Mohammed **KAIZ**● (Shanmugarajah **SANJEEV** 80), Philip Costa **PATABANDIGE**. Tr: **JUNG** Jang

HALCHOWK, KATHMANDU		
11-04-2011, Att: 1000, Ref: Abdul Baki OMA		
Korea DPR		2
Afghanistan		0

PRK - Choe Kum Chol [45], Ri Chol Myong [68]

PRK: **KIM** Myong Gil - **RI** Kwang Chon, **RI** Kwang Hyok (Ri Il Jin 62), **KIM** Song Gi, **PAK** Nam Chol, **KIM** Kuk Jin, **PAK** Song Chol (**JANG** Song Hyok 46), **RI** Chol Myong, **JON** Kwang Ik, **CHOE** Kum Chol (**RIM** Chol Min 66), **JONG** Il Gwan. Tr: **YUN** Jong Su

AFG: Mansur **FAQIRYAR** - Djelaludin **SHARITYAR**, Zohib Islam **AMIRI**● (Zakria **REZAI** 83), Faisal **SAKHIZADA**●, Abassin **ALIKHIL**, Harez Arian **HABIB**, Qays **SHAYESTEH** (Zubayr **AMIRI** 62), Israfeel **KOHISTANI**, Sidiq **WALIZADA** (Hashmatullah **BARAKZAI** 82), Mustafa **HADID**, Yusef **MASHRIQI**. Tr: Mohammad **KARGAR**

AFC CHALLENGUE CUP FINAL TOURNAMENT NEPAL 2012

First Round Group Stage

Group A	Pl	W	D	L	F	A	Pts	PLE	MDV	NEP
Turkmenistan	3	2	1	0	6	1	7	0-0	3-1	3-0
Palestine	3	2	1	0	4	0	7		2-0	2-0
Maldives	3	1	0	2	2	5	3			1-0
Nepal	3	0	0	3	0	6	0			

Group B	Pl	W	D	L	F	A	Pts	PHI	TJK	IND
Korea DPR	3	3	0	0	8	0	9	2-0	2-0	4-0
Philippines	3	2	0	1	4	3	6		2-1	2-0
Tajikistan	3	1	0	2	3	4	3			2-0
India	3	0	0	3	0	8	0	Held in Kathmandu, Nepal 8-03-2012 to 19-03-2012		

Semi-finals

Korea DPR	2
Palestine	0

Philippines	1
Turkmenistan	2

Final

Korea DPR	2
Turkmenistan	1

3rd Place Play-off

Philippines	4
Palestine	3

Top scorers (Finals only): **6** - Phil **YOUNGHUSBAND** PHI • **3** - **PAK** Nam Chol I PRK • **2** - Seven players with two goals

	GROUP A	PL	W	D	L	F	A	PTS		PLE	MDV	NEP
1	Turkmenistan	3	2	1	0	6	1	7		0-0	3-1	3-0
2	Palestine	3	2	1	0	4	0	7			2-0	2-0
3	Maldives	3	1	0	2	2	5	3				1-0
4	Nepal	3	0	0	3	0	6	0				

HALCHOWK, KATHMANDU
8-03-2012, 15:00, Att: 1000, Ref: Yousef Almarzouq KUW

Turkmenistan	3	Mingazov [33], Conkayev [78], Amanov [85]
Maldives	1	Adhuham [20]

TURKMENISTAN
Rahmanberdi ALYHANOV - Nazar CHOLIYEV (Guvanc ABYLOV 46), David SARKISOV, Shohrat SOYUNOV, Serdar ANNAORAZOV, Ahmet ATAYEV - Rahimberdy BALTAYEV, Ruslan MINGAZOV, Umidjan ASTANOV - Berdy SHAMURADOV (c) (Gahrymanberdi CONKAYEV 59), Arslanmyrat AMANOV (Didar DURDIYEV 88). Tr: Yazguly HOJAGELDIYEV

MALDIVES
Imran MOHAMED (c) - Akram ABDUL GHANI, Ahmed SHAFIU, Mohamed SIFAN - Mohamed UMAIR, Mohamed ARIF, Rilwan WAHEED• (Thasneem MOHAMED 82), Mukhthaar NASEER (Hussain Niyaz MOHAMED 66), Hassan ADHUHAM (Mohammad RASHEED 59) - Ibrahim FAZEEL, Ahmed THARIQ◆81. Tr: Istvan URBANYI

DASHRATH, KATHMANDU
8-03-2012, 17:00, Att: 12 300, Ref: Ryuji Sato JPN

Nepal	0	
Palestine	2	Alaa Atya [4], Fahed Attal [65]

NEPAL
Kiran CHEMZONG - Biraj MAHARJAN• (Jitendra KARKI 76), Sagar THAPA (c), Rabin SHRESTHA, Rohit CHAND, Sandeep RAI - Nirajan KHADKA• (Bhola SILWAL 46), Raju TAMANG - Anil GURUNG, Ju RAI, Bharat KHAWAS (Santosh SHAHUKHALA 46•). Tr: Graham ROBERTS

PALESTINE
Ramzi SALEH (c) - Khaled MAHDI, Hussam ABUSALAH, Hussam WADI• - Mousa ABU JAZAR, Mohamed SAMARA, Khader YOUSSEF, Ashraf ALFAWAGHRA (Khaled SALEM 90), Murad ISMAIL - Fahed ATTAL (Ahmed SALAMA 85), Alaa ATYA (Abdelhabib ABUHABIB 72). Tr: Jamal MAHMOUD

HALCHOWK, KATHMANDU
10-03-2012, 15:00, Att: 1000, Ref: Ko Hyung Jin KOR

Palestine	0	
Turkmenistan	0	

PALESTINE
Tawfiq ALI - Ahmed HARBI, Khaled MAHDI, Hussam ABUSALAH - Mousa ABU JAZAR, Mohamed SAMARA (Mohammed JEBREEN 83), Khader YOUSSEF, Ashraf ALFAWAGHRA, Murad ISMAIL (Hussam WADI 79) - Fahed ATTAL• (c), Alaa ATYA• (Abdelhamid ABUHABIB 61). Tr: Jamal MAHMOUD

TURKMENISTAN
Rahmanberdi ALYHANOV - David SARKISOV•, Shohrat SOYUNOV, Serdar ANNAORAZOV, Ahmet ATAYEV• - Ruslan MINGAZOV•, Bahtiyar HOJAAHMEDOV, Umidjan ASTANOV, Elman TAGAYEV• (Guvanc ABYLOV 57) - Berdy SHAMURADOV (c) (Gahrymanberdi CONKAYEV 46•), Arslanmyrat AMANOV. Tr: Yazguly HOJAGELDIYEV

DASHRATH, KATHMANDU
10-03-2012, 17:00, Att: 15 000, Ref: Dmitri Mashentsev KGZ

Maldives	1	Mohamed Rasheed [51]
Nepal	0	

MALDIVES
Imran MOHAMED - Akram ABDUL GHANI, Ahmed SHAFIU, Mohamed SIFAN - Mohamed UMAIR, Mohamed ARIF, Rilwan WAHEED, Ali ASHFAQ (c), Mohammad RASHEED (Faruhad ISMAIL 64), Hassan ADHUHAM (Ahmed NASHID 60) (Mukhthaar NASEER 91+) - Ali ASHADH. Tr: Istvan URBANYI

NEPAL
Ritesh THAPA - Biraj MAHARJAN, Sagar THAPA (c), Rabin SHRESTHA (Jitendra KARKI 40), Sandeep RAI - Raju TAMANG (Santosh SHAHUKHALA 58), Rohit CHAND, Bhola SILWAL - Anil GURUNG, Ju RAI, Bharat KHAWAS. Tr: Graham ROBERTS

DASHRATH, KATHMANDU
12-03-2012, 15:00, Att: 2400, Ref: Ali Sabbagh LIB

Nepal	0	
Turkmenistan	3	Tagayev [7], OG [79], Hangeldiyev [89]

NEPAL
Kiran CHEMZONG - Biraj MAHARJAN, Sagar THAPA (c), Deepak BHUSAL, Nirajan KHADKA (Sabindra SHRESTHA 89), Sandeep RAI - Rohit CHAND (Jitendra KARKI 82), Santosh SHAHUKHALA - Anil GURUNG, Ju RAI (Ganesh LAWATI 84), Bharat KHAWAS. Tr: Graham ROBERTS

TURKMENISTAN
Rahmanberdi ALYHANOV (c) - Nazar CHOLIYEV (Umidjan ASTANOV 46), Akmyrat JUMANAZAROV, Guvanc REJEPOV, Shohrat SOYUNOV, Serdar ANNAORAZOV - Bahtiyar HOJAAHMEDOV, Gahrymanberdi CONKAYEV, Elman TAGAYEV - Guvanc ABYLOV (Ruslan MINGAZOV 67), Arslanmyrat AMANOV (Guvanc HANGELDIYEV 60). Tr: Yazguly HOJAGELDIYEV

HALCHOWK, KATHMANDU
12-03-2012, 15:00, Att: 300, Ref: Dmitri Mashentsev KGZ

Maldives	0	
Palestine	2	Husam Wadi [59], Alfawaghra [94+]

MALDIVES
Imran MOHAMED - Akram ABDUL GHANI, Ahmed SHAFIU (Hussain Niyaz MOHAMED 86), Mohamed SIFAN - Mohamed UMAIR, Mohamed ARIF, Rilwan WAHEED (Ahmed NASHID 86), Ali ASHFAQ (c), Mohammad RASHEED• (Mukhthaar NASEER 63), Hassan ADHUHAM• - Ali ASHADH. Tr: Istvan URBANYI

PALESTINE
Ramzi SALEH (c) - Ahmed HARBI•, Khaled MAHDI, Hussam ABUSALAH - Hussam WADI• (Abdelhamid ABUHABIB 85), Mousa ABU JAZAR, Mohamed SAMARA• (Mohammed JEBREEN 89), Ashraf ALFAWAGHRA, Murad ISMAIL - Fahed ATTAL, Alaa ATYA (Khader YOUSSEF 77). Tr: Jamal MAHMOUD

AFC CHALLENGE CUP 2012 NEPAL

	GROUP B	PL	W	D	L	F	A	PTS		PHI	TJK	IND
1	Korea DPR	3	3	0	0	8	0	9		2-0	2-0	4-0
2	Philippines	3	2	0	1	4	3	6			2-1	2-0
3	Tajikistan	3	1	0	2	3	4	3				2-0
4	India	3	0	0	3	0	8	0				

HALCHOWK, KATHMANDU
9-03-2012, 15:00, Att: 1500, Ref: Pratap Singh IND

Korea DPR	2	Pak Nam Chol [58], Jang Kuk Chol [70]
Philippines	0	

KOREA DPR
RI Myong Guk - RI Kwang Chon (c), RI Kwang Hyok (JANG Song Hyok 87), PAK Nam Chol, JON Kwang Ik - PAK Nam Chol, PAK Song Chol, RI Chol Myong - JONG Il Gwan•, PAK Song Chol•, JANG Myong Il (JANG Kuk Chol 70). Tr: YUN Jong Su

PHILIPPINES
Neil ETHERIDGE• - Ray JONSSON, Juan GUIRADO (Robert Gier 76), Paul MULDERS (Emelio CALIGDONG 71), Jason SABIO - James YOUNGHUSBAND• (c), Marwin ANGELES (Lexton MOY 59), Philip YOUNGHUSBAND, Angel GUIRADO•, Misagh BAHADORAN - Carlos DE MURGA. Tr: Hans WEISS

DASHRATH, KATHMANDU
9-03-2012, 17:00, Att: 700, Ref: Ali Sabbagh LIB

India	0	
Tajikistan	2	Khamrakulov [61], Davronov [66]

INDIA
Karanjit SINGH - Syed Rahim NABI•, Adil KHAN, Samir NAIK, Raju GAIKWAD, Gouramangi SINGH - Anthony PEREIRA (Jewel RAJA 69), Francis FERNANDES, Rocus LAMARE - Sunil CHHETRI (c), Sushil SINGH (Joaquim ABRANCHES 81). Tr: Savio MADEIRA

TAJIKISTAN
Alisher TUYCHIEV - Davronjon ERGASHEV, Eraj RAJABOV, Sohib SAVANKULOV, Alexey NEGMATOV - Makhmadali SADYKOV (c), Fatkhullo FATKHULOEV (Dilshod VASIEV 86), Nuriddin DAVRONOV, Dzhakhongir DZHALILOV• - Farkhod TOKHIROV (Ilhomzhon ORTIKOV 78), Akhtam KHAMRAKULOV (Yusuf RABIEV 71). Tr: Kemal ALISPAHIC

HALCHOWK, KATHMANDU
11-03-2012, 15:00, Att: 1000, Ref: Yousef Almarzouq KUW

Tajikistan	0	
Korea DPR	2	Pak Nam Chol [4], Jang Kuk Chol [86]

TAJIKISTAN
Alisher TUYCHIEV - Davronjon ERGASHEV, Eraj RAJABOV, Sohib SAVANKULOV, Alexey NEGMATOV - Makhmadali SADYKOV (c), Fatkhullo FATKHULOEV, Nuriddin DAVRONOV (Dilshod VASIEV 46), Dzhakhongir DZHALILOV - Farkhod TOKHIROV (Yusuf RABIEV 60), Akhtam KHAMRAKULOV (Ibrahim RABIMOV• 67). Tr: Kemal ALISPAHIC

KOREA DPR
RI Myong Guk - RI Kwang Chon (c), RI Kwang Hyok, PAK Nam Chol, JON Kwang Ik - PAK Nam Chol, PAK Song Chol (KIM Ju Song 70), RI Chol Myong• - JONG Il Gwan, PAK Song Chol (JANG Song Hyok 87), JANG Myong Il (JANG Kuk Chol 35). Tr: YUN Jong Su

---

DASHRATH, KATHMANDU
11-03-2012, 17:00, Att: 300, Ref: Chaiya Mahapab THA

Philippines	2	James Younghusband 2 [10 73]
India	0	

PHILIPPINES
Neil ETHERIDGE - Ray JONSSON, Robert GIER, Juan GUIRADO, Paul MULDERS•, Jason SABIO - James YOUNGHUSBAND, Philip YOUNGHUSBAND, Angel GUIRADO (Marwin ANGELES 81) - Emelio CALIGDONG (c) (Misagh BAHADORAN 55), Carlos DE MURGA. Tr: Hans WEISS

INDIA
Karanjit SINGH - Syed Rahim NABI, Adil KHAN (Jewel RAJA 33), Samir NAIK, Raju GAIKWAD - Reisangmi VASHUM (Sushil SINGH 70), Joaquim ABRANCHES•, Gouramangi SINGH, Francis FERNANDES - Sunil CHHETRI (c). Tr: Savio MADEIRA

DASHRATH, KATHMANDU
13-03-2012, 15:00, Att: 200, Ref: Chaiya Mahapab THA

Korea DPR	4	Jon Kwang Ik [3], Ri Kwang Hyok [34], Pak Nam Chol [59], Ri Chol Myong [70]
India	0	

KOREA DPR
RI Myong Guk (KIM Myong Gil 62) - RI Kwang Chon (c), RI Kwang Hyok, PAK Nam Chol, JANG Song Hyok, JON Kwang Ik - PAK Nam Chol (RI Hyon Song 61), RI Chol Myong, JANG Kuk Chol - JONG Il Gwan, JANG Myong Il (KIM Ju Song 53). Tr: YUN Jong Su

INDIA
Subhasish CHOWDHURY - Syed Rahim NABI, Nirmal CHETTRI, Gouramangi SINGH, Raju GAIKWAD - Reisangmi VASHUM (Francis FERNANDES 24), Anthony PEREIRA, Jewel RAJA• (Lenny RODRIGUES 60), Rocus LAMARE - Sunil CHHETRI (c) (Chinadorai SABEETH 66), Sushil SINGH. Tr: Savio MADEIRA

HALCHOWK, KATHMANDU
13-03-2012, 15:00, Att: 800, Ref: Ryuji Sato JPN

Tajikistan	1	Negmatov [45]
Philippines	2	Phil Younghusband [54], Angel Guirado [80]

TAJIKISTAN
Alisher TUYCHIEV - Davronjon ERGASHEV, Sohib SAVANKULOV, Alexey NEGMATOV•, Akhtam NAZAROV (Kamil SAIDOV 88) - Makhmadali SADYKOV (c), Fatkhullo FATKHULOEV, Nuriddin DAVRONOV (Yusuf RABIEV 83), Dzhakhongir DZHALILOV• - Farkhod TOKHIROV (Ilhomzhon ORTIKOV 69), Akhtam KHAMRAKULOV. Tr: Kemal ALISPAHIC

PHILIPPINES
Neil ETHERIDGE - Ray JONSSON•, Robert GIER, Juan GUIRADO•, Paul MULDERS, Jason SABIO - James YOUNGHUSBAND•, Philip YOUNGHUSBAND, Angel GUIRADO• (Misagh BAHADORAN 90) - Emelio CALIGDONG (c) (Marwin ANGELES 66), Carlos DE MURGA. Tr: Hans WEISS

SEMI-FINALS

DASHRATH, KATHMANDU	
16-03-2012, 18:30, Att: 3000, Ref: Yousef Almarzouq KUW	
Korea DPR	2 Pak Kwang Ryong 2 [42] [68]
Palestine	0
KOREA DPR	
RI Myong Guk - RI Kwang Chon (c), RI Kwang Hyok, PAK Nam Chol, JON Kwang Ik - AN Yong Hak, PAK Nam Chol, RI Chol Myong - JANG Myong Il (JANG Kuk Chol 16), PAK Kwang Ryong, JONG Il Gwan (JANG Song Hyok 80). Tr: YUN Jong Su	
PALESTINE	
Ramzi SALEH• (c) - Ahmed HARBI, Khaled MAHDI, Hussam ABUSALAH - Mousa ABU JAZAR, Mohamed SAMARA• (Khaled SALEM 69), Khader YOUSSEF, Ashraf ALFAWAGHRA (Mohammed JEBREEN 84), Murad ISMAIL - Fahed ATTAL, Alaa ATYA (Mali KAWARE 47). Tr: Jamal MAHMOUD	

DASHRATH, KATHMANDU	
16-03-2012, 14:30, Att: 500, Ref: Ko Hyung Jin KOR	
Turkmenistan	2 Amanov [80], Conkayev [86]
Philippines	1
TURKMENISTAN	
Rahmanberdi ALYHANOV (c) - Akmyrat JUMANAZAROV, Guvanc REJEPOV, Serdar ANNAORAZOV, Ahmet ATAYEV• (Shohrat SOYUNOV 37) - Ruslan MINGAZOV•, Gahrymanberdi CONKAYEV, Bahtiyar HOJAAHMEDOV (Berdy SHAMURADOV 60), Umidjan ASTANOV•, Elman TAGAYEV (Guvanc ABYLOV 68) - Arslanmyrat AMANOV. Tr: Yazguly HOJAGELDIYEV	
PHILIPPINES	
Neil ETHERIDGE♦ [92+] - Ray JONSSON, Robert GIER, Juan GUIRADO, Paul MULDERS - Misagh BAHADORAN• (Lexton MOY 68), Philip YOUNGHUSBAND, Jason DE JONG, Marwin ANGELES - Carlos DE MURGA•, Emelio CALIGDONG (c) (Roel GENER 70). Tr: Hans WEISS	

THIRD PLACE PLAY-OFF

DASHRATH, KATHMANDU	
19-03-2012, 14:30, Att: 1000, Ref: Ali Sabbagh LIB	
Philippines	4 Phil Younghusband 2 [4] [25p], Angel Guirado [42], Juan Guirado [69]
Palestine	3 Abuhabib 2 [21] [67], Attal [78]
PHILIPPINES	
Eduard SACAPANO• - Ray JONSSON, Robert GIER (Jason DE JONG 75), Juan GUIRADO•, Paul MULDERS (Misagh BAHADORAN 93+), Jason SABIO - James YOUNGHUSBAND, Philip YOUNGHUSBAND, Angel GUIRADO - Carlos DE MURGA, Emelio CALIGDONG (c) (Marwin ANGELES 46). Tr: Hans WEISS	
PALESTINE	
Ramzi SALEH• (c) - Ahmed HARBI•, Khaled MAHDI, Hussam ABUSALAH• - Hussam WADI (Mohammed JEBREEN 35), Mousa ABU JAZAR•, Mohamed SAMARA (Ashraf ALFAWAGHRA• 51), Mali KAWARE (Nadim BARGHOUTHI 74), Khader YOUSSEF, Abdelhamid ABUHABIB - Fahed ATTAL. Tr: Jamal MAHMOUD	

FINAL

DASHRATH, KATHMANDU	
19-03-2012, 18:30, Att: 9000, Ref: Ryuji Sato JPN	
Korea DPR	2 Jong Il Gwan [36], Jang Song Hyok [87p]
Turkmenistan	1 Berdy Shamuradov [2]
KOREA DPR	
RI Myong Guk - RI Kwang Chon (c), RI Kwang Hyok, JON Kwang Ik•, JANG Kuk Chol (KIM Ju Song 53), PAK Nam Chol - AN Yong Hak (JANG Song Hyok 73), PAK Nam Chol, RI Chol Myong - PAK Kwang Ryong (PAK Song Chol 92+), JONG Il Gwan•. Tr: YUN Jong Su	
TURKMENISTAN	
Rahmanberdi ALYHANOV - David SARKISOV•, Shohrat SOYUNOV•, Serdar ANNAORAZOV• (Guvanc REJEPOV 64), Akmyrat JUMANAZAROV, Ahmet ATAYEV• - Bahtiyar HOJAAHMEDOV, Umidjan ASTANOV, Elman TAGAYEV (Ruslan MINGAZOV 42) - Guvanc ABYLOV (Arslanmyrat AMANOV 54), Berdy SHAMURADOV (c). Tr: Yazguly HOJAGELDIYEV	

WEST ASIAN FEDERATION CHAMPIONSHIP KUWAIT 2012

First Round Group Stage

	Pl	W	D	L	F	A	Pts	KUW	PLE	LIB
Oman	3	2	0	1	4	2	6	2-0	2-1	0-1
Kuwait	3	2	0	1	4	4	6		2-1	2-1
Palestine	3	1	0	2	3	4	3			1-0
Lebanon	3	1	0	2	2	3	3			

Semi-finals / Final

Semi-finals		Final	
Syria	1 5p		
Bahrain	1 4p		

	Pl	W	D	L	F	A	Pts	IRN	KSA	YEM
Bahrain	3	2	1	0	2	0	7	0-0	1-0	1-0
Iran	3	1	2	0	2	1	5		0-0	2-1
Saudi Arabia	3	1	1	1	1	1	4			1-0
Yemen	3	0	0	3	1	4	0			

Final	
Syria	1
Iraq	0

	Pl	W	D	L	F	A	Pts	IRQ	JOR
Syria	2	1	1	0	3	2	4	1-1	2-1
Iraq	2	1	1	0	2	1	4		1-0
Jordan	2	0	0	2	1	3	0		

Oman	0
Iraq	2

Held in Kuwait from 8-12-2012 to 20-12-2012 • Top scorers: **4** - Ahmad **AL DONI**, Syria & Qasim **HARDAN**, Oman • **2** - Jaycee **OKWUNWANNE**, Bahrain & Yousef **AL SULAIMAN**, Kuwait • **1** - 17 players with 1 goal and 1 own goal

GROUP A

	GROUP A	PL	W	D	L	F	A	PTS	KUW	PLE	LIB
1	Oman	3	2	0	1	4	2	6	2-0	2-1	0-1
2	Kuwait	3	2	0	1	4	4	6		2-1	2-1
3	Palestine	3	1	0	2	3	4	3			1-0
4	Lebanon	3	1	0	2	2	3	3			

AL SADAQUA WALSALAM, KUWAIT CITY
8-12-2012, 17:25, Att: 1500, Ref: Ali Sabah Adday IRQ

Kuwait	2	Yousef Al Sulaiman 2, Bader Al Mutwa 6p
Palestine	1	Ashraf Alfawaghra 45

KUWAIT
Nawaf **AL KHALDY**• - Fahad **SHAHEEN**•, Hussain **HAKEM**, Mohammad **AL RASHEDI**, Mohammed **RASHED**, Fahad **AL EBRAHIM**•, Waleed **JUMAH**, Talal **AL ENEZI** (Talal **AL AMER** 59), Hamad **AMAN** (Abdulaziz **AL ENEZI** 91+), Bader **AL MUTWA**, Yousef **AL SULAIMAN** (Abdulhadi **KHAMIS**• 75). Tr: Goran **TUFEGDZIC**

PALESTINE
Ramzi **SALEH**• - Omar **JAROON**• (Khaled **MAHDI** 70), Daniel **MUSTAFA**, Husam **ABUSALAH**•, Raed **FARES**, Mousa **ABU JAZAR**, Imad **ZATARA**•, Mali **KAWARE**, Khader **ABUHAMMAD**• (Khaldun **AL HALMAN** 90), Ashraf **ALFAWAGHRA**, Abdelhamid **ABUHABIB**• (Iyad **GHARQOUD** 71). Tr: Jamal **MAHMOUD**

AL SABAH, AL FARWANIYAH
8-12-2012, 19:30, Att: 2000, Ref: Abdulla Hassan Mohamed UAE

Oman	0	
Lebanon	1	Adnan Haidar 11

OMAN
Faiyz **AL RUSHEIDI** - Jaber **AL OWAISI**•, Ahmed **AL QURAINI** (Yaqoob **ABDUL KARIM** 77), Ali **AL JABRI**, Qasim **HARDAN**, Basim **AL RAJAIBI**, Mohamed **AL MAASHARI**, Hosni **AL BUSAIDY** (Nadhir **SLOUM** 67), Abdullah **AL HAMAR** (Abdullah **HADI** 59), Mohamed **AL SEYABI**•, Waleed **AL SAADI**. Tr: Paul **LE GUEN**

LEBANON
Abbas **HASSAN** - Ali **AL SAADI**, Mootaz **JOUNAIDI**, Walid **ISMAIL**• (Hassan **CHAITO** 90), Roda **ANTAR**, Abbas Ahmad **ATWI**, Adnan **HAIDAR**, Ahmad **ZREIK**, Nour **MANSOUR**• (Hassan **MEZHER** 74), Mahmoud **EL ALI** (Mouhamad **CHAMASS** 67), Mohamad **HAIDAR**••♦82. Tr: Theo **BUCKER**

AL SADAQUA WALSALAM, KUWAIT CITY
11-12-2012, 17:25, Att: 1400, Ref: Nasser Al Ghafari JOR

Kuwait	0	
Oman	2	Qasim Hardan 2 36 45

KUWAIT
Nawaf **AL KHALDY** - Fahad **SHAHEEN**, Hussain **HAKEM**, Mohammad **AL RASHEDI**, Mohammed **RASHED**, Fahad **AL EBRAHIM**•, Talal **AL AMER** (Abdulhadi **KHAMIS** 46), Waleed **JUMAH** (Abdulaziz **AL ENEZI** 80), Hamad **AMAN** (Abdulrahman **BANI** 64), Bader **AL MUTWA**, Yousef **AL SULAIMAN**. Tr: Goran **TUFEGDZIC**

OMAN
Mazin **AL KASBI** - Jaber **AL OWAISI**, Nadhir **SLOUM**•, Ali Salim **AL NAHAR** (Sami **BA OWAIN** 73), Ali **AL JABRI**, Qasim **HARDAN**, Basim **AL RAJAIBI**•, Mohamed **AL MAASHARI**, Mohamed **AL SEYABI**, Yaqoob **ABDUL KARIM** (Ahmed **AL SEYABI** 92+), Abdullah **HADI** (Waleed **AL SAADI** 88). Tr: Paul **LE GUEN**

AL SABAH, AL FARWANIYAH
11-12-2012, 19:30, Att: 2000, Ref: Ko Hyung Jin KOR

Lebanon	0	
Palestine	1	Iyad Gharqoud 74

LEBANON
Abbas **HASSAN** - Ali **AL SAADI**•, Mootaz **JOUNAIDI**, Walid **ISMAIL**• (Mahmoud **KOJOK** 73), Roda **ANTAR**••♦92+, Abbas Ahmad **ATWI**, Adnan **HAIDAR**, Ahmad **ZREIK**, Nour **MANSOUR** (Haytham **FAOUR** 79), Hassan **CHAITO**, Fayez **CHAMSINE** (Mahmoud **EL ALI** 58). Tr: Theo **BUCKER**

PALESTINE
Mohammed **SHBAIR** - Alexis **NORAMBUENA**•, Daniel **MUSTAFA**, Khaled **MAHDI**, Raed **FARES**, Mousa **ABU JAZAR** (Husam **ABUSALAH** 58), Imad **ZATARA**, Khader **ABUHAMMAD**, Ashraf **ALFAWAGHRA**, Mahmoud **SALAH**• (Mali **KAWARE** 69), Iyad **GHARQOUD** (Omar **JAROON** 80). Tr: Jamal **MAHMOUD**

AL SABAH, AL FARWANIYAH		
14-12-2012, 17:25, Att: 500, Ref: Minoru Tojo JPN		
Oman	2	Mohamed Al Seyabi [5], Qasim Hardan [33]
Palestine	1	Imad Zatara [40]

OMAN
Mazin AL KASBI - Jaber AL OWAISI, Nadhir SLOUM, Ali Salim AL NAHAR, Ali AL JABRI, Qasim HARDAN, Basim AL RAJAIBI, Mohamed AL MAASHARI, Mohamed AL SEYABI (Waleed AL SAADI 60), Yaqoob ABDUL KARIM (Abdullah AL HAMAR 83), Abdullah HADI. Tr: Paul LE GUEN

PALESTINE
Tawfiq ALI - Alexis NORAMBUENA (Mousa ABU JAZAR 68), Daniel MUSTAFA (Omar JAROON 73), Khaled MAHDI, Husam ABUSALAH (Ashraf ALFAWAGHRA 56), Raed FARES, Imad ZATARA, Mali KAWARE●, Khader ABUHAMMAD●, Abdelhamid ABUHABIB, Iyad GHARQOUD. Tr: Jamal MAHMOUD

AL SADAQUA WALSALAM, KUWAIT CITY		
14-12-2012, 17:25, Att: 4000, Ref: Ali Sabah Adday IRQ		
Kuwait	2	Yousef Al Sulaiman [8], Abdulhadi Khamis [79]
Lebanon	1	Abbas Ahmad Atwi [61p]

KUWAIT
Nawaf AL KHALDY - Fahad SHAHEEN, Hussain HAKEM, Mohammad AL RASHEDI●, Mohammed RASHED●●♦60, Fahad AL EBRAHIM, Talal AL ENEZI, Hamad AMAN (Amer AL FADHEL 68), Bader AL MUTWA, Abdulhadi KHAMIS (Talal AL AMER 83), Yousef AL SULAIMAN (Waleed JUMAH 86). Tr: Goran TUFEGDZIC

LEBANON
Abbas HASSAN - Ali AL SAADI, Mootaz JOUNAIDI●, Hassan MEZHER● (Fayez CHAMSINE 89), Abbas Ahmad ATWI, Adnan HAIDAR, Mouhamad CHAMASS (Ahmad ZREIK 81), Haytham FAOUR●, Nour MANSOUR●, Mahmoud EL ALI● (Hassan CHAITO 78), Mohamad HAIDAR●. Tr: Theo BUCKER

	GROUP B	PL	W	D	L	F	A	PTS	IRN	KSA	YEM
1	Bahrain	3	2	1	0	2	0	7	0-0	1-0	1-0
2	Iran	3	1	2	0	2	1	5		0-0	2-1
3	Saudi Arabia	3	1	1	1	1	1	4			1-0
4	Yemen	3	0	0	3	1	4	0			

AL SADAQUA WALSALAM, KUWAIT CITY		
9-12-2012, 17:25, Att: 1200, Ref: Minoru Tojo JPN		
Iran	0	
Saudi Arabia	0	

IRAN
Soosha MAKANI - Milad FAKHREDDINI●, Shoja KHALILZADEH, Milad NOORI●, Mehrdad POOLADI●, Payam SADEGHIAN (Omid EBRAHIMI 60), Yaghoub KARIMI (Ahmad HASANZADEH 71), Ghasem DEHNAVI●, Omid NAZARI, Mohammad KHANZADEH, Mehrdad OLADI (Mehdi NAZARI● 81). Tr: Carlos QUEIROZ

SAUDI ARABIA
Fawaz AL KHAIBARI - Osama HAWSAWI●, Abdullah AL DAWSARI, Abdulhakim AL FATIL, Ali AL ZUBAIDI, Ahmed AL FRAIDI● (Ibrahim AL IBRAHIM 77), Fahad HAMAD, Turky AL KHODAIR, Hussain AL MOGAHWI (Ahmed AL OUFI 83), Abdullah OTAYF, Bader AL KHAMES● (Hamad AL JUHAIM 89). Tr: Frank RIJKAARD

AL SABAH, AL FARWANIYAH		
9-12-2012, 19:30, Att: 150, Ref: Ali Sabbagh LIB		
Bahrain	1	Jaycee Okwunwanne [87]
Yemen	0	

BAHRAIN
Sayed JAFFER - Mohamed HUSAIN, Abdulla AL MARZOOQI, Dawood SAAD●, Rashed AL HOOTI, Mohamed SALMEEN, Sayed DHIYA (Jaycee OKWUNWANNE 63), Ali ABDULWAHAB, Issa MUTHANNA (Husain Salman MAKI 46), Abdulla YUSUF (Faisal BODAHOOM 46), Sami AL HUSAINI. Tr: Gabriel CALDERON

YEMEN
Saoud AL SOWADI - Hamada AL ZUBAIRI●, Abdulaziz AL GUMAEI, Mohammed FUAD, Najib AL HADDAD (Ayman AL HAGRI 55), Akram AL WORAFI, Khaled BALEID● (Mohammed BA ROWIS 73), Munassar BA HAJ, Nateeq HIZAM (Wahid AL KHYAT 73), Mohammed BOQSHAN●, Mohammed AL ABIDI. Tr: Tom SAINTFIET

AL SADAQUA WALSALAM, KUWAIT CITY		
12-12-2012, 17:25, Att: 1000, Ref: Banjar Al Dosari QAT		
Iran	0	
Bahrain	0	

IRAN
Ali HAGHIGHI - Pejman MONTAZERI, Shoja KHALILZADEH, Ehsan HAJSAFI● (Yaghoub KARIMI 46), Milad NOORI, Mehrdad POOLADI, Omid EBRAHIMI●, Mohammad KHANZADEH, Mehdi NAZARI● (Ghasem DEHNAVI 77), Mehrdad OLADI, Ahmad HASANZADEH (Payam SADEGHIAN 43). Tr: Carlos QUEIROZ

BAHRAIN
Sayed JAFFER - Mohamed HUSAIN, Faisal BODAHOOM (Mahmoud ABDULRAHMAN 61), Abdulla AL MARZOOQI, Dawood SAAD, Husain Salman MAKI, Mohamed SALMEEN●●♦26, Ali ABDULWAHAB, Hassan JAMEEL●, Sami AL HUSAINI (Abdulla YUSUF 73), Mohammed TAYEB (Rashed AL HOOTI 35). Tr: Gabriel CALDERON

AL SABAH, AL FARWANIYAH		
12-12-2012, 19:30, Att: 1000, Ref: Masoud Tufaylieh SYR		
Yemen	0	
Saudi Arabia	1	Abdullah Otayf [39]

YEMEN
Saoud AL SOWADI - Hamada AL ZUBAIRI●, Abdulaziz AL GUMAEI, Mohammed FUAD●, Najib AL HADDAD (Essam AL WORAFI 59), Akram AL WORAFI, Khaled BALEID● (Wahid AL KHYAT 75), Munassar BA HAJ (Ayman AL HAGRI 66), Nateeq HIZAM, Mohammed BOQSHAN, Mohammed AL ABIDI●. Tr: Tom SAINTFIET (Essam AL WORAFI 59)

SAUDI ARABIA
Fawaz AL KHAIBARI - Osama HAWSAWI●, Abdullah AL DAWSARI (Majed ASERI 42), Abdulhakim AL FATIL, Ali AL ZUBAIDI, Ahmed AL FRAIDI●, Fahad HAMAD, Turky AL KHODAIR (Ibrahim AL IBRAHIM 9), Hussain AL MOGAHWI, Abdullah OTAYF, Bader AL KHAMES (Hamad AL JUHAIM 81). Tr: Frank RIJKAARD

WEST ASIAN FEDERATION CHAMPIONSHIP KUWAIT 2012

AL SADAQUA WALSALAM, KUWAIT CITY
15-12-2012, 17:25, Att: 500, Ref: Ali Sabbagh LIB

Iran	2	Omid Nazari [41], Yaghoub Karimi [53]
Yemen	1	Essam Al Worafi [45]

IRAN
Hamed LAK - Pejman MONTAZERI, Mehrdad POOLADI, Yaghoub KARIMI, Ghasem DEHNAVI●, Mohammad ESMAEILI BEIGI● (Milad FAKHREDDINI 46), Omid EBRAHIMI●, Omid NAZARI, Mohammad KHANZADEH, Mehrdad OLADI (Shoja KHALILZADEH 92+), Ahmad HASANZADEH (Payam SADEGHIAN 46). Tr: Carlos QUEIROZ

YEMEN
Saoud AL SOWADI - Abdulaziz AL GUMAEI, Mudir ABDURABU, Mohammed FUAD, Najib AL HADDAD (Wahid AL KHYAT 59), Akram AL WORAFI, Munassar BA HAJ, Nateeq HIZAM● (Mohammed AL ABIDI 70), Mohammed BOQSHAN, Essam AL WORAFI (Kamel MOHAMMED 67), Ayman AL HAGRI. Tr: Tom SAINTFIET

AL SABAH, AL FARWANIYAH
15-12-2012, 17:25, Att: 200, Ref: Nasser Al Ghafari JOR

Bahrain	1	Jaycee Okwunwanne [77]
Saudi Arabia	0	

BAHRAIN
Sayed JAFFER - Mohamed HUSAIN, Faisal BODAHOOM (Sami AL HUSAINI 56), Abdulla AL MARZOOQI●, Dawood SAAD, Rashed AL HOOTI, Husain Salman MAKI, Hamad RAKEA● (Issa MUTHANNA 67), Mahmood ABDULRAHMAN, Hassan JAMEEL (Ali ABDULWAHAB● 55), Jaycee OKWUNWANNE. Tr: Gabriel CALDERON

SAUDI ARABIA
Fawaz AL KHAIBARI - Abdullah AL DAWSARI, Abdulhakim AL FATIL, Ali AL ZUBAIDI, Motaz HAWSAWI, Ahmed AL OUFI, Hussain AL MOGAHWI, Ibrahim AL IBRAHIM●, Abdullah OTAYF, Omar AL SUHAYMI (Salem AL DAWSARI 46), Bader AL KHAMES (Fahad HAMAD 58). Tr: Frank RIJKAARD

	GROUP C	PL	W	D	L	F	A	PTS		IRQ	JOR
1	Syria	2	1	1	0	3	2	4		1-1	2-1
2	Iraq	2	1	1	0	2	1	4			1-0
3	Jordan	2	0	0	2	1	3	0			

AL SABAH, AL FARWANIYAH
10-12-2012, 17:25, Att: 1600, Ref: Ali Shaban KUW

Iraq	1	Hammadi Ahmed [62]
Jordan	0	

IRAQ
JALAL HASSAN - KHALDOUN IBRAHIM, SAMAL SAEED, AHMED IBRAHIM, ALI BAHJAT●, Ali ADNAN, AHMED YASEEN, OSAMAH JABBAR (SAAD ABDULAMEER 63), Saif SALMAN (Nabeel SABAH 87), AMJED RADHI (MUTHANA KHALID 83), Hammadi AHMED. Tr: Hakeem SHAKIR

JORDAN
Abdallah ALZUBI - Ibrahim ZAWAHREH, Oday ZAHRAN●, Mohammad ALI●, Mohammad ALDMEIRI●, Saeed AL MURJAN, Raed FRAEH, Khalil BANI ATEYAH, Abdallah SALIM (Musab AL LAHAM 76), Hamza AL DARADREH, Ahmad SAMIR (Adnan ADOUS 65). Tr: Adnan AL ABBASI

AL SADAQUA WALSALAM, KUWAIT CITY
13-12-2012, 17:25, Att: 1300, Ref: Abdulla Hassan Mohamed UAE

Iraq	1	Al Massri OG [11]
Syria	1	Ahmad Al Doni [48]

IRAQ
JALAL HASSAN - SAMAL SAEED, AHMED IBRAHIM, ALI BAHJAT, Ali ADNAN●, KHALDOUN IBRAHIM, MUTHANA KHALID (OSAMAH JABBAR 74), AHMED YASEEN, Ammar AL ASAADI● (Saif SALMAN 52), AMJED RADHI (Amjed KHALAF 52), Hammadi AHMED. Tr: Hakeem SHAKIR

SYRIA
Mosab BALHOUS - Ahmad AL SALIH, Hamdi AL MASSRI, Hussein AL JWAYED, Mahmoud AL MAWAS, Oday Abd AL JAFAL, Khaled AL MBAYED, Mahmoud KHADOUJ (Qusay HABIB 58), Abd AL NASSER HASAN (Moayad AL AJAAN 73), Zahir AL MIDANI, Ahmad AL DONI (Omar KHRIBIN 91+). Tr: Hossam AL SAYED

AL SADAQUA WALSALAM, KUWAIT CITY
16-12-2012, 17:25, Att: 3000, Ref: Ko Hyung Jin KOR

Syria	2	Ahmad Al Doni 2 [62 82]
Jordan	1	Khalil Bani Ateyah [22]

SYRIA
Mosab BALHOUS● - Ahmad AL SALIH, Hamdi AL MASSRI, Hussein AL JWAYED, Moayad AL AJAAN, Mahmoud AL MAWAS, Qusay HABIB (Omar AL SOMAH 49), Oday Abd AL JAFAL (Omar KHRIBIN 59), Khaled AL MBAYED●, Zahir AL MIDANI, Ahmad AL DONI (Hamid DARWICH 91+). Tr: Hossam AL SAYED

JORDAN
Abdallah ALZUBI - Ibrahim ZAWAHREH, Oday ZAHRAN, Mohammad ALI, Mohammad ALDMEIRI●, Saeed AL MURJAN, Raed FRAEH● (Musab AL LAHAM 73), Khalil BANI ATEYAH, Adnan ADOUS (Ahmad ELIAS 58), Abdallah SALIM● (Mahmoud ZATARA 84), Hamza AL DARADREH●●◆95+. Tr: Adnan AL ABBASI

SEMI-FINALS

INTERNATIONAL, KUWAIT CITY		
18-12-2012, 19:30, Att: 6000, Ref: Ali Shaban KUW		
Bahrain	1 2p	Abdulwahab Ali 67
Syria	1 3p	Ahmad Al Doni 72
BAHRAIN		
Sayed **JAFFER** - Mohamed **HUSAIN**, Abdulla **AL MARZOOQI** (Dawood **SAAD** 16), Rashed **AL HOOTI**, Mahmoud **ABDULRAHMAN** (Husain Salman **MAKI** 46), Mohamed **SALMEEN**, Mohamed **DUAIJ**•, Ali **ABDULWAHAB**•, Issa **MUTHANNA**•, Jaycee **OKWUNWANNE** (Mohammed **TAYEB** 66), Sami **AL HUSAINI**. Tr: Gabriel **CALDERON**		
SYRIA		
Mosab **BALHOUS** - Ahmad **AL SALIH**, Hamdi **AL MASSRI**, Hussein **AL JWAYED**, Moayad **AL AJAAN**, Mahmoud **AL MAWAS**•, Omar **KHRIBIN** (Qusay **HABIB** 111), Khaled **AL MBAYED**, Zahir **AL MIDANI** (Mahmoud **KHADOUJ** 91), Ahmad **AL DONI**, Omar **AL SOMAH** (Oday Abd **AL JAFAL**• 74). Tr: Hossam **AL SAYED**		
PENALTIES		
Bahrain first: Husain ✓ • Jafal ✗ • Moosa ✗ • Salih ✓ • Saad ✗ • Habib ✓ • Tayeb ✗ • Khadouj ✗ • Salman ✓ • Douni ✓		

AL SABAH, AL FARWANIYAH		
18-12-2012, 17:30, Att: 500, Ref: Abdulla Hassan Mohamed UAE		
Oman	0	
Iraq	2	Amjed Radhi 6, Ahmed Yaseen 39
OMAN		
Mazin **AL KASBI** - Jaber **AL OWAISI**, Nadhir **SLOUM**, Ali Salim **AL NAHAR**, Ali **AL JABRI**, Qasim **HARDAN**, Basim **AL RAJAIBI**, Mohamed **AL MAASHARI** (Ahmed **AL SEYABI** 59), Mohamed **AL SEYABI** (Abdullah **AL HAMAR** 70), Yaqoob **ABDUL KARIM**, Abdullah **HADI** (Waleed **AL SAADI** 75). Tr: Paul **LE GUEN**		
IRAQ		
JALAL **HASSAN** - KHALDOUN **IBRAHIM**, AHMED **IBRAHIM**, ALI **BAHJAT**, ALI **ADNAN**•, AHMED **YASEEN** (MUTHANA **KHALID** 81), Saif **SALMAN**, Nabeel **SABAH**, AMJED **RADHI**• (HUSAM **IBRAHIM** 67), Hammadi **AHMED** (Amjad **KALAF** 77), WALEED **SALIM**. Tr: Hakeem **SHAKIR**		

THIRD PLACE PLAY-OFF

AL SABAH, AL FARWANIYAH		
20-12-2012, 16:10, Att: 100, Ref: Banjar Al Dosari QAT		
Oman	1	Qasim Hardan 68
Bahrain	0	
OMAN		
Faiyz **AL RUSHEIDI** - Nadhir **SLOUM**, Muheeb **ISSA**, Ahmed **AL QURAINI**, Ali Salim **AL NAHAR**, Sami **BA OWAIN** (Mohamed **AL MAASHARI** 91+), Basil **AL RAWAHI**, Ahmed **AL SEYABI** (Qasim **HARDAN** 54), Abdullah **AL HAMAR**, Yaqoob **ABDUL KARIM**, Waleed **AL SAADI** (Abdullah **HADI** 81). Tr: Paul **LE GUEN**		
BAHRAIN		
Sayed **JAFFER** - Faisal **BODAHOOM**, Abdulla **AL HAZAA**, Hamad **RAKEA** (Dawood **SAAD** 69), Mohamed **DUAIJ**•, Sayed **DHIYA**, Abdulwahab **AL MALOOD** (Husain Salman **MAKI** 54), Hassan **JAMEEL**, Abdulla **YUSUF**, Mohammed **TAYEB** (Mahmoud **ABDULRAHMAN** 46), Mohamed **AL MULLA**. Tr: Gabriel **CALDERON**		

FINAL

AL SADAQUA WALSALAM, KUWAIT CITY		
20-12-2012, 18:45, Att: 5000, Ref: Minoru Tojo JPN		
Syria	1	Ahmad Al Salih 74
Iraq	0	
SYRIA		
Mosab **BALHOUS**• - Ahmad **AL SALIH**, Hamdi **AL MASSRI**, Hussein **AL JWAYED**, Moayad **AL AJAAN**•, Mahmoud **AL MAWAS** (Qusay **HABIB** 70), Oday Abd **AL JAFAL**, Khaled **AL MBAYED** (Hamid **DARWICH** 22), Zahir **AL MIDANI**, Ahmad **AL DONI**, Omar **AL SOMAH**• (Omar **KHRIBIN** 87). Tr: Hossam **AL SAYED**		
IRAQ		
JALAL **HASSAN** - KHALDOUN **IBRAHIM**, AHMED **IBRAHIM** (SAMAL **SAEED** 67), Ali Bahjat, Ali **ADNAN**, AHMED **YASEEN** (Amjad **KALAF** 74), Saif **SALMAN**, Nabeel **SABAH**, AMJED **RADHI**, Hammadi **AHMED**, WALEED **SALIM** (HUSAM **IBRAHIM** 85). Tr: Hakeem **SHAKIR**		

ASEAN FOOTBALL CHAMPIONSHIP – AFF SUZUKI CUP 2012

Preliminary group

	LAO	TLS	BRU	CAM	Pts
Myanmar	0-0	2-1	1-0	3-0	10
Laos		1-3	3-1	1-0	7
Timor-Leste			1-2	5-1	6
Brunei				3-2	6
Cambodia					0

First round groups

Group A	PHI	VIE	MYA	Pts
Thailand	2-1	3-1	4-0	9
Philippines		1-0	2-0	6
Vietnam			1-1	1
Myanmar				1

Group B	MAS	IDN	LAO	Pts
Singapore	3-0	0-1	4-3	6
Malaysia		2-0	4-1	6
Indonesia			2-2	4
Laos				1

Semi-finals

Singapore	0	1
Philippines	0	0
Malaysia	0	0
Thailand	1	1

Final

Singapore	3	0
Thailand	1	1

Preliminary round held in Yangon, Myanmar, 5-10-2012 to 13-10-2012 • First round of the finals held in Malaysia and Thailand and then home and away for the semi-finals and final, 25-11-2012 to 22-12-2012 • Top scorers (incl preliminary round): **5** – Teerasil **DANGDA**, Thailand • **4** – Shahril **BIN ISHAK**, Singapore; Kyi **LIN**, Myanmar & Khampheng **SAYAVUTTHI**, Laos • **3** – Khairul **AMRI**, Singapore; **MURILO**, Timor-Leste; **ADE**, Timor-Leste; **ALAN**, Timor-Leste & Kirati **KEAWSOMBUT**, Thailand

	PRELIMINARY GROUP	PL	W	D	L	F	A	PTS	LAO	TLS	BRU	CAM
1	Myanmar	4	3	1	0	6	1	10	0-0	2-1	1-0	3-0
2	Laos	4	2	1	1	5	4	7		1-3	3-1	1-0
3	Timor-Leste	4	2	0	2	10	6	6			1-2	5-1
4	Brunei Darussalam	4	2	0	2	6	7	6				3-2
5	Cambodia	4	0	0	4	3	12	0				

THUWUNNA YTC, YANGON
5-10-2012, Att: 897, Ref: Al Yarimi YEM

Cambodia	1
Timor-Leste	5

CAM – Sokngon 91+ • **TLS** – Murilo 2 39 44, Ade 2 57 73, Alan 87p

CAM: Sou YATY - Sun SOPANHA (Chhun SOTHEARATH 60), Tieng TINY•, Om THAVRAK•, Touch PACHARONG, Khiev VIBOL, Chhin CHHOEUN (Tum SARAY 54), Prak UDOM (Teab VATHANAK 70), Sos SOUHANA - Khim BOREY, Keo SOKNGON. Tr: Hok SOCHETRA

TLS: EMERSON• - ANGGISU, ROCHA, ISAC, ADE (EUSEBIO 77), DIOGO, RAMON, Jose VIDE (NILO 87), HELBER, MURILO (OLIGARIO 90), ALAN. Tr: EMERSON ALCANTARA

THUWUNNA YTC, YANGON
5-10-2012, Att: 2552, Ref: Aslam MDV

Myanmar	1
Brunei Darussalam	0

MYA – Yan Aung Win 84

MYA: Thiha SITHU - Yan Aung Win, Zaw Min TUN, Aung Hein KYAW - Yan Aung KYAW, David HTAN, Kyi LIN (Khin Maung LWIN 93+), Thein Than WIN• - Yazar Win THEIN• (Paing SOE 94+), Kaung Si THU, Kyaw Zayar WIN•. Tr: PARK Sung Hwa

BRU: Wardun YUSOF - Affendy HAJI AKUP, Afi AMINUDDIN, Sairol SAHARI• (Haizul METUSIN 79) - Helmi ZAMBRIN, Rosmin KAMIS, Najib TARIF, Aminuddin TAHIR (Mohd IDRIS 72), Azwan ALI RAHMAN (Azwan SALLEH 69) - Shahrazen SAID, Adi SAID. Tr: KWON Oh Son

---

THUWUNNA YTC, YANGON
7-10-2012, Att: 4117, Ref: Shamsuz'man BAN

Timor-Leste	1
Myanmar	2

TLS – Alan 55 • **MYA** – Kyi Lin 2 38 74

TLS: EMERSON - ANGGISU, ROCHA•, ISAC, ADE•, DIOGO•, RAMON, PINTO (Jose VIDE 59), HELBER, MURILO•, ALAN. Tr: EMERSON ALCANTARA

MYA: Thiha SITHU - Moe WIN (Aung Hein KYAW 71), Yan Aung Win, Zaw Min TUN - Yan Aung KYAW, David HTAN (Paing SOE 57), Kyi LIN, Thein Than WIN - Yazar Win THEIN (Khin Maung LWIN 86), Kaung Si THU, Kyaw Zayar WIN. Tr: PARK Sung Hwa

---

THUWUNNA YTC, YANGON
7-10-2012, Att: 2110, Ref: Alzaabi UAE

Laos	1
Cambodia	0

LAO – Phapouvanin 40

LAO: Sengpchachan BOUNTHISANH - Saynakhonevieng PHOMMAPANYA•, Ketsada SOUKSAVANH, Kovanh NAMTHAVIXAY, Khamphoumy HANVILAY - Soukaphone VONGCHIENGKHAM•, Viengsavanh SAYYABOUN•, Khonesavanh SIHAVONG (Phatthana SYVILAY 57), Vilayout SAYYABOUNSOU (Khampheng SAYAVUTTHI 64) - Visay PHAPHOUVANIN (Kanlaya SYSOMVANG 79), Sopa SAYSANA. Tr: Kokichi KIMURA

CAM: Sou YATY - Sun SOPANHA •• ◆61, Lay RAKSMEY, Tieng TINY (Say PISETH 42), Om THAVRAK, Touch PACHARONG - Pung SOKSANA, Prak UDOM (Tum SARAY 82), Sos SOUHANA - Khim BOREY (Chhun SOTHEARATH 53), Keo SOKNGON. Tr: Hok SOCHETRA

THUWUNNA YTC, YANGON
9-10-2012, Att: 468, Ref: Takayama JPN

Cambodia	2
Brunei Darussalam	3

CAM – Udom 25, Borey 91+ • **BRU** – Tahir 56, Zambrin 62, Salleh 69

CAM: Oum VICHETH - Lay RAKSMEY• (Khiev VIBOL 65), Om THAVRAK•, Touch PACHARONG, Say PISETH - Chhun SOTHEARATH•, Pung SOKSANA (Teab VATHANAK 61), Prak Udom (Chhin CHHOEUN 58), Sos SOUHANA - Khim BOREY, Keo SOKNGON. Tr: Hok SOCHETRA

BRU: Wardun YUSOF - Affendy HAJI AKUP, Afi AMINUDDIN, Sairol SAHARI - Helmi ZAMBRIN, Azwan SALLEH (Hamizan SULAIMAN 80), Rosmin KAMIS, Najib TARIF, Aminuddin TAHIR (Mohd IDRIS 67) - Shahrazen SAID (Azwan ALI RAHMAN 77), Adi SAID. Tr: KWON Oh Son

---

THUWUNNA YTC, YANGON
9-10-2012, Att: 753, Ref: Aslam MDV

Timor-Leste	3
Laos	1

TLS – Murilo 43p, Ade 51, Alan 83 • **LAO** – Phapouvanin 77

TLS: EMERSON - ANGGISU•, ROCHA, ISAC, ADE, DIOGO, RAMON, PINTO (EUSEBIO 90), HELBER•, MURILO• (Jose VIDE 73), ALAN. Tr: EMERSON ALCANTARA

LAO: Sengpchachan BOUNTHISANH - Saynakhonevieng PHOMMAPANYA, Ketsada SOUKSAVANH, Khamla PINKEO•, Khamphoumy HANVILAY, Thotnilath SIBOUNHUANG (Soukaphone VONGCHIENGKHAM 50) - Kanlaya SYSOMVANG, Keoviengphet LITHTHIDETH (Sopa SAYSANA 57), Daoneua SYVIENGSAY, Vilayout SAYYABOUNSOU (Visay PHAPHOUVANIN 76) - Khampheng SAYAVUTTHI. Tr: Kokichi KIMURA

PART THREE – THE CONTINENTAL CONFEDERATIONS

THUWUNNA YTC, YANGON
11-10-2012, Att: 2251, Ref: Shamsuz'man BAN

Brunei Darussalam	1
Laos	3

BRU - Kamis [26] • LAO - Namthavixay [35], Sayavutthi [51p], Sysomvang [83p]

BRU: Wardun YUSOF - Affendy HAJI AKUP, Afi AMINUDDIN•, Sairol SAHARI - Helmi ZAMBRIN, Rosmin KAMIS (Nur OTHMAN 77), Najib TARIF (Nur OTHMAN 77), Aminuddin TAHIR (Azwan SALLEH 69), Azwan ALI RAHMAN (Nur OTHMAN 77) - Shahrazen SAID, Adi SAID (Mohd IDRIS 69). Tr: KWON Oh Son

LAO: Sengphachan BOUNTHISANH - Saynakhonevieng PHOMMAPANYA, Ketsada SOUKSAVANH, Kovanh NAMTHAVIXAY, Khamphoumy HANVILAY• - Phatthana SYVILAY, Soukaphone VONGCHIENGKHAM, Viengsavanh SAYYABOUN• (Kanlaya SYSOMVANG 62), Visay PHAPHOUVANIN - Sopa SAYSANA (Vilayout SAYYABOUNSOU 73), Khampheng SAYAVUTTHI (Phonepaseuth SYSOUTHAM• 79). Tr: Kokichi KIMURA

THUWUNNA YTC, YANGON
11-10-2012, Att: 3112, Ref: Al Yarimi YEM

Myanmar	3
Cambodia	0

MYA - Kyi Lin [60], Kaung Si Thu 2 [66 92+]

MYA: Thiha SITHU - Khin Maung LWIN, Yan Aung Win (Thet NIANG 51), Zaw Min TUN, Aung Hein KYAW, Pyaye Phyo AUNG - Yan Aung KYAW, David HTAN, Kyi LIN (Yazar Win THEIN 85), Thein Than WIN - Kyaw Zayar WIN (Kaung Si THU 60). Tr: PARK Sung Hwa

CAM: Oum VICHETH - Sun SOPANHA (Srey VEASNA 74), Lay RAKSMEY, Tieng TINY, Touch PACHARONG, Say PISETH• - Prak UDOM (Chhin CHHOEUN 54), Sos SOUHANA - Khim BOREY, Keo SOKNGON•, Srey UDOM (Chhun SOTHEARATH• 62). Tr: Hok SOCHETRA

THUWUNNA YTC, YANGON
13-10-2012, Att: 6234, Ref: Alzaabi UAE

Laos	0
Myanmar	0

LAO: Sengphachan BOUNTHISANH - Saynakhonevieng PHOMMAPANYA, Ketsada SOUKSAVANH, Kovanh NAMTHAVIXAY•, Khamphoumy HANVILAY• - Phatthana SYVILAY (Khonesavanh SIHAVONG 57), Kanlaya SYSOMVANG (Phonepaseuth SYSOUTHAM 77), Soukaphone VONGCHIENGKHAM, Visay PHAPHOUVANIN - Sopa SAYSANA• (Vilayout SAYYABOUNSOU 57), Khampheng SAYAVUTTHI. Tr: Kokichi KIMURA

MYA: Thiha SITHU - Khin Maung LWIN, Zaw Min TUN, Aung Hein KYAW (Moe WIN• 51), Pyaye Phyo AUNG - Yan Aung KYAW, David HTAN, Kyi LIN•, Thein Than WIN (Nyi Nyi MIN 46) - Thet NIANG, Kyaw Zayar WIN (Niang Lin OO 51). Tr: PARK Sung Hwa

THUWUNNA YTC, YANGON
13-10-2012, Att: 2423, Ref: Takayama JPN

Brunei Darussalam	2
Timor-Leste	1

BRU - Adi Said [16], Ali Rahman [74]
TLS - Pinto [79]

BRU: Wardun YUSOF• - Affendy HAJI AKUP, Haizul METUSIN, Afi AMINUDDIN - Helmi ZAMBRIN, Azwan SALLEH, Rosmin KAMIS (Mohd IDRIS 79), Fakharazzi HASSAN (Aminuddin TAHIR 71), Najib TARIF, Azwan ALI RAHMAN (Nur OTHMAN 84) - Adi SAID. Tr: KWON Oh Son

TLS: EMERSON• - ANGGISU, ROCHA•, ISAC•, ADE (Jose VIDE 46), DIOGO• (OLIGARIO 87), RAMON, PINTO, HELBER (CHIQUITO 69), ARY•, ALAN. Tr: EMERSON ALCANTARA

	GROUP A	PL	W	D	L	F	A	PTS	PHI	VIE	MYA
1	Thailand	3	3	0	0	9	2	9	2-1	3-1	4-0
2	Philippines	3	2	0	1	4	2	6		1-0	2-0
3	Vietnam	3	0	1	2	2	5	1			1-1
4	Myanmar	3	0	1	2	1	7	1			

RAJAMANGALA, BANGKOK
24-11-2012, 17:30, Att: 2312, Ref: Andre El Haddad LIB

Vietnam	1	Tan Tai Le [34]
Myanmar	1	Kyi Lin [53p]

VIETNAM
Hong Son DUONG - Van Hoan AU•, Gia Tu NGUYEN, Minh Duc NGUYEN (Van Bien NGUYEN 48) - Thanh Luong PHAM, Thanh Hung PHAN•, Tan Tai LE, Trong Hoang NGUYEN (Vu Phong NGUYEN 80), Quoc Anh HUYNH - Cong Vinh LE (Quang Hai NGUYEN 68). Tr: Thanh Hung PHAN

MYANMAR
Thiha SITHU - David HTAN, Zaw Min TUN, Aung Hein KYAW, Pyaye Phyo AUNG - Yan Aung KYAW (Thet NAING 78), Phyo Ko KO Thein (Zaw Zaw OO 46), Yan PAING (Kaung Si THU• 58), Naing Lin OO, Khin Maung LWIN - Kyi LIN. Tr: PARK Sung Hwa

RAJAMANGALA, BANGKOK
24-11-2012, 20:20, Att: 9503, Ref: Ryuji Sato JPN

Thailand	2	Pornsai [39], Kitpongsri [41]
Philippines	1	Mulders [77]

THAILAND
Kawin THAMSATCHANAN - Piyaphon BUNTAO (Nataporn PHANRIT 87), Panupong WONGSA, Cholnatit JANTAKAM, Theerathon BUTMATHAN - Jakkapan PORNSAI, Phichitphong CHOEICHIU•, Datsakorn THONGLAO (Sumanya PURISAY 71), Adul LAHSOH•, Anucha KITPONGSRI (Arthit SUNTHORNPHIT 89) - Teerasil DANGDA•. Tr: Winfried SCHAFER

PHILIPPINES
Eduard SACAPANO - Ray JONSSON, Robert GIER, Juan GUIRADO, Dennis CAGARA - Paul MULDERS•, James YOUNGHUSBAND (Patrick REICHELT 61), Jerry LUCENA, Emelio CALIGDONG (Jeffrey CHRISTIAENS 42) - Angel GUIRADO, Philip YOUNGHUSBAND (Marwin ANGELES 46). Tr: Hans WEISS

AFF SUZUKI CUP 2012

RAJAMANGALA, BANGKOK
27-11-2012, 17:30, Att: 6801, Ref: Ma Ning CHN

Vietnam	0	
Philippines	1	Caligdong [86]

VIETNAM
Hong Son DUONG - Van Bien NGUYEN, Gia Tu NGUYEN, Minh Duc NGUYEN• (Dinh Luat TRUONG 48), Dinh Dong TRAN - Thanh Luong PHAM (Van Quyet NGUYEN 72), Thanh Hung PHAN, Tan Tai LE•, Trong Hoang NGUYEN, Quoc Anh HUYNH - Cong Vinh LE (Quang Hai NGUYEN 70). Tr: Thanh Hung PHAN

PHILIPPINES
Eduard SACAPANO• - Ray JONSSON, Robert GIER•, Juan GUIRADO, Dennis CAGARA - Jason DE JONG, Paul MULDERS (Angel GUIRADO 55), Jerry LUCENA• - James YOUNGHUSBAND (Emelio CALIGDONG 75), Philip YOUNGHUSBAND• (Denis WOLF 65), Patrick REICHELT. Tr: Hans WEISS

RAJAMANGALA, BANGKOK
27-11-2012, 20:20, Att: 12 797, Ref: Yaqoob Abdul Baki OMA

Myanmar	0	
Thailand	4	Dangda 3 [20 82 89], Suntornpanavej [59]

MYANMAR
Thiha SITHU - Zaw Zaw OO (Thet NAING 69), Zaw Min TUN, Aung Hein KYAW, Pyaye Phyo AUNG - Yan Aung KYAW, Khin Maung LWIN, Yan PAING (Kaung Si Thu 68), Naing Lin OO (Aung MOE 73), David HTAN• - Kyi LIN•. Tr: PARK Sung Hwa

THAILAND
Kawin THAMSATCHANAN - Piyaphon BUNTAO, Panupong WONGSA, Cholnatit JANTAKAM•, Theerathon BUTMATHAN (Sompong SOLEB 83) - Jakkapan PORNSAI, Phichitphong CHOEICHIU• (Arthit SUNTHORNPHIT 71), Sumanya PURISAY (Apipoo SUNTORNPANAVEJ 58), Adul LAHSOH, Anucha KITPONGSRI - Teerasil DANGDA. Tr: Winfried SCHAFER

SUPACHALASAI, BANGKOK
30-11-2012, 20:20, Att: 3869, Ref: Yaqoob Abdul Baki OMA

Philippines	2	Phil Younghusband [47], Guirado [94+]
Myanmar	0	

PHILIPPINES
Eduard SACAPANO - Carlos DE MURGA, Robert GIER•, Juan GUIRADO, Dennis CAGARA• - James YOUNGHUSBAND (Demetrius OMPHROY 95+), Jason DE JONG•, Paul MULDERS, Patrick REICHELT (Emelio CALIGDONG 81) - Denis WOLF (Angel GUIRADO• 36), Philip YOUNGHUSBAND. Tr: Hans WEISS

MYANMAR
Thiha SITHU - Zaw Zaw OO, Zaw Min TUN, Khin Maung LWIN - Yan Aung KYAW, Aung MOE•, Yan PAING (Thet NAING 54), Thein Than WIN (Pyaye Phyo AUNG 54), David HTAN - Kaung Si THU (Soe Kyaw KYAW 76), Kyi LIN. Tr: PARK Sung Hwa

RAJAMANGALA, BANGKOK
30-11-2012, 20:20, Att: 13 196, Ref: Ryuji Sato JPN

Thailand	3	Keawsombut 2 [21 65], OG [82]
Vietnam	1	Van Quyet Nguyen [72]

THAILAND
Kawin THAMSATCHANAN - Piyaphon BUNTAO (Chanathip SONGKRASIN 43), Niwat SIRIWONG, Nataporn PHANRIT (Panupong WONGSA 67), Anucha KITPONGSRI (Theerathon BUTMATHAN 46) - Sompong SOLEB, Apipoo SUNTORNPANAVEJ, Prayat BUNYA, Arthit SUNTHORNPHIT♦71 - Sumanya PURISAY• - Kirati KEAWSOMBUT. Tr: Winfried SCHAFER

VIETNAM
Hong Son DUONG - Van Hoan AU•, Gia Tu NGUYEN, Minh Duc NGUYEN, Hong Tien NGUYEN (Ngoc Duy NGUYEN• 83) - Thanh Luong PHAM, Sy Cuong CAO, Tan Tai LE•, Trong Hoang NGUYEN (Vu Phong NGUYEN 77), Quoc Anh HUYNH (Quang Hai NGUYEN 46) - Van Quyet NGUYEN. Tr: Thanh Hung PHAN

	GROUP B	PL	W	D	L	F	A	PTS	MAS	IDN	LAO
1	Singapore	3	2	0	1	7	4	6	3-0	0-1	4-3
2	Malaysia	3	2	0	1	6	4	6		2-0	4-1
3	Indonesia	3	1	1	1	3	4	4			2-2
4	Laos	3	0	1	2	6	10	1			

BUKIT JALIL, KUALA LUMPUR
25-11-2012, 18:00, Att: 30 188, Ref: Ng Kai Lam HKG

Indonesia	2	Maitimo [43], Mofu [90]
Laos	2	Sayavutthi [30p], Liththideth [80]

INDONESIA
Endra PRASETYA♦26 - Raphael MAITIMO, Hamdi RAMDHAN• (Fachrudin WAHYUDI 72), Wahyu WIJIASTANTO•, Novan SASONGKO - Andik VERMANSYAH, Muhammad TAUFIQ, Tonnie CUSELL•, Oktavianus MANIANI (Wahyu NUGROHO 29), Irfan BACHDIM, Bambang PAMUNGKAS (Vendry MOFU 65). Tr: Nil MAIZAR

LAOS
Sengphachan BOUNTHISANH - Phattana SYVILAY, Khamphoumy HANVILAY, Ketsada SOUKSAVANH, Kovanh NAMTHAVIXAY - Soukaphone VONGCHIENGKHAM, Vilayout SAYYABOUNSOU (Keovienghet LITHTHIDETH• 31), Visay PHAPHOUVANIN (Khonesavanh SIHAVONG 73), Viengsavanh SAYYABOUN (Kanlaya SYSOMVANG 88), Sopa SAYSANA♦33 - Khampheng SAYAVUTTHI. Tr: Kokichi KIMURA

BUKIT JALIL, KUALA LUMPUR
25-11-2012, 20:45, Att: 51 478, Ref: Valentin Kovalenko UZB

Malaysia	0	
Singapore	3	Bin Ishak 2 [32 38], Duric [75]

MALAYSIA
Khairul BIN CHE - Bunyamin BIN UMAR, Mohamad AIDIL ZAFUAN, Mohamad MOHD SHAS, Mohamed BIN MUSLIM (Mahalli BIN JASULI 60) - Mohd BIN ZAMBRI (Wan BIN WAN NOR 46), Safiq BIN RAHIM, Amar BIN ROHIDAN (Azammuddin MOHD AKIL 78), Kunanlan SUBRAMANIAM - Mohd SALI, Norshahrul TALAHA. Tr: Krishnasamy RAJAGOBAL

SINGAPORE
Izwan BIN MAHBUD - Daniel BENNETT, Baihakki BIN KHAIZAN, Safuwan BAHARUDIN, Shaiful BIN ESAH (Irwan SHAH 69) - Jiayi SHI (Fazrul SHAHUL 91+), Mustafic FAHRUDIN, Hariss HARUN•, Shahdan BIN SULAIMAN - Shahril BIN ISHAK (Aleksandar DURIC 73), Khairul AMRI. Tr: Radojko AVRAMOVIC

BUKIT JALIL, KUALA LUMPUR		
28-11-2012, 18:00, Att: 12 676, Ref: Ali Abdulnabi BHR		
Indonesia	1	Vermansyah [88]
Singapore	0	

INDONESIA
Wahyu NUGROHO - Raphael MAITIMO, Fachrudin WAHYUDI, Wahyu WIJIASTANTO•, Novan SASONGKO - Elie AIBOY (Andik VERMANSYAH 47), Muhammad TAUFIQ•, Muhammad RACHMAT (Bambang PAMUNGKAS 57), Vendry MOFU, Oktavianus MANIANI• (Rashyid BAKRI 77) - Irfan BACHDIM. Tr: Nil MAIZAR

SINGAPORE
Izwan BIN MAHBUD - Daniel BENNETT, Baihakki BIN KHAIZAN•, Safuwan BAHARUDIN, Irwan SHAH••♦66 - Jiayi SHI•, Mustafic FAHRUDIN, Hariss HARUN• (Aleksandar DURIC 40), Shahdan BIN SULAIMAN - Shahril BIN ISHAK, Khairul AMRI• (Li QIU 76). Tr: Radojko AVRAMOVIC

BUKIT JALIL, KUALA LUMPUR		
28-11-2012, 20:45, Att: 38 415, Ref: Fan Qi CHN		
Laos	1	Sihavong [39]
Malaysia	4	Rahim [16], Sali [67], Wan Nor [76], Zambri [80]

LAOS
Sengphachan BOUNTHISANH - Phattana SYVILAY (Saynakhonevieng PHOMMAPANYA 76), Khonesavanh SIHAVONG (Vilayout SAYYABOUNSOU 54), Ketsada SOUKSAVANH, Kovanh NAMTHAVIXAY - Soukaphone VONGCHIENGKHAM, Keoviengphet LITHTHIDETH, Visay PHAPHOUVANIN (Daoneua SYVIENGSAY 70), Viengsavanh SAYYABOUN, Kanlaya SYSOMVANG - Khampheng SAYAVUTTHI. Tr: Kokichi KIMURA

MALAYSIA
Mohd BIN MARLIAS - Mahalli BIN JASULI, Mohamad AIDIL ZAFUAN, Mohamad MOHD SHAS, Mohamed BIN MUSLIM (Mohd AZMI 46) - Wan BIN WAN NOR, Safiq BIN RAHIM, Mohd Shakir BIN SHAARI, Kunanlan SUBRAMANIAM - Mohd SALI (Mohd BIN ZAMBRI 78), Norshahrul TALAHA (Baddrol BAKTHIAR 82). Tr: Krishnasamy RAJAGOBAL

SHAH ALAM, KUALA LUMPUR		
1-12-2012, 20:45, Att: 579, Ref: Ng Kai Lam HKG		
Singapore	4	Bin Ishak 2 [45] [53], Amri [63], Shahul [65]
Laos	3	Sayavutthi 2 [21] [81p], Liththideth [40]

SINGAPORE
Izwan BIN MAHBUD - Daniel BENNETT (Khairul AMRI 45), Baihakki BIN KHAIZAN, Safuwan BAHARUDIN, Fazrul SHAHUL• (Mohammad ABDUL 68) - Jiayi SHI, Mustafic FAHRUDIN•, Shahdan BIN SULAIMAN - Shahril BIN ISHAK, Aleksandar DURIC, Li QIU (Shaiful BIN ESAH 45). Tr: Radojko AVRAMOVIC

LAOS
Sengphachan BOUNTHISANH (Soukhtavy SOUNDALA 7) - Khamphoumy HANVILAY, Saynakhonevieng PHOMMAPANYA• (Phattana SYVILAY 72), Ketsada SOUKSAVANH, Kovanh NAMTHAVIXAY - Soukaphone VONGCHIENGKHAM, Keoviengphet LITHTHIDETH, Kanlaya SYSOMVANG - Khampheng SAYAVUTTHI, Visay PHAPHOUVANIN, Sopa SAYSANA (Vilayout SAYYABOUNSOU 67). Tr: Kokichi KIMURA

BUKIT JALIL, KUALA LUMPUR		
1-12-2012, 20:45, Att: 75 856, Ref: Valentin Kovalenko UZB		
Malaysia	2	Mohd Akil [27], Jasuli [30]
Indonesia	0	

MALAYSIA
Mohd BIN MARLIAS• - Mahalli BIN JASULI, Mohamad AIDIL ZAFUAN•, Mohamad MOHD SHAS, Mohd AZMI - Wan BIN WAN NOR, Safiq BIN RAHIM, Mohd Shakir BIN SHAARI• (Gary ROBBAT 40), Azammuddin MOHD AKIL (Ahmad BIN SAARANI 65) - Mohd SALI•, Norshahrul TALAHA (Amar BIN ROHIDAN 67). Tr: Krishnasamy RAJAGOBAL

INDONESIA
Wahyu NUGROHO - Raphael MAITIMO•, Fachrudin WAHYUDI, NOPENDI, Novan SASONGKO - Elie AIBOY (Andik VERMANSYAH 35), Muhammad TAUFIQ•, Vendry MOFU, Oktavianus MANIANI• (Tonnie CUSELL 58) - Samsul ARIF (Jhonny VAN BEUKERING 63), Irfan BACHDIM. Tr: Nil MAIZAR

SEMI-FINALS

RIZAL MEMORIAL, MANILA		
1st leg. 8-12-2012, 20:00, Att: 15 534, Ref: Abdullah Al Hilali OMA		
Philippines	0	
Singapore	0	

PHILIPPINES
Eduard SACAPANO - Carlos DE MURGA, Robert GIER, Juan GUIRADO, Dennis CAGARA• (Jeffrey CHRISTIAENS 88) - James YOUNGHUSBAND, Jason DE JONG (Marwin ANGELES 46), Paul MULDERS, Patrick REICHELT (Emelio CALIGDONG 77) - Angel GUIRADO, Philip YOUNGHUSBAND. Tr: Hans WEISS

SINGAPORE
Izwan BIN MAHBUD - Daniel BENNETT•, Baihakki BIN KHAIZAN, Safuwan BAHARUDIN•, Shaiful BIN ESAH - Mohammad ABDUL•, Mustafic FAHRUDIN, Shahdan BIN SULAIMAN - Khairul AMRI (Fazrul SHAHUL 79), Shahril BIN ISHAK, Aleksandar DURIC. Tr: Radojko AVRAMOVIC

JALAN BESAR, SINGAPORE		
2nd leg. 12-12-2012, 20:00, Att: 7613, Ref: Tan Hai CHN		
Singapore	1	Amri [19]
Philippines	0	

SINGAPORE
Izwan BIN MAHBUD - Daniel BENNETT, Baihakki BIN KHAIZAN, Safuwan BAHARUDIN, Shaiful BIN ESAH• - Mohammad ABDUL, Mustafic FAHRUDIN (Fazrul SHAHUL• 46), Shahdan BIN SULAIMAN - Khairul AMRI (Irwan SHAH 68), Shahril BIN ISHAK (Firdaus BIN KASMAN 90), Aleksandar DURIC. Tr: Radojko AVRAMOVIC

PHILIPPINES
Eduard SACAPANO - Carlos DE MURGA (Denis WOLF 83), Robert GIER, Juan GUIRADO, Dennis CAGARA - James YOUNGHUSBAND (Demetrius OMPHROY 61), Paul MULDERS, Jerry LUCENA, Patrick REICHELT (Emelio CALIGDONG 46) - Angel GUIRADO, Philip YOUNGHUSBAND. Tr: Hans WEISS

BUKIT JALIL, KUALA LUMPUR
1st leg. 9-12-2012, 20:00, Att; 87 410, Ref: Mohsen Torki IRN

Malaysia	1	Talaha [49]
Thailand	1	Dangda [79]

MALAYSIA
Mohd **BIN MARLIAS** - Mahalli **BIN JASULI**, Mohamad **AIDIL ZAFUAN**, Mohamad **MOHD SHAS**, Bunyamin **BIN UMAR**• (Mohd **AZMI** 85) - Baddrol **BIN BAKTHIAR** (Kunanlan **SUBRAMANIAM** 75), Safiq **BIN RAHIM**, Amar **BIN ROHIDAN** (Mohd **SALI** 75), Gary **ROBBAT** - Azammuddin **MOHD AKIL**, Norshahrul **TALAHA**. Tr: Krishnasamy **RAJAGOBAL**

THAILAND
Kawin **THAMSATCHANAN** - Piyaphon **BUNTAO**, Panupong **WONGSA**•, Cholnatit **JANTAKAM**, Theerathon **BUTMATHAN**• (Sompong **SOLEB** 52) - Jakkapan **PORNSAI**, Phichitphong **CHOEICHIU**, Datsakorn **THONGLAO** (Kirati **KEAWSOMBUT** 76), Adul **LAHSOH** (Apipoo **SUNTORNPANAVEJ** 59), Anucha **KITPONGSRI** - Teerasil **DANGDA**. Tr: Winfried **SCHAFER**

SUPACHALASAI, BANGKOK
2nd leg. 13-12-2012, 19:00, Att: 19 566, Ref: Lee Min Hu KOR

Thailand	2	Dangda [60], Butmathan [65]
Malaysia	0	

THAILAND
Kawin **THAMSATCHANAN** - Piyaphon **BUNTAO**, Panupong **WONGSA**, Cholnatit **JANTAKAM**, Theerathon **BUTMATHAN** (Arthit **SUNTHORNPHIT** 79) - Jakkapan **PORNSAI** (Sompong **SOLEB**• 70), Phichitphong **CHOEICHIU**• (Apipoo **SUNTORNPANAVEJ** 46), Datsakorn **THONGLAO**•, Adul **LAHSOH**, Anucha **KITPONGSRI** - Teerasil **DANGDA**. Tr: Winfried **SCHAFER**

MALAYSIA
Mohd **BIN MARLIAS** - Mahalli **BIN JASULI**•, Mohamad **AIDIL ZAFUAN**, Mohamad **MOHD SHAS**••♦44, Bunyamin **BIN UMAR** - Baddrol **BIN BAKTHIAR** (Mohd **SALI** 73), Safiq **BIN RAHIM**, Amar **BIN ROHIDAN**, Kunanlan **SUBRAMANIAM** (Mohd **BIN ZAMBRI** 53) - Azammuddin **MOHD AKIL**, Norshahrul **TALAHA**. Tr: Krishnasamy **RAJAGOBAL**

FINAL

JALAN BESAR, SINGAPORE
1st leg. 19-12-2012, 20:00, Att: 7613, Ref: Masaaki Toma JPN

Singapore	3	Fahrudin [10p], Amri [62], Bin Khaizan [91+]
Thailand	1	Lahso [65]

SINGAPORE
Izwan **BIN MAHBUD** - Daniel **BENNETT**, Baihakki **BIN KHAIZAN**, Safuwan **BAHARUDIN** (Irwan **SHAH** 93+), Shaiful **BIN ESAH** - Mohammad **ABDUL**, Mustafic **FAHRUDIN**•, Shahdan **BIN SULAIMAN** - Khairul **AMRI** (Firdaus **BIN MOHAMED** 87), Shahril **BIN ISHAK**, Aleksandar **DURIC**. Tr: Radojko **AVRAMOVIC**

THAILAND
Kawin **THAMSATCHANAN** - Piyaphon **BUNTAO**, Panupong **WONGSA** (Nataporn **PHANRIT** 27), Cholnatit **JANTAKAM**, Theerathon **BUTMATHAN** - Phichitphong **CHOEICHIU**, Datsakorn **THONGLAO** (Pipob **ON-MO** 79), Adul **LAHSOH** - Jakkapan **PORNSAI**, Teerasil **DANGDA**, Anucha **KITPONGSRI** (Arthit **SUNTHORNPHIT** 54). Tr: Winfried **SCHAFER**

SUPACHALASAI, BANGKOK
2nd leg. 22-12-2012, 19:00, Att: 23 158, Ref: Ravshan Irmatov UZB

Thailand	1	Keawsombut [45]
Singapore	0	

THAILAND
Kawin **THAMSATCHANAN** - Piyaphon **BUNTAO**, Panupong **WONGSA**, Cholnatit **JANTAKAM**, Theerathon **BUTMATHAN** - Jakkapan **PORNSAI** (Chanathip **SONGKRASIN** 75), Phichitphong **CHOEICHIU**•, Adul **LAHSOH**•, Datsakorn **THONGLAO** (Pipob **ON-MO** 69) - Kirati **KEAWSOMBUT**• (Apipoo **SUNTORNPANAVEJ** 79), Teerasil **DANGDA**. Tr: Winfried **SCHAFER**

SINGAPORE
Izwan **BIN MAHBUD** - Daniel **BENNETT**•, Baihakki **BIN KHAIZAN**, Safuwan **BAHARUDIN**, Shaiful **BIN ESAH** - Mohammad **ABDUL**•, Mustafic **FAHRUDIN**•, Shahdan **BIN SULAIMAN** (Fazrul **SHAHUL** 78) - Khairul **AMRI** (Li **QIU** 88), Shahril **BIN ISHAK**, Aleksandar **DURIC**. Tr: Radojko **AVRAMOVIC**

AFC U-19 CHAMPIONSHIP 2012 – QUALIFIERS

Qualifying Group A

(In Bangladesh)	Pl	W	D	L	F	A	Pts	KSA	OMA	BAN	MDV
Iraq	4	4	0	0	22	3	**12**	3-2	4-1	6-0	0-9
Saudi Arabia	4	3	0	1	21	3	**9**		4-0	4-0	11-0
Oman	4	2	0	2	6	8	6			1-0	4-0
Bangladesh	4	1	0	3	3	11	3				3-0
Maldives	4	0	0	4	0	27	0				

Qualifying Group B

(In Qatar)	Pl	W	D	L	F	A	Pts	KUW	JOR	BHR	TJK	BHU
Qatar	5	3	1	1	9	3	**10**	1-0	0-0	3-0	2-3	3-0
Kuwait	5	3	1	1	3	1	**10**		1-0	0-0	1-0	1-0
Jordan	5	3	1	1	11	2	**10**			3-0	4-1	4-0
Bahrain	5	2	1	2	7	6	7				4-0	3-0
Tajikistan	5	2	0	3	10	11	6					6-0
Bhutan	5	0	0	5	0	17	0					

Qualifying Group C

(In Iran)	Pl	W	D	L	F	A	Pts	UZB	IND	TKM	PAK
Iran	4	4	0	0	14	0	**12**	2-0	3-0	4-0	5-0
Uzbekistan	4	3	0	1	7	4	**9**		2-1	2-1	3-0
India	4	1	0	3	5	8	3			3-1	1-2
Turkmenistan	4	1	0	3	4	10	3				2-1
Pakistan	4	1	0	3	3	11	3				
Afghanistan				Withdrew							

Qualifying Group D

(In the UAE)	Pl	W	D	L	F	A	Pts	UAE	LIB	YEM	PLE
Syria	4	4	0	0	10	0	**12**	1-0	6-0	1-0	2-0
UAE	4	3	0	1	5	2	**9**		1-0	3-1	1-0
Lebanon	4	2	0	2	3	8	6			2-1	1-0
Yemen	4	1	0	3	4	7	3				2-1
Palestine	4	0	0	4	1	6	0				

Qualifying Group E

(In Thailand)	Pl	W	D	L	F	A	Pts	KOR	JPN	TPE	GUM
Thailand	4	3	1	0	15	0	**10**	1-0	0-0	1-0	13-0
Korea Republic	4	3	0	1	25	1	**9**		1-0	6-0	18-0
Japan	4	2	1	1	31	1	7			5-0	26-0
Chinese Taipei	4	1	0	3	11	12	3				11-0
Guam	4	0	0	4	0	68	0				
Hong Kong				Withdrew							

Qualifying Group F

(In Vietnam)	Pl	W	D	L	F	A	Pts	VIE	MAS	MYA	LAO
Korea DPR	4	3	1	0	10	3	**10**	2-2	4-1	2-0	2-0
Vietnam	4	1	3	0	8	4	**6**		0-0	2-2	4-0
Malaysia	4	1	2	1	5	5	5			0-0	4-1
Myanmar	4	0	3	1	4	6	3				2-2
Laos	4	0	1	3	3	12	1				

Qualifying Group G

(In Indonesia)	Pl	W	D	L	F	A	Pts	CHN	IDN	SIN	MAC
Australia	4	4	0	0	20	1	**12**	3-0	4-1	1-0	12-0
China PR	4	2	1	1	16	3	**7**		0-0	11-0	5-0
Indonesia	4	2	1	1	7	4	7			3-0	3-0
Singapore	4	0	1	3	0	15	1				0-0
Macau	4	0	1	3	0	20	1				

AFC U-19 CHAMPIONSHIP UAE 2012

First round groups

Group A	Pl	W	D	L	F	A	Pts	JPN	UAE	KUW
Iran	3	2	1	0	9	1	**7**	2-0	1-1	6-0
Japan	3	1	1	1	2	2	**4**		0-0	1-0
UAE	3	0	3	0	2	2	3			1-1
Kuwait	3	0	1	2	1	8	1			

Group B	Pl	W	D	L	F	A	Pts	KOR	THA	CHN
Iraq	3	2	1	0	5	1	**7**	0-0	3-0	2-1
Korea Republic	3	2	1	0	3	1	**7**		2-1	1-0
Thailand	3	1	0	2	3	6	3			2-1
China PR	3	0	0	3	2	5	0			

Group C	Pl	W	D	L	F	A	Pts	JOR	PRK	VIE
Uzbekistan	3	2	1	0	8	2	**7**	2-2	2-0	4-0
Jordan	3	1	2	0	8	5	**5**		1-1	5-2
Korea DPR	3	1	1	1	6	3	4			5-0
Vietnam	3	0	0	3	2	14	0			

Group D	Pl	W	D	L	F	A	Pts	SYR	KSA	QAT
Australia	3	1	2	0	3	2	**5**	1-1	1-1	1-0
Syria	3	1	1	1	7	4	**4**		5-1	1-2
Saudi Arabia	3	1	1	1	6	8	4			4-2
Qatar	3	1	0	2	4	6	3			

Quarter-finals

Korea Republic	4		
Iran	1		
Syria	2	0p	
Uzbekistan	2	3p	
Australia	3		
Jordan	0		
Japan	1		
Iraq	2		

Semi-finals

Korea Republic	3
Uzbekistan	1
Australia	0
Iraq	2

Final

Korea Republic	1	4p
Iraq	1	1p

Held in Ras Al Khaimah and Fujairah, UAE from 3-11-2012 to 17-11-2012 • Korea Republic, Iraq, Australia, Uzbekistan qualified for the 2013 FIFA U-20 World Cup in Turkey

AFC U-16 CHAMPIONSHIP 2012 – QUALIFIERS

Qualifying Group A
(In Iraq)

	Pl	W	D	L	F	A	Pts	IRN	QAT	PLE	BAN
Iraq	4	3	1	0	17	2	**10**	1-1	3-1	6-0	7-0
Iran	4	3	1	0	12	1	**10**		3-0	5-0	3-0
Qatar	4	2	0	2	9	6	6			4-0	4-0
Palestine	4	1	0	3	2	15	3				2-0
Bangladesh	4	0	0	4	0	16	0				
Sri Lanka	Withdrew										

Qualifying Group B
(In Kuwait)

	Pl	W	D	L	F	A	Pts	KUW	UAE	PAK	AFG	MDV
Yemen	5	4	1	0	15	2	**13**	2-1	1-1	4-0	3-0	5-0
Kuwait	5	4	0	1	14	3	**12**		3-1	2-0	3-0	5-0
UAE	5	3	1	1	13	4	10			2-0	3-0	6-0
Pakistan	5	2	0	3	7	9	6				3-1	4-0
Afghanistan	5	1	0	4	10	12	3					9-0
Maldives	5	0	0	5	0	29	0					

Qualifying Group C
(In Uzbekistan)

	Pl	W	D	L	F	A	Pts	IND	BHR	TJK	KGZ
Uzbekistan	4	4	0	0	20	1	**12**	9-0	2-0	2-1	7-0
India	4	3	0	1	13	11	**9**		2-1	4-1	7-0
Bahrain	4	1	1	2	7	7	4			2-2	4-1
Tajikistan	4	1	1	2	6	8	4				2-0
Kyrgyzstan	4	0	0	4	1	20	0				

Qualifying Group D
(In the Nepal)

	Pl	W	D	L	F	A	Pts	SYR	KSA	NEP
Oman	3	2	0	1	4	4	**6**	2-1	0-3	2-0
Syria	3	2	0	1	5	3	**6**		2-1	2-0
Saudi Arabia	3	1	1	1	5	3	4			1-1
Nepal	3	0	1	2	1	5	1			
Lebanon	Withdrew									

Qualifying Group E
(In Korea DPR)

	Pl	W	D	L	F	A	Pts	CHN	SIN	MAS	TLS
Korea DPR	4	4	0	0	16	2	**12**	1-0	1-0	3-0	11-2
China PR	4	3	0	1	8	3	**9**		3-1	3-1	2-0
Singapore	4	1	1	2	10	6	4			1-1	8-1
Malaysia	4	1	1	2	5	7	4				3-0
Timor-Leste	4	0	0	4	3	24	0				
Macau	Withdrew										

Qualifying Group F
(In Laos)

	Pl	W	D	L	F	A	Pts	KOR	LAO	VIE	CAM	TPE
Japan	5	4	0	1	21	6	**12**	2-4	6-0	5-2	4-0	4-0
Korea Republic	5	3	2	0	23	3	**11**		0-0	1-1	10-0	8-0
Laos	5	3	1	1	13	6	10			3-0	5-0	5-0
Vietnam	5	2	1	2	12	9	7				5-0	4-0
Cambodia	5	1	0	4	2	25	3					2-1
Chinese Taipei	5	0	0	5	1	23	0					

Qualifying Group G
(In Thailand)

	Pl	W	D	L	F	A	Pts	AUS	IDN	MYA	HKG	GUM
Thailand	5	5	0	0	28	6	**15**	3-2	4-1	4-1	6-2	11-0
Australia	5	4	0	1	22	5	**12**		5-2	4-0	1-0	10-0
Indonesia	5	3	0	2	26	10	9			4-1	2-0	17-0
Myanmar	5	2	0	3	13	14	6				4-2	7-0
Hong Kong	5	1	0	4	8	14	3					4-1
Guam	5	0	0	5	1	49	0					

AFC U-16 CHAMPIONSHIP IRAN 2012

First round groups

Group A	Pl	W	D	L	F	A	Pts	KUW	LAO	YEM
Iran	3	3	0	0	9	3	**9**	2-1	3-2	4-1
Kuwait	3	1	1	1	6	6	**4**		4-3	1-1
Laos	3	1	0	2	6	8	3			2-1
Yemen	3	0	1	2	3	7	1			

Group B	Pl	W	D	L	F	A	Pts	AUS	OMA	THA
Iraq	3	2	1	0	4	1	**7**	0-0	2-1	2-0
Australia	3	2	1	0	4	1	**7**		2-1	2-0
Oman	3	1	0	2	5	6	3			3-2
Thailand	3	0	0	3	2	7	0			

Group C	Pl	W	D	L	F	A	Pts	JPN	PRK	KSA
Korea Republic	3	3	0	0	7	1	**9**	3-1	3-0	1-0
Japan	3	2	0	1	6	3	**6**		3-0	2-0
Korea DPR	3	1	0	2	2	7	3			2-1
Saudi Arabia	3	0	0	3	1	5	0			

Group D	Pl	W	D	L	F	A	Pts	UZB	CHN	IND
Syria	3	1	2	0	2	1	**5**	1-0	1-1	0-0
Uzbekistan	3	1	1	1	4	4	**4**		1-1	3-2
China PR	3	0	3	0	4	4	3			2-2
India	3	0	2	1	4	5	2			

Quarter-finals

Uzbekistan	1 5p
Korea Republic	1 3p

Australia	1
Iran	5

Iraq	3
Kuwait	1

Syria	1
Japan	2

Semi-finals

Uzbekistan	3
Iran	2

Iraq	1
Japan	5

Final

Uzbekistan	1 3p
Japan	1 1p

Held in Tehran, Iran from 22-09-2012 to 6-10-2012 • Uzbekistan, Japan, Iran & Iraq qualified for the 2013 FIFA U-17 World Cup in the UAE.

CLUB TOURNAMENTS IN ASIA 2012

AFC CHAMPIONS LEAGUE 2012

First Round

Group A

		Pl	W	D	L	F	A	Pts	UAE	IRN	QAT	UZB
Al Jazira	UAE	6	5	1	0	18	10	16		1-1	3-2	4-1
Esteghlal Tehran	IRN	6	3	2	1	8	3	11	1-2		3-0	0-0
Al Rayyan	QAT	6	2	0	4	9	12	6	3-4	0-1		3-1
Nasaf Karshi	UZB	6	0	1	5	4	14	1	2-4	0-2	0-1	

Group B

		Pl	W	D	L	F	A	Pts	KSA	UAE	UZB	QAT
Al Ittihad	KSA	6	5	1	0	13	4	16		1-0	4-0	3-2
Bani-Yas	UAE	6	3	2	1	9	2	11	0-0		2-0	2-0
Pakhtakor Tashkent	UZB	6	2	1	3	6	10	7	1-2	1-1		3-1
Al Arabi	QAT	6	0	0	6	4	16	0	1-3	0-4	0-1	

Group C

		Pl	W	D	L	F	A	Pts	IRN	KSA	UAE	QAT
Sepahan	IRN	6	4	1	1	9	4	13		2-1	1-0	2-1
Al Ahli Jeddah	KSA	6	3	1	2	10	6	10	1-1		3-1	3-0
Al Nasr	UAE	6	2	0	4	6	11	6	0-3	1-2		2-1
Lekhwia	QAT	6	2	0	4	5	9	6	1-0	1-0	1-2	

Group D

		Pl	W	D	L	F	A	Pts	KSA	IRN	QAT	UAE
Al Hilal	KSA	6	3	3	0	10	7	12		1-1	2-1	2-1
Persopolis	IRN	6	3	2	1	14	5	11	0-1		1-1	6-1
Al Gharafa	QAT	6	1	3	2	7	10	6	3-3	0-3		2-1
Al Shabab	UAE	6	0	2	4	5	14	2	1-1	1-3	0-0	

Group E

		Pl	W	D	L	F	A	Pts	AUS	UZB	KOR	JPN
Adelaide United	AUS	6	4	1	1	7	2	13		0-0	1-0	2-0
Bunyodkor	UZB	6	3	1	2	8	7	10	1-2		1-0	3-2
Pohang Steelers	KOR	6	3	0	3	6	4	9	1-0	0-2		2-0
Gamba Osaka	JPN	6	1	0	5	5	13	3	0-2	3-1	0-3	

Group F

		Pl	W	D	L	F	A	Pts	KOR	JPN	AUS	CHN
Ulsan Hyundai	KOR	6	4	2	0	11	7	14		1-0	1-1	2-1
FC Tokyo	JPN	6	3	2	1	12	6	11	2-2		4-2	3-0
Brisbane Roar	AUS	6	0	3	3	6	11	3	1-2	0-2		1-1
Beijing Goan	CHN	6	0	3	3	6	11	3	2-3	1-1	1-1	

Group G

		Pl	W	D	L	F	A	Pts	KOR	JPN	AUS	CHN
Seongnam Ilhwa C'ma	KOR	6	2	4	0	13	5	10		1-1	5-0	1-1
Nagoya Grampus	JPN	6	2	4	0	10	4	10	2-2		3-0	0-0
Central Coast Mariners	AUS	6	1	3	2	7	11	6	1-1	1-1		5-1
Tianjin Teda	CHN	6	0	3	3	2	12	3	0-3	0-3	0-0	

Group H

		Pl	W	D	L	F	A	Pts	CHN	JPN	KOR	THA
Guangzhou Evergrande	CHN	6	3	1	2	12	8	10		3-1	1-3	1-2
Kashiwa Reysol	JPN	6	3	1	2	11	7	10	0-0		5-1	1-0
Jeonbuk Hy. Motors	KOR	6	3	0	3	10	15	9	1-5	0-2		3-2
Buriram United	THA	6	2	0	4	8	11	6	1-2	3-2	0-2	

Round of 16

Ulsan Hyundai *	3
Kashiwa Reysol	2
Bani-Yas	1
Al Hilal *	7
Adelaide United *	1
Nagoya Grampus	0
Seongnam Ilhwa Ch *	0
Bunyodkor	1
Al Ittihad *	3
Persopolis	0
FC Tokyo	0
Guangzhou Ev'grande *	1
Sepahan *	2
Esteghlal Tehran	0
Al Jazira *	3 2p
Al Ahli Jeddah	3 4p

AFC CHAMPIONS LEAGUE 2012

Quarter-finals		Semi-finals		Final	

Ulsan Hyundai *	1 4
Al Hilal	0 0

Ulsan Hyundai	3 2
Bunyodkor *	1 0

Adelaide United *	2 2
Bunyodkor	2 3

Ulsan Hyundai *	3
Al Ahli Jeddah	0

Al Ittihad *	4 1
Guangzhou Evergrande	2 2

Al Ittihad *	1 0
Al Ahli Jeddah	0 2

Sepahan *	0 1
Al Ahli Jeddah	0 4

* Home team/Home team in the first leg

Top scorers: **12** - **RICARDO OLIVEIRA** BRA, Al Jazira • **8** - Naif **HAZAZI** KSA, Al Ittihad • **7** - **RAFINHA** BRA, Gamba Osaka/Ulsan Hyundai & **VICTOR SIMOES** BRA, Al Ahli • **6** - Dario **COCA** ARG, Guangzhou & **KIM** Shin Wook KOR, Ulsan Hyundai • **5** - Eamon **ZAYED** LBY, Persepolis; **BRUNO CORREA** BRA, Sepahan; **LEANDRO DOMINGUES** BRA, Kashiwa Reysol, **YOO** Byung Soo KOR, Al Hilal & Amara **DIANE** CIV, Al Nasr

AFC CHAMPIONS LEAGUE 2011 QUALIFYING

West Asia Semi-finals

Esteghlal Tehran *	IRN	2
Zob Ahan	IRN	0

West Asia Final

Esteghlal Tehran *	IRN	3
Al Ittifaq	KSA	1

Al Shabab *	UAE	3
Neftchi Fergana	UZB	0

East Asia Finals

Pohang Steelers *	KOR	2
Chonburi	THA	0

Adelaide United *	AUS	3
Persipura Jayapura	IDN	0

* Home team • Esteghlal, Al Shabab, Pohang Steelers and Adelaide Utd qualified for the Group stage

West Asia Qualfying

Semi-Final. Azadi, Tehran
10-02-2012, 33 750, Tojo JPN

Esteghlal Tehran 2
Heyrdari [23], Borhani [67]
Mehdi RAHMATI - Khosro HEYDARI, Mehdi AMIRABADI, Hanif OMRANZADEH, Jlloyd SAMUEL, Ali HAMOUDI, Kianoush RAHMATI, Ferydoon ZANDI (Mohsen YOUSEFI 90), Pejman MONTAZERI, Arash BORHANI•, Goran JERKOVIC (Esmaeil SHARIFAT 62). Tr: Parviz MAZLOUMI

Zob Ahan 0
Mohamad BAGHER - Farsheed TALEBI, Mohammad Ali AHMADI (Hugo MACHADO 72), Mohammad SALSALI, Hossain MAHINI, Felipe ALVES, Davoud HAGHI, Sina ASHORI, Esmail FARHADI (Payam SADEGHIAN 43), Mohammad GHAZI (Hamid SHAFAAT 84), IGOR. Tr: Mansour EBRAHIMSADEH

Final. Azadi, Tehran
18-02-2012, 61 120, Kovalenko UZB

Esteghlal Tehran 3
Jerkovic [37], Heydari [62], Borhani [65]
Mehdi RAHMATI - Khosro HEYDARI, Mehdi AMIRABADI, Hanif OMRANZADEH, Jlloyd SAMUEL, Ali HAMOUDI, Kianoush RAHMATI, Mojtaba JABBARI, Pejman MONTAZERI, Arash BORHANI• (Mohsen YOUSEFI 88), Goran JERKOVIC• (Esmaeil SHARIFAT 68). Tr: Parviz MAZLOUMI

Al Ittifaq 1
Al Salem [59]
Fayez AL SABIAY - CARLOS SANTOS, Sayyaf AL BISHI, Ahmed Ali WALIBI, Mubarak Wajdi AL DOSSARI (Abdulmutalib AL TRAIDI 74), Saleh AL SAQRI, Yahya Mohammed OTAYN, Yahya AL SHEHRI, Hamad AL HAMAD (Zamil AL SALIM 74), Saleh Bashir AL DOSARI, Yousef AL SALEM. Tr: Branko IVANKOVIC

Final. Bin Rashid Al Maktoum, Dubai
18-02-2012, 2000, Torky IRN

Al Shabab 3
Obaid 2 [6 60], Haydarov [93+]
Ismail RABEE - Issa MOHAMMED, Mohammed MARZOOQ, Waleed ABBAS, Mahmoud QASSIM, Azizbek HAYDAROV, Adel ABDULLA, KIEZA (Naser MASOUD 90), Carlos VILLANUEVA (Suroor SALEM 90), Issa OBAID, CIEL• (Dawoud ALI 87). Tr: Paulo BONAMIGO

Neftchi Fergana 0
Khislat CHILMATOV - Fakhriddin KHOLMURADOV•, Shukurali PULATOV, Aybek NURBAEV, Dilyorbek IRMATOV, Yakubov BAHTIYORJON, Mansurjon SAIDOV, Aziz ALIJONOV, Sardor MIRZAYEV (Sherzod HAKIMOV 83), Ikboljon AKRAMOV• (Ghayrat DJUMAEV• 76), Anvar BERDIEV (Otabek ISROILOV• 46). Tr: Yuriy SARKISYAN

East Asia Qualfying

Final. Hindmarsh, Adelaide
16-02-2012, 5013, Toma JPN

Adelaide United 3
Boogaard [12], Levchenko [57], Van Dijk [84]
Eugene GALEKOVIC - Nigel BOOGAARD, CASSIO, Cameron WATSON, Osama MALIK, Evgeniy LEVCHENKO, Dario VIDOSIC (Jacob MELLING 75), Fabian BARBIERO•, Sergio VAN DIJK, Bruce DJITE (Zenon CARAVELLA 66), Iain RAMSAY (Evan KOSTOPOULOS 66). Tr: John KOSMINA

Persipura Jayapura 0
YOO Jae Hoon - Ricardo SALAMPESSY, Gerald PANGKALI, Yohanis TJOE (Imanuel WANGGAI 79), Paulin BIO, Imanuel PADWA (Zah KRANGAR 32), Moses BANGGO (Lukas MANDOWEN 57), BETO, Ian KABES, Tinus PAEW, Titus BONAI•. Tr: Jacksen F. TIAGO

Final. Steel Yard, Pohang
18-02-2012, 5344, Green AUS

Pohang Steelers 2
Hwang Jin Sung [28], Park Sung Ho [70]
SHIN Hwa Yong - KIM Gwang Seok, Zoran RENDULIC, SHIN Kwang Hoon, HWANG Jin Sung, KIM Tae Su, SHIN Hyung Min, KIM Dae Ho, Ianis ZICU (NO Byung Jun 57), Derek ASAMOAH (CHO Chan Ho 81), PARK Sung Ho (KIM Jin Yong 70). Tr: HWANG Sun Hong

Chonburi 0
Sinthaweechai HATHAIRATTANAKOOL - Suree SUKHA, Natthaphong SAMANA (Nurul SRIYANKEM 70), Suttinan PHUK-HOM, Anucha KITPONGSRI, Fode Bangaly DIAKITE, Cholratit JANTAKAM (Pipob ON-MO 38), Therdsak CHAIMAN, Geoffrey DOUMENG, Kazuto KUSHIDA, Ludovick TAKAM (Noppanon KACHAPLAYUK 79). Tr: Witthaya LADHAKUL

AFC CHAMPIONS LEAGUE 2012

GROUP A		Pl	W	D	L	F	A	Pts	UAE	IRN	QAT	UZB
Al Jazira	UAE	6	5	1	0	18	10	16		1-1	3-2	4-1
Esteghlal Tehran	IRN	6	3	2	1	8	3	11	1-2		3-0	0-0
Al Rayyan	QAT	6	2	0	4	9	12	6	3-4	0-1		3-1
Nasaf Karshi	UZB	6	0	1	5	4	14	1	2-4	0-2	0-1	

Ahmed bin Ali, Al Rayyan
6-03-2012, 5422, Williams AUS
Al Rayyan 0

Saud **AL HAJIRI** - Abdulrahman **MESBEH**, **CHO** Yong Hyung, Mosaab Mahmoud **AL HASSAN**, **NATHAN OTAVIO**, Abdulla **AFIFA**, **RODRIGO TABATA**, Daniel **GOMA** (Sayat **AL KORBI** 78), **AFONSO ALVES**, **LEANDRO** (Jaralla **AL MARRI** 78), Younes **ALI**. Tr: Diego **AGUIRRE**

Esteghlal Tehran 1
Jerkovic 91+
Mehdi **RAHMATI** - Khosro **HEYDARI**, Mehdi **AMIRABADI**•, Hanif **OMRANZADEH**, Jlloyd **SAMUEL**, Ali **HAMOUDI**•, Kianoush **RAHMATI**, Ferydoon **ZANDI** (Mohsen **YOUSEFI** 80), Pejman **MONTAZERI**, Milad **MEYDAVOUDI** (Goran **JERKOVIC** 81), Esmaeil **SHARIFAT**•. Tr: Parviz **MAZLOUMI**

Markaziy, Qarshi
7-03-2012, 13 000, Choi Myung Yong KOR
Nasaf Qarshi 2
Musaev 2, OG 18
Murad **ZUKHUROV** - Maksud **KARIMOV**, Botir **QORAEV**, Bojan **MALISIC**, Jahongir **DJIYAMURODOV**, Andrejs **PEREPLOTKINS** (Ivan **BOSKOVIC** 78), Artur **GEVORKYAN**, Fozil **MUSAEV**, Erkin **BOYDULLAEV**, Ilkhom **SHOMURODOV**, Kenja **TURAEV** (Nosirbek **OTAKUZIYEV** 69). Tr: Ruzikul **BERDIEV**

Al Jazira 4
Juma Abdullah 39, Mousa 68, Bare 75, Oliveira 88
Ali **KHASIF** - Lucas **NEILL**•, Juma **ABDULLAH**, Abdulla **MOUSA**, Khalid Sebil **LASHKARI**, Sami **RUBAIYA**, Abdulraheem **JUMAA** (**BARE** 65), Matias **DELGADO**• (Saleh **BASHEER** 90), Subait **KHATER** (Abdulsalam **JUMAA** 84), Ibrahim **DIAKY**, **RICARDO OLIVEIRA**. Tr: Frank **VERCAUTEREN**

Azadi, Tehran
20-03-2012, 41520, Al Hilali OMA
Esteghlal Tehran 0

Mehdi **RAHMATI** - Khosro **HEYDARI**, Mehdi **AMIRABADI**, Hanif **OMRANZADEH**, Jlloyd **SAMUEL**, Meysam **HOSSEINI**, Ali **HAMOUDI** (Mohsen **YOUSEFI** 85), Ferydoon **ZANDI**, Pejman **MONTAZERI**, Arash **BORHANI** (Esmaeil **SHARIFAT** 82), Goran **JERKOVIC** (Milad **MEYDAVOUDI** 67). Tr: Parviz **MAZLOUMI**

Nasaf Qarshi 0
Murad **ZUKHUROV** - Maksud **KARIMOV** (Sherzod **AZAMOV** 46), Botir **QORAEV**, Bojan **MALISIC**, Jahongir **DJIYAMURODOV**, Andrejs **PEREPLOTKINS** (Ilkhom **SHOMURODOV** 90), Artur **GEVORKYAN**, Fozil **MUSAEV**, Erkin **BOYDULLAEV**, Shoruh **GADOEV** (Mirzakamol **KAMALOV** 81), Ivan **BOSKOVIC**. Tr: Ruzikul **BERDIEV**

Mohamed bin Zayed, Abu Dhabi
20-03-2012, 2850, Abdulnabi BHR
Al Jazira 3
Oliveira 8, Diakey 54, Mousa 57
Ali **KHASIF** - Lucas **NEILL**•, Juma **ABDULLAH**, Abdulla **MOUSA**•, Salim Masoud **RASHID**, Yaser **MATAR**• (Sami **RUBAIYA** 71), Matias **DELGADO** (Sultan **BARGASH** 71), Subait **KHATER**, **BARE** (Abdulla **QASEM**• 69), Ibrahim **DIAKY**, **RICARDO OLIVEIRA**. Tr: **CAIO JUNIOR**

Al Rayyan 2
Goumou 65, Fabio Cesar 78
Saud **AL HAJIRI** - Abdulrahman **MESBEH** (Murad **NAJI** 72), **CHO** Yong Hyung, Mosaab Mahmoud **AL HASSAN**, **NATHAN OTAVIO**, **FABIO CESAR**, **RODRIGO TABATA**, Daniel **GOMA**, **AFONSO ALVES**, **LEANDRO**, Younes **ALI**. Tr: Diego **AGUIRRE**

Azadi, Tehran
3-04-2012, 36 735, Kim Dong Jin
Esteghlal Tehran 1
Zandi 68
Mehdi **RAHMATI** - Khosro **HEYDARI**, Mehdi **AMIRABADI**•, Hanif **OMRANZADEH**•, Jlloyd **SAMUEL**, Ali **HAMOUDI** (Goran **JERKOVIC** 63), Mohsen **YOUSEFI**, Ferydoon **ZANDI**, Pejman **MONTAZERI**, Arash **BORHANI** (Milad **MEYDAVOUDI** 71), Esmaeil **SHARIFAT**. Tr: Parviz **MAZLOUMI**

Al Jazira 2
Juma Abdullah 5, Bare 72
Ali **KHASIF**• - Juma **ABDULLAH**, Abdulla **MOUSA**, Salim Masoud **RASHID**, Ali **ABBAS**•, Sami **RUBAIYA**, Matias **DELGADO** (Saleh **BASHEER** 70), Subait **KHATER**, **BARE** (Sultan **BARGASH** 87), Ibrahim **DIAKY**, **RICARDO OLIVEIRA**. Tr: **CAIO JUNIOR**

Ahmed bin Ali, Al Rayyan
3-04-2012, 1877, Nishimura JPN
Al Rayyan 3
Tabata 9, Goumou 65, Al Aaeldin 88
Saud **AL HAJIRI** - **CHO** Yong Hyung•, Murad **NAJI**, Mosaab Mahmoud **AL HASSAN** (Hamid **ISMAIL** 46), **NATHAN OTAVIO**, Abdulla **AFIFA**, **RODRIGO TABATA**, Daniel **GOMA**, **AFONSO ALVES**, **LEANDRO** (Hamad **AL ABEDY**• 69), Younes **ALI** (Ahmed **AL AAELDIN** 86). Tr: Diego **AGUIRRE**

Nasaf Qarshi 1
Shomurodov 58
Murad **ZUKHUROV** - Sherzod **AZAMOV**, Botir **QORAEV**, Bojan **MALISIC**, Jahongir **DJIYAMURODOV**, Andrejs **PEREPLOTKINS** (Shoruh **GADOEV** 83), Artur **GEVORKYAN**, Fozil **MUSAEV**, Erkin **BOYDULLAEV**•, Mirzakamol **KAMALOV** (Ivan **BOSKOVIC** 55), Ilkhom **SHOMURODOV** (Shuhrat **MIRKHOLDIRSHOEV** 76). Tr: Ruzikul **BERDIEV**

Markaziy, Qarshi
18-04-2012, 7271, Lee Min Hu KOR
Nasaf Qarshi 0
Gayrat **HASANOV** - Maksud **KARIMOV**, Botir **QORAEV**, Bojan **MALISIC**, Jahongir **DJIYAMURODOV**•, Andrejs **PEREPLOTKINS** (Shoruh **GADOEV** 67), Artur **GEVORKYAN**, Fozil **MUSAEV**, Erkin **BOYDULLAEV** (Ilkhom **YUNUSOV** 17), Ilkhom **SHOMURODOV** (Kenja **TURAEV** 82), Nosirbek **OTAKUZIYEV**. Tr: Ruzikul **BERDIEV**

Al Rayyan 1
Tabata 62
Omar **BARI** - **CHO** Yong Hyung, Murad **NAJI**, Mosaab Mahmoud **AL HASSAN**, **NATHAN OTAVIO**, **FABIO CESAR**• (Hamad **AL ABEDY** 90), Abdulla **AFIFA**, **RODRIGO TABATA**, Daniel **GOMA**, **AFONSO ALVES**•, **LEANDRO** (Jaralla Al Marri 68). Tr: Diego **AGUIRRE**

Mohamed bin Zayed, Abu Dhabi
18-04-2012, 4562, Toma JPN
Al Jazira 1
Oliveira 63
Ali **KHASIF** - Lucas **NEILL**, Juma **ABDULLAH**•, Abdulla **MOUSA** (Saleh **BASHEER** 46), Salim Masoud **RASHID** (Khalid Sebil **LASHKARI** 62), Matias **DELGADO**, Subait **KHATER**, Khamis **ESMAAEL**, **BARE** (Ali **MABKHOUT** 82), Ibrahim **DIAKY**, **RICARDO OLIVEIRA**. Tr: **CAIO JUNIOR**

Esteghlal Tehran 1
Borhani 24
Mehdi **RAHMATI**• - Khosro **HEYDARI**, Hanif **OMRANZADEH**, Jlloyd **SAMUEL**, Meysam **HOSSEINI**, Ali **HAMOUDI**•, Mojtaba **JABBARI** (Esmaeil **SHARIFAT** 69), Andranik **TEYMOURIAN**•, Ferydoon **ZANDI**, Pejman **MONTAZERI**, Arash **BORHANI** (Goran **JERKOVIC** 84). Tr: Parviz **MAZLOUMI**

Azadi, Tehran
2-05-2012, 53774, Tan Hai CHN
Esteghlal Tehran 3
Borhani 2 23p 93+, Sharifat 76
Mehdi **RAHMATI**• - Khosro **HEYDARI**, Hanif **OMRANZADEH**, Jlloyd **SAMUEL**, Meysam **HOSSEINI**, Ali **HAMOUDI**•, Andranik **TEYMOURIAN** (Mohsen **YOUSEFI** 87), Ferydoon **ZANDI**• (Mojtaba **JABBARI** 68), Pejman **MONTAZERI**, Arash **BORHANI**, Milad **MEYDAVOUDI** (Esmaeil **SHARIFAT** 70). Tr: Parviz **MAZLOUMI**

Al Rayyan 0
Omar **BARI** - **CHO** Yong Hyung, Murad **NAJI**, Mosaab Mahmoud **AL HASSAN** (Hamid **ISMAIL** 56), **NATHAN OTAVIO**, **FABIO CESAR** (Mohamed **SALAH** 89), Abdulla **AFIFA**•, **RODRIGO TABATA**, Daniel **GOMA**, **AFONSO ALVES**, **LEANDRO** (Jaralla **AL MARRI** 56). Tr: Diego **AGUIRRE**

Mohamed bin Zayed, Abu Dhabi
2-05-2012, 820, Green AUS
Al Jazira 4
Bare 6, Oliveira 3 14p 33 42p
Ali **KHASIF** - Lucas **NEILL**, Juma **ABDULLAH**•, Abdulla **MOUSA**, Khalid Sebil **LASHKARI** (Salim Masoud **RASHID** 71), Matias **DELGADO**, Subait **KHATER**, Khamis **ESMAAEL**, **BARE** (Ali **MABKHOUT** 53), Ibrahim **DIAKY** (Sultan **BARGASH** 46), **RICARDO OLIVEIRA**. Tr: **CAIO JUNIOR**

Nasaf Qarshi 1
Shomurodov 69
Gayrat **HASANOV**• - Sherzod **AZAMOV**, Botir **QORAEV**, Bojan **MALISIC**•, Jahongir **DJIYAMURODOV**, Fozil **MUSAEV**, Mirzakamol **KAMALOV**, Shoruh **GADOEV**, Ilkhom **YUNUSOV**, Ildar **BAYMATOV**, Ilkhom **SHOMURODOV** (Sukhrob **NEMATOV** 80), Kenja **TURAEV** (Shuhrt **MIRKHOLDIRSHOEV** 51). Tr: Ruzikul **BERDIEV**

Markaziy, Qarshi
16-05-2012, 929, Tojo JPN
Nasaf Qarshi 0
Murad **ZUKHUROV** - Sherzod **AZAMOV**, Maksud **KARIMOV**, Bojan **MALISIC** (Alisher **YUSUPOV** 59), Jahongir **DJIYAMURODOV**•, Andrejs **PEREPLOTKINS**, Fozil **MUSAEV** (Shuhrat **MIRKHOLDIRSHOEV** 59), Erkin **BOYDULLAEV**•, Ilkhom **YUNUSOV**, Ilkhom **SHOMURODOV** (Nosirbek **OTAKUZIYEV** 69), Kenja **TURAEV**•. Tr: Ruzikul **BERDIEV**

Esteghlal Tehran 2
Jerkovic 10, Jabbari 50p
Mehdi **RAHMATI** - Khosro **HEYDARI**, Mehdi **AMIRABADI**••68, Jlloyd **SAMUEL**•, Meysam **HOSSEINI**, Javad **SHIRZAD**, Mojtaba **JABBARI** (Hamid **AZIZZADEH** 89), Ferydoon **ZANDI**, Pejman **MONTAZERI**, Arash **BORHANI** (Milad **MEYDAVOUDI** 79), Goran **JERKOVIC** (Esmaeil **SHARIFAT** 70). Tr: Parviz **MAZLOUMI**

Ahmed bin Ali, Al Rayyan
16-05-2012, 535, El Haddad LIB
Al Rayyan 3
Tabata 73, Leandro 76, Al Aaeldin 90
Omar **BARI** - Abdulrahman **MESBEH**, **CHO** Yong Hyung, Murad **NAJI** (Sayat **AL KORBI** 46), Mosaab Mahmoud **AL HASSAN** (Ahmed **AL AAELDIN** 46), **NATHAN OTAVIO**, **RODRIGO TABATA**, Daniel **GOMA**, Waheed **MOHAMMEDI**, **LEANDRO**, Mohamed **SALAH** 70. Tr: Diego **AGUIRRE**

Al Jazira 4
Oliveira 4 8 33 67 88
Khalid **EISA** - Lucas **NEILL**, Saleh **BASHEER**, Salim Masoud **RASHID** (Khalid Sebil **LASHKARI** 46), Sami **RUBAIYA**, Subait **KHATER**•, Khamis **ESMAAEL**, Sultan **BARGASH**, **BARE** (Ahmed **MUHAD** 59), Ibrahim **DIAKY** (Abdulraheem **JUMAA** 73), **RICARDO OLIVEIRA**. Tr: **CAIO JUNIOR**

GROUP B		Pl	W	D	L	F	A	Pts	KSA	UAE	UZB	QAT
Al Ittihad	KSA	6	5	1	0	13	4	16		1-0	4-0	3-2
Bani-Yas	UAE	6	3	2	1	9	2	11	0-0		2-0	2-0
Pakhtakor Tashkent	UZB	6	2	1	3	6	10	7	1-2	1-1		3-1
Al Arabi	QAT	6	0	0	6	4	16	0	1-3	0-4	0-1	

Bani-Yas, Abu Dhabi
6-03-2012, 1795, Faghani IRN

Bani-Yas 2
Jaber [45p], Yeste [77]
Mohamed KHALAF - Ismael BOUZID, Mohamed JABER, Thamir MOHAMED, Haboush SALBUKH (Fawaz AWANA 73), Fawzi BASHEER•, Sultan AL GHAFRI, Yousif JABER, Francisco YESTE (Adnan HUSSAIN 81), Andre SENGHOR, Fareed ISMAIL (Saleh AL MENHALI 88). Tr: Gabriel CALDERON

Al Arabi 0
Rajab KASSIM• - Waleed MOHYADEN, Ahmed DAD, Hadi AGHILI, Abdelaziz HATEM (Nasser Saleh AL KHALFAN 87), Mohammed SALEM, Leonardo PISCULICHI•, Majdi SIDDIQ, Abdulaziz AL SULAITI, Boualem KHOUKHI, Arafat DJAKO (Abdulla MAARAFIYA 76). Tr: Abdullah SAAD

Prince Abdullah Al Faisal, Jeddah
6-03-2012, 250, Tojo JPN

Al Ittihad 4
Adelghani [4], Abousaban 2 [31] [51], Omar [58]
Mabrouk ZAID - Osama AL HARBI, Mishal AL SAEED, Hamad AL MONTASHARI, Ibrahim HAZAZI, Saud KHARIRI•, Mohammed NOOR, Mohammed ABUSABAAN, Hosny ABD RABOU (Aiman SABER 63), Naif HAZAZI (Fabrice N'GUESSI 77), Faouzi ABDELGHANI (Abdullah OMAR 55). Tr: Raul CANEDA

Pakhtakor Tashkent 0
Temur JURAEV - Murod KHALMUKHAMEDOV, Aleksandr KLETSKOV••[37], Aleksey NIKOLAEV, Naoya SHIBAMURA, Kakhi MAKHARADZE•, Sanibal ORAHOVAC (Dilshod SHAROFETDINOV• (Vladimir KOZAK 61), Stanislav ANDREEV (Sherzodbek KARIMOV 46), Farhod TADJIYEV, Irakli KLIMIASHVILI (Oybek KILICHEV 46). Tr: Dejan Durdevic

JAR, Tashkent
20-03-2012, 2300, Choi Myung Yong KOR

Pakhtakor Tashkent 1
Sharofetdinov [29]
Temur JURAEV - Igor KRIMETS, Davronbek KHASHIMOV, Aleksey NIKOLAEV, Kakhi MAKHARADZE, Sanibal ORAHOVAC (Sherzodbek KARIMOV 46), Dilshod SHAROFETDINOV (Vladimir KOZAK• 57), Stanislav ANDREEV, Oybek KILICHEV, Irakli KLIMIASHVILI, Bakhriddin VAHOBOV (Temurkhuja ABDUKHOLIQOV 64). Tr: Dejan DURDEVIC

Bani-Yas 1
Fawzi [60]
Mohamed KHALAF - Ismael BOUZID, Nawaf MUBARAK, Mohamed JABER•, Thamir MOHAMED, Ibrahim SAEED (Haboush SALBUKH 46), Fawzi BASHEER - (Ahmed ALI 78), Sultan AL GHAFRI (Fareed ISMAIL 87), Yousif JABER, Mohamed FAWZI, Andre SENGHOR. Tr: Gabriel CALDERON

Grand Hamad, Doha
20-03-2012, 1855, Lee Min Hu KOR

Al Arabi 1
Pisculichi [26]
Rajab KASSIM - Mohammed AL ZEYARAH, Waleed MOHYADEN, Ahmed DAD, Hadi AGHILI, Mohammed SALEM, Leonardo PISCULICHI•, Majdi SIDDIQ, Abdulla MAARAFIYA (Abdelaziz HATEM 70), Boualem KHOUKHI•, Arafat DJAKO (Ali MEJBEL 75). Tr: Abdullah SAAD

Al Ittihad 3
Hazazi 2 [21] [82], Al Montashari [30]
Mabrouk ZAID - Rashid AL RAHEEB•, Osama AL HARBI, Mishal AL SAEED•, Hamad AL MONTASHARI, Saud KHARIRI•, Mohammed NOOR, Mohammed ABUSABAAN, Hosny ABD RABOU (Abdoh OTAIF 76), Naif HAZAZI•, Mohammed Ali AL RASHED (Ibrahim HAZAZI 68). Tr: Raul CANEDA

JAR, Tashkent
4-04-2012, 5532, Tan Hai CHN

Pakhtakor Tashkent 3
Karimov [9], Sharofetdinov [74], Abdukholiqov [93+]
Alexander LOBANOV - Igor KRIMETS•, Davronbek KHASHIMOV, Aleksey NIKOLAEV, Kakhi MAKHARADZE, Sanibal ORAHOVAC•, Sherzodbek KARIMOV (Abbosbek MAKHSTALIEV 71), Stanislav ANDREEV, Oybek KILICHEV (Dilshod SHAROFETDINOV 64), Temurkhuja ABDUKHOLIQOV, Irakli KLIMIASHVILI (Vladimir KOZAK 87). Tr: Dejan Durdevic

Al Arabi 1
Pisculichi [37]
Rajab KASSIM - Mohammed AL ZEYARAH, Waleed MOHYADEN, Ahmed DAD, Hadi AGHILI, Abdelaziz HATEM•, Mohammed SALEM (Ali MEJBEL 84), Leonardo PISCULICHI, Majdi SIDDIQ•, Abdulla MAARAFIYA• (Arafat DJAKO 78), Boualem KHOUKHI. Tr: Abdullah SAAD

Prince Abdullah Al Faisal, Jeddah
4-04-2012, 11 495, Abdulnabi BHR

Al Ittihad 1
Hazazi [79p]
Mabrouk ZAID - Rashid AL RAHEEB (Mishal AL SAEED 74), Redha TUKAR, Hamad AL MONTASHARI, Ahmed Hassan ASIRI, Ibrahim HAZAZI•, Mohammed ABUSABAAN•, Abdoh OTAIF, Naif HAZAZI, Ali AL ZUBAIDI• (Maan KHODARY 57), Faouzi ABDELGHANI (Fabrice N'GUESSI 90). Tr: Raul CANEDA

Bani-Yas 0
Mohamed KHALAF - Ismael BOUZID•, Mohamed JABER, Thamir MOHAMED• (Francisco YESTE 72), Haboush SALBUKH, Fawzi BASHEER, Fawaz AWANA•, Yousif JABER (Ibrahim SAEED 77), Ahmed ALI (Sultan AL GHAFRI 70), Mohamed FAWZI, Andre SENGHOR. Tr: Gabriel CALDERON

Bani-Yas, Abu Dhabi
17-04-2012, 6265, Kim Dong Jin KOR

Bani-Yas 1
Mohamed KHALAF - Nawaf MUBARAK (Haboush SALBUKH 71), Mohamed JABER•, Thamir MOHAMED•, Sultan AL GHAFRI, Fawaz AWANA, Francisco YESTE, Ahmed ALI (Yousif JABER 90), Mohamed FAWZI, Andre SENGHOR, Fareed ISMAIL (Amer ABDULRAHMAN 57). Tr: Gabriel CALDERON

Al Ittihad 0
Mabrouk ZAID - Redha TUKAR, Osama AL HARBI•, Hamad AL MONTASHARI, Saud KHARIRI, Mohammed ABUSABAAN, Hatan BABHIR (Hosny ABD RABOU 54), Abdoh OTAIF (Mishal AL SAEED• 73), Naif HAZAZI (Mohammed Ali AL RASHED 66), Faouzi ABDELGHANI. Tr: Raul CANEDA

Grand Hamad, Doha
17-04-2012, 500, Shukralla BHR

Al Arabi 0
Rajab KASSIM - Mohammed AL ZEYARAH• (Muaz ADAM•82), Waleed MOHYADEN, Ahmed DAD, Hadi AGHILI•, Abdelaziz HATEM, Leonardo PISCULICHI, Majdi SIDDIQ, Abdulla MAARAFIYA (Abdallah AL ORAIMI 82), Boualem KHOUKHI, Arafat DJAKO (Abdulla AL SULAITI 70). Tr: Abdullah SAAD

Pakhtakor Tashkent 1
Abdukholiqov [41]
Temur JURAEV - Igor KRIMETS, Davronbek KHASHIMOV•, Aleksey NIKOLAEV, Kakhi MAKHARADZE, Sherzodbek KARIMOV (Abbosbek MAKHSTALIEV 89), Dilshod SHAROFETDINOV• (Vladimir KOZAK 80), Stanislav ANDREEV, Oybek KILICHEV••[75], Temurkhuja ABDUKHOLIQOV (Bakhriddin VAHOBOV 84), Irakli KLIMIASHVILI•. Tr: Dejan DURDEVIC

JAR, Tashkent
2-05-2012, 4000, Torky IRN

Pakhtakor Tashkent 1
Klimiashvili [68]
Temur JURAEV - Igor KRIMETS⊛[69], Davronbek KHASHIMOV, Ilhomjon SUYUNOV, Kakhi MAKHARADZE, Sherzodbek KARIMOV, Stanislav ANDREEV, Vladimir KOZAK, Abbosbek MAKHSTALIEV (Alisher AZIZOV 63), Temurkhuja ABDUKHOLIQOV (Timur KHAKIMOV 85), Irakli KLIMIASHVILI•. Tr: Dejan DURDEVIC

Al Ittihad 1
Hazazi [60], Abousaban [93+]
Mabrouk ZAID - Redha TUKAR, Osama AL HARBI•, Hamad AL MONTASHARI, Ibrahim HAZAZI, Saud KHARIRI (Maan KHODARY 33), Mohammed ABUSABAAN• (Faouzi ABDELGHANI 60), Hosny ABD RABOU (Abdoh OTAIF (Ali AL ZUBAIDI 72), Naif HAZAZI•. Tr: Raul CANEDA

Grand Hamad, Doha
2-05-2012, 527, Sato JPN

Al Arabi 0
Rajab KASSIM - Muaz ADAM, Waleed MOHYADEN•, Hadi AGHILI (Abdulla AL SULAITI 43), Abdelaziz HATEM•, Mohammed SALEM, Leonardo PISCULICHI•, Majdi SIDDIQ•, Abdulaziz AL SULAITI (Abdallah AL ORAIMI 57), Boualem KHOUKHI, Arafat DJAKO (Nasser Saleh AL KHALFAN 70). Tr: Abdullah SAAD

Bani-Yas 4
Bashir [17], Yeste [39], Mubarak [52], Senghor [77]
Mohamed KHALAF - Ismael BOUZID, Nawaf MUBARAK, Fawzi BASHEER (Haboush SALBUKH 64), Sultan AL GHAFRI•, Fawaz AWANA (Amer ABDULRAHMAN 63), Yousif JABER, Francisco YESTE (Saleh AL MENHALI 78), Mohamed FAWZI, Andre SENGHOR, Fareed ISMAIL. Tr: Gabriel CALDERON

Bani-Yas, Abu Dhabi
16-05-2012, 3927, Bashir SIN

Bani-Yas 2
Senghor [13], Abdulrahman [71]
Mohamed KHALAF - Ismael BOUZID, Nawaf MUBARAK, Mohamed JABER, Thamir MOHAMED (Saleh AL MENHALI 76), Fawzi BASHEER, Yousif JABER, Francisco YESTE (Ibrahim Jaber NASER 77), Mohamed FAWZI, Andre SENGHOR, Fareed ISMAIL (Amer ABDULRAHMAN 59). Tr: Gabriel CALDERON

Pakhtakor Tashkent 0
Temur JURAEV - Davronbek KHASHIMOV, Ilhomjon SUYUNOV, Aleksey NIKOLAEV, Kakhi MAKHARADZE, Sherzodbek KARIMOV (Abbosbek MAKHSTALIEV 46), Stanislav ANDREEV (Alisher AZIZOV 66), Vladimir KOZAK, Oybek KILICHEV (Dilshod SHAROFETDINOV 56), Temurkhuja ABDUKHOLIQOV, Irakli KLIMIASHVILI. Tr: Dejan Durdevic

Prince Abdullah Al Faisal, Jeddah
16-05-2012, 9621, Al Hilali OMA

Al Ittihad 3
Abd Rabo [30], N'Guessi [64], Abdelghani [93+]
Mabrouk ZAID - Redha TUKAR, Mishal AL SAEED, Ahmed Hassan ASIRI, Maan KHODARY (Hatan BABHIR 62), Saud KHARIRI, Hosny ABD RABOU, Abdoh OTAIF (Mohammed NOOR 72), Abdullah OMAR, Fabrice N'GUESSI• (Mohammed Ali AL RASHED 86), Faouzi ABDELGHANI•. Tr: Raul CANEDA

Al Arabi 2
Khoukhi 2 [9] [45]
Masoud ZERAEI••[90] - Muaz ADAM, Mohammed AL ZEYARAH, Waleed MOHYADEN, Ahmed DAD•, Mohammed SALEM, Abdulaziz AL SULAITI (Ahmed Saleh AL KHALFAN 90), Abdulla MAARAFIYA (Meshal AL ENEZI 89), Boualem KHOUKHI•, Abdallah AL ORAIMI (Nasser Saleh AL KHALFAN 80), Arafat DJAKO. Tr: Abdullah SAAD

AFC CHAMPIONS LEAGUE 2012

GROUP C		Pl	W	D	L	F	A	Pts	IRN	KSA	UAE	QAT
Sepahan	IRN	6	4	1	1	9	4	13		2-1	1-0	2-1
Al Ahli Jeddah	KSA	6	3	1	2	10	6	10	1-1		3-1	3-0
Al Nasr	UAE	6	2	0	4	6	11	6	0-3	1-2		2-1
Lekhwia	QAT	6	2	0	4	5	9	6	1-0	1-0	1-2	

Foolad Shahr, Isfahan
7-03-2012, 6550, Tan Hai CHN

Sepahan 1
Correa 84

Rahman AHMADI - Hassan ASHJARI, Jalal HOSSEINI, Mohsen BENGAR, Abolhassan JAFARI•, Mehdi KARIMIAN, Omid EBRAHIMI, Fabio JANUARIO, Xhevair SUKAJ (Moharram NAVIDKIA 71), Bruno CESAR (Hadi TAMINI 90), Mehdi Seyed SALEHI (Emad MOHAMMED 78). Tr: Zlatko KRANJCAR

Al Nasr 0

Abdulla MOOSA (Ahmad SHAMBIH 86) - Masoud HASSAN, Mohammed Ali ABDULLA (Jamal Ibrahim HUSSEIN 88), Helal SAEED, Talal HAMAD, Mahmoud Hassan DARWISH, Humaid ABBAS• (Saeed MUBARAK 83), Mark BRESCIANO•, Leo LIMA•, Luca TONI, Amara DIANE. Tr: Walter ZENGA

Jassim Bin Hamad, Doha
7-03-2012, 4227, Abdulnabi BHR

Lekhwia 1
Nam Tae Hee 74

Baba MALICK - Dame TRAORE, Dame MUFTAH, Mohammed MUSA, Madjid BOUGHERRA, LUIZ CEARA, Hussain Ali SHEHAB•, Karim BOUDIAF•, NAM Tae Hee•, Bakari KONE, Moumouni DAGANO (Lassina DIABY 81). Tr: Djemal BELMADI

Al Ahli Jeddah 0

Yaser AL MOSAILEM - Kamel AL MOR (Abdulrahim JIZAWI 84), Kamil AL MOUSA, Jufain AL BISHI (Aqeel AL SAHIBI 30), Mansour AL HARBI, Jairo PALOMINO, Taisir AL JASSIM, MARCELO CAMACHO, Mohsen AL EISA (Mohammed AL MUWALLAD 52), VICTOR SIMOES•, Amad AL HOSANI•. Tr: Karel JAROLIM

Al Maktoum, Dubai
21-03-2012, 4720, Kim Dong Jin KOR

Al Nasr 2
Diane 2 37 92+

Abdulla MOOSA - Masoud HASSAN, Mohammed Ali ABDULLA, Helal SAEED, Mahmoud Hassan DARWISH•, Humair ABBAS•, Jamal Ibrahim HUSSAIN 76), Habib FARDAN, Mark BRESCIANO• (Younis Ahmad ABDULLA 64), Leo LIMA•, Luca TONI (Mana Sabil OBAID 88), Amara DIANE. Tr: Walter ZENGA

Lekhwia 1
Dagano 42

Baba MALICK - Dame TRAORE, Khaled MUFTAH•, Mohammed MUSA (Mousa Majid AL ALLAQ 77), Madjid BOUGHERRA, LUIZ CEARA (Ali Hasan YAHYA 23), Hussain Ali SHEHAB, Karim BOUDIAF•, Adel LAMY•, Bakari KONE (NAM Tae Hee 69), Moumouni DAGANO. Tr: Djemal BELMADI

Prince Abdullah Al Faisal, Jeddah
21-03-2012, 14247, Kovalenko UZB

Al Ahli Jeddah 1
Simoes 94+

Abdullah AL MUAIOUF - Kamel AL MOR•, Waleed BAKSHWN, Kamil AL MOUSA, Aqeel AL SAHIBI (Motaz AL MUSA 46), Mansour AL HARBI, Jairo PALOMINO, Taisir AL JASSIM, Mohsen AL EISA (Marcelo CAMACHO 60), Amad AL HOSANI, Mohammed MAJRASHI (VICTOR SIMOES 68). Tr: Karel JAROLIM

Sepahan 1
Correa 35

Rahman AHMADI - Hassan ASHJARI, Jalal HOSSEINI, Mohsen BENGAR, Abolhassan JAFARI•, Moharram NAVIDKIA, Mehdi KARIMIAN (Ahmad JAMSHIDIAN 70), Omid EBRAHIMI•, FABIO JANUARIO (Hadi TAMINI 46), BRUNO CESAR, Mehdi Seyed SALEHI (Mehdi JAFARPOUR 84). Tr: Zlatko KRANJCAR

Foolad Shahr, Isfahan
3-04-2012, 6732, Sato JPN

Sepahan 2
Hosseini 10, Correa 89

Rahman AHMADI, Jalal HOSSEINI, Mohsen BENGAR, Hashem BEIKZADEH, Abolhassan JAFARI, Moharram NAVIDKIA, Mehdi KARIMIAN (Xhevair SUKAJ•77), Omid EBRAHIMI, FABIO JANUARIO (Hossein PAPI 87), BRUNO CESAR, Mehdi Seyed SALEHI (Ahmad JAMSHIDIAN 67). Tr: Zlatko KRANJCAR

Lekhwia 1
Afif 55

Baba MALICK - Dame TRAORE, Khaled MUFTAH, Mohammed MUSA, Madjid BOUGHERRA, LUIZ CEARA, Hussain Ali SHEHAB, NAM Tae Hee (Adel LAMY 41), Ali Hasan YAHYA (Lassina DIABY 90), Moumouni DAGANO (Mohammed RAZAK 85). Tr: Djemal BELMADI

Al Maktoum, Dubai
3-04-2012, 4376, Tojo JPN

Al Nasr 1
Diane 52

Abdulla MOOSA - Masoud HASSAN, Mohammed Ali ABDULLA, Helal SAEED, Ali Salem Ahmed FARAJ, Mahmoud Hassan DARWISH, Humaid ABBAS (Jamal Ibrahim HUSSAIN 64), Habib FARDAN, Mana Sabil OBAID (Ali Ahmed HUSSAIN 54), Amara DIANE, Younis Ahmad ABDULLA (Salem KHAMIS 82). Tr: Walter ZENGA

Al Ahli Jeddah 2
Simoes 27, Al Jassim 50

Abdullah AL MUAIOUF - Waleed BAKSHWN, Kamil AL MOUSA, Mohammed AL MUWALLAD (Kamel AL MOR 64), Aqeel AL SAHIBI (Mohammed AL FATIL 82), Mansour AL HARBI, Motaz AL MUSA (Mohsen AL EISA 67), Taisir AL JASSIM•, Marcelo CAMACHO, VICTOR SIMOES, Yasir AL FAHMI. Tr: Karel JAROLIM

Jassim Bin Hamad, Doha
18-04-2012, 3423, Bashir SIN

Lekhwia 1
Kone 91+

Baba MALICK - Dame TRAORE, Khaled MUFTAH, Mohammed MUSA, Madjid BOUGHERRA, LUIZ CEARA, Karim BOUDIAF, NAM Tae Hee, Adel LAMY (Bakari KONE 58), Ali Hasan YAHYA (Lassina DIABY 80), Moumouni DAGANO (Mohammed RAZAK 65). Tr: Djemal BELMADI

Sepahan 0

Rahman AHMADI - Hassan ASHJARI, Jalal HOSSEINI, Mohsen BENGAR•, Abolhassan JAFARI, Moharram NAVIDKIA, Omid EBRAHIMI, FABIO JANUARIO (Mehdi KARIMIAN 70), Xhevair SUKAJ (Mehdi JAFARPOUR 68), BRUNO CESAR (Ahmad JAMSHIDIAN 89), Mehdi Seyed SALEHI. Tr: Zlatko KRANJCAR

Prince Abdullah Al Faisal, Jeddah
18-04-2012, 16386, Choi Myung Yong KOR

Al Ahli Jeddah 3
Jaizawi 55, Simoes 66, Al Mousa 73

Abdullah AL MUAIOUF - Waleed BAKSHWN• (Yasir AL FAHMI 46), Kamil AL MOUSA, Mohammed AL MUWALLAD, Mansour AL HARBI, Jairo PALOMINO, Motaz AL MUSA•, Taisir AL JASSIM, Marcelo CAMACHO, Abdulrahim JIZAWI (Kamel AL MOR 86), VICTOR SIMOES. Tr: Karel JAROLIM

Al Nasr 1
Diane 33

Abdulla MOOSA - Masoud HASSAN (Jamal Ibrahim HUSSAIN• 60), Mohammed Ali ABDULLA, Helal SAEED, Ali Salem Ahmed FARAJ, Mahmoud Hassan DARWISH, Humaid ABBAS (Younis Ahmad ABDULLA 71), Habib FARDAN, Mark BRESCIANO, Leo LIMA, Amara DIANE•. Tr: Walter ZENGA

Al Maktoum, Dubai
1-05-2012, 2264, Shukralla BHR

Al Nasr 0

Abdulla Moosa◆50 - Mohammed Ali ABDULLA, Helal SAEED, Ali Salem Ahmed FARAJ, Mahmoud Hassan DARWISH, Humaid ABBAS (Abdulla ABDULGHAFOOR 52), Habib FARDAN, Mark BRESCIANO•, LEO LIMA, Amara DIANE (Khaled Ali MATAR 88), Younis Ahmad ABDULLA (Jamal Ibrahim HUSSAIN 63). Tr: Walter ZENGA

Sepahan 3
Correa 44, Sukaj 69, Salehi 77

Rahman AHMADI• - Hassan ASHJARI, Jalal HOSSEINI, Mohsen BENGAR, Abolhassan JAFARI, Moharram NAVIDKIA, Mehdi KARIMIAN (Mehdi JAFARPOUR• 67), Omid EBRAHIMI, FABIO JANUARIO (Ahmad JAMSHIDIAN 78), Xhevair SUKAJ, BRUNO CESAR (Mehdi Seyed SALEHI 74). Tr: Zlatko KRANJCAR

Prince Abdullah Al Faisal, Jeddah
1-05-2012, 10214, Toma JPN

Al Ahli Jeddah 3
Jaizawi 9, Simoes 61, Al Jassi 91+

Abdullah AL MUAIOUF - Mohammed AL FATIL, Kamil AL MOUSA (Aqeel AL SAHIBI 90), Mohammed AL MUWALLAD, Mansour AL HARBI•, Motaz AL MUSA, Taisir AL JASSIM, Marcelo CAMACHO, Abdulrahim JIZAWI (Kamel AL MOR 83), VICTOR SIMOES•, Yasir AL FAHMI (Mohsen AL EISA 79). Tr: Karel JAROLIM

Lekhwia 0

Baba MALICK - Dame TRAORE•, Khaled MUFTAH, Mohammed MUSA, Madjid BOUGHERRA (Ahmed YASSER 64), LUIZ CEARA, Mohammed RAZAK (Moumouni DAGANO 46), Hussain Ali SHEHAB (Ali Hasan YAHYA 61), Karim BOUDIAF, NAM Tae Hee, Bakari KONE. Tr: Djemal BELMADI

Foolad Shahr, Isfahan
15-05-2012, 6371, Lee Min Hu KOR

Sepahan 2
Sukaj 19, Bengar 85

Rahman AHMADI - Jalal HOSSEINI, Mohsen BENGAR, Hashem BEIKZADEH, Abolhassan JAFARI (Mehdi JAFARPOUR 40), Moharram NAVIDKIA, Mehdi KARIMIAN, Omid EBRAHIMI, FABIO JANUARIO (Hadi TAMINI 85), Xhevair SUKAJ (Mehdi Seyed SALEHI 50), BRUNO CESAR. Tr: Zlatko KRANJCAR

Al Ahli Jeddah 1
Al Hosni 62

Yaser AL MOSAILEM - Waleed BAKSHWN, Mohammed AL MUWALLAD, Haidar AL AMER, Aqeel AL SAHIBI• (Jairo PALOMINO 46), Jufain AL BISHI, Motaz AL MUSA (Ahmed DARWESH• 69), Hamoud ABBAS, Hassan AL RAHEB, Amad AL HOSANI (Abdulrahim JIZAWI 63), Yasir AL FAHMI. Tr: Karel JAROLIM

Jassim Bin Hamad, Doha
15-05-2012, 643, Irmatov UZB

Lekhwia 1
Diaby 38

Amine LECOMTE - Mohammed MUDATHER, Dame TRAORE, Mousa Majid AL ALLAQ, Ismail MOHAMAD•, Karim BOUDIAF•, Ahmed YASSER, NAM Tae Hee, Bakari KONE, Ali Hasan YAHYA (Moumouni DAGANO 71), Lassina DIABY. Tr: Djemal BELMADI

Al Nasr 2
Diane 55, Humaid Abbas 57

Ahmad SHAMBIH - Masoud HASSAN, Mohammed Ali ABDULLA, Ali Salem Ahmed FARAJ, Mahmoud Hassan DARWISH, Humaid ABBAS (Jamal Ibrahim HUSSAIN 87), Habib FARDAN, Salem KHAMIS (Helal SAEED 68), LEO LIMA•, Luca TONI (Younis Ahmad ABDULLA 78), Amara DIANE. Tr: Walter ZENGA

GROUP D

		Pl	W	D	L	F	A	Pts	KSA	IRN	QAT	UAE
Al Hilal	KSA	6	3	3	0	10	7	12		1-1	2-1	2-1
Persepolis	IRN	6	3	2	1	14	5	11	0-1		1-1	6-1
Al Gharafa	QAT	6	1	3	2	7	10	6	3-3	0-3		2-1
Al Shabab	UAE	6	0	2	4	5	14	2	1-1	1-3	0-0	

Bin Rashid Al Maktoum, Dubai
7-03-2012, 3542, Bashir SIN

Al Shabab 0

Ismail RABEE - Mohammed MARZOOQ, Waleed ABBAS, Mahmoud QASSIM, Hamdan QASSIM (Abdulla DARWISH 80), Azizbek HAYDAROV•, Adel ABDULLA, KIEZA, Carlos VILLANUEVA, Issa OBAID (Naser MASOUD 80), CIEL. Tr: Paulo BONAMIGO

Al Gharafa 0

Qasem BURHAN (Abdulaziz ALI 35) - Ibrahim AL GHANIM, Hamed SHAMI•, George Kwesi SEMAKOR, Ahmed AL BINALI•, Lawrence QUAYE, Othmane EL ASSAS, Fahad AL SHAMMARI, DIEGO TARDELLI, Farhad MAJIDI, Muayed HASSAN (Mirghani AL ZAIN 58). Tr: Bruno METSU

Prince Faisal Bin Fahad, Riyadh
7-03-2012, 9574, Lee Min Hu KOR

Al Hilal 1

Al Shalhoub [53]

Khalid SHARAHELE - Sultan AL BISHI, Osama HAWSAWI•40, Abdullah AL ZORI, Majed AL MARSHADI, Mohammad AL SHALHOUB (Abdullatif AL GHANNAM 77), Salman AL FARAJ, Ahmed AL FRAIDI•, Adil HERMACH, YOO Byung Soo• (Youssef EL ARABI 76), Salem AL DOSSARI (Saad AL HARTHI 88). Tr: Ivan HASEK

Persepolis 1

Karimi [42p]

Asmir AVDUKIC - Mohammad NOSRATI, Sheys REZAEI, Mehrdad POULADI, Ali KARIMI, Maziar ZARE (Hadi NOROUZI 65), Hossein BADAMAKI, Mohammad NOURI, Hamidreza ALIASGARI, Gholamreza REZAEI, Javad KAZEMIAN (Amir FESHANGCHI 82). Tr: Mustafa DENIZLI

Azadi, Tehran
21-03-2012, 82700, Toma JPN

Persepolis 6

Zayed 3 [8 47 53], Rezaei.G [59], Karimi [62p], Feshangchi [87]

Asmir AVDUKIC - Mohammad NOSRATI, Sheys REZAEI, Mehrdad POULADI, Ali KARIMI (Mehdi MAHDAVIKIA 75), Mohammad NOURI, Saman AGHAZAMANI, Hamidreza ALIASGARI, Gholamreza REZAEI (Maziar ZARE 80), Eamon ZAYED, Javad KAZEMIAN (Amir FESHANGCHI• 58). Tr: Mustafa DENIZLI

Al Shabab 0

Ciel [56p]

Ismail RABEE - Mohammed MARZOOQ, Waleed ABBAS, Mohamed AHMED, Mahmoud QASSIM (Suroor SALEM 79), Carlos VILLANUEVA•, Issa OBAID (Naser MASOUD 80), CIEL. Tr: Paulo BONAMIGO

Al Gharafa, Doha
21-03-2012, 6092, Shukralla BHR

Al Gharafa 3

Tardelli 2 [44 78], El Assas [93+p]

Abdulaziz ALI (Galaleldeen OMER 28) - Ibrahim AL GHANIM, Hamed SHAMI, George Kwesi SEMAKOR, Ahmed AL BINALI, Lawrence QUAYE (Fahad AL SHAMMARI 90), Mohammad YASSER, Othmane EL ASSAS, DIEGO TARDELLI, Farhad MAJIDI, Mirghani AL ZAIN (Aruna DINDANE 71). Tr: PAULO SILAS

Al Hilal 3

Hermach [16], El Arabi [64], Al Zori [75]

Khalid SHARAHELE - Abdullah AL ZORI, Abdullah AL DOSSARI (Mohammed AL QARNI 87), Hasan KHAIRAT, Abdullatif AL GHANNAM, Christian WILHELMSSON, Mohammad AL SHALHOUB, Salman AL FARAJ•, Adil HERMACH (Nawaf AL ABED 53), YOO Byung Soo (Youssef EL ARABI• 63), Salem AL DOSSARI. Tr: Ivan HASEK

Bin Rashid Al Maktoum, Dubai
4-04-2012, 4522, Williams AUS

Al Shabab 1

Ciel [37]

Ismail RABEE - Mohammed MARZOOQ, Waleed ABBAS•, Sami ANBAR, Mohamed AHMED, Esam DHAHI, Hamdan QASSIM (Dawoud ALI• 60), Naser MASOUD (Suroor SALEM 78, Rashed HASSAN 88), Adel ABDULLA•, KIEZA, CIEL•. Tr: Paulo BONAMIGO

Al Hilal 1

Yoo Byung Soo [70]

Khalid SHARAHELE - Sultan AL BISHI•, Osama HAWSAWI, Abdullah AL DOSSARI (Mohammad AL SHALHOUB 46), Majed AL MARSHADI•, Abdullatif AL QARNI, Christian WILHELMSSON (Nawaf AL ABED 54), Salman AL FARAJ•, YOO Byung Soo (Saad AL HARTHI 83), Youssef EL ARABI, Salem AL DOSSARI. Tr: Ivan HASEK

Al Gharafa, Doha
4-04-2012, 2800, Al Hilali OMA

Al Gharafa 0

Galaleldeen OMER - Ibrahim AL GHANIM, Hamed SHAMI, George Kwesi SEMAKOR, Ahmed AL BINALI, Lawrence QUAYE, Mohammad YASSER (Mirghani AL ZAIN 85), Othmane EL ASSAS, Diego TARDELLI•, Farhad MAJIDI (Muayed HASSAN 77), Aruna DINDANE. Tr: Paulo SILAS

Persepolis 3

Rezaei.G [3], Zayed [6], Kazemian [73]

Asmir AVDUKIC - Mohammad NOSRATI, Sheys REZAEI, Mehrdad POULADI, Ali KARIMI•, Mohammad NOURI, Saman AGHAZAMANI (Maziar ZARE 38), Amir FESHANGCHI (Javad KAZEMIAN 67), Hamidreza ALIASGARI, Gholamreza REZAEI (Hossein BADAMAKI 84), Eamon ZAYED. Tr: Mustafa DENIZLI

Azadi, Tehran
17-04-2012, 96200, Irmatov UZB

Persepolis 1

Karimi [85]

Asmir AVDUKIC - Mohammad NOSRATI, Sheys REZAEI, Mehrdad POULADI, Ali KARIMI, Mohammad NOURI, Saman AGHAZAMANI, Amir FESHANGCHI, Gholamreza REZAEI (Vahid HASHEMIAN 83), Eamon ZAYED (Mehdi MAHDAVIKIA 67), Hadi NOROUZI (Javad KAZEMIAN 63). Tr: Mustafa DENIZLI

Al Gharafa 1

Mubarak [91+]

Qasem BURHAN - Ibrahim AL GHANIM, Hamed SHAMI•, George Kwesi SEMAKOR, Youssef RAMADAN•, Lawrence QUAYE, Othmane EL ASSAS•, Fahad AL SHAMMARI, Farhad MAJIDI•• ♦ 72, Muayed HASSAN (Diego TARDELLI 76), Aruna DINDANE (Mirghani AL ZAIN• 15). Tr: Paulo SILAS

Prince Faisal Bin Fahad, Riyadh
17-04-2012, 2118, El Haddad LIB

Al Hilal 2

El Arabi 2 [45 68]

Hassan AL OTAIBI - Sultan AL BISHI•89, Abdullah AL ZORI, Hasan KHAIRAT• (YOO Byung Soo 54), Majed AL MARSHADI, Abdullatif AL GHANNAM, Mohammad AL SHALHOUB (Mohammad NAMI 90), Adil HERMACH, Youssef EL ARABI, Nawaf AL ABED (Mohammed AL QARNI• 75), Salem AL DOSSARI. Tr: Ivan HASEK

Al Shabab 1

Kieza [28]

Salem AL HAMMADI - Waleed ABBAS, Sami ANBAR, Mohamed AHMED, Esam DHAHI• (Mohammed MARZOOQ 50), Hamdan QASSIM, Azizbek HAYDAROV (Naser MASOUD 68), Adel ABDULLA•, KIEZA, Issa OBAID (Dawoud ALI 77), CIEL•. Tr: Paulo BONAMIGO

Azadi, Tehran
1-05-2012, 73154, Kim Dong Jin KOR

Persepolis 0

Asmir AVDUKIC - Mohammad NOSRATI, Sheys REZAEI, Mehrdad POULADI, Ali KARIMI, Maziar ZARE, Hossein BADAMAKI, Amir FESHANGCHI• 56), Mohammad NOURI (Hadi NOROUZI 86), Hamidreza ALIASGARI• (Mamadou TALL• 90), Gholamreza REZAEI, Eamon ZAYED. Tr: Mustafa DENIZLI

Al Hilal 1

El Arabi [59]

Hassan AL OTAIBI - Osama HAWSAWI•, Abdullah AL DOSSARI, Majed AL MARSHADI, Abdullatif AL GHANNAM•, Mohammad AL SHALHOUB (Abdullah AL ZORI 80), Salman AL FARAJ (Saad AL HARTHI 90), Ahmed AL FRAIDI, Adil HERMACH, Youssef EL ARABI, Salem AL DOSSARI• (YOO Byung Soo 85). Tr: Ivan HASEK

Al Gharafa, Doha
1-05-2012, 641, Choi Myung Yong KOR

Al Gharafa 2

Dindane [81], El Assas [83p]

Qasem BURHAN - Ibrahim AL GHANIM•, George Kwesi SEMAKOR, Youssef RAMADAN (Mirghani AL ZAIN 61), Ahmed AL BINALI (Mohammed HAREES 78), Lawrence QUAYE, Mohammad YASSER (Aruna DINDANE 46), Othmane EL ASSAS, Fahad AL SHAMMARI, DIEGO TARDELLI•, Muayed HASSAN. Tr: PAULO SILAS

Al Shabab 1

Issa Mohammed [65]

Salem AL HAMMADI - Issa MOHAMMED, Abdulla DARWISH (Dawoud ALI 86), Waleed ABBAS, Sami ANBAR•, Mohamed AHMED (Ibrahim ABDULLA 88), Esam DHAHI•, Hassan IBRAHIM, KIEZA• (Naser MASOUD 86), Issa OBAID, CIEL•. Tr: Paulo BONAMIGO

Bin Rashid Al Maktoum, Dubai
15-05-2012, 5822, Tan Hai CHN

Al Shabab 1

Essa Obaid [7]

Ismail RABEE - Issa MOHAMMED, Sami ANBAR, Hamdan QASSIM•, Hassan IBRAHIM, Azizbek HAYDAROV (Rashed HASSAN 74), Fahad HASSAN (Ramadhan AL MAS 57), Ibrahim ABDULLA (Dawoud ALI 63), Naser MASOUD, Adel ABDULLA, Sanad ALI. Tr: Paulo BONAMIGO

Persepolis 3

Zayed [43], Pooladi [52], Badamaki [90]

Asmir AVDUKIC - Sheys REZAEI, Alireza NOORMOHAMADI, Mehrdad POULADI (Hossein BADAMAKI 83), Ali KARIMI, Mohammad NOURI•, Saman AGHAZAMANI• (Ebrahim SHAKOURI 33), Hamidreza ALIASGARI, Gholamreza REZAEI (Mehdi MAHDAVIKIA 90), Eamon ZAYED, Javad KAZEMIAN. Tr: Mustafa DENIZLI

Prince Faisal Bin Fahad, Riyadh
15-05-2012, 10275, Nishimura JPN

Al Hilal 2

Al Fraidi [48], Al Abed [65]

Hassan AL OTAIBI - Sultan AL BISHI, Osama HAWSAWI, Majed AL MARSHADI, Abdullatif AL GHANNAM, Christian WILHELMSSON (Mohammed AL QARNI 90), Salman AL FARAJ, Ahmed AL FRAIDI• (Salem AL DOSSARI 72), Adil HERMACH, YOO Byung Soo, Nawaf AL ABED (Essa AL MEHYANI 90). Tr: Ivan HASEK

Al Gharafa 1

OG [82]

Galaleldeen OMER - Hamed SHAMI (Muayed HASSAN 46), George Kwesi SEMAKOR, Youssef RAMADAN (Mohammed SAYYAR 72), Ahmed AL BINALI, Mohammad YASSER, Othmane EL ASSAS, Fahad AL SHAMMARI, Farhad MAJIDI (Mohammed HAREES 53), Mirghani AL ZAIN, Aruna DINDANE. Tr: PAULO SILAS

AFC CHAMPIONS LEAGUE 2012

GROUP E		Pl	W	D	L	F	A	Pts	AUS	UZB	KOR	JPN
Adelaide United	AUS	6	4	1	1	7	2	13		0-0	1-0	2-0
Bunyodkor	UZB	6	3	1	2	8	7	10	1-2		1-0	3-2
Pohang Steelers	KOR	6	3	0	3	6	4	9	1-0	0-2		2-0
Gamba Osaka	JPN	6	1	0	5	5	13	3	0-2	3-1	0-3	

Expo '70, Osaka
6-03-2012, 9101, Abdou QAT
Gamba Osaka 0

Yosuke FUJIGAYA - Sota NAKAZAWA, Hiroki FUJIHARU, Akira KAJI, Yasuhito ENDO•, Takahiro FUTAGAWA (Shinichi TERADA 74), Yasuyuki KONNO•, Tomokazu MYOJIN, Takuya TAKEI (LEE Seung Yeoul 46), RAFINHA, PAULINHO (Akihiro SATO 62). Tr: Jose Carlos SERRAO

Pohang Steelers 3
Kim Tae Su [19], Rendulic [22], Asamoah [76]

SHIN Hwa Yong - KIM Gwang Seok, Zoran RENDULIC (KIM Won Il 90), JUNG Hong Youn, SHIN Kwang Hoon, HWANG Jin Sung, KIM Tae Su, SHIN Hyung Min•, Derek ASAMOAH, PARK Sung Ho (CHO Chan Ho 88), NO Byung Jun• (KIM Jin Yong 70). Tr: HWANG Sun Hong

JAR, Tashkent
6-03-2012, 7000, El Haddad Lib
Bunyodkor 1
Murzoev [94+]

Ignatiy NESTEROV - Akmal SHORAKHMEDOV, Hayrulla KARIMOV, Anvar GAFUROV, Emil KENZHESARIEV (Jovlon IBROKHIMOV 46), Slavoljub DORDEVIC, David CARNEY (Shavkat SALOMOV 64), Lutfulla TURAEV, Viktor KARPENKO, Anvarjon SOLYIEV (Kamoliddin MIRZAEV 64), Bahodir PARDAEV. Tr: Mirdjalol KASIMOV

Adelaide United 2
Boogaard [12], Golec [53]

Eugene GALEKOVIC - Nigel BOOGAARD, Daniel MULLEN, Anthony GOLEC, Cameron WATSON, Osama MALIK, Zenon CARAVELLA (Francisco USUCAR 72), Dario VIDOSIC, Fabian BARBIERO (Jon MCKAIN 85), Bruce DJITE (Sergio VAN DIJK 62), Iain RAMSAY. Tr: John KOSMINA

Hindmarsh, Adelaide
20-03-2012, 5112, Al Zarooni UAE
Adelaide United 2
Mullen 2 [17] [24]

Eugene GALEKOVIC - Nigel BOOGAARD, Jon MCKAIN, Daniel MULLEN•, CASSIO, Osama MALIK, Zenon CARAVELLA, Dario VIDOSIC, Francisco USUCAR (Fabian BARBIERO 74), Bruce DJITE (Sergio VAN DIJK 80), Iain RAMSAY (Evan KOSTOPOULOS 78). Tr: John KOSMINA

Gamba Osaka 0

Yosuke FUJIGAYA - Sota NAKAZAWA•, Hiroki FUJIHARU, Akira KAJI•, Yasuhito ENDO, Yasuyuki KONNO, Tomokazu MYOJIN (Shinichi TERADA 71), Takuya TAKEI, RAFINHA, PAULINHO (Takahiro FUTAGAWA 77), LEE Seung Yeoul 64, Hayato SASAKI. Tr: Jose Carlos SERRAO

Steelyard, Pohang
20-03-2012, 3449, Albadwawi UAE
Pohang Steelers 0

SHIN Hwa Yong - KIM Gwang Seok, KIM Won Il•, JUNG Hong Youn, SHIN Kwang Hoon, HWANG Jin Sung, KIM Tae Su (KIM Chan Hee 82), SHIN Hyung Min, Ianis ZICU (NO Byung Jun 52), KO Moo Yeol, CHO Chan Ho (PARK Sung Ho 75). Tr: HWANG Sun Hong

Bunyodkor 2
Turaev [28], Murzoev [77]

Ignatiy NESTEROV - Hayrulla KARIMOV, Anvar GAFUROV, Artyom FILIPOSYAN, Sakhob JURAEV, David CARNEY, Emil KENZHESARIEV 90), Shavkat SALOMOV (Anvarjon SOLYIEV 90), Lutfulla TURAEV, Viktor KARPENKO, Jan KOZAK, Kamoliddin MIRZAEV (Ruslan MELZIDDINOV 90). Tr: Mirdjalol KASIMOV

Expo '70, Osaka
3-04-2012, 6100, Mahapab THA
Gamba Osaka 3
Endo [14], Rafinha 2 [58p] [82p]

Yosuke FUJIGAYA - Sota NAKAZAWA, Hiroki FUJIHARU, Akira KAJI (Daiki NIWA 83), Yasuhito ENDO•, Shinichi TERADA, Shu KURATA (Hayato SASAKI 67), Yasuyuki KONNO, Takuya TAKEI, RAFINHA, Akihiro SATO• (Tomokazu MYOJIN• 79). Tr: Masanobu MATSUNAMI

Bunyodkor 1
Soliev [88]

Ignatiy NESTEROV - Hayrulla KARIMOV, Anvar GAFUROV, Artyom FILIPOSYAN, Sakhob JURAEV• (Anvarjon SOLYIEV 81), David CARNEY (Emil KENZHESARIEV 68), Shavkat SALOMOV, Lutfulla TURAEV, Viktor KARPENKO, Jan Kozak•, Kamoliddin MIRZAEV (Bahodir PARDAEV 80). Tr: Mirdjalol KASIMOV

Steelyard, Pohang
3-04-2012, 2833, Al Ghamdi KSA
Pohang Steelers 1
Kim Dae Ho [68]

KIM Da Sol - KIM Gwang Seok, Zoran RENDULIC, PARK Hee Chul, HWANG Jin Sung (HWANG Ji Soo 87), KIM Tae Su (CHO Chan Ho 55), SHIN Hyung Min, KIM Dae Ho, Ianis ZICU, Derek ASAMOAH, KO Moo Yeol (PARK Sung Ho 68). Tr: HWANG Sun Hong

Adelaide United 0

Eugene GALEKOVIC - Nigel BOOGAARD, Jon MCKAIN, Daniel MULLEN, CASSIO, Osama MALIK•, Zenon CARAVELLA, Dario VIDOSIC, Fabian BARBIERO 39), Francisco USUCAR (Sergio VAN DIJK 72), Bruce DJITE, Iain RAMSAY (Evan KOSTOPOULOS 81). Tr: John KOSMINA

Hindmarsh, Adelaide
18-04-2012, 7659, Tan Hai CHN
Adelaide United 1
Djite [90]

Eugene GALEKOVIC - Nigel BOOGAARD, Jon MCKAIN, Daniel MULLEN, CASSIO, Osama MALIK, Zenon CARAVELLA, Francisco USUCAR (Fabian BARBIERO 79), Bruce DJITE, Iain RAMSAY, Evan KOSTOPOULOS (Teeboy KAMARA 84). Tr: John KOSMINA

Pohang Steelers 0

SHIN Hwa Yong - LEE Won Jae, Zoran RENDULIC, KIM Won Il•, HWANG Ji Soo• (LEE Myung Joo 67), SHIN Hyung Min•, KIM Dae Ho, Ianis ZICU, Derek ASAMOAH, KIM Jin Yong (CHO Chan Ho 74), NO Byung Jun (SHIN Jin Ho 83). Tr: HWANG Sun Hong

JAR, Tashkent
18-04-2012, 4000, Al Ghamdi KSA
Bunyodkor 3
Murzoev [14], Turaev [42], Soliev [84]

Ignatiy Nesterov - Hayrulla Karimov, Anvar Gafurov, Emil Kenzhesariev, Artyom Filiposyan, Jovlon Ibrokhimov, Shavkat Salomov, Lutfulla Turaev, Viktor Karpenko (Ruslan Melziddinov 90), Jan Kozak (Anvarjon Solyiev 80), Kamoliddin Mirzaev (Anvar Rajabov 58). Tr: Mirdjalol Kasimov

Gamba Osaka 2
Kurata [18], Abe [93+]

Yosuke Fujigaya - Sota Nakazawa, Hiroki Fujiharu, Akira Kaji, Hayato Sasaki (Rafinha 46), Takahiro Futagawa (Hiroyuki Abe 62), Shu Kurata (Paulinho 80), Yasuyuki Konno, Tomokazu Myojin, Takuya Takei, Akihiro Sato. Tr: Masanobu Matsunami

Hindmarsh, Adelaide
2-05-2012, 7794, Liu Kwok Man HKG
Adelaide United 0

Eugene GALEKOVIC - Nigel BOOGAARD, Jon MCKAIN, Daniel MULLEN, CASSIO, Iain FYFE 54), Zenon CARAVELLA (Evan KOSTOPOULOS• 73), Dario VIDOSIC (Teeboy KAMARA 84), Fabian BARBIERO, Bruce DJITE, Iain RAMSAY. Tr: John KOSMINA

Bunyodkor 0

Ignatiy NESTEROV - Akmal SHORAKHMEDOV•, Hayrulla KARIMOV, Anvar GAFUROV, Emil KENZHESARIEV, David CARNEY (Shavkat SALOMOV 86), Jovlon IBROKHIMOV, Lutfulla TURAEV, Viktor KARPENKO, Jan KOZAK (Alibobo RAKHMATULLAEV 87), Kamoliddin MIRZAEV• (Anvarjon SOLYIEV 89). Tr: Mirdjalol KASIMOV

Steelyard, Pohang
2-05-2012, 3825, Faghani IRN
Pohang Steelers 2
Kim Jin Yong [45], Asamoah [77]

SHIN Hwa Yong - KIM Gwang Seok, Zoran RENDULIC, SHIN Kwang Hoon, PARK Hee Chul•, HWANG Jin Sung, HWANG Ji Soo, LEE Myung Joo (SHIN Jin Ho 86), Derek ASAMOAH•, PARK Sung Ho (NO Byung Jun 70), KIM Jin Yong (KO Moo Yeol 65). Tr: HWANG Sun Hong

Gamba Osaka 0

Atsushi KIMURA - Sota NAKAZAWA, Hiroki FUJIHARU, Akira KAJI (Daiki NIWA• 46), Yasuhito ENDO, Shu KURATA, Yasuyuki KONNO, Tomokazu MYOJIN, Takuya TAKEI (Takahiro FUTAGAWA 72), RAFINHA (Kenta HOSHIHARA 61), Akihiro SATO. Tr: Masanobu MATSUNAMI

Expo '70, Osaka
16-05-2012, 7294, Shukralla BHR
Gamba Osaka 0

Yosuke FUJIGAYA - Sota NAKAZAWA, Daiki NIWA, Hiroyuki ABE (Kotaro OMORI 66), Tatsuya UCHIDA, Keigo NUMATA, Hayato SASAKI, Takahiro FUTAGAWA, Takuya TAKEI, RAFINHA (Akihiro SATO 76), LEE Seung Yeoul (Kenta HOSHIHARA 82). Tr: Masanobu MATSUNAMI

Adelaide United 2
Van Dijk [65], OG [88]

Eugene GALEKOVIC - Nigel BOOGAARD, Jon MCKAIN (Francisco USUCAR 77), Daniel MULLEN, CASSIO, Iain FYFE, Zenon CARAVELLA, Dario VIDOSIC, Fabian BARBIERO (Sergio VAN DIJK 60), Bruce DJITE•, Iain RAMSAY (Evan KOSTOPOULOS 85). Tr: John KOSMINA

JAR, Tashkent
16-05-2012, 5100, Balideh QAT
Bunyodkor 1
Gafurov [48]

Ignatiy NESTEROV - Akmal SHORAKHMEDOV, Hayrulla KARIMOV, Anvar GAFUROV (Emil KENZHESARIEV 67), Artyom FILIPOSYAN, Jovlon IBROKHIMOV, Shavkat SALOMOV (Ruslan MELZIDDINOV 81), Lutfulla TURAEV•, Viktor KARPENKO, Jan KOZAK, Kamoliddin MIRZAEV (Anvarjon SOLYIEV 90). Tr: Mirdjalol KASIMOV

Pohang Steelers 0

SHIN Hwa Yong - KIM Gwang Seok•, KIM Won Il, SHIN Kwang Hoon•, HWANG Jin Sung, KIM Tae Su, SHIN Hyung Min, KIM Dae Ho, Derek ASAMOAH (SHIN Jin Ho• 87), NO Byung Jun (KO Moo Yeol 67), CHO Chan Ho (PARK Sung Ho 46). Tr: HWANG Sun Hong

PART THREE – THE CONTINENTAL CONFEDERATIONS

GROUP F		Pl	W	D	L	F	A	Pts	KOR	JPN	AUS	CHN
Ulsan Hyundai	KOR	6	4	2	0	11	7	14		1-0	1-1	2-1
FC Tokyo	JPN	6	3	2	1	12	6	11	2-2		4-2	3-0
Brisbane Roar	AUS	6	0	3	3	6	11	3	1-2	0-2		1-1
Beijing Goan	CHN	6	0	3	3	6	11	3	2-3	1-1	1-1	

Suncorp, Brisbane
6-03-2012, 12 037, Kovalenko UZB
Brisbane Roar   **0**
Michael THEO - Matthew SMITH, Shane STEFANUTTO•, Ivan FRANJIC•, Sayed Mohamed ADNAN•, Erik PAARTALU, Massimo MURDOCCA (Luke BRATTAN 60), Thomas BROICH, Besart BERISHA, HENRIQUE (James MEYER 78), Rocky VISCONTE (Kofi DANNING 55). Tr: Ange POSTECOGLOU
FC Tokyo   **2**
Yazawa [45], Hasegawa [55]
Shuichi GONDA - Yuhei TOKUNAGA, Masato MORISHIGE, Hideto TAKAHASHI, Kenichi KAGA (JANG Hyun Soo 86), Kosuke OTA, Aria Jasuru HASEGAWA•, Naohiro ISHIKAWA (Hiroki KAWANO 90), Naotake HANYU (Sotan TANABE 76), Tatsuya YAZAWA, Kazuma WATANABE. Tr: Ranko POPOVIC

Ulsan Munsu, Ulsan
6-03-2012, 1515, Al Zarooni UAE
Ulsan Hyundai Motors   **2**
Kim Shin Wook [26], Go Seul Ki [34]
KIM Young Kwang - LEE Yong, KANG Min Soo•, KWAK Tae Hwi, CHOI Jae Soo, LEE Ho•, GO Seul Ki• (Akihiro IENAGA 43), Juan VELEZ, KIM Shin Wook, LEE Keun Ho, KIM Seung Yong (PARK Seung II 77). Tr: KIM Ho Gon
Beijing Goan   **1**
HOU Sen - ZHOU Ting, XU Yunlong•, ZHANG Xinxin•◆90, FRANCOIS, Darko MATIC, XU Liang, WANG Xiaolong, ZHU Yifan (PIAO Cheng 38), SHAO Jiayi (MAO Jianqing 75), REINALDO (Andrija KALUDEROVIC 82). Tr: Jaime PACHECO

National, Tokyo
20-03-2012, 14 110, Irmatov UZB
FC Tokyo   **2**
Tokunaga [37], Kajiyama [83]
Shuichi GONDA - Yuhei TOKUNAGA, Masato MORISHIGE, Hideto TAKAHASHI•, Kenichi KAGA, Kosuke OTA, Takuji YONEMOTO (Aria Jasuru HASEGAWA•, Yohei KAJIYAMA, Naohiro ISHIKAWA, Tatsuya YAZAWA (Naotake HANYU 69), Kazuma WATANABE (LUCAS 83). Tr: Ranko POPOVIC
Ulsan Hyundai Motors   **2**
Kim Seung Yong [80], Maranhao [88]
KIM Young Kwang - LEE Yong, KANG Min Soo•, KWAK Tae Hwi, LEE Ho•, Juan VELEZ (LEE Jae Seong 70), KANG Jin Ouk, Akihiro IENAGA (PARK Seung II 63), KIM Shin Wook (MARANHAO 57), LEE Keun Ho, KIM Seung Yong. Tr: KIM Ho Gon

Workers Stadium, Beijing
20-03-2012, 41 000, Abdou QAT
Beijing Goan   **1**
Piao Cheng [7]
HOU Sen - YU Yang, ZHOU Ting, XU Yunlong, Darko MATIC•, XU Liang, WANG Changqing (SHAO Jiayi 82), JIAO Zhe, PIAO Cheng•, Andrija KALUDEROVIC (REINALDO 58), MAO Jianqing (ZHANG Xizhe 73). Tr: Jaime PACHECO
Brisbane Roar   **1**
Nichols [20]
Michael THEO - Matthew SMITH, Shane STEFANUTTO•, Ivan FRANJIC, Sayed Mohamed ADNAN, Erik PAARTALU, Massimo MURDOCCA (James MEYER 73), Mitch NICHOLS, Thomas BROICH, Besart BERISHA, HENRIQUE (Kofi DANNING 89). Tr: Ange POSTECOGLOU

Ulsan Munsu, Ulsan
4-04-2012, 1673, El Haddad LIB
Ulsan Hyundai Motors   **1**
Lee Jae Seong [54]
KIM Seung Gyu - LEE Yong, LEE Jae Seong, KWAK Tae Hwi, CHOI Jae Soo, GO Seul Ki, Juan VELEZ, Akihiro IENAGA (KIM Shin Wook 59), MARANHAO (KIM Dong Suk 76), LEE Keun Ho, KIM Seung Yong (KIM Hyo Gi 88). Tr: KIM Ho Gon
Brisbane Roar   **1**
Fitzgerald [36]
Michael THEO - Matthew SMITH, Shane STEFANUTTO, Matthew JURMAN◆46, Ivan FRANJIC, Erik PAARTALU, Massimo MURDOCCA (Luke BRATTAN 66), Mitch NICHOLS (Rocky VISCONTE 86), Thomas BROICH, Nick FITZGERALD (Jack HINGERT 52), Besart BERISHA. Tr: Ange POSTECOGLOU

Workers Stadium, Beijing
4-04-2012, 31 256, Mozaffarizadeh IRN
Beijing Goan   **1**
Wang Xiaolong [10p]
SEN Hou - YU Yang•, ZHOU Ting, XU Yunlong•, Darko MATIC, XU Liang, WANG Changqing (MAO Jianqing 59), WANG Xiaolong (ZHANG Xizhe 75), JIAO Zhe, PIAO Cheng, Andrija KALUDEROVIC (REINALDO 59). Tr: Jaime PACHECO
FC Tokyo   **1**
Hasegawa [44]
Shuichi GONDA - Yuhei TOKUNAGA, Masato MORISHIGE, Hideto TAKAHASHI•, Kenichi KAGA (JANG Hyun Soo 10), Kosuke OTA, Aria Jasuru HASEGAWA•, Naohiro ISHIKAWA, Naotake HANYU (LUCAS 60), Tatsuya YAZAWA (Sotan TANABE 72), Kazuma WATANABE. Tr: Ranko POPOVIC

Suncorp, Brisbane
17-04-2012, 7200, Torky IRN
Brisbane Roar   **1**
Stefanutto [25]
Michael THEO - Matthew SMITH, Shane STEFANUTTO, Ivan FRANJIC, Sayed Mohamed ADNAN, Erik PAARTALU, Massimo MURDOCCA (Luke BRATTAN 63), Mitch NICHOLS (James MEYER 76), Thomas BROICH, Besart BERISHA• (Nick FITZGERALD 59), HENRIQUE. Tr: Ange POSTECOGLOU
Ulsan Hyundai Motors   **2**
Velez [11], Kwak Tae Hwi [73p]
KIM Seung Gyu - LEE Jae Seong, KANG Min Soo, KWAK Tae Hwi, LEE Ho, KIM Young Sam, GO Seul Ki (KIM Hyo Gi 90), Juan VELEZ, MARANHAO (Akihiro IENAGA• 50), LEE Keun Ho, KIM Seung Yong (CHOI Jae Soo 83). Tr: KIM Ho Gon

National, Tokyo
17-04-2012, 9537, Abdulnabi BHR
FC Tokyo   **3**
Watanabe [7], Otake [45], Yazawa [57]
Hitoshi SHIOTA - Yuhei TOKUNAGA, Masato MORISHIGE, Kosuke OTA, JANG Hyun Soo, Takuji YONEMOTO (Aria Jasuru HASEGAWA 51), Naohiro ISHIKAWA, Yohei OTAKE•, Sotan TANABE• (Yuichi MARUYAMA 90), Kazuma WATANABE (Sota HIRAYAMA 76). Tr: Ranko POPOVIC
Beijing Goan   **0**
SEN Hou - YU Yang, ZHOU Ting, LANG Zheng, ZHANG Xinxin, Darko MATIC•, XU Liang (ZHANG Xiaobin 63), ZHANG Xizhe, WANG Xiaolong• (MAO Jianqing 72), PIAO Cheng, REINALDO (Andrija KALUDEROVIC 61). Tr: Jaime PACHECO

National, Tokyo
2-05-2012, 8492, Balideh QAT
FC Tokyo   **4**
Takahashi [5], Mukuhara [20], Watanabe 2 [44p 60]
Shuichi GONDA - Yuhei TOKUNAGA, Masato MORISHIGE, Hideto TAKAHASHI•, JANG Hyun Soo, Kenta MUKUHARA, Aria Jasuru HASEGAWA•, Yohei KAJIYAMA (Naohiro ISHIKAWA 85), Naotake HANYU (Takuji YONEMOTO 78), Tatsuya YAZAWA, Kazuma WATANABE (LUCAS 73). Tr: Ranko POPOVIC
Brisbane Roar   **2**
Berisha [4], Broich [33]
Michael THEO - Matthew SMITH, Shane STEFANUTTO, Ivan FRANJIC, Sayed Mohamed ADNAN (Matthew JURMAN 67), Erik PAARTALU, Luke BRATTAN (Mitch NICHOLS 63), James MEYER (Rocky VISCONTE 63), Thomas BROICH, Nick FITZGERALD, Besart BERISHA. Tr: Rado VIDOSIC

Workers Stadium, Beijing
2-05-2012, 21 692, Al Hilali OMA
Beijing Goan   **2**
Zhang Xizhe [47], Shao Jiayi [92+]
BAI Xiaolei - XU Yunlong, LANG Zheng, XU Liang, ZHANG Xizhe, ZHANG Xiaobin, XU Wu (YU Yang 73), ZHU Yifan•, JIAO Zhe (PIAO Cheng 33), Andrija KALUDEROVIC (REINALDO◆86, 83), JIAYI Shao. Tr: Jaime PACHECO
Ulsan Hyundai Motors   **3**
Kim Shin Wook [17], Kim Seung Yong [20], Maranhao [79]
KIM Seung Gyu - LEE Jae Seong, KANG Min Soo, KWAK Tae Hwi, LEE Ho (MARANHAO 53), KIM Young Sam, GO Seul Ki, Juan VELEZ, KIM Shin Wook (KIM Seung Yong 68), LEE Keun Ho (Akihiro IENAGA◆ 84), KIM Seung Yong. Tr: KIM Ho Gon

Suncorp, Brisbane
16-05-2012, 5615, Albadwawi UAE
Brisbane Roar   **1**
Berisha [15]
Michael THEO - Matthew JURMAN, Ivan Franjic•, Sayed Mohamed ADNAN, Corey BROWN, Erik PAARTALU (Luke BRATTAN 81), Massimo MURDOCCA, Mitch NICHOLS• (James MEYER 75), Thomas BROICH, Besart BERISHA•, Kofi DANNING 74. Tr: Rado VIDOSIC
Beijing Goan   **1**
Li Hanbo [34]
BAI Xiaolei - YU Yang, YANG Yun (MAO Jianqing 77), LANG Zheng, ZHANG Xizhe, ZHANG Xiaobin•, XU Wu•, ZHU Yifan, LI Hanbo (WANG Changqing 73), JIAO Zhe•, SHAO Jiayi (Andrija KALUDEROVIC 49). Tr: Jaime PACHECO

Ulsan Munsu, Ulsan
16-05-2012, 5746, Al Ghamdi KSA
Ulsan Hyundai Motors   **1**
Kang Min Soo [37]
KIM Young Kwang - LEE Jae Seong, KANG Min Soo, KWAK Tae Hwi, KIM Young Sam•, KIM Dong Suk (LEE Ho 73), GO Seul Ki, Juan VELEZ, MARANHAO (CHOI Jae Soo 80), LEE Keun Ho, KIM Seung Yong (KIM Shin Wook 46). Tr: KIM Ho Gon
FC Tokyo   **0**
Hitoshi SHIOTA - Yuhei TOKUNAGA, Masato MORISHIGE, Hideto TAKAHASHI, JANG Hyun Soo (Yohei HAYASHI 84), Kenta MUKUHARA, Takuji YONEMOTO, Aria Jasuru HASEGAWA, Hiroki KAWANO (Yohei KAJIYAMA 49), Tatsuya YAZAWA (LUCAS 69), Kazuma WATANABE. Tr: Ranko POPOVIC

AFC CHAMPIONS LEAGUE 2012

GROUP G

		Pl	W	D	L	F	A	Pts	KOR	JPN	AUS	CHN
Seongnam Ilhwa C'ma	KOR	6	2	4	0	13	5	10		1-1	5-0	1-1
Nagoya Grampus	JPN	6	2	4	0	10	4	10	2-2		3-0	0-0
Central Coast Mariners	AUS	6	1	3	2	7	11	6	1-1	1-1		5-1
Tianjin Teda	CHN	6	0	3	3	2	12	3	0-3	0-3	0-0	

Mizuho, Nagoya
7-03-2012, 6686, Shukralla BHR
Nagoya Grampus 2
Kennedy [58p], Kanazaki [74]
Seigo NARAZAKI - Marcus Tulio TANAKA, Takahiro MASUKAWA, Shohei ABE•, Naoshi NAKAMURA (Kensuke NAGAI 67), Jungo FUJIMOTO•, Danilson CORDOBA, Mu KANAZAKI (DANIEL 75), Hayuma TANAKA•, Keiji TAMADA•, Joshua KENNEDY (Keiji YOSHIMURA 86). Tr: Dragan STOJKOVIC
Seongnam Ilhwa Chunma 2
Heverton 2 [47 93+]
HA Kang Jin - YUN Young Sun• (LIM Jong Eun 65), Sasa OGNENOVSKI•, PARK Jin Po, HONG Chul•, KIM Sung Hwan•, HAN Sang Woon (LEE Chang Hoon 83), HEVERTON, JEON Sung Chan• (YOON Bit Garam 58), EVERTON SANTOS, Vladimir JOVANCIC. Tr: SHIN Tae Yong

TEDA, Tianjin
7-03-2012, 19 800, Al Hilali OMA
Tianjin Teda 0

SONG Zhenyu - Milan SUSAK, LI Weifeng, Lucian GOIAN, BAI Yuefeng, CAO Yang, LI Benjian (HU Rentian 46), WANG Xinxin (MAO Biao 79), CHEN Tao, Velice SUMULIKOSKI, Ars SJOERD (HUI Jiakang 70). Tr: Josip KUZE
Central Coast Mariners 0

Mathew RYAN - Joshua ROSE, Pedj BOJIC•, Patrick ZWAANSWIJK, Alex WILKINSON, John HUTCHINSON, Oliver BOZANIC (Tom ROGIC 65), Daniel MCBREEN (Troy HEARFIELD 90), Adam KWASNIK• (Bernie IBINI-ISEI 77). Tr: Graham ARNOLD

Central Coast, Gosford
21-03-2012, 5130, Liu Kwok Man HKG
Central Coast Mariners 1
Zwaanswijk [28]
Mathew RYAN - Joshua ROSE, Pedj BOJIC, Patrick Zwaanswijk, Alex Wilkinson, John Hutchinson, Oliver BOZANIC, Troy HEARFIELD (Bernie IBINI-ISEI 72), Michael MCGLINCHEY, Tom ROGIC• (Daniel MCBREEN 78), Mustafa AMINI. Tr: Graham ARNOLD
Nagoya Grampus 1
Tulio [21]
Seigo NARAZAKI - Marcus Tulio TANAKA, Shohei ABE, DANIEL, Yosuke ISHIBITSU, Keiji YOSHIMURA (Taishi TAGUCHI 68), Danilson CORDOBA, Mu KANAZAKI (Teruki TANAKA 74), Keiji TAMADA, Joshua KENNEDY•, Kensuke NAGAI. Tr: Dragan STOJKOVIC

Tancheon, Seongnam
21-03-2012, 2553, Balideh QAT
Seongnam Ilhwa Chunma 1
Han Sang Woon [14]
HA Kang Jin - YUN Young Sun, Sasa OGNENOVSKI, PARK Jin Po, KIM Sung Hwan, NAMGUNG Woong (KIM Seong Jun 67), HAN Sang Woon, YOON Bit Garam (JEON Sung Chan 78), HEVERTON, EVERTON SANTOS, Vladimir JOVANCIC. Tr: SHIN Tae Yong
Tianjin Teda 1
Goian [69]
SONG Zhenyu - HE Yang• (ZHOU Liao 46), Milan SUSAK (NIE Tao 60), LI Weifeng•, Goian LUCIAN, BAI Yuefeng•, CAO Yang•, CHEN Tao (LIAO Bochao 87), Velice SUMULIKOSKI, HUI Jiakang, Ars SJOERD. Tr: Josip KUZE

Central Coast, Gosford
3-04-2012, 5018, Kovalenko UZB
Central Coast Mariners 1
Kwasnik [50]
Mathew RYAN - Joshua ROSE◆62, Pedj BOJIC, Patrick ZWAANSWIJK, Alex WILKINSON, John HUTCHINSON, Oliver BOZANIC, Michael MCGLINCHEY (Troy HEARFIELD 72), Daniel MCBREEN (Sam GALLAGHER 67), John SUTTON, Adam KWASNIK• (Bernie IBINI-ISEI 78). Tr: Graham ARNOLD
Seongnam Ilhwa Chunma 1
Santos [57]
HA Kang Jin - YUN Young Sun, PARK Jin Po, KIM Sung Hwan (HONG Chul 46), NAMGUNG Woong, LIM Jong Eun•, HAN Sang Woon (YOON Bit Garam 85), HEVERTON, EVERTON SANTOS, Vladimir JOVANCIC. Tr: SHIN Tae Yong

TEDA, Tianjin
3-04-2012, 12 249, Irmatov UZB
Tianjin Teda 0

SONG Zhenyu - Milan SUSAK, LI Weifeng•, Lucian GOIAN•, NIE Tao, CAO Yang, WANG Xinxin (HUI Jiakang 46), CHEN Tao•, Velice SUMULIKOSKI (BAI Yuefeng 77), ZHOU Liao•, MAO Biao (Ars SJOERD 46). Tr: Josip KUZE
Nagoya Grampus 3
Fujimoto [24], Tamada [49], Nagai [73]
Seigo NARAZAKI - Takahiro MASUKAWA, DANIEL, Yosuke ISHIBITSU, Jungo FUJIMOTO•, Danilson CORDOBA, Mu KANAZAKI (YOSHIMURA OGAWA 68), Hayuma TANAKA, Keiji TAMADA, Joshua KENNEDY (Yuki MAKI 75), Kensuke NAGAI (ALEX 80). Tr: Dragan STOJKOVIC

Mizuho, Nagoya
18-04-2012, 6006, Liu Kwok Man HKG
Nagoya Grampus 0

Seigo NARAZAKI - Takahiro MASUKAWA, DANIEL, Yosuke ISHIBITSU (Shohei ABE 68), Naoshi NAKAMURA (Yuki MAKI 46), Yoshizumi OGAWA• (Ryota ISOMURA 68), Danilson CORDOBA, Mu KANAZAKI, Hayuma TANAKA, Keiji TAMADA, Kensuke NAGAI. Tr: Dragan STOJKOVIC
Tianjin Teda 0

YANG Qipeng - HE Yang•, Milan SUSAK, Lucian GOIAN, BAO Bochao, NIE Tao, CAO Yang•, Velice SUMULIKOSKI (WANG Xinxin 73), HUI Jiakang, MAO Biao (ZHOU Liao• 78), Ars SJOERD (BAI Yuefeng 65). Tr: Josip KUZE

Tancheon, Seongnam
18-04-2012, 2017, Mozaffarizadeh IRN
Seongnam Ilhwa Chunma 5
Lee Chang Hoon [39], Santos 2 [43 73p], Kim Sung Hwan [69], Jovancic [84]
HA Kang Jin - YUN Young Sun, PARK Jin Po, KIM Sung Hwan•, NAMGUNG Woong (HONG Chul 77), LIM Jong Eun, KIM Seong Jun (YOON Bit Garam 77), HEVERTON, EVERTON SANTOS, Vladimir JOVANCIC, LEE Chang Hoon (LEE Hyun Ho 84). Tr: SHIN Tae Yong
Central Coast Mariners 0

Mathew RYAN - Patrick ZWAANSWIJK•, Alex WILKINSON, Sam GALLAGHER, Trent MCCLENAHAN, John HUTCHINSON, Daniel MCBREEN (Trent SAINSBURY 46), Michael MCGLINCHEY (Bernie IBINI-ISEI 66), Mustafa AMINI, John SUTTON, Adam KWASNIK (Troy HEARFIELD 46). Tr: Graham ARNOLD

Central Coast, Gosford
1-05-2012, 4155, Al Zarooni UAE
Central Coast Mariners 5
McBreen 2 [10 20], Rose [48], McGlinchey [71], Amini [85]
Mathew RYAN - Joshua ROSE, Pedj BOJIC• (Trent MCCLENAHAN 79), Patrick ZWAANSWIJK, Alex WILKINSON, John HUTCHINSON, Oliver BOZANIC, Michael MCGLINCHEY, Tom ROGIC (Mustafa AMINI 69), Daniel MCBREEN, Adam KWASNIK (Bernie IBINI-ISEI 90). Tr: Graham ARNOLD
Tianjin Teda 1
Liao Bochao [72]
YANG Qipeng - LI Hongyang•, Milan SUSAK•, LI Weifeng, Lucian GOIAN, LIAO Bochao, NIE Tao, BAI Yuefeng (LI Benjian 46), WANG Xinxin (HUI Jiakang 46), Velice SUMULIKOSKI (ZHENG Yi 63), Ars SJOERD. Tr: Josip KUZE

Tancheon, Seongnam
1-05-2012, 6379, Albadawi UAE
Seongnam Ilhwa Chunma 1
Han Sang Woon [12]
JUNG San•, Sasa OGNENOVSKI, PARK Jin Po, HONG Chul•, KIM Sung Hwan, NAMGUNG Woong (LEE Hyun Ho 66), LIM Jong Eun, KIM Seong Jun, HAN Sang Woon, YOON Bit Garam (KIM Hyun Woo 86), LEE Chang Hoon• (EVERTON SANTOS 79). Tr: SHIN Tae Yong
Nagoya Grampus 1
OG [72]
Seigo NARAZAKI - Marcus Tulio TANAKA, Shohei ABE (Keiji TAMADA 46), DANIEL, Naoshi NAKAMURA (Keiji YOSHIMURA 77), Jungo FUJIMOTO, Yoshizumi OGAWA, Danilson CORDOBA, Mu KANAZAKI (Yuki MAKI• 67), Hayuma TANAKA, Kensuke NAGAI. Tr: Dragan STOJKOVIC

Mizuho, Nagoya
15-05-2012, 5037, Abdou QAT
Nagoya Grampus 3
Tamada [19], Fujimoto [36], Tulio [87]
Seigo NARAZAKI - Marcus Tulio TANAKA, Takahiro MASUKAWA, Shohei ABE, Jungo FUJIMOTO• (Makito YOSHIDA 78), Yoshizumi OGAWA, Keiji YOSHIMURA, Mu KANAZAKI, Hayuma TANAKA, Teruki TANAKA (Kensuke NAGAI 63), Keiji TAMADA (Taishi TAGUCHI 63). Tr: Dragan STOJKOVIC
Central Coast Mariners 0

Mathew RYAN - Joshua ROSE, Patrick ZWAANSWIJK, Trent SAINSBURY, Alex WILKINSON, John HUTCHINSON•, Adriano PELLEGRINO• (Trent MCCLENAHAN• 59), Michael MCGLINCHEY, Tom ROGIC, Daniel MCBREEN• (Mitchell DUKE 78), Adam KWASNIK (Bernie IBINI-ISEI 59). Tr: Graham ARNOLD

TEDA, Tianjin
15-05-2012, BCD, Faghani IRN
Tianjin Teda 0

SONG Zhenyu - HE Yang, LI Hongyang•, LIAO Bochao, BAI Yuefeng, CAO Yang, LI Benjian (Velice SUMULIKOSKI 46), WANG Xinxin (Ars SJOERD• 46), ZHENG Yi•, ZHOU Liao•, HUI Jiakang (MAO Biao 69). Tr: Josip KUZE
Seongnam Ilhwa Chunma 3
Yoon Bit Garam [32], Jovancic 2 [48 69p]
HA Kang Jin - Sasa OGNENOVSKI, PARK Jin Po, KIM Sung Hwan, NAMGUNG Woong, LIM Jong Eun (YUN Young Sun 8), KIM Seong Jun, HAN Sang Woon, LEE Hyun Ho (KIM Deok Il 88), YOON Bit Garam, Vladimir JOVANCIC• (HEVERTON 72). Tr: SHIN Tae Yong

PART THREE – THE CONTINENTAL CONFEDERATIONS

GROUP H		Pl	W	D	L	F	A	Pts	CHN	JPN	KOR	THA
Guangzhou Evergrande	CHN	6	3	1	2	12	8	10		3-1	1-3	1-2
Kashiwa Reysol	JPN	6	3	1	2	11	7	10	0-0		5-1	1-0
Jeonbuk Hy. Motors	KOR	6	3	0	3	10	15	9	1-5	0-2		3-2
Buriram United	THA	6	2	0	4	8	11	6	1-2	3-2	0-2	

World Cup Stadium, Jeonju
7-03-2012, 7978, Mozaffarizadeh IRN

Jeonbuk Hyundai Motors 1
Jeong Seong Hoon [70]

KIM Min Sik – KIM Sang Sik, CHO Sung Hwan (SIM Woo Yeon 30), LIM You Hwan, CHOI Chul Soon, PARK Won Jae, JIN Kyung Sun•, ENINHO, KIM Jung Woo (LUIZ HENRIQUE 59), SEO Sang Min (JEONG Shung Hoon 65), LEE Dong Gook. Tr: LEE Heung Sil

Guangzhou Evergrande 5
Cleo 2 [27] [69], Conca 2 [41] [73], Muriqui [76]

YANG Jun•, FENG Xiaoting, ZHANG Linpeng•, ZHENG Zhi, Dario CONCA, CHO Won Hee•, SUN Xiang, ZHAO Xuri, CLEO, MURIQUI, GAO Lin. Tr: LEE Jang Soo

Thunder Castle, Buriram
7-03-2012, 15 089, Irmatov UZB

Buriram United 3
Jirawat 2 [10] [77], Jadigerov [38]

Sivaruck TEDSUNGNOEN – Theeraton BUNMATHAN, Pratum CHUTHONG, Yves EKWALLA, Apichet PUTTAN, Jakkraphan KAEWPROM, Suchao NUTNUM, Jirawat MAKAROM (Surat SUKHA 81), Asqar JADIGEROV (Sumanya PURISAI 65), Franck OHANDZA• (Adisak KRAISORN 88), Frank ACHEAMPONG. Tr: Attaphol BUSPAKOM

Kashiwa Reysol 2
Tanaka [55], Sakai [64]

Takanori SUGENO – Naoya KONDO, Hiroki SAKAI, Tatsuya MASUSHIMA, Hirofumi WATANABE, Hidekazu OTANI (AN Young Hak 46), LEANDRO DOMINGUES, JORGE WAGNER, Akimi BARADA, Hideaki KITAJIMA (Ricardo LOBO 46), Junya TANAKA (Masato KUDO 66). Tr: NELSINHO BAPTISTA

Hitachi, Kashiwa
21-03-2012, 8175, Green AUS

Kashiwa Reysol 5
Nasu [40], Domingues 2 [44p] [45], Tanaka [89], Barada [93+]

Takanori SUGENO – Hiroki SAKAI, Tatsuya MASUSHIMA, Daisuke NASU, Wataru HASHIMOTO, Hidekazu OTANI, LEANDRO DOMINGUES, JORGE WAGNER, Ryoichi KURISAWA, Junya TANAKA, Ricardo LOBO (Akimi BARADA 85). Tr: NELSINHO BAPTISTA

Jeonbuk Hyundai Motors 1
Huang Bowen [51]

LEE Bum Soo – KIM Sang Sik, CHOI Chul Soon•, PARK Won Jae•, JEON Kwang Hwan (LEE Dong Gook 46), JIN Kyung Sun•, ENINHO, LEE Seung Hyun, JUNG Hun•, KIM Jung Woo (KIM Dong Chan 57), HUANG Bowen (Hugo DROGUETT 79). Tr: LEE Heung Sil

Tianhe, Guangzhou
21-03-2012, 38 512, El Haddad LIB

Guangzhou Evergrande 1
Cleo [69]

YANG Jun•, FENG Xiaoting, ZHANG Linpeng• (FENG Junyan 37), ZHENG Zhi, Dario CONCA, CHO Won Hee, SUN Xiang, ZHAO Xuri, CLEO, MURIQUI, GAO Lin (WU Pingfeng 64). Tr: LEE Jang Soo

Buriram United 2
Suchao [61p], Acheampong [79]

Sivaruck TEDSUNGNOEN – Theeraton BUNMATHAN•, Pratum CHUTHONG, Yves EKWALLA, Apichet PUTTAN• (Surat SUKHA• 51), Jakkraphan KAEWPROM, Suchao NUTNUM, Jirawat MAKAROM (Suriya DOMTAISONG 87), Asqar JADIGEROV•, Franck OHANDZA, Frank ACHEAMPONG. Tr: Attaphol BUSPAKOM

Hitachi, Kashiwa
4-04-2012, 8787, Albadwawi UAE

Kashiwa Reysol 0

Takanori SUGENO – Naoya KONDO, Hiroki SAKAI, Tatsuya MASUSHIMA, Ryoji FUKUI•, Hidekazu OTANI, LEANDRO DOMINGUES, JORGE WAGNER, Ryoichi KURISAWA•, Junya TANAKA (Akimi BARADA 65), Masato KUDO (Ricardo LOBO 73). Tr: NELSINHO BAPTISTA

Guangzhou Evergrande 0

YANG Jun• – FENG Xiaoting, QIN Sheng, ZHENG Zhi, Dario CONCA, CHO Won Hee, SUN Xiang, ZHAO Xuri, CLEO, MURIQUI, GAO Lin. Tr: LEE Jang Soo

Thunder Castle, Buriram
4-04-2012, 22 700, Shukralla BHR

Buriram United 0

Sivaruck TEDSUNGNOEN – Theeraton BUNMATHAN•, Pratum CHUTHONG• , Yves EKWALLA, Apichet PUTTAN (Surat SUKHA 51), Jakkraphan KAEWPROM, Suchao NUTNUM, Jirawat MAKAROM, Asqar JADIGEROV (Somjed SUTTABUTH• 46), Franck OHANDZA (Suriya DOMTAISONG• 78), Frank ACHEAMPONG. Tr: Attaphol BUSPAKOM

Jeonbuk Hyundai Motors 2
Lee Seung Hyun [9], Seo Sang Min [34]

KIM Min Sik• – KIM Sang Sik, KIM Jae Hoan, CHOI Chul Soon•, PARK Won Jae, ENINHO•, LEE Seung Hyun, JUNG Hun•, HUANG Bowen, LUIZ HENRIQUE (SEO Sang Min 26) (HONG Ju Bin 85), LEE Dong Gook. Tr: LEE Heung Sil

World Cup Stadium, Jeonju
17-04-2012, 6432, Al Zarooni UAE

Jeonbuk Hyundai Motors 3
Lee Dong Gook 2 [25] [27], Park Won Jae [80]

KIM Min Sik – KIM Sang Sik (KIM Jung Woo 67), CHO Sung Hwan, LIM You Hwan•, PARK Won Jae•, JEON Kwang Hwan, ENINHO, LEE Seung Hyun (JEONG Shung Hoon 78), SEO Sang Min, LUIZ HENRIQUE (HUANG Bowen 67), LEE Dong Gook. Tr: LEE Heung Sil

Buriram United 2
Ohandza 2 [20] [56]

Sivaruck TEDSUNGNOEN – Pratum CHUTHONG, Yves EKWALLA, Apichet PUTTAN•, Surat SUKHA, Jakkraphan KAEWPROM, Sumanya PURISAI (Asqar JADIGEROV 37), Suchao NUTNUM (Sarif SAINUI 80), Jirawat MAKAROM, Franck OHANDZA, Frank ACHEAMPONG. Tr: Attaphol BUSPAKOM

Tianhe, Guangzhou
17-04-2012, 40 000, Abdou QAT

Guangzhou Evergrande 3
Conca [29p], Muriqui 2 [58] [84]

YANG Jun• – FENG Xiaoting, ZHANG Linpeng, QIN Sheng• (ZHAO Xuri• 46), ZHENG Zhi, Dario CONCA, CHO Won Hee (FENG Junyan 81), SUN Xiang, CLEO, MURIQUI, GAO Lin (LI Jianhua 90). Tr: LEE Jang Soo

Kashiwa Reysol 1
Sakai [50]

Takanori SUGENO – Hiroki SAKAI•, Tatsuya MASUSHIMA, Hirofumi WATANABE•, Masato FUJITA (Junya TANAKA 68), Hidekazu OTANI, LEANDRO DOMINGUES, JORGE WAGNER, Akimi BARADA (Masakatsu SAWA 46), Ryoichi KURISAWA, Masato KUDO (Ricardo LOBO 68). Tr: NELSINHO BAPTISTA

Hitachi, Kashiwa
1-05-2012, 8099, Al Ghamdi KSA

Kashiwa Reysol 1
Domingues [24]

Koji INADA – Hiroki SAKAI, Tatsuya MASUSHIMA, Wataru HASHIMOTO, Hirofumi WATANABE, LEANDRO DOMINGUES•, JORGE WAGNER, AN Young Hak, Akimi BARADA, Hideaki KITAJIMA (Masakatsu SAWA 70), Ricardo LOBO• (Masato KUDO 70). Tr: NELSINHO BAPTISTA

Buriram United 0

Sivaruck TEDSUNGNOEN – Theeraton BUNMATHAN, Pratum CHUTHONG, Yves EKWALLA•, •41, Surat SUKHA, Piyarat LAJUNGREED, Jakkraphan KAEWPROM, Suchao NUTNUM (Sarif SAINUI 73), Jirawat MAKAROM (Chalermpong KEDKAEW• 51), Franck OHANDZA (Suriya DOMTAISONG 81), Frank ACHEAMPONG. Tr: Attaphol Buspakom

Tianhe, Guangzhou
1-05-2012, 47 869, Kovalenko UZB

Guangzhou Evergrande 1
Conca [10p]

YANG Jun•, FENG Xiaoting, ZHANG Linpeng, ZHENG Zhi, Dario CONCA (JIANG Ning 60), CHO Won Hee, SUN Xiang, ZHAO Xuri (FENG Junyan 46), CLEO, MURIQUI, GAO Lin (WU Pingfeng 82). Tr: LEE Jang Soo

Jeonbuk Hyundai Motors 3
Lee Seung Hyun [43], Lee Dong Gook 2 [91+] [93+p]

KIM Min Sik – KIM Sang Sik (ENINHO 46, CHOI Chul Soon 88), CHO Sung Hwan•••65, LIM You Hwan, JEON Kwang Hwan, JIN Kyung Sun, LEE Seung Hyun• (Hugo DROGUETT 62), JUNG Hun, KIM Jung Woo, SEO Sang Min, LEE Dong Gook. Tr: LEE Heung Sil

World Cup Stadium, Jeonju
15-05-2012, 11 459, Abdulnabi BHR

Jeonbuk Hyundai Motors 0

KIM Min Sik – KIM Sang Sik, CHOI Chul Soon, PARK Won Jae•, JIN Kyung Sun• (LEE Seung Hyun 50) (JEONG Shung Hoon 72), ENINHO, JUNG Hun, KIM Jung Woo, Hugo DROGUETT (LUIZ HENRIQUE 56), SEO Sang Min, LEE Dong Gook. Tr: LEE Heung Sil

Kashiwa Reysol 3
Domingues [49], Tanaka [62]

Takanori SUGENO – Naoya KONDO, Hiroki SAKAI, Tatsuya MASUSHIMA•, Daisuke NASU, Hidekazu OTANI•, LEANDRO DOMINGUES, JORGE WAGNER, Akimi BARADA, Junya TANAKA (Koki MIZUNO 84), Masato KUDO (Ryohei HAYASHI 87). Tr: NELSINHO BAPTISTA

Thunder Castle, Buriram
15-05-2012, 18 000, Delovski AUS

Buriram United 1
Suriya [57]

Sivaruck TEDSUNGNOEN – Theeraton BUNMATHAN, Pratum CHUTHONG, Apichet PUTTAN, Surat SUKHA•, Jakkraphan KAEWPROM, Suchao NUTNUM• (Adisak KRAISORN 87), Ekkachai SUMREI (Suriya DOMTAISONG 20), Jirawat MAKAROM, Franck OHANDZA (Sarif SAINUI 55), Frank ACHEAMPONG. Tr: Attaphol BUSPAKOM

Guangzhou Evergrande 2
Gao Lin [49], Conca [91+p]

LI Shuai – FENG Xiaoting, ZHANG Linpeng• (FENG Junyan 81), ZHENG Zhi•, Dario CONCA, CHO Won Hee, SUN Xiang, ZHAO Xuri (MURIQUI 65), CLEO, JIANG Ning• (QIN Sheng• 46), GAO Lin. Tr: LEE Jang Soo

AFC CHAMPIONS LEAGUE 2012

ROUND OF SIXTEEN

Ulsan Munsu, Ulsan
30-05-2012, 14 341, Alzarooni UAE

Ulsan Hyundai 3
Kim Shin Wook [54], OG [71], Lee Keun Ho [88]

KIM Seung Gyu - LEE Jae Seong, KANG Min Soo, KWAK Tae Hwi, LEE Ho (KANG Jin Ouk 86), KIM Young Sam, GO Seul Ki, Juan VELEZ, KIM Shin Wook•, LEE Keun Ho, KIM Seung Yong (MARANHAO 67). Tr: KIM Ho Gon

Kashiwa Reysol 2
Leandro Domingues [66], Tanaka [92+]

Takanori SUGENO - Naoya KONDO, Hiroki SAKAI•, Tatsuya MASUSHIMA, Daisuke NASU, Hidekazu OTANI (Masakatsu SAWA 77), LEANDRO DOMINGUES•, JORGE WAGNER, Ryoichi KURISAWA, Junya TANAKA, Masato KUDO (Ryohei HAYASHI 86). Tr: NELSINHO BAPTISTA

Prince Faisal bin Fahd, Riyadh
23-05-2012, 22 518, Shukralla BHR

Al Hilal 7
Yoo 4 [23] [38] [53] [61], Wilhelmsson 2 [26] [59], Al Dawsari [86]

Khalid SHARAHELE - Sultan AL BISHI•, Osama HAWSAWI, Majed AL MARSHADI, Abdullatif AL GHANNAM, Christian WILHELMSSON, Salman AL FARAJ (Abdullah AL ZORI 82), Ahmed AL FRAIDI, Adil HERMACH, YOO Byung Soo (Youssef EL ARABI 84), Nawaf AL ABED (Salem AL DOSSARI 72). Tr: Ivan HASEK

Bani-Yas 1
Yeste [57p]

Mohamed KHALAF - Ismael BOUZID, Nawaf MUBARAK, Mohamed JABER (Fareed ISMAIL 36), Thamir MOHAMED•, Amer ABDULRAHMAN, Fawzi BASHEER (Saleh AL MENHALI◆89, 74), Sultan AL GHAFRI•, Yousif JABER, Mohamed FAWZI (Francisco YESTE 46), Andre SENGHOR. Tr: Gabriel CALDERON

Hindmarsh, Adelaide
29-05-2012, 9758, Abdul Bashir SIN

Adelaide United 1
McKain [42]

Eugene GALEKOVIC - Nigel BOOGAARD, Jon MCKAIN, Daniel MULLEN, CASSIO, Iain FYFE, Zenon CARAVELLA (Sergio VAN DIJK 68), Dario VIDOSIC (Evan KOSTOPOULOS 82), Fabian BARBIERO, Bruce DJITE• (Teeboy KAMARA 88), Iain RAMSAY. Tr: John KOSMINA

Nagoya Grampus 0

Seigo NARAZAKI - Marcus Tulio TANAKA, Takahiro MASUKAWA, Shohei ABE, DANIEL•, Jungo FUJIMOTO, Yoshizumi OGAWA, Taishi TAGUCHI (Hayuma TANAKA 68), Keiji TAMADA (Mu KANAZAKI 46), Joshua KENNEDY, Kensuke NAGAI (Teruki TANAKA 72). Tr: Dragan STOJKOVIC

Tancheon, Seongnam
29-05-2012, 3808, Torky IRN

Seongnam Ilhwa Chunma 0

HA Kang Jin - Sasa OGNENOVSKI, PARK Jin Po, HONG Chul (LEE Hyun Ho 78), KIM Sung Hwan, NAMGUNG Woong, LIM Jong Eun•, KIM Seong Jun, HAN Sang Woon (YUN Young Sun 90), YOON Bit Garam, HEVERTON (KIM Deok Il 66). Tr: SHIN Tae Yong

Bunyodkor 1
Karimov [53p]

Ignatiy NESTEROV - Akmal SHORAKHMEDOV, Hayrulla KARIMOV, Anvar GAFUROV•, Artyom FILIPOSYAN, David CARNEY (Anvar RAJABOV 90), Jovlon IBROKHIMOV, Shavkat SALOMOV (Alibobo RAKHMATULLAEV 66), Lutfulla TURAEV, Jan KOZAK (Ruslan MELZIDDINOV 87), Kamoliddin MIRZAEV. Tr: Mirdjalol KASIMOV

Prince Abdullah Al Faisal, Jeddah
23-05-2012, 15 300, Kovalenko UZB

Al Ittihad 3
Naif Hazazi [36p], Abdelghani [45], Otaif [87]

Mabrouk ZAID - Redha TUKAR, Osama AL HARBI, Hamad AL MONTASHARI, Saud KHARIRI, Mohammed ABUSABAAN (Maan KHODARY 83), Hosny ABD RABOU, Abdoh OTAIF, Abdullah OMAR, Naif HAZAZI (Fabrice N'GUESSI 59), Faouzi ABDELGHANI (Mohammed NOOR 81). Tr: Raul CANEDA

Persepolis 0

Asmir AVDUKIC - Sheys REZAEI, Alireza NOORMOHAMADI, Mehrdad POULADI, Ali KARIMI, Maziar ZARE (Amir FESHANGCHI 46), Hossein BADAMAKI• (Hadi NOROUZI 46), Mohammad NOURI (Vahid HASHEMIAN 79), Hamidreza ALIASGARI, Gholamreza REZAEI•, Eamon ZAYED. Tr: Mustafa DENIZLI

Tianhe, Guangzhou
30-05-2012, 39 560, Balideh QAT

Guangzhou Evergrande 1
Cleo [31]

YANG Jun - FENG Xiaoting, ZHANG Linpeng•, ZHENG Zhi, Dario CONCA (GAO Lin 75), CHO Won Hee, SUN Xiang, ZHAO Xuri•, CLEO (LI Jianhua 90), MURIQUI, JIANG Ning (FENG Junyan 62). Tr: LEE Jang Soo

FC Tokyo 0

Shuichi GONDA - Yuhei TOKUNAGA, Masato MORISHIGE•, Hideto TAKAHASHI, Kenta MUKUHARA (Yohei HAYASHI 85), Takuji YONEMOTO (Tatsuya YAZAWA 55), Aria Jasuru HASEGAWA, Yohei KAJIYAMA, Naohiro ISHIKAWA (Hiroki KAWANO 84), Kazuma WATANABE, LUCAS. Tr: Ranko POPOVIC

Foolad Shahr, Isfahan
22-05-2012, 12 351, Kim Dong Jin KOR

Sepahan 2
Correa [8], Bengar [34]

Rahman AHMADI - Jalal HOSSEINI, Mohsen BENGAR, Hashem BEIKZADEH, Moharram NAVIDKIA• (Ahmad JAMSHIDIAN 75), Mehdi JAFARPOUR, Mehdi KARIMIAN, Omid EBRAHIMI, FABIO JANUARIO, Xhevair SUKAJ (Mehdi Seyed SALEHI 61), BRUNO CESAR (Hossein PAPI 81). Tr: Zlatko KRANJCAR

Esteghlal 0

Mehdi RAHMATI - Khosro HEYDARI, Hanif OMRANZADEH•, Jlloyd SAMUEL•, Meysam HOSSEINI (Mohsen YOUSEFI 69), Ali HAMOUDI (Goran JERKOVIC 41), Mojtaba JABBARI, Andranik TEYMOURIAN•, Ferydoon ZANDI (Milad MEYDAVOUDI 80), Pejman MONTAZERI, Arash BORHANI. Tr: Parviz MAZLOUMI

Mohamed Bin Zayid, Abu Dhabi
22-05-2012, 13 355, Sato JPN

Al Jazira 3 2p
Oliveira 2 [33] [114], Delgado [62]

Ali KHASIF - Lucas NEILL, Juma ABDULLAH, Abdulla MOUSA, Salim Masoud RASHID, Matias DELGADO (Abdulraheem JUMAA 86), Subait Khater• (Sultan BARGASH 60), Khamis ESMAEEL, BARE (Ahmed MUHAD 71), Ibrahim DIAKY, Ricardo OLIVEIRA. Tr: CAIO JUNIOR

Al Ahli 3 4p
Camacho [22], Al Hosni [75], Victor Simoes [118]

Abdullah AL MUAIOUF - Waleed BAKSHWN (Amad AL HOSANI 65), Kamil AL MOUSA•, Mohammed AL MUWALLAD (Sultan AL SAWADI 115), Mansour AL HARBI, Jaire PALOMINO, Motaz AL MUSA, Taisir AL JASSIM, Marcelo CAMACHO, Abdulrahim JIZAWI (Yasir AL FAHMI• 73), VICTOR SIMOES. Tr: Karel JAROLIM

QUARTER-FINALS

Ulsan Munsu, Ulsan
19-09-2012, 5955, Sato JPN

Ulsan Hyundai 1
Rafinha [10]

KIM Young Kwang - LEE Yong, KANG Min Soo•, KWAK Tae Hwi, KIM Young Sam, KIM Dong Suk (LEE Jae Seong 79), Juan VELEZ, MARANHAO (KIM Shin Wook• 57), LEE Keun Ho, KIM Seung Yong (GO Seul Ki 68), RAFINHA. Tr: KIM Ho Gon

Al Hilal 0

Abdullah ALSDAIRY - Abdullah AL ZORI•, Mohammad NAMI•, Majed AL MARSHADI, Kader MANGANE•, Yasir AL SHAHRANI (Salem AL DOSSARI 87), Mohammed AL QARNI, Abdulaziz AL DOSARI, Adil HERMACH (Salman AL FARAJ 65), WESLEY, YOO Byung Soo (Yasser AL QAHTANI 78). Tr: Antoine KOMBOUARE

Prince Faisal bin Fahd, Riyadh
3-10-2012, 19 573, Torky IRN

Al Hilal 0

Abdullah ALSDAIRY - Sultan AL BISHI, Abdullah AL ZORI, Majed AL MARSHADI• (Ahmed AL FRAIDI 46), Kader MANGANE, Mohammed AL QARNI• (Nawaf AL ABED• 81), Abdulaziz AL DOSARI (Salem AL DOSSARI 58), Salman AL FARAJ, Adil HERMACH•, WESLEY, YOO Byung Soo. Tr: Antoine KOMBOUARE

Ulsan Hyundai 4
Rafinha 2 [24 27], Kim Shin Wook [54], Lee Keun Ho [65]

KIM Young Kwang - LEE Yong, KANG Min Soo•, KWAK Tae Hwi, LEE Ho• (KIM Dong Suk 71), KIM Young Sam, Juan VELEZ, KIM Shin Wook, LEE Keun Ho (Lee Seung Yeoul 80), KIM Seung Yong, RAFINHA (MARANHAO 38). Tr: KIM Ho Gon

Hindmarsh, Adelaide
19-09-2012, 10 366, Al Hilali OMA

Adelaide United 2
Ramsay [7], Kostopoulos [16]

Eugene GALEKOVIC - Nigel BOOGAARD♦[42], Iain FYFE•, CASSIO, Cameron WATSON, Daniel BOWLES, Dario VIDOSIC (Anthony GOLEC 53), Fabian BARBIERO, Bruce DJITE (Sergio VAN DIJK 74), Iain RAMSAY (Jeronimo NEUMANN 81), Evan KOSTOPOULOS•. Tr: John KOSMINA

Bunyodkor 2
Hasanov [44], Salomov [75]

Ignatiy NESTEROV - Akmal SHORAKHMEDOV, Hayrulla KARIMOV•, Anvar GAFUROV, Artyom FILIPOSYAN, Jovlon IBROKHIMOV•, Luttfulla TURAEV, Jasur HASANOV•, Viktor KARPENKO (Ilkhom SHOMURODOV 83), Jan KOZAK (Shavkat SALOMOV 66), Kamoliddin MIRZAEV• (Anvarjon SOLYIEV 76). Tr: Mirdjalol KASIMOV

JAR Stadium, Tashkent
3-10-2012, 7212, Abdulnabi BHR

Bunyodkor 3
Yuraev [20], Shorakhmedov [72], Rakhmatullaev [114]

Ignatiy NESTEROV - Akmal SHORAKHMEDOV, Hayrulla KARIMOV, Anvar GAFUROV••♦[100], Artyom FILIPOSYAN, Jovlon IBROKHIMOV•, Luttfulla TURAEV, Jasur HASANOV•, Viktor KARPENKO (Alibobo RAKHMATULLAEV 71), Jan KOZAK (Anvarjon SOLYIEV 67, Shavkat SALOMOV 95), Kamoliddin MIRZAEV. Tr: Mirdjalol KASIMOV

Adelaide United 2
Ramsay [4], Neumann [63]

Eugene GALEKOVIC - Jon MCKAIN, Iain FYFE••♦[120], CASSIO, Cameron WATSON, Daniel BOWLES•, Dario VIDOSIC•, Fabian BARBIERO••♦[88], Sergio VAN DIJK (Osama MALIK 90), Iain RAMSAY (Bruce DJITE 113), Evan KOSTOPOULOS• (Jeronimo NEUMANN• 61). Tr: John KOSMINA

Prince Abdullah Al Faisal, Jeddah
19-09-2012, 15 971, El Haddad LIB

Al Ittihad 4
Diego Souza [29], Noor [49p], Naif Hazazi 2 [61 88]

Mabrouk ZAID - Redha TUKAR•, Osama AL HARBI, Mishal AL SAEED (Anas SHARBINI 46), Hamad AL MONTASHARI, Ibrahim HAZAZI, Modeste M'BAMI•, DIEGO SOUZA (Fahad AL MUWALLAD 85), Saud KHARIRI, Mohammed NOOR, Naif HAZAZI. Tr: Raul CANEDA

Guangzhou Evergrande 2
Gao Lin [27], Huang Bowen [39]

YANG Jun - FENG Xiaoting, LI Jianhua (RONG Hao 72), KIM Young Gwon, QIN Sheng, ZHENG Zhi, Dario CONCA, SUN Xiang•, MURIQUI (HUANG Bowen• 36), Lucas BARRIOS, GAO Lin (FENG Junyan 85). Tr: Marcello LIPPI

Tianhe, Guangzhou
2-10-2012, 39 997, Kim Dong Jin KOR

Guangzhou Evergrande 2
Barrios [19], Conca [35p]

LI SHUAI - RONG Hao (JIANG Ning 81), FENG Xiaoting•, KIM Young Gwon, ZHANG Linpeng, FENG Junyan (LI Jianhua 72), QIN Sheng, ZHENG Zhi, Dario CONCA•, Lucas BARRIOS (ZHAO Xuri 76), GAO Lin. Tr: Marcello LIPPI

Al Ittihad 1
Al Muwallad [79]

Mabrouk ZAID - Redha TUKAR• (Ahmed Hassan ASIRI 42), Osama AL HARBI•, Hamad AL MONTASHARI•, Ibrahim HAZAZI, Modeste M'BAMI, DIEGO SOUZA, Anas SHARBINI, Saud KHARIRI, Mohammed NOOR (Fahad AL MUWALLAD 70), Mohammed ABUSABAAN (Naif HAZAZI 46). Tr: Raul CANEDA

Foolad Shahr, Isfahan
19-09-2012, 9280, Liu Kwok Man HKG

Sepahan 0

Reza MOHAMMADI - Hassan ASHJARI, Farsheed TALEBI, Mohammad ALI AHMADI, Moharram NAVIDKIA• (Mohamed GHOLAMI 86), Mehdi JAFARPOUR, Omid EBRAHIMI (Ahmad JAMSHIDIAN 62), Ervin BULKU, Adel KOLAHKAJ, Radomir DALOVIC (Xhevair SUKAJ 78), Mohammad KHALATBARI. Tr: Zlatko KRANJCAR

Al Ahli 0

Abdullah AL MUAIOUF - Kamel AL MOR, Waleed BAKSHWN•, Mansour AL HARBI, Kamil AL MOUSA, Jairo PALOMINO, Motaz AL MUSA•, Taisir AL JASSIM, Diego MORALES (Mohsen AL EISA 90), Abdulrahim JIZAWI (Yahya Mohammed OTAYN 80), Amad AL HOSANI (Essa AL MEHYANI 90). Tr: Karel JAROLIM

Prince Abdullah Al Faisal, Jeddah
2-10-2012, 16 838, Green AUS

Al Ahli 4
Victor Simoes [30p], Al Hosni 2 [35 45], Jaizawi [70]

Abdullah AL MUAIOUF - Kamel AL MOR, Waleed BAKSHWN, Mansour AL HARBI, Kamil AL MOUSA, Jairo PALOMINO, Motaz AL MUSA, Taisir AL JASSIM, Diego MORALES (Essa AL MEHYANI 71), VICTOR SIMOES (Abdulrahim JIZAWI• 46), Amad AL HOSANI (Bader AL KHAMIS• 80). Tr: Karel JAROLIM

Sepahan 1
Talebi [37]

Reza MOHAMMADI♦[27] - Hassan ASHJARI, Farsheed TALEBI, Mohammad Ali AHMADI, Moharram NAVIDKIA•, Mehdi JAFARPOUR (Xhevair SUKAJ 46), Omid EBRAHIMI•, Ervin BULKU, Adel KOLAHKAJ, Radomir DALOVIC (Ahmad JAMSHIDIAN 57), Mohammad KHALATBARI (Mohamad BAGHER 29). Tr: Zlatko KRANJCAR

SEMI-FINALS

JAR Stadium, Tashkent
24-10-2012, 7500, Albadwawi UAE

Bunyodkor   **1**
Ibrokhimov [5]

Ignatiy NESTEROV - Akmal SHORAKHMEDOV• (Bahodir PARDAEV 90), Hayrulla KARIMOV, Artyom FILIPOSYAN, Sakhob JURAEV•, Jovlon IBROKHIMOV, Lutfulla TURAEV, Jasur HASANOV, Viktor KARPENKO (Alibobo RAKHMATULLAEV 78), Jan KOZAK (Shavkat SALOMOV 68), Kamoliddin MIRZAEV. Tr: Mirdjalol KASIMOV

Ulsan Hyundai   **3**
Rafinha [31], Kim Shin Wook [53], Lee Keun Ho [72]

KIM Young Kwang - LEE Yong, KANG Min Soo•, KWAK Tae Hwi, LEE Ho, KIM Young Sam, Juan VELEZ, KIM Shin Wook (MARANHAO 83), LEE Keun Ho (LEE Seung Yeoul 90), KIM Seung Yong (GO Seul Ki 80), RAFINHA. Tr: KIM Ho Gon

---

Ulsan Munsu, Ulsan
31-10-2012, 7864, Abdou QAT

Ulsan Hyundai   **2**
Kim Shin Wook [53], Lee Keun Ho [75]

KIM Young Kwang - LEE Yong, KANG Min Soo, KWAK Tae Hwi (LEE Jae Seong 77), LEE Ho (GO Seul Ki 60), KIM Young Sam, Juan VELEZ, KIM Shin Wook (KO Chang Hyun 74), LEE Keun Ho, KIM Seung Yong, RAFINHA. Tr: KIM Ho Gon

Bunyodkor   **0**

Ignatiy NESTEROV - Akmal SHORAKHMEDOV, Hayrulla KARIMOV (Dilshod JURAEV• 81), Artyom FILIPOSYAN, Jovlon IBROKHIMOV, Shavkat SALOMOV, Lutfulla TURAEV•, Jasur HASANOV (Bahodir PARDAEV 64), Viktor KARPENKO (Alibobo RAKHMATULLAEV 77), Ruslan MELZIDDINOV, Kamoliddin MIRZAEV. Tr: Mirdjalol KASIMOV

Prince Abdullah Al Faisal, Jeddah
22-10-2012, 17 050, Balideh QAT

Al Ittihad   **1**
Naif Hazazi [67]

Mabrouk ZAID - Osama AL HARBI, Hamad AL MONTASHARI, Ahmed Hassan ASIRI, Ibrahim HAZAZI, Modeste M'BAMI, DIEGO SOUZA (Fahad AL MUWALLAD 81), Anas SHARBINI, Saud KHARIRI, Mohammed NOOR, Naif HAZAZI•. Tr: Raul CANEDA

Al Ahli   **0**

Abdullah AL MUAIOUF - Kamel AL MOR (Diego MORALES 76), Aqeel AL SAHIBI•, Mansour AL HARBI, Jairo PALOMINO, Motaz AL MUSA (Mohsen AL EISA 88), Taisir AL JASSIM, Yahya Mohammed OTAYN, Mustafa AL BASSAS, VICTOR SIMOES, Amad AL HOSANI. Tr: Karel JAROLIM

Prince Abdullah Al Faisal, Jeddah
31-10-2012, 17 200, Nisjimura JPN

Al Ahli   **2**
Moataz Al Musa [44], Victor Simoes [84]

Abdullah AL MUAIOUF - Kamel AL MOR, Aqeel AL SAHIBI, Mansour AL HARBI♦95+, Jairo PALOMINO, Motaz AL MUSA (Waleed BAKSHWN 84), Taisir AL JASSIM•, Diego MORALES (Mohammed AMAN 94+), Mustafa AL BASSAS, VICTOR SIMOES (Mohsen AL EISA 91+), Amad AL HOSANI•. Tr: Karel JAROLIM

Al Ittihad   **0**

Mabrouk ZAID - Osama AL HARBI•, Hamad AL MONTASHARI, Ahmed Hassan ASIRI, Ibrahim HAZAZI, Modeste M'BAMI, Anas SHARBINI, Saud KHARIRI, Mohammed NOOR, Fahad AL MUWALLAD•, Naif HAZAZI. Tr: Raul CANEDA

AFC CHAMPIONS LEAGUE FINAL
ULSAN MUNSU FOOTBALL STADIUM, ULSAN

Saturday, 10-11-2012, 19:30, Att: 42 153, Ref: Ben Williams AUS
Assistants: Luke Brennan AUS & Paul Cetrangolo AUS

ULSAN HYUNDAI   3   0   **AL AHLI**

Kwak Tae Hwi [13], Rafinha [68], Kim Seung Yong [75]

ULSAN HYUNDAI
Blue shirts blue shorts, blue socks

Tr: Kim Ho Gon

Kim Young Kwang

Lee Yong   Kwak Tae Hwi (c)†   Kang Min Soo [31]   Kim Young Sam [68] / Lee Jae Seong

[46] Lee Ho / Go Seul Ki   Julian Velez

Kim Seung Yong   Lee Keun Ho

Kim Shin Wook [88]   Rafinha [79] / Maranhao

Victor Simoes   Amad Al Hosani

[71] Waleed Bakshwn / Abdulrahim Jizawi   Taisir Al Jassim (c) [86] / Diego Morales

[72] Moataz Al Musa [79] / Mohsen Al Eisa   Mustafa Besas [92+]

Haidar Al Amer   Jairo Palomino   Aqeel Al Sahibi   Kamel Al Mor

Tr: Karel Jarolim   Abdullah Al Muaiouf

White shirts, green shorts, white socks
AL AHLI

MATCH STATS

Jeonbuk		Al Sadd
23	Shots	9
15	Shots on Goal	2
10	Fouls Committed	17
5	Corner Kicks	5
3	Caught Offside	0
55	Possession %	45

(C) Captain † Man of the Match

Ulsan have had to wait for a long time to come to the final so I told the players we must win the game and to do that we must play a normal game. The players created a lot of pressure in the first half and all of the players played their part. After the first goal the players felt they could win and they made some mistakes and allowed Al Ahli to create some attacks. I am so happy for the players. They wanted to play in the FIFA Club World Cup and it is the same for me.

Kim Ho Gon

Maybe we are expecting a lot from the players and it's true they didn't perform well, but it's not because they didn't want to but because Ulsan are a strong team and they played well. After the first goal I think we created a few chances to score at least one goal in the first half, but the strikers didn't score and they didn't work with the ball very well. Al Ahli is a very young team and these players have gained experience this season. The team has learned a lot.

Karel Jarolim

AFC PRESIDENT'S CUP 2012

First round groups

Group A (In Lahore, PAK)

		Pl	W	D	L	F	A	Pts		PAK	MGL
Kaohsiung Taipower	TPE	2	1	1	0	1	0	4		0-0	1-0
Khan Research Labs	PAK	2	0	2	0	0	0	2			0-0
Erchim	MNG	2	0	1	1	0	1	1			

Group B (In Phnom Penh, CAM)

		Pl	W	D	L	F	A	Pts		CAM	NEP	BHU
Dordoi Bishkek	KGZ	3	3	0	0	17	3	9		1-0	5-1	11-2
Phnom Penh Crown	CAM	3	2	0	1	9	1	6			1-0	8-0
Nepal Police Club	NEP	3	1	0	2	5	6	3				4-0
Yeedzin	BHU	3	0	0	3	2	23	0				

Group C (In Dushanbe, TJK)

		Pl	W	D	L	F	A	Pts		PLE	TKM
Esteghlal Dushanbe	TJK	2	2	0	0	3	1	6		1-0	2-1
Shabab Al Amari	PLE	2	1	0	1	2	2	3			2-1
Balkan Balkanabat	TKM	2	0	0	2	2	4	0			

Top scorer: **8** - Mirlan **MURZAEV** KGZ, Dordoi • **5** - Azamat **BAYMATOV** KGZ, Dordoi • **4** - Khim **BOREY** CAM, Phnom Penh Crown • **3** - **ANDERSON** BRA, Dordoi; Davron **ERGASHEV** TJK, Esteghlal; Dilshod **VASIEV** TJK, Esteghlal & Ahmed **KESHKESH** PLE, Shabab Al Amari

Final Tournament groups

	Pl	W	D	L	F	A	Pts		DB	PPC
Esteghlal Dushanbe	2	2	0	0	8	0	6		2-0	6-0
Dordoi Bishkek	2	1	0	1	8	2	3			8-0
Phnom Penh Crown	2	0	0	2	0	14	0			

	Pl	W	D	L	F	A	Pts		KT	KRL
Shabab Al Amari	2	1	1	0	6	2	4		1-1	5-1
Kaohsiung Taipower	2	1	1	0	4	2	4			3-1
Khan Research Labs	2	0	0	2	2	8	0			

Final

Esteghlal Dushanbe	2
Shabab Al Amari	1

AFC PRESIDENT'S CUP FINAL 2012

Central Stadium, Dushanbe, 30-09-2012, Att: 19 323, Ref: Fahad Almirdasi KSA

Esteghlal Dushanbe 2 Ergashev [69], Vasiev [78]
Shabab Al Amari 1 Keshkesh [21]

Esteghlal - Alisher **TUYCHIEV** - Sohib **SAVANKULOV**, Eraj **RAJABOV**, Davronjon **ERGASHEV** - Makhmadali **SADYKOV** (Alexander **FRANK** 46), Nuriddin **DAVRONOV**, Dzhakhongir **DZHALILOV**•, Dilshod **VASIEV** (c), Fatkhullo **FATKHULOEV**• - Yusuf **RABIEV** (Ibragim **RABIMOV** 46), Farkhod **TOKHIROV** (Umedzhon **SHARIPOV**• 81). Tr: Nikola **KANAZOVIC**

Al Amari - Abdallah **ALSIDAWI** - Khaled **MAHDI**, Ahmed **SALAMA**, Nour **OWDA**, Hamza **ZOUBI** - Ayed **JAMHOUR**• (c), Mali **KAWARE**•, Mahmoud **SHAIKHQASEM**, Sulaiman **OBAID** (Adham **ARAR** 73) - Jamal **ALIWISAT**, Ahmed **KESHKESH**. Tr: Raed **ASSAF**

AFC CUP 2012

First Round

Group A

		Pl	W	D	L	F	A	Pts	KUW	OMA	JOR	SYR
Al Qadisiya	KUW	6	3	1	2	14	7	10		2-0	1-2	5-2
Al Suwaiq	OMA	6	3	1	2	8	9	10	1-5		0-0	2-0
Al Faysali	JOR	6	2	3	1	10	7	9	1-1	2-3		1-1
Al Ittihad	SYR	6	1	1	4	5	14	4	1-0	0-2	1-4	

Group B

		Pl	W	D	L	F	A	Pts	IRQ	KUW	YEM	IND
Arbil	IRQ	6	4	2	0	11	5	14		1-1	2-1	2-0
Kazma	KUW	6	3	2	1	10	6	11	1-2		1-1	3-0
Al Urooba	YEM	6	2	2	2	10	8	8	2-2	1-2		4-1
East Bengal	IND	6	0	0	6	2	14	0	0-2	1-2	0-1	

Group C

		Pl	W	D	L	F	A	Pts	KSA	KUW	LIB	MDV
Al Ittifaq	KSA	6	4	2	0	18	7	14		2-2	0-0	2-0
Al Kuwait	KUW	6	3	2	1	17	10	11	1-5		1-0	7-1
Al Ahed	LIB	6	2	1	3	7	11	7	1-3	0-4		5-3
VB Sports	MDV	6	0	1	5	9	23	1	3-6	2-2	0-1	

Group D

		Pl	W	D	L	F	A	Pts	JOR	UZB	OMA	IND
Al Wihdat	JOR	6	4	0	2	15	9	12		3-1	2-1	5-0
Neftchi Fergana	UZB	6	3	2	1	11	7	11	2-1		3-1	3-0
Al Urooba	OMA	6	2	1	3	8	10	7	4-2	0-0		1-0
Salgoacar	IND	6	1	1	4	6	14	4	1-2	2-2	3-1	

Group E

		Pl	W	D	L	F	A	Pts	SYR	IRQ	LIB	YEM
Al Shorta	SYR	6	5	0	1	14	6	15		3-2	3-2	3-0
Al Zawra'a	IRQ	6	4	0	2	12	5	12	2-1		1-0	5-0
Safa	LIB	6	3	0	3	6	7	9	0-2	1-0		1-0
Al Tilal	YEM	6	0	0	6	1	15	0	0-2	0-2	1-2	

Group F

		Pl	W	D	L	F	A	Pts	HKG	MAS	VIE	SIN
Kitchee	HKG	6	3	2	1	9	4	11		2-2	2-0	3-1
Terengganu	MAS	6	3	1	2	10	8	10	0-2		6-2	0-2
Song Lam Nghe An	VIE	6	2	1	3	6	9	7	1-0	0-1		3-0
Tampines Rovers	SIN	6	1	2	3	3	7	5	0-0	0-1	0-0	

Group G

		Pl	W	D	L	F	A	Pts	THA	SIN	HKG	MYA
Chonburi	THA	6	4	2	0	10	5	14		1-0	2-0	1-0
Home United	SIN	6	3	1	2	9	6	10	1-2		3-1	3-1
Citizen	HKG	6	2	1	3	9	12	7	3-3	1-2		2-1
Yangon United	MYA	6	0	2	4	4	9	2	1-1	0-0	1-2	

Group H

		Pl	W	D	L	F	A	Pts	MAS	IDN	VIE	MYA
Kelantan	MAS	6	4	1	1	10	5	13		3-0	0-0	1-0
Arema	IDN	6	2	1	3	12	12	7	1-3		6-2	1-1
Navibank Saigon	VIE	6	2	1	3	10	12	7	1-2	3-1		4-1
Ayewawady United	MYA	6	2	1	3	7	10	7	3-1	0-3	2-0	

Round of 16

Al Kuwait	1	3p
Al Qadisiya *	1	1p

Kazma	1
Al Wihdat *	2

Arema	2
Kitchee *	0

Al Suwaiq	0
Al Ittifaq *	1

Chonburi *	1
Al Zawra'a	0

Home United	0
Al Shorta *	3

Kelantan *	3
Terengganu	2

Neftchi Fergana	0
Arbil *	4

Top scorers: 9 - Amjad **RADHI** IRQ, Arbil & Raja **RAFE** SYR, Shorta • 8 - Mohammed **GHADDAR** LIB, Kelantan; Sebastian **TAGLIABUE** ARG, Ittifaq & Edison **FONSECA** COL, Navibank Saigon • 7 - **ROGERINHO** BRA, Kuwait • 6 - Mahmoud **SHELBAIEH** JOR, Wihdat & Abdulhadi **KHAMIS** KUW, Kuwait

AFC CUP 2012

Quarter-finals			Semi-finals			Final		
Al Kuwait *	0	3						
Al Wihdat	0	0						
			Al Kuwait *	4	2			
			Al Ittifaq	1	0			
Arema *	0	0						
Al Ittifaq	2	2						
						Al Kuwait	4	
						Arbil	0	
Chonburi *	1	4						
Al Shorta	2	2						
			Chonburi	1	1			
			Arbil *	4	4			
Kelantan	1	1						
Arbil *	5	1						

* Home team/Home team in the first leg

AFC CUP FINAL 2012

Franso Hariri Stadium, Arbil, 3-11-2012, Att: 22 000, Ref: Valentin Kovalenko UZB

Arbil	0	
Al Kuwait	4	Hammami 2 [3p 90], Rogerio [42], Khamis [83]

ARBIL

Sarhank MOHSIN - Ahmad Ibrahim KHALAF, Nadim SABAGH, Ivan BUKENYA, Halkard Mulla MOHAMMAD, Salih SADIR (Mustafa KARIM 77), Saad ABDULAMEER, Nabeel SABAH (Luay SALAH 64), Ammar AL ASAADI (Sula MATOVO 46), Miran KHASRO, Amjad RADHI. Tr: Nizar MAHROUS

KUWAIT

Musab AL KANDARI - Husain Ali BABA, Fahad Awadh SHAHEEN, Husain AL SHAMMARI, Chedi HAMMAMI•, Waleed Ali JUMAH, Fahad AL ENEZI (Jarah AL ATEEQI 65), Sami AL SANEA, Shereedah AL SHEREEDAH, Issam JEMAA (Abdulhadi KHAMIS 54), ROGERINHO• (Abdullah AL DHAFEERI 88). Tr: Ion MARIN

CAF

CONFEDERATION AFRICAINE DE FOOTBALL

CAF MEMBER ASSOCIATIONS (54)

ALG - Algeria • ANG - Angola • BEN - Benin • BOT - Botswana • BFA - Burkina Faso • BDI - Burundi • CMR - Cameroon • CPV - Cape Verde Islands
CTA - Central African Republic • CHA - Chad • COM - Comoros • CGO - Congo • COD - Congo DR • CIV - Côte d'Ivoire • DJI - Djibouti
EGY - Egypt • EQG - Equatorial Guinea • ERI - Eritrea • ETH - Ethiopia • GAB - Gabon • GAM - Gambia • GHA - Ghana • GUI - Guinea
GNB - Guinea-Bissau • KEN - Kenya • LES - Lesotho • LBR - Liberia • LBY - Libya • MAD - Madagascar • MWI - Malawi • MLI - Mali
MTN - Mauritania • MRI - Mauritius • MAR - Morocco • MOZ - Mozambique • NAM - Namibia • NIG - Niger • NGA - Nigeria • RWA - Rwanda
STP - São Tomé e Príncipe • SEN - Senegal • SEY - Seychelles • SLE - Sierra Leone • SOM - Somalia • RSA - South Africa • SSD South Sudan
SDN - Sudan • SWZ - Swaziland • TAN - Tanzania • TOG - Togo • TUN - Tunisia • UGA - Uganda • ZAM - Zambia • ZIM - Zimbabwe

CAF ASSOCIATE MEMBER ASSOCIATIONS (2)

REU - Reunion • ZAN - Zanzibar • Neither of these two nations is affiliated to FIFA

Zambia's victory in the 2012 Africa Cup of Nations was one of the most remarkable and poignant in the history of the tournament but their reign as African champions was the shortest, lasting two days less than a full year. The decision to switch the tournament from the years in which the FIFA World Cup is played saw the 2014 tournament brought forward a year to the start of 2013. It also saw South Africa step in as hosts to replace Libya with the Libyans now aiming to host the 2017 tournament. At the finals in South Africa the Super Eagles of Nigeria won the tournament again after a 19-year gap, beating surprise finalists Burkina Faso 1-0 in the final at Soccer City. Coach Stephen Keshi became only the second person after Mahmoud El Gohary to win the title as both player and coach. It was a quiet year for African teams in the six FIFA tournaments played during 2012 although there were very encouraging signs in the two age restricted women's tournaments with Nigeria reaching the semi-finals of the FIFA U-20 Women's World Cup in Japan and Ghana beating Germany 1-0 in the play-off for third place at the FIFA U-17 Women's World Cup in Azerbaijan. In club football the often chaotic aftermath of the Arab Spring had ramifications for football with widespread disruption. In Libya there was little club football played at all while in Egypt the tense political situation spilled onto the football pitch with 72 people killed at a match between Al Masry and Al Ahly in Port Said. The league was suspended, a decision that left Egyptian clubs without any domestic football for a year and a half, but despite this Al Ahly still managed to win a record breaking seventh CAF Champions League title after beating Tunisia's Esperance 3-2 on aggregate in the final. There were surprise winners of the CAF Confederation Cup with Congo's AC Leopards beating Djoliba of Mali 4-3 on aggregate in the final. It was Congo's first trophy since CARA Brazzaville won the African Champions Cup back in 1974.

Confédération Africaine de Football (CAF)

PO Box 23, 3 Abdel Khalek Sarwat Street, El Hay El Motamayez, 6th October City, Egypt
Tel +20 2 8371000   Fax +20 2 8370006
info@cafonline.com   www.cafonline.com
President: Issa Hayatou CMR   General Secretary: Hicham El Amrani MAR
CAF Formed: 1957

CAF EXECUTIVE COMMITTEE

President: Issa Hayatou CMR   1st Vice-President: Seyi Memene TOG   2nd Vice-President: Molefi Oliphant RSA

ORDINARY MEMBERS OF THE EXECUTIVE COMMITTEE

Amadou Diakité MLI	Adoum Djibrine CHA	Amos Adamu NGA
Mohamed Raouraoua ALG	Suketu Patel SEY	Hani Abu Rida EGY
Almamy Kabele Camara GUI	Celestin Musabyimana RWA	Thierry Kamach CTA
	Magdi Shams El Din SUD	
Co-opted: Slim Aloulou TUN	FIFA Exco: Jacques Anouma CIV	General Secretary: Hicham El Amrani MAR

MAP OF CAF MEMBER NATIONS

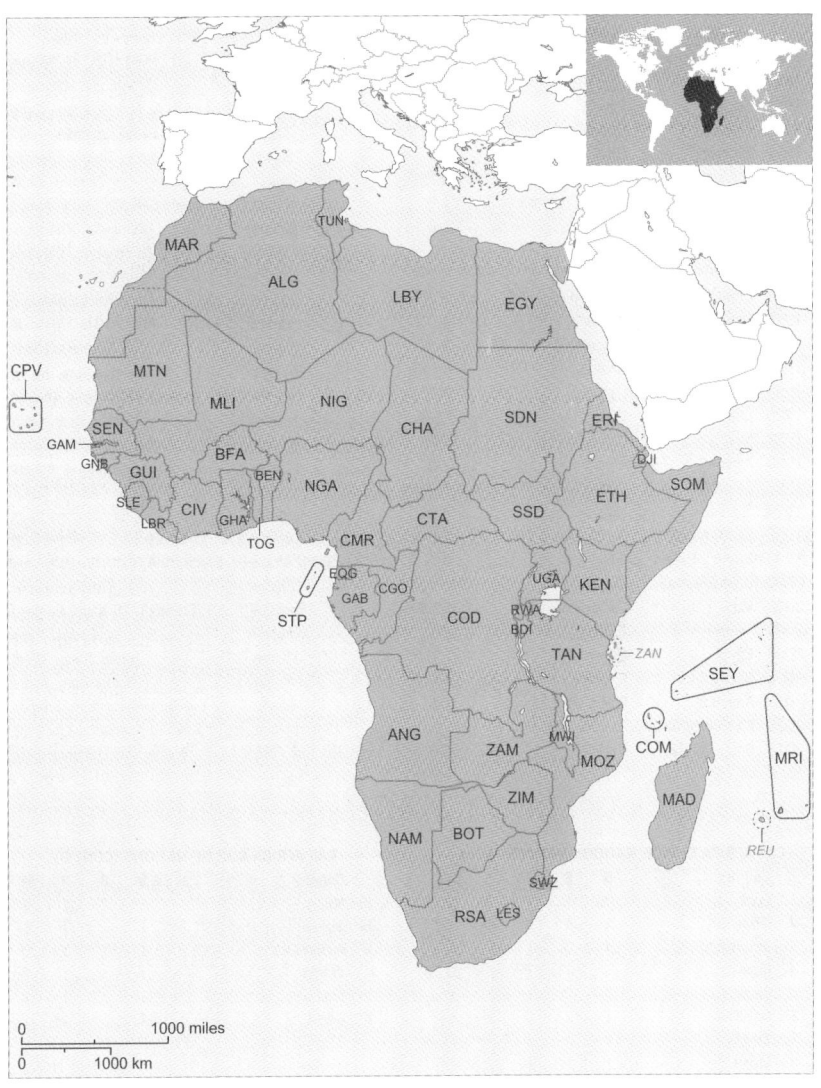

AFRICAN TOURNAMENTS

AFRICAN NATIONAL TEAM TOURNAMENTS

CAF AFRICA CUP OF NATIONS

Year	Host Country	Winners	Score	Runners-up	Venue
1957	Sudan	Egypt	4-0	Ethiopia	Municipal, Khartoum
1959	Egypt	Egypt	2-1	Sudan	Al Ahly Stadium, Cairo
1962	Ethiopia	Ethiopia	2-0	Egypt	Haile Selassie, Addis Abeba
1963	Ghana	Ghana	3-0	Sudan	Accra Stadium, Accra
1965	Tunisia	Ghana	3-2	Tunisia	Zouiten, Tunis
1968	Ethiopia	Congo Kinshasa	1-0	Ghana	Haile Selassie, Addis Abeba
1970	Sudan	Sudan	1-0	Ghana	Municipal, Khartoum
1972	Cameroon	Congo	3-2	Mali	Omnisports, Yaoundé
1974	Egypt	Zaire	2-2 2-0	Zambia	International, Cairo
1976	Ethiopia	Morocco	1-1	Guinea	Addis Abeba Stadium
1978	Ghana	Ghana	2-0	Uganda	Accra Stadium, Accra
1980	Nigeria	Nigeria	3-0	Algeria	Surulere, Lagos
1982	Libya	Ghana	1-1 7-6p	Libya	11th June Stadium, Tripoli
1984	Côte d'Ivoire	Cameroon	3-1	Nigeria	Houphouët Boigny, Abidjan
1986	Egypt	Egypt	0-0 5-4p	Cameroon	International, Cairo
1988	Morocco	Cameroon	1-0	Nigeria	Mohamed V, Casablanca
1990	Algeria	Algeria	1-0	Nigeria	Stade Olympique, Algiers
1992	Senegal	Côte d'Ivoire	0-0 11-10p	Ghana	Stade de l'Amite, Dakar
1994	Tunisia	Nigeria	2-1	Zambia	El Menzah, Tunis
1996	South Africa	South Africa	2-0	Tunisia	Soccer City, Johannesburg
1998	Burkina Faso	Egypt	2-0	South Africa	Stade du 4 Août, Ouagadougou
2000	Ghana/Nigeria	Cameroon	2-2 4-3p	Nigeria	Surulere, Lagos
2002	Mali	Cameroon	0-0 3-2p	Senegal	Stade du 26 Mars, Bamako
2004	Tunisia	Tunisia	2-1	Morocco	Rades, Tunis
2006	Egypt	Egypt	0-0 4-2p	Côte d'Ivoire	International, Cairo
2008	Ghana	Egypt	1-0	Cameroon	Ohene Djan, Accra
2010	Angola	Egypt	1-0	Ghana	Cidade Universitária, Luanda
2012	Eq.Guinea/Gabon	Zambia	0-0 8-7p	Côte d'Ivoire	Stade d'Angondje, Libreville
2013	South Africa	Nigeria	1-0	Burkina Faso	Soccer City, Johannesburg

CAF AFRICA CUP OF NATIONS MEDALS TABLE

	Country	G	S	B	F	SF
1	Egypt	7	1	3	7	11
2	Ghana	4	4	1	8	10
3	Cameroon	4	2	1	6	8
4	Nigeria	3	4	7	7	13
5	Congo DR	2		1	2	4
6	Côte d'Ivoire	1	2	4	3	8
7	Zambia	1	2	3	3	6
8	Tunisia	1	2	1	3	5
9	Sudan	1	2	1	3	2
10	Algeria	1	1	2	2	6
11	South Africa	1	1	1	2	3
12	Morocco	1	1	1	1	4
13	Ethiopia	1	1	1	1	3
14	Congo	1			1	2

CAF AFRICA CUP OF NATIONS (CONT'D)

	Country	G	S	B	F	SF
15	Mali		1	2	1	6
16	Senegal		1		1	3
17	Burkina Faso		1		1	2
	Uganda		1		1	2
19	Libya		1		1	1
20	Guinea		1			
		29	29	29	54	99

KEY
G = Gold (winners) • S = Silver (runners-up) • B = Bronze (semi-finalists) • F = appearances in the final • SF = appearances in the semi-final

FOOTBALL TOURNAMENT OF THE AFRICAN GAMES

Year	Host Country	Winners	Score	Runners-up	Venue
1965	Congo	Congo	0-0 †	Mali	Brazzaville
1973	Nigeria	Nigeria	2-0	Guinea	Lagos
1978	Algeria	Algeria	1-0	Nigeria	Algiers
1987	Kenya	Egypt	1-0	Kenya	Nairobi
1991	Egypt	Cameroon	1-0	Tunisia	Cairo
1995	Zimbabwe	Egypt	3-1	Zimbabwe	Harare
1999	South Africa	Cameroon	0-0 4-3p	Zambia	Johannesburg
2003	Nigeria	Cameroon	2-0	Nigeria	Abuja
2007	Algeria	Cameroon	1-0	Guinea	Algiers
2011	Mozambique	Ghana	1-1 4-2p	South Africa	Maputo

† Decided on number of corner-kicks awarded. Congo won 7-2

FOOTBALL TOURNAMENT OF THE AFRICAN GAMES MEDALS TABLE

	Country	G	S	B
1	Cameroon	4		1
2	Egypt	2		1
3	Nigeria	1	2	2
4	Ghana	1		2
5	Algeria	1		
	Congo	1		
7	Guinea		2	
8	South Africa		1	1
	Tunisia		1	1
10	Kenya		1	
	Mali		1	
	Zambia		1	
	Zimbabwe		1	
14	Côte d'Ivoire			1
	Mali			1
		10	10	10

COSAFA CUP

Year	Host Country	Winners	Score	Runners-up	Venue
1997	Home and away	Zambia	1-1	Namibia	Windhoek
1998	Home and away	Zambia	1-0	Zimbabwe	Harare
1999	Home and away	Angola	1-0 1-1	Namibia	Luanda & Windhoek
2000	Home and away	Zimbabwe	3-0 3-0	Lesotho	Maseru & Bulawayo
2001	Home and away	Angola	0-0 1-0	Zimbabwe	Luanda & Harare
2002	Home and away	South Africa	3-1 1-0	Malawi	Blantyre & Durban
2003	Home and away	Zimbabwe	2-1 2-0	Malawi	Blantyre & Harare
2004	Home and away	Angola	0-0 5-4p	Zambia	Lusaka
2005	Home and away	Zimbabwe	1-0	Zambia	Mafikeng
2006	Home and away	Zambia	2-0	Angola	Lusaka
2007	Home and away	South Africa	0-0 4-3p	Zambia	Bloemfontein
2008	South Africa	South Africa	2-1	Mozambique	Thulamahashe
2009	Zimbabwe	Zimbabwe	3-1	Zambia	Harare

COSAFA CUP MEDALS TABLE

	Country	G	S	B
1	Zimbabwe	4	2	
2	Zambia	3	4	2
3	Angola	3	1	1
4	South Africa	3		2
5	Namibia		2	

COSAFA CUP MEDALS TABLE (CONT'D)

	Country	G	S	B
6	Malawi		2	1
7	Mozambique		1	3
8	Lesotho		1	
9	Botswana			2
	Swaziland			2
		13	13	13

CECAFA CUP

Year	Host Country	Winners	Score	Runners-up	Venue
1973	Uganda	Uganda	2-1	Tanzania	
1974	Tanzania	Tanzania	1-1 5-3p	Uganda	
1975	Zambia	Kenya	0-0 5-4p	Malawi	
1976	Zanzibar	Uganda	2-0	Zambia	
1977	Somalia	Uganda	0-0 5-3p	Zambia	
1978	Malawi	Malawi	3-2	Zambia	
1979	Kenya	Malawi	3-2	Kenya	
1980	Sudan	Sudan	1-0	Tanzania	
1981	Tanzania	Kenya	1-0	Tanzania	
1982	Uganda	Kenya	1-1 5-3p	Uganda	
1983	Kenya	Kenya	1-0	Zimbabwe	
1984	Uganda	Zambia	0-0 3-0p	Malawi	Kampala
1985	Zimbabwe	Zimbabwe	2-0	Kenya	Rufaro, Harare
1986	Sudan	Not held			
1987	Ethiopia	Ethiopia	1-1 5-4p	Zimbabwe	
1988	Malawi	Malawi	3-1	Zambia	
1989	Kenya	Uganda	3-3 2-1	Malawi	Nyayo, Nairobi
1990	Zanzibar	Uganda	2-0	Sudan	
1991	Uganda	Zambia	2-0	Kenya	Kampala
1992	Tanzania	Uganda	1-0	Tanzania	Mwanza
1993	Uganda	Not held			
1994	Kenya	Tanzania	2-2 4-3p	Uganda	Nairobi
1995	Uganda	Zanzibar	1-0	Uganda	
1996	Sudan	Uganda	1-0	Sudan	
1997		Not held			
1998	Rwanda	Not held			
1999	Rwanda	Rwanda B	3-1	Kenya	Amahoro, Kigali
2000	Uganda	Uganda	2-0	Uganda B	Nakivubo, Kampala
2001	Rwanda	Ethiopia	2-1	Kenya	Amahoro, Kigali
2002	Tanzania	Kenya	3-2	Tanzania	Memorial, Arusha
2003	Sudan	Uganda	2-0	Rwanda	Khartoum
2004	Ethiopia	Ethiopia	3-0	Burundi	Addis Abeba
2005	Rwanda	Ethiopia	1-0	Rwanda	Amahoro, Kigali
2006	Ethiopia	Zambia	0-0 11-10p	Sudan	Addis Abeba
2007	Tanzania	Sudan	2-2 4-2p	Rwanda	Dar es Salaam
2008	Uganda	Uganda	1-0	Kenya	Kampala
2009	Kenya	Uganda	2-0	Rwanda	Nairobi
2010	Tanzania	Tanzania	1-0	Côte d'Ivoire	Dar es Salaam
2011	Tanzania	Uganda	2-2 3-2p	Rwanda	Dar es Salaam
2012	Uganda	Uganda	2-1	Kenya	Kampala

CECAFA CUP MEDALS TABLE

	Country	G	S	B
1	Uganda	13	5	7
2	Kenya	5	7	8
3	Ethiopia	4		1
4	Tanzania	3	5	4
5	Malawi	3	3	4
6	Sudan	3	2	3
7	Zambia	2	5	4
8	Rwanda	1	5	4
9	Zimbabwe	1	2	1
10	Zanzibar	1		4
11	Burundi		1	
12	Côte d'Ivoire B		1	
		36	36	40

COUPE CEMAC

Year	Host Country	Winners	Score	Runners-up	Venue
2003	Congo	Cameroon	3-2	Central African Rep.	Brazzaville
2005	Gabon	Cameroon	1-0	Chad	Libreville
2006	Equat. Guinea	Equatorial Guinea	1-1 4-2p	Cameroon	Bata
2007	Chad	Congo	1-0	Gabon	N'Djamena
2008	Cameroon	Cameroon	3-0	Congo	Yaounde
2009	Cent'l African Rep	Central African Rep.	3-0	Equatorial Guinea	Bangui
2010	Congo	Congo	1-1 9-8p	Cameroon	Brazzaville

COUPE CEMAC MEDALS TABLE

	Country	G	S	B
1	Cameroon	3	2	
2	Congo	2	1	1
3	Central African Republic	1	1	2
4	Equatorial Guinea	1	1	
5	Chad		1	2
6	Gabon		1	2
		7	7	7

COPA AMILCAR CABRAL

Year	Host Country	Winners	Score	Runners-up	Venue
1979	Guinea-Bissau	Senegal	1-0	Mali	Bissau
1980	Gambia	Senegal	1-0	Gambia	Banjul
1981	Mali	Guinea	0-0 6-5p	Mali	Bamako
1982	Cape Verde	Guinea	3-0	Senegal	Praia
1983	Mauritania	Senegal	3-0	Guinea-Bissau	Nouakchott
1984	Sierra Leone	Senegal	0-0 5-3p	Sierra Leone	Freetown
1985	Gambia	Senegal	1-0	Gambia	Banjul
1986	Senegal	Senegal	3-1	Sierra Leone	Dakar
1987	Guinea	Guinea	1-0	Mali	Conakry
1988	Guinea-Bissau	Guinea	3-2	Mali	Bissau
1989	Mali	Mali	3-0	Guinea	Bamako
1991	Senegal	Senegal	1-0	Cape Verde Islands	Dakar
1993	Sierra Leone	Sierra Leone	2-0	Senegal	Freetown
1995	Mauritania	Sierra Leone	0-0 4-2p	Mauritania	Nouakchott
1997	Gambia	Mali	1-0	Senegal	Banjul
2000	Cape Verde	Cape Verde Islands	1-0	Senegal	Praia
2001	Mali	Senegal	3-1	Gambia	Bamako
2005	Guinea	Guinea	1-0	Senegal	Conakry
2007	Guinea-Bissau	Mali	2-1	Cape Verde Islands	Bissau

COPA AMILCAR CABRAL MEDALS TABLE

	Country	G	S	B
1	Senegal	8	5	4
2	Guinea	5	1	4
3	Mali	3	4	6
4	Sierra Leone	2	2	1
5	Cape Verde Islands	1	2	2
6	Gambia		3	2
7	Guinea-Bissau		1	
8	Mauritania		1	
		19	19	19

AFRICAN CLUB TOURNAMENTS

CAF CHAMPIONS LEAGUE

Year	Winners	Country	Score	Country	Runners-up
1965	Oryx Douala	CMR	2-1	MLI	Stade Malien
1966	Stade Abidjan	CIV	1-3 4-1	MLI	AS Real Bamako
1967	Tout Puissant Englebert	COD	1-1 2-2	GHA	Asante Kotoko
1968	Tout Puissant Englebert	COD	5-0 1-4	TOG	Etoile Filante
1969	Al Ismaili	EGY	2-2 3-1	COD	Tout Puissant Englebert
1970	Asante Kotoko	GHA	1-1 2-1	COD	Tout Puissant Englebert
1971	Canon Yaoundé	CMR	0-3 2-0 1-0	GHA	Asante Kotoko
1972	Hafia FC Conakry	GUI	4-2 3-2	UGA	Simba FC
1973	AS Vita Kinshasa	COD	2-4 3-0	GHA	Asante Kotoko
1974	CARA Brazzaville	CGO	4-2 2-1	EGY	Mehalla Al Kubra
1975	Hafia FC Conakry	GUI	1-0 2-1	NGA	Enugu Rangers
1976	Mouloudia d'Algiers	ALG	3-0 0-3 4-1p	GUI	Hafia FC Conakry
1977	Hafia FC Conakry	GUI	1-0 3-2	GHA	Hearts of Oak
1978	Canon Yaoundé	CMR	0-0 2-0	GUI	Hafia FC Conakry
1979	Union Douala	CMR	0-1 1-0 5-3p	GHA	Hearts of Oak
1980	Canon Yaoundé	CMR	2-2 3-0	COD	AS Bilima
1981	JE Tizi-Ouzou	ALG	4-0 1-0	COD	AS Vita Kinshasa
1982	Al Ahly Cairo	EGY	3-0 1-1	GHA	Asante Kotoko
1983	Asante Kotoko	GHA	0-0 1-0	EGY	Al Ahly Cairo
1984	Zamalek	EGY	2-0 1-0	NGA	Shooting Stars
1985	FAR Rabat	MAR	5-2 1-1	COD	AS Bilima
1986	Zamalek	EGY	2-0 0-2 4-2p	CIV	Africa Sports
1987	Al Ahly Cairo	EGY	0-0 2-0	SUD	Al Hilal
1988	Entente Setif	ALG	0-1 4-0	NGA	Iwuanyanwu Owerri
1989	Raja Casablanca	MAR	1-0 0-1 4-2p	ALG	Mouloudia d'Oran
1990	JS Kabylie	ALG	1-0 0-1 5-3p	ZAM	Nkana Red Devils
1991	Club Africain	TUN	5-1 1-1	UGA	Nakivubo Villa
1992	Wydad Casablanca	MAR	2-0 0-0	SUD	Al Hilal
1993	Zamalek	EGY	0-0 0-0 7-6p	GHA	Asante Kotoko
1994	Espérance Tunis	TUN	0-0 3-1	EGY	Zamalek
1995	Orlando Pirates	RSA	2-2 1-0	CIV	ASEC Mimosas
1996	Zamalek	EGY	1-2 2-1 4-2p	NGA	Shooting Stars
1997	Raja Casablanca	MAR	0-1 1-0 5-4p	GHA	Obuasi Goldfields
1998	ASEC Mimosas	CIV	0-0 4-1	ZIM	Dynamos
1999	Raja Casablanca	MAR	0-0 0-0 4-3p	TUN	Espérance Tunis
2000	Hearts of Oak	GHA	2-1 3-1	TUN	Espérance Tunis
2001	Al Ahly Cairo	EGY	1-1 3-0	RSA	Mamelodi Sundowns
2002	Zamalek	EGY	0-0 1-0	MAR	Raja Casablanca
2003	Enyimba	NGA	2-0 0-1	EGY	Al Ismaili
2004	Enyimba	NGA	1-2 2-1 5-3p	TUN	Etoile du Sahel
2005	Al Ahly Cairo	EGY	0-0 3-0	TUN	Etoile du Sahel
2006	Al Ahly Cairo	EGY	1-1 1-0	TUN	CS Sfaxien
2007	Etoile du Sahel	TUN	0-0 3-1	EGY	Al Ahly Cairo
2008	Al Ahly Cairo	EGY	2-0 2-2	CMR	Cotonsport
2009	TP Mazembe	COD	1-2 1-0	NGA	Heartland
2010	TP Mazembe	COD	5-0 1-1	TUN	Espérance Tunis
2011	Espérance Tunis	TUN	0-0 1-0	MAR	Wydad Casablanca
2012	Al Ahly Cairo	EGY	1-1 2-1	TUN	Espérance Tunis

CAF CHAMPIONS LEAGUE MEDALS TABLE

	Country	G	S	B	F	SF
1	Egypt	13	5	9	18	27
2	Congo DR	5	5	6	10	16
3	Morocco	5	2	3	7	8
4	Cameroon	5	1	6	6	12
5	Tunisia	4	7	4	11	13
6	Algeria	4	1	5	5	10
7	Ghana	3	8	6	11	15
8	Guinea	3	2	3	5	8
9	Nigeria	2	5	11	7	18
10	Côte d'Ivoire	2	2	6	4	9
11	South Africa	1	1	1	2	3
12	Congo	1			1	1

CAF CHAMPIONS LEAGUE MEDALS TABLE (CONT'D)

	Country	G	S	B	F	SF
13	Sudan		2	4	2	6
14	Mali		2	1	2	3
	Uganda		2	1	2	3
16	Zambia		1	6	1	7
17	Togo		1	3	1	4
18	Zimbabwe		1	1	1	1
19	Senegal			5		5
20	Ethiopia			2		2
	Kenya			2		2
22	Angola			1	1	1
	Libya			1		1
	Tanzania			1		1
		48	48	88	96	176

CAF CHAMPIONS LEAGUE MEDALS TABLE

	Club		G	S	B
1	Al Ahly Cairo	EGY	7	2	3
2	Zamalek	EGY	5	1	2
3	TP Mazembe	COD	4	2	3
4	Hafia FC Conakry	GUI	3	2	
5	Raja Casablanca	MAR	3	1	1
6	Canon Yaoundé	CMR	3		2
7	Asante Kotoko	GHA	2	5	3
8	Esperance Tunis	TUN	2	4	3
9	Jeunesse Sportive Kabylie	ALG	2		3
10	Enyimba	NGA	2		2
11	Hearts of Oak	GHA	1	2	1
12	Etoile du Sahel	TUN	1	2	
13	ASEC Mimosas	CIV	1	1	5
14	Ismaily	EGY	1	1	3
15	AS Vita Club Kinshasa	COD	1	1	1
16	Wydad Casablanca	MAR	1	1	
17	FAR Rabat	MAR	1		2
18	Oryx Douala	CMR	1		1
	Union Douala	CMR	1		1
20	CARA Brazzaville	CGO	1		
	Mouloudia Alger	ALG	1		
	Club Africain	TUN	1		
	Entente Setif	ALG	1		
	Orlando Pirates	RSA	1		
	Stade Abidjan	CIV	1		
26	Al Hilal	SUD		2	4
27	Heartland Owerri	NGA		2	2
28	AS Bilima	COD		2	
	Shooting Stars	NGA		2	
30	Nkana Red Devils	ZAM		1	5
31	Enugu Rangers	NGA		1	3
32	Dynamos	ZIM		1	1
	Ghazl Al Mehalla	EGY		1	1
	Mouloudia Oran	ALG		1	1
	CS Sfaxien	TUN		1	1
36	Africa Sports	CIV		1	

CAF CHAMPIONS LEAGUE MEDALS TABLE (CONT'D)

	Club		G	S	B
	Cotonsport	CMR		1	
	Etoile Filante	TOG		1	
	Nakivubo Villa	UGA		1	
	AS Real Bamako	MLI		1	
	Obuasi Goldfields	GHA		1	
	Mamelodi Sundowns	RSA		1	
	Simba FC	UGA		1	
	Stade Malien	MLI		1	
45	US Goree	SEN			2
	AS Kaloum Star	GUI			2
	Lomé I	TOG			2
	Jeanne d'Arc	SEN			2
49	Bendel Insurance	NGA			1
	Kenya Breweries	KEN			1
	Cotton Club	ETH			1
	ASC Diaraf	SEN			1
	Djoliba AC	MLI			1
	Express FC	UGA			1
	Great Olympics	GHA			1
	DC Motema Pembe	COD			1
	Al Ittihad	LBY			1
	Kakimbo FC	GUI			1
	Kano Pillars	NGA			1
	AFC Leopards	KEN			1
	Leopard Douala	CMR			1
	FC Lupopo	COD			1
	Mufulira Wanderers	ZAM			1
	Petro Atlético	ANG			1
	Real Republicans	GHA			1
	St. Georges	ETH			1
	Semassi Sokode	TOG			1
	SC Simba	TAN			1
	Sunshine Stars	NGA			1
	Stationery Stores	NGA			1
	Tonnerre Yaoundé	CMR			1
	USM Alger	ALG			
			48	48	88

CAF CUP WINNERS' CUP

Year	Winners	Country	Score	Country	Runners-up
1975	Tonnerre Yaoundé	CMR	1-0 4-1	CIV	Stella Abidjan
1976	Shooting Stars	NGA	4-1 0-1	CMR	Tonnerre Yaoundé
1977	Enugu Rangers	NGA	4-1 1-1	CMR	Canon Yaoundé
1978	Horoya AC Conakry	GUI	3-1 2-1	ALG	MA Hussein-Dey
1979	Canon Yaoundé	CMR	2-0 6-0	KEN	Gor Mahia
1980	TP Mazembe	COD	3-1 1-0	CIV	Africa Sports
1981	Union Douala	CMR	2-1 0-0	NGA	Stationery Stores
1982	Al Mokaoulum	EGY	2-0 2-0	ZAM	Power Dynamos
1983	Al Mokaoulum	EGY	1-0 0-0	TOG	Agaza Lomé
1984	Al Ahly Cairo	EGY	1-0 0-1 4-2p	CMR	Canon Yaoundé
1985	Al Ahly Cairo	EGY	2-0 0-1	NGA	Leventis United
1986	Al Ahly Cairo	EGY	3-0 0-2	GAB	AS Sogara
1987	Gor Mahia	KEN	2-2 1-1	TUN	Espérance Tunis
1988	CA Bizerte	TUN	0-0 1-0	NGA	Ranchers Bees
1989	Al Merreikh	SUD	1-0 0-0	NGA	Bendel United
1990	BCC Lions	NGA	3-0 1-1	TUN	Club Africain
1991	Power Dynamos	ZAM	2-3 3-1	NGA	BCC Lions
1992	Africa Sports	CIV	1-1 4-0	BDI	Vital'O
1993	Al Ahly Cairo	EGY	1-1 1-0	CIV	Africa Sports
1994	DC Motema Pembe	COD	2-2 3-0	KEN	Kenya Breweries
1995	JS Kabylie	ALG	1-1 2-1	NGA	Julius Berger
1996	Al Mokaoulum	EGY	0-0 4-0	COD	Sodigraf
1997	Etoile du Sahel	TUN	2-0 0-1	MAR	FAR Rabat
1998	Espérance Tunis	TUN	3-1 1-1	ANG	Primeiro Agosto
1999	Africa Sports	CIV	1-0 1-1	TUN	Club Africain
2000	Zamalek	EGY	4-1 0-2	CMR	Canon Yaoundé
2001	Kaiser Chiefs	RSA	1-1 1-0	ANG	Inter Luanda
2002	Wydad Casablanca	MAR	1-0 1-2	GHA	Asante Kotoko
2003	Etoile du Sahel	TUN	0-2 3-0	NGA	Julius Berger

Discontinued after the 2003 tournament and replaced by the CAF Confederation Cup

CUP WINNERS CUP MEDALS TABLE

	Country	G	S	B	F	SF
1	Egypt	8		6	8	14
2	Tunisia	4	3	2	7	9
3	Nigeria	3	7	4	10	14
4	Cameroon	3	4	3	7	10
5	Côte d'Ivoire	2	3	2	5	7
6	Congo DR	2	1	2	3	5
7	Kenya	1	2	2	3	5
8	Algeria	1	1	4	2	6
9	Morocco	1	1	2	2	4
10	Zambia	1	1	2	2	4
11	Guinea	1		2	1	3
	Sudan	1		2	1	3
	South Africa	1		2	1	3
14	Angola		2		2	2
15	Ghana		1	2	1	3

CUP WINNERS CUP MEDALS TABLE (CONT'D)

	Country	G	S	B	F	SF
16	Burundi		1	1	1	2
	Gabon		1	1	1	2
	Togo		1	1	1	2
19	Libya			3		3
20	Burkina Faso			2		2
	Congo			2		2
	Mali			2		2
	Mozambique			2		2
	Reunion			2		2
25	Benin			1		1
	Madagascar			1		1
	Rwanda			1		1
	Senegal			1		1
	Zimbabwe			1		1
		29	29	58	58	116

CUP WINNERS CUP MEDALS TABLE

	Club		G	S	B
1	Al Ahly Cairo	EGY	4		
2	Mokawloon	EGY	3		1
3	Africa Sports	CIV	2	2	1
4	Etoile du Sahel	TUN	2		
5	Canon Yaoundé	CMR	1	3	1
6	Gor Mahia	KEN	1	1	1
7	BCC Lions	NGA	1	1	
	Power Dynamos	ZAM	1	1	
	Tonnerre Yaoundé	CMR	1	1	
	Esperance Tunis	TUN	1	1	
11	Horoya AC Conakry	GUI	1		2
	Al Merreikh	SUD	1		2
	Wydad Casablanca	MAR	1		2
14	Daring Club Motema Pembe	COD	1		1
	Shooting Stars	NGA	1		1
	Zamalek	EGY	1		1
17	CA Bizerte	TUN	1		
	Enugu Rangers	NGA	1		
	Jeunesse Sportive Kabylie	ALG	1		
	Kaiser Chiefs	RSA	1		
	TP Mazembe	COD	1		
	Union Douala	CMR	1		
23	Club Africain	TUN		2	1
24	Julius Berger	NGA		2	
25	NA Hussein-Dey	ALG		1	1
	Agaza Lomé	TOG		1	1
	Bendel Insurance	NGA		1	1
28	Asante Kotoko	GHA		1	
	FAR Rabat	MAR		1	
	Inter Clube	ANG		1	
	Kenya Breweries	KEN		1	
	Leventis United	NGA		1	
	Primeiro de Agosto	ANG		1	
	Ranchers Bees	NGA		1	
	Sodigraf	COD		1	
	AS Sogara	GAB		1	
	Stationery Stores	NGA		1	
	Stella Abidjan	CIV		1	
	Vital'O	BDI		1	

CUP WINNERS CUP MEDALS TABLE (CONT'D)

	Club		G	S	B
40	Djoliba AC	MLI			2
	Kadiogo	BFA			2
	Mufulira Wanderers	ZAM			2
	St Louisienne	REU			2
44	Abiola Babes	NGA			1
	APR FC	RWA			1
	ASEC Mimosas	CIV			1
	CR Belouizdad	ALG			1
	BFV FC	MAD			1
	Blackpool	ZIM			1
	Diamant Yaoundé	CMR			1
	Dragons de l'Ouème	BEN			1
	Al Ahly Tripoli	LBY			1
	Al Ittihad	EGY			1
	Al Ittihad	LBY			1
	Al Nasr	LBY			1
	CS Hammam-Lif	TUN			1
	Hearts of Oak	GHA			1
	Inter Club	CGO			1
	Inter Star	BDI			1
	Ismaily	EGY			1
	ASC Jeanne d'Arc	SEN			1
	Jomos Cosmos	RSA			1
	El Kanemi Warriors	NGA			1
	Kumbo Strikers	CMR			1
	AFC Leopards	KEN			1
	Mansoura	EGY			1
	Al Masry	EGY			1
	Desportivo Maputo	MOZ			1
	Maxaquene	MOZ			1
	Mbilinga	GAB			1
	Orlando Pirates	RSA			1
	AS Police	CGO			1
	Sekondi Hasaacas	GHA			1
	Entente Setif	ALG			1
	USM Alger	ALG			1
	AS Vita Club Kinshasa	COD			1
			29	29	58

CAF CUP

Year	Winners	Country	Score	Country	Runners-up
1992	Shooting Stars	NGA	0-0 3-0	UGA	Nakivubo Villa
1993	Stella Abidjan	CIV	0-0 2-0	TAN	SC Simba
1994	Bendel Insurance	NGA	0-1 3-0	ANG	Primeiro de Maio
1995	Etoile du Sahel	TUN	0-0 2-0	GUI	Kaloum Star
1996	Kawkab Marrakech	MAR	1-3 2-0	TUN	Etoile du Sahel
1997	Esperance Tunis	TUN	0-1 2-0	ANG	Petro Atlético
1998	CS Sfaxien	TUN	1-0 3-0	SEN	ASC Jeanne d'Arc
1999	Etoile du Sahel	TUN	1-0 1-2	MAR	Wydad Casablanca
2000	JS Kabylie	ALG	1-1 0-0	EGY	Al Ismaili
2001	JS Kabylie	ALG	1-2 1-0	TUN	Etoile du Sahel
2002	JS Kabylie	ALG	4-0 0-1	CMR	Tonnerre Youndé
2003	Raja Casablanca	MAR	2-0 0-0	CMR	Cotonsport Garoua

Discontinued after the 2003 tournament and replaced by the CAF Confederation Cup

CAF CUP MEDALS TABLE

	Country	G	S	B	F	SF
1	Tunisia	4	2	2	6	8
2	Algeria	3			3	3
3	Morocco	2	1		3	3
4	Nigeria	2		3	2	5
5	Côte d'Ivoire	1		3	1	4
6	Cameroon		2	2	2	4
7	Angola		2	1	2	3
8	Egypt		1	2	1	3
9	Tanzania		1	1	1	2
	Uganda		1	1	1	2
11	Guinea		1		1	1
	Senegal		1		1	1
13	Congo DR			2		2
14	Congo			1		1
	Ethiopia			1		1
	Kenya			1		1
	Mozambique			1		1
	Reunion			1		1
	Sudan			1		1
	Zambia			1		1
		12	12	24	24	48

CAF CUP MEDALS TABLE

	Club		G	S	B
1	JS Kabylie	ALG	3		
2	Etoile du Sahel	TUN	2	2	
3	Bendel Insurance	NGA	1		
	Espérance Tunis	TUN	1		
	Kawkab AC Marrakech	MAR	1		
	CS Sfaxien	TUN	1		
	Raja Casablanca	MAR	1		
	Shooting Stars	NGA	1		
	Stella Club Abidjan	CIV	1		
10	Cotonsport	CMR		1	1
11	Ismaily	EGY		1	
	Jeanne d'Arc	SEN		1	
	AS Kaloum	GUI		1	
	Nakivubo Villa	UGA		1	
	Petro Atlétco	ANG		1	
	Primeiro de Maio	ANG		1	
	Simba SC	TAN		1	
	Tonnerre Yaoundé	CMR		1	
	Wydad Casablanca	MAR		1	
20	Africa Sports	CIV			1
	Atletico Sport Aviacao	ANG			1
	CA Bizerte	TUN			1

CAF CUP MEDALS TABLE (CONT'D)

Club		G	S	B
Canon Yaoundé	CMR			1
Club Africain	TUN			1
DC Motema Pembe	COD			1
Enugu Rangers	NGA			1
Ferroviarrio Maputo	MOZ			1
Insurance	ETH			1
Inter Club	CGO			1
Iwuanyanwu Nationale	NGA			1
Jasper United	NGA			1
Kampala CC	UGA			1
Kenya Breweries	KEN			1
Malindi	TAN			1
Al Masry	EGY			1
El Mourada	SUD			1
Nchanga Rangers	ZAM			1
Saint Denis	REU			1
Satelitte	CIV			1
Stade Abidjan	CIV			1
AS Vita Kinshasa	COD			1
Zamalek	EGY			1
		12	12	24

CAF CONFEDERATION CUP

Year	Winners	Country	Score	Country	Runners-up
2004	Hearts of Oak	GHA	1-1 1-1 8-7p	GHA	Asante Kotoko
2005	FAR Rabat	MAR	0-1 3-0	NGA	Dolphin Port Harcourt
2006	Etoile du Sahel	TUN	1-1 0-0	MAR	FAR Rabat
2007	CS Sfaxien	TUN	4-2 1-0	SUD	Al Merreikh
2008	CS Sfaxien	TUN	0-0 2-2	TUN	Etoile du Sahel
2009	Stade Malien	MLI	0-2 2-0 3-2p	ALG	Entente Sétif
2010	FUS Rabat	MAR	0-0 3-2	TUN	CS Sfaxien
2011	Maghreb Fès	MAR	0-1 1-0 6-5p	TUN	Club Africain
2012	AC Léopards	CGO	2-2 2-1	MLI	Djoliba

CAF CONFEDERATION CUP MEDALS TABLE

	Country	G	S	B	F	SF
1	Tunisia	3	3		6	2
2	Morocco	3	1		4	2
3	Ghana	1	1		2	
	Mali	1	1		2	2
5	Congo	1			1	1
6	Sudan		1	3	1	3
7	Nigeria		1	2	1	2
8	Algeria		1		1	1
9	Egypt			1		1
	Libya			1		1
	Angola			1		1
		9	9	8	18	16

CAF CONFEDERATION CUP MEDALS TABLE

	Club		G	S	B
1	CS Sfaxien	TUN	2	1	
2	FAR Rabat	MAR	1	1	
	Etoile du Sahel	TUN	1	1	
4	FUS Rabat	MAR	1		
	Hearts of Oak	GHA	1		
	AC Léopards	CGO	1		
	Maghreb Fès	MAR	1		
	Stade Malien	MLI	1		
9	Al Merreikh	SUD		1	1
10	Asante Kotoko	GHA		1	
	Club Africain	TUN		1	
	Djoliba	MLI		1	
	Dolphin	NGA		1	
	Entente Sétif	ALG		1	
15	Al Hilal	SUD			2
16	Bayelsa United	NGA			1
	ENPPI	EGY			1
	InterClube	ANG			1
	Al Ittihad	LBY			1
	Sunshire Stars	NGA			1
			9	9	8

CECAFA CLUB CHAMPIONSHIP

Year	Winners	Country	Score	Country	Runners-up
1974	Simba SC	TAN	1-0 †	KEN	Abaluhya FC
1975	Young Africans	TAN	2-0	TAN	Simba SC
1976	Luo Union	KEN	2-1	TAN	Young Africans
1977	Luo Union	KEN	2-1	SOM	Horsed
1978	Kamapala City Council	UGA	0-0 3-2p	TAN	Simba SC
1979	Abaluhya FC	KEN	1-0	UGA	Kampala City Council
1980	Gor Mahia	KEN	3-2	KEN	Abaluhya FC
1981	Gor Mahia	KEN	1-0	TAN	Simba SC
1982	AFC Leopards	KEN	1-0	ZIM	Rio Tinto
1983	AFC Leopards	KEN	2-1	MWI	Admarc Tigers
1984	AFC Leopards	KEN	2-1	KEN	Gor Mahia
1985	Gor Mahia	KEN	2-0	KEN	AFC Leopards
1986	Al Merreikh	SDN	2-2 4-2p	TAN	Young Africans
1987	Nakivubo Villa	UGA	1-0	SDN	Al Merreikh
1988	Kenya Breweries	KEN	2-0	SDN	Al Merreikh
1989	Kenya Breweries	KEN	3-0	TAN	Coastal Union
1990	Not held				
1991	Simba SC	TAN	3-0	UGA	Nikivubo Villa
1992	Simba SC	TAN	1-1 5-4p	TAN	Young Africans
1993	Young Africans	TAN	2-1	UGA	Nakivubo Villa
1994	Al Merreikh	SDN	2-1	UGA	Express FC
1995	Simba SC	TAN	1-1 5-3p	UGA	Express FC
1996	Simba SC	TAN	1-0	RWA	APR FC
1997	AFC Leopards	KEN	1-0	KEN	Kenya Breweries
1998	Rayyon Sport	RWA	2-1	ZAN	Mlandege
1999	Young Africans	TAN	1-1 4-1p	UGA	SC Villa
2000	Tusker FC	KEN	3-1	RWA	APR FC
2001	Tusker FC	KEN	0-0 3-0p	KEN	Oserian
2002	Simba SC	TAN	1-0	BDI	Prince Louis
2003	SC Villa	UGA	1-0	TAN	Simba SC
2004	APR FC	RWA	3-1	KEN	Ulinzi Stars
2005	SC Villa	UGA	3-0	RWA	APR FC
2006	Police FC	UGA	2-1	TAN	Moro United
2007	APR FC	RWA	2-1	UGA	URA Kampala
2008	Tusker	KEN	2-1	UGA	URA Kampala
2009	ATRACO	RWA	1-0	SDN	Al Merreikh
2010	APR FC	RWA	2-0	ETH	Saint George
2011	Young Africans	TAN	1-0	TAN	Simba SC
2012	Young Africans	TAN	2-0	TAN	Azam

CECAFA CLUB CUP MEDALS TABLE

	Country	G	S
1	Kenya	15	7
2	Tanzania	11	11
3	Uganda	5	8
4	Rwanda	5	3
5	Sudan	2	3
6	Burundi		1
	Ethiopia		1
	Malawi		1
	Somalia		1
	Zanzibar		1
	Zimbabwe		1
		38	38

CECAFA CLUB CUP MEDALS TABLE

	Club		G	S
1	Simba SC	TAN	6	5
2	AFC Leopards	KEN	5	3
	Young Africans	TAN	5	3
4	Gor Mahia	KEN	5	1
	Tusker	KEN	5	1
6	APR FC	RWA	3	3
	SC Villa	UGA	3	3
8	Al Merreikh	SDN	2	3
9	Kampala CC	UGA	1	1
10	ATRACO	RWA	1	
	Police FC	UGA	1	
	Rwanda	RWA	1	
13	Express FC	UGA		2

CECAFA CLUB CUP MEDALS TABLE

	Club		G	S
	URA Kampala	UGA		2
15	ADMARC Tigers	MWI		1
	Azam	TAN		1
	Coastal Union	TAN		1
	Horsed	SOM		1
	Mlandege	TAN		1
	Moro United	TAN		1
	Oserian	KEN		1
	Prince Louis	BDI		1
	Rio Tinto	ZIM		1
	Saint George	ETH		1
	Ulinzi Stars	KEN		1
			38	38

AFRICAN YOUTH TOURNAMENTS

AFRICAN U-20 CHAMPIONSHIP

Year	Host Country	Winners	Score	Runners-up	Venue
1979		Algeria	2-1 2-3	Guinea	Algiers, Conakry
1981		Egypt	1-1 2-0	Cameroon	Douala, Cairo
1983		Nigeria	2-2 2-1	Côte d'Ivoire	Abidjan, Lagos
1985		Nigeria	1-1 2-1	Tunisia	Tunis, Lagos
1987		Nigeria	2-1 3-0	Togo	Lomé, Lagos
1989		Nigeria	2-1 2-0	Mali	Bamako, Lagos
1991	Egypt	Egypt	2-1	Côte d'Ivoire	Cairo
1993	Mauritius	Ghana	2-0	Cameroon	Bellevue
1995	Nigeria	Cameroon	4-0	Burundi	Lagos
1997	Morocco	Morocco	1-0	South Africa	Meknès
1999	Ghana	Ghana	1-0	Nigeria	Accra
2001	Ethiopia	Angola	2-0	Ghana	Addis Abeba
2003	Burkina Faso	Egypt	4-3	Côte d'Ivoire	Ouagadougou
2005	Benin	Nigeria	2-0	Egypt	Cotonou
2007	Congo	Congo	1-0	Nigeria	Brazzaville
2009	Rwanda	Ghana	2-0	Cameron	Kigali
2011	South Africa	Nigeria	3-2	Cameroon	Johannesburg

Played as a U-21 championship from 1979-2001

AFRICAN U-20 CHAMPIONSHIP MEDALS TABLE

	Country	G	S	B
1	Nigeria	6	2	4
2	Egypt	3	1	3
3	Ghana	3	1	1
4	Cameroon	1	4	1
5	Algeria	1		3
6	Morocco	1		1
7	Angola	1		
	Congo	1		
9	Côte d'Ivoire		3	3
10	Mali		1	1
	Guinea		1	1
12	South Africa		1	
	Tunisia		1	
	Togo		1	
	Burundi		1	
16	Ethiopia			2
17	Somalia			1
	Benin			1
	Gambia			1
		17	17	23

AFRICAN U-17 CHAMPIONSHIP

Year	Host Country	Winners	Score	Runners-up	Venue
1995	Mali	Ghana	3-1	Nigeria	Bamako
1997	Botswana	Egypt	1-0	Mali	Gaborone
1999	Guinea	Ghana	3-1	Burkina Faso	Conakry
2001	Seychelles	Nigeria	3-0	Burkina Faso	Victoria
2003	Swaziland	Cameroon	1-0	Sierra Leone	Mbabane
2005	Gambia	Gambia	1-0	Ghana	Bakau
2007	Togo	Nigeria	1-0	Togo	Lome
2009	Algeria	Gambia	3-1	Algeria	Algiers
2011	Rwanda	Burkina Faso	2-1	Rwanda	Kigali

AFRICAN U-17 CHAMPIONSHIP MEDALS TABLE

	Country	G	S	B
1	Ghana	2	1	2
2	Nigeria	2	1	1
3	Gambia	2		
4	Burkina Faso	1	2	1
5	Cameroon	1		
	Egypt	1		
7	Mali		1	2
8	Algeria		1	
	Rwanda		1	
	Sierra Leone		1	
	Togo		1	
12	Côte d'Ivoire			1
	Congo			1
	Guinea			1
		9	9	9

AFRICAN WOMEN'S TOURNAMENTS

CAF AFRICAN WOMEN'S CHAMPIONSHIP

Year	Host Country	Winners	Score	Runners-up	Venue
1991		Nigeria	2-0 4-0	Cameroon	
1995		Nigeria	4-1 7-1	South Africa	
1998	Nigeria	Nigeria	2-0	Ghana	Abeokuta
2000	South Africa	Nigeria	2-0	South Africa	Johannesburg
2002	Nigeria	Nigeria	2-0	Ghana	Lagos
2004	South Africa	Nigeria	5-0	Cameroon	Johannesburg
2006	Nigeria	Nigeria	1-0	Ghana	Warri
2008	Equatorial Guinea	Equatorial Guinea	2-1	South Africa	Malabo
2010	South Africa	Nigeria	4-2	Equatorial Guinea	Daveyton
2012	Equatorial Guinea	Equatorial Guinea	4-0	South Africa	Malabo

CAF AFRICAN WOMEN'S CHAMPIONSHIP MEDALS TABLE

	Country	G	S	B
1	Nigeria	8		1
2	Equatorial Guinea	2	1	
3	South Africa		4	2
4	Ghana		3	3
5	Cameroon		2	2
6	Angola			1
7	Congo DR			1
8	Guinea			1
	Zambia			1
		10	10	12

WOMEN'S FOOTBALL TOURNAMENT OF THE AFRICAN GAMES

Year	Host Country	Winners	Score	Runners-up	Venue
2003	Nigeria	Nigeria	1-0	South Africa	Abuja
2007	Algeria	Nigeria	4-0	South Africa	Algiers
2011	Mozambique	Cameroon	1-0	Ghana	Maputo

CAF AFRICAN WOMEN'S CHAMPIONSHIP MEDALS TABLE

	Country	G	S	B
1	Nigeria	2		
2	Cameroon	1		1
3	South Africa		2	
4	Ghana		1	1
5	Algeria			1
		3	3	3

AFRICAN U-20 CUP OF NATIONS FOR WOMEN

Year	Host Country	Winners	Score	Runners-up	Venue
2002	Home & away	Nigeria	6-0 3-2	South Africa	
2004	Home & away	Nigeria	1-0 0-0	South Africa	
2006	Home & away	Nigeria & Congo DR			
2008	Home & away	Nigeria		Congo DR	
2010	Home & away	Nigeria & Ghana			
2012	Home & away	Nigeria & Ghana			

AFRICAN U-17 CUP OF NATIONS FOR WOMEN MEDALS TABLE

	Country	G	S	B
1	Nigeria	6		
2	Ghana	2		1
3	Congo DR	1	1	3
4	South Africa		2	2
5	Equatorial Guinea			2
6	Central African Republic			1
	Morocco			1
	Tunisia			1
		9	3	11

AFRICAN U-17 CUP OF NATIONS FOR WOMEN

Year	Host Country	Winners	Score	Runners-up	Venue
2008	Home & Away	Nigeria	4-2 0-1	Ghana	
2010	Home & Away	Nigeria & Ghana			
2012	Home & Away	Nigeria/Ghana/Gambia			

AFRICAN U-17 CUP OF NATIONS FOR WOMEN MEDALS TABLE

	Country	G	S	B
1	Nigeria	3		
2	Ghana	2	1	
3	Gambia	1		
4	Cameroon			1
5	South Africa			1
		6	1	2

CAF AFRICA CUP OF NATIONS EQUATORIAL GUINEA/GABON 2012

Qualifying groups

Group A	Pl	W	D	L	F	A	Pts		MLI	CPV	ZIM	LBR
Mali	6	3	1	2	9	6	10			3-0	1-0	2-1
Cape Verde Isl	6	3	1	2	7	7	10		1-0		2-1	4-2
Zimbabwe	6	2	2	2	7	5	8		2-1	0-0		3-0
Liberia	6	1	2	3	7	12	5		2-2	1-0	1-1	

Group B	Pl	W	D	L	F	A	Pts		GUI	NGA	ETH	MAD
Guinea	6	4	2	0	13	5	14			1-0	1-0	4-1
Nigeria	6	3	2	1	12	5	11		2-2		4-0	2-0
Ethiopia	6	2	1	3	8	13	7		1-4	2-2		4-2
Madagascar	6	0	1	5	4	14	1		1-1	0-2	0-1	

Group C	Pl	W	D	L	F	A	Pts		ZAM	LBY	MOZ	COM
Zambia	6	4	1	1	11	2	13			0-0	3-0	4-0
Libya	6	3	3	0	6	1	12		1-0		1-0	3-0
Mozambique	6	2	1	3	4	6	7		0-2	0-0		3-0
Comoros	6	0	1	5	2	14	1		1-2	1-1	0-1	

Group D	Pl	W	D	L	F	A	Pts		MAR	CTA	ALG	TAN
Morocco	6	3	2	1	8	2	11			0-0	4-0	3-1
C. African Rep	6	2	2	2	5	5	8		0-0		2-0	2-1
Algeria	6	2	2	2	5	8	8		1-0	2-0		1-1
Tanzania	6	1	2	3	6	9	5		0-1	2-1	1-1	

Group E	Pl	W	D	L	F	A	Pts		SEN	CMR	COD	MRI
Senegal	6	5	1	0	16	2	16			1-0	2-0	7-0
Cameroon	6	3	2	1	12	5	11		0-0		1-1	5-0
Congo DR	6	2	1	3	10	11	7		2-4	2-3		3-0
Mauritius	6	0	0	6	2	22	0		0-2	1-3	1-2	

Group F	Pl	W	D	L	F	A	Pts		BFA	GAM	NAM
Burkina Faso	4	3	1	0	12	3	10			3-1	4-0
Gambia	4	1	1	2	5	6	4		1-1		3-1
Namibia	4	1	0	3	3	11	3		1-4	1-0	

Group G	Pl	W	D	L	F	A	Pts		NIG	RSA	SLE	EGY
Niger	6	3	0	3	6	8	9			2-1	3-1	1-0
South Africa	6	2	3	1	4	2	9		2-0		0-0	1-0
Sierra Leone	6	2	3	1	5	5	9		1-0	0-0		2-1
Egypt	6	1	2	3	5	5	5		3-0	0-0	1-1	

Group H	Pl	W	D	L	F	A	Pts		CIV	RWA	BDI	BEN
Cote d'Ivoire	6	6	0	0	19	4	18			3-0	2-1	2-1
Rwanda	6	2	0	4	5	15	6		0-5		3-1	0-3
Burundi	6	1	2	3	7	9	5		0-1	3-1		1-1
Benin	6	1	2	3	8	11	5		2-6	0-1	1-1	

Group I	Pl	W	D	L	F	A	Pts		GHA	SUD	CGO	SWZ
Ghana	6	5	1	0	13	1	16			0-0	3-1	2-0
Sudan	6	4	1	1	8	3	13		0-2		2-0	3-0
Congo	6	2	0	4	5	10	6		0-3	0-1		3-1
Swaziland	6	0	0	6	2	14	0		0-3	1-2	0-1	

Group J	Pl	W	D	L	F	A	Pts		ANG	UGA	KEN	GNB
Angola	6	4	0	2	7	5	12			2-0	1-0	1-0
Uganda	6	3	2	1	6	2	11		3-0		0-0	2-0
Kenya	6	2	2	2	4	4	8		2-1	0-0		2-1
Guinea-Bissau	6	1	0	5	2	8	3		0-2	0-1	1-0	

Group K	Pl	W	D	L	F	A	Pts		BOT	TUN	MWI	TOG	CHA
Botswana	8	5	2	1	7	3	17			1-0	0-0	2-1	1-0
Tunisia	8	4	2	2	14	6	14		0-1		2-2	2-0	5-0
Malawi	8	2	6	0	13	8	12		1-0			1-0	6-2
Togo	8	1	3	4	6	10	6		1-0	1-2	1-1		0-0
Chad	8	0	3	5	7	20	3		0-1	1-3	2-2	2-2	

Final Tournament first Round Group Stage

	Pl	W	D	L	F	A	Pts	EQG	LBY	SEN
Zambia	3	2	1	0	5	3	7	1-0	2-2	2-1
Equat'l Guinea	3	2	0	1	3	2	6		1-0	2-1
Libya	3	1	1	1	4	4	4			2-1
Senegal	3	0	0	3	3	6	0			

	Pl	W	D	L	F	A	Pts	SUD	ANG	BFA
Côte d'Ivoire	3	3	0	0	5	0	9	1-0	2-0	2-0
Sudan	3	1	1	1	4	4	4		2-2	2-1
Angola	3	1	1	1	4	5	4			2-1
Burkina Faso	3	0	0	3	2	6	0			

	Pl	W	D	L	F	A	Pts	TUN	MAR	NIG
Gabon	3	3	0	0	6	2	9	1-0	3-2	2-0
Tunisia	3	2	0	1	4	3	6		2-1	2-1
Morocco	3	1	0	2	4	5	3			1-0
Niger	3	0	0	3	1	5	0			

	Pl	W	D	L	F	A	Pts	MLI	GUI	BOT
Ghana	3	2	1	0	4	1	7	2-0	1-1	1-0
Mali	3	2	0	1	3	3	6		1-0	2-1
Guinea	3	1	1	1	7	3	4			6-1
Botswana	3	0	0	3	2	9	0			

Gabon and Equatorial Guinea qualified automatically as hosts • Togo were initially refused entry but were later re-admitted

NATIONAL TOURNAMENTS IN AFRICA 2012

CAF AFRICA CUP OF NATIONS EQUATORIAL GUINEA/GABON 2012

Quarter-finals		Semi-finals		Final	
Zambia	3				
Sudan	0				
		Zambia	1		
		Ghana	0		
Tunisia	1				
Ghana	2				
				Zambia	0 8p
				Côte d'Ivoire	0 7p
Mali	1 5p				
Gabon	1 4p				
		Mali	0		
		Côte d'Ivoire	1		
Equatorial Guinea	0				
Côte d'Ivoire	3				

Top scorers (qualifiers and finals): **7** - Cheick **DIABATE** MLI; Didier **DROGBA** CIV; Issam **JEMAA** TUN & **MANUCHO** ANG • **6** - Christopher **KATONGO** ZAM & Emmanuel **MAYUKA** ZAM • **5** - Mamadou **NIANG** MLI; Jerome **RAMATLHAKWANE** BOT; Moussa **SOW** SEN & Alain **TRAORE** BFA

QUALIFYING GROUP A

		Pl	W	D	L	F	A	Pts	MLI	CPV	ZIM	LBR
Mali	MLI	6	3	1	2	9	6	10		3-0	1-0	2-1
Cape Verde Islands	CPV	6	3	1	2	7	7	10	1-0		2-1	4-2
Zimbabwe	ZIM	6	2	2	2	7	5	8	2-1	0-0		3-0
Liberia	LBR	6	1	2	3	7	12	5	2-2	1-0	1-1	

ESTADIO DA VAREZA, PRAIA
4-09-2010, Ref: Benouza ALG

Cape Verde Islands	1
Mali	0

CPV - Tony Varela [44]

CPV: FOCK - Dario FURTADO, Nando NEVES, VARELA, STOPIRA, Ronny SOUTO, Marco SOARES, Elvis BABANCO (ZE LUIS), Vitor MORENO, DADY (Tony VARELA), LITO (HELDON). Tr: Lucio ANTUNES

MLI: Oumar SISSOKO - Adama COULIBALY, Bekaye DABO (Souleymane KEITA), Drissa DIAKITE, Amadou SIDIBE (Mustapha YATABARE), Ousmane BERTHE, Adama TAMBOURA, Mahamadou DIARRA, Sambou YATABARE (Ismael KEITA), Modibo MAIGA, Mamadou SAMASSA. Tr: Alain GIRESSE

NATIONAL COMPLEX, PAYNESVILLE
5-09-2010, Codjia BEN

Liberia	1
Zimbabwe	1

LBR -Oliseh [68] • ZIM - Musona [30]

LBR: Sunday SEAH - George BAYSAH, Jimmy DIXON, Solomon GRIMES, Emmanuel WENNAH, David GBEMIE (Theo WEEKS LEWIS 46), Steven MENNOH, Sekou OLISEH, Anthony LAFFOR, Isaac PUPO (Perry KOLLIE 85), Patrick DOEPLAH (James Koko LOMELL 60). Tr: Bertalan BICSKEI

ZIM: Washington ARUBI - Method MWANJALI, Thomas Langu SWESWE, Onismor BHASERA, Noel KASEKE, Justice MAJABVI, Ashley RAMBANAPASI (Lionel MTIZWA 79), Clemence MATAWU (Benjamin MARARE 86), Tafadzwa RUSIKE, Edward SADOMBA, Knowledge MUSONA (Nyasha MUSHEKWI 74).

STADE 26 MARS, BAMOKO
9-10-2010, Djaoupe TOG

Mali	2
Liberia	1

MLI - Abdou Traore [2], OG [51] • LBR - Weeks [42]

MLI: Oumar SISSOKO - Adama COULIBALY, Drissa DIAKITE, Adama TAMBOURA, Kalifa Cisse, Mahamadou DIARRA, Kalilou TRAORE, Abdou TRAORE, Modibo MAIGA (Mamadou SAMASSA 67), Mohamed TRAORE (Dramane TRAORE 83), Sigamary DIARRA (Mustapha YATABARE 55). Tr: Alain GIRESSE

LBR: Sunday SEAH (Saylee SWEN 45) - Jimmy DIXON, Gizzie DORBOR, Solomon GRIMES, Alex KARMO, Ben TEEKLOH (Francis DOE 70), Steven MENNOH, Theo WEEKS LEWIS, Sekou OLISEH, Anthony LAFFOR, Amadiya RENNIE (Patrick DOEPLAH 82). Tr: Bertalan BICSKEI

RUFARO, HARARE
10-10-2010, Ref: Ndume GAB

Zimbabwe	0
Cape Verde Islands	0

ZIM: Washington ARUBI - Method MWANJALI, Thomas Langu SWESWE, Onismor BHASERA, Noel KASEKE, Justice MAJABVI, Esrom NYANDORO, Clemence MATAWU (Nyasha MUSHEKWI 58), Tafadzwa RUSIKE, BENJANI (Edward SADOMBA 65), Knowledge MUSONA (Vuza NYONI 89). Tr: Tom SAINTFIET

CPV: Ernesto SOARES - Dario FURTADO (SIDNEI 63), Nando NEVES, Jose TAVARES DA MOURA, VARELA, Tony VARELA, Marco SOARES, Elvis BABANCO, Vitor MORENO, DADY (Ryan MENDES 71), LITO. Tr: Lucio ANTUNES

ESTADIO DA VAREZA, PRAIA
26-03-2011, Ref: Lemghaifry MTN

Cape Verde Islands	4
Liberia	2

CPV - Heldon 2 [14 45], Babanco [25], Odair Fortes [53] • LBR - Wleh [38], Keita [85]

CPV: FOCK - GEGE, Nando NEVES, VARELA, STOPIRA, Ronny SOUTO, Tony VARELA, Elvis BABANCO (SIDNEI 62), Odair FORTES (FABIO SILVA 83), HELDON (Ryan MENDES 76), LITO. Tr: Lucio ANTUNES

LBR: Sunday SEAH (Saylee SWEN 60) - Myers GARLO, Christopher GBANDI, Patrick GERHARDT (Leon POWER 55), Solomon GRIMES, Dennis TEAH, Solomon WESSEH, Alseny KEITA (James ROBERTS 88), Anthony LAFFOR, William JEBOR, Patrick WLEH. Tr: Roberto LANDI

STADE 26 MARS, BAMOKO
26-03-2011, Ref: Gassama GAM

Mali	1
Zimbabwe	0

MLI - Diabate [24]

MLI: Soumbeila DIAKITE - Drissa DIAKITE, Ousmane BERTHE, Abdoulaye MAIGA, Adama TAMBOURA, Kalilou TRAORE, Mahamadou DIARRA, Mahamane TRAORE (Sambou YATABARE 72), Cheick DIABATE, Modibo MAIGA (Abdou TRAORE 46), Tenema N'DIAYE (Samba SOW 68). Tr: Alain GIRESSE

ZIM: Tapuwa KAPINI - Method MWANJALI, Thomas Langu SWESWE, Guthrie ZHOKINYU, Vuza NYONI, Khama BILLIAT (Ovidy KARURU 70), Justice MAJABVI (Archieford GUTU 65), Tinashe NENGOMASHA, Benjamin MARARE (Denver MUKAMBA 45), Edward SADOMBA, Nyasha MUSHEKWI. Tr: Norman MAPEZA

RUFARO, HARARE
5-06-2011, Ref: Bennett RSA

Zimbabwe	2
Mali	1

ZIM - Musona 2 [45 90p] • MLI - Mahamane Traore [50]

ZIM: Tapuwa KAPINI - Method MWANJALI, Thomas Langu SWESWE, Gilbert MAPEMBA, Vuza NYONI, Khama BILLIAT, Justice MAJABVI (Willard KATSANDE 63), Tinashe NENGOMASHA, Ovidy KARURU, Nyasha MUSHEKWI (Edward SADOMBA 73), Knowledge MUSONA. Tr: Norman MAPEZA

MLI: Soumbeila DIAKITE - Mohamed FOFANA (Abdoulaye MAIGA 46), Cedric KANTE, Adama TAMBOURA, Ismael KEITA (Mahamadou DIARRA 63), Kalilou TRAORE, Bakaye TRAORE, Abdou TRAORE, Mahamane TRAORE, Cheick DIABATE (Tenema N'DIAYE 76), Modibo MAIGA. Tr: Alain GIRESSE

NATIONAL COMPLEX, PAYNESVILLE
5-06-2011, Ref: Lamptey GHA

Liberia	1
Cape Verde Islands	0

LBR - Doe [31]

LBR: Nathaniel SHERMAN (Louis CRAYTON 35) - Solomon GRIMES, Dennis TEAH, George GEBRO, Ben TEEKLOH (Solomon WESSEH 85), Alseny KEITA, Sekou OLISEH, Anthony LAFFOR, Joe NAGBE, Isaac PUPO (Zah KRANGAR 74), Francis DOE. Tr: Roberto LANDI

CPV: FOCK - GEGE, Nando NEVES, NHAMBU (Dario FURTADO 60), VARELA, STOPIRA (SIDNEI 76), Ronny SOUTO, Elvis BABANCO, Odair FORTES, HELDON, LITO (Ryan MENDES 60). Tr: Lucio ANTUNES

STADE 26 MARS, BAMOKO
3-09-2011, Ref: Diatta SEN

Mali	3
Cape Verde Islands	0

MLI - Diabate 2 [27 30], Mahamane Traore [50]

MLI: Soumbeila DIAKITE - Adama COULIBALY, Cedric KANTE, Drissa DIAKITE ◆ 90, Adama TAMBOURA, Kalilou TRAORE, Seydou KEITA, Abdou TRAORE (Mohamed FOFANA), Bakaye TRAORE (Samba SOW), Mahamane TRAORE (Sidy KONE), Cheick DIABATE. Tr: Alain GIRESSE

CPV: FOCK - GEGE, Nando NEVES, NIVALDO, VARELA, Ronny SOUTO (Dario FURTADO), Guy RAMOS (VALDO), Elvis BABANCO, Odair FORTES (Ryan MENDES), DADY, HELDON. Tr: Lucio ANTUNES

RUFARO, HARARE
4-09-2011, Ref: Benouza ALG

Zimbabwe	3
Liberia	0

ZIM - Katsande [16], Karuru [45], Billiat [85]

ZIM: Tapuwa KAPINI - Method MWANJALI (Archieford GUTU 80), Daniel VHEREMU, Gilbert MAPEMBA, Vuza NYONI, Khama BILLIAT, Tinashe NENGOMASHA (Lincoln ZVASIYA 64), Ovidy KARURU, Edward SADOMBA, Quincy ANTIPAS (Tafadzwa RUSIKE 35), Willard KATSANDE. Tr: Norman MAPEZA

LBR: Nathaniel SHERMAN - Solomon GRIMES, Dennis TEAH, Solomon WESSEH, George GEBRO, Alseny KEITA, Dulee JOHNSON (Samuel THOMPSON 87), Sekou OLISEH, Anthony LAFFOR (Patrick WLEH 61), Isaac PUPO (Ansu TOURE 46), Dioh WILLIAMS. Tr: Roberto LANDI

NATIONAL COMPLEX, PAYNESVILLE
8-10-2011, Ref: Cordier CHA

Liberia	2
Mali	2

LBR - Williams [2], Wleh [92+] • MLI - Diabate [16], Kante [87]

LBR: Nathaniel SHERMAN - Alpha JAMES, Dennis TEAH, Solomon WESSEH, Trokon ZEON, Martin KARNDU, Sekou OLISEH, Ansu TOURE, Dioh WILLIAMS, Patrick WLEH. Tr: Roberto LANDI

MLI: Soumbeila DIAKITE - Adama COULIBALY, Mohamed FOFANA, Cedric KANTE, Adama TAMBOURA, Samba SOW, Kalilou TRAORE, Seydou KEITA, Abdou TRAORE, Mahamane TRAORE, Cheick DIABATE. Tr: Alain GIRESSE

ESTADIO DA VAREZA, PRAIA
8-10-2011, Ref: Lemghaifry MTN

Cape Verde Islands	2
Zimbabwe	1

CPV - Valdo [3], Ryan Mendes [13] • ZIM - Musona [68p]

CPV: Ernesto SOARES - GEGE, Nando NEVES, NIVALDO, VARELA, Ronny SOUTO, Tony VARELA (Guy RAMOS 77), Elvis BABANCO (Dario FURTADO 69), Odair FORTES, VALDO, Ryan MENDES (HELDON 69). Tr: Lucio ANTUNES

ZIM: Tapuwa KAPINI - Method MWANJALI, Thomas Langu SWESWE, Gilbert MAPEMBA, Vuza NYONI, Khama BILLIAT, Tinashe NENGOMASHOA (Cuthbert MALAJILA 80), Ovidy KARURU, Willard KATSANDE, Nyasha MUSHEKWI (Tafadzwa RUSIKE 69), Knowledge MUSONA. Tr: Norman MAPEZA

QUALIFYING GROUP B

		Pl	W	D	L	F	A	Pts	GUI	NGA	ETH	MAD
Guinea	GUI	6	4	2	0	13	5	14		1-0	1-0	4-1
Nigeria	NGA	6	3	2	1	12	5	11	2-2		4-0	2-0
Ethiopia	ETH	6	2	1	3	8	13	7	1-4	2-2		4-2
Madagascar	MAD	6	0	1	5	4	14	1	1-1	0-2	0-1	

ADDIS ABEBA STADIUM
5-09-2010, Ref: Mnkantjo ZIM

Ethiopia	1
Guinea	4

ETH - Umed Ukuri [29] • GUI - Yattara [37], Kalabane [45], Cisse.K [61], Zayatte [75]

ETH: No line up available

GUI: Naby YATTARA - Ousmane BANGOURA, Mamadou DIALLO, Oumar KALABANE, Kamil ZAYATTE, Ibrahima CAMARA, Mamadou BAH, Ibrahima TRAORE, Ibrahima YATTARA (Amadou CISSE), Karamoko CISSE (Mohamed SACKO), Fode MANSARE. Tr: Michel DUSSUYER

UJ ESUENE STADIUM, CALABAR
5-09-2010, Ref: Jedidi TUN

Nigeria	2
Madagascar	0

NGA - Martins [19], Eneramo [45]

NGA: Vincent ENYEAMA - Danny SHITTU, Joseph YOBO, Valentine NWABILI, Chidi ODIAH, Oluwafemi AJILORE (Eneji OTEKPA 54), John Obi MIKEL (Ahmed MUSA 75), Michael ENERAMO (Stanley OKORO 68), Obafemi MARTINS, Peter ODEMWINGIE, Kalu UCHE. Tr: Augustine EGUAVOEN

MAD: Jean Chrysostome RAHARISON - Eric-Julien RAKOTONDRABE, Pascal RAZAKANANTENAINA, Lalaina NOMENJANAHARY, Juvet TSIAROVANA (Jose RAZAFIMANDIMBY 46), Julien LELEU, Paulin VOAVY, Ibrahim AMADA, Faneva Ima ANDRIATSIMA, Faed ARSENE (Tony MAMODALY 60), Dimitri Carlos ZOZIMAR (Carolus ANDRIAMAHITSINORO 74). Tr: Jean-Paul RABIER

MAHAMASINA, ANTANANARIVO
10-10-2010, Ref: Ngossi MWI

Madagascar	0
Ethiopia	1

ETH - Fikru Teferra [56]

MAD: Andriambelomasina KANDY - Eric-Julien RAKOTONDRABE, Mamy RANDRIANARISOA, Pascal RAZAKANANTENAINA (Carolus ANDRIAMAHITSINORO 60), Lalaina NOMENJANAHARY, Edgar NANDRASANA (Johann PAUL 55), Sedera RANDRIAMPARANY, Jose RAZAFIMANDIMBY, Paulin VOAVY, Faneva Ima Andriatsima (Tony MAMODALY 76), Faed ARSENE. Tr: Jean-Paul RABIER

ETH: Jemal SADAT - Mulualem REGASSA, Anwar SIRAJ, Tesfaye BEKELE, Mesfin ASSEFA, Teshome GETU, Ibrahim HUSSEIN, Tesfaye Tafese◆85, Girma ASHENAFI, Lemasse FIKRU, Andualem Nigussie. Tr:

STADE 28 SEPTEMBRE, CONAKRY
10-10-2010, Ref: El Ahrach MAR

Guinea	1
Nigeria	0

GUI - Constant [5]

GUI: Naby YATTARA - Ibrahima BANGOURA, Mamadou DIALLO, Oumar KALABANE, Kamil ZAYATTE, Ibrahima CAMARA (Mohamed SACKO 90), Mamadou BAH, Kevin CONSTANT (Habib BALDE 77), Ibrahima YATTARA (Ibrahima TRAORE 72), Karamoko CISSE, Fode MANSARE. Tr: Michel DUSSUYER

NGA: Vincent ENYEAMA - Ayodele ADELEYE, Joseph YOBO, Chidi ODIAH, Taye TAIWO, Ayila YUSSUF, SUNNY (John OWOERI 60), Victor OBINNA, Michael ENERAMO (Ahmed MUSA 66), Obafemi MARTINS, Kalu UCHE. Tr: Augustine EGUAVOEN

MAHAMASINA, ANTANANARIVO
27-03-2011, Ref: Mpanisi ZAM

Madagascar	1
Guinea	1

MAD - Rajoarimanana [17] • GUI - Bah.M [80]

MAD: Andriambelomasina KANDY - Jimmy RADAFISON, Solo Valery RAKOTOARINOSY, Mamy Gervais RANDRIANARISOA, Pascal RAZAKANANTENAINA, Lalaina NOMENJANAHARY, Tovo RABENANDRASANA (Tsiala Kennedy GANJA 90), Johann PAUL, Claudio RAMIADAMANANA (Edgar NANDRASANA 73), Faed ARSENE (Boto FAGNORENA 82), Yvan Rajoarimanana. Tr: MOSA

GUI: Naby YATTARA, Ibrahima BANGOURA, Boubacar DIALLO, Mamadou BAH 46), Oumar KALABANE, Kamil ZAYATTE, Ibrahima CAMARA, Kevin CONSTANT (Sadio DIALLO 87), Richard SOUMAH, Pascal FEINDOUNO, Karamoko CISSE◆49, Larsen TOURE (Ibrahima YATTARA 46). Tr: Michel DUSSUYER

ABUJA STADIUM, ABUJA
27-03-2011, Jedidi TUN

Nigeria	4
Ethiopia	0

NGA - Utaka 2 [2 53], Ikechwukw Uche 2 [77 90]

NGA: Dele AIYENUGBA - Efe AMBROSE, Joseph YOBO, Chibuzor OKONKWO, Taye TAIWO, Joel OBI (Kalu UCHE 83), John Obi MIKEL, Victor OBINNA, Victor ANICHEBE (Peter ODEMWINGIE 57), Peter UTAKA (Ikechukwu UCHE 69), Ahmed MUSA 70). Tr: Samoson SIASIA

ETH: No line up available

PART THREE – THE CONTINENTAL CONFEDERATIONS

ADDIS ABEBA STADIUM
5-06-2011, Ref:

Ethiopia	2
Nigeria	2

ETH - Salhadin Said 2 [45] [50] • NGA - Uche [27], Yobo [86]

ETH: Yedenakachew KIDANE BEYENE - Butako ABEBAW, Degu DEBEBE, Alula GIRMA MEKONNEN, Aynalem HAILU REDA, Adane GIRMA, Asrat MEGERSA GOBENA, Teshome BEYENE MINYAHILE, Tesfaye TAFESE, Oumed OUKRI, Salaheldin SAID. Tr: Tom SAINTFIET

NGA: Vincent ENYEAMA - Efe AMBROSE, Joseph YOBO, Chibuzor OKONKWO, Taye TAIWO, Joel OBI, John Obi MIKEL, Victor OBINNA (Fegor OGUDE), Ikechukwu UCHE (Victor ANICHEBE), Peter UTAKA (Ekigho EHIOSUN), Ahmed MUSA. Tr: Samson SIASIA

STADE 28 SEPTEMBRE, CONAKRY
5-06-2011, Ref: Codjia BEN

Guinea	4
Madagascar	1

GUI - Kalabane [6], Bngoura.I [17], Diallo.A [60], Habib Balde [62] • MAD - Faed Arsene [24]

GUI: Naby YATTARA - Morlaye CISSE, Oumar KALABANE, Ibrahima DIALLO, Habib BALDE, Mamadou BAH, Mohamed SACKO, Ibrahima TRAORE, PASCAL FEINDOUNO (Sadio DIALLO 46), Ibrahima YATTARA (Sory Ibrahima CONTE 60), Ismael BANGOURA. Tr: Michel DUSSUYER

MAD: Andriambelomasina KANDY - Eric-Julien RAKOTONDRABE, Mamy RANDRIANARISOA, Mamisoa RAZAFINDRAKOTO, Pascal RAZAKANANTENAINA, Edgar NANDRASANA (Jose RAZAFIMANDIMBY 54), Johann PAUL, Claudio RAMIADAMANANA (Boto FAGNORENA 60), Faed ARSENE, Tsiala Kennedy GANJA (Carolus ANDRIAMAHITSINORO 71), Yvan RAJOARIMANANA. Tr: MOSA

MAHAMASINA, ANTANANARIVO
4-09-2011, Ref: Kirwa KEN

Madagascar	0
Nigeria	2

NGA - Yobo [68], Obinna [72]

MAD: Robin Jean Claude RAKOTONIRINA - Urbain ANDRIAMAMPIONONA, Leonard BESABOTSY, Jean BOSCO, Ando MANOELANTSOA, Edgar NANDRASANA, Ferdinand RAMANAMAHEFA, Josoa Razafimahatratra, Jose RAZAFIMANDIMBY, Yvan RAJOARIMANANA, Jean-Jacques RAZANAJAFY. Tr: Franck RAJAONARISAMBA

NGA: Dele AIYENUGBA - Efe AMBROSE, Joseph YOBO, Elderson ECHIEJILE, Chibuzor OKONKWO, Joel OBI (Chinedu OBASI 72), John Obi MIKEL, Victor OBINNA, Victor ANICHEBE, Ikechukwu UCHE (Fegor OGUDE 66), Ahmed MUSA (Emmanuel EMENIKE 46). Tr: Samson SIASIA

STADE 28 SEPTEMBRE, CONAKRY
4-09-2011, Ref: Bennaceur TUN

Guinea	1
Ethiopia	0

GUI - Balde.B [33]

GUI: Naby YATTARA - Dianbobo BALDE, Kamil ZAYATTE, Sory Ibrahima CONTE (Ibrahima YATTARA 80), Ibrahima DIALLO, Habib BALDE, Mamadou BAH, Kevin CONSTANT, Ibrahima TRAORE, Pascal FEINDOUNO (Sadio DIALLO 75), Ismael BANGOURA. Tr: Michel DUSSUYER

ETH: No line up available

ADDIS ABEBA STADIUM
8-10-2011, Ref:

Ethiopia	4
Madagascar	2

ETH - Umed Ukuri [31], Aden Girma [56], Fikru Teferra [59], Shemeles Bekele [73] •
MAD - Razafimandimby [3], Nomenjanahary [57]

ETH: No line up available

MAD: No line up available

ABUJA STADIUM, ABUJA
8-10-2011, Ref: Doue CIV

Nigeria	2
Guinea	2

NGA - Obinna [63], Uche [77] • GUI - Bangoura.I [63], Traore.I [102+]

NGA: Dele AIYENUGBA - Efe AMBROSE, Joseph YOBO, Taye TAIWO, Joel OBI (Ekigho EHIOSUN 67), John Obi MIKEL, Fegor OGUDE, Victor OBINNA, Emmanuel EMENIKE, Chinedu OBASI, Peter ODEMWINGIE (Ikechukwu UCHE 61). Tr: Samson SIASIA

GUI: Naby YATTARA - Dianbobo BALDE, Morlaye CISSE, Kamil ZAYATTE, Ibrahima DIALLO (Alhassan BANGOURA 93+), Mamadou BAH, Kevin CONSTANT, Ibrahima TRAORE, Sadio DIALLO, Pascal FEINDOUNO, Ismael BANGOURA. Tr: Michel DUSSUYER

QUALIFYING GROUP C

		Pl	W	D	L	F	A	Pts	ZAM	LBY	MOZ	COM
Zambia	ZAM	6	4	1	1	11	2	13		0-0	3-0	4-0
Libya	LBY	6	3	3	0	6	1	12	1-0		1-0	3-0
Mozambique	MOZ	6	2	1	3	4	6	7	0-2	0-0		3-0
Comoros	COM	6	0	1	5	2	14	1	1-2	1-1	0-1	

KONKOLA, CHILILABOMBWE
5-09-2010, Ref: Eyob ERI

Zambia	4
Comoros	0

ZAM - Kalaba [5], Tembo [21], Chamanga [30], Mayuka [82]

ZAM: Kennedy MWEENE - Kampamba CHINTU, Joseph MUSONDA, Billy MWANZA, Emmanuel MBOLA, Noah CHIVUTA, Rainford KALABA (Isaac CHANSA 67), Felix KATONGO (Jonas SAKUWAHA 63), Fwayo TEMBO (Emmanuel MAYUKA 70), James CHAMANGA, Christopher KATONGO. Tr: Dario BONETTI

COM: Mahamoud MROIVILI - Mahamoud Ali MCHANGAMA, Damine ABDOULHANIOU, Mohamed MAHAMOUD, Bourhani SOILIHI, Mikikad DAOUD, Mohamed MOEGNI, Ahmed Ali SOILIHI. Tr: Chamite ABDEREMANE

MACHAVA, MAPUTO
5-09-2010, Bangoura GUI

Mozambique	0
Libya	0

MOZ: Joao Raphael KAPANGO - Dario Ivan KHAN, MANO, MEXER, Almiro LOBO, GENITO (Alberto Fanuel MASSINGUE 82), SIMAO, TONY, JUMISSE (MBINHO 68), DOMINGUES, Helder PELEMBE (JOSEMAR 46). Tr: Mart NOOIJ

LBY: Samir ABOUD - Younes AL SHIBANI, Osama CHTIBA, Ali SALAMA, Abdelaziz BELREESH, Mohamed EL MUGHRABY, Marwan MABROUK, Ibrahim EL HAASY, Abdul Nasser SALEEL, Ahmed SAAD OSMAN (Hussein AL IDRISSY 59), Ahmed ZUWAY. Tr: Marcos PAQUETA

STADE SAID CHEIKH, MITSAMIOULI
9-10-2010, Ref: Ibada TAN

Comoros	0
Mozambique	1

MOZ - Josemar [90]

COM: Mahamoud MROIVILI - David HUMBLOT, Mahamoud Ali M'CHANGAMA, Ali RASSOUL, Nadjim ABDOU, Ben Ahmed ATTOUMANI, Youssouf M'CHANGAMA, Aziz M'MADI, Ali M'MADI, Mohamed M'CHANGAMA, Mohamed MOEGNI (Yacine SAANDI 46). Tr: Chamite ABDEREMANE

MOZ: Joao Raphael KAPANGO - CAMPIRA, MANO, Alberto Fanuel MASSINGUE, PAITO (JOSEMAR 46), Almiro LOBO, Momed HAGY, GENITO (Daniel DANILHO 46), SIMAO, DOMINGUES, Antonio Afonso TONY (Jerry SITOE 46). Tr: Mart NOOIJ

CAF AFRICA CUP OF NATIONS 2012

JUNE 11 STADIUM, TRIPOLI
10-10-2010, Ref: Gassama GAM

Libya	1
Zambia	0

LBY - Ahmed Saad Osman [36]

LBY: Samir ABOUD - Younes AL SHIBANI (Omar DAWOOD 82), Osama CHTIBA, Ali SALAMA, Abdelaziz BELREESH, Mohamed EL MUGHRABY, Marwan MABROUK, Ibrahim EL HAASY (Reyad ELLAFI 61), Naser SALIL, Ahmed SAAD OSMAN, Ahmed ZUWAY (Mohamed ZUBYA 89). Tr: Marcos PAQUETA

ZAM: Kennedy MWEENE - Kampamba CHINTU, Joseph MUSONDA, Henry MULENGA (Rodgers KOLA 89), Stophira SUNZU, Noah CHIVUTA, Rainford KALABA, Fwayo TEMBO (Isaac CHANSA 46), James CHAMANGA, Jonas SAKUWAHA (Emmanuel MAYUKA 46), Jacob MULENGA. Tr: Dario BONETTI

MACHAVA, MAPUTO
27-03-2011, Ref: Ramocha BOT

Mozambique	0
Zambia	2

ZAM - Chamanga [15], Mayuka [92+]

MOZ: Joao Raphael KAPANGO - CAMPIRA (Dario Ivan KHAN 46), MANO (MEXER 46), PAITO, Almiro LOBO, GENITO, SIMAO, DOMINGUES, DARIO, Carlos FUMO, MBINHO (Helder PELEMBE 70). Tr: Mart NOOIJ

ZAM: Kennedy MWEENE - Kampamba CHINTU, Joseph MUSONDA, Francis KASONDE, Stophira SUNZU, Noah CHIVUTA (Henry MULENGA 60), Isaac CHANSA, Rainford KALABA, James CHAMANGA (Emmanuel MAYUKA 69), Christopher KATONGO, Collins MBESUMA (Given SINGULUMA 69). Tr: Dario BONETTI

STADE 26 MARS, BAMOKO
28-03-2011, Ref: Diatta SEN

Libya	3
Comoros	0

LBY - Al Khatroushi [20], Abdelkader [70], Mohamed [82]

LBY: Samir ABOUD - Younes AL SHIBANI, Abdelaziz BELREESH (Omar DAWOOD 86), Mohamed EL KHATROUSHI 19), Djamal MOHAMED, Ibrahim EL HAASY (Naser SALIL 86), Tariq Q'TAIT, Abdallah AL SHARIF, Ahmed ABDELKADER, Osama EL FAZZANI. Tr: Marcos PAQUETA

COM: Mahamoud MROIVILI (Mohamed MBALIA 46) - David HUMBLOT, Mahamoud Ali M'CHANGAMA, Kassim AHAMADA, Ben Ahmed ATTOUMANI, Youssouf M'CHANGAMA, Damine ABDOULHANIOU (Djahouari MBELIZI 65), Ali M'MADI, Mogni YOUSSOUF, Kemal BOURHANI, Mohamed M'CHANGAMA. Tr: Chamite ABDEREMANE

NKOLOMA, LUSAKA
4-06-2011, Ref: Ngobi UGA

Zambia	3
Mozambique	0

ZAM - Chris Katongo 2 [47] [68], Mbesuma [86]

ZAM: Kennedy MWEENE - Kampamba CHINTU, Joseph MUSONDA, Thomas NYRIENDA, Francis KASONDE, Stophira SUNZU, Isaac CHANSA, Rainford KALABA, Christopher KATONGO (William NJOVU 90), Emmanuel MAYUKA (Felix KATONGO 83), Collins MBESUMA (Rodgers KOLA 86). Tr: Dario BONETTI

MOZ: Joao Raphael KAPANGO - Dario Ivan KHAN, MANO, Zainadine JUNIOR, PAITO, Almiro LOBO (Jerry SITOE 68), GENITO, WHISKEY, JUMISSE (NELSINHO 88), DOMINGUES, DARIO (TCHITXO 80). Tr: Mart NOOIJ

STADE SAID CHEIKH, MITSAMIOULI
5-06-2011, Ref: Nampiandraza MAD

Comoros	1
Libya	1

COM - Mze Mbaba [83] • LBY - Boussefi [43]

COM: Mohamed Hassani MBALIA - David HUMBLOT, Salim MRAMBOINI, Yacine SAANDI, Ali RASSOUL, Nadjim ABDOU, Ben Ahmed ATTOUMANI, Youssouf M'CHANGAMA, Mogni YOUSSOUF, Mohamed M'CHANGAMA, Abdoulaide MZE MBABA. Tr: Chamite ABDEREMANE

LBY: Mohamed NASHNOUSH - Aziz ABADI, Ahmed AL ALWANI, Younes AL SHIBANI, El MUGHRALY, Mohamed EL MUGHRABY, Naser SALIL, Abdallah AL SHARIF, Tarek AL TAIB, Reyad ELLAFI, Ihaab BOUSSEFI. Tr: Marcos PAQUETA

PETRO SPORT STADIUM, CAIRO
3-09-2011, Ref: Omar EGY

Libya	1
Mozambique	0

LBY - Ellafi [30]

LBY: Samir ABOUD - Ahmed AL ALWANI, Ali SALAMA, Rabie ELLAFI, Mohamed EL MUGHRABY, Moataz BEN AMER (Walid EL KHATROUSHI 66), Mohamed ESNANI, Djamal MOHAMED, Mohamed AL GHANODI, Ahmed SAAD OSMAN, Ahmed ZUWAY. Tr: Marcos PAQUETA

MOZ: Joao Raphael KAPANGO – CAMPIRA, MANO, MEXER, Almiro LOBO, JOSEMAR, SIMAO, DOMINGUES, NELSINHO (Momed HAGY 53). Tr: Mart NOOIJ

STADE SAID CHEIKH, MITSAMIOULI
4-09-2011, Ref: Kagabo RWA

Comoros	1
Zambia	2

COM - Youssouf M'Changama [32] • ZAM - Felix Katongo [23], Mayuka [87]

COM: No line up available

ZAM: Kennedy MWEENE - Joseph MUSONDA, Thomas NYRIENDA (Fwayo TEMBO 46), Henry MULENGA, Francis KASONDE, Stophira SUNZU, Rainford KALABA, Justin ZULU, James CHAMANGA, Christopher KATONGO (Given SINGULUMA 78), Collins MBESUMA (Emmanuel MAYUKA 62). Tr: Dario BONETTI

NCHANGA STADIUM, CHINGOLA
8-10-2011, Ref: Mohamadou CMR

Zambia	0
Libya	0

ZAM: Kennedy MWEENE - Kampamba CHINTU, Joseph MUSONDA, Henry MULENGA, Stophira SUNZU, Isaac CHANSA, Justin ZULU, James CHAMANGA (Fwayo TEMBO 83), Christopher KATONGO, Collins MBESUMA (Emmanuel MAYUKA 65), Jacob MULENGA. Tr: Dario BONETTI

LBY: No line up available

MACHAVA, MAPUTO
8-10-2011, Ref: Nguluwe MWI

Mozambique	3
Comoros	0

MOZ - Maninho [6], Dario [18p], Domingues [39]

MOZ: Joao Raphael KAPANGO - Chico MUCHANGA, Zainadine JUNIOR, Almiro LOBO, Momed HAGY, WHISKEY, MAYUNDA (JOSEMAR 46), Stelio Ernesto TELINHO (Manuelito UETIMANE 83), DOMINGUES, DARIO, MANINHO (REGINALDO 61). Tr: Mart NOOIJ

COM: Mahamoud Mroivili - David Humblot, Mahamoud Ali Mchangama, Kassim Ahamada, Ali Rassoul, Ben Ahmed Attoumani, Ali M'Madi, Said Anfane Boura. Tr: Chamite ABDEREMANE

QUALIFYING GROUP D

		Pl	W	D	L	F	A	Pts	MAR	CTA	ALG	TAN
Morocco	MAR	6	3	2	1	8	2	11		0-0	4-0	3-1
Central African Republic	CTA	6	2	2	2	5	5	8	0-0		2-0	2-1
Algeria	ALG	6	2	2	2	5	8	8	1-0	2-0		1-1
Tanzania	TAN	6	1	2	3	6	9	5	0-1	2-1	1-1	

MUSTAPHA TCHAKER, BLIDA
3-09-2010, Ref: Djaoupe TOG

Algeria	1
Tanzania	1

ALG - Guedioura [44] • TAN - Rajabu [32]

ALG: Rais M'BOLHI - Madjid BOUGHERRA, Rafik HALLICHE (Carl MEDJANI 51), Nadir BELHADJ, Adlene GUEDIOURA, Hassan YEBDA, Ryad BOUDEBOUZ (Djamel ABDOUN 69), Karim ZIANI, Rafik DJEBBOUR, Abdelkader GHEZZAL, Abdelmalek ZIAYA (Chadli AMRI 71). Tr: Rabah SAADANE

TAN: Shaaban HASSAN - Nadir HAROUB, Aggrey MORRIS, Stephano MWASIKA (Jabir STIMA 56), Shadrack NSAJIGWA, Abdi KASSIM, Idrissa RAJABU, Henry Joseph SHINDIKA, Nizar KHALFAN, Danny MRWANDA (Seleman KASSIM 70), Mrisho NGASA. Tr: Jan POULSEN

MOULAY ABDELLAH, RABAT
4-09-2010, Ref: Coulibaly MLI

Morocco	0
Central African Rep	0

MAR: Nadir LAMYAGHRI - Mickael CHRETIEN, Mehdi BENATIA, Chakib BENZOUKANE, Hicham MAHDOUFI, Karim EL AHMADI (Youssouf HADJI 75), Adil HERMACH, Moubarek BOUSSOUFA, Mohamed BERRABEH, Marouane CHAMAKH, Mounir EL HAMDAOUI (Youssef EL ARABI 65). Tr: Dominique CUPERLY

CTA: Geoffrey LEMBET - Audin BOUTOU, Salif KEITA, Therence KETHEVOAMA, Vianney MABIDE, Foxi KETHEVOAMA (Bertrand KEMO 75), Clovis-Franklin ANZITE, Eloge Enza YAMISSI, Romaric LIGNANZI, Hilaire MOMI, Evans KONDOGBIA (Eudes DAGOULOU 71)

BENJAMIN MKAPA, DAR ES SALAAM
9-10-2010, Ref: Seechurn MRI

Tanzania	0
Morocco	1

MAR - El Hamdaoui [42]

TAN: Juma KASEJA - Nadir HAROUB, Aggrey MORRIS, Stephano MWASIKA, Shadrack NSAJIGWA, Shaban NDITI, Idrissa RAJABU (Salum MACHAKU 69), Henry Joseph SHINDIKA (Mohamed BANKA 60), Nizar KHALFAN (John Raphael BOCCO 86), Danny MRWANDA, Mrisho NGASA. Tr: Jan POULSEN

MAR: Nadir LAMYAGHRI - Mehdi BENATIA, Ahmed KANTARI, Mickael CHRETIEN, Adil HERMACH, Rachid SOULAIMANI, Karim EL AHMADI (Abdelmoulla BERRABEH 53), Houssine KHARJA, Moubarek BOUSSOUFA, Marouane CHAMAKH (Youssef EL ARABI 88), Mounir EL HAMDAOUI (Youssouf Hadji 79). Tr: Dominique CUPERLY

BARTHELEMY BOGANDA, BANGUI
10-10-2010, Ref: Carvalho ANG

Central African Rep	2
Algeria	0

CTA - Dopekoulouyen [81], Momi [85]

CTA: Geoffrey LEMBET - Therence KETHEVOAMA, Vianney MABIDE, Eloge Enza YAMISSI, Fernander KASSAI, Clovis-Franklin ANZITE, Romaric LIGNANZI, Foxi KETHEVOAMA (Eudes DAGOULOU 70), David MANGA (Audin BOUTOU 68), Charlie DOPEKOULOUYEN, Hilaire MOMI. Tr: Jules ACCORSI

ALG: Rais M'BOLHI - Madjid BOUGHERRA, Anthar YAHIA, Nadir BELHADJ (Abdelmalek ZIAYA 86), Carl MEDJANI, Djamel MESBAH (Lazhar Hadj AISSA 75), Mehdi LACEN, Hassan YEBDA (Khaled LEMMOUCHIA 72), Djamel ABDOUN, Rafik DJEBBOUR, Abdelkader GHEZZAL. Tr: Abdelhak BEN CHIKHA

BENJAMIN MKAPA, DAR ES SALAAM
26-03-2011, Ref: Kirwa KEN

Tanzania	2
Central African Rep	1

TAN - Nditi [49], Samatta [91+] • CTA - Mabide [13]

TAN: Shaaban HASSAN - Aggrey MORRIS, Shadrack NSAJIGWA, Nurdin BAKARI, Shaban NDITI, Idrissa RAJABU (Stephano MWASIKA 65), Henry Joseph SHINDIKA (Mbwana SAMATTA 65), Mohamed BANKA, John Raphael BOCCO, Mohamed Abdallah MACHUPA, Mrisho NGASA. Tr: Jan POULSEN

CTA: Geoffrey LEMBET - Salif KEITA, Nicaise OZINGONI, Vianney MABIDE, Eloge Enza YAMISSI, Fernander KASSAI, Clovis-Franklin ANZITE, Romaric LIGNANZI, Foxi KETHEVOAMA, David MANGA, Hilaire MOMI. Tr: Jules ACCORSI

STADE 19 MAI, ANNABA
27-03-2011, Ref: Seechurn MRI

Algeria	1
Morocco	0

ALG - Yebda [7p]

ALG: Rais M'BOLHI - Mehdi MOSTEFA, Ismael BOUZID, Anthar YAHIA (Carl MEDJANI 71), Djamel MESBAH, Khaled LEMMOUCHIA, Mehdi LACEN, Abdelkader GHEZZAL, Hassan YEBDA (Lazhar Hadj AISSA 90), Ryad BOUDEBOUZ (Nadir BELHADJ 81), Rafik DJEBBOUR. Tr: Abdelhak BEN CHIKHA

MAR: Nadir LAMYAGHRI - Mickael CHRETIEN, Mehdi BENATIA, Ahmed KANTARI, Rachid SOULAIMANI, Adil HERMACH, Houssine KHARJA, Moubarek BOUSSOUFA, Younes BELHANDA (Oussama ASSAIDI 91), Adel TAARABT (Youssef EL ARABI 71), Marouane CHAMAKH. Tr: Eric GERETS

STADE DE MARRAKECH
4-06-2011, Ref: Doue CIV

Morocco	4
Algeria	0

MAR - Benatia [27], Chamakh [39], Hadji [60], Assaidi [69]

MAR: Nadir LAMYAGHRI - Jamal ALIOUI, Mehdi BENATIA, Abdelhamid EL KAOUTARI, Badr EL KADDOURI, Adil HERMACH (Mohamed CHIHANI 71), Houssine KHARJA, Younes BELHANDA, Youssouf HADJI (Youssef EL ARABI 85), Marouane CHAMAKH, Oussama ASSAIDI (Moubarek BOUSSOUFA 81). Tr: Eric GERETS

ALG: Rais M'BOLHI - Madjid BOUGHERRA, Anthar YAHIA, Djamel MESBAH, Mehdi MOSTEFA, Khaled LEMMOUCHIA, Mehdi LACEN, Hassan YEBDA (Ryad BOUDEBOUZ 46), Karim ZIANI, Foued KADIR (Karim MATMOUR 46), Rafik DJEBBOUR (El Arbi SOUDANI 71). Tr: Abdelhak BEN CHIKHA

BARTHELEMY BOGANDA, BANGUI
5-06-2011, Ref: Alioum CMR

Central African Rep	2
Tanzania	1

CTA - Momi [38], Dopekoulouyen [89] • TAN - Nditi [76]

CTA: No line up available

TAN: Shaaban HASSAN (Shabane DIHILI 46) - Nadir HAROUB, Aggrey MORRIS, Shadrack NSAJIGWA, Nurdin BAKARI, Shaban NDITI, Mwinyi KAZIMOTO (Mohamed Abdallah MACHUPA 46), Idrissa RAJABU, Nizar KHALFAN, John Raphael BOCCO (Mbwana SAMATTA 46), Mrisho NGASA. Tr: Jan POULSEN

BENJAMIN MKAPA, DAR ES SALAAM
3-09-2011, Lemghaifry MTN

Tanzania	1
Algeria	1

TAN - Samatta [22] • ALG - Bouazza [52]

TAN: Juma KASEJA - Aggrey MORRIS, Juma Saidi NYOSO, Amir MAFTAH, Shadrack NSAJIGWA, Shaban NDITI (Idrissa RAJABU 76), Abdi KASSIM, Henry Joseph SHINDIKA, Nizar KHALFAN, Danny MRWANDA (Mrisho NGASA 67), Mbwana SAMATTA. Tr: Jan POULSEN

ALG: Rais M'BOLHI - Madjid BOUGHERRA, Ismael BOUZID, Abdelkader LAIFAOUI, Nadir BELHADJ (Hameur BOUAZZA 46), Carl MEDJANI (Hassan YEBDA 56), Djamel MESBAH, Mehdi LACEN, Karim ZIANI (Abdelkader GHEZZAL 77), Karim MATMOUR, Karim BENYAMINA. Tr: Abdelhak BEN CHIKHA

CAF AFRICA CUP OF NATIONS 2012

BARTHELEMY BOGANDA, BANGUI
4-09-2011, Ref: Jedidi TUN

Central African Rep	0
Morocco	0

CTA: Geoffrey LEMBET - Audin BOUTOU, Manasse Enza YAMISSI, Salif KEITA, Therence KETHEVOAMA, Vianney MABIDE, Clovis-Franklin ANZITE, Romaric LIGNANZI, David MANGA, Charlie DOPEKOULOUYEN (Eudes DAGOULOU 72), Hilaire MOMI. Tr: Jules ACCORSI

MAR: Nadir LAMYAGHRI - Mehdi BENATIA, Abdelhamid EL KAOUTARI, Mickael CHRETIEN, Badr EL KADDOURI, Houssine KHARJA, Younes BELHANDA, Moubarek BOUSSOUFA, Youssef EL ARABI (Mohamed CHIHANI 75), Oussama ASSAIDI (Mounir EL HAMDAOUI 80). Tr: Eric GERETS

STADE DE MARRAKECH
9-10-2011, Ref: Gassama GAM

Morocco	3
Tanzania	1

MAR - Chamakh [20], Taarabt [69], Boussoufa [89] •
TAN - Kassim [40]

MAR: Nadir LAMYAGHRI - Mehdi BENATIA, Abdelhamid EL KAOUTARI, Mickael CHRETIEN, Badr EL KADDOURI, Houssine KHARJA, Younes BELHANDA, Moubarek BOUSSOUFA, Adel TAARABT (Youssef EL ARABI 71), Marouane CHAMAKH (Said FATAH 89), Oussama ASSAIDI (Karim EL AHMADI 85). Tr: Eric GERETS

TAN: Juma KASEJA - Aggrey MORRIS, Erasto NYONI, Juma Saidi NYOSO, Shaban NDITI, Abdi KASSIM, Idrissa RAJABU, Henry Joseph SHINDIKA, Mohamed Abdallah MACHUPA (Mrisho NGASA 66), Danny MRWANDA, Mbwana SAMATTA (John Raphael BOCCO 80). Tr: Jan POULSEN

STADE 5 JUILLET, ALGIERS
9-10-2011, Ref: Fall SEN

Algeria	2
Central African Rep	0

ALG - Yebda [2], Kadir [30]

ALG: Rais M'BOLHI - Madjid BOUGHERRA, Ismael BOUZID, Djamel MESBAH, Mehdi MOSTEFA, Adlene GUEDIOURA, Hocine METREF, Hassan YEBDA (Khaled LEMMOUCHIA 79), Foued KADIR (Kamel GHILAS 85), Karim MATMOUR, Abdelkader GHEZZAL (Rafik DJEBBOUR 72). Tr: Abdelhak BEN CHIKHA

CTA: Prince SAMOLA - Audin BOUTOU, Nicaise OZINGONI, Vianney MABIDE, Eloge Enza YAMISSI, Fernander KASSAI, Clovis-Franklin ANZITE, Romaric LIGNANZI, Mamadi SAOUDI (Manasse Enza YAMISSI 46), Foxi KETHEVOAMA, Hilaire MOMI. Tr: Jules ACCORSI

QUALIFYING GROUP E

		Pl	W	D	L	F	A	Pts	SEN	CMR	COD	MRI
Senegal	SEN	6	5	1	0	16	2	**16**		1-0	2-0	7-0
Cameroon	CMR	6	3	2	1	12	5	**11**	0-0		1-1	5-0
Congo DR	COD	6	2	1	3	10	11	**7**	2-4	2-3		3-0
Mauritius	MRI	6	0	0	6	2	22	**0**	0-2	1-3	1-2	

STADE ANJALAY, BELLE VUE
4-09-2010, Ref: Damon RSA

Mauritius	1
Cameroon	3

MRI - Jonathan Bru [45p] • CMR - Eto'o 2 [39][47], Choupo-Moting [63p]

MRI: Ivahn MARIE-JOSEE - Johan CUNDASAMY, Bassanio DIOLLE, Giullano EDOUARD, Bruno RAVINA, Jonathan BRU, Stephane BADUL, Colin BELL (Christopher BAZERQUE 65), Kervin GODON (Jonathan ERNEST 65), Louis PITHIA, Andy Pierre SOPHIE. Tr: Akbar PATEL

CMR: Guy N'Dy ASSEMBE - Sebastien BASSONG, Benoit ASSOU-EKOTTO, Henri BEDIMO (Eyong ENOH 72), Aurelien CHEDJOU, Nicolas N'KOULOU, Marcel NDJENG (Vincent ABOUBAKAR 62), Jean II MAKOUN, Gilles BINYA, Maxim CHOUPO-MOTING (Henri Bienvenu NTSAMA 80), Samuel ETO'O. Tr: Javier CLEMENTE

STADE MALIBA, LUBUMBASHI
5-09-2010, Ref: Haimoudi ALG

Congo DR	2
Senegal	4

COD - Mihayo [42], Kabungu [71] • SEN - Sow [6], Niang 3 [12][22][57p]

COD: Muteba KIDIABA - Herita ILUNGA, Joel Andre SAMI, Cedric MONGONGU, Kazembe MIHAYO, Mbenza BEDI, Miala NKULUKUTA, Zola MATUMONA, Cedrick MAKIADI (Mulota KABANGU 23), Dieumerci MBOKANI (Yves Diba ILUNGA 70), Dioko KALUYITUKA. Tr: Robert NOUZARET

SEN: Khadim NDIAYE - Omar DAF (Alpha BA 23), Pape DIAKHATE, Kader MANGANE, Boukary DRAME, Issiar DIA (Souleymane CAMARA 70), Remi GOMIS, Mickael TAVARES, Deme N'DIAYE (Guirane N'DAW 77), Mamadou NIANG, Moussa SOW. Tr: Amara TRAORE

STADE ADJIA, GAROUA
9-10-2010, Ref: Maillet SEY

Cameroon	1
Congo DR	1

CMR - OG [54] • COD - Diba Ilunga [37]

CMR: Guy N'Dy ASSEMBE - Sebastien BASSONG, Benoit ASSOU-EKOTTO (Aloys NONG 70), Henri BEDIMO, Aurelien CHEDJOU, Nicolas N'KOULOU, Marcel NDJENG (Georges MANDJECK 83), Gilles BINYA, Eyong ENOH, Vincent ABOUBAKAR, Samuel ETO'O. Tr: Javier CLEMENTE

COD: Muteba KIDIABA - Joel KIMUAKI, Herita ILUNGA, Miala NKULUKUTA, Kazembe MIHAYO, Tiko Tshiolola TSHINYAMA, Zola MATUMONA (Marcel MBAYO 78), Mazowa N'SUMBU (Albert MILAMBO-MUTAMBA 60), Mbenza BEDI, Yves DIBA ILUNGA, Dioko KALUYITUKA (Lomana Tresor LUALUA 75). Tr: Robert NOUZARET

STADE SENGHOR, DAKAR
9-10-2010, Ref: Bennett RSA

Senegal	7
Mauritius	0

SEN - Papiss Cisse 3 [8][38][76], Niang 2 [22][62], Sow [47], OG [90]

SEN: Khadim NDIAYE - Omar DAF, Kader MANGANE, Pape DIAKHATE, Boukary DRAME (Jacques FATY 70), Guirane N'DAW, Papiss CISSE (Demba BA 80), Mickael TAVARES, Deme N'DIAYE (Mame Biram DIOUF 46), Mamadou NIANG, Moussa SOW. Tr: Amara TRAORE

MRI: Yannick MACOA - Johan CUNDASAMY, Christopher BAZERQUE, Bassanio DIOLLE, Viviadeo BOODHUN (Joye ESTAZIE 46), Giullano EDOUARD, Bruno RAVINA, Jonathan BRU, Kervin GODON, Louis PITHIA (Menzy COCO 46), Andy Pierre SOPHIE. Tr: Akbar PATEL

STADE SENGHOR, DAKAR
26-03-2011, Ref: Saadallah TUN

Senegal	1
Cameroon	0

SEN - Demba Ba [92+]

SEN: Khadim NDIAYE - Lamine SANE, Pape DIAKHATE, Kader MANGANE, Omar DAF, Mohamed DIAME, Guirane N'DAW, Papiss Biram DIOUF (Dame N'DOYE 56), Mamadou NIANG (Issiar DIA 82), Moussa SOW, Papiss CISSE (Demba BA 70). Tr: Amara TRAORE

CMR: Idriss KAMENI - Benoit ANGBWA, Stephane M'BIA, Aurelien CHEDJOU, Henri BEDIMO (Maxim CHOUPO-MOTING 61), Benoit ASSOU-EKOTTO, Eyong ENOH, Nicolas N'KOULOU, Landry N'GUEMO (Georges MANDJECK 87), Samuel ETO'O, Achille WEBO (Vincent ABOUBAKAR 75). Tr: Javier CLEMENTE

STADE DES MARTYRS, KINSHASA
27-03-2011, Ref: Wokoma NGA

Congo DR	3
Mauritius	0

COD - LuaLua [28p], Matumona [48], Diba Ilunga [61p]

COD: Muteba KIDIABA - Joel KIMUAKI, Landry MULEMO (Issama MPEKO 46), Patrick ILONGO, Youssuf MULUMBU, Kazembe MIHAYO, Tiko Tshiolola TSHINYAMA (Kiritsho KASUSULA 46), Zola MATUMONA, Mulota KABANGU, Yves DIBA ILUNGA, Lomana Tresor LUALUA (Christian KINKELA 79). Tr: Robert NOUZARET

MRI: No line up available

PART THREE – THE CONTINENTAL CONFEDERATIONS

AHMADOU AHIDJO, YAOUNDE
4-06-2011, Ref: Carvalho ANG

Cameroon	0
Senegal	0

CMR – Idriss KAMENI - Benoit ANGBWA, Stephane M'BIA, Nicolas N'KOULOU, Gaetan BONG, Eyong ENOH, Landry N'GUEMO (Henri BEDIMO 71), Vincent ABOUBAKAR, Maxim CHOUPO-MOTING (Aurelien CHEDJOU 71), Benjamin MOUKANDJO (Achille WEBO 84), Samuel ETO'O. Tr: Javier CLEMENTE

SEN – Bouna COUNDOUL - Lamine SANE♦90, Souleymane DIAWARA, Kader MANGANE (Moustapha BAYAL 83), Cheikh M'BENGUE, Mohamed DIAME (Guirane N'DAW 61), Remi GOMIS, Issiar DIA♦90, Moussa SOW, Mamadou NIANG, Papiss CISSE (Deme N'DIAYE 61). Tr: Amara TRAORE

STADE ANJALAY, BELLE VUE
5-06-2011, Ref: Ngosi MWI

Mauritius	1
Congo DR	2

MRI - Jonathan Bru [11p] • COD - Diba Ilunga [20], Kabungu [45]

MRI – Ivahn MARIE-JOSEE - Johan CUNDASAMY (Westley MARQUETTE 83), Joye ESTAZIE, Almondo FRICAIN, Joel JULES, Bruno RAVINA, Jonathan BRU, Kevin BRU, Jerry LOUIS, Fabien PITHIA, Andy Pierre SOPHIE. Tr: Akbar PATEL

COD – Muteba KIDIABA - Joel KIMUAKI, Herita ILUNGA, Landry MULEMO, Miala NKULUKUTA, Zola MATUMONA, Mbenza BEDI, Mulota KABANGU, Cedrick MAKIADI, Yves DIBA ILUNGA, Dioko KALUYITUKA (Christian KINKELA 73). Tr: Robert NOUZARET

AHMADOU AHIDJO, YAOUNDE
3-09-2011, Ref: Bangoura GUI

Cameroon	5
Mauritius	0

CMR - Kweuke [54], Mbuta [65], Eto'o [70p], N'Guemo [85], Choupo-Moting [93+]

CMR – Idriss KAMENI - Benoit ANGBWA, Henri BEDIMO (Leonard KWEUKE 46), Gaetan BONG, Aurelien CHEDJOU, Nicolas N'KOULOU, Alexandre SONG, Eric DJEMBA-DJEMBA (Landry N'GUEMO 64), Matthew MBUTA, Maxim CHOUPO-MOTING, Samuel ETO'O (Paul Alo'o EFOULOU 86). Tr: Javier CLEMENTE

MRI – Ivahn MARIE-JOSEE - Christopher BAZERQUE, Joye ESTAZIE, Bruno RAVINA, Chandrayah VEERANAH, Jonathan BRU, Stephane BADUL, Jimmy CUNDASAMY, Louis PITHIA, Fabien PITHIA, Gurty CALAMBE. Tr: Akbar PATEL

STADE SENGHOR, DAKAR
3-09-2011, Ref: Doue CIV

Senegal	2
Congo DR	0

SEN - Sow 2 [33] [53]

SEN – Bouna COUNDOUL - Jacques FATY, Kader MANGANE, Souleymane DIAWARA, Cheikh M'BENGUE, Mohamed DIAME, Remi GOMIS (El Hadji Makhtar THIOUNE 76), Papakouly DIOP (Pape DIAKHATE 60), Moussa SOW, Papiss CISSE, Deme N'DIAYE (Diomansy KAMARA 72). Tr: Amara TRAORE

COD – Muteba KIDIABA - Patrick ILONGO, Kazembe MIHAYO, Miala NKULUKUTA, Tiko Tshiolola TSHINYAMA (Patou Ebunga SIMBI 87), Mbenza BEDI (Daniel BAKONGOLIA 67), Mulota KABANGU, Deo KANDA, Joel KIMUAKI, Tresor MPUTU, Kiritsho KASUSULA. Tr: Claude LE ROY

STADE DES MARTYRS, KINSHASA
7-10-2011, Ref: Abdel Rahman SUD

Congo DR	2
Cameroon	3

COD - Kaluyituka [11], Kanda [40] •
CMR - Eto'o [18], Mbuta [75], Choupo-Moting [79]

COD – Thierry EBENGUI - Gladys BOKESE, Cedric MONGONGU (Ilifo ILONGA 20), Issama MPEKO, Kiritsho KASUSULA, Tiko Tshiolola TSHINYAMA (Yves Magola MAPANDA 78), Lema MABIDI (Patrick ILONGO 71), Zola MATUMONA, Deo KANDA, Dioko KALUYITUKA, Tresor MPUTU. Tr: Claude LE ROY

CMR – Idriss KAMENI - Sebastien BASSONG, Gaetan BONG, Nicolas N'KOULOU, Alexandre SONG, Eric DJEMBA-DJEMBA (Matthew MBUTA 70), Landry N'GUEMO, Eyong ENOH, Maxim CHOUPO-MOTING (Dany NOUNKEU 89), Samuel ETO'O (Leonard KWEUKE 80), Benjamin MOUKANDJO. Tr: Javier CLEMENTE

STADE ANJALAY, BELLE VUE
9-10-2011, Ref: Sikazwe ZAM

Mauritius	0
Senegal	2

SEN - N'Doye [9], Papiss Cisse [26]

MRI – Yannick MACOA - Bruno RAVINA, Almondo FRICAIN, Cedric PERMAL, Chandrayah VEERANAH, Colin BELL, Stephane BADUL♦16, Menzy COCO, Ashley LEMINCE (Christopher BAZERQUE 79), Louis PITHIA, Fabien PITHIA (Stephane NABAB 90). Tr: Akbar PATEL

SEN – Bouna COUNDOUL - Lamine SANE, Moustapha BAYAL, Souleymane DIAWARA, Armand TRAORE, Remi GOMIS (Lamine GASSAMA 83), Mohamed DIAME, Dame N'DOYE (Souleymane CAMARA 72), Mamadou NIANG, Diomansy KAMARA, Papiss CISSE (Mame Biram DIOUF 58). Tr: Amara TRAORE

QUALIFYING GROUP F

		Pl	W	D	L	F	A	Pts		BFA	GAM	NAM
Burkina Faso	BFA	4	3	1	0	12	3	10			3-1	4-0
Gambia	GAM	4	1	2	5	6	4		1-1		3-1
Namibia	NAM	4	1	0	3	3	11	3		1-4	1-0	

INDEPENDENCE STADIUM, BAKAU
4-09-2010, Ref: Ragab LBY

Gambia	3
Namibia	1

GAM - Nyassi [10], Momodou Ceesay [12], Jallow [34]
NAM - Risser [91+]

GAM – Pa Dembo TOURAY - Kebba CEESAY, Omar JAWO, Abdou JAMMEH, Pa Saikou KUJABI, Tijan JAITEH, Sainey NYASSI (Dawda BAH 75), Mustapha JARJU, Momodou CEESAY (Njogu DEMBA-NYREN 75), Aziz Corr NYANG (Ebrahima Ibou SAWANEH 80), Ousman JALLOW. Tr: Paul PUT

NAM – Athiel MBAHA - Richard GARISEB, Hartman TOROMBA (Steven GOAXAB 46), Collin BENJAMIN, Sydney PLAATJIES, Oliver RISSER, Quinton JACOBS, Alfred NDYENGE (Wilko RISSER 46), Jamuovandu NGATJIZEKO, Henrico BOTES, Tangeni SHIPAHU (Edwards ASINO 75). Tr: Tom SAINTFIET

STADE DU 4-AOUT, OUAGADOUGOU
9-10-2010, Ref: Osman EGY

Burkina Faso	3
Gambia	1

BFA - Dagano [16], Balima [57], Kabore [69] •
GAM - Momodou Ceesay [75]

BFA – Daouda DIAKITE - Ibrahim GNANOU, Mahamoudou KERE, Bakary KONE, Paul KOULIBALY, Charles KABORE, Saidou PANANDETIGUIRI, Alain TRAORE (Mohamed KOFFI 71), Habib BAMOGO (Wilfred BALIMA 20), Moumouni DAGANO (Aristide BANCE 66), Wilfried SANOU. Tr: Paulo DUARTE

GAM – Pa Dembo TOURAY - Kebba CEESAY, Omar JAWO, Abdou JAMMEH, Pa Saikou KUJABI (Pa Modou JAGNE 54), Tijan JAITEH, Ebrima SOHNA (Kenny MANSALLY 46), Sainey NYASSI, Mustapha JARJU, Aziz Corr NYANG (Momodou CEESAY 46), Ousman JALLOW. Tr: Paul PUT

STADE DU 4-AOUT, OUAGADOUGOU
26-03-2011, Ref: Cordier CHA

Burkina Faso	4
Namibia	0

BFA - Alain Traore 3 [25] [45] [80], OG [73]

BFA – Germain SANOU - Mahamoudou KERE, Bakary KONE, Mamadou TALL (Ibrahim GNANOU 77), Herve Xavier ZENGUE, Charles KABORE (Djakaridja KONE 67), Saidou PANANDETIGUIRI, Alain TRAORE, Jonathan PITROIPA, Moumouni DAGANO, Wilfried SANOU (Abdou TRAORE 72). Tr: Paulo DUARTE

NAM – Athiel MBAHA - Richard GARISEB, Hartman TOROMBA, Collin BENJAMIN (Wilko RISSER 78), Sydney PLAATJIES, Oliver RISSER, Razundara TJIKUZU, Ronald KETJIJERE, Jamuovandu NGATJIZEKO, Henrico BOTES♦65, Rudolph BESTER (Tangeni SHIPAHU 90). Tr: Brian ISAACS

CAF AFRICA CUP OF NATIONS 2012

INDEPENDENCE, WINDHOEK
4-06-2011, Ref: Damon RSA

| Namibia | 1 |
| Burkina Faso | 4 |

NAM - Shipahu [83] • BFA - Abdou Traore [12], Bance [57p], Alain Traore [80], Pitroipa [92+]

NAM: Virgil VRIES - Richard GARISEB, Denzil HAOSEB (Bradley WERMANN 61), Hartman TOROMBA, Sydney PLAATJIES (Jamuovandu NGATJIZEKO 66), Oliver RISSER, Ronald KETJIJERE, Johannes SEIBEB, Jordan HAIMBILI (Sidney URIKHOB 61), Tangeni SHIPAHU, Rudolph BESTER. Tr: Brian ISAACS

BFA: Germain SANOU - Ibrahim GNANOU, Mahamoudou KERE (Jonathan PITROIPA 74), Bakary KONE, Mamadou TALL, Herve Xavier ZENGUE, Charles KABORE, Alain TRAORE, Aristide BANCE, Yahia KEBE, Abdou TRAORE. Tr: Paulo DUARTE

INDEPENDENCE, WINDHOEK
3-09-2011, Ref: Mohamadou CMR

| Namibia | 1 |
| Gambia | 0 |

NAM - Shipahu [83]

NAM: Virgil VRIES - Da Costa ANGULA, Willem MWEDIHANGA, Steven SABATHA, Larry HORAEB, Heinrich ISAACKS, Ronald KETJIJERE, Willy STEPHANUS, Ananias GEBHARDT, Tangeni SHIPAHU, Rudolph BESTER. Tr: Brian ISAACS

GAM: No line up available

INDEPENDENCE STADIUM, BAKAU
8-10-2011, Ref: Saadallah TUN

| Gambia | 1 |
| Burkina Faso | 1 |

GAM - Danso [59] • BFA - Dagano [90]

GAM: Musa CAMARA - Mamadou DANSO, Omar JAWO, Abdou JAMMEH, Pa Modou JAGNE, Tijan JAITEH, Abdou DAMPHA (Ebrima SOHNA 78), Momodou CEESAY, Aziz Corr NYANG, Ousman JALLOW, Demba SAVAGE. Tr: Paul PUT

BFA: Daouda DIAKITE - Ibrahim GNANOU, Mahamoudou KERE (Djakaridja KONE 78), Paul KOULIBALY, Mamadou TALL, Mohamed KOFFI, Florent ROUAMBA, Wilfred BALIMA (Abdou TRAORE 60), Bertrand TRAORE (Aristide BANCE 68), Moumouni DAGANO, Yahia KEBE. Tr: Paulo DUARTE

QUALIFYING GROUP G

		Pl	W	D	L	F	A	Pts	NIG	RSA	SLE	EGY
Niger	NIG	6	3	0	3	6	8	9		2-1	3-1	1-0
South Africa	RSA	6	2	3	1	4	2	9	2-0		0-0	1-0
Sierra Leone	SLE	6	2	3	1	5	5	9	1-0	0-0		2-1
Egypt	EGY	6	1	2	3	5	5	5	3-0	0-0	1-1	

MOMBELA STADIUM, NELSPRUIT
4-09-2010, Ref: Abdel Rahman SDN

| South Africa | 2 |
| Niger | 0 |

RSA - Mphela [12], Parker [45]

RSA: Itumeleng KHUNE - Bongani KHUMALO, Aaron MOKOENA, Anele NGONGCA, Tsepo MASILELA, Macbeth SIBAYA, Thanduyise KHUBONI (Reneilwe LETSHOLONYANE 66), Steven PIENAAR (Teko MODISE 80), Siphiwe TSHABALALA, Katlego MPHELA (Kermit ERASMUS 77), Bernard PARKER. Tr: Pitso MOSIMANE

NIG: Kassaly DAOUDA - Koffi Dan KOWA, Moussa Bonkano DJIBRILLA, Chikoto MOHAMED, Amadou KADER, Jimmy BULUS, Parfait KOUASSI (Souleymane Dela SACKO 63), Idrissa LAOUALI, Alhassane ISSOUFOU, Daouda KAMILOU, Moussa MAAZOU (Karim Lancina KONATE 70). Tr: Harowna DOULLA

CAIRO INTERNATIONAL STADIUM
5Diatta SEN-09-2010, Ref:

| Egypt | 1 |
| Sierra Leone | 1 |

EGY - Fathallah [61] • SLE - Mustapha Bangoura [56]

EGY: Essam EL HADARY - Ahmed EL MOHAMADY, Wael GOMAA, Mahmoud FATHALLAH, Sayed MOAWAD, Ahmed FATHI, Ahmed HASSAN (Amr EL SOULIA 76), GEDO, Mohamed ABOUTRIKA, Ahmed MEKKY (Walid SOLIMAN 51), Ahmed ALI (Ahmed Abdel ZAHER 71). Tr: Hassan SHEHATA

SLE: Christian CAULKER - Ibrahim KARGBO, Umaru BANGURA, Ibrahim KOROMA, Sheriff SUMA, Rodney STRASSER, Samuel BARLAY, Kei KAMARA (David SIMBO 51), Mustapha BANGURA, Albert JARRETT, Mohamed BANGURA. Tr: Christian COLE

SEYNI KOUNTCHE, NIAMEY
10-10-2010, Ref: Doue CIV

| Niger | 1 |
| Egypt | 0 |

NIG - Maazou [34]

NIG: Kassaly DAOUDA - Moussa Bonkano DJIBRILLA, Amadou KADER, Koffi Dan KOWA, Delis AHOU, Idrissa LAOUALI, Karim Lancina KONATE, Boubacar TALATOU, Moussa MAAZOU, Daouda KAMILOU, Alhassane ISSOUFOU (Karim PARAISO 88). Tr: Harowna DOULLA

EGY: Essam EL HADARY - Mahmoud FATHALLAH, Sherif Abdel FADIL, Wael GOMAA, Ahmed EL MOHAMADY, Mohamed Abdel SHAFY, Ahmed FATHI, Hossam GHALY (Walid SOLIMAN 46), Mohamed ABOUTRIKA, Ahmed ALI (Mohamed FADL 46), Amr ZAKI (Ahmed MEKKY 68). Tr: Hassan SHEHATA

NATIONAL STADIUM, FREETOWN
10-10-2010, Ref: Lemghaifry MTN

| Sierra Leone | 0 |
| South Africa | 0 |

SLE: Christian CAULKER (Brima BANGURA 46) - Umaru BANGURA, Ibrahim KARGBO, David SIMBO, Rodney STRASSER, Alfred SANKOH, Samuel BARLAY, Julius WOOBAY, Mustapha BANGURA, Sheriff SUMA, Mohamed BANGURA. Tr: Christian COLE

RSA: Itumeleng KHUNE - Bongani KHUMALO, Aaron MOKOENA, Anele NGONGCA, Tsepo MASILELA, Macbeth SIBAYA, Thanduyise KHUBONI, Teko MODISE, Siphiwe TSHABALALA (Sthembiso NGCOBO 55), Katlego MPHELA (Morgan GOULD 70), Bernard PARKER (Reneilwe LETSHOLONYANE 70). Tr: Pitso MOSIMANE

ELLIS PARK, JOHANNESBURG
26-03-2011, Ref: Coulibaly MLI

| South Africa | 1 |
| Egypt | 0 |

RSA - Mphela [93+]

RSA: Itumeleng KHUNE - Anele NGONGCA, Morgan GOULD, Bongani KHUMALO, Siboniso GAXA (Ruben CLOETE 83), Daylon CLAASEN, Kagisho DIKGACOI, Steven PIENAAR (Reneilwe LETSHOLONYANE 82), Bernard PARKER (Davide SOMMA 61), Siphiwe TSHABALALA, Abel Katlego MPHELA. Tr: Pitso MOSIMANE

EGY: Essam EL HADARY - Wael GOMAA, Hossam GHALY, Mahmoud FATHALLAH, Ahmed EL MOHAMADY, Mohamed SHAWKY, Ahmed FATHI, Sayed MOAWAD, SHIKABALA (Mohamed ZIDAN 86), Hosny Abd RABO (GEDO 60), El Sayed HAMDI (Mohamed ABOUTRIKA 77). Tr: Hassan SHEHATA

SEYNI KOUNTCHE, NIAMEY
27-03-2011, Ref: Doue CIV

| Niger | 3 |
| Sierra Leone | 1 |

NIG - Issoufou [64], Sidibe [79], Kamilou [89] • SLE - Mohamed Bangura [11]

NIG: No line up available

SLE: Christian CAULKER - Ibrahim KOROMA, Umaru BANGURA (Kewullay CONTEH 64), Ibrahim KARGBO, Medo KAMARA, Rodney STRASSER, Julius WOOBAY, Mustapha BANGURA, Sheriff SUMA, Mohamed BANGURA, Mohamed KALLON (Kei KAMARA 73). Tr: Lars Olof MATTSSON

NATIONAL STADIUM, FREETOWN
4-06-2011, Ref: Coulibaly MLI

Sierra Leone	1
Niger	0

SLE - Teteh Bangura [50]

SLE: Christian CAULKER - Ibrahim KOROMA, Umaru BANGURA, David SIMBO, Medo KAMARA (Ibrahim KARGBO 60), Rodney STRASSER, Khalifa JABBIE, Sheriff SUMA, Mohamed BANGURA, Teteh BANGURA (Desmond WELLINGTON 81), Kei KAMARA. Tr: Lars Olof MATTSSON

NIG: Kassaly DAOUDA - Koffi Dan KOWA, Chikoto MOHAMED, Delis AHOU, Amadou KADER, Karim Lancina KONATE, Boubacar DJIBOLALAHOU, Idrissa LAOUALI (Abdoul Aziz HAMADOU 82), William NGOUNOU, Alhassane ISSOUFOU (Moussa MOHAMED 23) (Saidou IDRISSA 75), Daouda KAMILOU. Tr: Harowna DOULLA

CAIRO MILITARY STADIUM
5-06-2011, Ref: Jedidi TUN

Egypt	0
South Africa	0

EGY: Essam EL HADARY - Hossam GHALY, Wael GOMAA, Mahmoud FATHALLAH (Amr EL SOULIA 79), Ahmed EL MOHAMADY, Ahmed FATHI, Hosny Abd RABO, Sayed MOAWAD, SHIKABALA (Ahmed ALI 66), Mohamed ZIDAN (GEDO 57), Ahmed Abdel ZAHER. Tr: Hassan SHEHATA

RSA: Itumeleng KHUNE - Anele NGONGCA, Morgan GOULD, Siyabonga SANGWENI, Tsepo MASILELA, Reneilwe LETSHOLONYANE, Kagisho DIKGACOI, Bernard PARKER (Tlou SEGOLELA 74), Andile JALI, Siphiwe TSHABALALA (Bevan FRANSMANN 90), Abel Katlego MPHELA (Davide SOMMA 86). Tr: Pitso MOSIMANE

NATIONAL STADIUM, FREETOWN
3-09-2011, Ref: Alioum CMR

Sierra Leone	2
Egypt	1

SLE - Sheriff Suma [14], Mohamed Bangura [89p]
• EGY - Mohsen [44]

SLE: Christian CAULKER - David SIMBO, Ibrahim KOROMA, Umaru BANGURA, Sheriff SUMA, Rodney STRASSER (Medo KAMARA 46), Ibrahim KARGBO, Kei KAMARA, Alfred SANKOH (Samuel BARLAY 86), Teteh BANGURA, Mohamed BANGURA. Tr: Lars Olof MATTSSON

EGY: Mohamed Abo GABAL - Ahmed SOBHY, Ahmed HEGAZY, Mohamed Abdel FATTAH, Islam RAMADAN, Amr EL SOULIA, Mohamed EL NENY, Mohamed SALAH (Ali AFIFI 93), Ahmed HASSAN, Ahmed MAGDY (SHERWYDA 62), Marwan MOHSEN (Omar GABER 75). Tr: Hany RAMZY

SEYNI KOUNTCHE, NIAMEY
4-09-2011, Ref: Haimoudi ALG

Niger	2
South Africa	1

NIG - Kowa [10], Maazou [47] • RSA - Jali [71]

NIG: Kassaly DAOUDA - Koffi Dan KOWA, Moussa Bonkano DJIBRILLA, Chikoto MOHAMED, Amadou KADER, Karim Lancina KONATE, William NGOUNOU, Issoufou Boubacar GARBA, Boubacar TALATOU, Alhassane ISSOUFOU, Moussa MAAZOU. Tr: Harowna DOULLA

RSA: Itumeleng KHUNE - Morgan GOULD, Anele NGONGCA, Siyabonga SANGWENI, Tsepo MASILELA, Andile JALI, Thanduyise KHUBONI, Teko MODISE, Thulani SERERO (Lehlehonolo MAJORO 46), Siphiwe TSHABALALA (Daylon CLAASEN 70), Bernard PARKER. Tr: Pitso MOSIMANE

CAIRO INTERNATIONAL STADIUM
8-10-2011, Ref: Wokoma NGA

Egypt	3
Niger	0

EGY - Mohsen 2 [48 71], Mohamed Salah [56]

EGY: Ahmed EL SHENAWI - Omar GABER, Moaaz EL HENAWI, Ahmed HEGAZY, Islam RAMADAN, Mohamed EL NENY, Amr EL SOULIA, Mohamed SALAH, Ahmed HASSAN (Mohamed IBRAHIM 53), Ahmed MAGDY (Saleh GOMAA 69), Marwan MOHSEN (SHERWYDA 81). Tr: Hariy RAMZY

NIG: Kassaly DAOUDA - Amadou KADER, Chikoto MOHAMED, Koffi Dan KOWA♦84, Karim Lancina KONATE, William NGOUNOU, Issoufou GARBA (Daouda KAMILOU 53), Alhassane ISSOUFOU (Olivier BONNES 62), Boubacar TALATOU (Idrissa LAOUALI 68), Moussa MAAZOU, Johan MAZADOU. Tr: Harowna DOULLA

MOMBELA STADIUM, NELSPRUIT
8-10-2011, Ref: Ngosi MWI

South Africa	0
Sierra Leone	0

RSA: Itumeleng KHUNE - Morgan GOULD, Anele NGONGCA, Siyabonga SANGWENI, Siboniso GAXA, Daylon CLAASEN (Matthews Oupa MANYISA 77), Andile JALI, Thanduyise KHUBONI, Siphiwe TSHABALALA, Katlego MPHELA, Bernard PARKER (Reneilwe LETSHOLONYANE 63). Tr: Pitso MOSIMANE

SLE: Christian CAULKER - Umaru BANGURA, Ibrahim KARGBO, Medo KAMARA, Rodney STRASSER, Khalifa JABBIE (Samuel BARLAY 46), Alfred SANKOH, Sheriff SUMA, Teteh BANGURA (Sam Obi METZGER 62), Mohamed BANGURA, Kei KAMARA. Tr: Lars Olof MATTSSON

QUALIFYING GROUP H

		Pl	W	D	L	F	A	Pts	CIV	RWA	BDI	BEN
Cote d'Ivoire	CIV	6	6	0	0	19	4	18		3-0	2-1	2-1
Rwanda	RWA	6	2	0	4	5	15	6	0-5		3-1	0-3
Burundi	BDI	6	1	2	3	7	9	5	0-1	3-1		1-1
Benin	BEN	6	1	2	3	8	11	5	2-6	0-1	1-1	

HOUPHOUET-BOIGNY, ABIDJAN
4-09-2010, Ref: Maillet SEY

Côte d'Ivoire	3
Rwanda	0

CIV - Yaya Toure [10], Kalou [19], Eboue [39]

CIV: Daniel YEBOAH - Guy DEMEL (ROMARIC 65), Kolo TOURE, Arthur BOKA, Emmanuel EBOUE, Siaka TIENE (Abraham Guie GUIE 65), Didier ZOKORA, Yaya TOURE, Cheik TIOTE (Emerse FAE 74), GERVINHO, Salomon KALOU. Tr: Francois ZAHOUI

RWA: Jean-Luc NDAYISHIMIYE - Anwar KIBAYA, Boubakary SADOU (Ismael NSHUTINAMAGARA 45), Daddy BIRORI, Didier KAPET, Jean-Baptiste MUGIRANEZA, Harouna NIYONZIMA, Jerome SINA (Djamal MWISENEZA 46), Jean-Claude IRANZI, Lewis ANIWETA (Tumaine NTAMUHANGA 46), Albert NGABO. Tr: Sellas TETTEH

STADE DE L'AMITE, COTONOU
5-09-2010, Ref: Bennett RSA

Benin	1
Burundi	1

BEN - Pote [2] • BDI - Kavumbagu [86]

BEN: Ludovic Carlos ALLA - Khaled ADENON, Damien CHRYSOSTOME, Rachidi IMOROU, Cedric COREA, Djiman KOUKOU, Djamal FASSASSI (Arnaud SEKA 88), Ousmane MAKARIMI, Stephane SESSEGNON (Razak OMOTOYOSSI 63), Romuald BOCO, Mickael POTE. Tr: Jean-Marc NOBILO

BDI: Janvier NDIKUMANA - Henry MBAZUMUTIMA, Valery Twite NAHAYO, Floribert NDAYISABA, Karim NIIZIGIYIMANA, Henry MBAZUMUTIMA, Faty PAPY (Pierre KWIZERA 75), Claude NDAYISENGA, Hussein NZEYIMANA, Fwadi NDAYISENGA (Didier KAVUMBAGU 68), Ndabashinze DUGARY (Cedric AMISSI 53). Tr: Adel AMROUCHE

STADE RWAGASORE, BUJUMBURA
9-10-2010, Ref: El Raay LBY

Burundi	0
Côte d'Ivoire	1

CIV - Romaric [34]

BDI: Vladimir NIYONKURU - Mbanza HUSSEIN, Henry MBAZUMUTIMA (Pierre KWIZERA 60), Valery Twite NAHAYO, Floribert NDAYISABA (Cedric AMISSI 60), Karim NIIZIGIYIMANA, Hassan HAKIZIMANA, Faty PAPY, Fwadi NDAYISENGA (Didier KAVUMBAGU 30), Ndabashinze DUGARY, Saidi NTIBAZONKIZA. Tr: Adel AMROUCHE

CIV: Daniel YEBOAH - Kolo TOURE, Arthur BOKA, Emmanuel EBOUE, Siaka TIENE, Didier ZOKORA, Emerse FAE, ROMARIC (Seydou DOUMBIA 85), Cheik TIOTE, Kader KEITA (Abraham Guie GUIE 80), GERVINHO (Wilfried BONY 80). Tr: Francois ZAHOUI

CAF AFRICA CUP OF NATIONS 2012

STADE AMAHORO, KIGALI
9-10-2010, Ref: Haimoudi ALG

Rwanda	0
Benin	3

BEN - Tchomogo [68], Omotoyossi [81], Sessegnon [88]

RWA: Jean-Luc NDAYISHIMIYE - Clement MUTUNZI, Aimable RUCOGOZA, Abdul SIBOMANA, Daddy BIRORI, Didier KAPET, Jean-Baptiste MUGIRANEZA, Harouna NIYONZIMA, Jean-Claude IRANZI (Anwar KIBAYA 72), Kipson ATUHEIRE (Roger TCHOUASSI 46), Albert NGABO. Tr: Sellas TETTEH

BEN: Ludovic Carlos ALLA - Khaled ADENON, Damien CHRYSOSTOME, Rachidi IMOROU, Djiman KOUKOU, Seidah TCHOMOGO, Stephane SESSEGNON, Romuald BOCO, Mohamed AOUDOU (Nouihoum KOBENA 46), Razak OMOTOYOSSI (Jacques BESSAN 85), Mickael POTE (Isaac LOUTE 46). Tr: Jean-Marc NOBILO

STADE AMAHORO, KIGALI
26-03-2011, Ref: Abdel Rahman SDN

Rwanda	3
Burundi	1

RWA - Iranzi [34], Uzamukunda [45p], Gasana [88] • **BDI** - Faty Papi [37]

RWA: Jean-Luc NDAYISHIMIYE - Adolphe HAKUNDUKIZE, Ismael NSHUTINAMAGARA, Abuha SIBOMANA, Eric GASANA, Patrick MAFISANGO, Jean-Baptiste MUGIRANEZA, Harouna NIYONZIMA, Jean-Claude IRANZI, Jacques TUYISENGE, Elias UZAMUKUNDA. Tr: Sellas TETTEH

BDI: Vladimir NIYONKURU - Valery Twite NAHAYO, Karim NIIZIGIYIMANA, Hassan HAKIZIMANA, Faty PAPY, Pierre KWIZERA, Hussein NZEYIMANA, Fwadi NDAYISENGA (Henry MBAZUMUTIMA 70), Cedric AMISSI (Abdoul Razak FISTON 80), Ndabashinze DUGARY, Saidi NTIBAZONKIZA. Tr: Adel AMROUCHE

OHENE DJAN, ACCRA
27-03-2011, Ref: Kayindi UGA

Côte d'Ivoire	2
Benin	1

CIV - Drogba 2 [45][75] • **BEN** - Tchomogo [13]

CIV: Daniel YEBOAH - Guy DEMEL♦[79], Steve GOHOURI, Emmanuel EBOUE (Kafoumba COULIBALY 46), Siaka TIENE, Didier ZOKORA, ROMARIC (Kader KEITA 46), Cheik TIOTE, Didier DROGBA, GERVINHO, Salomon KALOU. Tr: Francois ZAHOUI

BEN: Guillaume BEMENOU - Khaled ADENON, Damien CHRYSOSTOME, Rachidi IMOROU, Iazadi FOUSSENI (Djiman KOUKOU 46), Jocelyn AHOUEYA, Nouihoum KOBENA (Daniel LANIGNAN 46), Seidah TCHOMOGO, Stephane SESSEGNON, Mohamed AOUDOU (Reda JOHNSON 68), Mickael POTE

STADE RWAGASORE, BUJUMBURA
5-06-2011, Ref: Abdel Rahman SDN

Burundi	3
Rwanda	1

BDI - Ntibazonkiza 2 [29][53], Kavumbagu [84] • **RWA** - Kamana [48]

BDI: Athanase NYABENDA - Albert KAZE, Karim NIZIGIYIMANA, Hassan HAKIZIMANA, Faty PAPY, Pierre KWIZERA, Hussein NZEYIMANA, Fwadi NDAYISENGA, Cedric AMISSI, Selemani NDIKUMANA, Saidi NTIBAZONKIZA. Tr:

RWA: Jean-Luc NDAYISHIMIYE - Mao KALISA, Abuba SIBOMANA, Eric GASANA, Patrick MAFISANGO, Jean-Baptiste MUGIRANEZA, Hussein SIBOMANA, Olivier KAREKEZI, Peter KAGABO, Jacques TUYISENGE, Elias UZAMUKUNDA. Tr: Sellas TETTEH

STADE DE L'AMITE, COTONOU
5-06-2011, Ref: Kayindi UGA

Benin	2
Côte d'Ivoire	6

BEN - Sessegnon 2 [45][60p] • **CIV** - Ya Konan [13], Drogba 2 [21][73], Gervinho 2 [30][79], Bony [86]

BEN: Guillaume BEMENOU - Khaled ADENON, Damien CHRYSOSTOME, Reda JOHNSON (Djiman KOUKOU 42), Emmanuel IMOROU (Nouihoum KOBENA 81), Seidah TCHOMOGO, Mouritala OGUNBIYI (Arsene MENESSOU 73), Stephane SESSEGNON, Romuald BOCO, Razak OMOTOYOSSI, Mickael POTE

CIV: Boubacar BARRY - Benjamin ANGOUA, Igor LOLO, Kafoumba COULIBALY, Emmanuel EBOUE, Jean-Jacques GOSSO, Yaya TOURE, Didier KONAN (Wilfried BONY 65), Seydou DOUMBIA (Max-Alain GRADEL 54), Didier DROGBA (ROMARIC 88), GERVINHO. Tr: Francois ZAHOUI

STADE AMAHORO, KIGALI
3-09-2011, Ref: Grisha ITA

Rwanda	0
Côte d'Ivoire	5

CIV - Kalou [33], Bony 2 [42][43], Ya Konan [68], Gervinho [83]

RWA: Jean-Luc NDAYISHIMIYE - Emery BAYISENGE, Ismael NSHUTINAMAGARA, Abdul SIBOMANA, Patrick MAFISANGO, Harouna NIYONZIMA, Charles Mwesigye TIBINGANA, Jean-Claude IRANZI, Labama Bokota KAMANA (Andrew BUTEERA 72), Jacques TUYISENGE, Albert NGABO. Tr: Sellas TETTEH

CIV: Boubacar BARRY - Guy DEMEL, Igor LOLO (Max-Alain GRADEL 71), Arthur BOKA, Emmanuel EBOUE, Siaka TIENE, Didier ZOKORA, Yaya TOURE (Didier KONAN 60), Wilfried BONY (Seydou DOUMBIA 54), GERVINHO, Salomon KALOU. Tr: Francois ZAHOUI

STADE RWAGASORE, BUJUMBURA
4-09-2011, Ref: Abdel Rahman SDN

Burundi	1
Benin	1

BDI - Faty Papy [92+] • **BEN** - Akpagba [55]

BDI: Janvier NDIKUMANA - Valery Twite NAHAYO, Floribert NDAYISHIMIYE, Karim NIZIGIYIMANA (Laudy MAVUGO 63), Hassan HAKIZIMANA, Faty PAPY, Hussein NZEYIMANA, Cedric AMISSI, Ndabashinze DUGARY (Didier KAVUMBAGU 59), Selemani NDIKUMANA, Saidi NTIBAZONKIZA. Tr: Adel AMROUCHE

BEN: Guillaume BEMENOU - Seidou BARAZE, Reda JOHNSON, Arsene MENESSOU, Junior SALOMON, Fabrice GOZO, Alain HOUNSA, Seidah TCHOMOGO (Guy AKPAGBA 46), Sidoine OUSSOU (Mohamed AOUDOU 73), Stephane SESSEGNON, Isaac LOUTE. Tr: Fortune GLELE

STADE DE L'AMITE, COTONOU
9-10-2011, Ref: Moukoko CGO

Benin	0
Rwanda	0

RWA - Kagere [6]

BEN: Guillaume BEMENOU - Seidou BARAZE (Jacques BESSAN 51), Reda JOHNSON, Arsene MENESSOU, Junior SALOMON, Fabrice GOZO, Alain HOUNSA, Djamal FASSASSI (Patmos ABOKI 70), Sidoine OUSSOU (Daniel LANIGNAN 43), Stephane SESSEGNON, Isaac LOUTE. Tr: Fortune GLELE

RWA: Jean-Claude NDORI - Mao KALISA, Eric GASANA, Jean-Baptiste MUGIRANEZA (Jacques TUYISENGE 93), Frederic NDAKA, Harouna NIYONZIMA, Hussein SIBOMANA, Charles Mwesigye TIBINGANA (Elias UZAMUKUNDA 76), Olivier KAREKEZI, Meddy KAGERE, Albert NGABO

HOUPHOUET-BOIGNY, ABIDJAN
9-10-2011, Ref: Otogo-Castane GAB

Côte d'Ivoire	2
Burundi	1

CIV - Kolo Toure [70], Gervinho [91+] • **BDI** - Nahimana [77]

CIV: Boubacar BARRY - Kolo TOURE (Emmanuel EBOUE 75), Arthur BOKA, Kafoumba COULIBALY, Didier ZOKORA, Yaya TOURE, Cheik TIOTE, Didier KONAN (Kader KEITA 55), Wilfried BONY (Didier DROGBA 48), GERVINHO, Salomon KALOU. Tr: Francois ZAHOUI

BDI: Vladimir NIYONKURU - Valery Twite NAHAYO, Floribert NDAYISABA, Karim NIZIGIYIMANA, Hassan HAKIZIMANA, Faty PAPY, Hussein NZEYIMANA, Cedric AMISSI, Ndabashinze DUGARY, Selemani NDIKUMANA, Saidi NTIBAZONKIZA. Tr: Adel AMROUCHE

QUALIFYING GROUP I

		Pl	W	D	L	F	A	Pts	GHA	SDN	CGO	SWZ
Ghana	GHA	6	5	1	0	13	1	16		0-0	3-1	2-0
Sudan	SDN	6	4	1	1	8	3	13	0-2		2-0	3-0
Congo	CGO	6	2	0	4	5	10	6	0-3	0-1		3-1
Swaziland	SWZ	6	0	0	6	2	14	0	0-3	1-2	0-1	

KHARTOUM STADIUM
4-09-2010, Ref: Kaoma ZAM
Sudan 2
Congo 0
SDN - El Tahir 2 [11] [90p]

SDN: No line up available

CGO: No line up available

SOMHLOLO NATIONAL, LOBAMBA
5-09-2010, Ref: Seechurn MRI
Swaziland 0
Ghana 3
GHA - Andre Ayew [13], Tagoe [69], Sarpei [80]

SWZ: Njabuliso SIMELANE - Eugene DLAMINI, Zakhele MANYATSI, Mxolisi MTHETHWA, Siyabonga MDLULI, Sifiso DLAMINI (Lwazi MAZIYA 32), Nkosingiphile TSABEDZE, Thulani TSABEDZE, Dennis MASINA (Phinda DLAMINI 80), Darren CHRISTIE (Mzwandile NDZIMANDZE 46), Siza DLAMINI

GHA: Richard KINGSON - Lee ADDY, John PAINTSIL, Isaac VORSAH, Hans Adu SARPEI, Anthony ANNAN, Kwadwo ASAMOAH, Kevin-Prince BOATENG (Emmanuel AGYEMANG BADU 63), Andre AYEW (Jordan AYEW 73), Asamoah GYAN (Samuel INKOOM 85), Prince TAGOE. Tr: Milovan RAJEVAC

STADE REVOLUTION, BRAZZAVILLE
10-10-2010, Ref: Ssegonga UGA
Congo 3
Swaziland 1
CGO - Mouko [21p], Sembolo 2 [35] [74] •
SWZ - Christie [37]

CGO: Barel MOUKO - Bruce ABDOULAYE, Francis N'GANGA, Fabry Destin MAKITA-PASSY (Patrick MOUAYA 17), Prince ONIANGUE, Delvin NDINGA, Olfaga OKIELE, Brunel Okana STASI (Franchel IBARA 70), Francky SEMBOLO, Ladislas DOUNIAMA (Jusly BOUKAMA-KAYA 52), Fabrice ONDAMA. Tr: Ivica TODOROV

SWZ: Sandile GININDZA - Eugene DLAMINI (Gumbi SAMKELO 63), Zakhele MANYATSI, Mxolisi MTHETHWA, Goodman THWALA, Dennis FAKUDZE, Mphile TSABEDZE, Thulani TSABEDZE (Mzwandile NDZIMANDZE 46), Dennis MASINA (Phinda DLAMINI 76), Mtanafuthi BHEMBE, Darren CHRISTIE

BABA YARA, KUMASI
10-10-2010, Ref: Damon RSA
Ghana 0
Sudan 0

GHA: Richard KINGSON - John MENSAH, John PAINTSIL, Isaac VORSAH, Hans Adu SARPEI, Anthony ANNAN, Kwadwo ASAMOAH, Bennard KUMORDZI (Emmanuel AGYEMANG BADU 71), Andre AYEW (Emmanuel CLOTTEY 76), Jordan AYEW (Prince TAGOE 56), Asamoah GYAN ♦ 80. Tr: James APPIAH

SDN: Elmuez MAHGOUB - Mohamed Ali SAFARI, Balla GABIR, Khalefa Ahmed HAMOUDA, Saifeldin MASAWI, Omer BAKHEBT, Raji ABDEL-AATI, Alaa Eldin YOUSIF, Muhannad EL TAHIR (Musaab MAAZ 66), Bader Eldin GALAG (Mohamed BASHIR 55), Mudathir EL TAHIR (Bakri Abdel KADER 94). Tr: MAZDA

STADE REVOLUTION, BRAZZAVILLE
27-03-2011, Ref: Bennett RSA
Congo 0
Ghana 3
GHA - Tagoe [24], Adiyiah [44], Muntari [82]

CGO: Barel MOUKO - Bruce ABDOULAYE, Igor NGANGA, Francis N'GANGA, Fabry Destin MAKITA-PASSY, Jean-Claude MPASSY (Ulrich KAPOLONGO 63), Prince ONIANGUE (Chardin MFOUTOU 65), Delvin NDINGA, Brunel Okana STASI (Franchel IBARA 55), Francky SEMBOLO, Fabrice ONDAMA. Tr: Robert CORFOU

GHA: Richard KINGSON - John MENSAH, John PAINTSIL, Isaac VORSAH, David ADDY (Lee ADDY 45), Anthony ANNAN, Emmanuel AGYEMANG BADU, Kwadwo ASAMOAH, Andre AYEW (Sulley Ali MUNTARI 82), Dominic ADIYIAH, Prince TAGOE (Samuel INKOOM 70). Tr: Goran STEVANOVIC

AL MERREIKH, OMDURMAN
27-03-2011, Ref: Raouf EGY
Sudan 3
Swaziland 0
SDN - Bashir 2 [2] [63], El Tahir [71]

SDN: No line up available

SWZ: No line up available

BABA YARA, KUMASI
3-06-2011, Ref: Haimoudi ALG
Ghana 3
Congo 1
GHA - Vorsah [62], Tagoe [66], Agyemang [78] •
CGO - Moussilou [75]

GHA: Richard KINGSON - John MENSAH, John PAINTSIL, Isaac VORSAH, Daniel OPARE, Emmanuel AGYEMANG BADU, Michael ESSIEN (Derek BOATENG 72), Kwadwo ASAMOAH, Kevin-Prince BOATENG (Dominic ADIYIAH 56), Sulley Ali MUNTARI (Andre AYEW 61), Prince TAGOE. Tr: Goran STEVANOVIC

CGO: Massa Cham MONKOLA - Bruce ABDOULAYE ♦ 50, Igor NGANGA, Francis N'GANGA, Fabry Destin MAKITA-PASSY, Delvin NDINGA, Chardin Madila MFOUTOU, Franci LITSINGI, Matt MOUSSILOU, Harris TCHILIMBOU, Fabrice ONDAMA. Tr: Robert CORFOU

SOMHLOLO NATIONAL, LOBAMBA
5-06-2011, Ref: Bennett RSA
Swaziland 1
Sudan 2
SWZ - Kunene [80] • SDN - Eldin Galag [64], Alaedin Yousif [88]

SWZ: Mphikeleli DLAMINI - Siboniso MALAMBE, Siyabonga MDLULI, Sifiso DLAMINI, Manqoba KUNENE, Welile MASEKO (Mtanafuthi BHEMBE 60), Sifiso NKAMBULE, Dennis MASINA, Zweli NXUMALO (Mbuso GINA 60), Sihawu DLAMINI, Mzwandile NDZIMANDZE (Felix BADENHORST 70) Tr: Obed MLOTSA

SDN: No line up available

OHENE DJAN, ACCRA
2-09-2011, Ref: Cordier CHA
Ghana 2
Swaziland 0
GHA - Gyan [8], Agyemang [78]

GHA: Adam LARSEN - Jonathan MENSAH, John PAINTSIL, Isaac VORSAH, Daniel OPARE, Emmanuel AGYEMANG BADU, Derek BOATENG, Sulley Ali MUNTARI (Kwadwo ASAMOAH 46), Andre AYEW (Samuel INKOOM 75), Dominic ADIYIAH, Asamoah GYAN (Prince TAGOE 41). Tr: Goran STEVANOVIC

SWZ: Sandile GININDZA - Siboniso MALAMBE, Ntobeko MTHINKHULU, Siyabonga MDLULI, Manqoba KUNENE, Celucolo MMEMA (Mtanafuthi BHEMBE 69), Sifiso NKAMBULE, Nkosingiphile TSABEDZE (Sabelo GAMEDZE 81), Dennis MASINA (Zweli MANDLA 81), Sihawu DLAMINI, Mbuso GINA

CAF AFRICA CUP OF NATIONS 2012

STADE REVOLUTION, BRAZZAVILLE
4-09-2011, Ref: Seechurn MRI
Congo 0
Sudan 1
SDN - Abdel Kader 77

CGO: Massa Cham MONKOLA - Bomassi DJODJO, Children MIANGOUNINA, Igor NGANGA, Francis N'GANGA (Harris TCHILIMBOU 79), Delvin NDINGA, Chardin MFOUTOU, Likibi TSOUMOU (Bienvenu KOMBO 50), Franci LITSINGI, Matt MOUSSILOU (Guelor Bebhey NDEY 65), Fabrice ONDAMA. Tr: Camille NGAKOSSO

SDN: No line up available

SOMHLOLO NATIONAL, LOBAMBA
8-10-2011, Ref: Kaoma ZAM
Swaziland 0
Congo 1
CGO - Nkolo 47

SWZ: No line up available

CGO: No line up available

KHARTOUM STADIUM
8-10-2011, Ref: Bennaceur TUN
Sudan 0
Ghana 2
GHA - Gyan 11, John Mensah 20

SDN: Elmuez MAHGOUB - Ahmed AL BASHA, Balla GABIR, Amir Rabei ABDELNABI, Khalefa Ahmed HAMOUDA, Saifeldin MASAWI, Nasr Eldin Omer EL SHIGAIL, Musaab MAAZ, Muhannad EL TAHIR, Bader Eldin GALAG, Bakri ABDEL KADER. Tr: MAZDA

GHA: Adam LARSEN - John MENSAH, John PAINTSIL, Isaac VORSAH, Samuel INKOOM, Daniel OPARE, Emmanuel AGYEMANG BADU, Derek BOATENG (Mohamed ABU 88), Kwadwo ASAMOAH (Lee ADDY 60), Sulley Ali MUNTARI (Anthony ANNAN 60), Asamoah GYAN. Tr: Goran STEVANOVIC

QUALIFYING GROUP J

		Pl	W	D	L	F	A	Pts	ANG	UGA	KEN	GNB
Angola	ANG	6	4	0	2	7	5	12		2-0	1-0	1-0
Uganda	UGA	6	3	2	1	6	2	11	3-0		0-0	2-0
Kenya	KEN	6	2	2	2	4	4	8	2-1	0-0		2-1
Guinea-Bissau	GNB	6	1	0	5	2	8	3	0-2	0-1	1-0	

NATIONAL STADIUM, KAMPALA
4-09-2010, Ref: Osman EGY
Uganda 3
Angola 0
UGA - Obua 35, Mwesigwa 57, Sserunkuma 88

UGA: Denis ONYANGO - Simeon MASSA, Andrew MWESIGWA, Ibrahim SEKAGYA, Godfrey WALUSIMBI, David OBUA (Brian UMONY 75), Musa MUDDE, Vincent KAYIZZI, Tony MAWEJJE, Geofrey MASSA (Geoffrey SSERUNKUMA 80), Mike SSERUMAGGA. Tr: Bobby WILLIAMSON

ANG: LAMA - ENOQUE (MINGO BILE 84), KALI, KIKAS, BERNARDO PATACA, ADAWA, GILBERTO, HUGO (GERALDO 57), DJALMA (TITI BUENGO 50), Ricardo JOB, MANUCHO. Tr: Herve RENARD

ESTADIO 24 SETEMBRO, BISSAU
4-09-2010, Ref: Bennaceur TUN
Guinea-Bissau 1
Kenya 0
GNB - Dionisio Mendez 76

GNB: Flaviano NANQUE - Saido BANJAI, Bruno FERNANDES, JOSE MONTEIRO, ZEZINHO, Bacar BALDE, Bocundji CA, Romisio DE BRAZETE, Emiliano TE, IVANILDO, Dionisio MENDEZ. Tr: Luis NORTON DE MATOS

KEN: No line up available

KASARANI, NAIROBI
9-10-2010, Ref: Diatta SEN
Kenya 0
Uganda 0

KEN: Wilson OBURU - Edgar OCHIENG, James SITUMA, Julius OWINO (Osborne MONDAY 15), George OWINO, Levy MUAKA (Allan WANGA 59), Patrick OSIAKO, McDonald MARIGA, Victor WANYAMA (George ODHIAMBO 81), Dennis OLIECH, Kevin OMONDI. Tr: Jacob MULEE

UGA: Denis ONYANGO - Andrew MWESIGWA, Ibrahim SEKAGYA, Joseph Nestroy KIZITO, Simon MASABA, Musa MUDDE, Steve BENGO (Geoffrey SSERUNKUMA 60), Vincent KAYIZZI, Tony MAWEJJE, Eugene SSEPPUYA (Geofrey MASSA 56), Mike SSERUMAGGA. Tr: Bobby WILLIAMSON

ESTADIO 11 NOVEMBRO, LUANDA
9-10-2010, Ref: Coulibaly MLI
Angola 1
Guinea-Bissau 0
ANG - Gilberto 22p

ANG: LAMA (WILSON 55) - KALI, BERNARDO PATACA, Francisco ZUELA, CHARA, ADAWA (OSORIO 64), DEDE (TITI BUENGO 80), GILBERTO, DJALMA, Ricardo JOB, MANUCHO. Tr: Zeca AMARAL

GNB: Flaviano NANQUE - Saido BANJAI (AILTON 75), Bruno FERNANDES, JOSE MONTEIRO, ZEZINHO (Dionisio MENDEZ 59), Bacar BALDE, Bocundji CA, EDNILSON (Bafode CARVALHO 70), Emiliano TE, Almani MOREIRA, CICERO. Tr: Luis NORTON DE MATOS

KASARANI, NAIROBI
26-03-2011, Ref: Djaoupe TOG
Kenya 2
Angola 1
KEN - Jamal Mohammed 53, Mariga 87 •
ANG - Manucho 18

KEN: Arnold Otieno ORIGI - Edgar OCHIENG, Joseph SHIKOKOTI, James SITUMA, Johanna OMOLO (Mohammed JAMAL 50), Joseph NYAGA (Victor WANYAMA 50), Dennis ODHIAMBO, McDonald MARIGA 88, Bob MUGALIA, George ODHIAMBO (Kevin OMONDI 76), Dennis OLIECH. Tr: Zedekiah OTIENO

ANG: LAMA - DANY AFONSO, MINGO BILE, Miguel QUIAMI (Jose Pierre VUNGUIDICA 87), CHARA, Dominique KIVUVU (GERALDO 80), DEDE, GILBERTO, DJALMA, MATEUS (JOAO MARTINS 62), MANUCHO. Tr: Lito VIDIGAL

ESTADIO 24 SETEMBRO, BISSAU
26-03-2011, Ref: Aguidissou BEN
Guinea-Bissau 0
Uganda 1
UGA - Obua 22

GNB: Emanuel Carmo NENE - Saido BANJAI, BRUNO FERNANDES, JOSE MONTEIRO, ZEZINHO (Mamadu CANDE 72), Bacar BALDE, ERIDSON (Abdul CARRUPT 80), Bocundji CA, Mustafa SILLA, CICERO, Dionisio MENDEZ (Basile DE CARVALHO 60). Tr: Luis NORTON DE MATOS

UGA: Denis ONYANGO - Andrew MWESIGWA, Ibrahim SEKAGYA, Joseph Nestroy KIZITO, Simon MASABA, Godfrey WALUSIMBI, David OBUA, Musa MUDDE, Vincent KAYIZZI (Joseph KABAGAMBE 46), Tony MAWEJJE, Geofrey MASSA (Geoffrey SSERUNKUMA 72). Tr: Bobby WILLIAMSON

NATIONAL STADIUM, KAMPALA
4-06-2011, Ref: Ruzive ZIM

Uganda	2
Guinea-Bissau	0

UGA - Walusimbi [43], Massa [62]

UGA: Denis ONYANGO - Andrew MWESIGWA, Joseph Nestroy KIZITO, Simon MASABA, Godfrey WALUSIMBI, David OBUA (Geoffrey SSERUNKUMA 65), Musa MUDDE, Hassan WASSWA, Vincent KAYIZZI (Joseph KABAGAMBE 75), Tony MAWEJJE, Geofrey MASSA (Robert SSENTONGO 75). Tr: Bobby WILLIAMSON

GNB: No line up available

ESTADIO 11 NOVEMBRO, LUANDA
5-06-2011, Ref: Maillet SEY

Angola	1
Kenya	0

ANG - Manucho [69]

ANG: CARLOS FERNANDES - DANY AFONSO, MINGO BILE (MARCO AIROSA 78), Miguel QUIAMI, Francisco ZUELA, Andre MACANGA, DEDE (CHARA 82), GILBERTO, DJALMA, MATEUS (Jose Pierre VUNGUIDICA 66), MANUCHO; Tr: Lito VIDIGAL

KEN: Boniface OLUOCH - Pascal OCHIENG, Edgar OCHIENG, James SITUMA, Osborne MONDAY (Mohammed JAMAL 64), Anthony KIMANI, Titus MULAMA, Kevin OPONDO (George ODHIOMBO 77), Allan WANGA (Patrick Oboya ONYANGO 56), Victor WANYAMA, Dennis OLIECH. Tr: Zedekiah OTIENO

KASARANI, NAIROBI
3-09-2011, Ref: Lamptey GHA

Kenya	2
Guinea-Bissau	1

KEN - Baraza [58], Oliech [93+] • GNB - Ailton [81]

KEN: Arnold Otieno ORIGI - Pascal OCHIENG, James SITUMA, Mohammed JAMAL, Anthony KIMANI, Titus MULAMA (Stephen WARURU 51), Dennis ODHIAMBO, Kevin OPONDO (John BARAZA 51), Victor WANYAMA, Bob MUGALIA (Collins OKOTH 66), Dennis OLIECH. Tr: Zedekiah OTIENO

GNB: Jonas MENDES - Saido BANJAI, EDSON CORREIA, Bacar BALDE, ERIDSON, Bocundji CA, LUCIANO TEIXEIRA, IVANILDO, AILTON, Basile DE CARVALHO, Dionisio MENDEZ. Tr: Luis NORTON DE MATOS

ESTADIO 11 NOVEMBRO, LUANDA
4-09-2011, Ref: El Ahrach MAR

Angola	2
Uganda	0

ANG - Manucho [57], Flavio [73]

ANG: CARLOS FERNANDES - DANY AFONSO, MARCO AIROSA, Miguel QUIAMI, AMARO (FLAVIO 52), Francisco ZUELA, Andre MACANGA, DEDE, DJALMA (OSORIO 92), MATEUS, MANUCHO (Jose Pierre VUNGUIDICA 78). Tr: Lito VIDIGAL

UGA: Denis ONYANGO - Andrew MWESIGWA, Ibrahim SEKAGYA, Joseph Nestroy KIZITO, Simon MASABA, Godfrey WALUSIMBI, David OBUA (Geoffrey SSERUNKUMA 70), Musa MUDDE, Tony MAWEJJE (Patrick OCHAN 81), Joseph KABAGAMBE (Vincent KAYIZZI 67), Geofrey MASSA. Tr: Bobby WILLIAMSON

NATIONAL STADIUM, KAMPALA
8-10-2011

Uganda	0
Kenya	0

UGA: Denis ONYANGO - Andrew MWESIGWA, Ibrahim SEKAGYA, Joseph Nestroy KIZITO, Simon MASABA, Musa MUDDE, Vincent KAYIZZI (Moses OLOYA 63), Tony MAWEJJE, Geofrey MASSA (Geoffrey SSERUNKUMA 77), Mike SSERUMAGGA (Michael MUTYABA 66), Brian UMONY. Tr: Bobby WILLIAMSON

KEN: Francis OCHIENG - Arnold Otieno ORIGI, James SITUMA, Osborne MONDAY, Collins OKOTH (Crispin OLANDO 88), Dennis ODHIAMBO, Kevin OPONDO (Stephen WARURU 75), McDonald MARIGA, Victor WANYAMA, Nyongesa Michael BARAZA (Bob MUGALIA 64), Dennis OLIECH. Tr: Zedekiah OTIENO

ESTADIO 24 SETEMBRO, BISSAU
8-10-2011

Guinea-Bissau	0
Angola	2

ANG - Manucho [8], Mateus [70]

GNB: Jonas MENDES - Saido BANJAI, BRUNO FERNANDES, EDSON CORREIA, Bacar BALDE, ERIDSON (Dionisio MENDEZ 67), Bocundji CA (Mamadu CANDE 78), Almani MOREIRA, IVANILDO, AILTON, SAMI (LUCIANO TEIXEIRA 76). Tr: Luis NORTON DE MATOS

ANG: CARLOS FERNANDES - DANY AFONSO, MARCO AIROSA, Miguel QUIAMI, Francisco ZUELA, Andre MACANGA, DEDE, DJALMA (Jose Pierre VUNGUIDICA 88), MATEUS (MINGO BILE 76), FLAVIO (GILBERTO 61), MANUCHO. Tr: Lito VIDIGAL

QUALIFYING GROUP K

		Pl	W	D	L	F	A	Pts	BOT	TUN	MWI	TOG	CHA
Botswana	BOT	8	5	2	1	7	3	17		1-0	0-0	2-1	1-0
Tunisia	TUN	8	4	2	2	14	6	14	0-1		2-2	2-0	5-0
Malawi	MWI	8	2	6	0	13	8	12	1-1	0-0		1-0	6-2
Togo	TOG	8	1	3	4	6	10	6	1-0	1-2	1-1		0-0
Chad	CHA	8	0	3	5	7	20	3	0-1	1-3	2-2	2-2	

STADE NATIONAL, N'DJAMENA
1-07-2010, Ref: Benouza ALG

Chad	2
Togo	2

CHA - Djem Nam [20], Mbaiam [28] • TOG - Mani [25], Aloenouvo [68]

CHA: Armel KOULARA - Mondesir ALLADJIM, Sitamadji ALLARASSEM, Macrada MADAWA, Asselme NASSAM, Karl Max BARTHELEMY, Leger DJEM NAM, Hilaire KEDIGUI, Yaya KERIM, Nekiambe Marius MBAIAM, Ezechiel NDOUASSEL. Tr: Sherif EL KHASHAB

TOG: Baba TCHAGOUNI - Dare NIBOMBE, Assimiou TOURE, Serge AKAKPO, Abdul-Gafar MAMAH, Guillaume BRENNER (Vincent BOSSOU 89), Moustapha SALIFOU (Kwami Kacla ENINFUL 30), Euloge AHODIKPE (Backer ALOENOUVO 50), Sapol MANI, Yao Junior SENAYA, Camaldine ABRAW. Tr: Thierry FROGER

EL MENZAH, TUNIS
1-07-2010, Ref: Diatta SEN

Tunisia	0
Botswana	1

BOT - Ramatlhakwane [31]

TUN: Aymen MATHLOUTHI - Karim HAGGUI, Bilal IFA, Mehdi MERIAH, Radhouene FELHI, Khaled KORBI, Hocine RAGUED, Fahid BEN KHALFALLAH, Oussama DARRAGI (Wissem BEN YAHIA 46), Issam JEMAA (Sami ALLAGUI 84), Youssef MSAKNI (Yassine CHIKHAOUI 74). Tr: Bertrand MARCHAND

BOT: Modiri MARUMO - Ndiapo LETSHOLATHEBE, Mosimanegape RAMOSHIBIDU, Ronnet THUMA, Patrick LENYELETSE, Ofentse NATO, Mogakolodi NGELE, Diphetogo SELOLWANE (Dirang MOLOI 85), Phenyo MONGALA, Mokgathi MOKGATHI (Joel MOGOROSI 46), Jerome RAMATLHAKWANE. Tr: Stanley TSHOSANE

STADE DE KEGUE, LOME
9-07-2010, Ref: Bennett RSA

Togo	1
Malawi	1

TOG - Aloenouvo [75] • MWI - Mwakasungula [18]

TOG: Kossi AGASSA (Baba TCHAGOUNI 46) - Kwami Kacla ENINFUL (Guillaume BRENNER 8), Dare NIBOMBE, Assimiou TOURE, Serge AKAKPO, Abdul-Gafar MAMAH, Moustapha SALIFOU, Sapol MANI, Serge GAKPE (Backer ALOENOUVO 72), Yao Junior SENAYA, Camaldine ABRAW. Tr: Thierry FROGER

MWI: Swadyk SANUDI - Elvis KAFOTEKA, Harry NYIRENDA, Peter MPONDA, Allan KAMANGA, Davi BANDA, Robert NGAMBI, Hellings MWAKASUNGULA, Fisher KONDOWE, Joseph KAMWENDO, Essau KANYENDA. Tr: Kinnah PHIRI

CAF AFRICA CUP OF NATIONS 2012

NATIONAL STADIUM, GABORONE
9-07-2010, Ref: Seechurn MRI

Botswana	1
Chad	0

BOT - Mongala [49]

BOT: Modiri MARUMO - Ndiapo LETSHOLATHEBE, Mmusa OHILWE, Mosimanegape RAMOSHIBIDU, Mompati THUMA, Ofentse NATO, Mogakolodi NGELE, Diphetogo SELOLWANE, Phenyo MONGALA (Othusitse PILANE 80), Mokgathi MOKGATHI, Jerome RAMATLHAKWANE. Tr: Stanley TSHOSANE

CHA: Dominique TEINKOR - Sitamadji ALLARASSEM, Cesar MADALANGUE, David MBAIHOULOUM, Asselme NASSAM, Karl Max BARTHELEMY, Leger DJEM NAM, Hilaire KEDIGUI, Yaya KERIM, Nekiambe Marius MBAIAM, Ezechiel NDEOUASSEL. Tr: Sherif EL KHASHAB

STADE NATIONAL, N'DJAMENA
11-08-2010, Ref: Doue CIV

Chad	1
Tunisia	3

CHA - N'Douassel [72] • TUN - Korbi [9], Ben Khalfallah 2 [43 81]

CHA: Ndakom Valerie NDEIDOUM (Armel KOULARA 28), Sitamadji ALLARASSEM, Armand DJERABE, Abbas MAIGUE (Majdi TRAOUI 75), Azrack MAHAMAT, Asselme NASSAM, Karl Max BARTHELEMY, Leger DJEM NAM, Hilaire KEDIGUI, Nekiambe Marius MBAIAM, Ezechiel NDOUASSEL. Tr: Sherif EL KHASHAB

TUN: Hamdi KASRAOUI - Karim HAGGUI, Ammar JEMAL, Alaeddine YAHIA, Anis BOUSSAIDI, Khaled KORBI, Mehdi NAFTI, Fahid BEN KHALFALLAH, Oussama DARRAGI (Yassine CHIKHAOUI 73), Zouheir DHAOUADI (Amine CHERMITI 63), Issam JEMAA. Tr: Bertrand MARCHAND

KAMUZU, BLANTYRE
11-08-2010, Ref: Carvalho ANG

Malawi	1
Botswana	1

MWI - Banda [75] • BOT - Ramatlhakwane [62]

MWI: Swadyk SANUDI - Allan KAMANGA, Peter MPONDA, James SANGALA, Elvis KAFOTEKA (Victor NYIRENDA 70), Davi BANDA, Hellings MWASUNGULA, Fisher KONDOWE, Joseph KAMWENDO (Essau KANYENDA 46), Chiukepo MSOWOYA, Russel MWAAFULIRWA (Atusaye NYONDO 70). Tr: Kinnah PHIRI

BOT: Modiri Marumo - Ndiapo Letsholathebe, Mmusa Ohilwe, Mosimanegape Ramoshibidu, Mompati Thuma, Joel Mogorosi (Mokgathi Mokgathi 51), Sekhana Koko, Boitumelo Mafoko, Patrick Motsepe, Diphetogo Selolwane (Onalethata Thekiso 51), Jerome RAMATLHAKWANE. Tr: Stanley TSHOSANE

UNIVERSITY STADIUM, GABORONE
4-09-2010, Ref: Kagabo RWA

Botswana	2
Togo	1

BOT - Mogorosi [6], Ramatlhakwane [47] • TOG - Gakpe [44]

BOT: Modiri MARUMO - Ndiapo LETSHOLATHEBE, Mmusa OHILWE, Mosimanegape RAMOSHIBIDU, Mompati THUMA, Joel MOGOROSI, Boitumelo MAFOKO (Patrick MOTSEPE 69), Ofentse NATO, Diphetogo SELOLWANE (Mokgathi MOKGATHI 71), Phenyo MONGALA (Pontsho MOLOI 35), Jerome RAMATLHAKWANE. Tr: Stanley TSHOSANE

TOG: Baba TCHAGOUNI - Senah MANGO (Sadat Ouro AKORIKO 69), Dare NIBOMBE, Serge AKAKPO, Abdul-Gafar MAMAH, Komlan AMEWOU, Moustapha SALIFOU, Floyd AYITE (Zakari MOROU 58), Serge GAKPE (Sapol MANI 58), Jonathan AYITE, Razak BOUKARI. Tr: Thierry FROGER

STADE 7 NOVEMBRE, TUNIS
4-09-2010, Ref: Lamptey GHA

Tunisia	2
Malawi	2

TUN - Jemaa 2 [11 26] • MWI - Msowoya [45], Kanyenda [82p]

TUN: Hamdi KASRAOUI - Karim HAGGUI, Alaeddine YAHIA, Anis BOUSSAIDI, Yassin MIKARI, Khaled KORBI, Mehdi NAFTI, Fahid BEN KHALFALLAH, Zouheir DHAOUADI (Youssef MSAKNI 70), Chaouki BEN SAADA, Issam JEMAA. Tr: Bertrand MARCHAND

MWI: Swadyk SANUDI - Allan KAMANGA, Peter MPONDA, Harry NYIRENDA, James SANGALA, Elvis KAFOTEKA, Robert NGAMBI (Limbikani MZAVA 64), Fisher KONDOWE (Atusaye NYONDO 64), Hellings MWASUNGULA◆45, Essau KANYENDA, Russel MWAAFULIRWA (Chiukepo MSOWOYA 42). Tr: Kinnah PHIRI

KAMUZU, BLANTYRE
9-10-2010, Ref: Kirwa KEN

Malawi	6
Chad	2

MWI - Zakazaka [13], Kanyenda 2 [21 52], Msowoya 2 [68 79], Ngambi [85] • CHA - N'Douassel [26], Mbaiam [81]

MWI: Swadyk SANUDI - Peter MPONDA, Limbikani MZAVA, James SANGALA, Elvis KAFOTEKA, Davi BANDA, Robert NGAMBI, Peter WADABWA, Essau KANYENDA, Grant LUNGU (Maupo MSOWOYA 60), Jimmy ZAKAZAKA. Tr: Kinnah PHIRI

CHA: Dominique TEINKOR - Sitamadji ALLARASSEM, Armand DJERABE, Abbas MAIGUE, Azrack MAHAMAT, Asselme NASSAM, Karl Max BARTHELEMY, Leger DJEM NAM, Hilaire KEDIGUI, Nekiambe Marius MBAIAM, Ezechiel NDOUASSEL. Tr: Sherif EL KHASHAB

STADE DE KEGUE, LOME
10-10-2010, Ref: Abdel Rahman SDN

Togo	1
Tunisia	2

TOG - Mani [40] • TUN - Jemaa [34], Chermiti [90]

TOG: Baba TCHAGOUNI - Dare NIBOMBE (Backer ALOENOUVO 74), Abdul-Gafar MAMAH, Alaixys ROMAO, Komlan AMEWOU, Zakari MOROU, Moustapha SALIFOU, Sapol MANI, Thomas DOSSEVI (Adekanmi OLUFADE 55), Serge GAKPE, Razak BOUKARI. Tr: Thierry FROGER

TUN: Wassim NAOUARA - Ammar JEMAL, Karim SAIDI, Alaeddine YAHIA, Anis BOUSSAIDI, Khaled KORBI, Majdi TRAOUI, Fahid BEN KHALFALLAH (Amine CHERMITI 73), Zouheir DHAOUADI (Oussama DARRAGI 57), Sami ALLAGUI (Wissem BEN YAHIA 90), Issam JEMAA. Tr: Bertrand MARCHAND

UNIVERSITY STADIUM, GABORONE
17-11-2010, Ref: Kaoma ZAM

Botswana	1
Tunisia	0

BOT - Ramatlhakwane [45]

BOT: Modiri MARUMO - MONISATEPE, MOGARA (Dirang MOLOI 79), Shinwe MISSA, Ndiapo LETSHOLATHEBE, Joel MOGOROSI, Tshepo MOTLHABANKWE, Ofentse NATO, Phenyo MONGALA, Diphetogo SELOLWANE (Mompati THUMA 77), Jerome RAMATLHAKWANE. Tr: Stanley TSHOSANE

TUN: Aymen MATHLOUTHI - Anis BOUSSAIDI, Khaled SOUISSI, Karim SAIDI, Ammar JEMAL, Khaled KORBI (Oussama DARRAGI 46), Majdi TRAOUI, Fahid BEN KHALFALLAH, Wissem BEN YAHIA, Zouheir DHAOUADI (Youssef MOUIHBI 53), Ahmed AKAICHI (Saber KHELIFA 78). Tr: Bertrand MARCHAND

STADE DE KEGUE, LOME
17-11-2010, Ref: Coulibaly MLI

Togo	0
Chad	0

TOG: Baba TCHAGOUNI - Dare NIBOMBE, Serge AKAKPO, Abdul-Gafar MAMAH, Komlan AMEWOU, Zakari MOROU, Moustapha SALIFOU, Sapol MANI, Backer ALOENOUVO, Jonathan AYITE, Razak BOUKARI. Tr: Thierry FROGER

CHA: No line up available

KAMUZU, BLANTYRE
26-03-2011, Ref: Mohamadou CMR

Malawi	1
Togo	0

MWI - Chavula [18]

MWI: Simplex NTHARA - Jacob NGWIRA, Harry NYIRENDA, James SANGALA, Moses CHAVULA, Elvis KAFOTEKA, Robert NGAMBI, Peter WADABWA (Maupo MSOWOYA 46), Joseph KAMWENDO (Frank BANDA 46), Essau KANYENDA, Jimmy ZAKAZAKA. Tr: Kinnah PHIRI

TOG: Juvenal PEDOMEY - Eric AKOTO, Senah MANGO, Assimiou TOURE, Abdul-Gafar MAMAH, Komlan AMEWOU (Vincent BOSSOU 46), Zakari MOROU (Lalawele ATAKORA 46), Sapol MANI, Dove WOME, Floyd AYITE, Saibou SAFIOU (Komi-Fovi AGUIDI 46). Tr: Stephen KESHI

STADE NATIONAL, N'DJAMENA
26-03-2011, Ref: Bichari ALG

Chad	0
Botswana	1

BOT - Ramatlhakwane [52]

CHA: No line up available

BOT: Modiri MARUMO - Ndiapo LETSHOLATHEBE, Mmusa OHILWE, Mosimanegape RAMOSHIBIDU, Mompati THUMA, Ofentse NATO, Diphetogo SELOLWANE (Joel MOGOROSI 69), Phenyo MONGALA (Boitumelo MAFOKO 69), Mogogi GABONAMONG, Moemedi MOATLHAPING, Jerome RAMATLHAKWANE. Tr: Stanley TSHOSANE

UNIVERSITY STADIUM, GABORONE
5-06-2011, Ref: Diatta SEN

Botswana	0
Malawi	0

BOT: Modiri MARUMO - Ndiapo LETSHOLATHEBE, Mmusa OHILWE, Mosimanegape RAMOSHIBIDU, Mompati THUMA, Joel MOGOROSI (Dirang MOLOI 79), Patrick MOTSEPE (Boitumelo MAFOKO 74), Diphetogo SELOLWANE (Moemedi MOATLHAPING 72), Phenyo MONGALA, Mogogi GABONAMONG, Jerome RAMATLHAKWANE. Tr: Stanley TSHOSANE

MWI: Simplex NTHARA - Harry NYIRENDA, James SANGALA, Moses CHAVULA, Elvis KAFOTEKA, Davi BANDA, Robert NGAMBI, Frank BANDA (Ndaziona CHATSALIRA 74), Peter WADABWA (Jimmy ZAKAZAKA 79), Chiukepo MSOWOYA, Atusaye NYONDO. Tr: Kinnah PHIRI

STADE OLYMPIQUE, SOUSSE
5-06-2011, Ref: Bangoura GUI

Tunisia	5
Chad	0

TUN - Jomaa 3 [22 44 53], Abdennour [35], Darragi [47]

TUN: Aymen MATHLOUTHI - Aymen ABDENNOUR, Walid HICHRI, Sameh DERBALI, Khalil CHEMMAM, Khaled KORBI (Wissem BEN YAHIA 72), Majdi TRAOUI, Oussama DARRAGI (Adel CHEDLI 63), Iheb MSAKNI, Sami ALLAGUI, Issam JEMAA (Lamjed CHEHOUDI 54). Tr: Sami TRABELSI

CHA: Armel KOULARA - Mondesir ALLADJIM, Sitamadji ALLARASSEM, Armand DJERABE, Abbas MAIGUE, Azrack MAHAMAT, Karl Max BARTHELEMY, Leger DJEM NAM, Hilaire KEDIGUI, Nekiambe Marius MBAIAM, Ezechiel NDOUASSEL. Tr: Sherif EL KHASHAB

KAMUZU, BLANTYRE
3-09-2011, Ref: Maillet SEY

Malawi	0
Tunisia	0

MWI: Simplex NTHARA - Chikumbutso KANYENDA (Maupo MSOWOYA 6), Limbikani MZAVA, Harry NYIRENDA, James SANGALA, Moses CHAVULA, Davi BANDA, Robert NGAMBI (Jacob NGWIRA 72), Frank BANDA, Russel MWAAFULIRWA, Atusaye NYONDO (Peter WADABWA 66). Tr: Kinnah PHIRI

TUN: Aymen MATHLOUTHI - Walid HICHRI, Ammar JEMAL, Anis BOUSSAIDI (Khaled SOUISSI 67), Khalil CHEMMAM, Hocine RAGUED, Adel CHEDLI, Majdi TRAOUI, Zouheir DHAOUADI (Lamjed CHEHOUDI 70), Sami ALLAGUI (Amine CHERMITI 79), Issam JEMAA. Tr: Sami TRABELSI

STADE DE KEGUE, LOME
4-09-2011, Ref: Dembele CIV

Togo	1
Botswana	0

TOG - Arimiyaou [23]

TOG: Mawugbe ATSOU - Kodjo DADZIE, Dare NIBOMBE (Sadat Ouro AKORIKO 70), Serge AKAKPO, Abdul-Gafar MAMAH, Alaixys ROMAO, Prince SEGBEFIA (Lalawele ATAKORA 90), Komlan AMEWOU, Dove WOME, Kondo ARIMIYAOU (Backer ALOENOUVO 71), Razak BOUKARI. Tr: Tchanile TCHAKALA

BOT: Modiri MARUMO - Ndiapo LETSHOLATHEBE, Mmusa OHILWE, Edwin OLERILE (Tshepo MOTLHABANKWE 28), Mompati THUMA, Joel MOGOROSI, Ofentse NATO, Diphetogo SELOLWANE, Lemponye TSHIRELETSO, Mogogi GABONAMONG, Onalethata THEKISO (Sekhana KOKO 75). Tr: Stanley TSHOSANE

STADE NATIONAL, N'DJAMENA
8-10-2011

Chad	2
Malawi	2

CHA - Labo [65], Barthelemy [94+] •
MWI - Ngambi [35], Nyirenda [81]

CHA: No line up available

MWI: No line up available

STADE 7 NOVEMBRE, TUNIS
8-10-2011, Ref: Haimoudi ALG

Tunisia	2
Togo	0

TUN - Hichri [19], Khelifa [79]

TUN: Aymen MATHLOUTHI - Aymen ABDENNOUR, Walid HICHRI, Khalil CHEMMAM, Hocine RAGUED, Jamel SAIHI, Wissem BEN YAHIA, Oussama DARRAGI (Iheb MSAKNI 43), Sami ALLAGUI (Zouheir DHAOUADI 63), Issam JEMAA, Saber KHELIFA. Tr: Sami TRABELSI

TOG: Baba TCHAGOUNI - Kodjo DADZIE♦[77], Sadat Ouro AKORIKO, Serge AKAKPO, Abdul-Gafar MAMAH, Alaixys ROMAO, Komlan AMEWOU, Lalawele ATAKORA (Prince SEGBEFIA 85), Zakari MOROU, Dove WOME, Serge GAKPE (Backer ALOENOUVO 56). Tr: Tchanile TCHAKALA

CAF AFRICA CUP OF NATIONS EQUATORIAL GUINEA/GABON 2012

First round groups	Pts	Quarter-finals		Semi-finals		Final	
Zambia	7						
Equatorial Guinea	6	Zambia	3				
Libya	4	Sudan	0				
Senegal	0						
				Zambia	1		
	Pts			Ghana	0		
Côte d'Ivoire	9						
Sudan	4	Tunisia	1				
Angola	4	Ghana	2				
Burkina Faso	0						
						Zambia	0 8p
	Pts					Côte d'Ivoire	0 7p
Gabon	9						
Tunisia	6	Mali	1 5p				
Morocco	3	Gabon	1 4p				
Niger	0						
				Mali	0		
	Pts			Côte d'Ivoire	1	3rd Place Play-off	
Ghana	7						
Mali	6	Equatorial Guinea	0			**Mali**	2
Guinea	4	**Côte d'Ivoire**	3			Ghana	0
Botswana	0						

Top scorers (finals only): **3** - **MANUCHO** ANG; Didier **DROGBA** CIV, Pierre-Emerick **AUBAMEYANG** GAB; Cheick **DIABATE** MLI; Houssine **KHARJA** MAR; Christopher **KATONGO** ZAM & Emmanuel **MAYUKA** ZAM

PART THREE – THE CONTINENTAL CONFEDERATIONS

GROUP A

		Pl	W	D	L	F	A	Pts	EQG	LBY	SEN
Zambia	ZAM	3	2	1	0	5	3	7	1-0	2-2	2-1
Equatorial Guinea	EQG	3	2	0	1	3	2	6		1-0	2-1
Libya	LBY	3	1	1	1	4	4	4			2-1
Senegal	SEN	3	0	0	3	3	6	0			

ESTADIO DE BATA
21-01-2012, 19:30, Att: 35 000, Ref: Doue CIV

EQUATORIAL GUINEA 1 – 0 **LIBYA**

Balboa 87

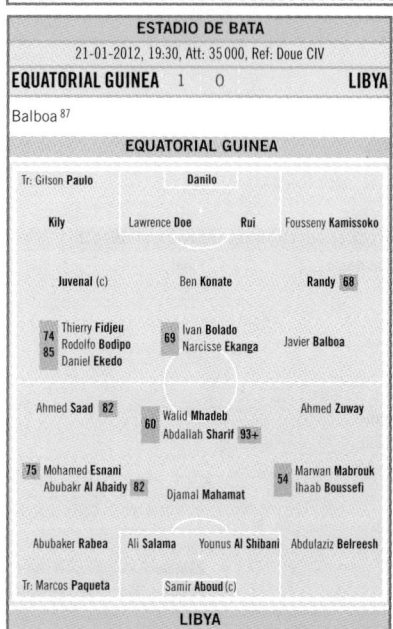

ESTADIO DE BATA
21-01-2012, 22:00, Att: 17 500, Ref: Alioum CMR

SENEGAL 1 – 2 **ZAMBIA**

N'Doye 73 — Mayuka 12, Kalaba 20

ESTADIO DE BATA
25-01-2012, 18:15, Att: 1500, Ref: Coulibaly MLI

LIBYA 2 – 2 **ZAMBIA**

Saad 2 5 48 — Mayuka 29, Katongo.C 54

ESTADIO DE BATA
25-01-2012, 21:15, Att: 35 000, Ref: Rahman SUD

EQUATORIAL GUINEA 2 – 1 **SENEGAL**

Randy 61, Kily 93+ — Sow 89

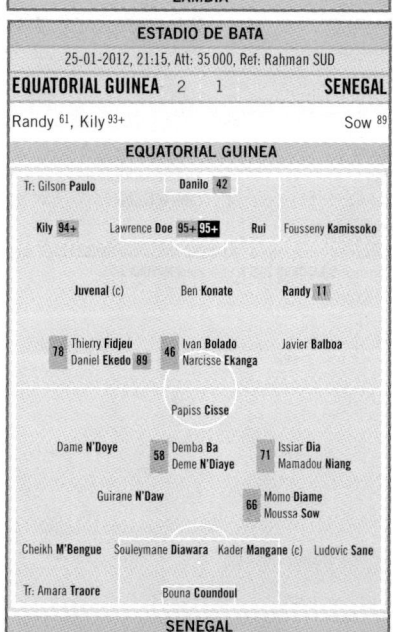

CAF AFRICA CUP OF NATIONS 2012

NUEVO ESTADIO DE MALABO
29-01-2012, 19:00, Att: 44 000, Ref: Benouza ALG

EQUATORIAL GUINEA 0 – 1 ZAMBIA

Katongo.C 68

ESTADIO DE BATA
29-01-2012, 19:00, Att: 10 000, Ref: Seechurn MRI

LIBYA 2 – 1 SENEGAL

Boussefi 2 5, 84 — Deme N'Diaye 10

GROUP B

		Pl	W	D	L	F	A	Pts	SDN	ANG	BFA
Côte d'Ivoire	CIV	3	3	0	0	5	0	9	2-0	1-1	1-0
Sudan	SUD	3	1	1	1	4	4	4		1-0	2-1
Angola	ANG	3	1	1	1	4	5	4			6-1
Burkina Faso	BFA	3	0	0	3	2	6	0			

NUEVO ESTADIO DE MALABO
22-01-2012, 17:00, Att: 5000, Ref: Seechurn MRI

COTE D'IVOIRE 1 – 0 SUDAN

Drogba 39

NUEVO ESTADIO DE MALABO
22-01-2012, 20:00, Att: 17 000, Ref: Benouza ALG

BURKINA FASO 1 – 2 ANGOLA

Alain Traore 58 — Mateus 48, Manucho 68

NUEVO ESTADIO DE MALABO
26-01-2012, 17:00, Att: 2500, Ref: Lemghaifry MTN

SUDAN	2 2	ANGOLA
Bashir 2 [32] [74]		Manucho 2 [4] [50p]

SUDAN
Tr: Mohamed **Abdalla**
Akram El Hadi **Salem**
Balla **Jabir** [95+], Saif **Masawi**, Najem **Abdullah**, Muawia **Bashir** [9]
Alaeldin **Yousif**, Hamid **Nazar**
Mohamed **Bashir**, Haitham **Mustafa** (c) [65] Bader **Galag**, Muhannad **Tahir**
Mudathir El **Tahir** [92+] Ramadan **Agab**

Flavio **Amado** [46] Nando **Rafael** [60] [73] Jose **Vunguidica**, **Manucho**
Djalma [83] Manucho **Barros**, **Gilberto** [24], Andre **Macanga** (c), **Mateus**
Miguel **Quiame**, **Dani**, Francisco **Zuela**, Marco **Airosa**
Tr: Lito **Vidigal**, **Carlos** [71]

ANGOLA

NUEVO ESTADIO DE MALABO
26-01-2012, 20:00, Att: 4000, Ref: Grisha EGY

COTE D'IVOIRE	2 0	BURKINA FASO
Kalou [16], Kone OG [82]		

COTE D'IVOIRE
Tr: Francois **Zahoui**
Boubacar **Barry**
Jean-Jacques **Gosso**, Kolo **Toure**, Sol **Bamba**, [75] Siaka **Tiene** [28] Arthur **Boka**
Didier **Zokora** [57]
Cheick **Tiote** [77], [81] Yaya **Toure** Wilfried **Bony**
Gervinho, Didier **Drogba** (c) [65] Salomon **Kalou** [40] Max **Gradel**

Jonathan **Pitroipa**, Moumouni **Dagano**, [78] Prejuce **Nakoulma** Aristide **Bance**
Alain **Traore** [87] Narcisse **Yameogo**
Mahamoudou **Kere** (c) [73] Florent **Rouamba**, Charles **Kabore** [32]
Saidou **Panandetiguiri**, Mamadou **Tall**, Bakary **Kone**, Mohamed **Koffi**
Tr: Paulo **Duarte**, Daouda **Diakite**

BURKINA FASO

ESTADIO DE BATA
30-01-2012, 19:00, Att: 132, Ref: Otogo-Castane GAB

SUDAN	2 1	BURKINA FASO
El Tahir 2 [33] [79]		Ouedraogo [95+]

SUDAN
Tr: Mohamed **Abdalla**
Akram El Hadi **Salem**
Ahmed Al **Basha**, [7] Najem **Abdullah**, Saif **Masawi** [67], Muawia **Bashir** Mosaab **Omer**
Alaeldin **Yousif**, Hamid **Nazar**
Haitham **Mustafa** (c)
[93+] Mohamed **Bashir** Ramadan **Agab**, Muhannad **Tahir** [96+] Amer **Kamal**
Mudathir El **Tahir**

Moumouni **Dagano** (c)
Jonathan **Pitroipa**, Narcisse **Yameogo** [66] Bertrand **Traore**, Prejuce **Nakoulma** [55] Issiaka **Ouedraogo**
Charles **Kabore**, Mohamed **Koffi**
Saidou **Panandetiguiri** [36], Ibrahim **Gnanou**
Mamadou **Tall**, [79] Djakaridja **Kone** Benjamin **Balima**
Tr: Paulo **Duarte**, Daouda **Diakite**

BURKINA FASO

NUEVO ESTADIO DE MALABO
30-01-2012, 19:00, Att: 1500, Ref: Jedidi TUN

COTE D'IVOIRE	2 0	ANGOLA
Eboue [33], Bony [64]		

COTE D'IVOIRE
Tr: Francois **Zahoui**
Boubacar **Barry**
[87] Igor **Lolo** [57] Benjamin **Angoua**, Kolo **Toure** (c), Sol **Bamba**, Arthur **Boka**
Kafoumba **Coulibaly**
Didier **Ya Konan**, [79] Seydou **Doumbia** Didier **Drogba**
Emmanuel **Eboue** [59] Abdul Kader **Keita** [93+], Max **Gradel**
Wilfried **Bony**

Manucho
[80] **Djalma** Jose **Vunguidica**, **Gilberto**, **Mateus**
Dede [66] Andre **Macanga** (c) [22] Nando **Rafael**
[83] Miguel **Quiame** Love, **Dani** [70], Francisco **Zuela**, Marco **Airosa**
Tr: Lito **Vidigal**, Wilson **Alegre**

ANGOLA

CAF AFRICA CUP OF NATIONS 2012

GROUP C

		Pl	W	D	L	F	A	Pts	TUN	MAR	NIG
Gabon	GAB	3	3	0	0	6	2	9	1-0	3-2	2-0
Tunisia	TUN	3	2	0	1	4	3	6		2-1	2-1
Morocco	MAR	3	1	0	2	4	5	3			1-0
Niger	NIG	3	0	0	3	1	5	0			

STADE D'ANGONDJE, LIBREVILLE
23-01-2012, 17:00, Att: 38 000, Ref: Maillet SEY

GABON 2 — 0 NIGER

Aubameyang [31], N'Guema [42]

GABON
Tr: Gernot Rohr — Didier Ovono (c)
Edmond Mouele, Remy Ebanega, Bruno Ecuele, Charly Moussono
Levy Madinda, Cedric Moubamba
Eric Mouloungui, Andre Biyogo Poko [91+] / Lloyd Palun
Pierre Aubameyang [84] / Daniel Cousin, Stephane N'Guema [75] / Zita Mbanangoye

NIGER
Moussa Maazou
Talatou Boubacar [63] / Amadou Moutari, Issoufou Alhassane [43] / Yacouba Seydou Ali, Issoufou Boubacar
Abdoul Karim Lancina, Idrissa Laouali (c), Sulliman Mazadou [57] / Jimmy Bulus
Mohamed Soumaila
Mohamed Chicoto, Amadou Kader
Tr: Harouna Gadbe — Kassaly Daouda

STADE D'ANGONDJE, LIBREVILLE
23-01-2012, 20:00, Att: 18 000, Ref: Bennett RSA

MOROCCO 1 — 2 TUNISIA

Kharja [86] — Korbi [34], Msakni [76]

MOROCCO
Tr: Eric Gerets — Nadir Lamyaghri
Mehdi Benatia [33], Ahmed Kantari
Michael Chretien [57], Badr El Kaddouri [81]
Houssine Kharja (c), Younes Belhanda
Nordin Amrabat, Mbark Boussoufa [60] / Youssouf Hadji, Oussama Assaidi [46] / Adel Taarabt
Marouane Chamakh [78] / Youssef El Arabi

TUNISIA
Saber Khelifa
Mejdi Traoui, Sami Allagui [57] / Youssef Msakni
Yassine Chikhaoui [65] / Hocine Ragued
Zouheir Dhaouadi [80] / Amine Chermiti, Khaled Korbi [26]
Ammar Jemal [86], Aymen Abdennour, Karim Haggui (c), Bilel Ifa [58]
Tr: Sami Trabelsi — Aymen Mathlouthi [93+]

STADE D'ANGONDJE, LIBREVILLE
27-01-2012, 17:00, Att: 20 000, Ref: Sikazwe ZAM

NIGER 1 — 2 TUNISIA

N'Gounou [9] — Msakni [4], Jemaa [90]

NIGER
Tr: Harouna Gadbe — Kassaly Daouda
Mohamed Chicoto, Kofi Dankowa
Jimmy Bulus [93+] / Issoufou Alhassane, Mohamed Soumaila
Yacouba Seydou Ali, Olivier Bonnes, Abdoul Karim Lancina (c) [45]
Issoufou Boubacar [84] / Idrissa Laouali, William N'Gounou [70] / Daouda Kamilou
Moussa Maazou

TUNISIA
Amine Chermiti [46] / Issam Jemaa
Youssef Msakni, Yassine Chikhaoui [66] / Sami Allagui, Zouheir Dhaouadi [50] / Oussama Darragi
Khaled Korbi, Mejdi Traoui [53]
Ammar Jemal, Aymen Abdennour, Karim Haggui (c) [78], Bilel Ifa [11]
Tr: Sami Trabelsi — Aymen Mathlouthi

STADE D'ANGONDJE, LIBREVILLE
27-01-2012, 20:00, Att: 35 000, Ref: Gassama GAM

GABON 3 — 2 MOROCCO

Aubameyang [76], Cousin [79], Mbanangoye [98+] — Kharja 2 [24 o.l.]

GABON
Tr: Gernot Rohr — Didier Ovono (c)
Edmond Mouele, Remy Ebanega, Bruno Ecuele, Charly Moussono
Andre Biyogo Poko [98+] / Cedric Moubamba / Lloyd Palun
Eric Mouloungui [85] / Zita Mbanangoye, Levy Madinda, Stephane N'Guema [46] / Daniel Cousin
Pierre Aubameyang

MOROCCO
Youssef El Arabi [46] / Nordin Amrabat
Mehdi Carcela [67] / Adel Taarabt, Youssouf Hadji, Younes Belhanda [54]
Houssine Kharja (c), Adil Hermach [28]
Badr El Kaddouri, Ahmed Kantari, Mehdi Benatia [96+] / [73] Michael Chretien / Jamal Alioui
Tr: Eric Gerets — Nadir Lamyaghri

STADE DE FRANCEVILLE, FRANCEVILLE
31-01-2012, 19:00, Att: 22 000, Ref: Doue CIV

GABON	1	0	TUNISIA

Aubameyang 61

STADE D'ANGONDJE, LIBREVILLE
31-01-2012, 19:00, Att: 4000, Ref: Nampiandraza MAD

NIGER	0	1	MOROCCO

Belhanda 78

GROUP D

		Pl	W	D	L	F	A	Pts	MLI	GUI	BOT
Ghana	GHA	3	2	1	0	4	1	7	2-0	1-1	1-0
Mali	MLI	3	2	0	1	3	3	6		1-0	2-1
Guinea	GUI	3	1	1	1	7	3	4			6-1
Botswana	BOT	3	0	0	3	2	9	0			

STADE DE FRANCEVILLE, FRANCEVILLE
24-01-2012, 17:00, Att: 5000, Ref: Diatta SEN

GHANA	1	0	BOTSWANA

John Mensah 25

STADE DE FRANCEVILLE, FRANCEVILLE
24-01-2012, 20:00, Att: 10 000, Ref: Jedidi TUN

MALI	1	0	GUINEA

Bakaye Traore 30

CAF AFRICA CUP OF NATIONS 2012

STADE DE FRANCEVILLE, FRANCEVILLE
28-01-2012, 17:00, Att: 4000, Ref: El Ahrach MAR

BOTSWANA 1 – 6 **GUINEA**

Selolwane 23p | Diallo.AS 2 15 27, Camara.A 42, Traore.I 45, Bah.M 83, Soumah 86

BOTSWANA

Tr: Stanley Tshosane — Adam Larsen Kwarasey

Ndiapo Letsholathebe — Mompati Thuma (c)

Tshepo Motlhabankwe 29 — Mmusa Ohilwe 52

Ofentse Nato 38 / Patrick Motsepe 45 — Mogogi Gabonamong

Pontsho Moloi 46 / Boitumelo Mafoko — Dipsy Selolwane — Phenyo Mongala 72 / Mogakolodi Ngele

Jerome Ramatlhakwane

Ismael Bangoura — Ibrahima Traore 68 / Alhassane Bangoura

Abdoul Camara

Pascal Feindouno 63 / Ibrahima Conte — Abdoulaye Sadio Diallo 80 / Naby Soumah

Mamadou Bah

Ibrahima Diallo — Bobo Balde — Kamil Zayatte (c) 22 — Thierno Bah

Tr: Michel Dussuyer — Naby Yattara 20

GUINEA

STADE DE FRANCEVILLE, FRANCEVILLE
28-01-2012, 20:00, Att: 7500, Ref: Haimoudi ALG

GHANA 2 – 0 **MALI**

Gyan 64, Andre Ayew 71

STADE D'ANGONDJE, LIBREVILLE
1-02-2012, 10:00, Att: 20000, Ref: Rahman SDN

BOTSWANA 1 – 2 **MALI**

Ngele 50 | Dembele 56, Seydou Keita 74

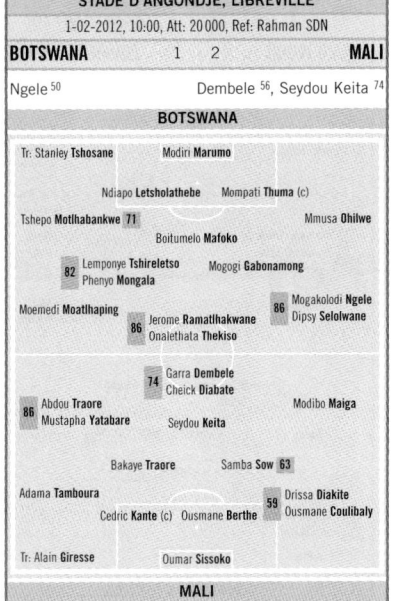

STADE DE FRANCEVILLE, FRANCEVILLE
1-02-2012, 19:00, Att: 5500, Ref: Bennett RSA

GHANA 1 – 1 **GUINEA**

Agyemang-Badu 27 | Abdoul Camara 45

QUARTER-FINALS

ESTADIO DE BATA
4-02-2012, 17:00, Att: 200, Ref: Gassama GAM

ZAMBIA 3 – 0 SUDAN

Sunzu [15], Katongo.C [66], Chamanga [86]

ZAMBIA

Tr: Herve Renard

Kennedy **Mweene**

Davies **Nkausu**, Stophira **Sunzu**, Hijani **Himoonde**, Joseph **Musonda**

[56] Chisamba **Lungu**, Nathan **Sinkala** [45]
Francis **Kasonde**

[89] Chris **Katongo** (c), Isaac **Chansa**, Rainford **Kalaba**
Jonas **Sakuwaha**

[64] Emmanuel **Mayuka**
James **Chamanga**

Mudathir **El Tahir**

Muhannad **Tahir** [45], [68] Haitham **Mustafa** [c], Ahmed **Al Basha**
Bader **Galag**

[42] Hamid **Nazar**, [30] Alaeldin **Yousif**
Ramadan **Agab**, Amer **Kamal**

Mosaab **Omer**, Muawia **Bashir**, Saif **Masawi** [34] [65] [65], Khalifa **Ahmed** [37]

Tr: Mohamed **Abdalla**   Akram El Hadi **Salem**

SUDAN

STADE DE FRANCEVILLE, FRANCEVILLE
5-02-2012, 20:00, Att: 8000, Ref: Alioum CMR

GHANA 2 – 1 TUNISIA

John Mensah [9], Andre Ayew [100]   Khelifa [41]

GHANA

Tr: Goran Stevanovic   Adam **Larsen Kwarasey**

Tr: Sami **Trabelsi**   Aymen **Mathlouthi**

TUNISIA

STADE D'ANGONDJE, LIBREVILLE
5-02-2012, 17:00, Att: 30 000, Ref: Haimoudi ALG

GABON 1 4p 1 5p MALI

Mouloungui [54]   Diabate [85]

GABON

Tr: Alain **Giresse**   Soumbeila **Diakite**

MALI

NUEVO ESTADIO DE MALABO
4-02-2012, 20:00, Att: 12 500, Ref: Maillet SEY

COTE D'IVOIRE 3 – 0 EQUATORIAL GUINEA

Drogba 2 [35] [69], Yaya Toure [81]
Drogba missed penalty [29]

COTE D'IVOIRE

Tr: Francois **Zahoui**   Boubacar **Barry**

Jean-Jacques **Gosso**, Kolo **Toure**, Sol **Bamba**, Arthur **Boka**

[87] Kafoumba **Coulibaly**, [77] Didier **Zokora**
Emmanuel **Eboue**, Wilfried **Bony**

Yaya **Toure**

Gervinho, [85] Max **Gradel**
Didier **Drogba** (c), Salomon **Kalou**

---

[71] Narcisse **Ekanga**, Javier **Balboa**
Ivan **Bolado**

Randy, Juvenal (c) [80], [46] Daniel **Ekedo**
Thierry **Fidjeu**

Ben **Konate**

[84] Fousseny **Kamissoko**, Rui, Lawrence **Doe**, Kily
Raul **Fabiani**

Tr: Gilson **Paulo**   Danilo

EQUATORIAL GUINEA

SEMI-FINALS

ESTADIO DE BATA		
8-02-2012, 17:00, Att: 12 000, Ref: Benouza ALG		
ZAMBIA	1 0	**GHANA**
Mayuka 78		Gyan missed penalty 7

ZAMBIA
Tr: Herve Renard
Kennedy Mweene
Davies Nkausu — Stophira Sunzu 52 — Hijani Himoonde — Joseph Musonda
Francis Kasonde 10 66 — Nathan Sinkala
Chisamba Lungu
Chris Katongo (c) — Isaac Chansa 69 — Rainford Kalaba
James Chamanga 46
Emmanuel Mayuka

Asamoah Gyan 74
Prince Tagoe
Jordan Ayew — Kwadwo Asamoah — Andre Ayew 86
Sulley Muntari
Anthony Annan — Derek Boateng 63 83 **83**
Lee Addy — John Mensah (c) 72 — John Boye 15 — Samuel Inkoom
Isaac Vorsah
Tr: Goran Stevanovic — Adam Larsen Kwarasey
GHANA

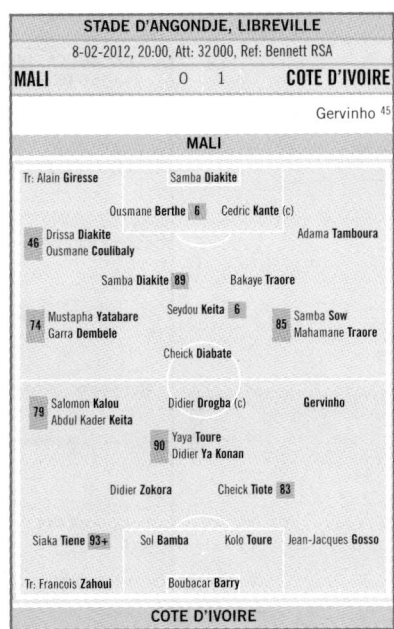

THIRD PLACE PLAY-OFF

FINAL

CAF AFRICA CUP OF NATIONS FINAL 2012
STADE D'ANGONDJE, LIBREVILLE

Sunday, 12-02-2012, 20:30, Att: 40 000, Ref: Badra Diatta SEN
Assistants: Bechir Hassani TUN & Evarist Menkouande CMR

ZAMBIA	0 8p 0 7p	COTE D'IVOIRE

Drogba Missed Penalty 71

ZAMBIA
Green shirts with a red/black/orange stripe, black shorts, green socks

Tr: Herve **Renard**

Kennedy **Mweene**

Davies **Nkausu**   Stophira **Sunzu**   Hijani **Himoonde**   12 74   Joseph **Musonda**
Nyambe **Mulenga** 69
Felix **Katongo**

Chisamba **Lungu**   Nathan **Sinkala**   Isaac **Chansa**   Rainford **Kalaba**

Chris **Katongo** (c)   Emmanuel **Mayuka**

Didier **Drogba** (c)

Salomon **Kalou** 63
Max **Gradel**

Gervinho

Cheick **Tiote** 63   87   Yaya **Toure**
Wilfried **Bony**   75   Didier **Zokora**
Didier **Ya Konan**

Siaka **Tiene**   Sol **Bamba** 66   Kolo **Toure**   Jean-Jacques **Gosso**

Tr: Francois **Zahoui**   Boubacar **Barry**

Orange shirts with white/green trimmings, orange shorts, orange socks
COTE D'IVOIRE

PENALTIES		
ZAM		CIV
	Tiote	✓
✓	Chris Katongo	
	Bony	✓
✓	Mayuka	
	Bamba	✓
✓	Chansa	
	Gradel	✓
✓	Felix Katongo	
	Drogba	✓
✓	Mweene	

	Tiene	✓
✓	Sinkala	
	Ya Konan	✓
✓	Lungu	
	Kolo Toure	✗[1]
✗[2]	Kalaba	
	Gervinho	✗[3]
✓	Sunzu	

[1] Saved • [2] Over crossbar
[3] Past post

(C) Captain

I told them if we got to the final we would play in Gabon where the plane crashed. There was a special significance in that. My players were magnificent. I know we're not the best but we have a strength and force that animated our team and made us African champions. They found the strength. I don't know where. You can see the talent. This is something enormous - something that appeared unrealisable before the competition began.

Herve Renard

We didn't expect such a challenging final but we go back to Abidjan with not too much shame. I think we played a good game. I congratulate Zambia. It is difficult, however, when you take part in a competition and you don't concede any goals and score nine! You feel the cup is within your reach. We didn't have much luck. We missed the penalty in normal time and then perhaps lost a bit of confidence. This is a big disappointment for us.

Francois Zahoui

REGIONAL TOURNAMENTS IN AFRICA 2012

CECAFA CUP UGANDA 2012

First round groups

Group A	Pl	W	D	L	F	A	Pts	KEN	ETH	SSD
Uganda	3	3	0	0	6	0	**9**	1-0	1-0	4-0
Kenya	3	2	0	1	5	2	**6**		3-1	2-0
Ethiopia	3	1	0	2	2	4	**3**			1-0
South Sudan	3	0	0	3	0	7	**0**			

Group B	Pl	W	D	L	F	A	Pts	TAN	SDN	SOM
Burundi	3	3	0	0	7	1	**9**	1-0	1-0	5-1
Tanzania	3	2	0	1	9	1	**6**		2-0	7-0
Sudan	3	1	0	2	1	3	**3**			1-0
Somalia	3	0	0	3	1	13	**0**			

Group C	Pl	W	D	L	F	A	Pts	MWI	ZAN	ERI
Rwanda	3	2	0	1	5	2	**6**	2-0	1-2	2-0
Malawi	3	2	0	1	5	4	**6**		2-0	3-2
Zanzibar	3	1	1	1	2	3	**4**			0-0
Eritrea	3	0	1	2	2	5	**1**			

Quarter-finals

Uganda	2
Ethiopia	0
Rwanda	0
Tanzania	2
Zanzibar	0 6p
Burundi	0 5p
Malawi	0
Kenya	1

Semi-finals

Uganda	3
Tanzania	0
Zanzibar	2 2p
Kenya	2 4p

Final

Uganda	2
Kenya	1

Third place play-off

Zanzibar	1 6p
Tanzania	1 5p

Played in Kampala, Uganda from 24-11-2012 to 8-12-2012 • Top scorers: **5** - John **BOCCO** TAN; Mrisho **NGASSA** TAN & Robert **SSENTONGO** UGA

CECAFA CUP FINAL 2012

Namboole Stadium, Kampala, 8-12-2012, Ref: Thierry Nkurunziza BDI

Uganda	2	Ssentongo [28], Kizito [90]
Kenya	1	Lavatsa [87]

UGANDA

Hamza **MUWONGE** - Dennis **IGUMA**, Henry **KALUNGI**, Isaac **ISINDE**, Godfrey **WALUSIMBI** - Moses **OLOYA** (Marico **KAWESA** 94+), Geoffrey **KIZITO**, Hassan **WASWA** (c), Joseph **OCHOYA** (Hamis **KIIZA** 54) - Robert **SSENTOGO**, Emmanuel **OKWI** (Said **KYEYNNE** 65). Tr: Bobby **WILLIAMSON**

KENYA

Duncan **OCHIENG** - Anthony Modo **KIMANI** (c), Jockins **ATUDO**, David **OWINO** (Kevin **OMONDI** 20) (Paul **WERE** 80), Abdallah **JUMA** - Clifford **MIHESO** (Rama **SALIM** 48), Humphrey **MIENO**, Anthony Muki **KIMANI**, David **OCHIENG** - Edwin **LAVATSA**, Mike **BARAZA**. Tr: James **NANDWA**

CAF AFRICA CUP OF NATIONS SOUTH AFRICA 2013

Qualifying groups

Cape Verde Islands	4 3				
Madagascar*	0 1	Cape Verde Islands*	2 1	South Africa	
Guinea-Bissau*	0 0	Cameroon	0 2	Cape Verde Islands	
Cameroon	1 1			Morocco	
Morocco	Bye			Angola	
		Morocco	0 4		
Tanzania*	1 1 6p	Mozambique*	2 0		
Mozambique	1 1 7p				
Angola	Bye				
		Angola	1 2		
Burundi*	2 0	Zimbabwe*	3 0		
Zimbabwe	1 1				
Ghana	Bye				
		Ghana*	2 1		
Chad*	3 0	Malawi	0 0		
Malawi	2 2				
Mali	Bye				
		Mali*	3 4		
		Botswana	0 1		
Botswana				Ghana	
Congo DR	4 3			Mali	
Seychelles*	0 0	Congo DR*	4 1	Congo DR	
		Equatorial Guinea	0 2	Niger	
Equatorial Guinea	Bye				
Niger	Bye				
		Niger	0 2		
		Guinea*	1 0		
Guinea	Bye				
Burkina Faso	Bye				
		Burkina Faso	0 3		
Egypt*	2 1	Central African Rep*	1 1		
Central African Rep	3 1				
Nigeria	0 2				
Rwanda*	0 0	Nigeria	2 6		
Namibia	0 0	Liberia*	2 1		
Liberia*	1 0				
Zambia	Bye				
		Zambia*	1 0 9p	Burkina Faso	
Congo*	3 0	Uganda	0 1 8p	Nigeria	
Uganda	1 4			Zambia	
Ethiopia*	0 1			Ethiopia	
Benin	0 1	Ethiopia	3 2		
		Sudan*	5 0		
Sudan	Bye				
Côte d'Ivoire	Bye				
		Côte d'Ivoire*	4 2		
		Senegal	2 0		
Senegal	Bye				
Togo	1 1				
Kenya*	2 0	Togo	1 2		
		Gabon*	1 1		
Gabon	Bye				
Tunisia	Bye				
		Tunisia	2 0		
São Tomé/Príncipe*	2 2	Sierra Leone*	2 0		
Sierra Leone	1 4			Côte d'Ivoire	
Algeria	2 4			Togo	
Gambia*	1 1	Algeria	1 2	Tunisia	
		Libya*	0 0	Algeria	
Libya	Bye				

Final Tournament first Round Group Stage

	Pl	W	D	L	F	A	Pts	CPV	MAR	ANG
South Africa	3	1	2	0	4	2	5	0-0	2-2	2-0
Cape Verde Islands	3	1	2	0	3	2	5		1-1	2-1
Morocco	3	0	3	0	3	3	3			0-0
Angola	3	0	1	2	1	4	1			

	Pl	W	D	L	F	A	Pts	MLI	COD	NIG
Ghana	3	2	1	0	6	2	7	1-0	2-2	3-0
Mali	3	1	1	1	2	2	4		1-1	1-0
Congo DR	3	0	3	0	3	3	3			0-0
Niger	3	0	1	2	0	4	1			

	Pl	W	D	L	F	A	Pts	NGA	ZAM	ETH
Burkina Faso	3	1	2	0	5	1	5	1-1	0-0	4-0
Nigeria	3	1	2	0	4	2	5		1-1	2-0
Zambia	3	0	3	0	2	2	3			1-1
Ethiopia	3	0	1	2	1	7	1			

	Pl	W	D	L	F	A	Pts	TOG	TUN	ALG
Côte d'Ivoire	3	2	1	0	7	3	7	2-1	3-0	2-2
Togo	3	1	1	4	3	4	4		1-1	2-0
Tunisia	3	1	1	1	2	4	4			1-0
Algeria	3	0	1	2	2	5	1			

Preliminary round: **Seychelles** w-o Swaziland • **São Tomé and Príncipe** 1-0 0-0 Lesotho • * Home team in the 1st leg

NATIONAL TOURNAMENTS IN AFRICA 2013

CAF AFRICA CUP OF NATIONS SOUTH AFRICA 2013

Quarter-finals

Nigeria	2
Côte d'Ivoire	1

South Africa	1 2p
Mali	1 3p

Ghana	2
Cape Verde Islands	0

Togo	0
Burkina Faso	1

Semi-finals

Nigeria	4
Mali	1

Ghana	1 2p
Burkina Faso	1 3p

Final

Nigeria	1
Burkina Faso	0

South Africa qualified automatically as hosts • Match details for both qualifiers and the finals will appear in Oliver's Almanack of World Football 2014

CAF AFRICA CUP OF NATIONS FINAL 2013

FNB Stadium 'Soccer City', Johannesburg, 10-02-2013, Att: 85 000, Ref: Djamel Haimoudi ALG

Nigeria	1	Sunday Mba 40
Burkina Faso	0	

NIGERIA
Vincent **ENYEAMA** (c) - Efe **AMBROSE**, Kenneth **OMERUO**•, Godfrey **OBOABONA**, Uwa Elderson **ECHIEJILE** (Juwon **OSHANIWA**• 66) - Ogenyi **ONAZI**•, Mikel John **OBI**• - Victor **MOSES**, Sunday **MBA** (Joseph **YOBO** 89), Brown **IDEYE**• - Ikechukwu **UCHE** (Ahmed **MUSA** 54). Tr: Stephen **KESHI**

BURKINA FASO
Daouda **DIAKITE** - Mohamed **KOFFI**, Bakary **KONE**, Paul **KOULIBALY** (Moumouni **DAGANO** 84), Saidou **PANANDETIGUIRI** - Djakaridja **KONE** (Abdou Razack **TRAORE** 90), Florent **ROUAMBA**• (Wilfried **SANOU** 65) - Prejuce **NAKOULMA**, Charles **KABORE** (c), Jonathan **PITROIPA** - Aristide **BANCE**. Tr: Paul **PUT**

CLUB TOURNAMENTS IN AFRICA IN 2012

ORANGE CAF CHAMPIONS LEAGUE 2012

First Round

Al Ahly	EGY	Bye	
Coin Nord *	COM	1	1
Ethiopian Coffee	ETH	0	4
Tonnerre d'Abomey	TOG	0	1
AS Garde Nationale *	NIG	0	0
Stade Malien	MLI	Bye	
Al Hilal Omdurman	SDN	Bye	
Les Astres Douala	CMR	0	2
DFC 8ème *	CTA	1	1
AS Vita Club *	COD	5	1
Atlético Olympique	BDI	0	4
ASFA Yennenga *	BFA	0	1
ASO Chlef	ALG	0	4
Etoile du Sahel	TUN	Bye	
Tusker *	KEN	0	0
APR FC	RWA	0	1
JSM Béjaïa	ALG	0	3
Foullah Edifice *	CHA	0	1
Diables Noirs	CGO	0	0
AFAD Djékanou *	CIV	1	1
Djoliba	MLI	Bye	
LCS Maseru	LES	0	0
URA Kampala *	UGA	3	0
Recreativo Libolo	ANG	3	1
Orlando Pirates *	RSA	1	1
Sunshine Stars	NGA	Bye	
TP Mazembe	COD	Bye	
Japan Actuel's *	MAD	1	0
Power Dynamos	ZAM	5	3
FC Platinum	ZIM	4	4
Green Mamba *	SWZ	2	0
Al Merreikh Omdurman	SDN	Bye	
Cotonsport Garoua	CMR	Bye	
CD Elá Nguema *	EQG	0	0
Dolphin	NGA	3	3
Raja Casablanca	MAR	Bye	
LISCR *	LBR	0	0
Berekum Chelsea	GHA	2	3
Zamalek	EGY	1	1
Young Africans *	TAN	1	0
Missile FC Libreville *	GAB	3	0
Africa Sports	CIV	2	2
Horoya AC	GUI	0	1
Ports Authority *	SLE	0	0
Maghreb Fès	MAR	Bye	
Dynamos	ZIM	Bye	
Mafunzo *	ZAN	0	0
Liga Muçulmana	MOZ	2	3
Brikama United *	GAM	0 1 3p	
US Ouakam	SEN	1 0 1p	
Espérance Tunis	TUN	Bye	

Second Round

Al Ahly	0	3
Ethiopian Coffee *	0	0
Tonnerre d'Abomey *	0	2
Stade Malien	0	5
Al Hilal Omdurman	3	5
DFC 8ème *	0	1
AS Vita Club	0	2
ASO Chlef *	0	3
Etoile du Sahel	0	3
APR FC *	0	2
JSM Béjaïa *	1	0
AFAD Djékanou	2	3
Djoliba	2	
URA Kampala *	0	
Recreativo Libolo	4	0
Sunshine Stars	1	3
TP Mazembe	1	6
Power Dynamos *	1	0
FC Platinum *	2	0
Al Merreikh Omdurman	2	3
Cotonsport Garoua	1	1
Dolphin *	2	0
Raja Casablanca	0	3
Berekum Chelsea *	5	0
Zamalek *	1	1
Africa Sports	0	2
Horoya AC *	1	0
Maghreb Fès	1	3
Dynamos	2	1
Liga Muçulmana *	2	0
Brikama United *	1	1
Espérance Tunis	1	3

Third Round

Al Ahly	0	3
Stade Malien *	1	1
Al Hilal Omdurman *	1 1 2p	
ASO Chlef	1 1 4p	
Etoile du Sahel *	4	0
AFAD Djékanou	1	1
Djoliba *	1	0
Sunshine Stars	1	1
TP Mazembe *	2	1
Al Merreikh Omdurman	0	1
Cotonsport Garoua	0	1
Berekum Chelsea *	0	2
Zamalek	2	2
Maghreb Fès *	0	0
Dynamos	0	1
Espérance Tunis *	6	1

* Home team in the first leg • Losing teams in the third round enter the Confederation Cup

ORANGE CAF CHAMPIONS LEAGUE 2012

Champions League Stage   Semi-finals   Final

Group A	Pl	W	D	L	F	A	Pts	EST	SS	ASO	ESS
Espérance Tunis	4	3	0	1	6	3	**9**		1-0	3-2	1-0
Sunshine Stars	4	2	0	2	4	4	**6**	0-2		2-0	-
ASO Chlef	4	1	0	3	4	7	**3**	1-0	1-2		0-1
Etoile du Sahel			Disqualified					0-2	0-0	-	

Al Ahly	3	1
Sunshine Stars *	3	0

Al Ahly *	1	2
Espérance Tunis	1	1

TP Mazembe *	0	0
Espérance Tunis	0	1

Group B	Pl	W	D	L	F	A	Pts	AA	TPM	BC	Za
Al Ahly	6	3	2	1	9	6	**11**		2-1	4-1	1-1
TP Mazembe	6	3	1	2	9	6	**10**	2-0		2-2	2-0
Berekum Chelsea	6	2	3	1	9	10	**9**	1-1	1-0		3-2
Zamalek	6	0	2	4	5	10	**2**	0-1	1-2	1-1	

Top scorers: **12** - Emmanuel **CLOTTEY** GHA, Berekum Chelsea • **6** - Mohamed **ABOUTRIKA** EGY, Al Ahly; Mbwana **SAMATA** TAN, TP Mazembe & Tresor **MPUTU** COD, TP Mazembe • **5** - **GEDO** EGY, Al Ahly; Izu **AZUKA** NGA, Sunshine Stars & Yannick **N'DJENG** CMR, Espérance Tunis • **4** - Karim Ali **HADJI** ALG, ASO Chlef; **RASCA** ANG, Recreativo Libolo; Mudather **EL TAHIR** SUD, Al Hilal & Youssef **MSAKNI** TUN, Espérance Tunis

FIRST ROUND

Stade Said Cheikh, Mitsamiouli, 18-02-2012
Coin Nord	1	Mahamoud Mohamed [30]
Ethiopian Coffee	0	

Addis Abeba Stadium, 4-03-2012
Ethiopian Coffee	4	Medhane Tadesse 2 [28 88], Daniel Deribe [75], Tafesse Tesfaye [80]
Coin Nord	1	Nazakali Issa [44]

Stade Seyni Kountche, Niamey, 18-02-2012
Garde Nationale	0	
Tonnerre Abomey	0	

Stade de l'Amitie, Cotonou, 4-03-2012
Tonnerre Abomey	1	Mohamed Aoudou [41]
Garde Nationale	0	

Barthelemy Boganda Stadium, Bangui, 19-02-2012
DFC 8ème	1	Terence Bimale [68]
Les Astres	0	

Stade de la Reunification, Doula, 4-03-2012
Les Astres	2	Christian Kabong [16], Augustine Taoga [46]
DFC 8ème	1	Moussa Limane [44]

Stade des Martyrs, Kinshasa, 10-03-2012
Vita Club	5	Tady Etekiama [19], Romaric Rongombe [41], Yves Magola 2 [44 78], OG [66]
At. Olympique	0	

Prince Louis Rwagasore, Bujumbura, 18-03-2012
At. Olympique	4	Chritophe Ndayishimiye 2 [13 62], Pierre Kwizera [36], Henri Mbazumutima [64]
Vita Club	1	Tady Etekiama [35]

Stade du 4-Août, Ouagadougou, 18-02-2012
ASFA Yennenga	0	
ASO Chlef	0	

Stade Mohamed Boumezrag, Chlef, 2-03-2012
ASO Chlef	4	Mohamed Seguer 3 [4 90 94+], Zakaria Haddouche [73]
ASFA Yennenga	1	Issouf Ouattara [45]

Nyayo, Nairobi, 18-02-2012
Tusker	0	
APR FC	0	

Stade Regional Nyamirambo, Kigali, 4-03-2012
APR FC	1	Faty Papy [52]
Tusker	0	

Stade Omnisports, N'Djamena, 18-02-2012
Foullah Edifice	0	
JSM Béjaïa	0	

Stade de l'Unité Maghrébine, Béjaïa, 2-03-2012
JSM Béjaïa	3	Ernest Yelemou 2 [22 68], Rafik Boulainceur [35]
Foullah Edifice	1	Abdel Aziz Aboubakar [80]

Stade Robert Champroux, Abidjan, 19-02-2012
AFAD Djékanou	1	Boblay Allegne [72]
Diables Noirs	0	

Stade Alphonse Massemba-Debat, Brazzaville, 6-03-2012
Diables Noirs	0	
AFAD Djékanou	1	Cheick Moukoro [92+]

Namboole National Stadium, Kampala, 18-02-2012
URA Kampala	3	Manco Kaweesa [12], Sula Bagala [55], Augustine Nsumba [60]
LCS Maseru	0	

Setsoto Stadium, Maseru, 4-03-2012
LCS Maseru	0	
URA Kampala	0	

Mandela Bay Stadium, Port Elizabeth, 19-02-2012
Orlando Pirates	1	Rooi Mahamutsa [92+]
Recreativo Libolo	3	Rasca 2 [12 17], Henry Camara [63]

Estádio Patrice Lumumba, Munenga, 3-03-2012
Recreativo Libolo	1	Rasca [34]
Orlando Pirates	1	Andile Jali [45]

Mahamasina, Antananarivo, 19-02-2012
Japan Actuel's	1	Rindra Rakotondrabe [75]
Power Dynamos	5	Mulenga Mukuka 2 [9 62], Simon Bwalya [68], Felix Nyaende 2 [74 87]

Arthur Davies Stadium, Kitwe, 4-03-2012
Power Dynamos	3	Govenda Simwala [11], Kennedy Mudenda [20], Felix Nyaende [30]
Japan Actuel's	0	

Somhlolo National Stadium, Lobamba, 19-02-2012
Green Mamba	2	Maseko [60], Mdluli [89]
FC Platinum	4	Donald Ngoma 2 [9 27], Allan Gahadzikwa [29], Sadiki Ali [84]

Mandava Stadium, Zvishavane, 3-03-2012
FC Platinum	4	Joel Ngodzo [7], Charles Sibanda 2 [29 45], Allan Gahadzikwa [37]
Green Mamba	0	

Nuevo Estadio de Malabo, Malabo, 19-02-2012
Elá Nguema	0	
Dolphin	3	Emmanuel Nwachi [16], Chidi Osuchukwu [26], Ifeanyi Egwim [50]

Liberation Stadium, Port Harcourt, 4-03-2012
Dolphin	3	Isiaka Olawale [2], Ifeanyi Egwim [20], Chidi Osuchukwu [72]
Elá Nguema	0	

Antoinette Tubman Stadium, Monrovia, 19-02-2012
LISCR	0	
Berekum Chelsea	2	Eric Agyeman [57], Prince Arko [79]

Golden City Park, Berekum, 4-03-2012
Berekum Chelsea	3	Jordan Opoku [44], Emmanuel Clottey 2 [66 70]
LISCR	0	

Benjamin Mkapa National Stadium, Dar es Salaam, 18-02-2012
Young Africans	1	Hamis Kiiza [36]
Zamalek	1	Amr Zaki [74]

Military Academy Stadium, Cairo, 3-03-2012
Zamalek	1	Mido [31]
Young Africans	0	

Stade de Franceville, Franceville, 19-02-2012
Missile	3	Gui Gosse 2 [3 34p], Cedric Mintsa [35]
Africa Sports	2	Stephane Iani [2], Tiemoko Konate [21]

Stade Felix Houphouet-Boigny, Abidjan, 4-03-2012
Africa Sports	2	Serge Kouakou [24], Tiemoko Konate [79]
Missile	0	

National Stadium, Freetown, 18-02-2012
Ports Authority	0	
Horoya	0	

Stade du 28 Septembre, Conakry, 4-03-2012
Horoya	1	Abraham Sylla [70]
Ports Authority	0	

Amaan Stadium, Zanzibar City, 19-02-2012
Mafunzo	0	
Liga Muçulmana	2	Muandro 2 [8 14]

Estádio Da Liga Muçulmana, Matola, 10-03-2012
Liga Muçulmana	3	Telinho 2 [1 37], Reginaldo [62]
Mafunzo	0	

Box Bar Mini Stadium, Brikama, 18-02-2012
Brikama United	0	
US Ouakam	1	Ngagne Diallo [60]

Stade Demba Diop, Dakar, 3-03-2012
US Ouakam	0	Brikama W 3-1p
Brikama United	1	Foday Trawally [70]

SECOND ROUND

Addis Abeba Stadium, 25-03-2012
Ethiopian Coffee	0	
Al Ahly	0	

Military Academy Stadium, Cairo, 8-04-2012
Al Ahly	3	Fabio Junior [8], Mohamed Aboutrika 2 [61p, 77]
Ethiopian Coffee	0	

Stade Rene Pleven d'Akpakpa, Cotonou, 1-04-2012
Tonnerre Abomey	0	
Stade Malien	0	

Stade 26 Mars, Bamako, 14-04-2012
Stade Malien	5	Oumar Kida 2 [10, 34], Mohamed Koumare [26], Moussa Coulibaly [77p], Abdoulaye Cissoko [85]
Tonnerre Abomey	2	Romuald Kiki [24], Mohamed Aoudou [51]

Barthelemy Boganda Stadium, Bangui, 24-03-2012
DFC 8ème	0	
Al Hilal	3	Mudather El Tahir [15], Edward Sadomba [54], Almadina [68]

Al Hilal Stadium, Omdurman, 6-04-2012
Al Hilal	5	Mudather El Tahir 2 [18, 40], Edward Sadomba 2 [48, 65], Saif Eldin Farah [67]
DFC 8ème	1	OG [90]

Stade Mohamed Boumezrag, Chlef, 23-03-2012
ASO Chlef	0	
Vita Club	0	

Stade des Martyrs, Kinshasa, 8-04-2012
Vita Club	2	Magola [54p], Ngudikama [94+]
ASO Chlef	3	Karim Ali Hadji 2 [1, 44], Hocine Achiou [85]

Stade Regional Nyamirambo, Kigali, 24-03-2012
APR FC	0	
Etoile du Sahel	0	

Stade Olympique, Sousse, 6-04-2012
Etoile du Sahel	3	Lasaad Jaziri 2 [9, 98+], Hamed Namouchi [89]
APR FC	2	Dan Wagaluka [39], Faty Papy [81]

Stade de l'Unité Maghrébine, Béjaïa, 23-03-2012
JSM Béjaïa	1	Ahmed Gasmi [55]
AFAD Djékanou	2	Mathieu Kadjo [5], Boblay Allegne [43]

Stade Robert Champroux, Abidjan, 7-04-2012
AFAD Djékanou	3	Kouakou Amoro 2 [15p, 60], Cheick Ahmed [75]
JSM Béjaïa	0	

Namboole National Stadium, Kampala, 24-03-2012
URA Kampala	0	
Djoliba	2	Alou Bagayoko [16], Bourahama Sidibe [25]

Estádio Patrice Lumumba, Munenga, 25-03-2012
Recreativo Libolo	4	Rasca [33], Adawa Mokanga [79], Dario [81], Chico Caputo [90]
Sunshine Stars	1	Izu Azuka [59]

International Stadium, Ijebu Ode, 8-04-2012
Sunshine Stars	3	Izu Azuka [20], Godfrey Oboabona [30p], Dele Olorundare [80]
Recreativo Libolo	0	

Arthur Davies Stadium, Kitwe, 24-03-2012
Power Dynamos	1	Kabwe Kamuzati [80]
TP Mazembe	1	Mbwana Samata [16]

Stade Frederic Kibassa Maliba, Lubumbashi, 8-04-2012
TP Mazembe	6	Rainford Kalaba [9], Tresor Mputu 3 [21, 66p, 72], Given Singuluma 2 [42, 44]
Power Dynamos	0	

Rufaro Stadium, Harare, 24-03-2012
FC Platinum	2	Mitchell Katsvairo [31], Joel Ngodzo [51]
El Merreikh	2	Saeed Mustafa [36], Mike Mutyaba [80]

Al Merreikh Stadium, Omdurman, 7-04-2012
El Merreikh	3	Kelechi Osunwa 2 [11, 43], Jonas Sakuwaha [19p]
FC Platinum	0	

Liberation Stadium, Port Harcourt, 25-03-2012
Dolphin	2	Ifeanyi Egwim [2], Owusu Addai [87]
Cotonsport	1	Jacques Haman [19]

Roumdé Adjia Stadium, Garoua, 8-04-2012
Cotonsport	1	Jacques Haman [21]
Dolphin	0	

Golden City Park, Berekum, 25-03-2012
Berekum Chelsea	5	Solomon Asante [34], Abdul Basit [66], Emmanuel Clottey 3 [53, 62p, 88]
Raja Casablanca	0	

Stade Mohamed V, Casablanca, 8-04-2012
Raja Casablanca	3	Mohamed Oulhaj [50], Hassan Tayr [70], Yassine Salhi [92+]
Berekum Chelsea	0	

Military Academy Stadium, Cairo, 25-03-2012
Zamalek	1	Razak Omotoyossi [2]
Africa Sports	0	

Stade Felix Houphouet-Boigny, Abidjan, 8-04-2012
Africa Sports	2	Soumaila Belem [57], Koffi Olie [68]
Zamalek	1	

Stade du 28 Septembre, Conakry, 25-03-2012
Horoya	1	Issiaga Sylla [36]
Maghreb Fès	1	Hamza Hajji [2]

Complexe Sportif de Fès, Fès, 8-04-2012
Maghreb Fès	3	Hamza Abourazzouk 2 [24, 71], Abdelhadi Halhoul [29]
Horoya	0	

Estádio Da Liga Muçulmana, Matola, 24-03-2012
Liga Muçulmana	2	Telinho [45], Muandro [80]
Dynamos	2	Takesure Chinyama 2 [21, 52]

Rufaro Stadium, Harare, 8-04-2012
Dynamos	1	Takesure Chinyama [17]
Liga Muçulmana	0	

Box Bar Mini Stadium, Brikama, 24-03-2012
Brikama United	1	Musa Bojang [12]
Espérance Tunis	1	Wajdi Bouazzi [4]

Stade Olympique de Radès, Tunis, 6-04-2012
Espérance Tunis	3	Wajdi Bouazzi [40], Youssef Msakni [45], Karim Aouadhi [72]
Brikama United	1	Saikou Sawo [25]

THIRD ROUND

Stade Modibo Keita, Bamako, 29-04-2012		
Stade Malien	1	Lamine Diawara [89]
Al Ahly	0	
Military Academy Stadium, Cairo, 14-05-2012		
Al Ahly	3	Mohamed Aboutrika 3 [54 82p 88]
Stade Malien	1	Oumar Kida [17]
Al Hilal Stadium, Omdurman, 29-04-2012		
Al Hilal	1	Mudather El Tahir [10]
ASO Chlef	1	Karim Ali Hadji [56]
Stade Mohamed Boumezrag, Chlef, 12-05-2012		
ASO Chlef	1	Karim Ali Hadji [81], Chelf W 4-2p
Al Hilal	1	Ala'a Eldin Yousif [33]
Stade Olympique, Sousse, 28-04-2012		
Etoile du Sahel	4	Lamjed Chehoudi [29], Lasaad Jaziri [55p], Mossaab Sassi [85], Hatem Bejaoui [90]
AFAD Djékanou	1	Krahire Yannick [61]
Stade Robert Champroux, Abidjan, 12-05-2012		
AFAD Djékanou	1	Konan Kouadio [59]
Etoile du Sahel	0	
Stade Modibo Keita, Bamako, 28-04-2012		
Djoliba	1	Bourahama Sidibe [71]
Sunshine Stars	1	Izu Azuka [1]
International Stadium, Ijebu Ode, 13-05-2012		
Sunshine Stars	1	Izu Azuka [40]
Djoliba	0	

Stade Frederic Kibassa Maliba, Lubumbashi, 29-04-2012		
TP Mazembe	2	Mbwana Samata [22], Tresor Mputu [70]
Al Merreikh	0	
Al Merreikh Stadium, Omdurman, 12-05-2012		
Al Merreikh	1	Kelechi Osunwa [75]
TP Mazembe	1	Nathan Sinkala [56]
Golden City Park, Berekum, 29-04-2012		
Berekum Chelsea	0	
Cotonsport	0	
Roumdé Adjia Stadium, Garoua, 13-05-2012		
Cotonsport	1	Jacques Haman [83p]
Berekum Chelsea	2	Mohamed Abdul Basit [30], Emmanuel Clottey [90]
Complexe Sportif de Fès, Fès, 28-05-2012		
Maghreb Fès	0	
Zamalek	2	Ahmed Hassan [78], Ahmed Gaafar [89]
Military Academy Stadium, Cairo, 13-05-2012		
Zamalek	2	Ibrahim Salah [2], Hazem Emam [48]
Maghreb Fès	0	
Stade Olympique de Radès, Tunis, 28-04-2012		
Espérance Tunis	6	Walid Hichri [8], Karim Aouadhi [14], Youssef Msakni 2 [38 93+], Yannick N'Djeng [77], Iheb Msakni [84]
Dynamos	0	
Rufaro Stadium, Harare, 8-04-2012		
Dynamos	1	Denver Mukamba [83]
Espérance Tunis	1	Khaled Ayari [48]

GROUP STAGE

GROUP A

		Pl	W	D	L	F	A	Pts	TUN	NGA	ALG	TUN
Espérance Tunis	TUN	4	3	0	1	6	3	9		1-0	3-2	1-0
Sunshine Stars	NGA	4	2	0	2	4	4	6	0-2		2-0	-
ASO Chlef	ALG	4	1	0	3	4	7	3	1-0	1-2		0-1
Etoile du Sahel	TUN				Disqualified				0-2	0-0	-	

Mohamed Boumezrag, Chlef 7-07-2012, Coulibaly MLI	
ASO Chlef	0
Match result annulled	
Mohamed GHALEM - Toufik BOUHAFER•, Chemseddine NESSAKH (Mohamed AMROUNE 77), Farid MELLOULI - Mohamed AOUAMERI, Maamar BENTOUCHA (Patrick KAMGAING 66), Mohamed ZAOUCHE, Sabri GHARBI, Kheireddine SELLAMA (Youcef MAAMAR• 46), Mohamed MESSAOUD - Karim Ali HADJI. Tr: Rachid BELHOUT	
Etoile du Sahel	1
Belaid [9]	
Aymen MATHLOUTHI - Rami BEDOUI•, Hatem BEJAOUI, Felhi RADHOUANE, Chamseddine DHAOUADI - Franck KOM, Wael BELLAKHAL, Mossab SASSI, Amen BELAID - SANTOS (Lamjed CHEHOUDI 83), Justin MENGOLO (Hamed NAMOUCHI 89). Tr: Mondher KBAIER	

International Stadium, Ijebu Ode 8-07-2012, Gassama GAM	
Sunshine Stars	0
Moses OCHEJE - Ofem INAH, Isaac HELE, Godfrey OBOABONA - Medrano TAMEN (Sunday EMMANUEL 46), Oluwasina ABE, Moses JAMES - Ibrahim AJANI, Izu AZUKA, Osas IDEHEN (Dele OLORUNDARE 56), Dayo OJO. Tr: Gbenga OGUNBOTE	
Espérance Tunis	2
Msakni.Y [20], N'Djeng [45]	
Moez BEN CHERIFA - Harrison AFFUL, Walid HICHERI, Mohamed BEN MANSOUR, Sameh DERBALI, Khalil CHEMMAM - Karim AOUADHI (Idrissa COULIBALY 86), Khaled MOUELHI, Mejdi TRAOUI• (Oussama BOUGHANMI 72), Youssef MSAKNI (Khaled AYARI 82) - Yannick N'DJENG. Tr: Nabil MAALOUL	

Stade Olympique de Radès, Tunis 20-07-2012, El Ahrach MAR	
Espérance Tunis	3
Mouelhi 2 [29p 87p], N'Djeng [93+]	
Moez BEN CHERIFA - Idrissa COULIBALY, Harrison AFFUL (Iheb MSAKNI 90), Mohamed BEN MANSOUR, Sameh DERBALI (Youcef BELAILI 76) - Karim AOUADHI, Khaled MOUELHI, Youssef MSAKNI• - Yannick N'DJENG, Idriss MHIRSI (Oussama BOUGHANMI 64). Tr: Nabil MAALOUL	
ASO Chlef	2
Mellouli [42], Messaoud [85]	
Mohemed GHALEM• - Toufik BOUHAFER (Youcef MAAMAR 76), Chemseddine NESSAKH•, Farid MELLOULI•, Samir ZAOUI, Samir ZAZOU• - Maamar BENTOUCHA•, Mohamed ZAOUCHE, Sabri GHARBI, Mohamed MESSAOUD•♦ [94+] - Anicet EYENGA (Mohamed AMROUNE 67). Tr: Rachid BELHOUT	

CAF CHAMPIONS LEAGUE 2012

Stade Olympique, Sousse
21-07-2012, Seechurn MRI

Etoile du Sahel   0
Match result annulled

Aymen MATHLOUTHI - Rami BEDOUI, Hatem BEJAOUI, Chamseddine DHAOUADI (Bilel BEN MESSAOUD 67), Felhi RADHOUANE - Franck KOM (Lamjed CHEHOUDI 75), Wael BELLAKHAL, Amen BELAID, Mossaab SASSI - SANTOS, Justin MENGOLO (Moussa MAAZOU 57). Tr: Mondher KBAIER

Sunshine Stars   0

Moses OCHEJE - Ado ALI, Alaba OSAWE, Godfrey OBOABONA - Jude EBITOGWA, Oluwasina ABE (Sunday EMMANUEL 36), Soga SAMBO - Ukeyima AKOMBO (Izu AZUKA 77), Ibrahim AJANI, Dayo OJO, Dele OLORUNDARE. Tr: Gbenga OGUNBOTE

International Stadium, Ijebu Ode
5-08-2012, Nampiandraza MAD

Sunshine Stars   2
Olorundare [48], Azuka [59]

Moses OCHEJE - Alaba OSAWE, Godfrey OBOABONA - Jude EBITOGWA, Moses JAMES, Soga SAMBO (Ofem INAH 46) - Izu AZUKA, Ukeyima AKOMBO (Sunday ABE 84), Ibrahim AJANI•, Dayo OJO• (Medrano TAMEN 76), Dele OLORUNDARE. Tr: Gbenga OGUNBOTE

ASO Chlef   0

Mohemed GHALEM - Toufik BOUHAFER•, Farid MELLOULI, Samir ZAOUI, Samir ZAZOU - Mohamed ZAOUCHE, Patrick KAMGAING (Mohamed AMROUNE 58), Sabri GHARBI - Karim Ali HADJI, Anicet EYENGA, Zakaria HADDOUCHE (Chemseddine NESSAKH• 55). Tr: Rachid BELHOUT

Stade Olympique de Radès, Tunis
5-08-2012, Alioum CMR

Espérance Tunis   1
Match result annulled   Mouelhi [41p]

Moez BEN CHERIFA - Harrison AFFUL (Wajdi BOUAZZI 76), Walid HICHERI, Mohamed BEN MANSOUR, Sameh DERBALI•, Khalil CHEMMAM - Khaled MOUELHI, Karim AOUADHI, Idriss MHIRSI (Youcef BELAILI 59) - Yannick N'DJENG (Khaled AYARI 89). Tr: Nabil MAALOUL

Etoile du Sahel   0

Aymen MATHLOUTHI - Rami BEDOUI, Hatem BEJAOUI, Felhi RADHOUANE, Chamseddine DHAOUADI - Franck KOM•, Wael BELLAKHAL (Bilel BEN MESSAOUD• 73), Mossaab SASSI• (Lamjed CHEHOUDI• 46), Amen BELAID - SANTOS (Justin MENGOLO 62), Moussa MAAZOU. Tr: Mondher KBAIER

Mohamed Boumezrag, Chlef
17-08-2012, Bangoura GUI

ASO Chlef   1
Eyenga [48]

Mohemed GHALEM - Youcef MAAMAR• (Patrick KAMGAING 46), Mohamed AOUAMRI, Samir ZAOUI, Samir ZAZOU - Mohamed BENTOUCHA, Sabri GHARBI••♦65 - Karim Ali HADJI, Anicet EYENGA, Mohamed AMROUNE (Zakaria HADDOUCHE 58). Tr: Rachid BELHOUT

Sunshine Stars   2
Tamen [45], Ukeyima [76]

Moses OCHEJE - Alaba OSAWE, Precious OSASCO, Ado ALI (Valentine IWUORIE 81), Godfrey OBOABONA - Jude EBITOGWA, Medrano TAMEN, Oluwasina ABE - Izu AZUKA• (Adeniyi ALABA 83), Ukeyima AKOMBO, Dele OLORUNDARE. Tr: Gbenga OGUNBOTE

Stade Olympique, Sousse
18-08-2012, Doue, CIV

Etoile du Sahel   0
Match abandoned after 72 minutes

Aymen MATHLOUTHI - Rami BEDOUI, Hatem BEJAOUI (Lamjed CHEHOUDI 46), Chamseddine DHAOUADI, Felhi RADHOUANE• - Bilel BEN MESSAOUD•, Amen BELAID, Abdel HABIB MEITE - Justin MENGOLO, Amor OMRANI. Tr: Mondher KBAIER

Espérance Tunis   2
Aouadhi [41], N'Djeng [71]

Moez BEN CHERIFA - Walid HICHERI, Mohamed BEN MANSOUR, Sameh DERBALI, Khalil CHEMMAM - Youssef MSAKNI, Houcine RAGUED• (Mejdi TRAOUI 63), Karim AOUADHI (Oussama BOUGHANMI• 46), Khaled MOUELHI, Wajdi BOUAZZI - Yannick N'DJENG. Tr: Nabil MAALOUL

Stade Olympique de Radès, Tunis
2-09-2012, Abdul Rahman SDN

Espérance Tunis   1
OG [52]

Moez BEN CHERIFA - Harrison AFFUL, Walid HICHERI, Mohamed BEN MANSOUR, Sameh DERBALI - Wajdi BOUAZZI (Idriss MHIRSI 70), Khaled MOUELHI, Youcef BELAILI (Chaker ZOUAGHI 89), Houcine RAGUED, Youssef MSAKNI (Didier LEBRI 92+) - Yannick N'DJENG. Tr: Nabil MAALOUL

Sunshine Stars   0

Moses OCHEJE - Alaba OSAWE•, Precious OSASCO, Solomon KWAMBE•, Ado ALI (Moses JAMES 81) - Jude EBITOGWA, Dayo OJO, Egbune HARRISON, Izu AZUKA, Ukeyima AKOMBO, Ibrahim AJANI (Medrano TAMEN 79). Tr: Gbenga OGUNBOTE

Stade Olympique, Sousse
Match not played

Etoile du Sahel   –

Match not played

ASO Chlef   –

Mohamed Boumezrag, Chlef
14-09-2012, Otogo Castane GAB

ASO Chlef   1
Eyenga [26]

Mohemed GHALEM - Toufik BOUHAFER, Mohamed AOUAMRI, Samir ZAOUI, Samir ZAZOU• - Maamar BENTOUCHA (Kheireddine SELAMA 85), Mohamed ZAOUCHE, Mohamed SAIDOUNE•, Chemseddine NESSAKH• - Karim Ali HADJI (Mohamed AMROUNE 93+), Anicet EYENGA (Zakaria HADDOUCHE 73). Tr: Rachid BELHOUT

Espérance Tunis   0

Wassim NAOUARA - Harrison AFFUL, Seifallah HOSNI, Mohamed BEN MANSOUR - Wajdi BOUAZZI•, Mejdi TRAOUI, Houcine RAGUED• - Oussama BOUGHANMI (Yannick N'DJENG 65), Chaker ZOUAGHI - Khaled AYARI (Youssef MSAKNI• 63), Youcef BELAILI (Iheb MSAKNI 82). Tr: Nabil MAALOUL

International Stadium, Ijebu Ode
Match not played

Sunshine Stars   –

Match not played

Etoile du Sahel   –

GROUP B

		Pl	W	D	L	F	A	Pts	EGY	COD	GHA	EGY
Al Ahly	EGY	6	3	2	1	9	6	11		2-1	4-1	1-1
TP Mazembe	COD	6	3	1	2	9	6	10	2-0		2-2	2-0
Berekum Chelsea	GHA	6	2	3	1	9	10	9	1-1	1-0		3-2
Zamalek	EGY	6	0	2	4	5	10	2	0-1	1-2	1-1	

Ohene Djan, Accra
7-07-2012, Diatta SEN

Berekum Chelsea 3
Clottey 3 [29 46 91+]

Ernest SOWAH - Richard Kissi BOATENG•, Prince ANOKYE (Mohamed MUSA 66), Edward KPODO, Ahmed ADAMS - Jordan OPOKU, Gladson AWAKO, Awudu MORO (Joseph Ato BISSAH 63), Solomon ASANTE (Ibrahim ISSAKA 77), Jackson OWUSU - Emmanuel CLOTTEY. Tr: Hans VAN DER PLUIJM

Zamalek 2
Cisse 2 [22 34]

Abdel WAHEED EL SAYED - Sabry RAHIL (Amr ZAKY 66), Mahmoud FATHALLA, Hani SAIED•, Alexis MENDOMO - Nour AL SAYED, Islam AWAD (Mohammed ABDEL SHAFI 41), Ibrahim SALAH, Hazem EMAM - Ahmed FATHY GAAFAR, Abdoulaye CISSE (Mohamed IBRAHIM 46). Tr: Hassan SHEHATA

Military Academy, Cairo
8-07-2012, Doue CIV

Al Ahly 2
Moteab [12], Gedo [92+]

Sherif EKRAMY• - Ahmed FATHY, Mohamed NAGUIB, Sherif ABDEL FADIL, Sayed MOAWAD• - Mohamed ABOUTRIKA (Abdallah SAIED 86), Hossam GHALY, Hossam ASHOUR•, Waleed SOLIMAN• (GEDO 72) - Mohamed BARAKAT, Emad MOTEAB (Anicet OUSSOU KONAN 59). Tr: Hossam EL BADRY

TP Mazembe 1
Samata [85]

Robert KIDIABA - Eric NKULUKUTA, Joel KIMWAKI•81, Jean KASUSULA, Felix Stophira SUNZU - Rainford KALABA (Guy LUSADISU 87), Patrick ILONGO, Nathan SINKALA• - Tresor MPUTU, Given SINGULUMA (Deo KANDA 70), Luka LUNGU• (Aly Mbwana SAMATA 65). Tr: Lamine N'DIAYE

Stade TP Mazembe, Lubumbashi
22-07-2012, Bennett RSA

TP Mazembe 2
Mputu 2 [11 32]

Robert KIDIABA - Eric NKULUKUTA, Pamphile MIHAYO, Jean KASUSULA, Felix Stophira SUNZU - Rainford KALABA (Deo KANDA 87), Patrick ILONGO• (Guy LUSADISU 59), Nathan SINKALA• - Tresor MPUTU, Given SINGULUMA, Aly Mbwana SAMATA (Francis KASONDE 75). Tr: Lamine N'DIAYE

Berekum Chelsea 2
Clottey 2 [70p 84]

Ernest SOWAH - Richard Kissi BOATENG•, Edward KPODO, Eric AGYEMANG•, Ahmed ADAMS - Jordan OPOKU (Ibrahim ISSAKA 68), Gladson AWAKO, Solomon ASANTE (Awudu MORO 95+), Jackson OWUSU - Mohamed MUSA, Emmanuel CLOTTEY. Tr: Hans VAN DER PLUIJM

Military Academy, Cairo
22-07-2012, Kirwa KEN

Zamalek 0

Abdel WAHEED EL SAYED - Ahmed SAMIR FARAG, Mahmoud FATHALLA, Mohammed ABDUL SHAFY, Alexis MENDOMO - Nour AL SAYED•, Ahmed HASSAN (Ahmed FATHY GAAFAR 61), Mohamed IBRAHIM (Hazem EMAM 76), Ibrahim SALAH - Hamada TOLBA•, Abdoulaye CISSE (Islam AWAD 71). Tr: Hassan SHEHATA

Al Ahly 1
Aboutrika [79]

Sherif EKRAMY - Ahmed FATHY•, Mohamed NAGUIB, Sherif ABDEL FADIL, Sayed MOAWAD - Mohamed ABOUTRIKA (Mahmoud HASSAN 89), Hossam GHALY (Abdallah SAIED 61), Hossam ASHOUR•, Waleed SOLIMAN - Mohamed BARAKAT, Emad MOTEAB (GEDO 67). Tr: Hossam EL BADRY

Stade TP Mazembe, Lubumbashi
4-08-2012, Abdel Rahman SDN

TP Mazembe 2
Kasongo [70], Samata [77]

Robert KIDIABA - Eric NKULUKUTA•, Pamphile MIHAYO (Hichani HIMOONDE 69), Jean KASUSULA, Felix Stophira SUNZU - Rainford KALABA, Patrick OCHAN (Ngandu KASONGO 66), Patrick ILONGO• - Tresor MPUTU, Given SINGULUMA (Deo KANDA• 67), Aly Mbwana SAMATA. Tr: Lamine N'DIAYE

Zamalek 0

Abdel WAHEED EL SAYED - Sabry RAHIL, Ahmed SAMIR FARAG (Hazem EMAM 62), Mahmoud FATHALLA, Alexis MENDOMO• - Nour AL SAYED, Ahmed HASSAN, Ibrahim SALAH (Mohamed IBRAHIM 75) - Ahmed FATHY GAAFAR (Razak OMOTOYOSSI 72), Hamada TOLBA, Abdoulaye CISSE. Tr: Ismail YOUSSEF

Military Academy, Cairo
4-08-2012, Haimoudi ALG

Al Ahly 4
Said [17], Nagieb [33], Soliman 2 [68 72]

Sherif EKRAMY - Wael GOMA••♦63, Mohamed NAGUIB, Sherif ABDEL FADIL, Sayed MOAWAD - Hossam GHALY, Hossam ASHOUR•, Waleed SOLIMAN (Mahmoud HASSAN 78) - Mohamed BARAKAT•, Abdallah SAIED (Dominique DA SILVA 86), Anicet OUSSOU KONAN (GEDO• 58). Tr: Hossam EL BADRY

Berekum Chelsea 1
Clottey [41p]

Ernest SOWAH - Richard Kissi BOATENG••♦45, Awudu NAFIU•, Eric AGYEMANG•, Ahmed ADAMS - Jordan OPOKU•, Gladson AWAKO (Alfred ARTHUR 71), Yaw BADOLO (Ibrahim ISSAKA 80), Jackson OWUSU - Abdul BASIT (Solomon ASANTE 71), Emmanuel Clottey. Tr: Hans VAN DER PLUIJM

Ohene Djan, Accra
19-08-2012, El Ahrach MAR

Berekum Chelsea 1
Opoku [52]

Iddrissu ABUBARKAR - Samuel KYERE, Edward KPODO•, Alfred ARTHUR•, Ahmed ADAMS - Jordan OPOKU, Solomon ASANTE, Jackson OWUSU - Awudu MORO (Abdul BASIT 67), Bismark IDAN (Ibrahim ISSAKA 78), Emmanuel CLOTTEY. Tr: Hans VAN DER PLUIJM

Al Ahly 1
Oussou Konan [43]

Sherif EKRAMY - Ahmed FATHY•, Mohamed NAGUIB, Sherif ABDEL FADIL, Sayed MOAWAD• - Mohamed ABOUTRIKA, Mahmoud HASSAN, Hossam GHALY, Waleed SOLIMAN (Mohamed BARAKAT• 80) - Anicet OUSSOU KONAN (Dominique DA SILVA 56), GEDO (Abdallah SAIED 73). Tr: Hossam EL BADRY

Military Academy, Cairo
19-08-2012, Jedidi TUN

Zamalek 1
Omotoyossi [36]

Abdel WAHEED EL SAYED - Sabry RAHIL, Ahmed SAMIR FARAG•, Mahmoud FATHALLA, Alexis MENDOMO• - Hazem EMAM (Said KOTTA 77), Hani SAIED, Ibrahim SALAH - Mohamed IBRAHIM (Islam AWAD 63), Razak OMOTOYOSSI (Ahmed FATHY GAAFAR 71), Abdoulaye CISSE. Tr: Jorvan VIEIRA

TP Mazembe 2
Himoonde [34], Samata [44]

Robert KIDIABA - Hichani HIMOONDE, Jean KASUSULA•, Francis KASONDE (Herve NDONGA 63), Felix Stophira SUNZU - Rainford KALABA, Patrick OCHAN (Ngandu KASONGO 63), Joel KIMWAKI - Tresor MPUTU, Given SINGULUMA, Aly Mbwana SAMATA (Deo KANDA 86). Tr: Lamine N'DIAYE

Military Academy, Cairo
1-09-2012, Coulibaly MLI

Zamalek 1
Ibrahim.M [13]

Abdel WAHEED EL SAYED - Sabry RAHIL, Ahmed SAMIR FARAG, Mahmoud FATHALLA, Hazem EMAM (Said KOTTA 84) - Hani SAIED, Mohamed IBRAHIM, Islam AWAD (Mohamed ABDUL SHAFY 67), Ibrahim SALAH - Omar GABER, Abdoulaye CISSE. Tr: Jorvan VIEIRA

Berekum Chelsea 1
Nafiu [24]

Ernest SOWAH - Samuel KYERE•, Awudu NAFIU•, Alfred ARTHUR, Ahmed ADAMS - Gladson AWAKO (Jordan OPOKU 76), Solomon ASANTE, Abdul BASIT, Jackson OWUSU - Bismark IDAN (Richard Kissi BOATENG 72), Emmanuel CLOTTEY. Tr: Hans VAN DER PLUIJM

CAF CHAMPIONS LEAGUE 2012

Stade TP Mazembe, Lubumbashi	Ohene Djan, Accra	Military Academy, Cairo
2-09-2012, Alioum CMR	16-09-2012, Gassama GAM	16-09-2012, Jedidi TUN
TP Mazembe 2	**Berekem Chelsea** 1	**Al Ahly** 1
Samata [49], Kanda [61]	Opoku [80]	Barakat [62]

Robert KIDIABA - Eric NKULUKUTA, Hichani HIMOONDE, Jean KASUSULA, Felix Stophira SUNZU - Rainford KALABA (Herve NDONGA 89), Deo KANDA (Thomas ULIMWENGU 67), Joel KIMWAKI - Tresor MPUTU, Given SINGULUMA, Aly Mbwana SAMATA (Ngandu KASONGO 72). Tr: Lamine N'DIAYE

Collins ADDO• - Samuel KYERE•, Richard Kissi BOATENG, Alfred ARTHUR, Kweku ANDOH, Ahmed ADAMS (Yaw ALEXANDER 31) - Joseph BISSAH (Ibrahim ISSAKA 62), Jordan OPOKU, Solomon ASANTE, Abdul BASIT• (Gladson AWAKO 82), Jackson OWUSU. Tr: Hans VAN DER PLUIJM

Sherif EKRAMY - Sayed MOAWAD, Rami RABIA, Sherif ABDEL FADIL (Ahmed SEDIK 32), Saad SAMIR - Hossam GHALY, Ahmed SHOKRI (Mohamed BARAKAT 48), TREZEGUET, Abdallah SAIED - GEDO, Anicet OUSSOU KONAN (Emad MOTEAB 78). Tr: Hossam EL BADRY

Al Ahly 0	**TP Mazembe** 0	**Zamalek** 1
		Ibrahim [43]

Sherif EKRAMY - Wael GOMA, Ahmed SHEDID, Sherif ABDEL FADIL, Saad SAMIR, Ahmed SEDIK (GEDO 58) - Mohamed ABOUTRIKA (Hossam GHALY 77), Hossam ASHOUR, Waleed SOLIMAN, Abdallah SAIED - Dominique DA SILVA (Anicet OUSSOU KONAN 64). Tr: Hossam EL BADRY

Robert KIDIABA - Eric NKULUKUTA, Hichani HIMOONDE, Jean KASUSULA, Felix Stophira SUNZU (Nathan SINKALA 46) - Rainford KALABA, Deo KANDA (Thomas ULIMWENGU 76), Joel KIMWAKI - Tresor MPUTU, Given SINGULUMA (Ngandu KASONGO 72), Aly Mbwana SAMATA. Tr: Lamine N'DIAYE

Abdel WAHEED EL SAYED - Alexis MENDOMO, Mohamed ABDUL SHAFY, Mahmoud FATHALLA, Ahmed HASSAN (Hazem EMAM 85) - Hani SAIED, Ahmed SAMIR, Mohamed IBRAHIM, Islam AWAD, Ibrahim SALAH - Ahmed GAAFAR (Abdoulaye CISSE 59). Tr: Jorvan VIEIRA

SEMI-FINALS

International Stadium, Ijebu Ode	30 June Stadium, Cairo
6-10-2012, Bennett RSA	21-10-2012, Alioum CMR
Sunshine Stars 3	**Al Ahly** 1
Temen [38], Olorundare [73p], Osasco [84]	Gedo [28]

Moses OCHEJE - Ofem INAH, Precious OSASCO, Valentine IWUORIE, Isaac HELE - Medrano TAMEN, Sunday EMMANUEL - Ukeyima AKOMBO, Izu AZUKA (Dele OLORUNDARE 42), Moses JAMES•, Dayo OJO (Ibrahim AJANI 44). Tr: Gbenga OGUNBOTE

Sherif EKRAMY - Ahmed FATHY, Wael GOMA, Mohamed NAGUIB, Ahmed SHEDID - Hossam GHALY, Hossam ASHOUR, Mohamed BARAKAT (Shehab AHMED 64), Abdallah SAIED (Rami RABIA 89) - Al Sayed HAMDY (Emad MOTEAB 61), GEDO. Tr: Hossam EL BADRY

Al Ahly 3	**Sunshine Stars** 0
Gedo 2 [18][74], Hamdy [32]	

Sherif EKRAMY• - Ahmed FATHY, Wael GOMA•, Mohamed NAGUIB, Ahmed SHEDID (Saad SAMIR 75) - Hossam GHALY, Hossam ASHOUR, Waleed SOLIMAN, Abdallah SAIED - Al Sayed HAMDY (Dominique DA SILVA 69), GEDO. Tr: Hossam EL BADRY

Henry AYODELE - Godfrey OBOABONA, Alaba OSAWE, Precious OSASCO, Ado ALI (Moses JAMES 83) - Jude EBITOGWA (Isaac HELE 47), Oluwasina ABE (Egbune HARRISON 63), Medrano TAMEN•, Ibrahim AJANI - Izu AZUKA•, Dele OLORUNDARE. Tr: Gbenga OGUNBOTE

Stade TP Mazembe, Lubumbashi	Stade Olympique de Radès, Tunis
7-10-2012, Doue CIV	20-10-2012, Diatta SEN
TP Mazembe 0	**Espérance Tunis** 1
	Ben Mansour [70]

Robert KIDIABA - Eric NKULUKUTA, Hichani HIMOONDE, Jean KASUSULA•, Felix Stophira SUNZU••♦92+ - Rainford KALABA (Ngandu KASONGO 62), Deo KANDA (Thomas ULIMWENGU 58), Joel KIMWAKI - Tresor MPUTU•, Given SINGULUMA, Aly Mbwana SAMATA (Nathan SINKALA 83). Tr: Lamine N'DIAYE

Moez BEN CHERIFA - Sameh DERBALI•, Walid HICHERI, Mohamed BEN MANSOUR, Khalil CHEMMAM - Harrison AFFUL (Youcef BELAILI 69), Walid HICHERI, Mohamed BEN MANSOUR, Khalil CHEMMAM - Harrison AFFUL, Khaled MOUELHI, Karim AOUADHI, Houcine RAGUED•, Youssef MSAKNI (Mejdi TRAOUI 85) - Yannick N'DJENG (Chaker ZOUAGHI 88). Tr: Nabil MAALOUL

Espérance Tunis 0	**TP Mazembe** 0

Moez BEN CHERIFA - Sameh DERBALI•, Walid HICHERI, Mohamed BEN MANSOUR, Khalil CHEMMAM - Harrison AFFUL (Khaled AYARI 77), Khaled MOUELHI, Karim AOUADHI (Chaker ZOUAGHI 81), Houcine RAGUED•, Mejdi TRAOUI• - Yannick N'DJENG (Youssef MSAKNI 85). Tr: Nabil MAALOUL

Robert KIDIABA (Vumi MATAMPI 76) - Eric NKULUKUTA, Hichani HIMOONDE, Jean KASUSULA, Joel KIMWAKI• - Guy LUSADISU (Thomas ULIMWENGU 67), Patrick ILONGO, Nathan SINKALA (Deo KANDA 83) - Tresor MPUTU, Given SINGULUMA, Aly Mbwana SAMATA. Tr: Lamine N'DIAYE

FINAL

CAF CHAMPIONS LEAGUE FINAL 2012 1ST LEG
BORGE EL ARAB STADIUM, ALEXANDRIA

Sunday, 4-11-2012, 19:00, Att: 25 000, Ref: Djamel Haimoudi ALG
Assistants: Mohamed Bechirene ALG & Bouabdalah Omari ALG

AL AHLY	1	1	ESPERANCE
Hamdy 88			Hichri 49

AL AHLY
Blue shirts, white shorts, red socks

Tr: Hossam El Badry — Sherif Ekramy

Ahmed Fathy 26, Wael Gomaa, Mohamed Nagieb 46 Sherif Adel-Fadil / Al Sayed Hamdy
Hossam Ghaly (c) 60 Mohamed Barakat, Hossam Ashour
Abdallah Saied, Mohamed Aboutrika, Walid Soliman
Gedo 82 Emad Moteab

ESPERANCE
Navy blue shirts, navy blue shorts, navy blue socks

Tr: Nabil Maaloul — Moez Ben Cherifia
Mohamed Ben Mansour, Walid Hichri
Khalil Chammam (c) 45, Khaled Mouelhi, Sameh Derbali 10
Wajdi Bouazzi, Houcine Ragued 86 Chaker Zouagi, Karim Aouadhi 9, Yannick N'Djeng 82 Khaled Ayari, Harrison Afful 55 Mejdi Traoui 73

CAF CHAMPIONS LEAGUE FINAL 2012 1ST LEG
STADE OLYMPIQUE DE RADES, TUNIS

Saturday, 17-11-2012, 18:30, Att: 31 000, Ref: Bouchaib El Ahrach MAR
Assistants: Redouane Achik MAR & Bouazza Rouani MAR

ESPERANCE	1	2	AL AHLY
N'Djeng 85			Gedo 43, Soliman 63

ESPERANCE
Yellow and gold striped shirts, black shorts, black socks

Tr: Nabil Maaloul — Moez Ben Cherifia
Walid Hichri, Mohamed Ben Mansour 93+
Chaker Zouagi, Khalil Chammam (c)
Houcine Ragued 73 Khaled Ayari, Khaled Mouelhi
Wajdi Bouazzi 56 Youcef Belaili, Karim Aouadhi 46 Iheb Msakni, Youssef Msakni
Yannick N'Djeng

AL AHLY
Blue and black striped shirts, white shorts, red socks

Tr: Hossam El Badry — Sherif Ekramy
Al Sayed Hamdy 66 Mohamed Aboutrika
Walid Soliman 71 Dominque Da Silva, Gedo 88 Ramy Rabia, Abdallah Saied
Hossam Ashour, Hossam Ghaly (c)
Ahmed Shedid, Mohamed Nagieb, Wael Gomaa, Ahmed Fathy

We were a lot better. We scored two goals and missed many other chances. The coach told us to pile pressure from the very beginning and even after the goal he urged us to keep on pressing to grab the second and kill off the game. We wanted this trophy so much to offer it to the families and the souls of the fans who died in the Port Said stadium disaster.
— Abdallah Al Saied

Ahly were the better side in this game and they deserved to win. We didn't produce a fine performance and I can't claim that the absent players were the reason. I think the result we had in the first leg affected us negatively contrary to what most people thought would be the case. I don't believe Msakni's participation after returning from injury was a wrong decision as he was one of the games' best players.
— Nabil Maaloul

CECAFA KAGAME INTER-CLUB CUP TANZANIA 2012

First round groups

Group A		Pl	W	D	L	F	A	Pts	COD	TAN	DJI
URA	UGA	3	3	0	0	8	2	**9**	3-1	2-0	3-1
AS Vita Club	COD	3	1	1	1	9	4	**4**		1-1	7-0
Simba SC	TAN	3	1	1	1	4	3	**4**			3-0
AS Port	DJI	3	0	0	3	1	13	**0**			

Group B		Pl	W	D	L	F	A	Pts	ZAN	KEN
Azam	TAN	2	0	2	0	1	1	**2**	1-1	0-0
Mafunzo	ZAN	2	0	2	0	1	1	**2**		0-0
Tusker	KEN	2	0	2	0	0	0	**2**		

Group C		Pl	W	D	L	F	A	Pts	TAN	RWA	SSD
At Olympique	BDI	3	2	1	0	7	0	**7**	2-0	0-0	5-0
Y. Africans	TAN	3	2	0	1	9	3	**6**		2-0	7-1
APR FC	RWA	3	1	1	1	7	2	**4**			7-0
Wau Salaam	SSD	3	0	0	3	1	19	**0**			

Quarter-finals
- Young Africans 1 5p
- Mafunzo 1 3p

- URA 1
- APR FC 2

- AS Vita Club 2
- At. Olympique 1

- Simba 1
- Azam 3

Semi-finals
- Young Africans 1
- APR FC 0

- AS Vita Club 1
- Azam 2

Final
- Young Africans 2
- Azam 0

Third place play-off
- AS Vita Club 2
- APR FC 1

Played in Dar es Salaam, Tanzania from 14-07-2012 to 28-07-2012
Top scorers: **7** - Said **BAHANUNZI** TAN, Yanga • **6** - Taddy **ETEKIAMA** COD, Vita Club & Hamis **KIZZA** UGA, Yanga • **5** - John **BOCCO** TAN, Azam

---

CECAFA KAGAME INTER-CLUB CUP FINAL 2012
National Stadium, Dar es Salaam, 28-07-2012, Ref: Thierry Nkurunziza BDI

Young Africans	2	Kizza [44], Bahanunzi [93+]
Azam	0	

YOUNG AFRICANS

Ally **MUSTAPHA** - Stephano **MWASIKA**, Oscar **JOSHUA**, Nadir **HAROUB** (c), Kelvin **YONDAN** - Athuman **IDD**, Rashid **GUMBO** (Juma **SEIF** 74), Haruna **NIYONZIMA** - David **LUHENDE** - Said **BAHANUNZI**, Hamis **KIZZA**. Tr: Tom **SAINTFIET**

AZAM

Deogratius **MUNISHI** - Ibrahim **SHIKANDA** (Samih **NUHU** 69), Erasto **NYONI**, Aggrey **MORRIS** (c), Said **MORADI** - Ramadhani **CHOMBO** - Ibrahim **MWAIPOPO**, Jabir **STIMA**, Salum **SALUM** - Kipre **TCHETCHE** (Mrisho **NGASSA** 67), John **BOCCO**. Tr: Stewart **HALL**

CAF CONFEDERATION CUP 2012

First Round

Léopards *	CGO	2	2
Tempête Mocaf	CTA	0	2
CS Sfaxien	TUN	Bye	
Unisport Bafang	CMR	1	0
Séwé Sports *	CIV	0	0
Heartland	NGA	Bye	
Al Amal Atbara	SDN	Bye	
Jamhuri *	ZAN	0	1
Hwange	ZIM	3	4
Tana FC	MAD	1	2
Extension Gunners *	BOT	2	0
InterClube	ANG	Bye	
Al Ahly Shendi	SDN	Bye	
Gor Mahia	KEN	0	0
Ferroviario Maputo *	MOZ	3	1
Entente Sétif	ALG	Bye	
Kiyovu Sport *	RWA	1	1
Simba	TAN	1	2
Warri Wolves	NGA	Bye	
Union Douala *	CMR	1	0
FC Kallon	SLE	0	2
St Eloi Lupopo	COD	Bye	
Motor Action	ZIM	1	0
Black Leopards *	RSA	1	2
Club Olympique	MLI	Bye	
Sahel SC Niamey	NIG	0	2
Renaissance *	CHA	2	2
LLB Academic *	BDI	3	2
Atlético Semu	EQG	0	0
ENPPI	EGY	Bye	
Real Bamako	MLI	Bye	
Casa Sport	SEN	0 1 3p	
Gamtel *	GAM	1 0 4p	
Invincible Eleven	LBR	w/o	
Desportivo Mansabá *	GNB		
Wydad Casablanca	MAR	Bye	
CODM Meknès	MAR	Bye	
Nania *	GHA		
FC Séquence	GUI	w/o	
Etoile Filante	BFA	0	2
Dragons de l'Ouémé *	BEN	1	0
ASEC Mimosas	CIV	Bye	
Royal Leopards	SWZ	0	1
Red Arrows *	ZAM	0	0
US Tshinkunku	COD	Bye	
Saint George	ETH	1	4
Mangasport *	GAB	0	0
Club Africain	TUN	Bye	

Second Round

Léopards *	1	2
CS Sfaxien	2	0
Unisport Bafang *	0	1
Heartland	0	2
Al Amal Atbara	1	0
Hwange *	1	0
Tana FC *	2 0 5p	
InterClube	0 2 6p	
Al Ahly Shendi	1	2
Ferroviario Maputo *	0	0
Entente Sétif	0	3
Simba *	2	1
Warri Wolves	0	2
FC Kallon *	0	0
St Eloi Lupopo	2	2
Black Leopards *	4	2
Club Olympique	2	3
Renaissance *	3	1
LLB Academic *	1	1
ENPPI	1	4
Real Bamako	0	3
Gamtel *	1	1
Invincible Eleven *	0	1
Wydad Casablanca	2	4
CODM Meknès	2	3
FC Séquence *	0	0
Etoile Filante *	2	0
ASEC Mimosas	2	2
Royal Leopards *	1	2
US Tshinkunku	1	1
Saint George *	1	0
Club Africain	1	2

Third Round

Léopards	2	2
Heartland *	3	1
Al Amal Atbara	1	0
InterClube *	4	2
Al Ahly Shendi	0 3 9p	
Simba *	3 0 8p	
Warri Wolves *	3	0
Black Leopards	1	2
Club Olympique	1	3
ENPPI *	3	0
Real Bamako	0	1
Wydad Casablanca *	3	0
CODM Meknès	1	0
ASEC Mimosas *	1	0
Royal Leopards *	0	2
Club Africain	1	5

CAF CONFEDERATION CUP 2012

Intermediate Round

Léopards	CGO	0	2
Maghreb Fès * †	MAR	1	0

Dynamos * †	ZIM	0	0
InterClube	ANG	0	1

Al Ahly Shendi	SDN	0	2
Cotonsport * †	CMR	1	0

Black Leopards	RSA	2	0
Al Merreikh * †	SDN	3	0

Al Hilal * †	SDN	2	1
Club Olympique	MLI	0	0

AFAD Djékanou * †	CIV	0	0
Wydad Casablanca	MAR	0	1

Stade Malien * †	MLI	3	1
CODM Meknès	MAR	0	1

Club Africain	TUN	0 2 3p	
Djoliba * †	MLI	2 0 4p	

Group Stage

Group A	Pts	AM	AH	IC	AA
Al Merreikh	14		3-2	1-0	2-0
Al Hilal	11	1-1		3-0	2-0
InterClube	5	0-0	1-1		0-1
Al Ahy Shendi	3	0-1	1-2	1-2	

Group B	Pts	Dj	Le	WAC	SM
Djoliba	13		1-1	2-1	2-1
AC Léopards	9	3-0		1-1	1-0
Wydad C'blanca	6	1-2	3-1		1-1
Stade Malien	3	0-2	1-1	3-3	

Léopards *	2	0
Al Merreikh	1	0

Final

Léopards *	2	2
Djoliba	2	1

Al Hilal *	2 0 6p	
Djoliba	0 2 7p	

* Home team in the first leg
† Champions League third round losers that entered at the Intermediate round

CONCACAF

CONFEDERATION OF NORTH, CENTRAL AMERICAN AND CARIBBEAN ASSOCIATION FOOTBALL

CONCACAF MEMBER ASSOCIATIONS (35)
AIA - Anguilla • ATG - Antigua and Barbuda • ARU - Aruba • BAH - Bahamas • BRB - Barbados • BLZ - Belize • BER - Bermuda
VGB - British Virgin Islands • CAN - Canada • CAY - Cayman Islands • CRC - Costa Rica • CUB - Cuba • DMA - Dominica
DOM - Dominican Republic • SLV - El Salvador • GRN - Grenada • GUA - Guatemala • GUY - Guyana • HAI - Haiti • HON - Honduras
JAM - Jamaica • MEX - Mexico • MSR - Montserrat • ANT - Netherlands Antilles • NCA - Nicaragua • PAN - Panama • PUR - Puerto Rico
SKN - St Kitts and Nevis • LCA - St Lucia • VIN - St Vincent/Grenadines • SUR - Suriname • TRI - Trinidad and Tobago
TCA - Turks and Caicos Islands • VIR - US Virgin Islands • USA - United States of America

CONCACAF ASSOCIATE MEMBER ASSOCIATIONS (5)
GYF - French Guiana • GLP - Guadeloupe • MTQ - Martinique • SMT - Saint Martin • SMX - Sint Maarten
None of these five nations are affiliated to FIFA

2012 proved to be another successful year for CONCACAF on the world stage with member nations winning three of the six world titles on offer during the course of the year. The highlight was the success of both the Mexican men's team and the American women's team at the London Olympics. While the USA gold medal winning performance may have been expected, the success of Mexico in claiming their gold was not. In the final at Wembley they beat the fancied Brazilians 2-1 to claim their first-ever medal in Olympic football and what was the nation's only gold of the entire games. In contrast the USA claimed their fourth gold in the five games that women's football has been played with their 2-1 victory over Japan securing a hat trick of Olympic titles. It was sweet revenge for their defeat at the hands of the Japanese in the previous year's FIFA Women's World Cup final. There was also success for the American team in the FIFA U-20 Women's World Cup after they beat Germany 1-0 in the final in Tokyo but there was little for Mexico's Monterrey to celebrate at the end of the year in the FIFA Club World Cup in Japan when they lost to Chelsea in the semi-finals. Earlier in the year they had beaten compatriots Santos Laguna 3-2 on aggregate in the CONCACAF Champions League final to retain the trophy that they had first won in 2011. It was also a busy year for football in the Caribbean with Trinidad's Caledonia AIA claiming the CFU club title for the first time while at the end of the year Antigua played host to the 16th edition of the Caribbean Cup where Cuba caused a huge sensation by beating eight times champions Trinidad and Tobago 1-0 in the final to claim the trophy for the first time.

Confederation of North, Central American and Caribbean Association Football (CONCACAF)
725, Fifth Avenue, Trump Tower, 17th Floor, New York, NY 1022, USA
Tel +1 212 3080 044   Fax +1 212 3081 851
mail@concacaf.net   www.concacaf.com
President: Jeffrey Webb CAY   General Secretary: Ted Howard USA
CONCACAF Formed: 1961

CONCACAF EXECUTIVE COMMITTEE
President: Jeffrey Webb CAY
Vice-President: Lisle Austin BRB   Vice-President: Alfredo Hawit Banegas HON   Vice-President: Justino Compean MEX

ORDINARY MEMBERS OF THE EXECUTIVE COMMITTEE
Horace Burrell JAM   Ariel Alvarado PAN   Sunil Gulati USA
FIFA Exco: Rafael Salguero GUA   FIFA Exco: Chuck Blazer USA

MAP OF CONCACAF MEMBER NATIONS

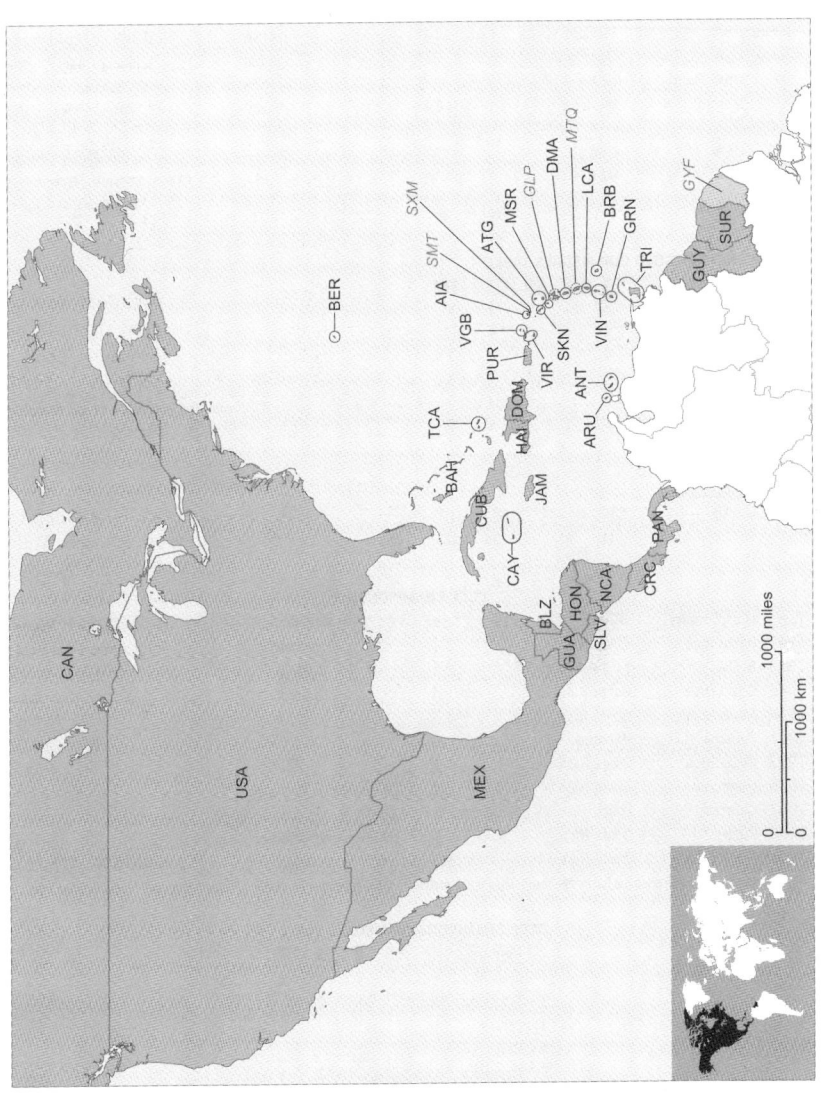

CENTRAL AMERICAN, NORTH AMERICAN AND CARIBBEAN NATIONAL TEAM TOURNAMENTS

CONCACAF GOLD CUP

Year	Host Country	Winners	Score	Runners-up	Venue
1991	USA	USA	0-0 4-3p	Honduras	Coliseum, Los Angeles
1993	Mexico/USA	Mexico	4-0	USA	Azteca, Mexico City
1995	USA	Mexico	2-0	Brazil	Coliseum, Los Angeles
1998	USA	Mexico	1-0	USA	Coliseum, Los Angeles
2000	USA	Canada	2-0	Colombia	Coliseum, Los Angeles
2002	USA	USA	2-0	Costa Rica	Rose Bowl, Pasadena
2003	Mexico/USA	Mexico	1-0	Brazil	Azteca, Mexico City
2005	USA	USA	0-0 3-1p	Panama	Giants Stadium, New Jersey
2007	USA	USA	2-1	Mexico	Soldier Field, Chicago
2009	USA	Mexico	5-0	USA	Giants Stadium, New Jersey
2011	USA	Mexico	4-2	USA	Rose Bowl, Pasadena

CONCACAF GOLD CUP MEDALS TABLE

	Country	G	S	B	F	SF
1	Mexico	6	1	1	7	8
2	USA	4	4	2	8	10
3	Canada	1		2	1	3
4	Honduras		1	3	1	4
5	Costa Rica		1	2	1	5
6	Panama		1	1	1	2
7	Jamaica			1		2
8	Guadeloupe			1		1
	Trinidad and Tobago			1		1
10	Guatemala					1
		11	8	12	19	37

KEY
G = Gold (winners) • S = Silver (runners-up) • B = Bronze (semi-finalists) • F = appearances in the final • SF = appearances in the semi-final

CCCF CHAMPIONSHIP

Year	Host Country	Winners	Score	Runners-up	Venue
1941	Costa Rica	Costa Rica	3-1	El Salvador	San José
1943	El Salvador	El Salvador	2-1	Guatemala	San Salvador
1946	Costa Rica	Costa Rica	1-4	Guatemala	San José
1948	Guatemala	Costa Rica	2-3	Guatemala	Guatemala City
1951	Panama	Panama	2-0	Costa Rica	Panama City
1953	Costa Rica	Costa Rica	4-1	Honduras	San José
1955	Honduras	Costa Rica	2-1	Netherlands Antilles	Tegucigalpa
1957	Curaçao	Haiti	3-1	Curaçao	Willemstad
1960	Cuba	Costa Rica	4-1†	Netherlands Antilles	Havana
1961	Costa Rica	Costa Rica	4-0	El Salvador	San José

All tournaments played on a league basis. The result listed is the match played between the top two • † Play-off after both teams finished level

CCCF CHAMPIONSHIP MEDALS TABLE

	Country	G	S	B
1	Costa Rica	7	1	1
2	El Salvador	1	2	
3	Panama	1		1
4	Haiti	1		
5	Guatemala		3	1
6	Curaçao		2	1
7	Honduras		1	5
8	Netherlands Antilles		1	
9	Nicaragua			1
		10	10	10

CONCACAF NATIONS CUP

Year	Host Country	Winners	Score	Runners-up	Venue
1963	El Salvador	Costa Rica	4-1	El Salvador	San Salvador
1965	Guatemala	Mexico	2-1	Guatemala	Guatemala City
1967	Honduras	Guatemala	1-0	Mexico	Tegucigalpa
1969	Costa Rica	Costa Rica	1-1	Guatemala	San José
1971	Trinidad & T	Mexico	0-0	Haiti	Port of Spain

All tournaments played on a league basis. The result listed is the match played between the top two

CONCACAF NATIONS CUP MEDALS TABLE

	Country	G	S	B
1	Mexico	2	1	
2	Costa Rica	2		2
3	Guatemala	1	2	
4	El Salvador		1	
	Haiti		1	
6	Netherlands Antilles			2
7	Honduras			1
		5	5	5

CARIBBEAN CUP

Year	Host Country	Winners	Score	Runners-up	Venue
1989	Barbados	Trinidad & Tobago	2-1	Grenada	Bridgetown
1990	Trinidad	Not completed			
1991	Jamaica	Jamaica	2-0	Trinidad & Tobago	Kingston
1992	Trinidad	Trinidad & Tobago	3-1	Jamaica	Port of Spain
1993	Jamaica	Martinique	0-0 6-5p	Jamaica	Kingston
1994	Trinidad	Trinidad & Tobago	7-2	Martinique	Port of Spain
1995	Cayman/Jamaica	Trinidad & Tobago	5-0	St Vincent/Grenadines	George Town
1996	Trinidad	Trinidad & Tobago	2-0	Cuba	Port of Spain
1997	Antigua/St Kitts	Trinidad & Tobago	4-0	St Kitts and Nevis	St John's
1998	Jamaica/Trinidad	Jamaica	2-1	Trinidad & Tobago	Port of Spain
1999	Trinidad	Trinidad & Tobago	2-1	Cuba	Port of Spain
2001	Trinidad	Trinidad & Tobago	3-0	Haiti	Port of Spain
2005	Barbados	Jamaica	1-0†	Cuba	Waterford
2007	Trinidad	Haiti	2-1	Trinidad & Tobago	Port of Spain
2008	Jamaica	Jamaica	2-0	Grenada	Kingston
2010	Martinique	Jamaica	1-1 5-4p	Guadeloupe	Fort-de-France
2012	Antigua	Cuba	1-0	Trinidad & Tobago	St John's

† Final tournament played as a league. The match listed is between the top two.

CONCACAF NATIONS CUP MEDALS TABLE

	Country	G	S	B
1	Trinidad and Tobago	8	4	2
2	Jamaica	5	2	2
3	Cuba	1	3	3
4	Haiti	1	1	3
	Martinique	1	1	3
6	Grenada		2	
7	Guadeloupe		1	2
8	St Kitts and Nevis		1	
	St Vincent/Grenadines		1	
10	St Lucia			1
		16	16	16

UNCAF CUP/COPA CENTROAMERICANA

Year	Host Country	Winners	Score	Runners-up	Venue
1991	Costa Rica	Costa Rica	2-0†	Honduras	San José
1993	Honduras	Honduras	2-0†	Costa Rica	Tegucigalpa
1995	El Salvador	Honduras	3-0	Guatemala	San Salvador
1997	Guatemala	Costa Rica	1-1†	Guatemala	Mateo Flores, Guatemala City
1999	Costa Rica	Costa Rica	1-0†	Guatemala	San José
2001	Honduras	Guatemala	2-0†	Costa Rica	Tegucigalpa
2003	Panama	Costa Rica	1-1†	Guatemala	Rommel Fernández, Panama City
2005	Guatemala	Costa Rica	1-1 7-6p	Honduras	Mateo Flores, Guatemala City
2007	El Salvador	Costa Rica	1-1 4-1p	Panama	Cuscatlán, San Salvador
2009	Honduras	Panama	0-0 5-3p	Costa Rica	Tiburcio Andino, Tegucigalpa
2011	Panama	Honduras	2-1	Costa Rica	Rommel Fernández, Panama City
2013	Costa Rica	Costa Rica	1-0	Honduras	

† Final tournament played as a league. The match listed is between the top two.

CONCACAF NATIONS CUP MEDALS TABLE

	Country	G	S	B
1	Costa Rica	7	4	
2	Honduras	3	3	2
3	Guatemala	1	4	3
4	Panama	1	1	2
	El Salvador			5
		12	12	12

CENTRAL AMERICAN, NORTH AMERICAN AND CARIBBEAN CLUB TOURNAMENTS

CONCACAF CHAMPIONS LEAGUE

Year	Winners	Country	Score	Country	Runners-up
1962	Guadalajara	MEX	1-0 5-0	GUA	Comunicaciones
1963	Racing Club Haïtienne	HAI	W-O	MEX	Guadalajara
1964	Not completed				
1965	Not completed				
1966	Not held				
1967	Alianza	SLV	1-2 3-0 5-3	ANT	Jong Colombia
1968	Toluca	MEX	W-O †		
1969	Cruz Azul	MEX	0-0 1-0	GUA	Comunicaciones
1970	Cruz Azul	MEX	W-O †		
1971	Cruz Azul	MEX	5-1	CRC	LD Alajuelense
1972	Olimpia	HON	0-0 2-0	SUR	Robinhood
1973	Transvaal	SUR	W-O †		
1974	Municipal	GUA	2-1 2-1	SUR	Transvaal
1975	Atletico Español	MEX	3-0 2-1	SUR	Transvaal
1976	Aguila	SLV	6-1 2-1	SUR	Robinhood
1977	América	MEX	1-0 0-0	SUR	Robinhood
1978	UAG Tecos	MEX	W-O †		
1979	Deportivo FAS	SLV	1-0 8-0	ANT	Jong Colombia

CONCACAF CLUB TOURNAMENTS

CONCACAF CHAMPIONS LEAGUE (CONT'D)

Year	Winners	Country	Score	Country	Runners-up
1980	UNAM Pumas	MEX	2-0 ‡	HON	Universidad de Honduras
1981	Transvaal	SUR	1-0 1-1	SLV	Atlético Marte
1982	UNAM Pumas	MEX	2-2 3-0	SUR	Robinhood
1983	Atlante	MEX	1-1 5-0	SUR	Robinhood
1984	Violette	HAI	W-O †		
1985	Defence Force	TRI	2-0 0-1	HON	Olimpia
1986	LD Alajuelense	CRC	4-1 1-1	SUR	Transvaal
1987	América	MEX	2-0 1-1	TRI	Defence Force
1988	Olimpia	HON	2-0 2-0	TRI	Defence Force
1989	UNAM Pumas	MEX	1-1 3-1	CUB	Piñar del Rio
1990	América	MEX	2-2 6-0	CUB	Piñar del Rio
1991	Puebla	MEX	3-1 1-1	TRI	Police FC
1992	América	MEX	1-0	CRC	LD Alajuelense
1993	Deportivo Saprissa	CRC	2-2 ‡	MEX	Leon
1994	Cartagines	CRC	3-2	MEX	Atlante
1995	Deportivo Saprissa	CRC	1-0 ‡	GUA	Municipal
1996	Cruz Azul	MEX	1-1 ‡	MEX	Necaxa
1997	Cruz Azul	MEX	5-3	USA	Los Angeles Galaxy
1998	DC United	USA	1-0	MEX	Toluca
1999	Necaxa	MEX	2-1	CRC	LD Alajuelense
2000	LA Galaxy	USA	3-2	HON	Olimpia
2001	Not completed				
2002	Pachuca	MEX	1-0	MEX	Monarcas Morelia
2003	Toluca	MEX	3-3 2-1	MEX	Monarcas Morelia
2004	LD Alajuelense	CRC	1-1 4-0	CRC	Deportivo Saprissa
2005	Deportivo Saprissa	CRC	2-0 1-2	MEX	UNAM Pumas
2006	América	MEX	0-0 2-1	MEX	Toluca
2007	Pachuca	MEX	2-2 0-0 7-6p	MEX	Guadalajara
2008	Pachuca	MEX	1-1 2-1	CRC	Deportivo Saprissa
2009	Atlante	MEX	2-0 0-0	MEX	Cruz Azul
2010	Pachuca	MEX	1-2 1-0	MEX	Cruz Azul
2011	Monterrey	MEX	2-2 1-0	USA	Real Salt Lake
2012	Monterrey	MEX	2-0 1-2	MEX	Santos Laguna

† 1968 Toluca were declared champions after Aurora GUA and Transvaal SUR were disqualified • 1970 Cruz Azul were declared champions after Deportivo Saprissa CRC and Transvaal SUR withdrew • 1973 Transvaal were declared champions after LD Alajuelense CRC and Deoprtivo Saprissa CRC withdrew • 1978 UAG Tecos were joint winners with Comunicaciones GUA and Defence Force TRI • 1984 Violette were declared champions after Guadalajara and New York Freedoms were disqualified • ‡ 1980 1993 1995 & 1996 finals played as a league with the match listed between the top two

CONCACAF CHAMPIONS LEAGUE MEDALS TABLE

	Country	G	S	B	F	SF
1	Mexico	28	13	16	41	57
2	Costa Rica	6	5	12	11	23
3	El Salvador	3	1	2	4	6
4	Surinam	2	8	3	10	13
5	Guatemala	2	3	7	5	12
6	Honduras	2	3	3	5	8
7	Trinidad and Tobago	2	3	2	5	7
8	USA	2	2	12	4	16
9	Haiti	2			2	2
10	Netherlands Antilles		2	4	2	6
11	Cuba		2		2	2
12	Martinique			3		3
13	Bermuda			1		1
	Puerto Rico			1		1
	Canada			1		1
		49	42	67	91	158

CONCACAF CHAMPIONS LEAGUE MEDALS TABLE

	Club		G	S	B
1	Cruz Azul	MEX	5	2	1
2	América	MEX	5		1
3	Pachuca	MEX	4		1
4	Deportivo Saprissa	CRC	3	2	7
5	UNAM Pumas	MEX	3	1	2
6	LD Alajuelense	CRC	2	3	4
7	Transvaal	SUR	2	3	
8	Toluca	MEX	2	2	2
9	Olimpia	HON	2	2	1
10	Defence Force	TRI	2	2	
11	Atlante	MEX	2	1	
12	Monterrey	MEX	2		3
13	Comunicaciones	GUA	1	2	3
14	Guadalajara	MEX	1	2	1
15	Municipal	GUA	1	1	1
	Necaxa	MEX	1	1	1
17	Los Angeles Galaxy	USA	1	1	
18	DC United	USA	1		6
19	Alianza	SLV	1		2
20	Aguila	SLV	1		
	Atlético Español	MEX	1		
	CS Cartaginés	CRC	1		
	Deportivo FAS	SLV	1		
	Puebla	MEX	1		
	Racing Club Haïtienne	HAI	1		
	UAG Tecos	MEX	1		
	Violette	HAI	1		
28	Robinhood	SUR		5	3
29	Jong Colombia	ANT		2	1

CONCACAF CHAMPIONS LEAGUE MEDALS TABLE

	Club		G	S	B
30	Piñar del Rio	CUB		2	
	Monarcas Morelia	MEX		2	
32	Leon	MEX		1	2
33	Santos Laguna	MEX		1	1
34	Atlético Marte	SLV		1	
	Police FC	TRI		1	
	Real Salt Lake	USA		1	
	Universidad de Honduras	HON		1	
38	Chicago Fire	USA			2
	Houston Dynamo	USA			2
	SUBT	ANT			2
	Trintoc	TRI			2
42	Aurora	GUA			1
	Herediano	CRC			1
	Kansas City Wizards	USA			1
	L'Aiglon	MTQ			1
	Marathon	HON			1
	Pembrooke	BER			1
	Philidelphia Ukrainians	USA			1
	Puerto Rico Islanders	PUR			1
	Real España	HON			1
	Riviere-Pilote	MTQ			1
	US Robert	MTQ			1
	Sithoc	ANT			1
	Suchitepequez	GUA			1
	Tigres UANL	MEX			1
	Toronto FC	CAN			1
	Xelaju	GUA			1
			49	42	67

CFU CLUB CHAMPIONSHIP

Year	Winners	Country	Score	Country	Runners-up
1997	United Petrotin	TRI	2-1	JAM	Seba United
1998	Joe Public	TRI	1-0	TRI	Caledonia AIA
2000	Joe Public	TRI	1-0 †	TRI	W Connection
2003	San Juan Jabloteh	TRI	2-1 1-2 4-2p	TRI	W Connection
2004	Harbour View	JAM	1-1 2-1	JAM	Tivoli Gardens
2005	Portmore United	JAM	1-2 4-0	SUR	Robinhood
2006	W Connection	TRI	1-0	TRI	San Juan Jabloteh
2007	Harbour View	JAM	2-1	TRI	Joe Public
2008	Not held				
2009	W Connection	TRI	2-1	PUR	Puerto Rico Islanders
2010	Puerto Rico Islanders	PUR	1-1 †	TRI	Joe Public
2011	Puerto Rico Islanders	PUR	3-1	HAI	Tempête FC
2012	Caledonian AIA	TRI	1-1 4-3p	TRI	W Connection

† Played on a league system. The match listed was between the top two

CONCACAF CLUB TOURNAMENTS

CFU CLUB CHAMPIONSHIP MEDALS TABLE

	Country	G	S	B
1	Trinidad and Tobago	9	8	2
2	Jamaica	3	3	1
3	Puerto Rico	2	1	2
4	Haiti		1	
5	Suriname		1	
6	Guyana			1
		14	14	6

CFU CLUB CHAMPIONSHIP MEDALS TABLE

	Club		G	S	B
1	W Connection	TRI	3	4	
2	Joe Public	TRI	2	2	
3	Puerto Rico Islanders	PUR	2	1	2
4	Harbour View	JAM	2		1
5	San Juan Jabloteh	TRI	1	1	2
6	Caledonia AIA	TRI	1	1	
7	Portmore United	JAM	1		
	Defence Force	TRI	1		
	United Petrotin	TRI	1		
10	Arnett Gardens	JAM		1	
	Robinhood	SUR		1	
	Seba United	JAM		1	
	Tempête	HAI		1	
	Tivoli Gardens	JAM		1	
15	Alpha United	GUY			1
			14	14	6

COPA INTERCLUBES DE UNCAF

Year	Winners	Country	Score	Country	Runners-up
1971	Comunicaciones	GUA	†	CRC	Deportivo Saprissa
1972	Deportivo Saprissa	CRC	†	GUA	Aurora
1973	Deportivo Saprissa	CRC	†	SLV	Aguila
1974	Municipal	GUA	†	CRC	Deportivo Saprissa
1975	Platense	SLV	†	GUA	Aurora
1976	Aurora	GUA	†	GUA	Comunicaciones
1977	Municipal	GUA	†	GUA	Comunicaciones
1978	Deportivo Saprissa	CRC	†	CRC	Cartiginés
1979	Aurora	GUA	1-0 0-0	HON	Real España
1980	Broncos	HON	†	SLV	Alianza
1981	Olimpia	HON	w/o		
1982	Real España	HON	2-1 0-0	GUA	Xelajú
1983	Comunicaciones	GUA	†	GUA	Aurora
1996	LD Alajuelense	CRC	†	CRC	Deportivo Saprissa
1997	Alianza	SLV	1-0	CRC	Deportivo Saprissa
1998	Deportivo Saprissa	CRC	2-1 1-1	GUA	Municipal
1999	Olimpia	HON	†	CRC	LD Alajuelense
2000	Olimpia	HON	†	CRC	LD Alajuelense
2001	Municipal	GUA	†	CRC	Deportivo Saprissa
2002	LD Alajuelense	CRC	†	PAN	Arabe Unido
2003	Deportivo Saprissa	CRC	3-2	GUA	Comunicaciones
2004	Municipal	GUA	†	CRC	Deportivo Saprissa
2005	LD Alajuelense	CRC	1-0 0-1 4-2p	HON	Olimpia
2006	Puntarenas FC	CRC	3-2 0-1 3-1p	HON	Olimpia
2007	CD Motagua	HON	1-1 1-0	CRC	Deportivo Saprissa

Discontinued • Known as the Copa Fraternidad 1971-83 • Torneo de Grandes de Centroamerica 1996-98 • † Played on a league basis

CFU CLUB CHAMPIONSHIP MEDALS TABLE

	Country	G	S
1	Costa Rica	9	10
2	Guatemala	8	8
3	Honduras	6	3
4	El Salvador	2	2
5	Panama		1
		25	24

COPA INTERCLUBES DE UNCAF
MEDALS TABLE

	Club		G	S
1	Deportivo Saprissa	CRC	5	7
2	Municipal	GUA	4	1
3	LD Alajuelense	CRC	3	2
	Olimpia	HON	3	2
5	Comunicaciones	GUA	2	3
	Aurora	GUA	2	3
7	Alianza	SLV	1	1
	Real España	HON	1	1
9	Motagua	HON	1	
	Puntarenas	CRC	1	
	Broncos	HON	1	
	Platense	SLV	1	
13	Aguila	SLV		1
	Arabe Unido	PAN		1
	Cartigines	CRC		1
	Xelajú	GUA		1
			25	24

CENTRAL AMERICAN, NORTH AMERICAN AND CARIBBEAN YOUTH TOURNAMENTS

CONCACAF U-20 TOURNAMENT

Year	Host Country	Winners	Runners-up
1954	Costa Rica	Costa Rica	Panama
1956	El Salvador	El Salvador	Neth. Antilles
1958	Guatemala	Guatemala	Honduras
1960	Honduras	Costa Rica	Honduras
1962	Panama	Mexico	Guatemala
1964	Guatemala	El Salvador	
1970	Cuba	Mexico	Cuba
1973	Mexico	Mexico	Guatemala
1974	Canada	Mexico	Cuba
1976	Puerto Rico	Mexico	Honduras
1978	Honduras	Mexico	Canada

CONCACAF U-20 TOURNAMENT (CONT'D)

Year	Host Country	Winners	Runners-up
1980	USA	Mexico	USA
1982	Guatemala	Honduras	USA
1984	Trinidad	Mexico	Canada
1986	Trinidad	Canada	USA
1988	Guatemala	Costa Rica	Mexico
1990	Guatemala	Mexico	Trinidad
1992	Canada	Mexico	USA
1994	Honduras	Honduras	Costa Rica
1996	Mexico	Canada	Mexico
2009	Trinidad & T	Costa Rica	USA
2011	Guatemala	Mexico	Costa Rica

CONCACAF U-17 TOURNAMENT

Year	Host Country	Winners	Runners-up
1983	Trinidad	USA	Trinidad
1985	Mexico	Mexico	Costa Rica
1987	Honduras	Mexico	USA
1988	Trinidad	Cuba	USA

CONCACAF U-17 TOURNAMENT (CONT'D)

Year	Host Country	Winners	Runners-up
1991	Trinidad	Mexico	USA
1992	Cuba	USA	Mexico
1994	El Salvador	Costa Rica	USA
1996	Trinidad	Mexico	USA
2011	Jamaica	USA	Canada

CENTRAL AMERICAN, NORTH AMERICAN AND CARIBBEAN WOMEN'S TOURNAMENTS

CONCACAF WOMEN'S GOLD CUP

Year	Host Country	Winners	Score	Runners-up	Venue
1991	Haiti	USA	5-0	Canada	Port au Prince
1993	USA	USA	1-0	Canada	Long Island
1994	Canada	USA	6-0	Canada	Montreal
1998	Canada	Canada	1-0	Mexico	Toronto
2000	USA	USA	1-0	Brazil	Foxboro, Boston
2002	USA/Canada	USA	2-1	Canada	Rose Bowl, Pasadena
2006	USA	USA	2-1	Canada	Home Depot Center, Los Angeles
2010	Mexico	Canada	1-0	Mexico	Quintana Roo, Cancun

CONCACAF WOMEN'S GOLD CUP MEDALS TABLE

	Country	G	S	B
1	USA	6		1
2	Canada	2	5	
3	Mexico		2	3
4	Trinidad and Tobago			2
5	Costa Rica			1
		8	7	7

CONCACAF WOMEN'S U-20 CHAMPIONSHIP

Year	Host Country	Winners	Score	Runners-up	Venue
2004	Canada	Canada	2-1	USA	Frank Clair, Ottawa
2006	Mexico	USA	3-2	Canada	Luis Fuentes, Veracruz
2008	Mexico	Canada	1-0	USA	Cuauhtémoc, Puebla
2010	Guatemala	USA	1-0	Mexico	Cementos Progreso, Guatemala City
2012	Panama	USA	2-1	Canada	Rommel Fernández, Panama City

CONCACAF WOMEN'S GOLD CUP MEDALS TABLE

	Country	G	S	B
1	USA	3	2	
2	Canada	2	2	
3	Mexico		1	3
4	Costa Rica			2
		5	5	5

CONCACAF WOMEN'S U-17 CHAMPIONSHIP

Year	Host Country	Winners	Score	Runners-up	Venue
2008	Trinidad & Tobago	USA	4-1	Costa Rica	Marvin Lee, Macoya
2010	Costa Rica	Canada	1-0	Mexico	Alejandro Morera Soto, Alajuela
2012	Guatemala	USA	1-0	Canada	Cementos Progreso, Guatemala City

CONCACAF WOMEN'S GOLD CUP MEDALS TABLE

	Country	G	S	B
1	USA	2		1
2	Canada	1	1	1
3	Mexico		1	1
4	Costa Rica		1	
		3	3	3

NATIONAL TEAM TOURNAMENTS 2012

CARIBBEAN CUP 2012 QUALIFYING TOURNAMENT

First Round Groups

Group 1 (In Haiti)	Pl	W	D	L	F	A	Pts	PUR	BER	SMT
Haiti	3	3	0	0	12	2	**9**	2-1	3-1	7-0
Puerto Rico	3	2	0	1	12	3	**6**		2-1	9-0
Bermuda	3	1	0	2	10	5	3			8-0
Saint Martin	3	0	0	3	0	24	0			

Group 2 (In St Lucia)	Pl	W	D	L	F	A	Pts	VIN	LCA	CUW
Guyana	3	2	0	1	6	3	**6**	1-2	3-0	2-1
St Vincent/Grenadines	3	2	0	1	6	2	**6**		0-1	4-0
Saint Lucia	3	2	0	1	6	4	6			5-1
Curaçao	3	0	0	3	2	11	0			

Group 3 (In Martinique)	Pl	W	D	L	F	A	Pts	SUR	MSR	VGB
Martinique	3	2	1	0	23	2	**7**	2-2	5-0	16-0
Suriname	3	2	1	0	13	3	**7**		7-1	4-0
Montserrat	3	1	0	2	8	12	3			7-0
British Virgin Islands	3	0	0	3	0	27	0			

Group 4 (In Barbados)	Pl	W	D	L	F	A	Pts	BRB	DMA	ARU
Dominican Republic	3	2	1	0	5	3	**7**	1-0	2-1	2-2
Barbados	3	2	0	1	3	2	**6**		1-0	2-1
Dominica	3	1	0	2	4	5	3			3-2
Aruba	3	0	1	2	5	7	1			

Group 5 (In St Kitts)	Pl	W	D	L	F	A	Pts	GYF	SKN	AIA
Trinidad and Tobago	3	3	0	0	15	1	**9**	4-1	1-0	10-0
French Guiana	3	2	0	1	8	5	**6**		3-0	4-1
St Kitts and Nevis	3	1	0	2	2	4	3			2-0
Anguilla	3	0	0	3	1	16	0			

Second Round Groups

Group 6 (In Grenada)	Pl	W	D	L	F	A	Pts	GYF	GRN	GUY
Haiti	3	2	0	1	3	1	**6**	0-1	2-0	1-0
French Guiana	3	1	1	1	5	5	**4**		1-1	3-4
Grenada	3	1	1	1	3	4	4			2-1
Guyana	3	1	0	2	5	6	3			

Group 7 (In Guadeloupe)	Pl	W	D	L	F	A	Pts	MTQ	GLP	PUR
Dominican Republic	3	2	1	0	6	2	**7**	1-1	2-0	3-1
Martinique	3	1	2	0	6	5	**5**		3-3	2-1
Guadeloupe	3	1	1	1	7	6	4			4-1
Puerto Rico	3	0	0	3	3	9	0			

Group 8	Pl	W	D	L	F	A	Pts	CUB	SUR	VIN
Trinidad and Tobago	3	2	1	0	5	1	**7**	1-0	3-0	1-1
Cuba	3	1	1	1	6	2	**4**		5-0	1-1
Suriname	3	1	0	2	1	8	3			1-0
St Vincent/Grenadines	3	0	2	1	2	3	2			

Grenada, Guadeloupe & Cuba received byes to the second round • Antigua qualified for the finals as hosts, Jamaica as holders
Top scorers (overall including finals): 13 - Kevin **PARSEMAIN** MTQ • 9 - Gary **PIGREE** GYF • 7 - Hector **RAMOS** PUR; Jonathan **FANA** DOM & Jean-Philippe **PEGUERO** HAI • 5 - Jamal **GAY** TRI & Marcel **HERNANDEZ** CUB • 4 - Tyrell **BURGESS** BER; Keon **DANIEL** TRI; Steeve **GUSTAN** MTQ; Vurlon **MILLS** GUY; Stefano **RIJSSEL** SUR & Cornelius **STEWART** VIN

QUALIFYING GROUP 1

		Pl	W	D	L	F	A	Pts	PUR	BER	STM
Haiti	HAI	3	3	0	0	12	2	9	2-1	3-1	7-0
Puerto Rico	PUR	3	2	0	1	12	3	6		2-1	9-0
Bermuda	BER	3	1	0	2	10	5	3			8-0
Saint Martin	STM	3	0	0	3	0	24	0			

SYLVIO CATOR, PORT-AU-PRINCE		SYLVIO CATOR, PORT-AU-PRINCE		SYLVIO CATOR, PORT-AU-PRINCE	
7-09-2012, Att: 2000, Ref: Taylor BRB		7-09-2012, Att: 10 000, Ref: Morrison JAM		9-09-2012, Att: 2000, Ref: Royal JAM	
Bermuda	1	Haiti	7	Puerto Rico	9
Puerto Rico	2	Saint Martin	0	Saint Martin	0
BER - Russell 78p • PUR - Marrero 68, Ramos 90		HAI - Jean-Philippe 3 4 40 45, Junior 2 22 41, LaFrance 70, Jean-Eudes 90		PUR - Ramos 4 14 43 46 81, Wilson 25, Arrieta 45, Marrero 2 69 83, Oikkonen 76	

BER: Frederick HALL - Tyrell BURGESS, Darius COX, Khano SMITH, Damon MING, Andre MANDERS (Seion DARREL 89), Antwan RUSSELL, Domico CODDINGTON (Ian COKE 88), Jahni RAYNOR (Reginald THOMPSON-LAMBE 72), Shakir SMITH, John Barry NUSUM (c). Tr: Andrew BASCOME

PUR: William GAUDETTE - Scott JONES••♦83 (Tyler WILSON 83), Noah DELGADO (c), Alexis RIVERA, Christian ARRIETA, Joseph MARRERO (Joshua HANSEN 89), John KRAUSE, Andres PEREZ (Samuel SOTO 70), Fernando GONZALEZ, Anthony VAZQUEZ•, Hector RAMOS. Tr: Jeaustin CAMPOS

HAI: Johny PLACIDE (c) - Reginald GOREUX, Pierre JEAN-JACQUES, Kevin LAFRANCE, Louis JEFF, Aveska JUDELIN, Peguero JEAN-PHILIPPE (James FRANCOIS 73), Maurice EUDES, Olrish SAUREL (Jean-Marc ALEXANDRE 60), Monuma JUNIOR, Joseph PETERSON (Peter GERMAIN 66). Tr: Israel CANTERO

STM: David SAINTIL - Henri EMILE (c), Richardson BERNARD, Jude SAINTVAL•, Samuel DE MOULIN, Francois MILCET, Bellechasse YANNICK, Nicola CHALMET (Omar MORALES 79), Eric DANIEL, Quentin MALLENGUERY (Jerome LLORENS 67), Cherubin JUNIOR (Victor RICHARDSON 62). Tr: Dominique RENIA

PUR: William GAUDETTE - Marco VELEZ (c), Noah DELGADO (Joshua HANSEN 46), Alexis RIVERA, Christian ARRIETA (Andres PEREZ 58), Joseph MARRERO, Tyler WILSON, Fernando GONZALEZ (Alex OIKKONEN 64), Anthony VAZQUEZ, Hector RAMOS, Samuel SOTO. Tr: Jeaustin CAMPOS

STM: David SAINTIL - Henri EMILE (c), Richardson BERNARD, Jude SAINTVAL, Samuel DE MOULIN, Victor YANNICK, Eric DANIEL♦51, Jerome LLORENS• (Quentin MALLENGUERY 60), Kevin GUINET•, Cherubin JUNIOR (Nicola CHALMET 73). Tr: Dominique RENIA

CARIBBEAN CUP 2012 – QUALIFYING TOURNAMENT

SYLVIO CATOR, PORT-AU-PRINCE	
9-09-2012, Att: 10 500, Ref: Skeete BRB	
Haiti	3
Bermuda	1

HAI - Saurel [30], Eudes [39], Jean-Philippe [41]•
BER - Russell [86]

HAI: Johny PLACIDE (c) - Reginald GOREUX (Rubin Jean GARRY 74), Kevin LAFRANCE, Louis JEFF (Peter GERMAIN 79), Aveska JUDELIN, Peguero JEAN-PHILIPPE, Maurice EUDES (Louis FRITZNEL 60), Olrish SAUREL, Monuma JUNIOR, Joseph PETERSON, Jean-Marc ALEXANDRE•. Tr: Israel CANTERO

BER: Frederick HALL - Tyrell BURGESS, Darius COX•, Khano SMITH, Damon MING (Jahni RAYNOR 79), Andre MANDERS, Antwan RUSSELL•, Domico CODDINGTON• (Lejaun SIMMONS 90), John Barry NUSUM (c), Shakir SMITH, Reginald THOMPSON-LAMBE•. Tr: Andrew BASCOME

SYLVIO CATOR, PORT-AU-PRINCE	
11-09-2012, Att: 3000, Ref: Royal JAM	
Saint Martin	0
Bermuda	8

BER - Burgess 4 [18 31 49 76], Russell [52], Manders [61], Coke [80], Simmons [87]

STM: David SAINTIL - Anthony MARICEL (Omar MORALES 52), Henri EMILE (c), Richardson BERNARD, Jude SAINTVAL, Francois MILCET, Bellechasse YANNICK, Yvon FANTILUS, Kevin GUINET (Victor RICHARDSON 46), Quentin MALLENGUERY (Nicola CHALMET 69), Cherubin JUNIOR. TD: Dominique RENIA

BER: Tahj BELL - Tyrell BURGESS (Clay DARRELL 78), Darius COX (Lejaun SIMMONS 65), Khano SMITH, Damon MING, Andre MANDERS (Ian COKE 65), Antwan RUSSELL, Domico CODDINGTON, Drewonde BASCOME, Shakir SMITH, John Barry NUSUM (c). Tr: Andrew BASCOME

SYLVIO CATOR, PORT-AU-PRINCE	
11-09-2012, Att: 12 000, Ref: Morrison JAM	
Haiti	2
Puerto Rico	1

HAI - Jean-Philippe [65p], Eudes [67]•
PUR - Delgado [73]

HAI: Johny PLACIDE (c) - Reginald GOREUX, Kevin LAFRANCE•, Louis JEFF, Aveska JUDELIN, Peguero JEAN-PHILIPPE• (Alain VUBERT 81), Maurice EUDES, Olrish SAUREL, Monuma JUNIOR (Pierre JEAN-JACQUES 55), Joseph PETERSON (Louis FRITZNEL 46), Jean-Marc ALEXANDRE. Tr: Israel CANTERO

PUR: Eric REYES - Richard MARTINEZ, Marco VELEZ• (c) (Joshua HANSEN 85), Noah DELGADO, Alexis RIVERA, Christian ARRIETA (Samuel SOTO 46), Joseph MARRERO (Tyler WILSON 85), John KRAUSE•, Fernando GONZALEZ, Anthony VAZQUEZ•, Hector RAMOS. Tr: Jeaustin CAMPOS

QUALIFYING GROUP 2

		Pl	W	D	L	F	A	Pts	VIN	LCA	CUW
Guyana	GUY	3	2	0	1	6	3	6	1-2	3-0	2-1
St Vincent/Grenadines	VIN	3	2	0	1	6	2	6		0-1	4-0
Saint Lucia	LCA	3	2	0	1	6	4	6			5-1
Curaçao	CUW	3	0	0	3	2	11	0			

BEAUSEJOUR, GROS ISLET	
21-10-2012, Att: 1200, Ref: Pinas SUR	
Guyana	1
St Vincent/Grenadines	2

GUY - Richardson [45p] • VIN - Myron Samuel [30], Stewart [79]

GUY: Ronson WILLIAMS - Dwight PETERS, Colin NELSON, Anthony ABRAMS (Sheldon HOLDER 68), Julien EDWARDS (Kelvin SMITH• 65), Konata MANNINGS (Anthony BENFIELD 75), Gregory RICHARDSON•, Charles POLLARD, Kester JACOBS, Trayon BOBB, Christopher NURSE (c). Tr: Jamal SHABAZZ

VIN: Kenyan LYNCH - Dorren HAMLET•, Roy RICHARDS, Odanza DENNIE•, Wesley CHARLES, Theon GORDON, Wendell CUFFY (Zenroy LEE 87), Cornelius STEWART (c), Myron SAMUEL (Nical STEPHENS 89), Shandel SAMUEL (Azinho SOLOMON 75), Shemol TRIMMINGHAM•. Tr: Cornelius HUGGINS

BEAUSEJOUR, GROS ISLET	
21-10-2012, Att: 1650, Ref: Willett ATG	
Curaçao	1
St Lucia	5

CUW - Isenia [48] • LCA - Paul [14], Valcin [44], Edin [51], Charlemagne [86], Frederick [90]

CUW: Rowendy SUMTER - Ashar BERNARDUS (c), Mirco COLINA, Shuremy FELOMINA, Hujoybert DELANDO•••90, Richendro KIRINDONGO, Christopher ISENIA, Nathan MARTINA, Vilyson LAKE, Lourens MARTINA (Randall WINKLAAR 76), Lendell JOHANNES (Richenel LOURENS 46). Tr: Ludwig ALBERTO

LCA: Randy POLEON - Magnam VALCIN, Kurt FREDERICK, Eligah JOSEPH• (c), Burton EMMANUEL, Pernal WILLIAMS, Rickson AUGUSTIN, Eden CHARLES (Guy GEORGE 89), Romiel FELIX (Tafari CHARLEMAGNE 75), Everton LAMBERT, Tremain PAUL•. Tr: Francis LASTIC

BEAUSEJOUR, GROS ISLET	
23-10-2012, Att: 750, Ref: Bogle JAM	
Curaçao	1
Guyana	2

CUW - OG [53] • GUY - Mills [1], Richardson [42p]

CUW: Rowendy SUMTER - Shuremy FELOMINA• (Rowendley POPPEN 82), Ruchendro KIERINDONGO, Christopher ISENIA, Nathan MARTINA•, Vilyson LAKE, Richenel LOURENS (Randall WINKLAAR 52), Lendell JOHANNES, Jurensley MARTINA (Quinston BARTHOLOMEUS 69••89), Mirco COLINA, Ashar BERNARDUS. Tr: Ludwig ALBERTO

GUY: Ronson WILLIAMS• - Walter MOORE, Charles POLLARD, Colin NELSON, Kelvin SMITH, Dwight PETERS, Konata MANNINGS, Christopher NURSE, Sheldon HOLDER (Trayon BOBB 70), Vurlon MILLS (Anthony ABRAMS 84), Gregory RICHARDSON. Tr: Jamaal SHABAZZ

BEAUSEJOUR, GROS ISLET	
23-10-2012, Att: 1652, Ref: Vazquez DOM	
St Lucia	1
St Vincent/Grenadines	0

LCA - Paul [69]

LCA: Randy POLEON, Pernal WILLIAMS•, Elijah JOSEPH, Sheldon EMMANUEL, Kurt FREDERICK, Tremain PAUL (Romiel FELIX (Tafari CHARLEMAGNE 68), Everton LAMBERT, Rickson AUGUSTIN, Eden CHARLES (Lawrence ST CROIX 61), Cliff VALCIN (Jamil JOSEPH 80). Tr: Francis LASTIC

VIN: Kenyan-Desmond LYNCH (Dwaine SANDY 62) - Dorren HAMLET•, Roy RICHARDS, Odanza DENNIE (Oscar NERO 46), Wesley CHARLES•, Theon GORDON, Wendell CUFFY, Cornelius STEWART, Myron SAMUEL, Shemol TRIMMINGHAM, Nical STEPHENS (Shandel SAMUEL 46). Tr: Cornelius HUGGINS

BEAUSEJOUR, GROS ISLET	
25-10-2012, Att: 852, Ref: Vazquez DOM	
St Vincent/Grenadines	4
Curaçao	0

VIN - Stewart 2 [8 76], Hamlet [58], Myron Samuel [78]

VIN: Dwaine SANDY - Oscar NERO, Wesley CHARLES, Azinho SOLOMON (Shandel Samuel 80), Roy RICHARDS, Nical STEPHENS, Shemol TRIMMINGHAM•, Dorren HAMLET (Theon GORDON 85), Wendell CUFFY (Zenroy LEE 62), Cornelius STEWART, Myron SAMUEL. Tr: Cornelius HUGGINS

CUW: Rowendy SUMTER - Shuremy FELOMINA (Richenel LOURENS), Ruchendro KIERINDONGO, Christopher ISENIA, Nathan MARTINA (Rowendley POPPEN 35), Vilyson LAKE•, Geryon ALBERTO (Abdiel PINEDO 64), Lendell JOHANNES, Jurensley MARTINA, Mirco COLINA•, Ashar BERNARDUS. Tr: Ludwig ALBERTO

BEAUSEJOUR, GROS ISLET	
25-10-2012, Att: 2500, Ref: Willett ATG	
St Lucia	0
Guyana	3

GUY - Mills 2 [14 34], Richardson [37]

LCA: Thaddeus FRANCIS - Pernal WILLIAMS, Guy GEORGE• (Elijah JOSEPH 39), Sheldon EMMANUEL•, Kurt FREDERICK, Tremain PAUL, Romiel FELIX, Everton LAMBERT, Rickson AUGUSTIN•, Eden CHARLES (Jamil JOSEPH 55), Cliff VALCIN. Tr: Francis LASTIC

GUY: Ronson WILLIAMS - Walter MOORE, Charles POLLARD, Colin NELSON, Kelvin SMITH, Dwight PETERS (Anthony ABRAMS 66), Konata MANNINGS, Christopher NURSE, Trayon BOBB• (Andrew MURRAY 87), Vurlon MILLS (Kester JACOBS 77), Gregory RICHARDSON. Tr: Jamaal SHABAZZ

QUALIFYING GROUP 3

		Pl	W	D	L	F	A	Pts	SUR	MSR	VGB
Martinique	MTQ	3	2	1	0	23	2	7	2-2	5-0	16-0
Suriname	SUR	3	2	1	0	13	3	7		7-1	4-0
Montserrat	MSR	3	1	0	2	8	12	3			7-0
British Virgin Islands	VGB	3	0	0	3	0	27	0			

GEORGES-GRATIANT, LE LAMENTIN
5-09-2012, Att: 188, Ref: Angela ARU

Montserrat	1
Suriname	7

MSR - Allen [48] • SUR - Waal 2 [3 11], Sordam [16], Vallei [39], Drenthe [45], Rijssel 2 [85 90]

MSR: Dean BYFIELD - Alexander BRAMBLE, Kendell ALLEN, Leovan O'GARRO, Terryl MILLER (Kelvin PONDE 46), Ellis REMY, Jay Lee HODGSON, Marlon CAMPBELL, Hildyard MENDES (c) (Dale LEE 89), Darryl ROACH (Nyron DYER 37), Dean MASON. Tr: Kenny DYER

SUR: Ronny ALOEMA (c) - Guillermo FAERBER, Jetro FER (Romano SORDAM 49), Guno KWASIE, Jurmen Eugene VALLEI•, Giovanni URENTHE (Ives VLIJTER 75), Emilio LIMON (Romano STEKKEL 64), Vitorinio PINAS, Romano SORDAM, Stefano RIJSSEL, Giovanni WAAL. Tr: Ricardo WINTER

GEORGES-GRATIANT, LE LAMENTIN
5-09-2012, Att: 800, Ref: Santos PUR

Martinique	16
British Virgin Islands	0

MTQ - Delem 2 [6 68], Gustan [12], Dondon [41p], Parsemain 6 [32 63 67 70 81 86], Mainge [37], Abaul 2 [46 54], Berdix [80p], Balmy [82], Sidney [87]

MTN: Emmanuel VERMIGNON - Stephane ABAUL (Gaetan SIDNEY 67), Jacky BERDIX•, Sebastien CRETINOIR (c), Jordy DELEM, Gerald DONDON, Marvin ESOR (Alex BALMY 75), Steeve GUSTAN (Jean-Emmanuel NEDRA• 67), Djenhael MAINGE, Kevin PARSEMAIN, Karl VITULIN•. Tr: Patrick CAVELAN

VGB: Vesquever FRETT - Gregory JAMES (c), Jevone DEMMING ♦ [38], Rushedo ROBINSON•- (Avondale WILLIAMS 41), Jamal SARGEANT, Troy CAESAR (Javier SMITH 71), Trevor PETERS, Jhon SAMUEL (Christopher TELEMAQUE 18), Carlos SEPTUS, Fladimir SEPTUS, James SHEARMAN. Tr: Avondale WILLIAMS

EN CAMEE, RIVIERE-PILOTE
7-09-2012, Att: 200, Ref: Anderson PUR

British Virgin Islands	0
Suriname	4

SUR - Rijssel 2 [35 42], Drenthe [36], Loswijk [81]

VGB: Vesquever FRETT - Gregory JAMES (c), Andre RYAN, Rushedo ROBINSON, Jamal SARGEANT, Troy CAESAR, Trevor PETERS (Joel FAHIE 66), Jhon SAMUEL• (Fladimir SEPTUS 58), Carlos SEPTUS, Christopher TELEMAQUE (Errol WELLINGTON 80), James SHEARMAN. Tr: Avondale WILLIAMS

SUR: Ronny ALOEMA (c) - Guillermo FAERBER•, Jctro FER, Naldo KWASIE, Jurmen Eugene VALLEI, Giovanni DRENTHE (Wilfried Armand GALIMO 78), Emilio LIMON (Romano STEKKEL 65), Vitorinio PINAS, Romano SORDAM, Stefano RIJSSEL (Donovan Jurmain LOSWIJK 56), Giovanni WAAL. Tr: Ricardo WINTER

EN CAMEE, RIVIERE-PILOTE
7-09-2012, Att: 400, Ref: Da Costa BAH

Martinique	5
Montserrat	0

MTQ - Parsemain 4 [5 20 59 61], Gustan [9]

MTQ: Emmanuel VERMIGNON - Stanley ANGLIO, Sebastien CRETINOIR (c), Jordy DELEM•, Marvin ESOR (Nicolas ZAIRE 62), Steeve GUSTAN (Alex BALMY 75), Sebastien LEPEL (Djenhael MAINGE, Jean-Emmanuel NEDRA, Kevin PARSEMAIN (Gaetan SIDNEY 74), Kevin TRESFIELD•. Tr: Patrick CAVELAN

MSR: Jermain SWEENEY - Alexander BRAMBLE, Leovan O'GARRO (Clifford NEWBY-HARRIS 75), Nyron DYER (Hildyard MENDES 60), Dale LEE (Darryl ROACH 57), Ellis REMY, Jay Lee HODGSON (c), Bradley WOODS, Marlon CAMPBELL•, Kelvin PONDE, Dean MASON. Tr: Kenny DYER

PIERRE-ALIKER, FORT-DE-FRANCE
9-09-2012, Att: 120, Ref: Anderson PUR

British Virgin Islands	0
Montserrat	7

MSR - OG [33], Campbell 2 [35 45], Roach [49], Woods [53], Remy 2 [71 87]

VGB: Montgomery BUTLER (Vesquever FRETT 68) - Gregory JAMES (c), Andre RYAN, Jevone DEMMING, Rushedo ROBINSON•♦[57], Javier SMITH (Christopher TELEMAQUE 36), Jamal SARGEANT, Troy CAESAR, Carlos SEPTUS, Fladimir SEPTUS (Errol WELLINGTON 59), James SHEARMAN. Tr: Avondale WILLIAMS

MSR: Jermain SWEENEY - Nyron DYER, Dale LEE, Terrell MILLER, Bradley WOODS (Jay Lee HODGSON 55), Marlon CAMPBELL, Clifford NEWBY-HARRIS, Hildyard MENDES (c), Darryl ROACH (Ellis REMY 70), Kelvin PONDE, Dean MASON. Tr: Kenny DYER

PIERRE-ALIKER, FORT-DE-FRANCE
9-09-2012, Att: 241, Ref: Angela ARU

Martinique	2
Suriname	2

MTQ - Parsemain [3], Mainge [22] •
SUR - Aloema [25], Loswijk [90p]

MTQ: Emmanuel VERMIGNON - Stephane ABAUL•, Jacky BERDIX (Alex BALMY 70), Sebastien CRETINOIR• (c) (Fabrice REUPERNE• 43), Jordy DELEM, Gerald DONDON•, Steeve GUSTAN (Kevin TRESFIELD 79), Djenhael MAINGE, Kevin PARSEMAIN, Karl VITULIN•, Nicolas ZAIRE. Tr: Patrick CAVELAN

SUR: Ronny ALOEMA (c) - Giovanni ALLEYNE, Guillermo FAERBER, Naldo KWASIE, Jurmen VALLEI, Emilio LIMON (Donovan LOSWIJK 84), Vitorinio PINAS (Giovanni WAAL 58), Romano STEKKEL, Ives VLIJTER (Romano SORDAM• 68), Wilfried GALIMO, Stefano RIJSSEL. Tr: Ricardo WINTER

QUALIFYING GROUP 4

		Pl	W	D	L	F	A	Pts	BRB	DMA	ARU
Dominican Republic	DOM	3	2	1	0	5	3	7	1-0	2-1	2-2
Barbados	BRB	3	2	0	1	3	2	6		1-0	2-1
Dominica	DMA	3	1	0	2	4	5	3			3-2
Aruba	ARU	3	0	1	2	5	7	1			

KENSINGTON OVAL, BRIDGETOWN
23-09-2012, Att: 300, Ref: Lancaster GUY

Aruba	2
Dominican Republic	2

ARU - Baten [6], Barradas [30] •
DOM - Ozuna 2 [13 76]

ARU: Eric ABDUL - Francois CROES (Martis JOMAR 88), Reinhard BREINBURG, Ronnie NOUWEN, Raymond BATEN (c), Rensy BARRADAS (Ulises NUNEZ GARCIA 70), Jean-Luc BERGEN (Brian SIEM 67), Rashidi GILKES, Frederick GOMEZ•, Luis Carlos CROES, Theric RUIZ. Tr: Elvis ALBERTUS

DOM: Wellington AGRAMONTE - Johan CRUZ, Cesar GARCIA, Heinz BARMETTLER, Solange GONZALEZ, Erick Junior OZUNA, Jonathan FANA FRIAS (c), Kerbi RODRIGUEZ (Gilberto ULLOA 87), Domingo PERALTA (Pedro NUNEZ 58), Rafael FLORES, Hansley MARTINEZ. Tr: Clemente HERNADNEZ

KENSINGTON OVAL, BRIDGETOWN
23-09-2012, Att: 300, Ref: Brizan TRI

Barbados	1
Dominica	0

BRB - Williams [35]

BRB: Jason BOXILL - Barry SKEETE, Raheim SARGEANT, Ranaldo MARQUES, Mario HARTE• (Malcolm MARSHALL 74), Kemar HEADLEY (Jason LOVELL 90), Rashida WILLIAMS• (c), Tristan PARRIS (Kyle GIBSON 58), Ramuel MILLER, Ricardo MORRIS, Andre BOURNE•. Tr: Colin FORDE

DMA: Glenson PRINCE (c) - Prince AUSTRIE• (Elmond DERRICK 69), Hubert PRINCE (Delbert DAILEY 11), Collin BERNARD, Kelrick WALTER, Lester LANGLAIS, Joel Etienne CLARK•, Kurlson BENJAMIN•, Shern DAILEY, Carlvin CHRISTOPHER, Chad BERTRAND (Eddie THOMAS 29). Tr: Kirt HECTOR

KENSINGTON OVAL, BRIDGETOWN
25-09-2012, Att: 150, Ref: Clarke LCA

Dominica	3
Aruba	2

DMA - Bertrand [36], Benjamin 2 [45 77] •
ARU - Bergen [40], Gomez [55]

DMA: Glenson PRINCE (c) - Delbert DAILEY, Collin BERNARD, Kelrick WALTER, Elmond DERRICK, Joel Etienne CLARK• (Andy St Rose 90), Kurlson BENJAMIN (Lester LANGLAIS 86), Shern DAILEY, Eddie THOMAS (Glenworth ELIZEE• 31), Carlvin CHRISTOPHER•, Chad BERTRAND. Tr: Kirt HECTOR

ARU: Eric ABDUL (Kendrick DANIA 90) - Francois CROES, Reinhard BREINBURG•♦♦[61], Theric RUIZ (Brian SIEM 67), Ronnie NOUWEN, Raymond BATEN• (c), Rensy BARRADAS, Jean-Luc BERGEN (Ulises NUNEZ GARCIA 85), Rashidi GILKES, Frederick GOMEZ, Luis Carlos CROES. Tr: Elvis ALBERTUS

CARIBBEAN CUP 2012 – QUALIFYING TOURNAMENT

KENSINGTON OVAL, BRIDGETOWN
25-09-2012, Att: 750, Ref: Elskamp SUR

Barbados	0
Dominican Republic	1

DOM - Nunez [80]

BRB: Jason BOXILL - Barry SKEETE•, Raheim SARGEANT• (Armando LASHLEY 85), Ranaldo MARQUES•, Mario HARTE (Carl JOSEPH 46), Kemar HEADLEY, Rashida WILLIAMS (c), Tristan PARRIS, Ramuel MILLER (Kyle GIBSON 90), Ricardio MORRIS, Andre BOURNE. Tr: Colin FORDE

DOM: Wellington AGRAMONTE• - Johan CRUZ, Cesar GARCIA•, Solange GONZALEZ, Kerbi RODRIGUEZ, Domingo PERALTA• (Jimmy REYES 90), Jonathan FANA FRIAS (c) (Pedro NUNEZ 46), Erick Junior OZUNA (Kerbi SEVERINO 90), Rafael FLORES•, Hansley MARTINEZ, Heinz BARMETTLER. Tr: Clemente HERNADNEZ

KENSINGTON OVAL, BRIDGETOWN
27-09-2012, Att: 300, Ref: Brizan TRI

Dominican Republic	2
Dominica	1

DOM - Fana Frias 2 [66] [90] • DMA - Langlais [39]

DOM: Wellington AGRAMONTE - Johan CRUZ, Cesar GARCIA, Solange GONZALEZ•, Kerbi RODRIGUEZ, Domingo PERALTA• (Jimmy REYES 82), Erick Junior OZUNA, Rafael FLORES, Pedro NUNEZ (Jonathan FANA FRIAS 58), Hansley MARTINEZ, Heinz BARMETTLER (c). Tr: Clemente HERNADNEZ

DMA: Glenson PRINCE (c) - Delbert DAILEY•, Collin BERNARD, Kelrick WALTER, Elmond DERRICK, Lester LANGLAIS, Shern DAILEY, Glenworth ELIZEE (Kurlson BENJAMIN 35), Eddie THOMAS (Malcolm JOSEPH 74), Chad BERTRAND••♦85, Carlvin CHRISTOPHER. Tr: Kirt HECTOR

KENSINGTON OVAL, BRIDGETOWN
27-09-2012, Att: 300, Ref: Lancaster GUY

Barbados	2
Aruba	1

BRB - Skeete [21], Harte [56] • ARU - Bergen [32]

BRB: Kerry HOLDER - Barry SKEETE•, Ranaldo MARQUES•, Mario HARTE (Tristan PARRIS 77), Kemar HEADLEY, Rashida WILLIAMS (c), Malcolm MARSHALL (Jason LOVELL 81), Ramuel MILLER, Armando LASHLEY (Raheim SARGEANT 70), Ricardio MORRIS, Andre BOURNE•. Tr: Colin FORDE

ARU: Kendrick DANIA - Francois CROES, Theric RUIZ (Brian SIEM 84), Ronnie NOUWEN•, Raymond Baten (c)••♦84, Rensy BARRADAS, Jean-Luc BERGEN (Ulises Nunez GARCIA 80), Rashidi GILKES, Frederick GOMEZ•, Ricangel DE LECA, Martis JOMAR. Tr: Elvis ALBERTUS

QUALIFYING GROUP 5

		Pl	W	D	L	F	A	Pts		GYF	SKN	AIA
Trinidad and Tobago	TRI	3	3	0	0	15	1	9		4-1	1-0	10-0
French Guiana	GYF	3	2	0	1	8	5	6			3-0	4-1
St Kitts and Nevis	SKN	3	1	0	2	2	4	3				2-0
Anguilla	AIA	3	0	0	3	1	16	0				

WARNER PARK, BASSETERRE
10-10-2012, Att: 400, Ref: Brea CUB

French Guiana	1
Trinidad and Tobago	4

GYF - Darcheville [16] • TRI - Hector [26], Gay [35], Daniel [72], Plaza [82]

GYF: Rudy MERILLE - Gary MARIGARD, Samuel SOPHIE•, Mickael RIMANE (Serge LESPERANCE 66), Marvin TORVIC, Albert AJAISO, Ludovic BAAL, Lesly MALOUDA, Rhudy EVENS (Stephan CLET 68), Nekie ADIPI (Gary PIGREE 75), Jean-Claude DARCHEVILLE. Tr: Steeve FALGAYRETTES

TRI: Jan-Michael WILLIAMS - Joevin JONES, Carlyle MITCHELL, Daneil CYRUS, Robert PRIMUS, Seon POWER, Keon DANIEL•, Densill THEOBALD, Kevon CARTER (Willis PLAZA 79), Hughton HECTOR (Clyde LEON 87), Jamal GAY• (Richard ROY 70). Tr: Hutson CHARLES♦46

WARNER PARK, BASSETERRE
10-10-2012, Att: 700, Ref: Johnson GUY

St Kitts and Nevis	2
Anguilla	0

SKN - Sawyers [15], Harris [20]

SKN: Julani ARCHIBALD - Thrizen LEADER, Patrice LIBURD, Tesfa ROBINSON•, Kareem HARRIS, Zephaniah THOMAS•, Devaughn MITCHOM 65), Romaine SAWYERS, Gerard WILLIAMS, Devaughn ELLIOTT (Aaron MOSES-GARVEY 78), Ian LAKE (Josh LEADER 88), Atiba HARRIS. Tr: Jeffrey HAZEL

AIA: Kelvin LIDDIE - Girdon CONNOR, Kevin HAWLEY, Khaloni RICHARDSON, Adonijah RICHARDSON, Leon JEFFERS, Germain HUGHES (Ashton DUMAS 80), Kenny WILLIAMS, Khalid BROOKS (Vershawn HODGES 86), Codero LAKE (Damian BAILEY 66), Terrence RODGERS. Tr: Colin JOHNSON

WARNER PARK, BASSETERRE
12-10-2012, Att: 600, Ref: Hidalgo DOM

French Guiana	4
Anguilla	1

GYF - Pigree 3 [3] [45] [50], Baal [74] • AIA - Rodgers [59]

GYF: Jean PETIT-HOMME - Gary MARIGARD, Marvin TORVIC, Albert AJAISO, Ludovic BAAL, Lesly MALOUDA (Warren Ho Meou CHOUNE 62), Rhudy EVENS (Francis SAMPAIN 79), Serge LESPERANCE, Nekie ADIPI (Stephan CLET 69), Gary PIGREE. Tr: Steeve FALGAYRETTES

AIA: Kelvin LIDDIE - Adonijah RICHARDSON• (Jermaine HODGE 84), Kevin HAWLEY, Khaloni RICHARDSON, Leon JEFFERS•, Germain HUGHES, Terrence RODGERS, Girdon CONNOR, Damian BAILEY (Ashton DUMAS 45), Kenny WILLIAMS, Khalid BROOKS (Kyle KENTISH 79). Tr: Colin JOHNSON

WARNER PARK, BASSETERRE
12-10-2012, Att: 1700, Ref: Rubalcaba CUB

St Kitts and Nevis	0
Trinidad and Tobago	1

TRI - Carter [51]

SKN: Julani ARCHIBALD - Zephaniah THOMAS (Errol O'LOUGLIN 75), Tesfa ROBINSON, Romaine SAWYERS, Patrice LIBURD•, Thrizen LEADER, Devaughn ELLIOTT (Orlando MITCHUM 61), Vaneer HARRIS, Atiba HARRIS•, Gerard WILLIAMS, Ian LAKE (Aaron MOSES-GARVEY 79). Tr: Jeffrey HAZEL

TRI: Jan-Michael WILLIAMS - Carlyle MITCHELL, Robert PRIMUS, Seon POWER•, Joevin JONES, Daneil CYRUS, Hughton HECTOR, Keon DANIEL (Curtis GONZALES 82), Clyde LEON, Densill THEOBALD (Kevon CARTER 43) (Willis PLAZA 84), Jamal GAY. Tr: Derek KING

WARNER PARK, BASSETERRE
14-10-2012, Att: 40, Ref: Johnson GUY

Trinidad and Tobago	10
Anguilla	0

TRI - Gay 4 [7] [21] [32] [38], Daniel 3 [11] [35] [40], Plaza 2 [53] [63], Tessdale [71]

TRI: Jan-Michael WILLIAMS - Carlyle MITCHELL (Kareem MOSES 54), Seon POWER, Joevin JONES, Daneil CYRUS, Sylvester TESSDALE, Hughton HECTOR, Keon DANIEL (Willis PLAZA 46), Kevon CARTER, Clyde LEON, Jamal GAY (Devon JORSLING 46). Tr: Hutson CHARLES

AIA: Kelvin LIDDIE (Kareem BURRIS 23) - Girdon CONNOR, Leon JEFFERS, Adonijah RICHARDSON (Kion LEE 46), Kevin HAWLEY, Kenny WILLIAMS, Khalid BROOKS (Jermaine HODGE 73), Terrence RODGERS, Damian BAILEY, Germain HUGHES, Ashton DUMAS. Tr: Colin JOHNSON

WARNER PARK, BASSETERRE
14-10-2012, Att: 200, Ref: Brea CUB

St Kitts and Nevis	0
French Guiana	3

GYF - Pigree 2 [7] [72], Darcheville [8]

SKN: Akil BYRON - Aaron MOSES (Devaughn ELLIOTT 64), Orlando MITCHUM, Tesfa ROBINSON (Akil GRIER 72), Romaine SAWYERS, Patrice LIBURD• (Errol O'LOUGLIN 52), Thrizen LEADER, Vaneer HARRIS, Atiba HARRIS•, Gerard WILLIAMS, Ian LAKE. Tr: Jeffrey HAZEL

GYF: Rudy MERILLE (Jean PETIT-HOMME• 27) - Warren Ho Meou CHOUNE, Rhudy EVENS, Serge LESPERANCE, Marvin TORVIC, Albert AJAISO, Jean-Claude DARCHEVILLE (Nekie ADIPI 46), Ludovic BAAL•, Gary PIGREE• (Stephan CLET 82), Samuel SOPHIE, Gary MARIGARD. Tr: Steeve FALGAYRETTES

QUALIFYING GROUP 6

		Pl	W	D	L	F	A	Pts		GYF	GRN	GUY
Haiti	HAI	3	2	0	1	3	1	6		0-1	2-0	1-0
French Guiana	GYF	3	1	1	1	5	5	4			1-1	3-4
Grenada	GRN	3	1	1	1	3	4	4				2-1
Guyana	GUY	3	1	0	2	5	6	3				

NATIONAL STADIUM, ST GEORGE'S
14-11-2012, Att: 1000, Ref: Skeete BRB

Haiti	1
Guyana	0

HAI - Saurel [47]

HAI: Johny PLACIDE (c) - Jeasony ALCENAT (Vaniel SIRIN 90), Jean RUBIN, Peter GERMAIN, Aveska JUDELIN, Leonel SAINT PREUX (Pascal MILLIEN 81), Peguero JEAN-PHILIPPE (James FRANCOISE 74), Monuma Constant JUNIOR, Ednerson RAYMOND, Jean-Marc ALEXANDRE, Olrish SAUREL. Tr: Israel CANTERO

GUY: Derrick CARTER - Jake NEWTON•, Walter MOORE, Dwain JACOBS (Clive NOBREGA 84), Christopher NURSE• (c), Charles POLLARD, Shawn BEVENEY (Daniel WILSON 81), Vurlon MILLS (Carey HARRIS 67), Kester JACOBS, Trayon BOBB, Jamaal SMITH. Tr: Jamaal SHABAZZ

NATIONAL STADIUM, ST GEORGE'S
14-11-2012, Att: 1500, Ref: Jauregui CUW

Grenada	1
French Guiana	1

GRN - Rocastle [33] • GYF - Pigree [90]

GRN: Shemel LOUISON - David CYRUS, Craig ROCASTLE (Kimron REDHEAD 86), Cassim LANGAIGNE, Marc MARSHALL, Clive MURRAY (Bradley BUBB 67), Kithson BAIN, Michael MARK, Anthony STRAKER•, Raymond ALLEYNE (Dwayne LEO• 51), Moron PHILLIP. Tr: Alister DEBELLOTTE

GYF: Laurent PETCHY - Gary MARIGARD, Marvin EDOUARD•, Serge LESPERANCE, Warren Ho Meou CHOUNE, Raymond JEAN-JACQUES, Jean-Claude DARCHEVILLE• (c), Marc-Frederic HABRAN (Stanley RIDEL 46), Gary PIGREE, Samuel SOPHIE (Eric MARTINON 75), David MARTINON (Stephan CLET 82). Tr: Comtout HUBERT

NATIONAL STADIUM, ST GEORGE'S
16-11-2012, Att: 750, Ref: Nunez CUB

French Guiana	1
Haiti	0

GYF - Pigree [55]

GYF: Laurent PETCHY - Gary MARIGARD••◆88, Marvin EDOUARD, Serge LESPERANCE•, Warren Ho Meou CHOUNE (Eric MARTINON 90), Raymond JEAN-JACQUES, Jean-Claude DARCHEVILLE (c) (Stanley RIDEL 67), Gary PIGREE, Samuel SOPHIE, David MARTINON (Marc-Frederic HABRAN 80), Marc EDWIGE•. Tr: Comtout HUBERT

HAI: Johny PLACIDE (c) - Jeasony ALCENAT, Jean RUBIN, Peter GERMAIN, Aveska JUDELIN•, Leonel SAINT PREUX (Pascal MILLIEN 68), Peguero JEAN-PHILIPPE (Fritznel Louis 62), Monuma Constant JUNIOR (Peterson JOSEPH 71), Ednerson RAYMOND•, Jean-Marc ALEXANDRE•, Olrish SAUREL. Tr: Israel CANTERO

NATIONAL STADIUM, ST GEORGE'S
16-11-2012, Att: 1400, Ref: Brizan TRI

Grenada	2
Guyana	1

GRN - Bain [46], Murray [81] • GUY - Wilson [48]

GRN: Shemel LOUISON - David CYRUS, Craig ROCASTLE (Kimron REDHEAD 65), Cassim LANGAIGNE, Marc MARSHALL, Clive MURRAY (Brian ANDREW), Kithson BAIN (Bradley BUBB 72), Michael MARK, Anthony STRAKER, Raymond ALLEYNE, Moron PHILLIP. Tr: Alister DEBELLOTTE

GUY: Derrick CARTER - Jake NEWTON, Walter MOORE (Sheldon HOLDER 89), Christopher NURSE• (c), Daniel WILSON (Carey HARRIS 71), Charles POLLARD, Shawn BEVENEY, Vurlon MILLS (Dwain JACOBS 62), Kester JACOBS, Trayon BOBB, Jamaal SMITH. Tr: Jamaal SHABAZZ

NATIONAL STADIUM, ST GEORGE'S
18-11-2012, Att: 1500, Ref: Nunez CUB

Guyana	4
French Guiana	3

GUY - Mills [12], Moore [46], Beveney [2 58 87p] •
GYF - Ridel 2 [34 63], Edwige [90]

GUY: Derrick CARTER - Jake NEWTON, Walter MOORE (c), Nicholas MILLINGTON• (Pernell SCHULTZ 88), Daniel WILSON (Carey HARRIS 79), Charles POLLARD (Dwain JACOBS 46), Shawn BEVENEY, Vurlon MILLS, Kester JACOBS, Clive NOBREGA, Trayon BOBB. Tr: Jamaal SHABAZZ

GYF: Jean-Beaunel PETIT-HOMME - Marvin EDOUARD•, Eric MARTINON, Serge LESPERANCE (c), Warren Ho Meou CHOUNE (Stephan CLET 55), Raymond JEAN-JACQUES, Gary PIGREE, Samuel SOPHIE•, Stanley RIDEL, David MARTINON (50: Marc-Frederic HABRAN), Marc EDWIGE. Tr: Comtout HUBERT

NATIONAL STADIUM, ST GEORGE'S
18-11-2012, Att: 3000, Ref: Brizan TRI

Grenada	0
Haiti	2

HAI - Alencat [36], OG [58]

GRN: Shemel LOUISON - David CYRUS, Craig ROCASTLE, Cassim LANGAIGNE, Marc MARSHALL (Kevin EDWARDS 45), Clive MURRAY, Kithson BAIN (Bradley BUBB 59), Michael MARK, Anthony STRAKER, Raymond ALLEYNE, Moron PHILLIP (Kimron REDHEAD 75). Tr: Alister DEBELLOTTE

HAI: Frandy MONTREVIL - Jeasony ALCENAT, Jean RUBIN, Peter GERMAIN, Peterson JOSEPH (Peguero JEAN-PHILIPPE 90), Aveska JUDELIN, Leonel SAINT PREUX (Monuma Constant JUNIOR 62), Pascal MILLIEN, Jean-Marc ALEXANDRE, James FRANCOISE (Fritznel LOUIS 82), Olrish SAUREL•. Tr: Israel CANTERO

QUALIFYING GROUP 7

		Pl	W	D	L	F	A	Pts		MTN	GLP	PUR
Dominican Republic	DOM	3	2	1	0	6	2	7		1-1	2-0	3-1
Martinique	MTN	3	1	2	0	6	5	5			3-3	2-1
Guadeloupe	GLP	3	1	1	1	7	6	4				4-1
Puerto Rico	PUR	3	0	0	3	3	9	0				

STADE NABAJOTH, LES ABYMES
23-10-2012, Att: 100, Ref: Baptiste DMA

Martinique	2
Puerto Rico	1

MTQ - Sabin 2 [38p 43] • PUR - Ramos [55]

MTQ: Wilfried BULGARE - Jacky BERDIX, Jordy DELEM, Steeve PENEL◆87, William SERY•, Gael GERMANY, Ludovic FARDIN• (Karl VITULIN 75), Steeve GUSTAN, Yoan PIVATY (Stephane ABAUL 75), Kevin PARSEMAIN, Cedric SABIN• (Anthony ANGELY 67). Tr: Patrick CAVELAN

PUR: Eric REYES - Scott JONES, Marco VELEZ•, Noah DELGADO, Alexis RIVERA•90, Fernando GONZALEZ•, John KRAUSE, Joshua HANSEN (Tyler WILSON• 80), Andres CABRERO (Samuel SOTO 67), Joseph MARRERO (Christopher MEGALOUDIS 46), Hector RAMOS. Tr: Jeaustin CAMPOS

STADE NABAJOTH, LES ABYMES
23-10-2012, Att: 1505, Ref: Cambridge VIN

Guadeloupe	0
Dominican Republic	2

DOM - Fana Frias 2 [45 90]

GLP: Franck GRANDEL - Pascal CHIMBONDA, Jean-Luc LAMBOURDE•, Eddy VIATOR, Cedric VANOUKIA (Gregory GENDREY 69), Dominique MOCKA (Loic LOVAL 57), Stephane AUVRAY, Larry CLAVIER, Teddy BACOUL, Fabien BERAL•, Mickael ANTOINE-CURIER (Wladimir PASCAL 65). Tr: Steve BIZASENE

DOM: Wellington AGRAMONTE - Cesar LEDESMA•, Cesar GARCIa, Heinz BARMETTLER, Solangel MILIANO•, Kerbi RODRIGUEZ• (Manuel PEREZ 90), Rafael FLORES, Jonathan FANA FRIAS, Pedro NUNEZ (Domingo PERALTA), Hansley MARTINEZ, Jimmy REYES (Erick OZUNA 65). Tr: Clemente HERNANDEZ

STADE NABAJOTH, LES ABYMES
25-10-2012, Att: 1800, Ref: Delves VIN

Dominican Republic	1
Martinique	1

DOM - Peralta [45] • MTQ - Zaire [72]

DOM: Wellington AGRAMONTE - Cesar LEDESMA•, Cesar GARCIA, Heinz BARMETTLER, Inoel NAVARRO (Pedro NUNEZ 60), Solangel MILIANO, Kerbi RODRIGUEZ (Jimmy REYES 87), Rafael FLORES, Jonathan FANA FRIAS, Domingo PERALTA• (Manuel PEREZ), Hansley MARTINEZ. Tr: Clemente HERNANDEZ

MTQ: Wilfried BULGARE - Jacky BERDIX, Jordy DELEM, GERMANY•, William SERY, Ludovic FARDIN•◆60, Nicolas ZAIRE•, Karl VITULIN (Stephane ABAUL• 70), Steeve GUSTAN•, Kevin PARSEMAIN•, Cedric SABIN (Anthony ANGELY 70). Tr: Patrick CAVELAN

CARIBBEAN CUP 2012 – QUALIFYING TOURNAMENT

STADE NABAJOTH, LES ABYMES	
25-10-2012, Att: 1800, Ref: Leslie DMA	
Guadeloupe	4
Puerto Rico	1

GLP - Loval [8], Mocka 2 [11 26], Pascal [69] •
PUR - Ramos [83]

GLP: Franck GRANDEL - Pascal CHIMBONDA, Jean-Luc LAMBOURDE, Eddy VIATOR, Mathias BABEL, Dominique MOCKA (Wilhem SEVERIN 74), Stephane AUVRAY (Mickael ANTOINE-CURIER 79), Larry CLAVIER (Wladimir PASCAL 63), Fabien BERAL, Gregory GENDREY, Loic LOVAL. Tr: Steve BIZASENE

PUR: Eric REYES - Anthony VAZQUEZ•, Scott JONES, Noah DELGADO (Andres CABRERO 63), Samuel SOTO, Fernando GONZALEZ (Victor PINTO 87), John KRAUSE•, Christopher MEGALOUDIS, Joseph MARRERO (Steven ESTRADA), Tyler WILSON, Hector RAMOS. Tr: Jeaustin CAMPOS

STADE NABAJOTH, LES ABYMES	
27-10-2012, Att: 2891, Ref: Cambridge VIN	
Puerto Rico	1
Dominican Republic	3

PUR - Velez [80] • DOM - Fana Frias 2 [19 70], Ulloa [86]

PUR: Eric REYES - Anthony VAZQUEZ, Scott JONES, Marco VELEZ, Alexis RIVERA, Fernando GONZALEZ, Samuel SOTO (Christopher MEGALOUDIS 46), Joseph MARRERO (Joshua HANSEN 70), Steven ESTRADA, Alex OIKKONEN (Noah DELGADO 46), Hector RAMOS. Tr: Jeaustin CAMPOS

DOM: Wellington AGRAMONTE• - Cesar LEDESMA, Cesar GARCIA, Heinz BARMETTLER, Jhoan CRUZ, Kerbi RODRIGUEZ, Rafael FLORES (Jimmy REYES 90), Jonathan FANA FRIAS, Erick OZUNA (Gilberto ULLOA), Hansley MARTINEZ, Domingo PERALTA• (Manuel PEREZ 75). Tr: Clemente HERNANDEZ

STADE NABAJOTH, LES ABYMES	
27-10-2012, Att: 2891, Ref: Leslie DMA	
Guadeloupe	3
Martinique	3

GLP - Clavier 2 [13 33], Pascal [74] •
MTQ - Germany [17], Gustan 2 [24 63]

GLP: Christophe OLOL - Pascal CHIMBONDA, Jean-Luc LAMBOURDE•, Eddy VIATOR, Mathias BABEL•, Stephane AUVRAY, Fabien BERAL•, Gregory GENDREY, Dominique MOCKA (Teddy BACOUL 65), Loic LOVAL• (Wladimir PASCAL 69), Larry CLAVIER (Mickael ANTOINE-CURIER 74). Tr: Steve BIZASENE

MTQ: Emmanuel VERMIGNON - Jacky BERDIX•, Jordy DELEM, Steeve PENEL (Nicolas ZAIRE 47), William SERY• (Stanley ANGLIO 85), Gael GERMANY, Stephane ABAUL, Steeve GUSTAN•, Kevin PARSEMAIN, Yoan PIVATY, Anthony ANGELY (Karl VITULIN 74). Tr: Patrick CAVELAN

QUALIFYING GROUP 8

		Pl	W	D	L	F	A	Pts	CUB	SUR	VIN
Trinidad and Tobago	TRI	3	2	1	0	5	1	7	1-0	3-0	1-1
Cuba	CUB	3	1	1	1	6	2	4		5-0	1-1
Suriname	SUR	3	1	0	2	1	8	3			1-0
St Vincent/Grenadines	VIN	3	0	2	1	2	3	2			

DWIGHT YORKE, SCARBOROUGH	
14-11-2012, Att: 200, Ref: Bedeau GRN	
Cuba	5
Suriname	0

CUB - Hernandez 4 [6 36 62 89], Martinez [46]

CUB: Odelin MOLINA - Carlos FRANCISCO, Jorge CORRALES• (Dairo MACIAS 79), Jorge CLAVELO (c), Marcel HERNANDEZ, Jaime COLOME• (Ruslan Batista 73), Ariel MARTINEZ, Alianni URGELLES, Renay MALBLANCHE•, Alexy ZUASNABAR (Yaudel LAHERA), Alberto GOMEZ. Tr: Walter BENITEZ

SUR: Ronny ALOEMA (c) - Jurmen VALLEI, Furgill ONG A FAT• (Joel BAJA 54), Jetro FER, Guno KWASIE, Stefan BANETI, Giovanni WAAL, Giovanni ALLEYNE (Romano STEKKEL 45), Stefano RIJSSEL (Iwan PINAS 60), Emilio LIMON, Giovanni DRENTHE. Tr: Eugene VERWEY

DWIGHT YORKE, SCARBOROUGH	
14-11-2012, Att: 800, Ref: Campbell JAM	
Trinidad and Tobago	1
St Vincent/Grenadines	1

TRI - Jorsling [3] • VIN - Myron Samuel [24]

TRI: Jan-Michael WILLIAMS - Clyde LEON (Kendell JAGDEOSINGH 53), Joevin JONES, Hughton HECTOR, Devon JORSLING (Hashim ARCIA 67), Atullah GUERRA (Keyon EDWARDS 53), Kevon CARTER, Curtis GONZALES, Denisl THEOBALD•, Carlyle MITCHELL•, Seon POWER•. Tr: Hutson CHARLES

VIN: Kenyan-Desmond LYNCH• - Wesley CHARLES (c) (Reginal RICHARDSON 43), Roy RICHARDS, Shemol TRIMMINGHAM, Cornelius STEWART, Dorren HAMLET•, Myron SAMUEL (Nical STEPHENS 78), Wendell CUFFY (Romano SNAGG 67), Emerald GEORGE, Theon GORDON, Keith JAMES. Tr: Cornelius HUGGINS

DWIGHT YORKE, SCARBOROUGH	
16-11-2012, Att: 300, Ref: Taylor BRB	
St Vincent/Grenadines	1
Cuba	1

VIN - Stewart [8] • CUB - Linares [48]

VIN: Kenyan-Desmond LYNCH - Roy RICHARDS (Jolanshoy MCDOALD 70), Shemol TRIMMINGHAM, Cornelius STEWART, Dorren HAMLET, Myron SAMUEL• (Nical Stephens 89), Wendell CUFFY (Romano SNAGG 81), Emerald GEORGE, Reginal RICHARDSON, Theon GORDON (c), Keith JAMES. Tr: Cornelius HUGGINS

CUB: Odelin MOLINA - Carlos FRANCISCO, Jorge CORRALES, Jorge CLAVELO (c), Marcel HERNANDEZ, Jaime COLOME, Roberto LINARES (Alexy Zuasnabar 87), Ariel MARTINEZ (Adonis RAMOS 78), Alianni URGELLES, Renay MALBLANCHE, Alberto GOMEZ (Ruslan BATISTA). Tr: Walter BENITEZ

DWIGHT YORKE, SCARBOROUGH	
16-11-2012, Att: 950, Ref: Georges HAI	
Trinidad and Tobago	3
Suriname	0

TRI - Power [35], Roy [50], David [88]

TRI: Jan-Michael WILLIAMS (c) - Joevin JONES, Kern CUPID, Hughton HECTOR, Aubrey DAVID, Richard ROY• (Clyde LEON 72), Hashim ARCIA (Atullah GUERRA 72), Keyon EDWARDS, Denisl THEOBALD, Carlyle MITCHELL• (Kareem MOSES 60), Seon POWER•. Tr: Hutson CHARLES

SUR: Ronny ALOEMA (c) - Guno KWASIE, Stefan BANETI (Jurmen VALLEI 62), Giovanni WAAL (Giovanni DRENTHE 67), Giovanni ALLEYNE, Stefano RIJSSEL, Emilio LIMON, Joel BAJA, Naldo KWASIE, Romano STEKKEL•, Wilfried GALIMO (Iwan PINAS 79). Tr: Eugene VERWEY

DWIGHT YORKE, SCARBOROUGH	
18-11-2012, Att: 200, Ref: Georges HAI	
Suriname	1
St Vincent/Grenadines	0

SUR - Aloema [42p]

SUR: Ronny ALOEMA (c) - Naldo KWASIE, Joel BAJA, Jurmen VALLEI•, Guno KWASIE, Giovanni ALLEYNE, Romano STEKKEL, Giovanni WAAL, Giovanni DRENTHE (Furgill ONG A FAT 90), Wilfried GALIMO (Stefan BANETI 77), Iwan PINAS• (Evani ESPERANCE 71). Tr: Eugene VERWEY

VIN: Kenyan-Desmond LYNCH - Keith JAMES•• ♦ [90], Jolanshoy MCDOWALD, Reginal RICHARDSON, Emerald GEORGE, Cornelius STEWART (Azinho SOLOMON 90), Wendell CUFFY• (Romano SNAGG 66), Shemol TRIMMINGHAM, Myron SAMUEL•, Dorren HAMLET, Theon GORDON (Nical STEPHENS 61). Tr: Cornelius HUGGINS

DWIGHT YORKE, SCARBOROUGH	
18-11-2012, Att: 1300, Ref: Campbell JAM	
Trinidad and Tobago	1
Cuba	0

TRI - Guerra [67]

TRI: Jan-Michael WILLIAMS (c) - Marvin PHILLIPS 53) - Joevin JONES, Kern CUPID, Kareem MOSES, Hughton HECTOR, Aubrey DAVID, Richard ROY (Curtis GONZALES 76), Hashim ARCIA (Atullah GUERRA• 66), Keyon EDWARDS, Denisl THEOBALD, Seon POWER••. Tr: Hutson CHARLES

CUB: Julio RAMOS - Carlos FRANCISCO, Jorge CORRALES, Jorge CLAVELO (c), Marcel HERNANDEZ (Yaudel LAHERA 62), Roberto LINARES (Alexy ZUASNABAR 76), Ariel MARTINEZ, Alianni URGELLES, Renay MALBLANCHE, Ruslan BATISTA (Adonis RAMOS 42), Alberto GOMEZ. Tr: Walter BENITEZ

CARIBBEAN CUP ANTIGUA AND BARBUDA 2012

First Round Group Stage

Group A	Pl	W	D	L	F	A	Pts	TRI	DOM	ATG
Haiti	3	2	1	0	3	1	7	0-0	2-1	1-0
Trinidad and Tobago	3	1	1	1	2	3	4		2-1	0-2
Dominican Republic	3	1	0	2	4	5	3			2-1
Antigua and Barbuda	3	1	0	2	3	3	3			

Group B	Pl	W	D	L	F	A	Pts	CUB	GYF	JAM
Martinique	3	2	1	0	4	1	7	1-0	3-1	0-0
Cuba	3	2	0	1	3	2	6		2-1	1-0
French Guiana	3	1	0	2	4	6	3			2-1
Jamaica	3	0	1	2	1	3	1			

Held in Antigua from 7-12-2012 to 16-12-2012 • Top scorers: **2** - Eight players with two goals
Cuba, Trinidad, Haiti and Martinique qualified for the CONCACAF Gold Cup 2013

Semi-finals

Martinique	1 4p
Trinidad & Tobago	1 5p

Cuba	1
Haiti	0

Final

Cuba	1
Trinidad & Tobago	0

Third place play-off

Haiti	1
Martinique	0

CARIBBEAN CUP ANTIGUA AND BARBUDA 2012

	GROUP A	PL	W	D	L	F	A	PTS		TRI	DOM	ATG
1	Haiti	3	2	1	0	3	1	7		0-0	2-1	1-0
2	Trinidad and Tobago	3	1	1	1	2	3	4			2-1	0-2
3	Dominican Republic	3	1	0	2	4	5	3				2-1
4	Antigua and Barbuda	3	1	0	2	3	3	3				

ANTIGUA RECREATION GROUND, ST JOHN'S
7-12-2012, 18:00, Att: 150, Ref: Valdin Legister JAM

Haiti 0
Trinidad and Tobago 0

HAITI
Johnny PLACIDE - Jean ALCENAT, Mechak JEROME, Judelin AVESKA, Olrish SAUREL•, Brunel FUCIEN, Peter GERMAIN, Monuma CONSTANT•, Fritznel LOUIS (Jean Philippe PEGUERO 77), Pascal MILIEN (Jean Garry RUBIN 63), Leonel SAINT-PREUX (Vaniel SIRIN 81). Tr: Israel CANTERO

TRINIDAD AND TOBAGO
Jan Michael WILLIAMS - Daneil CYRUS, Carlyle MITCHELL, Seon POWER, Joevin JONES, Aubrey DAVID, Kevin MOLINO•, (Keyon EDWARDS 80), Ataullah GUERRA (Kevon CARTER 74), Densill THEOBALD, Hughton HECTOR, Willis PLAZA (Lester PELTIER 46). Tr: Hutson CHARLES

ANTIGUA RECREATION GROUND, ST JOHN'S
7-12-2012, 20:00, Att: 150, Ref: Wilson Dacosta BAH

Antigua and Barbuda 1 Byers [17]
Dominican Republic 2 Garcia [74], Fana Frias [90]

ANTIGUA AND BARBUDA
Molvin JAMES - Karanja MACK, George DUBLIN, Akeem THOMAS, Ranja CHRISTIAN, Tamarley THOMAS, Kemoy ALEXANDER (Luke BLAKELY 61), Quentin GRIFFITH, Gayson GREGORY (Stephan SMITH 52), Randolph BURTON, Peter BYERS•. Tr: Rolston WILLIAMS

DOMINICAN REPUBLIC
Miguel LLOYD - Cesar LEDESMA, Cesar GARCIA, Heinz BARMETTLER, Eduardo ACEVEDO, Kerbi RODRIGUEZ (Carlos MARTINEZ 82), Rafael FLORES, Jonathan FANA FRIAS, Pedro Antonio NUNEZ (Erick OZUNA 67), Hansley MARTINEZ, Domingo PERALTA (Javier SANTANA 71). Tr: Clemente HERNANDEZ

ANTIGUA RECREATION GROUND, ST JOHN'S
9-12-2012, 17:00, Att: 800, Ref: Elmer Bonilla SLV

Dominican Republic 1 Rodriguez [12]
Haiti 2 Saint-Preux [10], Peguero [39]

DOMINICAN REPUBLIC
Miguel LLOYD - Eduardo ACEVEDO, Cesar GARCIA, Hansley MARTINEZ (Erick OZUNA 46), Cesar LEDESMA, Carlos MARTINEZ, Heinz BARMETTLER, Jonathan FANA FRIAS, Rafael FLORES, Domingo PERALTA (Inoel NAVARRO 71), Kerbi RODRIGUEZ (Javier SANTANA 86). Tr: Clemente HERNANDEZ

HAITI
Frandy MONTREVIL - Mechak JEROME, Peter GERMAIN, Judelin AVESKA, Olrish SAUREL, Vaniel SIRIN• (Brunel FUCIEN 86), Jean ALCENAT•, Monuma CONSTANT, Pascal MILIEN (Jean Garry RUBIN 59), Leonel SAINT-PREUX•, Jean Philippe PEGUERO (Jean Marc ALEXANDRE 64). Tr: Israel CANTERO

ANTIGUA RECREATION GROUND, ST JOHN'S
9-12-2012, 19:00, Att: 2000, Ref: Rubalcaba CUB

Antigua and Barbuda 2 Griffith [51], Byers [73]
Trinidad and Tobago 0

ANTIGUA AND BARBUDA
Molvin JAMES - Quentin GRIFFITH, George DUBLIN, Akeem THOMAS, Karanja MACK, Tamarley THOMAS, Kemoy ALEXANDER, Gayson GREGORY, Randolph BURTON (Teran WILLIAMS 75), Stephan SMITH, Peter BYERS (Lennox JULIAN 90). Tr: Rolston WILLIAMS

TRINIDAD AND TOBAGO
Jan Michael WILLIAMS - Daneil CYRUS, Carlyle MITCHELL, Seon POWER, Joevin JONES, Aubrey DAVID•, Kevin MOLINO (Kevon CARTER 69), Ataullah GUERRA, Densill THEOBALD, Hughton HECTOR (Richard ROY 80), Jamal GAY (Devon JORSLING 66). Tr: Hutson CHARLES

ANTIGUA RECREATION GROUND, ST JOHN'S
11-12-2012, 17:00, Att: 250, Ref: Kevin Thomas

Trinidad and Tobago 2 Carter [14], Molino [70]
Dominican Republic 1 Rodriguez [52]

TRINIDAD AND TOBAGO
Jan Michael WILLIAMS - Joevin JONES, Carlyle MITCHELL, Seon POWER, Aubrey DAVID•, Daneil CYRUS, Curtis GONZALES•, Densill THEOBALD, Kevon CARTER• (Kevin MOLINO 65), Ataullah GUERRA (Keyon EDWARDS 81), Devon JORSLING (Willis PLAZA 71). Tr: Hutson CHARLES

DOMINICAN REPUBLIC
Miguel LLOYD - Cesar LEDESMA, Cesar GARCIA, Hansley MARTINEZ, Eduardo ACEVEDO, Heinz BARMETTLER, Jonathan FANA FRIAS, Rafael FLORES (Carlos MARTINEZ 71), Kerbi RODRIGUEZ, Pedro Antonio NUNEZ (Erick OZUNA 62), Domingo PERALTA• (Jimmy REYES 73). Tr: Clemente HERNANDEZ

ANTIGUA RECREATION GROUND, ST JOHN'S
11-12-2012, 19:00, Att: 800, Ref: Marcos Brea CUB

Antigua and Barbuda 0
Haiti 1 Peguero [19]

ANTIGUA AND BARBUDA
Molvin JAMES - Quentin GRIFFITH, George DUBLIN•, Akeem THOMAS, Karanja MACK, Gayson GREGORY (Eugene KIRWAN 60), Kemoy ALEXANDER, Randolph BURTON (Lloyd JEREMY 81), Tamarley THOMAS, Stephan SMITH (Anton BLACKWOOD 69), Peter BYERS. Tr: Rolston WILLIAMS

HAITI
Johnny PLACIDE - Mechak JEROME•, Peter GERMAIN, Judelin AVESKA, Olrish SAUREL (Jean Garry RUBIN 90), Jean Marc ALEXANDRE, Jean ALCENAT, Monuma CONSTANT, Leonel SAINT-PREUX (Brunel FUCIEN 84), Jean Philippe PEGUERO (Frantz BERTIN 90). Tr: Israel CANTERO

	GROUP B	PL	W	D	L	F	A	PTS		CUB	GYF	JAM
1	Martinique	3	2	1	0	4	1	7		1-0	3-1	0-0
2	Cuba	3	2	0	1	3	2	6			2-1	1-0
3	French Guiana	3	1	0	2	4	6	3				2-1
4	Jamaica	3	0	1	2	1	3	1				

SIR VIVIAN RICHARDS STADIUM, NORTH SOUND
8-12-2012, 18:00, Att: 100, Ref: Enrico Wijngaarde SUR

Martinique 1 Piquionne 29
Cuba 0

MARTINIQUE
Kevin OLIMPA - Nicolas ZAIRE, Sebastien CRETINOIR, William SERY, Jacky BERDIX•, Daniel HERELLE, Nicolas MIRZA, Steeve GUSTAN• (Anthony ANGELY• 86), Gael GERMANY, Kevin PARSEMAIN (Jordy DELEM 90), Frederic PIQUIONNE• (Stephane ABAUL 83). Tr: Patrick CAVELAN

CUBA
Odelin MOLINA - Jorge Luis CORRALES, Carlos Domingo FRANCISCO• (Joel COLOME 79), Jorge Luis CLAVELO, Marcel HERNANDEZ, Jaime COLOME•, Alianni URGELLES, Alberto GOMEZ, Renay MALBLANCHE•, Ariel Pedro MARTINEZ (Adonis RAMOS 64), Yaudel LAHERA (Alexei ZUAZNABAR 56). Tr: Walter BENITEZ

SIR VIVIAN RICHARDS STADIUM, NORTH SOUND
8-12-2012, 20:00, Att: 100, Ref: Sandy Vazquez DOM

Jamaica 1 Stewart 22
French Guiana 2 Pigree 19, Evens 48

JAMAICA
Dwayne MILLER - Andrae CAMPBELL (Ricardo GARDNER 60), Shavar THOMAS•, Montrose PHINN, Xavian VIRGO, Demar PHILLIPS, Jason MORRISON, Jermaine HUE• (Darren MATTOCKS 54), Keammar DALEY, Ryan JOHNSON (Omar CUMMINGS 54), Tremaine STEWART. Tr: Theodore WHITMORE

FRENCH GUIANA
Laurent PETCHY - Gary MARIGARD, Samuel SOPHIE, Marvin TORVIC, Marc EDWIGE•, Serge LESPERANCE, Albert AJAISO, Rhudy EVENS, Lesly MALOUDA, Gary PIGREE (Stanley RIDEL 87), Jean-Claude DARCHEVILLE (Marc-Frederic HABRAN 79). Tr: Francois LOUIS-MARIE

SIR VIVIAN RICHARDS STADIUM, NORTH SOUND
10-12-2012, 17:00, Att: 225, Ref: William Anderson PUR

Cuba 2 Martinez 2 74 76
French Guiana 1 Pigree 16

CUBA
Odelin MOLINA - Jorge Luis CORRALES (Ariel MARTINEZ 68), Carlos Domingo FRANCISCO, Jorge Luis CLAVELO, Marcel HERNANDEZ (Alexei ZUAZNABAR 58), Alianni URGELLES, Jaime COLOME•, Alberto GOMEZ, Joel COLOME, Renay MALBLANCHE, Yaudel LAHERA (Adrian Arturo DIZ PE• 81). Tr: Walter BENITEZ

FRENCH GUIANA
Laurent PETCHY - Gary MARIGARD, Samuel SOPHIE, Albert AJAISO•, Marvin TORVIC, Marc EDWIGE, Serge LESPERANCE, Rhudy EVENS, Lesly MALOUDA•, Gary PIGREE, Jean-Claude DARCHEVILLE (Stanley RIDEL 85). Tr: Francois LOUIS-MARIE

SIR VIVIAN RICHARDS STADIUM, NORTH SOUND
10-12-2012, 19:00, Att: 225, Ref: Sherwin Johnson GUY

Jamaica 0
Martinique 0

JAMAICA
Dwayne MILLER - (Dwayne KERR 74) - Alvas POWELL, Shavar THOMAS (Ricardo GARDNER 65), Montrose PHINN, Lovel PALMER, Tremaine STEWART, Jason MORRISON, Jermaine HUE (Lamar NELSON 82), Demar PHILLIPS••♦62, Jermaine ANDERSON, Darren MATTOCKS. Tr: Theodore WHITMORE

MARTINIQUE
Kevin OLIMPA - Nicolas ZAIRE, William SERY, Jordy DELEM• (Fabrice REUPERNE 85), Jacky BERDIX, Daniel HERELLE, Sebastien CRETINOIR, Nicolas MIRZA, Gael GERMANY, Kevin PARSEMAIN• (Anthony ANGELY 90), Frederic PIQUIONNE (Josue JOSEPH-ROSE 82). Tr: Patrick CAVELAN

SIR VIVIAN RICHARDS STADIUM, NORTH SOUND
12-12-2012, 17:00, Att: 100, Ref: Sandy Vazquez DOM

French Guiana 1 Darcheville 81
Martinique 3 Piquionne 12, Parsemain 33, Angely 77

FRENCH GUIANA
Laurent PETCHY - Gary MARIGARD (Marc-Frederic HABRAN 52), Marvin TORVIC, Albert AJAISO, Lesly MALOUDA (Frederic ADINGE 51), Raymond JEAN-JACQUES•, Rhudy EVENS (Stanley RIDEL 59), Serge LESPERANCE, Samuel SOPHIE, Jean-Claude DARCHEVILLE, Gary PIGREE. Tr: Francois LOUIS-MARIE

MARTINIQUE
Kevin OLIMPA - Nicolas ZAIRE, William SERY, Sebastien CRETINOIR, Romain BANNAIS, Daniel HERELLE, Nicolas MIRZA (Lionel RAVI• 80), Steeve GUSTAN, Gael GERMANY (Anthony ANGELY 23), Kevin PARSEMAIN, Frederic PIQUIONNE (Daniel HERELLE 59). Tr: Patrick CAVELAN

SIR VIVIAN RICHARDS STADIUM, NORTH SOUND
12-12-2012, 19:00, Att: 200, Ref: Elmer Bonilla SLV

Jamaica 0
Cuba 1 Urgelles 57

JAMAICA
Dwayne KERR - Alvas POWELL•, Dicoy WILLIAMS, Lovel PALMER, Ricardo GARDNER, Tremaine STEWART (Lamar NELSON 66), Rohan REID, Jason MORRISON, Keammar DALEY (Omar CUMMINGS 53), Darren MATTOCKS, Ryan JOHNSON (Jermaine ANDERSON• 69). Tr: Theodore WHITMORE

CUBA
Odelin MOLINA - Jorge Luis CLAVELO, Carlos Domingo FRANCISCO, Jorge Luis CORRALES, Alianni URGELLES•, Jaime COLOME, Alberto GOMEZ (Adrian Arturo DIZ PE 61), Joel COLOME (Adonis RAMOS 71), Ariel MARTINEZ•, Renay MALBLANCHE, Yaudel LAHERA (Roberto LINARES 71). Tr: Walter BENITEZ

SEMI-FINALS

ANTIGUA RECREATION GROUND, ST JOHN'S
14-12-2012, 17:00, Att: 200, Ref: Enrico Wijngaarde SUR

Haiti	0	
Cuba	1	Joel Colome [9]

HAITI
Johnny PLACIDE - Jean Garry RUBIN (Vaniel SIRIN 56), Judelin AVESKA•, Peter GERMAIN (Wiselet SAINT-LOUIS 56), Mechak JEROME, Olrish SAUREL, Jean ALCENAT•, Jean Marc ALEXANDRE, Monuma CONSTANT (Brunel FUCIEN 71), Leonel SAINT-PREUX, Jean Philippe PEGUERO. Tr: Israel CANTERO

CUBA
Odelin MOLINA• - Jorge Luis CLAVELO, Carlos Domingo FRANCISCO, Renay MALBLANCHE, Ariel MARTINEZ, Jaime COLOME, Alberto GOMEZ, Alianni URGELLES, Joel COLOME (Jorge Luis CORRALES 90), Marcel HERNANDEZ (Adrian Arturo DIZ PE 77), Yaudel LAHERA (Roberto LINARES 61). Tr: Walter BENITEZ

ANTIGUA RECREATION GROUND, ST JOHN'S
14-12-2012, 20:00, Att: 200, Ref: Elmer Bonilla SLV

Martinique	1 4p	Parsemain [76]
Trinidad and Tobago	1 5p	Roy [90]

MARTINIQUE
Emmanuel VERMIGNON - Jacky BERDIX•, Sebastien CRETINOIR, Stanley ANGLIO, Romain BANNAIS, Jordy DELEM, Daniel HERELLE (Fabrice REUPERNE 87), Lionel RAVI• (Kevin PARSEMAIN 68), Steeve GUSTAN, Stephane ABAUL, Josue JOSEPH-ROSE (Frederic PIQUIONNE 68). Tr: Patrick CAVELAN

TRINIDAD AND TOBAGO
Jan Michael WILLIAMS - Curtis GONZALES, Seon POWER, Carlyle MITCHELL, Daneil CYRUS, Densill THEOBALD•, Keyon EDWARDS, Joevin JONES (Richard ROY 85), Kevon CARTER (Kevin MOLINO 76), Ataullah GUERRA•, Devon JORSLING (Jamal GAY 69). Tr: Hutson CHARLES

THIRD PLACE PLAY-OFF

ANTIGUA RECREATION GROUND, ST JOHN'S
16-12-2012, 14:00, Att: 100, Ref: Wilson Dacosta BAH

Haiti	1	Saint-Preux [94]
Martinique	0	

HAITI
Frandy MONTREVIL - Frantz BERTIN, Olrish SAUREL (Peter GERMAIN 100), Vaniel SIRIN, Mechak JEROME, Jean Garry RUBIN, Brunel FUCIEN•, Jean Marc ALEXANDRE•, Wiselet SAINT-LOUIS (Monuma CONSTANT 91), Jean Philippe PEGUERO, Fritznel LOUIS (Leonel SAINT-PREUX 76). Tr: Israel CANTERO

MARTINIQUE
Loic CHAUVET - William SERY, Fabrice REUPERNE• (Daniel HERELLE 71), Nicolas ZAIRE, Stanley ANGLIO•, Stephane ABAUL, Jordy DELEM•, Steeve GUSTAN (Frederic PIQUIONNE 81), Kevin PARSEMAIN, Djenael MAINGE• (Steven LECEFEL 81), Anthony ANGELY•. Tr: Patrick CAVELAN

SEMI-FINAL PENALTIES
TRINIDAD WON 5-4

MTQ			TRI
✓	Berdix		
	Theobald		✓
✓	Cretinoir		
	Molino		✓
✓	Gustan		
	Mitchell		✓
✓	Parsemain		
	Gonzales		✓
✗[1]	Piquionne		
	Guerra		✓

FINAL

ANTIGUA RECREATION GROUND, ST JOHN'S
16-12-2012, 17:00, Att: 750, Ref: Valdin Legister JAM

Cuba	1	Hernandez [113]
Trinidad and Tobago	0	

CUBA
Odelin Molina - Jorge Luis CLAVELO, Joel COLOME, Renay MALBLANCHE, Jaime COLOME, Alianni URGELLES, Carlos Domingo FRANCISCO, Marcel HERNANDEZ (Adrian Arturo DIZ PE 116), Alberto GOMEZ (Alexei ZUASNABAR 97), Ariel MARTINEZ, Yaudel LAHERA (Roberto LINARES 61). Tr: Walter BENITEZ

TRINIDAD AND TOBAGO
Jan Michael WILLIAMS• - Seon POWER•, Carlyle MITCHELL, Aubrey DAVID, Joevin JONES (Devon JORSLING 86), Densill THEOBALD, Ataullah GUERRA, Daneil CYRUS, Kevon CARTER• (Kevin MOLINO 83), Keyon EDWARDS, Jamal GAY (Curtis GONZALES 104). Tr: Hutson CHARLES

CLUB TOURNAMENTS 2011–12

CONCACAF CHAMPIONS LEAGUE 2011–12

Preliminary Round

Morelia	MEX	5	2
Tempête St Marc	HAI	0	0
Motagua	HON	4	0
Municipal	GUA	0	2
Santos Laguna	MEX	3	1
Olimpia	HON	1	2
Isidro Metapán	SLV	2	1
Puerto Rico Isl'ders	PUR	0	3
Toronto FC	CAN	2	2
Real Estelí	NCA	1	1
Alianza	SLV	0	0
FC Dallas	USA	1	1
San Francisco	PAN	1	0
Seattle Sounders	USA	0	2
Herediano	CRC	8	2
Alpha United	GUY	0	2

Group Phase

Group A

		Pl	W	D	L	F	A	Pts	USA	MEX	CRC	HON
Los Angeles Galaxy	USA	6	4	0	2	8	4	**12**		2-1	2-0	2-0
Morelia	MEX	6	4	0	2	11	5	**12**	2-1		2-1	4-0
LD Alajuelense	CRC	6	4	0	2	8	6	**12**	1-0	1-0		1-0
Motagua	HON	6	0	0	6	2	14	**0**	0-1	0-2	2-4	

Group B

		Pl	W	D	L	F	A	Pts	MEX	SLV	USA	HON
Santos Laguna	MEX	6	4	1	1	16	6	**13**		6-0	2-0	3-2
Isidro Metapán	SLV	6	3	0	3	10	15	**9**	2-0		1-3	3-2
Colorado Rapids	USA	6	2	1	3	9	12	**7**	1-4	3-2		1-2
Real España	HON	6	1	2	3	9	11	**5**	1-1	1-2	1-1	

Group C

		Pl	W	D	L	F	A	Pts	MEX	CAN	USA	PAN
Pumas UNAM	MEX	6	3	2	1	8	2	**11**		4-0	0-1	1-0
Toronto FC	CAN	6	3	1	2	7	7	**10**	1-1		0-1	1-0
FC Dallas	USA	6	2	1	3	6	11	**7**	0-2	0-3		1-1
Tauro	PAN	6	1	2	3	7	8	**5**	0-0	1-2	5-3	

Group D

		Pl	W	D	L	F	A	Pts	MEX	USA	GUA	CRC
Monterrey	MEX	6	4	0	2	11	4	**12**		0-1	3-1	1-0
Seattle Sounders	USA	6	3	1	2	10	7	**10**	1-2		4-1	0-1
Comunicaciones	GUA	6	2	1	3	8	13	**7**	1-0	2-2		2-0
Herediano	CRC	6	2	0	4	6	11	**6**	0-5	1-2	4-1	

CONCACAF CHAMPIONS LEAGUE 2011-12

Quarter-Finals

Monterrey	MEX	3	4
Morelia *	MEX	1	1

Isidro Metapán *	SLV	2	0
Pumas UNAM	MEX	1	8

Toronto FC *	CAN	2	2
Los Angeles Galaxy	USA	2	1

Seattle Sounders *	USA	2	1
Santos Laguna	MEX	1	6

Semi-finals

Monterrey *	3	1
Pumas UNAM	0	1

Toronto FC *	1	2
Santos Laguna	1	6

Final

Monterrey *	2	1
Santos Laguna	0	2

* Home team in the first leg

Top scorers: **7** - Humberto **SUAZO** CHI, Monterrey & Oribe **PERALTA** MEX, Santos Laguna • **6** - Jorge **BARBOSA** BRA, Herediano; Herculez **GOMEZ** USA, Santos Laguna & Joao **PLATA** ECU, Toronto • **5** - Dario **CARRENO** MEX, Monterrey; Ryan **JOHNSON** JAM, Toronto & Christian **SUAREZ** ECU, Santos Laguna • **4** - Martin **BRAVO** ARG, UNAM Pumas; Aldo **DE NIGRIS** MEX, Monterrey; Eduardo **HERRERA** MEX, UNAM Pumas; Carlos **QUINTERO** COL, Santos Laguna & Paolo **SUAREZ** URU, Isidro Metapán

PRELIMINARY ROUND

1st leg. Estadio Morelos, Morelia
28-07-2011, 6954, Rodriguez HON
Morelia 5
Huiqui [15], Sabah [63p], Rojas [67], Sepulveda [70], Lozano [76]
Federico VILAR (c) - Miguel SABAH (Damian MANSO 64), Joao ROJAS, Miguel SANSORES, Adrian ALDRETE, Jaime LOZANO, Diego JIMENEZ, Edgar LUGO, Marvin CABRERA, Aldo RAMIREZ (Felipe AYALA 59), Joel HUIQUI (Angel SEPULVEDA 68). Tr: Tomas BOY
Tempête St Marc 0

Guerry ROMONDT• - Mysson FENELUS•, William Soares FRANCA (Guilherme ROGER 55) (Frantz DALUSMA 81), Makendy DURVERGER, Vaniel SIRIN, Herold CHARLES, Thompson AMIUS (c), Itor DE PONTES (Fabien VORBE 17), Chedlin FRANCOEUR, Valdano PAUL, Elie PAUL. Tr: Danilo BARRIGA

2nd leg. Estadio Morelos, Morelia
3-08-2011, 6919, Santos PUR
Tempête St Marc 0

Guerry ROMONDT• - Mysson FENELUS, Guiherme SOUZA, Makendy DURVERGER, Jackson JEAN• (William Soares FRANCA• 46), Herold CHARLES (Gregory JOACHIM 64), Anoual ELIACIN (Itor DE PONTES 46), Thompson AMIUS (c), Changler CADET, Chedlin FRANCOEUR, Valdano PAUL. Tr: Danilo BARRIGA
Morelia 2
Sepulveda [31], Sansores [78]
Carlos RODRIGUEZ - Luis SILVA•, Luis NORIEGA, Felipe AYALA (Mario MORENO 57), Yasser CORONA, Angel SEPULVEDA, Jaime LOZANO (c) (Miguel SANSORES 59), Diego JIMENEZ, Edgar LUGO (Claudio BOY 62), Alejandro MUNOZ•, Julio ATILANO. Tr: Tomas BOY

1st leg. Tiburcio Andino, Tegucigalpa
28-07-2011, 6000, Moreno PAN
Motagua 4
Bengtson [42], Borjas [56], Guevara [69], Ramirez.G [76]
Donaldo MORALES - Odis BORJAS•, Junior IZAGUIRRE, Carlos DISCUA (Omar ELVIR 73), Jorge CLAROS, Guillermo RAMIREZ, Mario GUERRERO, Johnny LEVERON•, Amado GUEVARA (c) (Mario GIRON 80), Jerry BENGSTON (Aly ARRIOLA 80), Adan RAMIREZ. Tr: Ramon MARADIAGA
Municipal 0

Jaime PENEDO - Jaime VIDES, Yony FLORES (c), Eliseo QUINTANILLA•◆45, Oscar ISAULA (Evandro FERREIRA 46), Pedro SAMAYOA (Juan Jose CASTILLO 69), Marvin AVILA, Mario RODRIGUEZ (Manuel LEON 57), Cristian NORIEGA, Saul PHILLIP, Jose MONTERROSO. Tr: Javier DELGADO

2nd leg. Mateo Flores, Guatemala City
4-08-2011, 1500, Arellano MEX
Municipal 2
Romero 2 [32 43p]
Cristian ALVAREZ - Jaime VIDES, Yony FLORES, Gonzalo ROMERO (c) (Juan Jose CASTILLO 77), Evandro FERREIRA (Gregory RUIZ 66), Pedro SAMAYOA, Marvin AVILA, Pablo SOLORZANO, Mario RODRIGUEZ, Cristian NORIEGA, Saul PHILLIP (Oscar ISAULA 71). Tr: Javier DELGADO
Motagua 0

Donaldo MORALES• - Odis BORJAS•, Junior IZAGUIRRE, Carlos DISCUA (Sergio MENDOZA 79), Jorge CLAROS•, Guillermo RAMIREZ (Aly ARRIOLA 89), Mario GUERRERO, Johnny LEVERON•, Amado GUEVARA (c), Jerry BENGSTON•, Adan RAMIREZ (Emilson CRUZ 79). Tr: Ramon MARADIAGA

1st leg. Corona, Torreón
27-07-2011, 7500, Aguilar SLV
Santos Laguna 3
Peralta [29], Rodriguez [61p], Quintero [63]
Oswaldo SANCHEZ (c) - Carlos QUINTERO, Jorge ESTRADA, Jose CARDENAS (Carlos OCHOA 81), Juan Pablo RODRIGUEZ, Daniel LUDUENA (Rodolfo SALINAS 69), Christian SUAREZ (Jesus ESCOBOZA 66), Santiago HOYOS, Felipe BALOY, Oribe PERALTA•, Carlos MORALES. Tr: Diego COCCA
Olimpia 1
Bekeles [66]
Donis ESCOBER - Fabio DE SOUZA (c), Brayan BECKELES•, Juan Carlos GARCIA (Henry BERMUDEZ 50), Alexander LOPEZ (Nestor MARTINEZ 81), Walter CASTRO, Javier PORTILLO (Reynaldo TIGUATH 64), Johnny PALACIOS, Oscar GARCIA•, Washington BRUSCHI, Oliver MORAZAN•. Tr: Danilo TOSELLO

2nd leg. Tiburcio Andino, Tegucigalpa
3-08-2011, 10644, Marrufo USA
Olimpia 2
Rojas [16], Beckeles [86]
Noel VALLADARES (c) - Fabio DE SOUZA, Brayan BECKELES, Reynaldo TILGUATH (Carlos MEJIA• 62), Alexander LOPEZ, Walter CASTRO (Douglas MATTOSO 70), Roger ROJAS, Javier PORTILLO•, Johnny PALACIOS, Oscar GARCIA, Washington BRUSCHI (Nestor MARTINEZ 80). Tr: Danilo TOSELLO
Santos Laguna 1
Suarez [14]
Oswaldo SANCHEZ• (c) - Jose CARDENAS, Carlos OCHOA•, Christian SUAREZ (Carlos QUINTERO 61), Jaime TOLEDO (Jesus ESCOBOZA 82), Rodolfo SALINAS, Santiago HOYOS, Rafael FIGUEROA, Felipe BALOY, Jose OLVERA (Juan Pablo RODRIGUEZ 59), Carlos MORALES. Tr: Diego COCCA

1st leg. Jorge Suarez, Metapán
27-07-2011, 1658, Perea PAN
Isidro Metapán 2
Sanchez.E [65], Allan Kardec [87]
Miguel MONTES - Ernesto AQUINO (c), ALLAN KARDECK (Jose ALVARADO 90), Rodolfo SUAREZ, Christian BAUTISTA (Mark BLANCO 65), Edwin SANCHEZ (Milton MOLINA 90), Andres FLORES, Alfredo PACHECO, Ramon SANCHEZ, Alexander ESCOBAR, Hector MEJIA•. Tr: Edwin PORTILLO
Puerto Rico Islanders 0

Raymond BURSE - Richard MARTINEZ, Noah DELGADO (c) (Kevon VILLAROEL 86), David FOLEY•, Aaron PITCHKOLAN, Jonathan FANA FARIAS (Yaikel PEREZ 79), Matthew BOURAEE (Joseph SALEM 62), Osei TELESFORD, Logan EMORY•, Jamie CUNNINGHAM•, Jay NEEDHAM. Tr: Colin CLARKE

2nd leg. Juan Loubriel, Bayamón
3-08-2011, 1125, Legister JAM
Puerto Rico Islanders 3
Foley 2 [60p 68p], Richardson [95+]
Raymond BURSE - Scott JONES, Richard MARTINEZ, Noah DELGADO (Gregory RICHARDSON 64), David FOLEY•, Aaron PITCHKOLAN, Jonathan FANA FARIAS, Petter VILLEGAS (Nicholas ADDLERY 57), Osei TELESFORD (Leonardo LY 86), Logan EMORY, Jay NEEDHAM. Tr: Colin CLARKE
Isidro Metapán 1
Blanco [56]
Miguel MONTES - Ernesto AQUINO (c), Rodolfo SUAREZ•, Christian BAUTISTA• (Milton MOLINA 82), Edwin SANCHEZ (Jorge Luis MORAN 83), Andres FLORES, Alfredo PACHECO•, Ramon SANCHEZ, Mark BLANCO (Jose ALVARADO 90), Alexander ESCOBAR, Hector MEJIA•. Tr: Edwin PORTILLO

CONCACAF CHAMPIONS LEAGUE 2011-12

1st leg. BMO Field, Toronto
27-07-2011, 9241, Salazar USA

Toronto FC	2
	Plata 2 [56 72]

Milos KOCIC - Andrew IRO, Doneil HENRY, Ashtone MORGAN, Ryan JOHNSON (Javier MARTINA 77), Danny KOEVERMANS, Matthew STINSON (Julian DEGUZMAN 72), Nick SOOLSMA, Torsten FRINGS• (c), Richard ECKERSLEY, Gianluca ZAVARISE• (Joao PLATA 48). Tr: Aron WINTER

Real Estelí	1
	Calero [80]

Carlos MENDIETA - Jaime RUIZ• (Marlon MEDINA 87), Manuel ROSAS, Samuel WILSON (Wilber SANCHEZ 90), Elmer MEJIA (c), Francisco LOPEZ•, Franklin LOPEZ, Felix ZELEDON, Felix RODRIGUEZ, Salvador GARCIA, Jose FLORES (Rudel CALERO 62). Tr: Otoniel OLIVAS

2nd leg. Independencia, Estelí
2-08-2011, 4500, Castro HON

Real Estelí	1
	Rosas [45p]

Carlos MENDIETA - Jaime RUIZ, Luis GONZALEZ, Manuel ROSAS, Samuel WILSON (Wilber SANCHEZ 73), Rudel CALERO, Elmer MEJIA (c), Francisco LOPEZ, Franklin LOPEZ, Felix ZELEDON, Felix RODRIGUEZ (Jose FLORES 58). Tr: Otoniel OLIVAS

Toronto FC	2
	Johnson 2 [37 47]

Milos KOCIC - Andrew IRO, Doneil HENRY, Joao PLATA, Ryan JOHNSON (Ashtone MORGAN 59), Torsten FRINGS• (c), Terrence DUNFIELD•, Danleigh BORMAN (Danny KOEVERMANS 71), Richard ECKERSLEY, Javier MARTINA (Matthew STINSON 34), Perica MAROSEVIC. Tr: Aron WINTER

1st leg. Cuscatlán, San Salvador
28-07-2011, 7301, Gantar CAN

Alianza	0

Yimy CUELLAR - Edwin MARTINEZ, Marcelo MESSIAS, Rudis CORRALES, Christian CASTILLO• (c), Herbert SOSA•, Hector SALAZAR (Carlos AYALA 72), Jonathan BARRIOS, Leonardo DA SILVA (Rafael BURGOS 85), Jose ALVARADO, Elman RIVAS• (Abraham AMAYA 61). Tr: Roberto GAMARRA

FC Dallas	1
	Jackson [70]

Kevin HARTMAN - Daniel HERNANDEZ• (c), Ugochukwu IHEMELU, Jair BENITEZ, Jackson GONCALVES, Bruno GUARDA• (Andrew JACKSON 71), Ricardo VILLAR (Eric ALEXANDER 75), George JOHN, Marvin CHAVEZ• (Bobby WARSHAW 90), Zach LOYD, Brek SHEA. Tr: Schellas HYNDMAN

2nd leg. Pizza Hut Park, Frisco
3-08-2011, 3400, Wijngaarde SUR

FC Dallas	1
	Ihemelu [37]

Kevin HARTMAN - Daniel HERNANDEZ• (c), Ugochukwu IHEMELU, Jair BENITEZ, Jackson GONCALVES (Ruben LUNA 42), Bruno GUARDA•, Ricardo VILLAR, George JOHN, Marvin CHAVEZ (Andrew WIEDEMAN 71), Zach LOYD, Brek SHEA (Eric ALEXANDER 58). Tr: Schellas HYNDMAN

Alianza	0

Henry HERNANDEZ - Edwin MARTINEZ•, Mauricio QUINTANILLA, Ely SERRANO (Abraham AMAYA 56), Rudis CORRALES (Carlos AYALA 56), Rafael BURGOS•, Christian CASTILLO (c), Herbert SOSA, Jose ALVARADO, Elman RIVAS (Jose MARADIAGA 85). Tr: Roberto GAMARRA

1st leg. Rommel Fernández, Panama
26-07-2011, 700, Espana GUA

San Francisco	1
	Brown [28p]

Eric HUGHES - Rolando ALGANDONA, Manuel TORRES (c), Martin GOMEZ, Eybir BONAGA, Luis Felipe OLIVARDIA, Johann DE AVILA (Jose GARCES 70), Eduardo JIMENEZ (Edgardo PANEZO• 43), Amir WAITE, Roberto CHEN, Roberto BROWN• (Jefrey DIAZ 80). Tr: Leonardo PIPINO

Seattle Sounders	0

Kasey KELLER (c) - Patrick IANNI, Osvaldo ALONSO•, James RILEY, Erik FRIBERG (Patrick NOONAN 74), Mauro ROSALES, Leonardo GONZALEZ, Fredy MONTERO, Roger LEVESQUE (Michael FUCITO 58), Lamar NEAGLE (Alvaro FERNANDEZ• 58), Jeffrey PARKE•. Tr: Sigi SCHMID

2nd leg. Century Link Field, Seattle
3-08-2011, 21233, Solis CRC

Seattle Sounders	2
	Fernandez [41], Jaqua [98]

Kasey KELLER• (c) - Osvaldo ALONSO•, James RILEY, Erik FRIBERG• (Servando CARRASCO 112), Mauro ROSALES•, Leonardo GONZALEZ, Alvaro FERNANDEZ (Lamar NEAGLE 110), Fredy MONTERO, Zach SCOTT, Patrick NOONAN (Jonathan JAQUA 67), Jeffrey PARKE. Tr: Sigi SCHMID

San Francisco	0

Miguel TORRES - Rolando ALGANDONA, Manuel TORRES (c), Martin GOMEZ, Eybir BONAGA, Luis Felipe OLIVARDIA, Johann DE AVILA•, Edgardo PANEZO (Jefrey DIAZ 100), Amir WAITE (Fredy ARIZALA 84), Roberto CHEN, Roberto BROWN•. Tr: Leonardo PIPINO

1st leg. Estadio Nacional, San José
26-07-2011, 7335, Davila NCA

Herediano	8
	Vargas [10], Cancela [30], Arias [38], Salazar [59], Barbosa 3 [70 77 89], Cordero [94+]

Leonel MOREIRA - Cristian MONTERO (c), Olman VARGAS (Victor NUNEZ 56), Yosimar ARIAS, Marvin ANGULO, Jose CUBERO, Marvin OBANDO (Jose Luis CORDERO 72), Pablo SALAZAR, Carlos CASTRO•, Jose CANCELA, Anderson ANDRADE• (Jorge BARBOSA De Lima 65). Tr: Alejandro GUINTINI

Alpha United	0

Ronson WILLIAMS - Kris CAMACHO, Kirk DUCKWORTH, Cornelius HENRY (Jevon FRANCIS 55), Dwain JACOBS, Adrian MITCHELL, Anthony ABRAMS• (c), Selwyn ISAACS (Shavane SEAFORTH 49), Warren GILKES, Philbert MOFFATT (Travis GRANT 63), Kelvin MCKENZIE. Tr: Wayne DOVER

2nd leg. Providence, Providence
4-08-2011, 600, Skeete BRB

Alpha United	2
	Abrams [34], Grant [75]

Ronson WILLIAMS• - Shavane SEAFORTH, Kris CAMACHO, Kirk DUCKWORTH•, Dwain JACOBS, Adrian MITCHELL, Dwight PETERS (Warren GILKES 29), Anthony ABRAMS (c) (Cornelius HENRY 71), Travis GRANT•, Kelvin MCKENZIE♦44, Jevon FRANCIS (Thirzen LEADER• 89). Tr: Wayne DOVER

Herediano	2
	Hernandez [78], Barbosa [84]

Ronny FERNANDEZ - Michael RODRIGUEZ, Cristian MONTERO (c), Olman VARGAS, Yosimar ARIAS, Marvin ANGULO•• ♦ 79, Andres CASTRO (Carlos CASTRO 69), Carlos HERNANDEZ, Marvin OBANDO (Erick SANCHEZ 69), Jorge BARBOSA De Lima, Jose CANCELA. Tr: Alejandro GUINTINI

PART THREE – THE CONTINENTAL CONFEDERATIONS

GROUP A		Pl	W	D	L	F	A	Pts	USA	MEX	CRC	HON
Los Angeles Galaxy	USA	6	4	0	2	8	4	12		2-1	2-0	2-0
Morelia	MEX	6	4	0	2	11	5	12	2-1		2-1	4-0
LD Alajuelense	CRC	6	4	0	2	8	6	12	1-0	1-0		1-0
Motagua	HON	6	0	0	6	2	14	0	0-1	0-2	2-4	

Home Depot Center, Carson, LA
16-08-2011, 8196, Wijngaarde SUR
Los Angeles Galaxy 2
Cristman [13], Donovan [60]
Joshua SAUNDERS - Todd DUNIVANT, Gregg BERHALTER•, Omar GONZALEZ, Sean FRANKLIN (Christopher BIRCHALL 84), Landon DONOVAN (c), Adam CRISTMAN, Mike MAGEE (Miguel LOPEZ 88), JUNINHO, AJ DELAGARZA, David BECKHAM (Michael STEPHENS 75). Tr: Bruce ARENA
Motagua 0

Donaldo MORALES - Junior IZAGUIRRE, Carlos DISCUA (Brayan GARCIA 62), Jorge CLAROS, Guillermo RAMIREZ (Edras PADILLA 76), Mario GUERRERO♦70, Johnny LEVERON, Amado GUEVARA (c), Aly ARRIOLA (Emilson CRUZ 88), Sergio MENDOZA, Jerry BENGSTON. Tr: Ramon MARADIAGA

Alejandro Soto, Alajuela
16-08-2011, 7000, Moreno PAN
LD Alajuelense 1
McDonald [77]
Alfonso QUESADA• - Giancarlo GONZALEZ, Jose SALVATIERRA, Marcelo FAZZIO (Cristian OVIEDO 62), Pablo GABAS (c), Christopher MENESES, Allen GUEVARA, Kevin SANCHO (Jorge GATGENS 55), Jonathan MCDONALD•, Jhonny ACOSTA, Juan GUZMAN (Alejandro ALPIZAR 73). Tr: Oscar RAMIREZ
Morelia 0

Federico VILAR• (c) - Enrique PEREZ•, Rafael MARQUEZ LUGO (Miguel SABAH 56), Luis NORIEGA, Yasser CORONA•, Manuel PEREZ, Jaime LOZANO (Joao ROJAS 75), Diego JIMENEZ, Edgar LUGO (Luis SANDOVAL 46), Marvin CABRERA•, Aldo RAMIREZ. Tr: Tomas BOY

Home Depot Center, Carson, LA
25-08-2011, 9855, Rodriguez.M MEX
Los Angeles Galaxy 2
Gonzalez [38], Barrett [77]
Joshua SAUNDERS - Todd DUNIVANT, Gregg BERHALTER (Sean FRANKLIN 26), Omar GONZALEZ, Landon DONOVAN• (c), Robbie KEANE (Christopher BIRCHALL 90), Adam CRISTMAN (Chad BARRETT 71), Mike MAGEE•, JUNINHO♦87, AJ DELAGARZA, David BECKHAM•. Tr: Bruce ARENA
LD Alajuelense 0

Ivan GARCIA - Giancarlo GONZALEZ, Jose SALVATIERRA, Marcelo FAZZIO, Alejandro ALPIZAR (Carlos CLARK 74), Pablo GABAS (c), Christopher MENESES, Allen GUEVARA, Kevin SANCHO (Cristian OVIEDO 83), Jhonny ACOSTA•, Juan GUZMAN (Cristhian LAGOS 82). Tr: Oscar RAMIREZ

Estadio Morelos, Morelia
25-08-2011, 5463, Bonilla SLV
Morelia 4
Marquez Lugo [2], Rojas [50], Jimenez [70], Lugo [72]
Carlos RODRIGUEZ - Enrique PEREZ, Rafael MARQUEZ LUGO (Diego MEJIA 68),Joao ROJAS, Luis NORIEGA (Miguel SABAH 60), Felipe AYALA, Yasser CORONA, Manuel PEREZ (Aldo RAMIREZ 71), Diego JIMENEZ, Edgar LUGO, Marvin CABRERA. Tr: Tomas BOY
Motagua 0

Donaldo MORALES - Odis BORJAS, Junior IZAGUIRRE, Jorge CLAROS, Guillermo RAMIREZ (Sergio MENDOZA 62), Brayan GARCIA, Johnny LEVERON, Junior PADILLA, Amado GUEVARA, David MOLINA (Carlos DISCUA 46), Jerry BENGSTON. Tr: Ramon MARADIAGA

Estadio Morelos, Morelia
13-09-2011, 16 000, Pineda HON
Morelia 2
Aldrete [83], Sabah [92+]
Federico VILAR (c) - Luis SILVA, Rafael MARQUEZ LUGO, Jorge GASTELUM (Manuel PEREZ 77), Joao ROJAS, Luis SANDOVAL (Edgar LUGO 57), Alexei ALDRETE, Damian MANSO (Miguel SABAH• 46), Diego JIMENEZ, Marvin CABRERA, Aldo RAMIREZ. Tr: Tomas BOY
Los Angeles Galaxy 1
Keane [52]
Joshua SAUNDERS - Todd DUNIVANT, Omar GONZALEZ, Frankie HEJDUK, Christopher BIRCHALL (Jovan KIROVSKI 87), Landon DONOVAN (c), Robbie KEANE, Adam CRISTMAN (Chad BARRETT 63), Mike MAGEE (Bryan JORDAN 76), AJ DELAGARZA, Michael STEPHENS. Tr: Bruce ARENA

Tiburcio Andino, Tegucigalpa
15-09-2011, 1928, Delgadillo MEX
Motagua 0

Donaldo MORALES - Odis BORJAS, Jorge CLAROS, Guillermo RAMIREZ (Jhon PALACIOS 59), Mario GUERRERO•, Johnny LEVERON, Junior PADILLA (Carlos DISCUA 59), Amado GUEVARA• (c), Sergio MENDOZA, Jerry BENGSTON, Adan RAMIREZ. Tr: Ramon MARADIAGA
LD Alajuelense 4
Valle [41], McDonald [51], Guevara 2 [84 86]
Patrick PEMBERTON - Giancarlo GONZALEZ, Cristian OVIEDO (Juan GUZMAN 71), Verny RAMIREZ•, Marcelo FAZZIO, Pablo GABAS• (c) (Allen GUEVARA 79), Luis VALLE, Kevin SANCHO (Jose SALVATIERRA 84), Jonathan MCDONALD, Porfirio LOPEZ, Jhonny ACOSTA•. Tr: Oscar RAMIREZ

Alejandro Soto, Alajuela
21-09-2011, 13 377, Campbell JAM
LD Alajuelense 1
Gabas [28]
Patrick PEMBERTON• - Giancarlo GONZALEZ, Jose SALVATIERRA, Marcelo FAZZIO•, Pablo GABAS (c) (Juan GUZMAN• 86), Luis VALLE, Kevin SANCHO (Christopher MENESES 80), Luis SEQUEIRA (Allen GUEVARA 64), Jonathan MCDONALD, Porfirio LOPEZ•, Jhonny ACOSTA. Tr: Oscar RAMIREZ
Los Angeles Galaxy 0

Joshua SAUNDERS - Todd DUNIVANT, Omar GONZALEZ•, Landon DONOVAN (c), Chad BARRETT (Adam CRISTMAN 61), Robbie KEANE, Mike MAGEE, JUNINHO (Paolo CARDOZO 68), AJ DELAGARZA, David BECKHAM•, Bryan JORDAN•. Tr: Bruce ARENA

Tiburcio Andino, Tegucigalpa
22-09-2011, 1752, Santos PUR
Motagua 0

Donaldo MORALES - Odis BORJAS (Junior PADILLA 70), Junior IZAGUIRRE, Milton REYES, Jorge CLAROS•, Luis LOPEZ (Adan RAMIREZ 46), Guillermo RAMIREZ (Carlos MORAN 64), Mario GUERRERO, Amado GUEVARA (c), Sergio MENDOZA, Jerry BENGSTON. Tr: Luis Alberto REYES
Morelia 2
Corona [55], Manso [58]
Jesus URBINA - Luis SILVA, Miguel SANSORES (Julio ATILANO 74), Luis NORIEGA•, Felipe AYALA•, Yasser CORONA, Damian MANSO, Manuel PEREZ (Ernest NUNGARAY 86), Angel SEPULVEDA (Claudio BOY 90), Diego JIMENEZ, Marvin CABRERA. Tr: Tomas BOY

Home Depot Center, Carson, LA
28-09-2011, 7500, Aguilar MEX
Los Angeles Galaxy 2
Magee [21], Juninho [91+]
Joshua SAUNDERS - Todd DUNIVANT, Omar GONZALEZ, Frankie HEJDUK (Hector JIMENEZ 71), Landon DONOVAN (c), Adam CRISTMAN (Chad BARRETT 67), Mike MAGEE (Bryan JORDAN 46), JUNINHO, AJ DELAGARZA•, Michael STEPHENS, Paolo CARDOZO•. Tr: Bruce ARENA
Morelia 1
Marquez Lugo [59]
Federico VILAR - Enrique PEREZ, Rafael MARQUEZ LUGO (c) (Miguel SABAH 63), Luis NORIEGA (Adrian ALDRETE 53), Felipe AYALA (Aldo RAMIREZ 63), Yasser CORONA, Damian MANSO, Manuel PEREZ, Angel SEPULVEDA, Diego JIMENEZ•, Marvin CABRERA. Tr: Tomas BOY

Alejandro Soto, Alajuela
28-09-2011, 9099, Legister JAM
LD Alajuelense 1
McDonald [27]
Patrick PEMBERTON - Giancarlo GONZALEZ, Jose SALVATIERRA, Marcelo FAZZIO (Cristian OVIEDO 87), Pablo GABAS (c), Luis VALLE, Allen GUEVARA (Carlos CLARK• 79), Kevin SANCHO (Alejandro ALPIZAR 61), Jonathan MCDONALD•, Porfirio LOPEZ, Jhonny ACOSTA. Tr: Oscar RAMIREZ
Motagua 0

Kerpo DE LEON - Odis BORJAS, Milton REYES• (c), Emilson CRUZ• (Roger MONDRAGON 69), Carlos DISCUA (Guillermo RAMIREZ 46), Luis LOPEZ, Carlos MORAN, Johnny LEVERON, Sergio MENDOZA, Omar ELVIR (Junior PADILLA 46), Adan RAMIREZ. Tr: Jose TREVINO

Estadio Morelos, Morelia
18-10-2011, 15 000, Moreno PAN
Morelia 2
Rojas [56], Sabah [59]
Carlos RODRIGUEZ - Enrique PEREZ, Luis SILVA, Rafael MARQUEZ LUGO (c), Jorge GASTELUM (Aldo RAMIREZ• 46), Adrian ALDRETE, Yasser CORONA (Miguel SABAH 57), Manuel PEREZ•, Angel SEPULVEDA, Edgar LUGO (Joao ROJAS 46), Joel HUIQUI. Tr: Tomas BOY
LD Alajuelense 1
Gabas [36]
Patrick PEMBERTON - Giancarlo GONZALEZ•, Jose SALVATIERRA•, Marcelo FAZZIO•, Pablo GABAS (c), Luis VALLE, Allen GUEVARA (Diego CALVO 78), Luis SEQUEIRA• (Christopher MENESES 56), Porfirio LOPEZ, Jhonny ACOSTA, Juan GUZMAN• (Elias PALMA 83). Tr: Oscar RAMIREZ

Tiburcio Andino, Tegucigalpa
20-10-2011, 14 000, Lopez GUA
Motagua 0

Donaldo MORALES - Odis BORJAS, Emilson CRUZ (Guillermo RAMIREZ 75), Carlos DISCUA, Jorge CLAROS (c), Mario GIRON (Amado GUEVARA• 46), Johnny LEVERON, Roger MONDRAGON (Milton REYES• 46), Sergio MENDOZA, David MOLINA, Jerry BENGSTON. Tr: Jose TREVINO
Los Angeles Galaxy 1
Juninho [29]
Joshua SAUNDERS• - Todd DUNIVANT, Omar GONZALEZ, Frankie HEJDUK, Chad BARRETT (Christopher BIRCHALL 64), Mike MAGEE, JUNINHO, AJ DELAGARZA, David BECKHAM (c), Miguel LOPEZ (Landon DONOVAN 69), Paolo CARDOZO (Michael STEPHENS 80). Tr: Bruce ARENA

CONCACAF CHAMPIONS LEAGUE 2011-12

GROUP B		Pl	W	D	L	F	A	Pts	MEX	SLV	USA	HON
Santos Laguna	MEX	6	4	1	1	16	6	**13**		6-0	2-0	3-2
Isidro Metapán	SLV	6	3	0	3	10	15	**9**	2-0		1-3	3-2
Colorado Rapids	USA	6	2	1	3	9	12	**7**	1-4	3-2		1-2
Real España	HON	6	1	2	3	9	11	**5**	1-1	1-2	1-1	

Corona, Torreón
16-08-2011, 5500, Quesada CRC
Santos Laguna 3
Enriquez [28], OG [51], Suarez [74]
Miguel BECERRA (c) - Aaron GALINDO, Carlos OCHOA, Jaime TOLEDO (Juan Pablo RODRIGUEZ 78), Rafael FIGUEROA, Osmar MARES, Enrique LOPEZ, Jose OLVERA (Christian SUAREZ 69), Juan ENRIQUEZ, Jesus ESCOBOZA (Arnulfo GONZALEZ• 74), Luis GARCIA. Tr: Diego COCCA
Real España 2
Delgado [42], Lalin [68]
Marcelo MACIAS - Mario MARTINEZ, Julio RODRIGUEZ•, Christian MARTINEZ (Jairo PUERTO 65), Luis LOBO (Allan LALIN 52), Maynor MARTINEZ, Johnny CALDERON (Hilder COLON 80), Alfredo MEJIA (c), Daniel TEJEDA, Edder DELGADO, Sergio BICA. Tr: Mario ZANABRIA

Dick's SGP, Commerce City, Denver
17-08-2011, 4165, Taylor BRB
Colorado Rapids 3
Kandji 2 [16 45], Akpan [50]
Matt PICKENS - Drew MOOR•, Jeffrey LARENTOWICZ (c), Joseph NANE, Macoumba KANDJI (Brian MULLAN 71), Wells THOMPSON, Andre AKPAN, Marvell WYNNE (Michael HOLODY 78), Sanna NYASSI• (Quincy AMARIKWA 45), Kosuke KIMURA, Scott PALGUTA. Tr: Gary SMITH
Isidro Metapan 3
Alan Kardeck [2p], Suarez [25]
Miguel MONTES - Ernesto AQUINO• (c), Mario POSADAS• (Milton MOLINA 76), ALLAN KARDECK♦41, Rodolfo SUAREZ, Christian BAUTISTA (Mark BLANCO 56), Edwin SANCHEZ (Jorge MORAN 68), Andres FLORES, Alfredo PACHECO, Ramon SANCHEZ, Alexander ESCOBAR. Tr: Edwin PORTILLO

Francisco Morazán, San Pedro Sula
23-08-2011, 5841, Garcia MEX
Real España 1
Rodriguez [87]
Kevin HERNANDEZ - Mario MARTINEZ, Julio RODRIGUEZ•, Christian MARTINEZ (Jairo PUERTO 45), Maynor MARTINEZ, Allan LALIN, Johnny CALDERON (Carlos PAVON 66), Alfredo MEJIA (c), Daniel TEJEDA, Edder DELGADO, Sergio BICA (Hilder COLON 45). Tr: Mario ZANABRIA
Colorado Rapids 1
Larentowicz [45]
Steward CEUS - Danny EARLS, Jeffrey LARENTOWICZ (c), Joseph NANE, Omar CUMMINGS (Quincy AMARIKWA 71), Wells THOMPSON, Ross LABAUEX (Sanna NYASSI 81), Andre AKPAN, Michael HOLODY•, Kosuke KIMURA, Scott PALGUTA (Drew MOOR 69). Tr: Gary SMITH

Jorge Suarez, Metapán
24-08-2011, 3260, Bogle JAM
Isidro Metapan 2
Suarez [45], Bautista [52]
Miguel MONTES - Ernesto AQUINO (c), Rodolfo SUAREZ• (Mario POSADAS 83), Christian BAUTISTA (Milton MOLINA 89), Edwin SANCHEZ (Jorge MORAN 86), Andres FLORES, Alfredo PACHECO, Ramon SANCHEZ•, Mark BLANCO, Alexander ESCOBAR, Hector MEJIA. Tr: Edwin PORTILLO
Santos Laguna 0
Miguel BECERRA - Aaron GALINDO, Carlos OCHOA•, Jaime TOLEDO, Rafael FIGUEROA (c), Osmar MARES, Juan ENRIQUEZ (Carlos PARRA 72), Edson MORUA, Arnulfo GONZALEZ (Carlos QUINTERO 59), Jesus ESCOBOZA, Luis GARCIA• (Cesar IBANEZ• 59). Tr: Diego COCCA

Francisco Morazán, San Pedro Sula
13-09-2011, 3358, Lopez GUA
Real España 1
Pavon [80p]
Marcelo MACIAS - Jairo PUERTO, Mario MARTINEZ, Carlos PAVON (c), Luis LOBO (Allan LALIN 46), Maynor MARTINEZ (Gerson RODAS 46), Alfredo MEJIA (Christian MARTINEZ 68), Daniel TEJEDA, Edder DELGADO•, Sergio BICA•, Ever ALVARADO•. Tr: Mario ZANABRIA
Isidro Metapan 2
Aquino [8], Alan Kardeck [57]
Miguel MONTES - Ernesto AQUINO• (c), ALLAN KARDECK, Christian BAUTISTA (Rene RAMOS 89), Edwin SANCHEZ (Mario POSADAS• 80), Andres FLORES, Alfredo PACHECO•, Ramon SANCHEZ•, Alexander ESCOBAR•, Hector MEJIA•, Jose ALVARADO. TD: Edwin PORTILLO

Dick's SGP, Commerce City, Denver
13-09-2011, 9760, Morena PAN
Colorado Rapids 1
Mullan [77]
Steward CEUS - 2-Danny EARLS (Miguel COMMINGES 46), Drew MOOR, Jeffrey LARENTOWICZ, Macoumba KANDJI, Omar CUMMINGS, Wells THOMPSON (Brian MULLAN 56), Marvell WYNNE, Sanna NYASSI, Pablo MASTROENI (c) Joseph NANE 69), Scott PALGUTA. Tr: Gary SMITH
Santos Laguna 4
Ludena [14], Peralta [27], Quintero [64], Suarez [71]
Oswaldo SANCHEZ• (c) - Carlos QUINTERO, Jorge ESTRADA, Juan Pablo RODRIGUEZ• (Jaime TOLEDO 70), Daniel LUDUENA (Edson BICA 89), Christian SUAREZ•, Rodolfo SALINAS (Jose CARDENAS 49), Santiago HOYOS, Rafael FIGUEROA, Oribe PERALTA, Carlos MORALES. T: Eduardo RERGIS

Dick's SGP, Commerce City, Denver
21-09-2011, 4512, Wijngaarde SUR
Colorado Rapids 1
Akpan [18]
Steward CEUS - Joseph NANE (Jamie SMITH 64), Macoumba KANDJI (Sanna NYASSI• 68), Brian MULLAN (Omar CUMMINGS 79), Wells THOMPSON, Ross LABAUEX•, Andre AKPAN, Michael HOLODY, Kosuke KIMURA, Scott PALGUTA, Tyrone MARSHALL. Tr: Gary SMITH
Real España 2
Pavon 2 [12 33]
Marcelo MACIAS - Julio Pablo RODRIGUEZ•, Carlos PAVON (c) (Jesus MUNGUIA 70), Christian MARTINEZ (Clayvin ZUNIGA• 52), Juan ACEVEDO, Allan LALIN (Luis LOBO 86), Johnny CALDERON, Daniel TEJEDA, Edder DELGADO, Henry ACOSTA•, Sergio BICA. Tr: Mario ZANABRIA

Corona, Torreón
22-09-2011, 5500, Gantar CAN
Santos Laguna 6
Cardenas [21], Quintero 2 [28 55], Peralta 2 [38 86], Ochoa [79]
Miguel BECERRA• - Carlos QUINTERO, Jorge ESTRADA•, Jose CARDENAS, Juan Pablo RODRIGUEZ (Jaime TOLEDO 70), Santiago HOYOS (Carlos OCHOA• 58), Felipe BALOY, Oribe PERALTA, Jose OLVERA. Tr: Benjamin GALINDO
Isidro Metapan 0
Miguel MONTES (Fidel MONDRAGON 85) - Milton MOLINA, ALLAN KARDECK (Oscar ESCALANTE 81), Rodolfo SUAREZ, Christian BAUTISTA•, Edwin SANCHEZ (Jorge MORAN• 64), Andres FLORES (c), Mark BLANCO, Alexander ESCOBAR, Hector MEJIA, Jose ALVARADO. Tr: Edwin PORTILLO

Francisco Morazán, San Pedro Sula
28-09-2011, 6296, Rodas GUA
Real España 1
Mario Martinez [61]
Marcelo MACIAS - Mario MARTINEZ, Julio Pablo RODRIGUEZ, Carlos PAVON (c) (Luis LOBO 45), Christian MARTINEZ (Maynor MARTINEZ 74), Johnny CALDERON•, Alfredo MEJIA•, Daniel TEJEDA, Edder DELGADO, Henry ACOSTA, Sergio BICA. Tr: Mario ZANABRIA
Santos Laguna 1
Ochoa [51]
Miguel BECERRA - Jose CARDENAS (Arnulfo GONZALEZ 73), Carlos OCHOA, Cesar IBANEZ, Jaime TOLEDO, Rafael FIGUEROA, Jose OLVERA, Carlos MORALES (c) (Enrique LOPEZ• 81), Juan ENRIQUEZ (Carlos PARRA 69), Jesus ESCOBOZA, Luis GARCIA. Tr: Benjamin GALINDO

Jorge Suarez, Metapán
28-09-2011, 1920, Castro HON
Isidro Metapan 1
Pacheco [36]
Miguel MONTES - Ernesto AQUINO (c), Jorge MORAN (Edwin SANCHEZ• 55), ALLAN KARDECK, Rodolfo SUAREZ, Andres FLORES, Alfredo PACHECO, Ramon SANCHEZ, Mark BLANCO, Alexander ESCOBAR, Hector MEJIA• (Marvin MONTERROZA 78). Tr: Edwin PORTILLO
Colorado Rapids 1
Ababio [31], Amarikwa [49], Cummings [77]
Steward CEUS• - Danny EARLS•, Joseph NANE, Eddie ABABIO (David ARMSTRONG 61), Quincy AMARIKWA (Macoumba KANDJI 90), Wells THOMPSON, Ross LABAUEX•, Andre AKPAN (Omar CUMMINGS• 72), Michael HOLODY•, Scott PALGUTA•, Tyrone MARSHALL (c). Tr: Steve GUPPY

Corona, Torreón
19-10-2011, 6000, Campbell JAM
Santos Laguna 2
Galindo [55], Edcoboza [67]
Miguel BECERRA (c) - Aaron GALINDO, Jose CARDENAS, Carlos OCHOA (Carlos PARRA 66), Jaime TOLEDO, Enrique LOPEZ (Edson MORUA 75), Felipe BALOY•, Jose OLVERA, Juan ENRIQUEZ (Arnulfo GONZALEZ 68), Jesus ESCOBOZA•, Luis GARCIA. Tr: Benjamin GALINDO
Colorado Rapids 0
Steward CEUS - Drew MOOR, Jeffrey LARENTOWICZ•, Macoumba KANDJI (Omar CUMMINGS 62), Wells THOMPSON, Ross LABAUEX (Sanna NYASSI 58), Caleb FOLAN, Marvell WYNNE (Eddie ABABIO 78), Kosuke KIMURA, Scott PALGUTA, Miguel COMMINGES. Tr: Gary SMITH

Jorge Suarez, Metapán
20-10-2011, 2020, Quesada CRC
Isidro Metapan 3
Suarez 2 [50 82], Sanchez [68]
Miguel MONTES - Milton MOLINA (Christian BAUTISTA 63), Ernesto AQUINO (c), ALLAN KARDECK (Jose ALVARADO 78), Rodolfo SUAREZ•, Edwin SANCHEZ (Jorge MORAN 87), Andres FLORES, Alfredo PACHECO, Ramon SANCHEZ, Mark BLANCO, Alexander ESCOBAR. Tr: Edwin PORTILLO
Real España 2
Delgado [56], Maynor Martinez [92+]
Marcelo MACIAS - Mario MARTINEZ, Julio Pablo RODRIGUEZ, Carlos PAVON (c) (Allan LALIN• 60), Christian MARTINEZ (Jairo PUERTO 46), Maynor MARTINEZ, Johnny CALDERON, Alfredo MEJIA (Henry ACOSTA, c), Daniel TEJEDA•, Edder DELGADO•, Sergio BICA•. Tr: Mario ZANABRIA

GROUP C

GROUP C		Pl	W	D	L	F	A	Pts	MEX	CAN	USA	PAN
Pumas UNAM	MEX	6	3	2	1	8	2	11		4-0	0-1	1-0
Toronto FC	CAN	6	3	1	2	7	7	10	1-1		0-1	1-0
FC Dallas	USA	6	2	1	3	6	11	7	0-2	0-3		1-1
Tauro	PAN	6	1	2	3	7	8	5	0-0	1-2	5-3	

Olímpico Universitario, Mexico City
17-08-2011, 4000, Molina HON
Pumas UNAM 0

Odin PATIÑO - Michelle CASTRO, Eduardo GAMEZ, Juan Carlos CACHO (Eduardo BARRON 45), Humberto GONZALEZ (c), Salvador MEDINA (Martin BRAVO 55), Cesar SANCHEZ•, Raul SERVIN (Eduardo AGUIRRE 45), Jose GARCIA, Aaron SANDOVAL•, Carlos CAMPOS. Tr: Guillermo VASQUEZ

FC Dallas 1
Chavez [66]

Kevin HARTMAN - Daniel HERNANDEZ (c), Ugochukwu IHEMELU, Jair BENITEZ, Jackson GONCALVES• (Fabian CASTILLO• 70), Daniel CRUZ (Eric ALEXANDER 82), Ricardo VILLAR (Andrew JACKSON 76), George JOHN, Marvin CHAVEZ, Zach LOYD•, Brek SHEA•. Tr: Schellas HYNDMAN

Rommel Fernández, Panama City
18-08-2011, 1905, Brea CUB
Tauro 1
Moreno [76p]

Alvaro ANZOLA - Luis MORENO• (c), Juan PEREZ, Leonel PARRIS, Diego CANALI (Victor MENDIETA 64), Gabriel RIOS (Manuel VARGAS 33), Juan BARRERA, Auriel GALLARDO (Temistocles PEREZ 35), Marcos SANCHEZ, Carlos RODRIGUEZ, Reinel HERRERA. Tr: Juan Carlos CUBILLA

Toronto FC 2
Johnson [21], De Guzman [24]

Milos KOCIC• - Andrew IRO• (Dasan ROBINSON 37), Julian DEGUZMAN•, Joao PLATA, Ryan JOHNSON, Danny KOEVERMANS (Mikael YOURASSOWSKY• 58), Matthew STINSON• (Ashtone MORGAN 46), Robert HARDEN, Danleigh BORMAN, Richard ECKERSLEY•, Perica MAROSEVIC. Tr: Aron WINTER

BMO Field, Toronto
25-08-2011, 500, Santos PUR
Toronto FC 0

Milos KOCIC - Julian DEGUZMAN, Joao PLATA, Ryan JOHNSON, Matthew STINSON (Doneil HENRY 80), Robert HARDEN, Torsten FRINGS• (c), Danleigh BORMAN (Ashtone MORGAN 54), Richard ECKERSLEY••♦90, Gianluca ZAVARISE (Leandre GRIFFIT 56), Perica MAROSEVIC. Tr: Aron WINTER

FC Dallas 1
Stewart [45]

Kevin HARTMAN - Daniel HERNANDEZ (c), Ugochukwu IHEMELU, Jair BENITEZ•, Jackson GONCALVES (Fabian CASTILLO• 24), Daniel CRUZ (Bruno GUARDA• 63), Ricardo VILLAR (Bobby WARSHAW 76), Jeremy HALL, Marvin CHAVEZ, Brek SHEA•, Jack STEWART. Tr: Schellas HYNDMAN

Rommel Fernández, Panama City
25-08-2011, 1621, Navarro CAN
Tauro 0

Adnihell ARIANO♦29 - Luis MORENO (c), Manuel VARGAS, Temistocles PEREZ (Jean MCLEAN 77), Juan PEREZ, Leonel PARRIS, Diego CANALI (Alvaro ANZOLA 30), Juan BARRERA (Auriel GALLARDO 60), Marcos SANCHEZ, Carlos RODRIGUEZ, Reinel HERRERA•. Tr: Juan Carlos CUBILLA

Pumas UNAM 0

Odin PATIÑO - David CABRERA (c), Michelle CASTRO (Eduardo BARRON 63), Eduardo AGUIRRE, Neftali TEJA•, Alfonso NIETO, Erik VERA, Jose GARCIA, Kevin QUIÑONES (Cesar SANCHEZ 60), Aaron SANDOVAL•, Carlos CAMPOS (Salvador MEDINA• 46). Tr: Guillermo VASQUEZ

Pizza Hut Park, Frisco, Dallas
14-09-2011, 3001, Quesada CRC
FC Dallas 1
Cruz [1]

Kevin HARTMAN - Daniel HERNANDEZ (c), Ugochukwu IHEMELU, Andrew JACKSON, Jair BENITEZ•, Jackson GONCALVES, Daniel CRUZ (Maykel GALINDO 75), Ricardo VILLAR•, Zach LOYD•, George JOHN, Jeremy HALL (Andre WIEDEMAN 89). Tr: Schellas HYNDMAN

Tauro 1
Moreno [41p]

Alvaro ANZOLA - Luis MORENO (c), Manuel VARGAS (Jhoan MELO• 18), Temistocles PEREZ•, Juan PEREZ, Leonel PARRIS, Auriel GALLARDO 60), Juan BARRERA (Jean MCLEAN 90), Victor MENDIETA, Carlos RODRIGUEZ, Reinel HERRERA. Tr: Juan Carlos CUBILLA

Olímpico Universitario, Mexico City
14-09-2011, 3382, Bogle JAM
Pumas UNAM 4
Bravo 3 [17][33][42], Velarde [21]

Odin PATIÑO - Efrain VELARDE, Dario VERON, Diego DE BUEN (Neftali TEJA 74), Javier CORTES, David CABRERA, Martin BRAVO (Eduardo AGUIRRE 61), Luis FUENTES, Juan PALENCIA (David IZAZOLA 46), Carlos ORRANTIA, Juan Carlos RAMIREZ. Tr: Guillermo VASQUEZ

Toronto FC 0

Milos KOCIC - Andrew IRO (Eddy VIATOR 39), Doneil HENRY, Ashtone MORGAN, Julian DEGUZMAN, Ryan JOHNSON (Perica MAROSEVIC 49), Danny KOEVERMANS (Terrence DUNFIEL 56), Nicky SOOISMA•, Robert HARDEN, Torsten FRINGS• (c), Danleigh BORMAN. Tr: Aron WINTER

BMO Field, Toronto
20-09-2011, 10132, Vaughn USA
Toronto FC 1
Koevermans [40]

Milos KOCIC - Andrew IRO, Ashtone MORGAN, Ryan JOHNSON, Danny KOEVERMANS (Mikael YOURASSOWSKY• 79), Nicky SOOISMA (Julian DEGUZMAN 61), Robert HARDEN, Torsten FRINGS• (c), Terrence DUNFIELD• (Matthew STINSON 73), Richard ECKERSLEY, Perica MAROSEVIC. Tr: Aron WINTER

Tauro 0

Alvaro ANZOLA - Luis MORENO (c), Temistocles PEREZ, Juan PEREZ, Leonel PARRIS, Juan BARRERA (Gabriel RIOS 63), Marcos SANCHEZ (Auriel GALLARDO• 45), Victor MENDIETA (Diego CANALI 72), Jhoan MELO•, Carlos RODRIGUEZ•, Reinel HERRERA•. Tr: Juan Carlos CUBILLA

Pizza Hut Park, Frisco, Dallas
21-09-2011, 4985, Lopez GUA
FC Dallas 0

Kevin HARTMAN - Daniel HERNANDEZ (c), Ugochukwu IHEMELU, Jackson GONCALVES♦40, Daniel CRUZ (Andre WIEDEMAN 85), Ricardo VILLAR (Bobby WARSHAW 72), George JOHN, Fabian CASTILLO (Maykel GALINDO 46), Jeremy HALL, Brek SHEA•, Jack STEWART. Tr: Schellas HYNDMAN

Pumas UNAM 2
Herrera [84], Izazola [91+]

Odin PATIÑO - Efrain VELARDE, Dario VERON, Diego DE BUEN, Javier CORTES, David CABRERA• (David IZAZOLA 61), Martin BRAVO (Eduardo AGUIRRE 67), Luis FUENTES♦40, Juan PALENCIA (C. Carlos ORRANTIA 46), Juan Carlos RAMIREZ•, Neftali TEJA. Tr: Guillermo VASQUEZ

BMO Field, Toronto
27-09-2011, 9115, Brizan TRI
Toronto FC 1
Marosevic [35]

Milos KOCIC - Andrew IRO, Ashtone MORGAN•, Julian DEGUZMAN (c), Ryan JOHNSON, Danny KOEVERMANS (Doneil HENRY 46), Matthew STINSON•, Nicky SOOISMA (Javier MARTINA 65), Robert HARDEN, Richard ECKERSLEY (Matthew GOLD 74), Perica MAROSEVIC. Tr: Aron WINTER

Pumas UNAM 1
Palacios [51]

Odin PATIÑO - Marco PALACIOS, Dario VERON, Diego DE BUEN, David CABRERA (Javier CORTES 46), David IZAZOLA•, Michelle CASTRO, Eduardo AGUIRRE (Martin BRAVO 72), Neftali TEJA, Erik VERA, Kevin QUIÑONES (Carlos ORRANTIA 46). Tr: Guillermo VASQUEZ

Rommel Fernández, Panama City
28-09-2011, 316, Rodriguez MEX
Tauro 5
Moreno [12], Gallardo [33], Perez T 2 [77][86], Sanchez [81]

Alvaro ANZOLA - Luis MORENO• (c), Temistocles PEREZ, Juan PEREZ, Leonel PARRIS, Gabriel RIOS (Marcos SANCHEZ 46), Juan BARRERA (William AGUILAR 74), Auriel GALLARDO (Victor MENDIETA 59), Carlos RODRIGUEZ•♦90, Jean MCLEAN, Azmahar ARIANO•. Tr: Juan Carlos CUBILLA

FC Dallas 3
Benitez [23p], Luna 2 [84][93+p]

Kevin HARTMAN (c) - Jair BENITEZ♦58, Daniel CRUZ (Andrew JACKSON• 66), Zach LOYD, Maykel GALINDO (Bruno GUARDA 46), George JOHN, Fabian CASTILLO•♦89, Bobby WARSHAW (Ugochukwu IHEMELU 69), Marvin CHAVEZ, Jack STEWART, Ruben LUNA•. Tr: Schellas HYNDMAN

Pizza Hut Park, Frisco, Dallas
18-10-2011, 2578, Garcia MEX
FC Dallas 0

Kevin HARTMAN - Daniel HERNANDEZ• (c), Ugochukwu IHEMELU, Andrew JACKSON, Jackson GONCALVES, Ricardo VILLAR (Daniel CRUZ 46), Zach LOYD, George JOHN, Jeremy HALL (Ruben LUNA• 67), Marvin CHAVEZ, Brek SHEA (Bruno GUARDA 87). Tr: Schellas HYNDMAN

Toronto FC 3
Koevermans [29], Plata 2 [69][81]

Milos KOCIC - Andrew IRO•, Doneil HENRY, Ashtone MORGAN, Julian DEGUZMAN• (Terrence DUNFIELD 80), Joao PLATA (Perica MAROSEVIC 85), Ryan JOHNSON, Danny KOEVERMANS (Nathan STURGIS 89), Nicky SOOISMA•, Robert HARDEN, Torsten FRINGS (c). Tr: Aron WINTER

Olímpico Universitario, Mexico City
19-10-2011, 5522, Aguilar SLV
Pumas UNAM 1
Cacho [45]

Odin PATIÑO - Marco PALACIOS, Diego DE BUEN, Javier CORTES (Michelle CASTRO 46), David CABRERA (Carlos CAMPOS 80), Martin BRAVO (David IZAZOLA 55), Luis FUENTES, Juan Carlos CACHO•, Neftali TEJA, Erik VERA, Aaron SANDOVAL. Tr: Guillermo VASQUEZ

Tauro 0

Alvaro ANZOLA - Temistocles PEREZ (Diego CANALI 76), Juan PEREZ (c), Leonel PARRIS, Juan BARRERA (William AGUILAR 68), Auriel GALLARDO (Rolando BOTELLO 46), Marcos SANCHEZ, Victor MENDIETA•, Jean MCLEAN, Reinel HERRERA, Azmahar ARIANO•. Tr: Juan Carlos CUBILLA

CONCACAF CHAMPIONS LEAGUE 2011-12

GROUP D		Pl	W	D	L	F	A	Pts	MEX	USA	GUA	CRC
Monterrey	MEX	6	4	0	2	11	4	**12**		0-1	3-1	1-0
Seattle Sounders	USA	6	3	1	2	10	7	**10**	1-2		4-1	0-1
Comunicaciones	GUA	6	2	1	3	8	13	**7**	1-0	2-2		2-0
Herediano	CRC	6	2	0	4	6	11	**6**	0-5	1-2	4-1	

CenturyLink Field, Seattle
16-08-2011, 10017, Delgadillo MEX
Seattle Sounders — 4
Evans [35], Fucito 2 [61 67], OG [87]
Terence BOSS - Michael FUCITO, Bradley EVANS (c), Patrick IANNI• (Roger LEVESQUE 83), James RILEY•, Leonardo GONZALEZ• (Zach SCOTT 74), Alvaro FERNANDEZ, Fredy MONTERO (Mauro ROSALES 62), Servando CARRASCO, Lamar NEAGLE♦55, Jhon HURTADO•. Tr: Sigi SCHMID
Comunicaciones — 1
Arreola [2]
Juan PAREDES - Edgard MARTINEZ♦[80], Erwin MORALES, Carlos RAMIREZ•, Jean MARQUEZ (Rigoberto GOMEZ 76), Carlos CASTRILLO•, Fredy THOMPSON•, Transito MONTEPEQUE (Hernan SANDOVAL 77), Bryan ORDONEZ (Carlos MEJIA 69), Adolfo MACHADO•, Jairo ARREOLA•. Tr: Ivan SOPEGNO

Estadio Nacional, San Jose
17-08-2011, 8959, Mejia SLV
Herediano — 0
Leonel MOREIRA - Michael RODRIGUEZ, Jose Luis CORDERO (Olman VARGAS 46), Yosimar ARIAS, Jose CUBERO, Marvin OBANDO, Pablo SALAZAR, Victor NUNEZ•, Carlos CASTRO (Jean SANCHEZ GUTIERREZ• 46), Junior ALVARADO (Carlos HERNANDEZ 61), Jose CANCELA (c). Tr: Alejandro GUINTINI
Monterrey — 5
Carreno 3 [21 22 35], Corona [36], De Nigris [56]
Jonathan OROZCO (c) - Severo MEZA, Ricardo OSORIO (Luis RODRIGUEZ 63), Darvin CHAVEZ, Hector MORALES, Abraham CARRENO• (Aldo DE NIGRIS 46), Jesus ZAVALA, Walter AYOVI (Cesar DE LA PENA 46), Hiram MIER, Jesus CORONA, Marcelo CAZAUBON. Tr: Victor VUCETICH

Tecnológico, Monterrey
23-08-2011, 10234, Rodas GUA
Monterrey — 0
Jonathan OROZCO (c) - Severo MEZA (Ricardo OSORIO 81), Darvin CHAVEZ, Hector MORALES (Walter AYOVI 61), Luis PEREZ (c), Aldo DE NIGRIS, Jesus ZAVALA, Neri CARDOZO, Hiram MIER, Jesus CORONA (Abraham CARRENO 72), Humberto SUAZO. Tr: Victor VUCETICH
Seattle Sounders — 1
Fernandez [38]
Terence BOSS - Bradley EVANS (c), Tyson WAHL, James RILEY•, Alvaro FERNANDEZ (Leonardo GONZALEZ 76), Zach SCOTT, Jonathan JAQUA• (Osvaldo ALONSO 64), Servando CARRASCO, Roger LEVESQUE (Amadou SANYANG 83), Patrick NOONAN, Jeffrey PARKE•. Tr: Sigi SCHMID

La Pedrera, Guatemala City
24-08-2011, 726, Geiger USA
Comunicaciones — 2
Ceballos [73], Ordonez [94+]
Juan PAREDES - Erwin MORALES, Carlos RAMIREZ (Hernan SANDOVAL 61), Jean MARQUEZ•, Carlos CASTRILLO•, Rafael MORALES, Fredy THOMPSON•, Transito MONTEPEQUE (Bryan ORDONEZ 61), Marvin CEBALLOS, Adolfo MACHADO, Jairo ARREOLA (c) (Jose DEL AGUILA 76). TD: Ivan SOPEGNO
Herediano — 0
Daniel CAMBRONERO - Cristian MONTERO (c), Erick SANCHEZ, Olma VARGAS, Yosimar ARIAS (Carlos HERNANDEZ 63), Jean SANCHEZ GUTIERREZ (Marvin ANGULO 55), Jose CUBERO•, Marvin OBANDO, Pablo SALAZAR, Victor NUNEZ (Jorge BARBOSA De Lima 67), Jose CANCELA (c). Tr: Alejandro GUINTINI

Estadio Nacional, San Jose
14-09-2011, 514, Perea PAN
Herediano — 1
Cancela [45p]
Daniel CAMBRONERO - Cristian MONTERO, Jose Luis CORDERO, Olman VARGAS, Jose CUBERO, Marvin OBANDO, Pablo SALAZAR, Victor NUNEZ• (Jorge BARBOSA De Lima 74), Junior ALVARADO (Marvin ANGULO 77), Jose CANCELA (c), Anderson ANDRADE (Diego MADRIGAL 64). Tr: Jafet SOTO
Seattle Sounders — 2
Montero 2 [3 54]
Kasey KELLER (c) - Patrick IANNI, Leonardo GONZALEZ, Alvaro FERNANDEZ•, Fredy MONTERO, Zach SCOTT•, Jonathan JAQUA (Patrick NOONAN 73), Servando CARRASCO, Roger LEVESQUE (James RILEY 90), Lamar NEAGLE (Amadou SANYANG 83), Jhon HURTADO•. Tr: Sigi SCHMID

La Pedrera, Guatemala City
14-09-2011, 3552, Aguilar SLV
Comunicaciones — 1
Ramirez [45]
Juan PAREDES• - Edgard MARTINEZ•, Carlos MEJIA (Erwin MORALES 72), Carlos RAMIREZ, Abner TRIGUEROS, Carlos CASTRILLO•, Rafael MORALES, Transito MONTEPEQUE (Hernan SANDOVAL 72), Rigoberto GOMEZ• (c), Adolfo MACHADO, Marco Tulio CIANI• (Jorge APARICIO 90). Tr: Ivan SOPEGNO
Monterrey — 0
Jonathan OROZCO - Severo MEZA, Darvin CHAVEZ, Hector MORALES, Sergio SANTANA, Abraham CARRENO (Neri CARDOZO 67), Jose BASANTA (c), Jesus ZAVALA, Walter AYOVI, Eduardo GUEVARA (Humberto SUAZO 75), Marvin PINON (Aldo DE NIGRIS 55). Tr: Victor VUCETICH

Tecnológico, Monterrey
20-09-2011, 10578, Marrufo USA
Monterrey — 3
Santana [32], Perez [68], Suazo [86]
Jonathan OROZCO - Ricardo OSORIO, Darvin CHAVEZ, Luis PEREZ (c), Aldo DE NIGRIS (Luis RODRIGUEZ 90), Sergio SANTANA (Sergio PEREZ 80), Jose BASANTA, Jesus ZAVALA, Neri CARDOZO (Walter AYOVI 68), Hiram MIER•, Humberto SUAZO. Tr: Victor VUCETICH
Comunicaciones — 1
Mejia [83]
Juan PAREDES - Edgard MARTINEZ, Carlos MEJIA, Carlos RAMIREZ, Carlos CASTRILLO (Dagoberto ARRIOLA 68), Rafael MORALES, Fredy THOMPSON•, Transito MONTEPEQUE (Marvin CEBALLOS 55), Bryan ORDONEZ, Rigoberto GOMEZ (c) (Jose DEL AGUILA 75), Adolfo MACHADO•. Tr: Ivan SOPEGNO

CenturyLink Field, Seattle
20-09-2011, 10163, Brizan TRI
Seattle Sounders — 0
Kasey KELLER (c) - Patrick IANNI•, Leonardo GONZALEZ, Zach SCOTT (Samuel OCHOA 74), Jonathan JAQUA, Servando CARRASCO, Roger LEVESQUE (Fredy MONTERO 56), Patrick NOONAN, Lamar NEAGLE•, Amadou SANYANG (Osvaldo ALONSO 56), Jhon HURTADO•. Tr: Sigi SCHMID
Herediano — 1
Arias [25]
Daniel CAMBRONERO• - Cristian MONTERO (c), Erick SANCHEZ (Jose CUBERO 76), Jose Luis CORDERO•, Yosimar ARIAS• (Olman VARGAS 71), Marvin OBANDO, Jorge BARBOSA De Lima•, Pablo SALAZAR, Junior ALVARADO, Anderson ANDRADE (Marvin ANGULO 86), Francisco CALVO. Tr: Jafet SOTO

La Pedrera, Guatemala City
27-09-2011, 4500, Garcia MEX
Comunicaciones — 2
Montepeque [7], Morales.R [64]
Juan PAREDES - Dagoberto ARRIOLA, Edgard MARTINEZ, Erwin MORALES•, Carlos MEJIA, Carlos RAMIREZ, Rafael MORALES, Fredy THOMPSON, Transito MONTEPEQUE (Marvin CEBALLOS 56), Bryan ORDONEZ (Abner TRIGUEROS 76), Rigoberto GOMEZ (Jose DEL AGUILA 45). Tr: Ivan SOPEGNO
Seattle Sounders — 2
Alonso 2 [44 89]
Kasey KELLER - Michael FUCITO (Samuel OCHOA 65), Tyson WAHL, Osvaldo ALONSO, Erik FRIBERG (Servando CARRASCO 73), Alvaro FERNANDEZ, Fredy MONTERO, Zach SCOTT, Lamar NEAGLE (Jonathan JAQUA 90), Jeffrey PARKE, Jhon HURTADO•. Tr: Sigi SCHMID

Tecnológico, Monterrey
27-09-2011, 12445, Bonilla SLV
Monterrey — 1
De Nigris [30]
Juan DE DIOS IBARRA - Severo MEZA, Darvin CHAVEZ, Hector MORALES, Aldo DE NIGRIS, Jesus ZAVALA, Walter AYOVI (Neri CARDOZO 66), Hiram MIER, Sergio PEREZ, Jesus CORONA (Sergio SANTANA 54), Humberto SUAZO (c) (Luis PEREZ 74). Tr: Victor VUCETICH
Herediano — 0
Daniel CAMBRONERO - Cristian MONTERO (c), Jose Luis CORDERO (Diego MADRIGAL 66), Yosimar ARIAS•, Jose CUBERO, Marvin OBANDO, Jorge BARBOSA De Lima (Victor NUNEZ 46), Pablo SALAZAR, Junior ALVARADO, Anderson ANDRADE (Olman VARGAS 74), Francisco CALVO. Tr: Jafet SOTO

CenturyLink Field, Seattle
18-10-2011, 15866, Wijngaarde SUR
Seattle Sounders — 1
Montero [42]
Bryan MEREDITH - Tyson WAHL, Osvaldo ALONSO, James RILEY, Erik FRIBERG, David ESTRADA (Lamar NEAGLE 79), Fredy MONTERO (c), Samuel OCHOA (Michael FUCITO 71), Zach SCOTT•, Roger LEVESQUE, Jeffrey PARKE (Patrick IANNI 67). Tr: Sigi SCHMID
Monterrey — 2
Carreno [3], Delgado [60]
Jonathan OROZCO (Juan DE DIOS IBARRA 72) - Severo MEZA•, Ricardo OSORIO, Hector MORALES•, Luis PEREZ• (c), Sergio SANTANA, Abraham CARRENO, Jose BASANTA, Cesar DELGADO (Neri CARDOZO 80), Sergio PEREZ, Humberto SUAZO•. Tr: Victor VUCETICH

Estadio Nacional, San Jose
18-10-2011, 200, Navarro CAN
Herediano — 4
Barbosa 2 [13 41], Montero [49], Cordero [61]
Leonel MOREIRA - Cristian MONTERO, Erick SANCHEZ, Marvin ANGULO, Andres CASTRO, Carlos HERNANDEZ, Jorge BARBOSA De Lima (Anderson ANDRADE 71), Junior ALVARADO, Diego MADRIGAL (Jose Luis CORDERO 59), Jose CANCELA• (c) (Olman VARGAS 46), Francisco CALVO. Tr: Jafet SOTO
Comunicaciones — 1
Mejia [8]
Juan PAREDES - Edgard MARTINEZ, Erwin MORALES, Carlos MEJIA, Carlos RAMIREZ (Osmar LOPEZ 46), Rafael MORALES, Jose DEL AGUILA•, Transito MONTEPEQUE (Bryan ORDONEZ 46), Rigoberto GOMEZ (c) (Dagoberto ARRIOLA 69), Kendel HERRARTE•, Adolfo MACHADO. Tr: Ivan SOPEGNO

QUARTER-FINALS

Estadio Morelos, Morelia
6-03-2012, Att: 14 951, Ref: Chacon MEX

Morelia 1
Huiqui [60]

Federico VILAR (c) - Enrique PEREZ, Mauricio ROMERO, Rafael MARQUEZ LUGO (Luis SANDOVAL 58), Edinson TOLOZA (Jaime LOZANO 65), Felipe De Jesus AYALA (Diego MEJIA 76), Alexei ALDRETE•, Angel SEPULVEDA•, Edgar LUGO, Aldo RAMIREZ, Joel HUIQUI. TD: Tomas BOY

Monterrey 3
Suazo 2 [28 44], Carreno [91+]

Jonathan OROZCO - Severo MEZA, Darvin CHAVEZ, Luis PEREZ (Abraham CARRENO 83), Aldo DE NIGRIS (Othoniel ARCE 83), Angel REYNA, Jose BASANTA, Jesus ZAVALA, Cesar DELGADO (Walter AYOVI 75), Hiram MIER, Humberto SUAZO•. TD: Victor VUCETICH

Tecnológico, Monterrey
13-03-2012, Att: 33 000, Ref: Garcia MEX

Monterrey 4
Suazo 2 [44p 71], Perez [61p], Ayovi [83]

Jonathan OROZCO - Severo MEZA, Ricardo OSORIO, Hector MORALES, Luis PEREZ (c), Aldo DE NIGRIS (Neri CARDOZO 71), Angel REYNA, Jose BASANTA, Jesus ZAVALA (Sergio PEREZ 75), Cesar DELGADO• (Walter AYOVI 71), Humberto SUAZO. Tr: Victor VUCETICH

Morelia 1
Sepulveda [78p]

Federico VILAR (c) - Enrique PEREZ, Rafael MARQUEZ LUGO• (Edgar LUGO 46), Jorge GASTELUM•, Joao ROJAS, Luis SANDOVAL (Edinson TOLOZA 52), Alexei ALDRETE, Angel SEPULVEDA, Jaime LOZANO (Mauricio ROMERO 46), Aldo RAMIREZ, Joel HUIQUI•. Tr: Tomas BOY

Jorge Calero Suarez, Metapán
8-03-2012, Att: 4131, Ref: Lopez GUA

Isidro Metapan 2
Blanco 2 [27 49]

Miguel MONTES - Ernesto AQUINO, Rodolfo SUAREZ, Christian BAUTISTA (Jorge MORAN 88), Edwin SANCHEZ (Milton MOLINA 72), Alfredo PACHECO, Ramon SANCHEZ, Mark BLANCO (Allan KARDECK 62), Alexander ESCOBAR, Hector MEJIA, Jose ALVARADO. Tr: Edwin PORTILLO

Pumas UNAM 1
Herrera [67]

Miguel PALACIOS - Efrain VELARDE, Marco PALACIOS, Dario VERON•, Javier CORTES (Alonso NIETO 60), David CABRERA, Martin BRAVO (Eduardo AGUIRRE 54), Luis FUENTES•, Fernando ESPINOSA•, Juan Carlos CACHO (Carlos ORRANTIA 45), Jose GARCIA•. Tr: Guillermo VASQUEZ

Olímpico Universitario, Mexico City
15-03-2012, Att: 7800, Ref: Geiger USA

PUMAS UNAM 8
OG [25], Herrera 2 [26 63], Velarde [39], Bravo [54], Garcia [69], Espinoza [73], Cacho [88]

Odin PATINO - Efrain VELARDE, Marco PALACIOS, Dario VERON (c) (Erik VERA 49), Martin BRAVO (Juan Carlos CACHO• 56), Luis FUENTES•, Fernando ESPINOSA, Carlos ORRANTIA, Eduardo AGUIRRE (Diego DE BUEN 63), Jose GARCIA, Carlos CAMPOS. TD: Guillermo VASQUEZ

Isidro Metapan 0

Miguel MONTES - Ernesto AQUINO, Rodolfo SUAREZ (Jorge MORAN 38), Christian BAUTISTA, Edwin SANCHEZ (Allan KARDECK 57), Alfredo PACHECO (c), Ramon SANCHEZ, Mark BLANCO (Mario AGUILAR 46), Alexander ESCOBAR, Hector MEJIA, Jose ALVARADO•. Tr: Edwin PORTILLO

Rogers Centre, Toronto
7-03-2012, Att: 47 658, Ref: Campbell JAM

Toronto FC 2
Johnson [12], Silva [17]

Stefan FREI• - Miguel ACEVAL, Ashtone MORGAN, Joao PLATA (Reginald THOMPSON-LAMBE 58), Ryan JOHNSON, Luis SILVA (Aaron MAUND 88), Danny KOEVERMANS•, Robert HARDEN, Torsten FRINGS (c), Terrence DUNFIELD (Matthew STINSON 90), Richard ECKERSLEY. TD: Aron WINTER

LA Galaxy 2
Magee [29], Donovan [89]

Joshua SAUNDERS - Todd DUNIVANT, Sean FRANKLIN, Robbie KEANE, Landon DONOVAN (c), Edson BUDDLE, Mike MAGEE, JUNINHO (Michael STEPHENS 87), AJ DELAGARZA, David BECKHAM, Andrew BOYENS (Chad BARRETT 87). Tr: Bruce ARENA

Home Depot Center, Carson, LA
14-03-2012, Att: 7500, Ref: Moreno PAN

LA Galaxy 1
OG [55]

Joshua SAUNDERS - Todd DUNIVANT, Sean FRANKLIN• (Daniel KEAT 72), Robbie KEANE, Landon DONOVAN (c), Edson BUDDLE, Mike MAGEE (Paolo CARDOZO 72), JUNINHO, AJ DELAGARZA, Thomas MEYER (Chad BARRETT 84), David BECKHAM. TD: Bruce ARENA

Toronto FC 2
Johnson [34], Soolsma [67]

Milos KOCIC - Miguel ACEVAL•, Ashtone MORGAN, Julian DEGUZMAN (Luis SILVA 63), Joao PLATA (Terrence DUNFIELD 46), Ryan JOHNSON, Danny KOEVERMANS (Aaron MAUND 69), Nicky SOOISMA, Robert HARDEN, Torsten FRINGS• (c), Richard ECKERSLEY•. Tr: Aron WINTER

CenturyLink Field, Seattle
7-03-2012, Att: 23 433, Ref: Quesada CRC

Seattle Sounders 2
Estrada [12], Evans [63]

Michael GSPURNING - Bradley EVANS, Adam JOHANSSON, Osvaldo ALONSO, Mauro ROSALES (c), Leonardo GONZALEZ•, Alvaro FERNANDEZ (Edward JOHNSON 78), David ESTRADA• (Marc BURCH 90), Fredy MONTERO, Jeffrey PARKE, Jhon HURTADO•. Tr: Sigi SCHMID

Santos Laguna 1
Gomez [61]

Oswaldo SANCHEZ• - Jorge Ivan ESTRADA, Aaron GALINDO, Marc CROSAS, Juan Pablo RODRIGUEZ• (Rodolfo SALINAS 83), Daniel LUDUENA (Candido RAMIREZ 74), Christian SUAREZ, Herculez GOMEZ (Carlos OCHOA 84), Santiago HOYOS•, Osmar MARES•, Oribe PERALTA. Tr: Benjamin GALINDO

Corona, Torreón
14-03-2012, Att: 14 278, Ref: Aguilar SLV

Santos Laguna 6
Suarez 2 [8 76], Peralta [10], Gomez 2 [49 58], Ochoa [81]

Oswaldo SANCHEZ (c) - Jorge Ivan ESTRADA, Aaron GALINDO, Marc CROSAS (Rodolfo SALINAS 33), Juan Pablo RODRIGUEZ•, Daniel LUDUENA (Candido RAMIREZ 63), Christian SUAREZ, Herculez GOMEZ (Carlos OCHOA 70), Osmar MARES, Felipe BALOY•, Oribe PERALTA•. Tr: Benjamin GALINDO

Seattle Sounders 1
Fernandez [37]

Michael GSPURNING - Bradley EVANS, Adam JOHANSSON, Osvaldo ALONSO, Mauro ROSALES (c), Leonardo GONZALEZ• (Christian SIVEBAEK 77), Alvaro FERNANDEZ, David ESTRADA (Edward JOHNSON 62) (Roger LEVESQUE 86), Fredy MONTERO•, Jeffrey PARKE, Jhon HURTADO. Tr: Sigi SCHMID

SEMI-FINALS

Tecnológico, Monterrey
28-03-2012, Att: 26 716, Ref: Penaloza MEX
Monterrey 3
Morales [7], De Nigris 2 [60] [72]
Jonathan OROZCO - Ricardo OSORIO, Hector MORALES, Luis PEREZ (c), Aldo DE NIGRIS, Angel REYNA (Cesar DE LA PENA 79), Jose BASANTA, Jesus ZAVALA (Walter AYOVI 79), Neri CARDOZO, Sergio PEREZ (Alejandro GARCIA 87), Humberto SUAZO. Tr: Victor VUCETICH
Pumas UNAM 0

Miguel PALACIOS - Efrain VELARDE (c), Marco PALACIOS, Martin BRAVO (Juan Carlos CACHO•), David IZAZOLA (Michelle CASTRO 78), Fernando ESPINOSA, Eduardo AGUIRRE (Carlos ORRANTIA 78), Alfonso NIETO•, Jose GARCIA, Aaron SANDOVAL, Carlos CAMPOS. Tr: Guillermo VASQUEZ

Olímpico Universitario, Mexico City
4-04-2012, Att: 7300, Ref: Morales MEX
Pumas UNAM 1
Garcia [71]
Odin PATINO - Efrain VELARDE• (c), Marco PALACIOS, Diego DE BUEN, Javier CORTES (Manuel PEREZ 46), Martin BRAVO (Alfonso NIETO 65), Luis FUENTES•, Carlos ORRANTIA, Eduardo AGUIRRE, Jose GARCIA, Carlos Alberto CAMPOS (Fernando ESPINOSA• 46). Tr: Guillermo VASQUEZ
Monterrey 1
Reyna [35]
Jonathan OROZCO - Severo MEZA, Hector MORALES•, Angel REYNA (Cesar DE LA PENA• 46), Abraham CARRENO, Jose BASANTA (Ricardo OSORIO 67), Jesus Eduardo ZAVALA, Neri CARDOZO, Cesar DELGADO• (Othoniel ARCE 46), Walter AYOVI, Sergio PEREZ. Tr: Victor VUCETICH

BMO Field, Toronto
28-03-2012, Att: 18 950, Ref: Salazar USA
Toronto FC 1
Aceval [37]
Milos KOCIC - Miguel ACEVAL (Aaron MAUND 49), Ashtone MORGAN, Julian DEGUZMAN (c), Ryan JOHNSON, Danny KOEVERMANS•, Nicky SOOISMA (Joao PLATA 71), Reginald THOMPSON-LAMBE, Robert HARDEN, Terrence DUNFIELD, Richard ECKERSLEY. Tr: Aron WINTER
Santos Laguna 1
Gomez [30]
Oswaldo SANCHEZ (c) - Carlos QUINTERO♦90, Jorge Ivan ESTRADA (Cesar IBANEZ 45), Aaron GALINDO, Marc CROSAS•, Carlos OCHOA (Oribe PERALTA 61), Christian SUAREZ, Herculez GOMEZ (Candido RAMIREZ 67), Rodolfo SALINAS, Santiago HOYOS, Osmar MARES♦77. Tr: Benjamin GALINDO

Corona, Torreón
4-04-2012, Att: 26 843, Ref: Pineda HON
Santos Laguna 6
Gomez 2 [31] [45], Rodriguez 2 [56p] [64p], Peralta [66], Ludena [92+]
Oswaldo SANCHEZ (c) - Jorge Ivan ESTRADA, Aaron GALINDO, Marc CROSAS, Juan Pablo RODRIGUEZ, Daniel LUDUENA, Christian SUAREZ (Candido RAMIREZ 72), Herculez GOMEZ (Carlos OCHOA 69), Felipe BALOY, Oribe PERALTA•, Jose OLVERA (Carlos MORALES 27). Tr: Benjamin GALINDO
Toronto FC 2
Plata 2 [15] [43]
Milos KOCIC - Miguel ACEVAL• (Doneil HENRY 69), Ashtone MORGAN, Julian DEGUZMAN (c), Joao PLATA (Reginald THOMPSON-LAMBE 65), Ryan JOHNSON, Luis SILVA, Nicky SOOISMA, Robert HARDEN, Terrence DUNFIELD (Matthew STINSON 59), Richard ECKERSLEY. Tr: Aron WINTER

FINAL

CONCACAF CHAMPIONS LEAGUE FINAL 1ST LEG
ESTADIO TECNOLOGICO, MONTERREY
Wednesday, 25-04-2012, 19:00, Att: 28 000, Ref: Roberto Garcia MEX
Assistants: Jose Luis Carmargo MEX & Alberto Morin MEX

MONTERREY	2	0	SANTOS LAGUNA
Humberto Suazo 2 60 86			Neri Cardozo 82

MONTERREY
Blue shirts with white stripes on the front, white shorts, blue socks

Tr: Victor Vucetich

Jonathan Orozco

Severo Meza — Hiram Mier — Jose Maria Basanta — Darvin Chavez

Angel Reyna — Luis Ernesto Perez (c) [58] — Jesus Zavala — Neri Cardozo 10
Dario Carreno 71 — Walter Ayoui

Aldo de Nigris 88 — Humberto Suazo 4
Hector Morales

Herculez Gomez

Carlos Quintero 83 — Christian Suarez
Daniel Ludena

Candido Ramirez 63 — Marc Crosas 86
Carlos Morales — Rodolfo Salinas 88

Juan Pablo Rodriguez

Osmar Mares 73 — Aaron Galindo — Felipe Baloy 40 — Jorge Ivan Estrada

Oswaldo Sanchez (c)

Tr: Benjamin Galindo

Green and white hooped shirts, green shorts, green socks
SANTOS LAGUNA

CONCACAF CHAMPIONS LEAGUE FINAL 2ND LEG
ESTADIO CORONA, TORREON
Wednesday, 25-04-2012, 19:00, Att: 28 000, Ref: Roberto Garcia MEX
Assistants: Jose Luis Carmargo MEX & Alberto Morin MEX

SANTOS LAGUNA	2	1	MONTERREY
Daniel Ludena 45,			Neri Cardozo 82
Oribe Peralta 51			

SANTOS LAGUNA
Green and white hooped shirts, green shorts, green socks

Tr: Benjamin Galindo

Oswaldo Sanchez (c)

Jorge Ivan Estrada — Rafael Figueroa — Aaron Galindo — Cesar Ibanez

Juan Pablo Rodriguez

Rodolfo Salinas 84 — Daniel Ludena 45
Candido Ramirez — Herculez Gomez 57

Christian Suarez 73 — Carlos Quintero
Carlos Morales — Oribe Peralta

Aldo de Nigris 5 — Jesus Zavala 84
Hector Morales 87 — Dario Carreno

Neri Cardozo — Luis Ernesto Perez (c) 91+ — Jesus Zavala 33 — Angel Reyna 63
Walter Ayoui

Darvin Chavez — Jose Maria Basanta — Hiram Mier — Severo Meza

Tr: Victor Vucetich

Jonathan Orozco 7

Blue shirts with white stripes on the front, white shorts, blue socks
MONTERREY

MATCH STATS

Monterrey		Santos
16	Shots	15
6	Shots on Goal	5
9	Fouls Committed	18
4	Corner Kicks	2
2	Caught Offside	2
59	Possession (%)	41

(C) Captain

MATCH STATS

Santos		Monterrey
11	Shots	7
6	Shots on Goal	2
13	Fouls Committed	8
3	Corner Kicks	4
0	Caught Offside	0
47	Possession (%)	53

(C) Captain

This team had lots of personality, and that's how we won it. The key is to always work hard and to put together teams with a strong mentality and a constant desire to improve.
— Victor Manuel Vucetich

Sadly I couldn't play (because of the booking in the 1st leg). One feels really bad watching from the outside. We are deserving champions and now we can try to improve in Japan in the FIFA Club World Cup.
— Humberto Suazo

They are worthy champions. In Monterrey, they beat us through and through. Tonight we had a great opportunity in front of our fans. We accomplished the most difficult task... scoring two goals against them is very difficult to do. We created chances and played well, but we knew we were facing a great team, because man-to-man, they have a great roster.
— Benjamin Galindo

CFU CLUB CHAMPIONS CUP 2012

First Round Groups

Group 1 (In Cayman Islands)

		Pl	W	D	L	F	A	Pts	CAY	BER
George Town	CAY	2	1	1	0	2	1	4		2-1 0-0
Elite	CAY	2	1	0	1	3	3	3		2-1
North Village Rams	BER	2	0	1	1	1	2	1		

Group 2 (In Guyana)

		Pl	W	D	L	F	A	Pts	GUY	CUW	GUY
Inter Moengotapoe	SUR	3	3	0	0	11	3	9	1-0	3-2	7-1
Alpha United	GUY	3	2	0	1	5	2	6		3-1	2-0
Hubentut Fortuna	CUW	3	1	0	2	5	7	3			2-1
Milerock	GUY	3	0	0	3	2	11	0			

Group 3 (In Haiti)

		Pl	W	D	L	F	A	Pts	HAI	PUR
Victory	HAI	2	1	1	0	6	2	4		1-1 5-1
Baltimore	HAI	2	1	1	0	3	1	4		2-0
Bayamon	PUR	2	0	0	2	1	7	0		

Second round groups

Group 1 (In Cayman Isl)

		Pl	W	D	L	F	A	Pts	TRI	CAY
Puerto Rico Isl'ders		2	1	1	0	8	0	4	0-0	8-0
Caledonia AIA		2	1	1	0	5	0	4		5-0
George Town		2	0	0	2	0	13	0		

Group 2 (In Trinidad)

		Pl	W	D	L	F	A	Pts	TRI	HAI	SUR
Antigua Barracuda		3	2	1	0	5	1	7	2-1	0-0	3-0
W Connection		3	2	0	1	9	2	6		2-0	6-0
Victory		3	1	1	1	8	4	4			8-2
Inter Moengotapoe		3	0	0	3	2	17	0			

Final Tournament

Caledonia AIA	2	
Antigua Barracuda	0	

Caledonia AIA	1	4p
W Connection	1	3p

Puerto Rico Islanders	1
W Connection	4

3rd place play-off

Puerto Rico Islanders	2
Antigua Barracuda	0

26/03/2010 - 21/06/2012 • Puerto Rico Islanders PUR, Antigua Barracuda ATG, Caledonia TRI and W Connection TRI all received byes to the second round • Finals held in Trinidad • Top three qualify for the 2012-13 CONCACAF Champions League
Top scorers: **7** - Bony **PIERRE** HAI, Victory • **5** - Hachim **ARCIA** TRI, W Conection & Ricardo **CHARLES** HAI, Victory • **4** - Jonathan **FANA** DOM, Puerto Rico Islanders & Stefano **RUSSEL** SUR, Inter Moengotapoe • **3** - Anthony **ABRAHAMS** GUY, Alpha United; Rennie **BRITTO** TRI, W Connection; Devorn **JORSLING** TRI, Caledonia & Patrick **JIMMI** SUR, Inter Moengotapoe

FIRST ROUND GROUP MATCHES

TE McField SC, George Town
25-03-2012, Att: 250, Ref: Royal JAM
George Town SC 0

Miguel PITTA - Paul SMITH, Junior FISHER, Leighton ELLIOTT, Nicholas EBANKS, Garth ANDERSON, Ian LINDO (c), Kevin MOORE (Davelee COLE 83), Justin PIERRE (David HARDING 5) (Stanton CLARKE 63), Tex WHITLOCK, Fabian MALCOLM. Tr: Lee RAMOON

North Village Rams 0

Jason WILLIAMS - Tyrell BURGESS, Kofi DILL, Sean FUBLER, Devrae TANKARD, Jason DAVIS, Devaun DEGRAFF (c), Jemeiko JENNINGS (Pierre SMITH 90), Ralph BEAN JR., Lashun DILL (Keishan BEAN 54), Jason LEE (Vernon TANKARD 83). Tr: Shaun GOATER

TE McField SC, George Town
27-03-2012, Att: 1700, Ref: Thomas JAM
Elite 2
Carter 2 [13 66]

Dereck RIVERS - Alex BELCHER, Marvin BOOTHE• (Cardiel HYDES 72), Jose Luis BUSH (Chris WELCOME 84), Rene CARTER, Benjamin CUPID, Darvin CUPID, Darvin DIXON, Jedd EBANKS, Abijah RIVERS (c), Jairo SANCHEZ, Dwayne WRIGHT (Javier MEDINA 87). Tr: Gregory EBANKS

North Village Rams 1
Keishan Bean [60]

Jason WILLIAMS - Tyrell BURGESS, Kofi DILL•, Sean FUBLER, Logan ALEXANDER, Jason DAVIS, Devaun DEGRAFF (c) (Vernon TANKARD 66), Kaiwon DILL (Jemeiko JENNINGS 58), Ralph BEAN JR., Keishan BEAN•90, Jason LEE♦39. Tr: Shaun GOATER

TE McField SC, George Town
29-03-2012, Att: 590, Ref: Royal JAM
George Town SC 2
Malcolm [40], Cuevas-Ebanks [87]

Miguel PITTA - Paul SMITH, Junior FISHER, Leighton ELLIOTT, Nicholas EBANKS (Davelee COLE 35), Garth ANDERSON (Limberg CUEVAS-EBANKS 84), Ian LINDO (c), Kevin MOORE, Fabian MALCOLM, David HARDING (Tex WHITLOCK 72), Kirk ROWE•. Tr: Lee RAMOON

Elite 1
Wright [5]

Dereck RIVERS - Alex BELCHER, Marvin BOOTHE•, Jose Luis BUSH, Rene CARTER, Benjamin CUPID, Darvin DIXON, Jedd EBANKS, Abijah RIVERS (c), Jairo SANCHEZ, Dwayne WRIGHT (Javier MEDINA 74). Tr: Gregory EBANKS

National Stadium, Providence
17-04-2012, Att: 100, Ref: Angela ARU
Milerock 1
Sears [31]

Darius FRANK• - Keivin SULLIVAN (c), Ryan CRANDON, Deshawn JOSEPH•, Michael CRANDON, Kester JACOBS, Dwayne ALI, Clive NOBREGA (Jermaine FORDYLE 80), Steve BREWLEY (Delon MCALLISTER 69), Keon SEARS, Ray BOBBSEMPLE (Ron FREDTKON 62). Tr: Bryan JOSEPH

Hubentut Fortuna 2
Trenidad [69], Gomes Chacas [79]

Elfried WEIJMAN - Hairiks JANSEN•, Nellyson FLANEUR, Andreas AITATUS, Tomsjansen SORANLEY (c), Everon ESPACIA, Anthony ESPACIA, Rugin SNOIJL, Ronildo Souza DE MELO (Renato Souza DE MELO• 51), Lisandro TRENIDAD, Dwight BELLIOT (Jose Adriano GOMES CHACAS 61). Tr: Nicolau DE BARRIOS

National Stadium, Providence
17-04-2012, Att: 100, Ref: Santos PUR
Alpha United 0

Richard RENOLDS - Howard LOWE (c), Richard EDWARDS, Philbert MOFFATT• (Anthony BENFIELD 74), Andrew MURRAY, Dwight PETERS•75, Issa MCPHERSON, Daniel WILSON• (Dwain JACOBS 56), Quincy MADRAMOOTOO•, Kelvin MCKENZIE, Kris CAMACHO (Anthony ABRAMS 56). Tr: Wayne DOVER

Inter Moengotapoe 1
Rijssel [23]

Brayen DAMBA - Jerrel ADENSIBA, Petrus APANTA (Ricardo MISIEDJAN 82), Marlon BRON• (Junglo BRUNSWIYK 62), Patrick JIMMY (c), Naldo KWASIE, Nathan MISIEDJAN (Fabian JEROE 74), Claudio PINAS•, Stefano RIJSSEL•, Germain VAN DIJCK, Ives VLIJTER. Tr: Jeroe HESRON

National Stadium, Providence
19-04-2012, Att: 100, Ref: Stewart CAY
Inter Moengotapoe 7
Rijssel 2 [8 87], Adensiba [28], Pinas [52], Jimmy 2 [62p 76p], Plein [86]

Brayen DAMBA - Jerrel ADENSIBA (Stefan BANETI 72), Petrus APANTA, Marlon BRON (Kareem KWASIE 61), Patrick JIMMY (c), Naldo KWASIE, Nathan MISIEDJAN, Claudio PINAS, Germain VAN DIJCK, Stefano RIJSSEL, Ives VLIJTER (Clarence PLEIN• 82). TD: Jeroe HESRON

Milerock 1
Fordyce [45]

Darius FRANK - Ryan CRANDON (c), Michael CRANDON (Runic VELLOZA 80), Jermaine GRANDISON, Kester JACOBS, Clive NOBREGA, Dwayne ALI, Jermaine FORDYLE (Deon CHARTER 66), Andrae HECTOR, Steve BREWLEY (Ron FREDTKON 60), Kenard SIMON. Tr: Bryan JOSEPH

National Stadium, Providence
19-04-2012, Att: 150, Ref: Skeete BRB
Hubentut Fortuna 1
Flaneur [59]

Elfried WEIJMAN - Hairiks JANSEN•, Nellyson FLANEUR, Andreas AITATUS•, Tomsjansen SORANLEY (c), Everon ESPACIA, Anthony ESPACIA, Rugin SNOIJL, Renato Souza DE MELO (Marcos GIRIGORIE• 52), Jose Adriano GOMES CHACAS (Dwight BELLIOT 70), Lisandro TRENIDAD••85. Tr: Nicolau DE BARRIOS

Alpha United 3
Murray [5], Abrams [25], Wilson [84]

Richard RENOLDS - Howard LOWE (c), Richard EDWARDS, Julien EDWARDS• (Philbert MOFFATT 77), Andrew MURRAY (Daniel WILSON 64), Dwain JACOBS, Anthony ABRAMS, Issa MCPHERSON, Anthony BENFIELD 67), Quincy MADRAMOOTOO, Kelvin MCKENZIE, Kris CAMACHO. Tr: Wayne DOVER

National Stadium, Providence
21-04-2012, Att: 50, Ref: Santos PUR
Inter Moengotapoe 3
Jimmy [44], Vlijter [65], Rijssel [70]

Brayen DAMBA - Jerrel ADENSIBA, Clarence PLEIN [86], Petrus APANTA, Fabian JEROE, Patrick JIMMY (c), Kareem KWASIE (Stefan BANETI 62), Naldo KWASIE, Claudio PINAS (Sirano AMOEFERIE 45), Germain VAN DIJCK, Stefano PIJSSEL, Ives VLIJTER•. Tr: Jeroe HESRON

Hubentut Fortuna 2
Gomes Chacas [45], Belliot [60]

Elfried WEIJMAN - Nellyson FLANEUR••♦83, Rashid WINKLAAR•, Andreas AITATUS• (Marcos GIRIGORIE 90), Tomsjansen SORANLEY (c), Hairiks JANSEN•, Dwight BELLIOT••♦60, Martes IVANECK (Jose Adriano GOMES CHACAS 35). Tr: Nicolau DE BARRIOS

National Stadium, Providence
21-04-2012, Att: 50, Ref: Stewart CAY
Alpha United 2
Abrams 2 [7 80]

Richard RENOLDS - Howard LOWE (c), Richard EDWARDS, Julien EDWARDS, Andrew MURRAY (Daniel WILSON 45), Dwain JACOBS (Clarence BENFIELD 65), Anthony ABRAMS, Issa MCPHERSON•, Quincy MADRAMOOTOO, Kelvin MCKENZIE•, Dwight PETERS• (Kris CAMACHO 88). Tr: Wayne DOVER

Milerock 0

Darius FRANK - Keivin SULLIVAN (c), Michael CRANDON, Deshawn JOSEPH, Kester JACOBS, Jermaine FORDYCE•, Deon CHARTER, Ron FREDTKON (Benaekman SMARTT 79), Andrae HECTOR (Ronald CAPLE 71), Steve BREWLEY (Eon RODRIGUES 90), Randy JEROME. Tr: Bryan JOSEPH

Stade Emmanuel Sanon, St Marc
17-04-2012, Att: 2000, Ref: Brea CUB
Baltimore St Marc 2
Titin [7], Dieujuste [82]

James ELAN - Ricardo ADE, Junior ALEXANDRE (Jacquelin PRUDHOMME 69), Kesly JEAN-JACQUES, Johnny JEAN•, Tonio PIERRE, Angelo DIEUJUSTE (Ernst-Raymond FLEURINAT 89), Serge LOUIS, Kenzy TITIN, Ednerson RAYMOND (Gabriel MICHEL 67), Alain VUBERT (c). Tr: Herbo ODELUS

Bayamon 0

Balni Mercado CABRERA - Adrian FRACISCO (Carlos ROSARIO 63), Alan ACEVEDO, Andres CABRERO (Eloy MATOS 53), Carlos GRUESO, Daniel OJEDA, Javier LALONDRIZ (Alvaro GARCIA 46), John IBARGUEN•, Juan VELEZ, Julio MAYA, Stanley GUIRAND (c). Tr: David CABALLERO

Stade Emmanuel Sanon, St Marc
19-04-2012, Att: 250, Ref: Rubalcaba CUB
Victory 5
Bony Pierre 4 [21 57 75 82], Ricardo Charles [45]

Ronald ELUSMA - Philippe TOUSSAINT (Garpard BAPTISTE), Ricardo CHARLES, Walter JOSEPH, Jean FRANCOIS, Harold MILORD (Joseph BEAUGE 81), Parnel GUERRIER (c), Samuel JACQUES, Andersuntcha BEAUVIAS, Jean Fritz ST. GERMAIN, Bony PIERRE• (George CHERY 85). Tr: Wasbens PRINCIME

Bayamon 1
Rosario [64]

Balni Mercado CABRERA - Andres CABRERO, Carlos GRUESO (Alan ACEVEDO 19), Carlos ROSARIO, Daniel OJEDA, Eloy MATOS•63, John IBARGUEN• (Alvaro GARCIA 18), Raymond MENDA, Samuel CABRERA, Stanley GUIRAND• (c), Samuel SOTO (Javier LALONDRIZ 67). Booked: Tr: David CABALLERO

Stade Emmanuel Sanon, St Marc
21-04-2012, Att: 3500, Ref: Vasquez DOM
Baltimore St Marc 1
Peter Germain [90]

James ELAN (Ricardo LOUIS 46) - Ricardo ADE, Kesly JEAN-JACQUES•, Johnny JEAN, Angelo DIEUJUSTE (Junior ALEXANDRE 57), Louis SERGE (Jacquelin PRUDHOMME 65), Kenzy TITIN, Ednerson RAYMOND•, Alain VUBERT (c), Peter GERMAIN•, Cardjy SATURNE. Tr: Herbo ODELUS

Victory 1
Bony Pierre [86]

Ronald ELUSMA - Jean Fritz ST. GERMAIN, Walter JOSEPH, Joseph BEAUGE, Ricardo CHARLES, Bony PIERRE (Othniel ROSARD 90), Jean FRANCOIS•, Harold MILORD, Parnel GUERRIER (c), Samuel JACQUES (Philippe TOUSSAINT 89), Andersuntcha BEAUVIAS (Garpard BAPTISTE 78). Tr: Wabens PRINCIME

CFU CLUB CHAMPIONSHIP 2012 SECOND ROUND QUALIFYING GROUP 1

		Pl	W	D	L	F	A	Pts		TRI	CAY
Puerto Rico Islanders	PUR	2	1	1	0	8	0	4		0-0	8-0
Caledonia AIA	TRI	2	1	1	0	5	0	4			5-0
George Town	CAY	2	0	0	2	0	13	0			

TE McField SC, George Town
21-05-2012, Att: 100, Ref: Bogle JAM
Puerto Rico Islanders 0

Richard MARTIN - Jamie CUNNINGHAM, Jonathan FANA FRIAS, Justin FOJO, David FOLEY (Joshua HANSEN 72), Richard MARTINEZ, Jay NEEDHAM, Hector RAMOS (Noah DELGADO 75), Gregory RICHARDSON (Tyler WILSON 78), Alexis RIVERA, Jarad VAN SCHAIK•. Tr: Adrian WHITBREAD

Caledonia AIA 0

Ronson WILLIAMS - Radanfah ABU BAKR, Kareem JOSEPH•, Stephan DAVID, Devorn JORSLING• (Trevin CAESAR 85), Abdallah PHILLIPS (Cornelius STEWART 73), Keyon EDWARDS, Nuru MUHAMMAD, Trayon BOBB, Walter MOORE, Jamal GAY. Tr: Jamaal SHABAZZ

TE McField SC, George Town
23-05-2012, Att: 100, Ref: Cambridge VIN
Caledonia AIA 5
Jorsling 2 [47 70], Caesar 2 [72 76], Smith [85]

Ronson WILLIAMS - Radanfah ABU BAKR, Kareem JOSEPH, Stephan DAVID•, Devorn JORSLING, Keyon EDWARDS, Nuru MUHAMMAD, Trayon BOBB (Nathan LEWIS 82), Walter MOORE, Cornelius STEWART (Conrod SMITH 71), Jamal GAY (Trevin CAESAR 70). Tr: Jamaal SHABAZZ

George Town SC 0

Miguel PITTA - Garth ANDERSON (Limburg CUEVAS-EBANKS 67), Kemar BARTON, Nicholas EBANKS (Davelee COLE 26), Leighton ELLIOTT, David HARDING (Raheem ROBINSON 46), Fabian MALCOLM, Kevin MOORE, Kirk ROW, Paul SMITH, Tex WHITELOCKE. Tr: Lee RAMOON

TE McField SC, George Town
25-05-2012, Att: 300, Ref: Da Costa BAH
Puerto Rico Islanders 8
Ramos 2 [4 20], Fana Frias 3 [22 54 56], OG 2 [27 61], Robinson [61]

Cody LAURENDI - Giovanni EDWARD, Jonathan FANA FRIAS (Tyler WILSON 59), David FOLEY (Nyarkso DANSO 59), Richard MARTINEZ, Jay NEEDHAM, Andres PEREZ, Hector RAMOS• (Joshua HANSEN 44), Gregory RICHARDSON, Jarad VAN SCHAIK, Anthony VAZQUEZ. Tr: Adrian WHITBREAD

George Town SC 0

Miguel PITTA - Garth ANDERSON, Kemar BARTON•, Leighton ELLIOTT•, Junior FISHER (Raheem ROBINSON• 40), Ian LINDO (Dennis SMITH 81), Fabian MALCOLM, Kevin MOORE, Paul SMITH, Tex WHITELOCKE, Metchie WILLIAMS (David HARDING 54). Tr: Lee RAMOON

CFU CLUB CHAMPIONSHIP 2012 SECOND ROUND QUALIFYING GROUP 2

		Pl	W	D	L	F	A	Pts		TRI	HAI	SUR
Antigua Barracuda	ATG	3	2	1	0	5	1	7		2-1	0-0	3-0
W Connection	TRI	3	2	0	1	9	2	6			2-0	6-0
Victory	HAI	3	1	1	1	8	4	4				8-2
Inter Moengotapoe	SUR	3	0	0	3	2	17	0				

Manny Ramjohn, Marabella
6-05-2012, Att: 300, Ref: Taylor BRB
W Connection 2
Arcia 2 [16 77]

Jan-Michael Williams (c) - Eligah Joseph, Rennie Brito, Clyde Leon, Gerard Williams, Hashim Arcia (Kern Cupid 77), Andre Quashie, Leslie Joel Russell (Akeem Benjamin 46), Jerrel Britto (Christian Viveros 65), Joevin Jones, Shahdon Winchester. Tr: Stuart CHARLES-FEVRIER

Victory 0

Ronald ELUSMA - Jean Fritz ST. GERMAIN, Parnel GUERRIER (c), Philippe TOUSSAINT, Jean FRANCOIS, Harold MILORD•, Garpard BAPTISTE (Ricardo CHARLES 65), Bony PIERRE (Leopart Luxon JEAN 82), Andersuntcha BEAUVAIS, Walter JOSEPH, Othniel ROSARD (Nicodeme BEAUGE 62). Tr: Wasbens PRINCIME

Manny Ramjohn, Marabella
6-05-2012, Att: 260, Ref: Nunez CUB
Antigua Barracuda 3
Tamoley Thomas 2 [9 89], Griffith [43]

Molvin JAMES - Ranja CHRISTIAN, Luke BLAKELY, Kimoi ALEXANDER••♦82, Quinton GRIFFITH, Orlando MITCHUM•, Tamorley THOMAS, Peter BYERS (Stefan SMITH 46), George DUBLIN (c), Akeem THOMAS• (Karanja MACK 72), Lawson ROBINSON (Matthew ALDRED 46). T: Thomas CURTIS

Inter Moengotapoe 0

Brayen DAMBA - Nathan MISIEDJAN•, Naldo KWASIE, Patrick JIMMY• (c), Ives VLIJTER, Marlon BRON (Junglo BRUNSWIJK 66), Claudio PINAS, Jerrel ADENSIBA (Stefan BANETI 71), Stefano RIJSSEL, Germain VAN DIJCK, Petrus APANTA (Ricardo MISIEDJAN 85). Tr: Jeroe HESRON

Manny Ramjohn, Marabella
8-05-2012, Att: 200, Ref: Jauregui CUW
Victory 3

Ronald ELUSMA - Jean Fritz ST. GERMAIN, Parnel GUERRIER•, Philippe TOUSSAINT, Jean FRANCOIS, Harold MILORD•, Bony PIERRE•, Andersuntcha BEAUVIAS (Garpard BAPTISTE 78), Nicodeme BEAUGE, Walter JOSEPH•, Ricardo CHARLES. Tr: Wasbens PRINCIME

Antigua Barracuda 0

Keita DECASTRO - Karanja MACK, Luke BLAKELY, Stefan SMITH (Kerry SKEPPLE 74), Quinton GRIFFITH, Orlando MITCHUM, Tamorley THOMAS•, Peter BYERS (Lloyde JEREMY JR. 89), George DUBLIN (c), Matthew ALDRED (Akeem THOMAS 46), Lawson ROBINSON•. Tr: Thomas CURTIS

Manny Ramjohn, Marabella
8-05-2012, Att: 250, Ref: Johnson GUY
Inter Moengotapoe 0

Brayen DAMBA - Anduelo AMOEFERIE (Naldo KWASIE 37), Nathan MISIEDJAN•, Patrick JIMMY (c), Ives VLIJTER, Claudio PINAS•, Jerrel ADENSIBA, Stefano RIJSSEL, Stefan BANETI• (Junglo BRUNSWIJK 64), Germain VAN DIJCK, Petrus APANTA. Tr: Jeroe HESRON

W Connection 6
Winchester 2 [3 52], Arcia 2 [31 59], Cupid [42], Jerrel Britto [64]

Jan-Michael WILLIAMS (c) - Akeem BENJAMIN, Eligah JOSEPH (Christian VIVEROS 46), Kemuel RIVERS, Rennie BRITO, Clyde LEON, Gerard WILLIAMS, Kern CUPID, Hashim ARCIA (Jomal WILLIAMS 67), Joevin JONES•, Shahdon WINCHESTER (Jerrel BRITTO 56). Tr: Stuart CHARLES-FEVRIER

Manny Ramjohn, Marabella
10-05-2012, Att: 390, Ref: Taylor BRB
Inter Moengotapoe 2
Ricardo Misiedjan 2 [32 75]

Rudolf DANIEL - Naldo KWASIE (Anduelo AMOEFERIE 58), Patrick JIMMY (c), Fabian JEROE•, Marlon BRON (Stefan BANETI 55), Ricardo MISIEDJAN, Junglo BRUNSWIJK, Clarence PLEIN•, Jerrel ADENSIBA, Stefano RIJSSEL, Germain VAN DIJK. Tr: Jeroe HESRON

Victory 8
Ricardo Charles 4 [1 56 79 90], Toussaint [3], Bony Pierre 2 [32 75], Beauge [51]

Ronald ELUSMA - Jean Fritz ST. GERMAIN, Parnel GUERRIER (c), Samuel Alte JACQUES• (Garpard BAPTISTE 77), Philippe TOUSSAINT, Jean FRANCOIS, Bony PIERRE, Andersuntcha BEAUVIAS (Leopart JEAN 57) (Othniel ROSARD 90), Nicodeme BEAUGE, Walter JOSEPH, Ricardo CHARLES. Tr: Wasbens PRINCIME

Manny Ramjohn, Marabella
10-05-2012, Att: 400, Ref: Nunez CUB
W Connection 1
OG [21]

Aquelius SYLVESTER - Akeem BENJAMIN, Kemuel RIVERS, Kern CUPID (c), Andre QUASHIE, Christian VIVEROS, Jomal WILLIAMS, Jerrel BRITTO, Anthony PARRIS (Joevin JONES 69), Johan PELTIER• (Rennie BRITO 70), Neil BENJAMIN (Shahdon WINCHESTER 70). Tr: Stuart CHARLES-FEVRIER

Antigua Barracuda 2
Aldred [38], Byers [42]

Keita DECASTRO - Luke BLAKELY, Stefan SMITH, Kimoi ALEXANDER (Matthew ALDRED 37), Quinton GRIFFITH, Orlando MITCHUM, Tamorley THOMAS• (Karanja MACK 90), Peter BYERS (Lloyde JEREMY JR. 79), George DUBLIN (c), Akeem THOMAS, Lawson ROBINSON. Tr: Thomas CURTIS

SEMI-FINALS AND THIRD PLACE PLAY-OFF

Manny Ramjohn, Marabella
19-06-2012, Att: 305, Ref: Elskamp SUR
Antigua Barracudas 0

Molvin JAMES - George DUBLIN (c), Akeem THOMAS (Luke BLAKELY 75), Tamorley THOMAS•, Quinton GRIFFITH, Peter BYERS, Stefan SMITH (Ranja CHRISTIAN 77), Kimoi ALEXANDER, Kerry SKEPPLE (Matthew ALDRED 67), Orlando MITCHUM•, Lawson ROBINSON•. Tr: Thomas CURTIS

Caledonia AIA 2
Abu Bakar [65], Jorsling [86]

Ronson WILLIAMS - Nuru MUHAMMAD•, Radanfah ABU BAKR, Kareem JOSEPH, Walter MOORE, Stephan DAVID, Keyon EDWARDS, Cornelius STEWART (Nathan LEWIS 73), Trayon BOBB, Trevin CAESAR (Devorn JORSLING 58), Jamal GAY• (Conrod SMITH• 80). Tr: Jamaal SHABAZZ

Manny Ramjohn, Marabella
19-06-2012, Att: 400, Ref: Taylor BRB
Puerto Rico Islanders 1
Hansen [76]

Richard MARTIN - Noah DELGADO (c), Giovanni EDWARD (Cesar GARCIA 71), Jonathan FANA FRIAS, Justin FOJO, David FOLEY, Richard MARTINEZ, Anthony VAZQUEZ•, Jay NEEDHAM, Jarad VAN SCHAIK (Gregory RICHARDSON 63), Nicholas ADDLERY (Joshua HANSEN 70). Tr: Adrian WHITBREAD

W Connection 4
Rennie Britto 2 [28 66], Jerrel Britto [58], Arcia [90]

Jan-Michael WILLIAMS - Akeem BENJAMIN, Eligah JOSEPH•, Rennie BRITO, Clyde LEON, Gerard WILLIAMS, Kern CUPID (c), Hashim ARCIA•, Andrei PACHECO (Johan PELTIER 87), Jerrel BRITTO (Christian VIVEROS 77), Joevin JONES. Tr: Stuart CHARLES-FEVRIER

SEMI-FINALS AND THIRD PLACE PLAY-OFF

Manny Ramjohn, Marabella
21-06-2012, Att: 250, Ref: Skeete BRB
Antigua Barracudas 0

Keita DECASTRO - George DUBLIN (c), Akeem THOMAS, Tamorley THOMAS•, Quinton GRIFFITH, Peter BYERS•, Karanja MACK (Stefan SMITH 53), Orlando MITCHUM, Luke BLAKELY, Matthew ALDRED (Kerry SKEPPLE 64), Lawson ROBINSON (Kimoi ALEXANDER 74). Tr: Thomas CURTIS

Puerto Rico Islanders 2
Hansen [14], Fana Frias [52p]

Richard MARTIN• - Jonathan FANA FRIAS, Justin FOJO, David FOLEY, Joshua HANSEN (Noah DELGADO 57), Richard MARTINEZ•, Jay NEEDHAM, Gregory RICHARDSON (Nicholas ADDLERY 69), Alexis RIVERA• (c), Osei TELESFORD (Jarad VAN SCHAIK 61), Anthony VAZQUEZ. Tr: Adrian WHITBREAD

FINAL

Manny Ramjohn, Marabella
21-06-2012, Att: 400, Ref: Pinas SUR
Caledonia AIA 1 4p
Abu Bakar [97]

Glenroy SAMUEL - Nuru MUHAMMAD, Radanfah ABU BAKR, Kareem JOSEPH (Conrod SMITH 85), Walter MOORE, Stephan DAVID, Keyon EDWARDS•, Cornelius STEWART (Jamal GAY 62), Trayon BOBB, Nathan LEWIS (Abdallah PHILLIPS 63), Devorn JORSLING. Tr: Jamaal SHABAZZ

W Connection 1 3p
Leon [103p]

Jan-Michael WILLIAMS - Akeem BENJAMIN, Eligah JOSEPH•, Rennie BRITO (Neil BENJAMIN JR. 105), Clyde LEON, Gerard WILLIAMS, Kern CUPID, Hashim ARCIA, Andrei PACHECO (Christian Ocoro VIVEROS 68), Jerrel BRITTO (Johan PELTIER• 67), Joevin JONES. Tr: Stuart CHARLES-FEVRIER

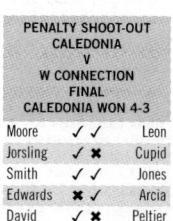

PENALTY SHOOT-OUT
CALEDONIA
V
W CONNECTION
FINAL
CALEDONIA WON 4-3

Moore	✓	✓	Leon
Jorsling	✓	✗	Cupid
Smith	✓	✓	Jones
Edwards	✗	✓	Arcia
David	✓	✗	Peltier

WOMEN'S TOURNAMENTS 2012

CONCACAF U-20 WOMEN'S CHAMPIONSHIP PANAMA 2012 QUALIFYING

Caribbean Groups

Group A	Pl	W	D	L	F	A	Pts	CUB	LCA
Jamaica†	2	2	0	0	6	0	**6**	2-0	4-0
Cuba†	2	1	0	1	9	2	**3**		9-0
St Lucia	2	0	0	2	0	13	**0**		

Group B	Pl	W	D	L	F	A	Pts	CAY	SUR
Trinidad and Tobago†	2	2	0	0	9	0	**6**	1-0	8-0
Cayman Islands†	2	1	0	1	4	1	**3**		4-0
Suriname	2	0	0	2	0	12	**0**		

Group C	Pl	W	D	L	F	A	Pts	PUR	SKN
Haiti†	2	2	0	0	8	0	**6**	4-0	4-0
Puerto Rico†	2	1	0	1	4	8	**3**		4-0
St Kitts and Nevis	2	0	0	2	0	8	**0**		

Group D	Pl	W	D	L	F	A	Pts	DOM	AIA	ATG
Guyana†	3	3	0	0	14	1	**9**	2-1	5-0	7-0
Dominican Republic†	3	2	0	1	15	3	**6**		5-0	9-1
Anguilla	3	1	0	2	1	10	**3**			1-0
Antigua and Barbuda	3	0	0	3	1	17	**0**			

Caribbean Second Round Groups

Group E	Pl	W	D	L	F	A	Pts	JAM	CAY	DOM
Haiti	3	3	0	0	8	0	**9**	1-0	3-0	4-0
Jamaica	3	2	0	1	6	1	**6**		2-0	4-0
Cayman Islands	3	0	1	2	0	5	**1**			0-0
Dominican Republic	3	0	1	2	0	8	**1**			

Group F	Pl	W	D	L	F	A	Pts	TRI	PUR	GUY
Cuba	3	1	2	0	7	3	**5**	1-1	1-1	5-1
Trinidad and Tobago	3	1	1	1	3	3	**4**		0-1	2-1
Puerto Rico	3	1	1	1	2	2	**4**			0-1
Guyana	3	1	0	2	3	7	**3**			

Central American Groups

Group 1 (In Honduras)	Pl	W	D	L	F	A	Pts	CRC	HON
Guatemala	2	2	0	0	6	2	**6**	3-1	3-1
Costa Rica	2	1	0	1	5	3	**3**		4-0
Honduras	2	0	0	2	1	7	**0**		

Group 2 (In Panama)	Pl	W	D	L	F	A	Pts	NCA	SLV
Panama	2	1	1	0	5	3	**4**	3-1	2-2
Nicaragua	2	1	0	1	4	5	**3**		3-2
El Salvador	2	0	1	1	4	5	**1**		

† Qualified for the Caribbean second round group • Canada, USA and Mexico qualified automatically for the finals

CONCACAF U-20 WOMEN'S CHAMPIONSHIP PANAMA 2012

First Round Group Stage

Group A	Pl	W	D	L	F	A	Pts	MEX	JAM	HAI
Canada	3	3	0	0	8	0	**9**	1-0	2-0	5-0
Mexico	3	2	0	1	13	2	**6**		3-1	10-0
Jamaica	3	0	1	2	1	5	**1**			0-0
Haiti	3	0	1	2	0	15	**1**			

Group B	Pl	W	D	L	F	A	Pts	PAN	GUA	CUB
USA	3	3	0	0	18	0	**9**	6-0	6-0	6-0
Panama	3	2	0	1	5	8	**6**		3-1	2-1
Guatemala	3	1	0	2	6	11	**3**			5-2
Cuba	3	0	0	3	3	13	**0**			

Semi-finals

USA	4
Mexico	0

Panama	0
Canada	6

Final

USA	2
Canada	1

3rd Place: **Mexico** 5-0 Panama

Finals held in Panama from 2-03-2012 to 11-03-2012 • USA, Canada & Mexico qualified for the 2012 FIFA U-20 Women's World Cup in Japan

CONCACAF U-17 WOMEN'S CHAMPIONSHIP GUATEMALA 2012 QUALIFYING

Caribbean Groups

Group A	Pl	W	D	L	F	A	Pts		BER	ATG
Bahamas†	2	2	0	0	12	0	**6**		2-0	10-0
Bermuda	2	1	0	1	5	2	**3**			5-0
Antigua and Barbuda	2	0	0	2	0	15	**0**			

Group B	Pl	W	D	L	F	A	Pts		DMA	SKN
Trinidad and Tobago†	4	4	0	0	46	0	**12**		13-0	11-0
Dominica	4	2	0	2	7	18	**6**	0-5		5-0
St Kitts and Nevis	4	0	0	4	0	35	**0**	0-17	0-2	

Group C	Pl	W	D	L	F	A	Pts		AIA	CUW
Guyana†	2	1	1	0	3	1	**4**		2-0	1-1
Anguilla	2	1	0	1	2	3	**3**			2-1
Curacao	2	0	1	1	2	3	**1**			

Group D	Pl	W	D	L	F	A	Pts		DOM	ARU
Jamaica†	2	2	0	0	12	0	**6**		3-0	9-0
Dominican Republic	2	1	0	1	7	3	**3**			7-0
Aruba	2	0	0	2	0	16	**0**			

Caribbean Second Round Group

Group E	Pl	W	D	L	F	A	Pts		JAM	BAH	GUY
Trinidad and Tobago	3	3	0	0	12	0	**9**		1-0	3-0	8-0
Jamaica	3	2	0	1	7	1	**6**			2-0	5-0
Bahamas	3	1	0	2	1	5	**3**				1-0
Guyana	3	0	0	3	0	14	**0**				

Central American Qualifiers

Panama	6	2
Nicaragua	0	1

Panama	1	2
Costa Rica	0	1

El Salvador	0	0
Costa Rica	2	0

† Qualified for the Caribbean second round group • Canada, USA and Mexico qualified automatically for the finals • Guatemala qualified as hosts

CONCACAF U-17 WOMEN'S CHAMPIONSHIP GUATEMALA 2012

First Round Group Stage

Group A	Pl	W	D	L	F	A	Pts	PAN	JAM	GUA
Canada	3	3	0	0	16	1	**9**	6-0	4-0	6-1
Panama	3	1	1	1	8	8	**4**		1-1	7-1
Jamaica	3	1	1	1	4	5	**4**			3-0
Guatemala	3	0	0	3	2	16	**0**			

Group B	Pl	W	D	L	F	A	Pts	MEX	TRI	BAH
USA	3	3	0	0	18	0	**9**	3-0	5-0	10-0
Mexico	3	2	0	1	8	3	**6**		2-0	6-0
Trinidad & Tobago	3	0	1	2	0	7	**1**			0-0
Bahamas	3	0	1	2	0	16	**1**			

Semi-finals

USA	7
Panama	0

Mexico	0
Canada	1

Final

USA	1
Canada	0

3rd Place: **Mexico** 6-0 Panama

Finals held in Guatemala from 2-05-2012 to 12-05-2012 • USA, Canada & Mexico qualified for the 2012 FIFA U-17 Women's World Cup in Azerbaijan

CONMEBOL
CONFEDERACION SUDAMERICANA DE FUTBOL

CONMEBOL MEMBER ASSOCIATIONS (10)
ARG - **Argentina** • BOL - **Bolivia** • BRA - **Brazil** • CHI - **Chile** • COL - **Colombia**
ECU - **Ecuador** • PAR - **Paraguay** • PER - **Peru** • URU - **Uruguay** • VEN - **Venezuela**

For a continent with such a rich history of football, South America has played host to the FIFA World Cup finals relatively infrequently. Indeed, since Brazil last hosted the tournament in 1950, just Chile in 1962 and Argentina in 1978 have played host and as preparations for the finals in Brazil in 2014 neared completion - with just the stadium in Manaus providing cause for concern - the South American qualifying tournament reached the halfway stage at the end of 2012 with Argentina, a resurgent Colombia and Ecuador staking strong claims for one of the four guaranteed places on offer. Without any qualifying matches, the Brazil national team has struggled to maintain its position in the FIFA/Coca-Cola World Ranking and in July 2012 fell out of the top ten for the first time in the history of the rankings, finishing the year in 18th place. There was also disappointment for the Brazilians in the football tournament of the 2012 London Olympic Games with defeat in the final against Mexico while the Brazil women's team failed to progress beyond the quater-finals - something both will be keen to redress when Rio hosts the games in 2016. In club football Corinthians became the 23rd club to win the Copa Libertadores when they beat Boca Juniors 3-1 on aggregate in the 2012 final, denying the Argentine club the opportunity to equal Independiente's record haul of seven titles. For Corinthians, who pride themselves on being one of the best supported clubs not only in Brazil but across the whole of South America, it was the realisation of a long cherished dream and there was a visible demonstration of the passion of their fans when 30,000 of them travelled to Tokyo to witness their triumph over European champions Chelsea in the final of the FIFA Club World Cup. It was the second time Corinthians had been crowned world champions - having won the first-ever title in 2000 on home soil as invited guests - and it brought to an end a run of five consecutive titles by European clubs. Just four days previously Brazil had made a clean sweep of South American club honours when Sao Paulo FC won the 2012 Copa Sudamericana. In the final they met Argentina's Tigre who, finding themselves 2-0 down in the second leg, refused to come out for the second half after claiming they had been attacked by security officials.

Confederación Sudamericana de Fútbol (CONMEBOL)
Autopista Aeropuerto Internacional y Leonismo Luqueño, Luque, Gran Asuncion, Paraguay
Tel +595 21 645781   Fax +595 21 645791
conmebol@conmebol.com.py   www.conmebol.com
President: Dr Nicolas Leoz PAR   Secretary General: Jose Luis Meiszner ARG
CONMEBOL Formed: 1916

CONMEBOL EXECUTIVE COMMITTEE
President: Dr Nicolas Leoz PAR

| Vice-President: Eugenio Figueredo URU | Secretary General: Jose Luis Meiszner ARG | Treasurer: Romer Osuna BOL |

DIRECTORS OF THE EXECUTIVE COMMITTEE

Rafael Esquivel VEN   Juan Angel Napout PAR   Marco Polo Del Nero BRA
Francisco Acosta ECU   Luis Bedoya COL   Alfredo Asfura CHI
                                 Manuel Burga PER

MAP OF CONMEBOL MEMBER NATIONS

SOUTH AMERICAN NATIONAL TEAM TOURNAMENTS

COPA AMERICA

Year	Host Country	Winners	Score	Runners-up	Venue
1910	Argentina ††	Argentina	4-1	Uruguay	‡ Racing Club, Buenos Aires
1916	Argentina †	Uruguay	0-0	Argentina	‡ Racing Club, Buenos Aires
1917	Uruguay	Uruguay	1-0	Argentina	‡ Parque Pereira, Montevideo
1919	Brazil	Brazil	1-0	Uruguay	§ Laranjeiras, Rio de Janeiro
1920	Chile	Uruguay	1-1	Argentina	* Sporting Club, Vina del Mar
1921	Argentina	Argentina	1-0	Brazil	* Sportivo Barracas, Buenos Aires
1922	Brazil	Brazil	3-0	Paraguay	§ Laranjeiras, Rio de Janeiro
1923	Uruguay	Uruguay	2-0	Argentina	‡ Parque Central, Montevideo
1924	Uruguay	Uruguay	0-0	Argentina	‡ Parque Central, Montevideo
1925	Argentina	Argentina	2-2	Brazil	‡ Bombonera, Buenos Aires
1926	Chile	Uruguay	2-0	Argentina	* Sport de Nunoa, Santiago
1927	Peru	Argentina	3-2	Uruguay	* Estadio Nacional, Lima
1929	Argentina	Argentina	4-1	Paraguay	* San Lorenzo, Buenos Aires
1935	Peru †	Uruguay	3-0	Argentina	‡ Estadio Nacional, Lima
1937	Argentina	Argentina	2-0	Brazil	‡ San Lorenzo, Buenos Aires
1939	Peru	Peru	2-1	Uruguay	‡ Estadio Nacional, Lima
1941	Chile †	Argentina	1-0	Uruguay	* Estadio Nacional, Santiago
1942	Uruguay	Uruguay	1-0	Argentina	‡ Centenario, Montevideo
1945	Chile †	Argentina	3-1	Brazil	* Estadio Nacional, Santiago
1946	Argentina †	Argentina	2-0	Brazil	‡ Monumental, Buenos Aires
1947	Ecuador	Argentina	6-0	Paraguay	* Estadio Capwell, Guayaquil
1949	Brazil	Brazil	7-0	Paraguay	§ Sao Januario, Rio de Janeiro
1953	Lima	Paraguay	3-2	Brazil	§ Estadio Nacional, Lima
1955	Chile	Argentina	1-0	Chile	‡ Estadio Nacional, Santiago
1956	Uruguay †	Uruguay	1-0	Argentina	‡ Centenario, Montevideo
1957	Peru	Argentina	3-0	Brazil	‡ Estadio Nacional, Lima
1959	Argentina	Argentina	1-1	Brazil	‡ Monumental, Buenos Aires
1959	Ecuador †	Uruguay	5-0	Argentina	* Modelo, Guayaquil
1963	Bolivia	Bolivia	5-4	Brazil	‡ Felix Capriles, Cochabamba
1967	Uruguay	Uruguay	1-0	Argentina	‡ Centenario, Montevideo
1975		Peru	0-1 2-0 1-0	Colombia	Bogota, Lima, Caracas
1979		Paraguay	3-0 0-0 1-0	Chile	Asuncion, Santiago, Buenos Aires
1983		Uruguay	2-0 1-1	Brazil	Montevideo & Salvador
1987	Argentina	Uruguay	1-0	Chile	Monumental, Buenos Aires
1989	Brazil	Brazil	1-0	Uruguay	‡ Maracana, Rio de Janeiro
1991	Chile	Argentina	3-2	Brazil	* Estadio Nacional, Santiago
1993	Ecuador	Argentina	2-1	Mexico	Monumental, Guayaquil
1995	Uruguay	Uruguay	1-1 5-3p	Brazil	Centenario, Montevideo
1997	Bolivia	Brazil	3-1	Bolivia	Hernando Siles, La Paz
1999	Paraguay	Brazil	3-0	Uruguay	Defensores del Chaco, Asuncion
2001	Colombia	Colombia	1-0	Mexico	El Campin, Bogota
2004	Peru	Brazil	2-2 4-2p	Argentina	Estadio Nacional, Lima
2007	Venezuela	Brazil	3-0	Argentina	Pachencho Romero, Maracaibo
2011	Argentina	Uruguay	3-0	Paraguay	Monumental, Buenos Aires

† Extraordinario tournaments are recognised as official tournaments though the teams did not compete for the Copa America • †† Unofficial tournament that is not part of the official records. CONMEBOL refer to it as The South American Championship although it was known at the time as the Copa Centenario • ‡ Tournament played on a league system. The final game was between the top two teams • * Tournament played on a league system. The game listed between the top two teams was not the final match in the tournament • § Tournament played on a league system. The game listed was a play-off after the top two teams finished level on points.

COPA AMERICA MEDALS TABLE

	Country	G	S	B	F	SF
1	Uruguay	15	6	7	5	9
2	Argentina	14	12	4	3	4
3	Brazil	8	11	7	6	8
4	Paraguay	2	6	8	2	3
5	Peru	2		5	1	5
6	Colombia	1	1	3	2	6
7	Bolivia	1	1		1	1
8	Chile		4	5	2	3
9	Mexico		2	3	2	5
10	Honduras			1		1
11	Ecuador					1
	United States					1
	Venezuela					1
		43	43	43	24	46

This table does not include the 1910 tournament and does not distinguish between official and extraordinario tournaments

KEY
G = Gold (winners) • S = Silver (runners-up) • B = Bronze (semi-finalists) • F = appearances in the final • SF = appearances in the semi-final

---

SOUTH AMERICAN CLUB TOURNAMENTS

COPA LIBERTADORES DE AMERICA

Year	Winners	Country	Score	Country	Runners-up
1960	Peñarol	URU	1-0 1-1	PAR	Olimpia
1961	Peñarol	URU	1-0 1-1	BRA	Palmeiras
1962	Santos	BRA	2-1 2-3 3-0	URU	Peñarol
1963	Santos	BRA	3-2 2-1	ARG	Boca Juniors
1964	Independiente	ARG	0-0 1-0	URU	Nacional Montevideo
1965	Independiente	ARG	1-0 1-3 4-1	URU	Peñarol
1966	Peñarol	URU	2-0 2-3 4-2	ARG	River Plate
1967	Racing Club	ARG	0-0 0-0 2-1	URU	Nacional Montevideo
1968	Estudiantes LP	ARG	2-1 1-3 2-0	BRA	Palmeiras
1969	Estudiantes LP	ARG	1-0 2-0	URU	Nacional Montevideo
1970	Estudiantes LP	ARG	1-0 0-0	URU	Peñarol
1971	Nacional Montevideo	URU	0-1 1-0 2-0	ARG	Estudiantes LP
1972	Independiente	ARG	0-0 2-1	PER	Universitario
1973	Independiente	ARG	1-1 0-0 2-1	CHI	Colo Colo
1974	Independiente	ARG	1-2 2-0 1-0	BRA	São Paulo FC
1975	Independiente	ARG	0-1 3-1 2-0	CHI	Union Española
1976	Cruzeiro	BRA	4-1 1-2 3-2	ARG	River Plate
1977	Boca Juniors	ARG	1-0 0-1 0-0 5-4p	BRA	Cruzeiro
1978	Boca Juniors	ARG	0-0 4-0	COL	Deportivo Cali
1979	Olimpia	PAR	2-0 0-0	ARG	Boca Juniors
1980	Nacional Montevideo	URU	0-0 1-0	BRA	Internacional
1981	Flamengo	BRA	2-1 0-1 2-0	CHI	Cobreloa
1982	Peñarol	URU	0-0 1-0	CHI	Cobreloa
1983	Grêmio	BRA	1-1 2-1	URU	Peñarol
1984	Independiente	ARG	1-0 0-0	BRA	Grêmio
1985	Argentinos Juniors	ARG	1-0 0-1 1-1 5-4p	COL	América Cali
1986	River Plate	ARG	2-1 1-0	COL	América Cali
1987	Peñarol	URU	0-2 2-1 1-0	COL	América Cali
1988	Nacional Montevideo	URU	0-1 3-0	ARG	Newell's Old Boys
1989	Atlético Nacional Medellín	COL	0-2 2-0 5-4p	PAR	Olimpia
1990	Olimpia	PAR	2-0 1-1	ECU	Barcelona
1991	Colo Colo	CHI	0-0 3-0	PAR	Olimpia

COPA LIBERTADORES DE AMERICA (CONT'D)

Year	Winners	Country	Score	Country	Runners-up
1992	São Paulo FC	BRA	1-0 0-1 3-2p	ARG	Newell's Old Boys
1993	São Paulo FC	BRA	5-1 0-2	CHI	Universidad Catolica
1994	Velez Sarsfield	ARG	1-0 0-1 5-3p	BRA	São Paulo FC
1995	Grêmio	BRA	3-1 1-1	COL	Atlético Nacional Medellin
1996	River Plate	ARG	0-1 2-0	COL	América Cali
1997	Cruzeiro	BRA	0-0 1-0	PER	Sporting Cristal
1998	Vasco da Gama	BRA	2-0 2-1	ECU	Barcelona
1999	Palmeiras	BRA	0-1 2-1 4-3p	COL	Deportivo Cali
2000	Boca Juniors	ARG	2-2 0-0 4-2p	BRA	Palmeiras
2001	Boca Juniors	ARG	1-0 0-1 3-1p	MEX	Cruz Azul
2002	Olimpia	PAR	0-1 2-1 4-2p	BRA	São Caetano
2003	Boca Juniors	ARG	2-0 3-1	BRA	Santos
2004	Once Caldas	COL	0-0 1-1 2-0p	ARG	Boca Juniors
2005	São Paulo FC	BRA	1-1 4-0	BRA	Atlético Paranaense
2006	Internacional	BRA	2-1 2-2	BRA	São Paulo FC
2007	Boca Juniors	ARG	3-0 2-0	BRA	Grêmio
2008	LDU Quito	ECU	4-2 1-3 3-1p	BRA	Fluminense
2009	Estudiantes LP	ARG	0-0 2-1	BRA	Cruzeiro
2010	Internacional	BRA	2-1 3-2	MEX	Guadalajara
2011	Santos	BRA	0-0 2-1	URU	Peñarol
2012	Corinthians	BRA	1-1 2-0	ARG	Boca Juniors

COPA LIBERTADORES MEDALS TABLE

	Country	G	S	B	F	SF
1	Argentina	22	9	32	31	63
2	Brazil	16	15	23	31	54
3	Uruguay	8	8	18	16	34
4	Paraguay	3	3	14	6	20
5	Colombia	2	7	18	9	27
6	Chile	1	5	15	6	21
7	Ecuador	1	2	9	3	12
8	Peru		2	6	2	8
9	Mexico		2	5	2	7
9	Bolivia			3		3
	Venezuela			3		3
		53	53	146	106	252

COPA LIBERTADORES MEDALS TABLE

	Club		G	S	B
1	Independiente	ARG	7		5
2	Boca Juniors	ARG	6	4	4
3	Peñarol	URU	5	5	10
4	Estudiantes La Plata	ARG	4	1	1
5	Nacional Montevideo	URU	3	3	7
6	Olimpia	PAR	3	3	5
7	São Paulo FC	BRA	3	3	3
8	Santos FC	BRA	3	1	4
9	River Plate	ARG	2	2	11
10	Grêmio	BRA	2	2	3
11	Cruzeiro	BRA	2	2	2
12	Internacional	BRA	2	1	2
13	SE Palmeiras	BRA	1	3	2

COPA LIBERTADORES MEDALS TABLE (CONT'D)

	Club		G	S	B
14	Colo Colo	CHI	1	1	3
15	At. Nacional Medellín	COL	1	1	2
16	Flamengo	BRA	1		2
	LDU Quito	ECU	1		2
	Racing Club Avellaneda	ARG	1		2
	Vélez Sarsfield	ARG	1		2
20	Argentinos Juniors	ARG	1		1
	Corinthians	BRA	1		1
22	Once Caldas	COL	1		
	Vasco da Gama	BRA	1		
24	América Cali	COL		4	6
25	Barcelona	ECU		2	5
26	Deportivo Cali	COL		2	2

COPA LIBERTADORES MEDALS TABLE (CONT'D)

	Club		G	S	B
27	Cobreloa	CHI		2	1
28	Newell's Old Boys	ARG		2	
29	Universidad Catolica	CHI		1	4
30	Universitario	PER		1	3
31	Chivas Guadalajara	MEX		1	2
32	Union Española	CHI		1	1
33	Atlético Paranaense	BRA		1	
	Cruz Azul	MEX		1	
	Fluminense	BRA		1	
	São Caetano	BRA		1	
	Sporting Cristal	PER		1	
38	Cerro Porteño	PAR			6
39	Universidad de Chile	CHI			4
40	CF América	MEX			3
	Millonarios	COL			3
	San Lorenzo de Almagro	ARG			3
43	Alianza	PER			2
	Botafogo	BRA			2
	Rosario Central	ARG			2
	Libertad	PAR			2
47	Atlético Junior	COL			1

COPA LIBERTADORES MEDALS TABLE (CONT'D)

Club		G	S	B
Atlético Mineiro	BRA			1
Atlético San Cristobal	VEN			1
Blooming	BOL			1
Bolivar	BOL			1
Cúcuta Deportiva	COL			1
Danubio	URU			1
Defensor Lima	PER			1
Deportes Tolima	COL			1
Emelec	ECU			1
Guarani Asuncion	PAR			1
Guarani Campinas	BRA			1
Huracán	ARG			1
Independiente Medellin	COL			1
Independiente Santa Fé	COL			1
Jorge Wilsterman	BOL			1
El Nacional Quito	ECU			1
O'Higgins	CHI			1
Palestino	CHI			1
Portuguesa	VEN			1
ULA Merida	VEN			1
		53	53	146

SUPERCOPA JOAO HAVELANGE

Year	Winners	Country	Score	Country	Runners-up
1988	Racing Club	ARG	2-1 1-1	BRA	Cruzeiro
1989	Boca Juniors	ARG	0-0 0-0 5-3p	ARG	Independiente
1990	Olimpia	PAR	3-0 3-3	URU	Nacional Montevideo
1991	Cruzeiro	BRA	0-2 3-0	ARG	River Plate
1992	Cruzeiro	BRA	4-0 0-1	ARG	Racing Club
1993	São Paulo FC	BRA	2-2 2-2 5-3p	BRA	Flamengo
1994	Independiente	ARG	1-1 1-0	ARG	Boca Juniors
1995	Independiente	ARG	2-0 0-1	BRA	Flamengo
1996	Velez Sarsfield	ARG	1-0 2-0	BRA	Cruzeiro
1997	River Plate	ARG	0-0 2-1	BRA	São Paulo FC

SUPERCOPA MEDALS TABLE

	Country	G	S	B	F	SF
1	Argentina	6	4	4	10	14
2	Brazil	3	5	6	8	14
3	Paraguay	1		2	1	3
4	Uruguay		1	4	1	5
5	Chile			2		2
	Colombia			2		2
		10	10	20	20	40

SUPERCOPA MEDALS TABLE

	Club		G	S	B
1	Cruzeiro	BRA	2	2	2
2	Independiente	ARG	2	1	
3	River Plate	ARG	1	1	2
4	São Paulo FC	BRA	1	1	1
5	Boca Juniors	ARG	1	1	
	Racing Club	ARG	1	1	
7	Olimpia	PAR	1		2
8	Velez Sarsfield	ARG	1		
9	Flamengo	BRA		2	1
10	Nacional Montevideo	URU		1	2
11	Colo Colo	CHI			2
	Peñarol	URU			2
	At. Nacional Medellin	COL			2
14	Argentinos Juniors	ARG			1
	Estudiantes LP	ARG			1
	Santos	BRA			1
	Grêmio	BRA			1
			10	10	20

COPA CONMEBOL

Year	Winners	Country	Score	Country	Runners-up
1992	Atlético Mineiro	BRA	2-0 0-1	PAR	Olimpia
1993	Botafogo	BRA	1-1 2-2 3-1p	URU	Peñarol
1994	São Paulo FC	BRA	6-1 0-3	URU	Peñarol
1995	Rosario Central	ARG	0-4 4-0 4-3p	BRA	Atlético Mineiro
1996	Lanús	ARG	2-0 0-1	COL	Independiente Santa Fé
1997	Atlético Mineiro	BRA	4-1 1-1	ARG	Lanús
1998	Santos	BRA	1-0 0-0	ARG	Rosario Central
1999	Talleres Córdoba	ARG	2-4 3-0	BRA	CSA

COPA CONMEBOL MEDALS TABLE

	Country	G	S	B	F	SF
1	Brazil	5	2	6	7	13
2	Argentina	3	2	4	5	9
3	Uruguay		2		2	2
4	Paraguay		1	1	1	2
	Colombia		1	1	1	2
6	Chile			2		2
7	Ecuador			1		1
	Peru			1		1
		8	8	16	16	32

COPA CONMEBOL MEDALS TABLE

	Club		G	S	B
1	Atlético Mineiro	BRA	2	1	2
2	Lanus	ARG	1	1	
3	Rosario Central	ARG	1	1	1
4	Botafogo	BRA	1		
	Santos	BRA	1		

COPA CONMEBOL MEDALS TABLE (CONT'D)

	Club		G	S	B
	São Paulo FC	BRA	1		
	Talleres Cordoba	ARG	1		
8	Peñarol	URU		2	
9	CSA	BRA		1	
	Independiente Santa Fé	COL		1	
	Olimpia	PAR		1	
12	Corinthians	BRA			1
	Deportes Concepcion	CHI			1
	Gimnasia y Esgrima	ARG			1
	El Nacional Quito	ECU			1
	San Lorenzo	ARG			1
	América Cali	COL			1
	Colón Santa Fé	ARG			1
	Atlético Colegiales	PAR			1
	Sampaio Correa	BRA			1
	São Raimundo	BRA			1
	Vasco da Gama	BRA			1
	Universitario	PER			1
	Universidad de Chile	CHI			1
			8	8	16

COPA MERCOSUR

Year	Winners	Country	Score	Country	Runners-up
1998	Palmeiras	BRA	1-2 3-1 1-0	BRA	Cruzeiro
1999	Flamengo	BRA	4-3	BRA	Palmeiras
2000	Vasco da Gama	BRA	2-0 0-1 4-3	BRA	Palmeiras
2001	San Lorenzo	ARG	0-0 1-1 4-3p	BRA	Flamengo

COPA MERCOSUR MEDALS TABLE

	Country	G	S	B	F	SF
1	Brazil	3	4	3	7	10
2	Argentina	1		3	1	4
3	Paraguay			1		1
	Uruguay			1		1
		4	4	8	8	16

COPA MERCOSUR MEDALS TABLE

	Club		G	S	B
1	Palmeiras	BRA	1	2	
2	Flamengo	BRA	1	1	
3	San Lorenzo	ARG	1		2
4	Vasco da Gama	BRA	1		
5	Cruzeiro	BRA		1	
6	Atlético Mineiro	BRA			1
	Corinthians	BRA			1
	Grêmio	BRA			1
	Olimpia	PAR			1
	Peñarol	URU			1
	River Plate	ARG			1
			4	4	8

COPA MERCONORTE

Year	Winners	Country	Score	Country	Runners-up
1998	Atlético Nacional Medellin	COL	3-1 1-0	COL	Deportivo Cali
1999	América Cali	COL	1-2 1-0	COL	Independiente Santa Fé
2000	Atlético Nacional Medellin	COL	0-0 2-1	COL	Millonarios
2001	Millonários	COL	1-1 1-1 3-1p	ECU	Emelec

COPA MERCONORTE MEDALS TABLE

	Country	G	S	B	F	SF
1	Colombia	4	3	1	7	8
2	Ecuador		1	2	1	3
3	Mexico				3	3
4	Peru				1	1
	Venezuela				1	1
		4	4	8	8	16

COPA MERCONORTE MEDALS TABLE

	Club		G	S	B
1	Atlético Nacional Medellin	COL	2		
2	Millonarios	COL	1	1	1
3	América Cali	COL	1		
4	Emelec	ECU		1	1
5	Deportivo Cali	COL		1	
	Independiente Santa Fé	COL		1	
7	Alianza Lima	PER			1
	Caracas FC	VEN			1
	Chivas Guadalajara	MEX			1
	El Nacional Quito	ECU			1
	Necaxa	MEX			1
	Santos Laguna	MEX			1
			4	4	8

COPA SUDAMERICANA

Year	Winners	Country	Score	Country	Runners-up
2002	San Lorenzo	ARG	4-0 0-0	COL	Atlético Nacional Medellin
2003	Cienciano	PER	3-3 1-0	ARG	River Plate
2004	Boca Juniors	ARG	0-1 2-0	BOL	Bolivar
2005	Boca Juniors	ARG	1-1 1-1 4-3p	MEX	Pumas UNAM
2006	Pachuca	MEX	1-1 2-1	CHI	Colo Colo
2007	Arsenal	ARG	3-2 1-2	MEX	America
2008	Internacional	BRA	1-0 1-1	ARG	Estudiantes LP
2009	LDU Quito	ECU	5-1 0-3	BRA	Fluminense
2010	Independiente	ARG	0-2 3-1 5-3p	BRA	Goiás EC
2011	Universidad de Chile	CHI	1-0 3-0	ECU	LDU Quito
2012	São Paulo FC	BRA	0-0 2-0	ARG	Tigre

COPA SUDAMERICANA MEDALS TABLE

	Country	G	S	B	F	SF
1	Argentina	5	3	5	8	13
2	Mexico	1	2	2	3	5
3	Brazil	2	2	5	4	9
4	Ecuador	1	1	2	2	4
5	Chile	1	1	2	2	4
6	Peru	1			1	1
7	Colombia		1	3	1	4
8	Bolivia		1	1	1	2
9	Paraguay				1	1
	Uruguay			1		1
		11	11	22	22	44

COPA SUDAMERICANA MEDALS TABLE

	Club		G	S	B
1	Boca Juniors	ARG	2		
2	LDU Quito	ECU	1	1	2
3	Internacional	BRA	1		1
	São Paulo FC	BRA	1		1
5	Arsenal	ARG	1		
	Cienciano	PER	1		
	Independiente	ARG	1		
	Pachuca	MEX	1		
	San Lorenzo	ARG	1		
	Universidad de Chile	CHI	1		
11	River Plate	ARG		1	2
12	Atlético Nacional Medellin	COL		1	1
	Bolivar	BOL		1	1
14	CF América	MEX		1	
	Colo Colo	CHI		1	
	Estudiantes LP	ARG		1	
	Fluminense	BRA		1	
	Goiás EC	BRA		1	
	Pumas UNAM	MEX		1	

SOUTH AMERICAN WOMEN'S TOURNAMENTS

COPA SUDAMERICANA MEDALS TABLE (CONT'D)

	Club		G	S	B
	Tigre	ARG		1	
21	Velez Sarsfield	ARG			2
22	Millonarios	COL			2
	Universidad Catolica	CHI			2
	Argentinos Juniors	ARG			1
	Atlético Paranaense	BRA			1
	Cerro Porteño	PAR			1

COPA SUDAMERICANA MEDALS TABLE (CONT'D)

Club		G	S	B
Guadalajara	MEX			1
Nacional Montevideo	URU			1
Palmeiras	BRA			1
Toluca	MEX			1
Vasco da Gama	BRA			1
		11	11	22

SOUTH AMERICAN YOUTH TOURNAMENTS

SUDAMERICANA SUB-20

Year	Host Country	Winners	Runners-up
1954	Venezuela	Uruguay	Brazil
1958	Chile	Uruguay	Argentina
1964	Colombia	Uruguay	Paraguay
1967	Paraguay	Argentina	Paraguay
1971	Paraguay	Paraguay	Uruguay
1974	Chile	Brazil	Uruguay
1975	Peru	Uruguay	Chile
1977	Venezuela	Uruguay	Brazil
1979	Uruguay	Uruguay	Argentina
1981	Ecuador	Uruguay	Brazil
1983	Bolivia	Brazil	Uruguay
1985	Paraguay	Brazil	Paraguay
1987	Colombia	Colombia	Brazil
1988	Argentina	Brazil	Colombia
1991	Venezuela	Brazil	Argentina
1992	Colombia	Brazil	Uruguay
1995	Bolivia	Brazil	Argentina
1997	Chile	Argentina	Brazil
1999	Argentina	Argentina	Uruguay
2001	Ecuador	Brazil	Argentina
2003	Uruguay	Argentina	Brazil
2005	Colombia	Colombia	Brazil
2007	Paraguay	Brazil	Argentina
2009	Venezuela	Brazil	Paraguay
2011	Peru	Brazil	Uruguay

SUDAMERICANA SUB-17

Year	Host Country	Winners	Runners-up
1985	Argentina	Argentina	Brazil
1986	Peru	Bolivia	Brazil
1988	Ecuador	Brazil	Argentina
1991	Paraguay	Brazil	Uruguay
1993	Colombia	Colombia	Chile
1995	Peru	Brazil	Argentina
1997	Paraguay	Brazil	Argentina
1999	Uruguay	Brazil	Paraguay
2002	Peru	Brazil	Argentina
2003	Bolivia	Argentina	Brazil
2005	Venezuela	Brazil	Uruguay
2007	Ecuador	Brazil	Colombia
2009	Chile	Brazil	Argentina
2011	Ecuador	Brazil	Uruguay

From 1985-1988 the championship was a U-16 tournament but since 1991 it has operated as an U-17 championship

SOUTH AMERICAN WOMEN'S TOURNAMENTS

SOUTH AMERICAN WOMEN'S CHAMPIONSHIP

Year	Host Country	Winners	Runners-up
1991	Brazil	Brazil	Chile
1995	Brazil	Brazil	Argentina
1998	Argentina	Brazil	Argentina
2003	Peru	Brazil	Argentina
2006	Argentina	Argentina	Brazil
2010	Ecuador	Brazil	Colombia

SOUTH AMERICAN WOMEN'S U-20 CHAMPIONSHIP

Year	Host Country	Winners	Runners-up
2004		Brazil	Paraguay
2006	Chile	Brazil	Argentina
2008	Brazil	Brazil	Argentina
2010	Colombia	Brazil	Colombia
2012	Brazil	Brazil	Argentina

SOUTH AMERICAN WOMEN'S U-17 CHAMPIONSHIP

Year	Host Country	Winners	Runners-up
2008	Chile	Colombia	Brazil
2010	Brazil	Brazil	Chile
2012	Bolivia	Brazil	Uruguay

CLUB TOURNAMENTS IN SOUTH AMERICA IN 2012

COPA SANTANDER LIBERTADORES 2012

Preliminary Round

Internacional *	BRA	1	2
Once Caldas	COL	0	2
Flamengo	BRA	1	2
Real Potosí *	BOL	2	0
Unión Española *	CHI	1	2
Tigres UANL	MEX	0	2
Arsenal *	ARG	3	1
Sport Huancayo	PER	0	1
Libertad	PAR	0	4
El Nacional *	ECU	1	1
Peñarol *	URU	4	1
Caracas	VEN	0	1

* Home team in the first leg

Group Stage

Grupo 1
		Pts	BRA	BRA	BOL	PER
Santos	BRA	13		3-1	2-0	2-0
Internacional	BRA	8	1-1		5-0	2-0
The Strongest	BOL	7	2-1	1-1		2-1
Juan Aurich	PER	6	1-3	1-0	1-0	

Grupo 2
		Pts	ARG	ECU	BRA	PAR
Lanús	ARG	10		1-0	1-1	6-0
Emelec	ECU	9	0-2		3-2	1-0
Flamengo	BRA	8	3-0	1-0		3-3
Olimpia	PAR	7	2-1	2-3	3-2	

Grupo 3
		Pts	CHI	BOL	COL	CHI
Unión Española	CHI	10		2-1	2-0	1-1
Bolívar	BOL	10	1-3		2-1	3-0
Atlético Junior	COL	7	2-1	0-1		3-0
Universidad Católica	CHI	6	2-1	1-1	2-2	

Grupo 4
		Pts	BRA	ARG	ARG	VEN
Fluminense	BRA	15		0-2	1-0	1-0
Boca Juniors	ARG	13	1-2		2-0	2-0
Arsenal	ARG	6	1-2	1-2		3-0
Zamora	VEN	1	0-1	0-0	0-1	

Grupo 5
		Pts	PAR	BRA	URU	PER
Libertad	PAR	13		1-1	2-1	4-1
Vasco da Gama	BRA	13	2-0		1-2	3-2
Nacional Montevideo	URU	6	1-2	0-1		1-0
Alianza Lima	PER	3	1-2	1-2	1-0	

Grupo 6
		Pts	BRA	MEX	PAR	VEN
Corinthians	BRA	14		1-0	2-0	6-0
Cruz Azul	MEX	11	0-0		4-1	4-0
Nacional Asunción	PAR	4	1-3	1-2		3-2
Deportivo Táchira	VEN	3	1-1	1-1	0-0	

Grupo 7
		Pts	ARG	ECU	URU	MEX
Velez Sarsfield	ARG	12		1-0	1-3	3-0
Deportivo Quito	ECU	10	3-0		2-0	5-0
Defensor Sporting	URU	9	0-3	2-0		1-0
Guadalajara	MEX	4	0-2	1-1	1-0	

Grupo 8
		Pts	CHI	COL	ARG	URU
Universidad de Chile	CHI	13		2-1	5-1	2-1
At. Nacional Medellín	COL	11	2-0		2-2	3-0
Godoy Cruz	ARG	5	0-1	4-4		1-0
Peñarol	URU	4	1-1	0-4	4-2	

COPA SANTANDER LIBERTADORES 2012

Round of 16			Quarter-finals			Semi-finals			Final		
Corinthians	0	3									
Emelec *	0	0									
			Corinthians	0	1						
			Vasco da Gama *	0	0						
Lanús	1 2	4p									
Vasco da Gama *	2 1	5p									
						Corinthians	1	1			
						Santos *	0	1			
Vélez Sarsfield	1	1									
At. Nacional *	0	1									
			Vélez Sarsfield *	1 0	2p						
			Santos	0 1	4p						
Bolívar *	2	0									
Santos	1	8									
									Corinthians	1	2
									Boca Juniors *	1	0
Univ. de Chile	1	6									
Deportivo Quito *	4	0									
			Univ. de Chile	1 1	5p						
			Libertad *	1 1	3p						
Cruz Azul *	1	0									
Libertad	1	2									
						Univ. de Chile	0	0			
						Boca Juniors *	2	0			
Fluminense	0	2									
Internacional *	0	1									
			Fluminense	0	1	* Home team in the first leg					
			Boca Juniors *	1	1						
Unión Española	1	2									
Boca Juniors *	2	3									

Top scorers: **8** - **NEYMAR** BRA, Santos & Matias **ALUSTIZA** ARG, Deportivo Quito • **7** - Dorlan **PABON** COL, At. Nacional • **6** - Junior **FERNANDES** CHI, Univ de Chile & **LEANDRO DAMIAO** BRA, Inter • **5** - Emanuel **HERRERA** ARG, Unión Española; Javier **OROZCO** MEX, Cruz Azul & **EMERSON** QAT, Corinthians

PRELIMINARY ROUND

Beira-Rio, Porto Alegre
25-01-2012, Att: 33 058, Ref: Vazquez URU

Internacional 1
Leandro Damiao [11]

MURIEL - INDIO, NEI, KLEBER, RODRIGO MOLEDO, Pablo GUINAZU, Mario BOLATTI, Andres D'ALESSANDRO, OSCAR• (JOAO PAULO 85), LEANDRO DAMIAO (JO 90), DAGOBERTO (MARCOS AURELIO 64). Tr: DORIVAL JUNIOR

Once Caldas 0

Neco MARTINEZ - Emanuel ACOSTA•, Jamell RAMOS, Diego AMAYA, Mauricio CASIERRA•, Avimiled RIVAS, Harrison HENAO• (David ALVAREZ 34), Jorge NUNEZ, Mario GONZALEZ, Jhon PAJOY (Ayron DEL VALLE 86), Jefferson CUERO (Guillermo BELTRAN 61). Tr: Luis PAEZ

Palogrande, Manizales
1-02-2012, Att: 14 295, Ref: Chacon MEX

Once Caldas 2
Nunez [2p], Gonzalez [24]

Neco MARTINEZ - Emanuel ACOSTA, David ALVAREZ (Ayron DEL VALLE 18), Jamell RAMOS, Diego AMAYA, Mauricio CASIERRA (Jefferson CUERO 66), Avimiled RIVAS, Jorge NUNEZ, Mario GONZALEZ, Guillermo BELTRAN (Jair REINOSO 52), Jhon PAJOY. Tr: Luis PAEZ

Internacional 2
D'Alessandro [11p], Tinga [21]

MURIEL• - INDIO, NEI•, KLEBER, RODRIGO MOLEDO, Pablo GUINAZU, TINGA (ELTON 64), Mario BOLATTI, Andres D'ALESSANDRO, OSCAR• (FABRICIO 88), LEANDRO DAMIAO (DAGOBERTO 80). Tr: DORIVAL JUNIOR

Victor Ugarte, Potosí
25-01-2012, Att: 19 100, Ref: Prudente URU

Real Potosí 2
Centurion [30], Brittes [57]

Henry LAPCZYK - Rony JIMENEZ•, Alberto ALARCON•, Claudio CENTURION, Rosauro RIVERO, Roly SEJAS, Eduardo ORTIZ, Jose MICHELENA (Nicolas TUDOR 86), Sebastian POL, Edgardo BRITES (Pastor TORREZ 87), Victor ANGOLA (Mario OVANDO 74). Tr: Victor ZWENGER

Flamengo 1
Luiz Antonio [28]

FELIPE - LEO MOURA•, WELINTON SOUZA, JUNIOR CESAR, DAVID•, AIRTON (Dario BOTTINELLI• 60), WILLIANS• (CAMACHO 86), RONALDINHO, RENATO, LUIZ ANTONIO, DEIVID (NEGUEBA 60). Tr: Vanderlei LUXEMBURGO

Engenhao, Rio de Janeiro
1-02-2012, Att: 32 004, Ref: Rivera PER

Flamengo 2
Leo Moura [39], Ronaldinho [92+]

FELIPE - LEO MOURA•, WELINTON SOUZA, JUNIOR CESAR, DAVID, WILLIANS•, RONALDINHO, RENATO• (MURALHA 74), Dario BOTTINELLI (CAMACHO 74), LUIZ ANTONIO, DEIVID (NEGUEBA 82). Tr: Vanderlei LUXEMBURGO

Real Potosí 0

Henry LAPCZYK - Gerardo YECEROTTE•, Rony JIMENEZ, Alberto ALARCON•, Claudio CENTURION••♦78), Rosauro RIVERO, Roly SEJAS, Mario OVANDO (Sebastian POL 53), Eduardo ORTIZ (Victor ANGOLA 81), Jose MICHELENA (Nicolas TUDOR 56), Edgardo BRITES•. Tr: Victor ZWENGER

Santa Laura, Santiago
25-01-2012, Att: 4567, Ref: Intriago ECU

Unión Española 1
Barriga [58]

Eduardo LOBOS - Jorge AMPUERO, Rafael OLARRA•, Braulio LEAL•, Gonzalo VILLAGRA, Emiliano VECCHIO (Mauro DIAZ• 46), Fernando CORDERO, Gonzalo BARRIGA (Jean Paul PINEDA 80), Dagoberto CURRIMILLA, Sebastian JAIME, Fabian SAAVEDRA (Emanuel HERRERA 46). Tr: Jose SIERRA

Tigres UANL 0

Aaron FERNANDEZ - Eder BORELLI, Jonathan BORNSTEIN, Fernando NAVARRO (Francisco ACUNA 83), Jose RIVAS••, Lampros KONTOGIANNIS, Abraham STRINGEL, Alberto ACOSTA (Edgar PACHECO 46), Jesus DUENAS•, Alan PULIDO, Emmanuel CERDA. Tr: Ricardo FERRETTI

Universitario, Monterrey
1-02-2012, Att: 18 926, Ref: Laverni ARG

Tigres UANL 2
Pulido [2] [14] [22]

Aaron FERNANDEZ - Eder BORELLI, Jonathan BORNSTEIN, Fernando NAVARRO (Victor GARZA 77), Jose RIVAS••♦37, Francisco ACUNA (Edgar PACHECO 46), Lampros KONTOGIANNIS•, Alberto ACOSTA, Jesus DUENAS, Alan PULIDO, Emmanuel CERDA (Jorge VALENCIA 40)•. Tr: Ricardo FERRETTI

Unión Española 1
Herrera [38p], Jaime [68]

Eduardo LOBOS• - Francisco ALARCON• (Diego SCOTTI 46), Jorge AMPUERO•, Rafael OLARRA, Braulio LEAL•, Gonzalo VILLAGRA, Fernando CORDERO, Gonzalo BARRIGA (Rodolfo MADRID 88), Mauro DIAZ••♦63, Emanuel HERRERA (Jean Paul PINEDA 84), Sebastian JAIME•. Tr: Jose SIERRA

Julio Grondona, Buenos Aires
24-01-2012, Att: 721, Ref: Oliveira

Arsenal 3
Cordoba [21], Zelaya [35], Mosca [87]

Christian CAMPESTRINI - Lisandro LOPEZ, Guillermo BURDISSO, Juan CAFFA (Hugo NERVO 65), Carlos CARBONERO••♦65, Damian PEREZ, Nicolas AGUIRRE•, Adrian GONZALEZ, Ivan MARCONE, Jorge CORDOBA (Gustavo BLANCO LESCHUK 65), Emilio ZELAYA (Claudio MOSCA 83). Tr: Gustavo ALFARO

Sport Huancayo 0

Leonel CUERDO - Anier FIGUEROA, Miguel ARAUJO, Rafael FARFAN, Renzo REANOS, Roman OJEDA, Blas LOPEZ•, Angelo CRUZADO, Luis HERNANDEZ (WELINGTON ADAO 46), Sergio IBARRA• (Ryan SALAZAR 71), Jair BAYLON•. Tr: Miguel COMPANY

Estadio Huancayo, Huancayo
31-01-2012, Att: 13 000, Ref: Vazquez URU

Sport Huancayo 1
Ibarra [44]

Leonel CUERDO - Anier FIGUEROA, Rafael FARFAN, Renzo REANOS, Enio NOVOA, WELINGTON ADAO, Blas LOPEZ•, Ryan SALAZAR (Angelo CRUZADO 46) (Yves ROACH 77), Luis HERNANDEZ• (Roman OJEDA 66), Sergio IBARRA, Jair BAYLON. Tr: Gustavo ALFARO

Arsenal 1
Leguizamon [85]

Christian CAMPESTRINI• - Lisandro LOPEZ, Guillermo BURDISSO, Hugo NERVO, Damian PEREZ, Nicolas AGUIRRE• (Juan CAFFA 71), Gaston ESMERADO, Adrian GONZALEZ, Ivan MARCONE•, Jorge CORDOBA (Luciano LEGUIZAMON 46), Emilio ZELAYA• (Gustavo BLANCO LESCHUK 83). Tr: Gustavo ALFARO

Olimpico Atahualpa, Quito
25-01-2012, Att: 7000, Ref: Rivera PER

El Nacional 1
Anangono [43]

Danny CABEZAS - Javier CHILA•, Juan Carlos ANANGONO, Flavio CAICEDO, Juan GOVEA (Fabricio GUEVARA 61), Ricardo LOPEZ•, Erik MINDA (Franklin GUERRA 46), Edison PRECIADO (Edmundo ZURA• 83), Marwin PITA, Jose MADRID, Juan Luis ANANGONO. Tr: Mario SARALEGUI

Libertad 0

Rodrigo MUNOZ• - Nery BAREIRO, Ismael BENEGAS•, Sergio AQUINO, Miguel SAMUDIO, Cristian MENENDEZ (Pablo VELAZQUEZ 64), Luciano CIVELLI, Victor CACERES, Carlos BONET, Ariel NUNEZ (Mauro CABALLERO JR 76), Rodolfo GAMARRA• (Marcos MELGAREJO 78). Tr: Jorge BURRUCHAGA

Nicolás Leoz, Asuncion
1-02-2012, Att: 301, Ref: Pezzota ARG

Libertad 4
Velazquez [1], Nunez [29], Gamarra [34], Civelli [93+]

Rodrigo MUNOZ• - Nery BAREIRO (Gustavo MENCIA• 27), Ismael BENEGAS, Sergio AQUINO, Miguel SAMUDIO, Luciano CIVELLI, Victor CACERES, Carlos BONET, Pablo VELAZQUEZ• (Mauro CABALLERO JR 81), Ariel NUNEZ, Rodolfo GAMARRA• (Victor AYALA 73). Tr: Jorge BURRUCHAGA

El Nacional 1
Minda [17]

Danny CABEZAS (Patricio GARCIA 46), Javier CHILA•, Juan Carlos ANANGONO, Flavio CAICEDO•, Franklin GUERRA, Ricardo LOPEZ, Erik MINDA (Juan GOVEA 61), Edison PRECIADO (Edmundo ZURA 73), Marwin PITA, Jose Madrid••♦88), Juan Luis ANANGONO. Tr: Mario SARALEGUI

Centenario, Montevideo
25-01-2012, Att: 40 870, Ref: Beligoy ARG

Peñarol 4
Freitas [35], Zalayeta [38], Joao Pedro [63], Estoyanoff [70]

Fabian CARINI - Juan ALVEZ, Alejandro GONZALEZ, Dario RODRIGUEZ•, Carlos VALDEZ, Nicolas FREITAS, Luis AGUIAR (Emiliano ALBIN 85), Sebastian CRISTOFORO, Fabian ESTOYANOFF• (Santiago SILVA 72), Marcelo ZALAYETA, Rodrigo MORA (JOAO PEDRO• 57). Tr: Gregorio PEREZ

Caracas FC 0

Renny VEGA - Fidel PEREZ•, Rohel BRICENO, Julio MACHADO•, AMARAL, Edgar JIMENEZ, Angelo PENA (Luis GONZALEZ 74), Jesus GOMEZ (Jesus MEZA• 54), Juan GUERRA•, Victor FERREIRA, Anthony URIBE (Romulo OTERO 62). Tr: Ceferonio BENCOMO

Olímpico, Caracas
1-02-2012, Att: 15 917, Ref: Ricci BRA

Caracas FC 1
Peraza [77]

Renny VEGA - Rohel BRICENO, Julio MACHADO•, Edwin PERAZA, AMARAL, Edgar JIMENEZ, Jesus GOMEZ (Romulo OTERO 74), Juan GUERRA (Luis GONZALEZ 84), Jesus MEZA, Victor FERREIRA, Anthony URIBE (Angelo PENA 64). Tr: Ceferonio BENCOMO

Peñarol 1
Estoyanoff [27]

Fabian CARINI - Juan ALVEZ, Alejandro GONZALEZ, Dario RODRIGUEZ, Carlos VALDEZ, Nicolas FREITAS•, Luis AGUIAR• (Emiliano ALBIN 46), Sebastian CRISTOFORO• (Joao PEDRO 85), Fabian ESTOYANOFF, Marcelo ZALAYETA, Rodrigo MORA (Marcel NOVICK 73). Tr: Gregorio PEREZ

COPA LIBERTADORES 2012

GRUPO 1		Pl	W	D	L	F	A	Pts	BRA	BRA	BOL	PER
Santos	BRA	6	4	1	1	12	5	**13**		3-1	2-0	2-0
Internacional	BRA	6	2	2	2	10	6	**8**	1-1		5-0	2-0
The Strongest	BOL	6	2	1	3	5	11	**7**	2-1	1-1		2-1
Juan Aurich	PER	6	2	0	4	4	9	**6**	1-3	1-0	1-0	

Beira-Rio, Porto Alegre
7-02-2012, Att: 28 968, Ref: Prudente URU
Internacional 2
Oscar [23], Datolo [89]
MURIEL - INDIO (BOLIVAR 46), KLEBER, RODRIGO MOLEDO, Pablo GUINAZU, Mario BOLATTI (Jesus DATOLO 74), Andres D'ALESSANDRO•, ELTON, OSCAR, LEANDRO DAMIAO, DAGOBERTO• (JOAO PAULO 79). Tr: DORIVAL JUNIOR

Juan Aurich 0

Diego PENNY - Leandro FLEITAS, Nelinho QUINA•, Luis GUADALUPE, Manuel UGAZ (Julio CAICEDO 62), Cesar ORTIZ••◆36, Jhon VALENCIA, Roberto GUIZASOLA, William CHIROQUE, Jorge MOLINA, Ysrael ZUNIGA (Israel KAHN 76). Tr: Diego UMANA

Hernando Siles, La Paz
15-02-2012, Att: 19 084, Ref: Vera ECU
The Strongest 2
Cristaldo [33], Ramallo [93+]
Daniel VACA - Delio OJEDA, Luis MENDEZ, Ernesto CRISTALDO (Rodrigo RAMALLO• 67), Enrique PARADA•, Nelvin SOLIZ, Jair TORRICO, Alejandro CHUMACERO, Luis Hernan MELGAR (Sebastian GONZALEZ• 82), Sacha LIMA•, Pablo ESCOBAR. Tr: Mauricio SORIA

Santos 1
Henrique [9]
RAFAEL• - Jorge FUCILE, EDU DRACENA, DURVAL, PARA, AROUCA•, HENRIQUE, GANSO, IBSON (ELANO 58), BORGES (ALAN KARDEC 67), NEYMAR•. Tr: MURICY RAMALHO

Hernando Siles, La Paz
23-02-2012, Att: 8257, Ref: Beligoy ARG
The Strongest 2
Gonzalez [26], Escobar [76]
Daniel VACA - Delio OJEDA, Luis MENDEZ•, Ernesto CRISTALDO, Nelvin SOLIZ•, Jair TORRICO, Alejandro CHUMACERO, Sacha LIMA, Sebastian GONZALEZ (Matias MARCHESINI 83), Pablo ESCOBAR• (Leonel REYES 90), Rodrigo RAMALLO (Ronaille CALHEIRA 51). Tr: Mauricio SORIA

Juan Aurich 1
OG [23]
Diego PENNY• - Leandro FLEITAS•, Nelinho QUINA, Luis GUADALUPE, Manuel UGAZ• (Orlando CONTRERAS 46), Jhon VALENCIA, Roberto GUIZASOLA, Jorge MOLINA, Anderson CUETO (Jeickson REYES 73), Ysrael ZUNIGA, Mauricio MONTES. Tr: Diego UMANA

Urbano Caldeira, Santos
7-03-2012, Att: 12 857, Ref: Roman BRA
Santos 3
Neymar 3 [18p 54 64]
RAFAEL - Jorge FUCILE (BRUNO RODRIGO 84), EDU DRACENA, DURVAL, JUAN•, AROUCA, HENRIQUE, GANSO, IBSON (ELANO• 79), BORGES (ALAN KARDEC 75), NEYMAR•. Tr: MURICY RAMALHO

Internacional 1
Leandro Damiao [63]
MURIEL - INDIO•, NEI, KLEBER, RODRIGO MOLEDO, Pablo GUINAZU, Mario BOLATTI• (TINGA• 62), Andres D'ALESSANDRO• (DAGOBERTO• 62), ELTON• (Jesus DATOLO 46), OSCAR, LEANDRO DAMIAO. Tr: DORIVAL JUNIOR

Beira-Rio, Porto Alegre
13-03-2012, Att: 25 098, Ref: Arias PAR
Internacional 5
Dagoberto [3], Leandro Damiao 3 [6 56 72], Jo [80]
MURIEL - INDIO, NEI, KLEBER•, RODRIGO MOLEDO, Pablo GUINAZU, Mario BOLATTI (JO 78), OSCAR, Jesus DATOLO (GILBERTO 79), LEANDRO DAMIAO (JO 81), DAGOBERTO. Tr: DORIVAL JUNIOR

The Strongest 0
Daniel VACA - Matias MARCHESINI, Delio OJEDA, Luis MENDEZ•, Ernesto CRISTALDO• Enrique PARADA• (Nelvin SOLIZ 46), Jair TORRICO, Alejandro CHUMACERO, Sacha LIMA (Marco PAZ 46), Sebastian GONZALEZ (Luis Hernan MELGAR 80), Pablo ESCOBAR. Tr: Mauricio SORIA

Elias Aguirre, Chiclayo
15-03-2012, Att: 10 264, Ref: Silvera URU
Juan Aurich 1
Tejada [14]
Diego PENNY - Leandro FLEITAS•, Nelinho QUINA, Luis GUADALUPE••◆57, Alfredo ROJAS, Jhon VALENCIA•, Israel KAHN, Roberto GUIZASOLA•, Anderson CUETO (Orlando CONTRERAS• 60), Luis TEJADA, Ysrael ZUNIGA. Tr: Diego UMANA

Santos 3
Fucile [35], Ganso [39], Borges [68]
RAFAEL - Jorge FUCILE•, Edu DRACENA, DURVAL, JUAN•, AROUCA, HENRIQUE (ADRIANO 90), GANSO, IBSON, BORGES (ALAN KARDEC 80), NEYMAR. Tr: MURICY RAMALHO

Hernando Siles, La Paz
21-03-2012, Att: 11 176, Ref: Ponce ECU
The Strongest 1
Ramallo [46]
Daniel VACA - Delio OJEDA, Luis MENDEZ•, Ernesto CRISTALDO, Gerson GARCIA, Jair TORRICO, Alejandro CHUMACERO, Sacha LIMA•, Sebastian GONZALEZ (Luis Hernan MELGAR 78), Pablo ESCOBAR, Rodrigo RAMALLO (Nelvin SOLIZ 68). Tr: Uber ACOSTA

Internacional 1
Gilberto [88]
MURIEL - INDIO, NEI, KLEBER, RODRIGO MOLEDO, Pablo GUINAZU (Mario BOLATTI 57), TINGA•, JOAO PAULO (JAJA 65), Jesus DATOLO•, LEANDRO DAMIAO, DAGOBERTO (GILBERTO 64). Tr: DORIVAL JUNIOR

Pacaembú, São Paulo
22-03-2012, Att: 24 435, Ref: Loustau ARG
Santos 2
Edu Dracena [15], Neymar [58]
RAFAEL - Jorge FUCILE, EDU DRACENA, DURVAL, JUAN, AROUCA•, HENRIQUE, GANSO, IBSON (ELANO 74), BORGES, NEYMAR. Tr: MURICY RAMALHO

Juan Aurich 0
Diego PENNY - Leandro FLEITAS, Orlando CONTRERAS, Nelinho QUINA, Diego MINAYA, Manuel UGAZ• (Jorge MOLINA 73), Alfredo ROJAS, Cesar ORTIZ (Jhon VALENCIA• 68), Israel KAHN, Anderson CUETO, Ysrael ZUNIGA• (Luis TEJADA 46). Tr: Diego UMANA

Beira-Rio, Porto Alegre
4-04-2012, Att: 35 530, Ref: Ricci BRA
Internacional 1
Nei [8]
MURIEL - INDIO, NEI•, KLEBER, RODRIGO MOLEDO••◆88, TINGA (GILBERTO 77), ELTON•, JESUS DATOLO (BOLIVAR 90), SANDRO SILVA•, LEANDRO DAMIAO, DAGOBERTO (JAJA 71). Tr: DORIVAL JUNIOR

Santos 1
Alan Kardec [64]
RAFAEL - Jorge FUCILE (ALAN KARDEC 64), EDU DRACENA•, DURVAL, JUAN, AROUCA, HENRIQUE, GANSO, IBSON, BORGES (ELANO 82), NEYMAR•. Tr: MURICY RAMALHO

Elias Aguirre, Chiclayo
5-04-2012, Att: 2038, Ref: Intriago ECU
Juan Aurich 1
Araujo [20]
Diego PENNY - Leandro FLEITAS, Orlando CONTRERAS•, Nelinho QUINA, Alfredo ROJAS, Cesar ORTIZ, Javier ARAUJO (Luis TEJADA 59), Israel KAHN, Roberto GUIZASOLA, William CHIROQUE, Ysrael ZUNIGA (Jhon VALENCIA 76). Tr: Diego UMANA

The Strongest 0
Daniel VACA- Matias MARCHESINI•, Luis MENDEZ, Ernesto CRISTALDO, Enrique PARADA, Nelvin SOLIZ, Jair TORRICO, Alejandro CHUMACERO, Sacha LIMA (Leonel REYES 46), Sebastian GONZALEZ (Luis Hernan MELGAR 80), Pablo ESCOBAR•. Tr: Eduardo VILLEGAS

Elias Aguirre, Chiclayo
19-04-2012, Att: 3000, Ref: Escalante ECU
Juan Aurich 1
Tejada [20]
Diego PENNY• - Leandro FLEITAS, Nelinho QUINA, Diego MINAYA, Luis GUADALUPE, Alfredo ROJAS•, William CHIROQUE, Jorge MOLINA• (Jhon VALENCIA 20), Anderson CUETO, Luis TEJADA, Ysrael ZUNIGA (Israel KAHN 83). Tr: Diego UMANA

Internacional 0
MURIEL - BOLIVAR, INDIO•, NEI, KLEBER, TINGA• (JOAO PAULO 83), Andres D'ALESSANDRO•, Jesus DATOLO (JO 64), SANDRO SILVA, LEANDRO DAMIAO, GILBERTO (JAJA 46). Tr: DORIVAL JUNIOR

Urbano Caldeira, Santos
19-04-2012, Att: 11 761, Ref: Quintana PAR
Santos 2
Alan Kardec [85], Neymar [87]
RAFAEL - EDU DRACENA, DURVAL, JUAN, AROUCA (IBSON 75), HENRIQUE• (ALAN KARDEC 67), ELANO (FELIPE ANDERSON 77), GANSO, ADRIANO•, BORGES, NEYMAR. Tr: MURICY RAMALHO

The Strongest 0
Daniel VACA• - Matias MARCHESINI, Luis MENDEZ, Ernesto CRISTALDO, Enrique PARADA•, Nelvin SOLIZ, Jair TORRICO, Alejandro CHUMACERO, Leonel REYES• (Rodrigo RAMALLO 85), Luis Hernan MELGAR (Sacha LIMA 76), Pablo ESCOBAR. Tr: Eduardo VILLEGAS

GRUPO 2

GRUPO 2		Pl	W	D	L	F	A	Pts	ARG	ECU	BRA	PAR
Lanús	ARG	6	3	1	2	11	6	10		1-0	1-1	6-0
Emelec	ECU	6	3	0	3	7	8	9	0-2		3-2	1-0
Flamengo	BRA	6	2	2	2	12	10	8	3-0	1-0		3-3
Olimpia	PAR	6	2	1	3	10	16	7	2-1	2-3	3-2	

George Capwell, Guayaquil
9-02-2012, Att: 10830, Ref: Roldan COL
Emelec 1
Figueroa [50p]
Esteban DREER - Oscar BAGUI, Gabriel ACHILIER, Enner VALENCIA (Walter IZA 81), Pedro QUINONEZ•, Jose QUINONEZ, Fernando GIMENEZ, Fernando GAIBOR, Marlon DE JESUS (Nicolas VIGNERI 59), Marcos MONDAINI (Carlos QUINONEZ 64), Luciano FIGUEROA. Tr: Julio FLEITAS
Olimpia 0
Martin SILVA - Sergio ARIOSA (Pablo ZEBALLOS 61♦90), Francisco NAJERA•, Enrique MEZA•, Adrian ROMERO, Fabio CABALLERO•, Sergio ORTEMAN, Vladimir MARIN, Osvaldo HOBECKER (Renzo REVOREDO 73), Maxi BIANCUCCHI (Sergio ALMIRON 89), Luis CABALLERO. Tr: Gerardo PELUSSO

Ciudad de Lanús, Buenos Aires
15-02-2012, Att: 12153, Ref: Silvera URU
Lanús 1
Carranza [74]
Agustin MARCHESIN - Paolo GOLTZ, Luciano BALBI, Carlos ARAUJO, Diego BRAGHIERI (Carlos IZQUIERDOZ 90), Matias FRITZLER, Mauricio PEREYRA (Cesar CARRANZA 73), Eduardo LEDESMA, Juan NEIRA (Silvio ROMERO 63), Diego VALERI, Mariano PAVONE. Tr: Gabriel SCHURRER
Flamengo 1
Leo Moura [45]
FELIPE - LEO MOURA, WELINTON SOUZA•, JUNIOR CESAR, DAVID, AIRTON (Dario BOTTINELLI• 72), WILLIANS, RONALDINHO, RENATO• (LUIZ ANTONIO 87), Claudio MALDONADO (DEIVID 90). Tr: Joel SANTANA

Nicolás Leoz, Asuncion
23-02-2012, Att: 6625, Ref: Ubriaco URU
Olimpia 2
Marin [24], Biancucchi [79]
Martin SILVA• - Renzo REVOREDO•, Enrique MEZA, Salustiano CANDIA, Eduardo ROMERO, Fabio CABALLERO (Carlos PAREDES 83), Sergio ORTEMAN, Vladimir MARIN, Osvaldo HOBECKER (Eduardo ARANDA 78), Luis CABALLERO (Sergio ALMIRON 69), Maxi BIANCUCCHI. Tr: Gerardo PELUSSO
Lanús 1
Araujo [71]
Agustin MARCHESIN• - Paolo GOLTZ•, Luciano BALBI, Carlos ARAUJO•, Diego BRAGHIERI•, Matias FRITZLER•, Mauricio PEREYRA (Silvio ROMERO 5), Mario REGUEIRO, Diego GONZALEZ, Diego VALERI (Juan NEIRA 35), Mariano PAVONE. Tr: Gabriel SCHURRER

Engenhao, Rio de Janeiro
8-03-2012, Att: 31859, Ref: Ubriaco URU
Flamengo 1
Vagner Love [48]
PAULO VICTOR - LEO MOURA (NEGUEBA 30), WELINTON SOUZA (DEIVID 46), Marcos GONZALEZ, JUNIOR CESAR, DAVID, RONALDINHO, MURALHA, Dario BOTTINELLI•, LUIZ ANTONIO, VAGNER LOVE. Tr: Joel SANTANA
Emelec 0
Esteban DREER - Oscar BAGUI, Gabriel ACHILIER, Enner VALENCIA, Pedro QUINONEZ•, Jose QUINONEZ• (Carlos QUINONEZ• 42), Fernando GIMENEZ, Fernando GAIBOR, Luciano FIGUEROA (Nicolas VIGNERI 62), Marlon DE JESUS♦45, Marcos MONDAINI (Walter IZA 46). Tr: Julio FLEITAS

Ciudad de Lanús, Buenos Aires
13-03-2012, Att: 3872, Ref: Carrillo PER
Lanús 1
Pavone [71]
Agustin MARCHESIN - Paolo GOLTZ, Luciano BALBI, Carlos ARAUJO•, Diego BRAGHIERI, Matias FRITZLER•, Mario REGUEIRO, Mauro CAMORANESI• (Eduardo LEDESMA 74), Diego GONZALEZ (Silvio ROMERO 64), Diego VALERI (Guido PIZARRO 87), Mariano PAVONE. Tr: Joel SANTANA
Emelec 0
Esteban DREER - Fulton FRANCIS•, Carlos QUINONEZ, Gabriel ACHILIER, Jose QUINONEZ♦37, Enner VALENCIA (Marcos MONDAINI 84), Pedro QUINONEZ (Polo WILA 85), Fernando GIMENEZ, Fernando GAIBOR•, Nicolas VIGNERI (Wilson MORANTE 43), Luciano FIGUEROA. Tr: Julio FLEITAS

Engenhao, Rio de Janeiro
15-03-2012, Att: 30755, Ref: Buitrago COL
Flamengo 3
Bottinelli [37], Ronaldinho [56p], Luiz Antonio [63]
PAULO VICTOR - Marcos GONZALEZ, JUNIOR CESAR, DAVID, RAFAEL GALHARDO•, RONALDINHO, MURALHA, Dario BOTTINELLI•, LUIZ ANTONIO, THOMAS (NEGUEBA•79), VAGNER LOVE. Tr: Joel SANTANA
Olimpia 0
Martin SILVA• - Francisco NAJERA, Enrique MEZA, Sergio ARIOSA, Adrian ROMERO•, Sergio ORTEMAN• (Osvaldo HOBECKER 73), Vladimir MARIN•, Fabio CABALLERO, Eduardo ARANDA• (Pablo ZEBALLOS), Luis CABALLERO•. Tr: Gerardo PELUSSO

George Capwell, Guayaquil
20-03-2012, Att: 12874, Ref: Osses CHI
Emelec 0
Esteban DREER - Oscar BAGUI, Gabriel ACHILIER, Wilson MORANTE•, Pedro QUINONEZ• (Polo WILA• 72), Angel MENA (Pablo PALACIOS 58), Enner VALENCIA•, Fernando GIMENEZ, Fernando GAIBOR• (Efren MERA 70), Marlon DE JESUS, Luciano FIGUEROA. Tr: Julio FLEITAS
Lanús 2
Regueiro 2 [5] [87p]
Agustin MARCHESIN - Paolo GOLTZ, Luciano BALBI (Maximiliano VELAZQUEZ 23), Carlos ARAUJO, Diego BRAGHIERI•, Matias FRITZLER, Mario REGUEIRO•, Mauro CAMORANESI (Diego GONZALEZ 81), Guido PIZARRO, Diego VALERI (Eduardo LEDESMA 77), Mariano PAVONE. Tr: Gabriel SCHURRER

Defensores del Chaco, Asuncion
28-03-2012, Att: 31154, Ref: Osses CHI
Olimpia 3
Orteman [6], Zeballos [52], Aranda [70]
Martin SILVA• - Sergio ARIOSA, Francisco NAJERA•, Enrique MEZA•, Adrian ROMERO•, Fabio CABALLERO (Carlos PAREDES 83), Eduardo ARANDA•, Sergio ORTEMAN, Vladimir MARIN (Osvaldo HOBECKER 87), Pablo ZEBALLOS (Maxi BIANCUCCHI 75), Luis CABALLERO•. Tr: Gerardo PELUSSO
Flamengo 2
Vagner Love [48], Bottinelli [77]
FELIPE - LEO MOURA, Marcos GONZALEZ, JUNIOR CESAR, DAVID• (WELINTON SOUZA 56), WILLIANS, RONALDINHO, MURALHA (DEIVID 71), Dario BOTTINELLI•, LUIZ ANTONIO, VAGNER LOVE. Tr: Joel SANTANA

Ciudad de Lanús, Buenos Aires
3-04-2012, Att: 12141, Ref: Rivera PER
Lanús 6
Pavone 2 [13] [54], Camoranesi [29], Regueiro [70], Valeri [77], Romero [84]
Agustin MARCHESIN - Paolo GOLTZ, Luciano BALBI, Carlos ARAUJO, Diego BRAGHIERI•, Matias FRITZLER, Mario REGUEIRO (Silvio ROMERO 76), Mauro CAMORANESI (Mauricio PEREYRA 71), Guido PIZARRO•, Diego VALERI, Mariano PAVONE (Cesar CARRANZA 79). Tr: Gabriel SCHURRER
Olimpia 0
Martin SILVA - Francisco NAJERA, Enrique MEZA•, Sergio ARIOSA, Adrian ROMERO•, Sergio ORTEMAN, Vladimir MARIN (Osvaldo HOBECKER 37), Fabio CABALLERO (Carlos PAREDES 81), Eduardo ARANDA, Pablo ZEBALLOS, Luis CABALLERO (Arnaldo CASTORINO 80). Tr: Gerardo PELUSSO

George Capwell, Guayaquil
4-04-2012, Att: 16701, Ref: Vazquez URU
Emelec 1
Figueroa 2 [33] [82], Gaibor [90p]
Esteban DREER - Oscar BAGUI, Gabriel ACHILIER•, Wilson MORANTE, Enner VALENCIA (Angel MENA 56), Pedro QUINONEZ (Mariano MINA 58), Jose QUINONEZ, Fernando GIMENEZ, Fernando GAIBOR•, Marlon DE JESUS, Marcos MONDAINI 65), Luciano FIGUEROA. Tr: Julio FLEITAS
Flamengo 2
OG [8], Deivid [42]
FELIPE - LEO MOURA, WELINTON SOUZA, Marcos GONZALEZ, JUNIOR CESAR, WILLIANS, RONALDINHO, MURALHA (LUIZ ANTONIO 80), Dario BOTTINELLI (MAGAL 82), DEIVID (GUSTAVO• 69), VAGNER LOVE. Tr: Joel SANTANA

Engenhao, Rio de Janeiro
12-04-2012, Att: 15932, Ref: Roldan COL
Flamengo 3
Welinton [17], Deivid [41], Luiz Antonio [49]
FELIPE - LEO MOURA, WELINTON SOUZA•, Marcos GONZALEZ, JUNIOR CESAR, WILLIANS (MURALHA 54), RONALDINHO, Dario BOTTINELLI, LUIZ ANTONIO, DEIVID (THOMAS 88), VAGNER LOVE. Tr: Joel SANTANA
Lanús 0
Agustin MARCHESIN - Paolo GOLTZ, Luciano BALBI, Carlos ARAUJO, Diego BRAGHIERI, Matias FRITZLER, Mario REGUEIRO, Guido PIZARRO, Diego GONZALEZ• (Eduardo LEDESMA 73), Diego VALERI (Mauricio PEREYRA 83), Mariano PAVONE. Tr: Gabriel SCHURRER

Defensores del Chaco, Asuncion
12-04-2012, Att: 26891, Ref: Silvera URU
Olimpia 2
Castorino [45], Zeballos [91+]
Martin SILVA (Victor CENTURION 64) - Francisco NAJERA (Maxi BIANCUCCHI 77), Enrique MEZA• (Salustiano CANDIA 50), Sergio ARIOSA, Adrian ROMERO, Sergio ORTEMAN, Vladimir MARIN, Fabio CABALLERO, Eduardo ARANDA, Pablo ZEBALLOS, Arnaldo CASTORINO. Tr: Gerardo PELUSSO
Emelec 3
Mondaini [66], Mena [87], Quinonez [92+]
Esteban DREER - Oscar BAGUI•, Gabriel ACHILIER•, Wilson MORANTE, Enner VALENCIA, Pedro QUINONEZ• (Polo WILA 75), Jose QUINONEZ•, Fernando GIMENEZ (Marlon DE JESUS 83), Fernando GAIBOR (Angel MENA• 59), Marcos MONDAINI, Luciano FIGUEROA. Tr: Julio FLEITAS

COPA LIBERTADORES 2012

GRUPO 3		Pl	W	D	L	F	A	Pts	CHI	BOL	COL	CHI
Unión Española	CHI	6	3	1	2	10	7	10		2-1	2-0	1-1
Bolívar	BOL	6	3	1	2	9	7	10	1-3		2-1	3-0
Atlético Junior	COL	6	2	1	3	8	8	7	2-1	0-1		3-0
Universidad Católica	CHI	6	1	3	2	6	11	6	2-1	1-1	2-2	

Santa Laura, Santiago
8-02-2012, Att: 4935, Ref: Quitana PAR
Union Española 2
Herrera [64], Cordero [65]
Eduardo LOBOS - Marco HIDALGO, Jorge AMPUERO (Francisco ALARCON 78), Braulio LEAL, Gonzalo VILLAGRA, Diego SCOTTI, Rodolfo MADRID, Fernando CORDERO, Gonzalo BARRIGA, Emanuel HERRERA, Sebastian JAIME (Jean Paul PINEDA 84). Tr: Jose SIERRA
Atlético Junior 0
Sebastian VIERA - Hector QUINONES, Daniel BRICENO, Braynner GARCIA•, Jaider ROMERO (Juan Gilberto NUNEZ• 56), Giovanni HERNANDEZ, Luis NARVAEZ•, Vladimir HERNANDEZ (Victor CORTES 76), Jossymar GOMEZ, Luis PAEZ• (Michael BALANTA• 59), Luis Carlos RUIZ. Tr: Jose HERNANDEZ

San Carlos de Apoquindo, Santiago
9-02-2012, Att: 10475, Ref: Loustau ARG
Universidad Católica 1
Ovelar [43]
Cristopher TOSELLI - Cristian ALVAREZ, David HENRIQUEZ, Francisco SILVA•, Felipe GUTIERREZ, Michael RIOS• (Hans MARTINEZ 65), Kevin HARBOTTLE (Nicolas CASTILLO 65), Matias CAMPOS TORO, Stefano MAGNASCO (Rodrigo VALENZUELA• 81), Roberto OVELAR, Nicolas TRECCO. Tr: Mario LEPE
Bolívar 1
Ferreira [37]
Marcos ARGUELLO - Edemir RODRIGUEZ, Gabriel VALVERDE•, Lorgio ALVAREZ (Leonel JUSTINIANO 74), Pablo FRONTINI, Jhasmani CAMPOS (Juan ARCE 62), Lucas SCAGLIA•, Abdon REYES (Damian LIZIO 52), Rudy CARDOZO, Walter FLORES••♦71, William FERREIRA. Tr: Guillermo HOYOS

Hernando Siles, La Paz
21-02-2012, Att: 11502, Ref: Caceres PAR
Bolívar 1
Rodriguez [1]
Marcos ARGUELLO - Edemir RODRIGUEZ, Gabriel VALVERDE•, Lorgio ALVAREZ, Pablo FRONTINI, Lucas SCAGLIA (Jeison SIQUITA 55), Abdon REYES, Rudy CARDOZO, Damian LIZIO (Jhasmani CAMPOS 72), Leonel JUSTINIANO (Juan ARCE 64), William FERREIRA. Tr: Guillermo HOYOS
Union Española 3
Diaz [62], Herrera [65], Pineda [85]
Eduardo LOBOS - Marco HIDALGO, Jorge AMPUERO, Braulio LEAL, Gonzalo VILLAGRA, Diego SCOTTI•, Fernando CORDERO, Gonzalo BARRIGA (Dagoberto CURRIMILLA 84), Mauro DIAZ (Rodolfo MADRID 65), Emanuel HERRERA, Sebastian JAIME (Jean Paul PINEDA 79). Tr: Jose SIERRA

San Carlos de Apoquindo, Santiago
23-02-2012, Att: 8861, Ref: Lunati ARG
Universidad Católica 2
Gutierrez 2 [19] [26]
Cristopher TOSELLI - Enzo ANDIA, Cristian ALVAREZ, Francisco SILVA (Matias MIER 86), Jorge ORMENO, Felipe GUTIERREZ, Kevin HARBOTTLE (Nicolas CASTILLO 77), Matias CAMPOS TORO, Stefano MAGNASCO•, Roberto OVELAR, Nicolas TRECCO (Francisco PIZARRO 65). Tr: Mario LEPE
Atlético Junior 2
Hernandez [52], Quinones [60]
Sebastian VIERA - Andres GONZALEZ, Anselmo DE ALMEIDA•, Hector QUINONES, Ivan VELEZ, Breiner BELALCAZAR•, Giovanni HERNANDEZ, Luis NARVAEZ• (Braynner GARCIA 83), Vladimir HERNANDEZ•, Sherman CARDENAS (Luis Carlos RUIZ 46), Luis PAEZ (Juan GILBERTO NUNEZ 77). Tr: Jose HERNANDEZ

Santa Laura, Santiago
6-03-2012, Att: 9593, Ref: Puga CHI
Union Española 1
Herrera [45]
Eduardo LOBOS - Jorge AMPUERO•, Braulio LEAL•, Gonzalo VILLAGRA, Diego SCOTTI•, Rodolfo MADRID, Dagoberto CURRIMILLA, Mauro DIAZ, Jean Paul PINEDA (Gonzalo BARRIGA 73), Emanuel HERRERA (Emiliano VECCHIO 89), Sebastian JAIME. Tr: Jose SIERRA
Universidad Católica 1
Andia [38]
Cristopher TOSELLI - Marko BISKUPOVIC•, Enzo ANDIA•, Matias PEREZ, Francisco SILVA••♦88, Rodrigo VALENZUELA•, Felipe GUTIERREZ• (Stefano MAGNASCO 90), Michael RIOS• (Jorge ORMENO 70), Kevin HARBOTTLE (Francisco PIZARRO 69), Matias CAMPOS TORO, Roberto OVELAR. Tr: Mario LEPE

Metropolitano, Barranquilla
8-03-2012, Att: 10320, Ref: Soto VEN
Atlético Junior 0
Sebastian VIERA - Andres GONZALEZ, Anselmo DE ALMEIDA, Hector QUINONES, Ivan VELEZ, Braynner GARCIA•, Giovanni HERNANDEZ, Cesar FAWCETT, Jossymar GOMEZ (Sherman CARDENAS 70), Luis PAEZ, Luis Carlos RUIZ (Victor CORTES• 75). Tr: Jose HERNANDEZ
Bolívar 1
Ferreira [80]
Marcos ARGUELLO - Edemir RODRIGUEZ (Ronald EGUINO 90), Gabriel VALVERDE, Pablo FRONTINI•, Jhasmani CAMPOS, Lucas SCAGLIA, Rudy CARDOZO•, Damian LIZIO (Abdon REYES 61), Walter FLORES, Juan ARCE (Lorgio ALVAREZ 76), William FERREIRA. Tr: Guillermo HOYOS

Hernando Siles, La Paz
20-03-2012, Att: 8608, Ref: Rivera PER
Bolívar 2
Alvarez [30], Campos [39]
Marcos ARGUELLO - Edemir RODRIGUEZ•, Gabriel VALVERDE, Lorgio ALVAREZ, Pablo FRONTINI, Lucas SCAGLIA• (Damir MIRANDA•74), Jhasmani CAMPOS (Ronald EGUINO 80), Rudy CARDOZO, Walter FLORES, Juan ARCE, William FERREIRA (Damian LIZIO 54). Tr: Guillermo HOYOS
Atlético Junior 1
Ruiz [67]
Sebastian VIERA - Andres GONZALEZ•, Anselmo DE ALMEIDA•, Hector QUINONES (Victor CORTES 63), Ivan VELEZ, Braynner GARCIA, Jaider ROMERO•, Giovanni HERNANDEZ (Cesar FAWCETT 46), Sherman CARDENAS (Norvey OROZCO 80), Michael BALANTA, Luis Carlos RUIZ. Tr: Jose HERNANDEZ

San Carlos de Apoquindo, Santiago
28-03-2012, Att: 9741, Ref: Polic CHI
Universidad Católica 2
Ovelar [7], Gazale [87]
Cristopher TOSELLI - Enzo ANDIA, Cristian ALVAREZ•, Felipe GUTIERREZ, Michael RIOS (Jorge ORMENO• 61), Matias CAMPOS TORO••♦78, Gonzalo SEPULVEDA, Stefano MAGNASCO, Roberto OVELAR•, Francisco PIZARRO (Daud GAZALE 70), Nicolas TRECCO (Marko BISKUPOVIC 81). Tr: Mario LEPE
Union Española 1
Villagra [85]
Eduardo LOBOS - Jorge AMPUERO•, Braulio LEAL, Gonzalo VILLAGRA, Diego SCOTTI, Fernando CORDERO, Gonzalo BARRIGA (Leonel MENA 71), Dagoberto CURRIMILLA, Mauro DIAZ (Emiliano VECCHIO 57), Emanuel HERRERA, Sebastian JAIME. Tr: Jose SIERRA

Metropolitano, Barranquilla
5-04-2012, Att: 6668, Ref: Oliveira BRA
Atlético Junior 3
Velez [45], Paez [85], Hernandez [90]
Carlos RODRIGUEZ - Anselmo DE ALMEIDA, Ivan VELEZ, Braynner GARCIA, Harold MACIAS•, Cesar FAWCETT, Breiner BELALCAZAR•, Juan GILBERTO NUNEZ (Michael BALANTA 57), Sherman CARDENAS (Luis PAEZ 67), Victor CORTES (Vladimir HERNANDEZ 46), Luis Carlos RUIZ. Tr: Jose HERNANDEZ
Universidad Católica 0
Cristopher TOSELLI - Marko BISKUPOVIC, Enzo ANDIA•, Cristian ALVAREZ, Francisco SILVA, Felipe GUTIERREZ (Jorge ORMENO 66), Michael RIOS (Matias MIER 66), Stefano MAGNASCO•, Roberto OVELAR, Francisco PIZARRO•, Nicolas TRECCO (Daud GAZALE• 46). Tr: Mario LEPE

Santa Laura, Santiago
10-04-2012, Att: 5297, Ref: Lopes BRA
Union Española 2
Leal [17], Herrera [66]
Eduardo LOBOS - Marco HIDALGO, Jorge AMPUERO, Braulio LEAL, Gonzalo VILLAGRA, Diego SCOTTI, Fernando CORDERO, Leonel MENA (Rodolfo MADRID 46), Mauro DIAZ (Dagoberto CURRIMILLA 90), Emanuel HERRERA, Sebastian JAIME (Jean Paul PINEDA 78). Tr: Jose SIERRA
Bolívar 1
Cantero [82]
Marcos ARGUELLO - Edemir RODRIGUEZ•, Gabriel VALVERDE, Lorgio ALVAREZ, Pablo FRONTINI•, Jhasmani CAMPOS•, Rudy CARDOZO, Damian LIZIO (Abdon REYES 76), Walter FLORES•, Ever CANTERO, Juan ARCE. Tr: Guillermo HOYOS

Metropolitano, Barranquilla
17-04-2012, Att: 3103, Ref: Beligoy ARG
Atlético Junior 2
Cardenas [22p], Paez [34p]
Carlos RODRIGUEZ♦30 - Hector QUINONES, Daniel BRICENO, Ivan VELEZ, Braynner GARCIA•, Harold MACIAS, Breiner BELALCAZAR, Juan GILBERTO NUNEZ (Vladimir HERNANDEZ 62), Sherman CARDENAS (Luis Carlos RUIZ 62), Luis PAEZ, Victor CORTES (Jose Luis CHUNGA• 32). Tr: Jose HERNANDEZ
Union Española 1
Vecchio [12]
Eduardo LOBOS• - Marco HIDALGO• (Emanuel HERRERA 46), Rafael OLARRA, Braulio LEAL• (Gonzalo VILLAGRA 66), Diego SCOTTI, Emiliano VECCHIO, Leonel MENA, Dagoberto CURRIMILLA, Mauro DIAZ, Jean Paul PINEDA, Sebastian JAIME (Fernando CORDERO 57). Tr: Jose SIERRA

Hernando Siles, La Paz
17-04-2012, Att: 15734, Ref: Vera ECU
Bolívar 3
Frontini [1], Flores [27], Lizio [48]
Marcos ARGUELLO (Romel QUINONEZ 85), Edemir RODRIGUEZ, Gabriel VALVERDE, Lorgio ALVAREZ, Pablo FRONTINI, Jhasmani CAMPOS, Rudy CARDOZO, Damian LIZIO (Ronald EGUINO 83), Walter FLORES, Ever CANTERO, Juan ARCE (Abdon REYES 82). Tr: Guillermo HOYOS
Universidad Católica 0
Cristopher TOSELLI - Enzo ANDIA, Cristian ALVAREZ•, Francisco SILVA (Kevin HARBOTTLE 46), Felipe GUTIERREZ, Michael RIOS, Matias CAMPOS TORO (Matias PEREZ 59), Daud GAZALE, Roberto OVELAR, Francisco PIZARRO (Gonzalo SEPULVEDA• 55). Tr: Mario LEPE

PART THREE – THE CONTINENTAL CONFEDERATIONS

GRUPO 4		Pl	W	D	L	F	A	Pts	BRA	ARG	ARG	VEN
Fluminense	BRA	6	5	0	1	7	4	**15**		0-2	1-0	1-0
Boca Juniors	ARG	6	4	1	1	9	3	**13**	1-2		2-0	2-0
Arsenal	ARG	6	2	0	4	6	7	**6**	1-2	1-2		3-0
Zamora	VEN	6	0	1	5	0	8	**1**	0-1	0-0	0-1	

Engenhao, Rio de Janeiro
7-02-2012, Att: 28 928, Ref: Arias PAR
Fluminense 1
Fred [2]
Diego CAVALIERI - Leandro EUZEBIO♦90, CARLINHOS, ANDERSON, EDINHO, DIGUINHO (DIGAO 90), WAGNER♦76, DECO• (WELLINGTON NEM 73), BRUNO, FRED•, RAFAEL SOBIS (THIAGO NEVES 65). Tr: ABEL BRAGA
Arsenal 0
Christian CAMPESTRINI• - Lisandro LOPEZ•, Guillermo BURDISSO, Hugo NERVO (Adrian GONZALEZ 81), Carlos CARBONERO, Damian PEREZ, Nicolas AGUIRRE♦76), Gaston ESMERADO (Diego TORRES• 65), Ivan MARCONE, Luciano LEGUIZAMON, Emilio ZELAYA (Jorge CORDOBA 73). Tr: Gustavo ALFARO

Agustin Tovar, Barinas
14-02-2012, Att: 14 853, Ref: Buitrago COL
Zamora 0
Alvaro FORERO - Jaime BUSTAMANTE•, Nelson SEMPERENA, Rennier RODRIGUEZ, Moises GALEZO, Engelberth BRICENO, Cesar Alexander GONZALEZ, Dario FIGUEROA (Gregory LANCKEN 90), Luis VARGAS•, Gabriel TORRES (Oscar NORIEGA 81), Luis YANEZ (Jhon CORDOBA 64). Tr: Oscar GIL
Boca Juniors 0
Agustin ORION - Rolando SCHIAVI, Clemente RODRIGUEZ, Facundo RONCAGLIA, Juan INSAURRALDE, Diego RIVERO (Cristian CHAVEZ 68), Roman RIQUELME, Walter ERVITI (Pablo LEDESMA• 77), Leandro SOMOZA, Tanque SILVA, Dario CVITANICH (Pablo MOUCHE 61). Tr: Julio FALCIONI

Julio Grondona, Buenos Aires
21-02-2012, Att: 390, Ref: Osses CHI
Arsenal 3
Ortiz [1], Carbonero [15], Leguizamon [43]
Christian CAMPESTRINI• - Lisandro LOPEZ•, Guillermo BURDISSO, Cristian TROMBETTA•, Jorge ORTIZ (Gaston ESMERADO 62), Juan CAFFA (Claudio MOSCA 62), Carlos CARBONERO, Gonzalo ESPINOZA, Adrian GONZALEZ, Jorge CORDOBA (Gustavo BLANCO LESCHUK 82), Luciano LEGUIZAMON. Tr: Gustavo ALFARO
Zamora 0
Alvaro FORERO• - Jaime BUSTAMANTE, Dollbys RODRIGUEZ, Nelson SEMPERENA, Rennier RODRIGUEZ (Cesar GONZALEZ 46), Moises GALEZO, Engelberth BRICENO, Dario FIGUEROA (Cesar Alexander GONZALEZ 60), Luis VARGAS•, Gabriel TORRES (Cesar MARTINEZ 83), Luis YANEZ•. Tr: Oscar GIL

La Bombonera, Buenos Aires
7-03-2012, Att: 35 592, Ref: Amarilla PAR
Boca Juniors 1
Somoza [47]
Agustin ORION - Clemente RODRIGUEZ, Matias CARUZZO, Facundo RONCAGLIA•, Juan INSAURRALDE•, Diego RIVERO (Cristian CHAVEZ 63), Roman RIQUELME•, Walter ERVITI (Orlando GAONA 70), Leandro SOMOZA, Pablo MOUCHE (Sergio ARAUJO 82), Tanque SILVA. Tr: Julio FALCIONI
Fluminense 2
Fred [9], Deco [54]
DIEGO CAVALIERI - CARLINHOS, DIGAO, ANDERSON, Edwin VALENCIA, THIAGO NEVES (RAFAEL SOBIS 72), DIGUINHO•, WELLINGTON NEM, DECO (EDINHO 82), BRUNO (JEAN 67), FRED•. Tr: ABEL BRAGA

Julio Grondona, Buenos Aires
14-03-2012, Att: 5829, Ref: Lunati ARG
Arsenal 1
OG [9]
Christian CAMPESTRINI• - Lisandro LOPEZ, Guillermo BURDISSO, Hugo NERVO, Carlos CARBONERO, Damian PEREZ, Gonzalo ESPINOZA (Jorge ORTIZ 70), Nicolas AGUIRRE (Juan CAFFA 76), Ivan MARCONE, Luciano LEGUIZAMON, Emilio ZELAYA (Gustavo BLANCO LESCHUK 70). Tr: Gustavo ALFARO
Boca Juniors 2
Mouche [28], Ledesma [67]
Agustin ORION - Rolando SCHIAVI, Clemente RODRIGUEZ, Facundo RONCAGLIA, Juan INSAURRALDE, Diego RIVERO (Pablo LEDESMA 63), Roman RIQUELME, Walter ERVITI (Cristian CHAVEZ 90), Leandro SOMOZA•, Pablo MOUCHE (Juan SANCHEZ MINO 90), Tanque SILVA. Tr: Julio FALCIONI

Engenhao, Rio de Janeiro
14-03-2012, Att: 24 769, Ref: Polic CHI
Fluminense 1
Anderson [57]
DIEGO CAVALIERI - LEANDRO EUZEBIO, CARLINHOS (CARLETO 82), ANDERSON, Edwin VALENCIA, THIAGO NEVES, WELLINGTON NEM, DECO (Manuel LANZINI 74), BRUNO, FRED•, RAFAEL SOBIS (SOUZA 46). Tr: ABEL BRAGA
Zamora 0
Alvaro FORERO• - Jaime BUSTAMANTE, Dollbys RODRIGUEZ (Josmar ZAMBRANO 67), Nelson SEMPERENA, Moises GALEZO, Layneker ZAFRA•, Engelberth BRICENO, Cesar Alexander GONZALEZ (Gabriel TORRES 62), Luis VARGAS, Luis YANEZ (Jhon CORDOBA 70), Cesar MARTINEZ. Tr: Oscar GIL

La Bombonera, Buenos Aires
29-03-2012, Att: 28 224, Ref: Loustau ARG
Boca Juniors 2
Ledesma [49], Sanchez Mino [67]
Agustin ORION• - Rolando SCHIAVI, Clemente RODRIGUEZ, Facundo RONCAGLIA•, Juan INSAURRALDE, Roman RIQUELME (Dario CVITANICH 62), Walter ERVITI, Pablo LEDESMA, Leandro SOMOZA•♦37, Pablo MOUCHE (Juan SANCHEZ MINO 75), Tanque SILVA (Nicolas BLANDI 90). Tr: Julio FALCIONI
Arsenal 0
Christian CAMPESTRINI - Guillermo BURDISSO•, Victor CUESTA•, Hugo NERVO (Adrian GONZALEZ• 70), Juan CAFFA, Carlos CARBONERO, Damian PEREZ, Gonzalo ESPINOZA (Emilio ZELAYA 56), Ivan MARCONE• (Jorge ORTIZ 46), Jorge CORDOBA, Luciano LEGUIZAMON. Tr: Gustavo ALFARO

Agustin Tovar, Barinas
29-03-2012, Att: 7000, Ref: Vera ECU
Zamora 0
Alvaro FORERO - Jaime BUSTAMANTE•, Dollbys RODRIGUEZ, Nelson SEMPERENA, Moises GALEZO (Gabriel TORRES 80), Cesar GONZALEZ, Layneker ZAFRA (Josmar ZAMBRANO (Luis YANEZ 67), Luis VARGAS•, Jhon CORDOBA (Cesar MARTINEZ 57), Oscar NORIEGA. Tr: Oscar GIL
Fluminense 1
Rafael Sobis [78]
DIEGO CAVALIERI - LEANDRO EUZEBIO•, CARLINHOS, ANDERSON, Edwin VALENCIA, THIAGO NEVES (Manuel LANZINI 74), DIGUINHO, WELLINGTON NEM (RAFAEL SOBIS 75), DECO, BRUNO, FRED (RAFAEL MOURA 85). Tr: ABEL BRAGA

Agustin Tovar, Barinas
10-04-2012, Att: 2853, Ref: Quintana PAR
Zamora 0
Alvaro FORERO - Jaime BUSTAMANTE•, Dollbys RODRIGUEZ, Nelson SEMPERENA, Cesar GONZALEZ (Jhon CORDOBA 46), Layneker ZAFRA, Dario FIGUEROA (Engelberth PEREZ 26), Luis VARGAS, Gabriel TORRES, Oscar NORIEGA (Cesar Alexander GONZALEZ 81), Luilly GARCIA. Tr: Oscar GIL
Arsenal 1
Caffa [29]
Christian CAMPESTRINI• - Danilo GERLO, Cristian TROMBETTA, Victor CUESTA•, Hugo NERVO, Juan CAFFA (Claudio MOSCA 67), Gonzalo ESPINOZA, Gaston ESMERADO, Diego TORRES•, Jorge CORDOBA (Nicolas AGUIRRE 64), Gustavo BLANCO LESCHUK (Ivan MARCONE•78). Tr: Gustavo ALFARO

Engenhao, Rio de Janeiro
11-04-2012, Att: 36 263, Ref: Ubriaco URU
Fluminense 0
DIEGO CAVALIERI - LEANDRO EUZEBIO•, CARLINHOS, ANDERSON, EDINHO (JEAN 46), THIAGO NEVES, DIGUINHO•, WELLINGTON NEM, DECO, BRUNO (Manuel LANZINI 76), FRED (RAFAEL MOURA 61). Tr: ABEL BRAGA
Boca Juniors 2
Cvitanich [33], Sanchez Mino [74]
Agustin ORION - Rolando SCHIAVI, Clemente RODRIGUEZ, Facundo RONCAGLIA•, Juan INSAURRALDE, Walter ERVITI (Juan SANCHEZ MINO 70), Pablo LEDESMA, Cristian CHAVEZ (Diego RIVERO 81), Cristian ERBES, Tanque SILVA, Dario CVITANICH (Pablo MOUCHE 68). Tr: Julio FALCIONI

La Bombonera, Buenos Aires
18-04-2012, Att: 31 705, Ref: Orosco BOL
Boca Juniors 2
Blandi [67], Riquelme [74]
Sebastian SOSA - Franco SOSA, Matias CARUZZO, Gaston SAURO, Diego RIVERO, Roman RIQUELME, Cristian CHAVEZ (Orlando GAONA 83), Cristian ERBES• (Pablo LEDESMA 76), Juan SANCHEZ MINO, Pablo MOUCHE (Sergio ARAUJO 65), Nicolas BLANDI. Tr: Julio FALCIONI
Zamora 0
Alvaro FORERO - Jaime BUSTAMANTE•, Dollbys RODRIGUEZ••♦81, Nelson SEMPERENA, Moises GALEZO, Layneker ZAFRA, Josmar ZAMBRANO (Cesar GONZALEZ 63), Luis VARGAS•, Gabriel TORRES (Luilly GARCIA 77), Luis YANEZ• (Cesar GONZALEZ 80), Oscar NORIEGA. Tr: Julio QUINTERO

Julio Grondona, Buenos Aires
18-04-2012, Att: 204, Ref: Silvera URU
Arsenal 1
Aguirre [80]
Christian CAMPESTRINI♦85 - Danilo GERLO, Cristian TROMBETTA, Victor CUESTA, Jorge ORTIZ (Gaston ESMERADO 76), Juan CAFFA• (Nicolas AGUIRRE 66), Gonzalo ESPINOZA, Adrian GONZALEZ•, Diego TORRES, Jorge CORDOBA, Claudio MOSCA (Gustavo BLANCO LESCHUK 46). Tr: Gustavo ALFARO
Fluminense 2
Carlinhos [34], Rafael Moura [92+]
DIEGO CAVALIERI - LEANDRO EUZEBIO (GUM 40), CARLINHOS, ANDERSON, EDINHO (Manuel LANZINI 90), THIAGO NEVES, DIGUINHO•, WELLINGTON NEM (RAFAEL SOBIS•17), DECO•, BRUNO, RAFAEL MOURA. Tr: ABEL BRAGA

COPA LIBERTADORES 2012

GRUPO 5		Pl	W	D	L	F	A	Pts	PAR	BRA	URU	PER
Libertad	PAR	6	4	1	1	11	7	**13**		1-1	2-1	4-1
Vasco da Gama	BRA	6	4	1	1	10	6	**13**	2-0		1-2	3-2
Nacional Montevideo	URU	6	2	0	4	5	7	**6**	1-2	0-1		1-0
Alianza Lima	PER	6	1	0	5	6	12	**3**	1-2	1-2	1-0	

São Januario, Rio de Janeiro
8-02-2012, Att: 27 300, Ref: Buitrago COL
Vasco da Gama 1
Alecsandro [73]
FERNANDO PRASS - THIAGO FELTRI, RODOLFO•, DEDE, MAX (FELLIPE BASTOS• 46), EDUARDO COSTA, FELIPE (Carlos TENORIO 61), JUNINHO PERNAMBUCANO•, DIEGO SOUZA, NILTON, ALECSANDRO. Tr: CRISTOVAO

Nacional Montevideo 2
OG [30], Sanchez [46]
Leonardo BURIAN - Andres SCOTTI• (JADSON 46), Alexis ROLIN, Diego PLACENTE•, Christian NUNEZ, Israel DAMONTE•, Maximiliano CALZADA, Santiago ROMERO (Mathias ABERO 67), Matias CABRERA•, Tabare VIUDEZ•, Vicente SANCHEZ (Alvaro RECOBA 70). Tr: Marcelo GALLARDO

Nicolás Leoz, Asuncion
9-02-2012, Att: 742, Ref: Vazquez URU
Libertad 4
Civelli [46], Aquino [66p], Caballero [78], OG [90]
Rodrigo MUNOZ - Joe BIZERA, Ismael BENEGAS•, Miguel SAMUDIO, Luciano CIVELLI, Victor CACERES, Carlos BONET, Sergio AQUINO, Pablo VELAZQUEZ (Cristian MENENDEZ 75), Ariel NUNEZ (Mauro CABALLERO JR 36), Rodolfo GAMARRA (Victor AYALA 81). Tr: Jorge BURRUCHAGA

Alianza Lima 1
Arroe [27]
Salomon LIBMAN - Manuel CORRALES, Christian RAMOS•, Carlos ASCUES (Jose FERNANDEZ 68), Walter IBANEZ, Johnnier MONTANO, Edgar GONZALEZ•, Joazinho ARROE (Jorge BAZAN 59), Paulo ALBARRACIN, Paolo HURTADO, Jonathan CHARQUERO (Cristofer SOTO 76). Tr: Jose SOTO

Parque Central, Montevideo
16-02-2012, Att: 18 589, Ref: Laverni ARG
Nacional Montevideo 1
Aguirre [23]
Leonardo BURIAN - Andres SCOTTI, Alexis ROLIN, Diego PLACENTE• (Alexander MEDINA 66), Christian NUNEZ, Israel DAMONTE•, Maximiliano CALZADA (Alvaro RECOBA 61), Marcos AGUIRRE (Mathias ABERO 46), Matias CABRERA, Tabare VIUDEZ, Vicente SANCHEZ•. Tr: Marcelo GALLARDO

Libertad 2
Samudio [58], Caballero [63]
Rodrigo MUNOZ - Joe BIZERA, Ismael BENEGAS, Jonathan SANTANA (Mauro CABALLERO JR• 55), Miguel SAMUDIO, Luciano CIVELLI, Victor CACERES•, Carlos BONET, Sergio AQUINO•, Pablo VELAZQUEZ (Cristian MENENDEZ 74), Rodolfo GAMARRA (Victor AYALA 62). Tr: Jorge BURRUCHAGA

São Januario, Rio de Janeiro
6-03-2012, Att: 29 900, Ref: Abal ARG
Vasco da Gama 3
OG [18], Dede [59], Juninho [80p]
FERNANDO PRASS - THIAGO FELTRI, RODOLFO (DOUGLAS 46), FAGNER, DEDE, EDUARDO COSTA (FELIPE 46), JUNINHO PERNAMBUCANO, DIEGO SOUZA, NILTON, ALECSANDRO, WILLIAM BARBIO. Tr: CRISTOVAO

Alianza Lima 2
Charquero [16], Ibanez [85]
Salomon LIBMAN - Manuel CORRALES, Christian RAMOS•, Walter IBANEZ, Johnnier MONTANO (Jose FERNANDEZ• 70), Giancarlo CARMONA♦48, Edgar GONZALEZ, Paulo ALBARRACIN, Paolo HURTADO, Jonathan CHARQUERO (Joazinho ARROE• 64), Jorge BAZAN (Edgar VILLAMARIN 51). Tr: Jose SOTO

Estadio Nacional, Lima
13-03-2012, Att: 17 038, Ref: Roldan COL
Alianza Lima 1
Fernandez.J [15]
Salomon LIBMAN - Manuel CORRALES• (Jesus RABANAL• 71), Christian RAMOS•, Carlos ASCUES, Walter IBANEZ, Johnnier MONTANO•, Edgar GONZALEZ, Henry QUINTEROS•, Paolo HURTADO, Jonathan CHARQUERO (Jorge BAZAN 63), Jose FERNANDEZ (Cristofer SOTO 77). Tr: Jose SOTO

Nacional Montevideo 0
Leonardo BURIAN - Alexis ROLIN, Diego PLACENTE♦70, Andres SCOTTI, Christian NUNEZ (Alvaro RECOBA 54), Israel DAMONTE•♦60, Maximiliano CALZADA•, Santiago ROMERO, Tabare VIUDEZ, Alexander MEDINA (Joaquin BOGHOSSIAN 15), Vicente SANCHEZ (Gonzalo BUENO 64). Tr: Marcelo GALLARDO

Nicolás Leoz, Asuncion
14-03-2012, Att: 3847, Ref: Osses CHI
Libertad 1
Nunez [69]
Rodrigo MUNOZ - Ismael BENEGAS, Nery BAREIRO, Miguel SAMUDIO, Cristian MENENDEZ (Mauro CABALLERO Jr• 68), Luciano CIVELLI, Victor CACERES, Carlos BONET, Sergio AQUINO• (Victor AYALA 79), Ariel Nunez•♦82, Rodolfo Gamarra (Pablo Velazquez 60. Tr: Jorge Burruchaga

Vasco da Gama 1
Diego Souza [16]
FERNANDO PRASS - THIAGO FELTRI (RODOLFO 62), FAGNER, DEDE, RENATO SILVA, FELIPE, EDUARDO COSTA•, FELIPE, DIEGO SOUZA♦53, NILTON (ROMULO 72), ALECSANDRO, WILLIAM BARBIO•. Tr: CRISTOVAO

São Januario, Rio de Janeiro
21-03-2012, Att: 15 799, Ref: Roldan COL
Vasco da Gama 2
Juninho [52], Alecsandro [61]
FERNANDO PRASS - THIAGO FELTRI, DEDE, RENATO SILVA, MAX, EDUARDO COSTA (JUNINHO PERNAMBUCANO 46), FELIPE (FELLIPE BASTOS 76), ROMULO, EDER LUIS, ALECSANDRO, WILLIAM BARBIO (ALLAN 46). Tr: CRISTOVAO

Libertad 0
Rodrigo MUNOZ - Ismael BENEGAS, Joe BIZERA, Victor AYALA (Nestor CAMACHO 75), Sergio AQUINO, Miguel SAMUDIO, Cristian MENENDEZ, Luciano CIVELLI• (Marcos MELGAREJO 75), Victor CACERES, Carlos BONET, Rodolfo GAMARRA (Pablo VELAZQUEZ 67). Tr: Jorge BURRUCHAGA

Centenario, Montevideo
27-03-2012, Att: 18 036, Ref: Pitana ARG
Nacional Montevideo 1
Viudez [68]
Leonardo BURIAN - Andres SCOTTI•, Alexis ROLIN, Darwin TORRES•, Christian NUNEZ, Maximiliano CALZADA, Tabare VIUDEZ•, Facundo PIRIZ (Alvaro RECOBA 55), Matias VECINO (Santiago ROMERO• 80), Vicente SANCHEZ, Gonzalo BUENO (Mathias ABERO 73). Tr: Marcelo GALLARDO

Alianza Lima 0
Salomon LIBMAN - Manuel CORRALES•, Carlos ASCUES•, Walter IBANEZ, Giancarlo CARMONA, Edgar GONZALEZ•, Henry QUINTEROS•, Joazinho ARROE (Cristofer SOTO 90), Paolo HURTADO (Miguel CURIEL 72), Jorge BAZAN• (Cesar VIZA 83), Jose FERNANDEZ. Tr: Jose SOTO

Alejandro Villanueva, Lima
3-04-2012, Att: 7736, Ref: Laverni ARG
Alianza Lima 1
Curiel [76]
Salomon LIBMAN - Manuel CORRALES (Jesus RABANAL• 16), Carlos ASCUES, Walter IBANEZ, Giancarlo CARMONA, Edgar GONZALEZ, Henry QUINTEROS, Joazinho ARROE, Paolo HURTADO (Miguel CURIEL 60), Jorge BAZAN (Cesar VIZA 53), Jose FERNANDEZ. Tr: Jose SOTO

Vasco da Gama 2
Felipe Bastos 2 [17 70]
Fernando PRASS - THIAGO FELTRI (RODOLFO 80), FAGNER, DEDE, RENATO SILVA, FELIPE (NILTON 83♦90), DIEGO SOUZA (ALLAN 71), FELLIPE BASTOS, ROMULO, EDER LUIS, ALECSANDRO. Tr: CRISTOVAO

Nicolás Leoz, Asuncion
5-04-2012, Att: 4541, Ref: Ponce ECU
Libertad 2
Velazquez [65], Caceres [90]
Rodrigo MUNOZ - Ismael BENEGAS, Cristian NASUTI•, Luciano CIVELLI (Cristian MENENDEZ 55), Victor CACERES•, Carlos BONET, Sergio AQUINO, Jonathan SANTANA, Miguel SAMUDIO, Ariel NUNEZ (Rodolfo GAMARRA 70), Pablo VELAZQUEZ (Nestor CAMACHO 87). Tr: Jorge BURRUCHAGA

Nacional Montevideo 1
Viudez [9]
Leonardo BURIAN - Alexis ROLIN•, Mathias ABERO, Andres SCOTTI, JADSON (Facundo PIRIZ• 68), Christian NUNEZ, Israel DAMONTE•, Maximiliano CALZADA, Tabare VIUDEZ, Matias VECINO (Gonzalo BUENO 80), Vicente SANCHEZ (Alvaro RECOBA 60). Tr: Marcelo GALLARDO

Alejandro Villanueva, Lima
12-04-2012, Att: 4626, Ref: Soto VEN
Alianza Lima 1
Hurtado [22]
Jorge RIVERA - Manuel CORRALES, Carlos ASCUES, Giancarlo CARMONA•, Edgar GONZALEZ (Henry QUINTEROS• 68), Carlos BELTRAN, Paulo ALBARRACIN, Paolo HURTADO (Joazinho ARROE 46), Jorge BAZAN, Cristofer SOTO, Miguel CURIEL• (Jonathan CHARQUERO 60). Tr: Jose SOTO

Libertad 2
Camacho [53], Nunez [74]
Rodrigo MUNOZ - Ismael BENEGAS, Cristian NASUTI, Carlos BONET•, Sergio AQUINO (Victor AYALA 65), Jonathan SANTANA, Miguel SAMUDIO, Cristian MENENDEZ (Pablo VELAZQUEZ 84), Luciano CIVELLI (Nestor CAMACHO 52), Victor CACERES, Ariel NUNEZ•. Tr: Jorge BURRUCHAGA

Parque Central, Montevideo
12-04-2012, Att: 4302, Ref: Lunati ARG
Nacional Montevideo 0
Jorge BAVA - Diego PLACENTE, Pablo ALVAREZ•, Mathias ABERO•, Santiago ROMERO (Israel DAMONTE• 63), Rafael GARCIA, Maximiliano CALZADA, Marcos AGUIRRE (Alvaro RECOBA 60), Facundo Piriz, Joaquin BOGHOSSIAN (Vicente SANCHEZ 60), Gonzalo BUENO. Tr: Marcelo GALLARDO

Vasco da Gama 1
Diego Souza [56]
FERNANDO PRASS - THIAGO FELTRI, RODOLFO, FAGNER (ALLAN 89), RENATO SILVA, EDUARDO COSTA, DIEGO SOUZA, FELLIPE BASTOS, ROMULO, EDER LUIS, ALECSANDRO• (WILLIAM BARBIO 76). Tr: CRISTOVAO

GRUPO 6

GRUPO 6		Pl	W	D	L	F	A	Pts	BRA	MEX	PAR	VEN
Corinthians	BRA	6	4	2	0	13	2	**14**		1-0	2-0	6-0
Cruz Azul	MEX	6	3	2	1	11	4	**11**	0-0		4-1	4-0
Nacional Asuncion	PAR	6	1	1	4	6	13	**4**	1-3	1-2		3-2
Deportivo Táchira	VEN	6	0	3	3	4	15	**3**	1-1	1-1	0-0	

Nicolás Leoz, Asuncion
8-02-2012, Att: 5000, Ref: Pitana ARG
Nacional Asuncion 0
Bogado 20
German CAFFA - David MENDOZA, Denis CANIZA•, Herminio MIRANDA, Raul PIRIS, Ricardo MAZACOTTE, Derlis ORUE (Javier GONZALEZ• 46), Javier VILLARREAL (Ramon CACERES 62), Silvio TORALES, Rodrigo TEIXEIRA (German CANO 69), Ariel BOGADO. Tr: Javier TORRENTE
Cruz Azul 2
Orozco 2 5 28
Jose CORONA - Nestor ARAUJO, Gerardo FLORES, Jair PEREIRA, Adrian CORTES, Gerardo TORRADO• (Yosgart GUTIERREZ 68), Israel CASTRO, Christian GIMENEZ, Alejandro VELA (Javier AQUINO 55), Javier OROZCO (Omar BRAVO 73), Emanuel VILLA. Tr: Enrique MEZA

Polideportivo, San Cristóbal
15-02-2012, Att: 12 532, Ref: Roldan COL
Deportivo Táchira 1
Herrera 21
Roberts RIVAS• - Wilker ANGEL, Andres ROUGA, Jackson CLAVIJO•, Gamadiel GARCIA (Federico MARTORELL 77), Angel CHOURIO (William ZAPATA 81), Diego GUERRERO, Jorge CASANOVA•, Gerzon CHACON•, Javier VILLAFRAZ•, Sergio HERRERA (Ruben AROCHA 89). Tr: Jaime DE LA PAVA
Corinthians 1
Ralf 94+
JULIO CESAR - ALESSANDRO•, CHICAO, FABIO SANTOS, LEANDRO CASTAN, RALF, PAULINHO, DANILO, LIEDSON (ALEX 57), EMERSON (ELTON 57), JORGE HENRIQUE (WILLIAN 74). Tr: TITE

Estadio Azul, Mexico City
21-02-2012, Att: 19 036, Ref: Machado COL
Cruz Azul 4
Cortes 18p, Perea 54, Orozco 78, Villa 82
Jose CORONA - Nestor ARAUJO, Gerardo FLORES, Jair PEREIRA, Adrian CORTES, Javier AQUINO (Christian GIMENEZ 73), Israel CASTRO, Hector GUTIERREZ, Edixon PEREA (Emanuel VILLA 81), Alejandro VELA (MARANHAO 73), Javier OROZCO. Tr: Enrique MEZA
Deportivo Táchira 0
Roberts RIVAS - Wilker ANGEL, Andres ROUGA•, Jackson CLAVIJO•, Gamadiel GARCIA•, Angel CHOURIO, Diego GUERRERO, Jorge CASANOVA (Ruben AROCHA• 65), Gerzon CHACON•, Javier VILLAFRAZ (Mauricio PARRA 68), Sergio HERRERA (William ZAPATA• 53). Tr: Jaime DE LA PAVA

Pacaembú, São Paulo
7-03-2012, Att: 32 336, Ref: Osses CHI
Corinthians 2
Danilo 38, Jorge Henrique 67
JULIO CESAR - CHICAO, FABIO SANTOS•, LEANDRO CASTAN•, RALF, PAULINHO, ALEX (DOUGLAS 80), DANILO, EDENILSON, LIEDSON (DOUGLAS 80), JORGE HENRIQUE (EMERSON 83). Tr: TITE
Nacional Asuncion 0
Ignacio DON - David MENDOZA, Denis CANIZA, Herminio MIRANDA, Ricardo MAZACOTTE, Javier VILLARREAL, Marcos RIVEROS, Derlis ORUE, Ramon CACERES (German CANO 63), Angel ORUE (Rodrigo TEIXEIRA 55), Javier GONZALEZ• (Ariel BOGADO 46). Tr: Javier TORRENTE

Defensores del Chaco, Asuncion
13-03-2012, Att: 399, Ref: Intriago ECU
Nacional Asuncion 3
Cano 2 50p 72, Torales 81
Ignacio DON - Denis CANIZA, Marcos MIERS, Herminio MIRANDA•, Ricardo MAZACOTTE (Angel ORUE 67), Gustavo CRISTALDO, Javier VILLARREAL, Marcos RIVEROS (Silvio TORALES 60), Derlis ORUE (Gustavo NOGUERA 21), German CANO, Rodrigo TEIXEIRA. Tr: Javier TORRENTE
Deportivo Táchira 2
Fernandez 30, Chourio 79
Roberts RIVAS - Wilker ANGEL, Andres ROUGA•, Jackson CLAVIJO• 50, Angel CHOURIO, Diego GUERRERO, Pedro FERNANDEZ• 87, Mauricio PARRA• (Gamadiel GARCIA 80), Jorge CASANOVA, Gerzon CHACON, William ZAPATA• (Cristian CASSERES 67). Tr: Jaime DE LA PAVA

Estadio Azul, Mexico City
14-03-2012, Att: 29 333, Ref: Vera ECU
Cruz Azul 0
Jose CORONA - Julio DOMINGUEZ (Manuel MARIACA 46), Gerardo FLORES, Jair PEREIRA, Adrian CORTES, Israel CASTRO (Omar BRAVO 61), Christian GIMENEZ, MARANHAO, Hector GUTIERREZ, Javier OROZCO, Emanuel VILLA (Edixon PEREA 80). Tr: Enrique MEZA
Corinthians 0
JULIO CESAR - CHICAO, FABIO SANTOS, LEANDRO CASTAN, RALF, PAULINHO•, ALEX, DANILO (ELTON 82), EDENILSON, LIEDSON (EMERSON 67), JORGE HENRIQUE (Luis RAMIREZ 90). Tr: TITE

Pacaembú, São Paulo
21-03-2012, Att: 29 931, Ref: Vazquez URU
Corinthians 1
Danilo 35
JULIO CESAR - CHICAO, FABIO SANTOS, LEANDRO CASTAN, RALF•, PAULINHO, ALEX (ELTON 86), DANILO•, EDENILSON, LIEDSON (EMERSON• 68), JORGE HENRIQUE. Tr: TITE
Cruz Azul 0
Jose CORONA - Fausto PINTO••♦70, Gerardo FLORES, Jair PEREIRA•, Manuel MARIACA•, Adrian CORTES, Israel CASTRO (MARANHAO 46), Christian GIMENEZ, Hector GUTIERREZ, Edixon PEREA (Alejandro VELA 77), Omar BRAVO (Emanuel VILLA 64). Tr: Enrique MEZA

Polideportivo, San Cristóbal
27-03-2012, Att: 3000, Ref: Orosco BOL
Deportivo Táchira 0
Roberts RIVAS - Wilker ANGEL•, Andres ROUGA, Gamadiel GARCIA (Miguel VIELMA 77), Angel CHOURIO, Diego GUERRERO•, Mauricio PARRA (Jorge CASANOVA 83), Ruben AROCHA, Gerzon CHACON, Javier VILLAFRAZ, Cristian CASSERES•. Tr: Jaime DE LA PAVA
Nacional Asuncion 0
German CAFFA - Denis CANIZA, Gustavo NOGUERA (Carlos Ruiz PERALTA 64), Marcos MIERS•, Herminio MIRANDA, Ricardo MAZACOTTE, Gustavo CRISTALDO (Angel ORUE 74), Javier VILLARREAL, Marcos RIVEROS, German CANO (Ariel BOGADO 68), Rodrigo TEIXEIRA. Tr: Javier TORRENTE

Polideportivo, San Cristóbal
3-04-2012, Att: 3640, Ref: Ubriaco URU
Deportivo Táchira 1
Parra 19
Roberts RIVAS - Wilker ANGEL, Andres ROUGA, Gamadiel GARCIA, Angel CHOURIO, Pedro FERNANDEZ•, Mauricio PARRA (Jorge CASANOVA 71), Ruben AROCHA, Gerzon CHACON, Javier VILLAFRAZ, Cristian CASSERES (Miguel VIELMA 87). Tr: Jaime DE LA PAVA
Cruz Azul 1
Gimenez 83
Jose CORONA - Jair PEREIRA•, Manuel MARIACA, Adrian CORTES, Israel CASTRO, Christian GIMENEZ, MARANHAO (Alejandro VELA 52), Hector GUTIERREZ (Inaki DOMINGUEZ 79), Francisco FLORES•, Edixon PEREA, Emanuel VILLA (Omar BRAVO 39). Tr: Enrique MEZA

Antonio Sarubbi, Ciudad del Este
11-04-2012, Att: 7000, Ref: Loustau ARG
Nacional Asuncion 1
Ruiz 70
Ignacio DON - Denis CANIZA, Marcos MIERS•, Herminio MIRANDA, Ricardo MAZACOTTE•, Javier VILLARREAL, Silvio TORALES, Marcos RIVEROS• (Carlos RUIZ PERALTA 65), Derlis ORUE• (Javier GONZALEZ 62), Rodrigo TEIXEIRA (Ariel BOGADO 75), German CANO. Tr: Javier TORRENTE
Corinthians 3
Jorge Henrique 28, Emerson 51, Elton 71
JULIO CESAR - CHICAO, FABIO SANTOS, LEANDRO CASTAN, RALF, PAULINHO, DANILO, EDENILSON (WELDER 86), LIEDSON (ELTON 68), EMERSON (WILLIAN 80), JORGE HENRIQUE. Tr: TITE

Estadio Azul, Mexico City
18-04-2012, Att: 13 903, Ref: Carrillo PER
Cruz Azul 4
Orozco 20, Maranhao 45, Bravo 65, Perea 80
Yosgart GUTIERREZ - Fausto Pinto, Nestor ARAUJO, Gerardo FLORES (Francisco FLORES 67), Manuel MARIACA, Javier AQUINO•, Israel CASTRO, MARANHAO, Hector GUTIERREZ• (Christian GIMENEZ 56), Omar BRAVO (Edixon PEREA 68), Javier OROZCO. Tr: Enrique MEZA
Nacional Asuncion 1
Cristaldo 43
Ignacio DON - Marcos MIERS•, Herminio MIRANDA, Raul PIRIS•, Ricardo MAZACOTTE, Carlos RUIZ PERALTA (Derlis ORUE 82), Gustavo CRISTALDO, Silvio TORALES, Marcos RIVEROS, Ariel BOGADO (Cesar FLORENCIANEZ 77), Angel ORUE (German CANO 57). Tr: Gustavo MORINIGO

Pacaembú, São Paulo
18-04-2012, Att: 27 379, Ref: Polic CHI
Corinthians 6
Danilo 17, Paulinho 26, Jorge Henrique 62, Emerson 70, Liedson 72, Douglas 83p
JULIO CESAR - CHICAO (WELDER 46), FABIO SANTOS, LEANDRO CASTAN, RALF, PAULINHO, DANILO (DOUGLAS 60), EDENILSON, LIEDSON, EMERSON (WILLIAN 79), JORGE HENRIQUE. Tr: TITE
Deportivo Táchira 0
Roberts RIVAS - Wilker ANGEL, Andres ROUGA♦36, Gamadiel GARCIA, Pedro FERNANDEZ, Mauricio PARRA• (William DIAZ• 39), Ruben AROCHA (Jackson CLAVIJO 52), Gerzon CHACON, Javier VILLAFRAZ (Diego GUERRERO 86), Anderson ARIAS, Cristian CASSERES. Tr: Jaime DE LA PAVA

COPA LIBERTADORES 2012

GRUPO 7		PJ	W	D	L	F	A	Pts	ARG	ECU	URU	MEX
Velez Sarsfield	ARG	6	4	0	2	10	6	12		1-0	1-3	3-0
Deportivo Quito	ECU	6	3	1	2	11	4	10	3-0		2-0	5-0
Defensor Sporting	URU	6	3	0	3	6	7	9	0-3	2-0		1-0
Guadalajara	MEX	6	1	1	4	2	12	4	0-2	1-1	1-0	

Luis Franzini, Montevideo
7-02-2012, Att: 6812, Ref: Osses CHI
Defensor Sporting 0

Yonatan IRRAZABAL - Ramon ARIAS (Pablo PINTOS 77), Nestor MOIRAGHI, Diego Manuel RODRIGUEZ, Diego ROLAN, Diego Martin RODRIGUEZ, Federico PINTOS•, Andres FLEURQUIN, Bryan ALEMAN, Nicolas OLIVERA (Gaston PUERARI 77), Ignacio RISSO (Maximiliano CALLORDA 67). Tr: Gustavo DIAZ

Vélez Sarsfield 3
Ramirez [41], Obolo [81], Dominguez [85]

Marcelo BAROVERO - Sebastian DOMINGUEZ, Fernando ORTIZ, Emiliano PAPA, Fabian CUBERO•, Augusto FERNANDEZ, David RAMIREZ (Ivan BELLA 83), Victor ZAPATA (Alejandro CABRAL 77), Francisco CERRO•, Juan MARTINEZ (Federico INSUA 62), Ivan OBOLO. Tr: Ricardo GARECA

Omnilife, Guadalajara
7-02-2012, Att: 4368, Ref: Soto VEN
Guadalajara 1
Arellano [92+]

Luis MICHEL - Hector REYNOSO•, Miguel PONCE•, Jonny MAGALLON (Antonio SALAZAR 78), Kristian ALVAREZ, Patricio ARAUJO• (Jorge MORA 46), Julio NAVA, Jorge ENRIQUEZ, Xavier BAEZ• (Alberto MEDINA 55), Omar ARELLANO, Carlos FIERRO. Tr: Ignacio AMBRIZ

Deportivo Quito 0

Marcelo ELIZAGA (Adrian BONE 90) - Giovanny ESPINOZA•, Isaac MINA•, Luis CHECA, Pedro VELASCO, Alex BOLANOS, Benito OLIVO•, Luis SARITAMA, Fidel MARTINEZ, Matias ALUSTIZA (Julio BEVACQUA 72), Juan Carlos PAREDES (Dixon ARROYO 87). Tr: Carlos ISCHIA

Luis Franzini, Montevideo
14-02-2012, Att: 3192, Ref: Lopes BRA
Defensor Sporting 2
Aleman [22p], Callorda [78]

Yonatan IRRAZABAL - Ramon ARIAS, Nestor MOIRAGHI, Diego Manuel RODRIGUEZ (Robert HERRERA 66), Diego FERREIRA•, Diego Martin RODRIGUEZ, Pablo PINTOS, Andres FLEURQUIN, Bryan ALEMAN (Juan AMADO 89), Nicolas OLIVERA (Federico PINTOS 78), Maximiliano CALLORDA. Tr: Gustavo DIAZ

Deportivo Quito 0

Marcelo ELIZAGA - Giovanny ESPINOZA, Isaac MINA, Luis CHECA•, Pedro VELASCO, Alex BOLANOS, Benito OLIVO• (Luis ESCALADA 81), Luis SARITAMA, Fidel MARTINEZ•, Matias ALUSTIZA, Juan Carlos PAREDES• (Edder VACA 71). Tr: Carlos ISCHIA

José Amalfitani, Buenos Aires
22-02-2012, Att: 8661, Vuaden BRA
Vélez Sarsfield 3
Obolo [67], Insua 2 [81] [82]

Marcelo BAROVERO - Sebastian DOMINGUEZ, Fernando ORTIZ•, Emiliano PAPA, Fabian CUBERO•, Augusto FERNANDEZ, Victor ZAPATA (Alejandro CABRAL 61), Francisco CERRO• (Hector CANTEROS 86), Federico INSUA, Juan MARTINEZ (Lucas PRATTO 73), Ivan OBOLO. Tr: Ricardo GARECA

Guadalajara 0

Luis MICHEL - Hector REYNOSO, Jonny MAGALLON, Kristian ALVAREZ, Patricio ARAUJO•, Marco FABIAN•, Jorge ENRIQUEZ (Antonio SALAZAR 79), Jesus SANCHEZ•, Xavier BAEZ•, Omar ARELLANO, Erick TORRES (Julio NAVA 71). Tr: Ignacio AMBRIZ

Olimpico Atahualpa, Quito
7-03-2012, Att: 9849, Ref: Buitrago COL
Deportivo Quito 3
Alustiza [45p], Martinez.F [48], Saritama [71]

Marcelo ELIZAGA - Giovanny ESPINOZA, Isaac MINA•, Luis CHECA, Pedro VELASCO, Alex BOLANOS, Luis SARITAMA, Fidel MARTINEZ, Matias ALUSTIZA (Luis ESCALADA 84), Juan Carlos PAREDES (Jorge FOLLECO 70), Julio BEVACQUA• (Benito OLIVO• 46). Tr: Carlos ISCHIA

Vélez Sarsfield 0

Marcelo BAROVERO - Sebastian DOMINGUEZ•, Fernando ORTIZ, Emiliano PAPA•, Fabian CUBERO• (Lucas PRATTO 58), Augusto FERNANDEZ (Ivan BELLA 23), Alejandro CABRAL, Hector CANTEROS, Francisco CERRO•, Federico INSUA, Ivan OBOLO (Juan MARTINEZ 72). Tr: Ricardo GARECA

Omnilife, Guadalajara
13-03-2012, Att: 7529, Ref: Escalante VEN
Guadalajara 1
Fierro [10]

Luis MICHEL - Hector REYNOSO•, Jonny MAGALLON, Kristian ALVAREZ, Patricio ARAUJO, Julio NAVA, Jesus SANCHEZ• (Giovani CASILLAS 80), Xavier BAEZ, Omar ARELLANO (Edgar MEJIA 64), Antonio SALAZAR, Carlos FIERRO (Jorge Mora 87). Tr: Ignacio AMBRIZ

Defensor Sporting 0

Yonatan IRRAZABAL - Ramon ARIAS, Nestor MOIRAGHI•, Diego Manuel RODRIGUEZ, Diego FERREIRA (Bryan ALEMAN 78), Diego Martin RODRIGUEZ• (Ignacio RISSO 84), Pablo PINTOS•, Andres FLEURQUIN, Diego ROLAN (Federico PINTOS 73), Matias BRITOS, Nicolas OLIVERA. Tr: Gustavo DIAZ

José Amalfitani, Buenos Aires
22-03-2012, Att: 7300, Ref: Seneme BRA
Vélez Sarsfield 1
Martinez.J [89]

Marcelo BAROVERO - Sebastian DOMINGUEZ, Fernando ORTIZ, Emiliano PAPA, Fabian CUBERO, Augusto FERNANDEZ, Victor ZAPATA (Alejandro CABRAL 90), Francisco CERRO, Federico INSUA• (Jonathan RAMIREZ 87), Juan MARTINEZ, Ivan OBOLO (Lucas PRATTO 67). Tr: Ricardo GARECA

Deportivo Quito 0

Marcelo ELIZAGA - Giovanny ESPINOZA, Isaac MINA•, Luis CHECA, Jorge FOLLECO, Pedro VELASCO, Alex BOLANOS•, Benito OLIVO, Luis SARITAMA, Fidel MARTINEZ, Matias ALUSTIZA (Dixon ARROYO 76). Tr: Carlos ISCHIA

Luis Franzini, Montevideo
28-03-2012, Att: 2597, Ref: Caceres PAR
Defensor Sporting 1
Olivera [70]

Yonatan IRRAZABAL - Ramon ARIAS, Nestor MOIRAGHI•, Diego Manuel RODRIGUEZ, Diego FERREIRA (Ignacio RISSO 46), Diego Martin RODRIGUEZ, Federico PINTOS•, Pablo PINTOS, Matias BRITOS•, Bryan ALEMAN• (Robert HERRERA 83), Nicolas OLIVERA (Juan AMADO 89). Tr: Gustavo DIAZ

Guadalajara 0

Luis MICHEL - Hector REYNOSO, Jonny MAGALLON, Kristian ALVAREZ•, Patricio ARAUJO, Julio NAVA•• ♦40, Jesus SANCHEZ (Edgar MEJIA 46), Xavier BAEZ, Omar ARELLANO (Alberto MEDINA 51), Antonio SALAZAR (Mario DE LUNA 46), Carlos FIERRO. Tr: Ignacio AMBRIZ

Olimpico Atahualpa, Quito
10-04-2012, Att: 5380, Ref: Carrillo PER
Deportivo Quito 2
Checa [36], Bevacqua [63]

Marcelo ELIZAGA - Giovanny ESPINOZA, Luis CHECA (Luis ROMERO 65), Jorge FOLLECO, Pedro VELASCO, Benito OLIVO (Edder VACA 85), Luis SARITAMA•, Fidel MARTINEZ•, Matias ALUSTIZA, Juan Carlos PAREDES (Dixon ARROYO 70), Julio BEVACQUA. Tr: Carlos ISCHIA

Defensor Sporting 0

Yonatan IRRAZABAL - Ramon ARIAS, Nestor MOIRAGHI, Diego Manuel RODRIGUEZ, Diego FERREIRA•, Diego Martin RODRIGUEZ, Federico PINTOS♦54, Pablo PINTOS (Mario RISSO 65), Matias BRITOS, Bryan ALEMAN (Diego ROLAN 56), Nicolas OLIVERA (Robert HERRERA 59). Tr: Gustavo DIAZ

Omnilife, Guadalajara
11-04-2012, Att: 16730, Ref: Gambetta PER
Guadalajara 0

Victor HERNANDEZ - Hector REYNOSO, Miguel PONCE (Antonio SALAZAR 67), Kristian ALVAREZ•, Patricio ARAUJO, Marco FABIAN, Jorge ENRIQUEZ (Giovani CASILLAS 45), Jesus SANCHEZ, Xavier BAEZ, Omar ARELLANO (Carlos FIERRO 75), Erick TORRES. Tr: Ignacio AMBRIZ

Vélez Sarsfield 2
Fernandez.A [69], Pratto [89]

Marcelo BAROVERO - Sebastian DOMINGUEZ, Fernando ORTIZ, Emiliano PAPA, Fabian CUBERO (Gino PERUZZI 74), Augusto FERNANDEZ (Francisco CERRO 88), Alejandro CABRAL, Hector CANTEROS, Victor ZAPATA, Juan MARTINEZ, Ivan OBOLO (Lucas PRATTO 71). Tr: Ricardo GARECA

Olimpico Atahualpa, Quito
17-04-2012, Att: 11000, Ref: Roldan
Deportivo Quito 5
Alustiza 4 [17] [27] [70] [86], Martinez.F [64]

Marcelo ELIZAGA - Giovanny ESPINOZA•, Luis CHECA (Isaac MINA 46), Jorge FOLLECO, Pedro VELASCO, Benito OLIVO (Edison VEGA 74), Luis SARITAMA, Fidel MARTINEZ, Matias ALUSTIZA, Juan Carlos PAREDES•, Julio BEVACQUA (Alex BOLANOS 62). Tr: Carlos ISCHIA

Guadalajara 0

Victor HERNANDEZ - Mario DE LUNA, Dionicio ESCALANTE, Hector REYNOSO•, Edgar MEJIA, Jorge ENRIQUEZ••♦58, Jesus SANCHEZ•, Xavier BAEZ (Abraham CORONADO 46), Giovani CASILLAS (Antonio SALAZAR• 64), Erick TORRES•, Carlos FIERRO (Patricio ARAUJO 59). Tr: Ignacio AMBRIZ

José Amalfitani, Buenos Aires
17-04-2012, Att: 8000, Ref: Ricci BRA
Vélez Sarsfield 1
Insua [63p]

German MONTOYA - Fernando TOBIO, Sebastian DOMINGUEZ, Mariano BITTOLO, Fabian CUBERO•, Augusto FERNANDEZ (Ivan BELLA 72), David RAMIREZ (Jonathan RAMIREZ 55), Victor ZAPATA, Francisco CERRO•, Juan MARTINEZ (Federico INSUA 55), Lucas PRATTO. Tr: Ricardo GARECA

Defensor Sporting 3
Olivera [6], Rodriguez [37], Britos [46]

Yonatan IRRAZABAL• - Ramon ARIAS, Nestor MOIRAGHI, Diego Manuel RODRIGUEZ, Robert HERRERA, Juan AMADO (Mario Risso 81), Diego FERREIRA•, Diego Martin RODRIGUEZ, Matias BRITOS (Ignacio RISSO 57), Bryan ALEMAN (Gaston SILVA 72), Nicolas OLIVERA•. Tr: Gustavo DIAZ

PART THREE – THE CONTINENTAL CONFEDERATIONS

GRUPO 8		Pl	W	D	L	F	A	Pts	CHI	COL	ARG	URU
Universidad de Chile	CHI	6	4	1	1	11	6	13		2-1	5-1	2-1
At. Nacional Medellin	COL	6	3	2	1	16	8	11	2-0		2-2	3-0
Godoy Cruz	ARG	6	1	2	3	10	16	5	0-1	4-4		1-0
Peñarol	URU	6	1	1	4	6	13	4	1-1	0-4	4-2	

Atanasio Girardot, Medellin
14-02-2012, 40 118, Carrillo PER
Atlético Nacional Medellin 2
Valencia [27], Pabon [80]
Gaston PEZZUTI - Alexis HENRIQUEZ, Elkin CALLE•, Cristian TULA (Oscar MURILLO 46), Juan VALENCIA (Farid DIAZ 46), Macnelly TORRES, Luis MOSQUERA (Alexander MEJIA 67), Jhersson CORDOBA•, John VALOY, Dorlan PABON, Diego ALVAREZ. Tr: Santiago ESCOBAR

Universidad de Chile 0
Johnny HERRERA - Eugenio MENA, Osvaldo GONZALEZ (Paulo MAGALHAES 46), Albert ACEVEDO, Jose ROJAS, Marcelo DIAZ, Pedro MORALES (Roberto CERECEDA 60), Charles ARANGUIZ•, Gustavo LORENZETTI (Raul RUIDIAZ 46), Junior FERNANDES, Francisco CASTRO. Tr: Jorge SAMPAOLI

Malvinas Argentinas, Mendoza
16-02-2012, 12 153, Orosco BOL
Godoy Cruz 1
Villar [52]
Sebastian TORRICO - Leonardo SIGALI, Roberto RUSSO, Zelmar GARCIA, Nicolas SANCHEZ, Nicolas OLMEDO, Diego VILLAR (Lucas CEBALLOS• 75), Federico LERTORA• (Juan Carlos FALCON 46), Ariel ROJAS, Ruben RAMIREZ•, Facundo CASTILLON (Leandro CARUSO 83). Tr: Nery PUMPIDO

Peñarol 0
Fabian CARINI - Juan ALVEZ (Joao PEDRO 66), Alejandro GONZALEZ••♦59, Dario RODRIGUEZ, Carlos VALDEZ, Nicolas FREITAS•, Luis AGUIAR (Jorge ZAMBRANA 81), Sebastian CRISTOFORO, Maximiliano PEREZ (Joaquin AGUIRRE 64), Fabian ESTOYANOFF, Marcelo ZALAYETA. Tr: Gregorio PEREZ

Centenario, Montevideo
21-02-2012, 33 713, Amarilla PAR
Peñarol 0
Fabian CARINI - Juan ALVEZ (Joao PEDRO 46), Joaquin AGUIRRE, Dario RODRIGUEZ, Carlos VALDEZ, Nicolas FREITAS, Luis AGUIAR, Sebastian CRISTOFORO•, Fabian ESTOYANOFF (Santiago SILVA• 59), Marcelo ZALAYETA, Rodrigo MORA (Maximiliano PEREZ 72). Tr: Gregorio PEREZ

Atlético Nacional Medellin 4
Cordoba 2 [8 49], Pabon 2 [64 77]
Gaston PEZZUTI - Alexis HENRIQUEZ, Elkin CALLE, Cristian TULA, Farid DIAZ, Macnelly TORRES (Juan QUINTERO 83), Luis MOSQUERA• (Diego ALVAREZ 83), Alexander MEJIA, Jhersson CORDOBA, John VALOY (Alejandro BERNAL 46), Dorlan PABON. Tr: Santiago ESCOBAR

Santa Laura, Santiago
22-02-2012, 14 230, Seneme BRA
Universidad de Chile 5
Fernandes 3 [29 45 72], Lorenzetti [34], Henriquez [90]
Johnny HERRERA - Eugenio MENA, Osvaldo GONZALEZ, Albert ACEVEDO, Matias RODRIGUEZ, Jose ROJAS, Marcelo DIAZ, Charles ARANGUIZ, Gustavo LORENZETTI (Pedro MORALES 88), Junior FERNANDES• (Angelo HENRIQUEZ 85), Francisco CASTRO (Roberto CERECEDA 74). Tr: Jorge SAMPAOLI

Godoy Cruz 1
Sigali [53]
Sebastian TORRICO - Leonardo SIGALI•, Zelmar GARCIA (Gonzalo CABRERA 66), Lucas CEBALLOS (Jorge CURBELO• 46), Nicolas SANCHEZ, Nicolas OLMEDO (Federico LERTORA 67), Juan Carlos FALCON•, Diego VILLAR, Ariel ROJAS, Ruben RAMIREZ, Facundo CASTILLON•. Tr: Nery PUMPIDO

Centenario, Montevideo
6-03-2012, 29 600, Ponce ECU
Peñarol 1
Freitas [21]
Fabian CARINI - Alejandro GONZALEZ, Marcelo SILVA, Dario RODRIGUEZ•, Carlos VALDEZ, Emiliano ALBIN (Maximiliano PEREZ 68), Nicolas FREITAS, Sebastian CRISTOFORO, Fabian ESTOYANOFF (Jorge ZAMBRANA 82), Marcelo ZALAYETA (Joao PEDRO 72), Rodrigo MORA. Tr: Jorge DA SILVA

Universidad de Chile 1
Fernandes [34]
Johnny HERRERA - Eugenio MENA•, Osvaldo GONZALEZ, Albert ACEVEDO•, Matias RODRIGUEZ•, Jose ROJAS, Marcelo DIAZ, Charles ARANGUIZ (Roberto CERECEDA 82), Angelo HENRIQUEZ (Raul RUIDIAZ 83), Junior FERNANDES•, Francisco CASTRO (Gustavo LORENZETTI• 46). Tr: Jorge SAMPAOLI

Malvinas Argentinas, Mendoza
8-03-2012, 5315, Vuaden BRA
Godoy Cruz 4
Caruso 3 [8 68 90], Ramirez [33]
Sebastian TORRICO - Leonardo SIGALI, Lucas CEBALLOS, Nicolas SANCHEZ, Jorge CURBELO• (Juan Carlos FALCON 34), Diego VILLAR•, Federico LERTORA, Armando COOPER (Facundo CASTILLON 58), Ariel ROJAS, Leandro CARUSO, Ruben RAMIREZ (Alvaro NAVARRO 80). Tr: Nery PUMPIDO

Atlético Nacional Medellin 4
Mosquera [13], OG [29], Pabon 2 [54 69]
Gaston PEZZUTI - Alexis HENRIQUEZ, Elkin CALLE, Cristian TULA, Farid DIAZ, Alejandro BERNAL (Sebastian PEREZ 76), Macnelly TORRES (Juan QUINTERO 86), Luis MOSQUERA, Alexander MEJIA, Jhersson CORDOBA, Dorlan PABON (Carlos RENTERIA 90). Tr: Santiago ESCOBAR

Atanasio Girardot, Medellin
22-03-2012, 37 602, Lopes BRA
Atlético Nacional Medellin 2
Mosquera 2 [2 61p]
Gaston PEZZUTI - Alexis HENRIQUEZ, Cristian TULA, Farid DIAZ, Alejandro BERNAL, Macnelly TORRES, Luis MOSQUERA, Alexander MEJIA, Jhersson CORDOBA, Dorlan PABON (Diego ALVAREZ 26) (Juan QUINTERO 69), Carlos RENTERIA. Tr: Santiago ESCOBAR

Godoy Cruz 2
Curbelo [23], Castillon [34]
Sebastian TORRICO - Leonardo SIGALI••♦90, Marcelo CARDOZO•, Lucas CEBALLOS•, Nicolas SANCHEZ•, Jorge CURBELO, Diego VILLAR• (Armando COOPER 82), Federico LERTORA, Ariel ROJAS (Juan Carlos FALCON 74), Leandro CARUSO (Sergio LOPEZ• 85), Facundo CASTILLON. Tr: Nery PUMPIDO

Estadio Nacional, Santiago
27-03-2012, 33 095, Vauden BRA
Universidad de Chile 1
Rodriguez 2 [2 91+]
Johnny HERRERA - Eugenio MENA, Osvaldo GONZALEZ, Albert ACEVEDO•, Matias RODRIGUEZ•, Jose ROJAS, Marcelo DIAZ, Felipe GALLEGOS (Emilio HERNANDEZ• 54), Charles ARANGUIZ (Raul RUIDIAZ 71), Gustavo LORENZETTI, Junior FERNANDES•. Tr: Jorge SAMPAOLI

Peñarol 2
Valdez [51]
Fabian CARINI - Alejandro GONZALEZ, Dario RODRIGUEZ•, Carlos VALDEZ• (Marcelo SILVA 70), Emiliano ALBIN, Nicolas FREITAS•, Luis AGUIAR, Joao PEDRO (Fabian ESTOYANOFF 61), Sebastian CRISTOFORO•, Marcelo ZALAYETA (Maximiliano PEREZ 23), Rodrigo MORA. Tr: Jorge DA SILVA

Malvinas Argentinas, Mendoza
4-04-2012, 11 628, Amarilla PAR
Godoy Cruz 0
Sebastian TORRICO - Marcelo CARDOZO (Armando COOPER• 62), Zelmar GARCIA, Lucas CEBALLOS, Nicolas SANCHEZ•, Jorge CURBELO (Nicolas OLMEDO• 74), Diego VILLAR•, Federico LERTORA, Ariel ROJAS•(Facundo CASTILLON 46), Leandro CARUSO, Ruben RAMIREZ. Tr: Nery PUMPIDO

Universidad de Chile 1
Henriquez [45]
Johnny HERRERA - Eugenio MENA, Osvaldo GONZALEZ, Albert ACEVEDO•, Matias RODRIGUEZ, Jose ROJAS, Marcelo DIAZ, Charles ARANGUIZ (Sebastian MARTINEZ 72), Gustavo LORENZETTI, Angelo HENRIQUEZ (Raul RUIDIAZ 80), Junior FERNANDES• (Roberto CERECEDA 64). Tr: Jorge SAMPAOLI

Atanasio Girardot, Medellin
10-04-2012, 24 306, Antequera BOL
Atlético Nacional Medellin 3
Murillo [7], Pabon [44], Alvarez [64]
Gaston PEZZUTI - Oscar MURILLO, Cristian TULA (Alexis HENRIQUEZ 73), Juan VALENCIA•, Alejandro BERNAL•, Macnelly TORRES, Alexander MEJIA, Sebastian PEREZ, Jhersson CORDOBA (Luis MOSQUERA 61), Dorlan PABON (Juan QUINTERO 76), Diego ALVAREZ. Tr: Santiago ESCOBAR

Peñarol 0
Danilo LERDA - Juan ALVEZ, Alejandro GONZALEZ•, Marcelo SILVA•, Emiliano ALBIN, Facundo GUICHON (Sebastian ROSANO 67), Nicolas FREITAS, Nicolas AMODIO (Joao PEDRO 60), Sebastian CRISTOFORO•, Maximiliano PEREZ (Jorge ZAMBRANA 78), Rodrigo MORA. Tr: Jorge DA SILVA

Centenario, Montevideo
19-04-2012, 24 011, Marques BRA
Peñarol 4
Zambrana 2 [37 73], Mora [50], Perez [61]
Leandro GELPI - Juan ALVEZ, Emilio MACEACHEN (Emiliano ALBIN 46), Marcelo SILVA, Facundo GUICHON (Sebastian CRISTOFORO 46), Marcel NOVICK, Jorge ZAMBRANA•, Joao PEDRO (Rodrigo MORA 46), Sebastian ROSANO, Nicolas AMODIO, Maximiliano PEREZ. Tr: Jorge DA SILVA

Godoy Cruz 2
Sanchez [12], Sevillano [19]
Sebastian TORRICO - Roberto RUSSO, Marcelo CARDOZO•, Nicolas SANCHEZ•, Nicolas OLMEDO, Emanuel AGUILERA•, Armando COOPER, Sergio LOPEZ (Gonzalo CABRERA 68), Sergio SANCHEZ• (Lucas CEBALLOS 77), Alvaro NAVARRO (Facundo CASTILLON 66), Sergio SEVILLANO. Tr: Daniel OLDRA

Estadio Nacional, Santiago
19-04-2012, 30 800, Rivera PER
Universidad de Chile 2
Rodriguez [10], Gonzalez [68]
Johnny HERRERA - Eugenio MENA, Osvaldo GONZALEZ, Matias RODRIGUEZ, Jose ROJAS, Marcelo DIAZ, Emilio HERNANDEZ• (Paulo MAGALHAES 82), Charles ARANGUIZ•, Sebastian MARTINEZ, Angelo HENRIQUEZ (Raul RUIDIAZ• 67), Junior FERNANDES (Felipe GALLEGOS 46). Tr: Jorge SAMPAOLI

Atlético Nacional Medellin 1
Pabon [62]
Gaston PEZZUTI - Oscar MURILLO, Elkin CALLE, Cristian TULA•, Juan VALENCIA (Diego ALVAREZ 56), Farid DIAZ, Alejandro BERNAL• (Juan QUINTERO 81), Macnelly TORRES, Alexander MEJIA, Sebastian PEREZ (Jhersson CORDOBA 67), Dorlan PABON. Tr: Santiago ESCOBAR

COPA LIBERTADORES 2012

ROUND OF SIXTEEN

George Capwell, Guayaquil
2-05-2012, Att: 16974, Ref: Buitrago COL
Emelec 0

Esteban DREER - Oscar BAGUI, Carlos QUINONEZ, Gabriel ACHILIER•, Enner VALENCIA, Pedro QUINONEZ, Jose QUINONEZ, Fernando GIMENEZ (Angel MENA 74), Fernando GAIBOR• (Efren MERA 53), Marcos MONDAINI (Marlon DE JESUS 64), Luciano FIGUEROA. Tr: Julio FLEITAS

Corinthians 0

CASSIO - CHICAO•, FABIO SANTOS, LEANDRO CASTAN•, RALF, PAULINHO, DANILO• (ALESSANDRO 84), EDENILSON•, WILLIAN (ALEX 58), EMERSON• (ELTON 79), JORGE HENRIQUE••♦52. Tr: TITE

Pacaembú, São Paulo
9-05-2012, Att: 32577, Ref: Ubriaco URU
Corinthians 3
Fabio Santos [7], Paulinho [64], Alex [85]

CASSIO - CHICAO•, FABIO SANTOS, LEANDRO CASTAN•, RALF, PAULINHO•, ALEX, DANILO, EDENILSON (ALESSANDRO 46), WILLIAN (LIEDSON 71), EMERSON (DOUGLAS 87). Tr: TITE

Emelec 0

Esteban DREER - Oscar BAGUI, Carlos QUINONEZ (Marlon DE JESU 68), Gabriel ACHILIER, Enner VALENCIA (Efren MERA 55), Pedro QUINONEZ•, Jose QUINONEZ•, Fernando GIMENEZ, Fernando GAIBOR•, Marcos MONDAINI, Luciano FIGUEROA. Tr: Julio FLEITAS

São Januário, Rio de Janeiro
2-05-2012, Att: 13017, Ref: Silvera URU
Vasco da Gama 2
Alecsandro [25], Diego Souza [42]

FERNANDO PRASS - THIAGO FELTRI, RODOLFO, JULINHO•, FAGNER•, RENATO SILVA, FELIPE (FELLIPE BASTOS 64), DIEGO SOUZA• CARLOS ALBERTO 70), ROMULO (EDUARDO COSTA 41), EDER LUIS, ALECSANDRO. Tr: CRISTOVAO

Lanús 1
Regueiro [62]

Agustin MARCHESIN - Paolo GOLTZ, Carlos ARAUJO, Diego BRAGHIERI, Maximiliano VELAZQUEZ•, Matias FRITZLER•, Mario REGUEIRO, Mauro CAMORANESI (Diego GONZALEZ 85), Guido PIZARRO•, Diego VALERI• (Silvio ROMERO 63), Mariano PAVONE (Teofilo GUTIERREZ 71). Tr: Gabriel SCHURRER

Fortaleza, Lanús, Buenos Aires
9-05-2012, Att: 6408, Ref: Amarilla PAR
Lanús 2 4p
Pavone [60], Gutierrez [78]

Agustin MARCHESIN - Paolo GOLTZ, Carlos ARAUJO, Diego BRAGHIERI•, Maximiliano VELAZQUEZ•, Matias FRITZLER•, Mario REGUEIRO, Mauro CAMORANESI, Guido PIZARRO• (Teofilo GUTIERREZ 46), Diego VALERI (Silvio ROMERO 71), Mariano PAVONE•. Tr: Gabriel SCHURRER

Vasco da Gama 1 5p
Nilton [18]

FERNANDO PRASS - THIAGO FELTRI, RODOLFO•, FAGNER, RENATO SILVA, JUNINHO PERNAMBUCANO, DIEGO SOUZA (ALLAN 67), NILTON (FELIPE 86), ROMULO, EDER LUIS (CARLOS ALBERTO 82), ALECSANDRO. Tr: CRISTOVAO

Atanasio Girardot, Medellin
1-05-2012, Att: 33242, Ref: Ubriaco URU
Atlético Nacional 0

Gaston PEZZUTI - Alexis HENRIQUEZ, Cristian TULA•, Farid DIAZ (Juan VALENCIA 86), Alejandro BERNAL, Macnelly TORRES, Luis MOSQUERA, Alexander MEJIA•, Sebastian PEREZ (Juan QUINTERO 35), Jhersson CORDOBA (Diego ALVAREZ 68), Dorlan PABON•. Tr: Juan Carlos OSORIO

Velez Sarsfield 1
Bella [8]

Marcelo BAROVERO - Sebastian DOMINGUEZ, Fernando ORTIZ, Emiliano PAPA, Fabian CUBERO•, Augusto FERNANDEZ, Victor ZAPATA (Leandro DESABATO 89), Francisco CERRO, Ivan BELLA• (Gino PERUZZI), Juan MARTINEZ (Federico INSUA 80), Lucas PRATTO. Tr: Ricardo GARECA

José Amalfitani, Buenos Aires
8-05-2012, Att: 10731, Ref: Quintana PAR
Velez Sarsfield 1
Fernandez [52]

Marcelo BAROVERO - Fernando TOBIO, Sebastian DOMINGUEZ•, Emiliano PAPA, Fabian CUBERO, Augusto FERNANDEZ, Alejandro CABRAL, Victor ZAPATA (Ivan BELLA 68), Francisco CERRO, Juan MARTINEZ (David RAMIREZ 90), Lucas PRATTO (Ivan OBOLO 81). Tr: Ricardo GARECA

Atlético Nacional 1
Mosquera [69]

Gaston PEZZUTI - Alexis HENRIQUEZ•, Cristian TULA, Farid DIAZ, Alejandro BERNAL•, Macnelly TORRES•, Luis MOSQUERA• (Juan VALENCIA 90), Alexander MEJIA, Jhersson CORDOBA• (Juan QUINTERO 81), Aviles HURTADO (Diego ALVAREZ 63), Dorlan PABON. Tr: Juan Carlos OSORIO

Hernando Siles, La Paz
25-04-2012, 20127, Ref: Osses CHI
Bolívar 2
OG [1], Campos [74]

Marcos ARGUELLO - Edemir RODRIGUEZ, Gabriel VALVERDE, Lorgio ALVAREZ, Pablo FRONTINI•, Jhasmani CAMPOS (Ronald EGUINO 90), Rudy CARDOZO, Damian LIZIO, Walter FLORES, William FERREIRA (Ever CANTERO 22), Juan ARCE•. Tr: Guillermo HOYOS

Santos 1
Maranhao [34]

RAFAEL• - EDU DRACENA•, DURVAL•, JUAN, MARANHAO, AROUCA, ELANO (IBSON 70), GANSO, ADRIANO, BORGES (ALAN KARDEC 65), NEYMAR. Tr: MURICY RAMALHO

Vila Belmiro, Santos
10-05-2012, Att: 15000, Ref: Vasquez URU
Santos 8
Elano 2 [6 50], Neymar 2 [21p 36], Ganso 2 [27 52], Alan Kardec [29], Borges [60]

RAFAEL - EDU DRACENA, DURVAL, JUAN, AROUCA (IBSON 63), HENRIQUE, ELANO (FELIPE ANDERSON 68), GANSO, ADRIANO, NEYMAR, ALAN KARDEC (BORGES 56). Tr: Muricy RAMALHO

Bolívar 0

Marcos ARGUELLO - Edemir RODRIGUEZ, Gabriel VALVERDE•, Lorgio ALVAREZ (Jeison SIQUITA 82), Pablo FRONTINI•, Jhasmani CAMPOS (Rudy CARDOZO (Damir MIRANDA 56), Damian LIZIO, Walter FLORES, Ever CANTERO (Abdon REYES 68), Juan ARCE. Tr: Guillermo HOYOS

Olímpico Atahualpa, Quito
3-05-2012, Att: 16540, Ref: Chacon MEX
Deportivo Quito 3
Alustiza 2 [30 56], Checa [45], Martinez [82]

Marcelo ELIZAGA - Giovanny ESPINOZA•, Isaac MINA, Luis CHECA (Luis ROMERO 72), Pedro VELASCO, Benito OLIVO•♦31, Luis SARITAMA, Fidel MARTINEZ, Matias ALUSTIZA•, Juan Carlos PAREDES (Edison VEGA 81), Julio BEVACQUA (Alex BOLANOS 35). Tr: Carlos ISCHIA

Universidad de Chile 1
Rodriguez [36]

Johnny HERRERA - Eugenio MENA, Osvaldo GONZALEZ••♦59, Matias RODRIGUEZ, Jose ROJAS•, Marcelo DIAZ, Igor LICHNOVSKY, Charles ARANGUIZ, Sebastian MARTINEZ (Paulo MAGALHAES• 46), Angelo HENRIQUEZ (Gustavo LORENZETTI 46), Junior FERNANDES. Tr: Jorge SAMPAOLI

Estadio Nacional, Santiago
10-05-2012, Att: 43211, Ref: Pitana ARG
Universidad de Chile 6
Fernandes 2 [20 27], Díaz [35], Mena [56], Henriquez 2 [70 73]

Johnny HERRERA - Eugenio MENA, Matias RODRIGUEZ, Jose ROJAS•, Paulo MAGALHAES, Marcelo DIAZ, Guillermo MARINO (Sebastian MARTINEZ 46), Charles ARANGUIZ, Gustavo LORENZETTI, Angelo HENRIQUEZ (Raul RUIDIAZ 81), Junior FERNANDES (Francisco CASTRO 88). Tr: Jorge SAMPAOLI

Deportivo Quito 0

Marcelo ELIZAGA - Giovanny ESPINOZA•, Isaac MINA, Luis CHECA (Luis ROMERO 88), Jorge FOLLECO (Edder VACA 72), Pedro VELASCO (Julio BEVACQUA 61), Alex BOLANOS•, Luis SARITAMA•, Fidel MARTINEZ, Matias ALUSTIZA•, Juan Carlos PAREDES•. Tr: Carlos ISCHIA

Estadio Azul, Mexico City
1-05-2012, Att: 29395, Ref: Pezzotta ARG
Cruz Azul 1
Orozco [26]

Jose CORONA - Fausto PINTO, Nestor ARAUJO, Gerardo FLORES•, Jair PEREIRA•, Israel CASTRO, Christian GIMENEZ, Hector GUTIERREZ (Javier AQUINO 46), Alejandro VELA, Omar BRAVO• (Edixon PEREA 58), Emanuel VILLA (Javier OROZCO 46). Tr: Enrique MEZA

Libertad 1
Velazquez [70]

Rodrigo MUNOZ - Ismael BENEGAS, Cristian NASUTI•, Carlos BONET, Sergio AQUINO, Victor AYALA, Miguel SAMUDIO (Joe BIZERA 85), Luciano CIVELLI, Victor CACERES•, Pablo VELAZQUEZ (Cristian MENENDEZ 74), Ariel NUNEZ (Rodolfo GAMARRA 72). Tr: Jorge BURRUCHAGA

Nicolás Leoz, Asuncion
8-05-2012, Att: 6505, Ref: Vauden BRA
Libertad 2
Nunez [9], Caceres [49]

Rodrigo MUNOZ - Cristian NASUTI•, Ismael BENEGAS, Victor AYALA, Miguel SAMUDIO (Joe BIZERA 85), Luciano CIVELLI, Victor CACERES•, Carlos BONET, Sergio AQUINO, Pablo VELAZQUEZ (Cristian MENENDEZ 74), Ariel NUNEZ (Rodolfo GAMARRA 72). Tr: Jorge BURRUCHAGA

Cruz Azul 0

Jose CORONA - Fausto PINTO, Nestor ARAUJO, Gerardo FLORES•, Jair PEREIRA•, Israel CASTRO, Christian GIMENEZ, Hector GUTIERREZ (Javier AQUINO 46), Alejandro VELA, Omar BRAVO• (Edixon PEREA 58), Emanuel VILLA (Javier OROZCO 46). Tr: Enrique MEZA

PART THREE – THE CONTINENTAL CONFEDERATIONS

Beira-Rio, Porto Alegre
25-04-2012, Att: 32 278, Ref: Oliveira BRA
Internacional 0
MURIEL - INDIO, NEI•, KLEBER (FABRICIO 43), RODRIGO MOLEDO, Pablo GUINAZU•, TINGA•, Jesus DATOLO (JO 85), SANDRO SILVA•, LEANDRO DAMIAO, DAGOBERTO (JAJA 46). Tr: DORIVAL JUNIOR
Fluminense 0
DIEGO CAVALIERI - GUM, CARLINHOS, ANDERSON, EDINHO•, THIAGO NEVES (Manuel LANZINI 79), DIGUINHO (JEAN 32), DECO•, BRUNO, FRED, RAFAEL SOBIS• (SOUZA 86). Tr: ABEL BRAGA

Engenhao, Rio de Janeiro
10-05-2012, Att: 33 386, Ref: Seneme BRA
Fluminense 2
Leandro Euzebio [15], Fred [45]
DIEGO CAVALIERI - GUM, LEANDRO EUZEBIO, CARLINHOS•, EDINHO, THIAGO NEVES, DECO (Edwin VALENCIA 73), JEAN•, BRUNO•, FRED (RAFAEL MOURA 69), RAFAEL SOBIS (MARCOS JUNIOR 82). Tr: ABEL BRAGA
Internacional 1
Leandro Damiao [13]
MURIEL - INDIO•, NEI, RODRIGO MOLEDO•, FABRICIO, Pablo GUINAZU (DAGOBERTO 71), TINGA (JO 80), OSCAR, Jesus DATOLO (JAJA 59), SANDRO SILVA, LEANDRO DAMIAO. Tr: Dorival JUNIOR

La Bombonera, Buenos Aires
2-05-2012, Att: 32 715, Carrillo PER
Boca Juniors 2
Riquelme [24], Silva [89]
Agustin ORION - Rolando SCHIAVI•, Clemente RODRIGUEZ•, Franco SOSA•, Juan INSAURRALDE, Roman RIQUELME, Walter ERVITI, Pablo LEDESMA (Diego RIVERO 46), Cristian ERBES• (Juan SANCHEZ MINO 83), Tanque SILVA, Dario CVITANICH (Pablo MOUCHE 66). Tr: Julio FALCIONI
Union Española 1
Jaime [72]
Eduardo LOBOS - Jorge AMPUERO•, Braulio LEAL, Gonzalo VILLAGRA (Rafael OLARRA 59), Diego SCOTTI♦90, Fernando CORDERO, Leonel MENA•, Dagoberto CURRIMILLA, Mauro DIAZ• (Emiliano VECCHIO 90), Emanuel HERRERA, Sebastian JAIME (Jean Paul PINEDA 83). Tr: Jose SIERRA

Santa Laura, Santiago
9-05-2012, Att: 18 454, Ref: Roldan COL
Union Española 2
Pineda [61], Jaime [70]
Eduardo LOBOS - Jorge AMPUERO, Rafael OLARRA, Braulio LEAL, Emiliano VECCHIO, Fernando CORDERO, Leonel MENA, Dagoberto CURRIMILLA, Mauro DIAZ (Jean Paul PINEDA 46), Emanuel HERRERA, Sebastian JAIME. Tr: Jose SIERRA
Boca Juniors 3
Insaurralde [25], Mouche [49], Riquelme [67]
Agustin ORION• - Rolando SCHIAVI, Clemente RODRIGUEZ• (Juan SANCHEZ MINO 78), Facundo RONCAGLIA (Franco SOSA• 46), Juan INSAURRALDE, Diego RIVERO, Roman RIQUELME, Walter ERVITI, Cristian ERBES, Pablo MOUCHE, Dario CVITANICH (Nicolas BLANDI 88): Tr: Julio FALCIONI

QUARTER-FINALS

São Januário, Rio de Janeiro
16-05-2012, Att: 20 510, Ref: Ricci BRA
Vasco da Gama 0
FERNANDO PRASS - THIAGO FELTRI, RODOLFO, FAGNER, RENATO SILVA, JUNINHO PERNAMBUCANO• (CARLOS ALBERTO 71), DIEGO SOUZA (FELIPE 71), NILTON•, ROMULO, EDER LUIS, ALECSANDRO. Tr: CRISTOVAO
Corinthians 0
CASSIO - ALESSANDRO•, CHICAO, FABIO SANTOS, LEANDRO CASTAN, RALF, PAULINHO, ALEX (DOUGLAS 79), DANILO (ELTON 87), EMERSON (WILLIAN 82), JORGE HENRIQUE•. Tr: TITE

Pacaembú, São Paulo
23-05-2012, Att: 35 974, Ref: Vuaden BRA
Corinthians 1
Paulinho [87]
CASSIO - ALESSANDRO•, CHICAO, FABIO SANTOS, LEANDRO CASTAN, RALF, PAULINHO•, ALEX, DANILO, EMERSON• (LIEDSON 78), JORGE HENRIQUE• (WILLIAN 72). Tr: TITE
Vasco da Gama 0
FERNANDO PRASS - THIAGO FELTRI (FELIPE 49), RODOLFO, FAGNER, RENATO SILVA•, JUNINHO PERNAMBUCANO•, DIEGO SOUZA, NILTON•, ROMULO, EDER LUIS• (CARLOS ALBERTO 70), ALECSANDRO. Tr: CRISTOVAO

José Amalfitani, Buenos Aires
17-05-2012, Att: 21 847, Ref: Amarilla PAR
Velez Sarsfield 1
Obolo [35]
Marcelo BAROVERO - Gino PERUZZI•, Sebastian DOMINGUEZ, Emiliano PAPA•, Fabian CUBERO, Augusto FERNANDEZ, Alejandro CABRAL (Ivan BELLA 86), Victor ZAPATA, Francisco CERRO• (David RAMIREZ 90), Juan MARTINEZ (Hector CANTEROS 90), Ivan OBOLO. Tr: Ricardo GARECA
Santos 0
RAFAEL• - Edu DRACENA•, DURVAL, JUAN•, AROUCA, HENRIQUE, ELANO (FELIPE ANDERSON 75), GANSO, ADRIANO•, NEYMAR•, ALAN KARDEC (BORGES 58). Tr: MURICY RAMALHO

Vila Belmiro, Santos
24-05-2012, Att: 13 908, Ref: Silvera URU
Santos 1 4p
RAFAEL - EDU DRACENA, DURVAL, JUAN (LEO 73), AROUCA•, HENRIQUE (MARANHAO 85), ELANO, GANSO, ADRIANO• (Wason RENTERIA 64), NEYMAR•, ALAN KARDEC•. Tr: MURICY RAMALHO
Velez Sarsfield 1 2p
Marcelo BAROVERO♦39 - Gino PERUZZI, Sebastian DOMINGUEZ, Fernando ORTIZ, Emiliano PAPA, Fabian CUBERO, Augusto FERNANDEZ• (Hector CANTEROS 89), Alejandro CABRAL (Ivan BELLA 81), Victor ZAPATA, Juan MARTINEZ, Ivan OBOLO (German MONTOYA 41). Tr: Ricardo GARECA

COPA LIBERTADORES 2012

Nicolás Leoz, Asuncion
16-05-2012, Att: 7189, Ref: Ubriaco URU

Libertad 1
Victor Caceres [7]
Rodrigo MUNOZ - Ismael BENEGAS•, Cristian NASUTI, Victor AYALA, Sergio AQUINO, Miguel SAMUDIO•, Luciano CIVELLI (Mauro CABALLERO JR 86), Victor CACERES•, Carlos BONET (Rodolfo GAMARRA 58), Pablo VELAZQUEZ (Cristian MENENDEZ 75), Ariel NUNEZ•. Tr: Jorge BURRUCHAGA

Universidad de Chile 1
Lorenzetti [55]
Johnny HERRERA - Eugenio MENA, Osvaldo GONZALEZ•, Matias RODRIGUEZ (Emilio HERNANDEZ 81♦90), Jose ROJAS, Marcelo DIAZ, Igor LICHNOVSKY, Felipe GALLEGOS (Paulo MAGALHAES 58), Charles ARANGUIZ, Gustavo LORENZETTI (Albert ACEVEDO 89), Angelo HENRIQUEZ. Tr: Jorge SAMPAOLI

Estadio Nacional, Santiago
24-05-2012, Att: 44 742, Ref: Roldan COL

Universidad de Chile 1 5p
Marcelo Diaz [17]
Johnny HERRERA - Eugenio MENA, Osvaldo GONZALEZ, Albert ACEVEDO, Matias RODRIGUEZ, Jose ROJAS, Marcelo DIAZ•, Charles ARANGUIZ, Gustavo LORENZETTI, Angelo HENRIQUEZ (Raul RUIDIAZ 80), Junior FERNANDES. Tr: Jorge SAMPAOLI

Libertad 1 3p
OG [22]
Rodrigo MUNOZ - Ismael BENEGAS, Cristian NASUTI•, Victor AYALA, Sergio AQUINO (Jonathan SANTANA 81), Miguel SAMUDIO•, Luciano CIVELLI•, Victor CACERES•, Carlos BONET (Rodolfo GAMARRA 81), Pablo VELAZQUEZ•, Ariel NUNEZ• (Nestor CAMACHO 87). Tr: Jorge BURRUCHAGA

La Bombonera, Buenos Aires
17-05-2012, Att: 45 320, Ref: Jose Buitrago COL

Boca Juniors 1
Mouche [51]
Agustin ORION - Rolando SCHIAVI, Clemente RODRIGUEZ•, Facundo RONCAGLIA, Juan INSAURRALDE, Diego RIVERO, Roman RIQUELME, Walter ERVITI•, Cristian ERBES (Nicolas BLANDI 46), Pablo MOUCHE, Dario CVITANICH (Sergio ARAUJO 88). Tr: Julio FALCIONI

Fluminense 0
DIEGO CAVALIERI - GUM, CARLINHOS••♦34, ANDERSON, EDINHO•, THIAGO NEVES (DIGAO 85), WAGNER•, JEAN, BRUNO, RAFAEL MOURA (MARCOS JUNIOR 66), RAFAEL SOBIS (CARLETO• 46). Tr: Abel BRAGA

Engenhao, Rio de Janeiro
23-05-2012, Att: 36 276, Ref: Osses CHI

Fluminense 1
Carleto [16]
DIEGO CAVALIERI - GUM, ANDERSON, CARLETO, EDINHO, THIAGO NEVES, WAGNER (WELLINGTON NEM 73), JEAN•, BRUNO, RAFAEL MOURA, RAFAEL SOBIS (MARCOS JUNIOR 89). Tr: Abel BRAGA

Boca Juniors 1
Silva [91+]
Agustin ORION - Rolando SCHIAVI, Clemente RODRIGUEZ•, Facundo RONCAGLIA, Juan INSAURRALDE, Diego RIVERO, Roman RIQUELME, Walter ERVITI (Matias CARUZZO 90), Cristian ERBES (Juan SANCHEZ MINO 80), Tanque SILVA, Dario CVITANICH (Pablo MOUCHE• 66). Tr: Julio FALCIONI

SEMI-FINALS

Vila Belmiro, Santos
13-06-2012, Att: 14 788, Ref: Marcelo BRA

Santos 0
RAFAEL - EDU DRACENA, DURVAL, JUAN, AROUCA (FELIPE ANDERSON 81), HENRIQUE, ELANO (BORGES 46), GANSO, ADRIANO, NEYMAR•, ALAN KARDEC (DIMBA 90). Tr: MURICY RAMALHO

Corinthians 1
Emerson [28]
CASSIO• - ALESSANDRO•, CHICAO, FABIO SANTOS, LEANDRO CASTAN•, RALF, PAULINHO, ALEX (WALLACE 90), DANILO, EMERSON••♦77, JORGE HENRIQUE. Tr: TITE

Pacaembú, São Paulo
20-06-2012, At: 35 873, Ref: Vuaden BRA

Corinthians 1
Danilo [47]
CASSIO - ALESSANDRO, CHICAO, FABIO SANTOS, LEANDRO CASTAN, RALF, PAULINHO, ALEX, DANILO, WILLIAN (LIEDSON 46), JORGE HENRIQUE. Tr: TITE

Santos 1
Neymar [39]
RAFAEL - EDU DRACENA, DURVAL, JUAN (LEO 75), AROUCA, HENRIQUE, GANSO, ADRIANO (ELANO 74), BORGES (DIMBA 80), NEYMAR, ALAN KARDEC. Tr: MURICY RAMALHO

La Bombonera, Buenos Aires
14-06-2012, Att: 42 983, Ref: Roldan COL

Boca Juniors 2
Silva [15], Sanchez Mino [54]
Agustin ORION - Rolando SCHIAVI, Facundo RONCAGLIA•, Juan INSAURRALDE•, Roman RIQUELME, Walter ERVITI, Pablo LEDESMA (Cristian CHAVEZ 78), Leandro SOMOZA•, Juan SANCHEZ MINO, Pablo MOUCHE (Dario CVITANICH 81), Tanque SILVA. Tr: Julio FALCIONI

Universidad de Chile 0
Johnny HERRERA - Eugenio MENA, Osvaldo GONZALEZ•, Albert ACEVEDO, Matias RODRIGUEZ (Paulo MAGALHAES 56), Jose ROJAS, Marcelo DIAZ, Charles ARANGUIZ, Gustavo LORENZETTI (Raul RUIDIAZ 81), Angelo HENRIQUEZ (Sebastian UBILLA 73), Junior FERNANDES. Tr: Jorge SAMPAOLI

Estadio Nacional, Santiago
21-06-2012, Att: 51 000, Ref: Ubriaco URU

Universidad de Chile 0
Johnny HERRERA• - Eugenio MENA, Osvaldo GONZALEZ (Paulo MAGALHAES 60), Matias RODRIGUEZ, Jose ROJAS•, Marcelo DIAZ, Guillermo MARINO, Charles ARANGUIZ, Angelo HENRIQUEZ, Junior FERNANDES (Raul RUIDIAZ 73), Francisco CASTRO (Sebastian UBILLA 46). Tr: Jorge SAMPAOLI

Boca Juniors 0
Agustin ORION• - Rolando SCHIAVI, Clemente RODRIGUEZ, Matias CARUZZO, Facundo RONCAGLIA•, Roman RIQUELME••, Walter ERVITI, Pablo LEDESMA (Diego RIVERO 90), Leandro SOMOZA, Pablo MOUCHE (Dario CVITANICH• 75), Tanque SILVA• (Lucas VIATRI 84). Tr: Julio FALCIONI

FINAL

MATCH STATS (1st Leg)

Boca		Corinthians
9	Shots	6
3	Shots on Goal	3
13	Fouls Committed	6
7	Corner Kicks	3
6	Caught Offside	1

MATCH STATS (2nd Leg)

Corinthians		Boca
7	Shots	3
5	Shots on Goal	2
11	Fouls Committed	16
4	Corner Kicks	4
1	Caught Offside	5

We totally deserved this. We did not lose any games. It is extraordinary for us to win this title, which Corinthians had never won in the past.

Danilo

We've won the title without losing a game. The other teams that have done this in the past only played seven or eight matches. So how does becoming champions without losing in 14 games compare? I can't quite grasp how much it means, but it's going to be a long time before another team does the same.

Tite

I've told the club president I'm not going to carry on. I feel empty. I haven't got anything else to give to the club. I can't play at half pace.

Juan Roman Riquelme

WOMEN'S TOURNAMENTS IN SOUTH AMERICA 2012

CAMPEONATO SUDAMERICANO FEMENINO SUB-20 BRAZIL 2012

First Round Group Stage

Group A	Pl	W	D	L	F	A	Pts	PAR	URU	BOL	PER
Brazil	4	4	0	0	16	1	**12**	2-0	7-0	2-1	6-0
Paraguay	4	2	1	1	6	3	**7**		3-1	0-0	3-0
Uruguay	4	2	0	2	5	12	6			2-1	2-1
Bolivia	4	0	2	2	2	4	2				0-0
Peru	4	0	1	3	1	9	1				

Group B	Pl	W	D	L	F	A	Pts	COL	CHI	ECU	VEN
Argentina	4	3	0	1	10	6	**9**	0-1	3-2	4-2	3-1
Colombia	4	3	0	1	7	3	**9**		1-0	2-0	0-1
Chile	4	2	0	2	9	5	6			3-1	4-0
Ecuador	4	1	0	3	6	11	3				3-2
Venezuela	4	1	0	3	4	10	3				

Final Round Group

	Pl	W	D	L	F	A	Pts	ARG	COL	PAR
Brazil	3	3	0	0	11	0	**9**	2-0	1-0	8-0
Argentina	3	1	1	1	5	5	4		3-1	2-2
Colombia	3	1	0	2	3	5	3			2-1
Paraguay	3	0	1	2	3	12	1			

Top scorer: **9** - Ketlen BRA • **7** - Thais BRA • **4** - Soriano ARG • **3** - Beatriz BRA; Glaucia BRA; Jetzabeth CHI; Florencia ARG & Cuevas PAR

Brazil, Argentina and Colombia qualified for the 2013 FIFA U-20 Women's World Cup in Japan
Tournament played in Curitiba, Ponta Grossa and Paranagua, Brazil from 20-01-2012 to 5-02-2012

CAMPEONATO SUDAMERICANO FEMENINO SUB-17 BOLIVIA 2012

First Round Group Stage

Group A	Pl	W	D	L	F	A	Pts	ARG	ECU	BOL	PER
Uruguay	4	4	0	0	13	5	**12**	1-0	7-2	2-1	3-2
Argentina	4	3	0	1	8	3	**9**		1-0	4-3	3-0
Ecuador	4	1	1	2	7	11	4			4-2	1-1
Bolivia	4	1	0	3	9	11	3				4-1
Peru	4	0	1	3	4	11	1				

Group B	Pl	W	D	L	F	A	Pts	COL	VEN	PAR	CHI
Brazil	4	4	0	0	24	1	**12**	5-1	3-0	7-0	9-0
Colombia	4	3	0	1	9	6	**9**		2-1	3-0	3-0
Venezuela	4	2	0	2	7	7	6			3-2	3-0
Paraguay	4	1	0	3	4	14	3				2-1
Chile	4	0	0	4	1	17	0				

Final Round Group

	Pl	W	D	L	F	A	Pts	URU	COL	ARG
Brazil	3	3	0	0	9	2	**9**	1-0	3-1	5-1
Uruguay	3	2	0	1	6	4	6		2-1	4-2
Colombia	3	1	0	2	6	5	3			4-0
Argentina	3	0	0	3	3	13	0			

Top scorer: **9** - Yamila Badell URU • **8** - Byanca Araujo BRA • **7** - Brenda Carolina BRA • **4** - Dayana Castilo COL & Carolina Birizamberri URU

Brazil, Uruguay and Colombia qualified for the 2013 FIFA U-17 Women's World Cup in Azerbaijan
Tournament played in Sucre, Santa Cruz and Montero, Bolivia from 9-03-2012 to 25-03-2012

COPA SUDAMERICANA 2012

First Round

São Paulo FC	BRA	Bye
EC Bahia	BRA	Bye
Nacional Montevideo	URU	0 4
Deportes Iquique *	CHI	2 0
Monagas *	VEN	0 2
LDU Loja	ECU	2 4
Emelec *	ECU	1 1
Universidad San Martin	PER	0 1
Danubio *	URU	0 1
Olimpia	PAR	0 2
Universidad de Chile	CHI	Bye
Independiente	ARG	Bye
Boca Juniors	ARG	Bye
Envigado	COL	0 2
Unión Comercio *	PER	0 0
Universitario Sucre	BOL	0 1
Liverpool *	URU	3 2
Atlético Goianiense	BRA	Bye
Figueirense	BRA	Bye
Deportes Tolima *	COL	3 0
Deportivo Lara	VEN	1 0
Blooming *	BOL	1 0
Universidad Católica	CHI	1 3
Millonarios	COL	0 3
Inti Gas Deportes *	PER	0 0
Oriente Petrolero	BOL	1 1
Guaraní *	PAR	0 2
Botafogo	BRA	Bye
Palmeiras	BRA	Bye
Barcelona	ECU	0 5
Deportivo Tachira *	VEN	0 1
Tacuary *	PAR	0 2
Cobreloa	CHI	1 2
Coritiba	BRA	Bye
Grêmio	BRA	Bye
Cerro Porteño	PAR	3 4
O'Higgins *	CHI	3 0
La Equidad *	COL	0 1
Mineros de Guyana	VEN	1 2
Racing Club	ARG	Bye
Colón Santa Fe	ARG	Bye
Deportivo Quito *	ECU	1 3
León de Huánuco	PER	0 2
Cerro Largo	URU	1 0
Aurora *	BOL	2 0
Argentinos Juniors	ARG	Bye
Tigre	ARG	Bye

Second round

São Paulo FC	2	2
EC Bahia *	0	0
Nacional Montevideo	1	1
LDU Loja *	0	2
Emelec	1	0
Olimpia *	0	0
Universidad de Chile	Bye	
Independiente	3	0
Boca Juniors *	3	0
Envigado *	1	0
Liverpool	1	1
Atlético Goianiense *	1 1	4p
Figueirense	1 1	2p
Deportes Tolima	0	3
Universidad Católica *	2	1
Millonarios	4	1
Guaraní *	2	1
Botafogo	0	3
Palmeiras *	2	1
Barcelona	0	4
Cobreloa *	0	3
Coritiba	0	3
Grêmio *	1	2
Cerro Porteño	2	4
Mineros de Guyana *	2	0
Racing Club	1	1
Colón Santa Fe *	3	2
Deportivo Quito *	2	3
Aurora	1	1
Argentinos Juniors *	1	1
Tigre	2	4

Round of 16

São Paulo FC	1	0
LDU Loja *	1	0
Emelec	2	0
Universidad de Chile *	2	1
Independiente *	2	2
Liverpool	1	1
Atlético Goianiense	0	3
Universidad Católica *	2	1
Millonarios	1	3
Palmeiras *	3	0
Barcelona *	0	1
Grêmio	1	2
Cerro Porteño	2	2
Colón Santa Fe *	1	1
Deportivo Quito *	2	0
Tigre	0	4

* Home team in the 1st leg

COPA SUDAMERICANA 2012

Quarter-finals	Semi-finals	Final

COPA SUDAMERICANA FINAL 2012 FIRST LEG
La Bombonera, Buenos Aires, 5-12-2012, Att: 49 000, Ref: Antonio Arias PAR

| Tigre | 0 |
| São Paulo FC | 0 |

TIGRE

Damian ALBIL - Norberto PAPARATTO•, Mariano ECHEVERRIA, Alejandro DONATTI♦15, Lucas ORBAN - Angel Gaston DIAZ, Diego FERREIRA - Martin GALMARINI (c), Ramiro LEONE, Ruben BOTTA• (Agustin TORASSA 87) - Ezequiel MAGGIOLO (Diego FTACLA 77). Tr: Nestor GOROSITO

SAO PAULO FC

ROGERIO CENI (c) - PAULO MIRANDA, RAFAEL TOLOI•, RHODLFO•, CORTEZ - WELLINGTON, DENILSON• - JADSON (CICERO 60) - LUCAS, OSVALDO, LUIS FABIANO♦14. Tr: NEY FRANCO

| São Paulo FC | 2 | 5 |
| Universidad de Chile * | 0 | 0 |

| São Paulo FC | 1 | 0 |
| Universidad Católica * | 1 | 0 |

| Independiente * | 2 | 1 |
| **Universidad Católica** | 2 | 2 |

| São Paulo FC | 0 | 2 |
| Tigre * | 0 | 0 |

| **Millonarios** | 0 | 3 |
| Grêmio * | 1 | 1 |

| Millonarios | 0 | 1 |
| **Tigre** * | 0 | 1 |

COPA SUDAMERICANA FINAL 2012 SECOND LEG
Morumbi, São Paulo, 12-12-2012, Att: 67 042, Ref: Enrique Osses CHI
Match abandoned at half-time after Tigre refused to play on. Result stood

| São Paulo FC | 2 | Lucas [22], Osvaldo [28] |
| Tigre | 0 | |

SAO PAULO FC

ROGERIO CENI (c) - PAULO MIRANDA♦45, RAFAEL TOLOI, RHODOLFO, CORTEZ - WELLINGTON, DENILSON• - JADSON - LUCAS, OSVALDO•, WILLIAN JOSE. Tr: NEY FRANCO

TIGRE

Damian ALBIL - Erik GODOY•, Norberto PAPARATTO, Mariano ECHEVERRIA, Lucas ORBAN - Angel Gaston DIAZ♦45, Diego FERREIRA - Martin GALMARINI• (c), Ramiro LEONE, Ruben BOTTA - Ezequiel MAGGIOLO. Tr: Nestor GOROSITO

| Cerro Porteño * | 1 | 2 |
| **Tigre** | 0 | 4 |

Top scorers: **5** - Jonathan Fabbro PAR, Cerro Porteño; Carlos Nunez URU, Liverpool; Fabio Renato BRA, LDU Loja; Wason Renteria COL, Millonarios & Michael Rios CHI, Un. Católica

OFC

OCEANIA FOOTBALL CONFEDERATION

OFC MEMBER ASSOCIATIONS (11)
ASA - **American Samoa** • COK - **Cook Islands** • FIJ - **Fiji** • NCL - **New Caledonia** • NZL - **New Zealand**
PNG - **Papua New Guinea** • SAM - **Samoa** • SOL - **Solomon Islands** • TAH - **Tahiti** • TGA - **Tonga** • VAN - **Vanuatu**

ASSOCIATE OFC MEMBER ASSOCIATIONS (5)
KIR - **Kiribati** • FSM - **Micronesia** • NIU - **Niue** • PLW - **Palau** • TUV - **Tuvalu**
None of these five nations are affiliated to FIFA

Oceania produced one of the best stories of 2012 when Tahiti surprised everyone - themselves included - by winning the 2012 OFC Nations Cup in the Solomon Islands. In the 39-year history of the tournament the trophy had only ever been won by either Australia or New Zealand but the decision by the Australians to join the Asian Football Confederation in 2006 has meant a more level playing field for the remaining members of the OFC. At the end of 2011 a preliminary group was held in Samoa for the four smallest nations in the OFC, a tournament that received worldwide attention when American Samoa won their first-ever international match by beating Tonga 2-1. They failed to claim the single berth on offer for the finals, however, and it was the hosts Samoa who booked their ticket to the Solomon Islands. There the two first round groups also formed part of the 2014 FIFA World Cup qualifying process, with the top two from each progressing not only to the semi-finals of the Nations Cup but also to a final round of World Cup qualifying to be played on a home and away basis in the second half of 2012. With everyone predicting a final between the Solomon Islands and New Zealand, the semi-finals turned expectations on their heads when New Caledonia beat New Zealand 2-0 and Tahiti knocked out hosts Solomon Islands 1-0. In the final an early goal by Steevy Chong was enough for Tahiti to create their own piece of history and also to book their place at the 2013 FIFA Confederations Cup in Brazil. There was consolation for New Zealand in the 2011-12 OFC Champions League when Auckland City prevented AS Tefana completing an unlikely double for Tahiti after beating them 3-1 on aggregate in the final. Tefana had come away from the first leg in Auckland with hopes of turning around a 2-1 defeat but lost the return leg 1-0 in Tahiti after a Manel Exposito goal just before half-time secured the trophy for Auckland for the fourth time in seven years.

Oceania Football Confederation (OFC)
Ericsson Stadium, 12 Maurice Road, Penrose, PO Box 62 586, Auckland 6, New Zealand
Tel +64 9 5258161   Fax +64 9 5258164
info@ofcfoot.org.nz   www.oceaniafootball.com
President: David Chung PNG
General Secretary: Tai Nicholas COK
Vice-President: Martin Alufurai SOL
OFC Formed: 1966

OFC EXECUTIVE COMMITTEE
President: David Chung PNG

Senior Vice-President: Martin Alufurai SOL	Vice-President: Lee Harmon COK	Treasurer: Dr MS Sahu Khan FIJ
	Fred de Jong NZL	
Lambert Matlock VAN	Toetu Petana SAM	Lord Ve'ehala TGA

MAP OF OFC MEMBER NATIONS

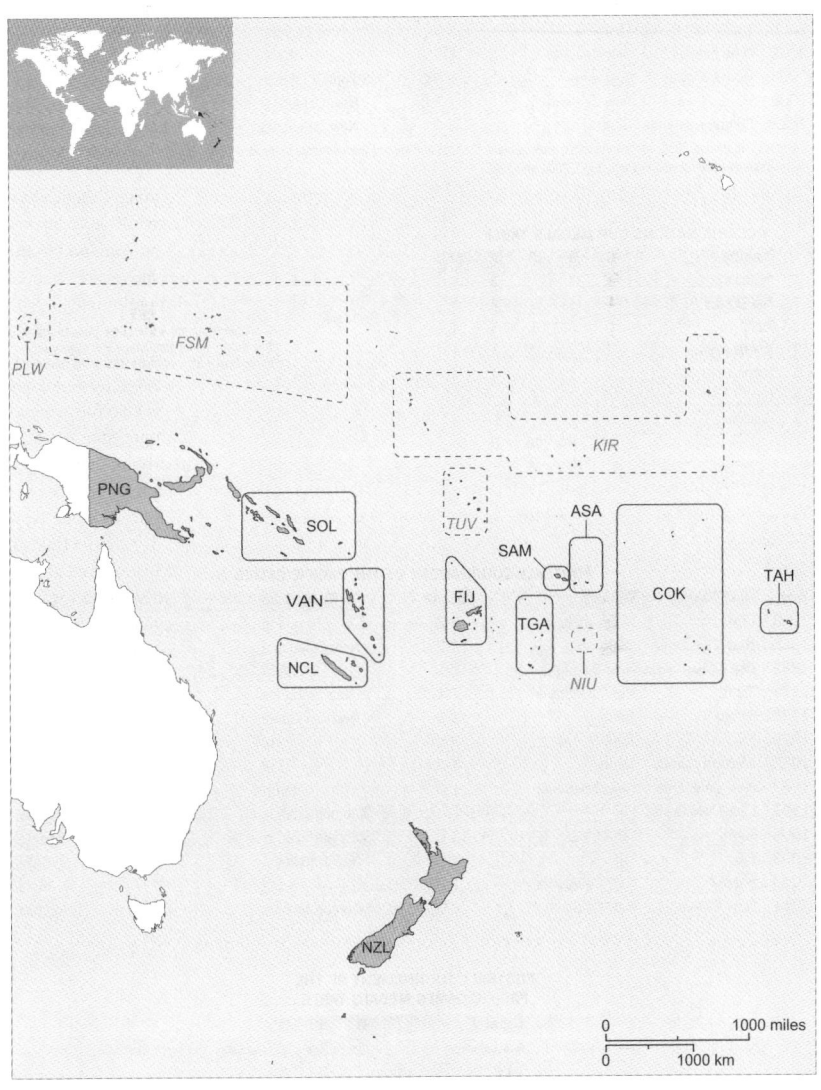

OCEANIA NATIONAL TEAM TOURNAMENTS

OCEANIA NATIONS CUP

Year	Host Country	Winners	Score	Runners-up	Venue
1973	New Zealand	New Zealand	2-0	Tahiti	Auckland
1980	New Caledonia	Australia	4-2	Tahiti	Nouméa
1996	Home & away	Australia	6-0 5-0	Tahiti	Papeete & Canberra
1998	Australia	New Zealand	1-0	Australia	Brisbane
2000	Tahiti	Australia	2-0	New Zealand	Stade de Pater, Papeete
2002	New Zealand	New Zealand	1-0	Australia	Ericsson Stadium, Auckland
2004	Home & away	Australia	5-1 6-0	Solomon Islands	Honaria & Sydney
2008	Home & away	New Zealand	3-1 3-0	New Caledonia	League system
2012	Solomon Islands	Tahiti	1-0	New Caledonia	Lawson Tama, Honiara

There was no final in 2008. The results listed were between the first and second placed teams in the FIFA World Cup qualifying group for Oceania. Semi-finals were not played in 1973, 1980, 2004 and 2008

OCEANIA NATIONS CUP MEDALS TABLE

	Country	G	S	B	F	SF
1	Australia	4	2		6	4
2	New Zealand	4	1	3	4	5
3	Tahiti	1	3	1	4	4
4	New Caledonia		2	2	1	1
5	Solomon Islands		1	2	1	3
6	Fiji			2		1
7	Vanuatu					2
		9	9	10	16	20

KEY
G = Gold (winners) • S = Silver (runners-up) • B = Bronze (semi-finalists) • F = appearances in the final • SF = appearances in the semi-final

FOOTBALL TOURNAMENT OF THE PACIFIC GAMES

Year	Host Country	Winners	Score	Runners-up	Venue
1963	Fiji	New Caledonia	8-2	Fiji	Suva
1966	New Caledonia	Tahiti	2-0	New Caledonia	Noumea
1969	Papua New Guinea	New Caledonia	2-1	Tahiti	Port Moresby
1971	Tahiti	New Caledonia	7-1	New Hebrides	Papeete
1975	Guam	Tahiti	2-1	New Caledonia	Guam
1979	Fiji	Tahiti	3-0	Fiji	Suva
1983	Western Samoa	Tahiti	1-0	Fiji	Apia
1987	New Caledonia	New Caledonia	1-0	Tahiti	Noumea
1991	Papua New Guinea	Fiji	1-1 ?-?p	Solomon Islands	Port Moresby
1995	Tahiti	Tahiti	2-0	Solomon Islands	Papeete
2003	Fiji	Fiji	2-0	New Caledonia	Suva
2007	Samoa	New Caledonia	1-0	Fiji	Apia
2011	New Caledonia	New Caledonia	2-0	Solomon Islands	Noumea

FOOTBALL TOURNAMENT OF THE PACIFIC GAMES MEDALS TABLE

	Country	G	S	B
1	New Caledonia	6	3	2
2	Tahiti	5	2	3
3	Fiji	2	4	1
4	Solomon Islands		3	2
5	Vanuatu		1	3
6	Papua New Guinea			2
		13	13	13

FOOTBALL TOURNAMENT OF THE SOUTH PACIFIC MINI GAMES

Year	Host Country	Winners	Score	Runners-up	Venue
1981	Solomon Islands	Tahiti	1-0	New Caledonia	Honiara
1985	Cook Islands	Tahiti	2-0	Fiji	Rarotonga
1989	Tonga	Papua New Guinea	0-0 4-3p	Fiji	Nuku'alofa
1993	Vanuatu	Tahiti	3-0	Fiji	Port Vila

FOOTBALL TOURNAMENT OF THE SOUTH PACIFIC MINI GAMES MEDALS TABLE

	Country	G	S
1	Tahiti	3	
2	Papua New Guinea	1	
3	Fiji		3
4	New Caledonia		1
		4	4

POLYNESIAN CUP

Year	Host Country	Winners	Score	Runners-up	Venue
1994	Western Samoa	Tahiti	1-0	Tonga	Apia
1996	Tonga	Tonga	1-0	Western Samoa	Nuku'alofa
1998	Cook Islands	Tahiti	5-0	Cook Islands	Rarotonga
2000	Tahiti	Tahiti	2-0	Cook Islands	Papete

Competitions have always been organised on a league basis. The result listed is the game between the top two in the league standings

POLYNESIAN CUP MEDALS TABLE

	Country	G	S	B
1	Tahiti	3		
2	Tonga	1	1	
3	Cook Islands		2	1
4	Samoa		1	3
		4	4	4

MELANESIAN CUP

Year	Host Country	Winners	Score	Runners-up	Venue
1988	Solomon Islands	Fiji	3-1	Solomon Islands	Solomon Islands
1989	Fiji	Fiji	3-0	New Caledonia	Fiji
1990	Vanuatu	Vanuatu	1-0	New Caledonia	Vanuatu
1992	Vanuatu	Fiji	2-2	New Caledonia	Vanuatu
1994	Solomon Islands	Solomon Islands	1-0	Fiji	Solomon Islands
1996	Papua New Guinea	Papua New Guinea	1-1	Solomon Islands	Papua New Guinea
1998	Vanuatu	Fiji	2-1	Vanuatu	Vanuatu
2000	Fiji	Fiji	2-2	Solomon Islands	Fiji

A final was played only in the first competition in 1988. The results listed after then are between the first two teams in the league standings

MELANESIAN CUP MEDALS TABLE

	Country	G	S	B
1	Fiji	5	1	1
2	Solomon Islands	1	3	3
3	Vanuatu	1	1	2
4	Papua New Guinea	1		1
5	New Caledonia		3	1
		8	7	8

OCEANIA CLUB TOURNAMENTS

OFC CHAMPIONS LEAGUE

Year	Winners	Country	Score	Country	Runners-up
1987	Adelaide City	AUS	1-1 4-1p	NZL	Mount Wellington
1999	South Melbourne	AUS	5-1	FIJ	Nadi
2001	Wollongong City Wolves	AUS	1-0	VAN	Tafea FC
2005	Sydney FC	AUS	2-0	NCL	AS Magenta
2006	Auckland City	NZL	3-1	TAH	AS Piraé
2007	Waitakere United	NZL	1-2 1-0	FIJ	Ba
2008	Waitakere United	NZL	1-3 5-0	SOL	Kossa
2009	Auckland City	NZL	7-2 2-2	SOL	Koloale
2010	Hekari United	PNG	3-0 1-2	NZL	Waitakere United
2011	Auckland City	NZL	2-1 4-0	VAN	Amicale
2012	Auckland City	NZL	3-1 1-0	TAH	AS Tefana

OFC CHAMPIONS LEAGUE MEDALS TABLE

	Country	G	S	B	F	SF
1	New Zealand	6	2	3	8	4
2	Australia	4			4	3
3	Papua New Guinea	1			1	
4	Tahiti		2	1	2	4
5	Vanuatu		2	1	2	2
6	Fiji		2		2	2
7	Solomon Islands		2		2	
8	New Caledonia		1		1	1
		11	11	5	22	16

OFC CHAMPIONS LEAGUE MEDALS TABLE

	Club		G	S	B
1	Auckland City	NZL	4		
2	Waitakere United	NZL	2	1	
3	Adelaide City	AUS	1		
	Hekari United	PNG	1		
	South Melbourne	AUS	1		

OFC CHAMPIONS LEAGUE MEDALS TABLE (CONT'D)

	Club		G	S	B
	Sydney FC	AUS	1		
	Wollongong City Wolves	AUS	1		
8	Tafea FC	VAN		1	1
9	Amicale	VAN		1	
	Ba	FIJ		1	
	Koloale	SOL		1	
	Kossa	SOL		1	
	AS Magenta	NCL		1	
	Mount Wellington	NZL		1	
	Nadi	FIJ		1	
	AS Pirae	TAH		1	
	AS Tefana	TAH		1	
18	Central United	NZL			1
	Napier City Rovers	NZL			1
	AS Venus	TAH			1
	YoungHeart Manawatu	NZL			1
			11	11	5

OCEANIA YOUTH TOURNAMENTS

OFC U–20 CHAMPIONSHIP

Year	Host Country	Winners	Score	Runners-up	Venue
1974	Tahiti	Tahiti	2-0	New Zealand	Papeete
1978	New Zealand	Australia	5-1 †	Fiji	Auckland
1980	Fiji	New Zealand	2-0	Australia	Suva
1982	Papua New Guinea	Australia	4-3	New Zealand	Port Moresby
1985	Australia	Australia	3-2 †	Israel	Sydney
1987	New Zealand	Australia	1-1 †	Israel	Auckland
1988	Fiji	Australia	1-0	New Zealand	Suva
1990	Fiji	Australia	6-0 †	New Zealand	Suva
1992	Tahiti	New Zealand	1-0 †	Tahiti	Papeete
1994	Fiji	Australia	1-0	New Zealand	Suva
1996	Tahiti	Australia	2-1	New Zealand	Papeete
1998	Samoa	Australia	2-0	Fiji	Apia

OFC U–20 CHAMPIONSHIP (CONT'D)

Year	Host Country	Winners	Score	Runners-up	Venue
2001	New Cal/Cook Is	Australia	1-2 3-1	New Zealand	Auckland & Coffs Harbour
2003	Vanuatu/Fiji	Australia	11-0 4-0	Fiji	Melbourne & Ba
2005	Solomon Islands	Australia	3-0	Solomon Islands	Honiara
2007	New Zealand	New Zealand	3-2	Fiji	Waitakere
2009	Tahiti	Tahiti	0-0	New Caledonia	Papeete
2011	New Zealand	New Zealand	3-1	Solomon Islands	Auckland

The 1978, 1985, 1987, 1990, 1992, 2007 and 2009 tournaments were played as leagues • The results shown are those between the top two teams

OFC U-20 CHAMPIONSHIP
MEDALS TABLE

	Country	G	S	B
1	Australia	12	1	
2	New Zealand	4	7	5
3	Tahiti	2	1	
4	Fiji		4	4
5	Solomon Islands		2	2
6	Israel		2	
7	New Caledonia		1	1
8	Vanuatu			3
9	Chinese Taipei			1
		18	18	16

OFC U–17 CHAMPIONSHIP

Year	Host Country	Winners	Score	Runners-up	Venue
1983	New Zealand	Australia	2-1	New Zealand	Mount Smart, Auckland
1986	Chinese Taipei	Australia	0-1	New Zealand	CKF Stadium, Kaohsiung
1989	Australia	Australia	5-1	New Zealand	
1991	New Zealand	Australia	1-1 1-0	New Zealand	Napier
1993	New Zealand	Australia	3-0	Soloman Islands	
1995	Vanuatu	Australia	1-0	New Zealand	
1997	New Zealand	New Zealand	1-0	Australia	
1999	Fiji	Australia	5-0	Fiji	Churchill Park, Lautoka
2001	Samoa/Cook Isl	Australia	3-0 6-0	New Zealand	Canberra & Auckland
2003	Home & away	Australia	3-1 4-0	New Caledonia	Nouméa
2005	New Caledonia	Australia	1-0	Vanuatu	Nouméa
2007	Tahiti	New Zealand	2-1	Tahiti	Papeete
2009	New Zealand	New Zealand	2-0	Tahiti	Auckland
2011	New Zealand	New Zealand	2-0	Tahiti	Auckland

From 1983 to 1991 and in 2007 and 2009 the tournaments were played as leagues • The results shown are those between the top two teams

OFC U-17 CHAMPIONSHIP
MEDALS TABLE

	Country	G	S	B
1	Australia	10	1	
2	New Zealand	4	6	
3	Tahiti		3	
4	Solomon Islands		1	4
5	Fiji		1	2
6	New Caledonia		1	1
7	Vanuatu		1	1
8	Chinese Taipei			3
		14	14	11

OCEANIA WOMEN'S TOURNAMENTS

OFC WOMEN'S CHAMPIONSHIP

Year	Host Country	Winners	Score	Runners-up	Venue
1983	New Caledonia	New Zealand	3-2	Australia	Nouméa
1986	New Zealand	Chinese Taipei	4-1	Australia	Christchurch
1989	Australia	Chinese Taipei	1-0	New Zealand	Brisbane
1991	Australia	New Zealand	1-0 0-1 †	Australia	Sydney
1995	Papua N. Guinea	Australia	1-2 1-0 †	New Zealand	Port Moresby
1998	New Zealand	Australia	3-1	New Zealand	Mount Smart, Auckland
2003	Australia	Australia	2-0 †	New Zealand	Belconnen, Canberra
2007	Papua N. Guinea	New Zealand	7-0	Papua New Guinea	Lae
2010	New Zealand	New Zealand	11-0	Papua New Guinea	Auckland

† The 1991, 1995, 2003 and 2007 tournaments were played as leagues • The results shown are those between the top two teams

OFC WOMEN'S CHAMPIONSHIP MEDALS TABLE

	Country	G	S	B
1	New Zealand	4	4	1
2	Australia	3	3	1
3	Chinese Taipei	2		
4	Papua New Guinea		2	4
5	New Caledonia			1
6	Tonga			1
7	Cook Islands			1
		9	9	9

OFC WOMEN'S U-20 CHAMPIONSHIP

Year	Host Country	Winners	Score	Runners-up	Venue
2002	Tonga	Australia	6-0	New Zealand	Nuku'alofa
2004	Papua New Guinea	Australia	14-1	Papua New Guinea	Lloyd Robson Oval, Port Moresby
2006	Samoa	New Zealand	6-0	Tonga	JS Blatter Complex, Apia
2010	New Zealand	New Zealand	8-0	Cook Islands	North Harbour, Auckland
2012	New Zealand	New Zealand	6-0	Papua New Guinea	Centre Park, Mangere

OFC WOMEN'S U-17 CHAMPIONSHIP

Year	Host Country	Winners	Score	Runners-up	Venue
2010	New Zealand	New Zealand	10-0	Solomon Islands	North Harbour, Auckland
2012	New Zealand	New Zealand	9-0	Papua New Guinea	Centre Park, Mangere

WOMEN'S FOOTBALL TOURNAMENT OF THE PACIFIC GAMES

Year	Host Country	Winners	Score	Runners-up	Venue
2003	Fiji	Papua New Guinea	†	Guam	Suva
2007	Samoa	Papua New Guinea	3-1	Tonga	Apia
2011	New Caledonia	Papua New Guinea	2-1	New Caledonia	Noumea

† Played on a league basis

OFC WOMEN'S U-20 CHAMPIONSHIP MEDALS TABLE

	Country	G	S	B
1	New Zealand	3	1	
2	Australia	2		
3	Papua New Guinea		2	1
4	Tonga		1	2
5	Cook Islands		1	
6	Solomon Islands			1
	New Caledonia			1
		5	5	5

OFC WOMEN'S U-17 CHAMPIONSHIP MEDALS TABLE

	Country	G	S	B
1	New Zealand	2		
2	Papua New Guinea		1	1
3	Solomon Islands		1	
4	Cook Islands			1
		2	2	2

WOMEN'S FOOTBALL TOURNAMENT OF THE PACIFIC GAMES MEDALS

	Country	G	S	B
1	Papua New Guinea	3		
2	Tonga		1	1
3	Guam		1	
4	New Caledonia		1	
5	Fiji			2
		3	3	3

OCEANIA NATIONAL TEAM TOURNAMENTS 2012

OFC NATIONS CUP SOLOMON ISLANDS 2012

First Round Group Stage

Group A	Pl	W	D	L	F	A	Pts	NCL	VAN	SAM
Tahiti	3	3	0	0	18	5	9	4-3	4-1	10-1
New Caledonia	3	2	0	1	17	6	6		5-2	9-0
Vanuatu	3	1	0	2	8	9	3			5-0
Samoa	3	0	0	3	1	24	0			

Group B	Pl	W	D	L	F	A	Pts	SOL	FIJ	PNG
New Zealand	3	2	1	0	4	2	7	1-1	1-0	2-1
Solomon Islands	3	1	2	0	2	1	5		0-0	1-0
Fiji	3	0	2	1	1	2	2			1-1
Papua New Guinea	3	0	1	2	2	4	1			

Top scorers: **6** - Jacques **HAEKO** NCL • **5** - Chris **WOOD** NZL & Lorenzo **TEHAU** TAH • **4** - Bertrand **KAI** NCL; Benjamin **TOTORI** SOL; Alvin **TEHAU** TAH & Jonathan **TEHAU** TAH • **3** - Robert **TASSO** VAN

Semi-finals

Tahiti	1
Solomon Islands	0

New Zealand	0
New Caledonia	2

Final

Tahiti	1
New Caledonia	0

3rd Place Play-off

New Zealand	4
Solomon Islands	3

GROUP A

		Pl	W	D	L	F	A	Pts	NCL	VAN	SAM
Tahiti	TAH	3	3	0	0	18	5	9	4-3	4-1	10-1
New Caledonia	NCL	3	2	0	1	17	6	6		5-2	9-0
Vanuatu	VAN	3	1	0	2	8	9	3			5-0
Samoa	SOL	3	0	0	3	1	24	0			

LAWSON TAMA, HONIARA
1-06-2012, Att: 3000, Ref: Gerald Oiaka SOL

Tahiti	10	Tehau.L 4 $^{8\ 82\ 84\ 85}$, Tehau.J 2 $^{16\ 78}$, Tehau.A 2 $^{18\ 40}$, Tehau.T ^{54}, Chong Hue ^{61}
Samoa	1	Malo ^{69}

TAHITI
Mikael **ROCHE** - Alvin **TEHAU** (Teaonui **TEHAU** 53), Tamatoa **WAGEMANN**, Lorenzo **TEHAU**, Angelo **TCHEN**, Nicolas **VALLAR** (C), Hiro **POROIAE**•, Steevy **CHONG HUE** (Manaraii **PORLIER** 73), Heimano **BOUREBARE** (Pierre **KOHUMOETINI** 57), Jonathan **TEHAU**, Vincent **SIMON**. Tr: Eddy **ETAETA**

SAMOA
Motu **HAFOKA** - Andrew **SETEFANO**• (C), Vaalii **FAALOGO**, Silao **MALO**, Jarrell **SALE**, Joseph **HOEFLICH** (Masei **AMOSA** 68), Luki **GOSCHE** (Amilale **ESAROMA** 64), Mike **SAOFALGA**•, Sapati **UMUTAUA** (Peni **KITIONA** 87), Sopo **FAKAUA**, Spencer **KELI**. Tr: Malo **VAGA**

LAWSON TAMA, HONIARA
1-06-2012, Att: 7000, Ref: Peter O'Leary NZL

New Caledonia	5	Kai 3 $^{32\ 58\ 76}$, Gope-Fenepej ^{66}, Kayara.R ^{87}
Vanuatu	2	Tasso ^{52}, Naprapol ^{61}

NEW CALEDONIA
Rocky **NYIKEINE** - Judikael **IXOEE**, Olivier **DOKUNENGO** (C), Dominique **WACALIE**, Marius **BAKO** (Miguel **KAYARA** 75), Bertrand **KAI**, Noel **KAUDRE** (Roy **KAYARA** 61), Dick **KAUMA**, Jean **WAKANUMUNE**, Joel **WAKANUMUNE**, Georges **GOPE-FENEPEJ** (Jacques **HAEKO** 92). Tr: Alain **MOIZAN**

VANUATU
Enest **BONG** - Selwin **SESE**, Robert **TOM**, Jean Robert **YELOU** (C) (Dominique **FRED** 70), Derek **MALAS**, Joseph **NAMARIAU** (Kensi **TANGIS** 63), Francois **SAKAMA** (Robert **TASSO** 39), Alphonse **BONGNAIM**, Jean **NAPRAPOL**, Roddy **LENGA**, Brian **KALTAK**. Tr: Percy **AVOCK**

LAWSON TAMA, HONIARA
3-06-2012, Att: 2200, Ref: John Saohu SOL

Vanuatu	5	Naprapol ^{29}, Kaltack.B ^{45}, Malas ^{47}, Tasso ^{74}, Vava $^{93+}$
Samoa	0	

VANUATU
Seiloni **IARUEL** - Kevin **SHEM**, Paul **YOUNG**, Fredy **VAVA**, Derek **MALAS** (Sailas **NAMATAK** 65), Jean **KALTACK** (Robert **TASSO** 71), Jean **NAPRAPOL** (Kensi **TANGIS** 80), Michell **KALTAK**, Lucien **HINGE**•, Dominique **FRED**, Brian **KALTAK** (C). Tr: Percy **AVOCK**

SAMOA
Ethan **ELISAIA** - Andrew **SETEFANO** (C), Vaalii **FAALOGO**, Silao **MALO**•, Jarrell **SALE**, Suivai **ATAGA** (Joseph **HOEFLICH** 77), Sapati **UMUTAUA** (Patrick **ASIATA** 70), Sopo **FAKAUA**, Amilale **ESAROMA**, Spencer **KELI**, Masei **AMOSA** (Mike **SAOFALGA** 51). Tr: Malo **VAGA**

LAWSON TAMA, HONIARA
3-06-2012, Att: 3500, Ref: Chris Kerr NZL

Tahiti	4	Tehau.A ^{19}, Vallar ^{28p}, Tehau.L ^{34}, Degage ^{86}
New Caledonia	3	Bako ^{76}, Haeko ^{83}, Kauma ^{89}

TAHITI
Mikael **ROCHE** - Alvin **TEHAU**• (Roihau **DEGAGE** 76), Teheivarii **LUDIVION**, Lorenzo **TEHAU** (Teaonui **TEHAU** 89), Henri **CAROINE**, Angelo **TCHEN**, Nicolas **VALLAR** (C) (Tamatoa **WAGEMANN** 66), Steevy **CHONG HUE**, Heimano **BOUREBARE**, Jonathan **TEHAU**, Vincent **SIMON**. Tr: Eddy **ETAETA**

NEW CALEDONIA
Rocky **NYIKEINE** - Judikael **IXOEE**• (Emile **BEARUNE** 46), Olivier **DOKUNENGO** (C) (Miguel **KAYARA** 74), Dominique **WACALIE**, Marius **BAKO**, Bertrand **KAI** (Jacques **HAEKO** 46), Roy **KAYARA**, Dick **KAUMA**, Jean **WAKANUMUNE**♦55, Joel **WAKANUMUNE**, Georges **GOPE-FENEPEJ**♦28. Tr: Alain **MOIZAN**

PART THREE – THE CONTINENTAL CONFEDERATIONS

LAWSON TAMA, HONIARA
5-06-2012, Att: 1000, Ref: Gerald Oiaka SOL

New Caledonia	9	Kayara.R [10], Haeko 5 [11 45 71 89 91+], Kabeu [22], Ixoee [25p], Gnipate [44]
Samoa	0	

NEW CALEDONIA
Marc OUNEMOA (C) - Judikael IXOEE, Emile BEARUNE, Georges BEARUNE, Kalaje GNIPATE, Miguel KAYARA (Bertrand KAI 57), Jacques HAEKO, Roy KAYARA (Joel WAKANUMUNE 57), Noel KAUDRE, Iamel KABEU, Jonathan KAKOU. Tr: Alain MOIZAN

SAMOA
Aukusotino AITUPE (Sopo FAKAUA 46), Andrew SETEFANO (C), Vaalii FAALOGO, Silao MALO, Jarrell SALE, Mike SAOFALGA, Sapati UMUTAUA (Patrick ASIATA 46), Amilale ESAROMA (Tamoto FENIKA 87), Spencer KELI, Masei AMOSA. Tr: Malo VAGA

LAWSON TAMA, HONIARA
5-06-2012, Att: 1000, Ref: Peter O'Leary NZL

Tahiti	4	Vallar [14p], Tehau.J [37], Tehau.A [57], Tehau.T [86]
Vanuatu	1	Tasso [95+]

TAHITI
Xavier SAMIN - Alvin TEHAU (Roihau DEGAGE 64), Teheivarii LUDIVION, Lorenzo TEHAU, Henri CAROINE, Angelo TCHEN, Teaonui TEHAU, Nicolas VALLAR (C), Heimano BOUREBARE (Tamatoa WAGEMANN• 88), Jonathan TEHAU (Pierre KOHUMOETINI 78), Edson LEMAIRE•. Tr: Eddy ETAETA

VANUATU
Enest BONG• - Kevin SHEM, Paul YOUNG, Jean Robert YELOU (C) (Fredy VAVA 19), Sailas NAMATAK, Derek MALAS, Robert TASSO, Joseph NAMARIAU, Alphonse BONGNAIM, Roddy LENGA (Michell KALTAK 53), Brian KALTAK (Kensi TANGIS 66). Tr: Percy AVOCK

GROUP B		Pl	W	D	L	F	A	Pts	SOL	FIJ	PNG
New Zealand	NZL	3	2	1	0	4	2	7	1-1	1-0	2-1
Solomon Islands	SOL	3	1	2	0	2	1	5		0-0	1-0
Fiji	FIJ	3	0	2	1	1	2	2			1-1
Papua New Guinea	PNG	3	0	1	2	2	4	1			

LAWSON TAMA, HONIARA
2-06-2012, Att: 15 000, Ref: Isidore A-Ambassa NCL

New Zealand	1	Smith [11]
Fiji	0	

NEW ZEALAND
Mark PASTON (Jake GLEESON 54), Tony LOCHHEAD, Ben SIGMUND, Tommy SMITH (C), Leo BERTOS•, Michael MCGLINCHEY, Shane SMELTZ, Chris KILLEN, Marco ROJAS (Chris WOOD 54), Ivan VICELICH•, Kosta BARBAROUSES (Rory FALLON• 80). Tr: Ricki HERBERT

FIJI
Simione TAMANISAU (C) - Avinesh SUWAMY, Samuela VULA, Taniela WAQA, Alvin SINGH• (Ilisoni TUINAWAIVUVU 61), Pita SENIBIAUKULA, Osea VAKATALESAU•, Alvin AVINESH, Roy KRISHNA, Remuero TEKIATE, Samuela KAUTOGA. Tr: Juan Carlos BUZZETTI

LAWSON TAMA, HONIARA
2-06-2012, Att: 15 000, Ref: Norbert Hauata TAH

Solomon Islands	1	Totori [5]
Papua N. Guinea	0	

SOLOMON ISLANDS
Junior RAY - Hardies AENGARI, Jeffery BULE, Henry FAARODO (C), Tome FAISI, Freddie KINI, James NAKA (Jack WETNEY 52), Leslie NATE, Joses NAWO (Mostyn BEUI 63), Nelson KILIFA, Benjamin TOTORI. Tr: Jacob MOLI

PAPUA NEW GUINEA
Leslie KALAI - Valentine NELSON, Daniel JOE, Kelly JAMPU•, Samuel KINI, Michael FOSTER (Jeremy YASASA 75), Kema JACK, Reginald DAVANI (Raymond GUNEMBA 46), David MUTA (C), Niel HANS (Eric KOMENG 46), Koriak UPAIGA. Tr: Frank FARINA

LAWSON TAMA, HONIARA
4-06-2012, Att: 3000, Ref: Bruce George VAN

New Zealand	2	Smeltz [2], Wood [52]
Papua N. Guinea	1	Hans [89p]

NEW ZEALAND
Jake GLEESON - Tony LOCHHEAD••♦89, Ben SIGMUND (Tim MYERS 87), Tommy SMITH (C), Michael MCGLINCHEY, Shane SMELTZ (Tim PAYNE 67), Chris KILLEN (Aaron CLAPHAM• 58), Ivan VICELICH, Jeremy BROCKIE, Kosta BARBAROUSES, Chris WOOD. Tr: Ricki HERBERT

PAPUA NEW GUINEA
Leslie KALAI - Kila IARAVAI, Valentine NELSON, Daniel JOE, Samuel KINI (Niel HANS 61), Raymond GUNEMBA (Jamal SEETO 61), Michael FOSTER, Kema JACK•, David MUTA (C), Eric KOMENG (Jeremy YASASA 85), Koriak UPAIGA. Tr: Frank FARINA

LAWSON TAMA, HONIARA
4-06-2012, Att: 12 000, Ref: Kader Zitouni TAH

Solomon Islands	0	
Fiji	0	

SOLOMON ISLANDS
Junior RAY - Mostyn BEUI (Jeffery BULE 28), Henry FAARODO (C), Tome FAISI, Abraham INIGA (Nicholas MURI 77), Joe LUWI, James NAKA, Leslie NATE (Jack WETNEY 49), Seni NGAVA, Loni QARABA, Nelson KILIFA. Tr: Jacob MOLI

FIJI
Simione TAMANISAU (C) - Avinesh SUWAMY, Samuela VULA• (Paulo POSIANO• 78), Taniela WAQA, Pita SENIBIAUKULA•, Osea VAKATALESAU, Alvin AVINESH, Roy KRISHNA (Maciu DUNADAMU 65), Remuero TEKIATE, Samuela KAUTOGA (Alvin SINGH 35), Ilisoni TUINAWAIVUVU•. Tr: Juan Carlos BUZZETTI

LAWSON TAMA, HONIARA		LAWSON TAMA, HONIARA	
6-06-2012, Att: 3000, Ref: Kader Zitouni TAH		6-06-2012, Att: 18 000, Ref: Norbert Hauata TAH	
Papua N. Guinea	1 Jack [85]	**Solomon Islands**	1 Totori [56]
Fiji	1 Dunadamu [13]	**New Zealand**	1 Wood [13]
PAPUA NEW GUINEA		**SOLOMON ISLANDS**	

Leslie KALAI - Kila IARAVAI, Valentine NELSON, Daniel JOE, Samuel KINI (Reginald DAVANI• 78), Raymond GUNEMBA (Jamal SEETO 65), Michael FOSTER, Kema JACK, David MUTA (C), Eric KOMENG (Jeremy YASASA 65), Koriak UPAIGA•. Tr: Frank FARINA

FIJI

Simione TAMANISAU• (C) - Avinesh SUWAMY, Samuela VULA, Taniela WAQA, Alvin SINGH•, Pita SENIBIAUKULA, Osea VAKATALESAU (Apisai SMITH 57), Alvin AVINESH, Roy KRISHNA (Misaele DRAUNIBAKA 82), Remuero TEKIATE•, Maciu DUNADAMU. Tr: Juan Carlos BUZZETTI

NEW ZEALAND

Jake GLEESON - Tim MYERS, Tommy SMITH• (C), Ian HOGG, Leo BERTOS (Jeremy BROCKIE 58), Marco ROJAS (Kosta BARBAROUSES 58), Rory FALLON (Adam MCGEORGE 63), Aaron CLAPHAM, Michael BOXALL, Chris WOOD, Tim PAYNE. Tr: Ricki HERBERT

SEMI-FINALS

LAWSON TAMA, HONIARA		LAWSON TAMA, HONIARA	
8-06-2012, Att: 15 000, Ref: Peter O'Leary NZL		8-06-2012, Att: 10 000, Ref: Norbert Hauata TAH	
Solomon Islands	0	**New Caledonia**	2 Kai [60], Gope-Fenepej [93+]
Tahiti	1 Tehau.J [15]	**New Zealand**	0
SOLOMON ISLANDS		**NEW CALEDONIA**	

Junior RAY (Shadrack RAMONI 27) - Hardies AENGARI, Jeffery BULE•, Henry FAARODO (C), Tome FAISI, James NAKA (Joses NAWO 46), Leslie NATE, Loni QARABA, Nelson KILIFA•, Benjamin TOTORI, Jack WETNEY (Joe LUWI 77). Tr: Jacob MOLI

TAHITI

Xavier SAMIN - Alvin TEHAU, Teheivarii LUDIVION, Lorenzo TEHAU•, Henri CAROINE•, Angelo TCHEN•, Nicolas VALLAR (C), Steevy CHONG HUE (Teaonui TEHAU 75), Heimano BOUREBARE, Jonathan TEHAU, Vincent SIMON. Tr: Eddy ETAETA

NEW CALEDONIA

Rocky NYIKEINE• - Judikael IXOEE, Emile BEARUNE, Olivier DOKUNENGO (C), Dominique WACALIE, Jacques HAEKO (Roy KAYARA 75), Marius BAKO, Bertrand KAI (Noel KAUDRE 87), Iamel KABEU, Joel WAKANUMUNE, Georges GOPE-FENEPEJ. Tr: Alain MOIZAN

NEW ZEALAND

Jake GLEESON - Tony LOCHHEAD (Rory FALLON 85), Ben SIGMUND•, Tommy SMITH (C), Leo BERTOS• (Marco ROJAS 63), Michael MCGLINCHEY, Shane SMELTZ, Chris KILLEN, Ivan VICELICH, Kosta BARBAROUSES, Chris WOOD (Jeremy BROCKIE 63). Tr: Ricki HERBERT

3RD PLACE PLAY-OFF AND FINAL

LAWSON TAMA, HONIARA. 3RD PLACE PLAY-OFF		LAWSON TAMA, HONIARA. FINAL	
3rd place. 10-06-2012, Att: 15 000, Ref: Kader Zitouni TAH		10-06-2012, 15:00, Att: 10 000, Ref: Peter O'Leary NZL	
Solomon Islands	3 Teleda [48], Totori 2 [54] [87]	**Tahiti**	1 Chong Hue [10]
New Zealand	4 Wood 3 [10] [24] [29], Smeltz [90]	**New Caledonia**	0
SOLOMON ISLANDS		**TAHITI**	

Shadrack RAMONI - Jeffery BULE, Henry FAARODO (C), Tome FAISI•, Abraham INIGA, Nicholas MURI (Benjamin TOTORI 31), Seni NGAVA (Leslie NATE 46), Nelson KILIFA, Himson TELEDA, Joshua TUASULIA (Hardies AENGARI 37), Vivian WICKHAM. Tr: Jacob MOLI

NEW ZEALAND

Jake GLEESON - Tim MYERS•, Tommy SMITH (C) (Ivan VICELICH 52), Ian HOGG•, Marco ROJAS (Shane SMELTZ 76), Jeremy BROCKIE•, Kosta BARBAROUSES, Aaron CLAPHAM, Michael BOXALL, Chris WOOD (Cameron HOWIESON 58), Tim PAYNE•. Tr: Ricki HERBERT

Xavier SAMIN - Alvin TEHAU, Teheivarii LUDIVION, Lorenzo TEHAU• (Manaraii PORLIER 89), Henri CAROINE, Angelo TCHEN•, Nicolas VALLAR (C), Steevy CHONG HUE, Heimano BOUREBARE (Teaonui DEGAGE 91), Jonathan TEHAU, Vincent SIMON. Tr: Eddy ETAETA

NEW CALEDONIA

Rocky NYIKEINE - Judikael IXOEE•, Emile BEARUNE•, Olivier DOKUNENGO• (C) (Roy KAYARA 66), Dominique WACALIE, Jacques HAEKO, Marius BAKO•, Bertrand KAI, Iamel KABEU, Joel WAKANUMUNE, Georges GOPE-FENEPEJ. Tr: Alain MOIZAN

CLUB TOURNAMENTS IN OCEANIA 2011-12

OFC CHAMPIONS LEAGUE 2011-12

First Round Groups

Group A		Pl	W	D	L	F	A	Pts	TAH	NZL	SOL	NCL
AS Tefana	TAH	6	4	1	1	15	12	**13**		3-0	4-1	2-0
Waitakere United	NZL	6	4	0	2	21	6	**12**	10-0		4-0	4-0
Ba	FIJ	6	3	0	3	7	16	**9**	0-5	3-2		2-1
AS Mont-Dore	NCL	6	0	1	5	2	11	**1**	1-1	0-1	0-1	

Final

Auckland City	2	1
AS Tefana	1	0

Group B		Pl	W	D	L	F	A	Pts	NZL	PNG	VAN	SOL
Auckland City	NZL	6	4	1	1	17	8	**13**		2-0	3-2	7-3
Hekari United	PNG	6	3	2	1	9	6	**11**	1-1		2-0	3-1
Amicale	VAN	6	2	1	3	6	7	**7**	1-0	1-1		2-0
Koloale	SOL	6	1	0	5	7	18	**3**	1-4	1-2	1-0	

Top scorers: 8 - Fenedy **MASAUVAKALO** VAN, Amicale • 3 - Daniel **KOPRIVCIC** CRO, Auckland City; Manuel **EXPOSITO** ESP, Auckland City; Henry **FA'ARODO** SOL, Hekari United; Benjamin **TOTORI** SOL, Koloale & Alan **PEARCE** NZL, Waitakere United

GROUP A

		Pl	W	D	L	F	A	Pts	TAH	NZL	SOL	NCL
AS Tefana	TAH	6	4	1	1	15	12	**13**		3-0	4-1	2-0
Waitakere United	NZL	6	4	0	2	21	6	**12**	10-0		4-0	4-0
Ba	SOL	6	3	0	3	7	16	**9**	0-5	3-2		2-1
AS Mont-Dore	NCL	6	0	1	5	2	11	**1**	1-1	0-1	0-1	

Fred Taylor Park, Waitakere
29-10-2011, Att: 900, Ref: Varman FIJ
Waitakere United 10
Pearce 2 [10p 44], De Vries 3 [14 37 75], Krishna 5 [33 40 49 70 90]
Danny **ROBINSON** - Jason **ROWLEY**, Aaron **SCOTT** • (Gagame **FENI** 64), Tim **MYERS**, Luke **ADAMS**, Martin **BULLOCK**•, Christopher **BALE** (Ross **MCKENZIE** 46), Jake **BUTLER**, Ryan **DE VRIES**, Allan **PEARCE** (Sean **LOVEMORE** 73), Roy **KRISHNA**. Tr: Neil **EMBLEN**
AS Tefana 0
Xavier **SAMIN**♦7 - Pierre **KUGOGNE**, Jean Claude **CHANG KOEI CHANG**, Taurua **MARMOUYET**• (Stephane **FAATIARAU** 75), Angelo **TCHEN**•, Heimano **BOUREBARE**, Larry **MARMOUYET** (Hiva **KAMOISE** 45), Stanley **ATANI** (Leonce **ROOMETUA** 8), Sebastien **LABAYEN**, Taufa **NEUFFER**, Axel **WILLIAMS**. Tr: Laurent **HEINIS**

Govind Park, Ba
30-10-2011, Att: 1500, Ref: Kerr NZL
Ba 2
Suwamy 2 [64 82]
Jone **RALULU** - Avinesh **SUWAMY**, Manueli **KALOU**, Jone **VESIKULA**, Alvin **SINGH**, Remueru **TEKIATE** (Rinal **PRASAD** 61), Isimeli **NARESIA**, Kini **VILIAME**, Malakai **TIWA**, Marika **MADIGI**•, Tuimasi **MANUCA** (Keni **DOIDOI** 76). Tr: Yogendra **DUTT**
AS Mont Dore 1
Hmae.J [33]
Jean-Jacques **WACHOU** - Dominique **SAWA**•, Jean-Patrick **WAKANUMUNE**, Georges **WADRENGES**, Pierre **NYIKEINE** (Jacques **WAMYTAN**• 79), Loic **Wakanumune**•, Olivier **DOKUNENGO**, Jose **HMAE** (Kalaje **GNIPATE** 63), Patrick **DIAKE**, Brian Rony **ATTI** (Fabrice **WACAPO** 65), Jean-Marc **HMALOKO**. Tr: Thierry **SARDO**

Stade Numa-Daly Magenta, Nouméa
12-11-2011, Att: 300, Ref: Cross NZL
AS Mont Dore 1
Hmae.M [70]
Jean-Jacques **WACHOU** - Dominique **SAWA**•, Jean-Patrick **WAKANUMUNE**, Pierre **NYIKEINE**, Loic **WAKANUMUNE**, Jose **HMAE** (Ricardo **PELLETIER** 71), Patrick **DIAKE**, Kalaje **GNIPATE**, Michel **HMAE**, Brian Rony **ATTI**••♦[83], Jean-Marc **HMALOKO** (Fabrice **WACAPO** 84). Tr: Thierry **SARDO**
AS Tefana 1
Kamoise [80]
Leonce **ROOMETUA** - Pierre **KUGOGNE**, Jean Claude **CHANG KOEI CHANG**, Taurua **MARMOUYET**, Angelo **TCHEN** (Stephane **FAATIARAU** 84), Heimano **BOUREBARE**•, Larry **MARMOUYET**, Hiva **KAMOISE** 71, Sebastien **LABAYEN**, Taufa **NEUFFER** (David **CHANG KOEI CHANG** 89), Axel **WILLIAMS**. Tr: Laurent **HEINIS**

Fred Taylor Park, Waitakere
20-11-2011, Att: 4000, Ref: Hauata TAH
Waitakere United 4
OG [56], McKenzie [60], Bale [71], Lovemore [93+]
Danny **ROBINSON** - Jason **ROWLEY**, Aaron **SCOTT** (Luke **ADAMS** 86), Tim **MYERS**, Martin **BULLOCK** (Sean **LOVEMORE** 64), Christopher **BALE**, Ross **MCKENZIE**, Jake **BUTLER**, Ryan **DE VRIES** (Gagame **FENI** 80), Allan **PEARCE**, Roy **KRISHNA**. Tr: Neil **EMBLEN**
Ba 0
Jone **RALULU** - Avinesh **SUWAMY**, Manueli **KALOU**, Jone **VESIKULA**, Alvin **SINGH**, Malakai **KAINIHEWE**•, Keni **DOIDOI** (Ronil **KUMAR** 68), Kini **VILIAME**, Malakai **TIWA**, Marika **MADIGI**♦47, Josaia Junior **BUKALIDI** (Isimeli **NARESIA** 74). Tr: Yogendra **DUTT**

Stade Numa-Daly Magenta, Nouméa
3-12-2011, Att: 400, Ref: Jacques TAH
AS Mont Dore 0
Jean-Jacques **WACHOU** - Jacques **WAMYTAN**, Georges **WADRENGES**•, Pierre **NYIKEINE**•, Loic **WAKANUMUNE**, Olivier **DOKUNENGO**, Jose **HMAE** 87), Romain **PAINBENI**, Patrick **DIAKE**, Kalaje **GNIPATE** (Pascal **KENON** 74), Michel **HMAE**, Jean-Marc **HMALOKO** (Loic **BESSIERES** 69). Tr: Thierry **SARDO**
Waitakere United 1
Bale [40]
Danny **ROBINSON** - Jason **ROWLEY**, Aaron **SCOTT**, Tim **MYERS**♦57, Martin **BULLOCK**, Christopher **BALE**•, Ross **MCKENZIE**, Jake **BUTLER**, Ryan **DE VRIES** (Sean **LOVEMORE** 86), Allan **PEARCE**, Roy **KRISHNA**. Tr: Neil **EMBLEN**

Stade Louis Ganivet, Fa'aa
2-12-2011, Att: 117, Ref: Waldron NZL
AS Tefana 4
Marmouyet 2 [1p], Degage 2 [38 77], Williams [85]
Xavier **SAMIN** - Stephane **FAATIARAU**•, Pierre **KUGOGNE**• (Luthy **BOHL** 90), Angelo **TCHEN**•, Larry **MARMOUYET**•, Hiva **KAMOISE** (Taurua **MARMOUYET** 79), Stanley **ATANI** (Axel **WILLIAMS**• 52), Sebastien **LABAYEN**, Manutahi **TEREMATE**•, Taufa **NEUFFER**•, Roihau **DEGAGE**. Tr: Laurent **HEINIS**
Ba 0
Vesikula [59p]
Jone **RALULU** - Avinesh **SUWAMY**♦79, Manueli **KALOU**•, Jone **VESIKULA**, Alvin **SINGH**•, Isimeli **NARESIA**••♦87, Shalen **LAL** (Meli **CODRO** 60), Kini **VILIAME**•, Rinal **PRASAD** (Josefata **NEIBULI** 67), Malakai **TIWA**♦70, Mavileko **NAKAMA** (Josaia Junior **BUKALIDI** 86). Tr: Yogendra **DUTT**

OFC CHAMPIONS LEAGUE 2011–12

Stade Numa-Daly Magenta, Nouméa
18-02-2012, Att: 100, Ref: O'Leary NZL
AS Mont Dore 0
Jean-Jacques WACHOU - Dominique SAWA, Jean-Patrick WAKANUMUNE, Georges WADRENGES•, Steeven LONGUE, (Loic WAKANUMUNE 55), Romain PAINBENI•, Pascal KENON (Loic BESSIERES• 64), Patrick DIAKE, Michel HMAE, Jean-Marc HMALOKO, Yoann GERBET (Pierre NYIKEINE• 46). Tr: Georges WADRENGES
Ba 1
Vakatalasau 36p
Jone RALULU - Manueli KALOU, Jone VESIKULA•, Alvin SINGH, Remueru TEKIATE, Ronil KUMAR, Laisenia RAURA, Aisea CODRO, Marika MADIGI•, Mavileko NAKAMA (Jone SALAUNEUNE 78), Osea VAKATALESAU. Tr: Yogendra DUTT

Stade Louis Ganivet, Fa'aa
17-02-2012, Att: 193, Ref: Ambassa NCL
AS Tefana 3
Tehau [1], Labayen [43], Neuffer [70]
Xavier SAMIN - Pierre KUGOGNE, Jean Claude CHANG KOEI CHANG, Taurea MARMOUYET, Angelo TCHEN•, Heimano BOUREBARE, Larry MARMOUYET• (Stephane FAATIARAU 65), Lorenzo TEHAU, Sebastien LABAYEN•, Taufa NEUFFER• (Hiva KAMOISE 85), Alvin TEHAU. Tr: Laurent HEINIS
Waitakere United 0
Matthew UPTON - Jason ROWLEY, Matt CUNNEEN, Martin BULLOCK• (Ross HAVILAND• 73), Christopher BALE, Ross MCKENZIE•, Neil EMBLEN, Jake BUTLER, Ryan DE VRIES•, Allan PEARCE (Sean LOVEMORE 60), Roy KRISHNA (Andrew BEVIN 88). Tr: Carl JORGENSEN

Stade Louis Ganivet, Fa'aa
2-03-2012, Att: 248, Ref: Achari FIJ
AS Tefana 2
Degage 47, Chang [71p]
Xavier SAMIN - Stephane FAATIARAU, Pierre KUGOGNE, Jean Claude CHANG KOEI CHANG, Heimano BOUREBARE, Stanley ATANI, Lorenzo TEHAU, Sebastien LABAYEN, Roihau DEGAGE (Hiva KAMOISE 58), Alvin TEHAU, Axel WILLIAMS. Tr: Laurent HEINIS
AS Mont Dore 0
Jean-Jacques WACHOU - Jacques WAMYTAN, Steeven LONGUE, Romain PAINBENI, Pascal KENON, Patrick DIAKE, Kalaje GNIPATE, Jean-Marc HMALOKO•, Fabrice WACAPO, Loic BESSIERES•, Yoann GERBET (Pierre WEINANE 86). Tr: Georges WADRENGES

Govind Park, Ba
4-03-2012, Ref: Hauata TAH
Ba 3
Tekiate 36, Salauneune 51, Kainihewe 73
Jone RALULU - Avinesh SUWAMY, Manueli KALOU, Remueru TEKIATE, Ronil KUMAR, Kini VILIAME, Malakai TIWA, Laisenia RAURA, Marika MADIGI•, Jone SALAUNEUNE (Malakai KAINIHEWE 69), Osea VAKATALESAU•. Tr: Yogendra DUTT
Waitakere United 2
Cunneen 31, Lovemore 83
Danny ROBINSON - Jason ROWLEY, Aaron SCOTT, Tim MYERS, Matt CUNNEEN, Christopher BALE•, Ross MCKENZIE (Rory TURNER 52), Jake BUTLER, Ryan DE VRIES (Sean LOVEMORE 57), Allan PEARCE (Neil EMBLEN 74), Roy KRISHNA. Tr: Ross HAVILAND

Fred Taylor Park, Waitakere
31-03-2012, Att: 150, Ref: Zitouni TAH
Waitakere United 4
McKenzie 68, Haviland 73, Pearce 82, Lovemore 87
Danny ROBINSON - Jason ROWLEY, Aaron SCOTT, Tim MYERS, Ross HAVILAND, Ross MCKENZIE (Jordan VALE 78), Jake BUTLER•, Ryan DE VRIES (Martin BULLOCK 76), Allan PEARCE, Roy KRISHNA (Rory TURNER•), Sean LOVEMORE•. Tr: Neil EMBLEN
AS Mont Dore 0
Jean-Jacques WACHOU - Dominique SAWA•, Jacques WAMYTAN, Georges WADRENGES•, Steeven LONGUE, Romain PAINBENI•, Pascal KENON (Pierre WEINANE 89), Patrick DIAKE (Fabrice WACAPO 60), Kalaje GNIPATE, Brian Rony ATTI (Yoann GERBET 70), Jean-Marc HMALOKO. Tr: Georges WADRENGES

Bill McKinlay Park, Auckland
15-04-2012, Ref: Oiaka SOL
Ba 0
Jone RALULU - Manueli KALOU, Jone VESIKULA (Laisenia RAURA 41), Alvin SINGH•, Remueru TEKIATE, Ronil KUMAR (Josefata NEIBULI 87), Kini VILIAME, Malakai TIWA, Marika MADIGI, Jone SALAUNEUNE• (Isimeli NARISIA 64), Osea VAKATALESAU•. Tr: Yogendra DUTT
AS Tefana 5
Tchen 2 [36] [42], Neuffer [53], Tehau [74], Williams [86]
Xavier SAMIN - Stephane FAATIARAU, Pierre KUGOGNE, Jean Claude CHANG KOEI CHANG, Angelo TCHEN, Heimano BOUREBARE, Larry MARMOUYET (Lorenzo TEHAU 72), Stanley ATANI, Sebastien LABAYEN•, Taufa NEUFFER (Roihau DEGAGE 77), Alvin TEHAU• (Axel WILLIAMS 85). Tr: Laurent HEINIS

GROUP B		Pl	W	D	L	F	A	Pts	NZL	PNG	VAN	SOL
Auckland City	NZL	6	4	1	1	17	8	**13**		2-0	3-2	7-3
Hekari United	PNG	6	3	2	1	9	6	**11**	1-1		2-0	3-1
Amicale	VAN	6	2	1	3	6	7	**7**	1-0	1-1		2-0
Koloale	SOL	6	1	0	5	7	18	**3**	1-4	1-2	1-0	

Korman, Port Vila
29-10-2011, Att: 6500, Ref: O'Leary NZL
Amicale 1
Masauvakalo [45]
Ernest BONG - Rexley TARIVUTI, Nelson SALE, Alphonse BONGNAIM, Jean Robert YELOU, Derek MALAS, Gibson DAUDAU, Alick MAEMAE, Joachim WAROI (Joe LUWI 70), Fenedy MASAUVAKOLO, Jack WETNEY (Young PAUL 60). Tr: Luke EROI
Hekari United 1
Jack [93+]
Leslie KALAI - Trevor IRE (Clifton AUMAE 46), John NAMANI•, Andrew LEPANI, Koriak UPAIGA, Samuel KINI (Wira WAMA 81), David MUTA, Eric KOMENG, Raymond GUNEMBA, Neil HANS (Nigel DABINGYABA 43), Kema JACK. Tr: Jerry ALLEN

Lawson Tama, Honiara
29-10-2011, Att: 18 000, Ref: Achari FIJ
Koloale 1
Totori [74p]
Shadrock RAMONI - Freddie KINI, Cecil BURU, Samson TAKAYAMA, Francis LAFAI, Lency SAENI (James NAKA 71), Mostyn BEUI (Molis GAGAME JNR 83), Henry FA'ARODO, Joses NAWO•, Benjamin TOTORI, Ian PAIA (Ezra SALE 90). Tr: Peter EKE
Auckland City 4
Exposito 2 [22p] [54], Mulligan 2 [86] [93+]
Jacob SPOONLEY - Ian HOGG, Angel BERLANGA, Chad COOMBES, Ivan VICELICH, David MULLIGAN, Daniel KOPRIVIC, Alex FENERIDIS, Albert RIERA• (ANDREU 50), Manel EXPOSITO (Emiliano TADE 69), Adam DICKINSON (Adam MCGEORGE 79). Tr: Ramon TRIBULIETX

Kiwitea Street, Auckland
19-11-2011, Att: 800, Ref: Varman FIJ
Auckland City 2
Exposito [49], Tade [72]
Jacob SPOONLEY - Ian HOGG, Angel BERLANGA•, James PRITCHETT, Ivan VICELICH, David MULLIGAN, Daniel KOPRIVIC (Emiliano TADE 61), Alex FENERIDIS, Albert RIERA (ANDREU 55), Manel EXPOSITO, Adam DICKINSON• (Adam MCGEORGE 72). Tr: Ramon TRIBULIETX
Hekari United 0
Leslie KALAI - Andrew LEPANI (John NAMANI 80), Pita BOLATOGA•, Koriak UPAIGA, David MUTA, Clifton AUMAE (Samuel KINI 71), Taniela WAQA, Raymond GUNEMBA (Ian YANUM 62), Maciu DUNADAMU, Wira WAMA•, Kema JACK. Tr: Jerry ALLEN

Korman, Port Vila
19-11-2011, Att: 6000, Ref: Waldron NZL
Amicale 2
Waroi 2 [3] [53]
Ernest BONG - Young PAUL (Rexley TARIVUTI 58), Selwyn SESE ALA•, Richard ANISUA (Jean Robert YELOU 55), Nelson SALE, Alphonse BONGNAIM, Derek MALAS, Gibson DAUDAU, Alick MAEMAE, Joachim WAROI• (Moffat DERAMOA 70), Fenedy MASAUVAKOLO. Tr: Luke EROI
Koloale 0
Shadrock RAMONI - Freddie KINI, Cecil BURU, Francis LAFAI (Israel FANAI 82), Mostyn BEUI, James NAKA• (Lency SAENI 70), Henry FA'ARODO, Joses NAWO, Molis GAGAME JNR (Willy DAUDAU 57), Benjamin TOTORI, Ian PAIA. Tr: Peter EKE

PMRL, Port Moresby
10-12-2011, Ref: Achari FIJ
Hekari United 3
Waqa [6], Lepani [16], Bolatoga [79]
Leslie KALAI - Andrew LEPANI, Pita BOLATOGA•, Koriak UPAIGA•, David MUTA, Eric KOMENG, Clifton AUMAE (Samuel KINI 60), Taniela WAQA, Maciu DUNADAMU• (Nigel DABINGYABA 87), Wira WAMA, Kema JACK (Raymond GUNEMBA 41). Tr: Jerry ALLEN
Koloale 1
Naka [82]
Shadrock RAMONI - Israel FANAI, Freddie KINI, Gideon OMOKIRIO, Francis LAFAI• (David LAFAI 21), Mostyn BEUI (Steven ANISI 90), James NAKA, Henry FA'ARODO, Joses NAWO, Benjamin TOTORI, Ian PAIA (Ezra SALE 75). Tr: Peter EKE

Kiwitea Street, Auckland
18-01-2012, Att: 800, Ref: Zitouni TAH
Auckland City 3
Exposito 2 [40p] [45], Dickinson [87]
Jacob SPOONLEY - Angel BERLANGA, James PRITCHETT, Ivan VICELICH, David MULLIGAN, Daniel KOPRIVIC, Alex FENERIDIS, Manel EXPOSITO (Emiliano TADE 62), Luis CORRALES (Adam MCGEORGE 64), Chad COOMBES 90), Adam DICKINSON. Tr: Ramon TRIBULIETX
Amicale 2
OG [23], Maemae [76]
Ernest BONG - Young PAUL (Rexley TARIVUTI 82), Selwyn SESE ALA, Richard ANISUA (Jean Robert YELOU 64), Nelson SALE, Alphonse BONGNAIM•, Derek MALAS•, Gibson DAUDAU, Alick MAEMAE, Joachim WAROI• (Moffat DERAMOA 57), Fenedy MASAUVAKOLO. Tr: Luke EROI

Semifinals

Kiwitea Street, Auckland
18-02-2012, Att: 850, Ref: Jacques TAH
Auckland City 7
Dickinson 2 7 59, Coombes 36, OG 40, Vicelich 58, Milne 62, Koprivic 83
Tamati WILLIAMS - Angel BERLANGA (Simon ARMS 63), Chad COOMBES, James PRITCHETT, Ivan VICELICH, Andrew MILNE, Daniel KOPRIVIC, Alex FENEREDIS, Albert RIERA (Iwa SHAKER 85), Manel EXPOSITO, Adam DICKINSON (Stephen CARMICHAEL 63). Tr: Ramon TRIBULIETX
Koloale 3
Anisi 16, Totori 65, Naka 93+
Shadrock RAMONI - Freddie KINI, Cecil BURU, Gideon OMOKIRIO (Israel FANAI 67), Francis LAFAI, Lency SAENI (Abraham EKE JR 89), Augustine SAMANI, James NAKA, Steven ANISI, Benjamin TOTORI, Ian PAIA (Ezra SALE 60). Tr: Jeffery ALLEN

PMRL, Port Moresby
18-02-2012, Att: 5000, Ref: Kerr NZL
Hekari United 2
Jack 2 11 79
Leslie KALAI - Ilatia TUILAU•, Andrew LEPANI, Koriak UPAIGA, Samuel KINI, David MUTA, Eric KOMENG, Taniela WAQA••♦46, Maciu DUNADAMU (Raymond GUNEMBA 90), Wira WAMA (Daniel JOE 84), Kema JACK. Tr: Jerry ALLEN
Amicale 0
Chikau MANSALE - Young PAUL (Moffat DERAMOA 74), Selwyn SESE ALA, Richard ANISUA (Jean Robert YELOU 59), Nelson SALE, Samuela KAUTOGA, Derek MALAS, Gibson DAUDAU (Rexley TARIVUTI 41), Alick MAEMAE, Fenedy MASAUVAKALO, Jean Nako NAPRAPOL. Tr: Luke EROI

Lawson Tama, Honiara
3-03-2012, Ref: Waldron NZL
Koloale 1
Sale 87
Shadrock RAMONI - Israel FANAI, Freddie KINI, Samson TAKAYAMA (Cecil BURU 18), Gideon OMOKIRIO, Lency SAENI•, Augustine SAMANI, Mostyn BEUI, James NAKA, Benjamin TOTORI (Ezra SALE 68), Ian PAIA (Abraham EKE JR• 73). Tr: Jeffery ALLEN
Amicale 0
Ernest BONG - Young PAUL, Selwyn SESE ALA, Richard ANISUA (Rexley TARIVUTI 70), Nelson SALE••♦79, Samuela KAUTOGA, Jean Robert YELOU, Gibson DAUDAU, Alick MAEMAE••♦72, Joachim WAROI (Jean Nako NAPRAPOL 58), Fenedy MASAUVAKALO. Tr: Luke EROI

PMRL, Port Moresby
3-03-2012, Ref: Oiaka SOL
Hekari United 1
Dunadamu 60
Leslie KALAI - Ilatia TUILAU•, Andrew LEPANI•, Pita BOLATOGA♦85, Koriak UPAIGA•, Samuel KINI, David MUTA, Ian YANUM (Raymond GUNEMBA 68), Maciu DUNADAMU, Wira WAMA (Clifton AUMAE 90), Kema JACK. Tr: Jerry ALLEN
Auckland City 1
Fenerdis 91+
Tamati WILLIAMS - Angel BERLANGA, James PRITCHETT, Ivan VICELICH•, David MULLIGAN (Andrew MILNE 57), Alex FENEREDIS•, Albert RIERA, Ivan DIAZ, Manel EXPOSITO, Luis CORRALES, Adam DICKINSON• (Adam MCGEORGE 57). Tr: Ramon TRIBULIETX

Korman, Port Vila
31-03-2012, Att: 5000, Ref: George VAN
Amicale 1
Tangis 60
Ernest BONG - Young PAUL• (Rexley TARIVUTI 84), Selwyn SESE ALA, Richard ANISUA, Alphonse BONGNAIM, Samuela KAUTOGA, Derek MALAS, Gibson DAUDAU, Roddy LENGA, Moffat DERAMOA•, Jean Nako NAPRAPOL (Kensi TANGIS 55). Tr: Luke EROI
Auckland City 0
Jacob SPOONLEY - Ian HOGG, Chad COOMBES (Albert RIERA 59), James PRITCHETT, Andrew MILNE, Simon ARMS, David MULLIGAN, Daniel KOPRIVIC, Adam MCGEORGE, Manel EXPOSITO, Luis CORRALES. Tr: Ramon TRIBULIETX

Lawson Tama, Honiara
31-03-2012, Att: 5000, Ref: Waldron NZL
Koloale 1
Totori 16
Shadrock RAMONI - Israel FANAI (Cecil BURU 80), Freddie KINI•, Samson TAKAYAMA, Gideon OMOKIRIO (Augustine SAMANI 46), Lency SAENI, Mostyn BEUI•, James NAKA, Steven ANISI, Benjamin TOTORI, Ian PAIA. Tr: Jeffery ALLEN
Hekari United 2
Dunadamu 45, Jack 75
Leslie KALAI - Koriak UPAIGA, Samuel KINI, Eric KOMENG, Clifton AUMAE, Ian YANUM (Nigel DABINGYABA 33), Taniela WAQA, Daniel JOE, Maciu DUNADAMU (Raymond GUNEMBA 80), Wira WAMA, Kema JACK. Tr: Jerry ALLEN

FINAL

Kiwitea Street, Auckland
29-04-2012, Att: 1500, Ref: John Saohu SOL
Auckland City 2
Mulligan 57, Koprivcic 60
Jacob SPOONLEY - Ian HOGG•, Angel BERLANGA, James PRITCHETT, Ivan VICELICH, David MULLIGAN (Luis CORRALES 65), Daniel KOPRIVIC, Alex FENEREDIS•, Albert RIERA, Manel EXPOSITO, Adam DICKINSON (Chad COOMBES• 80). Tr: Ramon TRIBULIETX
AS Tefana 1
Williams 72
Xavier SAMIN - Stephane FAATIARAU, Pierre KUGOGNE, Jean Claude CHANG KOEI CHANG, Angelo TCHEN (Tauraa MARMOUYET 81), Heimano BOUREBARE, Larry MARMOUYET, Stanley ATANI, Lorenzo TEHAU (Axel WILLIAMS 67), Taufa NEUFFER (Roihau DEGAGE 86), Alvin TEHAU. Tr: Laurent HEINIS

Stade Louis Ganivet, Fa'aa
12-05-2012, Att: 1900, Ref: A-Ambassa NCL
AS Tefana 0
Xavier SAMIN - Pierre KUGOGNE, Jean Claude CHANG KOEI CHANG, Tauraa MARMOUYET, Angelo TCHEN, Heimano BOUREBARE•, Larry MARMOUYET, Sebastien LABAYEN• (Hiva KAMOISE 77), Taufa NEUFFER (Stanley ATANI 72), Alvin TEHAU•, Axel WILLIAMS (Lorenzo TEHAU 56). Tr: Laurent HEINIS
Auckland City 1
Exposito 41
Jacob SPOONLEY• - Ian HOGG, Angel BERLANGA, James PRITCHETT, Ivan VICELICH, Daniel KOPRIVIC (Chad COOMBES 51), Alex FENEREDIS•69, Albert RIERA, Ivan DIAZ• (Adam MCGEORGE 73), Manel EXPOSITO (Andrew MILNE 90), Adam DICKINSON•. Tr: Ramon TRIBULIETX

WOMEN'S TOURNAMENTS IN OCEANIA 2012

OFC U-20 WOMEN'S CHAMPIONSHIP NEW ZEALAND 2012

	Pl	W	D	L	F	A	Pts	PNG	NCL	SAM
New Zealand	3	3	0	0	28	1	9	6-0	10-1	12-0
Papua N. Guinea	3	1	1	1	5	9	4		4-2	1-1
New Caledonia	3	1	0	2	8	15	3			5-1
Samoa	3	0	1	2	2	18	1			

New Zealand qualified for the 2012 FIFA U-20 Women's World Cup in Japan • Matches played at Centre Park, Mangere 10/04/2012 - 14/04/2012 • Top scorer: 8 - Rosie WHITE NZL

OFC U-17 WOMEN'S CHAMPIONSHIP NEW ZEALAND 2012

	Pl	W	D	L	F	A	Pts	PNG	COK	NCL
New Zealand	3	3	0	0	29	1	9	9-0	7-0	13-1
Papua N. Guinea	3	2	0	1	4	11	6		3-2	1-0
Cook Islands	3	1	0	2	5	10	3			3-0
New Caledonia	3	0	0	3	1	17	0			

New Zealand qualified for the 2012 FIFA U-17 Women's World Cup in Azerbaijan • Matches played at Centre Park, Mangere 9/04/2012 - 13/04/2012 • Top scorers: 6 - Hannah CARLSEN & Jasmine PEREIRA NZL

UEFA

UNION DES ASSOCIATIONS EUROPEENNES DE FOOTBALL

UEFA MEMBER ASSOCIATIONS (53)

ALB - **Albania** • AND - **Andorra** • ARM - **Armenia** • AUS - **Austria** • AZE - **Azerbaijan** • BLR - **Belarus** • BEL - **Belgium**
BIH - **Bosnia-Herzegovina** • BUL - **Bulgaria** • CRO - **Croatia** • CYP - **Cyprus** • CZE - **Czech Republic** • DEN - **Denmark** • ENG - **England**
EST - **Estonia** • FRO - **Faroe Islands** • FIN - **Finland** • FRA - **France** • GEO - **Georgia** • GER - **Germany** • GRE - **Greece** • HUN - **Hungary**
ISL - **Iceland** • IRL - **Republic of Ireland** • ISR - **Israel** • ITA - **Italy** • KAZ - **Kazakhstan** • LVA - **Latvia** • LIE - **Liechtenstein** • LTU - **Lithuania**
LUX - **Luxembourg** • MKD - **Macedonia FYR** • MLT - **Malta** • MDA - **Moldova** • MNE - **Montenegro** • NED - **Netherlands** • NIR - **Northern Ireland**
NOR - **Norway** • POL - **Poland** • POR - **Portugal** • ROU - **Romania** • RUS - **Russia** • SMR - **San Marino** • SCO - **Scotland** • SRB - **Serbia**
SVK - **Slovakia** • SVN - **Slovenia** • ESP - **Spain** • SWE - **Sweden** • SUI - **Switzerland** • TUR - **Turkey** • UKR - **Ukraine** • WAL - **Wales**

The Spanish national team re-wrote the history books when they beat Italy 4-0 in the final of Euro 2012 in Kyiv by becoming the first nation to successfully defend the title. The margin of victory was also the biggest of the 14 finals played so far and they became the first European team to win a hat trick of continental and world titles. Indeed, not since Uruguay in 1930 has a nation won such a high profile hat trick of international championships, a testament to the place this side has earned in the annals of the game. The finals in Poland and Ukraine proved to be a great success and have left both countries with a core of first class stadia that should serve them well in the future. They were also the last finals to be staged with 16 teams, a formula that has helped produce some excellent football since it was introduced at Euro 96. The finals in France in 2016 will feature a cumbersome 24 teams - nearly half of all the member associations of UEFA - while the 2020 finals are to be staged in various cities and countries across the continent. Only time will tell if it was a wise decision to change a winning formula. 2012 proved to be an extraordinary year for the city of London. Against the backdrop of Queen Elizabeth's Diamond Jubilee and the successful staging of the Olympic Games, Chelsea set the tone for a summer of celebrations by becoming the first club from the English capital to be crowned European champions. They did it the hard way by beating the reigning champions Barcelona in the semi-finals and then Bayern Munich who were playing at 'home' in the final. Beaten semi-finalists four times and losing finalists in 2008, Chelsea became the fifth different English team to win the title - more than any other nation. They fared less well, however, at the end of year FIFA Club World Cup after losing to Brazil's Corinthians in the final and overall Europe had a poor year in world tournaments. There were no European medals in the two Olympic football tournaments and the only world title claimed was by the French in the FIFA U-17 Women's World Cup in Azerbaijan.

Union des associations européennes de football (UEFA)
Route de Genève 46, 1260 Nyon, Switzerland
Tel +41 22 9944444   Fax +41 22 9944488
info@uefa.com   www.uefa.com
President: Michel Platini FRA   Secretary General: Gianni Infantino ITA
UEFA Formed: 1954

UEFA EXECUTIVE COMMITTEE

President: Michel Platini FRA	1st Vice-President: Senes Erzik TUR	2nd Vice-President: Geoffrey Thompson ENG
3rd Vice-President: Angel María Villar Llona ESP	4th Vice-President: Marios Lefkaritis CYP	5th Vice-President: Joseph Mifsud MLT

ORDINARY MEMBERS OF THE EXECUTIVE COMMITTEE

Giancarlo Abete ITA	Frantisek Laurinec SVK	Dr Gilberto Madail POR
Grigory Surkis UKR	Liutauras Varanavicius LTU	Allan Hansen DEN
Avraham Luzon ISR	Mircea Sandu ROU	Michael van Praag NED
Dr Theo Zwanziger GER		Hon President: Lennart Johansson SWE
FIFA Exco member: Michel D'Hooghe BEL	Secretary General: Gianni Infantino ITA	FIFA Exco member: Franz Beckenbauer GER

1020   PART THREE – THE CONTINENTAL CONFEDERATIONS

MAP OF UEFA MEMBER NATIONS

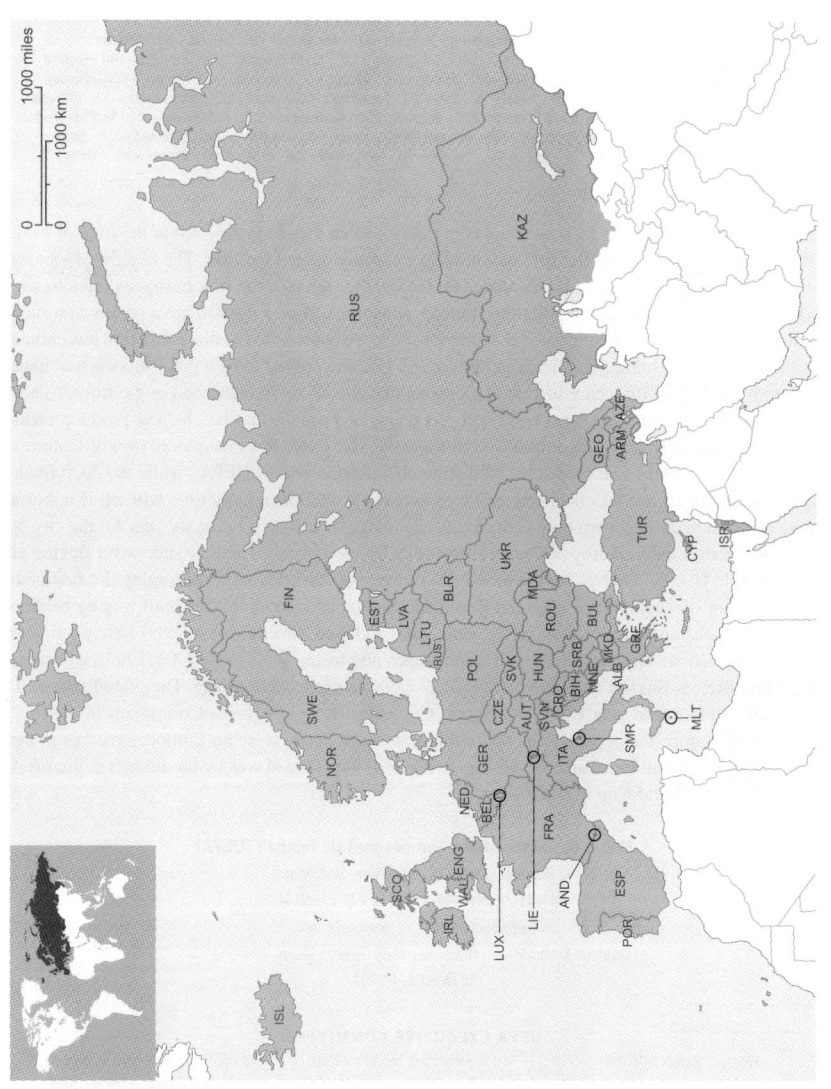

EUROPEAN NATIONAL TEAM TOURNAMENTS

UEFA EUROPEAN CHAMPIONSHIP

Year	Host Country	Winners	Score	Runners-up	Venue
1960	France	Soviet Union	2-1	Yugoslavia	Parc des Princes, Paris
1964	Spain	Spain	2-1	Soviet Union	Bernabeu, Madrid
1968	Italy	Italy	1-1 2-0	Yugoslavia	Stadio Olimpico, Roma
1972	Belgium	Germany FR	3-0	Soviet Union	Heysel, Brussels
1976	Yugoslavia	Czechoslovakia	2-2 5-4p	Germany FR	Crvena Zvezda, Belgrade
1980	Italy	Germany FR	2-1	Belgium	Stadio Olimpico, Rome
1984	France	France	2-0	Spain	Parc des Princes, Paris
1988	Germany FR	Netherlands	2-0	Soviet Union	Olympiastadion, Munich
1992	Sweden	Denmark	2-0	Germany	Nya Ullevi, Gothenburg
1996	England	Germany	2-1	Czech Republic	Wembley, London
2000	Belgium/Netherlands	France	2-1	Italy	Feijenoord Stadion, Rotterdam
2004	Portugal	Greece	1-0	Portugal	Estadio da Luz, Lisbon
2008	Austria/Switzerland	Spain	1-0	Germany	Ernst Happel, Vienna
2012	Poland/Ukraine	Spain	4-0	Italy	Olympic Stadium, Kyiv

UEFA EUROPEAN CHAMPIONSHIP MEDALS TABLE

	Country	G	S	B	F	SF
1	Germany	3	3	2	6	8
2	Spain	3	1		4	4
3	France	2		1	2	4
4	Soviet Union	1	3		4	5
5	Italy	1	2	1	3	4
6	Netherlands	1		4	1	5
7	Czechoslovakia	1		2	1	2
8	Denmark	1		1	1	3
9	Greece	1			1	1
10	Yugoslavia		2		2	3
11	Portugal		1	3	1	4
12	Belgium		1	1	1	2
	Czech Republic		1	1	1	2
14	England			2		2
15	Hungary			1		2
	Sweden			1		1
	Russia			1		1
	Turkey			1		1
		14	14	22	28	54

KEY
G = Gold (winners) • S = Silver (runners-up) • B = Bronze (semi-finalists) • F = appearances in the final • SF = appearances in the semi-final

EUROPEAN CLUB TOURNAMENTS

UEFA CHAMPIONS LEAGUE

Year	Winners	Country	Score	Country	Runners-up
1956	Real Madrid	ESP	4-3	FRA	Stade de Reims
1957	Real Madrid	ESP	2-0	ITA	Fiorentina
1958	Real Madrid	ESP	3-2	ITA	Milan
1959	Real Madrid	ESP	2-0	FRA	Stade de Reims
1960	Real Madrid	ESP	7-3	FRG	Eintracht Frankfurt

UEFA CHAMPIONS LEAGUE (CONT'D)

Year	Winners	Country	Score	Country	Runners-up
1961	Benfica	POR	3-2	ESP	Barcelona
1962	Benfica	POR	5-3	ESP	Real Madrid
1963	Milan	ITA	2-1	POR	Benfica
1964	Internazionale	ITA	3-1	ESP	Real Madrid
1965	Internazionale	ITA	1-0	POR	Benfica
1966	Real Madrid	ESP	2-1	YUG	Partizan Beograd
1967	Celtic	SCO	2-1	ITA	Internazionale
1968	Manchester United	ENG	4-1	POR	Benfica
1969	Milan	ITA	4-1	NED	Ajax
1970	Feyenoord	NED	2-1	SCO	Celtic
1971	Ajax	NED	2-0	GRE	Panathinaikos
1972	Ajax	NED	2-0	ITA	Internazionale
1973	Ajax	NED	1-0	ITA	Juventus
1974	Bayern München	FRG	1-1 4-0	ESP	Atlético Madrid
1975	Bayern München	FRG	2-0	ENG	Leeds United
1976	Bayern München	FRG	1-0	FRA	AS Saint-Étienne
1977	Liverpool	ENG	3-1	FRG	Borussia Mönchengladbach
1978	Liverpool	ENG	1-0	BEL	Club Brugge
1979	Nottingham Forest	ENG	1-0	SWE	Malmö FF
1980	Nottingham Forest	ENG	1-0	FRG	Hamburger SV
1981	Liverpool	ENG	1-0	ESP	Real Madrid
1982	Aston Villa	ENG	1-0	FRG	Bayern München
1983	Hamburger SV	FRG	1-0	ITA	Juventus
1984	Liverpool	ENG	1-1 4-2p	ITA	Roma
1985	Juventus	ITA	1-0	ENG	Liverpool
1986	Steaua Bucuresti	ROU	0-0 2-0p	ESP	Barcelona
1987	FC Porto	POR	2-1	FRG	Bayern München
1988	PSV Eindhoven	NED	0-0 6-5p	POR	Benfica
1989	Milan	ITA	4-0	ROU	Steaua Bucuresti
1990	Milan	ITA	1-0	POR	Benfica
1991	Crvena Zvezda Beograd	YUG	0-0 5-3p	FRA	Olympique Marseille
1992	Barcelona	ESP	1-0	ITA	Sampdoria
1993	Olympique Marseille	FRA	1-0	ITA	Milan
1994	Milan	ITA	4-0	ESP	Barcelona
1995	Ajax	NED	1-0	ITA	Milan
1996	Juventus	ITA	1-1 4-2p	NED	Ajax
1997	Borussia Dortmund	GER	3-1	ITA	Juventus
1998	Real Madrid	ESP	1-0	ITA	Juventus
1999	Manchester United	ENG	2-1	GER	Bayern München
2000	Real Madrid	ESP	3-0	ESP	Valencia
2001	Bayern München	GER	1-1 5-4p	ESP	Valencia
2002	Real Madrid	ESP	2-1	GER	Bayer Leverkusen
2003	Milan	ITA	0-0 3-2p	ITA	Juventus
2004	FC Porto	POR	3-0	FRA	Monaco
2005	Liverpool	ENG	3-3 3-2p	ITA	Milan
2006	Barcelona	ESP	2-1	ENG	Arsenal
2007	Milan	ITA	2-1	ENG	Liverpool
2008	Manchester United	ENG	1-1 6-5p	ENG	Chelsea
2009	Barcelona	ESP	2-0	ENG	Manchester United
2010	Internazionale	ITA	2-0	GER	Bayern München
2011	Barcelona	ESP	3-1	ENG	Manchester United
2012	Chelsea	ENG	1-1 4-3p	GER	Bayern München

UEFA CHAMPIONS LEAGUE MEDALS TABLE

	Country	G	S	B	F	SF
1	Spain	13	9	23	22	45
2	Italy	12	14	8	26	34
3	England	12	7	18	19	37
4	Germany	6	9	11	15	26
5	Netherlands	6	2	5	8	13
6	Portugal	4	5	2	9	11
7	France	1	5	8	6	14
8	Scotland	1	1	6	2	8
9	Romania	1	1	2	2	4
	Serbia	1	1	2	2	4
11	Belgium		1	3	1	4
12	Greece		1	2	1	3
13	Sweden		1	1	1	2
14	Hungary			3		3
	Switzerland			3		3
	Ukraine			3		3
17	Austria			2		2
	Bulgaria			2		2
	Poland			2		2
20	Czech Republic			1		1
	Russia			1		1
	Slovakia			1		1
	Turkey			1		1
		57	57	110	114	224

UEFA CHAMPIONS LEAGUE MEDALS TABLE

	Club		G	S	B
1	Real Madrid	ESP	9	3	11
2	Milan	ITA	7	4	2
3	Liverpool	ENG	5	2	3
4	Bayern München	GER	4	5	5
5	Barcelona	ESP	4	3	7
6	Ajax	NED	4	2	2
7	Manchester United	ENG	3	2	7
8	Internazionale	ITA	3	2	3
9	Juventus	ITA	2	5	3
10	Benfica	POR	2	5	1
11	FC Porto	POR	2		1
12	Nottingham Forest	ENG	2		
13	Chelsea	ENG	1	1	4
14	Glasgow Celtic	SCO	1	1	2
15	Hamburger SV	GER	1	1	1
	Olympique Marseille	FRA	1	1	1
	Steaua Bucuresti	ROU	1	1	1
18	Borussia Dortmund	GER	1		2

UEFA CHAMPIONS LEAGUE MEDALS TABLE (CONT'D)

	Club		G	S	B
	Crvena Zvezda Beograd	SER	1		2
	PSV Eindhoven	NED	1		2
21	Feyenoord	NED	1		1
22	Aston Villa	ENG	1		
23	Stade de Reims	FRA		2	
	Valencia	ESP		2	
25	Atlético Madrid	ESP		1	2
	Leeds United	ENG		1	2
	AS Monaco	FRA		1	2
	Panathinaikos	GRE		1	2
29	Arsenal	ENG		1	1
	Borussia Mönchengladbach	GER		1	1
	AS Saint-Étienne	FRA		1	1
32	Bayer Leverkusen	GER		1	
	Club Brugge	BEL		1	
	Eintracht Frankfurt	GER		1	
	Fiorentina	ITA		1	
	Malmö FF	SWE		1	
	Partizan Beograd	SRB		1	
	Roma	ITA		1	
	Sampdoria	ITA		1	
40	Dynamo Kyiv	UKR			3
41	RSC Anderlecht	BEL			2
	CSKA Sofia	BUL			2
	FC Zürich	SUI			2
44	FK Austria	AUT			1
	Girondins Bordeaux	FRA			1
	Deportivo La Coruna	ESP			1
	Derby County	ENG			1
	Dinamo Bucuresti	ROU			1
	Dukla Praha	CZE			1
	Dundee	SCO			1
	Dundee United	SCO			1
	Galatasaray	TUR			1
	IFK Göteborg	SWE			1
	Hibernian Edinburgh	SCO			1
	1.FC Köln	GER			1
	Legia Warszawa	POL			1
	FC Nantes	FRA			1
	Olympique Lyonnais	FRA			1
	Paris Saint-Germain	FRA			1
	Rába ETO Györ	HUN			1
	Glasgow Rangers	SCO			1
	SK Rapid Wien	AUT			1
	Real Sociedad	ESP			1
	Schalke 04	GER			1
	Spartak Moskva	RUS			1
	Spartak Trnava	SVK			1
	Standard CL	BEL			1
	Tottenham Hotspur	ENG			1
	Ujpesti TE	HUN			1
	Vasas Budapest	HUN			1
	Villarreal	ESP			1
	Widzew Lódz	POL			1
	Young Boys Berne	SUI			1
			57	57	110

EUROPEAN CUP WINNERS' CUP

Year	Winners	Country	Score	Country	Runners-up
1961	Fiorentina	ITA	2-0 2-1	SCO	Rangers
1962	Atlético Madrid	ESP	1-1 3-0	ITA	Fiorentina
1963	Tottenham Hotspur	ENG	5-1	ESP	Atlético Madrid
1964	Sporting CP	POR	3-3 1-0	HUN	MTK Budapest
1965	West Ham United	ENG	2-0	FRG	TSV München 1860
1966	Borussia Dortmund	FRG	2-1	ENG	Liverpool
1967	Bayern München	FRG	1-0	SCO	Rangers
1968	Milan	ITA	2-0	FRG	Hamburger SV
1969	Slovan Bratislava	CZE	3-2	ESP	Barcelona
1970	Manchester City	ENG	2-1	POL	Gornik Zabrze
1971	Chelsea	ENG	1-1 2-1	ESP	Real Madrid
1972	Rangers	SCO	3-2	URS	Dynamo Moskva
1973	Milan	ITA	1-0	ENG	Leeds United
1974	1.FC Magdeburg	GDR	2-0	ITA	Milan
1975	Dynamo Kyiv	URS	3-0	HUN	Ferencváros
1976	RSC Anderlecht	BEL	4-2	ENG	West Ham United
1977	Hamburger SV	FRG	2-0	BEL	RSC Anderlecht
1978	RSC Anderlecht	BEL	4-0	AUT	FK Austria
1979	Barcelona	ESP	4-3	FRG	Fortuna Düsseldorf
1980	Valencia	ESP	0-0 5-4p	ENG	Arsenal
1981	Dynamo Tbilisi	URS	2-1	GDR	Carl Zeiss Jena
1982	Barcelona	ESP	2-1	BEL	Standard CL
1983	Aberdeen	SCO	2-1	ESP	Real Madrid
1984	Juventus	ITA	2-1	POR	FC Porto
1985	Everton	ENG	3-1	AUT	SK Rapid Wien
1986	Dynamo Kyiv	URS	3-0	ESP	Atlético Madrid
1987	Ajax	NED	1-0	GDR	Lokomotive Leipzig
1988	KV Mechelen	BEL	1-0	NED	Ajax
1989	Barcelona	ESP	2-0	ITA	Sampdoria
1990	Sampdoria	ITA	2-0	BEL	RSC Anderlecht
1991	Manchester United	ENG	2-1	ESP	Barcelona
1992	Werder Bremen	GER	2-0	FRA	Monaco
1993	Parma	ITA	3-1	BEL	Royal Antwerp FC
1994	Arsenal	ENG	1-0	ITA	Parma
1995	Real Zaragoza	ESP	2-1	ENG	Arsenal
1996	Paris Saint-Germain	FRA	1-0	AUT	SK Rapid Wien
1997	Barcelona	ESP	1-0	FRA	Paris Saint-Germain
1998	Chelsea	ENG	1-0	GER	VfB Stuttgart
1999	Lazio	ITA	2-1	ESP	Real Mallorca

CUP WINNERS' CUP MEDALS TABLE

	Country	G	S	B	F	SF
1	England	8	5	8	13	21
2	Spain	7	7	5	14	19
3	Italy	7	4	9	11	20
4	Germany	4	4	9	8	17
5	Belgium	3	4	5	7	12
6	Scotland	2	2	4	4	8
7	Ukraine	2	-	-	2	2
8	France	1	2	6	3	9
9	German DR	1	2	3	3	6
10	Netherlands	1	1	6	2	8
11	Portugal	1	1	3	2	5
12	Georgia	1		1	1	2
13	Czechoslovakia	1			1	1

CUP WINNERS' CUP MEDALS TABLE (CONT'D)

	Country	G	S	B	F	SF
14	Austria		3	1	3	4
15	Hungary		2	1	2	3
16	Russia		1	5	1	6
17	Poland		1	1	1	2
18	Czech Republic			3		3
19	Croatia			2		2
	Serbia			2		2
	Bulgaria			2		2
22	Romania			1		1
	Wales			1		1
		39	39	78	78	156

CUP WINNERS' CUP MEDALS TABLE

	Club		G	S	B
1	Barcelona	ESP	4	2	
2	RSC Anderlecht	BEL	2	2	
3	Milan	ITA	2	1	
4	Chelsea	ENG	2		2
5	Dynamo Kyiv	UKR	2		
6	Atlético Madrid	ESP	1	2	2
	Arsenal	ENG	1	2	
8	Glasgow Rangers	SCO	1	2	
9	Sampdoria	ITA	1	1	1
	West Ham United	ENG	1	1	1
	Fiorentina	ITA	1	1	1
	Paris Saint-Germain	FRA	1	1	1
13	Ajax	NED	1	1	
	Hamburger SV	GER	1	1	
	Parma	ITA	1	1	
16	Bayern München	GER	1		3
17	Juventus	ITA	1		2
	Real Zaragoza	ESP	1		2
19	Aberdeen	SCO	1		1
	Dinamo Tbilisi	GEO	1		1
	Manchester City	ENG	1		1
	Manchester United	ENG	1		1
	KV Mechelen	BEL	1		1
	Sporting CP	POR	1		1
	Tottenham Hotspur	ENG	1		1
26	Borussia Dortmund	GER	1		
	Everton	ENG	1		
	Lazio	ITA	1		
	1.FC Magdeburg	GDR	1		
	Slovan Bratislava	SVK	1		
	Valencia	ESP	1		
	Werder Bremen	GER	1		
33	Real Madrid	ESP		2	
	SK Rapid Wien	AUT		2	
35	Dinamo Moskva	RUS		1	2
36	FK Austria	AUT		1	1
	Carl Ziess Jena	GDR		1	1
	AS Monaco	FRA		1	1
	Standard CL	BEL		1	1
	Liverpool	ENG		1	1
41	Ferencváros	HUN		1	
	Fortuna Düsseldorf	GER		1	
	Górnik Zabrze	POL		1	
	Leeds United	ENG		1	
	VfB Leipzig	GDR		1	
	Real Mallorca	ESP		1	
	MTK-VM Budapest	HUN		1	

CUP WINNERS' CUP MEDALS TABLE (CONT'D)

	Club		G	S	B
	TSV München 1860	GER		1	
	FC Porto	POR		1	
	Royal Antwerp FC	BEL		1	
	VfB Stuttgart	GER		1	
52	Feyenoord	NED			3
53	Benfica	POR			2
	Glasgow Celtic	SCO			2
	Lokomotiv Moskva	RUS			2
	PSV Eindhoven	NED			2
57	Atalanta	ITA			1
	Banik Ostrava	CZE			1
	Bayer Uerdingen	GER			1
	SK Beveren	BEL			1
	Girondins Bordeaux	FRA			1
	Borussia Mönchengladbach	GER			1
	Cardiff City	WAL			1
	Club Brugge	BEL			1
	CSKA Sofia	BUL			1
	Deportivo La Coruña	ESP			1
	1.FC Köln	GER			1
	Dukla Praha	CZE			1
	Dunfermline Athletic	SCO			1
	Berliner FC	GDR			1
	Dinamo Bucuresti	ROU			1
	Dinamo Zagreb	CRO			1
	Eintracht Frankfurt	GER			1
	Hajduk Split	CRO			1
	Legia Warszawa	POL			1
	Olympique Lyonnais	FRA			1
	Olympique Marseille	FRA			1
	FC Nantes	FRA			1
	Napoli	ITA			1
	1.FC Nürnberg	GER			1
	OFK Beograd	SER			1
	Crvena Zvezda Beograd	SER			1
	Roma	ITA			1
	FSV Zwickau	GDR			1
	FC Schalke 04	GER			1
	Slavia Sofia	BUL			1
	Sparta Praha	CZE			1
	Spartak Moskva	RUS			1
	Torino	ITA			1
	FC Twente Enschede	NED			1
	Ujpesti TE	HUN			1
	Racing Club Genk	BEL			1
	Vicenza	ITA			1
	Wolverhampton Wanderers	ENG			1
			39	39	78

FAIRS CUP

Year	Winners	Country	Score	Country	Runners-up
1958	Barcelona	ESP	2-2 6-0	ENG	London Select XI
1960	Barcelona	ESP	0-0 4-1	ENG	Birmingham City
1961	Roma	ITA	2-2 2-0	ENG	Birmingham City
1962	Valencia	ESP	6-2 1-1	ESP	Barcelona
1963	Valencia	ESP	2-1 2-0	YUG	Dinamo Zagreb

FAIRS CUP (CONT'D)

Year	Winners	Country	Score	Country	Runners-up
1964	Real Zaragoza	ESP	2-1	ESP	Valencia
1965	Ferencváros	HUN	1-0	ITA	Juventus
1966	Barcelona	ESP	0-1 4-2	ESP	Real Zaragoza
1967	Dinamo Zagreb	YUG	2-0 0-0	ENG	Leeds United
1968	Leeds United	ENG	1-0 0-0	HUN	Ferencváros
1969	Newcastle United	ENG	3-0 3-2	HUN	Ujpesti Dózsa
1970	Arsenal	ENG	1-3 3-0	BEL	RSC Anderlecht
1971	Leeds United	ENG	2-2 1-1	ITA	Juventus

FAIRS CUP MEDALS TABLE

	Country	G	S	B	F	SF
1	Spain	6	3	1	9	10
2	England	4	4	5	8	13
3	Italy	1	2	4	3	7
4	Hungary	1	2	2	3	5
5	Croatia	1	1		2	2
6	Belgium		1	2	1	3
7	Scotland			4		4
8	Germany			3		3
9	Serbia			2		2
10	Netherlands			1		1
11	Switzerland			1		1
12	Turkey			1		1
		13	13	26	26	52

FAIRS CUP MEDALS TABLE

	Club		G	S	B
1	Barcelona	ESP	3	1	
2	Leeds United	ENG	2	1	1
3	Valencia	ESP	2	1	
4	Ferencvaros	HUN	1	1	1
5	Dinamo Zagreb	CRO	1	1	
	Real Zaragoza	ESP	1	1	
7	Roma	ITA	1		1
8	Arsenal	ENG	1		
	Newcastle United	ENG	1		

FAIRS CUP MEDALS TABLE (CONT'D)

	Club		G	S	B
10	Birmingham City	ENG		2	1
11	Juventus	ITA		2	
12	RSC Anderlecht	BEL		1	
	London Select XI	ENG		1	
	Ujpesti TE	HUN		1	
15	Internazionale	ITA			2
	1.FC Köln	GER			2
17	Ajax	NED			1
	Atlético Madrid	ESP			1
	Belgrade Select XI	SRB			1
	Bologna	ITA			1
	Chelsea	ENG			1
	Crvena Zvezda	SRB			1
	Dundee	SCO			1
	Eintracht Frankfurt	GER			1
	Göztepe Izmir	TUR			1
	Hibernian	SCO			1
	Lausanne-Sports	SUI			1
	RFC Liège	BEL			1
	Liverpool	ENG			1
	Kilmarnock	SCO			1
	Manchester United	ENG			1
	MTK-VM Budapest	HUN			1
	Rangers	SCO			1
	Union St Gilloise	BEL			1
			13	13	26

UEFA CUP

Year	Winners	Country	Score	Country	Runners-up
1972	Tottenham Hotspur	ENG	2-1 1-1	ENG	Wolverhampton Wanderers
1973	Liverpool	ENG	3-0 0-2	FRG	Borussia Mönchengladbach
1974	Feyenoord	NED	2-2 2-0	ENG	Tottenham Hotspur
1975	Borussia Mönchengladbach	FRG	0-0 5-1	NED	FC Twente Enschede
1976	Liverpool	ENG	3-2 1-1	BEL	Club Brugge
1977	Juventus	ITA	1-0 1-2	ESP	Athletic Bilbao
1978	PSV Eindhoven	NED	0-0 3-0	FRA	SEC Bastia
1979	Borussia Mönchengladbach	FRG	1-1 1-0	YUG	Crvena Zvezda Beograd
1980	Eintracht Frankfurt	FRG	2-3 1-0	FRG	Borussia Mönchengladbach
1981	Ipswich Town	ENG	3-0 2-4	NED	AZ 67 Alkmaar
1982	IFK Göteborg	SWE	1-0 3-0	FRG	Hamburger SV
1983	RSC Anderlecht	BEL	1-0 1-1	POR	Benfica

UEFA CUP (CONT'D)

Year	Winners	Country	Score	Country	Runners-up
1984	Tottenham Hotspur	ENG	1-1 1-1 4-3p	BEL	RSC Anderlecht
1985	Real Madrid	ESP	3-0 0-1	HUN	Videoton SC
1986	Real Madrid	ESP	5-1 0-2	FRG	1.FC Köln
1987	IFK Göteborg	SWE	1-0 1-1	SCO	Dundee United
1988	Bayer Leverkusen	FRG	0-3 3-0 3-2p	ESP	Español
1989	Napoli	ITA	2-1 3-3	FRG	VfB Stuttgart
1990	Juventus	ITA	3-1 0-0	ITA	Fiorentina
1991	Internazionale	ITA	2-0 0-1	ITA	Roma
1992	Ajax	NED	2-2 0-0	ITA	Torino
1993	Juventus	ITA	3-1 3-0	GER	Borussia Dortmund
1994	Internazionale	ITA	1-0 1-0	AUT	Austria Salzburg
1995	Parma	ITA	1-0 1-1	ITA	Juventus
1996	Bayern München	GER	2-0 3-1	FRA	Bordeaux
1997	Schalke 04	GER	1-0 0-1 4-1p	ITA	Internazionale
1998	Internazionale	ITA	3-0	ITA	Lazio
1999	Parma	ITA	3-0	FRA	Olympique Marseille
2000	Galatasaray	TUR	0-0 4-1p	ENG	Arsenal
2001	Liverpool	ENG	5-4	ESP	CD Alavés
2002	Feyenoord	NED	3-2	GER	Borussia Dortmund
2003	FC Porto	POR	3-2	SCO	Glasgow Celtic
2004	Valencia	ESP	2-0	FRA	Olympique Marseille
2005	CSKA Moskva	RUS	3-1	POR	Sporting CP
2006	Sevilla	ESP	4-0	ENG	Middlesbrough
2007	Sevilla	ESP	2-2 3-1p	ESP	Espanyol
2008	Zenit St Petersburg	RUS	2-0	SCO	Rangers
2009	Shakhtar Donetsk	UKR	2-1	GER	Werder Bremen

UEFA CUP MEDALS TABLE

	Country	G	S	B	F	SF
1	Italy	9	6	12	15	27
2	Germany	6	8	22	14	36
3	England	6	4	4	10	14
4	Spain	5	4	10	9	19
5	Netherlands	4	2	2	6	8
6	Russia	2		1	2	3
7	Sweden	2			2	2
8	Belgium	1	2	3	3	6
9	Portugal	1	2	2	3	5
10	Ukraine	1		1	1	2
11	Turkey	1			1	1
12	France		4	5	4	9
13	Scotland		3		3	3
14	Austria		1	1	1	2
	Hungary		1	1	1	2
	Serbia		1	1	1	2
17	Czech Republic			2		2
	German DR			2		2
	Romania			2		2
20	Bosnia-Herzegovina			1		1
	Croatia			1		1
	Denmark			1		1
	Greece			1		1
	Switzerland			1		1
		38	38	76	76	152

UEFA CUP MEDALS TABLE

	Club		G	S	B
1	Internazionale	ITA	3	1	3
2	Juventus	ITA	3	1	1
3	Liverpool	ENG	3		
4	Borussia Mönchengladbach	GER	2	2	1
5	Tottenham Hotspur	ENG	2	1	1
6	Parma	ITA	2		1
	Real Madrid	ESP	2		1
8	Feyenoord	NED	2		
	IFK Göteborg	SWE	2		
	Sevilla	ESP	2		
11	RSC Anderlecht	BEL	1	1	
12	Bayern München	GER	1		3
13	Bayer Leverkusen	GER	1		1
	FC Schalke 04	GER	1		1
15	Ajax	NED	1		
	CSKA Moskva	RUS	1		
	Eintracht Frankfurt	GER	1		
	Galatasaray	TUR	1		
	Ipswich Town	ENG	1		
	Napoli	ITA	1		
	FC Porto	POR	1		
	PSV Eindhoven	NED	1		
	Shakhtar Donetsk	UKR	1		
	Valencia	ESP	1		
	Zenit St Petersburg	RUS	1		
26	Borussia Dortmund	GER		2	1
27	RCD Espanyol	ESP		2	

UEFA CUP MEDALS TABLE (CONT'D)

	Club		G	S	B
	Olympique Marseille	FRA		2	
29	1.FC Köln	GER		1	3
	Werder Bremen	GER		1	3
31	Hamburger SV	GER		1	2
	VfB Stuttgart	GER		1	2
33	AZ Alkmaar	NED		1	1
	Club Brugge	BEL		1	1
	Fiorentina	ITA		1	1
	Lazio	ITA		1	1
	Sporting CP	POR		1	1
	Twente Enschede	NED		1	1
39	Arsenal	ENG		1	
	Austria Salzburg	AUT		1	
	CD Alavés	ESP		1	
	Athletic Bilbao	ESP		1	
	SEC Bastia	FRA		1	
	Benfica	POR		1	
	Girondins Bordeaux	FRA		1	
	Glasgow Celtic	SCO		1	
	Crvena Zvezda Beograd	SRB		1	
	Dundee United	SCO		1	
	Middlesbrough	ENG		1	
	Glasgow Rangers	SCO		1	
	Roma	ITA		1	
	Torino	ITA		1	
	Videoton SC	HUN		1	
	Wolverhampton Wanderers	ENG		1	
55	Barcelona	ESP			4
56	Atlético Madrid	ESP			2
	1.FC Kaiserslautern	GER			2
	Milan	ITA			2
59	AEK Athens	GRE			1
	AJ Auxerre	FRA			1
	Boavista	POR			1

UEFA CUP MEDALS TABLE (CONT'D)

Club		G	S	B
Bohemians Praha	CZE			1
Bologna	ITA			1
Brondbyernes IF	DEN			1
Cagliari	ITA			1
MSV Duisburg	GER			1
1.FC Dynamo Dresden	GDR			1
Dynamo Kyiv	UKR			1
Ferencváros	HUN			1
Genoa 1893	ITA			1
Grasshopper-Club	SUI			1
Hajduk Split	CRO			1
Hertha BSC Berlin	GER			1
Karlsruher SC	GER			1
Leeds United	ENG			1
VfB Leipzig	GDR			1
Racing Club Lens	FRA			1
AS Monaco	FRA			1
RWD Molenbeek	BEL			1
Newcastle United	ENG			1
Nottingham Forest	ENG			1
Osasuna	ESP			1
Paris Saint-Germain	FRA			1
Radnicki Nis	SRB			1
Slavia Praha	CZE			1
FC Sochaux	FRA			1
Spartak Moskva	RUS			1
Steaua Bucuresti	ROU			1
Tenerife	ESP			1
FC Tirol	AUT			1
Universitatea Craiova	ROU			1
Villarreal	ESP			1
KSV Waregem	BEL			1
Zeljeznicar Sarajevo	BIH			1
		38	38	76

UEFA EUROPA LEAGUE

Year	Winners	Country	Score	Country	Runners-up
2010	Atlético Madrid	ESP	2-1	ENG	Fulham
2011	FC Porto	POR	1-0	POR	SC Braga
2012	Atlético Madrid	ESP	3-0	ESP	Athletic Bilbao

UEFA EUROPA LEAGUE MEDALS TABLE

	Country	G	S	B	F	SF
1	Portugal	1	1	2	2	4
2	Spain	2	1	2	3	5
3	England		1	1	1	2
4	Germany			1		1
		3	3	6	6	12

UEFA EUROPA LEAGUE MEDALS TABLE

	Club		G	S	B
1	Atlético Madrid	ESP	2		
2	FC Porto	POR	1		
3	SC Braga	POR		1	
	Fulham	ENG		1	
	Athletic Bilbao	ESP		1	
6	Benfica	POR			1
	Hamburger SV	GER			1
	Liverpool	ENG			1
	Sporting CP	POR			1
	Valencia	ESP			1
	Villarreal	ESP			1
			3	3	6

EUROPEAN YOUTH TOURNAMENTS

UEFA EUROPEAN U-21 CHAMPIONSHIP

Year	Host Country	Winners	Score	Runners-up	Venue
1978		Yugoslavia	1-0 4-1	German DR	Halle & Mostar
1980		Soviet Union	0-0 1-0	German DR	Rostock & Moscow
1982		England	3-1 2-3	Germany FR	Sheffield & Bremen
1984		England	1-0 2-0	Spain	Seville & Sheffield
1986		Spain	1-2 2-1 3-0p	Italy	Rome & Valladolid
1988		France	0-0 3-0	Greece	Athens & Besançon
1990		Soviet Union	4-2 3-1	Yugoslavia	Sarajevo & Simferopol
1992		Italy	2-0 0-1	Sweden	Ferrara & Växjö
1994	France	Italy	1-0	Portugal	Montpellier
1996	Spain	Italy	1-1 4-2p	Spain	Barcelona
1998	Romania	Spain	1-0	Greece	Bucharest
2000	Slovakia	Italy	2-1	Czech Republic	Bratislava
2002	Switzerland	Czech Republic	0-0 3-1p	France	St Jakob Park, Basel
2004	Germany	Italy	3-0	Serbia & Montenegro	Ruhrstadion, Bochum
2006	Portugal	Netherlands	3-0	Ukraine	Bessa, Oporto
2007	Netherlands	Netherlands	4-1	Serbia	Euroborg, Groningen
2009	Sweden	Germany	4-0	England	Swedbank Stadion, Malmö
2011	Denmark	Spain	2-0	Switzerland	Aarhus Stadion, Aarhus
2013	Israel				

UEFA U-21 CHAMPIONSHIP MEDALS TABLE

	Country	G	S	B
1	Italy	5	1	4
2	Spain	3	2	2
3	England	2	1	5
4	Soviet Union	2		1
	Netherlands	2		1
6	France	1	1	2
	Yugoslavia	1	1	2
8	Czech Republic	1	1	
	Germany	1	1	
10	Serbia		2	1
11	Greece		2	
	Germany DR		2	

UEFA U-21 CHAMPIONSHIP MEDALS TABLE (CONT'D)

	Country	G	S	B
13	Sweden		1	2
14	Portugal		1	1
	Switzerland		1	1
16	Ukraine		1	
17	Scotland			2
18	Belarus			1
	Belgium			1
	Bulgaria			1
	Denmark			1
	Hungary			1
	Norway			1
		18	18	30

UEFA EUROPEAN U-19 CHAMPIONSHIP

Year	Host Country	Winners	Score	Runners-up	Venue
1981	West Germany	Germany FR	1-0	Poland	Düsseldorf
1982	Finland	Scotland	3-1	Czechoslovakia	Helsinki
1983	England	France	1-0	Czechoslovakia	White Hart Lane, London
1984	Soviet Union	Hungary	0-0 3-2p	Soviet Union	Zentralny, Moscow
1986	Yugoslavia	German DR	3-1	Italy	Subotica
1988	Czechoslovakia	Soviet Union	3-1	Portugal	Frydek-Mistek
1990	Hungary	Soviet Union	0-0 4-2p	Portugal	Bekescsaba
1992	Germany	Turkey	2-1	Portugal	Bayreuth
1993	England	England	1-0	Turkey	City Ground, Nottingham
1994	Spain	Portugal	1-1 4-1p	Germany	Merida
1995	Greece	Spain	4-1	Italy	Katerini
1996	France/Luxemb	France	1-0	Spain	Besançon
1997	Iceland	France	1-0	Portugal	Reykjavík

UEFA EUROPEAN U-19 CHAMPIONSHIP (CONT'D)

Year	Host Country	Winners	Score	Runners-up	Venue
1998	Cyprus	Republic of Ireland	1-1 4-3p	Germany	Larnaca
1999	Sweden	Portugal	1-0	Italy	Norrköping
2000	Germany	France	1-0	Ukraine	Nürnberg
2001	Finland	Poland	3-1	Czech Republic	Helsinki
2002	Norway	Spain	1-0	Germany	Ullevaal, Oslo
2003	Liechtenstein	Italy	2-0	Portugal	Rheinpark Stadion, Vaduz
2004	Switzerland	Spain	1-0	Turkey	Colovray, Nyon
2005	Nth. Ireland	France	3-1	England	Windsor Park, Belfast
2006	Poland	Spain	2-1	Scotland	Miejski, Poznan
2007	Austria	Spain	1-0	Greece	Linzer, Linz
2008	Czech Republic	Germany	3-1	Italy	Strelnice, Jablonec nad Nisou
2009	Ukraine	Ukraine	2-0	England	Olympiyskiy, Donetsk
2010	France	France	2-1	Spain	Michel d'Ornano, Caen
2011	Romania	Spain	3-2	Czech Republic	Concordia, Chiajna
2012	Estonia	Spain	1-0	Greece	Lilleküla, Tallinn

Played as an U-18 tournament from 1981 to 2001

UEFA U-19 CHAMPIONSHIP MEDALS TABLE

	Country	G	S	B
1	Spain	7	2	5
2	France	6		4
3	Portugal	2	5	
4	Germany	2	3	4
5	Soviet Union	2	1	1
6	Italy	1	4	
7	England	1	2	4
8	Turkey	1	2	
9	Poland	1	1	1
	Ukraine	1	1	1
11	Scotland	1	1	
12	Republic of Ireland	1		2

UEFA U-19 CHAMPIONSHIP MEDALS TABLE (CONT'D)

	Country	G	S	B
13	Hungary	1		1
	Germany DR	1		1
15	Czech Republic		2	2
16	Greece		2	1
17	Czechoslovakia		2	
18	Serbia			3
19	Austria			2
	Croatia			2
21	Norway			1
	Slovakia			1
	Switzerland			1
		28	28	37

UEFA EUROPEAN U-17 CHAMPIONSHIP

Year	Host Country	Winners	Score	Runners-up	Venue
1982	Italy	Italy	1-0	Germany FR	Falconara
1984	Germany FR	Germany FR	2-0	Soviet Union	Ulm
1985	Hungary	Soviet Union	4-0	Greece	Budapest
1986	Greece	Spain	2-1	Italy	Athens
1987	France	Italy	1-0	Soviet Union	Paris
1988	Spain	Spain	0-0 4-2p	Portugal	Teresa Rivero, Madrid
1989	Denmark	Portugal	4-1	German DR	Vejle
1990	East Germany	Czechoslovakia	3-2	Yugoslavia	Erfurt
1991	Swtzerland	Spain	2-0	Germany	Wankdorf, Berne
1992	Cyprus	Germany	2-1	Spain	Ammokostos, Larnaca
1993	Turkey	Poland	1-0	Italy	Inönü, Istanbul
1994	Rep. Ireland	Turkey	1-0	Denmark	Tolka Park, Dublin
1995	Belgium	Portugal	2-0	Spain	Brussels
1996	Austria	Portugal	1-0	France	Wien
1997	Germany	Spain	0-0 5-4p	Austria	Celle
1998	Scotland	Republic of Ireland	2-1	Italy	McDiarmid Park, Perth

EUROPEAN WOMEN'S TOURNAMENTS

UEFA EUROPEAN U-17 CHAMPIONSHIP (CONT'D)

Year	Host Country	Winners	Score	Runners-up	Venue
2000	Israel	Portugal	2-1	Czech Republic	Ramat Gan
2001	England	Spain	1-0	France	Stadium of Light, Sunderland
2002	Denmark	Switzerland	0-0 4-2p	France	Farum Park, Farum
2003	Portugal	Portugal	2-1	Spain	Fontelo Municipal, Viseu
2004	France	France	2-1	Spain	Gaston Petit, Chateauroux
2005	Italy	Turkey	2-0	Netherlands	E. Mannucci, Pontedera
2006	Luxembourg	Russia	2-2 5-3p	Czech Republic	Josy Barthel, Luxembourg
2007	Belgium	Spain	1-0	England	RFC Tournai, Tournai
2008	Turkey	Spain	4-0	France	Mardan Sports Complex, Antalya
2009	Germany	Germany	2-1	Netherlands	Magdeburg Stadium, Magdeburg
2010	Liechtenstein	England	2-1	Spain	Rheinpark, Vaduz
2011	Serbia	Netherlands	5-2	Germany	Karadorde, Novi Sad
2012	Slovenia	Netherlands	1-1 5-4p	Germany	Stozice, Ljubljana

Played as an U-16 tournament prior to 2002

UEFA U-17 CHAMPIONSHIP MEDALS TABLE

	Country	G	S	B
1	Spain	8	5	3
2	Portugal	5	1	1
3	Germany	3	4	3
4	Italy	2	3	3
5	Netherlands	2	2	2
6	Turkey	2	2	
7	France	1	4	4
8	Soviet Union	1	2	1
	England	1	1	3
10	Poland	1	1	2
11	Switzerland	1		1
	Czechoslovakia	1		1
13	Republic of Ireland	1		

UEFA U-17 CHAMPIONSHIP MEDALS TABLE (CONT'D)

	Country	G	S	B
	Russia	1		
15	Czech Republic		2	
16	Austria		1	1
	Denmark		1	1
	Germany DR		1	1
	Greece		1	1
	Yugoslavia		1	1
21	Belgium			1
	Croatia			1
	Georgia			1
	Israel			1
	Ukraine			1
		30	30	36

EUROPEAN WOMEN'S TOURNAMENTS

UEFA EUROPEAN WOMEN'S CHAMPIONSHIP

Year	Host Country	Winners	Score	Runners-up	Venue
1984		Sweden	1-0 0-1 4-3p	England	Gothenburg & Luton
1987	Norway	Norway	2-1	Sweden	Ullevål, Oslo
1989	Germany FR	Germany FR	4-1	Norway	Osnabrück
1991	Denmark	Germany	3-1	Norway	Aalborg Stadion
1993	Italy	Norway	1-0	Italy	Dino Manuzzi, Cesena
1995	Germany	Germany	3-2	Sweden	Fritz Walter Stadion, Kaiserslautern
1997	Norway/Sweden	Germany	2-0	Italy	Ullevål, Oslo
2001	Germany	Germany	1-0	Sweden	Donaustadion, Ulm
2005	England	Germany	3-1	Norway	Ewood Park, Blackburn
2009	Finland	Germany	6-2	England	Olympiastadion, Helsinki

UEFA WOMEN'S CHAMPIONSHIP MEDALS TABLE

	Country	G	S	B	F	SF
1	Germany	7			7	8
2	Norway	2	3	3	5	8
3	Sweden	1	3	3	4	7
4	Italy		2	2	2	6
5	England		2	1	2	4
6	Denmark			4		4
7	Spain				1	1
8	Finland				1	1
9	Netherlands				1	1
		10	10	16	20	40

UEFA WOMEN'S CHAMPIONS LEAGUE

Year	Winners	Country	Score	Country	Runners-up
2002	1.FFC Frankfurt	GER	2-0	SWE	Umeå IK
2003	Umeå IK	SWE	4-1 3-0	DEN	Fortuna Hjørring
2004	Umeå IK	SWE	3-0 5-0	GER	1.FFC Frankfurt
2005	1.FFC Turbine Potsdam	GER	2-0 3-1	SWE	Djurgården/Alvsjö
2006	1.FFC Frankfurt	GER	4-0 3-2	GER	1.FFC Turbine Potsdam
2007	Arsenal	ENG	1-0 0-0	SWE	Umeå IK
2008	1.FFC Frankfurt	GER	1-1 3-2	SWE	Umeå IK
2009	FCR 2001 Duisburg	GER	6-0 1-1	RUS	Zvezda-2005
2010	1.FFC Turbine Potsdam	GER	0-0 7-6p	FRA	Olympique Lyonnais
2011	Olympique Lyonnais	FRA	2-0	GER	1.FFC Turbine Potsdam
2012	Olympique Lyonnais	FRA	2-0	GER	1.FFC Frankfurt

UEFA WOMEN'S CHAMPIONS LEAGUE MEDALS TABLE

	Country	G	S	B	F	SF
1	Germany	6	4	4	10	14
2	Sweden	2	4	4	6	10
3	France	2	1	4	3	7
4	England	1		4	1	5
5	Denmark		1	2	1	3
6	Russia		1		1	1
7	Norway			2		2
8	Finland			1		1
	Italy			1		1
		11	11	22	22	44

UEFA WOMEN'S CHAMPIONS LEAGUE MEDALS TABLE

	Club		G	S	B
1	1.FFC Frankfurt	GER	3	2	1
2	Umeå IK	SWE	2	3	2
3	1.FFC Turbine Potsdam	GER	2	2	1
4	Olympique Lyonnais	FRA	2	1	2
5	Arsenal LFC	ENG	1		4
6	FCR 2001 Duisburg	GER	1		2
7	Djurgården/Alvsjö	SWE		1	1
8	Fortuna Hjørring	DEN		1	
	Zvezda 2005 Perm	RUS		1	
10	Brøndby	DEN			2
11	HJK Helsinki	FIN			1
	Toulouse	FRA			1
	Malmö FF Dam	SWE			1
	Trondheims-Ørn	NOR			1
	Montpellier HSC	FRA			1
	Kolbotn	NOR			1
	Bardolino	ITA			1
			11	11	22

EUROPEAN WOMEN'S TOURNAMENTS

UEFA EUROPEAN WOMEN'S U-19 CHAMPIONSHIP

Year	Host Country	Winners	Score	Runners-up	Venue
1998		Denmark	2-0 2-3	France	Aabenraa & Niederbronn-les-Bains
1999	Sweden	Sweden	1-0	Germany	Bromölla
2000	France	Germany	4-2	Spain	La Libération, Boulogne
2001	Norway	Germany	3-2	Norway	Aråsen, Lillestrom
2002	Sweden	Germany	3-1	France	Olympia, Helsingborg
2003	Germany	France	2-0	Norway	Alfred Kunze Sportpark, Leipzig
2004	Finland	Spain	2-1	Germany	Pohjola Stadion, Vantaa
2005	Hungary	Russia	2-2 6-5p	France	ZTE, Zalaegerszeg
2006	Switzerland	Germany	3-0	France	Neufeld, Berne
2007	Iceland	Germany	2-0	England	Laugardalsvöllur, Reykjavík
2008	France	Italy	1-0	Norway	Vallée du Cher, Tours
2009	Belarus	England	2-0	Sweden	Gorodskoi, Borisov
2010	Macedonia	France	2-1	England	Gradski, Skopje
2011	Italy	Germany	8-1	Norway	Romeo Galli, Imola
2012	Turkey	Sweden	1-0	Spain	Mardan, Antalya

The first three tournaments were played as U-18 championships

UEFA WOMEN'S U-19 CHAMPIONSHIP MEDALS TABLE

	Country	G	S	B
1	Germany	6	2	4
2	France	2	4	2
3	Sweden	2	1	4
4	England	1	2	2
5	Spain	1	2	
6	Denmark	1		4
7	Italy	1		3
8	Russia	1		2
	Norway		4	1
10	Switzerland			2
11	Finland			1
	Netherlands			1
	Portugal			1
		15	15	27

UEFA EUROPEAN WOMEN'S U-17 CHAMPIONSHIP

Year	Host Country	Winners	Score	Runners-up	Venue
2008	Switzerland	Germany	3-0	France	Colovray, Nyon
2009	Switzerland	Germany	7-0	Spain	Colovray, Nyon
2010	Switzerland	Spain	0-0 4-1p	Republic of Ireland	Colovray, Nyon
2011	Switzerland	Spain	1-0	France	Colovray, Nyon
2012	Switzerland	Germany	1-1 4-3p	France	Colovray, Nyon

UEFA WOMEN'S U-17 CHAMPIONSHIP MEDALS TABLE

	Country	G	S	B
1	Germany	3		2
2	Spain	2	1	
3	France		3	1
4	Republic of Ireland		1	
5	Denmark			2
		5	5	5

UEFA EURO 2012 POLAND/UKRAINE

Qualifying groups

Group A — Pl W D L F A Pts GER TUR BEL AUT AZE KAZ
Germany 10 10 0 0 34 7 **30** — 3-0 3-1 6-2 6-1 4-0
Turkey 10 5 2 3 13 11 **17** 1-3 — 3-2 2-0 1-0 2-1
Belgium 10 4 3 3 21 15 **15** 0-1 1-1 — 4-4 4-1 4-1
Austria 10 3 3 4 16 17 **12** 1-2 0-0 0-2 — 3-0 2-0
Azerbaijan 10 2 1 7 10 26 **7** 1-3 1-0 1-1 1-4 — 3-2
Kazakhstan 10 1 1 8 6 24 **4** 0-3 0-3 0-2 0-0 2-1 —

Group B — Pl W D L F A Pts RUS IRL ARM SVK MKD AND
Russia 10 7 2 1 17 4 **23** — 0-0 3-1 0-1 1-0 6-0
Rep of Ireland 10 6 3 1 15 7 **21** 2-3 — 2-1 0-0 2-1 3-1
Armenia 10 5 2 3 22 10 **17** 0-0 0-1 — 3-1 4-1 4-0
Slovakia 10 4 3 3 7 10 **15** 0-1 1-1 0-4 — 1-0 1-0
Macedonia 10 2 2 6 8 14 **8** 0-1 0-2 2-2 1-1 — 1-0
Andorra 10 0 0 10 1 25 **0** 0-2 0-2 0-3 0-1 0-2 —

Group C — Pl W D L F A Pts
Italy 10 8 2 0 20 2 **26** — 3-0 3-0 1-0 3-0 5-0
Estonia 10 5 1 4 15 14 **16** 1-2 — 1-1 0-1 4-1 2-1
Serbia 10 4 3 3 13 12 **15** 1-1 1-3 — 1-1 2-1 3-1
Slovenia 10 4 2 4 11 7 **14** 0-1 1-2 1-0 — 0-1 5-1
Nth Ireland 10 2 3 5 9 13 **9** 0-0 1-2 0-1 0-0 — 4-0
Faroe Islands 10 1 1 8 6 26 **4** 0-1 2-0 0-3 0-2 1-1 —

Group D — Pl W D L F A Pts
France 10 6 3 1 15 4 **21** — 1-1 2-0 0-1 3-0 2-0
Bosnia-H'vina 10 6 2 2 17 8 **20** 0-2 — 2-1 1-0 2-0 5-0
Romania 10 3 5 2 13 9 **14** 0-0 3-0 — 2-2 1-1 3-1
Belarus 10 3 4 3 8 7 **13** 1-1 0-2 0-0 — 2-0 2-0
Albania 10 2 3 5 7 14 **9** 1-2 1-1 1-1 1-0 — 1-0
Luxembourg 10 1 1 8 3 21 **4** 0-2 0-3 0-2 0-0 2-1 —

Group E — Pl W D L F A Pts
Netherlands 10 9 0 1 37 8 **27** — 4-1 5-3 2-1 1-0 11-0
Sweden 10 8 0 2 31 11 **24** 3-2 — 2-0 5-0 2-1 6-0
Hungary 10 6 1 3 22 14 **19** 0-4 2-1 — 0-0 2-1 8-0
Finland 10 3 1 6 16 16 **10** 0-2 1-2 1-2 — 4-1 8-0
Moldova 10 3 0 7 12 16 **9** 0-1 1-4 0-2 2-0 — 4-0
San Marino 10 0 0 10 0 53 **0** 0-5 0-5 0-3 0-1 0-2 —

Group F — Pl W D L F A Pts
Greece 10 7 3 0 14 5 **24** — 2-0 2-1 1-0 1-1 3-1
Croatia 10 7 1 2 18 7 **22** 0-0 — 3-1 2-0 2-1 3-0
Israel 10 5 1 4 13 11 **16** 0-1 1-2 — 2-1 1-0 3-1
Latvia 10 3 2 5 9 12 **11** 1-1 0-3 1-2 — 1-1 2-0
Georgia 10 2 4 4 7 9 **10** 1-2 1-0 0-0 0-1 — 1-0
Malta 10 0 1 9 4 21 **1** 0-1 1-3 0-2 0-2 1-1 —

Group G — Pl W D L F A Pts
England 8 5 3 0 17 5 **18** — 0-0 2-2 1-0 4-0
Montenegro 8 3 3 2 7 7 **12** 2-2 — 1-0 1-0 1-1
Switzerland 8 3 2 3 12 10 **11** 1-3 2-0 — 4-1 3-1
Wales 8 3 0 5 6 10 **9** 0-2 2-1 2-0 — 0-1
Bulgaria 8 1 2 5 3 13 **5** 0-3 0-1 0-0 0-1 —

Group H — Pl W D L F A Pts
Denmark 8 6 1 1 15 6 **19** — 2-1 2-0 1-0 2-0
Portugal 8 5 1 2 21 12 **16** 3-1 — 1-0 5-3 4-4
Norway 8 5 1 2 10 7 **16** 1-1 1-0 — 1-0 3-1
Iceland 8 1 1 6 6 14 **4** 0-2 1-3 1-2 — 1-0
Cyprus 8 0 2 6 7 20 **2** 1-4 0-4 1-2 0-0 —

Group I — Pl W D L F A Pts
Spain 8 8 0 0 26 6 **24** — 2-1 3-1 3-1 6-0
Czech Rep 8 4 1 3 12 8 **13** 0-2 — 1-0 0-1 2-0
Scotland 8 3 2 3 9 10 **11** 2-3 2-2 — 1-0 2-1
Lithuania 8 1 2 5 4 13 **5** 1-3 1-4 0-0 — 0-0
Liechtenstein 8 1 1 6 3 17 **4** 0-4 0-2 0-1 2-0 —

Final Tournament first Round Group Stage

Pl W D L F A Pts GRE RUS POL
Czech Rep. 3 2 0 1 4 5 **6** 2-1 1-4 1-0
Greece 3 1 1 1 3 3 **4** — 1-0 1-1
Russia 3 1 1 1 5 3 **4** — — 1-1
Poland 3 0 2 1 2 3 **2**

Pl W D L F A Pts POR DEN NED
Germany 3 3 0 0 5 2 **9** 1-0 2-1 2-1
Portugal 3 2 0 1 5 4 **6** — 3-2 2-1
Denmark 3 1 0 2 4 5 **3** — — 1-0
Netherlands 3 0 0 3 2 5 **0**

Pl W D L F A Pts ITA CRO IRL
Spain 3 2 1 0 6 1 **7** 1-1 1-0 4-0
Italy 3 1 2 0 4 2 **5** — 1-1 2-0
Croatia 3 1 1 1 4 3 **4** — — 3-1
Rep. Ireland 3 0 0 3 1 9 **0**

Pl W D L F A Pts FRA UKR SWE
England 3 2 1 0 5 3 **7** 1-1 1-0 3-2
France 3 1 1 1 3 3 **4** — 2-0 0-2
Ukraine 3 1 0 2 2 4 **3** — — 2-1
Sweden 3 1 0 2 5 5 **3**

Qualifying play-offs
Bosnia 0-0 2-6 **Portugal** • Turkey 0-3 0-0 **Croatia** • **Czech Rep** 2-0 1-0 Montenegro • Estonia 0-4 1-1 **Rep Ireland**

NATIONAL TEAM TOURNAMENTS IN 2010–12

UEFA EURO 2012 POLAND/UKRAINE

Quarter-finals		Semi-finals		Final	
Spain	2				
France	0				
		Spain	0 4p		
		Portugal	0 2p		
Czech Republic	0				
Portugal	1				
				Spain	4
				Italy	0
Germany	4				
Greece	2				
		Germany	1		
		Italy	2		
England	0 2p				
Italy	0 4p				

Top scorers (Finals): **3** - Fernando **TORRES** ESP (Golden Boot Winner); Mario **MANDZUKIC** CRO; Mario **GOMEZ** GER; Mario **BALOTELLI** ITA; **CRISTIANO RONALDO** POR & Alan **DZAGOEV** RUS • **2** - Ten players scored twice
Top scorers (Overall incl qualifiers): **12** - Klaas-Jan **HUNTELAAR** NED • **10** - Miroslav **KLOSE** GER & **CRISTIANO RONALDO** POR • **9** - Mario **GOMEZ** GER • **7** - Mikael **FORSSELL** FIN; Robbie **KEANE** IRL; David **VILLA** ESP; Antonio **CASSANO** ITA & Robin **VAN PERSIE** NED

UEFA EURO 2012 POLAND/UKRAINE QUALIFYING TOURNAMENT

	GROUP A	PL	W	D	L	F	A	PTS	GER	TUR	BEL	AUT	AZE	KAZ
1	Germany	10	10	0	0	34	7	30		3-0	3-1	6-2	6-1	4-0
2	Turkey	10	5	2	3	13	11	17	1-3		3-2	2-0	1-0	2-1
3	Belgium	10	4	3	3	21	15	15	0-1	1-1		4-4	4-1	4-1
4	Austria	10	3	3	4	16	17	12	1-2	0-0	0-2		3-0	2-0
5	Azerbaijan	10	2	1	7	10	26	7	1-3	1-0	1-1	1-4		3-2
6	Kazakhstan	10	1	1	8	6	24	4	0-3	0-3	0-2	0-0	2-1	

Germany qualified directly for the finals • Turkey qualified for a play-off v Croatia • Turkey 0-3 0-0 **Croatia**

ASTANA ARENA, ASTANA
3-09-2010, 15 800, Vad HUN

Kazakhstan	0
Turkey	3

TUR - Arda Turan [24], Hamit Altintop [26], Nihat Kahveci [76]

KAZ: Andrey SIDELNIKOV - Renat ABDULIN, Aleksey POPOV, Aleksandr KISLITSYN (Mikhail ROZHKOV 85), Aleksandr KIROV, Andrey KARPOVICH• (Denis RODIONOV 64), Nurbol ZHUMASKALIEV•, Heinrich SCHMIDTGAL, Azat NURGALIEV, Maksim AZOVSKIY, Sergey OSTAPENKO (Gleb MALTSEV 72). Tr: Bernd STORCK

TUR: ONUR Kivrak - SABRI Sarioglu, OMER Erdogan, SERVET Cetin, HAKAN Balta, ARDA Turan, EMRE Belozoglu, Mehmet AURELIO (Colin KAZIM-RICHARDS 89), HAMIT Altintop, TUNCAY Sanli (HALIL Altintop 80), NIHAT Kahveci (SELCUK Inan 82). Tr: Guus HIDDINK

ROI BAUDOUIN, BRUSSELS
3-09-2010, 41 126, Hauge NOR

Belgium	0
Germany	1

GER - Klose [51]

BEL: Logan BAILLY - Toby ALDERWEIRELD, Daniel VAN BUYTEN, Vincent KOMPANY•, Thomas VERMAELEN, Jan VERTONGHEN, Timmy SIMONS (Jelle VOSSEN 83), Eden HAZARD (Steven DEFOUR 73), Marouane FELLAINI, Moussa DEMBELE, Romelu LUKAKU (Christian BENTEKE 73). Tr: Georges LEEKENS

GER: Manuel NEUER - Holger BADSTUBER, Per MERTESACKER, Philipp LAHM, Marcell JANSEN (Heiko WESTERMANN 46), Bastian SCHWEINSTEIGER•, Mesut OZIL (CACAU• 88), Thomas MULLER, Sami KHEDIRA, Lukas PODOLSKI (Toni KROOS 70), Miroslav KLOSE. Tr: Joachim LOW

SUKRU SARACOGLU, ISTANBUL
7-09-2010, 43 538, Skomina SVN

Turkey	3
Belgium	2

TUR - Hamit Altintop [48], Semih Senturk [66], Arda Turan [78] • **BEL** - Van Buyten 2 [28 69]

TUR: ONUR Kivrak - SABRI Sarioglu (GOKHAN Gonul 73), ISMAIL Koybasi, OMER Erdogan, SERVET Cetin, ARDA Turan, SELCUK Inan (SEMIH Senturk 46), EMRE Belozoglu•, Mehmet AURELIO, HAMIT Altintop, TUNCAY Sanli (SELCUK Sahin•82). Tr: Guus HIDDINK

BEL: Logan BAILLY - Toby ALDERWEIRELD•, Daniel VAN BUYTEN•, Vincent KOMPANY••♦64, Thomas VERMAELEN, Jan VERTONGHEN, Timmy SIMONS, Marouane FELLAINI, Guillaume GILLET (Eden HAZARD 82), Moussa DEMBELE (Kevin MIRALLAS 64), Romelu LUKAKU (Axel WITSEL 76). Tr: Georges LEEKENS

RB ARENA, SALZBURG
7-09-2010, 22 500, Strahonja CRO

Austria	2
Kazakhstan	0

AUT - Linz [91+], Hoffer [92+]

AUT: Jurgen MACHO - Ekrem DAG, Franz SCHIEMER, Sebastian PRODL, Emanuel POGATETZ, Christian FUCHS, Veli KAVLAK, Jakob JANTSCHER• (David ALABA 66), Roland LINZ, Marc JANKO (Stefan MAIERHOFER 79), Martin HARNIK (Erwin HOFFER 66). Tr: Dietmar CONSTANTINI

KAZ: Gleb MALTSEV (Sergey KHIZHNICHENKO 46) - Andrey SIDELNIKOV, Renat ABDULIN, Aleksey POPOV, Aleksandr KISLITSYN• (Mikhail ROZHKOV•75), Aleksandr KIROV, Evgenly AVERCHENKO, Nurbol ZHUMASKALIEV•, Azat NURGALIEV• (Maksim AZOVSKIY 59), Andrey KARPOVICH, Kazbek GETERIEV. Tr: Bernd STORCK

MUNGERSDORFER, COLOGNE
7-09-2010, 43 751, Strombergsson SWE

Germany	6
Azerbaijan	1

GER - Westermann [28], Podolski [44], Klose 2 [45 92+], OG [53], Badstuber [86] • **AZE** - Javadov [57]

GER: Manuel NEUER - Holger BADSTUBER, Per MERTESACKER (Heiko WESTERMANN 11), Philipp LAHM, Sami KHEDIRA, Bastian SCHWEINSTEIGER (CACAU 72), Sascha RIETHER, Mesut OZIL, Thomas MULLER (Marko MARIN 62), Miroslav KLOSE, Lukas PODOLSKI. Tr: Joachim LOW

AZE: Kamran AGAYEV - Elnur ALLAHVERDIYEV, Samir ABBASOV, Sasa YUNISOGLU (Vurgun HUSEYNOV 56), Mahir SHUKUROV, Maksim MEDVEDEV, Rail MALIKOV, Aleksandr CHERTOGANOV (Rasad A. SADIQOV 64), Rashad SADIKHOV, Vuqar NADIROV (Araz ABDULLAYEV 86), Vagif JAVADOV. Tr: Berti VOGTS

ASTANA ARENA, ASTANA
8-10-2010, 8500, Borski POL

Kazakhstan	0
Belgium	2

BEL - Ogunjimi 2 [52 70]

KAZ: Andrey SIDELNIKOV - Aleksey POPOV, Aleksandr KISLITSYN••♦69, Aleksandr KIROV, Renat ABDULIN, Nurbol ZHUMASKALIEV (Evgenly AVERCHENKO 87), Heinrich SCHMIDTGAL, Azat NURGALIEV (Mikhail ROZHKOV 74), Andrey KARPOVICH•, Kazbek GETERIEV, Sergey KHIZHNICHENKO. Tr: Bernd STORCK

BEL: Logan BAILLY - Daniel VAN BUYTEN, Jelle VAN DAMME (Jonathan LEGEAR 78), Nicolas LOMBAERTS, Olivier DESCHACHT, Toby ALDERWEIRELD, Axel WITSEL, Timmy SIMONS, Marouane FELLAINI•, Jelle VOSSEN•, Romelu LUKAKU (Marvin OGUNJIMI 46). Tr: Georges LEEKENS

ERNST-HAPPEL-STADION, VIENNA
8-10-2010, 26 500, Vollquartz DEN

Austria	3
Azerbaijan	0

AUT - Prodl [3], Arnautovic 2 [53 92+]

AUT: Jurgen MACHO - Franz SCHIEMER, Paul SCHARNER, Sebastian PRODL (Florian KLEIN, Christian FUCHS, Zlatko JUNUZOVIC (Julian BAUMGARTLINGER 78), Marko ARNAUTOVIC, Stefan MAIERHOFER, Roland LINZ (Erwin Hoffer 59), Martin HARNIK (Veli KAVLAK 55). Tr: Dietmar CONSTANTINI

AZE: Kamran AGAYEV - Sasa YUNISOGLU•, Mahir SHUKUROV, Elnur ALLAHVERDIYEV•, Samir ABBASOV, Rail MALIKOV, Rashad SADIKHOV, Elvin MAMMEDOV (Vuqar NADIROV 59), Rahid AMIRGULIYEV, Vagif JAVADOV (Rasad A. SADIQOV 74), Rauf ALIYEV•. Tr: Berti VOGTS

OLYMPIASTADION, BERLIN
8-10-2010, 74 244, Webb ENG

Germany	3
Turkey	0

GER - Klose 2 [42 87], Ozil [79]

GER: Manuel NEUER - Heiko WESTERMANN, Per MERTESACKER, Philipp LAHM, Holger BADSTUBER, Mesut OZIL (Marko MARIN 90), Thomas MULLER, Toni KROOS, Sami KHEDIRA, Lukas PODOLSKI (Christian TRASCH 86), Miroslav KLOSE (CACAU 90). Tr: Joachim LOW

TUR: VOLKAN Demirel - SABRI Sarioglu, GOKHAN Gonul, OMER Erdogan, SERVET Cetin•, NURI Sahin (SERCAN Yildirim 78), Mehmet AURELIO (TUNCAY Sanli 23), OZER Hurmaci, EMRE Belozoglu, HAMIT Altintop, HALIL Altintop (SEMIH Senturk 63). Tr: Guus HIDDINK

TOFIG BAHRAMOV, BAKU
12-10-2010, 29 500, Deaconu ROU

Azerbaijan	1
Turkey	0

AZE - Rashad Sadygov [38]

AZE: Kamran AGAYEV - Sasa YUNISOGLU, Mahir SHUKUROV•, Elnur ALLAHVERDIYEV, Rail MALIKOV (Aleksandr CHERTOGANOV• 45), Rashad SADIKHOV, Rahid AMIRGULIYEV•, Ruslan ABISOV, Farid GULIYEV (Rauf ALIYEV 71), Vuqar NADIROV, Vagif JAVADOV (Vurgun HUSEYNOV 85). Tr: Berti VOGTS

TUR: VOLKAN Demirel - IBRAHIM Toraman, GOKHAN Gonul, SERVET Cetin, HAKAN Balta•, SELCUK Inan (HALIL Altintop 82), OZER Hurmaci (NIHAT Kahveci 46), EMRE Belozoglu, HAMIT Altintop, TUNCAY Sanli (SERCAN Yildirim 63), SEMIH Senturk. Tr: Guus HIDDINK

UEFA EURO 2012 POLAND/UKRAINE QUALIFYING GROUP A

ASTANA ARENA, ASTANA
12-10-2010, 18 000, Tudor ROU

Kazakhstan	0
Germany	3

GER - Klose [48], Gomez [76], Podolski [85]

KAZ: Andrey SIDELNIKOV - Aleksey POPOV, Aleksandr KIROV, Renat ABDULIN•, Farkhadbek IRISMETOV• (Mikhail ROZHKOV 68), Nurbol ZHUMASKALIEV, Heinrich SCHMIDTGAL, Azat NURGALIEV (Evgeniy AVERCHENKO 63), Kazbek GETERIEV, Sergey KHIZHNICHENKO (Andrey FINONCHENKO 79), Maksim AZOVSKIY. Tr: Bernd STORCK

GER: Manuel NEUER - Heiko WESTERMANN, Per MERTESACKER, Philipp LAHM, Holger BADSTUBER, Mesut OZIL (CACAU 79), Thomas MULLER (Marko MARIN 71), Toni KROOS, Sami KHEDIRA, Lukas PODOLSKI, Miroslav KLOSE (Mario GOMEZ 55). Tr: Joachim LOW

ROI BAUDOUIN, BRUSSELS
12-10-2010, 24 231, Dean ENG

Belgium	4
Austria	4

BEL - Vossen [11], Fellaini [47], Ogunjii [87], Lombaerts [90] • AUT - Schiemer 2 [14 62], Arnautovic [29], Harnik [93+]

BEL: Logan BAILLY - Toby ALDERWEIRELD (Dedryk BOYATA 46), Nicolas LOMBAERTS•, Vincent KOMPANY, Axel WITSEL, Jan VERTONGHEN, Timmy SIMONS• (Romelu LUKAKU 73), Jonathan LEGEAR, Marouane FELLAINI (Eden HAZARD 81), Jelle VOSSEN, Marvin OGUNJIMI. Tr: Georges LEEKENS

AUT: Jurgen MACHO - Franz SCHIEMER•, Paul SCHARNER♦68, Sebastian PRODL, Florian KLEIN•, Christian FUCHS, Julian BAUMGARTLINGER, Veli KAVLAK (Erwin HOFFER 56), Zlatko JUNUZOVIC (Yasin PEHLIVAN 72), Marko ARNAUTOVIC (Martin HARNIK 88), Stefan MAIERHOFER•. Tr: Dietmar CONSTANTINI

ERNST-HAPPEL-STADION, VIENNA
25-03-2011, 44 300, Bezborodov RUS

Austria	0
Belgium	2

BEL - Witsel 2 [6 50]

AUT: Jurgen MACHO - Emanuel POGATETZ, Christian FUCHS, Aleksandar DRAGOVIC, Ekrem DAG, Zlatko JUNUZOVIC (Umit KORKMAZ 69), Julian BAUMGARTLINGER, David ALABA (Yasin PEHLIVAN 54), Marko ARNAUTOVIC, Marc JANKO (Stefan MAIERHOFER 54), Martin HARNIK. Tr: Dietmar CONSTANTINI

BEL: Simon MIGNOLET - Daniel VAN BUYTEN, Vincent KOMPANY•, Laurent CIMAN, Axel WITSEL, Jan VERTONGHEN, Timmy SIMONS, Steven DEFOUR, Nacer CHADLI, Marvin OGUNJIMI (Kevin MIRALLAS 80), Moussa DEMBELE. Tr: Georges LEEKENS

FRITZ-WALTER, KAISERSLAUTERN
26-03-2011, 47 849, Stavrev MKD

Germany	4
Kazakhstan	0

GER - Klose 2 [3 88], Muller.T 2 [25 43]

GER: Manuel NEUER - Holger BADSTUBER, Dennis AOGO, Per MERTESACKER, Philipp LAHM, Bastian SCHWEINSTEIGER (Mario GOTZE 78), Mesut OZIL, Thomas MULLER (Toni KROOS 78), Sami KHEDIRA, Lukas PODOLSKI (Mario GOMEZ 65), Miroslav KLOSE. Tr: Joachim LOW

KAZ: David LORIYA - Vladyslav CHERNYSHOV, Renat ABDULIN, Farkhadbek IRISMETOV•, Kayrat NURDAULETOV, Kazbek GETERIEV, Sergey OSTAPENKO 81), Anton CHICHULIN, Nurbol ZHUMASKALIEV (Maksat BAYZHANOV 46), Azat NURGALIEV (Zhambyl KUKEEV 10), Ulan KONYSBAEV, Sergey KHIZHNICHENKO. Tr: Miroslav BERANEK

SUKRU SARACOGLU, ISTANBUL
29-03-2011, 40 420, Kralovec CZE

Turkey	2
Austria	0

TUR - Arda Turan [28], Gokhan Gonul [78]

TUR: VOLKAN Demirel - SERDAR Kesimal, GOKHAN Gonul, SERVET Cetin, HAKAN Balta, HAMIT Altintop, ARDA Turan (MEHMET Topal 89), NURI Sahin, SELCUK Inan, MEHMET Ekici (MEHMET Topuz•63), BURAK Yilmaz (SEMIH Senturk 72). Tr: Guus HIDDINK

AUT: Jurgen MACHO - Paul SCHARNER•, Emanuel POGATETZ•, Christian FUCHS•, Aleksandar DRAGOVIC, Ekrem DAG, Yasin PEHLIVAN (Umit KORKMAZ 57), Julian BAUMGARTLINGER (Erwin HOFFER 46), David ALABA, Stefan MAIERHOFER, Martin HARNIK (Marko ARNAUTOVIC 69). Tr: Dietmar CONSTANTINI

ROI BAUDOUIN, BRUSSELS
29-03-2011, 34 985, Stalhammar SWE

Belgium	4
Azerbaijan	1

BEL - Vertonghen [12], Simons [32p], Chadli [45], Vossen [74] • AZE - Abishov [16]

BEL: Simon MIGNOLET - Laurent CIMAN, Daniel VAN BUYTEN (Jelle VAN DAMME 80), Nicolas LOMBAERTS, Steven DEFOUR (Vadis ODJIDJA-OFOE 90), Nacer CHADLI, Axel WITSEL, Jan VERTONGHEN, Timmy SIMONS, Jelle VOSSEN, Moussa DEMBELE (Eden HAZARD 64). Tr: Georges LEEKENS

AZE: Kamran AGAYEV - Mahir SHUKUROV, Vladimir LEVIN, Rail MALIKOV•, Ruslan ABISOV, Rashad SADIKHOV, Elvin MAMMADOV (Javid HUSEYNOV 78), Aleksandr CHERTOGANOV, Rahid AMIRGULIYEV, Rauf ALIYEV, Vagif JAVADOV (Vuqar NADIROV 75). Tr: Berti VOGTS

ASTANA ARENA, ASTANA
3-06-2011, 10 000, Norris SCO

Kazakhstan	2
Azerbaijan	1

KAZ - Gridin 2 [57 68] • AZE - Nadirov [63]

KAZ: Roman NESTERENKO - Mukhtar MUKHTAROV, Yuriy LOGVINENKO (Mikhail ROZHKOV 65), Kayrat NURDAULETOV, Samat SMAKOV, Heinrich SCHMIDTGAL•, Kazbek GETERIEV, Sergey KHAYRULLIN (Aleksandr KIROV 82), Sergey OSTAPENKO (Sergey KHIZHNICHENKO 78), Ulan KONYSBAEV, Sergey GRIDIN. Tr: Miroslav BERANEK

AZE: Kamran AGAYEV - Maksim MEDVEDEV, Vladimir LEVIN, Rail MALIKOV, Rashad SADIKHOV, Rasad A. SADIQOV, Afran ISMAYILOV, Ruslan ABISOV, Javid HUSEYNOV (Vuqar NADIROV 61), Vagif JAVADOV, Rauf ALIYEV (Murad HUSEYNOV 79). Tr: Berti VOGTS

ERNST-HAPPEL-STADION, VIENNA
3-06-2011, 47 500, Busacca SUI

Austria	1
Germany	2

AUT - OG [50] • GER - Gomez 2 [44 90]

AUT: Christian GRATZEI - Paul SCHARNER•, Emanuel POGATETZ, Florian KLEIN, Christian FUCHS, Ekrem DAG (Zlatko JUNUZOVIC 66), Stefan KULOVITS, Julian BAUMGARTLINGER•, David ALABA, Erwin HOFFER (Marc JANKO 88), Martin HARNIK (Daniel ROYER 81). Tr: Dietmar CONSTANTINI

GER: Manuel NEUER - Arne FRIEDRICH, Marcel SCHMELZER, Philipp LAHM, Mats HUMMELS, Mesut OZIL•, Thomas MULLER, Toni KROOS (Dennis AOGO 90), Sami KHEDIRA (Holger BADSTUBER 69), Lukas PODOLSKI (Andre SCHURRLE 67), Mario GOMEZ•. Tr: Joachim LOW

ROI BAUDOUIN, BRUSSELS
3-06-2011, 44 185, Rizzoli ITA

Belgium	1
Turkey	1

BEL - Ogunjimi [4] • TUR - Burak Yilmaz [22]

BEL: Simon MIGNOLET - Nicolas LOMBAERTS, Vincent KOMPANY, Toby ALDERWEIRELD, Eden HAZARD (Dries MERTENS 60), Steven DEFOUR• (Jelle VOSSEN 87), Nacer CHADLI, Axel WITSEL, Jan VERTONGHEN (Thomas VERMAELEN 46), Timmy SIMONS, Marvin OGUNJIMI. Tr: Georges LEEKENS

TUR: VOLKAN Demirel - SERDAR Kesimal, SERVET Cetin, CAGLAR Birinci, SABRI Sarioglu, Colin KAZIM-RICHARDS•, SELCUK Inan (MEHMET Topal 78), EMRE Belozoglu, ARDA Turan (SEMIH Senturk 85), SELCUK Sahin, BURAK Yilmaz (MEHMET Ekici 76). Tr: Guus HIDDINK

TOFIG BAHRAMOV, BAKU
7-06-2011, 29 858, Koukoulakis GRE

Azerbaijan	1
Germany	3

AZE - Huseynov [89] • GER - Ozil [29], Gomez [40], Schurrle [93+]

AZE: Kamran AGAYEV - Vurgun HUSEYNOV, Elnur ALLAHVERDIYEV, Rail MALIKOV, Rashad SADIKHOV, Afran ISMAYILOV (Arif ISAYEV 58), Aleksandr CHERTOGANOV (Rasad A. SADIQOV 86), Rahid AMIRGULIYEV, Ruslan ABISOV, Vuqar NADIROV•, Vagif JAVADOV (Murad HUSEYNOV 72). Tr: Berti VOGTS

GER: Manuel NEUER - Philipp LAHM, Mats HUMMELS, Benedikt HOWEDES•, Holger BADSTUBER, Dennis AOGO, Mesut OZIL (Mario GOTZE 78), Thomas MULLER (Lewis HOLTBY 88), Toni KROOS, Lukas PODOLSKI (Andre SCHURRLE 76), Mario GOMEZ. Tr: Joachim LOW

TOFIG BAHRAMOV, BAKU
2-09-2011, 9300, Probert ENG

Azerbaijan	1
Belgium	1

AZE - Aliyev [86] • BEL - Simons [55p]

AZE: Kamran AGAYEV - Elnur ALLAHVERDIYEV•, Mahir SHUKUROV, Vurgun HUSEYNOV, Ruslan ABISOV (Rahid AMIRGULIYEV 64), Rashad SADIKHOV, Agil NABIYEV•, Afran ISMAYILOV (Elvin MAMMADOV• 58), Aleksandr CHERTOGANOV (Branimir SUBASIC 83), Rauf ALIYEV, Vagif JAVADOV. Tr: Berti VOGTS

BEL: Simon MIGNOLET - Toby ALDERWEIRELD, Nicolas LOMBAERTS•, Vincent KOMPANY•, Eden HAZARD, Marouane FELLAINI•, Axel WITSEL, Jan VERTONGHEN, Timmy SIMONS, Dries MERTENS, Romelu LUKAKU (Igor DE CAMARGO 60). Tr: Georges LEEKENS

TURK TELECOM ARENA, ISTANBUL
2-09-2011, 47 756, Turpin FRA

Turkey	2
Kazakhstan	1

TUR - Burak Yilmaz [31], Arda Turan [96+] • KAZ - Konysbayev [55]

TUR: VOLKAN Demirel - SABRI Sarioglu•, EGEMEN Korkmaz, SERDAR Kesimal (UMUT Bulut 81), HAKAN Balta, ARDA Turan•, Colin KAZIM-RICHARDS, SELCUK Inan♦90, MEHMET Ekici (SELCUK Sahin 51), EMRE Belozoglu (GOKHAN Tore 60), BURAK Yilmaz. Tr: Guus HIDDINK

KAZ: Aleksandr MOKIN• - Mukhtar MUKHTAROV, Yuriy LOGVINENKO•, Aleksandr KIROV, Mark GORMAN, Kayrat NURDAULETOV, Marat SHAKHMETOV (Maksat BAYZHANOV 82), Heinrich SCHMIDTGAL, Marat KHAYRULLIN (Sergey OSTAPENKO 66), Ulan KONYSBAEV (Tanat NUSERBAEV•86), Sergey GRIDIN. Tr: Miroslav BERANEK

PART THREE – THE CONTINENTAL CONFEDERATIONS

VELTINS ARENA, GELSENKIRCHEN
2-09-2011, 53 313, Tagliavento ITA

Germany	6
Austria	2

GER - Klose [8], Ozil 2 [23 47], Podolski [28], Gotze [88], Schurrle [83] • **AUT** - Arnautovic [42], Harnik [51]

GER: Manuel NEUER – Philipp LAHM, Mats HUMMELS, Benedikt HOWEDES (Jerome BOATENG 46), Holger BADSTUBER, Bastian SCHWEINSTEIGER, Mesut OZIL, Thomas MULLER, Toni KROOS (Mario Gotze 85), Lukas PODOLSKI (Andre SCHURRLE 74), Miroslav KLOSE. Tr: Joachim LOW

AUT: Christian GRATZEI – Franz SCHIEMER, Emanuel POGATETZ, Florian KLEIN, Christian FUCHS, Ekrem DAG, Daniel ROYER (Erwin HOFFER 74), Julian BAUMGARTLINGER, David ALABA, Marko ARNAUTOVIC, Martin HARNIK. Tr: Dietmar CONSTANTINI

TOFIG BAHRAMOV, BAKU
6-09-2011, 9112, Hermansen DEN

Azerbaijan	3
Kazakhstan	2

AZE - Aliyev [53], Shukurov [62], Javadov [67] • **KAZ** - Ostapenko [20], Yevstigneev.V [77]

AZE: Kamran AGAYEV – Mahir SHUKUROV•, Vurgun HUSEYNOV, Rashad SADIKHOV, Agil NABIYEV (Sasa YUNISOGLU 13), Afran ISMAYILOV (Ruslan ABISOV 87), Aleksandr CHERTOGANOV (Branimir SUBASIC 46), Ufuk BUDAK, Rahid AMIRGULIYEV, Vagif JAVADOV, Rauf ALIYEV. Tr: Berti VOGTS

KAZ: Aleksandr MOKIN – Mikhail ROZHKOV (Vitaliy EVSTIGNEEV 77), Yuriy LOGVINENKO•, Aleksey KIROV, Mark GORMAN•, Kayrat NURDAULETOV, Marat SHAKHMETOV (Serikzhan MUZHIKOV 70), Zhambyl KUKEEV (Marat KHAYRULLIN 59), Sergey OSTAPENKO, Ulan KONYSBAEV, Sergey GRIDIN. Tr: Miroslav BERANEK

ERNST-HAPPEL-STADION, VIENNA
6-09-2011, 47 500, Undiano ESP

Austria	0
Turkey	0

AUT: Pascal GRUNWALD – Christian FUCHS, Ekrem DAG, Franz SCHIEMER, Paul SCHARNER, Emanuel POGATETZ, Daniel ROYER (Erwin HOFFER 67), Julian BAUMGARTLINGER, David ALABA, Marko ARNAUTOVIC (Stefan MAIERHOFER 90), Martin HARNIK. Tr: Dietmar CONSTANTINI

TUR: VOLKAN Demirel – EGEMEN Korkmaz, SERVET Cetin, HAKAN Balta, SABRI Sarioglu, ARDA Turan, MEHMET Topal, SELCUK Sahin, YEKTA Kurtulus•, UMUT Bulut, BURAK Yilmaz• (GOKHAN Tore 90). Tr: Guus HIDDINK

DALGA, BAKU
7-10-2011, 6000, Studer SUI

Azerbaijan	1
Austria	4

AZE - Nadirov [74] • **AUT** - Ivanschitz [34], Janko 2 [52 62], Junuzovic [91+]

AZE: Kamran AGAYEV – Vurgun HUSEYNOV, Elnur ALLAHVERDIYEV, Sasa YUNISOGLU♦ 27, Rashad SADIKHOV, Afran ISMAYILOV, Ufuk BUDAK, Ruslan ABISOV, Rasad A. SADIQOV (Rahid AMIRGULIYEV 46), Vagif JAVADOV (Vuqar NADIROV 57), Rauf ALIYEV•. Tr: Berti VOGTS

AUT: Pascal GRUNWALD – Christian FUCHS, Aleksandr DRAGOVIC, Ekrem DAG, Paul SCHARNER, Sebastian PRODL, Andreas IVANSCHITZ (Daniel ROYER 73), Julian BAUMGARTLINGER•, David ALABA•, Marko ARNAUTOVIC (Zlatko JUNUZOVIC 66), Marc JANKO (Philipp HOSINER 88). Tr: Willibald RUTTENSTEINER

TURK TELECOM ARENA, ISTANBUL
7-10-2011, 49 532, Atkinson ENG

Turkey	1
Germany	3

TUR - Hakan Balta [79] • **GER** - Gomez [35], Muller.T [66], Schweinsteiger [86p]

TUR: VOLKAN Demirel – SABRI Sarioglu, EGEMEN Korkmaz, GOKHAN Gonul, SERVET Cetin, HAKAN Balta, ARDA Turan (Colin KAZIM-RICHARDS 70), MEHMET AURELIO (UMUT Bulut 86), SELCUK Inan (GOKHAN Tore 46), HAMIT Altintop•, BURAK Yilmaz. Tr: Guus HIDDINK

GER: Manuel NEUER – Per MERTESACKER, Philipp LAHM, Jerome BOATENG (Benedikt HOWEDES 73), Holger BADSTUBER•, Bastian SCHWEINSTEIGER, Thomas MULLER, Sami KHEDIRA, Mario GOTZE (Marco REUS 90), Lukas PODOLSKI (Andre SCHURRLE 62), Mario GOMEZ. Tr: Joachim LOW

ROI BAUDOUIN, BRUSSELS
7-10-2011, 29 758, Mazic SRB

Belgium	4
Kazakhstan	1

BEL - Simons [40p], Hazard [43], Kompany [49], Ogunjimi [84] • **KAZ** - Nurdauletov [86p]

BEL: Simon MIGNOLET – Vincent KOMPANY, Laurent CIMAN, Daniel VAN BUYTEN•, Jan VERTONGHEN, Axel WITSEL, Timmy SIMONS (Steven DEFOUR 75), Dries MERTENS, Eden HAZARD (Vadis ODJIDJA-OFOE 63), Igor DE CAMARGO (Marvin OGUNJIMI 73), Moussa DEMBELE. Tr: Georges LEEKENS

KAZ: Vladimir LOGINOVSKIY – Mikhail ROZHKOV, Mukhtar MUKHTAROV, Nurtas KURGULIN♦ 59, Aleksandr KIROV, Vitaliy YEVSTIGNEEV, Zhambyl KUKEEV (Kayrat NURDAULETOV 61), Andrey KARPOVICH• (Marat SHAKHMETOV 75), Serikzhan MUZHIKOV, Daurenbek TAZHIMBETOV (Sergey OSTAPENKO 57), Sergey KHIZHNICHENKO. Tr: Miroslav BERANEK

ASTANA ARENA, ASTANA
11-10-2011, 11 000, Kaasik EST

Kazakhstan	0
Austria	0

KAZ: Andrey SIDELNIKOV – Mikhail ROZHKOV, Mukhtar MUKHTAROV, Aleksandr KIROV, Mark GURMAN• (Vitali YEVSTIGNEEV 77), Kayrat NURDAULETOV, Heinrich SCHMIDTGAL•, Azat NURGALIEV (Serikzhan MUZHIKOV 46), Marat KHAYRULLIN, Sergey OSTAPENKO•, Sergey GRIDIN. Tr: Miroslav BERANEK

AUT: Pascal GRUNWALD – Paul SCHARNER, Sebastian PRODL, Christian FUCHS, Aleksandar DRAGOVIC, Ekrem DAG, Stefan KULOVITS (Veli KAVLAK 74), Andreas IVANSCHITZ (Zlatko JUNUZOVIC 66), David ALABA, Marko ARNAUTOVIC (Stefan MAIERHOFER 83), Marc JANKO. Tr: Willibald RUTTENSTEINER

ESPRIT ARENA, DUSSELDORF
11-10-2011, 48 483, Moen NOR

Germany	3
Belgium	1

GER - Ozil [30], Schurrle [33], Gomez [48] • **BEL** - Fellaini [86]

GER: Manuel NEUER – Per MERTESACKER, Philipp LAHM (Ilkay GUNDOGAN 84), Mats HUMMELS, Benedikt HOWEDES, Mesut OZIL, Thomas MULLER (Marco Reus 71), Toni KROOS, Sami KHEDIRA•, Andre SCHURRLE, Mario GOMEZ (CACAU 77). Tr: Joachim LOW

BEL: Simon MIGNOLET – Laurent CIMAN, Nicolas LOMBAERTS, Vincent KOMPANY, Axel WITSEL•, Jan VERTONGHEN, Timmy SIMONS, Eden HAZARD, Marouane FELLAINI, Marvin OGUNJIMI (Romelu LUKAKU 46), Moussa DEMBELE (Dries MERTENS 64). Tr: Georges LEEKENS

TURK TELECOM ARENA, ISTANBUL
11-10-2011, 32 174, Rasmussen DEN

Turkey	1
Azerbaijan	0

TUR - Burak Yilmaz [60]

TUR: SINAN Bolat – GOKHAN Zan, SABRI Sarioglu, EGEMEN Korkmaz, HAKAN Balta, ARDA Turan, MEHMET Topal, Colin KAZIM-RICHARDS (SELCUK Inan 57), EMRE Belozoglu (GOKHAN Tore 78), HAMIT Altintop, BURAK Yilmaz (UMUT Bulut 87). Tr: Guus HIDDINK

AZE: Kamran AGAYEV – Mahir SHUKUROV, Vladimir LEVIN, Vurgun HUSEYNOV, Rashad SADIKHOV, Afran ISMAYILOV (Elvin MAMMADOV 46) (Arif ISAYEV 85), Aleksandr CHERTOGANOV, Ufuk BUDAK (Rahid AMIRGULIYEV 90), Ruslan ABISOV, Branimir SUBASIC, Vuqar NADIROV. Tr: Berti VOGTS

	GROUP B	PL	W	D	L	F	A	PTS	RUS	IRL	ARM	SVK	MKD	AND
1	Russia	10	7	2	1	17	4	23		0-0	3-1	0-1	1-0	6-0
2	Republic of Ireland	10	6	3	1	15	7	21	2-3		2-1	0-0	2-1	3-1
3	Armenia	10	5	2	3	22	10	17	0-0	0-1		3-1	4-1	4-0
4	Slovakia	10	4	3	3	7	10	15	0-1	1-1	0-4		1-0	1-0
5	Macedonia FYR	10	2	2	6	8	14	8	0-1	0-2	2-2	1-1		1-0
6	Andorra	10	0	0	10	1	25	0	0-2	0-2	0-3	0-1	0-2	

Russia qualified directly for the finals • Rep. Ireland qualified for a play-off v Estonia • Estonia 0-4 1-1 **Rep. Ireland**

UEFA EURO 2012 POLAND/UKRAINE QUALIFYING GROUP B

REPUBLICAN, YEREVAN
3-09-2010, 8600, Szabo HUN

Armenia	0
Republic of Ireland	1

IRL - Fahey [76]

ARM: Roman BEREZOVSKIY - Artak YEDIGARYAN• (Hovhannes HAMBARDZUMYAN 71), Sargis HOVSEPYAN, Robert ARZUMANYAN, Ararat ARAKELYAN, Artur YEDIGARYAN (David MANOYAN 68), Levon PACHAJYAN, Karlen MKRTCHYAN, Henrikh MKHITARYAN, Edgar MALAKYAN (Edgar MANUCHARYAN 79), Yura MOVSISYAN. Tr: Vardan MINASYAN

IRL: Shay GIVEN - Richard DUNNE, Sean ST LEDGER, John O'SHEA, Glenn WHELAN•, Liam LAWRENCE, Kevin KILBANE, Paul GREEN, Kevin DOYLE, Aiden MCGEADY (Keith FAHEY 69), Robbie KEANE (Andy KEOGH 85). Tr: Giovanni TRAPPATTONI

COMUNAL, ANDORRA LA VELLA
3-09-2010, 1100, Borg MLT

Andorra	0
Russia	2

RUS - Pogrebnyak 2 [14 64p]

AND: Fernando SILVA - Josep GOMES, Jordi RUBIO (Ivan LORENZO 57), Cristian MARTINEZ•, Ildefons LIMA•, Marc BERNAUS, Marcio VIEIRA, Marc PUJOL• (Daniel MEJIAS 88), Josep AYALA•, Sergi MORENO (Manolo JIMENEZ 76), Sebastian PEREZ. Tr: David RODRIGO

RUS: Igor AKINFEEV - Sergey IGNASHEVICH, Vasiliy BEREZUTSKIY, Aleksandr ANYUKOV, Igor SEMSHOV, Konstantin ZYRYANOV, Roman SHIROKOV, Vladimir BYSTROV (Alan DZAGOEV 61), Diniyar BILYALETDINOV•, Pavel POGREBNYAK (Roman PAVLYUCHENKO 86), Andrey ARSHAVIN. Tr: Dick ADVOCAAT

PASIENKY, BRATISLAVA
3-09-2010, 5980, Circhetta SUI

Slovakia	1
FYR Macedonia	0

SVK - Holosko [91+]

SVK: Jan MUCHA - Martin SKRTEL•, Kornel SALATA (Juraj KUCKA 76), Peter PEKARIK (Jakub SYLVESTR 90), Tomas HUBOCAN, Vladimir WEISS (Erik JENDRISEK 61), Zdeno STRBA, Marek SAPARA, Marek HAMSIK, Miroslav STOCH•, Filip HOLOSKO. Tr: Vladimir WEISS

MKD: Edin NUREDINOVSKI• - Nikolce NOVESKI, Igor MITRESKI, Vance SIKOV••♦85, Velice SUMULIKOSKI, Goran POPOV, Slavco GEORGIEVSKI, Filip DESPOTOVSKI• (Aleksandar LAZEVSKI 73), Ivan TRICKOVSKI (Boban GRNCAROV 80), Goran PANDEV•, Ilco NAUMOSKI (Stevica RISTIC 61). Tr: Mirsad JONUZ

LOKOMOTIV, MOSCOW
7-09-2010, 27 052, De Bleeckere BEL

Russia	0
Slovakia	1

SVK - Stoch [27]

RUS: Igor AKINFEEV - Vasiliy BEREZUTSKIY, Aleksandr ANYUKOV, Sergey IGNASHEVICH (Diniyar BILYALETDINOV 81), Igor SEMSHOV (Vladimir BYSTROV 60), Alan DZAGOEV, Konstantin ZYRYANOV, Yuriy ZHIRKOV•, Roman SHIROKOV, Andrey ARSHAVIN, Pavel POGREBNYAK (Roman PAVLYUCHENKO 71). Tr: Dick ADVOCAAT

SVK: Jan MUCHA - Tomas HUBOCAN, Radoslav ZABAVNIK, Martin SKRTEL, Kornel SALATA, Juraj KUCKA• (Erik JENDRISEK 58), Miroslav KARHAN (Marek SAPARA 73), Marek HAMSIK, Zdeno STRBA, Filip HOLOSKO, Miroslav STOCH (Mario PECALKA 90). Tr: Vladimir WEISS

NATIONAL ARENA FILIP II, SKOPJE
7-09-2010, 9000, Berntsen NOR

FYR Macedonia	2
Armenia	2

MKD - Gjurovski [42], Naumoski [96+p] •
ARM - Movsisyan [41], Manucharyan [91+]

MKD: Aleksandar TODOROVSKI - Nikolce NOVESKI, Igor MITRESKI, Velice SUMULIKOSKI, Goran POPOV, Mario GUROVSKI (Baze ILIJOSKI 75), Slavco GEORGIEVSKI (Filip DESPOTOVSKI 67), Ivan TRICKOVSKI, Stevica RISTIC (Ilco NAUMOSKI• 62), Goran PANDEV. Tr: Mirsad JONUZ

ARM: Roman BEREZOVSKIY - Artak YEDIGARYAN, Sargis HOVSEPYAN, Robert ARZUMANYAN, Ararat ARAKELYAN•, Levon PACHAJYAN (Artur YEDIGARYAN 70), Karlen MKRTCHYAN• (Hrayr MKOYAN 90), Henrikh MKHITARYAN, David MANOYAN, Edgar MALAKYAN (Edgar MANUCHARYAN 58), Yura MOVSISYAN•. Tr: Vardan MINASYAN

AVIVA STADIUM, DUBLIN
7-09-2010, 40 283, Trattou CYP

Republic of Ireland	3
Andorra	1

IRL - Kilbane [15], Doyle [41], Keane [54] •
AND - Martinez [45]

IRL: Shay GIVEN - Sean ST LEDGER, John O'SHEA (Stephen KELLY 75), Richard DUNNE•, Glenn WHELAN (Darron GIBSON 61), Liam LAWRENCE, Kevin KILBANE, Paul GREEN, Aiden MCGEADY, Robbie KEANE, Kevin DOYLE (Andy KEOGH 82). Tr: Giovanni TRAPPATTONI

AND: Fernando SILVA• - Josep GOMES, Cristian MARTINEZ•, Ildefons LIMA•, Jordi ESCURA, Marc BERNAUS, Marcio VIEIRA, Marc PUJOL (Oscar SONEJEE 86), Josep AYALA (Xavier ANDORRA 71), Sergi MORENO• (Manolo JIMENEZ 59), Sebastian PEREZ. Tr: David RODRIGO

REPUBLICAN, YEREVAN
8-10-2010, 8500, Orsato ITA

Armenia	3
Slovakia	1

ARM - Movsisyan [23], Ghazaryan [50], Mkhitaryan [89] • SVK - Weiss [37]

ARM: Roman BEREZOVSKIY - Sargis HOVSEPYAN, Artak YEDIGARYAN, Robert ARZUMANYAN (Ararat ARAKELYAN 79), Levon PACHAJYAN (Edgar MANUCHARYAN 46), Karlen MKRTCHYAN•, Henrikh MKHITARYAN, Hrayr MKOYAN, Gevorg GHAZARYAN, Yura MOVSISYAN, PIZELLI (Artur YEDIGARYAN 72). Tr: Vardan MINASYAN

SVK: Jan MUCHA - Radoslav ZABAVNIK (Filip SEBO 81), Martin SKRTEL•, Kornel SALATA, Peter PEKARIK, Vladimir WEISS, Kamil KOPUNEK• (Juraj KUCKA 56), Miroslav KARHAN, Marek HAMSIK, Miroslav STOCH (Filip HOLOSKO 57), Stanislav SESTAK 72). Tr: Vladimir WEISS

COMUNAL, ANDORRA LA VELLA
8-10-2010, 550, Mazeika LTU

Andorra	0
FYR Macedonia	2

MKD - Naumoski [42], Sikov [60]

AND: Fernando SILVA - Josep GOMES, Cristian MARTINEZ (Manolo JIMENEZ 74), Jordi ESCURA•, Marc BERNAUS, Josep AYALA (Samir BOUSENINE 86), Marcio VIEIRA, Marc VALES, Daniel MEJIAS (Ivan LORENZO 62), Sebastian GOMEZ, Sergi MORENO. Tr: David RODRIGO

MKD: Edin NUREDINOVSKI - Igor MITRESKI, Vlade LAZAREVSKI, Nikolce NOVESKI, Vance SIKOV, Slavco GEORGIEVSKI (Mario GUROVSKI 34), Filip DESPOTOVSKI, Velice SUMULIKOSKI (Boban GRNCAROV 83), Ilco NAUMOSKI (Armin IBRAIMI 73), Ivan TRICKOVSKI, Stevica RISTIC. Tr: Mirsad JONUZ

AVIVA STADIUM, DUBLIN
8-10-2010, 50 411, Blom NED

Republic of Ireland	2
Russia	3

IRL - Keane [72p], Long [78] • RUS - Kerzakhov [11], Dzagoev [29], Shirokov [50]

IRL: Shay GIVEN - Sean ST LEDGER•, John O'SHEA, Richard DUNNE, Glenn WHELAN (Darron GIBSON 66), Liam LAWRENCE (Shane LONG 61), Kevin KILBANE, Paul GREEN, Aiden MCGEADY, Robbie KEANE, Kevin DOYLE• (Keith FAHEY 71). Tr: Giovanni TRAPPATTONI

RUS: Igor AKINFEEV - Sergey IGNASHEVICH, Vasiliy BEREZUTSKIY, Aleksandr ANYUKOV•, Konstantin ZYRYANOV (Igor SEMSHOV 68), Yuriy ZHIRKOV, Roman SHIROKOV, Alan DZAGOEV (Aleksey BEREZUTSKIY 84), Andrey ARSHAVIN• 84), Andrey ARSHAVIN, Aleksandr KERZHAKOV (Pavel POGREBNYAK 80), Igor DENISOV•. Tr: Dick ADVOCAAT

REPUBLICAN, YEREVAN
12-10-2010, 12 000, Mikulski POL

Armenia	4
Andorra	0

ARM - Ghazaryan [4], Mkhitaryan [16], Movsisyan [33], Pizzelli [52]

ARM: Roman BEREZOVSKIY - Sargis HOVSEPYAN, Artak YEDIGARYAN, Robert ARZUMANYAN, Artur YEDIGARYAN, Henrikh MKHITARYAN, Hrayr MKOYAN, Edgar MANUCHARYAN, Gevorg GHAZARYAN (Edgar MALAKYAN 67), Yura MOVSISYAN (Hovhannes GOHARYAN 53), PIZELLI (Ara YUSPASHYAN 82). Tr: Vardan MINASYAN

AND: Fernando SILVA• - Josep GOMES, Cristian MARTINEZ (Jordi RUBIO 87), Ildefons LIMA•, Jordi ESCURA, Marc BERNAUS, Marcio VIEIRA•, Marc VALES (Xavier ANDORRA• 64), Josep AYALA, Sebastian GOMEZ, Sergi MORENO (Manolo JIMENEZ 52). Tr: David RODRIGO

POD DUBNOM, ZILINA
12-10-2010, 10 892, Undiano ESP

Slovakia	1
Republic of Ireland	1

SVK - Durica [36] • IRL - St Ledger [16]

SVK: Jan MUCHA• - Radoslav ZABAVNIK, Kornel SALATA, Tomas HUBOCAN•, Jan DURICA, Vladimir WEISS (Miroslav STOCH 70), Juraj KUCKA, Miroslav KARHAN•, Marek HAMSIK, Stanislav SESTAK• (Filip HOLOSKO 70), Erik JENDRISEK (Tomas ORAVEC 84). Tr: Vladimir WEISS

IRL: Shay GIVEN - Sean ST LEDGER, John O'SHEA, Richard DUNNE, Glenn WHELAN, Kevin KILBANE, Paul GREEN (Darron GIBSON 41), Keith FAHEY (Andy KEOGH 71), Aiden MCGEADY, Shane LONG, Robbie KEANE. Tr: Giovanni TRAPPATTONI

NATIONAL ARENA FILIP II, SKOPJE
12-10-2010, 10 500, Johannesson SWE

FYR Macedonia	0
Russia	1

RUS - Kerzakhov [8]

MKD: Edin NUREDINOVSKI - Nikolce NOVESKI•, Igor MITRESKI, Aleksandar LAZEVSKI, Vance SIKOV•, Armin ALIMI 80), Filip DESPOTOVSKI (Slavco GEORGIEVSKI 77), Velice SUMULIKOSKI, Ivan TRICKOVSKI, Ilco NAUMOSKI. Tr: Mirsad JONUZ

RUS: Igor AKINFEEV - Aleksandr ANYUKOV•, Sergey IGNASHEVICH•, Vasiliy BEREZUTSKIY, Konstantin ZYRYANOV, Yuriy ZHIRKOV, Roman SHIROKOV, Alan DZAGOEV (Aleksey BEREZUTSKIY 62), Andrey ARSHAVIN (Vladimir BYSTROV 81), Aleksandr KERZHAKOV (Pavel POGREBNYAK 79), Igor DENISOV. Tr: Dick ADVOCAAT

REPUBLICAN, YEREVAN
26-03-2011, 14800, Thomson SCO

Armenia	0
Russia	0

Roman BEREZOVSKIY - Sargis HOVSEPYAN, Robert ARZUMANYAN, Karlen MKRTCHYAN, Henrikh MKHITARYAN, Edgar MALAKYAN (Edgar MANUCHARYAN 48), Hrayr MKOYAN, Levon HAYRAPETYAN• (Artak YEDIGARYAN 67), Gevorg GHAZARYAN, PIZELLI (Artur YEDIGARYAN 57), Yura MOVSISYAN. Tr: Vardan MINASYAN

Igor AKINFEEV - Roman SHISHKIN•, Sergey IGNASHEVICH, Vasiliy BEREZUTSKIY, Konstantin ZYRYANOV, Yuriy ZHIRKOV, Roman SHIROKOV, Alan DZAGOEV, Andrey ARSHAVIN (Diniyar BILYALETDINOV 90), Aleksandr KERZHAKOV (Pavel POGREBNYAK 78), Igor DENISOV. Tr: Dick ADVOCAAT

COMUNAL, ANDORRA LA VELLA
26-03-2011, 850, Masiah ISR

Andorra	0
Slovakia	1

SVK - Sebo 21

Josep GOMES - Cristian MARTINEZ, Ildefons LIMA, Emili GARCIA, Marc BERNAUS, Jordi RUBIO, Manolo JIMENEZ• (Oscar SONEJEE 87), Josep AYALA (Juli SANCHEZ 81), Marc VALES, Sebastian GOMEZ (Marcio VIEIRA 72), Sergi MORENO•. Tr: David RODRIGO

Jan MUCHA• - Martin SKRTEL, Peter PEKARIK, Jan DURICA, Filip LUKSIK, Tomas KONA, Marek HAMSIK, Filip SEBO, Robert VITTEK (Juraj PIROSKA 78), Miroslav STOCH• (Kornel SALATA 90), Erik JENDRISEK (Filip HOLOSKO 87). Tr: Vladimir WEISS

AVIVA STADIUM, DUBLIN
26-03-2011, 33200, Vad HUN

Republic of Ireland	2
FYR Macedonia	1

IRL - McGeady 2, Keane 21 •
MKD - Trickovski 45

Keiren WESTWOOD• - Darren O'DEA, Kevin FOLEY, Richard DUNNE•, Glenn WHELAN, Kevin KILBANE, Darron GIBSON• (Keith FAHEY 77), Damien DUFF, Aiden MCGEADY, Robbie KEANE (James MCCARTHY 87), Kevin DOYLE (Shane LONG 20).Tr: Giovanni TRAPATTONI

Edin NUREDINOVSKI - Nikolce NOVESKI, Boban GRNCAROV•, Vance SIKOV, Darko TASEVSKI (Mario GUROVSKI 61), Velice SUMULIKOSKI, Goran POPOV•, Muhamed DEMIRI• (Slavco GEORGIEVSKI 84), Ivan TRICKOVSKI, Goran PANDEV, Ilco NAUMOSKI (Stevica RISTIC 67). Tr: Mirsad Jonuz

PETROVSKI, ST PETERSBURG
4-06-2011, 18000, Lannoy FRA

Russia	3
Armenia	1

RUS - Pavlyuchenko 3 26 59 73p •
ARM - Pizzelli 25

Igor AKINFEEV - Sergey IGNASHEVICH•, Vasiliy BEREZUTSKIY•, Aleksandr ANYUKOV (Renat YANBAEV 74), Dmitriy TORBINSKIY, Igor SEMSHOV (Denis GLUSHAKOV 69), Konstantin ZYRYANOV (Alan DZAGOEV 82), Yuriy ZHIRKOV, Roman PAVLYUCHENKO, Andrey ARSHAVIN, Igor DENISOV. Tr: Dick ADVOCAAT

Roman BEREZOVSKIY - Sargis HOVSEPYAN, Robert ARZUMANYAN•, Levon PACHAJYAN• (Edgar MANUCHARYAN 57), Karlen MKRTCHYAN (Artak YEDIGARYAN 89), Henrikh MKHITARYAN, Levon HAYRAPETYAN, Hrayr MKOYAN•, Gevorg GHAZARYAN, PIZELLI (Artur YEDIGARYAN• 67), Yura MOVSISYAN•. Tr: Vardan MINASYAN

PASIENKY, BRATISLAVA
4-06-2011, 4300, Jemini ALB

Slovakia	1
Andorra	0

SVK - Karhan 63

Marian KELLO - Tomas HUBOCAN, Jan DURICA, Marek CECH (Kornel SALATA 83), Juraj KUCKA (Stanislav SESTAK 46), Miroslav KARHAN, Robert JEZ•, Marek HAMSIK, Filip HOLOSKO (Igor ZOFCAK 74), Robert VITTEK, Filip SEBO. Tr: Vladimir WEISS

Fernando SILVA (Sebastian GOMEZ 64), Josep GOMES, Cristian MARTINEZ, Ildefons LIMA, Jordi RUBIO, Emili GARCIA, Marc BERNAUS, Manolo JIMENEZ (Joaquim BESORA 86), Josep AYALA (Xavier ANDORRA• 16), Marcio VIEIRA, Marc VALES•. Tr: David RODRIGO

NATIONAL ARENA FILIP II, SKOPJE
4-06-2011, 29500, Meyer GER

FYR Macedonia	0
Republic of Ireland	2

IRL - Keane 2 8 37

Martin BOGATINOV - Nikolce NOVESKI, Boban GRNCAROV, Vance SIKOV, Velice SUMULIKOSKI, Goran POPOV, Filip DESPOTOVSKI (Mario GUROVSKI 57), Muhamed DEMIRI (Dusan SAVIC 72), Ivan TRICKOVSKI, Goran PANDEV, Ilco NAUMOSKI (Ferhan HASANI 10). Tr: Mirsad JONUZ

Shay GIVEN - John O'SHEA, Darren O'DEA, Stephen KELLY, Glenn WHELAN, Kevin KILBANE, Stephen HUNT, Keith ANDREWS, Aiden MCGEADY, Robbie KEANE, Simon COX• (Shane LONG 64). Tr: Giovanni TRAPATTONI

COMUNAL, ANDORRA LA VELLA
2-09-2011, 750, Kostadinov BUL

Andorra	0
Armenia	3

ARM - Pizzelli 35, Ghazaryan 75, Mkhitaryan 91+p

Fernando SILVA (Sebastian GOMEZ 72), Josep GOMES, Cristian MARTINEZ, Ildefons LIMA♦90 Jordi RUBIO, Emili GARCIA, Marc BERNAUS, Marc VALES, Marc PUJOL•, Josep AYALA (Juli SANCHEZ 87), Sergi MORENO (Marcio VIEIRA 80). Tr: David RODRIGO

Roman BEREZOVSKIY - Sargis HOVSEPYAN, Karlen MKRTCHYAN, Henrikh MKHITARYAN, Artak ALEKSANYAN, Hrayr MKOYAN, Edgar MANUCHARYAN (Edgar MALAKYAN 78), Levon HAYRAPETYAN, Gevorg GHAZARYAN (Zaven BADOYAN 89), Artur SARKISOV•, PIZELLI (Artak YEDIGARYAN 84). Tr: Vardan MINASYAN

LUZHNIKI, MOSCOW
2-09-2011, 31028, Yildirim Bulent TUR

Russia	1
FYR Macedonia	0

RUS - Semshov 41

Vyacheslav MALAFEEV - Vasiliy BEREZUTSKIY, Aleksey BEREZUTSKIY, Aleksandr ANYUKOV, Igor SEMSHOV (Roman PAVLYUCHENKO 46), Konstantin ZYRYANOV (Dmitriy TORBINSKIY 60), Yuriy ZHIRKOV, Roman SHIROKOV•, Andrey ARSHAVIN, Aleksandr KERZHAKOV• (Denis GLUSHAKOV 88), Igor DENISOV•. Tr: Dick ADVOCAAT

Martin BOGATINOV - Nikolce NOVESKI•, Vance SIKOV, Daniel GEORGIEVSKI, Velice SUMULIKOSKI• (Muarem MUAREM 85), Goran POPOV, Muhamed DEMIRI•, Ivan TRICKOVSKI, Goran PANDEV•♦90, Mirko IVANOVSKI (Aleksandar TRAJKOVSKI 75), Agim IBRAIMI (Ferhan HASANI 66). Tr: John TOSHACK

AVIVA STADIUM, DUBLIN
2-09-2011, 35480, Proenca POR

Republic of Ireland	0
Slovakia	0

Shay GIVEN - Stephen WARD, Sean ST LEDGER•, John O'SHEA, Richard DUNNE•, Glenn WHELAN, Damien DUFF, Keith ANDREWS, Aiden MCGEADY (Stephen HUNT 84), Robbie KEANE, Kevin DOYLE (Simon COX 64). Tr: Giovanni TRAPATTONI

Jan MUCHA• - Martin SKRTEL, Peter PEKARIK, Jan DURICA, Marek CECH, Vladimir WEISS (Erik JENDRISEK 85), Juraj KUCKA• (Karim GUEDE 76), Miroslav KARHAN, Marek HAMSIK, Miroslav STOCH, Filip HOLOSKO (Robert VITTEK 88). Tr: Vladimir WEISS

LUZHNIKI, MOSCOW
6-09-2011, 49515, Brych GER

Russia	0
Republic of Ireland	0

Vyacheslav MALAFEEV - Aleksey BEREZUTSKIY, Aleksandr ANYUKOV•, Sergey IGNASHEVICH, Vasiliy BEREZUTSKIY, Igor SEMSHOV, Konstantin ZYRYANOV, Yuriy ZHIRKOV (Diniyar BILYALETDINOV 76), Roman SHIROKOV, Andrey ARSHAVIN, Aleksandr KERZHAKOV (Roman PAVLYUCHENKO 54). Tr: Dick ADVOCAAT

Shay GIVEN - Stephen WARD•, Darren O'DEA, Stephen KELLY, Richard DUNNE•, Keith ANDREWS, Glenn WHELAN, Damien DUFF (Stephen HUNT• 67), Kevin DOYLE (Simon COX 59), Aiden MCGEADY, Robbie KEANE. Tr: Giovanni TRAPATTONI

NATIONAL ARENA FILIP II, SKOPJE
6-09-2011, 5000, Whitby WAL

FYR Macedonia	1
Andorra	0

MKD - Ivanovski 59

Martin BOGATINOV - Daniel MOJSOV, Daniel GEORGIEVSKI, Vance SIKOV, Ferhan HASANI (Samir FAZLI 68), Velice SUMULIKOSKI, Goran POPOV, Ivan TRICKOVSKI, Muarem MUAREM• (Muhamedin HUSEINI• 77), Mirko IVANOVSKI, Agim IBRAIMI (Aleksandar TRAJKOVSKI 46). Tr: John TOSHACK

Fernando SILVA (Sebastian GOMEZ 73), Josep GOMES, Emili GARCIA•, Marc BERNAUS, Cristian MARTINEZ, Jordi RUBIO• (Alexandre GUTIERREZ• 26), Josep AYALA, Marcio VIEIRA (Marc RENOM 83), Marc VALES•, Oscar SONEJEE•, Sergi MORENO. Tr: David RODRIGO

POD DUBNOM, ZILINA
6-09-2011, 7238, Borski POL

Slovakia	0
Armenia	4

ARM - Movsisyan 57, Mkhitaryan 70, Ghazaryan 80, Sarkisov 91+

Jan MUCHA - Karim GUEDE• (Robert JEZ 55), Jan DURICA•, Marek CECH• (Erik JENDRISEK 78), Martin SKRTEL, Peter PEKARIK, Vladimir WEISS (Stanislav SESTAK• 71), Miroslav KARHAN, Marek HAMSIK•, Miroslav STOCH•, Filip HOLOSKO. Tr: Vladimir WEISS

Roman BEREZOVSKIY - Sargis HOVSEPYAN, Artur YEDIGARYAN (Artur YUSPASHYAN 90), Artak ALEKSANYAN, Karlen MKRTCHYAN, Henrikh MKHITARYAN, Hrayr MKOYAN•, Levon HAYRAPETYAN, Gevorg GHAZARYAN, PIZELLI• (Edgar MANUCHARYAN 73), Yura MOVSISYAN (Artur SARKISOV 85). Tr: Vardan MINASYAN

UEFA EURO 2012 POLAND/UKRAINE QUALIFYING GROUP C

REPUBLICAN, YEREVAN
7-10-2011, 14 403, Schorgenhofer AUT
Armenia 4
FYR Macedonia 1
ARM - Pizzelli [28], Mkhitaryan [34], Ghazaryan [69], Sarkisov [91+] • MKD - Sikov [86]
ARM: Roman BEREZOVSKIY - Sargis HOVSEPYAN, Artur YUSPASHYAN, Artur YEDIGARYAN, Karlen MKRTCHYAN• (Artur SARKISOV75), Henrikh MKHITARYAN, Artak ALEKSANYAN, Levon HAYRAPETYAN, Gevorg GHAZARYAN (Edgar MALAKYAN 83), PIZELLI (Edgar MANUCHARYAN 63), Yura MOVSISYAN. Tr: Vardan MINASYAN
MKD: Martin BOGATINOV - Nikolce NOVESKI, Vance SIKOV, Daniel GEORGIEVSKY (Vlade LAZAREVSKI 51), Velice SUMULIKOSKI••◆54, Goran POPOV•, Muhamed DEMIRI, Ivan TRICKOVSKI, Muarem MUAREM (Mario GUROVSKI 46), Mirko IVANOVSKI•, Filip IVANOVSKI (Igor MITRESKI 60). Tr: John TOSHACK

POD DUBNOM, ZILINA
7-10-2011, 10 087, Eriksson SWE
Slovakia 0
Russia 1
RUS - Dzagoev [71]
SVK: Jan MUCHA - Martin SKRTEL•, Peter PEKARIK, Tomas HUBOCAN, Jan DURICA, Juraj KUCKA (Karim GUEDE 73), Miroslav KARHAN (Filip SEBO 86), Marek HAMSIK, Miroslav STOCH•, Filip HOLOSKO (Vladimir WEISS 74), Erik JENDRISEK. Tr: Vladimir WEISS
RUS: Vyacheslav MALAFEEV - Sergey IGNASHEVICH, Vasiliy BEREZUTSKIY, Aleksandr ANYUKOV•, Konstantin ZYRYANOV•, Yuriy ZHIRKOV (Aleksey BEREZUTSKIY 90), Roman SHIROKOV, Alan DZAGOEV (Aleksandr SAMEDOV 90), Roman PAVLYUCHENKO (Pavel POGREBNYAK 87), Andrey ARSHAVIN, Igor DENISOV. Tr: Dick ADVOCAAT

COMUNAL, ANDORRA LA VELLA
7-10-2011, 860, Kovarik CZE
Andorra 0
Republic of Ireland 2
IRL - Doyle [8], McGeady [20]
AND: Fernando SILVA - Josep GOMES, Cristian MARTINEZ•, Ildefons LIMA (Oscar SONEJEE 80), Emili GARCIA, Marc BERNAUS, Alexandre GUTIERREZ (Ivan LORENZO 78), Marc PUJOL (Carlos PEPPE 60), Josep AYALA•, Marcio VIEIRA, Sergi MORENO. Tr: David RODRIGO
IRL: Shay GIVEN - Stephen WARD•, Sean ST LEDGER, John O'SHEA, Darren O'DEA, Glenn WHELAN (Keith FAHEY 65), Damien DUFF (Stephen HUNT 75), Keith ANDREWS, Aiden MCGEADY, Robbie KEANE, Kevin DOYLE (Shane LONG 71). Tr: Giovanni Trapattoni

LUZHNIKI, MOSCOW
11-10-2011, 38 790, Hacmon ISR
Russia 6
Andorra 0
RUS - Dzagoev 2 [5 44], Ignashevich [26], Pavlyuchenko [30], Glushakov [59], Bilyaletdinov [78]
RUS: Vyacheslav MALAFEEV - Roman SHISHKIN, Sergey IGNASHEVICH, Vasiliy BEREZUTSKIY, Aleksey BEREZUTSKIY, Igor SEMSHOV (Diniyar BILYALETDINOV 72), Denis GLUSHAKOV (Aleksandr SAMEDOV 80), Alan DZAGOEV, Roman PAVLYUCHENKO• (Pavel POGREBNYAK 73), Andrey ARSHAVIN, Igor DENISOV•. Tr: Dick ADVOCAAT
AND: Josep GOMES - Alexandre GUTIERREZ, Ildefons LIMA•, Emili GARCIA, Marc BERNAUS, Marcio VIEIRA, Marc VALES, Marc PUJOL• (Juli SANCHEZ 84), Carlos PEPPE (Ivan LORENZO 80), Sebastian GOMEZ (Fernando SILVA•70), Sergi MORENO. Tr: David RODRIGO

AVIVA STADIUM, DUBLIN
11-10-2011, 45 200, Iturralde ESP
Republic of Ireland 2
Armenia 1
IRL - OG [43], Dunne [59] • ARM - Mkhitaryan [62]
IRL: Shay GIVEN - Sean ST LEDGER•, John O'SHEA, Stephen KELLY•, Richard DUNNE, Glenn WHELAN (Keith FAHEY 76), Damien DUFF•, Keith ANDREWS•, Aiden MCGEADY (Stephen HUNT 67), Kevin DOYLE••◆81, Simon COX (Jon WALTERS 80). Tr: Giovanni TRAPATTONI
ARM: Roman BEREZOVSKIY◆26 - Sargis HOVSEPYAN, Karlen MKRTCHYAN, Henrikh MKHITARYAN, Edgar MALAKYAN (Arsen PETROSYAN• 28), Artak ALEKSANYAN•, Hrayr MKOYAN•, Levon HAYRAPETYAN, Gevorg GHAZARYAN (Artur SARKISOV 63), PIZELLI (Edgar MANUCHARYAN 53), Yura MOVSISYAN. Tr: Vardan MINASYAN

NATIONAL ARENA FILIP II, SKOPJE
11-10-2011, 4100, Chapron FRA
FYR Macedonia 1
Slovakia 1
MKD - Noveski [79] • SVK - Piroska [54]
MKD: Martin BOGATINOV - Nikolce NOVESKI, Daniel MOJSOV•, Aleksandar LAZEVSKI (Filip IVANOVSKI 64), Vlade LAZAREVSKI, Vance SIKOV, Vlatko GROZDANOSKI (Robert PETROV 46), Mario GUROVSKI, Muhamed DEMIRI, Ivan TRICKOVSKI, Samir FAZLI (Aleksandar TRAJKOVSKI 84). Tr: John TOSHACK
SVK: Jan MUCHA - Kornel SALATA, Peter PEKARIK, Lubomir MICHALIK, Tomas HUBOCAN (Marek CECH 46), Vladimir WEISS, Juraj KUCKA, Robert JEZ (Peter GRAJCIAR 88), Marek HAMSIK, Juraj PIROSKA (Filip HOLOSKO 87), Erik JENDRISEK•. Tr: Vladimir WEISS

	GROUP C	PL	W	D	L	F	A	PTS	ITA	EST	SRB	SVN	NIR	FRO
1	Italy	10	8	2	0	20	2	26		3-0	3-0	1-0	3-0	5-0
2	Estonia	10	5	1	4	15	14	16	1-2		1-1	0-1	4-1	2-1
3	Serbia	10	4	3	3	13	12	15	1-1	1-3		1-1	2-1	3-1
4	Slovenia	10	4	2	4	11	7	14	0-1	1-2	1-0		0-1	5-1
5	Northern Ireland	10	2	3	5	9	13	9	0-0	1-2	0-1	0-0		4-0
6	Faroe Islands	10	1	1	8	6	26	4	0-1	2-0	0-3	0-2	1-1	

Italy qualified directly for the finals • Estonia qualified for a play-off v Rep. Ireland • Estonia 0-4 1-1 **Rep. Ireland**

A LE COQ ARENA, TALLINN
11-08-2010, Att: 5470, Ref: Vucemilovic CRO
Estonia 2
Faroe Islands 1
EST - Saag [91+], Piiroja [93+] • FRO - Edmundsson [26]
EST: Sergei PAREIKO - Raio PIIROJA, Dmitriy KRUGLOV (Sander POST 70), Enar JAAGER, Alo BARENGRUB, Ragnar KLAVAN, Sander PURI (Ats PURJE 76), Aleksandr DMITRIJEV, Konstantin VASSILJEV, Andres OPER (Kaimar SAAG 62), Tarmo KINK. Tr: Tarmo RUUTLI
FRO: Gunnar NIELSEN• - Jonas NAES, Atli GREGERSEN, Johan DAVIDSEN, Hendrik RUBEKSEN, Christian HOLST•, Joan EDMUNDSSON•, Frodi BENJAMINSEN, Jann Ingi PETERSEN (Bogi LOKIN 85), Jakup a BORG• (Rogvi POULSEN 67), Simun SAMUELSEN (Justinus HANSEN 74). Tr: Brian KERR

TORSVOLLUR, TORSHAVN
3-09-2010, Att: 1847, Ref: Toussaint LUX
Faroe Islands 0
Serbia 3
SRB - Lazovic [14], Stankovic [18], Zigic [91+]
FRO: Gunnar NIELSEN• - Johan DAVIDSEN, Hendrik RUBEKSEN, Jonas NAES, Atli GREGERSEN, Joan EDMUNDSSON, Frodi BENJAMINSEN, Jann Ingi PETERSEN (Justinus HANSEN 72), Christian HOLST (Arnbjorn HANSEN 79), Daniel UDSEN (Christian MOURITSEN 46), Simun SAMUELSEN. Tr: Brian KERR
SRB: Andelko DURICIC - Nemanja VIDIC, Neven SUBOTIC, Antonio RUKAVINA•, Ivan OBRADOVIC• (Aleksandar LUKOVIC 46), Milos KRASIC, Dejan STANKOVIC (Radoslav PETROVIC 58), Zdravko KUZMANOVIC, Milan JOVANOVIC, Nikola ZIGIC, Danko LAZOVIC (Milos NINKOVIC 82). Tr: Radomir ANTIC

A LE COQ ARENA, TALLINN
3-09-2010, Att: 8600, Ref: Velasco ESP
Estonia 1
Italy 2
EST - Zenjov [31] • ITA - Cassano [60], Bonucci [63]
EST: Sergei PAREIKO - Taavi RAHN, Raio PIIROJA•, Dmitriy KRUGLOV (Tarmo KINK 82), Enar JAAGER, Ragnar KLAVAN•, Sander PURI (Ats PURJE 77), Aleksandr DMITRIJEV, Martin VUNK•, Konstantin VASSILJEV, Sergei ZENJOV (Kaimar SAAG 64). Tr: Tarmo RUUTLI
ITA: Salvatore SIRIGU - Cristian MOLINARO, Giorgio CHIELLINI, Mattia CASSANI, Leonardo BONUCCI, Simone PEPE (Fabio QUAGLIARELLA 59), Riccardo MONTOLIVO (Angelo PALOMBO 75), Daniele DE ROSSI, Andrea PIRLO, Giampaolo PAZZINI, Antonio CASSANO (Luca ANTONELLI 80). Tr: Cesare PRANDELLI

PART THREE – THE CONTINENTAL CONFEDERATIONS

LJUDSKI VRT, MARIBOR
3-09-2010, Att: 12 000, Ref: Balaj ROU

Slovenia	0
Northern Ireland	1

NIR - Evans 70

SVN – Samir HANDANOVIC - Matej MAVRIC, Bojan JOKIC, Miso BRECKO, Bostjan CESAR, Aleksander RADOSAVLJEVIC, Robert KOREN, Andraz KIRM (Josip ILICIC 75), Zlatan LJUBIJANKIC (Tim MATAVZ 88), Valter BIRSA, Milivoje NOVAKOVIC (Zlatko DEDIC 74). Tr: Matjaz KEK

NIR – Maik TAYLOR - Gareth MCAULEY, Aaron HUGHES, Stephen CRAIGAN, Craig CATHCART, Chris BAIRD, Grant MCCANN (Corry EVANS 67), Steven DAVIS, Chris BRUNT• (Johnny GORMAN 89), David HEALY• (Kyle LAFFERTY• 67), Warren FEENEY. Tr: Nigel WORTHINGTON

CRVENA ZVEZDA, BELGRADE
7-09-2010, Att: 24 028, Ref: Benquerenca POR

Serbia	1
Slovenia	1

SRB - Zigic 86 • SVN - Novakovic 63

SRB – Andelko DURICIC - Nemanja VIDIC•, Neven SUBOTIC, Antonio RUKAVINA, Aleksandar LUKOVIC•, Zoran TOSIC (Milos KRASIC 46), Dejan STANKOVIC• (Gojko KACAR71), Zdravko KUZMANOVIC•, Nikola ZIGIC•, Danko LAZOVIC, Milan JOVANOVIC (Milos NINKOVIC 64). Tr: Radomir ANTIC

SVN – Samir HANDANOVIC• - Matej MAVRIC•, Bojan JOKIC, Miso BRECKO, Bostjan CESAR, Aleksander RADOSAVLJEVIC•, Robert KOREN, Andraz KIRM• (Dalibor STEVANOVIC 89), Valter BIRSA (Josip ILICIC 78), Milivoje NOVAKOVIC, Zlatko DEDIC (Zlatan LJUBIJANKIC 77). Tr: Matjaz KEK

ARTEMIO FRANCHI, FLORENCE
7-09-2010, Att: 19 266, Ref: Kulbakov BLR

Italy	5
Faroe Islands	0

ITA - Gilardino 11, De Rossi 22, Cassano 27, Quagliarella 81, Pirlo 90

ITA – Emiliano VIVIANO - Lorenzo DE SILVESTRI, Giorgio CHIELLINI, Leonardo BONUCCI, Luca ANTONELLI, Andrea PIRLO, Riccardo MONTOLIVO, Daniele DE ROSSI (Angelo PALOMBO 76), Giuseppe ROSSI (Fabio QUAGLIARELLA 58), Alberto GILARDINO (Giampaolo PAZZINI 59), Antonio CASSANO. Tr: Cesare PRANDELLI

FRO – Gunnar NIELSEN - Hendrik RUBEKSEN, Atli GREGERSEN, Johan DAVIDSEN•, Egil a BO, Jann Ingi PETERSEN, Bogi LOKIN (Jonas NAES 74), Joan EDMUNDSSON (Daniel UDSEN 89), Frodi BENJAMINSEN, Christian MOURITSEN (Christian HOLST 75), Simun SAMUELSEN. Tr: Brian KERR

PARTIZAN, BELGRADE
8-10-2010, Att: 12 000, Ref: Layushkin RUS

Serbia	1
Estonia	3

SRB - Zigic 60 • EST - Kink 63, Vassiljev 73, OG 91+

SRB – Vladimir STOJKOVIC - Nemanja VIDIC•, Aleksandar LUKOVIC, Branislav IVANOVIC, Marko LOMIC, Dejan STANKOVIC, Zdravko KUZMANOVIC (Danko LAZOVIC• 79), Milos KRASIC•, Gojko KACAR (Zoran TOSIC 46), Nikola ZIGIC, Milan JOVANOVIC (Milos NINKOVIC 46). Tr: Vladimir PETROVIC

EST – Sergei PAREIKO - Taavi RAHN, Raio PIIROJA•, Dmitriy KRUGLOV, Enar JAAGER, Ragnar KLAVAN, Sander PURI (Ats PURJE 69), Aleksandr DMITRIJEV•, Konstantin VASSILJEV•, Tarmo KINK (Kaimar SAAG 64), Sergei ZENJOV (Martin VUNK 88). Tr: Tarmo RUUTLI

WINDSOR PARK, BELFAST
8-10-2010, Att: 15 200, Ref: Chapron FRA

Northern Ireland	0
Italy	0

NIR – Maik TAYLOR - Chris BAIRD, Gareth MCAULEY, Aaron HUGHES, Jonny EVANS, Stephen CRAIGAN, Chris BRUNT (Niall MCGINN 71), Grant MCCANN (Corry EVANS 80), Steven DAVIS, David HEALY (Kyle LAFFERTY 66), Warren FEENEY. Tr: Nigel WORTHINGTON

ITA – Emiliano VIVIANO - Domenico CRISCITO, Giorgio CHIELLINI, Mattia CASSANI, Leonardo BONUCCI, Andrea PIRLO, Simone PEPE (Giuseppe ROSSI 84), Stefano MAURI (Claudio MARCHISIO 79), Daniele DE ROSSI, Antonio CASSANO, Marco BORRIELLO (Giampaolo PAZZINI 74). Tr: Cesare PRANDELLI

STOZICE, LJUBLJANA
8-10-2010, Att: 15 750, Ref: Todorov BUL

Slovenia	5
Faroe Islands	1

SVN - Matavz 3 25 36 65, Novakovic 72p, Dedic 84
FRO - Mouritsen 93+

SVN – Samir HANDANOVIC - Miso BRECKO, Bostjan CESAR•, Marko SULER, Bojan JOKIC, Josip ILICIC, Aleksander RADOSAVLJEVIC (Armin BACINOVIC 59), Robert KOREN, Valter BIRSA (Andraz KIRM 51), Tim MATAVZ, Milivoje NOVAKOVIC (Zlatko DEDIC 73). Tr: Matjaz KEK

FRO – Jakup MIKKELSEN - Atli GREGERSEN•, Egil a BO, Hendrik RUBEKSEN•, Jonas NAES, Justinus HANSEN•, Joan EDMUNDSSON, Frodi BENJAMINSEN•, Bogi LOKIN (Hjalgrim ELTTOR 41), Christian HOLST (Jann Ingi PETERSEN 81), Daniel UDSEN (Christian MOURITSEN 81). Tr: Brian KERR

SVANGASKARD, TOFTIR
12-10-2010, Att: 1921, Ref: Zimmermann SUI

Faroe Islands	1
Northern Ireland	1

FRO - Holst 60 • NIR - Lafferty 76

FRO – Jakup MIKKELSEN - Jonas NAES•, Atli GREGERSEN•, Johan DAVIDSEN, Erling JACOBSEN, Christian HOLST (Justinus HANSEN 85), Hjalgrim ELTTOR, Joan EDMUNDSSON, Frodi BENJAMINSEN, Daniel UDSEN (Jann Ingi PETERSEN 68), Simun SAMUELSEN (Arnbjorn HANSEN• 78). Tr: Brian KERR

NIR – Maik TAYLOR - Gareth MCAULEY, Aaron HUGHES, Jonny EVANS, Stephen CRAIGAN, Chris BAIRD, Niall MCGINN (Corry EVANS 83), Steven DAVIS•, Chris BRUNT, Kyle LAFFERTY, Warren FEENEY (David HEALY 50). Tr: Nigel WORTHINGTON

A LE COQ ARENA, TALLINN
12-10-2010, Att: 5722, Ref: Skjerven NOR

Estonia	0
Slovenia	1

SVN - OG 67

EST – Sergei PAREIKO - Enar JAAGER, Taavi RAHN (Karl PALATU 55), Dmitriy KRUGLOV•, Ragnar KLAVAN, Aleksandr DMITRIJEV, Andrei SIDORENKOV, Sander PURI (Ats PURJE 69), Konstantin VASSILJEV, Tarmo KINK (Sergei ZENJOV 59), Kaimar SAAG 72. Tr: Tarmo RUUTLI

SVN – Samir HANDANOVIC - Miso BRECKO, Bostjan CESAR, Marko SULER, Bojan JOKIC, Aleksander RADOSAVLJEVIC•, Robert KOREN, Josip ILICIC (Andraz KIRM 67), Valter BIRSA• (Zlatan LJUBIJANKIC 90), Tim MATAVZ (Zlatko DEDIC 53), Milivoje NOVAKOVIC. Tr: Matjaz KEK

LUIGI FERRARIS, GENOA
12-10-2010, Att: 28 000, Ref: Thomson SCO

Italy	3
Serbia	0

Match abandoned after 6'. Italy awarded match 3-0

ITA – Emiliano VIVIANO - Domenico CRISCITO, Giorgio CHIELLINI, Leonardo BONUCCI, Gianluca ZAMBROTTA, Andrea PIRLO, Angelo PALOMBO, Stefano MAURI, Claudio MARCHISIO, Giampaolo PAZZINI, Antonio CASSANO. Tr: Cesare PRANDELLI

SRB – Zeljko BRKIC - Neven SUBOTIC, Slobodan RAJKOVIC•, Aleksandar LUKOVIC, Branislav IVANOVIC, Zoran TOSIC, Dejan STANKOVIC, Zdravko KUZMANOVIC, Milos KRASIC, Gojko KACAR, Dragan MRDJA. Tr: Vladimir PETROVIC

CRVENA ZVEZDA, BELGRADE
25-03-2011, Att: BCD, Ref: Gumienny BEL

Serbia	2
Northern Ireland	1

SRB - Pantelic 65, Tosic 74 • NIR - McAuley 40

SRB – Zeljko BRKIC - Neven SUBOTIC, Aleksandar KOLAROV, Branislav IVANOVIC, Milan BISEVAC, Zoran TOSIC, Dejan STANKOVIC•, Nenad MILIJAS (Milos NINKOVIC 47), Adem LJAJIC (Milan JOVANOVIC 47), Milos KRASIC• (Radoslav PETROVIC 86), Marko PANTELIC•. Tr: Vladimir PETROVIC

NIR – Lee CAMP - Gareth MCAULEY, Aaron HUGHES, Jonny EVANS• (Pat MCCOURT 86), Craig CATHCART, Chris BAIRD, Johnny GORMAN (Warren FEENEY 78), Corry EVANS, Sammy CLINGAN, Chris BRUNT, Kyle LAFFERTY (David HEALY• 46). Tr: Nigel WORTHINGTON

STOZICE, LJUBLJANA
25-03-2011, Att: 15 790, Ref: Brych GER

Slovenia	0
Italy	1

ITA - Thiago Motta 73

SVN – Samir HANDANOVIC - Marko SULER, Bojan JOKIC, Miso BRECKO (Sinisa ANDELKOVIC 69), Bostjan CESAR•, Aleksander RADOSAVLJEVIC, Robert KOREN, Andraz KIRM, Valter BIRSA (Josip Ilicic 74), Milivoje NOVAKOVIC, Zlatko DEDIC (Zlatan LJUBIJANKIC 56). Tr: Matjaz KEK

ITA – Gianluigi BUFFON - Christian MAGGIO, Giorgio CHIELLINI, Leonardo BONUCCI, Federico BALZARETTI, Thiago MOTTA•, Riccardo MONTOLIVO• (Claudio MARCHISIO 87), Stefano MAURI (Antonio NOCERINO 63), Alberto AQUILANI, Giampaolo PAZZINI, Antonio CASSANO (Giuseppe ROSSI 74). Tr: Cesare PRANDELLI

A LE COQ ARENA, TALLINN
29-03-2011, Att: 5185, Ref: Nijhuis NED

Estonia	1
Serbia	1

EST - Vassiljev 84 • SRB - Pantelic 38

EST – Sergei PAREIKO - Taavi RAHN•, Raio PIIROJA•, Dmitriy KRUGLOV, Enar JAAGER, Ragnar KLAVAN, Sander PURI (Ats PURJE• 29), Aleksandr DMITRIJEV, Konstantin VASSILJEV, Kaimar SAAG (Tarmo KINK 66), Jarmo AHJUPERA (Andres OPER 55). Tr: Tarmo RUUTLI

SRB – Zeljko BRKIC - Nemanja VIDIC, Aleksandar KOLAROV, Branislav IVANOVIC, Milan BISEVAC•, Zoran TOSIC, Radoslav PETROVIC, Milos NINKOVIC (Vesko TRIVUNOVIC 14), Nenad MILIJAS•, Marko PANTELIC, Milan JOVANOVIC (Nikola ZIGIC 74). Tr: Vladimir PETROVIC

UEFA EURO 2012 POLAND/UKRAINE QUALIFYING GROUP C

WINDSOR PARK, BELFAST
29-03-2011, Att: 14 200, Ref: Kuipers NED

Northern Ireland	0
Slovenia	0

NIR: Lee CAMP - Gareth MCAULEY, Jonny EVANS, Stephen CRAIGAN, Craig CATHCART, Chris BAIRD•, Grant MCCANN (Josh MCQUOID 71), Corry EVANS• (Liam BOYCE 90), Sammy CLINGAN, Chris BRUNT•, Warren FEENEY (Pat MCCOURT 82). Tr: Nigel WORTHINGTON

SVN: Samir HANDANOVIC - Marko SULER, Matej MAVRIC, Bojan JOKIC, Miso BRECKO, Robert KOREN•, Andraz KIRM, Josip ILICIC (Zlatan LJUBJANKIC 29), Armin BACINOVIC• (Goran SUKALO 90), Valter BIRSA, Milivoje NOVAKOVIC (Zlatko DEDIC 84). Tr: Matjaz KEK

SVANGASKARD, TOFTIR
3-06-2011, Att: 974, Ref: Drachta AUT

Faroe Islands	0
Slovenia	2

SVN - Matavz 29, OG 47

FRO: Jakup MIKKELSEN - Jonas NAES (Suni OLSEN 81), Pol JUSTINUSSEN, Einar HANSEN, Johan DAVIDSEN•, Christian HOLST (Christian MOURITSEN 76), Hjalgrim ELTTOR, Joan EDMUNDSSON•, Frodi BENJAMINSEN, Daniel UDSEN (Atli DANIELSEN 45), Rogvi BALDVINSSON. Tr: Brian KERR

SVN: Samir HANDANOVIC - Marko SULER♦25, Bojan JOKIC, Miso BRECKO, Bostjan CESAR, Robert KOREN, Josip ILICIC, Armin BACINOVIC, Tim MATAVZ (Andraz KIRM 77), Valter BIRSA (Matej MAVRIC 48), Milivoje NOVAKOVIC (Zlatan LJUBJANKIC 55). Tr: Matjaz KEK

ALBERTO BRAGLIA, MODENA
3-06-2011, Att: 19 434, Ref: Tudor ROU

Italy	3
Estonia	0

ITA - Rossi 21, Cassano 39, Pazzini 68

ITA: Gianluigi BUFFON - Andrea RANOCCHIA, Christian MAGGIO, Giorgio CHIELLINI, Federico BALZARETTI•, Andrea PIRLO, Riccardo MONTOLIVO, Claudio MARCHISIO, Alberto AQUILANI• (Antonio NOCERINO 24), Giuseppe ROSSI (Sebastian GIOVINCO 79), Antonio CASSANO (Giampaolo PAZZINI 65). Tr: Cesare PRANDELLI

EST: Sergei PAREIKO - Taavi RAHN, Raio PIIROJA, Dmitriy KRUGLOV, Enar JAAGER, Ragnar KLAVAN•, Martin VUNK•, Taijo TENISTE (Kaimar SAAG 59), Sander PURI, Tarmo KINK (Gert KAMS 78), Sergei ZENJOV (Jarmo AHJUPERA 58). Tr: Tarmo RUUTLI

SVANGASKARD, TOFTIR
7-06-2011, Att: 1715, Ref: Munukka FIN

Faroe Islands	2
Estonia	0

FRO - Benjaminsen 43p, Hansen.A 47

FRO: Jakup MIKKELSEN - Jonas NAES, Einar HANSEN, Pol JUSTINUSSEN••♦88, Atli GREGERSEN, Atli DANIELSEN, Christian HOLST (Christian MOURITSEN 84), Hjalgrim ELTTOR (Suni OLSEN 90), Frodi BENJAMINSEN, Rogvi BALDVINSSON, Arnbjorn HANSEN (Simun SAMUELSEN 69). Tr: Brian KERR

EST: Sergei PAREIKO• - Taavi RAHN, Raio PIIROJA, Dmitriy KRUGLOV, Enar JAAGER, Sander PURI••♦56, Konstantin VASSILJEV, Kaimar SAAG (Sergei MOSNIKOV 82), Tarmo KINK, Jarmo AHJUPERA (Gert Kams 67), Sergei ZENJOV•. Tr: Tarmo RUUTLI

WINDSOR PARK, BELFAST
10-08-2011, Att: 13 183, Ref: Aleckovic BIH

Northern Ireland	4
Faroe Islands	0

NIR - Hughes 5, Davis 66, McCourt 2 71 88

NIR: Lee CAMP - Gareth MCAULEY (Craig CATHCART 46), Aaron HUGHES, Jonny EVANS, Chris BAIRD•, Pat MCCOURT•, Grant MCCANN, Corry EVANS (Niall MCGINN 59), Steven DAVIS, Sammy CLINGAN, David HEALY (Jamie WARD 83). Tr: Nigel WORTHINGTON

FRO: Jakup MIKKELSEN - Jonas NAES, Atli GREGERSEN, Johan DAVIDSEN, Suni OLSEN (Atli DANIELSEN 75), Christian HOLST (Arnbjorn HANSEN 68), Hjalgrim ELTTOR (Christian MOURITSEN 75), Joan EDMUNDSSON, Frodi BENJAMINSEN, Daniel UDSEN, Rogvi BALDVINSSON. Tr: Brian KERR

TORSVOLLUR, TORSHAVN
2-09-2011, Att: 5654, Ref: Bognar HUN

Faroe Islands	0
Italy	1

ITA - Cassano 11

FRO: Rene TORGAR - Jonas NAES, Pol JUSTINUSSEN (Christian MOURITSEN 45), Atli GREGERSEN, Johan DAVIDSEN, Christian HOLST (Simun SAMUELSEN 87), Hjalgrim ELTTOR, Joan EDMUNDSSON, Frodi BENJAMINSEN, Suni OLSEN• (Atli DANIELSEN 76), Rogvi BALDVINSSON. Tr: Brian KERR

ITA: Gianluigi BUFFON - Christian MAGGIO, Domenico CRISCITO, Giorgio CHIELLINI, Andrea RANOCCHIA, Andrea PIRLO, Thiago MOTTA (Alberto AQUILANI 73), Riccardo MONTOLIVO, Daniele DE ROSSI, Antonio CASSANO (Mario BALOTELLI 86), Giuseppe ROSSI (Giampaolo PAZZINI 59). Tr: Cesare PRANDELLI

STOZICE, LJUBLJANA
2-09-2011, Att: 15 480, Ref: Studer SUI

Slovenia	1
Estonia	2

SVN - Matavz 78 • **EST** - Vassiljev 29p, Purje 81

SVN: Samir HANDANOVIC - Miso BRECKO, Bostjan CESAR, Bojan JOKIC, Branko ILIC, Aleksander RADOSAVLJEVIC (Dare VRSIC 56), Robert KOREN, Josip ILICIC (Nejc PECNIK 82), Valter BIRSA, Tim MATAVZ, Milivoje NOVAKOVIC (Zlatan LJUBJANKIC 56). Tr: Matjaz KEK

EST: Sergei PAREIKO - Enar JAAGER, Taavi RAHN, Raio PIIROJA (Andrei STEPANOV 74), Dmitriy KRUGLOV (Ats PURJE 69), Ragnar KLAVAN, Aleksandr DMITRIJEV•, Martin VUNK, Taijo TENISTE, Konstantin VASSILJEV, Sergei ZENJOV (Jarmo AHJUPERA 61). Tr: Tarmo RUUTLI

WINDSOR PARK, BELFAST
2-09-2011, Att: 15 148, Ref: Einwaller AUT

Northern Ireland	0
Serbia	0

SRB - Pantelic 67

NIR: Lee CAMP - Gareth MCAULEY, Aaron HUGHES, Jonny EVANS•, Craig CATHCART, Chris BAIRD, Grant MCCANN• (Warren FEENEY 71), Corry EVANS• (Niall MCGINN 59), Steven DAVIS, Chris BRUNT, David HEALY (Josh MCQUOID 84). Tr: Nigel WORTHINGTON

SRB: Bojan JORGACEVIC - Neven SUBOTIC, Slobodan RAJKOVIC•, Aleksandar KOLAROV, Branislav IVANOVIC, Zoran TOSIC (Adem LJAJIC 79), Dejan STANKOVIC, Milos NINKOVIC• (Radoslav PETROVIC• 74), Zdravko KUZMANOVIC (Ljubomir FEJSA 89), Marko PANTELIC, Milan JOVANOVIC. Tr: Vladimir PETROVIC

PARTIZAN, BELGRADE
6-09-2011, Att: 7500, Ref: Amirkhanyan ARM

Serbia	3
Faroe Islands	1

SRB - Jovanovic 6, Tosic 22, Kuzmanovic 69 •
FRO - Benjaminsen 37

SRB: Bojan JORGACEVIC - Neven SUBOTIC, Aleksandr KOLAROV, Branislav IVANOVIC, Milan BISEVAC (Nenad TOMOVIC 45), Zoran TOSIC, Dejan STANKOVIC (Radoslav PETROVIC 46), Milos NINKOVIC (Ljubomir FEJSA 82), Zdravko KUZMANOVIC, Marko PANTELIC, Milan JOVANOVIC. Tr: Vladimir PETROVIC

FRO: Rene TORGARD - Jonas NAES, Atli GREGERSEN, Johan DAVIDSEN, Atli DANIELSEN, Christian HOLST• (Christian MOURITSEN 78), Hjalgrim ELTTOR•, Joan EDMUNDSSON, Frodi BENJAMINSEN, Rogvi BALDVINSSON, Simun SAMUELSEN (Pol JUSTINUSSEN 73). Tr: Brian KERR

A LE COQ ARENA, TALLINN
6-09-2011, Att: 8660, Ref: Stalhammar SWE

Estonia	4
Northern Ireland	1

EST - Vunk 28, Kink 32, Zenjov 60, Saag 93+ •
NIR - OG 40

EST: Sergei PAREIKO - Taavi RAHN•, Raio PIIROJA, Dmitriy KRUGLOV, Enar JAAGER, Ragnar KLAVAN, Martin VUNK, Sander PURI (Ats PURJE 63), Konstantin VASSILJEV, Tarmo KINK (Kaimar SAAG 88), Jarmo AHJUPERA (Sergei ZENJOV 52). Tr: Tarmo RUUTLI

NIR: Lee CAMP - Gareth MCAULEY, Aaron HUGHES, Craig CATHCART, Chris BAIRD, Niall MCGINN (Josh MCQUOID 65), Grant MCCANN, Steven DAVIS, Sammy CLINGAN, Chris BRUNT, David HEALY (Warren FEENEY 65). Tr: Nigel WORTHINGTON

ARTEMIO FRANCHI, FLORENCE
6-09-2011, Att: 18 000, Ref: Moen NOR

Italy	1
Slovenia	0

ITA - Pazzini 85

ITA: Gianluigi BUFFON - Andrea RANOCCHIA, Giorgio CHIELLINI, Mattia CASSANI, Federico BALZARETTI•, Andrea PIRLO, Thiago MOTTA (Claudio MARCHISIO 46), Riccardo MONTOLIVO (Mario BALOTELLI 76), Daniele DE ROSSI, Giuseppe ROSSI, Antonio CASSANO (Giampaolo PAZZINI 61). Tr: Cesare PRANDELLI

SVN: Jasmin HANDANOVIC - Marko SULER, Bojan JOKIC, Miso BRECKO•, Bostjan CESAR•, Dare VRSIC (Nejc PECNIK• 76), Aleksandr RADOSAVLJEVIC, Robert KOREN•, Andraz KIRM (Zlatko DEDIC 86), Valter BIRSA (Josip ILICIC 57), Milivoje NOVAKOVIC. Tr: Matjaz KEK

WINDSOR PARK, BELFAST
7-10-2011, Att: 12 604, Ref: Grafe GER

Northern Ireland	1
Estonia	2

NIR - Davis 22 • **EST** - Vassiljev 2 77p 84

NIR: Lee CAMP• - Gareth MCAULEY, Lee HODSON, Craig CATHCART•, Chris BAIRD, Pat MCCOURT, Grant MCCANN (David HEALY 83), Steven DAVIS, Sammy CLINGAN (Corry EVANS 32), Chris BRUNT, Kyle LAFFERTY• (Warren FEENEY 69). Tr: Nigel WORTHINGTON

EST: Sergei PAREIKO - Andrei STEPANOV, Raio PIIROJA, Dmitriy KRUGLOV, Enar JAAGER, Ragnar KLAVAN, Martin VUNK, Sander PURI (Ats PURJE 57), Aleksandr DMITRIJEV, Tarmo KINK (Konstantin VASSILJEV 65), Jarmo AHJUPERA (Sergei ZENJOV• 46). Tr: Tarmo RUUTLI

PART THREE – THE CONTINENTAL CONFEDERATIONS

CRVENA ZVEZDA, BELGRADE
7-10-2011, Att: 35 000, Ref: Proenca POR

Serbia	1
Italy	1

SRB - Ivanovic [26] • ITA - Marchisio [2]

SRB: Bojan JORGACEVIC - Neven SUBOTIC, Slobodan RAJKOVIC, Aleksandar KOLAROV, Branislav IVANOVIC•, Zoran TOSIC•, Dejan STANKOVIC• (Milan JOVANOVIC 87), Milos NINKOVIC, Milos KRASIC (Nikola ZIGIC• 77), Ljubomir FEJSA (Radoslav PETROVIC 46), Marko PANTELIC. Tr: Vladimir PETROVIC

ITA: Gianluigi BUFFON - Christian MAGGIO•, Giorgio CHIELLINI, Leonardo BONUCCI, Andrea BARZAGLI, Andrea PIRLO, Riccardo MONTOLIVO (Alberto AQUILANI 82), Claudio MARCHISIO (Antonio NOCERINO 70), Daniele DE ROSSI, Antonio CASSANO (Sebastian GIOVINCO 66), Giuseppe ROSSI. Tr: Cesare PRANDELLI

STADIO ADRIATICO, PESCARA
11-10-2011, Att: 19 480, Ref: Mateu ESP

Italy	3
Northern Ireland	0

ITA - Cassano 2 [21] [53], OG [74]

ITA: Gianluigi BUFFON (Morgan DE SANCTIS 76), Giorgio CHIELLINI, Mattia CASSANI, Andrea BARZAGLI, Federico BALZARETTI, Andrea PIRLO, Riccardo MONTOLIVO, Daniele DE ROSSI, Alberto AQUILANI (Antonio NOCERINO 69), Sebastian GIOVINCO, Antonio CASSANO (Pablo OSVALDO 56). Tr: Cesare PRANDELLI

NIR: Maik TAYLOR - Ryan McGIVERN, Gareth McAULEY, Lee HODSON, Chris BAIRD, Oliver NORWOOD (Conor McLAUGHLIN 74), Johnny GORMAN (Niall McGINN 77), Corry EVANS, Steven DAVIS, Andy LITTLE, David HEALY (Warren FEENEY 65). Tr: Nigel WORTHINGTON

LJUDSKI VRT, MARIBOR
11-10-2011, Att: 9848, Ref: De Bleeckere BEL

Slovenia	1
Serbia	0

SVN - Vrsic [45]

SVN: Samir HANDANOVIC - Bojan JOKIC, Bostjan CESAR, Miso BRECKO (Branko ILIC 65), Marko SULER•, Aleksander RADOSAVLJEVIC, Andraz KIRM, Armin BACINOVIC• (Rene KRHIN 69), Dare VRSIC (Valter BIRSA 76), Tim MATAVZ•, Zlatan LJUBIJANKIC. Tr: Matjaz KEK

SRB: Bojan JORGACEVIC - Neven SUBOTIC, Aleksandar KOLAROV, Branislav IVANOVIC, Nemanja VIDIC, Dejan STANKOVIC, Radoslav PETROVIC (Marko PANTELIC 51), Milos NINKOVIC (Nenad MILIJAS 72), Zoran TOSIC, Dragan MRDJA, Milan JOVANOVIC• (Milos KRASIC 56). Tr: Vladimir PETROVIC

	GROUP D	PL	W	D	L	F	A	PTS	FRA	BIH	ROU	BLR	ALB	LUX
1	France	10	6	3	1	15	4	21		1-1	2-0	0-1	3-0	2-0
2	Bosnia-Herzegovina	10	6	2	2	17	8	20	0-2		2-1	1-0	2-0	5-0
3	Romania	10	3	5	2	13	9	14	0-0	3-0		2-2	1-1	3-1
4	Belarus	10	3	4	3	8	7	13	1-1	0-2	0-0		2-0	2-0
5	Albania	10	2	3	5	7	14	9	1-2	1-1	1-1	1-0		1-0
6	Luxembourg	10	1	1	8	3	21	4	0-2	0-3	0-2	0-0	2-1	

France qualified directly for the finals • Bosnia qualified for a play-off v Portugal • Bosnia 0-2 2-6 **Portugal**

CEAHLAUL, PIATRA NEAMT
3-09-2010, Att: 13 400, Ref: Schorgenhofer AUT

Romania	1
Albania	1

ROU - Stancu [80] • ALB - Muzaka [87]

ROU: Bogdan LOBONT - Razvan RAT•, Mirel Radoi, Gabriel TAMAS, Cosmin CONTRA (Gabriel MURESAN 56), George FLORESCU, Ciprian DEAC, Razvan COCIS (Ovidiu HEREA• 77), Gabriel TORJE, Daniel NICULAE (Bogdan STANCU 64), Ciprian MARICA. Tr: Razvan LUCESCU

ALB: Arian BEQAJ - Andi LILA, Armend DALLKU, Debatik CURRI, Kristi VANGJELI•, Klodian DURO (Gjergj MUZAKA 82), Lorik CANA, Ansi AGOLLI, Ervin SKELA (Gilman LIKA 79), Ervin BULKU, Erjon BOGDANI (Hamdi SALIHI 57). Tr: Josip KUZE

JOSY BARTHEL, LUXEMBOURG
3-09-2010, Att: 7327, Ref: Banari MDA

Luxembourg	0
Bosnia-Herzegovina	3

BIH - Ibricic [6], Pjanic [12], Dzeko [16]

LUX: Jonathan JOUBERT - Kim KINTZIGER, Mathias JANISCH, Eric HOFFMANN•, Tom SCHNELL, Dan COLLETTE (Daniel DA MOTA 76), Lars GERSON, Gilles BETTMER (Tom LATERZA 86), Rene PETERS, Mario MUTSCH, Stefano BENSI• (Joel KITENGE 46). Tr: Luc HOLTZ

BIH: Kenan HASAGIC - Emir SPAHIC, Miralem PJANIC (Ermin ZEC 78), Zvjezdan MISIMOVIC, Senad LULIC, Senijad IBRICIC (Haris MEDUNJANIN 72), Elvir RAHIMIC (Sanel JAHIC 67), Vedad IBISEVIC, Edin DZEKO. Tr: Safet SUSIC

STADE DE FRANCE, PARIS
3-09-2010, Att: 76 395, Ref: Collum SCO

France	0
Belarus	1

BLR - Kislyak [86]

FRA: Hugo LLORIS - Gael CLICHY, Bacary SAGNA, Adil RAMI, Philippe MEXES, Abou DIABY, Florent MALOUDA, Yann M'VILA, Guillaume HOARAU, Loic REMY (Matthieu VALBUENA 34), Jeremy MENEZ (Louis SAHA 69, Kevin GAMEIRO 80). Tr: Laurent BLANC

BLR: Yuriy ZHEVNOV - Aleksandr YUREVICH, Igor SHITOV, Sergey OMELYANCHUK, Aleksandr MARTINOVICH, Aleksandr KULCHIY, Aleksandr HLEB, Jan TIGOREV•, Vitaliy RODIONOV• (Sergey KORNILENKO 85), Vitaliy KUTUZOV (Sergey KISLYAK 74), Vyatcheslav HLEB (Anton PUTSILA 89). Tr: Bernd STANGE

DINAMO, MINSK
7-09-2010, Att: 26 354, Ref: Kralovec CZE

Belarus	0
Romania	0

BLR: Yuriy ZHEVNOV - Aleksandr YUREVICH, Igor SHITOV, Sergey OMELYANCHUK, Aleksandr MARTINOVICH, Aleksandr KULCHIY, Sergey KISLYAK, Aliaksandr HLEB (Anton PUTSILA 73), Vitaliy KUTUZOV (Sergey KRIVETS 87), Sergey KORNILENKO, Vitaliy RODIONOV 76), Vyatcheslav HLEB. Tr: Bernd STANGE

ROU: Costel PANTILIMON - Gabriel TAMAS, Razvan RAT, Mirel RADOI•, Vasile MAFTEI•, Cristian CHIVU, Gabriel TORJE (Razvan COCIS 46), George FLORESCU, Ciprian DEAC• (Ciprian MARICA 83), Bogdan STANCU (Daniel NICULAE 73), Marius BILASCO. Tr: Razvan LUCESCU

QEMAL STAFA, TITANA
7-09-2010, Att: 10 000, Ref: Trutz SVK

Albania	1
Luxembourg	0

ALB - Salihi [37]

ALB: Arian BEQAJ - Armend DALLKU, Debatik CURRI, Ervin SKELA, Gjergj MUZAKA (Jahmir HYKA 80), Klodian DURO (Andi LILA 90), Lorik CANA, Ansi AGOLLI, Ervin BULKU•, Hamdi SALIHI, Erjon BOGDANI•. Tr: Josip KUZE

LUX: Jonathan JOUBERT - Tom SCHNELL, Kim KINTZIGER, Eric HOFFMANN, Guy BLAISE, Rene PETERS•, Ben PAYAL, Gilles BETTMER (Dan COLLETTE 90), Mario MUTSCH••58, Tom LATERZA (Massimo MARTINO 81). Tr: Luc HOLTZ

KOSEVO, SARAJEVO
7-09-2010, Att: 28 000, Ref: Brych GER

Bosnia-Herzegovina	0
France	2

FRA - Benzema [72], Malouda [78]

BIH: Kenan HASAGIC - Emir SPAHIC, Safet NADAREVIC, Mensur MUJDZA, Elvir RAHIMIC (Sanel JAHIC 74), Miralem PJANIC•, Senad LULIC, Senijad IBRICIC•, Zvjezdan MISIMOVIC, Vedad IBISEVIC (Ermin ZEC 74), Edin DZEKO. Tr: Safet SUSIC

FRA: Hugo LLORIS - Bacary SAGNA, Adil RAMI, Philippe MEXES, Gael CLICHY, Florent MALOUDA (Blaise MATUIDI 80), Yann M'VILA, Alou DIARRA, Abou DIABY, Matthieu VALBUENA•, Karim BENZEMA. Tr: Laurent BLANC

UEFA EURO 2012 POLAND/UKRAINE QUALIFYING GROUP D

JOSY BARTHEL, LUXEMBOURG
8-10-2010, Att: 1857, Ref: Stavrev MKD

Luxembourg	0
Belarus	0

LUX: Jonathan JOUBERT - Eric HOFFMANN, Guy BLAISE, Tom SCHNELL, Kim KINTZIGER•, Gilles BETTMER (Lars GERSON 62), Rene PETERS, Ben PAYAL (Michel KETTENMEYER 77), Tom LATERZA, Charles LEWECK, Aurelien JOACHIM (Daniel DA MOTA 66). Tr: Luc HOLTZ

BLR: Yuriy ZHEVNOV - Aleksandr YUREVICH (Dmitriy MOLOSH 88), Igor SHITOV, Sergey OMELYANCHUK, Aleksandr MARTINOVICH, Sergey KISLYAK, Jan TIGOREV (Anton PUTSILA 68), Aleksandr KULCHIY•, Tsimafei KALACHEV•, Vyatcheslav HLEB (Vitaliy RODIONOV 67), Sergey KORNILENKO♦69. Tr: Bernd STANGE

QEMAL STAFA, TITANA
8-10-2010, Att: 14 220, Ref: Jakobsson ISL

Albania	1
Bosnia-Herzegovina	1

ALB - Duro [45] • **BIH** - Ibisevic [21]

ALB: Arian BEQAJ - Kristi VANGJELI, Andi LILA, Armend DALLKU•, Gjergj MUZAKA (Gilman LIKA 66), Klodian DURO, Lorik CANA, Ansi AGOLLI, Ervin BULKU, Hamdi SALIHI, (Jahmir HYKA 85), Erjon BOGDANI• (Ervin SKELA 47). Tr: Josip KUZE

BIH: Kenan HASAGIC (Asmir BEGOVIC 47), Emir SPAHIC•, Mensur MUJDZA, Adnan MRAVAC• (Boris PANDZA 47), Elvir RAHIMIC, Miralem PJANIC, Zvjezdan MISIMOVIC, Haris MEDUNJANIN, Senad LULIC•, Vedad IBISEVIC, Edin DZEKO (Senijad IBRICIC 90). Tr: Safet SUSIC

STADE DE FRANCE, PARIS
9-10-2010, Att: 79 299, Ref: Proenca POR

France	2
Romania	0

FRA - Remy [83], Gourcuff [93+]

FRA: Hugo LLORIS - Anthony REVEILLERE, Adil RAMI, Philippe MEXES•, Gael CLICHY, Florent MALOUDA, Yann M'VILA, Alou DIARRA•, Samir NASRI (Yoann GOURCUFF 74), Matthieu VALBUENA (Loic REMY 68), Karim BENZEMA (Dimitri PAYET 86). Tr: Laurent BLANC

ROU: Costel PANTILIMON - Cristian SAPUNARU•, Razvan RAT, Mirel RADOI, Cristian CHIVU, Gabriel TAMAS, George FLORESCU•, Razvan COCIS (Mihai ROMAN 87), Ianis ZICU (Ciprian DEAC 46), Bogdan STANCU, Daniel NICULAE (Ciprian MARICA 63). Tr: Razvan LUCESCU

DINAMO, MINSK
12-10-2010, Att: 7000, Ref: Rasmussen DEN

Belarus	2
Albania	0

BLR - Rodionov [10], Krivets [77]

BLR: Yuriy ZHEVNOV - Igor SHITOV, Sergey OMELYANCHUK, Dmitriy MOLOSH• (Aleksandr YUREVICH 87), Aleksandr MARTINOVICH, Aleksandr KULCHIY (Sergey KRIVETS 75), Sergey KISLYAK, Jan TIGOREV, Anton PUTSILA• (Vyatcheslav HLEB 83), Tsimafei KALACHEV•, Vitaliy RODIONOV. Tr: Bernd STANGE

ALB: Arian BEQAJ - Kristi VANGJELI, Admir TELI, Andi LILA, Armend DALLKU••♦90, Ansi AGOLLI, Ervin SKELA• (Edmond KAPLLANI 81), Gilman LIKA• (Elis BAKAJ 76), Klodian DURO, Ervin BULKU (Gjergj MUZAKA 59), Hamdi SALIHI. Tr: Josip KUZE

STADE SAINT-SYMPHORIEN, METZ
12-10-2010, Att: 24 710, Ref: Jug SVN

France	2
Luxembourg	0

FRA - Benzema [22], Gourcuff [76]

FRA: Hugo LLORIS - Adil RAMI•, Anthony REVEILLERE, Gael CLICHY, Philippe MEXES, Yoann GOURCUFF, Florent MALOUDA (Samir NASRI 62), Abou DIABY, Alou DIARRA, Guillaume HOARAU (Loic REMY 72), Karim BENZEMA (Dimitri PAYET 62). Tr: Laurent BLANC

LUX: Jonathan JOUBERT - Eric HOFFMANN, Guy BLAISE, Tom SCHNELL, Ben PAYAL, Gilles BETTMER (Daniel DA MOTA 83), Rene PETERS••♦55, Mario MUTSCH•, Tom LATERZA (Jeff STRASSER 66), Aurelien JOACHIM (Joel KITENGE 52), Charles LEWECK. Tr: Luc HOLTZ

JOSY BARTHEL, LUXEMBOURG
25-03-2011, Att: 8400, Ref: Hagen NOR

Luxembourg	0
France	2

FRA - Mexes [28], Gourcuff [72]

LUX: Jonathan JOUBERT - Eric HOFFMANN, Guy BLAISE, Tom SCHNELL, Lars GERSON, Daniel DA MOTA 71), Gilles BETTMER, Ben PAYAL, Mario MUTSCH•, Tom LATERZA (Massimo MARTINO 54), Charles LEWECK (Jacques PLEIN 90), Aurelien JOACHIM. Tr: Luc HOLTZ

FRA: Hugo LLORIS - Adil RAMI, Philippe MEXES, Patrice EVRA, Bacary SAGNA, Yann M'VILA, Alou DIARRA•, Florent MALOUDA, Yann M'VILA, Yoann GOURCUFF, Franck RIBERY, Karim BENZEMA. Tr: Laurent BLANC

BILINO POLJE, ZENICA
26-03-2011, Att: 13 000, Ref: Teixeira ESP

Bosnia-Herzegovina	2
Romania	1

BIH - Ibisevic [63], Dzeko [83] • **ROU** - Marica [29]

BIH: Kenan HASAGIC - Emir SPAHIC, Mensur MUJDZA, Adnan MRAVAC, Elvir RAHIMIC•, Miralem PJANIC, Zvjezdan MISIMOVIC (Senijad IBRICIC 81), Haris MEDUNJANIN (Darko MALETIC 71), Senad LULIC, Vedad IBISEVIC• (Zlatan MUSLIMOVIC 76), Edin DZEKO. Tr: Safet SUSIC

ROU: Costel PANTILIMON - Gabriel TAMAS, Razvan RAT, Cornel RAPA, Dorin GOIAN, George FLORESCU (Adrian ROPOTAN 76), Ciprian DEAC (Ianis ZICU 85), Dan ALEXA, Gabriel TORJE (Razvan COCIS 71), Adrian MUTU, Ciprian MARICA. Tr: Razvan LUCESCU

QEMAL STAFA, TITANA
26-03-2011, Att: 13 826, Ref: Strombergsson

Albania	1
Belarus	0

ALB - Salihi [62]

ALB: Samir UJKANI - Kristi VANGJELI, Admir TELI, Andi LILA, Ervin SKELA (Klodian DURO 80), Altin LALA•, Lorik CANA•, Ansi AGOLLI, Ervin BULKU, Hamdi SALIHI• (Gjergj MUZAKA 90), Erjon BOGDANI (Elis BAKAJ 75). Tr: Josip KUZE

BLR: Sergey VEREMKO - Igor SHITOV•, Sergey OMELYANCHUK, Dmitriy MOLOSH•, Aleksandr MARTINOVICH, Jan TIGOREV, Anton PUTSILA (Pavel SITKO 82), Aleksandr KULCHIY• (Aleksandr BYCHENOK 62), Sergey KRIVETS (Leonid KOVEL 46), Sergey KISLYAK, Vyatcheslav HLEB•. Tr: Bernd STANGE

CEAHLAUL, PIATRA NEAMT
29-03-2011, Att: 13 500, Ref: Gocek TUR

Romania	3
Luxembourg	1

ROU - Mutu 2 [24][68], Zicu [78] • **LUX** - Gerson [22]

ROU: Ciprian TATARUSANU - Gabriel TAMAS• (Dorin GOIAN 65), Cristian SAPUNARU, Razvan RAT, Florin GARDOS, Ianis ZICU, Adrian ROPOTAN•, Gabriel MURESAN, Bogdan STANCU (Gabriel TORJE 46), Adrian MUTU (Marius ALEXE 84), Ciprian MARICA. Tr: Razvan LUCESCU

LUX: Jonathan JOUBERT - Tom SCHNELL (Massimo MARTINO 90), Eric HOFFMANN, Guy BLAISE•, Rene PETERS, Ben PAYAL, Lars GERSON (Daniel DA MOTA 59), Gilles BETTMER (Tom LATERZA 81), Mario MUTSCH•, Charles LEWECK, Aurelien JOACHIM. Tr: Luc HOLTZ

STADIONUL GIULESTI, BUCHAREST
3-06-2011, Att: 8200, Ref: Eriksson SWE

Romania	3
Bosnia-Herzegovina	0

ROU - Mutu [37], Marica 2 [41][55]

ROU: Ciprian TATARUSANU - Gabriel TAMAS, Cristian SAPUNARU•, Razvan RAT, Paul PAPP, Gabriel MURESAN, Alexandru BOURCEANU, Gabriel TORJE•, Lucian SANMARTEAN (Cristian TANASE 64), Ciprian MARICA (Marius ALEXE 87), Adrian MUTU (Romeo SURDU• 83). Tr: Razvan LUCESCU

BIH: Kenan HASAGIC - Emir SPAHIC, Mensur MUJDZA, Adnan MRAVAC, Senijad IBRICIC (Sime STILIC• 64), Elvir RAHIMIC, Miralem PJANIC, Zvjezdan MISIMOVIC, Haris MEDUNJANIN (Vedad IBISEVIC 46), Senad LULIC, Edin DZEKO (Zlatan MUSLIMOVIC 64). Tr: Safet SUSIC

DINAMO, MINSK
3-06-2011, Att: 26 500, Ref: Fernandez ESP

Belarus	1
France	1

BLR - OG [20] • **FRA** - Malouda [22]

BLR: Sergey VEREMKO• - Dmitriy VERKHOVTSOV, Vitaliy TRUBILA, Igor SHITOV, Sergey OMELYANCHUK, Aleksandr MARTINOVICH, Maksim BORDACHEV, Jan TIGOREV, Anton PUTSILA (Sergey KISLYAK 86), Tsimafei KALACHEV• (Vyatcheslav HLEB 90), Andrey VORONKOV. Tr: Bernd STANGE

FRA: Hugo LLORIS - Eric ABIDAL, Mamadou SAKHO, Bacary SAGNA•, Adil RAMI•, Franck RIBERY, Samir NASRI, Florent MALOUDA, Alou DIARRA, Abou DIABY (Loic REMY 73), Karim BENZEMA. Tr: Laurent BLANC

DINAMO, MINSK
7-06-2011, Att: 9500, Ref: Salmanov AZE

Belarus	0
Luxembourg	2

BLR - Kornilenko [48p], Putilo [73]

BLR: Yuriy ZHEVNOV - Dmitriy VERKHOVTSOV, Vitaliy TRUBILA (Vyatcheslav HLEB 62), Igor SHITOV, Sergey OMELYANCHUK, Maksim BORDACHEV, Jan TIGOREV, Anton PUTSILA, Aleksandr KULCHIY (Sergey KISLYAK 87), Tsimafei KALACHEV, Andrey VORONKOV• (Sergey KORNILENKO 46). Tr: Bernd STANGE

LUX: Jonathan JOUBERT - Tom SCHNELL, Massimo MARTINO, Kevin MALGET (Joel KITENGE 61), Eric HOFFMANN, Guy BLAISE•, Rene PETERS, Ben PAYAL•, Lars GERSON, Charles LEWECK (Dan COLLETTE 84), Daniel DA MOTA (Tom LATERZA 77). Tr: Luc HOLTZ

PART THREE – THE CONTINENTAL CONFEDERATIONS

BILINO POLJE, ZENICA
7-06-2011, Att: 9000, Ref: Blom NED

Bosnia-Herzegovina	2
Albania	0

BIH - Medunjanin [67], Maletic [91+]

BIH: Kenan HASAGIC - Emir SPAHIC•, Boris PANDZA, Mensur MUJDZA (Darko MALETIC• 73), Elvir RAHIMIC, Miralem PJANIC (Muhamed BESIC 77), Zvjezdan MISIMOVIC, Haris MEDUNJANIN, Senad LULIC, Vedad IBISEVIC (Zlatan MUSLIMOVIC 61), Edin DZEKO. Tr: Safet SUSIC

ALB: Samir UJKANI - Kristi VANGJELI, Armend DALLKU, Debatik CURRI, Ervin SKELA, Altin LALA (Gjergj MUZAKA 72), Lorik CANA, Ansi AGOLLI (Andi LILA 60◆87), Ervin BULKU, Hamdi SALIHI, Erjon BOGDANI (Klodian DURO• 46). Tr: Josip KUZE

JOSY BARTHEL, LUXEMBOURG
2-09-2011, Att: 2812, Ref: Karasev RUS

Luxembourg	0
Romania	2

ROU - Torje 2 [34] [45]

LUX: Jonathan JOUBERT - Tom SCHNELL, Eric HOFFMANN (Ante BUKVIC 76), Guy BLAISE, Ben PAYAL, Lars GERSON, Gilles BETTMER, Mario MUTSCH, Charles LEWECK, Aurelien JOACHIM (Joel KITENGE 46), Daniel DA MOTA (Mathias JANISCH 61). Tr: Luc HOLTZ

ROU: Ciprian TATARUSANU - Razvan RAT, Alexandru MATEL, Dorin GOIAN•, George GALAMAZ (Vlad CHIRICHES 61), Gabriel TORJE• (Daniel NICULAE• 76), Cristian TANASE, Costin LAZAR, Razvan COCIS, Ciprian MARICA (Bogdan STANCU 86), Gheorghe BUCUR. Tr: Victor PITURCA

DINAMO, MINSK
2-09-2011, Att: 28 500, Ref: Kassai HUN

Belarus	0
Bosnia-Herzegovina	2

BIH - Salihovic [22p], Medunjanin [24]

BLR: Yuriy ZHEVNOV - Dmitriy VERKHOVTSOV, Vitaliy TRUBILA, Igor SHITOV, Aleksandr MARTINOVICH, Anton PUTSILA, Aleksandr KULCHIY, Sergey KISLYAK, Maksim ZHAVNERCHIK (Pavel SITKO 63), Tsimafei KALACHEV, Sergey KORNILENKO (Andrey VORONKOV 63). Tr: Bernd STANGE

BIH: Kenan HASAGIC - Emir SPAHIC•, Sasa PAPAC•, Boris PANDZA, Adnan ZAHIROVIC, Elvir RAHIMIC, Miralem PJANIC•, Haris MEDUNJANIN (Zlatan MUSLIMOVIC 88), Senad LULIC, Sejad SALIHOVIC (Darko MALETIC 72), Edin DZEKO (Zvjezdan MISIMOVIC 80). Tr: Safet SUSIC

QEMAL STAFA, TITANA
2-09-2011, Att: 15 600, Ref: Nikolaev RUS

Albania	1
France	2

ALB - Bogdani [46] • **FRA** - Benzema [11], M'Vila [18]

ALB: Samir UJKANI - Kristi VANGJELI, Admir TELI•, Armend DALLKU•, Debatik CURRI (Altin LALA 24), Ansi AGOLLI, Ervin SKELA (Jahmir HYKA 46), Lorik CANA•, Ervin BULKU (Elis BAKAJ 70), Hamdi SALIHI, Erjon BOGDANI. Tr: Josip KUZE

FRA: Hugo LLORIS - Eric ABIDAL, Anthony REVEILLERE•, Younes KABOUL, Patrice EVRA, Franck RIBERY, Samir NASRI, Florent MALOUDA (Marvin MARTIN 82), Yann M'VILA, Alou DIARRA, Karim BENZEMA. Tr: Laurent BLANC

BILINO POLJE, ZENICA
6-09-2011, Att: 12 000, Ref: Atkinson ENG

Bosnia-Herzegovina	1
Belarus	0

BIH - Misimovic 87

BIH: Asmir BEGOVIC - Sasa PAPAC, Boris PANDZA• (Zvjezdan MISIMOVIC 46), Mensur MUJDZA, Adnan ZAHIROVIC•, Elvir RAHIMIC, Haris MEDUNJANIN, Senad LULIC, Senijad IBRICIC (Ermin ZEC 64), Sejad SALIHOVIC• (Semir STILIC 19), Edin DZEKO. Tr: Safet SUSIC

BLR: Yuriy ZHEVNOV - Dmitriy VERKHOVTSOV, Vitaliy TRUBILA•, Aleksandr MARTINOVICH••◆85, Igor SHITOV•, Pavel SITKO (Andrey VORONKOV 77), Anton PUTSILA•, Aleksandr KULCHIY, Sergey KISLYAK, Tsimafei KALACHEV••◆34, Sergey KORNILENKO•. Tr: Bernd STANGE

JOSY BARTHEL, LUXEMBOURG
6-09-2011, Att: 2132, Ref: Kari FIN

Luxembourg	2
Albania	1

LUX - Bettmer [27], Joachim [78] • **ALB** - Bogdani [64]

LUX: Jonathan JOUBERT - Tom SCHNELL•, Mathias JANISCH, Ante BUKVIC, Guy BLAISE, Ben PAYAL (Joel PEDRO 88), Lars GERSON, Gilles BETTMER, Mario MUTSCH, Charles LEWECK (Aurelien JOACHIM 68), Daniel DA MOTA (Stefano BENSI 70). Tr: Luc HOLTZ

ALB: Samir UJKANI - Franc VELIU (Ervin BULKU 62), Kristi VANGJELI, Admir TELI•, Ervin SKELA, Altin LALA•, Klodian DURO (Gjergj MUZAKA 46), Ansi AGOLLI◆54, Hamdi SALIHI, Edmond KAPLLANI (Elis BAKAJ 46), Erjon BOGDANI••◆85. Tr: Josip KUZE

NATIONAL, BUCHAREST
6-09-2011, Att: 49 137, Ref: Webb ENG

Romania	0
France	0

ROU: Ciprian TATARUSANU - Cristian SAPUNARU, Razvan RAT, Dorin GOIAN•, Vlad CHIRICHES, Cristian TANASE•, Costin LAZAR (Bogdan STANCU 44), Razvan COCIS•, Alexandru BOURCEANU, Banel NICOLITA•, Ciprian MARICA (Gheorghe BUCUR 90). Tr: Victor PITURCA

FRA: Hugo LLORIS - Adil RAMI, Patrice EVRA, Eric ABIDAL, Bacary SAGNA, Marvin MARTIN, Yann M'VILA•, Yohan CABAYE (Samir NASRI 75), Matthieu VALBUENA (Loic REMY 71), Franck RIBERY, Karim BENZEMA. Tr: Laurent BLANC

BILINO POLJE, ZENICA
7-10-2011, Att: 12 000, Ref: Evans WAL

Bosnia-Herzegovina	5
Luxembourg	0

BIH - Dzeko [12], Misimovic 2 [15] [22p], Pjanic [36], Medunjanin [51]

BIH: Asmir BEGOVIC - Sasa PAPAC, Mensur MUJDZA, Emir SPAHIC, Miralem PJANIC, Zvjezdan MISIMOVIC, Haris MEDUNJANIN (Senijad IBRICIC 64), Senad LULIC (Darko MALETIC 66), Elvir RAHIMIC (Adnan ZAHIROVIC 59), Vedad IBISEVIC, Edin DZEKO. Tr: Safet SUSIC

LUX: Jonathan JOUBERT - Ante BUKVIC•, Guy BLAISE, Tom SCHNELL, Lars GERSON, Gilles BETTMER, Ben PAYAL, Mario MUTSCH•, Tom LATERZA (Mathias JANISCH 83), Charles LEWECK, Daniel DA MOTA (Aurelien JOACHIM 44). Tr: Luc HOLTZ

NATIONAL, BUCHAREST
7-10-2012, Att: 29 486, Kelly IRL

Romania	2
Belarus	2

ROU - Mutu 2 [19] [51p] • **BLR** - Kornilenko [45], Dragun [82]

ROU: Costel PANTILIMON - Gabriel TAMAS, Razvan RAT•, Cosmin MOTI•, Alexandru MATEL, Gabriel TORJE, Lucian SANMARTEAN (Adrian CRISTEA 28), Costin LAZAR (Razvan COCIS 70), Alexandru BOURCEANU, Adrian MUTU, Ciprian MARICA (Bogdan STANCU 80). Tr: Victor PITURCA

BLR: Yuriy ZHEVNOV - Dmitriy VERKHOVTSOV•, Sergey OMELYANCHUK, Egor FILIPENKO (Pavel PLASKONNY 20), Maksim BORDACHEV (Oleg VERETILO 90), Aleksandr KULCHIY, Sergey KRIVETS (Filipp RUDIK 60), Sergey KISLYAK, Pavel NEKHAYCHIK, Stanislav DRAGUN, Sergey KORNILENKO•. Tr: Bernd STANGE

STADE DE FRANCE, PARIS
7-10-2011, Att: 65 239, Ref: Koukoulakis GRE

France	3
Albania	0

FRA - Malouda [11], Remy [38], Reveillere [67]

FRA: Hugo LLORIS - Adil RAMI•, Younes KABOUL, Patrice EVRA (Anthony REVEILLERE 46), Mathieu DEBUCHY•, Samir NASRI, Florent MALOUDA, Yann M'VILA, Yohan CABAYE (Marvin MARTIN 47), Loic REMY•, Bafetimbi GOMIS (Djibril CISSE 79). Tr: Laurent BLANC

ALB: Samir UJKANI - Kristi VANGJELI•, Andi LILA•, Armend DALLKU, Odise ROSHI, Gjergj MUZAKA (Ahmed JANUZI 73), Gilman LIKA (Sabien LILAJ 81), Jahmir HYKA (Elis BAKAJ 63), Klodian DURO•, Lorik CANA•, Hamdi SALIHI. Tr: Josip KUZE

QEMAL STAFA, TITANA
11-10-2011, Att: 3000, Ref: Mazeika LTU

Albania	1
Romania	1

ALB - Salihi [24] • **ROU** - Luchin [77]

ALB: Samir UJKANI - Admir TELI, Andi LILA, Armend DALLKU, Lorik CANA, Odise ROSHI (Gjergj MUZAKA 77), Sabien LILAJ, Altin LALA, Erjon BOGDANI (Ahmed JANUZI• 46), Elis BAKAJ (Jahmir HYKA 67), Hamdi SALIHI. Tr: Josip KUZE

ROU: Silviu LUNG JR - Dorin GOIAN, Gabriel TAMAS•, Srdjan LUCHIN, Iasmin LATOVLEVICI, Razvan COCIS, Alexandru BOURCEANU, Banel NICOLITA• (Gabriel TORJE 63), Costin LAZAR (Gheorghe BUCUR 87), Adrian MUTU, Ciprian MARICA (Bogdan STANCU 49). Tr: Victor PITURCA

STADE DE FRANCE, PARIS
11-10-2011, Att: 78 467, Ref: Thomson SCO

France	1
Bosnia-Herzegovina	1

FRA - Nasri [78p] • **BIH** - Dzeko [40]

FRA: Hugo LLORIS - Patrice EVRA•, Eric ABIDAL, Anthony REVEILLERE•, Adil RAMI, Samir NASRI, Florent MALOUDA (Marvin MARTIN 61), Yann M'VILA, Yohan CABAYE• (Kevin GAMEIRO 61), Jeremy MENEZ, Loic REMY (Alou DIARRA• 82). Tr: Laurent BLANC

BIH: Kenan HASAGIC (Asmir BEGOVIC 46), Sasa PAPAC•, Boris PANDZA•, Mensur MUJDZA• (Darko MALETIC 61), Emir SPAHIC•, Miralem PJANIC, Zvjezdan MISIMOVIC, Haris MEDUNJANIN (Adnan ZAHIROVIC 71), Senad LULIC, Elvir RAHIMIC, Edin DZEKO. Tr: Safet SUSIC

UEFA EURO 2012 POLAND/UKRAINE QUALIFYING GROUP E

	GROUP E	PL	W	D	L	F	A	PTS	NED	SWE	HUN	FIN	MDV	SMR
1	Netherlands	10	9	0	1	37	8	27		4-1	5-3	2-1	1-0	11-0
2	Sweden	10	8	0	2	31	11	24	3-2		2-0	5-0	2-1	6-0
3	Hungary	10	6	1	3	22	14	19	0-4	2-1		0-0	2-1	8-0
4	Finland	10	3	1	6	16	16	10	0-2	1-2	1-2		4-1	8-0
5	Moldova	10	3	0	7	12	16	9	0-1	1-4	0-2	2-0		4-0
6	San Marino	10	0	0	10	0	53	0	0-5	0-5	0-3	0-1	0-2	

Netherlands qualified directly for the finals • Sweden qualified also as the second-placed team with the best record

---

ZIMBRU, CHISINAU
3-09-2010, Att: 10 300, Ref: Malek POL

Moldova	2
Finland	0

MDA - Suvorov [69], Doros [74]

MDA: Stanislav NAMASCO - Alexandru EPUREANU, Simeon BULGARU, Vitali BORDIAN, Igor TIGIRLAS• (Igor BUGAEV 69), Alexey SAVINOV, Nicolae JOSAN (Alexandru SUVOROV 58), Vadim BORET, Eugen CEBOTARU, Viorel FRUNZA, Anatoli DOROS (Valeriu ANDRONIC •75). Tr: Gavril BALINT

FIN: Otto FREDRIKSON - Petri PASANEN, Niklas MOISANDER, Sami HYYPIA♦36, Roman EREMENKO, Alexei EREMENKO (Mikael FORSSELL 81), Tim SPARV, Markus HEIKKINEN, Roni POROKARA (Mika VAYRYNEN 75), Jari LITMANEN (Kasper HAMALAINEN 46), Jonatan JOHANSSON. Tr: Stuart BAXTER

RASUNDA, STOCKHOLM
3-09-2010, Att: 32 304, Ref: Atkinson ENG

Sweden	2
Hungary	0

SWE - Wernbloom 2 [51] [73]

SWE: Andreas ISAKSSON (Johan WILAND 46), Behrang SAFARI, Olof MELLBERG, Daniel MAJSTOROVIC, Mikael LUSTIG, Pontus WERNBLOOM, Anders SVENSSON (Kim KALLSTROM 33), Emir BAJRAMI, Ola TOIVONEN•, Zlatan IBRAHIMOVIC, Johan ELMANDER (Sebastian LARSSON 49). Tr: Erik HAMREN

HUN: Gabor KIRALY• - Zoltan LIPTAK•, Pal LAZAR•, Roland JUHASZ, Krisztian VADOCZ, Zsolt LACZKO•, Vladimir KOMAN, Akos ELEK (Tamas PRISKIN 59), Balazs DZSUDZSAK (Szabolcs HUSZTI 46), Gergely RUDOLF (Tamas HAJNAL 82), Zoltan GERA. Tr: Sandor EGERVARI

STADIO OLIMPICO, SERRAVALLE
3-09-2010, Att: 4127, Ref: Evans WAL

San Marino	0
Netherlands	5

NED - Kuyt [16p], Huntelaar 3 [38] [48] [66], Van Nistelrooy [90]

SMR: Aldo SIMONCINI - Fabio VITAIOLI, Carlo VALENTINI, Davide SIMONCINI• (Simone BACCIOCCHI• 61), Alessandro DELLA VALLE•, Maicol BERRETTI•, Damiano VANNUCCI, Pier Filipo MAZZA, Andy SELVA, Manuel MARANI (Alex GASPERONI 76), Matteo VITAIOLI (Nicola CIACCI 82). Tr: Giampaolo MAZZA

NED: Maarten STEKELENBURG - Gregory VAN DER WIEL, Erik PIETERS, Joris MATHIJSEN, Hedwiges MADURO•, Mark VAN BOMMEL, Nigel DE JONG (Rafael VAN DER VAART 46), Wesley SNEIJDER, Dirk KUYT (Ruud VAN NISTELROOY 68), Klaas-Jan HUNTELAAR, Eljero ELIA (Ibrahim AFELLAY 59). Tr: Bert VAN MARWIJK

SWEDBANK STADION, MALMO
7-09-2010, Att: 21 083, Ref: McKeon IRL

Sweden	6
San Marino	0

SWE - Ibrahimovic 2 [7] [77], OG 2 [11] [26], Granqvist [51], Berg [92+]

SWE: Johan WILAND - Behrang SAFARI, Olof MELLBERG♦34, Daniel MAJSTOROVIC, Mikael LUSTIG, Pontus WERNBLOOM (Johan ELMANDER 69), Sebastian LARSSON, Kim KALLSTROM, Emir BAJRAMI, Ola TOIVONEN (Andreas GRANQVIST 47), Zlatan IBRAHIMOVIC (Marcus BERG 82). Tr: Erik HAMREN

SMR: Aldo SIMONCINI - Fabio VITAIOLI•, Davide SIMONCINI, Alessandro DELLA VALLE, Nicola CHIARUZZI (Alex GASPERONI 73), Simone BACCIOCCHI (Carlo VALENTINI 79), Damiano VANNUCCI, Pier Filipo MAZZA, Andy SELVA, Manuel MARANI• (Maicol BERRETTI 56), Matteo VITAIOLI. Tr: Giampaolo MAZZA

SZUSZA FERENC, BUDAPEST
7-09-2010, Att: 9209, Ref: Kovarik CZE

Hungary	2
Moldova	1

HUN - Rudolf [50], Koman [66] • MDA - Suvorov [79]

HUN: Gabor KIRALY - Zoltan LIPTAK•, Pal LAZAR•, Roland JUHASZ, Zsolt LACZKO, Vladimir KOMAN (Krisztian VADOCZ 88), Akos ELEK, Balazs DZSUDZSAK, Peter CZVITKOVICS (Adam SZALAI 46), Gergely RUDOLF (Vilmos VANCZAK 64), Zoltan GERA. Tr: Sandor EGERVARI

MDA: Stanislav NAMASCO - Alexandru EPUREANU, Simeon BULGARU, Vitali BORDIAN, Vadim BOLOHAN, Igor TIGIRLAS, Petru RACU, Nicolae JOSAN (Anatoli DOROS 59), Alexandru SUVOROV, Eugen CEBOTARU (Andrei COJOCARI 71), Viorel FRUNZA• (Igor BUGAEV 84). Tr: Gavril BALINT

DE KUIP, ROTTERDAM
7-09-2010, Att: 25 000, Ref: Nikolaev RUS

Netherlands	2
Finland	1

NED - Huntelaar 2 [7] [16p] • FIN - Forssell [18]

NED: Maarten STEKELENBURG - Gregory VAN DER WIEL, Joris MATHIJSEN, Johnny HEITINGA, Rafael VAN DER VAART (Eljero ELIA 64), Mark VAN BOMMEL, Nigel DE JONG, Wesley SNEIJDER, Ibrahim AFELLAY (Jeremain LENS 74), Vurnon ANITA, Klaas-Jan HUNTELAAR (Ruud VAN NISTELROOY 62). Tr: Bert VAN MARWIJK

FIN: Otto FREDRIKSON - Petri PASANEN, Veli LAMPI, Mika VAYRYNEN, Tim SPARV•, Daniel SJOLUND (Jonatan JOHANSSON 69), Markus HEIKKINEN•, Kasper HAMALAINEN (Roni POROKARA 46), Roman EREMENKO•, Mikael FORSSELL (Alexei EREMENKO 80). Tr: Stuart BAXTER

PUSKAS FERENC, BUDAPEST
8-10-2010, Att: 10 596, Ref: Kaasik EST

Hungary	8
San Marino	0

HUN - Rudolf 2 [11] [25], Szalai 3 [18] [27] [48], Koman [60], Dzsudzsak [89], Gera [93+p]

HUN: Gabor KIRALY - Krisztian VERMES, Vilmos VANCZAK, Roland JUHASZ, Zsolt LACZKO, Vladimir KOMAN (Peter CZVITKOVICS 78), Akos ELEK (Krisztian VADOCZ 63), Balazs DZSUDZSAK, Adam SZALAI (Tamas PRISKIN 63), Gergely RUDOLF, Zoltan GERA. Tr: Sandor EGERVARI

SMR: Aldo SIMONCINI - Fabio VITAIOLI, Alessandro DELLA VALLE•, Carlo VALENTINI••♦90, Maicol BERRETTI, Simone BACCIOCCHI (Nicola ALBANI 52), Damiano VANNUCCI, Fabio BOLLINI (Michele CERVELLINI 84), Paolo MONTAGNA, Manuel MARANI, Matteo VITAIOLI (Matteo BUGLI 77). Tr: Giampaola MAZZA

ZIMBRU STADIUM, CHISINAU
8-10-2010, Att: 10 500, Ref: Meyer GER

Moldova	0
Netherlands	1

NED - Huntelaar [37]

MDA: Stanislav NAMASCO - Alexandru EPUREANU, Simeon BULGARU, Vitali BORDIAN, Vadim BOLOHAN, Victor GOLOVATENCO, Petru RACU, Alexandru SUVOROV, Eugen CEBOTARU (Valeriu ANDRONIC 69), Viorel FRUNZA (Igor BUGAEV 46), Anatoli DOROS (Nicolae JOSAN 78). Tr: Gavril BALINT

NED: Maarten STEKELENBURG - Gregory VAN DER WIEL, Erik PIETERS, Joris MATHIJSEN, Johnny HEITINGA, Rafael VAN DER VAART, Mark VAN BOMMEL, Wesley SNEIJDER, Ibrahim AFELLAY (Urby EMANUELSON 90), Dirk KUYT, Klaas-Jan HUNTELAAR. Tr: Bert VAN MARWIJK

OLYMPIC, HELSINKI
12-10-2010, Att: 18 532, Ref: Kelly IRL

Finland	1
Hungary	2

FIN - Forssell [86] • HUN - Szalai [50], Dzsudzsak [94+]

FIN: Jussi JAASKELAINEN - Petri PASANEN, Niklas MOISANDER, Sami HYYPIA, Mika VAYRYNEN•, Tim SPARV, Alexei EREMENKO 71), Daniel SJOLUND (Shefki KUQI 81), Markus HEIKKINEN, Roman EREMENKO, Roni POROKARA (Jari LITMANEN 71), Mikael FORSSELL. Tr: Stuart BAXTER

HUN: Gabor KIRALY - Krisztian VERMES, Zoltan LIPTAK•, Vilmos VANCZAK, Krisztian VADOCZ (Adam PINTER 74), Zsolt LACZKO (Vilmos VANCZAK 87), Akos ELEK•, Balazs DZSUDZSAK, Adam SZALAI, Gergely RUDOLF (Vladimir KOMAN 47), Zoltan GERA. Tr: Sandor EGERVARI

AMSTERDAM ARENA, AMSTERDAM
12-10-2010, Att: 46 000, Ref: Lannoy FRA

Netherlands	4
Sweden	1

NED - Huntelaar 2 [4 55], Afellay 2 [37 59] •
SWE - Granqvist [69]

NED: Maarten STEKELENBURG - Gregory VAN DER WIEL, Erik PIETERS, Joris MATHIJSEN, Johnny HEITINGA, Rafael VAN DER VAART, Mark VAN BOMMEL (Wout BRAMA 72), Wesley SNEIJDER, Ibrahim AFELLAY, Dirk KUYT (Jeremain LENS 29), Klaas-Jan HUNTELAAR (Ruud VAN NISTELROOY 85). Tr: Bert Van MARWIJK

SWE: Andreas ISAKSSON - Behrang SAFARI (Oscar WENDT 46), Daniel MAJSTOROVIC, Mikael LUSTIG, Andreas GRANQVIST, Pontus WERNBLOOM (Kim KALLSTROM 54), Anders SVENSSON, Sebastian LARSSON•, Ola TOIVONEN• (Marcus BERG 79), Zlatan IBRAHIMOVIC, Johan ELMANDER. Tr: Erik HAMREN

STADIO OLIMPICO, SERRAVALLE
12-10-2010, Att: 714, Ref: Courtney NIR

San Marino	0
Moldova	2

MDA - Josan [20], Doros [86p]

SMR: Aldo SIMONCINI - Davide SIMONCINI, Simone BACCIOCCHI•, Fabio VITAIOLI, Damiano VANNUCCI, Michele CERVELLINI (Maicol BERRETTI 60), Fabio BOLLINI (Nicola CIACCI• 67), Pier Filipo MAZZA, Paolo MONTAGNA (Matteo COPPINI 82), Manuel MARANI, Matteo VITAIOLI•. Tr: Giampaolo MAZZA

MDA: Stanislav NAMASCO - Alexandru EPUREANU, Vitali BORDIAN, Victor GOLOVATENCO, Nicolae JOSAN (Denis ZMEU 69), Andrei COJOCARI• (Alexey SAVINOV 82), Vadim BORET, Valeriu ANDRONIC, Alexandru SUVOROV, Viorel FRUNZA, Igor BUGAEV (Anatoli DOROS 62). Tr: Gavril BALINT

OLYMPIC, HELSINKI
17-11-2010, Att: 8192, Ref: Matejek CZE

Finland	8
San Marino	0

FIN - Vayrynen [39], Hamalainen 2 [49 67], Forssell 3 [51 59 78], Litmanen [71p], Porokara [73]

FIN: Otto FREDRIKSON - Petri PASANEN, Niklas MOISANDER, Veli LAMPI, Mika VAYRYNEN, Daniel SJOLUND (Jari LITMANEN 46), Markus HEIKKINEN, Kasper HAMALAINEN (Roni POROKARA 70), Roman EREMENKO• Alexei EREMENKO (Shefki KUQI 80), Mikael FORSSELL. Tr: Olli HUTTUNEN

SMR: Aldo SIMONCINI - Fabio VITAIOLI (Damiano VANNUCCI 72), Alessandro DELLA VALLE, Maicol BERRETTI (Alex DELLA VALLE 67), Michele CERVELLINI, Matteo BUGLI, Matteo COPPINI, Andy SELVA•, Paolo MONTAGNA (Manuel MARANI 79), Nicola ALBANI•, Matteo VITAIOLI. Tr: Giampaolo MAZZA

PUSKAS FERENC, BUDAPEST
25-03-2011, Att: 25 311, Ref: Velasco ESP

Hungary	0
Netherlands	4

NED - Van der Vaart [8], Afellay [45], Kuyt [54], Van Persie [62]

HUN: Gabor KIRALY - Vilmos VANCZAK•, Zoltan LIPTAK•, Roland JUHASZ, Jozsef VARGA (Krisztian VADOCZ 46), Zsolt LACZKO, Vladimir KOMAN• (Peter CZVITKOVICS 46), Akos ELEK• (Tamas PRISKIN 79), Balazs DZSUDZSAK, Gergely RUDOLF, Zoltan GERA. Tr: Sandor EGERVARI

NED: Michel VORM - Gregory VAN DER WIEL, Erik PIETERS, Joris MATHIJSEN, Johnny HEITINGA, Rafael VAN DER VAART, Wesley SNEIJDER, Nigel DE JONG, Ibrahim AFELLAY (Eljero ELIA 63), Robin VAN PERSIE•, Dirk KUYT (Ruud VAN NISTELROOY 81). Tr: Bert VAN MARWIJK

RASUNDA, STOCKHOLM
29-03-2011, Att: 25 544, Ref: Kircher GER

Sweden	2
Moldova	1

SWE - Lustig [30], Larsson.S [82] •
MDA - Suvorov [92+]

SWE: Andreas ISAKSSON - Mikael ANTONSSON, Oscar WENDT, Mikael LUSTIG, Andreas GRANQVIST, Emir BAJRAMI (Martin OLSSON 72), Pontus WERNBLOOM• (Rasmus ELM 65), Sebastian LARSSON, Kim KALLSTROM•, Johan ELMANDER (Alexander GERNDT 89), Zlatan IBRAHIMOVIC. Tr: Erik HAMREN

MDA: Stanislav NAMASCO - Vadim BOLOHAN, Igor ARMAS, Victor GOLOVATENCO, Vadim BORET, Petru RACU, Alexandru GATCAN (Valeriu ANDRONIC 83), Alexandru SUVOROV, Eugen CEBOTARU, Viorel FRUNZA (Igor BUGAEV 46), Anatoli DOROS (Anatoli CHEPTINE 72). Tr: Gavril BALINT

AMSTERDAM ARENA, AMSTERDAM
29-03-2011, Att: 51 700, Ref: Moen NOR

Netherlands	5
Hungary	3

NED - Van Persie [13], Sneijder [61], V. Nistelrooy [73], Kuyt 2 [78 81] • HUN - Rudolf [46], Gera 2 [50 75]

NED: Michel VORM - Gregory VAN DER WIEL, Erik PIETERS (Urby EMANUELSON 64), Joris MATHIJSEN, Johnny HEITINGA, Rafael VAN DER VAART, Wesley SNEIJDER, Nigel DE JONG, Ibrahim AFELLAY, Robin VAN PERSIE (Ruud VAN NISTELROOY 46), Dirk KUYT (Eljero ELIA 90). Tr: Bert VAN MARWIJK

HUN: Marton FULOP - Vilmos VANCZAK, Adam PINTER• (Vladimir KOMAN 46), Pal LAZAR•, Roland JUHASZ•, Krisztian VADOCZ, Zsolt LACZKO, Balazs DZSUDZSAK, Gergely RUDOLF, Tamas PRISKIN, Zoltan GERA. Tr: Sandor EGERVARI

STADIO OLIMPICO, SERRAVALLE
3-06-2011, Att: 1218, Ref: Sipailo LVA

San Marino	0
Finland	1

FIN - Forssell [41]

SMR: Aldo SIMONCINI - Fabio VITAIOLI (Simone BACCIOCCHI 88), Davide SIMONCINI•, Alessandro DELLA VALLE•, Damiano VANNUCCI, Michele CERVELLINI, Fabio BOLLINI, Pier Filipo MAZZA (Maicol BERRETTI 77), Andy SELVA, Manuel MARANI, Matteo VITAIOLI (Paolo MONTAGNA 80). Tr: Giampaolo MAZZA

FIN: Lukas HRADECKY - Jukka RAITALA, Petri PASANEN, Niklas MOISANDER, Veli LAMPI, Mika Vayrynen, Perparim HETEMAJ (Daniel SJOLUND 84), Markus HEIKKINEN, Kasper HAMALAINEN, Alexei EREMENKO (Riku RISKI 68), Mikael FORSSELL (Berat SADIK 90). Tr: Mixu PAATELAINEN

ZIMBRU, CHISINAU
3-06-2011, Att: 10 500, Ref: Marriner ENG

Moldova	1
Sweden	4

MDA - Bugaev [61] • SWE - Toivonen [11], Elmander 2 [30 58], Gerndt [88]

MDA: Stanislav NAMASCO - Vadim BOLOHAN, Victor GOLOVATENCO, Petru RACU, Stanislav IVANOV, Alexandru GATCAN (Igor TIGIRLAS 46), Alexandru SUVOROV, Eugen CEBOTARU (Artur PATRAS 78), Igor BUGAEV, Anatoli DOROS (Gheorghe BOGHIU 63). Tr: Gavril BALINT

SWE: Andreas ISAKSSON - Olof MELLBERG, Daniel MAJSTOROVIC, Mikael LUSTIG, Oscar WENDT, Anders SVENSSON, Sebastian LARSSON, Kim KALLSTROM, Tobias HYSEN (Emir BAJRAMI 40), Ola TOIVONEN (Pontus WERNBLOOM 68), Johan ELMANDER (Alexander GERNDT 75). Tr: Erik HAMREN

RASUNDA, STOCKHOLM
7-06-2011, Att: 32 128, Ref: Gautier FRA

Sweden	5
Finland	0

SWE - Kallstrom [11], Ibrahimovic 3 [31 35 53], Bajrami [83]

SWE: Andreas ISAKSSON - Oscar WENDT, Olof MELLBERG, Daniel MAJSTOROVIC, Mikael LUSTIG, Anders SVENSSON, Sebastian Larsson (Christian WILHELMSSON 89), Kim KALLSTROM, Emir BAJRAMI, Ola TOIVONEN (Zlatan IBRAHIMOVIC 25), Johan ELMANDER (Pontus WERNBLOOM 81). Tr: Erik HAMREN

FIN: Anssi JAAKKOLA - Joona TOIVIO, Petri PASANEN, Niklas MOISANDER, Mika VAYRYNEN, Perparim HETEMAJ, Markus HEIKKINEN (Markus HALSTI 46), Kasper HAMALAINEN (Mika AARITALO 46), Roman EREMENKO, Alexei EREMENKO• (Alexander RING 79), Mikael FORSSELL. Tr: Mixu PAATELAINEN

STADIO OLIMPICO, SERRAVALLE
7-06-2011, Att: 1915, Ref: Radovanovic MNE

San Marino	0
Hungary	3

HUN - Liptak [40], Szabics [49], Koman [83]

SMR: Aldo SIMONCINI - Giacomo BENEDETTINI, Fabio VITAIOLI (Alex DELLA VALLE 46), Alessandro DELLA VALLE•, Michele CERVELLINI•, Fabio BOLLINI (Simone BACCIOCCHI 80), Damiano VANNUCCI, Pier Filipo MAZZA, Andy SELVA, Manuel MARANI (Maicol BERRETTI• 64), Matteo VITAIOLI. Tr: Giampaolo MAZZA

HUN: Gabor KIRALY - Vilmos VANCZAK•, Zoltan LIPTAK (Adam PINTER 87), Roland JUHASZ•, Tamas HAJNAL (Peter CZVITKOVICS 71), Akos ELEK, Balazs DZSUDZSAK, Zsolt LACZKO, Vladimir KOMAN, Imre SZABICS (Tamas KOLTAI 84), Krisztian NEMETH. Tr: Sandor EGERVARI

OLYMPIC, HELSINKI
2-09-2011, Att: 9056, Ref: Kakos GRE

Finland	4
Moldova	1

FIN - Hamalainen 2 [11 43], Forssell [52p], OG [70] •
MDA - Alexeev [85]

FIN: Lukas HRADECKY - Joona TOIVIO, Jukka RAITALA, Niklas MOISANDER, Daniel SJOLUND (Teemu PUKKI 61), Perparim HETEMAJ•, Kasper HAMALAINEN (Timo FURUHOLM 76), Roman EREMENKO, Kari ARKIVUO, Alexander RING (Mika VAYRYNEN 72), Mikael FORSSELL. Tr: Mixu PAATELAINEN

MDA: Nicolae CALANCEA - Alexandru EPUREANU•, Igor ARMAS, Victor GOLOVATENCO, Denis ZMEU, Alexey SAVINOV, Vadim BORET, Alexandru SUVOROV• (Vitali BORDIAN 55), Eugen CEBOTARU•, Georgi OVSYANNIKOV (Serghei ALEXEEV 69), Anatoli DOROS• (Anatoli CHEPTINE 55). Tr: Gavril BALINT

PUSKAS FERENC, BUDAPEST
2-09-2011, Att: 23 500, Ref: Skomina SVN

Hungary	2
Sweden	0

HUN - Szabics [44], Rudolf [90] •
SWE - Wilhelmsson [60]

HUN: Gabor KIRALY - Adam PINTER, Zoltan LIPTAK• (Gyorgy SANDOR 73), Zsolt KORCSMAR, Zsolt LACZKO, Vladimir KOMAN, Tamas HAJNAL (Zoltan STIEBER 65), Akos ELEK, Jozsef VARGA, Gergely RUDOLF, Imre SZABICS• (Tamas PRISKIN 80). Tr: Sandor EGERVARI

SWE: Andreas ISAKSSON - Daniel MAJSTOROVIC, Mikael LUSTIG, Andreas GRANQVIST, Oscar WENDT, Anders SVENSSON (Rasmus ELM 52), Sebastian LARSSON (Ola TOIVONEN 68), Kim KALLSTROM (Pontus WERNBLOOM 88), Christian WILHELMSSON•, Johan ELMANDER, Zlatan IBRAHIMOVIC•. Tr: Erik HAMREN

UEFA EURO 2012 POLAND/UKRAINE QUALIFYING GROUP E

PHILIPS STADION, EINDHOVEN
2-09-2011, Att: 35 000, Ref: Liany ISR

Netherlands	11
San Marino	0

NED - Van Persie 4 [7 65 67 79], Sneijder 2 [12 87], Heitinga [17], Kuyt [49], Huntelaar 2 [56 77], Wijnaldum [90]

NED: Maarten STEKELENBURG - Gregory VAN DER WIEL, Erik PIETERS, Joris MATHIJSEN, Johnny HEITINGA, Mark VAN BOMMEL (Hedwiges MADURO 74), Kevin STROOTMAN (Georginio WIJNALDUM 86), Wesley SNEIJDER, Robin VAN PERSIE, Dirk KUYT (Eljero ELIA 74), Klaas-Jan HUNTELAAR. Tr: Bert VAN MARWIJK

SMR: Aldo SIMONCINI - Fabio VITAIOLI, Davide SIMONCINI• (Simone BACCIOCCHI 82), Giacomo BENEDETTINI, Matteo ANDREINI, Damiano VANNUCCI, Michele CERVELLINI, Fabio BOLLINI (Alex GASPERONI• 68), Pier Filipo MAZZA (Matteo COPPINI 54), Andy SELVA, Matteo VITAIOLI. Tr: Giampaolo MAZZA

OLYMPIC, HELSINKI
6-09-2011, Att: 21 580, Ref: Grafe GER

Finland	0
Netherlands	2

NED - Strootman [29], De Jong [93+]

FIN: Lukas HRADECKY - Joona TOIVIO, Petri PASANEN (Jukka RAITALA 78), Niklas MOISANDER, Perparim HETEMAJ••◆60, Kasper HAMALAINEN, Roman EREMENKO, Kari ARKIVUO, Alexander RING, Mikael FORSSELL (Daniel SJOLUND 86), Teemu PUKKI (Mika VAYRYNEN 61). Tr: Mixu PAATELAINEN

NED: Maarten STEKELENBURG - Gregory VAN DER WIEL, Erik PIETERS, Joris MATHIJSEN, Johnny HEITINGA, Mark VAN BOMMEL, Kevin STROOTMAN, Wesley SNEIJDER, Robin VAN PERSIE (Eljero ELIA 68), Dirk KUYT, Klaas-Jan HUNTELAAR (Luuk DE JONG 67). Tr: Bert VAN MARWIJK

ZIMBRU, CHISINAU
6-09-2011, Att: 10 500, Ref: Bebek CRO

Moldova	0
Hungary	2

HUN - Vanczak [7], Rudolf [83]

MDA: Artiom GAIDUCHEVICI - Alexandru EPUREANU, Igor ARMAS, Victor GOLOVATENCO, Denis ZMEU (Igor BUGARU 46), Alexey SAVINOV, Anatoli CHEPTINE (Anatoli DOROS 62), Vadim BORET, Alexandru SUVOROV, Eugen CEBOTARU, Serghei ALEXEEV• (Igor TIGIRLAS 73). Tr: Gavril BALINT

HUN: Gabor KIRALY - Vilmos VANCZAK, Adam PINTER (Gyorgy SANDOR 64), Zsolt KORCSMAR (Zsolt LACZKO• 67), Roland JUHASZ•, Jozsef VARGA, Vladimir KOMAN, Tamas HAJNAL, Akos ELEK, Imre SZABICS (Krisztian VADOCZ 83), Gergely RUDOLF. Tr: Sandor EGERVARI

STADIO OLIMPICO, SERRAVALLE
6-09-2011, Att: 2946, Ref: McLean SCO

San Marino	0
Sweden	5

SWE - Kallstrom [64], Wilhelmsson 2 [70 93+], Olsson.M [81], Hysen [89]

SMR: Federico VALENTINI• - Fabio VITAIOLI•, Davide SIMONCINI••◆53, Simone BACCIOCCHI•, Damiano VANNUCCI, Michele CERVELLINI, Fabio BOLLINI• (Alex GASPERONI 83), Matteo COPPINI (Matteo ANDREINI 71), Andy SELVA, Manuel MARANI• (Giacomo BENEDETTINI 55), Matteo VITAIOLI. Tr: Giampaolo MAZZA

SWE: Andreas ISAKSSON - Martin OLSSON, Daniel MAJSTOROVIC, Mikael LUSTIG, Andreas GRANQVIST, Christian WILHELMSSON, Kim KALLSTROM, Rasmus ELM• (Anders SVENSSON 65), Ola TOIVONEN (Sebastian LARSSON 57), Zlatan IBRAHIMOVIC, Johan Elmander (Tobias HYSEN 67). Tr: Erik HAMREN

OLYMPIC, HELSINKI
7-10-2011, Att: 23 257, Ref: Clattenburg ENG

Finland	1
Sweden	2

FIN - Toivio [73] • SWE - Larsson.S [8], Olsson.M [52]

FIN: Lukas HRADECKY - Joona TOIVIO, Jukka RAITALA•, Niklas MOISANDER, Mika VAYRYNEN (Timo FURUHOLM 70), Tim SPARV, Kasper HAMALAINEN, Roman EREMENKO, Kari ARKIVUO•, Alexander RING, Teemu PUKKI (Mikael FORSSELL 60). Tr: Mixu PAATELAINEN

SWE: Andreas ISAKSSON - Martin OLSSON, Olof MELLBERG, Daniel MAJSTOROVIC•, Mikael LUSTIG, Christian WILHELMSSON (Anders SVENSSON 54), Sebastian LARSSON (Ola TOIVONEN 67), Kim KALLSTROM (Emir BAJRAMI 86), Rasmus ELM, Zlatan IBRAHIMOVIC•, Johan ELMANDER•. Tr: Erik HAMREN

DE KUIP, ROTTERDAM
7-10-2011, Att: 47 226, Ref: Jug SVN

Netherlands	1
Moldova	0

NED - Huntelaar [40]

NED: Michel VORM - Gregory VAN DER WIEL, Erik PIETERS, Joris MATHIJSEN, Jeffrey BRUMA, Rafael VAN DER VAART, (Eljero ELIA 77), Mark VAN BOMMEL, Kevin STROOTMAN•, Robin VAN PERSIE, Dirk KUYT, Klaas-Jan HUNTELAAR. Tr: Bert VAN MARWIJK

MDA: Stanislav NAMASCO - Alexandru EPUREANU, Simeon BULGARU, Igor ARMAS, Victor GOLOVATENCO, Petru RACU, Stanislav IVANOV, Anatoli CHEPTINE (Georgi OVSYANNIKOV 84), Alexandru SUVOROV (Denis ZMEU 58), Eugen CEBOTARU, Serghei ALEXEEV (Igor BUGAEV 69). Tr: Gavril BALINT

PUSKAS FERENC, BUDAPEST
11-10-2011, Att: 25 169, Ref: Undiano ESP

Hungary	0
Finland	0

HUN: Gabor KIRALY - Zsolt KORCSMAR, Roland JUHASZ, Vilmos VANCZAK, Vladimir KOMAN, Tamas HAJNAL (Zoltan STIEBER 88), Akos ELEK, Jozsef VARGA, Gyorgy SANDOR (Krisztian VADOCZ 61), Imre SZABICS, Tamas PRISKIN (Balazs DZSUDZSAK 59). Tr: Sandor EGERVARI

FIN: Otto FREDRIKSON - Jukka RAITALA, Niklas MOISANDER•, Joona TOIVIO, Tim SPARV, Kasper HAMALAINEN (Teemu PUKKI 84), Roman EREMENKO, Kari ARKIVUO (Veli LAMPI 55), Mika VAYRYNEN, Alexander RING, Mikael FORSSELL (Timo FURUHOLM 67). Tr: Mixu PAATELAINEN

ZIMBRU, CHISINAU
11-10-2011, Att: 6534, Ref: Reinert FRO

Moldova	4
San Marino	0

MDA - Zmeu [30], OG [62], Suvorov [66], Andronic.G [87]

MDA: Artiom GAIDUCHEVICI - Alexandru EPUREANU, Igor ARMAS, Victor GOLOVATENCO, Denis ZMEU, Petru RACU (Valeriu ANDRONIC 70), Anatoli CHEPTINE, Alexandru SUVOROV, Eugen CEBOTARU (Igor TIGIRLAS 78◆84), Serghei ALEXEEV (Igor BUGAEV 61), Anatoli DOROS. Tr: Gavril BALINT

SMR: Aldo SIMONCINI - Alessandro DELLA VALLE, Maicol BERRETTI (Matteo BUGLI 67), Giacomo BENEDETTINI, Simone BACCIOCCHI (Alessandro BIANCHI 89), Damiano VANNUCCI, Alex GASPERONI (Paolo MONTAGNA 76), Michele CERVELLINI, Matteo COPPINI, Andy SELVA, Matteo VITAIOLI•. Tr: Giampaolo MAZZA

RASUNDA, STOCKHOLM
11-10-2011, Att: 30 066, Ref: Cakir TUR

Sweden	3
Netherland	2

SWE - Kallstrom [14], Larsson.S [52p], Toivonen [53] • NED - Huntelaar [23], Kuyt [50]

SWE: Andreas ISAKSSON - Martin OLSSON, Olof MELLBERG, Daniel MAJSTOROVIC, Mikael LUSTIG, Rasmus ELM, Anders SVENSSON, Sebastian LARSSON, Kim KALLSTROM, Ola TOIVONEN (Pontus WERNBLOOM 71). Tr: Erik HAMREN

NED: Michel VORM - Jeffrey BRUMA, Gregory VAN DER WIEL, Erik PIETERS, Joris MATHIJSEN, Rafael VAN DER VAART, Mark VAN BOMMEL, Kevin STROOTMAN (Luuk DE JONG 81), Robin VAN PERSIE, Dirk KUYT (Eljero ELIA 73), Klaas-Jan HUNTELAAR. Tr: Bert VAN MARWIJK

	GROUP F	PL	W	D	L	F	A	PTS	GRE	CRO	ISR	LVA	GEO	MLT
1	Greece	10	7	3	0	14	5	24		2-0	2-1	1-0	1-1	3-1
2	Croatia	10	7	1	2	18	7	22	0-0		3-1	2-0	2-1	3-0
3	Israel	10	5	1	4	13	11	16	0-1	1-2		2-1	1-0	3-1
4	Latvia	10	3	2	5	9	12	11	1-1	0-3	1-2		1-1	2-0
5	Georgia	10	2	4	4	7	9	10	1-2	1-0	0-0	0-1		1-0
6	Malta	10	0	1	9	4	21	1	0-1	1-3	0-2	0-2	1-1	

Greece qualified directly for the finals • Croatia qualified for a play-off v Turkey • Turkey 0-3 0-0 **Croatia**

PART THREE – THE CONTINENTAL CONFEDERATIONS

RAMAT GAN STADIUM, RAMAT GAN
2-09-2010, Att: 17 365, Ref: Ennjimi FRA

Israel	3
Malta	1

ISR - Benayoun 3 [7 64p 75] • MLT - Pace [38]

ISR: Dudu AOUATE - Dani BONDARV, Dedi BEN DAYAN, Tal BEN HAIM, Lior REFAELOV, Biram KAYAL (Eyal GOLASA 86), Tamir COHEN, Almog COHEN, Yossi BENAYOUN•, Eran ZAHAVY (Gil VERMOUTH 51), Ben SAHAR (Shlomi ARBEITMAN 73). Tr: Luis FERNANDEZ

MLT: Andrew HOGG - Carlo MAMO, Jonathan CARUANA, Gareth SCIBERRAS, Jamie PACE•, Roderick BRIFFA (Clayton FAILLA 82), Shaun BAJADA, Andrei AGIUS, Michael MIFSUD, Edward HERRERA (Manny MUSCAT 80), Daniel BOGDANOVIC• (Andrew COHEN• 57). Tr: John BUTTIGIEG

SKONTO STADIUM, RIGA
3-09-2010, Att: 7600, Ref: Kuipers NED

Latvia	0
Croatia	3

CRO - Petric [43], Olic [51], Srna [82]

LVA: Andris VANINS - Oskars KLAVA, Deniss IVANOVS, Kaspars GORKSS, Andrejs RUBINS (Jurijs ZIGAJEVS 85), Maksims RAFALSKIS, Pavels MIHADJUKS•, Juris LAIZANS (Vitalijs ASTAFJEVS 87), Aleksandrs CAUNA, Maris VERPAKOVSKIS•, Girts KARLSONS (Artjoms RUDNEVS 63). Tr: Aleksandrs STARKOVS

CRO: Vedran RUNJE - Josip SIMUNIC, Vedran CORLUKA, Ivan STRINIC, Ognjen VUKOJEVIC• (Danijel PRANJIC 70), Darijo SRNA•, Ivan RAKITIC, Niko KRANJCAR, Mladen PETRIC (Mario MANDZUKIC 84), Ivica OLIC, EDUARDO (Nikica JELAVIC 62). Tr: Slaven BILIC

KARAISKAKIS, PIRAEUS
3-09-2010, Att: 14 794, Ref: Clos ESP

Greece	1
Georgia	1

GRE - Spiropoulos [72] • GEO - Iashvili [3]

GRE: Michail SIFAKIS - Vasilios TOROSIDIS, Nikos SPYROPOULOS, Georgios SEITARIDIS (Kostas MITROGLOU 71), Sokratis PAPASTATHOPOULOS, Avraam PAPADOPOULOS•, Kostas KATSOURANIS•, Giorgios KARAGOUNIS, Georgios SAMARAS• (Sotiris NINIS 59), Dimitrios SALPINGIDIS, Theofanis GEKAS. Tr: Fernando SANTOS

GEO: Nukri REVISHVILI - Dato KVIRKVELIA, Kakha KALADZE, Zurab KHIZANISHVILI•, Aleksandr AMISULASHVILI, Ucha LOBJANIDZE•, Levan KOBIASHVILI, Gogita GOGUA (Giorgi MEREBASHVILI 87), Malchaz ASATIANI, Aleksandr IASHVILI (Jano ANANIDZE 54), Vladimer DVALISHVILI (Nikoloz GELASHVILI 60). Tr: Temur KETSBAIA

BORIS PAICHADZE, TBILISI
7-09-2010, Att: 45 000, Ref: Kever SUI

Georgia	0
Israel	0

GEO: Nukri REVISHVILI - Ucha LOBJANIDZE•, Zurab KHIZANISHVILI, Kakha KALADZE, Aleksandr AMISULASHVILI, Levan KOBIASHVILI•, Gogita GOGUA (Tornike APTISAURI 75), Malchaz ASATIANI, Jano ANANIDZE, Aleksandr IASHVILI (David SIRADZE 46), Vladimer DVALISHVILI (Giorgi MEREBASHVILI 63). Tr: Temur KETSBAIA

ISR: Dudu AOUATE - Dekel KEINAN, Dani BONDARV•, Dedi BEN DAYAN, Tal BEN HAIM•, Lior REFAELOV (Gil VERMOUTH 75), Biram KAYAL, Tamir COHEN (Eran ZAHAVY 61), Almog COHEN, Yossi BENAYOUN, Ben SAHAR (Shlomi ARBEITMAN 53). Tr: Luis FERNANDEZ

TA'QALI STADIUM, TA'QALI
7-09-2010, Att: 6255, Ref: Asumaa FIN

Malta	0
Latvia	2

LVA - Gorkss [43], Verpakovskis [85]

MLT: Andrew HOGG - Manny MUSCAT (Daniel BOGDANOVIC• 59), Carlo MAMO (Ryan FENECH 77), Jonathan CARUANA, Gareth SCIBERRAS (Clayton FAILLA 77), Jamie PACE, Roderick BRIFFA, Shaun BAJADA, Andrei AGIUS•, Michael MIFSUD•, Andrew COHEN. Tr: John BUTTIGIEG

LVA: Andris VANINS - Oskars KLAVA•, Deniss IVANOVS, Kaspars GORKSS, Andrejs RUBINS, Maksims RAFALSKIS• (Vitalijs ASTAFJEVS 82), Pavels MIHADJUKS, Juris LAIZANS, Aleksandrs CAUNA, Maris VERPAKOVSKIS (Andrejs PEREPLOTKINS 90), Artjoms RUDNEVS (Girts KARLSONS 70). Tr: Aleksandrs STARKOVS

MAKSIMIR, ZAGREB
7-09-2010, Att: 24 399, Ref: Larsen DEN

Croatia	0
Greece	0

CRO: Vedran RUNJE - Josip SIMUNIC, Vedran CORLUKA, Ivan STRINIC, Ognjen VUKOJEVIC (Ivan RAKITIC• 57), Darijo SRNA•, Danijel PRANJIC, Luka MODRIC, Niko KRANJCAR, Mladen PETRIC (Nikica JELAVIC 46), Ivica OLIC (EDUARDO 73). Tr: Slaven BILIC

GRE: Michail SIFAKIS - Loukas VYNTRA, Giorgos TZAVELAS•, Vasilios TOROSIDIS• (Georgios SEITARIDIS 90), Sokratis PAPASTATHOPOULOS•, Avraam PAPADOPOULOS, Alexandros TZIOLIS, Kostas KATSOURANIS, Giorgios KARAGOUNIS (Sotiris NINIS 70), Georgios SAMARAS, Dimitrios SALPINGIDIS (Theofanis GEKAS 59). Tr: Fernando SANTOS

BORIS PAICHADZE, TBILISI
8-10-2010, Att: 38 000, Ref: Black NIR

Georgia	1
Malta	0

GEO - Siradze [91+]

GEO: Nukri REVISHVILI - Lasha SALUKVADZE, Zurab KHIZANISHVILI•, Kakha KALADZE, Aleksandr AMISULASHVILI, Giorgi MEREBASHVILI (David SIRADZE 46), Levan KOBIASHVILI, Gogita GOGUA, Malchaz ASATIANI, Jano ANANIDZE (Murtaz DAUSHVILI 73), Vladimer DVALISHVILI (Aleksandr IASHVILI 46). Tr: Temur KETSBAIA

MLT: Justin HABER - Carlo MAMO, Jonathan CARUANA, Gareth SCIBERRAS (Ryan FENECH 69), Jamie PACE, Roderick BRIFFA, Shaun BAJADA, Andrei AGIUS•, Andre SCHEMBRI• (Paul FENECH 80), Michael MIFSUD, Andrew COHEN• (Massimo GRIMA 90). Tr: John BUTTIGIEG

KARAISKAKIS, PIRAEUS
8-10-2010, Att: 13 520, Ref: Damato ITA

Greece	1
Latvia	0

GRE - Torosidis [58]

GRE: Michail SIFAKIS - Giorgos TZAVELAS, Vasilios TOROSIDIS•, Sokratis PAPASTATHOPOULOS, Avraam PAPADOPOULOS, Sotiris NINIS (Ioannis FETFATZIDIS 83), Kostas KATSOURANIS, Giorgios KARAGOUNIS (Pantelis KAFES 89), Alexandros TZIOLIS•, Kostas MITROGLOU (Dimitrios SALPINGIDIS 78), Georgios SAMARAS. Tr: Fernando SANTOS

LVA: Andris VANINS - Oskars KLAVA, Deniss IVANOVS, Kaspars GORKSS, Dzintars ZIRNIS•, Andrejs RUBINS (Jurijs ZIGAJEVS• 66), Juris LAIZANS (Andrejs PEREPLOTKINS 83), Aleksandrs CAUNA, Vitalijs ASTAFJEVS, Maris VERPAKOVSKIS•, Artjoms RUDNEVS (Girts KARLSONS 74). Tr: Aleksandrs STARKOVS

RAMAT GAN STADIUM, RAMAT GAN
9-10-2010, Att: 33 421, Ref: Stark GER

Israel	1
Croatia	2

ISR - Shechter [81] • CRO - Kranjcar 2 [36p 41]

ISR: Dudu AOUATE - Yoav ZIV, Dekel KEINAN•, Tal BEN HAIM•, Gil VERMOUTH, Bebars NATCHO, Tamir COHEN (Roberto COLAUTTI 51), Almog COHEN, Elroy COHEN (Eyal GOLASA• 69), Itay SHECHTER•, Elyaniv BARDA (Lior REFAELOV 56). Tr: Luis FERNANDEZ

CRO: Vedran RUNJE - Josip SIMUNIC, Gordon SCHILDENFELD, Vedran CORLUKA, Ivan STRINIC, Ivan RAKITIC (Ognjen VUKOJEVIC• 77), Danijel PRANJIC, Luka MODRIC, Niko KRANJCAR•, Ivica OLIC (Mate BILIC 72), EDUARDO (Mario MANDZUKIC 57). Tr: Slaven BILIC

SKONTO STADIUM, RIGA
12-10-2010, Att: 4330, Ref: Neves POR

Latvia	1
Georgia	1

LVA - Cauna [91+] • GEO - Siradze [74]

LVA: Andris VANINS - Oskars KLAVA•, Deniss IVANOVS, Kaspars GORKSS•, Dzintars ZIRNIS, Jurijs ZIGAJEVS (Andrejs PEREPLOTKINS 86), Andrejs RUBINS, Juris LAIZANS (Kristaps GREBIS 82), Aleksandrs CAUNA, Vitalijs ASTAFJEVS, Artjoms RUDNEVS. Tr: Aleksandrs STARKOVS

GEO: Nukri REVISHVILI• - Ucha LOBJANIDZE, Dato KVIRKVELIA (Gogita GOGUA• 69), Kakha KALADZE, Aleksandr AMISULASHVILI, David SIRADZE•, Levan KOBIASHVILI, Murtaz DAUSHVILI, Malchaz ASATIANI, Jano ANANIDZE (Lasha SALUKVADZE 79), Aleksandr IASHVILI (Aleksandre KOSHKADZE 88). Tr: Temur KETSBAIA

KARAISKAKIS, PIRAEUS
12-10-2010, Att: 16 935, Ref: Hansson SWE

Greece	2
Israel	1

GRE - Salpingidis [22], Karagounis [63p] • ISR - OG [59]

GRE: Michail SIFAKIS - Nikos SPYROPOULOS, Sokratis PAPASTATHOPOULOS, Loukas VYNTRA, Avraam PAPADOPOULOS, Sotiris NINIS (Ioannis FETFATZIDIS 16), Kostas KATSOURANIS, Giorgios KARAGOUNIS, Pantelis KAFES, Dimitrios SALPINGIDIS (Ioannis MANIATIS 87), Georgios SAMARAS (Kostas MITROGLOU 81). Tr: Fernando SANTOS

ISR: Dudu AOUATE - Dekel KEINAN, Rami GERSHON, Dani BONDARV, Lior REFAELOV, Eyal GOLASA, Almog COHEN, Tamir COHEN (Elroy COHEN• 69), Bebars NATCHO (Gil VERMOUTH 63), Itay SHECHTER•, Roberto COLAUTTI (Elyaniv BARDA 75). Tr: Luis FERNANDEZ

MAKSIMIR, ZAGREB
17-11-2010, Att: 9000, Ref: Gomes POR

Croatia	3
Malta	0

CRO - Kranjcar 2 [18 42], Kalinic [81]

CRO: Vedran RUNJE - Gordon SCHILDENFELD, Vedran CORLUKA, Darijo SRNA•, Ivan RAKITIC (Ivo ILICEVIC 69), Danijel PRANJIC, Luka MODRIC, Niko KRANJCAR, Tomislav DUJMOVIC, Mladen PETRIC (Nikola KALINIC 60), EDUARDO (Mario MANDZUKIC 78). Tr: Slaven BILIC

MLT: Andrew HOGG - Jonathan CARUANA, Gareth SCIBERRAS (Paul FENECH 88), Jamie PACE, John HUTCHINSON, Massimo GRIMA•, Roderick BRIFFA, Shaun BAJADA, Andre SCHEMBRI (Ryan FENECH 70), Michael MIFSUD, Daniel BOGDANOVIC (Kevin SAMMUT 83). Tr: John BUTTIGIEG

UEFA EURO 2012 POLAND/UKRAINE QUALIFYING GROUP F

BORIS PAICHADZE, TBILISI
26-03-2011, Att: 55 000, Ref: Tagliavento ITA

Georgia	1
Croatia	0

GEO - Kobiashvili [90]

Nukri REVISHVILI - Aleksandr AMISULASHVILI, Lasha SALUKVADZE, Akaki KHUBUTIA, Zurab KHIZANISHVILI, Kakha KALADZE, Murtaz DAUSHVILI (Gogita GOGUA 73), Levan KOBIASHVILI, Jaba KANKAVA, Vladimer DVALISHVILI (David SIRADZE 46), Aleksandr IASHVILI (Otari MARTSVALADZE• 62). Tr: Temur KETSBAIA

Vedran RUNJE - Vedran CORLUKA, Ivan STRINIC, Dejan LOVREN, Tomislav DUJMOVIC•, Darijo SRNA, Ivan RAKITIC (Ivan PERISIC 62), Luka MODRIC, Niko KRANJCAR• (Nikica JELAVIC 70), Mladen PETRIC (Danijel PRANJIC 84), Nikola KALINIC. Tr: Slaven BILIC

BLOOMFIELD, TEL AVIV
26-03-2011, Att: 10 801, Ref: Mazic SRB

Israel	2
Latvia	1

ISR - Barda [16], Kayal [81] • LVA - Gorkss [62]

Dudu AOUATE - Yoav ZIV (Ben SAHAR 66), Rami GERSHON, Itzhak COHEN, Tal BEN HAIM, Taleb TAWATHA•, Lior REFAELOV (Gil VERMOUTH 83), Bebars NATCHO•, Biram KAYAL, Omar DAMARI, Elyaniv BARDA (Maor BUZAGLO 69). Tr: Luis FERNANDEZ

Andris VANINS - Ritus KRJAUKLIS, Deniss IVANOVS, Kaspars GORKSS, Deniss KACANOVS•, Andrejs RUBINS (Andrejs PEREPLOTKINS 57), Maksims RAFALSKIS (Jurijs ZIGAJEVS 58), Artis LAZDINS, Ivan LUKJANOVS, Maris VERPAKOVSKIS (Danils TURKOVS 73), Artjoms RUDNEVS. Tr: Aleksandrs STARKOVS

TA'QALI STADIUM, TA'QALI
26-03-2011, Att: 10 605, Ref: Weiner GER

Malta	0
Greece	1

GRE - Torosidis [92+]

Justin HABER - Carlo MAMO, Jonathan CARUANA (Jamie PACE 46), Gareth SCIBERRAS, John HUTCHINSON, Roderick BRIFFA, Shaun BAJADA (Ryan FENECH 78), Andrei AGIUS, Andre SCHEMBRI (Andrew COHEN• 90), Michael MIFSUD, Daniel BOGDANOVIC. Tr: John BUTTIGIEG

Alexandros TZORVAS - Giorgos TZAVELAS•, Vasilios TOROSIDIS•, Sokratis PAPASTATHOPOULOS♦84, Avraam PAPADOPOULOS, Sotiris NINIS (Panagiotis KONE 81), Kostas KATSOURANIS, Giorgios KARAGOUNIS, Georgios SAMARAS, Dimitrios SALPINGIDIS (Ioannis FETFATZIDIS 61), Nikos LIBEROPOULOS (Kostas MITROGLOU 70). Tr: Fernando SANTOS

BLOOMFIELD, TEL AVIV
29-03-2011, Att: 13 716, Ref: Fautrel FRA

Israel	1
Georgia	0

ISR - Tal Ben Haim II [59]

Dudu AOUATE - Dekel KEINAN, Rami GERSHON, Dani BONDARY•, Tal BEN HAIM, Lior REFAELOV (Gil VERMOUTH 63), Bebars NATCHO (Tal BEN HAIM 52), Biram KAYAL, Almog COHEN•, Maor BUZAGLO, Elyaniv BARDA (Yossi BENAYOUN 71). Tr: Luis FERNANDEZ

Nukri REVISHVILI - Lasha SALUKVADZE, Akaki KHUBUTIA, Zurab KHIZANISHVILI, Kakha KALADZE, Aleksandr AMISULASHVILI•, Levan KOBIASHVILI•, Jaba KANKAVA, Murtaz DAUSHVILI (Dato KVIRKVELIA 46), Otari MARTSVALADZE• (David SIRADZE 72), Aleksandr IASHVILI (Vladimer DVALISHVILI 64). Tr: Temur KETSBAIA

POLJUD, SPLIT
3-06-2011, Att: 28 000, Ref: Johannesson SWE

Croatia	2
Georgia	1

CRO - Mandzukic [76], Kalinic [78] •
GEO - Kankava [17]

Vedran RUNJE - Josip SIMUNIC, Vedran CORLUKA, Ivan PERISIC (Ivan KLASNIC 70), Ognjen VUKOJEVIC (Tomislav DUJMOVIC 71), Darijo SRNA, Danijel PRANJIC, Luka MODRIC, Mario MANDZUKIC, Nikica JELAVIC (Nikola KALINIC• 46), EDUARDO. Tr: Slaven BILIC

Giorgi LORIA - Lasha SALUKVADZE, Dato KVIRKVELIA, Akaki KHUBUTIA•, Zurab KHIZANISHVILI, Guram KASHIA (Jano ANANIDZE 80), Kakha KALADZE, Gia GRIGALAVA, David Siradze (Vladimer DVALISHVILI 56), Jaba KANKAVA, Aleksandr IASHVILI• (Murtaz DAUSHVILI 61). Tr: Temur KETSBAIA

SKONTO STADIUM, RIGA
4-06-2011, Att: 6147, Ref: Kelly IRL

Latvia	1
Israel	2

LVA - Cauna [62p] • ISR - Benayoun [19], Tal Ben Haim I [43p]

Andris VANINS - Ritus KRJAUKLIS, Oskars KLAVA•, Deniss IVANOVS•, Kaspars GORKSS, Aleksejs VISNAKOVS (Ritvars RUGINS 71), Maksims RAFALSKIS (Jurijs ZIGAJEVS• 28), Artis LAZDINS, Aleksandrs CAUNA, Artjoms RUDNEVS, Andrejs PEREPLOTKINS (Edgars GAURACS 60). Tr: Aleksandrs STARKOVS

Dudu AOUATE - Yuval SHPUNGIN, Dekel KEINAN, Rami GERSHON, Tal BEN HAIM, Lior REFAELOV (Tal BEN HAIM• 79), Almog COHEN, Yossi BENAYOUN, Eran ZAHAVY (Eyal GOLASA 89), Tomer HEMED (Maor BUZAGLO, Bebars NATCHO 69). Tr: Luis FERNANDEZ

KARAISKAKIS, PIRAEUS
4-06-2011, Att: 14 746, Ref: Gil POL

Greece	3
Malta	1

GRE - Fetfatzidis 2 [7 63], Papadopoulos [26] •
MLT - Mifsud [54]

Demitrios KONSTANTOPOULOS - Vasilios TOROSIDIS, Nikos SPYROPOULOS, Vangelis MORAS, Kyriakos PAPADOPOULOS•, Alexandros TZIOLIS, Sotiris NINIS (Lazaros CHRISTODOULOPOULOS 79), Kostas KATSOURANIS, Giorgios KARAGOUNIS (Pantelis KAFES 70), Ioannis FETFATZIDIS, Dimitrios SALPINGIDIS (Kostas MITROGLOU 90). Tr: Fernando SANTOS

Andrew HOGG - Jonathan CARUANA, Gareth SCIBERRAS, John HUTCHINSON (Paul FENECH 87), Ryan FENECH, Roderick BRIFFA, Shaun BAJADA (Clayton FAILLA 80), Andrei AGIUS, Andre SCHEMBRI, Michael MIFSUD, Daniel BOGDANOVIC (Andrew COHEN 59). Tr: John BUTTIGIEG

BLOOMFIELD, TEL AVIV
2-09-2011, Att: 13 100, Ref: Thomson SCO

Israel	0
Greece	1

GRE - Ninis [60]

Dudu AOUATE - Omri BEN HARUSH•, Yuval SHPUNGIN, Rami GERSHON, Tal BEN HAIM, Lior REFAELOV•, Biram KAYAL•, Almog COHEN• (Bebars NATCHO• 61), Yossi BENAYOUN, Eran ZAHAVY• (Tomer HEMED 54), Itay SHECHTER (Omar DAMARI 55). Tr: Luis FERNANDEZ

Michail SIFAKIS - Giannis ZARADOUKAS, Vasilios TOROSIDIS, Kyriakos PAPADOPOULOS•, Avraam PAPADOPOULOS, Sotiris NINIS (Ioannis FETFATZIDIS 77), Kostas KATSOURANIS, Giorgios KARAGOUNIS, Pantelis KAFES• (Grigoris MAKOS 41), Georgios SAMARAS, Dimitrios SALPINGIDIS• (Ioannis MANIATIS• 84). Tr: Fernando SANTOS

MIKHEIL MESKHI, TBILISI
2-09-2011, Att: 15 422, Ref: Trattou CYP

Georgia	0
Latvia	1

LVA - Cauna [64]

Giorgi LORIA - Zurab KHIZANISHVILI, Guram KASHIA, Kakha KALADZE, Aleksandr AMISULASHVILI (Vladimer DVALISHVILI 71), David TARGAMADZE, Levan KOBIASHVILI, Jaba KANKAVA, Jano ANANIDZE (David SIRADZE 55), Otari MARTSVALADZE, Aleksandr IASHVILI (Shota GRIGALASHVILI 55). Tr: Temur Ketsbaia

Andris VANINS - Ritus KRJAUKLIS•, Oskars KLAVA, Deniss IVANOVS, Kaspars GORKSS•, Aleksandrs FERTOVS•, Aleksejs VISNAKOVS, Artis LAZDINS (Juris LAIZANS 88), Aleksandrs CAUNA, Ivan LUKJANOVS, Maris VERPAKOVSKIS• (Edgars GAURACS 77). Tr: Aleksandrs STARKOVS

TA'QALI STADIUM, TA'QALI
2-09-2011, Att: 6150, Ref: Chapron FRA

Malta	1
Croatia	3

MLT - Mifsud [38] • CRO - Vukojevic [11], Badelj [32], Lovren [68]

Andrew HOGG - Manny MUSCAT, Gareth SCIBERRAS, John Hutchinson, Ryan Fenech• (Carlo Mamo 88), Roderick Briffa (Jamie Pace 74), Andrei Agius, Andre Schembri, Michael Mifsud (Ivan Woods 82), Clayton Failla•, Andrew Cohen. Tr: John Buttigieg

Stipe PLETIKOSA - Vedran CORLUKA•, Sime VRSALJKO, Ivan STRINIC, Dejan LOVREN, Ognjen VUKOJEVIC, Darijo SRNA, Ivan PERISIC (Tomislav DUJMOVIC 67), Milan BADELJ (EDUARDO 81), Mario MANDZUKIC•, Ivan KLASNIC (Nikola KALINIC 46). Tr: Slaven BILIC

MAKSIMIR, ZAGREB
6-09-2011, Att: 13 688, Ref: Velasco ESP

Croatia	3
Israel	1

CRO - Modric [47], Eduardo 2 [55 57] •
ISR - Hemed [44]

Stipe PLETIKOSA - Vedran CORLUKA (Tomislav DUJMOVIC 46), Josip SIMUNIC, Ivan STRINIC•, Dejan LOVREN, Niko KRANJCAR, Ognjen VUKOJEVIC (EDUARDO 46), Darijo SRNA•, Luka MODRIC, Nikica JELAVIC (Nikola KALINIC 87), Mario MANDZUKIC. Tr: Slaven BILIC

Dudu AOUATE (Guy HAIMOV 46), Omri BEN HARUSH•, Eyad HUTAVA, Rami GERSHON, Tal BEN HAIM♦51, Yossi BENAYOUN, Taleb TAWATHA, Biram KAYAL, Tamir COHEN (Eyal GOLASA 57), Eran ZAHAVY• (Itay SHECHTER 68), Tomer HEMED. Tr: Luis FERNANDEZ

TA'QALI STADIUM, TA'QALI
6-09-2011, Att: 5000, Ref: Van Boekel NED

Malta	1
Georgia	1

MLT - Mifsud [25] • GEO - Kankava [15]

Andrew HOGG• - Jonathan CARUANA, Gareth SCIBERRAS, John HUTCHINSON, Ryan FENECH (Daniel BOGDANOVIC 59), Roderick BRIFFA, Andrei AGIUS, Andre SCHEMBRI (Jamie PACE 76), Michael MIFSUD, Clayton FAILLA, Andrew COHEN (Ivan WOODS 90). Tr: John BUTTIGIEG

Nukri REVISHVILI - Zurab KHIZANISHVILI•, Guram KASHIA•, Kakha KALADZE, Gia GRIGALAVA, David TARGAMADZE, Levan KOBIASHVILI, Jaba KANKAVA, Jano ANANIDZE (Aleksandr KOBAKHIDZE 77), Otari MARTSVALADZE (Shota GRIGALASHVILI 66), Aleksandr IASHVILI (Vladimer DVALISHVILI 61). Tr: Temur KETSBAIA

1052   PART THREE – THE CONTINENTAL CONFEDERATIONS

SKONTO STADIUM, RIGA
6-09-2011, Att: 5415, Ref: Todorov BUL

Latvia	1
Greece	1

LVA - Cauna 19 • GRE - Papadopoulos [84]

LVA: Andris VANINS• - Ritus KRJAUKLIS•, Oskars KLAVA, Deniss IVANOVS, Aleksandrs FERTOVS, Aleksejs VISNAKOVS (Jurijs ZIGAJEVS 83), Pavels MIHADJUKS, Juris LAIZANS•, Aleksandrs CAUNA, Ivan LUKJANOVS, Maris VERPAKOVSKIS (Artjoms RUDNEVS• 68). Tr: Aleksandrs STARKOVS

GRE: Michail SIFAKIS - Giannis ZARADOUKAS•, Sokratis PAPASTATHOPOULOS, Kyriakos PAPADOPOULOS•, Loukas VYNTRA (Ioannis MANIATIS• 71), Giorgios KARAGOUNIS, Grigoris MAKOS (Georgios GEORGIADIS 81), Ioannis FETFATZIDIS (Alexandros TZIOLIS 46), Dimitrios SALPINGIDIS, Georgios SAMARAS, Nikos LIBEROPOULOS. Tr: Fernando SANTOS

SKONTO STADIUM, RIGA
7-10-2011, Att: 4315, Ref: Trutz SVK

Latvia	2
Malta	0

LVA - Visnakovs.A [33], Rudnevs [83]

LVA: Andris VANINS - Oskars KLAVA, Deniss IVANOVS, Kaspars GORKSS, Aleksejs VISNAKOVS, Pavels MIHADJUKS, Juris LAIZANS (Ritvars RUGINS 75), Aleksandrs CAUNA, Ivan LUKJANOVS•, Maris VERPAKOVSKIS• (Andrejs RUBINS 90), Artjoms RUDNEVS (Edgars GAURACS 87). Tr: Aleksandrs STARKOVS

MLT: Andrew HOGG - Steve BORG, Gareth SCIBERRAS (Paul FENECH 83), Jamie PACE (Ivan WOODS 70), John HUTCHINSON, Ryan FENECH (Carlo MAMO 82), Roderick BRIFFA, Andrei AGIUS•, Andre SCHEMBRI, Clayton FAILLA•, Andrew COHEN•. Tr: John BUTTIGIEG

KARAISKAKIS, PIRAEUS
7-10-2011, Att: 27 200, Ref: Webb ENG

Greece	2
Croatia	0

GRE - Samaras [71], Gekas [79]

GRE: Alexandros TZORVAS• - Giannis ZARADOUKAS•, Vasilios TOROSIDIS (Loukas VYNTRA 44), Sokratis PAPASTATHOPOULOS, Avraam PAPADOPOULOS•, Kostas KATSOURANIS, Giorgios KARAGOUNIS• (Grigoris MAKOS 88), Alexandros TZIOLIS (Georgios FOTAKIS 62), Theofanis GEKAS, Georgios SAMARAS•, Dimitrios SALPINGIDIS. Tr: Fernando SANTOS

CRO: Stipe PLETIKOSA - Vedran CORLUKA (Domagoj VIDA 75), Josip SIMUNIC, Dejan LOVREN•, Ivan STRINIC, Niko KRANJCAR, Ognjen VUKOJEVIC, Luka MODRIC, Mario MANDZUKIC, Nikica JELAVIC• (Nikola KALINIC• 62), EDUARDO• (Ivan PERISIC 52). Tr: Slaven BILIC

MIKHEIL MESKHI, TBILISI
11-10-2011, Att: 7824, Ref: Orsato ITA

Georgia	1
Greece	2

GEO - Targamadze 19 • GRE - Fotakis [79], Charisteas [85]

GEO: Nukri REVISHVILI - Zurab KHIZANISHVILI, Guram KASHIA, Kakha KALADZE, Aleksandr AMISULASHVILI, David TARGAMADZE•, Levan KOBIASHVILI, Jaba KANKAVA• (Ucha LOBJANIDZE 42), Shota GRIGALASHVILI (Aleksandr IASHVILI 51), Otari MARTSVALADZE, Levan MCHEDLIDZE• (Aleksandre GURULI 65). Tr: Temur KETSBAIA

GRE: Alexandros TZORVAS - Loukas VYNTRA, Nikos SPYROPOULOS•, Sokratis PAPASTATHOPOULOS, Kyriakos PAPADOPOULOS, Alexandros TZIOLIS (Georgios FOTAKIS 56), Kostas KATSOURANIS, Giorgios KARAGOUNIS, Dimitrios SALPINGIDIS (Stefanos ATHANASIADIS• 68), Theofanis GEKAS (Panagiotis KONE 90), Angelos CHARISTEAS. Tr: Fernando SANTOS

TA'QALI STADIUM, TA'QALI
11-10-2011, Att: 2164, Ref: Paixao POR

Malta	0
Israel	1

ISR - Refaelov [11], Gershon [93+]

MLT: Andrew HOGG - Carlo MAMO, Jonathan CARUANA (Steve BORG 82), Gareth SCIBERRAS, John HUTCHINSON, Ryan FENECH, Paul FENECH (Edward HERRERA 64), Roderick BRIFFA, Andrei AGIUS•, Ivan WOODS• (Christian CARUANA 81), Michael MIFSUD. Tr: John BUTTIGIEG

ISR: Dudu AOUATE - Rami GERSHON, Dani BONDARV (Gil VERMOUTH 57), Taleb TAWATHA, Lior REFAELOV (Almog COHEN 49), Bebars NATCHO, Eyal GOLASA, Ben SAHAR (Tal BEN HAIM 78), Tomer HEMED, Maor BUZAGLO, Dudu BITON. Tr: Luis FERNANDEZ

KANTRIDA, RIJEKA
11-10-2011, Att: 8370, Ref: Gautier FRA

Croatia	2
Latvia	0

CRO - Eduardo [66], Mandzukic [72]

CRO: Stipe PLETIKOSA - Josip SIMUNIC, Vedran CORLUKA (Domagoj VIDA 32), Ivan STRINIC, Dejan LOVREN, Darijo SRNA, Ivan RAKITIC, Luka MODRIC, Niko KRANJCAR (Ivan PERISIC 60), Mario MANDZUKIC (Nikica JELAVIC 84), EDUARDO. Tr: Slaven BILIC

LVA: Andris VANINS - Oskars KLAVA•, Deniss IVANOVS, Kaspars GORKSS, Ritvars RUGINS• (Igors TARASOVS 81), Aleksejs VISNAKOVS (Andrejs RUBINS 88), Pavels MIHADJUKS, Juris LAIZANS, Aleksandrs CAUNA, Artjoms RUDNEVS, Andrejs PEREPLOTKINS (Edgars GAURACS 72). Tr: Aleksnadrs STARKOVS

GROUP G	PL	W	D	L	F	A	PTS	ENG	MNE	SUI	WAL	BUL
1 England	8	5	3	0	17	5	18		0-0	2-2	1-0	4-0
2 Montenegro	8	3	3	2	7	7	12	2-2		1-0	1-0	1-1
3 Switzerland	8	3	2	3	12	10	11	1-3	2-0		4-1	3-1
4 Wales	8	3	0	5	6	10	9	0-2	2-1	2-0		0-1
5 Bulgaria	8	1	2	5	3	13	5	0-3	0-1	0-0	0-1	

England qualified directly for the finals • Montenegro qualified for a play-off v Czech Republic
Czech Republic 2-0 1-0 Montenegro

POD GORICOM, PODGORICA
3-09-2010, Att: 7442, Ref: Kakos GRE

Montenegro	1
Wales	0

MNE - Vucinic [30]

MNE: Mladen BOZOVIC - Elsad ZVEROTIC, Savo PAVICEVIC•, Milan JOVANOVIC, Miodrag DZUDOVIC•, Marko BASA, Simon VUKCEVIC (Fatos BECIRAJ 87), Milorad PEKOVIC•, Branko BOSKOVIC (Vladimir BOZOVIC 73), Mirko VUCINIC, Radomir DALOVIC (Mitar NOVAKOVIC 83). Tr: Zlatko KRANJCAR

WAL: Wayne HENNESSEY - Chris GUNTER, James COLLINS (Craig MORGAN 75), Ashley WILLIAMS, Sam RICKETTS•, Dave EDWARDS (Robert EARNSHAW 63), David VAUGHAN, Joe LEDLEY, Gareth BALE•, Craig BELLAMY, Steve MORISON• (Simon CHURCH 78). Tr: John TOSHACK

WEMBLEY STADIUM, LONDON
3-09-2010, Att: 73 426, Ref: Kassai HUN

England	4
Bulgaria	0

ENG - Defoe 3 [3][61][86], Johnson.A [83]

ENG: Joe HART - Glen JOHNSON, Michael DAWSON (Gary CAHILL 57), Ashley COLE, Phil JAGIELKA, Gareth BARRY, James MILNER•, Steven GERRARD, Theo WALCOTT (Adam JOHNSON 74), Wayne ROONEY, Jermain DEFOE (Ashley YOUNG 87). Tr: Fabio CAPELLO

BUL: Nikolai MIHAILOV - Ilian STOYANOV, Zhivko MILANOV, Stanislav MANOLEV (Veselin MINEV 56), Ivan IVANOV, Stanislav ANGELOV•, Chavdar YANKOV, Stilian PETROV, Martin PETROV, Valeri BOJINOV (Dimitar RANGELOV 63), Ivelin POPOV• (Georgi PEEV 79). Tr: Stanimir STOILOV

VASIL LEVSKI, SOFIA
7-09-2010, Att: 9470, Ref: Bezborodov RUS

Bulgaria	0
Montenegro	1

MNE - Zverotic [36]

BUL: Nikolai MIHAILOV - Ivan IVANOV, Ilian STOYANOV, Veselin MINEV, Zhivko MILANOV (Stanislav GENCHEV 47), Stanislav ANGELOV•, Stilian PETROV•, Martin PETROV•, Georgi PEEV (Valeri DOMOVCHIYSKI 67), Dimitar RANGELOV (Valeri BOJINOV 47), Ivelin POPOV. Tr: Stanimir STOILOV

MNE: Mladen BOZOVIC - Marko BASA, Elsad ZVEROTIC (Mitar NOVAKOVIC 68), Savo PAVICEVIC, Milan JOVANOVIC, Miodrag DZUDOVIC, Branko BOSKOVIC• (Vladimir BOZOVIC 64), Simon VUKCEVIC, Milorad PEKOVIC•, Mirko VUCINIC, Radomir DALOVIC (Mladen KASCELAN 77). Tr: Zlatko KRANJCAR

UEFA EURO 2012 POLAND/UKRAINE QUALIFYING GROUP G

ST. JAKOB PARK, BASEL	POD GORICOM, PODGORICA	CARDIFF CITY STADIUM, CARDIFF
7-09-2010, Att: 37 500, Ref: Rizzoli ITA	8-10-2010, Att: 10 750, Ref: Iturralde ESP	8-10-2010, Att: 14 061, Ref: Eriksson SWE
Switzerland 1	Montenegro 1	Wales 0
England 3	Switzerland 0	Bulgaria 1
SUI - Shaqiri [71]	MNE - Vucinic [68]	BUL - Popov [48]
ENG - Rooney [10], Johnson.A [69], Bent [88]		
SUI: Diego BENAGLIO - Reto ZIEGLER, Steve VON BERGEN, Stephan LICHTSTEINER•♦[65], Stephane GRICHTING•, Pirmin SCHWEGLER (Moreno COSTANZO 83), Xavier MARGAIRAZ (Xherdan SHAQIRI 46), Gokhan INLER, David DEGEN (Marco STRELLER 64), Alexander FREI, Eren DERDIYOK. Tr: Ottmar HITZFELD	**MNE:** Mladen BOZOVIC - Elsad ZVEROTIC, Stefan SAVIC, Milan JOVANOVIC, Miodrag DZUDOVIC, Marko BASA, Simon VUKCEVIC• (Fatos BECIRAJ 85), Mitar NOVAKOVIC, Branko BOSKOVIC (Mladen KASCELAN 46), Mirko VUCINIC•, Radomir DALOVIC (Radoslav BATAK 90). Tr: Zlatko KRANJCAR	**WAL:** Wayne HENNESSEY - Ashley WILLIAMS, Sam RICKETTS•, Chris GUNTER•♦[90], James COLLINS, Danny COLLINS, David VAUGHAN, Joe LEDLEY (Andy KING 59), Dave EDWARDS (Simon CHURCH 68), Gareth BALE, Steve MORISON (Hal ROBSON-KANU 82). Tr: Brian FLYNN
ENG: Joe HART - Joleon LESCOTT, Glen JOHNSON, Ashley COLE•, Phil JAGIELKA, James MILNER•, Steven GERRARD, Gareth BARRY, Theo WALCOTT (Adam JOHNSON 13), Wayne ROONEY (Shaun WRIGHT-PHILLIPS 79), Jermain DEFOE (Darren BENT 73). Tr: Fabio CAPELLO	**SUI:** Marco WOLFLI - Reto ZIEGLER, Steve VON BERGEN, Scott SUTTER, Stephane GRICHTING, Valentin STOCKER (Hakan YAKIN 77), Xherdan SHAQIRI (Tranquillo BARNETTA 67), Pirmin SCHWEGLER, Gokhan INLER, Marco STRELLER (Eren DERDIYOK 67), Alexander FREI. Tr: Ottmar HITZFELD	**BUL:** Nikolai MIHAILOV - Petar ZANEV•, Ivan IVANOV, Valentin ILIEV (Pavel VIDANOV 37), Nikolay BODUROV•, Stilian PETROV, Martin PETROV•, Georgi PEEV (Dimitar RANGELOV 72), Blagoy GEORGIEV•, Ivelin POPOV, Dimitar MAKRIEV (Chavdar YANKOV 87). Tr: Lothar MATTHAUS

ST. JAKOB PARK, BASEL	WEMBLEY STADIUM, LONDON	MILLENNIUM STADIUM, CARDIFF
12-10-2010, Att: 26 000, Ref: Hamer LUX	12-10-2010, Att: 73 451, Ref: Grafe GER	26-03-2011, Att: 68 959, Ref: Benquerenca POR
Switzerland 4	England 0	Wales 0
Wales 1	Montenegro 0	England 2
SUI - Stocker 2 [8 89], Streller [21], Gokhan Inler [82p]		ENG - Lampard [7p], Bent [15]
WAL - Bale [13]		
SUI: Diego BENAGLIO (Marco WOLFLI 8), Steve VON BERGEN, Stephan LICHTSTEINER•, Stephane GRICHTING, Reto ZIEGLER, Valentin STOCKER, Pirmin SCHWEGLER (Gelson FERNANDES 90), Gokhan INLER, Tranquillo BARNETTA•, Marco STRELLER, Alexander FREI (Eren DERDIYOK 79). Tr: Ottmar HITZFELD	**ENG:** Joe HART - Joleon LESCOTT, Glen JOHNSON, Rio FERDINAND, Ashley COLE, Ashley YOUNG• (Shaun WRIGHT-PHILLIPS 74), Adam JOHNSON, Steven GERRARD, Gareth BARRY•, Wayne ROONEY•, Peter CROUCH (Kevin DAVIES• 70). Tr: Fabio CAPELLO	**WAL:** Wayne HENNESSEY - Ashley WILLIAMS, Chris GUNTER, Andrew CROFTS•, James COLLINS•, Danny COLLINS, Aaron RAMSEY, Joe LEDLEY•, Andy KING (Ched EVANS 65), Steve MORISON (David VAUGHAN 65), Craig BELLAMY•. Tr: Gary SPEED
WAL: Wayne HENNESSEY - Danny COLLINS, Andrew CROFTS, Ashley WILLIAMS, James COLLINS•, Darcy BLAKE (Christian RIBEIRO 54), Andy KING•, David VAUGHAN (Sam MACDONALD 89), Dave EDWARDS (Steve MORISON 77), Gareth BALE, Simon CHURCH. Tr: Brian FLYNN	**MNE:** Mladen BOZOVIC - Elsad ZVEROTIC, Stefan SAVIC•, Milan JOVANOVIC, Miodrag DZUDOVIC•, Marko BASA•, Simon VUKCEVIC•, Milorad PEKOVIC, Mitar NOVAKOVIC (Mladen KASCELAN• 62), Branko BOSKOVIC (Fatos BECIRAJ 83), Radomir DALOVIC (Andrija DELIBASIC 77). Tr: Zlatko KRANJCAR	**ENG:** Joe HART - John TERRY, Glen JOHNSON•, Michael DAWSON, Ashley COLE, Ashley YOUNG, Jack WILSHERE (Stewart DOWNING 82), Scott PARKER (Phil JAGIELKA 88), Frank LAMPARD, Wayne ROONEY• (James MILNER 70), Darren BENT. Tr: Fabio CAPELLO

VASIL LEVSKI, SOFIA	WEMBLEY STADIUM, LONDON	POD GORICOM, PODGORICA
26-03-2011, Att: 9600, Ref: Collum SCO	4-06-2011, Att: 84 459, Ref: Skomina SVN	4-06-2011, Att: 11 500, Ref: Yefet ISR
Bulgaria 0	England 2	Montenegro 1
Switzerland 0	Switzerland 2	Bulgaria 1
	ENG - Lampard [37p], Young [51]	MNE - Djalovic [53] • BUL - Popov [66]
	SUI - Barnetta 2 [32 35]	
BUL: Nikolai MIHAILOV - Kostadin STOYANOV•, Stanislav MANOLEV•, Ivan IVANOV, Ivan BANDALOVSKI, Petar ZANEV, Stilian PETROV, Blagoy GEORGIEV•, Spas DELEV (Zdravko LAZAROV 81), Dimitar MAKRIEV (Tzvetan GENKOV 52), Ivelin POPOV (Stanislav ANGELOV 85). Tr: Lothar MATTHAUS	**ENG:** Joe HART - Glen JOHNSON•, John TERRY, Rio FERDINAND•, Ashley COLE (Leighton BAINES 30), Scott PARKER, James MILNER, Jack WILSHERE•, Frank LAMPARD (Ashley YOUNG 46), Theo WALCOTT (Stewart DOWNING 78), Darren BENT. Tr: Fabio CAPELLO	**MNE:** Mladen BOZOVIC - Elsad ZVEROTIC (Stevan JOVETIC 72), Stefan SAVIC, Luka PEJOVIC, Savo PAVICEVIC• (Mladen KASCELAN 82), Marko BASA•, Milorad PEKOVIC•, Nikola DRINCIC, Vladimir BOZOVIC• (Ivan FATIC 76), Mirko VUCINIC, Radomir DALOVIC. Tr: Zlatko KRANJCAR
SUI: Marco WOLFLI - Steve VON BERGEN, Stephan LICHTSTEINER, Stephane GRICHTING, Reto ZIEGLER, Valentin STOCKER (Eren DERDIYOK• 67), Gokhan INLER, Blerim DZEMAILI, Valon BEHRAMI• (Gelson FERNANDES 17), Marco STRELLER (Mario GAVRANOVIC 77), Alexander FREI. Tr: Ottmar HITZFELD	**SUI:** Diego BENAGLIO - Johan DJOUROU•, Philippe SENDEROS, Stephan LICHTSTEINER, Reto ZIEGLER, Granit XHAKA, Xherdan SHAQIRI, Gokhan INLER, Valon BEHRAMI• (Blerim DZEMAILI 58), Tranquillo BARNETTA (Innocent EMEGHARA 90), Eren DERDIYOK (Admir MEHMEDI 75). Tr: Ottmar HITZFELD	**BUL:** Nikolai MIHAILOV - Petar ZANEV, Stanislav MANOLEV, Ivan IVANOV, Ivan BANDALOVSKI, Nikolay BODUROV, Hristo YANEV (Tzvetan GENKOV 84), Stilian PETROV (Chavdar YANKOV 46), Martin PETROV (Spas DELEV 88), MARQUINHOS•, Ivelin POPOV. Tr: Lothar MATTHAUS

VASIL LEVSKI, SOFIA	CARDIFF CITY STADIUM, CARDIFF	ST. JAKOB PARK, BASEL
2-09-2011, Att: 27 230, Ref: De Bleeckere BEL	2-09-2011, Att: 8194, Ref: Banti ITA	6-09-2011, Att: 16 880, Ref: Kralovec CZE
Bulgaria 0	Wales 2	Switzerland 3
England 3	Montenegro 1	Bulgaria 1
ENG - Cahill [13], Rooney 2 [21 45]	WAL - Morison [29], Ramsey [50] • MNE - Jovetic [71]	SUI - Shaqiri 3 [45 62 90] • BUL - Ivanov.I [9]
BUL: Nikolai MIHAILOV - Petar ZANEV, Zhivko MILANOV•, Ivan IVANOV, Ivan BANDALOVSKI (Georgi SARMOV• 46), Nikolaj BODUROV, Stilian PETROV, Martin PETROV, Blagoy GEORGIEV, Ivelin POPOV (MARQUINHOS 81), Tzvetan GENKOV (Georgi BOZHILOV 61). Tr: Lothar MATTHAUS	**WAL:** Wayne HENNESSEY - Neil TAYLOR, Chris GUNTER, Ashley WILLIAMS, Aaron RAMSEY (Andrew CROFTS 64), Joe LEDLEY, Darcy BLAKE, Craig BELLAMY•, Gareth BALE (Robert EARNSHAW 90), Steve MORISON (Hal ROBSON-KANU 83), Craig BELLAMY•. Tr: Gary SPEED	**SUI:** Diego BENAGLIO - Johan DJOUROU•, Philippe SENDEROS, Stephan LICHTSTEINER, Reto ZIEGLER, Granit XHAKA (Gelson FERNANDES 48), Xherdan SHAQIRI• (Nassim BEN KHALIFA 90), Gokhan INLER, Blerim DZEMAILI, Admir MEHMEDI (Innocent EMEGHARA 83), Eren DERDIYOK. Tr: Ottmar HITZFELD
ENG: Joe HART - Chris SMALLING, Gary CAHILL, John TERRY, Ashley COLE, Ashley YOUNG (James MILNER 61), Scott PARKER, Stewart DOWNING, Gareth BARRY (Frank LAMPARD 80), Theo WALCOTT (Adam JOHNSON 83), Wayne ROONEY. Tr: Fabio CAPELLO	**MNE:** Mladen BOZOVIC - Elsad ZVEROTIC, Stefan SAVIC, Radoslav BATAK, Sasa BALIC• (Milan JOVANOVIC 83), Simon VUKCEVIC, Milorad PEKOVIC, Nikola DRINCIC•, Mirko VUCINIC (Andrija DELIBASIC 79), Stevan JOVETIC, Radomir DALOVIC (Dejan DAMJANOVIC 57). Tr: Zlatko KRANJCAR	**BUL:** Nikolai MIHAILOV - Ivan IVANOV, Zhivko MILANOV•♦[65], Petar ZANEV, Valentin ILIEV, Georgi SARMOV, Stilian PETROV, Martin PETROV (Vladimir GADZHEV• 60), Blagoy GEORGIEV•, Ivelin POPOV, Tzvetan GENKOV (Nikolaj BODUROV 70). Tr: Lothar MATTHAUS

WEMBLEY STADIUM, LONDON
6-09-2011, Att: 77 128, Ref: Schorgenhofer AUT

England	1
Wales	0

ENG - Young [35]

ENG: Joe HART – John TERRY, Chris SMALLING, Ashley COLE, Gary CAHILL, Ashley YOUNG, James MILNER•, Stewart DOWNING (Adam JOHNSON 79), Gareth BARRY, Frank LAMPARD (Scott PARKER 73), Wayne ROONEY (Andy CARROLL 89). Tr: Fabio CAPELLO

WAL: Wayne HENNESSEY – Ashley WILLIAMS, Neil TAYLOR, Chris GUNTER, Andrew CROFTS, Aaron RAMSEY, Joe LEDLEY, Jack COLLISON (Andy KING 85), Darcy BLAKE, Gareth BALE, Steve MORISON (Robert EARNSHAW 67). Tr: Gary SPEED

LIBERTY STADIUM, SWANSEA
7-10-2011, Att: 12 317, Ref: Kuipers NED

Wales	2
Switzerland	0

WAL - Ramsey [60p], Bale [71]

WAL: Wayne HENNESSEY – Ashley WILLIAMS, Neil TAYLOR, Chris GUNTER, Andrew CROFTS (David VAUGHAN 81), Joe ALLEN, Aaron RAMSEY, Darcy BLAKE•, Gareth BALE, Craig BELLAMY, Steve MORISON (Simon CHURCH 81). Tr: Gary SPEED

SUI: Diego BENAGLIO – Timm KLOSE•, Steve VON BERGEN•, Reto ZIEGLER♦55, Stephan LICHTSTEINER, Granit XHAKA (Admir MEHMEDI 81), Fabian FREI (Innocent EMEGHARA 71), Valon BEHRAMI, Xherdan SHAQIRI (Ricardo RODRIGUEZ 62), Gokhan INLER, Eren DERDIYOK. Tr: Ottmar HITZFELD

POD GORICOM, PODGORICA
7-10-2011, Att: 11 340, Ref: Stark GER

Montenegro	2
England	2

MNE - Zverotic [45], Delibasic [91+]
ENG - Young [11], Bent [31]

MNE: Mladen BOZOVIC – Elsad ZVEROTIC, Stefan SAVIC, Miodrag DZUDOVIC, Simon VUKCEVIC, Milorad PEKOVIC•, Mladen KASCELAN (Milan JOVANOVIC• 46), Vladimir BOZOVIC (Andrija DELIBASIC• 79), Mirko VUCINIC•, Stevan JOVETIC•, Fatos BECIRAJ (Dejan DAMJANOVIC 64). Tr: Branko BRNOVIC

ENG: Joe HART – John TERRY, Phil JONES, Ashley COLE, Gary CAHILL, Ashley YOUNG (Stewart DOWNING 60), Scott PARKER, Gareth BARRY, Theo WALCOTT (Danny WELBECK 74), Wayne ROONEY♦74, Darren BENT (Frank LAMPARD 64). Tr: Fabio CAPELLO

VASIL LEVSKI, SOFIA
11-10-2011, Att: 11 340, Ref: Gil POL

Bulgaria	0
Wales	1

WAL - Bale [45]

BUL: Nikolai MIHAILOV – Petar ZANEV, Georgi TERZIEV, Yordan MILIEV, Stanislav MANOLEV (Spas DELEV 52), Ivan IVANOV•, Aleksandar TONEV, Stilian PETROV•, Vladimir GADZHEV•, Valeri DOMOVCHIYSKI (Valeri BOJINOV 62), Ivelin POPOV (Dimitar RANGELOV 70). Tr: Mihail MADANSKI

WAL: Wayne HENNESSEY – Ashley WILLIAMS, Neil TAYLOR, Chris GUNTER, Andrew CROFTS, Aaron RAMSEY, Darcy BLAKE (Adam MATTHEWS 41), Joe ALLEN•, Gareth BALE, Steve MORISON (Simon CHURCH 70), Craig BELLAMY. Tr: Gary SPEED

ST. JAKOB PARK, BASEL
11-10-2011, Att: 19 997, Ref: Benquerenca POR

Switzerland	2
Montenegro	0

SUI - Derdiyok [51], Lichtsteiner [65]

SUI: Diego BENAGLIO – Ricardo RODRIGUEZ, Johan DJOUROU, Stephan LICHTSTEINER•, Steve VON BERGEN, Granit XHAKA (Gelson FERNANDES 85), Xherdan SHAQIRI (David DEGEN 79), Gokhan INLER, Valon BEHRAMI•, Admir MEHMEDI, Eren DERDIYOK (Innocent EMEGHARA 69). Tr: Ottmar HITZFELD

MNE: Mladen BOZOVIC – Marko CETKOVIC•, Elsad ZVEROTIC, Stefan SAVIC, Luka PEJOVIC (Vladimir BOZOVIC 46), Radoslav BATAK, Nikola DRINCIC (Petar GRBIC 72), Drasko BOZOVIC, Radomir Dalovic• (Andrija DELIBASIC 66), Dejan DAMJANOVIC, Fatos BECIRAJ•. Tr: Branko BRNOVIC

	GROUP H	PL	W	D	L	F	A	PTS	DEN	POR	NOR	ISL	CYP
1	Denmark	8	6	1	1	15	6	19		2-1	2-0	1-0	2-0
2	Portugal	8	5	1	2	21	12	16	3-1		1-0	5-3	4-4
3	Norway	8	5	1	2	10	7	16	1-1	1-0		1-0	3-1
4	Iceland	8	1	1	6	6	14	4	0-2	1-3	1-2		1-0
5	Cyprus	8	0	2	6	7	20	2	1-4	0-4	1-2	0-0	

Denmark qualified directly for the finals • Portugal qualified for a play-off v Bosnia • Bosnia 0-2 2-6 **Portugal**

LAUGARDALSVOLLUR, REYKJAVIK
3-09-2010, Att: 6137, Ref: Banti ITA

Iceland	1
Norway	2

ISL - Helgusson [38] • NOR - Hangeland [58], Abdellaoue [75]

ISL: Gunnleifur GUNNLEIFSSON – Gretar STEINSSON (Veigar GUNNARSSON 76), Indridi SIGURDSSON, Solvi OTTESEN, Kristjan SIGURDSSON, Gylfi SIGURDSSON, Eggert JONSSON, Aron Gunnarsson•, Heidar HELGUSON (Arnor ADALSTEINSSON 76), Johann GUDMUNDSSON (Rurik GISLASON 87). Tr: Olafur JOHANNESSON

NOR: Jon KNUDSEN – Kjetil WAEHLER, John Arne RIISE, Tom HOGLI, Brede HANGELAND•, Bjorn Helge RIISE (Steffen IVERSEN 57), Morten PEDERSEN, Erik HUSEKLEPP (Espen RUUD 75), Henning HAUGER•, Christian GRINDHEIM, Mohammed ABDELLAOUE (Jan Gunnar SOLLI 88). Tr: Egil OLSEN

AFONSO HENRIQUES, GUIMARAES
3-09-2010, Att: 9100, Ref: Clattenburg ENG

Portugal	4
Cyprus	4

POR - Almeida [8], Meireles [29], Danny [50], Fernandes [60] • CYP - Aloneftis [3], Konstantinou [11], Okkas [57], Avraam [89]

POR: EDUARDO – MIGUEL, RICARDO CARVALHO, BRUNO ALVES, QUARESMA, NANI, RAUL MEIRELES, MANUEL FERNANDES (JOAO MOUTINHO 78), FABIO COENTRAO, DANNY (LIEDSON 61), HUGO ALMEIDA (YANNICK DJALO 84). Tr: Carlos QUEIROZ

CYP: Antonis GEORGALLIDES – Giorgios MERKIS, Marios ELIA (Savvas POURSAITIDIS 66), Marinos SATSIAS, Konstantinos MAKRIDES, Sinisa DOBRASINOVIC, Ilias CHARALAMBOUS•, Costas CHARALAMBIDES (Marios NICOLAOU 75), Michalis KONSTANTINOU, Andreas AVRAAM, Efstathios ALONEFTIS (Yiannis OKKAS 56). Tr: Angelos ANASTASIADIS

PARKEN, COPENHAGEN
7-09-2010, Att: 18 908, Ref: McDonald SCO

Denmark	1
Iceland	0

DEN - Kahlenberg [91+]

DEN: Anders LINDEGAARD – Simon KJAER, Leon JESSEN, Lars JACOBSEN, Daniel AGGER, Christian POULSEN, Thomas KAHLENBERG, Christian ERIKSEN (Mads JUNKER 56), Michael KROHN-DEHLI (Martin VINGAARD 76), Dennis ROMMEDAHL, Nicklas PEDERSEN (Morten SKOUBO• 71). Tr: Morten OLSEN

ISL: Gunnleifur GUNNLEIFSSON – Birkir SAEVARSSON, Indridi SIGURDSSON, Solvi OTTESEN, Kristjan SIGURDSSON, Gylfi SIGURDSSON•, Eggert JONSSON•, Aron GUNNARSSON, Rurik GISLASON•, Heidar HELGUSON (Kolbeinn SIGTHORSSON 77), Johann GUDMUNDSSON (Birkir BJARNASON 90). Tr: Olafur JOHANNESSON

UEFA EURO 2012 POLAND/UKRAINE QUALIFYING GROUP H

ULLEVAAL STADION, OSLO	ANTONIS PAPADOPOULOS, LARNACA	ESTADIO DO DRAGAO, PORTO
7-09-2010, Att: 24 535, Ref: Duhamel FRA	8-10-2010, Att: 7648, Ref: Gumienny BEL	8-10-2010, Att: 27 117, Ref: Braamhaar NED
Norway 1 — Portugal 0	Cyprus 1 — Norway 2	Portugal 3 — Denmark 1
NOR - Huseklepp [21]	CYP - Okkas [58] • NOR - Riise.JA [2], Carew [42]	POR - Nani 2 [29,30], Ronaldo [85] • DEN - OG [79]
NOR: Jon KNUDSEN - Kjetil WAEHLER (Vadim DEMIDOV 28), Espen RUUD, Tom HOGLI, Brede HANGELAND, Morten PEDERSEN, Erik HUSEKLEPP, Henning HAUGER, Christian GRINDHEIM (Ruben JENSSEN 86), Bjorn Helge RIISE•, John CAREW (Mohammed ABDELLAOUE 38). Tr: Egil OLSEN	**CYP:** Antonis GEORGALLIDES - Giorgios MERKIS (Demetris CHRISTOFI 81), Savvas POURSAITIDIS•, Konstantinos MAKRIDES, Sinisa DOBRASINOVIC, Ilias CHARALAMBOUS (Giorgos EFREM 86), Costas CHARALAMBIDES (Marinos SATSIAS• 46), Yiannis OKKAS, Michalis KONSTANTINOU, Andreas AVRAAM, Efstathios ALONEFTIS. Tr: Angelos ANASTASIADIS	**POR:** EDUARDO - JOAO PEREIRA, RICARDO CARVALHO, PEPE, CARLOS MARTINS (TIAGO 75), RAUL MEIRELES, NANI (VARELA 88), JOAO MOUTINHO, FABIO COENTRAO, HUGO ALMEIDA (HELDER POSTIGA 69), CRISTIANO RONALDO. Tr: PAULO BENTO
POR: EDUARDO - SILVIO, RICARDO CARVALHO, BRUNO ALVES, TIAGO (DANNY 71), RAUL MEIRELES•, QUARESMA (LIEDSON 83), NANI, MIGUEL VELOSO, MANUEL FERNANDES, HUGO ALMEIDA•. Tr: Carlos QUEIROZ	**NOR:** Jon KNUDSEN - Kjetil WAEHLER, John Arne RIISE•, Tom HOGLI, Brede HANGELAND, Bjorn Helge RIISE (Petter MOEN 75), Morten PEDERSEN, Erik HUSEKLEPP (Espen RUUD 80), Henning HAUGER, Christian GRINDHEIM, John CAREW• (Mohammed ABDELLAOUE 84). Tr: Egil OLSEN	**DEN:** Thomas SORENSEN (Anders LINDEGAARD 32), Per KROLDRUP, Simon KJAER, Lars JACOBSEN, William KVIST (Peter LOVENKRANDS 72), Daniel JENSEN (Christian ERIKSEN 58), Martin VINGAARD, Michael SILBERBAUER•, Christian POULSEN, Dennis ROMMEDAHL, Nicklas PEDERSEN. Tr: Morten OLSEN

PARKEN, COPENHAGEN	LAUGARDALSVOLLUR, REYKJAVIK	GSP, NICOSIA
12-10-2010, Att: 15 544, Ref: Muniz ESP	12-10-2010, Att: 9767, Ref: Einwaller AUT	26-03-2011, Att: 2088, Ref: Ceferin SVN
Denmark 2 — Cyprus 0	Iceland 1 — Portugal 3	Cyprus 0 — Iceland 0
DEN - Rasmussen [48], Lorentzen [81]	ISL - Helguson [17] — POR - Ronaldo [3], Meireles [27], Postiga [72]	
DEN: Anders LINDEGAARD - Simon KJAER, Leon JESSEN, Lars JACOBSEN, Daniel AGGER (Per KROLDRUP 39), Christian POULSEN, Kasper LORENTZEN, Michael KROHN-DEHLI (Christian ERIKSEN 65), Dennis ROMMEDAHL, Nicklas PEDERSEN•, Mads JUNKER (Morten RASMUSSEN 46). Tr: Morten OLSEN	**ISL:** Gunnleifur GUNNLEIFSSON - Gretar STEINSSON, Ragnar SIGURDSSON, Indridi SIGURDSSON (Arnor ADALSTEINSSON 86), Birkir SAEVARSSON (Veigar GUNNARSSON 85), Olafur SKULASON•, Kristjan SIGURDSSON, Helgi DANIELSSON, Birkir BJARNASON (Gunnar THORVALDSSON 68), Heidar HELGUSON, Eidur GUDJOHNSEN•. Tr: Olafur Johannesson	**CYP:** Antonis GEORGALLIDES - Valentinos SIELIS (Jason DEMETRIOU 46), Giorgios MERKIS•, Costas CHARALAMBIDES, Savvas POURSAITIDIS (Marios ELIA 61), Chrysis MICHAEL, Konstantinos MAKRIDES, Sinisa DOBRASINOVIC, Andreas AVRAAM, Efstathios ALONEFTIS, Demetris CHRISTOFI (Nektarios ALEXANDROU 73). Tr: Angelos ANASTASIADIS
CYP: Antonis GEORGALLIDES - Giorgios MERKIS, Marinos SATSIAS•, Savvas POURSAITIDIS, Konstantinos MAKRIDES, Sinisa DOBRASINOVIC, Ilias CHARALAMBOUS (Paraskevas CHRISTOU 28), Yiannis OKKAS, Michalis KONSTANTINOU, Andreas AVRAAM (Alexandros GARPOZIS 64), Efstathios ALONEFTIS (Costas CHARALAMBIDES 54). Tr: Angelos ANASTASIADIS	**POR:** EDUARDO - JOAO PEREIRA, PEPE, RICARDO CARVALHO, NANI (DANNY 88), JOAO MOUTINHO, RAUL MEIRELES, CARLOS MARTINS (TIAGO• 77), FABIO COENTRAO, CRISTIANO RONALDO, HUGO ALMEIDA (HELDER POSTIGA 66). Tr: PAULO BENTO	**ISL:** Stefan MAGNUSSON• - Hermann HREIDARSSON, Indridi SIGURDSSON•, Birkir SAEVARSSON, Kristjan SIGURDSSON•, Aron GUNNARSSON, Rurik GISLASON (Alfred FINNBOGASON 63), Gylfi SIGURDSSON (Birkir BJARNASON 90), Eggert JONSSON•, Heidar HELGUSON, Johann GUDMUNDSSON (Arnor SMARASON 58). Tr: Olafur Johannesson

ULLEVAAL STADION, OSLO	LAUGARDALSVOLLUR, REYKJAVIK	ESTADIO DA LUZ, LISBON
26-03-2011, Att: 24 828, Ref: Rocchi ITA	4-06-2011, Att: 7629, Ref: Aydinus TUR	4-06-2011, Att: 47 829, Ref: Cakir TUR
Norway 1 — Denmark 1	Iceland 0 — Denmark 2	Portugal 1 — Norway 0
NOR - Huseklepp [81] • DEN - Rommedahl [27]	DEN - Schone [60], Eriksen [75]	POR - Postiga [53]
NOR: Rune JARSTEIN - Brede HANGELAND, Kjetil WAEHLER•, Espen RUUD (Daniel BRAATEN 78), John Arne RIISE, Christian GRINDHEIM, Bjorn Helge RIISE, Morten PEDERSEN, Erik HUSEKLEPP (Steffen IVERSEN 89), Henning HAUGER, Mohammed ABDELLAOUE. Tr: Egil OLSEN	**ISL:** Stefan MAGNUSSON• - Hermann HREIDARSSON, Birkir SAEVARSSON, Bjarni EIRIKSSON, Olafur SKULASON• (Alfred FINNBOGASON 67), Kristjan SIGURDSSON•, Gylfi SIGURDSSON, Aron GUNNARSSON, Heidar HELGUSON (Johann GUDMUNDSSON 77), Eidur GUDJOHNSEN, Kolbeinn SIGTHORSSON. Tr: Olafur JOHANNESSON	**POR:** EDUARDO - PEPE, JOAO PEREIRA (SILVIO 73), BRUNO ALVES, RAUL MEIRELES, NANI (VARELA 86), JOAO MOUTINHO, CARLOS MARTINS (RUBEN MICAEL 69), FABIO COENTRAO, HELDER POSTIGA, CRISTIANO RONALDO. Tr: PAULO BENTO
DEN: Thomas SORENSEN - Daniel AGGER, William KVIST, Mathias JORGENSEN, Lars JACOBSEN•, Christian ERIKSEN, Michael SILBERBAUER, Christian POULSEN (Jakob POULSEN 69), Michael KROHN-DEHLI (Thomas ENEVOLDSEN 83), Nicklas BENDTNER, Dennis ROMMEDAHL (Daniel WASS 90). Tr: Morten OLSEN	**DEN:** Thomas SORENSEN - Bo SVENSSON•, Simon POULSEN, William KVIST (Christian POULSEN 60), Simon KJAER, Lars JACOBSEN, Niki ZIMLING, Christian ERIKSEN, Michael KROHN-DEHLI (Lasse SCHONE 46), Dennis ROMMEDAHL, Nicklas BENDTNER. Tr: Morten OLSEN	**NOR:** Rune JARSTEIN - John Arne RIISE, Tom HOGLI, Brede HANGELAND, Vadim DEMIDOV, Bjorn Helge RIISE, Morten PEDERSEN, Erik HUSEKLEPP (Daniel BRAATEN 75), Henning HAUGER, Christian GRINDHEIM (Markus HENRIKSEN 84), John CAREW (Mohammed ABDELLAOUE 60). Tr: Egil OLSEN

ULLEVAAL STADION, OSLO	GSP, NICOSIA	PARKEN, COPENHAGEN
2-09-2011, Att: 22 381, Ref: Hategin ROU	2-09-2011, Att: 15 444, Ref: Rocchi ITA	6-09-2011, Att: 37 167, Ref: Lannoy FRA
Norway 1 — Iceland 0	Cyprus 0 — Portugal 4	Denmark 2 — Norway 0
NOR - Abdellaoue [88p]	POR - Ronaldo 2 [35p,82], Almeida [84], Danny [92+]	DEN - Bendtner 2 [24,44]
NOR: Rune JARSTEIN - Kjetil WAEHLER, Espen RUUD, Tom HOGLI, Brede HANGELAND, Alexander TETTEY, Jonathan PARR (Daniel BRAATEN• 68), Erik HUSEKLEPP (Simen BRENNE 87), Henning HAUGER, Christian GRINDHEIM (John CAREW 80), Mohammed ABDELLAOUE. Tr: Egil OLSEN	**CYP:** Antonis GEORGALLIDES - Giorgios MERKIS, Jason DEMETRIOU, Paraskevas CHRISTOU, Savvas POURSAITIDIS, Konstantinos MAKRIDES• (Marios NICOLAOU 38), Sinisa DOBRASINOVIC•• 34, Costas CHARALAMBIDES (Nektarios ALEXANDROU 63), Yiannis OKKAS, Andreas AVRAAM, Demetris CHRISTOFI (Giorgos EFREM 80). Tr: Nikos NIOPLIAS	**DEN:** Thomas SORENSEN - William KVIST, Simon KJAER•, Lars JACOBSEN, Nicolai BOILESEN, Daniel AGGER, Niki ZIMLING, Christian ERIKSEN, Michael KROHN-DEHLI (Lasse SCHONE 69), Dennis ROMMEDAHL (Michael SILBERBAUER 65), Nicklas BENDTNER (Nicklas PEDERSEN 89). Tr: Morten OLSEN
ISL: Stefan MAGNUSSON• - Solvi OTTESEN, Indridi SIGURDSSON•, Birkir SAEVARSSON, Hjortur VALGARDSSON, Eggert JONSSON, Rurik GISLASON•, Helgi DANIELSSON (Birkir BJARNASON 90), Eidur GUDJOHNSEN, Kolbeinn SIGTHORSSON (Veigar GUNNARSSON 77), Johann GUDMUNDSSON (Steinþor THORSTEINSSON 80). Tr: Olafur JOHANNESSON	**POR:** RUI PATRICIO - JOAO PEREIRA, PEPE, BRUNO ALVES, RUBEN MICAEL• (MIGUEL VELOSO 63), NANI (DANNY 85), JOAO MOUTINHO, RAUL MEIRELES, FABIO COENTRAO, HELDER POSTIGA (HUGO ALMEIDA 76), CRISTIANO RONALDO•. Tr: PAULO BENTO	**NOR:** Rune JARSTEIN - Kjetil WAEHLER (Vadim DEMIDOV 46), Espen RUUD, John Arne RIISE (Daniel BRAATEN• 61), Havard NORDTVEIT•, Tom HOGLI•, Brede HANGELAND•, Alexander TETTEY, Erik HUSEKLEPP (John CAREW 67), Christian GRINDHEIM•, Mohammed ABDELLAOUE. Tr: Egil OLSEN

PART THREE – THE CONTINENTAL CONFEDERATIONS

LAUGARDALSVOLLUR, REYKJAVIK
6-09-2011, Att: 5267, Ref: Jovanetic SRB

Iceland	1
Cyprus	0

ISL - Sigthorsson [5]

ISL: Hannes HALLDORSSON - Hallgrimur JONASSON, Birkir SAEVARSSON, Hjortur VALGARDSSON, Kristjan SIGURDSSON, Eggert JONSSON•, Helgi DANIELSSON, Birkir BJARNASON• (Alfred FINNBOGASON 84), Eidur GUDJOHNSEN, Kolbeinn SIGTHORSSON (Bjorn SIGURDARSON 84), Johann GUDMUNDSSON (Matthias VILHJALMSSON 88). Tr: Olafur JOHANNESSON

CYP: Antonis GEORGALLIDES - Giorgios MERKIS, Jason DEMETRIOU•, Paraskevas CHRISTOU, Marinos SATSIAS, Savvas POURSAITIDIS, Costas CHARALAMBIDES (Kyriakos PAVLOU 83), Yiannis OKKAS• (Konstantinos MAKRIDES• 46), Andreas AVRAAM, Nektarios ALEXANDROU (Giorgos EFREM 61), Demetris CHRISTOFI. Tr: Nikos NIOPLIAS

GSP, NICOSIA
7-10-2011, Att: 2408, Ref: Strahonja CRO

Cyprus	1
Denmark	4

CYP - Avraam [45] • DEN - Jacobsen [7], Rommedahl 2 [11 22], Krohn-Dehli [20]

CYP: Antonis GEORGALLIDES - Giorgios PELAGIAS, Giorgios MERKIS, Jason DEMETRIOU (Marinos SATSIAS 71), Savvas POURSAITIDIS• (Athos SOLOMOU 47), Giorgos EFREM, Sinisa DOBRASINOVIC•, Costas CHARALAMBIDES, Michalis KONSTANTINOU (Demetris CHRISTOFI 62), Andreas AVRAAM•, Nektarios ALEXANDROU. Tr: Nikos NIOPLIAS

DEN: Thomas SORENSEN - Simon POULSEN, William KVIST, Simon KJAER, Lars JACOBSEN (Michael SILBERBAUER 82), Andreas BJELLAND•, Niki ZIMLING• (Martin JORGENSEN 68), Christian ERIKSEN, Michael KROHN-DEHLI, Dennis ROMMEDAHL (Christian POULSEN 71), Nicklas BENDTNER. Tr: Morten OLSEN

ESTADIO DO DRAGAO, PORTO
7-10-2011, Att: 35 715, Ref: Nijhuis NED

Portugal	5
Iceland	3

POR - Nani 2 [13 21], Postiga [44], Moutinho [81], Eliseu [87]
ISL - Jonasson 2 [48 68], Sigurdsson.G [94+p]

POR: RUI PATRICIO - ROLANDO•, JOAO PEREIRA, BRUNO ALVES, NANI, JOAO MOUTINHO, RAUL MEIRELES (MIGUEL VELOSO 60), CARLOS MARTINS• (RUBEN MICAEL 72), ELISEU, HELDER POSTIGA (NUNO GOMES 88), CRISTIANO RONALDO. Tr: PAULO BENTO

ISL: Stefan MAGNUSSON - Hallgrimur JONASSON (Matthias VILHJALMSSON 88), Birkir SAEVARSSON•, Solvi OTTESEN, Hjortur VALGARDSSON, Kristjan SIGURDSSON, Gylfi SIGURDSSON, Aron GUNNARSSON, Rurik GISLASON (Arnor SMARASON 88), Birkir BJARNASON, Johann GUDMUNDSSON (Alfred FINNBOGASON 81). Tr: Olafur JOHANNESSON

ULLEVAAL STADION, OSLO
11-10-2011, Att: 13 490, Ref: Collum SCO

Norway	3
Cyprus	1

NOR - Pedersen [25], Carew [34], Hogli [65]
CYP - Okkas [42]

NOR: Rune JARSTEIN - Kjetil WAEHLER, Espen RUUD• (Simen BRENNE 62), John Arne RIISE, Tom HOGLI, Vadim DEMIDOV, Alexander TETTEY (Ruben JENSSEN 80), Morten PEDERSEN (Jonathan PARR 46), Erik HUSEKLEPP, Christian GRINDHEIM, John CAREW. Tr: Egil OLSEN

CYP: Tasos KISSAS - Giorgios PELAGIAS (Stelios PARPAS 6), Giorgios MERKIS•, Jason DEMETRIOU, Athos SOLOMOU, Marinos SATSIAS, Sinisa DOBRASINOVIC, Ilias CHARALAMBOUS, Costas CHARALAMBIDES (Demetris CHRISTOFI 62), Yiannis OKKAS (Andreas STAVROU 81), Andreas AVRAAM. Tr: Nikos NIOPLIAS

PARKEN, COPENHAGEN
11-10-2011, Att: 37 012, Ref: Rizzoli ITA

Denmark	2
Portugal	1

DEN - Krohn-Dehli [13], Bendtner [63]
POR - Cristiano Ronaldo [92+]

DEN: Thomas SORENSEN - William KVIST, Simon KJAER, Lars JACOBSEN, Andreas BJELLAND, Niki ZIMLING (Christian POULSEN 70), Michael SILBERBAUER• (Simon POULSEN 76), Christian ERIKSEN, Michael KROHN-DEHLI, Nicklas BENDTNER, Dennis ROMMEDAHL• (Jakob POULSEN 87). Tr: Morten OLSEN

POR: RUI PATRICIO - BRUNO ALVES, ROLANDO, JOAO PEREIRA, CARLOS MARTINS (QUARESMA 65), RAUL MEIRELES, NANI, JOAO MOUTINHO, ELISEU (MIGUEL VELOSO 65), CRISTIANO RONALDO, HELDER POSTIGA (NUNO GOMES 78). Tr: PAULO BENTO

	GROUP I	PL	W	D	L	F	A	PTS	ESP	CZE	SCO	LTU	LIE
1	Spain	8	8	0	0	26	6	24		2-1	3-1	3-1	6-0
2	Czech Republic	8	4	1	3	12	8	13	0-2		1-0	0-1	2-0
3	Scotland	8	3	2	3	9	10	11	2-3	2-2		1-0	2-1
4	Lithuania	8	1	2	5	4	13	5	1-3	1-4	0-0		0-0
5	Liechtenstein	8	1	1	6	3	17	4	0-4	0-2	0-2	2-0	

Spain qualified directly for the finals • Czech Republic qualified for a play-off v Montenegro
Czech Republic 2-0 1-0 Montenegro

DARIUS & GIRENAS, KAUNAS
3-09-2010, Att: 5248, Ref: Cakir TUR

Lithuania	0
Scotland	0

LTU: Zydrunas KARCEMARSKAS - Marius STANKEVICIUS, Andrius SKERLA•, Deividas SEMBERAS, Tadas KIJANSKAS•, Darvydas SERNAS (Vytautas LUKSA 80), Ramunas RADAVICIUS•, Mindaugas PANKA, Saulius MIKOLIUNAS (Robertas POSKUS 71), Edgaras CESNAUSKIS, Tomas DANILEVICIUS (Kestutis IVASKEVICIUS• 90). Tr: Raimondas ZUTAUTAS

SCO: Allan MCGREGOR - Steven WHITTAKER (Christophe BERRA 90), David WEIR, Stephen MCMANUS, Alan HUTTON, Barry ROBSON (James MCFADDEN 69), Steven NAISMITH, Darren FLETCHER, Scott BROWN• (James MORRISON 76), Kenny MILLER, Lee MCCULLOCH•. Tr: Craig LEVEIN

RHEINPARK STADION, VADUZ
3-09-2010, Att: 6100, Ref: Yildirim TUR

Liechtenstein	0
Spain	4

ESP - Torres 2 [18 54], Villa [26], Silva [62]

LIE: Peter JEHLE - Michael STOCKLASA, Martin STOCKLASA, Yves OEHRI (Franz-Josef VOGT 46), Lucas EBERLE (Martin RECHSTEINER 45), Franz BURGMEIER, Sandro WIESER (Ronny BUCHEL 82), Michele POLVERINO, Ronny HASLER•, Mario FRICK, Philippe ERNE. Tr: Hans-Peter ZAUGG

ESP: Iker CASILLAS - Joan CAPDEVILA, SERGIO RAMOS, Gerard PIQUE, Carlos MARCHENA, Sergio BUSQUETS, XABI ALONSO, XAVI (Cesc FABREGAS 45), Andres INIESTA (PEDRO Rodriguez 65), DAVID VILLA, FERNANDO TORRES (DAVID SILVA 57). Tr: Vicente DEL BOSQUE

ANDRUV STADION, OLOMOUC
7-09-2010, Att: 12 038, Ref: Yefet ISR

Czech Republic	0
Lithuania	1

LTU - Sernas [27]

CZE: Petr CECH - Zdenek POSPECH, Michal KADLEC, Tomas HUBSCHMAN, Roman HUBNIK•, Tomas ROSICKY, Daniel PUDIL (Roman BEDNAR 83), Jan POLAK (Jiri STAJNER 69), Jaroslav PLASIL, Martin FENIN (Tomas NECID 59), Milan BAROS. Tr: Michal BILEK

LTU: Zydrunas KARCEMARSKAS - Marius STANKEVICIUS, Andrius SKERLA, Deividas SEMBERAS•, Tadas KIJANSKAS, Edgaras CESNAUSKIS•, Darvydas SERNAS• (Robertas POSKUS 61), Ramunas RADAVICIUS, Mindaugas PANKA, Saulius MIKOLIUNAS (Vytautas LUKSA 79), Tomas DANILEVICIUS (Kestutis IVASKEVICIUS 90). Tr: Raimondas ZUTAUTAS

UEFA EURO 2012 POLAND/UKRAINE QUALIFYING GROUP I 1057

HAMPDEN PARK, GLASGOW
7-09-2010, Att: 37 050, Ref: Shvetsov UKR

Scotland	2
Liechtenstein	1

SCO - Miller [63], McManus [97+] • LIE - Frick [47]

Allan MCGREGOR• - David WEIR, Lee WALLACE (Barry ROBSON 55), Stephen MCMANUS, Alan HUTTON•, Darren FLETCHER, Scott BROWN, Kenny MILLER, James MCFADDEN (James MORRISON 46), Lee MCCULLOCH•, Kris BOYD (Steven NAISMITH 66). Tr: Craig LEVEIN

Peter JEHLE - Michael STOCKLASA, Martin STOCKLASA•, Martin RECHSTEINER•, Yves OEHRI, Sandro WIESER• (Ronny BUCHEL 71), Michele POLVERINO•, Franz BURGMEIER•, David HASLER (Nicolas HASLER 90), Mario FRICK• (Fabio D'ELIA• 79), Philippe ERNE. Tr: Hans Peter ZAUGG

SYNOT TIP ARENA, PRAGUE
8-10-2010, Att: 14 922, Ref: Bebek CRO

Czech Republic	1
Scotland	0

CZE - Hubnik [69]

Petr CECH - Michal KADLEC, Tomas HUBSCHMAN•, Roman HUBNIK, Zdenek POSPECH, Marek SUCHY, Jaroslav PLASIL (Jan RAJNOCH 90), Tomas ROSICKY, Jan POLAK, Tomas NECID• (Mario HOLEK 84), Lukas MAGERA (Roman BEDNAR 59). Tr: Michal BILEK

Allan MCGREGOR - Stephen MCMANUS, Alan HUTTON, Steven WHITTAKER•, David WEIR•, Gary CALDWELL (Kenny MILLER 76), James MORRISON (Barry ROBSON 84), Darren FLETCHER, Graham DORRANS, Jamie MACKIE (Chris IWELUMO 76), Steven NAISMITH. Tr: Craig LEVEIN

EL HELMANTICO, SALAMANCA
8-10-2010, Att: 16 800, Ref: Rocchi ITA

Spain	3
Lithuania	1

ESP - Llorente 2 [47 56], Silva [79]
LTU - Sernas [54]

Iker CASILLAS - SERGIO RAMOS (Alvaro ARBELOA 83), Gerard PIQUE, Joan CAPDEVILA, Carles PUYOL, DAVID SILVA, Andres INIESTA, SANTI CAZORLA, Sergio BUSQUETS, DAVID VILLA (PABLO Hernandez 76), Fernando LLORENTE (Aritz ADURIZ 76). Tr: Vicente DEL BOSQUE

Zydrunas KARCEMARSKAS - Marius STANKEVICIUS, Andrius SKERLA, Deividas SEMBERAS, Tadas KIJANSKAS, Darvydas SERNAS, Ramunas RADAVICIUS, Mindaugas PANKA, Saulius MIKOLIUNAS (Deividas CESNAUSKIS 59), Edgaras CESNAUSKIS (Robertas POSKUS 84), Tomas DANILEVICIUS (Kestutis IVASKEVICIUS 82). Tr: Raimondas ZUTAUTAS

RHEINPARK STADION, VADUZ
12-10-2010, Att: 2555, Ref: Sukhina RUS

Liechtenstein	0
Czech Republic	2

CZE - Necid [12], Vaclav Kadlec [29]

Peter JEHLE - Yves OEHRI, Michael STOCKLASA, Martin STOCKLASA•, Martin RECHSTEINER•, Michele POLVERINO•, Franz BURGMEIER, Sandro WIESER• (Ronny BUCHEL 84), Mario FRICK, Thomas BECK (Nicolas HASLER 66), Philippe ERNE (Rony HANSELMANN 78). Tr: Hans-Peter ZAUGG

Petr CECH - Michal KADLEC, Tomas HUBSCHMAN•, Roman HUBNIK, Zdenek POSPECH, Marek SUCHY, Jan POLAK (Jiri STAJNER 59), Jaroslav PLASIL, Tomas ROSICKY, Tomas NECID (Milan PETRZELA 89), Vaclav KADLEC (Roman BEDNAR 64). Tr: Michal BILEK

HAMPDEN PARK, GLASGOW
12-10-2010, Att: 51 322, Ref: Busacca SUI

Scotland	2
Spain	3

SCO - Naismith [58], OG [66] • ESP - Villa [44p], Iniesta [65], Llorente [79]

Allan MCGREGOR - Steven WHITTAKER•♦ [89], David WEIR, Stephen MCMANUS, Phil BARDSLEY, Steven NAISMITH, James MORRISON (Shaun MALONEY 98), Darren FLETCHER, Graham DORRANS (Jamie MACKIE 80), Kenny MILLER•, Lee MCCULLOCH (Charlie ADAM 46). Tr: Craig LEVEIN

Iker CASILLAS - SERGIO RAMOS, Gerard PIQUE, Joan CAPDEVILA, Carles PUYOL, XABI ALONSO, Andres INIESTA, DAVID SILVA (Fernando LLORENTE 76), SANTI CAZORLA (PABLO Hernandez 71), Sergio BUSQUETS (Carlos MARCHENA 90), DAVID VILLA. Tr: Vicente DEL BOSQUE

NUEVO LOS CARMENES, GRANADA
25-03-2011, Att: 16 301, Ref: Kassai HUN

Spain	2
Czech Republic	1

ESP - Villa 2 [69 72p] • CZE - Plasil [29]

Iker CASILLAS - SERGIO RAMOS, Gerard PIQUE, Joan CAPDEVILA (SANTI CAZORLA 58), Alvaro ARBELOA•, XABI ALONSO• (FERNANDO TORRES 46), Andres INIESTA, Sergio BUSQUETS, XAVI, JESUS NAVAS (Carlos MARCHENA 86), DAVID VILLA. Tr: Vicente DEL BOSQUE

Petr CECH - Michal KADLEC, Tomas HUBSCHMAN•, Roman HUBNIK, Zdenek POSPECH•, Tomas SIVOK, Tomas ROSICKY, Daniel PUDIL (Adam HLOUSEK 78), Jaroslav PLASIL, Milan BAROS, Jan REZEK• (Tomas NECID 84). Tr: Michal BILEK

E.ON, CESKE BUDEJOVICE
29-03-2011, Att: 6600, Ref: Hategan ROU

Czech Republic	2
Liechtenstein	0

CZE - Baros [3], Michal Kadlec [70]

Petr CECH - Zdenek POSPECH, Michal KADLEC, Tomas HUBSCHMAN, Roman HUBNIK, Tomas SIVOK, Tomas ROSICKY (Jan POLAK 84), Jaroslav PLASIL•, Jan MORAVEC (Adam HLOUSEK 56), David LAFATA (Tomas NECID 59), Milan BAROS. Tr: Michal BILEK

Peter JEHLE - Michael STOCKLASA•, Martin STOCKLASA, Martin RECHSTEINER•, Nicolas HASLER, Franz BURGMEIER, Martin BUCHEL (Wolfgang KIEBER 10) (Andreas CHRISTEN 81), David HASLER, Mario FRICK•, Thomas BECK•, Philippe ERNE. Tr: Hans Peter ZAUGG

DARIUS & GIRENAS, KAUNAS
29-03-2011, Att: 9180, Ref: Duhamel FRA

Lithuania	1
Spain	3

LTU - Stankevicius [57] • ESP - Xavi [19], OG [70], Mata [83]

Zydrunas KARCEMARSKAS - Marius STANKEVICIUS, Andrius SKERLA, Deividas SEMBERAS, Tadas KIJANSKAS, Marius ZALIUKAS, Edgaras CESNAUSKIS, Darvydas SERNAS (Tadas LABUKAS 74), Mindaugas PANKA, Saulius MIKOLIUNAS (Ramunas RADAVICIUS 71), Tomas DANILEVICIUS (Dominykas GALKEVICIUS 85). Tr: Raimondas ZUTAUTAS

Iker CASILLAS - Alvaro ARBELOA, Raul ALBIOL, Gerard PIQUE (SERGIO RAMOS 89), Andoni IRAOLA, XABI ALONSO, XAVI, SANTI CAZORLA (Juan MATA 67), JAVI MARTINEZ, DAVID VILLA (DAVID SILVA 54), Fernando LLORENTE. Tr: Vicente DEL BOSQUE

RHEINPARK STADION, VADUZ
3-06-2011, Att: 1886, Ref: Kuchin KAZ

Liechtenstein	2
Lithuania	0

LIE - Erne [7], Polverino [36]

Benjamin BUCHEL - Martin STOCKLASA, Marco RITZBERGER, Daniel KAUFMANN•, Michele POLVERINO, Nicolas HASLER, Franz BURGMEIER, Martin BUCHEL, Benjamin FISCHER (Mathias CHRISTEN 72), Thomas BECK• (Andreas CHRISTEN 84), Philippe ERNE (Rony HANSELMANN 87). Tr: Hans Peter ZAUGG

Ernestas SETKUS - Deividas SEMBERAS, Tadas KIJANSKAS, Marius STANKEVICIUS (Deividas CESNAUSKIS 46), Andrius SKERLA, Darvydas SERNAS•, Ramunas RADAVICIUS•, Mindaugas PANKA, Saulius MIKOLIUNAS, Edgaras CESNAUSKIS (Mantas SAVENAS 68), Tomas DANILEVICIUS• (Tadas LABUKAS 46). Tr: Raimondas ZUTAUTAS

DARIUS & GIRENAS, KAUNAS
2-09-2011, Att: 3500, Ref: Johnsen NOR

Lithuania	0
Liechtenstein	0

Zydrunas KARCEMARSKAS - Deividas SEMBERAS, Arunas KLIMAVICIUS•, Tadas KIJANSKAS, Marius ZALIUKAS, Mindaugas PANKA (Mantas SAVENAS 88), Saulius MIKOLIUNAS (Marius PAPSYS 64), Edgaras CESNAUSKIS♦ 74, Deividas CESNAUSKIS, Arvydas NOVIKOVAS• (Tadas LABUKAS 46), Tomas DANILEVICIUS. Tr: Raimondas ZUTAUTAS

Peter JEHLE - Michael STOCKLASA, Martin STOCKLASA, Marco RITZBERGER, Martin RECHSTEINER•, Yves OEHRI• (Daniel KAUFMANN 52), Sandro WIESER• (Nicolas HASLER 46), Franz BURGMEIER, Martin BUCHEL (Wolfgang KIEBER 90), David HASLER, Mario FRICK•. Tr: Hans Peter ZAUGG

HAMPDEN PARK, GLASGOW
3-09-2011, Att: 51 564, Ref: Blom NED

Scotland	2
Czech Republic	2

SCO - Miller [45], Fletcher.D [82] • CZE - Plasil [78], Michal Kadlec [90p]

Allan MCGREGOR - Alan HUTTON, Christophe BERRA•, Gary CALDWELL, Phil BARDSLEY (Danny WILSON 76), Steven NAISMITH (Barry ROBSON 87), James MORRISON, Scott BROWN•, Charlie ADAM (Don COWIE 79), Kenny MILLER•, Darren FLETCHER. Tr: Craig LEVEIN

Jan LASTUVKA - Jan RAJNOCH, Michal KADLEC, Tomas HUBSCHMAN, Roman HUBNIK, Tomas SIVOK, Tomas ROSICKY, Jaroslav PLASIL•, Petr JIRACEK• (Tomas PEKHART• 78), Milan PETRZELA (Jan REZEK• 56), Tomas PEKHART• (Kamil VACEK 90). Tr: Michal BILEK

HAMPDEN PARK, GLASGOW
6-09-2011, Att: 34 071, Ref: Jakobsson ISL

Scotland	1
Lithuania	0

SCO - Naismith [50]

Allan MCGREGOR - Steven WHITTAKER, Christophe BERRA, Gary CALDWELL, Phil BARDSLEY (Stephen CRAINEY 70), Steven NAISMITH, James MORRISON (Graham DORRANS• 79), Darren FLETCHER, Don COWIE, Barry BANNAN (Robert SNODGRASS 84), David GOODWILLIE. Tr: Craig LEVEIN

Zydrunas KARCEMARSKAS - Deividas SEMBERAS•, Arunas KLIMAVICIUS, Tadas KIJANSKAS (Tomas DANILEVICIUS 61), Marius ZALIUKAS, Deividas CESNAUSKIS, Darvydas SERNAS, Ramunas RADAVICIUS, Linas PILIBAITIS, Saulius MIKOLIUNAS (Ricardas BENIUSIS 77), Tadas LABUKAS• (Arvydas NOVIKOVAS 46). Tr: Raimondas ZUTAUTAS

LAS GAUNAS, LOGROÑO
6-09-2011, Att: 15 660, Ref: Lechner AUT

Spain	6
Liechtenstein	0

ESP - Negredo 2 [33] [37], Xavi [44], Ramos [52], Villa 2 [59] [79]

ESP: Iker CASILLAS - Sergio RAMOS (THIAGO Alcantara 55), Alvaro ARBELOA, Raul ALBIOL, Sergio BUSQUETS, XABI ALONSO, Andres INIESTA, XAVI (Cesc FABREGAS 46), Alvaro NEGREDO (Fernando LLORENTE 62), DAVID VILLA, Juan MATA. Tr: Vicente DEL BOSQUE

LIE: Peter JEHLE - Martin STOCKLASA, Marco RITZBERGER, Michael STOCKLASA, Franz BURGMEIER•, Martin BUCHEL (Wolfgang KIEBER 82), Sandro WIESER (Nicolas HASLER• 72), Mario FRICK, Thomas BECK (Rony HANSELMANN 88), David HASLER. Tr: Hans Peter ZAUGG

GENERALI ARENA, PRAGUE
7-10-2011, Att: 18 800, Ref: Tagliavento ITA

Czech Republic	0
Spain	2

ESP - Mata [7], Xabi Alonso [23]

CZE: Petr CECH - Tomas HUBSCHMAN♦69, Roman HUBNIK, Theodor GEBRE SELASSIE, Petr JIRACEK, Daniel KOLAR (Kamil VACEK 77), Tomas SIVOK, Tomas ROSICKY, Daniel PUDIL, Milan BAROS (Tomas PEKHART 62), Vaclav KADLEC. Tr: Michal BILEK

ESP: Iker CASILLAS - Alvaro ARBELOA, SERGIO RAMOS (Carles PUYOL 46), Raul ALBIOL, Gerard PIQUE, DAVID SILVA, Sergio Busquets, XAVI, XABI ALONSO (JAVI MARTINEZ 71), FERNANDO TORRES (DAVID VILLA 61), Juan MATA. Tr: Vicente DEL BOSQUE

RHEINPARK STADION, VADUZ
8-10-2011, Att: 5636, Ref: Hagen NOR

Liechtenstein	0
Scotland	1

SCO - Mackail-Smith [32]

LIE: Peter JEHLE - Martin STOCKLASA•, Marco RITZBERGER, Martin RECHSTEINER, Daniel KAUFMANN, Michele POLVERINO•, Nicolas HASLER, Rony HANSELMANN (Lucas EBERLE 75), Martin BUCHEL (Wolfgang KIEBER 71), Mario FRICK, Thomas BECK•. Tr: Hans Peter ZAUGG

SCO: Allan MCGREGOR - Alan HUTTON, Christophe BERRA, Gary CALDWELL, Phil BARDSLEY, Steven NAISMITH, James MORRISON, Darren FLETCHER, Barry BANNAN (James FORREST 73), Charlie ADAM (Don COWIE 76), Craig MACKAIL-SMITH•. Tr: Craig LEVEIN

JOSE RICO PEREZ, ALICANTE
11-10-2011, Att: 27 559, Ref: Johannesson SWE

Spain	3
Scotland	1

ESP - Silva 2 [6] [44], Villa [54]
SCO - Goodwillie [66p]

ESP: VICTOR VALDES - SERGIO RAMOS•, Gerard PIQUE, Carles PUYOL (Alvaro ARBELOA 46), JORDI ALBA, DAVID SILVA (THIAGO Alcantara 55), SANTI CAZORLA, Sergio BUSQUETS, XAVI (Fernando LLORENTE 64), PEDRO Rodriguez, DAVID VILLA. Tr: Vicente DEL BOSQUE

SCO: Allan MCGREGOR - Alan HUTTON, Christophe BERRA, Gary CALDWELL, Phil BARDSLEY, James MORRISON•, Darren FLETCHER• (Don COWIE 85), Barry BANNAN (James FORREST 64), Charlie ADAM (David GOODWILLIE• 64), Steven NAISMITH, Craig MACKAIL-SMITH. Tr: Craig LEVEIN

DARIUS & GIRENAS, KAUNAS
11-10-2011, Att: 4000, Ref: Fernandez ESP

Lithuania	1
Czech Republic	4

LTU - Sernas [68p]
CZE - Michal Kadlec 2 [2p] [85p], Rezek 2 [16] [45]

LTU: Zydrunas KARCEMARSKAS - Marius STANKEVICIUS, Andrius SKERLA•, Marius ZALIUKAS, Saulius MIKOLIUNAS, Kestutis IVASKEVICIUS (Arvydas NOVIKOVAS 46), Darvydas SERNAS, Ramunas RADAVICIUS•, Linas PILIBAITIS (Ricardas BENIUSIS 74), Gediminas VICIUS, Robertas POSKUS (Mindaugas PANKA• 57). Tr: Raimondas ZUTAUTAS

CZE: Petr CECH - Roman HUBNIK♦67, Theodor GEBRE SELASSIE, Michal KADLEC, Daniel KOLAR, Tomas SIVOK, Jaroslav PLASIL, Petr JIRACEK, Milan BAROS (Tomas PEKHART 59), Jan REZEK (Zdenek POSPECH 82), Vaclav PILAR (Daniel PUDIL 70). Tr: Michal BILEK

PLAY-OFFS

BILINO POLJE, ZENICA
11-11-2011, Att: 15 292, Ref: Webb ENG

Bosnia-Herzegovina	0
Portugal	0

BIH: Asmir BEGOVIC - Sanel JAHIC•, Emir SPAHIC, Senad LULIC, Adnan ZAHIROVIC, Elvir RAHIMIC, Miralem PJANIC, Zvjezdan MISIMOVIC (Senijad IBRICIC 86), Haris MEDUNJANIN (Darko MALETIC 67), Sejad SALIHOVIC• (Vedad IBISEVIC 67), Edin DZEKO. Tr: Safet SUSIC

POR: RUI PATRICIO - JOAO PEREIRA, BRUNO ALVES, PEPE, JOAO MOUTINHO, RAUL MEIRELES (RUBEN MICAEL 82), NANI, MIGUEL VELOSO, FABIO COENTRAO, HELDER POSTIGA• (HUGO ALMEIDA 65), CRISTIANO RONALDO. Tr: PAULO BENTO

ESTADIO DA LUZ, LISBON
15-11-2011, Att: 47 728, Ref: Stark GER

Portugal	6
Bosnia-Herzegovina	2

POR - Ronaldo 2 [8] [53], Nani [24], Postiga 2 [72] [82], Veloso [80] • BIH - Misimovic [41p], Spahic [65]

POR: RUI PATRICIO - PEPE, JOAO PEREIRA, BRUNO ALVES, RAUL MEIRELES (RUBEN MICAEL• 64), NANI (QUARESMA 83), MIGUEL VELOSO, JOAO MOUTINHO, FABIO COENTRAO•, HELDER POSTIGA• (CARLOS MARTINS 84), CRISTIANO RONALDO. Tr: PAULO BENTO

BIH: Asmir BEGOVIC - Emir SPAHIC•, Sasa PAPAC•, Sanel JAHIC, Adnan ZAHIROVIC, Elvir RAHIMIC• (Darko MALETIC 56), Miralem PJANIC (Muhamed BESIC 65), Zvjezdan MISIMOVIC, Haris MEDUNJANIN•, Senad LULIC••♦54, Edin DZEKO•. Tr: Safet SUSIC

GENERALI ARENA, PRAGUE
11-11-2011, Att: 14 560, Ref: Fernandez ESP

Czech Republic	2
Montenegro	0

CZE - Pilar [63], Sivok [92+]

CZE: Petr CECH - Michal KADLEC, Theodor GEBRE SELASSIE, Petr JIRACEK, Tomas SIVOK, Tomas ROSICKY, Daniel PUDIL, Jaroslav PLASIL, Tomas PEKHART (Daniel KOLAR 90), Jan REZEK• (Zdenek POSPECH 81), Vaclav PILAR• (David LAFATA 90). Tr: Michal BILEK

MNE: Mladen BOZOVIC - Miodrag DZUDOVIC•, Stefan SAVIC, Savo PAVICEVIC•, Milan JOVANOVIC•, Nikola DRINCIC, Simon VUKCEVIC (Andrija DELIBASIC 89), Milorad PEKOVIC• (Elsad ZVEROTIC 80), Dejan DAMJANOVIC (Vladimir BOZOVIC 61), Mirko VUCINIC, Stevan JOVETIC. Tr: Branko BRNOVIC

POD GORICOM, PODGORICA
15-11-2011, Att: 10 100, Ref: Rizzoli ITA

Montenegro	0
Czech Republic	1

CZE - Jiracek [81]

MNE: Mladen BOZOVIC - Elsad ZVEROTIC, Stefan SAVIC•, Savo PAVICEVIC•, Miodrag DZUDOVIC, Nikola DRINCIC•, Vladimir BOZOVIC (Radomir DALOVIC 80), Mirko VUCINIC•, Stevan JOVETIC, Dejan DAMJANOVIC• (Simon VUKCEVIC 76), Fatos BECIRAJ (Andrija DELIBASIC 57). Tr: Branko BRNOVIC

CZE: Petr CECH - Michal KADLEC, Roman HUBNIK, Theodor GEBRE SELASSIE, Tomas SIVOK•, Tomas ROSICKY, Jaroslav PLASIL, Petr JIRACEK, Jan REZEK (Zdenek POSPECH 60), Vaclav PILAR (Daniel KOLAR 69), Tomas PEKHART (Milan BAROS• 84). Tr: Michal BILEK

TURK TELEKOM ARENA, ISTANBUL
11-11-2011, Att: 42 863, Ref: Brych GER

Turkey	0
Croatia	3

CRO - Olic [2], Mandzukic [32], Corluka [51]

TUR: VOLKAN Demirel - REMZI Kacar, SABRI Sarioglu•, EGEMEN Korkmaz, GOKHAN Gonul (Gokhan Tore 46), HAKAN Balta•, ARDA Turan•, SELCUK Inan (MEHMET Topal 69), EMRE Belozoglu•, HAMIT Altintop, BURAK Yilmaz (UMUT Bulut 81). Tr: Guus HIDDINK

CRO: Stipe PLETIKOSA - Domagoj VIDA, Josip SIMUNIC, Gordon SCHILDENFELD, Darijo SRNA, Ivan RAKITIC (Danijel PRANJIC 83), Luka MODRIC, Tomislav DUJMOVIC•, Ivica OLIC• (Nikica JELAVIC 85), Mario MANDZUKIC (EDUARDO 90). Tr: Slaven BILIC

MAKSIMIR, ZAGREB
15-11-2011, Att: 26 371, ref: Proenca POR

Croatia	0
Turkey	0

CRO: Stipe PLETIKOSA - Domagoj VIDA•, Josip SIMUNIC, Gordon SCHILDENFELD, Darijo SRNA, Luka MODRIC, Ognjen VUKOJEVIC (EDUARDO 88), Ivan RAKITIC, Danijel PRANJIC, Ivica OLIC (Ivan PERISIC 62), Mario MANDZUKIC• (Nikica JELAVIC 77). Tr: Slaven BILIC

TUR: SINAN Bolat - OMER Toprak, ISMAIL Koybasi, EGEMEN Korkmaz•, CANER Erkin• (GOKHAN Tore 36), SELCUK Inan•, HAMIT Altintop•, SERKAN Balci•, SELCUK Sahin, Colin KAZIM-RICHARDS, UMUT Bulut (HALIL Altintop 71). Tr: Guus HIDDINK

A. LE COQ ARENA, TALLINN
11-11-2011, Att: 10 500, Kassai HUN

Estonia	0
Republic of Ireland	4

IRL - Andrews [13], Walters [67], Keane 2 [71, 88p]

EST: Sergei PAREIKO• - Andrei STEPANOV••♦35, Raio PIIROJA••♦77, Dmitriy KRUGLOV, Enar JAAGER, Ragnar KLAVAN, Martin VUNK (Joel LINDPERE 61), Aleksandr DMITRIJEV, Konstantin VASSILJEV, Tarmo KINK (Ats PURJE 67), Jarmo AHJUPERA• (Vladimir VOSKOBOINIKOV 55). Tr: Tarmo RUUTLI

IRL: Shay GIVEN - Stephen WARD, Sean ST LEDGER, Stephen KELLY, Richard DUNNE, Glenn WHELAN (Keith FAHEY 78), Damien DUFF (Stephen HUNT 73), Keith ANDREWS, Jon WALTERS (Simon COX 83), Aiden MCGEADY, Robbie KEANE. Tr: Giovanni TRAPATTONI

AVIVA STADIUM, DUBLIN
15-11-2011, Att: 51 151, Ref: Kuipers NED

Republic of Ireland	1
Estonia	1

IRL - Ward [32] • EST - Vassiljev [57]

IRL: Shay GIVEN - Sean ST LEDGER, John O'SHEA, Richard DUNNE, Stephen WARD, Stephen HUNT (Aiden MCGEADY 59), Damien DUFF (Keith FAHEY 79), Keith ANDREWS, Glenn WHELAN, Robbie KEANE (Simon COX 67), Kevin DOYLE. Tr: Giovanni TRAPATTONI

EST: Pavel LONDAK - Taavi RAHN•, Dmitriy KRUGLOV (Sander PURI 18), Enar JAAGER, Ragnar KLAVAN, Taijo TENISTE, Joel LINDPERE (Tarmo KINK 54), Martin VUNK•, Konstantin VASSILJEV, Kaimar SAAG, Vladimir VOSKOBOINIKOV (Ats PURJE 73). Tr: Tarmo RUUTLI

UEFA EURO 2012 POLAND/UKRAINE FINAL TOURNAMENT

First round groups		Quarter-finals		Semi-finals		Final	
Group A							
Czech Republic	6						
Greece	4	**Spain**	2				
Russia	4	France	0				
Poland	2						
				Spain	0 4p		
Group B				Portugal	0 2p		
Germany	9						
Portugal	6	Czech Republic	0				
Denmark	3	**Portugal**	1				
Netherlands	0						
						Spain	4
Group C						Italy	0
Spain	7						
Italy	5	**Germany**	4				
Croatia	4	Greece	2				
Republic of Ireland	0						
				Germany	1		
Group D				**Italy**	2		
England	7						
France	4	England	0 2p				
Ukraine	4	**Italy**	0 4p				
Sweden	3						

UEFA EURO 2012 POLAND/UKRAINE GROUP A

GROUP A

		Pl	W	D	L	F	A	Pts	GRE	RUS	POL
Czech Republic	CZE	3	2	1	1	4	5	6	2-1	1-4	1-0
Greece	GRE	3	1	1	1	3	3	4		1-0	1-1
Russia	RUS	3	1	1	1	5	3	4			1-1
Poland	POL	3	0	2	1	2	3	2			

NATIONAL STADIUM, WARSAW
8-06-2012, 18:00, Att: 56826, Ref: Velasco ESP

POLAND 1 — 1 **GREECE**

Lewandowski 17 — Salpingidis 51
Karagounis missed pen 71

POLAND

Tr: Franciszek Smuda — Wojciech Szczesny [69]

Sebastian Boenisch — Marcin Wasilewski — Damien Perquis — Lukasz Piszczek

Eugen Polanski — Rafal Murawski

[70] Maciej Rybus — Jakub Blaszczykowski (c)
Przemysław Tyton

Ludovic Obraniak

Robert Lewandowski

[46] Sotiris Ninis — Fanis Gekas [68] — Giorgos Samaras
Dimitris Salpingidis — Kostas Fortounis

Giannis Maniatis — Kostas Katsouranis — Giorgos Karagounis (c) [54]

Jose Holebas [45] — Vassilis Torossidis

Sokratis Papastathopoulos [35] [44] [44] — Avraam Papadopoulos [37]
Kyriakos Papadopoulos

Tr: Fernando Santos — Kostas Chalkias

GREECE

MUNICIPAL STADIUM, WROCLAW
8-06-2012, 20:45, Att: 37348, Ref: Webb ENG

RUSSIA 4 — 1 **CZECH REPUBLIC**

Dzagoev 2 15 79, Shirokov 24, — Pilar 52
Pavlyuchenko 82

RUSSIA

Tr: Dick Advocaat — Vyacheslav Malafeev

Aleksandr Anyukov — Sergei Ignashevich — Aleksei Berezutski — Yuri Zhirkov

Roman Shirokov — Igor Denisov — Konstantin Zyryanov

[84] Alan Dzagoev — Aleksandr Kerzhakov [73] — Andrey Arshavin (c)
Aleksandr Kokorin — Roman Pavlyuchenko

[85] Milan Baros
David Lafata

[46] Jan Rezek — Tomas Rosicky (c) — Vaclav Pilar
Tomas Hubschman

[76] Petr Jiracek — Jaroslav Plasil
Milan Petrzela

Michal Kadlec — Tomas Sivok — Roman Hubnik — Theodor Gebre Selassie

Tr: Michal Bilek — Petr Cech

CZECH REPUBLIC

MUNICIPAL STADIUM, WROCLAW
12-06-2012, 18:00, Att: 35213, Ref: Lannoy FRA

GREECE 1 — 2 **CZECH REPUBLIC**

Gekas 53 — Jiracek 3, Pilar 6

GREECE

Tr: Fernando Santos — [23] Kostas Chalkias
Michalis Sifakis

Kyriakos Papadopoulos [56] — Kostas Katsouranis

Vassilis Torossidis [34] — Jose Holebas

[46] Giorgos Fotakis — Giannis Maniatis — Giorgos Karagounis (c)
Fanis Gekas

Dimitris Salpingidis [57] — Kostas Fortounis [71]
Giorgos Samaras — Kostas Mitroglou

[64] Milan Baros
Tomas Pekhart

Vaclav Pilar — [46] Tomas Rosicky (c) [27] — Petr Jiracek [36]
Daniel Kolar [65]
[90] Frantisek Rajtoral

Jaroslav Plasil — Tomas Hubschman

David Limbersky — Michal Kadlec — Tomas Sivok — Theodor Gebre Selassie

Tr: Michal Bilek — Petr Cech

CZECH REPUBLIC

NATIONAL STADIUM, WARSAW
12-06-2012, 20:45, Att: 53617, Ref: Stark GER

POLAND 1 — 1 **RUSSIA**

Blaszczykowski 57 — Dzagoev 37

POLAND

Tr: Franciszek Smuda — Przemyslaw Tyton

Lukasz Piszczek — Marcin Wasilewski — Damien Perquis — Sebastian Boenisch

[73] Dariusz Dudka — Eugen Polanski [79]
Adrian Mierzejewski — Adam Matuszczyk

Jakub Blaszczykowski (c) — Rafal Murawski — Ludovic Obraniak
[93+] Pawel Brozek

Robert Lewandowski [60]

Andrey Arshavin (c) — [73] Aleksandr Kerzhakov — [79] Alan Dzagoev [75]
Roman Pavlyuchenko — Marat Izmailov

Konstantin Zyryanov — Igor Denisov [60] — Roman Shirokov

Yuri Zhirkov — Sergei Ignashevich — Aleksei Berezutski — Aleksandr Anyukov

Tr: Dick Advocaat — Vyacheslav Malafeev

RUSSIA

PART THREE – THE CONTINENTAL CONFEDERATIONS

		Pl	W	D	L	F	A	Pts		POR	DEN	NED
Germany	GER	3	3	0	0	5	2	9		1-0	2-1	2-1
Portugal	POR	3	2	0	1	5	4	6			3-2	2-1
Denmark	DEN	3	1	0	2	4	5	3				1-0
Netherlands	NED	3	0	0	3	2	5	0				

UEFA EURO 2012 POLAND/UKRAINE GROUP B 1063

ARENA LVIV, LVIV
13-06-2012, 19:00, Att: 34 915, Ref: Thomson SCO

DENMARK 2 3 **PORTUGAL**

Bendtner 2 [41] [80] — Pepe [24], Postiga [36], Varela [87]

DENMARK

Tr: Morten Olsen — Stephan Andersen

Lars Jacobsen [81], Simon Kjær, Daniel Agger (c), Simon Poulsen

William Kvist, Niki Zimling / Jakob Poulsen [56] [16]

Dennis Rommedahl / Tobias Mikkelsen [60], Christian Eriksen, Michael Krohn-Dehli / Lasse Schøne [92+]

Nicklas Bendtner

PORTUGAL

Cristiano Ronaldo (c) [92+], Helder Postiga / Nelson Oliveira [64], Nani / Rolando [89]

Joao Moutinho, Miguel Veloso, Raul Meireles / Silvestre Varela [84] [29]

Fabio Coentrao, Pepe, Bruno Alves, Joao Pereira

Tr: Paulo Bento — Rui Patricio

PORTUGAL

METALIST STADIUM, KHARKIV
13-06-2012, 21:45, Att: 38 633, Ref: Eriksson SWE

NETHERLANDS 1 2 **GERMANY**

Van Persie [73] — Gomez 2 [24] [38]

NETHERLANDS

Tr: Bert van Marwijk — Maarten Stekelenburg

Gregory van der Wiel, John Heitinga, Joris Mathijsen, Jetro Willems [90]

Nigel de Jong [80], Mark van Bommel (c) / Klaas-Jan Huntelaar [46]

Arjen Robben / Dirk Kuyt [83], Wesley Sneijder, Ibrahim Afellay / Rafael van der Vaart [46]

Robin van Persie

GERMANY

Lukas Podolski, Mario Gomez / Miroslav Klose [72], Thomas Muller / Lars Bender [92+]

Mesut Ozil / Toni Kroos [81]

Bastian Schweinsteiger, Sami Khedira

Philipp Lahm (c), Holger Badstuber, Mats Hummels, Jerome Boateng [87]

Tr: Joachim Low — Manuel Neuer

GERMANY

METALIST STADIUM, KHARKIV
17-06-2012, 21:45, Att: 38 633, Ref: Rizzoli ITA

PORTUGAL 2 1 **NETHERLANDS**

Ronaldo 2 [28] [74] — Van der Vaart [11]

PORTUGAL

Tr: Paulo Bento — Rui Patricio

Joao Pereira [92+], Bruno Alves, Pepe, Fabio Coentrao

Raul Meireles / Custodio [72], Miguel Veloso, Joao Moutinho

Nani / Rolando [87], Helder Postiga / Nelson Oliveira [64], Cristiano Ronaldo (c)

NETHERLANDS

Klaas-Jan Huntelaar

Wesley Sneijder, Robin van Persie [69], Arjen Robben

Rafael van der Vaart (c), Nigel de Jong

Jetro Willems / Ibrahim Afellay [51] [67], Joris Mathijsen, Ron Vlaar, Gregory van der Wiel

Tr: Bert van Marwijk — Maarten Stekelenburg

NETHERLANDS

ARENA LVIV, LVIV
17-06-2012, 21:45, Att: 35 000, Ref: Velasco ESP

DENMARK 1 2 **GERMANY**

Krohn-Dehli [24] — Podolski [19], Bender [80]

DENMARK

Tr: Morten Olsen — Stephan Andersen

Lars Jacobsen, Simon Kjær, Daniel Agger (c), Simon Poulsen

William Kvist

Jakob Poulsen / Tobias Mikkelsen [62], Niki Zimling / Christian Poulsen [78]

Christian Eriksen, Michael Krohn-Dehli

Nicklas Bendtner

GERMANY

Mario Gomez / Miroslav Klose [74]

Lukas Podolski / Andre Schurrle [64], Mesut Ozil, Thomas Muller / Toni Kroos [84]

Bastian Schweinsteiger, Sami Khedira

Philipp Lahm (c), Holger Badstuber, Mats Hummels, Lars Bender

Tr: Joachim Low — Manuel Neuer

GERMANY

GROUP C

		Pl	W	D	L	F	A	Pts	ITA	CRO	IRL
Spain	ESP	3	2	1	0	6	1	7	1-1	1-0	4-0
Italy	ITA	3	1	2	0	4	2	5		1-1	2-0
Croatia	CRO	3	1	1	1	4	3	4			3-1
Republic of Ireland	IRL	3	0	0	3	1	9	0			

ARENA GDANSK, GDANSK
10-06-2012, 18:00, Att: 43 615, Ref: Kassai HUN

SPAIN 1 – 1 **ITALY**

Fabregas [64] — Di Natale [61]

SPAIN
Tr: Vicente Del Bosque
Iker Casillas (c)
Alvaro Arbeloa [84], Gerard Pique, Sergio Ramos, Jordi Alba [66]
Sergio Busquets
Xavi Hernandez, Xabi Alonso
David Silva [64], Cesc Fabregas [74], Andres Iniesta
Jesus Navas, Fernando Torres [84]

ITALY
Mario Balotelli [37] / Antonio Di Natale [56]
Antonio Cassano [65] / Sebastian Giovinco
Emanuele Giaccherini, Christian Maggio [89]
Thiago Motta [90] / Antonio Nocerino, Andrea Pirlo, Claudio Marchisio
Giorgio Chiellini [79], Daniele De Rossi, Leonardo Bonucci [79]
Gianluigi Buffon (c)
Tr: Cesare Prandelli

MUNICIPAL STADIUM, POZNAN
10-06-2012, 20:45, Att: 43 200, Ref: Kuipers NED

REP. OF IRELAND 1 – 3 **CROATIA**

St Ledger [19] — Mandzukic 2 [3,49], Jelavic [43]

REPUBLIC OF IRELAND
Tr: Giovanni Trapattoni
Shay Given
John O'Shea, Sean St Ledger, Richard Dunne, Stephen Ward
Glenn Whelan, Keith Andrews [45]
Aiden McGeady [54] / Simon Cox, Damien Duff
Kevin Doyle [53] / Jon Walters, Robbie Keane (c) [75] / Shane Long

CROATIA
Nikica Jelavic [72] / Niko Kranjcar [84], Mario Mandzukic
Ivan Perisic [89] / Eduardo, Luka Modric [53], Ivan Rakitic [92+] / Tomislav Dujmovic
Ognjen Vukojevic
Ivan Strinic, Gordon Schildenfeld, Vedran Corluka, Darijo Srna [84]
Stipe Pletikosa
Tr: Slaven Bilic

MUNICIPAL STADIUM, POZNAN
14-06-2012, 18:00, Att: 37 096, Ref: Webb ENG

ITALY 1 – 1 **CROATIA**

Pirlo [39] — Mandzukic [72]

ITALY
Tr: Cesare Prandelli
Gianluigi Buffon (c)
Leonardo Bonucci, Daniele De Rossi, Giorgio Chiellini
Claudio Marchisio, Andrea Pirlo, Thiago Motta [56] / Riccardo Montolivo [80]
Christian Maggio, Emanuele Giaccherini
Mario Balotelli [69] / Antonio Di Natale, Antonio Cassano [83] / Sebastian Giovinco

CROATIA
Mario Mandzukic [94+] / Niko Kranjcar, Nikica Jelavic [83] / Eduardo
Ivan Perisic [68] / Danijel Pranjic, Luka Modric, Ognjen Vukojevic, Ivan Rakitic
Ivan Strinic, Gordon Schildenfeld [86], Vedran Corluka, Darijo Srna [45]
Stipe Pletikosa
Tr: Slaven Bilic

ARENA GDANSK, GDANSK
14-06-2012, 20:45, Att: 36 572, Ref: Proenca POR

SPAIN 4 – 0 **REP. OF IRELAND**

Torres 2 [4,70], Silva [49], Fabregas [83]

SPAIN
Tr: Vicente Del Bosque
Iker Casillas (c)
Alvaro Arbeloa, Gerard Pique, Sergio Ramos, Jordi Alba
Sergio Busquets
Xavi Hernandez, Xabi Alonso [65] [54] / Javi Martinez [76]
David Silva, Fernando Torres [74] / Cesc Fabregas, Andres Iniesta [80] / Santi Cazorla

REPUBLIC OF IRELAND
Robbie Keane (c) [36], Simon Cox [46] / Jon Walters
Aiden McGeady [80] / Glenn Whelan [45] / Paul Green, Keith Andrews [76] / Damien Duff / James McClean
John O'Shea, Sean St Ledger [84], Richard Dunne, Stephen Ward
Shay Given
Tr: Giovanni Trapattoni

UEFA EURO 2012 POLAND/UKRAINE GROUP D

ARENA GDANSK, GDANSK			MUNICIPAL STADIUM, POZNAN		
18-06-2012, 20:45, Att: 38371, Ref: Stark GER			18-06-2012, 20:45, Att: 44416, Ref: Cakir TUR		
CROATIA	0 1	**SPAIN**	**ITALY**	2 0	**REP. OF IRELAND**
	Jesus Navas 88		Cassano 36, Balotelli 90		

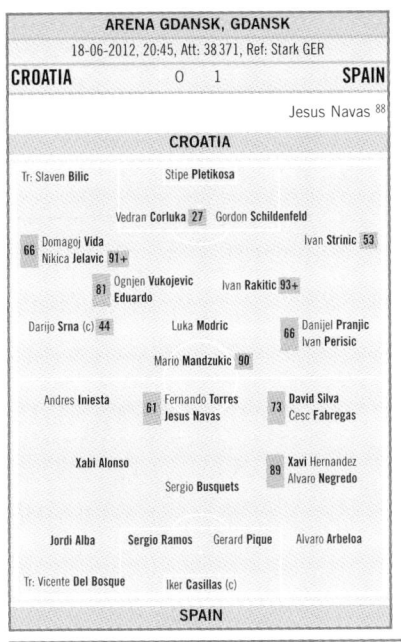

GROUP D										
		Pl	W	D	L	F	A	Pts	FRA	UKR	SWE
England	ENG	3	2	1	0	5	3	7	1-1	1-0	3-2
France	FRA	3	1	1	1	3	3	4		2-0	0-2
Ukraine	UKR	3	1	0	2	2	4	3			2-1
Sweden	SWE	3	1	0	2	5	5	3			

DONBASS ARENA, DONETSK			OLYMPIC STADIUM, KYIV		
11-06-2011, 19:00, Att: 42000, Ref: Rizzoli ITA			11-06-2011, 21:45, Att: 68000, Ref: Cakir TUR		
FRANCE	1 1	**ENGLAND**	**UKRAINE**	2 1	**SWEDEN**
Lescott 30		Nasri 39	Shevchenko 2 55 62		Ibrahimovic 52

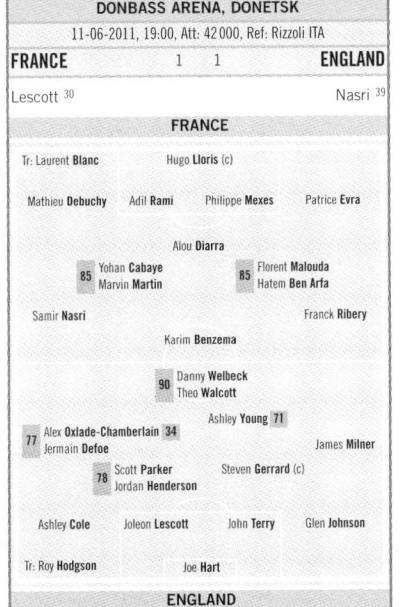

1066   PART THREE – THE CONTINENTAL CONFEDERATIONS

DONBASS ARENA, DONETSK
15-06-2011, 19:00, Att: 51 504, Ref: Kuipers NED

UKRAINE 0 – 2 **FRANCE**

Match suspended after 5 minutes due to a thunderstorm but resumed 58 minutes later

Menez 53, Cabaye 56

UKRAINE

Tr: Oleh Blokhin — Andriy Pyatov

Oleh Gusev — Taras Mikhalik — Yevhen Khacheridi — Yevhen Selin 55

Anatoliy Tymoshchuk 87 — 46 Andriy Voronin / Marko Devic

68 Andriy Yarmolenko / Olexandr Aliyev — 60 Serhiy Nazarenko / Artem Milevskiy — Yevhen Konoplyanka

Andriy Shevchenko (c)

FRANCE

Karim Benzema 76 / Olivier Giroud

Franck Ribery — 73 Jeremy Menez 40 / Marvin Martin

68 Yohan Cabaye / Yann M'Vila — Samir Nasri

Alou Diarra

Gael Clichy — Philippe Mexes 81 — Adil Rami — Mathieu Debuchy 79

Hugo Lloris (c)

Tr: Laurent Blanc

OLYMPIC STADIUM, KYIV
15-06-2011, 21:45, Att: 70 000, Ref: Skomina SVN

SWEDEN 2 – 3 **ENGLAND**

Johnson OG 49, Mellberg 59

Carroll 23, Walcott 64, Welbeck 78

SWEDEN

Tr: Erik Hamren — Andreas Isaksson

66 Andreas Granqvist / Mikael Lustig — Olof Mellberg 63 — Jonas Olsson 72 — Martin Olsson

Anders Svensson 91+ — Kim Kallstrom

Sebastian Larsson — Zlatan Ibrahimovic (c) — 81 Rasmus Elm / Christian Wilhelmsson

79 Johan Elmander / Markus Rosenberg

ENGLAND

60 Danny Welbeck / Alex Oxlade-Chamberlain — Andy Carroll

Ashley Young — Scott Parker — Steven Gerrard (c) — 61 James Milner 58 / Theo Walcott

Ashley Cole — Joleon Lescott — John Terry — Glen Johnson

Tr: Roy Hodgson — Joe Hart

DONBASS ARENA, DONETSK
19-06-2011, 21:45, Att: 51 504, Ref: Kassai HUN

ENGLAND 1 – 0 **UKRAINE**

Rooney 48

ENGLAND

Tr: Roy Hodgson — Joe Hart

Glen Johnson — John Terry — Joleon Lescott — Ashley Cole 78

70 James Milner / Theo Walcott — Steven Gerrard (c) 73 — Scott Parker — Ashley Young

87 Wayne Rooney / Alex Oxlade-Chamberlain

82 Danny Welbeck / Andy Carroll

UKRAINE

Marko Devic 70 / Andriy Shevchenko 86

77 Artem Milevskiy / Bohdan Butko

78 Denys Garmash / Serhiy Nazarenko

Yevhen Konoplyanka — Andriy Yarmolenko

Anatoliy Tymoshchuk (c) 63

Yevhen Selin — Yaroslav Rakitskiy 74 — Yevhen Khacheridi — Oleh Gusev

Tr: Oleh Blokhin — Andriy Pyatov

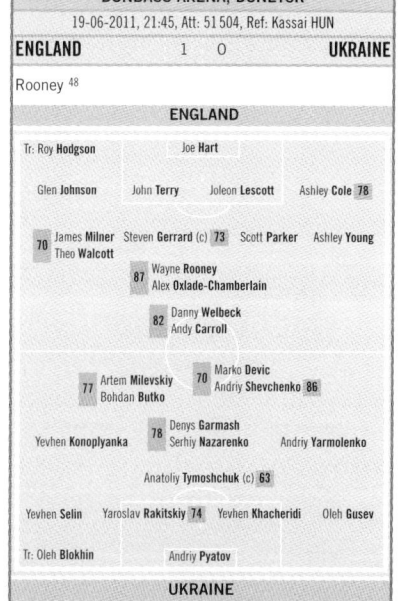

OLYMPIC STADIUM, KYIV
19-06-2011, 21:45, Att: 65 000, Ref: Proenca POR

SWEDEN 2 – 0 **FRANCE**

Ibrahimovic 54, Larsson 91+

SWEDEN

Tr: Erik Hamren — Andreas Isaksson

Andreas Granqvist — Olof Mellberg — Jonas Olsson — Martin Olsson

79 Anders Svensson 70 — Kim Kallstrom / Samuel Holmen 81

Sebastian Larsson — Zlatan Ibrahimovic (c) — 46 Emir Bajrami / Christian Wilhelmsson

78 Ola Toivonen / Pontus Wernbloom

FRANCE

Karim Benzema

Franck Ribery — 59 Hatem Ben Arfa / Florent Malouda

83 Yann M'Vila / Olivier Giroud — Alou Diarra — 77 Samir Nasri / Jeremy Menez

Gael Clichy — Philippe Mexes 68 — Adil Rami — Mathieu Debuchy

Tr: Laurent Blanc — Hugo Lloris (c)

QUARTER-FINALS

NATIONAL STADIUM, WARSAW
21-06-2012, 20:45, Att: 58 145, Ref: Webb ENG

CZECH REPUBLIC 0 1 PORTUGAL

Ronaldo 79

CZECH REPUBLIC
Tr: Michal Bilek — Petr Cech (c)

Theodor Gebre Selassie, Tomas Sivok, Michal Kadlec, David Limbersky 90

Tomas Hubschman 86, Jaroslav Plasil
Tomas Pekhart

Petr Jiracek, Vladimir Darida 61, Jan Rezek, Vaclav Pilar

Milan Baros

PORTUGAL
Cristiano Ronaldo (c), Helder Postiga 40, Hugo Almeida, Nani 84, Custodio 26

Miguel Veloso 27, Joao Moutinho, Raul Meireles 88, Rolando

Fabio Coentrao, Bruno Alves, Pepe, Joao Pereira

Tr: Paulo Bento — Rui Patricio

ARENA GDANSK, GDANSK
22-06-2012, 20:45, Att: 43 000, Ref: Skomina SVN

GERMANY 4 2 GREECE

Lahm 39, Khedira 61, Samaras 55,
Klose 68, Reus 74 Salpingidis 89p

GERMANY
Tr: Joachim Low — Manuel Neuer

Jerome Boateng, Mats Hummels, Holger Badstuber, Philipp Lahm (c)

Sami Khedira, Bastian Schweinsteiger

Marco Reus 80, Mesut Ozil, Andre Schurrle 67
Mario Gotze, Thomas Muller

Miroslav Klose 80
Mario Gomez

GREECE
Dimitris Salpingidis
Giorgos Samaras 14, Kostas Katsouranis (c), Sotiris Ninis 46, Fanis Gekas

Giannis Maniatis, Grigoris Makos 72, Nikos Liberopoulos

Giorgos Tzavellas 46, Vassilis Torossidis
Giorgos Fotakis

Kyriakos Papadopoulos, Sokratis Papastathopoulos 75

Tr: Fernando Santos — Michalis Sifakis

DONBASS ARENA, DONETSK
23-06-2011, 20:45, Att: 46 145, Ref: Rizzoli ITA

SPAIN 2 0 FRANCE

Xabi Alonso 2 19 91+p

SPAIN
Tr: Vicente Del Bosque — Iker Casillas (c)

Alvaro Arbeloa, Gerard Pique, Sergio Ramos 31, Jordi Alba

Sergio Busquets
Xavi Hernandez, Xabi Alonso

David Silva 65, Andres Iniesta 84
Pedro Rodriguez, Cesc Fabregas 67, Santi Cazorla
Fernando Torres

FRANCE
Karim Benzema
Franck Ribery, Mathieu Debuche 64, Jeremy Menez 76

Florent Malouda 65, Yohan Cabaye 42
Samir Nasri, Yann M'Vila 79, Olivier Giroud

Gael Clichy, Laurent Koscielny, Adil Rami, Anthony Reveillere

Tr: Laurent Blanc — Hugo Lloris (c)

OLYMPIC STADIUM, KYIV
24-06-2011, 20:45, Att: 56 500, Ref: Proenca POR

ENGLAND 0 2p 4p 0 ITALY

ENGLAND
Tr: Roy Hodgson — Joe Hart

Glen Johnson, John Terry, Joleon Lescott, Ashley Cole

Steven Gerrard (c), Scott Parker 94
Jordan Henderson

James Milner 60, Ashley Young
Andy Carroll, Wayne Rooney
Danny Welbeck 60
Theo Walcott

ITALY
Antonio Cassano 78, Mario Balotelli
Alessandro Diamanti

Daniele De Rossi 80, Riccardo Montolivo, Claudio Marchisio
Antonio Nocerino, Andrea Pirlo

Federico Balzaretti, Ignazio Abate 91+, Christian Maggio 93

Leonardo Bonucci, Andrea Barzagli 82

Tr: Cesare Prandelli — Gianluigi Buffon (c)

SEMI-FINALS

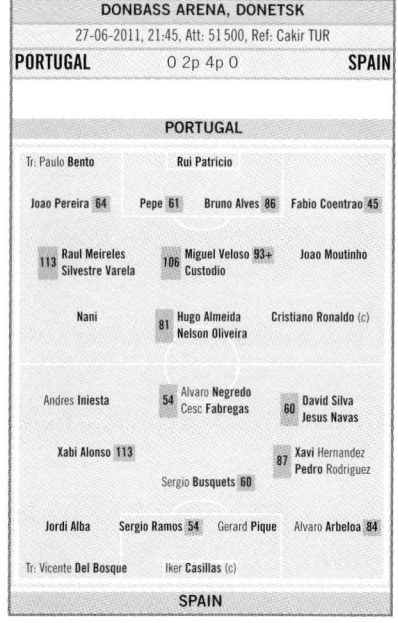

FINAL

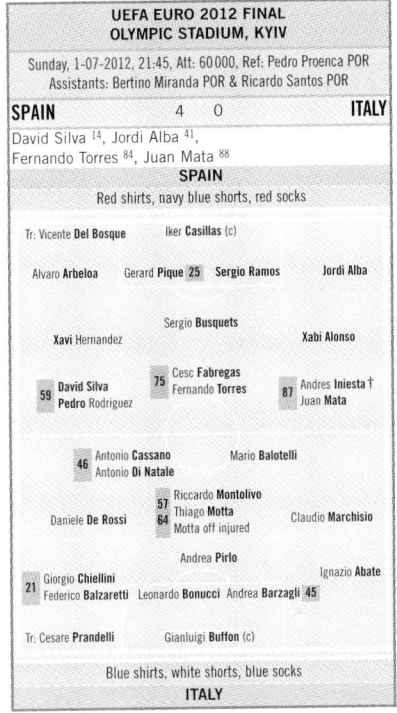

UEFA EURO 2012 FINAL
OLYMPIC STADIUM, KYIV

Sunday, 1-07-2012, 21:45, Att: 60 000, Ref: Pedro Proenca POR
Assistants: Bertino Miranda POR & Ricardo Santos POR

SPAIN 4 — 0 **ITALY**

David Silva [14], Jordi Alba [41],
Fernando Torres [84], Juan Mata [88]

SPAIN
Red shirts, navy blue shorts, red socks

Tr: Vicente **Del Bosque**   Iker **Casillas** (c)

Alvaro **Arbeloa**   Gerard **Pique** [25]   Sergio **Ramos**   Jordi **Alba**

Sergio **Busquets**
Xavi **Hernandez**   Xabi **Alonso**

David **Silva** [59]   Cesc **Fabregas** [75]   Andres **Iniesta** †
Pedro **Rodriguez**   Fernando **Torres**   Juan **Mata** [87]

Antonio **Cassano** [46]   Mario **Balotelli**
Antonio **Di Natale**

Riccardo **Montolivo** [57]
Daniele **De Rossi**   Thiago **Motta** [64]   Claudio **Marchisio**
Motta off injured

Andrea **Pirlo**
Giorgio **Chiellini** [21]   Ignazio **Abate**
Federico **Balzaretti**   Leonardo **Bonucci**   Andrea **Barzagli** [45]

Tr: Cesare **Prandelli**   Gianluigi **Buffon** (c)

Blue shirts, white shorts, blue socks
ITALY

Spain	MATCH STATS	Italy
14	Shots	11
9	Shots on Goal	6
17	Fouls Committed	10
3	Corner Kicks	3
3	Caught Offside	3
52	Possession (%)	48

(C) Captain † Man of the Match

This is a great generation of players. They have roots and know how to play because they come from a country that knows how to. This is a great era for Spanish football. We had an extraordinary match - everything went our way tonight. Italy had one fewer player, one less day of rest and they tried throughout but couldn't get into the game. We played our own game and were faithful to what we've done over the years. This is a great time for all the Spanish people.
Vicente del Bosque

Our only regret is that we were so tired. We were up against a great side, the world champions, and as soon as we went down to ten men it was game over. We had a couple of chances at the start of the second half but didn't take them and when Thiago Motta went off we had nothing left in the tank. When we did attack, we struggled to get back to cover. You have to pay credit to Spain. They have made history tonight and deservedly so.
Cesare Prandelli

UEFA CHAMPIONS LEAGUE 2011-12

Second Qualifying Round				Third Qualifying Round				Play-off Round				Group Stage			
								Bayern München	GER	2	1				
								FC Zürich	SUI	0	0				
				Standard CL	BEL	1	0								
				FC Zürich	SUI	1	1								
												Group A			Pts
				OB Odense	DEN	1	4					Bayern München	GER		13
				Panathinaikos	GRE	1	3	OB Odense	DEN	1	0	Napoli	ITA		11
								Villarreal	ESP	0	3	Manchester City	ENG		10
												Villarreal	ESP		0
				Twente Enschede	NED	2	0					Group B			Pts
				FC Vaslui	ROU	0	0					Internazionale	ITA		10
								Twente Enschede	NED	2	1	CSKA Moskva	RUS		8
				Benfica	POR	2	1	Benfica	POR	2	3	Trabzonspor	TUR		7
				Trabzonspor	TUR	0	1					Lille OSC	FRA		6
												Group C			Pts
												Benfica	POR		12
								Olympique Lyonnais	FRA	3	1	FC Basel	SUI		11
				Dynamo Kyiv	UKR	0	1	Rubin Kazan	RUS	1	1	Manchester United	ENG		9
				Rubin Kazan	RUS	2	2					Otelul Galati	ROU		0
Bangor City	WAL	0	0												
HJK Helsinki	FIN	3	10	HJK Helsinki	FIN	1	0					Group D			Pts
Dinamo Zagreb	CRO	3	0	Dinamo Zagreb	CRO	2	1					Real Madrid	ESP		18
Neftchi Baku	AZE	0	0					Dinamo Zagreb	CRO	4	0	Olympique Lyonnais	FRA		8
								Malmö FF	SWE	1	2	Ajax	NED		8
				Rangers	SCO	0	1					Dinamo Zagreb	CRO		0
Malmö FF	SWE	2	1	Malmö FF	SWE	1	1								
HB Tórshavn	FRO	0	1												
Maccabi Haifa	ISR	5	2									Group E			Pts
Borac Banja Luka	BIH	1	3	Maccabi Haifa	ISR	2	1					Chelsea	ENG		11
NK Maribor	SVN	2	3	NK Maribor	SVN	1	1					Bayer Leverkusen	GER		10
F91 Dudelange	LUX	0	1					Maccabi Haifa	ISR	2 1 1p		Valencia	ESP		8
				KRC Genk	BEL	2	1	KRC Genk	BEL	1 2 4p		KRC Genk	BEL		3
Partizan Beograd	SRB	4	1	Partizan Beograd	SRB	1	1								
Shkendija Tetovo	MKD	0	0												
												Group F			Pts
												Arsenal	ENG		11
								Arsenal	ENG	1	2	Olympique Marseille	FRA		10
								Udinese	ITA	0	1	Olympiacos	GRE		9
												Borussia Dortmund	GER		4
Mogren Budva	MNE	1	0												
Litex Lovech	BUL	2	3	Litex Lovech	BUL	1	1					Group G			Pts
Skonto Riga	LVA	0	0	Wisla Krakow	POL	2	3					APOEL Nicosia	CYP		9
Wisla Krakow	POL	1	2					Wisla Krakow	POL	1	1	Zenit St Petersburg	RUS		9
Skënderbeu Korçë	ALB	0	0					APOEL Nicosia	CYP	0	3	FC Porto	POR		8
APOEL Nicosia	CYP	2	4	APOEL Nicosia	CYP	0	2					Shakhtar Donetsk	UKR		5
Slovan Bratislava	SVK	2	1	Slovan Bratislava	SVK	0	0								
Tobol Kostanay	KAZ	0	1												
				FC København	DEN	1	2					Group H			Pts
Shamrock Rovers	IRL	1	0	Shamrock Rovers	IRL	0	0					Barcelona	ESP		16
Flora Tallinn	EST	0	0					FC København	DEN	1	1	Milan	ITA		9
Rosenborg BK	NOR	5	0					Viktoria Plzen	CZE	3	2	Viktoria Plzen	CZE		5
Breidablik	ISL	0	2	Rosenborg BK	NOR	0	2					BATE Borisov	BLR		2
Pyunik Yerevan	ARM	0	1	Viktoria Plzen	CZE	1	3								
Viktoria Plzen	CZE	4	5												
Valletta	MLT	2	0												
Ekranas Panevezys	LTU	3	1	Ekranas Panevezys	LTU							The home team in the first leg			
Linfield	NIR	0	1	BATE Borisov	BLR							of the qualifying round matches			
BATE Borisov	BLR	1	2					BATE Borisov	BLR	1	2	is listed above their opponents			
FC Zestafoni	GEO	3	0					SK Sturm Graz	AUT	1	0				
Dacia Chisinau	MDA	0	2	FC Zestafoni	GEO	1	0								
SK Sturm Graz	AUT	2	2	SK Sturm Graz	AUT	1	1								
Videoton	HUN	0	3												

First qualifying round: Tre Fiori 0-3 1-2 **Valletta** • FC Santa Coloma 0-2 0-2 **F91 Dudelange**

CLUB TOURNAMENTS IN EUROPE 2011–12

UEFA CHAMPIONS LEAGUE 2011–12

Round of 16			Quarter-finals			Semi-finals			Final		
Chelsea	1	4									
Napoli *	3	1									
			Chelsea	1	2						
			Benfica *	0	1						
Zenit St Petersburg *	3	0									
Benfica	2	2									
						Chelsea *	1	2			
						Barcelona	0	2			
Milan *	4	0									
Arsenal	0	3									
			Milan *	0	1						
			Barcelona	0	3						
Bayer Leverkusen *	1	1									
Barcelona	3	7									
									Chelsea	1	4p
									Bayern München	1	3p
Real Madrid	1	4									
CSKA Moskva *	1	1									
			Real Madrid	3	5						
			APOEL Nicosia *	0	2						
Olymp. Lyonnais *	1 0 3p										
APOEL Nicosia	0 1 4p										
						Real Madrid	1 2 1p				
						Bayern München *	2 1 3p				
Olymp. Marseille *	1	1									
Internazionale	0	2									
			Olymp. Marseille *	0	0						
			Bayern München	2	2						
FC Basel *	1	0									
Bayern München	0	7									

* Home team in the first leg

Top scorers: 14 - Lionel **MESSI** ARG, Barcelona • 12 - Mario **GOMEZ** GER, Bayern München • 10 - **CRISTIANO RONALDO** POR, Real Madrid • 7 - Karim **BENZEMA** FRA, Real Madrid • 6 - Didier **DROGBA** CIV, Chelsea • 5 - Jose **CALLEJON** ESP, Real Madrid; Roberto **SOLDADO** ESP, Valencia; Bafetimbi **GOMIS** FRA, Olymp. Lyonnais; Alexander **FREI** SUI, FC Basel; Seydou **DOUMBIA** CIV, CSKA Moskva; Roman **SHIROKOV** RUS, Zenit St Petersburg; Edinson **CAVANI** URU, Napoli & Zlatan **IBRAHIMOVIC** SWE, Milan

Europa League Qualifiers
Play-off round losers qualify for the Europa League group stage. Losers in the third qualifying round qualify for the play-off round while the third placed teams in the group stage qualify for the first knockout round

FIRST QUALIFYING ROUND

Comunal, Andorra la Vella
1st leg. 28-06-2011, 300, Pilav BIH
FC Santa Coloma   **0**

Ricardo FERNANDEZ - Genis GARCIA●, David RIBOLLEDA, Oscar SONEJEE, Javier SANCHEZ - Samir BOUSENINE, Christian XINOS, Manolo JIMENEZ - Alejandro ROMERO● (Mariano URBANI 60), Norberto URBANI (C) (Albert MERCADE 80), Renato MOTA (Cristopher POUSA 67). Tr: Luis BLANCO

F91 Dudelange   **2**
Legros [57], Caillet [79]

Jonathan JOUBERT (C) - Jeffrey RENTMEISTER, Jean-Philippe CAILLET, Ben PAYAL● (Stefano BENSI 82), Bryan MELISSE●, Paco SANCHEZ●, Daniel DA MOTA● (Romain OLLE-NICOLLE 70), Jean-Sebastien LEGROS, Aurelien JOACHIM (Thomas GRUSZCZYNSKI 52), Sofian BENZOUIEN●, Michael WIGGERS. Tr: Daniel THEIS

2nd leg. Jos Nosbaum, Dudelange
2nd leg. 5-07-2011, 1015, Rossi SMR
F91 Dudelange   **2**
Abdullei 2 [60 89]

Jonathan JOUBERT (C) - Michael WIGGERS, Julien TOURNUT (Ben PAYAL 73), Jean-Philippe CAILLET, Romain OLLE-NICOLLE - Paco SANCHEZ, Jeffrey RENTMEISTER - Stefano BENSI (Daniel DA MOTA 63), Jean-Sebastien LEGROS●, Bryan MELISSE - Thomas GRUSZCZYNSKI (Amadou ABDULLEI 55), Tr: Daniel THEIS

FC Santa Coloma   **0**

Ricardo FERNANDEZ - Luciano NASTRI● (Txema GARCIA 67), Christian XINOS, David RIBOLLEDA, Javier SANCHEZ - Oriol FITE, Cristopher POUSA, Manolo JIMENEZ, Norberto URBANI (C) (Juli SANCHEZ 57) - Mariano URBANI (Samir BOUSENINE 18), Alejandro ROMERO. Tr: Luis BLANCO

Olimpico, Serravalle
1st leg. 28-06-2011, 544, Muir SCO
Tre Fiori   **0**

Mauro BERTOZZI - Nicola CANAREZZA (C)●, Alessio BALLANTI, Giacomo BENEDETTINI, Matteo ANDREINI● - Federico MACINA (Gerhard ZENUNAY 57), Altin LISI, Paolo TARINI● (Nicolo GRINI 46) - Fabio VANNONI, Alessandro GIUNTA (Federico AMICI 65), Michael SIMONCINI. Tr: Paolo TARINI

Valletta   **3**
Denni [43], Effiong [50], Agius.G [70p]

Andrew HOGG - Dyson FALZON, Steve BORG, Jonathan CARUANA● (Kenneth SCICLUNA 71), Roderick BRIFFA● - DENNI, Edmond AGIUS, Jamie PACE (C), Ryan FENECH (Gilbert AGIUS 54) - William BARBOSA, Alfred EFFIONG (Ian ZAMMIT 60). Tr: Leonard FARRUGIA

Hibernians Ground, Paola
2nd leg. 6-07-2011, 1616, Pashaj ALB
Valletta   **2**
Zammit [58p], Barbosa [88]

Andrew HOGG - Edmond AGIUS, Steve BORG, Kenneth SCICLUNA, Dyson FALZON - Ousseni ZONGO (William BARBOSA● 58), Jamie PACE, Gilbert AGIUS (C), DENNI (Ryan FENECH 39) - Ian ZAMMIT, Alfred EFFIONG (Kevin SAMMUT 77). Tr: Leonard FARRUGIA

Tre Fiori   **1**
Lisi [21p]

Gianluca COLA - Nicola CANAREZZA (C) (Simone GRANA 78), Matteo VENDEMINI●●56, Nicolo GRINI, Matteo ANDREINI● - Fabio VANNONI, Altin LISI, Michael SIMONCINI - Federico AMICI (Gerhard ZENUNAY 65), Alessandro GIUNTA (Francesco STOLFI 91+), Maximiliano BAIZAN. Tr: Paolo TARINI

SECOND QUALIFYING ROUND

Belle Vue, Rhyl
1st leg. 13-07-2011, 1189, Genov BUL
Bangor City   **0**

Lee IDZI - Peter HOY, Chris ROBERTS, David MORLEY, James BREWERTON, Michael JOHNSTON, Chris JONES (Sion EDWARDS 68), Craig GARSIDE, Les DAVIES, Nicky WARD (Mark SMYTH 68), Alan BULL (Kyle WILSON 68). Tr: Neville POWELL

HJK Helsinki   **3**
Sadik 2 [14 55], Sorsa [89]

Ville WALLEN - Tuomas KANSIKAS●, Valtteri MOREN, Mathias LINDSTROM, Mikko SUMUSALO, Alexander RING, Sebastian MANNSTROM (Sebastian SORSA 63), Dawda BAH, Aki RIIHILAHTI, Berat SADIK● (Cheyne FOWLER 71), Teemu PUKKI (Jarno PARIKKA 83). Tr: Antti MUURINEN

Sonera, Helsinki
2nd leg. 19-07-2011, 5944, Kharitonashvili
HJK Helsinki   **10**
Ring [37], Sadik [44], Zeneli 2 [47 54], Rafinha [52], Pukki 2 [64 67], Kastrati 2 [66 88], Parikka [71]

Ville WALLEN - Valtteri MOREN, Mathias LINDSTROM, Mikko SUMUSALO, Alexander RING, RAFINHA, Dawda BAH, Aki RIIHILAHTI (Cheyne FOWLER 59), Erfan ZENELI, Berat SADIK (Kastriot KASTRATI 59), Teemu PUKKI (Jarno PARIKKA 69). Tr: Antti MUURINEN

Bangor City   **0**

Lee IDZI - Peter HOY (Michael WALSH 56), Chris ROBERTS, David MORLEY, James BREWERTON●, Michael JOHNSTON●, Chris JONES (Clive WILLIAMS 56), Les DAVIES (Craig GARSIDE 72), Nicky WARD, Alan BULL, Kyle WILSON. Tr: Neville POWELL

Maksimir, Zagreb
1st leg. 13-07-2011, 33266, Gautier FRA
Dinamo Zagreb   **3**
Badelj [37], Krstanovic 2 [46 65p]

Ivan KELAVA - Luis IBANEZ, TONEL, Sime VRSALJKO, Domagoj VIDA, Jerko LEKO●, SAMMIR, Milan BADELJ●, Mehmed ALISPAHIC (Mateo KOVACIC 88), Fatos BECIRAJ (Ante RUKAVINA 67), Ivan KRSTANOVIC● (Ivan TOMECAK 79). Tr: Krunoslav JURCIC

Neftchi Baku   **0**

Sasa STAMENKOVIC● - Rail MALIKOV, DENIS, Igor MITRESKI (Javid HUSEYNOV 44), ALESSANDRO●, Slavco GEORGIEVSKI, RODRIGUINHO● (Bakhodir NASIMOV● 71), FLAVINHO, Ruslan ABISOV, Rashad ABDULLAYEV (Javid IMAMVERDIYEV 77), Emile MPENZA. Tr: Arif ASADOV

Tofiq Bahramov, Baku
2nd leg. 19-07-2011, 7000, Kaasik EST
Neftchi Baku   **0**

Sasa STAMENKOVIC - Rail MALIKOV, DENIS, Ruslan AMIRJANOV, Slavco GEORGIEVSKI (Mirhuseyn SEYIDOV 85), RODRIGUINHO (Javid IMAMVERDIYEV 6), FLAVINHO, Ruslan ABISOV, Rashad ABDULLAYEV (Javid HUSEYNOV 46), Emile MPENZA, Bakhodir NASIMOV. Tr: Arif ASADOV

Dinamo Zagreb   **0**

Ivan KELAVA - Luis IBANEZ, TONEL●, Sime VRSALJKO●, Domagoj VIDA, Jerko LEKO, SAMMIR (Adrian CALELLO 89), Milan BADELJ, Mehmed ALISPAHIC (Mateo KOVACIC 79), Fatos BECIRAJ (Ante RUKAVINA 72), Ivan KRSTANOVIC. Tr: Krunoslav JURCIC

Swedbank, Malmö
1st leg. 13-07-2011, 12501, Panayi CYP
Malmö FF   **2**
Rexhepi [58], OG [77]

Dusan MELICHAREK - Markus HALSTI, Pontus JANSSON, RICARDINHO●, Daniel ANDERSSON, Ivo PEKALSKI (Miljan MUTAVDZIC 89), Jimmy DURMAZ, Daniel LARSSON, Wilton FIGUEIREDO, Dardan REXHEPI (Alex NILSSON 82), Agon MEHMETI (Omid NAZARI 88). Tr: Rikard NORLING

HB Tórshavn   **0**

Teitur GESTSSON● - Rogvi HOLM, Hendrik RUBEKSEN, Hans a LAG, Paetur JØRGENSEN, Hanus THORLEIFSSON● (Kristin MOURITSEN 90), Frodi BENJAMINSEN●, Kari NIELSEN, Rogvi POULSEN, Simun SAMUELSEN (Jon POULSEN 90), Andrew av FLOTUM (Jogvan NOLSOE 87). Tr: Sigfridur CLEMENTSEN

Gundadalur, Tórshavn
2nd leg. 19-07-2011, 688, Vukadinovic SRB
HB Tórshavn   **1**
Benjaminsen [70]

Teitur GESTSSON - Rogvi HOLM, Hendrik RUBEKSEN, Paetur JØRGENSEN, Hanus THORLEIFSSON (Jogvan DAVIDSEN 89), Frodi BENJAMINSEN, Kari NIELSEN, Rogvi POULSEN● (Kristin MOURITSEN 88), Vagnur MORTENSEN, Simun SAMUELSEN, Andrew av FLOTUM (Jogvan NOLSOE 74). Tr: Sigfridur CLEMENTSEN

Malmö FF   **1**
Figueiredo [91+]

Dusan MELICHAREK - Markus HALSTI, Pontus JANSSON, RICARDINHO, Daniel ANDERSSON, Ivo PEKALSKI, Jimmy DURMAZ, Daniel LARSSON, Wilton FIGUEIREDO, Dardan REXHEPI (Jiloan HAMAD 63), Agon MEHMETI● (Miljan MUTAVDZIC 85). Tr: Rikard NORLING

UEFA CHAMPIONS LEAGUE 2011-12

Kiryat Eliezer, Haifa
1st leg. 13-07-2011, 9750, Valeri ITA
Maccabi Haifa 5
Amashe 3 [45] [71] [73], Yampolsky [72], Golasa [80]
Nir DAVIDOVITCH - Jurica BULJAT•, Eyal MESHUMAR, Seidu YAHAYA, Gustavo BOCCOLI• (Vladimer DVALISHVILI 39), Taleb TAWATHA, Eyal GOLASA, Andriy PILYAVSKY, Idan VERED (Shlomi AZULAY 65), Wiyam AMASHE, Yaniv KATAN (Dela YAMPOLSKY• 60). Tr: Elisha LEVY

Borac Banja Luka 1
Raspudic [24]
Asmir AVDUKIC - Bojan MARKOVIC (Bojan PETRIC 69), Milan STUPAR, Boris RASPUDIC, Drasko ZARIC, Dragoslav STAKIC, Sasa KOVACEVIC, Srdan GRAHOVAC (Dusko SAKAN 64), Borislav MIKIC, Branislav KRUNIC, Dusko STAJIC (Nemanja VIDAKOVIC• 79). Tr: Velimir STOJNIC

Gradski, Banja Luka
2nd leg. 20-07-2011, 4000, Liesveld NED
Borac Banja Luka 3
Krunic 2 [9] [34], Vidakovic [84]
Asmir AVDUKIC - Bojan MARKOVIC, Boris RASPUDIC, Drasko ZARIC, Dragoslav STAKIC, Sasa KOVACEVIC• (Milan STUPAR 65), Srdan GRAHOVAC•, Borislav MIKIC• (Sinisa DUJAKOVIC 90), Nemanja VIDAKOVIC•, Petar KUNIC, Dusko STAJIC (Stefan DUJAKOVIC 87). Tr: Velimir STOJNIC

Maccabi Haifa 2
Dvalishvili 2 [24] [54]
Nir DAVIDOVITCH - Jurica BULJAT, Eyal MESHUMAR, Seidu YAHAYA•, Gustavo BOCCOLI• (Dela YAMPOLSKY 57), Taleb TAWATHA, Eyal GOLASA, Andriy PILYAVSKY, Vladimer DVALISHVILI, Idan VERED (Mohammad GHADIR 75), Wiyam AMASHE• (Shlomi AZULAY 68). Tr: Elisha LEVY

Ljudski vrt, Maribor
1st leg. 12-07-2011, 5500, Banari MDA
NK Maribor 2
Arghus [36], Ibraimi [45]
Marko PRIDIGAR - Ales MEJAC, Aleksander RAJCEVIC, ARGHUS (Jovan VIDOVIC 90), Zeljko FILIPOVIC (Goran CVIJANOVIC 66), Dejan MEZGA, Mitja VILER, Ales MERTELJ•, MARCOS TAVARES (Etien VELIKONJA 81), Agim IBRAIMI, Robert BERIC•. Tr: Darko MILANIC

F91 Dudelange 0
Jonathan JOUBERT• - Julien TOURNUT, Jean-Philippe CAILLET•, Romain OLLE-NICOLLE (Daniel DA MOTA 73), Ben PAYAL, Paco SANCHEZ, Jean-Sebastien LEGROS• (Thomas GRUSZCZYNSKI 78), Sofian BENZOUIEN, Michael WIGGERS•, Amodou ABDULLEI•, Bryan MELISSE•. Tr: Dany THEIS

Jos Nosbaum, Dudelange
2nd leg. 19-07-2011, 1152, Borg MLT
F91 Dudelange 1
Da Mota [54]
Jonathan JOUBERT - Julien TOURNUT, Jeffrey RENTMEISTER, Jean-Philippe CAILLET••[75], Ben PAYAL (Kevin MALGET 62), Paco SANCHEZ, Sofian BENZOUIEN, Michael WIGGERS•, Amodou ABDULLEI (Romain OLLE-NICOLLE 80), Daniel DA MOTA••[76], Stefano BENSI (Thomas GRUSZCZYNSKI 66). Tr: Dany THEIS

NK Maribor 3
Mezga 2 [26] [76p], Beric [72]
Marko PRIDIGAR - Ales MEJAC, Aleksander RAJCEVIC, ARGHUS•, Zeljko FILIPOVIC (GABRIEL 60), Martin MILEC, Dejan MEZGA, Goran CVIJANOVIC, Ales MERTELJ, Etien VELIKONJA (MARCOS TAVARES 64), Robert BERIC (Dalibor VOLAS 80). Tr: Darko MILANIC

Partizan, Belgrade
1st leg. 13-07-2011, 15324, Kuchin KAZ
Partizan Beograd 4
Vukic [48], Edu [58], Scepovic [74], OG [76]
Vladimir STOJKOVIC - Vladimir VOLKOV, Aleksandar RANKOVIC, Nikola AKSENTIJEVIC, Ivan IVANOV, MEDO, Zvonimir VUKIC•, Sasa ILIC (Nemanja TOMIC 67), Stefan BABOVIC•, EDUARDO (Vladimir JOVANCIC 76), Marko SCEPOVIC (Lazar MARKOVIC 87). Tr: Aleksandar STANOJEVIC

Shkendija Tetovo 0
Suat ZENDELI - Ardijan CUCULI, Ilir ELMAZOVSKI (Medzit NEZIRI 84), Vladimir NIKITOVIC, Sedat BERISHA•, Nebi MUSTAFI, Elmedin REDZEPI (Valmir NAFIU 67), Ferhan HASANI, Izair EMINI, Muhamedin HUSEINI (Jasir SELMANI 88), Ersen SALI•. Tr: Osmani CATIP

Philip II National, Skopje
2nd leg. 19-07-2011, 5000, Hategan ROU
Shkendija Tetovo 0
Suat ZENDELI - Medzit NEZIRI, Ardijan CUCULI•, Vladimir NIKITOVIC, Sedat BERISHA, Nebi MUSTAFI, Ferhan HASANI, Izair EMINI (Marjan BILBILOVSKI 86), Muhamedin HUSEINI••[90], Ersen SALI (Genc HYSENI 46), Jasir SELMANI (Gjelbrim TAHIPI 75). Tr: Osmani CATIP

Partizan Beograd 1
Jovancic [68]
Radisa ILIC - Vladimir VOLKOV, Aleksandar RANKOVIC, Nikola AKSENTIJEVIC, Ivan IVANOV, MEDO•, Nemanja TOMIC (Stefan BABOVIC 46), Zvonimir VUKIC (Nikola NINKOVIC 77), Sasa ILIC, EDUARDO (Vladimir JOVANCIC 64), Marko SCEPOVIC. Tr: Aleksandar STANOJEVIC

Pod Goricom, Podgorica
1st leg. 12-07-2011, 1500, Mazeika LTU
Mogren Budva 1
Zec.M [14]
Nemanja SCEKIC - Risto LAKIC, Janko SIMOVIC, Radoslav BATAK (Nikola BOGIC 46), Aleksandar KAPISODA, Bojan IVANOVIC, Drasko BOZOVIC•, Igor MATIC, Miodrag ZEC (Nikola VUJOVIC 62), Danilo CULAFIC• (Ratko ZEC 87), Vladimir GLUSCEVIC•. Tr: Branislav MILACIC

Litex Lovech 2
Todorov 2 [77] [79]
VINICIUS - Petar ZANEV, Dzemal BERBEROVIC•, Plamen NIKOLAY, Nikolaj BODUROV, Hristo YANEV, WELLINGTON, Georgi MILANOV (Robert FLORES 78), Nebojsa JELENKOVIC, Thiago MIRACEMA (Momchil TSVETANOV 71), Celio CODO (Svetoslav TODOROV 64). Tr: Luboslav PENEV

Gradski, Lovech
2nd leg. 19-07-2011, 4000, Marriner ENG
Litex Lovech 3
Zanev [3], Todorov [49p], Yanev [80]
VINICIUS - Petar ZANEV, Dzemal BERBEROVIC (Maxime JOSSE 77), Plamen NIKOLOV, Nikolaj BODUROV, Hristo YANEV, WELLINGTON (THIAGO MIRACEMA 67), Georgi MILANOV, Nebojsa JELENKOVIC, Svetoslav TODOROV (Robert FLORES 72), Momchil TSVETANOV. Tr: Luboslav PENEV

Mogren Budva 0
Miodrag TODOROVIC - Risto LAKIC•, Janko SIMOVIC, Radoslav BATAK (Vladan TATAR 59), Aleksandar KAPISODA•, Bojan IVANOVIC, Igor MATIC, Andrija MIRKOVIC•, Luka DORDEVIC (Nikola VUJOVIC 62), Danilo CULAFIC (Marko BAKIC 74), Vladimir GLUSCEVIC. Tr: Branislav MILACIC

Skonto, Riga
1st leg. 13-07-2011, 5200, Masiah ISR
Skonto Riga 0
Germans MALINS - Renars RODE, Vitalijs SMIRNOVS, Ruslan MINGAZOV, Deniss KACANOVS, Aleksandrs FERTOVS, Igors TARASOVS, Armands PETERSONS (Bally SMART 66), Juris LAIZANS••[83], Arturs KARASAUSKS (FABINHO 62), Valerijs SABALA (Kristaps BLANKS 76). Tr: Marian PAHARS

Wisla Krakow 1
Sergei PAREIKO - Kew JALIENS, Osman CHAVEZ, Michael LAMEY, Maor MELIKSON (Lukasz GARGULA 86), Radoslaw SOBOLEWSKI, Dragan PALJIC, Cezary WILK, Tzvetan GENKOV (Dudu BITON• 75), Patryk MALECKI, Ivica ILIEV. Tr: Robert MAASKANT

Miejski, Krakow
2nd leg. 19-07-2011, 19300, Mazic SRB
Wisla Krakow 2
Malecki [51], Iliev [64]
Sergei PAREIKO - Kew JALIENS, Osman CHAVEZ, Michael LAMEY (Marko JOVANOVIC 87), Maor MELIKSON, Radoslaw SOBOLEWSKI• (Gervasio NUNEZ 75), Dragan PALJIC, Cezary WILK, Tzvetan GENKOV, Patryk MALECKI, Ivica ILIEV• (Tomas JIRSAK 85). Tr: Robert MAASKANT

Skonto Riga 0
Germans MALINS - Renars RODE, Vitalijs SMIRNOVS, Vitalijs MAXIMENKO•, Ruslan MINGAZOV••[90], Deniss KACANOVS, Aleksandrs FERTOVS, Igors TARASOVS, Bally SMART (FABINHO 55), Nathan JUNIOR (Armands PETERSONS 72), Valerijs SABALA (Kristaps BLANKS 67). Tr: Marian PAHARS

Skënderbeu, Korçë
1st leg. 13-07-2011, 5000, Valasek SVK
Skënderbeu Korçë 0
Orges SHEHI - Eloy ROBLES (Marko RADAS 46), Endrit VRAPI, Nurudeen ORELESI•, Ditmar BICAJ, Renato ARAPI, Blendi SHKEMBI, Gjergj MUZAKA, Igli ALLMUCA• (Bernardo RIBEIRO 67), Davor BRATIC (Luko BISKUP 85), Marcos DOS SANTOS. Tr: Shpetim DURO

APOEL Nicosia 2
Nuno Morais [52], Manduca [56]
Dionisis CHIOTIS - Savvas POURSAITIDIS, PAULO JORGE, WILLIAM Boaventura, NUNO MORAIS, Costas CHARALAMBIDES (Nektarios ALEXANDROU 86), HELIO PINTO, Christos KONTIS, MARCINHO (Aldo ADORNO 72), Esteban SOLARI, Gustavo MANDUCA (Marinos SATSIAS• 82). Tr: Ivan JOVANOVIC

GSP, Nicosia
2nd leg. 20-07-2011, 11271, De Marco ITA
APOEL Nicosia 4
Solari [59], Aiton [66], Adorno [80], Charalambidis [86]
Dionisis CHIOTIS - Savvas POURSAITIDIS (Athos Solomou 80), MARCELO OLIVEIRA, WILLIAM Boaventura, NUNO MORAIS, Costas CHARALAMBIDES, HELIO PINTO (Sanel JAHIC 72), Christos KONTIS, Esteban SOLARI (AILTON 62), Aldo ADORNO, Gustavo MANDUCA. Tr: Ivan JOVANOVIC

Skënderbeu Korçë 0
Orges SHEHI - Endrit VRAPI•, Nurudeen ORELESI (Luko BISKUP• 46), Ditmar BICAJ, Renato ARAPI•, Blendi SHKEMBI, Gjergj MUZAKA (Igli ALLMUCA, Davor BRATIC, Marcos DOS SANTOS (Bernardo RIBEIRO 72). Tr: Shpetim DURO

1074 PART THREE – THE CONTINENTAL CONFEDERATIONS

Pasienky, Bratislava
1st leg. 12-07-2011, 5128, Shvetsov UKR
Slovan Bratislava 2
Sebo [41], Guede [81]

Matus PUTNOCKY - Martin DOBROTKA, Jiri KLADRUBSKY●, Mamadou BAGAYOKO●, Marian HAD, Erik GRENDEL (Marko MILINKOVIC 63), Igor ZOFCAK, Karim GUEDE, Peter STEPANOVSKY (Kristian KOLCAK 76), Juraj HALENAR◆67, Filip SEBO. Tr: Karel JAROLIM

Tobol Kostanay 0

Aleksandr PETUKHOV - Dumitru BOGDAN (Igor YURIN 70), Aleksandr KISLITSYN●, Evgeniy OVSHINOV, Ermek KUANTAEV, Stepan KUCERA, Vitaliy VOLKOV, Nenad SLIVIC●, Samir BEKRIC (Anatoliy BOGDANOV● 57), Robert ZEBELYAN, Bauyrzhan DZHOLCHIEV● (Sergey GRIDIN 64). Tr: Sergey PETRENKO

Central, Kostanay
2nd leg. 19-07-2011, 6800, Simunovic CRO
Tobol Kostanay 1
OG [62]

Aleksandr PETUKHOV - Dumitru BOGDAN●, Aleksandr KISLITSYN (Ermek KUANTAEV 60), Evgeniy OVSHINOV, Stepan KUCERA, Vitaliy VOLKOV, Nenad SLIVIC, Sergey KOSTYUK (Anatoliy BOGDANOV● 61), Sergey GRIDIN, Robert ZEBELYAN, Bauyrzhan DZHOLCHIEV●. Tr: Sergy PETRENKO

Slovan Bratislava 1
Kladrubsky [16]

Matus PUTNOCKY - Martin DOBROTKA●, Jiri KLADRUBSKY●, Mamadou BAGAYOKO (Erik CIKOS 85), Marian HAD, Milan IVANA (Filip KISS 65), Igor ZOFCAK, Marko MILINKOVIC (Marek KUZMA 76), Karim GUEDE, Peter STEPANOVSKY, Filip SEBO. Tr: Karel JAROLIM

Tallaght, Dublin
1st leg. 12-07-2011, 5026, Kehlet DEN
Shamrock Rovers 1
Turner [34]

Alan MANNUS - Pat SULLIVAN, Enda STEVENS, Craig SIVES, Ken OMAN, Stephen O'DONNELL (Gary O'NEILL 83), Chris TURNER● (Conor MCCORMACK 71), Billy DENNEHY, Ronan FINN, Gary TWIGG, Dean KELLY (Gary MCCABE 76). Tr: Michael O'NEILL

Flora Tallinn 0

Stanislav PEDOK - Nikita BARANOV, Gert KAMS, Karl PALATU, Sergei MOSNIKOV, Markus JURGENSON, Zakaria BEGLARISHVILI (Geir HERREM 46), Valeri MINKENEN, Rauno ALLIKU (Nikolai MASITSEV 71), Siim LUTS, Henri ANIER (Hannes ANIER 88). Tr: Martin REIM

A Le Coq Arena, Tallinn
2nd leg. 19-07-2011, 2970, Meckarovski MKD
Flora Tallinn 0

Stanislav PEDOK - Nikita BARANOV, Gert KAMS●, Karl PALATU, Sergei MOSNIKOV (Zakaria BEGLARISHVILI 72), Markus JURGENSON●, Nikolai MASITSEV (Meelis PEITRE 84), Valeri MINKENEN, Rauno ALLIKU (Alo DUPIKOV 10), Siim LUTS, Henri ANIER●. Tr: Martin REIM

Shamrock Rovers 0

Alan MANNUS - Pat SULLIVAN, Enda STEVENS●, Craig SIVES, Ken OMAN, Chris TURNER● (Stephen O'DONNELL 81), Billy DENNEHY, Ronan FINN, Conor MCCORMACK, Gary TWIGG, Dean KELLY. Tr: Michael O'NEILL

Lerkendal, Trondheim
1st leg. 13-07-2011, 4943, Yordanov BUL
Rosenborg BK 5
Skjelbred [43], Dorsin [48], Henriksen [72], Prica [76], Olsen [86]

Daniel ORLUND - Mikael LUSTIG, Mikael DORSIN, Jim LARSEN, Simen WANGBERG, Fredrik WINSNES, Per SKJELBRED, Markus HENRIKSEN, Jonas SVENSSON (Mushaga BAKENGA 70), Morten MOLDSKRED (Fredrik MIDTSJO 86), Rade PRICA (Trond OLSEN 79). Tr: Jan JONSSON

Breidablik 0

Ingvar Thor KALE - Jokull I ELISABETARSON, Kristinn JONSSON, Arnor ADALSTEINSSON, Tomas GARDARSSON (Andri YEOMAN 70), Finnur MARGEIRSSON (Olgeir SIGURGEIRSSON 90), Kari ARSAELSSON, Rafn HARALDSSON, Gudmundur KRISTJANSSON, Kristinn STEINDORSSON (Arnar BJORGVINSSON 90), Dylan MACALLISTER. Tr: Olafur KRISTJANSSON

Kópavogsvöllur, Kópavogur
2nd leg. 20-07-2011, 747, Virant BEL
Breidablik 2
Macallister [28], Steindorsson [82]

Ingvar Thor KALE - Jokull I ELISABETARSON, Kristinn JONSSON, Arnor ADALSTEINSSON, Tomas GARDARSSON (Arnar BJORGVINSSON 68), Finnur MARGEIRSSON●, Kari ARSAELSSON, Rafn HARALDSSON (Andri YEOMAN 74), Gudmundur KRISTJANSSON●, Kristinn STEINDORSSON (Viktor Unnar ILLUGASON 90), Dylan MACALLISTER. Tr: Olafur KRISTJANSSON

Rosenborg BK 0

Daniel ORLUND - Mikael LUSTIG, Mikael DORSIN, Jim LARSEN (Alejandro LAGO 63), Simen WANGBERG, Trond OLSEN, Fredrik WINSNES, Per SKJELBRED (Jonas SVENSSON 72), Markus HENRIKSEN, Mushaga BAKENGA (Morten MOLDSKRED 46), Rade PRICA. Tr: Jan JONSSON

Republican, Yerevan
1st leg. 12-07-2011, 3000, Lerjeus SWE
Pyunik Yerevan 0

Karen ISRAYELYAN - Varazdat HAROYAN, Sargis HOVSEPYAN, Artak YEDIGARYAN●, Kamo HOVHANNISYAN (Gagik POGHOSYAN 45), Edgar MALAKYAN, Artak ALEKSANYAN (David MANOYAN 46), Taron VOSKANYAN, Ghukas POGHOSYAN (Davit MINASYAN 64), Artur YUSPASHYAN, Hovhannes HOVHANNISYAN●. Tr: Vardan MINASYAN

Viktoria Plzen 4
Bakos 2 [7 40p], Horvath [28p], Kolar [72]

Roman PAVLIK - David BYSTRON (Frantisek SEVINSKY 70), Marian CISOVSKY, Petr TRAPP, Pavel HORVATH, Milan PETRZELA (Martin FILLO 83), Petr JIRACEK, Daniel KOLAR, Frantisek RAJTORAL, Vaclav PILAR (Michal DURIS 73), Marek BAKOS. Tr: Pavel VRBA

Struncovych sadech, Plzen
2nd leg. 19-07-2011, 5400, Munukka FIN
Viktoria Plzen 5
Bakos 2 [38 42], Kolar 2 [45 57], Pilar [91+]

Roman PAVLIK - David LIMBERSKY, David BYSTRON, Marian CISOVSKY, Pavel HORVATH, Milan PETRZELA (Michal DURIS 65), Petr JIRACEK, Daniel KOLAR (Vladimir DARIDA 81), Frantisek RAJTORAL, Vaclav PILAR, Marek BAKOS (Jakub HORA 74). Tr: Pavel VRBA

Pyunik Yerevan 1
Malakyan [49]

Karen ISRAYELYAN - Varazdat HAROYAN, Sargis HOVSEPYAN, Artak YEDIGARYAN, Edgar MANUCHARYAN, Kamo HOVHANNISYAN (Gagik POGHOSYAN 59), Edgar MALAKYAN, David MANOYAN (Vardan BAKALYAN 79), Artak ALEKSANYAN, Artur YUSPASHYAN, Hovhannes HOVHANNISYAN (Ghukas POGHOSYAN 54). Tr: Vardan MINASYAN

Hibernians Ground, Paola
1st leg. 12-07-2011, 1608, Radovanovic MNE
Valletta 2
Mifsud [43], Barbosa [91+p]

Andrew HOGG - Jonathan CARUANA●, Ian AZZOPARDI, Steve BORG, Ryan FENECH (Kevin SAMMUT 79), Edmond AGIUS●, Roderick BRIFFA●, Jamie PACE (Alfred EFFIONG 46), Gilbert AGIUS, WILLIAM, Michael MIFSUD. Tr: Leonard FARRUGIA

Ekranas Panevezys 3
Umeh [15], Gleveckas [22], Radavicius [41p]

Emilius ZUBAS - Dainius GLEVECKAS●, Andrius JOKSAS●, Ignas DEDURA●, Dusan MATOVIC●, Ramunas RADAVICIUS (Marius SKINDERIS 83), Aurimas KUCYS, Mauro ALONSO (Andrius VELICKA 80), Marko ANDELKOVIC, Aurimas VERTELIS, Uchenna UMEH (Tadas MARKEVICIUS 65). Tr: Valdas URBONAS

Aukstaitija, Panevezys
2nd leg. 19-07-2011, 3000, Constantin ROU
Ekranas Panevezys 1
Dedura [5]

Emilius ZUBAS - Andrius JOKSAS●, Ignas DEDURA, Dusan MATOVIC●, Ramunas RADAVICIUS, Aurimas KUCYS, Mauro ALONSO (Andrius VELICKA 70), Marko ANDELKOVIC●, Aurimas VERTELIS (Arnas RIBOKAS 83), Giedrius TOMKEVICIUS●, Uchenna UMEH (Jevgenij MOROZAS 89). Tr: Valdas URBONAS

Valletta 0

Andrew HOGG - Ian AZZOPARDI, Steve BORG●, Ryan FENECH, Edmond AGIUS, Dyson FALZON, Kevin SAMMUT● (DENNI● 55), Gilbert AGIUS, WILLIAM, Alfred EFFIONG (Ian ZAMMIT 67), Michael MIFSUD. Tr: Leonard FARRUGIA

Windsor Park, Belfast
1st leg. 13-07-2011, 1212, Gil POL
Linfield 1
Fordyce [5]

Alan BLAYNEY - David ARMSTRONG●, Jim ERVIN, Albert WATSON, Chris CASEMENT (Billy Joe BURNS 82), Philip LOWRY, Nathan HANLEY, Daryl FORDYCE, Robert GARRETT, Peter THOMPSON (Mark MCALLISTER 77), Michael CARVILL (Brian MCCAUL 90). Tr: David JEFFREY

BATE Borisov 1
Bressan [37p]

Aleksandr GUTOR - Aleksandr YUREVICH, Maksim BORDACHEV, Egor FILIPENKO, Marko SIMIC, Dmitriy LIKHTAROVICH (Edgar OLEKHNOVICH 77), Aleksandr VOLODKO, Renan BRESSAN, Pavel NEKHAYCHIK, Aleksandr PAVLOV (Filipp RUDIK 86), Maksim SKAVYSH (Artem KONTSEVOY 70). Tr: Viktor GONCHARENKO

Gorodskoi, Borisov
2nd leg. 19-07-2011, 5200, Kovarik CZE
BATE Borisov 2
Nekhaychik [58], Pavlov [61]

Aleksandr GUTOR - Igor SHITOV, Aleksandr YUREVICH●, Egor FILIPENKO, Marko SIMIC, Dmitriy LIKHTAROVICH (Edgar OLEKHNOVICH 78), Oleg PATOTSKIY, Renan BRESSAN (Aleksandr VOLODKO 64), Pavel NEKHAYCHIK●, Aleksandr PAVLOV, Artem KONTSEVOY● (Vitaliy RODIONOV 80). Tr: Viktor GONCHARENKO

Linfield 0

Alan BLAYNEY - David ARMSTRONG, Jim ERVIN, Albert WATSON, Chris CASEMENT (Billy Joe BURNS 69), Philip LOWRY, Nathan HANLEY, Daryl FORDYCE● (Brian MCCAUL 76), Robert GARRETT, Michael CARVILL, Mark MCALLISTER (Aaron BURNS 62). Tr: David JEFFREY

UEFA CHAMPIONS LEAGUE 2011-12

David Abashidze, Zestafoni
1st leg. 13-07-2011, 4458, Ozkahya TUR
FC Zestafoni 3
Gelashvili [14], Dvali 2 [23] [40]
Roin KVASKHVADZE - Temur GONGADZE, Georgi ONIANI, Giorgi KHIDESHELI, Zaali ELIAVA, Murtaz DAUSHVILI•, Irakli DZARIA (Tornike GORGIASHVILI 71), Shota GRIGALASHVILI, Tornike APTISAURI (Shota BABUNASHVILI 86), Nikoloz GELASHVILI (Rati TSINAMDZGVRISHVILI 68), Jaba DVALI. Tr: George Geguchadze
Dacia Chisinau 0
Artiom GAIDUCHEVICI - Lucian DOBRE, David GAMEZARDASHVILI, Goran DIMOVSKI, Alexandru ONICA (Ghenadie ORBU 78), Branislav ATANACKOVIC (Abdoul MAMAH 41), Slaven STJEPANOVIC, Janko TUMBASEVIC, Andrei COJOCARI•, Maxim MIHAILOV, Aleksandr NECHAEV (Aleksandru DEDOV 46). Tr: Igor DOBROVOLSKIY

Zimbru, Chisinau
2nd leg. 20-07-2011, 4000, Jug SVN
Dacia Chisinau 2
Popovici [20], Orbu [92+p]
Artiom GAIDUCHEVICI - Denis ILESCU•, Dumitru POPOVICI (Vasili PAVLOV 84), Abdoul MAMAH, Goran DIMOVSKI, Slaven STJEPANOVIC, Janko TUMBASEVIC (Aleksandr NECHAEV 77), Andrei COJOCARI, Ghenadie ORBU, Maxim MIHAILOV, Aleksandru DEDOV (Milos Krkotic 71). Tr: Igor DOBROVOLSKIY
FC Zestafoni 0
Roin KVASKHVADZE - Temur GONGADZE•-♦64, Georgi ONIANI•, Giorgi KHIDESHELI (Mamuka KOBAKHIDZE 86), Zaali ELIAVA, Murtaz DAUSHVILI, Irakli DZARIA, Shota GRIGALASHVILI, Tornike APTISAURI (Tornike GORGIASHVILI 82), Nikoloz GELASHVILI, Jaba DVALI (Kakhaber ALADASHVILI 69). Tr: George GEGUCHADZE

Hypo-Arena, Klagenfurt
1st leg. 13-07-2011, 11500, Attwell ENG
SK Sturm Graz 2
Szabics [68], Kienast [92+]
Christian GRATZEI - Dominic PURCHER•, Ferdinand FELDHOFER•, Thomas BURGSTALLER, Joachim STANDFEST, Manuel WEBER, Andreas HOLZL•, Haris BUKVA (Patrick WOLF 36), Samir MURATOVIC• (Roman KIENAST 62), Matthias KOCH (Sandro FODA 82), Imre SZABICS. Tr: Franco FODA
Videoton 0
Tomas TUJVEL - Alvaro BRACHI•, Zoltan LIPTAK•, Hector SANCHEZ, Gabor HORVATH•, Dusan VASILJEVIC (Gyorgy SANDOR 63), Attila POLONKAI (Daniel NAGY 82), Andras GOSZTONY (WALTER 73), Nikola MITROVIC, Akos ELEK•, Andre ALVES. Tr: PAULO SOUSA

Sóstói, Székesfehérvár
2nd leg. 20-07-2011, 8760, Stavrev MKD
Videoton 3
Elek [27], Sandor [32], Liptak [45]
Tomas TUJVEL - Alvaro BRACHI, Zoltan LIPTAK•, Hector SANCHEZ, Gabor HORVATH, Andras GOSZTONY (WALTER 79), Gyorgy SANDOR (Nemanja NIKOLIC 76), Nikola MITROVIC, Daniel NAGY, Akos ELEK (Attila POLONKAI 65), Andre ALVES•. Tr: PAULO SOUSA
SK Sturm Graz 2
Holzl [28], Feldhofer [39]
Christian GRATZEI• - Dominic PURCHER• (George POPKHADZE 46), Ferdinand FELDHOFER, Thomas BURGSTALLER, Joachim STANDFEST•, Manuel WEBER, Andreas HOLZL, Samir MURATOVIC, Matthias KOCH, Patrick WOLF• (Martin EHRENREICH 83), Imre SZABICS (Roman KIENAST 46). Tr: Franco FODA

THIRD QUALIFYING ROUND

Maurice Dufrasne, Liège
1st leg. 27-07-2011, 13727, Yefet ISR
Standard CL 1
Gonzalez [90]
SINAN Bolat - Dan OPARE, FELIPE, Sebastien POCOGNOLI (Christian BENTEKE 87), KANU, Jelle VAN DAMME•, Yoni BUYENS, Pape CAMARA (Nacho GONZALEZ 84), Mohammed TCHITE, Aloys NONG (Michy BATSHUAYI 84), Mbaye LEYE. Tr: Jose RIGA
FC Zürich 1
Mehmedi [79]
Johnny LEONI - JORGE TEIXEIRA, Ricardo RODRIGUEZ, Philippe KOCH•, Mathieu Beda, Xavier MARGAIRAZ (Stjepan KUKURUZOVIC 23), Silvan AEGERTER, Adrian NIKCI•, Dusan DURIC (Raphael KOCH 90), Alexandre ALPHONSE, Admir MEHMEDI• (Josip DRMIC 87). Tr: Urs FISCHER

Letzigrund, Zürich
2nd leg. 3-08-2011, 10500, Valeri ITA
FC Zürich 1
Mehmedi [58]
Johnny LEONI - JORGE TEIXEIRA, Ricardo RODRIGUEZ, Philippe KOCH•, Mathieu BEDA, Silvan AEGERTER, Stjepan KUKURUZOVIC, Adrian NIKCI, Dusan DURIC• (Heinz BARMETTLER 83), Alexandre ALPHONSE (Raphael KOCH 90), Admir MEHMEDI (Amine CHERMITI 80). Tr: Urs FISCHER
Standard CL 0
SINAN Bolat - Dan OPARE (Reginal GOREUX 34), FELIPE•, Sebastien POCOGNOLI (Pape CAMARA 61), KANU, Jelle VAN DAMME•, Nacho GONZALEZ, Yoni BUYENS♦21, Mohammed TCHITE, Aloys NONG (Christian BENTEKE 61), Mbaye LEYE•. Tr: Jose RIGA

Tre-For Park, Odense
1st leg. 27-07-2011, 10055, Gomez ESP
OB Odense 1
Reginiussen [90]
Stefan WESSELS - Espen RUUD, Anders MOLLER CHRISTENSEN, Tore REGINIUSSEN, Bernard MENDY (Rurik GISLASON 46) (Eric DJEMBA-DJEMBA 69), Hans ANDREASEN, Rasmus JENSEN (Daniel HOEGH 85), Andreas JOHANSSON, Peter UTAKA, Chris SORENSEN•, Bashkim KADRII. Tr: Henrik CLAUSEN
Panathinaikos 1
Leto [47]
Alexandros TZORVAS - Josu SARRIEGI, Jean-Alain BOUMSONG, Stergos MARINOS, Loukas VYNTRA, Nikos SPYROPOULOS•, Sotiris NINIS (Giorgios KARAGOUNIS 77), Sebastian LETO, SIMAO, Kostas KATSOURANIS, Antonis PETROPOULOS (Quincy OWUSU-ABEYIE 73). Tr: Jesualdo FERREIRA

Olympic, Athens
2nd leg. 2-08-2011, 24374, Marriner ENG
Panathinaikos 3
Boumsong [35], Toche [50], Petropoulos [95+]
Alexandros TZORVAS - Josu SARRIEGI, Jean-Alain BOUMSONG, Stergos MARINOS (TOCHE 20), Loukas VYNTRA, Nikos SPYROPOULOS, Sotiris NINIS, Sebastian LETO, SIMAO, Kostas KATSOURANIS• (Giorgios KARAGOUNIS 74), CLEYTON (Antonis PETROPOULOS 67). Tr: Jesualdo FERREIRA
OB Odense 4
Johansson [12], Ruud [58] Kadrii [80], Andreasen [88]
Stefan WESSELS• - Espen RUUD•, Anders MOLLER CHRISTENSEN, Tore REGINIUSSEN, Bernard Mendy••♦90, Hans ANDREASEN, Andreas JOHANSSON• (Daniel HOEGH 89), Eric DJEMBA-DJEMBA, Peter UTAKA (Kalilou TRAORE 87), Chris SORENSEN, Bashkim KADRII. Tr: Henrik CLAUSEN

GelreDome, Arnhem
1st leg. 26-07-2011, 12800, Bebek CRO
Twente Enschede 2
Janko 2 [34p] [57]
Nikolai MIHAILOV - Tim CORNELISSE, Peter WISGERHOF, DOUGLAS, Bart BUYSSE, Wout BRAMA•, Steven BERGHUIS (Theo VOGELSANG 80), Thilo LEUGERS, Luuk DE JONG, Emir BAJRAMI (Ola JOHN 71), Marc JANKO (Andrej RENDLA 85). Tr: Co ADRIAANSE
FC Vaslui 0
Vytautas CERNIAUSKAS - Paul PAPP•, Zhivko MILANOV, Gabriel CANU (Pavol FARKAS 60), Petar JOVANOVIC, Lucian SANMARTEAN•, Milos PAVLOVIC, Raul COSTIN• (Nemanja MILISAVLJEVIC 63), WESLEY•, ADAILTON•, Mike TEMWANJIRA (Yero BELLO 73). Tr: Viorel HIZO

Ceahlaul, Piatra Neamt
2nd leg. 3-08-2011, 5280, Fautrel FRA
FC Vaslui 0
Vytautas CERNIAUSKAS - Paul PAPP, Silviu BALACE, Pavol FARKAS, Petar JOVANOVIC (Zhivko MILANOV 73), Lucian SANMARTEAN (Nemanja MILISAVLJEVIC• 60), Raul COSTIN, WESLEY•, Razvan NEAGU• (Richard ANNANG 78), ADAILTON, Mike TEMWANJIRA. Tr: Viorel HIZO
Twente Enschede 0
Nikolai MIHAILOV - Tim CORNELISSE, Peter WISGERHOF, DOUGLAS, Dwight TIENDALLI•, Wout BRAMA, Steven BERGHUIS, Willem JANSSEN, Luuk DE JONG, Bryan RUIZ (Ola JOHN 74), Marc JANKO (Denny LANDZAAT 86). Tr: Co ADRIAANSE

Estádio da Luz, Lisbon 1st leg. 27-07-2011, 37 341, Studer SUI	Atatürk Olympic, Istanbul 2nd leg. 3-08-2011, 32 060, Stavrev MKD	Lobanovsky Dynamo, Kyiv 1st leg. 27-07-2011, 16 430, Borbalan ESP
Benfica **2**	**Trabzonspor** **1**	**Dynamo Kyiv** **0**
Nolito [71], Gaitan [88]	Paulo Henrique [32]	
ARTUR Moares - EMERSON, LUISAO, Ezequiel GARAY, RUBEN AMORIM• (MAXI PEREIRA 64), JAVI GARCIA•, Pablo AIMAR (Axel WITSEL 74), Nicolas GAITAN, Enzo PEREZ (NOLITO• 54), Oscar CARDOZO, Javier SAVIOLA. Tr: JORGE JESUS	TOLGA Zengin - Arkadiusz GLOWACKI, REMZI Kacar, Ondrej CELUSTKA, Adrian MIERZEJEWSKI◆58, Didier ZOKORA•, Gustavo COLMAN•, SERKAN Balci (HALIL Altintop 79), PAULO HENRIQUE (ALANZINHO 44), BURAK Yilmaz, Pawel BROZEK (MUSTAFA Yumlu 63). Tr: SENOL Gunes	Oleksandr SHOVKOVSKIY - DANILO SILVA, Pape DIAKHATE, Badr EL-KADDOURI, Evgen KHACHERIDI•, Ognjen VUKOJEVIC (Artem MILEVSKIY 55), Oleg GUSEV (Milos NINKOVIC 78), Roman EREMENKO (Aleksandr ALIEV 86), Lukman HARUNA, Andriy YARMOLENKO, Brown IDEYE. Tr: Yuriy SEMIN
Trabzonspor **0**	**Benfica** **1**	**Rubin Kazan** **2**
	Nolito [19]	Kasaev [6], Natkho [68p]
TOLGA Zengin - Arkadiusz GLOWACKI, REMZI Kacar•, Ondrej CELUSTKA, Adrian MIERZEJEWSKI (Pawel BROZEK 85), Didier ZOKORA•, Gustavo COLMAN, ALANZINHO (AYKUT Akgun 67), SERKAN Balci, PAULO HENRIQUE, BURAK Yilmaz. Tr: SENOL Gunes	ARTUR Moares - EMERSON, LUISAO, MAXI PEREIRA•, Ezequiel GARAY•, JAVI GARCIA, Pablo AIMAR•, (Nemanja MATIC 64), Nicolas GAITAN• (BRUNO CESAR 87), Axel WITSEL, NOLITO, Javier SAVIOLA (Franco JARA 75). Tr: JORGE JESUS	Sergey RYZHIKOV - Cristian ANSALDI, Salvatore BOCCHETTI, Solomon KVERKVELIA, Roman SHARONOV, Alan KASAEV (Pyotr NEMOV 69), Sergey KISLYAK, Christian NOBOA, Gokdeniz KARADENIZ•, Bebars NATCHO (Alisher DZHALILOV 90), Vladimir DYADYUN (Aleksey MEDVEDEV• 60). Tr: Kurban BERDIYEV

Central, Kazan 2nd leg. 3-08-2011, 19 820, Braamhaar NED	Sonera, Helsinki 1st leg. 27-07-2011, 10 153, Kovarik CZE	Maksimir, Zagreb 2nd leg. 3-08-2011, 25 370, Jakobsson ISL
Rubin Kazan **2**	**HJK Helsinki** **1**	**Dinamo Zagreb** **1**
Dyadyun [19], Medvedev [88]	Ring [14]	Ibanez [90]
Sergey RYZHIKOV - Vitaliy KALESHIN, Salvatore BOCCHETTI•, Solomon KVERKVELIA, Roman SHARONOV, Alan KASAEV (Pyotr NEMOV 73), Sergey KISLYAK, Christian NOBOA (Igor LEBEDENKO 89), Gokdeniz KARADENIZ, Bebars NATCHO, Vladimir DYADYUN (Aleksey MEDVEDEV 81). Tr: Kurban BERDIYEV	Ville WALLEN - Mathias LINDSTROM•, Juhani OJALA, Mikko SUMUSALO, Alexander RING, RAFINHA, Dawda BAH, Aki RIIHILAHTI, Erfan ZENELI (Sebastian SORSA 62), Berat SADIK (Jari LITMANEN 78), Teemu PUKKI• (Akseli PELVAS 82). Tr: Antti MUURINEN	Ivan KELAVA - Luis IBANEZ, TONEL, Sime VRSALJKO, Domagoj VIDA, Jerko LEKO, SAMMIR, Milan BADELJ, Mehmed ALISPAHIC• (Mateo KOVACIC 19), Fatos BECIRAJ (Leandro CUFRE 81), Ivan KRSTANOVIC (Ante RUKAVINA 55). Tr: Krunoslav JURCIC
Dynamo Kyiv **1**	**Dinamo Zagreb** **2**	**HJK Helsinki** **0**
Gusev [92+]	OG [19], Sammir [77]	
Oleksandr SHOVKOVSKIY - DANILO SILVA• (Andriy SHEVCHENKO 63), Goran POPOV, Pape DIAKHATE, Ognjen VUKOJEVIC•, Oleg GUSEV, Roman EREMENKO, Lukman HARUNA• (Denys GARMASH 46), Ayila YUSSUF, Andriy YARMOLENKO•, Brown IDEYE. Tr: Yuriy SEMIN	Ivan KELAVA - Luis IBANEZ•, TONEL, Sime VRSALJKO, Domagoj VIDA, Jerko LEKO, SAMMIR (Adrian CALELLO 89), Milan BADELJ, Mehmed ALISPAHIC• (Mateo KOVACIC 69), Fatos BECIRAJ• (Ante RUKAVINA 60), Ivan KRSTANOVIC. Tr: Krunoslav JURCIC	Ville WALLEN - Mathias LINDSTROM•, Juhani OJALA, Mikko SUMUSALO, Alexander RING•, RAFINHA, Dawda BAH, Aki RIIHILAHTI• (Sebastian MANNSTROM 62), Erfan ZENELI (Sebastian SORSA 57), Berat SADIK, Teemu PUKKI (Akseli PELVAS 75). Tr: Antti MUURINEN

Ibrox, Glasgow 1st leg. 26-07-2011, 28 828, Lahoz ESP	Swedbank, Malmö 2nd leg. 3-08-2011, 19 084, Bezborodov RUS	Kiryat Eliezer, Haifa 1st leg. 27-07-2011, 9600, Dias POR
Rangers **0**	**Malmö FF** **1**	**Maccabi Haifa** **2**
	Hamad [80]	Dvalishvili [8p], Yampolsky [70]
Allan MCGREGOR - David WEIR (JUANMA ORTIZ 28), Sasa PAPAC•, Lee WALLACE•, Steven WHITTAKER, Madjid BOUGHERRA, Lee MCCULLOCH, Maurice EDU, Steven DAVIS, Steven NAISMITH, Nikica JELAVIC. Tr: Ally MCCOIST	Dusan MELICHAREK - Pontus JANSSON•, RICARDINHO•◆73, Daniel ANDERSSON, Miljan MUTAVDZIC (Dardan REXHEPI 46) (Jeffrey AUBYNN 69), Jiloan HAMAD, Ivo PEKALSKI, Jimmy DURMAZ, Daniel LARSSON, WILTON FIGUEIREDO, Agon MEHMETI (Filip STENSTROM 34). Tr: Rikard NORLING	Bojan SARANOV (Nir DAVIDOVITCH• 46) - Jurica BULJAT, Eyal MESHUMAR, Taleb TAWATHA, Eyal GOLASA•, Ali OSMAN, Andriy PILYAVSKY (Sari FALAH 82), Vladimer DVALISHVILI, Idan VERED•, Wiyam AMASHE, Mohammad GHADIR (Dela YAMPOLSKY 46). Tr: Elisha LEVY
Malmö FF **1**	**Rangers** **1**	**NK Maribor** **1**
Larsson [18]	Jelavic [23]	Tavares [27]
Dusan MELICHAREK - Markus HALSTI, Pontus JANSSON, Daniel ANDERSSON, Miljan MUTAVDZIC, Jiloan HAMAD, Ivo PEKALSKI, Jimmy DURMAZ, Daniel LARSSON (Yago FERNANDEZ 80), WILTON FIGUEIREDO• (Dardan REXHEPI 69), Agon MEHMETI (Amin NAZARI 53). Tr: Rikard NORLING	Allan MCGREGOR - Sasa PAPAC•, Lee WALLACE, Steven WHITTAKER◆19, Madjid BOUGHERRA•◆66, Lee MCCULLOCH•, Maurice EDU•, Steven DAVIS, Steven NAISMITH•, Juanma ORTIZ (Kane HEMMINGS 84), Nikica JELAVIC•. Tr: Ally MCCOIST	Jasmin HANDANOVIC - Ales MEJAC, Aleksander RAJCEVIC, ARGHUS•, Martin MILEC, Dejan MEZGA (Zeljko FILIPOVIC 89), Goran CVIJANOVIC•, Ales MERTELJ, MARCOS TAVARES (Dalibor VOLAS 75), Agim IBRAIMI, Robert BERIC. Tr: Darko MILANIC

Ljudski vrt, Maribor 2nd leg. 3-08-2011, 12 000, Ennjimi FRA	Cristal Arena, Genk 1st leg. 26-07-2011, 12 735, Koukoulakis GRE	Partizan, Belgrade 2nd leg. 3-08-2011, 24 511, De Sousa POR
NK Maribor **0**	**KRC Genk** **2**	**Partizan Beograd** **1**
Tavares [32]	Vossen [70p], Ogunjimi [92+]	Tomic [40]
Jasmin HANDANOVIC - Jovan VIDOVIC, Ales MEJAC• (Dejan TRAJKOVSKI 80), Aleksander RAJCEVIC, Martin MILEC, Dejan MEZGA• (Etien VELIKONJA 81), Goran CVIJANOVIC (Dalibor VOLAS 66), Ales MERTELJ, MARCOS TAVARES, Agim IBRAIMI, Robert BERIC. Tr: Darko MILANIC	Laszlo KOTELES - Torben JONELEIT, Anele NGCONGCA◆32, NADSON•, David HUBERT (Elyaniv BARDA 71), Daniel TOZSER, Kevin DE BRUYNE, Thomas BUFFEL (Anthony VANDEN BORRE• 46), Kennedy NWANGANGA, Daniel PUDIL, Jelle VOSSEN (Marvin OGUNJIMI 85). Tr: Frank VERCAUTEREN	Vladimir STOJKOVIC - Aleksandar MILJKOVIC•, Vladimir VOLKOV, Ivan IVANOV, Nemanja RNIC, MEDO, Nemanja TOMIC (Dejan BABIC 51), Zvonimir VUKIC•, Sasa ILIC (Nikola NINKOVIC 86), EDUARDO, Marko SCEPOVIC (Lazar MARKOVIC 77). Tr: Aleksandar STANOJEVIC
Maccabi Haifa **1**	**Partizan Beograd** **1**	**KRC Genk** **1**
Vered [10]	Tomic [65]	Vossen [58p]
Nir DAVIDOVITCH - Sari FALAH, Jurica BULJAT•, Eyal MESHUMAR•, Seidu YAHAYA, Gustavo BOCCOLI, Taleb TAWATHA•, Eyal GOLASA, Vladimer DVALISHVILI• (Mohammad GHADIR 88), Idan VERED (Ali OSMAN 90), Wiyam AMASHE (Dela YAMPOLSKY 54). Tr: Elisha LEVY	Vladimir STOJKOVIC - Vladimir VOLKOV, Aleksandar RANKOVIC, Ivan IVANOV, Nemanja RNIC, MEDO, Zvonimir VUKIC (Sasa MARKOVIC 90), Sasa ILIC•, Stefan BABOVIC•◆48, EDUARDO (Vladimir JOVANCIC• 68), Marko SCEPOVIC (Nemanja TOMIC• 53). Tr: Aleksandar STANOJEVIC	Laszlo KOTELES - Torben JONELEIT, Anthony VANDEN BORRE•, NADSON, Timothy DURWAEL, David HUBERT, Daniel TOZSER, Kevin DE BRUYNE•, Daniel PUDIL, Jelle VOSSEN (Elyaniv BARDA 68), Marvin OGUNJIMI (Kennedy NWANGANGA 86). Tr: Frank VERCAUTEREN

UEFA CHAMPIONS LEAGUE 2011-12

Gradski, Lovech
1st leg. 26-07-2011, 6800, Skjerven NOR
Litex Lovech 1
Tom [45]
VINICIUS - Petar ZANEV, Dzemal BERBEROVIC•, Plamen NIKOLOV, Nikolaj BODUROV, Hristo YANEV, WELLINGTON, Georgi MILANOV• (Maxime JOSSE 86), Nebojsa JELENKOVIC, Svetoslav TODOROV (Celio CODO 65), Momchil TSVETANOV (Robert FLORES 73). Tr: Luboslav PENEV
Wisla Krakow 2
Lamey [19], Melikson [76]
Milan JOVANIC - Kew JALIENS, Osman CHAVEZ•, Junior DIAZ, Michael LAMEY, Maor MELIKSON, Radoslaw SOBOLEWSKI, Gervasio NUNEZ (Lukasz GARGULA 77), Cezary WILK, Tzvetan GENKOV (Marko JOVANOVIC 87), Ivica ILIEV• (Andraz KIRM 66). Tr: Robert MAASKANT

Miejski, Krakow
2nd leg. 3-08-2011, 23 050, Ref: Aydinus TUR
Wisla Krakow 3
Melikson 2 [42, 56p], Wilk [84]
Sergei PAREIKO - Kew JALIENS, Osman CHAVEZ, Junior DIAZ, Michael LAMEY (Marko JOVANOVIC 86), Maor MELIKSON• (Dragan PALJIC 84), Radoslaw SOBOLEWSKI, Gervasio NUNEZ, Andraz KIRM, Tzvetan GENKOV, Patryk MALECKI (Cezary WILK 75). Tr: Robert MAASKANT
Litex Lovech 1
Bodurov [68]
VINICIUS - Petar ZANEV, Iliya MILANOV, Plamen NIKOLOV, Nikolaj BODUROV, Hristo YANEV (Aleksandr TSVETKOV 62), WELLINGTON, Georgi MILANOV (Celio CODO 72), Nebojsa JELENKOVIC◆76, THIAGO MIRACEMA, Momchil TSVETANOV (Svetoslav TODOROV 52). Tr: Luboslav PENEV

GSP Nicosia
1st leg. 26-07-2011, 14 553, Boekel NED
APOEL Nicosia 0
Dionisis CHIOTIS - Savvas POURSAITIDIS•, PAULO JORGE, WILLIAM Boaventura, NUNO MORAIS, Costas CHARALAMBIDES, HELIO PINTO, Christos KONTIS, Esteban SOLARI (MARCINHO 59), Aldo ADORNO (Ivan TRICKOVSKI 72), Gustavo MANDUCA (AILTON 59). Tr: Ivan JOVANOVIC
Slovan Bratislava 0
Matus PUTNOCKY - Erik CIKOS (Milan IVANA 86), Martin DOBROTKA, Jiri KLADRUBSKY, Mamadou BAGAYOKO, Marian HAD, Erik GRENDEL• (Marko MILINKOVIC 61), Igor ZOFCAK, Karim GUEDE•, Peter STEPANOVSKY (Lukas PAUSCHEK 71), Filip SEBO. Tr: Karel JAROLIM

Pasienky, Bratislava
2nd leg. 3-08-2011, 9348, Sippel GER
Slovan Bratislava 0
Matus PUTNOCKY - Erik CIKOS (Akos SZARKA 85), Martin DOBROTKA, Jiri KLADRUBSKY, Mamadou BAGAYOKO, Marian HAD, Erik GRENDEL•◆60, Igor ZOFCAK, Karim GUEDE•, Peter STEPANOVSKY• (Marko MILINKOVIC 61), Filip SEBO. Tr: Karel JAROLIM
APOEL Nicosia 2
Ailton [58], Manduca [93+]
Dionisis CHIOTIS - Savvas POURSAITIDIS•, PAULO JORGE, WILLIAM Boaventura, NUNO MORAIS, HELIO PINTO, Christos KONTIS, MARCINHO (Sanel JAHIC 89), AILTON (Costas CHARALAMBIDES 79), Ivan TRICKOVSKI (Esteban SOLARI 84), Gustavo MANDUCA. Tr: Ivan JOVANOVIC

Parken, Copenhagen
1st leg. 27-07-2011, 11 577, Radovanovic MNE
FC København 0
Ottesen [4]
Johan WILAND - Pierre BENGTSSON, Solvi OTTESEN, ZANKA, CLAUDEMIR•, Christian GRINDHEIM, Johnny THOMSEN (Ragnar SIGURDSSON 46), Thomas DELANEY (Johan ABSALONSEN 61), Christian BOLANOS, Cesar SANTIN (Morten NORDSTRAND 70), Pape DIOUF. Tr: Roland NILSSON
Shamrock Rovers 0
Ryan THOMPSON - Pat SULLIVAN, Enda STEVENS, Craig SIVES, Ken OMAN (Dan MURRAY• 83), Stephen RICE (Ciaran KILDUFF 90), Billy DENNEHY, Ronan FINN, Conor MCCORMACK, Gary TWIGG, Dean KELLY (Gary MCCABE 54). Tr: Michael O'NEILL

Tallaght, Dublin
2nd leg. 2-08-2011, 5901, Ozkahya TUR
Shamrock Rovers 0
Ryan THOMPSON - Pat SULLIVAN, Enda STEVENS, Craig SIVES, Dan MURRAY, Gary MCCABE (Dean KELLY 65), Chris TURNER, Billy DENNEHY, Ronan FINN (Stephen RICE 75), Conor MCCORMACK•, Gary TWIGG (Ciaran KILDUFF 75). Tr: Michael O'NEILL
FC København 2
N'Doye [42], Bolanos [73]
Johan WILAND - Pierre BENGTSSON, Solvi OTTESEN, Ragnar SIGURDSSON, ZANKA, CLAUDEMIR, Christian GRINDHEIM, Thomas KRISTENSEN (Johan ABSALONSEN 90), Christian BOLANOS (Thomas DELANEY 79), Pape DIOUF (Cesar SANTIN 83), Dame N'DOYE. Tr: Roland NILSSON

Lerkendal, Trondheim
1st leg. 27-07-2011, 8028, Jug SVN
Rosenborg BK 0
Daniel ORLUND - Mikael LUSTIG, Mikael DORSIN•, Jim LARSEN•, Simen WANGBERG, Fredrik WINSNES, Per SKJELBRED, Markus HENRIKSEN, Jonas SVENSSON (Trond OLSEN 73), Morten MOLDSKRED• (Mushaga BAKENGA 82), Rade PRICA. Tr: Jan JONSSON
Viktoria Plzen 1
Pilar [33]
Roman PAVLIK (Michal DANEK 16), David LIMBERSKY, David BYSTRON, Marian CISOVSKY•, Pavel HORVATH, Milan PETRZELA (Michal DURIS 78), Petr JIRACEK•, Daniel KOLAR, Frantisek RAJTORAL, Vaclav PILAR (Frantisek SEVINSKY 88), Marek BAKOS•. Tr: Pavel VRBA

Struncovych sadech, Plzen
2nd leg. 3-08-2011, 5124, Strahonja CRO
Viktoria Plzen 3
Bakos [56], Kolar [60], Petrzela [78]
Michal DANEK - David LIMBERSKY, David BYSTRON, Marian CISOVSKY (Frantisek SEVINSKY 32), Pavel HORVATH, Milan PETRZELA (Martin FILLO 89), Petr JIRACEK•, Daniel KOLAR•, Frantisek RAJTORAL, Vaclav PILAR, Marek BAKOS• (Michal DURIS 82). Tr: Pavel VRBA
Rosenborg BK 2
Lustig [44], Prica [77]
Daniel ORLUND - Mikael LUSTIG, Mikael DORSIN, Jim LARSEN•, Simen WANGBERG, Fredrik WINSNES, Markus HENRIKSEN•, Jonas SVENSSON• (Fredrik MIDTSJO 80), Morten MOLDSKRED (Mushaga BAKENGA 68), Daniel HOLM (Trond OLSEN 85), Rade PRICA. Tr: Jan JONSSON

Aukstaitija, Panevezys
1st leg. 26-07-2011, 2989, Aytekin GER
Ekranas Panevezys 0
Emilius ZUBAS• - Ignas DEDURA, Mantas SAMUSIOVAS, Ramunas RADAVICIUS• (Marius SKINDERIS 72), Arnas RIBOKAS (Andrius VELICKA 46), Aurimas KUCYS, Mauro ALONSO (Jevgenij MOROZAS 59), Marko ANDELKOVIC◆58, Aurimas VERTELIS, Giedrius TOMKEVICIUS, Uchenna UMEH. Tr: Valdas URBONAS
BATE Borisov 0
Aleksandr GUTOR - Igor SHITOV, Aleksandr YUREVICH, Egor FILIPENKO, Marko SIMIC, Dmitriy LIKHTAROVICH (Filipp RUDIK 61), Oleg PATOTSKIY (Mikhail GORDEYCHUK• 76), RENAN BRESSAN (Vitaliy RODIONOV 67), Pavel NEKHAYCHIK, Edgar OLEKHNOVICH•, Artem KONTSEVOY•. Tr: Viktor GONCHARENKO

Gorodskoi, Borisov
2nd leg. 2-08-2011, 5360, Gocek TUR
BATE Borisov 3
Rodionov [18], Renan Bressan [35], Gordeychuk [89]
Aleksandr GUTOR - Igor SHITOV•, Aleksandr YUREVICH, Egor FILIPENKO, Marko SIMIC, Dmitriy LIKHTAROVICH (Edgar OLEKHNOVICH 73), Oleg PATOTSKIY (Mikhail GORDEYCHUK 46), RENAN BRESSAN••◆40, Pavel NEKHAYCHIK, Dmitriy BAGA (Filipp RUDIK 85), Vitaliy RODIONOV. Tr: Viktor GONCHARENKO
Ekranas Panevezys 1
Velicka [22]
Emilius ZUBAS - Andrius JOKSAS, Ignas DEDURA•, Mantas SAMUSIOVAS•, Ramunas RADAVICIUS (Jevgenij MOROZAS 61), Aurimas KUCYS, Mauro ALONSO, Aurimas VERTELIS, Giedrius TOMKEVICIUS (Arnas RIBOKAS 81), Andrius VELICKA (Tadas MARKEVICIUS 69), Uchenna UMEH. Tr: Valdas URBONAS

Boris Paichadze National, Tbilisi
1st leg. 26-07-2011, 14 700, Kakos GRE
FC Zestafoni 1
Gelashvili [74]
Roin KVASKHVADZE - Georgi ONIANI•, Mamuka KOBAKHIDZE, Zaali ELIAVA (Georgi CHANKOTADZE 88), Kakhaber ALADASHVILI• (Alex BENASHVILI 82), Murtaz DAUSHVILI (Tornike GORGIASHVILI 57), Irakli DZARIA, Shota GRIGALASHVILI, Tornike APTISAURI•, Nikoloz GELASHVILI, Jaba DVALI. Tr: George GEGUCHADZE
SK Sturm Graz 1
Wolf [78]
Christian GRATZEI - George POPKHADZE, Thomas BURGSTALLER, Florian NEUHOLD, Martin EHRENREICH, Manuel WEBER•, Samir MURATOVIC, Florian KAINZ (Stefan STANGL 90), Sandro FODA (Matthias KOCH 83), Patrick WOLF, Roman KIENAST (Mario HAAS 82). Tr: Franco FODA

UPC Arena, Graz
2nd leg. 3-08-2011, 10 058, Gautier FRA
SK Sturm Graz 1
Kienast [68]
Christian GRATZEI - George POPKHADZE, Milan DUDIC, Thomas BURGSTALLER, Martin EHRENREICH, Manuel WEBER, Andreas HOLZL, Samir MURATOVIC, Patrick WOLF• (Florian KAINZ 85), Imre SZABICS (Darko BODUL 74), Roman KIENAST (Mario HAAS 90). Tr: Franco FODA
FC Zestafoni 0
Roin KVASKHVADZE - Georgi ONIANI•, Mamuka KOBAKHIDZE, Zaali ELIAVA, Kakhaber ALADASHVILI•, Murtaz DAUSHVILI (Tornike GORGIASHVILI 72), Irakli DZARIA (Rati TSINAMDZGVRISHVILI 80), Shota GRIGALASHVILI•, Tornike APTISAURI (Shota BABUNASHVILI 76), Nikoloz GELASHVILI•, Jaba DVALI. Tr: George GEGUCHADZE

PLAY-OFF ROUND

Allianz Arena, Munich
1st leg. 16-08-2011, 66 000, Nikolaev RUS
Bayern München 2
Schweinsteiger [8], Robben [72]

Manuel NEUER - RAFINHA, Jerome BOATENG, Holger BADSTUBER, Philipp LAHM - LUIZ GUSTAVO, Bastian SCHWEINSTEIGER - Arjen ROBBEN, Toni KROOS (Thomas MULLER 57), Franck RIBERY - Mario GOMEZ•. Tr: Jupp HEYNCKES

FC Zürich 0

Johnny LEONI - Raphael KOCH, Mathieu BEDA••♦90, JORGE TEIXEIRA, Ricardo RODRIGUEZ - Heinz BARMETTLER (Oliver BUFF 67), Silvan AEGERTER - Marco SCHONBACHLER (Adrian NIKCI 55), Admir MEHMEDI, Dusan DURIC - Amine CHERMITI (Josip DRMIC 84). Tr: Urs FISCHER

Letzigrund, Zürich
2nd leg. 24-08-2011, 23 600, Duhamel FRA
FC Zürich 0

Johnny LEONI - Philippe KOCH, Heinz BARMETTLER, JORGE TEIXEIRA, Ricardo RODRIGUEZ - Marco SCHONBACHLER, Oliver BUFF•, Silvan AEGERTER (Milan GAJIC 65), Dusan DURIC (Maurice BRUNNER 66) - Amine CHERMITI, Admir MEHMEDI (Josip DRMIC 78). Tr: Urs FISCHER

Bayern München 1
Gomez [7]

Manuel NEUER - Jerome BOATENG, Daniel VAN BUYTEN, Holger BADSTUBER, Philipp LAHM - LUIZ GUSTAVO, Bastian SCHWEINSTEIGER - Thomas MULLER (David ALABA 72), Toni KROOS (Anatoliy TYMOSHCHUK 64), Franck RIBERY - Mario GOMEZ (Nils PETERSEN 46). Tr: Jupp HEYNCKES

Tre-For Park, Odense
1st leg. 17-08-2011, 13 002, Skomina SVN
OB Odense 1
Andreason [84]

Stefan WESSELS - Espen RUUD, Anders MOLLER CHRISTENSEN, Daniel HOEGH•, Chris SORENSEN - Andreas JOHANSSON•, Eric DJEMBA-DJEMBA, Kalilou TRAORE, Bashkim KADRII - Rurik GISLASON• (Rasmus JENSEN 81), Hans ANDREASEN. Tr: Henrik CLAUSEN

Villarreal 0

DIEGO LOPEZ - MARIO, Cristian ZAPATA, Mateo MUSACCHIO•, JOAN ORIOL• - CANI, Carlos MARCHENA (MARCO RUBEN 85), BRUNO Soriano•, BORJA VALERO• (Marcos SENNA 84) - NILMAR (Javier CAMUNAS 83), Giuseppe ROSSI. Tr: Juan GARRIDO

El Madrigal, Villarreal
2nd leg. 23-08-2011, 18 304, Thomson SCO
Villarreal 3
Rossi 2 [50 66], Marchena [82]

DIEGO LOPEZ - Cristian ZAPATA, Mateo MUSACCHIO•, BRUNO Soriano, JOAN ORIOL - Javier CAMUNAS• (Carlos MARCHENA 74), Marcos SENNA•, BORJA VALERO ♦[77], CANI• (GONZALO Rodriguez• 83) - NILMAR (MARCO RUBEN 84), Giuseppe ROSSI. Tr: Juan GARRIDO

OB Odense 0

Stefan WESSELS - Espen RUUD, Anders MOLLER CHRISTENSEN, Tore REGINIUSSEN, Bernard MENDY• (Peter UTAKA 80) - Andreas JOHANSSON•, Kalilou TRAORE• (Chris SORENSEN 80), Eric DJEMBA-DJEMBA•, Bashkim KADRII••♦[71] - Hans ANDREASEN - Rurik GISLASON (Rasmus JENSEN 57), Tr: Henrik CLAUSEN

De Grolsch Veste, Enschede
1st leg. 16-08-2011, 20 000, Undiano ESP
Twente Enschede 2
De Jong [6], Ruiz [80]

Nikolai MIHAILOV - Tim CORNELISSE, Peter WISGERHOF, DOUGLAS, Dwight TIENDALLI (Bart BUYSSE 75) - Willem JANSSEN, Wout BRAMA, Denny LANDZAAT (Marc JANKO 46) - Bryan RUIZ, Luuk DE JONG, Emir BAJRAMI (Ola JOHN 58). Tr: Co ADRIAANSE

Benfica 2
Cardozo [21], Nolito [35]

ARTUR Moares• - MAXI PEREIRA•, LUISAO, Ezequiel GARAY, EMERSON - Axel WITSEL, JAVI GARCIA - Nicolas GAITAN (RUBEN AMORIM 56), Pablo AIMAR (Javier SAVIOLA 64), NOLITO - Oscar CARDOZO (Nemanja MATIC 88). Tr: JORGE JESUS

Estádio da Luz, Lisbon
2nd leg. 24-08-2011, 48 353, Brych GER
Benfica 3
Witsel 2 [46 66], Luisao [59]

ARTUR Moares - MAXI PEREIRA•, LUISAO, Ezequiel GARAY, EMERSON - JAVI GARCIA, Axel WITSEL - Nicolas GAITAN (BRUNO CESAR 74), Pablo AIMAR, NOLITO (Nemanja MATIC 74) - Oscar CARDOZO (Javier SAVIOLA 84). Tr: JORGE JESUS

Twente Enschede 1
Ruiz [85]

Nikolai MIHAILOV - Tim CORNELISSE, Peter WISGERHOF, DOUGLAS•, Dwight TIENDALLI - Wout BRAMA (Denny LANDZAAT 76), Willem JANSSEN (Ola JOHN 60) - Bryan RUIZ, Luuk DE JONG, Steven BERGHUIS (Emir BAJRAMI 60) - Marc JANKO. Tr: Co ADRIAANSE

Stade de Gerland, Lyon
1st leg. 16-08-2011, 35 468, Rocchi ITA
Olympique Lyonnais 3
Gomis [10], OG [40], Briand [71]

Hugo LLORIS - Anthony REVEILLERE•, Bakary KONE, Dejan LOVREN, Aly CISSOKHO (Miralem PJANIC 52) - Jimmy BRIAND (Jeremy PIED 82), Maxime GONALONS, Kim KALLSTROM, MICHEL BASTOS - LISANDRO LOPEZ, Bafetimbi GOMIS. Tr: Remi GARDE

Rubin Kazan 1
Dyadyun [3]

Sergey RYZHIKOV - Oleg KUZMIN•, Solomon KVERKVELIA, Roman SHARONOV, Salvatore BOCCHETTI•, Vitaliy KALESHIN - GOKDENIZ Karadeniz, Christian NOBOA, Bebars NATCHO, Alan KASAEV (Igor LEBEDENKO 69) - Vladimir DYADYUN (Aleksey MEDVEDEV 36). Tr: Kurban BERDIYEV

Central, Kazan
2nd leg. 24-08-2011, 20 620, De Bleeckere BEL
Rubin Kazan 1
Natkho [77]

Sergey RYZHIKOV - Pyotr NEMOV, Solomon KVERKVELIA, Roman SHARONOV, Vitaliy KALESHIN, Sergey KISLYAK• - GOKDENIZ Karadeniz, Christian NOBOA, Bebars NATCHO, Igor LEBEDENKO (Obafemi MARTINS 69) - Vladimir DYADYUN (Aleksey MEDVEDEV 69. Tr: Kurban BERDIYEV

Olympique Lyonnais 1
Kone.B [87]

Hugo LLORIS - Anthony REVEILLERE, Bakary KONE, Dejan LOVREN, Aly CISSOKHO - Jimmy BRIAND•, Maxime GONALONS, Kim KALLSTROM, MICHEL BASTOS - LISANDRO LOPEZ (Jeremy PIED 90), Bafetimbi GOMIS (Miralem PJANIC 84). Tr: Remi GARDE

Maksimir, Zagreb
1st leg. 17-08-2011, 30 065, Proenca POR
Dinamo Zagreb 2
Sammir 2 [4 60p], Rukavina [56], Beciraj [84]

Ivan KELAVA - Sime VRSALJKO, TONEL, Domagoj VIDA, Luis IBANEZ - Jerko LEKO, Adrian CALELLO (Mateo KOVACIC 87), SAMMIR (Mario SITUM 90), Milan BADELJ - Ante RUKAVINA, Ivan KRSTANOVIC (Fatos BECIRAJ 62). Tr: Krunoslav JURCIC

Malmö FF 1
Mehmeti [17]

Dusan MELICHAREK• - Markus HALSTI, Pontus JANSSON, Daniel ANDERSSON, Jiloan HAMAD - Agon MEHMETI (Ulrich VINZENTS 74), Ivo PEKALSKI, Miljan MUTAVDZIC (Jeffrey AUBYNN 66), Jimmy DURMAZ• - WILTON FIGUEIREDO (Dardan REXHEPI 66) - Daniel LARSSON. Tr: Rikard NORLING

Swedbank, Malmö
2nd leg. 23-08-2011, 15 331, Rizzoli ITA
Malmö FF 1
Figueiredo [69], Jansson [86]

Dusan MELICHAREK - Ulrich VINZENTS•, Pontus JANSSON, Markus HALSTI, RICARDINHO - Jiloan HAMAD•, Ivo PEKALSKI (Jeffrey AUBYNN 81), WILTON FIGUEIREDO•, Jimmy DURMAZ• (Miiko ALBORNOZ 79) - Daniel LARSSON, Agon MEHMETI (Dardan REXHEPI 78). Tr: Rikard NORLING

Dinamo Zagreb 0

Ivan KELAVA - Sime VRSALJKO•[50], TONEL•, Domagoj VIDA, Leandro CUFRE• - Milan BADELJ, Jerko LEKO, Adrian CALELLO•, SAMMIR• (Mario SITUM 81) - Fatos BECIRAJ (Mateo KOVACIC 58), Ante RUKAVINA (Ivan KRSTANOVIC 87). Tr: Krunoslav JURCIC

Ramat Gan, Ramat Gan
1st leg. 17-08-2011, 19 170, Stark GER
Maccabi Haifa 2
Amashe [8], Dvalishvili [28]

Nir DAVIDOVITCH - Eyal MESHUMAR, Itzhak COHEN, Sari FALAH, Vladimer DVALISHVILI - Idan VERED, Gustavo BOCCOLI (Dela YAMPOLSKY 65), Seidu YAHAYA, Eyal GOLASA (Tamir COHEN 82) - Taleb TAWATHA, Wiyam AMASHE (Chen AZRIEL 73). Tr: Elisha LEVY

KRC Genk 1
Barda [61]

Laszlo KOTELES - Timothy DURWAEL, NADSON, Torben JONELEIT•, Daniel PUDIL - Khaleem HYLAND (Fabien CAMUS 89), David HUBERT, Daniel TOZSER - Kevin VOSSEN• (Thomas BUFFEL 79), Kennedy NWANGANGA, Elyaniv BARDA. Tr: Frank VERCAUTEREN

Cristal Arena, Genk
2nd leg. 23-08-2011, 13 753, Webb ENG
KRC Genk 2 4p
Vossen [35], Buffel [41]

Laszlo KOTELES - Anele NGCONGCA, NADSON, Torben JONELEIT, Daniel PUDIL - Thomas BUFFEL (Anthony LIMBOMBE 110), David HUBERT, Daniel TOZSER, Elyaniv BARDA (Anthony VANDEN BORRE 96) - Kennedy NWANGANGA (Marvin OGUNJIMI 68), Jelle VOSSEN. Tr: Pierre DENIER

Maccabi Haifa 1 1p
Golasa [37]

Nir DAVIDOVITCH - Eyal MESHUMAR•, Itzhak COHEN••♦[109], Sari FALAH - Taleb TAWATHA• - Idan VERED (Yaniv KATAN 79), Gustavo BOCCOLI (Dela YAMPOLSKY 46), Seidu YAHAYA•, Eyal GOLASA - Vladimer DVALISHVILI, Wiyam AMASHE (Tamir COHEN 112). Tr: Elisha LEVY

UEFA CHAMPIONS LEAGUE 2011-12

Emirates, London
1st leg. 16-08-2011, 58,159, Blom NED
Arsenal 1
Walcott [4]

Wojciech SZCZESNY - Bacary SAGNA, Laurent KOSCIELNY, Thomas VERMAELEN, Kieran GIBBS• (Johan DJOUROU 46) (Carl JENKINSON 56) - Alex SONG - Theo WALCOTT•, Aaron RAMSEY, Tomas ROSICKY (Emmanuel FRIMPONG 73), GERVINHO - Marouane CHAMAKH. Tr: Arsene WENGER

Udinese 0

Samir HANDANOVIC - Joel EKSTRAND•, Mehdi BENATIA, DANILO, NEUTON• (Giovanni PASQUALE 60) - Emmanuel AGYEMANG-BADU - Mauricio ISLA, Giampiero PINZI• (Almen ABDI 88), Kwadwo ASAMOAH, Pablo ARMERO• - Antonio DI NATALE. Tr: Francesco GUIDOLIN

Friuli, Udine
2nd leg. 24-08-2011, 26,031, Benquerenca POR
Udinese 1
Di Natale [39]

Samir HANDANOVIC - Joel EKSTRAND, Mehdi BENATIA• (Giovanni PASQUALE 87), DANILO, NEUTON - Emmanuel AGYEMANG-BADU - Mauricio ISLA• (German DENIS 83), Kwadwo ASAMOAH, Giampiero PINZI (Diego FABBRINI•), Pablo ARMERO - Antonio DI NATALE. Tr: Francesco GUIDOLIN

Arsenal 2
Van Persie [55], Walcott [69]

Wojciech SZCZESNY - Bacary SAGNA•, Thomas VERMAELEN•, Johan DJOUROU, Carl JENKINSON• - Emmanuel FRIMPONG (Tomas ROSICKY 46) - Theo WALCOTT• (Andrey ARSHAVIN 90), Alex SONG, Aaron RAMSEY, GERVINHO (Armand TRAORE 86) - Robin VAN PERSIE. Tr: Arsene WENGER

Miejski, Krakow
1st leg. 17-08-2011, 22,545, Lannoy FRA
Wisla Krakow 1
Malecki [71]

Sergei PAREIKO - Marko JOVANOVIC•, Kew JALIENS•, Osman CHAVEZ, Junior DIAZ - Radoslaw SOBOLEWSKI, Gervasio NUNEZ - Ivica ILIEV (Cezary WILK 68), Maor MELIKSON, Patryk MALECKI• (Andraz KIRM 90) - Tzvetan GENKOV. Tr: Robert MAASKANT

APOEL Nicosia 0

Dionisis CHIOTIS - Athos SOLOMOU, Christos KONTIS, PAULO JORGE, WILLIAM Boaventura - NUNO MORAIS, HELIO PINTO - Ivan TRICKOVSKI (Esteban SOLARI 85), MARCINHO (Sanel JAHIC 80), Gustavo MANDUCA• (Costas CHARALAMBIDES• 46) - AILTON. Tr: Ivan JOVANOVIC

GSP, Nicosia
2nd leg. 23-08-2011, 21,665, Kassai HUN
APOEL Nicosia 3
OG [29], Ailton 2 [54] [87]

Dionisis CHIOTIS - Savvas POURSAITIDIS, Christos KONTIS, PAULO JORGE, WILLIAM Boaventura (Nektarios ALEXANDROU 85) - NUNO MORAIS, HELIO PINTO• - Ivan TRICKOVSKI, MARCINHO (Sanel JAHIC 90), Gustavo MANDUCA• (Costas CHARALAMBIDES• 85) - AILTON. Tr: Ivan JOVANOVIC

Wisla Krakow 1
Wilk [71]

Sergei PAREIKO - Michael LAMEY•, Kew JALIENS (Marko JOVANOVIC 80), Osman CHAVEZ, Junior DIAZ• - Radoslaw SOBOLEWSKI• (Ivica ILIEV 58), Cezary WILK - Gervasio NUNEZ•, Maor MELIKSON•, Patryk MALECKI (Andraz KIRM 80) - Tzvetan GENKOV. Tr: Robert MAASKANT

Parken, Copenhagen
1st leg. 24-08-2011, 19,148, Atkinson ENG
FC København 1
Ottesen [69]

Johan WILAND - Johnny THOMSEN, Solvi OTTESEN, ZANKA, Pierre BENGTSSON - Christian BOLANOS•, Thomas KRISTENSEN, Christian GRINDHEIM•, Pape DIOUF (Morten NORDSTRAND 56) - CLAUDEMIR (Johan ABSALONSEN• 65) - Dame N'DOYE•. Tr: Roland NILSSON

Viktoria Plzen 3
OG [52], Pilar [59], Fillo [79]

Marek CECH - Frantisek RAJTORAL, Marian CISOVSKY, David BYSTRON, David LIMBERSKY - Petr TRAPP•, Pavel HORVATH - Milan PETRZELA• (Martin FILLO 76), Daniel KOLAR, Vaclav PILAR (Jakub HORA 90) - Michal DURIS• (Frantisek SEVINSKY 89). Tr: Pavel VRBA

Struncovych sadech, Plzen
2nd leg. 24-08-2011, 19,350, Carballo ESP
Viktoria Plzen 2
Bakos [67], Duris [93+]

Marek CECH - Frantisek RAJTORAL, Marian CISOVSKY, David BYSTRON, David LIMBERSKY• - Petr JIRACEK•, Pavel HORVATH (Petr TRAPP 86) - Milan PETRZELA (Martin FILLO 82), Daniel KOLAR, Vaclav PILAR - Marek BAKOS (Michal DURIS 77). Tr: Pavel VRBA

FC København 1
Bolanos [32]

Johan WILAND - Johnny THOMSEN (Ragnar SIGURDSSON 83), Solvi OTTESEN, ZANKA, Pierre BENGTSSON - Christian BOLANOS (Pape DIOUF 74), Christian GRINDHEIM•, Thomas DELANEY - Morten NORDSTRAND• - CESAR SANTIN (Johan ABSALONSEN• 64), Dame N'DOYE. Tr: Roland NILSSON

Dinamo, Minsk
1st leg. 16-08-2011, 15,550, Moen NOR
BATE Borisov 1
Simic [59]

Aleksandr GUTOR - Aleksandr YUREVICH, Egor FILIPENKO, Marko SIMIC, Maksim BORDACHEV (Aleksandr VOLODKO 82) - Edgar OLEKHNOVICH, Dmitriy BAGA - Oleg PATOTSKIY (Mikhail GORDEYCHUK 46), Vitaliy RODIONOV• (Filipp RUDIK• 69), Pavel NEKHAYCHIK - Artem KONTSEVOY. Tr: Viktor GONCHARENKO

SK Sturm Graz 1
Weber [12]

Christian GRATZEI - Joachim STANDFEST, Milan DUDIC, Thomas BURGSTALLER, George POPKHADZE - Andreas HOLZL (Martin EHRENREICH 88), Manuel WEBER, Jurgen SAUMEL•, Haris BUKVA - Imre SZABICS (Samir MURATOVIC 72), Roman KIENAST. Tr: Franco FODA

UPC Arena, Graz
2nd leg. 24-08-2011, 14,528, Eriksson SWE
SK Sturm Graz 0

Christian GRATZEI - Joachim STANDFEST•, Milan DUDIC, Thomas BURGSTALLER, George POPKHADZE - Jurgen SAUMEL, Manuel WEBER - Patrick WOLF• (Florian KAINZ 60), Haris BUKVA (Mario HAAS 46), Andreas HOLZL (Samir MURATOVIC 74) - Imre SZABICS. Tr: Franco FODA

BATE Borisov 2
Volodko [36], Simic [70]

Aleksandr GUTOR - Dmitriy BAGA•, Egor FILIPENKO, Marko SIMIC•, Aleksandr YUREVICH - Aleksandr VOLODKO•, Edgar OLEKHNOVICH - Artem KONTSEVOY (Mikhail GORDEYCHUK 67), RENAN BRESSAN (Filipp RUDIK 59), Pavel NEKHAYCHIK - Vitaliy RODIONOV• (Maksim BORDACHEV 77). Tr: Viktor GONCHARENKO

PENALTIES
PLAY-OFF ROUND
GENK 4-1 M. HAIFA

Genk		Maccabi	
✓	Vossen		
		Dvalishvili	✗
✓	Hubert		
		Golasa	✗
✓	Tozser		
		Twatiha	✓
✓	Pudil		

PART THREE - THE CONTINENTAL CONFEDERATIONS

GROUP A		Pl	W	D	L	F	A	Pts	GER	ITA	ENG	ESP
Bayern München	GER	6	4	1	1	11	6	13		3-2	2-0	3-1
Napoli	ITA	6	3	2	1	10	6	11	1-1		2-1	2-0
Manchester City	ENG	6	3	1	2	9	6	10	2-0	1-1		2-1
Villarreal	ESP	6	0	0	6	2	14	0	0-2	0-2	0-3	

Etihad Manchester
14-09-2011, 44026, Eriksson SWE
Manchester City 1
Kolarov 74
Joe HART - Pablo ZABALETA•, Vincent KOMPANY, Joleon LESCOTT, Aleksandar KOLAROV (Gael CLICHY 75) - DAVID SILVA, Yaya TOURE, Gareth BARRY, Samir NASRI (Adam JOHNSON 76) - Edin DZEKO (Carlos TEVEZ 81), Sergio AGUERO. Tr: Roberto MANCINI

Napoli 1
Cavani 69
Morgan DE SANCTIS - Hugo CAMPAGNARO, Paolo CANNAVARO•, Salvatore ARONICA• - Christian MAGGIO•, Gokhan INLER•, Walter GARGANO, Juan ZUNIGA - Marek HAMSIK (Mario SANTANA 89), Edinson CAVANI (Goran PANDEV 84), Ezequiel LAVEZZI (Blerim DZEMAILI 58). Tr: Walter MAZZARRI

El Madrigal, Villarreal
14-09-2011, 19168, Cakir TUR
Villarreal 0
DIEGO LOPEZ - MARIO, Cristian ZAPATA, Mateo MUSACCHIO, Jose Manuel CATALA - Carlos MARCHENA•, Marcos SENNA (CANI 46), BRUNO Soriano - Jonathan DE GUZMAN (Javier CAMUNAS 72) - NILMAR (MARCO RUBEN 58), Giuseppe ROSSI. Tr: Juan GARRIDO

Bayern München 1
Kroos 7, Rafinha 76
Manuel NEUER - Jerome BOATENG, Daniel VAN BUYTEN (RAFINHA 23), Holger BADSTUBER, Philipp LAHM - Anatoliy TYMOSHCHUK•, Bastian SCHWEINSTEIGER• - Thomas MULLER, Toni KROOS (LUIZ GUSTAVO 81), Franck RIBERY - Mario GOMEZ (Nils PETERSEN 46). Tr: Jupp HEYNCKES

Allianz Arena, Munich
27-09-2011, 66000, Kassai HUN
Bayern München 2
Gomez 2 38 45
Manuel NEUER - RAFINHA, Daniel VAN BUYTEN, Jerome BOATENG, Philipp LAHM - Bastian SCHWEINSTEIGER, LUIZ GUSTAVO - Thomas MULLER, Toni KROOS (Anatoliy TYMOSHCHUK 83), Franck RIBERY (Nils PETERSEN 90) - Mario GOMEZ (Arjen ROBBEN 90). Tr: Jupp HEYNCKES

Manchester City 0
Joe HART - Micah RICHARDS, Kolo TOURE•, Vincent KOMPANY, Gael CLICHY• - DAVID SILVA, Yaya TOURE•, Gareth BARRY (Aleksandar KOLAROV 73), Samir NASRI (James MILNER 69) - Edin DZEKO (Nigel DE JONG 56), Sergio AGUERO•. Tr: Roberto MANCINI

San Paolo, Naples
27-09-2011, 46747, De Bleeckere BEL
Napoli 2
Hamsik 15, Cavani 17p
Morgan DE SANCTIS - Hugo CAMPAGNARO, Paolo CANNAVARO•, Salvatore ARONICA• - Juan ZUNIGA, Gokhan INLER, Walter GARGANO, Andrea DOSSENA - Marek HAMSIK (Giuseppe MASCARA 79), Edinson CAVANI (Goran PANDEV 71), Ezequiel LAVEZZI (Mario SANTANA 88). Tr: Walter MAZZARRI

Villarreal 0
DIEGO LOPEZ - Cristian ZAPATA, GONZALO Rodriguez• (Javier CAMUNAS 33), Mateo MUSACCHIO, Jose Manuel CATALA - Jonathan DE GUZMAN (HERNAN PEREZ 83), CANI•, Marcos SENNA (Wakaso MUBARAK 83), BRUNO Soriano, CANI• - NILMAR, Giuseppe ROSSI•. Tr: Juan GARRIDO

San Paolo, Naples
18-10-2011, 60074, Benquerenca POR
Napoli 1
OG 39
Morgan DE SANCTIS - Hugo CAMPAGNARO, Paolo CANNAVARO•, Salvatore ARONICA• - Christian MAGGIO•, Gokhan INLER (Mario SANTANA 89), Walter GARGANO, Juan ZUNIGA• - Marek HAMSIK (Giuseppe MASCARA 90), Edinson CAVANI (Blerim DZEMAILI 81), Ezequiel LAVEZZI•. Tr: Walter MAZZARRI

Bayern München 1
Kroos 2
Manuel NEUER - Jerome BOATENG, Daniel VAN BUYTEN, Holger BADSTUBER•, Philipp LAHM - Anatoliy TYMOSHCHUK, Bastian SCHWEINSTEIGER• - Thomas MULLER•, Toni KROOS•, Franck RIBERY (David ALABA 90) - Mario GOMEZ (LUIZ GUSTAVO 90). Tr: Jupp HEYNCKES

Etihad Manchester
18-10-2011, 43326, Kralovec CZE
Manchester City 2
OG 43, Aguero 93+
Joe HART - Pablo ZABALETA, Vincent KOMPANY, Joleon LESCOTT, Aleksandar KOLAROV - Yaya TOURE, Nigel DE JONG (Sergio AGUERO 62) - Adam JOHNSON (Gareth BARRY 40), DAVID SILVA, Samir NASRI (James MILNER 80) - Edin DZEKO. Tr: Roberto MANCINI

Villarreal 1
Cani 4
DIEGO LOPEZ • - Cristian ZAPATA, GONZALO Rodriguez, Carlos MARCHENA, Jose Manuel CATALA• - BRUNO Soriano - HERNAN PEREZ (Wakaso MUBARAK 80), BORJA VALERO, Jonathan DE GUZMAN (Marcos GULLON 88), CANI (MARIO• 82) - Giuseppe ROSSI•. Tr: Juan GARRIDO

Allianz Arena, Munich
2-11-2011, 66000, Kuipers NED
Bayern München 3
Gomez 3 17 23 42
Manuel NEUER - Jerome BOATENG•, Daniel VAN BUYTEN, Holger BADSTUBER••♦77, Philipp LAHM - LUIZ GUSTAVO, Bastian SCHWEINSTEIGER (Anatoliy TYMOSHCHUK 53), Thomas MULLER, Toni KROOS, Franck RIBERY (David ALABA 80) - Mario GOMEZ. Tr: Jupp HEYNCKES

Napoli 2
Fernandez 2 45 79
Morgan DE SANCTIS - Hugo CAMPAGNARO, Federico FERNANDEZ•, Salvatore ARONICA (Andrea DOSSENA 42) - Christian MAGGIO, Gokhan INLER, Blerim DZEMAILI (Goran PANDEV 84), Juan ZUNIGA••♦70 - Marek HAMSIK, Edinson CAVANI• - Ezequiel LAVEZZI. Tr: Walter MAZZARRI

El Madrigal, Villarreal
2-11-2011, 19358, Proenca POR
Villarreal 0
DIEGO LOPEZ - MARIO, GONZALO Rodriguez, Mateo MUSACCHIO•, Jose Manuel CATALA - BORJA VALERO, Carlos MARCHENA•, - HERNAN PEREZ• (JOAN ORIOL 84), Jonathan DE GUZMAN (ANGEL 76), Wakaso MUBARAK• (GERARD BORDAS 77) - JOSELU. Tr: Juan GARRIDO

Manchester City 3
Toure.Y 2 30 71, Balotelli 45p
Joe HART - Pablo ZABALETA, Vincent KOMPANY, Stefan SAVIC, Gael CLICHY - James MILNER, Nigel DE JONG - DAVID SILVA (Adam JOHNSON 65), Yaya TOURE (Sergio AGUERO 74), Samir NASRI - Mario BALOTELLI• (Aleksandar KOLAROV 82). Tr: Roberto MANCINI

San Paolo, Naples
22-11-2011, 57575, Skomina SVN
Napoli 2
Cavani 2 17 49
Morgan DE SANCTIS - Hugo CAMPAGNARO, Paolo CANNAVARO•, Salvatore ARONICA - Christian MAGGIO, Gokhan INLER (Blerim DZEMAILI 59), Walter GARGANO, Andrea DOSSENA (Federico FERNANDEZ 89) - Marek HAMSIK, Edinson CAVANI (Goran PANDEV 83), Ezequiel LAVEZZI. Tr: Walter MAZZARRI

Manchester City 1
Balotelli 33
Joe HART - Pablo ZABALETA (Adam JOHNSON 86), Vincent KOMPANY•, Joleon LESCOTT, Aleksandar KOLAROV• - Nigel DE JONG (Samir NASRI 71) - DAVID SILVA•, James MILNER, Yaya TOURE, Mario BALOTELLI• - Edin DZEKO (Sergio AGUERO 81). Tr: Roberto MANCINI

Allianz Arena, Munich
22-11-2011, 66000, Strombergsson SWE
Bayern München 3
Ribery 2 3 69, Gomez 24
Manuel NEUER - RAFINHA, Jerome BOATENG, Daniel VAN BUYTEN, Philipp LAHM - Anatoliy TYMOSHCHUK, David ALABA - Arjen ROBBEN (Ivica OLIC 76), Toni KROOS, Franck RIBERY (Danijel PRANJIC 81) - Mario GOMEZ (Thomas MULLER 72). Tr: Jupp HEYNCKES

Villarreal 1
De Guzman 50
DIEGO LOPEZ - MARIO, Mateo MUSACCHIO, Carlos MARCHENA, JOAN ORIOL - ANGEL• (Marcos SENNA 70), BRUNO Soriano - Jonathan DE GUZMAN (Wakaso MUBARAK 63), BORJA VALERO (JOSELU 78), HERNAN PEREZ - MARCO RUBEN•. Tr: Juan GARRIDO

Etihad Manchester
7-12-2011, 46002, Lannoy FRA
Manchester City 2
Silva 36, Toure.Y 52
Joe HART - Stefan SAVIC, Vincent KOMPANY, Joleon LESCOTT, Gael CLICHY - Yaya TOURE (Mario BALOTELLI 81), Gareth BARRY - Samir NASRI, DAVID SILVA (Adam JOHNSON 84) - Edin DZEKO (Nigel DE JONG 77), Sergio AGUERO. Tr: Roberto MANCINI

Bayern München 0
Hans Jorg BUTT - RAFINHA, Jerome BOATENG, Holger BADSTUBER, Diego CONTENTO - LUIZ GUSTAVO, Anatoliy TYMOSHCHUK - David ALABA, Danijel PRANJIC, Ivica OLIC• - Nils PETERSEN (Takashi USAMI 81). Tr: Jupp HEYNCKES

El Madrigal, Villarreal
7-12-2011, 15350, Moen NOR
Villarreal 0
DIEGO LOPEZ - ANGEL•, Cristian ZAPATA•, (GONZALO Rodriguez 76), Mateo MUSACCHIO, JOAN ORIOL - BRUNO Soriano - HERNAN PEREZ•, Marcos SENNA (JOSELU 73), Jonathan DE GUZMAN• - NILMAR (Javier CAMUNAS 64), MARCO RUBEN•. Tr: Juan GARRIDO

Napoli 2
Inler 65, Hamsik 76
Morgan DE SANCTIS - Hugo CAMPAGNARO•, Paolo CANNAVARO•, Salvatore ARONICA - Christian MAGGIO, Gokhan INLER, Walter GARGANO, Juan ZUNIGA (Gianluca GRAVA 90) - Marek HAMSIK (Blerim DZEMAILI 79), Edinson CAVANI (Goran PANDEV 82), Ezequiel LAVEZZI. Tr: Walter MAZZARRI

UEFA CHAMPIONS LEAGUE 2011-12

GROUP B		Pl	W	D	L	F	A	Pts	ITA	RUS	TUR	FRA
Internazionale	ITA	6	3	1	2	8	7	10		1-2	0-1	2-1
CSKA Moskva	RUS	6	2	2	2	9	8	8	2-3		3-0	0-2
Trabzonspor	TUR	6	1	4	1	3	5	7	1-1	0-0		1-1
Lille OSC	FRA	6	1	3	2	6	6	6	0-1	2-2	0-0	

Metropole, Lille
14-09-2011, 15 274, Benquerenca POR
Lille OSC 2
Sow [44], Pedretti [57]
Mickael LANDREAU - Mathieu DEBUCHY, Marko BASA•, David ROZEHNAL, Franck BERIA - Florent BALMONT, Rio MAVUBA, Benoit PEDRETTI• (Idrissa GUEYE 76) - Eden HAZARD•, Ludovic OBRANIAK (Joe COLE 77) - Moussa SOW (Sylvio RODELIN 86). Tr: Rudi GARCIA
CSKA Moskva 2
Doumbia 2 [72 90]
Vladimir GABULOV - Kirill NABABKIN•, Vasiliy BEREZUTSKIY, Sergey IGNASHEVICH, Aleksey BEREZUTSKIY - Zoran TOSIC, Alan DZAGOEV•, Evgeniy ALDONIN (Pavel MAMAEV 80), Aleksandrs CAUNA (Sekou OLISEH 67) - Seydou DOUMBIA (Deividas SEMBERAS 90), VAGNER LOVE. Tr: Leonid SLUTSKIY

San Siro, Milan
14-09-2011, 24 444, Johannesson SWE
Internazionale 0
JULIO CESAR - JONATHAN, LUCIO, Andrea RANOCCHIA•, Yuto NAGATOMO• - Javier ZANETTI, Esteban CAMBIASSO, Joel OBI (Ricardo ALVAREZ 55) - Mauro ZARATE• (COUTINHO 77), Wesley SNEIJDER - Giampaolo PAZZINI (Diego MILITO 55). Tr: Gian Piero GASPERINI
Trabzonspor 1
Celustka [76]
TOLGA Zengin - Ondrej CELUSTKA, REMZI Kacar•, Arkadiusz GLOWACKI, Marek CECH• - Gustavo COLMAN, Didier ZOKORA - SERKAN Balci, ALANZINHO• (Marek SAPARA 64), HALIL Altintop• (AYKUT Akgun 87) - PAULO HENRIQUE (Robert VITTEK 74). Tr: SENOL Gunes

Luzhniki, Moscow
27-09-2011, 35 000, Thomson SCO
CSKA Moskva 2
Dzagoev [45], Vagner Love [77]
Vladimir GABULOV - Kirill NABABKIN, Vasiliy BEREZUTSKIY, Sergey IGNASHEVICH, Aleksey BEREZUTSKIY - Evgeniy ALDONIN - Sekou OLISEH, Pavel MAMAEV (Zoran TOSIC 68), Alan DZAGOEV - Seydou DOUMBIA, VAGNER LOVE. Tr: Leonid SLUTSKIY
Internazionale 3
Lucio [6], Pazzini [23], Zarate [79]
JULIO CESAR - Yuto NAGATOMO, LUCIO, Walter SAMUEL, Cristian CHIVU (Lorenzo CRISETIG 90) - Javier ZANETTI, Esteban CAMBIASSO•, Joel OBI• - Giampaolo PAZZINI (Mauro ZARATE 49), Diego MILITO (JONATHAN 84) - Giampaolo PAZZINI (Mauro ZARATE 49), Diego MILITO. Tr: Claudio RANIERI

Hüseyin Avni Aker, Trabzon
27-09-2011, 17 349, Kuipers NED
Trabzonspor 1
Colman [75p]
TOLGA Zengin - Ondrej CELUSTKA, REMZI Kacar•, Arkadiusz GLOWACKI, Marek CECH• (Marek SAPARA 82) - Gustavo COLMAN, Didier ZOKORA - SERKAN Balci•, ALANZINHO• (Adrian MIERZEJEWSKI 66), HALIL Altintop (Pawel BROZEK 90) - PAULO HENRIQUE. Tr: SENOL Gunes
Lille OSC 1
Sow [30]
Mickael LANDREAU - Mathieu DEBUCHY, Marko BASA•, David ROZEHNAL, Franck BERIA• - Florent BALMONT, Rio MAVUBA, Benoit PEDRETTI - Eden HAZARD, Joe COLE• (Ludovic OBRANIAK 76) - Moussa SOW. Tr: Rudi GARCIA

Luzhniki, Moscow
18-10-2011, 18 000, Clattenburg ENG
CSKA Moskva 3
Doumbia 2 [29 86], Cauna [76]
Vladimir GABULOV - Semen FEDOTOV, Vasiliy BEREZUTSKIY, Sergey IGNASHEVICH, Aleksey BEREZUTSKIY - Alan DZAGOEV, Evgeniy ALDONIN, Pavel MAMAEV• (Deividas SEMBERAS 70), Zoran TOSIC (Aleksandrs CAUNA 62) - Seydou DOUMBIA (Elvir RAHIMIC 87), VAGNER LOVE. Tr: Leonid SLUTSKIY
Trabzonspor 0
TOLGA Zengin - Ondrej CELUSTKA, REMZI Kacar•, Arkadiusz GLOWACKI•, Marek CECH• (Marek SAPARA 75) - Gustavo COLMAN•, Didier ZOKORA• - SERKAN Balci•, ALANZINHO (Pawel BROZEK 46), Adrian MIERZEJEWSKI - HALIL Altintop (AYKUT Akgun 90). Tr: SENOL Gunes

Metropole, Lille
18-10-2011, 16 996, Webb ENG
Lille OSC 0
Vincent ENYEAMA - Mathieu DEBUCHY, Marko BASA, Aurelien CHEDJOU•, Franck BERIA, Franck BALMONT (Idrissa GUEYE 81), Rio MAVUBA, Benoit PEDRETTI• (Dimitri PAYET 63) - Eden HAZARD, Joe COLE (Ludovic OBRANIAK 74)- Moussa SOW. Tr: Rudi GARCIA
Internazionale 1
Pazzini [21]
JULIO CESAR - MAICON, LUCIO, Cristian CHIVU•, Yuto NAGATOMO - Javier ZANETTI, THIAGO MOTTA•, Esteban CAMBIASSO - Wesley SNEIJDER (Dejan STANKOVIC 67) - Giampaolo PAZZINI (Diego MILITO 81), Mauro ZARATE (Joel OBI 63). Tr: Claudio RANIERI

Hüseyin Avni Aker, Trabzon
2-11-2011, 19 516, Undiano ESP
Trabzonspor 0
TOLGA Zengin - Ondrej CELUSTKA, REMZI Kacar•, Arkadiusz GLOWACKI, Marek CECH - Didier ZOKORA• - Adrian MIERZEJEWSKI• (AYKUT Akgun 81), Gustavo COLMAN, SERKAN Balci• (ALANZINHO 61), HALIL Altintop (PAULO HENRIQUE 61) - BURAK Yilmaz. Tr: SENOL Gunes
CSKA Moskva 0
Vladimir GABULOV - Aleksey BEREZUTSKIY, Vasiliy BEREZUTSKIY, Sergey IGNASHEVICH, Georgiy SCHENNIKOV (Kirill NABABKIN 46) - Pavel MAMAEV• (Deividas SEMBERAS 80), Evgeniy ALDONIN - Alan DZAGOEV, VAGNER LOVE•, Zoran TOSIC (Aleksandrs CAUNA 69) - Seydou DOUMBIA•• ♦ 74, Tr: Leonid SLUTSKIY

San Siro, Milan
2-11-2011, 24 299, Stark GER
Internazionale 2
Samuel [18], Milito [65]
Luca CASTELLAZZI - Javier ZANETTI, LUCIO, Walter SAMUEL•, Cristian CHIVU - Dejan STANKOVIC, THIAGO MOTTA, Esteban CAMBIASSO - Wesley SNEIJDER (Ricardo ALVAREZ 67) - Diego MILITO (Joel OBI 90), Mauro ZARATE (Giampaolo PAZZINI 80). Tr: Claudio RANIERI
Lille OSC 1
De Melo [83]
Mickael LANDREAU - Mathieu DEBUCHY, David ROZEHNAL•, Aurelien CHEDJOU, Franck BERIA - Benoit PEDRETTI, Rio MAVUBA - Joe COLE (Dimitri PAYET 71), Eden HAZARD, Moussa SOW (Ludovic OBRANIAK 60) - Ireneusz JELEN (TULIO 46). Tr: Rudi GARCIA

Luzhniki, Moscow
22-11-2011, 19 100, Kralovec CZE
CSKA Moskva 0
Vladimir GABULOV - Kirill NABABKIN•, Vasiliy BEREZUTSKIY, Sergey IGNASHEVICH (Georgiy SCHENNIKOV 74), Aleksey BEREZUTSKIY - Pavel MAMAEV, Evgeniy ALDONIN - Sekou OLISEH, Alan DZAGOEV, Aleksandrs CAUNA (Serder SERDEROV 87) - VAGNER LOVE. Tr: Leonid SLUTSKIY
Lille OSC 2
OG [49], Sow [64]
Mickael LANDREAU - Mathieu DEBUCHY•, David ROZEHNAL•, Aurelien CHEDJOU, Franck BERIA - Florent BALMONT, Rio MAVUBA, Idrissa GUEYE - Eden HAZARD (TULIO 90), Joe COLE (Dimitri PAYET 87) - Moussa SOW (Ireneusz JELEN 74). Tr: Rudi GARCIA

Hüseyin Avni Aker, Trabzon
22-11-2011, 21 611, Atkinson ENG
Trabzonspor 1
Halil Altintop [23]
TOLGA Zengin - Ondrej CELUSTKA, Arkadiusz GLOWACKI•, REMZI Kacar, Marek CECH - SERKAN Balci• (Adrian MIERZEJEWSKI 64), Didier ZOKORA, Gustavo COLMAN - HALIL Altintop, ALANZINHO (PAULO HENRIQUE 85) - BURAK Yilmaz. Tr: SENOL Gunes
Internazionale 1
Alvarez [18]
JULIO CESAR - Yuto NAGATOMO, LUCIO, Walter SAMUEL, Cristian CHIVU• - Ricardo ALVAREZ (Davide FARAONI 89), Javier ZANETTI, Esteban CAMBIASSO, Dejan STANKOVIC, Mauro ZARATE (COUTINHO 69) - Diego MILITO (Giampaolo PAZZINI 86). Tr: Claudio RANIERI

Metropole, Lille
7-12-2011, 16 375, Proenca POR
Lille OSC 0
Mickael LANDREAU - Mathieu DEBUCHY, Marko BASA, Aurelien CHEDJOU•, Franck BERIA - Florent BALMONT (Laurent BONNART 84) - Florent BALMONT•, Rio MAVUBA - Dimitri PAYET (Sylvio RODELIN 89), Eden HAZARD, Joe COLE (Ludovic OBRANIAK 74) - Moussa SOW. Tr: Rudi GARCIA
Trabzonspor 0
TOLGA Zengin - Ondrej CELUSTKA (Adrian MIERZEJEWSKI 33), REMZI Kacar, Arkadiusz GLOWACKI, Marek CECH - Didier ZOKORA - SERKAN Balci, Gustavo COLMAN, ALANZINHO (PAULO HENRIQUE 65), HALIL Altintop - BURAK Yilmaz (MUSTAFA Yumlu 90). Tr: SENOL Gunes

San Siro, Milan
7-12-2011, 23 295, Borbalan ESP
Internazionale 1
Cambiasso [51]
Luca CASTELLAZZI - Yuto NAGATOMO, Andrea RANOCCHIA, Walter SAMUEL, Cristian CHIVU (Luca CALDIROLA• 46) - Davide FARAONI, Javier ZANETTI, Esteban CAMBIASSO, Joel OBI (Ricardo ALVAREZ 70) - COUTINHO, Mauro ZARATE 46) - Diego MILITO. Tr: Claudio RANIERI
CSKA Moskva 2
Doumbia [50], Berezutski.V [86]
Vladimir GABULOV - Kirill NABABKIN•, Vasiliy BEREZUTSKIY, Sergey IGNASHEVICH, Aleksey BEREZUTSKIY - Sekou OLISEH (Evgeniy ALDONIN 77), Pavel MAMAEV•, Deividas SEMBERAS• (Aleksandrs CAUNA 77), Alan DZAGOEV - Seydou DOUMBIA (Georgiy SCHENNIKOV 90), VAGNER LOVE. Tr: Leonid SLUTSKIY

PART THREE – THE CONTINENTAL CONFEDERATIONS

GROUP C		Pl	W	D	L	F	A	Pts	POR	SUI	ENG	ROU
Benfica	POR	6	3	3	0	8	4	**12**		1-1	1-1	1-0
FC Basel	SUI	6	3	2	1	11	10	**11**	0-2		2-1	2-1
Manchester United	ENG	6	2	3	1	11	8	**9**	2-2	3-3		2-0
Otelul Galati	ROU	6	0	0	6	3	11	**0**	0-1	2-3	0-2	

St Jakob Park, Basel
14-09-2011, 30126, Collum SCO
FC Basel 2
Fabian Frei 39, Alexander Frei 84p
Yann SOMMER - Markus STEINHOFER, David ABRAHAM, Aleksandar DRAGOVIC, PARK Joo Ho - Fabian FREI (Radoslav KOVAC 90), Adilson CABRAL, Benjamin HUGGEL••87, Granit XHAKA (Jacques ZOUA 78) - Marco STRELLER•, Alexander FREI (PAK Kwang Ryong 90). Tr: Thorsten FINK
Otelul Galati 1
Pena 58
Branko GRAHOVAC• - Cornel RAPA•, Milan PERENDIJA, Sergiu COSTIN, Adrian SALAGEANU♦82 - Liviu ANTAL•, Ioan FILIP (Gabriel VIGLIANTI 86), Gabriel GIURGIU, Silviu ILIE (Sorin FRUNZA 89) - John Ike IBEH, Marius PENA (Gabriel PARASCHIV 71). Tr: Dorinel MUNTEANU

Estádio da Luz, Lisbon
14-09-2011, 63822, Skomina SVN
Benfica 1
Cardozo 24
ARTUR Moares - MAXI PEREIRA•, LUISAO, Ezequiel GARAY, EMERSON, RUBEN AMORIM (NOLITO 56), Axel WITSEL, JAVI GARCIA, Nicolas GAITAN• (BRUNO CESAR 90) - Pablo AIMAR• (Nemanja MATIC 75) - Oscar CARDOZO. Tr: JORGE JESUS
Manchester United 1
Giggs 42
Anders LINDEGAARD - FABIO (Phil JONES 77), Chris SMALLING, Jonny EVANS, Patrice EVRA - Darren FLETCHER (Javier HERNANDEZ 68), Michael CARRICK• - Antonio VALENCIA (NANI 69), Ryan GIGGS, PARK Ji Sung - Wayne ROONEY•. Tr: Alex FERGUSON

Old Trafford, Manchester
27-09-2011, 73115, Tagliavento ITA
Manchester United 3
Welbeck 2 16 17, Young 90
David DE GEA - FABIO (NANI 70), Rio FERDINAND, Phil JONES, Patrice EVRA - Antonio VALENCIA, Michael CARRICK, ANDERSON (Dimitar BERBATOV 82), Ashley YOUNG - Ryan GIGGS (PARK Ji Sung 61) - Danny WELBECK. Tr: Alex FERGUSON
FC Basel 3
Fabian Frei 58, Alexander Frei 2 61 76p
Yann SOMMER - Markus STEINHOFER, David ABRAHAM, Aleksandar DRAGOVIC, PARK Joo Ho - Fabian FREI (Scott CHIPPERFIELD 77), Granit XHAKA•, Adilson CABRAL, Jacques ZOUA - Marco STRELLER• (PAK Kwang Ryong 81), Alexander FREI• (Taulant XHAKA 89). Tr: Thorsten FINK

Stadionul National, Bucharest
27-09-2011, 6824, Borbalan ESP
Otelul Galati 0
Branko GRAHOVAC - Nejc SKUBIC, Milan PERENDIJA•, Sergiu COSTIN, Zoran LJUBINKOVIC - Ioan FILIP, Gabriel GIURGIU - Liviu ANTAL, John Ike IBEH (Gabriel VIGLIANTI 46), Laurentiu BUS (Sorin FRUNZA 65) - Marius PENA (Branislav PUNOSEVAC 69). Tr: Dorinel MUNTEANU
Benfica 1
Bruno Cesar 40
ARTUR Moares - MAXI PEREIRA•, LUISAO, Ezequiel GARAY, EMERSON, JAVI GARCIA - Nicolas GAITAN (RODRIGO Moreno 77), Axel WITSEL, BRUNO CESAR (RUBEN AMORIM 82) - Oscar CARDOZO, Javier SAVIOLA (NOLITO 63). Tr: JORGE JESUS

Stadionul National, Bucharest
18-10-2011, 28047, Brych GER
Otelul Galati 0
Branko GRAHOVAC - Cornel RAPA•, Milan PERENDIJA••♦89, Sergiu COSTIN•, Adrian SALAGEANU - Ioan FILIP - Liviu ANTAL, Ionut NEAGU• (Marius PENA 72), Gabriel GIURGIU•, Sorin FRUNZA (Silviu ILIE 84) - Branislav PUNOSEVAC (Gabriel VIGLIANTI 88). Tr: Dorinel MUNTEANU
Manchester United 2
Rooney 2 64p 92+p
Anders LINDEGAARD - FABIO (Phil JONES 76), Chris SMALLING, Nemanja VIDIC♦67, Patrice EVRA - Antonio VALENCIA (Jonny EVANS 71), Michael CARRICK•, ANDERSON, NANI - Wayne ROONEY - Javier HERNANDEZ. Tr: Alex FERGUSON

St Jakob Park, Basel
18-10-2011, 35831, Kassai HUN
FC Basel 0
Yann SOMMER - Markus STEINHOFER, David ABRAHAM, Aleksandar DRAGOVIC, PARK Joo Ho - Xherdan SHAQIRI•, Granit XHAKA (Adilson CABRAL 80), Benjamin HUGGEL• (Scott CHIPPERFIELD 85), Fabian FREI (Jacques ZOUA 66) - Marco STRELLER•, Alexander FREI•. Tr: Heiko VOGEL
Benfica 2
Bruno Cesar 20, Cardozo 75
ARTUR Moares• - MAXI PEREIRA (MIGUEL VITOR 78), LUISAO, Ezequiel GARAY, EMERSON••♦86 - Axel WITSEL, JAVI GARCIA - Nicolas GAITAN, Pablo AIMAR (NOLITO 67), BRUNO CESAR - RODRIGO Moreno (Oscar CARDOZO 70). Tr: JORGE JESUS

Old Trafford, Manchester
2-11-2011, 74847, Strahonja CRO
Manchester United 2
Valencia 8, OG 88
David DE GEA - Phil JONES, Rio FERDINAND, Jonny EVANS• (Ezekiel FRYERS 89), FABIO - Antonio VALENCIA, Wayne ROONEY, ANDERSON (PARK Ji Sung 80), NANI - Michael OWEN (Javier HERNANDEZ 11), Dimitar BERBATOV. Tr: Alex FERGUSON
Otelul Galati 0
Branko GRAHOVAC - Cornel RAPA, Cristian SARGHI, Sergiu COSTIN•, Adrian SALAGEANU - Ioan FILIP - Liviu ANTAL (Laurentiu IORGA 61), Ionut NEAGU, Gabriel GIURGIU (Gabriel PARASCHIV 81), Silviu ILIE (Sorin FRUNZA 53) - Marius PENA. Tr: Dorinel MUNTEANU

Estádio da Luz, Lisbon
2-11-2011, 39270, Carballo ESP
Benfica 1
Rodrigo 4
ARTUR Moares - MAXI PEREIRA•, LUISAO, Ezequiel GARAY•, LUIS MARTINS (MIGUEL VITOR• 64) - BRUNO CESAR, Axel WITSEL, Nemanja MATIC, Nicolas GAITAN (NOLITO 82) - Pablo AIMAR• (Oscar CARDOZO 73) - Rodrigo MORENO. Tr: JORGE JESUS
FC Basel 1
Huggel 64
Yann SOMMER - Markus STEINHOFER, David ABRAHAM, Aleksandar DRAGOVIC, PARK Joo Ho - Xherdan SHAQIRI, Benjamin HUGGEL•, Granit XHAKA (Adilson CABRAL 82), Fabian FREI - Scott CHIPPERFIELD (Generic KUSUNGA 89), Jacques ZOUA (PAK Kwang Ryong 90). Tr: Heiko VOGEL

Stadionul National, Bucharest
22-11-2011, 5787, Hagen NOR
Otelul Galati 2
Giurgiu 75, Antal 81
Branko GRAHOVAC - Cornel RAPA, Cristian SARGHI, Milan PERENDIJA, Adrian SALAGEANU• - Ioan FILIP - Liviu ANTAL, Ionut NEAGU (Gabriel VIGLIANTI 67) (Gabriel PARASCHIV 84), Gabriel GIURGIU, Laurentiu IORGA (Silviu ILIE 67) - Marius PENA. Tr: Dorinel MUNTEANU
Manchester United 3
Fabian Frei 10, Alexander Frei 14, Streller 37
Yann SOMMER - Markus STEINHOFER, David ABRAHAM, Aleksandar DRAGOVIC, PARK Joo Ho - Xherdan SHAQIRI (Jacques ZOUA 82), Benjamin HUGGEL (Adilson CABRAL• 44), Granit XHAKA, Fabian FREI - Marco STRELLER, Alexander FREI (Scott CHIPPERFIELD 74). Tr: Heiko VOGEL

Old Trafford, Manchester
22-11-2011, 74873, Cakir TUR
Manchester United 2
Berbatov 30, Fletcher 59
David DE GEA - FABIO (Chris SMALLING 82), Phil JONES, Rio FERDINAND, Patrice EVRA - Antonio VALENCIA (Javier HERNANDEZ 81), Michael CARRICK•, Darren FLETCHER•, NANI - Ashley YOUNG - Dimitar BERBATOV. Tr: Alex FERGUSON
Benfica 2
OG 3, Aimar 61
ARTUR Moares• - MAXI PEREIRA•, LUISAO (MIGUEL VITOR 56), Ezequiel GARAY•, EMERSON - Axel WITSEL, JAVI GARCIA - Nicolas GAITAN (Nemanja MATIC 68), Pablo AIMAR (RUBEN AMORIM 84), BRUNO CESAR - RODRIGO Moreno. Tr: JORGE JESUS

St Jakob Park, Basel
7-12-2011, 36000, Kuipers SUI
FC Basel 2
Streller 9, Alexander Frei 84
Yann SOMMER - Markus STEINHOFER, David ABRAHAM, Aleksandar DRAGOVIC, PARK Joo Ho - Xherdan SHAQIRI (Valentin STOCKER 90), Adilson CABRAL, Granit XHAKA• (Scott CHIPPERFIELD 83), Fabian FREI• - Marco STRELLER, Alexander FREI (Generic KUSUNGA 88). Tr: Heiko VOGEL
Manchester United 1
Jones 89
David DE GEA - Chris SMALLING, Nemanja VIDIC (Jonny EVANS 44), Rio FERDINAND, Patrice EVRA• - Phil JONES, Ryan GIGGS, NANI (PARK Ji Sung (Federico MACHEDA 82), Ashley YOUNG• (Danny WELBECK 64) - Wayne ROONEY. Tr: Alex FERGUSON

Estádio da Luz, Lisbon
7-12-2011, 35155, Grafe GER
Benfica 1
Cardozo 7
ARTUR Moares - RUBEN AMORIM, JARDEL, Ezequiel GARAY, EMERSON - JAVI GARCIA - Nicolas GAITAN, Axel WITSEL, Pablo AIMAR (RODRIGO Moreno 70), BRUNO CESAR (NOLITO 57) - Oscar CARDOZO (Javier SAVIOLA 78). Tr: JORGE JESUS
Otelul Galati 0
Branko GRAHOVAC - Cornel RAPA, Alexandru BENGA, Milan PERENDIJA, Silviu ILIE (Zoran LJUBINKOVIC• 21) - Ioan FILIP - Liviu ANTAL (Sorin FRUNZA 81), Ionut NEAGU (Marius PENA 70), Gabriel GIURGIU•, Laurentiu IORGA - Gabriel PARASCHIV. Tr: Dorinel MUNTEANU

UEFA CHAMPIONS LEAGUE 2011-12

GROUP D		Pl	W	D	L	F	A	Pts	ESP	FRA	NED	CRO
Real Madrid	ESP	6	6	0	0	19	2	18		4-0	3-0	6-2
Olympique Lyonnais	FRA	6	2	2	2	9	7	8	0-2		0-0	2-0
Ajax	NED	6	2	2	2	6	6	8	0-3	0-0		4-0
Dinamo Zagreb	CRO	6	0	0	6	3	22	0	0-1	1-7	0-2	

Maksimir, Zagreb
14-09-2011, 27 055, Moen NOR
Dinamo Zagreb 0

Ivan KELAVA - Jerko LEKO•, Domagoj VIDA, TONEL, Luis IBANEZ - Ivan TOMECAK, Milan BADELJ, Adrian CALELLO (Mario SITUM 87), Mateo KOVACIC (Nikola POKRIVAC• 62) - SAMMIR - Ante RUKAVINA (Fatos BECIRAJ 75). Tr: Krunoslav JURCIC

Real Madrid 1
Di Maria [53]
Iker CASILLAS - SERGIO RAMOS, PEPE•, Ricardo CARVALHO, MARCELO••♦73 - XABI ALONSO, FABIO COENTRAO - Angel DI MARIA (Gonzalo HIGUAIN 78), Mesut OZIL (Lassana DIARRA 78), CRISTIANO RONALDO - Karim BENZEMA (Alvaro ARBELOA 82). Tr: Jose MOURINHO

Amsterdam ArenA, Amsterdam
14-09-2011, 49 504, Stark GER
Ajax 0

Kenneth VERMEER - Gregory VAN DER WIEL, Toby ALDERWEIRELD, Jan VERTONGHEN, Nicolai BOILESEN - Theo JANSSEN (Vurnon ANITA 70) - Miralem SULEJMANI (Lorenzo EBECILIO 85), Siem DE JONG, Christian ERIKSEN, Derk BOERRIGTER - Kolbeinn SIGTHORSSON (Dmitriy BULYKIN 81). Tr: Frank DE BOER

Olympique Lyonnais 0

Hugo LLORIS - Anthony REVEILLERE, Bakary KONE, Dejan LOVREN•, Aly CISSOKHO - Maxime GONALONS, Kim KALLSTROM - Jimmy BRIAND, Clement GRENIER, MICHEL BASTOS - Bafetimbi GOMIS• (Ishak BELFODIL 85). Tr: Remi GARDE

Stade de Gerland, Lyon
27-09-2011, 34 432, Kralovec CZE
Olympique Lyonnais 2
Gomis [23], Kone [42]
Hugo LLORIS - Anthony REVEILLERE, Bakary KONE, Dejan LOVREN, Aly CISSOKHO - Maxime GONALONS, Kim KALLSTROM - Jimmy BRIAND, Clement GRENIER (Jeremy PIED 79), MICHEL BASTOS - Bafetimbi GOMIS (Alexandre LACAZETTE 63). Tr: Remi GARDE

Dinamo Zagreb 0

Ivan KELAVA - Jerko LEKO•, Domagoj VIDA, TONEL, Luis IBANEZ - Milan BADELJ (Ivan TOMECAK 46), Adrian CALELLO, Nikola POKRIVAC (Ante RUKAVINA 74), Mateo KOVACIC (Josip SIMUNIC 46) - SAMMIR• - Fatos BECIRAJ. Tr: Krunoslav JURCIC

Bernabéu, Madrid
27-09-2011, 70 320, Clattenburg ENG
Real Madrid 3
Ronaldo [25], Kaka [41], Benzema [49]
Iker CASILLAS - SERGIO RAMOS, Raphael VARANE, RICARDO CARVALHO•, Alvaro ARBELOA - Sami KHEDIRA, XABI ALONSO - Mesut OZIL (HAMIT Altintop 84), KAKA (Angel DI MARIA 75), CRISTIANO RONALDO - Karim BENZEMA (Gonzalo HIGUAIN 75). Tr: Jose MOURINHO

Ajax 0

Kenneth VERMEER - Gregory VAN DER WIEL, Toby ALDERWEIRELD, Jan VERTONGHEN, Vurnon ANITA - Siem DE JONG, Theo JANSSEN (Eyong ENOH 51) - Miralem SULEJMANI (Lorenzo EBECILIO 71), Christian ERIKSEN, Derk BOERRIGTER (Thulani SERERO 83) - Kolbeinn SIGTHORSSON. Tr: Frank DE BOER

Bernabéu, Madrid
18-10-2011, 70 028, Cakir TUR
Real Madrid 4
Benzema [19], Khedira [47], OG [55], Ramos [81]
Iker CASILLAS - Alvaro ARBELOA, PEPE, SERGIO RAMOS, MARCELO - Sami KHEDIRA (Lassana FABIO COENTRAO 61), XABI ALONSO• - Angel DI MARIA, Mesut OZIL (KAKA 66), CRISTIANO RONALDO - Karim BENZEMA (Gonzalo HIGUAIN 72). Tr: Jose MOURINHO

Olympique Lyonnais 0

Hugo LLORIS - Anthony REVEILLERE, Bakary KONE•, Dejan LOVREN, Aly CISSOKHO - Gueida FOFANA, Kim KALLSTROM - Jimmy BRIAND•, Yoann GOURCUFF (EDERSON 66), MICHEL BASTOS - Bafetimbi GOMIS (Mouhamadou DABO 80). Tr: Remi GARDE

Maksimir, Zagreb
18-10-2011, 25 714, Grafe GER
Dinamo Zagreb 0

Ivan KELAVA - Domagoj VIDA•, TONEL, Josip SIMUNIC•, Luis IBANEZ• - Jerko LEKO, Adrian CALELLO• (Ivan TOMECAK• 80), Milan BADELJ (Mateo KOVACIC 46) - SAMMIR• - Fatos BECIRAJ (Nikola POKRIVAC 69), Ante RUKAVINA. Tr: Krunoslav JURCIC

Ajax 2
Boerriger [49], Eriksen [90]
Kenneth VERMEER - Gregory VAN DER WIEL, Toby ALDERWEIRELD, Jan VERTONGHEN, Vurnon ANITA - Eyong ENOH• - Miralem SULEJMANI, Christian ERIKSEN (Nicolas LODEIRO 90), Theo JANSSEN, Derk BOERRIGTER• (Dmitriy BULYKIN 70), Siem DE JONG. Tr: Frank DE BOER

Stade de Gerland, Lyon
2-11-2011, 40 099, Rizzoli ITA
Olympique Lyonnais 0

Hugo LLORIS - Anthony REVEILLERE, CRIS•, Dejan LOVREN (Bakary KONE 38), Mouhamadou DABO - Maxime GONALONS, Jimmy BRIAND, Yoann GOURCUFF, Kim KALLSTROM•, EDERSON (Ishak BELFODIL) - Bafetimbi GOMIS (Alexandre LACAZETTE 75). Tr: Remi GARDE

Real Madrid 2
Ronaldo 2 [24 69p]
Iker CASILLAS - Lassana DIARRA•, PEPE, SERGIO RAMOS, FABIO COENTRAO (Raul ALBIOL• 64) - Sami KHEDIRA•, XABI ALONSO - Angel DI MARIA (Jose CALLEJON 83), Mesut OZIL, CRISTIANO RONALDO - Karim BENZEMA (Gonzalo HIGUAIN• 71). Tr: Jose MOURINHO

Amsterdam ArenA, Amsterdam
2-11-2011, 49 707, Atkinson ENG
Ajax 4
Van der Wiel [20], Sulejmani [25], De Jong [65], Lodeiro [92+]
Kenneth VERMEER - Gregory VAN DER WIEL, Toby ALDERWEIRELD, Jan VERTONGHEN, Vurnon ANITA• - Eyong ENOH• - Miralem SULEJMANI (Jody LUKOKI 72), Christian ERIKSEN (Nicolas LODEIRO 80), Theo JANSSEN, Derk BOERRIGTER (Lorenzo EBECILIO 77) - Siem DE JONG. Tr: Frank DE BOER

Dinamo Zagreb 0

Ivan KELAVA - Sime VRSALJKO, Domagoj VIDA•, Josip SIMUNIC, Luis IBANEZ• - Milan BADELJ, Jerko LEKO, Adrian CALELLO• (Ivan TOMECAK 46), Mateo KOVACIC - SAMMIR (Mario SITUM 72) - Ante RUKAVINA (Fatos BECIRAJ 56). Tr: Krunoslav JURCIC

Bernabéu, Madrid
22-11-2011, 65 415, Kelly IRL
Real Madrid 6
Benzema 2 2 [66], Callejon 2 [6 49], Higuain [9], Ozil [20]
ADAN - Lassana DIARRA, Raphael VARANE, SERGIO RAMOS (Raul ALBIOL 46), FABIO COENTRAO - NURI Sahin, XABI ALONSO (HAMIT Altintop 46) - Jose CALLEJON, Mesut OZIL (Esteban GRANERO 46), Karim BENZEMA - Gonzalo HIGUAIN. Tr: Jose MOURINHO

Dinamo Zagreb 2
Beciraj [81], Tomecak [90]
Ivan KELAVA - Domagoj VIDA (Arijan ADEMI 63), TONEL, Leandro CUFRE•, Luis IBANEZ - Mateo KOVACIC, Milan BADELJ, Adrian CALELLO, Mehmed ALISPAHIC (Jerko LEKO, 63) - SAMMIR (Ivan TOMECAK 82) - Fatos BECIRAJ•. Tr: Krunoslav JURCIC

Stade de Gerland, Lyon
22-11-2011, 35 070, Eriksson SWE
Olympique Lyonnais 0

Hugo LLORIS - Anthony REVEILLERE•, CRIS••, Dejan LOVREN, Aly CISSOKHO - Yoann GOURCUFF, Kim KALLSTROM - Jimmy BRIAND (Alexandre LACAZETTE 85), LISANDRO LOPEZ (EDERSON 73), MICHEL BASTOS - Bafetimbi GOMIS. Tr: Remi GARDE

Ajax 0

Kenneth VERMEER - Gregory VAN DER WIEL (Daley BLIND 60), Toby ALDERWEIRELD, Jan VERTONGHEN, Vurnon ANITA•, Eyong ENOH• - Miralem SULEJMANI, Christian ERIKSEN, Theo JANSSEN•, Lorenzo EBECILIO (Davy KLAASSEN 85) - Nicolas LODEIRO (Jody LUKOKI 89). Tr: Frank DE BOER

Maksimir, Zagreb
7-12-2011, 16 457, Clattenburg ENG
Dinamo Zagreb 1
Kovacic [40]
Ivan KELAVA - Sime VRSALJKO, Jerko LEKO••♦28, Domagoj VIDA, Luis IBANEZ• - Milan BADELJ, Arijan ADEMI, Adrian CALELLO, Mateo KOVACIC (Nikola POKRIVAC 80) - SAMMIR (Mehmed ALISPAHIC 66) - Fatos BECIRAJ (Mario SITUM 55). Tr: Krunoslav JURCIC

Olympique Lyonnais 7
Gomis 4 [45 48 52 70], Gonalons [47], Lisandro [64], Briand [75]
Hugo LLORIS - Mouhamadou DABO, Bakary KONE, Dejan LOVREN (LISANDRO LOPEZ 54), Aly CISSOKHO• - Gueida FOFANA•, Maxime GONALONS - Jimmy BRIAND, Yoann GOURCUFF, Alexandre LACAZETTE (EDERSON 75) - Bafetimbi GOMIS•. Tr: Remi GARDE

Amsterdam ArenA, Amsterdam
7-12-2011, 51 557, De Sousa POR
Ajax 0

Kenneth VERMEER - Gregory VAN DER WIEL, Jan VERTONGHEN, Daley BLIND, Vurnon ANITA - Eyong ENOH - Miralem SULEJMANI, Christian ERIKSEN, Theo JANSSEN (Davy KLAASSEN 76), Lorenzo EBECILIO - Nicolas LODEIRO (Dmitriy BULYKIN 74). Tr: Frank DE BOER

Real Madrid 3
Callejon 2 [14 92+], Higuain [41]
Antonio ADAN - Alvaro ARBELOA• (PEDRO MENDES 67), Raphael VARANE, Raul ALBIOL, FABIO COENTRAO - Esteban GRANERO (XABI ALONSO 59), NURI Sahin - Jose CALLEJON, KAKA, Karim BENZEMA (HAMIT Altintop 54) - Gonzalo HIGUAIN. Tr: Jose MOURINHO

PART THREE – THE CONTINENTAL CONFEDERATIONS

GROUP E		Pl	W	D	L	F	A	Pts	ENG	GER	ESP	BEL
Chelsea	ENG	6	3	2	1	13	4	**11**		2-0	3-0	5-0
Bayer Leverkusen	GER	6	3	1	2	8	8	**10**	2-1		2-1	2-0
Valencia	ESP	6	2	2	2	12	7	**8**	1-1	3-1		7-0
KRC Genk	BEL	6	0	3	3	2	16	**3**	1-1	1-1	0-0	

Stamford Bridge, London
13-09-2011, 33 820, Lannoy FRA
Chelsea 2
David Luiz 67, Mata 92+

Petr CECH - Jose BOSINGWA, Branislav IVANOVIC, DAVID LUIZ• (ALEX 76), Ashley COLE - John MIKEL - RAUL MEIRELES (Frank LAMPARD 64), Florent MALOUDA - Daniel STURRIDGE (Nicolas ANELKA 64), FERNANDO TORRES•, Juan MATA. Tr: Andre VILLAS BOAS

Bayer Leverkusen 0

Bernd LENO - Gonzalo CASTRO•, Stefan REINARTZ, OMER Toprak, Michal KADLEC - Lars BENDER• (Hanno BALITSCH 80), Simon ROLFES - Andre SCHURRLE, Michael BALLACK (RENATO AUGUSTO 66), Sidney SAM (Eren DERDIYOK• 73) - Stefan KIEßLING. Tr: Robin DUTT

Cristal Arena, Genk
13-09-2011, 20 248, Einwaller AUT
KRC Genk 0

Laszlo KOTELES - Anele NGCONGCA, NADSON, Jeroen SIMAEYS, Daniel PUDIL• - Dugary NDABASHINZE, David HUBERT, Daniel TOZSER, Thomas BUFFEL• (Fabien CAMUS 85) - Kennedy NWANGANGA (Marvin OGUNJIMI 64), Jelle VOSSEN (Elyaniv BARDA 80). Tr: Mario BEEN

Valencia 0

DIEGO ALVES - Luis MIGUEL•, Adil RAMI, VICTOR RUIZ, Jeremy MATHIEU - MEHMET Topal - Daniel PAREJO (Artiz ADURIZ 74), EVER BANEGA• - Sofiane FEGHOULI (PABLO HERNANDEZ 69), Roberto SOLDADO, Pablo PIATTI (Sergio CANALES 79). Tr: Unai EMERY

Mestalla, Valenca
28-09-2011, 33 791, Rizzoli ITA
Valencia 1
Soldado 87p

DIEGO ALVES - Luis MIGUEL, Adil RAMI, VICTOR RUIZ•, JORDI ALBA - David ALBELDA•, EVER BANEGA (Sofiane FEGHOULI 72) - PABLO HERNANDEZ (JONAS 72), Sergio CANALES, Jeremy MATHIEU (Pablo PIATTI 58) - Roberto SOLDADO. Tr: Unai EMERY

Chelsea 0

Petr CECH - Jose BOSINGWA, DAVID LUIZ, John TERRY, Ashley COLE• - John MIKEL - RAMIRES (RAUL MEIRELES 65), Frank LAMPARD (Salomon KALOU• 83) - Juan MATA•, FERNANDO TORRES (Nicolas ANELKA 71), Florent MALOUDA•. Tr: Andre VILLAS BOAS

BayArena, Leverkusen
28-09-2011, 25 138, Kelly IRL
Bayer Leverkusen 2
Bender 30, Ballack 91+

Bernd LENO - Gonzalo CASTRO•, Stefan REINARTZ, Omer TOPRAK•, Michal KADLEC• (Michael BALLACK 80) - Lars BENDER, Simon ROLFES - Sidney SAM, RENATO AUGUSTO (Hanno BALITSCH 65), Andre SCHURRLE - Stefan KIEßLING (Eren DERDIYOK 90). Tr: Robin DUTT

KRC Genk 0

Laszlo KOTELES - Anele NGCONGCA, Jeroen SIMAEYS, NADSON• (Khaleem HYLAND 69), Daniel PUDIL• - Thomas BUFFEL, David HUBERT (Kennedy NWANGANGA 78), Daniel TOZSER, Kevin DE BRUYNE - Jelle VOSSEN (Elyaniv BARDA 46), Marvin OGUNJIMI. Tr: Mario BEEN

BayArena, Leverkusen
19-10-2011, 26 384, Thomson SCO
Bayer Leverkusen 2
Schurrle 52, Sam 56

Bernd LENO - Gonzalo CASTRO, Stefan REINARTZ (Manuel FRIEDRICH 46), Omer TOPRAK, Michal KADLEC - Lars BENDER, Simon ROLFES• - Sidney SAM (Daniel SCHWAAB 90), Michael BALLACK, Andre SCHURRLE• - Stefan KIEßLING• (Eren DERDIYOK 81). Tr: Robin DUTT

Valencia 1
Jonas 24

DIEGO ALVES - Luis MIGUEL•, Adil RAMI, VICTOR RUIZ, JORDI ALBA (Sofiane FEGHOULI 65) - David ALBELDA• (Artiz ADURIZ 82), EVER BANEGA• - PABLO HERNANDEZ (Sergio CANALES 79), JONAS, Jeremy MATHIEU - Roberto SOLDADO. Tr: Unai EMERY

Stamford Bridge, London
19-10-2011, 38 518, Nikolaev RUS
Chelsea 5
Meireles 8, Torres 2 11 27, Ivanovic 42, Kalou 72

Petr CECH - Jose BOSINGWA (ALEX 78), Branislav IVANOVIC, DAVID LUIZ•, Ashley COLE (Paulo FERREIRA 46) - Oriol ROMEU - RAUL MEIRELES, Frank LAMPARD (Salomon KALOU 68) - Nicolas ANELKA, FERNANDO TORRES, Florent MALOUDA. Tr: Andre VILLAS BOAS

KRC Genk 0

Laszlo KOTELES - Anele NGCONGCA, Abel MASUERO (Fabien CAMUS 46), Daniel TOZSER, Daniel PUDIL• - Thomas BUFFEL, Anthony VANDEN BORRE, Khaleem HYLAND•, Kevin DE BRUYNE - Jelle VOSSEN (Kennedy NWANGANGA 81), Elyaniv BARDA (Dugary NDABASHINZE 71). Tr: Mario BEEN

Mestalla, Valenca
1-11-2011, 37 047, Eriksson SWE
Valencia 3
Jonas 1, Soldado 65, Rami 75

DIEGO ALVES - Luis MIGUEL, Adil RAMI, VICTOR RUIZ, Jeremy MATHIEU - MEHMET Topal, EVER BANEGA (TINO COSTA• 24) - PABLO HERNANDEZ, JONAS (JORDI ALBA 74), Sofiane FEGHOULI (Pablo PIATTI 59) - Roberto SOLDADO. Tr: Unai EMERY

Bayer Leverkusen 1
Kiessling 31

Bernd LENO - Daniel FRIEDRICH, Omer TOPRAK•, Michal KADLEC - Lars BENDER (Stefan REINARTZ 79), Simon ROLFES - Sidney SAM• (Nicolai JORGENSEN 84), Michael BALLACK•, Andre SCHURRLE - Stefan KIEßLING (Eren DERDIYOK 77). Tr: Robin DUTT

Cristal Arena, Genk
1-11-2011, 22 584, Moen NOR
KRC Genk 1
Vossen 61

Laszlo KOTELES - Anthony VANDEN BORRE, Khaleem HYLAND, NADSON, Anele NGCONGCA - Thomas BUFFEL (Dugary NDABASHINZE 69), Fabien CAMUS, Daniel TOZSER, Kevin DE BRUYNE• - Kennedy NWANGANGA (Anthony LIMBOMBE 82), Jelle VOSSEN (Elyaniv BARDA 87). Tr: Mario BEEN

Chelsea 1
Ramires 26

Petr CECH - Jose BOSINGWA, Branislav IVANOVIC, DAVID LUIZ, Ashley COLE - Oriol ROMEU (Juan MATA 77) - RAMIRES (Frank LAMPARD 66), RAUL MEIRELES• - Nicolas ANELKA (Daniel STURRIDGE 66), FERNANDO TORRES, Florent MALOUDA. Tr: Andre VILLAS BOAS

BayArena, Leverkusen
23-11-2011, 29 285, Kassai HUN
Bayer Leverkusen 2
Derdiyok 73, Friedrich 90

Bernd LENO - Daniel SCHWAAB (Andre SCHURRLE 57), Manuel FRIEDRICH, Omer TOPRAK, Michal KADLEC• (Eren DERDIYOK 71) - Lars BENDER, Simon ROLFES - Gonzalo CASTRO, Michael BALLACK•, Sidney SAM - Stefan KIEßLING• (Bastian OCZIPKA 83). Tr: Robin DUTT

Chelsea 1
Drogba 48

Petr CECH - Branislav IVANOVIC•, DAVID LUIZ (ALEX 69), John TERRY, Jose BOSINGWA - RAMIRES, RAUL MEIRELES• (John MIKEL 80) - Daniel STURRIDGE, Frank LAMPARD, Juan MATA (Florent MALOUDA 66) - Didier DROGBA. Tr: Andre VILLAS BOAS

Mestalla, Valenca
23-11-2011, 35 086, Chapron FRA
Valencia 7
Jonas 10, Soldado 3 13 36 39, Pablo 68, Aduriz 70, Costa 81

DIEGO ALVES - Luis MIGUEL, Adil RAMI, VICTOR RUIZ• (Daniel PAREJO 46), Jeremy MATHIEU - MEHMET Topal, TINO COSTA - PABLO HERNANDEZ, JONAS, Sofiane FEGHOULI (Pablo PIATTI 57) - Roberto SOLDADO. (Artiz ADURIZ 70). Tr: Unai EMERY

KRC Genk 0

Laszlo KOTELES - Anthony VANDEN BORRE, Khaleem HYLAND (Anthony LIMBOMBE 61), NADSON, Daniel PUDIL - Thomas BUFFEL, Fabien CAMUS, Daniel TOZSER, Kevin DE BRUYNE - Jelle VOSSEN (Mohamed SARR 46), Elyaniv BARDA (Kennedy NWANGANGA 71). Tr: Mario BEEN

Stamford Bridge, London
6-12-2011, 41 109, Rocchi ITA
Chelsea 3
Drogba 2 3 76, Ramires 22

Petr CECH - Branislav IVANOVIC, DAVID LUIZ, John TERRY, Ashley COLE - Oriol ROMEU• - Daniel STURRIDGE, RAMIRES (John MIKEL 65), RAUL MEIRELES, Juan MATA (Florent MALOUDA 83) - Didier DROGBA (Fernando TORRES 77). Tr: Andre VILLAS BOAS

Valencia 0

DIEGO ALVES - Antonio BARRAGAN, Adil RAMI, VICTOR RUIZ, JORDI ALBA (Artiz ADURIZ 54) - David ALBELDA, TINO COSTA• (Daniel PAREJO 76) - Sofiane FEGHOULI (PABLO HERNANDEZ 65), JONAS, Jeremy MATHIEU - Roberto SOLDADO. Tr: Unai EMERY

Cristal Arena, Genk
6-12-2011, 21 187, Tagliavento ITA
KRC Genk 1
Vossen 30

Laszlo KOTELES - Anthony VANDEN BORRE, Jeroen SIMAEYS•, NADSON, Daniel PUDIL - Anele NGCONGCA - Dugary NDABASHINZE, Fabien CAMUS, Daniel TOZSER, Anthony LIMBOMBE (Thomas BUFFEL 75) - Jelle VOSSEN• (Elyaniv BARDA 81). Tr: Mario BEEN

Bayer Leverkusen 1
Derdiyok 79

Bernd LENO - Gonzalo CASTRO, Daniel SCHWAAB, Stefan REINARTZ (Nicolai JORGENSEN 87), Michal KADLEC (Bastian OCZIPKA 73) - Lars BENDER, Simon ROLFES - Sidney SAM, Michael BALLACK, Andre SCHURRLE (Stefan KIEßLING 68) - Eren DERDIYOK•. Tr: Robin DUTT

UEFA CHAMPIONS LEAGUE 2011-12

GROUP F		Pl	W	D	L	F	A	Pts	ENG	FRA	GRE	GER
Arsenal	ENG	6	3	2	1	7	6	11		0-0	2-1	2-1
Olympique Marseille	FRA	6	3	1	2	7	4	10	0-1		0-1	3-0
Olympiacos	GRE	6	3	0	3	8	6	9	3-1	0-1		3-1
Borussia Dortmund	GER	6	1	1	4	6	12	4	1-1	2-3	1-0	

Karaiskakis, Piraeus, Athens
13-09-2011, 30 040, Proença POR
Olympiacos 0

Franco COSTANZO - Vasilios TOROSIDIS, Olof MELLBERG, Avraam PAPADOPOULOS•, Jose HOLEBAS - Ljubomir FEJSA (Ariel IBAGAZA 67), Francois MODESTO - Djamel ABDOUN, DAVID FUSTER (Jean MAKOUN 67), Francisco YESTE (Rafik DJEBBOUR 55) - Kevin MIRALLAS•. Tr: Ernesto VALVERDE

Olympique Marseille 1
Lucho [51]
Steve MANDANDA - Cesar AZPILICUETA, Nicolas N'KOULOU, Souleymane DIAWARA, Djimi TRAORE - Alou DIARRA, Benoit CHEYROU (Rod FANNI 81•90) - Morgan AMALFITANO•, LUCHO GONZALEZ (Charles KABORE 77), Jeremy MOREL• - Loic REMY (Jordan AYEW•68). Tr: Didier DESCHAMPS

Signal Iduna Park, Dortmund
13-09-2011, 65 590, Rocchi ITA
Borussia Dortmund 1
Perisic [88]
Roman WEIDENFELLER - Lukasz PISZCZEK, Neven SUBOTIC, Mats HUMMELS, Marcel SCHMELZER - Sven BENDER•, Sebastian KEHL (Ivan PERISIC 69) - Mario GOTZE, Shinji KAGAWA (Mohamed ZIDAN 85), Kevin GROBKREUTZ (Jakub BLASZCZYKOWSKI 69) - Robert LEWANDOWSKI. Tr: Jurgen KLOPP

Arsenal 1
Van Persie [42]
Wojciech SZCZESNY - Bacary SAGNA•, Per MERTESACKER, Laurent KOSCIELNY, Kieran GIBBS - Alex SONG - Theo WALCOTT (Emmanuel FRIMPONG 76), Yossi BENAYOUN, Mikel ARTETA, Gervinho (Marouane CHAMAKH 86) - Robin VAN PERSIE (ANDRE SANTOS 86). Tr: Arsene WENGER

Emirates, London
28-09-2011, 59 676, Carballo ESP
Arsenal 2
Oxlade-Chamberlain [8], Santos [20]
Wojciech SZCZESNY - Bacary SAGNA, Per MERTESACKER, Alex SONG, ANDRE SANTOS - Emmanuel FRIMPONG, Alex OXLADE-CHAMBERLAIN (Aaron RAMSEY 67), Mikel ARTETA•, Tomas ROSICKY•, Andrey ARSHAVIN (Kieran GIBBS 83) - Marouane CHAMAKH (Robin VAN PERSIE 70). Tr: Arsene WENGER

Olympiacos 1
Fuster [27]
Franco COSTANZO - Vasilios TOROSIDIS, Olof MELLBERG, Ivan MARCANO, Jose HOLEBAS• - Pablo ORBAIZ (Djamel ABDOUN 75) - DAVID FUSTER• (Marko PANTELIC 80), Ariel IBAGAZA, Ljubomir FEJSA, Kevin MIRALLAS (Francois MODESTO 75) - Rafik DJEBBOUR•. Tr: Ernesto VALVERDE

Vélodrome, Marseille
28-09-2011, 26 142, Eriksson SWE
Olympique Marseille 3
Ayew.A 2 [20 69p], Remy [62]
Steve MANDANDA - Cesar AZPILICUETA, Souleymane DIAWARA, Nicolas N'KOULOU, Jeremy MOREL• - LUCHO GONZALEZ (Morgan AMALFITANO 73), Alou DIARRA, Charles KABORE - Matthieu VALBUENA, Loic REMY (Jordan AYEW 72••90), Andre AYEW (Jean-Philippe SABO 81). Tr: Didier DESCHAMPS

Borussia Dortmund 0
Roman WEIDENFELLER - Lukasz PISZCZEK, Neven SUBOTIC, Mats HUMMELS, Marcel SCHMELZER - Sven BENDER, Sebastian KEHL - Mario GOTZE, Shinji KAGAWA (Jakub BLASZCZYKOWSKI 64), Kevin GROBKREUTZ (Ivan PERISIC 64) - Robert LEWANDOWSKI (Lucas BARRIOS 72). Tr: Jurgen KLOPP

Vélodrome, Marseille
19-10-2011, 33 258, Skomina SVN
Olympique Marseille 0
Steve MANDANDA - Cesar AZPILICUETA, Souleymane DIAWARA•, Nicolas N'KOULOU, Jeremy MOREL - Alou DIARRA - LUCHO GONZALEZ, Benoit CHEYROU (Charles KABORE 87) - Matthieu VALBUENA, Loic REMY (Andre-Pierre GIGNAC• 69), Andre AYEW•. Tr: Didier DESCHAMPS

Arsenal 1
Ramsey [92+]
Wojciech SZCZESNY - Carl JENKINSON (Johan DJOUROU• 62), Per MERTESACKER, Laurent KOSCIELNY, ANDRE SANTOS - Alex SONG• - Theo WALCOTT (GERVINHO 67), Mikel ARTETA, Tomas ROSICKY, Andrey ARSHAVIN (Aaron RAMSEY 78) - Robin VAN PERSIE. Tr: Arsene WENGER

Karaiskakis, Piraeus, Athens
19-10-2011, 29 638, Nijhuis NED
Olympiacos 3
Holebas [8], Djebbour [40], Modesto [78]
Franco COSTANZO - Francois MODESTO, Olof MELLBERG, Avraam PAPADOPOULOS, Ivan MARCANO - Jean MAKOUN (Ioannis MANIATIS 72), Pablo ORBAIZ - Kevin MIRALLAS (Ioannis FETFATZIDIS 80), Ariel IBAGAZA, Jose HOLEBAS - Rafik DJEBBOUR (Marko PANTELIC 87). Tr: Ernesto VALVERDE

Borussia Dortmund 1
Lewandowski [26]
Roman WEIDENFELLER - Lukasz PISZCZEK, Neven SUBOTIC, Mats HUMMELS, Marcel SCHMELZER• - Sven BENDER, Ilkay GUNDOGAN (Moritz LEITNER 56) - Mario GOTZE (Kevin GROBKREUTZ 82), Shinji KAGAWA (Jakub BLASZCZYKOWSKI 66), Ivan PERISIC - Robert LEWANDOWSKI. Tr: Jurgen KLOPP

Emirates, London
1-11-2011, 59 961, Tagliavento ITA
Arsenal 0
Wojciech SZCZESNY - Carl JENKINSON, Per MERTESACKER, Thomas VERMAELEN, ANDRE SANTOS - Alex SONG, Mikel ARTETA - Theo WALCOTT•, Aaron RAMSEY, Tomas ROSICKY• 66), GERVINHO (Andrey ARSHAVIN 77) - PARK Chu Young (Robin VAN PERSIE 62). Tr: Arsene WENGER

Olympique Marseille 0
Steve MANDANDA - Rod FANNI, Souleymane DIAWARA, Nicolas N'KOULOU, Jeremy MOREL - Alou DIARRA•, Benoit CHEYROU - Jordan AYEW (Andre-Pierre GIGNAC 84), Matthieu VALBUENA, LUCHO GONZALEZ 74), Andre AYEW - Loic REMY (Morgan AMALFITANO 69). Tr: Didier DESCHAMPS

Signal Iduna Park, Dortmund
1-11-2011, 65 590, Bezborodov RUS
Borussia Dortmund 1
Grosskreutz [7]
Roman WEIDENFELLER - Lukasz PISZCZEK, Neven SUBOTIC, Mats HUMMELS, Marcel SCHMELZER - Moritz LEITNER (FELIPE SANTANA 86), Sebastian KEHL - Ivan PERISIC• (Jakub BLASZCZYKOWSKI 66), Mario GOTZE (Shinji KAGAWA 66), Kevin GROBKREUTZ - Robert LEWANDOWSKI. Tr: Jurgen KLOPP

Olympiacos 1
Modesto [89]
Balazs MEGYERI - Francois MODESTO, Olof MELLBERG•, Avraam PAPADOPOULOS•, Ivan MARCANO - (Djamel ABDOUN 67) - Pablo ORBAIZ• - Kevin MIRALLAS, Ljubomir FEJSA (Jean MAKOUN 59), Ariel IBAGAZA (Marko PANTELIC 79), Jose HOLEBAS - Rafik DJEBBOUR. Tr: Ernesto VALVERDE

Vélodrome, Marseille
23-11-2011, 25 392, Rizzoli ITA
Olympique Marseille 0
Steve MANDANDA - Charles KABORE, Souleymane DIAWARA, Nicolas N'KOULOU, Djimi TRAORE - Matthieu VALBUENA (LUCHO GONZALEZ 73), Alou DIARRA, Benoit CHEYROU (Stephane MBIA 61), Andre AYEW - Loic REMY•, Jordan AYEW (Andre-Pierre GIGNAC 61). Tr: Didier DESCHAMPS

Olympiacos 1
Fetfatzidis [82]
Balazs MEGYERI - Vasilios TOROSIDIS, Olof MELLBERG, Avraam PAPADOPOULOS, Ivan MARCANO - DAVID FUSTER (Francisco YESTE 74), Francois MODESTO, Ioannis MANIATIS, Jose HOLEBAS (Ioannis FETFATZIDIS 75) - Kevin MIRALLAS, Rafik DJEBBOUR (Giannis POTOURIDIS 88). Tr: Ernesto VALVERDE

Emirates, London
23-11-2011, 59 531, De Bleeckere BEL
Arsenal 2
Van Persie 2 [49 86]
Wojciech SZCZESNY - Laurent KOSCIELNY (Johan DJOUROU 83), Per MERTESACKER, Thomas VERMAELEN, ANDRE SANTOS - Alex SONG - Theo WALCOTT• (Abou DIABY 86), Aaron RAMSEY•, Mikel ARTETA, GERVINHO (Yossi BENAYOUN• 74) - Robin VAN PERSIE. Tr: Arsene WENGER

Borussia Dortmund 1
Kagawa [92+]
Roman WEIDENFELLER - Lukasz PISZCZEK, FELIPE SANTANA, Mats HUMMELS, Marcel SCHMELZER• - Sven BENDER (Moritz LEITNER 25), Sebastian KEHL (Lucas BARRIOS 64) - Mario GOTZE (Ivan PERISIC 29), Shinji KAGAWA, Kevin GROBKREUTZ - Robert LEWANDOWSKI. Tr: Jurgen KLOPP

Karaiskakis, Piraeus, Athens
6-12-2011, 30 816, Undiano ESP
Olympiacos 3
Djebbour [16], Fuster [36], Modesto [89]
Balazs MEGYERI - Vasilios TOROSIDIS, Olof MELLBERG, Avraam PAPADOPOULOS•, Ivan MARCANO - Francois MODESTO, Ioannis MANIATIS - Kevin MIRALLAS, DAVID FUSTER (Djamel ABDOUN 64), Jose HOLEBAS• (Pablo ORBAIZ 37) - Rafik DJEBBOUR (Anastasios PAPAZOGLOU 90). Tr: Ernesto VALVERDE

Arsenal 1
Benayoun [57]
Lukasz FABIANSKI (Vito MANNONE 25) - Johan DJOUROU, Sebastian SQUILLACI, Thomas VERMAELEN, ANDRE SANTOS (Ignasi MIQUEL 51) - Emmanuel FRIMPONG•, Francis COQUELIN (Tomas ROSICKY 67) - Alex OXLADE-CHAMBERLAIN, Andrey ARSHAVIN, Yossi BENAYOUN - Marouane CHAMAKH. Tr: Arsene WENGER

Signal Iduna Park, Dortmund
6-12-2011, 65 000, Webb ENG
Borussia Dortmund 2
Blaszczykowski [23], Hummels [32p]
Roman WEIDENFELLER - Lukasz PISZCZEK, FELIPE SANTANA•, Mats HUMMELS, Chris LOWE - Sebastian KEHL (ANTONIO DA SILVA 32), Ilkay GUNDOGAN - Jakub BLASZCZYKOWSKI, Robert LEWANDOWSKI, Mario GOTZE (Ivan PERISIC 46) - Lucas BARRIOS (Shinji KAGAWA 63). Tr: Jurgen KLOPP

Olympique Marseille 2
Remy [45], Ayew.A [85], Valbuena [87]
Steve MANDANDA - Cesar AZPILICUETA, Souleymane DIAWARA, Djimi TRAORE - Alou DIARRA•, Stephane MBIA (Benoit CHEYROU 46) - Morgan AMALFITANO•, LUCHO GONZALEZ (Jordan AYEW 67), Andre AYEW• - Loic REMY (Matthieu VALBUENA• 73). Tr: Didier DESCHAMPS

PART THREE – THE CONTINENTAL CONFEDERATIONS

GROUP G		Pl	W	D	L	F	A	Pts	CYP	RUS	POR	UKR
APOEL Nicosia	CYP	6	2	3	1	6	6	9		2-1	2-1	0-2
Zenit St Petersburg	RUS	6	2	3	1	7	5	9	0-0		3-1	1-0
FC Porto	POR	6	2	2	2	7	7	8	1-1	0-0		2-1
Shakhtar Donetsk	UKR	6	1	2	3	6	8	5	1-1	2-2	0-2	

Estádio do Dragão, Porto
13-09-2011, 36 612, Brych GER
FC Porto 2
Hulk [28], Kleber [51]
HELTON – Jorge FUCILE, Nicolas OTAMENDI, MAICON, ALVARO PEREIRA• – Steven DEFOUR, FERNANDO (Fernando BELLUSCHI 61), JOAO MOUTINHO – HULK (VARELA 78), KLEBER (DJALMA 69), James RODRIGUEZ. Tr: VITOR PEREIRA
Shakhtar Donetsk 0
Luiz Adriano 12
Oleksandr RIBKA – Darijo SRNA•, Dmitro CHIGRINSKIY••♦90, Yaroslav RAKITSKIY♦40, Razvan RAT – FERNANDINHO, Henrikh MKHITARYAN – EDUARDO (Oleksandr KUCHER 42), JADSON (ALEX TEIXEIRA 64), WILLIAN (Tomas HUBSCHMAN 81) – LUIZ ADRIANO•. Tr: Mircea LUCESCU

GSP, Nicosia
13-09-2011, 21 269, Iturralde ESP
APOEL Nicosia 2
Manduca [73], Ailton [75]
Dionisis CHIOTIS – Savvas POURSAITIDIS (Athos SOLOMOU 74), MARCELO OLIVEIRA•, PAULO JORGE•, WILLIAM Boaventura – NUNO MORAIS•, HELIO PINTO – Ivan TRICKOVSKI, MARCINHO (Sanel JAHIC• 65), Gustavo MANDUCA (Nektarios ALEXANDROU 89), AILTON. Tr: Ivan JOVANOVIC
Zenit St Petersburg 1
Zyryanov [63]
Vyacheslav MALAFEEV – Aleksandr ANYUKOV, BRUNO ALVES••♦76, Tomas HUBOCAN (Aleksandr BUKHAROV 89), Nicolas LOMBAERTS, Domenico CRISCITO – Roman SHIROKOV (Viktor FAYZULIN 75), Igor DENISOV, Konstantin ZYRYANOV (Danko LAZOVIC 80) – DANNY•, Aleksandr KERZHAKOV. Tr: Luciano SPALLETTI

Petrovsky, St Petersburg
28-09-2011, 21 405, Webb ENG
Zenit St Petersburg 3
Shirokov 2 [20] [63], Danny [72]
Vyacheslav MALAFEEV – Aleksandr ANYUKOV, Tomas HUBOCAN•, Nicolas LOMBAERTS, Domenico CRISCITO – Konstantin ZYRYANOV (Szabolcs HUSZTI 86), Igor DENISOV, Roman SHIROKOV – Viktor FAYZULIN, Aleksandr KERZHAKOV (Aleksandr BUKHAROV 90), DANNY. Tr: Luciano SPALLETTI
FC Porto 1
Rodriguez.J [10]
HELTON – Jorge FUCILE••♦45, ROLANDO, Nicolas OTAMENDI•, ALVARO PEREIRA – FERNANDO – Fernando BELLUSCHI• (Steven DEFOUR 72), JOAO MOUTINHO – HULK, KLEBER (VARELA 33), James RODRIGUEZ (SOUZA 46). Tr: VITOR PEREIRA

Donbass Arena, Donetsk
28-09-2011, 47 014, Schorgenhofer AUT
Shakhtar Donetsk 1
Jadson [64]
Oleksandr RIBKA – Darijo SRNA•, Oleksandr CHIZHOV•, Oleksandr KUCHER, Razvan RAT• – Henrikh MKHITARYAN, Tomas HUBSCHMAN – ALEX TEIXEIRA (DOUGLAS COSTA 65), JADSON (EDUARDO 81), WILLIAN – LUIZ ADRIANO (Evgen SELEZNEV 76). Tr: Mircea LUCESCU
APOEL Nicosia 1
Trickovski [61]
Dionisis CHIOTIS – Savvas POURSAITIDIS, MARCELO OLIVEIRA, PAULO JORGE, WILLIAM Boaventura – NUNO MORAIS, Sanel JAHIC (MARCINHO• 58) – Ivan TRICKOVSKI, HELIO PINTO•, Gustavo MANDUCA (Costas CHARALAMBIDES 7) – AILTON (Esteban SOLARI 77). Tr: Ivan JOVANOVIC

Donbass Arena, Donetsk
19-10-2011, 50 578, De Bleeckere BEL
Shakhtar Donetsk 2
Willian [15], Luiz Adriano [45]
Oleksandr RIBKA – Darijo SRNA•, Oleksandr CHIZHOV• (Oleksandr KUCHER 72), Dmitro CHIGRINSKIY, Razvan RAT – FERNANDINHO, Tomas HUBSCHMAN – DOUGLAS COSTA (ALEX TEIXEIRA 75), JADSON (Henrikh MKHITARYAN 67), WILLIAN – LUIZ ADRIANO. Tr: Mircea LUCESCU
Zenit St Petersburg 2
Shirokov [33], Fayzulin [60]
Vyacheslav MALAFEEV – Tomas HUBOCAN•, BRUNO ALVES•, Nicolas LOMBAERTS, Domenico CRISCITO• – Roman SHIROKOV, Igor DENISOV, Konstantin ZYRYANOV (Sergey SEMAK 90) – Viktor FAYZULIN, Aleksandr BUKHAROV (Danko LAZOVIC 74), DANNY. Tr: Luciano SPALLETTI

Estádio do Dragão, Porto
19-10-2011, 32 512, Gautier FRA
FC Porto 1
Hulk [13]
HELTON – Cristian SAPUNARU•, ROLANDO•, Nicolas OTAMENDI•, ALVARO PEREIRA – FERNANDO (Fernando BELLUSCHI 76) – Fredy GUARIN•, JOAO MOUTINHO (Steven DEFOUR 78) – HULK•, KLEBER•, James RODRIGUEZ• (VARELA 69). Tr: VITOR PEREIRA
APOEL Nicosia 1
Ailton [19]
Dionisis CHIOTIS (Urko 52) – Savvas POURSAITIDIS, MARCELO OLIVEIRA, KAKA•, WILLIAM Boaventura – NUNO MORAIS, HELIO PINTO• – Costas CHARALAMBIDES, Ivan TRICKOVSKI• (Aldo ADORNO 90), Gustavo MANDUCA (Sanel JAHIC 72) – AILTON. Tr: Ivan JOVANOVIC

Petrovsky, St Petersburg
1-11-2011, 21 405, Lannoy FRA
Zenit St Petersburg 1
Lombaerts [45]
Vyacheslav MALAFEEV – Aleksandr ANYUKOV, Tomas HUBOCAN•, BRUNO ALVES, Nicolas LOMBAERTS, Domenico CRISCITO – Igor DENISOV•, Konstantin ZYRYANOV – Viktor FAYZULIN, Roman SHIROKOV, DANNY (Danko LAZOVIC• 85) – Aleksandr BUKHAROV (Sergey SEMAK 81). Tr: Luciano SPALLETTI
Shakhtar Donetsk 0
Oleksandr RIBKA – Darijo SRNA•, Oleksandr KUCHER, Yaroslav RAKITSKIY, Vyacheslav SHEVCHUK – Henrikh MKHITARYAN, Tomas HUBSCHMAN – ALEX TEIXEIRA (DOUGLAS COSTA 68), EDUARDO, WILLIAN• – LUIZ ADRIANO (Evgen SELEZNEV 77). Tr: Mircea LUCESCU

GSP, Nicosia
1-11-2011, 22 301, Rocchi ITA
APOEL Nicosia 2
Ailton [42p], Manduca [90]
URKO – Athos SOLOMOU, MARCELO OLIVEIRA, PAULO JORGE, Savvas POURSAITIDIS – Costas CHARALAMBIDES•, Ivan TRICKOVSKI (Esteban SOLARI 84), Gustavo MANDUCA• (Nektarios ALEXANDROU 90) – AILTON (Sanel JAHIC 76). Tr: Ivan JOVANOVIC
FC Porto 1
Hulk [89p]
HELTON – Jorge FUCILE, ROLANDO, Eliaquim MANGALA•, ALVARO PEREIRA – FERNANDO (Fredy GUARIN 59) – Fernando BELLUSCHI (Steven DEFOUR 76), JOAO MOUTINHO – HULK, KLEBER, VARELA• (James RODRIGUEZ 59). Tr: Vitor PEREIRA

Petrovsky, St Petersburg
23-11-2011, 21 500, Brych GER
Zenit St Petersburg 0
Vyacheslav MALAFEEV – Aleksandr ANYUKOV, Tomas HUBOCAN•, Nicolas LOMBAERTS•, Domenico CRISCITO – Konstantin ZYRYANOV (Vladimir BYSTROV 55), Igor DENISOV, Roman SHIROKOV (Danko LAZOVIC 88) – Viktor FAYZULIN, Aleksandr BUKHAROV, DANNY. Tr: Luciano SPALLETTI
APOEL Nicosia 0
URKO – Athos SOLOMOU, MARCELO OLIVEIRA, PAULO JORGE•, Nektarios ALEXANDROU• (Marios ELIA• 46) – NUNO MORAIS, HELIO PINTO – Costas CHARALAMBIDES, Ivan TRICKOVSKI (Aldo ADORNO 90), Gustavo MANDUCA – AILTON (Sanel JAHIC 67), Tr: Ivan JOVANOVIC

Donbass Arena, Donetsk
23-11-2011, 42 565, Thomson SCO
Shakhtar Donetsk 0
Oleksandr RIBKA – Vasiliy KOBIN• (DOUGLAS COSTA 87), Oleksandr KUCHER, Yaroslav RAKITSKIY, Razvan RAT – FERNANDINHO, Tomas HUBSCHMAN – EDUARDO• (JADSON• 59), Henrikh MKHITARYAN, WILLIAN (ALEX TEIXEIRA 69) – LUIZ ADRIANO. Tr: Mircea LUCESCU
FC Porto 2
Hulk [79], OG [92+]
HELTON – MAICON, ROLANDO, Nicolas OTAMENDI, ALVARO PEREIRA, FERNANDO – Fredy GUARIN•, DJALMA (Cristian RODRIGUEZ 74), Steven DEFOUR (SOUZA 88), James RODRIGUEZ• (VARELA 81) – HULK. Tr: VITOR PEREIRA

Estádio do Dragão, Porto
6-12-2011, 46 512, Carballo ESP
FC Porto 0
HELTON• – MAICON, ROLANDO, Nicolas OTAMENDI• (Fernando BELLUSCHI 82), ALVARO PEREIRA – FERNANDO, JOAO MOUTINHO – DJALMA (VARELA 68), Steven DEFOUR (KLEBER 46), James RODRIGUEZ – HULK•. Tr: VITOR PEREIRA
Zenit St Petersburg 0
Vyacheslav MALAFEEV – Aleksandr ANYUKOV, Tomas HUBOCAN, Nicolas LOMBAERTS, Domenico CRISCITO – Igor DENISOV – Sergey SEMAK, Viktor FAYZULIN• (Vladimir BYSTROV 58), Roman SHIROKOV (Konstantin ZYRYANOV 46), DANNY – Danko LAZOVIC (BRUNO ALVES 82). Tr: Luciano SPALLETTI

GSP, Nicosia
6-12-2011, 22 537, Hategan ROU
APOEL Nicosia 0
URKO – Savvas POURSAITIDIS, MARCELO OLIVEIRA•, PAULO JORGE, Nektarios ALEXANDROU• – NUNO MORAIS, Sanel JAHIC – Costas CHARALAMBIDES (Aldo ADORNO 77), MARCINHO (Tijani BELAID 60), Gustavo MANDUCA (Esteban SOLARI• 68) – Ivan TRICKOVSKI•. Tr: Ivan JOVANOVIC
Shakhtar Donetsk 2
Luiz Adriano [62], Seleznyov [78]
Oleksandr RIBKA – Darijo SRNA, Oleksandr KUCHER, Yaroslav RAKITSKIY•, Vyacheslav SHEVCHUK• – FERNANDINHO, Tomas HUBSCHMAN – DOUGLAS COSTA (EDUARDO 78), Henrikh MKHITARYAN•, WILLIAN (Marcelo MORENO 84) – LUIZ ADRIANO (Evgen SELEZNEV 73). Tr: Mircea LUCESCU

UEFA CHAMPIONS LEAGUE 2011-12

GROUP H		Pl	W	D	L	F	A	Pts	ESP	ITA	CZE	BLR
Barcelona	ESP	6	5	1	0	20	4	16		2-2	2-0	4-0
Milan	ITA	6	2	3	1	11	8	9	2-3		2-0	2-0
Viktoria Plzen	CZE	6	1	2	3	4	11	5	0-4	2-2		1-1
BATE Borisov	BLR	6	0	2	4	2	14	2	0-5	1-1	0-1	

Camp Nou, Barcelona
13-09-2011, 89 861, Atkinson ENG
Barcelona 2
Pedro [36], Villa [50]
VICTOR VALDES - DANI ALVES•, Javier MASCHERANO, Sergio BUSQUETS, Eric ABIDAL - XAVI, Andres INIESTA (Cesc FABREGAS 39) - PEDRO Rodriguez, Lionel MESSI, DAVID VILLA• (Ibrahim AFELLAY 84). Tr: Josep GUARDIOLA
Milan 2
Pato [1], Thiago Silva [92+]
Christian ABBIATI - Ignazio ABATE, Alessandro NESTA•, THIAGO SILVA, Gianluca ZAMBROTTA - Antonio NOCERINO, Mark VAN BOMMEL• (Alberto AQUILANI 78), Clarence SEEDORF - Kevin Prince BOATENG (Massimo AMBROSINI 34) - Antonio CASSANO (Urby EMANUELSON 62), Alexandre PATO. Tr: Massimiliano ALLEGRI

Eden, Prague
13-09-2011, 19 541, Duhamel FRA
Viktoria Plzen 1
Bakos [45]
Marek CECH - Frantisek RAJTORAL, Marian CISOVSKY, David BYSTRON, David LIMBERSKY (Petr TRAPP 79) - Pavel HORVATH, Petr JIRACEK - Milan PETRZELA (Michal DURIS 70), Daniel KOLAR•, Vaclav PILAR• (Jakub HORA 88) - Marek BAKOS. Tr: Pavel VRBA
BATE Borisov 1
Bressan [69]
Aleksandr GUTOR - Aleksandr VOLODKO, Egor FILIPENKO, Marko SIMIC•, Maksim BORDACHEV - Filipp RUDIK, Edgar OLEKHNOVICH• - RENAN BRESSAN• (Artem KONTSEVOY 72), Dmitriy BAGA, Mikhail GORDEYCHUK (Maksim VOLODKO 83) - Mateja KEZMAN (Alex PORFIRIO 76). Tr: Viktor GONCHARENKO

Dinamo, Minsk
28-09-2011, 29 555, Grafe GER
BATE Borisov 0
Aleksandr GUTOR - Aleksandr VOLODKO, Egor FILIPENKO, Marko SIMIC•, Maksim BORDACHEV - Dmitriy BAGA, Edgar OLEKHNOVICH, Filipp RUDIK (Kirill ALEKSIYAN 60), RENAN BRESSAN (Vadim KURLOVICH 81), Artem KONTSEVOY - Mateja KEZMAN (Maksim SKAVYSH 56). Tr: Viktor GONCHARENKO
Barcelona 5
OG [19], Pedro [22], Messi 2 [38,56], Villa [90]
VICTOR VALDES - DANI ALVES•, Javier MASCHERANO, Carles PUYOL, Eric ABIDAL (ADRIANO 61) - THIAGO Alcantara, XAVI (Cesc FABREGAS 59), Seydou KEITA - PEDRO Rodriguez (MAXWELL 68), Lionel MESSI, DAVID VILLA. Tr: Josep GUARDIOLA

San Siro, Milan
28-09-2011, 66 859, Meyer GER
Milan 2
Ibrahimovic [53p], Cassano [66]
Christian ABBIATI - Ignazio ABATE (Mattia DE SCIGLIO 87), Alessandro NESTA, THIAGO SILVA, Luca ANTONINI (Taye TAIWO 78) - Antonio NOCERINO, Mark VAN BOMMEL, Clarence SEEDORF (Alberto AQUILANI 70) - Urby EMANUELSON - Zlatan IBRAHIMOVIC, Antonio CASSANO. Tr: Massimiliano ALLEGRI
Viktoria Plzen 0
Marek CECH - Frantisek RAJTORAL, David BYSTRON, Marian CISOVSKY•, David LIMBERSKY - Petr JIRACEK, Pavel HORVATH• - Milan PETRZELA•, Daniel KOLAR (Vladimir DARIDA 90), Vaclav PILAR (Martin FILLO 76) - Marek BAKOS (Michal DURIS 67). Tr: Pavel VRBA

San Siro, Milan
19-10-2011, 66 040, Hagen NOR
Milan 2
Ibrahimovic [33], Boateng [70]
Christian ABBIATI - Ignazio ABATE, Alessandro NESTA (Philippe MEXES 85), Daniele BONERA•, Taye TAIWO - Alberto AQUILANI, Mark VAN BOMMEL, Antonio NOCERINO• - Kevin Prince BOATENG (Urby EMANUELSON 79) - Zlatan IBRAHIMOVIC, Antonio CASSANO (ROBINHO 62). Tr: Massimiliano ALLEGRI
BATE Borisov 0
Aleksandr GUTOR - Dmitriy BAGA, Artem RADKOV, Marko SIMIC•, Aleksandr YUREVICH - Aleksandr VOLODKO, Dmitriy LIKHTAROVICH (Edgar OLEKHNOVICH 66) - Artem KONTSEVOY, RENAN BRESSAN (Aleksandr PAVLOV 78), Maksim BORDACHEV• - Mateja KEZMAN (Maksim SKAVYSH 70). Tr: Viktor GONCHARENKO

Camp Nou, Barcelona
19-10-2011, 74 376, Stavrev MKD
Barcelona 2
Iniesta [10], Villa [82]
VICTOR VALDES - DANI ALVES, Javier MASCHERANO, ADRIANO, Eric ABIDAL - XAVI, Sergio BUSQUETS, Andres INIESTA (Seydou KEITA 85) - PEDRO Rodriguez, Lionel MESSI, DAVID VILLA (Isaac CUENCA 88). Tr: Josep GUARDIOLA
Viktoria Plzen 0
Marek CECH - Frantisek RAJTORAL, Marian CISOVSKY, David BYSTRON, David LIMBERSKY - Milan PETRZELA (Vladimir DARIDA 86), Pavel HORVATH, Petr JIRACEK, Vaclav PILAR (Martin FILLO 75) - Daniel KOLAR - Marek BAKOS (Michal DURIS 58). Tr: Pavel VRBA

Dinamo, Minsk
1-11-2011, 29 100, Rasmussen DEN
BATE Borisov 1
Bressan [55p]
Aleksandr GUTOR - Aleksandr YUREVICH, Artem RADKOV, Marko SIMIC, Maksim BORDACHEV - Aleksandr VOLODKO, Dmitriy LIKHTAROVICH (Edgar OLEKHNOVICH 63) - Artem KONTSEVOY (Mikhail GORDEYCHUK 84), Renan BRESSAN, Dmitriy BAGA (Aleksandr PAVLOV 76) - Maksim SKAVYSH. Tr: Viktor GONCHARENKO
Milan 1
Ibrahimovic [22]
Christian ABBIATI - Ignazio ABATE, Alessandro NESTA (Daniele BONERA 67), Mark VAN BOMMEL, Taye TAIWO - Alberto AQUILANI (Clarence SEEDORF 69), Massimo AMBROSINI•, Antonio NOCERINO - Kevin Prince BOATENG - Zlatan IBRAHIMOVIC, ROBINHO (Simone GANZ 83). Tr: Massimiliano ALLEGRI

Eden, Prague
1-11-2011, 20 145, Schorgenhofer AUT
Viktoria Plzen 0
Roman PAVLIK• - Frantisek RAJTORAL, Marian CISOVSKY♦22, David BYSTRON, David LIMBERSKY• - Pavel HORVATH• (Radim REZNIK 78), Petr JIRACEK• - Milan PETRZELA, Daniel KOLAR (Michal DURIS 68), Vaclav PILAR• - Marek BAKOS (Frantisek SEVINSKY 24). Tr: Pavel VRBA
Barcelona 4
Messi 3 [24p,45,92+], Fabregas [72]
VICTOR VALDES - DANI ALVES• (MAXWELL 70), Gerard PIQUE, Carles PUYOL, Eric ABIDAL (ALEXIS SANCHEZ 73) - THIAGO Alcantara, Sergio BUSQUETS (Seydou KEITA 65), Cesc FABREGAS - Isaac CUENCA, Lionel MESSI, ADRIANO. Tr: Josep GUARDIOLA

Dinamo, Minsk
23-11-2011, 26 520, Blom NED
BATE Borisov 0
Aleksandr GUTOR - Aleksandr YUREVICH, Egor FILIPENKO, Marko SIMIC, Aleksandr PAVLOV - Dmitriy BAGA, Aleksandr PAVLOV• (Mikhail GORDEYCHUK 69), Maksim VOLODKO, RENAN BRESSAN, Artem KONTSEVOY (Filipp RUDIK 75) - Maksim SKAVYSH (Mateja KEZMAN 77). Tr: Viktor GONCHARENKO
Viktoria Plzen 1
Bakos [42]
Marek CECH - Frantisek RAJTORAL, Frantisek SEVINSKY, David BYSTRON•, David LIMBERSKY, Petr JIRACEK - Milan PETRZELA (Martin FILLO 83), Daniel KOLAR, Vaclav PILAR (Radim REZNIK 90) - Marek BAKOS• (Michal DURIS 79). Tr: Pavel VRBA

San Siro, Milan
23-11-2011, 78 927, Stark GER
Milan 2
Ibrahimovic [20], Boateng [54]
Christian ABBIATI - Ignazio ABATE, Alessandro NESTA (Daniele BONERA 66), THIAGO SILVA, Gianluca ZAMBROTTA• - Alberto AQUILANI•♦♦30, Mark VAN BOMMEL• (Antonio NOCERINO 72), Clarence SEEDORF - Kevin Prince BOATENG - Zlatan IBRAHIMOVIC, ROBINHO (Alexandre PATO 46). Tr: Massimiliano ALLEGRI
Barcelona 3
OG [14], Messi [31p], Xavi [63]
VICTOR VALDES - Carles PUYOL•, Javier MASCHERANO•, Eric ABIDAL• - XAVI, Sergio BUSQUETS, Cesc FABREGAS (PEDRO Rodriguez 80), Seydou KEITA - THIAGO Alcantara (JONATHAN dos Santos 90), Lionel MESSI•, DAVID VILLA (ALEXIS SANCHEZ 68). Tr: Josep GUARDIOLA

Camp Nou, Barcelona
6-12-2011, 37 374, Collum SCO
Barcelona 4
Roberto [35], Montoya [60], Pedro 2 [63,89p]
Jose Manuel PINTO - Martin MONTOYA, Marc BARTRA, Andreu FONTAS, MAXWELL - SERGI ROBERTO (Marti RIVEROLA 80), JONATHAN dos Santos (Marc MUNIESA 59), THIAGO Alcantara - Isaac CUENCA, RAFINHA (Gerard DEULOFEU 71), PEDRO Rodriguez. Tr: Josep GUARDIOLA
BATE Borisov 0
Aleksandr GUTOR - Aleksandr YUREVICH•, Egor FILIPENKO, Marko SIMIC, Maksim BORDACHEV - Aleksandr PAVLOV (Mikhail GORDEYCHUK 64), Dmitriy BAGA, Dmitriy LIKHTAROVICH (Edgar OLEKHNOVICH 67), Maksim VOLODKO - RENAN BRESSAN (Mateja KEZMAN 78), Artem KONTSEVOY. Tr: Viktor GONCHARENKO

Eden, Prague
6-12-2011, 19 854, Vad HUN
Viktoria Plzen 2
Bystron [89], Duris [93+]
Marek CECH - Frantisek RAJTORAL, David BYSTRON, Marian CISOVSKY, David LIMBERSKY - Petr JIRACEK (Vladimir DARIDA 28), Pavel HORVATH - Milan PETRZELA, Daniel KOLAR (Michal DURIS• 67), Vaclav PILAR (Jakub HORA 84) - Marek BAKOS•. Tr: Pavel VRBA
Milan 2
Pato [47], Robinho [49]
Marco AMELIA - Mattia DE SCIGLIO, Philippe MEXES, Daniele BONERA, Taye TAIWO (Gianluca ZAMBROTTA 90) - Urby EMANUELSON, Massimo AMBROSINI•, Antonio NOCERINO (THIAGO SILVA 40) - Clarence SEEDORF, Alexandre PATO, ROBINHO (Bryan CRISTANTE 81). Tr: Massimiliano ALLEGRI

ROUND OF SIXTEEN

San Paolo, Naples
21-02-2012, Att: 52 495, Ref: Carballo ESP

Napoli 3
Lavezzi 2 [38] [65], Cavani [45]

Morgan DE SANCTIS - Hugo CAMPAGNARO, Paolo CANNAVARO, Salvatore ARONICA - Christian MAGGIO, Gokhan INLER, Walter GARGANO, Juan ZUNIGA - Marek HAMSIK (Goran PANDEV 82), Ezequiel LAVEZZI (Blerim DZEMAILI 74) - Edinson CAVANI•. Tr: Walter MAZZARRI

Chelsea 1
Mata [27]

Petr CECH - Branislav IVANOVIC, Gary CAHILL•, DAVID LUIZ, Jose BOSINGWA (Ashley COLE 12) - RAMIRES, RAUL MEIRELES• (Frank LAMPARD 70) - Daniel STURRIDGE, Juan MATA, Florent MALOUDA (Michael ESSIEN 70) - Didier DROGBA. Tr: Andre VILLAS BOAS

Stamford Bridge, London
14-03-2012, Att: 37 784, Ref: Brych GER

Chelsea 4
Drogba [28], Terry [47], Lampard [75p], Ivanovic [105]

Petr CECH - Branislav IVANOVIC, DAVID LUIZ, John TERRY (Jose BOSINGWA 98), Ashley COLE• - Michael ESSIEN, Frank LAMPARD• - Daniel STURRIDGE (FERNANDO TORRES 63), Juan MATA (Florent MALOUDA 95), RAMIRES - Didier DROGBA. Tr: Roberto DI MATTEO

Napoli 1
Inler [55]

Morgan DE SANCTIS - Hugo CAMPAGNARO•, Paolo CANNAVARO•, Salvatore ARONICA (Eduardo VARGAS 110) - Christian MAGGIO (Andrea DOSSENA• 37), Gokhan INLER•, Walter GARGANO, Juan ZUNIGA - Marek HAMSIK (Goran PANDEV 106), Ezequiel LAVEZZI - Edinson CAVANI. Tr: Walter MAZZARRI

Petrovsky, St Petersburg
15-02-2012, Att: 18 200, Ref: Eriksson SWE

Zenit St Petersburg 3
Shirokov 2 [27] [88], Semak [71]

Yuriy ZHEVNOV - Aleksandr ANYUKOV•, BRUNO ALVES•, Nicolas LOMBAERTS, Tomas HUBOCAN - Roman SHIROKOV, Igor DENISOV, Konstantin ZYRYANOV (Sergey SEMAK 46) - Maksim KANUNNIKOV (Vladimir BYSTROV 66), Aleksandr KERZHAKOV, Viktor FAYZULIN (Alessandro ROSINA 89). Tr: Luciano SPALLETTI

Benfica 2
Pereira [21], Cardozo [87]

ARTUR Moares - MAXI PEREIRA, LUISAO•, Ezequiel GARAY, EMERSON - Nemanja MATIC - Nicolas GAITAN (MIGUEL VITOR 90), Axel WITSEL, BRUNO CESAR• (NOLITO 76) - RODRIGO Moreno (Pablo AIMAR• 30), Oscar CARDOZO. Tr: JORGE JESUS

Estádio da Luz, Lisbon
6-03-2012, Att: 48 909, Ref: Webb ENG

Benfica 2
Pereira [45], Oliveira [93+]

ARTUR Moares - MAXI PEREIRA, LUISAO•, JARDEL, EMERSON - JAVI GARCIA• - BRUNO CESAR, Axel WITSEL, Nicolas GAITAN (Nemanja MATIC 72) - RODRIGO Moreno (NOLITO 62), Oscar CARDOZO (NELSON OLIVEIRA• 80). Tr: JORGE JESUS

Zenit St Petersburg 0

Vyacheslav MALAFEEV - Aleksandr ANYUKOV• (BRUNO ALVES 53), Tomas HUBOCAN, Nicolas LOMBAERTS, Domenico CRISCITO - Igor DENISOV• - Vladimir BYSTROV (Danko LAZOVIC 46), Roman SHIROKOV, Konstantin ZYRYANOV (Viktor FAYZULIN 70), Sergey SEMAK - Aleksandr KERZHAKOV. Tr: Luciano SPALLETTI

San Siro, Milan
15-02-2012, Att: 64 462, Ref: Kassai HUN

Milan 4
Boateng [15], Robinho 2 [38] [49], Ibrahimovic [79p]

Christian ABBIATI - Ignazio ABATE, Philippe MEXES•, THIAGO SILVA, Luca ANTONINI• - Antonio NOCERINO, Mark VAN BOMMEL, Clarence SEEDORF (Urby EMANUELSON 12), Kevin Prince BOATENG (Massimo AMBROSINI• 70) - Zlatan IBRAHIMOVIC, ROBINHO (Alexandre PATO 84). Tr: Massimiliano ALLEGRI

Arsenal 0

Wojciech SZCZESNY - Bacary SAGNA, Laurent KOSCIELNY (Johan DJOUROU• 44), Thomas VERMAELEN, Kieran GIBBS (Alex OXLADE-CHAMBERLAIN 66) - Alex SONG•, Mikel ARTETA - Theo WALCOTT (Thierry HENRY 46), Aaron RAMSEY, Tomas ROSICKY - Robin VAN PERSIE. Tr: Arsene WENGER

Emirates, London
6-03-2012, Att: 59 973, Ref: Skomina SVN

Arsenal 3
Koscielny [7], Rosicky [26], Van Persie [43p]

Wojciech SZCZESNY - Bacary SAGNA•, Laurent KOSCIELNY, Thomas VERMAELEN, Kieran GIBBS• - Alex SONG•, Alex OXLADE-CHAMBERLAIN (Marouane CHAMAKH 75) - Theo WALCOTT (PARK Chu Young 84), Tomas ROSICKY, GERVINHO - Robin VAN PERSIE. Tr: Arsene WENGER

Milan 0

Christian ABBIATI - Ignazio ABATE•, Philippe MEXES•, THIAGO SILVA, Djamel MESBAH (Daniele BONERA 90) - Antonio NOCERINO•, Mark VAN BOMMEL•, Urby EMANUELSON - ROBINHO, Zlatan IBRAHIMOVIC•, Stephan EL SHAARAWY (Alberto AQUILANI 70). Tr: Massimiliano ALLEGRI

BayArena, Leverkusen
14-02-2012, Att: 29 412, Ref: Thomson SCO

Bayer Leverkusen 1
Kadlec [52]

Bernd LENO - Vedran CORLUKA• (Danny DA COSTA 90), Daniel SCHWAAB•, Manuel FRIEDRICH, Michal KADLEC - Stefan REINARTZ - RENATO AUGUSTO, Lars BENDER, Simon ROLFES (Stefan KIEBLING 76), Gonzalo CASTRO• - Andre SCHURRLE (Karim BELLARABI 89). Tr: Robin DUTT

Barcelona 3
Sanchez 2 [41] [55], Messi [88]

VICTOR VALDES - DANI ALVES, Carles PUYOL, Javier MASCHERANO, Eric ABIDAL - Cesc FABREGAS, Sergio BUSQUETS, Andres INIESTA (THIAGO Alcantara• 60) - ALEXIS SANCHEZ (Isaac CUENCA 85), Lionel MESSI, ADRIANO (PEDRO Rodriguez 68). Tr: Josep GUARDIOLA

Camp Nou, Barcelona
7-03-2012, Att: 75 632, Ref: Moen NOR

Barcelona 7
Messi 5 [25] [43] [49] [58] [85], Tello 2 [55] [62]

VICTOR VALDES - DANI ALVES, Gerard PIQUE, Javier MASCHERANO, ADRIANO (Marc MUNIESA 63) - XAVI (Seydou KEITA 53), Sergio BUSQUETS, Cesc FABREGAS - PEDRO Rodriguez, Lionel MESSI, Andres INIESTA (Cristian TELLO 53). Tr: Josep GUARDIOLA

Bayer Leverkusen 1
Bellaribi [91+]

Bernd LENO - Gonzalo CASTRO•, Daniel SCHWAAB, OMER Toprak, Michal KADLEC - RENATO AUGUSTO (Bastian OCZIPKA 67), Stefan REINARTZ, Simon ROLFES•, Lars BENDER (Karim BELLARABI 55) - Stefan KIEBLING - Eren DERDIYOK (Andre SCHURRLE 55). Tr: Robin DUTT

Luzhniki, Moscow
21-02-2012, Att: 70 000, Ref: Kuipers NED

CSKA Moskva 1
Wernbloom [93+]

Sergey CHEPCHUGOV - Aleksey BEREZUTSKIY, Vasiliy BEREZUTSKIY, Sergey IGNASHEVICH, Georgiy SHCHENNIKOV - Pontus WERNBLOOM•, Evgeniy ALDONIN (Keisuke HONDA 68) - Ahmad MUSA (Sekou OLISEH 64), Alan DZAGOEV, Zoran TOSIC (Tomas NECID 82) - Seydou DOUMBIA. Tr: Leonid SLUTSKIY

Real Madrid 1
Ronaldo [28]

Iker CASILLAS - Alvaro ARBELOA, PEPE, SERGIO RAMOS•, FABIO COENTRAO• - Sami KHEDIRA, XABI ALONSO• - Jose CALLEJON (KAKA 75), Mesut OZIL (Raul ALBIOL 85), CRISTIANO RONALDO - Karim BENZEMA (Gonzalo HIGUAIN 16), Tr: Jose MOURINHO

Bernabéu, Madrid
14-03-2012, Att: 67 743, Ref: Lannoy FRA

Real Madrid 4
Higuain [26], Ronaldo 2 [55] [94+], Benzema [70]

Iker CASILLAS - Alvaro ARBELOA, PEPE, SERGIO RAMOS, MARCELO - Sami KHEDIRA, XABI ALONSO• - Mesut OZIL (Lassana DIARRA 88), KAKA (Esteban GRANERO 76), CRISTIANO RONALDO - Gonzalo HIGUAIN (Karim BENZEMA 69). Tr: Jose MOURINHO

CSKA Moskva 1
Tosic [77]

Sergey CHEPCHUGOV• - Aleksey BEREZUTSKIY, Vasiliy BEREZUTSKIY•, Sergey IGNASHEVICH, Georgiy SHCHENNIKOV - Ahmad MUSA• (Sekou OLISEH 60), Pontus WERNBLOOM, Evgeniy ALDONIN (Pavel MAMAEV• 46), Zoran TOSIC (Tomas NECID 81) - Alan DZAGOEV, Seydou DOUMBIA. Tr: Leonid SLUTSKIY

Stade de Gerland, Lyon
14-02-2012, Att: 32 010, Ref: Tagliavento ITA

Olympique Lyonnais 1
Lacazette [58]

Hugo LLORIS - Anthony REVEILLERE, Bakary KONE, CRIS, Aly CISSOKHO - Maxime GONALONS, Kim KALLSTROM - Alexandre LACAZETTE (Jimmy BRIAND 59), EDERSON (Yoann GOURCUFF 71), MICHEL BASTOS - LISANDRO LOPEZ. Tr: Remi GARDE

APOEL Nicosia 0

Dionisis CHIOTIS - Savvas POURSAITIDIS, PAULO JORGE, KAKA, WILLIAM Boaventura - NUNO MORAIS - Costas CHARALAMBIDES (Gustavo MANDUCA 82), HELDER SOUSA (MARCINHO 72), HELIO PINTO•, Ivan TRICKOVSKI, AILTON (Esteban SOLARI 68). Tr: Ivan JOVANOVIC

GSP, Nicosia
7-03-2012, Att: 22 701, Ref: Undiano ESP

APOEL Nicosia 1 4p
Manduca [9]

Dionisis CHIOTIS - Savvas POURSAITIDIS, MARCELO OLIVEIRA, PAULO JORGE, WILLIAM Boaventura - NUNO MORAIS, HELDER SOUSA (Nektarios ALEXANDROU 94) - Costas CHARALAMBIDES (MARCINHO 77), Esteban SOLARI• (Ivan TRICKOVSKI 74), Gustavo MANDUCA•• 115 - AILTON•. Tr: Ivan Jovanovic

Olympique Lyonnais 0 3p

Hugo LLORIS - Anthony REVEILLERE, Bakary KONE•, CRIS, Aly CISSOKHO - Maxime GONALONS•, Kim KALLSTROM - Jimmy BRIAND (Alexandre LACAZETTE 100), EDERSON (Bafetimbi GOMIS 73), MICHEL BASTOS• - LISANDRO LOPEZ. Tr: Reme GARDE

UEFA CHAMPIONS LEAGUE 2011-12

Vélodrome, Marseille
22-02-2012, Att: 37 646, Ref: Cakir TUR
Olympique Marseille 1
Ayew.A [93]

Steve MANDANDA - Cesar AZPILICUETA (Rod FANNI 80), Souleymane DIAWARA•, Nicolas N'KOULOU, Jeremy MOREL - Alou DIARRA, Benoit CHEYROU (Charles KABORE 84) - Morgan AMALFITANO, Matthieu VALBUENA, Andre AYEW - BRANDAO (Jordan AYEW 73). Tr: Didier DESCHAMPS

Internazionale 0

JULIO CESAR - MAICON (Yuto NAGATOMO 46), LUCIO, Walter SAMUEL, Cristian CHIVU• - Javier ZANETTI•, Dejan STANKOVIC•, Esteban CAMBIASSO - Wesley SNEIJDER - Diego FORLAN, Mauro ZARATE• (Joel OBI 63). Tr: Claudio RANIERI

San Siro, Milan
13-03-2012, Att: 62 632, Ref: Proenca POR
Internazionale 2
Milito [75], Pazzini [96+p]

JULIO CESAR - MAICON, LUCIO, Walter SAMUEL•, Yuto NAGATOMO - Javier ZANETTI•, Dejan STANKOVIC•, Andrea POLI (Esteban CAMBIASSO 74) - Wesley SNEIJDER (Joel OBI 58) - Diego FORLAN (Giampaolo PAZZINI 58), Diego MILITO. Tr: Claudio RANIERI

Olympique Marseille 1
Brandao [92+]

Steve MANDANDA••♦90 - Cesar AZPILICUETA, Souleymane DIAWARA•, Nicolas N'KOULOU, Jeremy MOREL - Alou DIARRA, Stephane MBIA - Morgan AMALFITANO, Matthieu VALBUENA (Benoit CHEYROU 76), Andre AYEW (Gennaro BRACIGLIANO 90), Loic REMY (BRANDAO 88). Tr: Didier DESCHAMPS

St Jakob-Park, Basel
22-02-2012, Att: 36 000, Ref: Rizzoli ITA
FC Basel 1
Stocker [86]

Yann SOMMER - Markus STEINHOFER, David ABRAHAM•, Aleksandar DRAGOVIC, PARK Joo Ho - Xherdan SHAQIRI (Jacques ZOUA 83), Benjamin HUGGEL, Granit XHAKA, Fabian FREI (Valentin STOCKER 65) - Marco STRELLER, Alexander FREI (Adilson CABRAL 89). Tr: Heiko VOGEL

Bayern München 0

Manuel NEUER - RAFINHA•, Jerome BOATENG, Holger BADSTUBER, Philipp LAHM - Anatoliy TYMOSHCHUK, David ALABA - Arjen ROBBEN, Toni KROOS (Ivica OLIC 88), Franck RIBERY (Thomas MULLER• 71) - Mario GOMEZ. Tr: Jupp HEYNCKES

PENALTIES
ROUND OF 16
APOEL 4-3 LYON

APOEL		Lyon
	Kallstrom	✓
✓ Ailton		
	Morais	✓
✓ Lisandro		
	Gomis	✓
✓ Alexandrou		
	Lacazette	✗
✓ Trickovski		
	Bastos	✗

Allianz Arena, Munich
13-03-2012, Att: 66 000, Ref: Clattenburg
Bayern München 7
Robben 2 [11 81], Muller [42], Gomez 4 [44 50 61 67]

Manuel NEUER - Philipp LAHM, Jerome BOATENG•, Holger BADSTUBER, David ALABA - LUIZ GUSTAVO, Toni KROOS - Arjen ROBBEN (Anatoliy TYMOSHCHUK 82), Thomas MULLER (Bastian SCHWEINSTEIGER 70), Franck RIBERY (Danijel PRANJIC 78) - Mario GOMEZ. Tr: Jupp HEYNCKES

FC Basel 0

Yann SOMMER - Markus STEINHOFER (Philipp DEGEN 70), David ABRAHAM, Aleksandar DRAGOVIC, PARK Joo Ho - Xherdan SHAQIRI (Jacques ZOUA 50), Adilson CABRAL•, Granit XHAKA, Fabian FREI (Valentin STOCKER 61) - Marco STRELLER•, Alexander FREI. Tr: Heiko VOGEL

PENALTIES
SEMI-FINAL
REAL 1-3 BAYERN

Real		Bayern
	Alaba	✓
✗ Ronaldo		
	Gomez	✓
✗ Kaka		
	Kroos	✗
✓ Alonso		
	Lahm	✗
✗ Ramos		
	Schweinsteiger	✓

QUARTER-FINALS

Estádio da Luz, Lisbon
27-03-2012, Att: 60 830, Ref: Tagliavento ITA
Benfica 0

ARTUR Moares - MAXI PEREIRA, LUISAO•, JARDEL, EMERSON - JAVI GARCIA• (NOLITO 81) - Nicolas GAITAN, Axel WITSEL, BRUNO CESAR• (Nemanja MATIC 69) - Pablo AIMAR (RODRIGO Moreno 69) - Oscar CARDOZO. Tr: JORGE JESUS

Chelsea 1
Kalou [75]

Petr CECH - PAULO FERREIRA (Jose BOSINGWA 80), DAVID LUIZ, John TERRY, Ashley COLE - RAUL MEIRELES• (Frank LAMPARD 68), John MIKEL - RAMIRES, Juan MATA, Salomon KALOU (Daniel STURRIDGE 82) - FERNANDO TORRES. Tr: Roberto DI MATTEO

Stamford Bridge, London
4-04-2012, Att: 37 264, Ref: Skomina SVN
Chelsea 2
Lampard [21p], Meireles [93+]

Petr CECH - Branislav IVANOVIC•, DAVID LUIZ, John TERRY (Gary CAHILL 60), Ashley COLE - John MIKEL•, Frank LAMPARD - RAMIRES•, Juan MATA (RAUL MEIRELES 80), Salomon KALOU, FERNANDO TORRES (Didier DROGBA 70). Tr: Roberto DI MATTEO

Benfica 1
Garcia [85]

ARTUR Moares - MAXI PEREIRA••♦40, JAVI GARCIA, EMERSON, Joan CAPDEVILA - Nemanja MATIC - BRUNO CESAR• (RODRIGO Moreno 72), Axel WITSEL, Nicolas GAITAN (Yannick DJALO 61) - Pablo AIMAR• - Oscar CARDOZO• (NELSON OLIVEIRA 57). Tr: JORGE JESUS

San Siro, Milan
28-03-2012, Att: 76 169, Ref: Eriksson SWE
Milan 0

Christian ABBIATI - Daniele BONERA, Philippe MEXES, Alessandro NESTA• (Djamel MESBAH 75), Luca ANTONINI - Antonio NOCERINO, Massimo AMBROSINI•, Clarence SEEDORF• - Kevin Prince BOATENG (Urby EMANUELSON 67) - Zlatan IBRAHIMOVIC, ROBINHO (Stephan EL SHAARAWY 52). Tr: Massimiliano ALLEGRI

Barcelona 0

VICTOR VALDES - Javier MASCHERANO, Gerard PIQUE, Carles PUYOL - DANI ALVES, Sergio BUSQUETS, Seydou KEITA• - XAVI - ALEXIS SANCHEZ (PEDRO Rodriguez 76), Lionel MESSI, Andres INIESTA (Cristian TELLO 65). Tr: Josep GUARDIOLA

Camp Nou, Barcelona
3-04-2012, Att: 94 629, Ref: Kuipers NED
Barcelona 3
Messi 2 [11p 41p], Iniesta [53]

VICTOR VALDES - Javier MASCHERANO•, Gerard PIQUE (ADRIANO 75), Carles PUYOL - XAVI (THIAGO Alcantara 63), Sergio BUSQUETS, Andres INIESTA - DANI ALVES, Cesc FABREGAS (Seydou KEITA 78), Isaac CUENCA• - Lionel MESSI. Tr: Josep GUARDIOLA

Milan 1
Nocerino [32]

Christian ABBIATI - Ignazio ABATE, Philippe MEXES•, Alessandro NESTA•, Luca ANTONINI• - Antonio NOCERINO•, Massimo AMBROSINI, Clarence SEEDORF• (Alberto AQUILANI 61) - Kevin Prince BOATENG (PATO 70) (MAXI LOPEZ• 83) - Zlatan IBRAHIMOVIC, ROBINHO•. Tr: Massimiliano ALLEGRI

GSP, Nicosia
27-03-2012, Att: 22 385, Ref: Brych GER
APOEL Nicosia 0

Dionisis CHIOTIS - Savvas POURSAITIDIS, MARCELO OLIVEIRA (KAKA 13), PAULO JORGE, WILLIAM Boaventura - Costas CHARALAMBIDES, NUNO MORAIS, HELIO PINTO (Esteban SOLARI 72), Nektarios ALEXANDROU (HELDER SOUSA 46) - Ivan TRICKOVSKI - AILTON, Tr: Ivan JOVANOVIC

Real Madrid 3
Benzema 2 [74][90], Kaka [82]

Iker CASILLAS - Alvaro ARBELOA, PEPE, SERGIO RAMOS, FABIO COENTRAO (MARCELO 64) - Sami KHEDIRA, Nuri SAHIN (Esteban GRANERO 84) - Karim BENZEMA, Mesut OZIL, CRISTIANO RONALDO - Gonzalo HIGUAIN (KAKA 63). Tr: Jose MOURINHO

Bernabéu, Madrid
4-04-2012, Att: 54 627, Ref: Rocchi ITA
Real Madrid 5
Ronaldo 2 [26][76], Kaka [37], Callejon [80], Di Maria [84]

Iker CASILLAS - SERGIO RAMOS, PEPE, Raphael VARANE, MARCELO (Jose CALLEJON 46) - Nuri SAHIN, Esteban GRANERO (Raul ALBIOL 65) - HAMIT Altintop, KAKA, CRISTIANO RONALDO - Gonzalo HIGUAIN (Angel DI MARIA 55). Tr: Jose MOURINHO

APOEL Nicosia 2
Manduca [67], Solari [82p]

URKO PARDO - Savvas POURSAITIDIS•, PAULO JORGE, KAKA, WILLIAM Boaventura - NUNO MORAIS, HELIO PINTO (Marinos SATSIAS 78) - Costas CHARALAMBIDES, MARCINHO, Gustavo MANDUCA (Aldo ADORNO 68) - AILTON (Esteban SOLARI 70). Tr: Ivan JOVANOVIC

Vélodrome, Marseille
28-03-2012, Att: 31 683, Ref: Carballo ESP
Olympique Marseille 0

Elinton ANDRADE - Cesar AZPILICUETA, Rod FANNI, Nicolas N'KOULOU, Jeremy MOREL - Alou DIARRA• (Benoit CHEYROU 71), Stephane MBIA• - Morgan AMALFITANO (BRANDAO 68), Matthieu VALBUENA, Andre AYEW - Loic REMY. Tr: Didier DESCHAMPS

Bayern München 2
Gomez [44], Robben [69]

Manuel NEUER - Philipp LAHM, Jerome BOATENG, Holger BADSTUBER, David ALABA• - LUIZ GUSTAVO•, Toni KROOS• (Anatoliy TYMOSHCHUK 63) - Arjen ROBBEN, Thomas MULLER (Bastian SCHWEINSTEIGER• 70), Franck RIBERY (Danijel PRANJIC 78) - Mario GOMEZ. Tr: Jupp HEYNCKES

Allianz Arena, Munich
3-04-2012, Att: 66 000, Ref: Moen NOR
Bayern München 2
Olic 2 [13][37]

Manuel NEUER - Philipp LAHM, Jerome BOATENG, Holger BADSTUBER, David ALABA• - Anatoliy TYMOSHCHUK, LUIZ GUSTAVO - Thomas MULLER (RAFINHA 39), Toni KROOS (Danijel PRANJIC 67), Franck RIBERY - Ivica OLIC (Mario GOMEZ 74). Tr: Jupp HEYNCKES

Olympique Marseille 0

Steve Mandanda - Cesar AZPILICUETA, Rod FANNI, Nicolas N'KOULOU, Jeremy MOREL (Morgan AMALFITANO 46) - Stephane MBIA•, Benoit CHEYROU - Loic REMY (Charles KABORE 63), Matthieu VALBUENA, Andre AYEW - BRANDAO (Andre-Pierre GIGNAC 74). Tr: Didier DESCHAMPS

SEMI-FINALS

Stamford Bridge, London
18-04-2012, Att: 38 039, Ref: Brych GER
Chelsea 1
Drogba [45]

Petr CECH - Branislav IVANOVIC, Gary CAHILL, John TERRY, Ashley COLE - John MIKEL - Juan MATA (Salomon KALOU 74), Frank LAMPARD, RAUL MEIRELES, RAMIRES• (Jose BOSINGWA 88) - Didier DROGBA•. Tr: Roberto DI MATTEO

Barcelona 0

VICTOR VALDES - DANI ALVES, Carles PUYOL, Javier MASCHERANO, ADRIANO - XAVI (Isaac CUENCA 87), Sergio BUSQUETS• - ALEXIS SANCHEZ (PEDRO Rodriguez• 66), Lionel MESSI, Cesc FABREGAS (THIAGO Alcantara 78), Andres INIESTA. Tr: Josep GUARDIOLA

Camp Nou, Barcelona
24-04-2012, Att: 95 845, Ref: Cakir TUR
Barcelona 2
Busquets [35], Iniesta [43]

VICTOR VALDES - Javier MASCHERANO, Gerard PIQUE (DANI ALVES 26), Carles PUYOL, XAVI, Sergio BUSQUETS - Isaac CUENCA (Cristian TELLO 67), Lionel MESSI•, Cesc FABREGAS (Seydou KEITA 74), Andres INIESTA• - ALEXIS SANCHEZ. Tr: Josep GUARDIOLA

Chelsea 2
Ramires [45], Torres [92+]

Petr CECH• - Branislav IVANOVIC•, Gary CAHILL (Bosingwa 12), John TERRY♦[37], Ashley COLE - Juan MATA (Salomon KALOU 58), Frank LAMPARD•, John MIKEL•, RAUL MEIRELES•, RAMIRES• - Didier DROGBA (FERNANDO TORRES 80). Tr: Roberto DI MATTEO

Allianz Arena, Munich
17-04-2012, Att: 66 000, Ref: Webb ENG
Bayern München 2
Ribery [17], Gomez [90]

Manuel NEUER - Philipp LAHM•, Jerome BOATENG, Holger BADSTUBER, David ALABA - LUIZ GUSTAVO, Bastian SCHWEINSTEIGER (Thomas MULLER 61) - Arjen ROBBEN•, Toni KROOS, Franck RIBERY - Mario GOMEZ. Tr: Jupp HEYNCKES

Real Madrid 1
Ozil [53]

Iker CASILLAS - Alvaro ARBELOA, PEPE, SERGIO RAMOS•, FABIO COENTRAO• - Sami KHEDIRA, XABI ALONSO• - Angel DI MARIA• (Esteban GRANERO 79), Mesut OZIL (MARCELO• 69), CRISTIANO RONALDO - Karim BENZEMA (Gonzalo HIGUAIN• 84). Tr: Jose MOURINHO

Bernabéu, Madrid
25-04-2012, Att: 71 654, Ref: Kassai HUN
Real Madrid 2 1p
Ronaldo 2 [6p][14]

Iker CASILLAS - Alvaro ARBELOA•, PEPE•, SERGIO RAMOS, MARCELO - Sami KHEDIRA, XABI ALONSO - Angel DI MARIA (KAKA 75), Mesut OZIL (Esteban GRANERO• 111), CRISTIANO RONALDO - Karim BENZEMA (Gonzalo HIGUAIN 105). Tr: Jose MOURINHO

Bayern München 1 3p
Robben [27p]

Manuel NEUER - Philipp LAHM, Jerome BOATENG, Holger BADSTUBER•, David ALABA•, LUIZ GUSTAVO•, Bastian SCHWEINSTEIGER - Arjen ROBBEN•, Toni KROOS, Franck RIBERY (Thomas MULLER 95) - Mario GOMEZ. Tr: Jupp HEYNCKES

FINAL

UEFA CHAMPIONS LEAGUE FINAL
ALLIANZ ARENA, MUNICH

Saturday, 19-05-2012, 20:45, Att: 62,500, Ref: Pedro Proenca POR
Assistants: Bertino Miranda POR & Ricardo Santos POR

BAYERN MUNCHEN 1 3p 1 4p **CHELSEA**

Thomas Muller 83 — Didier Drogba 88

BAYERN MUNCHEN
Red shirts, red shorts, red socks

Tr: Jupp Heynckes

Manuel Neuer

Philippe Lahm (c) — Jerome Boateng — Anatoliy Tymoshchuk — Diego Contento

Bastian Schweinsteiger 2 — Tony Kroos

Arjen Robben — Thomas Muller 87 — Franck Ribery
Daniel Van Buyten — Ivica Olic

Mario Gomez

Didier Drogba † 93

Ryan Bertrand 73 — Juan Mata — Salomon Kalou 84
Florent Malouda — Fernando Torres 120

Frank Lampard (c)

John Obi Mikel

Ashley Cole 81 — Gary Cahill — David Luiz 86 — Jose Bosingwa

Tr: Roberto Di Matteo — Petr Cech

Blue shirts, blue shorts, white socks

CHELSEA

MATCH STATS

Bayern		Chelsea
35	Shots	9
7	Shots on Goal	3
14	Fouls Committed	26
20	Corner Kicks	1
1	Caught Offside	2
56	Possession (%)	44

(C) Captain † Man of the Match

FINAL PENALTIES
CHELSEA WON 4-3

Bayern		Chelsea
✓	Philipp Lahm	
	Juan Mata	✗[1]
✓	Mario Gomez	
	David Luiz	✓
✓	Manuel Neuer	
	Frank Lampard	✓
✗[1]	Ivica Olic	
	Ashley Cole	✓
✗[2]	Schweinsteiger	
	Didier Drogba	✓

[1] Saved • [2] Saved onto post

My team played an outstanding match against opponents who played the way we expected and the way they'd played for the last few Champions League matches. We must blame ourselves for having so many opportunities without profiting. Chelsea were the lucky team today; they played the way they know best and I'd like to congratulate them on their performance. They put on a real fight, defensively they were very well organised and in the shoot-out they had the luck to win the Champions League.

Jupp Heynckes

Football, and life, is sometimes unpredictable and crazy. I don't think anyone could have predicted this. We've had a difficult season and to finish off like this is incredible. Obviously when Bayern scored there wasn't much time for us but the heart and passion these players have shown in this competition has been immense. Our preparation was very difficult with the suspended players and two defenders out, but the desire and motivation of the players has shown again tonight.

Roberto Di Matteo

UEFA EUROPA LEAGUE 2011–12
EARLY ROUNDS FOR TEAMS IN GROUPS A TO C

First Qualifying Round   **Second Qualifying Round**   **Third Qualifying Round**   **Play-off Round**

First Qualifying Round				Second Qualifying Round				Third Qualifying Round				Play-off Round			
				Vålerenga IF	NOR	1	1								
				Mika Ashtarak	ARM	0	0	Vålerenga IF	NOR	0	0				
								PAOK Thessaloníki	GRE	2	3	PAOK Thessaloníki	GRE	2	1
FC Koper	SVN	1	1					Karpaty Lviv	UKR	2	3	Karpaty Lviv	UKR	0	1
Shakhter K'gandy	KAZ	1	2	Shakhter Karagandy	KAZ	2	0	St Patrick's Athletic	IRL	0	1				
IBV Vestmannæyjar	ISL	1	0	St Patrick's Athletic	IRL	1	2								
St Patrick's Athletic	IRL	0	2									Rubin Kazan	RUS	Bye	
UE Santa Coloma	AND	0	0												
Paksi SE	HUN	1	4	Paksi SE	HUN	1	3								
Daugava D'vpils	LVA	0	1	Tromsø IL	NOR	1	0	Paksi SE	HUN	1	1				
Tromsø IL	NOR	5	2					Heart of Mid'thian	SCO	1	4	Heart of Mid'thian	SCO	5	0
												Tottenham Hotspur	ENG	0	0
												Shamrock Rovers†	IRL	1	2
												Partizan Beograd †	SRB	1	1
				Sant Julià	AND	0	0					Standard CL †	BEL	1	3
				Bnei Yehuda	ISR	2	2	Bnei Yehuda	ISR	1	0	Helsingborgs IF	SWE	0	1
								Helsingborgs IF	SWE	0	3				
												Hannover 96	GER	2	1
												Sevilla	ESP	1	1
												FC København	DEN	Bye	
Renova Cepciste	MKD	2 1 2p													
Glentoran	NIR	1 2 3p		Glentoran	NIR	0	0								
				Vorskla Poltava	UKR	2	3	Vorskla Poltava	UKR	0	2				
								Sligo Rovers	IRL	0	0	Vorskla Poltava	UKR	2	3
								Dinamo Bucuresti	ROU	2	2	Dinamo Bucuresti	ROU	1	2
				Iskra-Stal Rîbnita	MDA	1	1	Varazdin	CRO	2	1				
Varazdin	CRO	5	1	Varazdin	CRO	1	3	SV Ried	AUT	2	2				
Lusitanos	AND	1	0					Brøndby IF	DEN	0	4	SV Ried	AUT	0	0
AZAL Baku	AZE	1	1									PSV Eindhoven	NED	0	5
FK Minsk	BLR	1	2	FK Minsk	BLR	1	1								
				Gaziantepspor	TUR	1	4	Gaziantepspor	TUR	0	0				
								Legia Warszawa	POL	1	0	Legia Warszawa	POL	2	3
												Spartak Moskva	RUS	2	2
				FC Vaduz	LIE	0	3					Ekranas Pan'zys †	LTU	1	0
				Vojvodina Novi Sad	SRB	2	1	Hapoel Tel Aviv	ISR	4	1	Hapoel Tel Aviv	ISR	0	4
				Slask Wroclaw	POL	1	2	FC Vaduz	LIE	0	2				
				Dundee United	SCO	0	3	Slask Wroclaw	POL	0 0 4p					
				Metalurg Skopje	MKD	0	2	Lokomotiv Sofia	BUL	0 0 3p		Slask Wroclaw	POL	1	1
				Lokomotiv Sofia	BUL	0	3					Rapid Bucuresti	ROU	3	1

† Champions League 3rd qualifying round loser • Champions League play-off round losers qualified directly for the Europa League group stage
The home teams in the first leg are listed above their opponents

UEFA EUROPA LEAGUE 2011–12
EARLY ROUNDS FOR TEAMS IN GROUPS D TO F

First Qualifying Round	Second Qualifying Round	Third Qualifying Round	Play-off Round
			FC Nordsjælland DEN 0 1
			Sporting CP POR 0 2
	Anorthosis F'gusta CYP 3 0		Lazio ITA 6 3
	FC Gagra GEO 0 2	Anorthosis F'gusta CYP 0 2	Rabotnicki Skopje MKD 0 1
	Juvenes/Dogana SMR 0 0	Rabotnicki Skopje MKD 2 1	
Trans Narva EST 1 0	Rabotnicki Skopje MKD 1 3		
Rabotnicki Skopje MKD 4 3			Vaslui † ROU 2 0
		Sparta Praha CZE 5 2	Sparta Praha CZE 0 1
	Orebro SK SWE 0 0	FK Sarajevo BIH 0 0	
	FK Sarajevo BIH 0 2		
			FC Zürich Bye
			Besiktas TUR 3 0
		Alania Vladikavkaz RUS 1 1 4p	Alania Vladikavkaz RUS 0 2
	Kecskeméti TE HUN 1 0	FK Aktobe KAZ 1 1 2p	
	FK Aktobe KAZ 1 0	Palermo ITA 2 1	
	Vllaznia Shköder ALB 0 1	FC Thun SUI 2 1	FC Thun SUI 0 1
Birkirkara MLT 0 1	FC Thun SUI 0 2	Stoke City ENG 1 1	Stoke City ENG 1 4
Vllaznia Shköder ALB 1 1		Hajduk Split CRO 0 0	
			Litex Lovech † BUL 1 0
			Dynamo Kyiv † UKR 2 1
	Zeljeznicar BIH 1 0		
	Sheriff Tiraspol MDA 0 0	Zeljeznicar BIH 0 0	
	Maccabi Tel Aviv ISR 3 0	Maccabi Tel Aviv ISR 2 6	Maccabi Tel Aviv ISR 3 1
	Khazar Lenkoran AZE 1 0		Panathinaikos † GRE 0 2
			Athletic Bilbao ESP 0
			Trabzonspor † ‡ TUR 0
	Tauras Taurage LTU 2 0		
	ADO Den Haag NED 3 2	Omonia Nicosia CYP 3 0	
	Liepajas Metalurgs LVA 1 0	ADO Den Haag NED 0 1	Omonia Nicosia CYP 2 0
	RB Salzburg AUT 4 0	RB Salzburg AUT 1 3	RB Salzburg AUT 1 1
	Differdange 03 LUX 0 1	FK Senica SVK 0 0	
	Levadia Tallinn EST 0 0	Differdange 03 ‡‡ LUX 0 0	
	Rad Beograd SRB 0 1	Olympiakos Volou GRE 3 3	Differdange 03 LUX 0 0
Rad Beograd SRB 6 3	Olympiakos Volou GRE 1 1		Paris St-Germain FRA 4 2
Tre Penne SMR 0 1			
			Slovan Bratislava † SVK 1 1
			Roma ITA 0 1

† Champions League 3rd qualifying round loser • Champions League play-off round losers qualified directly for the Europa League group stage
The home teams in the first leg are listed above their opponents
‡ Trabzonspor withdrew to take part in the UEFA Champions League • ‡‡ Olympiakos Volou were disqualified

UEFA EUROPA LEAGUE 2011–12
EARLY ROUNDS FOR TEAMS IN GROUPS G TO I

First Qualifying Round				Second Qualifying Round				Third Qualifying Round				Play-off Round			
												Metalist Kharkiv	UKR	0	4
Ferencváros	HUN	3	2									Sochaux	FRA	0	0
Ulysses Yerevan	ARM	0	0	Ferencváros	HUN	2	1								
Aalesunds SK	NOR	4	2	Aalesunds SK	NOR	1	3	Aalesunds SK	NOR	4	1				
Neath	WAL	1	0	Suduva M'jampole	LTU	1	0	IF Elfsborg	SWE	0	1	Aalesunds SK	NOR	2	0
IF Elfsborg	SWE	4	1	IF Elfsborg	SWE	1	3	AZ Alkmaar	NED	2	1	AZ Alkmaar	NED	1	6
Fola Esch	LUX	0	1	Flamurtari Vlorë	ALB	0	1	FK Jablonec	CZE	0	1				
Buducnost P'gorica	MNE	1	2	FK Jablonec	CZE	2	5	Olimpija Ljubuljana	SVN	1	2				
Flamurtari Vlorë	ALB	3	1	Olimpija Ljubuljana	SVN	2	1	FK Austria Wien	AUT	1	3	FK Austria Wien	AUT	3	0
Siroki Brijeg	BIH	0	0	Bohemians	IRL	0	1	1.FSV Mainz	GER	1 1 3p		Gaz Metan Medias	ROU	1	1
Olimpija Ljubuljana	SVN	0	3	Rudar Pljevlja	MNE	0	0	Gaz Metan Medias	ROU	1 1 4p					
				FK Austria Wien	AUT	3	2								
				KuPS Kuopio	FIN	1	0					Malmö FF	SWE	Bye	
				Gaz Metan Medias	ROU	0	2								
												Zestafoni †	GEO	3	0
								Club Brugge	BEL	4	0	Club Brugge	BEL	3	2
				EB/Streymur	FRO	1	0	Karabakh Agdam	AZE	1	1				
Banga Gargzdai	LTU	0	0	Karabakh Agdam	AZE	1	0								
Karabakh Agdam	AZE	4	3	TPS Turku	FIN	0	0					Sporting Braga	POR	0	2
				Westerloo	BEL	1	0	BSC Young Boys	SUI	3	2	BSC Young Boys	SUI	0	2
				FH Hafnarfjördur	ISL	1	0	Westerloo	BEL	1	0				
UN Käerjeng 97	LUX	1	1	CD Nacional	POR	1	2	CD Nacional	POR	3	1				
BK Hacken	SWE	1	5	BK Hacken	SWE	1	2	BK Hacken	SWE	0	2	CD Nacional	POR	0	0
Honka Espoo	FIN	0	2	Honka Espoo	FIN	0	0					Birmingham City	ENG	0	3
Nomme Kalju	EST	0	0												
												NK Maribor †	SVN	2	1
												Rangers †	SCO	1	1
								Atlético Madrid	ESP	2	2				
								IF Strømgodset	NOR	1	0	Atlético Madrid	ESP	2	4
The New Saints	WAL	1	1					FC Midtjylland	DEN	0	1	Vitória Guimarães	POR	0	0
Cliftonville	NIR	1	0	The New Saints	WAL	1	2	Vitória Guimarães	POR	0	2				
				FC Midtjylland	DEN	3	5								
												Udinese	ITA	Bye	
												Celtic ‡	SCO	0	1
												FC Sion	SUI	0	3
				Shakhter Soligorsk	BLR	0	2								
Banants Yerevan	ARM	0	1	FK Ventspils	LVA	1	3	FK Ventspils	LVA	1	0				
Metalurgi Rustavi	GEO	1	1	Metalurgi Rustavi	GEO	1	2	Crvena Zvezda	SRB	2	7	Crvena Zvezda	SRB	1	0
Jagiellonia Bialystok	POL	1	0	Irtysh Pavlodar	KAZ	1	0	Metalurgi Rustavi	GEO	2	0	Stade Rennais	FRA	2	4
Irtysh Pavlodar	KAZ	0	2					Stade Rennais	FRA	5	2				

† Champions League 3rd qualifying round loser • Champions League play-off round losers qualified directly for the Europa League group stage
‡ Celtic later awarded both matches 3-0 after FC Sion were disqualified • The home teams in the first leg are listed above their opponents

UEFA EUROPA LEAGUE 2011-12
EARLY ROUNDS FOR TEAMS IN GROUPS J TO L

First Qualifying Round	Second Qualifying Round	Third Qualifying Round	Play-off Round
			HJK Helsinki † — FIN 2 1
			Schalke 04 — GER 0 6
			Steaua Bucuresti — ROU 2 1
			CSKA Sofia — BUL 0 1
			Maccabi Haifa — ISR Bye
	Floriana — MLT 0 0		Rosenborg BK † — NOR 0 1
	AEK Larnaca — CYP 8 1	**AEK Larnaca** — CYP 3 2	**AEK Larnaca** — CYP 0 2
		Mladá Boleslav — 0 2	
			Twente Enschede — NED Bye
			Wisla Krakow — POL Bye
	Domzale — SVN 1 1		
	Radniki Split — CRO 2 3	Radniki Split — CRO 0 0	
	Crusaders — NIR 1 0	**Fulham** — ENG 0 2	**Fulham** — ENG 3 0
Fulham — ENG 3 0	**Fulham** — ENG 3 4		D. Dnipropetrovsk — UKR 0 1
NSI Runavik — FRO 0 0			
			OB Odense — DEN Bye
		Bursaspor — TUR 2 3	
		FC Gomel — BLR 1 1	Bursaspor — TUR 1 2
			RSC Anderlecht — BEL 2 2
			Lokomotiv Moskva — RUS 2 1
		Levski Sofia — BUL 2 1 4p	Spartak Trnava — SVK 0 1
	KF Tirana — ALB 0 1	**Spartak Trnava** — SVK 1 2 5p	
Spartak Trnava — SVK 3 1	**Spartak Trnava** — SVK 0 3		**AEK Athens** — GRE 1 1
Zeta Golubovci — MNE 0 2	**KR Reykjavík** — ISL 3 0		Dinamo Tbilisi — GEO 0 1
IF Fuglafjørdur — FRO 1 1	MSK Zilina — SVK 0 2	KR Reykjavík — ISL 1 0	
KR Reykjavík — ISL 3 5	Llanelli — WAL 2 0	**Dinamo Tbilisi** — GEO 4 2	
Dinamo Tbilisi — GEO 2 3	**Dinamo Tbilisi** — GEO 1 5		
Milsami Orhei — MDA 0 1			SK Sturm Graz — AUT Bye

† Champions League 3rd qualifying round loser • Champions League play-off round losers qualified directly for the Europa League group stage
The home teams in the first leg are listed above their opponents

UEFA EUROPA LEAGUE 2011-12

Group Stage

Group A
		Pl	W	D	L	F	A	Pts
PAOK Thessaloníki	GRE	6	3	3	0	10	6	12
Rubin Kazan ‡	RUS	6	3	2	1	11	5	11
Tottenham Hotspur	ENG	6	3	1	2	9	4	10
Shamrock Rovers	IRL	6	0	0	6	4	19	0

GRE	RUS	ENG	IRL
	1-1	0-0	2-1
2-2		1-0	4-1
1-2	1-0		3-1
1-3	0-3	0-4	

Group B
		Pl	W	D	L	F	A	Pts
Standard CL	BEL	6	4	2	0	9	1	14
Hannover 96	GER	6	3	2	1	9	7	11
FC København ‡	DEN	6	1	2	3	5	9	5
Vorskla Poltava	UKR	6	0	2	4	4	10	2

BEL	GER	DEN	UKR
	2-0	3-0	0-0
0-0		2-2	3-1
0-1	1-2		1-0
1-3	1-2	1-1	

Group C
		Pl	W	D	L	F	A	Pts
PSV Eindhoven	NED	6	5	1	0	13	5	16
Legia Warszawa	POL	6	3	0	3	7	9	9
Hapoel Tel Aviv	ISR	6	2	1	3	10	9	7
Rapid Bucuresti	ROU	6	1	0	5	5	12	3

NED	POL	ISR	ROU
	1-0	3-3	2-1
0-3		3-2	3-2
0-1	2-0		0-1
1-3	0-1	1-3	

Group D
		Pl	W	D	L	F	A	Pts
Sporting CP	POR	6	4	0	2	8	4	12
Lazio	ITA	6	2	3	1	7	5	9
Vaslui	ROU	6	1	3	2	5	8	6
FC Zürich ‡	SUI	6	1	2	3	5	8	5

POR	ITA	ROU	SUI
	2-1	2-0	2-0
2-0		2-2	1-0
1-0	0-0		2-2
0-2	1-1	2-0	

Group E
		Pl	W	D	L	F	A	Pts
Besiktas	TUR	6	4	0	2	13	7	12
Stoke City	ENG	6	3	2	1	10	7	11
Dynamo Kyiv	UKR	6	1	4	1	7	7	7
Maccabi Tel Aviv	ISR	6	0	2	4	8	17	2

TUR	ENG	UKR	ISR
	3-1	1-0	5-1
2-1		1-1	3-0
1-0	1-1		3-3
2-3	1-2	1-1	

Group F
		Pl	W	D	L	F	A	Pts
Athletic Bilbao	ESP	6	4	1	1	11	8	13
RB Salzburg	AUT	6	3	1	2	11	8	10
Paris Saint-Germain	FRA	6	3	1	2	8	7	10
Slovan Bratislava	SVK	6	0	1	5	4	11	1

ESP	AUT	FRA	SVK
	2-2	2-0	2-1
0-1		2-0	3-0
4-2	3-1		1-0
1-2	2-3	0-0	

Group G
		Pl	W	D	L	F	A	Pts
Metalist Kharkiv	UKR	6	4	2	0	15	6	14
AZ Alkmaar	NED	6	1	5	0	10	7	8
FK Austria Wien	AUT	6	2	2	2	10	11	8
Malmö FF ‡	SWE	6	0	1	5	4	15	1

UKR	NED	AUT	SWE
	1-1	4-1	3-1
1-1		2-2	4-1
1-2	2-2		2-0
1-4	0-0	1-2	

Group H
		Pl	W	D	L	F	A	Pts
Club Brugge	BEL	6	3	2	1	12	9	11
Sporting Braga	POR	6	3	2	1	12	6	11
Birmingham City	ENG	6	3	1	2	8	8	10
NK Maribor	SVN	6	0	1	5	6	15	1

BEL	POR	ENG	SVN
	1-1	1-2	2-0
1-2		1-0	5-1
2-2	1-3		1-0
3-4	1-1	1-2	

Group I
		Pl	W	D	L	F	A	Pts
Atlético Madrid	ESP	6	4	1	1	11	4	13
Udinese ‡	ITA	6	2	3	1	6	7	9
Celtic	SCO	6	1	3	2	6	7	6
Stade Rennais	FRA	6	0	3	3	5	10	3

ESP	ITA	SCO	FRA
	4-0	2-0	3-1
2-0		1-1	2-1
0-1	1-1		3-1
1-1	0-0	1-1	

Group J
		Pl	W	D	L	F	A	Pts
Schalke 04	GER	6	4	2	0	13	2	14
Steaua Bucuresti	ROU	6	2	2	2	9	11	8
Maccabi Haifa ‡	ISR	6	2	0	4	10	12	6
AEK Larnaca	CYP	6	1	2	3	4	11	5

GER	ROU	ISR	CYP
	2-1	3-1	0-0
0-0		4-2	3-1
0-3	5-0		1-0
0-5	1-1	2-1	

Group K
		Pl	W	D	L	F	A	Pts
FC Twente Enschede ‡	NED	6	4	1	1	14	7	13
Wisla Krakow ‡	POL	6	3	0	3	8	13	9
Fulham	ENG	6	2	2	2	9	6	8
OB Odense ‡	DEN	6	1	1	4	9	14	4

NED	POL	ENG	DEN
	4-1	1-0	3-2
2-1		1-0	1-3
1-1	4-1		2-2
1-4	1-2	0-2	

Group L
		Pl	W	D	L	F	A	Pts
RSC Anderlecht	BEL	6	6	0	0	18	5	18
Lokomotiv Moskva	RUS	6	4	0	2	14	11	12
AEK Athens	GRE	6	1	0	5	8	15	3
SK Sturm Graz ‡	AUT	6	1	0	5	5	14	3

BEL	RUS	GRE	AUT
	5-3	4-1	3-0
0-2		3-1	3-1
1-2	1-3		1-2
0-2	1-2	1-3	

Round of 32

Atlético Madrid	3	1
Lazio *	1	0
Sporting Braga *	0	1
Besiktas	2	0
Standard CL	1	0
Wisla Krakow *	1	0
Club Brugge	1	0
Hannover 96 *	2	1
AZ Alkmaar *	1	1
RSC Anderlecht	0	0
PAOK Thessaloníki	0	0
Udinese *	0	3
PSV Eindhoven	2	4
Trabzonspor † *	1	1
Stoke City *	0	0
Valencia †	1	1
Sporting CP	2	1
Legia Warszawa *	2	0
FC Porto † *	1	0
Manchester City †	2	4
Olympiacos †	1	1
Rubin Kazan *	0	0
RB Salzburg *	0	1
Metalist Kharkiv	4	4
Schalke 04	1	3
Viktoria Plzen † *	1	1
Steaua Bucuresti *	0	0
FC Twente Enschede	1	1
Manchester United †	2	1
Ajax *	0	2
Lokomotiv Moskva *	2	0
Athletic Bilbao	1	1

UEFA EUROPA LEAGUE 2011-12

Round of 16	Quarter-Final	Semi-Final	Final

Atlético Madrid * 3 3
Besiktas 1 0

    Atlético Madrid * 2 2
    Hannover 96 1 1

Standard CL * 2 0
Hannover 96 2 4

        Atlético Madrid * 4 1
        Valencia 2 0

AZ Alkmaar * 2 1
Udinese 0 2

    AZ Alkmaar * 2 0
    Valencia 1 4

PSV Eindhoven 2 1
Valencia * 4 1

            Atlético Madrid 3
            Athletic Bilbao 0

Sporting CP * 1 2
Manchester City 0 3

    Sporting CP * 2 1
    Metalist Kharkiv 1 1

Olympiacos 1 1
Metalist Kharkiv * 0 2

        Sporting CP * 2 1
        Athletic Bilbao 1 3

Schalke 04 0 4
FC Twente Enschede * 1 1

    Schalke 04 * 2 2
    Athletic Bilbao 4 2

Manchester United * 2 1
Athletic Bilbao 3 2

* Home team in the first leg
‡ Qualified as a Champions League play-off round loser • † Qualified as a third placed team from the Champions League group stage

UEFA EUROPA LEAGUE FINAL 2012
Arena Nationala, Bucharest, 9-05-2012, Att: 52 347, Ref: Stark GER

Atlético Madrid 3 Falcao 2 [7],[34], Diego [85]
Athletic Bilbao 0

ATLETICO MADRID
Thibaut COURTOIS - JUANFRAN, Diego GODIN, MIRANDA, FILIPE LUIS - MARIO SUAREZ, GABI (c) - DIEGO (Eduardo SALVIO 90), ADRIAN LOPEZ (KOKE 88), ARDA Turan (Alvaro DOMINGUEZ 90) - Radamel FALCAO•. Tr: Diego SIMEONE

ATHLETIC BILBAO
Gorka IRAIZOZ - Andoni IRAOLA, JAVI MARTINEZ, Fernando AMOREBIETA•, Jon AURTENETXE (IBAI GOMEZ 46) - ANDER HERRERA• (Gaizka TOQUERO 63), Ander ITURRASPE (INIGO PEREZ• 46), Oscar DE MARCOS, Markel SUSAETA•, Fernando LLORENTE, Iker MUNIAIN. Tr: Marcelo BIELSA

YOUTH TOURNAMENTS IN EUROPE 2012

UEFA EUROPEAN U-17 CHAMPIONSHIP 2012

Qualifying Round Group 1

	Pl	W	D	L	F	A	Pts	BLR	NOR	AND
Hungary	3	3	0	0	11	3	9	4-1	3-2	4-0
Belarus	3	2	0	1	9	4	6		3-0	5-0
Norway	3	1	0	2	5	6	3			3-0
Andorra	3	0	0	3	0	12	0	Played in HUN		

Qualifying Round Group 2

	Pl	W	D	L	F	A	Pts	POR	ROM	FIN
Russia	3	2	1	0	5	2	7	1-1	1-0	3-1
Portugal	3	2	1	0	4	2	7		1-0	2-1
Romania	3	0	1	2	2	4	1			2-2
Finland	3	0	1	2	4	7	1	Played in POR		

Qualifying Round Group 3

	Pl	W	D	L	F	A	Pts	TUR	MKD	SMR
Scotland	3	2	1	0	5	1	7	1-1	1-0	3-0
Turkey	3	1	2	0	4	2	5		1-1	2-0
FYR Macedonia	3	1	1	1	6	2	4			5-0
San Marino	3	0	0	3	0	10	0	Played in MKD		

Qualifying Round Group 4

	Pl	W	D	L	F	A	Pts	IRL	KAZ	LIE
Czech Republic	3	3	0	0	9	0	9	1-0	2-0	6-0
Republic of Ireland	3	1	1	1	9	2	4		1-1	8-0
Kazakhstan	3	1	1	1	9	3	4			8-0
Liechtenstein	3	0	0	3	0	22	0	Played in KAZ		

Qualifying Round Group 5

	Pl	W	D	L	F	A	Pts	ITA	AUT	CYP
Denmark	3	3	0	0	11	3	9	4-1	2-1	5-1
Italy	3	2	0	1	7	6	6		3-2	3-0
Austria	3	1	0	2	5	5	3			2-0
Cyprus	3	0	0	3	1	10	0	Played in DEN		

Qualifying Round Group 6

	Pl	W	D	L	F	A	Pts	NED	BIH	LVA
England	3	3	0	0	7	0	9	1-0	2-0	4-0
Netherlands	3	2	0	1	7	2	6		3-0	4-1
Bosnia-Herzegovina	3	1	0	2	1	5	3			1-0
Latvia	3	0	0	3	1	9	0	Played in BIH		

Qualifying Round Group 7

	Pl	W	D	L	F	A	Pts	UKR	AZE	CRO
Belgium	3	2	0	1	5	5	6	0-2	1-0	4-3
Ukraine	3	1	1	1	2	1	4		0-0	0-1
Azerbaijan	3	1	1	1	2	2	4			2-1
Croatia	3	1	0	2	5	6	3	Played in CRO		

Qualifying Round Group 8

	Pl	W	D	L	F	A	Pts	GEO	BUL	MDA
Sweden	3	2	1	0	5	0	7	2-0	0-0	3-0
Georgia	3	2	0	1	5	5	6		3-2	2-1
Bulgaria	3	1	1	1	5	4	3			2-0
Moldova	3	0	0	3	1	7	0	Played in MDA		

Qualifying Round Group 9

	Pl	W	D	L	F	A	Pts	LTU	WAL	ARM
Serbia	3	3	0	0	10	3	9	2-0	6-1	2-1
Lithuania	3	1	0	2	4	4	3		0-2	4-0
Wales	3	1	0	2	5	9	3			2-3
Armenia	3	1	0	2	4	8	3	Played in SRB		

Qualifying Round Group 10

	Pl	W	D	L	F	A	Pts	LUX	NIR	FRO
France	3	3	0	0	11	0	9	2-0	4-0	5-0
Luxembourg	3	1	1	1	2	3	4		1-0	1-1
Northern Ireland	3	1	0	2	2	5	3			2-0
Faroe Islands	3	0	1	2	1	8	1	Played in LUX		

Qualifying Round Group 11

	Pl	W	D	L	F	A	Pts	POL	MNE	MLT
Spain	3	3	0	0	10	1	9	2-0	2-1	6-0
Poland	3	2	0	1	5	2	6		2-0	3-0
Montenegro	3	1	0	2	4	4	3			3-0
Malta	3	0	0	3	0	12	0	Played in MNE		

Qualifying Round Group 12

	Pl	W	D	L	F	A	Pts	ALB	SVK	EST
Germany	3	3	0	0	8	0	9	1-0	2-0	5-0
Albania	3	1	1	1	3	3	4		2-1	1-1
Slovakia	3	1	0	2	6	4	3			5-0
Estonia	3	0	1	2	1	11	1	Played in EST		

Qualifying Round Group 13

	Pl	W	D	L	F	A	Pts	SUI	GRE	ISR
Iceland	3	2	0	1	3	5	6	1-5	1-0	1-0
Switzerland	3	1	1	1	7	4	4		0-0	2-3
Greece	3	1	1	1	4	2	4			4-1
Israel	3	1	0	2	4	7	3	Played in ISR		

Elite Round Group 1

	Pl	W	D	L	F	A	Pts	SWE	ITA	SUI
France	3	3	0	0	6	2	9	3-1	1-0	2-1
Sweden	3	1	1	1	3	3	4		0-0	2-0
Italy	3	1	1	1	2	2	4			2-1
Switzerland	3	0	0	3	2	6	0	Played in FRA		

Elite Round Group 2

	Pl	W	D	L	F	A	Pts	CZE	BLR	LUX
Poland	3	3	0	0	7	1	9	2-0	2-0	3-1
Czech Republic	3	1	1	1	2	3	4		0-0	2-1
Belarus	3	0	2	1	1	3	2			1-1
Luxembourg	3	0	1	2	3	6	1	Played in LUX		

Elite Round Group 3

	Pl	W	D	L	F	A	Pts	ESP	ENG	UKR
Georgia	3	2	1	0	3	1	7	1-1	1-0	1-0
Spain	3	1	2	0	7	3	5		4-0	2-2
England	3	1	0	2	1	5	3			1-0
Ukraine	3	0	1	2	2	4	1	Played in GEO		

Elite Round Group 4

	Pl	W	D	L	F	A	Pts	POR	BUL	TUR
Germany	3	2	1	0	6	1	7	0-0	2-1	4-0
Portugal	3	1	2	0	3	0	5		0-0	3-0
Bulgaria	3	1	1	1	3	2	4			2-0
Turkey	3	0	0	3	0	9	0	Played in GER		

UEFA EUROPEAN U-19 CHAMPIONSHIP 2012

Elite Round Group 5

	Pl	W	D	L	F	A	Pts	SRB	ALB	IRL
Netherlands	3	2	1	0	7	2	7	1-1	4-0	2-1
Serbia	3	2	1	0	5	1	7		3-0	1-0
Albania	3	1	0	2	2	8	3			2-1
Republic of Ireland	3	0	0	3	2	5	0	Played in NED		

Elite Round Group 6

	Pl	W	D	L	F	A	Pts	DEN	SCO	LTU
Iceland	3	2	1	0	7	2	7	2-2	1-0	4-0
Denmark	3	2	1	0	8	5	7		3-2	3-1
Scotland	3	1	0	2	3	4	3			1-0
Lithuania	3	0	0	3	1	8	0	Played in SCO		

Elite Round Group 7

	Pl	W	D	L	F	A	Pts	HUN	RUS	WAL
Belgium	3	2	1	0	8	2	7	2-2	3-0	3-0
Hungary	3	2	1	0	10	5	7		3-2	5-1
Russia	3	1	0	2	4	7	3			2-1
Wales	3	0	0	3	2	10	0	Played in HUN		

UEFA EUROPEAN U-17 CHAMPIONSHIP SLOVENIA 2012

First Round Group Stage

Group A	Pl	W	D	L	F	A	Pts	GEO	FRA	ISL
Germany	3	3	0	0	5	0	9	1-0	3-0	1-0
Georgia	3	1	1	1	2	2	4		1-1	1-0
France	3	0	2	1	3	6	2			2-2
Iceland	3	0	1	2	2	4	1			

Group B	Pl	W	D	L	F	A	Pts	POL	BEL	SVN
Netherlands	3	1	2	0	3	1	5	0-0	0-0	3-1
Poland	3	1	2	0	2	1	5		1-0	1-1
Belgium	3	1	1	1	3	2	4			3-1
Slovenia	3	0	1	2	3	7	1			

Semi-finals

Netherlands	2
Georgia	0

Poland	0
Germany	1

Final

Netherlands	1 5p
Germany	1 4p

Finals held in Slovenia from 4-05-2012 to 16-05-2012

UEFA EUROPEAN U-19 CHAMPIONSHIP 2012

Qualifying Round Group 1

	Pl	W	D	L	F	A	Pts	HUN	FRO	SMR
Portugal	3	2	1	0	18	4	7	3-3	9-1	6-0
Hungary	3	2	1	0	11	4	7		3-1	5-0
Faroe Islands	3	1	0	2	6	12	3			4-0
San Marino	3	0	0	3	0	15	0	Played in POR		

Qualifying Round Group 2

	Pl	W	D	L	F	A	Pts	IRL	BUL	RUS
Bosnia-Herzegovina	3	3	0	0	6	1	9	2-0	2-1	2-0
Republic of Ireland	3	2	0	1	7	4	6		4-1	3-1
Bulgaria	3	1	0	2	3	6	3			1-0
Russia	3	0	0	3	1	6	0	Played in BUL		

Qualifying Round Group 3

	Pl	W	D	L	F	A	Pts	ITA	AZE	SWE
Romania	3	2	1	0	5	1	7	2-1	3-0	0-0
Italy	3	1	1	1	4	4	4		2-1	1-1
Azerbaijan	3	1	0	2	2	5	3			1-0
Sweden	3	0	2	1	1	2	2	Played in SWE		

Qualifying Round Group 4

	Pl	W	D	L	F	A	Pts	CYP	LVA	ISL
Norway	3	1	2	0	7	5	5	3-3	2-0	2-2
Cyprus	3	1	2	0	6	4	5		2-0	1-1
Latvia	3	1	0	2	2	4	3			2-0
Iceland	3	0	2	1	3	5	2	Played in CYP		

Qualifying Round Group 5

	Pl	W	D	L	F	A	Pts	SRB	ISR	LTU
Czech Republic	3	2	0	1	3	2	6	1-0	1-2	1-0
Serbia	3	1	1	1	1	1	4		1-0	0-0
Israel	3	1	1	1	4	4	4			2-2
Lithuania	3	0	2	1	2	3	2	Played in ISR		

Qualifying Round Group 6

	Pl	W	D	L	F	A	Pts	SUI	MKD	KAZ
Ukraine	3	2	1	0	6	1	7	1-1	3-0	2-0
Switzerland	3	2	1	0	6	1	7		3-0	2-0
FYR Macedonia	3	1	0	2	2	7	3			2-1
Kazakhstan	3	0	0	3	1	6	0	Played in MKD		

Qualifying Round Group 7

	Pl	W	D	L	F	A	Pts	MNE	NIR	BLR
Germany	3	2	1	0	10	4	7	2-0	5-1	3-3
Montenegro	3	1	1	1	2	3	4		2-1	0-0
Northern Ireland	3	1	0	2	5	8	3			3-1
Belarus	3	0	2	1	4	6	2	Played in NIR		

Qualifying Round Group 8

	Pl	W	D	L	F	A	Pts	SVN	SCO	WAL
Belgium	3	2	1	0	6	1	7	0-0	3-1	3-0
Slovenia	3	2	1	0	5	3	7		2-1	3-2
Scotland	3	1	0	2	5	6	3			3-1
Wales	3	0	0	3	3	9	0	Played in SVN		

Qualifying Round Group 9

	Pl	W	D	L	F	A	Pts	TUR	POL	LUX
Georgia	3	2	1	0	6	2	7	1-1	3-1	2-0
Turkey	3	1	2	0	6	3	5		2-2	3-0
Poland	3	1	1	1	5	6	4			2-1
Luxembourg	3	0	0	3	1	7	0		Played in TUR	

Qualifying Round Group 10

	Pl	W	D	L	F	A	Pts	ARM	SVK	AND
Greece	3	2	1	0	13	2	7	2-1	1-1	10-0
Armenia	3	2	0	1	4	3	6		2-1	1-0
Slovakia	3	1	1	1	3	3	4			1-0
Andorra	3	0	0	3	0	12	0		Played in ARM	

Qualifying Round Group 11

	Pl	W	D	L	F	A	Pts	NED	FIN	MDA
Croatia	3	2	1	0	8	2	7	0-0	4-2	4-0
Netherlands	3	2	1	0	5	0	7		2-0	3-0
Finland	3	1	0	2	6	8	3			4-2
Moldova	3	0	0	3	2	11	0		Played in NED	

Qualifying Round Group 12

	Pl	W	D	L	F	A	Pts	AUT	ALB	MLT
Denmark	3	2	1	0	5	0	7	0-0	1-0	4-0
Austria	3	1	2	0	3	0	5		0-0	3-0
Albania	3	1	1	1	4	1	4			4-0
Malta	3	0	0	3	0	11	0		Played in AUT	

Elite Round Group 1

	Pl	W	D	L	F	A	Pts	NED	NOR	CZE
France	3	3	0	0	11	2	9	6-0	3-1	2-1
Netherlands	3	2	0	1	5	7	6		2-1	3-0
Norway	3	1	0	2	3	5	3			1-0
Czech Republic	3	0	0	3	1	6	0		Played in CZE	

Elite Round Group 2

	Pl	W	D	L	F	A	Pts	MNE	SUI	SVN
England	3	2	1	0	7	1	7	1-1	1-0	5-0
Montenegro	3	1	1	1	4	2	4		3-0	0-1
Switzerland	3	1	0	2	2	4	3			2-0
Slovenia	3	1	0	2	1	7	3		Played in ENG	

Elite Round Group 3

	Pl	W	D	L	F	A	Pts	GER	ROU	HUN
Serbia	3	2	1	0	6	2	7	2-2	3-0	1-0
Germany	3	1	2	0	6	3	5		1-1	3-0
Romania	3	1	1	1	5	4	4			4-0
Hungary	3	0	0	3	0	8	0		Played in SRB	

Elite Round Group 4

	Pl	W	D	L	F	A	Pts	UKR	IRL	ISR
Portugal	3	3	0	0	11	1	9	3-0	1-0	7-1
Ukraine	3	2	0	1	5	3	6		3-0	2-0
Republic of Ireland	3	0	1	2	1	5	1			1-1
Israel	3	0	1	2	2	10	1		Played in POR	

Elite Round Group 5

	Pl	W	D	L	F	A	Pts	DEN	TUR	CYP
Greece	3	3	0	0	8	0	9	2-0	3-0	3-0
Denmark	3	2	0	1	9	5	6		3-1	6-2
Turkey	3	1	0	2	6	6	3			5-0
Cyprus	3	0	0	3	2	13	0		Played in DEN	

Elite Round Group 6

	Pl	W	D	L	F	A	Pts	GEO	AUT	BIH
Croatia	3	2	1	0	7	3	7	3-1	2-2	2-0
Georgia	3	2	0	1	7	6	6		2-1	4-2
Austria	3	1	1	1	5	4	4			2-0
Bosnia-Herzegovina	3	0	0	3	2	8	0		Played in CRO	

Elite Round Group 7

	Pl	W	D	L	F	A	Pts	ITA	BEL	ARM
Spain	3	3	0	0	6	3	9	2-1	2-1	2-1
Italy	3	2	0	1	7	4	6		2-1	4-1
Belgium	3	0	1	2	3	5	1			1-1
Armenia	3	0	1	2	3	7	1		Played in ITA	

UEFA EUROPEAN U-19 CHAMPIONSHIP ESTONIA 2012

First Round Group Stage

Group A	Pl	W	D	L	F	A	Pts	GRE	POR	EST
Spain	3	2	1	0	7	4	7	2-1	3-3	2-0
Greece	3	2	0	1	8	5	6		3-2	4-1
Portugal	3	1	1	1	8	6	4			3-0
Estonia	3	0	0	3	1	9	0			

Group B	Pl	W	D	L	F	A	Pts	FRA	CRO	SRB
England	3	2	1	0	5	3	7	2-1	1-1	2-1
France	3	2	0	1	5	2	6		1-0	3-0
Croatia	3	1	1	1	4	2	4			3-0
Serbia	3	0	0	3	1	8	0			

Semi-finals

Spain	3 4p		
France	3 2p		
England	1		
Greece	2		

Final

Spain	1
Greece	0

Finals held in Estonia from 3-07-2012 to 15-07-2012

WOMEN'S TOURNAMENTS IN EUROPE 2012

UEFA WOMEN'S U-17 CHAMPIONSHIP 2012

First Qualifying Round Group 1
	Pl	W	D	L	F	A	Pts	POL	LVA	GEO
Switzerland	3	3	0	0	34	2	9	2-1	15-0	17-1
Poland	3	2	0	1	19	2	6		6-0	12-0
Latvia	3	1	0	2	1	21	3			1-0
Georgia	3	0	0	3	1	30	0	Played in POL		

First Qualifying Round Group 2
	Pl	W	D	L	F	A	Pts	ROU	ITA	MKD
Republic of Ireland	3	2	1	0	10	3	7	3-2	1-1	6-0
Romania	3	2	0	1	11	6	6		3-2	6-1
Italy	3	1	1	1	9	4	4			6-0
FYR Macedonia	3	0	0	3	1	18	0	Played in MKD		

First Qualifying Round Group 3
	Pl	W	D	L	F	A	Pts	HUN	CRO	BUL
Sweden	3	3	0	0	21	0	9	5-0	6-0	10-0
Hungary	3	2	0	1	7	5	6		4-0	3-0
Croatia	3	0	1	2	2	12	1			2-2
Bulgaria	3	0	1	2	2	15	1	Played in HUN		

First Qualifying Round Group 4
	Pl	W	D	L	F	A	Pts	RUS	SVN	LTU
Norway	3	3	0	0	17	1	9	2-0	4-1	11-0
Russia	3	2	0	1	6	4	6		4-2	2-0
Slovenia	3	1	0	2	7	8	3			4-0
Lithuania	3	0	0	3	0	17	0	Played in LTU		

First Qualifying Round Group 5
	Pl	W	D	L	F	A	Pts	WAL	MDA	FRO
France	3	3	0	0	23	1	9	5-0	8-1	10-0
Wales	3	1	0	2	1	6	3		0-1	1-0
Moldova	3	1	0	2	2	9	3			0-1
Faroe Islands	3	1	0	2	1	11	3	Played in MDA		

First Qualifying Round Group 6
	Pl	W	D	L	F	A	Pts	FIN	ISR	NIR
England	3	3	0	0	10	4	9	4-2	4-1	2-1
Finland	3	2	0	1	13	6	6		7-0	4-2
Israel	3	1	0	2	3	12	3			2-1
Northern Ireland	3	0	0	3	4	8	0	Played in NIR		

First Qualifying Round Group 7
	Pl	W	D	L	F	A	Pts	SRB	TUR	GRE
Denmark	3	2	1	0	11	3	7	2-2	3-1	6-0
Serbia	3	2	1	0	9	5	7		4-3	3-0
Turkey	3	1	0	2	6	7	3			2-0
Greece	3	0	0	3	0	11	0	Played in SRB		

First Qualifying Round Group 8
	Pl	W	D	L	F	A	Pts	CZE	BLR	EST
Belgium	3	2	1	0	12	0	7	0-0	4-0	8-0
Czech Republic	3	2	1	0	11	0	7		5-0	6-0
Belarus	3	1	0	2	4	9	3			4-0
Estonia	3	0	0	3	0	18	0	Played in CZE		

First Qualifying Round Group 9
	Pl	W	D	L	F	A	Pts	BIH	UKR	AZE
Spain	3	3	0	0	20	0	9	6-0	7-0	7-0
Bosnia-Herzegovina	3	2	0	1	5	8	6		3-1	2-1
Ukraine	3	1	0	2	4	10	3			3-0
Azerbaijan	3	0	0	3	1	12	0	Played in AZE		

First Qualifying Round Group 10
	Pl	W	D	L	F	A	Pts	SCO	AUT	KAZ
Iceland	3	2	1	0	7	3	7	2-2	2-1	3-0
Scotland	3	1	2	0	6	3	5		1-1	3-0
Austria	3	1	1	1	13	3	4			11-0
Kazakhstan	3	0	0	3	0	17	0	Played in AUT		

UEFA EUROPEAN WOMEN'S U-17 CHAMPIONSHIP 2012

Second Qualifying Round

Group 1
	Pl	W	D	L	F	A	Pts	ISL	ENG	BEL
Switzerland	3	2	1	0	5	3	7	1-0	1-0	3-3
Iceland	3	2	0	1	4	2	6		1-0	3-1
England	3	1	0	2	1	2	3			1-0
Belgium	3	0	1	2	4	7	1			

Group 2
	Pl	W	D	L	F	A	Pts	NOR	IRL	POL
France	3	3	0	0	12	0	9	4-0	4-0	4-0
Norway	3	2	0	1	3	4	6		2-0	1-0
Republic of Ireland	3	1	0	2	1	6	3			1-0
Poland	3	0	0	3	0	6	0			

Group 3
	Pl	W	D	L	F	A	Pts	SWE	NED	FIN
Denmark	3	2	1	0	5	1	7	0-0	2-1	3-0
Sweden	3	1	1	1	4	4	4		1-2	3-2
Netherlands	3	1	0	2	4	3	3			1-2
Finland	3	1	0	2	4	7	3			

Group 4
	Pl	W	D	L	F	A	Pts	ESP	CZE	SRB
Germany	3	3	0	0	9	0	9	3-0	2-0	4-0
Spain	3	2	0	1	9	5	6		2-0	7-2
Czech Republic	3	0	1	2	2	6	1			2-2
Serbia	3	0	1	2	4	13	1			

Semi-finals
Switzerland 1 – France 5
Germany 2 – Denmark 0

Final
Germany 14p
France 13p

Third Place Play-off
Denmark 15p
Switzerland 14p

Finals in Nyon, Switzerland, 26-06-2012 to 29-06-2012

Group 1 in Belgium; Group 2 in Norway; Group 3 in Denmark; Group 4 in Spain

UEFA WOMEN'S CHAMPIONS LEAGUE 2011-12

First Qualifying Round

Group 1
		Pl	W	D	L	F	A	Pts	MKD	GRE	MDA
YB Frauen	SUI	3	2	1	0	11	2	7	3-1	1-1	7-0
ZFK Nase Taksi	MKD	3	2	0	1	8	3	6		1-0	6-0
PAOK	GRE	3	1	1	1	4	2	4			3-0
Goliador Chisinau	MDA	3	0	0	3	0	16	0	Played in MKD		

Group 2
		Pl	W	D	L	F	A	Pts	POR	HUN	LVA
ASA Tel Aviv Univ.	ISR	3	2	1	0	6	2	7	1-1	1-0	4-1
1° Dezembro	POR	3	1	2	0	5	1	5		0-0	4-0
MTK	HUN	3	1	1	1	12	1	4			12-0
Liepajas Metalurgs	LVA	3	0	0	3	1	20	0	Played in POR		

Group 3
		Pl	W	D	L	F	A	Pts	IRL	EST	SVN
Rayo Vallecano	ESP	3	3	0	0	9	1	9	1-0	4-1	4-0
Peamount United	IRL	3	2	0	1	12	2	6		5-1	7-0
Pärnu JK	EST	3	1	0	2	4	10	3			2-1
Krka	SVN	3	0	0	3	1	13	0	Played in SVN		

Group 4
		Pl	W	D	L	F	A	Pts	BIH	TUR	LTU
Olimpia Cluj	ROU	3	3	0	0	12	2	9	3-1	4-1	5-0
SFK 2000 Sarajevo	BIH	3	2	0	1	7	5	6		4-1	2-1
Atasehir Belediyesi	TUR	3	0	1	2	3	9	1			1-1
Gintra Universitetas	LTU	3	0	1	2	2	8	1	Played in BIH		

Group 5
		Pl	W	D	L	F	A	Pts	SRB	FRO	MLT
Glasgow City	SCO	3	3	0	0	17	0	9	4-0	5-0	8-0
Spartak Subotica	SRB	3	2	0	1	15	6	6		4-2	11-0
KI Klaksvík	FRO	3	1	0	2	3	9	3			1-0
Mosta	MLT	3	0	0	3	0	20	0	Played in SRB		

Group 6
		Pl	W	D	L	F	A	Pts	SVK	POL	ALB
PK-45 Vantaa	FIN	3	2	1	0	12	1	7	1-0	1-1	10-0
Slovan Bratislava	SVK	3	2	0	1	17	1	6		1-0	16-0
Unia Raciborz	POL	3	1	1	1	9	2	4			8-0
Ada Velipojë	ALB	3	0	0	3	0	34	0	Played in FIN		

Group 7
		Pl	W	D	L	F	A	Pts	UKR	WAL	LUX
Apollon Limassol	CYP	3	3	0	0	24	1	9	2-1	8-0	14-0
Lehenda-ShVSM	UKR	3	2	0	1	11	2	6		2-0	8-0
Swansea City	WAL	3	1	0	2	4	10	3			4-0
Progrès Niedercorn	LUX	3	0	0	3	0	26	0	Played in CYP		

Group 8
		Pl	W	D	L	F	A	Pts	BLR	BUL	NIR
Osijek	CRO	3	2	1	0	7	2	7	1-0	1-1	5-1
Bobruichanka	BLR	3	2	0	1	10	1	6		3-0	7-0
NSA Sofia	BUL	3	1	1	1	2	4	4			1-0
Newtownabbey	NIR	3	0	0	3	1	13	0	Played in CRO		

The top 22 ranked teams were given a bye to the round of 32

Round of 32

Olymp. Lyonnais	FRA	9	3
Olimpia Cluj *	ROU	0	0
Apollon Limassol *	CYP	2	1
Sparta Praha	CZE	2	2
Torres	ITA	2	3
ASA Tel Aviv Un. *	ISR	0	2
Standard CL *	BEL	0	4
Brøndby IF	DEN	2	3
Rossiyanka	RUS	2	1
Twente Enschede *	NED	0	0
Bristol Academy *	ENG	1	2
Energy Voronezh	RUS	1	4
Glasgow City *	SCO	1	3
Valur Reykjavík	ISL	1	0
Thor/KA *	ISL	0	2
Turbine Potsdam	GER	6	8
Arsenal	ENG	4	6
Bobruichanka *	BLR	0	0
PK-35 Vantaa *	FIN	1	0
Rayo Vallecano	ESP	4	3
Fortuna Hjørring	DEN	3	2
YB Frauen *	SUI	0	1
Osijek *	CRO	0	0
Göteborg FC	SWE	4	7
LdB Malmö	SWE	1	5
Tavagnacco *	ITA	2	0
CSHVSM *	KAZ	2	0
Neulengbach	AUT	1	5
Paris St-Germain	FRA	2	3
Peamount Utd *	IRL	0	0
Stabæk *	NOR	1	1
1.FFC Frankfurt	GER	0	4

Round of 16

Olymp. Lyonnais		6	6
Sparta Praha *		0	0
Torres		1	1
Brøndby IF *		2	3
Rossiyanka		4	3
Energy Voronezh *		0	3
Glasgow City		0	0
Turbine Potsdam *		10	7
Arsenal		1	5
Rayo Vallecano *		1	1
Fortuna Hjørring *		0	2
Göteborg FC		1	3
LdB Malmö		3	1
Neulengbach *		1	0
Paris St-Germain		0	2
1.FFC Frankfurt *		3	1

UEFA WOMEN'S CHAMPIONS LEAGUE 2011-12

Quarter-finals			Semi-finals			Final		
Olympique Lyonnais *	4	4						
Brøndby IF	0	0						
			Olympique Lyonnais *	5	0			
			Turbine Potsdam	1	0			
Rossiyanka	0	0						
Turbine Potsdam *	2	3						
						Olympique Lyonnais	2	
						1.FFC Frankfurt	0	
Arsenal *	3	0						
Göteborg FC	1	1						
			Arsenal *	1	0			
			1.FFC Frankfurt	2	2			
LdB Malmö *	1	0						
1.FFC Frankfurt	0	3						

* Home team in the first leg

UEFA WOMEN'S CHAMPIONS LEAGUE FINAL 2012

Olympiastadion, Munich, 17-05-2012, Att: 50 212, Ref: Jenny Palmqvist SWE

Olympique Lyonnais	2	Le Sommer [15p], Abily [28]
1.FFC Frankfurt	0	

OLYMPIQUE LYONNAIS
Sarah **BOUHADDI** - Wendie **RENARD**, Corine **FRANCO**, Sonia **BOMPASTOR** (c), Sabrina **VIGUIER** - Amandine **HENRY**•, Eugenie **LE SOMMER** (**ROSANA** 65), Louisa **NECIB** (Lara **DICKENMANN** 49), Shirley **CRUZ TRANA**, Camille **ABILY** - Lotta **SCHELIN** (Ami **OTAKI** 88). Tr: Patrice **LAIR**

1.FFC FRANKFURT
Desiree **SCHUMANN** - Gina **LEWANDOWSKI**, Saki **KUMAGAI**, Sara **THUNEBRO**, Meike **WEBER** (Ria **PERCIVAL** 61), Saskia **BARTUSIAK** - Melanie **BEHRINGER**, Dzsenifer **MAROZSAN**, Kerstin **GAREFREKES** - Svenja **HUTH** (Ana-Maria **CRNOGORCEVIC** 64), Sandra **SMISEK** (c) (Jessica **LANDSTROM** 83). Tr: Sven **KAHLERT**

UEFA WOMEN'S U-19 CHAMPIONSHIP 2012

First Qualifying Round Group 1

	Pl	W	D	L	F	A	Pts	NED	CRO	BUL
Norway	3	3	0	0	20	3	9	4-2	7-1	9-0
Netherlands	3	2	0	1	10	5	6		5-1	3-0
Croatia	3	1	0	2	3	12	3			1-0
Bulgaria	3	0	0	3	0	13	0			Played in BUL

First Qualifying Round Group 2

	Pl	W	D	L	F	A	Pts	POR	HUN	ISR
Republic of Ireland	3	3	0	0	12	1	9	1-0	6-0	5-0
Portugal	3	1	1	1	4	4	4		3-3	1-0
Hungary	3	1	1	1	4	9	4			1-0
Israel	3	0	0	3	1	7	0			Played in POR

First Qualifying Round Group 3

	Pl	W	D	L	F	A	Pts	POL	EST	CYP
Czech Republic	3	3	0	0	11	1	9	1-0	6-1	4-1
Poland	3	2	0	1	9	3	6		4-2	5-0
Estonia	3	0	1	2	6	13	1			3-3
Cyprus	3	0	1	2	4	12	1			Played in EST

First Qualifying Round Group 4

	Pl	W	D	L	F	A	Pts	WAL	SVN	KAZ
Iceland	3	3	0	0	7	1	9	2-0	2-1	3-0
Wales	3	2	0	1	7	3	6		4-1	3-0
Slovenia	3	1	0	2	5	6	3			3-0
Kazakhstan	3	0	0	3	0	9	0			Played in ISL

First Qualifying Round Group 5

	Pl	W	D	L	F	A	Pts	SRB	UKR	SVK
Sweden	3	3	0	0	11	0	9	7-0	3-0	1-0
Serbia	3	1	0	2	5	11	3		4-2	1-2
Ukraine	3	1	0	2	4	7	3			2-0
Slovakia	3	1	0	2	2	4	3			Played in SVK

First Qualifying Round Group 6

	Pl	W	D	L	F	A	Pts	ITA	MKD	ARM
Austria	3	2	1	0	12	1	7	0-0	5-1	7-0
Italy	3	2	1	0	11	0	7		4-0	7-0
FYR Macedonia	3	1	0	2	9	10	3			8-1
Armenia	3	0	0	3	1	22	0			Played in MKD

First Qualifying Round Group 7

	Pl	W	D	L	F	A	Pts	FIN	FRO	BLR
Scotland	3	2	1	0	14	2	7	1-1	9-0	4-1
Finland	3	2	1	0	5	1	7		3-0	1-0
Faroe Islands	3	1	0	2	2	13	3			2-1
Belarus	3	0	0	3	2	7	0			Played in FIN

First Qualifying Round Group 8

	Pl	W	D	L	F	A	Pts	RUS	GRE	LVA
Denmark	3	3	0	0	18	0	9	1-0	8-0	9-0
Russia	3	1	1	1	8	3	4		1-1	7-1
Greece	3	1	1	1	7	9	4			6-0
Latvia	3	0	0	3	1	22	0			Played in LVA

First Qualifying Round Group 9

	Pl	W	D	L	F	A	Pts	ROU	NIR	LTU
Belgium	3	2	1	0	9	2	7	2-0	1-1	6-1
Romania	3	2	0	1	10	2	6		3-0	1-0
Northern Ireland	3	1	1	1	5	4	4			4-0
Lithuania	3	0	0	3	1	17	0			Played in BEL

First Qualifying Round Group 10

	Pl	W	D	L	F	A	Pts	SUI	BIH	MDA
Spain	3	3	0	0	20	0	9	3-0	9-0	8-0
Switzerland	3	2	0	1	11	3	6		7-0	4-0
Bosnia-Herzegovina	3	1	0	2	2	16	3			2-0
Moldova	3	0	0	3	0	14	0			Played in BIH

Second Qualifying Round Group 1

	Pl	W	D	L	F	A	Pts	NOR	BEL	CZE
Portugal	3	2	0	1	7	5	6	3-1	2-1	2-3
Norway	3	2	0	1	7	5	6		3-0	3-2
Belgium	3	1	0	2	4	5	3			3-0
Czech Republic	3	1	0	2	5	8	3			Played in POR

Second Qualifying Round Group 2

	Pl	W	D	L	F	A	Pts	GER	NIR	POL
Sweden	3	3	0	0	7	1	9	1-0	3-0	3-1
Germany	3	2	0	1	4	1	6		2-0	2-0
Northern Ireland	3	1	0	2	3	5	3			3-0
Poland	3	0	0	3	1	8	0			Played in SWE

Second Qualifying Round Group 3

	Pl	W	D	L	F	A	Pts	FRA	NED	ISL
Romania	3	2	1	0	4	1	7	1-0	1-1	2-0
France	3	2	0	1	2	1	6		1-0	1-0
Netherlands	3	0	2	1	2	3	2			1-1
Iceland	3	0	1	2	1	4	1			Played in NED

Second Qualifying Round Group 4

	Pl	W	D	L	F	A	Pts	DEN	SUI	IRL
Serbia	3	3	0	0	7	2	9	4-2	1-0	2-0
Denmark	3	2	0	1	7	4	6		3-0	2-0
Switzerland	3	1	0	2	2	4	3			2-0
Republic of Ireland	3	0	0	3	0	6	0			Played in SRB

Second Qualifying Round Group 5

	Pl	W	D	L	F	A	Pts	ITA	SCO	RUS
Spain	3	3	0	0	11	2	9	4-0	3-2	4-0
Italy	3	2	0	1	6	6	6		4-2	1-0
Scotland	3	1	0	2	5	7	3			1-0
Russia	3	0	0	3	0	6	0			Played in RUS

Second Qualifying Round Group 6

	Pl	W	D	L	F	A	Pts	AUT	FIN	WAL
England	3	3	0	0	8	0	9	1-0	1-0	6-0
Austria	3	1	0	2	2	3	3		2-0	0-2
Finland	3	1	0	2	2	4	3			2-1
Wales	3	1	0	2	3	8	3			Played in ENG

UEFA EUROPEAN WOMEN'S U-19 CHAMPIONSHIP TURKEY 2012

First Round Group Stage

Group A	Pl	W	D	L	F	A	Pts	POR	TUR	ROU
Denmark	3	3	0	0	3	0	9	1-0	1-0	1-0
Portugal	3	1	1	1	1	1	4		0-0	1-0
Turkey	3	0	2	1	1	2	2			1-1
Romania	3	0	1	2	1	3	1			

Group B	Pl	W	D	L	F	A	Pts	SWE	ENG	SRB
Spain	3	2	1	0	7	0	7	0-0	4-0	3-0
Sweden	3	2	1	0	6	1	7		1-0	5-1
England	3	0	1	2	0	5	1			0-0
Serbia	3	0	1	2	1	8	1			

Semi-finals

Sweden 3 — Denmark 1
Portugal 0 — Spain 1

Final

Sweden 1 — Spain 0

Finals held in Turkey from 2-07-2012 to 14-07-2012